Botanica's
Roses

Botanica's Roses

The Encyclopedia of Roses
Foreword by David Austin
Introduced by William A. Grant

**Peter Beales, Dr Tommy Cairns, Walter Duncan,
Gwen Fagan, William Grant, Ken Grapes, Peter Harkness,
Kevin Hughes, John Mattock, David Ruston**

RAINCOAST BOOKS

Vancouver

1008 pages • 300 mm x 230 mm

Botanica

- A must for all gardeners
- An invaluable and enduring reference
- Over 10,000 plants
- Fully illustrated in color throughout

Botanica is the world's most authoritative, comprehensive and up-to-date single volume guide to plants for all gardeners and garden lovers that's lavishly illustrated throughout. Unrivalled in scope, **Botanica** features over 10,000 plants for you to choose from in its easy A to Z format that's fully illustrated in color throughout—from annuals, perennials, bulbs and roses, to trees and shrubs, ferns and palms, fruit and nut trees, orchids, cacti and succulents, lawns and ground covers, vegetables and herbs. Plus all the really practical information you need on care and cultivation from planting and propagating, to pests and diseases is at your fingertips. **Botanica** has been written in a fresh, easy-to-read style by a team of specialist plant experts and gardening writers.

A TO Z OF GARDEN PLANTS

PLANT HEADINGS
To make it easy to find the plant you are looking for, page headings on each spread indicate the first genus described on the left-hand page and the last genus on the right-hand page.

PHOTOGRAPHS
Photographs in Botanica illustrate colour, growth habits and other ornamental features of the plants.

CAPTIONS
Each photograph is captioned identifying the plant with its full botanical name.

MARGIN MARKERS
For ready reference, Botanica has been printed with colored alphabet tabs in the margin that move down the page to help you find the plant you are looking for.

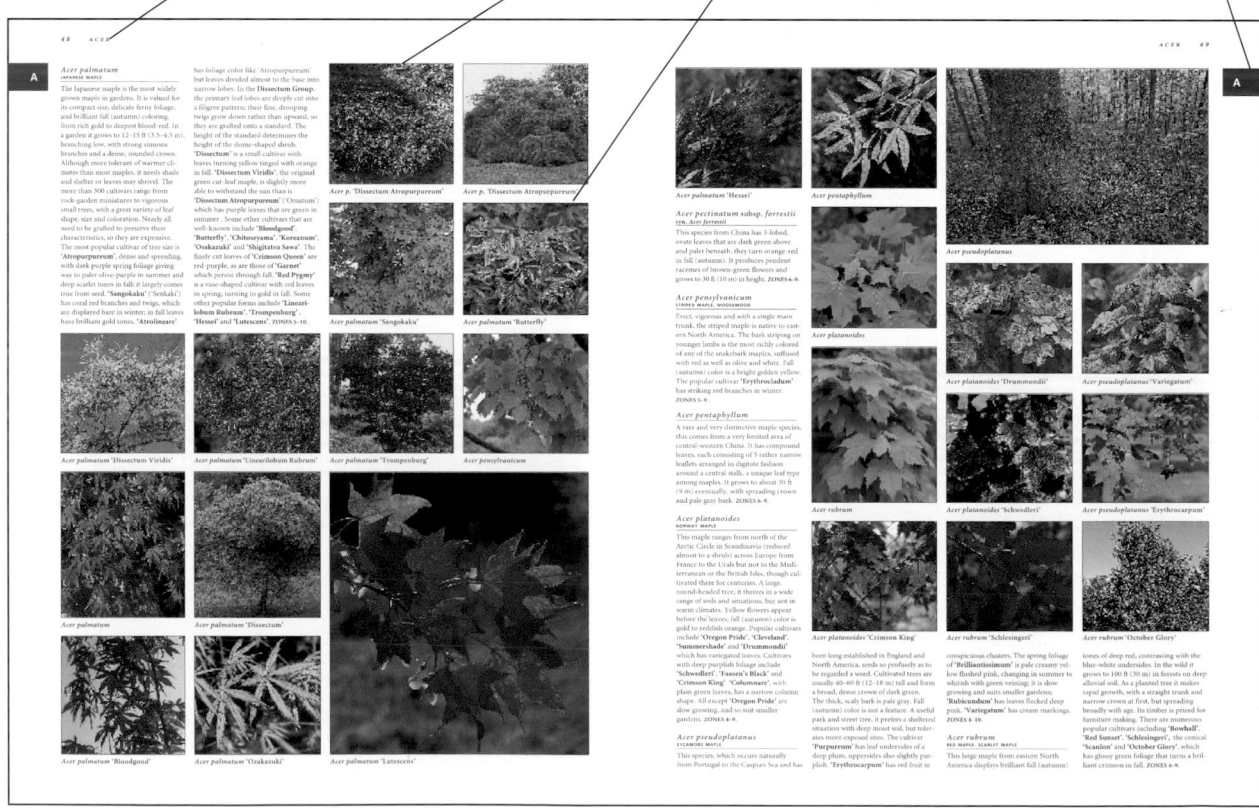

GENUS ENTRIES
In the A to Z section, plants are arranged in alphabetical order by genus. Entries include plant descriptions, geographical origin, cultivation, pests and diseases, height and spread and hardiness rating by zone.

Publisher	Gordon Cheers	First published in Canada in 1999 by
Managing editor	Margaret Olds	Raincoast Books
		8680 Cambie Street
Foreword by	David Austin	Vancouver, BC
		V6P 6M9
		(604) 323 7100
		www.raincoast.com
Consultants	Dr Tommy Cairns	
	William Grant	ISBN 1-55192-252-5
	Peter Harkness	
		First published in Australia in 1998 by
Writers	Peter Beales	Random House Australia Pty Ltd
	Dr Tommy Cairns	20 Alfred Street, Milsons Point, NSW Australia 2061
	Walter Duncan	Second edition, revised, published 1999
	Gwen Fagan	
	William Grant	All rights reserved. No part of this publication may be
	Ken Grapes	reproduced, stored in a retrieval system, or transmitted
	Peter Harkness	in any form or by any means, electronic, mechanical,
	Kevin Hughes	photocopying, recording or otherwise, without the prior
	John Mattock	written permission of the Publisher.
	David Ruston	
	Philip Sutherland	Photos © Random House Australia Pty Ltd 1998, 1999
	Thomas Williams	from the Random House Photo Library
Senior editor	Kate Etherington	Text © Random House Australia Pty Ltd 1998, 1999
Editors	Simon Maughan	Printed by Sing Cheong Printing Co. Ltd, Hong Kong
	Loretta Barnard	Film separation Pica Colour Separation, Singapore
	Lisa Foulis	
	Denise Imwold	
	Dee Rogers	
	Doreen Grézoux	
	Heather Jackson	
	Marie-Louise Taylor	

Picture research	Gordon Cheers	
Art directors	Stan Lamond	
	Bob Mitchell	Pages 2–3: 'Complicata'
		Page 5: 'L. D. Braithwaite'
Page layout	Joy Eckermann	Page 7: 'Rosamunde'
		Page 8: 'Leander'
Picture sizing	Jean Burnard	Pages 10–11: 'Rob Roy'
		Pages 14–15: 'Debut'
Publishing manager	Linda Watchorn	Pages 22–23: 'Iceberg'
		Pages 32–33: 'Pink Bassino'
Publishing coordinator	Sarah Sherlock	Pages 46–47: *Rosa glauca*
Publishing assistant	Olivia Kleindienst	Pages 62–63: 'Albertine'
		Pages 98–99: 'Bantry Bay'
Maps	Stan Lamond	Pages 136–137: 'Charles Austin'
	Graham Keane	Pages 188–189: 'Dorothy Peach'
		Pages 214–215: 'Étoile de Hollande'
Map zone consultant	Dr J. Gentilli	Pages 232–233: 'Frank Naylor'
		Pages 258–259: 'Gwen Swane'
Photo library	Susan Page	Pages 290–291: 'Iceberg'
		Pages 318–319: 'Jacqueline du Pré'
Chief photographer	James Young	Pages 342–343: 'Linda Thomson'
		Pages 374–375: 'Madame Caroline Testout'
Table compiled with		Pages 426–427: 'Orange Flame'
the assistance of	Steve Beck	Pages 446–447: 'Pat Austin'
		Pages 490–491: 'Red Devil'
Index	Joan Suter	Pages 528–529: 'Shona'
		Pages 582–583: 'The Compass Rose'
Typesetting	Dee Rogers	Pages 606–607: 'Vesper'
	Deanne Lowe	Pages 618–619: 'Will Scarlet'
	Joan Suter	

Consultants

PETER BEALES grew up in Norfolk and after leaving school he was apprenticed to LeGrice Roses of North Walsham. He now has a nursery in Norfolk and holds the National Collection of *Rosa* species in the UK. He is a regular exhibitor at British flower shows, and is a member of the Institute of Horticulture. He is a recipient of the Royal National Rose Society's most prestigious award, the Dean Hole Medal. He is the author of *Vision of Roses, Twentieth-Century Roses, Roses: An Illustrated Encyclopedia* and *Classic Roses*.

DR TOMMY CAIRNS is a chemistry graduate from the University of Glasgow and also holds two higher degrees, a PhD in analytical chemistry and a degree of Doctor of Science in Biochemistry and Toxicology. Roses are an all-embracing hobby: he grows over 1000 bushes, exhibits them internationally, and writes about their culture and history. He is the 1998 vice-president/president-elect of the American Rose Society, having edited a wide range of the society's publications including *Rose Exhibitor's Forum, Handbook for Selecting Roses, Growing Beautiful Roses* and *Modern Roses 10.* Currently Tommy is Editor of *World Rose News* as well as of *Modern Roses 11.*

WALTER DUNCAN was brought up in Adelaide where his passion for roses was fostered by his mother's love of gardening. In 1977 he began growing roses commercially in the Clare Valley of South Australia and today is a major supplier of plants to the Australian wholesale rose market. He is past president and a life member of the Rose Society of South Australia, has won two Banksian Medals for Horticulture from the Royal Horticultural Society, and is a member of the Advisory Committee of the Adelaide International Rose Garden. He also lectures on, and judges, a wide range of plants in both Australia and New Zealand.

GWEN FAGAN is a recognized rose expert in South Africa. Although she practised medicine for 20 years, since 1969 she has specialized in historical landscape restoration and design for which she has won many awards. Her thesis 'An Introduction to the man-made landscape at the Cape from the 17th to the 19th centuries' earned her a PhD from the University of Cape Town in 1995. She has published several articles regarding restoration projects including 'Roses at the Cape of Good Hope'. She has spoken at rose conferences around the world, as well as in South Africa where she is a prominent member of the rose community.

WILLIAM A. GRANT is a garden writer, photographer, and lecturer. After a long academic career during which he received two Fulbright awards, he retired to pursue his love of gardening. His long association with the University of California at Santa Cruz Arboretum has culminated in his role as president of its support group. His personal collection of plants is supplemented with a wide variety of Wild and Old Roses. He is the founder of the California Garden History Society and now lives and gardens in Aptos, California, on the Monterey Bay.

KEN GRAPES was born and brought up in Norfolk and served in the British Army for nearly 30 years. He acquired his love of gardening from his mother. For the past 15 years he has been Secretary General of the Royal National Rose Society. He has in his care the world-famous 'Gardens of the Rose' at St Albans where international trials for new roses are held, together with practical tests aimed at assessing the validity of many widely held perceptions about rose cultivation. In 1998 he was awarded the Society's highest honor, the Dean Hole Medal.

PETER HARKNESS is one in the long line of the Harkness family involved with rose breeding. In the 1980s he was chairman of the British Rose Growers' Association and also president of the British Association of Rose Breeders. In 1989 he retired from managing R. Harkness & Co., though he still assists his nephews in selecting new varieties for introduction. After five years as editor of *The Rose* and other Royal National Rose Society publications, he received, in 1996, the Society's Dean Hole Medal. He is currently on the council of the RNRS, and writes and lectures on roses. He also a judge at the International Rose Trials held in St Albans and Glasgow.

KEVIN HUGHES is an amateur rosarian whose obsession with gardening began in his birthplace of Lancashire. Thirty years in the British Army allowed him to garden in different parts of the world. On retiring in 1969 to Australia, he engaged in gardening and in university administration, while for the last 16 years has indulged his passion for Old Garden Roses. He has been the Heritage Rose Society co-ordinator for Sydney and is a member of the English and the American Rose Societies. He has travelled widely, photographing, lecturing and writing about roses.

JOHN MATTOCK is one of Britain's leading rose experts. He is also an acknowledged consultant on Mediterranean gardening and horticultural enterprises in the tropics. He grew roses commercially for his family company and introduced many new varieties. He served on the council of the Royal Horticultural Society for 15 years and was chairman of the Shows Committee responsible for the Chelsea Flower Show for 12 years. He holds the Society's highest award, the Victoria Medal of Honour, for services to horticulture. He is a vice-president of the Royal National Rose Society. John Mattock has written and contributed to several books on rose-growing.

DAVID RUSTON converted his family fruit property in Renmark, South Australia, into a commercial rose garden containing one of the largest collection of roses in the world. His expertise has been recognized with many awards, including the T. A. Stewart Memorial Award and the Australian Rose Award, both from the National Rose Society of Australia, as well as the highly regarded Dean Hole Medal from Britain's Royal National Rose Society. He was also presented with the Order of Australia for Services to Horticulture. A former president of the Rose Society of Australia and the founding president of the Australian Heritage Rose Society, he has also served as president of the World Federation of Rose Societies. Apart from running Ruston's Rose Garden, David Ruston tours the world giving lectures on roses and on the history of flower arranging.

Foreword

Of all the flowers to be found in gardens throughout the world, the rose is the most popular and the most widely grown. This has been true since the very dawn of civilization, at least in the Western world. Today, roses are to be found in every country, even where the climate is less than ideal. It is interesting to ask why this should be so.

First and foremost is the fact that although the beauty of the rose may vary from one variety to another, it is, at its best, the most beautiful of all flowers and, as if this were not enough, it nearly always has a delicious fragrance. Then there is the fact that it flowers over a very long season. So long as there is warmth and moisture, most roses will continue to flower until the arrival of winter. Roses are remarkably adaptable, being equally at home in warm climates, such as those of Australia and the southern United States, as in the cool, damp climate of Britain.

The rose is also a plant of incredible variety of form and growth—from the smallest Miniature Rose of just 6 inches (15 centimeters) in height to the vast Climbers of 40 or 50 feet (13 or 15 meters) in height—and every size in between those two extremes. Its foliage may be dark green and polished, as in the Large-flowered Roses (Hybrid Teas), or it may be a matt gray-green, as in the Alba Roses. The leaves of some roses may be small and almost fern-like, as in certain species roses, while in others they can be excessively large. Indeed, one of the great pleasures of roses is to see the various kinds of foliage develop early in the year before the flowers have arrived.

There are roses for just about every purpose and position in the garden—whatever size this may be. Roses may be short and compact, making them suitable for formal bedding, they may be shrub roses—small or large—ideal for the border; or they may be used to climb up walls or on trellis-work or to clamber into trees; or even to plant in wild areas where the garden meets the countryside. Other roses will creep along the ground to give ground cover. They may be grown in pots for the patio or elsewhere and small pot roses are excellent for the house—and, of course, no flower is more beautiful when arranged in bowls. Many roses are good companions for other plants in the mixed border, or they are beautiful in a border of their own. As well as all this, the rose is just about the only plant from which it is possible to create a whole garden for it alone.

Having said this, it is perhaps the individual flower that is the great glory of the rose. Few flowers can equal it for massed effect throughout the summer—but it is the individual bloom that makes it the 'Queen of Flowers'. These blooms may be almost as large as a peony, or no larger than a thimble. They may be in the form of a cup, a flat rosette, or domed—almost like a pincushion. With the exception of blue, almost every color is to be found—from brightest scarlet to richest yellow—but it is, perhaps, in the softer colors that roses are most at home.

To all this we must add the wonderful fragrance of the rose, which is also incredibly varied. Indeed, it sometimes seems that the rose, in one variety or another, is able to provide us with almost every fragrance in the garden. Besides the Old Rose fragrance, hints of musk, tea, jasmine, violet, myrrh, citrus and apple scents are to be found in roses of one kind or another. What we call the Old Rose scent is, perhaps, one of the most beautiful of these, and I am told this is the basis of most perfumes.

The cultivated rose is the result of centuries of plant breeding—first by simple selection and later by conscious hybridization. In fact, no flower has received so much attention from the plant breeder. This has resulted in a vast number of different varieties and it is this fact, together with the many qualities of the rose and its great popularity, that makes a book such as this a necessity.

Never before has there been an encyclopedia of roses on this scale. A team of leading experts has been gathered and they have written excellent descriptions. Not only this, but the photographs, too, are of a very high order. I am quite sure that *Botanica's Roses* is going to be an invaluable work of reference for rose lovers—both amateur and professional—throughout the world. It is certain, also, to be a source of pleasure in itself. I can only hope that it will remain in print for a very long time.

DAVID AUSTIN

Contents

How This Book Works

Botanica's Roses is an authoritative and comprehensive guide to more than 4000 roses. The book contains three sections.

The first section includes an introduction, information on the history of the rose—its origins and developments in breeding—as well as an explanation of the different types of rose and how they are classified. There is also detailed information on planning a rose garden, choosing roses (and plants to go with them), planting, cultivating and pruning roses. A climate map showing plant hardiness zones is also included with an explanation of how the zones are used.

The main section contains two fully illustrated A to Z sequences: one for the Wild (or species) Roses—the ancestors of all roses—and one for cultivated roses which makes up most of the book.

Each entry gives the rose's name; code name and synonyms where appropriate; horticultural classification; color classification; and notes if the rose is repeat-flowering. This is followed by a full description of the rose which also includes any interesting anecdotes and any specific cultivation requirements. The description then ends with a range of hardiness zones. For more

information on hardiness zones see page 21. The entries end with the breeder's name, country and date of registration; the rose's parentage; and any awards it has received.

The *code names* are usually composed of three capital letters (usually an abbreviation of the breeder's name) and lower case letters to give a unique word which identifies the rose.

The *horticultural classification* scheme used is described on page 26.

Our *color classification* given in the heading is based on the American Rose Society classification, except for the green roses—

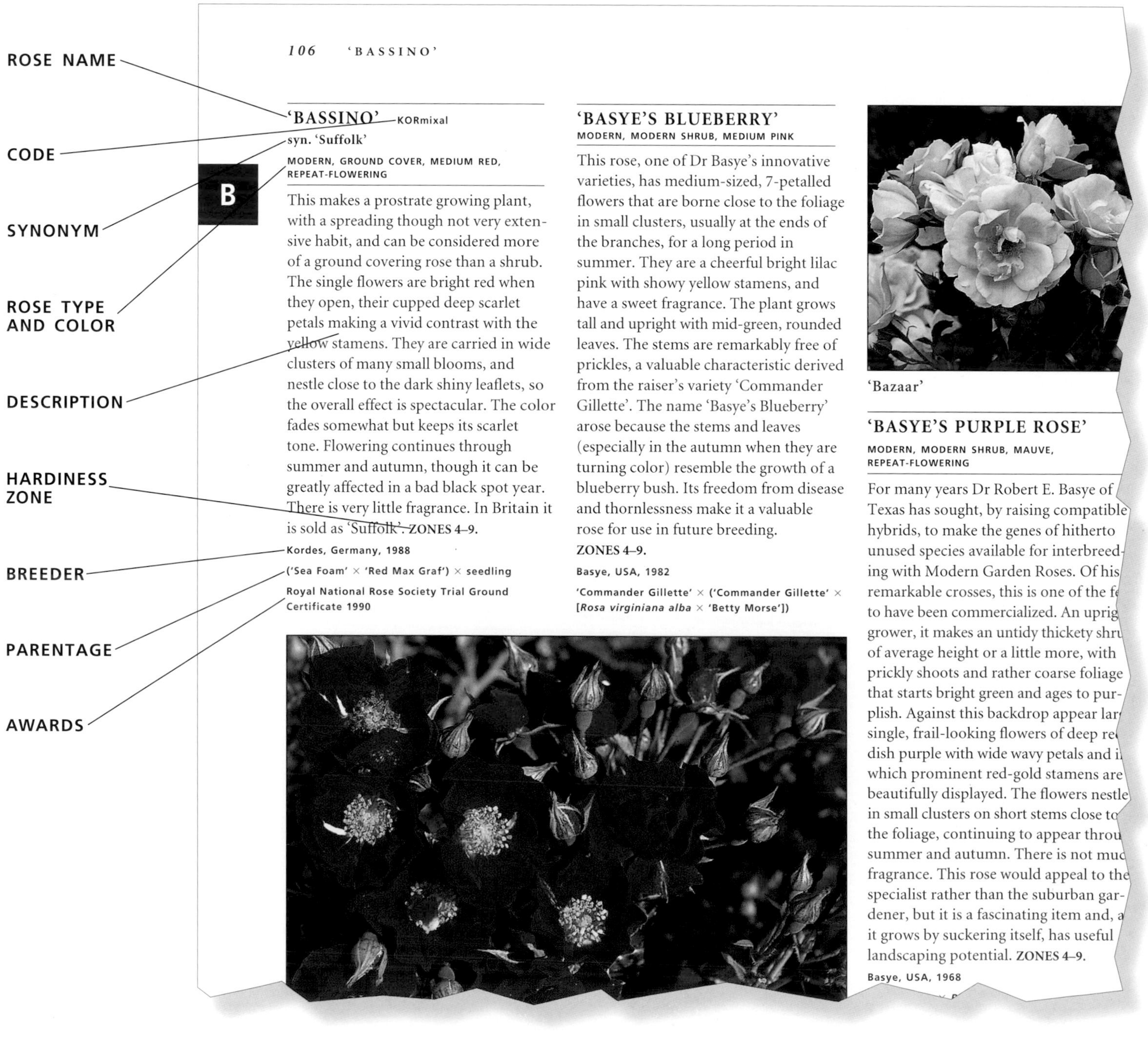

ROSE NAME

CODE

SYNONYM

ROSE TYPE AND COLOR

DESCRIPTION

HARDINESS ZONE

BREEDER

PARENTAGE

AWARDS

B

'BASSINO' —KORmixal
syn. 'Suffolk'
MODERN, GROUND COVER, MEDIUM RED, REPEAT-FLOWERING

This makes a prostrate growing plant, with a spreading though not very extensive habit, and can be considered more of a ground covering rose than a shrub. The single flowers are bright red when they open, their cupped deep scarlet petals making a vivid contrast with the yellow stamens. They are carried in wide clusters of many small blooms, and nestle close to the dark shiny leaflets, so the overall effect is spectacular. The color fades somewhat but keeps its scarlet tone. Flowering continues through summer and autumn, though it can be greatly affected in a bad black spot year. There is very little fragrance. In Britain it is sold as 'Suffolk'. ZONES 4–9.

Kordes, Germany, 1988
('Sea Foam' × 'Red Max Graf') × seedling
Royal National Rose Society Trial Ground Certificate 1990

'BASYE'S BLUEBERRY'
MODERN, MODERN SHRUB, MEDIUM PINK

This rose, one of Dr Basye's innovative varieties, has medium-sized, 7-petalled flowers that are borne close to the foliage in small clusters, usually at the ends of the branches, for a long period in summer. They are a cheerful bright lilac pink with showy yellow stamens, and have a sweet fragrance. The plant grows tall and upright with mid-green, rounded leaves. The stems are remarkably free of prickles, a valuable characteristic derived from the raiser's variety 'Commander Gillette'. The name 'Basye's Blueberry' arose because the stems and leaves (especially in the autumn when they are turning color) resemble the growth of a blueberry bush. Its freedom from disease and thornlessness make it a valuable rose for use in future breeding. ZONES 4–9.

Basye, USA, 1982
'Commander Gillette' × ('Commander Gillette' × [*Rosa virginiana alba* × 'Betty Morse'])

'Bazaar'

'BASYE'S PURPLE ROSE'
MODERN, MODERN SHRUB, MAUVE, REPEAT-FLOWERING

For many years Dr Robert E. Basye of Texas has sought, by raising compatible hybrids, to make the genes of hitherto unused species available for interbreeding with Modern Garden Roses. Of his remarkable crosses, this is one of the few to have been commercialized. An upright grower, it makes an untidy thickety shrub of average height or a little more, with prickly shoots and rather coarse foliage that starts bright green and ages to purplish. Against this backdrop appear large single, frail-looking flowers of deep reddish purple with wide wavy petals and in which prominent red-gold stamens are beautifully displayed. The flowers nestle in small clusters on short stems close to the foliage, continuing to appear through summer and autumn. There is not much fragrance. This rose would appeal to the specialist rather than the suburban gardener, but it is a fascinating item and, as it grows by suckering itself, has useful landscaping potential. ZONES 4–9.

Basye, USA, 1968

PAGE HEADINGS
These indicate the first rose described on the left-hand page and the last on the right-hand page. If the right-hand page has a full-page photo, the heading refers to the last rose on the left-hand page.

PHOTOGRAPHS
Superb color photographs illustrate the color, growth habit, and other ornamental features of the roses.

CAPTIONS
The captions clearly identify each picture, making it easy to find the rose you are looking for.

ENTRIES
Each entry gives the name of the rose, its synonyms, code name, classification, awards it has won, parentage, and a full description including flower color, size, foliage, flowering time, fragrance, cultivation, and hardiness rating by zone.

MARGIN MARKERS
For ready reference, colored alphabet tabs are printed in the margins of the cultivated roses section and move down the page to help you find the rose you are looking for.

Sample spread (pages 276–277), including entries for 'Gold Medal', 'Gold Rush', 'Gold Reef', 'Goldbusch', 'Golden Angel', 'Golden Bettina', 'Golden Anniversary', 'Golden Chersonese', 'Golden Anniversary', 'Golden Celebration', 'Golden Century', 'Golden Choice', and 'Golden Dawn'.

'Gold Medal'

'Goldbusch'

'Golden Angel'

'Gold Rush'

'Golden Celebration'

---

we have described them as green. In the ARS scheme, white is used for white, near white and white blend, and mauve for mauve and mauve blend. Where authorities differ, we have given both, for example apricot blend/light pink.

The *description* within the entry often uses colors that are slightly different to the color in the heading—this is because the color classification does not cater for the huge range of color hues roses exhibit; also colors can be quite subjective. Because the color of a rose can vary enormously, depending on the soil, the climate, and even as the bloom develops (the majority fade with

age), occasionally the photograph of a rose will not exactly match its description. Also, many bluish or lavender roses appear more in the pink tonal range when photographed.

Where no information appears for the breeder, country or date, this information was unavailable.

The *date* of introduction (instead of registration) has been given in some cases, for example when a rose has not been registered. For the Wild Roses the date given is generally the year the rose was first introduced to the Western world.

The rose's *parentage* gives the seed parent first, then the pollen parent. Where the par-

entage is not known, or the breeder does not wish to disclose the parentage, we have used the phrase 'Parentage unknown'.

The sections for Wild Roses and cultivated roses have been designed with dictionary-style page headings. The section on cultivated roses is so extensive that margin markers to help you find a particular rose quickly and easily have been incorporated.

The final section includes an extensive reference table, brief notes on some prominent rose breeders, a glossary of botanical and horticultural terms, a bibliography plus an index to all the roses, including cross references from code names and synonyms.

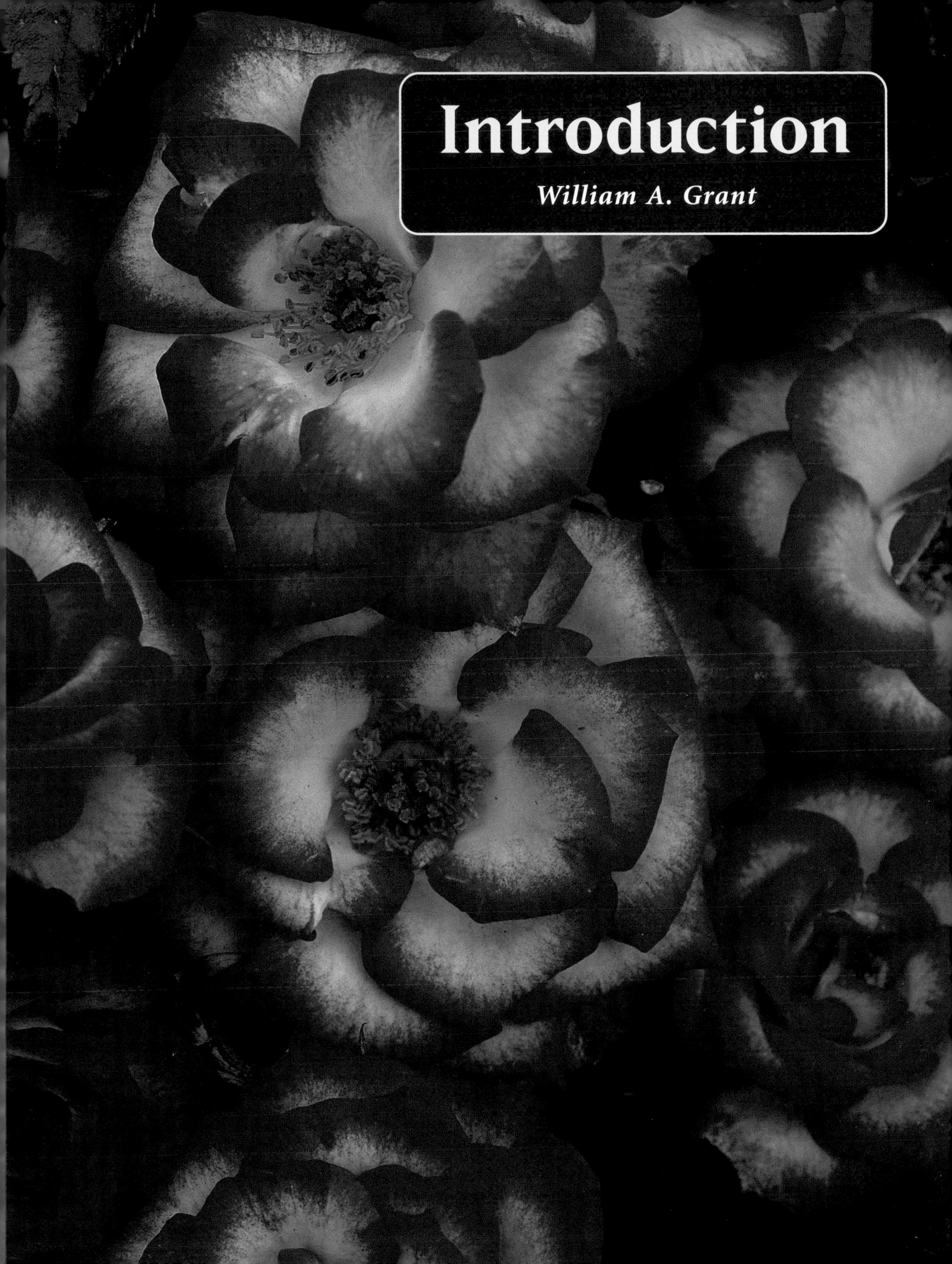

Introduction

William A. Grant

Readers of this book will find descriptions and photographs of roses from ancient times up to the present. No rose book can satisfy every demand of the inquisitive gardener, but this volume goes a long way to achieving that goal. However, for Canadians a bit more needs to be said about plants that can survive in Zones 1–4.

Gardeners everywhere are faced with challenges when they grow plants in difficult places. There are animals ready to devour them; diseases appear out of nowhere to weaken them; wind and sun wreak their damage; lack of care and nourishment will destroy them; and the strange weather patterns caused by global warming are creating new problems for them.

There are few countries in the world that have the hardiness zones of Canada. More than half of the country rests in Zone 2, where the average winter temperature ranges from –50°F to –40°F (–46°C to –40°C). Yet there are many plants that can survive in this zone with the winter protection of snow. And one of the hardiest is the rose. Roses are endemic to the Northern Hemisphere only, and there are 'polar' roses that have grown here since pre-historic times. Sadly, most gardeners either do not know of their existence or feel they would not be worth growing as they bloom but once a year.

The earliest settlers came in 1534 and would have brought types of roses that would survive well in this country—Gallicas, Albas, Damasks, and later, Centifolias. There must have been great disappointment when these colonists experienced the desperate winters when few plants could survive. Experience taught them that a great deal of effort was necessary to reproduce gardens they were used to from across the Atlantic. However, they adapted to the weather, finding native plants that survived and trading cuttings of them with each other

But of all plants, then and now, roses have usually headed the most popular list for people wishing to create their own Eden, either on the frontier or in the towns. And roses are tough—they can endure droughts and poor soils for longer than most perennials. Years ago gardeners put cuttings into potatoes, carried them across a continent in covered wagons, and planted them, knowing they would root with proper care.

The extremes of weather were finally overcome when cities created their own climates,

LEFT: *'Jens Munk', a Hybrid Rugosa from the Explorer Series, is a Canadian creation with soft lilac-pink blooms.*
BELOW LEFT: *The Shrub Rose 'Champlain', another member of the Explorer Series, commemorates Samuel de Champlain.*
BELOW CENTRE: *'Charles Albanel', also from the Explorer Series, is a Hybrid Rugosa with very disease-resistant foliage.*
BELOW: *'Henry Hudson', named for the English navigator, is among the most winter-hardy members of the Explorer Series.*

ABOVE: *The light pink flowers of 'John Davis', from the Explorer Series, have a strong spicy fragrance.*
RIGHT: *'William Baffin' bears its beautiful loose semi-double flowers from summer to autumn. It is also from the Explorer Series.*
BELOW RIGHT: *The medium red flowers of 'John Cabot' are borne on a shrub that almost grows tall enough to be classified as a small climber.*

indoors and out. Plants could be brought inside when the temperatures dropped or suddenly rose. Small glasshouses could be used to start seeds or cuttings. With the appearance of nurseries, gardeners had more choices in their selection of plants. And books could be consulted.

Today in Canada there are resources ready to help the avid gardener achieve goals that were difficult fifty years ago. Among the most dramatic changes has been the creation of winter-hardy roses. Several organizations and individuals have contributed greatly to making rose-growing possible in all temperature zones.

Explorer Series

The roses in this collection were developed between 1960 and 1990 by the Dominion Government in Ottawa at the Central Experimental Farm. The aim of this project was to produce roses that were disease-resistant, summer-flowering, requiring minimum care and no spraying. Most have a resistance to black spot and powdery mildew. And all are winter hardy down to Zones 2 or 3. They will survive if budded onto suitable understock such as *Rosa multiflora* or *R. canina*.

The winter-hardy Canadian Explorer roses, many of which are described in this book, include: 'Alexander MacKenzie'; 'Captain Samuel Holland'; 'Champlain'; 'Charles Albanel'; 'David Thompson'; 'De Montarville'; 'Frontenac'; 'George Vancouver'; 'Henry Hudson'; 'Henry Kelsey'; 'Jens Munk'; 'John Cabot'; 'John Davis'; 'John Franklin'; 'J. P. Connell'; 'Lambert Closse'; 'Louis Jolliet'; 'Marie-Victorin'; 'Martin Frobisher'; 'Nicolas'; 'Quadra'; 'Royal Edward'; 'Simon Fraser'; 'William Baffin' and 'William Booth'.

'Marie-Victorin' is named for a Christian Brother who founded the Montreal Botanical Garden, where there is a rose garden today.

Many of these roses are available from commercial nurseries either locally or by mail.

Parkland Series

These winter-hardy roses are creations of the Agriculture Research Station at Morden, Manitoba. The Parkland Series roses, many of which are described in this book, include: 'Adelaide Hoodless'; 'Cuthbert Grant'; 'Hope for Humanity'; 'Morden Amorette'; 'Morden Blush'; 'Morden Cardinette'; 'Morden Centennial'; 'Morden Fireglow'; 'Morden Ruby'; and 'Winnipeg Parks'. All of these roses are available at local nurseries or by mail. They are hardy down to –40°F (–40°C) with snow as protection.

Other Hybridizers

One of Canada's most famous rose hybridizers is Dr Felicitas Svejda (see page 679), whose creations have become bestsellers in many northern countries, especially in the United States. Her outstanding contributions include 'Henry Kelsey', 'John Cabot', 'John Davis' and 'William Baffin' from the Explorer Series. This octogenarian has just released a new rose 'William Booth' in honor of the Salvation Army's founder. Other Canadian hybridizers not mentioned elsewhere include Joyce Fleming, Georges Bugnet,

ABOVE: *'Jacques Cartier' was named for the first European to sail up the St Lawrence River.*
LEFT: *'Country Dancer' blooms repeatedly through the warmer months. It was created by Dr Griffith Buck.*
BELOW LEFT: *Each bloom on this hand-painted masterpiece, 'Little Artist', has different markings.*

Dr Frank L. Skinner, Percy H. Wright, George Mander, Dr Henry Marshall, and Keith Laver, known throughout the world for his Miniatures.

Over the past century, earlier hybridizers tried to create roses that did not need winter protection of any kind or those that could survive with some help. The earliest was Rudolf Geschwind, a forester in the last century who worked in what is now Czechoslovakia. He was ready to sacrifice perfume for hardiness, and his successes are still available today. Some of them are described in this book, the most outstanding being 'Geschwind's Nordlandrose'.

In the United States, two men worked to increase hardiness in roses: Drs Griffith Buck and Walter D. Brownell, whose creations have never really disappeared from nurseries, although they have experienced peaks and dips in popularity. The pressure to grow repeat-flowering Large-flowered/Hybrid Tea Roses, which are for the most part not winter-hardy, is so pervasive that the average gardener is attracted to what is advertised heavily, but not necessarily suitable. These hybridizers worked to change attitudes about what roses to grow to suit the local climate.

Buck Roses are now enjoying a renaissance because people have learned that beautiful, hardy, fragrant plants *can* exist in areas where the most popular new introductions of Large-flowered/Hybrid Teas and Cluster-flowered/Floribundas will fail. Buck was Professor of Horticulture at Iowa State University, where there is now a complete collection of his roses. This is a short list of those described in this book: 'Amiga Mia'; 'Applejack'; 'Bright Melody'; 'Carefree Beauty'; 'Country Dancer'; 'Distant Drums'; 'Prairie Harvest'; and 'Prairie Princess'

Brownell worked for the same goal, and his plants are called 'Sub-Zero Roses'. Three of them are described in *Botanica's Roses:* 'Elegance'; 'Nearly Wild'; and 'Lafter'.

The Wild Roses

The longest list of winter-hardy roses has been around since history began—namely, the species or Wild Roses. The hybridizers we have been listing above were aware of the strength, disease-resistance, and beauty of these plants. If you look at the parents of many of the Canadian-bred list you will mostly find that the following species were used in the breeding: *Rosa laxa; Rosa pimpinellifolia; Rosa arkansana; Rosa rugosa;* and *Rosa kordesii* (since 1952).

There are many more of these Wild Roses that would make good garden plants, especially in difficult situations. Some worth investigating are *Rosa acicularis, R. canina, R. glauca, R. fedtschenkoana, R. macrophylla, R. nitida, R. primula,* and many more. Those who complain that the species are difficult to control (not true of all of them), that they sucker greatly (some do), that they are almost all single roses (that is true) and their prickles can be intimidating (true), forget that there are other benefits from growing them.

Wild Roses require almost no care once they are established. Their habit of growth is important to know before planting them—most can be left alone in a woodland or wild garden. They are very healthy, rarely cursed with black spot, rust, or powdery mildew. They bloom early and some have a short season. But they return in the autumn to provide beautiful foliage and hips. And the benefit of hips is well known not only for their Vitamin C content but also for arranging in bouquets when little else in the garden is worth displaying.

But remember! Check with others who have grown these species to see what their experience has been. Some may need winter coverage or other protection.

Buying Roses

Most of the roses mentioned are available from mail-order nurseries. To find what outlets have them, consult the current paperback edition of *Combined Rose List* (see the Bibliography on the next page). It lists rose nurseries around the world that ship plants.

The two main sources in Canada for these roses are Pickering Nurseries in Ontario and Corn Hill Nursery Ltd in New Brunswick.

If roses are purchased by mail-order, send for catalogues first—they will state if the plants are grown on their own roots or budded onto understock. Own-root roses may arrive looking rather small, but with the right protection they will quickly catch up with the larger plants that you find in nursery centers.

Check to see if the mail-order companies guarantee the quality of their stock and will replace any rose that does not arrive in the best of health—or fails to survive because it is diseased.

Roses offered by stores other than nurseries are to be avoided as these usually offer seconds. Do not fall for the glamorous photographs or the 'latest' fashion. Roses that have been in the catalogues for years are tried and true.

The Canadian Rose Society is an essential source of information, not only through their

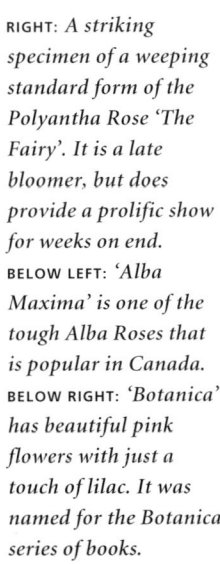

RIGHT: *A striking specimen of a weeping standard form of the Polyantha Rose 'The Fairy'. It is a late bloomer, but does provide a prolific show for weeks on end.*
BELOW LEFT: *'Alba Maxima' is one of the tough Alba Roses that is popular in Canada.*
BELOW RIGHT: *'Botanica' has beautiful pink flowers with just a touch of lilac. It was named for the Botanica series of books.*

publications, lectures, meetings, conferences, but also through their World Wide Web site, where questions can be filed to be read and answered by experts as well as experienced rose gardeners.

Rose societies in Canada, England, and the United States have published annuals for nearly 100 years, and many of these record the experiences of gardeners who faced the same problems of growing plants in difficult situations. The library of the Canadian Rose Society, as well as university, public, and private libraries, will make them available.

Planting roses and caring for them

A careful study of the site for planting roses is quite important where drainage is poor. Roses do not like wet feet so a hillside is far better than

a ravine where water may sit for long periods. Clay is superior to sand. Every property is different, so if there is a chance to have a soil analysis before planting, it is highly recommended.

Buy Canadian-grown plants on *Rosa multiflora* understock and then plant the bud union 2–4 inches (5–10 centimeters) below soil level. Mound with soil to a depth of 12 inches (30 centimeters) once the ground is frozen. Alternatively, take cuttings and grow them on their own roots. Where winters are harsh and summers are broiling and dry, mulching roses is extremely important. Refer to good gardening books for the varied methods of creating mulch and advice on the many kinds available commercially.

Conferring with local rose or horticultural societies may save much disappointment later. Visit other gardens in the area to see which roses are doing well and if possible ask the growers how they keep them healthy.

In Canada the use of chemical fertilizers has declined in recent years as research has proved that organic materials are far richer and friendlier to the rose and to the environment. Manures have proved their worth over the centuries but were replaced because the chemicals often offered quicker blooms and greener leaves. Remember, when we interfere, thinking that science alone can solve the problem, nature is disturbed.

Chemical sprays are used by nurseries to keep their plants healthy for sale to the public. This is understandable when plants are crowded so close together. But once the gardener puts a rose in the garden, there is little need for sprays unless the blooms are groomed for exhibition. Even then, it is possible, with the wise choice of plants, good soil and nutrients, careful maintenance of weeds, and sufficient water, to create a rose garden that requires little more than nature supplies.

Hardiness zone map

This book provides an excellent map for zone hardiness based on temperatures only, recorded by the USDA. However, you can also consult the Canadian Rose Society map. This is available from the society or at their website and gives more detail, being based on a combination of factors such as length of frost-free period, summer rainfall, maximum temperatures, snow cover, and wind. In addition, the American Horticulture Society website offers even more details based not on zones but on a much broader range of influences.

Public rose gardens

The Canadian Rose Society lists all the public gardens on its website and in its literature.

There are gardens in Alberta, British Columbia, Manitoba, Newfoundland, New Brunswick, Nova Scotia, Ontario, Prince Edward Island, and Quebec. The largest collections of Old and Modern Roses will be found at the Montreal Botanical Gardens, the Royal Botanical Gardens in Hamilton, Ontario, and at Butchart Gardens, outside Victoria, BC.

BIBLIOGRAPHY

Fillmore, Roscoe A., *Roses for Canadian Gardens.*

Hansen, N. E., *Hardy Roses for South Dakota,* published by the South Dakota State College at Brookings. Although this pamphlet was published in 1929 and may be hard to find, it has invaluable information about all classes of roses.

Osborne, Robert, *Roses for Canadian Gardens.*

Roses for the North, published by the Minnesota Agricultural Experiment Station.

Schneider, Peter, *Combined Rose List,* PO Box 677, Mantua, Ohio, USA 44255. It lists rose nurseries around the world that ship plants.

Shewchuk, George, *Rose Gardening on the Prairies.*

ABOVE LEFT: *The blooms of 'Pierre de Ronsard' (on the arch) repeat through summer and autumn.*
LEFT: *Roses make an excellent addition to a mixed border.*

Hardiness Zone Map

This map shows Canada divided into zones of expected minimum winter temperatures, which may limit the survival of cultivated plants. This system of Plant Hardiness Zones was originally developed by the US Department of Agriculture. The coldest zone is Zone 1, corresponding to a subarctic climate such as central Canada or Siberia; the warmest zone is Zone 12, which covers much of the equatorial tropics.

Each zone covers a range of 10 Fahrenheit degrees (5.5 Celsius degrees), as shown in the accompanying table (the Celsius rounded to the nearest degree). Zone 10 is the lowest zone in which frost and snow are not normally experienced.

For each rose listed in this book, both a minimum and maximum zone are indicated, for example Zones 4–9 for *Rosa* 'Peace'. This means that the rose will survive the average winter frosts expected in at least the warmer parts of Zone 4, in which temperatures fall below –20°F; but that it will also grow reasonably well in zones up to at least the cooler parts of Zone 9, where winter minimums are above 20°F. In fact, most roses will tolerate Zone 4 and above, while only the winter-hardy varieties will endure Zones 2 and 3. If you live in Zones 2–4, planting new roses in sites where there is falling cool air may bring disaster because the frosts are more severe. Wind is a great enemy of all plants but especially in frigid climates, so the protection provided by walls, shrubs, and fences may minimize the damage of gales or blizzards. Roses grown in Zones 4 and 5 will often require protection in winter to prevent excessive dieback. Giving a maximum zone goes beyond the original intent of the Plant Hardiness Zones, but we believe it serves a useful purpose, in that most roses have definite limits as to how warm a climate they will tolerate.

These zones indicate only one part of a plant's climatic requirements. Note that Zones 9–12 do not occur in Canada, but many of the roses may be grown in greenhouses.

Zone	°F	°C
1	below -50	below -46
2	-50 to -40	-46 to -40
3	-40 to -30	-40 to -34
4	-30 to -20	-34 to -29
5	-20 to -10	-29 to -23
6	-10 to 0	-23 to -18
7	0 to 10	-18 to -12
8	10 to 20	-12 to -7

Hardiness zones are based on the average minimum winter temperature for each zone.

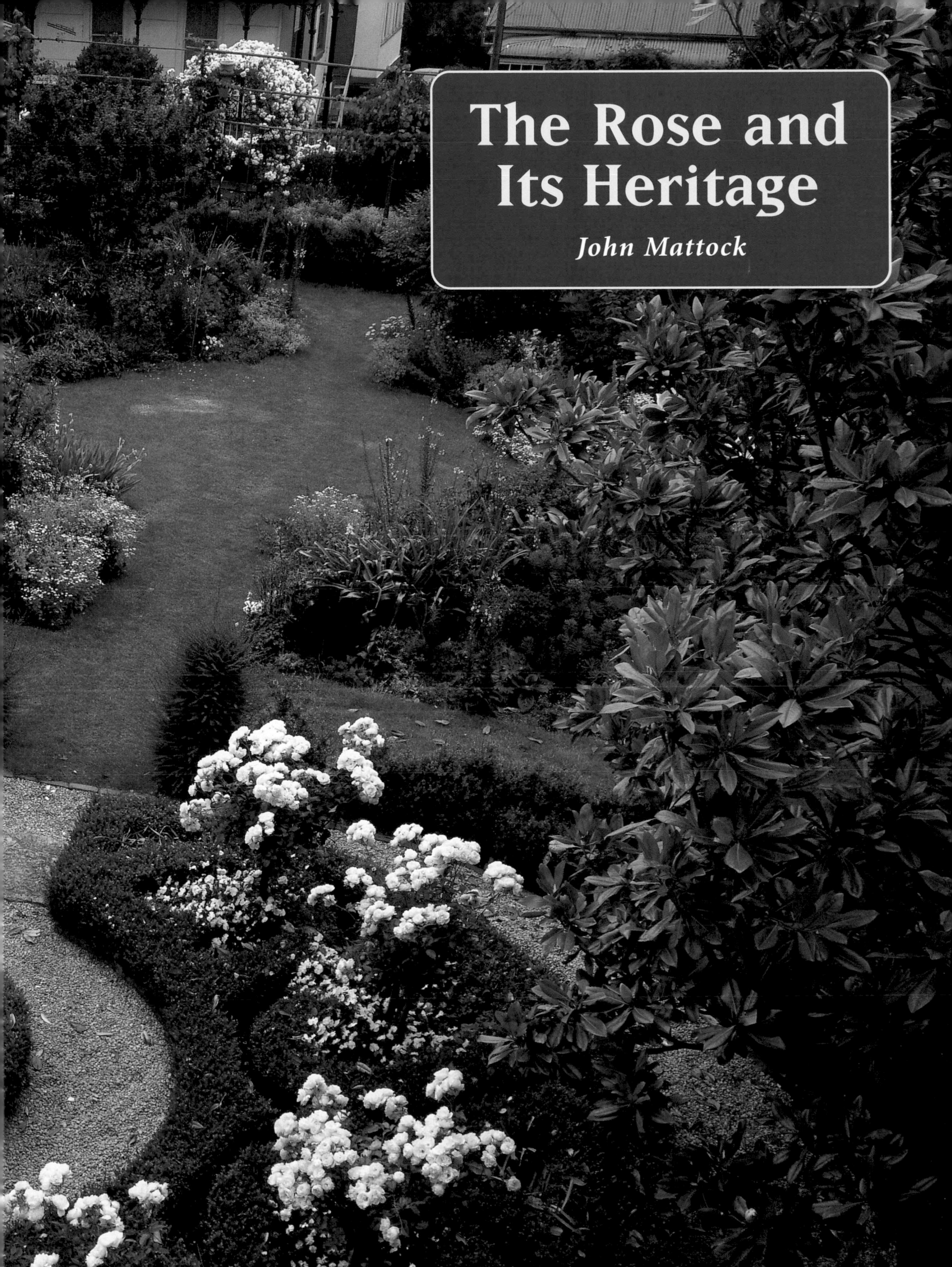

The Rose and Its Heritage

John Mattock

The History of the Rose

The rose is a phenomenal plant and is rightly known as 'the world's favorite flower'. No other flower has ever experienced the same popularity that the rose has enjoyed in the last fifty years. In temperate climates, roses are more widely grown than any other ornamental plant, and as cut flowers they are forever in fashion.

It has been estimated that 150 million plants are purchased by gardeners worldwide every year, and sophisticated breeding programs have produced a plant that dominates the world's cut-flower market; the annual crop is calculated in tons. Roses have also made a tremendous contribution to the perfume industry.

Roses boast an ancient lineage, and they are intricately entwined in our history and culture.

As a motif, the rose has been and still is depicted in many national emblems. It has been adopted by countless political factions, and even by businesses and several international events.

THE ORIGINS OF CULTIVATED ROSES

Roses species have a natural distribution throughout most parts of the Northern Hemisphere. Paleontologists inform us that they became established in the Tertiary Period, which began 70 million years ago. This means that the ancestors of the rose predate the evolution of humans.

Europe and the Middle East— the Dawn of Rose Breeding

Well before the Christian Era, the transportation of useful plants had played an essential part in the expansion of civilizations. The sprawling Roman Empire together with the excursions of Alexander the Great in Asia introduced many species never seen before in the Middle East and Europe. The dog rose *(Rosa canina)*, for example, was long thought to be a native of Britain, but was in fact brought there by the Romans.

By about AD 1200 the first five groups of domesticated roses had already begun to evolve in cultivation: Albas, Centifolias, Damasks, Gallicas and Scots Roses.

The Far East—the Birthplace of the Modern Garden Rose

Although rose growing enjoyed high popularity in the gardens of Europe for many hundreds of years, it was not until the end of the eighteenth century, with the discovery of *R. chinensis* in China, that a major step forward was achieved. The revolutionary characteristic of this rose is its ability to flower repeatedly from early summer to late autumn.

Some commentators have used the term 'perpetual flowering' but this can be misinterpreted and used too literally. 'Parson's Pink China',

'Slater's Crimson China', 'Hume's Blush Tea-scented China' and 'Parks' Yellow Tea-scented China'—the first cultivated varieties—opened up a new vista of roses with a modern classical shape, a true crimson color with a very pale hint of the early yellows and a repeat-flowering performance. The Far East became the birthplace of the Modern Garden Rose, and the rest is history.

East Meets West

The introduction of roses from the Far East coincided rather neatly with the advent of modern breeding techniques. Although the sexual function of the flower, in particular the function of the anthers and stigma, had been revealed in the seventeenth century, this discovery was not used in practical plant breeding for another two hundred years. Before this time, 'primitive' rose breeders would place two distinct varieties in pots together when both were in full bloom; they knew that there was a reasonable chance that the plants would cross-breed and produce seedlings with shared characteristics of the two parents.

In the early part of the nineteenth century, hybridists, primarily French amateurs, began a planned breeding program with very gratifying results. This was quickly followed up with some enthusiasm by rose-growing devotees all around the world. Soon, rose breeding without first planning the parentage became unthinkable.

The subsequent progeny produced were identified by groups usually named after their town or country of origin, the hybridist and, in some cases, a wealthy patron. Thus, collective terms such as Bourbons, Noisettes, Hybrid Perpetuals and Portlands came into existence with varying degrees of success. Eventually, the collective term Hybrid Teas was coined; 1867 is the date usually quoted when this modern group became a recognizable entity. Since that time, Hybrid Teas (also known as Large-flowered Roses), have progressed from strength to strength.

The Last Fifty Years

The early 1950s was a decisive time in the history of the rose. Gardening for leisure, rather than for food, became increasingly popular, and this coincided with the release of a new rose variety called 'Peace'. It is difficult to convey the impact this rose had on gardeners—simply put, everybody was growing it! 'Peace' almost single-handedly advanced the popularity of the rose out of all proportion to any other garden plant.

In the last decade there have been many new schools of thought on the role of the rose in the garden. No longer are we subjected to endless formal flowerbeds solely devoted to this single genus. It is not that gardeners have lost their appreciation of these superb blooms, rather it is that they have discovered how wonderful roses can look when grown informally among other plants such as clematis, honeysuckles, delphiniums, lavender, spring bulbs and geraniums.

Flower painting was popular in the nineteenth century. This is 'Princesse Mary of Cambridge'.

Although disease still rears its ugly head on certain occasions, the rose has become a much more adaptable plant; varieties are available that can be grown as shrubs, climbers, ground covers or in pots. Nowadays, the rose has a place in every garden, even the smallest back yard, and it is telling that the Patio Rose 'Sweet Dream' is one of the best-selling roses today.

THE ROSE IN HISTORY

As with most plants that have long been closely associated with the history of people, the rose has become deeply ingrained in our culture and beliefs. The Romans, who originally cultivated the rose as a medicinal plant, also used the blooms to enhance their festivities.

The Greeks, however, accepted the rose as a complement to the progress of their culture. Whenever a secret meeting was held, the Greeks used roses to decorate the ceilings of their conference rooms. This indicated that everything discussed was confidential, which is the origin of the phrase *sub rosa*.

In fifteenth century England, roses were chosen to represent the two rival royal factions: the white rose of the House of York (see 'White Rose of York') and the red rose of the House of Lancaster (see 'Apothecary's Rose'). The heraldic Tudor Rose emerged as the emblem of royalty. More recently, roses have been used as motifs to further the aspirations of political parties and national sporting teams.

THE ROSE IN THE ECONOMY

The rose was first introduced for its medicinal attributes: rosehips are a valuable source of vitamin C. Sadly, the specific uses of roses are never mentioned.

It is as a cut flower that the rose excels as an economic plant. Many millions of stems are cut and despatched every day. The center of this trade was originally in Aalsmeer in The Netherlands, where an extremely sophisticated distribution system was able to supply practically all the flower markets of the world. Intercontinental transport has now eliminated much of this trade; it is, for example, common practice for roses to be cut, graded and packaged in Kenya and to be on sale in the UK within 24 hours. The world's principal cut-rose nurseries are in The Netherlands, Denmark, Israel, Kenya, Zimbabwe, California and Colombia.

How Roses are Classified

The rose family, Rosaceae, is a large collection of many genera, with representatives from all over the world. They include many ornamental plants like spiraeas, cinquefoils and cotoneasters, and a great number of valuable crops, such as apples, plums, cherries, strawberries and quinces.

The group of true roses is known as the genus *Rosa*. It is made up of about 140 species: 95 of these are of Asian origin, 18 are North American and the remainder are from Europe and northwest Africa. Remarkably, no rose species have ever been found in the Southern Hemisphere.

ABOVE: *The introduction of 'Peace' in 1942 led to a sharp rise in the popularity of roses.*
RIGHT: *'Raubritter', a spectacular Modern Shrub Rose, grows informally here with* Convolvulus sabatius.
BELOW: *The green area denotes the natural distribution of the genus* Rosa.

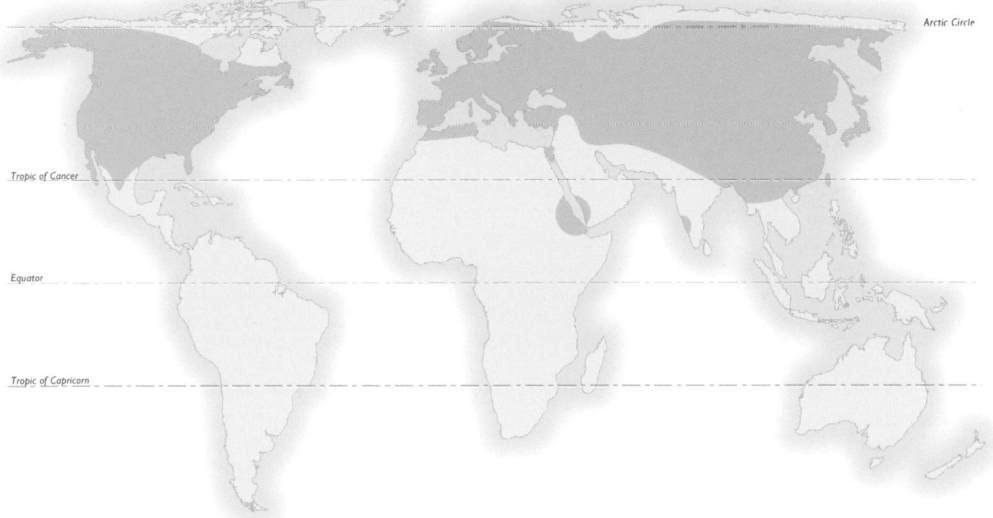

CLASSIFICATION SYSTEMS

In recent years, several attempts have been made to pigeonhole all the rose varieties available into an array of different categories. There are three principal institutions that have attempted this exercise, all with varying degrees of success.

The World Federation of Rose Societies has produced the most comprehensive, descriptive and wordy list. However, it has very little relevance to practical use, such as to nurseries who want to compile an easily read and informative catalogue.

The American Rose Society has compiled a classification system that is closely allied to the requirements of exhibitors and compilers of rose show schedules, although the botanical input is slightly misconceived. The American Rose Society also publishes *Modern Roses*, which is a comprehensive list of rose names.

The British Association Representing Breeders has published a list that is very relevant to hybridists. It is the work of the late Jack Harkness, and is probably the most succinct, but it is beginning to show signs of age and will probably have to be revised very soon.

The majority of rose gardeners simply want to grow good plants, and have little use for the complex botanical classification of the many thousands of rose cultivars. To this end, a simplified version of the World Federation of Rose Societies' system has been used in this book, which has been specifically designed to help the ordinary person answer some very basic questions about the size, shape, growth habit and flowering of popular roses.

BOTANICA'S ROSES
Rose Classes

ROSES

Modern Garden Roses
- **Bush Roses**
  - Large-flowered/Hybrid Tea
  - Cluster-flowered/Floribunda
  - Patio/Dwarf Cluster-flowered
  - Polyantha
- **Shrub Roses**
  - Modern Shrub
  - Hybrid Rugosa
  - Ground Cover
- **Climbing Roses**
  - Rambler
  - Large-flowered Climber
  - Cluster-flowered Climber
- **Miniature**
  - Climbing Miniature
  - Miniature

Old Garden Roses
- **Non-climbing**
  - Gallica
  - Damask
  - Centifolia (or Provence)
  - Moss
  - Alba
  - China
  - Tea
  - Portland
  - Bourbon
  - Hybrid Perpetual
  - Scots
  - Sweet Briar
  - Miscellaneous
- **Climbing**
  - Ayrshire
  - Climbing China
  - Laevigata
  - Sempervirens
  - Noisette
  - Boursault
  - Climbing Tea
  - Climbing Bourbon

Wild Roses

AMERICAN ROSE SOCIETY
Rose Classes

1	Alba	29	Hybrid Laevigata
2	Ayrshire	30	Hybrid Macounii
3	Bourbon	31	Hybrid Macrantha
4	Boursault	32	Hybrid Moyesii
5	Centifolia	33	Hybrid Musk
6	China	34	Hybrid Multiflora
7	Climbing Bourbon	35	Hybrid Nitida
8	Climbing China	36	Hybrid Nutkana
9	Climbing Floribunda	37	Hybrid Perpetual
10	Climbing Grandiflora	38	Hybrid Rugosa
11	Climbing Hybrid Perpetual	39	Hybrid Sempervirens
12	Climbing Hybrid Tea	40	Hybrid Setigera
13	Climbing Moss	41	Hybrid Spinosissima
14	Climbing Miniature	42	Hybrid Suffulta
15	Climbing Polyantha	43	Hybrid Tea
16	Climbing Tea	44	Kordesii
17	Damask	45	Large-flowered Climber
18	Eglantaria	46	Moss
19	Floribunda	47	Miniature
20	Gallica	48	Miscellaneous Old Garden Rose
21	Grandiflora	49	Noisette
22	Hybrid Alba	50	Portland
23	Hybrid Bracteata	51	Polyantha
24	Hybrid Blanda	52	Rambler
25	Hybrid Bourbon	53	Shrub
26	Hybrid China	54	Species
27	Hybrid Foetida	55	Tea
28	Hybrid Hugonis		

WORLD FEDERATION OF ROSE SOCIETIES
Rose Classes

MODERN GARDEN ROSES

1	Modern Shrub Recurrent Large-flowered	17	Large-flowered Climber Non-recurrent
2	Modern Shrub Recurrent Cluster-flowered	18	Cluster-flowered Climber Non-recurrent
3	Ground-cover Recurrent	19	Climbing Miniature Non-recurrent
4	Large-flowered		
5	Cluster-flowered		**OLD GARDEN ROSES**
6	Dwarf Cluster-flowered	20	Alba
7	Polyantha	21	Bourbon
8	Miniature	22	Boursault
9	Modern Shrub Non-Recurrent Large-flowered	23	China
		24	Damask
10	Modern Shrub Non-recurrent Cluster-flowered	25	Gallica
		26	Hybrid Perpetual
11	Ground-cover Non-recurrent	27	Moss
		28	Portland
12	Rambler Recurrent	29	Provence (Centifolia)
13	Large-flowered Climber Recurrent	30	Sweet Briar
		31	Tea
14	Cluster-flowered Climber Recurrent	32	Ayrshire
		33	Climbing Bourbon
15	Climbing Miniature Recurrent	34	Climbing Boursalt
		35	Climbing Tea
16	Rambler Non-recurrent	36	Noisette
		37	Sempervirens

WILD ROSES

38	Wild Roses Non-climbing
39	Wild Roses Climbing

BRITISH ASSOCIATION REPRESENTING BREEDERS
Rose Classes

1	Species and Groups
2	China
3	Noisette
4	Tea
5	Hybrid Tea
6	Floribunda
7	Florishrub
8	Miniature
9	Patio
10	Climbing Hybrid Tea
11	Climbing Floribunda
12	Climbing Miniature
13	Polyantha
14	Climbing Polyantha
15	Hybrid Musk
16	Wichuraiana Rambler
17	Wichuraiana Carpet
18	Wichuraiana Shrub
19	Gallica
20	Damask
21	Centifolia
22	Moss
23	Portland
24	Bourbon
25	Hybrid Perpetual
26	English
27	Scotch
28	Alba
29	Sweet Briar
30	Rugosa

TYPES OF WILD ROSE

The true species roses are often known as Wild Roses. Botanically, they are classified into four subgenera. Although these divisions are of little use to the practical gardener, they are of interest to anyone interested in the origins of garden roses.

Hulthemia

This very small subgenus from western Asia contains *Hulthemia persica* and *H. hardii*, which were used in Jack Harkness' breeding program and are being progressed by several other hybridists. They still have a long way to go before any forms are commercially viable.

Hesperhodes

This interesting group of only two species is native to southwestern USA. They are repeat-flowering and the hips show a remarkable affinity to gooseberry fruit.

Platyrhodon

Originating in southeastern China, this group contains *R. roxburghii*, which is more often called the chestnut rose because its hips resemble chestnuts.

Eurosa

Most rose species belong to this subgenus, which is itself divided into ten groups:

Banksianae is a group of six rose species. They are all climbers originating in China. The most popular is *R. banksiae lutea*, the yellow Banksian rose, a vigorous, almost thornless climber with sprays of very small, very double flowers. It is also one of the earliest roses to come into flower.

Laevigatae is a group of five species native to southeastern China. One of these, *R. laevigata* 'Cherokee Rose', has become so naturalized in southern USA that it is considered indigenous.

Bracteatae is a small group of three listed varieties. The most famous is 'Mermaid', an almost evergreen, very vigorous climber with large and repeat-flowering, single, sulfur yellow flowers. *R. bracteata*, a native of China, has become naturalized in frost-free areas of the USA.

Pimpinellifoliae is composed of eighteen species. Many of these are garden varieties. The most popular is the brilliant yellow 'Canary Bird', which originated in China.

Gallicanae forms the backbone of the European Old Garden Roses. It is a truly historical group, and the Centifolias, Moss Roses, Damasks and Gallicas all belong to this group.

Caninae is another European group. Curiously, it has contributed very little to the development of the cultivated rose.

Carolinae is exclusive to North America. *R. virginiana* is probably its most famous member; one of the prettiest shrubs in the garden today. It has never been developed.

Cinnamomea (Cassiorhodon) is a large group that includes many diverse species, such as *R. moyesii* and *R. rugosa*. Their principal contribution to

ABOVE: *The Wild Rose* Rosa multiflora cathayensis, *showing its characteristic light pink flowers.*
RIGHT: *'Dupontii' is an Old Garden Rose probably derived from a* Rosa gallica *and* R. moschata *cross.*

garden roses comes from the diversity of shape and the quality of the hips.

Synstylae were involved in the development of Cluster-flowered and Rambler Roses.

Chinenses is exclusive to China, and was the primary source of repeat-flowering in Modern Garden Roses. They have also contributed to the classical flower form, which is popular today.

TYPES OF OLD GARDEN ROSE

Grown in the gardens of Europe and Asia for many hundreds of years, Old Garden Roses were originally derived from Wild Roses.

Further changes came about with hybridization; travellers and adventurers brought species together that would never have met naturally. Through a continued process of mutation, selection and crossing over, many beautiful new roses came into existence.

Gallica Roses

The main member of this predominantly European and western Asian group is *R. gallica*, which has single red flowers. Gallica Roses have become known as the finest of the Old Garden Roses, and they flower once in summer.

Damask Roses

These were probably once prevalent in Damascus, hence the name. The Summer Damasks, which flower once only in summer, are derived from crosses between the Gallica Roses and *R. phoenicea*.

Hybridization of Gallica Roses with *R. moschata* produced the very similar Autumn Damasks,

which were the only Old Garden Roses of their time to deliver a limited second flowering.

Centifolia (or Provence) Roses

These 'one hundred-petalled roses' were raised in the seventeenth century by Dutch hybridists. They can be seen in the great Dutch flower paintings of that period. They flower for a brief period in summer.

Moss Roses

These are really aberrant Centifolia Roses, which appeared in the mid-seventeenth century. They have a mossy excrescence on the stems and the sepals. In the course of time, they became very popular. They are only once-flowering.

Alba Roses

Also known as 'white roses', the Albas make noble, once-flowering shrubs. The leaves have a characteristic blue-green appearance. The famous 'White Rose of York' is an Alba Rose.

China Roses

In China and east Asia, an extremely significant group of roses had developed in isolation: they flowered repeatedly throughout summer and autumn, not just in summer. In the late eighteenth and nineteenth centuries, four kinds in particular were brought to Europe, which culminated in the creation of the Modern Garden Roses.

Tea Roses

Developed from two tea-scented Chinas, a whole new repeat-flowering race called Tea Roses was introduced with beautiful and graceful blooms. They were grown mainly in France at first, since they are somewhat tender and unsuited to colder climates because of their *R. gigantea* ancestry.

Portland Roses

This repeat-flowering group is the result of a Gallica, Damask, Centifolia and China cross. The group is named for the Duchess of Portland.

Bourbon Roses

These were the first repeat-flowering roses to be created from the Chinas. This cross occurred initially on the Île de Bourbon in the Indian Ocean, hence the name of the group.

Hybrid Perpetual Roses

This repeat-flowering group was the result of intense hybridization and selection, mainly in

open-field cultivation. Hybrid Perpetuals were the dominant class of roses in Victorian England, and they bear a close affinity to Bourbons, from which they are derived.

Scots Roses

These hardy hybrids of *R. spinosissima* originated from northern Europe. They enjoyed a brief spell of popularity in the eighteenth century as bedding roses, flowering once only in summer.

Sweet Briar Roses

Developed from *R. eglanteria*, these non-repeat-flowering roses are valued for their small, apple-scented leaflets. Most Sweet Briars originate from the late nineteenth century onwards.

Ayrshire Roses

This group of rambling roses is apparently descended from *R. arvensis*, a trailing species of European hedgerows. They seem to have originated in Scotland, possibly by crossing with Sempervirens Roses. They do not repeat-flower.

Laevigata Roses

This small group of once-flowering, semi-rambling roses from China have become indigenous to the southern USA. They are characterized by dark green leaves and large, hooked thorns.

Sempervirens Roses

This small group of once-flowering ramblers are descendants of *R. sempervirens*, commonly known as the evergreen rose. All Sempervirens Roses have inherited this trait, being able to hold their foliage into winter.

LEFT: *The Bourbons were the first repeat-flowering roses to be bred from the Chinas. Seen here are the very double blooms of 'Reine Victoria'.*
BELOW: *Two lovely Cluster-flowered Roses, 'Allotria' (red) and 'Ivory Fashion' (white).*

Noisette Roses

This race of repeat-flowering climbers was developed by Philippe Noisette of Charleston, South Carolina. He introduced them in France when he moved there in 1817.

Boursault Roses

Originally raised by the distinguished French gardener who gave them his name, this small group of rambling roses was once thought to be derived from *R. pendulina* and *R. chinensis*, but because of their almost thornless stems and non-repeating blooms, some experts place them as derivatives of *R. blanda*.

TYPES OF MODERN GARDEN ROSE

Modern Garden Roses became possible when roses from China were brought back to Europe by traders and adventurers in the eighteenth and nineteenth centuries. Their value was recognized immediately, as they flowered regularly through the warmer months, unlike most of the European roses that only flowered once in early summer. The bush roses are the most significant of the Modern Garden Roses, and these are the ones people are most likely to grow in their gardens.

Large-flowered (or Hybrid Tea) Roses

In 1867, a new rose called 'La France' was introduced, bred by Jean-Baptiste Guillot. It was the first in a long line of Hybrid Teas, which later became known as Large-flowered Roses. Their principal characteristic is a large flower produced either singly or in small clusters of two or three. Another French grower, Pernet-Ducher, raised brilliant deep yellow, copper and bicolored Large-flowered Roses at the beginning of the twentieth century. The introduction of 'Peace' in 1942 really increased the rose's popularity with gardeners. In 1960, 'Tropicana' (syn. 'Super Star') burst on to the scene with its brilliant luminescent vermilion flowers; many progeny of this famous cultivar have been developed since.

Cluster-Flowered (or Floribunda) Roses

A consequence of crossing Large-flowered Roses with *R. multiflora*, a species characterized by large flower clusters, a very free-flowering bush rose was produced. For a long time, this category enjoyed a variety of names, which began with Polyantha Roses and finally Cluster-flowered Roses. They share the same broad color spectrum as Large-flowered Roses.

As many crosses have been made between Large-flowered and Cluster-flowered Roses, it has become more and more difficult to distinguish between them. In the USA, these in-between roses are often classified as Grandifloras.

Patio (or Dwarf Cluster-flowered) Roses

Almost custom made for the small garden, some nurseries like to describe Patio Roses as Dwarf Cluster-flowered Roses, although they have smaller flowers and leaves: a feature more akin to the perfection of Miniature Roses. Patio Roses freely produce bunches of well-formed flowers. They are sold in some countries as 'sweetheart' roses, and they are also easy to train as standards.

Polyantha Roses

'Pâquerette' is generally accepted as the first of the Polyantha Roses, introduced in 1875 by Jean-Baptiste Guillot. This Greek name literally means 'many flowers'. Although they are not much grown these days, some, like 'The Fairy', have never really lost their popularity.

Modern Shrub Roses

There are those roses that are perhaps a little bigger, more vigorous and spreading than bush roses and defy attempts to classify simply. These plants are called Modern Shrubs. They range in color and fragrance, and because they are easy to grow they are popular with both beginning rose growers and experienced rosarians.

Modern Shrub Roses are often further divided into more specific categories. Hybrid Musks were released in 1913 by the Reverend J. H. Pemberton. They are vigorous roses with attractive flowers. English Roses were bred specifically by David Austin to capture the fragrance and charm of Old Garden Roses on plants that also have the vigor, health, color range and repeat-flowering of Modern Garden Roses.

Hybrid Rugosa Roses

These attractive and large shrub roses are related to *R. rugosa*, an oriental species noted for its wrinkled, or rugose foliage. Hybrid Rugosas are noted for their hardiness and strong resistance to disease.

Ground Cover Roses

This group has been instrumental to roses being used to enhance the environment, whether in large public plantings or to give color to parts of the garden once considered inhospitable. The majority are repeat-flowering. 'Kent' was voted the best introduction of the last ten years.

Miniature Roses

The history of Miniature Roses is a mysterious one. Records reveal that a miniature form of rose was known about 170 years ago, and it was undoubtedly a miniature type of China Rose. By the 1850s it was a popular pot rose that could be propagated from seed, but it then passed into obscurity.

In 1917, a miniature species was found growing wild in Switzerland. It was named *R. rouletii* after its discoverer, Colonel Roulet. The first hybrid of this rose, called 'Peon', came from Jan de

ABOVE: *The ever-popular Polyantha Rose 'The Fairy' was first introduced in 1932.*
RIGHT: *'Wedding Day', a delightful Rambler, produces huge clusters of blooms.*

Wink in 1936. It was later marketed in the USA as 'Tom Thumb' and is still very popular. The work of Ralph Moore of the USA brought Miniature Roses into a league of their own. A legend in the rose world, his innovations have produced some extraordinary results such as 'Fairy Moss', 'Dresden Doll' and 'Lemon Delight'.

Climbing Miniatures can be the backbone of the small garden, lifting the eye and giving height. Some excellent varieties include 'Laura Ford', 'Nice Day' and 'Warm Welcome'.

Rambler Roses

With the introduction of *R. wichuraiana* and *R. multiflora* from Asia, this type of plant quickly became popular and appealed to the Victorian sense of big, sensuous and brash. Some of the most popular varieties, 'Albertine', 'American Pillar' and 'Dorothy Perkins', are still available.

Climber Roses

These roses are classified as either Large-flowered Climbers or Cluster-flowered Climbers. They are usually bred from bush roses, which have the peculiar tendency to throw climbing forms, properly called climbing mutations, and often have the word 'Climbing' added to their cultivar name. 'Climbing Mrs Sam McGredy' and 'Climbing Ena Harkness' are two examples, but there are many more, and they all share one impediment: they are only summer flowering. Their vigor, however, is prodigious and the quality of

the flower is very high. Without doubt, future advances in the flowering of climbing roses will have a tremendous impact in the small garden of tomorrow.

Recent Developments of the Modern Garden Rose

GENETICS AND ROSE BREEDING

The science of heredity is known as genetics. Significant recent advances in this field have helped plant breeders understand the inheritance of plant characteristics. Breeders are now able to be much more specific and innovative in the development of new varieties.

Occasionally, a cultivar will spontaneously produce a different color or form of growth. These are generally called sports, and are caused by mutation. Curiously, some cultivars are more prone to this deviation than others.

There are many examples of color mutations, many of which are never very successful. 'Queen Elizabeth' has pale red, white and yellow sports and the Patio Rose 'Sweet Dream' has many variations.

Climbing mutations are rare, a phenomenon to be valued. The odds of a climbing shoot appearing on a bush or shrub rose are astronomical, but if this does occur, the stem must be propagated vegetatively, usually by budding. Climbing sports tend to be summer-flowering only.

ABOVE: *The distinctive leaves, rosehips and flowers of the Hybrid Rugosa 'Frau Dagmar Hartopp'.*
LEFT: *When this previously unknown color was raised in 1960, 'Tropicana' became very popular.*

DOMINANT VARIETIES IN THE DEVELOPMENT OF THE ROSE

When studying the history of the cultivated rose, it is interesting to attempt to trace the influence of certain introductions on hybridizing. Initially, there is the tremendous influence of the China Roses, which introduced repeat-flowering to Western Europe, and at the end of the nineteenth century, *R. foetida* was responsible for the introduction of bright yellows and bicolors.

In the 1920s and 1930s the breeding houses of Dickson and McGredy used very reliable seedlings to perpetuate certain dominant characteristics. One of the seedlings raised by Sam McGredy's father contributed to the development of the enormously popular Large-flowered Rose 'Peace'.

Bred by Francis Meilland in 1942, 'Peace' was one of a handful of new varieties that went on to have tremendous influence. Concerted efforts were made to further develop these lines, although it took some time before an effective successor was bred from 'Peace'.

Many other momentous rose varieties have been raised over the last one hundred years. For example, 'Tropicana' (syn. 'Super Star') was an extremely popular luminous vermilion rose, and it was superseded ten years later by the even brighter 'Alexander'. 'Silver Jubilee', introduced in 1977, gave rise to a proliferation of very free-flowering Large- and Cluster-flowered Roses.

The Form and Fragrance of Roses

PLANT FORMS

Many aspects of the growth of roses are determined by climate. Many catalogue descriptions, therefore, can be quite variable, often only relevant to a particular country (or state).

Generally described, roses are shrubs that range from just a few inches to giant climbers and ramblers with the potential to grow up to 50 ft (15 m). They have upright, arching, scrambling or occasionally trailing stems. The usually deciduous leaves are alternately arranged, composed of an odd number of leaflets and are borne on generally prickly or thorny stems. The flowers are either carried singly or in corymbs of up to one hundred blooms; each flower has numerous stamens, styles and petals (most Wild Roses have single flowers with five petals). After flowering, the receptacle becomes fleshy to form a hip, which encloses a few to many seeds.

Thorns

Usually a consistent characteristic among roses, thorns may be absent altogether on some varieties. Those roses with *R. pimpinellifolia* and *R. rugosa* ancestry tend to have very small, needle-shaped bristles, and Large- and Cluster-flowered varieties have wing-shaped thorns that can be very large.

Leaves

Rose leaves mostly have five leaflets, as in Large- and Cluster-flowered Roses. Seven leaflets are typical of lines with *R. wichuraiana* and *R. multiflora* in their ancestry, and many Asiatic species can have as many as fifteen leaflets and appear almost fernlike. When bruised, the leaves of *R. eglanteria* and *R. primula* give a strong fragrance of apple and incense respectively.

Flower Shape and Size

Flowers are described as either being borne singly or in clusters. There is a tremendous variety of flower shapes and sizes; they are all described in relation to the number of petals and the way these are arranged. Single blooms mostly have five petals, and the double forms are divided into three categories: semi-double (10–20 petals), double (20–40 petals) and very double (over 40 petals).

Hips

Rosehips come in a variety of shapes and sizes, but are more easily classified into three types: subglobose, the hips so typical of roses with *R. rugosa* ancestry; globose, the small round hips usually associated with the majority of bush roses; and finally the dramatic flask-shaped hips so splendidly borne by descendants of *R. moyesii*.

FRAGRANCE IN ROSES

Modern physiologists emphasize that appreciation of scent is very subjective. In short, no two human beings have the same reaction to scent, which reveals a lot when it comes to explaining the enormous divide that exists between people when describing scent. With roses, what one person may describe as a sweet fragrance, another may pass off as a fetid odor.

Breeding for scent

Scent is a recessive factor that is easily lost through cross breeding. Recent successes by Sam McGredy suggest that this problem has been partially resolved, but not without a diminution of the color range. A long-established assumption that scent and a proneness to mildew go hand in hand has been disproved by Kordes in Germany: some of their very healthy Large-flowered Roses also have a wonderful scent. The Bourbons are the prime example of a class that collectively has much fragrance. 'Paul Neyron', a Hybrid Perpetual with a subtle scent of apple and lemon, is surely one of the sweetest smelling roses available today.

Attar of Roses

The essential oil of rose petals—attar of roses—is a precious commodity. In the Kazanlik Valley in Bulgaria, some 10 000 acres (4050 hectares) of land are cultivated with *R. damascena trigintipetala* (see 'Kazanlik'). The rose buds are harvested between sunrise and 10 a.m. in May and June, just as they are showing color before the essential oils dissipate. They are distilled almost immediately. An estimate for the quantities used is quite astronomical: about one million rose buds or 3 tons (3 tonnes) of flowers are required to produce just 2½ lbs (1.25 kg) of attar.

Potpourri

Rose petals also make a very good base for potpourri. They are collected during the heat of the day, sun dried and then stored in airtight containers to be used when required. Damask and Gallica Roses are very popular for this purpose, and some modern varieties, such as 'Fragrant Cloud' and 'Paul Sherville', are also suitable.

Some Famous Rose Gardens

There are very few gardens that have the reputation to be promoted on the quantity and quality of a single genus. The rose, however, enjoys so much celebrity that most countries in temperate regions can boast rose gardens that are well worth a visit.

Australia: Adelaide is rapidly becoming the rose capital of Australia. Its rose gardens are deserving of this title.

Austria: The rosarium at Baden near Vienna promotes the Austrian Rose Trials.

Canada: The Buchart Gardens in Vancouver demonstrate the wealth of the genus *Rosa*.

France: Paris has two famous rose gardens: Roseraie de l'Haÿ-les-Roses, which has tremendous historical significance, and Parc de Bagatelle, which holds the French Rose Trials.

Germany: The rosarium at Sangerhausen was once famed for having the world's most comprehensive collection. Sadly, it suffered from neglect under the East German regime, but it is well on the way to regaining its pre-war status.

The rose garden on Lake Konstanz enjoys a warm micro-climate, and the whole garden abounds with marvellous bougainvillea.

Zweibrücken has earned the nickname 'the City of Roses' because of its extremely successful rose garden.

Dortmund is presently the headquarters of the German Rose Society. The garden here is the home of the Baden-Baden Rose Trials.

Israel: The Wohl Rose Garden in Jerusalem is a perfect example of growing roses in an arid Mediterranean climate.

Italy: Cabriglea d'Arezzo, in the center of the Chianti Classico region, is the lifetime work of Professor Fineschi, an extremely distinguished Italian surgeon. Visitors are welcome, but a phone call is a courteous gesture.

New Zealand: The Parnell Gardens in Auckland include the Nancy Steen collection.

Republic of Ireland: St Anne's, on Dublin Bay, is the site of a fabulous rose garden. It is home to the Dublin Rose Trials.

Spain: The rose garden at the Parque de Oeste in Madrid is usually the first in Europe to be in full flower every spring.

Switzerland: With a backdrop of Lake Leman, the garden at Parc de la Grange is beautifully designed.

The Netherlands: The Westbroeckpark Rosarium in The Hague has a fine collection of new varieties. The Golden Rose of The Hague—a holy grail among rose breeders—is awarded here every year.

United Kingdom: The Gardens of the Rose at St Albans, the headquarters of the Royal National Rose Society, is home to the International Rose Trials, which are said to be the most rigorous in the world.

The Queen Mary Rose Garden in Regent's Park, London, is a demonstration of good municipal planting.

The Royal Horticultural Society's garden at Wisley in Surrey is beautifully kept, with a wide selection of all types of plants, not just roses. Rosemoor garden at Torrington in Devon has been planted with modern cultivars, as has the garden at Hyde Hall in Essex.

In Scotland, Aberdeen is known as the City of Roses, and in Northern Ireland the Lady Dixon Park has an immense selection of both historical roses and modern hybrids.

United States of America: The American Rose Center at Shreveport in Louisiana, the headquarters of the American Rose Society, boasts a well-structured and modern rose garden.

The Huntingdon Botanical Gardens in California has a wide selection of Old Garden Roses and a very fine botanical library.

The Brooklyn Botanic Gardens in New York and the Hershey Rose Gardens in Pennsylvania are just two examples of the wide variety of fine gardens across the USA.

The Future of the Rose

So how will the rose develop in the new millennium? Although the last one hundred years have seen an incredible development of the rose, it is not too hard to predict the next few years provided the objectives of rose breeders remain the same and there are no unexpected discoveries.

The development of a large shrub rose that freely bears high-quality blooms will probably be the first goal to be achieved. In fact many hybridists are well on the way to success, yet there is still a long way to go before they are a commercial proposition.

Fragrance and color are both a matter of fashion and will only be determined by the vagaries of change. Disappointingly, with the exception of an eagerly awaited blue rose and Sam McGredy's 'hand-painted' varieties, the gardening public has extremely conservative tastes. The perfect rose, according to public demand, is a Large-flowered Rose with classically shaped, red, yellow, pink or white, fragrant flowers that are also weatherproof and repeat-flowering. This has still to be achieved.

The greatest priority must go to the ultimate goal: freedom from disease. Most people today are not prepared to be slaves to the garden and there is a tremendous demand for a rose that is completely trouble free and demands the minimum of attention. This is not an impossible task, but it is fraught with impediments, such as the loss of flower quality.

There is a definite need to develop new types of rootstock. *R. laxa* may produce top-quality plants in some climates, but it is not very adaptable and an alternative needs to be found. Unfortunately, the search for a new rootstock has not proved fruitful in the last few years.

Only a fraction of the total number of rose species are used by hybridists. There must be around 140 species of Wild Roses, yet only about twenty have ever contributed to the development of the Modern Garden Rose. One certainty about the future of the rose is that there is still an extraordinary potential to be explored.

Roseraie de l'Haÿ-les-Roses, one of two famous rose gardens in Paris, has great historical significance.

Cultivating Roses

Lieutenant-Colonel Ken Grapes

The Myths and Misconceptions of Rose Cultivation

Roses are for enjoyment. They have a unique place in history, heraldry and literature and are a symbol of loyalty and love. It is not just for these reasons that roses have earned the tribute of 'The Queen of Flowers', but mainly because they are outstandingly good garden plants. How then can the maximum value and enjoyment be achieved from growing this model of excellence?

First and foremost, it must be emphasized that *roses are easy to grow*. One might not think so in view of the thousands of books, journals and articles that have been devoted to the business of growing roses over the past century. The myths and misconceptions that have grown up

The Gardens of the Rose at St Albans, the head-quarters of the UK Royal National Rose Society.

around this subject are a large part of its rich history. To understand this history is to understand that there is no mystery to growing roses.

Although roses are a very ancient genus—the UK Royal National Rose Society (RNRS) has some fossils of rose foliage considered to be many millions of years old—they were not commonly grown as ornamental garden plants until the early nineteenth century, particularly during the reign of Queen Victoria (1837–1901). The favorite roses of her time were the Hybrid Perpetuals, and with this popularity came the need for cultivation techniques—for their planting, feeding, training and pruning. Roses, they thought, needed the attention of a 'master' displaying considerable skills if they were to give of their best—perhaps one can see evolving here some form of Victorian job protection!

The Victorians worked out the best ways of growing their Hybrid Perpetuals, but at the same

time created the original rose-growing mystique or lore. Curiously, when looking at the tools and techniques of Victorian gardeners, there seems little actual difference from those of today. Yet the bulk of the roses grown today are quite different from those of the last century.

However, it is fair to say that the Victorians themselves did not make the subject too complicated. The great Dean Hole, first president of the RNRS, wrote an admirable *Book About Roses,* which went to many editions. Shorn of Victorian verbosity, the Dean set out clear and simple rules for growing roses. Where have we gone wrong since his time?

With the ever-increasing number of new roses and their cultivars, new techniques have been devised. As the millennium approaches, roses are probably the world's favorite flower. Everybody with a 'rosy axe' to grind has chipped in their own piece of expertise, along the lines of 'you

must do this and you must do that'—ever complicating what is, in fact, a matter of ease and simplicity. As a result, the general public's perception of roses is that they are complicated and tricky things to grow and look after.

Amateur rose societies, originally set up by members keen on exhibiting roses at shows, have not done much to alter this opinion; the distinguished Dean Hole was probably at the forefront of this. Although the Dean understood and wrote about roses for garden display, at heart he was an exhibitor, and the RNRS, over which he presided for 27 years, devoted much of its time and publications to the growing of roses for exhibition at shows. To some extent, exhibitor techniques still hold sway—all societies need exhibitors and they make the lovely shows which all enjoy— but it isn't necessary to follow demanding exhibitor techniques for good garden display.

Another reason for the adverse public perception of roses as good garden plants is because of the sheer conservatism of most gardeners. We either learned our gardening at our parent's knee, or we pick it up from books and magazines. In rose cultivation, there has seldom been any desire for experimentation or assessment of the established ways, to see if they are still valid and best. There have been plenty of trials by various government or scientific organizations, all aimed at solving problems for the professional grower, but apart from the chemical manufacturers who constantly seek more effective sprays and fertilizers, there has been little or no work to evaluate the techniques of the amateur gardener.

In recent years, all this has changed. The Royal National Rose Society (RNRS) and the American Rose Society (ARS) have both led the way in questioning every aspect of rose growing. They have been aided and abetted by the forward-looking consumer associations, who encourage the quest by always asking 'What if ...?'. Trials have encompassed planting, feeding, pruning, deadheading, searching for the most disease-resistant roses and more arcane matters such as soil sickness and the value of mulches. These trials, some of which have gone on for seven or more years, have been continued until the outcome becomes quite clear. Where useful lessons have been learnt from this process, they have been incorporated into the following sections of this chapter. Where there is any doubt, the old tried and tested methods have been retained.

Roses really are easy to grow and to look after. If the simple guidance in this chapter is followed, the gardener will be able follow the example of the Elizabethan poet Christopher Marlowe— 'I will make thee beds of roses and a thousand fragrant posies'.

PLANNING THE ROSE GARDEN

Home owners who inherit a garden with their new property are advised to see a summer through before making any major changes. The purpose of this is to get a proper 'feel' for the garden, and a clear idea of which plants are worth retaining in any new layout. They will also

Flat Single, semi-double and occasionally double flowers that are fully open and almost flat.

Cupped Open, single to double flowers with petals that curve out from the center.

High-centered Semi- to very double flowers with high, pointed centers that are tightly closed

Rosette Very double flowers with many slightly overlapping petals of different sizes.

Quartered-rosette Very double flowers with many overlapping petals packed into quarters.

Pompon Small and rounded, very double flowers filled with masses of tiny petals.

ROSE FLOWER SHAPES

be able to discover whether there are perennial weeds present, which can more easily be cleared before a new planting scheme is undertaken.

Garden owners who wish to redesign the area from scratch, such as purchasers of brand new houses, should also be in not too much of a hurry to get planting. Trees and shrubs in particular are not cheap, and are better planted after reflection on where the eventual shade will be cast. In some cases, it might be as well to hire a qualified garden designer. In this section are some general principles that should be considered before incorporating rose plantings in the new or redesigned garden.

THE USE OF ROSES IN GARDEN DESIGN

Roses come in an astonishing variety of shapes and sizes, which allows for great versatility in the garden: tiny roses can be grouped together and grown as focal points on their own, or in small containers or window boxes; low, spreading types are good for hanging baskets and larger containers; bush and shrub roses make fine hedges and screens, or can be grown in beds or mixed borders; climbing plants can be trained against walls and fences, or allowed to scramble up into even quite tall trees; and low, wide-growing varieties are useful for covering awkward places such as slopes, or for preventing the newspaper boy from riding his bicycle over the front garden! They can be used to complement any gardening style, be it relaxed cottage gardening or more formal bedding or courtyard schemes. In addition to this wonderful variety of plants are the blooms themselves. The flowers that roses bear come in a wide diversity of shape, color and—most importantly—scent.

Roses have a potentially long life, so it is very important that care be taken in their planting positions. Any rose that has been given a well-chosen site should flourish for many years, or even generations. There is a celebrated plant growing on the cathedral in Hildesheim, Germany, which is known to be over 900 years old.

PLANT ROSES WHERE THEY CAN RECEIVE PLENTY OF LIGHT

The main factor that will affect the planning of a new rose garden is sunlight. All plants need light for photosynthesis, the process that converts light into energy for growth. Roses do best in full sunshine, but conditions where they will receive around four hours of sunshine each day are perfectly satisfactory. This is not to say that roses cannot be grown in conditions with less light. Provided there is no dense shade, many roses will perform quite adequately in such positions, albeit with slightly less bloom. Climbing roses can be planted in the shade if they can reach up to flower in the sunshine.

A DRAFTY SITE CAN KILL A ROSE

Roses are tough and long-suffering plants, but they will not succeed in very cold, drafty spots, particularly as such places are often rather dry and out of the sun. In open and exposed conditions, it is advisable to provide some sort of windbreak, which could be either a solid fence or preferably a hedge or a planting of trees. A deciduous hedge is a surprisingly good windbreak, even in winter when the leaves have fallen. Care must be taken with the placing of solid fences, because in strong winds they can cause a great deal of turbulence on what is supposed to be the protected side.

A healthy specimen of the Large-flowered Rose 'Silver Jubilee'. Roses grow well in soil rich in organic matter.

WATER—THE IMPORTANCE OF IRRIGATION AND DRAINAGE SYSTEMS

Roses root quite deeply and do not need heavy watering. That said, the world is going through a spell of hot, dry summers, and water supplies are under increasing pressure from users. The installation of an irrigation system in the new (or old) garden will quickly repay the investment, particularly if use is made of drip hoses or buried 'leaky pipes' with a simple central control tap system for each particular area. A source of irrigation is also very important when a lot of plants are grown in containers. In high summer, these need watering at least once a day.

Where the garden is low lying or badly drained, it will be necessary to improve the drainage. The late Jack Harkness recommended the digging of a trial hole about 12 in (30 cm) deep in winter, which should then be filled with water. If the water soaks away in the following 24 hours, all should be well. If not, some form of drainage will be necessary. There are several ways in which this can be achieved, from the incorporation of garden compost, grit or other lightening material into the soil, to the digging of trenches and installation of clay pipes or similar drainage systems. The latter method requires quite a lot of hard work, and with large gardens, the easiest and most economical way is probably to hire a small excavator from the local DIY store. An alternative for those not inclined to major earthworks is to create raised beds with retaining walls, which may be made from brick, stone or old railway sleepers.

THE SOIL MUST BE DEEP AND RICH IN ORGANIC MATTER

Roses like a soil that is deep enough for the roots to hold the plant firmly in place. Where the top-soil overlays hard and impervious subsoil, the subsoil may have to be broken up to allow the roots to penetrate. The trial hole drainage test described previously will indicate whether or not this is necessary.

Roses draw their energy from sunlight, and nutrition from the soil through the roots. An ideal soil for roses is rich in organic matter— decayed vegetable matter or humus. Organic matter is usually introduced to the soil by the incorporation of manure, compost or mulches. Such soil is spongy in texture, holds water and encourages worms and bacteria to operate to the benefit of the plants. Levels of organic matter and reserves of plant food need to be replenished from time to time, and this is dealt with later.

There is a widely held belief that one must have a clay soil to grow good roses. This is quite untrue. Good roses can be grown in clay soils because they tend to retain moisture and nutrients, but they can be well grown in most other soils as well. Clay soils are hard work to dig, but if this is done in the winter, frosts will break down the clods into a much more workable form.

Light, sandy soils are the easiest to work, but are probably the most difficult for successful rose growing. They tend to dry out easily and be quick draining; plant food leaches away with the draining water. These problems are overcome by thorough incorporation of organic material into the soil, and the application of thick layers of almost any mulching material.

STRONGLY ACIDIC OR ALKALINE SOILS ARE UNSUITABLE FOR ROSES

The acidity or alkalinity of a soil directly affects the ability of plants to take up food. It is measured by the pH scale, of which pH 7 is neutral: anything less than pH 7 is acidic, and anything greater than pH 7 is alkaline. Roses will grow quite satisfactorily in acid or alkaline conditions, providing they are not at either extreme. It is best to aim for a slightly acid pH, 6 to 6.5. Simple soil test kits are available from garden centers, which will give amateur gardeners a very good idea of the pH of their soil.

Very acidic soils can be remedied by the addition of powdered lime or spent mushroom compost, which has a high chalk content. High alkalinity can be reduced by the addition of peat or manure, or by applying sulphate of ammonia as part of the feeding process.

Some Wild Roses grow naturally in very alkaline, chalky soils. In a garden at Highdown, England, there is a vigorous Wild Rose that grows strongly from roots embedded in solid white chalk! It is sensible to seek advice on varieties when roses must be grown in such conditions.

THE TIMING OF FLOWERING DISPLAYS IS IMPORTANT IN GARDEN DESIGN

If all roses flowered all the time, planning an interesting rose garden with a changing display throughout the year could be difficult indeed. Perhaps it is as well that the majority of the Old Garden Roses flower only in mid-summer like their Wild counterparts, since earlier or later flowering displays can be planned around them. Many of the Ramblers are also 'once-flowerers'. Modern Garden Roses mostly flower from early summer until the first frosts and could be thought to offer better garden value, although devotees of the Old Garden Roses would never allow such a suggestion. For sheer flower power, Cluster-flowered bush and climbing varieties take a lot of beating.

COLOR AND SCENT, AND ITS PLACE IN THE PLAN

Old Garden Roses range from deep purple through crimson and pink to white. Modern Garden Roses are of every color except blue— and who would want a blue rose, it wouldn't somehow seem right! Hot colors, like reds, oranges and strong yellows, are best planted near the house with the cooler colors of white and pale pink, purple or crimson further away. It is also a good idea to plant strongly scented roses where they can be appreciated near doors and windows, and around patios and garden seats. White and pale-colored flowers are especially valuable because they stand out in the dusk, enhancing the pleasure of an evening drink or alfresco supper.

FORMAL VERSUS INFORMAL DISPLAYS

For many gardeners, roses can only be planted in formal beds laid out with neat paths and edging. Such traditionalists are advised to plant their roses in clumps of five or six roses of a single variety, and to avoid using lots of small beds; smaller groups invariably give the garden a messy and unsatisfactory appearance. Simple planting schemes of a single variety are usually more impressive and can look very attractive. It is also a good idea to use standard roses to give variation and height to rose beds, but it is important to surround them with bush roses to conceal their (rather ugly) stems and posts.

The informal gardener, whether possessed of a grand or a cottage garden, will find that the use of companion plants will add immeasurably to the delights of informal schemes. Shrub roses in particular, both large and small, lend themselves well to mixed plantings with other shrubs and herbaceous plants. Rambler Roses (particularly the new repeat-flowering types) with thin, lax stems provide height, interest and elegance, especially when used on pergolas and arches.

OTHER PLANTS THAT ASSOCIATE WELL WITH ROSES

In his book *The Art of Planting,* Graham Stuart Thomas observes that the colors of Modern Garden Roses tend to be mainly on the yellow side of the red spectrum, whereas most roses raised before 1900 tend to be on the blue side of that spectrum. Most Wild Roses, apart from *Rosa moyesii, R. foetida* and the early yellow-flowered species such as 'Canary Bird', also belong to the blue side.

This division of roses into two separate color groups forms a very useful guideline, which helps gardeners to choose other plants that will associate well with roses. Coppery or yellowish foliage colors look well with Modern Garden Roses, and gray or silver foliage looks best with Old Garden or Wild Roses. As a rule, purple and magenta-colored plants are not suitable companions for Modern Garden Roses, and bright orange-red flowers are best avoided with Old Garden and Wild Roses.

The number of other plants that associate well with roses is almost limitless. They include clematis, especially the hybrids that flower in late summer, and the less vigorous honeysuckles. Both are glorious companions for Climber and Rambler Roses, in either contrasting or complementary color schemes. Honeysuckles add their appealing fragrance to that of scented roses, which is wonderful near doors and windows.

Herbaceous plants that are allowed to grow through or under roses add contrasting shapes, textures and colors. Spiky foxgloves are charming when they poke through shrub roses, and delphiniums and lupins add a similar statuesque dimension and contrast. Gray-foliaged plants are especially attractive and set off the richness of rose blooms to perfection. The gray form of the licorice plant *(Helichrysum petiolare),* for example, will spread under and through short-growing roses to give a solid and attractive base to mixed colors, which ties the planting into a harmonious whole. Many of the hardy geraniums combine well with roses as do self-seeding violas, deadnettles, lady's mantle, cosmos and some of the short polygonums. Even when not in flower, the foliage of geraniums can be neat and attractive. Santolinas and lavateras are also a pretty foil for roses.

Finally, there are spring bulbs, which not only provide color when the roses are possibly at their least attractive, but are also concealed by the burgeoning rose foliage when they have finished

RIGHT: *Two types of roses can be woven together to make a striking feature.*
BELOW: *Numerous other plants associate well with roses in mixed border displays.*

flowering. The bulbs can then stay in leaf as they build up the bulb for next season, without risk of premature removal by over-tidy gardeners.

Roses may also associate well with other roses, and can be interplanted to create superb displays. Climber and Rambler Roses, for example, can be woven together to charming effect, enhanced by the addition of a clematis when the roses have made sufficient growth.

FOLIAGE AND ROSEHIPS LENGTHEN A DISPLAY

Rose foliage varies considerably in color and texture and can be an attractive feature in the garden, even before the blooms appear. Colors vary from pale gray-green, through bright green to purple-bronze. Some roses, notably the Hybrid Rugosas, produce glorious autumn colors.

Most of the Wild Roses produce an array of hips in colors from yellow-green through red to

black. It is well worthwhile, towards the end of summer, to allow the last blooms to set hips, which may last well into winter. Many Modern Garden Roses will produce a splendid display of rosehips attractive to both garden and birds, and it causes no harm to the plants. The obsessive 'deadheader' will be deprived of this bonus.

ROSE BORDERS LOOK BEST WHEN EDGED

In both formal and informal plantings, maintenance will be easier where the roses and other plants can grow over a surrounding gravel or paved path. Where the surround is a lawn, a single row of small flagstones along the border will ensure that the plants look their best. It will also prevent damage by the lawnmower, and will avoid the need for edging the lawn.

How to Choose and Buy Roses

WHICH TO CHOOSE?

Since there is such a great variety of roses to choose from, in some countries thousands of different cultivars, how does one avoid picking poor varieties? There can be little doubt that some preliminary study will pay dividends here: decide on the type of planting required, such as formal, informal, climbing or ground cover. Once this is done it is best to consult the experts.

Most national rose or horticultural societies either run trials or publish appraisals of roses. The ARS and RNRS both give fair and unbiased opinions of roses in their publications, and produce lists of roses worthy of merit. These lists are aimed to help the novice gardener, and simply suggest varieties for particular locations in the garden. The UK Royal Horticultural Society gives its Award of Garden Merit to roses that have proved themselves to be good value garden plants. Be wary of growers' catalogues, however; the information is helpful, but it is wise to seek a second opinion as proud breeders sometimes understate the deficiencies of their creations!

CONFIRMATION OF THE CHOICE— FIND AN ESTABLISHED SPECIMEN

Although it may seem a bit tedious, it must be remembered that roses are long-lived, so this exercise is well worthwhile. The wise gardener, having first decided on the types and colors of the roses that are suitable, will then go to see established plants growing in a public or private garden, or nursery display garden, preferably one that is nearby. Only in this way can they be envisaged in one's own garden. Pictures in even the best catalogues and books do not always reproduce color correctly, and they can only describe growth habit, size and scent. The old military maxim that 'time spent on reconnaissance is never wasted' also applies to the selection of roses for the garden.

If possible, pay more than one visit to the garden or nursery to confirm that the selected varieties are the right height, size and color and, most importantly, are resistant to disease. When taking the (obligatory) sniff of the scent, examine the flowers for any discoloration due to sun or rain. All being well, the choice will have been made—now to acquire the plants.

ROSES FOR SALE ARE PRESENTED IN THREE DIFFERENT WAYS

Nowadays, roses can be bought in several ways. There are three types: bare-root, container-grown and pre-packed roses:

Bare-root plants have been lifted and despatched when they are dormant in winter. This is a very satisfactory and economical way to purchase roses, and they can be planted from mid-autumn to early spring. Watch out for shriveled or dried-out branches and roots. Such plants should be rejected.

Container-grown roses have been potted and grown on by the nursery. The best time to buy these is generally in late spring, or even mid-summer, when it is obvious from the new shoots that the plant is healthy and is growing well.

Pre-packed roses, like bare-root specimens, are also sold while the plants are dormant in winter. The roots are trimmed and usually wrapped in plastic, enclosing some compost. The stems may have been dipped in wax to help the plant retain moisture while it is distributed from producer to wholesaler to retailer. Most pre-packed roses are nicely boxed with color pictures of the variety and growing instructions. Like bare-root roses, they should be purchased and planted in winter, from mid-autumn to early spring, and any that appear dry and shriveled must be avoided. When planting, ignore the wax—it will eventually disappear.

Once a decision has been made on which varieties are required, it is a very good idea to place an order as soon as possible. Some varieties are in short supply and stocks can run out.

LEFT: *The color of a rose may vary with its position, the soil, the climate and even the age of the bloom.*
BELOW: *A good bare-root rose should have strong branches, a thick rootstock and abundant roots.*

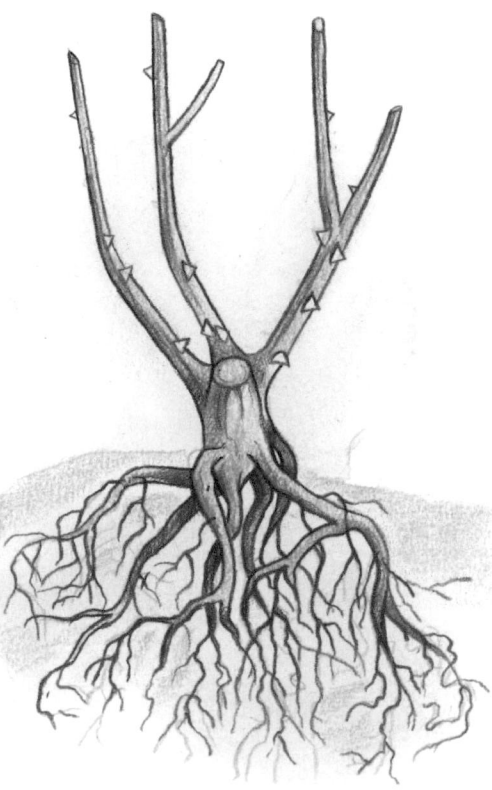

WHERE TO BUY ROSES

The best selection of varieties is to be found at specialist rose nurseries. Again, national rose societies can often help with nursery lists. Most garden centers sell limited varieties of roses, which are usually container grown, and the major DIY retailers sell container-grown and pre-packed roses. Container-grown roses tend to be more expensive than bare-root or pre-packed plants, because the nursery has had to pot them up and look after them for several months. As with any purchase, view bargains with suspicion!

HOW TO CHECK THE QUALITY OF PLANTS

What should a good rose plant look like? Overall, the plant should look fresh and healthy. There should be several thick and fibrous roots, and the rootstock or stem of the rose should be at least as thick as the average thumb. A healthy rose has top growth that consists of two or three good stout branches, the place where the branches grow from the stem is called the 'bud union'.

Avoid plants with few or very short roots, spindly rootstocks and branches, or where roots or branches are damaged. Just to complicate matters, there are a few rose varieties that only produce thin branches. Where these are found, seek expert advice.

HOW TO SPOT A HEALTHY CONTAINER PLANT

These should be actively growing and have healthy, well-spread branches. It is always a good idea to remove the plant from its pot to inspect the roots. Do this with care, and the plant should come out quite easily. If the compost in the pot is loose and starts to fall out, replace the plant and do not buy it unless the variety is unavailable elsewhere. In this instance, the plant can either be grown on at home in its container, or removed from the pot and treated like a bare-root rose. If the rootball lifts out cleanly, inspect it carefully and do not buy any where the roots have grown into a tight spiral leaving little or any of the compost on view. Such plants are 'pot bound', and seldom grow on well in the garden.

WHAT TO DO WHEN THE PLANTS COME HOME

If they are to be planted within a couple of days, bare-root and pre-packed roses should be placed, in their packaging, in a frost-free but cold place. If they are not to be planted for several days, it is worth 'heeling them in' by placing them in a dug-out hole in the garden, and covering the roots up to the rootstock. Take care not to lose the name label while doing this.

If the roots or branches look at all shriveled, they should be placed, up to and including the rootstock, in a bucket of cold water for a few days before planting. This is usually a good idea for pre-packed roses, where the roots have been shortened to fit in the box. Container-grown roses should also be kept in a cool, sheltered place prior to planting, and watered as needed.

How to Plant Roses

FIRST PREPARE THE SOIL

As discussed earlier in this chapter, the soil needs to be of sufficient depth for the roots, and prepared with the addition of manure or compost so it is rich in organic matter and retains moisture. It should not be too acid or too alkaline, and any perennial weeds should be removed, using weed killer if necessary. If a buried irrigation system is to be used, it should be installed at this time. 'Leaky pipe' and drip irrigation systems are the most effective and economical with water.

Where a large rose bed or planting is proposed, it is easier to spread a liberal thickness of manure or garden compost on the surface and then incorporate it into the soil as deeply and thoroughly as possible by using a motorized garden cultivator. A cultivator, not a rotovator, is required, and can be hired from a DIY store.

If an old rose bed is being replanted or only a single rose replaced, it is wise to assume that the soil will be 'rose-sick'. The causes of this sickness are not known for certain, but the problem can be overcome in any of the following ways: the first option is physically to relocate the rose bed to another place in the garden. If this is not feasible, an alternative method is to replace the soil to a depth of about 14 in (35 cm) with some that has not grown roses before, from the vegetable patch for example. A third option is to employ a professional garden contractor to sterilize the soil with a proprietary chemical.

Honey fungus is the only root disease likely to

Climbing roses add height, interest and elegance to the garden.

kill a rose. It is not specific, and will attack virtually any woody plant except yew. If honey fungus is in the garden, it might be wise to place a vertical barrier of a heavy gauge black plastic sheet around the new bed and have a professional sterilize the soil inside. The plastic edging sheet will need to be at least 18 in (45 cm) deep.

MARKING OUT PLANTING DISTANCES

The next step is to mark out the proposed positions of the roses by placing short canes or sticks in the soil. To make sure that the short sticks are spaced out correctly, it is always a good idea to cut two canes specifically for use as measures: one cane should equal the distance from the rose to the edge of the bed, and the other should equal the distance between plants.

The distances that roses should be planted apart depends not only on the type of rose, but also the climate in which they grow. It is therefore only possible to give an approximate guide here. Any rose planted as a specimen is fairly simple; just allow sufficient space for the plant at its mature width.

Most types will be grown in groups. They should all be spaced so that the ends of the branches intermingle with one another, especially for the purposes of ground cover, hedging or screening where a dense thicket is essential. Miniature Roses are best about 12 in (30 cm) apart, Climbing Miniatures need about 4 ft

(1.2 m) between plants and most Ramblers and Climbers like to be about 10 ft (3 m) apart. As a rule of thumb, most shrub or bush roses should be spaced about two-thirds of the eventual height. Bush roses can be subdivided into three types: large, 3–4 ft (1–1.2 m) apart; medium, 2–4 ft (60–120 cm) apart; and small, 12–24 in (30–60 cm) apart.

Where so desired, roses will look best if they overhang the edge of the bed or path. They should be planted about half the eventual height away from the edge. Any bare earth can easily be filled with appropriate companion plants, or smaller roses.

BARE-ROOT AND PRE-PACKED ROSES

This planting technique is essentially the same for every single type of rose. They should all be planted so that the bud union (where the first branches arise) is under the ground by about 2 in (5 cm). When the soil settles the bud union will be at the correct level, but even if it remains under the ground there is no need for concern; it may simply encourage extra branching.

First of all, reduce any exceptionally long roots to the general length. Cut off any broken roots or branches just before the damage and snip off any leaves, buds or hips. Then, dig out a hole large and deep enough to accommodate the roots *at the correct depth*. Lie a cane across the hole so that when the rose is placed it is easy to tell if the bud union will be underground.

Do not spread the roots by force. Many plants have roots that run in one direction. In this case, place the plant by the edge of the hole, and allow the roots to run across it. Fill in the hole with a planting mixture: two handfuls of sterilized bone meal or hoof and horn previously mixed up in a

large bucket full of damp peat or coir compost. When the hole is full, firm down *gently* and top up with the originally excavated soil, or the soil from the next planting hole. Then soak the plant in well with about 1 gallon (5 l) of water, using a can with the sprinkler removed. Finally, prune the branches hard so that they are about 4–6 in (10–15 cm) in length; this will allow the plant to direct its energy to making new roots without having to maintain a lot of top growth. The benefit of this will be seen the following summer.

CLIMBER AND RAMBLER ROSES

Climber and Rambler Roses should be planted in exactly the same way as bare-root and pre-packed roses. Climbers and Ramblers are often planted by walls, and it is *very important* that they should be planted well away, at least 18 in (45 cm) if possible, with the roots running away from the wall. Position them so that they lean towards the wall and can then be tied to the support *after* the soil has settled. Roses by walls need regular inspection for dryness. Water is most easily supplied by making a small wall of soil about 15 in (40 cm) or so in diameter around the plant and allowing a hose to trickle very gently overnight onto the roots. Climbers should not be pruned after planting.

STANDARD ROSES

These are planted as for bare-root and pre-packed roses, with the addition of a stout hardwood stake, which should be driven into the soil so that the top is just below the head of the standard rose. Then, fix the rose loosely to the stake with twine until the soil has settled and become firm. The stem of the rose should be wrapped with a small piece of hessian or similar

to prevent the stem chafing against the twine. The branches should then be pruned to about 6 in (15 cm) from the junction with the stem.

CONTAINER-GROWN ROSES

A hole should be dug about 3 in (7 cm) deeper than the pot the rose is in. The pot is best cut off the plant with scissors, a knife or secateurs so as not to disturb the rootball. Next, place a 2 in (5 cm) layer of planting mixture (the same used for bare-root and pre-packed roses) in the bottom of the hole and position the rootball carefully on top. Fill around the rootball with some more planting mixture, finally covering it with soil, which is then gently firmed down. It is much better to tempt the roots out of the rootball in this way rather than with the fingers as is sometimes recommended. If the roots are not attracted out of the rootball, they will fail to spread out and anchor the plant, which prevents it from picking up the nutrients and water essential for growth. If, for whatever reason, the soil is loose in the pot, it is best to shake it all off and plant the rose as described for a bare-root or pre-packed plant.

PLANTING ROSES INTO CONTAINERS

Roses can be very successful when grown in containers, which should be appropriate for the size of the rose when mature. A Climber, for example, will need a container at least 24 in (60 cm) in diameter and a minimum of 16 in (40 cm) deep. A layer of crocks or large stones should be placed in the bottom and the roses planted using a soil-based potting compost. This retains moisture and nutrients better than peat or coir composts, and the weight avoids the risk of the container being blown over by high winds.

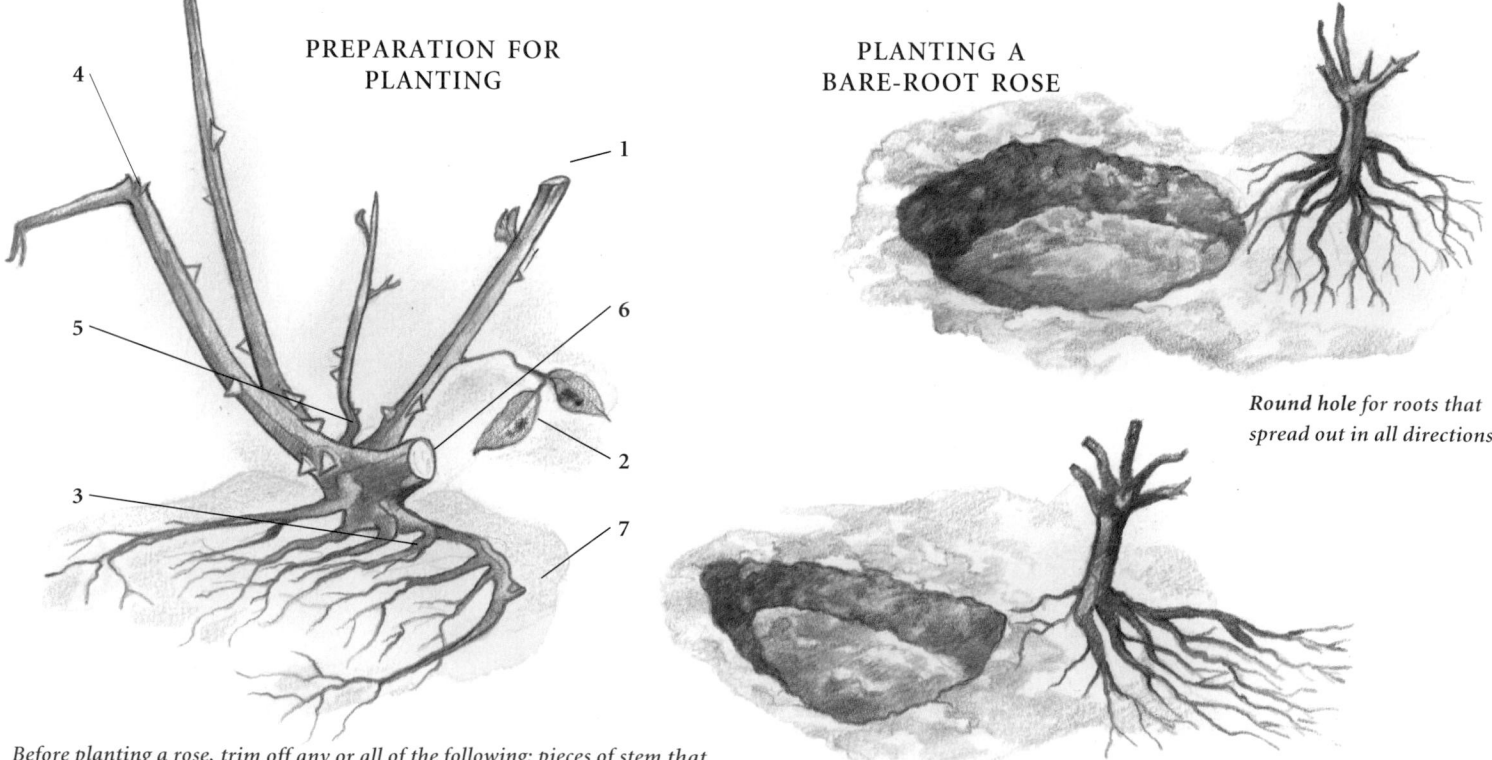

PREPARATION FOR PLANTING

PLANTING A BARE-ROOT ROSE

Round hole for roots that spread out in all directions.

Before planting a rose, trim off any or all of the following: pieces of stem that will die back to the eye (1), diseased or damaged leaves, roots or stems (2,3,4), shoots too thin to keep (5), rootstock 'snags' (6) and developing suckers (7).

Fan-shaped hole for roots that run in one direction only.

UNDERPLANTING ROSES WITH COMPANION SPECIES

Most companion plants can be added later, but bulbs are best planted at the same time as the roses, provided it is the right time of year to plant bulbs. It is easier to avoid damaging the roots of the roses, which encourages suckers, if done as the roses are planted. The taller daffodils and tulips make splendid companions. Most bulbs will naturalize and multiply if planted a little deeper than is generally recommended.

THE IMPORTANCE OF A MULCH

All mulches are valuable. They help retain moisture, deter weeds and in some cases add nutrients. Ignore any advice not to use materials such as dead leaves and grass clippings (except when the lawn has been treated with a weed killer). Other conventional materials include well-rotted manure, bark chips, coco shell and woven polypropylene ground cover sheeting. The RNRS has tested the latter material and found that it is particularly successful in helping newly planted roses to establish. The Society has also used shredded rose prunings and found them to make an excellent mulch, with no evidence whatsoever that it spreads fungal diseases. A good mulch will be about 4 in (10 cm) in depth. Applications of fertilizer will still be successful even if a mulch has been applied.

Pruning and Training Roses

There is probably more nonsense talked and written on this subject than any other specific horticultural task. It is really quite easy and straightforward. The exhibitor's view has prevailed for far too long in this matter, and it is simply *not necessary* to hard prune roses for good garden display. The exhibitor is after fine specimen blooms for the show; the gardener is not.

Very hard pruning necessitates heavy feeding to help the rose grow again. For the flower garden, this is a pointless exercise; the removal of about half the length of the old branches on bush roses is quite sufficient. Moreover, trials conducted over eight years have conclusively proved that the more foliage a rose carries, the better its per-

Tulips make excellent companion plants for roses.

formance. Gardeners are therefore advised not to remove the twiggy (non-flowering) growths when pruning; this 'exhibitor hard pruning' is counter-productive.

WHY PRUNE AND WHEN TO PRUNE?

Garden roses are pruned for two reasons: to keep them within bounds and to make them flower.

Despite the long-standing debate on the matter, there is little difference between pruning in the winter or the spring. The tidy gardener may prefer the winter, but the roses don't mind! On balance, it is best to wait for a sunny day and for the spirit to move the gardener.

It is usually worthwhile to reduce the height of tall bushes and shrubs by about a third in late autumn to avoid wind rock, especially in windy and exposed locations. Wind rock can create a small circular hole around the stem. If this fills with water and freezes, the plant may die.

Good gloves and secateurs are essential pruning tools. A pair of loppers and a pruning saw are also useful for cutting thick stems and stumps. Most older gardeners will find that a kneeling pad makes the task a lot easier. A good pair of scissors is best for Miniature Roses.

HOW TO PRUNE SHRUB ROSES, OLD GARDEN ROSES AND WILD ROSES

This group of roses can be left for three to five years with little or no pruning other than deadheading. Occasionally an old stem can be removed at the base to promote regeneration or to prevent the plant becoming too overcrowded or invasive. This technique of minimal pruning results in large and attractive plants. Alternatively, they can be pruned every year as though they were large bushes. Most shrub roses will, if left to grow, make very nice short- to medium-height climbers; Modern Shrub Roses are particularly useful for this purpose.

HOW TO PRUNE BUSH ROSES AND MINIATURE ROSES

First of all, remove all dead, diseased and damaged branches. Where there is disease, this usually shows as a discoloration in the pith in the branch. Remove sections of branch until the pith is white, even if this means the removal of the entire branch.

Woven plastic sheeting is particularly successful in helping newly planted roses to establish themselves.

The conventional method of pruning is to cut about ¼ in (6 mm) above a bud, sloping away from it at a slight angle.

Rough pruning of garden roses is often sufficient. Any dead 'snags' that result can be snipped off later.

Roses can be pruned using an electric hedge trimmer; however, they should only be used by experienced persons.

ABOVE: *To create attractive displays, Climbers and Ramblers must be trained properly.*
LEFT: *The removal of the oldest branch at its base each year promotes regeneration of the plant.*

In leaf, climbing roses are heavy and present considerable wind resistance, so they need strong supports. Galvanized wires retained by 'vine eyes' (available at most garden centers) are the best for walls and flat surfaces. Most commercially available trellises, however, are not strong enough for the job and arches and pillars need to be substantial and firmly fixed into the ground if they are not to be blown over.

Both Climber and Rambler Roses will look very attractive when supported on thick ropes hanging between short posts. A simple and effective 'pillar' for a climbing rose can easily be made by stapling a semi-rigid plastic mesh onto a stout wooden post.

HOW TO PRUNE STANDARD ROSES AND NEGLECTED PLANTS

Standard roses are simply roses that grow on top of a long stem. They only need moderate pruning to reduce the branches by no more than one-third, with the aim of creating a nice circular head. If the plant is a weeping standard, old flowered shoots should be shortened by half or removed entirely if there is plenty of new growth on the rose.

Neglected plants are usually inherited when people move into a new house. It can be quite difficult to identify the type, let alone the variety, of roses that have become very overgrown. If the roses cannot be identified, allow them to flower in the first summer, then decide whether or not they are worth keeping. If the plants are to be retained, they should be pruned back quite heavily, to about one-third of their normal height, removing all dead and diseased wood, and given fertilizer in early spring and again in summer.

Neglected standard roses should have the branches or shoots on the head of the plant reduced to about 6 in (15 cm) in length, and the side shoots cut back to a short stem 2 in (5 cm) long. For weeping standards, remove all old shoots at the base to leave up to six growths in all, then reduce these to about 10 in (25 cm) in length. Finally, feed the plant in early spring and summer as for other roses.

If neglected climbing roses flower reasonably well, it is only necessary to prune as normal. If the plant is very old, however, and does not produce good blooms, it may be as well to cut back all shoots to about 4 ft (1.2 m) from the base. After feeding and watering, it will either produce new shoots or expire.

Routine Care of Roses

If roses are to do well in the garden, they need some love and care. They need to be fed, mulched, deadheaded and any suckers that may be produced from the rootstocks or the standard stem need to be removed. Like many other garden plants, roses can be attacked by fungal diseases from time to time, and this requires some treatment. The famous rose breeder Sam McGredy likened disease on roses to tarnish on the family silver, which needs a little polishing to keep it in good order.

Each year, the oldest branch should be removed at its base, which promotes regeneration of the plant. Next, reduce the remaining branches by about half, but leave any thin, twiggy stems that will help the plant to make a good start in the next year. There is no need to differentiate between Large-flowered and Cluster-flowered Roses, and don't get too bothered about pruning to outward facing buds. These are sometimes difficult to see, and any resulting dead 'snags' can be snipped off later.

Where there are large beds of bush roses, the reduction by about half can be done by using an electric hedge trimmer. These are dangerous tools, however, and should only be used by experienced persons.

HOW TO PRUNE CLIMBER, RAMBLER AND GROUND COVER ROSES

On a well-trained climbing rose, pruning becomes a really simple matter: first, remove all dead, diseased and damaged wood, then reduce all side shoots, no matter how long, to stubs 2–3 in (5–8 cm) long. The main shoots are not pruned at all unless they end in flowers. In this case, they should be cut back to the first side shoot, which then takes over as leader. When the main shoot has filled its allotted space, the tip should be removed.

Every one or two years, or when there are sufficient shoots (more than three), remove the oldest at the base of the rose. This will cause the production of new shoots from the base. Sometimes it may be best to remove not the oldest shoot, but one where there is a new replacement shoot already available, which can be trained to fill the space.

Ignore the often proffered advice that, after flowering, stems of Rambler Roses should be removed. If this is done, the unfortunate plant then has to make a lot of regrowth for next year's bloom, which has to be encouraged by heavy feeding. There are some Ramblers that make plenty of new growths from the base, but Rambler Roses are best treated as lax-stemmed Climbers and pruned as such.

Ground Cover Roses need little or no pruning at all, other than to keep them within their allotted space.

HOW TO TRAIN CLIMBER AND RAMBLER ROSES

More important than their pruning, Climbers and Ramblers must be properly trained. On walls and fences, when the new growth is green and whippy, it can be easily bent and tied in; the main shoots should be trained as near horizontal as possible. Where the space on a wall is limited, between two windows for example, the shoots should be criss-crossed to cover the available area. On pillars and arches they should be trained in a spiral. These treatments will cause lots of flowering side-shoots to emerge from the main shoots and give the optimum display. Whatever the support, Climbers must not be allowed to grow vertically as this will result in ugly bare stems below a tangle of foliage and bloom.

FEEDING ROSES

Roses put a lot of effort into the production of flowers, so it is imperative that they be properly fed. The simplest way to do this is to give them a good dressing of a proprietary rose fertilizer twice a year: once in the spring and another in the summer. The fertilizer should be applied as instructed on the packet. Generally, it is not worth bothering with foliar feeds; they involve a lot of effort and give very little apparent benefit.

SOME COMMON NUTRITIONAL DEFICIENCIES AND REMEDIES

There are various signs that indicate malnutrition, best gauged by a study of the leaves. With regular applications of fertilizer there should be no problem, but the principal deficiencies and remedies are listed below. The severity of the problem will affect the dosage—consult with your nursery for exact directions.

ALWAYS ADD A MULCH

Many gardeners are concerned that mulches may upset the nutrient balance in the soil and that they act as a barrier to the addition of fertilizer. There need be no concern on either of these points, and fertilizer should be applied on top of the mulch. The rain will usually wash it through to the soil beneath, but during a very dry spell it can always be watered through. If there are any nutrient deficiencies, the application of the appropriate remedy on top of the mulch will eventually do the trick.

WATER ROSES ONLY DURING DRY SPELLS

Roses are deep rooted and, after new plants have become established, will seldom need any water. In the event of a prolonged dry spell, it is better to water using a drip-feed or 'leaky pipe' system that is left on long enough for the rose roots to be thoroughly soaked. Garden plants given small quantities of water will be encouraged to develop surface roots, which are more prone to drought damage. Roses growing in containers, window boxes and hanging baskets will need water at least once a day.

SYMPTOM	DIAGNOSIS	REMEDY
Young leaves are pale green	lack of nitrogen	Apply $1\frac{1}{2}$ oz/yd^2 (60 g/m^2) of hoof and horn, urea or blood and bone or $\frac{3}{4}$ oz/yd^2 (30 g/m^2) of sulphate of ammonia where the soil is not very acid
Small leaves with purplish undersides	lack of phosphorus	Apply $\frac{3}{4}$ oz/yd^2 (30 g/m^2) of superphosphate or $1\frac{1}{2}$ oz/yd^2 (60 g/m^2) of bone meal.
Purple or brown edges to leaves, and young leaves unnaturally red	lack of potassium	Apply $\frac{3}{4}$ oz/yd^2 (30 g/m^2) of sulphate of potash
Brown spots near the edges of leaves	lack of calcium	Apply $\frac{3}{4}$ oz/yd^2 (30 g/m^2) of nitro chalk or gypsum
Pale patches towards centers of leaves and areas of dead tissue near main vein	lack of magnesium	Apply $\frac{3}{4}$ oz/yd^2 (30 g/m^2) of epsom salts
Yellowish leaves	lack of iron	Apply 'Sequestrene' granules as directed on the packet, or iron chelates

REGULAR DEADHEADING ENCOURAGES MORE FLOWERS

After the flowers fade, the rose will set seed and cease to produce new flowering shoots. It is necessary, therefore, to remove these spent blooms, which is an activity called deadheading, and it fools the plant into producing more flowers. Deadheading is really a form of summer pruning, and used to involve the removal of spent blooms by cutting off the shoot some three to five leaves below the flower. Recent trials, however, have clearly established that the more foliage a rose plant bears, the better its performance, and it is now recommended that dead flowerheads should be snapped off at the abscission layer. This is a slightly swollen section in the stem below the bloom, normally where the first leaflets are found, and it is where the rosehip would naturally be shed. This is a revolutionary new method that applies to all Large-flowered Roses. Not only does the rose come back into flower between flushes more quickly, but with appreciably more flowers. This principle of retaining the maximum foliage on a rose should also be observed when deadheading Cluster-flowered Roses.

THE KEY TO GOOD HEALTH

Far too much has been written and spoken about the health problems of roses, and the need for spraying. There are just two really important factors that should be remembered: primarily, roses that are healthy and well cultivated will be better equipped to resist pests and diseases than unhealthy, badly treated specimens, and secondly, as with every other member of the plant kingdom, some varieties of roses are simply not worth growing because of their poor health.

If a rose performs poorly and continually gets disease, then it is a pain in the neck and should be thrown on the bonfire. In some countries they call this 'shovel pruning'. Too many gardeners persevere for far too long in trying to make something of losers, and it is simply not worth the bother. Instead, find out which roses are the best performers. Some helpful hints are given earlier in this chapter.

THE CHIEF FUNGAL DISEASES OF ROSES

There are three main villains so far as roses are concerned: black spot, mildew and rust. They are all quite simple to deal with, but the best tactic by far is prevention.

This flowering shoot has been deadheaded in the conventional but now outmoded way.

Dead flowerheads should be snapped off at the abscission layer. Here, new flowering shoots have already appeared.

Powdery mildew can be treated with a good rose fungicide, available from a garden center.

Black spot, a common disease of roses, is easily dealt with by preventive spraying with a fungicide.

Buy a bottle of good rose fungicide from the garden center. One containing bupirimate and triforine is recommended for black spot and mildew, and one with myclobutanil for mildew and rust. Sadly there is no panacea for all three fungi. Always use the chemicals as instructed, and remember to shake or stir the spray container at regular intervals while spraying the roses.

Roses should be sprayed early in the spring, as soon as there is enough foliage to make it worthwhile. Thoroughly cover both sides of the leaves and the branches themselves. Repeat the application at two week intervals, which should give good control for a long time. If the fungus continues to appear after this time, apply the occasional spray thereafter. A small amount of disease on the plants in autumn is not a matter of concern.

If the fungus appears during the growing season because spraying has been overlooked, the rose should be sprayed as soon as possible with two repeats at two week intervals. Most fungicide instructions permit the use of the spray at double strength in these cases. Further repeats may be necessary, which will help remind the gardener that it would have been easier to have applied a preventive spray in early spring.

Never use equipment that has been used for weed killer to spray roses. No matter how well washed the equipment is, there will always be traces of the weed killer left, which can damage roses. This is especially important where selective (hormone) weed killers are used. Selective sprays should only be used in windless conditions, when great care must be taken to prevent the spray drifting onto surrounding plants.

Although there is little evidence to suggest that fungicidal sprays harm the environment, some gardeners prefer not to use them. In this case, special care must be taken to choose good, disease-resistant varieties, and to feed them well. Any disease attack on a healthy rose should not be serious and can be tolerated.

COMMON ROSE PESTS

In most cases, an epidemic of any particular insect pest is likely to be followed by a build-up of its predators, so there is a perfectly good case for letting nature take its course. These predators, known as beneficial insects, include ladybirds, wasps and lacewings. Garden birds are also great allies, especially when there are the hungry young to be fed. The main insect pests of the rose garden, and the best means of eliminating them, are listed below:

Aphids (or greenfly) are best squashed by finger and thumb. Otherwise, spray with a pesticide that does not harm beneficial insects, such as one that contains pirimicarb.

Thrips may prevent blooms from opening; blooms that partially open have brown or black spots. As flowers must be inspected very carefully to find them, their effect is often undererstimated. They can be controlled by spraying buds and blooms with orthene, but this is an unpleasant procedure. Predators do not control them.

Leaf-rolling sawfly is worst where roses are growing in shade under trees. It is not really worth spraying because affected, rolled up leaves can be picked off and put in the dustbin, and plants given an extra dose of fertilizer.

Caterpillars (sometimes called rose slugworms) usually eat the surface of the leaves to create a skeleton effect. They are easily controlled either by picking off the caterpillars and affected leaves, or by spraying with an insecticide; one containing fenitrothion and permethrin is suitable.

Spider mites are worst in hot, dry conditions and cause a bronze discoloration on the uppersides of the leaves. The simplest remedy is to put an irrigation spray at ground level and thoroughly wet the undersides of the leaves.

'Cuckoo Spit' (the common froghopper) is not serious. Wash it off with a squirt from a hose.

SAFETY WITH CHEMICALS

Always read the label and follow instructions when using chemicals, and avoid skin contact, especially when they are undiluted. Remember to shake or stir the diluted chemical so that it is thoroughly mixed. A few squirts of a poorly diluted chemical can cause untold damage to a rose. Pets should be kept indoors and children kept occupied elsewhere when plants are being treated.

SUCKERS MUST BE REMOVED

These are unwanted growths from the rootstocks of budded plants. They should be removed. Suckers usually have leaves that are of different color and shape from the rest of the rose because the budded rootstock comes from a different type of rose; one selected for its healthy roots, not for its foliage and flowers. If the earth is scraped away, it will be seen that the suckers arise from the roots. To remove, uncover the source and pull it off, wearing a pair of gardening gloves. Roses that grow on their own roots do not produce unwanted suckers; any shoots from the roots will be of the actual rose, and are therefore welcomed. Standard roses sometimes also produce suckers from the stem below the bud union. Stem suckers are best rubbed off when small.

THE TREATMENT OF BLIND SHOOTS

These are shoots where the embryo flowers have been damaged in some way that prevents their development. In the past, the recommended procedure would be to cut the shoot back. The modern procedure is to remove only the tips of the blind shoot, or simply to leave it untouched.

How to Propagate Roses

CUTTINGS

Roses can most easily be propagated by cuttings in autumn. First, take pieces of stem about 8 in (20 cm) in length from well-ripened branches that have grown during the previous five or six months. The cuttings should have all but the top leaf snipped off so that it can be remembered which is the right way up. Then, make a slit in the ground by levering a spade to and fro to create a wedge-shaped hole about 6 in (15 cm) deep. It will help if a little sharp sand (available from any garden center) is placed in the bottom of the hole. Next, place the cuttings in the hole about 4 in (10 cm) apart and firm the soil around the hole with your foot. The cuttings should then be labeled and marked by a stick with a scrap of bright plastic or similar attached, to prevent the area being accidentally disturbed. Those cuttings that 'take' will eventually produce new shoots and can be transplanted one year later into a 'holding' bed, which is a cold frame or pot that is used to grow the cuttings on until they are large enough to plant into their final positions. Only some roses make cuttings, however, and this is a matter of trial and error.

LAYERING

Most roses with lax stems can be 'layered' into the soil to produce new plants. This is best done after summer flowering. First, choose a stem that is long and lax enough to be bent to ground level so that a section of it can be buried under the soil. Then, make a number of small cuts in the bark of the section that is to be buried. New roots will emerge from this 'damaged' part of the stem. Lightly cultivate the soil at the site, then place the cut part of the stem in a shallow hole and peg it down using one or two 'hairpins' made of galvanized wire. Finally, cover the stem with soil and mark the site with a cane or stick. By the following spring, the new plant should have rooted and be growing away happily. The new rose should be separated from its parent and transplanted.

SEED

Hybrid roses will not come true from seed, but Wild Roses do. In autumn, the ripe hips, which contain the seed, should be placed in a refrigerator for a month or so. The normal fridge temperature of 39°F (4°C) is fine. This treatment, called stratification, fools the seed into thinking that it has survived through winter, and it will then germinate when planted one seed to a pot. The pots should be kept in a cold frame or sheltered spot outdoors and, after germination, potted on to larger pots until the plants are big enough to plant out.

HYBRIDIZING NEW ROSE VARIETIES

This is quite a simple operation that involves the transfer of pollen from one rose (the pollen parent) to the stigma of another (the seed parent). This is normally done in insect-free conditions so that the breeder can guarantee the identity of both parents without the interference of insect pollinators. When the rosehip swells and matures, its seeds are sown in the same way as described previously. Professional nurseries may raise hundreds of thousands of new seedling roses in this way, from which good ones are selected on merit. Hybridizing roses is also a popular amateur hobby, and some rose societies have established their own special interest groups for this purpose.

BUDDING

Most commercially grown roses are propagated by budding. By this process, individual new rose seedlings can be increased in number by the insertion of a bud or 'eye' taken from the new rose into a T-shaped slit made in the stem of a Wild Rose rootstock. When the new bud or 'scion' takes and grows, the top growth of the original rootstock plant is cut off. Any gardener interested in budding roses is advised to pay a visit to a rose nursery in mid-summer to see it actually being done.

Miscellaneous Tasks

TRANSPLANTING OLD ROSES

All old roses can be moved, but it is seldom worth the effort unless the plant is extremely rare or precious. In this case, it might be a more sensible course to propagate by cuttings or layering, or to ask a rose nursery to bud new plants. The best time to move old plants is in autumn, although it can, with care, be done at any time.

First prepare the new planting hole and then cut back the branches on the old rose by three-quarters. Next, lift the old plant using a fork and shake off all the soil; two people holding opposite sides of the plant are better than one. Finally, trim off any damaged or overlong roots, and replant the specimen in its new position as soon as possible. Use planting compost and firm the soil down then water in. Regular watering should continue until the rose has become successfully established in its new home.

DAMAGE BY LARGE ANIMALS

There are several so-called 'repellents' on the market. They do not work for long, if at all, and neither does the application of unconventional materials such as tiger dung! The best and most effective deterrent is clear, heavy duty fishing line. String it tightly 3 ft (1 m) high along stout canes and it will put the animals off in a similar way as cotton on twigs helps to keep birds off the crocus bed. If the animals learn to leap the strand, add another at 6 ft (2 m) high. The advantage of this method is that it is comparatively cheap, easy to install and is more or less invisible from the house.

RIGHT: *New rose varieties can be hybridized by transferring pollen from one rose to the stigma of another.*
FAR RIGHT: *When propagating a rose by budding, a bud eye is slipped between a T-shaped incision in the root-stock, which is then bound above and below the eye with tape.*
BELOW: *Wild Roses will come true from seed, which is contained in the rosehips. Hybrid roses will not come true from seed.*

Wild Roses

Peter Beales

ROSA ACICULARIS NIPPONENSIS
DEEP PINK

This small, dense shrub to 3 ft (1 m) is armed with tiny prickles, although some of its older, dark green shoots may bear relatively few. The leaves are made up of matt green, elliptical, serrated leaflets, and the small, deep pink flowers, which are produced solitarily, appear in late spring. The ripe red hips are roundly pear-shaped and red when ripe. This is a very hardy species, which, as a garden plant, is superior in many ways to the North American and European *R. acicularis*. ZONES 4–11.

Japan, 1894

ROSA ARKANSANA
syns 'Arkansas Rose', *R. suffulta*
MEDIUM PINK

A short shrub with greenish stems up to 2 ft (60 cm) *R. arkansana* bears many

Rosa arvensis

Rosa arkansana

Rosa acicularis nipponensis

stems with thin prickles. These stems often die off each year and are replaced by new suckers. The leaves are made up to seven to eleven broadly elliptical, bright green, heavily serrated leaflets. Small flowers, about 1 in (2.5 cm) across, are produced in corymbs in early summer. The fruit are small, dark red and globular in shape. This is an interesting species, but is of little garden value. ZONES 4–11.

North America, 1896

ROSA ARVENSIS
syn. 'The Field Rose'
WHITE

A native of Europe, except for the cold north and the warmer Mediterranean regions, *R. arvensis* is commonly found in neglected hedgerows where it grows as a shade-tolerant and disease-free, relaxed scrambler or creeper up to 10 ft (3 m). Its flowers are creamy white, 1½ in (3 cm) across, with pronounced yellow stamens, and are produced solitarily or in small corymbs during early summer. Despite some descriptions to the contrary, this rose is slightly scented. The oval hips are red when ripe, and appear amid the serrated, deep green foliage mostly made up of seven leaflets. Numerous, hooked thorns cover the slender, dark green and flexible stems. This is a useful species for the natural garden; it was crossed with various Old Garden Roses in the early nineteenth century, which gave rise to a small group of ramblers known as the Ayrshires. The best known of these is

Rosa banksiae normalis

Rosa beggeriana

'Splendens', which is described in the main section of this book, and bears lovely double, silvery pink blooms. ZONES 4–10.

Europe, 1750

ROSA BANKSIAE NORMALIS
WHITE

Of the four forms of *R. banksiae* now in cultivation, this is considered to be the wild form. It is very vigorous—up to 30 ft (9 m)—in warm temperate climates or under glass. The scented flowers are white, single, small and borne in corymbs amid the light green broadly elongated leaves, which are composed of about five leaflets. All four varieties of *R. banksiae* are normally thornless and evergreen. **R. banksiae banksiae** (syns 'Banksiae Alba', 'Lady Banksia Snowflake', *R. banksiae alba plena*, 'White Lady Banks') was introduced in 1807. It is a cultivated form of the wild species, and its behavior is similar in all respects, except for its loosely double, white flowers. **R. banksiae lutea** (syn. 'Yellow Lady Banks'; Royal Horticultural Society Award of Garden Merit) is the best known and most widely grown form. Its corymbs of small, fully double, bright yellow flowers are produced in late spring in great profusion. They cover this vigorous and healthy, densely growing thornless Rambler, which grows up to 30 ft (9 m). **R. banksiae lutescens**, introduced in 1870, is a slightly less vigorous form with single, sulfur yellow flowers. It has a stronger perfume than

Rosa banksiae lutea

Rosa blanda (hip)

any of the others. **R.** × **fortuniana** *(syn. R. banksiae* × *R. laevigata)* is often used as a rootstock in warm climates. It has larger, double white flowers than the wild species, and unlike the purer forms of *R. banksiae normalis*, this rose is well armed with thorns. **Rosa cymosa** was introduced in 1904 and has many similarities to *R. banksiae normalis*. It is a rare rose, and has interesting, single white flowers. ZONES 4–10.

China, circa 1877

ROSA BEGGERIANA
WHITE

This tallish, densely branching shrub up to 8 ft (2.5 m) tall is scattered with numerous hooked thorns that are arranged in pairs. The leaves are made up of nine medium-sized, broadly elongated and serrated grayish green leaflets, and the flowers, which appear in early summer, are single, white and arranged in small, dense clusters. Individually, they are about 1 in (2.5 cm) across with little or no perfume. They are followed by small, rounded hips that ripen to deep reddish purple in the autumn. It is not common, but this shrub is well worth its space in the garden. ZONES 4–11.

Iran, 1868

ROSA BLANDA
syns 'Hudson's Bay Rose', 'Labrador Rose', *R. fraxinifolia*
MEDIUM PINK

This spring-blooming shrub grows to a height of 5 ft (1.5 m). Its stems are usually without thorns and prickles. The single, pink flowers are 2–2½ in (4–6 cm) wide and are usually borne several to a stem amid the foliage. Globular, sometimes elongated hips follow. ZONES 4–11.

Northern North America, 1773

ROSA BRACTEATA
syns 'Chicksaw Rose', 'Macartney Rose'
WHITE

A dense shrub or wall plant to 10 ft (3 m), *R. bracteata* has long, grayish brown stems that are well armed with hooked thorns, often arranged in pairs. There is a plentiful covering of dark green, roundish and glossy leaves that have tomentose undersides. There are nine leaflets. The white flowers, with pronounced stamens, sometimes have a hint of cream showing through. They are borne singly on the end of stubby laterals throughout summer, and are followed by

Rosa californica

Rosa bracteata

plumply rounded, orange hips. Although it is not suitable for cold climates, it makes an excellent shrub in temperate zones; it has, in fact become naturalized in the southern states of the USA. This is a superb wall plant, as it is evergreen and easy going. 'Mermaid', which is described in the main section of this book, is a famous offspring of this species and is much hardier. ZONES 4–11.

China, 1793

ROSA BRUNONII
syn. 'The Himalayan Musk'
WHITE

A very vigorous scrambler with brownish green unyielding wood and vicious hooked thorns, this rose can reach 40 ft (12 m) in height. The drooping leaves are long, narrowly oval and grayish green in color. Large corymbs of small, white flowers appear in mid-summer, followed by oval hips that quickly change from red to brown in maturity. This rose is

not totally hardy, and it has been widely distributed erroneously as *R. moschata* for many years. **R. brunonii 'La Mortola'** is a superior garden form that has longer, grayer leaves and bigger flowers. **R. moschata nepalensis** is a distinct form that is often incorrectly classed as a synonym of *R. brunonii*. ZONES 3–10.

Himalayas, circa 1823

ROSA CALIFORNICA
syn. 'California Wild Rose'
LIGHT PINK

This vigorous shrub grows up to 10 ft (3 m) and produces many young branches each year; like the older wood, these are well endowed with slender, hooked prickles. The soft dull green leaves have five to seven broadly elongated leaflets, and are a backdrop to the small corymbs of blooms that are produced over a fairly long period from early summer; the color is mid-pink with little or no scent. Plumply oval hips

Rosa brunonii (hips)

follow in autumn, which are red when ripe. *R. californica* is a useful shrub for wild gardens that appears to be hardy in all but the coldest areas. A semi-double form, 'Plena' is a much more useful and decorative garden shrub. It freely produces lilac-pink flowers and orange-red fruit. ZONES 3–10.

North America, circa 1878

ROSA CANINA
syns 'Briar Bush', 'Dog Rose'
LIGHT PINK

This common rose of hedgerows in central and western Europe, *R. canina* is a stoutly branching shrub that varies in

Rosa californica 'Plena'

Rosa canina

height from 6–12 ft (2–4 m). The thorny stems are adorned with mid-green leaves that have five to seven broadly elongated and serrated leaflets. The small, scented flowers are borne singly or in threes, and the color varies from blush white to pink. Oval, bright red hips follow, which are very conspicuous *en masse*; they are a valuable source of vitamin C and can be used to make superb syrup or jelly. It is not an auspicious garden shrub, perhaps, but makes an excellent ornamental hedge. For many years, this species was used in Europe as the main rootstock in commercial rose production. ZONES 3–10.

Europe, pre-1730

Rosa brunonii

Rosa brunonii

Rosa cinnamomea plena

Rosa carolina

Rosa carolina (hips)

ROSA CAROLINA
syns 'Caroline Rose', 'Pasture Rose'
MEDIUM PINK

Stout to medium in size, this rose is a dense, free-suckering shrub. Its young shoots are bristly, although the older stems only occasionally bear prickles, and are densely covered by leaves made up of five mostly elongated, elliptical and serrated, lightly glossy dark green leaflets. The pink flowers are borne in profusion in mid-summer. Like the flowers, the globular, bright red hips are produced one to a stem. *R. carolina glandulosa* was introduced in 1902. It is similar to *R. carolina* but with glandular leaf stalks. *R. carolina grandiflora* has both larger flowers and leaves, often with seven leaflets. *R. carolina* **'Plena'** is a double form that is slightly shorter in growth. *R. carolina alba*, as the name portrays, has white flowers. All of these make good dense, spreading shrubs for group planting and low hedges. They tolerate even the poorest soils. ZONES 4–11.
North America, 1826

ROSA CHINENSIS
syns 'Bengal Rose', 'China Rose',
R. chinensis indica
MEDIUM PINK/DARK RED

This rose was lost to cultivation for many years, and has only recently come back into circulation. Although it is not a true species, it is an important rose for its genes; in the eighteenth century, some of its early hybrids were crossed with European roses, such as the Damasks and Gallicas, which brought forth almost all the repeat-flowering now taken for granted in Modern Garden Roses. The growth is upright, to about 4–8 ft (1.2–2.5 m), and is irregularly armed with sizeable thorns. They are covered with mid- to dark green leaves made up of three to five leaflets that are reddish when young. The flowers are produced either singly or in large, well-spaced clusters and vary in color from pale pink to deep red. They usually deepen with age and there is little or no fragrance. Small, dull red hips follow the blooms. *R. chinensis* probably gave rise to *R. × odorata*, which is also variously known as *R. indica odorata* and *R. indica fragrans*. *R. indica* **'Major'** is now regarded as another offspring, which is used as a rootstock in warm climates. Each of these hybrids is probably the result of natural or even deliberate crossing with *R. gigantea*. Both are double and soft pink, and make useful repeat-flowering shrubs. 'Mutabilis', described in the main section of this book, is closely related. ZONES 5–11.
China, circa 1759

Rosa cinnamomea

ROSA CINNAMOMEA
syns 'Cinnamon Rose', R. majalis
MAUVE

This medium to tall shrub reaches 6 ft (1.8 m) in good soil. Its slim brownish stems are only partially armed with squat thorns. The leaves are matt dark green, gray beneath, and made up of five to seven leaflets. The single flowers are pinkish mauve, have no scent, and are produced singly or in small groups in late spring. The hips are small globular, smooth and dark red. Unfortunately, it is of little garden value. *R. cinnamomea plena*, (syns 'Rose de Mai', 'Rose de Plaquer', 'Rose du Saint-Sacrement') is a rarely seen double form. Graham Stuart Thomas tells us that it is one of the oldest of recorded roses. *R. cinnamomea foecundissima* is another double form with paler flowers. ZONES 4–11.
Europe, circa 1600

ROSA × CORYANA
syns 'Coryana', R. macrophylla ×
R. roxburghii
DEEP PINK

A strong growing shrub with reddish brown bark and lighter colored, strong and stout prickles, *R. × coryana* reaches a height of 8 ft (2.5 m). The dark green leaves are heavily veined, slightly downy and made up of between five and fifteen narrowly oval leaflets. The flowers are single, deep pink and are produced in early summer with no scent. The species seldom sets fruit. It is not a significant garden plant and is sometimes classified as a Modern Shrub. ZONES 4–11.
UK, 1926

ROSA DAVIDII
syn. 'Father David's Rose'
LIGHT PINK

This tall, stoutly arching shrub of firm stature grows up to 10 ft (3 m) or more in good soil. The stems are armed with long, sharp but broadly based thorns, and the leaves are broadly elongated, heavily veined with mid-green, smooth above, hairy beneath and have seven to nine leaflets. The flowers appear along the branches in small corymbs and are produced in mid-summer. They are mid-pink in color, scented and up to 1¼ in (5 cm) across with soft yellow stamens. Pendulous hips are borne in small clusters; although not large, each scarlet hip is an attractive, plump flagon shape, persistent long calyces. This species makes a superb shrub, and will fit into most gardens. *R. davidii elongata* has fewer flowers, but both the leaves and fruit are larger. ZONES 4–10.
Tibet, 1908

ROSA ECAE
syn. R. xanthina
DEEP YELLOW

A small, densely branching shrub up to 3 ft (1 m) tall in good soil, *R. ecae* has chocolate brown stems that are thickly populated with short and stubby, reddish colored, sharp thorns. The dark green leaves are made up of five to nine small, broadly oval, smooth leaflets. The single flowers are produced in late spring, and are approximately ¼ in (2 cm) across and bright buttercup yellow in color; there is no scent. The hips are small, round and bright red. This species needs a good soil and full sun to give of its best, although it is apparently quite hardy. It is best when only lightly pruned to keep in shape, and seems to do well grown in pots, tubs or urns. When *R. ecae* was crossed with 'Canary Bird' by A. E. Allen in the UK in 1963, it gave rise to the excellent shrub rose 'Golden Chersonese', which appears in the main section of this book. ZONES 4–11.
Afghanistan, 1880

Rosa ecae

Rosa × coryana

Rosa davidii elongata

Rosa foetida persiana

Rosa foetida persiana

ROSA EGLANTERIA

syns *R. rubiginosa,* 'Sweet Briar'
LIGHT PINK

This vigorous and tall shrub up to 10 ft (3 m) has densely prickly, fawny-green stems covered by strong and sharply hooked thorns. The dark green foliage smells strongly of apples, especially when crushed, and each leaf has five to seven leaflets. The single flowers, 1½ in (4 cm) in diameter, are soft clear pink, scented and very beautiful, followed by oval, slightly bristly and rich red hips. This species has many uses in the garden as a flowering shrub not least as a dense hedge, when it can be kept in shape by regular clipping; although this practice tends to reduce the yield of flowers, it encourages lots of new young aromatic shoots, which waft their scent into the surrounding air, especially on warm, early summer evenings after rain. ZONES 4–10.

Europe, circa 1594

Royal Horticultural Society Award of Garden Merit

ROSA ELEGANTULA 'PERSETOSA'

syns *R. farreri persetosa,* 'The Threepenny Bit Rose'
MEDIUM PINK

This broad and arching, wide-growing shrub grows to 5 ft (1.5 m). The young stems are densely covered in soft reddish brown bristles, yet the older stems are only sparsely prickled. The small and furry leaves are composed of seven to nine little leaflets, which are dark green,

burnished bronze and serrated; there is an excellent autumn coloring. Each flower is less than 1 in (3 cm) across, star-like in form and pinkish in color. They are not over conspicuous, even *en masse.* The fruit does not always set, but when it does it is small, drooping and broadly elliptical, orange when ripe. This shrub needs plenty of space to develop into its most graceful form. It is particularly attractive when covered with haw frost in midwinter. *R. elegantula* 'Persetosa' is still commonly listed in catalogues by its old name, *R. farreri persetosa.* ZONES 4–10.

China, 1900

ROSA FEDTSCHENKOANA

WHITE

This broadly upright, dense shrub to 6 ft (1.8 m) tall has reddish green stems that are moderately armed with long sharp spines. It is freely suckering, grows on its own roots and bears dense foliage that is soft to touch, oblong and made up of leaves with up to nine to fifteen, grayish green leaflets. The white flowers with golden stamens are borne either singly or in small clusters continuously, if spasmodically, throughout summer and autumn. The scent is almost repellent. The small and slender, elliptical, drooping, orange and bristly fruit look attractive

Rosa foetida

together with the flowers in early autumn. The agreeable nature of this shrub, together with the repeat-flowering ability makes this species a most useful garden plant. It is good as a broad and informal hedge. ZONES 4–11.

Central Asia, circa 1876

ROSA FILIPES

WHITE

In its wild form this species is seldom seen in gardens today. However, *R. filipes* 'Kiftsgate', which appears in the main A–Z sequence, has become exceedingly popular since it was introduced in 1938; the original plant still thrives as a giant among roses at Kiftsgate Court, Gloucestershire in the UK. ZONES 4–11.

China, 1908

ROSA FOETIDA

syn. 'Austrian Briar'
MEDIUM YELLOW

This upright shrub is capable of attaining 5 ft (1.5 m) in height. It bears rich dark green stems that are heavily overlaid with mahogany-brown and have many large, light-green thorns, becoming brown with age. The foliage is bright deep green—lighter beneath—smooth and downy with five to nine leaflets. The single flowers are produced mostly singly but generously on short stalks in early summer. They smell unpleasant, which gives the rose its name. *R. foetida bicolor*

Rosa eglanteria

(syn. 'Austrian Copper') is a popular sport of this species and is similar in all respects except for color, which is bright almost luminous orange-red. It was introduced in 1596. *R. foetida persiana* (syn. 'Persian Yellow') is a double yellow form that appeared in 1835. All of these roses are very prone to black spot, which is partly responsible for the proneness of many Modern Roses to this disease; it was *R. f. persiana* that was used as a pollen parent by French breeder Pernet-Ducher in the late nineteenth century to breed the first yellow and orange colored Large-flowered Rose called 'Soleil d' Or'. That was a significant event, which sadly had its downside, because black spot is an inherent affliction of many of its progeny even to this day. ZONES 4–11.

Asia Minor, pre-1596 or earlier

Rosa elegantula 'Persetosa'

Rosa fedtschenkoana

Rosa foetida bicolor

ROSA FOLIOLOSA
MEDIUM PINK

A low growing shrub to about 4 ft (1.2 m) *R. foliolosa* seems to prefer light, almost impoverished soils. It is best grown on its own roots, and is almost impossible to propagate vegetatively in any other way than from cuttings. The semi-glossy, dark green foliage is produced all along the wiry, greenish purple, thornless canes, and has seven to nine oblong leaflets that are soft and furry to touch. The flowers are mostly solitary and are deep bright cerise-pink in color

Rosa forrestiana

Rosa gigantea

Rosa giraldii

on short pedicels with very long sepals about 2 in (5 cm) across. They are produced later in the summer than many species. Small, rounded red hips develop from the early flowers only. It is an interesting rose, but of little garden value. There is also a white form. ZONES 4–10. USA, 1880

ROSA FORRESTIANA
DEEP PINK

This shrub carries only a few solitary flowers. They are deep rose pink in color and are usually borne singly. ZONES 4–10. Western China, 1918

ROSA GALLICA
syns 'French Rose', 'Rose of Provins'
DEEP PINK

Growing to 3 ft (1 m), this free-suckering rose is most certainly much older than indicated by its given date of introduction. Its dark green stems are almost thornless, and the foliage is light green, of medium to small size, somewhat rounded in shape and each leaf is made up of just five leaflets. The single flowers are only slightly scented and are produced in early summer. They are about 2½ in (6 cm) in diameter, clear mid-pink in color and have pronounced yellow stamens. The hips are a dull reddish

Rosa gigantea (hips)

color when ripe, held upright and are roundly urn shaped. This species is an easygoing plant that is ideal in a mixed border or with herbs. *R. gallica* was important in the early development of the cultivated rose. ZONES 5–11. Pre-1759

ROSA GENTILIANA
syn. *R. polyantha grandiflora*
WHITE

This vigorous climbing rose is capable of attaining heights of 20–30 ft (6–9 m). The thick and firm stems are dark green, mottled with reddish purple and moderately armed with large thorns. The leaves are large, shiny deep green, reddish when young and are made up of seven to nine broadly oblong leaflets. The flowers, which emerge from small creamy yellow buds in mid-summer, are pure white and single, and each is conspicuously endowed with deep yellow stamens and arranged in large clusters. They have a distinct smell of citrus. The orange-red hips are oval in shape. The species is a first class climber of distinction, and could have arisen as a chance hybrid. ZONES 4–11. China, circa 1907

ROSA GIGANTEA
syn. *R. × odorata gigantea*
WHITE

A medium to tall climber up to 20 ft (6 m), taller in its natural habitat, *R. gigantea* has long, arching branches of purplish-green that are randomly armed

Rosa foliolosa (hips)

Rosa glauca

Rosa gentiliana

with hooked thorns. The leaves are made up of seven prominently veined, long and narrow leaflets. The flowers are white, very large—up to 4 in (10 cm) in diameter at their best—sweetly scented and are produced in early summer. Yellowy orange, pear-shaped hips about 1 in (2.5 cm) long appear after the blooms. This tender species is unsuitable for cold climates. It is an ancestor of the early Tea Roses. ZONES 4–11. Burma and China, 1889

ROSA GIRALDII
MEDIUM PINK

A shrub to a height of some 6 ft (1.8 m) in good soil, *R. giraldii* bears long and arching shoots armed with sharp, slender prickles that are mostly arranged in pairs. The broadly oval, mid-green leaves are made up to seven to nine leaflets. Borne solitarily or a few together in small groups, the flowers are single, soft mid-pink in color and produced in mid-summer. The small, bright red, roundly oval hips follow. It is not the most conspicuous of Wild Roses, but it is an easygoing plant and worthy of space in any collection. ZONES 4–10. China, 1897

ROSA GLAUCA
syn. *R. rubrifolia*
MEDIUM PINK

This rose is probably much older than the given date. It is a very useful garden species making an open dense shrub of around 6 ft (1.8 m) tall. The arching, reddish purple, thornless shoots are well furnished with broadly oval, heavily serrated, grayish purple leaves that are made up of five to nine leaflets. Borne in small clusters, the flowers are little more than 1 in (2.5 cm) wide, single, star-like in formation and soft lilac-pink in color with soft creamy yellow stamens. They appear in early summer, and have no scent. The hips are at first red, then turn to burnished coppery purple in autumn. The species makes an excellent shrub that can be kept in bounds by regular pruning; this practice also encourages lots of colorful young shoots for the flower arranger, with whom this rose is very popular. It is also good as an informal hedge. 'Carmenetta', a hybrid between *R. glauca* and *R. rugosa* is more vigorous, but equally attractive and easygoing. ZONES 4–10.

Pre-1820

Royal Horticultural Society Award of Garden Merit

ROSA HELENAE
WHITE

Ever since the species was discovered by E. H. Wilson in Central China in 1907 and named for his wife, *R. helenae* has been one of the most popular of the Wild Roses for the garden. A large scrambler for climbing up into the branches of trees and covering large expanses of wall, *R. helenae* attains a height of some 20 ft (6 m) in fertile soils. The thick, grayish green stems are heavily mottled brown

Rosa hugonis

Rosa hugonis

Rosa holodonta (hips)

and have numerous strong, hooked thorns. The bark of the older stems is inclined to flake. Dark grayish green leaves, with seven to nine leaflets that are red when young, give good autumn color. The flowers are single, fragrant and white, and they appear in large corymbs in early to mid-summer. These are followed by drooping, oval and bright orange-red hips. Said to be tender, the species tolerates all but the most severe frosts. It is one of the most attractive tree scramblers, and is good in most soils. *Rosa helenae* seedlings (hybrids) are often sold as the original, so problems with identification have arisen. All of the hybrids are characterized by long, slender canes covered with corymbs of fragrant blossoms, 1–2 in (2.5–5 cm) across, which are white with pronounced yellow stamens. In autumn there is a spectacular display of red, oval hips. All forms of this rose are easy to train as climbers, and look especially good in trees. They do well on poor soil or in shade. If they are damaged by frost and need to be cut down they will readily produce new growth in spring. ZONES 4–11.

China, 1907

ROSA HEMISPHAERICA
syns *R. sulphurea*, 'Sulphur Rose'
MEDIUM YELLOW

Hardly a true species, this dense shrub grows to about 5 ft (1.5 m). Its brownish wood carries a sparse population of hooked brown thorns that are at first greenish yellow in color. The leaves have five to nine coarsely serrated, grayish green leaflets that are soft to touch. The double flowers often fail to open properly in wet weather and appear among

Rosa helenae

Rosa × kochiana

Rosa hemisphaerica

the foliage in early to mid-summer; they are held on very weak necks, and when the fruit sets, which is not often, it is globular and dark red. This is a fascinating rose that is depicted in several works of art by the seventeenth century Dutch Masters. It is why it was often referred to as a yellow Centifolia Rose. ZONES 4–11.

West Asia, 1625

ROSA HOLODONTA
syn. *R. moyesii rosea*
LIGHT PINK

This close relative of *R. moyesii* bears small clusters of pretty, light pink, single blooms. After the flowering season has ended, they develop into pear-shaped, glossy orange-red hips. The drooping fruits have persistent calyces, which give the appearance of short tentacles. ZONES 4–10.

Western China, 1908

ROSA HUGONIS
syns 'Father Hugo's Rose', 'Golden Rose of China'
MEDIUM YELLOW

John Mattock believes that this rose is much older than the given date. It is a tallish and upright, branching shrub to 7 ft (2.2 m) tall, and made up of brown stems with many sharp, flattish thorns. The fern-like leaves are composed of seven to thirteen leaflets. The flowers are single, bright yellow and borne singly all along the young, wiry lateral branches in

late spring and early summer; their texture is silky and sometimes they appear slightly crumpled. Approximately 2 in (5 cm) across, they are followed by small, purple-colored hips late in late summer and autumn. This species has much to commend it: it is more refined than most of the other single yellow roses. It does not seem to mind impoverished soil and is quite hardy in most climates. ZONES 4–10.

Circa 1899

Royal Horticultural Society Award of Garden Merit

ROSA × KOCHIANA
DEEP PINK/MAUVE

This short to medium-sized shrub grows to 3 ft (1 m) tall and has sturdy and dense, angular growth made up of bright green shoots with a few strong-pointed spines arranged in opposite pairs. The smooth and shiny, deep lime green leaves are each composed of seven to nine leaflets. The flowers are 1½ in (3 cm) across, can be rose-pink to mauve with bosses of creamy yellow stamens, and they are produced in mid-summer. Small, broadly pear-shaped, orange-red hips follow the blooms. *R. × kochiana* is probably the result of a cross between *R. pimpinellifolia* and *R. carolina*. The shrub is of excellent garden value, being easygoing in most soils, and it has richly colored foliage in autumn. ZONES 4–10.

North America, 1869

Rosa longicuspis

Rosa longicuspis

dark green leaves are oval and long. Relatively large, scented, single flowers are produced freely in small clusters in early summer; at first they are blush pink, then they fade to off white showing many creamy yellow stamens. The hips are dark red and round. Clearly not a true species, this rose is probably closely related to *R. gallica*. It makes a useful semi-procumbent shrub, although in some situations it is rather mildew prone. Despite this affliction, the plant always seems to grow well no matter what the soil. ZONES 4–11.

Found near La Flèche, France, 1923

ROSA LAEVIGATA
syn. 'The Cherokee Rose'
WHITE

This evergreen climber grows up to 15 ft (5 m) tall in warm climates. It needs protection or a sheltered warm position in cold areas. The mid-green stems have well-spaced, broad-hooked, reddish thorns and glossy dark green leaves that are made up of just three leaflets. The scented flowers, which appear in late spring for a short season only, are large, single, creamy white in color and have prominent yellow stamens. Very bristly, oval to pear-shaped, orange hips follow the flowers, but quickly change to brown with age. This species has become naturalized in several southern states of the USA. *R. laevigata* 'Cooperi' (syn. 'Cooper's Burmese') has darker green wood and foliage. It also seems to be more hardy. *R. anemonoides* 'Anemone Rose' and its sport 'Ramona' are both related to this species, as is the lovely, if shy blooming, 'Silver Moon.' They are described in the main section of this book. ZONES 4–10.

China, 1759

ROSA LONGICUSPIS
WHITE

A vigorous, almost evergreen climber to 20 ft (6 m) tall, *R. longiscuspis* has reddish wood with many sharply hooked thorns. The leaves are large, dark green and glossy, made up of five to seven broadly oblong, serrated leaflets that are tinted red until they mature. The flowers, which appear in mid-summer, are up to 2 in (5 cm) across; they are produced in tightly packed corymbs, which are white and waxy with a scent reminiscent of bananas. The small hips

are orange-red and oval in shape. Until recently, especially in the UK, *R. mulliganii* has been distributed under this name; it is a similar, but much hardier species. ZONES 4–11.

China, 1915

ROSA × MACRANTHA 'MACRANTHA'
LIGHT PINK/WHITE

This relaxed shrub has arching, dark green stems up to 4 ft (1.2 m) in height and almost twice as broad. The thorns are hooked and numerous, and the matt,

ROSA MAXIMOWICZIANA
syn. *R. glandulosa*
WHITE

This medium-sized, dense climbing shrub to 10 ft (3 m) tall bears slender branches with small, hooked prickles; the young shoots are bristly. The leaves are made up to seven to nine leaflets, smooth and semi-glossy with glandular stalks and mid-green in color. The flowers are scentless, white, single and about 2 in (5 cm) across. They come in small corymbs and are produced in early summer. The blooms are followed by small and oval, red hips. It is seldom seen

Rosa laevigata

Rosa × macrantha 'Macrantha'

except in the major collections, and is not of great value. **R. maximowicziana jackii** is almost thornless and has purplish wood. ZONES 4–10.

Korea, pre-1880

ROSA MICRANTHA
syns *R. floribunda, R. nemerosa, R. rubiginosa*
LIGHT PINK

Closely related to *R. eglanteria*, this species carries small, pale pink flowers. The plant will grow up to 6 ft (2 m) tall in ideal conditions. *R. micrantha* has become naturalized across North America. ZONES 4–10.

Mediterrarean, pre-1800

ROSA MOSCHATA
syn. 'The Musk Rose'
WHITE

A tall shrub or small climber to 10 ft (3 m) tall with firm, grayish green wood, *R. moschata* is sparsely populated with brown, hooked thorns. The gray-green leaves are soft to touch, downy on the undersides, especially on its prominent veins, inclined to droop and are made up of five to seven leaflets. The flowers are fragrant and creamy white, with well-spaced single petals; on hot days they reflex backwards. Each flower is about 1½ in (4 cm) across and loosely arranged in large corymbs that first appear in late summer, and repeat well into autumn. *R. moschata* is an ancestor of many Modern Garden Roses. Until it was rediscovered by Graham Stuart Thomas in 1963, the species was thought to be lost to cultivation. Prior to then, *R. brunonii* had been erroneously distributed through nurseries as *R. moschata*; a confusion that is still prevalent in some parts of the world to this day. It is an excellent

small climber or shrub. **R. moschata 'Plena'** is a seldom-seen, double form. ZONES 4–10.

Mediterranean Europe, 1614

ROSA MOYESII
MEDIUM RED

A sturdy and angular shrub to 10 ft (3 m) tall, this species has strong, reddish brown stems with numerous sharp, stout thorns often arranged in pairs. Each leaf has seven to eleven, mid-green to grayish green, serrated and oval leaflets. The flowers, which appear in early summer, are arranged in small groups and are dark glowing red in color and have very prominent golden colored stamens; the petals are often dusted with their profuse pollen. The hips appear in late summer and are drooping, flagon shaped and bright orange-red in color. These are probably of more garden value than its flowers. *R. moyesii* has brought forth several good Modern Shrubs over the years, including 'Eos', 'Geranium', 'Highdownensis' and 'Sealing Wax', which can be found in the main A–Z sequence. **R. moyesii fargesii** is a pink-flowered form that is similar to the species in all respects, except it is not as tall. ZONES 4–10.

China, circa 1890

ROSA MULLIGANII
WHITE

This vigorous scrambler of distinction produces long, dark green branches with broad strong thorns. It grows up to 20 ft (6 m) tall. The glossy dark green leaves are reddish purple when young, and are made up of five to seven large, elliptical leaflets. Fragrant flowers are borne in broad panicles in early summer, which are large for this type of climber attaining a size of up to 2½ in (6 cm) in good soil and an agreeable climate. The smooth

Rosa moyesii 'Geranium'

Rosa moschata (double form)

Rosa moyesii

Rosa moyesii (hips)

Rosa moyesii fargesii

Rosa mulliganii

Rosa multiflora cathayensis

Rosa nitida

Rosa multiflora carnea

and broadly oval hips have persistent sepals, and are orange-red in color. Quite hardy, this species is said to occasionally give a modest repeat-bloom in favorably warm conditions. It is an excellent garden-worthy species that has, until recently, been wrongly and widely distributed as *R. longicuspis*. ZONES 4–11.
China, 1917

ROSA MULTIFLORA
WHITE

This small climber, rambler or relaxed arching shrub is dense in habit with wiry, greenish brown branches that are only partially armed with darkish colored thorns. The leaves are made up of seven to nine leaflets, which are soft but leath-ery, mid-green in color and oblong in shape. Small single flowers with a distinctly fruity fragrance are produced in great profusion in mid-summer in upright conical clusters. The flowers are usually creamy white, but some are pink-edged. They are followed by small and rounded, inconspicuous orange hips each autumn. This species propagates easily from seeds or cuttings, so has been used widely as a hedging plant. It also makes a good rootstock; it is still commonly used for this purpose in commercial rose production, especially in warm climates. In some areas, especially in the USA, it has become so naturalized that it has become a despised weed. It is an important ancestor of many good summer-flowering Ramblers. *R. multiflora carnea*, introduced in 1804, is a stronger-growing, double, light pink form. *R. multiflora cathayensis*, which first appeared in 1902, is similar in most respects to the species except for its color, which is shade of soft blush pink. *R. multiflora watsoniana* (syn. 'Bamboo Rose') is treated as a novelty because of its creamy variegated leaves. It was introduced in 1870. 'De la Grifferaie' and 'Seven Sisters' are also descendants of *R. multiflora*, and both roses appear in the main A–Z sequence. ZONES 4–11.
Korea and Japan, 1862

ROSA NITIDA
MEDIUM PINK

This well-foliated, dense and short-growing shrub has many spines and prickles. It grows up to 3 ft (1 m) in good soils and is particularly good on its own roots as a free-suckering ground cover. The leaves are composed of seven to nine small, serrated, narrowly oblong leaflets, which are glossy dark green and dull and downy on the undersides; they change to brownish red in autumn. Single blooms—up to 2 in (5 cm) across—are produced in mid-summer. They are bright mid-pink, silky in texture and are followed in late summer and autumn by small, globular and slightly hairy bright red hips. This species grows readily from seed and is consequently used extensively for large-scale ground cover work. **'Corylus'** (*R. nitida* × *R. rugosa*) is a useful offspring that performs in much the same way as its parent, except that it grows a little taller and has more intense autumn coloring. ZONES 4–11.
North America, circa 1807

Rosa multiflora

Rosa nitida

ROSA NUTKANA
syn. 'Nutka Rose'
MEDIUM PINK

This medium-sized shrub to 5 ft (1.5 m) tall is upright in habit with slender stems of a purplish brown color. The thorns, which are generally found on older wood only, are straight and sharp. The young shoots are bristly, and the leaves are made up of five to nine smooth, broadly elliptical, dark green, serrated leaflets that have downy undersides. Produced singly, the flowers are single, lavender-purple in color with pronounced creamy yellow stamens. They are up to 2½ in (6 cm) across and appear in mid-summer. Very conspicuous, plumply oval, bright red hips follow. *R. nutkana* 'Cantab', introduced in 1927, is the best-known hybrid, being deep pink and flowering late in summer. It is slightly taller than the species. 'Schoener's Nutkana', another garden-worthy hybrid, appears in the main A–Z section of this book. ZONES 4–11.

North America, circa 1876

ROSA OMEIENSIS
WHITE

Although a species in its own right, it is so botanically similar to *R. sericea* that the two are now generally treated as the same. It is described under the heading of the latter. ZONES 4–11.

China, 1901

Rosa roxburghii plena

Rosa pisocarpa

ROSA PENDULINA
syns 'Alpine Rose', *R. alpina*
DEEP PINK/MAUVE

This upright, medium to tall shrub is about 6 ft (1.8 m) tall and has reddish purple, almost thornless stems. The leaves are composed of seven to nine slightly serrated, oblong leaflets, dark green in color with purple undertones. The blooms are produced singly or in small groups of up to five, and are deep mauve-pink with prominent creamy yellow stamens. They are produced in late spring and early summer. The slim and flask-shaped hips are bright orange-red. *R. pendulina* is a good shrub where a thornless rose is wanted, giving excellent, richly colored autumn foliage that combines nicely with the fruit. ZONES 4–10.

Europe, 1789

ROSA PHOENICIA
WHITE

This short to medium-growing climber or rambler has slender stems of darkish green, sparsely populated with small and hooked prickles. The grayish green leaves are made up of five to seven rounded and serrated, downy leaflets. Borne in corymbs, the white flowers are each about 1½ in (4 cm) across with no scent. The attractive hips are small and roundly oval in shape, and deep red in color.

Rosa pendulina

It is half hardy only and said to be the ancient parent of the Damask Roses. *R. moschata*, to which it bears much resemblance, is of far superior garden merit. ZONES 4–10.

Turkey, circa 1885

ROSA PISOCARPA
MEDIUM PINK

This summer flowering shrub bears small pink flowers, which are only about 1 in (2 cm) in diameter. They are carried on very short stalks in many flowered clusters, and are followed by globular hips. ZONES 4–10.

Western North America, circa 1882

ROSA POMIFERA
syns 'Apple Rose', *R. villosa*
MEDIUM PINK

This dense shrub to 6 ft (1.8 m) carries grayish green wood, sometimes slightly mottled with purple, that is randomly armed with straight sharp prickles. The young wood is reddish in color. The plentiful foliage made up of five to nine broadly oblong and generously serrated leaflets is dull grayish green in color and downy to touch. In mid-summer, usually in clusters of three, but sometimes only singly, clear pink, slightly fragrant flowers, some 2 in (5 cm) across, are borne. The hips are very bristly, globular to oval, medium sized, and deep red in color when fully ripe. 'Duplex', a semi-double form, which is more free-flowering, appears in the main A–Z. ZONES 4–11.

Europe and Asia

ROSA PRIMULA
syn. 'Incense Rose'
LIGHT YELLOW

The main characteristic of this rose is its fabulously incense-scented foliage that adorns a medium-sized shrub 2–4 ft (60–120 cm) tall. The leaves are small, and the thin, flexible stems are covered with many red prickles. In very early spring, *R. primula* carries a flush of

Rosa primula

yellowish white flowers. In North America, it was wrongly cultivated for a long time as *R. ecae*, which is a different species. ZONES 4–11.

Turkestan to Northern China, 1910
Royal Horticultural Society Award of Garden Merit

ROSA ROXBURGHII
syns 'Burr Rose', 'Chestnut Rose'
MEDIUM PINK

This is an interesting and somewhat un-rose-like shrub to 8 ft (2.5 m). It is angular and stiff in habit and the bark of the buffy brown stems flakes and peels with age; they are well armed with stout thorns that protrude from just below its leaves in pairs. The leaves are composed of seven to fifteen mid- to dark green, small, oblong leaflets, each distinctly hairy. In early summer, reasonably large, bright pink, satiny flowers are produced with prominent bosses of soft creamy yellow stamens. The fruits are very distinctive, like small chestnuts in their husks, turning from green to russet brown as they age. *R. roxburghii normalis* is similar in all respects, except it has blush pink to white flowers. *R. roxburghii plena*, introduced in 1814, is an excellent double, deep pink form that was known long before the species. Its beautiful flowers are often hidden by the foliage. ZONES 4–11.

China and Japan, 1908

Rosa roxburghii plena

Rosa rugosa alba

Rosa rugosa (hips)

Rosa sempervirens

Rosa rugosa

ROSA RUGOSA
syns 'Hedgehog Rose', 'The Japanese Rose'
MAUVE

This rose makes a dense, free-branching shrub to a height of 8 ft (2.5 m). Its fawny brown stems are heavily endowed with sharp, similar colored thorns. The leaves usually have seven to nine leaflets that are dark green and semi-glossy, broadly oval and serrated, often appearing wrinkled. They change to shades of rich yellow in the autumn. The single, scented flowers, produced solitarily or several together, open to 2½ in (6.5 cm) across and are bright deep pink in color with soft yellow stamens. They continue to appear from early summer through to autumn. The hips are large, globose, bright red and held on short stalks and are a major ornamental feature of this species and of its many forms and hybrids. **R. rugosa alba** is a white form that is particularly good with larger flowers up to 3 in (8 cm) across. Its fruit are more conspicuous both in size and color. **R. rugosa rubra** is a reddish purple form.

R. rugosa kamtchatica, introduced in 1770, is probably the result of a chance cross with *R. rugosa* and another species. It is less coarse than *R. rugosa* with greenish wood and fewer prickles, and its foliage is less wrinkly and brighter green. It has bright pink, single flowers. *R. rugosa* has been extensively hybridized over the years resulting in a wide selection of superbly healthy and hardy cultivars. 'Roseraie de l'Haÿ', 'Blanc Double de Coubert' and 'Frau Dagmar Hartopp' are just three of its better-known offspring, which can be found in the main A–Z. **ZONES 3–10.**
China and Japan, pre-1854

ROSA SEMPERVIRENS
WHITE

This vigorous climbing, evergreen species up to 20 ft (6 m) has flexible, long and trailing, dark green stems armed with moderate numbers of reddish prickles. The leaves are made up of five to seven long and pointed, oval and glossy leaflets. The single flowers are pro-duced in corymbs, and are up to 1½ in (4 cm) in diameter, white, fragrant and appear in mid-summer. The oval hips are bright red. *R. sempervirens* is important as the progenitor of several good Rambler Roses known collectively as 'The Evergreens'. The species is also significant in playing a part in the early development of the Ayrshires. It is not fully hardy, although its offspring appear to tolerate much lower temperatures. **ZONES 4–11.**
Mediterranean and Northern Africa, 1629

ROSA SERICEA
WHITE

This rose is seldom seen in cultivation. It differs little from the better known form *R. sericea pteracantha*, described below, except in its thorns, which are less spectacular. **ZONES 4–11.**
Himalayas, China, 1822

ROSA SERICEA PTERACANTHA
syns *R. omeiensis pteracantha*, 'Wingthorn Rose'
WHITE

This tall, angular shrub becomes stiff and rugged with age. Its older wood is brown with numerous fawny colored vicious thorns, and will reach a height of 10 ft

Rosa rugosa rubra

Rosa rugosa kamtchatica

Rosa setipoda

Rosa sherardii

(3 m) if left unpruned; however, the shrub is better kept to much lower proportions, for by so doing, its most ornamental features, which are displayed in the new growth each year, will be encouraged. The young shoots are purplish in color and armed with many large, translucent cherry red, wing-like thorns all along their length. The leaves are small, dark green and fern-like, and made up of seven to eleven small leaflets, hairy on their undersides. Composed of only four white petals, the flowers are about 1½ in (4 cm) across and appear in late spring. The fruit is small, plump and yellow-orange, and of little significance overall. **R. sericea chrysocarpa** has yellow fruits. ZONES 4–10.

China, 1890

ROSA SETIGERA
syn. 'Prairie Rose'
DEEP PINK

A shrub to 5 ft (1.5 m) tall with smooth, dark green wood and a moderate number of hooked prickles, *R. setigera* has leaves that are composed of three to five long, broadly oval, smooth and serrated, bright green leaflets with downy and grayish undersides. The flowers, which are deep pink paling with age, are well spaced in small groups, each 2½ in (6.5 cm) across. They never appear in large numbers together, but are produced over a long season from early to late summer. The fruit are round and of an insignificant greenish brown color. This rose is useful for its long flowering display and extreme hardiness. When used as a seed parent, it has given rise to some excellent progeny over the years, bringing forth climbers such as 'Baltimore Belle' and 'Long John Silver', both of which are described in the A–Z section. ZONES 4–11.

North America, 1810

ROSA SETIPODA
LIGHT PINK

This sturdy shrub up to 12 ft (4 m) unpruned has brownish colored older wood. It is very branching in habit, with sparsely arranged stout and pointed thorns. The leaves are composed of seven to nine, dark green, broadly oval and deeply serrated leaflets. The flowers, which appear in early summer, are about 2 in (5 cm) across, clear pink, paler in the centers, and have large bosses of creamy yellow stamens with profuse pollen. The petals are sometimes

notched on the outer edges. These blooms are arranged in clusters and are scented. It is the hips, though, that makes this rose so valuable as a garden plant; these can be up to 2½ in (6.5 cm) long and are plumply flagon shaped, whiskery, and bright orange-red in color. ZONES 4–10.

China, 1895

ROSA SHERARDII
syn. *R. omissa*
DEEP PINK

This dense shrub grows to 6 ft (1.8 m) tall, and is made up of short, muddled branches with randomly placed hooked and sharp prickles. The leaves are formed by seven to nine leaflets, which are bluish green in color and broadly elliptical in shape. The bright deep pink, single flowers, arranged in small clusters, are produced in late spring and early summer. Broadly oval, bright red hips follow. The density of this shrub makes it ideal for a tall, informal hedge or free-standing specimen shrub. ZONES 4–10.

Europe, 1933

ROSA SICULA
syn. *R. seraphinii*
DEEP PINK TO WHITE

A low-growing shrub up to 3 ft (1 m) in good soil, *R. sicula* suckers freely when grown on its own roots. It has reddish tinted branches amply armed with slender sharp prickles, and the leaves are made up of five to nine small roundish leaflets, slightly aromatic when crushed. Solitary, single flowers, ranging from pink to white, about 1 in (2.5 cm) in diameter, appear in late spring. These are followed by very small, globular to oval, red hips. It tolerates the most impoverished of soils, is quite hardy and looks good when planted in small groups. ZONES 4–10.

Europe and Northern Africa, circa 1894

Rosa sicula

ROSA SOULIEANA
WHITE

This tall shrub is capable of growing up to 15 ft (5 m) in good conditions. Its relaxed habit also provides it with a very broad girth. The long, grayish green stems are covered with an armature of long and slender, sharp yellowish prickles and the leaves, plentiful and soft grayish green, are made up of seven to nine leaflets, which are broadly elliptical, sharply serrated and slightly downy to touch. The flowers, about 1½ in (4 cm) across are single, white and fragrant and borne in tightly packed corymbs along the arching branches in mid-summer. They are quite a sight when a mature plant is in full flush. A great abundance of small round orange hips follow. *R. soulieana* is probably best in climates where severe frosts are not a regular occurrence. ZONES 4–10.

China, 1896

Royal Horticultural Society Award of Garden Merit

ROSA SPINOSISSIMA
syns 'Altaica', 'Burnet Rose', *R. pimpinellifolia*, 'Scots Rose'
WHITE

This short-growing, dense and prickly shrub suckers freely when grown on its own roots. The branches are upright or only slightly arching and greenish brown in color, thickly populated with both sharp thorns and bristles. There are five to eleven heavily serrated and broadly oval leaflets per leaf, which look almost fern-like *en masse*. They are darkish

green in color, changing to russet-brown in autumn. The flowers are produced in great profusion in late spring to early summer, and they are creamy white, single and quite beautiful with golden brown stamens. The globular hips are mahogany to black when ripe. **R. s. altaica**, (syn. *R. s.* 'Grandiflora'), introduced from western Asia in 1820, is a taller grower with larger, soft primrose flowers. It is a superior plant to the species, but both are worthwhile in any type of garden. In Victorian times, *R. spinosissima* was extensively used as a parent, giving rise to many double and single, short-growing shrub roses in a variety of colors. They include such varieties as 'Mary Queen of Scots', 'Single Cherry' and 'William III'. In the 1950s some excellent shrub roses were raised in Germany from this species, such as 'Frühlingsgold'. These can be found in the main A–Z. ZONES 3–11.

Europe, very ancient

Rosa spinosissima

Rosa spinosissima altaica

Rosa spinosissima (foliage)

Rosa sericea pteracantha

Rosa sweginzowii

Rosa sweginzowii (hips)

Rosa virginiana

ROSA STELLATA MIRIFICA
syns 'The Gooseberry Rose',
'The Sacramento Rose'
MAUVE

This unusual little shrub to 3 ft (1 m) is in many ways more like a gooseberry bush than a rose. It is dense and free branching, very prickly with slender pointed light green spines and many bristles. The leaves are made up of three to five grayish green, broadly oval and serrated leaflets. Single flowers are produced solitarily; they are lilac-pink with orange-yellow stamens and 1½ in (4 cm) across. Globular to urn-shaped, very bristly, inconspicuous red hips follow. It is quite a hardy rose, but is better grown in warm climates. **R. stellata**, introduced from southern USA in 1829, is shorter with deep purple flowers. ZONES 4–10.

Southwestern North America, 1916

Rosa tomentosa

ROSA SWEGINZOWII
MEDIUM PINK

This upright and sturdy shrub up to 15 ft (5 m) carries thick, brownish green wood with many bristles and large, flat, sharp thorns. The leaves are made up of seven to eleven oval to oblong, bright green, serrated leaflets, which have smooth uppersides and downy undersides with a prickly central rib. The flowers are 1½ in (4 cm) in diameter, and are produced singly or in threes together; they are bright pink with creamy yellow stamens, and appear in early summer. The hips are flagon shaped, slightly hairy and bright red. If space permits, this is a very showy shrub, for it is best left unpruned and allowed to develop its natural stature. **R. sweginzowii macrocarpa** is a superior form that came later from Germany. It has larger flowers and hips, and the color is much deeper. ZONES 3–10.

China, 1909

ROSA TOMENTOSA
syn. *R. cuspidata*
LIGHT PINK

Of upright and sturdy stature, this medium to tall shrub, 7 ft (2.2 m) tall, has greenish gray stems, that have stout, strong and sharp thorns. The leaves have five to seven leaflets that are broadly elliptical, dull grayish green, serrated and slightly furry to touch. The flowers are approximately 1½ in (4 cm) wide, single

Rosa webbiana

Rosa webbiana (hip)

and light pink in color. Small and oval red hips follow. *R. tomentosa* is of little importance as a garden plant, and is perhaps best grown as a hedge. ZONES 4–10.

Europe and Asia Minor, 1820

ROSA VIRGINIANA
syns *R. lucida*, 'Virginia Rose'
MEDIUM PINK

This upright-growing, small and free-suckering shrub to 5 ft (1.5 m) produces many reddish brown stems each with a few hooked brown thorns; the younger wood is often bristly. The leaves are made up of between seven and nine leaflets, which are glossy bright green at first,

Rosa woodsii

Rosa wichuraiana poteriifolia

then turn to rich russet-red and yellow in autumn, broadly elliptical in shape and generously serrated. Slightly scented, bright pink flowers, which are sometimes mottled slightly deeper and up to 2½ in (6.5 cm) across with many long yellow stamens, are produced either singly or in small groups over a long period during summer. The rounded hips are a shiny orange-red. This is an excellent garden shrub, which no serious rose lover should be without; it makes an excellent hedge. **R. virginiana** 'Alba' is a white form. Although it performs in much the same way as the pink species, it is less showy in most respects. ZONES 3–11.

North America, pre-1807

Royal Horticultural Society Award of Garden Merit

ROSA WEBBIANA
MEDIUM PINK

This graceful shrub attains a height and width of 5 ft (1.5 m). Its flexible stems are reddish purple in color, especially when young, later turning brownish; they develop long and sharp, straight, creamy yellow thorns as they age. The leaves are very small and broadly elliptical, bluish dark green, and made up of five to nine leaflets. The flowers are borne singly or in threes together, are lilac-pink, 1½ in (4 cm) in diameter and produced in early summer. Medium-sized, narrowly flask-shaped, bright scarlet and polished hips follow. This is a very ornamental species that tolerates all types of soil and climate. ZONES 4–11.

Himalayas and Turkey, 1879

ROSA WICHURAIANA
syns 'Memorial Rose', *R. luciliae*
WHITE

This semi-evergreen rambler or prostrate trailing rose up to 20 ft (6 m) tall is especially good in fertile soil. Its long and

Rosa woodsii

Rosa willmottiae

Rosa woodsii fendleri

Rosa woodsii fendleri (hip)

pliable, dark green stems are sparsely armed with hooked thorns. The plant is well foliated with glossy dark green leaves each with seven to nine rounded leaflets. Conical clusters of single white, fragrant flowers—1½ in (4 cm) wide—appear in mid- to late summer. Small, oval to round, dark red hips follow. This really is a first class garden plant in its own right, especially when allowed to expand as a ground cover, since it makes an impenetrable mound. It is also good when scrambling up into the branches of trees. *R. wichuraiana* was used extensively as a parent rose by breeders at the end of the nineteenth century, bringing forth such famous offspring as 'Dorothy Perkins', Albéric Barbier', 'Léontine Gervais', 'New Dawn' and 'Albertine', which are all described in the A–Z section of this book. **R. wichuraiana poteriifolia** is a compact form of the species. ZONES 3–11.
China and Japan, 1843

ROSA WILLMOTTIAE
MAUVE

Wider than tall, this shrub will attain a height of about 10 ft (3 m) in good soil. It produces long thin shoots that are purplish red in color and often covered in grayish bloom that is armed with tiny bristles and sharp prickles. The leaves are made up of three to nine, small and grayish, heavily serrated, oval leaflets. The flowers, which are borne all along the branches, are single, purplish pink and slightly scented, first appearing in early summer. Small, orange-red, pear-shaped hips follow. All these distinctive features make a charming, graceful shrub that is worthy of space in any garden. ZONES 3–11.
China, 1904

ROSA WOODSII
syn. 'Mountain Rose'
MEDIUM PINK

This shrub grows to 6 ft (1.8 m) in most situations, but it is not of great garden value. **R. woodsii fendleri**, introduced from North America in 1888, is superior to *R. woodsii* and more commonly grown. It is an upright shrub that freely produces stems of purplish gray with an abundance of slender prickles, although the slim and arching, flowering branches have fewer prickles. The leaflets are five to seven per leaf and are widely oval, serrated and grayish dark green in color. In mid-summer, flowers are produced singly or in twos and threes; they are lilac-pink in color and about 1½ in (4 cm) across. The fruit is about the size and shape of a cherry and bright red, their weight often causing the strong branches to arch over in an attractive way. It is a good shrub for hedging or for a wild garden. ZONES 3–11.
North America, 1820

ROSA XANTHINA
syn. 'Manchu Rose'
MEDIUM YELLOW

This is an upright, branching shrub to 6 ft (1.8 m) tall, with smooth mahogany brown stems and many thorns. The leaves are made up of seven to fifteen dark green leaflets. The flowers are bright yellow, single or occasionally semi-double, and they have golden brown stamens. They are borne in abundance in late spring, but there is only a small crop of oval, brownish red hips. **R. xanthina lindleyii** is a consistently semi-double form. **R. xanthina spontanea** is often confused with 'Canary Bird' (probably *R. hugonis* × *R. xanthina*), which is by far the best known of this group. It appears in the main A–Z. ZONES 3–11.
China and Korea, 1906

Rosa xanthina spontanea

Rosa xanthina lindleyii

A

'A COUNTRY WOMAN'
MODERN, LARGE-FLOWERED/HYBRID TEA,
DARK RED, REPEAT-FLOWERING

Released in Australia in 1997, 'A Country Woman' is named for the Country Women's Association, an organization that devotes much of its time to fund-raising and community support in Australian country regions. The deep red, fully double flowers are borne either singly or in small clusters. It is a tall-growing, strong bush rose with good disease resistance. So far, this rose has only been released in Australia. ZONES 4–9.

Zary, USA, 1997

'Ingrid Bergmann' × 'Olympiad'

'A LONGS PÉDONCULES'
OLD, MOSS, LIGHT PINK

This rose is aptly named for its long, narrow stalk (*pédoncule* is French for stalk), the area of the cane between the blossom and the first leaves. The small, mossy buds open to reveal a pink-lilac flush on

'A Country Woman'

the fragrant double blooms. It is a vigorous grower that performs best in part-shade and woodland settings. The foliage is an attractive light gray-green. It does well on its own roots and is resistant to most diseases. This is a tidy yet relaxed shrub that grows to a height of some 6 ft (1.8 m). Monsieur Robert of Angers, the hybridizer of 'Biarritz', produced some other still-famous roses such as 'Général Kléber' and 'Maréchal Davoust'. Sadly, its distribution and availability are limited. ZONES 5–10.

Robert, France, 1854

Parentage unknown

'AALSMEER GOLD'
syn. 'Bekola'

MODERN, LARGE-FLOWERED/HYBRID TEA,
DEEP YELLOW, REPEAT-FLOWERING

'Aalsmeer Gold' has been a cut-flower rose for growing under glass for 20 years. It is also an excellent garden rose, bearing its deep yellow 25-petalled flowers

'Aalsmeer Gold'

both singly and in small clusters. The buds are tinged with red on the outer petals when grown outdoors. The medium-sized, very well-formed blooms have high centers and hold well, both on the bush and when picked. The foliage is glossy dark green and abundant and the plant has a very bushy growth habit and a very quick repeat. There are no disease problems. ZONES 4–9.

Kordes, Germany, 1978

'Berolina' × seedling

'ABAILARD'
syns 'Abalard', 'Abaillard'
OLD, GALLICA, PINK BLEND

This rare Gallica is a survivor of a group that once numbered in the thousands. Typical of its kind, it is a low shrub that produces double blooms of medium size in late spring or early summer. The unusual-looking buds are surrounded by pointed leaves. The color is a marbled combination of pink and deep pink petals, making this a most attractive rose. ZONES 4–10.

Vibert, France, 1845

Parentage unknown

'ABBAYE DE CLUNY'   MEIbrinpay
MODERN, LARGE-FLOWERED/HYBRID TEA,
APRICOT BLEND, REPEAT-FLOWERING

This very free-blooming rose has fragrant flowers of an apricot blend that hold their form rather well. They are repeat-flowering. A bushy, healthy grower with dark green foliage, it is suitable as a bedding rose or as a standard. Propagation is by budding. This variety, which has a remarkable track record for awards in European trials, is curiously not as widely grown as it deserves to be. ZONES 4–9.

Meilland, France, 1996

'Just Joey' × (MEIresif × MEInan)

Monza Gold Medal 1993, Lyon Gold Medal 1994, Plus Belle de France 1994, Belfast Gold Medal 1995

'ABBEYFIELD ROSE'   COCbrose
MODERN, LARGE-FLOWERED/HYBRID TEA,
DEEP PINK, REPEAT-FLOWERING

'Abbeyfield Rose' has deep pink to rose red, very double and large, well-formed flowers consisting of 35 petals; they have a slight fragrance and are repeat-flowering. Mid-green, semi-glossy foliage appears on a bushy plant of medium height, which makes for a good bedding plant or a well-proportioned standard. It is hardy and moderately resistant to disease and should be propagated by budding. It was named to raise the profile of a charitable trust. ZONES 4–9.

Cocker, UK, 1985

'National Trust' × 'Silver Jubilee'

Glasgow Golden Prize 1990, Royal Horticultural Society Award of Garden Merit 1993

'ABBOTSWOOD'
MODERN, MODERN SHRUB, MEDIUM PINK

'Abbotswood' has pink double flowers that are slightly fragrant and which appear right throughout summer. With its tall and spreading habit it is perhaps better suited to the wild garden. It is a healthy, vigorous variety that is generally propagated from cuttings. ZONES 3–9.

Hilling, UK, 1954

A chance hybrid of *Rosa canina* × an unknown garden variety

'ABIGAILE'   TANelaigib
MODERN, CLUSTER-FLOWERED/FLORIBUNDA,
PINK BLEND

'Abigaile' is a short, bushy grower that is a useful plant for the small garden, in pots or window boxes or as a short

'Abbeyfield Rose'

standard. It has clusters of small double blooms that are a silvery pink and are tipped with carmine; they are very pretty but have little scent. It is moderately disease resistant and can be propagated from cuttings or by budding. ZONES 4–9.

Tantau, Germany, 1988

Parentage unknown

'ABRAHAM DARBY'   AUScot

syns 'Abraham', 'Country Darby'

MODERN, MODERN SHRUB, ORANGE-PINK, REPEAT-FLOWERING

The cup-formed, very large flowers of 'Abraham Darby' appear in small clusters; they are a peachy pink/apricot blend and have a strong, pronounced fragrance. The variety has dark green foliage and bushy growth that spreads slightly but is well shaped and tall. It enjoys moderate resistance to disease but can be susceptible to rust. Popular in a shrub border, it is repeat-flowering and was named after one of the founders of the Industrial Revolution. ZONES 4–9.

Austin, UK, 1985

'Aloha' × 'Yellow Cushion'

'ACAPULCO'   DICblender

MODERN, LARGE-FLOWERED/HYBRID TEA, RED BLEND, REPEAT-FLOWERING

The beautifully shaped long ivory yellow buds with scarlet tips on 'Acapulco' merge into classically shaped double flowers. The blooms, which are produced singly or in small clusters, are moderately fragrant. It is an upright grower with handsome dark green foliage and is reasonably disease resistant. Originally tested and launched as a cut-flower variety, it is gaining popularity as a very good garden plant. ZONES 4–9.

Dickson, UK, 1997

Parentage unknown

'Abraham Darby'

'Acey Deucy'

'Adam'

'ACEY DEUCY'   SAVathree

MODERN, MINIATURE, MEDIUM RED, REPEAT-FLOWERING

The vibrant electric red blooms contain about 20 petals, with a high-centered Large-flowered form suitable for exhibition. A black overlay on the reverse of the petals gives additional depth to the color. The bush may be slow to establish in cooler climates but the growth habit, 12–24 in (30–60 cm) tall, is relatively compact and is complemented by small, medium green, semi-glossy foliage. In warmer climates the florets are usually borne singly and have a light fragrance. It naturally grows one bloom per stem exclusively and can last between 3–5 days. 'Acey Deucy' is one of many great Miniatures developed during the late 1970s and early 1980s from experimenting with 'Sheri Anne' as pollen parent. ZONES 5–11.

Saville, USA, 1982

('Yellow Jewel' × 'Tamango') × 'Sheri Anne'

'ACHIEVEMENT'

MODERN, RAMBLER, DEEP PINK

This rose has small pink flowers and dainty leaves and is similar to 'Dorothy Perkins', although not as vigorous. It has no fragrance but is a great choice for pillars or pergolas. The foliage is variegated, so the bush remains attractive even after its early summer bloom. Formerly grown in New Zealand, it was reported to sport back frequently to 'Dorcas', a Rambler from 1922. ZONES 5–11.

English, UK, 1925

Sport of 'Dorcas'

'ACIDALIE'

OLD, BOURBON, WHITE, REPEAT-FLOWERING

'Acidalie' produces large, bowl-shaped blooms—nearly 3 in (8 cm) across—that

'Adair Roche'

'Acapulco'

appear at first as flesh-colored petals and then soften to white with a thin pink edge. Covered with prickles, the long canes make the rose suitable for a pillar or wall. It has some repeat bloom, but it is hard to find these days. Rousseau produced one great rose still in commerce, 'Général Jacqueminot', a Hybrid Perpetual. ZONES 5–11.

Rousseau, France, 1838

Parentage unknown

'ADAIR ROCHE'

MODERN, LARGE-FLOWERED/HYBRID TEA, PINK BLEND, REPEAT-FLOWERING

The large pink double flowers of 'Adair Roche', which are composed of 30 petals, have a silver reverse. They are well formed and slightly fragrant. The mid-green, glossy foliage is borne on a vigorous bush that is resistant to disease. Used as a bedding plant or as a standard, it is repeat-flowering. It was named for the architect who designed McGredy's house. ZONES 4–9.

McGredy, New Zealand, 1968

'Paddy McGredy' × seedling of 'Femina'

Belfast Gold Medal 1971

'ADAM'

OLD, TEA, MEDIUM PINK, REPEAT-FLOWERING

'Adam' helped to establish the reputation of the new class of Tea Roses. It was popular throughout the nineteenth century, having been raised by Monsieur Adam in his garden at Rheims, France. Semi-double, copper-pink, large globular blooms appear in clusters on short canes with hooked, purple prickles. The buds are very attractive. Its only weakness is a slight tendency to mildew in wet weather. 'Adam', a Tea Rose that really

'Adam Messerich'

smells like tea, is easy to grow and is stronger than most of its kin as it will survive in cooler climates. ZONES 5–10.

Adam, France, 1838

Possibly 'Hume's Blush' × 'Rose Edouard'

'ADAM MESSERICH'

OLD, BOURBON, MEDIUM RED, REPEAT-FLOWERING

This is one of the more popular Bourbons because of its disease resistance and abundant rebloom. The rose red blossoms are medium sized, semi-double and cupped and fade in strong sunlight. The growth is upright and vigorous, and the bush will reach 5 ft by 4 ft (1.5 m by 1.2 m) at maturity. There is a slight raspberry fragrance. It is frequently seen in bouquets because of its erect stems and flowers. When the rose opens, the lovely stamens vie for attention. This was very popular in Victorian England, and Bourbon Roses frequently appear in paintings of the time. ZONES 5–10.

Lambert, Germany, 1920

'Frau Oberhofgartner Singer' × (seedling of 'Louise Odier' × 'Louis Philippe')

'Adventure'

'Adélaïde d'Orléans'

'ADAM'S SMILE' SAVarend, SAVasmile
MODERN, MINIATURE, DEEP PINK, REPEAT-FLOWERING

What a sensational color this variety brings to a garden. Brilliant deep pink flowers, containing 23–27 petals, adorn an upright, compact bush sporting blooms of exquisite Large-flowered form. In most climates, the foliage is small, mid-green, semi-glossy and has unusual prickles that are characteristically gray-red and point downwards. 'Adam's Smile' gives neither fruit nor fragrance. In warm climates the flowers are borne singly with an occasional spray of 3–5 blooms. In cooler climates the deep pink color may become a muddy pink. The plant can provide an ample supply of cut flowers all season long. It was named by the hydridizer for one of his grandchildren. ZONES 4–11.

Saville, USA, 1991

('Rise 'n' Shine' × 'Sheri Anne') × 'Rainbow's End'

'ADÉLAÏDE D'ORLÉANS'
syn. 'Léopoldine d'Orléans'
OLD, SEMPERVIRENS, WHITE

The small buds of this gracious rambling rose are rosy pink before opening into pale white flowers that enfold striking yellow stamens. The clusters of loosely double blooms offer a delicate primrose scent. Sempervirens Roses are a result of the work of Monsieur Jacques, gardener to the Duc d'Orléans at the Chateau de Neuilly; the duke later became King Louis Philippe, after whom several roses were named. *Rosa sempervirens* blood gives them a strong constitution. In mid-summer, the long, slender canes with red prickles are covered with blooms. It looks wonderful on arches or pergolas—an attractive addition to any garden. ZONES 5–11.

Jacques, France, 1826

Parentage unknown

Royal Horticultural Society Award of Garden Merit 1993

'Admiral Rodney'

'ADÈLE PRÉVOST'
OLD, GALLICA, LIGHT PINK

This very rare Gallica was one of hundreds listed in nurseryman Prévost's catalogue in 1830. It was described as an upright, vigorous shrub with large, full blooms of blush pink with dark centers. The outer petals are reflexed while the inner ones are erect. ZONES 4–10.

Prévost, France, pre-1836

Parentage unknown

'ADMIRAL RODNEY'
MODERN, LARGE-FLOWERED/HYBRID TEA, PINK BLEND, REPEAT-FLOWERING

This very large-flowered variety is grown for its potential and for its appeal and almost exclusively for exhibition purposes. A robust grower, it has large, glossy dark green foliage. A bushy plant with very classically shaped, fragrant blooms of rose pink and a deeper reverse, composed of 45 petals, it is a respected favorite on the show bench. ZONES 4–9.

Trew, UK, 1973

Parentage unknown

'ADOLF HORSTMANN'
syn. 'Adolph Horstmann'
MODERN, LARGE-FLOWERED/HYBRID TEA, YELLOW BLEND, REPEAT-FLOWERING

This has rich yellow-orange, medium-sized, double flowers with a classic Large-flowered form. They are slightly fragrant. With its glossy foliage, vigorous upright form and repeat-flowering capacity it is a good subject for bedding or for growing as a standard. Reasonably

healthy and free flowering, it was named after the principal of a well-known nursery in northern Germany. ZONES 4–9.

Kordes, Germany, 1971

'Color Wonder' × 'Dr A. J. Verhage'

'ADVENTURE'
syn. 'Aventure'
MODERN, LARGE-FLOWERED/HYBRID TEA, ORANGE-RED, REPEAT-FLOWERING

The large orange-red flowers of 'Adventure' are composed of 55 petals and have a high center. They are slightly fragrant. The growth habit is bushy, upright and healthy, while the dark green foliage is very glossy. It is suitable as a bedder and for use in exhibitions. Propagation is by budding. ZONES 4–9.

Croix, France, 1964

('Corail' × 'Baccará') × seedling

'AENNCHEN VON THARAU'
syn. 'Annie of Tharau'
OLD, AYRSHIRE, WHITE

Named after the subject of a very romantic folk song, this once-blooming rose is the result of an unusual cross between 2 hardy roses. The medium-sized, double blossoms are creamy white, with a yellow-pink cast. The outer petals are reflexed; the large flower looks very much like a Centifolia Rose. This is a very hardy rose growing to a height of 9 ft (2.7 m) and is an excellent plant for the wild garden or at the back of the border. The dark green foliage sets off the bright blossoms. ZONES 4–10.

Geschwind, Hungary, 1886

Rosa alba × unknown Ayrshire

'Africa Star'

'Adolf Horstmann'

A

'Agatha Christie'

'Agathe Incarnata'

'Agnes'

'AFRICA STAR'

MODERN, LARGE-FLOWERED/HYBRID TEA, MAUVE, REPEAT-FLOWERING

This variety has very large, mauve, double blooms with 65 petals. It has a bushy growth habit with coppery foliage and is disease tolerant. 'Africa Star' can be grown in beds or as a standard and is propagated by budding. This rose owes its name to the fact that it was raised by Olga West of Que Que in what was then Rhodesia. ZONES 4–9.

West, Zimbabwe, 1965

Parentage unknown

'AFTERGLOW'

syn. 'Sam Buff'

MODERN, LARGE-FLOWERED/HYBRID TEA, ORANGE BLEND, REPEAT-FLOWERING

This Large-flowered variety produces long, pointed buds that open into golden yellow blooms with bright orange undersides. Slightly fragrant and double, the large flowers grow on long stems. The growth habit is bushy, while the glossy foliage is bluish green. ZONES 4–9.

LeGrice, UK, 1938

Sport of 'Mrs Sam McGredy'

'AGATHA'

syns Rosa × francofurtana agatha, R. gallica agatha

OLD, GALLICA, LIGHT PINK

'Agatha' is one of the survivors of a group from the eighteenth and nineteenth centuries called 'The Agathe Roses'; no one is sure why they have this name, though many theories are proposed. It is a broad-growing, dense, relaxed shrub to 5 ft (1.5 m) with dark greenish gray, almost thornless cane-like stems. The foliage is dark green, rather deeply veined, large, healthy and plentiful. The flowers are very fragrant, abundant and are up to 3 in (8 cm) across and borne in small clusters. These emerge

from tubby buds with feathery sepals in mid-summer and are made up of many beautifully arranged deep reddish pink petals each with paler reverses, often paling to softer pink especially around the outer edges of the fully open blooms. Completely disease resistant, this is a superb rose of distinction. ZONES 4–10.

France, circa 1800

Possibly Rosa gallica × R. pendulina

'AGATHA CHRISTIE' KORmeita

syn. 'Ramira'

MODERN, LARGE-FLOWERED CLIMBER, MEDIUM PINK, REPEAT-FLOWERING

This rose bears large, fragrant, glowing pink blooms. The foliage is dark green and glossy on a reasonably healthy plant. It is a great rose for walls or pillars, and it also makes an attractive large shrub. It was named for the British mystery writer who died in 1976. ZONES 4–9.

Kordes, Germany, 1990

Parentage unknown

'AGATHE INCARNATA'

OLD, GALLICA, MEDIUM PINK

Though the blossoms look fragile, this beautiful rose is a member of one of the hardiest groups of roses. The pale, soft pink blooms are very freely produced in sizeable clusters, each bloom about 1½ in (4 cm) across, perhaps slightly bigger in good fertile soil, which it prefers. The fragrant blooms, which appear in early summer, are composed of many narrow petals to form flat, often quartered flowers with a pronounced button eye in the center. The very thin petals are not happy in wet weather. This is a fairly prickly shrub of tidy habit to some 4 ft (1.2 m) in height. The foliage is grayish green and soft in texture. This Gallica has remained popular ever since its introduction. ZONES 3–9.

Pre-1811

Unknown Gallica × unknown Damask

'AGE TENDRE'

MODERN, LARGE-FLOWERED/HYBRID TEA, DEEP PINK, REPEAT-FLOWERING

'Age Tendre' produces long, pointed buds that open into large, double, high-centered pink flowers. They have little fragrance, but the variety is repeat-flowering and disease resistant. It is a vigorous, strongly stemmed plant that is useful as a specimen and for bedding. Propagation is by budding. ZONES 4–9.

Croix, France, 1966

'Queen Elizabeth' × 'Spartan'

'AGÉNA' DELcus

syn. 'Agenay'

MODERN, LARGE-FLOWERED/HYBRID TEA, ORANGE-PINK, REPEAT-FLOWERING

'Agéna' has long, pointed buds that become large, fragrant double blooms. Salmon pink in color, they appear singly and in small clusters. It has bushy, vigorous growth and leathery, glossy foliage. Suitable as a bedding variety, it is propagated by budding. ZONES 4–9.

Delbard-Chabert, France, 1966

'Chic Parisien' × ('Michele Meilland' × 'Mme Joseph Perraud')

'AGLAIA'

syn. 'Yellow Rambler'

MODERN, RAMBLER, LIGHT YELLOW

Although not popular with the critics, this is one of the most dependable Ramblers; it also has the distinction of being the first yellow-flowered one. It is known that Rosa multiflora, when used in crosses with yellow roses, reverts to its white origin, so the yellow in 'Aglaia' does fade rather quickly during its long blooming period. But the healthy foliage and profuse blooms, wedded to a strong

fragrance, are reasons enough to add it to a collection. Aglaia is one of the Three Graces in Greek mythology; the remaining two, Euphrosyne and Thalia, were used by the breeder to name other creations. 'Aglaia' is thought to be a parent of 'Trier', a very important breeding rose. ZONES 5–10.

Schmitt, France, 1896

Rosa multiflora × 'Rêve d'Or'

'AGNES'

MODERN, HYBRID RUGOSA, LIGHT YELLOW

Yellow Rugosas are few and far between and not particularly distinguished at present, although this one is more successful. The large double blooms are a pale amber with a deeper center, are fragrant and produced in small clusters. The foliage is typically rugose, that is, light, glossy and wrinkled. It is a vigorous healthy bush that is listed as being summer flowering, although in warm autumns there will be a second crop of color. It is propagated from cuttings or by budding. ZONES 3–9.

Saunders, Canada, 1900

Rosa rugosa × R. foetida persiana

'Age Tendre'

'Agéna'

A

'AGNES BERNAUER' KORnauer
MODERN, LARGE-FLOWERED/HYBRID TEA, LIGHT PINK, REPEAT-FLOWERING

'Agnes Bernauer' has light pink flowers with a slight fragrance. Very free flowering, it has a bushy, healthy growth habit and is an ideal plant for bedding and for growing as a standard. It has good repeat-flowering capabilities and is propagated by budding. ZONES 4–9.

Kordes, Germany, 1989
Parentage unknown

'AGREEMENT'
MODERN, CLUSTER-FLOWERED/FLORIBUNDA, PINK BLEND, REPEAT-FLOWERING

This is a very tall-growing rose with arching growth and clusters of very well-shaped, double blooms containing about 30 petals. These are a strong deep rose to orange-pink color with golden bases. The flowers are produced both singly and in small clusters. The abundant foliage is glossy bright green and the repeat is very good, although there is very little in the way of fragrance. This rose makes a very free-flowering tall hedge or can be used at the back of the border for background color. There is a slight tendency to mildew in autumn. ZONES 5–10.

LeGrice, UK, 1971
Parentage unknown

'AHOI'
MODERN, CLUSTER-FLOWERED/FLORIBUNDA, ORANGE-RED, REPEAT-FLOWERING

This low, bushy grower is very free flowering and produces its blooms in clusters. The bright orange-red, double flowers are urn shaped, on plants clothed with healthy foliage. Propagation is by budding. ZONES 4–9.

Tantau, Germany, 1964
Parentage unknown

'AÏCHA'
OLD, SCOTS, DEEP YELLOW

The special virtue of the Scots Roses is their hardiness and many hybrids have been bred from them for cool

'Akebono'

'Ahoi'

'Agreement'

conditions, notably by Kordes in Germany. 'Aïcha' has probably been pre-empted by a look-alike from Kordes, 'Frühlingsgold', which is better known. There are two main types of Scots Roses, the low-growing ones and the taller Asian types. This variety has deep yellow flowers that are large and very fragrant. It is a bushy, vigorous grower with light green foliage. ZONES 4–9.

Petersen, Denmark, 1966
'Souvenir de Jacques Verschuren' × 'Guldtop'

'AIMABLE AMIE'
OLD, GALLICA, DEEP PINK

The dark, pink petals in the center of this rose are surrounded by even darker outer petals that reflex. The well-formed, fully double blooms rise above a bush that grows to 5 ft (1.5 m) with dark green foliage. There is a strong fragrance to this amiable friend in the garden. This was one of the roses at Malmaison during the time of the Empress Josephine. ZONES 4–10.

The Netherlands, early 1800s
Parentage unknown

'AIMABLE ROUGE'
syn. 'Le Triomphe'
OLD, GALLICA, DEEP PINK, REPEAT-FLOWERING

There is an interesting rendering of this rose in a drawing by the French artist Redouté (1759–1840). The purple-pink blooms with some veining of deeper pink offer a strong perfume. They are almost serrated, rounded and well formed. The bush can reach 5 ft (1.5 m) and the flowers repeat well. It was very popular in Europe in the 1820s. ZONES 4–10.

Vibert, France, 1819
Parentage unknown

'Agnes Bernauer'

'Aimée Vibert'

'Aïcha'

'AIMÉE VIBERT'
syns 'Bouquet de la Mariée', 'Nivea'
OLD, NOISETTE, WHITE, REPEAT-FLOWERING

The buds and blooms together offer an enchanting scene, with the brilliant foliage adding to this charming rose. The outer petals are concave and the inner ones are small and tousled. The flowers are medium sized in umbel-like clusters, and the buds have a red flush. The strong musk scent helped this rose to become the most popular of the early Noisettes. Vibert raised the plant at his test grounds at Longjumeau near Paris, and he named it after his devoted daughter. 'Aimée Vibert' may take 3 years before it blooms as it expends its early energy in producing canes and bountiful foliage. It is at its best in autumn. ZONES 5–10.

Vibert, France, 1828
'Champneys' Pink Cluster' × hybrid of *Rosa sempervirens*

'AKEBONO'
MODERN, LARGE-FLOWERED/HYBRID TEA, YELLOW BLEND, REPEAT-FLOWERING

'Akebono' is a vigorous, upright plant with dark glossy foliage that is disease resistant. The high-pointed flowers are light yellow flushed with carmine, slightly fragrant and very double; they each have 56 petals. It is useful as a bedding rose and on the show bench, and is propagated by budding. ZONES 4–9.

Kawai, Japan, 1964
'Ethel Sanday' × 'Narzisse'

'ALAIN'
MODERN, CLUSTER-FLOWERED/FLORIBUNDA, MEDIUM RED, REPEAT-FLOWERING

This variety was the first of a notable collection of Cluster-flowered Roses bred by Francis Meilland, the distinguished breeder of 'Peace'. A very free-flowering plant growing to medium height, it has semi-double, large bright carmine red blooms that are slightly fragrant and each have 28 petals. Repeat-flowering, it has dark glossy foliage and is disease resistant; it makes a good bedding subject. Budding is the principle method of propagation. This rose was named after the son of Francis Meilland. ZONES 4–9.

Meilland, France, 1948

('Guineé' × 'Skyrocket') × 'Orange Triumph'

Geneva Gold Medal 1948

'Alain Blanchard' leaves

'Alain Blanchard' thorns

'ALAIN BLANCHARD'
OLD, GALLICA, MAUVE

This is a wide-growing shrub that in good soil can attain a height of 5 ft (1.5 m). The stems are a burnished, dark green and have several thorns. The foliage is mid-green and well serrated. The fragrant flowers are up to 3 in (8 cm) across when fully open, rather more than single in make-up and usually arranged in clusters. The first blooms appear in early summer, from when it goes on flowering spasmodically for about another month; they are rich deep crimson in color and mottled with blotches of purple and deep pink. A special feature of this rose is the prominent display of brilliant golden stamens, which set off the flowers to beautiful effect. This is an easy to grow shrub but is never one to give a mass display. ZONES 5–10.

Vibert, France, 1839

Rosa centifolia × R. gallica

'Alba Maxima'

'Alba Meidiland'

'ALAMEIN'
MODERN, CLUSTER-FLOWERED/FLORIBUNDA, ORANGE-RED, REPEAT-FLOWERING

This rose produces a continuous supply of large, 3 in (8 cm), semi-double flowers containing 10 petals that open flat and hold their color well. They are slightly fragrant and come in small clusters on a short stocky bush. It has a short to medium growth habit and good disease resistance. It was one of the first bright red Cluster-flowered Roses raised and is still a fine rose. ZONES 5–11.

McGredy, UK, 1963

'Spartan' × 'Queen Elizabeth'

'ALBA MAXIMA'
syns Rosa alba maxima, 'Great Double White', 'Maxima', 'The Jacobite Rose', 'Cheshire Rose'
OLD, ALBA, WHITE

This rose suffers from too many names, only a few of them listed above. Everyone wants to claim it and for good

'Alamein'

'Alain'

reason, as this is the creamiest of all the Albas. A popular rose for centuries, it grows to a large bush, reaching 8 ft (2.4 m) with a sparse habit. The flowers are 3–4 in (8–10 cm) in diameter, opening flat with a faint buff edge and a lovely fragrance. Pale, gray-green foliage covers the canes, which have a few large prickles. 'Alba Maxima' flowers in summer, is disease resistant and needs little pruning. ZONES 3–9.

Pre-1500

Possibly Rosa canina × R. gallica

Royal Horticultural Society Award of Garden Merit 1993

'ALBA MEIDILAND'   MEIflopan
syns 'Alba Meillandécor', 'Alba Sunblaze', 'Meidiland Alba'
MODERN, MODERN SHRUB, WHITE, REPEAT-FLOWERING

'Alba Meidiland' is a very pretty ground-cover shrub that has large clusters of

small, very double blooms with over 40 petals each; unfortunately they have little scent. Small, glossy, medium green foliage appears on a plant that will spread effectively to give color throughout summer and autumn. It is useful on banks and borders, makes a good subject for pots and window boxes and is very effective as a short weeping standard. It propagates very easily from cuttings and by budding. ZONES 4–9.

Meilland, France, 1987

Rosa sempervirens × 'Martha Carron'

Frankfurt Gold Medal 1989

'ALBA SEMI-PLENA'
syns Rosa × alba nivea, R. × alba suaveolens
OLD, ALBA, WHITE

The origin of the Albas is lost, but there are many conjectures as to their parentage. With nearly single blooms with significant anthers, the largest of the Albas has a sweet scent and pure white flowers.

'Albertine'

'Albertine'

The attractive gray-green leaves and autumn hips extend the season. Sometimes offered as simply 'Semi-plena', rosarians are divided over its worthiness. Some feel it is underrated and others feel that other Albas far outshine it. Michael Gibson, English rosarian, puts it on his list of favorite roses. It was introduced into the UK by invading Roman armies and shares the honor with the simple white Alba as the White Rose of York. ZONES 3–4.

Pre-1600

Possible sport of 'Alba Maxima'

Royal Horticultural Society Award of Garden Merit 1993

'ALBA SUAVEOLENS'

syn. 'Suaveolens'

OLD, ALBA, WHITE

Graham Thomas and Peter Beales claim this is the same rose as 'Alba Semi-plena', while historian Roy Shepherd and Gerry Krueger, who has the largest collection of Albas in the USA, say there is a difference. Photographs rarely help in these

'Albertine' leaves

disputes. Krueger states that the inner petals do not have the anthers found in 'Alba Semi-plena'; Trevor Griffiths concurs. All agree that it is sweetly scented. Very little work with the Albas has been done in the twentieth century, save for the German hybridizer Rolf Sievers, creator of the Blush series. They are bred with a mixture of old-fashioned and Kordesii roses. ZONES 3–9.

Pre-1750

Parentage unknown

'ALBÉRIC BARBIER'

MODERN, RAMBLER, WHITE

This very popular once-blooming Rambler has many uses—as a climber, as a tree and even as a ground cover. It has been used effectively as a weeping standard. Its creamy white flowers, rather large for a Rambler, have a yellow center, and the pliable, glossy branches are dotted with flower clusters outlined against the dark foliage. The vigorous, thin canes can be easily trained, while no real pruning is needed. The apple fragrance in early summer is strong, and blooms appear on lateral shoots as well as new ones. 'Albéric Barbier' does well in the shade and can grow to 20 ft (6 m) in a year. The Barbier nursery in Orléans produced the most popular Ramblers of the century, including 'Albertine',

'Alexandre Girault' and 'François Juranville'. He created 23 Climbers and Ramblers. ZONES 4–10.

Barbier, France, 1900

Rosa wichuraiana × 'Shirley Hibberd'

Royal Horticultural Society Award of Garden Merit 1993

'ALBERTINE'

MODERN, LARGE-FLOWERED CLIMBER, ORANGE-PINK

'Albertine' has been popular for some 75 years. A very vigorous plant with striking deep green, almost purple stems and foliage, it has semi-lax stems that require continuous securing as the plant grows. It does well on pergolas, while a position on a wall in full sun can encourage a magnificent plant; in some gardens it is grown as a weeping standard. The heavily scented flowers are deep pink to salmon with hints of copper, but sadly they flower only for about 3 weeks in

mid-summer. The cupped blooms are medium sized and appear in clusters. The foliage is prone to mildew but not to its detriment. ZONES 4–9.

Barbier, France, 1921

Rosa wichuraiana × 'Mrs Arthur Robert Waddell'

Royal Horticultural Society Award of Garden Merit 1993

'ALCHYMIST'

syns 'Alchemist', 'Alchymiste'

MODERN, MODERN SHRUB, APRICOT BLEND

'Alchymist' is an extremely vigorous, upright shrub with glossy bronze foliage that is very healthy. Its round buds produce very large, cupped flowers that are extremely fragrant; they are a yellow shaded orange color that is officially described as an apricot blend. It makes a good shrub or a short climber. ZONES 3–9.

Kordes, Germany, 1956

'Golden Glow' × *Rosa eglanteria* hybrid

'ALDO'

MODERN, CLUSTER-FLOWERED/FLORIBUNDA, ORANGE BLEND, REPEAT-FLOWERING

'Aldo' is a bit of a mystery. Not only is the breeder unknown but also its country of origin. It is a short-growing bush bearing semi-double, brightly colored orange flowers blended with red. Flowering is continuous and each bloom has 25 petals and lasts well on the bush without fading. It is quite disease resistant. 'Aldo' seems only to be available in Australia and is even hard to find there.

'Alba Semi-plena'

'Albéric Barbier'

'Alchymist'

'Aldo'

It is a good little rose for borders and beds where a bright color is needed. ZONES 5 10.

1986

Parentage unknown

'ALEC'S RED' COred

MODERN, LARGE-FLOWERED/HYBRID TEA, MEDIUM RED, REPEAT-FLOWERING

Most catalogues would describe the flowers on this rose as Turkey red, although they can easily discolor to a dirty red as they age. The large size (each flower has some 45 petals) and fantastic scent has enabled this variety to retain its popularity for many years. It is a vigorous, bushy plant with dark green foliage and is repeat-flowering, coming into flower very early in the season. It was named after a well-known Scottish rose grower who started breeding late in life, this being his first big success; it is now grown worldwide. It was named at a time when roses did not have code names, and every judge just knew it as 'Alec's Red'. A good bedding plant and also useful as a standard, it is propagated by budding. **'Climbing Alec's Red'** (Harkness, UK, 1975) is a very vigorous, climbing form that is identical to its parent in most other ways; like many sports, it is only summer flowering. ZONES 4–9.

Cocker, UK, 1970

'Fragrant Cloud' × 'Dame de Coeur'

Edland Fragrance Medal 1969, Royal National Rose Society President's International Trophy 1970, Belfast Frangrance Prize 1972, Anerkannte Deutsche Rose 1973

'ALEXANDER' HARlex

syn. 'Alexandra'

MODERN, LARGE-FLOWERED/HYBRID TEA, ORANGE-RED, REPEAT-FLOWERING

This extremely vigorous rose astonished every rose buff with its luminosity.

'Alexander'

Growing with the vigor of a Modern Shrub and having very healthy foliage that is glossy and bright green, it certainly has the potential to be a match for 'Queen Elizabeth'. The brilliant, bright vermilion large double flowers with 25 petals are produced in profusion on long stems in small clusters. Rather big for a bed, it is better grown as a specimen shrub. The breeder, Jack Harkness, named this after his commanding officer in northern Africa. It is propagated by budding. ZONES 4–9.

Harkness, UK, 1972

'Tropicana' × ('Ann Elizabeth' × 'Allgold')

Hamburg Gold Medal 1973, Belfast Gold Medal 1974, Anerkannte Deutsche Rose 1974, Royal National Rose Society James Mason Medal 1987, Royal Horticultural Society Award of Garden Merit 1993

'ALEXANDER HILL GRAY'

syns 'Yellow Maman Cochet', 'Yellow Cochet'

OLD, TEA, DEEP YELLOW, REPEAT-FLOWERING

Extremely popular when it was introduced, this rose is rarely seen today

'Alec's Red'

except in specialist nurseries. The large, full, high-centered blooms of dark yellow fading to creamy white have perfect form. The strong Tea fragrance and healthy foliage make it a good candidate for an open garden as it requires little maintenance. The blooms are very long lasting. It is an erect plant with excellent, light green foliage that is highly disease resistant. Six generations of the Dickson family have been offering roses from their base in County Down, Ireland; among their many popular roses are 'Shot Silk', 'Grandpa Dickson' and 'Precious Platinum'. ZONES 4–10.

Dickson, UK, 1911

Parentage unknown

'ALEXANDER MACKENZIE'
syn. 'Alexander Mackenzie'
MODERN, MODERN SHRUB, RED BLEND, REPEAT-FLOWERING

'Alexander MacKenzie' is a vigorous, upright shrub with yellow-green, leathery, glossy foliage and purple prickles. The medium red double blooms have a lighter reverse. They are of medium size, with 45 petals each and they are produced in clusters of 6–12. Repeat-flowering, this variety can withstand sub-zero temperatures and is propagated by budding or from cuttings. ZONES 3–9.

Svejda, Canada, 1985

'Queen Elizabeth' × ('Red Dawn' × 'Suzanne')

'Alexandre Girault'

'ALEXANDER VON HUMBOLDT'
MODERN, MODERN SHRUB, MEDIUM RED, REPEAT-FLOWERING

'Alexander von Humboldt' is a vigorous climbing shrub with medium glossy foliage that is suitable for pergolas and fences. It produces large clusters of crimson-scarlet blooms; the flowers have a slight fragrance. Repeat-flowering, it is considerably hardy and resistant to disease and can be propagated by budding. ZONES 3–9.

Kordes, Germany, 1960

Rosa kordesii × 'Cleopatra'

'ALEXANDRE GIRAULT'
MODERN, LARGE-FLOWERED CLIMBER, PINK BLEND

Those who have visited the great garden outside Paris, Roseraie de l'Haÿ, will remember the impressive display of this rose—800 plants spread on an enormous steel fence. The pink-carmine blend of the flowers in a mass demonstration is the largest of its kind in the world. The large, double blooms on pliable canes are ideal for training on pergolas and trellises. They have a strong apple scent. Although it blooms only once in mid-summer, this rose helped to establish the reputation of its breeder, Barbier, throughout Europe; it is not as popular elsewhere. It is very tolerant of shade and poor soil, and likes plenty of room. ZONES 5–10.

Barbier, France, 1909

Rosa luciae × 'Papa Gontier'

'Alexander von Humboldt'

'Alice Amos'

'ALEXANDRE LAQUEMENT'
syn. 'Alexander Laquemont'
OLD, GALLICA, MAUVE

This is a lax if fairly dense shrub that grows to about 3½ ft (1.1 m) high and almost as wide, and which is moderately armed with prickles. The mid-green foliage is fairly profuse. The flowers are borne in clusters and are about 2 in (5 cm) across. Each fragrant bloom has randomly arranged petals and forms a shallow cupped shape when fully open. They are deep red, brushed purple and pink, creating a most attractive effect, although various descriptions include dappled red and violet-crimson depending on whether it is planted in the shade or the sun. One reason that it may not have done as well as other Gallicas is that the foliage is prone to mildew. ZONES 5–10.

France, pre-1899

Parentage unknown

'ALFRED COLOMB'
OLD, HYBRID PERPETUAL, PINK BLEND, REPEAT-FLOWERING

Some call this a 'vulgar' rose, but it has stayed in the trade ever since its introduction. The strawberry red, reflexed crimson blooms are large, full and symmetrical, much like the Centifolias. It ranges from medium to vigorous in its growth and has a handsome, bushy appearance with large dark leaves. The wood is green and full of prickles. This rose blooms later than other Hybrid Perpetuals, even well into autumn. Many say it does best in heavy soils, it doesn't mind rain and it has very good disease resistance. It reached the peak of its popularity around the 1880s, when 800 of this breed were advertised in William Paul & Sons' catalogue. Lacharmé also produced such popular roses as 'Boule de Neige', 'Mme Lombard' and 'Salet'. ZONES 5–10.

Lacharmé, France, 1865

Seedling of 'Général Jacqueminot'

'Alida Lovett'

'ALFRED DE DALMAS'
syn. 'Mousseline'
OLD, MOSS, LIGHT PINK, REPEAT-FLOWERING

This very popular rose is a short-growing, densely branching tidy shrub to about 3 ft (1 m). It sends up strong thornless shoots that are completely clothed in gingery brown, tightly packed soft bristles. These shoots are well foliated with roundish mid-green leaves, which are bright green when young. The ample moss, which surrounds the receptacles and the calyx, is at first light green turning brownish green as the buds open. The fragrant flowers are creamy white heavily overlaid with silvery satiny pink, and can reach a diameter of up to 4 in (10 cm) in good soil; they first appear in early summer and continue almost without a break well into autumn. It repeats well. Being little more than semi-double, they show off rich

'Alfred de Dalmas'

golden anthers to advantage when fully open. This is a superb trouble-free old variety, useful for group planting or growing in containers. It tolerates shade. ZONES 4–10.

Laffay, France, 1855

Parentage unknown

'ALICE AMOS'
MODERN, CLUSTER-FLOWERED/FLORIBUNDA, PINK BLEND, REPEAT-FLOWERING

This very tough and vigorous Cluster-flowered Rose has good strong stems supporting mid-green, medium-sized foliage; unfortunately the foliage also has a poor health record. The long, pointed buds develop into mid-sized cerise flowers with a white eye. They have little fragrance. Repeat-flowering, it makes a good plant for bedding. Propagation is by budding. ZONES 4–9.

Spek, The Netherlands, 1922

'Tip Top' × seedling

'ALIDA LOVETT'
MODERN, LARGE-FLOWERED CLIMBER, LIGHT PINK

'Alida Lovett' is a very vigorous Climber that produces huge clusters of shell pink flowers with a sulfer-shaded base. The blooms have a slight fragrance, while the

'Alfred Colomb'

foliage is glossy and disease resistant. Summer flowering, it is useful for fences and pergolas and is very tolerant of semi-shade. Although bred by a famous American hybridist, it was introduced by J. T. Lovett, a nurseryman in Little Silver, New Jersey and named after his wife. Propagation is by budding. ZONES 4–9.

Van Fleet, USA, 1905

'Souvenir du President Carnot' × *Rosa wichuraiana*

'ALIKA'
syns *Rosa gallica* 'Grandiflora', 'Rose Pavot'
OLD, GALLICA, MEDIUM RED

Available only in the USA, this rose was brought to America from Russia by Professor N. E. Hansen in 1906 and introduced into commerce in 1930. Photographs helped establish its legendary charm. Large, semi-double (sometimes single) blooms of clear red are highlighted by golden stamens. It reaches 6 ft (1.8 m) in most situations and seems happiest in a woodland setting. Hansen worked in one of the coldest states in the USA, where he used this rose in his hybridizing program. ZONES 3–9.

USA, 1930

Parentage unknown

'Allen Chandler', right, at Sissinghurst Castle

'Allegro'

'Allgold'

'Alister Stella Gray'

'Alister Clark'

'ALISTER CLARK'

MODERN, POLYANTHA, LIGHT PINK,
REPEAT-FLOWERING

This lovely little rose occurred as a sport on a bush of 'Marjory Palmer' in Victoria, Australia. 'Marjory Palmer' had the Rambler 'Jersey Beauty' as a parent, and it is from this that 'Alister Clark' gets its large, extremely glossy, abundant foliage. The bush has a short and very spreading growth habit and the flowers are large for a Polyantha Rose. They come in clusters and have widely flaring outer petals surrounding a center packed with petals. Flowering is continuous and there are no disease problems. Laurie Newman asked the descendants of Alister Clark for permission to name the rose, which was introduced in 1990, after him. This was approved and it is a fitting tribute to Australia's greatest rose breeder. ZONES 4–10.

Newman, Australia, 1990

Sport of 'Marjory Palmer'

'ALISTER STELLA GRAY'

syn. 'Golden Rambler'

OLD, NOISETTE, LIGHT YELLOW,
REPEAT-FLOWERING

Long, pointed buds on this variety open to light yellow blooms with a dark yellow center. The beautiful, blowzy, quartered blossoms change color as they age. Thin canes hold few prickles, and the foliage is a healthy, dark green. It needs time to establish itself but will grow into a vigorous shrub, sometimes as high as 10 ft (3 m). Many who grow it say there is no other rose that will bloom so continuously, displaying cascades of beautifully formed blossoms in full sun. This Noisette should be deadheaded regularly. ZONES 5–10.

Gray, UK, 1894

Parentage unknown

Royal Horticultural Society Award of Garden Merit 1994

'ALL THAT JAZZ' TWOadvance

MODERN, MODERN SHRUB, ORANGE-PINK,
REPEAT-FLOWERING

The flowers of this variety are a coral-salmon blend, semi-double and with 12–15 petals; they have a pronounced Damask fragrance. Its pointed buds develop into cupped, loose and large blooms borne in sprays of 3–5. It has a shrubby, upright and bushy growth habit and dark green, glossy foliage that is disease resistant. Suitable as a specimen plant or a standard in a border, it flowers consistently through summer until late autumn. Propagation is by budding. ZONES 4–9.

Twomey, USA, 1991

'Gitte' × seedling

All-America Rose Selection 1992

'ALLEGRO' MEIarlo

MODERN, LARGE-FLOWERED/HYBRID TEA,
ORANGE-RED, REPEAT-FLOWERING

'Allegro' is a large-flowered, vigorous plant with glossy, leathery foliage and a bushy habit. The orange-red double blooms with 30 petals have a high center; they are slightly cupped as they develop and are lightly fragrant. Disease resistant, this variety has been a favorite for 30 years and is propagated by budding. ZONES 4–9.

Meilland, France, 1962

('Happiness' × 'Independence') × 'Soraya'

The Hague Gold Medal 1962, Rome Gold Medal 1962

'ALLELUIA' DELatur

syn. 'Hallelujah'

MODERN, LARGE-FLOWERED/HYBRID TEA,
RED BLEND, REPEAT-FLOWERING

'Alleluia' produces very large, heavy blooms with 30 petals that are velvety red with a silver reverse, which makes them a good subject for exhibition. They have little fragrance. A strong, robust, bushy plant with deep green glossy foliage, it is repeat-flowering and is suitable for bedding. It is propagated by budding. ZONES 4–9.

Delbard, France, 1980

(['Impeccable' × 'Papa Meilland'] × ['Gloire de Roma' × 'Impeccable']) × 'Corrida'

'ALLEN CHANDLER'

MODERN, LARGE-FLOWERED CLIMBER, MEDIUM
RED, REPEAT-FLOWERING

Brilliant crimson, semi-double, large flowers in clusters of 3–4 and with pointed buds are produced on this variety. Slightly fragrant, they are open and repeat their blooming from summer to autumn. It is a moderate grower with dark, leathery, glossy foliage that is suitable as a large shrub or to train up a pillar; it grows successfully on north walls. Historically it was one of the first of the repeat-flowering climbers. Although very healthy and tough, it has dropped out of popularity because it is such a reluctant bloomer. Propagation is by budding. ZONES 4–9.

Chandler, UK, 1923

'Hugh Dickson' × seedling

National Rose Society Gold Medal 1923

'ALLGOLD'

syn. 'All Gold'

MODERN, CLUSTER-FLOWERED/FLORIBUNDA,
MEDIUM YELLOW, REPEAT-FLOWERING

The deep, unfading, pure buttercup yellow, slightly fragrant, medium-sized

A

'Almost Sunset'

'Altissimo'

blooms with 15–20 petals on this variety are borne singly or in large trusses. They are a striking color; in fact 'Allgold' was the first Cluster-flowered Rose to possess an unfading yellow. A bushy plant with medium, pale green, glossy foliage, it is a nice bedding variety that makes a good subject as a standard. Its chief claim to fame is its ability to produce healthy progeny, although as a nursery plant it is disappointing because of the small proportion of saleable plants it actually produces. Propagation is by budding. The blooms of the climbing variant, **'Climbing Allgold'** (syns 'Grimpant Allgold', 'Grimpant All Gold'; Gandy, UK, 1961), are superior to its parent, although they only appear in summer and are very sparse. ZONES 4–9.

LeGrice, UK, 1956

'Goldilocks' × 'Ellinor LeGrice'

National Rose Society Gold Medal 1956

'ALLOTRIA' TANal
MODERN, CLUSTER-FLOWERED/FLORIBUNDA, ORANGE-RED, REPEAT-FLOWERING

Medium-sized flowers of brilliant orange-scarlet appear on 'Allotria' in large clusters. They are slightly fragrant and repeat their blooming from summer to autumn. It is a vigorous, healthy bush with dark glossy foliage that is suitable for bedding purposes, and is one of many Cluster-flowered Roses of this color that were bred at the same time. Propagation is by budding. ZONES 4–9.

Tantau, Germany, 1958

'Fanal' × seedling of 'Cinnabar'

'ALLSPICE' AROall
MODERN, LARGE-FLOWERED/HYBRID TEA, MEDIUM YELLOW, REPEAT-FLOWERING

This variety has large, double blooms with 35 petals that are colored deep yellow then age to medium yellow. The flowers have a very fragrant, sweet scent. The large, olive green foliage appears on a vigorous, upright, bushy plant that is disease resistant and is good for beds and as a specimen shrub. It is repeat-flowering. ZONES 4–9.

Armstrong, USA, 1977

'Buccaneer' × 'Peace'

'ALMOST SUNSET' JAColly
MODERN, LARGE-FLOWERED/HYBRID TEA, YELLOW BLEND, REPEAT-FLOWERING

The petals of 'Almost Sunset' are a blend of pink and yellow on the uppersides, and yellow at the base. They have yellow undersides. The medium-sized blooms are well formed and contain 20 petals. They are usually borne one to a stem and are perfect for picking. The plant grows to medium height and has dark, semi-glossy, disease-free foliage. The repeat-bloom is rather slow. ZONES 4–9.

Jackson and Perkins, USA, 1996

Parentage unknown

'ALOHA'
MODERN, LARGE-FLOWERED CLIMBER, MEDIUM PINK, REPEAT-FLOWERING

This widely grown variety is suitable as a short climber or as a free-flowering shrub. Its large, round buds develop into big multi-petalled blooms that are rose pink with a deeper reverse and have 58 petals. The flowers have a pronounced fragrance of apple blossom and are very hardy. Although slow to establish, 'Aloha' makes a fantastic shrub that is particularly good in sunless situations and is repeat-flowering. ZONES 3–9.

Boerner, USA, 1949

'Mercedes Gallart' × 'New Dawn'

'ALOUETTE'
MODERN, POLYANTHA, ORANGE-PINK, REPEAT-FLOWERING

'Alouette' produces clusters of small to medium-sized, salmon-orange semi-double blooms. The buds are long and pointed, and develop into cupped and very profuse flat flowers that are slightly fragrant and repeat their blooming. It has leathery foliage on a vigorous, healthy plant that is useful for borders and as a standard. ZONES 4–9.

Delforge, France, 1971

'Ambassadeur Baert' × seedling

'ALPINE SUNSET'
MODERN, LARGE-FLOWERED/HYBRID TEA, APRICOT BLEND, REPEAT-FLOWERING

This delightful rose is a restful combination of peaches, pinks, apricots, creams and yellows. The blooms, which are sweetly scented, very large and globular in form, are borne on firm stems close to the foliage on a neat compact plant. The leaves are light green and shiny and are large enough to furnish the bush well. Although repeat-flowering, there is usually a pause between the summer flowering and the next flush because the plant needs time to recover after producing its large blooms in quantity. New stems are not made freely; dieback will affect it in severe winters. ZONES 5–9.

Cant, UK, 1974

'Dr A. J. Verhage' × 'Grandpa Dickson'

Royal National Rose Society Trial Ground Certificate 1974, Belfast Certificate of Merit 1976, The Hague Fragrance Award 1976

'Alouette'

'ALTISSIMO' DELmur
syns 'Altus', 'Sublimely Single'
MODERN, LARGE-FLOWERED CLIMBER, MEDIUM RED, REPEAT-FLOWERING

This is an excellent climbing rose for walls and fences and to train up a pillar or on a pergola. The saucer-shaped, lightly scented blooms are fairly large, with about 7 petals, and open wide to show yellow stamens. A rich and bright deep scarlet, becoming crimson, they repeat-flower throughout summer and autumn against a background of large dark leaves. The plant grows vigorously with stiff branching stems to the average height one expects of a Climber, though it is apt to flower high unless trained to the horizontal. The flowers, which may appear one to a stem, are more often borne several together in wide clusters which explains why this variety can be described by the Royal National Rose Society as a Cluster-flowered Climber, and by the American Rose Society as a Large-flowered Climber. *Altissimo*, Italian for 'in the highest', is an appropriate name for this Climber. ZONES 4–9.

Delbard-Chabert, France, 1966

'Tenor' × seedling

Royal Horticultural Society Award of Garden Merit 1993

'Aloha'

'Alpine Sunset'

'AMADIS'
syns 'Crimson Boursault', 'Elegans'
OLD, BOURSAULT, DARK RED

Of the 50 Boursaults listed 200 years ago, there are only a few left. However, 'Amadis' has survived, surely because of its elegant, upright posture and large, cupped, semi-double flowers. They are deep crimson and purple and are borne in large, long-lasting clusters. The young wood is whitish green; the old wood is red-brown, and there are no prickles. Although it has neither perfume nor fruits, its deeply serrated leaves of brilliant green add to its winning traits. It blooms early in the season on old growth, and partial shade brings out the subtle colors. It is frequently found in old cemeteries as it was once used as an understock, and it was named for an amateur horticulturist. ZONES 5–10.

Laffay, France, 1829

Rosa pendulina × unknown

'AMALIA'   MEIcauf
syn. 'Fiord'
MODERN, LARGE-FLOWERED/HYBRID TEA,
DARK RED/LIGHT RED

This light to medium red Large-flowered Rose is very elegant—urn-shaped as the buds begin to swell and keeping well-proportioned, high-centered flowers as they open. It carries its blooms singly on long stems, making it good as a cut rose for decoration or exhibition as they last

'Ambassador'

'Amalia'

well. It is best grown in a part of the garden reserved for cut flowers because the habit is too tall to make it suitable for bedding. The flower production through summer and autumn is good, but there is little fragrance, always regrettable in a red rose. The leaves are large and furnish the lower part of the plant well. 'Amalia' is at its best in a sunny climate. ZONES 5–9.

Meilland, France, 1986

Parentage unknown

'AMANDA'   BEEsian
MODERN, CLUSTER-FLOWERED/FLORIBUNDA,
MEDIUM YELLOW, REPEAT-FLOWERING

Gardeners who enjoy a spectacle like this rose for its showy heads of lively yellow flowers. These medium-sized blooms have stiff, small petals, which crinkle at the edges and become suffused orange-pink as they age. There is a pleasant light fragrance. The growth is upright, inclined to be rather stiff and uneven, and there is a good coverage of small bright green leaves. 'Amanda' makes a useful bedding rose, with incidental blooms appearing between the summer and autumn flushes. It is not as popular as its merits may indicate, perhaps because the raiser's business was taken over not long after its introduction. ZONES 4–9.

Bees, UK, 1979

'Arthur Bell' × 'Zambra'

Royal National Rose Society Trial Ground Certificate 1979

'AMATSU-OTOME'
MODERN, LARGE-FLOWERED/HYBRID TEA,
YELLOW BLEND, REPEAT-FLOWERING

This variety is very popular in Japan, and has found favor abroad despite the mouthful of a name. At its best it is a beauty, bearing large, high-centered blooms of yellow with a hint of orange at the margins; however, these flowers are most likely to be seen in the exhibitors' classes at shows where they often win prizes, because they are constructed with wide firm petals that keep the blooms

'Amatsu-Otome'

in good shape until judging time is well past. There is a slight fragrance. As a garden rose 'Amatsu-Otome' is not nearly as popular, being tall and somewhat leggy and with mid-green, slightly glossy foliage that may need protection against black spot. The number of blooms produced in summer and autumn is respectable in view of their size, but it is as an exhibitor's rose not a gardener's one that most people plant it today. ZONES 5–9.

Teranishi, Japan, 1960

'Chrysler Imperial' × 'Doreen'

'AMATSU PINK'
MODERN, LARGE-FLOWERED/HYBRID TEA,
PINK BLEND, REPEAT-FLOWERING

The flowers of this rose are soft salmon pink and have good Large-flowered form. In spite of the weak necks, they are good for cutting, although the large booms tend to be heavy and are carried vertically. Like its parent, it is a medium-sized bush rose with a thick, strong growth habit that makes a good framework. It requires careful pruning—it is best to cut the canes to a well-developed eye on thick wood. This prevents the canes from dying back. The flower production is high, with very quick repeat. Disease resistance is good, and in warm areas flowers are produced well into winter. ZONES 5–9.

Teranishi , Japan, 1960

Sport of 'Amatsu Otome'

'Amadis'

'AMBASSADOR'   MEInuzeten
MODERN, LARGE-FLOWERED/HYBRID TEA,
ORANGE BLEND, REPEAT-FLOWERING

The flower color of this variety appears two-toned, because the outside of the petals is creamy yellow and the inside a strong shade of apricot. As the large conical buds open into moderately full, cupped blooms, the contrast shows to good effect until the color deepens and reddish apricot takes over. There is a light fragrance. 'Ambassador' is a long-stemmed variety bearing flowers through summer and autumn and is excellent for cutting and for exhibition, but would not be among the top choices as a bedding rose. The plant grows vigorously with dark foliage, which may on occasion need spraying against mildew. It does best in a warm climate. ZONES 5–9.

Meilland, France, 1979

Seedling × 'Whisky Mac'

'AMBER NECTAR'   MEHamber
MODERN, CLUSTER-FLOWERED/FLORIBUNDA,
APRICOT BLEND, REPEAT-FLOWERING

Plump buds on this variety open into cupped, rather loosely formed blooms of intensely rich amber yellow, which hold their color well through the life of the flowers. The color deepens to a bright orange-red in autumn, being responsive to the shorter daylight hours as are many apricot-hued roses. The petals are irregular in arrangement, and often scalloped round the edges. The large clusters of blooms appear through summer and autumn. The plant, which grows upright with a bushy, well-balanced habit to average height, will grow well in a bed and produce plentiful lime green foliage. ZONES 4–9.

Mehring, UK, 1997

'Alexander' × 'Sweet Magic'

'AMBER QUEEN'   HARroony
syn. 'Prinz Eugen von Savoyen'
MODERN, CLUSTER-FLOWERED/FLORIBUNDA,
APRICOT BLEND, REPEAT-FLOWERING

From the haul of awards it is clear there are special qualities that endear the judges to this rose. Its value as a garden item comes from the pure amber color, its ability to produce clusters of quite large well-formed blooms freely throughout summer and autumn, its neat bedding habit, generally robust health and sweet fragrance. There is in addition an appealing quality about 'Amber Queen', derived from the refreshing effect of the bright clean flowers against the dark leathery leaves. The growth habit is cushiony, and it normally grows to medium height. As a bedding rose it is splendid, it makes a fine standard, and is also seen in exhibition classes. 'Rosemary Harkness' was the name originally intended for this variety, but when it won Britain's Rose of the Year competition a change was made on grounds of commercial acceptability. The synonym comes from an Austrian national hero. ZONES 4–9.

Harkness, UK, 1984

'Southampton' × 'Typhoon'

Royal National Rose Society Certificate of Merit 1983, Lyons Rose du Siecle 1984, UK Rose of the Year 1984, Belfast Best Floribunda 1986, Genoa Rosa Euroflora 1986, Orléans Rose d'Or 1987, All-America Rose Selection 1988, New Zealand Gold Star 1988, Orléans Grand Prix d'Excellence 1989, The Hague Golden Rose and Silver Medal for Fragrance 1991, Royal National Rose Society James Mason Gold Medal 1993, Royal Horticultural Society Award of Garden Merit 1993

'AMBOSSFUNKEN'

syn. 'Anvil Sparks'

MODERN, LARGE-FLOWERED/HYBRID TEA, RED BLEND, REPEAT-FLOWERING

Many gardeners have been tempted to plant this eye-catching novelty, with its bizarrely flecked and stippled petals of yellow, apricot, carmine and orange-red. The enchantment rarely lasts, because beneath the pretty flowers is a vulnerable plant. The young flowers are urn shaped opening to middling-sized cupped blooms of loose form with a pleasing scent. They are carried upright on firm slim stems, and last well indoors if cut early. The plant grows to medium height or less and has dark foliage; sometimes this disguises the onset of black spot, to which the variety is susceptible. This rose is best in warm weather; it was discovered by Mr E. Meyer in his garden in East London, South Africa, from where it found its way to the Kordes nursery, who introduced it as 'a rose for the connoisseur'. ZONES 5–9.

Meyer, South Africa, 1961

Sport of 'Signora Piero Puricelli'

'AMBRIDGE ROSE' AUSwonder

MODERN, MODERN SHRUB, APRICOT BLEND, REPEAT-FLOWERING

This is a shrub rose of modest size, producing a good continuity of bloom through summer and autumn. The flowers are rounded and well filled with petals which crowd into each other, are carried in small clusters and have a noticeable fragrance. They are cupped at first, then expand to form rather loose rosettes, the color changing from apricot to apricot-pink and paling towards the outer edges. Growth is short, bushy and upright; medium-sized leaves are dark green and somewhat glossy. It was named after an English radio program called 'The Archers' about a fictional farming community. At the request of the BBC, an episode was written into the program wherein one of the characters went to see it at the Chelsea Show and talked to the breeder. ZONES 4–9.

Austin, UK, 1990

'Charles Austin' × seedling

'AMBROSIA'

MODERN, CLUSTER-FLOWERED/FLORIBUNDA, ORANGE BLEND, REPEAT-FLOWERING

When this rose was introduced it was heralded as a color break, because the vivid dark amber shade was indeed a novelty. The medium-sized flowers, composed of 7–10 petals, are borne in crowded heads and carry a slight fragrance. From pointed buds they open out almost flat, the petals reflexing and narrowing as they age, and appear with excellent continuity from summer to autumn. The growth habit is fairly vigorous, dwarf and bushy, with plentiful dark green foliage. This is a useful variety for a bed or low hedge. ZONES 4–9.

Dickson, UK, 1962

Seedling × 'Shepherd's Delight'

Royal National Rose Society Certificate of Merit, 1962

'AMÉLIA'

OLD, ALBA, MEDIUM PINK

'Amélia' is quite a short-growing rose for an Alba. The foliage is gray-green and plentiful, and although there are numerous thorns at least they are small. The flowers are up to 3 in (8 cm) across, semi-double to double and bright pink, and display golden stamens to stunning effect when fully open. They are highly scented and borne in small clusters in

'Amber Queen'

'Ambrosia'

'Ambossfunken'

mid-summer. It is hardy in difficult situations. Planted as an impenetrable hedge or in a woodland situation, it improves with the cutting back of old wood after flowering. This rose is really quite rare and could easily be classified as a Damask. ZONES 4–10.

Pre-1823

Parentage unknown

'AMERICA' JACclam

MODERN, LARGE-FLOWERED CLIMBER, ORANGE-PINK, REPEAT-FLOWERING

Few climbing roses have achieved the All-America Rose Selection award, and by its long commercial life this variety has shown that the judges were right. It flowers very freely in summer, with a reasonably good repeat bloom. The medium to large-sized blooms are full and prettily formed with overlapping petals, opening cupped from high-centered buds, and well scented. They appear in open clusters in a warm shade of coral-salmon, and pale as they age. The growth is vigorous and free branching, while the leaves are of medium size, semi-glossy and reasonably healthy. It makes an excellent climber of lower than average height so is suitable for walls, fences and pillars, and it does not resent being

pruned to form a big shrub. The name 'America' is significant because the rose was introduced in the bicentennial year of the USA. ZONES 4–9.

Warriner, USA, 1976

'Fragrant Cloud' × 'Tradition'

All-America Rose Selection 1976

'AMERICAN BEAUTY'

syn. 'Mme Ferdinand Jamin'

OLD, HYBRID PERPETUAL, DEEP PINK

In spite of its name, this is a French rose that became famous in the USA as a greenhouse variety that caused a revolution in the cut-flower industry. The buds are globular and develop into large, pink-carmine flowers. These blooms are composed of 50 petals to give a cup shape. The strong perfume and the long, stiff stems were the main reason for its commercial success. It sometimes repeats its flowers in late summer and autumn. Today it is no longer grown for cut flowers as others have replaced it. Its transition to the outdoors was successful in warm climates, although it is subject to rust and black spot. There is a climbing form but it is rarely grown. ZONES 5–10.

Lédéchaux, France, 1875

Parentage unknown

'Amélia'

'America'

'American Home'

'American Pillar'

'Americana'

'American Pillar'

'AMERICAN HERITAGE' LAMlam

MODERN, LARGE-FLOWERED/HYBRID TEA,
YELLOW BLEND, REPEAT-FLOWERING

There are many shapes and colors to be seen in this pretty rose, and it is delightful at every stage. Long pointed buds of cream and ivory open into large full-petalled blooms, producing a melange of ivory, salmon, pink and yellow shades in the broad petals. They open out wide to reveal an expanse of light yellow with pink tinges. This is a pleasing item for the garden and good to cut, the flowers being carried on long stems and appearing through summer and autumn. There is a light scent. The plant growth is upright and vigorous and it is well furnished with dark leathery leaves that should be checked for mildew. ZONES 4–9.

Lammerts, USA, 1965

'Queen Elizabeth' × 'Yellow Perfection'
All-America Rose Selection 1966

'AMERICAN HOME'

MODERN, LARGE-FLOWERED/HYBRID TEA,
DARK RED, REPEAT-FLOWERING

This variety is appreciated especially for its fragrance, which is rich and sweet and reminiscent of the Old Garden Roses.

The plump pointed buds open into large, dark red blooms of cupped form, moderately full of petals. They are carried on long stiff stems which makes them very suitable as cut flowers. 'American Home' makes a good garden rose as it is a steady performer, bearing flower on a vigorous, upright plant of average height through summer and autumn. The leaves are tough, mid-green and leathery, and it has a generally good health record. ZONES 4–9.

Morey, USA, 1960

'Chrysler Imperial' × 'New Yorker'

'AMERICAN PILLAR'

MODERN, RAMBLER, PINK BLEND

Its parentage makes this rose a candidate for pergolas, pillars and for climbing into trees. The carmine-pink blooms have a white eye and golden stamens. They are 3 in (8 cm) in diameter, and are frequently borne in large clusters. The thick canes are vigorous, reaching 20 ft (6 m) in a season, and are easily trained. The foliage is leathery, glossy, and subject to mildew. It blooms on old wood later than other ramblers and hates hot, dry weather but will tolerate partial shade. Although the single blossoms are unin-

teresting, collectively they are stunning. The rose is now enjoying a comeback—possibly because public gardens are using it again to great effect. ZONES 5–10.

Van Fleet, USA, 1902

(*Rosa wichuraiana* × *R. setigera*) × unnamed red
Hybrid Perpetual

'AMERICAN PRIDE' JACared

MODERN, LARGE-FLOWERED/HYBRID TEA,
DARK RED, REPEAT-FLOWERING

When people go up to a rose, their first action almost invariably is to bend forward to appreciate the fragrance. By that test it has to be said that this rose largely fails; in other respects it is very satisfactory in the garden. Oval-shaped buds on long stems open to large, full-petalled, velvety deep red flowers with high centers, which become rather charmingly confused as the blooms open out. They are borne freely over a long period in summer and autumn and are excellent for cutting except in mid-season, when the blooms tend to become malformed. The bush grows vigorously and upright to above average height, with large, dark green leaves. ZONES 4–9.

Warriner, USA, 1978

Parentage unknown

'AMERICANA'

MODERN, LARGE-FLOWERED/HYBRID TEA,
MEDIUM RED, REPEAT-FLOWERING

This rose enjoyed great popularity when it was introduced, because of the impact made by its bright and lively red color. It bears plump buds that open into very large, moderately full flowers with high centers and broad petals. As the blooms age the petals reflex to form a cup shape, holding the color tone to a late stage. The variety flowers freely through summer and autumn, and there is a light fragrance. The growth is vigorous and upright, with mid-green, leathery foliage. Gene Boerner had a resourceful answer if a visitor said a variety did not smell. He would put it under his hat for a few minutes, then retrieve it; the humidity in such a confined space never failed to activate the petal cells. 'Americana' is exactly the type of rose he would have played this trick with. ZONES 4–9.

Boerner, USA, 1961

Seedling of 'Poinsettia' × 'New Yorker'

'AMÉTHYSTE'

MODERN, RAMBLER, MAUVE

Trusses of intensely packed, double, crimson-violet blooms are arranged on long arching canes on this rose. The healthy foliage is glossy. Blooming only once, it is best as a tree climber or in the wild garden, and usually reaches 12 ft (3.5 m). Early critics called 'Améthyste' coarse and unmanageable as the flowers sometimes appear to be steel-blue with purplish undertones. It tolerates some shade. ZONES 5–10.

Nonin, France, 1911

Sport of 'Non-Plus Ultra'

'AMIGA MIA'

MODERN, MODERN SHRUB, MEDIUM PINK,
REPEAT-FLOWERING

This shrub rose grows like an extremely vigorous and tall bush variety, producing shell pink blooms freely from summer through to autumn. Plump, pointed buds open into large graceful flowers with up to 30 petals, with very good fragrance; sometimes they are borne singly, sometimes in an open cluster of several together. The leaves are dark and leathery and rate highly for disease resistance and hardiness. This rose was one of several raised by Professor Griffith Buck of Ames, Iowa, who specialized in breeding varieties that would withstand cold North American winters. *Amiga mia*

'American Heritage'

'American Pride'

'Amoretta'

'Amorosa'

means my friend; Buck named it for Californian rosarian Dorothy Stemler, whose eclectic eye for roses saved many that would otherwise have been lost to commerce. ZONES 4–9.

Buck, USA, 1978

'Queen Elizabeth' × 'Prairie Princess'

'AMORE'
MODERN, CLUSTER-FLOWERED/FLORIBUNDA, MEDIUM PINK, REPEAT-FLOWERING

This trouble-free small shrub has good dark green foliage and deep pink flowers with petals deeper pink on the outside than the inside. These appear in clusters freely through summer and autumn. The growth habit is medium and has a spreading tendency. 'Amore' is excellent as a shrub in a mixed border or among small shrubs and perennials. There is no scent. This variety and others such as 'Cara Bella', 'Gay Vista' and 'Honey Flow' were bred from 'Spring Song' by Frank Riethmuller of Sydney; they could easily be classed with 'Lavender Lassie' and 'Ballerina'. All are superb plants for landscaping. ZONES 5–11.

Riethmuller, Australia, 1957

'Orange Triumph' × 'Spring Song'

'AMORETTA'
MODERN, LARGE-FLOWERED/HYBRID TEA, APRICOT BLEND, REPEAT-FLOWERING

This rose carries very double flowers that are filled with many light apricot-pink petals. These blooms are usually carried singly against the shiny dark green foliage. ZONES 5–11.

Kordes, Germany, 1997

Parentage unknown

'AMORETTE'   AmoRU
syns 'Amoretta', 'Snowdrop'
MODERN, MINIATURE, WHITE, REPEAT-FLOWERING

This variety is one of the many Miniature masterpieces developed by an outstanding Dutch hybridizer. The ivory white double florets with 33–35 reflexed petals are borne in large clusters of 10–15 blooms. While the flowers may be large for a modern Miniature, the overall effect of large trusses of flowers is attractive, and this effect is prolonged by the long-lasting quality of these large sprays. The growth habit is quite compact and dense in most climates. The foliage is mid-green, long and narrow and the plant has red prickles. ZONES 4–11.

de Ruiter, The Netherlands, 1980

'Rosy Jewel' × 'Zorina'

'AMOROSA'   KORignale
MODERN, LARGE-FLOWERED/HYBRID TEA, WHITE, REPEAT-FLOWERING

This cut-flower variety is not normally recommended for garden use except in very warm climates, because the blooms are unlikely to open satisfactorily if they become damp. Grown in the right conditions, ideally under glass, it will be a boon for flower arrangers: the buds open slowly, the vase life is long and there is a good fragrance. The elegant flowers, which are carried on fairly long stems continuously from summer to autumn, are a delicate shade of blush white with pale apricot tints in the depths of the firm petals. The growth habit is upright, sturdy and very leafy, although the foliage is a little brittle and does not transport as well as some other varieties. 'Amorosa' is also quick to show thrip damage in spring. The variety is very attractive under night light. ZONES 5–10.

Kordes, Germany, 1995

Parentage unknown

'AMSTERDAM'   HAVam
MODERN, CLUSTER-FLOWERED/FLORIBUNDA, ORANGE-RED, REPEAT-FLOWERING

The International Rose Trials at The Hague are sited in a public park, and for a variety to win the gold medal there, as this one did, it needs to be an exceptionally good bedding rose. 'Amsterdam' flowers with freedom throughout summer and into autumn, and carries its blooms close to the foliage on a neat bushy plant of medium height. The blooms are a vivid deep orange-red, of medium to large size, cupped and rounded in form, with about 12 firm petals; the visual effect of so many blooms against the shining dark mahogany foliage is startling. Seasonal mildew, caused by rapid changes between day and night temperatures, usually in autumn, can sometimes cause a problem. ZONES 4–9.

Verschuren, The Netherlands, 1972

'Europeana' × 'Parkdirektor Riggers'

The Hague Gold Medal 1972

'AMY JOHNSON'
MODERN, LARGE-FLOWERED CLIMBER, MEDIUM PINK, REPEAT-FLOWERING

This is a very vigorous climber that produces an abundance of very fragrant, rosy pink blooms on long stems; they are scarce in summer, although a good flush is produced in the cool of autumn. They open out from plump buds into large, full-petalled, double, cupped flowers. The leaves are wrinkled. Amy Johnson was a pioneer aviator who, in 1930, achieved the feat of flying solo to Australia. It makes a good pillar rose, or can be grown over an arch or fence. ZONES 5–11.

Clark, Australia, 1931

'Souvenir de Gustav Prat' × unknown

'AMY ROBSART'
OLD, SWEET BRIAR, DEEP PINK

During a short period between 1890–95, Lord Penzance produced a group of roses that are still popular today. Although he was not the first to experiment with these hybrids he marketed them well, as they did not have an enthusiastic audience at first but gained a popularity they have not lost. An attractive, tall shrub, 'Amy Robsart' has large, semi-double, deep rose blossoms that are lovely when fully opened, the stamens adding to their beauty. In spite of its parentage the healthy foliage is not fragrant, although the rose is. Best in the background as its form is sprawling and rough, it tolerates shade. Red fruit adds to its usefulness as a hedge. It should be pruned lightly. ZONES 4–10.

Penzance, UK, 1894

Rosa eglanteria × Hybrid Perpetual or Bourbon

'ANABELL'   KORbell
syns 'Annabelle', 'Kordes' Rose Anabel'
MODERN, CLUSTER-FLOWERED/FLORIBUNDA, ORANGE BLEND, REPEAT-FLOWERING

This variety sometimes bears open clusters of blooms, with each flower on a short but distinct stem, and sometimes tight clusters with the flowers close together. The color is a warm shade of salmon-orange, deepening towards the petal edges. The blooms are large with a score of petals and open cupped, with a light fragrance. 'Anabell' is a good bedding rose as it bears flowers freely through summer and autumn. It grows upright, to average height for a bush rose, with attractive glossy foliage, coppery when young then becoming mid-green. ZONES 4–9.

Kordes, Germany, 1972

'Zorina' × 'Color Wonder'

Royal National Rose Society Trial Ground Certificate 1971

'Amy Johnson'

'Anabell'

'ANAÏS SÉGALAS'
OLD, GALLICA, PINK BLEND

This is a branching shrub up to about 3 ft (1 m) in height with very prickly gray-green stems, denoting some Centifolia influence. The foliage is light green, rounded and tidily presented all over the plant. The flowers, each about 1½ in (4 cm) across and beautifully formed, are arranged in clusters, and every petal seems to be groomed into place to create a flattish cushion with a central green eye. They are a rich deep mauve-pink in color, paling towards the edges. This is a free-flowering, healthy rose with a strong fragrance and it does well in poor soil. It is a good candidate for use as a pot plant. ZONES 4–10.

Vibert, France, or Parmentier, Belgium, 1837

Possibly unknown Gallica × unknown Centifolia

'ANASTASIA'
MODERN, LARGE-FLOWERED/HYBRID TEA, WHITE, REPEAT-FLOWERING

There is a striking contrast between the dark, rugged-looking foliage of this rose and the excellent white flowers. They are carried, usually one to a stem, on a strong-stemmed, vigorous, leafy plant that grows to average height or more. Plump, pointed buds open into large rounded blooms made up of about 30 wide petals, appearing through summer and autumn. There is little fragrance, however, the flowers of 'Anastasia' last well so they are good for flower arrangements and for exhibiting. This is a rose for drier climates, as the white flowers will mottle in damp conditions. ZONES 5–9.

Greff, USA, 1980

'John F. Kennedy' × 'Pascali'

'ANDALUSIEN'   KORdalu
MODERN, CLUSTER-FLOWERED/FLORIBUNDA, MEDIUM RED, REPEAT-FLOWERING

For a short bedding rose, this is an excellent performer that gives a good succession of bloom through summer and autumn on a neat, short, bushy plant. The flowers are set close together in sprays that stand a little above the foliage, and open from long slender buds into loosely formed, double flowers of medium size in a clear bright scarlet-crimson shade. When the blooms are fully open, the petals are often folded into each other. They carry no fragrance. The leaves are small and bright green, and clothe the vigorous plant plentifully to the base. It has exceptional frost hardiness. ZONES 3–9.

Kordes, Germany, 1977

Seedling × 'Zorina'

Anerkannte Deutsche Rose 1976

'Angel Face'

'Andalusien'

'Anaïs Ségalas'

'ANDENKEN AN ALMA DE L'AIGLE'
syns 'Isabella', 'Souvenir d'Alma de l'Aigle'

MODERN, CLUSTER-FLOWERED/FLORIBUNDA, LIGHT PINK, REPEAT-FLOWERING

This variety has blooms that are a delicate shade of light rosy salmon pink. The medium to large-sized flowers open cupped, with many petals, in nodding clusters and exude a light, pleasant fragrance. The plant grows vigorously and upright, with large, rather lax mid-green leaves, and although somewhat slow growing it can achieve average height or above. There is usually a pause in flowering between the prolific early to mid-summer crop and the autumn bloom. ZONES 4–11.

Kordes, Germany, 1948

Parentage unknown

'ANDRÉ LEROY D'ANGERS'
OLD, HYBRID PERPETUAL, MEDIUM RED, REPEAT-FLOWERING

Like so many Hybrid Perpetuals of more than a century ago, this rose is hard to find except in botanical gardens. The tall, vigorous bush with dark foliage offers large, rose-violet double blooms during a long season. ZONES 4–10.

Trouillard, France, 1866

Parentage unknown

'ANDREA STELZER'   KORfachrit
MODERN, LARGE-FLOWERED/HYBRID TEA, LIGHT PINK, REPEAT-FLOWERING

The light pink blooms on this variety are large, being made up of many wide petals, and succeed in holding their high centers as they open. Unfortunately there is not much scent. The variety is recommended as a tall narrow hedge with the object of cutting a supply of perfect blooms on tall stems, for flower arrangement and exhibition, through summer and autumn. The plant is well furnished with shiny leaves, but needs to be monitored for black spot. Andrea Stelzer was Miss South Africa in 1985 and Miss Germany in 1988, so it was most appropriate that the rose chosen for her should have been of German raising and introduced into commerce by Ludwigs of South Africa. ZONES 6–11.

Kordes, Germany, 1992

Parentage unknown

'ANDREWSII'
syn. 'Andrew's Rose'

OLD, SCOTS, MEDIUM PINK, REPEAT-FLOWERING

Named after Henry C. Andrews, an early rose writer, this rare rose has become popular again, with good reason—it is a member of a dependable, unique group. The pink flowers have a touch of cream at the stamens' base, and can range from semi-double to fully double. They are cupped, very large, and sometimes ruffled with veining. This quite floriferous rose makes an excellent dense shrub or hedge; it has also been successfully used as a ground cover. It is happiest in a woodland setting. 'Andrewsii' is described in some books as the double form of the Burnet rose (*Rosa pimpinellifolia*). It blooms in late spring with some repeat in autumn. ZONES 4–10.

1807

Hybrid of *Rosa spinosissima*

'ANEMONE'
syns *Rosa × anemonoides*, 'Anemone Rose', 'Pink Cherokee', *R. laevigata* 'Anemone'

MODERN, MODERN SHRUB, LIGHT PINK, REPEAT-FLOWERING

This is a most unusual-looking rose, with mauvish pink flowers that have been described as both silky and papery, qualities not usually ascribed to roses. They are made up of 5 large heart-shaped petals of uniform size, which form a setting for the pretty golden stamens in the center; the effect resembles a clematis rather than an anemone. There is a light fragrance, and in warmer climates there is likely to be some repeat-flowering. 'Anemone' is one of the earliest garden roses to come into bloom, and can be very early indeed if treated as a climber and sited against a warm wall; it will also tolerate shadier walls. When grown as a shrub it makes a stiff, branching grower of medium to large size with dark, rather sparse, shiny foliage and brownish stems. ZONES 5–9.

Schmidt, Germany, 1896

Possibly *Rosa laevigata* × unknown Tea Rose

'ANGEL DARLING'
MODERN, MINIATURE, MAUVE, REPEAT-FLOWERING

This variety is probably one of the first lavender Miniatures developed in the twentieth century by the master of hybridizing Miniatures. The charm of this variety is gauged by the adorable single form containing 10 petals, although some growers regard the size of the blooms, about 1½ in (35 mm), too large for the surrounding foliage. The contrasting yellow stamens on a fresh bloom are very beautiful, but that beauty is fleeting, lasting only a few days at best. This striking variety is a popular Miniature for garden display and exhibition. This vigorous plant is extremely productive and has leathery disease-resistant foliage. ZONES 4–11.

Moore, USA, 1976

'Little Chief' × 'Angel Face'

'ANGEL FACE'
MODERN, CLUSTER-FLOWERED/FLORIBUNDA, MAUVE, REPEAT-FLOWERING

This rose, highly popular in the USA for 30 years, has deep mauve-lavender flowers that darken with ruby flushes towards the edges and are formed of up to 40 prettily ruffled petals. They open

'Angel Darling'

with high centers, and become cup shaped as the firm petals reflex to show yellow stamens. There is a lemony fragrance and good continuity of bloom through summer and autumn. Sometimes the blooms are carried singly, sometimes in clusters of a few flowers. The growth habit is low and rounded, and the leaves are dark green, leathery and semi-glossy. Good for bedding and for cutting, it is better suited to warmer climates, perhaps because plenty of sunshine is needed to bring out the beauty of the color tones. ZONES 5–9.

Swim, USA, 1968

('Circus' × 'Lavender Pinocchio') × 'Sterling Silver'

All-America Rose Selection 1969, American Rose Society John Cook Medal 1971

'ANGELA' KORday
syn. 'Angelica'
MODERN, MODERN SHRUB, DEEP PINK, REPEAT-FLOWERING

This variety covers itself with heavy sprays of medium-sized, cupped flowers. They are predominantly deep rose pink in color with highlights of light pink, especially in the center of the blooms. The blossoms are carried on short stems close to the dark green foliage, and their combined weight causes the stems to bow, creating a pleasingly lax habit. There is a slight fragrance and good continuity of flowering. The plant has bright foliage, lots of vigor and a neat, robust habit. It is bushy, grows up to average height, and is very suitable to plant in a mixed flower border or to make a hedge or bed. ZONES 4–9.

Kordes, Germany, 1984

'Yesterday' × 'Peter Frankenfeld'

Anerkannte Deutsche Rose 1982

'ANGELA RIPPON' OcaRU
syn. 'Ocarina'
MODERN, MINIATURE, MEDIUM PINK, REPEAT-FLOWERING

The distinctive salmon-pink blooms of this variety are preceded by very attractive urn-shaped buds usually borne in large clusters. Some growers have labelled this variety more of a Patio Rose than a Miniature because of the large, very double blooms. These have a frilly effect when fully open. The compact bush grows as a vigorous plant in nearly all climatic zones and is adaptable enough to be grown in containers, or even for edging pathways. However, the repeat cycle is slow. This variety is a sister seedling to 'Amorette', gaining its

genealogy from the orange-red Cluster-flowered rose, 'Zorina', developed by Boerner in 1963. The variety was named for a famous British television personality. ZONES 4–11.

de Ruiter, The Nethrlands, 1977

'Rosy Jewel' × 'Zorina'

'ANGELINA'
MODERN, MODERN SHRUB, PINK BLEND, REPEAT-FLOWERING

This rather open shrub decorates itself with blooms in wide-spaced clusters with hardly a pause throughout summer and autumn. The flowers are saucer shaped, made up of about 12 fairly narrow petals. The petals are bright rose pink, paling to blush white towards the center, and array themselves around the golden stamens to charming effect. It is a small shrub with a rounded habit, so it is very suitable for the front of a border, especially as its delightful scent can readily be appreciated there. Growth is vigorous and the foliage dark green, and adequate rather than plentiful. The raiser, Alec Cocker, who was keen on Gilbert and Sullivan, named the plant after the plaintiff in *Trial By Jury*. ZONES 4–9.

Cocker, UK, 1975

('Tropicana' × 'Carine') × ('Cläre Grammerstorf' × 'Frühlingsmorgen')

Belfast Certificate of Merit 1977, Royal National Rose Society Trial Ground Certificate 1975

'ANGELIQUE' AnKORi, KORangeli
MODERN, LARGE-FLOWERED/HYBRID TEA, ORANGE BLEND, REPEAT-FLOWERING

This variety produces neatly formed individual flowers on long firm stems that should last a fortnight in a vase. They open from plump buds into fully petalled high-centered blooms of a luminous deep orange, with little variation in color. The outer petals are often frilled at the edges. The variety blooms prolifically through summer and autumn on a bushy, upright, rather tall plant, furnished with ample rich green foliage. There is little in the way of fragrance, as is normal with good cut-flower roses, because the petals of such varieties need to be hard so that the flowers will travel safely to market without bruising; when petals are hard the scent glands function poorly. The myth that roses have lost their scent probably arises from the commercial necessities of the florist trade, although thousands of garden roses have retained their fragrance. ZONES 4–7.

Kordes, Germany, 1980

'Mercedes' × seedling

'Angelique'

'ANGELITA' MACangel; MACangeli
syn. 'Snowball'
MODERN, MINIATURE, WHITE, REPEAT-FLOWERING

Small, very double flowers grace the spreading ground-cover traits of this variety. Its growth habit is truly spreading and has complementary dark green, glossy foliage. The creamy white rosette-shaped blooms are borne in clusters and the repeat-flowering cycle is fast. 'Angelita' is popular as a weeping standard or in a hanging basket where the massive bloom clusters bend elegantly to add to the dimension of the overall inflorescence. It is said to be a better plant than its pollen parent, 'Snow Carpet', as it carries twice as many florets. This variety represents an important evolutionary step in the hybridizing of miniature ground covers. ZONES 4–11.

McGredy, New Zealand, 1982

'Moana' × 'Snow Carpet'

Gold Star of the South Pacific in New Zealand, 1982, Gold Award at the International Trial Grounds in Dublin 1983

'ANGEL'S BLUSH' MICangel
MODERN, MINIATURE, APRICOT BLEND, REPEAT-FLOWERING

The elegant buds of this rose open to attractive apricot blend flowers where the darkest color tone is on the very edge of the petals. The double blooms have 15–25 petals and a light fragrance. They occasionally have high centers suitable for exhibition, but the flower form is quite informal. The blooms are borne singly on long straight stems and last a long time both on the bush and when picked. It is an upright plant with attractive, healthy foliage and is an easy rose to grow. ZONES 5–11.

Williams, USA, 1996

Seedling × select pollen

'ANITA'
MODERN, CLUSTER-FLOWERED/FLORIBUNDA, PINK BLEND, REPEAT-FLOWERING

There have been two Cluster-flowered Roses of this name, an earlier pink-with-yellow variety from Kordes of Germany, and this one from the USA. Neither has

'Angela Rippon'

had a long run in commerce, the first being grown today solely in India and the American variety not at all. Rather plump, pointed buds open into flowers that are a blend of pink shades; the flowers are large, with over 40 petals, and are usually carried in small clusters of 3–7 blooms. They have a light Tea fragrance. The plant continues flowering through summer and autumn, and usually grows to average height with large glossy leaves—and large prickles to beware of when pruning. ZONES 4–9.

Swim and Christensen, USA, 1982

'Rumba' × 'Marmalade'

'ANITA CHARLES' MORnita
MODERN, MINIATURE, ORANGE-PINK, REPEAT-FLOWERING

The florets on this variety are an unusual deep coral red that is almost tan with lighter undersides, which seem to fade in hot climates. The well-shaped blooms have a typical Large-flowered form containing 43 or more petals, making them suitable for exhibition and artistic arrangements. The variety is extremely vigorous, producing many blooms for an attractive garden display. While most of the blooms are naturally borne singly, a few sprays (2–3 blooms per cluster) can develop from time to time in cooler climates. The somewhat sprawling habit makes it a suitable candidate for a hanging basket. It was named for the famous American gospel singer. ZONES 5–11.

Moore, USA, 1981

'Golden Glow' × 'Over The Rainbow'

'Angela'

'Anita Charles'

'Anna Ford'

'Ann Endt'

'Anna de Diesbach'

'Anna Livia'

'ANN ABERCONWAY'

MODERN, CLUSTER-FLOWERED/FLORIBUNDA,
APRICOT BLEND, REPEAT-FLOWERING

There is a sense of well-being about this pretty garden rose. The flowers are large for a Cluster-flowered Rose, with many petals, and at first they display high centers, becoming cupped as the petals reflex. The color of the young flowers is on the yellow side of apricot, becoming suffused with apricot-pink as they open. After an excellent first flush the plants bear well in autumn, when the colors can be richer and deeper. There is a pleasing fragrance. It grows bushy and upright, with strong flower stems, to average height, and is clothed in dark leathery foliage that contrasts well with the blooms. The variety is useful for a bed and also for cut flowers, but it needs to be cut when the blooms are still at the yellowish stage otherwise the flowers will open fast and lose color. Ann Aberconway is the wife of Lord Aberconway, past President of Britain's Royal Horticultural Society. ZONES 4–9.

Mattock, UK, 1976

'Arthur Bell' × seedling

'ANN ENDT'

MODERN, HYBRID RUGOSA, DARK RED,
REPEAT-FLOWERING

The flowers of 'Ann Endt' are single and show a tuft of cream stamens that light up the flowers. The long, sepaled buds are an inheritance from *Rosa foliolosa*. There is a strong cinnamon scent. The foliage is small, soft and abundant and the plant has a good repeat cycle. It forms a very attractive small shrub that can be used as a hedge or border or combined with perennial plants. Ann Endt was a gardener, for many years, to Nancy

Steen, author of *Charm of Old Roses*. Ann then created a wonderful garden of her own where she was one of the pioneers of mass planting of roses with bulbs, perennials and shrubs. She lived in Auckland, New Zealand. ZONES 3–9.

Nobbs, New Zealand, 1978

Rosa rugosa × *R. foliolosa*

'ANNA DE DIESBACH'

syns 'Anna von Diesbach', 'Gloire de Paris'
OLD, HYBRID PERPETUAL, DEEP PINK,
REPEAT-FLOWERING

Although in the late nineteenth century the popularity of the Hybrid Perpetuals was overshadowed by the new Large-flowered Roses (Hybrid Teas), they are still around, and one of the most popular is 'Anna de Diesbach'. It has long, pointed, Large-flowered-like buds that open to large, double, cupped pink blooms with a darker pink center. The vigorous, tall shrub is covered with blooms from summer to autumn. Blooms can be 4 in (10 cm) across with long sepals that may be pointed or foliated. The leaves are glaucous green, the prickles small, and the canes large. The hybridizer dedicated the rose to the daughter of Countess Diesbach of Fribourg, Switzerland. ZONES 5–10.

Lacharmé, France, 1858

'La Reine' × seedling

'ANNA FORD'   HARpiccolo

MODERN, PATIO/DWARF CLUSTER-FLOWERED,
ORANGE BLEND, REPEAT-FLOWERING

The semi-double flowers of this plant are deep orange with a yellow eye, an attractive combination. This variety was one of the first to be referred to as a Patio or Dwarf Cluster-flowered Rose, resembling the Cluster-flowered Roses but

with flowers, leaves and stems neatly scaled down in size. The pointed buds open to cup-shaped blooms borne several to a stem with 10 petals and narrow, reddish brown thorns. There is a slight fragrance. It has bushy growth and repeats well; it is nearly always in bloom throughout the year. It was named for a British writer and television star. ZONES 4–11.

Harkness, UK, 1980

'Southampton' × 'Darling Flame'
Royal National Rose Society President's International Trophy 1981, Genoa Gold Medal 1987, Glasgow Gold Medal 1989

'ANNA LIVIA'   KORmetter

syns 'Sandton Smile', 'Trier 2000'
MODERN, CLUSTER-FLOWERED/FLORIBUNDA,
ORANGE-PINK, REPEAT-FLOWERING

There is not much orange in 'Anna Livia', despite the official color description. It is basically a clear and restful shade of rose pink, bearing sprays of full-petalled, high-centered blooms in good succession through summer and autumn. They are fairly large, rounded in form, and the placement of each bloom in the spray is particularly pleasing. There is a light refreshing scent. The habit is excellent, being bushy and rather spreading, to average height, and with plentiful leathery mid-green foliage. It is also useful for exhibition. Anna Livia is the main character of James Joyce's novel *Finnegans Wake*, set on the River Liffey in Dublin, and the rose was named to commemorate the Irish capital's millennium in 1998. ZONES 4–9.

Kordes, Germany, 1985

(Seedling × 'Tornado') × seedling
Belfast Certificate of Merit 1987, Orléans Gold Medal 1987, Glasgow Gold Medal 1991, Royal Horticultural Society Award of Garden Merit 1994

'ANNA LOUISA'

MODERN, CLUSTER-FLOWERED/FLORIBUNDA,
LIGHT PINK, REPEAT-FLOWERING

This rose is remembered by an older generation as a very satisfactory pink bedding variety of well-behaved habit—that is to say the growth is even, at or a little above medium height, and well furnished with semi-glossy mid-green leaves. The flowers are small, with plenty of petals, and borne in great profusion in large, well-filled clusters on firm stems through summer and autumn. They are pointed when young and open to a charming cupped shape, yielding a pleasant light fragrance. The color is an even shade of light pink with a hint of rosy salmon. ZONES 4–9.

de Ruiter, The Netherlands, 1967

'Highlight' × 'Valeta'

'ANNA OLIVIER'

OLD, TEA, PINK BLEND, REPEAT-FLOWERING

This fine old favorite has lovely, ruffled petals that are pink blended with a yellowish flesh color and changing to a shaded salmon with a reverse in rose. The blossoms are well formed, full, large, and high centered with frequent rebloom. The blossoms, which hang down on a vigorous, branching bush, exude a delicate Tea scent and make good cut flowers. It has light green pointed leaves and should be moderately pruned. ZONES 5–10.

Ducher, France, 1872

Parentage unknown

'ANNA PAVLOVA'

MODERN, LARGE-FLOWERED/HYBRID TEA,
LIGHT PINK, REPEAT-FLOWERING

The beauty of this rose lies in its wonderfully constructed flowers. They have many broad petals of the most subtle light pink shade, these making up huge high-centered flowers of rounded form. The rose is also exceptionally sweet scented. Unfortunately, however, the plant is not always worthy of the treasure it produces, as it has upright, rather spindly growth and large nondescript leaves. It is perhaps best kept in a part of the garden where it can be visited and admired, or cut to bring indoors, so that its beauty and fragrance can be enjoyed during the summer to autumn flowering season. It may need preventive spraying against black spot, and in poorer soils is best left unpruned. ZONES 4–9.

Beales, UK, 1981

Parentage unknown

'Anna Louisa'

'Anna Olivier'

'Anna Pavlova'

'Anne Diamond'

'ANNA ZINKEISEN' HARquhling
MODERN, MODERN SHRUB, LIGHT YELLOW, REPEAT-FLOWERING

The medium-sized flowers on this variety are pale gold in the bud stage, becoming ivory in the open blooms. They have the look of an Old Garden Rose, with many small overlapping petals that open wide to show a rounded outline and pretty gold stamens at the center. The scent has affinity with that of the Scots Roses, rather sweet like new-mown hay. The blooms are carried in big sprays on strong stems on a broad, vigorous, free-branching plant that grows to average height and width for a shrub rose. The leaves are plentiful, pointed and a bright shade of green. 'Anna Zinkeisen' flowers right through from summer to autumn, making it an admirable choice for mixed borders and for use in parks. ZONES 5–10.

Harkness, UK, 1983

Seedling × 'Frank Naylor'

Diploma Copenhagen 1982, Silver Medal Courtrai 1983, Royal National Rose Society Trial Ground Certificate 1983

'ANNE COCKER'
MODERN, CLUSTER-FLOWERED/FLORIBUNDA, ORANGE-PINK, REPEAT-FLOWERING

The color has neither true orange nor pink in it, so the official coding is misleading. It is an eye-catching scarlet, rich and bright. The small to medium-sized flowers are carried in wide sprays, each individual bloom being neat in all respects—in its roundelay form, the arrangement of its petals, and its placement relative to the other flowers. There is little scent. The flower stems are thick and strong and are covered with fine prickles. It is ideal for indoor display or for shows; exhibitors have found it useful because it comes into flower a little later than most roses. The blooming period then extends through to autumn. The growth habit is upright, rather stiff and narrow, and the leaves are plentiful and

'Anne de Bretagne'

dark green. It was named for the raiser's wife, who herself has bred many fine varieties. ZONES 4–9.

Cocker, UK, 1970

'Highlight' × 'Color Wonder'

Royal National Rose Society Certificate of Merit 1969

'ANNE DE BRETAGNE'
MElturaphar
syns 'Décor Rose', 'Meilland Décor Rose'
MODERN, MODERN SHRUB, DEEP PINK, REPEAT-FLOWERING

This vigorous shrub rose is well suited to modern parks and landscaping use. The flowers, carried in well-filled sprays on firm stems, are fairly full of petals, and open from cone-shaped buds into neatly formed blooms with high centers, in a rich shade of deep salmon-pink. As they open out they form loose cups and the color lightens. There is not much fragrance. There is good continuity of bloom through summer and autumn. The variety grows vigorously with an upstanding habit, and is well furnished with semi-glossy light green foliage. Anne of Brittany was the sole heiress of that duchy. ZONES 4–10.

Meilland, France, 1979

('Malcair' × 'Danse des Sylphes') × (['Zambra' × 'Zambra'] × Centenaire de Lourdes)

'ANNE DIAMOND' LANdia
MODERN, LARGE-FLOWERED/HYBRID TEA, APRICOT BLEND, REPEAT-FLOWRING

This is a rose that would be well served by the American term 'Grandiflora', because it bears fully double flowers of Large-flowered quality with the profusion one expects of a Cluster-flowered Rose. The urn-shaped buds show pink as the sepals part, but on the inside the petals are apricot, and this color predominates as the flowers expand. They fade off buff yellow in the fully open flowers, which are well scented. The blooms are usually carried in sprays of 3 or 4, appearing through summer and

'Anne Harkness'

autumn on stems long enough to cut for flower arrangement. The plant grows to above average height but is apt to branch awkwardly, so it is not ideal for bedding. The foliage is dark green. Anne Diamond is well known in England as a television presenter. ZONES 4–9.

Sealand, UK, 1988

'Mildred Reynolds' × 'Arthur Bell'

Royal National Rose Society Trial Ground Certificate 1987

'ANNE HARKNESS' HARkaramel
MODERN, CLUSTER-FLOWERED/FLORIBUNDA, APRICOT BLEND, REPEAT-FLOWERING

This is a remarkable rose by reason of its spectacular flower sprays, in which each perfect flower is evenly spaced to create a natural floral bouquet. They open cupped, with wavy petal edges filling the bloom, and hold their regular form for a long time before dropping cleanly. The double, medium-sized flowers are apricot, tinged with apricot pink as they age. There is little scent. The plant requires much energy to produce such large sprays and so the first flowering is distinctly later than that of other Cluster-flowered Roses though, once started, they flower on into autumn with hardly a pause. It grows tall and upright, with adequate mid-green foliage, and is suitable to group among other plants or to

'Anne Cocker'

grow as a hedge. The rose was named for the raiser's niece to mark her 21st birthday. ZONES 4–9.

Harkness, UK, 1980

'Bobby Dazzler' × seedling

Royal National Rose Society Trial Ground Certificate 1978, British Association of Rose Breeders Selection 1980

'ANNE LETTS'
MODERN, LARGE-FLOWERED/HYBRID TEA, PINK BLEND, REPEAT-FLOWERING

George Letts was a nurseryman in Suffolk, England, and a fellow breeder described this as 'his first and last good effort'. Thirty wide petals make up a bloom with a very high center, with the tips of the petals furled into points. The color is clear pale pink with creamy pink in the depths of the flower, creating a two-toned effect, and the scent is sweet without being strong. Flowering is maintained through summer and autumn, though in wet conditions the flowers are likely to ball due to their thick petals, and for this reason it is grown for sale today only in warmer climates. 'Anne Letts' grows to average height, making many side shoots, and is well clothed with large, glossy mid-green leaves. ZONES 5–9.

Letts, UK, 1954

'Peace' × 'Charles Gregory'

'Anna Zinkeisen'

'Anne Letts'

'Anne Morrow Lindbergh'

'Anne-Marie de Montravel'

'Anne's Delight'

'Anneka'

'ANNE-MARIE DE MONTRAVEL'

syn. 'Anna-Maria de Montravel'
MODERN, POLYANTHA, WHITE, REPEAT-FLOWERING

This is a very early survivor of the innovative breeding work done with dwarf forms of *Rosa multiflora* around Lyon in nineteenth-century France, and as such it would be worth growing as a curiosity. It is a most charming rose, making a dense, rather sprawling shrublet full of twiggy growth and graced with pointed dark green leaflets. The pure white flowers are small, and quite full of rather ragged petals that open out to reveal the stamens. Their scent is reminiscent of lily-of-the-valley, and they are borne profusely in big clusters in summer and more sparingly through to autumn. The raiser, a widow, was the mother-in-law of Francois Dubreuil, who himself raised many roses from the 1880s onwards. ZONES 4–9.

Rambaux, France, 1879
Dwarf strain of *Rosa multiflora* × 'Mme de Tartas'

'ANNE MARIE TRECHSLIN'

MEIfour
syn. 'Anne Marie'
MODERN, LARGE-FLOWERED/HYBRID TEA, DEEP PINK, REPEAT-FLOWERING

This rose catches the eye because of its pretty melange of colors, in which deep orange-pink predominates together with apricot, yellow and coral. The full-petalled flowers are carried on firm stems, long enough for cutting, and open from long, urn-shaped buds into high-centered blooms of good size. They do

not last for long, but the variety compensates the gardener by its good repeat-flowering, producing fresh cycles of growth and bloom throughout summer and autumn. The flowers also have a delightful fruity fragrance. The plant grows strongly with an upright habit, producing well-branched, rather smooth, reddish stems. The leaves are tinted red when young, before turning deep green and acquiring a leathery texture. Anne Marie Trechslin is one of this century's most accomplished rose painters. ZONES 4–9.

Meilland, France, 1968
'Sutter's Gold' × ('Demain' × 'Peace')
Monza Gold Medal for Fragrance 1968

'ANNE MORROW LINDBERGH' JACyap

syn. 'Melinda Gainsford'
MODERN, LARGE-FLOWERED/HYBRID TEA, PINK BLEND, REPEAT-FLOWERING

There are many color shades in this rose: pink predominates as the buds open, and blends with white and yellow in the high-centered flowers as the petals reflex. The blooms are large, fully double, and are normally borne individually on long stems, which makes them well suited for cutting. A good continuity of flower production is maintained through summer and autumn, and there is a pleasing fragrance. This is a variety built on generous lines, for as well as having large blooms its height is taller than average and the foliage is sizeable too, giving a good coverage of mid-green slightly glossy leaves on a vigorous, upstanding plant. After his astonishing

transatlantic flight in 1927, US aviator Charles Lindbergh made a goodwill tour to Mexico; here he met, wooed and subsequently married Miss Anne Morrow, daughter of the US ambassador to Mexico, to the great delight of the American public. ZONES 4–9.

Warriner, USA, 1994
Parentage unknown

'ANNE OF GEIERSTEIN'

OLD, SWEET BRIAR, DARK RED

Like a sun in a red sky, the center of this lovely rose is filled with stamens on a small white background surrounded by the semi-double, dark red petals. It blooms during summer, and reaches 10 ft (3 m) high and 8 ft (2.4 m) in width with vigorous canes, fragrant foliage and flowers. It does well in poor soil and makes an excellent hedge or woodland plant. It tolerates shade and should be pruned lightly; unfortunately, it is susceptible to black spot. ZONES 5–10.

Penzance, UK, 1894
Rosa eglanteria × unknown Hybrid Perpetual or Bourbon

'ANNEKA' HARronver

MODERN, LARGE-FLOWERED/HYBRID TEA, YELLOW BLEND, REPEAT-FLOWERING

There could be some doubt over whether to describe this as a Large-flowered or a Cluster-flowered Rose, because the flowers are of good size and it often produces a distinctive inflorescence, with longish stems radiating from a point on the main branch to give a very wide spray. The color is basically yellow, with a suffusion of reddish pink towards the

petal edges, and the flowers are fairly full, high centered, and have a pleasant light fragrance. They are borne with commendable freedom right through summer to autumn. The plant is very vigorous and free branching, of average height or a little less, and is well clothed with handsome bright green foliage. This is an excellent easy to grow bedding rose. It was named for Anneka Rice of BBC television at the suggestion of the Royal National Rose Society, in connection with her program 'Challenge Anneka'. ZONES 4–9.

Harkness, UK, 1990
'Goldbonnet' × 'Silver Jubilee'
Royal National Rose Society Trial Ground Certificate 1985

'ANNE'S DELIGHT'

MODERN, MINIATURE, MEDIUM PINK, REPEAT-FLOWERING

The fluorescent medium to dark pink color of the florets of 'Anne's Delight' is very attractive. However, the color can quickly fade in cool climates. Attractive buds open to Large-flowered type blooms containing about 40 petals, usually borne one to a stem. While the form of the florets may be of show quality, the weakness in this variety is perhaps the stingy bloom production and weak stems. The foliage is small, dark green and glossy and the growth habit has been described by many growers as 'like a cucumber plant with a spreading pattern'. The bush is susceptible to mildew and black spot. ZONES 4–11.

Williams, USA, 1981
'Little Darling' × 'Over The Rainbow'

'ANNIE VIBERT'

OLD, NOISETTE, WHITE BLEND, REPEAT-FLOWERING

After the double, pink, medium-sized blooms on this variety open they change to white. The flowers continue from summer until autumn and have a pleasant perfume; the long, arching canes reach up to 12 ft (3.5 m). Noisettes were crosses between *Rosa chinensis* and an *R. moschata* variety. The hybridizer, John Champneys of South Carolina, gave his neighbor, Philippe Noisette, seedlings of this rose, which the latter sent to his brother in Paris; many think it is a French rose, which it is not. All Noisettes require a warm climate. ZONES 5–10.

Vibert, France, 1828
Parentage unknown

'Anne Marie Trechslin'

'Annie Vibert'

'ANNIE'S SONG'

MODERN, CLUSTER-FLOWERED/FLORIBUNDA,
ORANGE-PINK, REPEAT-FLOWERING

'Annie's Song' is a short-growing rose
with shapely flowers that are cream and
are heavily margined with pink on the
outer petals; it is similar in coloring to
'Handel' but the pink is much deeper,
and it is more free flowering. The flowers, which have 30 tough petals each, are
good as cut flowers. Reaching 3 ft (1 m)
in height, it has large, profuse, very
disease-resistant foliage on thorny stems.
ZONES 5–10.

Spriggs, Australia, 1990

'Granada' × 'Kordes' Perfecta'

'ANOTHER CHANCE'

MODERN, LARGE-FLOWERED/HYBRID TEA, WHITE,
REPEAT-FLOWERING

The large, pointed buds of 'Another
Chance' are pure white and open to
creamy, very full flowers of exhibition
form. Flower production is good, the
flowers lasting well on the bush, and the
petals are tough and do not mark easily.
There is a mild perfume. This variety
grows to medium height and has bushy,
matt, dark green foliage that is resistant
to disease. The breeder gave this rose
'another chance', as it improves so much
after its initial flowering in the seed bed;
it deserves to be grown more widely than
it is. ZONES 4–10.

Heyes, Australia, 1994

'Mount Shasta' × 'Saffron'

'ANTHONY MEILLAND'

MEItalbaz, MEIbaltaz

MODERN, CLUSTER-FLOWERED/FLORIBUNDA,
MEDIUM YELLOW, REPEAT-FLOWERING

This variety bears fully petalled flowers
in a bright and cheerful shade of yellow.
They are often produced in clusters of
a few blooms, but they are so unusually
large for a Cluster-flowered Rose that,
when the blooms open, the heads may
be crowded together. It certainly makes
for a showy display, and the petals have
attractive folds and scalloped edges.
There is a pleasing fragrance, and the
repeat-flowering through summer to
autumn is good. This therefore makes
a very suitable rose for a bed, and the
bushy growth habit at or a little under
average height is in its favor. The leaves
of this variety are large, mid-green, and

'Another Chance'

somewhat glossy. The rose was named
after a member of the raiser's family.
ZONES 5–11.

Meilland, France, 1990

'Sunblest' × MEllenangal

'ANTIGONE' GAUti, GAhti

MODERN, LARGE-FLOWERED/HYBRID TEA,
YELLOW BLEND, REPEAT-FLOWERING

The Gaujard enterprise succeeded to a
famous name, for it took over Pernet-
Ducher's nursery in 1924. Members of

'Anthony Meilland'

the Gaujard family have a long
tradition of raising Large-flowered
Roses of classic form with broad petals
and high centers, and this one, raised
by Madame Jean Gaujard, is a fine
example. The pointed buds open on
strong stems to reveal large full-
petalled flowers. They are yellow and
shaded towards the petal margins with
orange-red, which tones down to

peach-pink as the flowers expand and
mature. They are carried on long stems,
and last well when cut for indoor display.
The fragrance is good, and there is a succession of flowers throughout the growing season: from summer well into
autumn. This variety is good for
bedding schemes and borders, as it
grows vigorously and is well furnished
with handsome bright green leaves. They

'Annie's Song'

are rather soft in texture, so the rose is likely to do better in warmer climates. 'Antigone' can easily be propagated by budding. ZONES 5–9.

Gaujard, France, 1969

'Rose Gaujard' × 'Guitare'

Bagatelle Gold Medal 1967

'ANTIGUA' JACtig

MODERN, LARGE-FLOWERED/HYBRID TEA, APRICOT BLEND, REPEAT-FLOWERING

The large blooms on this variety are an interesting blend of colors, opening from plump buds to reveal tints of pink on an apricot base, and admitting pale crimson at the petal edges as they age. They are fairly full of broad, rather soft petals, and do not retain their high-centered form for long before opening wide to show confused centers. There is a light fragrance, and the succession of flowers through summer and autumn is reasonably good. They are produced on long stems so are useful for cutting if they are taken at an early stage. The free-branching plant grows a little taller than average for a Large-flowered Rose, and is well furnished with leathery, dark green foliage. Despite its gold medal, it has never been widely grown. ZONES 4–9.

Warriner, USA, 1974

'South Seas' × 'Golden Masterpiece'

Geneva Gold Medal 1972

'Antigone'

'Antike 89'

'Antoine Rivoire'

'ANTIKE 89' KORdalen

syns 'Antique', 'Antique 89'

MODERN, LARGE-FLOWERED CLIMBER, PINK BLEND, REPEAT-FLOWERING

The flowers of this climbing rose are very full petalled, rounded in form, and open with confused centers, the petals enfolded against each other in all directions. The background color of the petals is blush, heavily overlaid with rose red, especially towards the petal margins. The flowers, which have only a modest fragrance, appear from summer to autumn on stiffly branching stems. This plant is useful for pillars, walls, fences and pergolas. The growth is vigorous, and there is a good coverage of tough leathery dark green foliage. ZONES 4–9.

Kordes, Germany, 1988

Parentage unknown

'ANTIQUE'

syn. 'Antike'

MODERN, CLUSTER-FLOWERED/FLORIBUNDA, RED BLEND, REPEAT-FLOWERING

The inside of the flower petals on this variety is a combination of rosy crimson with yellow in the middle, and the outside is all golden yellow. The blooms are quite large for a Cluster-flowered Rose, fairly full of petals, somewhat rounded in form, and without much fragrance. They are produced freely through summer and autumn. This rose is suitable for bedding, having an even growth habit to average height, vigorous, and with deep green, shiny leaves. ZONES 4–9.

Kordes, Germany, 1967

'Honeymoon' × 'Circus'

'ANTIQUE ROSE' MORcara; MORcana

MODERN, MINIATURE, MEDIUM PINK, REPEAT-FLOWERING

Pointed buds reveal old-fashioned-looking rose pink blooms on a vigorous, tall, upright-growing bush. The blooms are naturally produced one to a stem and have a high center and a slight fragrance. They tend to lose their brilliance of color and substance rather fast especially in dry climates. The foliage is dark green with brown prickles. This rose is well named as it has good color and form and resembles an Old Garden Rose. ZONES 4–11.

Moore, USA, 1980

'Baccara' × 'Little Chief'

'ANTIQUE SILK' KORampa

syn. 'Champagner'

MODERN, LARGE-FLOWERED/HYBRID TEA, WHITE, REPEAT-FLOWERING

This is an exception to the rule that florists' roses lack scent, because it does have a pleasant almond fragrance. The buds as they open are tightly coiled. They expand to create star-shaped blooms with several layers of petals, pointed at the tips and with high centers. The petals are very firm, ensuring the flowers will last well whether they are cut for arrangement or left to develop on the plant. The whiteness of the blooms is touched with cream and ivory, which imparts a silky sheen. 'Antique Silk' produces a good succession of flowers through summer and autumn carried on

'Antonia Ridge'

firm upright stems, which are pleasant to handle as there are few thorns. As well as being a good cut-flower variety, this performs well as a garden rose in warmer climates. Growth is upright and bushy, and the leaves medium green. ZONES 4–9.

Kordes, Germany, 1982

Seedling of 'Anabell' × seedling

'ANTOINE RIVOIRE'

MODERN, LARGE-FLOWERED/HYBRID TEA, LIGHT PINK, REPEAT-FLOWERING

This early Large-flowered Rose was for many years a standby for cutting, both commercially and in the garden. The color is a pretty blend of pale creamy yellow with flushes of rosy pink, and the rather flat blooms caused it to be likened to a camellia. Its numerous petals are substantial enough to hold the centers of the blooms in shape for several days, even in a warm climate, though they yield only a light fragrance. The growth is strong and upright though not many stems are produced, and flower production is very limited between the summer and autumn flushes. The foliage is bronzy green, large and leathery, and needs watching for black spot. Antoine Rivoire was the president of the Lyon Horticulturalists' Association. ZONES 4–7.

Pernet-Ducher, France, 1895

'Dr Grill' × 'Lady Mary Fitzwilliam'

'ANTONIA RIDGE' MEIparadon

MODERN, LARGE-FLOWERED/HYBRID TEA, MEDIUM RED, REPEAT-FLOWERING

This variety bears its blooms sometimes singly and sometimes several together. They are large, full petalled, carried upright on long stems, and open with high centers to display the rich deep red color. There is only a light fragrance which is disappointing in a red rose, but it is attractive, continuing in bloom through summer and autumn. The plant grows upright and bushy to average height, with sizeable mid-green leaves. Antonia Ridge wrote *For Love of a Rose*, a best seller which tells the fascinating story of the Meilland nursery. The raiser, professionally known as Marie-Louise Paolino, is Mme Marie-Louise Meilland. ZONES 4–9.

Paolino, France, 1976

('Chrysler Imperial' × 'Karl Herbst') × seedling

'ANTONINE D'ORMOIS'

syn. 'Antonia d'Ormois'

OLD, GALLICA, LIGHT PINK

This is a fairly tall though well-filled shrub that can attain a height of up to

'Antique Rose'

'Antique Silk'

6 ft (1.8 m), which is taller than most Gallicas. The stems are only sparsely armed with thorns. The profuse foliage is light green when young, ageing to darker green. The flowers, which are very shapely, are up to 2½ in (6 cm) in diameter. They are cushion like when fully open. The soft pink color pales to blush in hot sun. Blooming a little shyly, rather later than mid-summer, this lovely rose is blessed with a good sweet perfume. It is a little-known variety that makes up for its slight scarcity of flowers with quality, fragrance and health. ZONES 4–10.

Vibert, France, 1835

Parentage unknown

'ANUSHEH' PAYable

syn. 'Anushcar'

MODERN, CLUSTER-FLOWERED/FLORIBUNDA, RED BLEND, REPEAT-FLOWERING

This Modern Garden Rose bears large clusters of flowers in rather crowded heads that open into full-petalled medium-sized rosettes. The petals are strawberry red on the inside and a light yellow on the back, creating a pretty color combination as the young flowers unfold; the tones alter as the flowers age, but they manage to do so without the colors clashing unacceptably. The flowers have a modest but attractive fragrance. 'Anusheh' continues to flower

A

through summer and autumn. The plant grows bushy and upright to average height, with glossy mid-green leaves, and is useful for bedding and to cut for small arrangements. Archie Payne, who died in December 1997, was a keen amateur raiser with a discerning eye. ZONES 4–9.

Payne, UK, 1993

'Len Turner' × seedling

Royal National Rose Society Trial Ground Certificate 1990

'ANYTIME'

MODERN, MINIATURE, ORANGE-PINK, REPEAT-FLOWERING

This is a classic example of a single-petalled Miniature Rose. The bright orange-red blooms have a contrasting purplish blue eye and golden yellow stamens. A smoky tinge overlays the basic color, making this an attractive garden variety. The flowers are borne mostly in clusters of 5–10 blooms on strong straight stems. This vigorous plant is nearly always in bloom, and is resistant to diseases. In rose shows, it is hard to beat in the single-petalled class. As it sets hips easily, it has been a seed parent for two other great Miniatures by Sam McGredy, 'Kaikoura' and 'Wanaka'. ZONES 4–11.

McGredy, New Zealand, 1973

'New Penny' × 'Elizabeth of Glamis'

'APART'

MODERN, HYBRID RUGOSA, MAUVE BLEND, REPEAT-FLOWERING

There have been many excellent Hybrid Rugosas in recent years, and this one displays the rugged qualities that make them especially valuable for colder zones. It bears medium-sized, loosely double flowers with ruffled petals in a mauvish shade of pink over a long period through summer into autumn. The flowers are very fragrant. In autumn there is an outstanding display of

'Apple Blossom'

'Apollo'

'Apogée'

tomato-shaped hips. The plant grows to average height or more with the rounded shrubby habit typical of many Rugosas, and is healthy and hardy. ZONES 3–7.

Uhl, Germany, 1981

Parentage unknown

'APFELBLÜTE'

MODERN, GROUND COVER, WHITE, REPEAT-FLOWERING

There have been so many Ground Cover Roses introduced within recent years that it is difficult to choose between them. This variety can be expected to grow about half as wide again as its height, making it halfway between a shrub and a truly procumbent plant. It produces showy sprays of from 5–20 single flowers, opening wide to reveal the stamens. The young blooms are a delicate shade of pale pink, soon turning white, and are held on slightly bowing stems quite close to the foliage. There is not much scent. Overall the effect is spectacular because so many flowers are produced, and they are well set off against shiny bright green leaves. Flowering continues through to autumn. The name means 'apple blossom'. ZONES 4–9.

Noack, Germany, 1991

Parentage unknown

Anerkannte Deutsche Rose 1991

'APOGÉE' DELbaf, DELbal, DELbat

MODERN, LARGE-FLOWERED/HYBRID TEA, ORANGE BLEND, REPEAT-FLOWERING

This rose is interesting to have in the garden because the flower color varies in the course of the season, being basically coppery but blended sometimes with gentle peachy tones, and sometimes brighter with much more yellow. The richest tones are noticed in cooler weather. The flowers open from plump buds and are large and full petalled, becoming cupped as the petals reflex. They are freely

'Apothecary's Rose'

'Anusheh'

'Antonine d'Ormois'

'Anytime'

produced and have a light fragrance, and continuity of bloom is maintained through to autumn, making this a useful rose for cutting. The plant grows upright, to average or above average height, and is furnished with bronzy, glossy leaves. ZONES 4–9.

Delbard, France, 1966

('Queen Elizabeth' × 'Provence') × (seedling of 'Sultane' × 'Mme Joseph Perraud')

'APOLLO' ARMolo

MODERN, LARGE-FLOWERED/HYBRID TEA, MEDIUM YELLOW, REPEAT-FLOWERING

The flowers of this variety are a light and cheerful shade of yellow, opening from long tapered buds into fully double blooms. They have a pleasant fragrance and last well when cut. The plant grows bushy and upright, with dark leathery foliage, which needs watching for black spot. Although this rose achieved a very prestigious award, its record as a garden rose has proved disappointing and it achieved a lamentable 4.8 rating (out of 10) in the American Rose Society's National Rose Ratings. ZONES 4–9.

Armstrong, USA, 1971

'High Time' × 'Imperial Gold'

All-America Rose Selection 1972

'APOTHECARY'S ROSE'

syns Rosa gallica officinalis, 'Rose of Provins', 'Red Rose of Lancaster'

OLD, GALLICA, DEEP PINK

This is possibly the oldest rose to be cultivated in Europe. It has been used for medicinal purposes ever since its birth, and it is also part of the story of the War of the Roses. The semi-double blooms

with 4 rows of petals change from bright crimson to near purple, and are crowned with prominent stamens. The branching canes hold few prickles, and the dark green foliage is most attractive. It blooms later than its offspring and is highly disease resistant. The hips produce abundant seeds, ideal for naturalizing. It suckers readily when on its own roots and has an intense fragrance, the petals being ideal for potpourri. It serves well as erosion control on steep sites. ZONES 4–10.

Pre-1600

Parentage unknown

'APPLE BLOSSOM'

MODERN, RAMBLER, LIGHT PINK

Luther Burbank was a famed hybridizer of fruits, trees and plants, and this rose is his rose memorial. 'Apple Blossom' is the only one of his hybrids still in catalogues around the world. The vigorous canes support huge trusses of pink-white flowers with crinkled petals throughout summer. It is ideal for training up trees and on pergolas. The pliable stems are covered with dark green, healthy foliage and few prickles. ZONES 5–10.

Burbank, USA, 1932

'Dawson' × Rosa multiflora

'APPLEJACK'

MODERN, MODERN SHRUB, PINK BLEND, REPEAT-FLOWERING

This is a versatile rose equally at home in warm or cold climates. The flowers are showy, opening from pointed buds into loose, almost flat flowers formed of around 10 crumpled-looking petals. The color is rose pink with some rose red

A

'Apricot Nectar'

'Apricot Silk'

flushes. The blooms have a refreshing apple scent, from which the rose derives its name. They appear freely in summer, and the plant usually provides a scattering of later flowers nestling against the abundant leathery leaves. The growth is vigorous and untidy with arching stems, so it is suitable for growing as a big shrub in a naturalized setting where plants look after themselves, or it can be given a support and made into a climber. It is remarkably hardy. ZONES 3–9.

Buck, USA, 1973

'Goldbusch' × ('Josef Rothmund' × *Rosa laxa* 'Retzius')

'APPRECIATION'

MODERN, LARGE-FLOWERED/HYBRID TEA, MEDIUM RED, REPEAT-FLOWERING

This rose has inherited the robust upright habit of 'Queen Elizabeth' and produces its flowers on long stems, sometimes singly, sometimes in well-spaced clusters. They are light red in color, with some deeper crimson shading. The double flowers are quite large, opening to show a pointed shape and later becoming cupped as the petals reflex. They carry a slight fragrance, and flowering continues through summer and autumn. Glossy leaves effectively clothe the base of the vigorous plant. ZONES 4–9.

Gregory, UK, 1971

'Queen Elizabeth' × seedling

'APRICOT DELIGHT'

MODERN, LARGE-FLOWERED/HYBRID TEA, APRICOT BLEND, REPEAT-FLOWERING

'Apricot Delight' is a short, stocky grower that produces large double flowers of an intense apricot color similar to ripe apricots. The foliage is large, dark green and healthy and shows up the blooms well. Flower production is a bit stingy, with long periods between flushes, although the scent is strong and the buds are shapely at all stages of development; the buds are good for picking. There is some tendency to mildew in autumn. It does well where a low-growing variety is required. ZONES 4–10.

Delbard, France, 1978

Parentage unknown

'APRICOT GEM'

MODERN, CLUSTER-FLOWERED/FLORIBUNDA, APRICOT BLEND, REPEAT-FLOWERING

This small-growing rose was not registered when it was first released and has only been grown in limited quantities since. The strong, double, apricot flowers are borne in clusters that cover the bush, creating quite a charming effect. Its height at maturity is low, so it is ideal as a bush for a patio or at the edge of a bed. It has poor resistance to disease and needs care and attention throughout the season to keep it flowering and growing well. The plant does best in warm, dry conditions. It is not strong in cold, damp climates, although it is in these conditions that the most intense color is to be found in the blooms. ZONES 5–9.

Delbard and Chabert, France, 1978

Parentage unknown

'APRICOT NECTAR'

MODERN, CLUSTER-FLOWERED/FLORIBUNDA, APRICOT BLEND, REPEAT-FLOWERING

This has been a firm favorite since its beguiling flowers first appeared on the market over 30 years ago. The attraction is provided by a beautiful shade of golden apricot with just a hint of pink, the pretty cupped formation of the blooms, and their value for floral arrangement, because if cut at a young stage they will open slowly and give pleasure for many days. The flowers are full petalled, quite large so that especially in warmer climates they can become crowded in the cluster, and require disbudding. There is a pleasant fruity scent and a good succession of blooms through summer and autumn. Growth is

'Apricot Delight'

bushy and reasonably vigorous, and the plant is well covered in mid-green leaves. This is generally good as a garden rose but is not happy in dull cool conditions. ZONES 4–9.

Boerner, USA, 1965

Seedling × 'Spartan'

Royal National Rose Society Certificate of Merit 1965, All-America Rose Selection 1966

'APRICOT QUEEN'

MODERN, LARGE-FLOWERED/HYBRID TEA, APRICOT BLEND, REPEAT-FLOWERING

What was once a very popular rose is now quite hard to obtain, and the reason must lie partly in the deterioration that most varieties suffer after several decades of propagation, and partly in the fact that new roses have more appealing plant qualities than many of the old ones. 'Apricot Queen' produces slim buds, with elegantly furled petals, that open into well-filled scented flowers of rounded form. The color is basically apricot with salmon-pink shading, and the succession of bloom through summer and autumn is good. Two drawbacks are weak flower stems and skimpy leaf cover. Even so, this is a pretty item for the garden that performs well in warm climates. ZONES 5–9.

Howard, USA, 1940

'Mrs J. D. Eisele' × 'Los Angeles'

All-America Rose Selection 1941

'APRICOT SILK'

MODERN, LARGE-FLOWERED/HYBRID TEA, APRICOT BLEND, REPEAT-FLOWERING

The beauty of this rose lies in the color, a fusion of orange and orange-red shades in the high-centered flowers. The long buds open to full-petalled blooms that do indeed have a silky look, but they do not last long either on the plant or when cut nor do they have much scent. The bush grows upright to average height or less, and its covering of dark glossy leaves is hardly adequate, therefore giving the plant a spindly look. This is accentuated if black spot causes leaf loss, which is quite likely, and this in turn will affect the plant's repeat-flowering capabilities. Old-time catalogues used to give their customers a coded warning about roses of this nature with the words 'rewards good cultivation'. ZONES 4–9.

Gregory, UK, 1965

Seedling × 'Souvenir de Jacques Verschuren'

'APRICOT SUMMER'   KORpapiro

MODERN, PATIO/DWARF CLUSTER-FLOWERED, APRICOT BLEND, REPEAT-FLOWERING

Some nurseries classify this as a Miniature Rose because it is very short. Everything about the plant—flowers, stems, leaves—is scaled down in proportion. It produces clusters of many petite rosettes in a shade closer to pale salmon than true apricot, and repeats the cycle of growth and bloom very successfully throughout summer and autumn. There is no discernible scent. The leaflets are very small, pointed, dark green and shiny, and are produced on many vigorous shoots. Patio Roses are grown to fill up a small space, perhaps in a rockery, or for pots, so that they can be placed on display when coming into bloom and then put away to gather strength for the next reflowering. This variety can be grown from cuttings. ZONES 4–9.

Kordes, Germany, 1995

Parentage unknown

'Apricot Gem'

'APRICOT SUNBLAZE'

SAVamark

syns 'Mark One', 'Mark 1'

MODERN, MINIATURE, ORANGE-RED, REPEAT-FLOWERING

Brilliant orange-red flowers containing 43 or more petals start off cup shaped and then quickly change to flat, fully opened florets. Color fastness is noticeable, as the deep orange color does not fade in most climate zones. This is a real plus in landscaping design! Blooms can be borne singly but clusters of 10 or more florets are also common in cooler climates. The blooms have a spicy apple fragrance. ZONES 5–11.

Saville, USA, 1982

'Sheri Anne' × 'Glenfiddich'

'APRIL HAMER'

MODERN, LARGE-FLOWERED/HYBRID TEA, PINK BLEND, REPEAT-FLOWERING

This variety is an excellent garden and show rose that is magnificent for cutting and for the show bench. Consisting of 40 petals and with moderate fragrance, the flowers are very pale pink flushed much deeper pink at the petal edges. It is one of the best of all Australian-raised roses. The dark green foliage is plentiful and acts as a foil to the pale flowers. It is a strong healthy grower with upright growth, freedom from disease and the ability to produce high-quality flowers throughout the year. ZONES 6–11.

Bell, Australia, 1983

'Mount Shasta' × 'Prima Ballerina'

'AQUARIUS' ARMaq

MODERN, LARGE-FLOWERED/HYBRID TEA, PINK BLEND, REPEAT-FLOWERING

Also known as a Grandiflora Rose, this variety has high-centered flowers of medium size filled with quite broad petals, and carried singly or in sprays of several together. The color is a blend of reddish pink and cream, paling as the flowers open. They are good to cut as they last well; for this objective, the flower sprays should be thinned by removing some of the buds when they are very small. They do not carry much scent, but flower production is good through summer and autumn. The plant grows tall and vigorous, with tough leathery leaves. ZONES 4–9.

Armstrong, USA, 1971

('Charlotte Armstrong' × 'Contrast') × ('Fandango' × ['World's End' × 'Floradora'])

Geneva Gold Medal 1970, All-America Rose Selection 1971

'April Hamer'

'Aquarius'

'ARABIAN NIGHTS'

MODERN, CLUSTER-FLOWERED/FLORIBUNDA, ORANGE-PINK, REPEAT-FLOWERING

The color of this rose was startlingly novel in the 1960s, and hard to describe; one discerning grower called it 'orange-salmon' and another 'bright scarlet changing towards crimson'. They both caught something of the truth, for the color one sees depends much on how sunlight strikes the petals. The flowers are full and fairly large, open cupped, and are held aloft on strong stems, usually in clusters of 3–5. They withstand bad weather and are lovely to cut, but lack fragrance. The summer and autumn flowering is good, with only occasional flowers in between. The habit is bushy and upright, with ample dark green foliage, but it has a tendency towards mildew. ZONES 4–9.

McGredy, UK, 1963

'Spartan' × 'Beauté'

'ARAMIS'

MODERN, CLUSTER-FLOWERED/FLORIBUNDA, DARK RED, REPEAT-FLOWERING

This rose makes a vivid splash of color in the garden. Its semi-double flowers, of good size for a Cluster-flowered Rose, open cupped to display their glowing crimson scarlet petals. As they are normally borne in clusters of 7–8 blooms, the effect is eye-catching. The petals do not outstay their welcome, dropping cleanly before they decay, so that the plant always looks fresh and is very suitable for bedding. Blooming continues through summer and autumn, but the variety does not have much fragrance. Growth is vigorous, compact and very bushy to average height, and the plant has glossy, dark green foliage. ZONES 4–9.

Laperrière, France, 1964

'Bel Ami' × ('Java' × 'Alain')

'Arabian Nights'

'Archiduc Joseph'

'Archduke Charles'

'ARC ANGEL' FRYyorst

MODERN, LARGE-FLOWERED/HYBRID TEA, ORANGE BLEND, REPEAT-FLOWERING

Gareth Fryer has raised a series of excellent Large-flowered Roses in recent years, and this is one of his best. The blooms exhibit the classic form associated with the best of the class; elegant in bud, full of broad petals and forming a beautiful high center that will last for days in cool weather. The color is coppery orange in the bud, lightening to coppery yellow with veins of pale salmon as the blooms expand. There is some fragrance, and it blooms well through summer and autumn. The plant is bushy and vigorous, with dark green foliage. The ingenious name commemorates the diamond jubilee of ARC—the Arthritis and Rheumatism Council. ZONES 4–9.

Fryer, UK, 1996

Parentage unknown

'ARCHDUKE CHARLES'

syn. 'Archiduc Charles'

OLD, CHINA, RED BLEND, REPEAT-FLOWERING

The blossoms on this rose change color. Thomas Rivers remarked that it is a chameleon: the crimson outer petals with pink centers later deepen to solid crimson, and in full, hot sun everything turns red. The full, lasting blooms, which

'Aramis'

smell of bananas, are cupped with large 'guard' petals enclosing small petals of pale pink to white. Growing up to 6 ft (1.8 m), it has a neat, upright appearance and few prickles and is repeat-flowering. Frequent pruning is recommended to shape the lanky bush. For many years in Bermuda this was thought to be 'Seven Sisters'. ZONES 5–10.

Liffay, France, pre-1837

Seedling of Rosa chinensis 'Parson's Pink'

'ARCHIDUC JOSEPH'

OLD, TEA, PINK BLEND, REPEAT-FLOWERING

There has been much controversy over this rose as it has been incorrectly labeled as 'Monsieur Tillier' and vice versa— the two plants are very close in appearance. The buds of 'Archiduc Joseph' are dark pink, opening lighter and then turning copper, with strong pink overtones as well. Thin canes with glossy foliage are sometimes not strong enough to hold the quartered blooms upright. Colors vary depending on the weather and the location: the petals become purple-orange in humid climates but rose and pink in dry, hot weather. The canes are brownish red with dark, ashy green leaves. ZONES 7–8.

Nabonnand, France, 1892

Seedling of 'Mme Lombard'

'Arianna'

'Archiduchesse Elizabeth d'Autriche'

'Ardoisée de Lyon'

'ARCHIDUCHESSE ELIZABETH D'AUTRICHE'

OLD, HYBRID PERPETUAL, MEDIUM PINK, REPEAT-FLOWERING

The double, rose pink, very large, full blooms of this variety open flat. The petals resemble satin, and are medium pink with a lighter reverse. Vigorous and nearly thornless, this rose reaches 3 ft (1 m) and is quite floriferous in mid-summer. Hard pruning helps to shape its appearance. The archduchess was the daughter of Emperor Franz-Josef of the Austro-Hungarian Empire. Jack Harkness states that this rose is repeat-flowering, but it does not bloom continuously. ZONES 5–10.

Moreau et Robert, France, 1881

Parentage unknown

'ARCTIC SUNRISE'   BARarcsun

MODERN, MINIATURE, WHITE, REPEAT-FLOWERING

Bred from the original spreading Minia-ture Rose 'Snow Carpet', 'Arctic Sunrise' has the same characteristic spreading growth habit. Small, white, double florets with 30 petals are usually borne in large clusters of 40–60 blooms. The medium green foliage is small and disease resist-ant. This variety has no fragrance and does not set fruit as many of the descen-dants of its seed parent do. ZONES 4–11.

Barrett, UK, 1991

'Snow Carpet' × 'Tranquility'

'ARDOISÉE DE LYON'

OLD, HYBRID PERPETUAL, MAUVE, REPEAT-FLOWERING

Opening bright red and turning to a violet finish, the full, large and quartered blooms of this rose are rather muddled. In full sunlight they appear a rich cerise but the color is often criticized because of a blue reflection that detracts from the overall effect. The flowers have strong necks on a shrub that is 4 ft (1.2 m) high and 3 ft (1 m) wide. It has a sweet, rich fragrance, and the long hips that appear later in the season add to its charm. The foliage is dark, gray-green and rather coarse with brown prickles. Like so many Hybrid Perpetuals, it is subject to mildew and rust. ZONES 5–10.

Damaizin, France, 1858

Parentage unknown

'ARDS BEAUTY'   DICjoy

MODERN, CLUSTER-FLOWERED/FLORIBUNDA, MEDIUM YELLOW, REPEAT-FLOWERING

This is a cheerful rose that has pleased Britain's judges by its freedom of flower and continuity of bloom throughout the season. The double flowers are of small to average size, carried in clusters close to the foliage on a neat, short, bushy plant. The petals are firm and open cupped, displaying the canary yellow color to excellent effect and dispensing a pleasing fragrance. In very hot weather

'Arethusa'

the blooms may develop a disfiguring green center. The foliage complements the bush, being plentiful, glossy and rich green. The name refers to part of County Down, Northern Ireland, where the raiser lives. When the rose was launched, the mayor from the Ards district wore her splendid chain of office, made out of gold medals won by the Dickson nursery over the past 163 years. ZONES 4–9.

Dickson, UK, 1986

('Eurorose' × 'Whisky Mac') × 'Bright Smile'

Royal National Rose Society President's Inter-national Trophy 1983, Belfast Certificate of Merit 1988, Glasgow Certificate of Merit 1990

'ARDS ROVER'

OLD, HYBRID PERPETUAL, DARK RED

'Ards Rover' has large, crimson-velvet, globular blossoms with stiff petals that develop into a muddled form. The sparse and straggly, climbing growth does not detract from its value, however, because red climbers have always been scarce and there is a strong fragrance. It shares many characteristics of a Large-flowered Rose, and its flowers are good for cutting. It is slow to establish itself but, once estab-lished, the vigorous and rapid growth of the rigid canes needs little pruning except for the dead wood. It does not like hot sun and does well in shady situa-tions, flowering throughout summer. The Ards Peninsula is in Ireland, where the Dickson nursery was established well over 100 years ago. ZONES 4–10.

Dickson, UK, 1898

Parentage unknown

'ARETHUSA'

OLD, CHINA, YELLOW BLEND, REPEAT-FLOWERING

Clusters of clear yellow, blowzy blooms cover this short shrub from summer until autumn. Although it is gawky in appearance, it is a valuable plant in the border if it is surrounded by perennials.

The foliage is healthy, shiny and sparse. William Paul and Sons of England pro-duced scores of roses, including 'Hebe's Lip' and 'Magna Charta'. Arethusa was a famous spring in Syracuse, Sicily, in ancient times and, according to legend, a naiad of the same name made it her home. ZONES 5–10.

Paul, UK, 1903

Parentage unknown

'ARIANNA'   MEIdali

MODERN, LARGE-FLOWERED/HYBRID TEA, PINK BLEND, REPEAT-FLOWERING

This is a rose for warmer climates, where its large, high-centered flowers can be used to great effect as a hedge or large bed, because it is a very free-flowering variety. The blooms are double with about 36 petals, and are basically rose pink with a suffusion of coral-salmon, a soft and unusual tone. They have a light fragrance and, being long stemmed, are very suitable as cut flowers. The conti-nuity of bloom through summer and autumn is good, the autumn flowers being particularly fine. The growth is vigorous, to above average height and with an open, spreading habit, and there is an ample provision of dark leathery leaves. ZONES 5–9.

Meilland, France, 1968

'Charlotte Armstrong' × ('Peace' × 'Michèle Meilland')

Bagatelle Gold Medal 1965, Rome Gold Medal 1965, The Hague Gold Medal 1965

'ARIELLE DOMBASLE'

syn. 'Arielle Dombasie'

MODERN, LARGE-FLOWERED CLIMBER, ORANGE BLEND, REPEAT-FLOWERING

Without being particularly novel or remarkable, this makes a very effective and well-behaved climbing rose for all the usual purposes—wall, fence, pillar—for which a plant of average extent is re-quired. The official color code is perhaps misleading, because this rose is very much on the scarlet side of orange. The medium-sized flowers are double, borne in clusters of several together, and the petals open wide to display the bright warm color to good effect. As the flowers age they admit some reddish pink, but the tones of both old and new flowers go together well. There is a slight fragrance, and flowering continues through sum-mer and autumn. The leaves are plenti-ful, rugged and dark green. ZONES 4–9.

Meilland, France, 1991

Parentage unknown

'Arielle Dombasle'

'Ards Rover'

'ARISTIDE BRIAND'
MODERN, RAMBLER, MAUVE

This Rambler has bluish pink flowers that fade into light mauve-pink and white. The large clusters join thin canes that have shiny and healthy foliage. It once enjoyed great popularity but because it resembles 'Veilchenblau', another Rambler, it has become rare as the latter is stronger and more adaptable. Aristide Briand was a French statesman and an early advocate for the League of Nations who won the Nobel Prize in 1926 for his peace efforts. ZONES 5–10.

Penny, France, 1928

'Yseult Guillot' × seedling

'ARISTOBULE'
OLD, MOSS, DEEP PINK

On this variety crimson-purple blooms with a purple flush in the center appear quartered, with petals paler at the edge. It has lots of prickles and brown leaves and can grow to 5 ft (1.5 m). Unfortunately, it is no longer available in commerce. ZONES 5–10.

Foulard, France, 1849

Parentage unknown

'ARIZONA'   WErina
syn. 'Tocade'

MODERN, LARGE-FLOWERED/HYBRID TEA, ORANGE BLEND, REPEAT-FLOWERING

Like many roses with orange-salmon tones, this rose's color varies according to location. The base color is coppery orange, with salmon-red towards the petal edges and yellow in the petal depths; the tones are richer in cool climates. The flowers are of medium size, with sufficient petals to form shapely high-centered blooms of Large-flowered Rose character, opening from urn-shaped buds. In the USA it is regarded as a Grandiflora, presumably because it is tall and bears flowers on long stems with good continuity through summer and autumn. The blooms have a sweet fragrance. The plant is a vigorous, upright grower with crisp dark green foliage. It is sometimes affected by fungus troubles. ZONES 4–9.

Weeks, USA, 1975

(['Fred Howard' × 'Golden Scepter'] × 'Golden Rapture') × (['Fred Howard' × 'Golden Scepter'] × 'Golden Rapture')

All-America Rose Selection 1975

'ARIZONA SUNSET'
MODERN, MINIATURE, YELLOW BLEND, REPEAT-FLOWERING

Both the brilliant color combination and flower form of this rose have drawn rave reviews in both the UK and USA. The flowers are light yellow flushed orange-red, usually borne one to stem or in large clusters of 8 or more. The foliage is small, medium green and semi-glossy. However, this tall upright plant can suffer from disease, mainly mildew and black spot in cooler climate zones. Naming this Miniature was easy as the colors are evocative of the wonderful sunsets in the arid climate of Arizona, USA. ZONES 4–11.

Jolly, USA, 1985

'Orange Sweetheart' × 'Zinger'

'Armada'

'ARMADA'   HARuseful
syn. 'Trinity Fair'

MODERN, MODERN SHRUB, MEDIUM PINK, REPEAT-FLOWERING

'Armada' makes a modest-sized shrub, ideal for mixed borders or to plant as a small group or as a hedge. The flowers are a rich deep pink, of medium size with about 18 petals, cupped in form and appearing in big clusters on strong stems with good repeat-flowering. They have a pleasing scent. The plant is vigorous and free branching, with glossy green foliage, healthy and very hardy. The rose was named for a National Trust appeal in aid of Buckland Abbey, once the home of Sir Francis Drake, on the quatercentenary of the Spanish Armada's attempted invasion of Britain. ZONES 3–9.

Harkness, UK, 1988

'New Dawn' × 'Silver Jubilee'

Copenhagen Diploma 1988, Courtrai Silver Medal 1988, The Hague Gold Medal 1994

'ARNOLD'
syns 'Arnoldiana', 'The Arnold Rose'

MODERN, HYBRID RUGOSA, MEDIUM RED, REPEAT-FLOWERING

This variety holds perhaps more botanical interest than garden value. It is the result of crossing the very healthy and hardy *Rosa rugosa* strain with an Old Garden Rose, the identity of which is not entirely certain. The plant grows vigorously and upright to average height or more, bearing in early summer and sporadically later small to medium-sized deep red flowers made up of a few rather crumpled-looking petals. There is some fragrance, and the general character of the shrub in growth, foliage and hardiness shows its affinity to the *R. rugosa* parent. Jackson Dawson did his hybridizing at Arnold Arboretum. ZONES 3–9.

Dawson, USA, 1893

Rosa rugosa × 'Général Jacqueminot'

'ARRILLAGA'
OLD, HYBRID PERPETUAL, LIGHT PINK, REPEAT-FLOWERING

This California-born rose has big pink buds that open to very large, double blossoms with 50 petals. The bush can reach 10 ft (3 m) and has strong, green, healthy foliage. It has a strong perfume. It blooms in summer and frequently in

'Arizona'

autumn. One of the last Hybrid Perpetuals to be marketed, 'Arrillaga' was created by Father Georg Schoener (1864–1941), who worked in Oregon and California before World War II and is best remembered for his 'Schoener's Nutkana' from 1930. ZONES 5–10.

Schoener, USA, 1929

Seedling × 'Frau Karl Druschki'

'ARTHUR BELL'
MODERN, CLUSTER-FLOWERED/FLORIBUNDA, MEDIUM YELLOW, REPEAT-FLOWERING

This most satisfying garden rose has flowers that are clear yellow, bright in bud, opening paler and finishing almost primrose and transforming from pointed buds to pretty cups along the way. The 20 or so petals are firm and well able to withstand wet weather, which must have been needful on the Ulster breeder's nursery. The flower clusters are held above the foliage on upright, stiff stems, and the vigorous bush is handsomely clothed with shiny bright green leaves. The sweetly scented flowers repeat their bloom through summer and autumn, making this an excellent choice for a bed or group. They are also used for cutting and exhibition, as they last well. Bell's is a brand familiar to drinkers of Scotch, and Sam McGredy recalled that his reward for this rose was innumerable cases of whisky. **'Climbing Arthur Bell'** (Pearce, UK, 1978) freely bears flowers

'Arthur de Sansal'

'Arthur Bell'

just as lovely as the bush form, in summer and with some later bloom. The plant grows vigorously, putting out stiff stems that are best suited to being trained against a sizeable wall, where stems and shoots can be attached laterally or fanwise to a solid background. ZONES 4–9.

McGredy, UK, 1965

'Cläre Grammerstorf' × 'Piccadilly'

Royal National Rose Society Certificate of Merit 1964, Belfast Fragrance Prize 1967, Royal Horticultural Society Award of Garden Merit 1993

'ARTHUR DE SANSAL'
OLD, PORTLAND, MAUVE, REPEAT-FLOWERING

This is a short, almost spindly shrub that grows to a maximum height of 3 ft (1 m) and has dark, fairly thorny wood and very dark green foliage. The flowers are produced in large tightly packed clusters, starting in mid-summer and going on through to autumn. Each flower is some 2 in (5 cm) across and full of small layered petals, which creates a very flat effect when fully open. These richly perfumed flowers are deep maroon-red in color, ageing to a rather muddy purple. Time does not seem to have dealt any favors to this rose for it is now rather prone to both rust and mildew, but it can be most rewarding if these afflictions can be controlled or overlooked. ZONES 4–10.

Cochet, France, 1855

Seedling of 'Géant des Batailles'

'ARTHUR HILLIER'

MODERN, MODERN SHRUB, DEEP PINK,
REPEAT-FLOWERING

Arthur Hillier was the creator of the
Hillier Arboretum at Winchester in England, one of the most famous collections
of plants in the world. This rose named
after him is a cross between two species
from the Himalayas with single flowers
of 5 rich rosy crimson petals. They are
2½ in (6 cm) across, and are borne in
clusters on long arching canes with attractive ferny foliage. They are slightly
fragrant. There is some repeat-bloom.
This is a large shrub suitable for planting
in parks and wild gardens. ZONES 3–9.

Hillier, UK, 1961

Rosa macrophylla × R. moyesii

'ARTISTIC'

MODERN, CLUSTER-FLOWERED/FLORIBUNDA,
ORANGE BLEND, REPEAT-FLOWERING

Edward LeGrice raised several varieties
of most unusual coloring, in shades of
purple, lilac and brown. This belongs to
the brown group, and was offered as being of special interest to flower arrangers.
The blooms have around 12 rather stiff
petals, opening from pointed buds to
flowers of medium size that keep their
shape for a long time. They appear in
small clusters on wiry stems, and the
color undergoes a change from brownish
orange to reddish salmon as the petals
age. There is a rather sharp fragrance,
and flowering continues through summer and autumn. The leaves are small,
and from its general aspect it has to be
said that the plant is not a good garden
item, but as a resource in a cutting gar-

den and given generous treatment it
finds its rightful niche. ZONES 4–9.

LeGrice, UK, 1971

Parentage unknown

'ARTISTRY'   JACirst

MODERN, LARGE-FLOWERED/HYBRID TEA,
ORANGE BLEND, REPEAT-FLOWERING

The plump buds of this rose open into
fairly large blooms of reddish coral-
orange, which are usually borne singly
but sometimes in clusters. Each flower
has about 30 petals that hold a neat
center, which becomes cupped as the
outer petals reflex. They hold their shape
for a long time. There is a light fragrance,
which makes this a fine variety for cutting as well as for beds and borders. A
succession of bloom is well maintained
through summer and autumn. The
plant is vigorous, with an upright, well-
branched habit, and grows to average
height or more with mid-green, healthy
foliage. ZONES 4–9.

Zary, USA, 1996

Parentage unknown

All-America Rose Selection 1997

'ARUBA'   SPEcawijk

MODERN, LARGE-FLOWERED/HYBRID TEA,
MEDIUM RED, REPEAT-FLOWERING

'Aruba' is an excellent cut-flower variety
for greenhouse or outdoor production.
It has long-stemmed, smallish, very well-
formed flowers of bright red that are
continuously produced; the flowers have
a very long vase life when picked as the
tightly scrolled buds open slowly and
retain their color well at the fully open
stage. The growth habit is stocky on a

'Artistic'

'Artistry'

'Arthur Hillier'

'Aschermittwoch'

disease-free bush, and the foliage is rich
green and profuse. There are very few
thorns. ZONES 5–11.

Kordes, Germany, 1995

Sport of 'Calibra'

'ASCHERMITTWOCH'

syn. 'Ash Wednesday'

MODERN, LARGE-FLOWERED CLIMBER,
WHITE BLEND

The origin of this rose has been queried
because there is no scent from the leaves,
which a breeder would hope for in a
Rosa eglanteria (Sweet Briar) cross.
The flowers are an extraordinary color,
grayish white tinged with slate, lilac and
buff. They are large, appear in clusters
very freely in summer, and are packed
with petals that fold into each other
in the center of the blooms, creating a
quartered effect. There is little fragrance.
The plant grows strongly, making an upright, rather stiff climber of above average height, and is useful where a variety
is wanted that will associate with Old
Garden Roses or for those who like an
unusual item. The foliage is ample,
tough and healthy. ZONES 4–9.

Kordes, Germany, 1955

Possibly seedling of *Rosa eglanteria* × 'Ballet'

'ASCOT'

MODERN, CLUSTER-FLOWERED/FLORIBUNDA,
APRICOT BLEND, REPEAT-FLOWERING

The flowers of this rose open rather like
camellias. They are large for a Cluster-
flowered Rose, with about 18 wide petals,
and are borne in trusses on a fairly short
plant. The color is a pretty shade of pink,
usually with salmon tones, but in hot
weather admitting some apricot. It is a
useful variety for beds and at the front of
a border and is excellent for buttonholes,
as the petals are firm enough for the
flowers to hold their form and open
slowly. There is a light scent, and flowering continues through summer and
autumn. The plant is robust, dwarf and

'Aruba'

bushy, with large light green leaves that
may need to be checked regularly for
mildew. ZONES 4–9.

Dickson, UK, 1962

'Brownie' × seedling

'ASPEN'   POUlurt

syns 'Gold Magic Carpet', 'Gwent',
'Sun Cover'

MODERN, MODERN SHRUB, MEDIUM YELLOW,
REPEAT-FLOWERING

This is often sold as a Ground Cover
Rose and it will spread about twice as
wide as it grows high, the dimensions
both ways being modest; it is even recommended for a large hanging basket,
and if care is taken not to let it dry out
and a small rooted plant is chosen (one
grown on its own roots, for example)
then it will suit the purpose. The flowers
are semi-double, cupped, of small to
medium size and in a pleasing shade of
yellow. They are carried in pretty clusters
fairly close to the dark glossy foliage
through summer and autumn, and have
a light scent. Growth is vigorous, with
many shoots appearing. It will benefit
from preventive spraying where black
spot is prevalent. ZONES 4–9.

Olesen, Denmark, 1992

Parentage unknown

'ASSEMBLAGE DES BEAUTÉS'

syns 'Assemblage de Beauté', 'Rouge
Eblouissante'

OLD, GALLICA, DARK RED

This is an upright tidy-growing shrub to
4 ft (1.2 m) with darkish green burnished
wood, few thorns and leaves that are a
luxuriant mid-green. It produces abundant blooms on very dense, rich, gray-
green canes. The medium-sized buds
expand into double, medium-sized
blooms with a button eye, ranging in
color from crimson-scarlet to purple.
The very fragrant flowers are composed
of many petals, the inner ones incurving
towards a central small green pip each,
opening cushion shaped to a size of
about 2½ in (6.5 cm) in diameter. It is
outstanding as a cut flower and does well
in the shade and in mixed borders. This
is perhaps the brightest colored of all
the Gallicas. ZONES 5–10.

Delange, France, 1823

Parentage unknown

'ASSINIBOINE'

MODERN, MODERN SHRUB, DEEP PINK/
MEDIUM RED, REPEAT-FLOWERING

This is one of the many successful roses
bred in Canada for winter hardiness. The

'Aspen'

A

purplish red, semi-double flowers occur in clusters of 2–5 blooms on weak stems. They are borne in summer, and there is some repeat-flowering later in the season. There is a slight fragrance. It is a dense shrub with a spreading habit. It is also a very hardy rose, which is not surprising as it was bred to withstand the severe Canadian winters. 'Assiniboine' is strongly disease resistant and can be propagated on its own roots. It was named after a park in Winnipeg. ZONES 3–9.

Marshall, Canada, 1962

'Donald Prior' × *Rosa arkansana*

'ASSO DI CUORI'   KORred

syns 'Ace of Hearts', 'Toque Rouge'

MODERN, LARGE-FLOWERED/HYBRID TEA, DARK RED, REPEAT-FLOWERING

This variety is splendid for flower arrangers, because its firm petals keep the blooms in shape for many days and because the blooms are carried on long stems that are ideal for cutting and rarely have more than one flower to a stem. The large dark crimson buds open slowly into full-petalled flowers of classic Large-flowered shape, high centered, with symmetry of form and a rounded outline to the flowers. The open blooms are rich velvety crimson-scarlet, and often grace the show bench. They are produced with good succession through summer and autumn on an upstanding, vigorous bush well covered with dark green, glossy leaves. There is one imperfection, and that is the lack of a good fragrance, which in a red rose is greatly missed. ZONES 4–9.

Kordes, Germany, 1981

Parentage unknown

'ASTA VON PARPAT'

OLD, RAMBLER, MAUVE

This rose produces clusters of purple, medium-sized blooms that change to mauve-carmine in direct sun and which form on long branches during the summer flowering. The ruffled blossoms are double and sit erect on their stems. This vigorous shrub has dark, blue-green foliage and is one of a series of roses hybridized by Rudolf Geschwind in Hungary, where he used Wild Roses in his crosses. All of them carry the strong, disease-resistant genes of Wild Roses. He also created some still-popular shrubs, such as 'Gruss an Teplitz' and 'Gipsy Boy'. ZONES 5–10.

Geschwind, Hungary, 1909

Hybrid of *Rosa multiflora*

'Assemblage des Beautés'

'ASTRA'   BENstar

syns 'Little Star Rose', 'Soroptomist International'

MODERN, MINIATURE, MEDIUM PINK, REPEAT-FLOWERING

'Astra' has shrimp pink and ivory flowers with more than 40 petals. The fragrant blooms are star shaped. Sometimes they do not open properly and can just drop off the bush. The foliage is large, dark and glossy green on a tall, upright plant with no prickles. It has a very angular and spreading growth habit, and produces lots of branching which enhances the number of clustered sprays. The plant is not winter hardy and can suffer from die back. It is also susceptible to mildew and needs some protection during the growing season. ZONES 6–11.

Benardella, USA, 1995

'Party Girl' × 'Rosie'

'ASTRA DESMOND'

syn. 'White Flight'

MODERN, RAMBLER, YELLOW BLEND

This rose was originally named for an English opera star, but was lost with that name until Peter Beales discovered its true identity. The small, semi-double flowers of off-white to cream with yellow stamens crowd the long stems in great trusses. The plant is vigorous and healthy, blooming in summer and happiest growing around pillars. New Zealand rosarian Sally Allison described the perfume as being the same as orange blossoms. ZONES 5–10.

Possibly a seedling of 'White Mrs Flight'

'ASTRÉE'

MODERN, LARGE-FLOWERED/HYBRID TEA, PINK BLEND, REPEAT-FLOWERING

The legacy of 'Peace' has been logged by Dr Tommy Cairns of California, and up to 1995 he found that as a seed parent it had spawned 192 commercialized varieties. 'Astrée' is a fine rose in its own right, bearing large blooms of classic form. The buds are deep salmon-orange and open into fully double flowers, showing orange and pink as the petals expand. There is a satisfying fragrance, and the plant continues to bloom repeatedly through summer and autumn. It is fairly compact and well foliaged, making this a fine variety for a bed, and the flowers last well when cut. ZONES 4–9.

Croix, France, 1956

'Peace' × 'Blanche Mallerin'

Plus Belle Rose de France 1956

'Asta von Parpat'

'Astrée'

'Athena'

'Atlantis'

'ASTRID LINDGREN'

syn. 'Dream Sequence'

MODERN, MODERN SHRUB, LIGHT PINK, REPEAT-FLOWERING

This rose bears its flowers in large clusters. They are double and open cupped in a pure and even shade of mid-pink, and yield a light fragrance. Flowering begins in summer and continues over several weeks into autumn. The variety is very suitable for bedding where there is plenty of space for borders and as a hedge rose; the flowers cut well for small arrangements. The plant grows vigorously with an upright, free-branching habit to a little above average height. ZONES 4–9.

Poulsen, Denmark, 1991

Parentage unknown

Lyon First Prize

'ATHENA'   RühKOR

MODERN, LARGE-FLOWERED/HYBRID TEA, WHITE BLEND, REPEAT-FLOWERING

In many ways this fulfils the requirements of a good cut-flower rose: it bears a lot of flowering stems, and a high proportion carry just one plump bud. The buds open into shapely, high-centered blooms consisting of over 30 petals that are gleaming white in color with just a faint pink edge to the petals to make it interesting. The plant grows bushily to average height with a plentiful supply of leaves, unremarkably mid-green. As a bonus, there is a whiff of scent. In warmer climates this can be grown as a garden rose, but it is primarily a commercial item for the greenhouse. ZONES 4–9.

Kordes, Germany, 1984

Seedling × 'Helmut Schmidt'

'ATLANTIC STAR'   FRYworld

MODERN, CLUSTER-FLOWERED/FLORIBUNDA, ORANGE-PINK, REPEAT-FLOWERING

The attraction of this rose is its color, a bright salmon-orange, intense in the heart of the bloom and paling to salmon-coral towards the petal rims. The flowers, produced in big clusters, have about 20 wide petals. The plant continues in bloom through summer and autumn, grows upright and vigorously to average height, and is well clothed with dense, dark green foliage. There is a pleasant light scent. This makes a good bedding rose, and the individual flowers are useful to cut. 'Atlantic Star' was named to commemorate the 50th anniversary of the Battle of the Atlantic. ZONES 4–9.

Fryer, UK, 1993

Parentage unknown

'ATLANTIS'

MODERN, CLUSTER-FLOWERED/FLORIBUNDA, MAUVE, REPEAT-FLOWERING

The color of this rose is purplish lilac, paling to lilac as the petals expand. They soon reveal bright yellow stamens, a pretty sight when several flowers are clustered together; they are backed by dark shiny leaves. Flowering continues through summer and autumn on a plant of average height or less. Lovers of the unusual will find it useful. There is little fragrance. The raiser named it to symbolize the lights of Atlantis being engulfed by the sea, a thought prompted by the bright stamens surrounded by the 'blue' petals, which unfortunately tend to photograph pink. ZONES 5–9.

Harkness, UK, 1970

'Orangeade' × 'Lilac Charm'

Rome Gold Medal 1969

'Auckland Metro'

'Audie Murphy'

'AUCKLAND METRO'   MACbucpal
syns 'Métro', 'Precious Michelle'
MODERN, LARGE-FLOWERED/HYBRID TEA,
WHITE BLEND, REPEAT-FLOWERING

The flowers of this variety are made up of many overlapping petals, giving them a camellia-like appearance. They are creamy blush to white, well scented, and often produced in large trusses with the individual stems long enough to cut, a purpose for which the rose is well suited because the flowers are at their most beautiful when fully open. It is repeat-flowering, though after a prolific first flush there is often a pause before the next cycle of growth and bloom. The plant is sturdy and bushy, below average height and well furnished with glossy dark leaves, and good for bedding. It does best in warmer climates and is popular in New Zealand, and also in Australia where it is called 'Precious Michelle' in memory of a young lady named Michelle Joy Cowley from Queensland. ZONES 5–9.

McGredy, New Zealand, 1988

'Sexy Rexy' × (seedling × 'Ferry Porsche')

'AUDIE MURPHY'
MODERN, LARGE-FLOWERED/HYBRID TEA,
MEDIUM RED, REPEAT-FLOWERING

American rose buyers in the 1950s liked their Large-flowered Roses to re-flower quickly, even if the individual flowers were on the thin side; 'Audie Murphy' is a good example. It produces long stems topped by velvety crimson flowers, often 3 or 4 together, that open wide to make

'August Seebauer'

'Augustine Guinoisseau'

an eye-catching display. The succeeding crop follows quickly, helped by the fact that the plant has not been expending too much energy and by the variety's natural vigor. It is a good rose for cutting as well as for the garden, and has a spicy scent. The plant grows tall and robust with dark foliage that is bronzy green when young, and does best in warmer climates. It honors America's celebrated war hero and film star. ZONES 5–9.

Lammerts, USA, 1957

'Charlotte Armstrong' × 'Grande Duchesse Charlotte'

Portland Gold Medal 1957

'AUDREY HEPBURN'   TWOadore
MODERN, LARGE-FLOWERED/HYBRID TEA,
LIGHT PINK, REPEAT-FLOWERING

Audrey Hepburn was a garden lover with a special interest in roses, and this highly rated rose is named in her memory. It is very feminine in color, being a pretty shade of light pink with a rosy flush on the petal reverse. The flowers are full petalled, opening with pointed hearts and becoming rounded in form as the petals expand. They have a pleasant fruity scent, maintain a good succession of bloom through summer and autumn, and are good to cut or to grow in a bed. The plant grows to average height and is bushy and upright with crisp, dark green foliage. ZONES 4–9.

Twomey, USA, 1992

'Evening Star' × seedling

'AUGUST SEEBAUER'
syn. 'The Queen Mother'
MODERN, CLUSTER-FLOWERED/FLORIBUNDA,
DEEP PINK, REPEAT-FLOWERING

In the late 1940s this rose reached Britain, there winning admiration for its wonderful double flowers, most beautifully shaped to a high center and fragrant. The raiser had sent it to his

'Auguste Gervais'

agent in Norfolk, Ernest Morse, who wished to call it 'The Queen Mother', but the authorities made it clear that using a royal title as second choice in the UK would not do. The color is clear light rose in the bud, opening to deep pink as the petals expand, and some of the trusses are very large indeed. The habit is upright and bushy, but there is a tendency to mildew. The continuity of flowering through summer and autumn is excellent. The plant grows to average height, with glossy foliage. ZONES 4–9.

Kordes, Germany, 1944

'Break o' Day' × 'Else Poulsen'

Royal National Rose Society Trial Ground Certificate 1951

'AUGUSTE GERVAIS'
MODERN, LARGE-FLOWERED CLIMBER,
APRICOT BLEND

This vigorous grower is more of a Rambler than a Climber, because it produces long, flexible stems and is easy to train over pergolas and open fences, and to grow as a weeping standard. The flowers are moderately full of petals, which open out randomly to create large, informal-looking flowers. They have good scent, and change color from coppery yellow and salmon in the bud stage to almost white by the time the petals fall. The summer flowering is prolific but it does not repeat its bloom. The leaves are small, plentiful and shiny, though seasonal mildew may affect them. ZONES 4–9.

Barbier, France, 1918

Rosa wichuraiana × 'Le Progrés'

'AUGUSTE RENOIR'   MEItoifar
MODERN, LARGE-FLOWERED/HYBRID TEA,
MEDIUM PINK, REPEAT-FLOWERING

This new rose with an old-fashioned look has big flowers full of petals, opening with substantial quartered blooms to resemble a Hybrid Perpetual. They are a

'Aunty Dora'

warm shade of rosy pink, very fragrant, usually carried one bloom per stem, and flower on through summer and autumn. The plant grows to average height with a bushy habit, and is well clothed with slightly shiny leaves. One justification for naming a rose after Auguste Renoir (1841–1919) is that he is said to have used petals of his favorite roses as a skin tone guide when his models were away. ZONES 4–9.

Meilland, France, 1993

('Versailles' × 'Pierre de Ronsard') × 'Kimono'

'AUGUSTINE GUINOISSEAU'
syns 'Mademoiselle Augustine Guinoisseau', 'White La France'
MODERN, LARGE-FLOWERED/HYBRID TEA,
WHITE BLEND, REPEAT-FLOWERING

'La France' was recognized in 1867 as a remarkable landmark in roses, and became retrospectively the first Large-flowered Rose. It was so famous that any sport of it was assured of public interest. It resembles the parent except in color, which is not absolutely white but has blush tints, and in substance, being not quite so fully petalled. In other respects—scent, general habit and the ability to repeat the cycle of growth and flower—the two roses are similar. ZONES 4–9.

Guinoisseau, France, 1889

Sport of 'La France'

'AUNTY DORA'
MODERN, CLUSTER-FLOWERED/FLORIBUNDA,
MAUVE, REPEAT-FLOWERING

The flowers of this variety are that uncertain shade between magenta and pink, and appear quite early in the flowering season. They are of middling size with around 12 petals, and open slowly to reveal the stamens, yielding a pleasant light fragrance. The plant is repeat-flowering, grows to average height or a little below, and is suitable for bedding or as a gift—something the raiser must have had in mind, for when asked about the name his reply was: 'Everyone's got an Aunty Dora!' ZONES 4–9.

Deamer, UK, 1970

'Dearest' × 'Lilac Charm'

'AURIA SUNBLAZE'
syns 'Auria Meillandina', 'Savaje'
MODERN, MINIATURE, DEEP YELLOW,
REPEAT-FLOWERING

The 'Sunblaze' series of miniature roses was introduced by Meilland of France, primarily for growing in small pots in-

'Auria Sunblaze'

'Australia Felix'

'Australian Bicentennial'

side well-lit homes and offices. They are very small, compact plants with shiny foliage and flowers in flushes. Many of them are rather too small in growth in the open garden but are ideal in such areas as patios and window boxes. 'Auria Sunblaze' has shapely little buds that open to well-formed flowers containing 25–40 petals. The color is a clear yellow flushed with red at the petal edges. There is a quick repeat. The foliage is pale green and semi-glossy. ZONES 5–10.

Meilland, France, 1990

'Ferris Wheel' × 'Rainbow's End'

'AUSTRALIA FELIX'
MODERN, LARGE-FLOWERED/HYBRID TEA, MEDIUM RED, REPEAT-FLOWERING

The flowers of this variety open from small, rounded buds into moderately full blooms of cupped form. They are silvery pink with tints of lavender, have a pleasing fragrance, and appear through summer and autumn. The growth is average for a Large-flowered Rose, and it is reasonably vigorous, with a bushy habit and dark glossy foliage. ZONES 4–9.

Clark, Australia, 1919

'Jersey Beauty' × 'La France'

'AUSTRALIAN BICENTENNIAL'
syn. 'The Australian Bicentennial Rose'
MODERN, LARGE-FLOWERED/HYBRID TEA, MEDIUM RED, REPEAT-FLOWERING

This rose, as the name makes plain, commemorates the occasion in 1788 when the first British settlement was made in what is now Sydney. The flowers are very fragrant, fairly full, with substantial petals in a rich deep pink shade verging on rose red. They appear in summer and autumn and are held close to the dark green leaves on a plant of average size. At this stage it seems to be confined to gardens in its country of origin. ZONES 5–9.

Bell, Australia, 1988

('Daily Sketch' × 'Impeccable') × 'Red Planet'

'AUSTRALIAN CENTRE GOLD'
SAVacent
Syn. 'Center Gold'
MODERN, MINIATURE, MEDIUM YELLOW, REPEAT-FLOWERING

The blooms contain 30 petals of good form. These open to flat flowers of clear, rich yellow, although in cool weather they have a tendency to be a somewhat washed-out creamy color. The plant is tall, bushy and very free flowering. This is one of the healthiest and most prolific

Miniature Roses, but has lost popularity in recent years probably due to the less than appealing visual effect of the sometimes two-toned blooms. ZONES 4–9.

USA, 1986

'Rise 'n' Shine' × 'Kiskadee'

'AUSTRALIAN GOLD' KORmat
syn. 'Mona Lisa'
MODERN, CLUSTER-FLOWERED/FLORIBUNDA, APRICOT BLEND, REPEAT-FLOWERING

Plump buds of yellow and red open into a pretty combination of apricot-orange and peach-pink on this variety. The structure of the flowers is unusual: the center petals form a spiral that holds as the outer petals reflex, a characteristic that enables them to last well when cut. Clusters of about 5 blooms are produced through summer and autumn. They are moderately fragrant, and the petals drop cleanly. The plant grows with a bushy habit to average height with plentiful deep green, leathery leaves. ZONES 4–9.

Kordes, Germany, 1980

Parentage unknown

'AUSTRALIA'S OLYMPIC GOLD ROSE' WEKblagab
MODERN, CLUSTER-FLOWERED/FLORIBUNDA, DEEP YELLOW, REPEAT-FLOWERING

This rose is named for Sydney's 2000 Olympic Games. A mild fruity fragrance accompanies clusters of long-lasting, deep golden yellow flowers, which are carried on long strong stems above dark green foliage. The bush is upright, standing 4–5 ft (1.2–1.5 m) tall. It is a vigorous grower and the flowers repeat quickly through the season. ZONES 5–9.

'AUTUMN'
MODERN, LARGE-FLOWERED/HYBRID TEA, ORANGE BLEND, REPEAT-FLOWERING

The many-petalled flowers are a pretty mixture of apricot and gold, with flushes

'Australian Centre Gold'

of rosy red at the petal tips. The center petals remain tightly coiled while the outer rows reflex. 'Autumn' has a lovely sweet scent and makes an upright, sturdy bush of average height or more with big dark leaves and strong flower stems. There is some repeat-flowering. ZONES 4–9.

Coddington, USA, 1928

'Sensation' × 'Souvenir de Claudius Pernet'

'AUTUMN DAMASK'
syns 'Quatre Saisons', 'Four Seasons Rose', 'Rose of Castile', Rosa damascena semperflorens
OLD, DAMASK, MEDIUM PINK, REPEAT-FLOWERING

The shapely pink buds open to a crumpled bed of blowzy petals, darker pink in the center. The yellowish green serrated leaves cover a sparse and open plant. If it is happy, the rose will be covered with strongly perfumed blooms. It flowers in early summer and again in autumn and does not like any shade. This rose makes an attractive container plant and contributes a good share of perfume to potpourri. ZONES 4–10.

Possibly from Middle East to Italy, pre-1633

Possibly Rosa gallica × R. moschata or R. abyssinica

'AUTUMN DELIGHT'
MODERN, MODERN SHRUB, WHITE, REPEAT-FLOWERING

The buds of 'Autumn Delight' are pointed and apricot yellow in color, opening to near single flowers of very soft creamy yellow with beautiful stamens. The flowers fade quickly to white in hot weather, but are particularly beautiful in autumn when huge heads of 30–50 blooms appear on strong shoots. These are quite long lasting and retain their color well. It forms a large shrub with dark green, leathery, disease-resistant foliage and very few thorns and is useful for beds, borders, hedges and for planting in groups among perennials. It has a huge spring flush, rather sparse

'Australian Gold'

'Autumn Damask'

bloom in summer and then puts on a wonderful autumn display. ZONES 3–9.

Bentall, UK, 1933

Parentage unknown

'AUTUMN KISS' WALkiss
MODERN, MINIATURE, MEDIUM PINK, REPEAT-FLOWERING

This bushy plant is covered in small to medium salmon-pink flowers with 15–25 petals. The blooms are borne in small clusters and have a slight fragrance. The complementary foliage is small and dark green. 'Autumn Kiss' has an upright growth habit. ZONES 4–11.

Walsh, Australia, 1994

'Ginger Meggs' × 'Avandel'

'AUTUMN MAGIC' FOUtum
MODERN, MINIATURE, ORANGE BLEND, REPEAT-FLOWERING

The flowers are bright golden orange with just a tip of red at the edge of the petals and with a reverse yellow, on a compact medium-sized bush. The florets are double with over 35 petals and with exhibition form. Blooms are usually borne one to a stem and have an unusual characteristic—very long feathery sepals. The flowers have no fragrance and do not set fruit. ZONES 4–11.

Jacobs, USA, 1987

'Confetti' × 'Anita Charles'

'Australia's Olympic Gold Rose'

'Autumn Kiss'

'Autumn Delight'

A

'AUTUMN SUNBLAZE'   MEIferjac
MODERN, MINIATURE, ORANGE-RED,
REPEAT-FLOWERING

The bright orange-red flowers of
this rose are small and moderately full
with 15–25 petals, on a bushy plant with
medium-sized, dark green, semi-glossy
foliage. The flowers are borne in small
clusters on strong straight stems. The
plant is susceptible to mildew and black
spot in cooler climates. This is one of the
varieties in the 'Sunblaze' series by the
House of Meilland, specifically hybridized for simplicity of color and growth
pattern to encourage gardeners to grow
Miniature Roses. ZONES 5–11.

Meilland, France, 1996

('Bonfire Night' × 'MEininrut') × 'Orange Jewel'

'AUTUMN SUNLIGHT'
MODERN, LARGE-FLOWERED CLIMBER,
ORANGE-RED, REPEAT-FLOWERING

The flowers of this variety are of medium
size and rounded form, full of petals, and
are carried in large clusters on strong
stems with good continuity through
summer and autumn. They are pale vermilion and look rather dull until sunlight
catches the petals and brings out a beautiful luminous orange tone. There is a
pleasant fragrance. The plant grows to
average size for a climber and, being
vigorous and free branching, it is easy
to train on fences, walls, pillars and pergolas. The leaves are plentiful, glossy and
bright green. ZONES 4–9.

Gregory, UK, 1965

'Danse du Feu' × 'Climbing Goldilocks'

'Autumn Sunlight'

'Autumn Sunset'

'AUTUMN SUNSET'
MODERN, MODERN SHRUB, APRICOT BLEND,
REPEAT-FLOWERING

The difference between this rose and
its parent lies in the color, which in
'Autumn Sunset' is apricot with touches
of orange and deep yellow, whereas
'Westerland' is deeper orange with reddish flushes. This rose has loose, rather
shaggy-looking cupped flowers of middling size, fragrant and borne in clusters
on strong stems. It can make a hefty upright shrub, or be pruned to form a thick
hedge. The flowering period extends
through summer and autumn, and the
leaves are large, abundant and usually
very healthy. ZONES 4–9.

Lowe, USA, 1986

Sport of 'Westerland'

'AVALANCHE ROSE'   DELaval
MODERN, CLUSTER-FLOWERED/FLORIBUNDA,
MEDIUM RED, REPEAT-FLOWERING

This variety has blooms that are a warm
mixture of redcurrant and carmine. The
medium-sized flowers are borne in clusters of 5–14, each with about 24 well-ar-
ranged petals with open cups, becoming
flat. They last well, have a light fragrance,
and after a very prolific first flush of
bloom, will flower into summer and
autumn. This variety is a strong and
bushy grower, reaching average height
with a dense covering of handsome,
semi-glossy leaves. ZONES 4–9.

Delbard, France, 1986

('François et Josef Guy' × seedling of 'Sultane')
× ('Alain' × 'Étoile de Hollande')

'Avalanche Rose'

'Ave Maria'

'AVANDEL'   MORvandel
MODERN, MINIATURE, YELLOW BLEND,
REPEAT-FLOWERING

The long and pointed, elegant buds on
this upright, bushy plant yield beautiful
pink-yellow-peach flowers with 23 petals
and a cupped form. There is a strong
fruity fragrance. The best asset of this
variety is the color and substance of the
blooms, even though bloom production
is somewhat sparse and rare. The leathery
foliage is small and dark green. This
variety represents one of the many prize-
winning Miniatures that were borne
from the popular Cluster-flowered Rose
'Little Darling'. It needs winter protection to survive. ZONES 5–11.

Moore, USA, 1977

'Little Darling' × 'New Penny'

American Rose Society Award of Excellence 1978

'AVE MARIA'   KORav
syn. 'Sunburnt Country'
MODERN, LARGE-FLOWERED/HYBRID TEA,
ORANGE-PINK, REPEAT-FLOWERING

This is a rose for color impact. The
elegant buds are a rich salmon-orange,
and open into broad-petalled flowers of
lovely high-centered form with tints of
salmon-orange flushed salmon-red. It is
agreeably fragrant and is a good rose to
cut, because the flowers usually come
singly on long stems and the firmness of
the petals improves their holding qualities. The flowers repeat their bloom in
autumn and stand wet weather well. The
bush grows vigorously with an upright
habit and ample dark green foliage.
ZONES 4–9.

Kordes, Germany, 1981

'Uwe Seeler' × 'Sonia'

'AVIATEUR BLÉRIOT'
OLD, RAMBLER, YELLOW BLEND

A popular rose, this Rambler has coppery
orange buds that reveal large flowers of

'Avandel'

'Aviateur Blériot'

'Aviateur Blériot' leaves

saffron and gold that fade to white.
Large trusses of strongly fragrant blooms
crowd the vigorous canes. It has bright
green, glossy foliage with bronze overtones. This is a handsome plant, especially when used as a weeping standard.
Louis Blériot was the first aviator to
cross the English Channel. ZONES 4–10.

Fauque, France, 1910

Rosa wichuraiana × 'William Allen Richardson'

'AVIGNON'
MODERN, CLUSTER-FLOWERED/FLORIBUNDA,
MEDIUM YELLOW, REPEAT-FLOWERING

Although it has never been widely available, this is a pleasing variety by reason
of its cheerful yellow flowers carried in
well-spaced clusters on a dark-leafed
plant. They are quite fully petalled,
shaped like small-scale Large-flowered
Roses, and lightly scented. The stems are
almost free of thorns, which makes them
easy to handle when flowers are cut for
the house, a purpose for which they are
suited as they last well. The variety bears
its blooms through summer and autumn
on a sturdy upright plant, the only drawback being that the flowers are sometimes obscured by newly emerging
growths. The name was given to celebrate the town twinning of Avignon
with Colchester, the raiser's home.
ZONES 5–11.

Cants of Colchester Ltd, UK, 1974

'Zambra' × 'Allgold'

'AVOCET'   HARpluto
MODERN, CLUSTER-FLOWERED/FLORIBUNDA,
ORANGE BLEND, REPEAT-FLOWERING

The brilliant color of the young flowers
of this variety catches the eye. Stiff flower
stems support many buds that open to
show prettily waved petals of orange
edged with coppery vermilion, paling
to orange-pink. The plant is low and
spreading, and its dark lustrous leaves

make it look attractive in a bed or hedge even before flowering starts. It repeats its bloom well into autumn and withstands bad weather thanks to its firm petal texture, but there is not much fragrance. It is useful to cut and show. The avocet is the emblem of The Royal Society for the Protection of Birds; as there was no rose with black and white plumage their choice fell on this one. ZONES 4–9.

Harkness, UK, 1984

'Dame of Sark' × seedling

Courtrai Silver Medal 1981, Royal National Rose Society Trial Ground Certificate 1981

'AVON'

MODERN, LARGE-FLOWERED/HYBRID TEA, DARK RED, REPEAT-FLOWERING

This dark red rose has the virtue of holding its color tone, which has made it very popular in warmer countries, where reds so often turn purple. The flowers open on long stems to show elegant high-centered young flowers; they are good to cut at this stage. On the bush they develop into large, rather loosely formed flowers that give out a wonderful fragrance, flowering continuing through summer and autumn. The variety has an upright habit to above average height, so is suitable for a hedge or sizeable bed, and it is well furnished with leathery mid-green foliage. It seems happiest in warm dry climates, as in cool conditions it may mildew. ZONES 5–9.

Morey, USA, 1961

'Nocturne' × 'Chrysler Imperial'

'AWAKENING'

syn. 'Probuzini'

MODERN, LARGE-FLOWERED CLIMBER, LIGHT PINK, REPEAT-FLOWERING

In 1988 Mr Dick Balfour, former President of the Royal National Rose Society, paid a visit to Czechoslovakia where he noticed a rose similar to the lovely Rambler 'New Dawn', the only difference being that the bloom had double the usual number of petals. He brought back some wood for propagation by Peter Beales' nursery, and the rose was re-introduced in 1990 under the name 'Awakening'. With its muddled, petal-packed centers it is a charmer, with the good points of its parent: sweet scent, long flowering period, hardiness, excellent foliage and adaptability to being trained on or over almost anything one can think of. ZONES 3–9.

Blatna, Czechoslovakia, 1935

Sport of 'New Dawn'

'Aztec'

'AWARENESS'   FRYbingo

MODERN, LARGE-FLOWERED/HYBRID TEA, MEDIUM PINK, REPEAT-FLOWERING

Decent Large-flowered Roses are continually being raised, despite gloomy forecasts that their genetic possibilities are exhausted. This is a fragrant one, bearing bright pink flowers of classic high-centered form. They are borne sometimes singly and sometimes several together on sturdy upright stems, and continue to repeat the cycle of growth and bloom through summer and autumn. The bush is vigorous and well foliaged and grows to average height, making it suitable as a bedding rose as well as for cutting. It was named to assist a charity engaged in meningitis research in memory of Rachel Grant. ZONES 4–9.

Fryer, UK, 1997

Parentage unknown

'AYRSHIRE QUEEN'

OLD, AYRSHIRE, DARK RED

Although some people believe this rose is extinct, it still appears on a few nursery lists. The dark, purplish crimson, semi-double blooms appear in summer, covering barns and trees. It is hardy and does well in poor soil and enjoys some shade. The tiny canes can easily be trained and require little pruning except to keep them under control. It is often used for ground cover in cold climates. ZONES 4–10.

Rivers, UK, 1835

'Blush Ayrshire' × 'Tuscany'

'AZTEC'

MODERN, LARGE-FLOWERED/HYBRID TEA, ORANGE-RED, REPEAT-FLOWERING

An authority on roses of American origin notes that this variety is 'now rare'. The reason cannot lie in the flowers, for they are beautiful constructions: firm broad petals that create high-centered

'Avignon'

'Avocet'

blooms of wonderful symmetry, and the color a pure light vermilion-scarlet, a surprising shade, deep and gentle all at once. It was praised for the fact that it holds the vermilion tone without any trace of purple, which was the fault of 'Independence' and others in this novel color. There is a light fragrance and it is repeat-flowering, sometimes producing several perfect flowers together in a candelabra, though on the whole it does not flower freely. The bush is a disappointment, being short, lopsided and of sprawling habit, with the flowers too heavy for the stems. There is dark waxy foliage but not enough of it, and it does not make many new shoots. ZONES 4–9.

Swim, USA, 1957

'Charlotte Armstrong' × seedling

'AZURE SEA'   AROlala

MODERN, LARGE-FLOWERED/HYBRID TEA, MAUVE, REPEAT-FLOWERING

There have been many 'hopefully blue' roses over the years; this one bears medium-sized lavender-mauve flowers edged with pale ruby red, the outside of the petals being deeper in tone although in hot weather the color soon fades. The young blooms are fairly full with pointed centers, are carried on quite long stems so are good to cut, and have a little fragrance. They repeat their flowering, though mildew and black spot may cause leaf loss. The plant grows upright and bushy, to average height or above, with large dark leaves. ZONES 5–9.

Christensen, USA, 1983

('Angel Face' × 'First Prize') × 'Lady X'

'Avon'

'Awakening'

B

B

'BABE'
MODERN, POLYANTHA, PINK BLEND,
REPEAT-FLOWERING

This is a very short-growing Polyantha Rose that makes a good low border plant. The small pale pink flowers come in clusters of 5–15 and show up well against the mid-green foliage. It is disease free, although the repeat-flowering is average. The maximum effect will be gained if bushes are planted close together. There are very few thorns.
ZONES 5–9.

Miers, Australia, 1935

Parentage unknown

'BABY ALBERIC'
MODERN, POLYANTHA, LIGHT YELLOW,
REPEAT-FLOWERING

The color of this rose is yellow in the pointed buds, fading to almost creamy white as the small ruffled petals unfold.

'Baby Alberic'

'Babe'

They have a pleasant light fragrance and maintain a good succession of bloom through summer and autumn, the earlier flowering being particularly good. The plant grows vigorously with a low, spreading habit. Like the *Rosa wichuraiana* rambler from which it derives, 'Baby Alberic' has a good health record and is long lived. It appeared in Britain at a time when shrubby dwarf roses were going out of favor, and has never won recognition there. Today it is grown mostly in Australia. ZONES 4–9.

Chaplin, UK, 1932

Seedling of 'Albéric Barbier'

'BABY BACCARÀ'   MEIbyba
MODERN, MINIATURE, ORANGE-RED,
REPEAT-FLOWERING

This is one of the earliest Miniature Roses. It was produced in the same year as the mighty 'Starina' to attract rose growers to the newly evolved Miniature Roses. The small blooms are an attractive orange-scarlet color and are generally borne one bloom to a stem. Named to capture the popularity of 'Baccarà', a 1954 Large-flowered Rose also from Alain Meilland, this variety has slipped into obscurity due to increased interest in Miniatures with different color combinations and Large-flowered form. The flowers have a slight fragrance and are complemented by attractive dark green foliage. ZONES 5–11.

Meilland, France, 1965

'Callisto' × 'Perla de Alcañada'

'Baby Bettina'

'BABY BETSY McCALL'
MODERN, MINIATURE, LIGHT PINK,
REPEAT-FLOWERING

'Baby Betsy McCall' belongs to that classic group of Miniatures introduced in the 1960s where the bloom size was more important than flower form. Very small, cupped, light pink flowers (20 petals) adorn this compact dwarf bush which is only 8–10 in (20–25 cm) high and thus it is often classed as a micro-miniature. Its popularity has endured for almost four decades and it is grown today in all parts of the world. 'Baby Betsy McCall' is a good representative of the evolution of Miniature Roses, and is a favorite with flower arrangers. ZONES 4–11.

Morey, USA, 1960

'Cécile Brünner' × 'Rosy Jewel'

'BABY BETTINA'   MEIdacinu
MODERN, MINIATURE, ORANGE-RED,
REPEAT-FLOWERING

A sister seedling to 'Baby Baccara', this Miniature has elegant ovoid buds that open up to large vermilion flowers with a carmine reverse. There are 15–20 petals. The florets are cupped and are grown 3–5 blooms per cluster on strong stems. A slight fragrance is noted in warm climates. It is a dense vigorous bush with matt foliage. This rose, developed by Marie-Louisette Meilland, is one of the

'Baby Baccarà'

'Baby Betsy McCall'

many miniatures hybridized by the House of Meilland using as pollen parent the classic white Miniature, 'Perla de Alcañada', hybridized by Pedro Dot from Barcelona, Spain in 1945.
ZONES 4–11.

Meilland, France, 1977

'Callisto' × 'Perla de Alcañada'

'BABY BIO'
MODERN, PATIO/DWARF CLUSTER-FLOWERED,
DEEP YELLOW, REPEAT-FLOWERING

Because they are large in proportion to the plant, the cheerful bright yellow flowers, carried close to the foliage in big sprays, create a bold effect. They are full of petals, rounded in form, lightly scented, and keep flowering through summer and autumn. This variety is good in a bed or group, or as a neat hedge, where a short-growing rose is wanted. It has a vigorous, bushy habit and an ample coverage of dark shiny leaves. The raiser, an engine driver living in Derbyshire, raised it in his garden greenhouse; it is named for a plant food.
ZONES 5–9.

Smith, UK, 1977

'Golden Treasure' × seedling

Royal National Rose Society Certificate of Merit 1976, Rome Gold Medal 1976

'BABY BLANKET'   KORfullwind
syns 'Oxfordshire', 'Sommermorgen',
'Summer Morning'
MODERN, GROUND COVER, LIGHT PINK,
REPEAT-FLOWERING

Three gold medals speak for the plant quality of this rose. It produces many shoots, covering them with big

'Baby Eclipse'

flower-filled clusters from summer on into autumn. The cupped blooms are of small to medium size, fairly full, in pale pink shades with gold stamens and frilled petal edges, and are lightly scented. This vigorous plant puts out stems rather spikily in all directions, and is well furnished with leaves that are small, dark green and shiny with an excellent health record. It is very suitable for the front of a border, and is sold in Britain as one of a series named after counties. ZONES 4–9.

Kordes, Germany, 1991

'Surrey' × seedling

Courtrai Gold Medal, Monza Gold Medal, Royal National Rose Society Gold Medal 1993

'BABY CÉCILE BRÜNNER'

MORcebru

MODERN, MINIATURE, LIGHT PINK, REPEAT-FLOWERING

In all respects this variety is a miniature form of the ever-popular 'Cécile Brünner'. The small, soft pink flowers

'Baby Bio'

are borne in huge clusters with long peduncles that simply cascade from the tall upright bushy plant. Blooms open fairly quickly. With the complementary small foliage, 'Baby Cécile Brünner' can be considered a classic Miniature Rose. The florets sometimes possess a slight fragrance most noticeable on very warm days. It is suitable for hanging baskets or in containers. This Miniature really wants to be a climber like its mother! ZONES 4–11.

Moore, USA, 1981

'Climbing Cécile Brünner' × 'Fairy Princess'

'BABY DARLING'

MODERN, MINIATURE, APRICOT BLEND, REPEAT-FLOWERING

Elegant well-shaped apricot-pink buds yield beautiful double (20 petals) flowers with Large-flowered form. The florets have good color and substance and are suitable for exhibition. The bush is considered dwarf (12 in [30 cm] high)

'Baby Blanket'

in most climates. 'Baby Darling' is yet another fine example of the classic Miniature Roses that were developed in the early 1960s to capture the attention of the rose-growing public to this evolutionary step in the history of the rose. The extensive use by Moore of the yellow blend Cluster-flowered Rose, 'Little Darling' as seed parent resulted in dozens of award-winning Miniatures. Still grown and shown today, it has remained a popular variety for garden display. 'Climbing Baby Darling' (Trauger, USA, 1972) sends out long canes about 6 ft (1.8 m) long and the blooms occur in small clusters at almost every leaf axil on the horizontal plane. The bush is spreading and without cultivated annual pruning it will become somewhat unruly. ZONES 4–11.

Moore, USA, 1964

'Little Darling' × 'Magic Wand'

'Baby Darling'

'BABY ECLIPSE' MORecli

MODERN, MINIATURE, LIGHT YELLOW, REPEAT-FLOWERING

By using *Rosa wichuraiana* as seed parent, Ralph Moore succeeded in transmitting to most modern Miniatures the ability to root faster from cuttings. This led to a movement away from the mass production of plants from budding or grafting. The pollen parent is an equally famous Cluster-flowered Rose, having given rise to 'Queen Elizabeth'. From small buds, light yellow florets emerge that are themselves small and elegant. The bush is extremely vigorous and has a spreading habit if not kept in check. In fact many growers have commented that the plant spends 'more time growing than blooming'. ZONES 4–11.

Moore, USA, 1984

(*Rosa wichuraiana* × 'Floradora') × 'Yellow Jewel'

American Rose Society Award of Excellence 1984

'Climbing Baby Darling'

'Baby Katie'

'Baby Jayne'

'Baby Masquerade'

'BABY FAURAX'
MODERN, POLYANTHA, MAUVE, REPEAT-FLOWERING

This is said by some to be the nearest there is to a blue rose, the color having been described as amethyst and violet. The rosette-type blooms are small and packed together in dense clusters, which look large because the plant is short and stumpy, like a Miniature Rose. A little scent may be detectable, given a warm day and the exercise of supple limbs. It continues in bloom through summer and autumn. It is suspected of having *Rosa multiflora* ancestry because the petite dull green leaflets look to be of that type, and there are a number of purple-lilac ramblers in that family. This is a curious rose, good for small spaces, and has proved useful in breeding. ZONES 4–9.

Lille, France, 1924

Parentage unknown

'BABY GOLD STAR'
syn. 'Estrellita de Oro'
MODERN, MINIATURE, DEEP YELLOW, REPEAT-FLOWERING

This variety is a good example of the pioneering work done in the hybridizing of Miniature Roses by Pedro Dot. By crossing the progenitor of most modern Miniatures, 'Rouletii', with 'Eduardo Toda', he developed a Miniature with only 14 golden yellow petals. This marked a giant step forward in the early development of Miniature Roses and proved that miniature genes could be

passed on to a Large-flowered Rose. Many of Dot's achievements in hybridizing Miniature Roses were fundamental for the future successes of other hybridizers. The flowers are semi-double and are borne on a small compact bush. ZONES 5–11.

Dot, Spain, 1940

'Eduardo Toda' × 'Rouletii'

'BABY GRAND'   POUlit
MODERN, MINIATURE, MEDIUM PINK, REPEAT-FLOWERING

The flowers of this rose are clear pink and are borne in small clusters through summer and autumn. Each bloom contains 25–40 petals. The long-lasting blooms open to flat, quartered flowers, reminiscent of many Old Garden Roses. There is a slight apple fragrance. In hot climates, the pink becomes much deeper. It has small, matt mid-green foliage on a low, compact, well-rounded plant. It is extremely disease-resistant. This charming, old-fashioned kind of rose looks wonderful in a container where it can fill the space with flowers. ZONES 5–10.

Poulsen, Denmark, 1994

'Egeskov' × seedling

'BABY JAYNE'
syns 'Fairy Hedge', 'Pixie Hedge'
MODERN, CLIMBING MINIATURE, MEDIUM PINK, REPEAT-FLOWERING

This small Climbing Miniature produces clusters of small soft pink flowers

'Baby Faurax'

(45 petals). The bush grows no higher than 3–4 ft (1–1.2 m), and has small glossy green foliage. 'Baby Jayne' is an early example of the hybridizing exploration conducted by Ralph Moore to brings us the Modern Climbing Miniature Rose as we know it today. The extensive use by Moore of 'Zee', a Climbing Miniature never formally introduced commercially and derived from 'Tom Thumb', ensured that most crosses resulted in Climbing Miniatures. ZONES 4–11.

Moore, USA, 1957

'Violette' × 'Zee'

'BABY KATIE'
MODERN, MINIATURE, PINK BLEND, REPEAT-FLOWERING

Ovoid pointed buds on a compact, vigorous, bushy plant flower into lovely pastel cream and pink small florets (28 petals) with magnificent Large-flowered form. The blooms are show quality. This is a rose for everyone, as it has the basic charming features that epitomize the Miniature Rose. However, wide variation in color has been detected relative to climate zone. The foliage is matt green, complementing the blooms perfectly. 'Baby Katie' is just one of many successful seedlings that Harm Saville hybridized using 'Sheri Anne' as the seed parent. ZONES 4–11.

Saville, USA, 1978

'Sheri Anne' × 'Watercolor'

'BABY LOVE'   SCRIvluv
MODERN, PATIO/DWARF CLUSTER-FLOWERED, DEEP YELLOW, REPEAT-FLOWERING

This is a splendid dwarf shrublet, bearing with great freedom and continuity, cheerful saucer-shaped, butttercup yellow flowers. They are small, with 5 petals and borne one to a stem, close to the foliage at all levels on a low, rounded plant. They have a slight fragrance. The small, medium green, semi-glossy foliage is an ideal complement to the blooms. Flowers only last a few days but are well worth the wait! ZONES 4–11.

Scrivens, UK, 1992

'Sweet Magic' × seedling

Royal National Rose Society and Torridge Award 1993

'BABY MASQUERADE'   TANba; TANbakede
syns 'Baby Carnaval', 'Baby Carnival', 'Baby Maskarade', 'Baby Mascarade', 'Baby Maskerade'
MODERN, MINIATURE, RED BLEND, REPEAT-FLOWERING

This is a classic variety from the 1950s. The flowers open to golden yellow and age to a luminous but dull attractive red. The floret size is generally small—with about 23 petals. In modern rose shows it qualifies as a micro-miniature. Leathery foliage surrounds the slight blooms, which have a fruity fragrance, to give a

'Baby Gold Star'

'Baby Love'

'Ballerina' (hips)

'Ballerina'

compact low-growing bush about 8 in (20 cm) tall. The use of the classic 'Tom Thumb', hybridized by de Vink of Holland in 1936, as seed parent for this rose recognizes the evolutionary importance of such early varieties. ZONES 4–11.

Tantau, Germany, 1956

'Tom Thumb' × 'Masquerade'

'BABY PINOCCHIO'
MODERN, MINIATURE, PINK BLEND, REPEAT-FLOWERING

The flower size classifies this rose as a micro-miniature. Exquisite salmon-pink flowers open up from ovoid buds on a small, compact, vigorous bush. The florets turn a darker pink or a reddish tone when they are fully open. The foliage is equally small, and glossy and leathery, but it is quite susceptible to black spot and mildew. This is a forgotten variety that has slipped in the popularity ratings with the stream of new Miniatures in a rainbow of colors and form. ZONES 4–11.

Moore, USA, 1967

'Golden Glow' × 'Little Buckaroo'

'BACCARÁ' MEger
syn. 'Jaqueline'
MODERN, LARGE-FLOWERED/HYBRID TEA, ORANGE-RED, REPEAT-FLOWERING

The quoted parentage is a surprise as both the varieties named are poor doers, whereas 'Baccará' makes a vigorous, rangy plant. For years it was renowned as a foremost rose for florists, thanks to its long stems and the lasting qualities of the very full-petalled flowers. These open slowly and rather flat, showing a vivid deep vermilion color, with blackish shadings on the outer petals, and continue to flower well through summer and autumn. There is no fragrance. The dark leathery leaves are reddish when young, and clothe the plant reasonably well. This rose is best in a warm climate as rain spoils the flowers. ZONES 5–9.

Meilland, France, 1954

'Happiness' × 'Independence'

'BALLADE' TANedallab
MODERN, CLUSTER-FLOWERED/FLORIBUNDA, LIGHT PINK, REPEAT-FLOWERING

This is a gentle and kindly shade of light pink, and bears its blooms in clusters, although on occasion they may be borne singly. They are double and open cupped, with firm petals, but have very little fragrance. Blooming is consistent through summer and autumn. The main use of the variety is for bedding, in bor-

ders and as a hedge rose. The plant has a good health record and grows vigorously to form a bushy habit of average height, well furnished with large, bright green leaves. ZONES 4–9.

Tantau, Germany, 1991

Parentage unknown

'BALLERINA'
MODERN, MODERN SHRUB, MEDIUM PINK, REPEAT-FLOWERING

One of summer's treats is to see hundreds of small single, shallow-cupped light pink flowers cramming themselves all over 'Ballerina' like so many hydrangea heads. There is no scent to speak of, but in other respects it is hard to fault this rose. There is a pause after the first marathon blooming, and then a good second crop follows in autumn. This is a real enthusiast's rose, with a graceful rounded habit and abundant mid-green foliage, growing to average height. It can be planted on its own (in either shrub or standard form) where something special is wanted, or will make a splendid group or hedge. It does not mind being pruned to reduce the height. The parents are unknown, but the flowers remind one of the climbing rose 'Blush Rambler'. ZONES 4–9.

Bentall, UK, 1937

Parentage unknown

Royal Horticultural Society Award of Garden Merit 1993

'BALLET' KORflot
MODERN, LARGE-FLOWERED/HYBRID TEA, DEEP PINK, REPEAT-FLOWERING

The large, high-centered flowers of this rose, held firmly on upright stems, were a popular sight in many British gardens in the 1960s as few other roses with 50

'Baccará'

petals could withstand the rain so well. The bright deep pink blooms flower with good continuity through summer and autumn, and carry an elusive fragrance that some can detect but others fail to do. The upright and sturdy plant grows to average height, with light grayish green leaves. When Clean Air Acts started to change Britain's environment by removing chemicals from the atmosphere, 'Ballet' fell victim to black spot and gradually fell from favor. 'Climbing Ballet' (Kordes, Germany, 1962) is a vigorous grower recommended by the raiser for a high wall that faces the sun between noon and sunset. ZONES 4–9.

Kordes, Germany, 1958

'Florex' × 'Karl Herbst'

Royal National Rose Society Trial Ground Certificate 1956

'BALTIMORE BELLE'
syn. 'Belle de Baltimore'
OLD, MISCELLANEOUS, LIGHT PINK

This late summer-flowering Old Garden Rose bears clusters of many globular buds. They open into rather incurving, shaggy blossoms of average size, made up of dozens of small petals of the palest blush. There is slight to moderate scent. The plant inherits its vigor from *Rosa setigera*, the only climbing species native to North America, but is not quite as hardy.

'Bambula'

'Ballet'

'Climbing Ballet'

It is healthy, though, with fresh-looking mid-green leaves, growing to above average height with pliable stems. It is well suited for pergolas and places where it can extend itself, and be trained so it develops in a naturalistic way. ZONES 4–9.

Feast, USA, 1843

Rosa setigera × perhaps *R. noisette* or *R. gallica*

'BAMBULA'
MODERN, CLUSTER-FLOWERED/FLORIBUNDA, ORANGE-PINK, REPEAT-FLOWERING

This variety was introduced by Wheatcrofts in the UK at an unfortunate time, when the family firm was divided. The feud was soon healed, but 'Bambula' never received the attention it deserved. This free-flowering variety bears clusters of many large double flowers that open loosely to display pretty shades of salmon and orange. There is a slight fragrance. This rose is suitable for bedding and continues blooming through summer and autumn. The plant grows vigorously to below average height and has ample bright green glossy foliage. A bambula is a dance performed in the state of Louisiana in the US to the beating of a drum; perhaps the flowers were dancing in the wind when that particular naming inspiration came about. ZONES 4–9.

Tantau, Germany, 1970

'Schweizer Gruss' × 'Ahoi'

'Baron Girod de l'Ain'

'Barby'

'Banzai '83'

'BANTRY BAY'
MODERN, LARGE-FLOWERED CLIMBER, MEDIUM PINK, REPEAT-FLOWERING

Through summer and autumn this variety always seems to have something to show. The loosely double cupped flowers are deepish rose pink, a warm and kindly shade, showing their stamens as they open; they have a light fragrance. They are borne in clusters and appear at different levels on the plant, which clothes itself effectively in dark green foliage. This vigorous, free-branching rose is an excellent garden performer of restrained growth, with a good health record and suitable for all purposes. One of the best varieties to withstand wet weather, it is named after a scenic inlet in Ireland's County Cork. ZONES 4–9.

McGredy, UK, 1967

'New Dawn' × 'Korona'

Royal National Rose Society Certificate of Merit 1967, Belfast Certificate of Merit 1970

'BANZAI '83'   MEIzalitaf
syn. 'Spectra'

MODERN, LARGE-FLOWERED CLIMBER, YELLOW BLEND, REPEAT-FLOWERING

Although not widely grown, this is a most eye-catching climber. The high-centered young flowers are yellow with a rosy flush, and open to reveal pretty tints of orange-gold and pale crimson in the large, loosely double blooms, the balance of colors altering as the petals age. The flowers continue through summer and autumn, but there is not much scent. Of rather rigid upright habit, this looks well when trained against fences and walls or up a pillar. It grows to average height, with glossy, deep green foliage, and is likely to be giving of its best in a warm climate. ZONES 4–9.

Meilland, France, 1983

Parentage unknown

'BARBARA BUSH'   JACbush
MODERN, LARGE-FLOWERED/HYBRID TEA, PINK BLEND, REPEAT-FLOWERING

The elegant pointed buds of this pretty garden rose open slowly to reveal large full flowers, which develop rather low centers as the petals expand. The color is a blend of blush to ivory white and light rosy salmon-pink, the pink tones deepening where the petal surface is most exposed to the sun. The flowers are carried through summer and autumn on long stems suitable for cutting, and there is a light fragrance. The plant grows tall and vigorously, with dark green leaves, though it is sometimes affected by mildew. It is billed as 'the first choice of the First Lady', having been named for the wife of former US President George Bush. ZONES 4–9.

Warriner, USA, 1991

'Pristine' × 'Antigua'

'BARBY'   KORaby
MODERN, LARGE-FLOWERED/HYBRID TEA, MEDIUM PINK, REPEAT-FLOWERING

Plump reddish pink buds open on long stems on this variety to show full-petalled blooms which, as they slowly open, become very large and hold their centers while the outer petals reflex. The color is a warm rosy pink on the inner petal surface, while the reverse displays attractive pink veining on a silvery pink background. The blooms are useful for bedding and also for cutting, as they last well and withstand bad weather. Flowering continues through summer and autumn, with a little fragrance. The plant grows vigorously up to average height, with foliage that is reddish when young, becoming dark green and leathery when mature. ZONES 4–9.

Kordes, Germany, 1995

'Holsteinperle' × seedling

'BARON DE BONSTETTEN'
OLD, HYBRID PERPETUAL, DARK RED

This is one of the most elegant roses of its class; a robust, compact bush, it has velvety maroon, flat blooms that appear in summer on strong stems. The glossy flowers, tightly packed with 80 petals, turn from crimson to very dark purple, sun or shade determining the depth of color. The canes are armed with numerous prickles, and the foliage is rough. It has a strong fragrance. This rose hates hot weather, as the petals will crisp. The baron was a wealthy Swiss estate owner and rose fancier. ZONES 5–10.

Liabaud, France, 1871

'Général Jacqueminot' × 'Géant des Batailles'

'BARON DE WASSENAER'
OLD, MOSS, DEEP PINK

This is one of the few Mosses that can be used as a climber. It is a largely vigorous shrub to 7 ft (2.2 m) tall with dark prickly stems and equally dark green, coarse leaves. The flowers emerge from rounded, moderately mossed buds in mid-summer. The moss, like the foliage, is dark green, bordering on brown. When fully open the flowers attain a diameter of some 3 in (8 cm). They are each packed with many petals, at first bright red but quickly changing to a glowing crimson, slightly cupped until fully open and borne in clusters. Always a popular Moss, it requires little pruning and does well on poor soil. It occasionally repeats with an odd autumn bloom. There were three Verdiers—Charles, Victor and Eugene (who bred this rose). ZONES 5–10.

Verdier, France, 1854

Parentage unknown

'BARON GIROD DE L'AIN'
syns 'Baron Giraud de l'Ain', 'Princesse Christine von Salm'

OLD, HYBRID PERPETUAL, RED BLEND, REPEAT-FLOWERING

This is something of a novelty rose, looking as though someone has cut the edge of the petals with pinking shears. It has cupped, red blooms with a scalloped edge of white, which makes it a dramatic cut flower. The compact blooms are true crimson surrounded by broad, round, leathery leaves. The stiff, healthy green wood bears some prickles. It blooms all summer and may develop black spot in hot weather. The perfume is sweet. ZONES 5–10.

Reverchon, France, 1897

Sport of 'Eugene Fürst'

'Baron de Wassenaer'

'Bantry Bay'

B

'Baronne Henriette de Snoy'

'Baroness Rothschild'

'BARON J. B. GONELLA'

syns 'Baron G. B. Gonella', 'Baron J. G. Gonella'

OLD, BOURBON, PINK BLEND, REPEAT-FLOWERING

The rounded and cupped blooms of this rose are very double, about 3 in (8 cm) across, and are bright pink with compact, ruffled centers. Lilac shading appears on the large petals, which are smooth and thick. A rare Bourbon, it is vigorous and tall and has strong canes. It has a light fragrance, and blooms in summer only. The smooth, green bark is covered with red prickles. Guillot Père produced 80 varieties. ZONES 5–6.

Guillot Père, France, 1859

Seedling of 'Louise Odier'

'BARONESS ROTHSCHILD'

syn. 'Baronne Adolph de Rothschild'

OLD, HYBRID PERPETUAL, LIGHT PINK, REPEAT-FLOWERING

This marvellous cut flower looks as regal as its namesake; the very large buds open flesh pink with silver-edged petals. A full, cupped flower usually appears on a single cane. The vigorous bush is erect and hardy, with light green prickly canes; it blooms early and again in autumn. The gray-green foliage is most attractive. It should be pruned like a Large-flowered Rose. The only attribute this rose lacks is a strong perfume. Pernet and partners produced many successful roses from 1854 to 1931 that are still popular. ZONES 5–10.

Pernet, France, 1868

Sport of 'Souvenir de la Reine d'Angleterre'

'BARONNE EDMOND DE ROTHSCHILD'   MEIgriso

syns 'Baroness E. de Rothschild', 'Baronne de Rothschild'

MODERN, LARGE-FLOWERED/HYBRID TEA, RED BLEND, REPEAT-FLOWERING

Many bicolor roses are garish, but this one has subtler tones. It has broad petals,

'Baronne Prévost'

and reflex to reveal an expanse of ruby red verging on deep mauvish pink as the flowers age; this contrasts with a petal reverse that is basically white with reddish tints. The flowers are very large, double and high centered, and appear sporadically through summer and autumn, sometimes in wide clusters. They have a pleasing fragrance. Growth is taller than average, and the vigorous bush has an adequate cover of bronze green, leathery foliage. This is a good rose for the garden and to cut and is especially suited to warmer climates, but a watch needs to be kept for black spot. ZONES 4–9.

Meilland, France, 1969

('Baccará' × 'Crimson King') × 'Peace'

Lyon Gold Medal 1968, Monza Fragrance Prize 1968, Rome Gold Medal 1968, Belfast Fragrance Prize 1991

'BARONNE HENRIETTE DE SNOY'

syn. 'Baroness Henrietta Snoy'

OLD, TEA, PINK BLEND

Brent Dickerson characterizes this rose thus: 'Distressing at its worst, beautiful at its best, trial is merited.' In the right place in full sun the baroness can be quite charming. The peach, globular, very large blooms with a deeper pink reverse and a green eye are high centered. The foliage is bronze-green. Like so many Tea Roses, the bush is gawky and needs to be placed where its blooms show and not its feet. ZONES 7–11.

Bernaix, France, 1897

'Gloire de Dijon' × 'Mme Lombard'

'BARONNE PRÉVOST'

OLD, HYBRID PERPETUAL, MEDIUM PINK, REPEAT-FLOWERING

Extremely popular for many years, this early Hybrid Perpetual retains the shape of the Old Rose form. Large, globular buds open to full, flat, quartered, pink blooms that fade with age and make most attractive cut flowers. The stiff, stout canes are covered with attractive foliage and short red prickles. This tough, compact shrub blooms in summer with an occasional autumn repeat, and is best placed at the back of the border. It likes sun and rich soil. Desprez sold the ownership of the rose to Cochet senior for 100 francs; it is the oldest variety of its class still sold. ZONES 5–10.

Desprez, France, 1842

Parentage unknown

Royal Horticultural Society Award of Garden Merit 1993

'BAROQUE'   HARbaroque

MODERN, GROUND COVER, MAUVE, REPEAT-FLOWERING

There is a jewel-like quality about this most unusual rose. Pointed buds open to cupped blooms composed of about 15 petals, and when the petals are fully extended they show golden stamens against flowers of a startling mauve-pink. The flowers are carried close to the foliage, and given that there are several blooms to the cluster the effect is striking; the look is further enhanced by the purplish color of the leaves. There is a pleasant musky fragrance, and good continuity of flower is maintained through summer and autumn. It makes a useful ground cover rose of average height with a spreading, though not procumbent, habit and suits the front of a border or a large container. ZONES 4–9.

Harkness, UK, 1995

Bred from *Rosa eglanteria*, *R. bracteata* and *R. californica* lines

'BASILDON BOND'   HARjosine

MODERN, LARGE-FLOWERED/HYBRID TEA, APRICOT BLEND, REPEAT-FLOWERING

This rose was named after a quality writing paper by the makers, Britain's John Dickinson, to celebrate their centenary. Its bright deep apricot flowers contrast delightfully with plum red stems and dark shiny foliage. The blooms are of medium size, with many short petals, and open wide from pointed orange-red buds into cupped flowers of rather ragged form. They have a refreshing fruity fragrance, and bloom continually through summer and autumn. It looks well when planted in a bed or group, and grows with a neat upright habit. Its record for health and hardiness is better than that of many apricot roses, and it does not mind rain. ZONES 5–9.

Harkness, UK, 1980

('Sabine' × 'Circus') × ('Yellow Cushion' × 'Glory of Ceylon')

Belfast Gold Medal 1982

'Basildon Bond'

'Baronne Edmond de Rothschild'

'BASSINO' KORmixal
syn. 'Suffolk'
MODERN, GROUND COVER, MEDIUM RED,
REPEAT-FLOWERING

This makes a prostrate growing plant, with a spreading though not very extensive habit, and can be considered more of a ground covering rose than a shrub. The single flowers are bright red when they open, their cupped deep scarlet petals making a vivid contrast with the yellow stamens. They are carried in wide clusters of many small blooms, and nestle close to the dark shiny leaflets, so the overall effect is spectacular. The color fades somewhat but keeps its scarlet tone. Flowering continues through summer and autumn, though it can be greatly affected in a bad black spot year. There is very little fragrance. In Britain it is sold as 'Suffolk'. ZONES 4–9.

Kordes, Germany, 1988

('Sea Foam' × 'Red Max Graf') × seedling

Royal National Rose Society Trial Ground Certificate 1990

'Bassino'

'Bayadère'

'BASYE'S BLUEBERRY'
MODERN, MODERN SHRUB, MEDIUM PINK

This rose, one of Dr Basye's innovative varieties, has medium-sized, 7-petalled flowers that are borne close to the foliage in small clusters, usually at the ends of the branches, for a long period in summer. They are a cheerful bright lilac pink with showy yellow stamens, and have a sweet fragrance. The plant grows tall and upright with mid-green, rounded leaves. The stems are remarkably free of prickles, a valuable characteristic derived from the raiser's variety 'Commander Gillette'. The name 'Basye's Blueberry' arose because the stems and leaves (especially in the autumn when they are turning color) resemble the growth of a blueberry bush. Its freedom from disease and thornlessness make it a valuable rose for use in future breeding.
ZONES 4–9.

Basye, USA, 1982

'Commander Gillette' × ('Commander Gillette' × [*Rosa virginiana alba* × 'Betty Morse'])

'Bazaar'

'BASYE'S PURPLE ROSE'
MODERN, MODERN SHRUB, MAUVE,
REPEAT-FLOWERING

For many years Dr Robert E. Basye of Texas has sought, by raising compatible hybrids, to make the genes of hitherto unused species available for interbreeding with Modern Garden Roses. Of his remarkable crosses, this is one of the few to have been commercialized. An upright grower, it makes an untidy thickety shrub of average height or a little more, with prickly shoots and rather coarse foliage that starts bright green and ages to purplish. Against this backdrop appear large, single, frail-looking flowers of deep reddish purple with wide wavy petals and in which prominent red-gold stamens are beautifully displayed. The flowers nestle in small clusters on short stems close to the foliage, continuing to appear through summer and autumn. There is not much fragrance. This rose grows by suckering itself, and as such it has useful landscaping potential. ZONES 4–9.

Basye, USA, 1968

Rosa rugosa × *R. foliolosa*

'BAXTER BEAUTY'
OLD, TEA, APRICOT BLEND,
REPEAT-FLOWERING

Alister Clark, an Australian rose hybridizer who worked to develop roses that would rebloom in the warmer climate of his country, produced scores of roses that are still in commerce in Australia and are likely candidates for other countries. This is a *Rosa gigantea* hybrid that varies in color from light yellow to sulfur, with a hint of light salmon-pink. It can grow up to 6 ft (2 m) if lightly pruned. The semi-double blooms continue through a long season. It is good for winter blooms if pruned mid-autumn. Although many of Clark's roses were imported to such places as California before World War II, restrictions now prevent their distribution. ZONES 7–11.

Clark, Australia, 1939

Sport of 'Lorraine Lee'

'BAYADÈRE'
MODERN, LARGE-FLOWERED/HYBRID TEA, APRICOT
BLEND, REPEAT-FLOWERING

This variety bears flowers of great size made up of over 50 petals, which initially create a very high center as the blooms open and then subside as they reflex to create a quartered effect. They are a melange of salmon-orange to pink colors, with a canary yellow base and noticeable

'Baxter Beauty'

'Beauté'

veining on the petals. There is a light scent. Flowers appear during summer and autumn, though not with great freedom due to the energy the plant needs for their production. It is nevertheless a pleasing garden rose for cutting and to group in a border. The bush grows sturdily with a branching habit to average height and has dark bronzy foliage. It is reasonably hardy, but is better in warmer climates. The name may have been given with reference to the petal veining, because bayadère is a fabric in which the stripes run crosswise; it can also mean an Indian dancing girl. ZONES 5–9.

Mallerin, France, 1954

'RMS Queen Mary' × seedling

National Rose Society Gold Medal 1954

'BAZAAR'
MODERN, CLUSTER-FLOWERED/FLORIBUNDA,
MEDIUM PINK, REPEAT-FLOWERING

'Bazaar' sported from the vivid cerise Cluster-flowered Rose 'Vogue'. The shapely rose pink blooms are borne in well-spaced clusters. Each bloom contains 25 petals and has good high-centered form. There is a strong fragrance. The foliage is dark green on a neat plant. The flower production is average and the repeat-bloom cycle is rather slow. It is, however, a good bedding rose. 'Bazaar' is not well known outside Australia.
ZONES 4–9.

Australia, 1966

Sport of 'Vogue'

'BEAU NARCISSE'
OLD, GALLICA, MAUVE

Found today only in a few private collections and in some botanical gardens, this rose is striped purple-violet with the small flowers paler on the reverse. The fragrant, double clusters have green eyes and plenty of light green foliage fills the canes on a bush that grows to 5 ft by 4 ft

(1.5 m by 1.2 m). It blooms in summer only and was named after the mythological Narcissus, who was transformed into a flower after he drowned while gazing at his reflection in a pond. ZONES 5–10.

Miellez, France, 1850

Parentage unknown

'BEAUTÉ'
MODERN, LARGE-FLOWERED/HYBRID TEA, APRICOT BLEND, REPEAT-FLOWERING

Although not so widely grown today, for years after World War II many people considered this variety their first choice for its color, a lovely shade of apricot-yellow with some deeper flushes. The buds are long and open into high-centered flowers of elegant form. They are moderately full of petals, which soon reflex to give a cupped rose with a rounded outline, effectively displaying the pretty color. Flowering continues through summer and autumn, the blooms being carried singly or 3 to a stem, and there is a pleasant light scent. The growth is lower than average, and it spreads rather unevenly. The leaves are large and rich green but not plentiful; it becomes an open, rather bare-looking bush after a few years and seems reluctant to put out new stems. ZONES 5–9.

Mallerin, France, 1953

'Madame Joseph Perraud' × seedling

Royal National Rose Society Certificate of Merit 1954

'BEAUTIFUL BRITAIN'   DICfire
MODERN, CLUSTER-FLOWERED/FLORIBUNDA, ORANGE-RED, REPEAT-FLOWERING

The flowers of this variety are borne in rather uneven clusters, and open from neat rounded buds into cupped blooms of medium size, fairly well filled with petals that fall cleanly as they age. They are the color of not quite ripe tomatoes. This rose stands wet weather well, and

'Beautiful Britain'

'Beauty Secret'

continues to flower freely through summer and autumn. There is a light scent. The growth is upright, to a little below average height, with mid-green, rather sparse foliage that detracts from its value as a bedding rose. For planting in a group and as a source of buttonholes, it is a good performer. It is widely grown for sale in the UK, where it was named in connection with the Keep Britain Tidy Group. ZONES 4–9.

Dickson, UK, 1983

'Red Planet' × 'Eurorose'

UK Rose of the Year 1983, Belfast Certificate of Merit 1985

'BEAUTY OF ROSEMAWR'
OLD, TEA, PINK BLEND, REPEAT-FLOWERING

Upright, large, full flowers with overlapping petals and a raised center veined with carmine-crimson and white markings are the hallmarks of this rose. It is believed to be half-China and half-Tea. The twiggy, upright, dense foliage supports loosely formed, fragrant blooms. There is little foliage on this 4 ft x 2 ft (1.2 m x 60 cm) shrub. It blooms continuously through summer, does well in poor soil and enjoys the sun. It makes a good subject for a container or for hiding among perennials. ZONES 7–10.

Van Fleet, USA, 1903

Parentage unknown

'BEAUTY SECRET'
MODERN, MINIATURE, MEDIUM RED, REPEAT-FLOWERING

'Beauty Secret' is considered the classic Miniature Rose of the mid-1960s. The cardinal red flowers are high-centered with a characteristic point to the terminal edge of the petals. Grown on a vigorous bushy plant, the florets are mainly grouped in clusters of 4–10 blooms on strong straight stems. The color is fast and the blooms last a reasonably long time on the bush without serious fading. So attractive and well liked was this variety that when the American Rose Society award program started off in 1975, it was given the honor without hesitation. ZONES 4–11.

Moore, USA, 1965

'Little Darling' × 'Magic Wand'

American Rose Society Award of Excellence 1975

'BEGONIA'
MODERN, LARGE-FLOWERED/HYBRID TEA, PINK BLEND, REPEAT-FLOWERING

This variety produces very large blooms of a most attractive coral pink color on

'Beauty of Rosemawr'

usually long single stems. The petals are nicely ruffled and have the appearance of a tuberous begonia when fully open. Growing sturdily to medium height, 'Begonia' has dark green foliage. Flower production is very low and it does suffer from mildew, but visitors always ask its name when it is in flower. It looks most attractive when picked and arranged under night light. It was introduced by Treloar's Nursery and named for introduction into Australia; it is unknown in other countries. ZONES 5–9.

Gregory, UK

Parentage unknown

'BEHOLD'   SAVahold
MODERN, MINIATURE, MEDIUM YELLOW, REPEAT-FLOWERING

The long, urn-shaped buds of 'Behold' open to clear bright yellow flowers with a lighter reverse. The color is stunning and does not fade—even in strong sunlight. The double florets have 15–25 petals and are borne singly and in small, elegant clusters on long, straight stems. The flower form is high centered, so the blooms hold well for days. The foliage is a medium dull green on a vigorous, upright, compact bush. It is very easy to grow, but can suffer from mildew. It made its winning debut at the Royal National Rose Society National Miniature Show in 1997, where it caught the attention of both the judges and the audience. 'Behold' can brighten up any garden. ZONES 5–11.

Saville, USA, 1996

('Rise 'n' Shine' × 'Sheri Anne') × ('Heideröslein' × 'Nozomi')

'Bel Ange'

'BEL ANGE'
syns 'Bella Epoca', 'Belle Ange', 'Belle Epoque', 'Rosa Stern'
MODERN, LARGE-FLOWERED/HYBRID TEA, MEDIUM PINK, REPEAT-FLOWERING

This makes a vigorous upright plant, rather stiff in growth, but well endowed with handsome dark green foliage. The foliage acts as a good foil to the flowers, which open from dark red buds to show two color tones, the petals being rosy salmon on the inside with a deeper carmine-pink reverse. The blooms are full and open slowly, revealing classic exhibition form with high centers, and there is good fragrance. The flowers are freely borne through summer and autumn on a plant of average height or above, making this a good dual purpose rose for garden display in a bed and to cut for rose shows. ZONES 4–9.

Lens, Belgium, 1962

('Independence' × 'Papillon Rose') × ('Charlotte Armstrong' × 'Floradora')

Courtrai Gold Medal 1965

'Begonia'

B

'Belinda' (Tantau)

'Bella Rosa'

'Belle Amour'

'BELAMI'   KORhanbu
syn. 'Woods of Windsor'
MODERN, LARGE-FLOWERED/HYBRID TEA, ORANGE-PINK, REPEAT-FLOWERING

This rose gives a lot of pleasure, because it flowers and grows well. The buds are deep pink, and open to reveal wide petals in which cream, pale apricot and gentle shades of pink blend happily together, with deeper pink towards the petal rims. The blooms are full-petalled, maintain a high center and keep their symmetry as they open, so they are very suitable to cut for the house or to show. There is some fragrance, and flowering continues through summer and autumn. The plant grows strongly with an upright habit, and though it is on the tall side it is well rounded and balanced so that it looks good in a bed of one variety or as a hedge. The leaves start life reddish bronze and deepen to dark green as they mature. The British name, 'Woods of Windsor', refers to a firm of perfumers. ZONES 4–9.

Kordes, Germany, 1985

('Prominent' × 'Carina') × 'Emily Post'

Dublin Gold Medal 1983

'BELINDA'   TANbeedee
MODERN, MODERN SHRUB, ORANGE BLEND, REPEAT-FLOWERING

This is primarily a glasshouse rose, and indeed it was for some years a leader in that market; it is suitable for outdoor cultivation only in a warm climate. The flowers are borne in clusters of several together, and open from slender buds to display warm shades of orange-yellow with delicate flushes of copper. They are full-petalled and of medium size, carry a light fragrance, and appear with good continuity through summer and autumn. As is required of a greenhouse rose, they grow on firm upright stems of a good length for cutting and hold their form well when arranged in a vase. The plant grows vigorously and is bushy with an upright habit and glossy foliage. ZONES 5–9.

Tantau, Germany, 1971

Seedling × 'Zorina'

'BELINDA'
MODERN, MODERN SHRUB, MEDIUM PINK, REPEAT-FLOWERING

The semi-double flowers of this variety are a very warm shade of rose pink, with small areas of white at the base of the petals which, when they are seen from a distance, give them an airy effect. Although rather small, they make an impact because of the amount of bloom, the large pyramidal clusters being so crowded that the florets have to jostle for space to display their ruffled petals. After the first flush, there is good repeat bloom. There is a small amount of perfume, disappointingly so from a plant with such a brave display. It grows strongly to above average height unless kept down by pruning, and makes a good hedge rose or it can be grown up a pillar. It has healthy deep green leaves. The rose was raised by Ann Bentall, and her granddaughter is actually named after it; the following year her 'Ballerina' was introduced and its greater merit caused 'Belinda' to be rather unfairly undervalued. ZONES 4–9.

Bentall, UK, 1936

Parentage unknown

'BELINDA'S DREAM'
syn. 'Belinda's Rose'
MODERN, MODERN SHRUB, MEDIUM PINK, REPEAT-FLOWERING

This is perhaps a pointer to the way more roses will look in the future. It combines the vigor of a shrub with the quality bloom of a Large-flowered Rose and the quantity bloom of a Cluster-flowered Rose. Though carried on short stems, the blooms are large, with about 40 petals, and beautifully structured with the outer petals reflexing to display the high centers. A pretty shade of light pink, they have a sharp fruity scent and repeat their flower. The vigorous, upright plant grows to average size or more if lightly pruned, but keeps fairly compact and is well covered with healthy bluish green leaves. ZONES 4–9.

Basye, USA, 1988

'Tiffany' × 'Jersey Beauty'

'BELLA DONNA'
OLD, DAMASK, LIGHT PINK

This rose opens compactly with dark pink petals that develop into rather flat, muddled blooms with a yellow eye. The large, double clusters cover the pale green foliage and have a strong and haunting fragrance. It is best situated between other roses as an ornamental shrub and is strongly resistant to any diseases. Some confusion exists with its name as there are two other roses, an Alba and a Cluster-flowered Rose, with the same title. ZONES 5–10.

Pre-1848

Parentage unknown

'BELLA MINIJET'   MEllarac
MODERN, MINIATURE, YELLOW BLEND, REPEAT-FLOWERING

The flowers of this rose are peach colored and they hold their color well.

'Bella Minijet'

The very full blooms contain 50 petals and only reach a diameter of 1 in (25 mm). The foliage is small, mid-green and semi-glossy, on a plant with a bushy growth habit and high flower production. It has a very rapid repeat-bloom cycle. 'Bella Minijet' is one of a series of a dozen or so roses that make ideal pot plants. ZONES 5–10.

Meilland, France, 1992

Parentage unknown

'BELLA ROSA'   KORwonder
syn. 'Toynbee Hall'
MODERN, CLUSTER-FLOWERED/FLORIBUNDA, MEDIUM PINK, REPEAT-FLOWERING

This makes a splendid bedding rose where a neat short grower is required. The flowers are a warm rose pink, a very pure and even shade, and they are carried close to the foliage on short stems in very full clusters. The round buds open to disclose about 36 overlapping petals, which eventually part to frame the stamens. They flower with good continuity through summer and autumn, and have what the raiser described as a 'wild rose scent', which in this instance means light. The plant has a low, spreading habit, and is well clothed in small polished leaves. In England the rose is called 'Toynbee Hall', which refers to a social center in London that celebrated its centenary in 1984. ZONES 4–9.

Kordes, Germany, 1982

Seedling × 'Traumerei'

Copenhagen Gold Medal 1982, Baden-Baden Gold Medal 1983

'BELLARD'
syns 'Bellart', 'Bellert'
OLD, ALBA, LIGHT PINK

One of the lesser known Albas, 'Bellart' is a densely petalled rose with quartered flowers and button green eyes. The blush pink blooms rise above fresh green, pointed leaves. Its strong growth reaches 4 ft (1.2 m). As a thorny bush with prickles its leaves are typically Alba, but other characteristics point to a Gallica predecessor. It has a strong fragrance. ZONES 4–10.

Pre-1842

Parentage unknown

'BELLE AMOUR'
OLD, ALBA, LIGHT PINK

This is a medium-sized bushy shrub to 5 ft (1.5 m) with thorny stems. The foliage is mid- to dark green, serrated and coarse to touch. The fully double flowers are cushion shaped when fully open and arranged in small clusters, appearing in great profusion in early summer. The color is bright pink approaching salmon with an occasional paler petal. The spicy and pungent fragrance is reminiscent of myrrh. In autumn the thorny canes are decorated with oval, orange hips. This easy to grow shrub rose, even in the most impoverished of soils, was discovered by Englishwoman Nancy Lindsay in 1940 at a convent in Elboeuf, Normandy. Peter Beales considers it to be a Damask. ZONES 4–10.

Rosa alba × R. damascena

'Belle Blonde'

'Belle Isis'

'BELLE BLONDE' MEnap

MODERN, LARGE-FLOWERED/HYBRID TEA,
MEDIUM YELLOW, REPEAT-FLOWERING

The name of this rose was a happy choice, for the flower is wonderful, fashioned from 24 big petals in bright, unfading golden yellow, revealing deeper golden yellow in the heart of the flower as the petals reflex. There is good fragrance, and flowering continues through summer and autumn. More often than not the plant beneath belies the promise of the flower: liability to black spot is the most serious problem, but even in a fungus-free summer the plant is a slow mover, below average height and with only adequate leaf cover. Growing it could be justified on sentimental or historic grounds, with the understanding that if it looks a poor thing today then that is a measure of how far roses have improved since the middle of the century. ZONES 5–9.

Meilland, France, 1955

'Peace' × 'Lorraine'

'BELLE DE CRÉCY'

syn. 'Le Météore'
OLD, GALLICA, MAUVE

This rose produces large cerise and purple blooms that turn to lavender-gray or violet in hot weather. The full, flat flowers have a button eye that is surrounded by incurved center petals. A profuse bloomer and quite fragrant, it is a relaxed, slightly flimsy shrub with flexible green mottled brown stems that bear few thorns. The leaves are darkish green overlaid bluish gray, and a little coarse in texture. It is said that it came from Madame de Pompadour's chateau at Crécy, but is probably named after Crécy-en-Brie, where Roeser had his nursery. ZONES 4–10.

Roeser, France, pre-1836

Parentage unknown

Royal Horticultural Society Award of Garden Merit 1993

'BELLE DE SÉGUR'

syn. 'Joséphine de Beauharnais'
OLD, ALBA, LIGHT PINK

This rose has almost disappeared and is only found in a few collections. The soft, rosy flesh, which has blush edges, is cupped and double. The dark foliage grows on a vigorous, erect bush with few prickles. There are three roses with this name; two of them are Albas. Vibert created 600 hybrids during his career; two of the most famous are 'Jeanne d'Arc' and 'La Ville de Bruxelles'. ZONES 4–10.

Vibert, France, pre-1848

Parentage unknown

'BELLE DES JARDINS'

OLD, GALLICA, MAUVE BLEND

This is a complex, variegated bloom of purplish violet-red with stripes of white. The double, velvety flowers are strongly scented and are produced in midsummer. The dark leaves are prickly, and strong canes cover the 5 ft (1.5 m) bush. Other Guillot hybrids still popular in the trade are 'Etoile de Lyon' and 'Comtesse du Cayla'; the Guillot firm is one of the few old Lyons rose nurseries still in business. This rose is frequently sold under other names and has been the subject of some dispute for a long time. ZONES 4–10.

Guillot, France, 1872

'Village Maid' × seedling

'BELLE D'ORLÉANS'

MODERN, LARGE-FLOWERED CLIMBER,
ORANGE-RED, REPEAT-FLOWERING

The advent of 'Independence' in 1951 brought pelargonidin, the chemical that gives geraniums their scarlet coloring, into the service of rose breeders. When one allows for the time it takes to evaluate and then propagate new seedlings, it is evident that Marcel Robichon lost little time in using it, to be able to introduce

'Belle de Crécy'

its offspring after only 7 years. The rose is orange-red, with quite large full-petalled flowers borne in clusters, holding their color well except in wet weather which takes their beauty away. They have little scent, and continue to flower through summer and autumn. The plant is vigorous with glossy foliage, best suited for walls, fences and pillars where a climber of average growth is required. M. Robichon was perhaps unlucky in that 'Danse des Sylphes' in a similar color appeared the following year, and attracted more publicity. ZONES 5–9.

Robichon, France, 1958

Seedling × 'Independence'

'BELLE EPOQUE' FRYaboo

MODERN, LARGE-FLOWERED/HYBRID TEA,
ORANGE BLEND, REPEAT-FLOWERING

A beautiful feature of this large rose is the two-toned effect within the flower. The inside of the petals is a pretty golden-bronze, while the outside surface is deeper—the raiser calls it 'nectarine-bronze'. The colors make a delightful contrast as the flowers expand. They have long buds, big petals and the high-centered form of the classic Large-flowered Rose. The fragrant flowers continue to appear through summer and autumn on vigorous plants a little taller than average height, with ample dark green foliage and a good health record. This is suitable as a bedding variety, as a standard and for cutting. *La belle époque*, meaning 'fine period', refers to the period of comfortable living in France before World War I. ZONES 4–9.

Fryer, UK, 1994

'Remember Me' × 'Simba'

Royal National Rose Society Trial Ground Certificate 1995

'BELLE ISIS'

OLD, GALLICA, LIGHT PINK

This is a tidy 4 ft (1.2 m) shrub with clear, gray-green, toothed foliage. It has fat buds streaked with deep crimson and the double, quartered blossoms have reflexed outer petals, which slowly unfold to expose a white base. There is a strong myrrh perfume. This rose, which is ideal for the small garden, is frequently used in arrangements as the petals, arranged in tiers, are a photographer's delight. It is disease resistant and has prickles. Its outstanding character is reflected in an offspring, 'Constance Spry', one of the most popular of all David Austin's creations. ZONES 4–10.

Parmentier, Belgium, 1845

Probably a hybrid of *Rosa gallica* × *R.* × *centifolia*

'BELLE LYONNAISE'

OLD, CLIMBING TEA, LIGHT YELLOW,
REPEAT-FLOWERING

Although listed as a Tea, there are enough traits evident in this rose's blossoms and habit to fool many into thinking it is a Noisette. The large, full, quartered

'Belle Epoque'

'Belle d'Orléans'

blossoms are pale yellow fading into white—sometimes with a touch of salmon. Used as a pillar rose, it will bloom from summer through to autumn. The handsome foliage and sweet fragrance are best nurtured in a sunny, warm spot. ZONES 7–10.

Levet, France, 1870

Seedling of 'Gloire de Dijon'

'BELLE OF BERLIN'   TANireb
MODERN, LARGE-FLOWERED/HYBRID TEA, MEDIUM PINK, REPEAT-FLOWERING

The long slim buds on this variety open to reveal a pretty color contrast between the outer and inner surfaces of the petals. The outside is pale rosy pink with deeper veining, the inside a stronger shade. The effect is especially beautiful under artificial light, so it is as well the rose is ideal for cutting, the double, high-centered flowers being long lasting and carried on long firm stems. There is also a reasonable fragrance, and blooms continue to appear through the growing season. Growth is vigorous, the plant being an upright grower to average height or more. It is a rose for warmer climates, and is currently offered for sale only in Australia. ZONES 5–9.

Tantau, Germany, 1994

Parentage unknown

'BELLE POITEVINE'
MODERN, MODERN SHRUB, MEDIUM PINK, REPEAT-FLOWERING

While the parentage is not known, from the general appearance of its flowers,

growth and foliage it seems clear this is a *Rosa rugosa* hybrid. Long pointed buds open out into almost flat, quite large flowers with loosely crinkled petals. They are a cool shade of pale magenta pink, showing creamy stamens, and scented, and are produced over a long period in summer and autumn. The plant grows large and shrubby, with a more angular outline than that of wild Rugosas, and also with coarser foliage. Large dark red hips are sometimes produced. It is a good subject for a big hedge or shrubbery. The name translates as 'Beauty of Poitou', the region where the French raiser had his nursery. ZONES 3–9.

Bruant, France, 1894

Parentage unknown

Royal Horticultural Society Award of Garden Merit 1993

'BELLE PORTUGAISE'
syn. 'Belle of Portugal'
MODERN, LARGE-FLOWERED CLIMBER, LIGHT PINK

This very vigorous rose has become almost naturalized in parts of California. In other parts of North America it will not grow at all, as it is not frost hardy on account of the *Rosa gigantea* parentage. It is often considered a Climbing Tea, and the large flowers have the elegant pointed buds, silky petal texture and delicate fragrance associated with that group. A mixture of light salmon, pink, peachy and creamy shades, they open wide and rather loosely with reflexed petal rims and hang down on pendulous stems. The olive green leaves droop ele-

'Belle sans Flatterie'

gantly but are liable to seasonal mildew at times when the enormous amount of growth being made outstrips the food resources available. There is only one flowering, but in climates that suit it the sight of hundreds of blossoms on a high wall or fence is one of summer's horticultural treats. ZONES 6–10.

Cayeux, Portugal, 1903

Rosa gigantea × 'Reine Marie Henriette'

'BELLE SANS FLATTERIE'
OLD, GALLICA, MAUVE BLEND, REPEAT-FLOWERING

This was a very popular rose in France in the 1800s, and it is still not well known outside Europe. The double, quartered, mid-sized blooms appear in clusters. The lilac-pink petals at the edge are complemented with a rich pink at the center, while the outer petals are reflexed. There is some rebloom in late summer but little scent. The plant grows to a 4 ft (1.2 m) shrub and has dark green foliage. This rose was grown in the garden of Empress Josephine at Malmaison. ZONES 5–10.

Godefroy, The Netherlands, pre-1806

Parentage unknown

'BELLE STORY'   AUSelle, AUSspry
syn. 'Bienenweide'
MODERN, MODERN SHRUB, LIGHT PINK

The large flowers on this variety, borne in sprays, open to resemble peonies, with petals incurving towards the center and reflexing round the outer edges of the flower, revealing the red-gold stamens within. They are rose pink, the shade lightening towards the petal tips, fullpetalled, fragrant and bloom in summer. Growth is bushy and vigorous, to average height. The dark semi-glossy foliage is rather small and does not adequately clothe the plant, which needs welldrained, fertile soil to thrive. The name honors one of the first nursing sisters to join Britain's Royal Navy in 1864. It is also classified as an English Rose. ZONES 4–9.

Austin, UK, 1984

('Chaucer' × 'Parade') × ('The Prioress' × 'Iceberg')

'BELLE VICHYSOISE'
syn. 'Cornélie'
OLD, NOISETTE, LIGHT PINK, REPEAT-FLOWERING

The famous hybridizer Lévèque was taking the waters at Vichy when he saw this rose climbing on an orangery wall. Never having seen it before, he took a cutting to Eugene Verdier, another nurseryman, who propagated it, and it was ultimately identified. Light pink, small blooms in

'Belle Poitevine'

'Belle of Berlin'

clusters of 20–50 decorate the long canes on a vigorous bush. It loves full sun. The 15 ft (4.5 m) branches are best seen on a pillar. As with many Noisettes, it blooms all summer and into autumn. ZONES 7–10.

Lévèque, France, 1895

Parentage unknown

'BELLE VIRGINIE'
syn. 'Dauphine'
OLD, GALLICA, MAUVE BLEND

Only 2 gardens in the world still list this rose in their collections. The crimson buds open to a profusion of fragrant, lilac-violet flowers. It has an upright, bushy growth habit. ZONES 4–11.

France, pre-1826

Parentage unknown

'BELLONA'   KORilona
MODERN, CLUSTER-FLOWERED/FLORIBUNDA, MEDIUM YELLOW, REPEAT-FLOWERING

This is primarily a greenhouse rose, and likely to be successful in the garden only in warm climates. The flowers are beautifully constructed, with very firm petals keeping them in shape for many days of cut flower life. They are double, with high centers, in an eye-catching shade of bright yellow, and are quite large for a Cluster-flowered Rose. There is not much fragrance. The flowers continue through summer and autumn on a plant that grows vigorously with an upright habit and is clothed with ample bright green foliage. The name refers to the Roman goddess of war, whose progress was heralded by golden trumpets. ZONES 5–9.

Kordes, Germany, 1976

'New Day' × 'Minigold'

'BELVEDERE'
syn. 'Princesse Marie'
OLD, SEMPERVIRENS, MEDIUM PINK

This rose bears large trusses of double pink flowers that are carried in large

'Belle Story'

panicles. The flat blooms are surrounded by dark green foliage and have a lovely fragrance. The pliable stems have few prickles, making it an excellent rambler for walls, pergolas and over buildings. Able to reach 15 ft (4.5 m) in a season and capable of overwhelming a large tree, 'Belvedere' hates heat and does best in rich soil. The foliage may remain evergreen in warmer climates. M. Jacques, superintendent of the Chateau Neuilly gardens in the home of Louis Phillipe, is responsible for most of the Sempervirens hybrids. There has always been some disagreement among experts about the origin of this rose. **ZONES 4–10.**

Jacques, France, 1829
Parentage unknown

'BEN-HUR'
MODERN, LARGE-FLOWERED/HYBRID TEA, MEDIUM RED, REPEAT-FLOWERING

This is another example of a rose that in the USA is called a Grandiflora but internationally is considered to be a Large-flowered Rose. The large flowers may be carried singly or in clusters, opening out from long pointed buds into loosely double flowers with high centers. The blooms appear crimson tinged with carmine on the outside of the petals, and crimson as they open to reveal the inner surfaces. The flowers have some fragrance and they last well, as the petals are firm, which makes them useful for cutting as well as for use in the garden.

'Bengali'

'Bengale Rouge'

'Bellona'

The variety repeats its flower through summer and autumn, and grows vigorously and fairly compactly to above average height with a plentiful supply of glossy, leathery foliage. The release of the film *Ben-Hur* in 1960 coincided with the introduction of the rose. **ZONES 4–9.**

Lammerts, USA, 1960
'Charlotte Armstrong' × ('Charlotte Armstrong' × 'Floradora')

'BENDIGOLD'
MODERN, CLUSTER-FLOWERED/FLORIBUNDA, ORANGE-RED, REPEAT-FLOWERING

The red-tinted buds on this variety have a rounded shape and open into fairly full-petalled blooms of a lively shade of gold with orange highlights. They are quite large for a Cluster-flowered Rose, continue in bloom through summer and autumn and have a sharp but not unpleasing fragrance. The plant grows vigorously and upright to average height, with rather smooth stems and a good coverage of deep green leaves, which are bronzy red when they first appear. This Australian-bred rose was cleverly named by the raiser, whose home city of Bendigo in the state of Victoria was a focal point in the gold rush that began after the precious metal was first discovered there in 1851. **ZONES 4–9.**

Murley, Australia, 1979
'Rumba' × 'Redgold'

'BENGALE ROUGE'
OLD, CHINA, MEDIUM RED, REPEAT-FLOWERING

A prolific bloomer over a long period, this China is one of the most recent creations in that family. The ovoid buds of bright carmine open to double, large, red blooms of 35 petals. The abundant foliage is large and dark green on a plant that is taller than most Chinas. There are several roses with Bengale in their

'Ben-Hur'

names; all of them require a warm position and all are strongly resistant to diseases. **ZONES 7–10.**

Gaujard, France, 1955
'Grüss an Teplitz' × seedling

'BENGALI'   KORal
MODERN, CLUSTER-FLOWERED/FLORIBUNDA, ORANGE-RED, REPEAT-FLOWERING

As the plump buds unfold, the petals show a pretty shade of golden orange richly veined with orange-red. The flowers are of medium size, well filled with petals, and are borne in small, rather open clusters on firm stems. They open with high centers, and are excellent for buttonholes and small flower arrangements. There is light fragrance, and they appear with good continuity through summer and autumn, making this a good rose for bedding. The plant grows vigorously with a well-branched spreading habit to below average height, furnished with leaves that are reddish when young then becoming bright green and shiny. **ZONES 4–9.**

Kordes, Germany, 1969
'Dacapo' × seedling

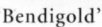

'Bendigold'

'Benson and Hedges Gold'

'Bennett's Seedling'

'BENITA' DICquarrel

MODERN, CLUSTER-FLOWERED/FLORIBUNDA,
DEEP YELLOW, REPEAT-FLOWERING

The pretty golden yellow blooms of this
variety have a frilled edge to the petals.
They open from urn-shaped buds into
full-petalled, fairly large-cupped flowers,
borne on firm stems in big, widely
spaced sprays like a candelabra, which
may include up to 12 blooms. A few
plants of 'Benita' will prove a useful
source for small flower arrangements
and for buttonholes. There is a light fragrance, and flowering continues through
summer and autumn. The growth habit
is uneven but overall it reaches average
height and is furnished with mid-green
leaves. By arrangement with the raiser it
was named by Mrs Barbel Abela in
memory of her mother. ZONES 4–9.

Dickson, UK, 1995

('Korresia' × 'Bright Smile') × seedling

Royal National Rose Society Trial Ground
Certificate 1990, Dublin Gold Medal 1992,
UK Breeders' Choice 1995

'BENJAMIN FRANKLIN'

MODERN, LARGE-FLOWERED/HYBRID TEA,
LIGHT PINK, REPEAT-FLOWERING

The plump buds of this rose open into
elongated full-petalled flowers of light
pink flushed with shades of golden
apricot. The blooms are high centered
and become cupped as the petals expand,
yielding some fragrance. They are carried
singly on long stems, and flower freely
over a long period. It has an upright
habit and grows to middling height, with
plentiful dark, leathery foliage that is
reddish green when young. It was named
to honor the American statesman
Benjamin Franklin (1706–90) and may
no longer be in commerce. ZONES 4–9.

Von Abrams, USA, 1969

Parentage unknown

'BENNETT'S SEEDLING'

syn. 'Thoresbyana'
OLD, AYRSHIRE, WHITE

This rose was discovered growing in a
hedge by the gardener of Earl Manvers at
Thoresby in Nottinghamshire in 1835.
Looking very much like a double form of
Rosa arvensis, the pure white blooms
have a faint perfume and continue over a
long period in summer. It can reach 20 ft
(6 m) and can be used as a climber or
ground cover. It is happy in sun or
shade. ZONES 5–11.

Bennett, UK, circa 1840

Believed to be a seedling of *Rosa arvensis*

'BENSON AND HEDGES GOLD' MACgem

MODERN, LARGE-FLOWERED/HYBRID TEA,
YELLOW BLEND, REPEAT-FLOWERING

This is a satisfying bedding rose, bearing
full-petalled flowers of high-centered

'Benvenuto'

form and good size, though the centers
are not held for long and the petals
dissolve into a pleasant muddle. The
blooms of rich deep yellow with flushes
of red have an enjoyable fragrance, and
give an excellent succession of bloom
through summer and autumn. The plant
usually grows vigorously with a bushy
habit, to below average height, with rugged leaves. It is happier in cooler climates,
because the color fades in hot sun. The
dedication of this rose to a brand of
cigarettes almost certainly harmed its
commercial prospects; history has come
a long way since tobacco was described
by Robert Burton in the seventeenth
century as 'a sovereign remedy to all
diseases'! ZONES 5–9.

McGredy, New Zealand, 1978

'Yellow Pages' × ('Arthur Bell' × 'Cynthia
Brooke')

Royal National Rose Society Trial Ground Certificate 1976, New Zealand Gold Star of the South
Pacific 1978

'BENVENUTO' MEIelpa

MODERN, LARGE-FLOWERED CLIMBER,
MEDIUM RED, REPEAT-FLOWERING

This cheerful garden rose bears well-filled
clusters of deep cherry red buds that open
to show light centers where the yellowish
petal bases surround the yellow stamens.
The color deepens to a crimson tone as
the petals unfold, and the shapely semi-
double flowers open out rather flat. They
are medium sized and lightly scented,
and the trusses are produced spasmodically through summer and autumn. It
makes vigorous, thorny growth, with an
upright free-branching habit and ample
deep green, shiny foliage, but it is of
modest size as climbers go and is best
suited where a restrained grower is
wanted for screening walls and fences or
to train up a pillar. ZONES 4–9.

Meilland, France, 1967

('Alain' × 'Guinee') × 'Cocktail'

'Berlin'

'BÉRÉNICE'

OLD, GALLICA, RED BLEND

The rich crimson-purple blooms of this
rose fade to magenta with a dark veining,
or in full sun they fade to mauve. They
are slightly quartered, globular and open
flat. The vigorous and spreading bush is
covered with rough, medium green
foliage. There is strong fragrance, and in
autumn there is a good crop of hips. It is
rare to find in commerce. 'Bérénice' was
a famous tragedy by French playwright
Racine. ZONES 4–10.

Vibert, France, 1818

Parentage unknown

'BERKELEY BEAUTY' MORberk

MODERN, MINIATURE, MAUVE BLEND,
REPEAT-FLOWERING

The blooms of 'Berkeley Beauty' are an
attractive combination of lacy white
edged with lavender to pink. The florets
are considered Large-flowered form and
are borne one bloom per stem. The plant
is a neat medium height bush with abundant semi-glossy foliage. The prickles
vary from green to brown. This rose was
named to honor the city of Berkeley,
home of the University of California.
ZONES 4–11.

Moore, USA, 1988

'Pink Petticoat' × 'Make Believe'

'BERLIN'

MODERN, MODERN SHRUB, ORANGE BLEND,
REPEAT-FLOWERING

Wilhelm Kordes raised a series of shrub
roses suitable for parks, naming them after German cities. As befits a park rose,
this is a vigorous, trouble-free grower,
tall, upright and shrubby with thick
leathery leaves and well armed with
prickles. The saucer-shaped flowers
appear very bright when their few petals
first open, the color being vivid orange-
scarlet with yellow at the base. As the
petals expand they become waved at the
edges, lose their brilliance of tone and
turn cherry red. The color impact is
considerable because the trusses are large
and contain many blooms, and flowering
continues through summer and autumn.
There is little scent. Sometimes this
has been called a Hybrid Musk Rose,
although it more closely resembles a
tough, overgrown Cluster-flowered
Rose. ZONES 4–9.

Kordes, Germany, 1949

'Eva' × 'Peace'

Royal National Rose Society Trial Ground
Certificate 1950

'Berkeley Beauty'

'Benita'

B

'Betsy Ross'

'Bernstein-Rose'

'BERMUDA KATHLEEN'
MODERN, MODERN SHRUB, MEDIUM RED,
REPEAT-FLOWERING

This is one of the mystery roses rescued from oblivion by the Bermuda Rose Society. It has spread round the islands from cuttings taken from the 1950s in Hilda Horsfield's garden, and produces open sprays of fairly small, single flowers on slender stems. They open apple-blossom pink and saucer-shaped, and darken to a dusty rose pink, becoming flat as they age. In Bermuda's climate the rose flowers all year round, yet still produces small light orange hips. The plant grows with an upright habit to average height, or taller if trained as a semi-climber on a wall. The leaflets are mid-green, pointed and shiny. There are points of similarity to 'Mutabilis', including a lack of scent, which make it seem likely that this is a chance seedling of that rose. ZONES 5–9.

Horsfield, Bermuda, 1993

Probably a seedling of 'Mutabilis'

'BERNINA'
MODERN, CLUSTER-FLOWERED/FLORIBUNDA,
WHITE, REPEAT-FLOWERING

The commercial availability of this rose is limited rather strangely to a single nursery in its country of origin and to two in Western Australia. It is a short grower, bearing white flowers like small replicas of Large-flowered Roses. They are fairly full of petals, neatly formed with high centers, and with the outer petals reflexing and scrolling to a point. There is some scent, and the blooms repeat their flower through summer and autumn. The plant is compact in growth with light green leaves, and is suitable for bedding and cutting for small arrangements. ZONES 4–9.

de Ruiter, The Netherlands, 1979

Parentage unknown

'BERNSTEIN-ROSE'   TANeitbar
syn. 'Amaroela'
MODERN, CLUSTER-FLOWERED/FLORIBUNDA,
DEEP YELLOW, REPEAT-FLOWERING

This is a Modern Garden Rose with an old-style flower. Its plump buds at first show red flushes, but when the flowers are open they are a pure and even shade of amber yellow. They are of medium size and full of petals, which are enfolded tightly against each other as the blooms open wide, the inner petals incurving and the outer ones reflexing in the manner of an Old Garden Rose. They continue in flower through summer and autumn, and stand up well to bad weather. The scent is light. For a bedding rose this is a useful and robust variety. A compact, vigorous plant, it grows to below average height and is furnished with dark green, rather narrow leaves. Bernstein is the German word for amber. ZONES 4–9.

Tantau, Germany, 1987

Parentage unknown

'BERT MULLEY'
syn. 'Edna Walling'
MODERN, POLYANTHA, MEDIUM PINK,
REPEAT-FLOWERING

This shrub rose grows to 5 ft (1.5 m) in height and width and produces airy clusters consisting of 5–20 rose pink flowers freely for many months of the year. The foliage is small, abundant and soft green in color and the bush is absolutely free from disease. 'Bert Mulley' makes an excellent hedge and is good for planting in groups; it is one of the best Australian-raised roses. The plant always looks neat as the foliage is very close jointed on the stems. It was named after a great rose grower and exhibitor and judge who lived at Camden in New South Wales, Australia. ZONES 4–9.

Pre-1990

Sport of 'Renae'

'BERYL BACH'   HARtesia
MODERN, LARGE-FLOWERED/HYBRID TEA,
YELLOW BLEND, REPEAT-FLOWERING

This is a prolific producer of large, high-pointed elegant blooms, full of petals in the tradition of Large-flowered Roses. The buds open light yellow, and as the petals expand they admit a random suffusion of creamy pink and pale crimson. There is a pleasant fragrance, and for a rose with such a big flower the continuity of bloom through summer and autumn is good, making it a useful item for cutting. Wet weather can spoil the flowers because of their soft petals. The growth habit is upright, taller than average, with ample matt foliage and a denser, shrubbier habit than is usual for this class. The name means 'little Beryl' in Welsh; Mr Emil Willemstyn of London named it after his late wife. Not long afterwards he passed away peacefully in his garden while enjoying the roses he had planted in her memory. ZONES 4–9.

Harkness, UK, 1985

'Korresia' × 'Silver Jubilee'

'BEST WISHES'   CHESnut
syn. 'Curiosity Climbing'
MODERN, LARGE-FLOWERED CLIMBER, RED BLEND,
REPEAT-FLOWERING

Many plant species have variegated leaf forms, so why not roses? There have been a few, such as the trailing rose 'Achievement', but it was nowhere near as attractive as the Large-flowered bush 'Curiosity', introduced by Cocker of Aberdeen in 1971. That rose, a sport of 'Cleopatra', bears scarlet-red and yellow full-petalled blooms on low, bushy plants, and the sporting lies not in its flowers but in its foliage, which is green and white, beautifully overlaid with pink flushes when young. Alec Cocker, through his local university, established that this was indeed a true sporting and not a virus. However, the growth on 'Curiosity' is rather stunted, presumably because the leaves, lacking the full quota of chlorophyll, are inefficient feeders. Now that a climbing sport is available greater vigor should be assured, and this novelty is therefore well worth trying. It grows upright to average height. ZONES 4–9.

Chessum, UK, 1996

Sport of 'Curiosity'

'BETSY MCCALL'
MODERN, CLUSTER-FLOWERED/FLORIBUNDA,
ORANGE-PINK, REPEAT-FLOWERING

Gene Boerner raised the breathtakingly beautiful salmon 'Fashion', the pollen parent of this rose, and he utilized it extensively in further breeding work even though it is an indifferent grower. One supposes that his intention was to use a vigorous seed parent in making the cross that produced 'Betsy McCall', in the hope that it would provide a stronger plant. What emerged is a rose that produces big clusters of large double shrimp pink flowers, prettily formed and fragrant, and maintains a fair succession of bloom through summer and autumn. The plant makes a bushy, rather spreading grower, sparsely furnished with large matt green leaves. Unfortunately, it has not proved a much better grower than its pollen parent, nor has it kept free of rust and black spot. ZONES 4–9.

Boerner, USA, 1956

Seedling × 'Fashion'

'BETSY ROSS'   DELup
syn. 'La Passionata'
MODERN, LARGE-FLOWERED/HYBRID TEA,
DARK RED, REPEAT-FLOWERING

This variety has appeared in catalogues more often as 'La Passionata'. It is on the deep scarlet side of crimson, and produces large full-petalled blooms, high centered in the young flower and retaining a pretty, regular outline as the wide petals reflex. There is only a light scent, which is disappointing in a rose of this color. Flowering continues through summer and autumn on plants of average height with a vigorous, upright habit and a rather skimpy cover of leathery foliage. It seems more at home in warm climates. Both names of the rose commemorate revolutionaries. Betsy Ross created the 'Stars and Stripes' in 1777, and La Passionata was a prominent communist in the Spanish Civil War. ZONES 5–9.

Delbard, France, 1969

('Gloire de Rome' × 'La Vaudoise') × 'Divine'

'Betsy McCall'

'Bert Mulley'

'Betty Harkness'

'BETTINA' MEIpal

MODERN, LARGE-FLOWERED/HYBRID TEA, ORANGE-PINK, REPEAT-FLOWERING

Among the magnificent roses launched in post-war Europe by Francis Meilland, few have attracted the eye more than 'Bettina'. The reason lies in the rare and beautiful colors it reveals, as its deep reddish orange buds give place to flowers in warm peach and cream, richly marked with pretty reddish veining. In cool weather rich orange replaces the base of peach and cream. The petals are firmly textured and so evenly contoured when the flower is fully open that a knife laid across them would touch nearly all the petal tips. There is a light scent, and flowering continues through summer to autumn. As they last well and are on long stems the flowers are excellent for cutting, but the plant is not a good garden rose since it is uneven, does not make new shoots freely and may get mildew and black spot. The foliage is leathery, dark and reddish when young, but rather sparse. **'Climbing Bettina'** (MEIpalsar; syn. 'Grimpant Bettina'; Meilland, France, 1958) needs to be sited so as to avoid spring frosts which are liable to nip the emerging shoots and therefore cause bloom loss. It needs plenty of space to grow tall and wide. The stems become very stiff after a few months and need to be trained in place while they are still young and pliable. ZONES 5–9.

Meilland, France, 1953

'Peace' × ('Madame Joseph Perraud' × 'Demain')

Royal National Rose Society Trial Ground Certificate 1953

'BETTY HARKNESS' HARette

MODERN, CLUSTER-FLOWERED/FLORIBUNDA, ORANGE BLEND, REPEAT-FLOWERING

The flowers are on the large size for a Cluster-flowered Rose, and are well spaced in the cluster. They make a good color impact, therefore, as they open in big, upright trusses of saucer-shaped, full-petalled flowers. The color is a pretty blend of coral-orange and copper, and there is a sweet fragrance which is unusual for varieties in this spectrum. After a plentiful first blooming, flowers appear with good continuity through summer and autumn. For a bed or a group in a border, or as a hedge rose, this is a suitable choice as the plants grow vigorously to average height, attaining a bushy habit and an ample provision of shiny, dark green leaves. The late Jack Harkness loved the combination of beauty, scent and good health in this rose, and named it for his wife. ZONES 4–9.

Harkness, UK, 1998

Parentage unknown

Courtrai Gold Medal 1997, Paris Silver Medal 1997

'BETTY PRIOR'

MODERN, CLUSTER-FLOWERED/FLORIBUNDA, MEDIUM PINK, REPEAT-FLOWERING

This is a remarkable survivor of the forerunners of the Cluster-flowered Roses, which were termed Hybrid Polyanthas. It produces large clusters of modest-sized 5-petalled blooms, which open out like so many saucers. The effect is cheerful, because the flowers are a pretty shade of pink, lighter on the inside of the petal, and with a whitish base to give them pale hearts. They are produced in continual cycles of growth and bloom through summer and autumn on upright plants of average height or more, with ample healthy matt green foliage. This is a dependable garden and parks rose, being long lived and hardy and, despite a lack of fragrance, these good qualities have enabled it to survive as a widely grown rose where most of its contemporaries have long since disappeared. Betty Prior was a member of the raiser's family at their nursery near Colchester in Essex. ZONES 4–9.

Prior, UK, 1935

'Kirsten Poulsen' × seedling

National Rose Society Gold Medal 1933

'BETTY UPRICHARD'

MODERN, LARGE-FLOWERED/HYBRID TEA, APRICOT BLEND, REPEAT-FLOWERING

'Apricot blend', the official description, reflects the novelty of this variety's coloring in the 1920s: 'a luminous glow, unequalled since' as an old nurseryman put it. Today it would surely be considered a 'pink blend', being salmon-pink with a copper flush on the inside of the petal with a carmine flush on the outside. The effect is a delightful two-toned flower, which opens its slender buds to display high centers while the outer petals slowly reflex. There are only 20 or so broad petals, and it is wonderful to see how they contrive to create so elegant, if fleeting, a bloom. The bush is quick to repeat its fragrant flowers through summer and autumn on vigorous upright plants that grow above average height and are clothed with leathery mid-green leaves. It was named after a friend of the Dickson family in County Down, Northern Ireland, who was a keen huntswoman. ZONES 4–9.

Dickson, UK, 1922

Parentage unknown

National Rose Society Gold Medal 1921

'BEVERLY HILLS' DELmator

syn. 'Malicorne'

MODERN, LARGE-FLOWERED/HYBRID TEA, ORANGE BLEND, REPEAT-FLOWERING

This is a lovely garden rose that produces long-lasting, dark orange, well-shaped flowers in clusters. Disease resistance is reasonable and the growth tall. Flower production is excellent, although the flowers have no scent. The foliage is dark green, large and profuse and acts as a foil to the flowers. 'Beverly Hills' is a good rose for bedding when a hot color is required. ZONES 5–9.

Delbard, France, 1986

('Zambra' × 'Orange Sensation') × ('Zambra' × ['Orange Triumph' × 'Floradora'])

'Betty Prior'

'Beverly Hills'

'Betty Uprichard'

'Bettina'

B

'BEWITCHED'

MODERN, LARGE-FLOWERED/HYBRID TEA,
MEDIUM PINK, REPEAT-FLOWERING

This child of 'Queen Elizabeth' remains, after over 30 years, a popular choice in warm climates. The flowers are large, with fairly full-petalled flowers of an even shade of phlox pink and they hold their color even in hot weather. They open with high centers and take on a pleasing rounded outline as the petals reflex, yielding a sweet Damask fragrance. Long stems make this an excellent rose for cutting as well as for general garden use, and it will provide a succession of blooms through summer and autumn. The plant is vigorous and grows upright to above average height, and is clothed with large apple-green leaves. It is at its best in warmer climates, as the soft petals are easily marked in cool wet conditions. ZONES 4–9.

Lammerts, USA, 1967

'Queen Elizabeth' × 'Tawny Gold'

All-America Rose Selection 1967, Portland Gold Medal 1967

'BIANCO' COCblanco

MODERN, MINIATURE, WHITE, REPEAT-FLOWERING

This pure white Miniature comes from the northern cold climates of Aberdeen in Scotland from the same hybridizer

'Bewitched'

'Big John'

who gave the world the award-winning pink blend Large-flowered rose, 'Silver Jubilee'. It has double flowers, containing about 35 petals. The blooms have no fragrance. The florets are usually borne one to a stem or in small clusters on a compact bush. ZONES 4–9.

Cocker, UK, 1983

'Darling Flame' × 'Jack Frost'

'BIBI MAIZOON' AUSdimindo

syn. 'Bibi Mezoon'

MODERN, MODERN SHRUB, DEEP PINK,
REPEAT-FLOWERING

The cupped flowers of this full-petalled rose are deep pink, the color in the depths of the center petals being intensely rich. They open from round buds to cupped flowers with low centers, which reveal many quartered and infolded petals. There is good fragrance, and for their individual beauty the blooms leave little to be desired. The plant is slow to establish itself. It is a bushy grower and can reach average size, bearing arching stems with large dark leaves that have their share of fungus troubles. This rose is also classified as an English Rose. It is named for a member of the Omani royal family. ZONES 4–9.

Austin, UK, 1989

'The Reeve' × 'Chaucer'

'Big Ben'

'BICOLETTE'

MODERN, LARGE-FLOWERED/HYBRID TEA,
RED BLEND, REPEAT-FLOWERING

Yellowish buds on this rose open to show medium-sized blooms with high centers, in which the purple red color of the inner petal surfaces contrasts rather startlingly with the saffron yellow on the reverse. The full-petalled flowers are borne singly, but little or no scent is detectable. They last well if cut for the house when they are at a young stage. This makes a good garden rose, especially in cool locations, as it stands bad weather well, sheds it petals cleanly and flowers through summer and autumn. The plant grows to above average height with a branching habit, and has leathery, dark green, glossy leaves. ZONES 4–9.

Tschanz, Switzerland, 1980

'Queen Elizabeth' × 'Baronne Edmond de Rothschild'

'BIDDULPH GRANGE'

FRYdarkeye

syn. 'Rosentanz'

MODERN, MODERN SHRUB, RED BLEND,
REPEAT-FLOWERING

Although the parentage is not disclosed, the mop-head clusters of this rose indicate the Polyantha ancestry of 'Ballerina'. Many flower sprays are produced; these are large, with conical buds opening to show small, velvety, bright red, single blooms with white at the petal base. They are carried close to the plant, making an eye-catching sight when the petals part to reveal golden stamens. The flowers darken as they age before dropping cleanly, and they repeat well all through summer and autumn. There is little scent. The plant grows densely and compactly, and is very well furnished with dark shiny leaves. This rose looks good in all weathers, and will make a first-rate small shrub for a border or bed. It is named for a property belonging to England's National Trust, where an old garden has recently been renovated. ZONES 4–9.

Fryer, UK, 1988

Parentage unknown

Rome Gold Medal 1988, Belfast Prize 1991, Glasgow Gold Medal 1991

'BIG BEN'

MODERN, LARGE-FLOWERED/HYBRID TEA,
DARK RED, REPEAT-FLOWERING

This tall-growing rose produces flowers of deep crimson-scarlet, of good size and with high centers. They are fully double and flower over a long period through

summer and autumn, though the blooms may burn in hot sun. Breeder Douglas Gandy achieved his aim of obtaining a good bloom by crossing two of the most fragrant red roses of the day, but how far did he consider the constitution of the offspring? 'Ena Harkness' has bowing stems and the much darker 'Charles Mallerin' has a dreadfully lanky habit of growth. In the event 'Big Ben', which is still grown commercially in Canada and parts of the USA, proved a better grower but failed to inherit the scent. Its name comes from the famous bell in St Stephen's tower at the Palace of Westminster. ZONES 4–9.

Gandy, UK, 1964

'Ena Harkness' × 'Charles Mallerin'

'BIG JOHN' STEteaw

MODERN, LARGE-FLOWERED CLIMBER, PINK BLEND,
REPEAT-FLOWERING

'Big John' could just as easily be classed as a large Shrub Rose. Growth is strong and bushy to about 6 ft (2 m). Foliage is plentiful, mid-green and semi-glossy and very closely jointed. Flowers are very full, of 35–40 petals, well-formed and have good substance. The color is cream base, heavily overlaid with carmine-pink in the manner of the Large-flowered/ Hybrid Tea 'Olympic Torch'. Flower production is extremely high with quick repeat and the flowers last well on the bushes. 'Big John' is disease resistant and a good choice where a small climbing rose is required. It is sufficiently compact in growth not to need support. ZONES 5–9.

Stephens, New Zealand, 1995

Parentage unknown

'BIJOU D'OR' TANledolg

syn. 'Golden Jewel'

MODERN, PATIO/DWARF CLUSTER-FLOWERED,
DEEP YELLOW, REPEAT-FLOWERING

In recent years there has been a great increase in the number of dwarf, compact roses grown for the garden trade, and many breeders are selecting seedlings with this market especially in mind. Such varieties need to have a bushy, vigorous habit, produce plenty of new shoots all round the plant so that they present a balanced appearance to the customer, flower freely and as often as possible and have presentable foliage. This low grower is ideal for growing in a container or to fill a small space. It bears clusters of rich yellow double blooms that resemble small-scale Large-flowered Roses when newly open, then become cupped as they age. There is a light fragrance and a good succession of flowers through summer and autumn. ZONES 4–9.

Tantau, Germany, 1995

Parentage unknown

'BILL SLIM' HARquito

MODERN, CLUSTER-FLOWERED/FLORIBUNDA,
ORANGE-PINK, REPEAT-FLOWERING

The flowers on this variety appear sometimes singly but more often in quite big clusters on strong upright stems; they need their strength because the individual blooms are large for a Cluster-flowered Rose and are full of sizeable

'Bill Slim'

B

petals. They open out into rounded blooms of an even salmony red color, like that of ripening tomatoes, which lightens, but keeps its tone through the life of the flower. There is a light fragrance, and the blooms, which stand wet weather well, repeat their flower through summer and autumn. They are held quite close to the foliage, which is plentiful, rich green and glossy, on a bushy upright plant of average height. The rose is named for Field-Marshal Slim, under whom the raiser served in Burma in World War II. ZONES 4–9.

Harkness, UK, 1989

(['Highlight' × 'Color Wonder'] × seedling) × 'Silver Jubilee'

Royal National Rose Society Certificate of Merit 1985

'BILL TEMPLE'
MODERN, LARGE-FLOWERED/HYBRID TEA, WHITE BLEND, REPEAT-FLOWERING

This is a good garden rose, and its substantial petals give reason to suppose it would also be good for exhibition, but though capable of giving superb flowers the variety does not do so with enough consistency. The blooms are creamy white and come to a high center with good symmetry of form before opening to show a rounded outline. They have a little scent, stand wet weather well, and flower on through summer and autumn. It grows upright to average height or less and is furnished with dark foliage, which shows off the cool color of the flowers to good effect. The variety was named for a friend of the raiser. ZONES 4–9.

Harkness, UK, 1975

'Crimson Halo' × 'Piccadilly'

'BILL WARRINER'   JACsur
MODERN, CLUSTER-FLOWERED/FLORIBUNDA, ORANGE-PINK, REPEAT-FLOWERING

'Sun Flare' and 'Impatient' are two roses raised by the late Bill Warriner that achieved the coveted All-America Rose Selection award, so it is fitting that a seedling bred from them by his pupil Keith Zary should be named in his honor. It is a pretty color in the salmon-orange-coral spectrum, and produces its flowers freely in well-spaced large clusters. They are large for a Cluster-flowered Rose, with the neatly structured form of small-scale Large-flowered Roses as they open, becoming cupped with a rounded outline as the petals reflex. They have a light fragrance, and appear freely through summer and autumn on a free-branching plant that grows upright to average height. Bill Warriner, who died in 1991 at the age of 69, is credited with the raising of well over 150 varieties during his 25 years with the Jackson & Perkins company. ZONES 4–9.

Zary, USA, 1996

'Sun Flare' × 'Impatient'

'BILLARD ET BARRÉ'
OLD, CLIMBING TEA, MEDIUM YELLOW, REPEAT-FLOWERING

'Billard et Barré' is now enjoying a comeback. Often called a Noisette because of its color and habit, this double rose is

'Billy Boiler'

golden yellow with the buds opening to full, glossy blooms. The canes are tough on a vigorous and erect bush with long and shiny leaves. Its fragrance is sweet and it has a long summer–autumn blooming period. It looks wonderful on a pillar or pergola, though it can also be grown as a 6 ft (1.8 m) shrub. It should be pruned lightly. ZONES 7–11.

Pernet-Ducher, France, 1898

'Mlle Alice Furon' × 'Duchesse d'Auerstädt'

'BILLY BOILER'
MODERN, LARGE-FLOWERED CLIMBER, MEDIUM RED, REPEAT-FLOWERING

This variety is a fairly vigorous climbing rose of a brilliant red color but with only 10 or 12 petals that are of good substance. Its color and strong fragrance are its chief assets. 'Billy Boiler' grows to 10 ft (3 m) in height and has attractive foliage, although it can suffer from mildew in autumn. Eye-catching in spring, it makes a good pillar rose and there is some repeat bloom, mainly in late autumn. It can also be used on a tripod or to cover a fence. ZONES 5–9.

Clark, Australia, 1927

'Oskar Kordell' × unknown

'BING CROSBY'
MODERN, LARGE-FLOWERED/HYBRID TEA, ORANGE BLEND, REPEAT-FLOWERING

This rose is a powerful dark orange or lively red, its appearance to the eye depending on the season and the light. The flowers are usually produced individually, are full of wide petals, and open from plump buds into large blooms of high-centered form that become cupped as the petals reflex. They last well so are useful for cutting, and have a light spicy scent. The cycle of growth and flower is repeated through summer and autumn, and the later displays are often found to give better blooms. 'Bing Crosby' makes a good bedding rose, growing tall and upright with a slowly spreading habit and a covering of leathery leaves, which when they first grow are wrinkled, with reddish tints, before turning olive green. The famous singer died in 1977 so did not live to see the rose achieve its high All-America Rose Selection award, nor the wiles of the catalogue writers, who aver that it will 'croon a sweet tune in the garden'. It is at its best in warm climates. ZONES 4–9.

Weeks, USA, 1981

Seedling × 'First Prize'

All-America Rose Selection 1981

'Bing Crosby'

'Birmingham Post'

'Birthday Present'

'BIRMINGHAM POST'
MODERN, CLUSTER-FLOWERED/FLORIBUNDA, DEEP PINK, REPEAT-FLOWERING

This rose is pink, with deeper pink flushes on the petal reverse, and produces large full-petalled flowers not far off Large-flowered Rose quality, but borne in strong clusters through summer and autumn. There is a good fragrance. The plant grows vigorously, is taller than average, and has abundant mid-green, leathery foliage. Despite its good garden qualities, this rose has never become popular. The raiser may well have wondered what better parents a rose could have than one of the strongest and one of the most fragrant varieties of the day, but the only headlines made by 'Birmingham Post' were in the pages of the newspaper whose name it bears. ZONES 4–9.

Watkins Roses, UK, 1968

'Queen Elizabeth' × 'Wendy Cussons'

'BIRTHDAY PRESENT'
MODERN, LARGE-FLOWERED CLIMBER, DARK RED, REPEAT-FLOWERING

Douglas Toogood of Melbourne found this seedling in his seedling patch on his birthday—hence the name. 'Birthday Present' is a vigorous climber producing an abundance of very dark red, highly scented double blooms composed of 20 or more petals on a 13 ft (4 m) high plant. Repeat bloom will occur in some seasons but not in others. It is one of the

'Bill Temple'

best of the Australian-raised climbing red roses and has dark, leathery foliage and excellent disease resistance. It is a good rose for a wall, pillar or tripod and is even strong enough for an archway. ZONES 5–9.

Toogood, Australia, 1950

'Guinée' × 'Rouge Mallerin'

'BISCHOFSSTADT PADERBORN'
syns 'Fire Pillar', 'Paderborn'
MODERN, MODERN SHRUB, ORANGE-RED, REPEAT-FLOWERING

The synonym 'Fire Pillar' summarizes this variety well, as its flowers are quite large in a fiery shade of orange-scarlet with whitish yellow petal bases. They do not have many petals so the golden stamens are quickly revealed, adding

'Black Ice'

'Black Beauty'

'Black Boy'

extra flamboyance to the heart of the saucer-shaped flowers. These are long lasting, and appear through summer and autumn with good continuity on a robust shrub of average height. For parks display and for hedges this rose is a good choice as it grows vigorously with a free-branching habit and is well furnished with deep green glossy leaves. Against a pillar it can be trained to make a short climber. Paderborn is an historic Hanseatic market town and the seat of an ancient bishopric. ZONES 4–9.

Kordes, Germany, 1964

'Korona' × 'Spartan'

Anerkannte Deutsche Rose 1968

'BISHOP DARLINGTON'
MODERN, MODERN SHRUB, APRICOT BLEND, REPEAT-FLOWERING

Out of some 40 named roses raised by Captain George C. Thomas, this is one of the most widely grown. The long, pointed buds are a pretty shade of coral-pink, and open in a blend of peach and cream with yellow bases to the flowers, which have a pleasing scent. They are semi-double and soon reveal prominent stamens, often half-obscured by a stray curled petal. The flowers make an effective display even when seen from a distance, and their repeat-flowering increases their value as a background shrub for mixed borders. It can also be grown with support as a climber. It is a substantial plant, larger than average for a shrub rose, with an upright habit and a good complement of bronze green foliage. ZONES 4–9.

Thomas, USA, 1926

'Aviateur Blériot' × 'Moonlight'

'BIT O' SPRING'
MODERN, MINIATURE, PINK BLEND, REPEAT-FLOWERING

'Bit O' Spring' has attractive, long, pointed buds which result in medium buff pink blooms with a lighter yellow reverse. The flowers, borne one to a stem, have about 45 petals and usually have a Large-flowered form. They have an interesting color, which holds well if they are given afternoon shade. The bloom cycle is very prolific and the plant repeats well. The plant is upright and clothed with deep green matt foliage and tan prickles. However, this variety is prone to mildew and black spot. ZONES 4–11.

Williams, USA, 1980

'Tom Brown' × 'Golden Angel'

'BIT O' SUNSHINE'
syn. 'Little Bit o' Sunshine'
MODERN, MINIATURE, DEEP YELLOW, REPEAT-FLOWERING

'Bit O' Sunshine' is another classic Miniature from the 1950s from Ralph Moore. The flowers are bright buttercup yellow and have 18–20 petals. They grow on an upright, low, bushy plant to 12–14 in (30–35 cm) tall. Even the buds are attractive before they open up. The plant is strong and healthy. However, it is susceptible to mildew if it is not sprayed for protection. It is a great rose, but has lost popularity in its color class mainly due to the explosion of other yellow Miniatures onto the market. ZONES 4–11.

Moore, USA, 1956

'Copper Glow' × 'Zee'

'Bishop Darlington'

'BLACK BEAUTY'
MODERN, LARGE-FLOWERED/HYBRID TEA, DARK RED, REPEAT-FLOWERING

More than 24 roses have been described as black, although none is truly so, for as far as is known black is not a pigment that exists in the rose family. This one appears black to the eye in the bud stage and opens to a rich crimson-scarlet with the reverse of the petals dark velvety blackish red. The blooms are full of petals that are on the short side, open cupped with rather muddled centers, and have disappointingly little fragrance. They keep blooming well through summer and autumn unless mildew has overtaken them. The plant is an uneven grower, bearing the flowers aloft on long stems, and has adequate mid-green foliage. Although it is not a great garden rose in cool conditions it is useful to have for cutting, because the color is so superb when good blooms come along. ZONES 5–9.

Delbard, France, 1973

('Gloire de Rome' × 'Impeccable') × 'Papa Meilland'

'BLACK BOY'
syn. 'Blackboy'
MODERN, LARGE-FLOWERED CLIMBER, DARK RED

This is a popular climber in Australia where it has been passed around through cuttings for many years. It is not as dark as the name implies, being a rich deep crimson, paler on the petal reverse, and lightening in color as the flowers age. They are carried in clusters that bow under the weight when several open together. They are large and fairly full, sweetly fragrant, and when they open there is an appealing informality about the arrangement of the petals. Since many blooms appear together this is a very effective climbing plant for the garden, best used in places where the vigorous canes can be accommodated such as a

pergola or large fence. After the main burst of summer flowering there is not usually any significant later bloom. The foliage is light olive green. ZONES 5–9.

Clark, Australia, 1919

'Etoile de France' × 'Bardou Job' (or vice versa)

'BLACK GARNET'
MODERN, LARGE-FLOWERED/HYBRID TEA, DARK RED, REPEAT-FLOWERING

The plump oval buds on this variety are very blackish red retaining that color on the backs of the petals which open to reveal a less intense dark red with brick red highlights. The flowers, produced singly or in 3s, are exceedingly full petalled and develop a charming raggedness of form as the petals crowd against each other. They are long lasting but lack the strong scent that one expects in a deep red rose. The flowers are borne through summer and autumn on an upright plant of a little over average height, equipped with rather grayish green leaves. This variety is confined to the US but rates poorly in the American Rose Society's handbook, which reflects the experience of gardeners in that country. The indications are that it suits warmer climates, disliking cool ones. ZONES 5–9.

Weeks, USA, 1980

'Mister Lincoln' × 'Mexicana'

'BLACK ICE'
MODERN, CLUSTER-FLOWERED/FLORIBUNDA, DARK RED, REPEAT-FLOWERING

The buds on this variety are indeed very blackish, and on opening reveal clusters of the darkest scarlet flowers which carry only very slight fragrance. They are full petalled and fairly large for a Cluster-flowered Rose, with many blooms in the truss; the flowers continue through summer and autumn. The growth is below average height, compact and sturdy, with glossy deep green foliage. The name is not intentionally meteorological, but was inspired by the fact that 'Iceberg' is in the parentage. In practice, the dark flowers and dark leaves give the plant a somewhat funereal aspect, especially when touched by mildew, and it is grown more for its curiosity value than for horticultural excellence. ZONES 4–9.

Gandy, UK, 1971

('Iceberg' × 'Europeana') × 'Megiddo'

'BLACK JACK' MINkco
MODERN, MINIATURE, DARK RED, REPEAT-FLOWERING

Very dark red blooms with golden stamens characterize this rose. The

'Bit o' Sunshine'

'Black Jade'

'Black Prince'

beautiful Large-flowered exhibition form is common and it has a petal count of 40+. Bloom production, however, is on the light side. 'Black Jack' is sometimes susceptible to mildew and black spot, as well as some fading in climates with strong sunlight all day long. The petals can burn in hot climates. The plant is a tall, upright bush with small dark green foliage. ZONES 4–11.

Williams, USA, 1983

'Tom Brown' × 'Over the Rainbow'

'BLACK JADE'   BENblack
MODERN, MINIATURE, DARK RED, REPEAT-FLOWERING

This rose is very close in color to black. The vigorous, upright plant supports clusters of 5–10 blooms on very strong, straight stems. The florets have good exhibition form. When the bloom is fully open, it sports very attractive bright golden yellow stamens, which contrast with the very dark red petal color. As a garden variety it has a fairly rapid repeat bloom cycle. So dark is the bloom that some show judges have taken to using a flashlight to shine into the bloom center to properly observe the actual form. The very glossy foliage provides a natural barrier to mildew and other diseases. ZONES 4–11.

Benardella, USA, 1985

'Sheri Anne' × 'Laguna'

American Rose Society Award of Excellence 1985

'BLACK MAGIC'
MODERN, LARGE-FLOWERED CLIMBER, DARK RED

'Black Magic' gets both its beautiful dark red color and its rich damask perfume from its parent 'Guinée'. The flowers are double and occur profusely, but like 'Guinée' the repeat bloom is poor. Growing to 10 ft (3 m) or so, it is a good choice for pillars and tripods; it is also effective when planted near a window where its perfume can be appreciated. The foliage is abundant and the growth disease free. It may be more widely planted if it produced more blooms in summer and autumn. ZONES 4–9.

Hamilton, Australia, 1953

Seedling of 'Guinée'

'BLACK PRINCE'
OLD, HYBRID PERPETUAL, DARK RED, REPEAT-FLOWERING

This rose has full, cupped, dark crimson flowers that appear to be black, especially in the shade. The 5 ft (1.5 m) bush is

'Blanc Double de Coubert'

armed with prickles, and the foliage is sometimes subject to mildew. It responds well to hard pruning. There were once some 3000 Hybrid Perpetuals, many of which disappeared with the introduction of the Large-flowered Roses; Laffay is credited with starting this class of rose as early as 1837. ZONES 5–10.

Paul, UK, 1866

Seedling of 'Pierre Notting'

'BLACK VELVET'
MODERN, LARGE-FLOWERED/HYBRID TEA, DARK RED, REPEAT-FLOWERING

Although it originated in the US, the only country in which this rose currently appears to be offered is Australia, where conditions evidently suit it best. The color is a deep burgundy red with a dark overlay that, when it reflects the light, gives the velvety effect described by the name. It normally bears its flowers one to a stem, and the plump oval buds open into large semi-double blooms that have a pleasing fragrance. They are high centered at first but soon become cupped in form, and repeat their flowering through summer and autumn. The plant grows with reasonable vigor, has an upright habit to average height and is well furnished with leathery, dark green foliage. ZONES 5–9.

Morey, USA, 1960

'New Yorker' × 'Happiness'

'BLAIRII NO. 1'
OLD, HYBRID CHINA, MEDIUM PINK

Blair produced three roses with the same name but different numbers, although the first and the third have always suffered from comparison with No. 2. The large, semi-double, cupped blooms of 'Blairii No. 1' are bright rose, sometimes tinged with red. It has a branching growth and though it is a bit shy, it gives some repeat flowers in late summer. Less hardy than 'Blairii No. 2', it is sometimes called a Bourbon because of its form. It is subject to mildew. ZONES 5–10.

Blair, 1844

Rosa chinensis × a Bourbon rose

'BLAIRII NO. 2'
OLD, HYBRID CHINA, LIGHT PINK

The 2 levels of pink in this flower are dramatic and elegant. The large, flat, globe-shaped blooms, which are pink at the edge and darker in the center, are cupped and full of petals. The luxuriant canes are mahogany in color when

young and have a branching habit. The lax growth can reach 15 ft (4.5 m) but it is easily trained on walls, fences or pergolas. There are horrid prickles. It blooms in early summer but rarely repeats, and requires little pruning. There is probably no rose that has received such universal praise. ZONES 5–10.

Blair, 1845

Rosa chinensis × a Bourbon rose

Royal Horticultural Society Award of Garden Merit 1993

'BLANC DE VIBERT'
syn. 'Blanche de Vibert'
OLD, PORTLAND, WHITE, REPEAT-FLOWERING

This rose would be more popular if its talents were better known. Large, very full, flat blooms open lemon-yellow at first, quickly fading to milky white. The medium-sized, cupped, upright flowers are crested at the center, on strong canes. The downy, light green foliage appears to have a Gallica background. Happier in the shade in rich soil, its 3 ft by 3 ft (1 m by 1 m) size makes it ideal for a container. It hates wet weather to the point where the flowers ball and can rot off, before opening. ZONES 4–10.

Vibert, France, 1847

Parentage unknown

'Black Magic'

'BLANC DOUBLE DE COUBERT'
MODERN, HYBRID RUGOSA, WHITE, REPEAT-FLOWERING

This shrub has such close affinity to Rosa rugosa from the appearance of its foliage, inflorescence and fine prickles that the raiser's claim that 'Sombreuil' was the pollen parent has been doubted, though the plant has a more open aspect than the wild R. rugosa. It bears clusters of large flowers with crumpled petals, the flowers being as white as one can imagine—unless spoiled by rain, for their texture is soft and they mark easily. The semi-double blooms open out flat at different levels on the plant, and diffuse a pervasive scent, detectable even at night. Flowering continues through summer and autumn, and though hips are not normally produced, if they do appear they are orange-scarlet. The foliage is dark, leathery and wrinkled, and the plant grows, usually quite vigorously, to about average height. 'Coubert' in the name refers to the raiser's home village. ZONES 3–9.

Cochet–Cochet, France, 1892

Possibly Rosa rugosa × 'Sombreuil' or R. rugosa alba × R. rugosa alba

Royal Horticultural Society Award of Garden Merit 1993

'Blairii No. 2'

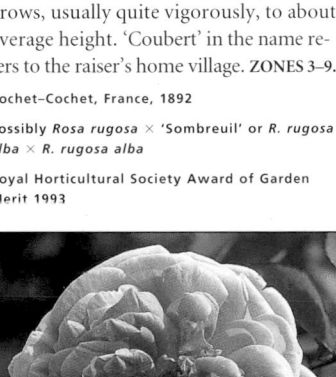

'Black Velvet'

B

'BLANCHE DE BELGIQUE'
syn. 'Blanche Superbe'
OLD, ALBA, WHITE

Often described as having the perfume of a white hyacinth, this rare Alba has double, large, blowzy, fragrant blooms that are borne in clusters of 5 or more. It is temperamental and often a shy bloomer. Similar in many respects to 'Maxima', with abundant loosely packed petals, it flowers in mid-summer only. Its growth is upright usually to 5 ft (1.5 m). The canes are covered with prickles, and the foliage is the standard gray-green for Albas. Although by no means common in today's gardens, it is well worth seeking out from the few specialist nurseries that still offer it. ZONES 4–10.

Vibert, France, 1848

Rosa alba hybrid

'BLANCHE LAFITTE'
syn. 'Mlle Blanche Lafitte'
OLD, BOURBON, WHITE BLEND, REPEAT-FLOWERING

This floriferous rose blooms in clusters and its white petals are tinged with a flesh color. The medium-sized flowers are full. A white Bourbon is rare, and this one is difficult to find today. Pradel, who is famous for his 'Maréchal Niel' (1864), produced 162 hybrids at his nursery in Montauban, France. ZONES 5–10.

Pradel, France, 1851

Parentage unknown

'Blanche Lafitte'

'Blanchefleur'

'BLANCHE MOREAU'
OLD, MOSS, WHITE

Although sired by a Damask rose, little of its influence shows through in the growth habit of this rose. Lovely in bud and surrounded by dark, heavy moss, it is the best white member of the Moss family. The very double, fragrant blooms are pure white with a pink center, and are arranged in clusters. The blooms are surrounded by a sea of dark green leaves, and the canes are bristly on a medium-sized shrub to about 5 ft (1.5 m). It flowers in mid-summer. It hates rain, but needs plenty of water in a warm summer. Unfortunately, when conditions dictate, it can suffer from bouts of mildew. ZONES 5–10.

Moreau-Robert, France, 1880

'Comtesse de Murinais' × 'Perpetual White Moss'

'BLANCHEFLEUR'
OLD, CENTIFOLIA, WHITE

This rose, which is probably related to the Gallicas, is a vigorous shrub of semi-relaxed habit that grows to some 5 ft (1.5 m) high and wide. The arching shoots are thorny but well foliated, with light grayish green leaves. The flowers are grouped in small clusters and open from reddish tinted buds to soft milky white with a distinct but soft blush in the center. Fragrant, fully double and often quartered, the outer petals fold back-

'Blaze'

wards when the flower is fully open to form a sort of ball effect that is most attractive. It flowers in early summer and looks wonderful in a rose border or mixed shrubbery. ZONES 4–10.

Vibert, France, 1835

Parentage unknown

'BLAZE'
MODERN, LARGE-FLOWERED CLIMBER, MEDIUM RED, REPEAT-FLOWERING

'Blaze' is extremely popular in the US, where its cheerful scarlet blooms form sheets of color in summer. They are carried in large clusters on strong stems, and open to fairly full-petalled blooms of neatly cupped form. There are often so many blooms that even though they are not large they become rather crowded and the stems may bow under the weight. There is a pleasant light scent. It is an easy plant to grow where an extensive, pliable, all-purpose climber is required, for it makes vigorous climbing shoots and covers itself with plentiful medium green leaves which are generally very healthy, though when introduced into Britain they proved prone to mildew. Some say 'Blaze' repeats its flowering in the autumn, but it may be that it has been confused with a selected form introduced a few years later. ZONES 4–9.

Kallay, USA, 1932

'Paul's Scarlet Climber' × 'Grüss an Teplitz'

'BLESSINGS'
MODERN, LARGE-FLOWERED/HYBRID TEA, ORANGE-PINK, REPEAT-FLOWERING

This rose bears urn-shaped rosy salmon buds, usually several together, on tall upright stems. They open cupped into quite large blooms of rosy pink, well filled with petals, so that they are able to display the color well. Because so many flowers come out together 'Blessings' makes a fine bedding rose; it is splendid to cut, though disbudding would be necessary if it were grown for that purpose alone. It is hardly ever troubled by wet weather, and flowering continues through summer and autumn. There is a pleasant though not pronounced fragrance. The plant grows taller than average and with an upright habit, and is well clothed in large dark leaves. ZONES 4–9.

Gregory, UK, 1968

'Queen Elizabeth' × seedling

Royal National Rose Society Certificate of Merit 1968, Baden-Baden Gold Medal 1971, Royal Horticultural Society Award of Garden Merit 1993

'Blessings'

'Bloomer Girl'

'Bloomfield Abundance'

'BLEU MAGENTA'
OLD, RAMBLER, MAUVE

Graham Stuart Thomas received this rose from Roseraie de l'Haÿ, the famous garden outside Paris, but has been unable to trace its origin. The blooms, which begin as violet-cerise fading to light violet, are double and occasionally have white streaks but, depending on its placement in sun or shade, the colors may range from deep red, crimson, violet and cerise. The yellow stamens add a touch of drama to this, the largest flower of any purple Rambler. The dainty blossoms are held aloft on thin canes. The foliage is dark and shiny. There are no prickles. ZONES 6–10.

Circa 1900

Parentage unknown

Royal Horticultural Society Award of Garden Merit 1994

'BLIZZARD' JACdrive
MODERN, MINIATURE, WHITE, REPEAT-FLOWERING

This beautiful rose has pure white flowers growing on a low-growing, compact bush. The flowers have 26–40 petals and are complemented by small, dark green, glossy foliage. The overall effect is an abundance of bloom sufficient to cover the entire plant. The clusters last for weeks and the plant is self-cleaning with a repeat cycle of 4–5 weeks. It is one of the few Miniatures hybridized by the late Bill Warriner who gave the world so many great Cluster-flowered roses while at Jackson & Perkins. ZONES 4–11.

Warriner, USA, 1991

'Petticoat' × 'Orange Honey'

'BLOOMER GIRL' TINgirl
MODERN, MINIATURE, ORANGE-PINK, REPEAT-FLOWERING

This rose has soft vermilion to medium pink blooms, grown one to a stem, on a bushy upright plant. The blooms have about 35 petals, open quickly, and have a slight fragrance. Occasionally the florets have exhibition form. This is a creation from one of the few Australian women rose hybridizers. Her experiments using the Large-flowered, 'Futura', as the seed parent really paid off, yielding many prize-winning varieties. ZONES 4–11.

Bennett, USA, 1983

'Futura' × 'Pink Petticoat'

'BLOOMFIELD ABUNDANCE'
syn. 'Spray Cécile Brünner'
MODERN, POLYANTHA, LIGHT PINK,
REPEAT-FLOWERING

The unmistakable features of this rose are the long, whiskery calyx lobes that hang down beneath the small light pink blooms. Apart from the sepals, the flowers resemble 'Cécile Brünner', having tiny urn-shaped buds that open into double pink rosettes. They are produced through summer and autumn and have a light scent. The plant grows upright, tall and arching, with thin brownish stems and small, shiny, sparse foliage that gives it a rather spindly aspect. With this rose no one is sure whether it is correctly named or whether another rose, 'Spray Cécile Brünner' from 1941 (which was a sport of 'Cécile Brünner') has usurped its place. **'White Bloomfield Abundance'** is a white sport. ZONES 4–9.

Thomas, USA, 1920

'Sylvia' × 'Dorothy Page-Roberts' or sport of 'Cécile Brünner'

'BLOOMFIELD COURAGE'
OLD, RAMBLER, RED BLEND

Of the 41 Bloomfield roses that were created by Captain George C. Thomas, this is one of 3 still popular with gardeners. He named them after his estate in Bloomfield, Pennsylvania. Small, single, dark velvety-red blossoms with white centers and prominent stamens completely hide the foliage. The open clusters hold 20 or more blooms at one time, but the color is rather hard and does not mix easily with others. The canes are easy to train and hold only a few prickles. It needs lots of room. There is some reflowering in autumn, and scarlet hips extend its season. It can climb a tree or cover an arch and blooms on old wood. ZONES 5–11.

Thomas, USA, 1925

Rosa wichuraiana × 'Crimson Rambler'

'Bloomfield Dainty'

'Bloomin' Easy'

'BLOOMFIELD DAINTY'
MODERN, MODERN SHRUB, MEDIUM YELLOW

Pointed orange buds on 'Bloomfield Dainty' open into pretty 5-petalled, saucer-shaped flowers of a fairly bright yellow, which soon turn light yellow and admit flushes of pink towards the petal tips as they age. There is a pleasant musky fragrance, and some repetition of bloom through summer and autumn. The variety is well named, since its flowers are indeed dainty, but they seem rather incongruous perched on the rugged canes that support them because the habit of the plant is to grow wide and tall, making a large, rather untidy shrub. It is well furnished with deep green glossy leaves and can, thanks to its flexible arching stems, be trained as a climber on a short fence or pillar. It seems happiest in a warm climate. ZONES 5–9.

Thomas, USA, 1924

'Danaë' × 'Madame Edouard Herriot'

'BLOOMIN' EASY'   AROtrusim
syn. 'Blooming Easy'
MODERN, MODERN SHRUB, MEDIUM RED,
REPEAT-FLOWERING

The buds on this variety open to cup-shaped flowers with about 24 petals in a clear bright red color. The flowers are of medium size, usually borne one to a stem, have a light fragrance, and repeat-flower through summer and autumn. The plant is of average growth for a shrub rose, with an upright, bushy habit, and it is well furnished with large, glossy mid-green foliage. Bright orange red hips appear in autumn. The name of this rose indicates the purpose for which it was recommended by the breeder, that is, for being grown in parks or by gardeners

'Bloomfield Courage'

who want a plant that is healthy, easy to grow, and can suffer a certain amount of neglect, including possible maltreatment at pruning time. It is more of a utilitarian rose than one that scores for its beauty, and its American Rose Society rating has remained low. ZONES 4–9.

Christensen, USA, 1988

'Trumpeter' × 'Simplicity'

'BLOSSOMTIME'
MODERN, LARGE-FLOWERED CLIMBER,
MEDIUM PINK, REPEAT-FLOWERING

The flowers of this rose are a little over middling size and very full of petals, and they combine two shades of china pink. The pretty oval buds are deep pink, and as they open they reveal the paler pink of the inner petal surfaces. They are high centered and fragrant, and are produced in well-spaced clusters of flowers with good continuity through summer and autumn. It can be grown short or tall depending on what is required and it can be kept as a pillar rose grown on to the average dimensions of a climbing rose or allowed to go higher and wider. In other words it is very adaptable, and will respond to whatever pruning and training it receives and always provide a satisfactory background of glossy, bronze green leaves. ZONES 4–9.

O'Neal, USA, 1951

'New Dawn' × seedling

'Blue Bajou'

'Blossomtime'

'BLUE BAJOU'   KORkultop
syns 'Blue Bayou', 'Blue-Bijou'
MODERN, CLUSTER-FLOWERED/FLORIBUNDA,
MAUVE BLEND, REPEAT-FLOWERING

There have been many roses incorporating the word 'blue' but so far no truly blue one has been developed, though geneticists are hoping to introduce delphinidin—the necessary pigment—into a rose from another flower, perhaps a petunia. Meanwhile, the rose world must make the best of the mauves and lilacs that come nearest to blue, some of which, in warm climates or under glass, can look close to the real thing. The Kordes firm has produced several, including this recent scented Cluster-flowered Rose, which produces very full silvery lilac flowers of rounded form. The petals are short, and as the outer ones reflex, those in the middle hold a tight center for some time before opening cupped. The pretty color contrasts beautifully with the glossy, dark green leaves, and the variety is very good for bedding and cutting and to grow in a container. 'Blue Bajou' continues to bear flowers, sometimes singly, sometimes in a spray, throughout summer and autumn on a neat, vigorous plant of below average height. ZONES 4–9.

Kordes, Germany, 1993

Parentage unknown

'Climbing Blue Moon'

'Blue Diamond'

'BLUE BOY'
MODERN, MODERN SHRUB, MAUVE

'Blue Boy' is a deep purple or violet, certainly funereal in tone. It bears double flowers of medium to large size, which open with high centers before losing their shape in a muddle of petals. They have good fragrance and appear in summer. The plant is vigorous, and grows to average height with an upright but untidy habit. The leaves are rather pale, semi-glossy and liable at times to mildew. This rose, despite the defects, is very interesting, because to obtain it the raiser crossed a bright pink Moss Rose of 1877 with his own brash vermilion 'Independence' of 1951, with this extra-ordinary result. 'Blue Boy' was, in fact, initially classified as a Moss Rose, and is grown more for curiosity and botanical interest than for its beauty. ZONES 4–9.
Kordes, Germany, 1958
'Louis Gimard' × 'Independence'

'BLUE DIAMOND'
MODERN, LARGE-FLOWERED/HYBRID TEA, MAUVE, REPEAT-FLOWERING

Early in the season this variety behaves like a Large-flowered Rose, bearing size-able flowers one to a stem, but the later blooms are produced in large trusses. They are a pretty shade of lavender mauve, full-petalled and of regular cupped form. They last well during the first inflorescence, but when the smaller blooms appear they are apt to open rather fast. There is little scent. The plant grows to below average height and has a bushy branching habit, purplish stems and dark bronzy foliage, which may need protection against black spot. This rose is useful as an occasional source of cut blooms and a curiosity. ZONES 4–9.
Lens, Belgium, 1963
'Purpurine' × ('Purpurine' × 'Royal Tan')

'BLUE MOON'   TANnacht
syns 'Blue Monday', 'Mainzer Fastnacht', 'Sissi'
MODERN, LARGE-FLOWERED/HYBRID TEA, MAUVE, REPEAT-FLOWERING

This is deservedly the most commercially successful of the 'blue' roses, being very

'Blue Boy'

'Blue Nile'

close to the blue side of lavender. The flowers are large and full-petalled, with high centers and good symmetry of form, and they last well, finally opening cupped to show the stamens. Usually there is one flower on the long stems, which makes them excellent for cutting. They are sweetly fragrant, and are produced through summer and autumn. The plant grows vigorously but it is somewhat splayed and reluctant to make new wood, and has a rather sparse cover of deep green foliage. Generally the plant is healthy and can overcome occasional mildew and black spot, but it is liable to die back in hard winters. 'Mainzer Fastnacht' refers to the Shrove Tuesday festival in the city of Mainz. Herr Tantau was persuaded to change the name to 'Sissi' as it was easier for non-Germans to pronounce, although 'sissy' means a

weakling in English, so a third alternative had to be found. **'Climbing Blue Moon'** (syn. 'Sissi, Climbing'; Mungia, USA, 1981) grows strongly to above average height. The most suitable site is a shel-tered high wall or fence. It also requires a fair amount of sunshine for good flower production; a warm climate suits it best. ZONES 4–9.
Tantau, Germany, 1965
Seedling × 'Sterling Silver'
Anerkannte Deutsche Rose 1964, Rome Gold Medal 1964, National Rose Society Certificate of Merit 1964

'BLUE NILE'   DELnible
syn. 'Nil Bleu'
MODERN, LARGE-FLOWERED/HYBRID TEA, MAUVE, REPEAT-FLOWERING

This is a substantial flower, thanks to its large broad petals. The plump pointed buds are usually produced singly, some-times 2 or 3 together, and they open on long stems into full-petalled blooms that can be good enough for exhibition. A faint magenta flush with delicate veining enlivens the lavender blue color. The flowers are strongly fragrant and good to cut, and repeat through summer and autumn. It is very vigorous with an up-right, spreading habit, grows to above average height and is well furnished with large olive green leaves. It prefers warmer climates. ZONES 4–9.
Delbard, France, 1976
('Holstein' × 'Bayadère') × ('Prelude' × 'Saint-Exupery')
Bagatelle Gold Medal

'BLUE PARFUM'   TANfifum,
TANfifume, TANtifum
syns 'Blue Perfume', 'Violette Parfum'
MODERN, LARGE-FLOWERED/HYBRID TEA, MAUVE, REPEAT-FLOWERING

The parentage of this rose is not dis-closed, as is usual with Tantau Roses, but it doubtless follows the line he used to obtain 'Blue Moon'. This is shorter and more compact in growth, leafier and not as vigorous. The flowers are quite large, full petalled and beautifully formed, in a

'Blue Moon'

B

'Blumenwunder'

'Bluesette'

color that varies subtly through the season, encompassing lilac, mauve, pale violet and blush. It is among the earliest of the Large-flowered Roses to come into bloom, and after a good initial display more blooms are produced through summer and autumn. They have an excellent fragrance and are good to cut. The plant grows to below average height with a neat, bushy upright habit and glossy dark green foliage. ZONES 4–9.

Tantau, Germany, 1978

Parentage unknown

'BLUE PETER' RUIblun
syns 'Azulabria', 'Bluenette'
MODERN, MINIATURE, MAUVE BLEND, REPEAT-FLOWERING

Deep lilac-purple blooms with contrasting yellow stamens make this rose a real talking point in the garden, as it is the bluest Miniature Rose yet. The flowers have about 20 petals and last for weeks on the bush. It is treasured by floral arrangers who love the color combination and the light green, semi-glossy foliage. The bush is compact and grows to 12–20 in (30–50 cm) high. ZONES 5–11.

de Ruiter, The Netherlands, 1983

'Little Flirt' × seedling

'BLUE RIVER' KORsicht
MODERN, LARGE-FLOWERED/HYBRID TEA, MAUVE BLEND, REPEAT-FLOWERING

This rose is another of those varieties that appear uncertain whether to

behave as Large-flowered or Cluster-flowered Roses, for the stems often carry several blooms. The rounded buds open to lovely lilac flowers that are randomly splashed with deep magenta-pink, especially towards the edges of the petals, providing, for a rose in this spectrum, an unusually strong color effect. The blooms are very fragrant, full of petals and last well when cut, and if the flowering shoots are disbudded early enough they are capable of producing quality exhibition blooms. The flowers continue to appear through summer to autumn on a vigorous and upright plant of average size and with dense dark green foliage. 'Blue River' does best in warmer climates. ZONES 5–9.

Kordes, Germany, 1984

'Blue Moon' × 'Zorina'

Baden-Baden Gold Medal

'BLUEBERRY HILL' WEKcryplag
MODERN, CLUSTER-FLOWERED/FLORIBUNDA, MAUVE

It is not just the color that will steal your heart—this lovely lilac rose also has a sweet apple fragrance. The blooms are large and semi-double and they smother the clean glossy foliage, much like an azalea bush in spring! 'Blueberry Hill' makes a medium sized rounded bush that stands 4 ft (1.2 m). ZONES 5–9.

'BLUESETTE' LENmau
MODERN, CLUSTER-FLOWERED/FLORIBUNDA, MAUVE, REPEAT-FLOWERING

This rose has an unusual character, bearing small flowers with up to 50 petals in clusters that may have as few as 3 or as many as 18 little flowers. They are lilac, and when they are fully open the petals lie almost flat, giving an appealing effect rather as if one were looking at an aster. There is a light fragrance, and the plant continues to produce flowers through summer and autumn. This is a useful rose to cut for small flower arrangements. It grows considerably below average height and has a bushy, upright habit

'Blue Peter'

and dark prickles and foliage. Like all the so-called 'blue' roses, 'Bluesette' tends to photograph pink. ZONES 4–9.

Lens, Belgium, 1984

'Little Angel' × ('Westmauve' × 'Blue Diamond')

'BLUMENSCHMIDT'
OLD, TEA, YELLOW BLEND, REPEAT-FLOWERING

Once popular, this rose is now rather hard to find. It is a somewhat tender Tea and prefers a warm situation in the sun. Primrose-yellow centers are surrounded by rose pink outer petals on blooms that are very large and full and have green centers. It is a low, compact bush with glossy, healthy foliage, and is quite disease resistant. ZONES 7–10.

Schmidt, Germany, 1906

Sport of 'Mlle Franziska Kruger'

'BLUMENWUNDER'
MODERN, MODERN SHRUB, DEEP PINK, REPEAT-FLOWERING

The loosely semi-double flowers (20–24 petals) of this rose are a glowing deep carmine-pink. The blooms are 3 in (8 cm) across and are borne in small to large clusters on a very bushy plant. There is a good repeat-flowering after a very plentiful spring flush. There is no fragrance. This strong growing, disease-resistant plant would make an ideal informal hedge in a large country garden. ZONES 4–9.

Kordes, Germany, 1994

Parentage unknown

'BLUSH BOURSAULT'
syns 'Calypso', 'Florida', 'Rose de l'Isle'
OLD, BOURSAULT, PINK BLEND

The very double, globular blooms of this rose are blush with a deep flesh center. They have a pendulous habit, hanging down over long, arching canes that have almost no prickles. The blowzy blooms, which tend to ball in damp weather, make attractive cut flowers. The dark green, oval leaves are serrated at the tips. This rose is best on a wall or fence, where it can be easily trained. French botanist Henri Boursault created many hybrid climbers from 1817 onwards. ZONES 5–11.

Pre-1838

Perhaps a China Rose × *Rosa pendulina* or *R. blanda*

'Blue River'

'BLUSH DAMASK'
syn. 'Blush Gallica'
OLD, DAMASK, LIGHT PINK

This is a dense broad twiggy shrub to 6 ft (1.8 m) that clearly has a Gallica influence. The stems are grayish green and moderately armed with short thorns; the foliage is dark green and plentiful. The flowers, which are produced in great numbers all over the bush in early summer, are fragrant and full and cushion-like, and when fully open attain a size of about 2 in (5 cm) across. The center of each bloom is mauve-pink and the outer petals are milky white, creating a very pretty effect. 'Blush Damask' is an easy-to-grow shrub that needs space to develop, but it will tolerate even the most dry and impoverished soil. ZONES 5–11.

Parentage unknown

'BLUSH HIP'
OLD, ALBA, LIGHT PINK

For many rosarians, this is the best of the Alba class. Classic in form and highly fragrant, 'Blush Hip' looks a great deal like 'Maiden's Blush' but it is taller. The bright red buds open to double blooms of soft pink with a button center and a green eye. This variety flowers early and there is no rebloom. The foliage is coarse with toothed leaves. ZONES 5–11.

Pre-1846

Parentage unknown

'Blush Damask'

'BLUSH NOISETTE'
OLD, NOISETTE, WHITE, REPEAT-FLOWERING

This was the first Noisette to be sold to the public and it is still highly regarded by rose gardeners; one of the American Noisettes, it started its life in South Carolina. Loosely double, perfectly formed blush-pink blooms open from dark pink buds. The dainty petals are supported on glossy, green foliage and have a perfume that many declare is strongly clove-like. It is often seen on pillars or as a hedge. The rose, which is vigorous and healthy and continues to bloom into autumn, does not mind light shade. Redouté has portrayed it as *Rosa noisettiana*. ZONES 7–10.

Noisette, USA, circa 1814

Seedling of 'Champney's Pink Cluster'

'BLUSH RAMBLER'
MODERN, RAMBLER, LIGHT PINK

This vigorous Rambler is often found in old cottage gardens. It is an almost thornless bush and has light green leaves. It has small cupped flowers which are light pink, and are borne in clusters. They have a very light scent, a trait derived from 'The Garland', a very early Musk/Multiflora cross. The other parent, nicknamed 'The Engineer' from the occupation of Albert Smith who found it in Japan and sent it to Turner of Edinburgh (the introducer), was very famous and set the trend for ramblers at the close of the nineteenth century.

'Blush Noisette'

'Bob Woolley'

Unfortunately, it suffered from mildew and was overtaken by the many other varieties which followed. ZONES 4–9.

Cant, UK, 1903

'Crimson Rambler' × 'The Garland'

'BLUSHING LUCY'
MODERN, LARGE-FLOWERED CLIMBER, LIGHT PINK, REPEAT-FLOWERING

This rose is cultivated now only in the UK and New Zealand, and might have become better known had its introduction not coincided with the beginning of World War II. It produces graceful stems bearing large clusters of pretty light pink flowers that are semi-double, with white at the base of the petals and a pleasant fragrance. 'Blushing Lucy' is rather late coming into bloom and, after an initial good display, it continues, unusually for a rambler, to produce more flower sporadically until autumn. The character of the plant suggests *Rosa wichuraiana* ancestry, for it is vigorous, has glossy foliage and will grow to a height slightly more than average. It does best in a sunny aspect, not, as did Wordsworth's original blushing Lucy, as 'A violet by a mossy stone Half hidden from the eye!' ZONES 4–9.

Williams, UK, 1938

Parentage unknown

'BOB HOPE'
MODERN, LARGE-FLOWERED/HYBRID TEA, MEDIUM RED, REPEAT-FLOWERING

The flowers on 'Bob Hope' open from urn-shaped buds into high-centered flowers, with a sufficiency of wide petals to create a large bloom but not enough to make it last for use as an exhibition rose. A bright cherry red, the flowers carry a mild fragrance and continue to appear through summer and autumn, although the mid-season blooms are often small and ragged. The plant grows upright, a little taller than average, and has dark green leathery leaves. Bob Hope was born in England in 1903, though long resident in the US. In 1998 he received a knighthood in the Queen's New Year's Honours list. ZONES 4–9.

Kordes, Germany, 1966

'Friedrich Schwartz' × 'Kordes' Perfecta'

'BOB WOOLLEY'
MODERN, LARGE-FLOWERED/HYBRID TEA, APRICOT BLEND, REPEAT-FLOWERING

As an exhibition rose this has been popular for many years, thanks to the holding qualities and size of its high-centered

'Blush Rambler'

'Blush Rambler'

flowers. There may be as many as 60 broad petals, which open to reveal peach-pink on the inner surfaces, the reverse being lemon yellow. There is a slight fragrance and flowering continues through summer and autumn, though with blooms this size the freedom with which the plant can produce them is limited. The foliage is matt green. The rose bears the name of a keen rosarian from the north of England; however his rose, because of its size, fares better in a climate less affected by rain. ZONES 4–9.

Sanday, UK, 1970

'Gavotte' × 'Spek's Yellow'

'BOBBIE JAMES'
MODERN, RAMBLER, WHITE

This rose has semi-double, small, slightly cupped blooms with creamy white petals and brilliant yellow stamens. The large clusters are borne on long, thin, attractive canes with troublesome prickles and full of glossy leaves with coppery edges. Because of its rampant growth, this rose needs plenty of room and a strong support, such as a tree. Although it blooms only in summer, it is a memorable event when the large clusters open and the extremely fragrant perfume permeates the garden. 'Bobbie James' was introduced by Graham Stuart Thomas, who named it in honor of a renowned Yorkshire horticulturist, 'one of the grand old men of gardening'. Its popularity has not flagged since its introduction. ZONES 5–10.

Sunningdale Nurseries, UK, 1960

Parentage unknown

Royal Horticultural Society Award of Garden Merit 1993

'Bob Hope'

'BOBBY CHARLTON'
MODERN, LARGE-FLOWERED/HYBRID TEA,
PINK BLEND, REPEAT-FLOWERING

This is among the best roses for exhibition, thanks to its very large full-petalled flowers which are borne singly on long stems. They open deep pink and have a silvery reverse to the petal but rain can spoil them, and exhibitors in damp climates have learned to protect their potential prize-winners. In warmer climates it ought to make a more acceptable garden rose, but because so much effort goes into producing each flower, blooms in late summer and autumn are not plentiful. There is a pronounced spicy fragrance. The plant grows to above average height, making an upright, rather leggy bush with dark leathery foliage. It is named for the soccer maestro who was capped for England 106 times. ZONES 4–9.

Fryer, UK, 1974

'Royal Highness' × 'Prima Ballerina'

Baden-Baden Gold Medal 1976, Portland Gold Medal 1980

'BOBBY DAZZLER'
syn. 'Rosella'

MODERN, CLUSTER-FLOWERED/FLORIBUNDA,
APRICOT BLEND, REPEAT-FLOWERING

'Bobby Dazzler' is a free-flowering rose that opens apricot and becomes flushed with orange-pink. It is full petalled, and as the plump buds open a few outer petals reflex while the center ones hold firm, making this a pretty rose to cut for small arrangements. The medium-sized flowers are carried sometimes singly, sometimes in clusters, and repeat their flower well throughout summer and autumn. They have a light fragrance. The plant grows to average height with a bushy, rather spreading habit, and is furnished with matt green foliage that is sometimes touched by seasonal mildew. Although raised in England, this rose has never been grown there commercially; the name 'Bobby Dazzler' commemorates a

'Bobby Dazzler'

'Bon Silène'

favorite dog owned by Alan Mason, the raiser's agent in New Zealand. ZONES 4–9.

Harkness, UK, 1973

('Vera Dalton' × 'Highlight') × ('Ann Elizabeth' × 'Circus')

New Zealand Certificate of Merit 1974

'BON SILÈNE'
OLD, TEA, DEEP PINK, REPEAT FLOWERING

This elegant rose has well-formed buds and deep rose, double blooms that are carmine-pink on the reverse of the petals. A cup shape is maintained by the stiff, upright petals. A strong tea-fruit perfume and elongated, leathery leaves complement this rampant grower. Its hardy growth will reach 5 ft (1.5 m). It has a few prickles and large hips, while the cut flowers are long lasting.

'Bonfire'

Slow to establish itself and much underrated, 'Bon Silène' likes a sunny, warm position and has been found in many southern US cemeteries, disease free and surviving neglect for over 100 years. The breeder, Alexandre Hardy, was the chief horticulturalist of the Luxembourg Palace in Paris. ZONES 5–10.

Hardy, France, pre-1837

Parentage unknown

'BON SILÈNE BLANC'
syn. 'White Bon Silène'
OLD, TEA, LIGHT YELLOW, REPEAT-FLOWERING

'Bon Silène Blanc' is no longer in commerce but can be found in only a few botanical gardens. It is a white form of 'Bon Silène' and has large, pale yellow blooms that fade to white. ZONES 5–10.

Morat, France, 1885

Parentage unknown

'BONFIRE'
MODERN, RAMBLER, MEDIUM RED

Brilliant red, double, cluster-flowered blooms of 20–25 crowd the long canes of this attractive rose. It was claimed at the

'Bobbie James'

time of its introduction that it was free from mildew, which had plagued many popular Ramblers, but it is rather rare and quite difficult to find today. ZONES 5–10.

Turbat, France, 1928

'Crimson Rambler' × Rosa wichuraiana

'Bobby Charlton'

B

'Bonfire Night'

'Bonnie Hamilton'

'BONFIRE NIGHT'

syn. 'Bonfire'

MODERN, CLUSTER-FLOWERED/FLORIBUNDA,
RED BLEND, REPEAT-FLOWERING

A bed of this rose at the height of summer provides a wonderful sight with the large semi-double flowers opening cupped to reveal a vivid blend of yellow with scarlet overlays. They are produced in well-spaced clusters that display the colors to great effect, especially when they are seen against a background of abundant dark foliage. There is a pleasant light fragrance, and the flowers continue to appear through summer and autumn come rain or shine, their prettily waved petals evoking a sense of warmth and well-being. The plant is vigorous and upright, growing fairly evenly to average height. Friends questioned the raiser's judgment in associating a rose with a bonfire, but the connection comes from the Bonfire Night celebrations in the UK on 5 November, the day King and Parliament were saved from being blown up in 1605. ZONES 4–9.

McGredy, UK, 1971

'Tiki' × 'Variety Club'

Royal National Rose Society Trial Ground
Certificate 1969

'BONICA'   MEIdomonac

syns 'Bonica 82', 'Demon', 'Bonica
Meidiland'

MODERN, MODERN SHRUB, MEDIUM PINK,
REPEAT-FLOWERING

Every garden should have this delightful rose. It bears sprays of clear rose pink flowers at different levels on a neat, spreading plant of modest size, covered in abundant rich green foliage that is attractive even before flowering starts. Once it does start, there is hardly any time when the plant is out of bloom until the winter frosts. The flowers are full of small petals and are cupped in form, and they have a light scent. For a specimen plant or a group, or to form a low mounded hedge, 'Bonica' is a lovely rose to have and a good one to recommend to people who say they 'can't grow roses', for its constitution and health are excellent. The name 'Bonica 82' is given to distinguish it from an earlier 'Bonica' from the same raiser. ZONES 4–9.

Meilland, France, 1981

Possibly (*Rosa sempervirens* × 'Mlle Marthe
Carron') × 'Picasso'

Anerkannte Deutsche Rose 1983, Belfast
Certificate of Merit 1983, All-America Rose
Selection 1987, Royal Horticultural Society
Award of Garden Merit 1993

'BONN'

MODERN, MODERN SHRUB, ORANGE-RED,
REPEAT-FLOWERING

The vigor, freedom of flower and health of 'Bonn' explain why it is so valuable for use in parks, although gardeners may feel these qualities do not compensate for its charmlessness. It has light to moderate scent and orange-scarlet flowers of good size, in clusters of up to 10, held aloft on strong stems. The flowers are semi-double, loosely formed and age to a pinky magenta. In growth the plant extends taller and wider than an average shrub rose, with light green glossy foliage. It is repeat-flowering, and when it was introduced half a century ago it was welcomed for this and its other good points. Choice has widened immensely since those days, and tastes in roses have changed. One rosarian summed up 'Bonn' by saying 'Rather crude for my taste, but at least you can see it.' It was named for the administrative capital of the German Federal Republic. ZONES 4–9.

Kordes, Germany, 1950

'Hamburg' × 'Independence'

Royal National Rose Society Certificate of Merit
1950

'BONNIE HAMILTON'

MODERN, CLUSTER-FLOWERED/FLORIBUNDA,
ORANGE-RED, REPEAT-FLOWERING

This well-behaved rose has no particular quality to differentiate it from others of similar character, which may explain why it has never been widely grown. It is vermilion in a kindly, not brash, shade, and it bears clusters of medium-sized double blooms that are beautifully neat in form, have high centers, and are maintained while the outer petals reflex, making it a superb rose for buttonholes. As a garden variety it is good in a bed, being free flowering, and it has a light fragrance. Blooming continues through summer and autumn on plants that are below average height with a bushy habit and dark green foliage. 'Bonnie Hamilton' was named for the historic town in Strathclyde, Scotland. ZONES 4–9.

Cocker, UK, 1976

'Anne Cocker' × 'Allgold'

'BONNY'

MODERN, MINIATURE, MEDIUM PINK,
REPEAT-FLOWERING

The small flowers of 'Bonny' are a deep pink with a lighter reverse, and the form of the florets is double (20+ petals) with globular form. There are abundant

blooms during the summer months with the plant producing small, long-lasting flowers similar to 'Dwarf King'. It has a dwarf stature with equally small, wrinkled foliage. The blooms have a light fragrance. ZONES 5–11.

Kordes, Germany, 1974

'Zorina' × seedling

'BONSOIR'   DICbo

MODERN, LARGE-FLOWERED/HYBRID TEA,
MEDIUM PINK, REPEAT-FLOWERING

For a perfect Large-flowered Rose, balanced for symmetry and size and with the petals furling away from a beautifully formed high center, 'Bonsoir' admirably suits the role—always provided that the weather is fine and warm. In these conditions the broad petals of light pink and peach-pink can function, and if they operate in time for a flower show, the other exhibitors will know they have a fight on their hands. For this rose to be introduced by a breeder from Northern Ireland, where rain often causes it to ball into a brown mess, was an act of faith. The faith was justified, for the continuing pleasure 'Bonsoir' gives in drier seasons and in warmer climates. It has a pleasant fragrance, is repeat-flowering, and grows to average height, with large dark leaves. ZONES 5–9.

Dickson, UK, 1968

Parentage unknown

Royal National Rose Society Certificate of Merit
1966

'BORDER KING'

syn. 'Roi des Bordures'

MODERN, CLUSTER-FLOWERED/FLORIBUNDA,
MEDIUM RED, REPEAT-FLOWERING

This is sometimes listed in reference books as a Polyantha but it really belongs with the Cluster-flowered Roses. The color is a brilliant strawberry red which is well displayed in large clusters of small

'Bonsoir'

'Bonica'

'Bonn'

'Borderer'

'Born Free'

semi-double flowers that appear freely through summer and autumn. There is very little fragrance. The growth is vigorous and the habit of the plant neat and bushy, to below average height, with a good covering of dark green glossy foliage which is usually healthy. Thanks to its good qualities it has been widely and effectively used as a bedding rose, though it appears not to be in commerce at the present time. ZONES 4–9.

de Ruiter, The Netherlands, 1952

Parentage unknown

'BORDER QUEEN'

syn. 'Reine des Bordures'

MODERN, CLUSTER-FLOWERED/FLORIBUNDA, ORANGE-PINK, REPEAT-FLOWERING

The flowers of 'Border Queen' are salmon-red with a shade of orange, which was considered a remarkable color at the time of introduction because it was different from that of any other Cluster-flowered Rose. Opening from small plump buds, they are carried very freely in large even trusses. The petals number just a few more than those of a true single rose, and as they reflex they reveal a light eye at the base and become slightly waved. The open flowers which are cup-shaped and show red-gold stamens in the center are only faintly scented but they appear freely through summer and autumn. A very popular bedding variety, its growth habit is strong and upright and, apart from being

troubled by seasonal mildew, the dark foliage has a good health record. ZONES 4–9.

de Ruiter, The Netherlands, 1951

Parentage unknown

Royal National Rose Society Gold Medal 1950

'BORDERER'

MODERN, POLYANTHA, PINK BLEND, REPEAT-FLOWERING

This was one of Alister Clark's earliest releases. The lightly formed flowers are cupped, and open to reveal attractive stamens among the mid-pink petals. The blooms continue throughout the season and it is rarely without flowers. The growth is small and thin, creating a tightly growing bush that makes a good hedge plant. It is also ideal for informal

edging of a rose bed. Clark's aim when breeding was to produce plants which were healthy and strong and that flowered continuously throughout the year in warmer climates. 'Borderer' was a pioneer in this style. ZONES 5–9.

Clark, Australia, 1918

'Jersey Beauty' × seedling

'BORDURE ROSE'   DELbara

syns 'Roslyne', 'Strawberry Ice'

MODERN, CLUSTER-FLOWERED/FLORIBUNDA, PINK BLEND, REPEAT-FLOWERING

The beauty of this rose lies in its unusual coloring, for its creamy petals are rimmed with pink as if dipped in strawberry juice, though they tend to lose their brilliance in cool wet conditions. Each well-spaced cluster holds many large blooms, fairly full of petals and opening cupped. They lack scent, but make an attractive sight in the garden and can be cut for exhibition despite the short flowering stems. It blooms continually through summer and autumn on a compact plant to average height with dense leathery dark green leaves; it has a good health record. This rose has been credited to Bees of England as well

'Border King'

as to Delbard, Bees introducing it in 1975 as 'Strawberry Ice' and Delbard in 1986 as 'Bordure Rose'. The award, recorded at the time, of a Gold Medal in Madrid in 1974 to 'Bordure Rose' raised by Mme Marie Delbard puts the issue of the raiser beyond doubt. ZONES 4–9.

Delbard, France, 1975

(['Goldilocks' × 'Virgo'] × ['Orange Triumph' × 'Yvonne Rabier']) × 'Fashion'

Baden-Baden Gold Medal 1973, Madrid Gold Medal 1974

'BORN FREE'

MODERN, MINIATURE, ORANGE-RED, REPEAT-FLOWERING

This rose has long pointed buds which cover the upright bushy plant and result in a massive display of brilliant orange-red, small double florets (20 petals). The foliage is dark green. The bloom repeats quickly, making it an ideal candidate for garden display. Contrasting yellow stamens stay fresh for weeks giving the variety an added visual bonus. This rose requires winter protection as it is sensitive to frost and snow. ZONES 5–11.

Moore, USA, 1978

'Red Pinocchio' × 'Little Chief'

'Border Queen'

'Bordure Rose'

'BOTANICA' TOMboy

MODERN, CLUSTER-FLOWERED/FLORIBUNDA,
LIGHT PINK, REPEAT-FLOWERING

'Botanica' has beautiful pink flowers
with just a touch of lilac. These are borne
in large clusters and have a delicious
fruity perfume. What sets this glorious
rose apart from the other Cluster-
flowered Roses is its ability to produce
blooms in profusion. The foliage is
healthy, matt and medium green on an
extremely vigorous, disease-resistant
bush with a slightly spreading habit. It
can reach between 3–4 ft (1–1.2 m) high

and about 3 ft (1 m) wide. The breeder,
George Thomson of Mount Barker in
South Australia, had long felt that the
flower size of many modern Cluster-
flowered Roses is too big, and he attempted various crosses to reduce the
size of the blooms. With this cross, his
dreams were realized, and 'Botanica' was
born. It was named for the successful
plant book *Botanica* which was published in 1997. This book is a companion volume to *Botanica*. **ZONES 5–9.**
Thomson, Australia

'Avandel' × 'Madam President'

'Bougainville'

'Botanica'

'BOTZARIS'

OLD, DAMASK, NEAR WHITE

This rose is not given the attention it
deserves, despite being a reliable,
versatile grower and is glorious at its
best. The creamy white, double, flat,
quartered blossoms emerge from pinkish
buds with long foliated sepals; these are
usually arranged in clusters and are
richly perfumed. The muddled petals
surround a button eye. It blooms only in
summer; its foliage is dark green and it
has prickles. A short, compact shrub to
about 4 ft (1.2 m), it makes an effective
hedge or an ornament in the wild
garden. This is a rose that rewards a
little extra loving care with much satis-
faction, especially in fine weather. Its
only flaw is that like many white double
roses 'Botzaris' dislikes too much rain.
ZONES 5–10.
Introduced by Robert, 1856

Parentage unknown

'BOUGAINVILLE'

OLD, NOISETTE, PINK BLEND

Like so many Noisettes, this vigorous
rose looks best on structures in open
ground. The red buds open to reveal
pink flowers tinged with lilac at the edge,
and turning pale with age. The very
double, cupped blossoms are medium in
size, while the narrow foliage is shiny
with a lacy appearance. It was named for
Admiral Bougainville (1729–1811), who
is also memorialized by the island in the
Solomons and the popular, tropical vine.
ZONES 7–11.
Cochet, France, 1822

Parentage unknown

'Boule de Neige'

'BOULE DE NEIGE'

syn. 'Snowball'

OLD, BOURBON, WHITE, REPEAT-FLOWERING

The opening buds of this rose are striped
with pink, and illustrate why old roses
have been the subject of so many wonderful paintings. The pure white blooms
are full and compact; the small clusters
of densely packed petals reflex quickly
into a ball. The dark, glossy foliage has a
leathery finish and there are some prickles. This is a good candidate for borders
or to use as a hedge, and it should be
pruned carefully. It has been successful
as a container plant and is tolerant of
shade. **ZONES 5–10.**
Lacharmé, France, 1867

'Mlle Blanche Lafitte' × 'Sappho'

'BOUQUET DE VÉNUS'

OLD, MISCELLANEOUS, DEEP PINK

This rare Old Garden Rose has large
semi-double flowers of cerise pink,
which are quartered. It is described as an
attractive bush with mid-green foliage.
There is some fragrance. **ZONES 5–10.**
Pre-1814

Parentage unknown

'BOUQUET D'OR'

OLD, NOISETTE, YELLOW BLEND,
REPEAT-FLOWERING

On the vigorous branches throughout
summer and into autumn, buff-yellow,
coppery salmon blooms crowd the stout
canes. The flowers are perfectly shaped,
double and quartered and have a strong
scent. Many claim that this rose is an
improvement over its parent, 'Gloire de
Dijon'. The half-open flower shows this
rose at its best. The foliage is dark green.
It likes a sunny spot in a large garden and
is highly disease resistant. **ZONES 7–11.**
Ducher, France, 1872

'Gloire de Dijon' × seedling

BOURBON ROSE

syn. *Rosa × bourboniana*

OLD, BOURBON

The name of this rose represents a group
of hybrids that are believed to have
resulted from a cross between *Rosa
chinensis* and *R. damascena semperflorens*.
The flowers are either double or semi-
double and come in red, pink or purple
and, when fully open, they are about 3 in
(8 cm) across. They are borne as solitary
blooms or occasionally in a small cluster.
Some are repeat-flowering. **ZONES 5–11.**
1817

Rosa chinensis × *R. damascena semperflorens*

'Bouquet d'Or'

'BOURGOGNE'
MODERN, MODERN SHRUB, MEDIUM RED

Rosa pendulina is a purplish pink species that has been little used by hybridizers. This variety is an interesting derivative, bearing medium to large-sized single pink blooms that open cupped and are borne freely in summer. They are followed in autumn by magnificent long scarlet hips, which appear in pendulous clusters at different levels on the plant and give off brilliant gleams of color when caught by the sun. The growth of the plant is interesting, being wide and bushy, and there are many slender stems that rise in an arch and then bow towards the ground under the weight of the hips and the leaves; the leaves are rather dark and narrow and are composed of 7 leaflets. ZONES 4–9.

Ilsink, The Netherlands, 1983

Derived from *Rosa pendulina*

'BOW BELLS'   AUSbells
MODERN, MODERN SHRUB, DEEP PINK, REPEAT-FLOWERING

This rose, also classified as an English Rose, bears large clusters of deep pink blooms. The medium-sized flowers have up to 24 petals that give the young blooms the shape of an artichoke before opening out into a cupped form. They are fragrant and are borne through summer and autumn. It is useful for a mixed border, growing to average height and

'Boys' Brigade'

width with an upright bushy habit; it has medium green, semi-glossy leaves. The raiser named it because of a fancied resemblance of the flowers to bells and with reference to the church at Bow, in London's east end. ZONES 4–9.

Austin, UK, 1991

Seedling × 'Graham Thomas'

'BOY O BOY'   DICuniform
MODERN, MODERN SHRUB, MEDIUM RED, REPEAT-FLOWERING

This makes a small, shrubby, uneven plant, bristling with many short shoots. The flowers are small, carried in clusters, and open from small pointed buds into 5-petalled cup-shaped blooms of bright red, making a vivid contrast with the golden stamens. There is not much scent, but the freedom of bloom and ability to continue flowering through summer and autumn make it excellent for a border or low spreading hedge. The plant is bushy with a dense cover down to the ground of many narrow bright green leaflets. It has a good health record. ZONES 4–9.

Dickson, UK, 1996

'Little Prince' × 'Eyeopener'

Royal National Rose Society Trial Ground Certificate 1994

'Bouquet de Vénus'

'Bow Bells'

'BOYS' BRIGADE'   COCdinkum
MODERN, PATIO/DWARF CLUSTER-FLOWERED, MEDIUM RED, REPEAT-FLOWERING

Bright red 5-petalled florets (carmine and crimson) literally cover this plant. The blooms have a lighter eye with dull yellow stamens. Usually borne in large clusters on strong straight stems, the blooms last for several weeks before falling off naturally and repeating the bloom cycle. This rose was named for the centenary of the UK Boys' Brigade. ZONES 4–11.

Cocker, UK, 1983

('Darling Flame' × 'Saint Alban') × ('Little Flirt' × 'Marlena')

Royal National Rose Society Trial Ground Certificate 1983

'BRADLEY CRAIG'   MACstewar
syn. 'Bradley Graig'
MODERN, CLUSTER-FLOWERED/FLORIBUNDA, ORANGE-RED, REPEAT-FLOWERING

Sam McGredy has raised a number of splendid bright orange-scarlet Cluster-flowered Roses, including 'Orangeade', 'Trumpeter' and 'City of Belfast'. 'Bradley Craig' has similar good qualities which include a neat habit, clean growth, freedom of bloom and repeat-flowering. The flowers are scarlet, of medium size, and have 24 petals with wavy fringes; they have golden stamens and a slight fragrance. The variety is well suited for beds and to make a hedge of up to average height. It is a bushy plant and is well clothed with mid-green, glossy leaves. ZONES 4–9.

McGredy, New Zealand, 1986

'Tojo' × 'Royal Occasion'

'BRANDENBURG'
MODERN, LARGE-FLOWERED/HYBRID TEA, ORANGE-RED, REPEAT-FLOWERING

Advertised as 'Big, Big, Brandenburg' when first offered, this variety fulfils the image expected of a Large-flowered Rose—a sizeable high-centered bloom of good proportions with a symmetrical arrangement of the petals. It falls down, though, on scent, which is only light. The color is deep salmon, shading to rich salmon-red. It bears its flowers on long stems, so they are good for cutting, and it has also been found useful for exhibition thanks to the breadth and firmness of its petals. It flowers sporadically through summer and autumn and opens reasonably well in all weathers, though it is at its best in a warmer climate. The leaves are large and medium green, reddish when young, and the habit is upright and taller than average. ZONES 4–9.

McGredy, UK, 1965

('Spartan' × 'Prima Ballerina') × 'Karl Herbst'

'Brandenburg'

B

'BRANDY'   AROcad

MODERN, LARGE-FLOWERED/HYBRID TEA, APRICOT BLEND, REPEAT-FLOWERING

'The richest apricot color yet in roses', say the catalogues. When 'Brandy' received its high award in the USA, the color certainly caught the judges' eyes, and the form of the young blooms is very elegant with 20 or more petals forming neat-looking high centers. As the petals open the large flowers become loose and informal in shape, and the bright golden stamens are soon revealed. There is a rather strong fruity scent and flowering continues through summer and autumn, so despite the fleeting nature of the blooms it is a suitable rose for a bed or hedge. It may prove vulnerable to black spot and, while it prefers cooler weather, it is not dependably frost hardy. The

'Brasilia'

growth is taller than average, with an upright habit and plentiful medium green glossy leaves of good size. ZONES 5–9.

Swim and Christensen, USA, 1981

'First Prize' × 'Dr A. J. Verhage'

All-America Rose Selection 1982

'BRASILIA'

MODERN, LARGE-FLOWERED/HYBRID TEA, RED BLEND, REPEAT-FLOWERING

In 'Piccadilly' Sam McGredy had bred such a superb bicolor rose that it was difficult to improve on. 'Brasilia' was raised from it, and a special feature that caught his eye was its handsome young blood-red foliage; unfortunately it appears to be restricted to a solitary grower in Hungary. It bears medium-sized blooms fairly full of petals that are light scarlet and yellow and form high centers in the young flower. They open rather loosely and do not mind rain. The variety continues to bloom through summer and autumn but does not have much scent. 'Brasilia' is satisfactory as a bedding rose except where black spot is likely to be troublesome. The growth is upright, usually to above average height, and it is furnished with the glossy red-colored young leaves referred to above which become a rich green as they age. ZONES 4–9.

McGredy, UK, 1968

'Kordes' Perfecta' × 'Piccadilly'

'Breath of Life'

'BRASS BAND'   JACcofl

MODERN, CLUSTER-FLOWERED/FLORIBUNDA, APRICOT BLEND, REPEAT-FLOWERING

This variety carries clusters of very full-petalled flowers that open from plump orange-yellow buds into medium to large-sized blooms of rounded form. As they open they reveal a fruit salad of colors, with melon, peach, papaya and apricot all displayed, and they yield a light fruity fragrance for added measure. The flowers continue to appear through summer and autumn and are especially good in cool weather, which helps bring out the deeper apricot tones. They make a good contrast with the large bright green leaves, an important factor to consider when choosing the most effective varieties to plant in a bed. The plant grows to average height with an upright bushy habit. Zones 4–9.

Christensen, USA, 1993

'Gold Badge' × seedling

All-America Rose Selection 1995

'BRASS RING'   DICgrow

syn. 'Peek-a-Boo'

MODERN, DWARF CLUSTER-FLOWERED/PATIO, ORANGE BLEND, REPEAT-FLOWERING

Masses of coppery orange flowers on a rounded bush are the hallmark of this rose. After opening, the orange florets fade to a wonderful rose pink, creating a masterpiece of color combination in the garden. The blooms possess only 21 petals and are at their best when fully open. The bush carries many short stems which tend to arch, so that it forms a leafy hummock. The plant tends to arch upward gaining considerable height over

'Bredon'

'Breathless'

the traditional compact Miniature bush. It is an excellent specimen for growing in containers. ZONES 5–11.

Dickson, UK, 1981

'Memento' × 'Nozomi'

Royal National Rose Society Certificate of Merit 1981, Belfast Certificate of Merit 1983

'BRAVE HEART'   HORbondsmile

MODERN, CLUSTER-FLOWERED/FLORIBUNDA, MEDIUM PINK, REPEAT-FLOWERING

It is necessary to specify the raiser's first name, because this talented family has three members currently active: father, mother and son. This rose from Heather Horner has sizeable loosely double flowers, carried in clusters of 3 or 5, that open with high-pointed centers. Salmon-pink with a moderate scent, they are excellent to cut for small arrangements as well as for a bed or group in the garden. The flowers appear through summer and autumn on an upright bushy plant of average height, with large semi-glossy mid-green leaves. The rose commemorates the late Joanne Gillespie and the work of a fund for the treatment of cancer set up in her name; *Brave Heart* was the title of her first book. ZONES 4–9.

Horner, UK, 1996

('Prominent' × 'Southampton') × 'Bright Smile'

'BREATH OF LIFE'   HARquanne

MODERN, LARGE-FLOWERED CLIMBER, APRICOT BLEND, REPEAT-FLOWERING

This climber has the unusual color of apricot skin, becoming apricot-pink as the flowers age. The medium to large-sized blooms are full petalled and develop like Cluster-flowered Roses, having high centers in the young flowers and becoming cupped with waved petals as they age. It is a very good rose for flower arrangements as the blooms are long lasting and hold their color when cut; old flowers on the plant are best deadheaded. Flowering continues through summer and autumn, and there is a pleasing fragrance. The growth is stiff and upright, to average size, and if it is to be trained sideways this needs to be done early while the long stems are still pliable. It has medium green leaves. Britain's Royal College of Midwives chose the name, which signifies both the Creator Spirit in Genesis and everybody's first vital act on coming into the world. ZONES 4–9.

Harkness, UK, 1982

'Red Dandy' × 'Alexander'

Japan Certificate of Merit 1983, New Zealand Certificate of Merit 1985

'Brandy'

'BREATHLESS' JACchry
MODERN, LARGE-FLOWERED/HYBRID TEA,
DEEP PINK, REPEAT-FLOWERING

This recent variety was introduced after
the death of its creator, which is always
likely to happen in the world of roses
because an interval of about 10 years
normally elapses between the pollination
and introduction of a new rose. Elegant
urn-shaped buds open into fairly full
flowers of excellent form, high centered
in the early stages, then becoming
rounded in form as the petals expand.
They are deep pink, paler on the outside
of the petals, of good size and are borne
usually one to a stem, which means they
are useful for cutting as well as for
garden display. There is a pleasing light
fragrance, and flowering continues
through summer and autumn. The plant
grows to above average height with an
upright habit, and is furnished with large
medium green leaves that are purplish
red when young. ZONES 4–9.

Warriner, USA, 1994

Seedling × 'Chrysler Imperial'

'BREDON' AUSbred
MODERN, MODERN SHRUB, APRICOT BLEND,
REPEAT-FLOWERING

The young flowers of 'Bredon' are a
delicate creamy pink with gentle apricot
shades in the depths of the petals; as they
open the apricot tones predominate,
growing paler as the blooms expand. They
are medium sized and beautifully formed,
with many petals infolding against one
another and creating muddled centers.
Flowering continues through summer
and autumn and there is a fruity scent. It
grows like a shrubby Cluster-flowered
Rose and is suitable for a border, preferably with shorter plants in front, because
the stems tend to be leggy and arching.
In winter they need to be pruned to keep
the plant tidy. The mid-green leaves are
large. Bredon is a scenic area in the west
of England. It is also classified as an English Rose. ZONES 4–9.

Austin, UK, 1984

'Wife of Bath' × 'Lilian Austin'

'BREEZE HILL'
MODERN, LARGE-FLOWERED CLIMBER,
APRICOT BLEND

This interesting rose is like a rambler
because it produces many flexible stems,
yet like a climber in the fairly large size of
its flowers and the dull, rounded character of its leaves. The quoted parentage
has been queried and descent from 'Dr
Van Fleet' suggested instead. The flowers,
usually borne in clusters of 3 or more,
are packed to the center with petals and
open rather flat, showing creamy blush
and apricot shades that pale to creamy
buff. Tolerating bad weather well, they
appear freely in summer with an occasional flower later and have a light apple
scent. Though a slow starter, the plant
can extend beyond the average for a
climbing rose or it may be trimmed and
grown as a big arching shrub. It is well
covered with rather small leaves and has
a good health record. 'Breeze Hill' was
named after the home of the eminent

'Brass Ring'

'Brenda'

rosarian Dr J. Horace McFarland in
Harrisburg, Pennsylvania. ZONES 4–9.

Van Fleet, USA, 1926

Rosa wichuraiana × 'Beauté de Lyon'

'BRENDA'
OLD, SWEET BRIAR, LIGHT PINK

Peach blossom to pink, single blooms
appear in spring on vigorous canes on
this rose. It does best in shade for bloom
color. The vigorous, attractive, tall shrub
is covered with hips in autumn. Lord
Penzance, an English judge, raised several hybrids using *Rosa eglanteria* as seed
parent for fragrance and habit, crossed
with pollen from Hybrid Perpetuals and
Bourbons to add color and size. His aim
was to raise repeat-flowering roses with
fragrance, but 'Brenda' never achieved
the widespread popularity of his other
hybrids. ZONES 5–11.

Penzance, UK, 1894

Parentage unknown

'Breeze Hill'

'BRENDA COLVIN'
syn. *Rosa filipes* 'Brenda Colvin'
MODERN, RAMBLER, LIGHT PINK

Where space is available this is a wonderfully rampageous plant to grow, as it is
capable of clothing several meters of
pergola or clambering up into a sizeable
tree. The flowers are small with up to
12 petals; they open light pink paling to
blush white, the flower form soon becoming cupped with the golden stamens
in full view, and are carried in dainty
sprays that nod under the weight. The
blooms usually appear later than most
climbing roses, and they continue to
flower with a delicate scent and extrava-
gant freedom for 3 or 4 weeks in the

summer. The long stems have large
prickles and arch towards the sky with
ample large, glossy, often wrinkled
foliage that is very healthy. In autumn
the plant carries small orange-colored
hips. ZONES 4–9.

Colvin, UK, 1970

Seedling of *Rosa filipes* 'Kiftsgate'

'BRENNUS'
syns 'Brutus', 'Queen Victoria',
'St Brennus'
OLD, HYBRID CHINA, DARK RED

Not well known except in warm climates,
this hybrid is either a Bourbon or a
China, depending on whom you trust.
The fully flat, brilliant crimson, globular

B

'Bridal Pink'

'Bright Beauty'

blooms are dark red, shaded violet. Very large in size, they are are cupped with wavy petals. Although it blooms only once, it does so over a long period, and its excellent foliage and flowers make it a good subject for a pillar. Brennus was a Gallic leader whose forces captured Rome around 329 BC, although historians state that his existence is probably a legend. ZONES 7–11.

Laffay, France, 1830

Parentage unknown

'BRIDAL PINK'   JACbri

MODERN, CLUSTER-FLOWERED/FLORIBUNDA, MEDIUM PINK, REPEAT-FLOWERING

The name indicates one purpose that this rose has served for 30 years, for the flower clusters are suitable for wedding bouquets. They open from elegant pointed buds into full-petalled, high-centered blooms of good size and perfection of form, and last well. The color is light pink with creamy tones and they have an appreciable scent. In warm climates it is rewarding in a sunny position, both as a pleasing border and to cut for small flower arrangements. The blooms are produced through summer and autumn, though wet or cool weather will spoil their beauty. It grows to average height with an upright habit and has leathery dark green foliage. ZONES 5–9.

Boerner, USA, 1967

Seedling of 'Summertime' × seedling of 'Spartan'

'BRIDAL WHITE'   JACwhy

syn. 'Tricia'

MODERN, CLUSTER-FLOWERED/FLORIBUNDA, WHITE, REPEAT-FLOWERING

This has similar traits to its parent rose and is the first of over 150 roses credited to Bill Warriner, although whether he actually found or discovered it personally is uncertain. Its name was changed to 'Tricia' in the early 1970s, and soon afterwards back again to 'Bridal White'. It has been widely grown for the florist trade but has never proved as popular with gardeners as its pink counterpart, reflecting the general rule that pink roses sell better than white ones. The flowers are more fully double than those of its parent, and open to reveal an informal, random arrangement of the petals. For their lasting qualities they are useful for cutting, but need a mild climate to make rewarding garden plants. ZONES 5–9.

Warriner, USA, 1970

Sport of 'Bridal Pink'

'BRIDE'   FRYyearn

MODERN, LARGE-FLOWERED/HYBRID TEA, LIGHT PINK, REPEAT-FLOWERING

Most people seeing the name in a bed of this rose would suppose it was bestowed with wedding bells in mind, but in fact it commemorates an ancient village on the Isle of Man, which lies between England and Ireland. It bears very large flowers of perfect form, high centered and with broad petals that reflex slowly, giving them a long life whether left on the plant or cut for indoors. They bloom through summer and autumn, and there is little variation in their delicate and pleasing light rose pink shade whatever the weather. The bush grows to average height with a fairly compact, bushy habit and has deep green foliage, purplish when young, against which the pale color of the roses shows up to beautiful effect. ZONES 4–9.

Fryer, UK, 1995

Parentage unknown

'Bride's Dream'

'BRIDE'S DREAM'   ROYroyness

syns 'Fairy Tale Queen', 'Marchenkonigin'

MODERN, LARGE-FLOWERED/HYBRID TEA, LIGHT PINK, REPEAT-FLOWERING

This is one of the best of pale pink roses. Bred from 'Royal Highness', it is the same soft pink color, but the buds are much longer, growth is much taller, and it does not suffer from mildew. The particularly long elegant buds open to large, double flowers with 30 high centered petals. There is slight fragrance. Flower production is very high and its very long stems make this an excellent rose for picking. The foliage is dark green and very profuse. The bush grows too tall for bedding, but it is a wonderful rose at the back of the border. ZONES 4–9.

Kordes, Germany, 1985

'Royal Highness' × seedling

'BRIGADOON'   JACpal

MODERN, LARGE-FLOWERED/HYBRID TEA, PINK BLEND, REPEAT-FLOWERING

This rose is popular because of the color of the flowers; these are a delightful blend of pink, cream and strawberry red, the deeper shades beautifully marked towards the petal tips. As the buds open, they reveal some 40 petals forming a tight coil in the heart of the flower. The petals slowly reflex to show a spiral center that slowly subsides as the blooms gradually open out. There is a spicy fragrance, and the flowers appear from summer to autumn. This is an attractive rose and it can prove useful for exhibition too, although the stems are too often on the short side to make it dependable for cutting. It grows tall and bushy and has a good coverage of large deep green glossy leaves, but it may die back in a hard winter. ZONES 5–9.

Warriner, USA, 1991

Seedling × 'Pristine'

All-America Rose Selection 1992

'BRIGHT BEAUTY'

MODERN, LARGE-FLOWERED/HYBRID TEA, ORANGE-RED, REPEAT-FLOWERING

Rose breeders send their new seedlings for trial to nurseries in different countries, because some do well in cool regions while others need the sun. This rose from France illustrates the point, for it has been grown in Australia since soon after its date of introduction but apparently nowhere else, and is one of those that is well suited to a warm climate. The lightly scented flowers are large and full, rather a dusky pale scarlet in color, and with firm broad petals that do not fly open too fast in hot weather. They appear through summer and autumn and are useful for cutting. The plant grows to average height or more and has large glossy leaves. ZONES 5–9.

Delbard, France, 1986

Parentage unknown

'BRIGHT FIRE'   PEAxi

syn. 'Brightfire'

MODERN, LARGE-FLOWERED CLIMBER, DARK RED, REPEAT-FLOWERING

The flowers of 'Bright Fire' are more fully petalled than the pure vermilion 'Alexander'. They are of medium to large size, and have high centers when they open, becoming more rounded as the petals reflex. There is not much scent. Blooming continues over a long period on a vigorous, stiffly branching plant that can go above average height and needs a firm support such as a wall, fence or tall pillar. It has large, leathery leaves. ZONES 4–9.

Pearce, UK, 1996

'Parkdirektor Riggers' × 'Guinée'

'BRIGHT MELODY'

MODERN, MODERN SHRUB, MEDIUM RED, REPEAT-FLOWERING

This variety has blooms of that shade where deep pink meets light red. They are borne usually in clusters of up to 10 blooms, which open from plump buds into fairly large saucer-shaped flowers composed of about 30 crumpled petals. The flowers have a slight fragrance, and continue through summer and autumn. The plant grows easily, making an upright bushy shrub of average height or more with dark olive green, leathery foliage. At present no nursery appears to be offering it for sale. ZONES 4–9.

Buck, USA, 1984

'Carefree Beauty' × ('Herz As' × 'Cuthbert Grant')

'Bride'

'Bright Smile'

'Brilliant Meillandina'

'BRIGHT SMILE' DICdance

MODERN, CLUSTER-FLOWERED/FLORIBUNDA,
MEDIUM YELLOW, REPEAT-FLOWERING

This is well named, for its cheerful
blooms always seem to give a welcome.
Its slender buds open out wide into fairly
large semi-double flowers, effectively
showing off the bright yellow petals and
prominent stamens. There is a pleasing
scent, and the plant always seems to have
flowers showing on it somewhere
throughout summer and autumn. The
growth is neat, bushy and spreading to
below average height and it has plenty of
shiny foliage, so it maintains an attractive
look even before the first flowers appear.
Occasionally the young shoots are
touched by seasonal mildew. ZONES 4–9.

Dickson, UK, 1981

'Eurorose' × seedling

British Association of Rose Breeders Selection
1980, Belfast Prize 1982, Glasgow Silver Medal
1989

'BRILLIANT MEILLANDINA'

MODERN, MINIATURE, ORANGE, REPEAT-FLOWERING

This rose has firm, ruffled, semi-double
flowers containing 15 petals. When fully
open they are orange-red and up to 1½ in
(35 mm) across. They are borne in clusters of 3–20. There is no scent. The short,
thick, rich green foliage is always healthy,
and this rose is spectacular in pots, on
patios and as standards. Care must be
taken to avoid damage from spider mite,
especially in the hotter months. Spray
regularly, making sure that the undersides
of the leaves is not forgotten. Dry mulching material should not be used as it also
encourages mite activity. This stylish
plant is an excellent addition to a well-
balanced collection of roses. ZONES 5–10.

Meilland, France, 1975

'Parador' × ('Baby Bettina' × 'Duchess of Windsor')

'BRISBANE BLUSH' PALock

MODERN, LARGE-FLOWERED/HYBRID TEA,
RED BLEND, REPEAT-FLOWERING

'Brisbane Blush' bears cerise flowers with
a silvery cream base. The full blooms
contain 25–40 petals and are borne in
small clusters. They have a lovely scent
which is inherited from 'Prima Ballerina'. The foliage is medium green, semi-
glossy and disease-resistant on a plant
with an upright growth habit. It has a
fairly quick repeat cycle, so these charming plants can be enjoyed throughout the
growing season. ZONES 4–9.

Long, Australia, 1993

('Golden Slippers' × 'Lavendula') × 'Prima Ballerina'

'Brisbane Blush'

'BRITANNIA'

MODERN, POLYANTHA, RED BLEND,
REPEAT-FLOWERING

The flowers of this cheerful little plant
are a pleasing shade of light crimson with
a whitish eye at the base of the petals.
There are only 5 petals and as many as
40 blooms in each flower spray, so it
makes a conspicuous sight. There is little
scent but flowering continues through
summer and autumn, making this a
useful garden plant where a low growing
hedge or an item to fill a small space is
required. Its leaves are leathery, semi-
glossy, small and narrow on a short,
compact and bushy plant. ZONES 4–9.

Burbage, UK, 1929

'Coral Cluster' × 'Eblouissant'

'BROADWAY' BURway

MODERN, LARGE-FLOWERED/HYBRID TEA,
YELLOW BLEND, REPEAT-FLOWERING

The color of 'Broadway' is delightful—
'orange suffused with gold' is how the
catalogues describe it. There is a good
deal of reddish pink towards the margins
of the petals, the coloring deepening and
extending in very sunny weather. The
blooms are fully double and quite large,
opening with high centers and holding a
pretty, regular shape as the petals reflex.
The flowers have a strong, spicy scent,
and continue to bloom through summer
and autumn, though the mid-season
ones are of lesser quality. The plant
grows to average height with an upright,
bushy habit and is furnished with shiny
dark green leaves. It makes a pleasing
bedding rose, and gives flowers suitable
for cutting which, by reason of their
color changes, are delightful to see as
they are opening in a vase. There is a risk
of die-back in severe winters. ZONES 5–9.

Anthony Perry, USA, 1985

('First Prize' × 'Gold Glow') × 'Sutter's Gold'

All-America Rose Selection 1986

'Broadway'

'BRONZE MASTERPIECE'

syn. 'Bronce Masterpiece'

MODERN, LARGE-FLOWERED/HYBRID TEA,
APRICOT BLEND, REPEAT-FLOWERING

The best flowers on this rose come early
in the flowering season, when the bronzy
orange tones are at their deepest. The
brownish amber buds open into high-
centered, full-petalled flowers that
become more orange-yellow in tone as
the petals reflex. They hold their form
for a long time in cooler weather, when
they can give exhibition blooms. They
have a rich fruity fragrance and continue
through summer and autumn, provided
there are no fungus troubles. The plant
grows to average height with an upright
habit and has leathery, glossy dark green
foliage. It is little grown today except in
warm climates. ZONES 5–9.

Boerner, USA, 1960

'Golden Masterpiece' × 'Kate Smith'

Geneva Gold Medal 1958

'BROTHER CADFAEL' AUSglobe

MODERN, MODERN SHRUB, MEDIUM PINK,
REPEAT-FLOWERING

A special attraction of this rose is the
shape of the flowers, deeply cupped with
an old-fashioned style like peonies. They
are fully double and have substantial
thick petals. The color is a rich shade of
rose pink and there is good fragrance. It
makes a sturdy upright bush of average

'Brother Cadfael'

height and has large dark leaves. It was
named after a monastic sleuth created by
Edith Pargeter, who wrote under the
name Ellis Peters. It is also classified as
an English Rose. ZONES 4–9.

Austin, UK, 1990

'Charles Austin' × seedling

'BROWN VELVET' MACcultra

syn. 'Colorbreak'

MODERN, CLUSTER-FLOWERED/FLORIBUNDA,
RUSSET, REPEAT-FLOWERING

Sam McGredy has constantly surprised
the rose world with his roses of extraordinary coloring; this one is a blend of
orange-red and brown. In cooler climates
the brownish tones predominate; in sun-
nier climes the brown becomes overlaid
with orange. Crowded clusters of round
buds open into double flowers with
quartered petals, which soon reflex to allow golden stamens to peep through. The
medium-sized, lightly scented flowers
continue blooming through summer and
autumn. It makes an upright bush of
average height with glossy dark green
leaves. ZONES 4–9.

McGredy, New Zealand, 1982

'Mary Sumner' × 'Kapai'

Gold Star of the South Pacific, New Zealand 1979

'Brown Velvet'

'Bronze Masterpiece'

B

'BROWNIE'

MODERN, CLUSTER-FLOWERED/FLORIBUNDA, RUSSET, REPEAT-FLOWERING

The work of Gene Boerner produced some extraordinary roses in the post-war years, including 'Lavender Pinocchio' which was a child of 'Grey Pearl'. When these two were crossed with one another, 'Brownie' resulted. It has tan-colored buds that open into cupped flowers of chocolate brown, with gold shading at the base and pinky red at the petal edges. Copper and creamy shades appear as the full-petalled flowers open out almost flat. The blooms appear sporadically through summer and autumn and are produced in well-spaced clusters, on upright plants that grow below average height, with leathery leaves. It is not constitutionally vigorous or healthy and needs good conditions to thrive. ZONES 4–9.

Boerner, USA, 1959

Seedling of 'Lavender Pinocchio' × 'Grey Pearl'

'BUCCANEER'

MODERN, LARGE-FLOWERED/HYBRID TEA, MEDIUM YELLOW, REPEAT-FLOWERING

In the USA this is called a Grandiflora, indicating a plant built on a more generous scale than most bushes; it fits that concept well, producing long urn-shaped buds in open clusters that open into cupped, rather loose blooms of bright yellow carried boldly on stiff stems and with a pleasant fragrance. The flowers have about 24 petals and make a bold and noticeable splash of color in the garden. They withstand bad weather well and it flowers through summer and

autumn. It can be difficult to site, because its habit is considerably taller than average. It can make a splendid pillar or semi-climber if trained on a stout pole or fence and lightly pruned. The plant is vigorous and usually very healthy, with an upright, free-branching habit and abundant deep bright green foliage. ZONES 4–9.

Swim, USA, 1952

'Geheimrat Duisberg' × ('Max Krause' × 'Captain Thomas')

Geneva Gold Medal 1952, Royal National Rose Society Trial Ground Certificate 1955

'BUFF BEAUTY'

MODERN, MODERN SHRUB, APRICOT BLEND, REPEAT-FLOWERING

This is a rose for the enthusiast, a desirable garden item even when not in bloom thanks to its gracefully rounded plant habit and ample covering of handsome dark shiny leaves. In summer and again in autumn it produces trusses of pale apricot blooms that show up tellingly against this dark background. The flowers have many petals that open out in the shape of powder puffs, showing charming muddled centers. They carry hints of buff yellow as well as apricot, have a pleasing fragrance and withstand bad weather well. It grows to average height or more, is excellent in borders or to plant against a low wall, and has a good health record. ZONES 4–9.

Bentall, UK, 1939

'William Allen Richardson' × unknown

Royal Horticultural Society Award of Garden Merit 1993

'Brownie'

'Buisman's Triumph'

'Buff Beauty'

'Bullata'

'BUFFALO GAL'   UHLwe

syns 'Foxi', 'Foxi Pavement', 'Foxy Pavement'

MODERN, MODERN SHRUB, DEEP PINK, REPEAT-FLOWERING

The color of this rose is a pretty shade of lavender-pink. The blooms are of medium size, have 5 crinkled petals and open out flat. They have a strong, spicy fragrance, and are produced with good continuity through summer and autumn. It grows to below average height for a shrub rose, and has many features that are characteristic of the Hybrid Rugosa Roses, such as a rounded habit of growth, prickly stems, wrinkled, leathery leaves and good health. The introducers in the USA decided they could not use the European name (listed here as a synonym) and adopted one with a Wild West connotation instead. ZONES 4–9.

Uhl, Germany, 1989

Parentage unknown

'BUISMAN'S TRIUMPH'

MODERN, CLUSTER-FLOWERED/FLORIBUNDA, MEDIUM PINK, REPEAT-FLOWERING

This rose makes a bold display, producing large trusses of up to 20 medium to large flowers that open from slender buds then become semi-double and cupped and rather loose in form. The color is in the spectrum where deep pink meets carmine-red, the flowers becoming lighter as they age. They have some fragrance. Though little grown today this used to be a popular choice for a hedge or single grouping, for the plant has vigor and hardiness, grows taller than average with an upright, bushy habit and is attractively furnished with dark green foliage, which is reddish tinted when young. In warm climates it is large enough to be considered a shrub rose. ZONES 4–9.

Buisman, The Netherlands, 1952

'Käthe Duvigneau' × 'Tantau's Triumph'

'Buccaneer'

'Bulls Red'

'BULLATA'

syns 'Lettuce-leaved Rose', *Rosa × centifolia bullata*, 'Rose à Feuilles de Laitue'

OLD, CENTIFOLIA, MEDIUM PINK

This is a lax shrub, to 5 ft (1.5 m) and almost as broad. The stems are long, arching, dark green and well populated with reddish thorns. The leaves of this rose make it interesting: each leaf is a clear rich green, large and very crinkled, like that of a lettuce. Very fragrant flowers emerge in mid-summer from tight round buds, arranged in small clusters. The fully opened flowers are a rich deep glowing pink and are made up of many tightly packed petals. They dislike rain, sometimes rotting off before opening in prolonged wet spells of weather, but this should not put anyone off this fascinating rose. It is identical to 'Centifolia', from which it probably sported or self-seeded in the distant past. ZONES 5–10.

Pre-1815

Parentage unknown

'BULLS RED'   MACrero

MODERN, LARGE-FLOWERED/HYBRID TEA, MEDIUM RED, REPEAT-FLOWERING

This rose is appreciated for its keeping qualities, which have made it very useful as a cut flower variety. It bears its flowers usually one to a stem, these opening out from plump buds into large broad-petalled blooms. They are double, with high centers, and in color are on the darker side of medium red; however they lack the rich fragrance one expects from a red rose. The plant flowers freely and maintains a good succession of bloom on long stems through summer and autumn. It is an upright grower, vigorous and taller than average, and has dark leaves. ZONES 4–9.

McGredy, New Zealand, 1977

'Sympathie' × 'Irish Rover'

'BURBANK'

syn. 'Santa Rosa'

OLD, TEA, MEDIUM PINK, REPEAT-FLOWERING

Internationally famous horticulturist Luther Burbank produced a number of roses at his nursery in Santa Rosa, California, at the turn of the century; few have remained in the catalogues. Confusion arose early when some claimed that 'Santa Rosa' was often sold as 'Burbank', which holds true to this day. 'Burbank' was described as a bright rose pink, very double bloom that turned lighter. The 3 in (8 cm) blossoms are held above the glossy foliage on strong canes. It needs a warm, sunny spot to do its best. Burbank was a controversial, self-promoting nurseryman who sold roses by mail. ZONES 7–11.

Burbank, USA, 1900

Derived from 'Hermosa' × 'Bon Silène'

St Louis World's Fair Gold Medal 1904

'BURGUNDIAN ROSE'

syns 'Burgundy Rose', 'Pompon de Burgogne', *Rosa burgundica*, *R. centifolia parvifolia*

OLD, CENTIFOLIA, PINK BLEND

This rose has a long but not very clear history; it requires a patient reader to find it in most books as it goes under a number of names. The small, deep pink blossoms suffused with purple, with a paler center, the dark, gray-green foliage and the few prickles make it a charming plant for a dense, low shrub or a pot. There is some fragrance. ZONES 4–10.

Burgundy, France, circa 1664

Parentage unknown

'BURMA STAR'

MODERN, CLUSTER-FLOWERED/FLORIBUNDA, APRICOT BLEND, REPEAT-FLOWERING

The color of 'Burma Star' is best described as yellow with a light flush of buff-orange, a clean and even shade that is well displayed in the large cupped blooms. They have a pleasant fragrance and appear occasionally singly but more often in showy long-stemmed clusters, with good continuity through summer and autumn. Growth is strong and upright, indeed somewhat narrow, to above average height, making this very suitable for a hedge as well as for planting in mixed borders. The foliage is dark and glossy and the variety has an excellent health record. The raiser named it for The Burma Star Association. ZONES 4–9.

Cocker, UK, 1974

'Arthur Bell' × 'Manx Queen'

Belfast Certificate of Merit 1976

'BURNABY'

syns 'Gold Heart', 'Golden Heart'

MODERN, LARGE-FLOWERED/HYBRID TEA, LIGHT YELLOW, REPEAT-FLOWERING

The parents of this rose do not carry very large flowers, so the raiser must have been surprised to conjure out of them a flower like 'Burnaby'. With over 50 big petals it makes a wonderful cabbage of a rose with high-centered form, opening majestically to show a rounded outline. Only a tendency to produce split blooms denies it a place among top-class roses

'Burgundian Rose'

'Burnaby'

for exhibition, but it is sufficiently vigorous and free flowering for the garden, maintaining a sporadic succession of lightly fragrant blooms through summer and autumn in a clear primrose yellow color, paling to cream. The plant grows to average height with a bushy habit and has rather sparse dark glossy foliage that needs watching for black spot. ZONES 4–9.

Eddie, Canada, 1954

'Phyllis Gold' × 'President Herbert Hoover'

National Rose Society Gold Medal 1954, Portland Gold Medal 1957

'BURNING LOVE'

syns 'Amour Ardent', 'Brennende Liebe'

MODERN, LARGE FLOWERED/HYBRID TEA, MEDIUM RED, REPEAT-FLOWERING

Often listed as a Grandiflora Rose in the USA, this is a vigorous grower that carries its flowers in trusses, usually 3 or 5 together. They are freely produced and fairly full and open to fair-sized blooms with high centers, before the petals reflex to display a loose, informal shape. The color is a glowing deep scarlet, and they have a slight fragrance. Though not now grown commercially, this has been chosen as a well-behaved bedding rose for many parks and gardens, growing to average height and noted for its bushy habit and dark glossy leaves. ZONES 4–9.

Tantau, Germany, 1956

'Fanal' × 'Crimson Glory'

Baden-Baden Gold Medal 1954

'BUTTERSCOTCH'   JACtan

MODERN, LARGE-FLOWERED CLIMBER, RUSSET

The flowers of 'Butterscotch' are light orange with a tan overlay. They are fairly large, opening from rounded buds into full-petalled flowers of somewhat loosely cupped form. They bloom freely in summer, give a modest show later in the flowering season, and yield a pleasant

'By Appointment'

'Burning Love'

'Buttons 'n' Bows'

'Burma Star'

light fragrance. The plant grows vigorously and branches freely, lending itself to being trained on fences, walls and pergolas. It is well furnished with semi-glossy medium green leaves. ZONES 4–9.

Warriner, USA, 1986

('Buccaneer' × 'Zorina') × 'Royal Sunset'

'BUTTONS'   DICmickey

MODERN, PATIO/DWARF CLUSTER-FLOWERED, PINK BLEND, REPEAT-FLOWERING

'Buttons' has urn-shaped buds in sprays which open to reveal salmon-pink blooms of exquisite form and grace. The foliage is a deep dark green providing a great background to the florets. The cut stems last for days. The medium-sized bushy plant is fairly disease-resistant and weatherproof. ZONES 4–11.

Dickson, UK, 1987

('Liverpool Echo' × 'Woman's Own') × 'Memento'

'BUTTONS 'N' BOWS'

syns 'Felicity II', 'Teeney-Weeny'

MODERN, MINIATURE, DEEP PINK, REPEAT-FLOWERING

Double flowers in shades of pink adorn this compact upright bush. They are usually borne singly or in small sprays and have a fruity fragrance. The form is high-centered and cupped, reflexing at

maturity. It is popular throughout the world providing a fast repeat-bloom cycle in most climates. ZONES 4–11.

Poulsen, Denmark, 1981

'Mini-Poul' × 'Harriet Poulsen'

'BY APPOINTMENT'   HARvolute

MODERN, CLUSTER-FLOWERED/FLORIBUNDA, APRICOT BLEND, REPEAT-FLOWERING

This rose is a creamy apricot color, very pale when the slim urn-shaped buds first open then deepening to show the subtle buff shades found in some Old Tea Roses. The double flowers are carried in rather crowded heads on upright stems, and at their best give wonderful sprays to cut and show because of the breathtaking effect of so many perfect tightly coiled young flowers seen together. Flowering starts late, and flowers appearing through the end of summer and into autumn are somewhat sparsely produced and rarely match the quality of the earlier ones. The plant grows upright and narrow to average height and has very dark leaves, which may be touched by mildew late in the season. It was named to commemorate the 150th anniversary of The Royal Warrant Holders' Association. ZONES 4–9.

Harkness, UK, 1990

'Anne Harkness' × 'Letchworth Garden City'

C

C

'Caid'

'Cabbage Rose'

'Cadillac'

'CABBAGE ROSE'
syns 'Centifolia', 'Provence Rose',
Rosa × centifolia
OLD, CENTIFOLIA, MEDIUM PINK

'The Rose of Painters' is the French name for this beautifully scented rose, which is seen in many Dutch still-life pictures and in Redouté's art as well. 'Cabbage Rose' is an unfortunate name, because a bloom in its full glory is a sight to behold. Medium pink, very double blooms with overlapping petals appear singly or in clusters in summer. The flowers tend to nod as there are so many petals, but not always 100 as some catalogues claim. It has coarse gray-green leaves and prickles and performs best in full sun. It reaches 6 ft (1.8 m) in maturity and is not particular about soil, but does not like wet weather. It needs pruning in late winter and some support if planted alone. ZONES 4–9.

The Netherlands, circa 1596

Parentage unknown

'CADILLAC' KORveril
MODERN, LARGE-FLOWERED/HYBRID TEA,
ORANGE-PINK, REPEAT-FLOWERING

'Cadillac' is an excellent cut-flower rose producing huge quantities of medium-sized pale salmon-pink flowers over a very long period. The buds are long and pointed and open slowly to flowers of

good substance that hold their color well. They are produced singly or several to a cluster on very long stems; they are long lasting when used for indoor decoration and show up well under artificial light. The plant is tall, upright and slender and is grown in large quantities under glass but is equally good as a garden rose when planted in the open. ZONES 5–11.

Kordes, Germany, 1991

Parentage unknown

'CAFÉ'
MODERN, CLUSTER-FLOWERED/FLORIBUNDA,
RUSSET, REPEAT-FLOWERING

Comment was sharply divided when this novel rose came on the market: 'We should hope never to be served coffee of this color' said one, while for another it was 'the precise color of café-au-lait'. Like many strangely colored roses, this one is affected by climate and season; if conditions are cool the coffee-with-cream coloring is pleasing, but where it is hot and dry the flowers become an unattractive fawnish brown. The slightly fragrant flowers are double, are borne in clusters and are fairly large, tending to hang their heads. They open saucer shaped, with the petals rather loosely disposed, but if cut young they will last well in flower arrangements. Despite the vigor evident from the seed parent line

the plant makes low growth and needs good cultivation to be worth keeping for its curiosity value. 'Café' has a sturdy and bushy habit and olive green foliage. ZONES 4–9.

Kordes, Germany, 1956

('Golden Glow' × *Rosa kordesii*) × 'Lavender Pinocchio'

'CAFÉ OLÉ' MORolé
MODERN, MINIATURE, RUSSET, REPEAT-FLOWERING

The pointed buds open with cupped form, to medium to large blooms with very double 40–50 petals. Borne singly or in sprays of 3–5 blooms, it has a spicy fragrance. It has medium to large foliage, which is medium green and dull to semi-glossy. The plant is vigorous and repeats well all year. The growth is upright, bushy and tall with slender prickles that are hooked downward. 'Café Olé' produces orange round fruit in autumn, giving the chance to plant the seed. ZONES 4–10.

Moore, USA, 1990

Sport of 'Winter Magic'

'CAID' DELsirp
MODERN, POLYANTHA, ORANGE BLEND,
REPEAT-FLOWERING

This variety appears today only in Australian nursery catalogues, halfway round the world from its place of origin. Whether it should be classified as a Polyantha is questionable, for if it were to appear today it would surely be counted as a Dwarf Cluster-flowered Rose. It has plump buds that open into brightly colored orange blooms, fairly full petalled and of medium size. They are carried in showy clusters on short stems, have a light fragrance and stand bad weather well. Flowering starts slightly later than for most varieties and continues sporadically through the rest of summer and autumn. For a plant near the front of a border or wherever a rose for a small space is required, this is an effective garden item. The growth is short and bushy, and it carries mid-green, leathery leaves. ZONES 4–9.

Delforge, Belgium, 1971

'Orangeade' × seedling

'CAIRNGORM'
MODERN, CLUSTER-FLOWERED/FLORIBUNDA,
ORANGE BLEND, REPEAT-FLOWERING

When they first open, the large clusters of buds on this variety promise a rich mêlée of tangerine and gold, but the effect is dimmed as the medium-sized,

double blooms age to a muted and indeterminate mix of salmon, reddish pink and yellow. There is a light fragrance in the rounded open flowers. In other respects the plant is well behaved, being a strong, upright grower of average height or above that is dependable for bedding, hedges and cutting, continuing in bloom through summer and autumn and being adequately furnished with healthy dark glossy leaves. ZONES 4–9.

Cocker, UK, 1973

'Anne Cocker' × 'Arthur Bell'

Royal National Rose Society Trial Ground Certificate 1971

'CAJUN SPICE'
MODERN, LARGE-FLOWERED/HYBRID TEA,
ORANGE-RED, REPEAT-FLOWERING

This recent introduction is currently offered by a few growers in the USA, and produces full-petalled, medium- to large-sized blooms on long stems. They are a colorful blend of orange-red and orange-yellow with a spicy fragrance, and are carried through summer and autumn on a plant that grows considerably taller than average. For a screen against a wall or fence where climbing roses are not appropriate, or for a tall hedge or towards the back of a border, this variety will be useful. It grows vigorously with an upright, branching habit. ZONES 5–9.

McMillan, USA, 1996

Parentage unknown

'CAL POLY' MORpoly
MODERN, MINIATURE, MEDIUM YELLOW,
REPEAT-FLOWERING

This is an excellent variety for the garden because it clothes itself in blooms all year. The medium yellow flowers are very long lasting and hold their color well even in the intense heat of summer. The moderately full 15–25 petal blooms come in small clusters and have a slight fragrance. The foliage is medium green and semi-glossy. It has very few prickles. It has an upright and bushy habit, is of medium height and is easy to maintain. Quite resistant to insects and fungal diseases, it is an ideal pathway border plant. This rose was named to honor the great horticultural school, California Polytechnic. ZONES 4–11.

Moore, USA, 1991

('Little Darling' × 'Yellow Magic') × 'Gold Badge'

American Rose Society Award of Excellence 1992

'Café'

'Calgold'

'Camaieux Fimbriata'

'CALDWELL PINK'
MODERN, POLYANTHA, MEDIUM PINK, REPEAT-FLOWERING

This mystery rose from the town of Caldwell in Texas has been re-introduced into commerce with a made-up name. It bears big clusters of small, double, lilac-pink flowers, composed of scores of narrow petals that form overlapping layers, leaving a small knot of incurved half-petals at the center. Flowering extends through summer and autumn but there is no scent. It is a graceful plant with a spreading, leafy habit that is useful in borders, near patios, to make an informal hedge and for use as a specimen plant. It grows to average size or less and has a dense cover of small narrow leaflets. ZONES 4–9.

Parentage unknown

'CALGOLD'
MODERN, MINIATURE, DEEP YELLOW, REPEAT-FLOWERING

'Calgold' is suitable for exhibition, with its pointed buds opening to deep clear yellow blooms with good high centers. The blooms are small with about 23 petals that hold very well, but in the heat they are often cupped and tend to lose that classic Large-flowered form. It is slightly fragrant and has small to medium glossy foliage. The growth habit is bushy; it is not very tall. It is easy to maintain and is a profuse bloomer. ZONES 4–11.

Moore, USA, 1977

'Golden Glow' × 'Peachy White'

'CALOCARPA'
MODERN, HYBRID RUGOSA, MEDIUM PINK, REPEAT-FLOWERING

This rose bears clusters of sizeable fragrant single flowers with crumpled petals and prominent golden stamens. They appear through summer and autumn and have a color that appears to vary from bright red to rich rose pink to rich lilac-crimson, according to reports from different countries, which suggests that either a mutating Chinese gene has been at work or that more than one variety is involved. The growth is average for a shrub rose; it has slender, bristly stems and is clothed with leaves that are large, coarse, medium green in color and slightly wrinkled. 'Calocarpa' makes a useful hedge, but its true attractions are the bunches of round scarlet hips that hang from it in autumn. ZONES 4–9.

Bruant, France, pre-1891

Possibly Rosa rugosa × unknown China

'Camélia Rose'

'CAMAIEUX'
OLD, GALLICA, MAUVE

'Camaieux' has sweetly scented, loosely double flowers that appear in mid-summer and have a magenta-pink background ageing to soft lavender or even soft purple; each petal is heavily splashed with white to give a very pleasing overall bicolor effect. Although its 3 ft (1 m) growth is short for a Gallica, it is vigorous and makes a fine pot plant or hedge, and is especially good for a small garden. On its own roots it can become invasive. It has attractive gray-green leaves and only a few prickles. ZONES 4–9.

Vibert, France, 1830

Parentage unknown

'CAMAIEUX FIMBRIATA'
OLD, GALLICA, MAUVE

This sport is one of the most attractive of all Gallicas and was found growing in a row of 'Camaieux' at Bell's Roses in Auckland, New Zealand. The color is the same, but instead of the blooms being striped and semi-double, they are marbled with purple and are very double. The many small petals are massed together to enclose a button eye, and the marbled effect is very attractive. Like all Gallicas, it only flowers once. The growth is dwarf and covered with a profusion of matt dark green foliage; there may be a little mildew late in the season. If planted with the bud union below ground level, the plant will form a thicket on its own roots. 'Camaieux Fimbriata' was imported into Australia where it has become more popular than it is in New Zealand. 'Camaieux' is probably the only Gallica to have ever produced a sport in the Southern Hemisphere; the sport is practically unknown in Europe or America. ZONES 5–9.

Bell's Roses, New Zealand, 1980

Sport of 'Camaieux'

'Camaieux'

'CAMARA' DELcama
MODERN, LARGE-FLOWERED/HYBRID TEA, ORANGE-RED, REPEAT-FLOWERING

In warm climates this rose is capable of giving individual blooms of exceptional beauty. They are large and full petalled, and open from rounded buds into high-centered flowers that hold their form as the outer petals reflex. The color is a vibrant blend of red, orange and vermilion, with a rim of dark red shading towards the petal edges where they have been exposed longest to the sun. There is a light fragrance, and flowering is maintained through summer and autumn. 'Camara' is useful for the cutting garden and will serve as a garden variety thanks to its vigorous, slightly spreading habit, though its foliage is sensitive to temperature changes and may need protection against mildew in some areas. ZONES 5–9.

Delbard, France, 1978

(['Chic Parisien' × 'Tropicana'] × ['Gloire de Rome' × 'Impeccable']) × ('Tropicana' × 'Samourai')

'CAMBRIDGESHIRE' KORhaugen
syn. 'Carpet of Color'
MODERN, MODERN SHRUB/GROUND COVER, RED BLEND, REPEAT-FLOWERING

This variety is claimed to be the first multi-colored ground-cover rose. 'Cambridgeshire' bears clusters of many pointed buds that open out into small semi-double blooms. As the petals reflex they disclose a mixture of colors, with gold, cerise, pink and scarlet all present in the small cupped flowers. As the flowers are crowded together and the clusters are borne with freedom all over the plant, the effect is startling rather than restful. Flowering continues through summer and autumn, with quiet intervals while the plant regathers its strength. There is little in the way of scent. The habit of growth is spreading but fairly compact, so this is a ground-cover rose suitable for a comparatively small space. The leaves are dark and shiny and furnish the plant well. ZONES 4–9.

Kordes, Germany, 1994

Parentage unknown

'CAMÉLIA ROSE'
syn. 'Camellia Rose'
OLD, CHINA, LIGHT PINK, REPEAT-FLOWERING

Because it looks like a camellia, this China Rose makes an attractive plant at the back of the border; a few writers list it as a Noisette. The bright, rosy pink, double, cupped flowers are of medium size, and tend to nod above the glossy leaves. There are occasional white streaks on the petals. It does well in a shady spot but must be warm. There are four other roses with the same name. ZONES 7–10.

Prévost, circa 1830

Parentage unknown

'CAMELOT'
MODERN, LARGE-FLOWERED/HYBRID TEA, ORANGE-PINK, REPEAT-FLOWERING

Regarded as a Grandiflora in the USA, this variety bears its flowers both one to a stem and in clusters. They are that shade often described as coral-pink or reddish salmon, and it is seen as a deep and rather hard tone on the young petals but lightens and softens as the flowers age. They are very full petalled, of medium to large size and open with high centers before becoming cupped as the petals unfold. There is a spicy scent, and blooms continue to appear through summer and autumn. This is a very suitable rose for cutting, because the flower stems are long, as well as for general garden display. The plant grows taller than average and has dark leathery foliage. ZONES 4–9.

Swim and Weeks, USA, 1964

'Circus' × 'Queen Elizabeth'

All-America Rose Selection 1965

'Calocarpa'

'Camelot'

C

'CAMEO'

MODERN, POLYANTHA, ORANGE-PINK,
REPEAT-FLOWERING

This variety was one of many Polyantha
sports that became very popular between
the two world wars. It bears crowded
clusters of small, rosette-shaped semi-
double blooms, which last well on
the plant and give good color impact.
The flowers are 'a peculiar mixture of
salmon, coral and orange', all of those
colors being present at some stage of the
season, the petals perhaps responding
to different light intensities as summer
turns to autumn. There is little fragrance
and some propensity to mildew, which
is one of the reasons why the Polyanthas
faded away in favor of the healthier and
bigger Cluster-flowered Roses from the
1940s onwards. The growth of 'Cameo'
is bushy and upright but short and very
compact, and it has petite, light gray-
green leaves. ZONES 4–9.

de Ruiter, The Netherlands, 1932

Sport of 'Orléans Rose'

'CAMP DAVID'

MODERN, LARGE-FLOWERED/HYBRID TEA,
DARK RED, REPEAT-FLOWERING

This rose from Germany is listed only in
Australia, where 7 nurseries offer it, as it

'Camp David'

'Canary'

is well suited to withstand the fierce sun
that causes the petals of many red roses
to discolor and 'burn'. The flowers
open with high centers, the firm petals
enabling them to hold their form. They
are fully double, of a dusky dark red
color, and are usually produced one to a
stem, which is convenient when they are
required for flower arrangement. There
is good fragrance, and the blooms withstand wet weather well. They are produced through summer and autumn on
a well-foliated plant that is sturdy and
free branching, growing to average
height or more. ZONES 5–9.

Tantau, Germany, 1984

Parentage unknown

'CAMPHILL GLORY' HARkreme

MODERN, LARGE-FLOWERED/HYBRID TEA,
PINK BLEND, REPEAT-FLOWERING

This cool-looking rose has plump buds
that open into large, creamy blush
flowers with a touch of light rose pink
on the petals. The blooms are carried on
long stems, sometimes 3 to a stem and
sometimes singly, and open with high-
pointed centers that hold this form to a
late stage. There is a light fragrance, and
blooming continues with good succession
for so large a rose through summer and

'Canary Bird'

'Can-Can'

autumn. Despite the pale color, 'Camphill
Glory' withstands bad weather well, and
it makes a useful bed or hedge with the
bonus that it can produce flowers good
enough to show. The plant's growth is
vigorous, to average height or more, and
the habit rather open, and it has reddish
stems and matt green leaves. The name
commemorates the work of the Camphill
Village Trust, which provides sheltered
communities for those who cannot live
in the wider world. ZONES 4–9.

Harkness, UK, 1980

'Elizabeth Harkness' × 'Kordes' Perfecta'

Royal National Rose Society Trial Ground Certificate 1981, Courtrai Certificate of Merit 1983

'CAN-CAN' LEGlow

MODERN, LARGE-FLOWERED/HYBRID TEA,
ORANGE BLEND, REPEAT-FLOWERING

There is something spritely about this
free-flowering rose, which perhaps inspired the thought behind the name.
The blooms, borne either singly or several
together, are fairly full with about 24
broad petals. As the outer ones reflex, the
rest maintain a high tight center, creating
an appealing flower shape that admits to
view a wide display of deep orange-red,
a rich, warm and even color until at the
last stages a glint of golden yellow is revealed at the petal base. The roses are
sweetly fragrant, drop their petals cleanly
and maintain a good succession of flower
through summer and autumn. For a bed,
'Can-Can' makes an excellent choice. It
grows slightly below average height with
a rather spreading habit, and is plentifully clothed with large, dark green,
semi-glossy leaves. ZONES 4–9.

LeGrice, UK, 1982

'Just Joey' × ('Superior' × 'Mischief')

Royal National Rose Society Trial Ground
Certificate 1981

'CANARY' TANcary

MODERN, LARGE-FLOWERED/HYBRID TEA,
YELLOW BLEND, REPEAT-FLOWERING

One might expect a canary to be pure
yellow, but this rose has orange as well in
the conical buds which open into large,
full-petalled blooms of sulfur yellow.
As the firm petals expand they become
suffused with reddish orange towards the
rims and finally open cupped, at which
stage some consider the blooms are at
their most beautiful. They are capable of
producing flowers of exhibition quality,
have a pleasing fragrance and continue
to bloom through summer and autumn,
though sometimes the second flowering

'Cameo'

'Camphill Glory'

is slow. As a garden rose this is a satisfactory performer, being generally healthy
and growing to about average height
with a strong, vigorous habit and rather
tough-looking olive green foliage that
is reddish when young. ZONES 4–9.

Tantau, Germany, 1976

Parentage unknown

'CANARY BIRD'

syn. *Rosa xanthina* 'Canary Bird'
MODERN, MODERN SHRUB, DEEP YELLOW

This is a spectacular rose in the right
place, where it has room to spread its
arching garlands of single bright yellow
flowers in late spring. The blooms are
small, are borne close to the brownish
red stems and nestle among light green,
ferny leaflets. They open saucer shaped
and have a pleasing scent. A few blooms
may appear towards the end of the
growing season. The plant can become
very large so giving it space is important,
because pruning will not only spoil its
natural grace but is also often resented,
resulting in die-back; the only pruning
needed is the removal of crossing shoots
and time-expired stems. 'Canary Bird'
is one of the healthiest roses, but a site
exposed to cold winds can cause injury
to tender buds in spring. Its parentage
must involve Chinese species, perhaps
Rosa hugonis crossed with *R. xanthina*.
ZONES 4–9.

Found in England, post-1907

Probably *Rosa hugonis* × *R. xanthina*

Royal Horticultural Society Award of Garden
Merit 1993

'CANDELLA' MACspeego

syn. 'Eternally Yours'
MODERN, LARGE-FLOWERED/HYBRID TEA,
RED BLEND, REPEAT-FLOWERING

The flowers of this variety are a rich
maroon-crimson with silvery white on
the reverse of the petals and are produced

in candelabra style, that is, in wide clusters, each bloom having a fairly long supporting stem. The pointed buds open into loosely formed blooms of medium size with about 20 petals, sometimes nodding on their stems. There is a light fragrance, and they repeat their flower reasonably well through summer and autumn. This variety makes a satisfactory garden rose for beds and borders, the growth being vigorous, if somewhat spindly, to average height or above. It is hardy and healthy except for occasional trouble with mildew, and has large, glossy dark green leaves. ZONES 4–9.

McGredy, New Zealand, 1990

'Howard Morrison' × 'Esmeralda'

'CANDEUR LYONNAISE'
OLD, HYBRID PERPETUAL, LIGHT YELLOW, REPEAT-FLOWERING

This rare rose was created at the start of World War I when many French hybridizers were breeding their last roses—a great number of these men died in the conflict. The white blossoms with yellow overtones have long, pointed buds. The flowers are double, large and, some say, more attractive than the parent. It blooms in mid-summer with some repeat. There are prickles, and the foliage is large and mid-green. A hardy, vigorous shrub that makes an excellent hedge, its upright canes reach 5 ft (1.2 m). ZONES 5–9.

Croibier, France, 1914

Seedling of 'Frau Karl Druschki'

'CANDLELIGHT' AROwedye
MODERN, LARGE-FLOWERED/HYBRID TEA, DEEP YELLOW, REPEAT-FLOWERING

Though it is no longer grown for sale in its country of origin, this sun-loving rose is more highly regarded in parts of Australia. The flowers are usually borne singly, and as the plump buds open they

'Candy Sunblaze'

'Candy Rose'

reveal deep yellow in the heart of the flowers, paling to lighter yellow and fringed with pink towards the circumference. The colors are deeper overall in hot weather. The inner petals are furled to form a spiral and, as they open, the center of the flowers becomes muddled. There is a pleasant fragrance, and blooming continues through summer and autumn. For a border and for cutting this is a useful rose in warmer climates, growing to average height or more with an upright, branching habit and being furnished with large, semi-glossy leaves. ZONES 5–9.

Swim and Christensen, USA, 1982

'Shirley Laugharn' × ('Bewitched' × 'King's Ransom')

'CANDY CANE'
MODERN, CLIMBING MINIATURE, PINK BLEND, REPEAT-FLOWERING

'Candy Cane' has dashing semi-double blooms of 13 petals that are deep pink dramatically striped with white. Normally, the florets come in loose clusters often containing 15–20 blooms that arch to form a hook like that of a walking cane—hence its name! This climbing variety can grow to 4–8 ft (1.2–2.4 m) tall in warm climatic zones. Very easy to maintain and disease resistant, it flowers from early spring to early autumn and is a magnificent background plant. It also looks wonderful against a garden wall. This rose can suffer from black spot in humid climates. Though an older variey, it is still a popular rose. ZONES 5–11.

Moore, USA, 1958

Seedling × 'Zee'

'CANDY FLO'
MODERN, LARGE-FLOWERED/HYBRID TEA, APRICOT BLEND, REPEAT-FLOWERING

This is one of Edward LeGrice's unusually colored roses. The flowers are an intriguing mixture of rose pink shaded with tan-apricot tints. The buds are long and pointed and the beautiful full blooms are quite unique. Flower production is good and the unusual color is most pronounced in cool weather; in fact, the color fades in hot sun. It has a dwarf and rather spreading habit, and the foliage is a dull matt green. 'Candy Flo' is wonderful for indoor decoration as its color always attracts attention. ZONES 5–11.

LeGrice, UK, 1973

Parentage unknown

'Candy Flo'

'Candella'

'Candlelight'

'Candy Stripe'

'CANDY ROSE' MEIranovi
MODERN, MODERN SHRUB, RED BLEND, REPEAT-FLOWERING

This sturdy plant produces big clusters of rather small pink blooms that have white eyes and are reddish pink on the petal reverse. They have about 10 petals and open out like saucers, giving a little fragrance. They are borne with great freedom in summer and there is good repeat flower through to autumn. The plant grows to average height but wider than average and with overhanging shoots. For use in the landscape as, for example, a large bed or hedge in a public park, this is an excellent rose, and it makes a good specimen or mixed border plant. The spreading plant is well covered with shining medium green leaves that are reddish when young. ZONES 4–9.

Meilland, France, 1983

(Rosa sempervirens × 'Mlle Marthe Carron') × (['Lilli Marleen' × 'Evelyn Fison'] × ['Orange Sweetheart' × 'Frühlingsmorgen'])

'CANDY STRIPE'
MODERN, LARGE-FLOWERED/HYBRID TEA, PINK BLEND, REPEAT-FLOWERING

This variety can give beautiful roses for cutting. Its plump buds open into huge, headily fragrant flowers of 60 petals,

among the largest in the rose world. They are a dusty, rather hard shade of pink, streaked or striped with blush and open to a cupped form that is held for a long time. The plant blooms through summer and autumn and grows vigorously with a dense habit to average height or more. It is well clothed with large, leathery dark green leaves. ZONES 4–9.

McCummings, USA, 1963

Sport of 'Pink Peace'

'CANDY SUNBLAZE' MEIdanclar
syn. 'Romantique Meillandina'
MODERN, MINIATURE, DEEP PINK, REPEAT-FLOWERING

The medium-sized, deep pink blooms of this rose are very full with over 20 petals, and have a slight fragrance. The foliage is medium sized, dark green and glossy. It has an upright growth habit and grows quite tall. One of the 'Sunblaze' series introduced by Meilland, it was specifically bred to provide a compact bush for landscaping purposes. It provides an abundance of attractive blooms with a fast recycle time, the result being a constant supply of florets which grace the bush all year long. ZONES 5–11.

Meilland, France, 1991

Sport of 'Lady Sunblaze'

'Cannes Festival'

'Canterbury'

'Capitaine John Ingram'

'CANNES FESTIVAL'
MODERN, LARGE-FLOWERED/HYBRID TEA,
YELLOW BLEND, REPEAT-FLOWERING

The flowers of this cultivar are yellow and amber. The young blooms are long and slender, made up of about 35 petals, which slowly reveal their centers and become cupped as they open out. There is a slight fragrance, and the flowering is maintained through summer and autumn. Although not currently in commerce, 'Cannes Festival' was for some years a useful garden rose for beds and borders, more successful in drier climates since wet weather can mark the petals. The plant grows vigorously to average height with an upright, branching habit, and is furnished with deep green foliage. The house of Meilland also produced another Large-flowered Rose called 'Cannes Festival' (MEIlicafal) in 1983, which is an apricot blend. ZONES 5–9.

Meilland, France, 1951

'Peace' × 'Prinses Beatrix'

National Rose Society Certificate of Merit 1951

'CANTABRIGIENSIS'
syn. 'The Cambridge Rose'
MODERN, MODERN SHRUB, LIGHT YELLOW

On a well-established plant hundreds of pale yellow flowers decorate the branches of this rose. They are single, are borne close to the small ferny leaflets on short stems, open cupped and have a pleasing scent. There is not normally any later flower, but in autumn small round orange-red hips appear; they can hardly be called decorative because they are not easy to see against the extensive growth the plant makes. Its main stems grow up erect and bristly then become bowed under the weight of side shoots and their foliage, by which time it is well above the average height for a shrub rose. The best place for 'Cantabrigiensis' is a naturalized garden where it can have plenty of space. The name means 'of Cambridge'. ZONES 4–9.

Cambridge Botanic Garden, UK, 1931

Probably *Rosa hugonis* × *R. sericea hookeri*

Royal Horticultural Society Cory Cup 1931, Royal Horticultural Society Award of Garden Merit 1994

'CANTERBURY'   AUSbury
MODERN, MODERN SHRUB, MEDIUM PINK,
REPEAT-FLOWERING

The large flowers of this rose may be considered single, having only about 8 petals, but they make the most of what they have by opening wide and revealing golden stamens set in an expanse of warm rose pink. The petals have a silky quality and yield a pleasant fragrance, and flowering continues sporadically through summer and autumn. The plant is not a strong grower, being considerably below average height, and it has a spreading habit of growth and dark green leaves. It is likely to thrive best in an open sunny location in fertile ground or in a warm climate such as that of Australia. ZONES 4–9.

Austin, UK, 1969

('Monique' × 'Constance Spry') × seedling

'CAPE COD'   POUlfan
syn. 'Johannesburg Garden Club'
MODERN, MODERN SHRUB, LIGHT PINK,
REPEAT-FLOWERING

In South Africa this rose is sold as a 'Colourscape Rose', meaning a variety whose flowers may have the shape of a Large-flowered or Cluster-flowered Rose or a Miniature, but with a less formal habit of growth. It makes a neat shrub, bearing large clusters of single blooms of medium size. They are a kindly shade of light pink, and in a breeze have the effect of butterflies hovering close to the leafy, spreading plant. There is no scent, but the variety flowers exceptionally well through summer and autumn. For any position where a free-flowering, wide-growing shrub of up to average height is required this is a suitable variety to try; it also lends itself to being grown in a container as it is well provided with small semi-glossy leaves. ZONES 4–9.

Olesen, Denmark, 1991

Parentage unknown

'CAPITAINE BASROGER'
OLD, MOSS, RED BLEND

Although lacking much moss on the big, tight buds, this rose is an attractive red blend with full, double blooms. The flowers, borne in sizeable clusters, are up to 3 in (8 cm) in diameter and have a strong fragrance. The apex flower of each cluster often opens well ahead of those surrounding it, nestling among the buds in an attractive fashion. The petals reflex, and the carmine may change to shades of purple depending on the weather and exposure to the sun. There are fearsome prickles. It reaches a height of 8 ft (2.4 m) and can be trained as a climber, looking very effective on a pillar; in any case it does need a support. ZONES 4–9.

Moreau-Robert, France, 1890

Parentage unknown

'CAPITAINE JOHN INGRAM'
OLD, MOSS, MAUVE

This rose has one of the richest colors in good weather. The pine-scented buds are well covered with reddish, sticky, dark greeny brown moss. They open to pompon, flat blooms that change color from dark purple to velvety crimson to reddish purple. There may be recurring bloom in late summer. The recurving blossoms have a button eye. Attaining about 5 ft (1.5 m) in good soils, this is a vigorous, dense shrub with many small prickles on its stems and lots of dark brownish red bristles. With its numerous dark green leaves of medium size, it makes an effective hedge. ZONES 4–9.

Laffay, France, 1854

Parentage unknown

'CAPRI'
MODERN, CLUSTER-FLOWERED/FLORIBUNDA,
ORANGE-PINK, REPEAT-FLOWERING

This free-blooming bush rose bears small clusters of fairly large blooms. They open from cone-shaped buds into high-centered, double flowers that become cupped as they expand to show about 35 petals. The color is a pretty combination of coral pink shades, which are deeper on the upperside of the petal surface and lighter on the underside. There is a light scent, and blooms continue to appear through summer and autumn. In the garden, 'Capri' is useful for beds and borders, although it appears no longer to be offered in commerce. The plant grows vigorously to average height, with glossy bright green, leathery foliage. ZONES 4–9.

Fisher, USA, 1956

'Fashion' × 'Floradora'

'CAPRICE'
syn. 'Lady Eve Price'
MODERN, LARGE-FLOWERED/HYBRID TEA,
PINK BLEND, REPEAT-FLOWERING

Fifty years ago the novel coloring of this rose made it a popular favorite, though

'Capri'

'Cantabrigiensis'

'Capitaine Basroger'

'Captain Christy' (foliage)

today only two growers, in France and Israel, are listing it. The flowers, often borne 3 or more to a shoot but sometimes singly, are bright carmine-pink to carmine-red inside and pinky cream to light yellow outside. They open from plump buds into semi-double, open-centered flowers that are quite large when the waved petals are fully expanded. The summer and autumn flowering is prolific, with some blooms between the main flushes. They withstand bad weather well, and there is a light scent. 'Caprice' makes a colorful bedding rose with vigorous, branching growth up to average height and a dense cover of glossy dark green leaves, which have coppery tints when young. Black spot can be troublesome in some years. ZONES 4–9.

Meilland, France, 1948

'Peace' × 'Fantastique'

'CAPRIOLE'

MODERN, CLUSTER-FLOWERED/FLORIBUNDA, MEDIUM PINK, REPEAT-FLOWERING

This variety displays its flowers in showy clusters of up to 40 blooms. They are cherry red in bud and open to large, semi-double blooms of vivid pure pink; they are lightened by prominent gold stamens. The flowers hold their color well whatever the weather, and continue to appear and add their sweet fragrance to the garden through summer and autumn. They look well in beds and borders, and as a hedge where a short grower is required. The habit of growth is vigorous, compact and bushy to below average height, and the plant is well furnished with dark green, semi-glossy foliage. Capriole means 'a leap': the flowering habit may have suggested this name. ZONES 4–9.

Tantau, Germany, 1956

'Red Favorite' × 'Fanal'

'CAPTAIN CHRISTY'

MODERN, LARGE-FLOWERED/HYBRID TEA, LIGHT PINK, REPEAT-FLOWERING

One of the earliest Large-flowered Roses still in cultivation, this variety is loved for the beauty of the flowers, its repeat-flowering ability and its continuing vigor. The large blooms are light rose pink, very full of petals and open out cupped and eventually rather flat, displaying charming muddled centers. In the depths of the petals the color is deeper, and in warmer conditions the flowers improve—they can be spoilt by rain, which may cause them to ball and

'Captain Christy'

refuse to open. Scent is present but is not strong. The height is average or above and the foliage is robust, reasonably plentiful and frequently likened to that of mahonias. For an historical garden this would be a good example of a successful early Large-flowered Rose, being easy to grow and giving a summer display followed by a dependable autumn show, with a few blooms in between. The raiser named it to honor a Londoner who was a keen amateur rosarian. **Climbing Captain Christy** (Ducher, France, 1881) has the same flower characteristics as its parent, and it also gives a certain amount of repeat bloom. In the climbing form the informality of the petal arrangement looks very appealing, and the attractive veining on the petals is also easier to appreciate. The plant grows strongly to average height or more for a climber, and has a good covering of foliage. It benefits from being sited in a sunny aspect, preferably against a wall where the vigorous growth can be spread out and well supported, because the blooms it carries are often on long heavy flower stems. ZONES 4–9.

Lacharme, France, 1873

'Victor Verdier' × 'Safrano'

'CAPTAIN HARRY STEBBINGS'

MODERN, LARGE-FLOWERED/HYBRID TEA, DEEP PINK, REPEAT-FLOWERING

This variety, which is mostly grown in the western USA and Canada, bears big pointed buds that open out into very large flowers of deep reddish pink. There are usually over 40 broad petals of firm texture, and the high-centered blooms therefore have interest for exhibitors. There is a good fruity fragrance, and flowering continues through summer and autumn. The plant grows upright to about average height and is well

'Caprice'

furnished with large, leathery leaves. The raiser, from Santa Rosa in California, gave it his own name, one way, as a commentator observed, of showing his faith in it. ZONES 4–9.

Stebbings, USA, 1980

Seedling of unknown sport

'CAPTAIN SAMUEL HOLLAND'

MODERN, MODERN SHRUB, MEDIUM RED, REPEAT-FLOWERING

This variety can be trimmed and grown as a big shrub, or the long shoots may be trained up to form a pillar. The flowers have about 24 petals and are carried singly or in clusters of up to 10. They are deep magenta in color and open rather flat, developing centers rather similar to camellias. There is a light fragrance, and the variety continues to bear flowers through summer and autumn. The plant is vigorous, producing long trailing branches, and is well clothed with glossy mid-green foliage. 'Captain Samuel Holland' was developed by the Canadian Department of Agriculture to serve the need for hardier roses in that country. ZONES 3–9.

Ogilvie, Canada, 1992

(*Rosa kordesii* × ['Red Dawn' × 'Suzanne']) × (*R. kordesii* × ['Red Dawn' × 'Suzanne'])

'CAPTAIN THOMAS'

MODERN, LARGE-FLOWERED CLIMBER, WHITE, REPEAT-FLOWERING

This attractive and unusual rose bears clusters of long pointed buds that open into simple 5-petalled blooms, which are a little over medium size. They are lemon yellow, fading creamy white towards the margins of the crinkled petals, and as they open they display prominent dark stamens. Although the variety does repeat its bloom, it only does so sporadically in late summer after the early flowering season. There is a light fragrance. The

growth is vigorous, with lustrous light green leaves, and the plant may be grown as a tall untidy shrub or trained up as a pillar. 'Captain Thomas' has proved a useful parent rose for breeders of yellow roses and was the pollen parent of 'Golden Showers'. It carries the name of its raiser, who was from California, and was put into commerce by Armstrong's, a well-known rose nursery in that state. ZONES 4–9.

Thomas, USA, 1935

'Bloomfield Completeness' × 'Attraction'

'CAPTAIN WATKINS'

MODERN, CLUSTER-FLOWERED/FLORIBUNDA, MEDIUM PINK, REPEAT-FLOWERING

This variety is a small-growing rose with a compact habit. It produces both small and large clusters of rather ragged-edged flowers of rose pink. The resistance to disease is good, but flower production is rather poor and there are long periods between flushes. For maximum effect, a number of these bushes need to be planted close together. The mid-green foliage of 'Captain Watkins' is somewhat sparse. ZONES 5–11.

Hyde, Australia, 1960

Parentage unknown

'Captain Watkins'

'Capriole'

'CARA MIA'

syns 'Dearest One', 'Maja Mauser', 'Natacha', 'Danima'

MODERN, LARGE-FLOWERED/HYBRID TEA, MEDIUM RED, REPEAT-FLOWERING

The round buds of this variety develop into large, double blooms that have a good fragrance. These are medium red in color and flower repeatedly throughout the summer months. The flowers contrast well with the dark green foliage, which is moderately resistant to disease. This rose has upright, vigorous growth and is popular as a bedding variety. It can be propagated by budding. ZONES 4–9.

McDaniel, USA, 1969

Parentage unknown

'CARABELLA'

MODERN, CLUSTER-FLOWERED/FLORIBUNDA, YELLOW BLEND, REPEAT-FLOWERING

The pointed apricot buds of this rose develop into creamy flowers that are edged with pink and have a pleasing fragrance. The single blooms are borne in clusters and, after the first flush, continue through summer and autumn. The plant is of moderate growth with glossy light green, healthy foliage and a bushy habit. It can be propagated by budding. ZONES 4–9.

Rietmuller, Australia, 1960

'Gartendirektor Otto Linne' × seedling

'CARDINAL DE RICHELIEU'

syns 'Cardinal Richelieu', 'Rose van Sian'

OLD, GALLICA, MAUVE

This is one of the most floriferous of the Gallicas, and its reputation and popularity are well merited. The long-lasting flowers, borne in small clusters, open from globular buds to a rich dark red that quickly change to royal purple, ageing to slate-gray. The central petals fold inwards to show off a lighter color on the reverse. 'Cardinal de Richelieu' is a medium-growing shrub to 4 ft (1.2 m), of tidy habit, and needs to be pruned well. The stems are burnished dark green with few or no thorns of consequence, and the leaves are a lush dark green, bordering on glossy. Cardinal Richelieu (1585–1642) was minister to Louis XIII. ZONES 4–9.

Parmentier, Belgium, pre-1847

Parentage unknown

Royal Horticultural Society Award of Garden Merit 1993

'CARDINAL HUME'   HARregale

MODERN, MODERN SHRUB, MAUVE BLEND, REPEAT-FLOWERING

This is an extremely popular and widely grown Modern Shrub that bears large clusters of magnificent medium-sized maroon-purple cupped blooms. They are produced throughout summer and autumn with excellent continuity, and have a strong fragrance of musk. The dark foliage in association with the color of the flowers makes this variety a very desirable plant, although it is a little prone to black spot. It has moderate, slightly spreading growth and is useful as a specimen plant in borders, where its distinct color adds a different spectrum. 'Cardinal Hume' has a complicated

'Carabella'

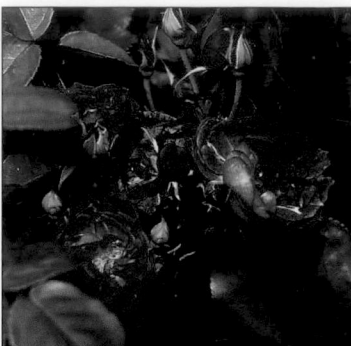

'Cardinal Hume'

pedigree and, like 'International Herald Tribune', was the start of a new type of rose bred from *Rosa californica*. The name was given to honor Basil Hume, the leading Roman Catholic cleric in England. It is easily propagated by budding or from cuttings. ZONES 4–9.

Harkness, UK, 1984

([Seedling × ('Orange Sensation' × 'Allgold')] × *Rosa californica plena*) × 'Frank Naylor'

Royal National Rose Society Certificate of Merit 1984, Courtrai Certificate of Merit 1986

'CARDINAL SONG'   MEImouslin

syn. 'Jacques Prévert'

MODERN, LARGE-FLOWERED/HYBRID TEA, MEDIUM RED, REPEAT-FLOWERING

Although in the USA this rose is called a Grandiflora (a classification not recognized by the World Federation of Rose Societies), the large size of the flowers qualifies it to be considered a Large-flowered rather than a Cluster-flowered Rose. The blooms average over 40 petals, and are often borne singly, sometimes in clusters. They open somewhat flat and carry a light fragrance, continuing to bloom through summer and autumn. In the garden this is a useful rose for beds and borders, and lasts well when cut. The plant grows to average height with a bushy, fairly upright habit, and is well furnished with large, glossy dark green leaves. ZONES 5–9.

Meilland, France, 1992

'Olympiad' × ('Michel Lis Le Jardinier' × 'Red Lady')

Lyon Gold Medal 1993

'CAREFREE BEAUTY'   BUCbi

syn. 'Audace'

MODERN, MODERN SHRUB, MEDIUM PINK, REPEAT-FLOWERING

This very popular shrub produces small clusters of pointed buds that open to a rich rose pink, but it rarely carries more

'Carefree Beauty'

'Carefree Delight'

than 4 flowers per stem. Each big and blowzy flower, to 4½ in (11 cm) wide, has 10–20 petals and gives a good fragrance. The blooms appear freely on their first flush, with repeat-flowerings later on. The foliage is smooth and olive green and wonderfully resistant to disease. It is an upright plant that is always covered in flowers and spreads readily, which makes it good as a low-maintenance hedge, but it is also fine on its own as a specimen plant. The orange-red hips that develop after the flowers add interest in winter. The growth is relatively winter hardy and can be propagated by budding. ZONES 4–9.

Buck, USA, 1977

Seedling × 'Prairie Princess'

'CAREFREE DELIGHT'   MEIpotal

syns 'Bingo Meidiland', 'Bingo Meillandecor'

MODERN, MODERN SHRUB, PINK BLEND, REPEAT-FLOWERING

Bred by Alain Meilland, 'Carefree Delight' gives a stunning display when planted *en masse*. The shrubs are literally covered with a haze of charming pink blooms continuously through the warmer months. Individually, the relatively small blooms are cup shaped and semi-double with a hint of cream, and are carried in clusters of up to 15. The growth is vigorous, spreading and well branched with an exceptional resistance to disease. The graceful, arching canes, covered with glossy green leaves during the growing season, are attractive even in winter and the pretty rosehips, which follow the flowers, bring hungry birds into the garden. ZONES 4–10.

Meilland, France, 1993

'Gitte' × seedling

Paris Gold Medal 1992, The Hague Gold Medal 1992, Anerkannte Deutsche Rose 1994, All-America Rose Selection 1996

'Cara Mia'

'Cardinal Song'

'Cardinal de Richelieu'

C

'CAREFREE WONDER' MEIpitac

syns 'Carefully Wonder', 'Dynastie'

MODERN, MODERN SHRUB, PINK BLEND,
REPEAT-FLOWERING

This repeat-flowering shrub rose bears
a profusion of small clusters of double
blooms, which cover the plant well with
an uninterrupted display of rich pink.
The wonderful flowers, which have 26
petals and are of medium size, have a
pale reverse and a slight fragrance. The
dense foliage is bright green and has
great resistance to disease. This variety
is a pretty, bushy growing, relatively
compact shrub with reddish prickles and
a good harvest of hips in autumn. It is
very useful for specimen planting or as
a hedge rose; it is especially spectacular
when planted in groups. ZONES 3–9.

Meilland, France, 1978

('Prairie Princess' × 'Nirvana') × ('Eyepaint' ×
'Rustica')

All-America Rose Selection 1991

'CARELESS LOVE'

MODERN, LARGE-FLOWERED/HYBRID TEA,
PINK BLEND, REPEAT-FLOWERING

This sport is a vigorous grower with a
good covering of large, leathery foliage.
There is a heavy fragrance, and the deep
pink blooms each have about 24 petals
that are streaked and splashed with
white. The flowers are large and well-
formed, which makes for a variety that
is very suitable in beds or borders, and
there is a good resistance to disease.
ZONES 4–9.

Conklin, USA, 1955

Sport of 'Red Radiance'

'CARELESS MOMENT'

MODERN, MINIATURE, PINK BLEND,
REPEAT-FLOWERING

The buds of this rose are long and
pointed, and produce florets with good
high centers. The blooms are usually

'Careless Moment'

'Carefree Wonder'

'Carla'

borne singly or occasionally in small
clusters all season long. In warmer
climates there is a slight fragrance.
It has a bushy and spreading growth
habit, and small, attractive, dark green
foliage that is resistant to diseases. It is
very easy to maintain and has an ample
supply of outstanding buds and quality
exhibition-form blooms—clear, clean,
with good color and substance on a very
dependable plant. At the American Rose
Society National Convention in Mobile,
Alabama, many years ago a fancy dress
contest was held where Rose Society
members were to come as their favorite
rose. The winner was a very pregnant
woman! ZONES 5–11.

Williams, USA, 1977

'Little Darling' × 'Over the Rainbow'

'CARIBBEAN' KORbirac

MODERN, LARGE-FLOWERED/HYBRID TEA,
APRICOT BLEND, REPEAT-FLOWERING

The large blooms of this variety each
have between 26 and 40 petals that are
apricot-orange in color with a yellow
blend. They are borne in small clusters
and give a pleasing fragrance. The large,
dark green, semi-glossy foliage makes
a good foil to the flowers and there is
a pronounced red mid-vein and leaf
margin on each new leaf. The plant
grows to medium height with many
thorns, and is resistant to disease. This
rose is useful as a bedding plant or as
a specimen in borders. It can be propagated by budding. ZONES 4–9.

Kordes, Germany, 1992

'Mercedes' × ('New Dawn' × seedling)

All-America Rose Selection 1994

'CARINA' MEIchim

MODERN, LARGE-FLOWERED/HYBRID TEA,
MEDIUM PINK, REPEAT-FLOWERING

The large, double blooms of this rose
each have about 40 petals that form a

'Carnaval'

'Carina'

'Carnaval'

beautiful flower with a high center and
a good form. They are medium pink and
fragrant, and are borne through summer
and autumn. The disease-resistant
foliage is deep green and leathery, and is
produced on an upright plant of medium
height. The variety is useful as a bedding
plant and a show rose and it can be
propagated by budding. ZONES 4–9.

Meilland, France, 1963

'White Knight' × ('Happiness' × 'Independence')

Anerkannte Deutsche Rose 1966

'CARLA'

MODERN, LARGE-FLOWERED/HYBRID TEA,
ORANGE-PINK, REPEAT-FLOWERING

This variety makes an excellent show
rose; the very large flowers are soft
salmon-pink in color, each with over
24 petals. There is also a pleasing
fragrance that persists as the blooms
continue to appear throughout summer
and autumn. The foliage is dark green,
which makes a good foil to the colorful
roses. The plant gives vigorous growth
that is resistant to disease, and can be
propagated by budding. ZONES 4–9.

de Ruiter, The Netherlands, 1963

'Queen Elizabeth' × 'The Optimist'

'CARMEN'

MODERN, HYBRID RUGOSA, MEDIUM RED

For a position where a disease-resistant
hedge rose is needed, 'Carmen' is a useful
variety. It produces large and single,
crimson flowers with yellow stamens
that give a modest scent. The dark green,
wrinkled leaves are borne on vigorous
growth that occasionally produces a few
flowers in autumn. It can be propagated
from cuttings or by budding. ZONES 4–9.

Lambert, Germany, 1907

Rosa rugosa rosea × 'Princesse de Béarn'

'CARNAVAL' KORfrilla

syns 'Carnival', 'Clip Rose'

MODERN, CLUSTER-FLOWERED/FLORIBUNDA,
RED BLEND, REPEAT-FLOWERING

This is an ideal variety for beds and borders, because the dark green, matt foliage
makes a striking color combination with
the white, red-edged flowers. These are
large, with up to 40 petals, and appear
through summer and autumn. There is
little fragrance. The growth is bushy and
has a moderate resistance to disease.
ZONES 4–9.

Kordes, Germany, 1987

Seedling × ('Die Krone' × 'Simona')

C

'Carol Ann'

'Carnival Parade'

'Carol-Jean'

'Carole Joy'

'CARNIVAL PARADE'
MODERN, MINIATURE, YELLOW BLEND, REPEAT-FLOWERING

'Carnival Parade' has very double golden yellow blooms edged red. The blooms have about 45 petals with high centers and are suitable for exhibition. Florets are borne singly and have a slight scent. The growth habit is bushy and upright with broad, firm, glossy foliage. A vigorous grower, it is very prolific, producing small blooms all year long. It is quick to repeat. ZONES 5–11.

Williams, USA, 1978

'Starburst' × 'Over the Rainbow'

'CAROL'
MODERN, LARGE-FLOWERED/HYBRID TEA, PINK BLEND, REPEAT-FLOWERING

The flowers of this variety are an attractive cyclamen rose with an apricot center. They are well formed blooms, each composed of about 45 petals, with a slight fragrance. Throughout summer and into autumn 'Carol' can be relied upon to produce its flowers in colorful clusters on a moderate-sized bush. The stems are almost thornless, and the moderate growth has good disease resistance. It is suitable as a bedding variety, and can be grown under glass for its cut flowers. ZONES 4–9.

Herholdt, South Africa, 1964

'Queen Elizabeth' × 'Confidence'

'CAROL AMLING'
syns 'Carol', 'Garnette Carol', 'Garnette Pink'
MODERN, CLUSTER-FLOWERED/FLORIBUNDA, MEDIUM PINK, REPEAT-FLOWERING

The Garnette family of roses has been developed principally for the cut-flower market, and do not make very successful garden plants as a result. This variety produces clusters of very small, double, rose pink blooms with a lighter edge, throughout summer and autumn. They are borne on a moderately upright bush that has some resistance to disease. The variety is propagated by budding or from cuttings. ZONES 4–9.

Amling and Beltran, USA, 1953

Sport of 'Garnette'

'CAROL ANN'
MODERN, POLYANTHA, ORANGE-PINK, REPEAT-FLOWERING

This dwarf plant epitomizes a whole host of varieties whose principal characteristics are a tendency to produce flowers that mutate into a wide spectrum of color. The colors are endless, and range from salmon to deep pink through to bright scarlet. 'Carol Ann' has flowers of orange-salmon that are very double and small, yet are packed with 35–45 petals. They are carried in big clusters all through summer, although this is only a very short bush. It is used extensively as an edging plant and pot rose. The variety is prone to mildew in autumn, and is propagated by budding or from cuttings. ZONES 3–9.

Kluis, The Netherlands, 1940

Sport of 'Marianne Kluis Superior'

'CAROL-JEAN'
MODERN, MINIATURE, DEEP PINK, REPEAT-FLOWERING

The blooms of this rose are a deep rosy pink on an upright, bushy plant. The florets with 25 petals are usually borne in clusters that are often too heavy for the stem to support, and so the fully opened clusters tend to droop. There is no lack of vigor in this rose and it repeats fairly well in most climates. While not an exhibition-type bloom, it can provide a stunning garden display. The bright color holds in hot weather. ZONES 5–11.

Moore, USA, 1977

'Pinocchio' × 'Little Chief'

'CAROLE JOY'
MODERN, LARGE-FLOWERED/HYBRID TEA, MEDIUM RED, REPEAT-FLOWERING

'Carole Joy' is a moderately strong grower with blood red, well-shaped flowers of 45 petals. They are large and sometimes of exhibition standard, and have a strong fragrance. The healthy foliage is dark green and glossy and new growth is purple tinged. Flower production is not as high as either parent and repeat bloom is rather slow. ZONES 5–9.

Allender, Australia, 1991

'Alec's Red' × 'Camp David'

'CAROLINE MARNIESSE'
OLD, NOISETTE, WHITE, REPEAT-FLOWERING

Sometimes mistaken for 'Félicité et Perpétue', this rather rare Noisette has small, globular blooms of pale flesh pink turning white. The clusters open over bronze-green foliage from late spring until autumn in warm situations. It is a good climber, and the 2 in (5 cm) blooms appear 'as neat as a pin and dainty as a French doll' according to Ethelyn Emery Keays, the noted American rose writer. ZONES 7–10.

Roeser, France, 1848

Parentage unknown

'CARROT TOP'   POUltop
MODERN, MINIATURE, ORANGE BLEND, REPEAT-FLOWERING

The fire engine orange color certainly makes this rose stand out in the garden crowd! The very shapely buds hold their brilliance from beginning to end on an attractive rounded bush surrounded with dark green foliage. The plant itself is very clean, easy to maintain and not too susceptible to diseases. The flowers have a high center and although there are not very many petals (20–25), they hold their form well for exhibition. An excellent repeat bloomer, the plant is almost always in flower. The blooms have a slight fragrance. ZONES 4–11.

Olesen, Denmark, 1994

Cluster-flowered seedling × Miniature seedling

C

'Carrot Top'

C

'CARROUSEL'

MODERN, LARGE-FLOWERED/HYBRID TEA,
MEDIUM RED, REPEAT-FLOWERING

This vigorous plant makes a good variety
for garden beds. It can be propagated by
budding. It produces double flowers that
consist of about 20 medium red petals
throughout summer and autumn. There
is a pleasant fragrance. The variety has a
bushy, vigorous, upright-growing habit
and dark green, leathery, healthy, glossy
foliage. ZONES 4–9.

Duehrsen, USA, 1950

Seedling × 'Margy'

Portland Gold Medal 1955, American Rose
Society Gold Medal 1956

'CARY GRANT' MEImainger

syn. 'Bushveld Dawn'

MODERN, LARGE-FLOWERED/HYBRID TEA,
ORANGE BLEND, REPEAT-FLOWERING

The large flowers of this rose each contain between 35–40 petals, and are borne
through summer with occasional later
blooms in autumn. The flowers are
a vivid orange blend with luminous
yellow-orange and scarlet-orange on
the margins of the basal petals. The high-
centered, well-formed blooms make this
a good variety for exhibition purposes.
There is a heavy, spicy fragrance. The
dark green foliage with a good health
record complements the bright flowers.

This is a good bedding and specimen
plant that is easily propagated by
budding. ZONES 4–9.

Meilland, France, 1987

('Pharaoh' × 'Königin der Rosen') × (['Zambĩa'] ×
'Suspense'] × 'King's Ransom')

'CASA BLANCA'

MODERN, LARGE-FLOWERED CLIMBER, WHITE,
REPEAT-FLOWERING

The white, semi-double, medium blooms
of this rose have a slight fragrance, and
are carried in small clusters. The overall
appearance of this moderate climber is
enhanced by dark green, glossy foliage
and vigorous growth, which flowers well
in summer and occasionally in autumn.
It is a very healthy plant. ZONES 4–9.

Sima, USA, 1968

'New Dawn' × 'Fashion'

'CASANOVA'

MODERN, LARGE-FLOWERED/HYBRID TEA,
LIGHT YELLOW, REPEAT-FLOWERING

The large, double, high-centered flowers
of this plant epitomize the whole host
of varieties that Sam McGredy produced
when he first embarked on the noble art
of rose breeding and assumed the mantle
of his ancestors. 'Casanova' has all the
attributes of a modern Large-flowered
Rose: a fashionable color and distinguished parents. The straw yellow,

'Cascabel'

fragrant blooms, each packed with about
38 petals, are produced on a healthy plant
that is popular with exhibitors. It is suitable for bedding. ZONES 4–9.

McGredy, New Zealand, 1964

'Queen Elizabeth' × 'Kordes' Perfecta'

'CASCABEL'

MODERN, CLUSTER-FLOWERED/FLORIBUNDA,
RED BLEND, REPEAT-FLOWERING

This compact plant with very vigorous
growth makes a good bedding rose. The
blooms emerge from globular buds, and
the 45–50 petals open flat. They are red
with a pearly underside, which turns to
carmine as they mature. There is only a
little scent, and the flowers will continue
to show through summer. The foliage
is glossy and dark green, with relatively
good health. The variety can be propagated by budding. ZONES 4–9.

Dot, Spain, 1957

'Méphisto' × 'Perla de Alcañada'

'CASINO' MACca

syn. 'Gerbe d'Or'

MODERN, LARGE-FLOWERED CLIMBER,
LIGHT YELLOW, REPEAT-FLOWERING

This really is one of the best yellow-
flowered climbing roses around; it is
good to grow on a warm wall, and its

'Casino'

floriferousness is quite remarkable. The
soft yellow, double, quartered blooms
are well formed, very full and fragrant;
they hold their large, old-fashioned
shape well and usually repeat superbly:
up to 5 times per year. The hips, if
deadheading is not completed, are large,
round and attractive. 'Casino' also makes
a good cut flower. The foliage is dark
green and healthy. Growers in regions
with hard winters may be discouraged
from growing this rose because it likes
warm climates. It has not received the
attention that it deserves. ZONES 5–9.

McGredy, New Zealand, 1963

'Coral Dawn' × 'Buccaneer'

National Rose Society Gold Medal 1963

'CASQUE D'OR' DELcasor

MODERN, LARGE-FLOWERED/HYBRID TEA,
MEDIUM YELLOW, REPEAT-FLOWERING

This upright bush with vigorous growth
bears medium-sized, cupped flowers
throughout the summer months. Each
bloom contains 30 yellow petals with
little fragrance. The foliage is a mid-
green. 'Casque D'Or' is a suitable variety
for bedding, or to grow as a standard.
It is easily propagated by budding.
ZONES 4–9.

Delbard, France, 1979

('Zambra' × 'Jean de la Lune') × ('Michèle
Meilland' × 'Tahiti')

'CASSANDRA'

MODERN, LARGE-FLOWERED/HYBRID TEA,
MEDIUM RED, REPEAT-FLOWERING

The large fragrant flowers of 'Cassandra'
are cherry red, high centered and consist
of 30–35 petals. Flower production is
below average and repeat bloom is slow.
The abundant foliage is large, dull green
and slightly serrated. 'Cassandra' is not
as good as any of its illustrious parents,
all of which are still readily available
in most countries. ZONES 5–9.

Dorieux, France, 1966

('Karl Herbst' × 'Ena Harkness') × ('Christian
Dior' × 'Peace')

'CASSANDRE' MEIdenji

MODERN, LARGE-FLOWERED CLIMBER,
MEDIUM RED, REPEAT-FLOWERING

This variety is mostly grown in warm
climates. It makes a useful pillar rose,
and is also suitable for growing on walls
and fences. The flowers are of medium
size, carried in clusters, with about
24 petals, and open cupped with a
rounded outline, showing light yellow
stamens. They are light red, ageing to

'Casque d'Or' below, with 'Swany' as a standard

'Carrousel'

'Casa Blanca'

rich carmine pink, with appreciable fragrance. Blooms appear through summer and autumn against a background of glossy dark green leaves. The plant grows vigorously to average height. ZONES 5–9.

Meilland, France, 1989

Parentage unknown

'CASTLE OF MEY' COClucid
MODERN, CLUSTER-FLOWERED/FLORIBUNDA, ORANGE BLEND, REPEAT-FLOWERING

This medium-sized, bushy grower bears small clusters of moderately full flowers during summer. Each bloom contains 15–20 orange-gold or apricot petals. There is a modest scent. The glossy leaves maintain good health, and this variety is suitable for growing in beds or borders. It can be propagated by budding. It was named after the northern Scottish retreat of the Queen Mother. ZONES 4–9.

Cocker, UK, 1992

'Anne Cocker' × ('Yellow Pages' × 'Silver Jubilee')

'CATERPILLAR' POUlcat
syns 'Charming Bells', Kiki Rose', 'Pink Drift'
MODERN, MINIATURE, LIGHT PINK

This is a low-growing, healthy Miniature Rose that spreads considerably, which makes it ideal as a ground cover. In summer it produces small, double, light pink blooms in medium to large clusters. There is only a little scent. The leaves are small, dark green and glossy, and the variety is easily propagated from cuttings or by budding. 'Caterpillar' is a development of the Bells varieties, and has a more sophisticated plant structure. However, it was quickly superseded by repeat-flowering forms. ZONES 4–9.

Olesen, Denmark, 1985

'Temple Bells' × seedling

'Caterpillar'

'Cassandre'

'CATHEDRAL'
syns 'Coventry Cathedral', 'Houston'
MODERN, CLUSTER-FLOWERED/FLORIBUNDA, APRICOT BLEND, REPEAT-FLOWERING

This is a free-flowering Cluster-flowered Rose with reddish apricot-shaded, salmon blooms. The large, slightly fragrant flowers are borne on a bushy plant with glossy olive green foliage in small clusters. Disease resistant and hardy, one of its names celebrates the rebuilding and re-dedication of the Coventry Cathedral, which was devastated during the blitz of World War II. It can be propagated by budding. ZONES 4–9.

McGredy, New Zealand, 1975

'Little Darling' × ('Goldilocks' × 'Irish Mist')

New Zealand Gold Medal 1974, Portland Gold Medal 1974, All-America Rose Selection 1976

'CATHEDRAL SPLENDOUR'
HARbell
MODERN, CLUSTER-FLOWERED/FLORIBUNDA, ORANGE-PINK, REPEAT-FLOWERING

This cultivar was named and promoted as a fund raiser for Westminster Cathedral's centenary. It bears sweetly scented, salmon pink, semi-double blooms. They have long stems, and continue to appear throughout summer. The leaves are a very healthy, glossy mid-green. This is a very good bedding variety that is also useful for cutting. Propagate by budding. ZONES 4–9.

Harkness, UK, 1995

Parentage unknown

'CATHERINE DE WÜRTEMBERG'
syn. 'Catherine von Wurtemberg'
OLD, MOSS, LIGHT PINK

This extremely rare rose has soft pink, flat, very full, globular blooms. The buds are well mossed then, when fully open, the slightly fragrant blossoms appear muddled in the center. The vigorous,

'Cathedral'

'Catherine Guillot'

'Catherine McAuley'

'Catherine Deneuve'

slender, erect bush can reach 6 ft (1.8 m). The young leaves are red and pointed; there are a few small prickles. ZONES 4–9.

Robert, France, 1843

Parentage unknown

'CATHERINE DENEUVE'
MEIpraserpi
MODERN, LARGE-FLOWERED/HYBRID TEA, ORANGE-PINK, REPEAT-FLOWERING

'Catherine Deneuve' grows into a strong, spreading bush with copious, large, matt mid-green foliage that is very disease resistant. The buds are produced mainly singly and are long, pointed and open fairly quickly to deep coral pink blooms of 20 petals. They are fragrant, have excellent substance and last well without fading; flower production is high and there is quick repeat. This variety is an excellent rose for bedding, borders and for use as a standard rose. ZONES 5–9.

Meilland, France, 1981

Parentage unknown

Rome Gold Medal 1979

'CATHERINE GUILLOT'
syn. 'Michel Bonnet'
OLD, BOURBON, DEEP PINK, REPEAT-FLOWERING

The carmine-rose blooms of 'Catherine Guillot' are quartered, full and very large, the smooth purple-pink petals

'Catherine Deneuve'

making a perfect cup. This is a vigorous bush reaching 6 ft (1.8 m) and even higher, and when used as a small climber it flowers freely throughout summer. The leaves are attractive, purple and long. It is an excellent cut flower with a strong fragrance. ZONES 5–9.

Guillot, France, 1860

Seedling of 'Louise Odier'

'CATHERINE McAULEY'
JACibras
MODERN, CLUSTER-FLOWERED/FLORIBUNDA, MEDIUM YELLOW, REPEAT-FLOWERING

Catherine McAuley was an Irish heiress who helped form the Sisters of Mercy, an order that spread through America to Australia and the Pacific Islands. This rose is a rich golden yellow with a delicate fragrance. The buds, which are well shaped and are produced in clusters of 4–5 blooms, are high centered and last well when cut. It is a very free-flowering plant that is quick to repeat. This is an ideal bedding rose and is also suitable for use as a hedge. ZONES 5–10.

Jackson & Perkins, USA, 1993

Parentage unknown

'Cavalcade'

'Catherine Mermet'

'CATHERINE MERMET'
OLD, TEA, LIGHT PINK, REPEAT-FLOWERING

This rose has high-centered, well-shaped buds that open to reveal fragrant, flesh pink blossoms edged in lilac. The large, globular, nodding blooms recur from spring until autumn, and look most attractive on their long stems. Their best moment is just after opening. 'Catherine Mermet', which is a valuable cut flower, likes warm weather and hates rain. ZONES 7–10.

Guillot, France, 1869

Parentage unknown

'CATHERINE SEYTON'
OLD, SWEET BRIAR, LIGHT PINK

One of the lesser-known Sweet Briar hybrids, 'Catherine Seyton' was named after a heroine of Scottish novelist Sir Walter Scott. The large, single, light pink blossoms are accented with attractive

yellow stamens. 'Catherine Seyton' is a vigorous bush that can reach 8 ft (2.4 m) and has prickles and orange-red hips. Both the blooms and the foliage are fragrant, the scent being strongest on a hot summer day or in the evening after rain. ZONES 5–9.

Penzance, UK, 1894

Parentage unknown

'CAVALCADE'
MODERN, CLUSTER-FLOWERED/FLORIBUNDA, RED BLEND, REPEAT-FLOWERING

This variety is suitable as a bedding plant and is valued for its pretty flowers, although they require constant dead-heading. Its round to oval buds develop into ox-blood red and yellow blooms, then turn to crimson-carmine and silvery pink in full sunlight. The medium-sized, double flowers have 32 petals each, and are carried in small clusters. There is a strong fragrance, like that of apples. The foliage is glossy, dark green and healthy, and the plant is vigorous and bushy. ZONES 4–9.

Verschuren-Pechtold, The Netherlands, 1950

Parentage unknown

'CÉCILE BRÜNNER'
syns 'Mme Cécile Brünner', 'Mlle Cécile Brünner', 'Mignon', 'Sweetheart Rose', 'Maltese Rose'

MODERN, POLYANTHA, LIGHT PINK, REPEAT-FLOWERING

This long-lived variety, which is classed as an Old Garden Rose, China, by some

'Cécile Brünner'

'Cécile Brünner'

authorities, patently has its origins in Asia, although authorities are divided between *Rosa multiflora* and *R. chinensis*. Almost thornless, it repeatedly produces large clusters of very small, perfectly shaped pink blooms. The long, pointed bud opens to pale, silvery pink blossoms. The perfectly formed, miniature blooms are double and rise above light red peduncles. The scent is sweet and slightly spicy. It is a small bush with sparse, dull green foliage of 3–5 leaflets, but it is very healthy. The shrub is low growing, which makes it ideal for small gardens or small beds. The continuous blooming is one reason that it has been so popular since its introduction. It was named for the daughter of Ulrich Brünner, renowned rose grower at Lausanne, Switzerland. It can be propagated by budding or from cuttings. **'Climbing Cécile Brünner'** (syns 'Climbing Mme Cécile Brünner', 'Climbing Mlle Cécile Brünner', 'Climbing Mignon', 'Climbing Sweetheart Rose'; Hosp, USA, 1894) is a very vigorous climber. Stronger growing than

'Cécile Brünner', it will grow to fantastic heights. It produces large clusters of very small, perfectly shaped pink blooms, reminiscent of those sometimes seen on China Roses. The scent is sweet and slightly spicy. Although technically a summer flower, it is a good plant on a warm wall and will flower spasmodically well into autumn. This is a long-lived variety with almost thornless stems. Although the dull green foliage is quite sparse, it is very healthy. The variety is occasionally misnamed 'Bloomfield Abundance', which is understandable because the blooms are almost identical. It is also very difficult to propagate because of the scarcity of budding eyes, although micropropagation may solve this problem. ZONES 4–9.

Ducher, France, 1881

Parentage disputed

Royal Horticultural Society Award of Garden Merit 1994

'CÉCILE LENS'   LENcil
MODERN, MINIATURE, MEDIUM PINK, REPEAT-FLOWERING

This rose deserves to be rediscovered as it has lots of charm and poise. The beautiful buds and the lovely pale pink blooms are often compared to another great Miniature Rose, 'First Love'. The small semi-double blooms with 20–25 petals open fairly quickly but this rose seems to win trophies when shown in the decorative class—that is when it is a quarter to half-open. The small clusters mainly consist of 3–5 blooms. ZONES 5–10.

Lens, Belgium, 1980

Parentage unknown

'Climbing Cécile Brünner'

'Climbing Cécile Brünner'

'Celestial'

'Centenary'

'CEE DEE MOSS' MORceedee, MORcd

MODERN, MODERN SHRUB, PINK BLEND, REPEAT-FLOWERING

This rose bears sprays of lightly scented, striped flowers and continues to bloom after the initial flush. The blooms are semi-double and medium sized, each with 15–25 pink petals that have an occasional white stripe and a pale underside. The growth is bushy, moderately spreading and disease resistant, with light green foliage. 'Cee Dee Moss' was raised by Ralph Moore, an amateur breeder who discovered that stripes in rose colors could be inherited. ZONES 4–9.

Moore, USA, 1990

'Carolyn Dean' × seedling

'CELEBRITY'

MODERN, LARGE-FLOWERED/HYBRID TEA, DEEP YELLOW, REPEAT-FLOWERING

The large, deep yellow flowers of this rose pale slightly as they age. They are well-formed and high-centered with a fruity fragrance and usually carried singly, which makes it a good variety for exhibition purposes. It is very free flowering with repeat blooms through summer. The foliage is dark green on an upright, bushy, disease-tolerant plant. ZONES 4–9.

Weeks, USA, 1989

('Sunbonnet' × 'Mister Lincoln') × 'Yellow Yo Yo'

'CELESTIAL'

syn. 'Céleste'
OLD, ALBA, LIGHT PINK

The buds of 'Celestial' are described as 'fabulous' and artists have painted it many times, especially Redouté and Alfred Parsons, illustrator of *The Genus Rosa*. The flowers are quite beautiful, especially in the furled bud stage; when open they are loosely semi-double and bright soft silvery pink in color, blending beautifully with the leaden gray foliage of

'Celsiana'

early summer. There are 5 rows of petals, which emit a strong fragrance during its summer season. This Old Garden Rose will do well in almost any situation in the garden, even in partial shade and impoverished soils. The dense, erect bush grows to 6 ft (1.8 m) and should not be pruned too much. There are three roses with this name. ZONES 5–9.

Pre-1848

Parentage unknown

Royal Horticultural Society Award of Garden Merit 1993

'CÉLINA'

OLD, MOSS, MAUVE

This is not the healthiest of shrub roses, but it is interesting nonetheless. Growing to about 4 ft (1.2 m), it has greenish red stems that are well foliated with mid- to dark green, coarsely serrated leaves. The flowers are no more than semi-double but are quite large, to almost 4 in (10 cm), and are borne in fragrant clusters. An appealing feature of 'Célina' is a generous display of golden yellow stamens. Something of a martyr to mildew, it may not be everyone's first choice of Moss Rose. ZONES 4–9.

Hardy, France, 1855

Parentage unknown

'CÉLINE DELBARD' DELceli, DELcélit, DELcet

MODERN, CLUSTER-FLOWERED/FLORIBUNDA, ORANGE BLEND, REPEAT-FLOWERING

This variety carries large, cupped flowers in small clusters. They each have about 24 salmon petals with silver undersides. There is no fragrance, but there are repeat-blooms through summer. The foliage is dark green, and the plant is a healthy moderate grower. ZONES 4–9.

Delbard-Chabert, France, 1986

Seedling × ('Milrose' × 'Legion d'Honneur')

Monza Gold Medal

'Céline Delbard'

'CÉLINE FORESTIER'

syns 'Liesis', 'Lusiades'
OLD, NOISETTE, LIGHT YELLOW, REPEAT-FLOWERING

This rose has pale yellow blooms, darkening at the center, that open from attractive buds. The quartered blossoms have a green, button eye, and the clusters have a spicy fragrance. Exquisite at maturity and repeating all summer, the large flowers need a happy, warm spot to show off well. The canes are spiny, reaching 6 ft (1.8 m), and the foliage is dark green and glossy. There are prickles. ZONES 7–10.

Trouillard, France, 1842

Noisette × *Rosa odorata*

Royal Horticultural Society Award of Garden Merit 1993

'CELSIANA'

OLD, DAMASK, LIGHT PINK

'Celsiana' has pale pink, semi-double, large blooms that occur in clusters on typically Damask-style short stalks in early summer. The nodding blossoms prefer semi-shade and have a strong musk fragrance. Impervious to weather, they are a delight to the eye, especially just before the fluted, crinkled petals fade to a delicate soft blush color before going over. This plant performs well in any type of soil or climate, growing to 4 ft (1.2 m) and is fairly dense in structure for a Damask. The gray-green foliage is smooth; sharp little prickles line the canes. It is mislabeled in Redouté's book as 'Incarnata Maxima'. The great Dutch painter Van Huysum often featured this rose in his floral paintings. ZONES 4–9.

Pre-1750

Parentage unknown

'CENTENAIRE DE LOURDES'

DELge
syns 'Centennaire de Lourdes', 'Mrs Jones'
MODERN, CLUSTER-FLOWERED/FLORIBUNDA, MEDIUM PINK, REPEAT-FLOWERING

Bred in France, 'Centenaire de Lourdes' is an exceptional variety that is very popular throughout Europe, probably because people fall in love with it at first sight. It was voted one of the world's top

ten roses at the World Rose Convention in 1994. It is an extremely vigorous and floriferous Cluster-flowered Rose that has never received the full recognition it deserves. It bears large, old-fashioned flowers of 15 soft rose petals in clusters that appear in huge numbers throughout summer, although there is little scent. The variety has a bushy habit, clothed with healthy, large mid-green foliage. It makes a fine bedding rose but is also suitable to grow as a standard. The beautiful crop of pear-shaped, orange hips that first appear in autumn are a bonus, and they last into winter. 'Centenaire de Lourdes Rouge' (DELflora) is a red-flowered mutation. ZONES 4–9.

Delbard-Chabert, France, 1958

('Frau Druschki' × seedling) × seedling

'CENTENARY' KORreldas

MODERN, CLUSTER-FLOWERED/FLORIBUNDA, MEDIUM PINK, REPEAT-FLOWERING

This rose has a good covering of glossy, dark green foliage that acts as a foil to the well-shaped clusters of rose pink, semi-double, medium-sized flowers. Its leafy habit will also suit it if grown as a standard. There is only a little scent. It has a good resistance to disease and is fine in beds or borders. 'Centenary' was named to celebrate the first 100 years of one of the UK's biggest nurseries. ZONES 4–9.

Kordes, Germany, 1997

Parentage unknown

Royal National Rose Society Trial Ground Certificate 1995

'Céline Forestier'

'Cécile Lens'

C

'CENTIFOLIA'

syn. *Rosa* × *centifolia*
OLD, CENTIFOLIA, MEDIUM PINK

'Centifolia' is frequently listed as a species rose but this is not so; according to Cambridge botanist C. C. Hurst, it is probably a complex hybrid with genealogy comprised of such diverse species as *Rosa rubra*, *R. phoenicia*, *R. moschata* and *R. canina*. This shrub rose can attain a height of some 6 ft (1.8 m) in good soil, producing long strong shoots with numerous reddish thorns and prickles. Its leaves are coarse, both in appearance and to touch, and are grayish green in color. The flowers, which appear in early to mid-summer, are arranged in small clusters and emerge from tight feathery buds. They are flattish, very double and very fragrant, and are a deep glowing pink in color. ZONES 4–9.

Pre-1596

Parentage unknown

'Centifolia Variegata'

'CENTIFOLIA MUSCOSA'

syn. *Rosa* × *centifolia muscosa*
OLD, MOSS, MEDIUM PINK

This lax shrub grows to 6 ft (1.8 m). It has many reddish colored thorns and small prickles, the latter like finely textured moss. The coarse foliage is grayish light green. The fragrant flowers are deep pink, and appear in mid-summer. They are very double, sometimes quartered and open flat from mossy buds.
ZONES 4–9.

Pre-1696

Possibly a sport of 'Centifolia'

'CENTIFOLIA VARIEGATA'

syns 'Belle des Jardins', 'Belle Villageois', 'Cottage Maid', 'Dometille Beccard', 'La Rubanee', *Rosa* × *centifolia variegata*, 'Village Maid'
OLD, CENTIFOLIA, PINK BLEND

This lovely rose is overburdened with too many names and an unknown

'Centurion'

background; those wishing to add it to their gardens must look under all the titles in the catalogues. Creamy white blossoms striped with pale lilac-pink on the thin petals offer a rich fragrance. Whether single or in clusters, the large blooms have given artists a perfect subject for their paintings. A robust shrub, it has dark green, coarsely toothed foliage, prickles and large hips and is free flowering during summer. It hates wet weather and makes a good hedge. It has been found naturalized in parts of New Zealand, where it has survived without help for 80 years. ZONES 4–9.

Vibert, France, 1845

Parentage unknown

'CENTRAL PARK' POUlpyg

MODERN, MODERN SHRUB, APRICOT BLEND, REPEAT-FLOWERING

This lowly plant grows twice as wide as it is high, so its habit is cushiony without being prostrate—enough for it to be considered a ground-cover rose. In the garden, it is useful for borders, beside pathways, on sloping ground and to form a low group or hedge. The color is a gentle and warm shade of peach, deeper in the heart of the blooms, which are of small to medium size, rounded in form, loosely double and borne freely in close clusters. They are lightly scented and continue to appear through summer and autumn on a compact plant. 'Central Park' is well below average height for a shrub rose, and a little over 3 ft (1 m) across in temperate climates. The small leaves are plentiful, bright green and shiny. ZONES 4–9.

Olesen, Denmark, 1995

Parentage unknown

'CENTURION'

MODERN, CLUSTER-FLOWERED/FLORIBUNDA, DARK RED, REPEAT-FLOWERING

'Centurion' is a bright crimson, blood red rose with some fragrance. The medium-sized, double blooms, each with 30 petals, are borne in small clusters, with repeat blooms during the summer season. They are produced on a bushy plant with dark green, glossy foliage that has a great resistance to disease. It was named to celebrate the centenary of John Mattock Roses, and is a good bedding variety that can be propagated by budding. ZONES 4–9.

Mattock, UK, 1975

'Evelyn Fison' × seedling

'Cerise Bouquet'

'Cerys Ann'

'CENTURY TWO'

MODERN, LARGE-FLOWERED/HYBRID TEA, MEDIUM PINK, REPEAT-FLOWERING

The long, pointed buds of this bushy rose develop into large, cupped, double flowers. The color is medium pink, and there is a considerable fragrance. This is a medium-sized rose with mid-green, leathery foliage. It makes a good bedding rose that can be propagated by budding. ZONES 4–9.

Armstrong, USA, 1971

'Charlotte Armstrong' × 'Duet'

'CERISE BOUQUET'

MODERN, MODERN SHRUB, DEEP PINK

This very free-flowering shrub produces an outstanding display of medium-sized, eye-catching blooms on very strong, slightly arching branches during summer. The flowers are bright cerise with a light fragrance. The growth is very vigorous and is clothed with dull green foliage. 'Cerise Bouquet' is a perfect subject for tall hedges and as a specimen plant. Propagation should be by budding or from cuttings. ZONES 4–9.

Tantau, Germany, 1958

Rosa multibracteata × 'Crimson Glory'

Royal Horticultural Society Award of Garden Merit 1993

'CERYS ANN' GUEscan

MODERN, LARGE-FLOWERED/HYBRID TEA, YELLOW BLEND, REPEAT-FLOWERING

The blooms of this variety are of classic Large-flowered form, with the high centers and symmetrical arrangement of their many firm petals beloved by rose exhibitors. They are basically a medium shade of yellow, with a suffusion of red towards the tips of the petals as they age. They are borne with reasonable freedom, considering their size, through summer and autumn and have a pleasant light fragrance. This is a useful variety for beds and borders, or to make a hedge. The plant grows somewhat unevenly to average height or less, is bushy and has shiny dark green foliage. The rose honors the memory of the raiser's granddaughter who, as a five year old, lost her life in tragic circumstances. Maurice Guest, an amateur breeder, vowed that if he ever produced an award-winning variety, it would bear her name. ZONES 4–9.

Guest, UK, 1997

'Fulton Mackay' × 'Freedom'

Royal National Rose Society Torridge Award and Trial Ground Certificate 1994

'Century Two'

'Champagne Cocktail'

'CÉSONIE'
OLD, MOSS, DEEP PINK

This compact Moss Rose bears its double pink flowers only once a year in early summer. They are large, fragrant and filled with many petals. 'Césonie' may be difficult to find as it is extremely rare in cultivation. ZONES 4–9.

Robert and Moreau, France, 1859

Parentage unknown

'CHABLIS'
MODERN, LARGE-FLOWERED/HYBRID TEA, WHITE, REPEAT-FLOWERING

The large blooms of this cultivar are packed with about 40 creamy white petals. There is a slight fragrance. This upright bush is furnished with large matt green foliage that is disease resistant. It is grown principally as an exhibition variety. ZONES 4–9.

Weeks, USA, 1983

Seedling × 'Louisiana'

'CHAMPAGNE'
MODERN, LARGE-FLOWERED/HYBRID TEA, YELLOW BLEND, REPEAT-FLOWERING

'Champagne' has buff yellow flowers with an apricot shade. The pointed buds develop into large, oval flowers with 28 petals that form a high center. There is a good fragrance and the blooms continue to appear after the initial flush. The foliage is dark green, leathery and disease resistant, and the habit is upright and bushy. This is a good variety both for bedding and exhibition. ZONES 4–9.

Lindquist, USA, 1961

'Charlotte Armstrong' × 'Duquesa de Peñaranda'

'CHAMPAGNE COCKTAIL'
HORflash

MODERN, CLUSTER-FLOWERED/FLORIBUNDA, YELLOW BLEND, REPEAT-FLOWERING

'Champagne Cocktail' has everything: shapely blooms, a gorgeous fragrance and a low susceptibility to disease. The pale yellow, medium-sized double flowers, strongly flecked and splashed with pink, and have 20 petals with yellow undersides. There is a reliable repetition of bloom after the first flush. It has a bushy habit and glossy mid-green foliage, and is suitable for bedding or can be grown as a standard. ZONES 4–9.

Horner, UK, 1983

'Old Master' × 'Southampton'

Royal National Rose Society Torridge Award and Trial Ground Certificate 1982, Belfast Certificate of Merit 1985, Glasgow Gold Medal 1990

'CHAMPAGNE PEARL'   KORopti
MODERN, CLUSTER-FLOWERED/FLORIBUNDA, APRICOT BLEND, REPEAT-FLOWERING

The large, dense clusters of warm creamy apricot flowers provide this medium-sized bush rose with a mist of color that gradually darkens and changes to green. The cupped flowers firmly retain their shape with age. 'Champagne Pearl' is a

'Champagne'

useful rose for cutting and arranging either as a single truss or for larger displays. It is also a good exhibition rose, but has only slight fragrance. The growth is compact and vigorous and is covered with variegated foliage. ZONES 4–10.

Kordes, Germany, 1994

Parentage unknown

'Champs-Elysées'

'Champion'

'CHAMPION'
MODERN, LARGE-FLOWERED/HYBRID TEA, YELLOW BLEND, REPEAT-FLOWERING

Packed with up to 55 petals per flower, 'Champion' is a rose for exhibitors, with very large, high-centered double blooms. They are yellow-cream, flushed with red and pink. The blooms are very fragrant, and give repeat displays through summer. It has large, pale green leaves. ZONES 4–9.

Fryer, UK, 1976

'Irish Gold' × 'Whisky Mac'

'CHAMPION OF THE WORLD'
syns 'Mrs DeGraw', 'Mrs de Graw'
OLD, HYBRID PERPETUAL, MEDIUM PINK, REPEAT-FLOWERING

This rose, which needs plenty of time to establish itself, is a vigorous shrub that likes to sprawl. The rose pink blooms are double, large and fragrant. The light green foliage is small, and the prickles are light brown. It grows to 4 ft (1.2 m) and makes a good pot plant. ZONES 5–9.

Woodhouse, UK, 1894

'Hermosa' × 'Magna Charta'

'CHAMPLAIN'
MODERN, MODERN SHRUB, DARK RED, REPEAT-FLOWERING

This repeat-flowering shrub gives moderately vigorous, bushy growth that is very healthy. It was bred to exist in the hard climate of North America, so tolerates extremely cold winters. It carries dark red, double flowers, each holding up to 30 petals, that are large, slightly fragrant and are borne in profusion on this compact plant. The leaves are small and dark yellow-green. Budding or cuttings are the best methods of propagation. ZONES 3–9.

Svelda, Canada, 1982

(Rosa kordesii × seedling) × ('Red Dawn' × 'Suzanne')

'Champneys' Pink Cluster'

'CHAMPNEYS' PINK CLUSTER'
syns 'Champneys' Rose', 'Champneyana'
OLD, NOISETTE, LIGHT PINK, REPEAT-FLOWERING

The lovely, dark pink buds of this rose open to small, double blooms that are gathered in clusters on purple canes. Highly fragrant, the blossoms repeat from spring until autumn. The foliage is light green. Many claim that this is the first Noisette, having originated in South Carolina. Like all of its clan it does best with lots of sun and good air circulation, and when used as a pillar, it can reach 10 ft (3 m). In 1986 it was unofficially renamed 'The Charleston Rose' in honor of its birthplace. ZONES 7–10.

Champneys, USA, circa 1811

Possibly 'Old Blush' × R. moschata

'Champion of the World'

'CHAMPS-ELYSÉES' MEIcarl,
MEIcari
MODERN, LARGE-FLOWERED/HYBRID TEA, DARK RED, REPEAT-FLOWERING

This rose has lovely red-crimson, double flowers with their 35 petals arranged to form a cup shape. They are slightly fragrant and continue to appear after the initial bloom. This is a vigorous plant that gives bushy and compact growth, clothed with dark green foliage. 'Champs-Elysées' has good resistance to disease and can be propagated by budding. The variety looks good in beds and borders, and is also suitable trained as a standard. The climbing sport, 'Climbing Champs-Elysées' (MEIcarlsar; 1969) has similar characteristics, although it is very rarely available now. It was bred in France in 1969. ZONES 4–9.

Meilland, France, 1957

'Monique' × 'Happiness'

Madrid Gold Medal 1957

'CHANELLE'
MODERN, CLUSTER-FLOWERED/FLORIBUNDA, ORANGE-PINK, REPEAT-FLOWERING

The large, peachy pink or pale pink flowers of this rose were named to commemorate the famous fashion house of Chanel. They are large, loose and double, and also have a shade of rose pink. Each flower has about 20 petals that hold a good form. They are carried in fragrant clusters that flower freely and repeatedly. This variety is a medium-sized bush with glossy dark green foliage. The growth is very healthy. ZONES 4–9.

McGredy, New Zealand, 1959

'Ma Perkins' × ('Fashion' × 'Mrs William Sprott')

National Rose Society Certificate of Merit 1958, Madrid Gold Medal 1959

'CHAPLIN'S PINK CLIMBER'
MODERN, LARGE-FLOWERED CLIMBER, MEDIUM PINK

The name of this variety is a slight contradiction, since technically the growth is somewhat lax and would be better associated with a rambler. It carries large clusters of big, bright pink blooms with golden stamens. They are semi-double, with over 24 petals, but will only flower in summer and give little scent. The mid-green foliage is plentiful, and the growth very vigorous. This was once a very popular variety in Britain and is still widely grown on the continent of Europe. ZONES 4–9.

Chaplin, UK, 1928

'Paul's Scarlet Climber' × 'American Pillar'

National Rose Society Gold Medal 1928

'CHAPLIN'S PINK COMPANION'
MODERN, LARGE-FLOWERED CLIMBER, LIGHT PINK

When this variety was first launched in 1961, it was purported to be repeat-flowering, but sadly this is not so. 'Chaplin's Pink Companion' is nevertheless a good example of the older type of floriferous, large-flowered Rambler. The flowers are silvery pink, medium sized and double, each with 22 petals. They are borne in fragrant clusters, but only flower during summer. The glossy green foliage clothes a very vigorous rose with a rambling habit. There is a considerable resistance to disease. ZONES 4–9.

Chaplin, UK, 1961

'Chaplin's Pink Climber' × 'Opera'

'CHARISMA' JELroganor
syn. 'Surprise Party'
MODERN, CLUSTER-FLOWERED/FLORIBUNDA, RED BLEND, REPEAT-FLOWERING

The slightly fragrant, medium-sized, double flowers of this rose are scarlet and yellow with up to 40 petals per bloom; they are carried in small clusters of 3–5 mostly in summer, but with later displays in autumn. The foliage is glossy green and leathery, and the bushy growth forms an upright habit. This is a bedding variety that also makes a good standard. ZONES 4–9.

Jelly, USA, 1977

'Gemini' × 'Zorina'

Portland Gold Medal 1977, All-America Rose Selection 1978

'Chanelle'

C

'Chaplin's Pink Climber'

'Chaplin's Pink Climber'

'Charisma'

'CHARLES ALBANEL'
MODERN, HYBRID RUGOSA, MEDIUM RED,
REPEAT-FLOWERING

'Charles Albanel' was developed by
its Canadian breeder for its hardiness.
The wrinkled foliage, grassy green and
leathery, is also very disease resistant.
The blooms are medium red and double,
with 20 petals per rose. They are fragrant
and give repeat displays after the first
bloom. This variety makes a good ground
cover, and it has been widely planted in
environmental landscaping; even when
not in flower, it is admired for its handsome foliage. ZONES 3–9.

Svejda, Canada, 1982

'Souvenir de Philemon Cochet' × seedling

'CHARLES AUSTIN'   AUSles,
AUSfather
MODERN, MODERN SHRUB, APRICOT BLEND

Named for the breeder's father, this rose
bears large, double blooms packed with
up to 70 apricot, pink-tinged petals that
pale with age. Although it is not repeat-

flowering, an occasional bloom may be
produced in autumn. Its flowers are carried singly or in clusters of up to 7 and
the petals are arranged to give a pinwheel
effect; there is a strong fruity fragrance.
It is best suited for planting in groups in
borders or for use as a pillar rose when
supported and lightly pruned. It grows
vigorously to form an upright plant, which
the raiser suggests should be cut down by
half early in spring. It is also classified as
an English Rose. **'Yellow Charles Austin'** (1981) is a yellow-flowered sport
that has similar characteristics. ZONES 4–9.

Austin, UK, 1973

'Aloha' × 'Chaucer'

'CHARLES DE GAULLE'
MEilaneIn
syn. 'Katherine Mansfield'
MODERN, LARGE-FLOWERED/HYBRID TEA,
MAUVE BLEND, REPEAT-FLOWERING

This is a strong-growing, medium-sized
rose with large, double flowers with
a good form and a unique warm lilac

color. They are very fragrant, as is the
case with many of the 'blue' roses, and
are mostly borne singly. Each flower
has about 38 petals per bloom to form
a globular or cupped shape. It is considered by many to be the finest of the
mauve Large-flowered Roses, but it does
not like damp or humid conditions. The
variety is useful in beds or borders and is
propagated by budding. 'Charles de
Gaulle' was named after the great French
statesman, but in New Zealand it is
better known as 'Katherine Mansfield',
one of their great writers. ZONES 4–9.

Meilland, France, 1974

('Sissi' × 'Prelude') × ('Kordes' Sondermeldung'
× 'Caprice')

Belfast Fragrance Prize 1978

'CHARLES DE LAPISSE'
MODERN, LARGE-FLOWERED/HYBRID TEA,
LIGHT PINK, REPEAT-FLOWERING

There have been several pale pink sports
of the famous 'Mme Caroline Testout',
the most notable perhaps being 'Admiral

Dewey' of 1899. This one came on the
scene later and appears to be no longer
available in commerce. It shares with
its famous parent the qualities of vigor,
freedom of bloom, hardiness and a similar form of flower, being large, globular
and full petalled but lighter in color. It is
useful for beds and borders, continuing
to bloom through summer and autumn
with a modest but pleasant scent. It makes
a freely branching plant of average height
and a stiff, upright habit, with prickly
stems and mid-green foliage. ZONES 4–9.

Laroulandie, France, 1910

Sport of 'Mme Caroline Testout'

'Charles de Lapisse'

'Charles Austin'

'Charles de Gaulle'

'CHARLES DE MILLS'
syns 'Charles Mills', 'Charles Wills',
'Bizarre Triomphant'
OLD, GALLICA, MAUVE

Often seen in photographs as the 'perfect
Old Garden Rose,' this Gallica is the
largest of its family. The flowers, which
are made up of a multitude of petals, are
quite large, and at their best often exceed
3 in (8 cm) in diameter. They emerge
in mid-summer from flat-topped buds,
at first cupped and then flatly saucer
shaped; their color is rich glowing purple
with subtle crimson highlights. The
petals, which have the feel of textured
velvet, are only slightly scented. The
arching canes reach 6 ft (1.8 m) on an
erect bush with very few prickles and
dark green leaves. It is sometimes found
in the wild. All Gallicas sucker freely
on their own roots. ZONES 4–9.

The Netherlands, pre-1700

Parentage unknown

Royal Horticultural Society Award of Garden
Merit 1993

'CHARLES GATER'
OLD, HYBRID PERPETUAL, MEDIUM RED,
REPEAT-FLOWERING

This rose has red, double blooms with
40 petals that are globular and extra large
and keep their color throughout their

'Charles de Mills'

'Charles Mallerin'

life. Often used as an exhibition rose,
the color sometimes appears a brownish
crimson under artificial light. Rare today,
it was named for the foreman at George
Paul's nursery, well known in the 1890s
as a pot rose grower. This nursery in
Cheshunt, England, produced the
famous 'Paul's Lemon Pillar.' ZONES 5–9.

George Paul and Son, UK, 1893

Parentage unknown

'CHARLES LAWSON'
OLD, BOURBON, DEEP PINK

During its short flowering season in mid-
summer, this vigorous shrub produces
fragrant, deep pink blooms, which are
veined and deeper in tone on the back of
the petals. Used as a climber, it can reach
8 ft (2.4 m). The handsome foliage is
large, and the prickles are hooked. It
needs the support of a pillar or fence.
ZONES 5–9.

Lawson, UK, 1853

Parentage unknown

'CHARLES LEFÈBVRE'
syns 'Paul Jamain', 'Marguerite Brassac'
OLD, HYBRID PERPETUAL, DARK RED,
REPEAT-FLOWERING

This rose has bright crimson blooms
with purple centers. They are cupped,
large and high centered; the full blossoms

'Charles Lefèbvre'

'Charles Lawson'

have as many as 70 petals and sit erect
on strong necks. Very popular at the
time of its introduction, Graham Thomas
calls this rose a landmark for its bright
crimson color. It is vigorous and tall,
and has smooth bark and some prickles,
and tolerates rain. Moderate pruning
is recommended. ZONES 5–9.

Lacharmé, France, 1861

'Général Jacqueminot' × 'Victor Verdier'

'CHARLES MALLERIN'
MODERN, LARGE-FLOWERED/HYBRID TEA,
DARK RED, REPEAT-FLOWERING

When first introduced, this rose was described as the darkest red ever launched.
The vigorous growth is sparse and erratic,
with disease-prone dark green, leathery
foliage; its scent, however, is still memorable. The long and pointed, elegant buds
develop into large, flat, double flowers
with 38 velvety, dark crimson petals. Its
unique coloring established this variety
as a good seller and it was named to
honor Francis Meilland's teacher, a retired railway engineer, who bred many
beautiful roses himself. 'Charles Mallerin'
has been a valuable parent, giving us
such roses as 'Papa Meilland', 'Mister
Lincoln' and 'Oklahoma'. ZONES 4–9.

Meilland, France, 1951

('Rome Glory' × 'Congo') × 'Tassin'

**'CHARLES RENNIE
MACKINTOSH'** AUSren
syns 'Glücksburg', 'Rosarium Glücksburg'
MODERN, MODERN SHRUB, PINK BLEND,
REPEAT-FLOWERING

The deep dusky lilac-purple, cupped
flowers of this rose turn to pure lilac and

'Charles Rennie Mackintosh'

'Charleston'

open wider as they age. They have an
old-fashioned style, a frilly appearance
and are very fragrant, flowering repeatedly through summer. It is reminiscent
of many incurved and cupped Bourbon
Roses with intriguing inner petals that
twist, which is typical of some Gallicas.
'Charles Rennie Mackintosh' forms
a shrub of many thin, wiry yet tough
stems and many spiky thorns, clothed
by many small, dark green leaves. It is
excellent for mixing with other colors
in arrangements. The variety was
named after the famous designer and
architect, and is very popular. Budding
is the best method of propagation. It
is also classified as an English Rose.
ZONES 4–9.

Austin, UK, 1988

('Chaucer' × 'Conrad F. Meyer') × 'Mary Rose'

'CHARLESTON' MEIridge
MODERN, CLUSTER-FLOWERED/FLORIBUNDA,
YELLOW BLEND, REPEAT-FLOWERING

Reminiscent of one of its distinguished
parents, this variety is more of a compact
plant with better quality flowers.
'Charleston' bears clusters of yellow
blooms flushed with red that then turn
red as they age in sunlight. Each flower
carries about 20 petals, and there is a
slight fragrance. The plant's growth is
compact and it has dark green foliage;
and can be propagated by budding.
There should be very few problems with
disease, but the rose will need to be
deadheaded to maintain its repeat-
flowering ability. ZONES 4–9.

Meilland, France, 1963

'Masquerade' × ('Radar' × 'Caprice')

'Charlie's Aunt'

'Charlotte' (Austin)

'CHARLIE'S AUNT'

MODERN, LARGE-FLOWERED/HYBRID TEA,
PINK BLEND, REPEAT-FLOWERING

The very large, creamy flowers of this
rose are heavily suffused with carmine,
and also give a pleasing fragrance. They
are high pointed, with 65 petals per
bloom, and develop into flowers of
exhibition quality. This is a vigorous
plant with dark green, healthy foliage.
It should be propagated by budding.
ZONES 4–9.

McGredy, New Zealand, 1965

'Golden Masterpiece' × 'Karl Herbst'

'CHARLOTTE'

MODERN, LARGE-FLOWERED/HYBRID TEA,
ORANGE-PINK, REPEAT-FLOWERING

This variety has long, pointed buds that
develop into high-centered, salmon-pink
and coral blooms. They are very fragrant
and bloom continuously. The foliage
is glossy green and clothes a vigorous,
healthy plant that can be propagated
by budding. ZONES 4–9.

Duehrsen, USA, 1941

'Joanna Hill' × 'Golden Dawn'

'CHARLOTTE'   AUSpoly

syn. 'Elgin Festival'

MODERN, MODERN SHRUB, LIGHT YELLOW,
REPEAT-FLOWERING

The parentage of 'Graham Thomas'
is evident in this variety, although the
flowers are a softer yellow, are rather
more cupped—becoming incurved
in late summer—and have a delicious
fragrance. It makes a bushy and healthy,
freely branching shrub that produces a
flush of bloom in mid-summer, followed
by intermittent color throughout
autumn. It is suitable as a specimen
shrub, and a few nurseries are apparently
developing this variety as a standard. It
should be propagated by budding. In
South Africa the variety is known as

'Charlotte Rampling'

'Elgin Festival', named after a town
about an hour's drive away from Cape
Town that is home to a successful rose
festival. It is also classified as an English
Rose. ZONES 4–9.

Austin, UK, 1993

Seedling × 'Graham Thomas'

'CHARLOTTE ARMSTRONG'

MODERN, LARGE-FLOWERED/HYBRID TEA,
DEEP PINK, REPEAT-FLOWERING

This highly acclaimed rose was one of
the parents of 'Queen Elizabeth'. The
large, pointed buds develop into deep
pink, double flowers with 35 petals. They
are fragrant and well formed. The foliage
is dark green and leathery on a vigorous
yet compact plant. ZONES 4–9.

Lammerts, USA, 1940

'Soeur Thérèse' × 'Crimson Glory'

All-America Rose Selection 1941, American Rose
Society David Fuerstenberg Prize 1941, ARS John
Cook Medal 1941, Portland Gold Medal 1941,
ARS Gertrude M. Hubbard Gold Medal 1945,
National Rose Society Gold Medal 1950

'CHARLOTTE RAMPLING'

MEIhirvin

syn. 'Thomas Barton'

MODERN, LARGE-FLOWERED/HYBRID TEA,
MEDIUM RED, REPEAT-FLOWERING

The large flowers of this variety are a
unique and striking color of wine red,
and produce a very good scent. They are
carried on an upright bush against dark
green foliage, and are repeat-flowering.
The unusual color of this variety makes
it a good bedding plant and a good
standard. It is propagated by budding.
ZONES 4–9.

Meilland, France, 1988

Parentage unknown

Monza Gold Medal 1987, Glasgow Fragrance
Award 1995

'CHARMIAN'   AUSmian

MODERN, MODERN SHRUB, MEDIUM PINK,
REPEAT-FLOWERING

This is a free-flowering shrub rose with
an arching habit; it bears large, rosette-

'Charmian'

shaped, medium pink, very fragrant
flowers that open flat, then curve in
slightly as they mature. The mid-green
foliage is semi-glossy and resistant to
disease. Because of its lax or spreading,
rather floppy growth, 'Charmian' lends
itself to growing in clumps in a border,

C

'Château de Chenonceaux'

'Châtelaine'

'Chattem Centennial'

or as a semi-climber on low fences and walls; its rather heavy flowers often weigh the branches down so that they touch the ground. The best method of propagation is by budding. It is also classified as an English Rose. ZONES 4–9.

Austin, UK, 1982

Seedling × 'Lilian Austin'

'CHASIN' RAINBOWS'

SAVachase

syn. 'Chasing Rainbows'

MODERN, MINIATURE, RED BLEND, REPEAT-FLOWERING

For gardenders who have a love of exotic rose colors, this is an excellent small and bright Miniature Rose to edge a bed of red and yellow roses. The tiny buds open to yellow flushed with red, then develop into full, muddled flowers with yellow centers and outer petals flushed bright red. They are not suitable for cutting nor are they fragrant, but for garden display or on patios in containers, the neat and compact shrub with its numerous blooms will provide a brilliant display throughout summer and autumn. ZONES 5–11.

Saville, USA, 1990

'Zorina' × 'Rainbow's End'

'CHÂTEAU DE CHENONCEAUX'

MODERN, LARGE-FLOWERED/HYBRID TEA, MEDIUM PINK, REPEAT-FLOWERING

'Château de Chenonceaux' is a good subject for shrub borders or specimen plants, with its large, pink flowers. They each have 45 petals, but there is little fragrance. The cultivar is a tall grower with large leaves, and flowers repeatedly after the initial flush. 'Château de Chenonceaux' is easily propagated by budding. ZONES 4–9.

Gaujard, France, 1973

'Americana' × 'Queen Elizabeth'

'CHÂTEAU DE CLOS VOUGEOT'

MODERN, LARGE-FLOWERED/HYBRID TEA, DARK RED, REPEAT-FLOWERING

The very dark, velvety red roses of 'Château de Clos Vougeot' have a powerful Damask fragrance. They are large, packed with as many as 75 petals per bloom. These are borne on a slightly lax, sprawling bush against dark green and leathery foliage. The variety is an old favorite and is still grown by connoisseurs. It was named after the splendid home of the finest clarets. Budding is the easiest method of propagation. **'Climbing Château de Clos Vougeot'** (Morse, UK, 1920) is a climbing form of the famous bush variety; a mutation that arose spontaneously in 1920. It is still widely grown and many plants are found in old gardens around the world. For maximum effect, this variety is best grown against a warm wall. ZONES 4–9.

Pernet-Ducher, France, 1908

Parentage unknown

'Château de Clos Vougeot'

'CHÂTELAINE'

MODERN, CLUSTER-FLOWERED/FLORIBUNDA, ORANGE-PINK, REPEAT-FLOWERING

The large, coral flowers of this rose are overcast with salmon, and give a good fragrance. They each have about 32 petals, and are carried in small clusters against the coppery and glossy foliage. The plant produces vigorous growth that is moderately resistant to disease. It can be propagated by budding. ZONES 4–9.

Lens, Belgium, 1957

('Peace' × seedling) × 'Fashion'

'CHATTEM CENTENNIAL'

MODERN, MINIATURE, ORANGE-RED, REPEAT-FLOWERING

The ovoid buds of this variety open to magnificent orange and red florets that hold their form well for exhibition. Considered an outstanding rose for cooler climates, its clear color has been compared with 'Starina' but this plant has a lot more vigor and is nearly always in bloom. The plant is upright and of medium height, and produces both single blooms as well as small clusters. Welcome in any garden because of its beauty and profuse flowering, it is quite easy to maintain and is usually resistant to pests and diseases. ZONES 4–11.

Jolly, USA, 1979

'Orange Sensation' × 'Zinger'

'CHAUCER' AUScer, AUScon

MODERN, MODERN SHRUB, MEDIUM PINK, REPEAT-FLOWERING

This is an early introduction from the Austin stable, which the raiser now considers to be passé. However, it fits well in a small garden and bears small clusters of deeply cupped, light pink blooms that pale towards the edges and show some stamens at the center. They give off a considerable myrrh-like scent that is delicious to some, but is not appreciated by all noses. Its repeat-flowering performance is somewhat surprising, given that 'Constance Spry' does not; the assumption is that one of the parents has a repeat-flowering ancestor. The foliage is matt mid-green, and the stems are covered in red thorns similar to those found on Gallica Roses. It has a bushy, upright, medium-sized habit, but is prone to mildew. 'Chaucer' is always suitable for the rose border or as a specimen plant, and can be propagated by budding; it has featured in the breeding of many good roses after 1970. It is also classified as an English Rose. ZONES 4–9.

Austin, UK, 1970

Seedling × 'Constance Spry'

'CHELSEA BELLE' TALchelsea

MODERN, MINIATURE, MEDIUM RED, REPEAT-FLOWERING

This rose brought a new color class to the world of Miniature Roses. The flowers are cherry red with a white base and whitish undersides. The high-centered blooms are borne either singly or in occasional clusters of 6–8 blooms on strong basal canes. The foliage is small, mid-green and semi-glossy. It has an upright habit, becoming a compact, dense bush, and is very vigorous. However, the plant can be susceptible to mildew if not sprayed regularly. The rose was named after Pete and Kay Taylor's favorite cocker spaniel and has been honored at the Royal National All-Miniature Rose Show as 'Best in Show', winning the coveted International Ralph Moore Award in 1993 with a bowl of 18 stems. ZONES 4–11.

Taylor, USA, 1987

'Azure Sea' × 'Party Girl'

'CHÉNÉDOLÉ'

OLD, CHINA, ORANGE-RED

This variety is one of those mystery Old Garden Roses that is difficult to identify. The growth habit, stems, foliage and

'Chaucer'

'Cherub'

'Cherry Meillandecor'

buds resemble Gallica Roses, but the flower color and form suggests a China link. It only flowers once in early summer. 'Chénédolé' bears single round buds, often in clusters of 2 or 3, with foliated glandular sepals that open one after the other to large, flat, quartered, light vermilion blooms with fragrant, silky petals. The leaves are dark green and brittle, and the shoots are covered with small, hooked thorns. The tall stems are inclined to be lax, so the shrub is best grown against a support. ZONES 4–11.

Thierry, France, pre-1841

Parentage unknown

'CHERISH' JACsal
MODERN, CLUSTER-FLOWERED/FLORIBUNDA, ORANGE-PINK, REPEAT-FLOWERING

One of a series of compact, slightly spreading roses, 'Cherish' bears short, flat buds that develop into flowers of coral pink, each with 28 petals. There is a slight fragrance. This is a good rose for the cutting garden: the flowers last well in a vase. The foliage is dark green and healthy, and it clothes a compact yet slightly spreading plant that can be propagated by budding. 'Love' and 'Honor' were also raised by Warriner, and they too won awards. ZONES 4–9.

Warriner, USA, 1980

'Bridal Pink' × 'Matador'

All-America Rose Selection 1980

'CHERRY BRANDY' TANryrandy
MODERN, LARGE-FLOWERED/HYBRID TEA, ORANGE BLEND, REPEAT-FLOWERING

The large, double flowers on this variety, borne singly or in clusters of 3–7, are fragrant with a good high-centered form; the 30 petals are a delightful shade of

'Cherub'

orange. Unfortunately there is no fragrance. Throughout summer and autumn there is good continuity of bloom against the glossy dark green, leathery foliage, which provides the necessary contrast to the flowers. This is a vigorous plant, with spreading but upright growth, that is good for bedding schemes. The variety maintains good health, and is easily propagated by budding. ZONES 4–9.

Tantau, Germany, 1985

Parentage unknown

Royal National Rose Society Trial Ground Certificate 1986, Belfast Gold Medal 1989

'CHERRY MEILLANDECOR'
MEIrumour
syn. 'Cherry Meidiland'
MODERN, MODERN SHRUB, RED BLEND, REPEAT-FLOWERING

A colorful addition to any garden, 'Cherry Meillandecor' bears single, bright red blooms that have bold white centers with golden yellow stamens. The petals are gently ruffled at the margins. It is a large, spreading shrub rose that has a good covering of shiny, dark green foliage topped by a continuous bloom through summer. In the garden, this rose is tolerant of poor soil and is extremely resistant to disease—most growers say it will never need spraying—and is ideal planted either in groups to form a hedge or simply on its own as a specimen. If the flowers are not deadheaded, they will develop into attractive rosehips that will continue to give interest into winter. ZONES 5–9.

Meilland, France, 1994

Parentage unknown

Geneva Gold Medal 1994

'Cherry-Vanilla'

'CHERRY SUNBLAZE' MEIbekarb
MODERN, MINIATURE, MEDIUM RED, REPEAT-FLOWERING

The medium red flowers of 'Cherry Sunblaze' are moderately full, with 15–25 petals. These smallish blooms are mainly borne in small clusters with little or no fragrance. The foliage is a lovely semi-glossy, mid- to dark green. Like the others in the 'Sunblaze' series from the House of Meilland, 'Cherry Sunblaze' has been deliberately cultivated to provide a medium-sized bush with an upright and dense character. This makes it suitable for easy incorporation into landscaping designs. ZONES 5–11.

Meilland, France, 1993

Sport of 'Début'

'CHERRY-VANILLA' ARMilla
MODERN, LARGE-FLOWERED/HYBRID TEA, PINK BLEND, REPEAT-FLOWERING

This big and floriferous variety with pink, cream-centered flowers is noted for

its high-centered, double blooms, which are fragrant and cupped in shape. It also has dark green, leathery foliage. The compact growth habit makes 'Cherry-Vanilla' suitable for bedding shemes, or for the front of a border. In the USA, it is classified as a Grandiflora. ZONES 4–9.

Armstrong, USA, 1973

'Buccaneer' × 'El Capitan'

'CHERUB'
MODERN, RAMBLER, PINK BLEND

This Australian Rambler, one of the creations of Alister Clark, flowers profusely in early summer. The salmon-pink blooms are semi-double, cupped and small, while the foliage is a rich glossy green and is wrinkled. The pliable canes make 'Cherub' a good rose for a pergola or for screening. Susan Irvine, an Australian garden writer, states that the blooms look like a China Rose. ZONES 6–10.

Clark, Australia, 1923

Seedling of 'Claire Jacquier'

'Cherish'

'Cherry Brandy'

C

C

'CHESHIRE LIFE'

MODERN, LARGE-FLOWERED/HYBRID TEA,
ORANGE-RED, REPEAT-FLOWERING

This large, vermilion rose has double, urn-shaped blooms composed of 36 petals. Some flowers may grow up to 5 in (13 cm) across. There is also a slight fragrance but it is hardly noticeable, and the foliage is dark green, leathery and resistant to disease. In the garden it is useful for bedding, and is valued for its summer blooms that repeat into autumn. ZONES 4–9.

Fryer, UK, 1972

'Prima Ballerina' × 'Princess Michiko'

'CHEVY CHASE'

MODERN, RAMBLER, DARK RED

This rose has small, full, dark crimson blooms with 65 petals that are borne in great clusters. They cover the vigorous canes, which can grow 15 ft (4.5 m) in one season, and are rather stiff and difficult to train. When in full flower this is a truly spectacular Rambler, although it is a high-maintenance plant that needs to be pruned for the best effect. The foliage

is light gray-green, wrinkled and dense, and the stems have hooked prickles. After its early summer blooming it should be deadheaded. Unfortunately, it is prone to rust. It is widely grown in the USA. ZONES 5–9.

Hansen, USA, 1939

Rosa soulieana × 'Eblouissant'

Dr W. Van Fleet Medal 1941

'CHIANTI'

MODERN, MODERN SHRUB, MAUVE BLEND

One of the first of David Austin's English Roses, 'Chianti' is a cross between a Modern Cluster-flowered Rose and an Old Garden Gallica Rose. The result has large, purplish maroon, semi-double, rosette-type flowers. They have a powerful old rose fragrance and are borne in small, rounded clusters, but sadly they are only summer flowering. It is a vigorous, very healthy grower with dark green, glossy foliage, and is suitable for shrub borders where there is plenty of room for it to develop. ZONES 4–9.

Austin, UK, 1967

'Dusky Maiden' × 'Tuscany'

'Chica'

'CHIC'

MODERN, CLUSTER-FLOWERED/FLORIBUNDA,
PINK BLEND, REPEAT-FLOWERING

The cupped flowers on this variety are medium sized and double, with some 68 tightly packed, coral pink petals. They are carried in small clusters, and have a slight fragrance. 'Chic' is repeat-flowering with vigorous growth and a branching habit; it is a good bedding variety that can be propagated by budding. There are very few plants remaining in cultivation, and some authorities consider it to be extinct altogether. ZONES 4–9.

Boerner, USA, 1953

'Pinocchio' seedling × 'Fashion'

'CHICA'

MODERN, LARGE-FLOWERED/HYBRID TEA,
LIGHT PINK, REPEAT-FLOWERING

'Chica' is an excellent cut-flower variety that is a good garden rose as well. The flowers are smallish in size, and are very double with many rows of petals. They are a lively clear soft pink color and are produced on long straight stems with few thorns. Flower production is extremely good and vase life is long. In the garden 'Chica' produces its attractive flowers over a very long period. The deep green foliage is ample, abundant and disease resistant. ZONES 5–11.

Kordes, Germany, 1996

Parentage unknown

'Cheshire Life'

'CHICAGO PEACE' JOHnago

MODERN, LARGE-FLOWERED/HYBRID TEA,
PINK BLEND, REPEAT-FLOWERING

This sport of the famous 'Peace' bears phlox pink, lightly perfumed, well-formed flowers that have a base of canary yellow. There is a good display in summer, with a reliable repeat performance in autumn. The growth is identical in many ways to the original, parent cultivar and should be propagated by budding, although the blooms are more intense. Like its parent, it needs protection from black spot. This is one of several mutations of 'Peace', which all appeared at about the same time. This particular form was discovered by a Chicago breeder, hence the name. A climbing form, **'Climbing Chicago Peace'**, is extremely reluctant to flower. ZONES 4–9.

Johnston, USA, 1962

Sport of 'Peace'

Portland Gold Medal 1962

'CHICK-A-DEE' MORchick

MODERN, MINIATURE, MEDIUM PINK, REPEAT-FLOWERING

What a complex and romantic parentage this rose has! However, its genealogy has been successfully and deliberately manipulated by Moore to produce this charming addition to the world of Miniature Roses. The pointed buds open

'Chic'

'Chianti'

'Chevy Chase'

up to produce medium pink, slightly fragrant florets that can have occasional stripes. The blooms are borne usually singly or in sprays of 3–9 florets with 40–50 petals, and have a high-centered exhibition form. The foliage is small, mid-green, matt to semi-glossy. The prickles are small, hooked downward, and brownish. It has a low growing, compact rounded habit. ZONES 4–11.

Moore, USA, 1990

'Cécile Brünner' × ('Dortmund' × ['Fairy Moss' × ('Little Darling' × 'Ferdinand Pichard')])

'CHILD'S PLAY'   SAVachild
MODERN, MINIATURE, WHITE, REPEAT-FLOWERING

This is one of the few Miniature Roses which is an All-America Rose Selection winner. The charming white blooms are framed with a delicate pink edge. The florets with more than 20 petals come singly or in small clusters of 3–6 blooms with excellent exhibition form—high centered with moderate stem length and small foliage. Low growing and round with a bushy growth habit, the plant is vigorous and bloom production is very fast. It is an excellent variety for garden display along a driveway or border as the plant is always in bloom. ZONES 4–11.

Saville, USA, 1991

('Yellow Jewel' × 'Tamango') × 'Party Girl'

All-America Rose Selection 1993, American Rose Society Award of Excellence 1993

'CHIMO'   INTercher
MODERN, MODERN SHRUB, MEDIUM RED, REPEAT-FLOWERING

This low-growing, spreading rose bears small, lightly fragranced blooms that are

'Chimo'

'China Doll'

'Chinatown'

red when they emerge and age to dark red. They are cupped and single with 5 wavy margined petals and a colorful boss of golden yellow stamens at the center. The plant is furnished with mid-green foliage, which makes an excellent back-drop to the stunning flowers that appear repeatedly through summer. ZONES 5–9.

Ilsink, The Netherlands, 1992

Seedling × 'Immensee'

'CHINA DOLL'
MODERN, POLYANTHA, MEDIUM PINK, REPEAT-FLOWERING

This once very popular, almost thornless variety still has its admirers. It is a compact and short, very free-flowering, up-right bush rose that bears large trusses of small, cupped, slightly fragrant flowers with 24 petals of rose with a base of mimosa yellow. The foliage is leathery with mostly 5 leaflets. It is a good, repeat-flowering subject for low-growing borders or as a short standard. 'China Doll' is quite healthy, and can be propagated by either budding or from cuttings It produces a constant display of flowers. **'Climbing China Doll'** (syn. 'Weeping China Doll'; Weeks, USA, 1977) is a climbing mutation. It is a very free-growing sport, but its repeat-flowering performance is open to doubt. It is a good subject for pergolas and as a lax-growing standard. ZONES 4–9.

Lammerts, USA, 1946

'Mrs Dudley Fulton' × 'Tom Thumb'

'CHINATOWN'
syn. 'Ville de Chine'
MODERN, CLUSTER-FLOWERED/FLORIBUNDA, DEEP YELLOW, REPEAT-FLOWERING

'Chinatown' is an extremely vigorous and outstanding plant that would properly be described as a shrub rose although most nurseries catalogue it as a Cluster-flowered bush rose; it does grow bigger

'Climbing China Doll'

'Chicago Peace'

'Climbing Chicago Peace'

'Chicago Peace'

if supported. Its long, strong stems are clothed in luxuriant, mid-green foliage and bear big clusters of large, yellow blooms that are edged with pink. This is a very fragrant rose with a heavy peach scent, and gives a continuous bloom of both single flowers and clusters through summer and into autumn. It should be pruned lightly to produce a balanced plant, and can be propagated by budding. 'Chinatown' is a wonderful rose in every way, as it is very resistant to disease, easy to grow and making a fine hedge. ZONES 3–9.

Poulsen, Denmark, 1963

'Columbine' × 'Cläre Grammerstorf'

Royal National Rose Society Gold Medal 1962, Royal Horticultural Society Award of Garden Merit 1993

'CHIQUITA'   MORkita
MODERN, MINIATURE, DARK RED, REPEAT-FLOWERING

The florets of 'Chiquita' are a very dark rich red but with a concurrent fluores-cent glow. The blooms are semi-double with 20 petals and are normally flat. They are borne singly. There is a slight fragrance to the blooms, which becomes especially pronounced in warm climates. This Miniature Rose inherited its fluorescent qualities from the famous seed parent 'Anytime'. The plant has an upright, dense habit of growth with small, matt mid-green foliage and has short, brown and hooked prickles. It bears few fruits. ZONES 4–11.

Moore, USA, 1988

'Anytime' × 'Happy Hour'

'Choo-Choo Centennial'

'Chivalry'

'CHIVALRY' MACpow
syn. 'Rittertum'
MODERN, LARGE-FLOWERED/HYBRID TEA,
RED BLEND, REPEAT-FLOWERING

The large double blooms of this rose are made up of 35 slightly incurved petals; they are red with yellowish undersides. There is only a little fragrance. This is a reasonable variety for beds or borders, and the foliage is dark green and glossy. The vigorous growth is disease resistant but sparse, and can be propagated by budding. ZONES 4–9.

McGredy, New Zealand, 1977

'Peer Gynt' × 'Brasilia'

'CHLORIS'
syn. 'Rosée du Matin'
OLD, ALBA, LIGHT PINK, REPEAT-FLOWERING

This vigorous rose is known poetically as 'Dew of the Morning'. It is very ancient, and grows to 6 ft (2 m) tall with very

'Chloris'

dark green leaves and few thorns. The flowers are similar to those of 'Celeste': double, with many reflexed petals that form a quartered arrangement with a button eye. They are gentle pink and look really bold against the dark foliage. ZONES 5–9.

Pre-1848

Parentage unknown

'CHOO-CHOO CENTENNIAL'
MODERN, MINIATURE, LIGHT PINK,
REPEAT-FLOWERING

The elegant ovoid buds of this rose flower to reveal luscious pastel-pink florets with an ivory reverse. The blooms have 68 petals; the bloom cycle extends for several weeks. The flower form is often regarded as similar to that of an Old Garden Rose. The florets are grouped in small clusters of 3–5. A very light fragrance can be detected when the

'Christine Wright'

blooms open up. This rose is best grown in hot climates to allow the blooms to reach full maturity before fading. The plant is small but prolific throughout the growing season. 'Choo-Choo Centennial' is just one of the many offspring generated by the classic seed parent 'Rise 'n' Shine'. ZONES 4–11.

Jolly, USA, 1980

'Rise 'n' Shine' × 'Grand Opera'

'CHORUS' MEIjulito, MEIjalita
MODERN, CLUSTER-FLOWERED/FLORIBUNDA,
ORANGE-RED

This extremely free-flowering variety deserves the highest recognition. It has healthy, glossy dark green foliage covered with medium-sized clusters of bright vermilion, double flowers. Each bloom consists of 35 petals and there is a slight fragrance of fruit. 'Chorus' certainly makes a brilliant splash of color in the garden and an even greater impact when planted *en masse*. It makes a good choice for a rose bed, or can be trained as a standard. This plant is not susceptible to pests or diseases and is propagated by budding. **'Climbing Chorus'** (MEIjulitasar; Meilland, France, 1986) is a mutation of this variety that is suitable for walls and pergolas. ZONES 4–9.

Paolino, France, 1977

'Tamango' × ('Sarabande' × 'Zambra')

Anerkannte Deutsche Rose 1977

'CHRISTIAN DIOR' MEIlie
MODERN, LARGE-FLOWERED/HYBRID TEA,
MEDIUM RED, REPEAT-FLOWERING

Named for the Parisian fashion designer, the large, well-formed, bright crimson,

double blooms of this rose have a lighter underside and a high-centered and pointed shape, although some open out into a cupped form. The exhibition standard flowers are packed with 55 petals each, and give a subtle fragrance. 'Christian Dior' flowers with great freedom, and these displays are repeated through the warmer months. It makes a bushy plant with glossy green, leathery foliage that is useful as a standard rose or in beds or borders. The long-stemmed blooms are good for cutting. When protected from powdery mildew, the growth is really healthy and can be propagated by budding. **'Climbing Christian Dior'** (Chang, 1966) is a popular form of this Large-flowered Rose. ZONES 4–9.

Meilland, France, 1958

('Independence' × 'Happiness') × ('Peace' × 'Happiness')

Geneva Gold Medal 1958, All-America Rose Selection 1962

'CHRISTINE, CLIMBING'
MODERN, LARGE-FLOWERED CLIMBER, DEEP
YELLOW

This rose is a climbing mutation of 'Christine', which was an extremely popular Large-flowered Rose in the 1940s. 'Christine, Climbing' produces a brilliant display of small, well-shaped, deep golden yellow blooms throughout summer. There is a lovely fragrance. The dark green glossy foliage is carried on a vigorous plant that is best propagated by budding. ZONES 4–9.

Willink, UK, 1936

Sport of 'Christine'

'CHRISTINE WRIGHT'
MODERN, LARGE-FLOWERED CLIMBER,
MEDIUM PINK, REPEAT-FLOWERING

This climber bears very large flowers in a warm shade of rose pink on long pendulous stems, usually in clusters but sometimes singly. They open from urn-shaped buds into cupped flowers of 20 or so overlapping petals that show prominent yellow stamens and give a generous early summer display at a time when few other roses are in bloom. There is a pleasing musky fragrance. Although some autumn blooms appear occasionally, deadheading should not be practised because the hips are attractive. In the garden, this is a suitable variety for walls, fences and for pergolas, or to grow into low-growing trees. It produces many new basal shoots so that old wood can be removed annually after flowering; if left

'Chorus'

'Christian Dior'

'Chromatella'

unchecked, it will extend up to twice the height of the average climbing rose. The plants are furnished with attractive glossy dark green leaves. 'Christine Wright' is very much a collector's item, being listed by only two nurseries: one in France and one in the USA. **ZONES 4–9.**

Hoopes Brothers and Thomas, USA, 1909

(*Rosa wichuraiana* × unknown Tea Rose) × 'Mme Caroline Testout'

'CHRISTOPHER'   COCopher
MODERN, LARGE-FLOWERED/HYBRID TEA,
MEDIUM RED, REPEAT-FLOWERING

The bright red, well-formed flowers of this cultivar are double and flower repeatedly after the first bloom. It is a compact plant with an upright habit that carries dark green, glossy foliage. It makes a good bedding rose, and is reputed to be very disease resistant. 'Christopher' immortalizes the name of a young boy, known to the breeder's grandparents, who was killed in a road accident. Propagate this plant by budding. **ZONES 4–9.**

Cocker, UK, 1993

'Anne Cocker' × 'National Trust'

'CHRISTOPHER COLUMBUS'
MEInronsse, MEIronsse

syns 'Christoph Colomb', 'Christoph Columbus', 'Columbas', 'Cristobal Colon', 'Cristoforo Colombo', 'Flamboyance'

MODERN, LARGE-FLOWERED/HYBRID TEA,
ORANGE BLEND, REPEAT-FLOWERING

The large, copper blooms of this rose are well formed and very full, with between 26–40 petals. Each flower is borne singly, but there are repeat flushes that give a light fragrance throughout summer and autumn. Dark green, semi-glossy foliage covers a rose that is otherwise very thorny. 'Christopher Columbus' has an upright growth habit, so is ideal for rose beds or borders. It should be propagated by budding, and is resistant to disease. **ZONES 4–9.**

Meilland, France, 1991

MEIgurani × ('Ambassador' × MEInaregi)

'CHRISTOPHER COLUMBUS'
POUlstripe

MODERN, CLUSTER-FLOWERED/FLORIBUNDA,
PINK BLEND, REPEAT-FLOWERING

This is a relatively short Cluster-flowered Rose, and could almost be classified as a Patio Rose. It bears medium to large clusters of small, cupped, double flowers that only have a subtle yet pleasant scent. They are pink with heavy scarlet stripes

'Chrysler Imperial'

and flower through summer with a reliable repeat display in autumn. The foliage is small, dark green and healthy. 'Christopher Columbus' is best propagated by budding. **ZONES 4–9.**

Poulsen, Denmark, 1992

Parentage unknown

Royal National Rose Society Trial Ground Certificate 1994

'CHROMATELLA'
syn. 'Cloth of Gold'

OLD, NOISETTE, LIGHT YELLOW,
REPEAT-FLOWERING

This variety bears single blooms in spring followed by clusters in autumn. The creamy white blooms with sulfur yellow centers are double and globular and have stiff petals. A vigorous, climbing rose that loves the sun, it can reach 12 ft (3.5 m) in maturity, but it takes a long time to establish itself. Many call it difficult, but patient growers are rewarded

with a wonderful late spring to autumn display. Sold more frequently under the name 'Cloth of Gold', it is rather disease prone and gangly, and only light pruning is recommended. Queen Victoria carried this rose when she opened the Crystal Palace in 1847. **ZONES 7–10.**

Coquereau, France, 1843

Seedling of 'Lamarque'

'CHRYSLER IMPERIAL'

MODERN, LARGE-FLOWERED/HYBRID TEA,
DARK RED, REPEAT-FLOWERING

This rose was an immensely popular variety when it was first introduced. 'Chrysler Imperial' is a compact, vigorous grower with dark green, semi-glossy leaves that enhance its overall appearance. It bears long, pointed buds developing into large, double, well-formed flowers with 45 velvety, rich crimson petals that turn bluish as they age. The blooms have a good fragrance and are repeat-flower-

'Christopher Columbus' (Meilland)

ing. This is a very good bedding variety that is also very popular as a standard, but it does suffer from die-back after a few years and mildew in cold weather. It should be propagated by budding. There was some dispute raised by the car company over the name, as it was originally intended to be named 'Chrysler'.

'Cicely Lascelles'

'Church Mouse'

'Circus'

'Climbing Chrysler Imperial' (syn. 'Grimp-ant Chrysler Imperial'; Begonia, USA, 1957) is a mutation that bears high-quality blooms, but only in summer. ZONES 4–9.

Lammerts, USA, 1952

'Charlotte Armstrong' × 'Mirandy'

Portland Gold Medal 1951, All-America Rose Selection 1953, Gamble Fragrance Award 1965

'CHURCH MOUSE'   FOUmouse
MODERN, MINIATURE, RUSSET, REPEAT-FLOWERING

The flowers of 'Church Mouse' are an unusual tan-brown with a yellow base ageing to a light lavender-brown. The color is loved by flower arrangers but often called 'muddy and bizarre' by detractors. The urn-shaped buds open to a rather loose-shaped bloom. The florets are usually borne singly or in small sprays of 3–4 blooms and have a marked sweet fragrance upon opening. The plant is winter tender and is not recommended for cooler climates. ZONES 6–11.

Jacobs, USA, 1989

'Angel Face' × 'Plum Duffy'

'CICELY LASCELLES'
MODERN, LARGE-FLOWERED CLIMBER, ORANGE-PINK, REPEAT-FLOWERING

This pink, semi-double variety is tall growing and suitable for use on veranda posts or when supported by a pole. Grown to the back of the rose bed, it will create interest by adding height. Alister Clark's aim as a breeder was to create ever-blooming plants that would continue to flower throughout the Australian winter, pruning being carried out in March to create a colorful display in the cooler months. 'Lorraine Lee' was his most successful attempt to capture this, while 'Cecily Lascelles' is best grown in the normal way, and left to flower in spring. The foliage is mid-green and healthy and growth is strong and vigorous. ZONES 5–9.

Clark, Australia, 1937

Probably 'Frau Oberhofgartner Singer' × 'Scorcher'

'CIDER CUP'   DIClalida
MODERN, MINIATURE, ORANGE BLEND, REPEAT-FLOWERING

This plant boasts deep apricot blend florets that have a glowing quality to them. Often described as one of the most attractive Miniatures in this color class, the plant is a prolific bloomer providing weatherproof flowers all season long. The florets are borne singly or in small sprays on a bushy, well-groomed plant. Because of the size of the blooms, some rose growers consider this a Patio Rose.

'Cinderella'

This has not dampened its popularity in England, where it is a favorite exhibition rose. It made its debut as a show winner in 1990 in Ohio, USA, where it was declared 'King of Show'. ZONES 4–11.

Dickson, UK, 1987

'Memento' × ('Liverpool Echo' × 'Woman's Own')

'CINDERELLA'
MODERN, MINIATURE, WHITE, REPEAT-FLOWERING

Satiny white tinged with a pale flesh tone is the best description of the blooms of 'Cinderella'. The very small florets with 55 petals, complemented by dainty, small foliage, definitely classify this classic rose as a micro-miniature. The plant always seems to be covered with blooms, mostly borne in large clusters. Introduced in 1953 by the Dutch pioneer of Miniature Roses, Jan de Vink, it is still very popular with arrangers. Cooler climates tend to enhance the fresh tone of the blooms. It is regarded by rosarian Nola Simpson of New Zealand as the standard by which she judges Miniatures. ZONES 4–11.

de Vink, The Netherlands, 1953

'Cécile Brünner' × 'Tom Thumb'

'CIRCUS'
MODERN, CLUSTER-FLOWERED/FLORIBUNDA, YELLOW BLEND, REPEAT-FLOWERING

This extremely free-flowering rose has yellow flowers flecked with pink, salmon and scarlet. The large, very full, double, high-centered blooms that develop from urn-shaped buds consist of about 50 petals, and are borne in large clusters on a vigorous, medium-sized bush. It has a spicy Tea fragrance and the foliage is semi-glossy and leathery. 'Circus' is moderately disease free. This repeat-flowering variety was a favorite for many years and still retains its popularity. It makes a good bedding variety that can be propagated by budding. **'Climbing Circus'** (House, USA, 1961) is a vigorous summer-flowering sport of 'Circus' that occasionally produces a few blooms in autumn. It is suitable for walls or pillars. ZONES 4–9.

Swim, USA, 1956

'Fandango' × 'Pinocchio'

Geneva Gold Medal 1955, Royal National Rose Society Gold Medal 1955, All-America Rose Selection 1956

'CITY GIRL'   HARzorba
MODERN, LARGE-FLOWERED CLIMBER, PINK BLEND, REPEAT-FLOWERING

This climbing rose bears showy masses of bright coral-pink, medium-sized, double blooms and has a reputation for flowering well into autumn. The later blooms are salmon-pink. The dark green, glossy foliage provides good cover for walls, pergolas and fences, and this also has the potential to make an attractive specimen shrub. 'City Girl' was named to celebrate the centenary of the City of London School for girls. It should be propagated by budding. ZONES 4–9.

Harkness, UK, 1994

'Armada' × 'Compassion'

Geneva Silver Medal 1995, Glasgow Silver Medal 1995

'CITY OF AUCKLAND'   MACtane
MODERN, LARGE-FLOWERED/HYBRID TEA, ORANGE BLEND, REPEAT-FLOWERING

This free-flowering cultivar is noted for its strong fragrance. The mid-green, semi-glossy foliage is covered by large, double flowers in shades of orange that bloom repeatedly after the first flush. The growth is bushy and disease resistant and can be propagated by budding. ZONES 4–9.

McGredy, New Zealand, 1981

'Benson and Hedges Gold' × 'Whisky Mac'

'Climbing Chrysler Imperial'

C

'City of Auckland'

'City of Goulburn'

yellow, copper and gold, open slowly from well-shaped buds and are excellent for cutting. The medium to tall-growing bush is very upright with dense green, disease-resistant foliage. ZONES 5–11.

Swane's Nursery, Australia, 1995

Parentage unknown

'CITY OF HEREFORD'
MODERN, LARGE-FLOWERED/HYBRID TEA, MEDIUM PINK, REPEAT-FLOWERING

The carmine-pink flowers of this rose seem to be very eager to impress. They are very large and very fragrant, and they repeatedly produce well-formed flowers throughout summer: pointed, with high centers of tightly packed petals. This is a very good bedding variety that carries dark green, plentiful foliage. ZONES 4–9.

LeGrice, UK, 1967

'Wellworth' × 'Spartan'

Belfast Fragrance Prize 1969

'City of Belfast'

'CITY OF BELFAST'   MACci
MODERN, CLUSTER-FLOWERED/FLORIBUNDA, ORANGE-RED, REPEAT-FLOWERING

This outstanding Cluster-flowered Rose has large clusters of brilliant orange to blood red or scarlet blooms. These have only a little scent, but are truly repeat-flowering. The bush itself has a slightly spreading habit and is covered with disease-tolerant, glossy green foliage; it is a favorite variety for bedding and as a standard. ZONES 4–9.

McGredy, UK, 1968

'Evelyn Fison' × ('Circus' × 'Korona')

New Zealand Gold Medal 1967, Royal National Rose Society President's International Trophy 1967, Belfast Gold Medal 1970, The Hague Gold Medal 1976

'CITY OF BENALLA'
MODERN, LARGE-FLOWERED/HYBRID TEA, ORANGE-PINK, REPEAT-FLOWERING

The large, double blooms of this rose are made up of 45 carmine petals, although the inner petals are closer to coral. These are closely arranged to give the flowers high centers; the lower, outer petals pale as they age. The flowers develop from pointed, globular buds, which are borne singly; there is a slight fragrance. 'City of Benalla' is a vigorous, tall-growing bush rose with brown prickles and a dense cover of glossy, dark green foliage. It is good for rose beds, borders or as a specimen plant. The best method of propagation is by budding. ZONES 4–9.

Dawson, Australia, 1983

'My Choice' × 'Extravaganza'

'CITY OF BIRMINGHAM'
KORholst

syns 'Esprit', 'Holstein 87', 'Kordes' Rose Holstein', 'Petite Marquis'

MODERN, MODERN SHRUB, DARK RED, REPEAT-FLOWERING

This cultivar is a very healthy and vigorous bush rose that grows to a moderate size. It carries semi-glossy foliage clothed with large clusters of semi-double flowers throughout summer and autumn. Each deep scarlet bloom only has about 12 petals. There is a slight fragrance. It was named to celebrate England's biggest industrial city, although gardeners in other parts of Europe may know it better by one of its synonyms; in Germany, it was named to acknowledge the province of Holstein. It can be propagated by budding. ZONES 4–9.

Kordes, Germany, 1987

Seedling × 'Chorus'

'City of Hereford'

'City of Benalla'

'CITY OF BRADFORD'
HARrotang

MODERN, CLUSTER-FLOWERED/FLORIBUNDA, ORANGE-RED, REPEAT-FLOWERING

This rose has orange-red, semi-double blooms made up of 15 petals with a wavy appearance, that form cup-shaped, small to medium-sized flowers. In warmer months, the flowers appear in large clusters against glossy, dark green foliage. A medium-sized, vigorous plant, it is used for bedding and as a standard. ZONES 4–9.

Harkness, UK, 1986

('Manx Queen' × 'Whisky Mac') × (['Highlight' × 'Colour Wonder'] × ['Parkdirektor Riggers' × 'Piccadilly'])

Dublin Certificate of Merit 1984, Courtrai Silver Medal 1988, Belfast Certificate of Merit 1988

'CITY OF GOULBURN'
MODERN, LARGE-FLOWERED/HYBRID TEA, YELLOW BLEND, REPEAT-FLOWERING

This rose was named by the Goulburn Rose Committee. The blooms are borne on long stems both singly and in clusters and flower production is profuse and continuous. The flowers are a mixture of

'City of Birmingham'

'City of Bradford'

C

'CITY OF LEEDS'

MODERN, CLUSTER-FLOWERED/FLORIBUNDA,
ORANGE-PINK, REPEAT-FLOWERING

Named for the city's Flower Show, this
variety has deep salmon-pink, medium-
sized to large, cupped to flat, double
flowers that are borne in clusters repeatedly through summer and autumn. The
well-formed blooms are slightly fragrant
and are made up of almost 20 petals. The
dark green, healthy foliage is an excellent
foil to the abundance of bloom that
appears in summer. This very good
bedding variety also excels as a standard
and is good for cut flowers. ZONES 4–9.

McGredy, UK, 1966

'Evelyn Fison' × ('Spartan' × 'Red Favorite')

Royal National Rose Society Gold Medal 1965,
Belfast Certificate of Merit 1968

'CITY OF LONDON'   HARukfore

MODERN, CLUSTER-FLOWERED/FLORIBUNDA,
LIGHT PINK, REPEAT-FLOWERING

Named for the 800th anniversary of the
city's charter, 'City of London' is a soft
pink rose that fades to blush. The cupped,
double flowers are large, becoming flat
with age. The small clusters of blooms
repeat continuously, and are noted for
their good fragrance during this time.
The glossy green foliage clothes sparsely
prickled stems. This vigorous, healthy,
well-rounded bush rose grows bigger on
a support and can be trained as a short
climber. ZONES 4–9.

Harkness, UK, 1988

'New Dawn' × 'Radox Bouquet'

LeRoeulx Gold Medal 1985, Belfast Gold Medal
1990, New Zealand Fragrance Award 1992, The
Hague Gold Medal 1993, Royal Horticultural
Society Award of Garden Merit 1993

'City of Leeds'

'CITY OF NEWCASTLE BICENTENNIAL'   JACopper

MODERN, LARGE-FLOWERED/HYBRID TEA,
MEDIUM RED, REPEAT-FLOWERING

This rose was named in honor of the
bicentenary of the city of Newcastle in
Australia. It has very well-formed exhibition-type flowers of clear crimson red.
There are 40 or more petals and a very
strong perfume. It is a tall and robust
plant with healthy dark green foliage.
This variety is good for bedding and also
makes a fine standard. Flowering is
profuse and continuous. ZONES 5–11.

Jackson and Perkins, USA, 1997

Parentage unknown

'CITY OF PRETORIA'   KORseubel

MODERN, CLUSTER-FLOWERED/FLORIBUNDA,
APRICOT BLEND, REPEAT-FLOWERING

This bush rose carries large trusses of
semi-double flowers that light up the
landscape with their brilliant apricot
color over summer and into autumn.
The long, shapely buds develop into
slightly fragrant blooms with cream
undersides. A bunch of half-open flowers
makes a cheerful indoor display; they are
popular with florists too, for they last
well. This attractive bedding plant has
vigorous, rounded growth to medium
height. ZONES 4–10.

Kordes, Germany, pre-1988

Parentage unknown

'CITY OF WANGARATTA'

MODERN, LARGE-FLOWERED/HYBRID TEA,
MEDIUM RED, REPEAT-FLOWERING

This variety was named for a rural city in
Victoria, Australia, and is only available in

'City of London'

'City of York'

'City of Newcastle Bicentennial'

that country. The blooms have 45 petals
and open flat from pointed buds, which
are smallish and are produced both
singly and in clusters. Repeat bloom is a
little slow. The plant is short and stocky
and moderately fragrant. The semi-
glossy, mid-green foliage is very healthy,
as is the case with all George Dawson's
introductions. ZONES 5–9.

Dawson, Australia, 1985

Parentage unknown

'CITY OF WARWICK'   AROfuto

MODERN, LARGE-FLOWERED/HYBRID TEA, RUSSET,
REPEAT-FLOWERING

'City of Warwick' was named by Swane's
Nursery after the rose and rodeo city of
Warwick in Queensland, Australia. It is
a bright red rose of 30 petals, producing
well-formed, high-centered blooms
that open slowly. The matt mid-green
foliage is large and the stems are long
and good for cutting. The plant is rather
slow to repeat. Swane's Nursery is the
Australian agent for the American firms
of Armstrong Nurseries and Jackson-
Perkins. They have introduced a number
of roses such as 'Mary MacKillop', 'Rose
of Wagga' and 'City of Goulburn', which
are considered ideal roses for Australian
conditions but are usually not available
in other countries. ZONES 5–10.

Christensen, USA, 1995

Parentage unknown

'CITY OF WORCESTER'

MODERN, LARGE-FLOWERED/HYBRID TEA,
MEDIUM RED, REPEAT-FLOWERING

This is a repeat-flowering variety with
medium to light red, very large, well-
formed blooms. They are fragrant and
double, filled with about 35 petals, and
have a high-centered shape. Strictly,
however, this is an exhibitor's rose
with little to commend it as a garden
variety; the growth is quite weak. 'City of

'City of Worcester'

'City of Wangaratta'

'City of Warwick'

Worcester' is believed to be extinct, but
if it is found it should be propagated by
budding. The foliage is matt and mid-
green. ZONES 4–9.

Scrivens, UK, 1983

'Red Planet' × ('Ena Harkness' × 'Fragrant
Cloud')

'CITY OF YORK'

syn. 'Direktör Benschop'
MODERN, LARGE-FLOWERED CLIMBER, WHITE

This vigorous plant is a suitable subject
to cover a pergola or a fence rather than
a wall, because its growth habit is more
similar to a Rambler than a climber. The
plant is clothed with leathery, glossy
green foliage. It displays large clusters of
up to 15 fragrant, creamy white flowers,
but only in early summer. In shape they
are large and slightly cupped, and are
made up of 15 petals with the stamens
exposed. Budding is the best method of
propagation. It was named for the city in
Pennsylvania. ZONES 4–9.

Tantau, Germany, 1945

'Professor Gnau' × 'Dorothy Perkins'

American Rose Society National Gold Medal
Certificate 1950

'CLAIR MATIN'   MEImont

syn. 'Grimpant Clair Matin'
MODERN, LARGE-FLOWERED CLIMBER,
MEDIUM PINK, REPEAT-FLOWERING

The pretty pink paler-centered flowers of
this rose have a very sweet fragrance.
They are medium sized and semi-double,
with 15 petals arranged in a flattened cup
shape. As the flowers unfurl from their
pointed buds to reveal attractive, gold
stamens, the leathery dark green foliage
is adorned with huge, rounded clusters
of up to 40 of these flowers. Very few
hips are produced, which leads to almost
continuous flowers from summer into
autumn; 'Clair Matin' is one of the most
free-blooming of all roses. The growth is

'Clair Matin'

vigorous and well branched with cocoa-colored stems—ideal for walls and pergolas, because it grows taller when supported and is easily propagated by budding. The huge panicles of flowers make excellent decorations, and in 1960 this rose won a thoroughly deserved Gold Medal at Bagatelle in Paris. Translated into English, the French name means 'morning light'. ZONES 4–9.

Meilland, France, 1960

'Fashion' × (['Independence' × 'Orange Triumph'] × 'Phyllis Bide')

Bagatelle Gold Medal 1960

'CLAIRE JACQUIER'
syn. 'Mlle Claire Jacquier'
OLD, NOISETTE, LIGHT YELLOW

Although it is delicate looking, the rampant growth of this rose can soon cover a large shed or a barn. The semi-double, numerous blossoms, which appear at the branch endings, are buff yellow but fade in the sun. It does not like to be tied down and prefers to roam on structures or into trees, and it flowers once in early summer. The pliable canes are covered with large, pointed, dark green leaves. A robust, healthy plant, 'Claire Jacquier' tolerates shade and is sweetly scented. ZONES 7–9.

Bernaix, France, 1888

Possibly *Rosa multiflora* × Tea Rose

'Claire Jacquier'

'CLAIRE ROSE'   AUSlight
MODERN, MODERN SHRUB, MEDIUM PINK, REPEAT-FLOWERING

This is one of the most exquisitely beautiful of the Modern Shrub Roses; it is also classified as an English Rose. The long-lasting sprays of flowers are large and repeat-flowering and of perfect old-fashioned form, in a delicate blush pink shade that fades attractively to almost white as they age. They are cupped at first, opening to flat, many-petalled, slightly incurved rosettes with a lovely perfume on a strong, reasonably big, upright plant. The branches spread a little

'Claire Rose'

and are covered with an abundance of pale green leaves. This is a variety that enjoys a hot, dry climate and can become marked by rain, but this is a small fault and it makes an excellent companion plant in a border; it is sometimes a little ungainly on its own, like its parent 'Charles Austin'. It can be propagated by budding. The superb flowers on long stems are ideal for cutting. David Austin named this rose for his daughter, Claire Calvert. ZONES 4–9.

Austin, UK, 1990

'Charles Austin' × (seedling × 'Iceberg')

C

'Claude Monet'

'Clarita'

'Cleo'

'CLARET CUP'

MODERN, MINIATURE, RED BLEND,
REPEAT-FLOWERING

This free-flowering, fragrant Miniature
Rose is a good subject for containers.
It bears small, dark red blooms, each
with a white eye; these emerge from
clusters of globular buds to give an attractive display. 'Claret Cup' is a vigorous yet compact, bushy rose that is
covered by leathery, dark green foliage.
ZONES 4–9.

Riethmuller, Australia, 1962

'Spring Song' × 'Eutin'

'CLARISSA'   HARprocrustes

MODERN, MINIATURE, APRICOT BLEND,
REPEAT-FLOWERING

The florets of this variety are rich yellow-
apricot and have classic Large-flowered
form. The blooms have 43 petals and are
normally borne in large trusses. The foliage is dark and glossy. It is good for cut
flowers, which last up to a week. Growth
can be tallish on an upright plant, but
leggy in colder climates. ZONES 4–11.

Harkness, UK, 1983

'Southampton' × 'Darling Flame'

New Zealand Gold Star of the Pacific 1982,
Geneva Prize 1982, Royal National Rose Society
Trial Ground Certificate 1981, Tokyo Certificate
of Merit 1983

'CLARITA'   MEIbyster

syn. 'Atoll'

MODERN, LARGE-FLOWERED/HYBRID TEA,
ORANGE-RED, REPEAT-FLOWERING

This cultivar has large, vermilion flowers
that carry a light fragrance. The blooms
are double and high centered, each filled
with up to 35 petals; they adorn the matt,
dark green foliage repeatedly through
summer. A good choice for rose beds or
mixed borders, 'Clarita' is a very vigorous, upright bush rose that is reliably
resistant to disease. The best method of
propagation is by budding. ZONES 4–9.

Meilland, France, 1971

'Tropicana' × ('Zambra' × 'Romantica')

Lyon Gold Medal 1971, Geneva Gold Medal 1971

'CLASS ACT'   JACare

syns 'First Class', 'White Magic'

MODERN, CLUSTER-FLOWERED/FLORIBUNDA,
WHITE, REPEAT-FLOWERING

Borne in sprays of 3–6, the creamy
flowers of this rose have a slight fragrance
of fruit. They are medium-sized and
semi-double, and have 25 flatly arranged,
loose petals. In summer, when the
blooms repeat continuously, the dark
green, semi-glossy, bushy foliage adds a
good color contrast, which serves to
highlight the flowers. This upright plant

grows to medium height and has long
prickles on its stems. It is a useful and
popular variety for beds and borders
or as a standard. It is propagated by
budding. ZONES 4–9.

Warriner, USA, 1988

'Sun Flare' × seedling

All-America Rose Selection 1989, Portland Gold
Medal 1989, New Zealand Gold Medal 1990

'CLASSIC SUNBLAZE'   MEIpinjid

syns 'Duc Meillandina', 'Duke Meillandina'

MODERN, MINIATURE, MEDIUM PINK,
REPEAT-FLOWERING

This compact, fast-blooming miniature
rose was the first of the 'Sunblaze' series
released by the House of Meilland. The
florets are a pure medium pink and are
borne singly or in small clusters. As
with all the roses in the series, 'Classic
Sunblaze' is easy to cultivate. It is a long-
lasting cut flower but has only a slight
fragrance. ZONES 4–11.

Meilland, France, 1985

Sport of 'Pink Meillandina'

'CLASSIC TOUCH'

MODERN, LARGE-FLOWERED/HYBRID TEA,
LIGHT PINK, REPEAT-FLOWERING

This is a tall, upright bush rose that can
be grown for exhibition. The large,
slightly fragrant flowers are light pink
and very full, packed with up to 46 petals
per bloom, and are borne throughout
the warmer months either singly or in
small clusters. The foliage is large, mid-
green and semi-glossy, and has a good
health record. Grown in the garden,
'Classic Touch' is suited to rose beds or
mixed borders. ZONES 4–9.

Hefner, USA, 1991

Sport of 'Touch of Class'

'CLAUDE MONET'   JACdesa

MODERN, LARGE-FLOWERED/HYBRID TEA,
RED BLEND, REPEAT-FLOWERING

The reason for growing this rose is its
color, or rather colors, for carmine red
buds open to a flamboyant mélange of
red, yellow and white on an orange-pink
base, with irregular patches, stripes and
dots on both sides of the petals—no two
flowers are the same. They are high
centered, of medium size, and open
loosely cupped, revealing brownish yellow
stamens. Some growers consider it a
Cluster-flowered Rose. Despite its attrac-
tiveness it appears to be currently offered
by only a few nurseries. In the garden it
is useful in beds and borders; it is excellent for cutting and bears blooms freely

through summer and autumn. The scent
is light and fruity, and the variety grows
vigorously to average height or above,
with mid-green foliage. It was named for
the French painter who lived from 1840–
1926. His countryman Henri Delbard
was right to claim that Monet would
have loved to welcome it into his garden
at Givenchy. ZONES 5–9.

Jackson and Perkins, USA, 1992

Parentage unknown

'CLAUS GROTH'

syn. 'Klaus Groth'

OLD, SCOTS, ORANGE BLEND

This vigorous, summer-flowering rose
bears attractive, salmon-orange flowers
that are shaded with apricot yellow.
They are full and very fragrant. Each
flower develops into a large hip, but
flowerheads should be picked if a long
flowering display is desired. The foliage
is dark green and clothes a bushy plant
that suits large borders or can be grown
as a specimen. 'Claus Groth' is best
propagated by budding or from cuttings.
ZONES 4–9.

Tantau, Germany, 1951

'RMS Queen Mary' × Rosa spinosissima

'CLEO'   BEEbop

MODERN, LARGE-FLOWERED/HYBRID TEA,
LIGHT PINK, REPEAT-FLOWERING

This showy and bushy rose is valued for
its large, high-centered, soft light pink
flowers. Each flower is filled with about
40 petals and there is a slight fragrance.
In summer these are borne continuously
against a backdrop of light green, semi-
matt foliage, either singly or in paired
clusters. This plant is easily propagated
by budding, although care should be
taken as it is covered with red prickles.
'Cleo' is a bedding variety that will make
a good exhibition rose. ZONES 4–9.

Bees, UK, 1981

'Kordes' Perfecta' × 'Prima Ballerina'

'CLIFFS OF DOVER'   POUlemb

MODERN, MODERN SHRUB, WHITE,
REPEAT-FLOWERING

The flowers of this shrub rose are white
and single, and open cupped to flat with
yellow stamens. They are small and are
borne in clusters close to the foliage,
sometimes becoming partly hidden by
fresher growth. In the garden, it is a useful variety for borders and sites where a
dense spreading shrub of modest size is
needed; it continues to bloom through
summer and autumn. Unfortunately, it

'Claret Cup'

'Class Act'

'Cockadoo'

'Clos Vougeot'

is almost entirely lacking in fragrance. The growth is vigorous to below average height for a shrub rose, and the plant is attractively clothed with small, glossy dark green leaves. This is one of a series of low-maintenance varieties that are offered on their own roots for ease of cultivation. ZONES 4–9.

Olesen, Denmark, 1995

Parentage unknown

'CLIMENTINA'
MODERN, LARGE-FLOWERED/HYBRID TEA, MEDIUM PINK, REPEAT-FLOWERING

This is a variety for rose beds or exhibition, and is very healthy. It produces large rosy pink flowers with a light scent on a bushy plant. Propagation is by budding. ZONES 4–9.

Klimenko, USSR, 1955

'Independence' × 'Peace'

'CLIO'
OLD, HYBRID PERPETUAL, LIGHT PINK, REPEAT-FLOWERING

The flowers of this rose are flesh colored, very double, globular and bloom in clusters. A silver-pink overtone and sweet perfume add to its charm. The graceful arching canes reach 4 ft (1.2 m) and are covered with rich green, leathery foliage and prickles. It flowers during a long period in summer, it hates the rain and will ball quickly in such weather. It should be pruned lightly. In Greek mythology Clio is the muse of history. ZONES 5–9.

William Paul and Son, UK, 1894

Parentage unknown

'CLIVIA' KORtag
MODERN, LARGE-FLOWERED/HYBRID TEA, ORANGE BLEND, REPEAT-FLOWERING

The round buds of this bush rose develop into large, double flowers filled with 30 salmon petals that are blended with orange-red. The high-centered blooms are fragrant and are of exhibition quality. This rose is suitable for a rose bed, and is clothed with matt green foliage. 'Clivia' is an upright, bushy plant that has brown prickles and can be propagated by budding. ZONES 4–9.

Kordes, Germany, 1985

'Mercedes' × ('Sonia' × 'Uwe Seeler')

'CLOS FLEURI BLANC' DELblan
syn. 'Snowy Summit'
MODERN, CLUSTER-FLOWERED/FLORIBUNDA, WHITE, REPEAT-FLOWERING

This plant is sufficiently vigorous for some catalogues to describe it as being a semi-climber; it is suitable either as a pillar rose or in a shrub border. 'Clos Fleuri Blanc' bears large white flowers that are double and delicately fragranced, packed with up to 40 petals. They bloom repeatedly throughout the summer months, which can be further encouraged by regular deadheading. The foliage is bright green. ZONES 4–9.

Delbard and Chabert, France, 1988

('Milrose' × 'Legion d'Honneur') × 'Candeur'

'CLOS VOUGEOT' DELific
syns 'Red Prolific', 'Rouge Prolific'
MODERN, CLUSTER-FLOWERED/FLORIBUNDA, MEDIUM RED, REPEAT-FLOWERING

This free-flowering plant bears clusters of medium-sized, double red flowers, each filled with over 24 petals. It has a bushy growth habit and bright green foliage, and is suitable for a rose bed; it blooms repeatedly through the warmer months. Unfortunately, there is no discernible fragrance. 'Clos Vougeot' should not be confused with 'Chateau de Clos Vougeot', a very fragrant Large-flowered Rose bred in 1908 that is still in commerce. ZONES 4–9.

Delbard-Chabert, France, 1983

('Alain' × 'Charles Mallerin') × ('Lafayette' × 'Walko')

'CLOTILDE SOUPERT'
MODERN, POLYANTHA, WHITE, REPEAT-FLOWERING

This short-growing variety is a forerunner of the modern Cluster-flowered and Patio Roses. It has been in cultivation for a long time, and is full of history. As a result, it is still listed in many catalogues. The large, pearly white flowers are very double and have soft rose pink centers. These are carried in fragrant clusters amid soft, rich green foliage that is relatively healthy. ZONES 4–9.

Soupert and Notting, Luxembourg, 1890

'Mignonette' × 'Mme Damaizin'

'Clos Fleuri Blanc'

'CLYTEMNESTRA'
MODERN, MODERN SHRUB, ORANGE-PINK, REPEAT-FLOWERING

The copper buds of this rose develop into small flowers with an interesting color. They are deep salmon-copper and gradually fade to chamois with age; the petals have a ruffled or crinkled appearance. Throughout summer, the blooms appear in fragrant clusters amid the leathery, dark green foliage. The rose has a spreading habit that shows its best as a specimen plant, particularly when planted in groups. Budding is the best method of propagation. 'Clytemnestra' is typical of the roses bred by Pemberton. ZONES 4–9.

Pemberton, UK, 1915

'Trier' × 'Liberty'

National Rose Society Gold Medal 1914

'COALITE FLAME'
MODERN, LARGE-FLOWERED/HYBRID TEA, ORANGE-RED, REPEAT-FLOWERING

Named to publicize the British coal industry, 'Coalite Flame' bears very large, very double flowers that are packed with up to 60 orange-red petals. The growth is vigorous and upright, clothed with large,

'Climentina'

'Clivia'

deep green, matt foliage. In summer, the bush is covered by the fragrant blooms. It makes a good bedding variety or can be planted in groups in borders. It is propagated by budding. ZONES 4–9.

Dickson, UK, 1974

'Fragrant Cloud' × 'Red Planet'

'COCKADOO' COCaquil
syn. 'Cock A Doo'
MODERN, PATIO/DWARF CLUSTER-FLOWERED, MEDIUM RED, REPEAT-FLOWERING

'Cockadoo' is one of the best of the low-bordering, small-flowered roses. The plant is very bushy, compact and low growing in habit, with dark green, glossy disease-free foliage. The flowers are multi-petalled and a clean, strong, vibrant red in color, and when fully open measure approximately 2½ in (6 cm) in diameter—not too small to be lost in the general pattern of the open garden, nor too large for the style of the bush. There is very little scent. It makes an excellent patio or half standard but is just as easily grown on the edge of the bed or in a pot. ZONES 5–9.

Cocker, UK, 1984

Parentage unknown

'Coalite Flame'

'COCKTAIL' MElmick
MODERN, MODERN SHRUB, RED BLEND,
REPEAT-FLOWERING

'Cocktail' is one of the brightest roses available, and although its parents either have double or semi-double flowers, this variety bears brilliant single flowers with just 5 petals. Borne in large clusters continually through summer and autumn, they emerge from pointed buds and are geranium red in color with a glowing, primrose yellow eye. There is a delicate, spicy fragrance. This is a vigorous, strong-growing rose clothed with glossy, leathery foliage that is generally treated as a semi-climber; it is suitable for use as a standard or in a shrub border, however, as well as a short climber or pillar rose. The variety is very spectacular because of the unusual intense color and the multitudinous flowers, perfect if a plant is needed to liven up a dismal part

'Colchester Beauty'

'Cognac'

of the garden. It can be propagated by budding, and is said to tolerate poor soils. ZONES 4–9.

Meilland, France, 1957

('Independence' × 'Orange Triumph') × 'Phyllis Bide'

'COCKTAIL '90'
MODERN, LARGE-FLOWERED/HYBRID TEA,
YELLOW BLEND, REPEAT-FLOWERING

This small bush rose is a cut-flower variety that produces large, semi-double blooms of a particularly clear deep yellow. There are only 20 petals, but these have amazing substance and the buds unfurl very slowly. At the half-open stage, 'Cocktail '90' is very beautiful. Flowers grown in the open garden usually become flushed with apricot on the petal edges and are carried on short stems. This makes it a far better rose under glass than it is in the garden. It should not be confused with 'Cocktail', also bred by Meilland and introduced in 1961; 'Cocktail' is more popular than 'Cocktail '90' and has huge panicles of single, bright red flowers with a yellow eye. The practice of giving a new rose the same name as one already in commerce should be discouraged. ZONES 5–9.

Meilland, France, 1986

Parentage unknown

'COCO'
MODERN, CLUSTER-FLOWERED/FLORIBUNDA,
YELLOW BLEND, REPEAT-FLOWERING

The deep golden yellow to orange-pink blooms of this rose are large, double and

'Colibri'

very fragrant. Each flower has about 20–25 petals. The foliage is glossy and bright green, and clothes a vigorous and free-growing bush. Budding is the best method of propagation. ZONES 4–9.

Fryer, UK, 1975

'Pernille Poulsen' × 'Redgold'

'COCORICO' MEllano
MODERN, CLUSTER-FLOWERED/FLORIBUNDA,
ORANGE-RED, REPEAT-FLOWERING

'Cocorico' was one of the earliest red Cluster-flowered Roses suitable for bedding displays in large parks and gardens. The buds are pointed, geranium red in color and open to large, almost single flowers of 8 petals that are borne in small and large clusters. The bush is vigorous and upright and bloom production is very high. Repeat-bloom is very rapid if spent flowers are removed. As with most single roses, hips are produced in abundance if trimming is not carried out regularly. The semi-glossy foliage is bright green and abundant. *Cocorico* is colloquial French for 'something to crow about'. After nearly 50 years in commerce, it is still a good bedding rose. ZONES 5–9.

Meilland, France, 1951

'Alain' × 'Orange Triumph'

Geneva Gold Medal 1951, National Rose Society Gold Medal 1951

'COCORICO 1989' MEllasso
syn. 'Birthday Girl'
MODERN, CLUSTER-FLOWERED/FLORIBUNDA,
PINK BLEND, REPEAT-FLOWERING

It is surprising that this variety is not more readily available after winning 5 gold medals in one year. The firm of Meilland has an unfortunate habit of naming new roses using the same name as that used for a former Meilland release still in commerce. Others are 'Rouge Meilland' and 'Mascotte'. 'Cocorico 1989' is an excellent bedding rose, something in the style of 'Seduction', with well-formed, semi-double blooms of 15 petals in a blend of soft coral pink with a cream base. The reverse of the petals is a creamy salmon color. The foliage is glossy, bright green and abundant and the bush is compact and of medium height. Disease resistance is good while bloom production is high and repeat-bloom is rapid. 'Cocorico 1989' is a

'Cocktail'

first-class rose for bedding and for use as a standard. There is some perfume. ZONES 5–9.

Meilland, France, 1989

Parentage unknown

Bagatelle Gold Medal 1989, Monza Gold Medal 1989, Rome Gold Medal 1989, Saverne Gold Medal 1989, Baden-Baden Gold Medal 1990, Belfast Gold Medal 1991, Glasgow Certificate of Merit 1996

'COGNAC'
MODERN, CLUSTER-FLOWERED/FLORIBUNDA,
APRICOT BLEND, REPEAT-FLOWERING

This cultivar is valued for its beautiful apricot flowers that have darker undersides. They are large and double with dark amber stamens, although there is little fragrance. The foliage is glossy and dark olive green. For a Cluster-flowered Rose the growth is of average height but is quite bushy, and it is covered with small clusters of flowers in summer. 'Cognac' is a rose bed variety or it can be grown as a standard. ZONES 4–9.

Tantau, Germany, 1956

'Alpine Glow' × 'Mrs Pierre S. duPont'

'COLCHESTER BEAUTY'
CANsend
MODERN, CLUSTER-FLOWERED/FLORIBUNDA,
DEEP PINK, REPEAT-FLOWERING

The candy pink, semi-double blooms of 'Colchester Beauty' are very fragrant. They are of medium size, and are mostly borne singly. In summer they decorate this medium-growing, bushy rose and look good against the dark green, semi-glossy foliage. The variety is popular in rose beds or as a standard; take care because there are some prickles. ZONES 4–9.

Pawsey, UK, 1989

'English Miss' × seedling

'COLIBRI' MElmal
syn. 'Colibre'
MODERN, MINIATURE, ORANGE BLEND,
REPEAT-FLOWERING

This is a Miniature Rose from the same magic hands that hybridized the famous Large-flowered Rose 'Peace', which changed the perception of Large-flowered form forever. The ovoid buds open to reveal orange-yellow double flowers that are color-fast in most climates. The blooms are characteristically small and occur in small clusters. They have only a light fragrance. The glossy

'Cocorico'

foliage complements the brightly colored blooms. It is no wonder this rose took the top award in The Netherlands in 1962. While no longer extensively grown, it must go down in the history books as one of the classic Miniatures of the century. ZONES 4–11.

Meilland, France, 1958

'Goldilocks' × 'Perla de Montserrat'

The Hague Golden Rose 1962

'COLIBRI 79'   MEIdanover

syn. 'Colibre 80'

MODERN, MINIATURE, ORANGE BLEND, REPEAT-FLOWERING

This rose is an improved release of the original 'Colibri'. While a sister seedling from the same cross, it has the same yellow-orange color combination that captured everyone's attention in 1958. 'Colibri 79' has the distinct advantage of having a more prolific bloom produc-tion. The blooms age to a golden orange at the edges with a bright yellow center—this makes for a spectacular display in the garden. ZONES 4–11.

Meilland, France, 1979

'Goldilocks' × 'Perla de Montserrat'

'COLIN'S SALMON'

MODERN, LARGE-FLOWERED/HYBRID TFA, PINK BLEND, REPEAT-FLOWERING

This sport appeared in a planting of 'Bel Ange' at Brundrett's rose farm in Australia. 'Colin's Salmon' has all the attributes of 'Bel Ange' except that the color is a rich salmon. The plump, oval buds open slowly to large, well-formed, double blooms that are filled with 35 petals and are fragrant. The foliage is very dark green, matt, profuse and particu-larly disease free. This is a good rose for cutting as the flowers last well when picked. ZONES 5–9.

Brundrett and Sons, Australia, 1970

Sport of 'Bel Ange'

Belfast Gold Medal 1981

'COLLEGIATE 110'   DICknowall

MODERN, CLUSTER-FLOWERED/FLORIBUNDA, MEDIUM YELLOW, REPEAT-FLOWERING

On the 110th anniversary of the Girl's Collegiate School in Pietermaritzburg, South Africa, the Old Girl's Guild arranged for a new yellow rose to commemorate the event—the chosen

'Colin's Salmon'

rose was 'Collegiate 110'. As Natal can be extremely hot and humid in summer, this rose was a good choice, since it had a proven resilience to such weather. The semi-double, clear yellow blooms appear in large trusses throughout the year on a neat bush of medium height. When used for mass display, it is a valuable landscape plant, but is also good for containers and smaller intimate areas. ZONES 5–12.

Dickson, UK, pre-1989

Parentage unknown

'COLLEGIATE PRIDE'

MODERN, LARGE-FLOWERED/HYBRID TEA, MEDIUM RED, REPEAT-FLOWERING

The foliage of 'Collegiate Pride' is small, mid-green, leathery and matt, and the wood is dark with very few thorns on new growth. The very double dark red blooms of 55 petals are usually borne one to a stem; they are on the small side but can occasionally be of exhibition standard. There is some fragrance. This variety was named after St Michael's Collegiate School in Hobart, Tasmania. ZONES 5–9.

Bell, Australia, 1988

'Melvena' × 'Red Planet'

'COLOR MAGIC'   JACmag

MODERN, LARGE-FLOWERED/HYBRID TEA, PINK BLEND, REPEAT-FLOWERING

As the long, apricot pink buds on this variety open during summer, they turn from ivory to rich deep rose. They are large and double, are filled with about 25 petals, and are almost flat in shape. 'Color Magic' flowers repeatedly through the warmer months and gives slight fragrance; the long stems encourage the

'Color Magic'

'Colour Wonder'

'Columbia'

use of this variety for cut flowers, for which it is ideally suited. This is a tall-growing rose with dark green, very healthy foliage, and is well suited to a rose bed or mixed border. ZONES 4–9.

Warriner, USA, 1978

Seedling × 'Spellbinder'

All-America Rose Selection 1978

'COLORAMA'   MEIrigalu

syns 'Colourama', 'Dr R. Magg'

MODERN, LARGE-FLOWERED/HYBRID TEA, RED BLEND, REPEAT-FLOWERING

This rose bears fragrant flowers continu-ously through summer on a plant that is vigorous, bushy and upright. The large, double, cup-shaped blooms are red and yellow and emerge from oval buds. It has very glossy green leaves and is a good bedding variety for rose beds or mixed borders. It can be propagated by bud-ding. ZONES 4–9.

Meilland, France, 1968

'Suspense' × 'Confidence'

'COLOUR WONDER'   KORbico

syns 'Königin der Rosen', 'Queen of Roses', 'Reine des Roses'

MODERN, LARGE-FLOWERED/HYBRID TEA, ORANGE BLEND, REPEAT-FLOWERING

The large, coral-orange double blooms of this rose have cream undersides and are packed with up to 50 petals. They emerge from oval buds in early summer

and continue to flower for as long as the weather remains warm. There is also a light fragrance. Also quite curious is the glossy bronze foliage that covers this vigorous, upright bush rose. 'Colour Wonder' can boast a lineage of two of the most widely grown roses in this century as its parents; it, too, has become a parent of many new varieties. ZONES 4–9.

Kordes, Germany, 1964

'Kordes' Perfecta' × 'Tropicana'

Anerkannte Deutsche Rose 1964, Belfast Gold Medal 1966

'COLUMBIA'

MODERN, LARGE-FLOWERED/HYBRID TEA, MEDIUM PINK, REPEAT-FLOWERING

The glistening, very bright rose pink, large, double flowers of this variety are very fragrant. They are also very full, with about 65 petals per bloom. In summer, the flowers emerge from long, pointed buds to decorate this vigorous, bushy plant, which is also covered with dark green foliage. It is a popular bed-ding rose that is propagated by budding. 'Columbia' is a famous parent, an important variety in the development of the rose. ZONES 4–9.

Hill, USA, 1916

'Ophelia' × 'Mrs George Shawyer'

American Rose Society Gertrude M. Hubbard Gold Medal 1919, Portland Gold Medal 1919

'Colorama'

C

'Commandant Beaurepaire'

'Columbine'

'Columbus'

'Columbus Queen'

'COLUMBINE'
syn. 'Colombine'
MODERN, CLUSTER-FLOWERED/FLORIBUNDA,
YELLOW BLEND, REPEAT-FLOWERING

The open clusters of very fragrant, creamy yellow, pink-tinged flowers on this variety are well formed and enhanced by the glossy, dark green foliage. This is a vigorous bush rose that flowers repeatedly through the warmer months. In the garden 'Columbine' is good in rose beds, and should be propagated by budding. ZONES 4–9.

Poulsen, Denmark, 1956

'Danish Gold' × 'Frensham'

'COLUMBUS' WEKuz
MODERN, CLUSTER-FLOWERED/FLORIBUNDA,
DEEP PINK, REPEAT-FLOWERING

The deep rose pink, double blooms of 'Columbus' emerge from pointed, oval buds and keep their color well, fading very little, but there is not much in the way of fragrance. They make splendid exhibition roses; the 28 petals are

arranged well to give flowers with high centers. Throughout summer, this variety produces a plentiful display of large, single blooms, sometimes in clusters of 3–5, that liven up the dull, mid-green, large foliage. This is a bushy, Cluster-flowered Rose of average size and growth that is good in either a mixed border or rose bed. Budding is the best method of propagation but take care with the prickles, which are slightly hooked but almost straight and pinkish brown in color. ZONES 4–9.

Carruth, USA, 1990

Seedling × 'Bridal Pink'

'COLUMBUS QUEEN'
MODERN, LARGE-FLOWERED/HYBRID TEA,
PINK BLEND, REPEAT-FLOWERING

The slightly fragrant, light pink blooms of this rose are double and are filled with 30 petals; they have darker undersides and are high centered to cupped. Throughout summer there is a continuous display of bloom as new flowers emerge from oval buds. This upright, vigorous bush rose is well furnished with dark green, leathery foliage. It suits beds and borders, and should be propagated by budding. ZONES 4–9.

Armstrong, USA, 1962

'La Jolla' × seedling

Geneva Gold Medal 1961

'COMANCHE'
MODERN, LARGE-FLOWERED/HYBRID TEA,
ORANGE-RED, REPEAT-FLOWERING

The long, pointed buds of this rose develop into large, double, orange-red flowers. They have high centers and are

'Comanche'

lightly fragranced. The upright plant with dark green, leathery foliage is adorned with repeat displays of these beautiful flowers throughout summer and autumn. 'Comanche' grows quite vigorously, and can be propagated by budding. For the garden it makes a fine standard, but it is just as pretty in a rose bed. ZONES 4–9.

Swim and Weeks, USA, 1968

'Spartan' × ('Carrousel' × 'Happiness')

All-America Rose Selection 1969

'COMMAND PERFORMANCE'
MODERN, LARGE-FLOWERED/HYBRID TEA,
ORANGE-RED, REPEAT-FLOWERING

The medium-sized, high-centered, orange-red blooms of 'Command Performance' emerge from oval buds and release a good fragrance. They are borne on a vigorous-growing, tall bush that is clothed with dark green, leathery foliage. It was once a popular variety, and is good in rose beds. The best method of propagation is by budding. ZONES 4–9.

Lindquist, USA, 1970

'Tropicana' × 'Hawaii'

All-America Rose Selection 1971

'COMMANDANT BEAUREPAIRE'
syn. 'Panachée d'Angers'
OLD, BOURBON, PINK BLEND

This is an elegant plant in any situation, and is often proclaimed the best of striped roses. The rose pink blooms are streaked with purple-violet and marble white. They are cupped and upright and offer a strong fragrance. The foliage is light green with long, pointed leaves and the plant has prickly canes that need to

be thinned after blooming has finished. 'Commandant Beaurepaire' does well in cool weather in the shade where it can reach 5 ft (1.5 m) high, which makes it a good candidate for a hedge. ZONES 5–9.

Moreau-Robert, France, 1879

Seedling of an unnamed Hybrid Perpetual

'COMMUNIS'
syns 'Common Moss', 'Mousseau Ancien',
'Old Pink Moss', 'Pink Moss'
OLD, MOSS, MEDIUM PINK

Some authorities equate this old rose with 'Centifolia Muscosa'; there may well be differing clones of both cultivars around the world, yet this one seems to be distinct and is one of the best Moss Roses. It is bushy, dense and upright in habit to 4 ft (1.2 m) with well-mossed dark green stems. The leaves are lush mid-green and coarsely serrated. Appearing in mid-summer, the flowers emerge from mossy buds quite slowly at first, but eventually attain a diameter of some 3 in (8 cm). They are a constant rich deep pink, very fragrant and very double and more often than not quartered with a button eye. ZONES 5–9.

France, pre-1700

Improved form of 'Centifolia Muscosa'

Royal Horticultural Society Award of Garden Merit 1993

'COMPASSION'
syn. 'Belle de Londres'
MODERN, LARGE-FLOWERED CLIMBER,
ORANGE-PINK, REPEAT-FLOWERING

This is one of the all-time greats in rose breeding, and has deservedly won many awards. Its combination of high-quality

'Command Performance'

'Communis'

'Complicata'

'Complicata' (hips)

blooms and wonderfully sweet fragrance on a plant that grows to the size of a big shrub makes it a perfect subject for a garden, equally at home on a fence, pergola or wall. It is the most popular climbing rose in England. Throughout summer and autumn, 'Compassion' is completely repeat-flowering. It bears large salmon-pink, apricot-shaded blooms that are filled with about 36 petals. They are borne either singly or in clusters of 3 amid the large, dark green, leathery foliage. The plant itself is an extremely healthy variety with reasonably vigorous growth and a bushy, branching habit that can be propagated by budding. ZONES 4–9.

Harkness, UK, 1973

'White Cockade' × 'Prima Ballerina'

Baden-Baden Gold Medal 1975, Geneva Gold Medal 1975, Orléans Gold Medal 1979, Royal National Rose Society Fragrance Medal 1973, Anerkannte Deutsche Rose 1976, Royal Horticultural Society Award of Garden Merit 1993

'COMPLICATA'

syn. 'Ariana d'Algier'
OLD, GALLICA, PINK BLEND

This is a broad, dense, vigorous shrub attaining a height of 6 ft (1.8 m) or even more if given something to scramble on or into, such as a small tree. It has strong, gray-green, partially thorned stems that are abundantly clothed in large, durable foliage. The flowers appear

in early summer only and are up to 4 in (10 cm) in diameter at their best. Very bright, clear pink and single, they are moderately fragrant and are considerably enhanced with a lovely boss of bright creamy yellow stamens. Apart from making a superb specimen shrub, this rose will also do well as an informal hedge. It is very healthy, tolerant of impover-ished soils and very hardy. ZONES 5–9.

Parentage may involve Rosa canina or R. macrantha

'COMTE BOULA DE NANTEUIL'

syns 'Boule de Nanteuil', 'Comte de Nanteuil'
OLD, GALLICA, MAUVE

The large, crimson-purple blooms of this rose have silver overtones and crimson

'Comtesse Cécile de Chabrillant'

'Compassion'

centers. They are filled with many petals, compact, flat and quartered, and are admirably set off by prominent stamens. Its manageable size and Damask-like fragrance make it an ideal candidate for a pot plant. It can also be used as a low hedge and is quite tolerant of shade. Some confusion exists between this rose and one sold as 'Comte de Nanteuil'; both are popular cut flowers. ZONES 4–9.

Roeser, France, 1834

Parentage unknown

'COMTE DE CHAMBORD'
OLD, PORTLAND, PINK BLEND, REPEAT-FLOWERING

This is a sturdy shrub to 4 ft (1.2 m) with strong, grayish green stems well populated with reddish prickles and thorns. The light gray-green foliage is serrated and slightly downy. The flowers are borne in small clusters or singly, and in great profusion from early summer to autumn. In the late stage of bud they are beautifully high centered and scrolled, then later densely packed with petals; they go through a cupped stage to become fully flat, often quartered and up to 3 in (8 cm) across when fully open. These powerfully perfumed flowers are dense rich pink, with hints of lilac and lavender. 'Comte de Chambord' is ideal for group planting; it also makes a good hedge and is excellent as a container plant. Some think this rose is actually 'Mme Boll' (Boll, France, 1859).
ZONES 5–9.

Robert and Moreau, France, 1863

Perhaps 'Baronne Prévost' × 'Duchess of Portland'

Royal Horticultural Society Award of Garden Merit 1993

'COMTE DE NANTEUIL'
OLD, HYBRID PERPETUAL, PINK BLEND, REPEAT-FLOWERING

This rose has light rose pink blooms with dark pink edges and green centers. They are full, cupped and large. It is a vigorous shrub but is often confused with 'Comte Boula de Nanteuil'.
ZONES 5–11.

Quetier, France, 1852

Parentage unknown

'COMTESSE CÉCILE DE CHABRILLANT'
OLD, HYBRID PERPETUAL, PINK BLEND, REPEAT-FLOWERING

This rare rose bears fragrant, satiny rose pink flowers with silver undersides over a long period. They are full, globular and of medium size with petals shaped like shells. The tall canes have leathery, dark green foliage and tiny prickles. ZONES 5–9.

Marest, France, 1858

Seedling of 'Jules Margottin'

'COMTESSE DE LACÉPÈDE'
OLD, MISCELLANEOUS, LIGHT PINK

This delicate rose has silvery blush outer petals that blend to pink petals in the center. The blooms are double, large and cupped, and appear in early summer. The shrub has attractive foliage and a moderate rate of growth. ZONES 5–10.

1840

Probably Gallica Rose × China Rose

'COMTESSE DE MURINAIS'
OLD, MOSS, WHITE

This tall shrub grows well as a small climber; it is equally good as a shrub. The leaves are bright green and slightly crinkled. The buds have finely textured moss or tightly packed, small prickles, and the fragrant flowers are pure white with a hint of blush. ZONES 5–9.

Vibert, France, 1843

Parentage unknown

'Comtesse de Murinais'

'Comte Boula de Nanteuil'

'COMTESSE DE ROCQUIGNY'
OLD, BOURBON, WHITE

The medium-sized blooms of 'Comtesse de Rocquigny' are white with an overtone of rosy salmon. They are filled with many petals and are globular in shape. Unfortunately, this rose is no longer in commerce; it has probably been lost forever. ZONES 5–10.

Vaurin, France, 1874

Parentage unknown

'COMTESSE DU CAŸLA'
OLD, CHINA, ORANGE BLEND, REPEAT-FLOWERING

For many, this is the best of all the Chinas. It has purple, nodding stems that carry large, loosely cupped, flat blooms of carmine tinted orange with yellow undersides. The highly scented blooms are reminiscent of sweet peas and tea, and the flowering season lasts as long as the warm summer weather permits. 'Comtesse du Caŷla' does best in full sun, looking rather straggly in the shade, and

the thin canes and glossy bronze-green foliage form a compact bush to 3 ft (1 m) tall. This is an excellent rose to plant among perennials because of its handsome appearance and constant bloom. The cut flowers, especially if taken when in bud, last a long time indoors. The countess, for which this rose was named, was a mistress of Louis XVI of France. ZONES 7–11.

Guillot, France, 1902

(Seedling of 'Rival de Paestum' × 'Mme Falcot') × 'Mme Falcot'

'COMTESSE RIZA DU PARC'
syn. 'Comtesse Risa du Parc'

OLD, TEA, MEDIUM PINK/PINK BLEND, REPEAT-FLOWERING

This rose has sometimes been called 'the metallic rose' because of the strong, coppery yellow, slightly cupped appearance of its flowers. These are large and globular blooms; they are usually borne singly on long stems. 'Comtesse Riza du Parc'

'Comtesse du Caŷla'

'Comtesse Riza du Parc'

'Comtesse de Rocquigny'

has a strong but uneven growth habit, made up of reddish canes that are covered with hooked prickles and healthy foliage. It is repeat-flowering but not a heavy bloomer, and requires a warm spot in the garden. ZONES 7–11.

Schwartz, France, 1876

Seedling of 'Comtesse de Labarthe'

'COMTESSE VANDAL'
syns 'Comtesse Vandale', 'Countess Vandal'

MODERN, LARGE-FLOWERED/HYBRID TEA, PINK BLEND, REPEAT-FLOWERING

This was an extremely popular, Large-flowered Rose in the 1930s. Throughout summer it bears large, double, salmon-pink flowers that have coppery pink undersides; the 30 petals are neatly arranged to give a high center. There is a delightful fragrance. The foliage is leathery and clothes an upright plant that can be propagated by budding. A climbing form, **'Climbing Comtesse Vandal'** (syns 'Climbing Comtesse Vandale', 'Climbing Countess Vandal', 'Grimpant Comtesse Vandal'; Jackson and Perkins, USA, 1936) is good for walls and screens. It only flowers in summer, but the blooms are of a very high quality. ZONES 4–9.

Leenders, The Netherlands, 1932

('Ophelia' × 'Mrs Aaron Ward') × 'Souvenir de Claudius Pernet'

Bagatelle Gold Medal 1931, National Rose Society Trial Ground Certificate

'CONCERTINO'   MEIbinosor
MODERN, CLUSTER-FLOWERED/FLORIBUNDA, ORANGE-RED, REPEAT-FLOWERING

The loosely flat to cupped, double flowers of this rose are a bright cherry red and bloom repeatedly through the warmer months. There are 20 petals per flower and a light fragrance persists. In the garden, 'Concertino' is popular for rose beds or borders; the dark green foliage is

'Concerto'

'Comtesse Vandal'

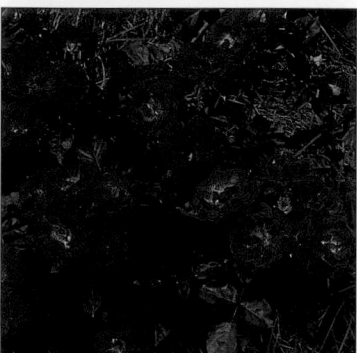

'Concertino'

a pleasing accompaniment to the sizeable clusters, which do not fade. It has an upright, bushy habit that should be propagated by budding. ZONES 4–9.

Meilland, France, 1976

(['Fidélio' × 'Fidélio'] × ['Zambra' × 'Zambra']) × 'Marlena'

'CONCERTO'
MODERN, CLUSTER-FLOWERED/FLORIBUNDA, MEDIUM RED, REPEAT-FLOWERING

Brilliant, medium red flowers emerge from pointed, oval buds on this variety to form loosely cup-shaped, semi-double blooms with 12–15 petals. There is a light fragrance. In summer, sizeable clusters of blooms that keep their color well cover the dark green foliage. 'Concerto' makes a good bedding rose that can be propagated by budding. The habit is upright and bushy. ZONES 4–9.

Meilland, France, 1953

'Alain' × 'Floradora'

National Rose Society President's International Trophy 1953

'CONDESA DE SÁSTAGO'
MODERN, LARGE-FLOWERED/HYBRID TEA, PINK BLEND, REPEAT-FLOWERING

This was the first bright, bicolored rose to be widely grown. 'Condesa de Sástago' has brilliant reddish orange, fragrant flowers with yellow undersides that emerge from oval buds. They are large and double, filled with about 55 petals to form the shape of a cup. This plant may be slightly prone to disease, but otherwise it is a strong, tall, upright grower that is furnished with glossy dark green foliage. **'Climbing Condesa de Sástago'** (Vestal, USA, 1936) is a useful climbing rose for training on walls. ZONES 4–9.

Dot, Spain, 1932

('Souvenir de Claudius Pernet' × 'Maréchal Foch') × 'Margaret McGredy'

Rome Gold Medal 1933, National Rose Society Trial Ground Certificate

C

'CONDITORUM'

syns 'Hungarian Rose', *Rosa gallica conditorum*, 'Tidbit Rose'
OLD, GALLICA, DARK RED

With a bushy and reasonably dense habit, this rose grows to about 3 ft (1 m) high. It has dark green stems, which are moderately thorny, and the plentiful foliage is gray-green and a little coarse. The very fragrant flowers are held upright in sizeable clusters and at their best are up to 3 in (8 cm) across when fully open. Appearing in early summer, they are slightly more than semi-double and somewhat disorderly in structure. They are cerise-crimson with strong magenta tints showing through; the display of bright yellow stamens is an added attraction. 'Conditorum' has many similarities to 'Officinalis'. ZONES 5–9.

1629

Parentage unknown

'CONFETTI'   AROjechs
MODERN, CLUSTER-FLOWERED/FLORIBUNDA, RED BLEND, REPEAT-FLOWERING

This rose is valued for its classically shaped, deep yellow blooms that have the fragrance of an old-fashioned Tea Rose. They develop from oval buds and

'Confidence'

'Confetti'

are double with about 24 petals. Borne in clusters of 3–7, they age to orange-red. Through summer this bushy, medium-sized rose is sprinkled with these flowers, which combine well with the mid-green foliage. 'Confetti' is a good healthy variety for a rose bed and can be propagated by budding. The stems are covered with prickles that are hooked downward. ZONES 4–9.

Swim and Christensen, USA, 1980

'Jack O'Lantern' × 'Zorina'

'CONFIDENCE'

MODERN, LARGE-FLOWERED/HYBRID TEA, PINK BLEND, REPEAT-FLOWERING

The large, double blooms of this variety are a pearly light pink with a hint of yellow at the base. The 38 petals unfurl from oval buds to form flowers with high centers and good fragrance. Throughout summer this upright and bushy Large-flowered Rose carries these blooms amid the dark green, leathery foliage. 'Confidence' is a relatively healthy rose that should be propagated by budding. It was the first successful variety to be bred from the enormously popular 'Peace' although it performs better in hot, dry climates, appreciating neither wet weather nor hard pruning. ZONES 4–9.

Meilland, France, 1951

'Peace' × 'Michèle Meilland'

Bagatelle Gold Medal 1951

'Condesa de Sástago'

'Conditorum'

'CONGRATULATIONS'   KORlift
syns 'Kordes' Rose Sylvia', 'Sylvia'
MODERN, LARGE-FLOWERED/HYBRID TEA, ORANGE-PINK, REPEAT-FLOWERING

'Congratulations' is a valuable addition to any collection of Modern Roses. It freely bears perfectly formed, medium pink blooms either singly or in small clusters on a bushy plant with large, dark green, healthy foliage. Each flower develops from a long, pointed bud and is filled with about 42 petals to form a double urn shape with a high center. It gives a nice fragrance and is a very good variety for grouping in a border. The long, upright flower stems are ideal for cutting; disbudding causes the plant to produce even larger blooms. Propagation is best achieved by budding. ZONES 4–9.

Kordes, Germany, 1979

'Carina' × seedling

Anerkannte Deutsche Rose 1977, British Association of Rose Breeders Selection 1977

'CONQUEROR'S GOLD'
HARtwiz
syn. 'Donauwalzer'
MODERN, CLUSTER-FLOWERED/FLORIBUNDA, YELLOW BLEND, REPEAT-FLOWERING

This medium-sized bush rose has semi-glossy, dark green foliage that forms a fine backdrop to the small clusters of up to 7 yellow blooms that appear repeatedly through summer. The flowers are average size and have petals edged with orange-red. 'Conqueror's Gold' should be propagated by budding. ZONES 4–9.

Harkness, UK, 1986

'Amy Brown' × 'Judy Garland'

Courtrai Certificate of Merit 1986, Belfast Gold Medal 1988

'Conqueror's Gold'

'Congratulations'

C

'Conservation'

'CONRAD FERDINAND MEYER'

MODERN, HYBRID RUGOSA, LIGHT PINK, REPEAT-FLOWERING

This widely grown cultivar can almost be classed as a semi-climber. It is a rampant, haggard, arching rose with its stems clothed with a plethora of thorns; it makes a good pillar rose or tall shrub. The freely borne flowers are double and very fragrant with soft silvery pink, cupped petals. The quality of the flowers improves each time they repeat through summer, although autumn blooms are unreliable. 'Conrad Ferdinand Meyer' should either be propagated by budding or from cuttings, and the coarse, leathery foliage can be prone to rust. ZONES 4–9.

Müller, Germany, 1899

('Gloire de Dijon' × 'Duc de Rohan') × *Rosa rugosa* 'Germanica'

'CONSERVATION'   COCdimple

MODERN, MINIATURE, PINK BLEND, REPEAT-FLOWERING

Although its official color is listed as a pink blend, the florets of 'Conservation' are more of a salmon-red to orange. The blooms contain only 18 petals, but their staying power is remarkable. Usually borne in clusters, the sprays appear as mounds of color against the glossy green foliage. There is a light fragrance on the opening day of the blooms but it dissipates quickly. The plant has a dense bushy habit and is disease resistant. This rose was named to celebrate the 50th anniversary of the World Wildlife Fund. The city of Aberdeen in Scotland has mass public plantings of this home-grown Miniature. ZONES 4–11.

James Cocker & Sons, UK, 1986

(['Sabine' × 'Circus'] × 'Maxi') × 'Darling Flame'

Dublin Gold Medal 1986, Glasgow Certificate of Merit 1990

'CONSTANCE'

MODERN, LARGE-FLOWERED/HYBRID TEA, MEDIUM YELLOW, REPEAT-FLOWERING

The double, high-centered blooms of this rose are a pretty yellow, turning to golden yellow as they age. During this time they release a light fragrance as the blooms repeat through summer. This Large-flowered Rose has a bushy growth habit and is well clothed with rich green, glossy foliage. It is a suitable subject for a rose bed. It should be propagated by budding. ZONES 4–9.

Pernet-Ducher, France, 1915

'Rayon d'Or' × seedling

Bagatelle Gold Medal 1916

'Constance Spry'

'CONSTANCE FINN'   HAReden

MODERN, CLUSTER-FLOWERED/FLORIBUNDA, LIGHT PINK, REPEAT-FLOWERING

This is a vigorous rose with growth that throws out long shoots bearing large trusses of flowers. These are blush pink to light rose pink with crimson bases. 'Constance Finn' is repeat-flowering and has a pleasing fragrance, which makes it good in a rose bed, as a shrub in a mixed border or among specimen plants if lightly pruned. Budding is the best method of propagation. ZONES 4–9.

Harkness, UK, 1997

Parentage unknown

'CONSTANCE SPRY'

syn. 'Constanze Spry'
MODERN, MODERN SHRUB, LIGHT PINK

This variety was the very first of its kind—the ancestor of all those Modern Shrubs that some breeders classify as English Roses (the reds excluded, being mainly derived from the 'Chianti'/'Tuscany' line). It has proved to be enormously popular. For anyone who wishes to grow roses, 'Constance Spry' would be a premier choice for every garden that has the room for this exceptional, lax-growing, rampant plant with large, soft luminous pink, cup-shaped, double flowers. Being a cross between a Modern Cluster-flowered Rose and an Old Garden Gallica Rose, it is not repeat-flowering, but this is not really a drawback because the single summer blooms are long lasting, spectacular and have a delicious fragrance of myrrh, a feature that has been passed on to many of its progeny. The growth is covered with large, dark green foliage that is very winter-hardy and has a good health record. It is useful in groups at the back of a mixed border, but because it can be quite sprawling it is better trained as a climber on walls to attain its best. This graceful rose was named after the famous pioneer of flower arranging of the 1950s and 1960s. ZONES 4–9.

Austin, UK, 1961

'Belle Isis' × 'Dainty Maid'

Royal Horticultural Society Award of Garden Merit 1993

'CONTRAST'

MODERN, LARGE-FLOWERED/HYBRID TEA, PINK BLEND, REPEAT-FLOWERING

The contrasting flowers of this rose have China pink and bronze uppersides and white and bronze undersides. They are double, with the petals tightly arranged to form a high center. Throughout summer 'Contrast' repeatedly produces very fragrant blooms on its compact yet extremely vigorous growth, which is covered with glossy, leathery foliage. The variety is a good bedding rose that also makes a nice standard. ZONES 4–9.

Howard and Smith, USA, 1937

Seedling × 'Talisman'

'COOPER'S BURMESE'

syns 'Gigantea Cooperi', *Rosa* × *cooperi*
OLD, LAEVIGATA, WHITE

This beautiful rose is best appreciated in a warm climate, where it bears large,

'Conrad Ferdinand Meyer'

'Constance Spry' growing on a trellis, with digitalis

saucer-shaped, single, creamy white flowers with prominent yellow stamens, and diffuses a pleasing fragrance. They appear quite freely in summer but are not dependably repeat-flowering. The delicacy of the blooms is in contrast with the character of the plant, for it produces prickly branching stems and can extend three times as far as the average climbing rose. The leaves are large and green and make a handsome foil to the pale, silky looking flowers. The use of this variety is limited in cooler climates due to its tenderness; for it to succeed, it will need a large wall that can give shelter from frost and cold winds. The original plant was grown by Roland Cooper, curator of the Royal Botanic Garden in Edinburgh, Scotland, who collected the seed in Burma. ZONES 6–9.

Cooper, UK, 1927

Possibly *Rosa laevigata* × *R. gigantea*

'COPACABANA'

MODERN, LARGE-FLOWERED CLIMBER, ORANGE-RED, REPEAT-FLOWERING

'Copacabana' inherits its rich orange-red color with dark red shading on the petal edges from the brilliantly colored 'Coup de Foudre'. The double flowers have 40 petals and are globular and large; they are produced both singly and in clusters on long stems and are fragrant. There is quite good repeat-bloom after a very profuse spring display. The autumn blooms are produced on very strong stems. The glossy dark green foliage is profuse and disease resistance is excellent. 'Copacabana' is a most useful rose for pillars and tripods as it never grows too large. Growth is rather thorny. ZONES 5–9.

Dorieux, France, 1966

'Coup de Foudre' × seedling

Royal National Rose Society Trial Ground Certificate 1968

'COPENHAGEN'

syn. 'Kobenhavn'

MODERN, LARGE-FLOWERED CLIMBER, MEDIUM RED, REPEAT-FLOWERING

This repeat-flowering climbing rose bears large, crimson-scarlet, semi-double, well-formed blooms that each have about 20 petals. They are produced in small clusters and there is a reasonable fragrance. Although the growth is some-times vigorous, 'Copenhagen' could be termed as a low-growing climber, ideal for pillars or small walls. The foliage is dark green with a coppery tinge and healthy. This was one of the first Modern Climbing Roses to be repeat-flowering, but it has now been superseded by more vigorous varieties that sadly do not have the same quality bloom. It can be propa-gated by budding. ZONES 4–9.

Poulsen, Denmark, 1964

Seedling × 'Ena Harkness'

National Rose Society Certificate of Merit 1963

'COPPÉLIA'

MODERN, CLUSTER-FLOWERED/FLORIBUNDA, ORANGE BLEND, REPEAT-FLOWERING

'Coppélia was originally introduced as a Large-flowered Rose, although it is correctly classed as a Cluster-flowered Rose. The blooms are medium sized, cupped and double, made up of 25 petals of good substance. They are a luminous rosy pink color with a hint of orange in the pink, and there is a slight fragrance. The foliage is mid-green and semi-glossy, and the bush is tall, spreading and extremely free flowering over a long period. 'Coppélia' is good as a bedding rose, and can also be planted as an informal hedge. ZONES 5–9.

Meilland, France, 1952

'Peace' × 'Europa'

'COPPER GEM'

MODERN, LARGE-FLOWERED/HYBRID TEA, APRICOT BLEND, REPEAT-FLOWERING

This variety is well named: of all the roses, its flowers are nearest in color to burnished copper. They are very well formed, high centered in the early stages and open to full blooms of 30–35 petals with a moderate perfume. The foliage is small, very bronze-purple in the early stages and semi-glossy; the flowers look superb against it. 'Copper Gem' is moderate and very bushy in growth and flower production is high with quick repeat. Unfortunately, the variety is very prone to black spot and to a lesser extent mildew—it is at its best in dry climate. This is a lovely rose for cutting and for growing in copper containers. It has a long vase life. ZONES 5–9.

Cocker and Son, UK, 1983

Parentage unknown

'COPPER POT'   DICpe

MODERN, CLUSTER-FLOWERED/FLORIBUNDA, ORANGE BLEND, REPEAT-FLOWERING

A tall plant for bedding, 'Copper Pot' bears large, orange-yellow, semi-double, flowers, each having 15 petals with deeper undersides. The fragrant blooms are repeat-flowering and are borne in trusses amid glossy bronze foliage. It can be propagated by budding. ZONES 4–9.

Dickson, UK, 1968

Seedling × 'Golden Scepter'

Royal National Rose Society Trial Ground Certificate 1968

'COPPER SUNSET'   SAVacop

MODERN, MINIATURE, ORANGE BLEND, REPEAT-FLOWERING

The long, pointed buds on this variety open to coppery orange flowers flushed with orange-red and a medium red reverse. The lightly fragrant, double blooms contain 21 petals. On occasions the blooms can have high centers, but the flowers open too quickly to preserve the form for any length of time. Even so, it is at its most attractive at the fully open stage when it shows off its attractive golden stamens against the complex coppery orange. The blooms come one to a stem as well as in sprays with an ever-changing range of colors—burnt orange and yellow, which gives the impression of burnished copper. In cool climates the flowers tend to ball. It is a medium-sized plant but the habit is angular if left unchecked. ZONES 4–11.

Saville, USA, 1988

'Acey Deucy' × 'Rainbow's End'

'COQUETTE DES ALPES'

OLD, BOURBON, WHITE, REPEAT-FLOWERING

The white, semi-cupped and semi-double blooms of this rose are filled with many pink-flushed petals, and usually occur in clusters. There is a pleasant fragrance. It is a vigorous, hardy bush covered with attractive foliage. One nurseryperson has described it as having an 'iron-clad constitution'. 'Coquette des Blanches' is a close relative of this rose, as can be seen by their common heritage. ZONES 5–10.

Lacharme, France, 1867

'Mlle Blanche Lafitte' × 'Sappho'

'COQUETTE DES BLANCHES'

OLD, BOURBON, WHITE, REPEAT-FLOWERING

The white blooms of this rose are lightly washed with pink. They are double and open to medium-sized cups, becoming somewhat flat as they age. It flowers freely in trusses, which are borne grace-fully on long stems, and there is some fragrance. 'Coquette des Blanches' is an upright, vigorous shrub with symmetri-cal branches that reaches 5 ft (1.5 m) in height. It is covered with elegant foliage and the branches have few prickles. Some rosarians doubt the parentage given by the breeder. ZONES 5–10.

Lacharme, France, 1871

'Mlle Blanche Lafitte' × 'Sappho'

'CORA MARIE'   KORlimit

syn. 'Dallas'

MODERN, LARGE-FLOWERED/HYBRID TEA, MEDIUM RED, REPEAT-FLOWERING

This is the ideal red florist rose: it has beautifully pointed buds on long thin stems that open to perfectly shaped blooms with firm petals. These last well when cut and are also sweetly fragrant. The velvety red flowers do not lose their luster in the sun, neither do they darken with age, so they can be depended on to give a long-lasting, brilliant display both in a vase and in the landscape. 'Cora Marie' is vigorous and very tall growing, so it is advisable to stake new branches. It is a well-loved garden bush rose, not only for its constant production of flowers, but also because it displays good resistance to disease. 'Cora Marie' is from the German firm of Kordes, which was founded in 1887 and has been an important contributor to rose breeding. ZONES 5–11.

Kordes, Germany, 1986

'Ankori' × seedling

'CORAL CLUSTER'

MODERN, POLYANTHA, ORANGE-PINK, REPEAT-FLOWERING

This is a typical example of the repeat-flowering pompon-type Polyanthas that were popular before the introduction of Cluster-flowered Roses. They were very prone to mutation, producing flowers in a variety of colors ranging from pale pink through to crimson. 'Coral Cluster' bears small, coral pink, double blooms throughout summer amid the pale green foliage. It is a very hardy cultivar, although it is prone to mildew from mid-summer. To propagate, take cuttings or remove the buds. ZONES 4–9.

Murrell, UK, 1920

Sport of 'Orléans Rose'

National Rose Society Gold Medal 1921

'Coral Cluster'

'Copenhagen'

'Copper Pot'

C

'CORAL DAWN'
MODERN, LARGE-FLOWERED CLIMBER,
MEDIUM PINK, REPEAT-FLOWERING

This is a vigorous climbing rose that bears beautiful rose pink, double flowers. They emerge from oval buds in summer to reveal large, well-formed blooms that are composed of 35 petals arranged into the shape of a cup. With repeat blooms throughout summer and autumn, the heavily fragranced flowers are carried in small clusters amid the healthy, leathery foliage. This is a slightly lax plant with stiff, branching stems that will greatly enhance low fences, walls or as a good subject for pillars. 'Coral Dawn' can be propagated by budding. ZONES 4–9.

Boerner, USA, 1952

('New Dawn' seedling × yellow Large-flowered Rose) × Orange-red Polyantha

'CORAL SATIN'
MODERN, LARGE-FLOWERED CLIMBER,
ORANGE-PINK, REPEAT-FLOWERING

The large, double, coral flowers of 'Coral Satin' emerge from oval buds and are reliably repeat-flowering through summer. They have a very good form; each flower has about 25 petals arranged to form a high center. This is a moderate-growing climbing rose that is very fragrant, very

'Coral Satin'

'Cordon Bleu'

healthy and well furnished with large, leathery foliage. It is a suitable subject for pillars and walls. Budding is the most reliable method of propagation. ZONES 4–9.

Zombory, USA, 1960

'New Dawn' × 'Fashion'

'CORAL SPIRE'   KORkragor
MODERN, LARGE-FLOWERD/HYBRID TEA,
MEDIUM PINK, REPEAT-FLOWERING

This is one of those tall-growing, upright roses chosen by Ludwig Taschner to use as background hedges or in beds with other tall-growing shrubs; he calls them 'spire roses'. The flowers develop from pointed buds into typical Large-flowered shape with tight, full centers and outer petals that curl back, all in shades of coral. They are carried high up on the tops of the tall branches and appear repeatedly through summer. The tall bush gives a good supply of cut flowers, which last a long time indoors; they are good for exhibiting, too, but have no fragrance. The growth is not only vigorous, but also disease resistant, and the plant mixes well with companion plants like blue ceanothus, puce-colored berberis or tall, blue sages. ZONES 4–10.

Kordes, Germany, 1994

Parentage unknown

'Cornelia'

'Cordelia'

'CORAL TREASURE'
MODERN, MINIATURE, ORANGE BLEND,
REPEAT-FLOWERING

This rose has ovoid buds that reveal coral-orange double flowers against a background of glossy green foliage. Described by growers as vigorous but short on blooms, this rose does best in warmer climates as it is susceptible to black spot in damp weather. The florets can be of show quality as they possess good color balance and vibrance. Sprays of 5–12 blooms are common and are usually borne from basal canes. The plant is extremely tall growing. ZONES 5–11.

Moore, USA, 1971

Seedling × 'Little Buckaroo'

'CORALIE'
OLD, DAMASK, LIGHT PINK

This fairly thorny shrub grows to 4 ft (1.2 m) high and has plenty of grayish dark green foliage. It flowers profusely in mid-summer, producing many medium-sized, fragrant, fully double blooms that are cupped; they take on a cushion shape when fully open. The color is soft mid-pink, later paling at the outer edges to a softer pink, then to blush, especially in hot sun. This is a lesser-known, but very good, Damask Rose. ZONES 5–9.

Pre-1848

Parentage unknown

'CORALIN'
syns 'Carolin', 'Carolyn', 'Karolyn'
MODERN, MINIATURE, ORANGE-RED,
REPEAT-FLOWERING

This classic Miniature Rose was developed in the 1950s. It boasts coral-red florets with 40 petals on a low-growing, compact plant. The pollen parent had been successfully used by Francis Meilland in the development of the prize-winning 'Colibri'. This rose was one of the first modern Miniatures but is no longer commercially available. It is, however, still grown in many countries via exchange of cuttings, and so continues to survive extinction. ZONES 5–11.

Dot, Spain, 1955

'Méphisto' × 'Perla de Alcañada'

'CORDELIA'
MODERN, LARGE-FLOWERED/HYBRID TEA,
APRICOT BLEND, REPEAT-FLOWERING

This is a tall plant that bears large, pointed, double flowers with 20 petals each. They are peach in color, and fade to a deeper shade as they age. There is a good fragrance. In the garden, 'Cordelia'

'Cordula'

makes a good bedding rose that has splendid, dark green foliage; it flowers well throughout summer. It can be propagated by budding. ZONES 4–9.

LeGrice, UK, 1975

Parentage unknown

'CORDON BLEU'   HARubasil
MODERN, LARGE-FLOWERED/HYBRID TEA,
APRICOT BLEND, REPEAT-FLOWERING

The pointed buds of this variety develop into medium-sized, double blooms that are usually carried singly or in small sprays. Each flower has about 20 apricot petals with begonia pink undersides; they age to deep apricot. Throughout summer these flowers repeat their display again and again, giving a pleasing fruity fragrance. 'Cordon Bleu' is an upright, medium-growing bush rose with dark green, glossy foliage—it makes a good standard or can be sited in a rose bed. Budding is the best method of propagation, but take care to avoid the reddish prickles, which curve downwards. It was named for the famous cookery school. ZONES 4–9.

Harkness, UK, 1992

'Basildon Bond' × 'Silver Jubilee'

Royal National Rose Society Trial Ground Certificate 1986

'CORDULA'   KORtri
MODERN, CLUSTER-FLOWERED/FLORIBUNDA,
ORANGE-RED, REPEAT-FLOWERING

The large clusters of orange-red, medium-sized, double blooms of this rose develop from globular buds and yield a light fragrance. They bloom repeatedly through summer and contrast well with the bronze-tinged, dark green, leathery foliage. The plant is a dwarf, with bushy growth that can be propagated by budding. 'Cordula' is suitable for a rose bed and makes a good standard. ZONES 4–9.

Kordes, Germany, 1972

'Europeana' × 'Marlena'

'CORNELIA'
MODERN, MODERN SHRUB, PINK BLEND,
REPEAT-FLOWERING

Raised by the Revered Joseph Pemberton of Essex, possibly from a seedling of 'Aglaia', 'Cornelia' has been popular ever since its release in 1925. The color of its flowers ranges from pale apricot-copper to salmon-pink or strawberry flushed yellow; the base is usually orange. They are small, very double, rosette shaped and are borne in large, arching trusses. The fragrance is distinctly musky.

C

'Cornelia' is a superb, strong-growing shrub rose that produces a continual bloom well into autumn. It has immense beauty and can look very effective cascading down a low wall or veranda, or trained around a pillar. There are no thorns, the foliage is dark green, bronze tinged and glossy and it prefers a sunny spot out of the wind. To propagate, take cuttings or retrieve the buds. ZONES 4–9.

Pemberton, UK, 1925

Parentage unknown

Royal Horticultural Society Award of Garden Merit 1993

'CORNSILK' SAVasilk

MODERN, MINIATURE, LIGHT YELLOW, REPEAT-FLOWERING

Beautiful creamy pastel-yellow flowers are the hallmark of this award-winning rose. The florets have 40+ petals and are of high exhibition quality. It is a vigorous plant covered with small, semi-glossy, disease-resistant foliage. Depending on climatic conditions the color of the blooms can change quite dramatically to much paler tones, and the color tends to fade faster in the heat of summer. Although the repeat bloom is slow, this rose is an outstanding Miniature for garden display. It is yet another offspring from the great yellow rose, 'Rise 'n' Shine'. ZONES 4–10.

Saville, USA, 1982

'Rise 'n' Shine' × 'Sheri Anne'

American Rose Society Award of Excellence 1983

'CORONADO'

MODERN, LARGE-FLOWERED/HYBRID TEA, RED BLEND, REPEAT-FLOWERING

This bicolored rose produces large red blooms with yellow undersides from long, pointed buds. They are filled with about 40 petals that form a high center and are reasonably fragrant. 'Coronado' is a vigorous, repeat-flowering rose with dark green, glossy foliage on an upright plant. It makes a good bedding variety and can be propagated by budding. ZONES 4–9.

Abrams, USA, 1961

('Multnomah' × 'Peace') × ('Multnomah' × 'Peace')

'Coronation Gold'

'CORONATION GOLD'
syn. 'Maja Oetker'

MODERN, CLUSTER-FLOWERED/FLORIBUNDA, APRICOT BLEND, REPEAT-FLOWERING

The clusters of golden yellow blooms with rich apricot shading that are carried on the upright stems of this plant make a bright and gaudy display. The flowers are large for a Cluster-flowered Rose, filled with about 25 petals, and open from globular buds into high-centered flowers with a rounded outline; they become cupped before the petals fall. They have a light fragrance, and maintain good continuity of bloom through summer and autumn and can withstand a reasonable amount of bad weather. In the garden, this is an excellent performer for a hedge or bed, and to group in a border. The plant grows vigorously with a neat, upright habit to a little below average height and is well clothed in bright green, shiny foliage. The raiser's firm holds the Royal Warrant from Queen Elizabeth II, and this rose commemorates the silver jubilee of her coronation. A more logical name would have been 'Coronation Silver'. ZONES 4–9.

Cocker, UK, 1978

('Sabine' × 'Circus') × ('Anne Cocker' × 'Arthur Bell')

'CORONET'

MODERN, CLUSTER-FLOWERED/FLORIBUNDA, DARK RED, REPEAT-FLOWERING

The clusters of large, semi-double blooms on this variety have 17 petals and are deep crimson. They repeat through

'Corvette'

'Corso'

the summer months and contrast well with the dark green, glossy foliage. The plant is vigorous and upright, but produces little in the way of scent. Budding is usually the most reliable method of propagation. ZONES 4–9.

de Ruiter, The Netherlands, 1957

'Independence' × 'Red Wonder'

'CORRIE' KORproha

MODERN, LARGE-FLOWERED/HYBRID TEA, DEEP PINK, REPEAT-FLOWERING

A rose for greenhouse production, 'Corrie' is equally good in warm climates as a garden rose. The buds are oval and open to smallish, well-formed flowers of deep rose pink with 35–40 closely packed petals. The bush is disease free and is covered with abundant, mid-green, semi-glossy foliage. There is a very quick repeat, so flower production is high. 'Corrie' is an excellent rose for picking; the blooms are extremely long lasting and hold their color well. It is also a good bedding rose, providing color over a long period. ZONES 5–9.

Kordes, Germany, 1992

Parentage unknown

'CORSO'

MODERN, LARGE-FLOWERED/HYBRID TEA, ORANGE BLEND, REPEAT-FLOWERING

This vigorous, upright variety had the potential to be a popular subject for cut

'Cornsilk'

flowers, but never became successful on the international market due to its liability to mildew. In the garden, however, 'Corso' produces lovely coppery orange, double blooms that are borne on long stems and have a good, classic form. The flowers are composed of 33 petals and are large, to $4\frac{1}{2}$ in (11 cm) across. They are repeat-flowering and have a light fragrance. The foliage is dark green and glossy and budding is the recommended method of propagation. ZONES 4–9.

Cocker, UK, 1976

'Anne Cocker' × 'Dr A. J. Verhage'

'CORVETTE' KORveco

MODERN, LARGE-FLOWERED/HYBRID TEA, ORANGE-RED, REPEAT-FLOWERING

This lovely, double, red-flowering rose was bred in Germany for release as a commercial cut-flower variety ideal for greenhouse production. Although only recently released, it is already proving to be popular with gardeners as the plant is easily grown, freely producing large numbers of flowers. The stems are long and strong, so that the large blooms are not easily broken in windy weather, and have few thorns. The healthy plant is well worth growing and will perform well in most situations. ZONES 5–10.

Kordes, Germany, 1997

Parentage unknown

'Corrie'

C

'Cosimo Ridolfi'

'Cottage Rose'

'Corylus'

'CORYLUS'
MODERN, MODERN SHRUB, MEDIUM PINK, REPEAT-FLOWERING

This bushy plant makes a beautiful shrub when not in bloom. Throughout summer it bears repeat displays of medium pink, saucer-shaped flowers that are fragrant and proudly show off their bright golden yellow stamens. These are borne either singly or in small trusses of up to 4, and if they are not deadheaded they develop into round, medium-sized, bright scarlet hips in autumn. The fruits are complemented by the impressive foliage: dark green, medium sized and willowy like its *Rosa rugosa* parent and which turns a beautiful bronze in autumn. Visitors will no doubt be impressed by the late display. 'Corylus' is easy to grow, and forms an upright, spreading plant that is very useful in shrub borders. To propagate, either take cuttings or remove the buds, but beware of the small, light brown prickles. *Corylus* is Latin for hazel, which is the breeder's first name. ZONES 4–9.

Le Rougetel, UK, 1988

Rosa nitida × *R. rugosa rubra*

'COSETTE'   HARquillypond
syn. 'Blue Carpet'

MODERN, CLUSTER-FLOWERED/FLORIBUNDA, MEDIUM PINK, REPEAT-FLOWERING

This is a true Patio Rose, a low and spreading plant ideal for small beds, borders, containers or as a short standard. It bears small pink flowers that are double and are filled with up to 60 quilled petals per bloom. There is a light fragrance.

Throughout summer clusters of blooms appear repeatedly amid the small, mid-green, matt foliage. It is propagated by budding or from cuttings, and is armed with dark prickles. ZONES 4–9.

Harkness, UK, 1983

Seedling × 'Esther's Baby'

'COSIMO RIDOLFI'
OLD, GALLICA, MAUVE

With a tidy and compact habit, this shrub seldom grows taller than 3 ft (1 m) and has stems that are gray-green with few thorns. The rich green foliage has some gray overlay, and is soft to touch. The medium-sized flowers open from firm round buds; they are fully double with a button eye and mostly saucer shaped with perfect symmetry. The color is violet-cerise, sometimes appearing almost blue in hot weather, and they are well scented. Unfortunately, this delightful rose is seldom seen. It is named for an Italian agricultural scientist (1794–1865). ZONES 5–9.

Vibert, France, 1842

Parentage unknown

'COSMIC'   BRIcos
MODERN, MINIATURE, ORANGE BLEND, REPEAT-FLOWERING

The long, pointed buds on this variety open slowly to reveal light to medium orange flowers with a light yellow reverse. The color intensifies to orange-pink in hot climate zones. The double florets with 26–40 petals have a light fragrance. They are borne singly as well as in small clusters, usually on strong straight stems,

'Cosette'

and have classical high-centered form suitable for exhibition and floral arrangements. The foliage is large, mid-green and semi-glossy with a vigorous and upright habit. It is subject to powdery mildew. 'Cosmic' was hybridized by an amateur rose grower, and is a worthy entry into the wonderful world of Miniature Roses. ZONES 5–11.

Bridges, USA, 1997

'Suzy' × seedling

'COTTAGE GARDEN'   HARyamber
MODERN, PATIO/DWARF CLUSTER-FLOWERED, ORANGE BLEND, REPEAT-FLOWERING

This rose is another great creation from the House of Harkness. The florets are a deep rich orange and the petal count can vary according to climate from 26–40 petals. The blooms are of a sufficiently large size for this variety to be classified as a Patio Rose. In warm climates, it constantly flowers in very large clusters, covering the entire bush with blossoms. The upright growth makes it an ideal container-grown plant for the patio. 'Cottage Garden' inherited its disease resistance and glossy foliage from its pollen parent, the Cluster-flowered Rose 'Amber Queen'. ZONES 4–11.

Harkness, UK, 1992

'Clarissa' × 'Amber Queen'

Glasgow Certificate of Merit 1994

'COTTAGE ROSE'   AUSglisten
syn. 'The Cottage Rose'

MODERN, MODERN SHRUB, MEDIUM PINK, REPEAT-FLOWERING

Also classified as an English Rose, this is a good shrub rose for a small garden. Its shallowly cupped, quartered-rosette, warm glowing pink flowers are borne during summer and autumn. Soon after the first flush appears, the next is in bud and ready to burst into bloom. This is a

'Cottontail'

charming, small, bushy plant useful for small beds or in a container, although it has little scent. It can be propagated by budding or from cuttings. For any gardener looking for a Modern Rose with the character of an Old Garden Rose, 'Cottage Rose' is without comparison. ZONES 4–9.

Austin, UK, 1991

'Wife of Bath' × 'Mary Rose'

'COTTONTAIL'   TINtail
MODERN, MINIATURE, WHITE, REPEAT-FLOWERING

Unusually fluffy white blooms with a slight fragrance occur in large clusters on this low-growing plant. This rose makes an ideal garden display, providing an abundance of bloom throughout the growing season. It is quite fast to repeat even without deadheading. Leslie Strawn is an amateur hybridizer who runs a Miniature Rose nursery in Southern California. She named 'Cottontail' for the rabbits which frequent her nursery and seem to be Miniature Rose fanciers themselves! ZONES 4–11.

Strawn, USA, 1983

'Pink Petticoat' × 'Pink Petticoat'

'COUNTESS OF STRADBROKE'
MODERN, LARGE-FLOWERED CLIMBER, DARK RED, REPEAT-FLOWERING

This free-flowering, dark crimson-red climbing rose is perfect for training up walls. The flowers seem to glow with color, and are large, globular and well shaped. They emerge from coral buds and emit a strong fragrance. Throughout summer, these are borne repeatedly amid the rich green, wrinkled foliage that covers this vigorous plant. 'Countess of Stradbroke' can be propagated by budding. ZONES 5–9.

Clark, Australia, 1928

'Walter C. Clark' × seedling

'COUNTRY DANCER'
MODERN, MODERN SHRUB, DEEP PINK, REPEAT-FLOWERING

This is an upright, dwarf shrub rose that produces large, rose red, double blooms repeatedly through the warmer months. The foliage is big, dark green and glossy. 'Country Dancer' is a useful plant for the front of a mixed border or in pots and has a reasonable fragrance. The growth habit is vigorous. ZONES 4–9.

Buck, USA, 1973

'Prairie Princess' × 'Johannes Boettner'

'Countess of Stradbroke'

'Country Dancer'

'Coupe d'Hébé'

give a good fragrance. 'Countrywoman' is suitable for rose beds and can be propagated by budding. ZONES 5–9.

Dawson, Australia, 1978

Seedling × 'Peace'

'COUP DE FOUDRE'
MODERN, CLUSTER-FLOWERED/FLORIBUNDA, ORANGE-RED, REPEAT-FLOWERING

The medium-sized, cupped blooms of this rose open throughout summer from well-formed buds and are a fiery red with only a little scent. This is a vigorous plant that is suitable for bedding and which is clothed with leathery, glossy bronze foliage. ZONES 4–9.

Hémeray-Aubert, France, 1956

('Peace' × 'Independence') × 'Oiseau de Feu'

'COUPE D'HÉBÉ'
OLD, BOURBON, DEEP PINK

With a name like this, one would be right to assume that the rose has cupped flowers. They are deep pink, very double and have waxy textured petals with wavy, crumpled edges. There is a strong, heady fragrance. This is a free-flowering rose but only in the first part of the season, and the blooms are heavy and hang down in an attractive manner. They last well when cut. Looking best in shade, the bush is vigorous and upright and can be used for a pillar if left unpruned. It does

well even in poor soil. The foliage is glossy and light green but is subject to mildew. ZONES 5–10.

Laffay, France, 1840

Bourbon hybrid × China hybrid

'COURTOISIE'   DELcourt
MODERN, CLUSTER-FLOWERED/FLORIBUNDA, ORANGE BLEND, REPEAT-FLOWERING

The large, double, orange blooms of 'Courtoise' have undersides that are blended with yellow. They appear repeatedly in small clusters throughout the warmer months and have a pleasing scent. It is a medium-sized, bushy bedding rose with mid-green foliage. ZONES 5–9.

Delbard-Chabert, France, 1984

'Avalanche Rose' × seedling of 'Fashion'

'Coup de Foudre'

'COUNTRY LIVING'   AUScountry
MODERN, MODERN SHRUB, LIGHT PINK, REPEAT-FLOWERING

Also classified as an English Rose, 'Country Living' is a must for any gardener who collects this sort of rose. The breeder claims that it is 'more old rose than old rose', yet it is a Modern Garden Rose that repeatedly produces perfectly shaped, medium-sized, delicate blooms freely through summer and into autumn. At times, each of these rosette-type flowers has a green eye at its confused center, although they are mostly blush to flesh pink fading to palest pink. There is a pleasing scent. 'Country Living' is a small-leaved variety with a twiggy, bushy character probably better described as a bush rose rather than a shrub rose; it is good at the front of a rose bed or in containers in a small garden. Some shoots do not appear to be winter hardy because they sometimes die back, but this is not a problem since the plant quickly recovers with new shoots at the base. Budding is the best method of propagation; take care of the small thorns. It was named for the magazine *Country Living*. ZONES 4–9.

Austin, UK, 1991

'Wife of Bath' × 'Graham Thomas'

'COUNTRY JOY'   MORcojo
MODERN, MINIATURE, PINK BLEND, REPEAT-FLOWERING

Another masterpiece from Ralph Moore, this rose was developed during his investigation into the use of 'Yellow Jewel' as a potential parent for transmission of the yellow genes. The small flowers have 40 petals and are light pink and yellow, and have a slight fragrance. The small complementary foliage is matt mid-green and is disease-resistant. This rose is not always easy to find, but is worthy of a place in any garden. ZONES 4–11.

Moore, USA, 1984

'Pinocchio' × 'Yellow Jewel'

'COUNTRY LADY'   HARtsam
MODERN, LARGE-FLOWERED/HYBRID TEA, ORANGE BLEND, REPEAT-FLOWERING

The medium-sized blooms of this tall, vigorous plant have a burnt look: reddish salmon-pink with undersides suffused pale scarlet, fading to orange-salmon then pink. They are borne with good continuity through summer and into autumn, usually singly or in small clusters. Each flower is urn shaped to pointed with about 24 loosely arranged petals. There is a spicy fragrance. If the flowers are not deadheaded, attractive oval fruits appear in autumn. 'Country Lady' was named for the Country Gentlemen's Association and is furnished with mid-green, healthy foliage and reddish, downward curving prickles. It can be propagated by budding. ZONES 4–9.

Harkness, UK, 1987

'Alexander' × 'Bright Smile'

Geneva Certificate of Merit 1985, Royal National Rose Society Trial Ground Certificate 1986

'COUNTRYWOMAN'
MODERN, LARGE-FLOWERED/HYBRID TEA, MEDIUM YELLOW, REPEAT-FLOWERING

This is a Large-flowered variety with globular buds that open to lemon yellow, flat, double blooms. These are borne on a bushy plant with leathery foliage and

'Courtoisie'

'Country Living'

'Country Joy'

'Countrywoman'

C

'Courvoisier'

'Cream Delight'

'COURTSHIP'

MODERN, LARGE-FLOWERED/HYBRID TEA,
MEDIUM PINK, REPEAT-FLOWERING

This repeat-flowering variety carries large,
double, high-centered to cup-shaped
flowers throughout summer. They
emerge from conical buds and have 28
cerise-pink petals per bloom with lighter
undersides. The foliage is dark green and
there is little fragrance. In the garden,
'Courtship' makes a vigorous and bushy
plant suitable for bedding. ZONES 4–9.

Shepherd, USA, 1955

'Mme Henri Guillot' × 'Peace'

'COURVOISIER'   MACsee

MODERN, CLUSTER-FLOWERED/FLORIBUNDA,
DEEP YELLOW, REPEAT-FLOWERING

The deep yellow double blooms of
this Cluster-flowered Rose have a shape
that is more characteristic of a Large-
flowered Rose. They are large, filled with
up to 50 petals, very fragrant and appear
in attractive trusses throughout summer.
This is an upright rose, with glossy dark
green foliage, that makes a fine bedding
plant. ZONES 5–9.

McGredy, New Zealand, 1970

'Elizabeth of Glamis' × 'Casanova'

Royal National Rose Society Trial Ground
Certificate 1969

'CRAMOISI PICOTÉ'
OLD, GALLICA, RED BLEND

This stiffly upright, medium-sized Gallica
grows up to 4 ft (1.2 m) high and has
cane-like, dark green stems and few
thorns. The small foliage is dark green
and coarse to touch, and the flowers
are arranged in tight clusters. These are
pompon shaped, deep pink and have
reddish touches to the edges of the petals.
This rose, which is bright and cheerful
rather than just beautiful, is moderately
fragrant and very useful in mixed
borders or even in pots. ZONES 5–9.

Vibert, France, 1834

Parentage unknown

'CRAMOISI SUPÉRIEUR'
syns 'Agrippina', 'Lady Brisbane'
OLD, CHINA, MEDIUM RED, REPEAT-FLOWERING

The small, semi-double flowers of this
China Rose are cupped and a clear and
unfading red, sometimes with a white
streak. They appear in clusters, repeat
regularly throughout the year and give a
raspberry fragrance. The small foliage is
rather spare on a wiry 6 ft (1.8 m) shrub,
but can be cut back regularly to promote
bushiness and continual flowering; it is
an excellent plant for the border or in a
container. Known to some as the 'old
Bermuda red rose', it has naturalized
itself on that island, which proves that it
can grow well under adverse conditions.
'Climbing Cramoisi Supérieur'
(Couturier, 1885) can reach 15 ft (4.5 m)
if properly trained. *Cramoisi* is the
French word for crimson. ZONES 6–11.

Coquereau, France, 1832

Seedling of 'Salter's Crimson China'

'CRAZY QUILT'   MORtrip

MODERN, MINIATURE, RED BLEND,
REPEAT-FLOWERING

This is just one of many striped Miniature Roses developed by Ralph Moore in

'Cramoisi Supérieur'

his quest to perfect the hybridizing
technique of striping. The cross between
'Fairy Moss' and Moore's striped seedling #26 produced a striped seedling he
named 'Striped #33', which eventually
became the pollen parent for this variety,
as well as many others. The flowers
with 25+ petals are red with random
creamy white stripes produced on a very
compact plant. The florets are borne in
small clusters or 1–3 blooms. Ageing
introduces a fading of the blooms that
enhances the overall color effect of the
plant. ZONES 4–11.

Moore, USA, 1980

'Little Darling' × Miniature seedling

'CREAM DELIGHT'   DUGcream,
SUNcredal
syn. 'Darling'
MODERN, LARGE-FLOWERED/HYBRID TEA,
LIGHT PINK, REPEAT-FLOWERING

This is a mutation of the very popular
and successful cut-flower variety 'Sonia'.
Although 'Cream Delight' is more widely
cultivated as a forcing variety it gives
good service as a garden plant, particularly in hot, dry climates. The flowers
are light pink, standing out well against
the deep green foliage. It should be
propagated by budding. ZONES 4–9.

Schuurman, New Zealand, 1983

Sport of 'Sonia'

'CREAM GOLD'

MODERN, MINIATURE, MEDIUM YELLOW,
REPEAT-FLOWERING

The long pointed buds of this rose
develop into elegant high-centered
blooms that are medium to light yellow,
depending on the climate. In some
climates the blooms appear to be white
rather than yellow. The florets have
about 38 petals and are often fragrant;
again, this is dependent on climate. The
bush is compact, with a low-spreading
growth. ZONES 5–11.

Moore, USA, 1978

'Golden Glow' × seedling

'CREAM PUFF'

MODERN, MINIATURE, PINK BLEND,
REPEAT-FLOWERING

This lovely addition to Miniature Roses
by an Australian-born hybridizer, Dee
Bennett, has flowers that are cream,
blushed pink. The florets contain 18
petals and are at their best when fully
opened, when the bright yellow stamens
are revealed. The natural growth habit
produces clusters of 3–5 blooms per
stem. The bloom size is large, as is the
foliage on a spreading bush. This makes
it a suitable candidate for Patio Rose
classification. ZONES 4–11.

Bennett, USA, 1981

'Little Darling' × 'Elfinesque'

'Cream Delight'

'Courtship'

'Crépuscule'

'CRÉPUSCULE'
OLD, NOISETTE, APRICOT BLEND,
REPEAT-FLOWERING

For warmer climates, perhaps no rose
enjoys more acclaim as a climber than this
one. It blooms from early spring until
the first frost, and has become popular
simply because it is hardy, floriferous
and quite beautiful. The apricot-yellow
blooms develop from perfect buds into
clusters of silky petals. The young leaves
are tinged with bronze ageing to light
green and the plant has few prickles.
It apparently does as well in shade as it
does in the sun. The sweet fragrance adds
another dimension to its worth, and is
especially suited to pergolas or as a floral
blanket on a fence. ZONES 6–11.

Dubreuil, France, 1904
Parentage unknown

'CRESSIDA'   AUScress
MODERN, MODERN SHRUB, APRICOT BLEND,
REPEAT-FLOWERING

One of the tallest roses in the Austin range
and also classified as an English Rose,
this variety makes very strong, upright
growth and is covered with big, rough-
textured, light green leaves. It carries

'Cressida'

small clusters of very large, very full,
cupped flowers that have a strong scent
of myrrh. They are apricot-pink in the
center, graduating to pale pink towards
the margins and apricot on the undersides; these colors mingle together very
well. 'Cressida' requires plenty of room
to grow, in a shrub border or against a
wall for example. If properly cultivated
the variety has the potential of producing
two flushes of flowers in a season.
ZONES 4–9.

Austin, UK, 1983
'Rugosa Conrad F. Meyer' × 'Chaucer'

'Cream Puff'

C

'CRESTED JEWEL'
OLD, MOSS, MEDIUM PINK

'Crested Jewel' is one in a series of roses produced by the revered hybridizer Ralph Moore of Visalia, California. He has experimented a lot with Moss Roses, and this is his most successful result. Its long, mossed buds open to bright pink, semi-double, high-centered blooms on a

'Crested Moss'

3 ft (1 m) bush. There is a slight scent. The foliage is tough and leathery, and the rose makes an ideal container plant. ZONES 5–11.

Moore, USA, 1971

'Little Darling' × 'Crested Moss'

'CRESTED MOSS'
syns 'Chapeau de Napoléon', 'Cristata'
OLD, MOSS, MEDIUM PINK

This is not perhaps a true Moss Rose as there is little or no moss anywhere on the plant, except on that part which takes the shape of a cocked hat on the calyxes of the flowers; this gives the rose its name. It is an angular, rather sparsely foliated, open shrub that grows to 5 ft (1.5 m) high and almost as wide. The stem is moderately populated with sharply pointed spines, and the gray-green leaves are heavily serrated. The flowers are similar to those of a Centifolia, both in form and size, but of a slightly brighter pink color. This very healthy and

easygoing shrub rose is often found listed by its other popular name 'Cristata'. ZONES 4–9.

Fribourg, Switzerland, pre-1820

Probably seedling of *Rosa* × *centifolia*

Royal Horticultural Society Award of Garden Merit 1993

'CRICKET'   AROket
MODERN, MINIATURE, ORANGE BLEND, REPEAT-FLOWERING

'Cricket' has tangerine buds that open to light orange florets, decorating a healthy, compact, completely disease-resistant bush. This rose is a winner for bloom production and ease of maintenance. Since the pollen parent is a deep yellow Cluster-flowered Rose, one might have expected some transmission of color and yet there is none. Instead, the pollen parent transmitted its great form and substance. While the flowers only contain 25 petals and the form is globular, 'Cricket' managed to win 'Queen of Show' at a popular all Miniature show in Southern California in 1989. It has leathery foliage. ZONES 4–11.

Christensen, USA, 1978

'Anytime' × 'Katherine Loker'

'Cricket'

'CRICRI'   MEIcri
syns 'Cri-Cri', 'Gavolda'
MODERN, MINIATURE, ORANGE BLEND, REPEAT-FLOWERING

'Cricri' has small globular buds that become small, full, open, very double rose-carmine blooms borne several together. This is another classic Miniature Rose developed by Francis Meilland just before his untimely death. The pollen parent, 'Perla de Alcañada', has deep pink flowers, and in some warm climates the flowers of 'Cricri' have been described as salmon-shaded coral blooms. The blossoms are long lasting on the bush and they also last well as cut flowers for indoors. The plant has a dwarf but bushy habit of growth. ZONES 4–11.

Meilland, France, 1958

('Alain' × 'Independence') × 'Perla de Alcañada'

'CRIMSON CASCADE'
FRYclimbdown
MODERN, LARGE-FLOWERED CLIMBER, DARK RED, REPEAT-FLOWERING

The bright crimson blooms of 'Crimson Cascade' are borne in small clusters on the ends of stiff, branching stems. They are cupped, double and bloom repeatedly through summer and into autumn. There is a light scent. This is a vigorous grower with glossy leaves that is suitable for training around pillars or on walls. It is a valuable addition to climbing roses as a whole, and can be propagated by cuttings. ZONES 4–9.

Fryer, UK, 1991

Parentage unknown

'CRIMSON CONQUEST'
syn. 'Climbing Red-Letter Day'
MODERN, LARGE-FLOWERED CLIMBER, DARK RED

Although many people describe this rose as a Climber, its slightly relaxed growth is closer to that of a Rambler, which makes it suitable for pergolas and pillars. The foliage is sage green and makes an interesting combination with the small, velvety scarlet-crimson, semi-double

'Crested Moss'

'Cricket'

'Crested Jewel'

blooms. These are carried in large clusters and give a light scent. The vigorous and spreading growth is best propagated by budding. ZONES 4–9.

Chaplin Bros, UK, 1931

Sport of 'Red-Letter Day'

'CRIMSON DESCANT'
MODERN, LARGE-FLOWERED CLIMBER, MEDIUM RED, REPEAT-FLOWERING

Suitable for pillars and walls, 'Crimson Descant' is a vigorous plant with deep green foliage and large, double, crimson blooms made up of about 30 petals. The flowers repeat their bloom through summer, and give a slight fragrance. Budding is the recommended method of propagation. ZONES 4–9.

Cant, UK, 1972

'Dortmund' × 'Etendard'

'CRIMSON GLOBE'
syn. 'Dr Rocques'
OLD, MOSS, DARK RED

This once-popular Moss Rose displays enormous buds that open to large, globular, deep crimson blooms; during early summer they produce a lovely fragrance. It is a vigorous bush that can reach a height of 4 ft (1.2 m) and is suitable for bedding displays. Unfortunately, the leaves are subject to mildew and in wet weather the blooms ball. It only needs moderate pruning. ZONES 5–11.

Paul, UK, 1890

Parentage unknown

'CRIMSON GLORY'
MODERN, LARGE-FLOWERED/HYBRID TEA, DARK RED, REPEAT-FLOWERING

For many years 'Crimson Glory' was the most reliable dark red Large-flowered Rose available. It bears large, deep velvety crimson blooms that emerge from long, pointed buds and is truly repeat-flowering right through summer and into autumn. There is an exceptionally pronounced, strong damask fragrance. In shape, the double flowers each consist of 30 petals arranged to form a rounded cup. It is a bushy variety with vigorous, slightly spreading growth and dark green, leathery leaves, making a good bedding rose that will also flourish as a standard. It can be propagated by budding, but is very prickly, so wear gloves when handling the stems. Many hybridists have attempted to use 'Crimson Glory' as a parent; the most

'Crimson Glory'

famous and successful result is 'Ena Harkness'. **'Climbing Crimson Glory'** was discovered by Millar of South Africa in 1941. It is similar to the parent, but it is only summer flowering and has stiff, branching growth that is best trained on a cool wall where it will not burn. Both forms of this variety are fairly vulnerable to mildew. ZONES 4–9.

Kordes, Germany, 1935

'Cathrine Kordes' seedling × 'W. E. Chaplin'

National Rose Society Gold Medal 1936, James Alexander Gamble Rose Fragrance Award 1961

'CRIMSON MOSS'
syn. 'Tinwell Moss'
OLD, MOSS, DARK RED

The buds of this rose are heavily mossed but the flowers do not always open

'Cricri'

properly. They are crimson and double. The rose's name, given by the clergyman of Tinwell in England who discovered it, is loosely used to describe other Moss Roses; this often leads to some confusion about this group. ZONES 4–10.

Lee, UK, pre-1846

Parentage unknown

'Crimson Glory'

'CRIMSON RAMBLER'
syns 'Shi Tz-mei', 'Soukara-Ibara', 'The Engineer's Rose', 'Turner's Crimson Rambler'

MODERN, RAMBLER, MEDIUM RED

This was the first red climber to be introduced to Europe from the Far East. It carries double, bright crimson, irregular

'Crimson Descant'

blooms that fade towards blue and occur in large pyramidal clusters. There is no fragrance. The mildew-susceptible foliage is light green and leathery, and covers a vigorous bush that can reach 25 ft (8 m) high. The British engineer, Robert Smith, saw it in a Japanese garden and sent it to friends in Edinburgh, Scotland; they called it 'The Engineer's Rose' because of Smith's occupation. In 1893, Charles Turner purchased the rose and the sales were enormous; it was so popular that even Queen Victoria traveled to Slough to see it. Today it has been surpassed by healthier Ramblers. **ZONES 5–11.**

From Japan, Turner, UK, 1893

Parentage unknown

'Crystal Palace'

'Crimson Shower'

'CRIMSON ROSETTE'
MODERN, CLUSTER-FLOWERED/FLORIBUNDA, DARK RED, REPEAT-FLOWERING

Clusters of small, double, dark crimson blooms emerge from small, oval buds on this variety to decorate it through the summer season. Each flower carries 30 petals and gives off a light fragrance. 'Crimson Rosette' is a good bedding rose with a dwarf and very bushy growth habit that is covered with dark green, leathery foliage. It can be propagated by budding. **ZONES 4–9.**

Krebs, USA, 1948

Parentage unknown

'CRIMSON SHOWER'
MODERN, RAMBLER, MEDIUM RED

The flowers produced on this rose are carried in large, dense clusters on a very vigorous but lax plant. The small, scarlet-crimson, double blooms are made up of 20 petals to form a rosette shape and are slightly fragrant. Although the variety is not repeat-flowering, the first flush begins late after mid-summer to early autumn, which can give the wrong impression. The trailing stems of this rose makes it a very suitable subject for pergolas and pillars, but it really excels as a weeping standard or 'umbrella rose'. 'Crimson Shower' is remarkably free of

disease for this type of plant, which can be propagated either by budding or from cuttings. The light green foliage is made up of many small leaflets. **ZONES 4–9.**

Norman, UK, 1951

Seedling of 'Excelsa'

National Rose Society Trial Ground Certificate 1951, Royal Horticultural Society Award of Garden Merit 1993

'CRIMSON WAVE' MEIperator
syn. 'Imperator'
MODERN, CLUSTER-FLOWERED/FLORIBUNDA, MEDIUM RED, REPEAT-FLOWERING

The large clusters on this vigorous, upright variety are cardinal red shaded cherry. They are large, double and happily repeat through summer. There is a slight fragrance of apple. The foliage of 'Crimson Wave' is semi-matt and dark green, and the plant is propagated by budding. **ZONES 4–9.**

Meilland, France, 1971

'Zambra' × ('Sarabande' × ['Goldilocks' × 'Fashion'])

'CRITERION'
MODERN, LARGE-FLOWERED/HYBRID TEA, DEEP PINK, REPEAT-FLOWERING

This bedding variety bears large, double, rose red flowers that are very fragrant. They have good form and are repeat-flowering. 'Criterion' is a vigorous and tall plant with dark green foliage, easily propagated by budding. **ZONES 4–9.**

de Ruiter, The Netherlands, 1966

('Independence' × 'Signal Red') × 'Peace'

'CRUMBLE BAR'
MODERN, CLUSTER-FLOWERED/FLORIBUNDA, DEEP YELLOW, REPEAT-FLOWERING

Treloar Roses of Portland tested a number of unnamed seedlings sent by Edward LeGrice. Ted Treloar was most

'Crimson Rosette'

'Crimson Wave'

'Crumble Bar'

impressed with the orange-brown color of this rose and was given permission to release it. He wanted to call it 'Violet Crumble', because the color was so similar to the center of a Violet Crumble Bar. This could have been an infringement of naming rights, so he settled for 'Crumble Bar'. The plant is very short and spreading with quite a few thorns and a good covering of matt mid-green foliage. The lightly fragranced flowers are very double, filled with 50–60 petals, and open quartered in the manner of the rose 'Café'. They develop from plump and oval buds. The color is at its best in warm weather, although flower production is actually low and repeat-bloom slow; in spring the blooms can be an unattractive straw yellow. 'Crumble Bar' is a rose for the flower arranger along with other unusual colors bred by Edward LeGrice: varieties such as 'News', 'Great News', 'Purple Splendour', 'Vesper', 'Artistic', 'Jocelyn', 'Amberlight', 'Tom Brown' and 'Ripples' come to mind. Because of its spreading habit, 'Crumble Bar' makes an unusual standard rose. Unfortunately, it is only available in Australia, where it is quite a popular rose. **ZONES 5–9.**

LeGrice, UK, 1982

Parentage unknown

'CRYSTAL PALACE' POUlrek
syn. 'Cristel Palace'
MODERN, PATIO/DWARF CLUSTER-FLOWERED, APRICOT BLEND, REPEAT-FLOWERING

Valued for its light peachy cream, double blooms that repeat through summer and autumn, 'Crystal Palace' is a compact plant that grows to about 24 in (60 cm) tall. The shiny, mid-green leaves make a perfect backdrop to the lovely cup-shaped, medium-sized flowers. There is a light scent. **ZONES 5–9.**

Olesen, Denmark, 1995

Parentage unknown

'CRYSTALLINE' ARObipy
MODERN, LARGE-FLOWERED/HYBRID TEA, WHITE, REPEAT-FLOWERING

A variety that excels as an exhibition rose, 'Crystalline' bears large white blooms filled with 35 petals tightly arranged to give a high center. There is a spicy fragrance. Usually borne singly on strong, upright stems, the flowers repeat through the warmer months. If the old blooms are not deadheaded they develop into large, globular orange hips that decorate this tall, bushy plant through autumn and into winter. The foliage is medium sized and semi-glossy. When handling it, be careful of the light green-tan prickles. **ZONES 4–9.**

Christensen and Carruth, USA, 1987

'Bridal Pink' × ('Blue Nile' × ['Ivory Tower' × 'Angel Face'])

'CUDDLES'
MODERN, MINIATURE, ORANGE-PINK, REPEAT-FLOWERING

This rose has ovoid buds, opening to deep coral-pink flowers that contain in excess of 55 petals, making it a natural for very hot climates. The florets have Large-flowered form and are slightly fragrant. Repeat bloom is fast with good production of both single blooms and small sprays. It is one of the few Miniatures with a Cluster-flowered Rose as its seed parent. The hybridizer died the year before this rose was honored by the American Rose Society. **ZONES 4–11.**

Schwartz, USA, 1978

'Zorina' × seedling

American Rose Society Award of Excellence 1979

'CUISSE DE NYMPHE EMUÉ'
syns 'Belle Therese', 'Incarnata', 'La Royale', 'La Séduisante', 'La Virginale', 'Maiden's Blush'

OLD, ALBA, MEDIUM PINK

This is one of the oldest of the popular roses in England and France, and its history is crowded with names. The earliest forms may date from the fifteenth century. The name is translated from French as the 'thigh of a passionate nymph', which prompted the Victorians to give it a new set of labels. It bears distinctive, fat, rich pink blooms that are beautiful as they open, becoming reflexed with age and paling at the edges. There is a strong but refined fragrance. The strong, arching canes are covered with blue-gray leaves. **ZONES 4–10.**

Parentage unknown

'Cymbaline'

'Crystalline'

'Cupid'

'CUPCAKE' SPIcup
MODERN, MINIATURE, MEDIUM PINK, REPEAT-FLOWERING

This lovely rose is still one of the best-selling varieties in the USA today. The clear pink blooms containing about 60 petals have the traditional high center characteristic of modern Large-flowered Roses, and this accounts for the success of this rose on the show tables. The florets are produced in small clusters of 1–5 blooms and have no fragrance whatsoever. The foliage is a glossy dark green indicating a high degree of resistance to diseases. It is one of the few Miniature Roses bred by an amateur hybridizer to win the American Rose Society Award of Excellence. **ZONES 4–11.**

Spies, USA, 1981

'Gene Boerner' × ('Gay Princess' × 'Yellow Jewel')

American Rose Society Award of Excellence 1983

'CUPID'
MODERN, LARGE-FLOWERED CLIMBER, LIGHT PINK

Although only summer flowering, the very large, cupped flowers on this variety glow with color. The blooms are pale pink tinted with peach and display golden stamens. The blooms are borne singly on stiff, branching stems amid large leaves, and if left uncut will develop into large, decorative hips that provide autumn and winter color. Vigorous and upright, 'Cupid' is suitable for pillars. **ZONES 4–9.**

Cant, UK, 1915

Parentage unknown

'CURIOSITY' COCty
MODERN, LARGE-FLOWERED/HYBRID TEA, RED BLEND, REPEAT-FLOWERING

As the name implies, this is a curious variety. When he discovered this rose,

'Cupcake'

'Curiosity'

'Cuddles'

Cocker claimed it was the only rose variety at the time to have such peculiar foliage; remarkably the leaves are patterned with dark, glossy green and white that contrasts well with the ruby red, young foliage. The well-formed, large, rounded to cup-shaped blooms are quite conventional, however, being scarlet on the uppersides and yellow on the undersides. They appear repeatedly through summer and autumn and give a light fragrance. As the variegated foliage is the main attraction, plant this stumpy bush rose where it can be admired. The foliage is also admired by flower arrangers. 'Curiosity' can be propagated by budding. **ZONES 4–9.**

Cocker, UK, 1971

Sport of 'Cleopatra'

'CUTHBERT GRANT'
MODERN, MODERN SHRUB, DARK RED, REPEAT-FLOWERING

This bushy grower gives an intermittent display of deep purplish red, semi-double, large, cupped blooms through the summer season. They emerge from oval buds and give a slight fragrance. The

plant is vigorous and upright, and is decorated with glossy green foliage. It is propagated by either budding or from cuttings. **ZONES 4–9.**

Marshall, Canada, 1967

('Crimson Glory' × 'Assiniboine') × 'Assiniboine'

'CYMBALINE' AUSlean
syns 'Cymbelene', 'Cymbeline'

MODERN, MODERN SHRUB, LIGHT PINK, REPEAT-FLOWERING

Although the flowers of this shrub rose may not please all tastes because of their unusual color, they can be used to beautiful effect in most color scheme. The breeder describes them as 'gray-pink', although they can be almost ashy. They are large and double and are filled with about 35 petals. There is a pronounced fragrance of myrrh, and the variety is truly repeat-flowering. 'Cymbaline' is an elegant rose with arching growth that spreads to ground level, showing its flowers to full effect. It can be propagated by budding. Unfortunately, it is a little prone to black spot. **ZONES 4–9.**

Austin, UK, 1982

Seedling × 'Lilian Austin'

D

D

'Dagmar Späth'

'Daily Sketch'

'Daily Mail Scented Rose'

'DAGMAR SPÄTH'

syns 'Blanc Lafayette', 'White Lafayette'
MODERN, CLUSTER-FLOWERED/FLORIBUNDA,
WHITE, REPEAT-FLOWERING

This exhibition variety has white, semi-double flowers edged and flushed pink, fading to pure white. Very large in size, the blooms appear in clusters from summer to autumn and have a slight scent. It is a bushy plant that is well furnished with rich green glossy foliage. ZONES 4–9.

Wirtz and Eicke, Germany, 1936

Sport of 'Lafayette'

'D'AGUESSEAU'

OLD, GALLICA, MEDIUM RED

Upright and vigorous with strong stems and few thorns, this fine rose can reach

5 ft (1.5 m) high and has plentiful foliage, which is a luscious dark green. The nicely scented flowers are borne in tight clusters from fat, dark red buds. They are very full of vibrant cerise petals with paler undersides, and form full, flat flowers that are quartered in form with tight buttons in the center. The color neither fades nor deepens with age. It is well scented and flowers in mid-summer. Vibert, the giant of French rose hybridizing, grew up in Paris during the Revolution and served as a soldier in Napoleon's army. Shortly before he died aged 89, he told his young grandson, 'I have loved only Napoleon and roses.' ZONES 4–10.

Vibert, France, 1837

Parentage unknown

'DAILY MAIL SCENTED ROSE'

MODERN, LARGE-FLOWERED/HYBRID TEA,
RED BLEND, REPEAT-FLOWERING

Pronounced the best scented rose when it was introduced in 1927, this variety has crimson flowers that are shaded maroon and vermilion and have dark crimson undersides. The blooms are very fragrant and appear through summer and autumn. A vigorous plant with dark green foliage, it is propagated by budding. ZONES 4–9.

Archer, UK, 1927

'Château de Clos Vougeot' × 'Kitchener of Khartoum'

'DAILY SKETCH'   MACai

MODERN, CLUSTER-FLOWERED/FLORIBUNDA,
PINK BLEND, REPEAT-FLOWERING

'Daily Sketch' has large blooms of silvery pink edged deep pink. They are each composed of 46 petals, are fragrant and appear in clusters from summer to autumn. It is a good bedding variety with dark foliage. ZONES 4–9.

McGredy, UK, 1961

'Ma Perkins' × 'Grand Gala'

National Rose Society Gold Medal 1960

'DAINTY BESS'

MODERN, LARGE-FLOWERED/HYBRID TEA,
LIGHT PINK, REPEAT-FLOWERING

'Dainty Bess' has been described as one of the loveliest roses ever bred. It has large single blooms that are a soft rose

pink with very distinct maroon stamens which give an added beauty. The flowers, which are fragrant, continue to bloom through summer and autumn on a plant that has vigorous, upright growth and deep green leathery foliage. It is propagated by budding. **'Climbing Dainty Bess'** (van Barneveld, USA, 1935) is summer flowering, and a good variety to grow on a wall. ZONES 4–9.

Archer, UK, 1925

'Ophelia' × 'Kitchener of Khartoum'

'DAINTY DINAH'   COCamond

MODERN, PATIO/DWARF-CLUSTER FLOWERED,
ORANGE-PINK, REPEAT-FLOWERING

Medium salmon-pink semi-double blooms (20 petals) with a slight spicy fragrance grace this compact, dense plant. As the florets age they turn a lovely orange-red. The blooms are well-formed but tend to open rather quickly in warm climates. It tends to be self-cleaning—it drops its flowers and immediately begins the next bloom cycle. This charming rose is an excellent choice for a border. ZONES 5–11.

Cocker, UK, 1981

'Anne Cocker' × 'Wee Man'

'DAINTY MAID'

MODERN, CLUSTER-FLOWERED/FLORIBUNDA,
PINK BLEND, REPEAT-FLOWERING

'Dainty Maid' has silvery pink, single flowers with carmine undersides. They

'D'Aguesseau'

'Dainty Bess

'Dairy Maid'

'Dallas'

open from pointed buds and appear in clusters with little scent. It is an upright, bushy, compact variety with dark, leathery foliage, and was outstanding when it was first introduced. **ZONES 4–9.**

LeGrice, UK, 1940

'D. T. Poulsen' × seedling

Portland Gold Medal 1941, National Rose Society Trial Ground Certificate

'DAIRY MAID'

MODERN, CLUSTER-FLOWERED/FLORIBUNDA, LIGHT YELLOW, REPEAT-FLOWERING

The buds on this rose are yellow splashed carmine, opening into flowers that are yellow fading to white. Large and single, they are produced in big clusters from summer to autumn. It is an upright grower with glossy foliage. **ZONES 4–9.**

LeGrice, UK, 1957

('Poulsen's Pink' × 'Ellinor LeGrice') × 'Mrs Pierre S. duPont'

National Rose Society Certificate of Merit 1957

'DALE FARM'

MODERN, CLUSTER-FLOWERED/FLORIBUNDA, ORANGE-RED, REPEAT-FLOWERING

This large rose has clusters of double, fragrant blooms. Bright vermilion in color, they are produced from summer to autumn. 'Dale Farm' is good for bedding, having dark green foliage and growing vigorously to medium height. **ZONES 4–9.**

Smith, UK, 1973

Parentage unknown

'DALLAS'

MODERN, LARGE-FLOWERED/HYBRID TEA, RED BLEND, REPEAT-FLOWERING

This variety has large, crimson-carmine flowers with a base of primrose yellow. These blooms, which are double with 40 petals, continue to appear throughout summer and autumn, but there is only a little fragrance. It is a large, vigorous plant, with dark green and glossy foliage, that makes a good bedding subject. **ZONES 4–9.**

Hunter, USA, 1963

Sport of 'Peace'

'Dale Farm'

D

'DAME BLANCHE'
MODERN, RAMBLER/GROUND COVER, WHITE

In an age when French hybridizers were creating a flock of new Ramblers, Turbat raised 50 cultivars, one of which, 'Ghislaine de Féligonde', is still in the catalogues. Although very rare these days, 'Dame Blanche' was a popular white rambler that was also used as a ground cover. The greenish white blooms are crowned with yellow stamens. It blooms only once in late spring, and the vigorous canes are easy to train on structures. ZONES 4–11.

Turbat, France, 1923

Parentage unknown

'DAME DE COEUR'
syns 'Dama di Cuori', 'Herz-Dame', 'Queen of Hearts'

MODERN, LARGE-FLOWERED/HYBRID TEA, MEDIUM RED, REPEAT-FLOWERING

This variety has very large, cherry red, double blooms with considerable fragrance that appear through summer and autumn with good continuity. The growth is vigorous and upright, and it has glossy dark green foliage. An important variety in the history and development of the rose, 'Dame de Coeur' is a reliable bedding plant. ZONES 4–9.

Lens, Belgium, 1958

'Peace' × 'Independence'

National Rose Society Trial Ground Certificate 1958

'DAME EDITH HELEN'
MODERN, LARGE-FLOWERED/HYBRID TEA, MEDIUM PINK, REPEAT-FLOWERING

The very large, glowing pink double blooms of 'Dame Edith Helen' have a

'Dame Prudence'

strong fragrance. Although not very free in appearance, they are borne continuously from summer to autumn on long, strong stems. A suitable plant for bedding, it has vigorous bushy growth and leathery foliage. ZONES 4–9.

Dickson, UK, 1926

Parentage unknown

National Rose Society Gold Medal 1926

'DAME OF SARK'
MODERN, CLUSTER-FLOWERED/FLORIBUNDA, ORANGE BLEND, REPEAT-FLOWERING

Its large, double flowers are orange flushed red and have yellow undersides. They are slightly fragrant and have about 33 petals. This bushy grower with its dark foliage is a good bedding variety and a reliable subject for growing as a standard. ZONES 4–9.

Harkness, UK, 1976

('Pink Parfait' × 'Masquerade') × 'Tablers' Choice'

Royal National Rose Society Trial Ground Certificate 1976, British Association of Rose Breeders Breeder's Choice 1976, Courtrai Silver Medal 1978

'Dame de Coeur'

'DAME PRUDENCE'
MODERN, MODERN SHRUB, LIGHT PINK

Also classified as an English Rose, 'Dame Prudence' was developed in the 1960s and has since been discarded by the breeder, yet it is still widely grown. The double flowers are soft pink with lighter undersides, and have 65 petals with a good fragrance. It has loose, floppy growth that is slightly prone to disease; it is best planted as a specimen. ZONES 4–9.

Austin, UK, 1969

'Ivory Fashion' × ('Constance Spry' × 'Ma Perkins')

'DAME WENDY'   CANson
MODERN, CLUSTER-FLOWERED/FLORIBUNDA, MEDIUM PINK, REPEAT-FLOWERING

The medium-sized, double flowers of 'Dame Wendy' are clear pink and mildly scented. They are borne from summer to autumn on a moderately growing, slightly spreading plant. A good subject for bedding or as a standard, it has glossy dark green, healthy foliage. ZONES 4–9.

Cants, UK, 1991

'English Miss' × 'Memento'

Royal National Rose Society Trial Ground Certificate 1990

'Dame of Sark'

'Dame Wendy'

D

'DANAË'

MODERN, MODERN SHRUB, LIGHT YELLOW, REPEAT-FLOWERING

The clusters of medium-sized double blooms on this variety are deep yolk yellow fading white as they age. They have little scent, although they do continue to appear through summer and autumn. 'Danaë' is a healthy medium-sized shrub with rich green shining foliage, that is a good subject for a shrub border when planted in groups. ZONES 4–9.

Pemberton, UK, 1913

'Trier' × 'Gloire de Chédane-Guinoiseau'

'DANCE OF JOY'

MODERN, CLUSTER-FLOWERED/FLORIBUNDA, MEDIUM RED, REPEAT-FLOWERING

This variety (dating from earlier this century) has large, double flowers that are a vivid scarlet-crimson in color. They are fragrant, and appear on a vigorously growing plant with dark green foliage. ZONES 5–9.

Sauvageot, France, 1931

'Paul's Scarlet Climber' × seedling

Bagatelle Gold Medal 1931

'DANIEL LACOMBE'

MODERN, RAMBLER, YELLOW BLEND

This rose is best remembered as the seed parent of the successful Rambler,

'Danse des Sylphes'

'Dapple Dawn'

'Tausendschön', but today it can only be found in a few botanical collections in Europe. The pale yellow, full blooms are flat and medium in size; the yellow is washed with pink. Although it is vigorous, it lacks hardiness, which may explain why it has been superseded by other Ramblers. ZONES 5–10.

Allard, 1885

'Général Jacqueminot' × *Rosa multiflora*

'DANSE DES SYLPHES'   MALcair

syn. 'Grimpant Danse de Sylphes'

MODERN, LARGE-FLOWERED CLIMBER, ORANGE-RED, REPEAT-FLOWERING

This vigorous Climber has flowers that are rich red suffused with geranium red. Globular and medium sized, they appear in large clusters and have little scent. A good healthy plant for walls and pillars, it has glossy deep green foliage on upright stems. ZONES 4–9.

Mallerin, France, 1959

'Spectacular' ('Dance du Feu') × ('Peace' × 'Independence')

'DAPHNÉ'

OLD, GALLICA, MEDIUM PINK

'Daphné', a rare Gallica, offers medium-sized, rosette blooms in rich lilac pink. Each flower has a small yellow eye of stamens. The colors are more pronounced in the shade and there is a strong scent. The 5 ft (1.2 m) bush has gray-green, ribbed foliage and prickly hips. If not pruned it will sprawl in all directions, and so is suitable as a ground cover or for falling over walls. Daphné was a young girl loved by the god Apollo; she fled his advances and escaped him by being changed into a laurel, afterwards his favorite tree. ZONES 4–10.

Vibert, France, 1819

Parentage unknown

'DAPPLE DAWN'   AUSapple

syn. 'English Dawn'

MODERN, MODERN SHRUB, LIGHT PINK, REPEAT-FLOWERING

Probably one of the most floriferous of the English Roses, 'Dapple Dawn' has

'Dance of Joy'

large single blooms that are a delicate shade of pink. They have little scent, but the flowers appear in big clusters that are produced in profusion throughout summer and autumn. It is a good subject for borders and as a specimen plant and is propagated by budding. ZONES 4–9.

Austin, UK, 1983

Sport of 'Red Coat'

'DARLING FLAME'   MEliucca

syns 'Minuette', 'Minuetto'

MODERN, MINIATURE, ORANGE-RED, REPEAT-FLOWERING

The blooms on this rose are mandarin red to vermilion with yellow anthers. They are double with 25 petals, globular, small and have a slight fragrance. The foliage is glossy dark green on a vigorous plant. 'Darling Flame' has been used extensively in borders and in containers for patios. The bloom cycle is fairly rapid during the growing season. This is one of the few Miniatures used as a tree, as it usually blooms in clusters that cover the entire bush. Jack Harkness used it in his hybridizing program for new Miniature Roses. ZONES 5–11.

Meilland, France, 1971

('RImosa' × 'Josephine Wheatcroft') × 'Zambra'

'DAVID THOMPSON'

MODERN, HYBRID RUGOSA, MEDIUM RED, REPEAT-FLOWERING

This rose has double flowers with yellow stamens that open from oval buds. The blooms have 25 medium red petals and quite a strong fragrance, and appear through summer and autumn. It is an upright, winter-hardy shrub with wrinkled foliage—a suitable subject for hedging. ZONES 4–9.

Svejda, Canada, 1979

('Schneezwerg' × 'Frau Dagmar Hartopp') × seedling

'Darling Flame'

'DAVID WHITFIELD'   GANa

MODERN, CLUSTER-FLOWERED/FLORIBUNDA, MEDIUM PINK, REPEAT-FLOWERING

With its large double blooms, which appear in open clusters, and its light scent, this variety makes a good bedding subject. The flowers are deep china pink and continue to appear throughout summer and autumn. 'David Whitfield' has a moderate growth habit and large, dark green leaves; it was named after a well-known entertainer. ZONES 4–9.

Gandy, UK, 1991

Seedling of 'Kerryman'

'DAWN CHORUS'   DICquaser

MODERN, LARGE-FLOWERED/HYBRID TEA, ORANGE BLEND, REPEAT-FLOWERING

Medium-sized, classically shaped blooms of deep orange appear very freely on short stems on this bushy variety. There is a continuity of bloom through summer and autumn, the flowers having a light scent. It has reddish leaves and is a suitable subject for bedding or as a well-furnished standard. ZONES 4–9.

Dickson, UK, 1993

'Wishing' × 'Peer Gynt'

Dublin Gold Medal 1993, Rose of the Year 1993, Glasgow Certificate of Merit 1995

D

'Dawson's Delight'

'Day Light'

'DAWSON'

syn. 'The Dawson Rose'
MODERN, RAMBLER, MEDIUM PINK

The hybridizer of this rose was attempting to create hardiness in ramblers, and this was his greatest success; it was the first multiflora hybrid produced in the USA by Jackson Dawson of the Arnold Arboretum. The small, bright rose pink blooms are fragrant and double, and form in clusters of 10–20 along the strong canes, which can reach 25 ft (8 m). This rose is impervious to frost and neglect, and is good when used as a tree climber or on a stone pile. It does not repeat-flower and has been superseded by roses with better color and reblooming strength. ZONES 4–11.

Dawson, USA, 1888

'Général Jacqueminot' × *Rosa multiflora*

'DAWSON'S DELIGHT'

MODERN, LARGE-FLOWERED/HYBRID TEA,
DEEP PINK, REPEAT-FLOWERING

This is one of George Dawson's best roses. The strong, healthy bush has large, glossy deep green foliage that is very disease free. The flowers are large, to 5 in (12 cm) across, and very full with 40–50 petals; they keep well both on the bush and when picked. They are a strong deep pink color with a hint of coral and have a good fragrance. ZONES 5–11.

Dawson, Australia, 1978

Parentage unknown

'DAY LIGHT'   INTerlight

syn. 'Daylight'
MODERN, CLUSTER-FLOWERED/FLORIBUNDA,
APRICOT BLEND, REPEAT-FLOWERING

The large clusters of big apricot-yellow, double flowers of this bush rose make a delightful display in summer. The plant would be especially suited to either a mixed shrub border or massed planting. The foliage is quite a deep green. 'Day Light' is reasonably healthy and can be propagated by budding. ZONES 4–9.

Ilsink, The Netherlands, 1991

Parentage unknown

Belfast Gold Medal 1992

'DAYBREAK'

syn. 'Day Break'
MODERN, MODERN SHRUB, MEDIUM YELLOW,
REPEAT-FLOWERING

'Daybreak' has clusters of golden yellow flowers that turn light yellow and have

'Daydream'

dark golden stamens. They are just semi-double (almost single), have a rich musk fragrance and appear through summer and autumn. It is a tidy shrub with very dark chocolate brown foliage that turns dark green with age, and is a good subject to plant as a specimen shrub. Propagation is by budding or from cuttings. ZONES 4–9.

Pemberton, UK, 1918

'Trier' × 'Liberty'

'DAYDREAM'

MODERN, CLUSTER-FLOWERED CLIMBER,
LIGHT PINK

This climbing variety has large, semi-double flowers. The blooms are a very pale pink to almost white, and have a slight scent. 'Daydream' has medium green glossy foliage. Free flowering, it is suitable for growing on a trellis or as a pillar rose. From the famous Australian breeder Alister Clark, it is now only available from Australian nurseries. ZONES 5–10.

Clark, Australia, 1925

Probably seedling × 'Rosy Morn'

'DAZZLER'   KELdaz

MODERN, MINIATURE, YELLOW BLEND,
REPEAT-FLOWERING

The flowers of 'Dazzler' are light yellow with much paler undersides and light red outer edges. The blooms are medium sized, borne mostly singly and have a light fragrance. While the flowers are an extremely attractive color, they are no match for the beauty of its parents. The plant is an upright bush with disease-resistant foliage. While the blooms may remain on the bush for a long time, they fade quickly to a muddy color; because of this they are unsuitable for cutting. ZONES 5–11.

Kelly, USA, 1997

'Rainbow's End' × 'Kristin'

'DE CANDOLLE'

MODERN, RAMBLER, LIGHT PINK

This is an extremely rare rose that was raised during a high period for Ramblers both before and after World War I. The flowers are red, medium in size and full. The only place that continues to have this rose in its collection is Sangerhausen in former East Germany, which is currently the largest rose garden in the world with a list of nearly one thousand roses. ZONES 4–11.

Robichon, France, 1913

Parentage unknown

'DE LA GRIFFERAIE'

MODERN, RAMBLER, DEEP PINK

Found in wild places, ruined buildings and old cemeteries, this rampant rose suckers vigorously on its own roots, which may explain why it has naturalized so readily. The trusses are filled with fully double, magenta-cerise blooms that are quite pink in the sun and tend to be shapeless and scentless. The 6 ft (1.8 m) shrub has long, arching branches of dark wood and is almost free of prickles. Used widely as root stock, it is not considered of much value in regular gardens; however, when it is discovered thriving on its own and with a delicious perfume, a second opinion may be warranted. The former residence of the de la Grifferaie family is in Normandy. ZONES 4–11.

Vibert, France, 1845

Possibly *Rosa multiflora* × unknown Gallica or Damask

'DE LA MAÎTRE-ÉCOLE'

syn. 'Rose du Maître d'École'
OLD, GALLICA, MAUVE

This rose was named after a village near Angers in France and for many years was wrongly named 'Rose du Maître d'Ècole'. It is a relaxed, dense shrub up to about 3 ft (1 m) high and wide. The stems are arching, dark grayish to green and practically thornless, and the foliage is dark green and profuse. The highly scented flowers are very large, 4 in (10 cm) in diameter and even larger in good soils. They are very double and almost always quartered, with a little green pip in the center surrounded by a button of infolding petals. The color is difficult to describe—it is basically deep pink with silvery highlights and shadings of mauve and soft purple. For a few weeks in mid-summer it is a sheer delight. ZONES 5–11.

Coquereau, France, 1831

Parentage unknown

Royal Horticultural Society Award of Garden Merit 1993

'DE MEAUX'

syns *Rosa centifolia pomponia*, 'Rose de Meaux'
OLD, CENTIFOLIA, MEDIUM PINK

This is one of the smallest of the Centifolia Roses, both in stature and size of flower. It seldom grows above 3 ft (1 m) high, sending up lots of gray-green shoots with numerous prickles. The light greenish gray foliage is small, firm and rugged. The small, full, scented flowers are rather like frilly pompons; they are arranged in sizeable bright pink clusters and are at their best quality early in summer. This rose makes a useful short dividing hedge and is excellent for group planting. It is also a good container plant. There is a white form available, generally listed as 'White de Meaux'. ZONES 5–11.

Sweet, UK, pre-1789

Parentage unknown

'DEAREST'

MODERN, CLUSTER-FLOWERED/FLORIBUNDA,
PINK BLEND, REPEAT-FLOWERING

An extremely popular variety, 'Dearest' has rosy salmon-pink double flowers

'Deb's Delight'

'Dearest'

with golden stamens. Appearing through summer and autumn, they are well shaped and fragrant. The growth habit is fairly bushy and to medium size; it has dark glossy foliage and prefers a position in full sun, and is suitable for bedding or to grow as a standard. **'Climbing Dearest'** (Ruston, Australia, 1970) is vigorous and mostly summer flowering, although some blooms will appear intermittently in autumn. ZONES 4–9.

Dickson, UK, 1960

Seedling × 'Spartan'

National Rose Society Gold Medal 1961

'DEBBIE THOMAS'
MODERN, LARGE-FLOWERED/HYBRID TEA, RED BLEND, REPEAT-FLOWERING

'Debbie Thomas' is a very new rose that produces large, exhibition-type blooms of 30 petals in a pink to red blend of colors. The flowers hold well on the showbench and were shown successfully at the Hampton Court Rose Show in England in July 1996. Like many of the newer varieties suitable for exhibition purposes, it was bred by an amateur. At the moment, it is only available from a few nurseries in England. ZONES 4–9.

Thomas, UK, 1992

'City of Gloucester' × 'My Joy'

'DEB'S DELIGHT'   LEGsweet
MODERN, CLUSTER-FLOWERED/FLORIBUNDA, PINK BLEND, REPEAT-FLOWERING

This low-growing, bushy variety is a good subject for small borders and pots and to grow as a short standard. Its silvery salmon-pink, double flowers appear very freely through summer and autumn; they each have 35 petals and they are

'Débutante'

fragrant. 'Deb's Delight' has mid-green, semi-glossy foliage and is propagated from cuttings or by budding. ZONES 4–9.

LeGrice, UK, 1983

'Tip Top' × seedling

Royal National Rose Society Trial Ground Certificate 1978

'DÉBUT'   MEIbarke
syns 'Douce Symphonie', 'Sweet Symphony'
MODERN, MINIATURE, RED BLEND, REPEAT-FLOWERING

The complex coloring of this rose's flowers is probably best described as luminous scarlet, blending to cream to yellow at the petal bases. They age to cherry red, white at the bases, giving the bush a profusion of changing color. The flowers are double, large, borne singly and have high centers for exhibition. The complementary foliage is semi-glossy and resistant to disease. 'Début' can be slow to establish, but the striking color makes it worth the wait. It is one of the few Miniatures to have the USA's most prestigious award. ZONES 4–11.

Mouchotte, France, 1988

'Coppélia' × 'Magic Carrousel'

All-America Rose Selection 1989

'DEBUTANTE'
MODERN, RAMBLER, LIGHT PINK

Those who have seen this rose paired with 'Bleu Magenta' at Mottisfont will understand why Graham Thomas holds such a high opinion of this *Rosa wichuraiana* hybrid; rose pink blossoms on short stems adorn the long canes, and the clusters fade quickly in the sun. It has a delicious apple fragrance. The healthy, dark green glossy foliage is not subject to

'Declic'

mildew, which makes it a stronger rose than its more famous relative 'Dorothy Perkins'; in fact, New Zealand rose author Sally Allison says it is 'more beautiful and refined'. It has been submerged in the fame of the older rose. It is easy to grow and can reach 15 ft (4.5 m), depending on how it is pruned and trained. ZONES 4–11.

Walsh, USA, 1902

'Baroness Rothschild' × *Rosa wichuraiana*

'DECLIC'
MODERN, MODERN SHRUB, MAUVE BLEND

A winner of two highly sought-after awards, 'Declic' is an excellent shrub rose with charming flowers that give a light fragrance. These are semi-double and open flat to reveal a cluster of golden stamens at the center. The slightly ruffled, very pale petals are soft pink closer to the margins and have more intense undersides. In summer, these blooms adorn a well-foliaged shrub, which is suitable for

a mixed border especially where its scent can be appreciated. It should be propagated by budding. ZONES 4–11.

Croix, France, 1988

Parentage unknown

Baden-Baden Gold Medal 1987, Bagatelle Fragrance Award 1987

'DECOR ARLEQUIN'
MODERN, MODERN SHRUB, APRICOT BLEND

Although classed as a Modern Shrub, 'Decor Arlequin' could just as easily have been classified as a Climber. The bush is very tall and upright and the light green foliage is semi-glossy, abundant and disease free. The semi-double, slightly fragrant flowers are apricot flushed with yellow and pink; there are 15 petals. The blooms are produced very freely in spring, but summer and autumn production is poor. It can be used on a pillar or tripod or treated as a large shrub. ZONES 4–11.

Meilland, France, 1975

Parentage unknown

'Decor Arlequin'

'Début'

D

'DEE BENNETT' SAVadee
MODERN, MINIATURE, ORANGE BLEND,
REPEAT-FLOWERING

Double, vibrant orange-red flowers with high exhibition centers characterize this prize-winning rose. They are usually borne one to a stem or in very small clusters of 3–5, and have excellent holding qualities. A fruity fragrance can be detected in warm climates. The plant has a vigorous growth habit and medium-sized, dark green, semi-glossy foliage. The rose was named to honor Dee Bennett, the Australian-born hybridizer, who created many great exhibition Miniature Roses. ZONES 4–11.

Saville, USA, 1988

'Zorina' × ('Sheri Anne' × ['Yellow Jewel' × 'Tamango'])

American Rose Society Award of Excellence 1989

'DEEP SECRET'
syn. 'Mildred Scheel'

MODERN, LARGE-FLOWERED/HYBRID TEA,
DARK RED, REPEAT-FLOWERING

The very deep crimson flowers of this variety are double with 40 petals, large

'Delicious'

'Deep Secret'

and very fragrant; they appear continuously throughout summer and autumn. It has upright growth to medium height and glossy dark green foliage, and is a good subject for a bedding scheme. ZONES 4–9.

Tantau, Germany, 1977

Parentage unknown

Anerkannte Deutsche Rose 1978

'DEEP VELVET'
MODERN, MINIATURE, DARK RED,
REPEAT-FLOWERING

Urn-shaped dark red flowers with 33 petals adorn this vigorous, healthy plant. The florets are considered exhibition type with their high centers, and are grown naturally one to a stem or in small clusters (2–3 florets). The blooms have a tendency to open quite quickly in the heat of the day. The foliage is tiny and an attractive medium green. Bloom production is a little on the sparse side, but their super form on super long stems makes this rose ideal for cutting for floral arrangements. The plant is susceptible to mildew. ZONES 5–11.

Jolly, USA, 1981

('Grand Opera' × 'Jimmy Greaves') × 'Baby Katie'

'DELAMBRE'
OLD, PORTLAND, DEEP PINK, REPEAT-FLOWERING

Portland Roses have always been praised for their brilliant scarlet flowers, and 'Delambre' is no exception—the carmine, deeply reddish pink blooms fade to lilac-pink and are fully double and quartered. The many clusters are packed with petals. The blooms are produced freely through summer and autumn, and are very fragrant. The upright, compact

'Delambre'

shrub bears healthy foliage and a few prickles and is particularly attractive when dressed in autumn foliage and hips. This rose, which will repeat its display of flowers if given rich soil and frequent feeding, is a good subject for a container. The firm of Moreau–Robert of Angers, France, produced many outstanding roses, some of which have been in the catalogues since their creation. ZONES 4–11.

Moreau and Robert, France, 1863

Parentage unknown

'DELICADO'
MODERN, LARGE-FLOWERED/HYBRID TEA,
ORANGE-PINK, REPEAT-FLOWERING

'Delicado' has shell pink flowers that are shaded peach and have some scent. The blooms are very large and appear in succession through summer and autumn. A good variety for bedding or for exhibition, it produces mid-green foliage on a plant that grows to medium height. ZONES 4–9.

Lowe, UK, 1954

Parentage unknown

'DELICATA'
MODERN, HYBRID RUGOSA, LIGHT PINK,
REPEAT-FLOWERING

'Delicata' has lilac-pink, semi-double flowers with a light scent. It has 10 petals, and flowering continues through summer and autumn. One of the shorter-growing Hybrid Rugosas, it has deep green wrinkled foliage. In the past this variety has proved notoriously difficult to propagate, although modern methods may have circumvented this problem. ZONES 4–9.

Cooling, UK, 1898

Parentage unknown

'Delicata'

'Delicado'

'Deep Velvet'

'DELICIOUS'
MODERN, MINIATURE, MEDIUM PINK,
REPEAT-FLOWERING

This aptly named Miniature Rose has small, rose pink flowers which emerge from elegant oval buds on a tall and upright bush. The blooms are full, with 26–40 petals and have a strong fragrance. The foliage is medium green and semi-glossy. ZONES 5–11.

Walsh, Australia, 1995

'Avandel' × ([seedling × 'Friesia'] × seedling)

'DELILLE'
OLD, MOSS, WHITE

The buds of 'Delille' are well-mossed and open to blush white, semi-double blooms with mauve overtones which appear in early summer. There may be later blooms. Moss Roses have stalks, sepals and sometimes leaves that have small, globular glands containing fragrant oils and often bristly stems. They are an offshoot of the Centifolia Rose. This rose, which is rather hard to find today, was a creation of the man who took over Vibert's nursery when he retired in 1851. ZONES 4–11.

Robert, France, 1852

Parentage unknown

'DELLA BALFOUR' HARblend
MODERN, LARGE-FLOWERED CLIMBER,
APRICOT BLEND, REPEAT-FLOWERING

This Climber has large blooms of peach and primrose that have a pleasing lemon fragrance. The flowers are big petalled and healthy and are produced on a robust plant with abundant large, dark green leaves. It is a very good variety for pillars and walls, and was named after the wife of a well-known, enthusiastic amateur rose lover. ZONES 4–9.

Harkness, UK, 1994

'Rosemary Harkness' × 'Elina'

Orléans Certificate of Merit 1997

'DEMOKRACIE'
syns 'Blaze Improved', 'Blaze Superior', 'New Blaze'

MODERN, LARGE-FLOWERED CLIMBER, DARK RED, REPEAT-FLOWERING

When 'Blaze' was originally marketed its chief claim to fame was that it was a repeat-flowering 'Paul's Scarlet'; unfortunately, it never fulfilled this expectation. There have been several pretenders since then, and this variety's claims are probably the closest to the original concept. 'Demokracie' produces large clusters of intense red flowers with a good form, appearing in procession through summer and autumn on lateral growth. They are semi-double but have virtually no scent. It is a vigorous plant for walls, pergolas and pillars. ZONES 4–9.

Böhm, Czechoslovakia, 1935

Parentage unknown

'DENISE GREY'   MEIxetal
syns 'Caprice', 'Make-Up'
MODERN, MODERN SHRUB, LIGHT PINK

A winner of two prestigious awards, 'Denise Grey' is a very floriferous shrub valued for its large bunches of medium-sized, gentle pink flowers. They are semi-double, flat to cupped in shape and show off a mass of dark stamens at the center. This is a medium-growing, healthy rose that is well furnished with reasonably large, glossy green foliage. For a mixed border, it makes a beautiful, summer-flowering shrub. It is disease resistant. ZONES 5–9.

Meilland, France, 1988

Parentage unknown

Bagatelle Gold Medal 1992, Frankfurt Gold Medal 1992

'DENTELLE DE BRUXELLES'
MODERN, MODERN SHRUB, LIGHT PINK, REPEAT-FLOWERING

'Dentelle de Bruxelles' grows into a large shrub, often wider than it is tall. It grows with great freedom in the spring, covering itself in pale pink blooms in small and large clusters. There is some repeat bloom. The mid-green foliage is abundant and right down to ground level. This variety is an excellent choice for planting in large gardens and parks where its pale-colored flowers show up very well from a distance. It also makes a good, tall informal hedge. There are no disease problems. So far it is not well known outside Europe. ZONES 4–11.

Lens, Belgium, 1988

Parentage unknown

'Denise Grey'

'Desert Charm'

'DENTELLE DE MALINES'
syn. 'Lens Pink'
MODERN, MODERN SHRUB, MEDIUM PINK

This shrub with its pretty pink flowers is reminiscent of a Hybrid Musk but it is only summer flowering and the blooms have a light scent. It is a medium to tall grower with dark green foliage that looks its best when planted in groups in a big border. ZONES 4–9.

Lens, Belgium, 1986

Parentage unknown

'DENVER'S DREAM'   SAVaden
MODERN, MINIATURE, ORANGE BLEND, REPEAT-FLOWERING

The flowers of this rose are a bright orange with a red reverse. The florets are double with 15–25 petals and have no fragrance. The blooms are mostly borne one to a stem with mid- to dark green, semi-glossy foliage on a medium-sized, upright bush. This is an excellent garden rose since it produces a myriad of dazzling coppery orange flowers that attract attention, and the unique color combination can add a bright spot to any garden design. The plant is tall, vigorous and very prolific, grows without much attention and is extremely winter hardy. This rose was named to commemorate the American Rose Society Spring National Convention held in Denver, Colorado, in 1995. ZONES 4–11.

Saville, USA, 1995

'Gingersnap' × 'Klima'

'DESCHAMPS'
syn. 'Longworth Rambler'
OLD, NOISETTE, MEDIUM RED, REPEAT-FLOWERING

This rose bears large, cupped, cherry red blossoms that fade to pink. It is a profuse bloomer that will repeat in autumn and it has a slight fragrance. The lovely muddled blooms are quite spectacular, and the buds are also attractive. It is a

'Dentelle de Malines'

'Demokracie'

'Dentelle de Bruxelles'

medium-sized plant with evergreen foliage that, like all Noisettes, needs a warm, sunny spot, and it is especially happy on pergolas and walls. It will tolerate some shade. ZONES 6–11.

Deschamps, France, 1877

Parentage unknown

'DESERT CHARM'
MODERN, MINIATURE, DARK RED, REPEAT-FLOWERING

Blazing red flowers with high centered, Large-flowered form are the hallmark of this rose. The blooms are large, slightly fragrant and weatherproof. The foliage is dark leathery green and disease-resistant. The plant has a compact, dense habit and is medium height, but it is difficult to grow and takes a couple of seasons to establish properly. Winter protection is a necessity if the plant is to survive. One of the best features of 'Desert Charm' is

that it is sun-proof, with a glowing color that holds well even in hot climates. ZONES 5–11.

Moore, USA, 1973

'Baccará' × 'Magic Wand'

'DESERT PEACE'   MEInomad
MODERN, LARGE-FLOWERED/HYBRID TEA, YELLOW BLEND, REPEAT-FLOWERING

This variety has medium-sized flowers that are yellow tinged with red and have a slight fragrance. They are double, with 25 petals, and appear singly on tall strong stems throughout summer and autumn. The attractive flowers can be cut for indoor decoration. 'Desert Peace' has a tall and upright growth habit, and glossy dark green foliage and is suitable for bedding schemes. ZONES 4–9.

Meilland, France, 1992

('Sonia' × 'Rumba') × ('Piccadilly' × 'Chicago Peace')

D

'Diablotin'

'Diamond Jubilee'

'Deuil de Paul Fontaine'

'DEUIL DE PAUL FONTAINE'
syn. 'Paul de Fontaine'
OLD, MOSS, MAUVE, REPEAT-FLOWERING

This rose is sadly rather prone to mildew, but if this is controlled it will give some of the most sumptuous blooms of any Moss Rose. Reaching only about 3 ft (1 m), the shrub is bushy and fairly tidy in habit although it is quite thorny. The leaves are red at first, ageing to dark green, and are relatively smooth for a Moss Rose. The buds are well endowed with finely textured, dark green moss. The fragrant flowers, which are very dark red to purple with unusual chocolate-colored shadings, are cupped until fully open when the blooms become flat and cushion like. Some repeat-flowering can be seen in late summer. If it is dead-headed regularly, it will bloom until autumn. ZONES 4–11.

Fontaine, France, 1873

Parentage unknown

'DEVONIENSIS'
syns 'Magnolia Rose', 'Victoria'
OLD, TEA, WHITE, REPEAT-FLOWERING

This shrub rose would be extinct now if a climbing sport had not shown up; **'Climbing Devoniensis'** is now more popular than the shrub. Both bloom early and profusely and have buds that are tinged red and open to very large, white blooms with yellow centers. The inner petals are curled and there is a strong Tea or lemon fragrance. As the first Tea Rose to be bred in England it has not found a warm home there, but it has been extraordinarily popular in mild climates. Brilliant dark green foliage covers the long canes, which have few prickles. It repeats from spring until autumn and has been one of the parents of some important roses, such as 'Lady Mary Fitzwilliam'. ZONES 6–11.

Foster, UK, 1838

'Smith's Yellow China' × 'Parks' Yellow Tea-scented China'

'DIABLOTIN'   DELpo
syn. 'Little Devil'
MODERN, CLUSTER-FLOWERED/Floribunda,
MEDIUM RED, REPEAT-FLOWERING

This variety has brilliant medium red, semi-double flowers with 17 petals that

'Devoniensis'

are produced in small clusters and have a slight fragrance. They appear freely throughout summer and autumn on a compact-growing plant. 'Diablotin' deserves to be more widely acknowledged but is now unfortunately only available in France. ZONES 4–9.

Delbard-Chabert, France, 1961

'Orléans Rose' × 'Fashion'

'DIADEM'   TANmeda
syn. 'Diadeem'
MODERN, CLUSTER-FLOWERED/FLORIBUNDA,
MEDIUM PINK, REPEAT-FLOWERING

This relatively small-growing bush rose bears long-stemmed clusters of rounded, clear pink blooms. There is a light scent and the foliage is dark green. 'Diadem' would be a suitable choice near the front of a bed or border, where it will repeat-flower through summer and autumn. The relatively healthy growth can be propagated by budding. ZONES 4–9.

Tantau, Germany, 1986

Parentage unknown

Durbanville Gold Medal 1990

Belfast Certificate of Merit 1994, Glasgow Certificate of Merit 1995

'DIAMANT'   KOReb
MODERN, CLUSTER-FLOWERED/FLORIBUNDA,
ORANGE-RED, REPEAT-FLOWERING

'Diamant' has round buds that develop into slightly fragranced, bright orange-scarlet, double flowers with 40 petals. They are produced in clusters of 3–7 throughout summer and autumn. The dark glossy foliage covers a plant with a vigorous, upright growth habit that makes a good bedding rose. ZONES 4–9.

Kordes, Germany, 1962

Parentage unknown

'DIAMOND JUBILEE'
MODERN, LARGE-FLOWERED/HYBRID TEA,
LIGHT YELLOW, REPEAT-FLOWERING

This variety has buff yellow, double, cupped flowers with 28 petals. They are strongly fragrant and continue to appear through summer and autumn. Suitable as a bedding subject, 'Diamond Jubilee' has an upright, compact growth habit and leathery foliage. ZONES 4–9.

Boerner, USA, 1947

'Maréchal Niel' × 'Feu Pernet-Ducher'

All-America Rose Selection 1948, Royal National Rose Society Trial Ground Certificate 1952

'DIANA'   TANdinadi
MODERN, CLUSTER-FLOWERED/FLORIBUNDA,
MEDIUM YELLOW, REPEAT-FLOWERING

'Diana' has round buds that open into globular, double, medium yellow blooms. They have a slight fragrance and appear in succession throughout summer and autumn. This variety is a medium-sized, upright grower with glossy mid-green foliage; it is good for bedding or to grow as a standard. ZONES 4–9.

Tantau, Germany, 1977

Parentage unknown

'DIANE'
MODERN, LARGE-FLOWERED/HYBRID TEA,
YELLOW BLEND, REPEAT-FLOWERING

The clear yellow flowers of this rose have darker yellow centers. They are large and well formed, and bloom through summer and autumn. 'Diane' is a tall-growing, vigorous plant that is good for bedding schemes. There is little scent. ZONES 5–9.

Gaujard, France, 1958

'Peace' × (seedling × 'Opera')

'Diana'

'Diamant'

'Diane'

'Dicky'

'DIAPASON'   DELpoc

MODERN, LARGE-FLOWERED/HYBRID TEA,
MEDIUM PINK, REPEAT-FLOWERING

Appearing in succession throughout
summer and autumn, the globular,
double flowers of this variety are a pretty
porcelain pink. They are fragrant and
have 40 petals. A suitable bedding plant,
'Diapason' is vigorous and bushy and
has bronze-green foliage. ZONES 5–9.

Delbard-Chabert, France, 1966

'Chic Parisien' × ('Sultane' seedling × 'Mme
Joseph Perraud')

'DICK KOSTER'

MODERN, POLYANTHA, DEEP PINK,
REPEAT-FLOWERING

This variety, one of a whole host of the
Koster family of roses, bears profuse
clusters of cup-shaped, deep pink blooms.
It is short and compact in stature and is
used extensively as a subject for the pot-
rose trade; it is very prone to producing

color sports. The foliage is typical for a
Polyantha: light green and susceptible
to mildew in autumn. Propagation is by
budding or from cuttings. ZONES 5–9.

Koster, The Netherlands, 1929

Sport of 'Anneke Koster'

'DICKSON'S FLAME'

MODERN, CLUSTER-FLOWERED/FLORIBUNDA,
ORANGE-RED, REPEAT-FLOWERING

This variety has medium-sized, scarlet
flame-colored flowers with a light
fragrance. Double and with 20 petals
each, they are beautifully formed and
continue to appear in trusses freely
throughout summer and autumn.
'Dickson's Flame' is a vigorous, branching plant that grows to medium height
and has mid-green foliage. ZONES 4–9.

Dickson, UK, 1958

'Independence' seedling × 'Nymph'

National Rose Society President's International
Trophy 1958

'DICKY'   DICkimono

syns 'Anisley Dickson', 'Münchner Kindl'

MODERN, CLUSTER-FLOWERED/FLORIBUNDA,
ORANGE-PINK, REPEAT-FLOWERING

This extraordinarily free-flowering Cluster-flowered Rose has long, pointed buds
that develop into reddish salmon-pink
flowers with a lighter reverse. Slightly
fragrant and double with 35 petals, they

are produced in clusters of 5-10 on gold
stems. 'Dicky' is a bushy variety that
grows to medium height and has glossy
green foliage. ZONES 4–9.

Dickson, UK, 1983

'Cathedral' × 'Memento'

Royal National Rose Society President's International Trophy 1984, Belfast Certifcate of Merit
1985, Royal Horticultural Society Award of
Garden Merit 1993

'Dickson's Flame'

'Diapason'

D

'Dirigent'

'Diorama'

'DIE WELT' DIEkor
syn. 'The World'

MODERN, LARGE-FLOWERED/HYBRID TEA,
ORANGE BLEND, REPEAT-FLOWERING

Large, perfectly formed flowers that
are slightly fragrant and are a blend of
orange, red and yellow appear through
summer and autumn on this variety.
They are double, with 25 petals, and high
centered, which makes 'Die Welt' a very
popular exhibition rose. It is a very tall
plant with glossy foliage that can sometimes be prone to mildew in autumn.
ZONES 4–9.

Kordes, Germany, 1976

Seedling × 'Peer Gynt'

'DIMPLES'

MODERN, CLUSTER-FLOWERED/FLORIBUNDA,
LIGHT YELLOW, REPEAT-FLOWERING

This Cluster-flowered Rose bears trusses
of canary yellow flowers that fade to
ivory. Semi-double and slightly fragrant,
they appear in succession through sum-

mer and autumn. It is a very healthy
spreading plant with glossy foliage; it
makes a superb standard. ZONES 4–9.

LeGrice, UK, 1968

Parentage unknown

'DIORAMA'

MODERN, LARGE-FLOWERED/HYBRID TEA,
YELLOW BLEND, REPEAT-FLOWERING

Appearing with good continuity through
summer and autumn, the large flowers
of this variety are high-centered and
apricot-yellow. They open loose and
flat and are very fragrant. 'Diorama' is
a healthy, large-growing plant with big,
mid-green, semi-glossy foliage. It is good
for bedding schemes. ZONES 4–9.

deRuiter, The Netherlands, 1965

'Peace' × 'Beauté'

Royal National Rose Society Trial Ground
Certificate 1965

'Dimples'

'Dr A. J. Verhage'

'DIRECTEUR ALPHAND'
syn. 'Alsace-Lorraine'

OLD, HYBRID PERPETUAL, MAUVE

The blackish purple blooms of this rose
are full, large and highlighted by velvety
brown and bright fiery red petals. It has a
full cup shape and is very fragrant. Unlike
other Hybrid Perpetuals, it does not have
a bluish cast to it. The bush has vigorous
canes and dark green foliage. ZONES 5–11.

Duval, France, 1879

Parentage unknown

'DIRIGENT'
syn. 'The Conductor'

MODERN, MODERN SHRUB, MEDIUM RED,
REPEAT-FLOWERING

This shrub has blood red semi-double
blooms that have a slight fragrance. They
appear in clusters made up of as many as
28 blooms. 'Dirigent' is a vigorous plant
with very healthy, leathery foliage that is
good for borders or as a specimen shrub.
ZONES 4–9.

Tantau, Germany, 1956

'Fanal' × 'Karl Weinhaüsen'

Anerkannte Deutsche Rose 1958

'DISCO DANCER' DICinfra

MODERN, CLUSTER-FLOWERED/FLORIBUNDA,
ORANGE-RED, REPEAT-FLOWERING

This bush bears sprays of orange-scarlet,
cupped, double flowers repeatedly from
spring to autumn. They appear on a

dense, rounded plant that produces a
mass of glossy green foliage. This variety
is suitable for bedding and as a standard.
There is a slight fragrance. ZONES 4–9.

Dickson, UK, 1984

'Cathedral' × 'Memento'

The Hague Gold Medal 1982, Royal National Rose
Society Trial Ground Certificate 1982, Belfast
Cetificate of Merit 1985

'DISTANT DRUMS'

MODERN, MODERN SHRUB, MAUVE,
REPEAT-FLOWERING

This variety bears large double blooms
with 40 overlapping petals in clusters
of up to 10 flowers from summer to
autumn. Rose purple in color, they have
an intense myrrh fragrance. 'Distant
Drums' is a vigorous plant with an erect
growth habit and leathery, dark green
foliage. It is suitable for borders and
to grow as a specimen. ZONES 4–9.

Buck, USA, 1984

'September Song' × 'The Yeoman'

'DR A. J. VERHAGE'
syn. 'Golden Wave'

MODERN, LARGE-FLOWERED/HYBRID TEA,
DEEP YELLOW, REPEAT-FLOWERING

This variety, which set the standard for
greenhouse roses when it appeared in
1963, was bred from the poor-growing
but brilliantly colored 'Tawny Gold' and
the slow-opening greenhouse variety
'Baccará'; it gained its gorgeous old-gold
coloring from the former and its strength
from the latter. The short-growing bush
produces great quantities of lovely buds
that open to show amber stamens and
strongly fragrant flowers with 22–30
nicely waved petals. 'Dr A. J. Verhage' is
still a lovely rose for cutting, although it
does not travel as well to overseas markets
as more recent yellows. The dark foliage
is prone to mildew. ZONES 5–11.

Verbeek , The Netherlands, 1963.

'Tawny Gold' × ('Baccará' × seedling)

Royal National Rose Society Trial Ground
Certificate 1960

'Disco Dancer'

D

'Die Welt'

'DOCTOR DICK' COCbaden
syn. 'Dr Dick'
MODERN, LARGE-FLOWERED/HYBRID TEA, ORANGE-PINK, REPEAT-FLOWERING

The very large blooms on this variety are orange-coral, double with 40 petals and have a slight fragrance. They appear in succession throughout summer and winter and their size and form make them a good flower for exhibition. An upright-growing plant suitable for bedding, it has matt green foliage and was named after a well-known Scottish surgeon and keen rose grower. ZONES 4–9.

Cocker, UK, 1986

'Fragrant Cloud' × 'Corso'

Belfast Certificate of Merit 1987

'DR ECKENER'
MODERN, HYBRID RUGOSA, PINK BLEND, REPEAT-FLOWERING

'Dr Eckener' forms a tall, vigorous shrub with huge, coarse, *Rosa rugosa*-like leaves and huge thorns. The flowers are yellow tinged with coppery rose fading to soft pink, their unique color probably being the reason for this variety's continued use in gardens. The large, fragrant blooms are cupped and semi-double and appear on the plant from summer through to autumn. ZONES 4–11.

Berger, Germany, 1930

'Golden Emblem' × unknown Hybrid Rugosa

'DR EDWARD DEACON'
MODERN, LARGE-FLOWERED/HYBRID TEA, ORANGE BLEND, REPEAT-FLOWERING

'Dr Edward Deacon', which obtains its color from its parent 'Mme Edouard Herriot', was one of the first coppery salmon Large-flowered Roses bred. The flowers are a salmon-orange to shrimp-pink, double, globular and highly scented on a medium-sized vigorous bush. Bloom production is good and the foliage is adequate, with some tendency to mildew. This rose, one of the forerunners of the brilliant copper and flamed-

'Dr Edward Deacon'

colored roses of today, is still a good rose for bedding schemes. ZONES 5–11.

Morse, UK, 1926

'Mme Edouard Herriot' × 'Gladys Holland'

'DOCTOR GRILL'
OLD, TEA, ORANGE-PINK, REPEAT-FLOWERING

This rose displays a dazzling array of colors as the pointed buds open to rose pink, slightly quartered blooms with shaded coppery tones. These flowers, which are prolific throughout a long season, are good cut flowers and last well in a vase. The branching habit and 3 ft (1 m) growth make it a suitable pot plant. It requires a warm spot and full sun and has been a good seed parent for other roses. It was named in honor of an avid gardener. ZONES 7–11.

Bonnaire, France, 1886

'Ophirie' × 'Souvenir de Victor Hugo'

'DR HARRY UPSHALL'
MODERN, MODERN SHRUB, PINK BLEND

Rosa foetida persiana was used by Pernet-Ducher to produce 'Soleil d'Or', which led to the Pernetiana Roses named after him and are in the breeding of all the bright yellow, strong orange, bright red and bicolored roses of today. It has been used very seldom since because of its lack of fertility, which makes 'Dr Harry Upshall' a very interesting rose. The medium-sized, fragrant flowers are a pink blend and have 30–40 petals. The foliage is small, mid-green and matt on a plant with a bushy, spreading habit. ZONES 5–11.

Fleming, USA, 1993

'Liverpool Echo' × *Rosa foetida persiana*

'DR HUEY'
syn. 'Shafter'
MODERN, LARGE-FLOWERED CLIMBER, DARK RED

An extremely strong grower, 'Dr Huey' covers itself very early in the season with

'Dr Harry Upshall'

masses of small, 2 in (5 cm) across, semi-double blooms with 10–15 petals. The flowers only appear once, but they have some fragrance and are a grand spectacle for a short period. 'Dr Huey', which is much used in Australia and elsewhere as an understock and crops up growing strongly in lots of old gardens, is very handy when a strong-growing, dark-colored Climber with flexible canes is required. It looks superb growing through and cascading down from an old tree. ZONES 4–11.

Thomas, USA, 1920

'Ethel' × 'Grüss an Teplitz'

American Rose Society Gold Medal, Gertrude M. Hubbard Gold Medal 1924

'DR J. H. NICHOLAS'
MODERN, LARGE-FLOWERED CLIMBER, MEDIUM PINK, REPEAT-FLOWERING

A short-growing climber with large, 50-petalled globular rose pink blooms borne singly and in clusters, this variety gets its fragrance and color from the famous old Hybrid Perpetual 'Georg Arends'. The foliage is dark and leathery and the flower production is good. 'Dr J. H. Nicholas', which makes a good pillar rose or is suitable for growing on a tripod, usually grows to around 8 ft (2.5 m) in height. ZONES 5–11.

Nicholas, USA, 1940

'Charles P. Kilham' × 'Georg Arends'

'DR JACKSON' AUStdoctor
MODERN, MODERN SHRUB, MEDIUM RED, REPEAT-FLOWERING

Also classified as an English Rose, 'Dr Jackson' has 5-petalled scarlet flowers with a central boss of golden stamens; they are borne singly and in small clusters and have no fragrance, but they do repeat-flower. With its mid-green foliage, few thorns and medium-sized, spreading growth, it makes a good shrub for landscape planting, especially if pruned lightly. There are no disease problems. ZONES 4–11.

Austin, UK, 1987

Parentage unknown

'DR JOHN SNOW'
MODERN, LARGE-FLOWERED/HYBRID TEA, WHITE, REPEAT-FLOWERING

With a name like 'Dr John Snow' it is not surprising that this variety is white. It produces creamy, double, up to 40-petalled flowers of exhibition form with good durability and fragrance. The foliage is light green on a tall-growing plant with

'Dr Huey'

'Dr Jackson'

'Dr John Snow'

'Dr W. Van Fleet'

excellent disease resistance, a factor probably inherited from the healthy and reliable 'Helen Traubel', and respectable flower production. ZONES 5–11.

Gandy, UK, 1979

'Helen Traubel' × seedling

'DR McALPINE' PEAfirst
syn. 'Seafirst'

MODERN, CLUSTER-FLOWERED/FLORIBUNDA, DEEP PINK, REPEAT-FLOWERING

This low-growing, bushy rose bears rose pink, double flowers with 30 petals. Of excellent form and produced in clusters of up to 10 blooms, they have a particularly strong fragrance and appear continuously. The foliage is dark, sets the flowers off well, and the disease resistance is good. This variety, with its red prickles, makes a good subject for a border or low hedge. ZONES 5–11.

Pearce, UK, 1983

Parentage unknown

'DR W. VAN FLEET'
MODERN, LARGE-FLOWERED CLIMBER, LIGHT PINK

This historically important rose, which sported the repeat-flowering 'New Dawn', has pointed buds that open to large, double, crisp blooms with stamens. The flowers are a soft pink ageing to flesh white and are fragrant. It is a vigorous climber to 20 ft (6 m) or

'Dr McAlpine'

more with good dark green glossy foliage that is spectacular in full bloom. It looks particularly effective when cascading from a tree or covering a shed. ZONES 4–11.

Van Fleet, USA, 1910

(*Rosa wichuraiana* × 'Safrano') × 'Souvenir du Président Carnot'

'DOLCE VITA' DELdal
syn. 'Niagara Pride'

MODERN, LARGE-FLOWERED/HYBRID TEA, ORANGE-PINK, REPEAT-FLOWERING

'Dolce Vita' has very large, salmon-colored, double blooms with 37 petals each. Appearing from summer to autumn, they are slightly fragrant and have high centers, and all in all a fine form that makes a very good exhibition

'Dolce Vita'

variety. The plant is vigorous and has an upright growth habit. ZONES 5–9.

Delbard, France, 1971

'Voeux de Bonheur' × ('Chic Parisien' × ('Michèle Meilland' × 'Mme Joseph Perraud'))

'DOLLY'
syn. 'Springs 75'

MODERN, CLUSTER-FLOWERED/FLORIBUNDA, ORANGE-PINK, REPEAT-FLOWERING

This very free-flowering variety bears clusters of 3–5 dark pink, medium-sized,

double blooms with 20 petals. They appear continuously through summer and autumn, but there is only a little fragrance. The foliage is dark and glossy on a medium-sized, bushy plant that is a very good bedding choice. It is also suitable as a standard. ZONES 4–9.

Poulsen, Denmark, 1975

('Nordia' × 'Queen Elizabeth') × (seedling × 'Mischief')

Baden-Baden Gold Medal 1973, Anerkannte Deutsche Rose 1987

'Dolly Parton'

'Don Marshall'

'DOLLY PARTON'

MODERN, LARGE-FLOWERED/HYBRID TEA, ORANGE-RED, REPEAT-FLOWERING

This rose produces large, luminous orange-red, double blooms with good continuity from summer to autumn. They each have 35 petals and are very fragrant. A medium-height, upright grower, it has semi-glossy green foliage. ZONES 4–9.

Winchel, USA, 1984

'Fragrant Cloud' × 'Oklahoma'

'DOMSTADT FULDA'   KORtanken

syns 'Cathedral City', 'Domstadt Fuida'

MODERN, CLUSTER-FLOWERED/FLORIBUNDA, DARK RED, REPEAT-FLOWERING

The clusters of red flowers on this bush are quite stunning against the backdrop of shiny dark green, leathery foliage. The urn-shaped to pointed, double flowers have a good shape and appear throughout summer. ZONES 4–9.

Kordes, Germany, 1994

Parentage unknown

'DON JUAN'

MODERN, LARGE-FLOWERED CLIMBER, DARK RED, REPEAT-FLOWERING

Appearing in succession throughout summer and autumn, the large, double blooms of this Climber are dark velvety red. They are particularly fragrant and have 35 petals. 'Don Juan' reaches a moderate height and is furnished with glossy dark green, leathery foliage. It is a good subject for growing on walls and up pillars. ZONES 4–9.

Malandrone, USA, 1958

'New Dawn' seedling × 'New Yorker'

'DON MARSHALL'   MORblack

MODERN, MINIATURE, DARK RED, REPEAT-FLOWERING

The flowers of 'Don Marshall' are medium red, with blackish red undersides. The blooms have about 35 petals with Large-flowered form and a light fragrance. The small, matt dark green foliage covers this spreading Miniature. Unfortunately, in hot climates the blooms will burn easily, in cooler climates the form will 'ball' and the growth is reasonably susceptible to mildew. This variety is one of a pair of Miniature Roses named by Ralph Moore for Don and Mary Marshall, in honor of their friendship and their dedication to roses. ZONES 4–10.

Moore, USA, 1982

'Baccará' × 'Little Chief'

'Donau'

'Domstadt Fulda'

'DONALD PRIOR'

MODERN, LARGE-FLOWERED/HYBRID TEA, MEDIUM RED, REPEAT-FLOWERING

This variety has bright scarlet flushed crimson, semi-double flowers with some fragrance. The large clusters of bloom are very showy, and flowering continues through summer and autumn. It has a bushy habit to medium height and dark leathery foliage, and does well in beds. ZONES 4–9.

Prior, UK, 1938

Seedling × 'D. T. Poulsen'

National Rose Society Certificate of Merit 1936

'DONAU'

MODERN, LARGE-FLOWERED CLIMBER, MAUVE

The mauve flowers of this beautiful climbing variety are borne in small clusters in summer. They are semi-double and open flat; the very centers are almost white where there is also a tiny clump of stamens. This is a lovely Large-flowered Climber for walls and pillars, covered with delicate, glossy green foliage that is often admired when the plant is not in flower. ZONES 4–9.

Praskac, Czechoslovakia, 1913

Parentage unknown

'DONCASTERI'

syn. *Rosa macrophylla doncasteri*

MODERN, MODERN SHRUB, DEEP PINK

'Doncasteri' produces flowers that are deep pink in color and are composed of 5 petals, which are followed in autumn by big flask-shaped hips. The foliage is purplish green and the stems plum colored on a large, arching shrub that is a very good subject for large borders or as a specimen plant. It is propagated by budding or from cuttings. ZONES 4–9.

Hurst, UK, 1930

Seedling of *Rosa macrophylla*

'DONNA MARIE'

syn. 'Donna Maria'

OLD, SEMPERVIRENS, WHITE

It is surprising that the evergreen Wild Rose *Rosa sempervirens* has not been used more often in hybridizing as it is healthy and vigorous. This pure white, very double rose is tinged with yellow at its base. Clusters of blossoms crowd the 7 ft (2.1 m) canes, and there are few prickles. There is some rebloom after its late spring outing. The pale green foliage and restrained habit make it ideal for smaller gardens. Those who grow this rose, which should really be classified as a Rambler, say that its sterling qualities are often overlooked. ZONES 4–11.

Vibert, France, 1830

Hybrid of *Rosa sempervirens*

'DORIS DOWNES'

MODERN, LARGE-FLOWERED CLIMBER, PINK BLEND

This vigorous climbing rose has very large, semi-double, cupped flowers that are pink shaded red. They are strongly

'Donald Prior'

Don Juan'

'Dorothy Dennison'

'Dorothy Dennison'

fragrant and appear from spring to early summer. It has healthy foliage and does best on walls or pergolas. ZONES 6–10.

Clark, Australia, 1932

Parentage unknown

'DORIS TYSTERMAN'

syn. 'Doris Tijsterman'

MODERN, LARGE-FLOWERED/HYBRID TEA, ORANGE BLEND, REPEAT-FLOWERING

This bush bears large, double, tangerine and gold blooms with 28 petals throughout summer and autumn. They have a light fragrance. A good bedding variety, it has an upright growth habit and disease-resistant, glossy foliage. ZONES 4–9.

Wisbech Plant Co, UK, 1975

'Peer Gynt' × seedling

'DORNRÖSCHEN'   HACicularis

syn. 'Sleeping Beauty'

MODERN, MODERN SHRUB, PINK BLEND, REPEAT-FLOWERING

Well-shaped blooms of salmon to deep pink with a reverse of yellow are produced on this variety from summer to autumn. They are double and fragrant and appear in large clusters. It is a good subject for growing as a specimen or in small groups in borders. ZONES 4–9.

Kordes, Germany, 1960

'Pikes Peak' × 'Ballet'

'DOROLA'   MACshana

syns 'Benson & Hedges Special', 'Parkay'

MODERN, MINIATURE, DEEP YELLOW, REPEAT-FLOWERING

Deep yellow flowers, each with 26 petals, literally cover this vigorous bush. It grows like a small Cluster-flowered Rose with lots of clusters of blooms that do not fade with age even in strong sunlight. The flowers have a strong fragrance when they first open up. The foliage is a semi-glossy mid-green. Growing this rose can be a rewarding experience as it provides

'Doris Tysterman'

a constant supply of blooms throughout the season, and the bush needs minimum maintenance and is disease-resistant. One of the alternatives for this charming Miniature is the name of a well-known cigarette! ZONES 4–11.

McGredy, New Zealand, 1982

'Darling Flame' × 'New Day'

Royal National Rose Society Certificate of Merit 1980

'DOROTHY DENNISON'

MODERN, RAMBLER, LIGHT PINK

When 'Dorothy Perkins' was introduced in the USA in 1901 it caused a sensation, and created in its wake an audience waiting for more of the same; it wasn't long before sports started to appear on the market, 'White Dorothy' and 'Lady Godiva' being the most successful of these. 'Dorothy Dennison', with its pale pink blossoms, tried its best but could not compete with the others and has almost disappeared. ZONES 4–11.

Dennison, USA, 1909

Sport of 'Dorothy Perkins'

'Dorothy Perkins'

'Dorothy Perkins'

'DOROTHY PEACH'

MODERN, LARGE-FLOWERED/HYBRID TEA, YELLOW BLEND, REPEAT-FLOWERING

'Dorothy Peach' has large, double flowers of deep yellow flushed with pink, each with 37 petals. Appearing continuously throughout summer and autumn, the blooms have a high center and are well shaped, and there is good fragrance. A vigorous bushy variety suitable for bedding, it has dark, glossy foliage and is propagated by budding. ZONES 4–9.

Robinson, UK, 1957

'Lydia' × 'Peace'

National Rose Society Gold Medal 1959

'DOROTHY PERKINS'

MODERN, RAMBLER, LIGHT PINK

This rose was very popular from the start, in part because it did well in a wide

'Doris Downes'

'Dorothy Peach'

range of climates. 'Dorothy Perkins' is full of rose pink blooms for one month in summer. Its small flowers with fragrant, quilled petals appear in huge clusters supported by glossy dark green foliage. The flexible canes with hooked prickles are easy to train, but when left to itself, the plant can ramble over barns, banks and buildings; it can reach up to 20 ft (6 m) in a single growing season. The rose was named for the granddaughter of the founder of the nursery firm of Jackson & Perkins, and it became an overnight success. It has a strong tendency to mildew, but the German hybridizer Hetzel developed a mildew-free cultivar called 'Super Dorothy'. ZONES 4–11.

Miller, USA, 1901

'Madame Gabriel Luizet' × *Rosa wichuraiana*

'Dorola'

'DOROTHY WHEATCROFT'

MODERN, LARGE-FLOWERED/HYBRID TEA,
MEDIUM RED, REPEAT-FLOWERING

Perhaps better described as a repeat-flowering shrub suitable for borders or as an attractive specimen plant, this variety has oriental red, semi-double flowers with darker shades. They each have 18 petals and are only slightly fragrant. 'Dorothy Wheatcroft' is a very strong upright-growing plant with bright green foliage that is propagated by budding. ZONES 4–9.

Tantau, Germany, 1960

Parentage unknown

National Rose Society Gold Medal 1960

'DORTMUND'

MODERN, LARGE-FLOWERED CLIMBER,
MEDIUM RED, REPEAT-FLOWERING

The large open flowers of this variety, with 5–10 petals, are scarlet-red with a white eye. They have a light scent and are borne in clusters from spring to autumn on a vigorous plant with dark green glossy foliage. The growth habit is upright although it may be pruned to make

a shrub; because it is so adaptable it may also be grown as a pillar rose or on a north wall. It needs regular and heavy deadheading. ZONES 4–9.

Kordes, Germany, 1955

Seedling × Rosa kordesii

Anerkannte Deutsche Rose 1954, Portland Gold Medal 1971

'DOUBLE CHARM'   HARango

syn. 'G. P. & J. Baker'

MODERN, CLUSTER-FLOWERED/FLORIBUNDA,
YELLOW BLEND, REPEAT-FLOWERING

'Double Charm' is a most unusual Cluster-flowered form. The flowers are very full with 80 petals that are so tightly packed in the blooms that they are crinkled. The color is a suffusion of red, orange and yellow. The unscented blooms are produced in large clusters on a short, stocky bush. The abundant foliage is glossy dark green and disease free. When the flowers open well, they can be most attractive but sometimes blooms open confused and misshapen. ZONES 5–11.

Harkness, UK, 1984

'Bobby Dazzler' × (seedling × 'Marion Harkness')

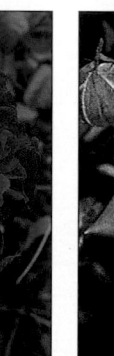

'Dorothy Wheatcroft'   'Double Joy'

'Double Delight'

'Dortmund'

'DOUBLE DELIGHT'   ANDeli

MODERN, LARGE-FLOWERED/HYBRID TEA,
RED BLEND, REPEAT-FLOWERING

This very bushy variety has large and double, high-centered blooms that are unique and immensely popular. They are creamy white turning to strawberry red, have a considerable spicy scent and appear from spring to autumn. It is a fine bedding rose although its disease resistance is suspect. It has an upright and spreading growth habit. **Climbing Double Delight** (AROclidd; syn. 'Grimpant Double Delight'; Christensen, USA, 1982) has precisely the same coloring as the bush variety. Summer flowering, it grows well on walls. ZONES 4–9.

Swim and Ellis, USA, 1977

'Granada' × 'Garden Party'

Baden-Baden Gold Medal 1976, Rome Gold Medal 1976, All-America Rose Selection 1977, Belfast Fragrance Prize 1980, James Alexander Gamble Rose Fragrance Medal 1986

'DOUBLE JOY'

MODERN, MINIATURE, ORANGE-PINK,
REPEAT-FLOWERING

This rose has elegant, long pointed buds that reveal fragrant, double pink flowers. They hold their color in even the hottest climates. The flower form is strictly for garden display and the foliage is small with an attractive matt texture. In general, the bush is easy to maintain and disease-resistant. This compact bush bears prolific sprays, each with 5–12 florets and is a wonderful addition to the garden. On occasions a cluster can win at a rose show. ZONES 5–11.

Moore, USA, 1979

'Little Darling' × 'New Penny'

'Double Delight'

'Double Charm'

'Douceur Normande'

'DOUBLE TREAT'   MORtreat

MODERN, MINIATURE, YELLOW BLEND,
REPEAT-FLOWERING

The mossy buds of this rose are possibly derived from 'Ferdinand Pichard', one of its Old Garden Rose parents. The flowers are double with a spectacular color combination—bright red and orange-yellow stripes. The florets are usually borne in small clusters of 3–5 and have a slight fragrance. Foliage is small, medium green and semi-glossy, and the bush is of medium height, upright but not very vigorous. Bloom production is poor. This rose, however, stands out in any garden because of the intriguing color combination of red and yellow with the value-added of the charm of mossing. Unfortunately the color can fade quickly to a dull-looking finish. ZONES 5–11.

Moore, USA, 1986

('Arizona' × ['Fairy Moss' × 'Fairy Moss']) × ('Little Darling' × 'Ferdinand Pichard')

'DOUBLE WHITE'

syns 'Double White', 'Double White Burnet', 'Elegans', Rosa spinosissima

OLD, SCOTS, WHITE

There are some problems with the name of this rose as it is easily used to describe other plants, especially 'Alba Maxima'. The double, sometimes semi-double, white blossoms are loosely cupped and have a perfume that strongly suggests lilies of the valley. It blooms in late spring and does not like rainy weather. The bush can reach 6 ft (1.2 m) and will sucker on its own root, and there are dark hips. It has been used effectively as a ground cover and hedge for it has the additional charm of good autumn foliage. Gertrude Jekyll used it at her home in Munstead on a low wall. ZONES 4–11.

Pre-1800

Parentage unknown

'Dream'

'Douceur Normande'

'DOUCEUR NORMANDE'
MEIpopul
syns 'Coral Meidiland', 'Goose Fair',
'Sandton City', 'Stadt Hildescheim'

MODERN, MODERN SHRUB, MEDIUM PINK,
REPEAT-FLOWERING

This landscape rose, bred for hardiness
and for growing in difficult areas, grows
strongly to 6 ft by 13 ft (2 m by 4 m) and
forms a dense prickly barrier, which
makes it good for planting along median
strips and difficult steep banks. The
single flowers are a coral-pink and come
in both large and small clusters. Hips
do form but the plant will continue to
flower over a long period. It is very
colorful in spring and keeps flowering well
into autumn. If it grows too big it can
be hard pruned in winter and it will
still produce good spring blooms. It
is immune to disease. ZONES 4–9.

Meilland, France, 1993

Hybrid of *Rosa wichuraiana*

'DOVE'   AUSdove
syn. 'Dovedale'

MODERN, MODERN SHRUB, LIGHT PINK,
REPEAT-FLOWERING

'Dove' is a delightful little rose of the palest pink coloring on a small, stocky bush.
The lightly scented flowers are most attractive in the bud at all stages of development and open to a 40-petalled bloom
4 in (10 cm) across. Flower production
is very high and it repeat-flowers rapidly.
The spreading growth makes it ideal as a
standard or for bedding, while the thin
wiry stems make the blooms ideal for
posies. The disease-free foliage is small,
dark green and semi-glossy, acting as a
foil for the delicacy of the flowers and
appearing on a plant that performs very
well in extremely high heat. It is also
classified as an English Rose. ZONES 4–9.

Austin, UK, 1984

'Wife of Bath' × seedling of 'Iceberg'

'Dove'

'DREAM'

MODERN, LARGE-FLOWERED/HYBRID TEA,
LIGHT PINK, REPEAT-FLOWERING

This well-named variety from Kordes is
grown all over the world under glass for
the cut-flower trade. The buds open very
slowly to show tints of the palest pink
flushed pale apricot and salmon. The
medium-sized blooms, which have many
petals and keep extremely well when cut,
are produced quite profusely. The glossy
dark green foliage has an excellent resistance to disease. 'Dream' has produced
several very good sports. ZONES 5–11.

Kordes, Germany, 1979

Parentage unknown

'DREAM GIRL'
syn. 'Dreamgirl'

MODERN, LARGE-FLOWERED CLIMBER, PINK BLEND,
REPEAT-FLOWERING

This variety has salmon-pink flowers
that are overlaid with apricot. They are
large, to 4 in (10 cm), very double with
55–65 petals and extremely fragrant and
there is good repeat bloom. The foliage
is glossy green and the growth is moderate to 10 ft (3 m), making 'Dream Girl'
a good rose for growing on a tripod or
up a pillar. There are not many climbing
roses in this color range, so it is a welcome addition, but it is not very well
known outside the USA. ZONES 4–11.

Jacobus, USA, 1944

'Dr W. Van Fleet' × 'Senora Gari'

Royal Horticultural Society Award of Garden
Merit 1993

'DREAM LOVER'   RENlover

MODERN, MINIATURE, LIGHT PINK,
REPEAT-FLOWERING

The full, pale pink flowers of 'Dream
Lover' contain 25–40 petals. The blooms
are medium-sized, with a diameter of
1½ in (35 mm), and are borne mostly
singly. They have a light raspberry

'Dream Time'

fragrance. The glossy, mid-green foliage
is disease resistant on a plant with an
upright, bushy habit. The repeat-bloom
cycle is very rapid. ZONES 5–10.

Rennie, Canada, 1995

'Pink Sheri' × 'Innocent Blush'

'DREAM TIME'
syn. 'Dreamtime'

MODERN, LARGE-FLOWERED/HYBRID TEA,
MEDIUM PINK, REPEAT-FLOWERING

Bred from two well-formed parents,
'Dream Time' has large, to 5 in (13 cm),
double, high-centered, pink flowers with
38 petals and a strong perfume. It lacks
the magnificent dark green foliage and
the strong growth of 'Prima Ballerina',
being only a moderately vigorous plant
with light green foliage. It is a suitable
subject for bedding. ZONES 5–11.

Bees, UK, 1977

'Kordes' Perfecta' × 'Prima Ballerina'

'DREAMER'   SAVadream

MODERN, MINIATURE, MEDIUM PINK,
REPEAT-FLOWERING

Pointed ovoid buds open to give dusty
pink cupped double blooms (20 petals).
The florets are borne one to a stem or in
small sprays of 3–5 blooms. This rose has
no fragrance. Foliage is semi-glossy dark
green on an upright compact round
bush. The bush always seems to be in
bloom with good, constant, vigorous
growth. The color of the florets is its best
asset and blooms can be of show quality,
although they tend to open too quickly
in hot weather. If this rose only had 6–10
more petals it would be knockout!
'Dreamer' is a good candidate for a container-grown plant for the patio. It can
be susceptible to mildew, so spray regularly. ZONES 4–11.

Saville, USA, 1992

'Baby Katie' × 'Shocking Blue'

'DREAMGLO'

MODERN, MINIATURE, RED BLEND,
REPEAT-FLOWERING

Emerging from long pointed buds, the
flowers of 'Dreamglo' are silvery white,
edged with deep currant red that be-

comes more predominant as they age.
The blooms have almost 50 petals with
classic Large-flowered form, but there
is only a slight fragrance. Each flower is
small, under 1 in (25 mm) in diameter,
and is complemented by the equally
small, dark green leaves. The eye-catching color of this rose makes it an ideal
candidate for selection as a garden or
exhibition variety. Because of the high
number of petals, it can hold its Large-
flowered form even on hot days, and
has won numerous awards in rose shows
across America. This rose has remained
popular since its introduction in 1978.
ZONES 4–11.

Williams, USA, 1978

'Little Darling' × 'Little Chief'

'DREAMING PARADE'

MODERN, MINIATURE, CORAL/SALMON,
REPEAT-FLOWERING

Poulsen's Nurseries of Denmark have
developed a series of about twelve
Miniature Roses with 'Parade' in their
names. They have called them 'Rosa
Nova' to distinguish them from similar
roses from other breeders, just as
Meilland's of France have called their
Miniatures 'Meillandina' or 'Sunblaze'.
The 'Rosa Nova' series are all very small,
bushy growers that are suited to pot
culture. The blooms are small with
well-formed little buds that open to
flat, double blooms of about two dozen
petals. The salmon-pink flowers of
'Dreaming Parade' occur both singly and

'Dreaming Parade'

'Dreamglo'

D

'Dresden'

'Dresden Doll'

'Drummer Boy'

'Duc de Fitzjames'

in small clusters and last well on the plant. The repeat-bloom cycle is very quick. ZONES 4–9.

Poulsen, Denmark, 1992

Parentage unknown

'DREAMING SPIRES'

MODERN, LARGE-FLOWERED CLIMBER,
DEEP YELLOW, REPEAT-FLOWERING

With two rich yellow parents, the former so strong as to be very nearly a climbing rose, it is not surprising to find that 'Dreaming Spires' is a deep yellow Large-flowered Climber. The richly fragrant flowers are well formed, double with two dozen petals and of medium size to 3 in (8 cm) in diameter. The repeat-flowering performance is excellent. 'Dreaming Spires' was named by John Mattock after the university city of Oxford, which is close to where he lives. The rose has dark green foliage that sets the flowers off to good advantage. Unfortunately it has

been largely overlooked in spite of winning a gold medal in Northern Ireland in 1977. ZONES 4–11.

Mattock , UK, 1973

'Buccaneer' × 'Arthur Bell'

Belfast Gold Medal 1977

'DRESDEN'

syn. 'Mathé Altéry'

MODERN, LARGE-FLOWERED/HYBRID TEA, WHITE,
REPEAT-FLOWERING

This variety has ovoid buds that open to large, to 5 in (13 cm), high-centered, well-formed flowers with 60 or more petals that are the palest pink in color. They are strongly fragrant but because of the amount of petals, they tend to ball in cool, damp spring weather; however, in summer the flowers are magnificent when most other varieties are burning in the hot sun. A good rose for inland Australia and southern California, 'Dresden' is an extremely vigorous, upright-growing plant with dark green, leathery foliage that is disease free. ZONES 5–11.

Robichon, France, 1961

'Ophelia' × 'Catherine Kordes'

'DRESDEN DOLL'

MODERN, MINIATURE, LIGHT PINK,
REPEAT-FLOWERING

The flowers of this rose are a soft but delicate dusty pink. The cupped blooms are small, with only 18 petals, and have a medium fragrance. When fully opened the blooms display another attractive feature—golden stamens, which add to the quality and appearance of the florets.

'Duc de Cambridge'

The bush is compact and throws lots of large clusters that are architecturally attractive, but quite large for a Miniature. In fact, the plant seems to want to grow outward rather than upward. This rose has won its share of awards at rose shows in the fully opened bloom class. It is a second generation of repeat-flowering Moss Miniatures borne from 'Fairy Moss'. Moore struggled for almost 25 years to introduce the Moss Rose characteristics of the once-blooming Old Garden Roses into repeat-flowering Miniature Roses. ZONES 4–11.

Moore, USA, 1975

'Fairy Moss' × seedling of unknown Moss

'DRUMMER BOY'   HARvacity

MODERN, CLUSTER-FLOWERED/FLORIBUNDA,
DARK RED, REPEAT-FLOWERING

With three small growers in its pedigree, it is not surprising that 'Drummer Boy' is a spreading, low-growing bush. The semi-double, cup-shaped flowers with 15 petals are a vivid intense scarlet; they come in small sprays and have a spicy fragrance. If spent flowers are not deadheaded then small and oval, greenish hips will form, these contrasting well with the later flowers. It is a good choice where low color is required, especially when planted *en masse* for maximum effect. The variety has mid-green, semi-glossy foliage and purplish red thorns. ZONES 5–11.

Harkness, UK, 1987

('Wee Man' × ['Southampton' × 'Darling Flame']) × 'Red Sprite'

Dublin Certificate of Merit 1986, Royal National Rose Society Trial Ground Certificate 1987, Baden-Baden ÖRP 1990, Glasgow Silver Medal 1990

'DUBLIN BAY'   MACdub

MODERN, LARGE-FLOWERED CLIMBER,
MEDIUM RED, REPEAT-FLOWERING

One of the best red Climbers available today, 'Dublin Bay' has oval buds and well-shaped, intensely bright red, fragrant flowers produced singly and in clusters. The repeat-flowering is outstanding: no sooner has one crop of flowers finished than another is on the way. It has dark green glossy foliage and good disease resistance. It is one of the most popular Climbers in New Zealand, also gaining great acclaim in Australia. ZONES 4–11.

McGredy, New Zealand, 1975

'Bantry Bay' × 'Altissimo'

Royal Horticultural Society Award of Garden Merit 1993

'DUC DE CAMBRIDGE'

syn. 'Duchesse de Cambridge'

OLD, DAMASK, MAUVE

Although the prickly canes of this rose look ominous, when it blooms, all bad thoughts are discarded as the flowers are quite impressive. This Damask has deep, purple-rose petals forming double, full, large blossoms. It is probably the darkest of all Damask flowers. The bush has a sprawling growth habit and can reach 6 ft (1.8 m) without pruning, but if it is pruned after the summer flush it will respond better the next year. The foliage is dark and reddish when young. ZONES 4–11.

Pre-1848

Parentage unknown

'DUC DE FITZJAMES'

OLD, GALLICA, DARK RED/DEEP PINK

This rose is sometimes classified as a Centifolia. It is a dense, vigorous, thorny and upright shrub that can reach 6 ft (1.8 m) high, covered with large and lush gray-green foliage. The highly fragrant flowers, borne in sizeable clusters in midsummer, are very large and full, up to 4 in (10 cm) across. They develop from round buds through a high-centered stage to become quartered and cupped in form when fully open. The color is a consistent deep glowing pink with paler undersides. It was named for Duc Edouard de Fitzjames (1776–1836), a supporter of the Bourbon Kings. ZONES 4–11.

Pre-1837

Parentage unknown

'Dublin Bay'

D

'Dreaming Spires'

'DUC DE GUICHE'
syns 'Senat Romain', 'Senateur Romain'
OLD, GALLICA, MAUVE

This is a dense, rather sprawling shrub to about 4 ft (1.2 m) with moderately armed darkish green stems. The clear rich green foliage is plentiful, roundly oval and almost glossy. The flowers, which emerge from small clusters of feathery buds, are about 3 in (8 cm) across, very double when open and flatly cushion-shaped around a prominent green central eye. The color is reddish magenta, sometimes overlaid with violet. The outer petals reflex as they age, and the center ones change to a deep purple in hot weather. They are very fragrant. Many of the de Guiche family served as diplomats and as politicians in France, especially during the nineteenth century. **ZONES 4–11.**

France, pre-1810

Parentage unknown

'DUC DE SUSSEX'
OLD, DAMASK, LIGHT PINK

The creamy white-pink flowers of this rose open large and full. The center petals are erect, while the outer ones fall away until the mature flower looks blowzy. There is a light fragrance. This once-blooming rose reaches 4 ft (1.2 m) at maturity and is found today in a few collections such as at Sangerhausen. Damask Roses are used for distillation of attar for perfume. **ZONES 4–11.**

Roseraie de l'Haÿ, France, 1856

Parentage unknown

'DUC DE VALMY'
OLD, GALLICA, MAUVE

The light purplish roses of this fragrant variety have an interesting marbled effect made up of purple veins. The large blooms are filled with many petals to form a neat cup shape. **ZONES 4–11.**

Parentage unknown

'Duc de Guiche'

D

'Duchess of Portland'

'Duchess of Wellington'

'Duchesse d'Angoulême'

'Duchesse d'Auerstädt'

'DUCHER'
syn. 'Bengale Ducher'
OLD, CHINA, WHITE, REPEAT-FLOWERING

This knee-high plant bears its blooms either singly or in clusters. The white outer petals are large, while the inner ones are smaller and folded. The 4 in (10 cm) flowers are flat on very short stems and tend to nod. One critic has praised this white rose as an excellent bedding plant because it drops its white flowers when it has finished blooming. The slender branches are smooth with lots of long, red prickles and the glossy foliage is light green, which adds further charm to this rose. It makes an ideal container plant. Jean-Claude Ducher (1820–74) was one of the most esteemed hybridizers during the golden age of rose production in Lyon, France. **ZONES 7–11.**

Ducher, France, 1869

Parentage unknown

'DUCHESS OF PORTLAND'
syns 'Duchesse de Portland', 'Portland Rose', *Rosa paestana, R. portlandica*, 'Scarlet Four Seasons'

OLD, PORTLAND, MEDIUM RED, REPEAT-FLOWERING

This rose inaugurated the Portland class of roses, also known as Damask Perpetuals. The fragrant blooms appear from mid-summer to late autumn. The large, semi-double, cupped flowers of deep rose and sometimes bright scarlet have yellow stamens with conspicuous anthers. Occasional white streaks on the petals indicates a China background. It is a low, compact shrub, and is good as a bedding plant, hedge, or in a container. The oval-shaped foliage is light green; there are hooked prickles. Deadheading keeps the plant attractive. Jack Harkness said 'the Portlands were the first hint of what the China rose was about to do', which implies that reblooming roses were on the horizon. **ZONES 4–10.**

Pre-1800

Possibly unknown red China × 'Autumn Damask'

'DUCHESS OF WELLINGTON'
MODERN, LARGE-FLOWERED/HYBRID TEA, LIGHT YELLOW, REPEAT-FLOWERING

The chief virtues of this variety are its long, elegant buds and its soft buff yellow fragrant flowers. In shape the buds are reminiscent of 'Lady Hillingdon' and, with only 15 or so petals, they open very quickly to show stamens. The stems are long and strong, the foliage is large and leathery and the growth habit is moderate and bushy. 'Duchess of Wellington', a rose that may be hard to find today, associates well with Tea Roses. **ZONES 5–10.**

Dickson , UK, 1909

Parentage unknown

'DUCHESSE D'ANGOULÊME'
syns 'Duc d'Angoulême', 'Wax Rose'
OLD, GALLICA, LIGHT PINK

This is a small, arching shrub that grows to 3 ft (1 m). The shoots are very green and almost unarmed, and the light to mid-green foliage is of superb quality. The pointed buds are arranged in small clusters. The flowers, which appear in mid-summer, are rather more than semi-double and are held on quite weak necks. Each flower is about 3½ in (9 cm) across, is richly endowed with fragrance and is made up of sizeable petals and remains consistently bright blush-pink shaded slightly deeper. At times they seem to have a translucent quality and so are very beautiful. This is a rewarding and healthy shrub for any situation; few of its kind are so refined. **ZONES 5–10.**

Vibert, France, 1821

Parentage unknown

'DUCHESSE D'AUERSTÄDT'
syn. 'Madame la Duchesse d'Auerstädt'
OLD, NOISETTE, YELLOW, REPEAT-FLOWERING

Blooming in the spring and autumn, this Noisette starts with round, pointed, yellow buds which open into globular, full blooms 5 in (12 cm) across. The golden yellow petals are quartered; the center ones have a hint of apricot. The blooms appear on the strong stalks either singly or in 3s. It is a disease-free mature plant which can reach 20 ft (6 m) high and is happiest in full sun. The vigorous, branching stems hold a few hooked prickles and beautiful, dark, serrated, leathery leaves. The flowers do not like rain. The Duchess was the wife of the Duc d'Auerstädt, Prince of Eckmuehl,

Maréchal de France, whose strategic talents and high morality made him Napoleon's best officer. **ZONES 7–11.**

Bernaix, France, 1887

Sport of 'Rêve d'Or'

'DUCHESSE DE BERRY'
syn. 'Duchesse de Berri'
OLD, GALLICA, PINK BLEND

This is a tall, vigorous Gallica with no prickles. There are near rosettes of wavy, pink petals forming slightly double flowers. The large, flat blooms are lilac-rose with mauve-crimson streaks. They have a strong fragrance. The duchess was the wife of the duke of the same name. He was the youngest son of the Comte d'Artois, brother of Louis XVI, who himself became king in 1824 as Charles X. The duchess was involved in many plots to put her son on the throne but all of them failed. **ZONES 4–11.**

Vibert, France, 1820

Parentage unknown

'DUCHESSE DE BRABANT'
syns 'Comtesse de Labarthe', 'Comtesse Ouwaroff', 'Countess Bertha', 'The Shell Rose'

OLD, TEA, LIGHT PINK, REPEAT-FLOWERING

This vigorous, spreading bush produces free-flowering blooms from late spring until autumn. The large, soft pink, very double, cupped blooms are shaped like tulips. The lovely buds open to 45 upright petals that have a salmon-pink flush. It is a slow-growing bush with light green, pointed leaves, which are prone to mildew in the spring. It grows to a height of 4 ft (1.2 m) and looks best when planted in 3s or 4s. President Theodore Roosevelt helped to widen the fame of this rose by wearing the buds in his coat buttonhole. It is also a good cut flower. **'Climbing Duchesse de Brabant'** has all the characteristics of its parent, but needs a warm spot to do its best. **ZONES 5–11.**

Bernède, France, 1857

Parentage unknown

'DUCHESSE DE BUCCLEUGH'
OLD, GALLICA, RED BLEND

This late-blooming Gallica has full, cupped, large blooms that range in color from pink to lavender to strong crimson,

'Duchesse de Brabant'

'Duchesse de Buccleugh'

'Duchesse de Montebello'

'Duftrausch'

depending on the weather, soil and light. The color of the blooms is quite unusual. The dark edges fade, and the flattened, quartered blooms have a green eye. This rose bears its flowers prolifically. The vigorous bush has gray-green foliage and hardly any prickles. Like most Gallicas, it tolerates poor soil. It should be placed where its colors match the other flowers in the garden. ZONES 4–10.

Vibert, France, 1837

Parentage unknown

'DUCHESSE DE CAMBACÉRÈS'

syn. 'Madame de Cambacérès'

OLD, HYBRID PERPETUAL, MAUVE BLEND, REPEAT-FLOWERING

The dark, strongly toothed leaves are both a wonderful background and a support to the flat layers of lilac-pink petals. The well-formed blooms are double, large and cupped and appear sometimes in clusters but often alone. The inner petals are muddled. They are borne abundantly in summer and autumn and have a strong fragrance. This is a vigorous but lax shrub; the bark is smooth and there are lots of slightly hooked prickles. A crop of narrow hips appears at the end of the season. This once very popular rose is found today only in a few gardens, such as Sangerhausen in eastern Germany. The duchess's husband was Bonaparte's second Consul and was exiled from 1815 to 1818. ZONES 5–11.

Fontaine, France, 1854

Parentage unknown

'DUCHESSE DE GRAMMONT'

OLD, NOISETTE, WHITE, REPEAT-FLOWERING

Blooming from spring until late summer, the small, pleasantly fragrant flowers of this rose are full, flesh-colored and proliferous. They appear as clusters on the

6 ft (1.8 m) canes. It is less rampant than other Noisettes, but enjoys a warm place in the garden. Dating old roses is always a risky business. It is possible to find that 3 or 4 different years are offered as the date of the rose's birth. In this case, some believe it is a rose created by Cels in 1825. The earliest reference to it is in Catherine Frances Gore's *The Book of Roses* (1838). ZONES 7–11.

Circa 1825

Parentage unknown

'DUCHESSE DE MONTEBELLO'

OLD, GALLICA, PINK

This beautiful Gallica has always been a popular cut flower, although it needs some extra care. The coral-rose or shell pink blooms are double, quartered, medium-sized, and often look like pink saucers with white centers. They have a light, sweet perfume. The flowers fade to flesh pink in the sun; the inner petals are reflexed around a green eye. It blooms in summer, and is a compact, erect bush with gray-green foliage and long sprays on its 5 ft (1.5 m) form. It is attractive at the back of a border or as a hedge. It tolerates poor soil, and should be given room to relax. Pruning improves its shape. ZONES 4–10.

Laffay, France, 1824–25

Unknown Gallica × unknown China

'DUCHESSE DE ROHAN'

syn. 'Duc de Rohan'

OLD, HYBRID PERPETUAL, PINK BLEND

This plant, which is rather coarse in habit, grows to about 5 ft (1.5 m) high. Its dark green, plentiful foliage is clearly Centifolia-like. The first flowers, which appear in mid-summer, are large when

'Duet'

fully open, flat and have many closely packed petals. There may be some later bloom. They are a rich warm pink color that fades slightly with age. This very fragrant, exceptionally beautiful shrub does not seem to mind growing in famished soil, but it certainly rewards good husbandry with excellence. Some rose growers class this rose as a Centifolia. ZONES 4–11.

France, pre-1848

Parentage unknown

'DUCHESSE DE VERNEUIL'

OLD, MOSS, PINK BLEND

This variety, one of the best Moss Roses, grows to 5 ft (1.5 m) high and has an upright habit. It is well branched, making a sturdy, structured shrub that seldom suffers from any disease. The thick stems are moderately thorny and there are lots of bristles. The leaves are abundant, clear mid-green and coarsely serrated. The full and very fragrant flowers, which emerge in mid-summer from well-mossed buds, are quite large in size, up to 3½ in (9 cm) in diameter. They are bright pink in color with softer highlights that are created by glimpses of the paler undersides of some of the petals as they unfold to form the fully open flowers. ZONES 4–10.

Portemer, France, 1856

Parentage unknown

'DUET'

MODERN, LARGE-FLOWERED/HYBRID TEA, MEDIUM PINK, REPEAT-FLOWERING

One of this century's greatest roses for sheer exuberance, health and continuity of flowers, 'Duet' has few equals. It produces oval, well-formed buds that open into high-centered, large—to 4 in (10 cm)—double flowers that are light pink on the uppersides and deep pink on the undersides. The blooms, which have 30 petals, come in clusters of 3–5 and are slightly fragrant; they appear all over the bush, with sometimes six flushes per year in warm countries. The growth habit is vigorous and upright and the foliage is leathery, and it has superb resistance to

disease . Extremely popular in warm climates and well deserving its two awards, this variety is great as a bedding rose. ZONES 5–11.

Swim, USA, 1960

'Fandango' × 'Roundelay'

Baden-Baden Gold Medal 1959, National Rose Society Trial Ground Certifcate 1960, All-America Rose Selection 1961

'DUFTRAUSCH'   TANschaubud

syns 'Olde Fragrance', 'Senteur Royale'

MODERN, LARGE-FLOWERED/HYBRID TEA, MEDIUM PINK, REPEAT-FLOWERING

This bush bears magnificent, deep mauve-pink double flowers with over 40 petals, which are neatly arranged and open flat. It has disease-resistant and upright growth with semi-glossy green foliage. There is a superb Damask perfume. ZONES 5–11.

Tantau, Germany, 1986

Parentage unknown

'DUKE OF EDINBURGH'

OLD, HYBRID PERPETUAL, DARK RED, REPEAT-FLOWERING

This rose needs a lot of cosseting to show its best, and it dislikes wet weather. The deep crimson, full, large blooms are veined with dark red. They are semi-double, well-formed and fragrant and look their best in semi-shade. The upright shrub is 2 ft (60 cm) tall and wide with large leaves. It prefers a rich soil. ZONES 5–11.

Paul, UK, 1868

'Général Jacqueminot' × seedling

'Duke of Edinburgh'

'Duet'

D

D

'Dupontii'

'Duke of Windsor'

'Duke Sunblaze'

'DUKE OF WELLINGTON'

syn. 'Duc de Wellington'

OLD, HYBRID PERPETUAL, DARK RED, REPEAT-FLOWERING

The hybridizer must have admired military men as he also created 'General Washington'. The large, well-shaped, high-centered blooms of deep crimson have a velvety texture. They are full and cupped with a strong scent and appear from summer until autumn. The dark foliage, which acts as a complement, covers thick and stout, upright and prickly canes. Because the blooms burn readily, it should be planted in the shade. The 'Iron Duke', as Wellington was known, scored his greatest military victory with the defeat of Napoleon at Waterloo. ZONES 5–11.

Granger, UK, 1864

'Lord Macaulay' × unknown

'DUKE OF WINDSOR'

syn. 'Herzog von Windsor'

MODERN, LARGE-FLOWERED/HYBRID TEA, ORANGE BLEND, REPEAT-FLOWERING

'Duke of Windsor' produces brilliant fluorescent orange flowers on an up-

right-growing, very vigorous, very thorny plant with magnificent large, glossy dark green leaves. Strangely enough, the thorns and canes but not the foliage are very prone to mildew. Flower production is poor but their fragrance is very strong, which is unusual in a rose of this color. The blooms are well formed and double, with 27 petals. ZONES 4–9.

Tantau, Germany, 1969

Parentage unknown

Edland Fragrance Award 1968, Anerkannte Deutsche Rose 1970

'DUKE OF YORK'

OLD, CHINA, PINK BLEND, REPEAT-FLOWERING

The China rose plays a great part in the history of modern roses as it has given them their everblooming genes. The Chinas tend to be small, bushy plants for smaller gardens. The double, large, rosy pink and white blooms of this China may have a crimson blush. The flower color is quite variable. The blooms are quartered and floriferous over a very long period. As with all Chinas, it performs best in a warm spot. The low, branching canes are dark with shiny

foliage. This is an ideal plant for a container. It deserves to be better known as few roses can claim to be so healthy, attractive, and perfumed, from spring to late autumn. ZONES 6–11.

Paul, UK, 1894

Parentage unknown

'DUKE SUNBLAZE'   MEIpinjid

syn. 'Duke Meillandina'

MODERN, MINIATURE, MEDIUM PINK, REPEAT-FLOWERING

This variety is a small-growing Miniature Rose with light green, semi-glossy foliage and nicely shaped buds that mature to small blooms only 1 in (25 mm) across. Each flower has 25–50 petals; the cooler the weather, the higher the petal count. These flowers, which last well on the plant, are a candy pink color and are borne in flushes with a quick repeat. 'Duke Sunblaze' is a wonderful little plant for use on a patio or in an enclosed area, but it is rather too small a bush to be suitable for a spot in the open garden. ZONES 5–11.

Meilland, France, 1996

Parentage unknown

'Dundee Rambler'

'DUNDEE RAMBLER'

OLD, AYRSHIRE, WHITE

This hardy and robust rose with a rambling habit can reach 20 ft (6 m) high. The double, milky white blooms appear in large clusters. A pink flush covers the small, fragrant flowers, which have many tightly packed petals. Its dense growth makes it a good woodland plant. There are large prickles. Careful pruning when training it on an arch, pillar or pergola increases its attraction during the summer-blooming period. ZONES 5–10.

Martin, UK, 1837

Rosa arvensis × unknown Noisette

'DUPLEX'

syns 'Apple Rose', Rosa pomifera duplex, R. villosa duplex, 'Wolley-Dod's Rose'

OLD, MISCELLANEOUS, MEDIUM PINK

This rose, which was discovered in the garden of the Reverend Wolley-Dod in Cheshire in 1900, is a double-flowered form of Rosa pomifera known for its very gray leaves and very large apple-shaped hips which are covered in bristles and turn red in autumn. The flowers are clear pink and semi-double and the foliage is downy and gray-green. Strong and gaunt growth to 10 ft (3 m) tall and 6 ft (2 m) wide makes this a good shrub for the back of a border. ZONES 4–11.

Vibert, France, pre-1838

Rosa pomifera × unknown Garden Rose

'DUPONTII'

syns 'Dupont Rose', Rosa × dupontii, 'Snow-Bush Rose'

OLD, MISCELLANEOUS, WHITE, REPEAT-FLOWERING

This vigorously healthy shrub is attractive as a hedge or a tree climber, or as a screen on fences. The blooms appear in clusters on arching canes in early summer. The pink buds unfold to blushed snow-white blooms. Overlapping petals surround the showy, golden stamens. The fragrance is rich, for some the smell of bananas. The long lasting blooms are excellent when cut for indoors. Gray-green leaves line the arching canes, and there are orange hips in the autumn. It prefers full sun. Dupont was the founder of the Luxembourg Gardens in Paris, and Empress Josephine commissioned him to aid her in creating the Malmaison rose collection. Susan Verrier lists this rose as a Gallica: a late-flowering cross between Rosa gallica and R. moschata. ZONES 4–11.

Pre-1817

Parentage unknown

'Duplex'

'Dusty Rose'

'Dutch Gold'

'DUPUY JAMAIN'
OLD, HYBRID PERPETUAL, MEDIUM RED, REPEAT-FLOWERING

This once popular rose lays claim to a very strange blend of colors—from red to cherry to cerise. The large and double, well-formed blooms flower freely from summer to autumn; they are at their best if the autumn is a cool season. They contain about 30 petals, which can easily burn under a hot sun. The vigorous, stiff and stout canes reach 5 ft (1.5 m) high and display a few prickles and gray-green foliage. This rose does well in poor soil and needs to be pruned to keep its shape. Monsieur Dupuy Jamain, who died in 1888 in Paris, was regarded as a distinguished nurseryman. ZONES 5–11.

Jamain, France, 1868

Parentage unknown

'DUSKY MAIDEN'
MODERN, CLUSTER-FLOWERED/FLORIBUNDA, DARK RED, REPEAT-FLOWERING

'Dusky Maiden' has proved to be an important factor in the breeding of most of David Austin's dark red English Roses. It has very dusky scarlet-crimson flowers with brilliant gold stamens that light up the flower. The single blooms are large, to 3 in (8 cm), are borne in trusses and are strongly fragrant. The dark green foliage appears on a vigorous bush that is excellent for low borders or hedges and associates well with matching perennial plants. ZONES 5–11.

LeGrice, UK, 1947

('Daily Mail Scented Rose' × ''Étoile de Hollande') × 'Else Poulsen'

National Rose Society Gold Medal 1948

'DÜSTERLOHE'
MODERN, RAMBLER, DEEP PINK

When this rose is in full bloom in midsummer, no other plant will outshine its beauty. Semi-double, rose pink blooms flower freely on the sprawling canes. The fragrant, globular blooms flatten and turn lilac-pink as they age; the center petals curve inwards around the attractive yellow stamens. A vigorous bush to 8 ft (2.4 m) high, it can be trained as a climber. The canes are prickly, and in autumn plump, pear-shaped, orange hips appear, decorating the bush throughout winter. Raised by Wilhelm Kordes II (1891–1976), head of the famous nursery, it is but one of his many roses that has achieved worldwide fame. Dr A. S. Thomas of Australia has said of Kordes that he was 'possibly the greatest rose man of all time'. ZONES 6–11.

Kordes, Germany, 1931

'Dance of Joy' × 'Daisy Hill'

'DUSTY ROSE'
MODERN, MINIATURE, MAUVE, REPEAT-FLOWERING

This rose has reddish purple, double flowers with high centers that are suitable for exhibition. There is a wonderful spicy fragrance. The low-spreading bush yields a generous number of blooms with just a touch of pink mixed in to give a dusty look; the color is long lasting. 'Dusty Rose' is an attractive plant for the garden since it blooms continuously all year, but it does need winter protection for survival. The small, dark green foliage is fairly disease resistant. ZONES 6–11.

Morey, USA, 1974

'Amy Vanderbilt' × 'Cécile Brünner'

'DUTCH GOLD'
MODERN, LARGE-FLOWERED/HYBRID TEA, MEDIUM YELLOW, REPEAT-FLOWERING

This rose, which was bred in England from two well-known parents, has double flowers with 30–35 rich golden yellow petals. They are large, to 5 in (15 cm), and have a good fragrance. The growth is strong and healthy and the flower production fair, the blooms standing up well to bad weather and keeping their color well both on the bush and when picked for indoor decoration. The foliage is glossy dark green. ZONES 5–11.

Wisbech Plant Company, UK, 1978

'Peer Gynt' × 'Whisky Mac'

The Hague Gold Medal

'DYNAMITE' JACsat
syn. 'High Flyer'
MODERN, LARGE-FLOWERED CLIMBER, DARK RED, REPEAT-FLOWERING

This promising rose has 40-petalled, dark red flowers that are 4 in (10 cm) wide and are produced in small clusters. They are slightly fragrant and appear profusely in spring although the repeat-flowering is a little slow. The superb foliage is plentiful, glossy dark green and disease free on a tall, upright, spreading plant. One of the easiest climbing red roses to grow, it is excellent as a pillar rose or on a fence or tripod. ZONES 4–10.

Warriner, USA, 1992

Seedling × 'Sympathie'

D

'Dupuy Jamain'

'Düsterlohe'

'Dupontii'

E

E

'EARL OF ELDON'

syn. 'Lord Eldon'
OLD, NOISETTE, ORANGE BLEND

'Earl of Eldon' is a vigorous climber and
a sun lover. The yellow buds open to full,
middle-sized flat flowers that range in
color from gold to copper to orange and
have a strong rose-purple overtone.
There is a strong fragrance during the
long summer flowering period. Unfortunately, it is no longer in commerce.
ZONES 5–9.

Eldon-Copin, UK, 1872
Parentage unknown

'EARTH SONG'

MODERN, LARGE-FLOWERED/HYBRID TEA,
DEEP PINK, REPEAT-FLOWERING

Griffith Buck has produced many roses
at the University of Iowa that will withstand the cold Canadian and central
USA winters. This variety has long
urn-shaped to pointed buds that open to

'Easter Morning'

'Easlea's Golden Rambler'

'Echo'

strong tyrian rose-colored, double blooms
with 25 petals. They are large, to 4 in
(10 cm), cupped and fragrant. The glossy
dark green, leathery foliage is resistant to
both cold weather and disease and appears on an upright, bushy plant. While
not readily available outside North
America, 'Earth Song' fills a great need in
extremely cold conditions where winter
hardiness is the most important consideration when ordering roses. ZONES 3–9.

Buck, USA, 1975
'Music Maker' × 'Prairie Star'

'EARTHQUAKE'   MORquake

MODERN, MINIATURE, RED BLEND,
REPEAT-FLOWERING

Brilliant bright striped red and yellow
flowers with a yellow reverse literally
cover this plant. The blooms are small
and have about 40 petals and there is no
fragrance. This rose loves the heat but it
does better in part shade, where the magnificent blooms keep their color. There is
no doubt that the striped effect is more
pronounced if it is given shade rather
than full sun—it is a real eye catcher in
the garden. The plant is winter tender
and may need protection to survive. This
rose was named after an earthquake hit
the small town of Coalinga in Central
California near Moore's home base,
Sequoia Nursery in Visalia. **'Climbing
Earthquake'** (MORshook) was introduced by Moore in 1990. It produces
long arching canes, with each leaf axil
throwing up small clusters of 3–5 florets.
The elevated splash of bloom color that

'Earthquake'

'Éclair'

the plant creates against a wall or fence
in the first spring flush is spectacular;
later in the season, however, bloom
production on the climbing version is
somewhat reduced. ZONES 6–11.

Moore, USA, 1983
'Golden Angel' × seedling

'EASLEA'S GOLDEN RAMBLER'

syn. 'Golden Rambler'
MODERN, LARGE-FLOWERED CLIMBER,
YELLOW BLEND/MEDIUM YELLOW

'Easlea's Golden Rambler' was a late-
comer to the list of rambling roses, most
of which were bred early in the twentieth
century. It has rich yellow flowers sometimes marked with red that are 4 in (10 cm)
across and bloom in clusters. They are
double with 35 petals, and strongly
fragrant, but the yellow color fades
quickly in hot climates and there is no
repeat bloom after the copious early
flush. The vigorous climbing growth to
10–13 ft (3–4 m) supports leathery,
rich olive green foliage. This variety
looks magnificent growing into purple-
foliaged trees and also looks good on
arbors and arches, the canes being very
pliable and easy to train. ZONES 4–9.

Easlea, UK, 1932
Parentage unknown
National Rose Society Gold Medal 1932

'EASTER MORNING'

syn. 'Easter Morn'
MODERN, MINIATURE, NEAR WHITE, REPEAT-
FLOWERING

The flowers of 'Easter Morning' are ivory
white and have 60–70 petals. The foliage
is a leathery, glossy dark green. It is an
excellent compact bush that tends to
spread, in most climates being a vigorous
grower with a haunting fragrance that it
is not always noticeable at first whiff. Because of the petal count, the florets last a
long time on the bush. This is an excellent choice of plant for a border or a window box. After 40 years in commerce this
rose is still popular worldwide. ZONES 5–11.

Moore, USA, 1960
'Golden Glow' × 'Zee'

'EASY GOING'   HARflow

MODERN, CLUSTER-FLOWERED/FLORIBUNDA,
MEDIUM YELLOW, REPEAT-FLOWERING

The flowers of this variety are a bright
and cheerful yellow with a hint of golden
bronze. They are large and open cupped,
carried close to the foliage but not concealed by it, in stiff, well-spaced clusters
that show a bold display of color. The

'Eclipse'

petals are waved and the blooms yield a
pleasant fragrance. The first flowering is
remarkably free, and more roses appear
through summer and autumn. This is a
useful rose for either a bed of one variety
or for a group; it is also suitable for exhibition and can be grown as a standard.
The vigorous, bushy plant is of average
height, and is furnished with plentiful
glossy, dark green leaves. ZONES 4–9.

Harkness, UK, 1998
Sport of 'Fellowship'
Dublin Gold Medal 1996, Monza Silver Medal
1997, Royal National Rose Society Trial Ground
Certificate 1998

'ECHO'

syn. 'Baby Tausendschön'
OLD, CHINA, PINK BLEND, REPEAT-FLOWERING

This offspring of a very popular rose
does best in partial shade. It has prolific,
large, semi-double blooms that are
cupped, and change from white to deep
pink. The outer curved petals shape the
rose like a bowl. The large trusses of
blooms cover the strong, erect stems,
which can reach 3 ft (1 m) on a compact
bush with glossy foliage. It is prone to
mildew where there is no air circulation.
There are no prickles. The shrub needs
deadheading during its flowering from
summer until autumn. It is an ideal subject for a container or the border, and it
also makes a long-lasting cut flower.
China Roses are ancestors of the modern
Cluster-flowered Roses. ZONES 4–9.

Lambert, Germany, 1914
Sport of 'Tausendschön'

'ÉCLAIR'

syn. 'Gärtendirektor Lauche'
OLD, HYBRID PERPETUAL, DARK RED,
REPEAT-FLOWERING

This outstanding member of the Hybrid
Perpetual family has folded outer petals
like rich velvet that surround the quartered center, and a strong perfume. The
well-shaped, dark red blossoms are
shaded black and open to form a large,
flat circle of color. It is a tall, vigorous
bush that produces flowers from summer to autumn and has little foliage but
many prickles. This is a rose that needs
to be given plenty of water and fertilized
regularly; it will repay this care accord-
ingly. It is a lovely cut flower. Lacharmé
of Lyons, France, produced many roses;
among the most notable are 'Salet' and
'Victor Verdier'. ZONES 4–9.

Lacharmé, France, 1883
'Général Jacqueminot' × seedling

'Eddie's Jewel'

'ECLIPSE'
MODERN, LARGE-FLOWERED/HYBRID TEA, LIGHT YELLOW, REPEAT-FLOWERING

The medals indicate that 'Eclipse' set a high standard for yellow roses in the 1930s; it has long, elegant, pointed buds of cadmium yellow shading to old gold with interesting long narrow sepals that took the florist world by storm. The double blooms have 28 petals and open to a rather loose shape and are very fragrant. The growth habit is strong and bushy, making it an excellent bedding plant, and the foliage is dark and leathery. ZONES 5–9.

Nicolas, USA, 1935

'Joanna Hill' × 'Federico Casas'

Portland Gold Medal 1936, Rome Gold Medal 1935, Bagatelle Gold Medal 1936, American Rose Society David Fuerstenberg Prize 1938

'EDDIE'S CRIMSON'
MODERN, MODERN SHRUB, MEDIUM RED

'Eddie's Crimson' is very similar to *Rosa moyesii* even though it has the single red Cluster-flowered Rose, 'Donald Prior' as a parent. The flowers are red, semi-double and 4 in (10 cm) across and the fruit is magnificent, being large and globular and persisting on the bush for a long time; it sets best in cold climates. The growth is vigorous, to 10 ft (3 m), on a bush that is rather gaunt and bare at the base. In hot areas there can be some scald of the limbs as the small, ferny foliage is rather sparse; nevertheless this variety can take its place in a shrub planting for autumn color. ZONES 4–9.

Eddie, Canada, 1956

'Donald Prior' × *Rosa moyesii* hybrid

'EDDIE'S JEWEL'
MODERN, MODERN SHRUB, MEDIUM RED, REPEAT-FLOWERING

'Eddie's Jewel' has fiery red flowers and red thorns; it looks quite dramatic when in full flower against a blue sky. It grows vigorously to 8 ft (2.5 m) and is repeat-flowering, although hips are not freely produced. It suffers from sun scald in hot climates. ZONES 4–9.

Eddie, Canada, 1962

'Donald Prior' × *Rosa moyesii* hybrid

'EDEN ROSE'
MODERN, LARGE-FLOWERED/HYBRID TEA, DEEP PINK, REPEAT-FLOWERING

This variety should not to be confused with the climbing rose 'Pierre de Ronsard' also bred by Meilland which is known as 'Eden Rose' in the UK. The

'Eden Rose'

plant described here has ovoid buds that open to deep tyrian rose flowers with 60 petals. They are cupped, 4 in (10 cm) wide and fragrant and hold their color and shape extremely well. 'Eden Rose' has a vigorous, upright growth habit and reasonably disease-resistant glossy dark green foliage. ZONES 4–9.

Meilland, France, 1950

'Peace' × 'Signora'

National Rose Society Gold Medal 1950

'EDITH BELLENDEN'
OLD, SWEET BRIAR, MEDIUM PINK

This rose produces a prolific, mid-summer flush of blooms. Although the pale pink, single blossoms are fragrant, the leaves offer a stronger perfume. True to its parents, it is a healthy, hardy, vigorous plant that is happy in poor soil and shade and enjoys a light pruning. Because of its hardiness and fragrance, it makes an ideal high hedge. ZONES 4–9.

Penzance, UK, 1895

Rosa foetida × *R. eglanteria*

'EDITH CLARK'
MODERN, LARGE-FLOWERED/HYBRID TEA, MEDIUM RED, REPEAT-FLOWERING

Named after the breeder's wife and one of the few of Alister Clark's Large-flowered Roses that is a dwarf grower in habit, this variety has double, globular, crimson red flowers that are slightly fragrant and are produced continuously. It has rich green foliage. ZONES 5–9.

Clark, Australia, 1928

'Mme Abel Chatenay' × seedling

'EDITH HOLDEN'   CHEwlegacy
syns 'Edwardian Lady', 'The Edwardian Lady'

MODERN, CLUSTER-FLOWERED/FLORIBUNDA, RUSSET, REPEAT-FLOWERING

This upright grower is quite unique in color; in cool weather the young flowers

'Edith Clark'

are a russet golden brown color with a yellow center while the reverse of the petals is pale; they age to gray and fawn. Semi-double with 15 petals and urn shaped, the slightly fragrant flowers are borne in long sprays of 10–20, appearing both profusely and continuously. This unique rose is lovely for flower arranging. In warm climates it grows to 10 ft (3 m) in height and is ideal for pillars or tripods, but it is also sturdy enough to be used without support as a free-standing shrub rose. The mid-green glossy foliage is large and plentiful and disease free. ZONES 4–9.

Warner, UK, 1988

'Belinda' × ('Elizabeth of Glamis' × ['Galway Bay' × 'Sutter's Gold'])

'EDITOR McFARLAND'
MODERN, LARGE-FLOWERED/HYBRID TEA, MEDIUM PINK, REPEAT-FLOWERING

This variety, which was named after Dr Horace McFarland of the *American Rose Annual* of the 1930s and under whose guidance the American Rose Society membership grew very rapidly, is one of 3 roses named after editors of rose annuals, the other two being 'Editor Stewart' for the editor of the *Australian Rose Annual*, 1939 and 'Editor Tommy Cairns', for the editor of the *American Rose Annual* in the 1990s and of *Modern Roses 10*; Dr Tommy Cairns is also a contributor to this book. 'Editor McFarland' has very fragrant, rich pink flowers with gold at the base of each of the 30 petals. The buds are well formed and open to long-lasting full blooms, the repeat-flowering is good and it suffers only rarely from disease. The climbing form is an excellent plant with very strong growth. ZONES 5–9.

Mallerin, France, 1931

'Pharisaer' × 'Lallita'

'Editor McFarland'

'Edith Holden'

'Eddie's Crimson'

E

'EDITOR STEWART'

MODERN, LARGE-FLOWERED/HYBRID TEA,
MEDIUM RED, REPEAT-FLOWERING

This short-growing climber has deep
cherry red, semi-double, large flowers
that open to reveal gold stamens. After a
prolific spring blooming, flowering continues through summer and autumn, a
rare thing in red climbing roses. The
foliage is bronze in the early stages then
turns to dark green as it matures. 'Editor
Stewart' is a good rose for a tripod or
pillar or it can be used as a very large,
free-standing shrub; it is one of the best
roses bred in Australia. **ZONES 5–9.**

Clark, Australia, 1939

Parentage unknown

'EDNA MARIE'   MORed

MODERN, MINIATURE, LIGHT PINK,
REPEAT-FLOWERING

'Edna Marie' has very soft pink flowers
with a softer yellow at the base of the
petals. Ageing turns the blooms almost
pure white. The florets, which are naturally borne one to a stem or in small
clusters, have a light fragrance. The
small, light green foliage with brown
prickles complements the blooms. The
plant has an upright, bushy and compact
habit, and can be successfully grown as a
small hedge. Ralph Moore, who named
this rose for Mary Marshall's mother on
the occasion of her 90th birthday, loves
to name roses for people he admires.
Edna was one such person! **ZONES 5–11.**

Moore, USA, 1988

'Pinocchio' × 'Peachy White'

'Edna Marie'

'Editor Stewart'

'EGLANTYNE'   AUSmak

syn. 'Eglantyne Jebb'

MODERN, MODERN SHRUB, LIGHT PINK,
REPEAT-FLOWERING

One of the best of David Austin's newer
roses, 'Eglantyne' is moderately tall and
extremely bushy with excellent disease
resistance and a continuous display of
large, very cup-shaped blooms composed
of many petals. They are the palest
pink in color and have beautiful form,
showing up well against the most attractive green foliage and they are strongly
scented. The flowers last very well on the
bush, their vase life being exceedingly
long. This variety is well suited to being
planted in groups. It is also classified as
an English Rose. **ZONES 4–9.**

Austin, UK, 1994

Parentage unknown

'EGOLI'   KORamaget

MODERN, LARGE-FLOWERED/HYBRID TEA,
DEEP YELLOW, REPEAT-FLOWERING

This rose was named for the popular
television series set in Johannesburg, the
City of Gold, that ran for many years and
which was watched by thousands of
South African housewives. 'Egoli' is
naturally a beautiful golden color, large
and showy. Three buds develop at the
ends of the flower stems into fully double
blooms with pointed centers and many
rows of frilly cut-out petals, so that the
shrub is covered in flowers like a Cluster-
flowered Rose. Specimen blooms, however, can be cultivated by removing side
buds. The flowers last well when cut, but

'Eglantyne'

'Eiffel Tower'

have little fragrance. The medium to tall
shrub is healthy and vigorous, and its
large, dark green leaves are an asset.
ZONES 5–11.

Kordes, Germany, 1995

Parentage unknown

'EIFFEL TOWER'

syns 'Eiffelturm', 'Tour Eiffel'

MODERN, LARGE-FLOWERED/HYBRID TEA,
MEDIUM PINK, REPEAT-FLOWERING

'Eiffel Tower', a magnificent rose in
warm, dry climates, has extremely long,
urn-shaped buds that open into mid-
pink, high-centered double flowers with
35 petals. The blooms are large, to 3–5 in
(8–13 cm) wide and are very fragrant;
crops of them appear profusely in quick
succession. This variety resents rain and
cold and does not perform so well in
cold climates, although in warmer areas
it is one of the best roses. The growth
habit is extremely strong and upright,
and the foliage is semi-glossy and leathery; new growth can burn in heatwave
conditions. **ZONES 4–9.**

Armstrong, USA, 1963

'First Love' × seedling

Geneva Gold Medal 1963, Rome Gold Medal 1963

'EKSTASE'

MODERN, LARGE-FLOWERED/HYBRID TEA,
DARK RED, REPEAT-FLOWERING

'Ekstase' is a good dark red rose that
shows great promise. The buds are long
and elegant and open to 40-petalled
flowers that have wonderful substance
and last very well both on the bush and
as cut flowers. Flower production is high
and constant and the fragrance is very
strong, which is unusual in a rose that is

'Ekstase'

suitable for greenhouse production. The
tall, upright plant has large, dark green,
disease-resistant foliage and extremely
long stems. Just as good a garden rose as
it is under glass, this variety is becoming
popular in Australia. **ZONES 5–9.**

Kordes, Germany, 1994

Parentage unknown

'EL CAPITAN'

MODERN, LARGE-FLOWERED/HYBRID TEA,
MEDIUM RED, REPEAT-FLOWERING

Called a Grandiflora in the USA, this
disease-free variety has very glossy dark
foliage on a vigorous, upright bush plant
that produces masses of deep cherry red
flowers both singly and in clusters. They
are shapely in the bud but open quickly
to large—to 4 in (10 cm)—high-
centered, double with 30 petals, slightly
fragrant blooms. One of the most free
flowering of all red roses and the first red
variety to flower each spring, it is an
excellent plant for bedding. The petite
buds look lovely in wedding bouquets.
ZONES 4–9.

Swim, USA, 1959

'Charlotte Armstrong' × 'Floradora'

Portland Gold Medal 1959

'ELECTRON'

syns 'Elektron', 'Mullard Jubilee'

MODERN, LARGE-FLOWERED/HYBRID TEA,
DEEP PINK, REPEAT-FLOWERING

'Electron' is an excellent garden rose and
obviously, with all these awards to its
credit, it is also good on the show bench.
The flowers are deep rose pink, very
double with 30 petals, of perfect form
and slow opening. When full they are
very beautiful and have a classic form,

'El Capitan'

and they are strongly fragrant. The bush is moderately tall and well foliaged to ground level, its magnificent foliage being inherited from 'Prima Ballerina'. The wood is thorny and the flower production fair, and the flowers hold their color well. ZONES 4–9.

McGredy, UK, 1970

'Paddy McGredy' × 'Prima Ballerina'

Royal National Rose Society Gold Medal 1969, The Hague Gold Medal 1970, Belfast Gold Medal 1972, Portland Gold Medal 1973, All-America Rose Selection 1973

'Elégance'

'ELEGANCE'

MODERN, LARGE-FLOWERED CLIMBER, MEDIUM YELLOW, REPEAT-FLOWERING

'Elegance' is a good climbing rose with dark green glossy foliage and large mid-yellow blooms that fade to white at the edges. The flowers are double with 40–50 petals and are large for a climbing rose, and there is not much repeat bloom. This variety, which does best in cooler climates as the yellow color of the blooms bleaches out in hot conditions, is excellent for pillars, tripods, arbors and fences where a disease-free, well-foliaged rose is needed. It has a vigorous growth habit. ZONES 4–9.

Brownell, USA, 1937

'Glenn Dale' × ('Mary Wallace' × 'Miss Lolita Armour')

'Elfin Charm'

'ELÉGANCE'

MODERN, LARGE-FLOWERED/HYBRID TEA, PINK BLEND

With large, fragrant, rose-copper flowers that emerge from globular buds, 'Elégance' is beautiful bush rose for a bedding scheme. The dark green, leathery foliage makes a good backdrop to the bright, double blooms. The moderate growth can be propagated by budding. ZONES 5–9.

Buyl, Belgium, 1955

Parentage unknown

'ELEGANT BEAUTY'   KORgatum

syns 'Delicia', 'Kordes' Rose Delicia'

MODERN, LARGE-FLOWERED/HYBRID TEA, LIGHT YELLOW, REPEAT-FLOWERING

'Elegant Beauty' produces lovely long buds on long stems, hence the name. The flowers are a very soft yellow flushed with pink and have only 20 petals. They make good cut flowers as the buds open slowly in spite of there being few petals. The large foliage is dark matt green on a plant with an upright, bushy growth habit. This variety is not well known in Australia or New Zealand, although it is rose of great refinement. ZONES 5–9.

Kordes, Germany, 1982

'New Day' × seedling

'Elegant Beauty'

'ELEGY'   MEIlucre

syn. 'Arturo Toscanini'

MODERN, LARGE-FLOWERED/HYBRID TEA, ORANGE-RED, REPEAT-FLOWERING

'Elegy', a breathtakingly beautiful rose at the half-open stage, has brilliant vermilion flowers, each petal being touched with dark red at the edges; the color comes from 'Independence', the first of the cinnabar roses. The slightly fragrant flowers are large, to 4 in (10 cm) across, double with 30 petals, and last well. They are also beautiful at the full bloom stage. This variety forms a small bush of sturdy growth with dark green semi-matt foliage but is not very free with its blooms. However, what it lacks in quantity it makes up for in quality. ZONES 5–9.

Meilland, France, 1971

(['Happiness' × 'Independence'] × 'Sutter's Gold') × (['Happiness' × 'Independence'] × 'Suspense')

'ELFIN CHARM'

MODERN, MINIATURE, PINK BLEND, REPEAT-FLOWERING

The short buds of 'Elfin Charm' reveal small, fragrant phlox pink flowers. The

'Elfinglo'

'Elegy'

small florets have a real old-fashioned charm, and the attractive blooms occur mostly in large clusters. Perhaps its most outstanding quality is its great early season display—the bush is covered with decorative flowers. The neat growing habit and medium size make 'Elfin Charm' a good contender for a prominent spot in the garden landscape. ZONES 5–11.

Moore, USA, 1974

(Rosa wichuraiana × 'Floradora') × 'Fiesta Gold'

'ELFINGLO'

MODERN, MINIATURE, MAUVE, REPEAT-FLOWERING

The ovoid buds on this variety open to reveal flowers described as reddish purple and double, with 25–40 petals. The bloom form is generally cupped to flat, and extremely small florets make this rose a micro-miniature. The beautiful blooms are usually borne in clusters in quite extraordinary abundance and with great holding capacity. Unfortunately, this rose is very susceptible to attack by spider mites. ZONES 5–11.

Williams, USA, 1977

'Little Chief' × 'Little Chief'

'Electron'

'Elizabeth of Glamis'

'Elina'

'Eliza'

'Eliza Dorothy'

'ELIE BEAUVILLAIN'

OLD, CLIMBING TEA, MEDIUM PINK,
REPEAT-FLOWERING

Climbing Tea Roses are treasured in
warm settings because of their health,
fragrance, form, vigor, and repeat-
blooming qualities, and this rose is no
exception. The copper-pink, full, large
blooms have a silvery blush and somewhat muddled petals, and appear from
late spring until autumn. Its vigorous
growth can cover a pergola or arch in a
few seasons, and the canes are covered
with large, bright green foliage and many
prickles. It is easily grown from cuttings
and is disease resistant. ZONES 5–9.

Beauvillain, France, 1887

'Gloire de Dijon' × 'Ophirie'

'ELINA'   DICjana

syn. 'Peaudouce'

MODERN, LARGE-FLOWERED/HYBRID TEA,
LIGHT YELLOW, REPEAT-FLOWERING

This variety is a strong, vigorous bush
with excellent dense, glossy dark green,
disease-resistant foliage that acts as a foil
to the huge, magnificently formed deep
cream blooms. The flowers, which are
often 6 in (15 cm) across and have 35
petals, last particularly well when picked
and are beautiful at all stages of development from bud to full bloom, forming

perfect exhibition subjects. The first
flush is a little later than most varieties, a
bonus that extends the spring flowering
season, and flower production is excellent. The flowers have a slight fragrance.
ZONES 4–9.

Dickson, UK, 1983

'Nana Mouskouri' × 'Lolita'

Anerkannte Deutsche Rose 1987, New Zealand
(Gold Star) Gold Medal 1987, Glasgow Silver
Medal 1991, Royal Horticultural Society Award
of Garden Merit 1993, James Mason Gold Medal
1994

'ÉLISA BOËLLE'

syn. 'Élise Boëlle'

OLD, HYBRID PERPETUAL, WHITE,
REPEAT-FLOWERING

Few roses can boast the perfect form of
this medium-sized, cupped, white and
flesh-colored variety. The circular, highly
scented blooms have incurved central
petals. The sometimes nodding blooms
are held on vigorous, long, slender stems.
It thrives best where summers are cool
and offers a second flush in autumn. A
compact bush at best on its own roots,
deadheading during the blooming
season will help to keep its form. Guillot
Père developed about 80 varieties from
his nursery in Lyons. ZONES 5–9.

Guillot, France, 1869

'M. Recamier' × unknown

'ELIZA'   KORlis

MODERN, LARGE-FLOWERED/HYBRID TEA,
MEDIUM PINK, REPEAT-FLOWERING

'Eliza', a new cut flower for the florist
trade, is a tall bush with thick dark
green foliage and very healthy growth.
The flowers, which are medium sized,
come both singly and in clusters. They
are a very clear deep pink, extremely
long lasting and open slowly both on the
bush and when picked. They have about
40 petals that pale a little at the outer
edges as the blooms age and there is little
scent. Flower production is continuous
with plenty of basal growth; the stems
are long and there are few thorns.
ZONES 5–9.

Kordes, Germany, 1996

Parentage unknown

'ELIZA DOROTHY'

MODERN, LARGE-FLOWERED/HYBRID TEA,
MEDIUM YELLOW, REPEAT-FLOWERING

The well-shaped buds of 'Eliza Dorothy'
open to 25-petalled blooms that can vary
in color from maize yellow to rich yellow,
always being attractive and holding their
shape well. The maize yellow color is
similar to that of its parent 'Marjorie
Atherton'. There is a strong perfume,
flower production is well above average
and the repeat-bloom is rapid. The rich
green, glossy foliage acts as a good foil to
the flowers on a plant with a tall or pillar
growth habit. This is a good garden rose.
ZONES 5–9.

Allender, Australia, 1984

'Marjorie Atherton' × 'Red Devil'

'ELIZABETH ARDEN'

MODERN, LARGE-FLOWERED/HYBRID TEA, NEAR
WHITE, REPEAT-FLOWERING

The plump buds of this rose open to
reveal medium- to large-sized flowers
of rounded form, with many petals of
good texture and substance. Their whiteness is not absolute, for there is cream
shading, and a touch of lemon at the
petal base. From the 1930s to the 1950s
this was one of the most popular pale-
colored Large-flowered Roses for beds
and borders, deservedly loved for its
sweet fragrance as well as for the freedom that it carries its flowers through
summer and autumn. The blooms are
good for cutting, although not quite
large enough for the show bench. 'Elizabeth Arden' grows to below average
height, with grayish green foliage that
looks sparse by modern standards, and
sometimes mildews. It was named for

the Canadian-born beautician who lived
1884–1966, and is still in commerce in
Australia. ZONES 5–9.

Prince, UK, 1929

'Edith Part' × 'Mrs Herbert Stevens'

National Rose Society Gold Medal 1929

'ELIZABETH HARKNESS'

MODERN, LARGE-FLOWERED/HYBRID TEA,
LIGHT YELLOW, REPEAT-FLOWERING

This most refined rose with some of the
form and delicacy of 'Ophelia' and
'Michèle Meilland' has 30 petals of lovely
form that open to offwhite to buff, often
with yellow and pink tones. Its color
is distinct from all other varieties and
it can be variable according to the season
and weather conditions, but it is always
beautiful. Flowering is profuse and the
fragrance strong on an upright, bushy
plant with dark, plentiful foliage. 'Elizabeth Harkness' was named after Jack and
Betty Harkness's only daughter to mark
her 21st birthday, and she carried the
rose in her wedding bouquet. ZONES 4–9.

Harkness, UK, 1969

'Red Dandy' × 'Piccadilly'

Royal National Rose Society Certificate of Merit
1969

'ELIZABETH OF GLAMIS'

MACel

syns 'Elisabeth', 'Irish Beauty'

MODERN, CLUSTER-FLOWERED/FLORIBUNDA,
ORANGE-PINK, REPEAT-FLOWERING

'Elizabeth of Glamis' was named after
Queen Elizabeth the Queen Mother,
whose ancestral home was Glamis Castle
in Scotland. It is an excellent Cluster-
flowered Rose with lush dark green,
plentiful foliage on a bushy, medium-
sized plant that is very quick to repeat-
flower. The buds are well shaped and
open to show stamens and 35 petals that
are a luminous salmon-orange. This is
an excellent bedding rose as the flowers

'Elizabeth Harkness'

'Elmshorn'

'Ellen'

and foliage appear from ground level and completely cover the bush. In some climates it can be difficult to transplant. ZONES 5–9.

McGredy, UK, 1964

'Spartan' × 'Highlight'

National Rose Society President's International Trophy 1963

'ELIZABETH TAYLOR'

MODERN, LARGE-FLOWERED/HYBRID TEA, DEEP PINK, REPEAT-FLOWERING

This exhibitor's rose has double flowers with 35 petals that are deep pink in color and extremely high centered. They are large, are usually borne singly and open to full blooms of excellent substance. The large, dark, semi-glossy foliage shows up the flowers well on an upright, disease-free plant. ZONES 4–9.

Weddle, USA, 1985

'First Prize' × 'Swarthmore'

'ELLEN'   AUScup

MODERN, MODERN SHRUB, APRICOT BLEND, REPEAT-FLOWERING

This variety (also classified as English Rose), has rich but soft apricot flowers tinged with brown. They are beautifully cupped in the bud stage and open to a loose quartered formation. Strongly scented, they have short stems and about 40 petals in cool weather but fewer in summer heat. After an excellent performance in spring, flowering is continuous but sparse in summer and then more profuse in autumn. The leaves are large and rather coarse and there are quite a few thorns. The growth is bushy but rather ungainly with long shoots towering above shorter growth. ZONES 4–9.

Austin, UK, 1984

'Charles Austin' × seedling

'ELLEN POULSEN'

MODERN, POLYANTHA, MEDIUM PINK, REPEAT-FLOWERING

'Ellen Poulsen' is a very bushy plant of low to medium height with dense glossy foliage, the leaves being packed very close together on the stems. The double, fragrant, bright cherry pink flowers appear in tight trusses continuously; they are large, have a good form and hold their shape well. This variety, which is resistant to mildew, can be pruned hard or lightly to form a small shrub; it makes a good border or small hedge because of the dense foliage cover. ZONES 4–9.

Poulsen, Denmark, 1911

'Mme Norbert Levavasseur' × 'Dorothy Perkins'

'ELLEN WILLMOTT'

MODERN, LARGE-FLOWERED/HYBRID TEA, YELLOW BLEND, REPEAT-FLOWERING

W. E. B. Archer produced some excellent single Large-flowered Roses in the 1930s, and this was one of the best. It was named after Miss Willmott of Warley Place in Essex, famous for her book *The Genus Rosa* and for her gardens at Warley Place and in the south of France; at one stage she employed 65 gardeners. The flowers are soft pink tinted yellow with pronounced stamens that are claret in color. The strong, healthy bush has good dark green, leathery foliage. ZONES 4–9.

Archer, UK, 1936

'Dainty Bess' × 'Lady Hillingdon'

'ELLINOR LEGRICE'

MODERN, LARGE-FLOWERED/HYBRID TEA, MEDIUM YELLOW, REPEAT-FLOWERING

This rose has a vigorous, upright growth habit and plenty of dark green glossy foliage. The flowers, which are large and full and a clear unfading yellow, have a fruity fragrance; they repeat-flower quite well. The stems are thorny and the wood is inclined to die back, but it is a good bedding rose. ZONES 4–9.

LeGrice, UK, 1949

'Mrs Beatty' × 'Yellowcrest'

National Rose Society Trial Ground Certificate 1947

'ELMHURST'

MODERN, LARGE-FLOWERED/HYBRID TEA, PINK BLEND, REPEAT-FLOWERING

By crossing 2 well-formed roses the breeder produced a rose with 35 petals of high-centered form and in a blending of pink and gold. They have a good scent, but repeat-flowering is rather slow. The foliage is mid-green and growth is upright and of medium height. ZONES 5–9.

Perry, USA, 1985

'Granada' × 'Helmut Schmidt'

'Ellen Willmott'

'ELMSHORN'

MODERN, MODERN SHRUB, DEEP PINK, REPEAT-FLOWERING

This variety, one of the strongest growing and most free flowering of all shrub roses, has small, cupped, double, well-formed flowers that are borne in huge well-spaced trusses. They have a slight scent, and the autumn display on huge arching shoots is deeper in color than it is in spring. Disease resistance is very high, and the foliage is glossy light green, most profuse and wrinkled. 'Elmshorn' can be used most effectively either singly or in groups set in grass or lawns for continuous color; it is repeat-flowering and deserves to be more widely grown where a large plant is required. ZONES 4–9.

Kordes, Germany, 1951

'Hamburg' × 'Verdun'

Anerkannte Deutsche Rose 1950, National Rose Society Certificate of Merit 1950

'ELSE POULSEN'

syn. 'Joan Anderson'

MODERN, CLUSTER-FLOWERED/FLORIBUNDA, MEDIUM PINK, REPEAT-FLOWERING

'Else Poulsen' is one of the earliest Cluster-flowered Roses bred by Poulsen of Denmark, who saw the potential of this class in gardens. It is a vigorous and bushy plant with dark glossy bronze foliage in the young stages. The bright pink flowers have 10 petals, open to reveal good stamens and they come in clusters of 3–12 or so. Simple but charming, they are some 2 in (5 cm) wide and are slightly fragrant. This variety is a good rose to plant among bulbs and perennials where its soft color and continuous bloom is very effective; it

also looks good with silver-foliaged plants, although it can suffer from mildew in autumn. ZONES 4–9.

Poulsen, Denmark, 1924

'Orléans Rose' × 'Red Star'

'ELVESHÖRN'   KORbotaf

MODERN, MODERN SHRUB, MEDIUM PINK, REPEAT-FLOWERING

This wonderful small shrub rose has a moderate and spreading growth habit and healthy dark green, semi-glossy foliage. The flowers, which come in well-spaced, elongated panicles have 35 petals. They retain their cherry pink color very well and have excellent substance. Flowering is extremely profuse in spring and then continuous in summer and autumn. 'Elveshörn' makes a very colorful low hedge or border or can be used in groups among herbaceous plants. ZONES 4–9.

Kordes, Germany, 1985

'The Fairy' × seedling

'ELYSIUM'   KORumelst

MODERN, CLUSTER-FLOWERED/FLORIBUNDA, MEDIUM PINK, REPEAT-FLOWERING

This variety has long, pointed buds that open to double, salmon-pink flowers with a boss of stamens. The buds are attractive at all stages of development and the nicely fragrant flowers look good when arranged under artificial light. They have 35 petals. The foliage is glossy and disease free on a profusely blooming, vigorous, tall plant. 'Elysium' makes an excellent bedding rose. ZONES 5–9.

Kordes, Germany, 1961

Parentage unknown

National Rose Society Certificate of Merit 1961

'Elysium'

'Ellinor LeGrice'

'Ellen Poulsen'

'EMANUEL' AUSuel
syn. 'Emmanuelle'
MODERN, MODERN SHRUB, APRICOT BLEND,
REPEAT-FLOWERING

This variety has very full flowers composed of 100 or more petals that open to form a flat rosette and are borne in small clusters. Like many Austin roses it can vary a great deal in color: in cool weather it is quite apricot whereas in summer heat it is quite pink with apricot tones at the base of the petals. Whatever the color it is attractive at all times. The blooms are large and very fragrant. 'Emanuel' is a medium-height, bushy, spreading plant with small, mid-green, semi-glossy, extremely dense foliage. It looks attractive in groups in perennial borders with other plants and is an excellent choice in both large and small gardens; it is also ideal for growing as a standard. 'Emanuel',

'Emanuel'

which is also classified as an English Rose, was named after the dress designers responsible for Princess Diana's wedding gown. ZONES 4–9.

Austin, UK, 1985

('Chaucer' × 'Parade') × (seedling × 'Iceberg')

'EMBASSY'
MODERN, LARGE-FLOWERED/HYBRID TEA, PINK
BLEND, REPEAT-FLOWERING

The well-shaped flowers of 'Embassy' are soft gold veined with carmine at the petal edges; they are strongly fragrant but are a little slow to repeat-flower. The foliage is glossy, abundant and disease free on an average-height plant. This variety is an excellent rose for exhibition purposes in cool climates, and is also a good bedding rose. ZONES 4–9.

Sanday, UK, 1967

'Gavotte' × ('Magenta' × 'Golden Scepter')

'Embassy'

'Embers'

'Emily'

'EMBER' SAVember
MODERN, MINIATURE, ORANGE-RED,
REPEAT-FLOWERING

When the small orange-red flowers containing about 15–20 petals emerge from the tiny buds of this variety, it is truly a sight to see. The florets, which are borne one bloom per stem, have no fragrance. The foliage is small and semi-glossy and the plant is of medium height, with an upright, compact, bushy habit. 'Ember' provides a constant supply of seemingly glowing orange-red blooms and is a popular cut flower. It also makes a good container-grown plant. ZONES 5–11.

Saville, USA, 1994

'Copper Sunset' × ('Zorina' × 'Baby Katie')

'EMBERS'
MODERN, CLUSTER-FLOWERED/FLORIBUNDA,
MEDIUM RED, REPEAT-FLOWERING

The glowing scarlet color suggested the name of this Cluster-flowered Rose. It bears strong-stemmed clusters of quite large blooms with up to 25 petals. They open from plump buds into high-centered flowers which become cupped as they open. There is a spicy scent, and blooming is maintained through summer and autumn. This rose is useful for beds, hedges and borders, although it is doubtful whether it is still commercially available. The compact bush grows vigorously to average height with dark green, semi-glossy foliage. ZONES 5–9.

Swim, USA, 1953

'World's Fair' × 'Floradora'

'EMILY' AUSburton
MODERN, MODERN SHRUB, LIGHT PINK,
REPEAT-FLOWERING

'Emily', a most refined little rose, has soft pink flowers that are at first cup shaped then become a rosette shape. They open to show a core of small petals that are paler on the outside then become deeper

'Emily Gray'

in color in the center. There is a very strong fragrance. The small, upright bush produces a lot of blooms, their unique shape making them ideal for cutting for use in arrangements. It is a good rose for small gardens but needs extra treatment to perform well. It is also classified as English Rose. ZONES 4–9.

Austin, UK, 1992

'The Prioress' × 'Mary Rose'

'EMILY GRAY'
MODERN, LARGE-FLOWERED CLIMBER, DEEP
YELLOW

This lovely yellow rambler has deep gold flowers infused with buff shades and with yellow stamens. They have 25 petals and are borne in clusters; there is little repeat bloom. One of the healthiest of all yellow climbing roses, it has glossy, dark, bronze foliage on an extremely vigorous plant with pliable canes. 'Emily Gray' is a good rose for pergolas and arches and for growing into trees. ZONES 4–9.

Williams, UK, 1918

'Jersey Beauty' × 'Comtesse du Cayla'

National Rose Society Gold Medal 1916

'EMILY LOUISE' HARwilla
MODERN, PATIO/DWARF CLUSTER-FLOWERED,
DEEP YELLOW, REPEAT-FLOWERING

'Emily Louise' is a very small plant with dark green glossy foliage that produces an abundant supply of small, single, 5-petalled flowers in both large and small clusters. The widely spaced petals give a star-like look, which is emphasized by a large boss of orange stamens. The flowers are held on extremely upright growth which adds to its charm. ZONES 4–9.

Harkness, UK, 1990

'Judy Garland' × 'Anna Ford'

Royal National Rose Society Certificate of Merit 1988, Rome Certificate of Merit 1989, New Zealand Certificate of Merit 1990, Glasgow Silver Medal 1993

'ÉMINENCE' GAXence
MODERN, LARGE-FLOWERED/HYBRID TEA, MAUVE,
REPEAT-FLOWERING

This sturdy, moderately vigorous bush has light green, leathery foliage. The large, double flowers with 40 petals are dark lavender. At their best the strongly scented flowers are well formed and attractive, but in cold wet weather they can ball and open to a dirty gray mauve color; however, they do last very well on the bush and when cut. This variety is best suited to warm, dry climates. ZONES 5–9.

Gaujard, France, 1962

'Peace' × ('Viola' × seedling)

'Emily Louise'

'EMMIE GRAY'
OLD, CHINA (TEA), MEDIUM RED,
REPEAT-FLOWERING

This is a provisional name for one of the
Bermuda Mystery Roses. These 'mystery
roses', which survived two world wars,
have not all been identified. Bermuda's
tropical climate makes it an ideal place
for growing Teas and Chinas such as this
everblooming rose, which has pink buds
with foliated petals that open to single,
bright pink to reddish flowers which
darken at the center. The dramatic yellow
stamens offer a delightful contrast on a
vigorous, upright bush with finely serrated, glossy leaves; there is a good crop
of hips. The flowers close at night. Emmie
Gray was a high school teacher in Bermuda for more than 30 years. ZONES 6–9.

Parentage unknown

'EMOTION'
syn. 'Souvenir d'Aline Fontaine'
OLD, BOURBON, PINK BLEND, REPEAT-FLOWERING

Two roses with this name were introduced in France last century, this one
from Guillot, and the other from
Fontaine in 1879. This rose is a very pale
pink with a delicate fragrance. The foliage is pale green and the bush needs to
be carefully tended. ZONES 4–9.

Guillot, 1862

Parentage unknown

'EMPEREUR DU MAROC'
syn. 'Emperor of Morocco'
OLD, HYBRID PERPETUAL, RED, REPEAT-FLOWERING

This rose, which has never lost its
popularity, has double, crimson-tinged
purple blooms containing 40 petals that
are borne in large clusters of 5–10. The

'Ena Harkness'

'Empress Michiko'

'Emmie Gray'

intensely fragrant flowers are small,
compact and muddled, and turn almost
black with age. A low, compact bush, it
needs rich cultivation to do its best. The
foliage is sparse but there are strong
prickles; hard pruning will strengthen its
performance. This rose is ideal for a small
garden or the border because of its color
and fragrance but it is prone to mildew,
and the flowers can easily burn in the
sun. ZONES 4–9.

Guinoisseau, France, 1858

'Géant des Batailles' seedling

'EMPRESS JOSÉPHINE'
syns 'Francofurtana', 'Souvenir de
l'Impératrice Josephine', 'The Frankfurt
Rose'
OLD, GALLICA, MEDIUM PINK

The origin of 'Empress Josephine' is so
shrouded in mystery that it has collected
a long list of names. It is an improved
form honoring Napoleon's first wife, who
was really the patroness of old roses. The
rich pink, veined, semi-double, loosely
shaped blooms are large and appear during summer; the wavy, textured petals
appear translucent. Although it has little
scent, its fame rests on its beauty as a cut
flower. The sprawling, well-branched 5 ft
(1.5 m) shrub has coarse, deeply veined
grayish leaves, some prickles and large
hips. It prefers the shade in warm areas
and may need support. ZONES 3–9.

Descemet, France, pre-1815

Rosa cinnamomea × R. gallica

Royal Horticultural Society Award of Garden
Merit 1993

'EMPRESS MICHIKO'   DICnifty
MODERN, LARGE-FLOWERED/HYBRID TEA,
LIGHT PINK, REPEAT-FLOWERING

'Empress Michiko', named after the
Empress of Japan, has lovely colorings of
pastel pinks, creams and even pale apricots. The buds are high centered and the

'Ena Baxter'

'Éminence'

'Empress Joséphine'

'Emotion'

outer petals attractively pointed. The
buds hold well and open to flowers of excellent substance. Flower production is
good. Growth is moderate, and the dark
green foliage is resistant to disease.
ZONES 4–9.

Dickson, UK, 1992

'Silver Jubilee' × ('Bright Smile' × 'Peer Gynt')

Royal National Rose Society Trial Ground
Certificate 1987, Glasgow Certificate of Merit
1994

'ENA BAXTER'   COCbonne
MODERN, LARGE-FLOWERED/HYBRID TEA,
MEDIUM PINK, REPEAT-FLOWERING

The well-formed, salmon-pink flowers of
'Ena Baxter' are produced in great quantities. They come in small, well-spaced
clusters that show up nicely against the
dark foliage. The dense, disease-resistant
foliage is glossy green and profuse. This
is a great rose for hedges and for borders
and is also a wonderful bedding rose.
There is some fragrance. ZONES 4–9.

Cocker & Son, UK, 1990

Seedling × 'Silver Jubilee'

Royal National Rose Society Trial Ground
Certificate 1987, Glasgow Gold Medal 1994

'ENA HARKNESS'
MODERN, LARGE-FLOWERED/HYBRID TEA,
MEDIUM RED, REPEAT-FLOWERING

'Ena Harkness' was bred by an amateur
hybridist, A. Norman, and introduced by

the Harkness firm; it was named after a
prominent flower arranger. This variety
was bred for cool climates where blooms
can be of the highest exhibition quality.
Of the purest unfading crimson and with
the true Damask perfume of its parent
'Crimson Glory', it was grown in most
rose gardens of the world in the 1950s.
The rather weak leaf stalks and sparse
leathery foliage led to a loss of popularity, but it is still grown in Tasmania,
Australia. The growth habit is moderately strong and upright and it is disease
resistant. 'Climbing Ena Harkness'
(1954) is a powerfully scented climbing
sport that is wonderful for a high trellis
or for growing up the walls of houses. It
flowers reasonably continuously after an
abundant spring flush. ZONES 4–9.

Norman, UK, 1946

'Crimson Glory' × 'Southport'

National Rose Society Gold Medal 1945, National
Rose Society Clay Cup for Fragrance 1945,
Portland Gold Medal 1955

'ENCHANTRESS'
OLD, TEA, WHITE, REPEAT-FLOWERING

This rose is frequently confused with the
Large-flowered Rose of the same name.
Its middle-sized blooms are round and
double, while the delicate, cream-white
petals have a buff center and are folded
at the edge. The trusses of fragrant
blooms, which appear from summer

through to autumn, are long lasting and enjoy a sunny, warm position. A bushy shrub that can reach 5 ft (1.5 m) and should be pruned moderately, it makes a good landscaping plant with its upright form and round leaves. ZONES 5–9.

Paul, UK, 1896

Parentage unknown

'ENFANT DE FRANCE'
OLD, HYBRID PERPETUAL, LIGHT PINK, REPEAT-FLOWERING

Produced on the eve of the birth of the Large-flowered or Hybrid Tea class of roses, this repeat-blooming variety has proved its worth over a long period. The blowzy, pink-white, fragrant blooms are double and sometimes quartered and there is a silvery pink cast to them. A velvet texture adds to the charm of the petals. The upright, strong bush does well in poor soil and has abundant leaves. ZONES 4–9.

Lartay, France, 1860

Parentage unknown

'ENGLISH ELEGANCE'   AUSleaf
MODERN, MODERN SHRUB, PINK BLEND, REPEAT-FLOWERING

This variety, which is also classified as an English Rose, has flowers that are an unusual combination of pink, copper

'English Garden'

'English Holiday'

and salmon. The large blooms have loosely arranged inner petals of a deeper color displayed within a ring of large outer petals of a lighter tint, but there is not much perfume. Flowering is profuse and the repeat bloom is good, particularly in cooler autumn weather where the lovely color combination is more pronounced. The large, spreading plant lends itself to espalier work; it is strong enough in habit to form a wide, arching shrub without support or it can be trained as a small climber. The foliage is light green and disease free and the nodes are very close together. ZONES 4–9.

Austin, UK, 1986

Parentage unknown

'ENGLISH GARDEN'   AUSbuff
syn. 'Schloss Glücksburg'
MODERN, MODERN SHRUB, APRICOT BLEND, REPEAT-FLOWERING

This small, upright plant is more like a Large-flowered Rose in growth than a shrub and has plentiful pale green foliage. The flowers are very variable in color and deepen in hot weather, changing from soft yellow to buff to pale apricot. The blooms are flat with a many small petals and often a quartered center, and they are wonderful as cut flowers and last well when picked. 'English Garden', which is

'Erfurt'

'English Elegance'

also classified as an English Rose, blends happily with most other flowers in the bed. It is proving to be popular in gardens throughout the world. ZONES 4–9.

Austin, UK, 1986

('Lilian Austin' × seedling) × ('Iceberg' × 'Wife of Bath')

'ENGLISH HOLIDAY'
MODERN, CLUSTER-FLOWERED/FLORIBUNDA, YELLOW BLEND, REPEAT-FLOWERING

The flowers of this variety, which are an attractive blend of yellow and salmon, are double with 30 petals, large and fragrant. It is a low-growing bush with large, glossy, disease-free foliage that makes a good bedding rose. ZONES 4–9.

Harkness, UK, 1977

'Bobby Dazzler' × 'Gold Bonnet'

Royal National Rose Society Trial Ground Certificate 1976

'ENGLISH MISS'
MODERN, CLUSTER-FLOWERED/FLORIBUNDA, LIGHT PINK, REPEAT-FLOWERING

With two excellent pink Cluster-flowered Roses as parents, it is not surprising that 'English Miss' has soft, clear pale pink flowers. They are extremely double with up to 60 petals, open from exquisite buds to large, flat, full blooms, and come in well-spaced clusters. There is a strong perfume. The very dark green to purple foliage acts as a nice background to the flowers. This popular, compact-growing bush has no disease problems. ZONES 4–9.

Cant, UK, 1978

'Dearest' × 'Sweet Repose'

Royal National Rose Society Trial Ground Certificate 1977, British Association of Rose Breeders Selection 1978

'EOS'
MODERN, MODERN SHRUB, RED BLEND

This tall, gaunt shrub to 6 ft (2 m) in height has small, ferny foliage. Its ovoid

'Ernest H. Morse'

'Eos'

buds open to semi-double, cupped, medium blooms that are sunset red with white centers and which are borne several together on a stem. There is a slight fragrance but no repeat bloom. 'Eos' appears to only set fruit in cold climates, which is a pity as the chief beauty of forms of *Rosa moyesii* are the long, flagon-shaped hips. ZONES 4–9.

Ruys, The Netherlands, 1950

Rosa moyesii × 'Magnifica'

'ERFURT'
MODERN, MODERN SHRUB, PINK BLEND, REPEAT-FLOWERING

'Erfurt' has a trailing, bushy growth habit and leathery, wrinkled, rich bronze-tinted disease-free foliage. Flowering is continuous despite a large crop of medium-sized round hips that turn from green to orange-red and which are produced after the first flush of flowers. The blooms are pink and develop from attractively scrolled buds that open to reveal cream to yellow towards the base of the petals and prominent stamens. The open flowers are attractive, particularly in summer and autumn when the hips appear among them to add to the effect; the hips are very effective for indoor decoration, lasting a number of months on the bush and not seeming to be devoured by birds. ZONES 4–9.

Kordes, Germany, 1939

Eva' × 'Réveil Dijonnais'

'ERNEST H. MORSE'
MODERN, LARGE-FLOWERED/HYBRID TEA, MEDIUM RED, REPEAT-FLOWERING

'Ernest H. Morse' was bred in Germany and named after the nurseryman in England who introduced it. The flowers are bright Turkey red, well formed with 30 petals and large, to 4 in (10 cm) across. They are extremely fragrant, retain their color well in the full blooms, and appear continuously. The plant is of medium height and has good leathery, disease-resistant foliage. This variety is still being sold by nurseries after 30 years in commerce because of its color, perfume and reliability. ZONES 4–9.

Kordes, Germany, 1964

Parentage unknown

Royal National Rose Society Gold Medal 1965

'Ernest's Blue'

'Erotika'

'ERNEST'S BLUE'

MODERN, LARGE-FLOWERED/HYBRID TEA, MAUVE, REPEAT-FLOWERING

'Ernest's Blue' is an unusual-colored rose, being a silvery blue-mauve shade. The slowly opening buds are well formed and strongly scented, and the flowers keep well when picked and blend well with other roses. This variety has a healthy, medium tall growth habit and abundant, disease-free foliage. **ZONES 5–9.**

Parentage unknown

'EROTIKA'

syns 'Eroica', 'Eroika', 'Erotica'

MODERN, LARGE-FLOWERED/HYBRID TEA, DARK RED, REPEAT-FLOWERING

'Erotika' is a respectable dark red rose with a very strong perfume. The well-shaped buds develop into large blooms containing 35, firm-textured petals with a velvety sheen. The disease-free foliage is glossy dark green on a tallish, vigorous, upright plant. It is popular in Germany where its color, strength, vigor and continuity of bloom earned it an award in 1969. It is grown worldwide and deserves to be more popular. **ZONES 4–9.**

Tantau, Germany, 1968

Parentage unknown

Anerkannte Deutsche Rose 1969

'ESCAPADE'   HARpade

MODERN, CLUSTER-FLOWERED/FLORIBUNDA, MAUVE, REPEAT-FLOWERING

There are not many roses that can be identified from a distance, but 'Escapade' is one of them. Breeder Jack Harkness said that its flowers were so full of nectar that there was usually a bee in almost every bloom. The soft mauve-pink semi-double flowers, which have 12 petals, a central boss of yellow stamens and a white eye, come in large clusters and look lovely against the glossy pale green, dense foliage. Flowering is prolific, although the flowers do fade rather quickly in hot climates. With its shrubby growth habit this plant is perfect for a hedge, and its lovely simple flowers also blend happily with herbaceous borders. **ZONES 4–9.**

Harkness, UK, 1967

'Pink Parfait' × 'Baby Faurax'

Baden-Baden Gold Medal 1968, Belfast Gold Medal 1968, Copenhagen First Prize 1970, Anerkannte Deutsche Rose 1973, Royal Horticultural Society Award of Garden Merit 1994

'ESKIMO'   KORcilmo

syn. 'Escimo'

MODERN, LARGE-FLOWERED/HYBRID TEA, WHITE, REPEAT-FLOWERING

'Eskimo', which is a very good cut-flower variety, has medium-sized blooms that open very slowly and last well on the bush and when picked. They are borne singly or in clusters. Flower production is good, the blooms appearing reasonably well in all seasons, but there is not

'English Miss'

'Escapade'

'Eskimo'

'Essex'

much scent. This variety can be grown to perfection under greenhouse conditions but it also a good performer in the garden. ZONES 5–9.

Kordes, Germany, 1991

Parentage unknown

'ESME EUVRARD' KORelgas
MODERN, LARGE-FLOWERED/HYBRID TEA, LIGHT PINK, REPEAT-FLOWERING

Named for a popular South African radio personality, 'Esme Euvrard' has inherited the well-shaped long pointed buds, that are such a pleasure to pick, from its famous parent. The buds unfold their strong petals slowly to form a symmetrical, delicate pink bloom of great quality, but with only a slight fragrance. It is a popular exhibition rose. In the garden, the shrub grows to a medium height, and is good for bedding schemes. ZONES 4–10.

Kordes, Germany, 1992

Hybrid of 'Bride's Dream'

'ESPECIALLY FOR YOU'
FRYworthy

MODERN, LARGE-FLOWERED/HYBRID TEA, MEDIUM YELLOW, REPEAT-FLOWERING

'Especially For You' is a new rose with a very strong perfume. The bright mimosa-yellow, double flowers have

'Espéranza'

25 petals; they are large and well formed, and are borne both singly and in clusters. The foliage is dark green and disease free and flower production is high with very good repeat. This rose is suitable for bedding and for borders. ZONES 4–9.

Fryer, UK, 1996

Seedling × 'Johnnie Walker'

'ESPÉRANZA'
MODERN, CLUSTER-FLOWERED/FLORIBUNDA, MEDIUM RED, REPEAT-FLOWERING

'Espéranza' is a tall-growing Cluster-flowered rose that can also be used as a shrub. The abundant foliage is dark, bronze, leathery and highly disease resistant on an upright, strong-growing

'Esther Geldenhuys'

'Estima'

plant. The flowers are bright red, double and come in huge clusters that completely cover the bush. The variety is most suitable as a bedding plant where a massed effect is required. The spent flowers should be removed or a large crop of round red hips will form, although these can look most attractive among later flowers. ZONES 4–9.

Delforge, France, 1966

'Donald Prior' × 'Reverence'

Baden-Baden Gold Medal 1968, The Hague Gold Medal 1968

'ESSEX' POUlnoz
syns 'Aquitaine', 'Pink Cover'
MODERN, GROUND COVER, MEDIUM PINK, REPEAT-FLOWERING

'Essex' is one of the County Series of ground cover roses bred by Poulsen of Denmark and Kordes of Germany and introduced by Mattock of England; there are nearly 20 of these short-growing roses named after English counties. This variety grows about 2 ft (60 cm) high and 5 ft (1.5 m) across, and its dark green foliage is covered with small, single blooms of a rich deep pink. Repeat-blooming is continuous, especially if the spent blooms are removed, and there are no disease problems. If the plants is left for a number of years without pruning and becomes too woody, then a hard cut back in winter will not affect the next spring display. ZONES 4–9.

Poulsen, Denmark, 1988

Parentage unknown

Royal National Rose Society Certificate of Merit 1987, Gold Medal Dublin 1987, Glasgow Certificate of Merit 1995

'ESTHER'
syns 'Duchesse d'Oldenbourg', 'Grande Esther'
OLD, GALLICA, PINK BLEND

'Esther' has full, medium-sized blooms that are loosely double; some have purple-crimson stripes. The yellow stamens are often hidden by the ragged, quilled petals. A strong fragrance marks the presence of this shrub in the garden. It is no longer in commerce. ZONES 4–9.

Vibert, France, 1845

Parentage unknown

'ESTHER GELDENHUYS'
KORskipei
MODERN, LARGE-FLOWERED/HYBRID TEA, ORANGE-PINK, REPEAT-FLOWERING

Nurseryman Ludwig Taschner of South Africa was most impressed with this rose from Kordes when he tested it in his trial grounds. The breeder was reluctant to introduce it but Taschner asked permission to release it in South Africa, naming it after a president of the rose society there. Grown both outside and under cover for cut-flower production, this variety has very long buds that open to clam-shaped, large, double flowers with 32 petals. They are soft coral-pink, moderately fragrant and appear quite profusely. The bush is very tall and well branched, the foliage is glossy purple to mid-green with yellow-brown thorns. A good garden and bedding rose, it is also excellent for arranging indoors as the stems are long and the color shows up very well under artificial light. ZONES 5–9.

Kordes, Germany, 1985

Seedling × seedling

'ESTIMA'
MODERN, MINIATURE, ORANGE BLEND

'Estima' forms a small, bushy plant with small, mid-green, semi-glossy foliage that is disease resistant. The small, very full flowers are deep orange with a salmon tint and have densely packed petals that open flat from ovoid buds. They keep for a very long time and last well when picked. It has been superseded by more modern varieties. ZONES 5–9.

de Ruiter, The Netherlands, 1986

Parentage unknown

'Especially For You'

'Etain'

'Étude'

'ETAIN'
MODERN, RAMBLER, ORANGE-PINK

This is a very useful rose for climbing smaller trees or stretching over arches. It bears salmon-pink trusses that offer some perfume during the summer flush. An added feature to its charms is the glossy, evergreen foliage. As the foliage truly is evergreen in milder climates, it makes an attractive plant throughout the year and looks wonderful as a backdrop to a perennial border. Its thin, pliable canes make it an easy rose to train, but be careful of the prickles. It requires little maintenance and is never touched by disease. Offered by the English nursery firm of Cants in 1953, it deserves to be more popular. **ZONES 4–9.**

Cants, UK, 1953

Parentage unknown

'ÉTERNA'   DELic
MODERN, LARGE-FLOWERED/HYBRID TEA, LIGHT PINK, REPEAT-FLOWERING

Despite having five terrific roses in the cross, 'Éterna' has not quite lived up to its pedigree. The buds are long and attractive and open to well-shaped, light salmon-pink flowers that are double with 30–35 petals. They have some fragrance and flower production is good, but as a cut flower this variety has lost popularity even though the blooms keep very well both on the bush and when picked. It is a vigorous, upright plant with foliage that is slightly prone to mildew. **ZONES 5–9.**

Delbard-Chabert, France, 1978

(['Michèle Meilland' × 'Carla'] × ['Dr Schweitzer' × 'Tropicana']) × ('Queen Elizabeth' × 'Provence')

'ETHEL'
MODERN, RAMBLER, LIGHT PINK

A catalogue of 1912 describes this as 'a delightful shade of flesh pink with semi-double flowers', yet a 1998 catalogue calls

'Éterna'

it mauve-pink with double flowers—this makes one wonder if the variety now in commerce is the correct rose. Turner's creation flowered in profusion in large trusses, and was noted for its light green foliage and vigorous habit. It, and its present-day counterpart, make suitable subjects for scrambling up and over pergolas, fences and substantial arches; it grows to twice the average extent for a climbing rose, and forms an excellent weeping standard. It flowers in summer only. **ZONES 4–9.**

Turner, UK, 1912

Seedling of 'Dorothy Perkins'

'ETHEL AUSTIN'   FRYmestin
MODERN, CLUSTER-FLOWERED/FLORIBUNDA, DEEP PINK, REPEAT-FLOWERING

Thanks to its two well-known and free-flowering parents, 'Ethel Austin' is a continuously blooming Cluster-flowered Rose with deep pink double flowers with 20 petals that are borne in clusters. There is a good fragrance and growth is upright, and the foliage is large, mid-green and disease resistant. **ZONES 4–9.**

Fryer, UK, 1984

'Pink Parfait' × 'Redgold'

'ETHEL DAWSON'
MODERN, LARGE-FLOWERED/HYBRID TEA, MEDIUM RED, REPEAT-FLOWERING

George Dawson raised some very good long-stemmed, glossy foliaged, disease-resistant roses, this one named for his wife being no exception. The flowers, which are mid-red with a white base, are medium sized, well formed and open slowly to full blooms that retain their color well. They have a pleasant perfume, and a good repeat cycle. 'Ethel Dawson' is a vigorous plant with deep green foliage. **ZONES 6–9.**

Dawson, Australia, pre-1978

Parentage unknown

'Ethel Dawson'

'ETNA'
OLD, MOSS, DARK RED

Its fiery color no doubt suggested the name of this variety to Laffay. The mossy, dark purple buds are followed by brilliant carmine, very full, fragrant blossoms. The thick petals create large flounces of color supported by rough, serrated leaves. The mossy leaves enclose perfectly formed red buds; when open, the blossoms are composed of tightly packed petals. **ZONES 4–9.**

Laffay, France, 1845

Parentage unknown

'ÉTOILE DE HOLLANDE'
MODERN, LARGE-FLOWERED/HYBRID TEA, MEDIUM RED, REPEAT-FLOWERING

'Étoile de Hollande' has been a popular rose for nearly 80 years, and is still widely grown. The flowers are bright red and fairly double, with 30–35 petals that are cupped at first and later open to large, full blooms. There is a very strong, true Damask fragrance. The foliage is rather soft, mid-green and not over-abundant on a moderately growing open plant. Many new red roses have been introduced with a fanfare of trumpets and then disappeared from commerce, but this one is still seen in most large rose collections; its color, velvety texture and perfume are its great attributes. **'Climbing Étoile de Hollande'** (1931; Royal Horticultural Society Award of Garden Merit, 1993) is a vigorous climbing sport that is excellent for pillars, tripods or arbors or for growing against the walls of houses where its perfume can be appreciated. **ZONES 4–9.**

Verschuren, The Netherlands, 1919

'General MacArthur' × 'Hadley'

'ÉTOILE DE LYON'
OLD, TEA, MEDIUM YELLOW, REPEAT-FLOWERING

No rose works harder throughout the year than this one, which produces blooms from early spring through to

winter. It has a strong Tea fragrance and is very healthy. Although the outer petals sometimes look poor, when the rose opens the saffron yellow petals cover any flaws. The globular, full, open blossoms are quite heavy, and they may droop on the thin canes. At first glance the buds indicate a Large-flowered Rose because of their long, pointed shape. Easy to establish, especially on its own roots, the vigorous bush will grow in shade or sun, hot or cold weather with equal force. One of the many roses named after the famous French center of rose breeding in the past century, it is quite resistant to all diseases and requires little care. **ZONES 6–9.**

Guillot, France, 1881

Seedling of 'Madame Charles'

'ÉTUDE'
MODERN, LARGE-FLOWERED CLIMBER, DEEP PINK, REPEAT-FLOWERING

'Étude', a good small climbing rose for a pillar or tripod, has dark green, very abundant foliage that is disease free. The flowers are deep rose pink, semi-double and open in all weathers; they come both singly and in clusters, have a very strong fragrance and bloom continuously. This variety is a thoroughly reliable rose and, although its blooms are not spectacular,

'Étoile de Lyon'

'Étoile de Hollande'

they appear in such abundance that a spectacular effect is obtained. If the spent blooms are not removed a large crop of big round hips will be produced, looking attractive among the later flowers. **ZONES 4–9.**

Gregory, UK, 1965

'Spectacular' × 'New Dawn'

National Rose Society Certificate of Merit 1964

'EUGENE DE BEAUHARNAIS'

syn. 'Prince Eugène'
OLD, CHINA, MAUVE, REPEAT-FLOWERING

'It nods like Zeus with grace and imposing majesty'—thus rose author Brent Dickerson quotes from an early commentator on this rose. The cupped, full, double blooms open on a small, bushy, upright plant. Depending on its placement in the garden, in sun or shade, the dark, rich crimson to red petals are slightly reflexed at the edge. Quite floriferous, the shrub is heavily covered with prickles; the small gray-green leaves are purple at the edges. It blooms from summer through to autumn, its only

flaw being its tendency to mildew. Prince Eugene (1781–1824) was the brother of Empress Josephine, creator of Malmaison. **ZONES 4–9.**

Hardy, France, 1838

Parentage unknown

'EUGÈNE FURST'

syn. 'General Korolkow'
OLD, HYBRID PERPETUAL, DEEP RED, REPEAT-FLOWERING

Grown around the world for its glowing color and healthy habit, this upright, tall, vigorous shrub produces flowers from spring until autumn, the autumn flush often being better than the spring flowering. The fragrant crimson-purple blooms are full, globular and large and, when viewed from the side, they appear to be goblets. The 5 ft (1.5 m) bush has handsome leaves that are subject to mildew. This rose is a parent of 'Reveil Dijonnais' and 'Baron Girod de l'Ain'. **ZONES 4–9.**

Soupert and Notting, France, 1875

'Baron de Bonstetten' × seedling

'Euphrosyne'

'Eugène Fürst'

'Europa'

'EUGÈNE VERDIER'

OLD, MOSS, DEEP PINK

'Eugène Verdier' should not be confused with the Large-flowered Rose of the same name (Guillot, 1863). Verdier's version needs the best growing conditions to show off its sterling qualities. The crimson to light red, well-formed blooms are double with a deeper red at the center; when fully open, the center is rather muddled. The buds are well mossed, and the outer petals are reflexed. A vigorous, bushy plant, it needs to be pruned moderately for the best effect and is a rose that responds quickly to fertilizer and a rich soil. The fragrant blooms make excellent cut flowers. **ZONES 4–9.**

Verdier, France, 1872

Parentage unknown

'EUGÉNIE GUINOISEAU'

syn. 'Eugénie de Guinoisseau'
OLD, MOSS, MEDIUM RED

Although a Moss Rose usually stays close to the ground, this one can be used as a climber. Reaching over 6 ft (2 m) at maturity, the vigorous, upright plant needs support. The cherry red to violet-purple blooms are full, large and flat and are marked with small white streaks. The mossy buds are fat, and the petals change from dark to light if planted in the sun. The bristly stems are covered with attractive leaves, and are serrated and dark. Long, narrow hips add charm in autumn, the end of its blooming period. **ZONES 4–9.**

Guinoisseau, France, 1864

Parentage unknown

'EUPHORIA'   INTereup

MODERN, GROUND COVER, YELLOW BLEND, REPEAT-FLOWERING

The blooms open from pointed buds into wide saucer-shaped, medium-sized, single blooms. They are freely borne in clusters, with each yellow petal gener-

'Euphrates'

'Europeana'

'Eurorose'

ously rimmed orange-red, fading through orange-salmon to salmon-pink as the blooms age. The effect is bright and pleasing, and there is a light fragrance. Flowering is maintained through summer and autumn on vigorous plants of low habit, which spread out about 5 times wider than their height. The mid-green foliage is shiny and plentiful. It makes a delightful addition to the front of a border, as well as for general ground cover uses. The precise details of the parentage are not disclosed, but it is known to have *Rosa persica* ancestry. **ZONES 4–9.**

Ilsink, The Netherlands, 1996

Parentage unknown

British Association of Rose Breeders, Breeders' Choice 1998

'EUPHRATES'   HARunique

MODERN, MODERN SHRUB, PINK BLEND

This unique little rose has single, slightly fragrant pale salmon-pink flowers with a deep pink eye that last well in water and always create a talking point. They have 5 petals and appear in clusters along the branches of the previous season's growth, flowering only in spring. When in bloom the plant looks more like a flowering *Cistus* than it does a rose. 'Euphrates', which is not very strong growing and performs best in hot, dry climates and lighter soils, has small, long, narrow pale green foliage. **ZONES 4–9.**

Harkness, UK, 1986

Rosa persica × seedling

'EUPHROSYNE'

syn. 'Pink Rambler'
MODERN, RAMBLER, MEDIUM PINK

This variety likes a shady spot best. Its bright carmine buds appear in clusters and open to pure dark pink, full, small blooms. The flat flowers change from a rich pink to pink to pale pink. The Tea fragrance is strong. A vigorous climber,

'Eurostar'

it looks best on an arch or a pillar and has pale green foliage that covers the pliable canes, which should be pruned lightly. It requires at least 3 years to establish itself, and was favored by Gertrude Jekyll in her garden designs. Euphrosyne is one of the 3 Graces of Greek mythology; 'Aglaia' and 'Thalia', the other 2, are also offered as ramblers by Schmitt, and all are still grown today. ZONES 4–9.

Schmitt, France, 1895

Rosa multiflora × 'Mignonette'

'EUROPA'   KORtexung
syn. 'Fleurop'

MODERN, LARGE-FLOWERED/HYBRID TEA, MEDIUM PINK, REPEAT-FLOWERING

'Europa' is a medium-growing, fairly disease-free rose that produces smallish, very well-formed rose pink flowers both singly and in clusters over an extremely long period. The buds are of a good shape and open slowly to very double blooms with good lasting qualities but little perfume. A tendency to mildew is probably the reason that this greenhouse rose has lost favor; it is quite a good garden variety that is spoilt by the fact that the full blooms tend to fade very quickly. ZONES 5–9.

Kordes, Germany, 1976

Parentage unknown

'EUROPEANA'
MODERN, CLUSTER-FLOWERED/FLORIBUNDA, DARK RED, REPEAT-FLOWERING

For many years 'Europeana' has set the standard for judging red Cluster-flowered Roses. The flowers are dark crimson, double with a rosette shape, large to 3 in (8 cm) across and come in big clusters of up to 30 blooms. They have some fragrance, flower production is excellent and the well-spaced heads are lovely for exhibition purposes. The plant is vigorous and has large, plentiful, bronze-green foliage after maturing from plum purple new growth. There can be some mildew at times and the very heavy, large trusses are inclined to blow over in windy weather. 'Europeana' well deserved its awards and is still popular today after more than 30 years in commerce. ZONES 4–9.

deRuiter, The Netherlands, 1963

'Ruth Leuwerik' × 'Rosemary Rose'

The Hague Gold Medal 1962, All-America Rose Selection 1968, Portland Gold Medal 1970

'EUROROSE'
MODERN, CLUSTER-FLOWERED/FLORIBUNDA, YELLOW BLEND, REPEAT-FLOWERING

The unusual flowers of this variety are yellow brown flushed with red, giving an overall golden brown effect. The blooms are double with 25 petals, shapely in the bud and, like the parent 'Redgold', open fairly quickly to be nicely shaped and full. They repeat-flower very quickly. Growth is short to moderate and the foliage is healthy, but there can be occasional mildew problems. This is a good bedding rose whose interesting color makes it useful for picking, especially for autumnal arrangements. ZONES 4–9.

Dickson, UK, 1973

'Zorina' × 'Redgold'

'EUROSTAR'   POUlreb
MODERN, CLUSTER-FLOWERED/FLORIBUNDA, MEDIUM YELLOW, REPEAT-FLOWERING

'Eurostar' produces large, golden yellow flowers both singly and in clusters on an upright plant with dark green, glossy foliage. There is a deeper color in the center of the blooms, which are many petalled and open to globular, cupped, old-fashioned type flowers. They are fragrant, look attractive both close up and at a distance and last well. Disease resistance is good and the repeat-bloom is quick. It is an excellent bedding rose and is also good for borders. ZONES 4–9.

Olesen, Denmark, 1994

Parentage unknown

'Eutin'

'Evangeline'

'EVANGELINE'
MODERN, RAMBLER, PINK BLEND

Evangeline, the long narrative poem by American poet Henry Wadsworth Longfellow, was a very popular work in the nineteenth century. This variety has rose-white single blooms that are veined pink. They appear as clusters on long stems, much like pyramids of apple blossoms. The large yellow anthers highlight the 2 in (5 cm) blooms, which are sweetly scented. It is a vigorous rambler that will reach 15 ft (4.5 m) and has dark, leathery foliage. There are hooked prickles and plenty of attractive hips. It likes to climb trees, but if it is to be used on a pergola then intelligent, regular pruning is necessary. This rose does well in the shade. Walsh produced a series of successful ramblers from his home in Woods Hole, Massachusetts, between 1901 and 1920. ZONES 4–9.

Walsh, USA, 1906

Rosa wichuraiana × 'Crimson Rambler'

'EVELYN'   AUSsaucer
MODERN, MODERN SHRUB, APRICOT BLEND, REPEAT-FLOWERING

'Evelyn', which is also classified as an English Rose, gets its color from 'Tamora' and its vigor from 'Graham Thomas'. The huge, very full blooms with over 40 petals open from a very broad shallow cup to a rosette form at maturity and have a most delicious perfume. They are usually rich apricot with a yellow base but can be much more pink in hot weather, a color change inherited from 'Gloire de Dijon'. This variety is a strong, upright-growing, medium-sized shrub that flowers both continuously and profusely. The firm of Crabtree and Evelyn chose it to advertise their perfume company. ZONES 4–9.

Austin, UK, 1992

'Graham Thomas' × 'Tamora'

'Evelyn Fison'

'EVELYN FISON'   MACev
syn. 'Irish Wonder'
MODERN, CLUSTER-FLOWERED/FLORIBUNDA, MEDIUM RED, REPEAT-FLOWERING

'Evelyn Fison' is a compact, robust bush with plentiful glossy dark green disease-resistant foliage. The slightly fragrant blooms are large, to 3 in (8 cm) across, and are produced singly and in well-spaced clusters of up to 20. The buds are well shaped and open to long-lasting, semi-double flowers of excellent substance, the scarlet color of which does not fade in heat or cold. The growth is rather thorny, but this variety well deserved its gold medal and is still widely grown today in spite of stiff opposition from more modern varieties. ZONES 4–9.

McGredy, UK, 1962

'Moulin Rouge' × 'Korona'

National Rose Society Gold Medal 1963

'EVENING STAR'   JACven
MODERN, CLUSTER-FLOWERED/FLORIBUNDA, WHITE, REPEAT-FLOWERING

This nice little rose bred from the lovely cream-tipped 'Saratoga' has white blooms with pale yellow at the base of the petals. They are double with a beautiful form, large and high centered. The foliage is plentiful, dark green and leathery on an upright, vigorous bush with very good repeat-bloom. There are no disease problems and the flowers have a slight fragrance. ZONES 6–9.

Warriner, USA, 1974

'White Masterpiece' × 'Saratoga'

Belfast Gold Medal and Fragrance Prize 1977, Portland Gold Medal 1977

'EVENSONG'
MODERN, LARGE-FLOWERED/HYBRID TEA, ORANGE-PINK, REPEAT-FLOWERING

The pretty flowers of 'Evensong', which are a blend of rose and salmon-pink, are double with 25 petals and open fairly

'Everest Double Fragrance'

'Eva'

'Evelyn'

'EUTIN'
syn. 'Hoosier Glory'
MODERN, CLUSTER-FLOWERED/FLORIBUNDA, DARK RED, REPEAT-FLOWERING

'Eutin' is an early Cluster-flowered Rose well known for its enormous heads of lightly perfumed, small, dark carmine-red double flowers. The buds are globular and pointed, and the trusses can have 50 or more blooms in the spring flush. The growth is vigorous and is covered by glossy, dark, abundant, leathery, disease-resistant foliage. The repeat-bloom is good. This variety makes an ideal hedge, is excellent for bedding and can also be used in the perennial border. It gets its huge flower clusters from its parent 'Eva'. ZONES 4–9.

Kordes, Germany, 1940

'Eva' × 'Solarium'

'EVA'
MODERN, MODERN SHRUB, RED BLEND, REPEAT-FLOWERING

This great shrub rose, which is used extensively in landscape planting, bears huge panicles of 75 or more flowers. They are semi-double and carmine-red in color with a white center that lights up the flower. Flowering is continuous if spent blooms are removed, but if they are left on the bush a wonderful crop of unusually colored pinkish red hips are produced in large clusters; these are ideal for flower arranging. 'Eva' has large, lush, disease-free foliage on a vigorous bush. It is excellent for use among flowering shrubs or as a background to perennials and bulbs. ZONES 4–9.

Kordes, Germany, 1933

'Robin Hood' × 'J. C. Thornton'

'Evensong'

'Excellenz von Schubert'

'Excelsa'

quickly to large, 5 in (13 cm) flowers of good substance. Flower production is fair, with rather long periods between flushes. The bush is moderately vigorous and the disease-free foliage is dark green. ZONES 4–9.

Arnot, UK, 1963

'Ena Harkness' × 'Sutter's Gold'

National Rose Society Certificate of Merit 1963

'EVEREST'
OLD, HYBRID PERPETUAL, WHITE

The cream-white blossoms of this variety have a green-lemon center. The immense, fragrant, double flowers with 25 petals are arranged in clusters on a low, spreading bush. Used as a hedge, the 3 ft (1 m) rose does well in poor soil but it is full of blooms during its summer season. Obviously named for the highest mountain in the world, the blooms do not like wet weather. Walter Easlea and Sons of Essex, England, produced a long list of successful roses, among them the excellent 'Easlea's Golden Rambler'. ZONES 5–9.

Easlea, UK, 1927

'Candeur Lyonnaise' × 'Mme Caristie Martel'

National Rose Society Gold Medal 1927

'EVEREST DOUBLE FRAGRANCE'
MODERN, CLUSTER-FLOWERED/FLORIBUNDA, LIGHT PINK, REPEAT-FLOWERING

This rose has heavily veined foliage that is dark green and nicely shows up the very pale pink flowers, which are borne in clusters of 3–7 blooms. The buds are long and pointed, and the full blooms have good substance and attractive stamens. They are extremely fragrant. This is a good rose for bedding purposes and as a hedge or border. It is particularly disease free and flowers continuously. ZONES 4–9.

Beales, UK, 1980

'Dearest' × 'Elizabeth of Glamis'

'Exploit'

'EXCELLENZ VON SCHUBERT'
MODERN, POLYANTHA, DEEP PINK, REPEAT-FLOWERING

'Excellenz von Schubert' has carmine-rose flowers that are shaded lilac and come in enormous clusters on long, arching canes. They are double and are set amid dark green foliage on a vigorous bush. Small round hips are produced in large clusters if spent blooms are not removed, the hips looking most attractive among the huge sprays of flowers that are produced in autumn. This rose is late to come into flower in spring, but flowering is continuous until early winter. It is ideal where a large shrub is required and can be used in groups or as a tall hedge. ZONES 4–9.

Lambert, Germany, 1909

'Mme Norbert Levavasseur' × 'Frau Karl Druschki'

'EXCELSA'
syn. 'Red Dorothy Perkins'
MODERN, RAMBLER, MEDIUM RED

'Excelsa' has bright red, double, cupped blooms with a white center that appear in irregular, large clusters. Often these clusters are pendent. The color is variable depending on placement in sun or shade. Pliable stems make it possible to train the plant on pergolas, and when this Rambler is seen tumbling down a wall or structure it is easy to see why it earned its gold medal. The vigorous, climbing canes are covered with prickles. Often found in old cemeteries, where it has naturalized, it is used in Europe as a weeping standard. If pruned severely, this rose makes an effective hedge. To prevent mildew, ensure good air circulation. An improved form of the rose, 'Super Excelsa', is also popular. ZONES 6–9.

Walsh, USA, 1909

American Rose Society Gold Medal 1914

'EXCITING'
syns 'Queen of Bermuda', 'Roter Stern'
MODERN, LARGE-FLOWERED/HYBRID TEA, MEDIUM RED, REPEAT-FLOWERING

This is a popular rose for the cut-flower trade mainly because of its strikingly narrow and pointed red buds that are borne on long sturdy stems. They open to medium-sized, semi-double flowers of a dullish red. These have no scent, but they last well. 'Exciting' is a tall, vigorous and healthy shrub that is covered with flowers for most of the year. ZONES 4–10.

Meilland, France, 1958

'Happiness' × 'Independence'

'EXPLOIT'   MEIlider
syns 'All In One', 'Grimpant Exploit'
MODERN, LARGE-FLOWERED CLIMBER, DEEP PINK/ MEDIUM RED

'Exploit' is an eye-catching rose in spring when its deep pink to red double flowers with 20 petals completely cover the vigorous growth. Flowering is sparse after the spring flush. The small, mid-green foliage is disease free on a plant that is good for pillars and fences. ZONES 4–9.

Meilland, France, 1985

'Fugue' × 'Sparkling Scarlet'

'EXPLORER'S DREAM'
MICdream, MICexplore
MODERN, MINIATURE, ORANGE-PINK, REPEAT-FLOWERING

This rose bears clusters of small pompon-style blooms made up of about 25 petals. They are deep orange-pink, with a hint of yellow at the petal base, and pale to salmon-pink as they age. It is suitable for a small space in the garden or to grow in containers. It has an upright habit and semi-glossy, dark green leaves. ZONES 4–9.

Williams, USA, 1992

Miniature seedling × 'Homecoming'

'EYECATCHER'
MODERN, CLUSTER-FLOWERED/FLORIBUNDA, PINK BLEND

The flowers of 'Eyecatcher' are pink flushed apricot with a silvery pink reverse. They are double, medium sized and fragrant. The foliage is pale and glossy and tones in well with the flowers, while the growth is shortish. ZONES 4–9.

Cant, UK, 1976

'Arthur Bell' × 'Pernille Poulsen'

'EYEOPENER'   INTerop
syns 'Erica', 'Eye Opener', 'Tapis Rouge'
MODERN, MODERN SHRUB, MEDIUM RED, REPEAT-FLOWERING

As both parents have a distinctive white eye to each flower, it is no surprise that the single, vivid red flowers of 'Eyeopener' have a white eye and gold stamens. They come in large and small clusters on a big, arching plant, broader than it is tall. Late in the season, large shoots bear hundreds of blooms on long stems with many lateral shoots also bearing blooms. The foliage is small, dark and plentiful. Disease resistance is good except for black spot in moist climates. ZONES 4–9.

Ilsink, The Netherlands, 1987

(Seedling × 'Eyepaint') × (seedling × 'Dortmund')

Royal National Rose Society Certificate of Merit 1986, Belfast Prize 1989

'EYEPAINT'   MACeye
syns 'Eye Paint', 'Tapis Persan'
MODERN, CLUSTER-FLOWERED/FLORIBUNDA, RED BLEND, REPEAT-FLOWERING

'Eyepaint' can be classed as hand painted since the bright red, single flowers with 5–6 petals and a white eye and golden stamens have streaks of white through them. The medium-sized flowers come in large and small clusters. Strong in growth and having disease-free, plentiful glossy foliage, can be used in groups plantings and even as a short pillar rose. ZONES 4–9.

McGredy, New Zealand, 1975

Seedling × 'Picasso'

Royal National Rose Society Trial Ground Certificate 1973, Baden-Baden Gold Medal 1974, Belfast Gold Medal 1978

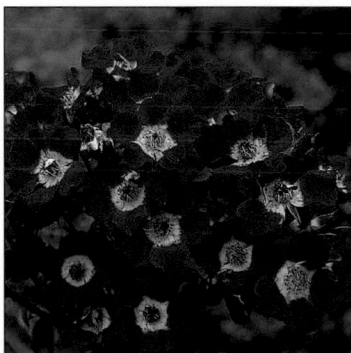

'Eyepaint'

'Eyecatcher'

'Eyeopener'

F

F

'F. J. Grootendorst'

'Fair Bianca'

'Fair Dinkum'

'F. J. GROOTENDORST'

syns 'Grootendorst', 'Grootendorst Red', 'Nelkenrose'

MODERN, HYBRID RUGOSA, MEDIUM RED, REPEAT-FLOWERING

This is a good thorny shrub with largish wrinkled leaves and a tall spreading habit. The small, bright crimson flowers, which have serrated edges like a carnation, are very double and come in clusters of up to 20 in a head, and have a slight fragrance. Flowering is continuous and no hips are produced. This rose, together with 'Pink Grootendoorst' and 'Grootendoorst Supreme', are sometimes known as the carnation roses; all make impenetrable hedges that are quite good for security purposes. ZONES 3–9.

de Goey, Germany, 1918

Rosa rugosa rubra × possibly 'Mme Norbert Levavasseur'

'FABVIER'

syn. 'Général Fabvier'
OLD, CHINA, MEDIUM RED, REPEAT-FLOWERING

The crimson-scarlet, semi-double flowers of this rose are borne singly or in clusters. They are open, of medium size and have heart-shaped petals with white streaks and a white center. Prominent yellow stamens add extra charm to this fragrant, repeat-blooming old favorite, which makes an excellent cut flower. The new foliage is tinted bronze. Strong stems on

a 4 ft (1.2 m), twiggy bush support the flowers, and prickles crowd the old canes. The plant is not bothered by rain. Fabvier was a distinguished French general. ZONES 4–9.

Laffay, France, 1832

Parentage unknown

'FAIR BIANCA'   AUSca

MODERN, MODERN SHRUB, WHITE, REPEAT-FLOWERING

'Fair Bianca', the first of David Austin's white roses, is also classified as an English Rose. It has lovely, medium-sized flowers that are flat and quartered, forming full rosettes. They appear in clusters, are very double with 60 or more petals and have a variable color, being quite pink in the center of the bloom in hot weather and buff in autumn. There is a strong myrrh fragrance and flowering is continuous. An average-sized upright plant, it looks charming with perennial plants and bulbs in borders. Clumps of 3, 5 or 7 plants look far more pleasing than single specimens. ZONES 4–9.

Austin, UK, 1982

Descended from 'Belle Isis'

'FAIR DINKUM'   TINdink

MODERN, MINIATURE, PINK BLEND, REPEAT-FLOWERING

The flowers of 'Fair Dinkum' are soft pink with an attractive darker petal

'Fairy Dancers'

margin, a white reverse and creamy centers. Although it is a Miniature, the blooms have exquisite Large-flowered form. The slightly fragrant flowers are framed with attractive, small, semi-glossy, dark green foliage and the bush is upright. This rose makes an ideal addition to the garden as it is quick to repeat, is disease resistant and has very few thorns. Dee Bennett often chose names to reflect her ancestry, coming as she does from Australia. ZONES 4–11.

Bennett, USA, 1983

Seedling × 'Coral Treasure'

'FAIR PLAY'   INTerfair

MODERN, MODERN SHRUB, MAUVE, REPEAT-FLOWERING

'Fair Play' has some of the color of the Harkness shrub rose 'Yesterday' but is much more prostrate in growth. The flowers are mauve, semi-double with 18 petals and come in large clusters. They have some fragrance. The foliage is smallish and dark green on a plant that blooms from summer through to autumn. It can be grown as a tall-growing ground cover and will cover quite a lot of space. ZONES 4–9.

Ilsink, The Netherlands, 1977

'Yesterday' × seedling

'FAIRHOPE'   TALfairhope

MODERN, MINIATURE, LIGHT YELLOW, REPEAT-FLOWERING

Pointed buds on this variety open to reveal flowers that are a soft, light pastel yellow. With only 16–28 petals the florets are of exceptional quality both in substance and form. The high-centered, exhibition-type blooms are borne naturally one to a stem but on occasions can occur as small clusters. They have a very

'Fairlane'

light fragrance. The long, straight stems of this rose are worthy of mention, as they are covered with dark green foliage that support the florets. American rose growers from coast to coast gave this rose an unprecedented score of 10 points out of 10! The plant is winter tender and was named by the Taylors after a small town in rural Alabama. ZONES 5–11.

Taylor, USA, 1989

'Azure Sea' × seedling

'FAIRLANE'

MODERN, MINIATURE, LIGHT YELLOW, REPEAT-FLOWERING

'Fairlane' has urn-shaped blooms with 20 petals that are near white, flushed with pink and yellow. The florets are borne one bloom per stem; in cooler climates they are borne in small sprays. A light fragrance is evident in warm climates. The foliage is glossy medium green and deeply serrated, with prickles slanted downward and the plant has a compact, dense, bushy habit. Vigor is not a quality of this rose, but the exquisite form and color can make one forget how few and far between the blooms are. The flowers are often said to resemble fine porcelain or a delicate jewel. The plant is quite tender and prone to black spot in damp humid climates. ZONES 5–11.

Schwartz, USA, 1980

'Charlie McCarthy' × seedling

'FAIRY CHANGELING'   HARnumerous

MODERN, POLYANTHA, MEDIUM PINK, REPEAT-FLOWERING

Jack Harkness used 'The Fairy' to produce a number of small, dense-growing Polyantha Roses, for example 'Fairy Crystal', 'Fairy Damsel', 'Fairy Maid', 'Fairy Like', 'Fairyland' and 'Fairy Snow'. All are excellent disease-free bushes with small, dense foliage and little trusses of pompon-shaped flowers. 'Fairy Changeling' has buds that open to double, magenta-rose flowers of 22 petals that are cupped in shape like older Polyantha Roses. The plant grows wider than it is tall, to about knee height. ZONES 4–9.

Harkness, UK, 1981

'The Fairy' × 'Yesterday'

Tokyo Certificate of Merit 1981

'FAIRY DAMSEL'   HARneatly

MODERN, POLYANTHA, DARK RED, REPEAT-FLOWERING

From the same crossing as 'Fairy Changeling', this variety has double,

'Fairy Changeling'

'Fairy Moss'

'Fairy Tale'

variety can be used for a border to taller varieties where white flowers are required. Disease resistance is good and repeat bloom excellent, the flowers lasting a long time on the bush. ZONES 4–9.

Harkness, UK, 1979

'The Fairy' × 'Yesterday'

'FAIRY TALE'
MODERN, MINIATURE, LIGHT PINK, REPEAT-FLOWERING

This rose has ovoid buds that open to reveal small, decorative flowers that fade to a delicate light pink. The double-style florets are slightly fragrant. The foliage is dark, glossy green and the plant has a vigorous, upright growth habit. This rose, one of the few varieties developed from 'The Fairy', is unfortunately no longer in commerce. ZONES 5–11.

Thompson, USA, 1960

'The Fairy' × 'Goldilocks'

'FAIRYLAND'   HARlayalong
MODERN, POLYANTHA, LIGHT PINK, REPEAT-FLOWERING

'Fairyland' is probably the best known of the little Polyantha Roses and is the one most like 'The Fairy' in color and growth habit, which is shrub-like and spreading,

growing wider than it does tall with many slender stems. It is, however, not so vigorous. Fat little buds open to light pink flowers that are double, with 24 petals, and cupped. The fragrance is strong and the repeat-flowering good. It has disease-free, glossy foliage. ZONES 4–9.

Harkness, UK, 1980

'The Fairy' × 'Yesterday'

Royal National Rose Society Trial Ground Certificate 1978, Baden-Baden Silver Medal 1980, New Zealand Silver Medal 1982

'FALKLAND'
OLD, SCOTS, WHITE

Scots Roses, as these species hybrids are known, are tough plants. This one has pale pink petals fading to white. The double, fragrant blooms gather in clusters on low canes. The late spring flush lasts for several weeks. The 3 ft by 3 ft (1 m by 1 m) prickly shrub has upright stems and small gray leaves. In autumn a good crop of maroon hips adds interest to this rose, which is excellent for a hedge or container. Extremely healthy and suckering readily, it was possibly named for Viscount Lucius Falkland (1610–43), an English statesman. ZONES 4–9.

Hybrid of *Rosa spinosissima*

dark red flowers composed of 24 petals on a low, spreading bush. The foliage is plentiful and disease free and flowering is continuous. This rose is suitable for use as a low hedge or as an edging to taller-growing varieties. ZONES 4–9.

Harkness, UK, 1981

'The Fairy' × 'Yesterday'

Munich IGA Silver Medal 1983

'FAIRY DANCERS'
MODERN, LARGE-FLOWERED/HYBRID TEA, APRICOT BLEND, REPEAT-FLOWERING

Although classed as a Large-flowered Rose, 'Fairy Dancers' could just as easily be a Cluster-flowered Rose in spite of having two tall-growing Large-flowered Roses as parents. It is a low, spreading bush with quite large thorns, rather sparse foliage and medium-sized flowers produced singly and in small clusters. The fragrant blooms are a beautiful buff apricot and of excellent form, opening slowly to a nicely formed full shape. Repeat bloom is a little slow, but disease resistance is fair. This is a good rose for cutting, the soft color showing up very well under artificial light. ZONES 5–9.

Cocker & Sons, UK, 1969

'Wendy Cussons' × 'Diamond Jubilee'

'FAIRY MOSS'
MODERN, MINIATURE, MEDIUM PINK, REPEAT-FLOWERING

The buds of 'Fairy Moss' have a moss character. The flowers are medium pink and semi-double and there is attractive, small, light green foliage on a vigorous dwarf bush. There is really no transition

between the buds and the blooms—they open very quickly. It is a fascinating little rose and certainly a conversation piece because of its historical and evolutionary place in Miniature Rose hybridizing. The rose is Ralph Moore's crowning achievement—a repeat-blooming Moss Miniature Rose. The moss character is sometimes difficult to detect, but the offspring of 'Fairy Moss' certainly are Moss Miniatures. ZONES 4–11.

Moore, USA, 1969

('Pinocchio' × 'William Lobb') × 'New Penny'

'FAIRY PRINCE'   HARnougette
MODERN, POLYANTHA, MEDIUM RED, REPEAT-FLOWERING

This variety, another Harkness rose from the same cross as 'Fairy Changeling' and 'Fairy Damsel', has geranium red, double blooms composed of 25 petals and cupped in shape. They come in small clusters and cover the bush. The plant spreads low and wide enough to be considered a ground cover rose, and flowering is continuous. ZONES 4–9.

Harkness, UK, 1981

'The Fairy' × 'Yesterday'

Copenhagen First Prize 1980

'FAIRY PRINCESS'
syn. 'Lilibet'
MODERN, CLUSTER-FLOWERED/FLORIBUNDA, LIGHT PINK, REPEAT-FLOWERING

This well-named variety is a short, stocky grower that bears small to medium sprays of elegant, well-shaped buds. They open to semi-double flowers of porcelain rose with 25 petals. The foliage is glossy and disease free and the repeat-bloom is fairly quick. 'Fairy Princess' is a charming rose for borders or bedding, and the color shows up well under artificial light when used for inside decoration. ZONES 4–9.

Lindquist, USA, 1953

'Floradora' × 'Pinocchio'

All-America Rose Selection 1954

'FAIRY SNOW'   HARlittle
MODERN, POLYANTHA, WHITE, REPEAT-FLOWERING

'Fairy Snow' is a small, neat grower with cupped little flowers of 20–25 petals that open flat. A low, spreading bush, this

'Fairyland'

'Falkland'

'Fairy Princess'

F

'FANCY PRINCESS'
syn. 'Otohime'

MODERN, LARGE-FLOWERED/HYBRID TEA,
DEEP PINK, REPEAT-FLOWERING

'Fancy Princess' is a good grower with
dark green glossy foliage on a medium-
sized bush that bears a continuous
supply of well-formed, deep pink flowers.
The buds open to full blooms that hold
their color well, and the plant has quite
reasonable disease resistance. ZONES 5–9.

Keisei, Japan, 1977

Parentage unknown

'FANDANGO'
MODERN, LARGE-FLOWERED/HYBRID TEA,
ORANGE-RED, REPEAT-FLOWERING

The chief virtue of 'Fandango' is its
color, which is a brilliant flame orange-
red with coral tones. The lovely color
fades quickly in hot climates, so it is a
better rose under cooler conditions. It
has pretty buds that open very quickly
in warm climates to loose, fragrant
flowers of 20 petals. The foliage is glossy,
leathery and plentiful on a bush that is
vigorous and upright in growth habit.
There is some repeat bloom after a prolific spring flowering. ZONES 4–9.

Swim, USA, 1950

'Charlotte Armstrong' × seedling

National Rose Society Trial Ground Certificate
1952

'Fantasia' (Kordes)

'Fancy Princess'

'FANNY BIAS'
syns 'Duchesse de Reggio', 'Fanny Parissot'
OLD, GALLICA, MEDIUM PINK

Suzanne Verrier states that this rose was
confused with 'Gloire de France' because
of their similarities; but Professor Joyaux
considers them distinct. The fragrant,
blush-to-flesh blooms have a rosy center.
The 3 in (8 cm) blooms are double, and
the petals have a tissue-like appearance.
ZONES 4–9.

Descemet, France, pre-1811

Parentage unknown

'FANTASIA'   KORfan
syn. 'Fantázia'

MODERN, LARGE-FLOWERED/HYBRID TEA,
PINK BLEND, REPEAT-FLOWERING

Described as either a Cluster-flowered or
Large-flowered Rose, this variety could
probably be classed as a cross between
the two. It bears pretty lilac-red to lilac-
pink, double flowers with much paler
centers that develop from oval buds into
globular blooms; they become urn-
shaped as they age and the petals curve
back. There is a good fragrance in the
warmer months when the flowers appear.
'Fantasia' is a fast-growing bush rose
with leathery, glossy green foliage.
ZONES 5–9.

Kordes, Germany, 1974

'Silver Star' × 'Tradition'

'Fantasia' (Dickson)

'Fascination'

'FANTASIA'
MODERN, LARGE-FLOWERED/HYBRID TEA,
MEDIUM YELLOW, REPEAT-FLOWERING

'Fantasia' and 'Eclipse' were the two
great garden roses of the 1940s, both
having long, pointed buds of great refinement. The bright yellow buds of
'Fantasia' open to double, clear bright
yellow flowers of 30–35 petals. Of medium size, they open to reveal stamens
when in full bloom and are borne on
long stems. Flower production is good
and it is one of the most highly perfumed
of all yellow roses. This variety is stated
as extinct in *Modern Roses 10*, but this is
not so; it is still grown in quite a few
Australian gardens as a bedding rose. It
has pale to mid-green foliage. ZONES 4–9.

Dickson, UK, 1943

Seedling × 'Lord Lonsdale'

National Rose Society Certificate of Merit 1949

'FANTIN-LATOUR'
OLD, CENTIFOLIA, LIGHT PINK

The sumptuous powdery pink blooms of
this rose appear in mid-summer, and can
be 3 in (8 cm) across when fully open.
At first they are cupped; later the outer
petals reflex to expose a central button of
tightly packed smaller petals. The scent is
intoxicating and there are few prickles.
The shrub usually reaches about 4 ft

'Fandango'

'Fantin-Latour'

(1.2 m); if not pruned it can climb to
10 ft (3 m). Pruning after flowering increases the number of blooms for the
following year. It is not bothered by hot,
dry weather but doesn't get as big as it
does when cooler, and it is prone to some
mildew. Henri Fantin-Latour (1836–
1904) was a famous French painter renowned for still lifes and flowers, many
of them Old Garden Roses. ZONES 4–9.

Parentage unknown

Royal Horticultural Society Award of Garden
Merit 1993

'FASCINATION'   JACoyel
MODERN, LARGE-FLOWERED/HYBRID TEA,
ORANGE-PINK, REPEAT-FLOWERING

'Fascination' is a very full rose composed
of 60 petals that are a blend of orange
and rosy pink. The globular buds open
to large, high-centered flowers borne
singly on upright stems. There is very
little perfume. The large, semi-glossy foliage is huge and the prickles are large and
hooked. This rose won a gold medal in
New Zealand in 1976, its size, unusual
color and abundant foliage being its
chief attributes. ZONES 4–9.

Warriner , USA, 1982

Seedling × 'Spellbinder'

New Zealand Gold Medal 1976

'FASHION'
MODERN, CLUSTER-FLOWERED/FLORIBUNDA,
PINK BLEND, REPEAT-FLOWERING

With all of its awards it is clear that
'Fashion' was a unique Cluster-
flowered Rose; it was an entirely new

color bred by Eugene Boerner, recognized as one of the best breeders of that class of roses of all time. Its buds are a deep peachy coral color, opening to flowers of 23 petals that are a glowing coral-peach. The fragrance is very strong from the highly perfumed parent 'Crimson Glory'. The flowers come in clusters on a bushy plant, with foliage that is slightly prone to mildew and is very prone to rust. 'Fashion' was much used for bedding and for borders in the 1950s and 1960s and is still available for sale in most countries; there is a very free-flowering climbing form. The unique color and free-flowering capacity of this variety led to an upsurge in demand for Cluster-flowered Roses throughout the world. ZONES 4–9.

Boerner, USA, 1949

'Pinocchio' × 'Crimson Glory'

National Rose Society Gold Medal 1948, Bagatelle Gold Medal 1949, Portland Gold Medal 1949, All-America Rose Selection 1950, David Fuerstenberg Prize 1950, American Rose Society Gold Medal 1954

'FASHION FLAME'
MODERN, MINIATURE, ORANGE-PINK, REPEAT-FLOWERING

Coral-orange florets develop from the attractive, pointed, ovoid buds of this rose. The blooms contain about 35 petals and are high centered. In cooler climates, the bloom size can increase to the Patio size range, and many growers comment that this rose is 'too big for a miniature'. The brilliant color holds well in hot climates. A vigorous plant with a fast repeat bloom cycle, it tends to grow out rather than up. For some reason, this rose attracts mite and mildew—as an early warning system in the garden. The Queensland

'Felicia'

'Félicité Bohain'

'Faust'

Rose Society in Australia has listed it as one of their all-time favorites. ZONES 5–11.

Moore, USA, 1977

'Little Darling' × 'Fire Princess'

'FAUST'
syn. 'Dr Faust'
MODERN, CLUSTER-FLOWERED/FLORIBUNDA, YELLOW BLEND, REPEAT-FLOWERING

'Faust', the first of the bicolored roses bred from 'Masquerade', has double blooms with 25 petals that appear in large clusters like its parent. The flowers are at first golden yellow with coral-orange shading to the outer petals, then turn a rather dull coral-pink at maturity, staying on the bush rather too long. The influence of *Rosa chinensis mutabalis* can be seen in these roses which change color as they develop and darken as they age. The fragrant blooms are freely produced on a bush with dark glossy foliage that is inclined to mildew, especially on the calyx and leaf stalks. ZONES 4–9.

Kordes, Germany, 1957

'Masquerade' × 'Golden Scepter'

National Rose Society President's International Trophy 1956

'FEE'
MODERN, LARGE-FLOWERED/HYBRID TEA, LIGHT PINK, REPEAT-FLOWERING

'Fee' is an extremely tall and vigorous bush that is quick to repeat bloom. The buds are pointed and very shapely, and open slowly to large very well-formed flowers with 40–50 petals that are borne on long, slender stems. The buds are very good for picking, open slowly and last particularly well. The plant should be hard pruned in winter or it can become top heavy and suffer from wind damage; there can also be some mildew in autumn. ZONES 4–9.

Kordes, Germany, 1989

Sport of 'Sylvia'

'Félicité Parmentier'

'Fashion Flame'

'Fashion'

'Fashion'

'FELICIA'
MODERN, MODERN SHRUB, PINK BLEND, REPEAT-FLOWERING

'Felicia' has strongly fragrant flowers that are the delicate soft pink and cream color of 'Ophelia' fading to almost white. Flowering is most profuse in spring and rather sparse in summer, followed in autumn by huge panicles bearing the most highly colored and longest lasting flowers of the year. If spent blooms are not removed, large round hips are produced; these stay green a long time before slowly turning to red, and look most attractive among the autumn flowers. This strong-growing plant has disease-resistant, plentiful foliage and close-jointed stems. It is a good free-standing shrub if pruned lightly; if trimmed hard in winter, it produces a medium-sized spreading bush. ZONES 4–9.

Pemberton, UK, 1928

'Trier' × 'Ophelia'

National Rose Society Certificate of Merit 1927, Royal Horticultural Society Award of Garden Merit 1993

'FÉLICITÉ BOHAIN'
syn. 'Félicité Bohan'
OLD, MOSS, DEEP PINK

This rose has pink blooms that pale as they age. The crinkled petals often hide

the button eye. The small, full double flowers have a quartered arrangement, and the petals reflex as the roses age during their summer flush. The 4 ft (1.2 m) shrub has bright green, small leaves that are edged in moss when young. ZONES 4–9.

Pre-1866

Parentage unknown

'FÉLICITÉ PARMENTIER'
OLD, ALBA, LIGHT PINK

The fat buds of this rose have a trace of yellow before opening to reveal soft, flesh pink blossoms that are white at the edges, fading to almost white in hot climates. A magnificent cut flower, the petals appear to swirl in circles. After opening flat the double, sweetly scented blooms reflex during the late spring–early summer flowering. A compact, sturdy if slightly sprawling rose, it grows to 4 ft (1.2 m) with stout, moderately thorny stems and profuse light grayish green foliage. It is ideal for a small garden or to grow in containers, and is happiest in partial shade; it will do well in poor soil. The strong perfume and its disease resistance make it a great landscaping plant. ZONES 4–9.

Pre-1834

Parentage unknown

Royal Horticultural Society Award of Garden Merit 1993

F

'Femina'

'Felicity Kendal'

'Ferdinand Pichard'

'FÉLICITÉ-PERPÉTUE'

syn. 'Félicité et Perpétue'
OLD, HYBRID SEMPERVIRENS, WHITE

The breeder named this rose for his new-born twin daughters, their names commemorating Christians martyred together in 203. It is one of the most popular ramblers, because of its vigor and disease resistance. The flowers have a delicate primrose scent. The pale pink

'Félicité-Perpétue'

blooms, which quickly turn white during the summer flush, are very double and flat and are borne in clusters that cover the bright green canes. These are armed with slender red prickles. When used as a ground cover it will form pyramid mounds; it is happy in any weather and it resents pruning. It was found recently on Alcatraz, the prison island, climbing old walls without any assistance years after it was planted. **ZONES 4–9.**

Jacques, France, 1828

Rosa sempervirens × Noisette

Royal Horticultural Society Award of Garden Merit 1993

'FELICITY KENDAL'   LANken

MODERN, LARGE-FLOWERED/HYBRID TEA, ORANGE-PINK, REPEAT-FLOWERING

'Felicity Kendal', named after the star of the delightful English comedy *The Good Life*, has slightly fragrant, salmon-orange, double flowers with 35 petals that are large and of good form. The foliage is dark green and abundant but is slightly

prone to mildew on a medium height bush. Flower production is fair with rather lengthy gaps between flushes, but the flowers are long lasting and keep well when picked. **ZONES 4–9.**

Sealand Nurseries, UK, 1985

'Fragrant Cloud' × 'Mildred Reynolds'

'FELLENBERG'

syns 'Fellemberg', 'La Belle Marseillaise'
OLD, NOISETTE, MEDIUM RED, REPEAT-FLOWERING

In this variety, dramatic color changes occur during the long summer to autumn blooming period; the bright crimson may sometimes change to cerise. The double, cupped, fragrant flowers have 36 petals and appear as trusses on vigorous canes. There are usually 3–4 blooms in a corymb at the ends of new shoots. Easy to grow from cuttings, it has a spreading habit and can easily reach 7 ft (2.1 m) on a rich site. Small red prickles and dark foliage make it an ideal candidate to grow around a pillar. There is a lovely drawing of this rose by Alfred Parsons in *The Genus Rosa*, the famous book produced by Ellen Willmott in the Edwardian years. **ZONES 4–9.**

Fellemberg, France, 1835

Parentage unknown

'FEMINA'

MODERN, LARGE-FLOWERED/HYBRID TEA, ORANGE-PINK, REPEAT-FLOWERING

'Femina' is a strong-growing rose with good leathery, disease-free foliage. The buds are long and pointed and of nice form, turning to large, very well-formed flowers of clear salmon-pink with a yellow base. Flower production is

respectable and the blooms are good for picking. Disease resistance is excellent on a vigorous, upright plant that is a suitable subject for bedding. **ZONES 4–9.**

Gaujard, France, 1963

'Ferdinand Arles' × 'Mignonne'

'FERDINAND PICHARD'

OLD, HYBRID PERPETUAL, RED BLEND, REPEAT-FLOWERING

One of the last Hybrid Perpetuals put on the market, this striped, cupped rose has stayed on the bestseller list since its birth. The 25 scarlet, streaked, clear pink petals change to a blush purple as they age. The tight clusters are cupped and may reach 4 in (10 cm) across. It likes the sun, but very hot weather may crisp the blooms. It is a vigorous, tall, upright bush that is suitable for a small garden; however, if it is pegged down it will produce twice the amount of blooms. The foliage is smooth and light green. This rose makes an effective hedge as long as it is deadheaded and fed well. **ZONES 4–9.**

Tanne, France, 1921

Parentage unknown

Royal Horticultural Society Award of Garden Merit 1993

'FERDY'   KEltoli

syn. 'Ferdi'
MODERN, MODERN SHRUB, DEEP PINK

This variety was one of the first ground-cover roses of very spreading habit. The foliage, which is mid-green and is closely packed on very long arching stems, has excellent disease resistance. The blooms are produced on small laterals along the canes of the previous season's growth; because of this the plant should not be pruned in winter. The double flowers are deep pink in color, have 20 petals, are small in size and come in clusters, the effect in spring being that of a mass of bloom completely covering the bush. Unfortunately, the flowers fade to a dirty color and remain on the bush for too long and there is very little repeat bloom. 'Ferdy' is sufficiently cascading in growth to make a superb weeping rose when grafted onto a tall standard stock, where after a few years it will cascade down to ground level and provide a wonderful sight in spring. **ZONES 4–9.**

Suzuki, Japan, 1984

Climbing seedling × 'Petite Folie' seedling

'Ferdy'

'FERIA'

MODERN, LARGE-FLOWERED/HYBRID TEA,
ORANGE-PINK, REPEAT-FLOWERING

With three bicolored roses in its breeding it is not surprising that 'Feria' is a bicolor rose. It is strong coral with a pink reverse to the petals. The strongly fragrant flowers are double and rather globular in shape, opening to very well-formed blooms with 35 petals. The foliage is leathery, mid-green and prolific; flower production is excellent, and there are no disease problems. This variety is a good rose for cutting, the color looking especially effective under night light. ZONES 4–9.

Meilland, France, 1968

('Grand Gala' × 'Premier Bal') × 'Love Song'

'FERLINE'   LAPdarle

MODERN, LARGE-FLOWERED/HYBRID TEA,
MEDIUM RED, REPEAT-FLOWERING

This lovely red rose produces double flowers that develop from pointed buds in summer. They combine well with the mid-green foliage. 'Ferline' is a bush rose suitable for bedding schemes, and can be propagated by budding. ZONES 5–9.

Lapièrre, France, 1984

Parentage unknown

'FERRY PORSCHE'

MODERN, LARGE-FLOWERED/HYBRID TEA,
MEDIUM RED, REPEAT-FLOWERING

One of the best crimson-red roses for outdoor flower production, 'Ferry Porsche' produces very long stems on a tall and vigorous, upright bush. The buds are long and pointed and open slowly to double blooms with 30–35 petals. The slightly fragrant flowers are high centered and long lasting and appear one to a stem. This variety, which can suffer a little from mildew in autumn, is an excellent rose for cutting as the flowers last particularly well when picked. ZONES 4–9.

Kordes, Germany, 1971

'Tropicana' × 'Americana'

'FERVID'

MODERN, CLUSTER-FLOWERED/FLORIBUNDA,
ORANGE-RED, REPEAT-FLOWERING

'Fervid' is a strong-growing, upright, healthy Cluster-flowered Rose with very large, profuse dark green foliage. The flowers, which are almost single with 7 ruffled petals of an intense orange-scarlet color, are large—up to 3 in (8 cm) across—and come in very well-spaced clusters. The color stability is good and the flowers last well. When lightly pruned this variety can make a good shrub rose; it is also useful planted in groups as a hedge or for use in a border. 'Fervid' is one of only a few roses that would be worth trying in sandy soil. ZONES 4–9.

LeGrice, UK, 1960

'Pimpernell' × 'Korona'

National Rose Society Trial Ground Certificate 1961

'FESTIVAL'   KORdialo

MODERN, PATIO/DWARF CLUSTER-FLOWERED,
RED BLEND, REPEAT-FLOWERING

'Festival' produces large clusters of semi-double blooms of glowing crimson with a silvery white reverse that cover a disease-resistant compact bush with luxurious foliage—a hallmark of Kordes. The bloom cycle on this rose is fairly fast, producing a rich abundance of florets that start off a rich crimson-scarlet and then age with a gold and silver center. The plant is a low-growing bush in the tradition of Kordes. It is rounded, compact and dense and has great foliage. ZONES 4–11.

Kordes, Germany, 1993

'Regensberg' × seedling

Royal National Rose Society Trial Ground Certificate 1994, UK Rose of the Year 1994, RNRS Rose Day Award 1998

'FEU PERNET-DUCHER'

MODERN, LARGE-FLOWERED/HYBRID TEA,
MEDIUM YELLOW, REPEAT-FLOWERING

This variety is an important rose, because it is one of the parents of the ever popular 'Diamond Jubilee', which is a Large-flowered Rose that was named to commemorate Jackon & Perkins' sixtieth year of rose growing. The very large and double, open flowers of 'Feu Pernet-Ducher' are deep cream with buff or apricot centers, and have a rather fruity fragrance and an old-fashioned look. Like 'Diamond Jubilee', 'Feu Pernet-Ducher' is upright in habit, although it makes a taller bush. The flowering is profuse and the disease resistance is good. ZONES 4–9.

Mallerin, France, 1935

'Julien Potin' × 'Margaret McGredy'

Portland Gold Medal 1936

F

'Fervid'

'Ferry Porsche'

'Feria'

'Ferline'

'Feu Pernet-Ducher'

'FEUERWERK'

syns ' Feu d'Artifice', 'Fireworks', 'Magneet'
MODERN, MODERN SHRUB, ORANGE BLEND

This lovely shrub rose bears clusters of bright orange-red, medium-sized blooms. They are semi-double and open from pointed buds in summer to form flat flowers centered with a mass of golden yellow stamens. 'Feuerwerk' is upright and bushy in habit, covered with glossy green leaves. Some sources incorrectly describe this rose as extinct. ZONES 5–9.

Tantau, Germany, 1962

Parentage unknown

'Feuerwerk'

'Feverball'

'FEUERZAUBER'   KORfeu

syns 'Fire Magic', 'Magic de Feu'
MODERN, LARGE-FLOWERED/HYBRID TEA,
ORANGE-RED, REPEAT-FLOWERING

'Feuerzauber' has large, bright orange-red flowers with a lighter reverse to the petals. They are double, containing 30 petals, and are high centered and of good form. The buds open rather quickly to well-formed, long-lasting blooms that retain their color well. The foliage is dark, glossy and disease resistant, and flower production is continuous. Strangely enough, from a child of the highly scented 'Fragrant Cloud' there is not much scent; however, this variety with its vigorous upright growth habit is an excellent rose for bedding or for borders where a strong color is desired. ZONES 4–9.

Kordes, Germany, 1973

'Fragrant Cloud' × seedling

'FEVERBALL'

MODERN, LARGE-FLOWERED/HYBRID TEA,
MEDIUM RED, REPEAT-FLOWERING

Very little is known about this variety other than it being a Large-flowered bush rose that produces a fine display of bright red, fully double flowers in summer. The blooms are either borne singly or in small clusters of up to 3 amid the mid-green foliage. It can be propagated by budding. ZONES 5–9.

Parentage unknown

'Fidélio'

'FIDÉLIO'   MEIchest

MODERN, CLUSTER-FLOWERED/FLORIBUNDA,
ORANGE-RED, REPEAT-FLOWERING

This excellent Cluster-flowered Rose has brilliant red flowers with dark shading on the outer petals which has been inherited from 'Fire King'. The buds are very shapely and open very slowly, being exquisite at the half-open stage, to brilliantly colored full blooms with 35 petals of wonderful substance. The bush is strong and spreading and has bronze-green young foliage that turns green at maturity. The flowers completely cover the bush from ground level upwards, which makes 'Fidélio' unsurpassed as a bedding or border rose; it is also an excellent standard. ZONES 4–9.

Meilland, France, 1964

('Radar' × 'Caprice') × 'Fire King'

'FIESTA'

MODERN, LARGE-FLOWERED/HYBRID TEA,
RED BLEND, REPEAT-FLOWERING

'Fiesta' has flowers that are double, large to 5 in (13 cm) and fragrant. The color is unusual, as the bright vermilion of the petals is splashed with cream, giving a striped effect. This rose is very difficult to obtain because its constitution is not very robust. It is moderate and bushy in growth habit and has glossy dark green foliage. There is another 'Fiesta' on the market which is more readily available. Recently released by Sam McGredy in New Zealand, this beautiful Cluster-flowered Rose is one of his 'hand-painted' roses. It too is a red blend. ZONES 5–9.

Hansen, USA, 1940

Sport of 'The Queen Alexandra Rose'

'Feuerzauber'

'Figurine'

'FIESTA GOLD'

MODERN, MINIATURE, YELLOW BLEND, REPEAT-FLOWERING

'Fiesta Gold' has long pointed buds that open to show off wonderful yellow and orange double blooms. These are cupped and have a slight fragrance. The buds are often considered the most attractive feature of this rose, as they open very quickly and the blooms age rather rapidly. If it is grown in half-shade the color effect will last longer. In wet climates, the blooms tend to ball and spot. The bush is a vigorous dwarf type covered with small, glossy, leathery foliage. ZONES 5–11.

Moore, USA, 1970

'Golden Glow' × 'Magic Wand'

'FIESTA RUBY'

MODERN, MINIATURE, MEDIUM RED, REPEAT-FLOWERING

This variety has double, medium, high-centered red florets with only a slight fragrance, surrounded by dark green foliage. The stable color survives even the hottest days or coolest nights; if the color does fade, it is usually to a weak purple tone. The florets have 35–45 petals and are slow to open, and the form is cabbage-like. This rose, an all-season variety with fast repeat bloom cycles, is vigorous, prolific and compact. ZONES 4–11.

Moore, USA, 1977

'Red Pinocchio' × 'Little Chief'

'FIGURINE'   BENfig

MODERN, MINIATURE, WHITE, REPEAT-FLOWERING

This aptly named rose has flowers that are ivory white, tinged with pink, on a medium, upright, dense plant. In tropical climates the blooms are light pink all over. 'Figurine' truly has elegant buds and a classic bloom form. The florets have only 15–25 petals yet the form is stunning—a classic Miniature Rose in all respects. The blooms are normally borne one to a stem. There is no doubt that these stems were made for cutting—it is grown in South Africa in greenhouses, and the cut flowers are shipped all over the world. The long stems are the hallmark of this rose, and represent Benardella's achievement in producing a Miniature strictly hybridized for the cut flower trade. 'Figurine' made a stunning appearance at the Royal National Rose

'Fiesta' (McGredy)

Society All Miniature Show, winning the basket class. ZONES 4–11.

Benardella, USA, 1991

'Rise 'n' Shine' × 'Laguna'

American Rose Society Award of Excellence 1992

'FIMBRIATA'

syns 'Diantheflora', 'Dianthiflora', 'Phoebe's Frilled Pink'

MODERN, MODERN SHRUB, LIGHT PINK, REPEAT-FLOWERING

This unusual little rose has pale pink flowers from 'Mme Alfred Carrière' and large rugose leaves from *Rosa rugosa*. The flowers are small and fringed like a carnation, extremely fragrant, and blooming is continuous. Strong enough a plant to use in the shrub or perennial border, it has good disease resistance. ZONES 4–9.

Morlet, France, 1891

Rosa rugosa × 'Mme Alfred Carrière'

'FINALE'   KORam

syn. 'Ami des Jardins'

MODERN, CLUSTER-FLOWERED/FLORIBUNDA, ORANGE BLEND, REPEAT-FLOWERING

'Finale', one of the earliest, low-growing Cluster-flowered Roses, has clusters of salmon-orange, double, large flowers to $3\frac{1}{2}$ in (9 cm) across. The flowers, which have 20 petals, are rather large in comparison to the bush. For maximum effect

'Fiesta Ruby'

this variety should be planted no less than 18 in (45 cm) apart. With its light green foliage it can provide a very colorful low border or small hedge. ZONES 4–9.

Kordes, Germany, 1964

'Nordlicht' × 'Meteor'

'FINANCIAL TIMES CENTENARY'   AUSfin

MODERN, MODERN SHRUB, DEEP PINK

Commemorating the centenary of the *Financial Times*, this rose has a rich Old Garden Rose fragrance. The flowers are large and of great depth, globular in shape and resemble an old Centifolia Rose. The petals curve inwards, enclosing the center of the blooms. The plant is

'Finale'

'Firecracker'

'Financial Times Centenary'

'Fiona'

upright in growth and of moderate vigor but, in warmer climates, many rose enthusiasts have been disappointed in its growth and flower production. It can suffer from die-back, and appears to grow much more strongly in cooler areas. 'Financial Times Centenary' is also classified as an English Rose. **ZONES 4–9.**

Austin, UK, 1989

Seedling × seedling

'FIONA' MEIbeluxen
MODERN, MODERN SHRUB, DARK RED, REPEAT-FLOWERING

'Fiona', a rose of all seasons, has dark rose red flowers that are double, smallish and are produced continuously in well-spaced clusters. They have 20 petals and some fragrance. The foliage is small, dark, semi-glossy and extremely free of disease on a plant with a spreading growth habit. If spent flowers are not removed an amazing display of large, round, extremely long-lasting hips are produced that persist until late winter if they are not picked for indoor decoration, where they can last for several months. In autumn, flowers and fruit can cover the bush at the same time and look most effective. This variety is a good little rose that grows wider than it does tall. **ZONES 4–9.**

Meilland, France, 1979

'Sea Foam' × 'Picasso'

'FIRE FESTIVAL'
MODERN, MINIATURE, YELLOW BLEND

A good rose at the front of a border or as part of a container display, 'Fire Festival' has very double, light yellow flowers that fade to a very light pink. They unfurl from pointed buds to form globular to urn-shaped blooms that are filled with many petals: those at the edge pale first so that middle-aged blooms appear to have yellow centers. The foliage is midgreen and the plant can be propagated by budding. **ZONES 4–11.**

de Ruiter, The Netherlands, 1992

Parentage unknown

'FIRE KING' MEIkans
MODERN, CLUSTER-FLOWERED/FLORIBUNDA, ORANGE-RED, REPEAT-FLOWERING

'Fire King' gets its bright scarlet-red color, which it retains extremely well, from its parent 'Moulin Rouge'. The plant is very vigorous, upright and bushy and produces large, rounded clusters of well-shaped double blooms with 50–60 petals continuously. The buds are attractive and open to $2\frac{1}{2}$ in (6 cm) blooms that are well spaced and well formed, making them good roses for exhibiting. Disease resistance is excellent and growth is rather thorny. This variety makes an excellent bedding rose or it can be used in a border; it has dark leathery foliage. **ZONES 4–9.**

Meilland, France, 1958

'Moulin Rouge' × 'Fashion'

All-America Rose Selection 1960

'FIRE PRINCESS'
MODERN, MINIATURE, ORANGE-RED, REPEAT-FLOWERING

The small, very double florets of 'Fire Princess' are characterized by their bright orange-red color against a backdrop of small, glossy green foliage. The florets are usually borne one to a stem naturally, or in small clusters that are highly floriferous. This plant is a strong grower and has no problems even in the coolest climate zones. The blooms tend to be judged as too big for a Miniature but growing it in a container can reduce the blooms to a more acceptable size. This pretty rose has been the parent of many other outstanding Miniature Roses. **ZONES 4–11.**

Moore, USA, 1969

'Baccarà' × 'Eleanor'

'FIRECRACKER'
MODERN, CLUSTER-FLOWERED/FLORIBUNDA, MEDIUM RED, REPEAT-FLOWERING

The color of 'Firecracker' is most unusual: it starts off orange flame with a pink base and becomes more pink as it ages, and there is a yellow base to the petals and prominent yellow stamens. The flowers are large, to 4 in (10 cm) across, semi-double with 12–15 petals and fragrant, and occur in small to medium clusters. The foliage is leathery, light green and copious on a plant with a bushy, moderate growth habit. This variety with its boss of yellow stamens is a rewarding little rose that should be planted more often; it has good disease resistance and continuous flower production. **ZONES 4–9.**

Boerner, USA, 1956

'Pinocchio' seedling × 'Numa Fay' seedling

National Rose Society Certificate of Merit 1955

'FIREFLY' MACfrabra
MODERN, MINIATURE, ORANGE BLEND, REPEAT-FLOWERING

This rose has been praised by many growers as one of the most beautiful garden varieties. Small, multi-petalled blooms adorn the vigorous, compact bush. Indeed the florets improve as the blooms become fully open and age, providing glorious color in the garden. The plant is remarkably resistant to insects and disease. Repeat-flowering is fast so that it is nearly always in bloom. **ZONES 4–11.**

McGredy, New Zealand, 1985

'Mary Sumner' × 'Ko's Yellow'

'Firefly'

'Fire Festival'

'Fire Princess'

'First Edition'

'FIREWORKS' SAVafire
MODERN, MINIATURE, RED BLEND, REPEAT-FLOWERING

Brilliant orange-yellow flowers with high classical Large-flowered centers borne singly or in small clusters are the hallmark of this rose. The spectacular color of the blooms is complemented by medium, glossy dark green foliage; American growers have written that 'it lights up like the 4th of July'. The plant is slow to start and the good form fizzles unless the stems are kept disbudded. The vigor of the bushy, compact plant is also questionable. The florets are often used by flower arrangers, who love the color. ZONES 4–11.

Saville, USA, 1991

('Rise 'n' Shine' × 'Sheri Anne') × 'Rainbow's End'

'FIRST EDITION' DELtep
syn. 'Arnaud Delbard'
MODERN, CLUSTER-FLOWERED/FLORIBUNDA, ORANGE-PINK, REPEAT-FLOWERING

Consideriding that there are four Cluster-flowered Roses and a Polyantha

'First Kiss'

'First Federal Gold'

Rose in this variety's breeding, it is not surprising that 'First Edition' is a brightly colored rose, the flowers being a luminous coral with orange shading. They are double with 28 petals and of medium size, to 2½ in (6 cm) across. The flowers open from buds that are well shaped and pointed and are most attractive . The foliage is glossy light green in color and acts as a foil to the brightly colored blooms. This plant has good disease resistance, is upright in growth and produces flowers in abundance. 'First Edition' is still a popular rose in the USA, well deserving its prestigious award. ZONES 5–9.

Delbard, France, 1976

('Zambra' × ['Orléans Rose' × 'Goldilocks']) × ('Orange Triumph' seedling × 'Floradora')

All-America Rose Selection 1977

'FIRST FEDERAL GOLD'
MODERN, LARGE-FLOWERED/HYBRID TEA, DEEP YELLOW, REPEAT-FLOWERING

'First Federal Gold' has pale yellow, very well-formed flowers consisting of 50 or more petals. The blooms, which are high centered, large and fragrant and are produced singly and in small clusters, keep their form very well, making this a rose excellent for cutting. This variety has foliage which is glossy and leathery on a vigorous, upright-growing bush and the disease resistance is good. ZONES 4–9.

Boerner, USA, 1967

'Golden Masterpiece' seedling × 'Golden Masterpiece' seedling

'FIRST KISS' JACling
MODERN, CLUSTER-FLOWERED/FLORIBUNDA, PINK BLEND, REPEAT-FLOWERING

'First Kiss' is one of the more recent Cluster-flowered Roses. It produces clusters of pale pink, moderately full flowers with 25 petals that are shaded yellow at the base. They have a slight fragrance and come in small clusters, giving them an appealing simple charm. This variety has mid-green foliage which is bushy to ground level. It is a compact plant that is quite disease resistant, and is excellent for bedding schemes. ZONES 4–9.

Warriner, USA, 1991

'Sun Flare' × 'Simplicity'

'FIRST LADY'
MODERN, LARGE-FLOWERED/HYBRID TEA, DEEP PINK, REPEAT-FLOWERING

'First Lady' was named in 1961 in honor of Jacqueline Kennedy, the wife of President John F. Kennedy and consequently the First Lady of the USA. It is a shortgrowing, healthy bush that produces semi-double flowers with 20 petals that are a rose to clear soft pink color, although its 'official' color is deep pink. The flowers are large and well formed, 3–4½ in (8–11.5 cm) across and they open to very attractive full blooms with a slight fragrance. The foliage is leathery, dark and free of disease on a medium-sized plant with an upright growth habit. The blooms, which are produced continuously, are excellent for cutting as they show up well under artificial light. The breeder, American Herbert Swim, was a dominant figure in rose breeding in the 1950s and 1960s. ZONES 4–9.

Swim, USA, 1961

'First Love' × 'Roundelay'

'First Lady'

F

'FIRST LIGHT' DEVrudi

MODERN, MODERN SHRUB, LIGHT PINK,
REPEAT-FLOWERING

This variety is an attractive shrub rose
with bright pink single flowers. They
each have 5 large petals and show off a
center that is massed with stamens and
anthers. 'First Light' is decorated with
healthy, mid-green foliage and should be
propagated by budding. ZONES 5–9.

Marciel, USA, 1998

'Bonica' × 'Ballerine'

All-America Rose Selection 1998

'FIRST LOVE'

syn. 'Premier Amour'

MODERN, LARGE-FLOWERED/HYBRID TEA, LIGHT
PINK, REPEAT-FLOWERING

'First Love' is a much loved rose admired
by all for the elegance of its small, beautifully formed pale pink buds shaded with
a deeper tone. The long, pointed buds
open to semi-double, slightly fragrant
blooms with 20–30 petals. The foliage is

'First Light'

small, leathery and light green. It is one
of the first roses to flower each spring
and repeats quickly, giving up to 6 flushes
of flowers per year in warmer districts.
The blooms are borne in enormous
quantities and completely cover the bush.
Unfortunately, older plants do not produce basal breaks and old trunks can become very gnarled and woody, but this
does not seem to affect flower production. The plant, which seems to grow
more strongly in cooler areas than it does
in warmer areas, has set a standard of refinement in the bud stage. It has very few
thorns. ZONES 4–9.

Swim, USA, 1951

'Charlotte Armstrong' × 'Show Girl'

National Rose Society Certificate of Merit 1952

'FIRST PRIZE'

MODERN, LARGE-FLOWERED/HYBRID TEA,
PINK BLEND, REPEAT-FLOWERING

'First Prize' is quite distinct from 'First
Love': the latter is refined, while the

'Fisher Holmes'

'First Love'

former is very large with huge, fat buds
that develop to large, double, high-
centered flowers of rose pink shading towards ivory at the center. The flower
color tends to bleach quickly, particularly
on hot days that follow dewy nights, but
there is a good fragrance. In keeping
with the size of the flowers the dark and
leathery foliage is very large, with good
disease resistance apart from some mildew in autumn. The growth habit is vigorous and upright and the heavy stems
are covered with huge thorns. ZONES 5–9.

Boerner, USA, 1970

Seedling of 'Enchantment' × Seedling of 'Golden
Masterpiece'

All-America Rose Selection 1970, American Rose
Society Gertrude M. Hubbard Gold Medal 1971

'FISHER HOLMES'

syn. 'Fisher & Holmes'

OLD, HYBRID PERPETUAL, DARK RED,
REPEAT-FLOWERING

This was one of the most popular roses
during the Victorian period, and it still
has its admirers. The long, pointed buds
open to reveal reddish scarlet blooms
shaded deep velvety crimson. The double
blooms contain 30 petals; they are large
and cupped, and are supported by long,
strong stems. The 3 ft (1 m) bush is upright and vigorous; pegging it down will
increase the number of blooms during
the long flowering season. The autumn
flush is even better than the summer
one, although it is subject to mildew and
rust. 'Fisher Holmes' has been used as an
effective container plant. ZONES 4–9.

Verdier, France, 1865

Seedling of 'Maurice Bernardin'

'Fisherman's Friend'

'FISHERMAN'S FRIEND'

AUSchild

syn. 'Fisherman'

MODERN, MODERN SHRUB, DARK RED,
REPEAT-FLOWERING

'Fisherman's Friend', named after a
brand of throat lozenge on behalf of children in need, is also classified as an English Rose. It is a huge, tall-growing
variety with enormous prickles and very
thick canes but it produces one of the
most beautifully formed and largest of all
the roses of this class. The buds are large,
cupped at first and later open to a rosette
shape. The blooms, filled with 60 or
more petals, open to a confused center
and are deep garnet-crimson becoming
more purple with age; in cold weather
they can be 6–7 in (15–18 cm) across and
are extremely beautiful. They have a
heavy damask fragrance. 'Fisherman's
Friend' is somewhat susceptible to mildew
and black spot but in spite of this, it is
worth a place in the garden. It flowers
very well in spring if the long canes are
trained horizontally on a fence or support, and probably does best in warmer,
drier areas of the world. ZONES 4–9.

Austin, UK, 1987

'Lilian Austin' × 'The Squire'

'FIVE-COLORED ROSE'

syn. 'Fortune's Five-Colored Rose'
OLD, TEA, WHITE, REPEAT-FLOWERING

The great English plant hunter Robert
Fortune discovered this rose in 1844 in a
Ning Po garden in China; he was also responsible for introducing several other
important roses to the West. The buds of
this variety are pale buff-white and open
to small, cupped, semi-double blossoms
that are white with red streaks or dots of
red. Sometimes a rose will be entirely
pink or red. The open shrub is 6 ft
(1.8 m) high and has pale green, dainty
foliage and bristly peduncles, hooked
prickles and orange-yellow hips. It
blooms continuously in warmer climates,
and is a handsome plant for any place in
the garden. There is some inconclusive
evidence that 'Smith's Parish', found in
Bermuda, might be the same rose.
ZONES 5–9.

Fortune, UK, 1844

Parentage unknown

'First Prize'

'FLAIR'

MODERN, LARGE-FLOWERED/HYBRID TEA,
ORANGE-PINK, REPEAT-FLOWERING

'Flair' is one of the many descendants of
'Ophelia' and was a greenhouse rose in
the 1950s. The buds are shapely and refined and of an unusual coral-blush
color shading to salmon; there are few
roses with this coloring. The blooms are
double, with 35 petals, high centered,
large—to 4 in (10 cm)—and come singly
and in small clusters. The plant has
moderate growth, mid-green foliage and
continuous flower production and is a
good choice for bedding, also looking
well when picked and arranged under artificial light. ZONES 4–9.

Verschuren-Pechtold, The Netherlands, 1951

'Lady Sylvia' × seedling

'FLAME SUNBLAZE'   MEItralur

syn. 'Flame Meillandina'

MODERN, MINIATURE, MEDIUM RED,
REPEAT-FLOWERING

The shapely buds of this rose open to
very double, flat red flowers containing
25–40 petals. They last very well on the
bush without fading, and there is a white
basal spot to each petal. The flowers
come in flushes with quick repeat.
'Flame Sunblaze' makes a very bushy
plant when grown in a container. It has
abundant medium-sized, semi-glossy
foliage, the new shoots having red tips
that turn green at maturity. There are
few thorns. ZONES 4–11.

Meilland, France, 1987

Sport of 'Prince Meillandina'

'FLAMENCO'

MODERN, CLUSTER-FLOWERED/FLORIBUNDA,
LIGHT PINK, REPEAT-FLOWERING

This variety has salmon-pink flowers
with a luminous quality. The blooms are
double, with 25 petals, up to 4 in (10 cm)
across, large for a Cluster-flowered Rose,
and come in clusters. 'Flamenco' is a
strong-growing bush with plentiful dark
green foliage, good flower production
and excellent disease resistance. It is suitable for cutting, the color looking
favorable at night. ZONES 4–9.

McGredy, UK, 1960

'Cinnabar' × 'Spartan'

'FLAMING BEAUTY'

MODERN, LARGE-FLOWERED/HYBRID TEA,
RED BLEND, REPEAT-FLOWERING

'Flaming Beauty', which is a very poor
grower, has double flowers of exhibition
form that are large, very high centered

'Flamenco'

'Flaming Sunset'

'Flame Sunblaze'

and have 35 petals. There are only a few
of them, but there is some fragrance.
The foliage is matt green and the growth
bushy. It is strange that such a meagre
grower should have such good growers
as parents; it is a rose for the exhibitor,
not for the garden. ZONES 5–9.

Winchell, USA, 1978

'First Prize' × 'Piccadilly'

'FLAMING PEACE'   MACbo

syn. 'Kronenbourg'

MODERN, LARGE-FLOWERED/HYBRID TEA,
RED BLEND, REPEAT-FLOWERING

'Flaming Peace' has all the fine qualities
of its parent 'Peace' except that the color
is a dull red shaded purple; however, the
reverse is yellow and this helps to give
life to the flowers. The blooms are very
well formed and beautiful at the full
bloom stage, where the petals of great
substance are arranged very evenly. The
plant has a tall growth habit, magnificent
glossy foliage, good disease resistance
and fair continuity of bloom. Its unique
color will assure its place in the gardens
of the future—there is no other rose
quite like it. ZONES 4–9.

McGredy, UK, 1966

Sport of 'Peace'

'Flamingo'

'Flaming Peace'

'FLAMING SUNSET'

MODERN, LARGE-FLOWERED/HYBRID TEA,
ORANGE BLEND, REPEAT-FLOWERING

The deep orange, ruffled flowers of this
rose fade to pink as they age and make an
interesting combination with the leaves,
which have a hint of light bronze. Each
bloom develops from a pointed bud and
has up to 40 petals that have lighter
undersides. 'Flaming Sunset' has reasonably vigorous growth and should be
propagated by budding. ZONES 5–9.

Eddie, Canada, 1948

Sport of 'McGredy's Sunset'

National Rose Society Certificate of Merit 1949

'FLAMINGO'   KORflüg

syns 'Margaret Thatcher', 'Porcelain',
'Veronica', 'Veronika'

MODERN, LARGE-FLOWERED/HYBRID TEA, LIGHT
PINK, REPEAT-FLOWERING

'Flamingo', a great greenhouse and
garden rose, has large, long, pointed buds
that open slowly to well-formed double
blooms with 25 thick petals. The high-
centered blooms are borne mainly singly
on thick, very thorny stems, are moderately fragrant and last well when cut. The
foliage is matt mid-green, the growth
habit is vigorous and upright and the
plant repeat blooms very quickly. There
can be mildew in autumn, but the main
fault is the numerous thorns. ZONES 4–9.

Kordes, Germany, 1979

Seedling × 'Lady Like'

'Flamingo'

'FLAMMENTANZ'   KORflata

syn. 'Flame Dance'

MODERN, LARGE-FLOWERED CLIMBER, MEDIUM RED

This variety has very large, double, high-
centered crimson flowers that are borne
in clusters and have good fragrance. The
foliage is dark and leathery on an extremely vigorous plant that does not
repeat bloom. 'Flammentanz' is very
hardy in cold climates and is most attractive in full bloom, especially where there
is sufficient space for it to grow to its full
size. ZONES 4–9.

Kordes, Germany, 1955

Rosa eglanteria hybrid × R kordesii

Anerkannte Deutsche Rose 1952

F

F

'Flashlight'

'Fleur Cowles'

'Flora' (Maarse)

'Floradora'

'FLASHLIGHT'

MODERN, CLUSTER-FLOWERED/FLORIBUNDA,
ORANGE-RED, REPEAT-FLOWERING

The orange-scarlet flowers of 'Flashlight' have a brownish undertone inherited from 'Vesper'. They are double, containing 28 petals, large at up to 4 in (10 cm) across, and fragrant, and open to reveal handsome golden stamens that light up the flower. The foliage is large, bronze in the early stages and blends well with the flowers, the growth tall and the repeat bloom adequate. This disease-resistant variety is a little bit different, a characteristic of many of Edward LeGrice's roses. ZONES 4–9.

LeGrice, UK, 1974

'Vesper' × seedling

'FLEUR COWLES'

MODERN, CLUSTER-FLOWERED/FLORIBUNDA,
LIGHT YELLOW, REPEAT-FLOWERING

The flowers of 'Fleur Cowles', which are cream shading to buff in the center, are double, large to 3 in (8 cm) across, and have 35 petals and a spicy fragrance. The foliage is dark and glossy on a compact bush. The delicate coloring of the flowers blends very well with parchment-tone roses such as 'Julia's Rose', 'Apricot Nectar', 'Champagner' and 'Cubana' and look lovely under artificial light. This variety is a flower arranger's rose and was in fact named after an English flower arranger. ZONES 5–9.

Gregory, UK, 1972

'Pink Parfait' × seedling

'FLORA'

MODERN, LARGE-FLOWERED/HYBRID TEA,
ORANGE-PINK, REPEAT-FLOWERING

Although two roses share the name, this 'Flora' is a Modern Garden Rose, bred more than a century after the original, by Maarse in The Netherlands. It is an upright and vigorous bush rose that is valued for its very fragrant, large double blooms, which adorn its branches in summer. They are pink, often tinted salmon, and show a center filled with golden yellow stamens. ZONES 5–9.

Maarse, The Netherlands, 1957

'Independence' × 'Charlotte Armstrong'

'FLORA'

syn. 'Flore'
OLD, HYBRID SEMPERVIRENS, MAUVE

The Roman goddess of flowers is memorialized in this summer-blooming Sempervirens hybrid. It grows to 12 ft by 8 ft (3.5 m by 2.4 m) and can be used as a rambler if it is not pruned. The lilac-pink blossoms, which have a darker center, are double, small, cup shaped, open flat and appear to be filled with petals. It is a fragrant, profusely flowering plant, and is a perfect candidate for a pergola; it also loves to romp over barns and up trees. The reddish stems and dark green, pointed leaves should be pruned lightly. This rose does well in poor soil; where the weather is hot, it is best planted in light shade. ZONES 4–9.

Jacques, France, circa 1830

Rosa sempervirens hybrid

'FLORADORA'

MODERN, CLUSTER-FLOWERED/FLORIBUNDA,
ORANGE-RED, REPEAT-FLOWERING

'Floradora' was one of the first of the new color group of salmon-orange roses that was to lead to the brilliant coloring of 'Super Star' and 'Fragrant Cloud'. This variety bears globular buds, opening double blooms of 25 petals with rather incurving central petals. These are produced in sprays of 3–12 blooms and there is some perfume. The bush has an upright growth habit, is disease resistant and the foliage is leathery and glossy. There is very little evidence of the very double, ferny-foliaged *Rosa roxburghii* in 'Floradora'. The color now looks rather dull compared with more modern varieties, but it is an important rose in an historical sense. Its novel color must have helped in winning the All-America Rose Selection in 1945. The blooms fade rather badly and this fault has been inherited by many of its progeny. ZONES 4–9.

Tantau, Germany, 1944

'Baby Chateau' × *Rosa roxburghii*

All-America Rose Selection 1945

'FLORENCE'

MODERN, LARGE-FLOWERED/HYBRID TEA,
LIGHT PINK, REPEAT-FLOWERING

'Florence' is an excellent rose under glass, producing large quantities of small to medium-sized blooms of a very soft pink. The abundant, tightly packed petals open slowly; the buds have very good transport qualities and hold well under refrigeration. The foliage is small, abundant and disease free. This variety is at its best when planted under cover and needs heavy disbudding in the garden to produce sizeable blooms. It has an excellent vase life. ZONES 5–9.

Kordes, Germany, 1987

Sport of 'Europa'

'FLORENCE MARY MORSE'

MODERN, CLUSTER-FLOWERED/FLORIBUNDA,
MEDIUM RED, REPEAT-FLOWERING

Bred in Germany, this rose was named after Mrs Morse of the English firm Henry Morse & Sons, and proved an excellent red rose suitable for beds and borders. A tall grower with good disease-resistant foliage, 'Florence Mary Morse' bears bright red flowers from spring to early winter. They are 3 in (8 cm) across with 15 petals. Trusses can be very large, with up to 20–30 blooms. The flowers last well but do not shed their petals after they have faded—a fault inherited from 'Baby Chateau'. If lightly pruned, this variety may be treated as a shrub; if pruned in the normal manner it makes a free-flowering Cluster-flowered Rose. If spent blooms are not removed, a good crop of bright red hips are produced and look good among the late blooms. ZONES 5–9.

Kordes, Germany, 1951

'Baby Chateau' × 'Magnifica'

National Rose Society Certificate of Merit 1950

'FLOWER CARPET'   NOAtraum

syns 'Blooming Carpet', 'Emera', 'Emera Pavement', 'Heidetraum', 'Pink Flower Carpet'

MODERN, MODERN SHRUB, DEEP PINK,
REPEAT-FLOWERING

'Flower Carpet' was launched in most countries with great publicity, claiming that it flowers continuously for 10 months of the year; it completely covers the soil; and smothers all weeds. This is a highly exaggerated claim—because of its rambler blood, the variety flowers later than most roses and has long periods without flowers between flushes. Also, it does not flower well into winter as it was claimed. It is, however, a very good ground cover rose with deep pink globular flowers with 15 petals of good substance, borne in sprays of 10–25. There is a slight scent. The globular fruit are small and do not seem to inhibit any flowering if spent blooms are not removed, while the spring flowering is particularly profuse, making 'Flower Carpet' a most attractive ground cover rose. If it gets too woody a hard winter prune every few years will bring back vigor without much loss of flower production. Black spot can occur in moist climates. ZONES 4–9.

Noack, Germany, 1989

'Immensee' × 'Amanda'

Glasgow Gold Medal 1993, Royal Horticultural Society Award of Garden Merit 1993

'Florence Mary Morse'

'Flower Carpet'

'Flying Doctor'

'FLOWER POWER'   KORpon

syns 'Blühwunder', 'Ponderosa'

MODERN, CLUSTER-FLOWERED/FLORIBUNDA, ORANGE-RED, REPEAT-FLOWERING

'Flower Power', which inherits its small bush size from 'Marlena', has globular buds and orange-red, double, cupped flowers of medium size on very short but sturdy growth. There are many thorns. The foliage is leathery and abundant with particularly short nodes, and it contrasts well with the flowers. It makes a very good low-growing hedge or is suitable as an edging to taller roses where a strong color is desired, especially when planted close together. ZONES 4–9.

Kordes. Germany. 1970

Seedling × 'Marlena'

Anerkannte Deutsche Rose 1971

'FLUTTERBYE'   WEKplasol

MODERN, MODERN SHRUB, YELLOW BLEND

This rose is fascinating. The large, single flowers are a deep yellow, changing to pinks and golds as they open. There is a red zone in the center of the flower and the effect of all these colors together on the plant is quite unique. The color changes are more pronounced than in *Rosa chinensis mutabilis*. The foliage is rich green and plentiful as is its parent 'Playboy', and the leaves on both varieties are extremely glossy. Tall in growth habit, 'Flutterbye' can be used as a freestanding shrub or trained onto a pillar or tripod as a small climber. Becoming popular in America, 'Flutterbye' will be much in demand when it becomes better known. ZONES 5–9.

Carruth, USA, 1996

'Playboy' × *Rosa soulieana* seedling

'FLYING COLORS'   SAVapaint

MODERN, MINIATURE, RED BLEND, REPEAT-FLOWERING

The red and yellow blend florets of this rose provide a lovely color combination that tends to fade with age to pink and white. The blooms are semi-double and small. The florets have a slight fragrance and are shown off to perfection by the small, medium green, semi-glossy foliage on an upright, compact bush. This rose

qualifies as a Micro-miniature. It has two outstanding qualities—the prolific way it produces a continuous display of blooms, and the overall vigor of the plant. While the blooms may offer some exhibition potential, their most beautiful stage is when the florets are fully open. This is essentially a trouble-free plant. ZONES 5–11.

Saville, USA, 1982

('Yellow Jewel' × 'Tamango') × 'Sheri Anne'

'FLYING DOCTOR'

syn. 'Flambo'

MODERN, LARGE-FLOWERED/HYBRID TEA, ORANGE-RED, REPEAT-FLOWERING

'Flying Doctor' produces very well-formed blooms of brilliant orange-red on an extremely healthy, medium-sized bush. The buds open slowly and keep their color well and flower production is continuous, which makes this rose ideal for cut-flower growing both under glass and outside; vase life is long and the color is retained until petal fall. The foliage is large, dark green and abundant. ZONES 4–9.

Kordes, Germany, 1990

Parentage unknown

'FOLIACÉE'

syn. 'Caroline de Berry'

OLD, CENTIFOLIA, MEDIUM PINK

Ethelyn Keays, noted American rosarian, states in her book *Old Roses* that this rose 'has most remarkably long and compounded foliate sepals which decorate its circumference in a charming way,

'Folklore'

like lace on an old-fashioned bonnet ...'. It is a light rose, fading to lilac-pink. The very large, loosely double blooms are full and globular, have button eyes and most attractive muddled centers. 'Foliacée' looks far more delicate than it really is. It is quite floriferous during the late spring blooming season, and there is a fine Old Rose fragrance. It is a compact bush with light green leaves and a few prickles that will reach 4–5 ft (1.2–1.5 m) in height. ZONES 4–9.

Descemet, France, 1810

Parentage unknown

'FOLIES-BERGÈRE'

MODERN, LARGE-FLOWERED/HYBRID TEA, YELLOW BLEND, REPEAT-FLOWERING

'Folies-Bergère' has large double flowers of a glowing yellow and copper blend that pale with age; in fact the rich color is its major asset. The flowers have a strong fragrance. The leathery foliage is tough and disease resistant and pale in color. With its vigorous, erect growth it makes a suitable subject for bedding. ZONES 5–9.

Gaujard, France, 1948

'Souvenir de Claudius Pernet' × seedling

'FOLKLORE'   KORlore

MODERN, LARGE-FLOWERED/HYBRID TEA, ORANGE BLEND, REPEAT-FLOWERING

'Folklore' is a great rose with extremely strong growth, almost reaching climbing proportions with stems up to 3 ft (1 m) in length. The fragrant flowers are large and particularly well formed, with between 45–50 thick petals each, making it an excellent variety for exhibiting. The blooms, which hold their shape remarkably well, are a beautiful glowing salmon-orange in color; they are excellent for picking and have a good vase life. The foliage is very large, disease free and glossy. Because of its height it should be planted at the back of the border or bed. It has produced a soft creamy biscuit sport called 'Delores'. ZONES 4–9.

Kordes, Germany, 1977

'Fragrant Cloud' × seedling

'FOLKSINGER'

MODERN, MODERN SHRUB, YELLOW BLEND, REPEAT-FLOWERING

Hybridized by Dr Griffith Buck of Iowa State University in the USA, 'Folksinger' is a shrub rose with yellow flowers flushed with dark apricot-peach tones. The fragrant blooms are double and large with 25 petals and are borne in both large and small clusters. The foliage is dark red, leathery and glossy and disease resistance is excellent. The growth is bushy and the repeat bloom excellent. It could be just as easily classified as a Cluster-flowered Rose. ZONES 3–9.

Buck, USA, 1985

'Carefree Beauty' × 'Sunsprite'

'FOREVER YOUNG'   BRIyoung

MODERN, MINIATURE, PINK BLEND, REPEAT-FLOWERING

This rose has small pointed buds of soft pink and white that open to medium pink flowers with perfect high centers. The lightly fragrant, double blooms contain 26–40 petals and are borne one to a stem. The eye-catching color tends to intensify in strong sunlight. It has dark green, semi-glossy foliage on a low, compact, well-rounded bush that grows to 14 in (34 cm) high. It is vigorous, disease resistant and very easy to maintain and is suitable for borders. ZONES 5–10.

Bridges, USA, 1997

'Trickster' × select pollen

'Flower Power'

F

'Flying Colors'

'FORNARINA'
OLD, GALLICA, PINK BLEND

This rose has medium-sized, double, cupped blooms of rich rose with a deeper shade at the center. They are spotted with blush-white, creating a very marbled effect. The compact shrub will reach 4 ft (1.2 m). 'Fornarina' has been confused with 2 older roses—'Belle Flore' with similar marbling, and one from Vétillard in 1826 which is deep purple. **ZONES 4–9.**

Possibly Vibert, France, circa 1841

Parentage unknown

'FORTUNE COOKIE'   SAVacook
MODERN, MINIATURE, APRICOT BLEND, REPEAT-FLOWERING

The elegant buds of this variety open to reveal apricot blend flowers with creamy outer petals. The double blooms have 15–25 petals, are produced both singly and in small clusters and have no scent. The foliage is semi-glossy mid-green on an upright, compact bush that is vigorous and very disease resistant. This is ideal for a mass planting, providing a carpet of consistent color. Its growth habit also makes it a good choice as a container plant, as it has a well-rounded architectural look. **ZONES 5–11.**

Saville, USA, 1995

'Baby Katie' × 'Mazurka'

'Fornarina'

'Fortune's Double Yellow'

'FORTUNE TELLER'   JACheir
MODERN, LARGE-FLOWERED/HYBRID TEA, MAUVE, REPEAT-FLOWERING

This rose, a respectable newcomer to the deep mauve to purple class, has full blooms with 40 petals that are large, to 5 in (13 cm) across, and are usually produced on single stems. Like most roses of this color they are intensely fragrant. Prickles are few and the foliage is dark green and semi-glossy on a tall, spreading bush. Flower production is high and the repeat bloom occurs quickly on a plant with excellent disease resistance. **ZONES 4–9.**

Warriner and Zary, USA, 1995

Seedling × 'Heirloom'

'FORTUNE'S DOUBLE YELLOW'

syns 'Beauty of Glazenwood', 'Gold of Ophir', *Rosa × odorata pseudindica*, 'San Rafael Rose'

OLD, MISCELLANEOUS, YELLOW BLEND, REPEAT-FLOWERING

An extremely popular, easy-to-grow rose in warm climates, this variety was discovered by plant hunter Robert Fortune (1812–80) in the Chinese garden of a wealthy mandarin. The short, fat, round buds are followed by apricot-yellow, semi-double blooms on short stems; as they age, the outer petals reflex. There is a slight flush of red on the outside petals. The fragrant blooms last well when cut, and the long, pliable canes are easily trained on pergolas or up trees. Brown, hooked prickles and serrated leaves line the stems. It can be used as a ground cover, tumbling down a bank or wall, but its most spectacular role is as a tree climber. In warm climates it blooms early and profusely with some intermittent flowers until late autumn. **ZONES 5–9.**

Fortune, UK, 1845

Parentage unknown

'Climbing Forty-niner'

'FORTUNIANA'
syns 'Double Cherokee', 'Fortuneana', *Rosa × fortuniana*

OLD, MISCELLANEOUS, WHITE

Often seen covering a small barn or arch, this variety is probably one of the healthiest roses around today. The small, double, creamy white blooms have a violet scent and are usually solitary on short, bristly pedicules. The canes are gawky and need support. Glossy, attractive foliage with few prickles makes it a handsome plant even when not in bloom. It has been used as understock in humid areas and in early summer, in the right spot and even in poor soil, this healthy rose will produce hundreds of blooms on well-established plants. It was introduced into England by Robert Fortune in 1845 and is quite similar to *Rosa banksiae* except that all its parts are larger. **ZONES 6–7.**

Fortune, UK, 1845

Rosa banksiae × *R. laevigata*

'FORTY-NINER'
MODERN, LARGE-FLOWERED/HYBRID TEA, RED BLEND, REPEAT-FLOWERING

'Forty-niner', which was named for the people who flocked to the Californian goldfields in 1849, is an unusual-colored rose bred from 'Contrast', which has something of the same coloring. The only Modern Rose to approach this red with purple undertones and straw yellow reverse is the sport of 'Peace' called 'Kronenbourg'. The buds are long and pointed and the double blooms with 30 petals are fairly large; they open quickly and fade to a rather dirty cerise-plum color. The glossy foliage is rather prone to black spot and mildew, while the plant appears to have lost vigor and is not widely grown nowadays. Its two gold medals were probably due to its unusual color. **'Climbing Forty-niner'** was introduced by Moffet in 1952; its red flowers with a yellow-orange reverse appear profusely in spring on a disease-free plant that is suitable as a pillar rose or for growing on tripods or fences. **ZONES 4–9.**

Armstrong, USA, 1949

'Contrast' × 'Charlotte Armstrong'

Portland Gold Medal 1947, All-America Rose Selection 1949, National Rose Society Trial Ground Certificate 1949

'FOUNTAIN'
syns 'Fontaine', 'Red Prince'

MODERN, LARGE-FLOWERED/HYBRID TEA, MEDIUM RED, REPEAT-FLOWERING

'Fountain' gained two premier awards in the one year but does not seem to have lived up to its early promise. Although not now available in many countries, it is a good rose with a shrubby habit that freely produces large, cupped, double flowers with 35 petals. The fragrance is very strong. The dark green foliage is glossy and disease resistant on a plant that is a good bedding rose. **ZONES 4–9.**

Tantau, Germany, 1970

Parentage unknown

Royal National Rose Society President's International Trophy 1971, Anerkannte Deutsche Rose 1971

'FOUNTAIN SQUARE'   JACmur
MODERN, LARGE-FLOWERED/HYBRID TEA, WHITE, REPEAT-FLOWERING

'Fountain Square' is similar to 'Pristine' except that the flowers are white instead of pale pink. The bushes are tall with large, dark green, abundant, disease-resistant foliage. The stems are very long and thick and the buds are long, large and develop into large flowers of great substance. These open rather quickly and at the half-open stage the form is superb. There are up to 28 very thick petals. Repeat bloom is a little slow. 'Fountain Square' is a splendid rose in cool weather when the flowers open more slowly. ZONES 5–9.

Humenick, USA, 1986

Sport of 'Pristine'

'FOXY LADY'   AROshrim
MODERN, MINIATURE, ORANGE-PINK, REPEAT-FLOWERING

The ovoid buds on 'Foxy Lady' reveal pointed double flowers that are orange-pink with paler petals in the center. The petals of the medium-sized florets overlap, and the foliage is attractively small compared with the bloom size. Regarded by many growers as 'a real beauty', the color can be salmon and cream in some warmer climates. Bloom production is sparse and the Large-flowered form is rare. Some people regard the choice of an adult name for a miniature rose somewhat peculiar. ZONES 5–11.

Christensen, USA, 1980

'Gingersnap' × 'Magic Carrousel'

'FRAGRANCE'
MODERN, LARGE-FLOWERED/HYBRID TEA, DEEP PINK, REPEAT-FLOWERING

'Charlotte Armstrong' has been used more often in breeding new roses in the USA than practically any other rose; the long pointed buds so often seen in American-bred roses such as 'Eiffel Tower', 'First Love' and 'First Lady' are an inheritance from it, as is the scent. The flowers of 'Fragrance' are deep carmine, double, high centered, large and extremely fragrant. The foliage is bronze at the early stages, later becoming green, on a healthy, disease-resistant plant with a tall, compact growth habit. ZONES 4–9.

Lammerts, USA, 1965

'Charlotte Armstrong' × 'Merry Widow'

'Fragrant Delight'

'FRAGRANT CLOUD'   TANellis
syns 'Duftwolke', 'Nuage Parfumé'
MODERN, LARGE-FLOWERED/HYBRID TEA, ORANGE-RED, REPEAT-FLOWERING

'Fragrant Cloud', one of the best loved roses of the twentieth century, has extremely fragrant blooms as one would expect from a rose bred from 'Prima Ballerina'. The flowers are an unusual coral-red to geranium red in color, are double with 30 petals and are very well formed; it is a particularly clear color and there is very little fading. The large foliage is a rich, glossy dark green on a vigorous bush that is very quick to repeat bloom. Mildew can be a problem in autumn, black spot can occur in damp weather and die-back can crop up in some strains. This variety is an excellent rose for bedding and for borders. ZONES 4–9.

Tantau, Germany, 1967

Seedling × 'Prima Ballerina'

National Rose Society President's International Trophy 1964, Portland Gold Medal 1966, James Alexander Gamble Rose Fragrance Award 1970, World's Favorite Rose 1981

'FRAGRANT DELIGHT'
MODERN, CLUSTER-FLOWERED/FLORIBUNDA, ORANGE-PINK, REPEAT-FLOWERING

'Fragrant Delight' is an excellent Cluster-flowered Rose in cold climates, where its light orange-salmon pink double flowers with 22 petals retain their color well. The flowers fade very quickly in hot climates in summer, but do quite well in spring and autumn in these areas. It is extremely

'Foxy Lady'

'Fragrant Cloud'

'Fragrant Dream'

'Fountain Square'

'Fragrant Hour'

fragrant, an inheritance from 'Whisky Mac', and is extremely popular in the UK where it won the James Mason Gold Medal. The foliage is glossy, healthy apart from some seasonal mildew and red tinted in the early stages. ZONES 4–9.

Wisbech Plant Company, UK, 1978

'Chanelle' × 'Whisky Mac'

Edland Fragrance Award 1976, James Mason Gold Medal 1988

'FRAGRANT DREAM'   DICodour
MODERN, LARGE-FLOWERED/HYBRID TEA, APRICOT BLEND, REPEAT-FLOWERING

The parents of this variety are all in apricot-orange tones, as is the case with 'Fragrant Dream'; it is a most attractive color. The blooms are double with 20 petals and are very fragrant. The foliage is large and mid-green on an upright, bushy plant that blooms continuously and has good disease resistance. ZONES 4–9.

Dickson, UK, 1989

('Eurorose' × 'Typhoon') × 'Bonfire'

Belfast Fragrance Prize 1991

'FRAGRANT GOLD'   TANduft
syn. 'Duftgold'
MODERN, LARGE-FLOWERED/HYBRID TEA, DEEP YELLOW, REPEAT-FLOWERING

The flowers of 'Fragrant Gold' are deep apricot, semi-double, large and fragrant and are set amid dark green glossy foliage. The growth is upright but flower production is rather low as the bush is slow to repeat. The flowers have excel-

lent substance but fade fairly quickly in hot sun, while the disease resistance is excellent. ZONES 5–9.

Tantau, Germany, 1982

Parentage unknown

Belfast Fragrance Prize 1984

'FRAGRANT HOUR'
MODERN, LARGE-FLOWERED/HYBRID TEA, ORANGE-PINK, REPEAT-FLOWERING

'Fragrant Hour' has double, 35-petalled flowers which are an unusual shade of peachy apricot-pink. They open quickly to full blooms of good substance on long stems and have a very strong scent. The foliage is light green and abundant and disease resistance is good, but repeat bloom is a little slow. This variety is good for bedding. ZONES 4–9.

McGredy, New Zealand, 1973

'Arthur Bell' × ('Spartan' × 'Grand Gala')

Belfast Gold Medal and Fragrance Prize 1975

'Fragrant Plum'

'Fragrant Plum'

'Fragrant Surprise'

'FRAGRANT PLUM'   AROplumi

MODERN, LARGE-FLOWERED/HYBRID TEA, MAUVE, REPEAT-FLOWERING

'Fragrant Plum' forms an upright, very strong-growing bush that produces large candelabra-like heads of flowers where the side arms have long enough stems for cutting. The sweet-scented flowers are very double, high centered and last well with little fading of color either in the vase or on the bush. Bloom production is high. Lush new growth can burn on very hot days in hot climates, which applies to other roses such as 'Paradise', 'First Love', 'Josephine Bruce' and 'Thäis'. ZONES 5–9.

Christensen, USA, 1990

'Shocking Blue' × ('Blue Nile' × 'Ivory Tower')

'FRAGRANT SURPRISE'

HARverag

syn. 'Samaritan'

MODERN, LARGE-FLOWERED/HYBRID TEA, APRICOT BLEND, REPEAT-FLOWERING

This comparatively recent rose from Harkness has the fruity scent and rich

gold color of its parent 'Dr A. J. Verhage'. The reddish apricot buds open to quartered blooms with 45 petals in a strong apricot shade merging to pink. They are borne singly and in small clusters and are freely produced, the best blooms occurring in spring and autumn; summer flowers open too quickly and the lovely apricot bleaches quickly in hot conditions. A good bedding rose, 'Fragrant Surprise' is not subject to disease, apart from some seasonal mildew; it has mid-green semi-glossy foliage, broad prickles and bushy, medium growth. ZONES 4–9.

Harkness, UK, 1991

'Silver Jubilee' × 'Dr A. J. Verhage'

Orléans Rose d'Or 1990, Baden-Baden Silver Medal 1992

'FRANÇAIS'

MODERN, CLUSTER-FLOWERED/FLORIBUNDA, ORANGE-PINK, REPEAT-FLOWERING

'Français' is a little known rose bred from the very early Cluster-flowered Rose 'Orange Triumph' and the single

red 'Holstein'. The semi-double flowers are bright pink tinted with orange, and borne in clusters. The growth habit is vigorous and spreading and disease resistance is good, while flower production occurs over a long period. ZONES 4–9.

Mallerin, France, 1951

'Holstein' × 'Orange Triumph'

'FRANCE INTER'   DELkri

MODERN, LARGE-FLOWERED/HYBRID TEA, MEDIUM RED, REPEAT-FLOWERING

With 'Rome Glory' as a parent and 'Dame Edith Helen' as a grandparent, it is not surprising that 'France Inter' has very large, double flowers with 45 petals that are magenta-red. The buds are large and there is some fragrance, while flower production is poor although the blooms last extremely well. ZONES 5–9.

Delbard, France, 1969

('Rome Glory' × 'La Vaudoise') × 'Divine'

'FRANCES PHOEBE'

syn. 'Francis Phoebe'

MODERN, LARGE-FLOWERED/HYBRID TEA, WHITE, REPEAT-FLOWERING

'Frances Phoebe' was sent by Edward LeGrice to Treloar Roses in Australia for testing; Ted Treloar was very impressed with the very full, white, beautifully

formed flowers and asked for permission to name the rose after his mother. The buds are long and develop slowly into 50-petal flowers of the highest exhibition quality that appear on short to moderate length stems. Flower production is very high on a disease-resistant bush with a reasonably tall growth habit. ZONES 4–9.

LeGrice, UK, 1979

Parentage unknown

'FRANCESCA'

MODERN, MODERN SHRUB, APRICOT BLEND, REPEAT-FLOWERING

'Francesca' gets its buff apricot color from the very early Large-flowered Rose

'Frances Phoebe'

'Français'

'France Inter'

'Francis E. Lester'

'Sunburst' and its spreading habit of growth from the shrub 'Danaë'. The lightly fragrant, almost single flowers come on long sprays on a tall, spreading bush with healthy, soft green foliage. Flower production is excellent in spring, the plant then blooms continuously from summer until autumn. An excellent shrub rose, 'Francesca' combines well with bulbs and perennials of similar coloring in a mixed border; in warmer areas it retains its foliage in winter in the manner of the Noisette Roses. ZONES 4–9.

Pemberton, UK, 1922

'Danaë' × 'Sunburst'

'FRANCINE AUSTIN'   AUSram
MODERN, MODERN SHRUB, WHITE,
REPEAT-FLOWERING

'Francine Austin', which was named after the breeder's daughter, is a small, spreading, heavily foliaged shrub that grows much wider than it does tall. The slightly fragrant flowers are white, very double pompons on extremely tall, arching canes. The leaves are very pale green and the leaflets long, narrow and widely spaced. This variety seems to grow far more compact and bushy in the UK than it does in warmer climates such as Australia, where the horizontal canes can suffer from sunburn in hot areas. It is good for picking and is excellent for cascading downwards in church pedestal arrangements. ZONES 4–9.

Austin, UK, 1988

'Alister Stella Gray' × 'Ballerina'

Glasgow Certificate 1990

'FRANCIS DUBREUIL'
syn. 'François Dubreuil'
OLD, TEA, DARK RED, REPEAT-FLOWERING

One of the darkest blooms in the rose world, this handsome rose needs part-shade to prevent its delicate, blood-red petals from scorching. The long, pointed buds open to reveal large, full, cupped flowers looking very much as if they were cut from velvet. The thick petals are peony-like and are quite destroyed in wet weather. The 3 ft (1 m), upright, somewhat lanky shrub is an ideal container plant, although it does have some prickles. It should be placed where its lovely scent can be enjoyed during its long blooming period. Dubreuil was a tailor in Lyons, France, before he took up rose hybridizing; he was the grand father of Francis Meilland. ZONES 4–9.

Dubreuil, France, 1894

Parentage unknown

'FRANCIS E. LESTER'
MODERN, MODERN SHRUB, WHITE

'Francis E. Lester' is a very vigorous climbing rose growing to 13–16 ft (4–5 m) that has thorny stems and pliable canes. The blooms, which appear rather late in spring in large panicles of up to 60 blooms, are white flushed with pale pink, single, 2 in (5 cm) across and look like huge heads of apple blossom. The huge hips that follow the flowers also appear in big clusters and last right through winter as birds do not seem to like them. Some growers get repeat bloom, but this is not common. In Odile Masquelie's garden, La Bon Maison in Lyons, a repeat-flowering seedling has occurred under 'Francis E. Lester' that is an excellent rose which flowers through summer and autumn and remains shrub-like. 'Francis E. Lester' itself is an excellent rose for growing into trees, where it can cascade downwards and show its huge sprays of flowers and hips to perfection. ZONES 4–9.

Lester Rose Gardens, USA, 1946

'Kathleen' × seedling

'Francine Austin'

'FRANÇOIS COPPÉE'
OLD, HYBRID PERPETUAL, DARK RED,
REPEAT-FLOWERING

The long, large, fragrant buds of this rose look very much like the buds of a Large-flowered Rose, as they stand erect on long, rigid stems. This profuse bloomer throughout its long season is a vigorous, erect plant covered with dark crimson, double, large flowers. In warm areas it is best to plant it in partial shade as the petals burn in direct, hot sun. The erect canes can reach 5 ft (1.5 m); the leaves are dark green and there are many short, straight prickles. ZONES 4–9.

Lédéchaux, France, 1895

Seedling of 'Victor Verdier'

'FRANÇOIS FOUCARD'
MODERN, RAMBLER, MEDIUM YELLOW

Rather rare today, this member of the large Barbier family of ramblers was a successful yellow rose when there were not too many of that color available. The medium-sized, long-lasting, lemon yellow blooms are semi-double and appear in clusters. They start as strong yellow but fade away to cream white on long, strong stems and they have a strong fragrance. The very vigorous canes can reach 12 ft (3.5 m) in a season. The shiny, healthy foliage is an added asset during the summer flowering with some autumn rebloom. Barbier of Orléans, France, was an outstanding hybridizer of ramblers, including 'Léontine Gervais', 'Paul Transon' and 'Albéric Barbier'. ZONES 4–9.

Barbier, France, 1900

Rosa wichuraiana × 'L'Idéal'

'FRANÇOIS GUILLOT'
MODERN, RAMBLER, WHITE

This rose has faintly yellow buds that open to milk white, double blossoms with a pink hue. The fairly large, fragrant flowers are long lasting and appear in clusters. Effective on an arch or pergola, this rampant climber will reach 18 ft (5.5 m) and has glossy, light green leaves. This rose is quite healthy, and should be pruned lightly after its summer blooming. ZONES 4–9.

Barbier, France, 1907

Rosa wichuraiana × 'Mme Laurette Messimy'

'FRANÇOIS JURANVILLE'
MODERN, RAMBLER, ORANGE-PINK

The late Jack Harkness praised this rose as the most beautiful of all the wichuraiana hybrids. The bright salmon-pink blooms appear as clusters over a long flowering period in summer. They are flat and a deeper pink in the center with a yellow base. The petals are quilled and quartered, and the fragrance is reminiscent of apples. Reaching almost 25 ft (8 m) at maturity, it has upright, very vigorous canes with shiny dark leaves, which are bronze-green at the edges, and a few prickles. It seems happiest climbing a tree although it is often used as a ground cover. ZONES 4–9.

Barbier, France, 1906

Rosa wichuraiana × 'Mme Laurette Messimy'

Royal Horticultural Society Award of Garden Merit 1993

'Francesca'

'Francis Dubreuil'

'FRANK NAYLOR'

MODERN, MODERN SHRUB, RED BLEND,
REPEAT-FLOWERING

The parentage of this rose must be as complicated as any rose cross ever made. 'Frank Naylor' is a tall shrub rose with small red-tinted foliage and small, single dark red flowers with a distinctive yellow eye. There is a musky fragrance. It flowers all through the season with the look of an Austrian briar and was named after Major-General Frank Naylor, who was president of the Royal National Rose Society. ZONES 4–9.

Harkness, UK, 1977

(['Orange Sensation' × 'Allgold'] × [{'Little Lady'
× 'Lilac Charm'} × {'Blue Moon' × 'Magenta'}]) ×
([{'Cläre Grammerstorf' × 'Frühlingsmorgen'} ×
{'Little Lady' × 'Lilac Charm'}] × [{'Blue Moon' ×
'Magenta'} × {'Cläre Grammerstorf' ×
'Frühlingsmorgen'}])

Royal National Rose Society Trial Ground
Certificate 1976

'FRANKLIN ENGLEMANN'

MODERN, CLUSTER-FLOWERED/FLORIBUNDA,
DARK RED, REPEAT-FLOWERING

'Franklin Englemann' has dark red double flowers with 36 petals that appear

'Frank Naylor'

'Frau Dagmar Hartopp'

in clusters and have excellent substance. New growth is bronze-red and plentiful and acts as a foil to the flowers, which are particularly long lasting. Flower production is good and disease resistance excellent on a vigorous bush. ZONES 4–9.

Dickson, UK, 1970

'Heidelberg' × ('Detroiter' × seedling)

'FRAU ASTRID SPÄTH'

syns 'Astrid Späth', 'Direktör Rikala'

MODERN, CLUSTER-FLOWERED/FLORIBUNDA,
DEEP PINK, REPEAT-FLOWERING

Both this rose and 'Lafayette' are shortish roses with good foliage and heads of flowers in clusters. The foliage is dark and glossy and there are plenty of blooms in a clear carmine rose color. This variety was used for low borders and bedding for many years in Europe and is still seen in many large parks and country gardens today. Disease resistance is excellent and the plant is particularly hardy to winter cold, which is probably the reason why 'Frau Astrid Späth' is still grown in abundance today. ZONES 4–9.

Späth, Germany, 1930

Sport of 'Lafayette'

'Frau Dagmar Hartopp'

'Franklin Englemann'

'FRAU DAGMAR HARTOPP'

syn. 'Fru Dagmar Hastrup'

MODERN, MODERN SHRUB, MEDIUM PINK,
REPEAT-FLOWERING

There is a lot of controversy as to the correct spelling of the name of this rose, but be that as it may it is an excellent shrub that produces large single flowers of a very clear silvery pink continuously from spring until winter that show up very well against the healthy rich green wrinkled foliage. A short, stocky grower, it produces a large crop of bright red, round hips, the first lot ripening for Christmas and able to be used for Christmas decorations in lieu of holly, which of course is not in fruit in summer in the Southern Hemisphere. 'Frau Dagmar Hartopp' suckers and forms a small thicket if the bud union is planted below ground level. It makes a lovely low hedge when the flowers and fruit are on the bush at the one time, and it can also be planted in the woodland or shrub border as a foreground to large-growing species roses. This variety is a simple yet sophisticated rose of a beautiful color and is very popular in all countries. ZONES 3–9.

Hastrup, Denmark, 1914

Parentage unknown

Royal Horticultural Society Award of Garden
Merit 1993

'FRAU KARL DRUSCHKI'

syns 'F. K. Druschki', 'Reine des Neiges',
'Schneekoenigen', 'Snow Queen', 'White
American Beauty'

OLD, HYBRID PERPETUAL, WHITE,
REPEAT-FLOWERING

For many this is the best of all the white roses, both as a bloom in the garden and as an elegant cut flower; the synonyms were used during World War I when German titles were anathema. The solitary snow white blooms, which have 35 petals, are cupped with promised

'Frau Karl Druschki

'Fred Edmunds'

stamens and appear in summer with a strong repeat in early autumn. The blooms do not like wet weather. The 6 ft (1.8 m) robust shrub is covered with handsome foliage and brutal prickles and there are many round, red hips. It needs careful pruning and is a good subject for pegging down. The husband of Frau Druschki was president of the German Rose Society. 'Climbing Frau Karl Druschki' is identical to its parent except that the flowers are smaller; it will reach 15 ft (4.5 m) and needs to be pruned annually of dead wood. ZONES 4–9.

Lambert, Germany, 1901

'Merveille de Lyon' × 'Mme Caroline Testout'

'FRÄULEIN OCTAVIA HESSE'

MODERN, RAMBLER, LIGHT YELLOW

If this rose and the rambler 'Albéric Barbier' were planted together it would be hard to tell the difference between them from their appearance, but the fruity apple fragrance of the former distinguishes it clearly. Not as popular as the French rose, it has charming yellow-white blossoms that are deeper yellow at the center; they are semi-double and cupped and appear in clusters, blooming over most of summer. Reaching 12 ft (3.5 m), the upright, wiry canes are covered with dark green leaves. Because it is tolerant of poor soil, it can be used as a ground cover. It blooms longer in a warm situation. ZONES 4–9.

Hesse, Germany, 1910

Rosa wichuraiana × 'Kaiserin Auguste Viktoria'

'FRED EDMUNDS'

syn. 'L'Arlésienne'

MODERN, LARGE-FLOWERED/HYBRID TEA,
ORANGE BLEND, REPEAT-FLOWERING

The firm of Meilland named 'Fred Edmunds' after a prominent nurseryman in the USA. It has long, pointed buds that open rather quickly to fairly double flowers with 25 petals; they are 5 in (13 cm) across and of a particularly vivid coppery orange color, a shade that was unique when introduced in 1943. The blooms are very fragrant. The attractive foliage is leathery and extremely glossy on a medium height, extremely bushy plant. This variety thoroughly deserved its 2 gold medals and seems to be staging a comeback in Australia after 45 years in commerce. ZONES 4–9.

Meilland, France, 1943

'Duquesa de Peñaranda' × 'Marie-Claire'

Portland Gold Medal 1942, All-America Rose
Selection 1944

'FRED GIBSON'
MODERN, LARGE-FLOWERED/HYBRID TEA,
APRICOT BLEND, REPEAT-FLOWERING

'Fred Gibson' was named after one of the
Royal National Rose Society's best
known and most successful exhibitors
who was amateur champion on numerous occasions. His rose is, of course, an
exhibition variety with lovely flowers of
maize-apricot with very high-pointed
centers. The double flowers, which have
30 petals and are slightly fragrant, open
very slowly and make good cut flowers.
The dark green foliage is disease-free.
It is a vigorous grower and of moderate
height. It has much more substance in
the petals than its parent, the soft-
petalled 'Gavotte'. ZONES 4–9.

Sanday, UK, 1968.

'Gavotte' × 'Buccaneer'

Royal National Rose Society Trial Ground
Certificate 1968

'FRED HOWARD'
MODERN, LARGE-FLOWERED/HYBRID TEA,
YELLOW BLEND, REPEAT-FLOWERING

This excellent garden rose is extremely
tall and produces continuous supplies of
very long-stemmed roses from spring to
winter. The buds are long and pointed,
and the double flowers of 55 petals are
high centered in the bud stage and open
flat at the full bloom stage. The color is
an apricot buff shaded pink, which is
unique to this variety. Growth is bronze
in the young stage, maturing to light
green; new growth can burn a little in
hot weather. 'Fred Howard' is an excellent rose for picking because of its long
stems, unusual color and good substance, although it has not received
the acclaim it deserves. ZONES 4–9.

Howard, USA, 1952

'Pearl Harbor' × seedling

National Rose Society Trial Ground Certificate
1950, All-America Rose Selection 1952

'FRED LOADS'
MODERN, CLUSTER-FLOWERED/FLORIBUNDA,
ORANGE-RED, REPEAT-FLOWERING

'Fred Loads' gets is vigor from its parent,
'Dorothy Wheatcroft'. It produces
enormous clusters of single 3 in (8 cm)
blooms at the top of extremely long
canes with abundant, glossy foliage. If it

'Freedom'

is pruned hard to reduce its ungainly
height in winter it then produces enormous heads of flowers that can often win
prizes in shows; the only other contender
for such huge trusses is 'Sally Holmes'. It
can make an impenetrable tall hedge and
is also suitable for bright color at the
back of a mixed border combined with
such flowers as kniphofias, golden rod
and sunflowers. ZONES 4–9.

Loads, UK, 1967

'Dorothy Wheatcroft' × 'Orange Sensation'

National Rose Society Gold Medal 1967, Royal
Horticultural Society Award of Garden Merit 1993

'FREDERIC MISTRAL' MEItebros
syn. 'The Children's Rose'
MODERN, LARGE-FLOWERED/HYBRID TEA,
LIGHT PINK, REPEAT-FLOWERING

As a winner of so many awards for its
fragrance, gardeners can expect a lot
from this rose. As well as their scent, the
flowers have an excellent shape: fully
double, filled with many petals to form
an urn shape with a tight center.
'Frederic Mistral' is covered with mid-
green foliage and makes a good bedding
variety. Budding is the recommended
method of propagation. ZONES 5–9.

Meilland, France, 1996

('Perfume Delight' × 'Prima Ballerina') ×
MEIzeli

Baden-Baden Fragrance Award 1993, LeRoeuix
Fragrance Award 1994, Monza Fragrance Award
1994, Belfast Fragrance Award 1996

'Freegold'

'Fred Gibson'

'Fred Howard'

'FREEDOM' DICjem
MODERN, LARGE-FLOWERED/HYBRID TEA,
DEEP YELLOW, REPEAT-FLOWERING

'Freedom' has very well formed, fragrant,
large blooms with 35 petals. The color is
a rich chrome yellow, probably inherited
from its parent, 'Bright Smile'. The foliage is mid-green and glossy on a medium
bush. Flower production is excellent and
there is a quick repeat between flushes.
This superb rose for bedding or for
hedges is very popular in the UK and its
gold medal was well deserved. ZONES 4–9.

Dickson, UK, 1984

('Eurorose' × 'Typhoon') × 'Bright Smile'

Royal National Rose Society Gold Medal 1983,
Glasgow Certificate of Merit 1989, Royal Horti-
cultural Society Award of Garden Merit 1993,
James Mason Award 1977

'FREEGOLD' MACfreego
syns 'Free Gold', 'Penelope Keith'
MODERN, MINIATURE, DEEP YELLOW, REPEAT-
FLOWERING

'Freegold' has small deep yellow blooms
with 20 petals and with a gold reverse
that cover an upright plant. The florets
are fragrant and can have Large-flowered
form. This rose loves full sun, responding by producing more color-fast
blooms. The plant, however, may be
slow to start. This is an excellent choice

'Frederic Mistral'

for growing in a container to give a
bright color splash to a patio or border.
'Freegold' is a grandchild of 'Anytime'.
ZONES 5–11.

McGredy, New Zealand, 1983

'Seaspray' × 'Dorola'

'FREIHERR VON MARSCHALL'
OLD, TEA, MEDIUM RED, REPEAT-FLOWERING

This very fragrant Tea Rose prefers warm
weather, where it will bloom over a long
season. The pointed buds open to dark
carmine, double blooms that are sometimes blood red in the shade but turn
blue with age. The floriferous, vigorous,

'Fred Loads'

F

'French Lace'

'Frenzy'

'French Lace'

'Frensham'

gawky shrub has fine foliage tinted red. Lambert ran the main German rose nursery at the turn of the century, producing such gems as 'Aglaia', 'Frau Karl Druschki' and 'Trier'. ZONES 4–9.

Lambert, Germany, 1903

'Princesse Alice de Monaco' × 'Rose d'Evian'

'FREISINGER MORGENRÖTE'
KORmarter

syns 'Morgenröte', 'Sunrise'

MODERN, LARGE-FLOWERED CLIMBER, ORANGE BLEND, REPEAT-FLOWERING

The flowers of this rose are red blended with orange. They have 25 petals, and are borne profusely in spring on a tall plant. The foliage is small and dark and the growth quite free. There is some repeat bloom. ZONES 4–9.

Kordes, Germany, 1988

Seedling × 'Lichtkönigen Lucia'

'FRENCH LACE'   JAClace

MODERN, CLUSTER-FLOWERED/FLORIBUNDA, WHITE, REPEAT-FLOWERING

'French Lace', which is as beautifully formed as its parents, is a lovely little rose with the most delicate coloring of tints of ivory, buff and palest apricot.

The flowers have 30 petals and are borne usually singly or in clusters of up to 5 blooms. There is, unfortunately, very little scent, which is surprising as 'Dr A. J. Verhage' is very well scented. The foliage is small and dark on a very bushy plant of low to medium height. This rose makes a lovely border or low hedge and is an excellent low bedding rose. In spite of the short growth, flower production is excellent and regrowth is very rapid. It is very popular in Australia, New Zealand and the USA. It is an excellent rose for indoor decoration when a small arrangement of delicate coloring is required. ZONES 4–9.

Warriner, USA, 1980

'Dr A. J. Verhage' × 'Bridal Pink'

All-America Rose Selection 1982, Portland Gold Medal 198

'FRENCH PERFUME'   KElbian

MODERN, LARGE-FLOWERED/HYBRID TEA, YELLOW BLEND, REPEAT-FLOWERING

'French Perfume' is one of several excellent roses bred by Mr Suzuki. Not many Japanese roses are released outside Japan, which is a pity because Japanese breeders have produced some first-class

roses. The flowers are pale pink flushed rose pink with a yellow base. They are very full (30 petals), are borne mostly singly and are very fragrant. There are small soft prickles on the back of the sepals, which is unusual in Modern Garden Roses and may trace back to the Old Garden Roses. The large foliage is purple-red when young turning to mid-green at maturity. It is a tall, upright and spreading plant. ZONES 5–9.

Suzuki, Japan, 1993

('Todoroki' × 'Montana') × seedling

'Friedrich Heyer'

'FRENSHAM'

MODERN, CLUSTER-FLOWERED/FLORIBUNDA, DARK RED, REPEAT-FLOWERING

This rose set the standard of excellence for red Cluster-flowered Roses for over 30 years. The medium-sized flowers are deep scarlet red, semi-double with 15 petals and come in large clusters. The growth is very vigorous and spreading. There is only a little perfume, which is strange for a rose with 'Crimson Glory' as a parent. 'Frensham' is a good rose for bedding and for hedges that lost favor because of mildew problems on young growth and its thorns, of which it has its fair share, but over the years it seems to have come back into favor. One of the great roses of the late 1940s and 1950s, it was probably the first really popular red Cluster-flowered Rose. ZONES 4–9.

Norman, UK, 1946

Probably 'Miss Edith Cavell' × 'Edgar Andrew'

National Rose Society Gold Medal 1949

'FRENZY'   MEIhigor

syn. 'Prince Igor'

MODERN, CLUSTER-FLOWERED/FLORIBUNDA, RED BLEND, REPEAT-FLOWERING

This rose gets its stunning color from a combination of colors from all its parents. It is a short-growing rose with blooms of a particularly brilliant nasturtium red with a vivid apricot-yellow reverse. Borne singly and in small clusters, they are well formed in the bud, opening to semi-double blooms of 25 petals that are 2 in (5 cm) across. The fragrance is fruity, and the foliage is matt, dark green and acts as a good background for the flowers. It makes an excellent low border or hedge and also looks good arranged with rosehips and autumn foliage for display in the home. ZONES 4–9.

Meilland, France, 1970

('Sarabande' × 'Dany Robin') × 'Zambra'

'FRESH PINK'

MODERN, MINIATURE, LIGHT PINK, REPEAT-FLOWERING

This rose has delicate ovoid buds that open to reveal light pink florets tipped with salmon. The florets are double with 25 petals, cupped and usually occur in very floriferous clusters (in excess of 20 blooms per stem). They have a light fragrance and are nicely complemented by leathery, glossy foliage. The bush thrives on neglect—it tends to clean itself and restart the bloom cycle. As the name suggests, the florets are quite a refreshing pink and look lovely in the garden. It is

'Frolic'

certainly a decorative rose. The seed parent is the key seedling developed by Moore to carry the ease of propagation into Miniature Roses. ZONES 4–11.

Moore, USA, 1964

(*Rosa wichuraiana* × 'Floradora') × 'Little Buckaroo'

'FREUDE'   DeKORat

syn. 'Decorat'

MODERN, LARGE-FLOWERED/HYBRID TEA, ORANGE-RED, REPEAT-FLOWERING

'Freude' is an extremely strong-growing rose with fragrant, vermilion flushed gold blooms with a gold reverse to the petals. They are of very good form, opening slowly to exhibition-type flowers. Growth is free and flower production is good, although flushes are a fair way apart. It is good for cutting and for use where a strong color is desired. Too tall for bedding but suitable for the back row of a rose bed, this variety deserved its German Rose Society award. ZONES 4–9.

Kordes, Germany, 1975

'Fragrant Cloud' × 'Peer Gynt'

Anerkannte Deutsche Rose 1975

'FRIEDRICH HEYER'

MODERN, MODERN SHRUB, ORANGE BLEND, REPEAT-FLOWERING

This shrub has big heads of brilliant orange-scarlet, semi-double flowers produced on a large, spreading bush with dark green, semi-glossy foliage that is disease free. Bloom production is abundant in spring, fair in summer and then quite good in autumn. When lightly pruned 'Friedrich Heyer' makes a plant of moderate size or it can be hard pruned like a Cluster-flowered Rose and still be effective in a bed or border. ZONES 4–9.

Tantau, Germany, 1956

Parentage unknown

National Rose Society Certificate of Merit 1957

'FRIEND FOR LIFE'   COCnanne

MODERN, CLUSTER-FLOWERED/FLORIBUNDA, PINK BLEND, REPEAT-FLOWERING

The flowers of this rose, which are borne in large clusters, are medium in size, semi-double with 10–14 petals and clear rose pink in color. They have good substance and last well. The foliage is dark green and glossy on a plant with a compact growth habit. A good rose for bedding or as an edging for taller varieties, it has no disease problems. ZONES 4–9.

Cocker, UK, 1994

(Seedling × 'Anne Cocker') × 'Silver Jubilee'

Glasgow Golden Prize 1997

'Frisco'

'FRIENDSHIP'   LINrick

MODERN, LARGE-FLOWERED/HYBRID TEA, DEEP PINK, REPEAT-FLOWERING

This rose makes a strong bush with an upright growth habit and large, leathery, dark green, very profuse foliage. The flowers on long stems, are an unusual color—deep pink flushes with coral pink. They are double with 28 petals and open slowly to large, flat, well-formed blooms that are extremely fragrant. Flower production is good and continuous, and the flowers last well both on the bush and when used inside where their color is enhanced by artificial light. It has excellent disease resistance. ZONES 4–9.

Lindquist, USA, 1978

'Fragrant Cloud' × 'Maria Callas'

'FRILLY DILLY'   MURfri

MODERN, CLUSTER-FLOWERED/FLORIBUNDA, DEEP PINK, REPEAT-FLOWERING

The flowers of this rose are a light magenta-pink and are borne in small sprays of 5–7 blooms. They have a slight scent. The blooms have unusual form—with 80–90 petals they appear to be long and thin in relation to their width. Some growers have likened the form to that of a dahlia with the stacking of layers of petals on top of each other. 'Frilly Dilly' needs a lot of heat to open fully and be really appreciated so it is recommended only for warm climates. Bloom production is good and the color holds well even in strong sunlight. The foliage is large and medium green with brown prickles on an upright bush. ZONES 6–11.

Murray, New Zealand, 1986

'Red Lion' × 'Magenta'

'FRILLY DILLY'

MODERN, MINIATURE, LIGHT PINK, REPEAT-FLOWERING

Some confusion may exist over this rose, which shares its name with a Cluster-

flowered Rose. This 'Frilly Dilly', however, is quite distinct: it is a Miniature Rose with soft pink, double flowers and small foliage. It is a good, summer-flowering rose for containers and small gardens. ZONES 5–9.

Cocker, UK, 1986

Parentage unknown

'FRISCO'   KORflapei

syn. 'Pamela'

MODERN, CLUSTER-FLOWERED/FLORIBUNDA, MEDIUM YELLOW, REPEAT-FLOWERING

'Frisco' is a very popular rose for greenhouse growing for cut flowers but is equally good as a colorful bedding rose outdoors in warmer climates, the color being a very rich yellow that deepens with hotter weather. The bush is small and very compact and flowers are produced abundantly over a very long period. They are double with 30–40 petals and excellent substance, and develop fairly slowly to very well-formed full blooms with little scent. The abundant, medium-sized foliage is dark green. Black spot can occur in moist climates. This rose, which produces strong basal growth topped with large heads of flowers with lateral growth long enough for picking, is one of the most free flowering of all roses. It lasts particularly well when cut. ZONES 4–9.

Kordes, Germany, 1986

('New Day' × 'Mini Gold') × ('Banzai' × 'Champagner')

'FRITZ NOBIS'

MODERN, MODERN SHRUB, PINK BLEND

This is one of the most aesthetically satisfying roses ever raised, seeming to have every leaf, petal and flower in the right place. It produces arching branches and covers them with an abundance of leathery grayish green leaves, then produces a show of flower in summer that creates as lovely a shrub as you could find in any species. The blooms are like small-scale Large-flowered Roses in the young flower then open cupped. They are double, of medium size, are borne in clusters of up to 20 and are chiefly light rose and salmon-pink in color, though cream and yellow hints are also present.

There is a pleasing fragrance, but, unfortunately, no extension of the flowering period beyond the first wonderful flush. For a shrubbery or mixed border this is a splendid rose to grow. It needs room, being about twice the size of an average shrub rose, and is remarkably healthy and hardy. ZONES 4–9.

Kordes, Germany, 1940

'Joanna Hill' × 'Magnifica'

Royal Horticultural Society Award of Garden Merit 1993

'FROLIC'

MODERN, CLUSTER-FLOWERED/FLORIBUNDA, MEDIUM PINK, REPEAT-FLOWERING

In spite of its age, 'Frolic' is still a good Cluster-flowered Rose where a very strong, bright, slightly mauve-pink color is desired . The flowers, which are medium sized, double with 20–25 petals and slightly fragrant, come in small and large well-filled sprays. It is a vigorous bush with pale green matt foliage that blooms very freely. This variety is an excellent rose for bedding schemes and is also good for borders. There are very few Cluster-flowered Rose in this color. ZONES 5–9.

Swim, USA, 1953

'World's Fair' × 'Pinocchio'

'FRONTIER TWIRL'

MODERN, MODERN SHRUB, PINK BLEND, REPEAT-FLOWERING

This interesting rose was bred from one of Professor Buck's own shrubs and a popular English-raised Large-flowered Rose and has features of both. The

'Fritz Nobis'

'Frilly Dilly' (Murray)

'Friendship'

blooms are double, and may be borne singly or several together in a combination of a warm shade of rose pink with yellow shading lower down the petals. The outer petals reflex while the rest hold a neat center, until finally they, too, open to create the form of a shallow cup. There is a satisfactory fragrance and blooms continue through summer and autumn, making it a useful plant for borders. The shrub grows upright but not very large and has leathery, bronzy green foliage. It is very hardy. **ZONES 4–9.**

Buck, USA, 1984

'Sevilliana' × 'Just Joey'

'FROSTY'
MODERN, MINIATURE, WHITE, REPEAT-FLOWERING

Incestuous breeding resulted in this lovely white Miniature Rose that blooms in small clusters of 3–10 flowers and has 45 petals per bloom. There is a strong honeysuckle scent. The florets are greenish white and have a button eye. This rose is a profuse bloomer and is ideal for growing in a container where the sprays can drape over the container as the plant grows outwards. It is easy to maintain and is free from disease. **ZONES 4–11.**

Moore, USA, 1953

(*Rosa wichuraiana* × seedling) × (*R. wichuraiana* × seedling)

'FRÜHLINGSANFANG'
syn. 'Spring's Beginning'
MODERN, MODERN SHRUB, WHITE

This variety produces large, white, single flowers that open out like shallow saucers to reveal prominent creamy yellow stamens. The blooms appear in spring, when the arching branches are laden with flowers and with their scent, but they do not give a repeat performance although by autumn there are maroon hips. The growth habit is very large, and it is such a dominating kind of plant that it needs a position with plenty of room where it can be allowed to grow naturally. The leaves are dark green and healthy and attractive when they turn color in autumn. **ZONES 4–9.**

Kordes, Germany, 1950

'Joanna Hill' × *Rosa pimpinellifolia altaica*

'FRÜHLINGSDUFT'
syn. 'Spring Fragrance'
MODERN, MODERN SHRUB, PINK BLEND

Wilhelm Kordes' crossing of the Large-flowered 'Joanna Hill' with a tough rose from the Altai mountain region in central Asia produced a remarkably large and vigorous plant. This variety bears fully double Large-flowered-type blooms that are light yellow to cream with some pink tints. They are freely produced in clusters of up to 5 fairly large blooms and open out loosely cupped, with muddled centers. The synonym indicates correctly that this variety is strongly scented, but the show of bloom occurs in spring only. Growth is very vigorous, to 2 or 3 times that of the average shrub rose, and the plant is well furnished with large, leathery leaves. **ZONES 4–9.**

Kordes, Germany, 1949

'Joanna Hill' × *Rosa pimpinellifolia altaica*

'Frühlingsanfang'

'FRÜHLINGSGOLD'
syn. 'Spring Gold'
MODERN, MODERN SHRUB, MEDIUM YELLOW

This variety is easily recognized in parks and gardens by its open, tree-like growth, decorated lavishly along the arching branches with big pale yellow semi-double flowers that open like saucers and have prominent sulfur yellow stamens. They are among the earliest roses to bloom, in springtime, and have a pleasing refreshing scent. There is scarcely any later bloom, but it is an excellent rose where space is available for it. Spent and crossing stems should be pruned out but otherwise it is best left alone, because blooms are produced along side shoots made in previous years and pruning will mean loss of potential flower. The young basal shoots have a downy fuzz of red-gold prickles, a magical sight when they are caught by the sun. The plant grows about double the size of an average shrub rose and has light green, rather wrinkled leaves and round purplish black hips in autumn which are interesting but are not particularly decorative. **ZONES 4–9.**

Kordes, Germany, 1937

'Joanna Hill' × *Rosa pimpinellifolia hispida*
Royal Horticultural Society Award of Garden Merit 1993

'FRÜHLINGSMORGEN'
syn. 'Spring Morning'
MODERN, MODERN SHRUB, PINK BLEND

'Frühlingsmorgen' is not as dominating a grower as most members of the 'Frühlings' group, and perhaps for that reason it is more often seen in gardens. The flowers are large, single and strikingly beautiful, being pale primrose in

'Frosty'

the center rimmed with cherry pink. Particularly fine are the maroon stamens, which are well displayed as the petals open wide. The flowers have a pleasant scent, and after the main flush in spring a few appear sporadically during the course of summer and autumn. The plant makes a rather open, freely branching shrub with ample, dark grayish green foliage, growing up to twice the dimensions of an average shrub rose. The hips are maroon and fairly large. **ZONES 4–9.**

Kordes, Germany, 1941

('E. G. Hill' × 'Cathrine Kordes') × *Rosa pimpinellifolia altaica*

'FRÜHLINGSSCHNEE'
MODERN, MODERN SHRUB, WHITE

This variety bears clusters of up to 10 medium-sized blooms that are not truly as white as snow (as the German name implies) but also have some ivory and cream in their flowers, which are fairly full of petals and are not single as is sometimes stated. They are well formed, opening with a rather random petal arrangement to allow a glimpse of the reddish gold stamens, and have a pleasing fragrance. The flowering period does not extend beyond spring. As this is a more modest grower than some in the 'Frühlings' group it would be more suitable as a garden plant, but in fact it is less well known than the others, perhaps lacking their individuality and charm. It grows about half as big again as the average shrub rose, has wrinkled, leathery foliage and is very healthy and hardy. **ZONES 4–9.**

Kordes, Germany, 1954

'Golden Glow' × *Rosa pimpinellifolia altaica*

'Frühlingsduft'

'Frühlingsgold'

'Frühlingszauber'

'Frühlingsmorgen'

'FRÜHLINGSZAUBER'
MODERN, MODERN SHRUB, MEDIUM PINK

This rose is similar to 'Frühlingsmorgen', which is not surprising since they have the same parentage; the differences lie in the number of petals and the habit of growth. 'Frühlingszauber' has semi-double, eye-catching blooms like big saucers that open to show rich cerise petal margins with prominent whitish yellow centers. They appear freely in spring in clusters of up to 10 blooms and carry a moderate fragrance, but do not repeat their bloom. The plant is upright, growing to about twice average size, but is open in habit to the extent of appearing spindly; it has a good covering of mid-green leaves. The name means 'spring magic', but its popularity has not equalled that of others in this group.
ZONES 4–9.

Kordes, Germany, 1942

('E. G. Hill' × 'Cathrine Kordes') ×
Rosa pimpinellifolia altaica

'FRUITÉ'   MEIfructoz
syn. 'Fruitee'

MODERN, CLUSTER-FLOWERED/FLORIBUNDA,
ORANGE BLEND, REPEAT-FLOWERING

'Fruité' makes a wonderful bedding rose, laden as it is with clusters of flowers. They are semi-double and open cupped to reveal a blend of apricot-yellow, salmon and orange-red in a cheerful melange of colors. They are lightly fragranced, are borne very freely on the first flowering and continue to provide cycles of growth and bloom through summer and autumn. As well as its usefulness for bedding, this variety is a pleasing rose to cut for the home or to show, withstanding bad weather well.

'Fugue'

'Fugue'

The growth habit is neat and fairly even to average height, and it is well clothed in glossy green leaves and has a good health record. Only the superb abundance of good roses can explain why it is not more widely known and grown.
ZONES 4–9.

Meilland, France, 1985

Parentage unknown

Belfast Gold Medal 1987

'FUCHSIA MEIDILAND'
MEIpelta

syns 'Cyclamen Meillandécor', 'Fuchsia Meillandécor'

MODERN, MODERN SHRUB, DEEP PINK,
REPEAT-FLOWERING

The Meilland rose-breeding station has developed many varieties with parks use in mind, and this rose answers that purpose well. It is very free blooming, bearing flowers of 12 or so petals in large clusters. They are medium sized in a deep pink shade, open cupped and repeat their bloom very satisfactorily through summer and autumn, though they do not have much fragrance. The growth is low and spreading so that it is sometimes considered a ground cover rose, but it is hardly procumbent enough to fit happily with that group. The leaves are light green and glossy, of medium size and plentiful. ZONES 4–9.

Meilland, France, 1991

'Bordurella' × 'Clair Matin'

'FUGUE'   MEItam
MODERN, LARGE-FLOWERED CLIMBER, DARK RED,
REPEAT-FLOWERING

This variety would have been a much more sought after dark red climbing rose if only it had a good scent; unfortunately, it is only slightly fragrant. Clusters of round buds open into flowers of dark scarlet with about 30 firm petals that last well if cut for the house. They are cupped in form, becoming flat before the petals fall, and withstand bad weather well. There is a profusion of bloom in summer and an intermittent flowering through summer and autumn. The plant grows vigorously to average height and is well suited for growing on walls, fences and pillars, although dry walls should be avoided as mildew can be troublesome. 'Fugue' is well furnished with leathery, deep green foliage.
ZONES 4–9.

Meilland, France, 1958

'Alain' × 'Guinée'

Madrid Gold Medal 1958

'Fruité'

'Fulgurante'

'FULGURANTE'
MODERN, LARGE-FLOWERED/HYBRID TEA,
MEDIUM RED

Although very little is known about 'Fulgurante', it is valued for its superbly urn-shaped, double, velvety red flowers. It is a good bedding variety, which can be propagated by budding. ZONES 5–9.

Parentage unknown

'FULTON MACKAY'   COCdana
syns 'Maribel', 'Senteur des Iles'

MODERN, LARGE-FLOWERED/HYBRID TEA,
YELLOW BLEND, REPEAT-FLOWERING

The beauty of this rose lies in the outstanding quality of the flowers, which open from long buds to classically shaped Large-flowered blooms with high centers, surrounded by broad reflexing petals. They are rich apricot-yellow with pink veining, with reddish salmon tints on the outer petals. There is a pleasing spicy perfume, and after a prolific first flush of bloom more flowers appear through summer and autumn. This rose is good for cutting and for a bed or group. It is not immune to black spot in a bad year but is vigorous enough to overcome it. The plant has a bushy, upright habit and plentiful glossy mid-green foliage. It was named for a distinguished Scottish actor.
ZONES 4–9.

Cocker & Son, UK, 1989

'Silver Jubilee' × 'Jana'

Royal National Rose Society Trial Ground
Certificate 1984, Glasgow Gold Medal 1992

'FUTURA'   KORoketto
MODERN, CLUSTER-FLOWERED/FLORIBUNDA,
MAUVE, REPEAT-FLOWERING

Ludwig Taschner of South Africa devised rose classes of his own in order to market some varieties effectively; this is one of his 'Flora Teas', so named because they combine the best qualities of Large-flowered and Cluster-flowered Roses. The flowers, which are a kindly shade of lavender-pink, open from tight buds into starry shaped blooms thanks to their having several layers of sharply pointed

'Fyvie Castle'

petals. The flowers have a long vase life and are excellent for cutting. There is a light almond scent, and flowering continues through summer and autumn. The plant grows upright to average height or more and has mid-green, semi-glossy foliage. ZONES 5–9.

Kordes, Germany, 1994

Sport of 'Antique Silk'

'FYVIE CASTLE'   COCbamber
syns 'Amberlight', 'Cocker's Amber'

MODERN, LARGE-FLOWERED/HYBRID TEA, PINK
BLEND, REPEAT-FLOWERING

This variety can bear really large flowers, sometimes of exhibition quality, and yet it also blooms freely enough to make it an excellent choice for a bed. The fully double, high-centered blooms are of rounded form, in a harmonious blend of light apricot, amber and pink. They have a pleasing scent, and continue through summer and autumn. The plant is shorter than average, neat and compact in growth and has large, mid-green, healthy foliage. 'Fyvie Castle' withstands wet weather well, and was named for a highland property belonging to the National Trust for Scotland. ZONES 4–9.

Cocker & Sons, UK, 1985

('Sunblest' × ['Sabine' × 'Dr A. J. Verhage']) ×
'Silver Jubilee'

New Zealand Gold Star of the South Pacific 1985,
Baden-Baden Silver Plate 1985

F

'Gabriella'

'Gabriella'

'Galia'

'Gail Borden'

'GABRIEL NOYELLE'

syn. 'Gabrielle Noyelle'
OLD, MOSS, APRICOT BLEND, REPEAT-FLOWERING

When the small, shapely, oval buds of this variety open fully, they reveal double orange-salmon blooms with a yellow base. The cupped blossoms have a strong scent. The foliage is dark green and leathery on an upright, bushy plant that grows to a height of 4 ft (1.2 m). This popular Moss blooms later than most and sometimes repeats in autumn. The firm of Buatois also created the climbing Large-flowered Rose 'Reveil Dijonnais'. ZONES 4–9.

Buatois, France, 1933

'Salet' × 'Souvenir de Mme Kreuger'

'GABRIELLA' BERgme

syn. 'Gabrielle'
MODERN, CLUSTER-FLOWERED/FLORIBUNDA, MEDIUM RED, REPEAT-FLOWERING

This is a rose grown by the thousands for the cut flower industry, having been discovered by a Swedish grower as a sport on a plant of another celebrated florists' rose, 'Mercedes'. It is medium red in color, providing through summer and autumn a good supply of flowers on short, wiry, almost thornless stems and needing little disbudding to obtain them. The flowers open in roundelay fashion, with overlapping petals, and last for ages. They have little scent. There is little point in growing 'Gabriella' in the garden except in very warm climates, but in a greenhouse it is rewarding. The bush grows to medium height or above and has olive green, leathery leaves. ZONES 5–9.

Berggren, Sweden, 1977

Sport of 'Mercedes'

'GAIL BORDEN'

MODERN, LARGE-FLOWERED/HYBRID TEA, PINK BLEND, REPEAT-FLOWERING

This rose has always been remarkable for the consistently high quality of its blooms. These are large and double with broad petals and open from plump buds into blooms of rounded outline and symmetrical form, the petals forming a fine cone in the center. The color is warm salmon inside the petals which can fade to yellowish cream outside. The whole bloom fades somewhat as the flowers age. There is a light sweet scent, and blooms continue to appear through summer and autumn. They may be produced singly or in 3s and 5s, and are resistant to bad weather. For a single-variety bed this is an excellent choice, though it has become something of a collectors' item as only 3 growers are at present listing it. The bush grows to average height with a slightly spreading habit, and has dark green, leathery leaves. ZONES 4–9.

Kordes, Germany, 1957

'Mevrouw H. A. Verschuren' × 'Viktoria Adelheid'

National Rose Society Gold Medal 1957

'GALAXY' MORgal

MODERN, MINIATURE, DARK RED, REPEAT-FLOWERING

The long, pointed buds of this rose develop into deep velvety red, double flowers made up of 23 petals. The small, non-fragrant blooms possess typical Large-flowered form and occur either singly or in small clusters of 5–10 blooms. There is a nice color contrast between the vivid red petals and the heavy yellow stamens at the fully open stage—a stunning combination, which can be disappointingly muddy in cool weather. It really takes the heat to bring out the sparkle. This ever-blooming bush can be planted as a hedge to give constant color throughout the growing season; it is also covered with small leaves and slightly downward-curving prickles. The plant has vigorous growth and is upright in habit. ZONES 4–11.

Moore, USA, 1980

'Fairy Moss' × 'Fairy Princess'

'GALIA' MEItinirol

MODERN, LARGE-FLOWERED/HYBRID TEA, ORANGE-RED, REPEAT-FLOWERING

This variety is a very bright and showy color, best described as vermilion with a gloss on it. It bears large blooms, composed of around 40 petals, that open from plump buds to show a cupped form. Usually the flowers are carried one to a stem, and as the stems are long this is a good variety to cut, all the more so because the blooms are very freely borne. There is, however, no detectable scent. Flowering continues through summer and autumn, on a plant that grows vigorously to average height and has a dense covering of large, matt deep green leaves. ZONES 4–9.

Meilland, France, 1977

MEIretni × 'Elegy'

'GALWAY BAY' MACba

MODERN, LARGE-FLOWERED CLIMBER, ORANGE-PINK, REPEAT-FLOWERING

The given color classification of this variety is misleading, because the rose is a rich deep cerise-pink; it holds its color through the life of the flower, with little obvious hint of orange about it. It is a vigorous climber that bears clusters of several blooms in summer and continues to flower through late summer and autumn. The flowers are of medium size, fairly full of petals and open cupped, the petals overlapping in an attractive way. There is a pleasant light scent. The growth is stiff and branching to average height, and it is best trained against a wall, fence or pillar. The foliage is dark green, oval in shape, plentiful and usually very healthy. Galway Bay is off the windswept and beautiful west coast of Ireland. ZONES 4–9.

McGredy, UK, 1966

'Heidelberg' × 'Queen Elizabeth'

'GARDEN CHARM'

MODERN, CLUSTER-FLOWERED/FLORIBUNDA, MEDIUM RED, REPEAT-FLOWERING

'Garden Charm' is a short, stocky Cluster-flowered Rose with an ample covering of dark green, semi-glossy foliage. The bright red blooms are produced in small to medium clusters and are particularly long lasting. The buds are shapely and open to a fine display of semi-double blooms, each with about 20 petals, and there is a fairly quick repeat. 'Garden Charm' is a very healthy bush suitable for bedding and for borders and low hedges, but there is no fragrance. ZONES 5–9.

Kordes, Germany, 1965

Parentage unknown

'Galia'

'Galaxy'

'Garden Charm'

'GARDEN PARTY'

MODERN, LARGE-FLOWERED/HYBRID TEA, WHITE, REPEAT-FLOWERING

Both parents of this rose have rewarded rose breeders with some excellent children, and 'Garden Party' is a fine example. The blooms are beautifully constructed, opening from urn-shaped buds into large, full flowers of delicate and graceful appearance. They are double, with long petals that form a high center, and become prettily waved as they reflex to form a wide bowl-shaped flower. The color is basically ivory merging into creamy yellow, with flushes of pink; these cool shades look soothing among brighter hued roses whether the variety is cut for the house or used for bedding in the garden. The first flush of bloom is very free for so large a rose, and flowering continues through summer and autumn. There is a pleasant light fragrance. The plant grows bushily to average height or more, and is well clothed in dark foliage. ZONES 4–9.

Swim, USA, 1959

'Charlotte Armstrong' × 'Peace'

Bagatelle Gold Medal 1959, All-America Rose Selection 1960

'GARDENIA'

MODERN, RAMBLER, WHITE

This Rambler has recently regained its popularity as one of the best white roses in its class. The pointed yellow buds develop into creamy white flowers with a yellow center. The large, full, cupped blooms appear in small sprays on short, strong stems during a prolonged blooming period; muddled and fragrant, the flowers will stay yellow if planted in the shade. The foliage is small, dark and glossy. It makes a stunning display on an arch or pergola or climbing up a tree, reaching 20 ft (6 m). The same nursery produced 'Jersey Beauty'. ZONES 7–10.

Manda, USA, 1899

Rosa wichuraiana × 'Perle des Jardins'

'GARNETTE'

syns 'Garnet', 'Garnette Red', 'Red Garnette'

MODERN, CLUSTER-FLOWERED/FLORIBUNDA, DARK RED, REPEAT-FLOWERING

'Leave it to the florists' is the advice of one expert regarding this rose that, although it has been immensely popular as a cut rose in all parts of the world, denies attempts to replicate the dainty well-spaced sprays of garnet red flowers out of

'Garnette'

doors. There the sprays arrange themselves less obligingly, the stems failing to grow to the required length, and mildew is likely to ruin the whole ensemble. When it is grown for the florist, the sprays open slowly to show cupped flowers of regular form, with each row of firm petals neatly lapping its neighbor and maintaining perfect shape and color tone for many days. Flowering continues through summer and autumn, but there is very little scent. Under glass the rose grows to above average height, but it is shorter in the open garden. The leaves are purplish when young, becoming deep green. ZONES 4–9.

Tantau, Germany, 1951

('Rosenelfe' × 'Eva') × 'Heros'

'GARTENDIREKTOR OTTO LINNE'

MODERN, MODERN SHRUB, DEEP PINK, REPEAT-FLOWERING

Except in one important respect, this is a rose with all the virtues. It is vigorous, healthy and easy to grow, is handsomely foliaged, flowers very freely and has the sort of habit that pleases fastidious gardeners who look to the outline and appearance of the whole plant. Where it falls down is in lack of scent, which is a considerable drawback for a rose with its appearance of old-fashioned charm. The modest-sized blooms are deep pink with a little yellow at the base, shaped like pompons with many small petals, and appear in big clusters of up to 30 flowers. They continue to appear, with rest periods in between, through summer and autumn. It will give good value as a garden plant, growing to about average height, with many light green leaves. ZONES 4–9.

Lambert, Germany, 1934

'Robin Hood' × 'Rudolph Kluis'

'Garden Party'

'GARTENZAUBER' KORnacho

syn. 'Gartenzauber 84'

MODERN, CLUSTER-FLOWERED/FLORIBUNDA, MEDIUM RED, REPEAT-FLOWERING

This is a bushy plant with bright flowers, much favored for use in parks. The blooms are dark red with a shining quality, borne sometimes singly and sometimes in small trusses, and develop from plump buds into very large flowers. There are over 30 petals, which on first opening provide a high center to the blooms; this effect is lost as they reflex randomly into the form of a cup, finally allowing a glimpse of gold stamens at the base. They have a Wild Rose fragrance, stand bad weather well, and are freely produced in summer with good continuity of flower through to autumn. These qualities make for a rose that is good for bedding and lasts well when cut. It grows to average height with an upright and bushy, branching habit, puts out many shoots and is well foliaged with dark green, semi-glossy leaves. The name means 'garden magic'. ZONES 4–9.

Kordes, Germany, 1984

(Seedling × 'Tornado') × 'Chorus'

'GARY LINEKER' PEArobin

MODERN, CLUSTER-FLOWERED/FLORIBUNDA, ORANGE BLEND, REPEAT-FLOWERING

This cheerful variety bears bright orange-vermilion blooms with yellow eyes in clusters of several together on long stems. They are open-cupped, medium-sized, semi-double and yield a light fragrance. If cut early, the young flowers will be very useful for small arrangements, and in the garden the variety is suitable for a bed where a bright splash of color is needed, or in a border where its tendency to uneven growth will be less noticeable. It withstands bad weather well and has excellent continuity of flower through summer and autumn. The plant grows to average height with an upright but slightly rangy habit, and is well provided with glossy mid-green leaves. The rose was named for England's popular soccer star in aid of

the Parkinson's Disease Society; 'Gary Lineker' deserves to be more widely grown. ZONES 4–9.

Pearce, UK, 1991

Parentage unknown

Glasgow Certificate of Merit 1994

'GAVNØ' POUlgav

syn. 'Bucks Fizz'

MODERN, CLUSTER-FLOWERED/FLORIBUNDA, ORANGE BLEND, REPEAT-FLOWERING

This is grown by several British nurseries under its synonym, which in this case refers to a pop music group rather than the popular drink. The roses are a cheerful and rather gentle shade of orange, borne in clusters of several together and shaped like small-scale Large-flowered blooms. They are of middling size and have about 20 broad petals, sufficient to create a high center as the petals begin to unfold and later becoming cupped. There is little scent and the flowers continue to appear through summer and autumn. Despite its Scandinavian origin, the variety seems liable to frost damage in a severe winter, and therefore a site protected from cold spring winds is advisable. The plant grows upright to average height or a little less, and has dark foliage that is reddish when young. ZONES 5–9.

Olesen, Denmark, 1988

Seedling × 'Mary Sumner'

Royal National Rose Society Trial Ground Certificate 1987

'Gavnø'

'Galway Bay'

'GAVOTTE'

MODERN, LARGE-FLOWERED/HYBRID TEA,
PINK BLEND, REPEAT-FLOWERING

'Gavotte' bears enormous full-petalled blooms with classic high centers and petals that open slowly and symmetrically, creating a perfect flower for exhibition. That is the prime reason for growing this rose, because if considered as a garden variety it has serious defects, namely failure of the broad petals to open due to rain, an awkward habit of growth and liability to black spot and rust. The blooms are a deep clear pink with silvery undersides and are borne freely, considering their size, and with reasonable continuity through summer and autumn. The plant grows vigorously to average or above average height with a rather splayed habit, and has large semi-glossy, deep green leaves. ZONES 4–9.

Sanday, UK, 1963

'Ethel Sanday' × 'Lady Sylvia'

National Rose Society Certificate of Merit 1962

'GAY DEBUTANTE'

MODERN, LARGE-FLOWERED/HYBRID TEA,
PINK BLEND, REPEAT-FLOWERING

There have been at least 18 sports of 'Peace', from 'Dorothy Goodwin' in 1954 to 'Julie Anne Ashmore' in 1985, but very few have endured as commercially grown varieties, 2 exceptions being

'Chicago Peace' and 'Flaming Peace' (also known as 'Kronenbourg'). 'Gay Debutante' is distinguished from the original rose by the blooms, which are light pink instead of light yellow, with yellow at the base of the petals. In other respects it shares the characteristics of 'Peace', having very large flowers of over 40 petals that open out into a delightful cupped shape, the flowers lasting wonderfully either on the plant or when cut. It flowers on through summer and autumn. The growth is vigorous and upright, and it has large leathery glossy leaves. ZONES 4–9.

Curtis, USA, 1960

Sport of 'Peace'

'GAY PRINCESS'

MODERN, CLUSTER-FLOWERED/FLORIBUNDA,
LIGHT PINK, REPEAT-FLOWERING

Although the parents of 'Gay Princess' are Cluster-flowered varieties and its blooms are borne in clusters as well as singly, the flowers have much of the appearance of Large-flowered Roses. Plump buds open into large, double, cupped blooms, light pink in color, and with a pleasing though at times elusive fragrance. They hold their centers well and are useful for cutting and for garden display. Flowering is well maintained through summer and autumn. The plant

'Gay Debutante'

'Gay Princess'

'Gavotte'

'Geisha'

grows to a little below average height with an upright, bushy habit and glossy leaves, and though usually healthy it may need watching for black spot. Despite its high award this rose is apparently only grown commercially today by two nurseries, both in warmer parts of the USA. ZONES 5–9.

Boerner, USA, 1967

'Spartan' × 'The Farmer's Wife'

All-America Rose Selection 1967

'GAY VISTA'

MODERN, MODERN SHRUB, LIGHT PINK,
REPEAT-FLOWERING

This variety can make quite a spectacle as it produces very large sprays of bloom on a substantial plant. The medium-sized flowers are single and open out from pointed buds to reveal petals that are rose pink to deeper pink at the edges with creamy white centers. There can be as many as 50 pleasantly fragrant blooms in the cluster, and flowers continue to appear through summer and autumn. Suitable to grow in a border, as a specimen plant or as a hedge, it is vigorous, has an arching habit, and in the warm climates where it is mostly grown for sale it will grow about shoulder height with an adequate provision of tough green foliage. ZONES 4–9.

Riethmuller, Australia, 1957

Parentage unknown

'GÉANT DES BATAILLES'

syn. 'Giant of Battles'
OLD, HYBRID PERPETUAL, MEDIUM RED

This rose was extraordinarily popular in the late 1800s, and it still retains its place as a fine cut flower. The round, fat buds

'Gay Vista'

'Géant des Batailles'

open to full (85 petals), flat, deep crimson blooms that turn maroon with age. The inner petals fold upon themselves. Groups of blossoms appear at the ends of branches, supported by sturdy pedicels. It is a moderately vigorous, erect but low-growing bush with robust stalks, dark green, serrated leaves and prickles that line the canes. It is susceptible to mildew and rust. ZONES 5–9.

Nérard, France, 1846

Hybrid of 'Gloire des Rosomanes'

'GEE GEE' BENgee

MODERN, MINIATURE, LIGHT YELLOW,
REPEAT-FLOWERING

This Miniature Rose will grow to almost 3 ft (1 m) high and produces many flowering stems that cover the bush with creamy yellow blooms throughout summer and autumn. Although the flowers are small, they are of perfect exhibition-standard shape and slightly fragranced, and will last a long time when picked. The color intensifies in autumn, and the flowers become flushed with apricot; the shrubs are at their best at this time of year. Grown in a bed with another Miniature like 'Rise 'n' Shine', a bright display can be ensured for most of the year. ZONES 5–11.

Benadella, USA, 1987

'Rise 'n' Shine' × 'Patricia'

'GEISHA'

syn. 'Pink Elizabeth Arden'
MODERN, CLUSTER-FLOWERED/FLORIBUNDA,
MEDIUM PINK, REPEAT-FLOWERING

There is a bed of this variety in the Gardens of the Rose in St Albans in England, which has continued to look splendid

'Geisha'

'Gem'

ever since it was planted some 20 years ago. In spite of that it has never become well known in the UK, perhaps because other good roses of similar color such as 'Dearest' and 'Vera Dalton' were already on the market. 'Geisha' produces many clusters of up to 20 pointed buds that open into quite large semi-double blooms of a very pure rose pink shade, set off by dark stamens. They are lightly scented, and continue to bloom with excellent continuity through summer and autumn, opening cleanly in all weathers. The plant grows evenly and bushily to average height and is well endowed with deep green glossy leaves. The raiser wanted to call it 'Elizabeth Arden', but there was a white rose of that name already and, as 'Pink Elizabeth Arden' is such a mouthful, it is more often sold as 'Geisha'. ZONES 4–9.

Tantau, Germany, 1964

Parentage unknown

'GEM'

MODERN, LARGE-FLOWERED/HYBRID TEA, MEDIUM PINK, REPEAT-FLOWERING

In the mind of the raiser was doubtless the hope that the classic shape and beauty and color of the crimson-scarlet 'Ena Harkness' would be united with the freedom of flower, good constitution and firm flower stem of the light pink 'Madame Butterfly', with the bonus of breathtaking fragrance from them both. The outcome did not fulfil all these expectations, giving a semi-double flower of moderate size in a gentle, deep pink tone that opens with a high center before becoming cupped. The flowers do have good fragrance and are produced

through summer and autumn on vigorous, upright plants, with matt mid-green foliage. ZONES 4–9.

Walker, Australia, 1960

'Ena Harkness' × 'Madame Butterfly'

'GENE BOERNER'

MODERN, CLUSTER-FLOWERED/FLORIBUNDA, MEDIUM PINK, REPEAT-FLOWERING

'Gene Boerner' has pink flowers of exceptional size and quality for a Cluster-flowered Rose. They open from plump buds into double, deep pink roses with centers of beautiful symmetry, which hold their form while the outer petals slowly reflex. In the depths of the flower deeper pink tones are seen. This is a good variety for cutting and bedding, though the old flowers are liable to be

'Général Jacqueminot'

blemished as they age. It continues to give a display through summer and autumn. The plant grows vigorously with an upright, slender habit to above average height and has a good complement of mid-green, glossy and healthy foliage. Eugene Boerner (1893–1966), known affectionately as 'Papa Floribunda' for his major contributions to this group of roses, was in charge of hybridizing for the Jackson & Perkins nursery. ZONES 4–9.

Boerner, USA, 1968

'Ginger' × ('Ma Perkins' × 'Garnette Supreme')

All-America Rose Selection 1969

'GÉNÉRAL GALLIÉNI'

OLD, TEA, RED BLEND

The fresh Tea fragrance of this rose becomes obvious on a warm day as the blowzy, coppery red blooms open. The cupped flowers change color depending on the weather and whether it is placed in sun or shade. The color range during

the long blooming season includes apricot, pink, yellow, blood red and maroon. It is a fine cut flower. The vigorous shrub displays dark green foliage and hooked red prickles, and does best in a warm position. This rose was named for the Governor-General of Madagascar, then part of the French empire. ZONES 7–9.

Nabonnand, France, 1899

'Souvenir de Thérèse Levet' × 'Reine Emma des Pays-Bas'

'GÉNÉRAL JACQUEMINOT'

syns 'General Jack', 'Jack Rose', 'La Brilliante', 'Mrs Cleveland Richard Smith', 'Triomphe d'Amiens'

OLD, HYBRID PERPETUAL, RED BLEND, REPEAT-FLOWERING

There are at least 500 seedlings and up to 60 sports of this honored Hybrid Perpetual on the books, and most of today's red roses can trace their ancestry to it. Scarlet-crimson buds open to immense, dark red flowers that rest on long, strong stems and the fragrant, velvety, double blooms have 27 petals. The large outer petals are closely packed with occasional white streaks. It flowers freely from summer until autumn, but the blooms do not like hot sun. The foliage is tinged with red on a bushy plant, and prickles line the stout stems. Mildew and rust may be a problem. Amateur breeder Roussel of Meudon, France named this rose for a French general of the early nineteenth century. ZONES 5–9.

Roussel, France, 1853

Seedling of 'Gloire des Rosomanes'

First Prize Versailles Exhibition 1854

G

'Général Galliéni'

G

'GÉNÉRAL KLÉBER'
OLD, MOSS, MEDIUM PINK

This outstanding Moss Rose in all respects has flowers that appear only once in early to mid-summer and are full, shapely and large, up to 4 in (10 cm) across. They are arranged in small clusters and are a soft silvery pink but, despite this pale coloring, the blooms stand up well to wet weather. There is a most delicious perfume. It grows up to 5 ft (1.5 m) in good soils. Both the bright green leaves and numerous buds and flower stalks are generously covered with bright green, soft-to-touch moss; the stems are also amply mossed but have few thorns. Général Kléber was in charge of Napoleon's army during the Egypt campaign. ZONES 4–9.

Robert, France, 1856

Parentage unknown

'GENERAL MACARTHUR, CLIMBING'
MODERN, LARGE-FLOWERED CLIMBER, DEEP PINK, REPEAT-FLOWERING

The flowers of this sport of the bush form are rose red, fairly large and full, with broad petals that open cup shaped and hold their form before dropping cleanly. The Damask fragrance is wonderful, and although most of the flowering is in summer there is a sporadic show

'Général Kléber'

'Général Schablikine'

extending through to autumn. Growth is vigorous, with branching stems capable of growing twice as far as the average size for a climber, and the plant is well furnished with dark leathery leaves. It is lovely on a high wall, big fence or pergola, where it can travel some distance. It was named for an American general, who lived from 1845 to 1912. ZONES 4–9.

Dickson, UK, 1923

Sport of 'General MacArthur'

'GÉNÉRAL SCHABLIKINE'
OLD, TEA, ORANGE-PINK, REPEAT-FLOWERING

This rose has fat buds of strong purple-pink that open to coppery pink, fragrant blossoms that are double, flat and quartered. The outer petals curl away from the paler, inner ones. Only occasionally nodding, the blooms sit on firm stems and love the sun. The 3 ft (1 m) bush has plum-colored shoots with medium-sized, blue-green leaves; there are tiny prickles under the leaf stalks. It requires little pruning and can be groomed well with constant deadheading, and makes a fine bedding plant as it is strongly disease resistant. The Nabonnand family created a dynasty of roses at their Riviera nursery from 1872–1924. Schablikine was a Crimean war hero. ZONES 6–9.

Nabonnand, France, 1878

Parentage unknown

'Général Schablikine'

'General Washington'

'GENERAL TESTARD'
syn. 'General Tetard'
MODERN, RAMBLER, RED BLEND

This rose bears small, semi-double flowers that are red with a white center. Borne in clusters, the blooms resemble those of its parent and make lovely cut flowers. The twiggy growth makes this rambler a good candidate for training on a pergola or a fence. ZONES 6–9.

Pajotin-Chédane, France, 1918

Sport of 'American Pillar'

'GENERAL WASHINGTON'
OLD, HYBRID PERPETUAL, DARK RED

The full, deep crimson blooms of this rose are packed with an astonishing number of flat, large petals: 150 in total. The fragrant petals reflex maroon and the autumn blooms are the best of the season. It has a moderate growth habit. Theopile Granger produced Hybrid Perpetuals for over 30 years, naming another after President Lincoln. ZONES 5–9.

Granger, USA, 1861

Sport of 'Triomphe de l'Exposition'

'GENTLE MAID'   HARvilac
MODERN, PATIO/DWARF CLUSTER-FLOWERED, MAUVE

This short-growing plant bears clusters of about 8 pointed buds that develop into rather surprising flowers: pink with a lilac tone, they have as many as 50–60 small quilled petals and open out into rosette-type blooms of small to medium size in which the petals lie back on one another, layer upon layer. The blooms continue to appear through summer and autumn and withstand bad weather well, but they do not give off much fragrance. This is an unusual and interesting item for the front of a border, a container or anywhere that a rose is required for a small space. It makes a low, spreading plant, compact in habit and has small, narrow dark green leaves. ZONES 4–9.

Harkness, UK, 1988

('Blue Moon' × ['Lilac Charm' × 'Sterling Silver']) × ([seedling × (seedling × Rosa californica)] × [seedling × 'Mozart'])

Baden-Baden Silver Medal 1992

'Gentle Touch'

'GENTLE TOUCH'   DIClulu
MODERN, PATIO/DWARF CLUSTER-FLOWERED, LIGHT PINK, REPEAT-FLOWERING

The light pink, double flowers of this rose have about 20 petals, and are small, urn-shaped and neatly formed. The blooms are produced in clusters as long as the weather remains warm, which makes it an ideal candidate for a small garden. It is particularly attractive in a container. There is a slight fragrance. The foliage is small compared with the blooms, and is mid-green and semi-glossy. ZONES 4–11.

Dickson, UK, 1986

('Liverpool Echo' × 'Woman's Own') × 'Memento'

UK Rose of the Year 1986, Royal Horticultural Society Award of Garden Merit 1993

'GEOFF HAMILTON'   AUSham
MODERN, MODERN SHRUB, LIGHT PINK, REPEAT-FLOWERING

Lovers of the old style of rose form, where the petals squeeze one another for space and become charmingly infolded in the process, will enjoy the large quartered blooms of this variety. It opens out from a plump bud into a cupped rose pink flower, then the outer ring of petals drops back and fades to white, providing a very attractive effect. The fragrant flowers are borne over a long period through summer and autumn. It is better in warm settled weather, as rain and wind can cause nodding stems. It is very suitable for a mixed border, being slightly larger in growth than average for a shrub rose. The leaves are long, matt and light green. Geoff Hamilton, who died in 1995, shared his love of gardening with millions who watched and enjoyed his programs on British television. ZONES 4–9.

Austin, UK, 1997

Parentage unknown

'GEORDIE'   HORkorblush
syn. 'Geordie Lad'

MODERN, LARGE-FLOWERED/HYBRID TEA, RUSSET, REPEAT-FLOWERING

The flowers of 'Geordie' have inherited some of the patterned coloring found in 'Champagne Cocktail', being mahogany red with a yellow base on the inside of the petals and lighter red on the outside. They are carried sometimes in sprays, sometimes singly, and open from plump buds into double blooms of middling size which, as the petals reflex, become cupped. They have a pleasant fruity scent, and flowering continues through summer and autumn. The plant growth is average, the habit upright, and the foliage matt and medium green. This is a useful if little known variety for general garden display and for cutting. The name refers to a native of Tyneside, a region of northeast England; it was introduced by Battersby Roses, whose nursery is close to that area. ZONES 4–9.

Horner, UK, 1990

'Prominent' × ('Champagne Cocktail' × 'Alpine Sunset')

'Georges Vibert'

'Georges Vibert'

'Georgette'

'GEORG ARENDS'

syns 'Fortuné Besson', 'George Arends', 'Rose Besson'

OLD, HYBRID PERPETUAL, MEDIUM PINK, REPEAT-FLOWERING

This variety has large buds that open to very big and blowzy, high-centered, pink and lilac blooms that appear singly on erect stems from mid-summer to autumn. The petals roll back, creating a cabbage rose effect. The blooms do best in cool weather or in the shade, and they make excellent cut flowers. This 5 ft (1.5 m) bush has large, gray-green foliage and few prickles. 'Georg Arends' does well in poor soil and ranks highly as a hedge, although it is subject to mildew. Hinner changed the original name, which was 'Fortune Besson', and he also produced 'Gruss an Aachen'. ZONES 6–9.

Hinner, Germany, 1910

'Frau Karl Druschki' × 'La France'

'GEORGE DICKSON'

MODERN, LARGE-FLOWERED/HYBRID TEA, MEDIUM RED, REPEAT-FLOWERING

Named after the founder of the still-flourishing nursery, 'George Dickson' enjoyed great popularity when it was first released. The large, perfectly formed, fragrant flowers, which are 5 in (12 cm) across, are medium red, and the undersides of the petals have very dark red veining. The foliage is dull green. Although this variety has been criticized by some as 'a large bloom on a weak stem', it won a valued medal at its inaugural showing and stayed on top of the English exhibition rose list for 20 years. George Dickson (1832–1914), a pioneer

'Geraldine'

breeder, was followed by four sons and their offspring in running the nursery. ZONES 5–9.

Dickson, UK, 1912

Parentage unknown

National Rose Society Gold Medal 1911

'GEORGES VIBERT'
OLD, GALLICA, RED BLEND

This striped rose is elegant both in the garden and in a vase. The small, compact, crimson buds reveal fragrant, loosely double blooms that are striped pale pink. When the petals recurve, they surround a center of gold stamens. The quilled and quartered flowers change in color according to the weather and light availability; sometimes they revert to light purple. The 4 ft (1.2 m) bush is compact and upright, and has dark green foliage, numerous small leaves and prickly canes. It is an ideal plant for a small garden or for a hedge, and was named for the grandson of one of the most renowned rose hybridizers. ZONES 4–9.

Robert, France, 1853

Parentage unknown

'GEORGETTE'

MODERN, MINIATURE, MEDIUM PINK/DEEP PINK, REPEAT-FLOWERING

The oval buds of this rose open to reveal medium pink flowers with darker veins on the 30 petals. They are borne singly and have a slight fragrance. This is a densely foliaged, upright and compact bush that has a prolific bloom; this is a useful feature, since the blooms are good for cutting and last well indoors. In the garden, the color ranges from deep fuchsia pink to pale pink. The darker veining also gives the blooms a dramatic look. 'Georgette' is proof positive that a Large-flowered Rose such as 'Electron' can give rise to a Miniature Rose. This

'Georg Arends'

hybridizing technique was used successfully by Dee Bennett to produce well over 100 new Miniature Rose varieties of exhibition quality. ZONES 4–11.

Bennett, USA, 1981

'Electron' × 'Little Chief'

'GERALDINE'   PEAhaze

MODERN, CLUSTER-FLOWERED/FLORIBUNDA, ORANGE BLEND, REPEAT-FLOWERING

The flowers of this variety are orange, of an unusually clear tone, although in strong sun they are liable to fade. Clusters of plump buds open into double flowers of medium size, the petals in the center being tightly coiled and holding this form for some time before reflexing to form a cup. When taken young they are useful for small flower arrangements, and the variety is also suitable for a bed or border. The flowers have a light scent, and maintain a good continuity of bloom through summer and autumn. The growth habit is upright, with some splayed shoots, to average height or less, and the plant has light green, semi-glossy leaves. Raiser Colin Pearce of Devon named it for his wife. ZONES 4–9.

Pearce, UK, 1984

Seedling × seedling

G

'Geranium'

'Geranium Red'

'Gerdo'

'GERANIUM'

syn. *Rosa moyesii* 'Geranium'
MODERN, MODERN SHRUB, MEDIUM RED

There are many forms of *Rosa moyesii* and this is one of the best for gardens, being slightly more compact in habit than the species. The small to medium-sized, single flowers are a brilliant geranium red, with creamy stamens, opening freely along the branches in summer. They do not repeat their flower and there is very little scent. In autumn there is a striking display of bright hips, slightly larger and smoother than in the wild form and deep orange-red in color. This rose will go well in a mixed border or where plants can be allowed to grow naturally, reaching nearly twice the height of an average shrub rose with arching stems. It has dainty, rather light green leaves. The variety was selected at the Royal Horticultural Society garden at Wisley 'some time before 1937' and introduced in 1938. ZONES 4–9.

Royal Horticultural Society, UK, 1938
Variety of Rosa *moyesii*
Royal Horticultural Society Award of Garden Merit 1993

'GERANIUM RED'

MODERN, CLUSTER-FLOWERED/FLORIBUNDA, ORANGE-RED, REPEAT-FLOWERING

The flowers of 'Geranium Red' are quite often borne singly as well as in clusters and are large, rounded at first then becoming flat. They have so many petals that when they are fully open their ruffled, quartered shape puts one in mind of the old Centifolia Roses. The color, as the name implies, is a deep and bright orange-red. There is a spicy, geranium-type of fragrance, and the flowers appear with good continuity through summer and autumn. This is a useful rose for cutting for small arrangements and to group in a border. The plant grows to average height with a bushy habit and is furnished with semi-glossy, dark olive green leaves, that are reddish when young. ZONES 4–9.

Boerner, USA, 1947
'Crimson Glory' × seedling

'GERBE ROSE'

MODERN, LARGE-FLOWERED CLIMBER, LIGHT PINK, REPEAT-FLOWERING

This is a charming variety, bearing up to 10 rose pink blooms per cluster. They are fully double, of medium to large size, and open cupped with ruffled, crinkled petals, allowing a glimpse of yellow stamens in the depths of the flower. They have a fragrance like peonies, especially noticeable in the evening. The main flush of flower is in early summer, and it continues to provide a few blooms later in the season. As this makes a less vigorous plant than most ramblers it is well suited to be grown up a pillar, on a wall (although not in full sun), or even trimmed and made into a specimen bush. It has smooth, reddish wood, and the leaves are dark green, glossy and generally healthy. ZONES 4–9.

Fauque, France, 1904
Rosa wichuraiana × 'Baroness Rothschild'

'Gerbe Rose'

'GERDO'

MODERN, CLUSTER-FLOWERED/FLORIBUNDA, APRICOT BLEND, REPEAT-FLOWERING

Because it is very durable, this rose is grown in vast quantities under glass for the cut-flower trade. The plump buds open slowly to flowers of a unique soft apricot-fawn color that are produced both singly and several to a stem, and are slightly frilled at the edges. It looks charming under night light when the color becomes very luminous. Basal growths often produce candelabra-like heads, with each lateral shoot long enough for cutting. There is no scent. It forms a low bush with glossy dark green foliage and is prone to black spot. As a garden rose, it is best in spring and autumn, because the flowers are short-lived in summer heat. ZONES 5–9.

Kordes, Germany, 1991
Sport of 'Mercedes'

'GERMANIA-AFRICANA'

KORtechna

MODERN, LARGE-FLOWERED/HYBRID TEA, ORANGE BLEND, REPEAT-FLOWERING

The South African-German Cultural Association organised a festival in 1992 and introduced this splendid rose during the festivities. The rich warm colors of an African sunset are reflected in these shapely blooms, which are cream flushed with apricot-yellow and orange on the undersides and edges of the broad petals. A strong fragrance lends further enchantment. This shrub is of medium height and is good for bedding schemes, since it continually produces new shoots with new flowers. The blooms of 'Germanica-Africana' are superb for cutting and exhibition. ZONES 4–10.

Kordes, Germany, 1992
Parentage unknown

'GERMISTON GOLD'   KORtake

MODERN, LARGE-FLOWERED/HYBRID TEA, DEEP YELLOW, REPEAT-FLOWERING

The pointed, urn-shaped buds on this variety are sometimes carried in sprays of 3, sometimes individually, on long stems, opening to large, golden yellow blooms formed out of 30 or so broad wavy-edged petals. They have a spicy fragrance and hold their color and form well even in a warm climate. It flowers freely through summer and autumn. As it grows with a neat, even, free-branching habit to average height it is suitable for a bed of one variety, the only fault being that the flowers do not drop cleanly so that deadheading is necessary. The leaves are mid-green. Germiston in the Transvaal is a major South African goldmining center; the rose is named to commemorate the city's centenary. ZONES 4–9.

Kordes, Germany, 1986
Seedling × seedling

'GERTRUDE JEKYLL'   AUSbord

MODERN, MODERN SHRUB, MEDIUM PINK, REPEAT-FLOWERING

The large full-petalled flowers of 'Gertrude Jekyll' open in the random fashion associated with Old Garden Roses, and the comparison is enhanced by their sweet scent and rich deep pink color. The flowering period extends right

'Gertrude Jekyll'

'Gertrude Jekyll'

'Geschwind's Orden'

'Gidget'

through summer and autumn. Raiser David Austin used the old Portland Rose 'Comte de Chambord' to achieve this, one of his best creations, which is splendid in a mixed bed or border; it looks especially effective grown with 'Jacqueline du Pré'. In cool climates the plant grows vigorously to average height with a somewhat uneven and lanky habit, but in warm conditions it makes much taller growth and is best treated as a climber. It is well furnished with grayish green leaves. The rose bears the famous name of Miss Jekyll (1843–1932), whose writings and practical example did much to influence garden design especially in the grouping of plants for color effect. ZONES 4–9.

Austin, UK, 1986

'Wife of Bath' × 'Comte de Chambord'

Royal Horticultural Society Award of Garden Merit 1994

'GERTRUDE RAFFEL'
MODERN, CLUSTER-FLOWERED/FLORIBUNDA, DEEP PINK, REPEAT-FLOWERING

This rose bears large clusters of semi-double flowers of good form. They are of medium size, and rosy pink in color. There is a slight fragrance, and blooming continues through summer and autumn. The plant is vigorous, has a bushy habit, and is well furnished with dark green leaves. Frank Raffel of California raised a number of varieties that were introduced through his Port Stockton nursery, and thought highly enough of this one to bestow on it a family name. 'Gertrude Raffel' has not been widely distributed, and does not appear to be currently listed by growers. ZONES 4–9.

Raffel, USA, 1956

Parentage unknown

'GESCHWIND'S NORDLANDROSE'
syn. 'Geschwind's Northern Rose'
MODERN, RAMBLER, MEDIUM PINK

This Rambler was the result of a long search by Geschwind for roses that can easily survive periods of severe frost, and was the first of a series of long-blooming shrubs or climbers. The early summer flowering produces many light pink, very double blooms that are full and long lasting, occurring in clusters on vine-like canes. The healthy plant looks best in a woodland setting or among other big shrubs. There are prickles, but no scent. ZONES 2–9.

Geschwind, Hungary, 1884

Parentage unknown

'GESCHWIND'S ORDEN'
syn. 'Decoration de Geschwind'
MODERN, RAMBLER, MAUVE

Until recently, all of Geschwind's creations were suffering a decline in favor, but with a renewed interest in winter-hardy roses they have developed a new popularity. This is one of a series he produced with hardiness in mind—almost at the cost of other qualities. However, this very healthy, disease-resistant rose is a valued addition to any garden, especially in drought-prone or hard-winter areas. The purple-violet, double blooms have a white edge and are borne in medium-sized clusters that can cover a 9 ft (2.7 m) plant. There is no perfume. The foliage, which is wrinkled and dull, is reminiscent of the Rosa rugosa side of the family. The rugged bush is covered with prickles. ZONES 4–9.

Geschwind, Hungary, 1886

Rosa rugosa × 'De la Grifferaie'

'GESCHWIND'S SCHÖNSTE'
syn. 'Geschwind's Most Beautiful'
MODERN, RAMBLER, DARK RED

The only quality lacking in this beautiful rose is perfume. Otherwise, the intense, strong red blooms are medium sized, double and flat, and occur in clusters; the red is a true shade and will not fade. It is a sprawling, 9 ft (3 m) shrub that is overwhelmed with blooms in early summer and can be trained on a fence or left to wander where it will. Geschwind was one of the few hybridizers who has used Rosa setigera in his crosses; 'Prairie Rose' (R. setigera's American name) provides its offspring with glossy, healthy foliage and late-blooming flowers. ZONES 4–9.

Geschwind, Hungary, 1900

Possibly a Rosa setigera hybrid

'GHISLAINE DE FÉLIGONDE'
MODERN, RAMBLER, LIGHT YELLOW, REPEAT-FLOWERING

This pretty rose has small, bright yellow, fragrant flowers tinged with orange that age to yellow-white tinted flesh. They are borne in clusters of 10–20. The flowers may also change from yellow to pink, orange, salmon and red. It is a moderately vigorous shrub growing to 8 ft (2.4 m) with few prickles and an attractive crop of red hips. If treated as a shrub or climber, it will do equally well in rich or poor soil and in sun or shade. G. A. Stevens wrote that it is the 'loveliest of all the multiflora ramblers', and anyone who has seen it tumbling down an

embankment or over a wall would agree. It produces blooms profusely in early summer and occasional clusters in autumn. ZONES 6–9.

Turbat, France, 1916

'Goldfinch' × seedling

'GIDGET'
MODERN, MINIATURE, ORANGE-PINK, REPEAT-FLOWERING

The pointed buds of this variety open up to flowers that range from coral-pink to coral-red depending on the climate zone. The flowers are small, decorative and slightly fragrant, and appear on a vigorous bush with small, mid-green foliage. It is best used in hanging baskets or as a standard. It is a profuse bloomer and easy to maintain. ZONES 4–11.

Moore, USA, 1975

Rosa wichuraiana × 'Floradora'

'GIGGLES'
KINgig
MODERN, MINIATURE, MEDIUM PINK, REPEAT-FLOWERING

The flowers of this rose are large for a Miniature, formed with high centers and usually borne singly, sometimes in small sprays. They are a pretty combination of rose pink shades, being deeper on the outside of their 18 or so petals, and fade to creamy pink as they age. There is a slight fragrance. It grows vigorously to above average height with matt mid-green leaves. ZONES 5–9.

King, USA, 1987

'Vera Dalton' × 'Rose Window'

'Gilda' (Geschwind)

'GILBERT BECAUD'
MEIridorio
MODERN, LARGE-FLOWERED/HYBRID TEA, YELLOW BLEND, REPEAT-FLOWERING

Fat conical buds on this variety give promise of a yellow flower to come, because yellow is the color of the outside of the petals. When the blooms open and reflex to reveal the inner surfaces a beautiful mix of orange and copper is seen in addition to the yellow, together with delicate pale red veining on the petals. The large double flowers are high centered and neatly formed, and are very suitable for cutting if taken young. They have a slight fragrance. The plant has an upright bushy habit of growth, making it suitable for bedding, with attractive matt foliage that is bronzy when young, then becomes medium green. ZONES 5–9.

Meilland, France, 1979

('Peace' × 'Mrs John Laing') × 'Bettina'

'GILDA'
MODERN, RAMBLER, DARK RED/MAUVE

This rose has very double, medium-sized striped blooms that are a combination of red and violet as they age, and finally change color to gray-mauve. Direct sunlight bleaches the red as the blooms open. It is a large and rambling shrub with an upright form, and the long canes support a floriferous production of blooms in mid-summer. There is no scent. This is one of Geschwind's many winter-hardy creations. ZONES 4–9.

Geschwind, Hungary, 1887

Parentage unknown

'Gertrude Raffel'

'Gilbert Becaud'

G

'GILDA'   PEAhigh
syns 'Daily Telegraph', 'The Daily Telegraph'

MODERN, CLUSTER-FLOWERED/FLORIBUNDA, LIGHT PINK, REPEAT-FLOWERING

The flowers of this rose are a very light color, usually described as pale shell pink, and they are prettily formed with high centers before opening out cupped. Medium sized and semi-double, they are usually borne in clusters of several blooms together. There is good fragrance, and the flowering continues through summer and autumn. It is suitable for cutting and can make a pleasing bed, but the habit is rather splayed. It is normally considered healthy, but will benefit from preventive spraying against fungus troubles. The plant grows with a bushy, spreading habit and has mid-green, leathery leaves. The *Daily Telegraph* is a British newspaper that for several years has sponsored the British Rose Festival in summer. ZONES 4–9.

Pearce, UK, 1988

Seedling × seedling

Belfast Certificate of Merit 1990

'GINA'
MODERN, CLUSTER-FLOWERED/FLORIBUNDA, DARK RED, REPEAT-FLOWERING

Breeders were anxious to make use of the genetic opportunities offered by 'Independence' with its novel cinnabar coloring, but this rose was not perhaps

'Gina' (Kordes)

'Ginger Meggs'

what Monsieur Kriloff was aiming for. It is a deep velvety crimson, with 6-petalled blooms borne in clusters of several together on spreading stems. It is a free-flowering rose, and continues to give a good display through summer and autumn, having the advantage that a rose of few petals is likely to be able to repeat its bloom more rapidly than one with many petals. It therefore makes a useful bedding rose, though there is very little fragrance. The leaves are glossy and the plant grows vigorously with an upright habit. ZONES 4–9.

Kriloff, France, 1960

'Alain' × 'Independence'

'GINA'   KORgiral, KORspenon
syn. 'Gina 1988'

MODERN, CLUSTER-FLOWERED/FLORIBUNDA, DARK RED, REPEAT-FLOWERING

Using the same name for different roses makes for confusion, but although registrars of rose names have tried to prevent it happening there is no law against it. The Kordes variety described here sometimes, but not always, carries the date after its name, to distinguish it from Kriloff's earlier 'Gina'. This one is an upright plant of slightly above average height that bears clusters of small to medium-sized blood red blooms on sturdy stems. The flowers are fully double, neatly formed with tight hearts, and hold that shape for some time before opening out

'Gina Lollobrigida'

to reveal confused centers. It is cultivated for the long life and color-holding ability of the flowers, because it is a greenhouse variety intended for the florist's shop rather than the garden. There is no scent to speak of. The plant grows upright with dark green foliage, and is worth trying out of doors only in a warm climate. ZONES 5–9.

Kordes, Germany, 1987

Parentage unknown

'GINA LOLLOBRIGIDA'
MEilivar
syns 'Children's Rose', 'The Children's Rose'

MODERN, LARGE-FLOWERED/HYBRID TEA, DEEP YELLOW, REPEAT-FLOWERING

The flowers of this rose, like huge golden orbs, seem much better suited to the film star than to their association with children, though it has to be added that sales have benefited The Children's Hospital in Britain. The blooms are a deep and unfading golden yellow, and very double with broad thick petals. They open into the shape of cabbages, making a bold show of bright color in the garden and lasting well when cut for the house. The petals may stick in wet weather. The variety is better in a border than a bed because it grows taller than average, holding the flowers aloft on long stiff stems like so many lollipops; this ungainly habit can be masked by using shorter plants in front. There is a light fragrance, and flowering is well maintained through summer and autumn considering the size of the flower. The leaves are large and a rich deep green. ZONES 4–9.

Meilland, France, 1990

MEidragelac × MEikinosi

'GINGER'
MODERN, CLUSTER-FLOWERED/FLORIBUNDA, ORANGE-RED, REPEAT-FLOWERING

This rose is an attractive reddish orange, a vivid color that stands out from a distance. Plump buds open into large double flowers, which open cupped and seem able to hold their color tone in all weather conditions. They are carried in rather irregular clusters, and continue to appear through summer and autumn. As is usual with such brightly colored roses there is some fragrance, but it is slight. The variety is suitable to cut for use in small arrangements and for corsages and buttonholes, and is also recommended to make a low hedge. It grows below

'Ginger'

'Ginger Rogers'

average height with a vigorous, compact habit, and is attractively furnished with glossy deep green foliage. ZONES 4–9.

Boerner, USA, 1962

Seedling of 'Garnette' × 'Spartan'

'GINGER MEGGS'
MODERN, CLUSTER-FLOWERED/FLORIBUNDA, ORANGE BLEND, REPEAT-FLOWERING

To see this rose it may be necessary to travel to Australia, where Brundretts, one of the nation's longest established growers, appear to be the only nursery in the world offering it today. It is a distinctive color, very close to carrot red, and the flowers are large, approaching Large-flowered quality, and borne sometimes singly but more usually in clusters. They are attractive at every stage, from the emerging high-centered young flowers to the cupped, fully open blooms. They have a light fragrance. This is a suitable rose for a bed and to cut for small arrangements as it bears flowers freely through summer and autumn. It grows to average height with a freely branching, leafy habit. ZONES 4–9.

Tantau, Germany, 1962

Parentage unknown

'GINGER ROGERS'
syn. 'Salmon Charm'

MODERN, LARGE-FLOWERED/HYBRID TEA, ORANGE-PINK, REPEAT-FLOWERING

This rose is a warm and pleasing reddish salmon tone, deeper in color towards the petal rims. The blooms have about 24 broad petals, and open from tightly furled plump buds into high-centered young flowers before becoming cupped and loosely formed with an irregular outline. They have a slight fragrance and maintain a succession of blooms through summer and autumn. The chief use of this rose is for bedding, and it grows vigorously with an upright habit to average height or above with matt, light to mid-green leaves. When Ginger Rogers took a stage role in London in 1969, the raiser named this variety for her. ZONES 4–9.

McGredy, UK, 1969

'Super Star' × 'Miss Ireland'

Royal National Rose Society Trial Ground Certificate 1968

'GINGER TODDLER'   PEAvesta
MODERN, CLUSTER-FLOWERED/FLORIBUNDA, ORANGE BLEND, REPEAT-FLOWERING

'Toddler roses' are a new group of bush roses with compact growth of short to medium height and double, medium-sized flowers. They produce a continuous show of flowers after regular clipping of the bush. 'Ginger Toddler', which was introduced by Ludwig's Nurseries in Pretoria, produces shapely, dark orange blooms. It is useful for mass planting, but can be grown on its own, with companion plants or as edgings or hedges, when the planting distance should be about 12 ft (4 m). ZONES 5–11.

Pearce, UK, 1996

Parentage unknown

'GINGERBREAD MAN'   POUlxas
MODERN, MINIATURE, APRICOT BLEND, REPEAT-FLOWERING

The decorative apricot-amber blooms cover this bush with color, which is most intense in cool climates. The medium-sized flowers generally occur in clusters on strong straight stems. There is a definite fruity fragrance. In the garden, this color is eye catching and is complemented by the glossy mid-green foliage. The bush is at its best when the clusters are fully open, which gives an expansive dome of color to the upright compact bush. It is disease resistant and an excellent choice for containers. ZONES 4 11.

Olesen, Denmark, 1995

Seedling × 'Texas'

'GINGERNUT'   COCcrazy
MODERN, PATIO/DWARF CLUSTER-FLOWERED, RUSSET, REPEAT-FLOWERING

The colors in this rose are unusual, being deep reddish orange on the outside of the petals and bronzy orange with pinky orange tints towards the petal tips on the inside. The flowers, though fairly small, have more than 40 petals, which lie back row upon row in neat array, disclosing all these pretty shades to view. They are carried in well-spaced clusters of many blooms, which appear with good continuity through summer and autumn. They withstand bad weather well, and there is a light spicy fragrance. 'Gingernut' is an interteresting rose to grow for any small space or in a container. The plant is compact, free

branching and very short, with small mid-green glossy leaflets. ZONES 4–9.

Cocker, UK, 1989

('Sabine' × 'Circus') × 'Darling Flame'

'GINGERSNAP'
syns 'Apricot Prince', 'Prince Abricot'
MODERN, CLUSTER-FLOWERED/FLORIBUNDA, ORANGE BLEND, REPEAT-FLOWERING

The shape of the open flowers on this rose is appealing. Long urn-shaped buds develop into large, fully double blooms with broad petals, which overlap one another and become very ruffled as they open out. The color is a lively shade of deep tangerine, with orange-red shading towards the petal rims. The roses have a fruity fragrance, and the continuity of flower is well maintained through summer and autumn. It is useful for beds and borders, and as the flowers are borne on long stems they give scope for cutting. The plant grows upright with a bushy habit to average height or even more, and has ample deep green glossy foliage. Seeming to do best in warm climates, it does not appear to be grown commercially outside the USA. ZONES 4–9.

Delbard-Chabert, France, 1978

('Zambra' × ['Orange Triumph' × 'Floradora']) × ('Jean de la Lune' × ['Spartan' × 'Mandrina'])

'GIPSY BOY'
syn. 'Zigeunerknabe'
OLD, BOURBON, DARK RED

This Bourbon Rose has stayed at the top of the list of favorite shrubs for nearly a century. Some classify it as a China and others as a Tea, because it combines the qualities of both of these. The reflexing, violet-purple blooms are semi-double, flat and medium sized with golden stamens at the center crowned with lemon anthers. There is also a slight scent. The wrinkled foliage covers this arching, graceful plant that can be treated as either a shrub or a climber. This variety also makes an attractive and useful boundary hedge since it has prickly stems and orange-red hips. New canes are always appearing from the base. It is strongly disease resistant, and

'Gingersnap'

with 'Gruss an Teplitz' comprises the outstanding creations of this Bohemian hybridizer. ZONES 4–9.

Geschwind, Hungary, 1909

Hybrid of 'Russelliana'

'GITTE'   KORita
syn. 'Peach Melba'
MODERN, LARGE-FLOWERED/HYBRID TEA, APRICOT BLEND, REPEAT-FLOWERING

This rose seems to enjoy warmer climates, where its long pointed buds open into cheerful copper-apricot flowers, deepening to orange-red at the petal tips and blending into light yellow and pink towards the center. The flowers are quite large with about 30 firm petals, enough to maintain a symmetrical high center while the petals unfold, curling prettily at the tips. They are carried on firm stems, have good fragrance, and are very suitable for cutting and for bedding, as flow-

ers continue through summer and autumn. The plant grows to average height on bushy, free-branching stems, and has dark semi-glossy leaves. ZONES 4–9.

Kordes, Germany, 1978

('Fragrant Cloud' × 'Peer Gynt') × (['Dr A.J. Verhage' × 'Color Wonder'] × 'Zorina')

'Gipsy Boy'

'Gitte'

'Gitte'

'Gladsome'

'Glastonbury'

'Givenchy'

'Gladsome'

'GIVENCHY' AROdousna
syn. 'Paris Pink'

MODERN, LARGE-FLOWERED/HYBRID TEA, RED BLEND, REPEAT-FLOWERING

The coloring of this rose varies considerably, depending on the amount of sunlight the plant receives. It is usually cyclamen pink in garden conditions, with paler pink on the petal reverse, but blendings of orange, yellow and red can also be seen as well as the 'raspberry juice' rimming of the petals found in its pollen parent, 'Double Delight'. The flowers have around 30 petals but they are substantial enough for this high-centered rose to be used for exhibition. Disbudding will be necessary for this purpose because the blooms often come more than one to a stem. There is excellent scent, as one would expect of a rose named for a Parisian parfumier, and

flowering continues through summer and autumn, making this a very rewarding variety for the garden. The plant grows to average height with a bushy habit and is clothed in dark green foliage. ZONES 4–9.

Christensen, USA, 1986

'Gingersnap' × 'Double Delight'

'GLAD TIDINGS' TANtide
syns 'Lübecker Rotspon', 'Peter Wessel'

MODERN, CLUSTER-FLOWERED/FLORIBUNDA, DARK RED, REPEAT-FLOWERING

This variety bears showy clusters of deep velvety crimson blooms on firm upright stems. The flowers are of medium size, with about 20 crisp petals, and open into neatly cupped rosettes that show the attractive stamens. There is little scent, but the continuity of flower through summer and autumn is good, and they withstand

wet weather exceedingly well. This variety is useful for exhibition and cutting, because the blooms last well, and it can make a splendid bed, although protective spraying against black spot is advisable. The plant is upright, with a bushy habit and grows to a little below average height; it has glossy dark green leaves. ZONES 4–9.

Tantau, Germany, 1989

Seedling × seedling

Royal National Rose Society Trial Ground Certificate 1988, UK Rose of the Year 1989, Durbanville Gold Medal 1991

'GLADSOME'
MODERN, RAMBLER, MEDIUM PINK

This lovely Rambler bears clusters of bright pink, single blooms that look very attractive against the abundant, mid-green foliage. Each bloom has a central boss of golden yellow stamens, and the petals are almost white at their bases. 'Gladsome' is a useful variety for disguising unattractive walls or fences; alternatively it can be trained as a pillar rose. ZONES 5–9.

Clark, Australia, 1937

Parentage unknown

'GLAMIS CASTLE' AUSlevel
MODERN, MODERN SHRUB, WHITE, REPEAT-FLOWERING

The flowers on 'Glamis Castle' are carried in small clusters, and individually are quite large with as many as 40 petals or more. They open out into wide shallow cups, showing the pointed petal edges to endearing effect. The basic color is creamy white, with buff tints in the heart of the blooms. The flowers which have a sharp myrrh scent, are not spoilt by wet weather, and the plant continues to produce flowers through summer and autumn—all qualities that make this rose suitable for a mixed border. The

plant grows to average height, making a twiggy but productive shrub. The leaves are semi-glossy and mid-green, and are rather prone to seasonal mildew. The rose was named for the Scots seat of the Bowes Lyon family, where Queen Elizabeth the Queen Mother spent some of her childhood and where Princess Margaret was born. The breeder regards this as his best white rose, and it is also classified as an English Rose. ZONES 4–9.

Austin, UK, 1992

'Graham Thomas' × 'Mary Rose'

'GLASTONBURY'
MODERN, MODERN SHRUB, RED BLEND, REPEAT-FLOWERING

Although a comparatively recent rose, this is available from only a few nurseries today and is not offered by its originator, having been superseded by later introductions. It produces globular buds, sometimes one to a stem, sometimes up to 5 in a cluster, that open into double dark crimson to deep purple flowers. There can be over 50 petals, making for a heavy flower that can be adversely affected if rain causes it to ball and fail to open or the stem to bow under the extra weight of moisture. There is a pungent fragrance, and flowers continue to appear during summer and autumn. It grows with an open, rather spreading habit to average height or less, with sparse mid-green foliage. It is also classified as an English Rose. ZONES 4–9.

Austin, UK, 1981

'The Knight' × seedling

'GLENARA'
MODERN, LARGE-FLOWERED/HYBRID TEA, DEEP PINK, REPEAT-FLOWERING

After the death of Alister Clark, this rose which he raised was introduced through the National Rose Society of Victoria, and named after his home. It produces flower stems 24 in (60 cm) in length bearing large semi-double blooms of deep rosy pink, each petal reflexing away from the center and furling to a point, revealing attractive golden stamens. The flowers are lightly scented, and maintain an excellent continuity of flower through summer and autumn. In the garden this makes a useful large bush, or it can be trained against a strong support to form a pillar. The plant is vigorous, with a bushy, upright habit, and is furnished with large leathery leaves. ZONES 5–9.

Clark, Australia, 1951

Parentage unknown

'Glad Tidings'

'Glamis Castle'

'Glenshane'

'Glenara'

'GLENDORA'   KORhuba
syn. 'Glendore'

MODERN, LARGE-FLOWERED/HYBRID TEA,
APRICOT BLEND, REPEAT-FLOWERING

This rose bears its flowers both singly and in clusters. The honey-colored pointed buds part to reveal high-centered blooms made up of about 30 wide petals. The open flowers are a pale creamy buff, toning to deeper buff in the center. As the petals reflex they fold back at the edges, and the flower becomes loose and ragged in form before dropping cleanly. The fragrance is sweet and enduring. There is a prolific first blooming, after which flowers continue to appear through summer and autumn, making this a rewarding rose for a bed or group. The plant grows vigorously to average height with an upright habit, and is clothed with mid-green, semi-glossy foliage. ZONES 4–9.

Huber, Germany, 1995

'Harmonie' × unknown

'GLENFIDDICH'

MODERN, CLUSTER-FLOWERED/FLORIBUNDA,
DEEP YELLOW, REPEAT-FLOWERING

Despite the official color coding the true color is a light amber yellow, a clear and soothing tone, acceptably close to that of the raiser's favorite malt whisky for which the rose was named. The flowers have about 24 large petals and open loosely double, with sizeable flowers for a Cluster-flowered Rose. They are carried on firm straight stems either singly or several together in open sprays, and contrast well with the glossy dark green leaves. The continuity of flower is very good, though in quality the blooms seem larger and finer in cooler areas; hot sun turns them pale yellow. There is a pleasing sweet fragrance, and for a hedge or bed or group this is a satisfactory rose, giving flowers for cutting also. It grows vigorously to average height with an upright habit. ZONES 4–9.

Cocker, UK, 1976

'Arthur Bell' × ('Sabine' × 'Circus')

'GLENGARRY'

MODERN, CLUSTER-FLOWERED/FLORIBUNDA,
ORANGE-RED, REPEAT-FLOWERING

This rose inherited something of the brilliant color of 'Evelyn Fison' and of the size of 'Wendy Cussons', the end result being a rose of a pure and even tone of vermilion-red with flowers like modest-sized Large-flowered Roses carried in clusters of several blooms together. In calm weather it looks a winner, but unfortunately the necks of the flowers are weak and inclined not just to bow but to be snapped off altogether in a strong breeze. It is also disappointing that there is little fragrance. This would be a good rose for a site protected from wind during the flowering period through summer and autumn, both for

'Glenfiddich'

the garden and to cut for small arrangements. It is healthy and well furnished with light to mid-green, semi-glossy leaves. ZONES 4–9.

Cocker, UK, 1969

'Evelyn Fison' × 'Wendy Cussons'

Royal National Rose Society Certificate of Merit 1968

'GLENN DALE'
syn. 'Glendale'

MODERN, LARGE-FLOWERED CLIMBER, LIGHT
YELLOW

This is a rose to grow for moments of loveliness, such as when its big clusters of up to 20 blooms attain their mid-summer glory. The flowers are sizeable and very double with about 40 petals, and open from plump buds into young flowers of yellowish white, fading to white as they open out with muddled centers. They have a light scent, and do not repeat their flower in autumn. The plant grows vigorously to average height, and is best suited to being grown on a fence or as a pillar rose on a strong support. The leaves are dark and leathery. Glenn Dale in Maryland was the raiser's place of residence. ZONES 4–9.

Van Fleet, USA, 1927

Perhaps *Rosa wichuraiana* × 'Isabella Sprunt'

Portland Gold Medal 1920

'GLENSHANE'   DICvood

MODERN, GROUND COVER, MEDIUM RED,
REPEAT-FLOWERING

'Glenshane' is the first of a ground cover series developed by Dicksons and being

'Glengarry'

sold as 'The Irish Glen Collection', taking their names after one of Ulster's scenic glories. This rose has small rosette-style flowers that are produced in lovely large trusses which may hold up to 36 evenly spaced blooms. They are bright red and semi-double with a slight fragrance, withstand bad weather well and continue in flower from summer right through to late autumn. This would be a suitable variety for the front of a border or a modest area that needs covering. It can be expected to grow up to knee height in cool climates and up to hip height in warm ones, and half as wide again, so though not truly procumbent it is spreading in its character. ZONES 4–9.

Dickson, UK, 1997

Seedling × 'Star Child'

Royal National Rose Society Trial Ground Certificate 1995, British Association of Rose Breeders Breeders' Choice 1998

'Glendora'

G

'Gloire de Dijon'

'Gloire de Chédane-Guinoisseau'

'GLETSCHER'

MODERN, CLUSTER-FLOWERED/FLORIBUNDA, MAUVE, REPEAT-FLOWERING

This is an interesting rose, though it appears to be no longer available from nurseries. Its plump buds open into double flowers of a clear pale lilac color, with high centers. They are quite large, sweetly scented, and flower at the end of graceful arching stems. More blooms are produced intermittently through summer and autumn. The plant may be lightly pruned and grown as a shrub, in which form it is suitable for a border, or it can be kept down to a little more than average height for a bush rose. It grows vigorously with an upright, bushy habit, and is furnished with glossy foliage.

Gletscher is the German word for glacier, and the name refers to this rose's cool bluish color tone. ZONES 4–9.
Kordes, Germany, 1955
Seedling × 'Lavender Pinocchio'

'GLOIRE DE BRUXELLES'

syn. 'Gloire de l'Exposition de Bruxelles'
OLD, HYBRID PERPETUAL, MAUVE, REPEAT-FLOWERING

This rose bears strongly fragrant, large, mauve blooms with muddled centers. The base of the petals is a brilliant red, and the flowers are full and flat with a rosette form. They appear in summer with some repeat in autumn. This is a vigorous, upright bush to 4 ft (1.2 m) high, but it does need support as it becomes untidy with age. The foliage is healthy, but is susceptible to mildew. ZONES 5–9.
Soupert and Notting, France, 1889
'Souvenir de William Wood' × 'Lord Macaulay'

'GLOIRE DE CHÉDANE-GUINOISSEAU'

OLD, HYBRID PERPETUAL, MEDIUM RED

The flowers of this rose are bright crimson-red, double and give an occasional repeat display. They are cupped and very large, filled with about 40 petals. The bush is strong, upright, tall and thorny with dark green leaves and strong flower

'Gletscher'

stems. It was originally recommended for pot culture and for exhibition. It is still available to gardeners, although not as freely as its parent, 'Gloire de Ducher'. ZONES 5–9.
Chédane-Pajotin, France, 1907
'Gloire de Ducher' × seedling

'GLOIRE DE DIJON'

syn. 'Old Glory'
OLD, CLIMBING TEA, ORANGE-PINK, REPEAT-FLOWERING

So many have praised this beautiful Climbing Tea over the past 140 years that it still stands with the most favored roses in the world. Fat, squat buds open to reveal large, rich buff pink blooms that are large, full, globular, quartered and quilled. The center petals are apricot and the outer petals fade quickly in the sun. There is a pleasant scent. The vigorous, climbing growth is best on a wall or a pillar, and it is wise to bend down the stalks to develop laterals and more blooms. The reddish canes have hooked prickles. It blooms from summer until the first frost; the flowers do not like wet weather and it is prone to mildew and black spot. ZONES 5–9.
Jacotot, France, 1853
'Souvenir de la Malmaison' × 'Desprez à Fleurs Jaunes'
First Prize Dijon Horticultural Fair 1852, Paris Gold Medal 1853, Royal Horticultural Society Award of Garden Merit 1993

'GLOIRE DE DUCHER'

syn. 'Germania'
OLD, HYBRID PERPETUAL, DARK RED, REPEAT-FLOWERING

David Austin, the creator of the English Roses, praises this one for the splendor of its flowers. The abundant, 4 in (10 cm)

'Gloire de Ducher'

blooms are dark red, full and large, and have maroon centers. The quilled petals are folded around a button eye. Flowers appear in summer although the best crops are seen if flowering extends into autumn. The arching canes reach 7 ft (2.1 m), and the strong branches have light, reddish bark and hooked prickles. Its lanky growth is best on a wall or pillar; pegging down produces more blooms. It is subject to mildew. ZONES 5–9.
Ducher, France, 1865
Parentage unknown

'GLOIRE DE FRANCE'

syn. 'Glory of France'
OLD, GALLICA, LIGHT PINK

Changing its colors in shade or sun, this Gallica appears to be a Centifolia hybrid. The double, informally quartered, pink blooms have cerise centers, and the pink edges fade to light purple. The vigorous, well-formed canes create a spreading and arching thicket that becomes covered with flowers in early summer. It has soft, gray-green foliage. Recent research indicates that this rose was bred by an amateur who was a Court official at Angers and that it is not synonymous with 'Fanny Bias' as once thought. ZONES 4–9.
Bizard, France, 1828
Parentage unknown

'GLOIRE DE GUILAN'

OLD, DAMASK, LIGHT PINK

This rose was discovered in the Middle East by Nancy Lindsay. The medium-sized, fragrant flowers, which are at first cupped, open flat and quartered and appear in mid-summer. They are rich clear pink with softer highlights, created by the many reflexing petals. It is a tallish but relaxed shrub that can, in good conditions and when left unpruned, attain a height of 6 ft (1.8 m) and a similar width. It has many small, hooked thorns and mid- to bright green, finely textured leaves. This very floriferous variety needs space to develop its pleasing personality and is tolerant of poor soils. ZONES 5–9.
Introduced by Hilling, UK, 1949
Parentage unknown

'GLOIRE DES JARDINS'

syn. 'La Gloire des Jardins'
OLD, GALLICA, MAUVE

The golden stamens are prominent on the deep purple-crimson blooms of this rose. In early summer, 'Gloire des Jardins' is covered with double, cupped flowers, which have incurved petals that are silver

'Gloire de France'

'Gloire de Guilan'

on the undersides. The bushy growth is compact and medium-sized, and covered with dark green leaves. ZONES 4–9.

Descement, France, pre-1815

Parentage unknown

'GLOIRE DES MOUSSEUX'
syns 'Gloire des Mousseuses', 'Madame Alboni'

OLD, MOSS, MEDIUM PINK

The flower buds and calyces of this rose are heavily covered with light green moss. The flowers are large   4 in (10 cm) across—and very full of pink petals that give a cushion effect when fully open. They pale to almost blush as the flowers mature. It is a tall shrub to 6 ft (1.8 m) and is sturdy in habit, with plentiful light to mid-green foliage. This is an excellent shrub with much to recommend it, not least a healthy disposition. ZONES 4–9.

Laffay, France, 1852

Parentage unknown

'GLOIRE DES POLYANTHA'
MODERN, POLYANTHA, MEDIUM PINK, REPEAT-FLOWERING

This rose is among the earliest Polyanthas, and bears panicles crowded with up to as many as 80 little blooms that open from conical buds into small double flowers. They are usually described as bright pink, but there is a good deal of carmine tone present and the pigment is seen on a pale background that enhances the overall effect. The middle of each petal is often striped deep pink or red, a reminder of the instability of color in this Polyantha strain. Flowering continues through summer and autumn and there is no scent to speak of. This variety is unlikely to be sought after, since it is apt to mildew. It grows to average height with plentiful leaflets that are dull and finely toothed like those of its wild *Rosa multiflora* ancestor. ZONES 4–9.

Guillot, France, 1887

Seedling of 'Mignonette'

'GLOIRE DES ROSOMANES'
syns 'Jupiter's Lightning', 'Ragged Robin', 'Red Robin'

OLD, CHINA, MEDIUM RED, REPEAT-FLOWERING

One of the hardiest roses ever created, this China is placed in the Bourbon class

'Gloire de Guilan' (hips)

by some rosarians. Blooming from spring until autumn, the fragrant rose begins with dainty, pointed buds that develop into sparkling maroon or glowing crimson flowers with white streaks. The semi-double, very large, widely cupped blooms appear in clusters and turn purple in hot weather. This rose has been the parent of many other varieties and is often used as an understock. 'Gloire des Rosomanes' is

a vigorous, upright bush to 5 ft (1.5 m) covered with prickles on its long branches. It does well on poor soil and produces many orange hips. ZONES 7–9.

Vibert, France, 1825

Parentage unknown

'GLOIRE D'UN ENFANT D'HIRAM'
OLD, HYBRID PERPETUAL, MEDIUM RED, REPEAT-FLOWERING

Although almost extinct, this rose has strong links with history. It was adopted by a Masonic society in Melun, France and named for a famous architect who constructed the first temple in Jerusalem in 985 BC. The bright red buds are followed by full, fragrant, abundant blooms ranging in color from vermilion, red and carmine. They age from vermilion-red to carmine to a velvety violet. The vigorous, upright plant can reach 7 ft (2.1 m) and looks best on a fence or wall. It is sparsely covered with handsome, gray-green leaves and a few large prickles; in

autumn there is a crop of large hips. Deadheading is highly recommended to extend the flowering period. ZONES 5–9.

Vilin, France, 1899

Seedling of 'Ulrich Brunner Fils'

'GLOIRE LYONNAISE'
OLD, HYBRID PERPETUAL, WHITE, REPEAT-FLOWERING

There are many roses with reference to Lyon in their names, which is not surprising as Lyon was the center of rose breeding in the nineteenth century. This is a cupped, creamy white, very double rose with 84 thin petals. The very large, fragrant blooms are somewhat flat and of medium size, and in the shade are chrome yellow. It is a floriferous shrub with dark green, leathery foliage, some prickles and good disease resistance. It should be pruned moderately. The 4 ft (1.2 m) canes make it an ideal shrub for the back of the border. ZONES 5–9.

Guillot, France, 1885

'Baroness Rothschild' × 'Mme Falcot'

'Gloire des Rosomanes'

'Gloire des Mousseux'

'Gloire des Mousseux'

'Gloire Lyonnaise'

G

'GLORIA MUNDI'
MODERN, POLYANTHA, ORANGE-RED, REPEAT-FLOWERING

Before World War II this rose was offered by nurseries as an orange variety, and it is a measure of the progress made by breeders that such a description now seems utterly misleading. Today it would be considered a scarlet-red, but at the time the label 'orange' or 'orange-red' certainly helped sell the roses. It was an important color break, due to a chemical change whereby pelargonidin, common in pelargoniums, entered the kingdom of the rose, and even though 'Gloria Mundi' was not the rose destined to carry that innovation forward it became amazingly popular. Its small double rosettes are born in clusters of many blooms, and it continues in flower throughout summer and autumn. It was formerly used for hedges and beds in parks and gardens everywhere. Some shoots tended to revert back to a parent form, showing an ugly clash of scarlet and magenta, one of the reasons why Polyanthas were ousted in favor of the healthier and color-fast Cluster-flowered Roses. ZONES 4–9.

de Ruiter, The Netherlands, 1929
Sport of 'Superb'

'Gloriana 97'

'Gloriana 97'

'GLORIANA 97' CHEwpope
MODERN, CLIMBING MINIATURE, MAUVE, REPEAT-FLOWERING

The double, medium-sized blooms of this rose each bear 15–25 mauve-pink petals with dark lilac undersides. The flowers are usually borne in small clusters amid the semi-glossy, mid-green foliage, and give a slight fragrance. 'Gloriana 97' is a tall Climbing Miniature that is one of the latest varieties to come from the winning hybridizing program of Chris Warner in England. ZONES 5–11.

Warner, UK, 1997
Parentage unknown

'GLORY BE' SAVabe
MODERN, MINIATURE, DEEP YELLOW, REPEAT-FLOWERING

The flowers of this variety are a bright shade of deep yellow, neatly formed with up to 25 petals. They are small in size, even for a Miniature. Usually, they are carried one to a stem, with no appreciable fragrance. 'Glory Be' is useful for a container or small space, as well as for exhibitions. The plants have an upright, bushy habit with small, semi-glossy, dark green leaves. ZONES 5–9.

Saville, USA, 1995
'Party Girl' × 'Sonnenkind'

'Goethe'

'Gold Badge'

'GLORY OF EDSELL'
syn. 'Glory of Edzell'
OLD, SCOTS, LIGHT PINK

This is one of the first roses to bloom in spring. It offers clear pink, single blooms with white centers that open flat and display large, attractive stamens. It is a 6 ft (1.8 m) tall shrub that does well in the shade. Small, dense, ferny foliage covers the upright, spiny canes; its growth habit makes it a good plant either for the woodland garden or as a hedge. Like other Scots Roses, it blooms only in spring. ZONES 5–9.

Pre-1900
Parentage unknown

'GLOWING'
MODERN, LARGE-FLOWERED/HYBRID TEA, PALE YELLOW, REPEAT-FLOWERING

This very tall-growing, upright rose of upright habit produces long, elegant, pointed blooms of soft maize yellow, sometimes lightly tinged with pink on the outer petals. The blooms open to very double flowers of 35 petals with the inner petals slightly quilled. There is a slight scent. The foliage is mid-green, matt and very plentiful, and there are no disease problems. 'Glowing' is a good rose for a tall hedge. ZONES 5–9.

LeGrice, UK, 1986
Parentage unknown

'GLOWING AMBER' MANglow
MODERN, MINIATURE, RED BLEND, REPEAT-FLOWERING

The flowers of this variety are scarlet-red with deep yellow undersides and bright yellow centers. They are double, made up of 26–40 petals, and have elegant high

'Glory of Edsell'

'Glowing'

centers that give it great exhibition potential. The blooms unfurl slowly to reveal the dramatic scarlet and yellow coloration that does not fade. The small flowers are borne singly on long stems and match the petite, dark green foliage. 'Glowing Amber' is a very prolific, vigorous bush that is easy to grow. The variety made its winning debut at the Royal National Rose Society National Miniature Show in 1997 where a vase of 6 impeccable blooms in the Dr Tommy Cairns Class took first prize. ZONES 5–10.

Mander, Canada, 1996
'June Laver' × 'Rubies 'n' Pearls'

'GOETHE'
OLD, MOSS, MAUVE BLEND

This is a tall, very vigorous bush as befits a hybrid of such unusual parentage. *Rosa multiflora* was normally used to produce Ramblers, and this may have been Lambert's original intention since he admired them. It is very prickly and there is lots of brownish moss on the buds. The deep magenta-pink flowers with yellow stamens are single, or almost so, and only bloom once in early summer. There are not many single Mosses around now, so it may be worth growing 'Goethe' as a curiosity, although Graham Thomas disparages it. ZONES 5–9.

Lambert, Germany, 1911
Rosa multiflora × unidentified Moss Rose

'GOLD BADGE' MEIgronuri
syns 'Gold Bunny', 'Rimosa 79'
MODERN, CLUSTER-FLOWERED/FLORIBUNDA, MEDIUM YELLOW, REPEAT-FLOWERING

This is a very popular yellow rose in warmer climates, praised for its clear unfading color, pleasant scent, freedom of flower and ability to maintain a good succession of bloom. It opens from conical buds into lemon yellow flowers full of petals that undulate into each other, which explains the use of the Latin word *rimosa* as one of the names, indicating the many chinks and crevices glimpsed between them. The flowers have the classic Large-flowered form, and when fully expanded are almost as big. They last well, so are useful to cut as well as for a bed or hedge in the garden. In cooler climates, although the blooms withstand bad weather well they seem to lose color and become liable to black spot and rust. The plant grows vigorously to less than average height and is amply provided with dark green glossy leaves. **'Climbing Gold Badge'** (MEIgro-nurisar; syns 'Climbing Gold Bunny', 'Climbing Rimosa'; Meilland, France, 1991) is a sport of 'Gold Badge'. It won the Baden-Baden Gold Medal and the Saverne Gold Medal in 1991. **ZONES 4–9.**

Paolino, France, 1978

'Poppy Flash' × ('Charleston' × 'Allgold')

'GOLD COIN'

MODERN, MINIATURE, DEEP YELLOW, REPEAT-FLOWERING

Bright buttercup yellow blooms are the hallmark of this classic golden oldie! The fragrant flowers are a little large for the typical Miniature, decorative in form, and are produced in large clusters. The blooms are exquisite when they open and give wonderful flat bursts of color through the summer and autumn, even in hot climates. 'Gold Coin' is often used as a border in the garden, but is quite winter tender and needs protection if there is snow. It looks best in the autumn because it gives a finale of color at the end of the growing season. **ZONES 5–11.**

Moore, USA, 1967

'Golden Glow' × 'Magic Wand'

'GOLD COUNTRY'   SEAgold

MODERN, MINIATURE, MEDIUM YELLOW, REPEAT-FLOWERING

The good-looking, medium yellow blooms of this rose are borne singly on an attractive, compact bush with light green, semi-glossy foliage. Although the flowers are a great color, they are a little

'Gold Fever'

'Gold Crown'

too big for a Miniature Rose; they are double, with about 20 petals, and are very fragrant. The variety is not that tolerant to heat, but in half shade the blooms retain much of their color and do not bleach out to a poor white shade. It is one of the many hybridizing efforts from that great Irish garden writer and speaker, Sean McCann. **ZONES 5–11.**

McCann, Ireland, 1987

'Rise 'n' Shine' × ('Rise 'n' Shine' × 'Casino')

'GOLD CROWN'

syns 'Corona de Oro', 'Couronne d'Or', 'Gold Krone', 'Goldkrone'

MODERN, LARGE-FLOWERED/HYBRID TEA, DEEP YELLOW, REPEAT-FLOWERING

On this variety, some 36 large, substantial petals create much bigger flowers than might be expected. They are very high-centered, and are borne, sometimes singly, sometimes in 3s, on lanky thick stems like lollipops. At their best the flowers are potential prize-winners at shows, but some develop split centers and the first flush sometimes fails to

'Gold Badge'

appear on time due to frost or cold winds in spring. Considering the size of the blooms, their ability to repeat their flower through summer and autumn is good, and there is some fragrance. For a group in a border it has its uses in the garden, though as a plant it somehow lacks grace. It grows vigorously to above average height and has tough foliage, dark and semi-glossy, that may be affected by seasonal mildew. **ZONES 5–9.**

Kordes, Germany, 1960

'Peace' × 'Spek's Yellow'

Royal National Rose Society Certificate of Merit 1960

'GOLD FEVER'   MORfever

MODERN, MINIATURE, MEDIUM YELLOW, REPEAT-FLOWERING

This rose has elegant, pointed buds that finally open to medium yellow blooms that age to a much lighter pale yellow. The cupped florets have 40–50 petals and a spicy fragrance. The blooms are usually borne one to a stem, but in early spring clusters can develop. They hold their color well in the heat. The foliage is of medium size, semi-glossy and has slender prickles, and the plant has a vigorous, compact, upright habit. It is ideal as a container-grown plant. **ZONES 4–11.**

Moore, USA, 1990

'Sheri Anne' × 'Gold Badge'

'Gold Glow'

'GOLD GLOW'

MODERN, LARGE-FLOWERED/HYBRID TEA, DEEP YELLOW, REPEAT-FLOWERING

This rose was credited to H. A. Conklin in the 1960 *American Rose Annual*, and to Anthony Perry in editions of *Modern Roses* since then. It has up to an incredible 120 petals in its bright yellow flowers, which open up like double dahlias with ruffled petal edges and may fade in very hot weather. The medium to large-sized blooms are borne singly and last well. There is a modest fragrance. The plant grows vigorously with an upright habit and has a covering of dark and glossy leathery leaves. **ZONES 5–9.**

Perry/Conklin, USA, 1959

'Fred Howard' × 'Sutter's Gold'

'Gold Coin'

'Gold Medal'

'GOLD MEDAL' AROyqueli
syn. 'Golden Medal'
MODERN, LARGE-FLOWERED/HYBRID TEA,
MEDIUM YELLOW, REPEAT-FLOWERING

This is a fine yellow rose for warmer countries. In the USA it is called a Grandiflora, but the flower size qualifies it to be accepted as a Large-flowered Rose elsewhere. The blooms are carried usually in open trusses, sometimes singly, and open from plump pointed buds into flowers of classic Large-lowered shape, with high centers that are maintained for some time while the outer petals reflex. The color is basically a shining deep yellow, sometimes streaked with orange and light red, and there is a pleasing fruity fragrance. For a bed or group or hedge where a large growing rose is wanted, and one that will keep blooming through summer and autumn, this is an excellent choice, and it gives splendid flowers for cutting. The plant grows tall and vigorously to above average height and is well furnished with deep green foliage. ZONES 5–9.

Christensen, USA, 1982

'Yellow Pages' × 'Shirley Langhorn'

New Zealand Gold Star of the South Pacific 1983

'GOLD REEF' POUldom
MODERN, CLUSTER-FLOWERED/FLORIBUNDA,
DEEP YELLOW, REPEAT-FLOWERING

This beautiful bush rose produces a continuous show of bright yellow, medium-sized, double flowers. The blooms are carried either singly or in small clusters and can be cut for indoor arrangements. There is a slight fragrance. 'Gold Reef' is a useful shrub because of its vigorous, carefree growth; it can be grown in groups with other tall roses or companion plants, or by themselves in clumps or as hedges to screen unsightly areas. ZONES 4–10.

Poulsen, Denmark, 1994

Parentage unknown

'GOLD RUSH'
MODERN, LARGE-FLOWERED CLIMBER, YELLOW
BLEND

The flowers of this light golden yellow rose have about 24 petals, which open to reveal high-centered young flowers that open out into cupped, rather loosely formed blooms with only a moderate fragrance. The flowering is usually confined to the summer only, though there may be a smattering of late bloom. This variety is suitable for growing against a warm wall or on a trellis or pergola. 'Gold Rush' makes vigorous growth and will extend a little beyond the average height expected of a climbing rose. There is a respectable covering of glossy, ivy green foliage. The plant is a rather rare item now and is offered only by nurseries in the USA, Canada and Israel.
ZONES 4–9.

Duehrsen, USA, 1941

Parentage unknown

'GOLDBUSCH'
MODERN, MODERN SHRUB, MEDIUM YELLOW,
REPEAT-FLOWERING

This is an interesting shrub to grow where there is plenty of space. It produces clusters of up to 20 pinkish buds, which develop into medium to

'Gold Rush'

'Goldbusch'

large-sized semi-double flowers in a pretty shade of pale gold. The blooms are loosely formed, and open cupped with ruffled petals half concealing the attractive gold stamens. They have a pleasant light fragrance, and are carried on arching stems freely in summer and sporadically later. For a garden where plants can be allowed to grow naturally this is a useful item, reaching double the size of an average shrub rose with an arching, sprawling habit. In warmer climates the growth is extensive enough to make it suitable for training as a climbing or pillar rose. The foliage is light green and leathery and has barely a hint of the scent the raiser no doubt hoped for through his use of *Rosa eglanteria*, the wild sweet briar. ZONES 4–9.

Kordes, Germany, 1954

'Golden Glow' × *Rosa eglanteria* hybrid

'GOLDEN ANGEL'
MODERN, MINIATURE, DEEP YELLOW,
REPEAT-FLOWERING

The short buds of 'Golden Angel' yield mature, pointed, deep yellow flowers containing 65 petals. The bush produces mostly large clusters of small, fragrant flowers with a long-lasting quality. It is at its most beautiful stage of bloom when fully opened, when the attractive petal formations are more obvious. The seed parent, the Large-flowered Rose 'Golden Glow', has been used extensively by Ralph Moore in his hybridizing program; it gives strength and vigor to its

offspring, but unfortunately not the small bloom size nor the Large-flowered form. ZONES 5–11.

Moore, USA, 1975

'Golden Glow' × ('Little Darling' × seedling)

'GOLDEN ANNIVERSARY'
MODERN, LARGE-FLOWERED/HYBRID TEA,
DEEP YELLOW, REPEAT-FLOWERING

There have been two roses of this name, providing a convenient solution to the problem of what to give to mark fiftieth celebrations. This one may still live on in gardens, though it is no longer commercially available. It bears plump buds that open into large rounded flowers with up to 60 petals. The flowers are yellow with high centers, and have good fragrance. Flowering continues through summer and autumn, though in really hot weather the blooms lose their color and become whitish, and in very wet conditions they sometimes ball and fail to open at all. The variety has performed satisfactorily as a bedding and exhibition rose, though it suffers in a bad black spot year. It is vigorous and grows taller than average with an upright, bushy habit. ZONES 4–9.

Mordigan Evergreen Nursery, USA, 1948

Sport of 'Good News'

'GOLDEN BETTINA'
MODERN, LARGE-FLOWERED/HYBRID TEA,
DEEP YELLOW, REPEAT-FLOWERING

This sport bears deep chrome yellow flowers, instead of the deep salmon-

'Golden Angel'

'Gold Medal'

'Golden Anniversary'

orange of its parent. The fragrant, double blooms each have 35 petals and develop from attractive oval buds that open to well-formed, rather flat flowers. The foliage is dark green, glossy and abundant, and the growth habit is vigorous with good flower production. Disease resistance is excellent. Both 'Bettina' and 'Golden Bettina' are good roses for bedding schemes and borders, and make bushy standards. ZONES 5–9.

Ruston, Australia, 1970

Sport of 'Bettina'

'GOLDEN CELEBRATION'

AUSgold

MODERN, MODERN SHRUB, DEEP YELLOW, REPEAT-FLOWERING

The round buds of this rose open into large flowers of cupped form, recessed in the center. They are fully double and intricately formed, with the larger petals forming a ring and overlapping each other round the outside while the base of the cup is filled with smaller petals, creased and folded. The deep yellow color is more golden than most roses that lay such a claim in their title. There is a strong fragrance and the variety continues to bloom through summer and autumn, though in wet weather the arching stems may be bowed down by the heavy flowers. It is very suitable for a border, making a rounded shrub of average height with dark glossy leaves. 'Golden Celebration' is also classified as an English Rose. ZONES 4–9.

Austin, UK, 1992

'Charles Austin' × 'Abraham Darby'

'GOLDEN CENTURY'

MODERN, CLIMBING MINIATURE, ORANGE BLEND, REPEAT-FLOWERING

The pointed buds of 'Golden Century' develop into flowers best described as cadmium red to nasturtium red, with some veining on the petals. The blooms are double, with 35 petals, medium sized and fragrant. The foliage is leathery and glossy green, and covers a moderately sized climber. During the first 2 years after planting it is slow to climb and there is little bloom production, but in the third year watch out for a breathtakingly big splash of color in the spring. The raiser was abe to obtain this result by using a special seedling of his own breeding. ZONES 4–11.

Moore, USA, 1978

(Rosa wichuraiana × 'Floradora') × ('Sister Thérèse' × Miniature seedling)

'GOLDEN CHERSONESE'

HILgold

MODERN, MODERN SHRUB, MEDIUM YELLOW

This is an interesting cross between Rosa ecae, a species not easy to establish in cooler countries, and 'Canary Bird', a species hybrid that is more vigorous. The offspring combines the vividly bright yellow of the first with the vigor of the second. The flowers are like brilliant buttercups, borne close to the branches on tall arching stems and are pleasantly fragrant. They appear in spring; this is one of the first roses to bloom. The wood is reddish and the small light green leaflets have a dainty ferny shape. The plant is best grown where it does not need pruning, except to remove dead wood. It makes an upright, somewhat narrow, arching plant up to about twice the average height for a shrub rose. It should be grown where it is not exposed to the risk of dieback caused by frost-bearing winds in early spring. The name is an ancient one referring to the Malay Peninsula. ZONES 5–9.

Allen, UK, 1969

Rosa ecae × 'Canary Bird'

'GOLDEN CHOICE'

MODERN, LARGE-FLOWERED/HYBRID TEA, MEDIUM YELLOW, REPEAT-FLOWERING

This variety bears lemon yellow flowers and in other respects resembles the variety from which it sported, having large full-petalled flowers that open to reveal high centers, with the outer petals reflexing back to create the classic Large-flowered form, a combination of size, symmetry and grace. There is a very sweet fragrance, and roses continue to appear through summer and autumn. It is capable of providing quality exhibition blooms if they are cut young, and it makes a good bedding or border rose. The plant grows upright with a bushy habit to average height or a little less, and is clothed in leathery leaves. Bardill's Nursery near Nottingham discovered the sport, and asked LeGrice of Norfolk, the breeders of 'My Choice', to introduce it. ZONES 4–9.

Bardill, UK, 1967

Sport of 'My Choice'

'GOLDEN DAWN'

MODERN, LARGE-FLOWERED/HYBRID TEA, MEDIUM YELLOW, REPEAT-FLOWERING

Only a very pale rising sun is needed to match the color of 'Golden Dawn', which is closer to primrose than gold; this is not to decry the great virtues of this rose, a standby for nurseries in the days before 'Peace' brought real strength into yellow roses. Its light-colored blooms, tinged with pink on the outer petals, are rounded and full and have a surprising ability to shrug off bad weather. Theirs are among the very first Large-flowered Roses to bloom in summer; again a surprise in view of their large size. The scent is sweet and enduring, and in its heyday the variety was one of the best choices for a bed as well as being useful for exhibition. All that tells against it by comparison with post-war yellows is that the dark gray-green foliage, good by the standards of that era, looks skimpy now—another measure of how the work of breeders has raised standards in recent years. There have been at least 3 climbing sports (Armstrong, USA, 1935; Knight, Australia, 1937; LeGrice, UK, 1946) of 'Golden Dawn' introduced into commerce and there is, not surprisingly, no record of a comparative trial of them all together having been made. The UK

'Golden Chersonese'

'Golden Bettina'

'Golden Celebration'

G

'Climbing Golden Dawn' is one that came from LeGrice of Norfolk. It was awarded the National Rose Society Trial Ground Certificate in 1946 and was re-leased that year. It is like the bush form in all respects save in its climbing growth, which will extend to about aver-age, and in the amount of late summer and autumn bloom, of which there is some but not nearly as much as in the bush form. ZONES 4–9.

Grant, Australia, 1929

'Elegante' × 'Ethel Somerset'

'GOLDEN DAYS'   RUgolda, RUggolda

MODERN, LARGE-FLOWERED/HYBRID TEA, DEEP YELLOW, REPEAT-FLOWERING

This is a rose with large flowers of classic form, made up of 36 wide petals. They are usually borne one to a stem and open with high centers, the petals recurving prettily so that their tips form an array of points around the circumference of the bloom. The color is bright yellow, tend-ing to fade and admit some pink at the edges as the flowers age. There is a pleas-ing fragrance, and blooms continue to appear through summer and autumn. The plant grows with a bushy habit to average height and has plentiful leathery foliage. The introducers intended it to be

used as a gift for golden weddings. Only in the UK is it commercially available at the time of writing. ZONES 4–9.

De Ruiter, The Netherlands, 1980

'Peer Gynt' × seedling

'GOLDEN DELIGHT'

MODERN, CLUSTER-FLOWERED/FLORIBUNDA, MEDIUM YELLOW, REPEAT-FLOWERING

'Golden Delight' has a compact habit with shorter than average growth. The flowers have a substantial number of petals, nearly 60 in all. The cheerful yellow blooms are carried in crowded clusters, and when fully open are cupped with the petals infolded against each other and the stamens peeping through. They have a sweet fragrance, and more flowers appear through summer and autumn. Given a fertile soil and good cultivation it makes a fine bedding rose, as it has a neat habit and attractive glossy dark green foliage. ZONES 4–9.

LeGrice, UK, 1956

'Goldilocks' × 'Ellinor LeGrice'

'GOLDEN FLEECE'

syn. 'Toison d'Or'

MODERN, CLUSTER-FLOWERED/FLORIBUNDA, MEDIUM YELLOW, REPEAT-FLOWERING

Gene Boerner used two of his own crea-tions as the parents of this rose, which is

'Golden Fleece'

a somewhat pallid buff yellow color, deeper in the center. The blooms are large, with nearly 40 waved petals, and they are borne in sizeable clusters on stiff stems. They have a pleasant fruity scent and flower repeatedly through summer and autumn, yet they are intolerant of prolonged wet weather. In the garden, this is a suitable rose for beds, borders and hedges, though only one grower ap-pears to be offering it today. The plants grow vigorously with a bushy, upright habit to average height, and have an ample covering of dark green, leathery leaves. ZONES 4–9.

Boerner, USA, 1955

'Diamond Jubilee' × 'Yellow Sweetheart'

Bagatelle Gold Medal 1955, National Rose Society Certificate of Merit 1955

'GOLDEN FRIENDSHIP'

HARtellody

MODERN, LARGE-FLOWERED/HYBRID TEA, MEDIUM YELLOW, REPEAT-FLOWERING

When the raiser saw this rose among his seedlings it reminded him of the beauti-ful old Large-flowered 'Golden Melody', and that thought inspired the choice of code name. The color is that of Jersey cream, a rich pale yellow with creamy blush towards the petal tips. The flowers have elegant long buds opening to blooms with very high centers, and, thanks to the breadth and firmness of the petals, they compose a larger bloom than one would think possible from only 26 or so of these. They are good for cutting as well as for general garden use, have a delicate fragrance and continue in bloom through summer and autumn. The

'Golden Gardens'

growth is upright and bushy, with dark green leaves. The variety was named and introduced in Australia on behalf of a women's friendship group, Beta Sigma Phi. ZONES 4–9.

Harkness, UK, 1982

'Basildon Bond' × 'Anne Harkness'

'GOLDEN GARDENS'   MORgogard

MODERN, MINIATURE, MEDIUM YELLOW, REPEAT-FLOWERING

The oval buds of this lovely rose mature into bright, clear yellow flowers with lighter undersides. These small, decora-tive blooms are double and cupped, with 28 petals, and usually occur in small clusters of 3–5 blooms. It is a very floriferous rose and tends to grow like a climber rather a bush. In the garden, it is best grown as a small shrub or a short climber. 'Golden Gardens' gains most of its attributes from the Cluster-flowered Roses 'Little Darling' and 'Gold Badge'. ZONES 5–11.

Moore, USA, 1989

('Little Darling' × 'Yellow Magic') × 'Gold Badge'

'GOLDEN GIANT'   KORbi

syns 'Fièvre d'Or', 'Gold Rausch', 'Goldrausch'

MODERN, LARGE-FLOWERED/HYBRID TEA, DEEP YELLOW, REPEAT-FLOWERING

With nearly 48 wide petals, this variety forms large high-centered blooms, and it is not unusual for up to 5 of them to be carried in one heavy truss. The raiser considered it to be a Cluster-flowered Rose, and in that company it would in-deed appear a 'giant'. The flowers are a rich bright yellow, paling towards the

'Golden Delight'

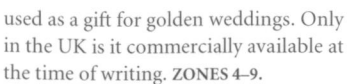

'Golden Friendship'

'Golden Days'

'Golden Giant'

edges and with veining on the petals. There is a pleasing fragrance, and flowers continue to appear with excellent continuity through summer and autumn. The flowers are good for exhibition if disbudded, and for cutting. In the garden this is best sited in a border behind other plants, because it is a tall, ungainly grower. Mildew can be a problem on the leaves, which are matt and medium green. The German name means 'gold rush' and the French name 'gold fever'. **ZONES 4–9.**

Kordes, Germany, 1961

('Condesa de Sástago' × 'Walter Bentley') × 'Buccaneer'

National Rose Society Gold Medal 1960

'GOLDEN GIRL' MEIvirgi
MODERN, LARGE-FLOWERED/HYBRID TEA, MEDIUM YELLOW, REPEAT-FLOWERING

In the USA this rose is sometimes called a Grandiflora, but it is close in character to a Large-flowered Rose. It bears bright yellow flowers on very long stems, sometimes singly and sometimes in a candelabra of several together. They are full petalled, well formed with high centers, and finally open cupped, giving a better display in cooler weather as hot sun causes them to pale to cream or white. The repeat-flowering is not particularly free, but flowers do appear through summer and autumn. They are moderately fragrant, and are good for cutting as they last well, or to group in a border. The plant grows vigorously with an upright habit and has leathery light green leaves that may at times be affected by black spot or mildew. **ZONES 4–9.**

Meilland, France, 1959

('Joanna Hill' × 'Eclipse') × 'Michèle Meilland'

'GOLDEN GLOVES'
MODERN, CLUSTER-FLOWERED/FLORIBUNDA, DEEP YELLOW, REPEAT-FLOWERING

The blooms of this rose are produced in small clusters. They are double, with rather small petals; on first opening they have tight centers like small-scale Large-flowered Roses, but then they become cupped, with the petals reflexing to reveal the stamens. There is a delicate fragrance, and flowering is maintained through summer and autumn. The plant is bushy and is furnished with bright green leaves, and it seems to be commercially available only in Western Australia though it was raised in California. The precise connection between a rose and the world of amateur boxing is difficult to follow, but therein lies the reason for the name, for the Golden Gloves Award is a high accolade in that branch of sport. **ZONES 4–9.**

Bear Creek, USA, 1991

('Korresia' × 'Katherine Loker') × 'Gingersnap'

'GOLDEN HALO' SAVahalo
MODERN, MINIATURE, MEDIUM YELLOW, REPEAT-FLOWERING

This prize-winning rose starts off with oval buds that develop into bright yellow flowers with 24–26 petals; there is a red touch to the outer petals as they reflex. They are of exhibition, Large-flowered

'Golden Harvest'

form and only have a slight fragrance. The plant has a very upright habit with no desire to spread out, and it is easy to grow and maintain. The foliage is glossy dark green and very disease resistant. This color created a lot of excitement when the rose first appeared, as good yellow Miniature Roses are difficult to find. The extra red blush to the outer petals is a real plus. In spite of its low petal count, 'Golden Halo' has traveled well to rose exhibitions around the world. **ZONES 4–11.**

Saville, USA, 1991

'Arthur Bell' × 'Rainbow's End'

American Rose Society Award of Excellence 1991

'GOLDEN HANDSHAKE'
CHEwsunford
MODERN, CLIMBING MINIATURE, DEEP YELLOW, REPEAT-FLOWERING

The flowers of 'Golden Handshake' are, as one would expect, a clear bright yellow and contain about 15–25 petals. The dainty flowers are borne in small clusters; they have a good form and a light fragrance. The plant has a tall, upright habit. **ZONES 5–11.**

Warner, UK, 1996

'Pam Ayres' × 'Laura Ford'

'GOLDEN HARVEST'
MODERN, LARGE-FLOWERED/HYBRID TEA, DEEP YELLOW, REPEAT-FLOWERING

The flowers of this variety open from urn-shaped buds into large high-centered blooms, made up of some 36 wide petals. The blooms hold their form and open slowly in hot weather, though this may cause a fading in their clear yellow color, admitting cream and white towards the petal margins. There is a light fragrance, and blooming continues through summer and autumn, making this rose suitable for beds and borders as well as for cutting. The plant grows vigorously to about average height and has a bushy habit, and it is well furnished with leathery textured glossy foliage that is reddish when young. **ZONES 4–9.**

Mallerin, France, 1943

'McGredy's Ivory' × seedling

'GOLDEN HOLSTEIN' KORtikel
syn. 'Surprise'
MODERN, CLUSTER-FLOWERED/FLORIBUNDA, DEEP YELLOW, REPEAT-FLOWERING

This is a lovely and unusual rose, bearing bright golden yellow flowers that look almost single, having only 12 or so rather small wavy petals. From pointed buds

'Golden Masterpiece'

'Golden Holstein'

they open out like little saucers, and they are perched closely together in clusters at the top of the stem with their attractive stamens exposed to view. They have a light scent, maintain an excellent succession of bloom, and withstand bad weather, though they fade in hot sun. For a group in a mixed border this rose is very suitable, though a watch needs to be kept for mildew. It grows strongly with a vigorous, upright habit to average height and has dark green shiny leaves. **ZONES 4–9.**

Kordes, Germany, 1989

Parentage unknown

'GOLDEN JUBILEE' COCagold
MODERN, LARGE-FLOWERED/HYBRID TEA, MEDIUM YELLOW, REPEAT-FLOWERING

This is a fine rose, handsome in its proportions, being fully double with about 30 firm petals. It carries its blooms upright on stiff stems, usually singly but sometimes in 3s, the flowers opening with high centers and developing into large flowers of symmetrical form as the petals reflex. The color is a medium shade of yellow, with touches of pink. For cutting, as a bedding rose or for a group in a border this is very suitable. The flowers have a light fragrance, and blooming continues through summer and autumn though usually with an interval after the first generous flush while the plant regathers its strength. It grows vigorously with an upright, lanky habit and has large mid-green leaves that may show seasonal mildew. **ZONES 4–9.**

Cocker, UK, 1981

'Peer Gynt' × 'Gay Gordons'

'Golden Girl'

'GOLDEN MASTERPIECE'
MODERN, LARGE-FLOWERED/HYBRID TEA, MEDIUM YELLOW, REPEAT-FLOWERING

The petals of this lemon yellow rose are long and broad; they open well in good weather but can ball up and spoil in the rain. Even when the sun shines there can be split centers and color fading, but when it is behaving well its 30 petals form elegant high centers as the young flowers emerge from long pointed buds. They have some fragrance. In its heyday it was a successful rose for a bed or border. It is an upright, vigorous grower but needs watching for black spot. **ZONES 4–9.**

Boerner, USA, 1954

'Mandalay' × 'Spek's Yellow'

National Rose Society Certificate of Merit 1954

'GOLDEN MOMENTS' FRYtranquil
MODERN, LARGE-FLOWERED/HYBRID TEA, DEEP YELLOW, REPEAT-FLOWERING

The color of this rose is not truly deep yellow as the official coding suggests but more of a golden amber, a warm and gentle shade, with blush pink touching the petal margins. It bears full-petalled flowers on long stems; the flowers open with tight centers, which are held for some time as the outer petals reflex. The blooms generally withstand wind and rain well and there is a pleasing fragrance. It grows to average height with a vigorous, bushy habit and has mid- to deep green leaves. **ZONES 4–9.**

Fryer, UK, 1991

Parentage unknown

The Hague First Class Certificate 1990, Rome Bronze Medal 1992, Belfast Certificate of Merit 1993

G

'Golden Slippers'

'Golden Ophelia'

'Golden Scepter'

'Golden Showers'

'GOLDEN OPHELIA'

MODERN, LARGE-FLOWERED/HYBRID TEA,
MEDIUM YELLOW, REPEAT-FLOWERING

The pretty shape of 'Ophelia' has set a standard for decorative (that is, modest-sized) Large-flowered Roses. Such roses retain their high center while the outer petals are reflexing to form a rounded outline to the flower, thus creating a form of beautiful symmetry. 'Golden Ophelia' does this to perfection, though its blooms are a little smaller and shorter than those of its parental namesake. The heart of the flower is yellow, paling to almost white towards the outer petals. There is a light fragrance, and it continues to blossom satisfactorily through summer and autumn. For cutting and as

a buttonhole it is excellent. The growth is slender, up to average height, and the glossy foliage cover is adequate rather than ample, but as an example of a .vintage decorative rose it is well worth having in the rose border. ZONES 4–9.

Cant, UK, 1918

Said to be 'Ophelia' × 'Mrs Aaron Ward'

National Rose Society Gold Medal 1918

'GOLDEN SCEPTER'

syn. 'Spek's Yellow'

MODERN, LARGE-FLOWERED/HYBRID TEA,
DEEP YELLOW, REPEAT-FLOWERING

The brilliance of the rich golden yellow color, and its unfading quality even in the hottest weather, tended to blind rosarians to the faults of this early post-war rose. The habit of growth is un-gainly, and the blooms are produced in wide sprays on stems not quite firm enough for so many roses, each with 36 petals all set to construct a sizeable flower. In spite of this it became, due to its freedom of bloom, general good health and, above all, its incomparable yellowness, one of the most popular roses of the 1950s, used for beds, borders and for cutting. There is a little scent, flowering is well maintained through summer and autumn, and it grows vig-orously, if gawkily, to above average height, with glossy leathery leaves.

'Climbing Golden Scepter' (syn. 'Climbing Spek's Yellow; Walters, USA, 1956) is a sport of 'Golden Scepter'. The disadvantages of the bush form of this rose are less of a problem in the climber because, when they are elevated, the flowers bowing on their long sprays are brought conveniently into the gardener's view. This vigorous plant is difficult to control, for it is capable of growing twice the size of the average climber. Also, the growth becomes very stiff after the first season, so training needs to be done early while the wood is still pliable. A high wall is the best and perhaps the only sensible site for this rose, because it can provide a firm support and many points of attachment. Shoots need to be trained laterally or slantwise, otherwise the base will become bare very quickly. Both the flowers and foliage are identical to those of the bush, but after the main summer flush the climbing form does not normally produce further flowers. ZONES 4–9.

Verschuren-Pechtold, The Netherlands, 1950

'Geheimrat Duisberg' 3 seedling

National Rose Society Trial Ground Certificate 1947

'GOLDEN SHOWERS'

MODERN, LARGE-FLOWERED CLIMBER,
MEDIUM YELLOW, REPEAT-FLOWERING

The virtues of 'Golden Showers' are its cheerful blooms, elegant in the young bud; the sweet scent of its wide opening semi-double flowers and the way they drop cleanly when they are done; its con-tinuance in bloom almost without pause from summer to late autumn; its pleas-ing glossy foliage; its compliance in growing as far as gardeners wish it to, and not sulking however badly it is pruned; and its comparative smoothness, which makes it an easy rose to handle. Against the assets must be weighed the snags—the fleeting nature of the flowers, their loss of color as they age, and a tinge of seasonal mildew. On balance, and lacking serious competition, this all-purpose climber must be considered still a front rank rose. ZONES 4–9.

Lammerts, USA, 1956

'Charlotte Armstrong' × 'Captain Thomas'

All-America Rose Selection 1957, Portland Gold Medal 1957, Royal Horticultural Society Award of Garden Merit 1993

'GOLDEN SLIPPERS'

syn. 'Orange Slippers'

MODERN, CLUSTER-FLOWERED/FLORIBUNDA,
YELLOW BLEND, REPEAT-FLOWERING

This rose is not widely grown today, but a generation ago it enhanced many planting schemes around the world with its beds of bright flowers. They are orange-flame on the inside of the petal, with pale gold on the reverse, so when the flowers are opening, the mix of colors is wonderful to behold. The young flowers are semi-double, open cupped and then become flat, the small petals narrowing and fading before they fall. The blooms carry a pleasant scent, though because the rose is a low grower the fragrance is often missed. After the

first generous flush more flowers are produced through summer and autumn, and for a small space or a container this has been a valuable rose. Today one would choose a better foliaged variety, for the covering of glossy green leaves that 'Golden Slippers' provides looks skimpy to modern eyes. ZONES 4–9.

Von Abrams, USA, 1961

'Goldilocks' × seedling

Portland Gold Medal 1960, All-America Rose Selection 1962

'GOLDEN STATE'

MODERN, LARGE-FLOWERED/HYBRID TEA,
DEEP YELLOW, REPEAT-FLOWERING

After more than 60 years this variety is still available in California, the 'Golden State' after which it was named, and also in Western Australia. The flowers are not as golden as the title of the rose suggests; they open light lemon yellow with a tawny cast, deepening in color as they open. The flowers are carried on firm upright stems, sometimes several to-gether, sometimes singly. They open from urn-shaped young flowers into cupped blooms full of ruffled petals, and have a sharp fruity scent. Blooming con-tinues through summer and autumn, and in a collection of pre-war Large-flowered Roses this variety can still hold its own for vigor. It has dark green leaves that are large, leathery and generally healthy. ZONES 5–9.

Meilland, France, 1937

'Souvenir de Claudius Pernet' × ('Charles P. Kilham' × seedling)

Bagatelle Gold Medal 1937, Portland Gold Medal 1937

'GOLDEN SURPRISE'

MODERN, CLUSTER-FLOWERED/FLORIBUNDA,
DEEP YELLOW, REPEAT-FLOWERING

There are been two good sports of 'Woburn Abbey', both of which were raised in Australia; 'Woburn Gold' by Robinson of New South Wales in 1970 and 'Golden Surprise' by Hamilton in Victoria in the same year. 'Woburn Gold' is very similar to 'Woburn Abbey', whereas 'Golden Surprise' seems to be a considerably shorter grower. The flowers are golden yellow and are produced in both small and large clusters. The blooms fade to rather a dirty color and persist on the bush. There can be some mildew problems, and 'Woburn Gold' is defi-nitely the better of the two. ZONES 5–9.

Hamilton, Australia, 1970

Sport of 'Woburn Abbey'

'Golden Surprise'

'Golden Wings'

'GOLDEN TIMES' KORtime

MODERN, CLUSTER-FLOWERED/FLORIBUNDA,
MEDIUM YELLOW, REPEAT-FLOWERING

This variety is unlikely to be successful in
the garden except in very warm climates,
because it is grown primarily for the
florists' trade with the special treatments
and growing conditions that entails. Its
plump buds are packed with over 40
petals, which open out into medium-
sized blooms of regular form in an even
shade of yellow. They are freely produced,
sometimes in clusters, sometimes one to
a stem, and are scented. It goes without
saying that flower production continues
through summer and autumn, since this
is a prime requirement of commercial
cut flower growing. It is vigorous, reaching average height or a little less, and has
a bushy habit. It has dark green semi-
glossy leaves of middling size. ZONES 4–9.

Kordes, Germany, 1976

'New Day' × 'Minigold'

'GOLDEN VISION'

MODERN, LARGE-FLOWERED CLIMBER,
MEDIUM YELLOW

Neither of the parents of this rose is very
hardy, so would-be growers need to be
living in a warm climate like that of its
country of origin, where it is still commercially available. It is one of many
crosses made by Alister Clark using the
vigorous *Rosa gigantea*. It is a strong
arching grower that carries semi-double
blooms that open yellow and fade almost
white. They are beautifully formed with
thin petals, with the outside ones
reflexing almost flat and the rest creating
a confused pattern of their own in the
heart of the flower. There is a pleasant
scent, but the plants are limited to just
one copious flowering each year, in late
spring. The leaves are coppery when
young. ZONES 6–10.

Clark, Australia, 1922

'Maréchal Niel' × *Rosa gigantea*

'GOLDEN WEDDING' AROkris

MODERN, CLUSTER-FLOWERED/FLORIBUNDA,
DEEP YELLOW, REPEAT-FLOWERING

This well-behaved rose produces its
lightly scented flowers usually in small
clusters, but sometimes singly, on firm
upright stems. They are a bold and
cheerful shade of yellow, full petalled and
of excellent form, holding their centers
while the outer petals reflex to form a
bloom of classic symmetry. Although a
Cluster-flowered Rose, some of the
blooms are as big as on many Large-

'Golden Wings'

flowered Roses. Flowering is maintained
through summer and autumn, and for
cutting, bedding and group planting this
is a rose that will give great pleasure. The
mid-green foliage is shiny and plentiful,
and the plant grows compactly and with
a vigorous habit to average height.
ZONES 4–9.

Christensen, USA, 1992

'Souvenir de H.A. Verschuren' × seedling

'GOLDEN WINGS'

MODERN, MODERN SHRUB, LIGHT YELLOW,
REPEAT-FLOWERING

Roy Shepherd was an eminent rose historian who died in 1962, and it is fitting
that his inspiration lives on in this remarkable variety. It produces large, pale
yellow flowers with only a few petals that
open like saucers, showing dark stamens.
They look frail but in fact withstand
wind and rain very well. Deadheading
will help bring on more blooms. There
is a light and pleasing scent, and for a
mixed border this is an excellent healthy
garden plant. The bush is vigorous and
prickly, with many twiggy stems and
light green leaves, and it grows to average
height or more. ZONES 4–9.

Shepherd, USA, 1956

'Soeur Therese' × (*Rosa pimpinellifolia altaica* ×
'Ormiston Roy')

American Rose Society Gold Medal 1958, Royal
Horticultural Society Award of Garden Merit 1993

'GOLDEN YEARS' HARween

MODERN, CLUSTER-FLOWERED/FLORIBUNDA,
MEDIUM YELLOW, REPEAT-FLOWERING

The flowers on 'Golden Years' open with
tight centers, but as the petals expand
they take on an old-fashioned appearance with over 40 petals crowding one
another in the cupped blooms. They are
carried in small clusters and present a
bold show of color, a rich golden yellow
with a bronze tint. There is a fruity scent,

'Goldener Olymp'

and it flowers freely and withstands bad
weather well, although mildew is sometimes a problem. It grows with vigor to
just below average height with a neat upright habit and dark green pointed
leaves. It was named for the centenary of
the Girls' Grammar School in the raiser's
home town of Hitchin. ZONES 4–9.

Harkness, UK, 1990

'Sunblest' × 'Amber Queen'

Hradec Golden Rose 1989, Orléans Gold Medal
1990

'GOLDENER OLYMP'

KORschnuppe

syn. 'Olympic Gold'

MODERN, LARGE-FLOWERED CLIMBER, DEEP
YELLOW, REPEAT-FLOWERING

This rose gives a generous first flush of
bloom, bearing several flowers together
on arching stems. They are a deep yellow
when the young flowers first open, but
after that the petals turn bronzy yellow
and become paler as they reflex to form
large shallow-cupped blooms. There is a
light fragrance. More flowers appear
through summer and autumn, but not in
generous numbers. It is best treated as a
short climber or pillar rose, suitable for
a fence or stout post. It grows with a stiff
and upright habit, and has large dark
green semi-glossy leaves. ZONES 4–9.

Kordes, Germany, 1984

Seedling × 'Goldstern'

'Golden Years'

'GOLDENER SOMMER 83'

MODERN, CLUSTER-FLOWERED/FLORIBUNDA,
MEDIUM YELLOW, REPEAT-FLOWERING

The young flowers on this rose are bright
golden yellow, fading to medium yellow
as the flowers age. They are large and
fully double, and open from plump buds
into well-formed blooms with neat
centers. Up to 10 blooms appear in the
clusters, but have little scent. Flowering
continues through summer and autumn,
and it is very suitable for bedding or
planting in a group. It grows below average height with a bushy, spreading habit,
is normally healthy and is well furnished
with matt dark green foliage. ZONES 5–9.

Noack, Germany, 1983

Parentage unknown

Anerkannte Deutsche Rose 1985

G

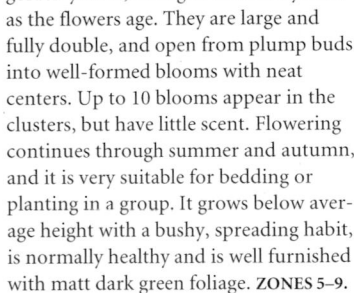

'Golden Wedding'

'Goldener Sommer 83'

'Goldener Sommer 83'

'GOLDFINCH'
MODERN, RAMBLER, LIGHT YELLOW

The brief mid-summer flowering has not stopped this rose from becoming extremely popular, its demure color being part of its charm. The small, oval, fat buds of deep yellow open to small, semi-double blooms that are borne in clusters. The blowzy petals surround many stamens and there is a slight fruity fragrance of oranges or bananas. The flowers fade fast in the sun, so planting it in light shade is recommended. It is easy to train the vigorous, angular growth onto a pillar or pergola, yet it can simply be left as a sprawling bush in a wild setting. There are glossy, pointed leaves and a few hooked prickles. ZONES 7–9.

Paul, UK, 1907

'Hélène' × seedling

'GOLDILOCKS'
syn. 'Goldie Locks'
MODERN, CLUSTER-FLOWERED/FLORIBUNDA, MEDIUM YELLOW, REPEAT-FLOWERING

When this rose was introduced, it had no obvious rival among Cluster-flowered Roses due to its novel features. The most important of these were its color, deep yellow in the round buds, paling when fully open, combined with its blooms, very full petalled and shaped like small-scale Large-flowered Roses. It also scored well for freedom of bloom in its first flush, for flowering on through summer and autumn, for having some fragrance, and for its neat lowly habit of growth, with the flowers nestling close against the foliage. For beds and the front of borders 'Goldilocks' was a favorite for several years, until supplanted by its own descendants such as 'Allgold' and 'Golden Delight'. It has small glossy leaves, which may be affected by black spot. ZONES 4–9.

Boerner, USA, 1945

Seedling × 'Doubloons'

American Rose Society John Cook Medal 1947, National Rose Society Certificate of Merit 1948

'GOLDMARIE 82'   KORfalt
syn. 'Goldmarie'
MODERN, CLUSTER-FLOWERED/FLORIBUNDA, DEEP YELLOW, REPEAT-FLOWERING

The synonym illustrates the confusion caused by the re-use of an old name. There was an earlier 'Goldmarie' from the same raiser in 1958 but the registration authorities ruled it extinct, enabling the name to be applied to a new variety. In fact the 1958 version is still commercially available, making a nonsense of the ruling. The newer form is of very similar character, bearing big clusters of deep yellow flowers on firm upright stems. They are large, fully double, have prettily waved petals and show some pinky red marking on the outside of the blooms. The delicately scented blooms are produced freely from summer through to autumn. For a bed, hedge or group this is a good choice; it has a vigorous bushy habit and glossy mid-green foliage. ZONES 4–9.

Kordes, Germany, 1984

(['Arthur Bell' × 'Zorina'] × ['Honeymoon' × 'Dr A.J. Verhage']) × (seedling × 'Korresia')

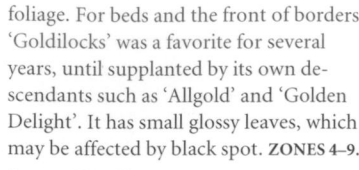

'Goldfinch'

'Goldilocks'

'Goldmarie 82'

'Goldy'

'GOLDSTAR'   CANdide
syns 'Disque d'Or', 'Gold Star', 'Golden Star', 'Goldina', 'Point de Jours'
MODERN, LARGE-FLOWERED/HYBRID TEA, DEEP YELLOW, REPEAT-FLOWERING

Young urn-shaped flowers on 'Goldstar' open into bright yellow blooms with high centers, the outer petals showing cream around the margins as they reflex. The flowers are of medium to large size and appear on upright stems, both singly and in small clusters. They are fully double and have a pleasant light scent. The plant continues to produce blooms through summer and autumn and is useful in a bed or border, though because it carries its blooms high on the plant it is advisable to grow a shorter variety in front. The plant grows vigorously with a compact, upright habit and has matt olive green foliage. ZONES 4–9.

Cant, UK, 1984

'Yellow Pages' × 'Dr A. J. Verhage'

The Hague Gold Medal 1984, Belfast Certificate of Merit 1986

'GOLDSTERN'   TANtern
syn. 'Gold Star', 'Goldstar'
MODERN, MODERN SHRUB, MEDIUM YELLOW, REPEAT-FLOWERING

The young flowers of this shrub rose are rounded in form and develop into large, full-petalled blooms of clear deep golden yellow that become flat as they expand. They are often borne in clusters, sometimes singly, have a modest scent and continue to show color through summer and autumn. The plant makes a useful addition to the border—it grows larger than the average shrub rose—and it can also be made to serve as a climber for walls, fences and pillars. The growth is vigorous with a plentiful cover of glossy, leathery, dark green leaves. ZONES 4–9.

Tantau, Germany, 1966

Parentage unknown

'Goldtopas'

'Golestan'

'GOLDTOPAS'   KORgo, KORtossgo
syns 'Gold Topaz', 'Goldtopaz'
MODERN, CLUSTER-FLOWERED/FLORIBUNDA, MEDIUM YELLOW, REPEAT-FLOWERING

This rose has an attractive and unusual color, a pleasing blend of amber, tan and yellow that is not evident at first, as the long young buds are apricot. The buds open into sizeable double flowers of cupped form, sometimes borne singly and sometimes in a cluster. There can be as many as 10 blooms to a stem which, when it happens, makes for ungainly, overcrowded flowerheads. The petals show wavy edges as they reflex, and there is a sharp fragrance. It is suitable for beds and borders where a shorter than average grower is needed. The habit is bushy, and the ample foliage is dark green and very glossy. ZONES 4–9.

Kordes, Germany, 1963

'Doctor Faust' × 'Circus'

Anerkannte Deutsche Rose 1963

'GOLDY'   KORbeen
MODERN, LARGE-FLOWERED/HYBRID TEA, DEEP YELLOW, REPEAT-FLOWERING

This very low-growing rose with very double, strongly fragranced flowers filled with up to 60 intense yellow petals, gives a display over a very long period. Unfortunately, many blooms emerge malformed, but when they do open properly they are most attractive—the stems are short so they do not make good cut flowers. The leaves are a dull green and there are sometimes problems with black spot. It has been superseded by more reliable deep yellow varieties. ZONES 5–9.

Kordes, Germany, 1981

Seedling of 'Berolina'

'GOLESTAN'   MEIsadina
MODERN, LARGE-FLOWERED/HYBRID TEA, ORANGE-RED, REPEAT-FLOWERING

This decorative rose has a modest-sized flower that retains the classic high-centered form. Slender buds open into double blooms of vivid vermilion. They have little scent, but continue to bloom through summer and autumn. If cut when the flowers are young, this is a useful variety but its garden value is limited, due to fungus problems. The plant grows upright with an uneven, branching habit and has dark glossy leaves. There seems to be no current commercial source of this variety. ZONES 4–9.

Meilland, France, 1975

('Tropicana ' × 'Tropicana') × ([seedling × 'Rouge Meilland'] × 'Independence')

'GOOD AS GOLD' CHEwsunbeam
MODERN, CLIMBING MINIATURE, DEEP YELLOW, REPEAT-FLOWERING

The deep yellow flowers of this rose are moderately full with about 24 petals per bloom. Like many of the offspring of the pollen parent 'Laura Ford', the florets are large and borne in small clusters. The blooms have a deeper golden yellow center and a sweet fragrance. The foliage is a fine semi-glossy, light green but there are some prickles. It takes a few years to establish. The plant is well suited for a pillar or narrow wall space. It has good disease resistance. ZONES 5–11.

Warner, UK, 1994

'Anne Harkness' × 'Laura Ford'

Royal National Rose Society Trial Ground Certificate 1993, British Association of Rose Breeders Selection 1995, RNRS Rose Day Award 1998

'GORDON'S COLLEGE' COCjabby
MODERN, CLUSTER-FLOWERED/FLORIBUNDA, ORANGE-PINK, REPEAT-FLOWERING

The large, pleasantly scented flowers of this rose are well supported on strong stems. They are a rich reddish salmon color, fully double, well-formed with high centers in the young flowers, and maintain an attractive shape through the life of the blooms. They are freely borne during the first flush and continue to show color through summer and autumn. This rose is suitable for a bed or to group in a border. The copious blackish young foliage turns purple-green with age. It is compact and grows vigorously to average height. It was named for the college in Aberdeen founded by Robert Gordon (1668–1731) and attended by generations of the raiser's family. ZONES 4–9.

Cocker, UK, 1993

'Abbeyfield Rose' × 'Roddy McMillan'

Royal National Rose Society Trial Ground Certificate 1989, Glasgow Silver Medal 1995, RNRS Rose Day Award 1998

'GOURMET PHEASANT'
MODERN, GROUND COVER, MEDIUM RED, REPEAT-FLOWERING

This rose was listed in their 1995 catalogue by Heirloom Old Garden Roses in Oregon, USA but without a disclosure of its origin. It is claimed to be a ground cover rose of the procumbent type, spreading about 7 times as far sideways as its height above the ground. The blooms are in that color range where rich red meets deep cherry pink, and open semi-double to show golden stamens.

They are borne in massive clusters on arching shoots that lie along the ground under the weight of the blooms and foliage. There is little scent, but a good succession of bloom through summer and autumn. It suits banks, the tops of walls and anywhere that a fast-growing ground cover is required. The leaves are bright green and glossy. ZONES 4–9.

USA, 1995

Parentage unknown

'GOURMET POPCORN' WEOpop
syn. 'Summer Snow'
MODERN, MINIATURE, WHITE, REPEAT-FLOWERING

This floriferous, semi-double Miniature Rose has been consistently voted by US growers as one of their favorites. The bush is vigorous, compact and cushion-like, covered by massive cascading clusters of 30–60 short-stemmed, pure white flowers with contrasting golden yellow stamens. The flowering season lasts through summer and autumn, and the fragrance is like rose honey. It is complemented by deep green, disease-resistant foliage. This dainty garden rose is ideal for mass plantings and is easily grown in containers, hanging baskets or any small space. ZONES 4–9.

Desamero, USA, 1986

Sport of 'Popcorn'

Royal National Rose Society Trial Ground Certificate 1995

'GOYA'
MODERN, CLUSTER-FLOWERED/FLORIBUNDA, WHITE, REPEAT-FLOWERING

This variety was named after the Spanish painter famous for his voluptuous nudes. It bears large, double blooms that are filled with about 30 white petals to form a good, high centered shape and are tinged with cream in the centers. There is some perfume. The abundant foliage is dark green, semi-glossy and covers a tall and upright bush. The long and pointed buds, produced on long stems either singly or in small clusters, give a good supply of flowers with a rather slow repeat. 'Goya' is a good rose for cutting. There are no disease problems. ZONES 5–9.

Bees Ltd, UK, 1976

'Mildred Reynolds' × 'Arthur Bell'

'GRACE ABOUNDING'
MODERN, CLUSTER-FLOWERED/FLORIBUNDA, WHITE, REPEAT-FLOWERING

White is not a fair color description, for this rose forms great clusters of open

'Goya'

saucer-like flowers in a variety of shades: off-white, cream, wheat or even pink. They are semi-double and of medium size, and so neatly spaced that, as well as being useful in the garden, the rose is grown by some specifically for exhibition. There is a light scent. The plant grows vigorously with a shrub-like habit to average height and is clothed with ample light green, semi-glossy foliage. The raiser named it with reference both to the plant's general character and to its generous supply of blooms, borrowing the title from one of the works of John Bunyan. ZONES 4–9.

Harkness, UK, 1968

'Pink Parfait' × 'Penelope'

Royal National Rose Society Trial Ground Certificate 1970

'GRACE DARLING'
OLD, TEA, NEAR WHITE

Grace Darling (1815–42) became an international celebrity in 1838 when she and her father rescued the crew of a

'Grace Darling'

shipwreck off the English coast. This compact bush is covered with large, creamy white shaded pink blooms in late spring, and there is some autumn flowering. The fragrant, cupped, globular blooms have peach-pink petals. The shrub is covered with gray green leaves. ZONES 6–9.

Bennett, UK, 1884

Parentage unknown

'Grace Abounding'

'Gourmet Pheasant'

'Good As Gold'

'Grafin Sonja'

'Grace de Monaco'

'Graham Thomas'

'Grand Hotel'

'GRACE DE MONACO' MEImit

MODERN, LARGE-FLOWERED/HYBRID TEA,
LIGHT PINK, REPEAT-FLOWERING

This rose is little grown today but a generation ago it was widely available, reflecting the popularity of Grace Kelly as she ceased to be a film star and became a royal. She was a lover of roses, and 'Grace de Monaco' was a wedding gift from the breeder. It has splendid flowers, large, full petalled, rounded in form and very fragrant. The color is a clear rose pink, a kindly, warm and even shade, though because the big petals are soft they are liable to be marked and spoilt by rain. They are borne freely and continue to give a show through summer and autumn, making this a good garden rose for drier climates and for cutting. It grows strongly to average height or more and has tall, branching stems that sometimes bow over under the weight of a heavy load of blooms. It is well supplied with large leathery leaves. ZONES 4–9.

Meilland, France, 1956

'Peace' × 'Michèle Meilland'

'GRACELAND' JACel

MODERN, LARGE-FLOWERED/HYBRID TEA,
MEDIUM YELLOW, REPEAT-FLOWERING

This variety scored highly in The Hague trials, where its performance as a bedding rose in a parks setting impressed the judges. The long-stemmed flowers are fairly large, full petalled and regular in form, with wavy edged outer petals disposed symmetrically around a neat center. As the petals reflex the blooms become loosely cupped; they are a cheerful shade of yellow, ageing lighter towards the margins. Flower production is good but scent is sadly lacking. Apart from that, this is a satisfactory rose for the garden and for cutting, making a plant rather above average height with smooth, dark green foliage. It bears the name of Elvis Presley's home. ZONES 4–9.

Warriner, USA, 1989

'New Day' × seedling

The Hague Gold Medal 1988

'GRACILIS'

OLD, BOURSAULT, MEDIUM RED

Boursault Roses were popular in France in the early 1900s when there were some 50 varieties; many of these have now disappeared. The cherry-shaded, lilacblush, semi-double blooms are cupped as they open and then become flat. They appear in early summer and prefer shade; their gorgeous, pendent form appeals to flower arrangers. The dark green foliage clothes vigorous branches, and the smooth stems are covered with large, long prickles. ZONES 6–9.

Wood, UK, 1830

Parentage unknown

'GRAFIN SONJA' KORfeimot

syn. 'Countess Sonja'

MODERN, LARGE-FLOWERED/HYBRID TEA,
PINK BLEND, REPEAT-FLOWERING

This is a charming rose of two colors: the long buds are cherry red, and when they open they reveal inner petal surfaces that are mainly silvery pink with a generous margin of deep cherry pink, a gentle but lively contrast. The medium-sized blooms are usually borne one to a stem, and are neatly formed with high centers. They are good for cutting, because the petals are firm and hold their shape, and they have a light wild rose fragrance. For the garden this is useful in beds and borders, and it continues to show color through summer and autumn. It make vigorous, free-branching growth to average height and is well furnished with shiny dark green leaves. ZONES 4–9.

Kordes, Germany, 1994

Parentage unknown

'GRAHAM THOMAS' AUSmas

syns 'English Yellow', 'Graham Stuart Thomas'

MODERN, MODERN SHRUB, DEEP YELLOW,
REPEAT-FLOWERING

When this rose was introduced it was a complete novelty, because it was the first real yellow rose to resemble in form and petal arrangement the hardy Old Garden Roses of the previous century whose color range had been limited to reds, purples, pinks and pale shades. 'Graham Thomas' is a clear yellow, deeper in the heart of its cupped blooms, which are borne with remarkable freedom considering their size and full petallage. They are carried on long arching stems, which often bow over under their weight. There is a pleasant fragrance, and flowering continues through summer and autumn, making this a good garden shrub for a border; it can also make a fine standard. In cool climates it usually grows to average height, but in warmer countries it extends much further and can be treated as a climber on a wall, fence or tall pillar. The rose was named to honor one of England's foremost rosarians, and is also classified as an English Rose. ZONES 4–9.

Austin, UK, 1983

'Charles Austin' × ('Iceberg' × seedling)

Royal Horticultural Society Award of Garden Merit 1993

'GRANADA'

syn. 'Donatella'

MODERN, LARGE-FLOWERED/HYBRID TEA,
RED BLEND, REPEAT-FLOWERING

The blooms on 'Granada' are sometimes borne singly but often appear several together in a wide cluster, so although called a Large-flowered Rose, this resembles an oversized Cluster-flowered Rose. The flowers have about 24 petals which form a neat high center, then reflex so that the old blooms are loosely cupped. They are a colorful blend of pink, orange red and light yellow. After the initial generous flush, flowers continue to appear through summer and autumn; they carry a spicy scent, making this an admirable garden rose where a tall plant is required. 'Granada' is not reliably winter hardy. It will grow nearly double average height with vigorous, upright growth. Its dark green leaves have a crinkled, leathery appearance and can be subject to powdery mildew. ZONES 5–9.

Lindquist, USA, 1963

'Tiffany' × 'Cavalcade'

All-America Rose Selection 1964, Gamble Fragrance Award 1968

'GRAND HOTEL' MACtel

syn. 'Grandhotel'

MODERN, LARGE-FLOWERED CLIMBER,
MEDIUM RED, REPEAT-FLOWERING

A feature of many older climbers was the excessive growth they made in relation to their short period of flower. This is a good example of how a modern climber sacrifices some of the growth but more than makes up for that by continuing to bear flowers after the main flush, right through summer and autumn. The sizeable blooms are fairly full, borne in clusters, and open loosely cupped. They withstand bad weather well, but have only a light fragrance. The growth is stiff and branching, making it easy to train on a wall or fence; it needs a good circulation of air if mildew and black spot are to be avoided, so a well-supported trellis is the best option of all. It grows to average height and can be kept shorter by pruning with no ill effects. It has a good covering of dark leaves. ZONES 4–9.

McGredy, UK, 1972

'Brilliant' × 'Heidelberg'

Anerkannte Deutsche Rose 1977

'GRAND MASTERPIECE'

JACpie

MODERN, LARGE-FLOWERED/HYBRID TEA,
MEDIUM RED, REPEAT-FLOWERING

The assets of this bright red variety are its freedom of flower, for after the first flush there continues to be a good show through summer and autumn, and the value of the rose for cutting, since the medium to large-sized blooms are carried on distinctly long stems. They are fully double and open from attractive long, slender buds into neatly formed flowers with high centers, the petals slowly parting to form a cup of regular outline. They last so well as cut flowers because the petals are firm and hard, but petals of that character do not exude any fragrance. It grows vigorously with a tall, upright habit to above average height and has mid-green leaves. ZONES 4–9.

Warriner, USA, 1978

Seedling × 'Tonight'

'GRAND NORD' DELgrord

syns 'Great Nord', 'Great North'

MODERN, LARGE-FLOWERED/HYBRID TEA, WHITE,
REPEAT-FLOWERING

When does a bush become a shrub? It has been said of this variety that 'the

'Grand Siècle'

'Grand Nord'

great north implies mountains and that is also the appearance of this rose.' This comment is based on its performance in South Africa, and the writer adds that a mature plant in that climate can be 10 ft (3 m) high and wide and covered with over 100 blooms suitable for cutting. In cooler climates it outstrips other Large-flowered Roses, but by a less dramatic margin, reaching twice the average height for a bush rose. Elegant pointed buds open into high-centered, double white blooms with a noticeable scent. They open slowly, preserving good symmetry of form. On established plants flowers continue to appear through summer and autumn. As a garden rose 'Grand Nord' is suitable for the back of a border; it is vigorous, producing many short flowering branches to give a fairly dense, dark-leafed effect. ZONES 4–9.

Delbard-Chabert, France, 1975

(['Queen Elizabeth' × 'Provence'] × ['Virgo' × 'Carina'])× (['Voeux de Bonheur' × 'Virgo'] × ['Virgo' × 'Peace'])

Paris Gold Medal 1970, Rome Gold Medal 1973

'GRAND SIÈCLE'   DELegran
syn. 'Great Century'
MODERN, LARGE-FLOWERED/HYBRID TEA, PINK BLEND, REPEAT-FLOWERING

'Feminine, elegant, beautiful' says the raiser of this, one of his favorite roses. The large flowers are made up of over 30 wide petals in the classic Large-flowered Rose tradition, forming blooms of grace and symmetry as they slowly expand. The color is a gentle blend of cream and pink, with rose pink showing in the depths of the flower as the petals open wide. There is a refreshing scent, in which notes of raspberry, apple and rose are to be found. This is a good rose for cutting as well as for garden display, bearing its flowers singly or in wide sprays through summer and autumn and growing to average height or a little more. It is vigorous and free branching and is furnished with large, mid- to dark green leaves. ZONES 4–9.

Delbard-Chabert, France, 1987

(['Queen Elizabeth' × 'Provence'] × ['Michèle Meilland' × 'Bayadère'])× (['Voeux de Bonheur' × MEImet] × ['Peace' × 'Dr Débat'])

Bagatelle Gold Medal

'GRANDMA'S PINK'   MORbouquet
MODERN, MODERN SHRUB, MEDIUM PINK, REPEAT-FLOWERING

Ralph Moore has introduced many innovative roses in his long career, and this one has a bloom like that of an old-fashioned shrub rose, on a repeat-flowering plant of modest size. The blooms are medium pink and very full of petals. They are of average size, and are borne in clusters of a few blooms. There is little scent. It is useful for a bed or border; it is also very well suited for planting in a tub or large pot, and for cutting. The plant grows to a little below the average height of a typical Cluster-flowered Rose, with an upright, bushy habit and matt, mid-green leaves. ZONES 4–9.

Moore, USA, 1991

'Shakespeare Festival' × 'Marchioness of Londonderry'

'GRANDMASTER'
syn. 'Grand Master'
MODERN, MODERN SHRUB, APRICOT BLEND, REPEAT-FLOWERING

The raiser, describing this, acknowledges its value 'where it does well', because it does not suit all localities. The flowers are apricot, shaded buff and orange, and quite large. They are semi-double and open flat, with a loose arrangement of ruffled petals. The flowerheads are very big and may hold up to 50 roses. There is a pleasing fragrance, and blooming continues through summer and autumn. It has been recommended for use in a group, as a hedge rose or specimen shrub, but newer roses of similar coloring, and with better constitutions, have usurped its place. The growth is upright and rather straggly, to average height or more, and the light green foliage can be prone to black spot. ZONES 5–9.

Kordes, Germany, 1954

'Sangerhausen' × 'Sunmist'

National Rose Society Gold Medal 1952

'GRAND'MÈRE JENNY'
syn. 'Grem'
MODERN, LARGE-FLOWERED/HYBRID TEA, YELLOW BLEND, REPEAT-FLOWERING

This daughter of 'Peace' has a beautiful flower made up of subtle shades, basically light yellow with tinges of pink on the outer petals and peach-yellow towards the middle. The blooms appear singly or several to a stem, and open from pointed buds into fully double flowers with long petals that create a well-formed cone at the center before reflexing fairly soon and dropping cleanly. The variety is free flowering and quick to repeat the cycle of growth. There is a sweet fragrance, and the blooms withstand bad weather very well. Its liability to black spot has, however, caused it to fall out of favor. It is a

moderately vigorous plant with an upright habit and handsome dark leaves. François Meilland named this rose for Jeanne Meilland, his grandmother, who helped and encouraged him in his work during good and bad times, and died in 1943, aged 87. **'Climbing Grand'mère Jenny'** (syn. 'Gremsar', 1958) is a sport of 'Grand'mère Jenny'. It repeat-flowers only sporadically, but in growth it is strong and vigorous. It is therefore best suited to a high wall or big fence or a pergola, where the branches have plenty of space to be trained. ZONES 5–9.

Meilland, France, 1950

'Peace' × 'Signora'

National Rose Society Gold Medal 1950, Rome Gold Medal 1955

'GRANNY'S BONNET'   JACflare
MODERN, CLUSTER-FLOWERED/FLORIBUNDA, PINK BLEND

The flowers of this rose are deep rose pink with pale lemon to white undersides. As they open, they show the underside color first, followed by the deep rose as the blooms open to show a boss of golden stamens. They appear in clusters, and the 'hand-painted' effect is most attractive. The foliage is dark green and semi-glossy, and covers these small- to medium-height bushes. 'Granny's Bonnet' is an excellent rose for beds or low borders, and can be used to good effect with bulbs and perennials in a mixed border. ZONES 5–9.

Jackson & Perkins, USA, 1996

Parentage unknown

'Great News'

'GREAT MAIDEN'S BLUSH'
OLD, ALBA, LIGHT PINK

The blush pink flowers of this large, arching shrub are finely perfumed, the color aptly described in the name. The foliage is grayish in the Alba fashion. There is also a 'Small Maiden's Blush', which was recorded and perhaps raised at Kew Gardens in 1797. These roses are inclined to sport variations, and there is a deeper-flowered version named 'Cuisse de Nymphe Emué'. Thrips and wet weather can damage this rose considerably. ZONES 5–9.

Circa 1400

Parentage unknown

'GREAT NEWS'
MODERN, CLUSTER-FLOWERED/FLORIBUNDA, MAUVE, REPEAT-FLOWERING

The flowers are so sizeable and sufficiently full, having nearly 36 petals, that the raiser considered it a Large-flowered Rose. They are deep plum-purple, with silvery tones on the outside of the petals, which become delightfully waved and ruffled as they open wide to give a good display of this warm and unusual color. There is a good scent, and the blooms appear through summer and autumn. The variety is suitable for lovers of curious roses, in either a bed or a border. It is a reasonably vigorous plant, but its uneven growth makes the height variable. The leaves are large and olive green. ZONES 4–9.

LeGrice, UK, 1973

'Rose Gaujard' × 'City of Hereford'

'Great Maiden's Blush'

'Grand'mère Jenny'

'GREAT VENTURE'

MODERN, LARGE-FLOWERED/HYBRID TEA, YELLOW BLEND, REPEAT-FLOWERING

'Great Venture' is an excellent rose. The plants are very strong and upright with plentiful large, dark green, leathery leaves that are very resistant to disease. The long buds open slowly to large, fragrant, double flowers of 30 petals. The color is rich apricot-yellow flushed with deep pink. With its long stems and abundant foliage, it is good for cutting. ZONES 5–9.

Dawson, Australia, 1970

'Daily Sketch' × 'Impeccable'

'GREAT WESTERN'

OLD, BOURBON, MAUVE

This fragrant rose starts with round, fat buds; there are so many of them that thinning is recommended to help them open. The double, globular, rounded blossoms are by turns deep red, magenta-crimson or purple-maroon. They appear in early summer in clusters of 10–15 and look their best in the shade. It is a vigorous shrub that grows to 6 ft (1.8 m) high, and has branching stalks and canes that are covered with prickles. It does well on poor soil. ZONES 5–9.

Laffay, France, 1840

Parentage unknown

'GREEN DIAMOND'

MODERN, MINIATURE, PINK, REPEAT-FLOWERING

The pointed buds of 'Green Diamond' open to reveal dusty pink blooms that mellow with age to a soft green. They are double, cupped and very small. The foliage is a diminutive, leathery, mid-

green and the plant is compact and very leafy. This is a repeat-flowering novelty rose. It starts the bloom cycle with pink florets and by the time the tiny blooms open they have turned chartreuse green. This rose is suitable to grow in a container for the patio or deck. ZONES 5–11.

Moore, USA, 1975

Polyantha seedling × 'Sheri Anne'

'GREEN FIRE'

MODERN, CLUSTER-FLOWERED/FLORIBUNDA, DEEP YELLOW, REPEAT-FLOWERING

This is quite well named, for the bright yellow roses seem to flicker in the breeze. Tidy trusses of small, neat buds open to reveal medium-sized, saucer-shaped flowers with striking deep yellow stamens. There is a slight fragrance. The plant flowers freely, making it a good subject for beds and borders. It grows upright with a compact, bushy habit to below average height, and has small, light green leaves. The foliage can be troubled by black spot. ZONES 5–9.

Swim, USA, 1958

'Goldilocks' × seedling

National Rose Society Trial Ground Certificate 1958

'GREEN ICE'

MODERN, MINIATURE, WHITE, REPEAT-FLOWERING

White pointed buds open to white to soft green flowers. These small, double blooms are complemented by equally small, attractive, glossy foliage. The flower form is decorative with the fully open blooms reminiscent of Old Garden Roses. Large trusses of flowers start off

white with just a hint of pink and as the blooms mature, they gradually acquire an attractive light green hue. The plant has a sprawling and spreading habit, which makes it an excellent choice for a hanging basket. ZONES 5–11.

Moore, USA, 1971

(Rosa wichuraiana × 'Floradora') × 'Jet Trail'

'GREEN ROSE'

syns Rosa chinensis viridiflora, 'Rosa Monstrosa', R. viridiflora

OLD, CHINA, GREEN, REPEAT-FLOWERING

This curious rose, which sports green sepals instead of petals, has long been a favorite with flower arrangers. The small oval buds of blue-green open to double, leaf-like sepals that are bronze at the tips. It is free flowering over a long period. 'Green Rose' is an upright, 4 ft (1.2 m) bush that is easy to grow and does well in poor soil. It is suitable for containers and is disease resistant. ZONES 7–9.

Pre-1833

Perhaps a sport of 'Old Blush'

'GREEN SNAKE' LENwich, LENwiga

syn. 'Serpent Vert'

MODERN, GROUND COVER, WHITE

'Green Snake' bears a host of small and single white flowers on a prostrate plant. The clusters hold up to 24 blooms on short stems, so that the overall effect is a meandering sheet of flower. There is a light scent. This rose is the result of hybridizing a species of the West (Rosa arvensis) with an Oriental one (R. wichuraiana). It only flowers briefly in summer, so it is never likely to be widely grown, but for its curiosity value it is well worth a place in the garden. This is a short plant, but in extent it is likely to travel eight times as far. The leaves are small and spoon shaped. ZONES 4–9.

Lens, Belgium, 1987

Rosa arvensis × R. wichuraiana

'GREENALLS GLORY' KIRmac

MODERN, CLUSTER-FLOWERED/FLORIBUNDA, PINK BLEND, REPEAT-FLOWERING

The flowers of this variety are a pretty shade, silvery white with a pale blush-pink center. They are lightly fragranced and are large, particularly in relation to the size of the plant, and appear in well-filled clusters with excellent continuity through summer and autumn. When they open, the centers are neatly furled, and the blooms slowly expand until they finally become almost flat. This creates a good display of color and enhances the value of the variety. It is suitable for beds where a low grower is required, or at the front row of a border or in a container. The buds are ideal for buttonholes and corsages. The plants grow very short, and are considered by some as Patio Roses. They have a vigorous, spreading habit and abundant glossy, mid-green foliage. The rose is named for an English brewing concern. ZONES 4–9.

Kirkham, UK, 1989

Sport of 'Regensberg'

'GREENMANTLE'

OLD, SWEET BRIAR, RED BLEND

This is one of the lesser known hybrids bred by Lord Penzance at the end of the nineteenth century. He also tried crosses between Rosa eglanteria and Hybrid Perpetuals as well as Bourbons to create extremely robust roses. The dark red buds open to clear pink, sometimes rosy red blooms with a white eye. The crinkled, 2 in (5 cm) petals surround golden stamens. Blooming only once in summer, it is a vigorous, healthy bush that creates an impenetrable barrier when used as a hedge. 'Greenmantle' has strong prickles and fragrant leaves, and is good as a woodland plant. The bright red, long-lasting hips are attractive in autumn. ZONES 4–9.

Penzance, UK, 1895

Hybrid of Rosa eglanteria

'GREENSLEEVES' HARlenten

MODERN, CLUSTER-FLOWERED/FLORIBUNDA, GREEN, REPEAT-FLOWERING

The main reason for growing this variety is to obtain flowers for cutting. If taken at the young stage, just as the pinky buds are opening, the blooms will hold their shape and display a beautiful chartreuse-green color, with a vase life so long that they may well require a dusting before the time comes to throw them out. If cut at this time, the flowers will remain fresh and saucer shaped, with crinkled petals. In the garden, the ageing flowers open flat, and are likely to become mottled and discolored. The plant carries its flower clusters on tall, upright stems, and blooms through summer and autumn. There is very little scent. This variety grows to above average height, with leathery foliage that looks tough but is not resistant to black spot. ZONES 4–9.

Harkness, UK, 1980

('Rudolph Timm' × 'Arthur Bell') × (['Pascali' × 'Elizabeth of Glamis'] × ['Sabine' × 'Violette Dot'])

Baden-Baden Special Prize 1979, Rome Certificate of Merit 1979

'Great Western'

'Green Ice'

'Greensleeves'

'Green Rose'

'Great Venture'

'GREY DAWN'
MODERN, CLUSTER-FLOWERED/FLORIBUNDA, MAUVE, REPEAT-FLOWERING

This rose is listed only by four growers, two European and two Californian. The large flowers, with over 40 petals, are carried in clusters. The color is grayish pink, with some light peach-yellow on the undersides of the petals. The flowers are substantial, high centered, and open wide as the petals reflex. Flowers continue sporadically through summer and autumn, and there is a light fragrance. The plant grows short with a bushy habit, and has glossy, dark green foliage. ZONES 5–9.

LeGrice, UK, 1975

'Brownie' × 'News'

'GRISELDIS'
OLD, BOURBON, MEDIUM PINK

This is one of the so-called 'northern' roses produced by this Bohemian hybridizer to withstand severe winter frosts. The large, full, flat pink blossoms appear in clusters on long canes and have no scent. It makes a 9 ft (3 m) shrub covered with healthy, bright green foliage and prickles. The floriferous blooms more than make up for its attitude. ZONES 3–9.

Geschwind, Hungary, 1895

Hybrid of *Rosa canina*

'GROOTENDORST SUPREME'
MODERN, HYBRID RUGOSA, DARK RED, REPEAT-FLOWERING

This variety carries clusters of many small, dark garnet red roses. They are fully double, with attractively serrated petals, and there is very little scent. It is best used in a border, where a very tough and easy plant is wanted. Alternatively, it can be sited in a cutting garden, because the dainty flowers are useful in small arrangements and will last many days. The variety makes a gaunt and prickly shrub

'Griseldis'

'Grootendorst Supreme'

'Gros Provins Panaché'

that grows to or above average height for a shrub rose. It has a good complement of small leathery leaves, although they are not sufficient to clothe its twiggy, spiky appearance. It has an exemplary record for good health. ZONES 4–9.

Grootendorst, The Netherlands, 1936

Sport of 'F. J. Grootendorst'

'GROS CHOUX D'HOLLANDE'
OLD, BOURBON, LIGHT PINK

The name of this rose literally means 'big cabbage of Holland', yet the flowers are neither big nor cabbage-like: they are fragrant, full, cupped and soft pink in color, and there do not seem to be many repeats. The bush is extremely vigorous and covers quite a lot of ground, growing up to 6 ft (2 m) high. ZONES 5–9.

Parentage unknown

'GROS PROVINS PANACHÉ'
OLD, GALLICA, MAUVE

This 5 ft (1.5 m) shrub blooms once in early spring and bears large, double, highly fragrant flowers. The purple-rose petals are blotched with white, making it of the best-looking 'striped' roses. It is disease-resistant and suits a mixed border or a woodland setting. ZONES 4–9.

Fontaine, France, pre-1855

Probably a Gallica × China hybrid

GRUSS AN AACHEN'
syn. 'Salut d'Aix la Chapelle'
MODERN, CLUSTER-FLOWERED/FLORIBUNDA, LIGHT PINK, REPEAT-FLOWERING

This rose bears large clusters of medium-sized blooms, which are pale orange-red with yellow in the bud stage, and open to a soothing blend of pearly blush and cream. Before becoming cupped, they display well-formed centers, with many petals folding in upon one another in a charming random fashion. There is a pleasing scent. It is normally short, mak-

'Gros Choux d'Hollande'

'Gruss an Aachen'

ing it useful to edge a border, or for a small bed or group. The leathery foliage is a rich dark green. The name means 'greetings to Aachen', which was the raiser's home city. ZONES 4–9.

Geduldig, Germany, 1909

'Frau Karl Druschki' × 'Franz Deegen'

'GRUSS AN BERLIN'
syn. 'Greetings'
MODERN, LARGE-FLOWERED/HYBRID TEA, MEDIUM RED, REPEAT-FLOWERING

The plump buds of this rose open to substantial blooms. The high-centered flowers are made up of 40 pure red petals. Disappointingly for a red rose, they have only a slight scent. The plants grow vigorously with a bushy, upright habit and glossy dark green foliage. Although not apparently currently offered for sale, it has been widely used for beds and borders in gardens and parks. ZONES 4–9.

Kordes, Germany, 1963

Parentage unknown

'GRUSS AN COBURG'
MODERN, LARGE-FLOWERED/HYBRID TEA, APRICOT BLEND, REPEAT-FLOWERING

Plump buds open into loosely double flowers of rounded form. The young flowers are a lively blend of light yellow with flushes of apricot, with coppery pink on the petal undersides. Medium-sized blooms, sometimes nodding on their stems, are freely borne in summer, with sporadic flowering later. There is a strong fragrance, and for cutting, or to plant in a border, this is a useful rose. It

'Gruss an Berlin'

'Gruss an Teplitz'

has reasonable vigor, making an angular plant to above average height. The foliage is deep green when mature and bronzy green when young. ZONES 4–9.

Felberg-Leclerc, Germany, 1927

'Alice Kaempff' × 'Souvenir de Claudius Pernet'

'GRUSS AN FREUNDORF'
MODERN, RAMBLER, DARK RED

This rose was recently re-introduced into cultivation. This vigorous Rambler bears shiny bright green, disease-free foliage. The single crimson blooms with white centers appear in large trusses and make a spectacular show for about six weeks. However, the small, oval, bright red hips bring their own charm in autumn. It has a strong fragrance. ZONES 3–10.

Praskac, Czechoslovakia, 1913

Hybrid of *Rosa wichuraiana* × 'Crimson Rambler'

'GRUSS AN TEPLITZ'
syn. 'Virginia R. Coxe'
OLD, BOURBON, MEDIUM RED, REPEAT-FLOWERING

This rose has been on the most popular rose list for over 100 years for its long blooming season and lovely perfume. Pointed buds open to shiny red, double, blooms that darken with age and have prominent stamens. The cupped flowers hang in loose clusters, which change color in bright sun. Used as a climber or a shrub, it is easy to grow or train. The young purple foliage matures to green. ZONES 5–9.

Geschwind, Hungary, 1897

(['Sir Joseph Paxton' × 'Fellenberg'] × 'Papa Gontier') × 'Gloire des Rosomanes'

G

G

'Guitare'

'Guillaume Gillemot'

'Guinée'

'GRUSS AN ZABERN'
MODERN, RAMBLER, WHITE

The white, fragrant, double blooms of this variety appear only once in early summer. They are medium sized and are gathered together in flat clusters. This rose can be trained easily as a climber, as the canes are thin and pliable; it looks wonderful on a pergola or an arch. It is healthy and disease resistant and is covered with small prickles. **ZONES 7–9.**

Lambert, France, 1904

'Euphrosine' × 'Madame Ocker Ferencz'

'GUIDING SPIRIT'   HARwolave
MODERN, PATIO/DWARF CLUSTER-FLOWERED, DEEP PINK, REPEAT-FLOWERING

Becuase they are carried several together in short-stemmed clusters, the small flowers appear to perch on the bushes. They are deep pink verging on rose red, with 20 or so small and narrow, fluted petals, which lie neatly arranged around golden stamens as the blooms unfold. There is a light scent, and flowers appear through summer and autumn. This short, compact plant is best used at the front of a border, or in a container. It has small, semi-glossy, dark green foliage. It is named for the World Association of Girl Guides and Girl Scouts, the year of introduction being the centenary of the birth of Olave, Lady Baden-Powell, who is referred to in the code name. **ZONES 4–9.**

Harkness, UK, 1989

([{'Blue Moon' × 'Lilac Charm'} × 'Sterling Silver'] × [seedling × {seedling × *Rosa californica*}]) × 'Little Prince'

Courtrai Certificate of Merit 1989

'GUILLAUME GILLEMOT'
OLD, HYBRID PERPETUAL, MEDIUM RED

In summer, this rose bears cherry red blossoms with pale silver overtones, the color darkening in shade. These round, very large and globular blooms cover the compact bush, and there is some repeat-bloom in autumn. Known today only in botanical collections, it was bred by the same hybridist who developed the famous rose 'Mme Alfred Carrière'. **ZONES 5–9.**

Schwartz, France, 1880

Seedling of 'Madame Charles Wood'

'GUINÉE'
MODERN, LARGE-FLOWERED CLIMBER, DARK RED, REPEAT-FLOWERING

This is perhaps the best of the blackish red climbing roses, combining great beauty with ease of cultivation. The intensely dark flowers have a velvety sheen on the young petals, which open into fairly large, full-petalled, cupped to flat blooms, with golden stamens half revealed as they open wide. There is a good fragrance on warm days, but it becomes hard to detect in windy or cool weather. It is best grown on a fairly sunny wall or strong fence where there is room to train the main stems sideways and slantwise. This will produce the maximum yield of flowers, which normally appear in summer with a few token blooms later on. The plant is vigorous and stiffly branching, with leathery, dark green foliage that may form mildew if the roots do not get enough moisture. **ZONES 4–9.**

Mallerin, France, 1938

'Souvenir de Claudius Denoyel' × 'Ami Quinard'

'Guinevere'

'GUINEVERE'
MODERN, LARGE-FLOWERED/HYBRID TEA, MEDIUM PINK, REPEAT-FLOWERING

This is a cool shade of rose pink, lighter on the petal undersides. On their first flush, the double flowers are very large, like round well-formed cabbages, their broad petals reflexing with elegant symmetry. They are carried on firm stems close to the foliage and give a light scent. The later blooms are smaller, but appear with good succession through summer and autumn. This is a useful rose for beds, borders and for cutting, although it appears to be no longer commercially available. It grows upright to average height, with a compact, bushy habit and somewhat rounded, deep green leaves. It was named after King Arthur's queen as one of a series of 'Round Table' roses. **ZONES 4–9.**

Harkness, UK, 1967

'Red Dandy' × 'Peace'

Royal National Rose Society Trial Ground Certificate 1966, Baden-Baden Gold Medal 1969

'GUITARE'   GAegui
MODERN, CLUSTER-FLOWERED/FLORIBUNDA, ORANGE BLEND, REPEAT-FLOWERING

This is a bright and cheerful rose, and bears clusters of plump buds that open to show full-petalled flowers of rounded form. They are of medium size, and display a colorful mixture of gold and orange, with coral-red shading towards the petal margins, and orange on the petal undersides. They have a good scent. It is well suited for bedding and planting in a border, and owing to its firm petals the flowers last well when cut. The plant grows vigorously with a bushy habit to reach an average height with leathery, light green leaves. **ZONES 4–9.**

Gaujard, France, 1963

Bagatelle Gold Medal 1966

'Vendôme' × 'Golden Slippers'

'GÜTERSLOH 85'
MODERN, MODERN SHRUB, MEDIUM RED, REPEAT-FLOWERING

The color of this variety is a fiery scarlet red, with glowing orange highlights on some of the petals as they expand. The flowers are of small to medium size, with about two dozen petals, and open loosely cupped. They are borne freely in well-spaced sprays, and continue to show color through summer and autumn. There is little fragrance. For planting in a mixed border, hedge rose or as a specimen plant, this is a suitable variety, albeit an uncommon one that is only listed by the raiser's nursery. The plant grows a little over the average height for a shrub rose, with an upright, free- branching habit and dark green foliage that is reddish when young. **ZONES 4–9.**

Noack, Germany, 1985

Parentage unknown

'GUY DE MAUPASSANT'
MEIsocrat

MODERN, CLUSTER-FLOWERED/FLORIBUNDA, MEDIUM PINK, REPEAT-FLOWERING

Although this is classified as a Cluster-flowered Rose, it is marketed by the raiser as a 'Romantica Rose', one of several offered that combine the confused, quartered shape of some Old Garden Roses with the upright habit and repeat-flowering of many modern ones. The flowers of this rose open from globe-shaped buds into very full blossoms that are packed with 100 or so infolded petals. They are light carmine-pink in both bud and open flower, and have a tart and spicy apple scent. Individual flowers in the cluster are suitable to cut for small arrangements. The plants will give color through summer and autumn in a bed or border behind shorter growing roses; they grow tall, up to twice the average height of a Modern bush rose, with a vigorous bushy, leafy habit. It is named for the French writer. **ZONES 4–9.**

Meilland, France, 1994

Parentage unknown

'GUY LAROCHE'   DELgorg, DELricos
syns 'Château de Versailles', 'Gorgeous George', 'La Tour d'Argent'

MODERN, LARGE-FLOWERED/HYBRID TEA, RED BLEND, REPEAT-FLOWERING

Although it has four names, not many nurseries list this rose, which is at its best in warm climates. The flowers are a brilliant red, with a silvery underside to the petals. They are full petalled and

'Gruss an Zabern'

'Guy de Maupassant'

'Guy Laroche'

'Gwen Nash'

usually carried singly. As they open, the blooms show high centers, but become shallowly cupped as the rather short petals reflex. The fully open flower has a symmetrical pattern, with the firm petals neatly arranged layer upon layer. They last well, and are therefore good for cutting as well as for the garden. There is a light scent, and flowering is maintained through summer and autumn. The plant grows to average height or above, with an upright, bushy habit and a covering of mid- to dark green leaves. ZONES 5–9.

Delbard, France, 1986

Seedling × ('Michèle Meilland' × 'Carla')

'GWEN FAGAN'   POUlgewfa
MODERN, MODERN SHRUB, LIGHT PINK, REPEAT-FLOWERING

This rose is named for the author of *Roses at the Cape of Good Hope* in which the roses collected in old gardens, cemeteries and along roadsides in South Africa are recorded. She is also a contributor to this book. Some of these, thought to be extinct, have been brought back into cultivation. 'Gwen Fagan' is an exquisitely fragrant shrub rose that continues to produce buds that expand into voluptuous pink blooms when all other roses have retired for the winter. The flowers are filled with many petals to form a rosette, quartered or muddled arrangement. This healthy shrub grows tall, and as branches are inclined to arch they are better supported or grown along a fence or wall. The best blooms appear from the second year onwards; when the shrub is covered in a mass of fragrant pink blooms, it is unbeatable. ZONES 4–11.

Poulsen, Denmark, 1991

Parentage unknown

'GWEN MAYOR'   COCover
syn. 'Gwen Meyer'
MODERN, LARGE-FLOWERED/HYBRID TEA, APRICOT BLEND, REPEAT-FLOWERING

Breeding work done by members of the Cocker family extends over a century, but became of major importance when Alec Cocker restarted it 30 years ago. His 'Silver Jubilee' of 1978 proved a valuable parent thanks to its flower and foliage qualities, and 'Gwen Mayor' is another from that stable. It bears high-centered flowers of classic Large-flowered Rose form, in a combination of peach and apricot shades. They are carried singly or in large clusters, and flower through summer and autumn. This is a good

garden rose with a pleasing fragrance, suitable for beds and borders, and also useful for cutting. The plant grows to average height or slightly less, with an upright, bushy habit and an excellent complement of glossy, dark green leaves. The rose is named in memory of the teacher who was killed in March 1996 with several of her pupils by a gunman in Dunblane, Scotland. ZONES 4–9.

Cocker, UK, 1997

'Silver Jubilee' × 'Remember Me'

'GWEN NASH'
MODERN, LARGE-FLOWERED CLIMBER, PINK BLEND, REPEAT-FLOWERING

This variety bears long, pointed buds that open to rather silky-looking blooms of a gentle rose pink, with yellowish white towards the base of the petals, and prominent golden stamens. The flowers are large, with 12 or more big, waved petals, and eventually develop a cupped form. The raiser said that he believed this rose to be 'the most beautiful thing in decorative pinks I can hope to produce'. There is a light fragrance. It requires a warm climate to thrive, and is best suited to a pergola or trellis where it is not limited for space. The plant grows vigorously with clambering stems,

'Gypsy Jewel'

'Gypsy Moth'

with large wrinkled leaves that are grayish green in color. ZONES 6–10.

Clark, Australia, 1920

'Rosy Morn' × seedling

'GWEN SWANE'   MACwhaka
MODERN, MODERN SHRUB, MEDIUM PINK, REPEAT-FLOWERING

This variety bears clusters of neatly formed roses of small to medium size. They are an even shade of pink, and composed of up to 40 small petals. There is a slight fragrance, and flowering continues through summer and autumn. It is suitable wherever a spreading shrub rose of below average height is required, and its trailing shoots make it particularly useful for growing as a weeping standard. The small, matt green foliage makes a good complement to the blooms. The variety is named for the late Mrs. E. N. Swane, a member of the long-established firm of rose growers in Australia. At the present time it appears to be available in that country only. ZONES 5–9.

McGredy, New Zealand, 1987

'Macbroey' × 'Snow Carpet'

'GYPSY'
MODERN, LARGE-FLOWERED/HYBRID TEA, ORANGE-RED, REPEAT-FLOWERING

The attraction of this rose is its flamboyant, eye-catching, scarlet-orange flowers that start out as large pointed buds, then open to full-petalled, tulip-shaped blooms, and finally become loosely cupped. They are carried on long stems, sometimes singly, in clusters at other times, and last well, making this a useful source of roses for cutting. Primarily, it is used as a showy garden plant, as a hedge rose or in a group wherever a tall plant is wanted that will give good continuity of bloom through summer and autumn. The scent is spicy but not very pronounced. This plant will grow above

average height, with an upright, well-branched habit and large, leathery, glossy leaves. ZONES 4–9.

Swim and Weeks, USA, 1972

(['Happiness' × 'Chrysler Imperial'] × 'El Capitan') × 'Comanche'

All-America Rose Selection 1973

'GYPSY JEWEL'
MODERN, MINIATURE, DEEP PINK, REPEAT-FLOWERING

The deep rose pink color and double flowers make this rose a real charmer. The small flowers are packed with over 50 petals and have a distinctive high center of exhibition standard. The blooms, which usually come in small clusters on a bush that is only 2 ft (60 cm) tall, are particularly long lasting. The growth habit is vigorous and bloom production is prolific. It has a tendency to spread rather than grow upright, and the low habit can be exploited to make an attractive border. ZONES 5–11.

Moore, USA, 1975

'Little Darling' × 'Little Buckaroo'

'GYPSY MOTH'
MODERN, CLUSTER-FLOWERED/FLORIBUNDA, ORANGE-PINK, REPEAT-FLOWERING

The flowers are a very pure and delicate shade of light salmon-pink with a light scent. They are carried on firm stems, sometimes singly but usually in clusters, and open from long buds into high-centered flowers of medium size. They hold a classic Large-flowered Rose shape, with the outer petals slowly reflexing to finally become open cupped. 'Gypsy Moth' is suitable for bedding and to cut for small arrangements. It grows vigorously to an average height with a bushy habit, and has long, glossy mid-green leaves. ZONES 4–9.

Tantau, Germany, 1968

Parentage unknown

'Gwen Swane'

HI

'HADLEY, CLIMBING'
MODERN, LARGE-FLOWERED CLIMBER, MEDIUM RED

This sport found in Germany came from a Large-flowered Rose raised in Hadley, Massachusetts, and 'Hadley' was one of the most popular reds of the years between the wars. The flowers are a warm but not deep shade of crimson, with a velvety texture, and open into large, loosely double, cupped flowers that have a good fragrance. The summer blooms are freely borne, of good size and quality, and there may be a few later flowers. They are long stemmed and therefore good to cut. For a wall, fence or tall pillar this is a suitable climber that grows to average height, but avoid a site exposed to chilling wind in spring, as this may cause blind shoots. The plant has rich green foliage, and is liable to seasonal mildew, therefore a dry site should also be avoided. ZONES 4–9.

Teschendorff, Germany, 1927

Sport of 'Hadley'

'HAKUUN'
syn. 'White Cloud'
MODERN, PATIO/DWARF CLUSTER-FLOWERED, WHITE, REPEAT-FLOWERING

This low grower bears masses of rounded, semi-double blooms in closely packed, short-stemmed sprays. They are of medium size and open from long pointed buds into neatly formed young flowers, which become cupped. The color in the early stages is buff-orange, paling to white, sometimes with pink

'Hadley, Climbing'

'Halali'

flecks as the petals expand. There is a light scent, and after the first flush, when the stems and leaves are almost lost to sight by the amount of bloom, flowers continue through summer and autumn. To edge a border or for any small space this is an excellent garden rose, especially useful where a cool color is required. It grows very short with a bushy, slightly spreading habit, and has light green leaves. The name is Japanese, and 'White Cloud' is a direct translation. ZONES 4–9.

Poulsen, Denmark, 1962

Seedling × ('Pinocchio' × 'Pinocchio')

'HALALI'
MODERN, CLUSTER-FLOWERED/FLORIBUNDA, DEEP PINK, REPEAT-FLOWERING

This variety can be considered more of a shrub than a bush, which is to be expected considering that its parents are both strong growers. It carries its large blooms on long stems, with several grouped together to form big clusters. They open from plump buds into loosely double flowers and become cupped in form with a rounded outline. The color is rosy pink, and there is a light fragrance. After the first flush, flowering continues through summer and autumn, which makes this a good choice where a tall rose is wanted, say for the back of a mixed border or for a strong hedge. It has a vigorous habit that grows considerably above average height, and has very large, dense, leathery leaves. ZONES 4–9.

Tantau, Germany, 1956

'Marchenland' × 'Peace'

'HALO DOLLY'   MORwateye
MODERN, MINIATURE, PINK BLEND, REPEAT-FLOWERING

The flowers of this rose are best described as bicolor, with the petals a reddish color on the outside and a pink on the inside surface with a reddish lavender at the base of the petals. The small florets have 6–14 petals and occur in small clusters on straight stems. The blooms have no scent. The foliage is small, mid-green and semi-glossy, and the rounded plant has an attractive, upright, bushy habit

which often tends to grow wider than taller. The color combination tends to last a lot longer if the plant is given afternoon shade. This rose is a hybridizing achievement by Ralph Moore, who introduced a series of these 'halo' varieties where the bloom center gives the effect of a central halo of contrasting color. ZONES 5–11.

Moore, USA, 1992

'Anytime' × seedling ('Anytime' × 'Angel Face')

'HALO RAINBOW'   MORrainbow
MODERN, MINIATURE, PINK BLEND, REPEAT-FLOWERING

There are only 5 petals on this rose, but what a wonderful color display. The creamy white flowers have a pink edging to the petals and the floret base has a picotte halo in the center. The blooms are borne in small clusters and have a light scent. The foliage is semi-glossy, mid-green and has no prickles. It has a spreading habit. This rose is a charming addition to the single-petalled class. As with its relatives in the series, the popularity of this type of Miniature Rose has fallen off in recent years. ZONES 5–11.

Moore, USA, 1995

Seedling × 'Make Believe'

'HALO STAR'   MORanyface
MODERN, MINIATURE, ORANGE BLEND, REPEAT-FLOWERING

With flowers that are red on the outside of the petals but orange to pink on the inside, all complemented by a rich contrasting lavender at the base, this is a truly lovely rose. The floret is a true single-petalled rose, having only 5 petals and a great red halo surrounding the golden yellow stamens. The small blooms are usually borne in small clusters. They have no fragrance. The color fades quickly and the petals, on ageing, curl up into informal star-shaped blooms. This small, upright plant is winter tender and is not suitable for climates with snowfall and frost. ZONES 6–11.

Moore, USA, 1992

Seedling ('Anytime' × 'Angel Face') × seedling ('Anytime' × 'Angel Face')

'HALO TODAY'   MORtoday
MODERN, MINIATURE, ORANGE-PINK, REPEAT-FLOWERING

The very distinct pink flowers with lavender at the base of each petal on this rose gives the center of the floret the desired 'halo' effect of the series. The blooms have 6–14 single petals and no

'Hakuun'

fragrance whatsoever. The florets tend to be borne in small clusters and are surrounded with semi-glossy, medium green foliage. This rose makes a small, upright, well-rounded bush suitable for growing in a container on the patio. Like the other members of the 'halo' series, it represents the control of color and form in the hybridizing process. However, the color combinations have not attracted wide popularity. ZONES 6–11.

Moore, USA, 1994

('Anytime' × 'Gold Badge') × ('Anytime' × 'Lavender Jewel')

'HAMBURGER PHOENIX'
MODERN, MODERN SHRUB, MEDIUM RED, REPEAT-FLOWERING

This rose can also be described as a climber, since it can be trained up a tall pillar or a wall or fence as well as making a strong specimen shrub of above average size. It is a rose to plant for overall color impact rather than for the individual beauty of the semi-double blooms. They are large and dark crimson and are carried in big clusters, opening cupped to show a glimpse of whitish yellow around the stamens in the heart of the flowers. There is a light fragrance, and blooms constantly appear through summer and autumn. The plant grows freely with arching stems, has a fine health record and appears dense in character thanks to its ample covering of large, shiny leaves. ZONES 4–9.

Kordes, Germany, 1954

Rosa kordesii × seedling

National Rose Society Trial Ground Certificate 1950

'HAMPSHIRE'   KORhamp
MODERN, GROUND COVER, MEDIUM RED, REPEAT-FLOWERING

For a position where a ground-cover rose of modest size is wanted, this is a useful variety. The flowers are borne in well-filled clusters, and their bright color catches the eye as the single, scarlet flowers unfold, especially when the petals open out flat to reveal golden yellow stamens. There is excellent continuity of bloom through summer and autumn, and attractive orange hips will follow if the spent trusses are not removed. There is only a light scent. The plant forms a low, spreading mound, two and a half times wide as it is high, and has glossy, mid-green leaves. The name was given by the English introducers to celebrate the centenary of Hampshire County Council. ZONES 4–9.

Kordes, Germany, 1989

Parentage unknown

'HAND IN HAND'   HARaztec
MODERN, PATIO/DWARF-CLUSTER FLOWERED, ORANGE-RED, REPEAT-FLOWERING

This is a dense, bushy, upright grower with very full rosette-type blooms of light scarlet. There is little scent. The blooms are freely produced, usually in clusters of many flowers. Repeat bloom is rapid and disease resistance is good. This is a good choice for a group or small bed where a leafy, compact bush of below average height is required. It was named to benefit a major British charity, the National Children's Home. ZONES 5–9.

Harkness, UK, 1994

'Little Prince' × 'Memento'

Geneva Certificate of Merit 1994, Courtrai and Glasgow Certificate of Merit 1995

'HANDEL' MACha

syns 'Haendel', 'Händel'

MODERN, LARGE-FLOWERED CLIMBER, RED BLEND, REPEAT-FLOWERING

This rose bears many blush flowers rimmed with pinky red, in wide clusters on upright stems. The slender buds open into loosely double blooms of small to medium size. Neatly formed with high centers in the young flower, they open cupped, and look their very best in cooler weather. There is little scent, and the continuity of bloom through summer and autumn is excellent, though mid-season blooms are often ragged. Apart from its value as a good climber with a moderate extent, 'Handel' is one of the best varieties to grow as a source of buttonholes. The well-spaced clusters of flowers are also valued by exhibitors. The plant is stiff and branching, so it needs to be planted on a wall, fence or trellis where it can spread out, or it can be grown up a pillar like an extra tall bush. It has glossy mid-green leaves, which can be affected by black spot. ZONES 4–9.

McGredy, New Zealand, 1965

'Columbine' × 'Heidelberg'

Royal National Rose Society Trial Ground Certificate 1965, Portland Gold Medal 1975, Royal Horticultural Society Award of Garden Merit 1993

'HANNAH GORDON' KORweiso

syn. 'Raspberry Ice'

MODERN, CLUSTER-FLOWERED/FLORIBUNDA, PINK BLEND, REPEAT-FLOWERING

The flowers of this rose are a delightful combination of blush and cherry-pink, the petals being mostly blush with a generous decoration of the deeper color along their rims. They are well proportioned, and develop from plump buds into double, cupped blooms that are quite large when fully open and yield a pleasant light fragrance. Because the clusters are well spaced and each flower has room to display itself, the overall effect is very colorful. Flowering continues through summer and autumn. This is a useful rose for a bed or border, and the flowers last well if cut. This is a vigorous plant with a rather open habit, growing to less than average height, and has large, dark green leaves. ZONES 4–9.

Kordes, Germany, 1983

Seedling × 'Bordure'

Royal National Rose Society Trial Ground Certificate 1983

'HANNE'

syn. 'Hannah'

MODERN, LARGE-FLOWERED/HYBRID TEA, MEDIUM RED, REPEAT-FLOWERING

'Peace' has been a prolific parent but not many roses have been raised from 'Ena Harkness', and although this variety is considered one of the best reds in northern Europe, it has never become well known elsewhere. It has some of the vigor and firm flower stems of 'Peace' allied to the fragrance of 'Ena Harkness', but the blooms are not as big. The color is crimson-scarlet, and the full-petalled flowers open from long buds into well-formed, high-centered blooms that continue through summer and autumn. They stand bad weather well, and are useful in beds, borders and for cutting. The bush grows vigorously with an upright habit to average height and has leathery foliage. ZONES 4–9.

Soenderhousen, Denmark, 1959

'Ena Harkness' × 'Peace'

'HANSA'

syn. 'Hansen's'

MODERN, HYBRID RUGOSA, MEDIUM RED, REPEAT-FLOWERING

The sizeable double blooms of this rose are reddish violet with mauve highlights, a striking and unusual color, and have attractively crinkled petals. They are heavy enough to cause the short necks to bow. The flowers have a strong clove-like scent, and are produced freely in summer with good continuity through to autumn, by which time the hips will have become large and red. This decorative variety is suitable for a shrubbery or mixed border where it will grow to above the average height for a shrub rose. It is very hardy. In milder climates it can become leggy and lose color. Its close relationship to *Rosa rugosa* is manifest in the general growth habit and strong, leathery leaves, which are veined and wrinkled. ZONES 3–9.

Schaum and Van Tol, The Netherlands, 1905

Parentage unknown

'Hampshire'

'Handel'

H

'HANSA-PARK' KORfischer
syn. 'Hanza Park'

MODERN, MODERN SHRUB, MAUVE, REPEAT-FLOWERING

This rose is soft pink, deeper on the outside of the petals. The flowers are of middling size, very full petalled and carried in well-spaced clusters. They have a light fragrance and are good for cutting, since the high-centered blooms open slowly to develop a symmetrical, rounded form that displays the warm color to good effect as the petals reflex. Flowering is well maintained through summer and autumn, and the plant grows vigorously with an upright habit to above average height with an ample covering of large, semi-glossy leaves. ZONES 4–9.

Kordes, Germany, 1994

Parentage unknown

'HANSALAND' KORhassi
syns 'Charles', 'Charles Notcutt'

MODERN, HYBRID RUGOSA, DARK RED, REPEAT-FLOWERING

This handsome shrub is derived from *Rosa rugosa* and it bears medium-sized blooms of an eye-catching, bright, deep

'Happiness'

'Happy Day'

scarlet. They open from clusters of slim, pointed buds into semi-double cupped flowers that show yellow stamens, with a light and pleasing fragrance. The plant is very free flowering, and continues to show color throughout summer and autumn. This rose is useful in the garden to form a hedge or for planting in a mixed border. It makes a dense bush of average height with a well-spread habit, and is generously furnished with light green leaves that are rounded, semi-glossy and display good autumn tints. In naming this rose the English introducers honor the horticulturalist Charles Notcutt. ZONES 4–9.

Kordes, Germany, 1993

Parentage unknown

Royal National Rose Society Certificate of Merit 1996, Belfast Certificate of Merit 1997

'HAPPENSTANCE'
syn. 'Baby Mermaid'

MODERN, MODERN SHRUB, LIGHT YELLOW, REPEAT-FLOWERING

Either a dwarf sport or seedling of the huge climber 'Mermaid', 'Happenstance' forms a small, thorny bush, wider than it

'Hansa-Park'

is tall, with shiny evergreen foliage. The flowering season starts late and continues well into autumn or until the frost. This variety forms very compact little mounds that show off the single, pale yellow flowers with amber stamens. 'Happenstance' is gaining popularity in the USA, but is practically unknown elsewhere. Like 'Mermaid', it revels in hot climates and hates the cold. This unique little rose gives a good fragrance and is very useful in small gardens. ZONES 5–9.

Buss, Germany, circa 1950

Derived from 'Mermaid'

'HAPPINESS'
syns 'Rim', 'Rouge Meilland'

MODERN, LARGE-FLOWERED/HYBRID TEA, MEDIUM RED, REPEAT-FLOWERING

This rose was launched with considerable eclat. As a greenhouse variety it was highly successful and gave perfectly formed, hard-petalled, long-lasting blooms for florists the world over, with a good yield of flowers through the cutting season. The blooms are large, brilliant crimson at first, then pale to medium red with a little 'blueing' in the color tone. They are full of petals and open rather flat. There is no fragrance and the foolish notion that garden roses have 'lost their scent' may be due to this and other widely distributed florists' roses. In cooler climates out of doors the rose rarely thrives, being reluctant to grow or flower freely. It is therefore recommended for garden use only in warmer countries, but not in areas where rust may be troublesome. The plant grows upright and branches well, with matt green foliage. ZONES 5–9.

Meilland, France, 1949

('Rome Glory' × 'Tassin') × ('Charles P. Kilham' × ['Charles P. Kilham' × 'Capucine Chambard'])

'HAPPY'
syn. 'Alberich'

MODERN, POLYANTHA, MEDIUM RED, REPEAT-FLOWERING

The flowers of this variety have been variously described as crimson and currant red. They appear as a sheet of color, because the clusters have scores of buds that open into small rosettes packed close together. The blooms are fairly double, with stiff petals, and will outlast their beauty if the heads are not removed once they start to fade. The first flowering is lavish, after which there is a pause while the plant regains strength to

'Happy'

'Happy Child'

produce more blooms in late summer and autumn. Before the advent of Ground Cover and Patio Roses, 'Happy' and its associated 'Compacta' roses were recommended for rockeries and small spaces, but they are little grown today. The plant is cushion-like in habit, very low and spreading, with small, dark, glossy leaves. ZONES 4–9.

de Ruiter, The Netherlands, 1954

'Robin Hood' × 'Katharina Zeimet' seedling

'HAPPY CHILD' AUScomp

MODERN, MODERN SHRUB, MEDIUM YELLOW, REPEAT-FLOWERING

This variety from David Austin is also classified as an English Rose. It has quite large flowers that are bright yellow in the center and pale towards the petal margins. They open from plump buds into wide-cupped blooms full of petals, most of them infolded against each other to create attractively confused centers, which are held for a long time while a few of the outer petals reflex to give a rounded outline to the flowers. There is a pleasing scent, and blooming continues through summer and autumn. The variety is suitable for a mixed border, being of average size for a shrub rose with a bushy habit and shiny, camellia-like mid-green leaves. It was named to help raise funds for the charity Population Concern. ZONES 4–9.

Austin, UK, 1993

(Seedling × 'Iceberg') × 'Hero'

'HAPPY DAY' SIMpalno
syn. 'Velvet Lustre'

MODERN, LARGE-FLOWERED/HYBRID TEA, RED BLEND, REPEAT-FLOWERING

There have been three roses called 'Happy Days', but only one 'Happy Day' has so far been recorded. This variety bears its flowers one to a stem and they open from long, pointed buds into full-petalled flowers of classic form, finally opening cupped. They are a blend of medium red and salmon-pink shades, with a light but pleasing fragrance. The flowers continue to bloom sporadically through summer and autumn. This variety is suitable for general garden use in beds and borders, though at present time it appears not to be commercially available. It grows vigorously with a bushy habit to average height, and has large, semi-glossy, dark green leaves. ZONES 4–9.

Simpson, New Zealand, 1979

'First Prize' × 'Gypsy Moth'

'HAPPY DAYS'   MACseatri
MODERN, LARGE-FLOWERED/HYBRID TEA, PINK BLEND, REPEAT-FLOWERING

The medium-sized flowers on this variety are a blend of gentle pink shades, blush on the uppersides of the petals and light rose pink, prettily veined, on the undersides. As the broad petals reflex the deeper shades become more visible to create a pleasing color contrast. The blooms are often borne in clusters and are fairly double with about 20 petals, which form high centers in the young flowers. There is a refreshing fragrance, and a succession of bloom is well maintained through summer and autumn. The flowers last well and are excellent for cutting; for garden display it is a useful rose. The plant grows to average height, with a bushy habit and dark green foliage. ZONES 4–9.

McGredy, New Zealand, 1988

(Poulsen seedling × 'Picasso') × 'Paradise'

'HAPPY THOUGHT'
MODERN, MINIATURE, ORANGE-PINK, REPEAT-FLOWERING

Elegant pointed buds on this rose open to reveal flowers that are pink, subtly blended with coral and yellow. The blooms are double with 40 petals and are surrounded by small, medium green foliage. The florets are a glowing color with a decorative informal form and bloom production is prolific. It repeats well. The plant tends to spread rather than grow tall, making it suitable for a hanging basket. 'Happy Thought' has many sister seedlings bred from the same cross that injected the improved ability of modern Miniatures to be propagated from cuttings. ZONES 5–11.

Moore, USA, 1978

(Rosa wichuraiana × 'Floradora') × 'Sheri Anne'

'HAPPY WANDERER'
MODERN, CLUSTER-FLOWERED/FLORIBUNDA, MEDIUM RED, REPEAT-FLOWERING

Although it has never become popular, this short-growing rose attracts many favorable comments. It produces short-stemmed sprays, so that they bloom close to the plant. Cone-shaped buds open into neatly formed flowers in a warm and even shade of crimson-scarlet. They are of medium size, with about 30 petals, and in warm climates they open fast enough to show a contrast with the golden stamens. There is a light scent, and after a very free first blooming more flowers appear during summer and

autumn. For a small space or a bed where a really short plant is wanted, this is a good choice. The bush is compact, vigorous and bushy, with slightly glossy, small leaves. ZONES 4–9.

McGredy, New Zealand, 1974

Seedling × 'Marlene'

Anerkannte Deutsche Rose 1975

'HAREWOOD'   TANinaso
syn. 'Snow Cloud'
MODERN, MODERN SHRUB, WHITE, REPEAT-FLOWERING

The color of the flowers on this variety in cooler climates is a definite light rose pink, with blush white towards the petal base. The semi-double blooms are fairly small with narrow petals and are carried in big clusters, opening cupped to show the stamens. They have a light fragrance and appear very freely in summer with good repeat flushes through summer and autumn. The plant is fairly short, and spreads twice as wide as it is high, with short, arching shoots. It is suitable as a ground-cover rose where there is limited space, and also to grow in a container, when it can be allowed to trail over the sides. The leaves are small and mid-green. ZONES 4–9.

Tantau, Germany, 1993

Parentage unknown

British Association of Rose Breeders Breeder's Choice 1995

'HARISON'S YELLOW'
syns 'Harisonii', 'Pioneer Rose', Rosa × harisonii, 'Yellow Rose of Texas'
OLD, MISCELLANEOUS, DARK YELLOW

The small, semi-double blooms of bright yellow on this variety produce a brief but spectacular spring show, and they have a fruity fragrance. The long canes create a bushy, open shrub with many prickles. This rose is one of the hardiest in the family and spreads quickly by suckers; in fact, the best way to propagate it is by planting the runners. There are black, bristly oval hips. Reaching 10 ft by 12 ft (3 m by 3.5 m) in two seasons, it produces more blooms when in dry, cool positions. After it appeared in the garden of attorney and amateur hybridist George F. Harison in 1830 in what is today downtown Manhattan, it was carried by many pioneers on their journey west. ZONES 4–9.

Harison, USA, circa 1830

Perhaps Rosa spinosissima × R. foetida

Royal Horticultural Society Award of Garden Merit 1993

'Harold Macmillan'

'Happy Wanderer'

'Harmonie'

'HARLEKIN'   KORlupo
syns 'Arlequin', 'Harlequin', 'Kiss of Desire'
MODERN, LARGE-FLOWERED CLIMBER, PINK BLEND, REPEAT-FLOWERING

This Climber bears clusters of large flowers that have creamy white bases and are generously margined with rose red. The flowers are very full petalled and have neatly formed centers at the young stage, to become cupped as the petals open wide. The stems bow under the weight of the blooms. There is a wild rose scent, and after the main flush more flowers appear sporadically through summer and autumn. For a wall, fence or pillar, this is a suitable rose that will grow to average extent. The plant is well furnished with dark green, shiny foliage. ZONES 4–9.

Kordes, Germany, 1986

Parentage unknown

'HARMONIE'   KORtember
MODERN, LARGE-FLOWERED/HYBRID TEA, ORANGE-PINK, REPEAT-FLOWERING

This variety has long, pointed buds that are borne in both clusters and singly, and open into elegantly formed flowers with high centers and good scent. There are only about 20 petals but they are so broad and firm that the flowers hold their shape, which makes them useful for cutting as well as in beds and borders. The color is basically a glowing salmon-

pink, a tone that holds well through the life of the bloom. A good succession of flowers is maintained through summer and autumn, the later blooms being particularly good. The plant grows vigorously to above average height and has an upright, bushy habit, well endowed with leaves that are large, leathery and semi-glossy. ZONES 4–9.

Kordes, Germany, 1981

'Fragrant Cloud' × 'Uwe Seeler'

Baden-Baden Gold Medal 1981

'HAROLD MACMILLAN'
HARwestsun
MODERN, CLUSTER-FLOWERED/FLORIBUNDA, ORANGE-RED, REPEAT-FLOWERING

The color of this rose is an eye-catching shade of orange-red. It bears very big clusters on firm stems, which open into neatly formed flowers that are perfect for buttonholes at the young stage. They only have about 18 petals, but these are firm enough for the flowers to last well. It is very suitable as a hedge, in a bed or to group in a border. There is a light fragrance, and flowers continue to appear through summer and autumn. The bush grows to average height and is well clothed with dark, glossy leaves. It was named in memory of a former British Prime Minister. ZONES 4–9.

Harkness, UK, 1989

'Avocet' × 'Remember Me'

Courtrai Silver Medal 1991

'Happy Thought'

'Harison's Yellow'

H

'Harvest Fayre'

'Harriny'

'Hawa Mahal'

'Harry Wheatcroft'

'HARRINY'

MODERN, LARGE-FLOWERED/HYBRID TEA, MEDIUM PINK, REPEAT-FLOWERING

This variety has fairly large blooms in a soft, pleasing shade of light rose pink which can vary with age. The blooms are perhaps over supplied with petals, of which there are about 40, because the high-centered flowers are easily spoiled by rain. Sometimes they are borne singly but often in threes, a characteristic inherited from 'Pink Favorite'. They have a good fragrance, described as a mixture of Damask and lemon. The variety is useful for bedding and planting in a group, and also for cutting. The flowers appear through summer and autumn, the late blooms being particularly fine. 'Harriny' grows a little above average height with an upright habit, and bears an abundance of healthy, dark green foliage. ZONES 4–9.

LeGrice, UK, 1967

'Pink Favorite' × 'Lively'

Belfast Fragrance Prize 1974

'HARRY EDLAND'

MODERN, CLUSTER-FLOWERED/FLORIBUNDA, MAUVE, REPEAT-FLOWERING

Although it has never become popular, this is one of the easiest of the lilac-pink roses to grow. The flowers are large and full petalled, often carried 3 to a stem,

and open with high centers, becoming rounded and cupped as the petals reflex. They have an excellent fragrance, and blooms continue to appear through summer and autumn. For those who like unusual colors this is a useful rose to grow as a group in a mixed border, and the flowers last well when cut. In New Zealand this is considered a Large-flowered Rose, and its flowers are noticeably bluer in tone in a warm climate. The plant grows strongly with a branching habit to average height and bears large, dark green leaves. When this rose won a medal named after the late secretary of Britain's Royal National Rose Society, Jack Harkness decided to name it in his memory. ZONES 4–9.

Harkness, UK, 1978

('Lilac Charm' × 'Sterling Silver') × ('Blue Moon' × ['Sterling Silver' × 'Africa Star'])

Royal National Rose Society Edland Medal for Fragrance and Trial Ground Certificate 1975

'HARRY WHEATCROFT'

syns 'Caribia', 'Harry'

MODERN, LARGE-FLOWERED/HYBRID TEA, YELLOW BLEND, REPEAT-FLOWERING

The blooms on this variety are similar to those of 'Piccadilly', which is yellow on the undersides of the petals and orange-red on the uppersides, except that the

orange-red surfaces appear to be rather bizarrely striped and streaked. A freak of nature has caused the color pigment to be missing in these areas, to show the natural blush of the unpigmented petal given a yellowish tone by the color on the undersides. For lovers of the unusual this is a pretty rose to grow; it is also lightly scented and free flowering, continuing to bloom through summer and autumn. It grows to a little less than average height with a bushy habit and handsome, glossy, dark green leaves. It bears the name of one of Britain's most successful nurserymen, who lived from 1898 to 1977, and whose extrovert behavior cloaked a shrewd head and kind heart. ZONES 5–9.

Wheatcroft & Sons, UK, 1972

Sport of 'Piccadilly'

'HARVEST FAYRE'   DICnorth

MODERN, CLUSTER-FLOWERED/FLORIBUNDA, ORANGE BLEND, REPEAT-FLOWERING

This variety produces flowers of yellowish apricot, a luminous shade that makes them stand out well in the garden from a considerable distance, especially as the clusters are evenly spaced so that each bloom stands a little apart from the rest. They are of medium size with about 20 firm petals and open from long, pointed buds to show pretty conical centers before they become rounded in outline, with the petals randomly arranged. There is a light fragrance, and flowering continues through summer and autumn. This rose will add sparkle to either a border or a bed. The plant grows sturdily but rather unevenly, so that some flowers are lost to sight among overgrowing shoots. The height of the plant is a little below average, and it has shiny, light green leaves. ZONES 4–9.

Dickson, UK, 1990

Seedling × 'Bright Smile'

UK Rose of the Year 1990

'HARVEST HOME'   HARwesi

syn. 'Harwest Home'

MODERN, HYBRID RUGOSA, MEDIUM PINK, REPEAT-FLOWERING

The long buds of this variety develop into loosely double blooms, which open wide to show the stamens. They are large and rather ragged looking, owing to their creased and furled petals. The color is a pleasing shade of mauve-pink and there is excellent fragrance. Flowering continues with good continuity through summer and autumn and there is a good display of tomato-shaped hips in autumn. For a mixed border, especially where growing conditions are not ideal, this is a useful medium-sized shrub rose to grow. With its rounded, dense habit, prickly stems, leathery, wrinkled foliage and general health and hardiness, the variety takes after the *Rosa rugosa* parentage. It was raised by Mrs Spicer of Hitchin from an unusually shaped hip she noticed on her 'Scabrosa' rose. She later became Mrs Rock, and in some works of reference the rose is credited to her under that name. ZONES 4–9.

Spicer, UK, 1983

Rosa rugosa scabrosa × seedling

Royal National Rose Society Trial Ground Certificate 1977

'HAWA MAHAL'

MODERN, LARGE-FLOWERED/HYBRID TEA, ORANGE-PINK, REPEAT-FLOWERING

Although not able to withstand the rain and cool summers of its country of origin, this has proved a satisfactory performer in warmer climates. The large flowers are a blend of salmon-pink and rose pink, and are borne singly or in small clusters. They have broad, rather soft petals, and exude a good fragrance as they open cupped from the high-centered young blooms. The continuity of flower through summer and autumn is well maintained, which makes this a suitable variety for beds and borders. The plant grows with an upright habit to average height and is well provided with large, dark green leaves. Hawa Mahal is an Indian name meaning 'The Palace of Winds', referring to an ornate structure built in 1799 with latticed screens and arches through which blow currents of air. ZONES 4–9.

Harkness, UK, 1976

'Fragrant Cloud' × 'Kordes' Perfecta'

'HAWAII'

MODERN, LARGE-FLOWERED/HYBRID TEA, ORANGE-RED, REPEAT-FLOWERING

A distinctive feature of this rose is the way it holds very high centers to the flowers while the outer petals furl themselves to narrow points. Long buds open into very large, full-petalled flowers with an iridescent bright color that is variously described as orange-coral or reddish salmon. They appear singly or sometimes in a candelabra (especially later in the season), and last well provided the weather stays cool. The fragrance has been likened to raspberries.

'Hawkeye Belle'

Blooms continue to appear sporadically through summer and autumn, though they fade and burn in hot sun and can be spoiled by rain. This is a suitable rose for a group in a border, and is best behind other plants because it grows tall and rather spindly. The leaves are leathery and mid-green, and liable to mildew. **ZONES 4–9.**

Boerner, USA, 1960

'Golden Masterpiece' × seedling

'HAWKEYE BELLE'

MODERN, MODERN SHRUB, WHITE, REPEAT-FLOWERING

The flowers of this rose are large and beautiful in their construction, and are borne in clusters on strong stems. The plump, pointed buds open to show high centers at first then, as they expand, the many petals resemble a coiled spring at the heart of the bloom. The petals gradually part to create overlapping layers, which give a charming effect at the fully open stage. The color is ivory white, lightly suffused with azalea pink as the flowers open. There is a sweet scent and flowering continues through summer and autumn, which makes this a good subject for mixed borders where a vigorous shrub of average growth is required. The plant grows as wide as it does tall, with an abundance of healthy, dark green, leathery foliage. **ZONES 4–9.**

Buck, USA, 1975

('Queen Elizabeth' × 'Pizzicato') × 'Prairie Princess'

'HEADLINER' JACtu

MODERN, LARGE-FLOWERED/HYBRID TEA, PINK BLEND, REPEAT-FLOWERING

This rose is a confection of blush white and cherry red, the red suffusing most of the petal surface towards the rims. The big flowers have all the elegant form of a classic Large-flowered Rose, holding their high centers while the outer petals reflex to create the symmetrical, balanced effect that will win prizes at the shows. In the garden the spiral patterns of color displayed as the blooms open will attract the eye, but it is a variety for warmer climates as it will spoil in rain. Flowering continues through summer and autumn, and there is a slight

'Heartbeat'

fragrance. The plant grows strongly with an upright habit to above average height, and has large, shiny leaves. **ZONES 5–9.**

Warriner, USA, 1985

'Love' × 'Color Magic'

'HEART OF GOLD' MACyelkil

MODERN, LARGE-FLOWERED/HYBRID TEA, YELLOW BLEND/DEEP YELLOW, REPEAT-FLOWERING

This well-formed, double rose bears beautiful yellow flowers throughout summer and autumn. The color is also enhanced by the backdrop of glossy dark green foliage, which makes this rose an ideal candidate for brightening up uninspiring parts of the garden. **ZONES 5–9.**

McGredy, New Zealand, 1995

'Solitaire' × 'Remember Me'

'HEARTBEAT'

MODERN, CLUSTER-FLOWERED/FLORIBUNDA, ORANGE BLEND, REPEAT-FLOWERING

The orange shades seen in the young, orange-red flowers of this rose become less dominant as they age and the petals fold back. However, the colors remain attractive, and combine well with the mid-green foliage that covers this bush rose. 'Heartbeat' can be propagated by budding. **ZONES 5–9.**

Dickson, UK, 1970

('Castanet' × 'Castanet') × ('Cordelia' × seedling)

'HEARTBEAT 97' COCorona

syn. 'Heartbeat 96'

MODERN, CLUSTER-FLOWERED/FLORIBUNDA, APRICOT BLEND, REPEAT-FLOWERING

This is a rose of cheerful colors, the uppersides of the petals being apricot with reddish flushes and the undersides creamy apricot, which provides a lively contrast as the blooms expand. They open from long buds into high-centered, full-petalled flowers with the outer petals

'Heart of Gold'

neatly reflexing to maintain a pretty shape. The flowers are carried in large clusters, and continue to show color through summer and autumn on a vigorous, upright plant that grows to average height or a little below with an abundance of dark green, glossy foliage. There is a light fragrance, and the variety is well suited to beds, borders and as a hedge. The rose was initially sold to benefit the Scots branch of Tenovus, which is involved in medical research projects of an innovative nature in universities and hospitals. **ZONES 4–9.**

Cocker, UK, 1997

'Coronation Gold' × 'British Concorde'

'HEARTBREAKER' WEKsybil

MODERN, MINIATURE, PINK BLEND, REPEAT-FLOWERING

When the pointed buds on this variety open, lightly scented deep pink flowers with a white base are revealed. The florets are of good exhibition form, having extremely high-spiralled centers. They are petite, borne either one bloom per stem or in small clusters. They can be larger in cooler climates. The foliage is small, dark green and glossy and the bush habit is upright. The eye-catching color makes a great garden display, but

'Hawaii'

the color tends to fade rather rapidly as the blooms age. Its vigorous growth potential ensures a constant supply of blooms throughout the year. The rose deserved its 'Queen of Show' award at the Royal National Rose Society National All Miniature Show in St Albans, England in 1994. **ZONES 5–11.**

Carruth, USA, 1989

'Crystalline' × 'Magic Carrousel'

Queen of Show, Royal National Rose Society National All Miniature Show 1994

'HEARTLAND' SAVsay

MODERN, MINIATURE, ORANGE-PINK, REPEAT-FLOWERING

The short buds of 'Heartland' open to pointed orange-pink flowers. The florets are double with 38 petals and have good exhibition Large-flowered form. The blooms can occur one per stem or in small sprays. The best attributes of this rose are its good clear color and the fact that it is always in bloom. The plant has excellent vigor and hardiness in all climates. This rose can be grown in a container on a patio or in the backyard. It is another great addition to Miniature Roses from 'Sheri Anne'. **ZONES 5–11.**

Saville, USA, 1982

'Sheri Anne' × 'Watercolor'

'Heartland'

'Headliner'

H

'HEARTS A'FIRE' BRIheart

syn. 'Hearts of Fire'

MODERN, MINIATURE, DARK RED,
REPEAT-FLOWERING

This rose carries dark red, well-shaped
flowers on a small, compact, disease-free
plant. The foliage is glossy dark green
and acts as a good background to the
flowers. 'Hearts A'Fire' gives a reliable,
continuous display of flowers with a
quick repeat. ZONES 5–9.

Bridges, USA, 1997

'Merrimac' × seedling

'HEAT WAVE'

syn. 'Mme Paula Guisez'

MODERN, CLUSTER-FLOWERED/FLORIBUNDA,
ORANGE-RED, REPEAT-FLOWERING

This is a dazzling brilliant orange-red
variety that produces sizeable flowers
in well-spaced clusters on stiff upright
stems. They open with neatly formed
centers that become cupped as they age.
In cool weather the orange-red tone is
little changed; the variety is not nearly as
attractive in hot climates, which makes
the color dull and harsh. Flowering is
well maintained through summer and
autumn, although there is not much
scent. 'Heat Wave' is suitable for a bed or
the front of a border. The plant grows to
below average height with an upright,
bushy, slightly spreading habit and semi-
glossy, dark green foliage. ZONES 4–9.

Swim, USA, 1958

Seedling × 'Roundelay'

'Heather Honey'

'Heat Wave'

'HEATHER AUSTIN' AUScook

MODERN, MODERN SHRUB, RED BLEND,
REPEAT-FLOWERING

This variety has flowers of deep rose pink
that open out from round buds into
large, full-petalled flowers. They are
unusual and interesting to look at because the petals are incurved, retaining
the shape of a globe flower when fully
open, and show off the golden stamens
in the depths of the deeply cupped
blooms. There is a pleasant fragrance,
and some repeat bloom through summer
and autumn. This is an attractive rose to
include in a shrub rose border, and is a
vigorous grower of slightly less than average height and width, with a bushy
habit. The leaves are large, matt and
mid-green. Heather Austin is the sister of
the raiser. ZONES 4–9.

Austin, UK, 1996

Parentage unknown

'HEATHER HONEY' HORsilbee

MODERN, LARGE-FLOWERED/HYBRID TEA, APRICOT
BLEND, REPEAT-FLOWERING

Although this Large-flowered Rose has
only 24 petals, they are long and contrive
to form young blooms of high-centered
classic form. The color is a clean and refreshing tone of apricot yellow, which is
deeper on the petal undersides. The
flowers have a fruity scent and are carried on firm stems, sometimes singly,
in sprays of up to 7. They continue to
produce blooms during summer and

autumn, and are useful for cutting or to
cultivate in beds and borders, though excessive rain can mark and spoil them. It
grows to average height, with a bushy
habit and a covering of glossy mid-green
leaves. ZONES 4–9.

Horner, UK, 1988

'Silver Jubilee' × ('Honey Favorite' ×
'Southampton')

Royal National Rose Society Torridge Award and
Trial Ground Certificate 1987

'HEAVEN' JACfon

MODERN, LARGE-FLOWERED/HYBRID TEA, WHITE,
REPEAT-FLOWERING

This large rose has long, urn-shaped
white buds, delicately rimmed with light
cyclamen pink. They open into high-
centered blooms that are packed with
wide petals of pale blush white and
touches of a slightly deeper blush. There
is a light and pleasing fragrance. The
flowers appear on long stems and are
good for cutting as well as for general
garden display, particularly in a border
where this tall grower can be planted behind shorter items. It is best in warmer
climates and fine weather. The plant
grows to above average height with an
upright, free-branching habit and large,
matt, dark green leaves. ZONES 4–9.

Warriner, USA, 1995

'Honor' × 'First Prize'

'HEAVENLY ROSALIND'

AUSmash

MODERN, MODERN SHRUB, PINK BLEND,
REPEAT-FLOWERING

Also classified as an English Rose,
'Heavenly Rosalind' inherits its charming, single, soft pink flowers from
'Shropshire Lass'. The outer petals
deepen to medium pink to give a Wild
Rose effect. The blooms are of medium
size and are produced in clusters. There
is a slight fragrance, prickles are few and
the foliage is medium size, dull dark
green, leathery and disease free. This
plant is a medium-growing, bushy rose
with a reliable repeat-bloom; it would
make a good free-flowering hedge, or
could either be used as part of a mixed
border or planted in groups. ZONES 5–9.

Austin, UK, 1995

'Shropshire Lass' × 'Heritage'

'HEBE'

MODERN, CLUSTER-FLOWERED/FLORIBUNDA, DEEP
PINK, REPEAT-FLOWERING

This very early Cluster-flowered Rose
has deep pink, well-shaped flowers that
have lighter undersides. The blooms are
produced both singly and in small clusters over a long period in summer. Compared with the vast numbers of red,
orange and salmon Cluster-flowered
Roses, it is surprising how few deep pink
like 'Hebe' are currently available. 'Hebe'
is reasonably resistant to disease. ZONES 5–9.

Leenders, The Netherlands, 1941

Parentage unknown

'HEBE'

MODERN, LARGE-FLOWERED/HYBRID TEA, ORANGE-
PINK, REPEAT-FLOWERING

This rose reminds one of the old Tea
Roses, because of its long petals, slender

neck, gaunt open habit and sweet scent.
The flowers are a pretty shade in which
salmon and orange come together, with
a hint of apricot yellow. They have 24
large petals, and in a newly opened
bloom the inner ones form a high cone
while the outer ones reflex to become
waved and crinkled. Because they are
soft in texture, the petals are easily
damaged by rain. The variety is a good
example of a type of rose voted worthy
of the highest award in 1949, when the
flower was all and the plants were not
seriously judged. It is doubtful if a
breeder would consider introducing
'Hebe' today, due to its frail stems and
lack of foliage. The plant is upright, with
glossy, bronzy foliage. ZONES 4–9.

Dickson, UK, 1949

Parentage unknown

National Rose Society Gold Medal 1949

'HÉBÉ'S LIP'

syns 'Reine Blanche', 'Rubrotincta'
OLD, SWEET BRIAR, WHITE

The scented flowers of this rose are
borne singly or in small clusters. They
are cupped, shapely and tidy semi-
double blooms with the golden stamens
shown off superbly by the creamy white
petals that are brushed crimson at the
outer edges. Flowering in early to mid-
summer, each flower can attain a diameter of up to 3 in (8 cm) in good soil.
This is a tidy, compact shrub that grows
to 4 ft (1.2 m). The leaves are fresh mid-
green, coarse to touch and well serrated.
It is thought to be a cross between a
Damask and Rosa eglanteria, but there
is no detectable scent from its foliage
which one might expect from such
parentage. It is very healthy. ZONES 4–9.

Lee, UK, pre-1846; reintroduced by Paul, UK, 1912

Rosa eglanteria × a Damask Rose

'HECTOR DEANE'

MODERN, LARGE-FLOWERED/HYBRID TEA, RED
BLEND, REPEAT-FLOWERING

The slender, high-centered flowers of
this variety are 'a mixture of orange,
cochineal, carmine and salmon-pink,
flushed and veined saffron yellow at the
base, in the words of the raiser. This
vivid combination of colors is accompanied by a sweet, fruity scent, and these
twin assets made 'Hector Deane', when a
novelty, a highly sought after rose. It
flowers through summer and autumn,
and used to be a popular choice for beds
and borders, with the added advantage
of having elegant, medium-sized blooms
on long stems that are ideal for cutting.
It grows vigorously with an upright, free-
branching habit to average height, with
glossy, dark green leaves. Unfortunately,
this variety is prone to rust, which has
been largely responsible for its fall from
favor. Hector Deane was the name of the
doctor who took out the tonsils of a
small boy who survived the ordeal to become, in due course, Sam McGredy IV.
ZONES 4–9.

McGredy, UK, 1938

'McGredy's Scarlet' × 'Lesley Dudley'

National Rose Society Clay Vase for Fragrance,
Royal Horticultural Society Clay Cup for
Fragrance

'Hébé's Lip'

'Hector Deane'

'Heidekind'

'HEIDEKIND' KORiver

syn. 'Esterel'

MODERN, MODERN SHRUB, DARK RED, REPEAT-FLOWERING

This tough rose bears crowded clusters of rich cherry red flowers on long bowing stems. The blooms are of middling size, and open out flat with frilled edges in big heads of 20 petals. The color is well maintained, with little fading as the flowers mature, and after the first flush they continue to appear through summer and autumn. There is a slight scent. For a hedge rose of modest height, or in a border, this would be a suitable rose to grow. It makes a sturdy, vigorous plant of somewhat less than average height for a shrub rose, and grows upright with arching stems, well-covered with attractive dark green leaves, which are small and shiny. ZONES 4–9.

Kordes, Germany, 1985

'The Fairy' × seedling

'HEIDEKÖNIGIN' KORdapt

syns 'Palissade Rose', 'Pheasant'

MODERN, GROUND COVER, LIGHT PINK, REPEAT-FLOWERING

The lightly fragrant flowers of this variety are large, light pink and double, each with 35 petals. The foliage is semi-glossy and medium green. The plant is disease resistant and has a spreading habit, making it very suitable as a ground cover or for training on a pillar. It is interesting to note that the work by Moore using *Rosa wichuraiana* to pass on its vigor and rambler habit to its progeny has also been employed by Kordes in producing this lovely Miniature Rose. ZONES 5–11.

Kordes, Germany, 1985

'Zwerkönig '78' × Seedling of *Rosa wichuraiana*

Royal National Rose Society Certificate of Merit 1986

'Heidelberg'

'HEIDELBERG' KORbe

syn. 'Gruss an Heidelberg'

MODERN, MODERN SHRUB, MEDIUM RED, REPEAT-FLOWERING

The flowers on this variety are carried on strong stems in clusters of up to 10, and they are quite large and full of petals, opening cupped to flat. The color is deep crimson as the buds begin to part, then open to a rich shade of crimson, finally paling with age. The scent is light and pleasant and, after a prolific first flush of bloom, there is a sporadic repeat-bloom through summer and autumn. For a shrubbery or to train on a pillar or against a wall not facing the full heat of the sun, this is a vigorous and upright rose with moderate lateral spread to above average height. There is an ample covering of large, leathery, semi-glossy leaves. ZONES 4–9.

Kordes, Germany, 1959

'World's Fair' × 'Floradora'

Royal National Rose Society Certificate of Merit 1958

'HEIDERÖSLEIN'

MODERN, CLUSTER-FLOWERED CLIMBER, YELLOW BLEND, REPEAT-FLOWERING

The pointed, pinky red buds of this variety develop into flowers of delicate rosy

'Heideröslein'

'Heidekönigin'

pink, with sulfur yellow at the base of the petals. They are of medium size, with 5 crinkled petals, and are borne in great clusters of up to as many as 60 blooms that open out flat to show attractive golden stamens. There is a good scent. This repeat-flowering rose can be kept pruned and grown as a shrub, or trained against a wall, fence or pillar. Round hips ripen in autumn to orange-red, and persist right through winter. The plant grows wide and bushy, with dark green leaves. ZONES 4–9.

Lambert, Germany, 1932

'Chamisso' × 'Amalie de Greiff'

'HEIDESCHNEE' KORconta

syns 'Moon River', 'Snow on the Heather'

MODERN, GROUND COVER, WHITE, REPEAT-FLOWERING

This is a prolific ground-covering variety which bears long, ground-hugging

'Heideschnee'

stems. It produces great numbers of medium-sized, pure white flowers in summer, borne close to the stems in large clusters. The blooms have 5 petals and become like little stars as they mature, with their tips furling into narrow points. After the first flush more flowers appear through summer and autumn, and they withstand bad weather well. There is a light fragrance. The variety is useful on banks, where the long canes will readily root themselves. It is also particularly effective in weeping standard form. The plant has a low, spreading habit and attractive shiny, dark green leaves. ZONES 4–9.

Kordes, Germany, 1990

Parentage unknown

'Heideschnee'

'Heidekönigin' growing on post, with 'Anna Livia' in the foreground

'HEIDESOMMER' KORlirus
syns 'Cevennes', 'Heidi Sommer'
MODERN, CLUSTER-FLOWERED/FLORIBUNDA,
WHITE, REPEAT-FLOWERING

The classification of this variety is a
problem, because it is not extensive
enough to be called a Ground Cover
Rose yet it is more spreading than most
Cluster-flowered Roses. It is useful to
plant in a group at the front of a border,
to cover a fairly small area or to grow in
a container. The plant has small, semi-
double, creamy white flowers borne with
great freedom in dense sprays, and they
open flat to show golden stamens. The
blooms contrast well against a background of small, dark, shiny leaves. They
continue to appear through summer and
autumn, and have a pleasant scent that
becomes sweet and pervasive in warm
settled weather and is attractive to bees.
Perhaps they are led astray by the name
label, for *Heidesommer* means 'summer
in the heather'. ZONES 4–9.

Kordes, Germany, 1985

'The Fairy' × seedling

'HEIDI' NOAheid
MODERN, MODERN SHRUB, MEDIUM PINK,
REPEAT-FLOWERING

In bud this is deep pink, and becomes
clear pink as it opens out. The small to
medium-sized flowers are borne in
immense heads, each with up to 100

'Heidesommer'

'Heidi'

blossoms that are carried on rigid stems
above the foliage. They open with just a
few petals to reveal prominent golden
stamens. This is a suitable rose for garden display in beds and borders, and
flowering continues through summer
and autumn. There is little scent. The
plant grows below the average height for
a shrub rose with a vigorous, spreading
habit, and is well furnished with semi-
glossy, bright green leaves that become
darker as they mature. Black spot may be
a problem in a season when conditions
favor the fungus. ZONES 4–9.

Noack, Germany, 1987

'Fairy Moss' × 'Iceberg'

Freiland Gold Medal 1987

'HEIKE' KORundum
MODERN, LARGE-FLOWERED/HYBRID TEA, MEDIUM
YELLOW, REPEAT-FLOWERING

One of the most stunning yellow roses
ever to be introduced to the modern rose
garden and florist trade, 'Heike' has enjoyed a great deal of popularity from
South African rose lovers. Its tight yellow
buds are tinged with green and develop
into perfectly shaped, open flowers with
petals that curl back from the firm
pointed centers in a classical way. The
color remains clear, and so many blooms
are repeatedly being formed that the
bush might be mistaken for a Cluster-
flowered Rose. There is a pleasing

'Heinz Erhardt'

'Heinzelmännchen'

fragrance, which adds to its popularity.
'Heike' is a medium-sized bush rose with
vigorous and remarkably disease-free
growth. It is therefore excellent for bedding schemes. ZONES 5–10.

Kordes, Germany, 1993

Parentage unknown

'HEINRICH MÜNCH'
syn. 'Pink Frau Karl Druschki'
OLD, HYBRID PERPETUAL, MEDIUM PINK,
REPEAT-FLOWERING

The round, pointed buds of this rose
become large, double, soft pink blooms
suffused with silvery pink. The full,
fragrant blooms, which contain 50 petals
and are slow to open, appear singly on
long, upright canes. When fully open
they look like cabbage roses, and they are
fine cut flowers. The 6 ft (1.8 m) shrub,
covered with soft green foliage, is vigorous and pegging down the canes will
produce a better crops of flowers. There
may be some autumn rebloom. It was
named after its discoverer, who gave it to
Hinner. ZONES 4–9.

Introduced by Hinner, Germany, 1911

'Frau Karl Druschki' × ('Mme Caroline Testout' ×
'Mrs W. J. Grant')

'HEINRICH SCHULTHEIS'
OLD, HYBRID PERPETUAL, LIGHT PINK, REPEAT-
FLOWERING

A prize-winning rose when it was introduced in England well over a century
ago, this Hybrid Perpetual is still valued
as a cut flower, especially just after it
opens. The soft pink, full, very large
blooms open cupped and then turn
blowzy. The 3 in (8 cm) flowers have
heavy, large petals. It is a branching,
upright bush that grows to 4 ft (1.2 m)
high and produces occasional blooms in
autumn. It was named for the founder
of the famous—and still flourishing—
German rose nursery. ZONES 4–9.

Bennett, UK, 1882

'Mabel Morrison' × 'E. Y. Teas'

'HEINZ ERHARDT'
MODERN, CLUSTER-FLOWERED/FLORIBUNDA,
MEDIUM RED, REPEAT-FLOWERING

This excellent bright red Cluster-
flowered Rose, of which there are so
many, bears large, double flowers made
up of 25 petals that are produced in
small to fairly large clusters. They last
very well in both extremes of heat and
cold and give a slight fragrance. The foliage is dark green and copper tinted when
young, and covers the very profuse,

vigorous growth that forms a bushy
plant. The disease resistance is good,
except for the occasional bout of mildew.
After all these years 'Heinz Erhardt' is
still a good rose for bedding schemes and
mixed borders, and its bushy habit
makes it ideal for growing as a mixed
standard. The Gold Medal at Baden-
Baden was well deserved. ZONES 5–9.

Kordes, Germany, 1962

Parentage unknown

Baden-Baden Gold Medal 1961, National Rose
Society Trial Ground Certificate 1962

'HEINZELMÄNNCHEN'
KORnuma
syn. 'Red Pixie'
MODERN, CLUSTER-FLOWERED/FLORIBUNDA,
MEDIUM RED, REPEAT-FLOWERING

This very low and compact plant, with
abundant rich green, glossy foliage, produces blooms in well-spaced clusters of
5–10. The color is a strong rich crimson
and the flowers have 20–30 petals of
great substance. They last a long time on
the bush in all weather conditions, without fading; the plant is quick to repeat
bloom and is particularly healthy. This is
one of the best bright red, low-growing
Cluster-flowered Roses for use as a low
border—plant it close together for maximum effect. It is also very suitable for
growing in containers. ZONES 4–9.

Kordes, Germany, 1984

('Satchmo' × seedling) × ('Messestadt Hannover'
× 'Hamburg')

'HEIRLOOM' JACloom
MODERN, LARGE-FLOWERED/HYBRID TEA, MAUVE,
REPEAT-FLOWERING

This is offered by a number of nurseries
in North America, but hardly anywhere
else. It produces fairly large flowers of
deep lilac-purple with darker shading towards the rims, and they fade to a paler
lilac tone as they age. They are borne
singly, sometimes in clusters, and are full
petalled, opening with low centers soon
forming a cupped shape and giving off a
strong, sweet fragrance. Flowering continues through summer and autumn.
The variety is suitable for inclusion in
beds and borders as an item of unusual
coloring; it can also be cut for domestic
arrangements, the stems not usually being long enough for large-scale florists'
work. The plant grows to average height
or less with a bushy habit and dark green
leaves. ZONES 4–9.

Warriner, USA, 1972

Seedling × seedling

H

'HELEN KNIGHT'
MODERN, MODERN SHRUB, MEDIUM YELLOW

This rose bears 5-petalled, saucer-shaped, bright yellow flowers of small to medium size. They appear in profusion in late spring or early summer to create a picture of beauty against arching, reddish stems and light green, fern-like foliage. The scent is faint, and there is not normally any later bloom in summer and autumn. The plant can be grown as a free-standing shrub, and is best left to grow naturally without having to be pruned, apart from the removal of dead or crossing branches. It can also be trained against a wall, but a site liable to suffer the effects of frost should be avoided. 'Helen Knight' grows slightly taller and wider than the average shrub rose, and was named by its raiser, Frank Knight of the Royal Horticultural Society Gardens at Wisley, after his wife, who helped him rear the original seedling. The pollen parent's identity is a guess; it was the only other rose in flower anywhere near *Rosa ecae*. ZONES 5–9.

Knight, UK, 1970

Rosa ecae × *Rosa ecae*

Royal Horticultural Society Award of Garden Merit 1994

'HELEN NAUDÉ'   KORdiena
syn. 'New Pristine'
MODERN, LARGE-FLOWERED/HYBRID TEA, WHITE BLEND, REPEAT-FLOWERING

This rose is named for a popular South African announcer on Radio Jacaranda. The creamy white flowers with pink-flushed outer petals have a delicate beauty of their own; they hold their shape for a long time and the bush produces many successive flowerings. 'Helen Naudé' is useful either as bedding, for cut flowers or on the exhibition bench. There is a slight fragrance. The plant is vigorous and usually medium sized, but can grow taller. ZONES 5–10.

Kordes, Germany, 1992

Parentage unknown

'HELEN TRAUBEL'
MODERN, LARGE-FLOWERED/HYBRID TEA, PINK BLEND, REPEAT-FLOWERING

The flowers on this variety are a fetching combination of warm peach-pink with flushes of yellow at the base, fading slightly as they age. Borne sometimes singly but quite often in 3s, they open from long buds into elegant flowers made up of 24 petals, and sustain high centers for a short period before they become cupped. They have a sweet scent, and appear with good continuity through summer and autumn. Weak flower stems often cause the blooms to nod, especially in windy conditions, which detracts from its value as a bedding rose on its own, but in a border among other plants it fits in well. The plant grows vigorously to average height with a bushy, branching habit and dark green, semi-glossy foliage. ZONES 4–9.

Swim, USA, 1951

'Charlotte Armstrong' × 'Glowing Sunset'
Rome Gold Medal 1951, All-America Rose Selection 1952, National Rose Society Trial Ground Certificate 1953

'HELENA'
MODERN, LARGE-FLOWERED/HYBRID TEA, LIGHT YELLOW, REPEAT-FLOWERING

'Helena' has long buds that reveal double, high-centered blooms of soft maize yellow, with 20–25 petals, opening to large flat flowers showing stamens. There is a good fragrance, the foliage is leathery and matt mid-green, and the growth habit is vigorous with quick repeat-bloom. Disease resistance is good. 'Helena' is good for bedding schemes and for use as a standard. ZONES 5–9.

1982

Sport of 'Helen Traubel' × ('Charlotte Armstrong' × 'Glowing Sunset')

'HELLO'   COChello
MODERN, PATIO/DWARF CLUSTER-FLOWERED, MEDIUM RED, REPEAT-FLOWERING

'Hello' has flowers that are a crimson red with a contrasting white eye to the center of the blooms. The florets are large with 6–14 single petals and are borne as large clusters. Because of its increased bloom size in cool climates, this rose is an attractive addition to the Patio classification. The foliage is semi-glossy, medium green and fairly disease resistant. This rose is another great creation from the talented Scottish hybridizer, the late James Cocker from Aberdeen. ZONES 5–11.

Cocker, UK, 1990

'Darling Flame' × seedling
Glasgow Gold Medal 1992

'HELMUT SCHMIDT'   KORbelma
syns 'Goldsmith', 'Simba'
MODERN, LARGE-FLOWERED/HYBRID TEA, MEDIUM YELLOW, REPEAT-FLOWERING

The large, pointed buds of this variety give promise of big flowers to come, and they are beauties. The urn-shaped, young blooms develop high centers around which the outer petals are arranged with wonderful symmetry. They usually appear one per strong, upright stem, which makes the variety an excellent cutting rose, especially as the blooms hold their shape and last well. It is a good rose for general garden use, flowering on through summer and autumn though tending to produce a flush of bloom followed by a pause. The plant grows neat and upright to below average height, with matt green foliage. In Germany this was introduced to honor a former chancellor; in the USA it is called 'Goldsmith', and the British name commemorates a dog—a golden labrador owned by the raiser's agent, Mark Mattock—called Simba (the Swahili word for lion) because of the color of its coat. ZONES 4–9.

Kordes, Germany, 1979

'New Day' × seedling
Courtrai Gold Medal 1979, Geneva Gold Medal 1979, Royal National Rose Society Trial Ground Certificate 1979

'HELPMEKAAR ROOS'
KORogesa
MODERN, LARGE-FLOWERED/HYBRID TEA, APRICOT BLEND, REPEAT-FLOWERING

The 'Helpmekaar' ('Help Each Other') was an organisation formed by prominent Afrikaaners in the depression years after World War I to provide study loans to students from poor families. The rose that commemorates this body has a very special warm burnt orange color to the flowers, which develop from pointed buds to fully open blooms. The flowers are looser than typical Large-flowered Roses, and are carried on long and sturdy flower stems; they make good cutting roses, with the added advantage of a pleasant perfume. 'Helpmekaar Roos' is a medium-sized shrub that is good for bedding schemes. ZONES 5–10.

Kordes, Germany, 1993

Parentage unknown

'HENKELL ROYAL'
MODERN, LARGE-FLOWERED/HYBRID TEA, MEDIUM RED, REPEAT-FLOWERING

This is a handsome, blood red rose. The flowers open from long buds into medium- to large-sized, full-petalled, high-centered blooms of good form. There is a splendid fragrance, and the variety continues to flower through summer and autumn, holding its color tone well even in hot weather. It is well suited for beds and borders and also for cutting, thanks to its stiff, upright stems and the long-lasting qualities of the bloom. The plant grows vigorously with a freely branching, bushy habit to average height and has large, glossy, dark green leaves. If black spot is about, it is likely to be affected. ZONES 4–9.

Kordes, Germany, 1964

Parentage unknown

Baden-Baden Gold Medal 1964

'HENRI BARRUET'
MODERN, LARGE-FLOWERED CLIMBER, PINK BLEND

The Barbier nursery firm in Orléans raised over 50 roses during the early twentieth century, including such masterpieces as 'Albéric Barbier' and 'Albertine', but this is one of their less well-known offerings. It is still obtainable commercially from a few specialist growers. It produces its lightly scented blooms in clusters of up to 15. They have coppery and yellow tones on the undersides of the petals and open pink, showing tints of white as the flowers develop. The summer blooming is very profuse. The growth is average for a Climber, with arching stems and olive green leaves. It is a suitable subject for fences and pillars, needing a free circulation of air for best results. ZONES 4–9.

Barbier, France, 1918

Parentage unknown

'HENRI FOUQUIER'
syn. 'Henri Foucquier'
OLD, GALLICA, MEDIUM PINK

Although this pink Gallica Rose is hard to find today, it really is worth the effort to locate it. The pure rose pink blossoms darken as they age or when the bush is planted in the shade. The fragrant petals reflex around a button eye. Dark foliage covers the spreading, sprawling shrub, which has few prickles. It was named for a French politician and writer who lived from 1838 to 1901. ZONES 4–9.

Pre-1842

Parentage unknown

'Helen Traubel'

'Helena'

'Helmut Schmidt'

'HENRI MARTIN'
syn. 'Red Moss'
OLD, MOSS, MEDIUM RED

The double flowers of this rose, which are loosely arranged in large clusters, open flat and are up to 3 in (8 cm) across. They are rich claret red to crimson and pale slightly to a softer red before going over. They are very fragrant. It is a vigorous, wide-growing shrub to 6 ft (1.8 m) with few thorns but many soft bristles on gracefully arching stems. The foliage is rich green, as is the moss on the flower buds and calyces; the moss is aromatic and smells like balsam. 'Henri Martin' does not mind poor soil, but needs space to develop as it can get considerably broad. It needs support of some kind, such as a tripod or trellis, to give its best. ZONES 4–9.

Laffay, France, 1863

Parentage unknown

Royal Horticultural Society Award of Garden Merit 1993

'HENRY FONDA'   JACyes
MODERN, LARGE-FLOWERED/HYBRID TEA, DEEP YELLOW, REPEAT-FLOWERING

There are only about 24 petals in this Large-flowered Rose but they are firm, so that the rich yellow flowers hold their form and last well. They open from pointed buds into medium- to large-sized blooms with neatly formed centers.

'Henry Nevard'

'Henry Kelsey'

The outer petals furl at the tips to create a flower of symmetry and beauty. There is a light scent, and a good succession of bloom is maintained through summer and autumn. This is a pretty rose for the garden, to use in beds, borders and small flower arrangements for which the length of stem is suited. The plant grows upright to above average height, and is well furnished with deep green, glossy foliage, which provides an excellent complement to the bright flowers. The rose commemorates the American actor who lived from 1905–82. ZONES 4–9.

Jackson & Perkins, USA, 1995

Parentage unknown

'HENRY HUDSON'
MODERN, HYBRID RUGOSA, WHITE, REPEAT-FLOWERING

Dr Felicitas Svejda and the Canadian Department of Agriculture have worked for many years to introduce roses hardy enough to withstand severe winter conditions, and this is one of the most successful. It makes a low, suckering plant, bearing pink-tipped buds that open into double white flowers. These become cupped as the petals expand to display golden stamens. They are of medium size with a good scent and, after the first generous flush, more blooms appear through summer and autumn. The old flowers do not fall readily and should be

'Heritage'

removed. This is very suitable as a low, bedding plant, and has an abundance of tough, deep green foliage. It is remarkably hardy and very healthy. The rose commemorates the explorer who died vainly seeking the Northwest Passage, and whose name lives on in a bay, straits and river, none of which were actually discovered by him. ZONES 3–9.

Svejda, Canada, 1976

Seedling of 'Schneezwerg'

'HENRY KELSEY'
MODERN, MODERN SHRUB, MEDIUM RED, REPEAT-FLOWERING

This is an exceptionally hardy rose for cold climates. The flowers are borne in heavy clusters of up to 18 medium to large-sized flowers. They are full petalled and are a warm, bright shade of red. As the petals reflex, the blooms become cupped to reveal prominent golden stamens. There is a sharp, spicy scent. The flowers age to rose red before dropping their petals cleanly, and they repeat-bloom through summer and autumn. This can be planted in a border to make an arching, pendulous shrub of lower than average height, but spreading in habit, with trailing stems. It can be more easily controlled if trained on a trellis, arch or fence as a modest-sized climber. It has glossy foliage that withstands mildew. ZONES 3–9.

Svejda, Canada, 1984

Hybrid of *Rosa kordesii* × seedling

'HENRY NEVARD'
OLD, HYBRID PERPETUAL, DARK RED, REPEAT-FLOWERING

One of the last Hybrid Perpetuals introduced to the trade, this vigorous bush is covered with large round buds that open to dark red, double blooms with 30 petals during summer. The large, cupped, highly fragrant flowers hold together well in warm weather. The bush has dark, leathery green foliage, and should be pruned lightly. ZONES 4–9.

Cant, UK, 1924

Parentage unknown

'HER MAJESTY'
OLD, HYBRID PERPETUAL, MEDIUM PINK

This rose has clear, rose-carmine blooms that are 6 in (15 cm) across and reflex toward the center as they open. They are very large and high centered, with thick petals, but critics cannot agree on whether they have perfume or not. This rose blooms later than others in its class. The vigorous, upright bush displays gray-green, glossy foliage and huge prickles. It needs time to establish itself and does well in rich soil. Mildew may be a problem. Henry Bennett was one of the first nurserymen to breed Large-flowered Roses. ZONES 4–9.

Bennett, UK, 1885

'Mabel Morrison' × 'Canary'

'HERBSTFEUER'
syn. 'Autumn Fire'
OLD, SWEET BRIAR, DARK RED, REPEAT-FLOWERING

This variety has dark red, semi-double, large, fragrant blooms that appear in

clusters on arching branches throughout the season from early summer until autumn. It is a 6 ft (1.8 m) shrub that produces large, pear-shaped, red-yellow hips, which add to its value as a landscaping rose. The autumn foliage is most attractive, the light green, pointed long leaves adding charm as they change color. This excellent candidate for the woodland or for hedges does equally well in shade or sun. ZONES 5–9.

Kordes, Germany, 1961

Hybrid of *Rosa eglanteria*

'HERERO'   HERbic
MODERN, LARGE-FLOWERED/HYBRID TEA, RED BLEND, REPEAT-FLOWERING

The Hereros are a tribe of tall, elegant people who live in Namibia, and this rose named for them reflects the colors of the Namib desert. When the pointed buds open into double flowers, the 35 petals have a most amazing range of warm colors, from gold to orange, tangerine and burnt amber. They are carried in small clusters of 3–8, and these can be successfully cut for indoor arrangements and for the show bench. There is no fragrance. 'Herero' is a tall and healthy shrub that makes its mark in the garden. ZONES 5–11.

Herholdt, South Africa, 1981

'Angel Bells' × 'Southern Sun'

'HERITAGE'   AUSblush
syn. 'Roberta'
MODERN, MODERN SHRUB, LIGHT PINK, REPEAT-FLOWERING

The plump buds of this rose open into big, cupped flowers that are full of petals that crowd the center of the blooms, randomly folding in upon one another in the style of an Old Garden Rose. They display a variety of light pink shades, from palest blush to warm rose pink deep in the center of the blooms. There is a good lemon fragrance, and after the first flush of flower the plant continues to show color through summer and autumn. This is a good rose for a border, bed or as a hedge. It grows vigorously and fairly compactly on its bowing branches, to average height for a shrub rose, with a good covering of dark green, semi-glossy leaves. From David Austin, it is also classified as an English Rose. ZONES 4–9.

Austin, UK, 1984

Seedling × ('Wife of Bath' × 'Iceberg')

'HERMAN STEYN'   KORfolklori
MODERN, LARGE-FLOWERED/HYBRID TEA, RED BLEND, REPEAT-FLOWERING

Herman Steyn has been head of the philately section in the South African Post Office for the last 25 years, and has been responsible for the release of many very beautiful stamps. His own rose is quite spectacular: it is full, with the classical Large-flowered Rose shape, but the combination of bright carmine petals painted on the undersides with bright yellow is the most striking characteristic. The flowers of this variety last well when cut, and when arranged in a copper or brass vase they can look really exotic.

There is a slight fragrance. 'Herman Steyn' is a tall and sturdy bush rose that is most often grouped in the garden with spire roses to form a backdrop to a bed of roses. ZONES 5–11.

Kordes, Germany, 1994

Parentage unknown

'HERMOSA'

syns 'Armosa', 'Mme Neumann', 'Mélanie Lemaire'

OLD, CHINA, LIGHT PINK, REPEAT-FLOWERING

This is a rose without any critics; it is healthy and vigorous, and fine as a bedding plant as well as by itself. 'Hermosa' has flourished in cultivation ever since its introduction. The pointed, attractive buds open to reveal light pink, highly centered, small blooms containing 35 petals. The cupped, globular flowers are nearly white at the base, and the outer petals reflex as the blooms age. The bushy growth is covered with blue-green, smooth leaves and a few prickles. This variety produces fragrant flowers, and it should be planted in groups of 3 or more. ZONES 5–9.

Marchesseau, France, pre-1837

Probably China × Bourbon

'HERO'   AUShero

MODERN, MODERN SHRUB, MEDIUM PINK, REPEAT-FLOWERING

The flowers of this rose are of middling size and prettily formed, the outer petals reflexing while the inner ones part to form a deep cup. The color is a soothing blend of light to medium pink shades, and there is a sharp myrrh fragrance. The plant grows leggy and arching, with its branches shooting out in a gawky fashion; the raiser recommends planting it in a group for a better visual effect, and in warmer climates it can be trained on a support as a climber. The flowers continue to appear in widely spaced, small sprays through summer and autumn. The overall height and width are slightly above the average for a shrub rose, and the leaves are semi-glossy. Hero was the priestess of Aphrodite, for whom Leander swam the Hellespont and drowned. ZONES 4–9.

Austin, UK, 1982

'The Prioress' × seedling

'HEROÏCA'

MODERN, LARGE-FLOWERED/HYBRID TEA, DARK RED, REPEAT-FLOWERING

The deep velvety red blooms of this rose become lighter as they age. They are full-

'Heroïca'

petalled with high centers and are produced freely in summer, repeating their show satisfactorily through summer and autumn. There is a light fragrance. Though little grown today, this variety has proved its effectiveness in beds and borders and as a hedge. The plant grows vigorously to average height, but does not match the standard of the flowers, having a somewhat open and straggly habit. It is furnished with large, mid-green leaves, which are not resistant to mildew. ZONES 4–9.

Lens, Belgium 1960

'Rome Glory' × 'Independence'

Rotterdam Gold Medal 1960

'HEROÏNE DE VAUCLUSE'

OLD, BOURBON, MEDIUM PINK

After the red buds on this variety open, clusters of large, quartered, globular, bright pink flowers appear on lax canes. They are filled with many fragrant petals that reflex during the profuse summer blooming period. The vigorous canes are lined with hips. 'Heroïne de Vaucluse' was named for Laure de Noves of Vaucluse, near Avignon, France, the object of the Italian poet Petrarch's love. ZONES 4–9.

Moreau, France, 1863

Parentage unknown

'HERTFORDSHIRE'   KORtenay

syn. 'Tommelise'

MODERN, MODERN SHRUB, DEEP PINK, REPEAT-FLOWERING

During several years of trials for disease resistance at The Gardens of the Rose in England, conducted without spray protection, 'Hertfordshire' emerged with an unblemished record for good health. The flowers are small and single, and are produced in great abundance in short-stemmed clusters. They soon open out into flat, carmine-pink flowers with pale

'Hertfordshire'

centers, displaying attractive stamens, to resemble scores of cheerful yellow eyes nestling against small, bright, shiny leaves. After the main flush it is rare for a plant to be without some flowers through summer and autumn. The habit of growth is low, undulating and somewhat spiky, which adds to the unusual character of this interesting rose. In the garden, it is suitable to be grown near the front of a border or to cover small spaces. This plant is so densely foliaged that a group can serve as ground-cover plants, suppressing weeds during the growing season. It is prickly, however, so weeding, when necessary, can be painful. ZONES 4–9.

Kordes, Germany, 1991

Parentage unknown

'HI HO'

MODERN, CLIMBING MINIATURE, ORANGE-PINK, REPEAT-FLOWERING

Deep pink and double flowers are borne in large clusters on this vigorous climber. What an abundant bloom display it offers! One to two years after planting, the bush takes off and sends up great strong canes to support the massive clusters that cover the bush. The bloom cycle repeat time is fast, so the plant tends to be self-cleaning. The foliage is a glossy green and has excellent disease resistance. These flowers are good for cutting and make great bouquets for indoors, as they are very long lasting. The abundant bloom production of this rose has ensured its popularity for well over 30 years. ZONES 5–11.

Moore, USA, 1964

'Little Darling' × 'Magic Wand'

'HIAWATHA'

MODERN, RAMBLER, RED BLEND

Named for the Indian hero of Longfellow's narrative poem, this Rambler has retained its popularity even after other, superior forms have been introduced. The tiny, round buds appear in mid-summer and are followed by deep

'Hidalgo'

crimson, single, cupped blooms in large trusses that feature white centers and golden anthers. Bright yellow stamens crown the flowers. This plant grows well in shade or sun, and the vigorous, lanky canes can sometimes reach 20 ft (6 m) in height. They are lined with leathery, rich green, glossy leaves. 'Hiawatha' does well on poor soil and looks best when climbing trees. M. H. Walsh of Woods Hole, Massachusetts, produced 40 ramblers between 1901 and 1920. ZONES 4–9.

Walsh, USA, 1904

'Crimson Rambler' × 'Paul's Carmine Pillar'

'HIDALGO'   MEItulandi

syn. 'Michel Hidalgo'

MODERN, LARGE-FLOWERED/HYBRID TEA, MEDIUM RED, REPEAT-FLOWERING

The cone-shaped buds of this variety part to reveal currant red flowers of some 30 petals, which open into very large, cupped blooms carried on long stems. The fragrance is excellent and the flowers last well. Continuity of bloom is well maintained through summer and autumn. When planted in a group as a source of flowers for cutting, 'Hidalgo' can be a useful rose. Ornamentally it is less merited, tending to have an untidy, straggling, albeit vigorous habit, with a ration of crooked flower stems and weak necks. The bush is well furnished with large, leathery, bronzy green foliage and

'Heroïne de Vaucluse'

'Hi Ho'

'High Summer'

'Highlight'

has a good health record. Miguel Hidalgo was a Mexican revolutionary hero who lived from 1753 to 1811. ZONES 4–9.

Meilland, France, 1979

(['Queen Elizabeth' × 'Karl Herbst'] × ['Lady' × 'Pharaon']) × (MEIcesar × 'Papa Meilland')

Baden-Baden Fragrance Award 1978

'HIGH ESTEEM'

MODERN, LARGE-FLOWERED/HYBRID TEA, PINK BLEND, REPEAT-FLOWERING

This rose has big flowers, each composed of up to 50 petals. They open from pointed buds into high-centered blooms, which are phlox pink on the uppersides of the petals and silvery pink on the undersides. They have a good fruity fragrance. Following a prolific initial flush of bloom, more flowers are

produced intermittently through summer and autumn. The flowers last well and are useful for cutting or grouping in a border, although as the variety is quite susceptible to mildew, an open sunny site is desirable. The plant grows vigorously with a compact, upright habit, and is furnished with leathery, light green leaves. ZONES 4–9.

Von Abrams, USA, 1961

('Charlotte Armstrong' × 'Mme Henri Guillot') × ('Multnomah' × 'Charles Mallerin')

'HIGH HOPES'   HARyup

MODERN, LARGE-FLOWERED CLIMBER, MEDIUM PINK, REPEAT-FLOWERING

The light rose pink flowers of this variety are double and provide a fine display through all of spring and autumn. The flowers are moderately sweetly scented and adorn this strong, vigorous plant, which has smaller stems than most climbers but without any thick heaviness. The foliage is strong and healthy although it tends to suffer mildly from black spot. 'High Hopes' is excellent for growing on all arches, pergolas and frames of average height that need a special rose over them; it is a most rewarding specimen to grow and sure to bring delight. ZONES 5–9.

Harkness, UK, 1992

'Compassion' × 'Congratulations'

The Hague First Class Certificate 1992, Tokyo Gold Medal 1992, Auckland Best Climber 1996

'Highdownensis'

'HIGH NOON'

MODERN, LARGE-FLOWERED CLIMBER, MEDIUM YELLOW, REPEAT-FLOWERING

This variety has semi-double yellow flowers with some pink shading. Strongly scented and decorative in style, they have 25–35 petals and are excellent as cut flowers as they are produced on good long stems. A moderately vigorous rose, 'High Noon' is a prolific bloomer with attractive rich green, disease-resistant foliage that is suitable for growing on veranda posts or on pillars. ZONES 5–9.

Lammerts, USA, 1946

'Soeur Thérèse' × 'Captain Thomas'

All-America Rose Selection 1948, National Rose Society Trial Ground Certificate

'HIGH SHERIFF'   HARwellington

MODERN, LARGE-FLOWERED/HYBRID TEA, ORANGE-RED, REPEAT-FLOWERING

Released only in 1992, this unusual-colored bush is one that will be sure to please. The flowers are orange-red, with some slight intensifying of the color on the outer petals; the blooms are reasonably full and strongly scented, and adorn a bush with little or few thorns. 'High Sheriff' is vigorous and disease resistant and has glossy dark green leaves. Although it is not the tallest of bushes, it is a useful height and is highly recommended for use as a hedge or border, or for a place in the garden that needs a lot of brightening up. ZONES 5–9.

Harkness, UK, 1992

(Seedling × ['Sabine' × 'Circus']) × 'Silver Jubilee'

Dublin Gold Medal 1989

'HIGH SUMMER'   DICbee

MODERN, CLUSTER-FLOWERED/FLORIBUNDA, ORANGE-RED, REPEAT-FLOWERING

'High Summer' has flowers that are orange-red on the uppersides of the petals but more pink to light pink on the undersides. The blooms are cupped and quite quaint, as the petals bend outwards to reveal the center petals still unfurling. It is a medium-sized bush that is prone to mildew in cooler and damper climates and suffers its fair share of black spot. It is, however, vigorous and has healthy, dark green foliage. ZONES 5–9.

Dickson, UK, 1978

'Zorina' × 'Ernest H. Morse'

'HIGHDOWNENSIS'

syn. *Rosa highdownensis* 'Hillier'
MODERN, MODERN SHRUB, MEDIUM RED

This variety is a hybrid seedling from *Rosa moyesii*. 'Highdownensis' has

single, oriental red flowers, purpling with age, with contrasting lighter fresh red, golden-tipped stamens. The orange rose hips are a magnificent bottle shape and hang on the branches from the end of their early flowering season until mid-winter, when they rot and fall. It is a vigorous, tall, upright growing plant that is best grown as a shrub, with small, neat foliage. It is hard to propagate by budding in the nursery, but once it has established itself in the garden it is extremely hardy and is best left unpruned. ZONES 5–9.

Stern, UK, 1928

Seedling of *Rosa moyesii*

Royal Horticultural Society Award of Garden Merit 1994

'HIGHFIELD'   HARcomp

syn. 'Lemon Sunbeam'
MODERN, LARGE-FLOWERED CLIMBER, LIGHT YELLOW, REPEAT-FLOWERING

The tight buds on this variety open out to semi-double flowers that are strong yellow in color then fade with pink blushes. They always have a good scent and appear with succession from spring to the later parts of autumn. It is a strong, vigorous climber with good tolerance to disease and healthy glossy leaves. It grows to medium height and is ideal for planting onto walls in a sunny position. ZONES 5–9.

Harkness, UK, 1980

Sport of 'Compassion'

Geneva Prize and Silver Medal 1980, Courtrai Certificate of Merit 1980

'HIGHLIGHT'

MODERN, CLUSTER-FLOWERED/FLORIBUNDA, ORANGE-RED, REPEAT-FLOWERING

This extremely free-flowering variety carries blooms of vivid geranium red but intensified with orange. It was one of the best varieties of the late 1950s as the flowers do not fade in summer sun; the older petals fall quickly and thereby the flowerhead always presents a 'clean' finish. The blooms are fragrant and are found in large clusters on this strong, vigorous plant with healthy green foliage. ZONES 5–9.

Robinson, UK, 1957

Seedling × 'Independence'

National Rose Society Gold Medal 1957

'HILDA HEINEMANN'

MODERN, LARGE-FLOWERED/HYBRID TEA, RED BLEND, REPEAT-FLOWERING

'Hilda Heinemann' never became popular in spite of its remarkable coloring. The buds are large and oval of a fiery nasturtium red color with a chrome yellow base to the petals. The blooms open fairly quickly and hold their color well. The bush grows to average height and has abundant rich green, very glossy foliage that is most attractive. Flower production is good with a particularly colorful autumn display. Disease resistance is good. It is an excellent rose for bedding as the flowers show up well against the foliage. ZONES 5–9.

Meilland, France, 1972

Parentage unknown

'HILDA MURRELL' AUSmurr
MODERN, MODERN SHRUB, MEDIUM PINK

Also classified as an English Rose, this beautiful variety has deep glowing pink flowers that may dull with age. They have a flat, symmetrical, rosette formation and are strongly scented. 'Hilda Murrell' is a moderately disease-resistant, thorny, strong bush that reaches average height and has large, leathery foliage. The rose was named for Miss Hilda Murrell, one of the pioneers of the re-introduction of Old Garden Roses after World War II. **ZONES 5–9.**

Austin, UK, 1984

Seedling × ('Parade' × 'Chaucer')

'HIMMELSAUGE'
syn. 'Francesco Dona'
MODERN, RAMBLER, MAUVE

One of the darkest and hardiest of the Ramblers, this 'eye of heaven' is a late bloomer. The large, dark purple, fragrant flowers do best in shade or partial shade as the sun can be harsh on the petals. Easy to train on a fence or over an arch, an autumn display of hips adds to its charm. **ZONES 4–9.**

Geschwind, Austria, 1894

Rosa setigera × *R. rugosa*

'HINRICH GAEDE'
MODERN, LARGE-FLOWERED/HYBRID TEA, ORANGE BLEND, REPEAT-FLOWERING

The large, fragrant blooms of this variety are bright red with orange at the base and on the outsides of the petals. The form is not classical, rather confused and muddled in its confirmation. 'Hinrich Gaede', a vigorous bush that is suitable only for warmer areas and dry climates, can be grown as a climber and has glossy bright green foliage that is susceptible to black spot. **ZONES 5–9.**

Kordes, Germany, 1931

'Lady Margaret Stewart' × 'Charles P. Kilham'

'Hilda Heinemann

'Hilda Murrell'

'Himmelsauge'

'HIPPOLYTE'
syn. 'Souvenir de Kean'
OLD, GALLICA, MAUVE

The fat buds of this rose open to vivid, carmine-shaded violet blossoms. Globular at first, the flowers reflex and change color to a deep wine red. Tiers of petals cascade down the arching canes, and the deep fragrance adds another dimension to its charms. Varying in its form from other Gallicas, this compact bush reaching 5 ft (1.5 m) high with neat, small leaves and no prickles is an ideal choice for a small garden or as a hedge. Hippolyte was the Amazon queen in Greek mythology. **ZONES 4–9.**

Pre-1842

Probably Gallica × China

'HIPPOLYTE JAMAIN'
OLD, HYBRID PERPETUAL, DEEP PINK

This rare old rose has intense, purplish red, double blooms containing 38 petals. The flowers are well-formed, semi-globular and large. The foliage is red when young, and covers a vigorous bush with an upright habit. **ZONES 4–9.**

Lacharme, France, 1874

Seedling of 'Victor Verdier'

'HIROSHIMA'S CHILDREN'
HARmark
MODERN, CLUSTER-FLOWERED/FLORIBUNDA, YELLOW BLEND, REPEAT-FLOWERING

The flowers of this variety blend warm shades of cream and pale coral pink and are ever-changing according to the season; they become more intense with cool weather. The lightly scented blooms have 35 petals, are suitable for cutting and are a generous size when in full bloom. The foliage is matt mid-green, and the plant has an open and bushy growth habit. **ZONES 5–9.**

Harkness, UK, 1985

Seedling of 'Bobby Dazzler'

'Hippolyte'

'Hiroshima's Children'

'Hippolyte Jamain'

'HOAGY CARMICHAEL'
MACtitir
MODERN, LARGE-FLOWERED/HYBRID TEA, MEDIUM RED, REPEAT-FLOWERING

This stylish red rose of exhibition standard has thinly textured petals, that encourage the blooms to open quickly. They do not last well when used as cut flowers. The blooms are slightly fragrant, with 26–40 petals, and are produced on strong, upright, bushy growth that is moderately disease resistant. The medium-sized foliage is matt dark green. It is not widely planted in Australia as there are other red roses that are superior. **ZONES 5–9.**

McGredy, New Zealand, 1990

('Sir Harry Pilkington' × 'Elegy') × 'Pounder Star'

'HOFGÄRTNER KALB'
OLD, CHINA, PINK BLEND, REPEAT-FLOWERING

Like most Chinas, this rose is long blooming but does not like wet weather. The large, well-formed flowers are bright rose carmine with yellow centers, while the outer petals are shaded red. The double flowers, with 35 petals, repeat from spring through until autumn; the fragrance is strong if the bush is planted in a warm position. This upright, vigorous bush has coppery foliage, and as

'Hokey Pokey'

with most Chinas, it is very healthy. The nursery that produced this rose also has 'Gruss an Coburg' to its credit. **ZONES 7–9.**

Felberg-Leclerc, France, 1914

'Souvenir de Mme Eugène Verdier' × 'Gruss an Teplitz'

'HOKEY POKEY'
MODERN, MINIATURE, APRICOT BLEND, REPEAT-FLOWERING

Long, pointed, elegant buds on this variety open to reveal flowers that are a deep apricot color fading to paler pinks. The florets are double with 28 petals, have a light spicy fragrance and can have high centers suitable for exhibition. In most warm climates, however, it tends to have a decorative type form rather than the Large-flowered form. Larger blooms are usually borne one per stem in cool climates, with small flowers in sprays a dominant feature in warmer climate zones. The foliage is finely serrated. This rose has been compared with the famous Miniature Rose, 'Holy Toledo'. While the color is charming on a fresh bloom, it can fade rather rapidly in the hot sun. It is a vigorous and well-branched plant. **ZONES 5–11.**

Saville, USA, 1980

'Rise 'n' Shine' × 'Sheri Anne'

H

'HOLLIE ROFFEY' HARramin

MODERN, MINIATURE, MEDIUM PINK, REPEAT-FLOWERING

The flowers of this rose are medium clear pink and double with 35 petals. The floret form is a pretty rosette with lots of clear pink petals filled with tiny petals at the center of the bloom. The long-lasting quality makes this rose a favorite with floral arrangers. The small blooms are usually borne in clusters and have a light fragrance. The foliage is pointed and mid-green. In warmer climate zones the plant can spread. ZONES 5–11.

Harkness, UK, 1985

('Tip Top' × ['Manx Queen' × 'Golden Masterpiece']) × 'Darling Flame'

'HOLSTEINPERLE' KORdiam

syns 'Heidi Kabel', 'Testa Rossa'

MODERN, LARGE-FLOWERED/HYBRID TEA, ORANGE-PINK, REPEAT-FLOWERING

The large flowers of this variety are orange-pink and fully double, with 40 or more petals per bloom. Unfortunately, they have little or no fragrance. The plant is medium in height and the clean foliage covers the bushy, upright frame well. ZONES 5–9.

Kordes, Germany, 1987

Seedling × 'Flamingo'

'Hollie Roffey'

'Holtermann's Gold'

'HOLTERMANN'S GOLD'

AROyeht

MODERN, LARGE-FLOWERED/HYBRID TEA, MEDIUM YELLOW, REPEAT-FLOWERING

This golden yellow rose is a vigorous, medium-sized plant with glossy green foliage that is highly resistant to black spot. The flowers are sweetly scented and neatly formed, with high-pointed centers in the very traditional Large-flowered form. The rose was named after Bernhard Holtermann, who donated the land on which the Sydney Church of England Grammar School was built in North Sydney, Australia, and it was released in 1989 to celebrate the centenary of the school. 'Holtermann's Gold' is a good rose but it is outclassed by 'Friesia', one of its parents. ZONES 5–9.

Armstrong, USA, 1989

('Friesia' × 'Katherine Loker') × 'Gingersnap'

'HOLY TOLEDO' ARObri

MODERN, MINIATURE, APRICOT BLEND, REPEAT-FLOWERING

'Holy Toledo' has ovoid buds that open to flowers that are apricot-orange with a yellow-orange reverse. The florets are double with 28 petals, overlap and are suitably complemented by small, dark green, disease-resistant foliage. It is a

'Holy Toledo'

vigorous and bushy plant. This Miniature Rose is a much admired variety, mainly for its wonderful color range, pretty flower shape, growth habit and clean foliage. The unique color combination is striking and needs to be seen to be believed. The blooms can come in large trusses on very strong stems that are resistant to damage from wind or rain. This award-winning rose has maintained its popularity worldwide for two decades. ZONES 5–11.

Christensen, USA, 1978

'Gingersnap' × 'Magic Carrousel'

American Rose Society Award of Excellence 1980

'HOMBRE'

MODERN, MINIATURE, PINK BLEND, REPEAT-FLOWERING

The blooms of this variety are a light apricot-pink with a reverse light pink. The double florets have more than 40 petals and those high-spiralled centers characteristic of Large-flowered Roses. On opening fully the blooms tend to be rather flat. They can have Large-flowered form in some climates, especially where there is high humidity. The color, however, can fade quite quickly, yielding an uninteresting washed beige tone. The small foliage is semi-glossy and dark green. 'Hombre' is an upright, vigorous bush but is prone to disease. ZONES 5–11.

Jolly, USA, 1983

'Humdinger' × 'Rise 'n' Shine'

'HOMÈRE'

OLD, TEA, PINK BLEND, REPEAT-FLOWERING

The lovely buds of this variety open to pale pink, cupped, full blossoms with a white center; the crinkled petals are flecked with lilac. The erect stems make this rose a fine cut flower. 'Homère' is a bushy plant that doesn't mind the rain and has sturdy branches with finely serrated leaves and red, curved prickles. It should be pruned lightly and is an ideal plant for the border or a container. It has a pleasant Tea fragrance, and is quite popular as a buttonhole flower. It was named in honor of the great Greek epic poet. ZONES 7–9.

Robert et Moreau, France, 1858

Possibly seedling of 'David Pradel'

'HONEY BUNCH' COCglen

syn. 'Honeybunch'

MODERN, CLUSTER-FLOWERED/FLORIBUNDA, YELLOW BLEND, REPEAT-FLOWERING

This Cluster-flowered Rose is considered by some authorities as a Patio/Dwarf

'Homère'

'Honey Favorite'

Cluster-flowered Rose. It has quite a good scent. It was released in 1989 and makes an ideal plant for a pot. The color, which is quite overpowering and is best used by itself in a single variety planting or a bed, is orange-yellow with salmon-pink and red undersides to the petals. The flowers are open and double on a small, compact-growing plant with dark green, healthy leaves with moderate disease resistance. ZONES 5–9.

Cocker, UK, 1989

(['Sabine' × 'Circus'] × 'Maxi') × 'Bright Smile'

'HONEY CHILE'

MODERN, CLUSTER-FLOWERED/FLORIBUNDA, LIGHT PINK, REPEAT-FLOWERING

This variety has pointed buds that open into double and cupped, soft salmon-pink flowers that are borne in clusters and are lightly fragrant. It is an upright-growing, vigorous bush although it is susceptible to black spot and mildew early and late in the season. The foliage is leathery. 'Honey Chile' is not widely grown in many countries but makes an excellent subject for a specimen group planting. ZONES 5–9.

Thomson, USA, 1964

'Fashion' × 'Queen Elizabeth'

'HONEY FAVORITE'

syn. 'Honey Favourite'

MODERN, LARGE-FLOWERED/HYBRID TEA, LIGHT PINK, REPEAT-FLOWERING

This rose is best grown in cooler climates; where summers are too hot, the double blooms tend to become small and out of proportion to the strength of the stem, and as they are delicate in color, the flowers only fully develop their soft yellowish pink tones in gentle conditions. 'Honey Favorite' is a vigorous plant that is very suitable for garden display as the healthy foliage is particularly resistant to black spot. It is too good to overlook for temperate gardens. ZONES 5–9.

Von Abrams, USA, 1962

Sport of 'Pink Favorite'

'HONEYFLOW'

MODERN, CLUSTER-FLOWERED/FLORIBUNDA, PINK BLEND, REPEAT-FLOWERING

This small, low-growing but spreading plant is well worth growing in a larger garden where there is enough space to make a worthwhile planting. It should be planted in long rows on either side of a formal path. The wood is thin and masses of shoots are produced from the base, each one carrying a large head of small, single, off-white flowers with the palest touch of pink. The foliage is pale green. Free flowering and hardy, it is very disease resistant and shows only some mildew. ZONES 5–9.

Riethmuller, Australia, 1957

'Spring Song' × 'Gartendirektor Otto Linne'

'HONIGMOND'

syn. 'Honeymoon'

MODERN, CLUSTER-FLOWERED/FLORIBUNDA, MEDIUM YELLOW, REPEAT-FLOWERING

'Honigmond' grows best in colder areas, where the yellow color holds longer and the plant is more compact; in warmer climates it may grow too tall and vigorous. The originator used hardy Sweet Briars heavily in its breeding in an effort to gain hardiness and disease resistance. This produced a free-flowering Cluster-flowered Rose that plays a more important role in breeding programs than it does as a decorative plant in the garden. This variety has canary yellow, slightly fragrant double flowers with 40 petals that appear in small clusters. It is a vigorous, bushy, upright-growing plant with dark-veined foliage. ZONES 5–9.

Kordes, Germany, 1960

'Cläre Grammerstorf' × 'Golden Scepter'

National Rose Society Trial Ground Certificate 1959

'HONOR'   JAColite

syns 'Honour', 'Michèle Torr'

MODERN, LARGE-FLOWERED/HYBRID TEA, WHITE, REPEAT-FLOWERING

The graceful, long, pointed buds of 'Honor' open to reveal delicate soft white flowers with golden stamens in the full-blown stage. The blooms are large, carrying 25–30 petals, are borne on long stems and are lightly fragrant. 'Honor' was released in 1980 to complete a series that also contained 'Love' and 'Cherish', and was easily the best; its awards stand testament to its excellence. A repeat-flowering, vigorous, tall and upright-growing

'Honeyflow'

plant, it has a high level of disease resistance both to black spot and mildew. It is an excellent plant in the garden, and the flowers are good for cutting as they last well in arrangements and stand out on the show bench. ZONES 5–9.

Warriner, USA, 1980

Parentage unknown

Portland Gold Medal 1978, All-America Rose Selection 1980

'HONORABLE LADY LINDSAY'

syn. 'Honorine Lady Lindsay'

MODERN, MODERN SHRUB, PINK BLEND, REPEAT-FLOWERING

This variety is not very strong growing and has probably only persisted in cultivation because of its flowers. An early pre-war hybrid, the full, double flowers are pink with darker undersides. It is repeat-flowering and there is a slight fragrance, although it tends to flower better in hot conditions than it does in cooler climates. 'Honorable Lady Lindsay' is a bushy plant that grows as tall as it does wide. ZONES 5–9.

Hansen, USA, 1939

'New Dawn' × 'Reverend F. Page-Roberts'

'HONORÉ DE BALZAC'

MEIparnin

MODERN, LARGE-FLOWERED/HYBRID TEA, PINK BLEND, REPEAT-FLOWERING

The plump buds of 'Honoré de Balzac' open into big blooms of rounded form. These are filled with many wide petals that, having a somewhat soft texture, tend to ball in wet weather. This variety is therefore best suited for drier climates. The color is a cool shade of light pink in the center of the flowers, fading to blush white on the outer petals. There is a pleasant light peach fragrance, and blooms are produced through summer and autumn. The plant grows strongly, with an uneven habit, to above average height with dark shiny leaves. In the garden, the variety is useful

'Honorable Lady Lindsay'

'Honorine de Brabant' (hip)

'Honorine de Brabant'

in beds and mixed borders. The name commemorates the celebrated French novelist who lived from 1799–1850. ZONES 4–9.

Meilland, France, 1993

Parentage unknown

'HONORINE DE BRABANT'

OLD, BOURBON, PINK BLEND, REPEAT-FLOWERING

Regal and temperamental, this rose bears blush pink, fragrant flowers that are spotted and striped; in the shade they may change to mauve and crimson. Not as brash as other striped roses, the large, loosely cupped blossoms have many petals in a quartered arrangement. The mid-summer blooms are the best and there is some autumn flowering. Lush, leathery foliage covers the vigorous, compact bush and, under the leaves, there are some prickles. 'Honorine de Brabant' does well on poor soil and is ideal at the back of the border or on a fence. It is one of the most popular roses in the world. ZONES 4–9.

Sport of 'Commandant Beaurepaire'

'HOOT OWL'   MORhoot

MODERN, MINIATURE, RED BLEND, REPEAT-FLOWERING

When the pointed buds on this variety finally open, they reveal red flowers with a dramatic white eye. The florets are single petalled (5 petals) and are usually borne singly or in small clusters. They have no fragrance. The plant has a compact, low-growing habit. 'Hoot Owl' is a great name for this rose, because the attractive color combination is reminiscent of an owl's eye. It sports long-lasting

blooms. The smaller size of the bush can be an asset to a garden where space is at a premium. ZONES 5–11.

Moore, USA, 1990

'Orangeade' × 'Little Artist'

'HORACE VERNET'

OLD, HYBRID PERPETUAL, DARK RED, REPEAT-FLOWERING

This very fragrant rose starts the growing season with fat buds that open to rich, velvety crimson blooms. These double flowers are high centered with 40 large petals, and appear profusely throughout its long blooming season. They also make fine, long-lasting cut flowers. This strong, erect, 4 ft (1.2 m) bush has smooth wood and attractive foliage that adds to its good qualities. This rose was named for French painter Horace Vernet (1789–1863). ZONES 5–9.

Guillot, France, 1866

'Général Jacqueminot' × seedling

'HORSTMANN'S ROSENRESLI'

MODERN, CLUSTER-FLOWERED/FLORIBUNDA, WHITE, REPEAT-FLOWERING

This excellent variety has soft pink buds that open fully to almost pure white, semi-double flowers that are freely produced in large clusters. The flowering is almost continuous, so there are few times in the season that it does not have blooms. A medium-sized, healthy, bushy plant, 'Horstmann's Rosenresli' has glossy mid-green leaves and moderate disease resistance. It is ideal for hedging. ZONES 5–9.

Kordes, Germany, 1955

'Rudolph Timm' × 'Lavender Pinocchio'

'Hot Pewter'

'Hot Chocolate'

'Hot Shot'

'HOT CHOCOLATE' SIMcho
MODERN, CLUSTER-FLOWERED/FLORIBUNDA, RUSSET, REPEAT-FLOWERING

Bred by an amateur breeder from New Zealand, this variety created a sensation when released because it was a brand new color—a deep rich orange, so dark that as the flowers age it could be described as a soft brown. This color, like many unusual informal flowers, requires cool weather to fully intensify; hot weather does not allow sufficient time for the full browning effect since the blooms open and fall too quickly. 'Hot Chocolate' is a hardy, disease-resistant, medium-sized plant that looks best when planted in a bed of its own to avoid color clashes. ZONES 5–9.

Simpson, New Zealand, 1986

'Princess' × ('Tana' × 'Mary Sumner')

New Zealand Gold Medal 1986

'HOT LIPS' TINlips
MODERN, MINIATURE, ORANGE-PINK, REPEAT-FLOWERING

This cheery variety produces deep coral to orange, fully double flowers that are high centered with 25–30 petals arranged in classic exhibition form. Carried singly or in sprays of 3–5, the slight fruity fragrance is an added attraction. The

blooms tend to fade in hot weather, but do age in an attractive manner. 'Hot Lips' is a vigorous, healthy plant with mid-green, semi-glossy leaves. It can be grown in a pot, although care should be taken to keep it in full sun as it will not thrive indoors for more than a couple of days. Spider mite can be a problem in very hot weather, and care must be taken to avoid defoliation. ZONES 5–9.

Bennett, USA, 1988

'Futura' × 'Why Not'

'HOT PEWTER'
syns 'Crucencia', 'Crucenia'
MODERN, LARGE-FLOWERED/HYBRID TEA, ORANGE-RED, REPEAT-FLOWERING

'Hot Pewter' produces double, bright red-orange flowers singly on a bushy plant with dark green leaves. It opens to full bloom stage quickly in warmer climates and is better suited to general garden planting rather than as a cutting variety. It is a vigorous rose that grows to moderate height and is not prone to disease. Because of its petal texture and delicate formation, it is more suitable for cool climates. ZONES 5–9.

Harkness, UK, 1978

'Alec's Red' × 'Red Dandy'

Freiland Silver Medal 1977

'Hot Lips'

'HOT SHOT'
syn. 'Hotshot'
MODERN, MINIATURE, ORANGE-RED, REPEAT-FLOWERING

'Hot Shot' has flowers that are a brilliant non-fading vermilion. The florets are double with 28 petals and can have Large-flowered form in warm, dry climates. The blooms can be a bit large, and they can suffer from 'balling' and ugly vegetative centers if they are fed too much nitrogen. Spent blooms tend to hang on too long. The flowers are at their most beautiful when fully open. The foliage is small and medium green on an upright, compact bush. This rose has some historical relevance—it was the first of many award-winning sister seedlings from the seed parent, the orange Large-flowered Rose 'Futura', and was created at a time when it was generally thought that Miniatures could only be bred from other Miniatures or from Cluster-flowered Roses. Bennett's work has rectified that misconception. This rose won Dee Bennett's first Award of Excellence. ZONES 5–11.

Bennett, USA, 1982

'Futura' × 'Orange Honey'

American Rose Society Award of Excellence 1984

'HOT TAMALE' JACpoy
syn. 'Sunbird'
MODERN, MINIATURE, YELLOW BLEND, REPEAT-FLOWERING

The flowers of this variety are an eye-catching yellow-orange blend that age dramatically to yellow-pink providing almost an electric glow to the blooms. This attractive color combination lasts for a long time, even in the midday sun of southern California. The florets have consistent Large-flowered form, making 'Hot Tamale' a frequent winner on the show tables. Blooms are borne mostly singly but small clusters can develop in

'Hot Tamale'

cooler climates. They have a light scent. The foliage is a highly complementary semi-glossy, dark green which is disease resistant on a compact, tall-growing plant. This rose was a hit at the Royal National Rose Society National Miniature show in St Albans, England in 1997 where a basket of over 100 blooms caught everyone's attention. What a pity it cannot trace back its characteristics to its parents. ZONES 5–11.

Zary, USA, 1993

Parentage unknown

American Rose Society Award of Excellence 1994

'HUGH DICKSON'
OLD, HYBRID PERPETUAL, MEDIUM RED, REPEAT-FLOWERING

Jack Harkness hated it, but Graham Thomas loves it: 'Hugh Dickson' has been popular for nearly 100 years, especially as a cut flower and a bedding plant. The thick, round buds open to show dark red, double, high-centered blooms containing 38 petals. These enormous, fragrant blossoms are carried erect on long stems and the large, rounded petals open to reveal an exposed center. It likes sun or shade and produces a lovely harvest of autumn blooms. The thick canes are covered with foliage that is red when young; they look best trained horizontally on a wall or pegged down to create a hedge. It should be deadheaded regularly and was named for the son of the founder of Dickson Nursery. ZONES 5–9.

Dickson, UK, 1905

'Lord Bacon' × 'Gruss an Teplitz'

'HUGH WATSON'
OLD, HYBRID PERPETUAL, ORANGE-PINK, REPEAT-FLOWERING

Except for some botanical garden collections, this rose has all but disappeared. The fragrant, double blooms are deep pink, tinged salmon, and open flat. Each bloom has 24 broad, thick, silver-pink petals that are medium in size. It is a vigorous bush that has branching canes and blooms throughout summer and into autumn. ZONES 5–9.

Dickson, UK, 1905

Parentage unknown

'HUGO ROLLER'
OLD, TEA, YELLOW BLEND, REPEAT-FLOWERING

The dainty, fragrant flowers of this variety are lemon yellow strongly infused with crimson. The double, well-formed blooms hang from weak stems and have petals that are a deeper shade of red in

'Hugh Dickson'

'Hugo Roller'

autumn. This rose likes a warm spot and is not bothered by heat. Small, rich green foliage covers this compact bush; its low growth makes it a good choice for a border, where it should be planted in groups of three or more. ZONES 7–9.

Paul, UK, 1907

Parentage unknown

'HUGUENOT 300' DELteb

MODERN, CLUSTER-FLOWERED/FLORIBUNDA, ORANGE BLEND, REPEAT-FLOWERING

This rose commemorates the immigration of hundreds of Huguenots from Europe to South Africa in 1688; through their diligence and knowledge, especially of viticulture, they were a great asset to the farming community already there. This little rose has become a great garden asset. There is a constant production of large trusses of highly colorful flowers throughout summer and autumn, as the fat buds open into semi-double blooms of brilliant orange-salmon. The cut flowers last long indoors and make good exhibition material, but have no scent. This medium-sized bush rose sometimes grows taller. When it is clipped, it will immediately produce reddish young leaves and more trusses of flowers. ZONES 5–11.

Delbard, France, 1985

('Zambra' × [Orléans Rose' × Goldilocks']) × (seedling of 'Orange Triumph' × 'Floradora')

'HULA GIRL'

MODERN, MINIATURE, ORANGE BLEND, REPEAT-FLOWERING

The long pointed buds on this variety open to double, deep orange or salmon-pink flowers with a touch of yellow at the base of the 45 petals. The blooms have a fruity fragrance. The foliage is small, dark green and glossy and the plant has a vigorous, tall growth habit. Bloom production is profuse in all climates and there is a good repeat cycle time. This award-winning rose was bred from two unusual parents rarely used for hybridizing by other breeders. ZONES 5–11.

Williams, USA, 1975

'Miss Hillcrest' × 'Mabel Dot'

American Rose Society Award of Excellence 1976

'HULA HOOP' MORhoop

MODERN, CLUSTER-FLOWERED/FLORIBUNDA, PINK BLEND, REPEAT-FLOWERING

The name of this variety gives the game away: it has pink flowers edged with darker pink, almost red, on the outer part of the petals, just like a hula hoop.

'Hula Girl'

The blooms are semi-double and have no real fragrance, which is not a surprise as 'Dortmund' is part of the parentage. The leaves are mid-green and dull on a medium bush. ZONES 5–9.

Moore, USA, 1990

('Dortmund' × seedling) × self

'HUME'S BLUSH TEA-SCENTED CHINA'

syns 'Odorata', 'Spice'
OLD, TEA, LIGHT PINK, REPEAT-FLOWERING

As the first Tea Rose introduced to the West from China, this variety has been the center of much speculation in recent years. It was thought to be lost entirely, but plants growing in Bermuda, which had been named 'Spice', have since been recognized as the real thing. The pale, creamy, flesh pink, full, flat blossoms are large and double, and they line the long branches. In the sun, the very fragrant flowers turn to white. It can be grown as a shrub or trained as a climber. It has attractive, glossy, evergreen foliage. ZONES 7–9.

Hume, UK, pre-1809

Rosa × odorata variety

'HUNTER'

syn. 'The Hunter'
MODERN, HYBRID RUGOSA, MEDIUM RED, REPEAT-FLOWERING

This rose bears clusters of faintly scented, bright crimson flowers with the main flush in spring but with continuous repetition in a lesser way until autumn. It is a tall, vigorous, bushy shrub with dark green foliage; the wrinkled veining so typical of these roses has been overshadowed by the influence of the pollen parent, 'Independence'; the leaves, while rough, bear a close resemblance to this parent. ZONES 5–9.

Mattock, UK, 1961

Rosa rugosa rubra × 'Independence'

'Hunter'

'HURDY GURDY' MACpluto

syn. 'Pluto'
MODERN, MINIATURE, RED BLEND, REPEAT-FLOWERING

The white stripes on the dark red flowers of this variety make it unusually appealing. They are small and double blooms and have a slight fragrance. 'Hurdy Gurdy' is a Miniature Rose with an upright habit and glossy green leaves that have a medium resistance to disease. ZONES 5–9.

McGredy, New Zealand, 1986

'Matangi' × 'Stars 'n' Stripes'

'ICE WHITE'

syn. 'Vision Blanc'
MODERN, CLUSTER-FLOWERED/FLORIBUNDA, WHITE

When Sam McGredy produced 'Ice White' he had been hoping to introduce a shorter, compact white Cluster-flowered Rose to complement 'Iceberg'; it had to be stronger than 'Irene of Denmark' but not as vigorous as 'Iceberg'. The clean white semi-double flowers of 'Ice White' are freely produced in small clusters. They have a faint scent. A medium-sized plant, it is healthy and disease resistant and suitable for garden edges. It has been overshadowed by 'Iceberg' even though it is quite a good variety. ZONES 4–9.

McGredy, New Zealand, 1966

'Mme Léon Cuny' × ('Orange Sweetheart' × 'Cinnabar')

Portland Gold Medal 1970

'Hume's Blush Tea-scented China'

'ICEBERG' KORbin

syns 'Fée des Neiges', 'Schneewittchen'
MODERN, CLUSTER-FLOWERED/FLORIBUNDA, WHITE, REPEAT-FLOWERING

It is hard to believe that 40 years have elapsed since 'Iceberg' was first introduced by Reimer Kordes. It is a unique variety that is head and shoulders above its peers and counterparts, a most shapely, dainty bloom that is rain resistant and long lasting, both as a cut flower and on the bush. The flowers are semi-double and well formed, pure white with occasional pinkish flushes in the bud stage, especially in early spring and autumn when the nights are cold and damp. Some pink spotting may occur on the petals at this time, caused by rain or dewdrops remaining on the petals overnight and then being color activated by

'Ice White'

'Iceberg'

'Hurdy Gurdy'

the morning sunshine. The blooms are produced in clusters of up to 15 per spray and they have a moderate but not overpowering rose fragrance. This variety can be used as a bedding plant for massed display; it is almost entirely resistant to mildew and suffers only mildly from black spot. All in all it is one of the best roses produced this century. **'Climbing Iceberg'** (syn. 'Climbing Fée des Neiges'; Cant, UK, 1968), which is never without bloom, is a disease-resistant, healthy, robust plant although it

sometimes fails to climb, a fault of the propagation technique when the incorrect buds or eyes have been chosen for propagation. It is not too rampant and can be used to cover small fences or garden outbuildings, being particularly suitable for use on feature poles in the garden or on veranda posts. **ZONES 4–9.**

Kordes, Germany, 1958

'Robin Hood' × 'Virgo'

National Rose Society Gold Medal 1958, Baden-Baden Gold Medal 1958, World's Favorite Rose 1983, Royal Horticultural Society Award of Garden Merit 1993

'Climbing Iceberg'

'Iced Parfait'

'ICED GINGER'

MODERN, CLUSTER-FLOWERED/FLORIBUNDA, ORANGE BLEND, REPEAT-FLOWERING

Pat Dickson created a winner when he bred 'Iced Ginger', an enchanting variety with its blends of pink and copper and delicate fragrance. The flowers, which are produced in small, even clusters on strong, short growth, can be picked and used as cut flowers, the coppery pink tones mixing well in most arrangements. A short-growing bush that requires careful pruning to correct its awkward growth habit, it is probably best suited for use in massed bedding or as an edging plant. The foliage is healthy and dark green and reasonably resistant to mildew, although it does succumb to black spot especially in wet areas. **ZONES 5–9.**

Dickson, UK, 1971

'Anne Watkins' × seedling

'ICED PARFAIT'

MODERN, CLUSTER-FLOWERED/FLORIBUNDA, LIGHT PINK, REPEAT-FLOWERING

Sister Mary Xavier of Launceston, Tasmania, crossed 'Pink Parfait' and 'Iceberg' in 1972 to produce this ever-charming rose. The blooms are a blend of the very palest pink and are produced during a flowering period that stretches from early spring until the coldest part of winter, and they have a sweet fragrance. 'Iced Parfait' is a reliable plant that grows to medium height and has pale green foliage and strong disease tolerance. It can be used as a bedding plant. **ZONES 5–9.**

Xavier, Australia, 1972

'Pink Parfait' × 'Iceberg'

'IDA ELIZABETH'   WELiz

MODERN, LARGE-FLOWERED/HYBRID TEA, MEDIUM RED, REPEAT-FLOWERING

Eric Welsh from Gosford, New South Wales, has been a prominent amateur rose breeder for many years. He has

'Iced Ginger'

'Ida Elizabeth'

concentrated his breeding efforts on Large-flowered Roses, producing with 'Ida Elizabeth' large, mid-red flowers of exhibition quality and form that are one of the best of the recent Australian-bred releases. The blooms also do well as cut flowers. The plant is strong and vigorous and has healthy, dark green foliage that is resistant to mildew. **ZONES 5–9.**

Welsh, Australia, 1987

'Red Lion' × 'Mainauperle'

'IGA 83 MÜNCHEN'   MEIbalbika

syns 'Meilland Rosiga '83', 'München 83', 'Rose IGA', 'The Wyevale Rose'

MODERN, CLUSTER-FLOWERED/FLORIBUNDA, MEDIUM RED, REPEAT-FLOWERING

Released in 1984, this rose is no longer widely available; red-flowering Cluster-flowered Roses must be good to make an impression and continue to be grown in gardens, otherwise they tend to simply fade away and be relegated to obscurity. 'Iga 83 München' has average-sized, double blooms of mid-red. Its growth habit is upright and of medium size, while the foliage is large and glossy dark green. **ZONES 4–9.**

Meilland, France, 1984

MEIgurami × ('Cruosa' × 'City of Leeds')

'ÎLE DE FRANCE'

MODERN, RAMBLER, RED BLEND

This Rambler, which is found today only in botanical collections, looks very much like its parent and has bright scarlet blooms with white centers borne in early to mid-spring. These are semi-double and open, and are borne in huge clusters on the end of short stems. The slightly fragrant blooms last a long time and do not fade quickly. The vigorous 20 ft (6 m) canes are lined with large, dark, leathery leaves and many prickles. Ideal for growing on a wall, it is disease resistant, tough and easily able to withstand many different climates and soil types. **ZONES 4–9.**

Nonin, France, 1922

Seedling of 'American Pillar'

'ILSE HABERLAND'

MODERN, MODERN SHRUB, MEDIUM PINK, REPEAT-FLOWERING

This shrub rose produces large, double, crimson pink flowers that are fragrant and pleasing to look upon. Released in 1956, it has slipped from the growing lists of many nurseries and is now quite hard to locate. The growth habit is upright, and it is a vigorous, strong, bushy variety. **ZONES 4–9.**

Kordes, Germany, 1956

'Obergärtner Wiebicke' × 'Peace'

'ILSE KROHN SUPERIOR'

MODERN, MODERN SHRUB, WHITE

This very sprawling, vigorous plant has some very useful applications. The flowers, which are only abundant in spring as it spends the rest of its time growing, are double and white, lovely as buds, and have a mild scent. It has healthy, glossy dark green leaves and a rampant, long, spreading habit that makes it ideal to grow over walls or even to climb up a tree. It is hardy and

'Climbing Iceberg'

resistant to black spot, all of which make it worth a try in a large garden that needs a tough plant. **ZONES 4–9.**

Kordes, Germany, 1964

Sport of 'Ilse Krohn'

'IMAGINATION'   WEKmar

MODERN, LARGE-FLOWERED/HYBRID TEA, APRICOT BLEND, REPEAT-FLOWERING

The large flowers on this variety are well worth a look. Beautiful in shape, they start an orange-apricot color and open to show a paler reverse to the petals. They are found on the bush in both singles and clusters and have only a slight fragrance. The growth is medium and compact, and it has mid-green glossy leaves. 'Imagination' can be grown successfully as a bush or a tree or as a standard rose; it will delight whichever way it is used. Disease resistance is average. **ZONES 5–9.**

Winchel, USA, 1992

'Marmalade' × seedling

'IMMENSEE'   KORimro

syns 'Grouse', 'Lac Rose', 'Kordes' Rose Immensee'

MODERN, MODERN SHRUB/GROUND COVER, LIGHT PINK

This charming rose was one of the first roses bred specifically as a ground cover; others of course have followed, but with this rose a new trend appeared.

'Immensee' covers the soil densely and is suitable to cover and stabilize sloping earth banks when planted in pockets created especially to retain water. It spreads rapidly. Early in the season it covers itself along the entire length of the newer shoots with single, bright pink buds that open to light pink, slightly scented flowers that fade more to white as they age. The foliage is dark and glossy and mostly disease resistant. **ZONES 4–9.**

Kordes, Germany, 1983

'The Fairy' × seedling of *Rosa wichuraiana*

Royal National Rose Society Gold Medal 1984

'IMMORTAL JUNO'   AUSjuno

MODERN, MODERN SHRUB, DEEP PINK, REPEAT-FLOWERING

David Austin, the raiser of 'Immortal Juno', has dropped this lovely warm pink rose from his catalogue as it marks badly in wet weather in Europe. This does not happen in Australia, however, where it is admired for its unusual beauty. The large, fragrant, cupped flowers are full and are formed in the Old Garden Rose style. They appear in clusters on a tall, vigorous bush that is wide and sprawling and has smooth, healthy green leaves. It sometimes suffers from mildew late in the season, and should not be confused with two other roses called 'Juno'. **ZONES 5–9.**

Austin, UK, 1983

Parentage unknown

'Immensee'

'Imagination'

'Immensee'

'Imp'

'Impatient'

'Impératrice Farah'

'Imp'

'IMP'

MODERN, CLUSTER-FLOWERED/FLORIBUNDA, RED BLEND, REPEAT-FLOWERING

This Australian-raised rose was selected after a worldwide search for a rose to feature on an English postage stamp that was used to mark the centenary of the Royal National Rose Society. The flowers are a blend of striking red and white marked on tough, healthy petals with only faint traces of scent. The color, however, is quite harsh and blending this variety with other plants is sometimes difficult. The growth is strong and the plant makes a vigorous stocky specimen with very healthy green leaves. It is a good rose for low plantings. ZONES 5–9.

Dawson, Australia, 1971

'Daily Sketch' × 'Impeccable'

'IMPATIENT'   JACdew

MODERN, CLUSTER-FLOWERED/FLORIBUNDA, ORANGE-RED, REPEAT-FLOWERING

This variety is strong in color, having unfading brick red flowers that, on fully opening, show rings of golden stamens. The blooms are not high centered, opening as flat saucer-like flowers. They have very little scent. It is a strong bush that grows to medium height and has glossy dark green leaves that are disease resistant. It is hard to propagate by budding, as much time is spent de-thorning the wood to avoid the numerous prickles

that would otherwise cause the budders much distress. It is not widely grown in Australia. ZONES 4–9.

Warriner, USA, 1982

'America' × seedling

All-America Rose Selection 1984

'IMPÉRATRICE EUGÉNIE'

OLD, MOSS, MAUVE

The flowers of this tall variety are lilac-pink, of medium size and very fragrant. They only bloom in summer, but in profusion. It is usually only available from specialist growers. Eugénie was the wife of the Emperor Napoleon III of France, who was overthrown in 1870 after his defeat in the Franco-Prussian War. She spent a long exile in England. ZONES 4–9.

Guillot, France, 1856

Parentage unknown

'IMPÉRATRICE FARAH'

DELivour

MODERN, LARGE-FLOWERED/HYBRID TEA, WHITE BLEND/PINK BLEND, REPEAT-FLOWERING

In warm climates, the unfolding creamy white petals of this variety become coral red at their tips and edges where they are exposed to the heat of the sun, giving a very beautiful effect. The blooms are large, of neat, regular form with many crisp petals, and good for cutting as they last well. There is a slight fragrance, and flowering is maintained through summer

and autumn. In the garden this rose needs careful placement, since it grows considerably above average height. It is useful towards the back of a bed or mixed border, and for screening walls and fences where climbing roses are not appropriate. The growth is upright and very vigorous, with a covering of large leathery leaves. The raiser's father met Queen Farah of Iran in 1974 when he named the rose 'Vivre' for a children's charity of which she was the President, and this led to an ongoing friendship. The Delbard family dedicated it to her. ZONES 4–9.

Delbard, France, 1992

Parentage unknown

Geneva Gold Medal 1992, Rome Gold Medal 1992

'IMPROVED CÉCILE BRÜNNER'

syn. 'Rosy Morn'

MODERN, CLUSTER-FLOWERED/FLORIBUNDA, ORANGE-PINK, REPEAT-FLOWERING

As can be seen by its parentage, this rose has no real relationship to the famous 'Cécile Brünner'. It bears clusters of salmon-pink to pink, double flowers made up of about 30 petals and develop from long, pointed buds. There is a light fragrance. The growth is very vigorous and upright, and is covered by leathery, dull green foliage. ZONES 5–9.

Duehrsen, USA, 1948

'Dainty Bess' × Rosa gigantea

'IN THE PINK'

MODERN, CLUSTER-FLOWERED/FLORIBUNDA, MEDIUM PINK, REPEAT-FLOWERING

The flowers on this Cluster-flowered Rose are fully double with around 58–60 petals and are usually found in groups of

4 or more. The color is a mid-pink and there is some slight musk fragrance. It is a medium-growing plant with a bushy habit and very hooked prickles, which can sometimes help in its identification. The leaves are glossy green and disease resistance is fair. ZONES 4–9.

Ryan, Australia, 1988

'Baby Faurax' × seedling

'INA'   TALina

MODERN, MINIATURE, WHITE, REPEAT-FLOWERING

This variety produces a profusion of flowers that are white with soft pink petal edges. They are moderately full with 15–25 petals—a number that depends on the weather—have good form, and are usually produced singly with a quick repeat. There is a slight fragrance. 'Ina' is a medium-sized, upright and healthy plant that is covered with semi-glossy, mid-green foliage. ZONES 5–9.

Taylor, USA, 1994

'Party Girl' × 'Fairhope'

'INCOGNITO'   BRIincog

MODERN, MINIATURE, MAUVE, REPEAT-FLOWERING

This variety has unique mauve blend flowers with a yellow reverse that are unlike any other rose in the garden. The lightly fragrant, double blooms have 15–25 petals, and are borne one bloom to a stem. They have good high centers and size for exhibition in rose shows. This outstanding rose attracts the eye with its wonderful color—dusky light mauve with a hint of yellow and pink and even russet, depending on the climatic conditions. It is also excellent as a garden variety as the plant bears lots of blooms throughout the growing season. It is a vigorous, tall, upright bush that is relatively disease resistant. In 1996, 'Incognito' won the New England Rose Trials held in Boston, Massachusetts, USA. ZONES 4–11.

Bridges, USA, 1995

'Jean Kenneally' × 'Twilight Trail'

New England Rose Trials USA 1996

'INDEPENDENCE'

syns 'Geranium', 'Kordes' Sondermeldung', 'Reina Elisenda', 'Sondermeldung'

MODERN, CLUSTER-FLOWERED/FLORIBUNDA, ORANGE-RED, REPEAT-FLOWERING

Sondermeldung is a German word that means 'special report', and what is

'Improved Cécile Brünner'

'In the Pink'

'Inner Wheel'

special about this rose is its color, which was brought about by pelargonidin, the chemical that gives geraniums their scarlet color. This was the first use of pelargonidin in a Cluster-flowered Rose. It was hailed (not by the raiser, who was a prudent, modest man) as 'the rose of the century', but drawbacks were soon apparent: the neatly formed, full-petalled, medium-sized blooms turned a hideous clashing purple as they age, and the rich scent genes of 'Crimson Glory' passed them by. The stems were not able to support the wide, heavy flower clusters, and the plant was only moderately vigorous. It bears flowers through summer and autumn on a plant below average height, with a skimpy cover of semi-glossy, dark green leaves. ZONES 5–9.

Kordes, Germany, 1951

F2 seedling ('Baby Château' × 'Crimson Glory')

Bagatelle Gold Medal 1943, National Rose Society Gold Medal 1950, Portland Gold Medal 1953

'INDIAN SUMMER'   PEAperfume
MODERN, LARGE-FLOWERED/HYBRID TEA, ORANGE BLEND, REPEAT-FLOWERING

The creamy orange flowers on this variety are full petalled, symmetrical in form, and open cleanly in all weathers. There is a good scent, and bloom continues through summer and autumn. The flower stems are stiff and rather short, and the growth of the plants somewhat uneven, but low enough to make this a good variety for the front of a border. The shiny dark green leaves can be subject to black spot. ZONES 5–9.

Pearce, UK, 1991

Parentage unknown

Glasgow Fragrance Prize and Certificate of Merit 1993, Royal Horticultural Society Award of Garden Merit 1994

'INDIGO'
OLD, PORTLAND, MAUVE, REPEAT-FLOWERING

This, the largest and darkest Portland, has very fragrant, double flowers that are arranged together in evenly spaced clusters and that are individually up to 3 in (8 cm) in diameter. The color is a deep purple, splashed or flushed crimson and with an occasional white fleck, and is enhanced by the golden yellow stamens in the center. It is an upright plant to 4 ft (1.2 m) with dark spiny wood and long, smooth, dark green foliage. There is an autumn crop of hips. 'Indigo' does well

in poor soil and makes an excellent hedge, and is also attractive in the border. It flowers from mid-summer to autumn. ZONES 4–9.

Laffay, France, 1830

Parentage unknown

'INGRID BERGMAN'   POUlman
MODERN, LARGE-FLOWERED/HYBRID TEA, DARK RED, REPEAT-FLOWERING

This wonderful rose has been acclaimed in rose trials all over the world, which gives a good indication of its performance. The high-quality flowers are velvet red, fully double and very fragrant. The color holds well, and new flowering shoots appear freely after each flush of bloom. It has vigorous, upright growth and dark green leathery leaves. 'Ingrid Bergman' is a strong plant, almost entirely disease resistant and worth a place in any rose garden as it gives so much pleasure. ZONES 4–9.

Poulsen, Denmark, 1985

Seedling × seedling

Royal National Rose Society Trial Ground Certificate 1983, Belfast Gold Medal 1985, Madrid Gold Medal 1986, Golden Rose of The Hague 1987, Royal Horticultural Award of Garden Merit 1993

'INNER WHEEL'   FRYjasso
MODERN, CLUSTER-FLOWERED/FLORIBUNDA, PINK BLEND, REPEAT-FLOWERING

A mass planting of this variety produces a wonderful effect, for as the flowers age an interesting range of color is produced. They begin bright salmon-pink on the outer edge of the flowers with ivory in the center; then, as the blooms fade, they become a delicate pink color that endures. They don't have much scent, but 'Inner Wheel' has been well received as a

'Innocence' (Chaplin Brothers)

decorative garden rose. It is a low, bushy plant with good dark green foliage and reasonable disease resistance, and it is suitable to a lot of climates. It was introduced to honor the Association of Rotarian Ladies in the UK. ZONES 4–9.

Fryer's Nursery, UK, 1984

'Pink Parfait' × 'Picasso'

'INNOCENCE'
MODERN, LARGE-FLOWERED/HYBRID TEA, WHITE, REPEAT-FLOWERING

'Innocence' has attractive, almost single, white, semi-double flowers with fine eye-catching stamens. Unfortunately, as with many of the early Large-flowered Roses, the frequency of flowering leaves much to be desired, and modern counterparts flower far more frequently and are more rewarding in the garden. It is a vigorous, medium-sized bush with healthy green foliage and moderate disease resistance, although it is susceptible to some problems in cooler climates. ZONES 4–9.

Chaplin Brothers, UK, 1921

Parentage unknown

'INNOCENCE'   SAVinn
MODERN, MINIATURE, WHITE, REPEAT-FLOWERING

The flowers of this variety are light yellow in the center with white on the outer edges and a light yellow reverse at the petal base. The double florets with 26–41 petals have a light fragrance. They are borne one to a stem or in small clusters, and bloom production is prolific. The foliage is dark green and there are only a few prickles on the stem. It has a vigorous, tall and spreading habit and is extremely winter hardy. The flowers are

'Ingrid Bergman'

used extensively for floral arrangements, boutonnieres or wedding bouquets. With its massive display of elegant informal white blooms, this a wonderful rose for the garden. ZONES 4–9.

Saville, USA, 1997

'High Jinks' × 'Rainbow's End'

'INTERNATIONAL HERALD TRIBUNE'   HARquantum
syns 'Margaret Isobel Hayes', 'Violetta', 'Viorita'
MODERN, CLUSTER-FLOWERED/FLORIBUNDA, MAUVE BLEND, REPEAT-FLOWERING

The unusual varieties Jack Harkness used to develop 'International Herald Tribune' resulted in a deep violet-colored, cupped, medium-sized bloom—a novelty in a Modern Garden Rose, especially one with such a gentle scent. It flowers constantly all over summer and is rarely without bloom, and was introduced in 1985 to honor the famous newspaper. The semi-glossy dark green foliage covers a vigorous low-growing bush that does not develop much height so it is good for the edge of the garden or a bed where the view over the top does not want to be hindered. ZONES 4–9.

Harkness, UK, 1984

Seedling × (['Orange Sensation' × 'Allgold'] × Rosa californica)

Geneva Rose D'Or, Geneva Gold Medal 1983, Monza Gold Medal 1984, Tokyo Gold Medal 1983, Belfast Certificate of Merit 1986

'International Herald Tribune'

'Ingrid Bergman'

'INTERVIEW'
syn. 'Interflora'

MODERN, LARGE-FLOWERED/HYBRID TEA,
ORANGE-PINK, REPEAT-FLOWERING

'Interview', bred from a strong cut-flower parent ('Baccarà') and introduced by the great French hybridist Alain Meilland, is a good dual-purpose rose. When first introduced it was extensively grown for cut bloom in the trade, but it soon established itself as a good garden plant and was widely cultivated and admired for its unusual color. The fully double flowers are apricot-salmon-pink with thick, heavy petals. They are medium sized and are held aloft on vigorous healthy growth that, in late autumn when new growth is soft, is prone to mildew. Nonetheless this variety is a worthy addition to the garden and will perform well in most areas. ZONES 5–9.

Meilland, France, 1968

(['Baccarà' × 'White Knight'] × ['Baccarà' × 'Jolie Madame']) × ('Baccarà' × 'Paris-Match')

'INTERVILLES'

MODERN, LARGE-FLOWERED CLIMBER,
MEDIUM RED, REPEAT-FLOWERING

Although popular in France at the time of its release, 'Intervilles' is not now widely grown. A moderately vigorous scarlet-flowered climbing rose, it produces masses of color all through the season, from spring to autumn. The blooms grow in clusters of 6–7 on a stem

and are of medium size and, while the strong texture of the petals enhances their lasting qualities, it is best used as a garden plant rather than a cut flower as the blooms lack delicacy and sharpness of form. It is not a vigorous Climber, probably best described as a pillar rose, and is well suited to small spaces or a pole or on the veranda post of a house. It is healthy, is tolerant of black spot and mildew and covers itself with glossy green leaves. ZONES 5–9.

Robichon, France, 1968

'Étendard' × seedling

'INTRIGUE' JACum

MODERN, CLUSTER-FLOWERED/FLORIBUNDA,
MAUVE, REPEAT-FLOWERING

'Intrigue' has lemon-scented, well-formed blooms like small-scale Large-flowered Roses, made up of some 20 petals. The rich reddish purple color makes it reminiscent of a nineteenth century rose. The bush grows to average height with an upright habit. The flowers are good for cutting, and it blooms through summer and autumn. It is well furnished with glossy dark green leaves. The warm coloring of this rose goes well with many other garden flowers, so it is good to plant in mixed borders as well as in beds of one variety. ZONES 4–9.

Warriner, USA, 1984

'White Masterpiece' × 'Heirloom'

All-America Rose Selection 1984

'Interview'

'Intervilles'

'Intervilles'

'Irène'

'INVINCIBLE' RUnatru
syn. 'Fennica'

MODERN, CLUSTER-FLOWERED/FLORIBUNDA,
DARK RED, REPEAT-FLOWERING

This rose is popular in Europe, but it is not widely grown in other countries. Dark crimson in color, the large blooms are symmetrical in shape but have a muddled center that covers golden stamens. The flowers hold their shape well and are good for cutting, lasting for a long time when picked. The bush is tall and compact and the disease-resistant foliage is glossy dark green. It is a shame that this variety is not more widely grown as it is worth its place in the garden. ZONES 4–9.

de Ruiter, The Netherlands, 1983

'Rubella' × 'National Trust'

'IPSILANTÉ'
syn. 'Ypsilante'

OLD, GALLICA, MAUVE

A popular Gallica, this rose offers a strong, rich perfume in addition to its attractive mauve-pink flowers. Round, fat buds open in mid-summer to large, cupped, double blooms with crinkled petals that twist in different directions. The outer petals fade with age. This sprawling, vigorous shrub will reach 5 ft (1.5 m) and has dense, rough, dark green foliage and red prickles. It does well on poor soil and is disease resistant. This variety was named for the Greek patriot and general Prince Alexandr Ypsilante who lived from 1792–1828. ZONES 4–9.

Vibert, France, 1821

Parentage unknown

'IRÈNE' MEIridol

MODERN, CLUSTER-FLOWERED/FLORIBUNDA,
DEEP PINK, REPEAT-FLOWERING

The clusters of deep pink blooms on this rose are incredibly vibrant. This rose would therefore liven up any garden dis-

'Ipsilanté'

'Irene of Denmark'

'Irène Watts'

play. These flowers rather dominate the mid-green foliage, and have eyes of many golden stamens. 'Irène' should be propagated by budding. ZONES 5–9.

Meilland, France, 1983

Parentage unknown

'IRENE OF DENMARK'
syns 'Irene au Danmark', 'Irène de Danemark', 'Irene von Dänemark',

MODERN, CLUSTER-FLOWERED/FLORIBUNDA,
WHITE, REPEAT-FLOWERING

The white flowers of this variety are borne in clusters, and often show traces of soft pink either as spots on the petals or as a pink infusion in cool, damp weather. It is a delicate plant that is useful for edging rose beds as it is low and compact in growth. The wood is light in color but hard in texture, while the leaves are a pale, shiny glossy green and are mildew resistant. Black spot may present problems when conditions are favorable. ZONES 4–9.

Poulsen, Denmark, 1948

'Orléans Rose' × ('Mme Plantier' × 'Edina')

National Rose Society Certificate of Merit 1952

'IRÈNE WATTS'

OLD, CHINA, LIGHT PINK/WHITE, REPEAT-FLOWERING

This rose, which is hardier than many Chinas, has long apricot buds that reveal pale pink, double blooms with large petals and a button eye. When fully open the flowers resemble large carnations. Small, dark green leaves cover a bushy, short, low-growing shrub that usually reaches 2 ft (60 cm). This is an excellent plant for the container or in the border, and is also effective as a low hedge. It blooms from spring until autumn. ZONES 5–9.

Guillot, France, 1896

Seedling of 'Mme Laurette Messimy'

Royal Horticultural Society Award of Garden Merit 1993

'Invincible'

'Irish Mist'

'Irish Elegance'

'Irish Gold'

'IRISH ELEGANCE'

MODERN, LARGE-FLOWERED/HYBRID TEA, ORANGE
BLEND/APRICOT BLEND, REPEAT-FLOWERING

The survival of this variety has probably
been guaranteed by its uniqueness—it
has long buds that open to wide, flat,
yellow-bronze flowers that are gently
smudged with pale pink. The blooms are
scented and are produced prolifically. A
tall, vigorous grower, 'Irish Elegance' has
semi-glossy green leaves and is remarkably disease resistant, especially as it was
bred over 90 years ago. The best results
have been gained by growing it as a small
shrub, as this removes coarseness from
the flowers. ZONES 4–9.

Dickson, UK, 1905

Parentage unknown

'IRISH GOLD'

syn. 'Grandpa Dickson'

MODERN, LARGE-FLOWERED/HYBRID TEA,
MEDIUM YELLOW, REPEAT-FLOWERING

This popular Large-flowered Rose has
certainly stood up well against newer
roses. Its fully double blooms are well
formed from the bud all the way through
to opening, and they have been widely
used on the rose show bench for exhibition purposes and have won many
prizes for their crispness of style. The
blooms are a pleasing yellow, without
any harshness of tone, while the outer
petals sometimes carry some tinges of
pink and the open flowers can often be
seen with an edged overlay of pink. A
good bush for any garden, it is not always a strong grower and the wood is
covered with many thorns. The mid-
green leaves are extremely glossy on
growth that is strong and stout. Like all
yellow roses it sometimes reacts badly
to black spot, and should be sprayed
regularly in spring. ZONES 5–9.

Dickson, UK, 1966

('Kordes' Perfecta' × 'Governador Braga da
Cruz') × 'Piccadilly'

Royal National Rose Society President's International Trophy 1965, Golden Rose of The Hague
1966, Belfast Gold Medal 1968, Portland Gold
Medal 1970

'IRISH MIST'

syns 'Irischer Regen', 'Irish Summer'

MODERN, CLUSTER-FLOWERED/FLORIBUNDA,
ORANGE-PINK, REPEAT-FLOWERING

This delightful variety has large clusters
of orange-salmon flowers. Like many
Cluster-flowered Roses in this color
group there is little or no fragrance,
which is a shame as it fares well in the
garden where it is best grown for overall
effect rather than as a cut flower. The

'Irish Rich Marbled'

plant growth is healthy and the dark
green semi-glossy leaves are disease
resistant, particularly to black spot and
mildew. It is not widely grown now as
other recent introductions have taken
its place, especially as they flower more
often through the season. ZONES 4–9.

McGredy, NZ, 1966

'Orangeade' × 'Mischief'

'IRISH RICH MARBLED'

OLD, SCOTS, RED BLEND

This rose has soft, rounded, pink buds
that are followed by deep pink flowers
with a lilac-pink reverse. Three rows of
petals outline a yellow center around the
stamens, and the outer petals reflex. As
they age, the blooms fade towards the
center. There is a musky scent. It is a
very prickly shrub to 3 ft (1 m) high
with small, dark, ferny leaves and round,
black hips. It suckers freely and should
be planted either in a container or where
it will not interfere with other plants.
Scots roses were popular between 1790
and 1830 when there were several hundred in commerce. ZONES 4–9.

Parentage unknown

'IRRESISTIBLE' TINresist

MODERN, MINIATURE, WHITE, REPEAT-FLOWERING

The wonderfully named 'Irresistible' has
ovoid buds that open to reveal flowers
that are near white with a pale pink
center. The florets are certainly double
having almost 45 petals. The blooms
have exquisite Large-flowered form and
are grown both one bloom per stem as
well as in small clusters. They have a
long-lasting quality and the florets develop a charming pink or green tinge on
the outer petals, depending on the
climate zone. The flowers have long
stems suitable for exhibition or just as
cut flowers for the home. The growth
habit is prolific with consistently strong
stems. There is nothing weak about this
tall, upright plant. In hot climates
a sunken center or small 'hole' in the
bloom form center can be produced.
This rose is a good example of Dee
Bennett's commitment to produce
healthy exhibition-type Miniature Roses.
ZONES 5–11.

Bennett, USA, 1989

'Tiki' × 'Brian Lee'

'ISABEL DE ORTIZ'

syn. 'Isabel Ortiz'

MODERN, LARGE-FLOWERED/HYBRID TEA,
PINK BLEND, REPEAT-FLOWERING

The parentage of this variety suggests
large blooms, and large they are. The
huge flowers are deep pink with a silvery
reverse and are held upright on strong,
light green stems. They have an added
bonus in that they are fragrant, fitting for
blooms of this size, and they last well as
cut flowers. However, in extremely cool,
wet conditions the blooms can 'ball',
with the outer petals being affected with
botrytis and failing to open. 'Isabel de
Ortiz' can be used for massed planting
and has been extremely eye-catching
when planted in public gardens. It is a
vigorous plant with healthy, shiny dark
green leaves and should be pruned to
encourage open growth. ZONES 4–9.

Kordes, Germany, 1962

'Peace' × 'Kordes' Perfecta'

Madrid Gold Medal 1961, National Rose Society
Gold Medal 1962

'Isabelle de France'

'Isabella Skinner'

'Isobel Harkness'

'ISABELLA GRAY'
OLD, NOISETTE, DEEP YELLOW, REPEAT-FLOWERING

'Isabella Gray' is no longer in commerce. Its charm is its fragrance, which is much stronger than its parent's. The bright, golden yellow blooms are large and globular. The buds hate rain and find it difficult to open except in warm, sunny weather, doing best against a wall or on a fence. Andrea Gray, a gardener in Charleston, South Carolina, collected hips from 'Chromatella' and chose this seedling; he named it for his daughter. ZONES 6–9.

Gray, USA, 1854

Seedling of 'Chromatella'

'ISABELLA SKINNER'
MODERN, MODERN SHRUB, MEDIUM PINK

This shrub rose produces well-formed pink flowers on new wood all summer long on a bushy plant. The parentage is unusual, and the breeder has been successful in producing a rose that is worthy of being included in a selection of Old Garden Roses. It is not widely grown in Australia. ZONES 4–9.

Pre-1965

(*Rosa laxa* × Tea) × Cluster-flowered seedling

'ISABELLE DE FRANCE'
MODERN, LARGE-FLOWERED/HYBRID TEA, ORANGE-RED, REPEAT-FLOWERING

'Isabelle de France' has large, orange-scarlet slightly scented flowers and is generally only grown by enthusiasts with a special interest in roses of the mid 1950s. The blooms are double and high centered and have a good form. The growth habit is strong and vigorous and the foliage is mid-green; however, it is prone to both black spot and mildew. ZONES 5–9.

Mallerin, France, 1956

'Peace' × ('Mme Joseph Perraud' × 'Opéra')

'ISOBEL DERBY'   HORethel
MODERN, LARGE-FLOWERED/HYBRID TEA, PINK BLEND, REPEAT-FLOWERING

The peach-pink flowers of this variety open from tight stylish buds and the petals deepen in color as they unfold.

Fully double, the blooms are borne singly or in groups of up to 5 and have a strong, unusual fruit scent. A medium-sized bush, it freely produces abundant growth and has good tolerance to most diseases. It is ideal for mass planting or as an individual specimen. ZONES 4–9.

Horner, UK, 1992

'Champagne Cocktail' × (['Honey Favorite' × 'Dr A. J. Verhage'] × 'Pot of Gold')

Royal National Rose Society Certificate of Merit and Torridge Award 1989, Dublin Gold Medal 1994, Glasgow Certificate of Merit 1996

'ISOBEL HARKNESS'
MODERN, LARGE-FLOWERED/HYBRID TEA, DEEP YELLOW, REPEAT-FLOWERING

'Isobel Harkness' has big, bullet-like buds that open into large, fully double, bright yellow flowers that have a good scent. The blooms tend to age lighter but do so gracefully. Rare or hard to find, the bush has good growth and solid canes on a medium-sized, stout plant with healthy glossy green leaves. Resistance to black spot and mildew is unfortunately not good. It was named for the daughter of rosarian Bill Harkness. ZONES 5–9.

Norman, UK, 1957

'McGredy's Yellow' × 'Phyllis Gold'

'ISPAHAN'
syns 'Pompon des Princes', 'Rose d'Isfahan'
OLD, DAMASK, MEDIUM PINK

The flowers of this rose appear in clusters in early summer and continue through to late summer. They are full and almost modern looking, at first being high

'Ita Buttrose'

centered and shapely and later becoming loosely double and muddled when fully open, but always with the most delicate texture. The fragrant blooms are up to 2½ in (6.5 cm) across and are consistently bright clear pink. The bush can reach about 5 ft (1.5 m) with an erect and fairly dense habit. The stems are grayish green and there are few thorns. The foliage is smooth, semi-glossy and mid-green with hints of gray. It is seldom afflicted by any disease other than an occasional touch of mildew. ZONES 4–9.

Pre-1832

Parentage unknown

Royal Horticultural Society Award of Garden Merit 1993

'ITA BUTTROSE'   ACOuule
MODERN, LARGE-FLOWERED/HYBRID TEA, ORANGE-PINK, REPEAT-FLOWERING

This medium-flowered variety has peachy orange blooms that sometimes have a darker look to the outside of the petals. Fully double, they have a pleasant tone that mixes well with pastel colors. The flowers are usually found singly on strong stems, and are ideal for cutting. The disease-resistant plant is of medium height and has dark green leaves and can be prone to black spot. It has fallen from many growers' lists and is now hard to find. ZONES 5–9.

Armstrong, USA, 1984

Parentage unknown

'Isobel Derby'

'Ispahan'

'IVORY FASHION'
MODERN, CLUSTER-FLOWERED/FLORIBUNDA, NEAR WHITE, REPEAT-FLOWERING

The buds on this variety begin ivory white and change to a more creamy white as the blooms open. They are high pointed, shapely and appear in clusters; when they open they cover the bush well. The flowers are semi-double, with some slight spice fragrance in the early stages that diminishes quickly, and they have attractive red stamens. It is ideal as a standard or patio standard. ZONES 5–9.

Boerner, USA, 1958

'Sonata' × 'Fashion'

National Rose Society Certificate of Merit 1957, All-America Rose Selection 1959

'IVORY PALACE'   MORivory
MODERN, MINIATURE, WHITE, REPEAT-FLOWERING

The ovoid buds of this rose mature into ivory white, very double flowers with almost 60 petals per bloom. In cool climates the florets can have the characteristic Large-flowered form. The blooms are borne in small sprays of 3–8 and have a light scent. The foliage is semi-glossy, mid-green and disease resistant on a medium plant. 'Ivory Palace' has been exhibited at its best as wonderful sprays of crystal clear white blooms. The flowers are extremely long lasting, both on the bush and as cut flowers. ZONES 5–11.

Moore, USA, 1990

'Sheri Anne' × 'Pinocchio'

'Ivory Fashion'

I

JK

'J. P. CONNELL'

MODERN, MODERN SHRUB, MEDIUM YELLOW/
LIGHT YELLOW, REPEAT-FLOWERING

This is the first yellow rose to be released in the Canadian breeding program for winter-hardy roses. The double, high-centered blooms, with 30–70 petals, are 3 in (8 cm) across and occur in small clusters. The inner petals are pale to medium yellow; the outer petals are yellow-white. There is a strong Tea scent during the summer flush. Later blooms occur intermittently. The abundant foliage is dark yellow-green on a bushy, spreading shrub that reaches 5 ft (1.5 m) in two years. There are no prickles. This rose needs time to establish itself before the bloom count increases. It is very disease resistant. ZONES 3–9.

Svedja, Canada, 1987

'Arthur Bell' × 'Von Scharnhorst'

'JACARANDA'   JacaKOR

syn. 'Jackaranda'

MODERN, LARGE-FLOWERED/HYBRID TEA,
MEDIUM PINK, REPEAT-FLOWERING

Probably better known to cut-flower growers, this useful tall rose is a good example of the direction that breeding is taking for the mass cut-flower market. Its strong scent and quickness for repeat-flowering make it a good greenhouse

'Jacqueline Nebout'

'Climbing Jackie'

proposition. The flowers are held on very long, strong stems and are medium pink, the color remaining constant even as the flowers age. A strong and healthy plant with large, mid-green leaves, it has good disease resistance and little susceptibility to mildew. ZONES 5–10.

Kordes, Germany, 1985

('Mercedes' × 'Emily Post') × seedling

'JACK FROST'

MODERN, CLUSTER-FLOWERED/FLORIBUNDA,
WHITE, REPEAT-FLOWERING

With its long stems and wonderful scent, this is still a popular cut-flower rose under glass. The flowers are full and double with very pointed and attractive buds. The bush is vigorous and upright and the leaves are dark green, and it has a fair resistance to mildew and black spot. 'Jack Frost' is most popular in the Americas; it has not always been widely grown around the world. ZONES 5–10.

Jelly, USA, 1962

'Garnette' × seedling

'JACKIE'

MODERN, MINIATURE, LIGHT YELLOW,
REPEAT-FLOWERING

This rose has beautifully shaped buds that open to straw yellow flowers, which change to white on full maturity. The

'Jacaranda'

'Jack Frost'

flowers are very double with more than 60 petals, possess Large-flowered form and have a delicate fragrance. The lovely, soft yellow blooms are shown to advantage against the glossy dark green foliage on a vigorous, dwarf spreading plant. The bloom cycle is quite fast so the plant is nearly always in bloom throughout the year. It is an excellent choice for growing indoors or in shade, as flowers tend to fade to white very quickly in full sun. It is disease-resistant and self-cleaning. Sadly, being an older variety, it is not as popular as it once was. **'Climbing Jackie'** is a sister seedling from the same cross, and bears generous floriferous clusters of soft yellow to creamy white 60-petalled blooms. It has very sharp thorns for a Miniature. 'Climbing Jackie' can grow to 10 ft (3m) in warm zones. Like 'Jackie' and all light yellow flowers, it needs a little shade during the day to preserve its color. ZONES 6–11.

Moore, California, 1955

'Golden Glow' × 'Zee'

'JACQUELINE DU PRÉ'

HARwanna

MODERN, MODERN SHRUB, WHITE,
REPEAT-FLOWERING

This variety, which keeps flowering for the whole season until the weather stops it, has clusters of loose blooms that appear freely. Cupped and semi-double, they show golden yellow stamens well when fully open and are a creamy white with a blushing of pink in cooler weather that is more pronounced in the bud than in the full-blown flower. They have a pronounced musk scent. The moderately

'Jacaranda'

'Jacqueline du Pré'

disease-resistant bush is average height and has a good covering of glossy green leaves. ZONES 4–10.

Harkness, UK, 1988

'Radox Bouquet' × 'Maigold'

Le Roeuix Gold Medal 1988, Royal National Rose Society Trial Ground Certificate 1994, Royal Horticultural Society Award of Garden Merit 1994

'JACQUELINE NEBOUT'

MEIchoiju

syns 'City of Adelaide', 'Sanlam-Roos'

MODERN, CLUSTER-FLOWERED/FLORIBUNDA,
MEDIUM PINK, REPEAT-FLOWERING

The full, double, mid-pink flowers of this variety have an abundance of color and style. Opening quite well but not fully, they have long stems and good lasting ability as cut flowers and appear exceptionally freely in late autumn, when the full richness of the color develops. It is a healthy, medium-sized bush, with thick, glossy dark green leaves, that is suitable for border planting or as a standard. The synonym 'City of Adelaide' was used to celebrate the first Rose Festival in Adelaide, South Australia. ZONES 5–10.

Meilland, France, 1989

Parentage unknown

Dublin Gold Medal 1988

'JADIS'   JACdis

syn. 'Fragrant Memory'

MODERN, LARGE-FLOWERED/HYBRID TEA,
MEDIUM PINK, REPEAT-FLOWERING

This old-style Large-flowered Rose has a charm of its own. The flowers are double without being overly full of petals, while the bud formation is stylish, and they make good picking specimens for the house. The blooms, which are wonderfully rich in scent and repeat-flower well over the season, are mid-pink with a deepening towards the center. It is a medium-sized, vigorous bush with an upright habit. Unfortunately, it is particularly prone to mildew and black spot but is worth a try if you like this type of flower. ZONES 5–10.

Warriner, USA, 1974

'Chrysler Imperial' × 'Virgo'

'JAMAICA'

MODERN, LARGE-FLOWERED/HYBRID TEA,
MEDIUM RED, REPEAT-FLOWERING

With a title suggesting the bright colors associated with the country for which it is named, 'Jamaica' has large, double, bright cherry red flowers that are cupped and have a good scent that is always a pleasure. The bush is upright growing in habit and it has glossy dark green leaves, but unfortunately it suffers from black spot and mildew and disease control is essential. **ZONES 5–10.**

Lindquist, USA, 1965

('Charlotte Armstrong' × 'Floradora') × 'Nocturne'

'JAMES MASON'
OLD, GALLICA, MEDIUM RED

This lovely Gallica Rose was named to honor the famous actor (1909–1984). It has a tremendous fragrance, but like all Gallicas is not repeat-flowering. The large bright blood red flowers are striking and bear only 2 rows of petals, while the yellow stamens show out clearly on the flat, open blooms. The medium-sized bush is upright in habit, spreading only a little; it enjoys good health and makes an ideal plant for growing in a spot that receives little attention through the year. The new growth is fresh and quick to shoot both after and during flowering on a plant that will always provide a good late spring show. **ZONES 5–11.**

Beales, UK, 1982

'Scharlachglut' × 'Tuscany Superb'

'JAMES MITCHELL'
OLD, MOSS, DEEP PINK

The flowers of 'James Mitchell' are produced very freely in mid-summer and are seldom more than 2 in (5 cm) across. They emerge from small and rounded, heavily mossed buds, and they are bright glowing pink, fading slightly with age. Each highly scented bloom is full of small petals, which creates a pompon effect. It is a wide, dense shrub growing to a height of some 5 ft (1.5 m) and has stems that are densely covered with tiny soft spines; these are a darkish green to brown color. The plentiful, well-serrated foliage is a grayish dark green. This is an exceptionally healthy rose for any situation. **ZONES 4–10.**

Verdier, France, 1861

Parentage unknown

'JAMES VEITCH'
OLD, MOSS, MAUVE, REPEAT-FLOWERING

This rose is good for the front of a border, since it has a low-growing, reasonably vigorous habit to 3 ft (1 m) tall. The stems are very thorny, covered with bristly moss and carry full, dark magenta, double blooms. It is very free flowering and is one of the 'perpetual' forms, which display throughout the season providing deadheading is carried

'Jamaica'

out. It is important, though, to feed this rose well if a good second flowering is to be expected. The rose is either named for James Veitch the son (1792–1863), or James Veitch the grandson (1815–1869) (or both) of the founder of the famous Veitch nursery in England, which was responsible for many plant hunting expeditions—most notably those of Wilson and Lobb. **ZONES 5–9.**

Verdier, France, 1865

Parentage unknown

'JANE ASHER'   PEApet
MODERN, PATIO/DWARF CLUSTER-FLOWERED, MEDIUM RED, REPEAT-FLOWERING

Large clusters of bright scarlet flowers ageing to a slightly paler tone provide a dome of color all year round. The florets are large, double and have no fragrance whatsoever and the foliage is small, semi-glossy and medium green. The plant has

'James Mitchell'

'James Veitch'

a low and compact habit. Because of its flower size, this rose is a classed as a Patio—larger than a Miniature but smaller than a Cluster-flowered Rose. It is best suited to a small bed or border, or as a container grown plant for the backyard or patio. It was named for the British actress on behalf of the National Autistic Society. **ZONES 5–11.**

Pearce, UK, 1987

'Hula Girl' × (['Vesper' × 'Aloha'] × 'Trumpeter')

'JANE ISOBELLA LINTON'
OLD, TEA, PINK BLEND, REPEAT-FLOWERING

This rose is one of five Tea Roses discovered at Bishop's Lodge in New South Wales, Australia. It was given the name of the wife of the first Anglican Bishop of the Riverina from 1885 to 1896. 'Jane Isobella Linton' produces long, slim buds that develop into a very full, quartered blooms of 60–70 petals that are light pink in color with an occasional deeper pink stripe. Darker shades of pink can be glimpsed at the base of the crowded inner petals. The thorny bush is of medium size with mid-green, semi-glossy foliage; the new growth is typically red. Like most Tea Roses, the size of the blooms and number of petals within them is reduced in hot weather with the best blooms of the year produced in the cool autumn weather. Since the color of the blooms can change from season to season, Tea Roses are practically impossible to identify, especially in the second half of the nineteenth century when well over 2000 varieties were available. This rose

'Jane Isobella Linton'

performs best in climates where there is little or no frost. Under these conditions, it will flower through winter. **ZONES 5–10.**

Australia

Parentage unknown

'JANET B. WOOD'
OLD, AYRSHIRE, WHITE

This 'lost' rose, one of the small group of Ayrshire ramblers, was discovered by Mrs McQueen in Scotland in 1984 and reintroduced by Peter Beales. The small, semi-double white blooms appear in small clusters during summer. There is a slight scent. The wire-like stems are covered with dark leaves and many prickles. If left unpruned, it can reach 30 ft (9 m) in several seasons. It is a hardy, robust plant that does well in poor soil and will grow easily up into trees; it can also be used as a ground cover. **ZONES 5–10.**

Reintroduced by Beales, UK, 1990

Hybrid of *Rosa arvensis*

'Janina'

'Janice Heyes'

'JANET MORRISON'
MODERN, LARGE-FLOWERED CLIMBER, DEEP PINK

Alister Clark raised this Climber, which bears deep pink, medium-sized flowers on long stems. They are semi-double and have a good scent. The growth is rampant, and it will grow quite large if left unpruned. The disease resistance is fair, although it is prone to some mildew in cooler weather. ZONES 6–11.

Clark, Australia, 1936

'Black Boy' × seedling

'JANET'S PRIDE'
OLD, SWEET BRIAR, PINK BLEND

This Sweet Briar Rose has white, semi-double blossoms that are edged with rose carmine, and have a strong apple scent. The once-blooming flowers look their best in shade. This is a vigorous bush that will reach 5 ft (1.5 m) high and is covered with dull, coarse foliage. It does well in poor soil. 'Janet's Pride' is good for the woodland garden, and it also makes an effective hedge. It was found in a hedgerow in Cheshire, England, by the Reverend C. Wolley-Dod. ZONES 5–10.

Paul, UK, 1892

Perhaps Rosa eglanteria × R. damascena

'JANICE HEYES'
MODERN, LARGE-FLOWERED/HYBRID TEA, LIGHT PINK, REPEAT-FLOWERING

The high-centered flowers on 'Janice Heyes' are typical of the line that George Dawson took in his breeding. The moderately large, scented, light pink flowers are double and have up to 50 petals in each bloom, appearing repeatedly from summer to autumn. It is a vigorous shrub with an upright growth habit and average disease resistance. ZONES 5–10.

Dawson, Australia, pre-1986

Parentage unknown

'JANINA'   TANija
MODERN, LARGE-FLOWERED/HYBRID TEA, ORANGE BLEND, REPEAT-FLOWERING

The deep salmon-rose pink flowers of 'Janina' have deeper maize yellow undersides to the petals that gives an overall effect of apricot. The buds are short and firm. This rose has an upright growth habit, very few thorns and fair disease resistance; it only needs attention in early spring to ensure the health of the glossy mid-green leaves. ZONES 5–10.

Tantau, Germany, 1974

Parentage unknown

'JANNA'
MODERN, MINIATURE, PINK BLEND, REPEAT-FLOWERING

'Janna' is an excellent rose for use in a border or in small containers. The bright rose pink flowers with white undersides have good substance (there is starch in the petals), are double and occur usually in small clusters with a cupped bloom form. The foliage is small, leathery and disease resistant. It has a dwarf and bushy growth habit. ZONES 5–11.

Moore, USA, 1970

'Little Darling' × ('Little Darling' × [Rosa wichuraiana × seedling of unknown Miniature])

'JAQUENETTA'   AUSjac
syn. 'Jacquenetta'
MODERN, MODERN SHRUB, APRICOT BLEND

Also classified as an English Rose, 'Jaquenetta' is unreliable in its repeat-bloom, and for this reason it has been withdrawn from some Austin lists. However, it is an attractive shrub with Old Garden Rose style, healthy in leaf and stem. ZONES 5–10.

Austin, UK, 1983

Parentage unknown

'JARDINS DE BAGATELLE'
MEImafris

syns 'Drottning Silvia', 'Gardin de Bagatelle', Karl Heinz Hanisch', 'Queen Silvia', 'Sarah'

MODERN, LARGE-FLOWERED/HYBRID TEA, WHITE, REPEAT-FLOWERING

The beautiful pale cream-white flowers of this variety have a pale pink flush in cool weather. They are fully double, have a sweet scent and are good for picking. It is a strong-growing, medium-sized upright plant with large, glossy green leaves with good disease resistance; it is easy to prune and maintain. Named after famous gardens in France, this rose is ideal for any gardener who wants either a single or mass planting, as it is quite hardy and tolerates a range of different conditions. ZONES 6–11.

Meilland, France, 1986

('Queen Elizabeth' × 'Eleg') × MEIdragelac

Bagatelle Fragrance Award 1984, Geneva Gold Medal 1984, Poitiers Gold Medal 1986, Genoa Gold Medal 1987

'JASON'   SHEricc
MODERN, LARGE-FLOWERED/HYBRID TEA, DEEP PINK, REPEAT-FLOWERING

The color of this variety is a strong and warm shade between cerise-pink and light coral-red, and the flowers are carried singly on firm stems. They open with high centers, and become cupped as the 30 or so petals reflex. There is also a pleasant light scent, and blooms appear through summer and autumn, which makes this a useful garden rose for beds and borders. The upright plant grows to a little above average height, with matt green foliage. In the Royal National Rose Society 1987 Trials, the amateur raiser scored a double success with this rose, named for his son, and with 'Emma May', named for his daughter. ZONES 4–9.

Sheridan, UK, 1994

'Silver Jubilee' × ('Golden Slippers' × 'Redgold')

Royal National Rose Society Trial Ground Certificate 1987

'Jaquenetta'

'Jardins de Bagatelle'

'Janet Morrison'

'JAUNE DESPREZ'

syns 'Desprez à Fleur Jaune', 'Jean Desprez', 'Noisette Desprez'

OLD, NOISETTE, YELLOW BLEND, REPEAT-FLOWERING

The pink buds of this rose open to reveal pale yellow blooms overshot with pink. Silky, fragrant petals smelling of bananas form large, cupped blooms. Sometimes the deep yellow is shaded peach, buff or apricot; it can produce a range of colors, depending on soil, weather, shade or sun. The flowers appear on short stems with the inner petals muddled. There is a long blooming season and some late repeat-flowering. It can reach 20 ft (6 m) in a few seasons, has few prickles, does well in poor soil and is best used on a wall or trellis or climbing a tree; it likes shade in hot weather. It has been said that the creator was handed this rose just before he died. ZONES 4–9.

Desprez, France, 1830

'Blush Noisette' × 'Parks' Yellow Tea-scented China'

Royal Horticultural Society Award of Garden Merit 1993

'JAYNE AUSTIN'   AUSbreak

MODERN, MODERN SHRUB, MEDIUM YELLOW, REPEAT-FLOWERING

Also classified as an English Rose, 'Jayne Austin' was named after the breeder's daughter-in-law, and it has a most delightful softness. The apricot and yellow shades are worked well over the petals, with delicacy in the outer petals and strength in the center. It has an upright habit and will quickly develop into a small shrub. The growth is vigorous with some occasional longer shoots. ZONES 5–10.

Austin, UK, 1994

'Graham Thomas' × 'Tamora'

'JAZZ'

MODERN, CLUSTER-FLOWERED/FLORIBUNDA, ORANGE BLEND, REPEAT-FLOWERING

This Cluster-flowered Rose has double, medium-sized, orange-yellow flowers with a pink-crimson blushing over the whole bloom. They have a slight rose fragrance and give repeat displays throughout summer. The variety has glossy dark green foliage that is moderately resistant to disease. 'Jazz' has an openness that can be a problem, as it tends to expose the center of the plant; this can be overcome with careful pruning and tidying up during the year. The rose is vigorous and healthy. ZONES 5–11.

de Ruiter, The Netherlands, 1960

'Masquerade' × seedling

'Jaune Desprez'

'Jayne Austin'

'Jazz'

'Jason'

'JEAN BACH SISLEY'
OLD, CHINA, PINK BLEND, REPEAT-FLOWERING

The long buds of this variety open to upright pink blooms whose outer petals are salmon-rose. They are veined carmine. The bicolor blooms have a tea fragrance and are happiest in cool weather. It blooms from late spring until autumn and is a moderately sized, sturdy, sprawling shrub with new leaves that are purple before turning dark green. 'Jean Bach Sisley' should only be pruned occasionally, and is an excellent bedding plant. ZONES 5–10.

Dubreuil, France, 1889

Parentage unknown

'JEAN DE LA LUNE'   DELbut, DELcro
syns 'Moon Magic', 'YelloGlo'

MODERN, CLUSTER-FLOWERED/FLORIBUNDA, DEEP YELLOW, REPEAT-FLOWERING

This low-growing variety has deep yellow, double flowers, which are found in clusters over the bush and have a slight

'Jean Mermoz'

'Jean Bach Sisley'

'Jean Kenneally'

fragrance that is easily washed out in poor weather. They are produced with good continuity from summer to autumn. The foliage is dull green and the overall bush height is low. ZONES 5–10.

Delbard-Chabert, France, 1965

('Orléans Rose' × 'Goldilocks') × ('Fashion' × seedling of 'Henri Mallerin')

'JEAN DUCHER'
syns 'Comte de Sembui', 'Ruby Gold'

OLD, TEA, ORANGE-PINK, REPEAT-FLOWERING

As a cut flower or in full bloom, this Tea Rose is one of the hardiest of its kind. The globular blooms are full and large and range in color from salmon to peach to pink, a factor that depends on the weather. The fragrant, blowzy blooms have red centers and hate wet weather. It is quite vigorous for a Tea, reaching 4 ft (1.2 m) high and as much across. It should only be pruned lightly. 'Jean Ducher' makes an effective container plant as it is highly disease resistant. ZONES 5–11.

Ducher, France, 1874

Parentage unknown

'JEAN GIONO'   MEIrokoi
MODERN, LARGE-FLOWERED/HYBRID TEA, YELLOW BLEND, REPEAT-FLOWERING

This is one of the raiser's 'Romantica' roses, which combines Old-style flower form with freedom of bloom over a long period through summer and autumn. The flowers are a vibrant blend of golden yellow with a suffusion of tangerine orange. They are of medium size, opening from round buds into rather shaggy,

'Jean de la Lune'

low-centered blooms of uneven shape, crowded with petals (about 120 in an average flower). The center petals are often quilled. The growth is vigorous, to average height or a little below, and the habit bushy, with lush and plentiful dark green foliage. There is a light spicy scent and the plants are suitable for beds and borders. ZONES 4–9.

Meilland, France, 1994

Parentage unknown

'JEAN GUICHARD'
MODERN, RAMBLER, PINK BLEND

Created during the craze for Ramblers early this century, this rose has all but disappeared except in public or private collections. The crimson-bronze buds open to become copper-pink blooms that appear in clusters along the wiry canes. The foliage is light green. Easily trained, it is best on a pergola or trellis. ZONES 4–10.

Barbier, France, 1905

Rosa wichuraiana × 'Souvenir de Catherine Guillot'

'JEAN KENNEALLY'   TINeally
MODERN, MINIATURE, APRICOT BLEND, REPEAT-FLOWERING

'Jean Kenneally' is a true star among Miniature Roses. In every respect it is as close to perfection as anyone can hope for—it has vigor, form, color, size and profusion, and is a must for serious exhibitors. Perhaps one of the most popular Miniature Roses in the USA, it was named by the breeder for a friend, a great rosarian of the San Diego Rose Society. The small, double flowers are pale to medium apricot and have very high quality Large-flowered form. The bloom can have a light fragrance. In cold climates a slight pink tinge may develop on the petals. The foliage is a semi-glossy mid-green, and the plant has a very upright habit, with large clusters of 10–12 blooms and the occasional single bloom being normal. It is one of the many sister seedlings derived from the same cross that ended up being award winners—'Futura' was a great seed parent for Bennett. This rose is a consistent winner on the show tables with perhaps its greatest achievement, the Interna-

'Jean Ducher'

tional Ralph Moore Trophy at the Royal National Rose Society National Miniature Show in 1997 for a basket of 125 blooms! ZONES 5–11.

Bennett, USA, 1984

'Futura' × 'Party Girl'

American Rose Society Award of Excellence 1986, International Ralph Moore Trophy, Royal National Rose Society National Miniature Show 1997

'JEAN MERMOZ'
syn. 'Jean Marmoz'

MODERN, POLYANTHA, MEDIUM PINK, REPEAT-FLOWERING

This lovely, free-flowering little Polyantha is a delight in any garden. The large clusters of mid-pink, cupped blooms are well placed away from the bush and have a slight sweet fragrance. Ideal for mass plantings or a border along a path or drive, 'Jean Mermoz' flowers well through most of the season. It is a small, low-growing bush with glossy dark green leaves on a stout, vigorous frame. Disease resistance is good and it needs little care, but it will need to be watched for mildew as the cool of autumn overtakes the summer days. ZONES 5–11.

Chenault, France, 1937

Rosa wichuraiana × seedling

'JEAN RAMEAU'
OLD, BOURBON, DEEP PINK, REPEAT-FLOWERING

The long, pink, full buds on this variety open to reveal large, shiny rose pink blooms that appear in clusters with the petals reflexing like a Large-flowered Rose. Some rosarians like the color of this rose better than its parent. It is quite floriferous throughout a long season and is a hardy, vigorous, upright bush that will reach 5 ft (1.5 m). It is disease resistant. Jean Phillipe Rameau (1683–1764) was a French composer who created operas and chamber works in the rococo style. ZONES 4–10.

Darclanne and Turbat, France, 1918

Sport of 'Madame Isaac Pereire'

'JEAN ROSENKRANTZ'
OLD, HYBRID PERPETUAL, ORANGE-RED, REPEAT-FLOWERING

This rose has large, coral-red flowers that are full and globular. The glowing color fades to deep pink as they age, and the fragrant petals are rolled. It has an open and upright form, and each bloom has a high center. Large prickles and handsome foliage cover this 4 ft (1.2 m) shrub, and the blooming season runs from late spring to autumn. It has not retained its original popularity. ZONES 5–10.

Portemer, France, 1864

Seedling of 'Victor Verdier'

'JEAN SOUPERT'
syn. 'Grand Mogul'
OLD, HYBRID PERPETUAL, DARK RED, REPEAT-FLOWERING

The fragrant, sometimes camellia-like blooms of 'Jean Soupert' are crimson-maroon. They are full, large, and sometimes turn almost black with a button eye. The floriferous bush is upright with dark green leaves and forbidding thorns, and it is prone to mildew. There is some autumn flowering. Jean Soupert (1834–1910) and his brother-in-law Pierre Notting raised such famous roses as 'Tour de Malakoff' and 'Violacée'. ZONES 5–10.

Lacharmé, France, 1875

'Charles Lefèbvre' × 'Souvenir du Baron de Sémur'

'JEANIE'
MODERN, LARGE-FLOWERED/HYBRID TEA, WHITE BLEND, REPEAT FLOWERING

The official color code for this variety is fairly misleading for there are distinct cream, blush pink, pale yellow and buffish tints present in the blooms, but the overall effect is pallid. They are large and substantial, with over 60 petals that give a high-centered form. There is a reasonable fragrance and blooming continues during summer and autumn, though not with great freedom, and in bad weather the flowers may fail to open altogether. The variety is otherwise good for cutting, as the long-stemmed blooms last well, and it is best sited in a mixed border. The bush grows vigorously with a spreading, rangy and somewhat shrubby habit to average height, and is furnished with dark green, leathery leaves. ZONES 5–9.

Eddie, Canada, 1959

'Condesa de Sástago' × 'Mme Edmond Labbé'

'Jeanne d'Arc'

'Jeanne LaJoie'

'JEANIE WILLIAMS'
MODERN, MINIATURE, RED BLEND, REPEAT-FLOWERING

The flowers of 'Jeanie Williams' are an unusual combination of orange-red tinted salmon with straw yellow undersides. They are produced in small, well-spaced clusters on a small bushy plant with rather dull, matt mid-green foliage. The repeat-bloom is quick and resistance to disease is good. ZONES 5–11.

Moore, USA, 1965

'Little Darling' × 'Magic Wand'

'JEANNE D'ARC'
OLD, ALBA, WHITE

This is a tall and sprawling shrub with flowers that are rather muddled in the center and fade quickly from cream to white in the sun. The characteristic blue-gray look in the older leaves may have been inherited from *Rosa canina*. It can best be described as a smaller version of the Jacobite rose, 'Alba Maxima'. ZONES 4–9.

Vibert, France, 1818

Parentage unknown

'JEANNE DE MONTFORT'
OLD, MOSS, MEDIUM PINK, REPEAT-FLOWERING

The fragrant flowers of this rose are arranged in large clusters, each opening to slightly less than fully double blooms of clear pink, with bright golden yellow stamens showing through the petals when fully open. It is a tall shrub or even a small climber, and reaches a height of some 8 ft (2.5 m), especially if allowed to grow unpruned. The long stout stems are covered in purplish, stubble-like moss, as are the flower buds. The profuse foliage is slightly glossy and mid-green. Given plenty of space, it is an excellent rose that will sometimes oblige with a repeat-flowering in autumn. ZONES 4–10.

Robert, France, 1851

Parentage unknown

'Jeanie'

'Jeanne de Montfort'

'Jennifer'

'JEANNE LaJOIE'
MODERN, CLIMBING MINIATURE, MEDIUM PINK, REPEAT-FLOWERING

This popular rose has long pointed buds which open to medium pink, exhibition type blooms. The flowers are double with 40 or more petals, and have just a hint of fragrance. The foliage is small, glossy, dark green and embossed. The tall canes can be easily trained to assume the lateral horizontal position to optimize bloom production along the cane. Trained on a fence or trellis, the bloom production is staggering! The non-fading florets have good form and substance making it one of the best climbers around. It has a vigorous nature and is an excellent choice when a huge display of color against a wall is desired. ZONES 5–11.

Sima, USA, 1975

'Casa Blanca' × 'Independence'

American Rose Society Award of Excellence 1977

'JEANNIE DEANS'
OLD, SWEET BRIAR, DARK RED

This is one of Lord Penzance's more popular creations, bred during his creation of Sweet Briar Roses. The brilliant crimson-scarlet, semi-double blooms are fragrant, as are the leaves. There is a long mid-summer bloom. It is a robust plant that produces strong prickles, so it should be given plenty of room. Penzance was one of the first hybridizers to employ controlled pollination in his work. This rose was named after a sensible heroine in Sir Walter Scott's novel *Heart of Midlothian*. ZONES 5–10.

Penzance, UK, 1895

Parentage unknown

'Jenny Brown'

'JENNIFER'   BENjen
MODERN, MINIATURE, PINK BLEND, REPEAT-FLOWERING

The small double florets (35 petals or fewer) have great classic form at all stages of bloom. The flowers are a light pink to light mauve with a white reverse. Great form and color are hallmarks of this rose but in some climates the blooms open very quickly. However, the porcelain-like flowers win everyone over and the color does not fade in the hot midday sun. Blooms usually occur in small clusters and have a light fragrance. The foliage is medium, semi-glossy and dark green. This is a great exhibition rose whether exhibited as one bloom per stem or in sprays. The stems are straight and strong. This rose brought amateur hybridizer, Frank Benardella, his first of many Awards of Excellence. ZONES 5–11.

Benardella, USA, 1985

'Party Girl' × 'Laguna'

American Rose Society Award of Excellence 1985

'JENNY BROWN'
MODERN, LARGE-FLOWERED/HYBRID TEA, ORANGE-RED/PINK BLEND, REPEAT-FLOWERING

This bright flowering bush originated from Australia and is not widely known around the world. The large and single, salmon-pink flowers start as long, pointed buds then open flat to show red and yellow stamens. The petals fade towards the

'Jessika'

'Jenny Duval'

'Jens Munk'

'Jersey Beauty'

'Jet Trail'

'Jenny's Rose'

center of the flowers and have similar undersides. There is a good fragrance that holds well. It is a vigorous, healthy, medium-height bush with fair disease resistance, although it is susceptible to black spot and mildew if it is not properly maintained. ZONES 5–11.

Parkes, Australia, 1974

('Pink Favorite' × 'Dorothy Peach') × 'Dainty Bess'

'JENNY DUVAL'
syn. 'Jenny'
OLD, GALLICA, MAUVE

Color changes occur so frequently in this rose, which is probably caused by variations in weather, soil and temperature, that it has often been confused with 'Président de Sèze', but Gallica authorities Suzanne Verrier and François Joyaux state that the two are entirely different roses. Colors range from rose, pink, violet and smoky lavender to mauve. This rose has large, loosely double blooms with undulating petals with deep centers of yellow stamens. The very fragrant flowers appear attractively on bending canes. The 5 ft (1.5 m) shrub, which is erect with gray-green leaves and stalwart prickles, does well in poor soil and is an effective hedge. Verrier believes it is a Gallica–China cross. ZONES 5–10.

Pre-1842

Parentage unknown

'JENNY WREN'
MODERN, CLUSTER-FLOWERED/FLORIBUNDA, APRICOT BLEND, REPEAT-FLOWERING

The gentle flowers on this variety have a special ruffled quality that is enjoyable and friendly. They are a light cream apricot that is blushed on the outside with a little pink; they are small and double and are held in groups. It has dark foliage that is susceptible to black spot and mildew and will need to be watched and is an upright, light grower that will seldom exceed 3 ft (1 m) in height. 'Jenny Wren' is a delicately flowered plant that will be sure to add to the depth of any rose collection. ZONES 5–11.

Ratcliffe, UK, 1957

'Cécile Brünner' × 'Fashion'

'JENNY'S ROSE'   CANsit
MODERN, CLUSTER-FLOWERED/FLORIBUNDA, LIGHT PINK, REPEAT-FLOWERING

This very fragrant variety has old-fashioned flowers that are soft blush pink, the inner part of the flowers being creamy white and the undersides of the petals a silver-white shade. The buds have a pointed look, then the blooms open almost flat to expose lovely golden stamens. There are only 2 or 3 rows of petals. It is a strong-growing bush to average height and has good disease resistance. ZONES 5–10.

Cants, UK, 1996

'Matangi' × 'Margaret Merrill'

'JENS MUNK'
MODERN, HYBRID RUGOSA, MEDIUM PINK, REPEAT-FLOWERING

Released from Canada, the hardiness of this rose is obvious, with good cold weather bringing out the best it has to offer. Its semi-double flowers are a soft pink with a tone of lilac thrown over the blooms. The stamens are yellow and add a good definition to the flowers' depth, while the fragrance is slight. 'Jens Munk' is a vigorous, medium-height plant that tends to be sprawling and unshapely when young but, as the bush matures, it makes a good disease-resistant shrub for the garden or parks. ZONES 3–9.

Svejda, Canada, 1974

'Schneezwerg' × 'Frau Dagmar Hartopp'

'JERSEY BEAUTY'
MODERN, RAMBLER, LIGHT YELLOW

Jack Harkness rated this a two-star rose, which is a rare accolade from the late, great rosarian who rarely gave any stars. Prominent yellow stamens radiate to the creamy, pale yellow petals that form large, very fragrant, single blooms, which appear in clusters. The flowers fade to white in the sun and there is no rebloom. The variety is a rampant rambler reaching 15 ft (4.5 m) when established, and it loves a warm spot in the garden, doing well on structures as well as on banks. The glossy, handsome leaves are evergreen in milder climates. The famous Australian hybridizer, Alister Clark, used this rose several times in his crosses. ZONES 4–10.

Manda, USA, 1899

Rosa wichuraiana × 'Perle des Jardins'

'JESSIE CLARK'
MODERN, LARGE-FLOWERED CLIMBER, MEDIUM PINK

This variety is a pink Rosa gigantea seedling with large, single flowers that are exquisite, lasting well as cut flowers. It has a very strong, compact growth habit and dark green foliage that is tinted a rich red when young. 'Jessie Clark' is a refined and attractive flower and was one of the forerunners of an entirely new range of Australian garden roses, with the main crop appearing when the weather is cold. In the initial years all proceeds for sales of this rose were donated to the National Rose Society of Victoria; it is not widely sought after today but is available at most specialist rose nurseries. ZONES 5–10.

Clark, Australia, 1915

Rosa gigantea × 'Mme Martignier'

'JESSIKA'   TANjeka
syns 'Jehoca', 'Jehoka', 'Jessica'
MODERN, LARGE-FLOWERED/HYBRID TEA, ORANGE-PINK, REPEAT-FLOWERING

The salmon and pink shades in the buds of this variety open into an apricot-yellow with a pink brushing of the petals. They are attractive flowers on strong stems and are produced abundantly. A strong, upright-growing bush with medium-sized, mid-green foliage, it is an all-purpose plant that will provide a good show, especially if disease prevention is undertaken in spring. ZONES 5–11.

Tantau, Germany, 1971

'Color Wonder' × 'Piccadilly'

'JET TRAIL'
MODERN, MINIATURE, WHITE, REPEAT-FLOWERING

White flowers sometimes tinted with green open from pointed buds. The florets are double with over 40 petals and

'Joasine Hanet'

can have Large-flowered form. The foliage is small and medium green on a compact and bushy plant. The rose is a good dependable white that is relatively disease-free. Cut flowers last a long time. It has been used extensively as a container grown plant for placement on patios. This classic rose from 1964, a sister seedling to 'Hi Ho', was named after the puffy white clouds created by jet aircraft. ZONES 5–11.

Moore, USA, 1964

'Little Darling' × 'Magic Wand'

'JEWEL BOX' MORbox
MODERN, MINIATURE, PINK BLEND, REPEAT-FLOWERING

The flowers of 'Jewel Box' are a light to deep pink blend with lighter undersides. The florets are double with 20 petals and have a light fragrance. Although the blooms tend to open quickly, the 'hand-painted' effect on the petals (presumably derived from its Cluster-flowered pollen parent) makes a significant color contribution to any garden. Colors and markings are more defined in hot weather. In cooler climates the blooms can grow much larger. The foliage is semi-glossy and medium green on a bushy plant with a pleasing shape and architecture. Once again, Ralph Moore has gone beyond the bounds of selecting parents to create a new type of masterpiece. ZONES 5–11.

Moore, USA, 1984

'Avandel' × 'Old Master'

'JOANNA HILL'
MODERN, LARGE-FLOWERED/HYBRID TEA, LIGHT YELLOW, REPEAT-FLOWERING

This rose has a wonderful scent that is rich and full, and no doubt caused quite a following when it was released in 1928. The flowers are delicate cream-yellow with a base flushed orange and are found in singles or very small groups on the bush. It is a vigorous, small-growing bush with sometimes poor health and it will need a lot of attention and care to ensure that the best blooms are produced. The foliage is leathery. For all of

that, though, the perfume will certainly please everyone and it is worth trying if only for that reason. ZONES 5–10.

J. H. Hill Co., USA, 1928

'Mme Butterfly' × 'Miss Amelia Gude'

'JOASINE HANET'
OLD, PORTLAND, MAUVE, REPEAT-FLOWERING

This early blooming rose, rare today, is one of the survivors in a class that briefly held the center of attention. The deep rose blooms are tinged with violet, turning almost purple-red depending on its site in the garden. The heavy, full, quartered blooms, which are 3 in (8 cm) across and appear in clusters, are strongly scented. This is a vigorous shrub that is quite hardy and disease resistant. Some would classify it as a Damask–Perpetual, a term that has become increasingly popular because of its repeat-flowering quality. ZONES 5–10.

Vibert, France, 1847

Parentage unknown

'JOCELYN'
MODERN, CLUSTER-FLOWERED/FLORIBUNDA, RUSSET, REPEAT-FLOWERING

This delightful rose has wonderful, unusual flowers. Large and double, the blooms have a quartered effect that is more old-fashioned than modern; they are deep red with a mahogany finish, although unfortunately the rich color is only seen in cooler climates as summer heat washes it back to a light red. The

'Johann Strauss'

glossy leaves are tough and reasonably disease resistant on a low-growing bush that is easy to manage but needs to be sited with thought as it can easily become lost in a garden. It is not suitable for hot, dry climates. ZONES 5–10.

LeGrice, UK, 1972

Parentage unknown

'JOHANN STRAUSS' MEIoffic
syns 'Forever Friends', 'Sweet Sonata'
MODERN, CLUSTER-FLOWERED/FLORIBUNDA, PINK BLEND, REPEAT-FLOWERING

'Johann Strauss' produces fully double blooms with 40 or more petals that are well scented and slightly globular. A soft salmon-pink in color, they appear singly or in small clusters on moderate length stems from early spring and are quick to repeat their bloom. Glossy bright green leaves produce a thick covering canopy on a medium-height bush that is mildew tolerant and only slightly troubled by black spot. This variety is a good all-round performer both for picking and for garden display, growing well as a bush and as a full standard. ZONES 4–10.

Meilland, France, 1994

(MEIturaphar × 'Mrs John Laing') × 'Egeskov'

'JOHN CABOT'
MODERN, MODERN SHRUB, MEDIUM RED, REPEAT-FLOWERING

A free-flowering shrub with a multitude of uses, this variety can be grown in

'Joanna Hill'

tough conditions and will require little maintenance. The semi-double, medium red flowers fade as they age and show their stamens well. These blooms are found in clusters, and they are not at all fragrant. 'John Cabot' is very tolerant of disease and is suitable for use as a hedge or for any place where little attention will be paid to it. It has plentiful, dense leaf coverage and will grow quite tall in warm climates, almost enough to be classified as a small climber. ZONES 3–9.

Svejda, Canada, 1978

Rosa kordesii × seedling

'JOHN CLARE' AUScent
MODERN, MODERN SHRUB, DEEP PINK, REPEAT-FLOWERING

This David Austin rose, which is also classified as an English Rose, has the most free-flowering habit of all the Austin roses released to date. The cupped, light crimson flowers are not for the purist rose form lover as they are a little informal and are prone to be very loose. They fade only a little as they open and develop to the full-blown stage, and the petals fall cleanly. 'John Clare' is not a tall grower and has a low-growing, spreading habit that is suited to its flower. It was named after the poet, John Clare, for The John Clare Society in the UK. ZONES 5–10.

Austin, UK, 1994

'Wife of Bath' × 'Giant Meyer'

'John Clare'

'Jocelyn'

'JOHN DAVIS'

MODERN, MODERN SHRUB, MEDIUM PINK, REPEAT-FLOWERING

This rose produces large heads of mid-pink flowers with cream to yellow at the base of the petals. They are double, with around 40 petals, and have a strong spicy fragrance. It has a strong, healthy growth habit, tough leaves and long canes that flow well and tend to run or trail along the ground. Disease resistance is good and it needs little care in most normal circumstances, with some attention being paid to mildew and black spot in those areas that suffer from heavy infestation. ZONES 3–9.

Svejda, Canada, 1986

(*Rosa kordesii* × seedling) × seedling

'JOHN F. KENNEDY'

syns 'JFK', 'President John F. Kennedy'

MODERN, LARGE-FLOWERED/HYBRID TEA, WHITE, REPEAT-FLOWERING

This variety bears tall, elegant buds that open into pure white flowers with some slight green tinges in the early bud stage. They are ideal as cut flowers and are produced quite freely on a strong, upright-growing bush with good disease resistance. The leaves are thick and tough, although in cool climes they can sometimes suffer a little from mildew. Obvi-

ously named after the former American president John F. Kennedy, this rose did not win any awards when released, although it still stands up well against newer white introductions. ZONES 5–11.

Boerner, USA, 1965

Seedling × 'White Queen'

'JOHN FRANKLIN'

MODERN, MODERN SHRUB, MEDIUM RED, REPEAT-FLOWERING

John Franklin has double medium red flowers that appear in small clusters of 2–5. They are slightly fragrant and are produced from summer to autumn. It is a medium-sized, upright-growing shrub with fair health that is best suited to colder areas as the blooms can withstand frost and snow, although it will still give joy to growers in warmer areas. The foliage is round, and it has yellow-green prickles with purple hues. ZONES 4–10.

Svejda, Canada, 1980

'Lilli Marleen' × seedling

'JOHN HOPPER'

OLD, HYBRID PERPETUAL, PINK BLEND, REPEAT-FLOWERING

A compact Hybrid Perpetual, this variety has bright rose blooms edged in lilac. The large, cupped, double flowers have 70 petals each with a carmine center; the

'Johnnie Walker'

outer petals fade with age. They appear on short stems, are very fragrant and cover the shrub in summer; there is some autumn repeat. The 4 ft (1.2 m) canes create an erect and bushy plant, and are covered with large leaves and light red, hooked prickles. It should be deadheaded to encourage the autumn blossoms. 'John Hopper' makes an effective hedge. ZONES 5–10.

Ward, UK, 1862

'Jules Margottin' × 'Madame Vidot'

'JOHN S. ARMSTRONG'

MODERN, LARGE-FLOWERED/HYBRID TEA, DARK RED, REPEAT-FLOWERING

Also classified as a Grandiflora Rose, 'John S. Armstrong' is a fine, free-flowering bush rose that bears very deep red blooms. They have high centers made up of about 48 petals that are arranged with precise symmetry. While not a true exhibition style, the variety makes an excellent cutting rose for general use. The scented flowers keep well when picked, and they are produced on long stems. The bush is tall and strong in growth, and it is well covered with shiny dark green leaves. There is minimal trouble with fungus disease. 'John S. Armstrong' is very well suited to hot conditions. ZONES 5–10.

Swim, USA, 1961

'Charlotte Armstrong' × seedling

National Rose Society Trial Ground Certificate 1961, All-America Rose Selection 1962

'John S. Armstrong'

'JOHN WATERER'

MODERN, LARGE-FLOWERED/HYBRID TEA, DARK RED, REPEAT-FLOWERING

This variety is a jolly good dark red that has a good production of flowers and quickly and freely reproduces each crop of bloom. It has many top points: the perfume is good without being strong, it has a classic form and, with an above-average-sized bloom, it has a presence rarely found in a rose. The flowering shoots tend to be weak and the flowers too heavy for this new growth, but they last well when picked. It suffers a little from mildew, although the growth is otherwise strong. It is still being grown in large numbers even though it was released in 1970. ZONES 5–10.

McGredy, UK, 1970

'King of Hearts' × 'Hanne'

Royal National Rose Society Certificate of Merit

'JOHNNIE WALKER'   FRYgran

MODERN, LARGE-FLOWERED/HYBRID TEA, APRICOT BLEND, REPEAT-FLOWERING

This rose has a lovely apricot whisky tone, hence the name. The large free flowers are more attractive when half open than when fully blown. Well formed and semi-double with around 20 petals, they have a slight fragrance that lasts well when cut. 'Johnnie Walker' is a strong grower with an up-right style and matt green leaves that cover the small shrub well. Disease needs to be carefully watched for and preventive measures taken early to

'John F. Kennedy'

'John Waterer'

'John Davis'

'John Hopper'

ensure the best blooms. Although only released in 1982, this variety may be difficult to find. ZONES 5–10.

Fryer's Nursery, UK, 1982

'Sunblest' × ('Arthur Bell' × 'Belle Blonde')

Royal National Rose Society Trial Ground Certificate 1980

'JOIE DE VIVRE'

MODERN, LARGE-FLOWERED/HYBRID TEA, PINK BLEND, REPEAT-FLOWERING

This bush has large, well-shaped flowers, which are both fragrant and colorful. Classic in form, they are found alone or in small groups and are pink with some gold at the bases. Although not large, this variety is strong and vigorous and moderately resistant to disease, although the younger bronze-green growth does suffers some mildew late in the season. ZONES 5–10.

Gaujard, France, 1949

Parentage unknown

National Rose Society Certificate of Merit 1950

'JOLLY ROGER'

MODERN, CLUSTER-FLOWERED/FLORIBUNDA, ORANGE BLEND, REPEAT-FLOWERING

The strong bright orange, red-tinged, cupped blooms of this variety are quite a difficult color to blend in the garden. They are semi-double and of average size with an almost ruffled appearance. There is no real fragrance. 'Jolly Roger' is not a big grower; it has a bushy, upright style and habit and a little wrinkling to its leaves. Better suited to a mass planting, it has good disease resistance. ZONES 5–10.

Armstrong, USA, 1973

'Spartan' × 'Angelique'

'Joseph's Coat'

'Josephine Bruce'

'Joie de Vivre'

'JOSEPHINE BAKER'   MEImaur

syn. 'Velvet Flame'

MODERN, LARGE-FLOWERED/HYBRID TEA, DARK RED, REPEAT-FLOWERING

This is an excellent disease-resistant, dark red rose that has been overlooked, never really becoming popular. The long, pointed buds open to double flowers containing 25 petals of very good substance. Flower production is excellent and the repeat cycle is reliable. It has a strong and upright growth. 'Josephine Baker' was named after the flamboyant American entertainer who made her home in France in the 1930s. ZONES 5–10.

Meilland, France, 1973

'Tropicana' × 'Papa Meilland'

'JOSEPHINE BRUCE'

MODERN, LARGE-FLOWERED/HYBRID TEA, DARK RED, REPEAT-FLOWERING

This lovely dark red variety repeat-flowers very well, being both free and abundant. The blooms are very strongly fragrant. Its low growth is wide and sprawling, and it needs special care to keep it healthy and safe from mildew. Special pruning is also required, cutting to an inward-pointing eye to try and rectify the spreading growth habit. **'Climbing Josephine Bruce'**, a sport discovered by the same breeder in 1954, is superior to the bush. Although not every garden has room for a Climber of this size, it is well worth finding some space for it to grow. The flowers are similar to those of the parent. ZONES 5–10.

Bees, UK, 1949

'Crimson Glory' × 'Madge Whipp'

National Rose Society Trial Ground Certificate 1953

'Jolly Roger'

'Joy of Health'

'JOSEPH'S COAT'

MODERN, LARGE FLOWERED CLIMBER, RED BLEND, REPEAT-FLOWERING

Best described as a yellow and red blend, this rose is a good example of a small, multi-colored Climber. 'Joseph's Coat' grows upright, and it is best suited to being layered out for the maximum amount of bloom, which is best in spring. The average-sized flowers are double and open almost flat to show the stamens clearly. ZONES 4–10.

Armstrong and Swim, USA, 1964

'Buccaneer' × 'Circus'

National Rose Society Trial Ground Certificate 1963, Bagatelle Gold Medal 1964

'JOY OF HEALTH'   HARxever

MODERN, CLUSTER-FLOWERED/FLORIBUNDA, MEDIUM PINK, REPEAT-FLOWERING

The flowers of this variety, which are full and double, are found in clusters. They are a soft salmon-pink with peach tones and old-fashioned in shape, being cupped and opening slowly without exposing the center entirely, keeping that form until falling. For smaller gardens, this healthy, vigorous bush is ideal. It has dark green matt leaves and was named and released in Australia in 1996 to benefit the Australian Rotary Health Research Fund. ZONES 5–10.

Harkness, UK, 1996

Seedling × 'Amber Queen'

'Josephine Baker'

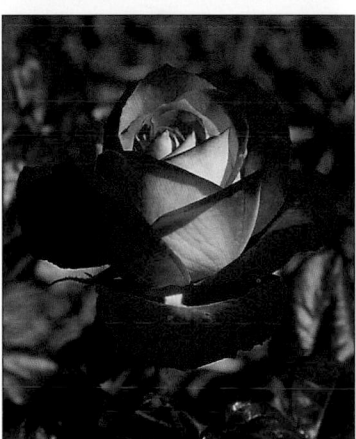

'Joy of Life'

'JOY OF LIFE'   TANmixa

MODERN, LARGE-FLOWERED/HYBRID TEA, RED BLEND, REPEAT-FLOWERING

The flowers of 'Joy of Life' appear in an unusual color combination that is best described as a red blend. The centers of the flowers are white with the outer edges of the petals margined with medium red, the effect being quite striking and a spectacular sight as a mass planting. The blooms are found singly over a healthy, strong-growing bush that is reasonably resistant to disease and which has good repeat-flowering. ZONES 5–10.

Tantau, Germany, 1996

Parentage unknown

J

'Joyfulness' (Kordes)

'Joyfulness' (Kordes)

'Joyce Edmonds'

'JOYBELLS'

syns 'Cubana', 'Joy Bells'

MODERN, CLUSTER-FLOWERED/FLORIBUNDA, MEDIUM PINK, REPEAT-FLOWERING

Well regarded by those who know it, this variety produces clusters of fully double, mid-pink flowers, fading with age, that exhibit a wonderful perfection in the arrangement of their petals. There is some scent and sometimes a little white through the flowers and they can be picked all through the season, which continues throughout summer and autumn. The glossy leaves are hardy, and the bush is moderately disease resistant. It is not a well-known variety, but a pleasure to have in the garden. ZONES 5–10.

Robinson, Australia, 1961

Seedling × 'Fashion'

'JOYCE EDMONDS'

MODERN, CLUSTER-FLOWERED/FLORIBUNDA, ORANGE-PINK, REPEAT-FLOWERING

The flowers of this variety are double and slightly cupped and strong in color, being an attractive mid-pink and showing golden stamens when they are fully open. There have little scent but last well when cut for indoor use. 'Joyce Edmonds' was introduced by the Australian rose grower and nurseryman John Nieuwesteeg in 1992. It is a vigorous grower that forms a strong, upright plant with glossy green leaves that are tough and disease resistant both to mildew and black spot. Growth is quick to repeat and flowering is continuous from spring until autumn. ZONES 5–10.

Nieuwesteeg, Australia, 1992

Sport of 'Scarlet Queen Elizabeth'

'JOYCE NORTHFIELD'

MODERN, LARGE-FLOWERED/HYBRID TEA, ORANGE BLEND, REPEAT-FLOWERING

This variety produces large, deep orange flowers on a vigorous, shrubby bush. Full and double, the flowers are high centered and have some fragrance. The dark green foliage is able to withstand some disease, but it does need attention to keep it entirely disease free for the whole flowering season. Dropped from many lists, 'Joyce Northfield' may be difficult to locate. ZONES 5–10.

Northfield, UK, 1977

'Fred Gibson' × 'Vienna Charm'

'Joyce Northfield'

'JOYCIE' MORjoyce

MODERN, MINIATURE, ORANGE BLEND, REPEAT-FLOWERING

Orange-apricot flowers with a much lighter reverse make this rose worthy of inclusion in the garden. The florets are double, with high centered Large-flowered form, borne usually one bloom per stem or in small sprays. The bloom size is moderate for a Miniature but can be larger in cooler climates. The foliage is mid-green and disease free. Its bright color and floriferous growth of sprays make this rose a good garden plant. It is, however, winter tender and will need protection for survival in cold climates. This rose was named by Ralph Moore to honor the retiring assistant to the Executive Director of the American Rose Society, Joyce Schimschock. ZONES 6–11.

Moore, USA, 1988

('Little Darling' × 'Yellow Magic') × 'Gold Badge'

'JOYFULNESS'

syn. 'Frohsinn'

MODERN, CLUSTER-FLOWERED/FLORIBUNDA, APRICOT BLEND, REPEAT-FLOWERING

This rose did well in its trials in Britain, being admired for its display of light coppery salmon flowers with orange and peach shading. They are fairly full and are carried in crowded clusters on upright stems. They open cupped and are pretty at this stage, but the colors soon become subdued. There is a light fragrance, and flowers appear through summer and autumn. For beds and borders this is a pleasing variety, and it also provides plenty of short-stemmed blooms for small arrangements; if cut young they will hold their color. The plant grows bushy and upright and has glossy dark green leaves; it may need protection from black spot. ZONES 4–9.

Tantau, Germany, 1961

'Hortsmann's Jubiläumsrose' × 'Circus'

National Rose Society Certificate of Merit 1963

'JOYFULNESS'

syn. 'Frohsinn '86'

MODERN, LARGE-FLOWERED/HYBRID TEA, APRICOT BLEND, REPEAT-FLOWERING

Although bred in Germany, this rose has not received much recognition anywhere other than Australia. There, however, it is one of the most popular roses. The flowers are of 25–30 petals, aging to a lovely medley of soft apricot/cream and peach tones, and show superb exhibition form. Flower production is high, and repeat bloom rapid. Disease resistance is good and the lovely buds last well when picked. There can be some confusion with the 1961 'Joyfulness' from Tantau, a Cluster-flowered/Floribunda with similar coloring. ZONES 5–9.

Kordes, Germany, 1986

Parentage unknown

'JUBILANT'

MODERN, CLUSTER-FLOWERED/FLORIBUNDA, LIGHT PINK, REPEAT-FLOWERING

This medium-sized rose has unusual flowers with a freeness of form and petals that open awkwardly. Short orange-pink buds give rise to soft cream blushed pink and yellow flowers that appear in clusters then open to a cupped shape. They have a light fragrance. The bush is small to medium with good repeat-flowering and glossy leaves and stout stems that make the framework a delight to prune in winter. Care must be taken to ensure that it does not suffer black spot early in the season, as this will hold back a good first flush of bloom. Mildew can be a problem in some climates. ZONES 5–10.

Dickson, UK, 1967

'Dearest' × 'Circus'

Royal National Rose Society Certificate of Merit 1965

'Joybells'

'Jubilant'

'Jules Margottin'

'Judy Fischer'

'Julia Mannering'

'JUDE THE OBSCURE' AUSjo

**MODERN, MODERN SHRUB, MEDIUM YELLOW,
REPEAT-FLOWERING**

The full rich yellow blooms of this variety are usually found either singly or in
very small clusters. The flowers, which
are loose and loosely cupped, sometimes
fail to open if the flowering season is
cool. They are strongly perfumed. It is an
average-growing bush with dull leaves
and pink-red new growth shoots more
like a Large-flowered Rose; it is robust
and shows reasonable disease resistance.
It is from David Austin and is also classified as an English Rose. ZONES 4–10.

Austin, UK, 1995

'Abraham Darby' × 'Windrush'

'JUDY FISCHER'

**MODERN, MINIATURE, MEDIUM PINK,
REPEAT-FLOWERING**

Pointed high centered pink buds open
slowly to small, double, deep rose pink
flowers which hold their color well. In
hot weather, the deep rose pink petals
may be a shade lighter. The florets are
complemented by small, dark green,
leathery foliage. The bush is a vigorous,
low growing compact plant that is easy
to establish. Often described as an all
weather variety, the bloom cycle is fast
no matter what the climate—sun, rain
or high water. It is easy to maintain as
it is completely disease resistant. What's
more, is that quality blooms are always
available for a rose show. ZONES 5–11.

Moore, USA, 1968

'Little Darling' × 'Magic Wand'

American Rose Society Award of Excellence 1975

'JUDY GARLAND' HARking

**MODERN, CLUSTERED-FLOWERED/FLORIBUNDA,
YELLOW BLEND, REPEAT-FLOWERING**

The bright flowers of 'Judy Garland'
are yellow, with the outer petals edged a
light red or orange. Medium sized and

fully double, the blooms look better as
shapely buds than they do as loose, fully
blown flowers, when they become a little
washed out and unattractive. The bush
is of average height with a spreading
growth habit and good healthy growth.
This rose is best suited to mass planting
and should be given consideration ahead
of some of its parents. ZONES 5–11.

Harkness, UK, 1978

(['Tropicana' × 'Circus'] × ['Sabine' × 'Circus'])
× 'Pineapple Poll'

Royal National Rose Society Trial Ground
Certificate 1977, Tokyo Silver Medal 1978

'JULES MARGOTTIN'

**OLD, HYBRID PERPETUAL, MEDIUM PINK,
REPEAT-FLOWERING**

The blooms of this rose can vary
from semi-double to very full, with
up to 90 petals, although a lesser
number is more common. The large,
pink flowers are like swirls of color,
and appear on long stems. It is a
vigorous and robust bush with light
green, oval, pointed leaves and dark
red prickles. It grows to 6 ft (1.8 m) tall,
but can be pruned to half that height.

'Julia's Rose'

There is a good crop of autumn
blooms. It is prone to mildew in wet
weather. Jacques Margottin (1817–92),
the creator of the famous 'Louise
Odier', named this rose for his oldest
son; there is also a climbing form.
ZONES 5–10.

Margottin, France, 1853

Seedling of 'La Reine'

'JULIA MANNERING'
OLD, SWEET BRIAR, LIGHT PINK

One of the 16 *Rosa eglanteria* hybrids
that Lord Penzance created in 5 years,
'Julia Mannering' has pearly, flesh pink,
single to semi-double blooms veined
with deeper pink; the colors are stronger
in the shade. They are borne on long
canes and both the dark green foliage
and the blooms are redolent with an
apple fragrance. This once-blooming
shrub is vigorous and needs plenty of
space. It does well in poor soil and makes
a strong hedge with bristly canes or an
attractive shrub in a woodland setting.
The rose was named after a character in
Sir Walter Scott's novel *Guy Mannering*.
ZONES 5–11.

Penzance, UK, 1895

Parentage unknown

'JULIA'S ROSE'

**MODERN, LARGE-FLOWERED/HYBRID TEA, RUSSET,
REPEAT-FLOWERING**

This is a most popular plant simply
for its color—the flowers are various
shades of copper, parchment and
brown, all mixed into a handsome
tone that intensifies dramatically in
cool to cold conditions. 'Julia's Rose'
has a place in every collection, even
though it is not a strong bush and
needs to be looked after; the rewards
are there for those who take the
challenge, as it flowers well for most of
the season and provides a unique color
for floral arrangements. The growth is
upright, and the foliage is reddish. It is
only recommended for gardeners who
are willing to take the time to control
disease, as it is not a strong grower.
ZONES 5–10.

Wisbech Plant Co., UK, 1976

'Blue Moon' × 'Dr A. J. Verhage'

Baden-Baden Gold Medal 1983

'JULIE'

**MODERN, LARGE-FLOWERED/HYBRID TEA,
DARK RED**

'Julie' bears long, pointed dark red
buds that open to brighter red blooms.

J

'Julia's Rose'

It has good retention of color and a pleasant scent. It has upright growth and soft, dark green foliage. This rose has been superseded by a lot of other red roses and has been dropped from many nursery lists; however, it is a strong-growing rose with reasonable disease resistance. ZONES 5–10.

Kordes, Germany, 1970

Seedling × 'Red American Beauty'

'JULIE DE MERSAN'

syn. 'Julie de Mersent'
OLD, MOSS, MEDIUM PINK

This rose bears medium-sized flowers that are double and striped with pink and white. 'Julie de Mersan' would be difficult to find nowadays; it seems only to be available on the continent of Europe, mainly in France. ZONES 4–9.

Thomas, France, 1854

Parentage unknown

'Julie Y'

'JULIE Y' HARbinger

syn. 'Julie Youell'
MODERN, LARGE-FLOWERED/HYBRID TEA, ORANGE-RED, REPEAT-FLOWERING

A very good cut-flower variety, 'Julie Y' is unavailable in many parts of the world. The medium red color of the fully double flowers is very good, without the hard brightness of some orange-reds. There is a noticeable fragrance. The bush itself is ideal for borders and in groups in beds, or for use as a standard. Not a tall grower, it still keeps an upright shape and spreads only a little. ZONES 5–10.

Harkness, UK, 1994

'Silver Jubilee' × 'Just Joey'

Belfast Certificate of Merit 1997, Glasgow People's Choice 1997, Orléan's Gold Medal 1997

'JULIET'

OLD, HYBRID PERPETUAL, PINK BLEND, REPEAT-FLOWERING

An early bloomer, this fragrant rose begins with golden yellow globular buds

'Julischka'

that develop into rich, rosy red blooms that are double and large; the weather may influence the intensity of the color. The undersides of the petals are old gold. 'Juliet' is an excellent cut flower, but it does not like wet or humid weather; there are occasional repeat-blooms. The 4 ft (1.2 m) tall, vigorous and bushy shrub has curiously curled leaves, and should be pruned lightly. ZONES 5–10.

Paul, UK, 1910

'Captain Hayward' × 'Soleil d'Or'

'JULISCHKA' TANjuka

syn. 'Juleschke'
MODERN, CLUSTER-FLOWERED/FLORIBUNDA, MEDIUM RED, REPEAT-FLOWERING

An unusual but excellent rose that produces good-quality Cluster-flowered heads, this bush has medium red flowers that are semi-double with about 20 petals. The perfume is pleasing. Not widely grown, specialist rose nurseries still grow 'Julischka' for the collectors who appreciate a unique rose. It is a clean, healthy, disease-free bush with fresh new glossy bronze growth. ZONES 5–11.

Tantau, Germany, 1974

Parentage unknown

New Zealand Gold Medal 1976, The Hague Golden Rose 1982

'JUNE BRIDE'

MODERN, LARGE-FLOWERED/HYBRID TEA, WHITE, REPEAT-FLOWERING

The large flowers of this rose start green-white but soon open into cream-white double flowers that are fragrant, high centered and cupped. They are produced throughout summer and autumn. The strong, vigorous, upright growth of this shrub is easily pruned into a desirable shape. The foliage is crinkled and leathery. The disease resistance is adequate only; some attention is needed to keep it entirely disease free. 'June Bride' has a wonderful first flush that will inspire and motivate. ZONES 5–11.

Shepherd, USA, 1957

('Mme Butterfly' × 'New Dawn') × 'Crimson Glory'

'JUNE LAVER' LAVjune

MODERN, MINIATURE, DEEP YELLOW, REPEAT-FLOWERING

'June Laver', named by the hybridizer for his wife, has flowers of exquisite Large-flowered form which are a dark yellow ageing to creamy yellow. The florets are double with 20–25 petals, borne singly or in small sprays of 3–5 blooms. They have no fragrance but are so elegant and

'June Bride'

'June Time'

resemble miniature Large-flowered blooms. The foliage is dark green with an attractive matt finish. It is an extremely low grower, rarely getting above 12 in (30 cm) tall even in the best growing conditions. The bloom repeat cycle is also poor. This rose is very prone to die back in winter and needs protection for survival, but in spite of its faults, it is a wonderful plant in the garden because it produces marvellous blooms of great exhibition quality. ZONES 6–11.

Laver, Canada, 1987

'Helmut Schmidt' × 'Gold Mine'

'JUNE PARK'

MODERN, LARGE-FLOWERED/HYBRID TEA, DEEP PINK, REPEAT-FLOWERING

'June Park' has fine, very pointed flowers of exhibition form, with thick petals that are arranged evenly. The pink color intensifies and becomes darker in cold weather—there is no translucency or variation of tone. There is a very strong, very sweet and very enticing fragrance, and the flowers appear early in the season and continue until late autumn. It has disease-resistant leaves and should be planted on the edges of beds as it is low growing. June Park was the daughter of Bertram Park, OBE, VMH, author, rosarian and long-time editor of *The Rose Annual* produced by the National Rose Society of Great Britain. ZONES 5–10.

Sanday, UK, 1958

'Peace' × 'Crimson Glory'

National Rose Society Gold Medal and Clay Vase for Fragrance 1959

'JUNE TIME'

MODERN, MINIATURE, LIGHT PINK, REPEAT-FLOWERING

The flowers are light pink with a darker pink reverse and have almost 75 petals, borne mainly in small clusters. 'June Time' is noted for its display of attractive sprays of little flat pompons bathed in rose pink. Unfortunately the blooms have no scent. The plant is a vigorous miniature rambler with a spreading habit sporting an over-abundance of glossy and essentially disease-resistant foliage. This rose is a clean and dependable plant with little or no maintenance required. Once again, this hybridizing effort illustrates the reach of Ralph Moore to explore the unknown and produce this wonderful Miniature Rose. ZONES 5–11.

Moore, USA, 1963

(*Rosa wichuraiana* × 'Floradora') × ([seedling of 'Etoile Luisante' × 'Red Ripples'] × 'Zee')

'June Park'

J
K

'JUNE WHITFIELD' HARchutzpah

MODERN, LARGE-FLOWERED/HYBRID TEA,
PINK BLEND, REPEAT-FLOWERING

This lovely new rose has tones that are bright and happy and are best described by the breeders as bold tones of 'scarlet and gold on an underlay of peachy pink', a strong color indeed. The bush itself is vigorous, healthy and able to survive most climates and soils. It is best suited to mass planting, and it was named for the British star of stage, television and radio. ZONES 5–10.

Harkness, UK, 1995

'Avocet' × 'Prima Ballerina'

'JUNIOR GEISHA'

MODERN, CLUSTER-FLOWERED/FLORIBUNDA,
ORANGE-RED, REPEAT-FLOWERING

One of the first, very low-growing, bushy Cluster-flowered Roses, 'Junior Geisha' is particularly useful for edging beds of roses and low borders if planted close together. The medium-sized, double flowers are made up of 20 bright orange-red petals, and are produced in clusters of 8–15 that stand well above the mass of small, dull matt green leaves. There is a good resistance to disease. Although the bloom is adequate, the repeat can be a little slow. ZONES 5–9.

Parentage unknown

'JUNIOR MISS'

syn. 'America's Junior Miss'

MODERN, CLUSTER-FLOWERED/FLORIBUNDA,
LIGHT PINK, REPEAT-FLOWERING

With such parents, the name of this rose seems as though it must have been pre-ordained. The plump buds open into pale coral-pink, full-petalled blooms of medium size. They are well formed and attractive at the young stage, but become faded and discolored with age. There is a modest fragrance, and blooms continue to appear through summer and autumn.

'Junior Geisha'

'Just Joey'

Only one nursery in the USA appears to be offering this variety. 'Junior Miss' grows vigorously with a bushy habit, and is furnished with glossy green leaves; it is suitable for a mixed border. ZONES 5–9.

Boerner, USA, 1964

'Seventeen' × seedling of 'Demure'

'JUNO'

OLD, CHINA, LIGHT PINK

This rose is non-repeating, and was perhaps accidentally created when Laffay was seeking a Hybrid Perpetual. The globular buds open to fine, flat, 3 in (8 cm) blush pink flowers, each with a central button eye. It is a beautiful rose and has a delicious fragrance. Its growth is lax and arching with large dark green foliage, smoother than most others of its type except 'Fantin-Latour' and with only a few thorns. Given space towards the front of a border, it can make a gracefully sturdy, very rewarding shrub. ZONES 5–10.

Laffay, France, 1847

Parentage unknown

'JUST FOR YOU' MORyou

MODERN, MINIATURE, DEEP PINK,
REPEAT-FLOWERING

Beautiful deep pink to light red flowers are the hallmark of this award-winning Miniature Rose. Although the florets can be a trifle large, they have consistent Large-flowered form all year long—even in temperatures of 90°F (30°C). Blooms occur singly or in small clusters and are often slow to open. The substance of the blooms can diminish in hot dry climates. 'Just For You' has a smallish, upright habit with a slow repeat-bloom cycle. ZONES 5–11.

Moore, USA, 1990

'Orangeade' × 'Rainbow's End'

American Rose Society Award of Excellence 1991

'Just Joey'

'Kabuki'

'JUST JOEY'

MODERN, LARGE-FLOWERED/HYBRID TEA,
ORANGE BLEND, REPEAT-FLOWERING

Looking at the two parents of this variety, it gives little indication of the offspring, and what a rose it is: an ever-popular variety that will still be so for many years to come. It has big, loose, double flowers that are an orange blend. and they are usually found in small clusters. They are well recommended both for cutting or for garden display. The bush is sprawling and grows to medium height, while the leaves are dark green. It is hard to compare 'Just Joey' with other Large-flowered Roses, as the richness of the flower and the looseness of the form make it so exciting and unusual. ZONES 5–10.

Cant, UK, 1972

'Fragrant Cloud' × 'Dr A. J. Verhage'

Royal National Rose Society James Mason Gold
Medal 1986, Royal Horticultural Society Award of
Garden Merit 1993, World's Favorite Rose 1994

'KABUKI' MEIgold

syn. 'Golden Prince'

MODERN, LARGE-FLOWERED/HYBRID TEA,
DEEP YELLOW, REPEAT-FLOWERING

'Kabuki' has rich deep yellow flowers that show a darker pink tinge in cool

'Kagayaki'

weather. They are fully double and open well, falling freely as they age. An upright grower of medium height, the bush is strong and has large leaves with stout frameworks. It is slightly susceptible to some dieback after pruning and needs light cutting to help it overcome this problem. ZONES 5–10.

Meilland, France, 1968

('Monte Carlo' × 'Bettina') × ('Peace' × 'Soraya')

'KAGAYAKI'

syn. 'Brilliant Light'

MODERN, CLUSTER-FLOWERED/FLORIBUNDA,
RED BLEND, REPEAT-FLOWERING

'Kagayaki' was released under the name 'Brilliant Light' and, when the rose is viewed, the color certainly is bright. The slightly fragrant flowers, which are mostly bright scarlet with a mesmerizing intensity, are large and double and have high centers. A strong bush with an upright nature, it is ideal for mass plantings or borders and will add a splash of color to any garden. Disease control is advised to maintain a healthy plant that is profuse in growth all season. ZONES 5–10.

Suzuki, Japan, 1970

(Seedling of 'Aztec' × ['Spectacular' × 'Aztec'])
× seedling of 'Cover Girl'

'Junior Miss'

'Karen Julie'

'Kambala'

'Kaikoura'

'KAIKOURA' MACwalla
MODERN, MINIATURE, ORANGE BLEND, REPEAT-FLOWERING

Large, bright orange-red flowers identify this rose even a mile away! The florets are double with about 27 petals and can be a little larger than the traditional Miniature Rose. This rose is popular in New Zealand where it wins at rose shows consistently. The blooms open to beautiful, flat, neon orange florets that hold onto their color for a long time, whatever the climate. The foliage is an attractive, glossy, dark green. This is a vigorous, compact bush with a good resistance to disease. 'Kaikoura' is a masterpiece from the hybridizing program of Sam McGredy where he has taken two of his other masterpieces and successfully transmitted both their desirable characteristics. It is named after a town in New Zealand. ZONES 5–11.

McGredy, New Zealand, 1978

'Anytime' × 'Matangi'

'KAISERIN AUGUSTE VIKTORIA'
syns 'K. A. Victoria', 'K. A. Viktoria'
MODERN, LARGE-FLOWERED/HYBRID TEA, WHITE, REPEAT-FLOWERING

The flowers of this variety are white, although in autumn they may show pink tinges at the edges of the petals. They are well formed with high, pointed centers and have evenly distributed petals that form a circular outline. It is a very healthy plant that grows vigorously to

form a large bush, and has shiny green leaves. Young growth is red and soft, then it quickly hardens to form strong branches. 'KAV', as it was fondly known in the nursery trade, was widely used as a cut flower at the turn of the century; it is still readily available today in specialist rose nurseries. ZONES 5–10.

Lambert, Germany, 1891

'Coquette de Lyon' × 'Lady Mary Fitzwilliam'

'KAKWA'
MODERN, MODERN SHRUB, WHITE

This rose has one enthusiastic flowering in spring, blooming before all the other roses in the garden. The blooms appear white from a distance, pale pink up close. There is an intense fragrance and the double flowers nearly blot out the foliage. This is an ideal candidate for a hedge as it does well in either poor or rich soil, and has a compact, bushy habit. Its wild rose background means that it does equally well in sun or in shade. Although 'Kakwa' was created for severe winter conditions, it is quite happy in other climates. It is also disease resistant. With all these good qualities, it is surprising that it is not more popular. ZONES 3–9.

Wallace, Canada, 1973

Hybrid of *Rosa spinosissima*

'KAMBALA' AROheddo
MODERN, LARGE-FLOWERED/HYBRID TEA, APRICOT BLEND, REPEAT-FLOWERING

This rose has not been released all over the world; available in Australia, it was

named after Kambala College in Sydney and may have been kept exclusively for them. The single flowers, which are large and fully double, are a lovely yellow with soft apricot toning. The scent is good and the keeping ability of the blooms fair. The bush is quite upright and needs care in warm humid areas to keep it free of black spot. ZONES 5–10.

Armstrong, USA, 1988

'Gingersnap' × 'Brandy'

'KARDINAL' KORlingo
MODERN, LARGE-FLOWERED/HYBRID TEA, MEDIUM RED, REPEAT-FLOWERING

Most people will have seen this rose on display in their local florists but would not be aware of its name. The flowers are rich cardinal red and are lightly scented. They usually appear singly on long stems and can be easily arranged. In the greenhouse and in the open 'Kardinal' grows to a medium-tall bush and has a good resistance to mildew and black spot. The repeat-flowering intervals are short but it is a wonderful rose for all purposes. ZONES 5–10.

Kordes, Germany, 1986

Seedling × 'Flamingo'

'KAREN BLIXEN' POUlari
syn. 'Silver Anniversary'
MODERN, LARGE-FLOWERED/HYBRID TEA, WHITE, REPEAT-FLOWERING

This variety has large, pure white flowers that have great presence about them and make wonderful exhibition roses. They are well formed and open with almost a loose manner and have a strong scent that keeps well with age. It was named to honor a great woman with a pioneering spirit who suffered the hardships of Africa. ZONES 5–10.

Poulsen, Denmark, 1992

Parentage unknown

'KAREN JULIE'
MODERN, LARGE-FLOWERED/HYBRID TEA, ORANGE-RED, REPEAT-FLOWERING

This rose, which is excellent for exhibition, has well-shaped blooms that are deep orange and contain 45 petals. There is a salmon-orange reverse to the petals. The flowers keep their form and color well on a medium-sized, bushy plant with matt and mid-green foliage, and the flowering is quite good for an exhibition-type rose. There are no disease problems. It is a fine rose for picking. ZONES 5–10.

Allender, Australia, 1979

'Alexander' × 'Vienna Woods'

'KAREN POULSEN'
MODERN, CLUSTER-FLOWERED/FLORIBUNDA, MEDIUM RED, REPEAT-FLOWERING

The 5-petalled cupped blooms of this rose are borne in clusters of 3–12, and when introduced it was said to have few rivals with regard to color, being 'a glorious fiery crimson, that lasts right up to the time the petals fall'. A well-behaved variety, it does not mind rain or sun; the only serious drawback is its need for deadheading, otherwise hips form that delay the next cycle of growth and bloom. With proper care it blooms through summer and autumn, the autumn sprays being especially strong and fine. There is little scent. 'Karen Poulsen' was one of the most popular pre-war hybrid polyanthas, as Cluster-flowered Roses were then called, and it was used extensively for beds in public parks because of its striking massed color effect. The plant grows unevenly and with moderate vigor to about average height, and it has semi-glossy, mid-green leaves. Karen was the niece of raiser Svend Poulsen. ZONES 4–9.

Poulsen, Denmark, 1932

'Kirsten Poulsen' × 'Vesuvius'

National Rose Society Gold Medal 1933, Portland Gold Medal 1935

'KARL FÖRSTER'
OLD, SCOTS, WHITE, REPEAT-FLOWERING

As a revered plantsman and author in Germany between the wars, Karl Förster is remembered today mostly for his work with grasses, and for this rose named in his honor. The slightly fragrant, snow white flowers emerge from pointed buds and are supported on long, gracefully arching stems. The large, almost double blooms are high centered, and present a lovely display of golden stamens. It is a vigorous bush covered with ferny, gray-green foliage. The young, bristly stems are red. It reaches 5 ft (1.5 m) high, and does well in poor soil and shade; deadheading will help promote bloom in autumn. It needs room to look its best and is an ideal rose for the woodland garden. ZONES 5–10.

Kordes, Germany 1931

'Frau Karl Druschki' × *Rosa spinosissima altaica*

'KARL HERBST'
syn. 'Red Peace'
MODERN, LARGE-FLOWERED/HYBRID TEA, MEDIUM RED, REPEAT-FLOWERING

The enormous flowers of a well-grown specimen of this rose have graced many a

'Karl Herbst'

'Karen Blixen'

'Kardinal'

'Kassel'

show, for with 60 broad petals it combines size and symmetry of form to a rare degree. The high-centered blooms open slowly, revealing a rather dull deep red color, darker on the inside of the petal. Blooming is well maintained through summer and autumn, although the flowers are impatient of rain and tend to ball. There is a light fragrance, and for a mixed bed or border this is a sturdy and reliable rose, still fairly widely grown after nearly half a century. The plant grows very vigorously with a branching habit to above average height, and is well furnished with large, leathery leaves that are semi-glossy and dark green. Karl Herbst was a lifelong friend of Wilhelm Kordes, both of them having been interned as enemy aliens by the British in World War I. ZONES 4–9.

Kordes, Germany, 1950

'Independence' × 'Peace'

National Rose Society Gold Medal 1950

'KARLSRUHE'
MODERN, CLUSTER-FLOWERED CLIMBER, DEEP PINK, REPEAT-FLOWERING

The flowers of 'Karlsruhe' are large, carried in clusters of up to 10, full-petalled and globular at first, becoming cupped as they open out. They are rose pink in color and have a slight scent. Following a prolific early flush the blooms are produced intermittently through summer and autumn on a well-branched plant. The variety grows with a spreading, climbing habit to average extent and is best suited for growing up pillars and on walls where the situation is not too dry. The leaves are plentiful and glossy. Karlsruhe is a city near the French border in southwest Germany, the name meaning 'Charles's Peace' with reference to Charlemagne. ZONES 4–9.

Kordes, Germany, 1957

Rosa kordesii × 'Golden Glow'

'KAROO ROSE'   POUlkaros
syn. 'Karoo'
MODERN, CLUSTER-FLOWERED/FLORIBUNDA, ORANGE-RED, REPEAT-FLOWERING

The most arid part of South Africa is called the Karoo, but although hot and dry, it has its own interesting plants, that can give a spectacular show after heavy rains. One needs a tough rose if it is to thrive in the long hot dry summer and frosty winters of the Karoo, and 'Karoo Rose' is exactly that. The medium-sized bush rose grows quickly and easily into a neat round shrub, which continuously

sprouts new flowering branches. The pointed buds develop into well-shaped, dark orange-red blooms with a crimson color reminiscent of a Karoo sunset. This is an excellent bedding variety and because it is long lasting, it is a popular cut-flower and exhibition rose. It has the added advantage of being fragrant. ZONES 4–11.

Poulsen, Denmark, 1988

Seedling × seedling

'KASSEL'
MODERN, LARGE-FLOWERED CLIMBER, ORANGE-RED, REPEAT-FLOWERING

There seems to be disagreement on the parentage of this variety. The blooms are scarlet red, fairly large, and are borne in clusters of up to 10 semi-double flowers. The young blooms are neatly formed with high centers, becoming wide and loosely cupped as they open. They have an appreciable fragrance and appear freely in summer, with sporadic later bloom through summer and autumn. This rose has a vigorous, arching habit and can be grown as a shrub or trained on a light support such as a short pillar or low fence, since it extends more than the average expected of a shrub and less than that of a climber. The leathery leaves are large, matt and reddish when young. This is one of many Kordes' roses named for a German city. ZONES 4–9.

Kordes, Germany, 1957

'Hamburg' × 'Scarlet Else'

National Rose Society Certificate of Merit 1957

'KATHARINA ZEIMET'
syn. 'White Baby Rambler'
MODERN, POLYANTHA, WHITE, REPEAT-FLOWERING

This dainty rose bears double white flowers in airy sprays of up to 50 blooms, making a very free display on the first flush of bloom with a good continuance of blossom throughout summer and autumn. There is a delicate fragrance, and the flowers are remarkably tolerant of bad weather. 'Katharina Zeimet' is suitable to group in beds or near the front of a border, beside a path, to make a low dense hedge and in a container. The plant is normally dwarf and compact but can become sizeable if not pruned. It grows vigorously with many twiggy shoots to average height or above for a Polyantha, and is well provided with many small, rich dark green leaflets. ZONES 4–9.

Lambert, Germany, 1901

'Étoile de Mai' × 'Marie Pavié'

'KATHLEEN'
MODERN, MODERN SHRUB, LIGHT PINK, REPEAT-FLOWERING

The pale color of this variety was modestly described by the raiser as 'pink blush, after the shade of *Rosa canina*'. The flowers are small and single, each with a charming arrangement of 5 separated petals and showing yellow stamens. They are carried in big clusters so that the overall effect is of apple blossom, and from them wafts a light fragrance, sweet and musky. The blooms appear very freely during the first flush, and more flowers are produced intermittently through summer and in autumn, when the blooms can be accompanied by sprays of orange hips. 'Kathleen' makes an excellent addition to a shrub border, having a somewhat sprawling habit and growing larger than the average shrub rose while in milder climates it grows big enough to make a useful climber. The leaves are long, drooping and dark green. ZONES 4–9.

Pemberton, UK, 1922

'Daphne' × 'Perle des Jardins'

'KATHLEEN FERRIER'
MODERN, CLUSTER-FLOWERED/FLORIBUNDA, ORANGE-PINK, REPEAT-FLOWERING

The semi-double flowers on 'Kathleen Ferrier' are a picture of simplicity and charm as they open like saucers to show prominent yellow stamens. These blooms are light salmon-pink with white towards the bases of the petals, have a pleasing scent and are carried in well-filled sprays on long stems throughout summer and autumn. This bush rose reaches shrub proportions in mild climates: it is also excellent as a hedge. 'Kathleen Ferrier' is vigorous and bushy to above average height, and is well supplied with shiny dark green leaves. The variety commemorates the popular British contralto who lived 1912–53

and inspired many through her glorious voice, warm personality and faith in times of adversity. ZONES 4–9.

Buisman, The Netherlands, 1952

'Gartenstolz' × 'Shot Silk'

National Rose Society Trial Ground Certificate 1955

'KATHLEEN HARROP'
OLD, BOURBON, LIGHT PINK, REPEAT-FLOWERING

Retaining all the good points of its parent, this popular rose is one of the last Bourbon Roses introduced. The large buds open to soft, shell pink blooms that are semi-double and are marked with transparent veins; the petals are dark on the undersides, although the color fades in direct sunlight. Some blooms appear in clusters. It reaches 10 ft (3 m) high as a climber, or half that as a shrub, and has no prickles and is covered by gray-green, pointed leaves. The plant is not bothered by wet weather, but during its mid-summer to autumn flowering it needs good air circulation to prevent mildew. The Dickson firm has been managed by six generations of the same family. ZONES 4–10.

Dickson, UK, 1919

Sport of 'Zéphirine Drouhin'

K

'Kathleen'

'Kathleen Harrop'

'KATHRYN McGREDY'

MACaucklad

MODERN, LARGE-FLOWERED/HYBRID TEA,
ORANGE-PINK, REPEAT-FLOWERING

The flowers of this variety combine symmetry of form and size of flower in the best traditions of the Large-flowered Rose. They are large, high centered and full of petals which combine several shades of pink, from blush on the outer petals to pale salmon in the depths of the bloom. On the first flowering the scented blooms are usually borne one to a stem, but the later summer and autumn flowers often come in clusters. This is a pretty plant for beds and borders, growing vigorously with an upright, bushy habit to average height. It has an ample cover of dark glossy leaves, which are reddish when young and effectively complement the flowers. Sam McGredy named this rose for his eldest daughter. ZONES 4–9.

McGredy, New Zealand, 1995

'City of Auckland' × 'Lady Rose'

'KATHRYN MORLEY'   AUSclub,

AUSvariety

MODERN, MODERN SHRUB, LIGHT PINK,
REPEAT-FLOWERING

The flowers of 'Kathryn Morley' are of medium to large size and very full, with over 40 petals. They are borne singly or in small clusters and open into pale pink flowers of charming old-fashioned appearance, the outer petals reflexing while the remainder are enfolded and slightly incurved, giving what has been described as a 'cup and saucer' effect. There is a pleasant scent, and flowering continues through summer and autumn. The plant makes a somewhat uneven, rangy grower with long canes as well as shorter stems, and it is best grown in a border where the beauty and scent of the flowers can be appreciated, but with lower growing plants in front. It grows vigorously and is furnished with large, mid- to dark green leaves. The rose was named in memory of the 17-year old daughter of Mr and Mrs Eric Morley. It is from David Austin and is also classified as an English Rose. ZONES 4–9.

Austin, UK, 1990

'Mary Rose' × 'Chaucer'

'KATHY'

MODERN, MINIATURE, MEDIUM RED,
REPEAT-FLOWERING

'Kathy' has pointed buds which open to small, medium red blooms with good form and substance. They have excellent color tone and are fragrant. The foliage is small and leathery in texture and the plant has a dwarf, compact growth habit.

'Kazanlik'

'Kazanlik' (hips)

'Kathryn Morley'

'Keepsake'

This winter hardy plant has a tendency to mildew. 'Kathy' is a sister seedling to 'Hi Ho', 'Jet Trial', and 'Judy Fischer' proving that the marriage between 'Little Darling' and 'Magic Wand' was a productive one! ZONES 5–11.

Moore, USA, 1970

'Little Darling' × 'Magic Wand'

'KAZANLIK'

syns *Rosa damascena trigintipetala*,
'Trigintipetala'

OLD, DAMASK, DEEP PINK

This plant is extensively grown in Kazanlik, Bulgaria because it is one of the varieties used to make the famous 'attar of roses'. The flowers, which are arranged in loose clusters on short thin stalks and appear in early to mid-summer, are soft pink in color and a bit more than semi-double when fully open; each is about 2 in (5 cm) across and exposes many creamy colored stamens. They are deliciously fragrant. 'Kazanlik' is an angular shrub to some 6 ft (1.8 m) high and almost as wide, with a twiggy growth habit and moderately thorny, brownish green wood. The light gray-green, serrated leaves are soft to touch. ZONES 5–11.

Pre-1700

Parentage unknown

'KEEPIT'

MODERN, LARGE-FLOWERED/HYBRID TEA,
LIGHT PINK, REPEAT-FLOWERING

The buds of 'Keepit' are long and elegant and open to large, exhibition-form flowers that are borne on very long stems. Each bloom containing 40 petals is pale pink in color, deepening a little at the petal edges. The foliage is mid-green, semi-glossy and abundant on a spreading plant that grows to medium height. George Dawson showed this rose to a friend from the Victorian Rose Society, saying that he was about to discard it.

'Keepit'

'Keepsake'

The friend said 'Keep it'—hence the name. It is one of the best exhibition varieties bred in Australia. ZONES 5–10.

Dawson, Australia, 1988

Parentage unknown

'KEEPSAKE'   KORmalda

syns 'Esmeralda', 'Kordes' Rose Esmeralda'

MODERN, LARGE-FLOWERED/HYBRID TEA,
PINK BLEND, REPEAT-FLOWERING

The flowers of this variety are large and full with 40 petals, and open with high centers. In color they are deep pink, admitting hints of light carmine and blush. There is a light fragrance, and flowering is well maintained through summer and autumn, the blooms being sometimes borne singly and sometimes in clusters of 3. The stems are of medium length and occasionally have crooked pedicels. 'Keepsake' is often used for bedding and it is suitable to group in a border and to grow for showing as the flowers last well, holding their form to a late stage and withstanding bad weather. The plant grows to average height or less with a bushy, rather untidy habit and has mid- to dark green, glossy and robust foliage. ZONES 4–9.

Kordes, Germany, 1981

Seedling × 'Red Planet'

Royal National Rose Society Trial Ground Certificate 1980, Portland Gold Medal 1987

'KEITH KIRSTEN'   TANsirk

MODERN, CLUSTER-FLOWERED/FLORIBUNDA,
ORANGE-RED, REPEAT-FLOWERING

The flowering stems of 'Keith Kirsten' carry well-filled clusters of pointed buds that open out into neatly formed, cupped, semi-double flowers. They are on the orange side of vermilion, lasting well and maintaining a good color tone in spite of hot sunshine; indeed, they seem happiest in a warm climate. There is not very much fragrance, as is to be expected in a firm-petalled variety of this color. This is a useful variety for beds and borders, and the long flower stems make it excellent for cutting. The flowers continue to appear through summer and autumn on a vigorous, bushy plant that grows to average height or above and is well furnished with glossy dark green foliage. The rose is named in honor of a South African horticulturalist in recognition of his valuable contributions to the nursery industry in that country. ZONES 4–9.

Tantau, Germany, 1990

Parentage unknown

'KENT'   POUlcov
syns 'Pyrenees', 'Sparkler', 'White Cover'
MODERN, GROUND COVER, WHITE,
REPEAT-FLOWERING

This is a spreading dwarf shrub with a low, rounded outline, rather than a true Ground Cover Rose, but in a limited space it is most useful either as a specimen plant, in a small group or near the front of a shrub border. The plant produces large trusses of small semi-double white flowers that open cupped then become flat. They are borne close to the plant, effectively providing a cushion of white at the height of the flowering season and maintaining a good succession of bloom through the rest of summer and autumn. There is a light fragrance, and the flowers look fresh and clean whatever the weather. It is as wide as an average shrub rose but half the height, and is well covered with small, shiny dark green leaves. ZONES 4–9.

Poulsen, Denmark, 1988

Parentage unknown

Baden-Baden Gold Medal 1990, Royal National Rose Society President's International Trophy 1990, Glasgow Certificate of Merit 1992, Royal National Rose Society British Rose Award 1998

'KENTUCKY DERBY'   AROder
MODERN, LARGE-FLOWERED/HYBRID TEA,
DARK RED, REPEAT-FLOWERING

The dark red flowers of this variety, though not particularly large, are well formed with high centers and last well even in warm climates. They are freely produced in summer and autumn, maintaining a good standard of quality throughout, and holding their color tone well in the hot sun. The scent, though, is not as strong as one hopes for in a red rose. This is a useful variety for beds and borders; it can also be cut for the house. It grows vigorously to average height with an upright, bushy habit. The glossy leaves are large and leathery. ZONES 4–9.

Armstrong, USA, 1972

'John S. Armstrong' × 'Grand Slam'

'KERRY GOLD'

MODERN, CLUSTER-FLOWERED/FLORIBUNDA,
YELLOW BLEND, REPEAT-FLOWERING

'Kerry Gold' almost qualifies as a Patio Rose, being a short grower, but its habit is too open, narrow and upright for it to fit in with this newer group; it is more like a scaled-down version of a Cluster-flowered Rose. The flowers are bright deep yellow, often with splashes or veinings of red on the outer petals. They are neatly formed and open to double,

'Kentucky Derby'

crisp-petalled, cupped blooms and, although of medium size, they look quite large in relation to the plant and stand upright on firm stems. The variety appears to have dropped out of growers' lists, which is a pity, for there is nothing else that resembles it, and as a cheerful ingredient in the garden for the front of a border or a small bed it has much to commend it. The succession of flower after the main flush is rather slow and this, together with its lack of scent and rather skimpy foliage, are the likely reasons for its eclipse. ZONES 4–9.

Dickson, UK, 1967

'Circus' × 'Allgold'

'KERRYMAN'

MODERN, CLUSTER-FLOWERED/FLORIBUNDA,
PINK BLEND, REPEAT-FLOWERING

The flowers of this variety are a pretty shade of salmon-pink in the center, paling to rosy salmon towards the margins. They are large for a Cluster-flowered Rose and are made up of 24 broad petals, so that the combined weight of the blooms in their clusters tends to bow down the stems, giving the plant a pleasing rounded effect. This works in its favor, especially when it is required for bedding. 'Kerryman' is a good rose for a border and low hedge also, though it is likely to be troubled by black spot in seasons when that fungus is prevalent. Flowering through summer and autumn is well maintained, and there is a light scent. The plant grows to average height or below and has a well-spread, bushy habit and semi-glossy leaves. The raiser named the rose to reflect his love of that part of Ireland. ZONES 4–9.

McGredy, UK, 1971

'Paddy McGredy' × ('Mme Léon Cuny' × 'Columbine')

Royal National Rose Society Certificate of Merit 1971

'Kiese'

'Kerry Gold'

'KEW RAMBLER'
MODERN, RAMBLER, MEDIUM PINK

The pointed, bright pink buds of this rampant Rambler open to reveal pink-white, single blooms with paler centers. They bloom later than most in its class and appear in trusses on the long, pliable canes. The large, moderately fragrant clusters are highlighted by the gold stamens. The attractive, gray-green foliage covers both the prickles and the orange-red hips. This summer-blooming rose can be used as a large shrub in the wild garden or trained on a pergola or high fence. It reaches 18 ft (5 m) in two years. ZONES 4–11.

Kew Gardens, UK, 1913

Rosa soulieana × 'Hiawatha'

'KIESE'
MODERN, MODERN SHRUB, MEDIUM RED

'Not a rose for the fainthearted' warns Britain's Keith Jones, one of the few nurserymen to offer this undisciplined vigorous shrub. It produces heads of semi-double or almost single, medium-sized blooms on strong prickly stems. They are a bright and cheery shade of cherry red, fading with age, with a yellowy white eye, large golden stamens and slight scent. It flowers in summer only, but bears large, round red hips in autumn. It is especially suited to areas where plants are allowed to become naturalized and look after themselves, for it needs no maintenance apart from trimming to keep it in bounds. Of an arching, free-branching habit, this rose will make a thicket up to twice as large as the average

'Kerryman'

shrub rose, and could be trained to create a pillar. The leaves are dark green, bright and glossy. The raiser's original intention was to create a rootstock, and as a standard stem it is excellent and long lived, though quite prickly. ZONES 4–9.

Kiese, Germany, 1910

'Général Jacqueminot' × *Rosa canina*

'KIFTSGATE'
syn. *Rosa filipes* 'Kiftsgate'
MODERN, LARGE-FLOWERED CLIMBER, WHITE

Among rose enthusiasts in the USA 'rose rustling' has become a popular pastime, and one of the most successful varieties acquired in this way came from Murrell's nursery, who obtained 'Kiftsgate' from a well-established plant growing in the Gloucestershire garden whose name it bears. It has spectacular clusters of many single, creamy white flowers on vigorous arching canes, and a pleasing scent that wafts around on still days. The best place for this variety is where it can grow naturally, and it is often planted to clamber into a large tree. It can be grown on big walls, but since one English specimen on a tithe barn has extended to over 148 ft (45 m), caution is clearly needed in siting it. The blooms appear *en masse* in mid-summer only, succeeded by small round hips. The leaves are large and shiny, and the canes carry large prickles that can make pruning an uncomfortable task; apart from the removal of dead branches, it is best to leave this rose to nature. ZONES 4–9.

Murrell, UK, 1954

Seedling of *Rosa filipes*

Royal Horticultural Society Award of Garden Merit

'Kew Rambler'

'Kiftsgate'

K

'King Arthur'

'Kimono'

'King's Ransom'

'Kiskadee'

'KIM'

MODERN, CLUSTER-FLOWERED/FLORIBUNDA,
MEDIUM YELLOW, REPEAT-FLOWERING

This variety has flowers that are large in proportion to the plant, having over 30 petals; they open from clusters of plump buds into rounded flowers of canary yellow and become cupped as the petals reflex, then admit flushes of pink as they age, to a marked degree in hot weather. The blooms are carried quite close to the foliage, giving the plant a compact appearance, and they repeat their flower with good continuity through summer and autumn. There is a pleasant light fragrance, and the flowers open cleanly in all weathers. 'Kim' is good for small spaces of every kind, to edge a bed and in a container. The growth is compact and bushy, much shorter than the average for a bush rose, and the plant is well provided with small, matt mid-green leaves. Kim Mulford died in childhood, and the rose is named in his memory. ZONES 4–9.

Harkness, UK, 1973

('Orange Sensation' × 'Allgold') × 'Elizabeth of Glamis'

Royal National Rose Society Certificate of Merit 1970

'KIMONO'

MODERN, CLUSTER-FLOWERED/FLORIBUNDA,
PINK BLEND, REPEAT-FLOWERING

The flowers of this rose are rounded in outline and of medium size and are carried in broad clusters. They are fully double, with over 40 small petals, and open out flat when fully expanded. The color is a kindly shade of salmon-pink, there is a pleasing fragrance, and flowers continue to appear through summer and autumn. This is an effective and dependable all-round performer for beds, borders and hedges, and it is still widely available after nearly 40 years in commerce. The plant grows vigorously, maintaining a uniform habit of growth to average height, and it is plentifully supplied with medium green foliage that is coppery when young. ZONES 4–9.

de Ruiter, The Netherlands, 1961

'Cocorico' × 'Frau Anny Beaufays'

Royal National Rose Society Trial Ground Certificate 1961

'KIND REGARDS' PEAtiger

MODERN, CLUSTER-FLOWERED/FLORIBUNDA,
MEDIUM RED, REPEAT-FLOWERING

The blooms are bright red, fully double and open with neatly coiled centers before becoming cupped, displaying stiff, elegantly fluted petals. They hold their color tone well in all weathers, but as is normal with this type of petal there is only a slight fragrance. The plant flowers well through summer and autumn, though its willowy growth habit makes it a less than ideal subject for a bed of one variety. However, if planted in a mixed border with other short plants in front it will mingle perfectly well with other subjects. The bush grows to below average height with bronze to deep green foliage. ZONES 4–9.

Pearce, UK, 1995

Parentage unknown

'KING ARTHUR'

MODERN, CLUSTER-FLOWERED/FLORIBUNDA,
ORANGE-PINK, REPEAT-FLOWERING

The blooms on this variety are big and heavy, with over 40 large petals, and are carried in candelabra-like open clusters. They are salmon-pink without much variation in color, except that the petals may become mottled as they age. There is a light fragrance. Considering the size of bloom the continuity of flowering is well maintained through summer and autumn, and for beds, hedges and borders this rose has been widely used, though currently it does not appear to be commercially available. Flowers intended for cutting need to be taken young, otherwise they may not open. The bush grows vigorously with an upright, free-branching habit to medium height and has large, matt green leaves. ZONES 4–9.

Harkness, UK, 1967

'Pink Parfait' × 'Highlight'

Royal National Rose Society Certificate of Merit 1966

'KING RICHARD' GENruby

MODERN, MODERN SHRUB, MAUVE,
REPEAT-FLOWERING

This is one of a series of 'Regal' roses, which are described as 'classical small-flowered shrub roses with good flower cover'. The color is somewhere between purple and magenta: a rich hue recalling the Rambler 'Violette', with white at the petal base. The virtually single flowers are produced in big showy clusters, and they open cupped, yielding a pleasant fragrance. This is a spectacular and unusual rose that looks good in a mixed border. It continues to provide blooms throughout summer and into autumn. The growth is somewhat spreading and open, with many vigorous and arching shoots. Overall, 'King Richard' grows to average height and as wide as it is high. There are many glossy green leaves. ZONES 4–9.

Genesis, UK, 1995

Parentage unknown

Royal National Rose Society Trial Ground Certificate 1995

'KING'S RANSOM'

MODERN, LARGE-FLOWERED/HYBRID TEA,
DEEP YELLOW, REPEAT-FLOWERING

This rose has been a standby for gardeners and nurseries for many years and remains popular. Its strengths are the good quality of the large double blooms, which open from urn-shaped buds into high-centered blooms before becoming cupped and falling cleanly; the clear color, which shows little variation in its bright and cheerful yellow tone from start to finish; the neat habit, upright and bushy, which makes it suitable for beds, hedges, borders and as a standard; its additional value as a rose for cutting and showing; its long flowering period through summer and autumn and tolerance of bad weather; and its foliage, dark green, glossy and reasonably plentiful. There is some scent, and the plant grows to average height or a little more. ZONES 4–9.

Morey, USA, 1961

'Golden Masterpiece' × 'Lydia'

All-America Rose Selection 1962

'KIRSTEN POULSEN'

MODERN, CLUSTER-FLOWERED/FLORIBUNDA,
MEDIUM RED, REPEAT-FLOWERING

This survivor of the hybrid polyanthas, which preceded the Cluster-flowered Roses, is still listed by several growers. The color is carmine-red to deep pink, with golden anthers showing in the heart of the medium-sized 5-petalled flowers. They are borne aloft in well-filled clusters on erect stems and, provided the plant is prevented from producing seed pods by removal of the old flowerheads, they will continue to appear through summer and autumn. The color impact made by these massed heads of flower was a novelty at the time, and this rose was for years a favorite choice for beds, borders and hedges. The plant grows vigorously with an upright, free-branching habit to above average height and has leathery foliage. It was named for the raiser's niece. ZONES 4–9.

Poulsen, Denmark, 1924

'Orléans Rose' × 'Red Star'

'KISKADEE'

MODERN, CLUSTER-FLOWERED/FLORIBUNDA,
MEDIUM YELLOW, REPEAT-FLOWERING

The flowers of this variety are like small-scale Large-flowered Roses, with about 25 petals, are borne sometimes singly and sometimes in small clusters and open to reveal high centers. They are clear yellow, with a pleasant light scent, and continue to bloom with good continuity through summer and autumn. Though little grown today, 'Kiskadee' has been a popular choice for beds, borders and hedges as it withstands bad weather well and the color of the blooms lasts without any significant fading, contrasting well with the deep green glossy leaves. The plant grows vigorously with an upright habit, usually to a little under average height. The kiskadee is an attractive yellow-breasted bird named from its call. ZONES 4–9.

McGredy, New Zealand, 1973

'Arthur Bell' × 'Cynthia Brooke'

K

'Kitty Kininmonth'

'Klaus Störtebeker'

'KISS'   KORikis, KORokis
MODERN, CLUSTER-FLOWERED/FLORIBUNDA,
ORANGE-PINK, REPEAT-FLOWERING

'Kiss' has pale salmon-pink, full-petalled flowers that are carried on long wiry stems either singly or in a cluster so open that each flower develops with a stem long enough to cut. They have the high-centered form of a Large-flowered Rose and last for ages. It performs well in warm climates, being vigorous and easy to grow, and continues to produce lightly fragrant blooms over a long period through summer and autumn. The plant grows to above average height and has dark green leaves. ZONES 4–9.

Kordes, Germany, 1988

Seedling × seedling

'KITTY KININMONTH'
MODERN, LARGE-FLOWERED CLIMBER, DEEP PINK,
REPEAT-FLOWERING

The semi-double flowers of this variety are very large and open cupped, showing golden stamens in the heart of the deep pink blooms. They have a slight scent, and there are likely to be sporadic flowers after the generous main flush has ended. This is another of Alister Clark's beautiful roses. It needs a warm climate and frost-free conditions to thrive, so in cooler countries it should be grown against a large, sheltered wall. It has wrinkled, dark green foliage. ZONES 5–9.

Clark, Australia, 1922

Parentage unknown

'KLAUS STÖRTEBEKER'
MODERN, LARGE-FLOWERED/HYBRID TEA,
MEDIUM RED, REPEAT-FLOWERING

On this variety the flowers are a blood red color and are very large, made up of 40 or so broad petals that form high centers and hold this shape to a late

'Kleopatra'

stage. There is some fragrance. Because of the size of the flowers bloom production is not as continuous as with most Large-flowered Roses, but the autumn offerings can be of excellent quality provided they are not spoiled by rain. 'Klaus Störtebeker' can be used for bedding, but the main reason for its cultivation is to exhibit it at shows, where it has won many prizes. It grows with a vigorous, upright habit to below average height and has deep green leaves. ZONES 4–9.

Kordes, Germany, 1962

'Montezuma' × 'Schlösser's Brillant'

'KLEOPATRA'   KORverpea
syns 'Cleopatra', 'New Cleopatra', 'Peace of Vereeniging'
MODERN, LARGE-FLOWERED/HYBRID TEA,
RED BLEND, REPEAT-FLOWERING

This variety produces fairly large double blooms that open with high centers, becoming rounded in shape as the petals reflex. Their colors make a striking contrast, as the uppersides of the petals are rich scarlet and the undersides golden yellow. The lightly scented flowers appear freely in summer, and they continue to bloom through to autumn, which makes this a very suitable garden rose for beds, borders and hedges. It grows to average height with a vigorous upright habit, and is well furnished with dark shiny leaves that are reddish when young. There was a similarly colored 'Kleopatra' from the same raiser in 1955. ZONES 4–9.

Kordes, Germany, 1992

Parentage unknown

'KOBA'   MEIroverna
MODERN, LARGE-FLOWERED/HYBRID TEA,
ORANGE-RED, REPEAT-FLOWERING

The plump buds of this rose open into cupped flowers of some 40 petals. The

'Königin Beatrix'

blooms are of medium size and are colored a luminous rich scarlet, and there is a light fragrance. The first flush of flower is particularly prolific, and a good succession is maintained through summer and autumn. This is primarily a garden rose, and it is good for beds and borders, though the flowers may spoil in wet weather. The plant grows vigorously with an upright habit to average height, and it is supplied with a good covering of large dark leaves. The variety does not appear to be currently in commerce. ZONES 4–9.

Meilland, France, 1979

([Seedling × 'Rouge Meilland'] × 'Independence') × 'Queen Elizabeth'

'KÖLNER KARNEVAL'   KORgi
syns 'Blue Girl', 'Cologne Carnival'
MODERN, LARGE-FLOWERED/HYBRID TEA, MAUVE,
REPEAT-FLOWERING

'Kölner Karneval' has large, full flowers with about 40 rather short petals that open to display neatly formed centers before the petals reflex and the shape becomes loosely cupped. They are borne either singly or in clusters in a pleasing shade of lilac-mauve, which shows bluish notes in periods of warm sunny weather. There is a light scent. It is one of the better garden performers in this color range, and is suitable for beds and borders. The plant grows vigorously with a bushy habit to average height or less, and has dark, leathery, glossy leaves. ZONES 4–9.

Kordes, Germany, 1964

Parentage unknown

Rome Gold Medal 1964

'Kölner Karneval'

'KÖNIGIN BEATRIX'   HetKORa
syn. 'Queen Beatrix'
MODERN, LARGE-FLOWERED/HYBRID TEA,
ORANGE BLEND, REPEAT-FLOWERING

This rose has flowers of peach and copper shades made up of 36 broad petals which form a larger bloom than the size of the buds leads one to expect. They are attractively formed, holding high centers for a long period while the outer petals reflex. Because of their lasting qualities they are useful for cutting and exhibition as well as for beds and borders. There is pleasant fragrance, considered by one judge to surpass that of the Old Garden Roses, and the blooms continue to appear through summer and autumn on wiry stems. The plant grows with an upright, bushy habit to average height and is well furnished with dark green, semi-glossy foliage. The variety was named in honor of the Queen of the Netherlands, who succeeded to the throne in 1980. ZONES 4–9.

Kordes, Germany, 1983

Seedling × 'Patricia'

'KÖNIGIN VON DÄNEMARK'
syn. 'Queen of Denmark'
OLD, ALBA, MEDIUM PINK

The flowers of this rose open from tight, stubby buds to flattish flowers packed full of bright deep pink petals. These can be up to 3 in (8 cm) across and exude an exquisite fragrance. The blooms appear in mid-summer in heavy clusters, sometimes so heavy that they bend the branches over in an arching fashion so that they almost touch the ground. It is a very thorny shrub to about 4 ft (1.2 m),

'Koba'

'Kiss'

K

covered with deep bluish green leaves—an attraction in themselves. While comparisons may be odious, this has to be one of the best of the Albas; it is an easy going rose that always exceeds expectations—except in very wet seasons when it does not fully open—even in the poorest soils. ZONES 4–10.

Booth, Denmark, 1826

Rosa alba × hybrid of unknown Damask

Royal Horticultural Society Award of Garden Merit 1993

'KONRAD ADENAUER'
syn. 'Konrad Adenauer Rose'

MODERN, LARGE-FLOWERED/HYBRID TEA, DARK RED, REPEAT-FLOWERING

Roses named for statesmen do not always measure up to expectations, and in one respect this variety falls literally short, for Adenauer was a big man and his namesake is a low grower. In other respects it is a pleasing rose, giving a good succession of well-formed deep blood red blooms through summer and autumn. They are of medium to large size, are borne singly or in small open clusters and open cupped, and they have a strong fragrance. In a bed or border and for cutting this is a useful variety, and it is also capable of providing exhi-

'Königin von Dänemark'

'Konrad Henkel'

bition blooms. It grows sturdily to below average height with an upright habit and has a covering of glossy light green foliage. From 1949 to 1963 Konrad Adenauer served as the first Chancellor of the West German Republic. ZONES 4–9.

Tantau, Germany, 1955

'Crimson Glory' × 'Hens Verschuren'

'KONRAD HENKEL'   KORjet
syn. 'Avenue's Red'

MODERN, LARGE-FLOWERED/HYBRID TEA, MEDIUM RED, REPEAT-FLOWERING

When the sun catches them there is a beautiful velvety sheen on the deep red petals of this variety, which form large, full-petalled roses borne sometimes singly and often in small open clusters on strong stems. The flowers have a pleasant light fragrance and continue to bloom freely through summer and autumn, being suitable for cutting as well as for use in beds and borders and as hedges. The plant grows vigorously with a stiff upright habit to average height and has dark green, semi-glossy leaves. The rose was named to mark the 75th birthday of one of the main architects of the post-war German economic revival. ZONES 4–9.

Kordes, Germany, 1983

Seedling × 'Red Planet'

'Konrad Adenauer'

'Kordes' Perfecta Superior'

'KORDES' BRILLANT   KORbisch
syn. 'Kordes' Brilliant'

MODERN, MODERN SHRUB, ORANGE BLEND, REPEAT-FLOWERING

The fully double flowers of 'Kordes' Brillant' are borne in big sprays and are quite large, neatly formed and of a most vibrant orange-red hue. They open cupped and, having stiff petals, hold their shape for a long time. There is a slight fragrance. The first flush of bloom is very prolific, and flowers continue to appear through summer and autumn. This gives good value in the garden where a hot color tone is required, and it also looks well in mixed borders and makes an effective screening plant. The plant grows strong and bushily to average height or more and has attractive bright green shiny leaves. ZONES 4–9.

Kordes, Germany, 1983

Seedling of 'Sympathie' × seedling

'KORDES' PERFECTA   KORalu
syn. 'Perfecta'

MODERN, LARGE-FLOWERED/HYBRID TEA, PINK BLEND, REPEAT-FLOWERING

A lady, seeing a bowl of this rose, commented 'They're not real, are they?', and on closer examination she and her friend decided they were not. The story proves how well this rose deserved its name, for at its best the symmetry of form is indeed 'perfect'. It needs fine warm weather, though, as it readily spoils in rain. The large blooms are blush pink edged pinky red, with up to 70 substantial petals forming high-pointed centers. There is a pleasant fragrance, which is evidently much stronger in warm climates than in cool ones. The plant continues to flower with remarkable freedom through summer and autumn, considering the size of its blooms. Having an upright and fairly compact habit it is very suitable for hedges, and also for beds, borders, as

'Kordes' Perfecta'

KORliam

standards and for cutting and exhibition. It grows vigorously to above average height and has lustrous dark foliage. **'Climbing Kordes' Perfecta'** (Japan Rose Society, Japan, 1962) is only currently listed by two growers, both of them in Australia, where the climate brings out the best of its fragrance and where wet weather is not likely to affect the blooms. It makes a vigorous plant and is likely to extend twice as far as the average climbing rose. In respect of flowers and leaves it is similar to the bush form. The Japan Rose Society, which discovered the sport, carries out its trials in Jindai Botanical Park, near Tokyo. The climbers to be assessed are trained on structures built like slatted tables, thus occupying lateral rather than vertical space, which encourages more flower and makes the plant easier both to prune and control and to judge. With a variety as vigorous as 'Climbing Kordes' Perfecta', this is obviously an advantageous method. ZONES 4–9.

Kordes, Germany, 1957

'Spek's Yellow' × 'Karl Herbst'

National Rose Society President's International Trophy 1957, Portland Gold Medal 1958

'KORDES' PERFECTA SUPERIOR'
syn. 'Perfecta Superior'

MODERN, LARGE-FLOWERED/HYBRID TEA, MEDIUM PINK, REPEAT-FLOWERING

This variety's claim of superiority is not reflected in its history, for it no longer appears to be in commerce whereas its parent is listed by over 30 growers. It is bright pink, and being a self color lacks the blush and pinky red marking that makes the original stand out so distinctively from other roses. Apart from the color it is similar. Sports rarely prove more popular than the rose they have originated from, though there are exceptions such as 'Lady Sylvia' (from 'Ophelia') and a number of climbing sports such as those from 'Étoile de Hollande' and 'Mrs Sam McGredy'. ZONES 4–9.

Kordes, Germany, 1963

Sport of 'Kordes' Perfecta'

KORLIAM

MODERN, LARGE-FLOWERED/HYBRID TEA, YELLOW BLEND, REPEAT-FLOWERING

KORliam is a large, exhibition rose containing 40 petals. The buds are huge and open to very well-formed blooms of deep cream flushed with pale pink and

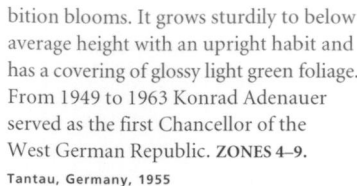

K

salmon. The growth is bronze maturing to pale green, but it is prone to black spot. The blooms are also inclined to ball in wet weather. It is a warm, dry-weather rose that appears to be available only in Australia and even then is only suitable for growing in warmer areas. ZONES 5–10.

Kordes, Germany, 1987

Parentage unknown

'KORONA'   KORnita

syn. 'Orange Korona'

MODERN, CLUSTER-FLOWERED/FLORIBUNDA, ORANGE-RED, REPEAT-FLOWERING

This rose's orange-scarlet blooms brought a bright and cheerful color to many gardens in the 1950s, and it was notable at the time because as they aged to salmon-pink they still toned in with the younger flowers. Up to that time the bright reds nearly all turned purple, creating a dreadful color clash. The lightly scented cupped blooms are fairly double, of medium to large size, and are carried boldly in trusses. They appear freely in summer and continue to repeat their flower through to autumn, performing well whatever the weather and giving excellent garden value as hedges and in beds and borders. The plant grows upright with a bushy habit to average height or more and is well furnished with olive green, semi-glossy leaves. ZONES 4–9.

Kordes, Germany, 1955

'Obergärtner Wiebicke' × 'Independence'

National Rose Society Gold Medal 1954

'KOROVO'

MODERN, LARGE-FLOWERED/HYBRID TEA, MEDIUM PINK, REPEAT-FLOWERING

The eye is attracted to the colorful petals of this variety, which are a pretty combination of light peach-pink with salmon-pink and tints of golden yellow. The large double blooms are shapely, opening from pointed buds to show high centers, and have a sweet and refreshing Tea fragrance. They appear freely in summer and continue to produce flowers through to autumn. 'Korovo' appears to be listed by only one nursery, although it is worth growing as a good example of a Large-flowered Rose that between the wars was a popular choice for garden and exhibition use. The plant grows vigorously with a bushy habit to average height and has thick olive green leaves. ZONES 4–9.

Leenders, The Netherlands, 1931

'Mrs T. Hillas' × 'Étoile de Hollande'

National Rose Society Trial Ground Certificate 1932

'Korona'

'Korovo'

'KO'S YELLOW'   MACkosyel

MODERN, MINIATURE, YELLOW BLEND, REPEAT-FLOWERING

The flowers of the rose are yellow, edged with red or deep pink fading to cream. The double florets with 39 petals have classic form. In warm weather the large blooms have a wonderful fragrance even the dullest of senses can detect. The large foliage is glossy mid- to dark green on a well-rounded, compact bush. Parentage of this rose is a complex combination of unusual breeding lines experimented with by Sam McGredy during the 1970s. It was named for Ko Schuurman, the wife of a close colleague and friend of the hybridizer. ZONES 5–11.

McGredy, New Zealand, 1978

('New Penny' × 'Banbridge') × ('Border Flame' × 'Manx Queen')

'KRISTIN'   BENmagic

MODERN, MINIATURE, RED BLEND, REPEAT-FLOWERING

'Kristin' has white flowers with a dramatic broad red edging on each and every petal. They are double (27–30 petals) and have a terrific consistent Large-flowered form. Blooms are usually borne one to a stem, or in small clusters on strong, straight stems. The foliage is semi-glossy and dark green, and it is a little large for the bloom size. This rose requires warm weather for the bloom to open fully and the color is more intense in hot climates, with the edging transcending deeper into each petal. The color combination is very striking with the edging giving definition to the classic shape of the blooms. In cooler climates only the outer petals seem to move, which leaves a cup and saucer shape to the florets. 'Kristin' is an award-winning variety that made its international exhibition debut in St Albans, England at the Royal National

'Kronprincessin Viktoria'

'Kristin'

'Ko's Yellow'

'Kwinana'

Rose Society National Miniature Show in 1995. It gathered up several key awards. ZONES 5–11.

Benardella, USA, 1992

DICmickey × 'Tinseltown'

American Rose Society Award of Excellence 1993

'KRISTO PIENAAR'   HERpot

MODERN, LARGE-FLOWERED/HYBRID TEA, YELLOW BLEND, REPEAT-FLOWERING

Professor Kristo Pienaar was a dynamic character who inspired not only his many students but also those where he lived. He was a most enthusiastic botanist and public-spirited man, and he stimulated improvement of the environment wherever he went. He also had a great interest in indigenous South African plants, which he promoted wherever he could. The rose named for him is striking for its beautiful bronze flowers that abundantly cover the medium-sized bush in summer. They are also very popular cut flowers, although there is no fragrance. ZONES 5–12.

Herholdt, South Africa, 1990

'Vienna Charm' × seedling

'KRONPRINCESSIN VIKTORIA'

syn. 'Kronprincessin Viktoria von Pruessen'

OLD, BOURBON, WHITE, REPEAT-FLOWERING

This rose has pure white, oval buds that are followed by milk white, large blooms with a light yellow center. During the flowering period from summer until autumn there are abundant blooms with

a strong Alba scent that are cupped and ruffled and 4 in (10 cm) across, and remain open for a long time. Like its parent, the flowers easily ball in wet weather. It is a vigorous, erect bush with short branches and light green leaves, and is an excellent choice for a small garden as it only reaches 3–4 ft (1–1.2 m). The crown princess (1840–1901) later became Empress Frederick of Prussia; she was the daughter of Queen Victoria of England. ZONES 4–10.

Volvert, Germany, 1887

Sport of 'Souvenir de la Malmaison'

'KWINANA'

MODERN, CLUSTER-FLOWERED/FLORIBUNDA, RED BLEND, REPEAT-FLOWERING

This variety makes an impact in the garden on account of its big clusters of brightly colored, single flowers. They are borne stiffly on strong and upright stems after the manner of the parent rose, 'Orange Triumph', and they open cupped from small plump buds; the color is crimson overlaid with carmine. There is a light fragrance, and the flowering display is well maintained through summer and into autumn. 'Kwinana' is still cultivated by one nursery in its country of origin, where it can be used to advantage in mixed borders. It makes a vigorous plant, taller than average, and it has ample leathery, matt green foliage. ZONES 4–9.

Riethmuller, Australia, 1962

'Orange Triumph' × seedling

'L. D. BRAITHWAITE' AUScrim
syns 'Braithwaite', 'Leonard Dudley Braithwaite'

MODERN, MODERN SHRUB, DARK RED, REPEAT-FLOWERING

The flowers of this variety are attractively formed. They are fairly large in size and have 40 or more petals, and they open to show a rounded form, with many petals infolded one against another in the center. The color is a rich even tone of dark crimson, and it holds well through the whole life of the flowers, which are borne singly and in wide-spaced clusters on firm, upright stems. They have a pleasing fragrance. The blooms continue to appear through summer and autumn and they withstand wet weather well. 'L. D. Braithwaite' makes a good rose to group in a border, the flower color consorting particularly well with older roses. Unfortunately the plant grows unevenly, so some flowers become lost amidst the younger growth, but generally this is a worthwhile variety, which grows sturdily to below average height and has gray-green leaves. ZONES 4–9.

Austin, UK, 1988

'The Squire' × 'Mary Rose'

'L. D. Braithwaite'

'La Belle Sultane'

'LA BELLE DISTINGUÉE'
syns 'La Petite Duchesse', 'Lee's Duchess', 'Scarlet Sweet Brier'

OLD, SWEET BRIAR, MEDIUM RED

A truly distinguished and popular rose, 'La Belle Distinguée' has fully double, small, flat, bright crimson blooms. Although there is no rebloom, the slightly fragrant rose makes up for it by providing a spectacular display in early summer. Reaching 5 ft (1.5 m), the compact, upright shrub displays dainty foliage that does not have much of the typical scent of this family. There are a few prickles and some small hips. It is a good candidate for a hedge or a woodland garden. ZONES 4–10.

Pre-1837

Parentage unknown

'LA BELLE SULTANE'
syns 'Belle Sultane', 'Gallica Maheca', 'Violacea'

OLD, GALLICA, DARK RED

The haunting color of this rose has helped to make its reputation. The spectrum of change includes mauve, purple, crimson, maroon and reddish violet, and the flowers pale to white at the base. After the round buds open, flat, almost single blooms with heart-shaped petals form around a crown of golden stamens. At times the fragrant petals appear to swirl. It is a tall shrub with an arching form and long canes covered with red bristles. 'La Belle Sultane' is an outstanding plant for the mixed border or for use as a hedge. A crop of round, red hips appears after the summer flowering. ZONES 4–10.

Probably from The Netherlands, 1700s, introduced in France by Dupont pre-1811

Parentage unknown

'LA BICHE'
OLD, NOISETTE, WHITE, REPEAT-FLOWERING

Although it is rarely seen today, this Noisette dramatically demonstrates how soil and climate can affect the color of a rose. Purple canes support white, well-

'La France'

formed blooms with a center of flesh pink. The cupped, large, globular flowers rise above long stems, and there is a pronounced Tea scent. The blooms are much lighter in full sun and poor soil. It is a vigorous rambler that takes at least 3 years to establish itself and continues to bloom from the end of spring until autumn. The name means 'The Doe' in English. It has a tendency to develop black spot. ZONES 4–10.

Trouillet, France, 1832

Parentage unknown

'LA BONNE MAISON'
MODERN, MODERN SHRUB, PINK BLEND, REPEAT-FLOWERING

Observant gardeners have been responsible for many improved rose forms and this is a good example, for it was noted by Mme Odile Masquelier of the Association les Roses Anciennes de La Bonne Maison. It resembles 'Francis E. Lester' in all particulars save one, and that is the period of flowering. Whereas the parent rose has a glorious burst of bloom in summer and, at best, just a few sporadic blooms in autumn, the seedling continues to give a good display after the main flush is over. The flowers are creamy white, single, borne in clusters, open cupped and are fragrant, and they appear on a very vigorous plant that extends twice as far as an average climbing rose. It has dark glossy leaves. 'La Bonne Maison' needs space, and is best grown where it can romp and look after itself. ZONES 4–9.

Masquelier, France, 1997

Seedling of 'Francis E. Lester'

'LA FOLLETTE'
MODERN, LARGE-FLOWERED CLIMBER, MEDIUM PINK, REPEAT-FLOWERING

The flowers of 'La Follette' open from long slender buds into urn-shaped flowers with the high centers and elegant form associated with Tea Roses. The earlier summer blooms are light rose pink, the color deepening to a kindly shade of carmine with the onset of warm weather. The scented flowers appear prolifically on their first flush and sporadically thereafter through summer and autumn. This variety needs protection from frost, so it is suitable in warm climates but difficult to establish out of doors elsewhere unless it is given a very large sheltered wall or big greenhouse. The growth is very vigorous, about three times the normal extent of a Climber,

'La France'

with many long, arching, free-branching stems. The best quality flowers are carried on new shoots made the previous year, so these should not be pruned. The plant is furnished with leaves that are large, long and somewhat limp. The French name means a lively, giddy young woman. ZONES 5–9.

Busby, France, pre-1867

Seedling of *Rosa gigantea*, perhaps crossed with 'Belle Portugaise'

'LA FRANCE'
MODERN, LARGE-FLOWERED/HYBRID TEA, LIGHT PINK, REPEAT-FLOWERING

This variety has long pointed buds that open into full-petalled light pink flowers with flushes of deeper pink on the petal reverse. They are high centered, have a fragrance that many praise and others find elusive, and continue in bloom through summer and autumn. The shape and texture of the flower, as well as the general refinement of the growth, sufficiently impressed 50 rosarians for it to be chosen out of 1000 candidates to bear their country's name, and it later came to be considered the first Large-flowered Rose. The plant grows vigorously to average height or below and has mid-green, semi-glossy foliage. Queries have been raised about the true identity of the rose offered by some growers; the variety sold by Ralph Moore of the USA was grown by his grandmother and has been known to him as 'La France' for over 80 years. **'Climbing La France'** was discovered in 1893 by Henderson in the USA. Since the full-petalled flowers of 'La France' tend to nod on their stems, it is therefore quite an advantage to plant the climber so that they can be viewed from below. ZONES 4–9.

Guillot, France, 1867

Perhaps 'Mme Victor Verdier' × 'Mme Bravy'; or a seedling of 'Mme Falcot'

'LA JOLLA'
MODERN, LARGE-FLOWERED/HYBRID TEA, PINK BLEND, REPEAT-FLOWERING

Today there are so many roses with blended coloring that it is hard to grasp what a novelty this one was 40 years ago. There is nothing strident about it though, for on a light peach-tinted base the petals are shaded and veined with rosy pink, yellow and red, all in gentle, pastel tones. The long elegant flowers are large and very full with over 60 petals, the outer ones seeming to outgrow those in the center and curling back at the tips to admit the heart of the flower to view. The lightly scented blooms withstand wet weather and continue to appear through summer and autumn. Though not apparently now in commerce, this was a good border rose and it is suitable for cutting. It grows with vigor to average height and has dark glossy leaves. It is named for a town in California (pronounced 'La Hoya'). ZONES 4–9.

Swim, USA, 1954

'Charlotte Armstrong' × 'Contrast'

National Rose Society Trial Ground Certificate 1955

'LA LOUISE'
syn. 'Louise'
OLD, GALLICA, DARK RED

This rose has semi-double, purple-crimson blooms that surround the yellow stamens. The fragrant petals pale to white at the base. In many ways this rose looks very much like 'La Belle Sultane', which may be the reason it has almost disappeared (at least under this name). ZONES 5–9.

Parmentier, Belgium, 1840

Parentage unknown

'LA MACULÉE'
OLD, GALLICA, RED BLEND

The large, full, semi-double, purple-crimson flowers of this rose are streaked with pink and are highly scented. It is a large shrub formed by slender, prickly canes. 'La Maculée', which has been a good seed parent for spotted and streaked Gallicas, was in Empress Josephine's collection at Malmaison. ZONES 5–9.

Dupont, France, 1810

Parentage unknown

'LA MARNE'
MODERN, POLYANTHA, PINK BLEND, REPEAT-FLOWERING

Many Polyantha Roses have disappeared, but this example has survived thanks to its vigor and general charm. The semi-double flowers, borne freely in well-filled clusters, are reminiscent of apple blossom, being rosy blush with bright salmon-rose towards the edges of the petals. They continue in bloom through summer and autumn but do not have much fragrance. This variety is particularly useful for borders and as a specimen plant in a container, and it is well worth including as a fine example of its type in a garden of rose history. The plant is vigorous, growing evenly to above average height, and it has a shrubby habit. It is almost thornless, with dark green shiny leaves that are held on the plant to a late stage in winter. ZONES 4–9.

Barbier, France, 1915

'Mme Norbert Levavasseur' × 'Comtesse du Cayla'

'LA MARSEILLAISE'   DELgeot
syn. 'Isobel Champion'
MODERN, LARGE-FLOWERED/HYBRID TEA, DARK RED, REPEAT-FLOWERING

The plump buds of this variety correctly indicate that a big flower is on the way.

The blooms have about 40 petals and are well formed, opening with high centers and maintaining a good symmetry of form as the petals expand. They are velvety deep scarlet in color and have a pleasing fragrance. After the first flush blooming is well maintained through summer and autumn, making this suitable in beds and borders and also to grow for cutting. It seems to do particularly well in warmer climates, making a handsome vigorous bush of average height or more with light green foliage. ZONES 4–9.

Delbard-Chabert, France, 1976

(['Glory of Rome' × 'Impeccable'] × ['Rouge Meilland' × 'Soraya']) × (MEIsar × 'Walko')

'LA MORTOLA'
syn. *Rosa brunonii* 'La Mortola'
MODERN, LARGE-FLOWERED CLIMBER, WHITE

This is an extra fine form of *Rosa brunonii*, with clusters of small silky petalled white flowers that open wide to display yellow stamens. There is a good musky fragrance. The summer blooming is spectacular, but it does not repeat its flower. This variety should be grown where there is ample space, for its vigor is such that it can extend 4 times as far as the average climbing rose, producing very long arching growths that will bush out over trees, walls and hedgerows. It is not tolerant of frost and therefore needs careful placement, since the right conditions for so large a plant are hard to provide. The leaves are long, limp, gray-green and downy. It is named after the Hanburys' famous garden in Italy, from where E. A. Bunyard brought stock to the UK; it was introduced some years later by Graham Thomas. ZONES 5–9.

Hanbury, UK, 1954

Form of *Rosa moschata nepalensis*

'LA NEIGE'
OLD, GALLICA, WHITE

The experts on Gallicas agree that this is a confusing item. Susan Verrier thinks it may be the same as a Gallica-Centifolia hybrid of 1838 called 'Boule de Neige', and François Joyaux points out that the raiser's firm listed it as a Centifolia, and that a completely white rose cannot be classified as a Gallica. 'La Neige' is described as having double white blooms with a hint of green in the petals. The flowers are fragrant. ZONES 5–10.

Robert, France, 1853

Parentage unknown

'LA NOBLESSE'
OLD, CENTIFOLIA, LIGHT PINK

This rose, which deserves to be better known, has flowers that are at first rather high centered but open flat and fairly full to about 3 in (8 cm) across. They are bright deep pink, paling with age to softer shades, and when fully open they expose brownish stamens. The petals are of a silky texture, which adds considerably to their charm, and are superbly scented. A broad, upright shrub that grows to about 5 ft (1.5 m) high, it has plentiful dark green, rather coarse foliage in the typical Centifolia mold. Little is

'La Perla'

'La Marne'

'La Marseillaise'

known about this rose and it may have been introduced under a different name, but whatever its provenance it is well worth space in any garden. ZONES 5–10.

Circa 1856

Parentage unknown

'LA PALOMA 85'   TANamola
syn. 'The Dove'
MODERN, CLUSTER-FLOWERED/FLORIBUNDA, WHITE, REPEAT-FLOWERING

'La Paloma 85' has brilliant creamy white flowers that reveal glimpses of gold in the depths of the petals as they open. The first flowers are often borne singly, but later ones frequently appear in close clusters of up to 12 blooms. They are full petalled, not very fragrant, and stand up well to wet weather; they continue to appear through summer and autumn. This is a useful rose for beds and borders, and to grow for cutting. It grows vigorously with an upright, bushy habit to below average height, and is well furnished with leathery, shiny and robust leaves. The name means, as the synonym reveals, 'The Dove'. ZONES 4–9.

Tantau, Germany, 1985

Parentage unknown

'LA PERLA'   KORlaper
MODERN, CLUSTER-FLOWERED/FLORIBUNDA, LIGHT PINK, REPEAT-FLOWERING

This is one of Kordes' pink cut-flower varieties that is also a great garden rose in warmer climates. The beautifully formed buds open slowly to lovely flowers of a soft pink slightly flushed with carmine. They last very well when picked, and do not lose their delicate coloring. Flower production is good, as

the repeat cycle is very fast. It is a healthy plant that is low to medium in height. 'La Perla' is a fine rose for bedding and for borders. ZONES 5–10.

Kordes, Germany, 1994

Parentage unknown

'LA PERLE'
MODERN, RAMBLER, LIGHT YELLOW

A strange brownish tint covers the buds of this rose before they open to reveal pale yellow to white blooms. The double, large flowers, which are cupped at first and then open flat, have quilled, fragile-looking petals. There is a strong, green apple fragrance during the early summer blooming. This is a tall, vigorous bush covered in shiny, dark green foliage, the young leaves being edged with carmine. The pliable, 30 ft (9 m) canes are easily trained on a trellis or arch, or are happy climbing a tree. ZONES 4–11.

Fauque and Fils, France, 1905

'Madame Hoste' × *Rosa wichuraiana*

'LA PLUS BELLE DES PONCTUÉES'
OLD, GALLICA, PINK BLEND

The large, loosely flat, deep rose blooms of this rose are spotted with a pale pink. The crumpled blossoms have muddled centers, and there is a strong fragrance during its summer flowering. The color only remains true in the shade; it fades in the sun. This is a robust shrub of 4–6 ft (1.2–1.8 m) that produces abundant, bright green foliage. It does well in poor soil. ZONES 4–10.

Probably 1800s; sometimes credited to Hebert, 1829, the name is not recorded before 1929

Parentage unknown

L

'La Reine'

'La Sévillana'

'LA REINE'
syns 'Reine des Français', 'Rose de la Reine'
OLD, HYBRID PERPETUAL, MEDIUM PINK,
REPEAT-FLOWERING

'La Reine' has indeed reigned ever since
its introduction in France over a century
and a half ago; its outstanding quality as
a cut flower during a long blooming
season may account for this popularity.
After the fat, high-centered buds open,
glossy rose pink blooms appear that are
tinged with lilac. The large globular
flowers with 78 petals have inner petals
that fold back upon themselves. The
plant reaches 4 ft (1.2 m), and needs support when young. The pale green leaves
have wavy edges, and there are some
prickles on the smooth bark. This rose
thrives best in rich soil, and deadheading
will help increase the autumn flowering.
Laffay produced many lovely roses, including 'Cardinal de Richelieu' and 'La
Vésuve'. ZONES 5–10.

Laffay, France, 1842

Possibly a seedling of 'William Jesse'

'La Sévillana'

'LA SÉVILLANA'   MEIgekanu
syn. 'Sévillana'
MODERN, CLUSTER-FLOWERED/FLORIBUNDA,
ORANGE-RED, REPEAT-FLOWERING

This rose produces lightly scented deep
bright vermilion flowers in clusters of up
to 5 on long flexible stems. They are of
medium size, are formed with neat
centers, and become cupped as they
open. The first flush of flower is very
colorful and showy, and more blooms
are produced with good continuity
through summer and autumn. The
growth is dense, leafy and shrubby, making this a good variety for hedges as well
as beds and borders. It grows somewhat
taller and wider than the average Cluster-flowered Rose. The leaves are dark
green and glossy. ZONES 4–9.

Meilland, France, 1978

([MEIbrim × 'Jolie Madame'] × ['Zambra' ×
'Zambra']) × (['Tropicana' × 'Tropicana'] ×
['Poppy Flash' × 'Rusticana'])

Anerkannte Deutsche Rose 1979, Belfast
Certificate of Merit 1984

'LA VILLE DE BRUXELLES'
OLD, DAMASK, DEEP PINK

This variety has large flowers, up to 3 in
(8 cm) wide when fully open. The
blooms are arranged in well-spaced clusters and appear in mid-summer. They

are consistently clear bright pink in color
and are fragrant. Each bloom is full of
reflexing petals and usually has a tight
button eye in the center. This upright
though dense shrub grows to some 5 ft
(1.5 m) high with dark green, fairly
thorny stems. The substantial foliage is a
rich mid-green. It is not too happy in wet
weather, but the little extra care required
is well worth it. ZONES 5–10.

Vibert, France, 1849

Parentage unknown

Royal Horticultural Society Award of Garden
Merit 1993

'L'ABONDANCE'
OLD, NOISETTE, WHITE/LIGHT PINK

'L'Abondance' is one of the lesser-known
Noisettes, producing flesh pink, double
blooms that are borne in well-spaced
clusters of 50–100 flowers. There is some
fragrance. The plant is an extremely vigorous rambler, reaching 10 ft (3 m) in
2 years, that can be used as a climber on
pillars or pergolas; it does well in poor
soil. The foliage is shiny and light green.
The firm of Moreau et Robert has produced other famous roses including
'Marbrée' and 'Homère'. ZONES 5–10.

Moreau et Robert, France, 1877

Parentage unknown

'LACE CASCADE'   JACarch
MODERN, LARGE-FLOWERED CLIMBER, WHITE,
REPEAT-FLOWERING

Bill Warriner raised 17 white or near
white varieties, and this is the only
Climber among them. The lightly
scented blooms are full and of medium
to large size. They are produced usually
in clusters on short stems and they open
out wide showing the stamens, with the
petals layered one row upon another,
giving a charming effect. Blooming continues through summer and autumn.
This climber, which looks good against a
wall or fence or on an arch or pillar,
grows sturdily with long arching canes
but does not extend much beyond the
average height and width expected of a
climber, renewing itself by means of new
shoots from near the base. The foliage is
glossy and dark green. ZONES 4–9.

Warriner, USA, 1992

'Iceberg' × 'Prairie Fire'

'LADY ALICE STANLEY'
MODERN, LARGE-FLOWERED/HYBRID TEA, PINK
BLEND, REPEAT-FLOWERING

An old Large-flowered Rose still commercially available after 90 years must
have something special about it. Vigor
and general good health are two reasons,
and another is surely the pretty formation of the flowers, in which the many
petals—sometimes numbering over
70—overlap and support one another
in regular formation. The color is deep
coral rose on the outside of the petals
and pale flesh pink inside and the fragrant
blooms maintain good continuity of
flowering through summer and autumn.
This variety lasts well when cut, and deserves a place in a garden of historic
roses. The plant grows with an upright,
branching habit to average height and
has rather sparse, rich green leathery foliage. ZONES 4–9.

McGredy, UK, 1909

Parentage unknown

National Rose Society Gold Medal 1908

'La Ville de Bruxelles'

'Lady Alice Stanley'

'L'Abondance'

'Lady Barbara'

'LADY BARBARA'   CHEwba

MODERN, LARGE-FLOWERED CLIMBER, ORANGE BLEND, REPEAT-FLOWERING

There are not many climbers of a warm orange tone; this one is tangerine on the inside of the petals, with an orange-yellow reverse. The blooms are double with about 20 petals, are often borne in clusters, and are formed like medium-sized Large-flowered Roses, which when taken young are useful for cutting. There is some fragrance, and flowers continue to appear sporadically through summer and autumn after the main flush has ended. In hot weather the flower color is liable to fade. This makes an ideal pillar rose, being stiff in its growth, or it can be trained on a wall or fence. The habit is upright, and it does not spread to the same extent as many climbing roses. The leaves are mid-green and semi-glossy. ZONES 4–9.

Warner, UK, 1987

'Red Planet' × ('Elizabeth of Glamis' × ['Galway Bay' × 'Sutter's Gold'])

Geneva Certificate of Merit 1984

'LADY CURZON'

MODERN, HYBRID RUGOSA, MEDIUM PINK, REPEAT-FLOWERING

The rose pink blooms of this variety are large and open their 5 crinkled petals like shallow saucers, displaying handsome golden stamens. Their refinement and delicacy is at odds with the character of the plant, which is very vigorous, producing prickly, arching stems that are capable of clambering through bushes and low trees and of being trained up as a climber on a strong support. It therefore needs plenty of space, and is suitable for a border among big plants for it is twice as high and 3 times as wide as the average shrub rose. The flowers are produced freely in summertime and have a light scent, and the foliage is rough, robust and mid- to dark green. This prickly, tangly, coarse-looking shrub can hardly be termed ladylike, and one wonders what Lady Curzon, the wife of the Viceroy of India, really thought of it. ZONES 4–9.

Turner, UK, 1901

Rosa macrantha × R. rugosa rubra

'LADY DIANA'

syn. 'Lady Di'

MODERN, LARGE-FLOWERED/HYBRID TEA, LIGHT PINK, REPEAT-FLOWERING

'Lady Diana' is grown mainly for the cut-flower trade. The blooms, of a very

'Climbing Lady Hillingdon'

delicate light pink shade, are borne singly or in small sprays. When young they are long and slender, and as their 30 or so petals expand they create a fairly large flower of classic Large-flowered form. There is a slight fragrance, and the continuity of bloom through summer and autumn, is good. In warmer climates this can be cultivated out of doors. The plant growth is tall and upright, and it has matt medium green leaves. ZONES 5–9.

Hoy, USA, 1986

'Sonia' × 'Caress'

'LADY ELGIN'   MEmaj

syn. 'Thaïs'

MODERN, LARGE-FLOWERED/HYBRID TEA, YELLOW BLEND, REPEAT-FLOWERING

The plump buds of 'Lady Elgin' give a true indication of the large flowers that follow. They are borne on long firm stems, are very full with about 40 petals and open with high centers, later becoming cupped. The color, a light orange-yellow with a pinkish overlay, is well held as the petals age. There is some scent, and flowering continues through summer and autumn. For general garden use in beds and borders this has been widely used in the past, though it is little grown today. The plant is moderately vigorous and grows with a bushy, upright habit to below average height. It has dark leathery leaves. ZONES 4–9.

Meilland, France, 1954

'Mme Kriloff' × ('Peace' × 'Genève')

'LADY GAY'

MODERN, RAMBLER, ORANGE-PINK

The breeder of 'Lady Gay' felt it was an improvement over his other creation, 'Dorothy Perkins', but the former never achieved the popularity of its stablemate. The double, salmon-pink blooms are small to medium sized and appear both in sprays and clusters on the long, pliable canes. Fragrant and proliferous, the flowers resemble 'Dorothy Perkins' but have a stronger resistance to mildew, which has always plagued the other rose. The glossy foliage is small and dark green, and and it has a vigorous growth habit, reaching 20 ft (6 m) in two years. Experts find it difficult to tell the difference between the two roses except for the fact that 'Lady Gay' is stronger and healthier. Walsh also created 'Evangeline', 'Excelsa' and 'Minnehaha'. ZONES 4–10.

Walsh, USA, 1905

Rosa wichuraiana × 'Bardou Job'

'LADY GODIVA'

MODERN, RAMBLER, LIGHT PINK

Discovered by Paul, this is another offspring of 'Dorothy Perkins', and there are white and red sports as well. Clusters of small, very double flowers appear on the 30 ft (9 m) canes during its summer season; it has been described by some as one of the finest Cluster-flowered Ramblers. The cameo-pink blooms are delicately shaded and deeper in the center. Almost evergreen, this vigorous Rambler can easily cover a pillar or pergola in a few seasons. ZONES 4–10.

Paul, UK, 1908

Sport of 'Dorothy Perkins'

'LADY HILLINGDON'

OLD, TEA, YELLOW BLEND, REPEAT-FLOWERING

Popular around the world, this Tea Rose offers a wide range of colors during its extended blooming period. The long, pointed buds open to flat, deep apricot-yellow blooms that fade in the sun. The large, thin petals are semi-double and hang down in a blowzy fashion. There are attractive stamens, a few prickles and a strong, tea fragrance. Red-bronze when young, the somewhat sparse, attractive foliage lines the thin canes. It is one of the healthiest of roses and is a lovely cut flower. **'Climbing Lady Hillingdon'**, (Hicks, USA, 1917) blooms from late spring until the approach of winter. Although easy to train on a structure it takes time to establish itself. ZONES 5–10.

Lowe and Shawyer, UK, 1910

'Papa Gontier' × 'Mme Hoste'

'LADY HUNTINGFIELD'

MODERN, LARGE-FLOWERED/HYBRID TEA, MEDIUM YELLOW, REPEAT-FLOWERING

The flowers of this rose are yellow with a touch of golden apricot, paler on the reverse. They are rounded in form and are well filled with spoon-shaped, rather soft-textured petals that jostle for space in the open blooms, creating a pleasingly informal, muddled center. There is an appreciable fragrance, and continuity of bloom is well maintained through summer and autumn. This variety is currently offered only in Australia, where there has been a revival of interest in the varieties raised by Alister Clark. The warmer climate there suits its use for general garden purposes. The plant grows vigorously with a bushy habit to average height and has glossy olive green leaves. ZONES 5–9.

Clark, Australia, 1937

'Busybody' × 'Aspirant Marcel Rouyer'

'Lady Huntingfield'

'Lady Curzon'

'Lady Elgin'

'Lady Elgin'

'LADY ILIFFE'

MODERN, LARGE-FLOWERED/HYBRID TEA, MEDIUM
RED, REPEAT-FLOWERING

An important feature of this rose is its
scent, which is rich, sweet and enduring.
The flowers are a bold strong color
usually described as tyrian rose, on the
border between dark pink and red, and
they are large, with nearly 40 broad
petals making up the high-centered,
long-lasting blooms. Flowering continues through summer and autumn.
This is a useful rose to plant by a path
or near the front of a border where the
scent can best be appreciated. 'Lady
Iliffe' grows to average height with a
bushy habit and is generously furnished
with large olive green foliage. The variety
was chosen by the lady whose name it
bears. ZONES 4–9.

Gandy, UK, 1976

'Saul' × 'Wendy Cussons'

'LADY IN RED'   JACopper

MODERN, LARGE-FLOWERED/HYBRID TEA, MEDIUM
RED, REPEAT-FLOWERING

This variety bears large, velvety, bright
red florets with outstanding symmetry
and substance. They are double, with a
light fragrance, and appear singly on
strong, straight, long stems that are suitable for cutting. The flowers last a long

time on the tall, upright bush, and the
repeat-cycle time is excellent. 'Lady in
Red' is disease resistant and weatherproof. ZONES 5–11.

Warriner, USA, 1997

Parentage unknown

'LADY LIKE'   TANekily

MODERN, LARGE-FLOWERED/HYBRID TEA, PINK
BLEND, REPEAT-FLOWERING

'Lady Like' has pointed buds that open
into somewhat low-centered flowers that
are made up of over 30 petals. The color
is a rich shade of deep pink, and they
have a touch of yellow at their base.
The petals open wide, which creates a
colorful effect on the free-flowering
bushes during the main season's flush,
after which a satisfactory continuity of
bloom is maintained through summer
and autumn. The flowers have a moderate fragrance and are able to withstand
bad weather well. 'Lady Like' is a dependable rose to use in beds and borders
and it is good to cut for the house,
thanks to its long flower stems. The plant
has a bushy and fairly even growth habit
to about average height and has a good
covering of glossy deep green, leathery
leaves. ZONES 4–9.

Tantau, Germany, 1989

Parentage unknown

'Lady Iliffe'

'Lady Mann'

'Lady Mavis Pilkington'

'Lady Mary Fitzwilliam'

'LADY MACROBERT'   COClent

MODERN, CLUSTER-FLOWERED/FLORIBUNDA,
APRICOT BLEND, REPEAT-FLOWERING

The flowers of this rose look like small-
scale Large-flowered Roses, being full of
petals and neatly formed. They are carried in large, well-spaced clusters and
open to show light apricot with deeper
shades. There is a modest fragrance, and
the continuity of bloom through summer and autumn is well maintained. As
a bedding and border rose this is a good
performer, and the number of blooms it
carries makes it a very useful resource for
cutting for small flower arrangements.
The plant is a vigorous grower, with an
upright compact habit to average height
or below, and it bears light green, semi-
glossy leaves. It was named to mark the
golden jubilee of the MacRobert Trusts,
established by Lady MacRobert in 1943,
which serves a variety of charitable
causes in the UK. ZONES 4–9.

Cocker, UK, 1993

'Clydebank Centenary' × seedling

Glasgow Silver Medal 1996

'LADY MANN'

MODERN, LARGE-FLOWERED/HYBRID TEA, PINK
BLEND, REPEAT-FLOWERING

This is one of the few roses bred from
'Lorraine Lee', and it has much of its
parent's growth habit. It is a strong bush
with abundant, large matt green foliage.
The attractive, pointed buds open to
rather loose full blooms. The flowers are
a deep coral pink and there is a strong
fragrance. Flower production is extremely high and repeat-bloom is very
rapid. This rose can be lightly pruned to
form a large shrub covered with blooms
5 or 6 times a year, or it can be pruned
hard in autumn in mild climates to en-
able it to flower in winter, where its long
buds take much longer to develop and
last longer. 'Lady Mann' makes a first-
class hedge or can be used in the shrubbery. ZONES 5–10.

Clark, Australia, 1940

'Lorraine Lee' × seedling

'LADY MARY FITZWILLIAM'

MODERN, LARGE-FLOWERED/HYBRID TEA, LIGHT
PINK, REPEAT-FLOWERING

This is one of the best known names in
the history of the modern rose, but the
impressions it made at the time of its introduction were mixed. It tends to put
much strength into forming perfect
flowers at the expense of growth, and
therefore it delighted rose exhibitors.

'Lady MacRobert'

The Secretary of Britain's National Rose
Society gave his opinion of its worth as a
garden plant by saying that it would be
difficult to find a weaker and more unsatisfactory grower than 'Lady Mary
Fitzwilliam'. In view of that, it is surprising first that it should have become one
of the most influential pollen parents
behind the modern roses of today, and
second that it could survive for more
than a century and still be found in nursery lists, though it is hard to be certain if
the variety offered is the right one. It has
pale flesh pink blooms of regular form
that are globular, full, long lasting and
scented. They are repeat-flowering and
are borne on short branches on a plant
of below average height that has matt
green foliage. ZONES 5–9.

Bennett, UK, 1882

'Devoniensis' × 'Victor Verdier'

'LADY MAVIS PILKINGTON'

KORlitze

MODERN, LARGE-FLOWERED/HYBRID TEA, YELLOW
BLEND, REPEAT-FLOWERING

The flowers of 'Lady Mavis Pilkington'
are large and high centered, with many
broad petals in cheerful shades of
orange-yellow with flushes of red on
the inner petal surfaces, giving a two-
toned effect as the blooms unfold. The
flowers are borne on long stems with
surprising freedom considering their
size, and are excellent for cutting as well
as for growing in beds and borders.
There is a light fragrance, and the continuity of bloom is well maintained
through summer and autumn. The plant
grows vigorously with an upright,
branching habit to average height or
more and is well furnished with shiny
dark green foliage. This rose was named
for a keen rose lover who is a Vice Patron
of the Royal National Rose Society.
ZONES 4–9.

Kordes, Germany, 1992

(Seedling × 'Sunblest') × 'Yankee Doodle'

'LADY MEILLAND'   MEIalzonite

MODERN, LARGE-FLOWERED/HYBRID TEA, ORANGE-
PINK, REPEAT-FLOWERING

The flowers on this rose are a gentle
shade of salmon with hints of vermilion-
orange. Urn-shaped, the blooms are of

medium size for a Large-flowered Rose and are well filled with large petals that open to show high centers and symmetrical form. They are borne on long stems and last well so are excellent to cut, as well as being useful in the garden where the vigor of the plant makes it good in borders and bedding schemes. The continuity of flower is well maintained through summer and autumn, though the blooms can be spoilt in wet weather. This variety grows sturdily with a spreading, free-branching habit, usually to above average height, and has ample dark green shiny foliage that sometimes proves susceptible to rust. ZONES 4–9.

Meilland, France, 1986

Parentage unknown

New Zealand Gold Medal 1982

'LADY MITCHELL'   HARyearn

MODERN, LARGE-FLOWERED/HYBRID TEA, MEDIUM RED, REPEAT-FLOWERING

Deep red pointed buds on this variety open into flowers of large size, made up of 50 petals that are an even and rich shade of rose red. They are borne usually singly, sometimes in 3s, on long firm stems and are good for cutting as they last well. They become cupped as they open, with the petal tips attractively arrayed layer upon layer. There is a pleasant light fragrance, and bloom production through summer and autumn is very well maintained both in quantity and quality. The neat growth of this variety makes this a good choice for bedding as well as for borders and hedges. The plant grows vigorously with a bushy habit to average height or less and has a generous provision of semi-glossy leaves. It was chosen by Peter Green of Bermuda to be named for his mother-in-law. ZONES 4–9.

Harkness, UK, 1990

'Dr Darley' × 'Silver Jubilee'

'LADY OF SKY'

MODERN, LARGE-FLOWERED/HYBRID TEA, ORANGE-RED, REPEAT-FLOWERING

This oddly named rose enjoyed only a few years in commerce, despite good qualities of growth inherited from its seed parent and its repeat-flowering ability. It is orange-red in color and bears high-centered blooms of over 30 petals, which become cupped as they open out. The blooms, which withstand wet weather well and have a light fragrance,

'Lady Meilland'

'Lady Roberts'

are carried on long stems so are useful for cutting. This variety is suitable for use as a hedge as well as for planting in borders or to make a bed where a taller variety is required. The plant grows vigorously with an upright habit to above average height and has a covering of large dark green leaves. ZONES 4–9.

Gregory, UK, 1974

'Queen Elizabeth' × seedling

'LADY OF THE DAWN'

INTerlada

MODERN, CLUSTER-FLOWERED/FLORIBUNDA, LIGHT PINK, REPEAT-FLOWERING

This rose is variously described as a Cluster-flowered Rose and as a Modern Shrub. It produces long stiff shoots that become bowed under the weight of the blossoms, which can easily number 20 or more in the cluster. The lightly scented flowers are creamy blush and rimmed pink around the petal edges. They are fairly large, semi-double and open like saucers to reveal red and gold stamens. Blooming continues through summer and autumn. This is very suitable for making a hedge, including in a border or planting in a bed where a sizeable grower is required, for it is capable of growing to the dimensions of an average shrub rose. It grows vigorously with an upright, arching habit and has dark green leathery leaves. ZONES 4–9.

Ilsink, The Netherlands, 1984

INTerdress × 'Stadt den Helder'

'LADY PENZANCE'

OLD, SWEET BRIAR, ORANGE-PINK

Looking quite elegant, 'Lady Penzance' is the best of the large crop of Sweet Briar hybrids created by Lord Penzance at the end of the nineteenth century. The cupped, single, salmon-pink blooms are flushed with a coppery pink and grow

'Lady of Sky'

'Lady of the Dawn'

'Lady Rachel'

yellow towards the edges, and they are studded with yellow stamens. There is little evidence of the apple scent associated with these hybrids, except in the foliage. The 6 ft (1.8 m) shrub has an arching form with dark, dense foliage and bright red hips. It is prone to black spot during the summer flowering, but is nevertheless a vigorous bush that is an ideal subject for a tall hedge or in a woodland garden. ZONES 5–10.

Penzance, UK, 1894

Rosa eglanteria × R. foetida bicolor

'LADY RACHEL'   CANdoodle

MODERN, CLUSTER-FLOWERED/FLORIBUNDA, NEAR WHITE, REPEAT-FLOWERING

The charm of this rose lies in the form of the flowers, which have incurving, waxen-looking petals towards the center of the blooms that part sufficiently to reveal golden stamens at their heart. They do particularly well in a warm climate, where they grow large and open almost flat, looking attractive at each stage. They are creamy white and yield a pleasing fragrance; flowering continues through summer and autumn. This is very effective for bedding and for near the front of a border with taller subjects behind. The

plant grows with an upright habit to average height or less and has light green leaves. It was named to honor the memory of Lady Alport, well known for her involvement in the Girl Guide movement, who died in 1983. ZONES 4–9.

Cant, UK, 1990

'English Miss' × 'Margaret Merril'

'LADY ROBERTS'

OLD, TEA, APRICOT BLEND, REPEAT-FLOWERING

This rose loves a warm spot in the garden, and will repay any effort to please it with abundant blooms from late spring until autumn. The long, pointed buds open to reveal rich, reddish apricot blooms with a coppery base. Sometimes the petals appear orange at the edge, the colors varying depending on their placement in sun or shade. The big, blowzy blooms have a strong tea fragrance and nod on the bushy plant, the olive green leaves being an attractive background to them. Its usual size is 4 ft (1.2 m), but if left unpruned it can be trained as a small climber. It also does well as a container plant. This rose does not mind wet weather. ZONES 5–10.

Cant, UK, 1902

Bud sport of 'Anna Olivier'

'Lady Meilland'

L

'Lady Rose'

'Lady Romsey'

'LADY ROMSEY'

MODERN, CLUSTER-FLOWERED/FLORIBUNDA,
NEAR WHITE, REPEAT-FLOWERING

The flowers of this variety begin as rather squat buds with reddish tints, which give little idea of the beauty to come. They open into fully double, high-centered creamy white blooms that become large and saucer shaped as the petals reflex, disclosing a hint of golden stamens. As the flowers age they sometimes admit touches of blush pink, and there is a light fragrance; the blooms continue to appear through summer and autumn. A short grower, it can be used to front a border or for a bed and is also suitable for growing under glass and to cut for small floral arrangements. The plant grows with a bushy, upright growth habit to not much more than half average height and has glossy light green leaves that have a pinkish tinge when young. Lady Romsey is from Broadlands in Hampshire. ZONES 4–9.

Beales, UK, 1985

('Fragrant Cloud' × 'Pascali') × seedling

'LADY ROSE'   KORlady

MODERN, LARGE-FLOWERED/HYBRID TEA,
ORANGE-PINK, REPEAT-FLOWERING

This variety produces long pointed buds, borne singly or several together, that open into large high-centered blooms. They consist of over 30 petals, which reflex so that the flowers become cupped as they open out. They are salmon-red with an orange cast, a warm and bright color, appear with remarkable freedom through summer and autumn, and have a pleasant fragrance. They are also good to cut for floral arrangements. It is an excellent garden plant for hedges, beds and borders and is especially well suited for growing in standard form. It makes a vigorous plant with an upright habit, growing to above average height, and is well furnished with dark green, semi-glossy leaves. ZONES 4–9.

Kordes, Germany, 1979

Seedling × 'Traumerei'

Belfast Gold Medal 1981

'LADY STUART'

OLD, CHINA, LIGHT PINK, REPEAT-FLOWERING

'Lady Stuart' has large, fresh pink blooms that open with the outer petals reflexing. The full, quartered flowers are globular, and the color deepens towards the center. In the sun the blooms fade to white. In any weather or temperature this is one of the most attractive China Roses in the garden. It is a vigorous, bushy, upright shrub that is covered with dull green leaves and prickles. The blooming season is long and finishes with a crop of small hips. ZONES 5–10.

Portemer, France, 1851

Parentage unknown

'LADY SUNBLAZE'   MEllarco

syns 'Lady Meillandina', 'Peace
Meillandina', 'Peace Sunblaze'

MODERN, MINIATURE, LIGHT PINK,
REPEAT-FLOWERING

This rose, raised by Marie-Louisette Meilland, has pale orient pink to light coral pink, fully double flowers with 40 petals which have no fragrance. The delicate blooms are usually borne on short stems and the repeat cycle is fast. The color is excellent on first opening but unfortunately fades all too quickly. The foliage is an attractive glossy dark green on a plant with a compact, bushy, yet upright growth habit. All in all, 'Lady Sunblaze' makes a great garden display because of its ability to resist most rose diseases, its quick repeat cycle and the fact that it is nearly always in bloom. It is an ideal choice for growing in a container. ZONES 5–11.

Meilland, France, 1985

('Fashion' × 'Zambra') × 'Belle Meillandina'

'LADY SYLVIA'

MODERN, LARGE-FLOWERED/HYBRID TEA, LIGHT
PINK, REPEAT-FLOWERING

The creamy rose pink flowers of this sweet-scented rose are among the loveliest one could wish to see. The young petal tips part to reveal deeper tints of pink and a hint of gold at the heart of the bloom which, although it opens rather fast, maintains a pleasing rounded outline until the petals fall. This is a rose much grown formerly by florists, and many brides have carried it in their bouquets. It is worth its place in the border as a historic rose and is a great resource for buttonholes and as a cut flower. The plant blooms through summer and autumn and grows quite vigorously, with a branching habit, to average height or more. It is long lived and sometimes survives in old gardens where other roses have disappeared. The leaves are dark green and by modern standards rather sparse. 'Climbing Lady Sylvia' (1933) is a marketable, vigorous but low-growing climbing sport with pink-blended flowers. ZONES 4–9.

Stevens, UK, 1926

Sport of 'Mme Butterfly'

'Lady Sunblaze'

'Lady Sylvia'

'Lady Waterlow'

'LADY TAYLOR'   SMltling
MODERN, CLUSTER-FLOWERED/FLORIBUNDA, ORANGE-RED, REPEAT-FLOWERING

This little-grown variety is a soothing shade of light vermilion on the inside of the petals, with orange-yellow veined red on the reverse. The flowers, which are made up of some 36 petals, are like small-scale Large-flowered Roses and appear large for the size of the plant. They are carried in clusters and are lightly scented, and flowering is maintained through summer and autumn with good continuity. This rose is useful for small spaces, to front a border or to plant in a container. It is sturdy and has a bushy growth habit, growing to about half average height. It has matt green foliage. ZONES 4–9.

Smith, UK, 1984

'Elizabeth of Glamis' × 'Topsi'

'LADY TRENT'
syn. 'Julia Ferran'
MODERN, LARGE-FLOWERED/HYBRID TEA, ORANGE BLEND, REPEAT-FLOWERING

The flowers of 'Lady Trent' are a unique shade of copper-orange. They are large, double and high centered, made up of 45 petals, and are very fragrant. The foliage is very glossy dark green and disease free, and covers a moderate-growing bush rose that produces an average yield of flowers. The blooms can be of exhibition standard and are good for cutting. The Spanish breeder, Pedro Dot, produced a large number of brightly colored roses that were all superb in hot climates. They mostly have 'Pernetiana' blood and are not hardy in areas that suffer from frost. This is probably the reason why they have not become as popular as they deserve. However, they are still superb roses for regions with similar climates, such as California, South Africa and Australia. ZONES 7–11.

Dot, Spain, 1940

'Rosieriste Gaston Lévêque' × 'Federico Casas'

'LADY VERA'
MODERN, LARGE-FLOWERED/HYBRID TEA, PINK BLEND, REPEAT-FLOWERING

The color of this rose is pale pink flushed with deeper pink at the petal edges. It has true exhibition form, very like that of 'Christian Dior'. 'Lady Vera' is a tall grower producing flowers on very long stems that have some perfume. The foliage is matt green and abundant and free of disease. This is an excellent rose for picking, especially when long stems are needed; it is also an ideal rose to provide height at the back of the rose bed. Flower production is average and there is a fair time between flushes. ZONES 5–10.

Smith, Australia, 1974

'Royal Highness' × 'Christian Dior'

'LADY WATERLOW'
MODERN, LARGE-FLOWERED CLIMBER, PINK BLEND

This old climber bears pleasantly scented, light salmon-pink blooms, singly or in small clusters, that open loosely cupped. They are semi-double with petals of a rather silky texture, and are quite large when fully open. They appear freely in summer, with sometimes a few blooms later in the year. This variety is useful for most purposes appropriate to a climber, such as on walls, fences, arches, pillars and pergolas. The growth habit is stiff and branching and, although it is not a rapid grower, the plant is capable of extending slightly further than the average climbing rose. It is reasonably well furnished with large, pointed, mid-green leaves. ZONES 4–9.

Nabonnand, France, 1903

'La France de '89' × 'Mme Marie Lavalley'

'LADY X'   MEIfigu
MODERN, LARGE-FLOWERED/HYBRID TEA, MAUVE, REPEAT-FLOWERING

The mauve coloring on the flowers of this variety is not very pronounced, for

'Lady X'

this is on the pink side of it, a light and even shade that looks attractive early in the life of the flower but becomes rather pallid by the time the petals fall. The blooms are fairly large, full petalled and prettily formed with high centers. Most of them are produced one to a stem and they possess a light sweet scent, and there is a good succession of flowers through summer and autumn. This rose is suitable for the middle or back of a border, since it is a taller than average grower. It has an upright, free-branching habit and vigorous growth, and its prickly stems carry rather sparse, leathery, semi-glossy leaves. ZONES 4–9.

Meilland, France, 1965

Seedling × 'Simone'

Portland Gold Medal 1968

'LAFAYETTE'
syns 'August Kordes', 'Joseph Guy'
MODERN, CLUSTER-FLOWERED/FLORIBUNDA, DEEP PINK, REPEAT-FLOWERING

Currently this rose appears to be listed by only one nursery, in California; it played a role as a parent of some early Cluster-flowered sports when that class of rose was in its infancy. The large semi-double blooms in a rich deep shade of cherry red are carried in immense clusters of up to 40 blooms and open like saucers, displaying the bold color well. They have a light scent and maintain a good succession of bloom through summer and autumn. For a historic collection this is an interesting rose to have, deserving a place near the front of a

'Lady Trent'

border where its colorful sprays can be enjoyed. The plant grows vigorously with a bushy, compact habit to less than average height and is supplied with glossy rich green leaves. The Marquis de Lafayette played a role in French politics and the American War of Independence. ZONES 4–9.

Nonin, France, 1924

'Rödhätte' × 'Richmond'

'LAFTER'
MODERN, LARGE-FLOWERED/HYBRID TEA, YELLOW BLEND, REPEAT-FLOWERING

The flower color on this variety is a mixture of orange-yellow on the outside of the petals and salmon-pink within and, as the petals reflex, the flowers appear progressively more pink. There are about 24 petals, making up a large but loosely formed bloom. The fragrance is good, and after the main flush more flowers are produced through summer and autumn. The unusual combination of genes in the breeding has resulted in a plant that grows like a shrub with Large-flowered blooms, and some growers list it among their shrubs and even suggest, in milder climates, that it be trained up as a pillar rose. Certainly its unconventional character will add interest in a border or a collection of unusual roses. The plant grows vigorously to the dimensions of an average shrub rose and has shiny pale green foliage. ZONES 4–9.

Brownell, USA, 1948

('V for Victory' × ['Général Jacqueminot' × 'Dr W. Van Fleet']) × 'Pink Princess'

'Lady Vera'

'Lady Taylor'

L

'LAGERFELD' AROlaqueli
syn. 'Starlight'
MODERN, LARGE-FLOWERED/HYBRID TEA, MAUVE,
REPEAT-FLOWERING

'Lagerfeld' has flowers that are a strange shade of grayish lavender, are made up of some 30 petals and open with high centers, becoming rounded in outline as they develop and maintaining good symmetry of form. Because they are fairly large and are carried in candelabra-style sprays of 5–15 blooms they tend to nod on the flower stems under their own weight, creating an untidy effect. There is good fragrance, especially on warm days, and blooming continues through summer and autumn. This rose, called a Grandiflora in the USA, is an interesting subject to include in a mixed border or bed but is best grown in a cutting garden where the growth defects will matter less and the blooms can be taken for arrangements, a purpose for which they are very well suited. The plant grows vigorously with a bushy, uneven habit to average height and has large, mid-green leaves. It was named for a Parisian couturier. **ZONES 4–9.**

Christensen, USA, 1986

'Blue Nile' × ('Ivory Tower' × 'Angel Face')

'L'AIMANT' HARzola
syn. 'Doux Parfum'
MODERN, CLUSTER-FLOWERED/FLORIBUNDA,
MEDIUM PINK, REPEAT-FLOWERING

The flowers of 'L'Aimant' are a warm shade of salmon-pink, fading to rose pink, and are carried sometimes singly but usually in clusters of several blooms which open like small-scale Large-flowered Roses, with 30 or so petals forming neat centers. The blooms become cupped as the petals reflex, yielding an excellent fragrance; in warmer countries the quality of bloom and fragrance is considerably enhanced. It flowers with good continuity through summer and autumn, standing bad weather well, is splendid for cutting and is a useful garden plant in beds and borders. The growth is vigorous, though somewhat uneven and with many branching shoots, to average height or more, while the leaves are leathery, olive green and shiny. The variety is named after the Coty perfume. **ZONES 4–9.**

Harkness, UK, 1994

'Southampton' × ('Radox Bouquet' ×
'Margaret Merril')

Bagatelle Fragrance Prize 1991, Royal National
Rose Society Edland Medal for Fragrance 1992,
RNRS British Rose Fragrance Award 1998

'Lancôme'

'Lamarque'

'L'Aimant'

'LAMARQUE'
syns 'General Lamarque', 'The Marshal'
OLD, NOISETTE, WHITE, REPEAT-FLOWERING

An amateur hybridizer raised this valuable Noisette in a window box in Angers, France, little knowing that it would become one of the most popular ramblers in rose history. The high-centered buds are followed by pure white, double blooms with a lemon-yellow center. The large, full, loose flowers have muddled centers and are pendulous. The violet fragrance is very strong, especially in the sun. Once established, this hardy climber will grow 20 ft (6 m) in a single season. The long, trailing canes are covered with smooth, gray-green foliage and there are small, hooked, red prickles. It is quite lovely on a trellis or large arch and was named in honor of a French general. **ZONES 4–10.**

Maréchal, France, 1830

'Blush Noisette' × 'Parks' Yellow Tea-scented
China'

'LAMBADA' KORdaba
MODERN, LARGE-FLOWERED/HYBRID TEA,
ORANGE-PINK, REPEAT-FLOWERING

South African florists love this very popular cut-flower variety, not only for its distinctive salmon-orange color, but also because the flowers are perfectly shaped from bud to open flower stage. The blooms are carried on thin but strong, medium-length stems and new flowers are produced throughout summer and autumn. Unfortunately, there is no fragrance. The shrub is healthy, of medium height and vigorous, and therefore good for bedding. 'Lambada' is not particularly suitable for exhibition. **ZONES 4–10.**

Kordes, Germany, 1992

Parentage unknown

'LANCASHIRE' KORstesgli
MODERN, MODERN SHRUB, MEDIUM RED,
REPEAT-FLOWERING

This variety has cherry red, semi-double flowers of small to medium size and carried close to the foliage in well-filled clusters. There is little scent, but flower production is very satisfactory as continuing cycles of growth and bloom appear through the summer and autumn months. The old-fashioned coloring of this rose will blend well with other plants including Old Garden Roses, making it

'Lagerfeld'

useful for planting near the front of mixed borders. The actual habit is a half-way house between that of a shrub and that of a ground-cover rose, for it forms a mound nearly twice as wide as it is high, the height being lower than the average for a shrub rose. The rich green leaves are plentiful and glossy. 'Lancashire' is one of a series named for English counties. **ZONES 4–9.**

Kordes, Germany, 1998

Parentage unknown

'LANCÔME' DELboip
MODERN, LARGE-FLOWERED/HYBRID TEA, DEEP
PINK, REPEAT-FLOWERING

This is primarily a greenhouse rose grown for the cut-flower trade, but in warmer climates it can give good results in the garden. The buds are long and elegant and open into large, full-petalled blooms of a rich and clear deep pink, which even in hot sunshine maintain their depth of color with little sign of fading. The hard petal texture, which makes the flowers marketable to florists, unfortunately prevents the scent glands from operating, which is especially disappointing in a rose of this color. Flower arrangers will nonetheless accept it for the value it gives them in beauty of form, long-lasting quality and length of stem. It flowers freely through summer and autumn and grows sturdily to above average height, and has glossy deep green leaves. It was named for a leading French cosmetic company. **ZONES 4–9.**

Delbard-Chabert, France, 1973

('Dr Albert Schweitzer' × ['Michèle Meilland' ×
'Bayadère']) × (MEImet × 'Présent Filial')

'LANEII'
syns 'Lane', 'Lane's Moss'
OLD, MOSS, MEDIUM RED

The flowers of this rose emerge in early to mid-summer from large, round, moss-covered buds, which are grouped together in tight clusters on strong stems. Each bloom is quite big, up to 3½ in (9 cm) across. The very double, fragrant flowers are a deep mauve-pink. It is a somewhat ungainly shrub reaching some 6 ft (1.8 m) in height and, if left unpruned, almost as wide. The stems are sparsely covered with dark green, stubble-like moss. The foliage is leathery, coarse and dark green. It does not mind impoverished soil and seems almost to thrive on neglect. **ZONES 4–10.**

Laffay, France, 1845

Parentage unknown

'LANGFORD LIGHT' LANnie
MODERN, MINIATURE, WHITE,
REPEAT-FLOWERING

This plant bears big clusters of small, white, semi-double blooms that show glimpses of bright yellow stamens beneath the center petals. The flowers are fairly small and carry a light scent. The weight of the blooms causes them to bow close to the ground, and after heavy rain they are likely to be marked by mud splashes. Flowering is well maintained through summer and autumn. This variety, which was named for the British actress Bonnie Langford, can be grown near the front of a border or in a small bed. It grows with a semi-prostrate, branching habit to well below average height and has shiny dark green leaves. The parentage given is that quoted by the raiser, but *Modern Roses 10* has it the other way round. ZONES 4–9.

Sealand, UK, 1984

'Little Flirt' × 'Ballerina'

'LANVIN'   AROlemo
MODERN, LARGE-FLOWERED/HYBRID TEA, LIGHT YELLOW, REPEAT-FLOWERING

The flowers of 'Lanvin' are a pleasing shade of clear light yellow with noticeable veining on the petals, which have a silky sheen. They are borne usually in sprays of 3 or 5 on long slim stems and are fairly large, with up to 30 petals, and neatly formed with high centers, becoming loosely cupped as they open but not yielding much fragrance. The length of stem and holding quality of the bloom make this a useful rose to grow for cutting as well as for general garden use, and flowering is well maintained through summer and autumn. The bush grows vigorously with an upright, bushy habit to average height and has semi-glossy, dark green foliage that is red tinted when young. The raiser introduced this as one of a trio of new roses named for Parisian couturiers. ZONES 4–9.

Christensen, USA, 1986

Seedling × 'Katherine Loker'

'LAS VEGAS'   KORgane
MODERN, LARGE-FLOWERED/HYBRID TEA, ORANGE BLEND, REPEAT-FLOWERING

This rose is an attractive confection of orange and yellow, the inside of the petals being orange-vermilion and the reverse chrome yellow with red veining, so that both colors are seen together as the flowers unfold. The effect is gaudy but fortunately more restrained than the lights of the city whose name it bears. The blooms are of medium to large size and fairly full with about 24 broad petals. They open loosely with low centers, the rows of petals overlapping one another and maintaining a neat attractive form throughout the life of the flower, although the weight of the blooms sometimes

causes them to nod. There is a light fragrance, good continuity of bloom is maintained through summer and autumn and they are suitable for cutting. This is a rewarding performer in beds and borders and as a hedge, for the growth is vigorous and upright, with plenty of basal growth to produce a well-filled, rounded plant. It grows to average height or a little more and has an ample provision of dark green, semi-glossy foliage. ZONES 4–9.

Kordes, Germany, 1981

'Ludwigshafen am Rhein' × 'Feuerzauber'

Geneva Gold Medal 1985, Portland Gold Medal 1988

'LAUGHTER LINES'   DICkerry
MODERN, CLUSTER-FLOWERED/FLORIBUNDA, PINK BLEND, REPEAT-FLOWERING

There are many colors in the medium to large-sized flowers on this variety, which open from clusters of pointed buds into semi-double cupped blooms of red, gold and white on a rosy pink background, the golden stamens showing up noticeably in the center. The lightly scented blooms continue through summer and autumn. 'Laughter Lines' gives a colorful garden display as a bedding, border or hedge rose and is delightful to cut for inclusion in small arrangements. It grows vigorously with a bushy, leafy habit to average height or less and has attractive dark green, shiny foliage. ZONES 4–9.

Dickson, UK, 1987

('Pye Colour' × 'Sunday Times') × 'Eyepaint'

Royal National Rose Society Gold Medal 1984, Belfast Certificate of Merit 1989

'LAURA'   MEldragelac
syns 'Laura 81', 'Natilda'
MODERN, LARGE-FLOWERED/HYBRID TEA, ORANGE BLEND, REPEAT-FLOWERING

The color of the flowers on this variety is a pastel shade of salmon pink with an

'Las Vegas'

'Laura Ashley'

'Laughter Lines'

'Lanvin'

'Laura Chantal'

orange tinge, paler on the petal reverse. The blooms are double with about 30 petals and are carried on firm stems, often several together in open sprays. They open with high centers before becoming loosely cupped as the petals reflex. There is a light fragrance and, after the initial generous flush, flowers continue to appear through summer and autumn. This rose is useful for cutting and for use in beds and borders and to form a hedge. It grows vigorously with an upright habit to average height and is well supplied with fresh green semi-glossy leaves. ZONES 4–9.

Meilland, France, 1981

('Pharaoh' × 'Color Wonder') × (['Suspense' × 'Suspense'] × 'King's Ransom')

Japan Gold Medal 1981

'LAURA ASHLEY'   CHEWharla
MODERN, MODERN SHRUB, MAUVE, REPEAT-FLOWERING

When the pointed buds of this rose open, lilac-mauve to pink flowers with a pink reverse and lots of golden yellow stamens are revealed. The flowers, mostly 5-petalled, occur as massive sprays of 10–30 blooms. They have a fruity fragrance. The foliage is semi-glossy and mid-green, with hooked prickles on a plant with a spreading, low

growth habit. What is wonderful about this rose is that the large trusses, when in peak bloom, literally cover the plant from head to toe! In some cooler climates the blooms are more of a rosy violet color with a white base to each petal. Although sometimes mistakenly classified as a Climbing Miniature, 'Laura Ashley' makes an ideal ground cover and is better there rather than against a trellis. It was named in memory of the celebrated clothes and fabric designer. ZONES 5–11.

Warner, UK, 1989

'Marjorie Fair' × 'Nozomi'

'LAURA CHANTAL'
MODERN, MINIATURE, PINK BLEND, REPEAT-FLOWERING

'Laura Chantal' is quite a tall-growing Miniature Rose that bears flowers of several shades of pink blended together. The plant is bushy and has matt foliage and very few thorns. Flower production is good, and the blooms have a strong fruity perfume. This rose was launched in aid of the South Australian Childhood Cancer Association and named after a little girl suffering from cancer. It is one of the best of the tall-growing Miniature Roses on the market today. ZONES 5–10.

Thomson, Australia, 1997

'Avandel' × 'Mme President'

'Laura'

L

'Lavaglut'

'Laura Ford'

'LAURA FORD' CHEWarvel
syn. 'Normandie'

MODERN, CLIMBING MINIATURE, MEDIUM YELLOW, REPEAT-FLOWERING

On this variety, pointed buds open up to medium yellow flowers with a lighter yellow reverse with ageing bringing on a pink flush to the petals. The florets are double with 22 petals, have good Large-flowered form and are normally borne in small, neatly formed clusters of 5–10 florets with a definite fruity scent. The foliage is light green. This plant is a vigorous, upright, tall bush and a great choice as a climber against a wall, fence or trellis where it will provide an eye-catching display all year round. 'Laura Ford' is weatherproof, providing an abundance of bloom throughout the year on an easy to maintain and disease-resistant plant. ZONES 5–11.

Warner, UK, 1989

('Anna Ford' × ('Elizabeth of Glamis' × ['Galway Bay' × 'Sutter's Gold'])

Royal National Rose Society Certificate of Merit 1988, Royal Horticultural Society Award of Garden Merit 1993

'LAURÉ DAVOUST'
syns 'Abondonnata', 'Marjorie W. Lester'

MODERN, MISCELLANEOUS, LIGHT PINK

Spectacular as a weeping standard or as a tree climber, 'Lauré Davoust' has frequently been given other names. The well-formed, double, pink blooms have a flesh tint. The pompon flowers turn lavender with age and appear in clusters on the thin canes. This variety is quite floriferous during its summer flourish. The 15 ft (4.5 m) stalks can easily be trained and have very few prickles. ZONES 4–10.

Laffay, France, 1834

Parentage unknown

'LAURETTE'
OLD, TEA, LIGHT PINK, REPEAT-FLOWERING

Little is known about the origins of 'Laurette', which is one of the most free-flowering and healthy of all the Tea Roses. Its buds are long and pointed, and open to very full, quartered, flat blooms of 40–45 petals with twisted petaloids in the center. There is a flush of deeper pink on the outer petals. The plant has a strong and spreading growth habit with plenty of mid-green, semi-glossy foliage. The flowering is continuous with a particularly fine autumn display; in warm climates, 'Laurette' will flower well into the winter. It makes a fine standard. ZONES 5–10.

France, 1886

Parentage unknown

'LAVAGLUT' KORlech
syns 'Intrigue', 'Lavaglow'

MODERN, CLUSTER-FLOWERED/FLORIBUNDA, DARK RED, REPEAT-FLOWERING

The velvety textured petals of this intensely deep red Cluster-flowered Rose are a beautiful sight when lit up by the sun. There are about 24 of them to each medium-sized flower, and many flowers make up the freely produced, evenly spaced clusters. The overall color impact is therefore considerable. The blooms themselves are shaped like camellias and hold this form to a late stage. They have little scent. Flowering is well maintained

'Lauré Davoust'

through summer and autumn, the blooms withstanding the effects of hot sun and rain much better than other dark reds. As a rose for bedding it is outstanding, thanks to its even growth habit, and it is also excellent in a border and as a hedge. It has, however, proven to be vulnerable to black spot in some areas. The plant grows strongly with a bushy, spreading habit to a little below average height and has ample glossy purplish green glossy foliage. This variety, widely planted under its English name, should not be confused with the reddish purple 'Intrigue' raised by Warriner of the USA in 1984. ZONES 4–9.

Kordes, Germany, 1978

'Gruss an Bayern' × seedling

Royal National Rose Society Trial Ground Certificate 1980

'LAVENDER CRYSTAL' ASAlar, ASAlav
syn. 'Blue Crystal'

MODERN, MINIATURE, MAUVE, REPEAT-FLOWERING

Warm sunny skies accentuate the bluish tones of this rose, which led Ralph Moore of California to describe it as 'nearest to blue'. The color is actually a light and clear shade of mauve. The young flowers are double and of regular form, holding tight centers as the outer petals expand to display ruffled edges, finally admitting gold stamens to view. They are on the large size for a Miniature Rose, and have a sweet fragrance. The blooms continue to display through summer and autumn, which makes 'Lavender Crystal' a useful item for small spaces in the garden, or for growing in a container. The plant grows bushily to average height, with mid-green foliage. ZONES 5–9.

Asami, Japan, 1985

Parentage unknown

'LAVENDER DREAM' INTerlav

MODERN, MODERN SHRUB, MAUVE, REPEAT-FLOWERING

This is a beautiful shrub rose that covers itself in big close clusters of small, deep lilac-pink blossoms, showing golden stamens. They are semi-double with about 16 petals, and after a very free initial blooming they continue to produce flowering shoots through the rest of summer and autumn. There is little fragrance. This is a fine variety for a specimen plant, to mix with others in a border or to use for a bed of one variety. The plant grows vigorously, making many shoots, spreading out wide and building up to the shape of a low mound. In height it grows to about half the average height for a shrub rose. The foliage, which is matt and light green, is sometimes touched by seasonal mildew. ZONES 4–9.

Ilsink, The Netherlands, 1984

'Yesterday' × 'Nastarana'

Anerkannte Deutsche Rose 1987

'LAVENDER JEWEL'

MODERN, MINIATURE, MAUVE, REPEAT-FLOWERING

As the name suggests, the flowers of this variety are a wonderful clear lavender-mauve. They are double with 38 petals and can have Large-flowered form in certain warm climates. When the soft lavender buds open they usually have an attractive magenta marking on the edge of the petals. The foliage is dark green and disease free. This plant has a low, compact, bushy growth habit that may tend to sprawl but it responds well to discipline, continuing to be vigorous. It loves climates with high humidity where the vigor is more marked than usual. ZONES 5–11.

Moore, USA, 1978

'Little Chief' × 'Angel Face'

'LAVENDER LACE'
MODERN, MINIATURE, MAUVE, REPEAT-FLOWERING

The clear lavender flowers tend to open too fast on this plant and so lose form and substance. However, the color can be improved by growing in partial shade. The flowers are double, have Large-flowered form and are fragrant. The foliage is small and glossy dark green. Borne in trusses with high centers at first, the blooms quickly open to flat, fully open florets with good yellow stamens. While the flowers are attractive the quality is unpredictable. It has a dwarf, vigorous

'Laurette'

'Lavender Dream'

'Lavender Mist'

'Lavender Jewel'

growth habit and tends to sulk in cold climates. Winter protection is required if plant is to survive frost or snow. ZONES 5–11.

Moore, USA, 1968

'Ellen Poulsen' × 'Debbie'

'LAVENDER LASSIE'

MODERN, MODERN SHRUB, MAUVE, REPEAT-FLOWERING

'Lavender Lassie' produces long stems that arch under the weight of big clusters of 60-petalled blooms. They are of medium size, open cupped and become flat with muddled centers as the petals reflex, finally resembling oversized rosettes. The color is a pleasing shade of pink with a hint of lavender, though in some seasons it loses much of the lavender tone and appears to be rose pink. There is a good fragrance, and a succession of bloom appears through summer and autumn. This variety is admirable in a shrub border, and the shape and color ensure that it consorts well with older roses. The plant is strong growing, freely branching and rather open in habit, giving the effect of an overgrown Cluster-flowered Rose and achieving the average height of a shrub rose. In warm climates the long canes can be trained on a pillar,

fence or wall, thus converting it into a climber. The foliage on this variety is rather sparse, semi-glossy and mid-green. ZONES 4–9.

Kordes, Germany, 1960

'Hamburg' × 'Mme Norbert Levavasseur'

Royal Horticultural Society Award of Garden Merit 1993

'LAVENDER MIST'

syn. 'Mystic Mauve'

MODERN, LARGE-FLOWERED/HYBRID TEA, MAUVE, REPEAT-FLOWERING

Plump buds on this variety open into blooms of some 36 petals that are lilac-mauve and are usually borne 3 to the cluster. They are quite large and open cupped to diffuse a refreshing light tea fragrance. After the main flush the plant continues to carry some bloom through summer and autumn, and in the garden it can be utilised on pergolas, arches, walls and fences, being quite vigorous with long, arching, prickly canes and big leaves. For some reason 'Lavender Mist' has never become widely grown under either of its two names, and it appears to be offered nowadays only in Australia. ZONES 4–9.

Christensen, USA, 1981

'Angel Face' × 'Allspice'

'Lavender Lassie'

'LAVENDER PINOCCHIO'

MODERN, CLUSTER-FLOWERED/FLORIBUNDA, MAUVE, REPEAT-FLOWERING

The raiser's use of unusually colored parents for this rose was rewarded, for it has buds of light chocolate brown that open in a shade of deep lavender with brownish centers, tinged with yellow at the base. As the flowers mature they take on mauve tints, finally fading to grayish pink before the ruffled petals fall. They are full-petalled, fairly large, loosely formed and change from cupped to almost flat form as they age. There is a pleasing fragrance, and flowers continue to appear through summer and autumn. This variety remains widely available after 50 years in commerce, which speaks as well of its plant qualities as of its endearing character. The plant is compact, growing below average height, and has leathery mid-green leaves. ZONES 4–9.

Boerner, USA, 1948

'Pinocchio' × 'Grey Pearl'

'LAVENDULA'

MODERN, CLUSTER-FLOWERED/floribunda, MAUVE, REPEAT-FLOWERING

This variety bears big clusters of buds that open into magenta flowers, becom-

ing more purplish as the petals mature. They are large for a Cluster-flowered Rose, rather low centered and open out flat. The blooms have good fragrance, and after a prolific early display the plant provides a good succession of bloom through summer and autumn. It can be used in beds and borders, though it is not widely grown today, being apparently offered only in Australia where the warm climate tends to intensify its color. It grows to below average height and has dark green foliage. ZONES 4–9.

Kordes, Germany, 1965

'Magenta' × 'Sterling Silver'

'Lavender Lace'

'Lavender Pinocchio'

'Lavendula'

'LAWINIA' TANklawi, TANklevi, TANklewi

syn. 'Lavinia'

MODERN, LARGE-FLOWERED CLIMBER, MEDIUM PINK, REPEAT-FLOWERING

This is an attractive climber, bearing 20-petalled blooms of loosely cupped, rounded form. They are fairly large, an even shade of pink, and appear singly or sometimes in clusters of a few or many flowers. There is a pleasant fragrance, and blooming continues through summer and autumn. This is an all-purpose variety for walls, fences, arches, pergolas and especially pillars, and it can be expected to grow to the average extent of a climbing rose. The plant is vigorous with stiff, upright, branching stems that are well furnished with mid-green leaves. It was named to honor Lavinia, Duchess of Norfolk, who lived from 1916 to 1995 and devoted much of her life to charitable work. ZONES 4–9.

Tantau, Germany, 1980

Parentage unknown

Royal Horticultural Society Award of Garden Merit 1995

'Le Havre'

'LAWRENCE JOHNSTON'

syn. 'Hidcote Yellow'

MODERN, LARGE-FLOWERED CLIMBER, MEDIUM YELLOW

This climber bears a lavish crop of strongly scented flowers in an eye-catching bright clear yellow that open loosely cupped. They are semi-double with about 15 petals, are quite large and are borne in clusters. Usually the flowering is restricted to summertime, but occasionally a few later blooms appear. As the plant is very vigorous it requires plenty of space, where the long arching stems can rampage over a roof, or a very high wall. It is likely to extend 2 or 3 times as much as an average climber. The leaves are light green and glossy and are prone to black spot, due doubtless to *Rosa foetida* genes in the pollen parent. This variety was raised, but not commercialized, by Pernet-Ducher, and the only plant was later bought from him by the owner of Hidcote Manor, whose name it bears. ZONES 4–9.

Pernet-Ducher, France, 1923

'Mme Eugène Verdier' × 'Persian Yellow'

'Le Soleil'

'Lawrence Johnston'

'LE CID'

MODERN, HYBRID RUGOSA, MEDIUM RED, REPEAT-FLOWERING

This strong-growing Hybrid Rugosa with very prickly wood bears bright crimson, double flowers repeatedly through the warmer months. Very few hips are produced. 'Le Cid' makes a good hedge plant, with foliage that usually turns gold in autumn. It grows well in poor, sandy soil and is resistant to disease. ZONES 5–10.

Vigneron, France, 1908

'Conrad Ferdinand Meyer' × 'Belle Poitevine'

'LE HAVRE'

OLD, HYBRID PERPETUAL, MEDIUM RED, REPEAT-FLOWERING

This variety, which was named for a seaport in northern France, has large,

overlapping vermilion, double blooms paling to purplish. It is quite floriferous during a long flowering period and displays attractive, leathery foliage and only a few prickles. Its bushy, 6 ft (1.8 m) form makes it a good candidate for the back of the border. ZONES 5–10.

Eudes, France, 1870

Parentage unknown

'LE RÊVE'

MODERN, LARGE-FLOWERED CLIMBER, LIGHT YELLOW

Clusters of pointed yellow buds on this variety open into light canary yellow, loosely formed, single or semi-double blooms of medium to large size. They open wide like saucers, and the petals pale to primrose yellow before they fall. The blooms are pleasantly scented and are usually borne rather early in summertime, giving a prolific display but not repeating their bloom. The plant is strong stemmed and vigorous and is suitable for pergolas, fences and arches; it can extend twice as far as the average climber. It is well furnished with rich green glossy foliage. Pernet-Ducher introduced this, his 'dream' rose, in preference to 'Lawrence Johnston', which he derived from the same parents, and it does have an altogether better health record. ZONES 4–9.

Pernet-Ducher, France, 1923

'Mme Eugène Verdier' × 'Persian Yellow'

'LE ROUGE ET LE NOIR'

DELcart

MODERN, LARGE-FLOWERED/HYBRID TEA, DARK RED, REPEAT-FLOWERING

It goes without saying that the petals of this variety are not actually black, but when the sun strikes their surface when the flowers are young they reflect what to the eye appears as a blackish sheen. The blooms are rich deep red and are made up of numerous rather short petals, which reflex so that each ring overlays the one below, giving the effect of an outsize glowing red rosette relieved by a glimpse of yellow stamens in the center. They have a light scent. This rose is suitable for beds and borders, though its distribution appears to be limited to

'Le Rouge et Le Noir'

'Lawinia'

France only. It grows strongly with an upright habit to average height and has dark green leaves that are reddish when young. The name may refer to a novel by Stendhal or to the red and black of the roulette wheel. ZONES 4–9.

Delbard, France, 1973

Parentage unknown

'LE SOLEIL'
MODERN, CLUSTER-FLOWERED/FLORIBUNDA, ORANGE-RED, REPEAT-FLOWERING

This variety produces small, well-shaped blooms in few-flowered clusters. They are luminous orange-red with black-red shading on the outer petals, which adds to the overall effect. The plant is short and stocky and is covered with large, glossy rich green foliage that is very attractive and acts as a foil to the brilliantly colored flowers. The foliage is disease free but the blooms are rather sparse and the repeat is rather slow. 'Le Soleil' is good for cutting and brings a vibrant color to any indoor display. ZONES 5–9.

Mallerin, France. 1959

Parentage unknown

'LE VÉSUVE'
syn. 'Lemesle'
OLD, CHINA, PINK BLEND, REPEAT-FLOWERING

'La Vésuve' has shapely, pointed buds that open to loose blooms of carmine to pink and sometimes to fiery red. They are very large, full flowers and are delicately veined. The blowzy flowers, with a wide center, will change color depending on whether it is planted in the sun or shade. Thriving best in a warm position, 'Le Vésuve' is a vigorous, small shrub of

'Le Vésuve'

'Léda'

'Legacy Jubilee'

'Legend'

'Lelia Laird'

'Leander'

4–5 ft (1.2–1.5 m) with an angular growth pattern. The foliage changes from coppery to shiny green as it ages. The mounded shape makes it an ideal bedding plant, and it is also successful as a container plant. Large red prickles and a delicate Tea scent add to its charm. **ZONES 6–10.**

Laffay, France, 1825

Parentage unknown

'LEANDER'   AUSlea
MODERN, MODERN SHRUB, APRICOT BLEND

Also classified as an English Rose, 'Leander' has pink to apricot flowers, more intense in the center depths. They are darker in bud. The blooms open flat and are closely packed with petals all enfolded together as they seek to expand into the space available, for this is a plant with rather small flowers. In terms of growth it is very large, especially in warm climates, where it can reach half as tall again as an average shrub rose or be supported and grown as a sizeable climber on a wall, fence or pillar. It therefore

needs careful placement so that it has enough room. The blooms are scented, are borne in wide sprays on slim stems and give of their best in summer, for the production of later flowers is limited. It has a somewhat open growth habit and smooth, mid-green foliage. **ZONES 4–9.**

Austin, UK, 1982

'Charles Austin' × seedling

'LEAPING SALMON'   PEAmight
syn. 'Emmanuelle'
MODERN, LARGE-FLOWERED CLIMBER, ORANGE-PINK, REPEAT-FLOWERING

This variety bears large double salmon-pink flowers of classic Large-flowered quality, having high centers, opening with graceful symmetry and lasting well either on the plant or when cut for floral arrangement. There is a pleasing fragrance, and following the main flush there is a steady succession of later blooms through summer and autumn, sometimes borne singly, sometimes in clusters. This rose is suitable for most purposes appropriate to a climber of average extent, especially on walls and fences where its stiff branches can be spread out and given firm support, and on a pillar. It is well furnished with large, semi-glossy leaves. **ZONES 4–9.**

Pearce, UK, 1983

(['Vesper' × 'Aloha'] × ['Paddy McGredy' × 'Maigold']) × 'Prima Ballerina'

'LÉDA'
syn. 'Painted Damask'
OLD, DAMASK, WHITE BLEND

Still a popular rose after 170 years, 'Léda' has red-brown buds that open to reveal a button eye, with the inner petals reflexing into a ball. The milky white petals finish with a crimson edge. Although it sprawls, it can be kept as a compact plant. The foliage is dark green, downy and semi-glossy on a shrub of

about 3 ft (1 m) in height. If pruned of old wood after flowering, this hardy, disease-resistant rose will produce highly perfumed flowers during late spring with some repeat in autumn. Some say it is not a Damask but should rather be in the Portland class. It was named for the mythological queen who was seduced by Zeus when he appeared in the form of a swan. There is also a pink form known as 'Pink Léda'. **ZONES 4–10.**

Pre-1827

Parentage unknown

'LEGACY JUBILEE'
MODERN, LARGE-FLOWERED/HYBRID TEA, YELLOW BLEND, REPEAT-FLOWERING

The long pointed buds on this variety open into colorful blooms of yellow, with a border of red along the petal edges. The flowers are quite large, finally open cupped, and yield a rather sharp but satisfying fragrance. Blooming continues with good succession through summer and autumn, the flowers withstanding the warm conditions of Australia well and being suitable for general garden purposes there; it is doubtful if the variety has ever been tested in cooler climates. The plant grows vigorously with an upright habit and is furnished with large glossy leaves. The name commemorates a special date in the history of a Legacy Club in the raiser's home state of Victoria. **ZONES 4–9.**

Dawson, Australia, 1974

'Great Venture' × 'Fred Streeter'

'LEGEND'   JACtop
syn. 'Top Star'
MODERN, LARGE-FLOWERED/HYBRID TEA, MEDIUM RED, REPEAT-FLOWERING

'Legend' has pointed, plump buds that open to reveal large flowers composed of about 30 broad petals. The young blooms are high centered but become rounded in outline as they mature, with the petals symmetrically arranged. The flowers are bright red and are usually borne singly, and their lasting quality and long stems make them good for cutting as well as serving the usual garden purposes in beds, borders and as hedges. There is some scent, and blooms continue to appear through summer and autumn. The plant grows vigorously with a stately, upright, bushy habit to above average height and has matt dark green leaves. **ZONES 4–9.**

Warriner, USA, 1992

'Grand Masterpiece' × seedling

'LELIA LAIRD'
MODERN, MINIATURE, ORANGE BLEND, REPEAT-FLOWERING

This rose bears an abundance of double, orange-red flowers with a yellow eye and 38 petals. The blooms have a strong Tea fragrance and can often exhibit good Large-flowered form although they open rather quickly in most climates. The flowers are considered to be a bit large for the traditional Miniature Rose. The foliage is mid-green with a lovely red edging on a plant that is generally tall and upright, but can be sprawling in cooler climates. **ZONES 5–11.**

Bennett, USA, 1979

'Contempo' × 'Sheri Anne'

'LEMON BLUSH'   SIElemon
MODERN, MODERN SHRUB, LIGHT YELLOW

This variety was raised in northern Germany as one of a series of hardy roses, the stated breeding line including Albas and roses developed from *Rosa kordesii*. The blooms are pale yellow shading to cream and open rather flat, with dozens of small petals enfolded together. The petals are soft textured and sweetly fragrant, and there is a prolific summer blooming but no repeat bloom later in the year. The plant grows with a strong shrubby habit, producing vigorous upright shoots that then begin to arch over under the weight of the stems and the leaves. It does well in a border among substantial plants, for the growth is appreciably larger and wider than that of an average shrub rose, and it has robust mid-green foliage. **ZONES 4–9.**

Sievers, Germany, 1988

Parentage unknown

'LEMON DELIGHT'
MODERN, MINIATURE, MEDIUM YELLOW, REPEAT-FLOWERING

Long, pointed, mossy buds on this variety open to reveal wonderful 10-petalled small blooms that are a bright butter yellow. The lovely florets have a strong lemon fragrance. The plant is free blooming, vigorous, bushy and upright and very hardy. The color is generally fast in most climates and the mossing adds an extra charm. 'Lemon Delight' is another outstanding achievement by Moore—the successful introduction of mossing into Miniature Roses with retention of the repeat-blooming characteristics. **ZONES 5–11.**

Moore, USA, 1978

'Fairy Moss' × 'Goldmoss'

'Lemon Blush'

'Lemon Delight'

'Leander'

'LEMON ELEGANCE'
MODERN, LARGE-FLOWERED/HYBRID TEA, MEDIUM YELLOW, REPEAT-FLOWERING

The buds of this variety are long and pointed and open into large flowers of lemon yellow. They are well formed with high centers in the young bloom, and are made up of nearly 40 petals. There is a pleasant fragrance, and blooms continue to appear after the initial flush is ended through summer and autumn. They are long stemmed and are suitable for cutting. 'Lemon Elegance' is best suited for borders and hedges, though obtaining it could be difficult since it appears to be no longer commercially available. The plant grows vigorously with upright stems to more than average height and is supplied with small leathery leaves. ZONES 4–9.

Jones, USA, 1960

Parentage unknown

'LEMON GLOW'
MODERN, LARGE-FLOWERED/HYBRID TEA, MEDIUM YELLOW, REPEAT-FLOWERING

'Lemon Glow' has long, pointed buds that open into very large blooms composed of up to 60 petals. They are lemon yellow, are borne singly or in clusters of 3 on long, strong stems, and are well formed with high centers. There is appreciable fragrance, and after a generous first blooming flower production

'Lemon Elegance'   'Lemon Glow'

'Lemon Sherbet'

continues intermittently through summer and autumn. This has been a useful rose for cutting and exhibition as well as general garden cultivation, but it does not now appear to be in commerce nor to have been grown outside North America. The plant grows strongly with an upright habit to average height or above and is furnished with light green, rather soft foliage. ZONES 4–9.

Schwartz, USA, 1964

'Sunlight' × 'Golden Masterpiece'

'LEMON HONEY' DICkindle
MODERN, CLUSTER-FLOWERED/FLORIBUNDA, LIGHT YELLOW, REPEAT-FLOWERING

This variety is one of the many that is hard to classify, for although it does bloom in clusters the individual flowers are the size of some Large-flowered Roses. The blooms are yellow, pale towards the petal edges and deeper in the center, with a tinge of pink on the outer petal rims as they age. They have a light fragrance and maintain a good succession of bloom through summer and autumn. This rose is useful for beds and borders or to make a hedge. It grows vigorously to average height, making many shoots from the base, and is equipped with dark leaves that contrast well with the light colored flowers. ZONES 4–9.

Dickson, UK, 1986

Parentage unknown

'Lemon Honey'

'LEMON SHERBET'
MODERN, LARGE-FLOWERED/HYBRID TEA, LIGHT YELLOW, REPEAT-FLOWERING

This variety sported from a white rose and it has a lot of white in it, the yellow coloring being confined to the center of the bloom. The flowers open from plump buds and are large with about 36 petals. They are high centered and are borne on upright stems of cuttable length and, since the flowers last well, they are suitable for floral arrangement and also for showing. They can give very satisfactory value in the garden, for blooms appear with good continuity through summer and autumn. There is a light fragrance. The plant grows vigorously with an upright habit to average height and has large leathery leaves. ZONES 4–9.

Kern, USA, 1973

Sport of 'Florence'

'LEMON SPICE'
MODERN, LARGE-FLOWERED/HYBRID TEA, LIGHT YELLOW, REPEAT-FLOWERING

The name of this rose has reference to the fruity, spicy scent, described as 'heavy, unusual but likeable', which seems to be the chief reason for growing it. The elegant pointed buds develop into large full-petalled blooms with high centers, which become rounded as the petals expand. A pale yellow color, the flowers are attractively formed but often prove too heavy for the slim stems and bow down, which detracts from its value as a garden plant and for use for cutting. The initial flowering is prolific, and more blooms are produced intermittently through summer and autumn. The plant grows with a spreading habit to average height and has dark, leathery textured leaves. ZONES 4–9.

Armstrong & Swim, USA, 1966

'Helen Traubel' × seedling

'LEN TURNER' DICjeep
syn. 'Daydream'
MODERN, CLUSTER-FLOWERED/FLORIBUNDA, RED BLEND, REPEAT-FLOWERING

This variety bears clusters of modest-sized flowers made up of about 36 small petals, which are blush and prettily rimmed with rich reddish pink. The blooms open like pompons, with many petal edges arrayed layer upon layer to give a delightful color effect. There is a light scent, and when the main flush is ended the plant rarely seems to be without signs of bloom throughout the rest

'Lemon Spice'

'Len Turner'

of summer and autumn. The unusual and distinctive character of the flowers makes this an interesting variety for beds and borders or for a low hedge, and it is good to cut for small arrangements. The plant grows quite vigorously with a free-branching, bushy habit to below average height and has a plentiful cover of dark green, semi-glossy leaves. The name honors a British rosarian who served the Royal National Rose Society as its secretary for 18 years. ZONES 4–9.

Dickson, UK, 1984

'Electron' × 'Eyepaint'

Royal National Rose Society Certificate of Merit 1983

'LEON LECOMTE'
OLD, DAMASK, DEEP PINK

This extremely rare Damask Rose is a rich pink with lemon yellow at the base of the petals. The large, double blooms fade in full sun so do best in partial shade. It will bloom throughout summer and has a sweet perfume. The lead green leaves cover the bush, which can reach 5–6 ft (1.5–1.8 m). As a compact shrub it can be used effectively as a hedge or in a border. A good crop of round hips appears in autumn. Damasks are used for the distillation of attar for perfume; some say they are the best of the scented roses. ZONES 5–10.

Parentage unknown

'LÉONARDO DE VINCI'
MEIdeauri

syns 'Léonard de Vinci', 'Leonardo da Vinci'

MODERN, CLUSTER-FLOWERED/FLORIBUNDA, LIGHT PINK, REPEAT-FLOWERING

This variety is one of a group of roses marketed by Meilland and named after artists and poets to meet a perceived need for roses 'that are characteristically old fashioned in style while imbued with modern day qualities of disease resistance and repeat flowering'. The lightly scented blooms of 'Léonardo de Vinci' are large and well filled and have over 40 petals, those in the center enfolded against one another as the flowers open. They are borne in clusters on firm stems and continue to flower through summer and autumn. This rose, which is useful for borders as well as for hedges and beds, grows vigorously with a bushy habit to average height or more and is well furnished with dark green glossy leaves. ZONES 4–9.

Meilland, France, 1994

'Sommerwind' × (MEIrose × 'Rosamunde')

Monza Gold Medal 1993

'LÉONIE LAMESCH'

MODERN, POLYANTHA, ORANGE BLEND, REPEAT-FLOWERING

'Léonie Lamesch' seems surprisingly flamboyant for a nineteenth-century rose. The American introducers informed their customers that 'ten distinctly colored flowers are frequently shown on the bush at one time, varying from cochineal red in the bud to glowing coppery red tinged with orange when the flower opens'. The spicy scented blooms are loosely double, are carried on long springy stems either singly or in clusters of up to 24 and open wide to display their brilliance. They continue flowering through summer and autumn. This rose is worth growing for its beauty and history in any small space where a somewhat stalky habit is acceptable. The bush is vigorous and grows upright to above average height for a Polyantha; it has rich green foliage that is reddish when young. It is long lived, which is why this old variety has endured. ZONES 5–9.

Lambert, Germany, 1899

'Aglaia' × 'Kleiner Alfred'

'Léonie Lamesch'

'Léonor de March'

'LÉONOR DE MARCH'

MODERN, LARGE-FLOWERED/HYBRID TEA, DARK RED, REPEAT-FLOWERING

The buds of this variety are long and pointed, and open into large, high-centered deep blood red flowers with broad petals that reflect the sun with a velvety sheen. The blooms, which have a good fragrance, are borne on firm stems, making this a useful rose for cutting as well as for general garden use in beds and borders. The continuity of flower is well maintained through summer and autumn. In habit the plant grows upright to average height or more, and it has glossy foliage. 'Léonor de March' does best in warmer climates, but at the present time it does not appear to be commercially available. ZONES 4–9.

Camprubi, Spain, 1957

'J. M. Lopez Pico' × 'Poinsettia'

Rome Gold Medal 1958

'LÉONTINE GERVAIS'

MODERN, LARGE-FLOWERED CLIMBER, APRICOT BLEND

The coppery red buds of this rose open to cupped blooms that develop into semi-double flowers of salmon and yellow that fade with age. The dramatic trusses gather in clusters of 3–10, and the mixture of colors in the large, fragrant blooms is most attractive. The young growth is bronzy, maturing to dark glossy foliage. Easily reaching 20 ft (6 m) in 3 or 4 years, it is ideal for pergolas, walls and trees and will tolerate some shade. In warm areas it will have some rebloom. This rose was one of 30 varieties created by Barbier and Compaigne of Orléans, France, during the first quarter of the twentieth century. ZONES 4–10.

Barbier, France, 1903

Rosa wichuraiana × 'Souvenir de Catherine Guillot'

'LES AMOUREUX DE PEYNET'   MEItobla

syns 'Efekto 21', 'Simply Magic'

MODERN, CLUSTER-FLOWERED/FLORIBUNDA, DEEP PINK, REPEAT-FLOWERING

This variety has a low and spreading habit, and could almost be described as a scaled-down Ground Cover Rose. It is very suitable for small gardens and patio areas, where the maximum of color is required and space is limited, and can also be used to advantage in more extensive plantings. The semi-double flowers are a warm shade of pinky red, which is deeper on the undersides of the petals,

'Léontine Gervais'

'Les Amoureux de Peynet'

so that as the blooms expand there is overall a bicolor effect. They are cupped with slightly ruffled petal tips, of small to medium size with a pleasant light scent, and are produced in large clusters through summer and autumn. The plant grows vigorously to below average height and is covered with glossy bright green leaves. ZONES 5–9.

Meilland, France, 1992

Parentage unknown

Bagatelle Gold Medal 1991, Lyon Rose of the Century 1992

'LES SJULIN'

MODERN, LARGE-FLOWERED/HYBRID TEA, PINK BLEND, REPEAT-FLOWERING

The flowers of this variety show coral pink on the inner petal surfaces and light red on the reverse. They are urn shaped, are borne sometimes singly or in clusters of up to 8 blooms, and open with cupped form to show a pretty arrangement of petals layered one row upon another. They have a pleasant fragrance, light and sweet, continue to appear through summer and autumn and last well when cut. The plant grows vigorously with an upright habit to above average height and can be used in a border, or to form a screening hedge. The leaves are dark olive green. Known for its hardiness, this rose is only available from nurseries in the cooler parts of the USA. ZONES 4–9.

Buck, USA, 1981

'Country Dancer' × (['Dornröschen' × 'Peace'] × 'Pink Peace')

'Leslie's Dream'

'LESLIE'S DREAM'   DICjoon

MODERN, LARGE-FLOWERED/HYBRID TEA, RED BLEND/MEDIUM RED, REPEAT-FLOWERING

The large rich crimson blooms of 'Leslie's Dream' are carried on long stems, making them very suitable for cutting and also as potential candidates for exhibition. There is not a great deal of fragrance, but the continuity of bloom through summer and autumn is well maintained. This variety is very suitable for a group in a border; it grows with an upright, branching habit to average height and is furnished with large dark green glossy leaves. The dream in the name refers to the vision of the late Leslie Mitchell, a much respected and loved Dubliner. ZONES 4–9.

Dickson, UK, 1994

'Bonfire Night' × 'Typhoon'

Royal National Rose Society Trial Ground Certificate 1983

'Liebeszauber'

'Leverkusen'

'Lilac Rose'

'Leveson Gower'

'LEUCHTSTERN'
MODERN, RAMBLER, PINK BLEND

This 'shining star' has almost disappeared from the world, with only one nursery offering it today. The slightly fragrant, single, deep rose blooms are medium in size and appear in clusters.

The centers of the blooms are white. It has a profuse flowering during one long period in early summer, which is followed by a heavy crop of red hips. The short, strong stems appear on a tall, hardy, bushy plant that is covered with healthy foliage. It does well in poor soil, and is perhaps best classified as a short rambler. **ZONES 4–10.**

Schmidt, Germany, 1899

'Daniel Lacombe' × 'Crimson Rambler'

'LEVERKUSEN'
MODERN, CLUSTER-FLOWERED CLIMBER, LIGHT YELLOW, REPEAT-FLOWERING

The medium-sized flowers of this variety are semi-double and appear in well-filled clusters, opening out into rosettes of light yellow. The main summer flush on a well-grown 'Leverkusen' is one of summer's treats, for the gentle pale color of the flowers contrasts beautifully with the bright, shiny, light green foliage. There is a pleasant light scent, and a few sporadic blooms are likely to appear in late summer and autumn. This climber lends itself to being trained on arches, pillars, fences and walls, producing many slender arching stems that can readily be tied in place. It extends to the average dimensions expected of a climber, to around 8 ft (2.4 m), and it can also be grown without support and allowed to make a sprawling, tangled shrub of greater width than height. It is one of

several of Kordes' roses named for a German town. **ZONES 4–9.**

Kordes, Germany, 1954

Rosa kordesii × 'Golden Glow'

'LEVESON GOWER'
syns 'Leverson Gower', 'Leweson Gower', 'Souvenir de la Malmaison Rose'
OLD, BOURBON, ORANGE-PINK, REPEAT-FLOWERING

This rose from Lyons, France, is often confused with the red form of 'Souvenir de la Malmaison', which might explain why it is sometimes seen under that name. It looks a lot like a Modern Large-flowered Rose, with pointed buds that open to full, cupped, very large blooms with red shaded salmon petals. The fragrant flowers are held above smooth, light green foliage. It is a robust bush, growing to 6 ft (1.8 m) high, and although it has a tendency to mildew in wet weather it has few prickles, and a large crop of hips appears in autumn. G. G. Leveson-Gower (1773–1846), first Earl Granville, was the English ambassador to France. **ZONES 5–10.**

Béluze, France, 1845

Parentage unknown

'LICHTKÖNIGIN LUCIA'
KORlilub
syns 'Lucia', 'Reine Lucia'
MODERN, MODERN SHRUB, MEDIUM YELLOW, REPEAT-FLOWERING

'Probably the most underrated yellow shrub that has ever been raised' is the verdict of one authority about this rose. The blooms, borne in clusters of several together on strong stems, are an intense shade of lemon yellow. They are of middling to large size with about 18 petals and open like shallow saucers, with their pretty red stamens half-hidden in the centers. There is a pleasing fragrance and, after a prolific first flush, continuity of flowering is well maintained through summer and autumn. This is an excellent subject for a mixed border, and in milder climates it can be grown on a pillar or as a short climbing rose. The plant grows tall with an upright, free-branching habit to the average height expected of a shrub rose. The stems are prickly and the leaves large, wrinkled and rather glossy. The name means 'Lucia, Queen of Light'. **ZONES 4–9.**

Kordes, Germany, 1966

'Zitronenfalter' × 'Cläre Grammerstorf'
Anerkannte Deutsche Rose 1968

'LIEBESZAUBER' KORmiach
syn. 'Crimson Spire'
MODERN, LARGE-FLOWERED/HYBRID TEA, MEDIUM RED, REPEAT-FLOWERING

On this variety the flowers are fairly large and a rich blood red color, and they are freely produced and normally carried one to a stem. After opening with high centers, they become loosely cupped with wavy, infolded petals in the middle of the bloom, looking attractive at each stage. The petals fall cleanly when they are spent. There is a noticeable fragrance, and after the first flowering is finished the succession of bloom through summer and autumn is well maintained. The

plant grows very vigorously, making many shoots, with a stiff, upright habit to taller than average height. In South Africa the variety is termed a 'Spire' rose, one of several roses recommended on account of their vigor and flower freedom for growing on as extra tall bushes. The leaves, reddish when young, become dark green as they mature. The name means 'love's magic', for which of course a red rose has to be first choice. **ZONES 4–9.**

Kordes, Germany, 1990

Seedling × 'Pink Panther'

'LIFESTYLE' MORdarain
MODERN, MINIATURE, PINK BLEND, REPEAT-FLOWERING

'Lifestyle' has moderately full flowers of 15–25 petals. They have a light fragrance, and the pink blend color holds well in most climates. The blooms can have good exhibition Large-flowered form, and are borne one bloom per stem with excellent repeat cycle times. The foliage is a semi-glossy, mid-green on a well rounded, upright plant. This is an excellent rose for the patio landscape as a container-grown bush. **ZONES 5–11.**

Moore, USA, 1992

'Little Darling' × 'Rainbow's End'

'LIGHTS OF BROADWAY'
SAValights
MODERN, MINIATURE, RED BLEND, REPEAT-FLOWERING

The blooms of this rose are very full, with 40 or more petals that are crammed into small flowers of lively shades of red with orange-yellow. The blooms are usually borne singly, and are likely to be more useful for exhibition work than in the garden. Flowering continues through summer and autumn, but there is no appreciable scent. The plant grows upright to average height, with semi-glossy, mid-green leaves. **ZONES 5–9.**

Saville, USA, 1993

('Tamango' × 'Yellow Jewel') × 'Party Girl'

'LILAC CHARM'
MODERN, CLUSTER-FLOWERED/FLORIBUNDA, MAUVE, REPEAT-FLOWERING

The flowers of 'Lilac Charm' are a pretty shade of pale lilac-mauve, showing prominent red stamens. Composed of 5–7 large petals, they are saucer-shaped open blooms that appear big for a Cluster-flowered Rose. They have a pleasing fragrance and flower with good continuity through summer and autumn. Despite the lapse of over 30 years since its introduction this variety is still widely available, especially in warmer countries where cold and rain cannot so easily wash out the lilac tones within the flowers, and it makes an unusual and beautiful addition to a bed or border. It is also good to cut if taken young, when the mauvish color is at its best. The very spreading plant grows with moderate vigor to less than average height and has matt dark green leaves. **ZONES 4–9.**

LeGrice, UK, 1962

Seedling of 'Lavender Pinocchio'
Royal National Rose Society Gold Medal 1961

'LILAC ROSE' AUSlilac
syn. 'Old Lilac'
MODERN, MODERN SHRUB, PINK BLEND, REPEAT-FLOWERING

This variety bears large flowers of lilac-pink, with over 40 petals. The blooms are borne in small clusters and open out wide like big rosettes, though they may ball and fail to open in wet conditions. There is a strong fragrance, and the variety blooms through summer and autumn. It can add interest towards the front of a shrub border, the color according well with Old Garden Roses and many other garden plants. 'Lilac Rose' grows with a bushy, upright habit to a little below average size and has olive green semi-glossy leaves. It is also classified as an English Rose. **ZONES 4–9.**

Austin, UK, 1990

Seedling × 'Hero'

'LILAC TIME'
MODERN, LARGE-FLOWERED/HYBRID TEA, MAUVE, REPEAT-FLOWERING

'Lilac Time' has flowers that are shapely and high centered when they open, becoming fairly large and finally loosely cupped and with an informal arrangement of their 36 petals. While undergoing trial in Britain the color of this rose was likened to lavender, and it drew the comment that it was 'probably the best yet in this range'. However, the color appears nearer to rose pink than anything else, though warm sunny weather may help to bring out the lilac tones. It is sweetly fragrant and produces its blooms after the first flush through summer and autumn. Collectors of 'hopefully blue' roses will doubtless wish to add it to their collection. It grows with moderate vigor and an upright habit to below average height and has small mid-green leaves. **ZONES 4–9.**

McGredy, UK, 1956

'Golden Dawn' × 'Luis Brinas'

National Rose Society Certificate of Merit 1955

'LILIAN AUSTIN' AUSli
MODERN, MODERN SHRUB, ORANGE-PINK, REPEAT-FLOWERING

The blooms of this variety are large and full, with 30 or so ruffled petals in a warm shade of rosy salmon pink, revealing a glimpse of stamens as well as a good expanse of color as they open out wide. They are sometimes borne singly, sometimes with up to 5 per cluster, and they have a pleasing fragrance. After the initial flush more flowers appear during the rest of summer and autumn. This variety sits well in borders among other plants, being of spreading but fairly compact habit and of average size for a shrub rose. In warm climates the stems grow longer with an arching habit, and can be trained on a fence to form a low climber. The plant is amply furnished with dark semi-glossy foliage. The raiser, David Austin, thought highly enough of this rose to name it for his mother. It is also classified as an English Rose. **ZONES 4–9.**

Austin, UK, 1973

'Aloha' × 'The Yeoman'

'Lilian Austin'

'Lilac Time'

'LILIAN BAYLIS' HARdeluxe
MODERN, CLUSTER-FLOWERED/FLORIBUNDA, LIGHT YELLOW, REPEAT-FLOWERING

The flowers of this variety are carried in well-spaced clusters and open with tighter centers. They expand slowly and become flat, as scores of reflexing petals lie back layer upon layer to reveal many petal tips. The color is a cool and subtle pale buff yellow, deeper in the heart of the blooms, and there is a pleasing fragrance. As a variety for bedding and to group in a border this is a useful plant, and the flowers are excellent to cut because they last well and are neatly spaced, and each stem forms a floral bouquet. Blooming continues through summer and autumn on this spreading, vigorous

'Lilian Austin'

plant, which grows to a little below average height, with plentiful rich green foliage. **ZONES 4–9.**

Harkness, UK, 1996

Seedling of 'Amber Queen'

'LILLI MARLEEN' KORlima
syns 'Lili Marléne', 'Lilli Marlene'
MODERN, CLUSTER-FLOWERED/FLORIBUNDA, MEDIUM RED, REPEAT-FLOWERING

'Lilli Marleen' is a good rose for a continuous display of low color. The ovoid buds open to fragrant, double flowers with 25 petals; at 3 in (8 cm) across they are large for a Cluster-flowered Rose. The rich red flowers, which completely smother the bush in spring, have a velvety sheen and stand up very well to both

'Lilli Marleen'

hot and cold conditions. They come in small clusters of 10–15 blooms and last very well on the bush. The foliage is leathery and dark green on a rather thick and stocky plant that is still a very popular rose after nearly 40 years in commerce. **Climbing Lilli Marleen** (PEKlimasar; syns 'Grimpant Lilli Marleen', 'Climbing Lili Marlene', 'Climbing Lilli Marlene'; Pekmez, France 1983) is a shortish, stocky climber that completely covers itself in shapely, long-lasting red flowers. **ZONES 5–10.**

Kordes, Germany, 1959

('Our Princess' × 'Rudolph Timm') × 'Ama'

Royal National Rose Society Certificate of Merit 1959, Anerkannte Deutsche Rose 1960, Golden Rose of The Hague 1966

'Lincoln Cathedral'

'Limona'

'Limelight'

'LILLIAN GIBSON'
MODERN, MODERN SHRUB, MEDIUM PINK

The large, double blooms of this rose appear in clusters of 15–25. Each bloom is 3 in (8 cm) across. They appear on long arching canes during summer and are extremely fragrant. This very hardy rose can reach 9 ft (2.7 m) in 2 years but has a slight tendency to rust. 'Lillian Gibson' was one of the early successes in the quest to breed winter-hardy roses; the Minnesota Agricultural Experiment Station has produced the most complete study of winter hardiness for roses. ZONES 4–11.

Hansen, USA, 1938

Rosa blanda × 'Red Star'

'LILY FREEMAN'
MODERN, MODERN SHRUB, MEDIUM PINK, REPEAT-FLOWERING

The single flowers of this variety are rose pink in color with a slight mauve tint to the pink, and are produced in small clusters from late spring until late autumn. The flowers are sweetly scented. Shining red hips are produced in abundance and look stunning among the later flowers, especially towards the end of autumn when the foliage turns to bronze, yellow and gold before falling. The bush is very compact and is immune to disease. This is an excellent rose for use as a low hedge or among bulbs and perennials in a mixed border. It was bred by Ian Huxley of Gilford in Victoria, Australia, and named after his mother. ZONES 5–10.

Huxley, Australia, 1998

'Schneezwerg' × seedling

'LIME KILN'
MODERN, RAMBLER, WHITE

This very vigorous plant was found growing in an old garden at Lime Kiln in Suffolk, England, which is now a rosarium; its origin is unknown. The flowers are small and semi-double, and have a silky whiteness about their petals. They are borne in big sprays in summer, and open cupped to show yellow stamens and diffuse a delicate fragrance.

'Linda Campbell'

'Lily Freeman'

This large plant produces reddish brown canes that are well armed with hooked prickles, which make it well suited for scrambling through trees. It extends twice as far as the average Rambler and forms a dense canopy; it is covered with many long, semi-glossy leaves of mid-green. ZONES 5–9.

UK, re-introduced 1970

Parentage unknown

'LIMELIGHT'   KORikon
syn. 'Golden Medaillon'
MODERN, LARGE-FLOWERED/HYBRID TEA, LIGHT YELLOW, REPEAT-FLOWERING

This well-named rose has light yellow flowers that can be tinged with soft green. At the half open stage, 'Limelight' has the formal elegance of a double camellia with petals of great substance in a very symmetrical arrangement. The double, high-centered blooms have 35 petals and are very fragrant. The foliage is dark green and semi-glossy on an upright, medium-sized bush. This variety is excellent to pick for indoor decoration as the green in the flower retains its color very well. ZONES 5–10.

Kordes, Germany, 1984

'Peach Melba' × seedling

'LIMONA'
MODERN, LARGE-FLOWERED/HYBRID TEA, LIGHT YELLOW, REPEAT-FLOWERING

'Limona' has long, large buds that open very slowly to huge, very well-formed flowers of the softest lemon coloring. The flower production is excellent and repeat is very quick. It is a very tall and upright plant that produces flowers on long stems. It is equally as good under glass as it is outside, and it should become one of the most popular of deep cream roses when it is better known. The vase life is extremely long. ZONES 5–10.

Kordes, Germany, 1996

Parentage unknown

'LINCOLN CATHEDRAL'
GLAnlin
syn. 'Sarong'
MODERN, LARGE-FLOWERED/HYBRID TEA, ORANGE BLEND, REPEAT-FLOWERING

One of several roses such as 'Winchester Cathedral' and 'Coventry Cathedral' named after English cathedrals, 'Lincoln Cathedral' has double flowers of 28 petals that are large and very well formed. The outer petals are pink, the inner ones orange with a yellow reverse—the mixture of colors giving the rose its synonym. The foliage is dark green and glossy and there are many red prickles on the bushy plant. This excellent garden rose is suitable for bedding, the combination of color in the flowers always attracting attention. In spite of its gold medal it is not often seen in gardens. ZONES 5–11.

Langdale, UK, 1985

'Silver Jubilee' × 'Royal Dane'

Royal National Rose Society Gold Medal 1985

'LINDA CAMPBELL'   MORten
syn. 'Tall Poppy'
MODERN, HYBRID RUGOSA, MEDIUM RED, REPEAT-FLOWERING

This rose was named after a former editor of the *American Rose Annual*, who died of cancer at a young age. The offspring of a Hybrid Rugosa crossed with a Miniature, it is a rose of very dense Rugosa-like growth that bears medium-sized flowers which repeat very quickly. The buds are pointed, and are medium red in color ageing to a paler shade. They are cupped, have 25 petals, and come in dense sprays of 5–20 blooms. There is no fragrance. The foliage is dark green and abundant. It is extremely hardy in very cold areas where temperatures fall well below zero. A bush of 'Linda Campbell' in full bloom is indeed a very colorful sight. ZONES 4–11.

Moore, USA, 1990

'Anytime' × 'Rugosa Magnifica'

'Linda Thomson'

'Linden Heath'

'Liselle'

'LINDA THOMSON' TOMtwo

MODERN, CLUSTER-FLOWERED/FLORIBUNDA,
DEEP PINK, REPEAT-FLOWERING

This Cluster-flowered Rose has fragrant, dusky pink, ruffled-edged flowers of good substance. It is a tough, disease-resistant bush with very beautiful dark green foliage that grows to medium height. Flowering is profuse and the repeat cycle is very rapid. This rose was named after the wife of the breeder. ZONES 5–11.

Thomson, Australia, 1996

'Fidelio' × 'Showbiz'

'LINDEN HEATH'

MODERN, MODERN SHRUB, MEDIUM PINK,
REPEAT-FLOWERING

'Linden Heath' is a bushy Cluster-flowered Rose that grows much wider than it grows tall. It produces masses of small, double rose pink flowers in small and large clusters over a very long period, and the repeat is very quick. The foliage is mid-green and plentiful but can be prone to black spot. This rose is good for a border as it is most compact and very free flowering, and the flowers last very well on the bush. ZONES 5–10.

Kordes, Germany, 1994

Parentage unknown

'LINVILLE'

MODERN, MINIATURE, WHITE BLEND,
REPEAT-FLOWERING

This is a useful rose for exhibitors, since it carries high-centered flowers of two dozen or so petals that hold their form well. The flowers are light pink, becoming palest blush white as they age. They are larger than most Miniature blooms, and are often borne singly. The period of flowering is maintained through summer and autumn, though not very freely, which reduces its value as a garden rose. There is a slight fruity scent, and the plant grows upright with moderate vigor to average height. Mid-green, semi-glossy foliage covers the plant. ZONES 6–9.

Bridges, USA, 1990

Seedling × seedling

'LISA MARÉE'

syn. 'Lisa'

MODERN, LARGE-FLOWERED/HYBRID TEA, DEEP
PINK, REPEAT-FLOWERING

This is an excellent rose with all the wonderful cut-flower attributes of the rose from which it sported. The buds are long and pointed and most elegant and open to extremely well-formed deep pink

flowers with a paler reverse to the petals. They last a very long time when cut. 'Lisa Marée', one of the few greenhouse roses that is equally good in the garden, has glossy foliage excellent good disease resistance. It has an amazing flower production and is grown by the tens of thousands under shadecloth in Zimbabwe for the European cut-flower market. ZONES 5–11.

Cowper, Zimbabwe, 1989

Sport of 'Esther Geldenhuys'

'LISELLE' RUlis

syn. 'Royal Romance'

MODERN, LARGE-FLOWERED/HYBRID TEA, ORANGE
BLEND, REPEAT-FLOWERING

This tall grower has plentiful dark green, disease-resistant foliage and flowers that are large and shapely and of a strong salmon-peach color. The blooms have excellent substance and last very well on the bush, and flower production is good. With its excellent foliage and brightly colored flowers this rose makes a good bedding rose, or it can be used as a hedge where strong but not garish color is required. ZONES 5–11.

de Ruiter, The Netherlands, 1981

'Whisky Mac' × 'Matador'

'LITTLE ARTIST' MACmanly

syn. 'Top Gear'

MODERN, MINIATURE, RED BLEND,
REPEAT-FLOWERING

The flowers of this 'hand-painted' masterpiece have bold splashes of red with random white markings. The florets are semi-double with 14–21 petals and quite large for a Miniature Rose. The low, spreading, disease-resistant plant blooms all year long providing a canopy of glorious blooms, each one with different markings. As the blooms age the color markings disappear to give an equally attractive, solid, medium red coloration to the petals. The bush is a well-rounded plant with mostly upright growth that looks wonderful as a container-grown plant on the patio or in the backyard. ZONES 5–11.

McGredy, New Zealand, 1982

'Eyepaint' × 'Ko's Yellow'

'LITTLE BO-PEEP' POUllen

syns 'Gentle Cover', 'Natchez', 'White
Carpet'

MODERN, MINIATURE, MEDIUM PINK,
REPEAT-FLOWERING

'Little Bo-Peep' has medium pink blooms borne in small clusters on a low-growing,

compact bush. The florets are double, with 26–40 petals depending on climate, and have a light fragrance. The foliage is small and a semi-glossy dark green with few prickles. It is relatively easy to maintain and has good disease resistance. This rose is an ideal choice for a border or container as the small clusters of blooms provide a very floriferous display. ZONES 5–11.

Olesen, Demark, 1991

'Caterpillar' × seedling

Royal National Rose Society President's
International Trophy 1991

'LITTLE BUCKAROO'

MODERN, MINIATURE, MEDIUM RED,
REPEAT-FLOWERING

The flowers on this classic rose are bright red with a fresh apple fragrance and appear in profusion on a vigorous, tall, upright bush that resists mildew and black spot. The florets are double with 23 petals surrounded by bronze, glossy, leathery foliage, making it an ideal plant for the garden. The genealogy of this rose is steeped in classical breeding lines using, as it does, one of the earliest

Miniatures known this century, 'Oakington Ruby'. This variety is propagated from cuttings. ZONES 5–11.

Moore, USA, 1956

(Rosa wichuraiana × 'Floradora') ×
('Oakington Ruby' × 'Floradora')

Certificate at International Rose Trials,
The Hague 1965

'LITTLE DARLING'

MODERN, CLUSTER-FLOWERED/FLORIBUNDA,
YELLOW BLEND, REPEAT-FLOWERING

'Little Darling' is considered one of the best introductions of the 1950s. This vigorous, spreading plant has glossy dark green, disease-resistant foliage. It produces large elongated sprays of 20–30 flowers that are a soft salmon-pink blend with yellow at the base of the petals. The medium-sized, double blooms are well formed, have 25 petals, and are spicily fragrant. The long panicles are good for cutting as the soft color shows up well indoors. ZONES 5–10.

Duehrsen, USA, 1956

'Captain Thomas' × ('Baby Château' × 'Fashion')

Portland Gold Medal 1958, All-America Rose
Society David Fuerstenberg Prize 1964

'Little Artist'

'Little Artist'

L

'LITTLE ESKIMO' MORwhit

MODERN, MINIATURE, NEAR WHITE, REPEAT-FLOWERING

The blooms of 'Little Eskimo' have been described as 'whiter than snow' or resembling small igloos because the near white flowers with almost 55 petals cover the plant in tiny puffy balls. The clusters of 3–7 blooms have no fragrance. The foliage is small, semi-glossy dark green and has long slender prickles. It has an upright growth habit, but has been used as a substantial ground cover when allowed to sprawl rather than grow upward. The rambler characteristics of this rose are obviously gained from one of its seed parents. ZONES 5–11.

Moore, USA, 1981

(*Rosa wichuraiana* × 'Floradora') × 'Jet Trail'

'LITTLE FLIRT'

MODERN, MINIATURE, RED BLEND, REPEAT-FLOWERING

The fragrant double flowers of 'Little Flirt' have 42 petals and are orange-red with a distinctive yellow reverse and a gold base. This is a very attractive color combination for garden display. The flowers do, however, have a sort of loose form. The plant has a vigorous, upright habit with light green foliage that is susceptible to mildew. This rose is now all but forgotten among the many new color combinations. ZONES 5–11.

Moore, USA, 1961

(*Rose wichuraiana* × 'Floradora') × ('Golden Glow' × 'Zee')

'Little Eskimo'

'Little Flirt'

'LITTLE GEM'

syn. 'Valide'
OLD, MOSS, DEEP PINK, REPEAT-FLOWERING

The buds of this rose are only slightly mossed, and are arranged either singly on short stalks or a few together in small clusters. The fragrant, many-petalled flowers open full to form a flat cushion, and are consistently reddish pink in color. Each flower is about 3 in (8 cm) in diameter, and they regularly repeat their bloom each autumn. The foliage is relatively small, darkish green and prolific on a dense, free-flowering shrub that attains a height of some 4 ft (1.2 m) in good soils. The almost thornless stems are liberally covered with mossy stubble. This shrub rose is of considerable garden merit and also makes a great container plant. This rose should not be confused with the Schuurman-bred Miniature of the same name. ZONES 4–10.

Paul, UK, 1880

Parentage unknown

'LITTLE GIRL'

MODERN, CLIMBING MINIATURE, ORANGE-PINK, REPEAT-FLOWERING

'Little Girl' has long pointed buds that reveal shapely coral to salmon-pink blooms on a plant with a climbing habit. The double florets have excellent form and substance, and are borne in profusion mostly in small clusters. The foliage is glossy mid-green. This rose grows more like a traditional pillar rose than a spreading climber. Its hallmarks

'Little Gem'

'Little Jackie'

are vigor, the profusion of bloom, color fastness, ease of maintenance and the fact that it is almost thornless. This rose is still one of the most popular climbing Miniatures in the USA. ZONES 5–11.

Moore, USA, 1973

'Little Darling' × 'Westmont'

'LITTLE JACKIE' SAVor

MODERN, MINIATURE, ORANGE BLEND, REPEAT-FLOWERING

The flowers on this award-winning rose are a light orange-red with a yellow reverse. The florets are double, with more than 20 petals, and have outstanding exhibition-style Large-flowered form. Bloom cycle repeat times are generally fast in most climates. The foliage is semi-glossy, mid-green and can develop mildew if it is not protected. The plant has a vigorous, upright growth habit with remarkable foliage density. 'Little Jackie' created quite a sensation at the first Royal National Rose Society National Miniature Show in St Albans, England in 1991, when it captured the newly created International Ralph Moore Trophy with a basket entry containing over 100 blooms. ZONES 5–11.

Saville, USA, 1982

('Prominent' × 'Sheri Anne') × 'Glenfiddich'

American Rose Society Award of Excellence 1984

'LITTLE LINDA'

MODERN, MINIATURE, LIGHT YELLOW, REPEAT-FLOWERING

The high pointed buds of 'Little Linda' open to semi-double yellow flowers of 17 petals with a tipped pink tinge in cooler climates. They are best described as micro-miniature because of their smallish size. The foliage is susceptible to mildew if not given appropriate protection, but the plant is vigorous and compact and provides an ample supply of blooms. When grown under good con-

'Little Girl'

'Little Opal'

'Little Paradise'

ditions, this rose shows off with mounds of sunshine yellow florets although the blooms tend to open too quickly. Generally, however, it is regarded as 'nothing special', finding patronage in only a few lonely gardens. ZONES 5–11.

Schwartz, USA, 1976

'Gold Coin' seedling × seedling

'LITTLE OPAL' SUNpat

MODERN, MINIATURE, LIGHT PINK, REPEAT-FLOWERING

The small flowers of 'Little Opal' are pale pink and fairly full, with 15–25 petals. They open rather quickly and there is a slight fragrance. Repeat-flowering occurs fairly quickly. The foliage is small, mid-green and glossy. The growth habit is upright and bushy, and the plant has good disease resistance. ZONES 5–10.

Schuurman, New Zealand, 1992

'White Dream' × 'Dicky Bird'

'LITTLE PARADISE' WEKlips

MODERN, MINIATURE, MAUVE BLEND, REPEAT-FLOWERING

'Little Paradise' has flowers of a deep lavender or blushing purple with a deeper lavender reverse, ageing to lighter tones. The double flowers with 20 petals have exquisite Large-flowered form. The blooms are usually borne one to stem and are fragrant. When fully open, the blooms have yet an additional asset—bright deep yellow contrasting stamens. Because the stems are normally strong and straight, this rose is an ideal cut flower for the home or rose show and its dependable bloom production makes it a great choice for a bright garden display. It was named by Tom Carruth to capture the form exhibited by its larger cousin, the mauve Large-flowered Rose 'Paradise'. ZONES 5–11.

Carruth, USA, 1988

'Shocking Blue' × 'Helen Boehm'

'LITTLE RAMBLER' CHEwramb
syn. 'Baby Rambler'

MODERN, CLIMBING MINIATURE, LIGHT PINK, REPEAT-FLOWERING

Delicate, porcelain pale pink, double flowers with 26–40 petals are the hallmark of this very fragrant rose. The blooms are borne in massive clusters on strong stems, and in full bloom 'Little Rambler' gets top marks. The foliage is small, dark green and semi-glossy. This plant is like a climber and can reach 7 ft (2.1 m) tall; its tendency to spread makes it an ideal candidate to train against a wall or trellis. It needs several seasons to establish but is a worthwhile rose, being clean and disease free. ZONES 5–11.

Warner, UK, 1995

('Cécile Brünner' × 'Baby Faurax') × ('Marjorie Fair' × 'Nozomi')

Royal National Rose Society Certificate of Merit 1991

'LITTLE RED DEVIL' AROvidil

MODERN, MINIATURE, MEDIUM RED, REPEAT-FLOWERING

This rose has ovoid buds that open to deep velvet red, long-lasting double blooms with 44 petals and a good scent. The blooms generally occur in small clusters of about 8 florets and the flower production is best in summer. The foliage is small and irregularly serrated. Its one glaring horticultural characteristic is the rather lengthy internodal distance between the sets of foliage. The plant has a tall, upright growth habit but can get a little rangy. Because it is winter tender, it must be protected if it is to survive. ZONES 5–11.

Christensen, USA, 1980

'Gingersnap' × 'Magic Carrousel'

'LITTLE SCOTCH'

MODERN, MINIATURE, LIGHT YELLOW, REPEAT-FLOWERING

Buff cream, petite, long buds open to straw yellow to white flowers on this variety. The florets are double, have 55 petals and are fragrant. The flower form is very informal. Color is maintained if it is given partial shade in the garden. However, this rose is susceptible to mildew and black spot and if grown in shade needs protection, probably best achieved by spraying. In full sun, the color quickly fades to a pure white. The foliage is leathery dark green on a compact, bushy plant. ZONES 5–11.

Moore, USA, 1958

'Golden Glow' × 'Zee'

'Little Red Devil'

'LITTLE SIZZLER' JACiat
syn. 'Patio Jewel'

MODERN, MINIATURE, MEDIUM RED, REPEAT-FLOWERING

The buds of 'Little Sizzler' are very pointed and open to medium red, cupped double flowers with 35 petals. They are borne both singly or in medium to large sprays, stand well above the foliage and last well without fading. The foliage, which is large for a Miniature, is dark green and semi-glossy and has hooked prickles. The plant grows to a medium height and is bushy. Flower production is good, which makes this rose excellent for mass planting in a small area. ZONES 5–10.

Warriner, USA, 1988

Seedling × 'Funny Girl'

'LITTLE SUNSET'

MODERN, MINIATURE, PINK BLEND, REPEAT-FLOWERING

'Little Sunset' has flowers that are star-shaped, with petals carrying salmon-pink on yellow. The decorative florets are usually borne in small clusters surrounded by small, light green foliage. The blooms are long lasting but the color fades rapidly in the sun. The foliage is subject to attack by mildew and black spot. It has a spreading habit if not disciplined. This rose is one of the early attempts at hybridizing Miniatures using one of the classical Miniature varieties of the time, 'Tom Thumb'. ZONES 5–11.

Kordes, Germany, 1967

Seedling × 'Tom Thumb'

'LITTLE TIGER' MORshaki

MODERN, MINIATURE, RED BLEND, REPEAT-FLOWERING

On this variety, short pointed buds open to striped flowers of varying patterns using red, yellow and white with the reverse dominant in yellow and white. The

'Lively'

florets are very double with more than 90 petals and have no fragrance. They do have a high center, but quickly collapse to decorative on opening and are generally grouped on the plant as small clusters of 3–5 blooms. Ageing blooms change color dramatically, giving the bush the appearance of a painter's messy, colorful palette. The plant habit is low, rounded and compact. 'Little Tiger' is another example of the brilliance of master miniature hybridizer, Ralph Moore, who pioneered stripes in Miniature Roses. ZONES 5–11.

Moore, USA, 1989

'Golden Angel' × 'Pinstripe'

'LITTLE WALLACE'

MODERN, CLUSTER-FLOWERED/FLORIBUNDA, PINK BLEND, REPEAT-FLOWERING

This charming little rose has an amazing capacity to flower extremely prolifically for a small-growing bush. Its buds are small, exceedingly long and pointed and very slim, making it ideal for use in posies and small arrangements. The color is soft rose pink with a yellow base to the petals. The tiny flowers are double with 25 petals, high centered and borne singly or in small clusters. The foliage is leathery and dark green. With its only fault being a tendency to mildew in late autumn, it is still grown as a cut-flower rose and can easily be propagated from cuttings. ZONES 5–10.

Beall Greenhouse Co., USA, 1952

Sport of 'Elfe'

'LITTLE WOMAN' DIClittle

MODERN, PATIO/DWARF CLUSTER-FLOWERED, PINK BLEND, REPEAT-FLOWERING

The warm pink blend blooms on the variety have 15–25 petals, Large-flowered form, and are fragrant. The blooms occur in medium-sized clusters carried on strong stems, providing a grand display

'Little Sunset'

of color all season long. In certain climates, the color varies to a rose pink or rosy salmon-pink against dark green foliage. There is no doubt that 'Little Woman' makes a wonderful choice for a container on the patio. It is also a natural choice for a small hedge or border design as the plant habit is very upright. ZONES 5–11.

Dickson, UK, 1987

'Memento' × ('Liverpool Echo' × 'Woman's Own')

Dublin Certificate of Merit 1984

'LIVELY'

MODERN, LARGE-FLOWERED/HYBRID TEA, DEEP PINK, REPEAT-FLOWERING

'Lively', one of the first roses to bloom in spring, has extremely fragrant flowers that are very full with 40 petals and are a rather harsh shade of deep pink. They can reach 6 in (15 cm) in diameter in cool weather and have exhibition form. The bush is low to medium in height, and the foliage is dark green and glossy. Flower production is good and the blooms last a long time on the bush without fading. This rose has quite good disease resistance. ZONES 5–10.

LeGrice, UK, 1959

'Wellworth' × 'Ena Harkness'

'Little Wallace'

'Little Scotch'

'Liverpool Echo'

'Living Fire'

'Lolita'

'Livin' Easy'

'Lola Montez'

'Lollipop'

'Long John Silver'

'LIVERPOOL ECHO'
syn. 'Liverpool'

MODERN, CLUSTER-FLOWERED/FLORIBUNDA,
ORANGE-PINK, REPEAT-FLOWERING

'Liverpool Echo' gets its very large
elongated panicles of flowers from its
parent 'Little Darling'. They are salmon-
pink, double with 25 petals, have good
Large-flowered form, are up to 4 in
(10 cm) across and have extremely good
substance to the petals. The plant is very
tall and bushy and can be used as a shrub
rose. The foliage is large, light green, extremely plentiful and comes up to flower
level in the manner of the Portland
Roses. Spring blooming is abundant
and continuity good. ZONES 5–10.

McGredy, UK, 1971

('Little Darling' × 'Goldilocks') × 'München'

Portland Gold Medal 1979

'LIVERPOOL REMEMBERS'
FRYstar

syn. 'Beauty Star'

MODERN, LARGE-FLOWERED/HYBRID TEA,
ORANGE-RED, REPEAT-FLOWERING

This rose bears large flowers of 40 petals
each that are a glowing vermilion color,
very large and are borne mostly singly on
very long stems. The foliage is mid-green
and glossy on a plant that is extremely

tall and upright, with an almost climbing
habit. There are many prickles. This is a
good rose for the back of the border,
blending well with such roses as 'Freude'
and 'Folklore'. It is great for cutting, as
the long stems add extra charm to the
bright color scheme. ZONES 5–10.

Fryer, UK, 1990

'Corso' × seedling

Belfast Certificate of Merit 1992

'LIVIN' EASY'   HARwelcome
syn. 'Fellowship'

MODERN, CLUSTER-FLOWERED/FLORIBUNDA,
ORANGE-BLEND

'Livin' Easy' is an excellent Cluster-
flowered Rose with flowers of a particularly glowing salmon-orange color. The
well-formed buds open to cup-shaped
blooms that reveal a central boss of
stamens. This is a vigorous and spreading bush with dark green, glossy, disease-
resistant foliage. It makes an excellent
bedding rose. There are good beds of
this rose in Regents Park in London.
ZONES 4–9.

Harkness, UK, 1992

'Southampton' × 'Remember Me'

Royal National Rose Society Gold Medal 1990,
All-America Rose Selection 1996, Portland Gold
Medal 1998

'LIVING FIRE'
MODERN, CLUSTER-FLOWERED/FLORIBUNDA,
ORANGE BLEND, REPEAT-FLOWERING

This is a very well-named rose, as the
flowers are orange suffused with orange-
red. They are double with 33 petals, have
rosette form and are medium in size. The
flowers, which are fragrant (which is
unusual in a rose of this color), come
singly and in small clusters on a moderately sized bush with dark green foliage
that nicely complements the flowers.
Flower production is continuous and the
plant has good disease resistance. 'Living
Fire' is a good rose to use where a luminous color is required. ZONES 5–11.

Gregory, UK, 1973

'Tropicana' × seedling

Royal National Rose Society Certificate of Merit
1973

'L'OBSCURITÉ'
OLD, MOSS, DARK RED

Not only is this rose obscure it is almost
impossible to obtain, the only contemporary supplier being in Denmark. It
bears large, semi-double, dark garnet-
crimson flowers. ZONES 4–9.

Lacharme, France, 1848

Parentage unknown

'LOLA MONTEZ'
syn. 'Lola Montes'

MODERN, LARGE-FLOWERED/HYBRID TEA, MEDIUM
RED, REPEAT-FLOWERING

Named after the exotic dancer, this is another brilliantly colored rose bred in
Spain for growing in a hot climate. The
blooms are a vivid orange-red with
about 20 petals, and they have great
substance. The foliage is large, rich green
and glossy. The growth is strong and upright, but there is no perfume. Flower
production is average, although they last
a long time and retain their color well
and the repeats are a little slow. 'Lola
Montez' makes a good, disease-resistant
bedding rose where a bright color is
needed. ZONES 5–9.

Dot, Spain, 1967

Parentage unknown

'LOLITA'   KORlita, LITakor
MODERN, LARGE-FLOWERED/HYBRID TEA, APRICOT
BLEND, REPEAT-FLOWERING

The soft apricot-bronze color of this rose
is unique. The very large, double flowers
with 28 petals open to large blooms with
quartered centers much like a peony.
The buds are large and ovoid and come
on very long stems with large bronze-

green foliage in the early stages, maturing to mid-green. There is a strong
perfume. With its long stems and lovely
flowers, 'Lolita' is a superb rose for cutting and lasts well indoors; it looks particularly good when used against dark
wooden panelling. It grows a little tall for
use as a bedding rose but is excellent as a
tall hedge or for planting at the back of a
rose bed. It can be affected in climates
with very cold winters, and there are no
disease problems. ZONES 5–10.

Kordes, Germany, 1972

'Colour Wonder' × seedling

Anerkannte Deutsche Rose 1973

'LOLLIPOP'
MODERN, MINIATURE, MEDIUM RED,
REPEAT-FLOWERING

These bright red flowers love the heat!
The florets are double with 35 petals and
have a light fragrance. The blooms have
good Large-flowered form and the fascinating neon red color makes this a stunning addition to the garden. Excellent
disease-resistant foliage covers the whole
plant. In general, the flowers are long
lasting and weatherproof. 'Lollipop' is
one of many sister seedlings bred from
Moore's pioneer use of a Rambler and a
Cluster-flowered Rose. ZONES 5–11.

Moore, USA, 1959

(Rosa wichuraiana × 'Floradora') × 'Little
Buckaroo'

'LONG JOHN SILVER'
MODERN, LARGE-FLOWERED CLIMBER, WHITE

This fine once-blooming climbing rose
bred from the cold-hardy, disease-free
Rosa setigera has large, white, cupped,
long-lasting fragrant flowers. They come
in clusters and are extremely double with
muddled centers like an old Centifolia
Rose. The growth is vigorous and the
plant has very large leathery leaves. After
an enormous spring flowering, an occasional bloom may be produced in summer and autumn. This is a good rose to
grow into trees, where its strong stems
soon hook onto a support. With the extremely late-flowering R. setigera in its
heritage, the rose season is extended.
ZONES 4–10.

Horvath, USA, 1934

Seedling of Rosa setigera × 'Sunburst'

'LORD GOLD'   DELgold
MODERN, LARGE-FLOWERED/HYBRID TEA, DEEP
YELLOW, REPEAT-FLOWERING

'Lord Gold' produces a continuous supply of large, shapely, clear yellow, double
flowers with 25–30 petals. Opening from
well-formed buds, the slightly perfumed
flowers are produced both singly and
several together. The foliage is a healthy
dark green on a strong bush that is medium to tall in height. This makes a good
bedding rose. ZONES 5–10.

Delbard, France, 1980

Parentage unknown

'LORD PENZANCE'
OLD, SWEET BRIAR, YELLOW BLEND

The hybridizer of many Sweet Briar
Roses is remembered in this attractive,
summer-blooming shrub. Dainty, single

'Lord Gold'

petals of soft, rosy yellow surround attractive yellow stamens. Both the flowers and the small dark leaves are fragrant, and bright red hips appear in autumn. It is a vigorous bush that does well in poor soil, and is a good choice for a woodland garden or a hedge. It has a tendency to black spot. Lord Penzance began his breeding program in 1890; he was nearly 80 when his hybrids were introduced.
ZONES 5–10.

Penzance, UK, 1894

Rosa eglanteria × 'Harison's Yellow'

'LORD RAGLAN'

OLD, HYBRID PERPETUAL, DARK RED,
REPEAT-FLOWERING

Typical of most Hybrid Perpetuals, this rose has very large blooms that are perfectly formed. The bright, velvety flowers are crimson turning to a burgundy with age, and they bloom throughout summer. Today, lost among the scores of similar roses, Lord Raglan' is still a good choice for its attractive, young red foliage and prickles and red wood. There is a strong fragrance. It is subject to mildew. Lord Raglan (1788–1855) was a British general who lost an arm at the Battle of Waterloo; he was commander-in-chief of the army in the Crimean war.
ZONES 5–10.

Guillot, France, 1854

Seedling of 'Géant des Batailles'

'LORDLY OBERON'   AUSron

MODERN, MODERN SHRUB, LIGHT PINK,
REPEAT-FLOWERING

The flowers of this rose are very double, cupped, large and extremely fragrant. They are similar in color and shape to its parent 'Chaucer', but there the similarity ends; 'Chaucer' is a shortish, stocky grower while 'Lordly Oberon' is very tall and has an almost climbing habit. The flowers are produced on tall, arching canes rather later in spring than most shrub roses. The foliage is large, matt, mid-green and very profuse on an upright plant with good disease resistance. It makes a suitable pillar rose in warm climates, or it can be used on a tripod. 'Lordly Oberon' repeat-blooms but because of its long stems takes a long time to do so; the flowers are excellent for picking, especially when long-stemmed pale pinks are required. It is also classified as an English Rose.
ZONES 4–10.

Austin, UK, 1982

'Chaucer' × seedling

'Lord Penzance'

'L'ORÉAL TROPHY'   HARlexis
syn. 'Alexis'

MODERN, LARGE-FLOWERED/HYBRID TEA, ORANGE
BLEND, REPEAT-FLOWERING

This sport of 'Alexander' shares the characteristics of that rose except in color, which is a luminous shade of reddish salmon overlaid with orange. Medium sized and double, they have a pleasant light scent and are at their best in cool weather, when they open with neatly formed high centers on long stems; they also last well. In hot conditions they fly open and develop scalloped petals. The flowers are freely produced through summer and autumn, and they are good for cutting provided they are taken young, just as the sepals are parting. This plant makes a suitable subject for a tall hedge or bed, and it looks good in a border. It is a vigorous, easy grower with an upright, free-branching habit, to above average height, and has a good complement of dark green shiny leaves. 'L'Oréal Trophy' was named by arrangement with the internationally known cosmetics enterprise.
ZONES 4–9.

Harkness, UK, 1982

Sport of 'Alexander'

Bagatelle Gold Medal 1982, Royal National Rose Society Certificate of Merit 1982, Belfast Gold Medal 1984, Courtrai Golden Rose 1986

'LORENA'   KORenlo
syn. 'Lorina'

MODERN, CLUSTER-FLOWERED/FLORIBUNDA,
MEDIUM PINK, REPEAT-FLOWERING

This respectable greenhouse rose produces large numbers of soft salmon-pink flowers on clean growth with few thorns. The double blooms have 35 petals and hold well in the bud stage, opening to well-formed full blooms of a particularly clear color. Production of blooms is very

'Lordly Oberon'

profuse, but there is no fragrance. The foliage is mid-green, semi-glossy and inclined to black spot. Although 'Lorena', which has an upright growth habit, has been superseded by better salmon-pink greenhouse varieties, it is still a good garden rose in cooler climates where the color does not bleach in the heat.
ZONES 5–11.

Kordes, Germany, 1984

'Angelique' × seedling

'LORRAINE LEE'
OLD, TEA, PINK BLEND, REPEAT-FLOWERING

One of the most famous of all Australian-bred roses, 'Lorraine Lee' is a second generation *Rosa gigantea* hybrid. Clark spent years producing roses suited to the warm Australian climate zones. The pointed buds open to double, cupped, rosy, apricot-pink blooms. It is fragrant and will bloom from early spring until the first frost. The rich green foliage has a leathery, glossy finish. A vigorous shrub, it can reach 6 ft (2 m) in 2 years; it can also be grown as a hedge. Australian rosarian Susan Irvine says that Clark created roses for the garden and not for the show table; however, he won the highest award for rose lovers—the Dean Hole Medal of the

'L'Oréal Trophy'

Royal National Rose Society. **'Climbing Lorraine Lee'** (McKay, 1932) is identical in all respects to the parent except that it reaches 18 ft (5 m) in 3 seasons.
ZONES 5–10.

Clark, Australia, 1924

'Jessie Clark' × 'Capitaine Millet'

'LOTTE GÜNTHART'

MODERN, LARGE-FLOWERED/HYBRID TEA,
MEDIUM RED, REPEAT-FLOWERING

The large, ovoid buds of 'Lotte Günthart' open very slowly to extremely double roses of 90 petals that are tightly packed in regular formation and resemble a peony. The flowers, which last a long time on the bush, also last extremely well when picked and look wonderful in mixed flower arrangements, where they can take the place of out-of-season peonies. The foliage is leathery and the growth habit is tall and upright, and disease resistance is excellent. This rose was named after one of the world's great flower painters; she lives in the medieval village of Regensberg in Switzerland, a town that has not changed in the last 400 years and specializes in painting old and new roses. ZONES 5–11.

Armstrong, USA, 1964

'Queen Elizabeth' × 'Bravo'

'Lorraine Lee'

L

'Lotte Günthart'

L

'L'OUCHE'

OLD, CHINA, PINK BLEND/LIGHT PINK, REPEAT-FLOWERING

This rose has double, perfectly cupped flowers that emerge from large, full, conical buds. The blooms are rose, sometimes shaded yellow, have thin petals and yellow stamens, and usually appear in clusters during a long flowering season. The 4 ft (1.2 m) shrub is thick and well branched, and has a compact, upright form. The dark green, thick foliage has a shading of bronze. ZONES 5–10.

Buatois, France, 1901

Parentage unknown

'LOUIS DE FUNÈS'   MEIrestif

syn. 'Charleston 88'

MODERN, LARGE-FLOWERED/HYBRID TEA, ORANGE BLEND, REPEAT-FLOWERING

This rose produces flowers of an intense apricot-orange color with a cadmium yellow reverse. They are fairly double, with 15–25 petals, and open very quickly from long elegant buds. The foliage is medium, very dark, glossy and plentiful on a strong and upright bush. The buds open too quickly for the show bench or for indoor decoration. ZONES 5–10.

Meilland, France, 1987

('Ambassador' × 'Whisky Mac') × ('Arthur Bell' × 'Kabuki')

Geneva Gold Medal 1983, Monza Gold Medal 1983

'Louis Gimard'

'Louis de Funès'

'LOUIS XIV'

OLD, CHINA, DARK RED, REPEAT-FLOWERING

Created during the high period of China Rose production in France, this royal namesake has been in the trade ever since it was introduced. It requires a warm climate and sun, which is fitting when one remembers that the king after whom the rose was named was known as The Sun King (1638–1715). The very fragrant, dark crimson, double blooms with 25 petals are globular, medium sized and full. They nod in the hot sun, and turn a bright red shaded maroon. There is sparse foliage on the compact, bushy plant. ZONES 5–10.

Guillot, France, 1859

Perhaps a seedling of 'Général Jacqueminot'

'LOUIS GIMARD'

OLD, MOSS, MEDIUM PINK

The flowers of this rose are arranged in tight clusters, and emerge from large mossy buds in mid-summer. They are very full and double and reach some 3 in (8 cm) across when fully open. The fragrant blooms are a rich cerise, brushed and highlighted magenta and pink. It is a sturdy shrub with stems that are well covered with purplish mossy stubble. The oval leaves are dark green. ZONES 5–10.

Pernet, France, 1877

Parentage unknown

'Louis XIV'

'L'Ouche'

'LOUIS PHILIPPE'

syns 'Louis Philippe d'Angers', 'Purple', 'Prince Eugene'

OLD, CHINA, RED BLEND, REPEAT-FLOWERING

This everblooming China has round, red buds that open to small, double, globular dark crimson blooms. White streaks are sometimes found on the thin, curved, fimbriated petals. It has a sweet scent and will bloom from late spring until frost. Shiny green foliage covers the bushy, rugged shrub, and the thin canes hold many small prickles. The bush can become untidy. This healthy rose can be grown easily from cuttings. ZONES 5–10.

Guérin, France, 1834

Parentage unknown

'LOUIS VAN HOUTTE'

OLD, HYBRID PERPETUAL, DARK RED, REPEAT-FLOWERING

This fragrant rose displays its best features in summer. The large, full, well-formed blooms have 40 petals. The double and crimson-maroon flowers are also cupped and mottled. The bush is quite floriferous, and the heavy blooms tend to nod. It is a vigorous 6 ft (1.8 m) bush with dark green branches and medium-sized canes; the long stems have some prickles. The leaves are glossy, and there is some repeat in autumn. This rose is named for a famous Belgian horticulturist (1810–76) known as 'the prince of nineteenth-century horticulture'. ZONES 5–10.

Lacharme, France, pre-1866

'Général Jacqueminot' × seedling

'LOUISA JANE'

MODERN, LARGE-FLOWERED/HYBRID TEA, MAUVE/PINK BLEND, REPEAT-FLOWERING

'Louisa Jane' is a sport that was found in a South Australian garden. The ground color is much paler than its parent but the petal edges are flushed with the same

'Louisa Jane'

'Louise d'Arzens'

cyclamen color, the petal reverse being almost white. This is an excellent grower with large, dark green, abundant, glossy foliage and a strong perfume. A great bedding rose, its unique color makes it very popular in Australia. The full blooms of both varieties are particularly attractive and hold their color well; both are good for cutting, combining very well with lavender and plum-toned roses. ZONES 5–10.

Ross, Australia, 1976

Sport of 'Baronne Edmond de Rothschild'

'LOUISA STONE'   HARbadge

MODERN, MODERN SHRUB, APRICOT BLEND, REPEAT-FLOWERING

'Louisa Stone' is also classified as an English Rose. With Poulsen's of Denmark introducing 'Renaissance Roses', Gaujard in France calling such roses 'Generosas' and Meilland in France calling his introductions 'Romanticas', there is some confusion over how to classify these roses, which all look like David Austin's English Roses. 'Louisa Stone' has fragrant, double flowers with 30–35 petals. They are the softest apricot color, paling to blush apricot at the petal edges, and are produced in clusters. The growth is shrubby with arching canes that will tumble attractively if not supported. It is excellent for bedding and borders and makes a good cut flower. ZONES 5–10.

Harkness, UK, 1997

Parentage unknown

'LOUISE CRETTÉ'

OLD, HYBRID PERPETUAL, WHITE, REPEAT-FLOWERING

Patience is required in establishing this rather rare rose if it is to perform to its best. The snow white, fragrant blooms, with a creamy white center and a slight yellow tint, are double with 55 petals. They are quite large, to 6 in (15 cm) across. It is an upright shrub with long stems that are covered with dark leaves and a few prickles. This offspring of 'Frau Karl Druschki' is claimed by some to be superior to the parent. ZONES 5–10.

Chambard, France, 1915

'Frau Karl Druschki' × 'Climbing Kaiserin Auguste Viktoria'

'LOUISE D'ARZENS'

OLD, NOISETTE, WHITE, REPEAT-FLOWERING

Enjoying a revival in popularity in recent years, this modest climber has attractive cream and pink buds that open to double, creamy white flowers that are full and medium sized. There is some fragrance during its repeat-flowering. This robust shrub with glossy light green foliage can reach 10 ft (3 m) in a few years. François Lacharme of Lyons, France, produced a long series of popular roses that are still in the catalogues, including 'Saland' and 'Louis van Houtte'. ZONES 5–10.

Lacharme, France, 1861

Parentage unknown

'LOUISE GARDNER' MACerupt
syn. 'Orana Gold'
MODERN, LARGE-FLOWERED/HYBRID TEA, YELLOW BLEND, REPEAT-FLOWERING

This rose produces large, double flowers with 25 petals that are yellow flushed coral on the outer petals. The petals have great texture, and the buds hold well before opening to very well-formed full blooms. There is little fragrance. The foliage is medium sized, mid-green and matt on an average-sized bushy plant. Although flower production is a little sparse, they are good for picking as they last well and hold their color. Disease resistance is good. ZONES 5–10.

McGredy, New Zealand, 1987

'Freude' × seedling of 'Sunblest'

'LOUISE ODIER'
syn. 'Mme de Stella'
OLD, BOURBON, DEEP PINK, REPEAT-FLOWERING

A first-rate cut flower and a reliable repeat bloomer, this rose has long been popular. The round buds open to reveal large, very double, warm pink flowers. It is a perfect shape for a Bourbon—cupped at first, then becoming flat and round. The ragged center petals have a lavender tint. This is one of the most floriferous of the Old Garden Roses and the flowers are held on long stems. The arching canes are covered with soft, olive green leaves and maroon prickles. If left unpruned it can be used as a climber, although more often it is a valuable addition to the border. It tolerates some shade, and its rich perfume makes it an excellent cut flower. It is the parent of many popular French roses. ZONES 4–10.

Margottin, France, 1851

Seedling of 'Emile Courtier'

'LOVE' JACtwin
MODERN, LARGE-FLOWERED/HYBRID TEA, RED BLEND, REPEAT-FLOWERING

Three roses bred by William Warriner named 'Love', 'Honor' and 'Cherish' all won the All-America Rose Selection for 1980—a remarkable feat. 'Love'

'Louise Odier'

produces rather stumpy buds of a deep cerise color with a silvery white reverse. They are double with 40 or more tightly packed petals and open slowly to well-formed exhibition-type blooms that last for a long time. Flower production is fairly good. It is a disease-resistant plant with an upright, stocky habit, and lots of large thorns. Red and silver bicolors are not very common; this is one of the best of them. ZONES 5–10.

Warriner, USA, 1980

Seedling × 'Redgold'

All-America Rose Selection 1980, Portland Gold Medal 1980

'LOVE ME' WALlove
MODERN, MINIATURE, WHITE, REPEAT-FLOWERING

The flowers of 'Love Me' are a creamy white with a marked pink edge. The double florets with 15–25 petals have a light fragrance. Although the blooms are on the small side they are complemented by equally small, matt mid-green foliage. The stems have few prickles. It has a low growing but upright habit. ZONES 5–11.

Walsh, Australia, 1994

'Magic Carrousel' × 'Old Master'

'LOVE POTION' JACsedi
syn. 'Purple Puff'
MODERN, CLUSTER-FLOWERED/FLORIBUNDA, MAUVE, REPEAT-FLOWERING

'Love Potion' produces deep clear lavender flowers in profusion. A low-spreading bush, it has medium dark green and glossy foliage that acts as a good foil to the large 30–40 petalled blooms, which are produced in small clusters. There are few prickles. There is a strong fragrance. This variety is good for small beds and borders and for inside decoration as it keeps well when picked. ZONES 5–10.

Christensen, USA, 1995

Seedling × 'Dilly Dilly'

'Love Potion'

'Loving Memory'

'LOVELY FAIRY' SPEvu
MODERN, POLYANTHA, DEEP PINK, REPEAT-FLOWERING

'Lovely Fairy' is a deep pink sport of 'The Fairy', with the same habit of growth and large clusters of small, double flowers. It is ideal for planting in warmer areas where the darker flowers keep their color better. Because of its rambler blood, it flowers later than most varieties but does so continuously through summer and autumn through to early winter. The abundant foliage is glossy, mid-green and disease free. This rose makes an ideal standard and is also useful for low hedges and for cascading over rocks and low walls. ZONES 5–10.

Spek, The Netherlands, 1990

Sport of 'The Fairy'

'LOVELY LADY' DICjubell
syn. 'Dickson's Jubilee'
MODERN, LARGE-FLOWERED/HYBRID TEA, MEDIUM PINK, REPEAT-FLOWERING

The double blooms of this rose develop slowly from large, oval buds into well-formed, fragrant flowers filled with about 35 petals. The color is a lively medium pink with a tint of coral-pink that is most attractive and lasts well. The blooms are good for cutting. 'Lovely Lady' makes a fine bedding variety, and is also excellent as a standard rose. The glossy rich green foliage is particularly healthy; it makes a dense cover to ground level over a compact bush. ZONES 5–10.

Dickson, UK, 1986

'Silver Jubilee' × ('Eurorose' × 'Anabell')

Royal National Rose Society Certificate of Merit 1983, Belfast Gold Medal 1988, Royal Horticultural Society Award of Garden Merit 1993, The Hague Silver Medal 1998

'LOVELY LOUISE'
MODERN, CLUSTER-FLOWERED/FLORIBUNDA, APRICOT BLEND, REPEAT-FLOWERING

'Lovely Louise' produces salmon-apricot, well-shaped flowers both singly and in clusters of 10 or more. Flowering continues over a long period on a short to medium-sized plant with good dark green, disease-resistant foliage. This rose is suitable for bedding where a bright but not harsh color is required. The blooms keep their color well. ZONES 5–10.

Dickson, UK, 1990

Parentage unknown

'Lovely Louise'

'Lovely Lady'

'LOVERS' MEETING'
MODERN, LARGE-FLOWERED/HYBRID TEA, ORANGE BLEND, REPEAT-FLOWERING

The long, pointed buds of this rose open fairly quickly to double flowers with 25 petals that are a clear bright orange color. The blooms, which are fragrant, are borne both singly and in clusters. The foliage is bronze in the young stages and growth is medium and upright. The plant has good disease resistance and the blooms hold their color well. This is an ideal rose for bedding where a bright color is required. ZONES 5–10.

Gandy, UK, 1980

Seedling × 'Egyptian Treasure'

Royal National Rose Society Trial Ground Certificate 1982

'LOVING MEMORY' KORgund 81
syns 'Burgund 81', 'Red Cedar'
MODERN, LARGE-FLOWERED/HYBRID TEA, MEDIUM RED, REPEAT-FLOWERING

This rose is one of the best red garden and exhibition roses available. The tall plant produces long stems carrying large abundant, semi-glossy, rich green foliage. The well-formed buds open slowly to huge full blooms with 40 symmetrically arranged petals that are high centered with excellent exhibition form. There is a slight fragrance and disease resistance is particularly good. The bush is rather too tall for bedding but is excellent for the back of a rose border; it can also be used as a very tall hedge. It is known as 'Red Cedar' in Australia, 'Loving Memory' in the UK and New Zealand, and 'Burgund 81' in Germany. ZONES 5–10.

Kordes, Germany, 1981

Seedling × seedling of 'Red Planet'

L

'Lucky Lady'

'Loving Touch'

'Lucetta'

'LOVING TOUCH'
MODERN, MINIATURE, APRICOT BLEND,
REPEAT-FLOWERING

The double, fragrant flowers of 'Loving Touch' have 25 petals and are a wonderful deep apricot in cool climates and a lighter apricot in hot climates. The large flowers are high centered and are borne one to a stem or in small clusters of 3–5. It has attractive foliage on a well-rounded, healthy, disease-resistant bush. The bloom cycle is very fast on a vigorous and easy to maintain plant. ZONES 5–11.

Jolly, USA, 1983

'Rise 'n' Shine' × 'First Prize'

American Rose Society Award of Excellence 1985

'LÜBECK'
syn. 'Hansestadt Lübeck'
MODERN, CLUSTER-FLOWERED/FLORIBUNDA,
ORANGE-RED, REPEAT-FLOWERING

This rose produces large, double, orange-red blooms in small clusters over a long period. There is very profuse bloom in spring, and the flowers hold their color well on the bush. The foliage is dark green and disease resistant on a plant with a tall habit. ZONES 5–10.

Kordes, Germany, 1962

Parentage unknown

National Rose Society Certificate of Merit 1962

'LUCETTA'   AUSemi
syn. 'English Apricot'
MODERN, MODERN SHRUB, APRICOT BLEND,
REPEAT-FLOWERING

This elegant rose has arching growth and leaves that are large, polished and very healthy. The saucer-shaped flowers are 5 in (12 cm) across and open to flat, loose, semi-double blooms that keep their color extremely well. The very clear pink buds open slowly and have a strong fragrance. Flower production is good and continuous. It is also classified as an English Rose. ZONES 4–10.

Austin, UK, 1983

Parentage unknown

'LUCKY CHARM'   MORain
MODERN, MINIATURE, YELLOW BLEND,
REPEAT-FLOWERING

The striped flowers of this rose are a combination of dominant yellow with red tinting. The unusual, double florets with 50–60 petals have high centers, but the blooms are small. The flowers are normally borne in small sprays of 3–5. The foliage is small and matt green and the plant has a low-growing habit. ZONES 5–11.

Moore, USA, 1989

'Rumba' × 'Pinstripe'

'LUCKY LADY'   ARMlu
MODERN, LARGE-FLOWERED/HYBRID TEA,
LIGHT PINK, REPEAT-FLOWERING

This rose has elegant, long, pointed buds. The double flowers have 28 petals, are a light pink color with a paler reverse, and are large, high centered and slightly fragrant. The foliage is dark green, glossy and disease resistant and the plant has an upright growth habit. Deserving its All-America Rose Selection award, 'Lucky Lady' has proved a good bedding rose over the years; the buds make very lovely cut flowers. ZONES 5–10.

Armstrong & Swim, USA, 1966

'Charlotte Armstrong' × 'Cherry Glow'

All-America Rose Selection 1967

'LUCKY PIECE'
MODERN, LARGE-FLOWERED/HYBRID TEA,
PINK BLEND, REPEAT-FLOWERING

This rose was found in an American garden in 1962 producing attractive colorful flowers of pink and yellow on a bush similar to 'Peace'. It was propagated for general sale, but the lovely new color did not remain stable as most plants reverted back to 'Peace'. Those that have not reverted have all the great attributes of 'Peace' as well as the rich coloring; however, other sports of 'Peace' such as 'Speaker Sam', 'Narre Peace' and 'White Peace' have likewise reverted to the original. Only the vivid 'Chicago Peace' has remained stable. ZONES 5–10.

Gordon, USA, 1962

Sport of 'Peace'

'LUCY ASHTON'
OLD, SWEET BRIAR, WHITE

This rose is one of the most successful roses produced by Lord Penzance in a short period at the end of the nineteenth century. When most would have given up the detailed work of hybridization, he continued into his eighties to produce 15 new roses; his use of Wild Roses had a profound effect on hybridization. This vigorous bush, covered with dark green foliage and pure white flowers edged in pink, is a candidate for a hedge or a woodland garden. It does well in poor soil and in the shade, and produces a big crop of hips soon after the end of flowering. Lucy Ashton is the tragic heroine of Sir Walter Scott's novel *The Bride of Lammermoor*, adapted by Donizetti for his opera *Lucia di Lammermoor*. ZONES 5–10.

Penzance, UK, 1894

Hybrid of *Rosa eglanteria*

'LUCY BERTRAM'
OLD, SWEET BRIAR, RED BLEND

This Penzance hybrid bears dark, shining crimson blooms with a white center. It is a vigorous bush with dark, fragrant foliage and makes an excellent hedge when planted in groups or in a woodland garden. If kept trimmed it will form a hedge of 6 ft (1.8 m) that will provide a strong barrier; it is also valuable as a pillar rose. There is an attractive crop of hips. Lucy Bertram is a romantic character in Sir Walter Scott's novel *Guy Mannering*. ZONES 5–10.

Penzance, UK, 1895

Hybrid of *Rosa eglanteria*

'LUCY CRAMPHORN'
syns 'Maryse Kriloff', 'Lucie Crampton'
MODERN, LARGE-FLOWERED/HYBRID TEA,
ORANGE-RED, REPEAT-FLOWERING

This variety has large, double flowers with 40 petals that are a strong signal red color; well formed and fragrant, they retain their color well, which makes 'Lucy Cramphorn' a good bedding rose. The foliage is glossy on a disease-resistant, vigorous and upright plant. The flowers last well both on the bush and when picked. One parent, 'Baccarà', was the first of the great greenhouse roses bred by the House of Meilland. ZONES 5–10.

Kriloff, France, 1960

'Peace' × 'Baccarà'

National Rose Society Certificate of Merit 1960

'LUIS DESAMERO'   TINluis
MODERN, MINIATURE, LIGHT YELLOW,
REPEAT-FLOWERING

This popular pastel yellow Miniature Rose is regarded internationally as one of the few truly colorfast varieties, especially in hot climates. The exhibition-type blooms, containing about 28 petals, are normally borne one to a stem but often in colder climates in small sprays of 3–5 blooms. Perhaps the most spectacular feature of this rose is the complementary deep green foliage with a shorter than normal internodal variance. Given space, this vigorous rose will grow tall and proud in all climates zones. It is regarded as fairly disease resistant and can possess a fruity fragrance. Named for a notable Southern California rose exhibitor by Dee Bennett, it has earned its place in rose history as one of the favorite exhibition Miniature Roses on both sides of the Atlantic. ZONES 5–11.

Bennett, USA, 1989

'Tiki' × 'Baby Katie'

'Lucky Charm'

'Lucky Piece'

L

'Lutin'

'LULU'
MODERN, CLUSTER-FLOWERED/FLORIBUNDA, ORANGE-PINK, REPEAT-FLOWERING

'Lulu' was bred from 'Zorina', a rose that was used a great deal for the breeding of greenhouse roses because of its durability, good form and strong color. This variety has double flowers of orange-pink that are smallish, well formed and slightly fragrant. The foliage is dark bronze in the early stages and growth is vigorous and upright. Flower production is very high and the plant is disease resistant. ZONES 5–11.

Kordes, Germany, 1973

'Zorina' × seedling

'LUSTIGE'   LuKOR
syn. 'Jolly'
MODERN, LARGE-FLOWERED/HYBRID TEA, RED BLEND, REPEAT-FLOWERING

'Lustige' produces flowers of an intense coppery flame red color with a yellow reverse that are large, double, cupped and very fragrant. The buds are also very attractive in color, but open rather quickly to well-formed full blooms. The color is most attractive and can be enjoyed over a long period as the flowers are produced in abundance. The foliage is large, glossy and leathery on a plant with a vigorous and upright growth habit with no disease problems. ZONES 5–10.

Kordes, Germany, 1973

'Peace' × 'Brandenburg'

'LUTIN'
MODERN, MINIATURE, DEEP PINK, REPEAT-FLOWERING

This is a fine little Miniature Rose with 58 pointed petals making up a well-shaped bloom. Flowers are produced in small, well-filled clusters. This dwarf bushy plant reaches 12–15 in (30–38 cm) in height. Flower production is well above average and the repeat bloom is rapid. Disease resistance is good. 'Lutin' is an excellent rose for a very low border or for planting in a pot or container. ZONES 5–10.

Breeder unknown, 1970

Sport of 'Scarlet Gem'

'LYDA ROSE'   LETlyda
MODERN, MODERN SHRUB, WHITE BLEND

This rose was bred by Kleine Lettunich, the breeder of 'Mateos Pink Butterflies', and was named after her daughter and the song from 'Music Man'. 'Lyda Rose' has single, 2½ in (6 cm) wide flowers that are white edged with delicate pink.

'Lyda Rose'

They are borne in large clusters to give an apple blossom-like appearance. The fragrance is very strong. It is a disease-free and spreading plant with rich green foliage that will even flower well in the shade. It makes an excellent bushy, free-flowering hedge. ZONES 5–10.

Lettunich, USA, 1994

Seedling of 'Francis E. Lester'

'LYDIA'
MODERN, LARGE-FLOWERED/HYBRID TEA, DEEP YELLOW, REPEAT-FLOWERING

There are three roses named 'Lydia', one from 1933, another from 1973 and this variety from 1949, possibly the most durable of them. The long, pointed buds are an intense saffron yellow color. They are high centered, very double and of medium size, and are produced prolifically. The foliage is dark green, leathery and glossy and growth is vigorous. After some 50 years in commerce 'Lydia' is still remembered as a good rose for bedding; it has stood the test of time for a rose in the yellow color range. ZONES 5–10.

Robinson, UK, 1949

'Phyllis Gold' × seedling

'LYKKEFUND'
MODERN, RAMBLER, WHITE BLEND

This Danish rambler follows its parent by producing huge fragrant trusses of semi-double blooms in one great flush in mid-summer. The medium-sized flowers are creamy yellow, darker at the center, and are tinged with pink; in the sun they fade to white. There are attractive orange-yellow stamens. This 'lucky find' is aptly named as it will cover a pergola or a fence with 18 ft (5 m) canes, or will arch over a pergola. The small, glossy, dark foliage has bronze edges. ZONES 5–10.

Olesen, Denmark, 1930

Seedling of Rosa helenae × 'Zéphirine Drouhin'

'LYNETTE'   KORlyn
MODERN, LARGE-FLOWERED/HYBRID TEA, WHITE, REPEAT-FLOWERING

'Lynette' has very long pointed buds that are cream blended with coral pink. They are double, well formed, open slowly and are produced singly or in small clusters. There is no fragrance. The plant is tall and the foliage dark. A popular rose in South Africa but not well known elsewhere, it is a popular rose for cutting and lasts well indoors. ZONES 5–10.

Kordes, Germany, 1983

'Clivia' × MEItakilor

'LYNN ANDERSON'   WEKjoe
syn. 'Oh My God'
MODERN, LARGE-FLOWERED/HYBRID TEA, PINK BLEND, REPEAT-FLOWERING

This rose has large flowers that are white edged deep pink. They have 35–40 petals and are borne singly on long stems. The plant is strong, tall and upright and has very large, mid-green foliage. There are few prickles. Although the flowers open very slowly, they hold their form and color well. ZONES 5–10.

Winchel, USA, 1995

Seedling × 'Gold Medal'

'LYNNE GOLD'   MORlyn
MODERN, MINIATURE, MEDIUM YELLOW, REPEAT-FLOWERING

'Lynne Gold' has tiny pointed buds that open to equally tiny yellow flowers. The florets are double with 25 petals and have a light fragrance. They are borne in small clusters with a good inflorescence. The open blooms are not quite as attractive and should be removed from the bush. The plant is vigorous, well branched and spreading. ZONES 5–11.

Moore, USA, 1983

'Ellen Poulsen' × 'Yellow Jewel'

'LYON RAMBLER'
MODERN, RAMBLER, DEEP PINK

No longer in commerce, this variety has rose pink blooms flushed with carmine. The semi-double, fragrant flowers are medium sized and appear in clusters during a long flowering period in summer. It is a vigorous plant with vine-like canes that is full of prickles and is disease resistant. The city of Lyons was the center of the rose world from 1830 until World War I, and many roses bear the name of the city. ZONES 4–10.

Dubreuil, France, 1909

Seedling of 'Crimson Rambler'

'LYON ROSE'
syn. 'Lyon's Rose'
MODERN, LARGE-FLOWERED/HYBRID TEA, ORANGE-PINK, REPEAT-FLOWERING

'Lyon Rose' is of great importance historically as it is one of the Pernetiana strain of roses bred from Rosa foetida persiana—the rose that was the ancestor of all the rich yellow, bright red and bicolor varieties of today. It has rather poor-textured flowers of pink shaded coral-red and yellow in the center. They are double with 44 petals, large and very fragrant. The bush is rather low and very spreading and the foliage is matt, pale green and not very abundant. This rose caused a sensation in the early part of this century because of its unique color. ZONES 5–10.

Pernet-Ducher, France, 1907

'Mme Mélanie Soupert' × seedling of 'Soleil d'Or'

Bagatelle Gold Medal 1909

'LYRIC'
MODERN, MODERN SHRUB, MEDIUM PINK

This rose has fragrant, rose pink, double flowers with 28 petals, medium in size and produced in large clusters. The foliage is healthy on a vigorous and upright plant. It was once used a lot for hedges and borders, but it is not seen very much these days. ZONES 4–10.

de Ruiter, The Netherlands, 1951

'Sangerhausen' × seedling

'Lustige'

'Lyon Rose'

'Lykkefund'

'MA PERKINS'

MODERN, CLUSTER-FLOWERED/FLORIBUNDA,
PINK BLEND, REPEAT-FLOWERING

'Ma Perkins' gets its cupped flowers
with central petals turning inwards
from 'Red Radiance' and some of its shell
pink color from 'Fashion'. The fragrant
flowers are double, cupped and large to
3½ in (9 cm) across. When they are
open, the lovely full blooms are a clear
pink color shaded with salmon. These
last well both on the bush and when
picked. The foliage is rich green and
glossy on a tall and vigorous plant. David
Austin saw the potential of the cupped,
old world form flowers of this rose and
used it in the breeding of 'Wife of Bath',
which he has also used widely in the
breeding of other varieties. ZONES 5–10.

Boerner, USA, 1952

'Red Radiance' × 'Fashion'

National Rose Society Certificate of Merit 1952,
All-America Rose Selection 1953

'MA TULIPE'

OLD, TEA, DARK RED, REPEAT-FLOWERING

This old and forgotten rose was found
growing in South Africa in an old garden
in the Langkloof by Gwen Fagan. It was
identified from descriptions in nineteenth-century South African catalogues.
The shrub has many of the typical qualities of Tea Roses: dark maroon, shiny
new leaves, angular growth and a lovely
fresh fragrance. The full, pointed buds
open into cup-shaped, crimson blooms;
the flower cup looks like a tulip because

the petals are quite long. They keep their
shape until the petals suddenly relax and
drop within a day. The blooms are produced in relays throughout the summer
and it is often the last rose in bloom in
the autumn garden. ZONES 5–12.

Parentage unknown

'MAB GRIMWADE'

MODERN, LARGE-FLOWERED/HYBRID TEA,
YELLOW BLEND, REPEAT-FLOWERING

'Mab Grimwade' is a small-growing
bush that bears flowers of a rich chrome
yellow shaded with apricot tints in the
center. The buds are very pretty and
open very quickly to double blooms.
Most of Alister Clark's roses are very
strong growers, but this one suffers badly
in cold winters. It is small to medium in
size. The mid-green foliage is disease
free, and the repeat bloom is good. This
was a popular rose in Australian gardens
in the 1940s when there was a shortage of
apricot and yellow roses. ZONES 5–10.

Clark, Australia, 1937

'Souvenir de Gustave Prat' × seedling

'MABEL MORRISON'

syn. 'White Baroness'

OLD, HYBRID PERPETUAL, WHITE,
REPEAT-FLOWERING

Always considered an excellent white
rose and cut flower, 'Mabel Morrison'
has been popular ever since its introduction. The handsome buds open to flesh
white, well-formed blooms with streaks
of pink appearing in hot weather. The

'Ma Perkins'

'Mab Grimwade'

'McGredy's Yellow'

MACspice

cupped, very fragrant small flowers are
double with 30 petals and appear in clusters. It is an upright bush with a stout,
erect form that does well in poor soil.
The beautiful foliage hides many prickles.
Growing to 4 ft (1.2 m) high and wide,
it is an excellent choice for a hedge or a
container plant, and will bloom during
summer with some autumn repeat.
Graham Thomas believes that this rose
is closer to a Portland because of the
grayish leaves, erect form and the Damask-like hips. ZONES 5–10.

Broughton, 1878

Sport of 'Baroness Rothschild'

'McGREDY'S SUNSET'

MODERN, LARGE-FLOWERED/HYBRID TEA,
ORANGE BLEND, REPEAT-FLOWERING

There are at least 20 roses with
'McGredy' in their name; 'McGredy's
Sunset' and 'McGredy's Yellow' are two
that have stood the test of time. This variety has long, pointed buds that are
chrome yellow usually stained with
peach and scarlet, with a clear yellow reverse to the petals. They are fragrant,
double, globular and open flat, and are at
their most attractive when about a third
open even though they are rather loose.
The flowers appear early in spring and
the repeat-bloom is very quick. The
young growth is bronze, maturing to
green on a dense and spreading bush.
This is still an obtainable rose after over
60 years in commerce. There is a climbing form, which unfortunately usually
reverts back to the bush. ZONES 5–10.

McGredy, UK, 1936

'Margaret McGredy' × 'Mabel Morse'

'McGREDY'S YELLOW'

MODERN, LARGE-FLOWERED/HYBRID TEA,
MEDIUM YELLOW, REPEAT-FLOWERING

This rose is one of the best available in
the pale yellow range. The long, pointed

'McGredy's Sunset'

'Madam President'

buds open to large, slightly cupped
double flowers containing 30 petals. The
color is a clear soft yellow, which is rare
in roses; the Modern Garden Rose 'Elina'
is something of the same shade. There
is a slight fragrance. The foliage is glossy
and bronze in the early stages turning
to mid-green on a vigorous, very free-
flowering plant that continues to flower
well into winter in warmer areas.
Mildew can occur at times. 'Climbing
McGredy's Yellow' (Western Rose Co.,
USA, 1937) is a particularly strong
climbing rose with lush, large green
leaves and thick thorny canes. It produces an enormous crop of flowers in
spring, especially if the canes are tied
down into a horizontal position at
pruning. ZONES 5–10.

McGredy, UK, 1933

'Mrs Charles Lamplough' × ('The Queen
Alexandra Rose' × 'J. B. Clark')

National Rose Society Gold Medal 1930, Portland
Gold Medal 1956

MACSPICE MACspike

MODERN, MINIATURE, MAUVE, REPEAT-FLOWERING

The basically mauve-pink flowers on this
variety are borne on larkspur-like sprays
that are about 12 in (30 cm) long. The
semi-double florets have a light scent.
These long flowering spikes are gracefully tipped with many small mauve
blooms (almost 50 per stem), giving the
overall appearance of a shrub rather than
a Miniature Rose. The foliage is small
and semi-glossy. This plant creates the
most beautiful display in the garden with
spreading arches covered with massive
trusses of blooms. It is a great addition
to the class, adding architectural beauty
beyond the normal bush habit.
ZONES 5–11.

McGredy, New Zealand, 1983

'Anytime' × 'Gardendirektor Otto Linne'

'MADAM PRESIDENT'

syn. 'Madame President'

MODERN, CLUSTER-FLOWERED/FLORIBUNDA,
PINK BLEND, REPEAT-FLOWERING

'Madam President' has some of the
most beautiful flowers of any rose. The
buds are beautifully shaped and open
slowly to very full blooms of camellia-
like perfection that have 30 petals and
are soft rose pink with a cream base.
The flowers hold their form and color
well and come singly or in small clusters
on a moderately sized bush. 'Madam
President' is particularly quick to repeat
bloom. The foliage is smallish, dark

M

green and profuse and disease resistance is good except for occasional black spot; it is an excellent rose for picking and lasts well inside; it is also superb as a standard because of its bushy nature. This rose seems to be mainly grown in New Zealand and Australia, where it is a recommended rose for general purposes. It has some fragrance. ZONES 5–10.

McGredy, New Zealand, 1975

Seedling × 'Handel'

'MME ABEL CHATENAY'
MODERN, LARGE-FLOWERED/HYBRID TEA, PINK BLEND, REPEAT-FLOWERING

'Mme Abel Chatenay' has had her 100th birthday and is still one of the most loved and popular of the very early Large-flowered Roses. With the Tea Rose 'Doctor Grill' as one parent and a Hybrid Perpetual as another, this could be just as easily classed as a Tea Rose. The pale pink buds are pointed and open to full, double, pale pink blooms with a deeper center and strong carmine pink on the reverse. They are fragrant. The foliage is bronze when young, maturing to green. It is surprising that such a lovely rose received no awards, but in 1895 the only awards available were from the National Rose Society in England and that appeared to be for the quality of the flower with no regard for the bush or habit of growth. 'Climbing Mme Abel Chatenay' (Page, UK, 1917) is still one of the best and most repeat-flowering of all pink climbing roses. ZONES 5–10.

Pernet-Ducher, France, 1895

'Doctor Grill' × 'Victor Verdier'

'MME ALFRED CARRIÈRE'
OLD, NOISETTE, WHITE, REPEAT-FLOWERING

Known for its reliable health, this rampant climber produces a continuous display of pale, pinkish white blooms over a long period. There is yellow at the base below the curly central petals. The large,

full, globular blooms have a Tea-like fragrance. The light, pale green foliage has well-serrated edges, and the flexible canes make it easy to train on a fence, wall, or pergola. It doesn't mind shade and can be propagated easily from cuttings. This popular rose was a creation of Joseph Schwartz, whose widow carried on his work—producing such famous plants as 'Mme Ernst Calvat' and 'Roger Lambelin'. In 1908 it was proclaimed 'the best white climber' with 62 out of 83 votes of the National Rose Society in England. ZONES 4–10.

Schwartz, France, 1879

Parentage unknown

Royal Horticultural Society Award of Garden Merit 1993

'MME ALFRED DE ROUGEMONT'
OLD, HYBRID PERPETUAL, LIGHT PINK, REPEAT-FLOWERING

This rose is classified by some as a Bourbon. It is a vigorous, tall-growing bush that bears medium-sized flowers, which open white with a tint of flesh pink that is deeper in the centers. The blooms are cupped and have been described as having a dainty and modest appearance. It blooms early in the growing season, with an occasional repeat, and is very floriferous. This rose produces vigorous growth. ZONES 5–9.

Lacharme, France, 1862

'Blanche Lafitte' × 'Sappho'

'MME ALICE GARNIER'
syn. 'Brownlow Hill Rambler'
MODERN, RAMBLER, PINK BLEND

The first part of the twentieth century found hybridizers in France creating a long list of wichuraiana climbers. This rampant Rambler bears many clusters of open, bright rose flowers with a center of yellow and light pink. The blooms are formed on long, slender branches. The

'Mme Alfred Carrière'

'Mme Abel Chatenay'

'Mme Antoine Mari'

flat rosettes of quilled and quartered petals have a strong fragrance of apples. It reaches 15 ft (4.5 m) and is covered with abundant small, dark, glossy foliage when the young bronze shoots mature. It does well in poor soil and tolerates shade. ZONES 5–10.

Fauque, France, 1906

Rosa wichuraiana × 'Mme Charles'

'MME ANTOINE MARI'
OLD, TEA, PINK BLEND, REPEAT-FLOWERING

Antoine Mari of Nice, France, produced this reliable Tea Rose during the period when Teas and Chinas were very popular. The camellia-like blooms are rosy flesh shaded lilac; sometimes there are cream-white stripes. The quilled petals create shapely, fragrant blooms that are double, full and large. The buds are particularly beautiful later in the season. This is a tidy plant suitable for a container or for being trained on a warm wall. It has plum-colored canes lined with light green leaves; there are prickles. It does best in the sun but in a protected spot. ZONES 6–11.

Mari, France, 1901

Parentage unknown

'MME ARTHUR OGER'
OLD, CLIMBING BOURBON, MEDIUM PINK, REPEAT-FLOWERING

No longer in commerce, it appears that this rose has also disappeared from botanical collections; like so many 'lost' roses, it may someday be found in a cem-

etery or an abandoned house. It has very large, double, brilliant pink blooms tinged with salmon. One writer described it as a stand-in for 'Zéphirine Drouhin', which may explain why that famous rose has overshadowed this one. It is bushy in form, hardy and quite vigorous. Pierre Oger introduced 95 hybrids with only 'Mme Pierre Oger', which was named after his wife, still in the catalogues. ZONES 4–10.

Oger, France, 1899

Seedling of 'Mme Isaac Pereire'

'MME BÉRARD'
OLD, CLIMBING TEA, ORANGE BLEND, REPEAT-FLOWERING

Looking very much like 'Gloire de Dijon', this rose is salmon-yellow shaded salmon-rose. It is double, large and cupped, and the petals unfold in scrolls with muddled centers. In full sun the flowers fade to pink and yellow. It will bloom from late spring until the first frost, and critics have claimed that this fragrant rose is one of the best Climbing Teas. It reaches 10 ft (3 m) high and wide, and is covered in dark green leaves. Hardier than most Tea Roses, it likes a sunny spot. Antoine Levet of Lyons, France, created many well-known roses between 1866 and 1889, among them 'Paul Neyron' and 'Perle des Jardins'. This one is sometimes listed with the Noisettes. ZONES 5–10.

Levet, France, 1872

'Mme Falcot' × 'Gloire de Dijon'

'Mme Alice Garnier'

M

'Mme Boll'

'Mme Berkeley'

'Mme Butterfly'

'Mme Bollinger'

'Mme Bravy'

'MME BERKELEY'
OLD, TEA, PINK BLEND, REPEAT-FLOWERING

This rose is well known as an excellent cut flower. It is very double, well shaped and long in the bud. The petals are arranged very much like a Large-flowered Rose, and the centers of the blooms are salmon with a blowzy form. The lightly scented blooms appear all summer and into autumn. It is a compact, bushy plant that should be pruned regularly to keep its shape, and is a good candidate for the border or a container. It does best in the sun. ZONES 5–10.

Bernaix, France, 1898

Parentage unknown

'MME BOLL'
OLD, PORTLAND/HYBRID PERPETUAL, DEEP PINK, REPEAT-FLOWERING

There is some dispute about the lineage of this rose, with one source giving a Hybrid Perpetual and 'Belle Fabert' as the parents and another classifying it as a Portland. It has been popular for nearly 150 years. The plump, carmine-rose blooms are large and open well. They are 4 in (10 cm) across, with large outer petals and many muddled inner ones. The very fragrant flowers appear late in spring and continue until the first frost. It has vigorous, stout canes that are covered with large leaves and dark gray prickles. The stems are short, bristly and glandular. ZONES 5–10.

Boll and Boyau, France, 1859

Probably 'Baronne Prévost' × 'Portlandica'

'MME BOLLINGER'
MODERN, CLUSTER-FLOWERED/FLORIBUNDA, ORANGE-PINK, REPEAT-FLOWERING

This is another rose bred from the beautifully formed 'Little Darling'. The flowers are deep salmon-orange, double with 25 petals, and are of good Large-flowered form. They are large—up to 3 in (8 cm) across— and are slightly fragrant. They come in nicely shaped trusses that hold their form and color well. Growth is moderately vigorous and the plant has good disease resistance. It makes a good bedding rose. ZONES 5–10.

McGredy, New Zealand, 1972

('Little Darling' × 'Goldilocks') × 'Bobbie Lucas'

'MME BRAVY'
syns 'Adèle Pradel', 'Danzille', 'Mme de Sertat'
OLD, TEA, NEAR WHITE, REPEAT-FLOWERING

Known for its raspberry-scented blooms, this rose has cupped, globular flowers that are creamy white sometimes shaded pink. These double blooms have short, folded center petals. This floriferous bloomer is a hardy bush covered with light green leaves. Its 3 ft (1 m) size makes it a good container plant. ZONES 6–11.

Guillot, France, 1846

Parentage unknown

'MME BUTTERFLY'
MODERN, LARGE-FLOWERED/HYBRID TEA, LIGHT PINK, REPEAT-FLOWERING

This rose is very similar to 'Ophelia', from which it sported; in the 1920s and 1930s exhibitors were not allowed to show both varieties as the judges could not tell them apart! The elegant buds are long and pointed and open to fragrant, double flowers with 28 petals. The foliage is leathery, and the growth is moderate. 'Climbing Mme Butterfly' (Smith, UK, 1926) is one of the best climbing roses, producing masses of lovely buds in large clusters in spring. If spent blooms are removed it flowers through summer and into autumn, where the color is richer and the blooms are larger and last longer. It is excellent growing over an arch or on a wall. The flowers can be damaged by thrips in spring. ZONES 5–10.

Hill & Company, USA, 1918

Sport of 'Ophelia'

'MME CAROLINE TESTOUT'
syn. 'City of Portland'
MODERN, LARGE-FLOWERED/HYBRID TEA, MEDIUM PINK, REPEAT-FLOWERING

This rose was named after a Parisian couturière and, although well over a century old, it is still grown in gardens throughout the world. The buds are large and globular, and the large flowers are bright rose with a darker center tinted carmine. They are very double and very fragrant. The petals are inclined to turn inwards at the center, giving a globular look. This rose was used by David Austin to produce 'Wife of Bath' and is in the pedigree of many of his Modern Shrub Roses (also classified as English Roses). It is a tough and hardy bush but the flowers are perhaps a little lacking in substance, a trifle papery in texture and they can ball in wet weather. 'Climbing Mme Caroline Testout' (Chauvry, France, 1901) is excellent on arches, pillars or pergolas or the walls of houses, where its large, globular blooms and strong scent can be appreciated. It is disease free. ZONES 5–11.

Pernet-Ducher, France, 1890

'Mme de Tartas' × 'Lady Mary Fitzwilliam'

'Climbing Mme Butterfly'

'Mme de Sancy de Parabère'

'MME CHARLES'
OLD, TEA, YELLOW BLEND/PINK BLEND, REPEAT-FLOWERING

This is one of the earlier French Teas. It has handsome buds that usually open to pink blooms, although some growers have reported it as having yellow blooms with a salmon center. They are full, semi-globular and appear in clusters. In the hot sun the color turns to sulfur. The shrub has no prickles, likes a warm position in the garden and will bloom throughout summer and into autumn. One early writer stated that it is an improved strain of 'Safrano'. ZONES 6–11.

Damaizin, France, 1864

'Mme Damaizin' × seedling

'MME CHARLES BALTET'
OLD, BOURBON, LIGHT PINK, REPEAT-FLOWERING

Rarely seen today, the strongly fragrant flowers of this Bourbon Rose appear in large clusters of 4–6. They overlap, are very full and are a delicate pink color, and are best in autumn if the summers are hot. It starts to bloom in early summer and is a vigorous, healthy shrub that reaches 5 ft (1.5 m) in maturity. Bourbons were named after the Ile de Bourbon in the Indian Ocean, which today is called Réunion; they have a very complicated and confusing origin. All Bourbons have large, wide, silky petals, and between 1830 and 1870 they were the most popular roses. Eugene Verdier produced an astonishing 222 hybrids in his Paris nursery. ZONES 5–10.

Verdier, France, 1865

Parentage unknown

'MME CORNÉLISSEN'
OLD, BOURBON, WHITE, REPEAT-FLOWERING

This rose never achieved the popularity of its parent. Its flowers are fragrant, small, nearly full and flat. The white blooms are suffused with pink, and there are attractive yellow anthers. There is some repeat-bloom. The foliage is large and pointed on a plant with a medium growth habit that is subject to black spot, especially in wet weather. 'Mme Cornélissen' lacks the charm and beauty of its parent. ZONES 5–10.

Cornélissen, 1865

Sport of 'Souvenir de la Malmaison'

'MME DE LA RÔCHE-LAMBERT'
OLD, MOSS, MAUVE, REPEAT-FLOWERING

This rose flowers continuously throughout summer and autumn, the blooms

'Mme Charles'

emerging from shapely, feathery buds that are well covered with light green moss. The rich deep burgundy-colored flowers are made up of many scrolled and fluted petals. These are highly scented and up to 3½ in (8 cm) across. It is a broadly growing shrub to about 4 ft (1.2 m) high. The stems are heavily mossed with soft stubble and bear few thorns of consequence. The bright green leaves are round, soft and smooth. This is a classic among the Moss Roses, if a slight propensity to mildew can be overlooked. ZONES 4–10.

Robert, France, 1851

Parentage unknown

Royal Horticultural Society Award of Garden Merit 1993

'MME DE SANCY DE PARABÈRE'
syns 'Mme Sancy de Parabère', 'Virginian Lass'
OLD, BOURSAULT, LIGHT PINK

This variety is one of four Boursaults cultivated today, a class of rose that originated in Paris. The clear, soft pink blooms are double, with the outer petals larger than the inside ones. The sweetly fragrant flowers are 5 in (12 cm) across, loose, circular and flat—they appear in large clusters. It blooms only once. This is called the largest flowered form of its class, and can easily reach 15 ft (4.5 m) high. It does best in partial shade, is quite hardy and does well in poor soil and all kinds of weather. The autumn foliage is particularly attractive and there are no prickles. The experts cannot agree on its classification. ZONES 4–10.

Bonnet, France, 1874

Parentage unknown

'MME DE SÉVIGNÉ'
OLD, BOURBON, PINK BLEND, REPEAT-FLOWERING

The blooms of this rose are bright rose in the center and lighter at the edges. They are full, large, double, and the petal edges are blush white. There is some perfume. There is a profuse flowering in summer with some repeat later. It is a vigorous shrub with attractive, large leaves. Marie de Rabutin-Chantal, Marquise de Sévigné (1626–96), was a famous French correspondent whose letters to her daughter are still popular reading. She is remembered as a highly principled, intelligent and delightful woman, the perfect subject for a rose like this. ZONES 5–11.

Moreau et Robert, France, 1874

Parentage unknown

'MME DE TARTAS'
syn. 'Mme de Thartas'
OLD, TEA, LIGHT PINK, REPEAT-FLOWERING

The large, cupped, blush pink blooms of this rose appear from early summer until the first frost. They are fully double, slightly fragrant, blowzy, and in the shade are an intense pink. It can be treated as a vigorous shrub or climber, or as a sprawling ground cover. The leathery, dark green foliage covers the large prickles. This is a most under-rated beautiful rose in mild climates that is an important ancestor of many Large-flowered Roses created during Victorian times. Jack Harkness believed it was the pollen parent for 'Mermaid'. ZONES 6–11.

Bernède, France, 1859

Parentage unknown

'MME DE WATTEVILLE'
OLD, TEA, YELLOW BLEND, REPEAT-FLOWERING

The buds of 'Mme de Watteville' are held on long stalks and open to full, free, well-formed flowers. The large, very fragrant blooms are lemon usually edged in pale pink; they resemble tulips on first opening and bloom throughout summer and into autumn. Small, dark green, dense foliage covers the branching, low-growing shrub. It does best in full sun, which will help it avoid a tendency to mildew. This modest rose is an ideal candidate for a container, as it is more tender than other Tea Roses. ZONES 6–11.

Guillot, France, 1883

Parentage unknown

'MME D'HÉBRAY'
syn. 'Unique Panachée'
OLD, GALLICA, PINK BLEND

This rose bears large, well-formed, full, white blooms with rose overtones sometimes with pink stripes. The fragrant flowers, flaunting golden stamens at their centers, are borne singly on arching canes. The blooms become blowzy as they age during the early summer blooming. The bristly canes harbor a few prickles and small hips. The light green foliage is healthy and attractive. This rose has also been classified as a Centifolia. ZONES 5–10.

Probably Pradel, France, 1857

Parentage unknown

'MME DIEUDONNÉ'
syn. 'Mme L. Dieudonné'
MODERN, LARGE-FLOWERED/HYBRID TEA, RED BLEND, REPEAT-FLOWERING

With four fiery red and orange roses in its pedigree, it is no surprise that this variety bears luminous orange-red flowers with gold undersides. The long, pointed buds, which are a beautiful rich bicolor, open quickly to double blooms of 30 petals that are high centered, large and fragrant. The full blooms lose their intense color rather quickly. The foliage is dark and glossy on a medium-sized, vigorous bush that can suffer from mildew. ZONES 5–10.

Meilland, France, 1949

('Mme Joseph Perraud' × 'Brazier') × ('Charles P. Kilham' × 'Capucine Chambard')

National Rose Society Certificate of Merit 1950

M

'Mme de Watteville'

'Mme Dieudonné'

'Mme de Tartas'

'MME DORÉ'
OLD, BOURBON, LIGHT PINK

Rare in its appearances in public or private gardens, this Bourbon Rose has large, light pink blooms that are full and fragrant. Its vigorous growth habit makes it ideal for a hedge or the woodland. Like most of its class, the petals are fragile and do not like wet weather. François Fontaine of Clamart, France, produced many Hybrid Perpetuals and several Bourbons. ZONES 5–10.

Fontaine, France, 1863

Parentage unknown

'MME DRIOUT'
syn. 'Mme Dreout'
OLD, CLIMBING TEA, PINK BLEND, REPEAT-FLOWERING

Sometimes classed as a Climbing Large-flowered Rose, this variety has shapely, beautiful buds that open to flat, quartered blooms of bright rose (deep red in the shade) striped carmine; the striping is more pronounced in spring. The full, large flowers are fragrant and repeat throughout spring and summer in warmer climates. It is a vigorous shrub that can easily be trained on a small pergola or a wall with full sun. The foliage is large and dark. Those who have grown this rose for some time say that it is fussy and needs lots of attention. It was discovered by Bolut and Thirat on a visit to Saint Dizier gardens, home of Monsieur Driout, mayor of that city. It is sometimes classified as a Noisette Rose. ZONES 5–10.

Thirat, France, 1902

Possible sport of 'Reine Marie Henriette'

'Mme Driout'

'Mme Edouard Ory'

'MME EDOUARD HERRIOT'
syn. 'Daily Mail Rose'
MODERN, LARGE-FLOWERED/HYBRID TEA, ORANGE BLEND, REPEAT-FLOWERING

This rose caused a sensation when it was introduced because of its color. The pointed buds open to flowers that are coral-red shaded yellow fading to pink, semi-double, large and fragrant. The full blooms are rather loose and quickly lose their color. The foliage is bronze in the early stages of growth and the bush has a spreading habit. Although bred in France and named after the wife of a French statesman, this variety won a competition in England run by the *Daily Mail* newspaper for a rose to call the 'Daily Mail Rose', and in fact it is still known by that name in England. **'Climbing Mme Edouard Herriot'** (syn. 'Climbing Daily Mail Rose') was introduced in 1921 by the Ketten Brothers of Luxembourg; it is a good free-flowering climber producing an excellent crop in spring and flowering through to autumn. It is rather thorny but is disease free. ZONES 5–10.

Pernet-Ducher, France, 1913

'Mme Caroline Testout' × Large-flowered Rose

National Rose Society Gold Medal 1913

'MME EDOUARD ORY'
OLD, MOSS, DEEP PINK, REPEAT-FLOWERING

The bright pink, fragrant flowers of this variety are full, globular and medium sized. As they age they fade to pale pink. There is a profuse blooming in late spring, with some further flowering later. It is an upright bush that is full of strong prickles. Moss Roses are actually Centifolia and Damask Roses that have

'Mme Ernst Calvat'

'Mme Fernandel'

developed a distinctive fragrant moss-like growth on the sepals, adding great elegance to the flower. They come in all colors, and some are repeat-flowering. ZONES 4–10.

Robert, France, 1854

Parentage unknown

'MME EMILIE CHARRON'
syn. 'Mme Emilie Charrin'
OLD, TEA, MEDIUM PINK, REPEAT-FLOWERING

This is an extremely rare rose that can only be found today in a few private collections. The delicate flesh pink flowers are cupped, large and very double, and have good form. The colors fade in the sun. It has a long blooming season and is an upright, vigorous, branching shrub that is good for the woodland and makes a good hedge. There are some prickles. The breeder was one of many hybridizers from Lyons, where most of the old roses in that period were created. ZONES 6–11.

Perrier, France, 1895

Parentage unknown

'MME ERNST CALVAT'
syns 'Mme Ernest Calvat', 'Pink Bourbon'
OLD, BOURBON, MEDIUM PINK, REPEAT-FLOWERING

This rose has large, cabbage-like blooms that are pink shaded darker pink. They are flat, quartered, and become blowzy as they open. There are many yellow anthers. It does well in the shade, especially where there are hot summers, and makes an excellent cut flower. It also does well in poor soil, but it needs to be established before it will perform at its best; it is subject to mildew. The arching canes can reach 6 ft (1.8 m) and are covered with dark green leaves that are red un-

'Mme Georges Bruant'

'Mme Gabriel Luizet'

derneath. Ernest Calvat, who died in 1910, was a glove manufacturer and amateur horticulturist. This rose was discovered by the hybridizer's widow, Mme Schwartz, who continued her husband's work and also produced two famous roses: 'Roger Lambelin' and 'La Tosca'. ZONES 4–10.

Schwartz, France, 1888

Sport of 'Mme Isaac Pereire'

'MME EUGÈNE RÉSAL'
OLD, CHINA, PINK BLEND, REPEAT-FLOWERING

A rainbow of colors is produced when these roses open, including bright pink, red and orange. The semi-double, cupped blooms develop from lovely elongated buds. Blooming with good continuity from summer to late autumn, the flowers are striking for their golden stamens. It is a well-groomed 4 ft (1.2 m) bush covered with dark green, glossy leaves, and is an ideal subject for massing. The flowers are fragrant, healthy and long lasting. ZONES 5–10.

Guillot, France, 1894

Sport of 'Mme Laurette Messimy'

'MME FALCOT'
OLD, TEA, MEDIUM YELLOW, REPEAT-FLOWERING

Beautiful buds on this variety open to reveal a variety of colors ranging from deep orange to clear yellow. The quilled, double, thick petals are 3 in (8 cm) across and the inner petals are folded. The cupped blooms are darker in the center and sometimes upon opening resemble tulips. The best blooms appear in autumn. This fragrant Tea needs time to establish itself before growing to a mature 5 ft (1.5 m) in height. The shiny

M

green leaves cover the many hooked prickles. 'Mme Falcot' is a parent of the popular 'Perle d'Or'. The Guillot nursery produced scores of famous roses for over a century, among them 'La France' and 'Belle des Jardins'. ZONES 6–11.

Guillot, France, 1858

Seedling of 'Safrano'

'MME FERNANDEL' MEIsunaj
syn. 'Fernandel'
MODERN, CLUSTER-FLOWERED/FLORIBUNDA, DEEP PINK, REPEAT-FLOWERING

Lyon Rose of the Century is an award that is much sought after, although it is not as prestigious as it sounds, for five varieties are so designated at Lyon every year. 'Mme Fernandel' was among them in 1989, and makes a good item for the garden when used in beds, borders or as a hedge. The blooms are neatly formed, urn shaped when young then becoming rounded with tight centers and finally cupped as their 30 or so petals expand. They are deep pink verging on light red with a shining quality, lightly scented, and appear in small clusters on firm stems through summer and autumn. This plant grows with an upright, bushy habit to average height or slightly below, and there is an ample covering of crisp dark green foliage. ZONES 5–9.

Meilland, France, 1989

Parentage unknown

Bagatelle Gold Medal 1988, Lyon Rose of the Century 1989

'MME GABRIEL LUIZET'
OLD, HYBRID PERPETUAL, LIGHT PINK, REPEAT-FLOWERING

Still a popular member of its class, this rose is bright silvery pink, paler at the edges. The pointed buds open to large, double flowers with 34 petals that are sometimes quartered. The plant blooms early and is quite fragrant and floriferous; there may also be later blooms. Stout, strong canes support the 6 ft (1.8 m) shrub and the attractive foliage serves as a good background for the flowers. It does well in poor soil. This rose should be lightly pruned and shaped. Gabriel Luizet (1794–1872) was an arborculturist who developed the practice of budding fruit trees for the first time. ZONES 5–10.

Liabaud, France, 1877

Seedling of 'Jules Margottin'

'MME GEORGES BRUANT'
MODERN, HYBRID RUGOSA, WHITE, REPEAT-FLOWERING

There does not seem to be much of the lovely Tea Rose 'Sombreuil' in the make-up of 'Mme Georges Bruant' except for the color of the flowers and the delicacy of the petal texture. The buds are long and pointed, and the white flowers are semi-double, loose in form and are borne in clusters on a thorny, spreading, heavily foliaged shrub. They are fragrant and repeat very well. There are a few hips produced but they are not as plentiful as most other Rugosa roses. The plant makes a good thick, impenetrable hedge with the advantage of blooms through-

'Mme Edouard Herriot'

'Mme Georges Delbard'

'Mme Grégoire Staechelin'

'Mme Grégoire Staechelin'

out spring, summer and into autumn. The foliage is healthy. ZONES 4–10.

Bruant, France, 1887

Rosa rugosa × 'Sombreuil'

'MME GEORGES DELBARD'
DELadel
syns 'Mme Delbard', 'Mrs G. Delbard'
MODERN, LARGE-FLOWERED/HYBRID TEA, DARK RED, REPEAT-FLOWERING

This outstanding rose has rich dark red flowers with magnificent substance to the broad petals. The large buds open to a very big, high-centered flowers with 40 petals. They are suitable for exhibition. There is no fragrance. The stems are very long and blooms come mainly singly, opening very slowly to full

blooms of great intensity of color and durability that keep particularly well when picked. The foliage is large, mid-green and semi-glossy, and the growth is tall and strong. ZONES 5–11.

Delbard, France, 1982

('Tropicana' × 'Samourai') × ('Tropicana' × ['Rome Glory' × 'Impeccable'])

'MME GRÉGOIRE STAECHELIN'
syn. 'Spanish Beauty'
MODERN, LARGE-FLOWERED CLIMBER, PINK BLEND

This is a great rose even though it flowers but once. The long, elegant buds open to soft delicate pink flowers stained crimson mainly on the back of the petals. They are ruffled, come singly and in

small clusters and are fragrant. If spent blooms are not removed, very large pear-shaped fruits are produced that change slowly from green to yellow-gold. It is an excellent pillar rose or can be used to cover an arch where its trusses of pale pink blooms show up well against its dark green foliage. ZONES 5–10.

Dot, Spain, 1927

'Frau Karl Druschki' × 'Château de Clos Vougeot'

Bagatelle Gold Medal 1927, American Rose Society John Cook Medal 1929, Royal Horticultural Society Award of Garden Merit 1993

M

'Mme Hardy'

'Climbing Mme Henri Guillot'

'Mme Isaac Pereire'

'MME HARDY'
OLD, DAMASK, WHITE

This is certainly one of the most beautiful whites of the summer-flowering roses. The freely produced flowers appear in early summer and are arranged both in clusters and solitarily all over the plant for about 3 weeks. They are very fragrant and exquisitely formed, at first cupped and finally opening very flat. The blooms are consistently pure white and each has a central green pip. It is a tall, dense, prickly shrub with dark brownish wood and is generously endowed with soft, light green leaves. Sadly, in some weather conditions the foliage can sometimes be marred by brown blotches (probably scorch marks when hot sun follows rain), but this is by no means a serious fault. It is very easy to grow. ZONES 4–11.

Hardy, France, 1832

Parentage unknown

Royal Horticultural Society Award of Garden Merit 1993

'MME HENRI GUILLOT'
MODERN, LARGE-FLOWERED/HYBRID TEA, RED BLEND, REPEAT-FLOWERING

This early rose makes a good show in spring. The flowers are of a unique blend of orange, coral and red, are double with 25 petals and open very quickly to large, orange, flat flowers of good substance.

There is a little fragrance and some rebloom after the spring flush. The very rich green foliage is particularly large and extremely glossy. The bush form has lost its vigor, a fault that has occurred in many of the brightly colored roses of the early part of this century. **'Climbing Mme Henri Guillot'** (Meilland, France, 1942) is a climbing form of 'Mme Henri Guillot'. ZONES 5–10.

Mallerin, France, 1938

'Rochefort' × seedling of *Rosa foetida bicolor*

Bagatelle Gold Medal 1936, Portland Gold Medal 1938

'MME ISAAC PEREIRE'
syn. 'Le Bienheureaux de la Salle'
OLD, BOURBON, DEEP PINK, REPEAT-FLOWERING

This famous rose has enjoyed almost universal praise. The huge, deep rose pink blooms are full and well formed upon opening, later becoming blowzy; a purple tint adds to the charm, especially in autumn. The very fragrant flowers are sometimes cupped and sometimes quartered, and they usually appear in clusters. It is a vigorous shrub to 7 ft (2.1 m) tall, and it is best pegged down or trained on a pillar, where it produces many laterals and more blooms. The long canes are covered with small prickles and deep green leaves. It does well in poor soil and in cool shade where summers are warm,

but is subject to mildew. Mme Pereire was a member of a banking family during the reign of Napolean III. ZONES 5–10.

Garçon, France, 1881

Parentage unknown

Royal Horticultural Society Award of Garden Merit 1993

'MME JEAN DUPUY'
OLD, TEA, YELLOW BLEND, REPEAT-FLOWERING

This rose has long, pointed buds on long, erect stems that open to reveal large, full, golden yellow blooms with pink overtones and reddish centers. The outer petals are edged in pink. The flowering period lasts from late spring until the first frost; the perfume has been described as 'delicious'. The vigorous canes are lined with pretty foliage and a few prickles. This healthy, neat, compact bush can grow into a large shrub if it is not controlled. Peter Lambert (1859–1939) was a successful German hybridizer who introduced many roses that are still in commerce today, among them 'Frau Karl Druschki', 'Trier' and 'Kaiserin Auguste Victoria'. This rose is dedicated to the wife of the French Minister of Agriculture. ZONES 6–11.

Lambert, Germany, 1902

Parentage unknown

'MME JOSEPH PERRAUD'
syn. 'Sunburst'
MODERN, LARGE-FLOWERED/HYBRID TEA, YELLOW BLEND, REPEAT-FLOWERING

This rose was introduced into Australia as 'Sunburst', and it soon became a favorite rose there. The large flowers are yellow with a deeply veined coppery center, are double with 30 petals and are fragrant. The buds of yellow flushed copper are long and pointed and particularly attractive, but the copper color in the center of the bloom fades quickly in hot weather. The foliage is glossy and disease free and flower production is good. ZONES 5–11.

Gaujard, France, 1934

'Julien Potin' × seedling

Bagatelle Gold Medal 1934

'MME JOSEPH SCHWARTZ'
syn. 'White Duchesse de Brabant'
OLD, TEA, WHITE, REPEAT-FLOWERING

Still a popular rose after more than a century, this is one of the best white Teas still in commerce. The pure white blooms have pink overtones and are full, medium sized and cupped. The compact, fragrant, well-formed flowers, which have muddled centers, bloom through-

out summer into autumn and are excellent cut flowers. The low-growing shrub has evergreen foliage and likes a cool, sunny position, and is good for container cultivation. It hates wet weather, when it is prone to black spot. ZONES 6–11.

Schwartz, France, 1880

Sport of 'Comtesse de Labarthe'

'MADAME JULES BOUCHÉ'
MODERN, LARGE-FLOWERED/HYBRID TEA, WHITE, REPEAT-FLOWERING

This rose can always be recognized by its zigzag growth habit, produced by the stems between each node turning to the left and then to the right. The buds are slender and dainty and open to very large double flowers, with the centers of the blooms shading to pale blush. The strongly fragrant flowers open flat like a Tea Rose and there are many overlapping petals like a camellia. Growth is tall and flower production is very high. There has been no reduction in vigor over the years. ZONES 5–11.

Croibier, France, 1911

'Pharisäer' × seedling

'MME JULES GRAVEREAUX'
OLD, CLIMBING TEA, APRICOT BLEND, REPEAT-FLOWERING

As a cut flower this rose has no superior. The long and pointed buds open to very large, very double, very full flesh-peach blooms that are compact and sometimes quartered. Yellow overtones are apparent when the blooms have opened fully. It is a bushy, lanky plant with lush, large, dark, glossy foliage that can reach 12 ft (3.5 m) in height and prefers dry, warm weather. It is subject to mildew. This rose was named for the wife of an administrator of a large Paris department store. ZONES 5–10.

Soupert & Notting, France, 1901

'Rêve d'Or' × 'Viscountess Folkestone'

'MME JULES THIBAUD'
MODERN, POLYANTHA, ORANGE-PINK, REPEAT-FLOWERING

This rose is similar to 'Cécile Brünner' except in color, which is a strong coral-pink. The flowers can be a bit larger and growth a little stronger. The blooms are borne in small clusters and rise well above the sparse, mid-green foliage, holding their color very well. It is disease free and makes an excellent hedge or low border. ZONES 4–11.

Post-1881

Sport of 'Cécile Brünner'

'Madame Jules Bouché'

'Mme Jules Gravereaux'

'Mme Jules Thibaud'

'Mme Knorr'

'MME KNORR'

syn. 'Mme de Knorr'

OLD, PORTLAND, MEDIUM PINK,
REPEAT-FLOWERING

The large, full, flat blooms on this variety are light rose with white undersides and dark centers. They are medium sized and semi-double, rather loose in form and have a very sweet fragrance. There is some repeat-flowering after the summer flush. It does well in poor soil and is a good, small hedging plant as its strong perfume will permeate the planting area. The healthy and abundant matt green foliage provides a strong background to the flowers. Portlands are also known as Damask Perpetuals; there were 150 varieties at the height of their popularity between 1800 and 1850. ZONES 5–11.

Verdier, France, 1855

Parentage unknown

Royal Horticultural Society Award of Garden Merit 1993

'MME KRILOFF'

MODERN, LARGE-FLOWERED/HYBRID TEA,
YELLOW BLEND, REPEAT-FLOWERING

The flowers of this variety are large and rounded in form with over 30 wide petals, and they have a good fragrance. The color is orange-yellow strongly veined with carmine. As one of the first seedlings of 'Peace' to be marketed, it gave a foretaste of the extraordinary influence that Meilland's most famous rose would exercise in the second half of the twentieth century. 'Mme Kriloff' is no longer commercially available. It flowers through summer and autumn and grows vigorously to an average height or above, with an upright habit and a good cover of large, leathery leaves. ZONES 5–9.

Meilland, France, 1944

'Peace' × 'Signora'

Bagatelle Gold Medal 1944, National Rose Society Gold Medal 1948

'MME LAURETTE MESSIMY'

syn. 'Laurette Messimy'

OLD, CHINA, DEEP PINK, REPEAT-FLOWERING

This attractive rose has long, salmon-colored buds that turn into rose pink blooms with yellow centers. The loose, semi-double, fragrant flowers are large. It does well in cool summers, as the flowers fade in hot weather. It is a bushy, upright plant covered with many gray-green, glossy leaves. It is an excellent bedding plant and is suitable as a container plant, and is full of blooms from late spring to autumn. ZONES 6–11.

Guillot, France, 1887

'Rival de Paestum' × 'Mme Falcot'

'Mme Legras de St Germain'

'Mme Lauriol de Barny'

'MME LAURIOL DE BARNY'

OLD, BOURBON, LIGHT PINK, REPEAT-FLOWERING

As a cut flower, this has to be the most gorgeous garden variety. Blooming earlier than any of its clan, this rose has silvery pink, full, quartered blooms that are large and very flat. The heavy, drooping sprays of sweetly scented flowers on long stems are frequently the target of photographers. The arching canes are covered with smooth leaves and, if pegged down, the result is a bounty crop of blooms. This is also a good candidate for a pillar as it easily reaches 7 ft (2.1 m) in two years. It does well in the shade and in poor soil. ZONES 5–10.

Trouillard, France, 1868

Hybrid of *Rosa arvensis*

'MME LEGRAS DE ST GERMAIN'

OLD, ALBA, WHITE

The flowers of this rose appear in clusters. Each bloom is cup shaped at first, opening to flat, perfectly formed, very double, cushion-like rosettes that are about 2 in (5 cm) across. There is a lovely fragrance. The color is glowing pure white with soft lemony yellow centers. 'Mme Legras de St Germain' can grow to 8 ft (2.5 m) tall in good soil, and it is made up of long, light to mid-green, almost thornless branches with plentiful soft, light green foliage. Clearly related to the Damasks, this outstanding rose is easy to grow. Although like many white, fully double roses it dislikes the rain, it is still worthy of a place in the garden either as a free-standing shrub or a climber. ZONES 4–10.

1846

Parentage unknown

'MME LÉON PAIN'

MODERN, LARGE-FLOWERED/HYBRID TEA,
PINK BLEND, REPEAT-FLOWERING

This rose produces pointed buds that open to flowers of flesh pink with an orange-yellow center and salmon-pink undersides to the petals. The flowers are double with 45 petals and are fragrant. The full blooms lose their color rather quickly. 'Mme Léon Pain' has a bushy and vigorous growth habit. ZONES 5–11.

Guillot, France, 1904

'Mme Caroline Testout' × 'Souvenir de Catherine Guillot'

'Mme Léon Pain'

'Mme Laurette Messimy'

'Mme Kriloff'

'Mme Kriloff'

M

'MME LINE RENAUD'
MODERN, LARGE-FLOWERED/HYBRID TEA,
MEDIUM RED, REPEAT-FLOWERING

This rose has the strong perfume of its parent 'Crimson Glory'. The color of the double, well-formed flowers is a rich velvety red. The foliage is light green and flower production is good. 'Mme Line Renaud' can sometimes suffer from mildew. ZONES 5–10.

Mondial Roses, France, 1956

'Crimson Glory' × seedling

'MME LOMBARD'
syns 'Mme Lambard', 'Mme Lambart'
OLD, TEA, ORANGE-PINK, REPEAT-FLOWERING

This rose is often called the 'cemetery rose' because it is found in cemeteries in great numbers; it has an amazing ability to stay alive in desperate situations. The long, crimson buds open to very double, large, globular, rosy salmon blooms with dark centers. The cupped, fragrant flowers vary in color as they age, deepening when fully open and in the shade. The blooming period extends from late spring until the first frost in warm areas. The flowers are best in autumn, when the colors are richer. It can be pruned to 5 ft (1.5 m) or be allowed to ramble to twice that height. The leathery, dark

'Mme Louis Laperrière'

'Mme Line Renaud'

green leaves hide numerous hooked prickles, and in autumn there is a large crop of red hips. ZONES 6–11.

Lacharme, France, 1878

Seedling of 'Mme de Tartas'

'MME LOUIS LAPERRIÈRE'
MODERN, LARGE-FLOWERED/HYBRID TEA,
MEDIUM RED, REPEAT-FLOWERING

Still one of the best dark red bedding roses today, this variety has very well-formed flowers of medium size that have 40–50 petals and are a rich dark crimson-red color. They have the wonderful fragrance of 'Crimson Glory'. The abundant foliage is dark green and disease free on a bush that grows to a moderate size. There are many flowers produced continuously. Its bushy habit lends itself to use as a standard. It thoroughly deserved its gold medal at Bagatelle. ZONES 5–10.

Laperrière, France, 1951

'Crimson Glory' × seedling

Bagatelle Gold Medal 1950, National Rose Society Certificate of Merit 1952

'MME LOUIS LÉVÊQUE'
OLD, MOSS, MEDIUM PINK, REPEAT-FLOWERING

The buds of this rose are large, round and sparsely mossed and open to large, consistently silvery pink flowers of

'Mme Louis Lévêque'

superb quality, especially in dry weather. The blooms are packed with crumpled petals; some can attain a diameter of 4 in (10 cm). They are richly endowed with scent, and flowers continue to appear well into autumn. The abundant foliage is large, rich dark green and smooth on an upright plant that grows to some 4 ft (1.2 m) high. The stems have few thorns and little or no moss. This aristocratic rose is unrivalled among the paler colored Moss Roses for charm and general good behavior. ZONES 5–10.

Lévêque, France, 1898

Parentage unknown

'MME MARIE CURIE'
syn. 'Québec'
MODERN, LARGE-FLOWERED/HYBRID TEA,
DEEP YELLOW, REPEAT-FLOWERING

This was one of the earliest roses to be patented in the USA. The high-centered and very well-formed flowers, which open from very attractive, long, pointed buds, are a rich yellow and contain 25 petals. They are of moderate size and have a slight fragrance and retain their color well. The foliage is dark green and healthy on a vigorous, compact bush that blooms profusely. There are no disease problems. This rose was named after Madame Curie, who was awarded the Nobel Prize for research into cancer. ZONES 5–11.

Gaujard, France, 1943

Parentage unknown

All-America Rose Selection 1944

'MME MOREAU'
OLD, MOSS, PINK BLEND

This Moss Rose has been lost among all the other more popular roses that came out of the period of their great popularity in France in the last half of the nineteenth century. The rosy pink blooms are edged in white. The fragrant

'Mme Lombard'

'Mme Pierre Oger'

'Mme Marie Curie'

flowers are full, large and moderately mossy and will frequently have a stripe on the petals. There is only one blooming period in late spring. ZONES 4–10.

Moreau et Robert, France, 1872

Parentage unknown

'MME PIERRE OGER'
OLD, BOURBON, PINK BLEND, REPEAT-FLOWERING

Its porcelain-like blooms have made this one of the most popular of the Old Garden Roses. The blush, creamy white blooms, with a lilac reverse, are cupped and loose and have dappled petals. The colors intensify in the sun. It has a long blooming season that extends from spring to the first frost. Narrow, upright branches support the heavy, delicately scented blooms. The abundant, light green leaves are oval and pointed, and dark prickles line the stalks. This is an ideal candidate for a container or for the back of a border. ZONES 4–10.

Oger, France, 1878

Sport of 'La Reine Victoria'

'MME PLANTIER'
OLD, ALBA, WHITE

The fragrant flowers of this rose are borne in large clusters. They are creamy at first, becoming mostly pure white with a little green pip in the center. It is a vigorous shrub or climber sometimes classified as a Damask. As a climber it can attain a height of at least 20 ft (6 m), but it is more commonly seen as a relaxed shrub to about 10 ft (3 m) high. The gray-green stems are long, arching and almost thornless, and the grayish leaves are soft to touch. Unfortunately the individual blooms can easily shatter in the wind, but this is a minor fault. ZONES 4–10.

Plantier, France, 1835

Thought to be Rosa alba × R. moschata

'MME SCIPION COCHET'
OLD, TEA, PINK BLEND, REPEAT-FLOWERING

Too many hybridizers named a rose after this lady, and as a result the two Teas and one Hybrid Perpetual are often confused with one another. This fragrant rose has ovoid buds that open to pale pink blooms that turn white with a yellow center. They are full and tulip shaped and appear on erect stems. The center petals of the very double blooms are rather blowzy. It is one of the most floriferous Teas, blooming constantly in warm climates. A lanky shrub, it has thick, glossy leaves and many prickles and is a good container plant, as it rarely gets larger than 3 ft (1 m). It was named after the wife of a famous breeder in Grisy-Suisnes, France. ZONES 5–10.

Bernaix, France, 1872

'Anna Olivier' × 'Comtesse de Brabant'

'MME SCIPION COCHET'
OLD, HYBRID PERPETUAL, MAUVE, REPEAT-FLOWERING

This rose was named by the breeder for his wife. A floriferous summer bloomer, the very fragrant purplish pink flowers are edged a soft pink. They are full, cupped, large and well formed. The petals are silvery on the back and form a rosette in the center that is rather frazzled. The large, strong branches are covered with light green foliage, and the bush can reach 5 ft (1.5 m) in a few seasons. It is subject to mildew in hot weather. The family nursery produced many roses in the second half of the nineteenth century. This rose is hard to find and only two nurseries in the world still offer it. ZONES 5–10.

Cochet, France, 1873

Parentage unknown

'MME SOUCHET'
OLD, BOURBON, PINK BLEND, REPEAT-FLOWERING

This extremely rare rose is not listed in any botanical collection today. It is a pale, very full, fragrant rose with blush white blooms. It has a long flowering period in summer, with some autumn flowers. The upright, bushy shrub is covered with handsome foliage. ZONES 5–10.

Souchet, France, 1843

Parentage unknown

'MME SOUVETON'
OLD, PORTLAND, PINK BLEND, REPEAT-FLOWERING

The delicate, semi-double, pink blooms with white overtones of this variety are medium sized, full and cupped. Some-

'Mme Scipion Cochet' (Bernaix)

times striped, they are usually borne on short stems. It is an early bloomer, and the fully opened flowers have a light fragrance. It is a medium-sized shrub with short branches with handsome foliage. Legend has it that the first rose in this family was brought from Italy by the Duchess of Portland, who found it near Naples. ZONES 5–10.

Pernet, France, 1874

Parentage unknown

'MME VICTOR VERDIER'
OLD, HYBRID PERPETUAL, MEDIUM RED, REPEAT-FLOWERING

An outstanding cut flower, this rose is 3 in (8 cm) across when in full bloom. The clear crimson, double flowers are large, with 75 petals, flat and cupped. The outer petals are larger than the inner ones, and the blooms appear in clusters during summer and autumn. The second crop of blossoms is considered more handsome. Attractive spring foliage fills the long canes, and there are some prickles. Disbudding the shrub carefully in spring will increase the beauty of the bush and the flowers. ZONES 5–10.

Verdier, France, 1863

'Senateur Vaise' × seedling

'MME VIOLET'
MODERN, LARGE-FLOWERED/HYBRID TEA, MAUVE, REPEAT-FLOWERING

The flowers of this rose are large, double and deep mauve in color. The flower production is average and the repeat cycle is rather slow. The blooms have a pleasant perfume. It has dark green, plentiful foliage and grows to medium height. 'Mme Violet' is not known in many countries but is a welcome addition to the mauve varieties. ZONES 5–11.

Teranishi, Japan, 1981

(['Lady' × 'Sterling Silver'] × ['Lady' × 'Sterling Silver']) × self

'Mme Violet'

'Mme Victor Verdier'

'Mme Victor Verdier'

'MME WAGRAM, COMTESSE DE TURENNE'
OLD, TEA, PINK BLEND, REPEAT-FLOWERING

This popular Tea Rose has very large, ovoid buds that open to satiny pink blooms that turn a rosy red with a yellow base. The full, large flowers are 4–5 in (10–12 cm) across and have a red reverse on the petals. When open the fragrant, long-lasting blooms have a rather blowzy form. It is a healthy, bushy plant with superb dark foliage and small prickles that likes hot weather. It reaches 3 ft (1 m) at maturity, making an ideal candidate as a container plant, is strongly resistant to disease and will bloom from late spring until autumn. ZONES 6–10.

Bernaix, France, 1894

Parentage unknown

'MME WILLIAM PAUL'
syns 'Mrs W. Paul', 'Mrs William Paul'
OLD, MOSS, DEEP PINK, REPEAT-FLOWERING

The bright rose red blooms of 'Mme William Paul' are full, cupped and large, and are at their most attractive in the shade. This floriferous rose blooms in spring with some autumn repeat. It has an erect habit and strong canes, and grows to 4 ft (1.2 m) at maturity. Moss

Roses need the best of growing conditions as some of them are tender, as this one is. They do not produce any seeds. Mrs Paul was the wife of a famous English rose hybridizer who created many lovely roses in his long lifetime (1812–1905). ZONES 6–10.

Moreau-Robert, France, 1869

Parentage unknown

'MME ZÖETMANS'
OLD, DAMASK, WHITE

The lovely flowers of this rose are very full and fragrant. They are blush pink at first, paling to milky white, usually with a button of incurling petals in the center and finishing rather flat and cushion-like. Each flower is about 2½ in (6 cm) across and arranged as one of a small cluster, appearing in abundance in early summer for a relatively short season. It is a compact shrub that grows to about 4 ft (1.2 m) and has dark green, fairly thorny wood and copious bright mid-green foliage. It is probably closely related to the Gallicas. This is a first-class variety, not least for its tidy disposition as a shrub. ZONES 4–10.

Marest, France, 1830

Parentage unknown

'Mme Wagram, Comtesse de Turenne'

'Mme Zöetmans'

'Maestro'

'Madelon'

'MADELEINE SELZER'

syns 'Mme Selzer', 'Yellow Tausendschön'
OLD, RAMBLER, LIGHT YELLOW

Pale lemon blooms that fade to white as they age appear in trusses on this rampant Rambler. The flowers are fully double and fragrant and make a strong impression when cascading down a trellis or tree during their summer flowering. It has bronze green foliage in spring and few prickles, and reaches 10 ft (3 m) in several years. 'Madeleine Selzer' is a good climber or rambler for a small garden, but it does need strong support when mature. Ludwig Walter of Severne in Alsace, France, was an amateur rose breeder. ZONES 5–11.

Walter, France, 1926

'Tausendschön' × 'Mrs Aaron Ward'

'MADELON' RUImeva
MODERN, LARGE-FLOWERED/HYBRID TEA,
ORANGE-RED, REPEAT-FLOWERING

Introduced as an orange cut-flower rose, 'Madelon' carries well-formed flowers with 30 petals that are slow to open, but last well when cut. Unfortunately, the rose is susceptible to both mildew and black spot, and because of this it has been superseded by better vermilion roses for the cut flower trade, and it has

lost popularity as a garden rose as well. However, in warm weather it can produce extremely beautiful flowers. ZONES 5–10.

de Ruiter, The Netherlands, 1981

'Varlon' × MEIgenon

'MLLE ANNIE WOOD'
syn. 'Annie Wood'
OLD, HYBRID PERPETUAL, MEDIUM RED,
REPEAT-FLOWERING

This rose has completely disappeared from any public collection and from commerce. The fragrant, crimson-scarlet blooms are full and large, and appear in clusters. The color darkens in shade; sometimes there is striping on the petals, especially in autumn. 'Mlle Annie Wood' is a vigorous bush with reddish canes covered by large dark leaves and reddish prickles. The rose is subject to mildew and rust. ZONES 5–10.

Verdier, France, 1866

Parentage unknown

'MLLE CLAIRE TRUFFAUT'
OLD, BOURBON, MEDIUM PINK, REPEAT-FLOWERING

This rose has almost disappeared and is found in only a few collections today. The elegant, medium-sized blooms are silvery pink and have a rather delicate appearance. Very fragrant, they sometimes appear alone or in clusters and continue throughout summer. One parent is supposed to have been *Rosa chinensis* and the other maybe 'Rose d'Quatre Saisons'; together they gave the rose a reblooming trait. ZONES 5–11.

Verdier, France, 1887

Parentage unknown

'MLLE FRANZISKA KRÜGER'
syn. 'Grand Duc Heritier de Luxembourg'
OLD, TEA, ORANGE-PINK, REPEAT-FLOWERING

When Nabonnand crossed two Tea Roses, he produced this popular,

floriferous rose that blooms well in a warm site. The copper-yellow and pink fragrant blooms open as cups and then reflex into half globes. The large flowers have white outer petals and a green eye. If grown where the blooms can be seen from below, it is an excellent climber that can reach 7 ft (2.2 m) on a wall. It also makes a compact shrub if pruned regularly. The foliage is plentiful and leathery with dark red at the leaf edges. This plant is highly disease resistant, although the blooms ball in wet weather. ZONES 5–10.

Nabonnand, France, 1880

'Catherine Mermet' × 'Général Schablikine'

'MLLE MARIE DAUVESSE'
OLD, HYBRID PERPETUAL, MEDIUM PINK,
REPEAT-FLOWERING

This was one of the many hybrids that were popular in the mid-nineteenth century, although they were soon superseded by the growing passion for Large-flowered Roses. 'Mlle Marie Dauvesse' is commercially unavailable nowadays, and is very rare in cultivation. It carries bright light pink blossoms of medium size. They are double and filled with many thick petals to create large, fragrant blooms. The summer flowering is followed by some repeat. The shrub can reach 4 ft (1.2 m) tall, and is covered with large, dull green leaves. Jacques Vigneron raised many other Hybrid Perpetuals. ZONES 5–10.

Vigneron, France, 1859

Parentage unknown

'MLLE MARIE DRIVON'
OLD, BOURBON, PINK BLEND, REPEAT-FLOWERING

This very vigorous, repeat-flowering rose is a poppy pink color, sometimes marbled or spotted carmine and lilac. The medium-sized blooms are very full and have pointed centers. The Bourbons continued to be produced in small numbers late into the nineteenth century, no doubt because of their usefulness as column and pillar roses. ZONES 5–9.

Schwartz, France, 1887

Seedling of 'Apolline'

'MLLE MARTHE CARRON'
MODERN, RAMBLER, WHITE

This is a very vigorous rambling rose with very long canes which produce large clusters of small, double, white-tinted pink flowers. The clusters can carry 40–50 blooms. This is a good rambling rose to cover unsightly fences or buildings and is sufficiently vigorous to grow into

trees where the long canes can cascade downwards, creating a wonderful display in late spring. There is no repeat bloom. The plant is disease free and the foliage is most attractive. ZONES 5–10.

Mermet, France, 1931

Sport of *Rosa wichuraiana* × *R. wichuraiana*

'MADHATTER' TINhat
syns 'G'day', 'Gidday'
MODERN, MINIATURE, MEDIUM YELLOW,
REPEAT-FLOWERING

The flowers of 'Madhatter' are double with 25–30 petals, cupped and have a heavy Damask fragrance. They are medium yellow. The exhibition-type blooms are borne singly or in small sprays. This rose is most noted for its long-lasting bright yellow blooms, which are often referred to as a yellow chrysanthemum color. The blooms have lots of substance in the petals allowing them to remain on the bush and hold their color for weeks. The foliage is semi-glossy and mid-green on a plant with a medium to compact growth habit. It is fairly disease resistant. What a pity the breeder did not leave the registered name as 'G'day'—at least to please those fans who watch Australian television programs! ZONES 5–11.

Bennett, USA, 1988

'Autumn' × 'Avandel'

'MADIBA' KORandpunk
MODERN, LARGE-FLOWERED/HYBRID TEA, MAUVE,
REPEAT-FLOWERING

This very special rose was named for Nelson Mandela, who is affectionately referred to by South Africans as *Madiba*, which means 'king' in the Xhosa language. The long pointed buds open into spectacular large blooms of deep maroon and lilac, and turn slowly into fawn as they age. These make good cut flowers and exhibition blooms, and have the added attraction of being fragrant. The shrub is tall, sturdy and thornless, and grows with great vigor. Throughout summer and into autumn 'Madiba' repeatedly produces its attractive large roses with their interesting color. ZONES 4–11.

Kordes, Germany, 1996

('Esther Geldenhuys' × 'Belami') × seedling

'MAESTRO' MACkinju, MACinju
MODERN, LARGE-FLOWERED/HYBRID TEA,
RED BLEND, REPEAT-FLOWERING

This variety has oval buds that open to medium red flowers with a painting of white washed through the petals. The

'Madhatter'

'Magic Carrousel'

undersides of the petals is a light silvery red. The double blooms have 28 petals and are borne singly and in small clusters. There is a slight fragrance. The flowers are very variable in color—in hot weather the color is almost pure red, but in cooler conditions the hand painting is much more evident. The red shade can be quite smoky, which adds greatly to the effect. The foliage is matt olive green and lush. This is a most interesting and unique rose. ZONES 5–10.

McGredy, New Zealand, 1980

Seedling of 'Picasso' × seedling

'MAGALI'

MODERN, LARGE-FLOWERED/HYBRID TEA, DEEP PINK, REPEAT-FLOWERING

This rose carries deep carmine flowers: a color that does not fade in the heat but is sometimes considered rather harsh, which may be the cause of the lack of popularity of this rose. The blooms are double with 35–40 petals, of medium size and slightly fragrant. There is a good production, and the repeat-bloom is quick. The foliage is abundant, mid-green and leathery on a vigorous and upright plant. ZONES 5–11.

Mallerin, France, 1952

'Charles P. Kilham' × 'Brazier'

'MAGENTA'

syn. 'Kordes' Magenta'
MODERN, LARGE-FLOWERED/HYBRID TEA, MAUVE, REPEAT-FLOWERING

This spreading grower carries the most unusual flowers of rosy lavender with overtones of brown. Although they fade to a slate-mauve color, they are attractive at all times; some of the subtle color of 'Lavender Pinocchio' can be seen in the open flower. The full flowers come in large clusters on tall, arching growth and, like most mauve roses, they are very fragrant. The foliage is dark green, leathery and profuse, and the growth is very vigorous. 'Magenta' seems to prefer cool climates; the old wood can burn in summer in hot climates if exposed to the sun. ZONES 4–11.

Kordes, Germany, 1954

Unknown yellow Cluster-flowered Rose × 'Lavender Pinocchio'

'MAGGIE'

syn. 'Pacific'
OLD, BOURBON, MEDIUM RED, REPEAT-FLOWERING

This rose was found by William Welch in Louisiana and has become very popular in the USA. Most agree that there is

some China in its background. The full, globular, bright red flowers have overlapping petals that darken in cool weather. There is a pronounced spicy scent and it makes a fine cut flower. It has a bushy growth habit, reaching 4–6 ft (1.2–1.8 m) high, is almost thornless and does well in rich soil. This rose, which makes a wonderful hedge or pillar rose, was found by Welch at a farm of his wife's grandmother, Maggie. Some claim it is one of the roses created by Rudolf Geschwind, like 'Gruss an Teplitz' or 'Eugene E. Marlitt'. ZONES 5–10.

Found in 1980

Parentage unknown

'MAGGIE BARRY'   MACoborn

syn. 'Maggy Barry'
MODERN, LARGE-FLOWERED/HYBRID TEA, PINK BLEND, REPEAT-FLOWERING

This rose from Sam McGredy is named after a popular television newsreader in New Zealand. The bush produces a continuous supply of very shapely buds in a distinct coral-orange color. As they open, they change to coral-salmon and the two colors combine together in the open blooms to very good effect. Growth is upright, bushy and vigorous and the plant is very free flowering and disease free. This is an excellent rose for bedding as the color is bright but not harsh. ZONES 5–10.

McGredy, New Zealand, 1993

'Louise Gardener' × 'West Coast'

'MAGIC'

MODERN, LARGE-FLOWERED/HYBRID TEA, MEDIUM RED, REPEAT-FLOWERING

The buds of 'Magic' are long and pointed and open to double flowers of 24 petals that are high centered, of medium size and usually borne one to a stem. The foliage is mid-green and matt, and there are slender prickles along the stems.

'Magic Dragon'

Growth is tall and upright. If the flowers are not removed, attractive pear-shaped fruits are produced that turn from green to orange and persist for a considerable time. They are certainly very attractive when mature and ideal for home decoration as they last in water for many weeks. ZONES 5–11.

Strahle, USA, 1987

MACvolar × 'Tonight'

'MAGIC CARPET'   JAClover

MODERN, GROUND COVER, MAUVE, REPEAT-FLOWERING

This rose has small, semi-double lavender flowers with a spicy fragrance. It is a very vigorous plant that grows 18–24 in (45–60 cm) high and twice as broad. The foliage is dark green, glossy and very resistant to disease. This is an attractive garden rose because the repeat-flowering is good and the foliage is held well into winter. It is ideal for growing over rocks or low walls, or for mass planting in more difficult positions where other roses would not prosper. ZONES 5–10.

Zary/Warriner, USA, 1992

'Immensee' × 'Class Act'

Rose of the Year 1996

'MAGIC CARROUSEL'   MORrousel

MODERN, MINIATURE, RED BLEND, REPEAT-FLOWERING

'Magic Carrousel' holds a treasured place in Miniature Rose history as the first of many varieties to attain Award of Excel-

lence status. The double flowers are creamy white with a vivid red edge and a well-formed high center, a feature cloned from the Cluster-flowered parent. This striking color combination took the rose-buying public by storm when it was introduced and its popularity has not diminished. When the blooms are fully open the plant is at its best, displaying florets with bright golden stamens. Small, glossy green foliage covers this vigorous and bushy plant. ZONES 5–11.

Moore, USA, 1972

'Little Darling' × 'Westmont'

American Rose Society Award of Excellence 1975

'MAGIC DRAGON'

MODERN, CLIMBING MINIATURE, DARK RED, REPEAT-FLOWERING

This is one of the few dark red Climbing Miniatures. The short, pointed buds open to dark red, double and decorative flowers. The foliage is small and leathery, and the plant is vigorous with an upright growth habit. The flowers tend to appear in small clusters with a loose form, but the plant is slow to repeat. The canes can be trained over either a fence, wall or trellis—good coverage might be slow to establish, but within a few years the canopy is dense and compact. It is a shame that this rose has been all but forgotten. ZONES 5–11.

Moore, USA, 1969

([Rosa wichuraiana × 'Floradora'] × seedling) × 'Little Buckaroo'

M

'Magenta'

'Maggie Barry'

'Magic Carpet'

'MAGIC LANTERN' STArqueli
syn. 'Rémy Martin'
MODERN, LARGE-FLOWERED/HYBRID TEA, ORANGE BLEND, REPEAT-FLOWERING

Five years elapsed between the introduction of this rose in Europe under its French name and in the USA under its English one. The large, high-centered flowers, with up to 40 petals, are a lively mixture of copper, orange and gold. They are usually borne singly, sometimes in small clusters, have a slight fruity fragrance and continue to show color through summer and autumn. The plant is slightly tender, but in a warm climate it serves well in beds, borders and hedges. 'Magic Lantern' grows with a bushy, upright habit to above average height with mid- to dark green, semi-glossy leaves that may require protection where black spot is a problem. ZONES 6–9.
Royon, France, 1989
Sport of 'Gold Medal'

'MAGIC MEIDILAND' MEIbonrib
syn. 'Magic Meillandecor'
MODERN, GROUND COVER, MEDIUM PINK, REPEAT-FLOWERING

This is a Ground Cover Rose in a new color. The flowers, which are very double, small and deep magenta pink,

'Mahina'

'Magic Sunset'

are produced in clusters of 3–7 blooms. There is a spicy freesia-like fragrance according to Louise Coleman of Heirloom Roses in the USA. The very glossy foliage is bronze when young and growth is very spreading, to some 10 ft (3 m) across. It flowers for a very long period and is exceptionally disease free. ZONES 5–10.
Meilland, France, 1993
Rosa sempervirens × ('Milrose' × 'Bonica')
Anerkannte Deutsche Rose 1995

'MAGIC SUNSET'
MODERN, CLUSTER-FLOWERED/FLORIBUNDA, ORANGE BLEND, REPEAT-FLOWERING

'Magic Sunset', quite a recent Cluster-flowered Rose, is shortish in growth with dark green matt foliage. The attractive deep copper buds open to full blooms with the inner petals hiding the stamens and creating an old-fashioned quartered look. This is a good rose for picking as its unique color holds well both as a cut flower and when left on the bush. Disease resistance is good and flower production continuous. ZONES 5–10.
Tantau, Germany, 1995
Parentage unknown

'MAGNA CHARTA'
syns 'Casper', 'Magna Carta'
OLD, HYBRID PERPETUAL, MEDIUM PINK, REPEAT-FLOWERING

This rose bears clusters of bright pink blooms with overtones of red. They are double, globular and quite large, and are held upright. Yielding a rich scent, the flowers cover the bush in summer with some autumn rebloom. Heavy, dark, glossy green leaves cover the vigorous bush, which usually reaches 10 ft (3 m) if left unpruned. There are fearsome prickles on an otherwise compact, erect, tidy shrub that does well in poor soil. Unfortunately, the blooms will ball in wet weather, and it is subject to mildew

'Mainauperle'

and black spot. 'Magna Charta' was named for one of the most important documents in English social and legal history. ZONES 5–11.
Paul, UK, 1876
Parentage unknown

'MAGNIFICA'
syns *Rosa eglanteria duplex* 'Weston', *R. rubiginosa magnifica*
OLD, SWEET BRIAR, MAUVE

The cupped, purple-red, semi-double blooms of this variety have white centers and prominent stamens. Both the flowers and the foliage are fragrant, although the leaves are not as heavily scented as expected from a Sweet Briar. It is a hardy shrub with dark, dense foliage that will reach 6 ft (2 m) at maturity. It does well in poor soil and is a good choice for a woodland garden or for a hedge. Both the flowers and bush do well in the shade. ZONES 4–11.
Hesse, Germany, 1916
Seedling of 'Lucy Ashton'

'MAHINA'
MODERN, LARGE-FLOWERED/HYBRID TEA, APRICOT BLEND, REPEAT-FLOWERING

There have been two apricot roses with the name 'Mahina', both introduced by Meilland in France—one in 1952 and the other in 1982. The former has reddish apricot, double flowers that contain 25 petals that are very large and fragrant. It inherits its form of flower from 'Peace' and its golden apricot color from the brilliant apricot-orange 'Fred Edmunds'. The growth is bushy and vigorous and disease free. ZONES 5–11.
Meilland, France, 1952
'Peace' × 'Fred Edmunds'
Bagatelle Gold Medal 1952

'Maigold'

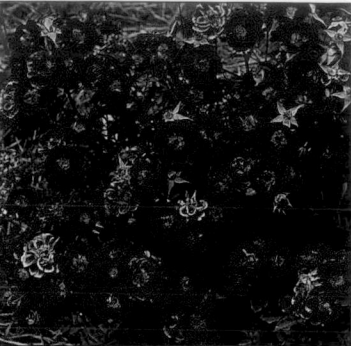
'Majorette'

'MAIDEN'S BLUSH'
syn. 'Small Maiden's Blush'
OLD, ALBA, WHITE

This tall and upright shrub bears soft, double, globular, medium-sized flowers that are blush in color. It does not repeat-flower. It is a fine shrub suitable for cottage gardens. The French called it 'Cuisse de Nymphe'. There are several variants of this rose; for a deeper colored one, the French added the qualification 'emué'. They are all sweetly scented. ZONES 4–11.
Kew Gardens, UK, 1797
Rosa alba × *R. centifolia*

'MAIGOLD'
syn. 'Maygold'
MODERN, MODERN SHRUB, DEEP YELLOW

This variety can be used as a shrub or as a climbing rose. The flowers appear very early, which is an inheritance from 'Frühlingstag' or 'Frühlingsgold'. The semi-double blooms are a rich orange-bronze, and have only 14 petals. They are large, 4 in (10 cm) across, cupped and very fragrant. The upright growth is very thorny, and there are next to no flowers after the initial burst. The glossy foliage can be susceptible to black spot. This rose holds its color best in cool climates; it is fleeting but lovely in warm areas and heralds the rose season. ZONES 4–11.
Kordes, Germany, 1953
'Poulsen's Pink' × 'Frühlingstag' or 'McGredy's Wonder' × 'Frühlingsgold'
National Rose Society Trial Ground Certificate

'MAINAUPERLE' KORmai
MODERN, LARGE-FLOWERED/HYBRID TEA, DARK RED, REPEAT-FLOWERING

The large, oval buds of this rose open to very dark red flowers with a velvety sheen. They are double with 35–40 petals, high centered, large and very fragrant. The foliage is large, dense, dark green and healthy on a tall, healthy, upright bush. Growth is very strong and basal growth produces candelabra-like heads with individual side shoots long enough for picking. It deserved its award but it has a few faults, like an abundance of large thorns and a slightly weak neck on smaller shoots. It was named after the great German garden of Count Bernadotte at Mainau on Lake Constance, one of Germany's most beautiful rose gardens. ZONES 5–10.
Kordes, Germany, 1969
Seedling × 'Americana'
Anerkannte Deutsche Rose 1966

M

'MAJORETTE' MEIpiess
syn. 'Majorette 86'
MODERN, MINIATURE, MEDIUM RED,
REPEAT-FLOWERING

Wonderful cardinal red flowers with
yellowish white centers are borne on this
rose in small clusters against a backdrop
of glossy green, healthy foliage. The
florets can be larger in cool climates,
which makes the rose a candidate for
classification as a Patio Rose. The clusters
are supported by strong, straight stems.
The repeat bloom cycle time is fast
(about 23 days) and the color is weatherproof in most climates. ZONES 5–11.

Meilland, France, 1986

'Magic Carrousel' × ('Grumpy' × 'Scarletta')

Glasgow Silver Medal 1992

'MALA RUBINSTEIN'
MODERN, LARGE-FLOWERED/HYBRID TEA,
MEDIUM PINK, REPEAT-FLOWERING

Coming from the coral and cream Cluster-flowered 'Sea Pearl' and the bright
salmon-orange Large-flowered 'Colour
Wonder', it is a surprise to find that this
rose has flowers of deep pink with just a
suggestion of orange. These large double
flowers have 45 petals, are high pointed,
5½ in (13 cm) across and very fragrant.
The blooms are at their most attractive
at the fully open stage. The flower production is good and disease resistance is
excellent. The foliage is large and matt
and rather dull green. ZONES 5–10.

Dickson, UK, 1971

'Sea Pearl' × 'Colour Wonder'

Edland Fragrance Medal 1972, Belfast Gold
Medal and Fragrance Prize 1973

'MALAGA'
MODERN, LARGE-FLOWERED CLIMBER, DEEP PINK,
REPEAT-FLOWERING

The blooms of this cultivar are reddish
pink, with about 36 large petals that
open from neat buds into flowers of
somewhat ragged form. They are often
carried in short-stemmed clusters, sometimes singly, and have a good fragrance.
This makes a fine pillar rose—also very
suitable for a wall or fence—repeatedly
flowering through summer and autumn.
'Malaga' grows up to average extent with
an upright, free-branching habit that
is well furnished with glossy dark green
foliage. ZONES 4–9.

McGredy, UK, 1971

('Hamburger Phoenix' × 'Danse du Feu') ×
'Copenhagen'

'Mala Rubinstein'

'MALCOLM SARGENT' HARwharry
syn. 'Natascha'
MODERN, LARGE-FLOWERED/HYBRID TEA,
MEDIUM RED, REPEAT-FLOWERING

The flowers of this rose are a bright
luminous crimson red. They are double
with 25 petals, are urn shaped in the bud
then open to loosely formed blooms at
the fully open stage. They are usually
borne singly on long strong stems and
they have a slight spicy fragrance. The
foliage is medium-sized, glossy dark green
and there are small reddish prickles on a
medium-sized, bushy plant that is quite
disease resistant. If spent blooms are not
removed dark green fruit are produced,
which look good against the bright
autumn flowers. ZONES 5–10.

Harkness, UK, 1988

'Herbstfeuer' × 'Trumpeter'

Belfast Gold Medal 1990, Courtrai Silver Medal
1990

'MAMAN COCHET'
OLD, TEA, PINK BLEND, REPEAT-FLOWERING

This popular rose has pointed buds that
open to light pink blooms with a darker
center and a yellow base. The double,
high-centered flowers are large, to 4 in
(10 cm) across, and cupped. The center
petals form a rosette; in humid weather
the thin petals ball. Some say it has a
fresh Tea scent, while others say it is
orris scented. 'Maman Cochet' does well
in poor soil and is suitable as a container
plant. Olive green, leathery leaves line
the canes, which are covered with
hooked prickles. If left unpruned it will
reach 7 ft (2.1 m). It is an excellent cut
flower. **'Climbing Maman Cochet'**
(Upton, 1909) easily reaches 12 ft (3.5 m)
tall. ZONES 5–10.

Cochet, France, 1893

'Marie van Houtte' × 'Mme Lombard'

'Mandarin'

'Malaga'

'MAMITA'
MODERN, LARGE-FLOWERED/HYBRID TEA,
MEDIUM RED, REPEAT-FLOWERING

This rose was raised by Monsieur
Robichon in the little town of Pithiviers,
which is now famous for the garden of
André Eve. 'Mamita' has very fragrant,
large, garnet red flowers on a vigorous
bush. The flower production is good,
and its resistance to disease is excellent.
ZONES 5–10.

Robichon, France, 1958

'Dickson's Red' × seedling

'MANDARIN'
MODERN, CLUSTER-FLOWERED/FLORIBUNDA,
MEDIUM RED, REPEAT-FLOWERING

This is one of the many roses bred by
Gene Boerner, who was affectionately
known as 'Papa Floribunda' because of
the number of first class Cluster-flowered
Roses that he bred. These were released
by the firm of Jackson and Perkins. The
buds of 'Mandarin' are ovoid, and the
semi-double flowers are a lively mandarin red. They have 18 petals, are high
centered, occur in large clusters and are
fragrant. The foliage is healthy and glossy
on a vigorous and upright plant. The
flower production is good. 'Mandarin'
is an excellent rose for hedges and for
borders but it is not seen much nowadays. ZONES 5–10.

Boerner, USA, 1951

Sport of 'Lilette Mallerin' × seedling of a red
Cluster-flowered Rose

'Mamita'

'MANDARIN' KORcelin
MODERN, MINIATURE, ORANGE BLEND,
REPEAT-FLOWERING

The attractive orange-pink, double
blooms of this rose give a classic cupped
shape when they burst into flower. They
become much flatter as they open and
the outer petals gradually lose their
orange tint, becoming much pinker.
They are accentuated by the very dark
green foliage. ZONES 5–10.

Kordes, Germany, 1987

Parentage unknown

Glasgow Gold Medal 1994, Dublin Certificate
of Merit

'MANETTII'
syn. *Rosa × noisettiana manettii*
OLD, NOISETTE, LIGHT PINK

This attractive shrub was found at the
famous rose garden in Monza, Italy, by
the director Signor Manetti. The delicate
pink flowers with a purplish tinge fill this
vigorous shrub, which is often found in
cemeteries. The leaves are deeply scented
and appear on smooth, dark brown,
gracefully arching canes. 'Manettii' is
easy to propagate from cuttings, and the
plant suckers; it is still sometimes used
for grafting and it began life as a rootstock for other roses. It may be a hybrid
of 'Slater's Crimson China' and *Rosa
moschata*. ZONES 4–11.

Manetti, Italy, 1820s; introduced by Rivers, UK,
1835

Parentage unknown

'Manettii'

'Maman Cochet'

'Many Thanks'

'Manou Meilland'

'Many Happy Returns'

'Marbrée'

'MANNHEIM'

MODERN, MODERN SHRUB, DARK RED, REPEAT-FLOWERING

This is one of Kordes' many shrub roses of the 1950s and 1960s that he named after German cities. 'Mannheim' produces a continuous display of double crimson flowers in large clusters on an upright bushy plant. The repeat-flowering is good. This rose, which could equally be classed as a Cluster-flowered Rose, is healthy and has leathery dark green foliage. It is a good rose for hedges and for use among perennials and shrubs in a mixed border. ZONES 4–11.

Kordes, Germany, 1958

'Rudolph Timm' × 'Fanal'

'MANNING'S BLUSH'

OLD, SWEET BRIAR, WHITE, REPEAT-FLOWERING

The white blooms of this rose are flushed pink and open flat. The fragrant, double blooms have many petals, and the leaves are also fragrant. Like most Sweet Briar Roses, this one will bloom early in spring and have some repeat in autumn. It is a dense, stalwart shrub covered with small leaves that line the arching canes. It does well in poor soil, and reaches 5 ft (1.5 m) if left unpruned. This is a good candidate for the wild garden and is equally happy in the sun or shade. It is strongly disease resistant. ZONES 4–11.

Pre-1799

Parentage unknown

'MANOU MEILLAND'   MEItulimon

MODERN, LARGE-FLOWERED/HYBRID TEA, MAUVE/ DEEP PINK, REPEAT-FLOWERING

This rose is like 'Baronne Edmond de Rothschild', with the same rich cyclamen pink flowers with silver undersides, but the growth is much shorter and more spreading. The large, double flowers have 50 petals, are fully cupped and appear in small clusters; they last very well without losing color. The abundant foliage is very dark green and glossy. 'Manou Meilland' makes an excellent border with 'Baronne de Rothschild', the only two roses of this color. Both are very popular. ZONES 5–11.

Meilland, France, 1980

('Baronne Edmond de Rothschild' × 'Baronne Edmond de Rothschild') × ('Ma Fille' × 'Love Song')

Paris Gold Medal 1977, Madrid Gold Medal 1978, New Zealand Gold Medal 1980

'MANY HAPPY RETURNS'

HARwanted

syn. 'Prima'

MODERN, MODERN SHRUB, PINK BLEND/LIGHT PINK, REPEAT-FLOWERING

This spreading and bushy rose bears large clusters of semi-double, soft pink flowers, which last well. The mid-green foliage acts as a foil to the pale flowers. If the spent blooms are not removed a large crop of roundish bright red hips are produced; these can look very effective with the autumn flowers. The flower production is very high, blooms being produced over a particularly long period. Its disease resistance is astonishing. This is a good rose for use with perennials and bulbs in a mixed border, where the flowers can show their unsophisticated charm. ZONES 5–10.

Harkness, UK, 1991

'Herbstfeuer' × 'Pearl Drift'

Courtrai Silver Medal 1987, Geneva Gold Medal and Prize 1987, Monza Silver Medal and Prize 1987, Royal National Rose Society Trial Ground Certificate 1988

'MANX QUEEN'

syn. 'Isle of Man'

MODERN, CLUSTER-FLOWERED/FLORIBUNDA, ORANGE BLEND, REPEAT-FLOWERING

The flowers of 'Manx Queen' have some of the richness of 'Shepherd's Delight', but they come in much smaller clusters. The semi-double blooms with 18 petals are rich gold flushed bronze-red. They are produced in medium-sized, well-spaced clusters, are fragrant and last well on the bush. The foliage is dark green and disease free on a plant with a bushy, compact growth habit, growing a similar size to its parent 'Circus'. This is an excellent bedding rose that continues to flower over a long period. ZONES 5–10.

Dickson, UK, 1963

'Shepherd's Delight' × 'Circus'

Royal National Rose Society Certificate of Merit 1963

'MANY THANKS'

MODERN, MINIATURE, APRICOT BLEND, REPEAT-FLOWERING

Identical to its parent except for the color of its petals, which are pale salmon-apricot with yellow bases and paler undersides, 'Many Thanks' carries long and pointed buds opening to double flowers. They are beautifully formed, high centered and very free flowering with a quick repeat. This healthy variety is vigorous and bushy, and in summer it is covered by well-spaced flower clusters. It is excellent for use in pots and for massed display in small beds. ZONES 5–10.

Geytenbeek, Australia, 1976

Sport of 'Mary Marshall'

'MARBRÉE'

OLD, PORTLAND, RED BLEND, REPEAT-FLOWERING

The marbled flowers of this rose come in sizeable clusters on longish stems. They are almost fully double and as much as 3 in (8 cm) across, with each large, purple-crimson petal smudged or speckled soft pink. When fully open an array of yellow stamens show through to effect. After the first generous flush of flowers in mid-summer this rose takes a little rest before giving a repeat performance in early autumn. The fragrance is of attar. It is tall for a Portland, and has ample, dark green, long, pointed foliage. It can be used in the border or as a hedge. It is a healthy and reliable landscaping plant. ZONES 5–10.

Moreau et Robert, France, 1858

Parentage unknown

'MARCEL BOURGOUIN'

syn. 'Le Jacobin'

OLD, GALLICA, MAUVE

The rich red velvet blooms of this rose age to gray-violet; the undersides of the petals is much paler. The somewhat flat flowers, which appear in early summer, are loosely double and blowzy, and are at their best after fully opening. The fragrance is very rich. The foliage is dark and velvety on an erect shrub that will reach 5 ft (1.5 m) high. It likes a rich soil. Those who have grown this rose say it is rather temperamental and needs cosseting, but it is effective as a hedge and tolerates some shade. ZONES 4–10.

Corboeuf, France, 1899

Seedling of 'Blanche Moreau'

'Marcel Bourgouin'

'Mannheim'

'Maréchal Davoust'

'Marchesa Boccella'

'MARCELLA'

MODERN, LARGE-FLOWERED/HYBRID TEA,
ORANGE BLEND, REPEAT-FLOWERING

This is a short-growing rose with shapely buds that are golden yellow lightly flushed with pink. The flowers are borne on short stems over a long period and retain their color well. 'Marcella' has a compact growth habit and good disease resistance, but the flower production is low. This rose is a good choice for a spot in the garden where a smaller bush is desired, such as at the front of a border. ZONES 5–10.

LeGrice, UK, 1986

Parentage unknown

'MÄRCHENLAND'

syn. 'Exception'

MODERN, CLUSTER-FLOWERED/FLORIBUNDA,
ORANGE BLEND, REPEAT-FLOWERING

This rose bears lovely rose-colored flowers tinted with salmon. The semi-double blooms have 18 petals and come in large clusters of up to 40. The large heads of fragrant flowers are quite eye-catching in spring, and there is repeat-bloom in summer and autumn. The foliage is dark green and plentiful on a plant with a vigorous and upright growth habit. 'Märchenland' makes an excellent hedge or border and can be used to great effect with perennial plants in mixed borders or in shrubberies. ZONES 5–10.

Tantau, Germany, 1951

'Swantje' × 'Hamburg'

National Rose Society Trial Ground Certificate 1952

'MARCHESA BOCCELLA'

syns 'Jacques Cartier', 'Marquise Boccella',
'Marquise Boçella'

OLD, HYBRID PERPETUAL, LIGHT PINK,
REPEAT-FLOWERING

The flowers of this rose develop from firm buds with feathery sepals and are borne in tight clusters; they open to fully double and quartered flowers often with button eyes. They are up to 3 in (8 cm) across and are soft pink. The very fragrant blooms are produced in succession from mid-summer to late autumn. It is an up-right, sturdy shrub to 4 ft (1.2 m) high, occasionally throwing up a taller shoot to 5 ft (1.5 m) or more. The stems are stout and strong and there are ample thorns. The foliage is light green when young

deepening to a blue-green with age; it is sometimes crinkly. This excellent rose makes both a good bedding variety and a fine hedge. In the USA, this rose is sold as 'Jacques Cartier', but it must be exhibited at rose shows there as 'Marchesa Boccella'. Most authorities now believe 'Jacques Cartier' is the same rose as 'Marchesa Boccella'. ZONES 4–9.

Desprez, France, 1842

Parentage unknown

'MARCHIONESS OF LONDONDERRY'

OLD, HYBRID PERPETUAL, LIGHT PINK,
REPEAT-FLOWERING

This rose is ivory white suffused with pink. The 50-petalled, cupped, full blooms are high centered, large, globular and fragrant. The flowers, which are carried on erect stalks, have large, thick, reflexed petals and look very much like Large-flowered Roses. This is a strong shrub covered with large, dull green leaves that will reach 6 ft (2 m) at maturity. The bush responds well to nourishment with a good repeat-bloom. This rose makes a superb cut flower. ZONES 5–10.

Dickson, UK, 1893

Seedling of 'Baronne Adolphe de Rothschild'

'MARCHIONESS OF LORNE'

OLD, HYBRID PERPETUAL, PINK BLEND,
REPEAT-FLOWERING

During a long flowering season, this floriferous rose flaunts its large petals. The full, cupped blooms are a rich, rosy pink, joined by a vivid carmine overtone. Its strong fragrance and erect stance make it a good cut flower. It has dark green foliage and some prickles and will reach 5 ft (1.5 m) if left unpruned. It does well in poor soil, but hates wet weather during the blooming period. The rose was named for Princess Louise, (1848–1939), sixth child of Queen Victoria. ZONES 5–10.

Paul, UK, 1889

Parentage unknown

'MARCHIONESS OF SALISBURY'

MODERN, LARGE-FLOWERED/HYBRID TEA,
DARK RED, REPEAT-FLOWERING

This was one of the first really deep red Large-flowered Roses produced; before

this, all dark red roses were either Teas or Hybrid Perpetuals. The large, globular blooms are held erect on the stems. The blooms fade as they age. There is a strong scent. The foliage is abundant with very dark green leaves with short nodes. The growth habit is like a Hybrid Perpetual, but the high-centered flowers are a more Large-flowered form. Blooming is continuous from spring until autumn. The Salisbury family garden at Hatfield House in Hertfordshire is still one of the greatest gardens in England, and the present Marchioness is one of England's most knowledgeable gardeners. ZONES 5–10.

Pernet, France, 1890

Parentage unknown

'MARCIA GANDY'

MODERN, LARGE-FLOWERED/HYBRID TEA,
RED BLEND, REPEAT-FLOWERING

This rose produces rosy crimson flowers with rosy salmon undersides. The attractive buds open quickly to full blooms. The flower production is fairly sparse but

growth is vigorous, and there is a very strong perfume. The foliage is dull green but quite sparse. The plant is fairly disease resistant. ZONES 5–11.

Verschuren, The Netherlands, 1957

Parentage unknown

'MARCO POLO'

MODERN, LARGE-FLOWERED/HYBRID TEA,
LIGHT PINK, REPEAT-FLOWERING

The color of 'Marco Polo' is similar to 'Memoriam'. The double flowers have good exhibition form, are high centered, large and fragrant. The foliage is glossy on a vigorous and upright plant. Bred by an amateur breeder who also bred 'Elizabeth Fankhauser' and 'Betano Beach', it has good disease resistance. ZONES 5–11.

Fankhauser, Australia, 1971

'Memoriam' × 'Elizabeth Fankhauser'

'MARÉCHAL DAVOUST'

syn. 'Maréchal Davout'

OLD, MOSS, MEDIUM PINK

The highly scented blooms of this rose are deep crimson deepening to almost purple. They are packed with petals, each with a softer colored underside which, when reflexed, gives the overall effect of mottling. It flowers freely during summer and is a disease-resistant shrub of sturdy, relatively tidy stature to some 5 ft (1.5 m) high in good soil. The stems are covered with brownish purple stubble, and the dark green foliage is a little coarse. It makes an effective hedge as it does well in poor soil, and it can also be pruned as a container plant. ZONES 4–11.

Robert, France, 1853

Parentage unknown

'Marchioness of Salisbury'

'Marcia Gandy'

'Marcella'

M

'MARÉCHAL FOCH'

syn. 'Red Orléans Rose'

MODERN, POLYANTHA, DEEP PINK, REPEAT-FLOWERING

This Polyantha rose has a vigorous, short, bushy growth habit and abundant foliage. The semi-double flowers can be deep pink to cherry red, and are borne in compact clusters of 5–20 fragrant blooms. 'Orléans Rose', which is deep pink with a white center, sported a number of times, producing roses varying in color in shades of pink and salmon. All make good low borders or short hedges and can be used where flowering over a long period is needed. There can be mildew in autumn. ZONES 4–11.

Levavasseur, France, 1918

Sport of 'Orléans Rose'

'MARÉCHAL NIEL'

OLD, NOISETTE, MEDIUM YELLOW, REPEAT-FLOWERING

This popular rose has large, golden yellow blooms that appear in clusters on weak stems, so they are best grown where they can be seen from below. It does well on a trellis or pergola. The blooms are very strongly Tea scented and make excellent cut flowers. It is used mostly as a climber, and it has soft, dark green leaves, smooth bark and many dark red, hooked prickles. It does well in partial shade, but one must have patience with this beauty. Henri Pradel of Montauban, France, made customers buy 12 other plants before he would give them this rose, as it was in such demand. It was named for a French general, minister of war for Napoleon III. ZONES 6–11.

Pradel, France, 1864

Seedling of 'Isabella Gray'

'MARGARET'

MODERN, LARGE-FLOWERED/HYBRID TEA, PINK BLEND, REPEAT-FLOWERING

'Margaret' is still a good garden rose even after over 40 years in commerce. The buds are large and well formed and open to well-shaped, long-lasting very double blooms. They are slightly globular, rose pink with silvery pink undersides and are very fragrant. The flower production is excellent and there are no disease problems. The plant, which is vigorous and has ample foliage, is a good bedding rose or it can be used as a hedge or border. ZONES 5–11.

Dickson, UK, 1954

Seedling of 'May Wettern' × 'Souvenir de Denier van der Gon'

National Rose Society Gold Medal 1954

'Margaret'

'Maréchal Foch'

'Maréchal Niel'

'Margaret'

'MARGARET MERRIL'   HARkuly

MODERN, CLUSTER-FLOWERED/FLORIBUNDA, WHITE, REPEAT-FLOWERING

This is a remarkable rose, as its many awards testify. The double, high-centered, white flowers have a faint blush tint in the center. There are 28 petals. It is large for a Cluster-flowered Rose, being up to 4 in (10 cm) across. The petals have very heavy substance and are very fragrant. The abundant foliage is big and glossy and the leaves come very close to the flower, giving a high-shouldered effect that shows the crisp flowers to perfection. It is at its best in cooler climates but will tolerate a wide range of climates, and is a superb bedding rose with no disease problems. Flower production is exceptionally high on short to medium-length stems and repeat bloom is quite remarkable. ZONES 5–11.

Harkness, UK, 1978

('Rudolph Timm' × 'Dedication') × 'Pascali'

Geneva Gold Medal 1978, Monza Gold Medal 1978, Rome Gold Medal 1978, Royal National Rose Society Edland Fragrance Award 1978, New Zealand Gold Medal & Fragrance Award 1982, RNRS James Mason Medal 1990, Auckland Fragrance Award 1992

'MARGARET TURNBULL'

MODERN, LARGE-FLOWERED CLIMBER, YELLOW BLEND, REPEAT-FLOWERING

'Margaret Turnbull' produces flowers of a very soft pink with a yellow base which becomes visible as the flowers open. They are double, cupped and large, and are produced very freely in spring, rather sparsely in summer and then more abundantly in autumn. There is a slight fragrance. The foliage is pale, wrinkled and a little sparse. This is a fairly vigorous rose that is ideal for use on a pillar or tripod. Disease resistance is good. The autumn flush is attractive and the blooms show up well from a distance. ZONES 4–11.

Clark, Australia, 1931

Parentage unknown

'MARGARET WASSERFALL'

KORoberfinz

MODERN, LARGE-FLOWERED/HYBRID TEA, WHITE BLEND, REPEAT-FLOWERING

Margaret Wasserfall is the editor of the South African magazine *Garden and Home*. Ludwig Taschner chose this rose from his trial grounds in Pretoria, which was an improvement of Margaret's favorite, 'Antique Silk'. Where 'Antique Silk' produces its best cut flowers under greenhouse conditions, this rose is a stronger, more carefree and vigorous tall shrub that flowers repeatedly. The fragrant blooms are large and full, star-shaped when open, and they have a delicate pinkish fawn tint that florists find very alluring. ZONES 5–10.

Kordes, Germany, 1994

Parentage unknown

'MARGO KOSTER'

syn. 'Sunbeam'

MODERN, POLYANTHA, ORANGE BLEND, REPEAT-FLOWERING

This rose is a sport of 'Dick Koster', which is in turn a sport of 'Annike Koster', which is a sport of 'Greta Kluis',

'Margaret Turnbull'

which is a sport of 'Echo', which is a sport of the climbing rose 'Tausendschön'! The flowers of 'Margo Koster' are salmon-pink, small and cupped and are produced in small, tightly packed clusters. As with most Polyanthas, mildew can be a problem. The plant is short and vigorous, and it flowers well into autumn after a late start in the season. ZONES 4–11.

Koster, The Netherlands, 1931

Sport of 'Dick Koster'

'MARGUERITE HILLING'
syn. 'Pink Nevada'

MODERN, MODERN SHRUB, MEDIUM PINK, REPEAT-FLOWERING

This variety has all the attributes of 'Nevada', from which it sported at Hillings Nursery. It grows into a large spreading bush and produces enormous quantities of almost single, dark pink flowers along the arching canes. The wood is dark plum colored and the foliage is light green and abundant. It flowers freely through spring until autumn and is one of the best of all shrub roses. It needs little pruning except for an occasional removal of some old wood to encourage new growth. 'Nevada' was bred by Pedro Dot, who also introduced an amazing selection of very brightly colored modern roses. ZONES 4–11.

Hilling, UK, 1959

Sport of 'Nevada'

Royal Horticultural Society Award of Garden Merit 1993

'Maria Teresa Bordas'

'Marguerite Hilling'

'MARIA LISA'
OLD, RAMBLER, PINK BLEND

This is a late member of the Rambler crowd, and has almost disappeared from public and even private gardens. Large clusters of small, single, fragrant blooms cover the vigorous plant. The flowers are clear rose pink with white centers. It has pliable canes that can easily be trained on pergolas or trellises. It has dark, leathery leaves with some prickles, blooms during early summer and is strongly disease resistant. ZONES 4–11.

Liebau, France, 1936

Parentage unknown

'MARIA MATHILDA'   LENmar
MODERN, MINIATURE, WHITE, REPEAT-FLOWERING

This rose is one of the few Miniature Roses hybridized by the Belgian master, Louis Lens. The white flowers are shaded with pink and usually grow in small clusters. They are double with 24 petals and are very fragrant. The foliage is glossy and very dark green. This prolific plant has an upright habit and is suitable as a container-grown plant. The blooms are long lasting and the repeat cycle is relatively fast. 'Maria Mathilda' is an all-round winner, bringing ease of maintenance with the reward of plenty of bloom and color. ZONES 5–11.

Lens, Belgium, 1980

Seedling of a Miniature × ('New Penny' × 'Jour De Fete')

Golden Rose of The Hague 1981

'Marguerite Hilling'

'MARIA TERESA BORDAS'
MODERN, LARGE-FLOWERED/HYBRID TEA, MEDIUM PINK, REPEAT-FLOWERING

This rose produces flowers in lovely shades of rose pinks, creams and soft yellows. The shapely, ovoid buds open to very double, high-centered flowers that have good exhibition form and 50 petals. The blooms are beautiful at all stages of development, particularly in the heat of summer when the coloring is at its loveliest. The plant has a medium to tall and upright growth habit, with very clean wood almost devoid of thorns. It was bred to do well in a hot climate like that of Spain. ZONES 5–11.

Bordas, Spain, 1953

'Sensation' × 'Peace'

'MARIANDEL'   KORpeahn
syns 'Carl Philip Kristian IV', 'The Times Rose'

MODERN, CLUSTER-FLOWERED/FLORIBUNDA, MEDIUM RED, REPEAT-FLOWERING

There are many good scarlet-crimson Cluster-flowered Roses, but 'Mariandel' is one of the very best. The semi-double flowers are produced in well-spaced clusters. The color is an intense bright red and the blooms hold their form and color well in both very hot and very cold conditions. The trusses of flowers also

'Margo Koster'

stand up to windy conditions very well. The abundant foliage is dark green, semi-glossy and red tinged in the early stages of growth. This rose is superb as a hedge or a bedding rose and is equally good in a border. It has become popular in many countries. ZONES 5–10.

Kordes, Germany, 1986

'Tornado' × 'Redgold'

Royal National Rose Society President's International Trophy 1982, Belfast Certificate of Merit 1986, Golden Rose of The Hague 1990, Royal Horticultural Society Award of Garden Merit 1993

'MARIE-ANTOINETTE'
MODERN, LARGE-FLOWERED/HYBRID TEA, DEEP PINK

It is interesting to note that a rose named after the beheaded Queen of France has the rose 'Queen Elizabeth' as one parent! This rose is not to be confused with the Gallica of 1829. 'Marie-Antoinette' produces well-formed rose pink flowers with a darker reverse to the petals. The vigorous upright plant has abundant dark green matt foliage. Disease resistance is good. Long, pointed buds open to blooms of 25–30 petals. There is a slight fragrance. ZONES 5–10.

Armstrong, USA, 1968

'Queen Elizabeth' × 'Chrysler Imperial'

'Marie-Antoinette'

'Mariandel'

M

'Marie de Blois'

'Marie de Saint Jean'

'MARIE DE BLOIS'
OLD, MOSS, MEDIUM PINK

Reddish moss covers the buds of this rose before they open to reveal pink blooms with reflexed petals. The frilled blooms are globular, full and blowzy, and appear in random clusters then repeat throughout the season. Bright green leaves cover the strongly disease-resistant bush, which does well in poor soil and is effective as a hedge if pruned to 5 ft (1.5 m). Moss Roses are mutations of the Centifolias; the moss covers the stem of the flower, the calyx, the sepals and even the leaflets. Robert created 'Sombreuil', another famous rose, at his nursery in Angers. ZONES 4–10.

Robert, France, 1852

Parentage unknown

'MARIE DE BOURGOGNE'
OLD, MOSS, MEDIUM PINK

Most people forget to rub the buds that are covered with the moss; this is another fragrant part of the rose, and to most it has a pleasant smell—which is true of this very rare rose. The fragrant, dark pink flowers are double, large and globular. To appear at their best, Moss Roses need the best growing conditions. Some roses are heavily covered with moss, which can be a light color or a dark

color. These roses appeared first in The Netherlands or France and were sold at exorbitant prices. ZONES 4–10.

Robert, France, 1853

Parentage unknown

'MARIE DE SAINT JEAN'
syn. 'Marie de St Jean'
OLD, PORTLAND, WHITE, REPEAT-FLOWERING

The exquisite white buds shaded dark pink on this variety open to pure white, full, plump blooms. The outside petals are larger than the rest, and the center of the bloom is muddled. Traces of dark pink edge the rose when it is fully open. The strongly fragrant flowers measure 3 in (8 cm) across. It blooms for a long period in summer with some autumn rebloom, and has gray-green foliage on an upright, vigorous plant. The bark is light green and the thin canes hold lots of prickles. Portlands belong to a small class with strong characteristics—form, beauty, color and fragrance; they are also known for their short stems. ZONES 5–11.

Damaizin, France, 1869

Parentage unknown

'MARIE DERMAR'
OLD, NOISETTE, LIGHT YELLOW, REPEAT-FLOWERING

The cream and flesh-colored blooms on 'Marie Dermar' have a yellowish tinge when fully open. The petals of the full, medium-sized, double blooms reflex, and there is a pleasant scent. The upright growth habit of this modest climber makes it a good choice for a small pillar or pergola. It has handsome foliage and a long summer-blooming period. This is a less famous creation of Geschwind (1829–1910), a genius at hybridizing who aimed to create winter-hardy roses that needed no protection. He produced two all-time popular roses—'Gruss an Teplitz' and 'Gipsy Boy'. ZONES 5–10.

Geschwind, Hungary, 1889

Seedling of 'Louise d'Arzens'

'Marie Dermar'

'MARIE D'ORLÉANS'
OLD, TEA, MEDIUM PINK, REPEAT-FLOWERING

Like so many Teas, this rose changes colors—copper red, salmon-pink and coral are some of the shades. The full, flat, fragrant blooms are quartered at first and become rather blowzy. They hold well, especially when used in bouquets. A hardy shrub covered with bronze-green foliage in spring, its sprawling growth is best controlled by using it as a bedding plant or in the border as it will bloom from spring until the first frost. The Nabonnand family created a long list of roses during the time that Gilbert, Paul and Clement worked in their Riviera nursery between the years 1872–1924. ZONES 6–11.

Nabonnand, France, 1883

Parentage unknown

'MARIE GOUCHAULT'
syn. 'Marie Gauschault'
MODERN, RAMBLER, MEDIUM RED

This early bloomer is clear red with salmon overtones. It is double and small and looks much like 'Dorothy Perkins'. The large clusters of 30–40 blooms, which begin as bright red and fade to pink, are long lasting but are not fragrant. It is a vigorous and hardy Rambler that is ideal for climbing trees or for covering sheds or barns; it can also be trained on a wall. It is disease free and there may be some rebloom. Most Ramblers are easy to train as their canes are thin and pliable. ZONES 4–11.

Turbat, France, 1927

Parentage unknown

'MARIE-JEANNE'
MODERN, POLYANTHA, WHITE, REPEAT-FLOWERING

The flowers of 'Marie-Jeanne' are pale blush and come in large clusters of up to 60. These well-formed blooms last well on the bush. The flowering is profuse in

spring, fairly continuous through summer and is followed by a very good crop in autumn. There is a light scent. This is a tall grower for a Polyantha, and it is also very spreading. The foliage is glossy light green with bronze tints in the early stages of growth. It is a vigorous bush that can be left unpruned to form a small shrub, or it can be treated in the normal way. This is a good rose for a border or hedge, and it can be mixed among perennial plants of similar coloring. ZONES 4–11.

Turbat, France, 1913

Parentage unknown

'MARIE LAMBERT'
syns 'Priscilla', 'Snowflake', 'White Hermosa'
OLD, TEA, WHITE, REPEAT-FLOWERING

An early bloomer, this fragrant rose begins with well-formed buds that open to pure white, medium-sized flowers, which age to pale flesh white. It is well formed, globular and floriferous and is a healthy, free and open shrub with plentiful foliage. Its 3 ft (1 m) growth makes it a good choice for a container but, if planted in a bed, it is best grown in groups of 3 or more to give the best effect. This is a creation of the French hybridizer and not of the more famous German rosarian. ZONES 6–11.

Lambert, France, 1886

Sport of 'Mme Bravy'

'MARIE LEONIDA'
syn. 'Leonida'
MODERN, LARGE-FLOWERED CLIMBER, WHITE, REPEAT-FLOWERING

'Marie Leonida' is a most distinctive rose. It has the vigor, glossy foliage and vicious thorns of *Rosa bracteata*, and unique, double, cream flowers that are so quartered that they are divided into four complete segments. Flowering is late but continues through autumn to winter. The foliage is bronze in the early stages, ageing to bronze green, and it is very glossy. The strong growth and evergreen foliage make it suitable for covering unsightly buildings or for growing into trees. It is sufficiently sturdy to grow as a huge mound without support and is particularly suited for large country gardens. It can also make a quite impenetrable hedge and need never be pruned until it gets out of control. ZONES 4–11.

1835

Reputedly *Rosa bracteata* × *R. laevigata* but more likely *R. bracteata* × a yellow Tea Rose

'Marie-Jeanne'

'Marie Lambert'

'Marie van Houtte'

'Marie Robert'

'MARIE LOUISE'
OLD, DAMASK, MEDIUM PINK

Thought by some to have originated in Empress Josephine's Malmaison garden around 1811 under a different name, this early flowering rose is pink with mauve overtones. The deliciously perfumed, double blooms are flat with a button eye. They are borne in fairly large clusters on the ends of the arching branches, which are often weighed to the ground by the size and number of the flowers, especially in rain. The blooms age to white. It is a lax shrub with dark greenish brown, moderately thorny branches and profuse foliage that does well in poor soil. Its 4 ft (1.2 m) height makes it an attractive container plant, and it has been known to survive years of neglect. Empress Josephine was the first wife of Napoleon and has become possibly the most famous woman in rose history. 'Marie Louise' is named after his second wife. ZONES 5–10.

Pre-1813

Parentage unknown

'MARIE PAVIÉ
MODERN, POLYANTHA, WHITE, REPEAT-FLOWERING

The buds of this rose are small and very well formed. The flowers appear in small clusters above the foliage and are pale pink with a slightly deeper tint in the center. It is a particularly free-flowering plant and blooms over a very long period. The growth habit and shape of the flower clusters fit better in the China class than in the Polyantha class. It is bushy in growth with dark green foliage and very few thorns. This rose, which can be put to many uses in large or small gardens, is an excellent plant for low hedges, borders or small beds and is a wonderful addition to a mixed border. It is still popular after all these years. ZONES 4–11.

Alégatière, France, 1888

Parentage unknown

'MARIE ROBERT'
OLD, PORTLAND, PINK BLEND, REPEAT-FLOWERING

Less well known than other Portlands, this rose has mauve-pink blooms that are of a medium to large size. The full blooms take on a lilac coloring as they age. The bushy, compact plant is ideal for small gardens or for containers, and is also effective in mass planting or in the border. Although assigned to oblivion in recent rose books, there are two nurseries in France that still offer it. Moreau et Robert bred 123 cultivars in their Angers nursery. ZONES 5–10.

Moreau et Robert, France, 1860

Parentage unknown

'MARIE VAN HOUTTE'
syns 'Mlle Marie van Houtte', 'The Gem'
OLD, TEA, PINK BLEND, REPEAT-FLOWERING

With two excellent parents, a rose like this could hardly fail to win public approval. The waxy buds open to wonderful deep cream blooms suffused pink with a buff yellow base; in the sun the color deepens to a dark pink. The fragrant flowers are very double, high centered and large. They are long lasting and floriferous, and the strong stems on the sprawling plant hold the blooms well. The foliage is leathery dark green and there are many prickles. It loves the sun and hates rain, and its short growth makes it a good candidate for a container. This was once considered the most valuable white rose by professional gardeners. It is dedicated to Mademoiselle Marie van Houtte of Ghent, Belgium. **'Climbing Marie van Houtte'** (Thomasville Nurseries Inc, USA, 1936) is the same as its parent in every way except that it will grow to 10 ft (3 m) in a short time. It is no longer in commerce. ZONES 6–11.

Ducher, France, 1871

'Mme de Tartas' × 'Mme Falcot'

'Marie Pavié'

'MARIETTA SILVA TAROUCA'
syn. 'Marietta Grafin Silva Tarouca'
MODERN, RAMBLER, MEDIUM PINK

This rather rare Rambler produces large, bright rose blooms that are borne in huge clusters on vigorous, *Rosa multiflora*-like canes. The flowers are small, frilled and purplish pink and have no fragrance. Rich green leaves line the slender growth, and there are small prickles. It blooms only in early summer. This very healthy rose is not prone to any diseases, and is perfect for a pergola or for climbing a tree. It originated in the Dendrological Gardens of Count Silva Tarouca at Pruhonice in central Europe. ZONES 4–11.

Tarouca, 1925

'Colibri' × 'Crimson Rambler'

'MARIJKE KOOPMAN'
MODERN, LARGE-FLOWERED/HYBRID TEA, MEDIUM PINK, REPEAT-FLOWERING

This rose was named by the raiser to honor the memory of his friend's daughter who lost her life in a road accident. The long and pointed buds open to double flowers with 25 petals that are mid-pink. These fragrant blooms are produced continuously both singly and in small clusters, and they last well on the bush. The dark green, leathery foliage is resistant to disease, and the plant has a tall and upright habit of growth. ZONES 5–11.

Fryer, UK, 1979

Parentage unknown

The Hague Gold Medal 1978, Le Roeuix Gold Medal 1978

'MARILYN'
MODERN, MINIATURE, LIGHT PINK, REPEAT-FLOWERING

The flowers of this variety have an unusual color combination—light pink with a purple base to each petal. They are very double, with 60 or more petals, and occur mainly in small clusters. These rosette-like flowers cover the entire compact bush, which makes 'Marilyn' a great choice for garden display. It is, however, susceptible to mildew if not protected. This rose is one of the earliest Miniatures Roses ever hybridized by the House of Dot in their pioneering progress to develop a genetic pool for other workers to follow. ZONES 5–11.

Dot, Spain, 1955

'Perla de Montserrat' × 'Bambino'

Le Roeuix Gold Medal 1978

'Marie Louise'

'Marie Leonida'

M

'MARINA' RinaKOR
MODERN, CLUSTER-FLOWERED/FLORIBUNDA, ORANGE BLEND, REPEAT-FLOWERING

This is a charming garden rose that is also perfect for cutting. The shapely flower buds are a vivid pure orange with a yellow base to each petal. The double, medium-sized blooms, which have 30 petals and are fragrant, come in clusters of up to 15 blooms and hold their color very well. The foliage is very glossy dark green on a bush that is of medium height and has an upright growth habit. Flower production is good and the plant is disease free. 'Marina' is suitable as a bedding plant or for a border or a hedge. ZONES 5–10.

Kordes, Germany, 1974

'Colour Wonder' × seedling

All-America Rose Selection 1981

'MARINETTE' AUScam
MODERN, MODERN SHRUB, MEDIUM PINK, REPEAT-FLOWERING

The unusual quality of this variety, which is also classified as an English Rose, is in the form of the young buds; they are described by the raiser as 'long, thin, almost pencil like'. The young blooms are rose pink with hints of cream and open fully into almost flat, semi-double flowers—the pink tones become increasingly mottled with cream as the petals expand. The blooms are quite large with a pleasing scent, and continue to flower through summer and autumn.

'Marjorie Atherton'

For a border 'Marinette' is an interesting addition to the garden because the airy character of the plant gives the effect of a shrub covered with butterflies. It grows with a bushy, well-proportioned habit to average height with mid-green foliage, and was named for Marina 'Marinette' Berry to assist the work of the charity Children in Hospital. ZONES 4–9.

Austin, UK, 1995

'Lucetta' × 'Red Coat'

'MARION HARKNESS' HARkantabil
MODERN, LARGE-FLOWERED/HYBRID TEA, YELLOW BLEND, REPEAT-FLOWERING

'Marion Harkness' has double flowers of creamy yellow flushed orange-red on the outer petals. They have 20–25 petals and a slight fragrance. It is a bushy plant with abundant mid-green foliage to ground level and excellent disease resistance that makes a good bedding variety as the foliage is abundant to ground level. The flowers hold their color well, looking particularly effective from a distance. ZONES 5–10.

Harkness, UK, 1979

(['Manx Queen' × 'Prima Ballerina'] × ['Chanelle' × 'Piccadilly']) × 'Piccadilly'

'MARIONETTE'
MODERN, CLUSTER-FLOWERED/FLORIBUNDA, WHITE BLEND, REPEAT-FLOWERING

This is a good low-growing bushy rose with double flowers containing 25–30 petals. They are creamy yellow, a color that fades to cream in hot weather, and are produced in well-spaced clusters of up to 20 blooms that are very pretty in spring and summer. The buds are nicely shaped, the flowers are fragrant, and blooming is profuse and continuous. 'Pinocchio', 'Red Pinocchio', 'Yellow Pinocchio' and 'White Pinocchio' were all excellent bedding roses in the 1940s and 1950s and helped to make Cluster-flowered Roses popular throughout the world. ZONES 5–10.

DeVor, USA, 1944

Sport of 'Pinocchio'

'Marjory Palmer'

'MARJORIE ATHERTON'
MODERN, LARGE-FLOWERED/HYBRID TEA, MEDIUM YELLOW, REPEAT-FLOWERING

This rose has the strong upright growth of 'Mount Shasta' and the plump buds and excellent foliage of 'Peace'. The color is soft maize yellow and keeps well. The large, oval buds open to long-lasting, double flowers with 25 petals and a beautiful rounded shape. The flower production is fairly good and there are no disease problems. The foliage is pale green. 'Marjorie Atherton' is one of the best Australian-raised roses. ZONES 5–10.

Bell, Australia, 1977

'Mount Shasta' × 'Peace'

'MARJORIE CHASE' KORamator
MODERN, LARGE-FLOWERED/HYBRID TEA, APRICOT BLEND, REPEAT-FLOWERING

Marjorie Chase, who has been producing ice-skating shows in South Africa for 25 years, had this rose named for her 75th birthday. The colors are not those associated with ice, however, for the fat and pointed golden buds open to full flowers with yellow bases that blend with apricot and copper in the petals to create a glowing warmth. The blooms make good cut flowers and are fragrant. This vigorous bush rose is of medium height and new shoots provide a constant show of flowers on short stems. ZONES 5–11.

Kordes, Germany, 1996

Parentage unknown

'MARJORIE FAIR' HARhero
syns 'Red Ballerina', 'Red Yesterday'
MODERN, LARGE-FLOWERED/HYBRID TEA, RED BLEND, REPEAT-FLOWERING

This excellent crimson shrub rose has small, single flowers with 5 petals each with a distinct white eye. They come in both small and very large clusters and blooming is continuous. The flowers, which hold well and do not fade, have a slight fragrance. The profuse foliage is light green and semi-glossy on a plant with a very dense and bushy habit that grows to moderate height. It makes a good hedge and is also useful among perennials and shrubs in a mixed border; it can also be used as a large shrub if not pruned. It can suffer from mite attack in hot weather. ZONES 4–10.

Harkness, UK, 1977

'Ballerina' × 'Baby Faurax'

Copenhagen First Prize 1977, Nordrose Gold Medal 1977, Rome Gold Medal 1977, Royal National Rose Society Trial Ground Certificate 1977, Baden-Baden Gold Medal 1979, Anerkannte Deutsche Rose 1980, Paris Paysage Prize 1988

'Marjorie Fair'

'MARJORIE MARSHALL' HARdenier
MODERN, MODERN SHRUB, APRICOT BLEND, REPEAT-FLOWERING

The flowers of 'Marjorie Marshall' are deep apricot paling at the petal edges. The well-formed blooms, which have 30–35 attractive rounded petals and open flat, are produced in small and large clusters and show up well against the dark green foliage. The repeat-bloom cycle is rapid. The strong and bushy growth of this rose is between that of an English Rose and a Cluster-flowered Rose. It is disease resistant. The flowers are good for picking. ZONES 5–10.

Harkness, UK, 1996

Seedling of 'Sexy Rexy'

Dublin Gold Medal 1997

'MARJORIE MAY' HORsunpegy
MODERN, CLUSTER-FLOWERED/FLORIBUNDA, ORANGE-PINK, REPEAT-FLOWERING

The flowers of this rose are basically a rich orange shade, with subtle blendings of pink and yellow. They are fairly large, with up to 40 petals, and usually appear in small clusters, maintaining a good succession of bloom through summer and autumn. There is a slight fragrance. 'Marjorie May' is appropriate for a hedge, bed or to group in a border. It grows with an upright habit to average height or above for a bush rose, with leathery, semi-glossy leaves. ZONES 4–9.

Horner, UK, 1993

'Playgroup' × 'Peer Gynt'

'MARJORY PALMER'
MODERN, POLYANTHA, MEDIUM PINK, REPEAT-FLOWERING

This is one of the best low-growing roses bred by Australia's most famous hybridist. The plant is very spreading and has large, attractive, glossy green foliage and heads of rich pink, double flowers that open flat and quartered. The disease resistance is excellent and repeat-blooming usually quick. There is an exceptional fragrance. It makes an excellent border rose and can be used as a low hedge, flowering over a very long period. A pale pink sport of this rose called 'Alister Clark' has recently been introduced. ZONES 4–11.

Clark, Australia, 1936

'Jersey Beauty' × seedling

'Marina'

'Marjorie May'

'Marmalade'

'Marquise de Balbiano'

'Martin Frobisher'

'MARK SULLIVAN'

syn. 'Président Chaussé'

MODERN, LARGE-FLOWERED/HYBRID TEA, ORANGE-PINK, REPEAT-FLOWERING

This rose inherits its rich coloring from both its parents. The flowers are a blend of cerise and apricot, pink and yellow, are double with 30–35 petals, and are high centered to cupped. They are up to 4 in (10 cm) across and are fragrant. The foliage is dark, leathery and glossy on a plant with an upright and vigorous growth habit. Although the flowers do lose some of their bright color upon opening, this is still a very attractive rose in the garden. ZONES 5–11.

Mallerin, France, 1942

'Luis Brinas' × 'Brazier'

'MARLENA'

MODERN, CLUSTER-FLOWERED/FLORIBUNDA, MEDIUM RED, REPEAT-FLOWERING

This is one of the best low-growing Cluster-flowered Roses. The semi-double flowers have 18 petals and are crimson-scarlet. They are well formed in the bud, opening to flat full blooms of great substance that hold their color extremely well. The blooms come in small clusters of 5–15 flowers and completely cover the bush. 'Marlena' is superb planted as a low border or hedge, placing the plants no further than 18 in (45 cm) apart for

maximum effect where a ribbon of red is desired. The flowers look wonderful against the very glossy, disease-resistant foliage. ZONES 5–10.

Kordes, Germany, 1964

'Gertrud Westphal' × 'Lilli Marleen'

Baden-Baden Gold Medal 1962, Belfast Gold Medal 1966, Anerkannte Deutsche Rose 1964

'MARMALADE'

MODERN, LARGE-FLOWERED/HYBRID TEA, ORANGE BLEND, REPEAT-FLOWERING

The buds of this unusually colored rose are long, pointed and elegant. They open to very well-formed double blooms of great substance that are a rich orange-brown color with deep yellow undersides. They are large and have a Tea Rose perfume. The foliage is very large, glossy and dark on a plant that is disease free, strong and very upright. Flower production is good, but there is a rather long period between flushes. ZONES 5–10.

Swim and Ellis, USA, 1977

'Arlene Francis' × 'Bewitched'

'MARONDO' KORtitut

MODERN, MODERN SHRUB, MEDIUM PINK, REPEAT-FLOWERING

During summer, this variety makes a wonderful sight laden with clusters of medium-sized, semi-double blooms. They are a warm shade of rosy salmon-

'Mary Adair'

pink, with white towards the petal bases, and open like saucers to reveal attractive golden stamens. There is a light scent. This rose can be used as a ground cover where a moderate-sized plant is required, as it spreads twice as wide as it does high. It is well furnished with handsome, shiny bright green leaves. ZONES 4–9.

Kordes, Germany, 1991

Parentage unknown

Anerkannte Deutsche Rose 1989

'MARQUISE DE BALBIANO'

OLD, BOURBON, MAUVE, REPEAT-FLOWERING

This rose has full, large, cupped, crimson blooms suffused with satiny pink. They are well formed and make excellent cut flowers. A strong fragrance and hardy disposition add to their charm. The stout, handsome-leafed shrub, which can reach 6 ft (2 m) tall, gives a floriferous first bloom and repeats well in autumn. If treated generously with water and fertilizer, it produces superb flowers. ZONES 5–10.

Lacharme, France, 1855

Parentage unknown

'MARRY ME' DICwonder

MODERN, PATIO/DWARF CLUSTER-FLOWERED, MEDIUM PINK, REPEAT-FLOWERING

Introduced in 1998 at the Chelsea Flower Show in London, 'Marry Me' combines double, camellia pink flowers with a dwarf, bushy, free-flowering growth habit, which also has a good disease resistance. The nicely shaped buds open to well-formed flowers that retain their color well as they age. ZONES 5–9.

Dickson, UK, 1998

('Bright Smile' × 'Robin Redbreast') × 'Cider Cup'

British Association of Rose Breeders, Breeders' Choice 1998

'MARTHA'

syn. 'Marthe'

OLD, BOURBON, PINK BLEND, REPEAT-FLOWERING

From early summer into autumn this wonderful variety, one of the most popular of all garden roses, bears deep pink to mauve-pink, double, free-flowering blooms all over the long canes. These thornless stalks can be easily trained on trellises or fences. The dark green, shiny foliage further adds to its charm; it does well in poor soil and tolerates some shade. There is a strong fragrance, and the variety is both cold hardy and disease resistant. ZONES 5–10.

Knudsen, France, 1912

Sport of 'Zéphirine Drouhin'

'MARTHA GONZALES'

OLD, CHINA, MEDIUM RED, REPEAT-FLOWERING

Rose rustlers in Texas have discovered or recovered many roses over the past twenty years, some of which have been identified and others given trial names. 'Martha Gonzales' is one of the most popular of these in the trade today, and it was discovered in Navasota, Texas, by Joe Woodard. It was named for the woman in whose garden it was found, but there has since been continuing dispute over its identity. The variety bears bright scarlet, nearly single blooms that open flat and display prominent stamens. There is an occasional white streak on the petals, which are usually 2 in (1 cm) across. It is a low-growing plant reaching 3 ft (1 m) at most, and the new foliage is dark red. The small and pointed dark green leaves sparsely cover the thin canes. ZONES 7–10.

Woodward, USA

Parentage unknown

'Marlena'

'Mary'

'MARTHA'S VINEYARD' POUlans

MODERN, MODERN SHRUB, DEEP PINK,
REPEAT-FLOWERING

The semi-double flowers of this rose are
up to 2 in (5 cm) across and are borne
in small clusters. There are few prickles.
The foliage is small, light green and
semi-glossy on a plant with a spreading
growth. The flowering is profuse and
continuous, and there are no disease
problems. ZONES 4–11.

Olesen, Denmark 1995

Seedling × seedling

'MARTIN FROBISHER'

MODERN, HYBRID RUGOSA, LIGHT PINK,
REPEAT-FLOWERING

This Canadian variety was bred using
roses that were hardy in Arctic winters,
and it is one of the best of all roses for
cold climates; it also performs well in hot
areas. The plant is tall and upright with
distinctive gray-green foliage. The well-
shaped buds open to fragrant, double
flowers with 25 or so pale pink petals.
The foliage and flowers look like an Alba
Rose, and it would be interesting to find
out if there is any Alba blood in the seedling parent. There are very few thorns.
It makes an excellent hedge. ZONES 3–11.

Svedja, Canada, 1968

'Schneezwerg' × seedling

'MARTINI'

MODERN, LARGE-FLOWERED/HYBRID TEA,
DARK RED, REPEAT-FLOWERING

'Martini' is a good red rose that has often
been overlooked. The dark red flowers
have a velvety texture, are very full and
contain 50 or more petals which open
slowly to well-formed blooms that hold
their color well. The fragrance is strong.
The plant is tall and healthy with mid-
green foliage and good disease resistance.
ZONES 5–10.

Delforge, France, 1967

Parentage unknown

'MARTONE'

MODERN, MINIATURE, PINK BLEND,
REPEAT-FLOWERING

Interest in growing Miniature Roses
for exhibition has increased during the
1990s, and this rose is well suited for
that purpose. Its pointed buds open to
medium pink flowers of average size
that are lighter at the base. They are well
formed with high centers, have 30 small
petals, and are often borne singly. There
is a light damask scent. 'Martone' has
an upright habit and mid-green, semi-
glossy foliage. ZONES 5 9.

Bridges, USA, 1989

'Queen City' × seedling

'MARY'

MODERN, POLYANTHA, ORANGE-PINK,
REPEAT-FLOWERING

This rose has all the characteristics of
'Orange Triumph', but is much more
pink in color. The strong, vigorous plant
produces huge heads of cupped, semi-
double flowers with petals inclined to
turn inwards to give a globular effect,
something often seen in Polyanthas. The
foliage is glossy and the bush has good

'Mary Delahunty'

disease resistance. 'Mary' and 'Orange
Triumph' were much used for hedging
when first introduced, although their
popularity is now on the wane. 'Mary'
is still a good rose for cutting as it holds
its color well. ZONES 5–10.

Qualm, The Netherlands, 1947

Sport of 'Orange Triumph'

'MARY ADAIR'

MODERN, MINIATURE, APRICOT BLEND,
REPEAT-FLOWERING

The double flowers of this rose are a
beautiful soft apricot color, and they
have good substance; the color will fade
under hot sun. The blooms are on the
smallish side and have a light fragrance.
They are of exhibition standard and are
borne on short stems on a plant that is
dwarf and bushy. The vigor is variable
and depends on the microclimate. Ralph
Moore chose the name in honor of a
great friend. ZONES 5–11.

Moore, USA, 1966

'Golden Glow' × 'Zee'

'MARY CAVE' HARamity

MODERN, CLUSTER-FLOWERED/FLORIBUNDA,
MEDIUM YELLOW, REPEAT-FLOWERING

The bright yellow flowers of this rose are
freely produced on a neat, upright plant
that makes a fine bedding variety in the

garden, and particularly in public parks,
where maximum color impact is desired.
The blooms are produced in well-spaced
clusters of 5–7, have up to 20 wide petals,
and yield a light spicy scent. 'Mary Cave'
flowers with good continuity through
summer and autumn. It is a little below
average height for a bush rose, and is
adorned with plenty of crisp and shiny
foliage that can be affected by seasonal
mildew. ZONES 4–9.

Harkness, UK, 1995

'Rosemary Harkness' × 'Golden Years'

Royal National Rose Society Trial Ground
Certificate 1994

'MARY DELAHUNTY'

MODERN, LARGE-FLOWERED/HYBRID TEA,
DARK RED, REPEAT-FLOWERING

The shapely buds of this rose open slowly
to large, full blooms that hold their color
well. The fragrant, dark red blooms are
borne on long stems on a tall and healthy
bush with abundant dark green foliage.
Flower production is well above average
and disease resistance is excellent. This,
possibly the best dark red rose bred in
Australia, was named after a very popular Australian television newsreader.
ZONES 5–10.

Bell, Australia, 1990

('Daily Sketch' × 'Impeccable') × 'Red Planet'

'Martini'

'MARY DONALDSON' CANana

MODERN, LARGE-FLOWERED/HYBRID TEA,
MEDIUM PINK, REPEAT-FLOWERING

The double flowers of this rose have 40
rose pink petals. They are of exhibition
form with a lovely fragrance. The foliage
is large and glossy dark green on an
upright plant that has excellent disease
resistance. This is a good rose for bedding and cutting; indoors, under artificial light, its color is shown to advantage.
The blooms last well and keep their color
until the petals fall. ZONES 5–10.

Cant, UK, 1983

'Kathleen O'Rourke' × seedling

Royal National Rose Society Trial Ground
Certificate 1984

M

'Mary MacKillop'

'Mary MacKillop'

'Mary Kay'

'MARY GUTHRIE'

MODERN, POLYANTHA, MEDIUM PINK,
REPEAT-FLOWERING

This rose has single flowers with prominent stamens. The fragrant blooms come
in small to large clusters and are cerise
in color. They flower profusely and continuously, and the foliage is a rather dull
green on a low, stocky plant. It is disease
resistant. ZONES 5–11.

Clark, Australia, 1929

'Jersey Beauty' × 'Scorcher'

'MARY HART, CLIMBING'

MODERN, LARGE-FLOWERED CLIMBER,
MEDIUM RED, REPEAT-FLOWERING

This cerise-red and gold bicolored rose
has tightly scrolled buds that open to
rather loose, flat flowers with 25 petals.
They are fragrant. The flowering is very
profuse early in the season and good in
autumn. The abundant foliage is light
green and healthy. ZONES 5–11.

Western Rose Company, USA, 1937

Sport of 'Talisman'

'MARY HAYLEY BELL'

KORparall, KORparau

syn. 'Abundancia'

MODERN, MODERN SHRUB, MEDIUM PINK,
REPEAT-FLOWERING

This compact rose has an uneven growth
habit and carries clusters of dainty, semi-
double, pink rosettes. There is a pleasing
scent. It was name for the distinguished
British playwright. ZONES 5–10.

Kordes, Germany, 1989

'Zwergkönig 78' × seedling

Royal National Rose Society President's International Trophy 1987

'MARY-JEAN'   HARyen

syn. 'Mary Jean'

MODERN, LARGE-FLOWERED/HYBRID TEA, APRICOT
BLEND

This variety has pointed, ovoid buds that
open to cupped, double, apricot flowers
containing 35 petals. They usually come
singly and are good for picking. There
is a very sweet perfume. The foliage is
abundant, large, medium green and
semi-glossy on a medium-sized plant
of bushy habit. It is an ideal rose for
bedding or for borders. ZONES 5–11.

Harkness, UK, 1990

'Dr Darley' × 'Amber Queen'

Courtrai Certificate of Merit 1994

'MARY KAY'   MINoco

MODERN, MINIATURE, LIGHT PINK,
REPEAT-FLOWERING

The blooms of 'Mary Kay' are pale pink,
double with 35 petals and small. There
is a slight fragrance. The foliage is small,
dark and glossy and growth is upright
and bushy. The buds of 'Mary Kay' are
attractive and open slowly to full blooms
that last well both on the bush and when
picked. Disease resistance is good and
repeat-bloom fairly rapid. ZONES 5–11.

Williams, USA, 1984

'Tom Brown' × 'Over the Rainbow'

'MARY MacKILLOP'

syn. 'Mother Mary McKillop'

MODERN, LARGE-FLOWERED/HYBRID TEA,
PINK BLEND, REPEAT-FLOWERING

Mary MacKillop was the founder of the
St Joseph's Order in Australia. The variety produces enormous quantities of
well-formed, soft pink roses over a very
long period—no sooner is one crop over
than another is on the way, which makes
'Mary MacKillop' a superb rose for bedding and borders. The flowers are produced both singly and in small,
well-spaced clusters on a plant that is
extremely dense and well foliaged, and
has an excellent resistance to disease.
There is some fading in the older
blooms. ZONES 5–10.

Swane, Australia, 1989

Parentage unknown

'MARY MANNERS'

MODERN, HYBRID RUGOSA, WHITE BLEND,
REPEAT-FLOWERING

This excellent sport of 'Sarah Van Fleet'
has white flowers slightly shaded with
pale pink. It is a very tall-growing bush
with extremely profuse rich and leathery
rugose foliage. The flowers are semi-
double, large and very fragrant and,
when fully open, reveal a boss of striking
stamens. Blooming is profuse and continuous. The flowers are most attractive
in the garden but, like most Hybrid
Rugosas, do not last well when picked.
'Mary Manners' grows into a tall,
extremely thorny bush. ZONES 5–10.

Leicester Rose Company, USA, 1970

Sport of 'Sarah Van Fleet'

'MARY MARSHALL'

MODERN, MINIATURE, ORANGE BLEND,
REPEAT-FLOWERING

The long, pointed buds of this rose open
to beautifully shaped, orange-pink flowers
with attractive yellow bases. These
blooms are double, cupped and fragrant,
and they have a good show quality about
them. It is an excellent rose for beginners,
because it grows well with lots of basal
activity and is completely disease resistant. The foliage is small and leathery in
texture, and it covers the plant, which
has a dwarf growth habit. The repeat
bloom cycle is fast . ZONES 5–11.

Moore, USA, 1970

'Little Darling' × 'Fairy Princess'

American Rose Society Award of Excellence 1975

'Mary Marshall'

'Mary Guthrie'

'MARY MATTHEWS'
MODERN, LARGE-FLOWERED/HYBRID TEA,
LIGHT PINK, REPEAT-FLOWERING

Named after a daughter of Bishop
Anderson of Hay in New South Wales,
Australia, the real name of this rose
is not known, but it must be of early
twentieth century vintage. The buds are
pointed and open to well-formed flowers
of pale pink. There are 20–30 petals, and
the profuse blooms mainly come one
to a stem, last well on the bush and give
a quick repeat. The disease-free growth
is upright with dark green, semi-glossy
foliage. Bishop Anderson was the second
Bishop of the Riverina in New South
Wales and was famous for his rose garden.
Most of his roses survived after 30 years
of neglect and very few of them can be
identified. ZONES 5–10.

Australia

Parentage unknown

'MARY POPE'
MODERN, CLUSTER-FLOWERED/FLORIBUNDA,
YELLOW BLEND, REPEAT-FLOWERING

The flowers of 'Mary Pope' are golden
yellow tinged with pink. They are double
with 25 petals and large—up to 3 in (8 cm)
in diameter—and are borne singly and
in clusters amid dark glossy foliage. Mary
Pope was the founder of the National
Association of Flower Arrangers in
England, a group that now has well over
100 000 members both there and abroad.
This rose is a vigorous grower with a
plentiful supply of flowers that are
suitable for picking. ZONES 5–10.

Sanday, UK, 1965

Seedling × 'Independence'

'MARY QUEEN OF SCOTS'
OLD, SCOTS, MEDIUM PINK

This is one of the most popular survivors
of the hundreds of Scots Roses that were
produced during their heyday between
1790 and 1830. In recent years, these
roses have grown in popularity because
of their beauty and hardiness. 'Mary
Queen of Scots' carries plum-tinted,
gray-lilac buds that open to reveal contrasting light and dark, fragrant pink
petals crowned with prominent stamens.
The small, exquisite blooms smother
the foliage in late spring. It is a compact,
round plant, reaching 3 ft (1 m) at maturity, and is covered with ferny, dense
foliage of tiny leaves. There is a small
number of awesome prickles. Round,
dark maroon hips follow the flowers in
autumn. According to legend, the Queen

of Scots brought this rose from France,
and it was rediscovered by Lady Moore
in Ireland. Jack Harkness, however, says
this is not possible on historical grounds.
Regardless of its origin, this frost-hardy
rose is a perfect candidate as a small
hedge or in a container, and is especially
happy in seaside settings. ZONES 4–9.

Parentage unknown

'MARY ROSE'   AUSmary
MODERN, MODERN SHRUB, MEDIUM PINK,
REPEAT-FLOWERING

The slightly fragrant flowers of this
popular rose, which are a strong rose
pink with a touch of lavender, occur over
a long period. The blooms open a little
loose, and are borne at the end of long,
arching shoots. It is a healthy bush that
is as broad as it is tall and which has produced two excellent sports—the almost
white 'Winchester Cathedral' and the
much softer pink 'Redouté'. Unfortunately the blooms shatter rather quickly
after they have reached the full blown
stage. This self-shedding is good for garden display but means that this is not
a good rose for picking. Also known as
an English Rose, it was named after the
flagship of Henry VIII which was raised
from the Solent River 400 years after it
sank. ZONES 4–11.

Austin, UK, 1983

Probably 'Wife of Bath' × 'The Miller'

'MARY SUMNER'   MACstra
MODERN, CLUSTER-FLOWERED/FLORIBUNDA,
ORANGE-RED, REPEAT-FLOWERING

This rose, which was raised by Sam
McGredy, is a tall, upright grower with
particularly disease-resistant foliage and
a continuous supply of orange-red, semi-
double flowers that do not fade. Each
bloom has 15 petals. The flowers are
slightly fragrant, and when in full flower
they completely cover the bush. 'Mary
Sumner' was named after the founder
of the Mothers' Union in England. This
is a rose for bedding and for borders.
ZONES 5–10.

McGredy, New Zealand, 1976

Seedling × seedling

'Mary Queen of Scots'

'Mary Rose'

'Mary Rose'

'Mary Matthews'

'Mary Sumner'

M

'MARY WALLACE'

MODERN, LARGE-FLOWERED CLIMBER,
MEDIUM PINK, REPEAT-FLOWERING

The pointed buds of this rose open to cupped, semi-double, fragrant flowers of a clear rose pink color. They are very large for a climbing rose. Blooming is most plentiful early in the season; there are few flowers in summer, but autumn blooming is more profuse. The flowers hold their color very well. This rose is a very famous yard rose in the USA because of its tidy growth habit, to 10 ft (3 m) or so. The foliage is a rich green and very glossy, and there are no disease problems. It is suitable for a pillar or tripod or for growing into a small tree. ZONES 4–11.

Van Fleet, USA, 1924

Rosa wichuraiana × a pink Large-flowered Rose

'MARY WEBB' AUSwebb

MODERN, MODERN SHRUB, APRICOT BLEND,
REPEAT-FLOWERING

'Mary Webb' produces large, deeply cupped, many-petalled flowers of a particularly pleasing soft apricot. There is a delicious fragrance. Flowering is continuous, but there is rather a long period between flushes. The blooms are borne on a bushy plant with long stems and large, pale green leaves that are disease resistant. This rose, which is also known as an English Rose, was named after a Shropshire novelist who lived from 1881 to 1927. 'Mary Webb' is an excellent rose for picking as its soft color

'Mascara'

'Mascara'

fits into most color schemes. It is also very versatile in the garden—both in soft color schemes or as a harmonizing agent for use between bright colors. ZONES 4–11.

Austin, UK, 1985

Seedling × 'Chinatown'

'MARYLÈNE'

MODERN, LARGE-FLOWERED/HYBRID TEA,
MEDIUM PINK, REPEAT-FLOWERING

This variety has been overlooked as a garden rose. Its long, pointed buds open slowly to flowers of a particularly fresh pearly pink color. The well-formed, double blooms contain 35 petals and hold their color well. It has a strong fragrance. The abundant foliage is dark, glossy and disease resistant on a plant with a tall and upright growth habit. Its long stems make this a good rose for cutting. ZONES 5–11.

Gaujard, France, 1965

'Mignonne' × 'Queen Elizabeth'

'MASCARA' MEIdalnu

MODERN, MINIATURE, MAUVE BLEND,
REPEAT-FLOWERING

This Miniature Rose carries a large number of light pinkish mauve flowers in summer. They have a lovely double form and the petals are edged with a much deeper color. When fully open, a center of golden stamens can be seen. The foliage is dull mid-green. ZONES 5–10.

Meilland, France, 1992

Parentage unknown

'Mary Wallace'

'Mascotte'

'MASCOTTE'

MODERN, LARGE-FLOWERED/HYBRID TEA,
MEDIUM PINK, REPEAT-FLOWERING

The firm of Meilland has produced two roses with this name; this is the earlier introduction. The buds, which are soft pink tinted with lilac, are long and pointed and open to blooms of great refinement. The large, extremely fragrant blooms have 35 petals and are borne on long stems. The open flowers are particularly attractive, as the lilac tint is very pronounced at the edge of the petals. The foliage is dark, healthy and profuse, and the plant has good disease resistance. ZONES 5–11.

Meilland, France, 1951

'Michèle Meilland' × 'President Herbert Hoover'

'MASQUERADE'

MODERN, CLUSTER-FLOWERED/FLORIBUNDA,
RED BLEND, REPEAT-FLOWERING

'Masquerade' was the first of the Cluster-flowered Roses that changed to a deeper color as the flowers matured, a feature inherited from the China Roses. The ovoid buds open to small, semi-double flowers that are produced in huge clusters of up to 30 on very strong stems. They are light yellow changing to salmon-pink and finally to a rather muddy red, a quite striking effect. It is a strong-growing, disease-resistant rose with large, dark green, very profuse foliage that makes a wonderful hedge as it flowers over a very long period. If spent blooms are not removed, a large crop of round red hips is produced, these looking most attractive among the multicolored flowers. **'Climbing Masquerade'** (Dillan, UK, 1958) is a particularly vigorous climber that suits a very tall pillar or fence. ZONES 5–11.

Boerner, USA, 1949

'Goldilocks' × 'Holiday'

National Rose Society Gold Medal 1952

'Mary Webb'

'Master Hugh'

'Matador'

'MASTER HUGH'

MODERN, MODERN SHRUB, DEEP PINK

The flowers of this delicate rose are rich rose pink and appear in clusters. Attractive orange-red, flagon-shaped hips follow, but in warm climates these are sparse. Its parent, *Rosa macrophylla*, comes from the Himalayas, so it is not surprising that 'Master Hugh' suffers in hot, dry climates. The foliage is a little meager on a very tall, upright bush. This is an excellent rose in cold climates where it can be spectacular in full flower. ZONES 4–10.

Mason, UK, 1970

Seedling of *Rosa macrophylla*

Royal Horticultural Society Award of Garden Merit 1993

'MATADOR' KORfarim

syns 'Esther o'Farim', 'Esther Ofarim'

MODERN, CLUSTER-FLOWERED/FLORIBUNDA,
ORANGE BLEND, REPEAT-FLOWERING

Bred from 'Zorina', a rose that is in the pedigree of Kordes' cut-flower varieties, 'Matador' produces very well-shaped, high-centered flowers of a brilliant scarlet-orange with golden undersides to the petals; the intensity of the color is quite eye-catching. The flowers have 30 petals and keep very well both on the bush and when picked. The foliage is dark and leathery and growth is on the shortish side, its short growth habit meaning it needs to be planted more closely together than other Cluster-flowered Roses. It is an excellent rose for bedding and for borders. ZONES 4–9.

Kordes, Germany, 1972

'Colour Wonder' × 'Zorina'

'MATANGI' MACman

MODERN, CLUSTER-FLOWERED/FLORIBUNDA,
RED BLEND, REPEAT-FLOWERING

'Matangi' is one of Sam McGredy's most beautiful 'hand-painted' roses. The oval

'Masquerade'

buds open to orange-red blooms with a silvery white eye and silver undersides to the petals. The color is more intense in cooler weather. The double flowers with 30 petals are large—up to 3½ in (9 cm) across—and are slightly fragrant. The foliage is small but profuse, and growth is strong, upright and bushy. Flower production is excellent and there are no disease problems. It unique color makes this rose a particularly lovely cut flower. ZONES 5–10.

McGredy, New Zealand, 1974

Seedling × 'Picasso'

Rome Gold Medal 1974, Belfast Gold Medal 1976, Portland Gold Medal 1982, Royal National Rose Society President's International Trophy 1974

'MATEO'S SILK BUTTERFLIES' LETsilk
OLD, CHINA, MEDIUM PINK, REPEAT-FLOWERING

This rose was a seedling found under a bush of *Rosa chinensis mutabilis* in Kleine Lettunich's amazing garden at Corralitos, California. It has a similar spreading habit to its parent, and grows quite large. It bears an amazing crop of single soft pink flowers in spring that continue until early winter. It is a superb plant for the mixed border or for the woodland because of its hardiness, its

'Matangi'

freedom of flowering and its disease resistance. This is a remarkable rose that is becoming very popular in the USA; hopefully it will soon be available to the rest of the world. ZONES 5–11.

Lettunich, USA, 1992

Seedling of *Rosa chinensis mutabilis*

'MATILDA' MElbeausai
syns 'Charles Aznavour', 'Pearl of Bedfordview', 'Seduction',

MODERN, CLUSTER-FLOWERED/FLORIBUNDA, WHITE, REPEAT-FLOWERING

This rose, which is excellent for climates with coolish summers, has well-formed buds that open very quickly to white

'Matilda'

'Max Colwell'

'Matilda'

'Matthias Meilland'

blooms edged with the softest rose pink. These fade extremely quickly to white in hot weather. The large, double blooms have 15–20 petals and no fragrance. The disease-resistant foliage is dark green and semi-glossy on a short to medium bushy plant. Flower production is remarkable, with an extraordinarily quick repeat cycle. 'Matilda' is ideal for use as a standard rose and is lovely in the cool weather of late autumn and early winter, where its delicate coloring remains for a much longer time. It is useful for indoor decoration where soft colors are desired. ZONES 5–10.

Meilland, France, 1998

MEIgurami × 'Nirvana'

Bagatelle Gold Medal 1987, Courtrai Gold Medal 1987

'MATTERHORN' ARMma

MODERN, LARGE-FLOWERED/HYBRID TEA, WHITE, REPEAT-FLOWERING

One of the world's best cream roses, 'Matterhorn' bears large, oval buds that open to very large, high-centered blooms, which contain 25 petals. The abundant foliage is tough and leathery on a tall, upright plant that produces very long, thick stems with numerous large thorns. Because of its tall growth, it should be planted at the back of the rose bed; it is too tall for bedding purposes. ZONES 5–10.

Armstrong, USA, 1965

'Buccaneer' × 'Cherry Glow'

Portland Gold Medal 1964, All-America Rose Selection 1966

'MATTHIAS MEILLAND' MEIfolio

MODERN, CLUSTER-FLOWERED/FLORIBUNDA, MEDIUM RED, REPEAT-FLOWERING

The Meilland family always names good roses after members of the family, such as 'Papa Meilland', 'Michèle Meilland', 'Manou Meilland' and 'Mme Meilland' ('Peace'). 'Matthias Meilland' certainly lives up to expectations, being one of the very best bright red Cluster-flowered Roses. The unfading blooms, which have great substance, are double with 20–25 petals and come in small and large well-spaced clusters. The extremely abundant foliage is medium sized, dark green, very glossy and disease resistant. Growth is strong and upright and flower production is excellent, which makes it one of the best roses for beds where a strong color is required. ZONES 5–10.

Meilland, France, 1985

('Mme Charles Sauvage' × 'Fashion') × ('Poppy Flash' × 'Parador')

Frankfurt Gold Medal 1989

'MAUDE SUMNER'

MODERN, CLUSTER-FLOWERED/FLORIBUNDA, ORANGE BLEND, REPEAT-FLOWERING

The South African artist Maude Sumner enjoyed painting still-lifes, especially of flowers. The rose named for her appears to have been created by a forgetful artist who took double white flowers, dipped them into a light salmon paint, then forgot to add the fragrance. This bush rose is of medium growth and useful for bedding schemes, perhaps planted with 'J. H. Pierneef', which has similar but

more intense coloring. It is floriferous and the blooms are good for both table decoration and exhibitions as they have strong stems and last for a long time when cut. ZONES 5–11.

Introduced by Ludwig, South Africa, 1994

Parentage unknown

'MAUREEN LIPMAN' FRAntier

MODERN, PATIO/DWARF CLUSTER-FLOWERED, ORANGE-PINK, REPEAT-FLOWERING

Judging by the performance of this rose in the garden, both the classification and the official color code seem misleading. It makes a vigorous, arching plant of low and spreading habit, nearly three times wider than its height; it may therefore be considered a Ground Cover Rose. The flowers are prettily formed, fairly large and full petalled, open to irregularly shallow cups and have a good fragrance. They are a kindly light shade of pink, nearer to flesh pink than orange-pink, and are borne in clusters through summer and autumn; the early flowering is particularly free. This is a good choice to grow in a position where a wide grower of modest height is required, for the variety has charm and unusual character. It grows vigorously with many matt mid-green leaves. Maureen Lipman is a British actress and keen rose lover. ZONES 4–9.

Cowlishaw, UK, 1997

Parentage unknown

'MAURICE BERNARDIN'

syns 'Exposition de Brie', 'Ferdinand de Lesseps'

OLD, HYBRID PERPETUAL, MEDIUM RED, REPEAT-FLOWERING

There were hundreds of Hybrid Perpetuals produced at the time Granger offered this rose to the trade, but only a small portion are still in commerce. 'Maurice Bernardin' is found today in only a few collections. The cerise-purple, lavender, or bright crimson blooms— sun or shade affects the color—appear in clusters on vigorous canes in summer with some autumn rebloom. The large, almost full, globular blossoms have high centers, much like the Centifolias. There is a strong fragrance and, like many of this class, it is subject to mildew. The shrub will reach 4 ft (1.2 m) tall, and has dark green foliage. Theophile Granger of France also created 'General Washington' and 'Duc de Wellington'. ZONES 5–10.

Granger, France, 1861

'Général Jacqueminot' × seedling

'MAUVE MELODÉE'

MODERN, LARGE-FLOWERED/HYBRID TEA, MAUVE

The mauve-purple buds of this rose are long and pointed, and open to 20-petalled flowers that are 4–5 in (10–12 cm) across. They usually appear in small clusters and are very fragrant. The blooms are attractive at all stages and retain their color better than most varieties in this color range. It is a stronger grower than its parent 'Sterling Silver'. The foliage is dark and leathery on a vigorous, upright, disease-resistant plant. ZONES 5–11.

Raffel, USA, 1962

'Sterling Silver' × seedling

'MAX COLWELL'

MODERN, MINIATURE, ORANGE-RED, REPEAT-FLOWERING

The long, pointed buds of this variety open to orange-red flowers that age to a dull red. Each small, fragrant flower bears about two dozen petals to give an informal shape that ends up in flat, open blooms with the yellow stamens showing. This rose received high ratings in its day for its garden display, as the vigorous plant produces a large number of sprays of rich orange-red blooms that last for days. It brings a bright and cheery look to the garden. The growth habit, if left unchecked, tends to be a bit spreading rather than growing upwards. 'Max Colwell' is rarely grown these days, due to the competition from more modern Miniatures in the same color class. ZONES 5–11.

Moore, USA, 1969

Seedling of a Cluster-flowered Rose × ('Little Darling' × seedling of a Miniature Rose)

'MAX GRAF'

MODERN, HYBRID RUGOSA, PINK BLEND

This is a very important rose as it is in the ancestry of most of the Modern Ground Cover Roses as well as many shrub roses. It was used by the great hybridist Kordes for breeding over a great many years. One of the earliest Ground Cover Roses, it has long, prostrate, trailing shoots with very attractive, disease-resistant wrinkled foliage. The shapely, single flowers are soft rose pink with golden stamens. It flowers only once in the season and, unlike most Hybrid Rugosas, does not set hips. It is an excellent rose for covering banks and difficult slopes, and is extremely hardy in cold climates. ZONES 4–11.

Bowditch, USA, 1919

Probably Rosa rugosa × R. wichuraiana

'Mauve Melodée'

'Max Graf'

'Mayor of Casterbridge'

'Meg'

'MAY QUEEN'
MODERN, RAMBLER, MEDIUM PINK

This rose bears short-stemmed, rosy pink flowers with a hint of lilac, which appear in great profusion during the earlier part of summer. They are full petalled, of medium size, rounded in form and open quartered with an old-fashioned look. There is a modest fruity fragrance, and they give a beautiful show whatever the weather. Because the stems are flexible, the variety lends itself to many uses in the garden; it is especially suited for garlanding trellises, pergolas and pillars, to trail over low walls and fences or to grow in a place where it can naturalize itself as a hummocky ground-covering plant. 'May Queen' is a vigorous and arching plant that extends a little further than is average for a climbing rose. The leaves are plentiful, glossy and dark, and create a handsome backcloth for the blooms. ZONES 4–9.

Manda, USA, 1898

Rosa wichuraiana × 'Champion of the World'

'MAYOR OF CASTERBRIDGE'
AUSbrid

MODERN, MODERN SHRUB, LIGHT PINK, REPEAT-FLOWERING

The flowers of this rose are medium sized, very full with 40 petals and a lovely light pink color. The blooms have Old Garden Rose form, are borne in small clusters and are very fragrant. Flower production is extremely high. The foliage is medium sized, light green and leathery on a disease-resistant plant with an up-right habit. The stems are moderately thorny. This rose, which is also known as an English Rose and which makes a nice rounded shrub in the garden, was named after the 1886 novel by Thomas Hardy. ZONES 5–10.

Austin, UK, 1996

Parentage unknown

'MAZEPPA'
syn. 'Mazzeppa'
OLD, GALLICA, RED BLEND

Both Mottisfont and Sangerhausen gardens still grow this Gallica Rose, although it has completely disappeared from commerce. The loosely double, ragged blooms are red with marbled white edges. The fat buds open to large blossoms with reflexed, rolled, and quartered petals and large, golden button eyes. There is a strong perfume. The large bush reaches 5 ft (1.5 m) tall and produces strong branches covered with fine, large leaves of deep green. A Polish nobleman, Ivan Mazeppa (1644–1707), is memorialized in Lord Byron's poem. He had fantastic adventures in Poland, served under Peter the Great in Russia and ended his career in Sweden. The rose is first mentioned in the Verdier catalogue of 1841. ZONES 4–9.

Pre-1841

Parentage unknown

'MÉCÈNE'
OLD, GALLICA, PINK BLEND

Only a few nurseries still supply this lovely Gallica Rose, and some European botanical gardens have preserved it. Its white petals with rose stripes create a double flower of rosette form. These fragrant blossoms appear singly or in groups of 2–5, and each has an attractive button eye. This compact and upright bush is outlined with smooth canes and covered with small, dark green foliage. It will reach 4–5 ft (1.2–1.5 m) at maturity. The rose was named after a consul under Augustus Caesar who became a protector of the famous Roman authors Virgil and Horace. ZONES 4–9.

Vibert, France, 1845

Parentage unknown

'MEDALLION'
MODERN, LARGE-FLOWERED/HYBRID TEA, APRICOT BLEND, REPEAT-FLOWERING

This rose, which was bred from two excellent garden roses, produces long, pointed buds of soft apricot that are double, large and full, like its parent 'South Seas'. The buds open slowly to well-shaped, full blooms that have a pleasant fragrance. The foliage is dark, leathery and abundant and growth is vigorous, upright and very healthy. 'Medallion' unfortunately does not seem to have been introduced into many countries outside the USA. ZONES 5–10.

Warriner, USA, 1973

'South Seas' × 'King's Ransom'

Portland Gold Medal 1972, All-America Rose Selection 1973

'MEDEO'   KORcremkis
MODERN, CLUSTER-FLOWERED/FLORIBUNDA, WHITE, REPEAT-FLOWERING

This sport of the salmon-pink 'Kiss' is, like its parent, primarily a greenhouse rose, but it can be grown in the garden in warm climates. The color is cream, and the crisp petals ensure that when the flowers are cut they 'seem to last forever', as one writer puts it. There is little scent due to the hardness of the petals. The flowers are of medium size, high centered when young and open slowly with regular form through summer and autumn.

'May Queen'

'Medeo'

In the garden, the place for this rose is towards the back of a border, for it grows tall; a group in a cutting garden would be useful, as the long, wiry stems make it ideal for floral arrangements. The plant grows to above average height with an upright habit and is well furnished with mid-green leaves. ZONES 6–10.

Kordes, Germany, 1991

Sport of 'Kiss'

'MEG'
MODERN, LARGE-FLOWERED CLIMBER, APRICOT BLEND, REPEAT-FLOWERING

This rose gets its climbing growth from 'Paul's Lemon Pillar' and some of its lovely soft salmon-apricot color and red stamens from 'Mme Butterfly'. The flowers have 10 petals that are very large for a single rose, up to 5½ in (13 cm) across. They come in small and large clusters. The foliage is dark and glossy on a strong and upright plant. The repeat-flowering is fair in summer and slightly more profuse in autumn. It is a great rose for a pillar, a tripod or an arch and looks stunning growing against a brick house; it is popular in all climates. If spent blooms are not removed, a good crop of large round hips is produced in autumn. ZONES 5–10.

Gosset, UK, 1954

'Paul's Lemon Pillar' × 'Mme Butterfly'

National Rose Society Gold Medal 1954

M

'Medallion'

'MEG MERRILIES'
OLD, SWEET BRIAR, DEEP PINK/MEDIUM RED

This Old Garden Rose carries single flowers with dark pink or carmine petals that have a deep notch at the edges. They also have white bases that highlight the central boss of contrasting golden yellow stamens. The long, arching canes are happiest in part shade where the colors are shown to best effect during the summer flowering. It is a perfect candidate for the woodland garden or as hedging. The canes are covered with prickles, and in autumn a fine crop of hips appears. Both the flowers and foliage are fragrant and highly disease resistant. Named after a wild creature in Sir Walter Scott's novel *Guy Mannering*, Meg is the leader of the gypsies and nurse of Harry Pertram. ZONES 4–9.

Penzance, UK, 1894

Rosa eglanteria × unknown Hybrid Perpetual or Bourbon Rose

'Meg Merrilies'

'Megiddo'

'MEGAN LOUISE'
MODERN, LARGE-FLOWERED/HYBRID TEA, PINK BLEND, REPEAT-FLOWERING

This rose has oval buds that are strong pink, deepening at the petal edges. They open to high-centered, double flowers with 48 petals and are of true exhibition form. The blooms are borne singly and also in small, well-spaced clusters. There is a strong fragrance, and they make lovely cut flowers. The foliage is matt green and tough but a little dull and the plant is short and bushy. The flower production is adequate and the repeat-bloom is fair. ZONES 5–10.

Welsh, Australia, 1981

'Red Lion' × 'Silver Lining'

'MEGIDDO'
MODERN, CLUSTER-FLOWERED/FLORIBUNDA, ORANGE-RED, REPEAT-FLOWERING

The profuse flowers of 'Megiddo' are brilliant orange-red. They are double

'Megan Louise'

with 25 petals, large—up to 4½ in (12 cm) across—and come in well-spaced clusters. They have excellent substance and hold their color for a long time. There is a slight fragrance. The foliage is dark green, large and very healthy, and covers the tall and upright growth. This is a fine bedding rose, whose merit has been overlooked in many countries. ZONES 5–10.

Gandy, UK, 1970

'Coup de Foudre' × 'Saint-Agaro'

Royal National Rose Society Trial Ground Certificate 1970

'MEILLANDINA'   MEIrov, MEIroy
MODERN, MINIATURE, MEDIUM RED, REPEAT-FLOWERING

'Meillandina', from Marie-Louisette Meilland, has scarlet flowers with an attractive contrasting yellow center. The bright yellow eye in each bloom is an eye-catching quality that makes this rose quite spectacular in the garden setting. The bush is vigorous and healthy. The name has since been used by the House of Meilland to describe a range of Miniature Roses of different colors, but with the same growth habits: a sort of series of clones with differing colors. ZONES 5–11.

Meilland, France, 1975

'Rumba' × ('Dany Robin' × 'Fire King')

'MELODY'   KORbolak
MODERN, LARGE-FLOWERED/HYBRID TEA, LIGHT PINK, REPEAT-FLOWERING

'Melody' makes an excellent cut flower, particularly under greenhouse conditions. The shapely, slender buds open slowly to very well-formed blooms that are soft light pink flushed with rose pink. They are medium in size and have slender stems, which makes them ideal for cutting; commercially, there are pack-

'Melody'

'Meillandina'

'Melody Maker'

aged for overseas markets, since their keeping qualities are outstanding. This tall, almost thornless bush rose produces a profusion of flowers both singly and in clusters over a very long period. They look particularly attractive when cut and arranged under artificial light. ZONES 5–11.

Kordes, Germany, 1991

Parentage unknown

'MELODY MAKER'   DICqueen
MODERN, CLUSTER-FLOWERED/FLORIBUNDA, ORANGE-RED, REPEAT-FLOWERING

This excellent Cluster-flowered Rose bears very full, brilliant orange-red blooms that have an excellent color stability, and the repeat-bloom is very rapid. There is a light scent. The foliage is medium sized, dark green and semi-glossy. It is an excellent rose for bedding schemes since it gives color over a very long period, but it can also be used as a low hedge or border. An amazing number of really good Cluster-flowered Roses like this one, with disease-free foliage and abundant flower production, have been produced by Pat and Colin Dickson. ZONES 5–10.

Dickson, UK, 1990

'Anisley Dickson' × 'Wishing'

Rose of the Year 1991, Glasgow Certificate of Merit 1996

'MEMENTO'   DICbar
MODERN, CLUSTER-FLOWERED/FLORIBUNDA, RED BLEND, REPEAT-FLOWERING

This good all-rounder from Pat Dickson has a profusion of large and globular buds that develop into strong salmon-red blooms. These cupped, double flowers have 20 petals, and are quite large for a Cluster-flowered Rose—up to 3 in (8 cm) across. They occur singly and in small to medium-sized clusters, and hold their color particularly well. The bushy plant is of medium height, and has an abundance of sage green, disease-resistant foliage. 'Memento', like most of Pat Dickson's Cluster-flowered Roses, makes an excellent bedder—especially among bright-colored bulbs and perennials—and is equally good as a hedge or border. There is a fine bed of it at the Lady Dickson Park in Belfast, Northern Ireland, where it won a gold medal in 1980. ZONES 5–10.

Dickson, UK, 1978

'Bangor' × 'Anabell'

Royal National Rose Society Trial Ground Certificate 1977, Belfast Gold Medal 1980

'Memento'

'MEMOIRE'   KORzuri
syn. 'Ice Cream'

MODERN, LARGE-FLOWERED/HYBRID TEA, WHITE,
REPEAT-FLOWERING

This is a wonderful cut-flower rose for
the garden. The flowers are very large
with up to 60 petals, have superb form
and are high centered, like the white rose
'Tineke'. There can be cream tints in the
center of each bloom. The foliage is plentiful, dark green and disease free, and
flower production is outstanding. The
stems are moderately long and the buds
open very slowly to exhibition-type
blooms that hold for days; they are best
under glass, but the variety is perfectly
happy in the open garden. ZONES 5–10.

Kordes, Germany, 1992

Parentage unknown

Belfast Gold Medal 1994, Glasgow Certificate
of Merit 1996, The Hague Fragrance Prize 1998

'MEMORIAM'

MODERN, LARGE-FLOWERED/HYBRID TEA,
LIGHT PINK, REPEAT-FLOWERING

This terrific rose has long, pointed buds
that open to clear pale pink double
blooms filled with 55 petals that give a
high center. These fragrant flowers are
very large—up to 6 in (15 cm) across—
and have superb exhibition form. In
cool, wet weather the color becomes very
pale. The foliage is dark and healthy, but
a little prone to black spot. The plant is
on the short side, although flower production is very high and the repeat cycle
is quick. The blooms lose their substance
rather quickly when cut. ZONES 5–10.

Von Abrams, USA, 1961

('Blanche Mallerin' × 'Peace') × ('Peace' × 'Frau
Karl Druschki')

Portland Gold Medal 1960, Royal National Rose
Society Certificate of Merit 1961

'Memoire'

'MEMORY BELLS'   POUkleioma

MODERN, GROUND COVER, DEEP PINK,
REPEAT-FLOWERING

The side branches of this plant spread
with many upright stems that carry dense
clusters of tiny round buds, which unfold

'Memoriam'

into small, bright pink flowers. It is a
healthy and compact ground cover that
is covered with shiny leaves. It can also
be grown as a small standard ZONES 4–10.

Poulsen, Denmark, 1994

Seedling × 'Rosenholm'

'Mercedes'

'Memory Lane' (Pearce)

'MEMORY LANE'
MODERN, MINIATURE, LIGHT PINK, REPEAT-FLOWERING

The oval buds of this variety open to rose pink, very double flowers packed full of petals. They are small and have a slight fragrance. The foliage is healthy on a plant with a vigorous, dwarf and bushy habit. ZONES 5–10.

Moore, USA, 1973

('Pinocchio' × 'William Lobb') × 'Little Chief'

'MEMORY LANE'   PEAvoodoo
MODERN, CLUSTER-FLOWERED/FLORIBUNDA, APRICOT BLEND, REPEAT-FLOWERING

The long and pointed buds of this rose open to fully double flowers made up of many light peach-yellow petals. They form a tight center, and the outer petals become reflexed as the flower matures. The color combines well with the mid-green foliage. ZONES 5–10.

Pearce, UK, 1995

('Geraldine' × seedling) × seedling

Royal National Rose Society Trial Ground Certificate 1993

'MENJA'
MODERN, MODERN SHRUB, MEDIUM PINK, REPEAT-FLOWERING

Not much is known about the breeding of 'Menja'. It is a most unusual and

'Menja'

beautiful little rose with large trusses of almost single, extremely cupped flowers that stay cupped until they fall. They are borne in great panicles, and from a distance resemble 'Kalmia'. It is a very bushy grower with plentiful light green, disease-resistant foliage. This is a rose that has been overlooked and should be much more widely planted for its unique beauty. It repeats extremely well and always attracts the attention of rose lovers when they see it for the first time. It is excellent as a hedge, or it can be used to great effect among bulbs, perennials and other shrubs. ZONES 5–10.

Petersen, Denmark, 1960

'Eva' × Rosa filipes

'MERCEDES'   MerKOR
MODERN, CLUSTER-FLOWERED/FLORIBUNDA, ORANGE-RED, REPEAT-FLOWERING

This variety was the first of the orange-red, medium-sized, durable roses for growing under glass. The buds are bright orange-red, and open to double flowers with 30–35 very high-centered petals. The flowers develop very dark edges to the petals in intense sunlight when grown outdoors; this is not a burning of the petals but a dark shading. The full blooms slowly fade in the garden to a dull, unattractive color. 'Mercedes' is

quick to repeat and lasts a very long time when cut; the fragrance is only slight. The foliage is large and leathery and growth is moderate, and there is some tendency to black spot and mildew. There are newer varieties from Kordes that are better growers and are more disease resistant. ZONES 5–11.

Kordes, Germany, 1974

'Anabell' × seedling

'MERMAID'
OLD, MISCELLANEOUS, LIGHT YELLOW, REPEAT-FLOWERING

The fragrant flowers of this rose are soft creamy yellow and are 5–6 in (12–15 cm) across. It comes into flower later than most varieties, but the display continues through summer and autumn and into winter. In warm areas it is gigantic—to 30 ft (9 m) or more across and 20 ft (6m) high if given sufficient support. The dark foliage is glossy and the plant has large, red, hooked thorns. It needs no pruning but can be cut back when it gets out of control, which makes it a great rose for covering unsightly sheds and old trees. It should not be planted near paths because of the vicious thorns. The growth is much less vigorous in cold climates. ZONES 4–11.

Paul, UK, 1918

Rosa bracteata × double yellow Tea Rose

National Rose Society Gold Medal 1917, Royal Horticultural Society Award of Garden Merit 1993

'MERRY ENGLAND'
syn. 'Merrie England'
OLD, HYBRID PERPETUAL, MEDIUM RED, REPEAT-FLOWERING

One of the earliest of Harkness roses, this is a sport of a very popular Bennett hybrid of 1882. Unfortunately, no record of this rose has been found in recent years. The medium red blooms are shaded carmine with a satiny finish; they are double with about 50 petals and are fragrant. The vigorous bush is healthy, and the flowering period is late spring. Many hybrids of this type were lost, since they were over-produced and followed by the introduction of the Hybrid Teas (or Large-flowered Roses), which took over in popularity. ZONES 5–10.

Harkness, UK, 1897

Sport of 'Heinrich Schultheis'

'MERVEILLE DE LYON'
OLD, HYBRID PERPETUAL, WHITE, REPEAT-FLOWERING

A favorite cut flower, this sport of an outstanding rose is pure white with a flush of soft pink at the petal edges. The double, large, cupped blossoms are free flowering and always appear as solitary offerings. The fragrant flowers appear in summer with some autumn rebloom. The strong, stout stems appear on a sturdy, upright bush that can reach 4 ft (1.2 m) at maturity. Its large, thick gray-green leaves and numerous prickles line the canes. The bush is prone to mildew. So many roses were named for Lyon in France, which was the center of rose hybridizing during a good part of the nine-teenth century. An international heritage rose conference was arranged there in 1999 to celebrate this achievement. ZONES 5–10.

Pernet, France, 1882

Sport of 'Baroness Rothschild'

'METEOR'
OLD, NOISETTE, DEEP PINK, REPEAT-FLOWERING

This is one of the few German-produced Noisettes. It has large, double, deep pink blooms that are larger than many others in that class. The blowzy flowers appear on long, pliable canes with Gallica-like foliage and have a heavy, rich fragrance and an ample reblooming in autumn. The shrub can reach 9 ft (2.7 m) in two years, looking its best in a woodland set-ting. Geschwind was famous in his time for his winter-hardy roses. ZONES 5–11.

Geschwind, Hungary, 1887

Parentage unknown

'Mermaid'

'Mermaid'

'Meteor' (Kordes)

'METEOR'

MODERN, CLUSTER-FLOWERED/FLORIBUNDA,
ORANGE-RED, REPEAT-FLOWERING

This very low-growing bushy rose bears
large, intense orange-scarlet flowers.
They are double with 40 petals, up to 3 in
(8 cm) across and occur in clusters of up
to 10. The huge heads of flowers completely cover the bush in spring. The foliage is light green and glossy. To achieve
the maximum effect it should be planted
very close together, and it makes a very
colorful low border where a bright color
is required; it is also useful as a foreground to taller growing varieties. The
blooms last particularly well on the bush.
ZONES 5–11.

Kordes, Germany, 1959

'Feurio' × 'Gertrud Westphal'

National Rose Society Certificate of Merit 1958,
Anerkannte Deutsche Rose 1966

'MEVROUW G. A. VAN ROSSEM'

syn. 'Mrs G. A. van Rossem'

MODERN, LARGE-FLOWERED/HYBRID TEA,
ORANGE BLEND, REPEAT-FLOWERING

This rose was much sought after in its
heyday due to the rich color of the
blooms. They are a beautiful orange with
much reddish veining, with the undersides of the petals often darker or even
bronze. The flowers are of medium size,
full of rather short petals, open cupped
with a rounded outline and have a good
fruity scent. They appear freely through
summer and autumn, and fifty years ago
they were noted for continuing in bloom
after other garden roses of the time had
ceased. In a rosarium, this is a good

'Mevrouw G. A. van Rossem'

Large-flowered Rose to grow as a worthy
representative of its period. The plant is
upright and bushy, growing a little below
average height, and has dark green leaves
that look sparse by the standards of today. **'Climbing Mevrouw G. A. van
Rossem'** (syn. 'Climbing Mrs G. A. van
Rossem'; Gaujard, France, 1937) is an
excellent variety, with apricot and orange
flowers that have yellow bases and are attractively veined with red. The undersides of the petals is dark orange-bronze.
This was a most unusual color in the
1920s when the bush form was introduced, and it is still a color unique to this
variety. The flowers are double with 35–
40 petals, large and very fragrant. After a
plentiful spring flush flowering is sparse
through summer and autumn. The foliage is large, dark green and very healthy.
ZONES 5–10.

Van Rossem, The Netherlands, 1929

'Souvenir de Claudius Pernet' × 'Gorgeous'

National Rose Society Certificate of Merit 1928

'MEVROUW NATHALIE NYPELS'

syn. 'Nathalie Nypels'

MODERN, POLYANTHA, MEDIUM PINK,
REPEAT-FLOWERING

One of the best of all the Polyanthas, this
variety gives a constant supply of pretty
little pink flowers borne in small elegant
clusters. They are sweetly scented. The
flower production is excellent and the repeat-bloom is rapid. It is quite low growing, to about 2 ft (60 cm) tall, and is very
spreading. The unassuming clear pink
florets make it a useful companion plant
in mixed borders, where it never clashes

'Mevrouw Nathalie Nypels'

or looks out of place. It can be used in a
mixed border, in a bed or as a hedge. It is
remarkable that this pretty plant with no
special distinctions is still grown today.
ZONES 5–10.

Leenders, The Netherlands, 1919

'Orléans Rose' × ('Comtesse du Cayla' × *Rosa
foetida bicolor*)

Royal Horticultural Society Award of Garden
Merit 1993

'MEVROUW VAN STRAATEN VAN NES'

syns 'Duchess of Windsor', 'L'Indéfrisible',
'Mrs van Nes', 'Permanent Wave', 'Van Nes'

MODERN, CLUSTER-FLOWERED/FLORIBUNDA,
MEDIUM RED, REPEAT-FLOWERING

The blooms of this rose have unique,
extremely wavy petals, hence one of its
synonyms. The semi-double, deep carmine flowers are borne in large clusters
and are slightly fragrant, and there are
long gaps between flushes. The foliage is
dark and leathery and growth is moderate. Mildew can be a problem, particularly in cool autumn weather. It is still
popular in most countries. ZONES 5–10.

Leenders, The Netherlands, 1932

Sport of 'Else Poulsen'

Bagatelle Gold Medal 1933, Rome Gold Medal 1934

'MEXICANA'

MODERN, LARGE-FLOWERED/HYBRID TEA,
RED BLEND, REPEAT-FLOWERING

'Mexicana' gets its lovely form from
'Kordes' Perfecta'. The buds are large
and ovoid and the flowers are an unusual
crimson-red touched with deeper plum
red tones. The undersides of the petals
are silvery. The large, double flowers
have 30–35 high-centered petals and are
very fragrant. The foliage is dark, glossy
and extremely healthy on a vigorous
and upright plant with good flower production. This rose is easy to identify because of its unusual color. ZONES 5–10.

Boerner, USA, 1966

'Kordes' Perfecta' × seedling

'MICHELANGELO'   MACtemaik

syn. 'The Painter'

MODERN, CLUSTER-FLOWERED/FLORIBUNDA,
ORANGE BLEND, REPEAT-FLOWERING

This rose has more subdued coloring
than the other 'painted' roses from
Sam McGredy; it is described as 'either
a creamy lemon with bold orange stripes
or blotches, or occasionally all orange
with lemon striping and blotching'. The
random pigments give an unusually re-
alistic 'hand-painted' effect. The flowers

'Mexicana'

'Mevrouw van Straaten van Nes'

'Meteor' (Geschwind)

M

are carried on firm stems in clusters, although their form is more like that of a Large-flowered Rose: high centered in the young blooms and becoming cupped as the many petals reflex. They are of good size, appear through summer and into autumn and have a light fragrance. 'Michelangelo' is suitable for beds, borders and hedges, and the individual blooms look most attractive when cut for small indoor arrangements. The variety grows vigorously with an upright habit to above average height, and it is well clothed with dense, glossy dark green foliage, which is reddish when young. ZONES 5–9.

McGredy, New Zealand, 1995

'Loiuse Gardner' × ('Auckland Metro' × seedling of 'Stars 'n' Stripes'

'Michèle Meilland'

'MICHÈLE MEILLAND'
MODERN, LARGE-FLOWERED/HYBRID TEA, LIGHT PINK, REPEAT-FLOWERING

The long and slender buds of this rose have a most refined shape. The color of the moderately sized blooms can vary from a soft salmon-pink to rose pink to a soft lilac, or they can be pale pink with a yellow base. Whatever the color it is always beautiful, and is particularly free flowering. The bush is of medium size with rather plum-colored wood, and the abundant foliage is medium green and disease free. This is an excellent rose for bedding, and its bushy growth and freedom of flower make it a splendid rose for standards. **'Climbing Michèle Meilland'** (syn. 'Grimpant Michèle Meilland'; 1951) is an excellent climbing rose that flowers from spring until autumn. It has moderately vigorous growth, which makes it ideal for a pillar or tripod. Its only fault is that some bushes are inclined to revert back to the bush form when planted out. ZONES 5–11.

Meilland, France, 1945

'Joanna Hill' × 'Peace'

National Rose Society Certificate of Merit 1958

'MICHELLE JOY'　AROshrel
MODERN, LARGE-FLOWERED/HYBRID TEA, ORANGE-PINK, REPEAT-FLOWERING

This is a strong-growing rose with long buds of deep salmon-pink produced

'Michelle Joy'

singly and in small clusters on very long stems. The buds open slowly and keep their color well. There is a light fragrance. 'Michelle Joy' has large, healthy, dark green foliage, and it is good for cutting, looking very attractive under artificial light. ZONES 5–10.

Armstrong, USA, 1991

Seedling × 'Shreveport'

'MICRUGOSA'
syn. Rosa × micrugosa 'Henkel'
MODERN, MODERN SHRUB, LIGHT PINK

This rose forms a large spreading shrub with excellent dense ferny leaves and single light pink flowers. These are produced on shortish shoots along the branches. The fruit is orange-red, round and most attractive; they ripen in late

'Micrugosa'

'Micrugosa Alba'

summer and do not persist very long on the plant. The rose produces good clear yellow autumn foliage in cold climates. It makes a good shrub rose for the shrubbery or can be planted in parks and woodland areas for its flowers, its fruit and its autumn foliage. The hips are covered with bristly hairs. ZONES 4–11.

Pre-1905

Rosa roxburghii × R. rugosa

'MICRUGOSA ALBA'
syn. Rosa × micrugosa alba
MODERN, MODERN SHRUB, WHITE, REPEAT-FLOWERING

Dr C. C. Hurst was a geneticist and outstanding contributor to the world's knowledge of rose development. He raised this seedling, which differs from 'Micrugosa' in color, being white with prominent stamens, and in flowering period, for it will continue blooming through summer and autumn. The growth is more erect, and the foliage lighter green. 'Micrugosa Alba' will serve the same purpose as its parent, yet has greater garden value. ZONES 4–9.

Hurst, England, post-1900

Seedling of 'Micrugosa'

'MIDAS TOUCH'　JACtou
MODERN, LARGE-FLOWERED/HYBRID TEA, DEEP YELLOW, REPEAT-FLOWERING

This well-named rose is a particularly bright yellow. The buds are moderately full and open to large, fragrant blooms that hold their color very well. It is quick to repeat and flowers extremely freely over a long period. The foliage is large, abundant, matt mid-green, and there are small prickles on the peduncles. The growth is tallish, upright and bushy, and the disease resistance good. ZONES 5–11.

Christensen, USA, 1992

'Brandy' × 'Freisensohne'

All-America Rose Selection 1994

'Michelangelo'

M

'Midas Touch'

'MIGNONETTE'

MODERN, POLYANTHA, LIGHT PINK,
REPEAT-FLOWERING

This variety, one of the earliest Polyantha
Roses, is still in most major rose collections after 120 years in commerce. The
flowers, which are rosy blush in color,
are 1 in (25 mm) across and come in
small and large tightly packed clusters.
The foliage is dark green on the upper
surface of the leaf and reddish beneath,
a characteristic inherited from China
Roses. The leaves are small and glossy
and there are red hooked prickles. It has
a very dwarf and compact growth habit,
but flower production is good. Bushes
of 'Mignonette' should be planted very
close together for maximum effect,
which makes a useful low border.
ZONES 4–11.

Guillot, France, 1880

Parentage unknown

'MIKADO'

syns 'Kohsai', 'Koh-sai'

MODERN, LARGE FLOWERED/HYBRID TEA,
RED BLEND, REPEAT-FLOWERING

This variety gets its brilliant flame red
color from the Japanese-bred Cluster-
flowered Rose 'Kagayaki'. The double
flowers each have 25 petals with a yellow

'Mignonette'

'Milord'

'Millie Walters'

base. These high-centered blooms are
of exhibition form and are usually borne
singly. The foliage is glossy mid-green on
a tall and upright bush with good disease
resistance. The flower production is
excellent. 'Mikado' is a lovely bush rose
for bedding schemes where a bright color
is required, and it also can also be used
effectively when trained as a standard.
ZONES 5–10.

Suzuki, Japan, 1987

'Fragrant Cloud' × 'Kagayaki'

All-America Rose Selection 1988

'MILESTONE' JACles

MODERN, LARGE-FLOWERED/HYBRID TEA,
RED BLEND, REPEAT-FLOWERING

The flowers of 'Milestone' are crimson-
red with silvery red undersides to the
petals. The buds open to coral-pink,
well-formed and full blooms that age to
a darker color. These large and cupped,
double flowers have 40 petals, and there
is a slight fragrance. The foliage is large
and glossy mid-green on an upright-
growing plant. This variety is one of the
very few red and silver bicolors available
today; others include 'Fortyniner',
'Mexicana', 'Love' and 'Osiria'.

'Milkmaid'

'MILLIE WALTERS' MORmilli

MODERN, MINIATURE, ORANGE-PINK,
REPEAT-FLOWERING

On this variety, the deep pink-coral,
double flowers with 45 petals are delicately small and have a light fragrance.
The plant is an upright, vigorous and
compact bush sporting equally small,
mid-green, matt foliage. This rose has
consistently good exhibition-type form
and the striking vivid color holds well
under sun and high humidity. The profusion of blooms is indeed a strength for
this highly-recommended rose. It is considered outstanding both for the garden
and as an exhibition rose. However, the

Unfortunately, 'Milestone' is not very
well known outside the USA, so it may
be a difficult rose to acquire. ZONES 5–10.

Warriner, USA, 1983

'Sunfire' × 'Spellbinder'

'MILKMAID'

OLD, NOISETTE, WHITE

Known to be almost exclusive to Australia but deserving of a far wider audience, 'Milkmaid' is one of the happiest
creations of Alister Clark, who became a
famous hybridizer during the first half of
the twentieth century. The small, semi-
double blooms range from creamy yellow to white, with a hint of yellowish
brown, and they appear in clusters during the late spring season. These fragrant
blossoms are complemented by rich,
dark green foliage. A vigorous climber,
the variety is an ideal subject for pergolas, trellises, or fences. Highly disease
resistant, this Noisette Rose is fast growing and is well suited to a warm position.
ZONES 6–11.

Clark, Australia, 1925

'Crépuscule' × seedling

plant can suffer from mildew if it is not
given the proper protection. 'Millie
Walters' was named after one of the
great first ladies of the American Rose
Society. ZONES 5–11.

Moore, USA, 1983

'Little Darling' × 'Galaxy'

'MILORD'

MODERN, LARGE-FLOWERED/HYBRID TEA,
MEDIUM RED, REPEAT-FLOWERING

This rose bears well-formed, crimson-
red, double flowers with 35 petals. The
blooms, which are up to 5 in (12 cm)
across, open slowly and last well both
on the bush and when picked. Flower
production is a little sparse, with long
intervals between flushes. They are very
fragrant, the intense perfume being inherited from the old carmine-red rose
'Rubaiyat' bred by McGredy in 1946.
The foliage is dark and leathery and the
growth habit is upright. ZONES 5–10.

McGredy, UK, 1962

'Rubaiyat' × 'Karl Herbst'

National Rose Society Certificate of Merit 1962

'MILROSE' DELbir

MODERN, CLUSTER-FLOWERED/FLORIBUNDA,
MEDIUM PINK, REPEAT-FLOWERING

The medium-sized flowers of 'Milrose'
are soft pink, semi-double and cupped
and are borne in clusters of 5–15. There
is a slight fragrance. This variety, which
has light green glossy foliage and vigorous growth, is a good bedding rose as the
flowers retain their color well; its bushy
growth also makes it suitable for use as
a standard. It is not well known outside
France. ZONES 5–10.

Delbard-Chabert, France, 1965

'Orléans Rose' × ('Francais' × 'Lafayette')

Baden-Baden Gold Medal 1964, Golden Rose
of The Hague 1978

M

'Mini Magic'

'Minijet'

'Minilights'

'MINI MAGIC'

MODERN, MINIATURE, YELLOW BLEND,
REPEAT-FLOWERING

The flowers of this rose are mainly
yellow when they first open, with pink
tones mainly on the edge of the petals.
As the flowers age, the yellow fades and
the pink intensifies to a light red almost
through the approximately 25 petals.
This deepening of color with age is inherited from 'Masquerade'. The flowers
are borne freely, both singly and in small
clusters, on a compact, healthy plant
about 8 in (20 cm) high. Foliage is medium green and glossy. It repeats quickly
and is suitable as a border plant or pot
specimen. It should not be confused with
the American rose of the same name, another miniature, that was bred by Ernest
Williams. ZONES 5–10.

Walsh, Australia, 1994

'Avandel' × ('Masquerade' × 'Pink Parfait')

'MINIJET'   MEirotego
syn. 'Mini Jet'

MODERN, MINIATURE, MEDIUM PINK,
REPEAT-FLOWERING

This tall-growing, spreading Miniature
produces large, semi-double flowers with
15 petals. A warm salmon-rose shade, the
flowers have good substance and thick
petals and open flat to show a boss of
golden stamens. The buds are very long
and pointed but open rather quickly.
The blooms are produced in small to
large sprays over a long period with
quick repeat, and are most attractive at
all stages of development. The foliage,
which is rather large for a Miniature, is

light green and semi-glossy. Disease resistance is good, and this attractive plant
is suitable for growing as a short standard. There is no fragrance. ZONES 5–10.

Meilland, France, 1977

Parentage unknown

'MINILIGHTS'   DICmoppet
syns 'Mini Lights', 'Goldfächer'

MODERN, MODERN SHRUB, MEDIUM YELLOW,
REPEAT-FLOWERING

'Minilights' gets its bright color from
'Bright Smile' and its spreading growth
and freedom of flower from the excellent
Cluster-flowered Rose 'White Spray'.
The small, semi-double, medium yellow
flowers have 5–15 petals. The blooms
come in small clusters on most attractive
small, glossy, dark green foliage. It is a
particularly free-flowering plant with
very quick repeat. A good border rose
and excellent as a standard, 'Minilights'
can also be used with bulbs and perennial
plants in the mixed border. Its disease
resistance is very good. ZONES 5–10.

Dickson, UK, 1987

'White Spray' × 'Bright Smile'

Royal National Rose Society Trial Ground
Certificate 1985

'MINNA'

OLD, SWEET BRIAR, WHITE

The pure white, semi-double blooms of
this rose have a clear salmon-rose flush
and appear at their best in the shade.
Both the blossoms and the foliage are
fragrant. The vigorous bush with dark
green foliage displays its flowers on
long, prickly canes. Like so many of the

Penzance hybrids, this creation is useful
as a tall hedge or attractive shrub in a
woodland setting. 'Minna' has disappeared from commerce and from most
public gardens. It was named for one of
the two beautiful daughters of Magnus
Troil, a character in Sir Walter Scott's
novel *The Pirate*. ZONES 4–10.

Penzance, UK, 1895

Parentage unknown

'MINNEHAHA'

MODERN, RAMBLER, LIGHT PINK

The rose world has much to thank Dr
Wichura of Germany for: he discovered
the beautiful creeping white species that
bears his name. Many superb Ramblers
were raised from it in the early twentieth
century and one, 'Dorothy Perkins',
became a household name. 'Minnehaha'
resembles it in many ways; the pink
rosettes, however, are a little larger, and
less stable in color, passing from rosy
pink to blush white as they age. They
are carried in clusters in great profusion.
As the stems are lax, the variety makes a
wonderful weeping standard, as well as
being good for pillars, open fences, pergolas, arches and anywhere that its trailing habit and cascading flowers can serve
to cover unsightly objects. It does require
a free circulation of air to lessen the risk
of mildew, and there is not much scent.
The plant makes many stems, and old
spent ones can be cut out completely
after flowering to allow space for new
growth. The leaves are small, glossy dark
green and plentiful. M. H. Walsh, of
Woods Hole, Massachusetts, raised forty
climbing roses between 1901 and 1920;
many are still popular, including 'Lady
Gray' and 'Excelsa'. He named this rose
for the wife of Hiawatha, the main character in Longfellow's poem. ZONES 4–9.

Walsh, USA, 1905

Rosa wichuraiana × 'Paul Neyron'

'MINNIE FRANCIS'

OLD, NOISETTE, DEEP PINK

Born in the original home of Noisette
Roses, South Carolina, USA, this plant
has disappeared from trade and is only
found in a few gardens. The deep pink,
often light red flowers open from long
and pointed buds. These blooms are

extra large, fragrant and full. There is
a long summer flowering. This modest
climber can reach 6 ft (2 m) tall and is
disease resistant. It can be trained as a
large shrub. Noisettes were the first roses
bred in the United States. ZONES 6–11.

Griffing Nursery, USA, 1895

Parentage unknown

'MINNIE PEARL'   SAVahowdy

MODERN, MINIATURE, PINK BLEND,
REPEAT-FLOWERING

The long, elegant buds of this rose open
to beautifully shaped, light pink flowers
with much darker undersides and the
ideal high-centered form of their larger
relatives, the Large-flowered Roses. The
blooms are borne singly or in large clusters, always on strong, straight stems.
This, together with the exquisite color
combination, makes 'Minnie Pearl' the
archetype of excellence in Miniature
Roses. The foliage is semi-glossy and
mid-green on this vigorous, upright
plant that keeps its color and form better
if it is given some relief from intense
heat. This rose has never received any
awards but is certainly a most worthy
candidate. It was named for an American
country and western entertainer, who
was also a great comedienne. ZONES 5–10.

Saville, USA, 1982

('Little Darling' × 'Tiki') × 'Party Girl'

'MINNIE WATSON'

MODERN, LARGE-FLOWERED/HYBRID TEA,
LIGHT PINK, REPEAT-FLOWERING

This variety, one of the best roses bred
in Australia, was bred by an amateur and
named after his mother. The large, well-

'Minnie Watson'

'Minnie Pearl'

'Mireille Matheiu'

'Mireille Matheiu'

shaped buds open to well-formed flowers of bright salmon-pink that are borne both singly and in small clusters. They are semi-double and retain their color well on the bush and there is some fragrance. The color is particularly luminous and the flowers look wonderful when arranged and used under artificial light. Flower production is amazing, with rapid regrowth and very small gaps between flushes. The foliage is rich green and extremely glossy and profuse, and the plant has excellent disease resistance. This is a great rose for use as a standard as its flowers completely cover the bush. ZONES 5–10.

Watson, Australia, 1965

'Dickson's Flame' × 'Dickson's Flame'

'MINUETTE'   LAMinuette
syn. 'La Minuette'

MODERN, CLUSTER-FLOWERED/FLORIBUNDA,
RED BLEND, REPEAT-FLOWERING

This is a really good little rose for greenhouse production for the cut-flower trade; it is also a first-class garden variety. The large, ovoid buds are a creamy white color and open very slowly to medium-sized, full blooms with 50 petals that are tipped with rose red on each petal edge. In hot weather the creamy white base to the petals can become much darker and turn to yellow tones. There is a slight fragrance. The flowers come both singly and in small and large well-spaced clusters and last very well both on the bush and when picked. It is a plant of medium growth and flower production is good,

although there can be mildew on the pedicels and leaf stalks and black spot can appear at times. It is excellent for hedges and is suitable for as a standard. ZONES 5–10.

Lammerts, USA, 1969

'Peace' × 'Rumba'

'MIO MAC'
syn. 'Mic Mac'

MODERN, CLUSTER-FLOWERED/FLORIBUNDA,
DEEP YELLOW, REPEAT-FLOWERING

'Mio Mac' is an excellent rose, producing attractive buds that open to full blooms of 40 petals. The enormous, well-formed flowers are apricot flushed with salmon-pink, a color that they hold well. The heads of flowers produce laterals that are long enough for picking as individual stems. The bush is very strong and has plentiful mid-green foliage that is very disease resistant. 'Mio Mac' makes a good show in the garden and is very suitable for bedding. ZONES 4–11.

Tantau, Germany, 1973

Parentage unknown

'MIRANDA'

OLD, PORTLAND, MEDIUM PINK/LIGHT PINK,
REPEAT-FLOWERING

Still a popular rose, 'Miranda' is often classified as a Damask Perpetual by some authorities. The medium, satiny pink, very double blooms are cupped, large and full. The thin petals are happiest in a warm site and dislike wet weather. The fragrant blossoms appear in early summer

'Mirato'

with some repeat in early autumn. 'Miranda' is a compact shrub of medium size with light gray-green foliage that has serrated edges. It is an ideal plant for a small garden or as a hedge. The famous French hybridizer Cochet also named a popular Portland after Arthur de Sansal in 1855. ZONES 4–9.

de Sansal, France, 1869

Parentage unknown

'MIRANDY'

MODERN, LARGE-FLOWERED/HYBRID TEA,
DARK RED, REPEAT-FLOWERING

'Mirandy', which was bred from 'Charlotte Armstrong', has dark red, double flowers with 45 petals. They are large, up to 5 in (12 cm) across, and have a strong Damask perfume inherited from 'Night'. Flower production is a little sparse with long intervals between flushes. This rose is still grown today after 50 years in commerce because of its dark red color and wonderful perfume. ZONES 5–11.

Lammerts, USA, 1945

'Night' × 'Charlotte Armstrong'

All-America Rose Selection 1945

'MIRATO'

MODERN, LARGE-FLOWERED/HYBRID TEA,
MEDIUM PINK, REPEAT-FLOWERING

The ovoid buds of 'Mirato' open slowly to very well-formed flowers of a clear soft salmon-rose color. The double blooms contain 30 petals and are very fragrant. The foliage is large and glossy on an upright and bushy plant with good disease resistance. This rose has not become popular as there are not enough flowers each flush and too long an interval between flushes. It is, nevertheless, a good rose for picking and looks wonderful under artificial light. ZONES 5–11.

Tantau, Germany, 1974

Seedling × seedling

'MIREILLE MATHEIU'   KORdehn

MODERN, CLUSTER-FLOWERED/FLORIBUNDA,
ORANGE-RED, REPEAT-FLOWERING

This is a good orange-red rose bearing ovoid buds that open to double flowers containing 27 petals. They are high

centered and large for a Cluster-flowered Rose—up to 3½ in (9 cm) across. The blooms come in well-shaped clusters on strong stems and have a slight fragrance. The foliage is soft and dark green, very plentiful and disease free. The plant displays vigorous and upright growth. ZONES 5–11.

Kordes, Germany, 1973

'Fragrant Cloud' × 'Peer Gynt'

'MIRIAM WILKINS'

OLD, HYBRID PERPETUAL, LIGHT PINK,
REPEAT-FLOWERING

Named for the founder of the international heritage rose movement, this variety was discovered in a Santa Rosa cemetery in California, USA growing on a wall about ten years ago. Unable to identify it, Philip Robinson decided to honor Miriam Wilkins. The deep pink,

'Miriam Wilkins'

'Mio Mac'

'Minuette'

M

full flowers look a great deal like an Autumn Damask. Lacy sepals cover the buds. There is a strong fragrance, and the blooms appear throughout summer and into autumn. Quite healthy, the 4 ft (1.2 m) shrub has large, dark green leaves that are not subject to any disease. Miriam Wilkins is responsible for the enormous growth of Old Rose societies in the USA, Australia, New Zealand, England and France. ZONES 5–10.

Robinson, USA, 1981

Seedling

'MIRIANA' MEIburgana

MODERN, LARGE-FLOWERED/HYBRID TEA, MEDIUM RED, REPEAT-FLOWERING

The large, double flowers of this variety are medium red and have 40 petals, the substance of the petals being very tough

'Miriana'

'Mischief'

and durable. There is no fragrance. The foliage is medium, semi-glossy and very abundant on an upright plant with excellent disease resistance. The flowers of 'Miriana' last very well on the bush and production is very good, but the color is a rather dull red and lacks life. ZONES 5–11.

Meilland, France, 1981

([Seedling × 'Independence'] × 'Suspense') × ([{'Alain' × *Rosa chinensis mutabilis*} × 'Caprice'] × 'Pharaoh')

'MISCHIEF' MACmi

MODERN, LARGE-FLOWERED/HYBRID TEA, ORANGE-PINK, REPEAT-FLOWERING

'Mischief' is a lovely little rose that gets its freedom of flower and color from the great Cluster-flowered Rose 'Spartan'. The well-formed, medium-sized flowers are a strong silvery salmon-pink. They are double, with 28 petals, hold their color well and are fragrant. The flower production is amazing and the repeat cycle is exceptionally rapid. The foliage is light green and semi-glossy on a vigorous and upright plant of medium height. This rose, which is excellent for bedding and for use as a standard, has lost popularity over the last decade or so, which is a great pity as it is one of the best roses of the 1960s. ZONES 5–11.

McGredy, UK, 1961

'Peace' × 'Spartan'

Portland Gold Medal 1965, National Rose Society President's International Trophy 1961

'Miss Edith Cavell'

'MISS ALL-AMERICAN BEAUTY' MEIdaud

syn. 'Maria Callas'

MODERN, LARGE-FLOWERED/HYBRID TEA, DEEP PINK, REPEAT-FLOWERING

'Miss All-American Beauty' is a great rose with deep rich pink flowers. The extremely fragrant blooms are double with 55 petals, large and cupped and hold their color well. The autumn blooms are magnificent, but growth is a little on the short side in summer heat. It gets its bushy habit and very healthy, disease-free foliage from its parent 'Karl Herbst'. **'Climbing Miss All-American Beauty'** (MEIudsur; syn. 'Climbing Maria Callas') was introduced by Meilland in 1969 and is one of the best deep pink climbing roses available. It has a copious supply of well-formed flowers in spring. ZONES 5–10.

Meilland, France, 1965

'Chrysler Imperial' × 'Karl Herbst'

Portland Gold Medal 1966, All-America Rose Selection 1968

'MISS ALL-AUSTRALIAN BEAUTY'

MODERN, LARGE-FLOWERED/HYBRID TEA, DEEP PINK, REPEAT-FLOWERING

This rose gets its very double flowers of excellent form from both parents. Like its parent 'Impeccable', 'Miss All-Australian Beauty' has many petals and extremely long-lasting form. The oval buds are very large and open to slightly fragrant flowers that are either light red or very deep pink with darker undersides. There are about 60 petals. The growth is tall and upright with plentiful dark green, very disease-resistant foliage, but flower production is rather poor and regrowth slow. However, the large, very well-formed flowers last very well. ZONES 5–10.

Ambrust, Australia, 1969

'Aztec' × 'Impeccable'

'Miss Daisy'

'Miss All-American Beauty'

'Miss All-Australian Beauty'

'MISS CYNTHIA FORDE'

MODERN, LARGE-FLOWERED/HYBRID TEA, DEEP PINK, REPEAT-FLOWERING

'Miss Cynthia Forde', a difficult rose to find today, has very bright deep pink, double flowers containing 35 petals. They are large and well formed. The undersides of the the petals are a lighter shade and there is a pleasant fragrance. This vigorous and bushy plant was a good bedding rose in the early part of this century but has been superseded by newer but not necessarily better varieties. ZONES 5–10.

Dickson, UK, 1909

Parentage unknown

National Rose Society Gold Medal 1909

'MISS DAISY' JACflare

MODERN, MINIATURE, DEEP YELLOW, REPEAT-FLOWERING

The lovely deep yellow flowers of 'Miss Daisy' are colorfast, even in hot climates. The double flowers, with up to 40 petals, have a light fragrance and are carried amid the small, glossy dark green foliage on a large and bushy, compact plant. This is a relatively disease-resistant variety that is easy to maintain. This rose is one of the few Miniatures hybridized by one of the masters of Cluster-flowered Roses. ZONES 5–10.

Warriner, USA, 1991

Seedling × 'Sun Flare'

'MISS EDITH CAVELL'

syns 'Edith Cavell', 'Nurse Cavell'

MODERN, POLYANTHA, DARK RED, REPEAT-FLOWERING

Edith Cavell was executed by the Germans in 1915, and to commemorate the 70th anniversary of her death the vicar of Swardeston in Norfolk, England, asked Peter Beales to try to find the rose named after her. One gnarled old plant was found out of six that had been planted in

1934 in the garden of Mrs Doris Levine of Brundell near the Norfolk Broads. 'Miss Edith Cavell' is a lovely little rose that produces small, globular flowers of rich crimson. There is little scent. The flowering is fairly continuous, but the plant can suffer from mildew. It makes a nice little border if planted close together. ZONES 4–11.

de Ruiter, The Netherlands, 1917

Sport of 'Orléans Rose'

'MISS FLIPPINS' TUCKflip
MODERN, MINIATURE, MEDIUM RED, REPEAT-FLOWERING

The double flowers of this rose are made up of 15–25 medium red petals with deep pink undersides. There is no fragrance, but the long-lasting flower form is excellent, with a high center suitable for exhibition in rose shows. The color is stable with minimal fading in hot weather. The blooms are naturally borne singly, amid the medium-sized, glossy dark green foliage on a compact bush to 24 in (60 cm) high. The growth is vigorous with a dense covering of foliage due to the very short distance between each leaf. 'Miss Flippins' is extremely easy to grow, yet it can suffer from mildew. It is an excellent red Miniature that has become a favorite of exhibitors since it won the Queen of Miniatures award at the American Rose Society National Show in 1996. ZONES 5–11.

Tucker, USA, 1997

'Elizabeth Taylor' × 'Kristin'

'MISS LOWE'
OLD, CHINA, MEDIUM RED, REPEAT-FLOWERING

Bright red, single blooms cover this small plant, and the quilled petals and stamens add their beauty. 'Miss Lowe' will tolerate poor conditions but improves a great deal in rich soil. The 3 ft (1 m) bush does best in full sun and is an ideal candidate for the border or in a container. There is never a hint of any disease. Some have classified it as 'Sanguinea', but this has been discounted. Jack Harkness, a noted English rosarian, states that it is not so much a sport as a reversion. ZONES 5–10.

1887

Sport of 'Slater's Crimson China'

'MISS MARION MANIFOLD'
syn. 'Marion Manifold'
MODERN, LARGE-FLOWERED CLIMBER, MEDIUM RED, REPEAT-FLOWERING

For many years 'Marion Manifold' was the most popular red climbing rose in

'Miss Marion Manifold'

Australia and it is still grown widely there in the cooler areas. The double flowers have 25 petals and are crimson-scarlet, globular and large, to 5 in (12 cm) across. They are very fragrant. The foliage is large, deep green and leathery on a vigorous plant that grows to 10–14 ft (3–4 m) high. This is a good rose for a pillar or tripod. There is some repeat-bloom. ZONES 5–10.

Adamson, Australia, 1913

Parentage unknown

'MISSION BELLS'
MODERN, LARGE-FLOWERED/HYBRID TEA, PINK BLEND, REPEAT-FLOWERING

The buds of 'Mission Bells' are long and pointed and an unusual orange-pink color. The double flowers have 40 high-centered petals and are large and fragrant. The foliage is dark and rather soft on a vigorous and very spreading bush. This is a rose of unusual color that is useful for bedding as it retains its color until petal fall. However, the stems are rather weak, which makes it unsuitable for picking. Flower production is extremely good and the repeat cycle is very rapid. ZONES 5–10.

Morris, USA, 1949

'Mrs Sam McGredy' × 'Mälar-Ros'

All-America Rose Selection 1950

'MR BLUEBIRD'
MODERN, MINIATURE, MAUVE, REPEAT-FLOWERING

The oval buds of 'Mr Bluebird' open to charming, lavender-blue, semi-double flowers made up of 15 petals. Unfortunately, the form is loose and the blooms often shatter too quickly; the small florets are therefore at their best when the blooms first open. The foliage is dark and somewhat coarse, and the plant is free flowering, clean and easy to maintain. It is hard to understand how a Miniature could be created from the incestuous

'Mr Chips'

'Mission Bells'

breeding of an Old Garden Rose. 'Old Blush' is believed to be 'The Last Rose of Summer' immortalized by Thomas Moore, the Irish poet. ZONES 4–11.

Moore, USA, 1960

'Old Blush' × 'Old Blush'

'MR CHIPS'
MODERN, LARGE-FLOWERED/HYBRID TEA, YELLOW BLEND, REPEAT-FLOWERING

'Mr Chips' is a combination of the colors of its parents. The shapely buds are deep yellow flushed with orange and pink on the outer petals. They open to medium-sized blooms with 45 very high-centered petals that hold their shape and color extremely well. The foliage is dark and glossy and repeat-flowering is very rapid. This rose flowers earlier than most varieties in spring. The flowers are very good for picking and it is a shame that 'Mr Chips' has not gained the popularity it deserves. ZONES 5–10.

Dickson, UK, 1970

'Grandma Dickson' × 'Miss Ireland'

'MR E. E. GREENWELL' HARjoobily
MODERN, CLUSTER-FLOWERED/FLORIBUNDA, ORANGE-PINK, REPEAT-FLOWERING

The semi-double flowers of this rose are rosy salmon. They have 18 petals and open flat, and at 3 in (8 cm) across are large for a Cluster-flowered Rose. It is a vigorous and spreading bush with abundant dark green foliage and few disease problems. This is a good rose for hedges

'Mister Lincoln'

'Mister Lincoln'

and for borders and can be used with bulbs and perennials in a mixed planting. It does not appear to be grown very much outside of the UK. ZONES 5–11.

Harkness, UK, 1978

'Jove' × 'City of Leeds'

Royal National Rose Society Trial Ground Certificate 1978, Courtrai Silver Medal 1978

'MISTER LINCOLN'
MODERN, LARGE-FLOWERED/HYBRID TEA, DARK RED, REPEAT-FLOWERING

This splendid rose has urn-shaped buds that open to dark red flowers with superb petal substance. The buds can open rather quickly in summer. The full blooms are at first cupped and then flat, and there are 35 huge petals that are extremely fragrant. The foliage is leathery,

'Mr E. E. Greenwell'

'Mr Bluebird'

M

matt and dark. Growth is extremely vigorous, making 'Mister Lincoln' unsuitable for bedding but superb for the back row of a rose bed. This is a very popular rose in Mediterranean-type climates. **'Climbing Mister Lincoln'** (Ram, India, 1974) is a magnificent Climber that flowers well through spring, summer and autumn. It can be used on a pillar or tripod but is too upright in growth and the shoots are too strong to be trained horizontally. ZONES 5–11.

Swim & Weeks, USA, 1964

'Chrysler Imperial' × 'Charles Mallerin'

All-America Rose Selection 1965

'Mrs Dudley Cross'

'Mrs Doreen Pike'

'Mrs Dudley Cross'

'Mrs B. R. Cant'

'MRS AARON WARD'
MODERN, LARGE-FLOWERED/HYBRID TEA, YELLOW BLEND, REPEAT-FLOWERING

This rose is a collector's item, as it is difficult to obtain nowadays. The buds are long, pointed and elegant and open to flowers that are quite variable in color, ranging from yellow to tones of salmon-pink. They are double, high centered and fragrant. The flowers are produced over a long period, and appear on a compact, dwarf bush. There can be a long gap between flushes. **'Climbing Mrs Aaron Ward'** (Dickson, UK, 1922) occurred 15 years after the bush form was introduced. It has yellow flowers that are washed with salmon-pink and is a moderate and bushy grower that is suitable for pillars or tripods. ZONES 5–10.

Pernet-Ducher, France, 1907

Parentage unknown

'MRS ALBERT NASH'
MODERN, LARGE-FLOWERED/HYBRID TEA, DARK RED, REPEAT-FLOWERING

This rose has very dark red, semi-double, extremely fragrant flowers. The buds are long and pointed and open fairly quickly. It has dark green, healthy, profuse foliage and is a strong and upright

'Mrs Bushby'

plant. The flower production is good but it is susceptible to black spot. ZONES 5–10.

Clark, Australia, 1929

Parentage unknown

'MRS ALSTON'S ROSE'
MODERN, POLYANTHA, RED BLEND, REPEAT-FLOWERING

This is a particularly good free-flowering Polyantha, and it is one of the few of this type produced by Alister Clark. The carmine-red flowers appear in small to medium-sized clusters on a very strong-growing plant. The blooms hold their color well. They are not as prone to mildew as most Polyanthas. ZONES 5–10.

Clark, Australia, 1940

Parentage unknown

'MRS ANTHONY WATERER'
MODERN, HYBRID RUGOSA, DARK RED, REPEAT-FLOWERING

'Mrs Anthony Waterer' shows very little influence of 'Général Jacqueminot' except in the foliage and the color of the flowers. The foliage is dark green and plentiful and in appearance is halfway between a Hybrid Perpetual and a Rugosa. The flowers are deep crimson, semi-double with 20 petals and open flat. They are very fragrant. It is a vigorous, bushy and cold-hardy plant with some repeat-bloom. It is excellent for a medium-sized hedge, and does not set hips. ZONES 4–11.

Waterer & Sons, UK, 1898

Rosa rugosa × 'Général Jacqueminot'

'MRS B. R. CANT'
OLD, TEA, MEDIUM PINK, REPEAT-FLOWERING

One parent of this rose is thought to be 'Red Safrano' (1867), a sport of the well-known 'Safrano', which this in no way resembles. This is a popular, reliable and successful Tea that has stood the test of

'Mrs Aaron Ward'

'Mrs Albert Nash'

'Mrs Alston's Rose'

time. The medium-sized, fully double flowers are rich red and silvery rose, tinged with blush at the bases of the petals. There is a pleasing Tea fragrance. 'Mrs B. R. Cant' forms a medium to high bush and repeats well throughout the season, as well as in winter in suitable climates. It is vigorous and easy to grow. **'Climbing Mrs B. R. Cant'** (Hjort, USA, 1960) is a sport of the original. It is similar to the parent, but difficult to find these days. ZONES 7–9.

Cant, UK, 1901

Parentage unknown

'MRS BUSHBY'
OLD, BOURBON, DEEP PINK

Discovered in Australia, the correct identity of this rose is not known. It carries fully double blooms that are filled with a great number of rich pink petals; they are arranged to give a flat flower with a confused center. The blooms develop from plump buds on long, thorny stems and mid-green foliage. 'Mrs Bushby' can be seen growing at David Ruston's nursery in South Australia. ZONES 5–10.

Parentage unknown

'MRS DOREEN PIKE' AUSdor
MODERN, HYBRID RUGOSA, MEDIUM PINK, REPEAT-FLOWERING

This rose bred by David Austin has large, very ruffled flowers that form rosettes of 40 petals. They are a warm rose pink and are strongly fragrant. Growth is low and bushy and there is plenty of small, pale green foliage. It makes an excellent border or a low hedge and it can also be used with bulbs and perennials in a mixed planting in the garden. Repeat-flowering is good and the plant is disease free. ZONES 5–10.

Austin, UK, 1993

'Martin Frobisher' × 'Roseraie de l'Haÿ'

M

'MRS DUDLEY CROSS'

OLD, TEA, YELLOW BLEND, REPEAT-FLOWERING

This plant grows to a bush of medium size. The flowers are light yellow with some pink, which predominates as the blooms age. It is a good rose for cutting, and the flowers are long lasting. They are quite large and repeat well throughout the season. Mildew can be a problem in some areas. ZONES 7–9.

Paul, UK, 1907

Parentage unknown

'MRS F. W. FLIGHT'

MODERN, LARGE-FLOWERED CLIMBER, DEEP PINK

The flowers of this rose are rose pink and semi-double and are borne in small and large clusters. The foliage is large, rich green and rather soft and can occasionally suffer from mildew. It is a good rose for a short pillar or tripod as it rather exceeds 10 ft (3 m) in height. Flowering is very profuse early in the season but there is no repeat-bloom. ZONES 5–10.

Cutbush, UK, 1905

'Crimson Rambler' × seedling

'MRS F. W. SANDFORD'

syn. 'Pride of the Valley'

OLD, HYBRID PERPETUAL, LIGHT PINK, REPEAT-FLOWERING

This rose resembles its parent, a vigorous large-flowered, rather gross Hybrid Perpetual. The blooms are somewhat cabbage-like and are good for exhibition. They are pale blush pink, fading to white. ZONES 5–9.

Curtis & Sandford, UK, 1898

Sport of 'Mrs John Laing'

'MRS FOLEY HOBBS'

OLD, TEA, WHITE/PINK BLEND, REPEAT-FLOWERING

The flowers of this rose are perhaps better suited for exhibition than to the rigors of the garden. They are creamy white with variable pink at the tips of the petals. They are of considerable form and substance, perhaps too much for the stems to bear. This is a conventional and reliable Tea Rose with a vigorous and robust growth habit. ZONES 6–9.

Dickson, UK, 1910

Parentage unknown

National Rose Society Gold Medal 1910

'MRS FRED DANKS'

MODERN, LARGE-FLOWERED/HYBRID TEA, MAUVE, REPEAT-FLOWERING

This variety, one of Alister Clark's best roses, has very long, slender buds that are an unusual deep rosy lilac color.

'Mrs Herbert Stevens'

'Mrs Georgia Chobe'

They open to large, semi-double flowers containing 20–25 petals, and there is a strong perfume. Flower production is continuous and blooms are quite often available in the winter months. The foliage is large, leathery, extremely plentiful and disease free on a plant with a very tall and upright habit. It is so tall that it can be used as a pillar rose or as a tall hedge. It is not available outside Australia. ZONES 5–10.

Clark, Australia, 1951

Parentage unknown

'MRS GEORGIA CHOBE'

MODERN, LARGE-FLOWERED/HYBRID TEA, LIGHT PINK, REPEAT-FLOWERING

This great exhibition rose has large, plum-colored buds that open to pale pink flowers that are extremely double, high centered and of magnificent form. They take a long time to open because of the number of petals (60), and because of their size. The foliage is leathery and pale green and growth is upright and fairly vigorous, but it is not a very productive bush and regrowth is slow to appear. ZONES 5–10.

Howard & Smith, USA, 1937

'Miss Rowena Thom' × 'Renault'

'MRS HAROLD ALSTON'

MODERN, LARGE-FLOWERED CLIMBER, MEDIUM PINK, REPEAT-FLOWERING

This strong-growing and upright, mid-pink rose carries long, pointed buds that open fairly quickly to double flowers with 20–25 petals. The blooming is profuse in spring and again in autumn. There is a lovely scent. It is disease free and looks wonderful on a pillar or tripod. The variety is one of the very many medium to deep pink climbing roses of 20 or so petals bred by Alister Clark. ZONES 5–10.

Clark, Australia, 1940

Parentage unknown

'Mrs Hugh Dettmann'

'Mrs Fred Danks'

'Mrs F. W. Flight'

'Mrs Foley Hobbs'

'MRS HERBERT STEVENS'

MODERN, LARGE-FLOWERED/HYBRID TEA, WHITE, REPEAT-FLOWERING

This rose has long, pointed, elegant buds that are pure white and which open to full, high-centered, fragrant blooms. The foliage is very pale green and disease free. Its growth is very dense and bushy and flower production is extremely profuse. This rose is still very popular in the warmer countries of the world where it usually flowers well into winter. '**Climbing Mrs Herbert Stevens**' (syns 'Grimpant Mrs Herbert Stevens', 'Stevens'; Pernet-Ducher, France, 1922) has long pliable canes that are not as stiff as most climbing roses, which makes it ideal for use on arches and pergolas where the pure white flowers show up well against the backdrop of pale green foliage. ZONES 5–10.

McGredy, UK, 1910

'Frau Karl Druschki' × 'Niphetos'

National Rose Society Gold Medal 1910

'MRS HUGH DETTMANN'

MODERN, LARGE-FLOWERED CLIMBER, APRICOT BLEND

Alister Clark's roses were mainly in pink and red shades, so this is a welcome addition in apricot-yellow. 'Mrs Hugh Dettmann' is a vigorous climbing rose producing a copious supply of nicely shaped buds opening to double flowers

with 17–22 petals that fade rather quickly. There is a slight scent. Growth is strong and healthy and there is some repeat. The plant has no disease problems. This rose can be grown on pillars, tripods and arches and is probably a better variety in cooler climates where there is not so much bleaching of the petal color. It flowers early in spring and heralds the rose season. ZONES 7–11.

Clark, Australia, 1930

Parentage unknown

'MRS IRIS CLOW'   HARbrite

MODERN, CLUSTER-FLOWERED/FLORIBUNDA, LIGHT PINK

The flowers of 'Mrs Iris Clow' are blush pink with pale pink undersides to the petals. The double flowers contain 28 petals and have a spicy fragrance. They are cupped, open to a rather loose formation and are borne in small clusters. The foliage is large, dark green, glossy and abundant and sets the flowers off nicely. It has an upright growth habit and is of medium height. This is a good rose for bedding and for use with pastel-toned bulbs and perennials in a mixed border. ZONES 5–10.

Harkness, UK, 1994

'Memento' × 'Princess Alice'

Courtrai Silver Medal 1997, Orléans Prix d'Or 1997, Orléans Crystal Prize 1997

M

'Mrs Norman Watson'

'Mrs Oakley Fisher'

'Mrs R. M. Finch'

'MRS JOHN LAING'
OLD, HYBRID PERPETUAL, MEDIUM PINK,
REPEAT-FLOWERING

'François Michelon' is a seedling of the famous 'La Reine', one of the first Hybrid Perpetuals from Jean Laffay, who created the class. The flowerheads resemble cabbages; they are cupped, large, fully double and very fragrant, and the color is silvery lilac-pink. The stems are nearly thornless. 'Mrs John Laing' is a healthy plant with a vigorous growth habit and is able to grow in poor soils. It is free from mildew. Bennett is said to have received $45 000 for the US distribution rights of this rose. John Laing was a London horticulturalist who died in 1901. ZONES 5–9.

Bennett, UK, 1887

'François Michelon' × seedling

National Rose Society Gold Medal 1885

'MRS MARY THOMSON'   TOMone
MODERN, MODERN SHRUB, PINK BLEND,
REPEAT-FLOWERING

The semi-double flowers of this rose, which occur in very large clusters, are lilac pink with cream centers and prominent golden stamens. The flower form is informal and decorative and there is a very distinctive fragrance. The foliage is matt green and the stems are thornless.

It has a bushy habit and is very disease resistant. This rose was described by Australian rose breeder Ian Spriggs as 'the sort of rose we should all be trying to breed'. It was named in honor of the mother of the breeder, George Thomson of Mount Barker, South Australia. ZONES 5–10.

Thomson, Australia, 1996

'Dapple Dawn' × 'Ophelia'

'MRS MYLES KENNEDY'
OLD, TEA, PINK BLEND, REPEAT-FLOWERING

This is another rose better suited to exhibition rather than to garden display. The flowers are very large; they are silvery white with buff shading and pink undersides, and the edges are sometimes picotee. The growth is only fair—it needs a good deal of nurturing and it can be a shy bloomer. It may be difficult to come by these days. ZONES 7–9.

Dickson, UK, 1906

Parentage unknown

'MRS NORMAN WATSON'
MODERN, LARGE-FLOWERED CLIMBER, DEEP PINK,
REPEAT-FLOWERING

The deep cherry pink flowers of this rose have no fragrance. The large florets have an informal form, and are borne in small clusters on a very vigorous bush that prefers to grow as a pillar rather than a true climber. This old world rose is winter hardy with a long repeat-bloom cycle. It is disease resistant. Almost forgotten among the wide variety of more modern climbers, it retains the majesty of an era gone by. ZONES 5–10.

Clark, Australia, 1930

'Radiance' × 'Gwen Nash'

'MRS OAKLEY FISHER'
MODERN, LARGE-FLOWERED/HYBRID TEA,
DEEP YELLOW, REPEAT-FLOWERING

This rose has buds of rich orange with random red flushes that open to buff copper flowers with golden stamens. The fragrant, single florets are borne in clusters on stems that often appear to have a weak appearance. It can be trained to resemble a lower-growing shrub rather than a tall Large-flowered Rose. 'Mrs Oakley Fisher' has endured for almost 75 years because of its charming flowers, which are set against a background of beautiful bronze, disease-resistant foliage. This classic rose has been described by various writers as a Large-flowered Rose, a Cluster-flowered Rose and a shrub rose. ZONES 5–10.

Cant, UK, 1921

Parentage unknown

National Rose Society Certificate of Merit 1921,
Royal Horticultural Society Award of Garden
Merit 1993

'MRS PAUL'
OLD, BOURBON, LIGHT PINK, REPEAT-FLOWERING

The flowers of 'Mrs Paul' are blush white, shaded rosy peach and resemble camellias. Its parent 'Mme Isaac Pereire' was one of the most famous Bourbons and has passed on its vigor and repeat-flowering qualities to its offspring. This is a somewhat slow grower to about 6 ft (1.8 m) under normal conditions. The

'Mrs John Laing'

Pauls, George and his uncle William, were considerable rose nurserymen and breeders in the nineteenth century. ZONES 5–9.

Paul, UK, 1891

Seedling of 'Mme Isaac Pereire'

'MRS PIERRE S. DUPONT'
MODERN, LARGE-FLOWERED/HYBRID TEA,
MEDIUM YELLOW, REPEAT-FLOWERING

This variety has long, pointed, reddish gold buds that open to flowers that are clear golden yellow then gradually change to a lighter yellow with exposure to the sun. The double florets have 40 petals and a fruity fragrance. The foliage is a rich dark green on a plant with moderate height, vigor and disease resistance. Bred by a well-known French hybridizer and named to honor the wife of a famous American industrialist of French descent, it was boldly introduced to the American rose-buying public by Robert Pyle of Conard-Pyle in 1929; Pyle later introduced the classic Large-flowered Rose 'Peace' to the USA. 'Climbing Mrs Pierre S. duPont' (Hillock, USA, 1933) is covered with small clusters of florets on long stems, and displays all the charming features of the variety. The petals tend to shed too quickly but the mass of yellow flowers are magnificent in the first flush of spring. It is not winter hardy. ZONES 6–11.

Mallerin, France, 1929

('Ophelia' × 'Rayon d'Or') × ('Ophelia' ×
['Constance' × 'Souvenir de Claudius Pernet'])

Bagatelle Gold Medal 1929

'MISTRESS QUICKLY'   AUSky
MODERN, MODERN SHRUB, MEDIUM PINK,
REPEAT-FLOWERING

The small, medium pink, very full flowers of this variety, which have 40 petals, come in large clusters. There is a slight fragrance. The foliage is small,

'Mrs Paul'

'Mrs Mary Thomson'

M

'Mrs Reynolds Hole'

'Mrs Sam McGredy'

'Mrs Richard Turnbull'

mid-green and semi-glossy, and there are a few prickles. Growth is bushy and medium. 'Mistress Quickly' will form a nicely rounded shrub and is useful in the shrub or perennial border or as a low hedge. It is also classified as an English Rose. ZONES 5–10.

Austin, UK, 1995

'Blush Noisette' × 'Martin Frobisher'

'MRS R. M. FINCH'
MODERN, POLYANTHA, MEDIUM PINK, REPEAT-FLOWERING

The rosy pink flowers on this variety become much lighter as they age and on exposure to the sun. The double florets are borne in compact clusters on this fairly disease-resistant plant. When 'Mrs R. M. Finch' was introduced in America, it won many admirers because its large, bushy habit and the loads of lovely clusters of rosy pink blooms make it ideal for garden display. ZONES 5–10.

Finch, Australia, 1923

'Orléans Rose' × seedling

'MRS REYNOLDS HOLE'
OLD, TEA, PINK BLEND, REPEAT-FLOWERING

This is a vigorous, floriferous and fragrant rose with long-stemmed deep purplish pink flowers that are good for cutting. It was named, of course, for the wife of the celebrated Dean Samuel Reynolds Hole, the first President of the (Royal) National Rose Society from its inception in 1876 until his death in 1904. ZONES 7–9.

Nabonnand, France, 1900

'Archiduc Joseph' × 'André Schwartz'

'MRS RICHARD TURNBULL'
MODERN, LARGE-FLOWERED CLIMBER, WHITE BLEND

Handsome, creamy white, single-petalled flowers are the hallmark of this classic example of a climber from the middle of the twentieth century. The florets are large and are borne in small clusters. It can be grown either as a pillar or a climber, but bloom production is best when it is trained as a true climber. It is an extremely vigorous plant and will easily grow to 30 ft (10 m). ZONES 5–10.

Clark, Australia, 1945

Hybrid of *Rosa gigantea*

'MRS SAM McGREDY'
MODERN, LARGE-FLOWERED/HYBRID TEA, ORANGE-PINK, REPEAT-FLOWERING

This rose has urn-shaped, pointed buds that open to large, scarlet-copper-orange flowers, with the undersides of the petals heavily flushed with red. The double florets have 40 petals and are very fragrant. The flower form begins as high centered, with the petals opening to show an inner lower center of symmetry. The plant is vigorous and tall and has beautiful reddish bronze foliage. Before World War II this rose was the talk of the town; it held its lofty position as a most popular rose until the appearance of 'Peace' in 1945 and has a prominent place in the history of roses. **'Climbing Mrs Sam McGredy'** (Guillaud, France, 1938; Royal Horticultural Society Award of Garden Merit 1993), which has tremendous vigor and bloom capacity, is a perfect climbing clone of its parent. It looks wonderful against a high wall or fence. ZONES 5–10.

McGredy, UK, 1929

('Donald Macdonald' × 'Golden Emblem') × (seedling × 'The Queen Alexandra Rose')

National Rose Society Gold Medal 1929, Portland Gold Medal 1956

'MRS WAKEFIELD CHRISTIE-MILLER'
MODERN, LARGE-FLOWERED/HYBRID TEA, PINK BLEND, REPEAT-FLOWERING

This rose has fragrant, double flowers that are a blush-shaded salmon color

'Misty'

with vermilion-rose undersides. The foliage is light green and leathery on a plant with a dwarf growth habit. In 1909, when this rose was introduced, the naming of roses reflected nineteenth-century Victorian formality. Its popularity was revived some years ago when it was wrongly identified as the long-lost 'Lady Mary Fitzwilliam'. However, it is delightful on its own merits. The large, fragrant, two-toned pink blooms look typically Edwardian. ZONES 5–10.

McGredy, UK, 1909

Parentage unknown

'MISTY'
MODERN, LARGE-FLOWERED/HYBRID TEA, WHITE, REPEAT-FLOWERING

This variety is the offspring of two popular white roses, but it has not become as well known as either of its parents. The buds are long, oval and pointed, and they open to creamy white flowers. These are double with 35 petals, cupped and are up to 4 in (10 cm) in diameter. There is a pleasant Tea Rose fragrance. The foliage is large, healthy and abundant on a vigorous and upright plant. Its flower production is not as profuse as either parents, and the repeat cycle is rather slow, which probably explains its lack of popularity. ZONES 5–10.

Armstrong, USA, 1965

'Mount Shasta' × 'Matterhorn'

'Mixed Marriage'

'Mrs Wakefield Christie-Miller'

'MIXED MARRIAGE'
MODERN, CLUSTER-FLOWERED/FLORIBUNDA, LIGHT PINK, REPEAT-FLOWERING

This rose, which sported from 'Bridal Pink', has soft pink flowers striped with a much deeper pink. The striping can be very variable: some blooms can be almost all pale pink, while others can be mostly deep pink. The attractive, pointed buds open to large, well-shaped blooms. Flower production is high and there is a quick repeat, although in hot weather 'Mixed Marriage' can lose much of its color and look rather bleached out. The bush has an identical growth habit to the original rose, and occasionally it will revert back to the original. 'Mixed Marriage' is a good rose for those who are keen on striped varieties. ZONES 5–10.

Ruston, Australia, 1987

Sport of 'Bridal Pink'

'MODEL OF PERFECTION'
MODERN, CLUSTER-FLOWERED/FLORIBUNDA, ORANGE BLEND, REPEAT-FLOWERING

This is a great rose for warm climates. The large, globular buds are a mixture of rich yellow, pink and strong bronze and open to long-lasting, double, exhibition-type blooms with 50 petals. The blooms are rich yellow in the center and each petal is edged with golden orange, then they slowly age to a dull dusky pink color. The fragrant flowers hold their

M

'Model of Perfection'

form extremely well and occur both singly and in small and large clusters, covering the bush from ground level upwards. It is a strong, bushy plant with mid-green, glossy foliage that can occasionally get mildew in autumn. The late autumn and early winter crop of flowers is truly magnificent. The bush is excellent for bedding and for borders, and the large heads of flowers are excellent on the show bench. ZONES 5–10.

Dickson, UK, 1977

'Zorina' × 'Arthur Bell'

'MODERN ART'   POUlart
syn. 'Prince de Monaco'

MODERN, LARGE-FLOWERED/HYBRID TEA, RED BLEND, REPEAT-FLOWERING

'Modern Art' and 'Maestro' were the first two hand-painted Large-flowered Roses. This rose produces medium red flowers that are suffused with orange-red. The underside of the petals is much paler, and this adds to the attractive hand-painted effect. The double blooms have 25 petals. The flowers are borne on long stems both singly and several to a cluster. There is only a slight fragrance. The healthy foliage is medium, dark green and matt on an upright, bushy plant. ZONES 5–10.

Olesen, Denmark, 1985

Seedling × seedling

Rome Gold Medal 1984

'Modern Art'

'Molineux'

'MOJAVE'

MODERN, LARGE-FLOWERED/HYBRID TEA, ORANGE BLEND, REPEAT-FLOWERING

This rose bred from 'Charlotte Armstrong' has the characteristic very long, pointed buds. They are apricot-orange tinted red and have prominent veining; the novel color makes this a popular rose. The very fragrant, double flowers have 25 petals and are large—up to 4½ in (12 cm) across. They open rather quickly in warm weather to attractive blooms that slowly turn pink as they age. The upright bush has profuse glossy foliage. Each flush produces lots of flowers and the repeat-bloom is rapid. **'Climbing Mojave'** (Trimper, Australia, 1964) also has good repeat-bloom through summer and autumn. ZONES 5–10.

Swim, USA, 1954

'Charlotte Armstrong' × 'Signora'

Bagatelle Gold Medal 1953, Geneva Gold Medal 1953, All-America Rose Selection 1954, National Rose Society Trial Ground Certificate 1955

'MOJE HAMMARBERG'

MODERN, HYBRID RUGOSA, MAUVE, REPEAT-FLOWERING

This rose has double flowers of reddish violet that are very fragrant and come on short weak stems. The fruit is large, red and abundant—an uncommon occurrence in very double Hybrid Rugosa roses. There is repeat-bloom. Its healthy

'Mojave'

'Molly McGredy'

and vigorous growth makes it an ideal rose to stand up to very cold winter conditions. The hips look attractive in autumn when they are interspersed with late flowers, and the autumn foliage is an added bonus. ZONES 3–9.

Hammarberg, Sweden, 1931

Parentage unknown

'MOLINEUX'   AUSmol

MODERN, MODERN SHRUB, DEEP YELLOW, REPEAT-FLOWERING

The flowers of 'Molineux' are very rich yellow and have a strong Tea scent. They open flat, hold their color well, and are produced singly and in small clusters. It flowers profusely on a short to medium-sized, bushy plant with upright growth that has no disease problems. This rose has an ideal bedding habit and is a good selection where a rich yellow color is desired. It was the first of David Austin's roses to win the President's Trophy of the Royal National Rose Society for the best new seedling rose of the year. It is useful to plant in a position where David Austin's other two great yellow roses, 'Graham Thomas' and 'Golden Celebration', would be too tall. 'Molineux' is also classified as an English Rose. ZONES 5–11.

Austin, UK, 1994

'Graham Thomas' × 'Golden Showers'

Royal National Rose Society President's International Trophy 1996, RNRS Henry Edland Medal for Fragrance 1996

'MOLLY McGREDY'   MACmo

MODERN, CLUSTER-FLOWERED/FLORIBUNDA, RED BLEND, REPEAT-FLOWERING

This rose, which was named after the breeder's sister, has flowers that are a most unusual carmine-red. The silver undersides to the petals provide a dramatic contrast. The large, well-formed, double blooms have 35 petals, and ap-

'Moje Hammarberg' (rosehips)

'Molly McGredy'

'Mon Cheri'

'Molly Sharman-Crawford'

pear in medium and small-sized clusters. There is some fragrance. The foliage is dark and glossy but not over-plentiful. 'Molly McGredy', a lovely rose for use in beds or in borders, is disease free. However it is rather slow to repeat-bloom. ZONES 5–11.

McGredy, UK, 1969

'Paddy McGredy' × ('Mme Léon Cuny' × 'Columbine')

Royal National Rose Society President's International Trophy 1968, Belfast Gold Medal 1971, Portland Gold Medal 1971

'MOLLY SHARMAN-CRAWFORD'

OLD, TEA, WHITE, REPEAT-FLOWERING

This is a low-growing Tea Rose with large, full, high-centered, fragrant flowers. They are white tinged with green. The plant has an upright and bushy growth habit. The rich green foliage is a little sparse. ZONES 7–9.

Dickson, UK, 1908

Parentage unknown

'MON CHERI'   AROcher

MODERN, LARGE-FLOWERED/HYBRID TEA, RED BLEND, REPEAT-FLOWERING

This distinctive rose has large, pointed buds that are a medium pink color with a yellow base to each of the 38 petals. The double blooms are usually borne singly or in small clusters on very long stems and there is a light fragrance. On opening, the rose changes to dark red and the effect of the three colors (pink, yellow and red) on the bush together is very striking. The large, abundant foliage is semi-glossy and medium green on a medium to tall, upright plant. The influence of 'Double Delight' can be seen in the deepening of the color of the full blooms. ZONES 5–10.

Christensen, USA, 1981

('White Satin' × 'Bewitched') × 'Double Delight'

All-America Rose Selection 1982

M

'MONA LISA'

MODERN, LARGE-FLOWERED CLIMBER, PINK BLEND, REPEAT-FLOWERING

This is an excellent small-growing climbing rose. The buds are ovoid and open to warm salmon-rose flowers. The blooms are double with 35 petals, and are cupped at first but open flat. They are large—4–4½ in (10–12 cm)—and are borne singly and in small clusters. The fragrance is very strong. The foliage is dark and leathery and there is good repeat-bloom. 'Mona Lisa' makes an excellent pillar rose or it can be grown on a tripod, and it is also strong enough to be grown as a large, free-standing bush without support. It is one of the best climbers for an area where a reliable, continuously flowering rose is desired. ZONES 5–10.

Malandrone, Italy, 1956

'Mrs Sam McGredy' × ('Mrs Sam McGredy' × [seedling × 'Captain Thomas'])

'MONCTON'

MODERN, HYBRID RUGOSA, LIGHT PINK, REPEAT-FLOWERING

This rose was bred to withstand very cold winter temperatures. It produces pale pink double flowers with 20 small petals. The very fragrant blooms are 2 in (5 cm) across and there is some repeat. The foliage is gray-green on a plant with an upright and bushy growth habit. 'Moncton' is unavailable in many countries outside North America. ZONES 4–11.

Svedja, Canada, 1977

'Schneezwerg' × Rosa chinensis

'MONDIALE'   KORozon

MODERN, LARGE-FLOWERED/HYBRID TEA, PINK BLEND, REPEAT-FLOWERING

The buds of this rose are plump and pointed, which gives promise of the full-petalled blooms that follow. They are deep coral-pink in the center of the

'Monique'

'Mona Lisa'

'Monsieur Tillier'

blooms, with yellow shading that flows from the base into each of the crisp petals. The outer petals fade to light pink as they age. There is little fragrance, and flowers are borne freely through summer and autumn. In warm climates and under glass, the growth becomes very tall; it is recommended for a hedge, the back of a border or to screen unsightly walls. It performs well as a cutting rose in all conditions. The habit is upright, with a dense cover of glossy leaves that are reddish when young. ZONES 5–9.

Kordes, Germany, 1993

Parentage unknown

'MONIKA'   TANaknom

syn. 'Monica'

MODERN, LARGE-FLOWERED/HYBRID TEA, PINK BLEND/ORANGE BLEND, REPEAT-FLOWERING

'Monika' has extremely long, elegant buds that open to well-formed flowers of bright vermilion with a golden base. This rich color holds well. The blooms are usually produced singly on long stems, making this a good rose for cutting, and they last well when picked. The bush grows tall and has very healthy, profuse, dark green, glossy foliage with very good disease resistance. Flower production is excellent. It makes a superb hedge and can be used for continuous color at the back of a rose bed. ZONES 5–10.

Tantau, Germany, 1985

Parentage unknown

'MONIQUE'

MODERN, LARGE-FLOWERED/HYBRID TEA, ORANGE-PINK, REPEAT-FLOWERING

'Monique' is still a lovely, reliable garden rose after nearly 50 years in commerce. The very long, pointed buds are a clear rosy salmon color, rather more rose than salmon. They open to shapely, double flowers with 25 petals that are up to 5 in (12 cm) across and are very fragrant. It is

'Montezuma'

'Monika'

'Moncton'

a vigorous and upright bush with few thorns that has pale green, medium-sized foliage. This is an excellent rose for bedding and for borders and is good for cutting. ZONES 5–10.

Paolino, France, 1949

'Lady Sylvia' × seedling

National Rose Society Gold Medal 1950

'MONSIEUR A. MAILLÉ'

OLD, BOURBON, RED BLEND, REPEAT-FLOWERING

This is a very vigorous Bourbon with very fragrant carmine-red blooms that deepen with age. It is a very robust plant that can best be trained as a climber. 'Monsieur A. Maillé' has been compared with 'Mme Isaac Pereire', the very popular Bourbon so disliked by Jack Harkness. ZONES 5–9.

Moreau-Robert, France, 1889

Parentage unknown

'MONSIEUR CORDEAU'

OLD, BOURBON, DEEP PINK, REPEAT-FLOWERING

This rose has been described variously as bright scarlet-crimson and as bright carmine-red shaded vermilion. Color, like smell, is an extremely subjective business! The flowers are very large and very fragrant. It is a vigorous, tall plant and is quite thorny. It is floriferous and has a good repeat-bloom cycle. This rose is uncommon nowadays, but is worth a spot in any garden. ZONES 5–9.

Moreau-Robert, France, 1892

Parentage unknown

'Mondiale'

'MONSIEUR TILLIER'

syn. 'Archiduc Joseph'

OLD, TEA, ORANGE PINK/PINK BLEND, REPEAT-FLOWERING

This rose has deep rose to purple flowers with orange and russet shades, and they open flattish. 'Monsieur Tillier' is a vigorous shrub of medium height, but it can grow to enormous heights if planted in a shrubbery. Like most Tea Roses, this rose is too tender to survive cold winters. ZONES 7–9.

Bernaix, France, 1891

Parentage unknown

'MONTEZUMA'

MODERN, LARGE-FLOWERED/HYBRID TEA, ORANGE-PINK, REPEAT-FLOWERING

This rose is variously described as orange-pink or salmon-red, both being apt descriptions. However, the full blooms fade to a rather dirty color, a fault inherited from 'Floradora'. The shapely buds open slowly to double flowers of 36 petals with high centers. They are about 4 in (10 cm) across and there is some fragrance. The repeat-bloom is very quick and flower production is excellent. The foliage is leathery and semi-glossy on a vigorous and compact plant. This is still an excellent garden rose although the color is now considered a trifle dull. ZONES 5–10.

Swim, USA, 1955

'Fandango' × 'Floradora'

Geneva Gold Medal 1955, National Rose Society Gold Medal 1956, Portland Gold Medal 1957

M

'Moonbeam'

'Moon River'

'Moonsprite'

'Moonlight'

'MOON RIVER'
MODERN, MINIATURE, MAUVE, REPEAT-FLOWERING

This attractive Miniature Rose is valued for its well-formed, double flowers. They are borne singly and the color is accentuated by the dark green foliage. It is only grown by two nurseries: one in the USA and one in Australia. As a result, it is a difficult variety to obtain. ZONES 5–10.

Bernadella, USA, 1997

Parentage unknown

'MOONBEAM'   AUSbeam
MODERN, MODERN SHRUB, APRICOT BLEND, REPEAT-FLOWERING

'Moonbeam' is very free flowering. It covers itself with flowers at frequent intervals and has very long, pointed buds that are a soft apricot-pink color, more pink than apricot. The color is particularly clear and fresh. The buds open to large, semi-double flowers containing 15–20 petals and a boss of golden stamens. The medium-sized bush has copious pale green foliage and no disease problems. This rose is excellent for a hedge or for bedding and also associates particularly well with bulbs and perennials. It is a lovely rose for picking, as the long buds hold well in the bud stage in cool weather. It is also known as an English Rose. ZONES 4–11.

Austin, UK, 1983

Parentage unknown

'MOONLIGHT'
MODERN, MODERN SHRUB, LIGHT YELLOW, REPEAT-FLOWERING

The fragrant flowers of 'Moonlight' are palest yellow fading to white, and have prominent yellow stamens. They are single and come in small and large well-spaced clusters. The foliage is dark and glossy, acting as a good foil to the flowers. Growth is bushy and the repeat cycle is very good. The flowers are particularly attractive in autumn, when they keep their yellow color for a longer period. This variety makes an excellent hedge and is good with bulbs and perennials. There are no disease problems except for a touch of seasonal mildew. If the spent blooms are not removed a copious supply of hips is produced that lasts for several months; these look very attractive among the late flowers. ZONES 4–11.

Pemberton, UK, 1913

'Trier' × 'Sulphurea'

National Rose Society Gold Medal 1913

'MOONSPRITE'
MODERN, CLUSTER-FLOWERED/FLORIBUNDA, LIGHT YELLOW, REPEAT-FLOWERING

This delightful little rose has never gained the popularity it deserves. The oval buds open to very full, very fragrant flowers of creamy white, shading to amber yellow in the center. There are 80 petals and blooms occur in small and large clusters. They are cupped at first and then open flat. The foliage is leathery and semi-glossy on a medium-sized, bushy plant with excellent flower production and quick repeat. It is still gaining popularity after over 40 years in commerce. ZONES 5–10.

Swim, USA, 1956

'Sutter's Gold' × 'Ondine'

Baden-Baden Gold Medal 1955, Rome Gold Medal 1956

'MOORE'S YELLOW'
MODERN, MINIATURE, MEDIUM YELLOW, REPEAT-FLOWERING

'Moore's Yellow' is a free-flowering yellow Miniature that produces large, oval buds that develop into well-formed double blooms with 20–25 petals. The flowers open flat and retain their color well; they repeat quickly. This variety has a small, spreading growth habit and pale green, semi-glossy foliage that is disease free. It makes a good standard and is ideal for use in pots and for small beds. ZONES 5–10.

Moore, USA, 1990

Parentage unknown

'MORDEN BLUSH'
MODERN, MODERN SHRUB, LIGHT PINK, REPEAT-FLOWERING

Bred by the Department of Agriculture in Canada for winter hardiness, 'Morden Blush' has flowers of light pink fading to ivory. The small, double blooms have 50 petals and open flat, and come in sprays of 1–5. The foliage is medium green and matt on a low, bushy plant with repeat-bloom. This is an excellent small shrub where winter hardiness is an important factor, although it is not well known outside Canada and the colder areas of the USA. ZONES 3–9.

Colicutt & Marshall, Canada, 1988

('Prairie Princess' × 'Morden Amorette') × ('Prairie Princess' × ['White Bouquet' × {*Rosa arkansana* × 'Assiniboine'}])

'MORDEN CENTENNIAL'
MODERN, MODERN SHRUB, MEDIUM PINK, REPEAT-FLOWERING

This rose bred by the Department of Agriculture in Canada for severe winter conditions has double, medium pink flowers that occur in clusters of up to 15. Each bloom has 50 petals and there is a slight fragrance. The foliage has 7 leaflets

'Moore's Yellow'

and is slightly glossy on a bushy shrub. The flowers always occur on new growth, and there is repeat-bloom. 'Modern Centennial' is able to withstand very cold winters without die-back of the canes. ZONES 3–9.

Marshall, Canada, 1980

'Prairie Princess' × ('White Bouquet' × ['J. W. Fargo' × 'Assiniboine'])

'MORDEN FIREGLOW'
MODERN, MODERN SHRUB, ORANGE-RED, REPEAT-FLOWERING

'Morden Fireglow' has bright orange-red flowers, a color that is rare in cold-hardy roses. The buds are pointed and open to loosely formed, fragrant blooms. The cupped, double flowers, which have 28 petals with red undersides, are borne in small clusters. It is a low, bushy plant with a good repeat cycle. Globular hips are produced if spent blooms are not removed. ZONES 3–9.

Colicutt & Marshall, Canada, 1989

Seedling × 'Morden Cardinette'

'MORDEN RUBY'
MODERN, MODERN SHRUB, PINK BLEND, REPEAT-FLOWERING

The buds of 'Morden Ruby' are oval, and they open to very double, pink blend flowers. They are 3 in (8 cm) in diameter, and the early blooming is very heavy on a vigorous plant that repeats well. This rose is not well known outside the colder areas of Canada and northern USA. ZONES 3–9.

Marshall, Canada, 1977

'Fire King' × ('J. W. Fargo' × 'Assiniboine')

'MORGENGRUSS'
syn. 'Morning Greeting'
MODERN, MODERN SHRUB, ORANGE-PINK, REPEAT-FLOWERING

This is an extremely vigorous shrub rose growing to 9–10 ft (2.7–3 m) high and

'Morden Ruby'

'Morden Blush'

'Moth'

'Moulin Rouge'

nearly as much across. The abundant foliage is glossy and light green. The ovoid buds open to very double blooms that occur in clusters and which are pale pink tinted with orange-yellow. They are very fragrant. 'Morgengruss' is an excellent shrub for planting in parks for a colorful spring display; it needs a lot of room to develop its full potential. It is particularly good in cold climates. ZONES 4–11.

Kordes, Germany, 1962

Parentage unknown

'MORGENROT' KORheim
MODERN, MODERN SHRUB, RED BLEND, REPEAT-FLOWERING

This is an excellent shrub rose from a complicated crossing using Cluster-flowered, Large-flowered and shrub roses. 'Morgenrot' is a medium-sized shrub bearing copious supplies of single, 5-petalled, bright red flowers in spring. The foliage is small, dark and matt and there is a light fragrance. If spent flowers are not removed a good display of round, dull red hips are produced in clusters; the hips persist into winter. ZONES 4–11.

Kordes, Germany, 1985

('Marlena' × 'Europeana') × (['Tropicana' × 'Carina'] × ['Cläre Grammerstorf' × 'Frühlingsmorgen'])

Paris Gold Medal 1983

'MORLETII'
syns 'Inermis Morletii', *Rosa pendulina plena*
OLD, BOURSAULT, MAUVE

The Boursaults are thought, without great confidence, to be a cross between *Rosa pendulina* and *R. chinensis*. They have few if any thorns (*inermis* is Latin for 'unarmed'), and there are now only four Boursaults freely available; 'Morletii' was the last of them to be introduced. The plant grows in an arching way, normally to about 6 ft (1.8 m) tall and wide, and bears many clusters of smallish, double magenta flowers in early summer. It can be trained as a climber. The leaves and stems color well in spring and autumn, when they become coppery orange. ZONES 7–9.

Morlet, France, 1883

Parentage unknown

'MORNING BLUSH'
OLD, ALBA, LIGHT YELLOW

Tall and upright in the center, flowing outward from the base like a fountain, this shrub needs plenty of room to offer its best features. The semi-double blooms of light yellow edged with dark pink line the strong canes for about a month during early summer, and the large, glossy dark green leaves act as a contrast to the velvet-like petals. There is some perfume. Like all Albas, this is a very healthy rose not at all afflicted with mildew or black spot. As a landscaping plant, 'Morning Blush' makes a fine rose for the back of a border or as a hedge. Sievers is the first modern breeder to successfully create large numbers of Albas; they are all reasonably winter hardy. ZONES 4–9.

Sievers, Germany, 1988

Parentage unknown

'MORNING JEWEL'
MODERN, LARGE-FLOWERED CLIMBER, MEDIUM PINK, REPEAT-FLOWERING

This is an excellent small, neat, climbing rose suitable for pillars or tripods. The large, fragrant flowers are rose pink and semi-double and have 20 petals. The blooms are borne both singly and in clusters. The foliage is glossy and abundant and the repeat-bloom is excellent. There are no disease problems. 'Morning Jewel' is one of the best fragrant pink climbing roses available for growing where a small climber is desired. It is found in many gardens in the UK and Europe. ZONES 5–11.

Cocker, UK, 1968

'New Dawn' × 'Red Dandy'

Anerkannte Deutsche Rose 1975, Royal Horticultural Society Award of Garden Merit 1993

'MOTH'
syn. 'The Moth'
MODERN, MODERN SHRUB, MAUVE, REPEAT-FLOWERING

'Moth', which is also known as an English Rose, is a large, very thorny shrub rose with very thick canes. The slim,

'Morletii'

elegant buds open to semi-double, pale pink blooms of 15 or so petals with a central boss of stamens. They come on short laterals on the last season's growth and completely cover the bush in spring. The repeat cycle is rather slow. The bush has a rather ungainly growth habit with large thorny wood and very angular spreading growth. In cool weather, the flowers can be beautiful but they open very quickly and do not hold well in hot weather. Moth was a fairy in Shakespeare's *A Midsummer Night's Dream*. ZONES 5–10.

Austin, UK, 1983

Parentage unknown

'MOTHER'S LOVE' TINlove
MODERN, MINIATURE, PINK BLEND, REPEAT-FLOWERING

The oval buds of this variety open to reveal pastel pink, double flowers with about two dozen petals that have soft yellow bases. There is a distinct fruity fragrance and the blooms normally occur singly or in small sprays. In hot, sunny climates the color can fade quite quickly. The foliage is a semi-glossy, mid-green and covers a medium-sized, compact plant. 'Mother's Love' is a remarkably beautiful variety that adds grace and charm to the garden with its carpet of color. This rose is a sister variety to many other outstanding winners produced by Dee Bennett using the same parents. ZONES 5–10.

Bennett, USA, 1989

'Futura' × 'Party Girl'

'MOTHERSDAY'
syns 'Fête Des Mères', 'Morsdag', 'Mothers Day', 'Muttertag'
MODERN, POLYANTHA, DARK RED, REPEAT-FLOWERING

A great many Polyantha Roses are sports of 'Orléans Rose' or 'Dick Koster'; 'Mothersday' is a sport of the latter. The small, many-petalled flowers are deep red and globular and come in clusters of 5–20. The foliage is small and glossy on a plant with a very dwarf habit. Flower production is good, but the repeat-bloom is a little slow. As with most Polyanthas, there can be mildew problems. This rose was grown in large quantities in pots in the past for forcing into flower in time for Mother's Day in Europe. ZONES 4–11.

Grootendorst, Germany, 1949

Sport of 'Dick Koster'

'MOULIN ROUGE'
syn. 'Sans Souci'
MODERN, CLUSTER-FLOWERED/FLORIBUNDA, MEDIUM RED, REPEAT-FLOWERING

This rose gets its color from 'Alain' and its large flower clusters from 'Orange Triumph'; the flowers last a very long time, another trait inherited from 'Orange Triumph'. The fragrant, rich red flowers are medium sized, double with 20 petals, and are cupped at first before opening flat. They are 2 in (5 cm) across and come in very well-spaced clusters. It has glossy foliage and an upright growth habit. This was one of the first really good Cluster-flowered Roses that was splendid for bedding, which led to an upsurge in popularity of this class for use in parks and gardens. It is susceptible to crown gall of the bud union in hot climates. ZONES 5–11.

Meilland, France, 1952

'Alain' × 'Orange Triumph'

Geneva Gold Medal 1952, National Rose Society President's International Trophy 1952

'Morning Blush'

M

'Morgengruss'

'MOUNT HOOD' MACmouhoo
syns 'Foster's Melbourne Cup', 'Foster's Wellington Cup'
MODERN, LARGE-FLOWERED/HYBRID TEA, WHITE, REPEAT-FLOWERING

The flowers of this rose are ivory white with a light fragrance. They are very double, containing 40–45 petals, with good high symmetrical centers. The blooms occur mainly as clusters, giving the bush a snow-capped appearance. The foliage is glossy deep green on a full-branching, tall, upright plant that has excellent vigor and disease resistance. It has an amazing capacity for bloom production, but the flowers usually require a little heat to open fully. This rose is a sister seedling of another famous rose, 'Singin' in the Rain'. It was appropriately named by the hybridizer to recognize the majestic snow-capped Mount Hood, which rises above the Columbia Gorge on the Oregon Trial in northwestern USA. **ZONES 5–10.**

McGredy, New Zealand, 1991

'Sexy Rexy' × 'Pot O' Gold'

New Zealand Gold Medal 1992, All-America Rose Selection 1996

'MOUNT SHASTA'
MODERN, LARGE-FLOWERED/HYBRID TEA, WHITE, REPEAT-FLOWERING

'Mount Shasta' is still one of the best white roses available. The buds are very large, long and pointed and most attractive. They open to well-formed, double flowers containing 20–25 petals. The fragrant, cupped blooms are up to 5 in

(12 cm) across, and are produced on very long stems that are excellent for picking at the bud stage. The leathery foliage is an unusual gray-green color that complements the flowers well. Growth is very vigorous and upright. This rose is whiter than 'Pascali' and 'Tineke' and is suitable for a wedding bouquet. **ZONES 5–10.**

Swim & Weeks, USA, 1963

'Queen Elizabeth' × 'Blanche Mallerin'

'MOUNTBATTEN' HARmantelle
MODERN, CLUSTER-FLOWERED/FLORIBUNDA, MEDIUM YELLOW, REPEAT-FLOWERING

This is a particularly strong-growing, healthy rose with extremely abundant foliage and dense growth. The clear soft yellow, double flowers with 45 petals are cupped at first, opening flat in the full bloom stage. They are borne singly and several together on long stems and are fragrant. The foliage is large, dark green and glossy. The first flush is very heavy and the repeat cycle is good. Although it has won many awards, it has not become as popular as might have been expected. It was named after Lord Mountbatten, who was killed in a bomb blast in Northern Ireland. **ZONES 5–10.**

Harkness, UK, 1982

'Peer Gynt' × (['Anne Cocker' × 'Arthur Bell'] × 'Southampton')

Royal National Rose Society Certificate of Merit 1979, Lyon Rose of the Century 1980, UK Rose of the Year 1982, Belfast Gold Medal, Orléans Gold Medal 1984, Courtrai Gold Medal 1986, Golden Rose of The Hague 1986, Royal Horticultural Society Award of Garden Merit 1993

'MOVIE STAR' TANeivom
MODERN, LARGE-FLOWERED/HYBRID TEA, PINK BLEND, REPEAT-FLOWERING

Very little is known about this greenhouse variety, which is only listed by one supplier in the USA. It bears double, high-centered blooms, and the coral-salmon petals reflex as the flowers mature. 'Movie Star' is covered with glossy dark green foliage and the flowers are borne one to a stem. **ZONES 5–10.**

Tantau, Germany, 1995

Parentage unknown

'MOZART'
MODERN, MODERN SHRUB, PINK BLEND, REPEAT-FLOWERING

This excellent shrub rose has fragrant, single flowers that are deep pink with a large white eye. They are small and come in small to very large clusters. There is good repeat-bloom, especially in autumn

'München'

'MOUSSEUX DU JAPON'
syns 'Japonica', 'Moussu du Japon', 'Muscosa Japonica'
OLD, MOSS, MAUVE

The fragrant flowers of this rose are loosely double. They are about 2½ in (6.5 cm) across and are magenta-pink ageing to softer shades of lilac-pink. It is a short to medium shrub to 4–5 ft (1.2–1.5 m) high with an angular growth habit. It sends up stiff, heavily mossed branches with laterals that carry well-spaced flower clusters. The leaves are broadly oval, leathery and dark green overlaid with purplish gray. It is probably the most heavily mossed rose of its kind—the moss extends all over the plant, including the leaf stalks, flower buds and calyxes; it is bright green in color, dense and soft to touch. Without this profuse moss this rose would have little to recommend it. **ZONES 4–11.**

Parentage unknown

'Mutabilis'

when enormous trusses of flowers are produced; these last a long time. The growth is very vigorous and spreading, and the plant has excellent resistance to disease. It looks rather like Harkness's 'Marjorie Fair', and both are excellent shrub roses. **ZONES 4–11.**

Lambert, Germany, 1937

'Robin Hood' × 'Rote Pharisäer'

'MULTIFLORE DE VAUMARCUS'
OLD, NOISETTE, LIGHT PINK, REPEAT-FLOWERING

This is not a very well-known variety but it is available from specialist growers in Europe and the UK. The plant has a medium growth habit. It is bushy and healthy and bears soft pink, medium to large flowers in big trusses. It blooms continuously. **ZONES 7–9.**

Menet, France, 1875

Parentage unknown

'MÜNCHEN'
MODERN, MODERN SHRUB, DARK RED, REPEAT-FLOWERING

This variety has long, pointed buds that open to semi-double, scarlet-crimson flowers with a light fragrance. The blooms are normally borne in small clusters on strong stems. The color of the blooms starts out as a very attractive cardinal red that acquires a lighter shading with exposure to full sun. The foliage is glossy dark green on a plant with a trailing growth habit. This is an extremely vigorous rose with a good repeat-bloom. **ZONES 4–10.**

Kordes, Germany, 1940

'Eva' × 'Reveil Dijonnais'

'MUTABILIS'
syns *Rosa chinensis mutabilis*, 'Tipo Idéale'
OLD, CHINA, YELLOW BLEND, REPEAT-FLOWERING

This rose was first probably introduced to horticulture in 1934 by Swiss botanist Henri Correvon of Geneva, who obtained it from Prince Ghilberto Borromeo's garden at Isola Bella. It normally makes a large, spreading bush but can go up to the eaves on a house wall in time. The flowers are butterfly-like and are borne in masses. They open yellow, turn to pink and then crimson and have a long flowering period. 'Masquerade' seems to be derived from this rose. **ZONES 5–10.**

Probably from China and introduced to Italy, pre-1894

Parentage unknown

Royal Horticultural Society Award of Garden Merit 1993

'Mount Hood'

'Mount Shasta'

'Movie Star'

'Mountbatten'

M

'MY CHOICE'

MODERN, LARGE-FLOWERED/HYBRID TEA,
PINK BLEND, REPEAT-FLOWERING

The double flowers of this variety have
33 petals and are pink with a pale primrose yellow reverse. There is a very noticeable damask fragrance. The buds
tend to be unattractive at the beginning
but mature into wonderfully formed
flowers with good substance and color.
The blooms are exceptionally large, at
4–5 in (12–14 cm) across, while the foliage is a very attractive leathery green on
a vigorous, tall-growing plant. It is not
winter hardy and can suffer from powdery mildew and black spot if left unprotected during the growing season. This
rose is best grown in warmer climates for
peak performance. Curiously, it has been
neglected by the rose-buying public in
spite of its gold medals. ZONES 5–11.

LeGrice, UK, 1958

'Wellworth' × 'Ena Harkness'

National Rose Society Gold Medal 1958, NRS Clay
Cup for Fragrance 1958, Portland Gold Medal 1961

'MY GIRL'

syn. 'Cunosa'

MODERN, CLUSTER-FLOWERED/FLORIBUNDA,
ORANGE BLEND, REPEAT-FLOWERING

'My Girl' has deep salmon flowers that
are borne in medium-sized clusters. They
are large and double, with 30 petals, and
have no fragrance. The flowers are
cupped, and there are golden stamens.
The foliage is dark green on a vigorous,
upright bush that is fairly disease resistant and affords the home gardener an
opportunity to use it as an explosive
landscape color. Winning the Gold
Medal award at the International Rose
Trials at The Hague in 1963 brought
this rose into prominence; it has subsequently been forgotten as a popular
international choice and is now mainly
grown in Europe. ZONES 5–10.

de Ruiter, The Netherlands, 1964

'Dacapo' × seedling of a Cluster-flowered Rose
The Hague Gold Medal 1963

'MY GRANNY' POUloma

syns 'Granny', 'Meine Oma', 'My Ouma'

MODERN, GROUND COVER, MEDIUM PINK,
REPEAT-FLOWERING

The name of this rose was suggested by
a visitor to Ludwig's Nursery in Pretoria,
South Africa. It has the shape and delicate coloring of heritage roses, so in this

'My Valentine'

regard 'My Granny' was a very clever
choice. The rose grows quickly and it is
covered by glossy dark green leaves that
are healthy and make a nice backdrop
to the numerous flowers, which are produced in successive bursts of color. The
open flowers are like small, clear pink rosettes; they have no fragrance. When new
basal branches appear, they grow out and
up until this healthy shrub is knee high
and double that in width. ZONES 4–11.

Poulsen, Denmark, 1991

Seedling × 'The Fairy'

'MY JOY'

MODERN, LARGE-FLOWERED/HYBRID TEA,
MEDIUM PINK, REPEAT-FLOWERING

Elegant, long, pointed buds on this variety open to rose pink, perfectly formed
flowers that are nearly always borne one
bloom to a stem. The long-lasting flowers
are supported on lengthy stems suitable
for cutting or exhibition. It requires a
little heat to allow all its petals to reflex
to the fully open stage. The glossy, dark
green foliage is a natural complement
to the quality blooms on a very vigorous,
upright grower. It was discovered by Len
Wood, who was President of the Royal
National Rose Society from 1987–88 and
is a keen exhibitor himself. He named it
for his wife. ZONES 5–11.

Wood, UK, 1976

Sport of 'Red Devil'

'MY LOVE'

MODERN, LARGE-FLOWERED/HYBRID TEA,
DARK RED, REPEAT-FLOWERING

The flowers on this variety are an attractive deep red that is non-fading as the
blooms open. The large florets have
45 petals and are very fragrant, even
in cooler climates. The high-centered

'My Choice'

flower form makes it suitable for exhibition. The blooms tend to be borne one
to a stem, but in cool climates clustering
has been observed. The foliage is dark
green on a vigorous, tall plant that is
disease resistant and winter hardy. This
is another remarkable offspring bred
from the award-winning Large-flowered
Rose 'Ena Harkness'. ZONES 4–11.

Anderson, UK, 1960

'Bayadère' × 'Ena Harkness'

'MY PLEASURE'

MODERN, CLUSTER-FLOWERED/FLORIBUNDA,
MEDIUM RED, REPEAT-FLOWERING

'My Pleasure' is a respectable Cluster-
flowered Rose that has been overlooked.
The flowers, which are produced in small
to large clusters and completely cover the
bush, are a bright glowing red that does
not fade. The buds are attractive and
open to full blooms of good substance;
the repeat-bloom is good. The foliage is
abundant, dark green and semi-glossy.
'My Pleasure' is suitable for bedding and
for borders, as the plant is of medium
size and is very compact, and there are
no disease problems. ZONES 5–11.

LeGrice, UK, 1988

Parentage unknown

'MY VALENTINE' MORmyval

MODERN, MINIATURE, DARK RED,
REPEAT-FLOWERING

The small buds of this rose open to dark
red flowers that are a little lighter once
they have unfolded fully. The blooms
possess a large number of petals—up to
65—to form high centers, and are normally borne in clusters surrounded with
glossy, bronze-tinted foliage. The habit is
vigorous and upright. 'My Valentine'
was specifically bred for the Valentine
Day's celebration and makes a lovely
potted plant that is vigorous and blooms
freely through the growing season.
ZONES 5–10.

Moore, USA, 1975

'Little Chief' × 'Little Curt'

'My Pleasure'

'MYRA STEGMAN'

MODERN, LARGE-FLOWERED/HYBRID TEA,
ORANGE-PINK, REPEAT-FLOWERING

Myra Stegman has done much for rose
promotion in South Africa, and this variety named in her honor has the same
constant supply of exciting salmon-apricot, double flowers that made its parent
famous. These can be successfully cut
for informal arrangements, but they lack
fragrance. The bush is of medium height,
sometimes quite tall, and it looks stunning
when grown with companion plants of
the same stature, such as blue ceanothus
or purple petreas. ZONES 4–11.

Introduced by Taschner, South Africa, 1991

Sport of 'Duet'

'MYRIAM' COCgrand

MODERN, LARGE-FLOWERED/HYBRID TEA,
LIGHT PINK, REPEAT-FLOWERING

This rose has large, light rose pink, very
fragrant flowers. They are very double
with 44 petals, and are borne one bloom
per stem with no clustering observed.
The foliage is medium green and semi-
glossy and there are some prickles on
the stems. It is a tall, upright grower.
The parents of this rose are both famous
in their own right, and the hybridizer
has successfully transmitted their best
qualities to this offspring. ZONES 5–10.

Cocker, UK, 1992

'Typhoo Tea' × 'Grandpa Dickson'

'My Girl'

'My Joy'

M

NO

'NANA MOUSKOURI'

MODERN, CLUSTER-FLOWERED/FLORIBUNDA, WHITE, REPEAT-FLOWERING

This rose has creamy white flowers with a pink flush in the bud stage prior to opening. In warm climates the flowers are almost pure white. The double florets have about 30 petals and are fragrant. The flower form is symmetrical with the high centers making it a suitable variety for exhibition purposes. The blooms, borne in small to medium-sized clusters, cover the bush, making for a beautiful garden display. The foliage is medium dark green on an upright, compact bush. It is a vigorous plant with good disease resistance to mildew and black spot. It was named to honor the celebrated Greek singer. ZONES 5–10.

Dickson, UK, 1975

'Redgold' × 'Iced Ginger'

'NANCY GARDINER'   KORkeindor

MODERN, CLUSTER-FLOWERED/FLORIBUNDA, ORANGE-PINK, REPEAT-FLOWERING

Nancy Gardiner is an esteemed South African garden writer and photographer. The rose chosen for her is a popular garden bush that forms a neat, thornless plant of medium height. It is disease and maintenance free and excellent for bed-

ding schemes. 'Nancy Gardiner' continuously forms new stems that produce either single blooms or clusters that bring with them a slight fragrance. When cut, the flowers are long lasting and good for exhibiting. The small buds, perfect for buttonholes, open to full, light coral-salmon blooms with tight centers and reflexing outer petals. It is a gentle rose suitable for both the landscape and the house. ZONES 4–10.

Kordes, Germany, 1994

Parentage unknown

'NANCY HAYWARD'

MODERN, LARGE-FLOWERED CLIMBER, MEDIUM RED, REPEAT-FLOWERING

The flowers of this variety are a bright cerise-red fading to a carmine-red. The large florets are single petalled with only a faint fragrance. The medium green foliage is very disease resistant. The plant has a vigorous climbing habit and needs training to spread out over a fence or high wall to maximize its bloom production at each lateral. When in full bloom this rose can stop traffic! It lasts well as a cut flower for indoors and needs little or no attention during the season except for removal of spent blooms. 'Nancy Hayward' has been successfully used on bal-

'Nancy Steen'

'Nancy Steen'

'National Trust'

'Nancy Hayward'

cony railings where it can bloom constantly, providing color throughout the growing season. ZONES 5–10.

Clark, Australia, 1937

'Jessie Clark' × seedling

'NANCY STEEN'

MODERN, CLUSTER-FLOWERED/FLORIBUNDA, PINK BLEND, REPEAT-FLOWERING

The large, fragrant, double flowers of this rose have 30 petals that are a blush pink with a pale cream center. The blooms have a flat informal form against a backdrop of dark green, glossy foliage. It is a strong-growing plant bearing an abundance of blooms that are always in clusters. While it has been registered as a Cluster-flowered Rose, it does resemble a Modern Shrub. The hybridizer named this rose after one of New Zealand's most notable rose growers who worked diligently to revive interest in Old Garden Roses. ZONES 5–10.

Sherwood, New Zealand, 1976

'Pink Parfait' × ('Ophelia' × 'Parkdirektor Riggers')

'NARROW WATER'

OLD, NOISETTE, LIGHT PINK, REPEAT-FLOWERING

This rose is a medium to tall Noisette with delicate, small, rosette-style lavender-pink flowers that are borne in sprays. It is reminiscent of 'Blush Noisette', the original Noisette rose. It really is a very desirable rose to have in the garden. Narrow Water Castle stands on a narrowing section of the Carlingford River between Newry and Warrenpoint. This river marks the boundary between Eire and Northern Ireland. ZONES 4–10.

Daisy Hill Nursery, Ireland, circa 1883

Sport of 'Nastarana'

'Nana Mouskouri'

'Nancy Hayward'

'Narrow Water'

'NATIONAL TRUST'

syn. 'Bad Nauheim'

MODERN, LARGE-FLOWERED/HYBRID TEA, DARK RED, REPEAT-FLOWERING

The bright red, weatherproof flowers of this variety have classic Large-flowered form and are supported by strong stems. The flowers are large—with a 4 in (10 cm) diameter—and very double with 53 petals but have no fragrance. They are borne one to a stem on a vigorous, compact bush with a short, neat habit. The foliage is medium to dark green and disease resistant. This rose is as near perfect as any red Large-flowered Rose could be, although many agree with the hybridizer that his 'Olympiad' introduced in 1982 was a step closer to that idea of perfection. It was named for the 75th Anniversary of the National Trust in Great Britain. ZONES 4–11.

McGredy, UK, 1970

'Evelyn Fison' × 'King of Hearts'

Royal National Society Trial Ground Certificate 1969, Belfast Certificate of Merit 1972

'NEARLY WILD'

MODERN, CLUSTER-FLOWERED/FLORIBUNDA, MEDIUM PINK, REPEAT-FLOWERING

Small pointed buds open to rose pink, single-petalled flowers. They are borne in clusters on long straight stems and are fragrant. The plant has a bushy, compact growth habit and reasonable disease resistance. Although this classic rose is nearly extinct and is no longer in commerce, it can still be observed growing is many old museum gardens and estates. The seed parent, 'Dr W. Van Fleet', was used extensively in rose hybridizing but its most famous contribution came in 1997 when the World Federation of Rose

Societies entered the climbing sport 'New Dawn' into the Rose Hall of Fame as one of the world's favorite roses. ZONES 4–10.

Brownell, USA, 1941

'Dr W. Van Fleet' × 'Leuchtstern'

'NELLIE NEIL'

MODERN, LARGE-FLOWERED/HYBRID TEA, WHITE BLEND, REPEAT-FLOWERING

Named after the mother of John Neil, one of Australia's best-known growers of cut roses, this rose has large, cupped blooms of creamy white flushed with deep pink on the outer petals. There are 25–30 broad petals of good substance. The blooms are borne both singly and in small clusters and the foliage is very dark green, large, glossy and very abundant. Flower production is average with a rather slow repeat. 'Nellie Neil' has an excellent record. ZONES 5–9.

Dawson, Australia, 1975

Parentage unknown

'NÉMÉSIS'

OLD, CHINA, DARK RED, REPEAT-FLOWERING

'Nemesis' bears pompon-style flowers which are a rich plum-crimson with coppery shadings. The blooms are small and double, and are borne in small clusters in early summer and larger heads later in the season. 'Némésis' is a dwarf plant, growing only to about 3 ft (1 m) high, and has twiggy stems and small leaves. ZONES 7–9.

Vibert, France, 1834

Parentage unknown

'NEON'

MODERN, CLUSTER-FLOWERED/FLORIBUNDA, ORANGE BLEND, REPEAT-FLOWERING

As its name implies, the flowers of this variety are a rich and intensive blend of pink and orange tints. They are neatly formed, with about two dozen petals, of small to medium size and without much scent. In summer they appear freely on their first bloom, and continue to show color through to late autumn. The variety is not commercially available today; in its prime it was suitable for

'Nevada'

the front of a border or for a small bed as it is compact in habit, with mid-green foliage. 'Neon' needs to be watched carefully for signs of black spot. ZONES 5–9.

Waterhouse Nursery Ltd, UK, 1971

Parentage unknown

'NESTOR'

OLD, GALLICA, MEDIUM RED

The flowers of 'Nestor' are very double, flat, cupped and quartered. The color of the blooms is magenta with the outer petals a charming lilac-pink. This is a fine rose worthy of a spot in any garden. The foliage is light green on a plant of medium height. One can only speculate on the naming of the rose—it is probable that it was named after a Frenchman, and not the king of Pylos who accompanied the Greeks to the Trojan war. ZONES 4–9.

Pre-1848

Parentage unknown

'NEUE REVUE'   KORiev

syn. 'News Review'

MODERN, LARGE-FLOWERED/HYBRID TEA, RED BLEND, REPEAT-FLOWERING

The flowers are sensational—large and perfectly formed with a rich blending of gold, pink and touches of coral. The double florets have 30 petals and are very fragrant. The foliage is typical of roses from the master hybridizer, Reimer Kordes—dark green, glossy and disease resistant. There are many large prickles

'Neue Revue'

'Nellie Neil'

and thorns on the stem, another characteristic of the works of Reimer Kordes. It is a vigorous upright bush, however, it does not get top marks as it inherits its soft wood from its grandparent, 'Perfecta'. 'Neue Revue' was named after a popular and well-respected German magazine of the time. ZONES 5–10.

Kordes, Germany, 1962

'Colour Wonder' × seedling

Anerkannte Deutsche Rose 1969

'NEVADA'

MODERN, MODERN SHRUB, WHITE, REPEAT-FLOWERING

'Nevada' has pink to apricot ovoid buds that open to large white flowers that are 4 in (10 cm) diameter with a reverse that is sometimes splashed carmine. The weatherproof, single-petalled blooms are borne in clusters on short stems and cover the bush. The foliage is medium green and usually disease resistant; in some wet climates black spot will develop if the plant is not protected by spraying. It is a tall, vigorous plant growing to 7 ft (2 m) in most climates. Rarely without blooms, this rose has the grace and majesty of a Wild Rose combined

'Neville Gibson'

with a Modern Shrub. As to its pollen parentage, there has been discussion that perhaps *Rosa moyesii fargesii*, a tetraploid form, was used. ZONES 4–10.

Dot, Spain, 1927

Reported to be 'La Giralda' × hybrid of *Rosa moyesii*

Royal Horticultural Society Award of Garden Merit 1993

'NEVILLE GIBSON'   HARportly

MODERN, LARGE-FLOWERED/HYBRID TEA, MEDIUM PINK, REPEAT-FLOWERING

These flowers are a clear and attractive medium pink with 40 petals. They are large, 4 in (10 cm) in diameter, and their high symmetrical centers make them suitable for exhibition. The fragrant flowers grow one bloom per strong, elegant, straight stem. They really need heat to open properly. The foliage is semi-glossy and medium green on a tall, upright, vigorous plant. It is generally disease free and easy to maintain in most climates. The color blends well with most plants in the garden. ZONES 5–10.

Harkness, UK, 1982

'Red Planet' × ('Carina' × 'Pascali')

Geneve Rose d'Or Gold Medal

'Neon'

N

'New Beginning'

'New Daily Mail'

'NEW BEGINNING' SAVabeg

MODERN, MINIATURE, ORANGE BLEND, REPEAT-FLOWERING

The bright orange-yellow, bicolored flowers of this variety have decorative form; they are double, made up of 40–50 petals, of medium size and are usually borne singly or in small sprays. It has no fragrance and the compact bush is covered with semi-glossy, mid-green foliage. This is best as a garden rose because it carries a constant production of blooms that do not fade too quickly in hot climates, although in cooler weather the color and form are much improved. The brilliant color makes it a suitable candidate for hanging baskets, borders and as a ground cover. This was the first Miniature Rose to be awarded the prestigious All-America Rose Selection award, which was previously reserved for large rose

categories—a well-deserved honor for the hybridizer, Harm Saville. It is interesting to note that 'Zorina' was also the parent of many other prize-winning Cluster-flowered Roses. ZONES 5–11.

Saville, USA, 1988

'Zorina' × seedling

All-America Rose Selection 1989

'NEW DAILY MAIL'

syn. 'Pussta'

MODERN, CLUSTER-FLOWERED/FLORIBUNDA, DARK RED, REPEAT-FLOWERING

This rose has globular buds that open to large, semi-double, dark red flowers with golden stamens. There is no fragrance. The foliage is a semi-glossy dark green on a vigorous, upright plant. This rose has two predecessors—the 1913 orange blend Large-flowered Rose, 'Daily Mail Rose', hybridized by Pernet-Ducher, and the crimson Large-flowered Rose, 'Daily Mail Scented Rose', bred by Archer in England in 1927. Furthermore, **'Climbing New Daily Mail'** was registered in 1989 by B. K. Patil of Bangalore, India. ZONES 5–10.

Tantau, Germany, 1972

'Letkis' × 'Walzertraum'

'NEW DAWN'

syns 'Everblooming Dr W. Van Fleet', 'The New Dawn'

MODERN, LARGE-FLOWERED CLIMBER, LIGHT PINK, REPEAT-FLOWERING

'New Dawn' has no faults and some great attributes that make it an all-time

'New Day'

favorite of many rose growers. Large, double, fragrant, cameo pink flowers fading to a flesh-toned white are the hallmarks of this rose. The foliage is glossy, dark green and disease resistant on a bush that climbs to about 20 ft (6 m). It is winter hardy and blooms all year long with an exceptional crop of flowers, both in small clusters and one bloom per stem whatever the climate zone. The sweet scent of the blooms is another plus. The canes and stems are pliable enough to accommodate any garden design. It was discovered in a Connecticut nursery owned by Henry Dree and holds the first plant patent ever issued in the USA. After almost 67 years in existence, it was elected to the World Rose Hall of Fame in 1997 by the members of the World Federation of Rose Societies at their Triennial Convention in Benelux. ZONES 4–10.

Dreer, USA, 1930

Sport of 'Dr W. Van Fleet'

Royal Horticultural Society Award of Garden Merit 1993, World Federation of Rose Societies World's Favorite Rose 1997

'NEW DAY' KORgold

syn. 'Mabella'

MODERN, LARGE-FLOWERED/HYBRID TEA, MEDIUM YELLOW, REPEAT-FLOWERING

The ovoid buds of this rose open to mimosa yellow, classic-shaped flowers. They are 4–5 in (10–12 cm) in diameter, double with 30 petals, very fragrant, and seem immune to weather damage. The flower form can, depending on climate, be high centered with excellent symmetry, but it is mostly decorative and informal. The non-fading blooms generally last well, making them suitable for cut flowers. It is an upright, vigorous bush

that prefers cool weather and has large, light green foliage. Those in the cut-flower trade refer to it by the synonym 'Mabella'. This rose is another example of the huge commitment by Reimer Kordes to produce disease-resistant plants that are winter hardy. ZONES 4–10.

Kordes, Germany, 1977

'Arlene Francis' × 'Roselandia'

'NEW FACE' INTerclem

MODERN, MODERN SHRUB, YELLOW BLEND, REPEAT-FLOWERING

Peter Ilsink has produced a fascinating range of shrub roses, and this one is particularly suitable for gardens where there is ample space, for it is capable of growing to twice the extent of the average shrub rose. The single blooms are creamy yellow, with bright pink edging towards the petal rims. They are of small to medium size and appear in large sprays with excellent continuity through summer and autumn. For a big border or naturalized garden this is a good rose, and the young flower sprays are suitable to cut for indoor flower arrangements. The plant grows upright with a dense, well-spread habit, and has prickly stems and medium-sized, semi-glossy leaves. ZONES 4–9.

Ilsink, The Netherlands, 1978

Parentage unknown

Bagatelle Gold Medal 1981

'NEW HORIZON' DICplay

MODERN, CLUSTER-FLOWERED/FLORIBUNDA ORANGE BLEND, REPEAT-FLOWERING

The color of this variety is difficult to describe: it is basically salmon, with random shades of pink and yellow in the young flowers, which admit reddish tints

'New Dawn'

'New Dawn'

'New Horizon'

'New Zealand'

'News'

as they expand and age. They are of medium size, borne on upright stems in tight clusters, and fairly full of petals, which form neat and conical centers before reflexing to reveal the stamens. There is little scent. In the garden, the variety can be used for a group in a border, or as a bed on its own. It blooms through summer and autumn on an upright, bushy plant of below average height that is well furnished with glossy mid-green leaves. ZONES 4–9.

Dickson, UK, 1991

'Disco Dancer' × 'Bonfire Night'

Royal National Rose Society Trial Ground Certificate 1989, Belfast Gold Medal 1993, Glasgow Certificate of Merit 1993

'NEW PENNY'

MODERN, MINIATURE, ORANGE-RED, REPEAT-FLOWERING

The short, pointed buds of this rose open variably to either orange-red or coral pink, semi-double flowers made up of about 20 petals; it is at its most beautiful when fully open. The color is dependent on the weather conditions. The flowers are fragrant with attractive stamens, and are borne in large clusters on strong, straight stems. This is an attractive compact bush with leathery, glossy foliage. The foliage color is more attractive and the blooms last longer if the bush is grown in partial shade. Its seed parent, *Rosa wichuraiana* × 'Floradora', has been used frequently by Moore in many of his Miniature masterpieces. ZONES 4–10.

Moore, USA, 1962

(*Rosa wichuraiana* × 'Floradora') × seedling

'NEW STAR'

MODERN, LARGE-FLOWERED/HYBRID TEA, MEDIUM YELLOW, REPEAT-FLOWERING

An excellent medium yellow bedding rose, 'New Star' carries many shapely buds that develop slowly into well-formed blooms of 30–35 petals. They are large, to 5 in (12 cm) across, and hold their shape and color well. The foliage is very dark green, glossy and extremely disease free on a tall and upright bush. Flower production is high with a quick repeat, and the petals are pointed, which may be the reason behind the name. The blooms are good for cutting. Many excellent roses now being bred in Japan, 'New Star' is one of the few that has been introduced in other countries. ZONES 5–9.

Keisei, Japan, 1987

Parentage unknown

'NEW YEAR' MACnewye
syn. 'Arcadian'

MODERN, LARGE-FLOWERED/HYBRID TEA, ORANGE BLEND, REPEAT-FLOWERING

The flowers of 'New Year' are a delightful blend of clear orange and golden yellow. The shapely florets have 20 petals and a light fragrance. They are borne in small clusters and sometimes one to a stem. In hot weather the blooms tend to open rather quickly but the prolific production compensates for this. The foliage is large and dark green on a tall, upright, vigorous bush that is also disease free. It is not winter hardy. Because of its dense bushy growth, it is an ideal garden variety providing color throughout the growing season. In 1995 a climbing sport with 6–14 petals was discovered by Joe Burks of Texas, USA. ZONES 5–10.

McGredy, New Zealand, 1983

'Mary Sumner' × seedling

All-America Rose Selection 1987

'NEW YORKER'

MODERN, LARGE-FLOWERED/HYBRID TEA, MEDIUM RED, REPEAT-FLOWERING

The 35-petalled flowers are a velvety bright scarlet-red and show no evidence of fading in any climatic zones. The florets are large—almost 5 in (12 cm) in diameter. They have classical high centers with good symmetry and a wonderful fruity fragrance, and are grown one per stem with little or no clustering. It is a vigorous bush with many branches. It is winter hardy, but it can suffer from powdery mildew if left unprotected. 'New Yorker' was popular in its day, but has disappeared from commerce. ZONES 4–10.

Boerner, USA, 1947

'Flambeau' × seedling

National Rose Society Certificate of Merit 1950

'NEW ZEALAND' MACgenev
syn. 'Aotearoa New Zealand'

MODERN, LARGE-FLOWERED/HYBRID TEA, LIGHT PINK, REPEAT-FLOWERING

This rose has large, soft warm pink blooms with excellent shape and form that are borne one to a stem on strong straight stems. The double florets have 30–35 petals with a strong honeysuckle fragrance. The foliage is glossy, dark green on a vigorous, upright bush with good overall shape and architecture. It prefers consistent temperatures on the warm side to show off its best characteristics. The real winner among its many attributes is the great fragrance. The plant takes a year to establish in the garden and then it performs beautifully. 'New Zealand' is a stunning credit to Sam McGredy who attained the zenith of perfection in breeding Large-flowered Roses of exceptional character and quality. ZONES 4–10.

McGredy, New Zealand, 1991

'Harmonie' × 'Auckland Metro'

Portland Gold Medal and Fragrance Award 1996

'NEWPORT FAIRY'
syn. 'Newport Rambler'

MODERN, RAMBLER, PINK BLEND, REPEAT-FLOWERING

The small single-petalled flowers are a deep rose pink with a white eye and golden stamens. They are borne in huge clusters on a vigorous rambler stretching 20 ft (6 m) in all directions if allowed to do so. The clusters resemble hydrangeas in their inflorescence and structure and in that first early flush literally cover the bush. These clusters contain up to 50 florets, which extend the bloom display for several weeks. It is fairly disease resistant but can suffer from spider mite in warmer climates. The repeat-bloom is not as prolific as the first bloom. Many rose growers allow this rose to take over an entire wall or even a roof. ZONES 4–10.

Gardener, USA, 1908

Rosa wichuraiana × 'Crimson Rambler'

'NEWS' LEGnews

MODERN, CLUSTER-FLOWERED/FLORIBUNDA, MAUVE, REPEAT-FLOWERING

The semi-double, fragrant flowers of this rose are a non-fading purple with contrasting golden yellow stamens. They are borne in clusters against attractive glossy, olive green foliage. The large blooms are weatherproof with good staying power on the bush. It is a vigorous, medium-sized, upright bush with a tendency to spread, and has excellent repeat-cycle times. It is easy to maintain and disease resistant—characteristics acquired from both its parents. After its introduction in 1970, a large bed was established in Queen Mary's Rose Garden in Regent's Park, London. It became the talk of the town and helped promote this rose, and rose growing, to the public. ZONES 4–10.

LeGrice, UK, 1968

'Lilac Charm' × 'Superb Tuscany'

Royal National Rose Society Gold Medal 1970, Belfast Certificate of Merit 1970

'New Year'

'New Star'

'New Yorker'

'Nice Day'

'Night Light'

'NICCOLO PAGANINI'   MEIcairma

syns 'Courage', 'Paganini'

MODERN, CLUSTER-FLOWERED/FLORIBUNDA, MEDIUM RED, REPEAT-FLOWERING

The buds of this variety are long with a graceful urn shape, and they open into rounded blooms with neatly coiled centers, that become quite large as the petals expand. They are a rich bright shade of red, with a shining, velvety look about them, but do not have more than a slight fragrance. The flower clusters appear with excellent continuity through summer and autumn, making this a popular choice for beds and borders or for a hedge. In warm climates it grows to average height with plentiful, crisp deep green foliage. ZONES 5–9.

Meilland, France, 1991

Parentage unknown

Geneva Gold Medal 1989, Rose of the Century 1990, Lyon Plus Belle Rose de France 1990

'NICE DAY'   CHEwsea

MODERN, CLIMBING MINIATURE, ORANGE-PINK, REPEAT-FLOWERING

The small, fragrant, salmon-pink flowers that adorn this rose each contain about 15–25 petals to form a neat rosette. They are borne in large and decorative clusters that are complemented by small, glossy bronze- to mid-green foliage. Its habit is decidedly climbing, but the plant can take several seasons to establish for maximum performance. The color holds well in sunny climates, but it seems to prefer cooler conditions where it can hold its color and bloom a lot longer. This is another major achievement by Chris Warner, who has developed a range of climbers in most color combinations. ZONES 5–10.

Warner, UK, 1992

'Seaspray' × 'Warm Welcome'

British Association of Rose Breeders Selection 1994

'NICOLE'   KORicole

MODERN, CLUSTER-FLOWERED/FLORIBUNDA, WHITE, REPEAT-FLOWERING

'Nicole' has large, double, white flowers that look their best at the fully open stage when the flowers adopt a flat form showing off the golden stamens amid a set of impeccable petals with deep cerise-red edges. There is just a hint of fragrance. They generally grow in medium-sized clusters of 5–9 blooms on very strong straight stems covered with thorns. The foliage is large, glossy and dark green on an extremely tall, vigorous plant. It sends

'Niccolo Paganini'

up strong new canes throughout the growing season and needs plenty of room to grow. This is one of several sister seedlings produced by Kordes all with the same colors, shape and form. In 1983 Kordes introduced 'Hannah Gordon' (syn. 'Raspberry Ice'). ZONES 4–10.

Kordes, Germany, 1985

Seedling × 'Bordure Rose'

'NICOLETTE'   LUDswenic

MODERN, LARGE-FLOWERED/HYBRID TEA, APRICOT BLEND, REPEAT-FLOWERING

This tall-growing rose is popular for its perfectly shaped buds and blooms that are excellent for cutting and exhibition, even though they are not fragrant. The color varies from a soft buff apricot in summer to darker shades of the same in autumn, and as the flowers are repeatedly formed on new basal branches, a bed of 'Nicolette' always provides color in the garden. ZONES 5–12.

Taschner, South Africa, 1995

Sport of 'Esther Geldenhuys'

'NIGEL HAWTHORNE'

HARquibbler
MODERN, MODERN SHRUB, PINK BLEND

The pointed buds open to lovely single-petalled flowers of pale salmon-rose with a deep scarlet eye at the base. They are borne singly or in clusters and have a light fruity fragrance. The stems tend to be a bit wiry, with wrinkled rich green foliage. It is a spreading, low grower. The cross is the first record of a successful union between two different species. It was named for the fine British actor who declared, when asked what type of rose he preferred, 'I am going to be a bit of a problem, because the kind of roses I like are unperfect roses.' The only imperfect trait is that flowering is brief. ZONES 4–10.

Harkness, UK, 1989

Hulthemia persica × 'Harvest Home'

'Nikki'

'NIGHT'

syn. 'Lady Sackville'

MODERN, LARGE-FLOWERED/HYBRID TEA, DARK RED, REPEAT-FLOWERING

This variety has long pointed buds that open to beautiful double, fragrant flowers of rich violet-crimson with black velvet shadows. The blooms have classic symmetrical high centers and tend to show a bluish red color after 2 or 3 days on the bush. The foliage is a glossy dark green and can mildew in certain climates. It has an overall bushy habit and is at its best in the first spring bloom. 'Night' was the forerunner of this color class of very dark crimson Large-flowered Roses with good form and habit. Unfortunately it is no longer in commerce and is available only in a few select locations in the world. ZONES 5–10.

McGredy, UK, 1930

Parentage unknown

'NIGHT LIGHT'   POUllight

syn. 'Night Life'

MODERN, LARGE-FLOWERED CLIMBER, DEEP YELLOW, REPEAT-FLOWERING

This rose has red-tinted pointed buds that open to reveal flowers of deep yellow ageing to orange-yellow. The double florets have 27 petals and a light sweet scent. They are borne in sprays of 3–5 florets against large, glossy, dark green foliage on a tall, spreading bush that can grow to 8 ft (2.4 m) high in one season in warmer climates. The flowers can be up to 5 in (12 cm) in diameter. The form is more decorative than formal. ZONES 5–10.

Poulsen, Denmark, 1982

'Westerland' × 'Pastorale'

'NIGHTINGALE'   HERgale

syn. 'Goliath'

MODERN, LARGE-FLOWERED/HYBRID TEA, PINK BLEND, REPEAT-FLOWERING

These flowers are an attractive rose pink which, on ageing, is more of a blended lighter color. They are 4–5 in (10–12 cm) in diameter, double with 25 petals and have a light fragrance. The high centers with good symmetry make it suitable as a top exhibition rose. The plant is vigorous and the blooms grow on long strong stems. It likes cooler weather and is mildew-prone if not protected by regular spraying with a fungicide. 'Nightingale' was rediscovered in the 1980s by American exhibitors, who admired its classical Large-flowered form. ZONES 5–10.

Herholdt, South Africa, 1970

'Rina Herholdt' × 'Tiffany'

'Niphetos'

'Nobilo's Chardonnay'

'NIKKI'

MODERN, CLUSTER-FLOWERED/FLORIBUNDA, ORANGE BLEND, REPEAT-FLOWERING

These semi-double flowers are pale pink with vermilion-orange veining and a hand-painted blotch with a white eye and reverse. There is no fragrance. The blooms are borne in small clusters of 3–5 florets with good overall inflorescence. The foliage is semi-glossy and medium green on a round, compact, bushy plant. It is vigorous and prolific, providing an abundance of sprays that cover the bush for most of the growing season. 'Nikki' is easy to grow and is disease resistant. It was hybridized by an amateur rose exhibitor, Tony Bracegirdle, who has subsequently been a Royal National Rose Society National Amateur Champion. ZONES 5–10.

Bracegirdle, UK, 1981

'Dusky Maiden' × 'Eyepaint'

'NINA WEIBULL'

MODERN, CLUSTER-FLOWERED/FLORIBUNDA, DARK RED, REPEAT-FLOWERING

The dark red flowers of 'Nina Weibull' do not fade easily. The florets are double and have an informal open form. They come in small clusters of 3–5 florets. The foliage is dark green on a compact bush with a short growth habit. It is generally prolific in bloom production, very disease resistant and very easy to grow. This rose is a great choice for a mass planting in the garden because of its consistent and uniform growth habit and constant color. ZONES 5–10.

Poulsen, Denmark, 1962

'Fanal' × 'Masquerade'

'NIPHETOS'

OLD, TEA, WHITE, REPEAT-FLOWERING

This is a classic Tea Rose with very elongated, tapering buds that open to pure white blooms. They are quite remarkably delicate and are somewhat reminiscent of 'Maréchal Niel'. There is a pronounced tea fragrance. The foliage is pale green on a plant with a medium growth habit. In colder climates, this is a rose for the greenhouse. **'Climbing Niphetos'** sported from 'Niphetos' and was introduced by William Keynes and Co. in 1889. It is more vigorous than its parent and bears bigger flowers. ZONES 7–9.

Bougère, France, 1843

Parentage unknown

'NOBILO'S CHARDONNAY'

MACrelea

syns 'Chardonnay', 'Chardony', 'Peachy'

MODERN, LARGE-FLOWERED/HYBRID TEA, MEDIUM YELLOW, REPEAT-FLOWERING

This rose has brilliant orange-yellow flowers. The large, double blooms have 35 petals, are 4–5 in (10–12 cm) in diameter, and are high centered and symmetrical. The foliage is small and an attractive light green on a well-rounded, compact bush. The pollen parent is the result of crossing Kordes' 1974 orange-pink Large-flowered Rose 'Wienerwald' with Sam McGredy's 1979 yellow blend Large-flowered Rose 'Benson & Hedges Gold'. This cross succeeded in passing on the desirable characteristics of both these great roses. ZONES 5–10.

McGredy, New Zealand, 1984

'Freude' × ('Wienerwald' × 'Benson & Hedges Gold')

'NOBLE ANTONY'   AUSway

syn. 'Noble Anthony'

MODERN, MODERN SHRUB, MEDIUM RED, REPEAT-FLOWERING

The flowers of this rose are handsome, beautifully formed and full of petals, which reflex to make what the raiser describes as a 'deeply domed' flower of unusual shape. They are deep magenta-crimson and appear freely through summer and autumn on an upright plant, growing below the average height for a shrub rose. It therefore makes a useful and striking addition near the front of a shrub border. The variety yields a pleasing scent, which seems to vary in strength according to the stage of the bloom, and it grows upright with a rather uneven habit, furnished with somewhat sparse foliage. It may need protection in areas where black spot is likely to be a problem. 'Noble Antony' is also classified as an English Rose. ZONES 4–9.

Austin, UK, 1995

Parentage unknown

'NOBLESSE'

MODERN, LARGE-FLOWERED/HYBRID TEA, ORANGE-RED, REPEAT-FLOWERING

These clear orange-red flowers have 28 petals, are 4–5 in (10–12 cm) in diameter and have a light fragrance. The bloom form is decorative—it does not have classical high centers. The foliage is mid-

N

green and glossy on a short to medium bush. It is a winter-tender plant and lacks vigor. While the blooms are large and attractive, the foliage and height are poor, and it has disappeared from commerce. Perhaps the reason for the apparent weaknesses is the incestuous cross! ZONES 6–10.

Spek, The Netherlands, 1969

'Coloranja' × 'Coloranja'

'NOËLLA NABONNAND'
OLD, CLIMBING TEA, DARK RED

The large flowers of 'Noëlla Nabonnand' are semi-double with 21 petals and do not last long, either on the bush or as a cut flower. The sweetly scented blooms are a velvety crimson color and the petals have a soft velvety texture. This vigorous, medium climber is well-foliated. There is a considerable early flush and lighter periodical flowering thereafter. In warmer climates, there can also be winter blooms. It was named for a member of the breeder's family. ZONES 7–9.

Nabonnand, France, 1901

'Reine Marie Henriette' × 'Bardou Job'

'NORA CUNNINGHAM'
MODERN, LARGE-FLOWERED CLIMBER, LIGHT PINK, REPEAT-FLOWERING

These lovely pink flowers have paler centers. They are semi-double, cupped and fragrant and have an informal loose flower form. The blooms are borne in abundance on long straight stems.

'Nora Cunningham'

'Noëlla Nabonnand'

The wrinkled foliage is light green. It is a vigorous, free-blooming Climber spreading 10–12 ft (3–3.5 m), and repeat-flowers in certain climates. This rose is just one of many hybridized by Australian-born Alister Clark, who also gave the world 'Kitty Kininmonth', 'Daydream' and 'Scorcher', all of which became well loved in Australia. ZONES 5–11.

Clark, Australia, 1920

Seedling of 'Gustav Grünerwald'

'NORFOLK' POUlfolk
MODERN, GROUND COVER, MEDIUM YELLOW, REPEAT-FLOWERING

These small, delicately scented flowers are a medium non-fading bright yellow. The double blooms come in weatherproof clusters. The foliage is glossy green on a compact, low-growing plant that grows to about 18–24 in (45–60 cm). Because it produces an abundance of color throughout the growing season and indeed flowers all year long, this rose is a welcome addition to the Ground Cover classification. It suits small spaces and containers. ZONES 5–10.

Poulsen, Denmark, 1990

Parentage unknown

'NORRIS PRATT'
MODERN, LARGE-FLOWERED/HYBRID TEA, MEDIUM YELLOW, REPEAT-FLOWERING

These deep golden yellow flowers are large, double and star shaped when open. The foliage is medium green,

'Norfolk'

'Norris Pratt'

leathery and disease resistant. This is a very low-growing bush only attaining some 18 in (45 cm) in height. With the advent of superior yellow Large-flowered Roses, 'Norris Pratt' has entered the history books and is rarely grown now. ZONES 5–10.

Buisman, The Netherlands, 1964

'Mrs Pierre S. duPont' × 'Marcelle Gret'

'NORTHAMPTONSHIRE'
MATtdor
MODERN, GROUND COVER, WHITE/LIGHT PINK, REPEAT-FLOWERING

The pearly pink flowers of this rose have a light sweet fragrance. The florets are 1–2 in (25–50 mm) in diameter; they have a cupped form and are borne in large clusters on strong stems. A carpet of attractive semi-glossy, mid-green foliage is produced in abundance. This rose blooms all year long, providing a long-lasting tapestry of color in the garden, and is ideal for a sunny bank or just cascading over a terrace. It was named by John Mattock for a wonderful county north of London. ZONES 5–10.

Mattock, UK, 1990

Parentage unknown

Royal National Rose Society Certificate of Merit 1988

'NORTHERN LIGHTS'
MODERN, LARGE-FLOWERED/HYBRID TEA, YELLOW BLEND, REPEAT-FLOWERING

This variety has canary lemon flowers with a suffusion of rose pink on the outer petals. The large blooms are over 5 in (12 cm) across, have 50 petals and are very fragrant. They have perfect classical high centers with great symmetry. The blooms are borne one to a stem and later in the growing season in small

'Northamptonshire'

'Northern Lights'

clusters and trusses. They are ideal for exhibition at rose shows or cutting for indoors since, because of the large petal count, they are extremely long lasting. The foliage is deep green and very glossy on a vigorous plant of medium height. The hybridizer lived in an area of Scotland where the Northern Lights could be seen. ZONES 4–10.

Cocker, UK, 1969

'Fragrant Cloud' × 'Kingcup'

'NORWICH CASTLE'
MODERN, CLUSTER-FLOWERED/FLORIBUNDA, ORANGE BLEND, REPEAT-FLOWERING

Shapely buds on this variety open to rich copper-orange flowers that gradually change with age to a soft apricot. The double florets have 30 petals, a faint but detectable fruity fragrance, and are borne in small dense clusters. The blooms open from high centers to reveal a charming flat rosette. They are excellent cut flowers and there is a consistent supply of blooms throughout the growing season. The foliage is shiny medium green on a vigorous, upright plant. It is winter hardy and can tolerate most soil types including clay. In naming this rose Peter Beales paid homage to the great Norman castle, now a museum that dominates the East Anglian capital of Norwich, his home town. ZONES 5–10.

Beales, UK, 1980

('Whisky Mac' × 'Arthur Bell') × 'Bettina'

'NORWICH UNION'
MODERN, CLUSTER-FLOWERED/FLORIBUNDA, MEDIUM YELLOW, REPEAT-FLOWERING

The flowers of this rose are a cheerful deep clear yellow, which pales to lemon with age. They are quite large, borne in clusters on upright stems, and open cupped, with a pleasant, refreshing fragrance. As a garden rose, this can be used for bedding, in borders and to make a neat hedge, and is suitable to cut for the house. The flowers continue to appear through summer and autumn on a plant of below average height with a stocky, upright habit and bright green, glossy leaves. It was named for an international insurance company founded in Norwich in 1797. ZONES 4–9.

Beales, UK, 1976

'Arthur Bell' × (seedling × 'Allgold')

'NOUVEAU VULCAIN'
OLD, GALLICA, MAUVE

This rose, which flowers after midsummer, has very full, flat blooms that

'Norwich Union'

'Nozomi'

'Nozomi'

are rich crimson flushed and veined with purple. They are very fragrant. It is a typical Gallica of medium to tall height, and is prone to suckering. The oldest surviving catalogues which list it are those of Belgian growers in the 1840s. ZONES 4–9.

Pre-1843

Parentage unknown

'NOVA ZEMBLA'
MODERN, HYBRID RUGOSA, WHITE

The flowers of this flesh pink to nearly white rose are strongly fragrant. The double florets are large—4 in (10 cm) across—and come in large clusters on strong stems that need no additional support. The foliage is deep dark green on a vigorous plant that can grow to 9 ft (2.7 m) high, making it ideal as a pillar rose. Although it blooms only once at the very beginning of the season, the display of rosehips later in autumn provides a dramatic tapestry of orange-red for most of winter. ZONES 4–10.

Mees, UK, 1907

Sport of 'Conrad Ferdinand Meyer'

'Norwich Castle'

'NOZOMI'
syn. 'Heideröslein Nozomi'
MODERN, CLIMBING MINIATURE, LIGHT PINK

The buds on this rose open to little, pale pink, single flowers that lighten to pearly pink. They are borne in trusses amid the small, glossy dark foliage, and have a light scent. The plant has a trailing habit and can be used as a climber or a ground cover. The blooms are produced on the previous year's wood, so only light pruning is recommended. 'Nozomi' means hope and was the name of the raiser's niece who died aged four. ZONES 5–10.

Onodera, Japan, 1968

'Fairy Princess' (1955 variety) × 'Sweet Fairy'

Royal Horticultural Society Award of Garden Merit 1993

'Nova Zembla'

'Nur Mahal'

'Nuits de Young'

'Nyveldt's White'

N O

'NUITS DE YOUNG'
OLD, MOSS, DARK RED

This is one of the darkest colored of all roses. The mossy buds open to small, roundly oval flowers that are borne in small clusters. The fragrant blooms are about 1½ in (4 cm) across. They are deep blackcurrant purple with grayish overtones, and the whole effect of each fully open flower is that of velvet. When fully open they reveal a small group of golden yellow stamens. It is a slender growing though dense shrub, relaxed in habit, to around 4 ft (1.2 m) high and wide. The stems are thornless but are densely covered with purplish brown, stubbly moss, and the leaves are rich dark green. This is a superb old variety that is most rewarding in spite of its relatively short flowering season in early summer. ZONES 4–10.

Laffay, France, 1845

Parentage unknown

'NUR MAHAL'
MODERN, MODERN SHRUB, MEDIUM RED, REPEAT-FLOWERING

The bright crimson flowers have a strong musk scent. The semi-double florets are borne in clusters on strong straight stems. The small foliage is dark green on a vigorous bush with pillar-type growth to 8–10 ft (2.4–3 m). It is a very pleasing bush that with pruning can be trained to be a medium-sized plant that is disease free. Pemberton named this rose after the powerful wife of Emperor Jahangir of India, whom legend credits with the discovery of 'Attar of Roses'. ZONES 5–10.

Pemberton, UK, 1923

'Château de Clos Vougeot' × Seedling of Hybrid Musk

'NURIA DE RECOLONS'
OLD, HYBRID PERPETUAL, WHITE, REPEAT-FLOWERING

This is now an obscure rose and therefore very hard to come by. The date of origin is very late for a Hybrid Perpetual, a class that had long been out of fashion by the 1930s. Although the white flowers have good form, they lack fragrance. 'Nuria de Recolons' reportedly has the greatest thrip resistance of any white rose. ZONES 5–9.

Dot, Spain, 1933

'Canigo' × 'Frau Karl Druschki'

'NYMPHENBURG'
MODERN, MODERN SHRUB, ORANGE-PINK, REPEAT-FLOWERING

Apricot-pink buds on this variety open to flowers that are a soft salmon-pink shaded orange towards the outer edges of the petals. The center is yellow. The blooms tend to fade with age to a paler blended color. The fragrant florets are large, semi-double, and come in small and large clusters. The foliage is large, glossy and dark green on a vigorous, upright bush growing 10 ft (3 m) tall or more. It is free flowering and easy to maintain and provides an abundance of blooms, as the repeat-flowering is good. When he named this rose, Wilhelm Kordes paid tribute to the palace and gardens of the city of Nymphenburg which is just outside Munich and which has become a popular tourist attraction. ZONES 4–10.

Kordes, Germany, 1954

'Sangerhausen' × 'Sunmist'

National Rose Society Trial Ground Certificate 1954

'Nymphenburg'

'NYVELDT'S WHITE'
MODERN, HYBRID RUGOSA, WHITE, REPEAT-FLOWERING

These beautiful single-petalled snow-white flowers have golden yellow stamens. The blooms are large and have a very sweet fragrance. The foliage is dark green on a vigorous plant that reaches 7 ft (2.1 m) high. It flowers continuously but if left ungroomed a tremendous crop of orange-red hips will appear. This rose is winter hardy and shade tolerant, making it suitable for hedge architecture. ZONES 4–10.

Nyveldt, The Netherlands, 1955

(Rosa rugosa rubra × R. cinnamomea) × R. nitida

'OAKINGTON RUBY'
MODERN, MINIATURE, MEDIUM RED, REPEAT-FLOWERING

The buds of 'Oakington Ruby' open to deep crimson petals that unfurl into ruby-crimson flowers with a white eye. These double blooms grow on a dwarf, compact bush that will only grow to 12 in (30 cm) high in cool climates. This rose has played a key role in the development of modern Miniature Roses. As the story goes, an old lady living in Oakington, England, found the plant growing in the gardens of the nearby Cathedral at Ely. In those early days, Miniature Roses were a largely undiscovered group, and so this rose, named for its color and place of discovery, was a precious find. 'Oakington Ruby' subsequently played a pivotal role in breeding along with 'Rouletii' and 'Tom Thumb'. Although the true parentage is unknown, it has been suggested that it was the result of crossing 'Rouletii' with a red Polyantha. Whatever its genesis, it certainly has a great historical significance. ZONES 4–10.

1933

Parentage unknown

'OAKMONT'
OLD, HYBRID PERPETUAL, PINK BLEND

This is one of the tall-growing Hybrid Perpetual Roses that flowers profusely in early summer. The flowers are a clear pink. It is not easily obtainable these days. ZONES 5–9.

May, 1893

Parentage unknown

'OCTAVIA HILL'   HARzeal
MODERN, CLUSTER-FLOWERED/FLORIBUNDA, MEDIUM PINK, REPEAT-FLOWERING

The clear medium pink flowers of this variety contain an astonishing 75 petals. They have a moderate Damask fragrance and come in small sprays of neatly spaced blooms. The blooms are about 3 in (8 cm) in diameter and have a double quartered form. The foliage is a semi-glossy, dark green on a medium-sized compact bush. It is a fairly vigorous plant, but requires removal of spent blooms to initiate the next bloom cycle and promote new growth. The flowers are ideal for cutting as they last a long time. ZONES 5–10.

Harkness, UK, 1995

'Armada' × 'Cornelia'

Courtrai Silver Medal 1995, The Hague Certificate of Merit 1998

'OCTAVIUS WELD'
OLD, TEA, PINK BLEND, REPEAT-FLOWERING

'Octavius Weld' was found on a grave in Blakiston, South Australia, and given the name on the tombstone. In the late nineteenth century, South Australian gardeners imported bare-root roses from England and vied with one another over their collections of all kinds of plants. 'Octavius Weld' was probably imported in the 1890s. It grows quickly into a huge bush as wide as it is tall, with matt mid-green pointed leaflets. The flowers are very variable; in spring they can be rose pink, in summer soft pink tinged with cream, and in autumn and winter the color of clotted cream. They are produced continuously, both singly and in small clusters. Long buds develop into very flat blooms with short petaloids in the center. The petal count varies from 25 to 40. The scent is typically Tea Rose. Repeat-bloom is rapid, even when spent blooms are not removed. In mild winters it may continue to flower. Mildew can be a slight problem in autumn. This is a lovely Tea Rose, but it is not grown outside Australia. ZONES 5–9.

Parentage unknown

'Octavia Hill'

'Oakmont'

'Octavius Weld'

'Octavius Weld'

'ŒILLET FLAMAND'
OLD, GALLICA, PINK BLEND

This rose resembles a pink carnation in shape. It is a conventional once-flowering Gallica. The flowers are pale pink, striped white and brighter pink. They are very double and very fragrant. The foliage is coarse and dark green on a plant with a vigorous, upright growth habit. Peter Beales has called it an 'interesting' rose. ZONES 4–9.

Vibert, France, 1845

Parentage unknown

'ŒILLET PANACHÉE'
syn. 'Striped Moss'
OLD, MOSS, PINK BLEND

The fragrant flowers of this rose are small, pale pink, and striped with vivid crimson ('panachée' means 'striped'). It is a small, upright shrub that grows to about 3 ft (1 m) and resembles a mossy Gallica. It is not very vigorous. This rose is suitable for growing in a container. ZONES 4–10.

Verdier, France, 1888

Parentage unknown

'ŒILLET PARFAIT'
OLD, GALLICA, PINK BLEND

'Œillet Parfait' is a good if little-grown rose. The fragrant flowers are 1½–2 in (4–5 cm) across and are borne in small erect clusters. They are rich pink, paling to soft pink, and are fully double and cushion-like when fully open. This is a compact, tidy, fairly upright shrub to 3 ft (1 m) high, marginally taller in good soil. The thin, dark green shoots are well endowed with thorns and prickles, and the foliage is round, mid- to light green and quite small. It seems to prefer good soil and some mollycoddling to give of its best. ZONES 4–10.

Foulard, France, 1841

Parentage unknown

'OKLAHOMA'
MODERN, LARGE-FLOWERED/HYBRID TEA, DARK RED, REPEAT-FLOWERING

This rose has long, pointed, ovoid buds that open to very dark red flowers with high centers and excellent symmetry. The florets are 5 in (12 cm) across, double with 45 petals and are very fragrant. They are borne one to a stem. The foliage is dark matt green on an extremely vigorous bush that grows as high as 7–8 ft (2.1–2.4 m) in one season. It does best in temperate climates: too much heat will scorch the dark red blooms and too much cold will turn them magenta. Its color and heavy scent have made this a very popular rose. It derives its name from the state of Oklahoma in the USA; the translation is 'Red Man's Land'. There are two versions of 'Climbing Oklahoma'; in 1968 the

'Œillet Flamand'

original breeders came out with the first climber, then in 1972 A. Ross & Son in Australia introduced the second. The vigor and performance of both climbers is excellent. ZONES 5–10.

Swim and Weeks, USA, 1964

'Chrysler Imperial' × 'Charles Mallerin'

Japan Gold Medal 1963

'OLAVE BADEN-POWELL'
MODERN, LARGE-FLOWERED/HYBRID TEA, MEDIUM RED, REPEAT-FLOWERING

The lovely flowers of this rose are a scarlet cardinal red. The blooms reach over 5 in (12 cm) across and have a very light fragrance. The foliage is dark green and leathery in texture. 'Olave Baden Powell' is no longer available commercially and can only be observed in the gardens of certain museums and estates. ZONES 4–10.

Tantau, Germany, 1972

Parentage unknown

'OLD BLUSH'
syns 'Common Blush China', 'Common Monthly', 'Old Pink Daily ', 'Old Pink Monthly', 'Parsons' Pink China'
OLD, CHINA, MEDIUM PINK, REPEAT-FLOWERING

This is the most common of the China Roses that were brought to Europe from China, initiating the great revolution in rose breeding by introducing the repeat-flowering factor into once-flowering old European roses. The light pink, semi-double flowers are smallish and muddled and they have a slight fragrance that is reminiscent of sweet peas. It is a slow-growing, medium-sized, twiggy bush that is almost thornless. 'Old Blush' is said to be Thomas Moore's 'last rose of summer'. 'Climbing Old Blush' is the same as its parent in all respects, except that it climbs very high and is suitable for pergolas and arches. ZONES 6–9.

Mid-1700s

Parentage unknown

'OLD GLORY'   BENday
MODERN, MINIATURE, MEDIUM RED, REPEAT-FLOWERING

The stunning bright red flowers of this rose age gracefully to blood red then to crimson, and when fully opened they look gorgeous with contrasting yellow stamens. The blooms are double, with about two dozen petals, and have perfect symmetry of form, which makes them suitable for exhibition. They are normally borne singly, but small sprays can develop in warm climates. In some climates the red color is replaced with a deep pink; in warmer weather the flowers open with the speed of light. The foliage is semi-glossy and dark green on a tall, vigorous, compact plant. 'Old Glory' won Champion Miniature Bloom at Rose World 1994 in Christchurch, New Zealand. It had been brought there all the way from sunny California by an enthusiastic exhibitor. ZONES 4–10.

Benardella, USA, 1988

'Rise 'n' Shine' × 'Harmonie'

American Rose Society Award of Excellence 1988

'Olave Baden-Powell'

'Old Blush'

'Œillet Panachée'

O

'Olé'

'Old Port'

'OLD JOHN'   DICwillynilly

MODERN, CLUSTER-FLOWERED/FLORIBUNDA, ORANGE-RED, REPEAT-FLOWERING

This new, vibrant and fiery orange-red Cluster-flowered Rose was named as a tribute to John Mattock, who has spent a lifetime in growing roses in the UK. Its blooms come in medium-sized clusters of 5–10, and appear against dark green foliage. The golden yellow stamens give a value-added effect when the blooms are fully open. ZONES 5–10.

Dickson, UK, 1998

Dublin Certificate of Merit 1997

'Sunseeker' × 'New Horizon'

'OLD MASTER'   MACesp

MODERN, CLUSTER-FLOWERED/FLORIBUNDA, RED BLEND, REPEAT-FLOWERING

The flowers of this variety are a striking combination of carmine with a silver eye and reverse. The florets have only 15 petals but what a color display—this is one of the first hand-painted creations from pioneer Sam McGredy. The fragrant blooms are large and reach about 4–5 in (10–12 cm) in diameter. They are borne in medium-sized sprays that add a bright color display to any garden. The foliage is semi-glossy, medium green on a vigorous bushy plant with good disease-resistant characteristics. It is winter hardy and will tolerate most soil types and climates. With 'Old Master', Sam McGredy opened up a new avenue of breeding, bringing the rose world yet another dimension in color to admire. ZONES 4–10.

McGredy, New Zealand, 1974

'Maxi' × ('Evelyn Fison' × ['Orange Sweetheart' × 'Frühlingsmorgen'])

Royal National Rose Society Trial Ground Certificate 1973

'OLD PORT'   MACkati

MODERN, CLUSTER-FLOWERED/FLORIBUNDA, MAUVE, REPEAT-FLOWERING

The flowers of 'Old Port' are a wonderful blend of red and mauve rather than purple. The double florets have 26–40 petals and an interesting flower form—old-fashioned quartered. The blooms are

'Oldtimer'

very fragrant. In hot climates the color can fade to a grayish blend and most rose growers plant this in partial shade to help sustain the beautiful color. The foliage is matt medium green on a bushy plant. In some cool climates vigor has been reported as poor; it does much better in temperate zones. Spraying to protect the plant from black spot is recommended. ZONES 5–10.

McGredy, New Zealand, 1990

(['Anytime' × 'Eyepaint'] × 'Purple Splendour') × 'Big Purple'

'OLDTIMER'   KORol

syns 'Coppertone', 'Old Time', 'Old Timer'

MODERN, LARGE-FLOWERED/HYBRID TEA, ORANGE BLEND, REPEAT-FLOWERING

The alternative name, 'Coppertone', is probably a better one, as the blooms often appear as a copper-tan color with orange highlights. The long pointed buds open to high-centered, old gold colored flowers with excellent symmetry. They are 5 in (12 cm) across and have a sweet fragrance. The foliage is glossy medium green on a vigorous, well-rounded plant. It is easy to grow and maintain but it prefers a warm spot in full sun in the garden, where it can perform at its best. This rose is winter hardy and has excellent disease resistance. It has been popular with rose growers all over the world for more than 30 years. ZONES 4–10.

Kordes, Germany, 1969

'Chantré' × 'Bronze Masterpiece'

'OLÉ'

MODERN, LARGE-FLOWERED/HYBRID TEA, ORANGE-RED, REPEAT-FLOWERING

'Olé' is also classified as a Grandiflora. The fragrant, ruffled flowers are a bright lipstick orange-red. The flowers are very double with more than 50 petals, and usually have classical high centers with good symmetry but can be cupped and

informal in warm climates. They tend to grow as elegant clusters of 5–8 blooms on strong, straight, upright stems. The color can range from warm crimson overlaid with orange to various luminous hues of red. The ruffled petals resemble carnations and the flowers are long lasting. The holly-like foliage is very disease resistant. **'Climbing Olé'** was discovered in 1982 by George Haight from San Jose, California. It grows to a height of 10–12 ft (3–3.5 m) and can be trained to cover a fence, wall or railing. ZONES 5–10.

Armstrong, USA, 1964

'Roundelay' × 'El Capitan'

'OLIVE'   HARpillar

MODERN, CLUSTER-FLOWERED/FLORIBUNDA, MEDIUM RED, REPEAT-FLOWERING

These double flowers are a rich ox-blood red color with the outer petals often ruffled. Each bloom has 36 petals and there is a spicy fragrance. The weatherproof blooms are large and have good high symmetrical centers. They are borne in small clusters with a pleasing inflorescence. They are long lasting as cut flowers. The foliage is large and glossy green on a vigorous bush with lots of branching growth, which promotes increased flower production. In some climates it wants to grow like a small pillar. ZONES 5–10.

Harkness, UK, 1982

(['Vera Dalton' × 'Highlight'] × seedling) × 'Dublin Bay'

Geneva Prize 1978

'OLYMPIAD'   MACauck

syn. 'Olympiode'

MODERN, LARGE-FLOWERED/HYBRID TEA, MEDIUM RED, REPEAT-FLOWERING

These flowers are a brilliant medium red that does not fade in the heat. They are double with 35 petals and have no fragrance. The blooms are large and elegantly shaped and come one to a stem, making it a great variety for entering in rose shows. The petals tend to burn a little in very hot climates. The foliage is medium matt green on a vigorous, bushy, disease-resistant plant. It made a stunning debut in 1984 when thousands of plants graced the streets and public gardens of Los Angeles, California, for everyone attending the Olympic Games to admire. ZONES 5–10.

McGredy, New Zealand, 1982

'Red Planet' × 'Pharaoh'

All-America Rose Selection 1984, Portland Gold Medal 1985

'Olympiad'

'Olympiad'

'Old Master'

'OLYMPIC TORCH'

syns 'Sei-ka', 'Seika'

MODERN, LARGE-FLOWERED/HYBRID TEA, RED BLEND, REPEAT-FLOWERING

The long pointed buds of this rose open to red and white flowers with a touch of gold at the center becoming all red with age. The flower form is high centered with good symmetry, but the double flowers have no fragrance. The foliage is glossy bronze and leathery on a very vigorous medium-sized, winter-hardy bush. In Japan 'Seika', the alternative name, means 'sacred fire'. This large and shapely rose honored the holding of the 1966 Olympic Games in Tokyo in both languages. ZONES 5–10.

Suzuki, Japan, 1966

'Rose Gaujard' × 'Crimson Glory'

New Zealand Gold Medal 1971

'OLYMPIC TRIUMPH'

MODERN, CLUSTER-FLOWERED/FLORIBUNDA, RED BLEND, REPEAT-FLOWERING

These red and yellow flowers open to salmon-orange flat blooms. They are double and have a faint scent. The blooms can be quite large, reaching a size of 4–5 in (10–12 cm) across, and are borne one to a stem or in small clusters. The foliage is sage green on an upright, vigorous plant. This wonderful rose never really became popular outside Europe and is unfortunately all but forgotten. ZONES 5–10.

Dickson, UK, 1973

'Shiralee' × 'Apricot Nectar'

'Olympic Torch'

'OMAR KHAYYÁM'

OLD, DAMASK, LIGHT PINK

The double flowers of this rose emerge from feathery buds and are about 2 in (5 cm) across. The rather spiky petals are sometimes arranged to give a quartered effect. The fragrant flowers display a prominent button eye when fully open. Seldom achieving a height of 3 ft (1 m), this twiggy upright shrub has a somewhat erratic growth habit. Its gray-green shoots are viciously armed with variously sized thorns. The soft foliage is a grayish light green. It is excellent as a container plant, and looks great in mixed borders. Over 100 years ago, seeds from the rose on Omar Khayyam's grave in Nashipur in Iran were brought to England and planted on the grave of his translator, Edward Fitzgerald. ZONES 4–10.

1893

Parentage unknown

'Olympic Triumph'

'OMBRÉE PARFAITE'

OLD, GALLICA, MAUVE

The flowers of this rose are quite variable, the same trusses bearing blooms of different shades ranging from pink to purple. The scented blooms are very double. It is a short-growing, tidy bush, suitable for a border. ZONES 4–9.

Vibert, France, 1823

A Gallica × a Centifolia

'ONDELLA'   MEIvanama

MODERN, LARGE-FLOWERED/HYBRID TEA, ORANGE-RED, REPEAT-FLOWERING

'Ondella' has conical buds that open to large vermilion-colored flowers. The double florets have 33 petals and only a little scent. The flower form is elegant and shapely. The foliage is dark green on a vigorous, tall, upright plant. This rose was bred essentially for the cut-flower trade and is rarely seen growing in an

'Ondella'

'Ondella'

outdoor setting. Meilland released a second **'Ondella'** (MEIrokad) in 1994 that is a dark red Cluster-flowered Rose. ZONES 5–10.

Meilland, France, 1979

('Elegy' × 'Arturo Toscanini') × ('Peace' × 'Demain')

'ONKAPARINGA'

MODERN, MODERN SHRUB, APRICOT BLEND, REPEAT-FLOWERING

'Onkaparinga' produces clusters of large, well-formed, apricot-pink flowers that turn pink as they age. Flower production is good with pleasing continuity and fragrance. The plant has matt foliage, a tall and very spreading growth habit, and is disease resistant. ZONES 5–10.

Thomson, Australia, 1987

'Cymbaline' × 'Troilus'

'OPAL BRÜNNER'

MODERN, CLUSTER-FLOWERED CLIMBER, LIGHT PINK

The light pink to rose, double flowers of this rose from California develop from very small buds. They appear in large clusters that have a slight musky scent. 'Opal Brünner' was introduced as a 'Cécile Brünner' look-alike. ZONES 4–10.

Marshall, USA, 1948

Parentage unknown

'OPEN ARMS'   CHEwpixcel

MODERN, RAMBLER, LIGHT PINK, REPEAT-FLOWERING

The flowers of this rose have 6–14 shell pink petals, and are carried in huge, fragrant clusters much like a hydrangea. The foliage is glossy dark green and disease resistant, and there are prickles on the stems. The variety can spread out nicely in all directions. ZONES 4–10.

Warner, UK, 1996

'Mary Sumner' × 'Laura Ashley'

Royal National Rose Society Certificate of Merit 1993

'Opening Night'

'Onkaparinga'

'OPENING NIGHT'   JAColber

MODERN, LARGE-FLOWERED/HYBRID TEA, RED BLEND, REPEAT-FLOWERING

The clear crimson buds of this rose unfold to reveal a lush display of velvety red petals that age to an attractive deep pink. The double florets have 25–30 petals and a light fragrance, and grow singly on strong straight stems. They are quite long lasting. The blooms are high centered and have a very symmetrical form, especially in cooler climates. The foliage is dark green and disease resistant and the plant has a vigorous, tall, upright habit. This is a great overall performer in the garden. Bred from two great red Large-flowered Roses, it has captured the attention of the rose-buying public in the USA. ZONES 5–10.

Zary, USA, 1998

'Olympiad' × 'Ingrid Bergman'

All-America Rose Selection 1998

'OPERA'

MODERN, LARGE-FLOWERED/HYBRID TEA, RED BLEND, REPEAT-FLOWERING

The long, pointed buds of this rose open to reveal light scarlet-red flowers with a yellow base to the petals. The double florets are loose and informal. They are large, with a diameter of 6 in (15 cm), and are supported by extremely strong stems. Bloom production is fairly abundant, but the color can fade in hot sun. The foliage is light green and leathery on an erect and vigorous plant. Susceptible to mildew and black spot if left unprotected, it needs regular spraying. 'Opera' is winter hardy, responding well to

'Orange Bunny'

severe pruning in most climates, and makes a lovely cut flower for indoors. ZONES 4–10.

Gaujard, France, 1950

'La Belle Irisée' × seedling

National Rose Society Gold Medal 1949

'OPHELIA'

MODERN, LARGE-FLOWERED/HYBRID TEA, LIGHT PINK, REPEAT-FLOWERING

'Ophelia' has elegant, double, marshmallow pink flowers with lemon centers. The fragrant blooms have 28 petals and are borne on long, straight, strong stems in clusters. The foliage is leathery on a vigorous, upright plant; the exact origin and parentage is a mystery. Whatever its source, it was extensively used to create

'Orange Flame'

'Orange Fire'

'Ophelia'

even more great roses. It also has 35 sports to its credit. Named after Shakespeare's tragic heroine, this rose has achieved immortality. **'Climbing Ophelia'** (Dickson, UK, 1920) grows to 10–12 ft (3–3.5 m). ZONES 5–10.

William, Paul & Son, UK, 1912

Possibly a chance seedling of 'Antoine Rivoire'

'ORANGE BUNNY'   MEIrianopur

MODERN, CLUSTER-FLOWERED/FLORIBUNDA, ORANGE-RED, REPEAT-FLOWERING

This rose has pointed buds that open to orange-red flowers with a darker reverse. The florets are semi-double with 13 petals and a cupped form and are borne in clusters of up to 25 blooms. They have a light fragrance and are surrounded by matt bronze foliage. The upright, compact bush is disease resistant. ZONES 5–10.

Meilland, France, 1979

'Scherzo' × ('Sarabande' × 'Frenzy')

'ORANGE CASCADE'

MODERN, CLIMBING MINIATURE, ORANGE BLEND, REPEAT-FLOWERING

'Orange Cascade' has pointed buds that open to give yellow-orange, double flowers of 20 petals. They are fragrant and are borne in small clusters on a willowy plant. It develops into a plant that produces sufficient flowers to make a pleasing display. The blooms tend to open fast and shatter quickly. ZONES 5–10.

Moore, USA, 1979

Yellow seedling × 'Magic Wand'

'ORANGE FIRE'

MODERN, MINIATURE, ORANGE-PINK, REPEAT-FLOWERING

The short pointed buds develop into small flowers that are a mixture of orange and shades of pink to carmine. They are double, with 40 petals, and are produced in small, well-spaced clusters amid the glossy, leathery, dark foliage. The growth is bushy and upright, and flower production is adequate with a quick repeat. Unfortunately, the older flowers fade to a rather dirty color—a fault that was inherited from 'Floradora'. ZONES 5–9.

Moore, USA, 1974

(*Rosa wichuraiana* × 'Floradora') × 'Fire Princess'

'ORANGE FLAME'
MODERN, LARGE-FLOWERED/HYBRID TEA, ORANGE-RED, REPEAT-FLOWERING

The pointed, ovoid buds of 'Orange Flame' open to reveal fresh orange-red flowers. The double florets are large at 5 in (12 cm) across. They have 33 petals and are fragrant. The bloom form is high centered and symmetrical, but the flowers often lose their form and can ball and show split centers, especially in cool and wet climates. The foliage is leathery and glossy on a tall, vigorous plant covered with vicious thorns. It needs heat to perform well. Although the blooms have good substance, the plant really needs several seasons to establish itself to produce abundant blooms all year long. ZONES 5–10.

Meilland, France, 1963

'Monte Carlo' × 'Radar'

'ORANGE HONEY'
MODERN, MINIATURE, ORANGE BLEND, REPEAT-FLOWERING

This rose carries pointed buds that open to reveal yellow-amber petals that unfurl to pure orange-yellow, double flowers of about 23 petals. They have a fruity fragrance and symmetrical high centers, but are usually more cupped. As the blooms age they develop a reddish color, which gives the rose an autumn effect. Flower production is prolific and the plant is covered in brilliant orange at most times. It has a spreading habit, which makes it an ideal choice for an eye-catching hanging basket. If grown in partial shade the bright orange color can be maintained for weeks. ZONES 5–11.

Moore, USA, 1979

'Rumba' × 'Over the Rainbow'

'ORANGE MIST'
MODERN, CLUSTER-FLOWERED/FLORIBUNDA, ORANGE BLEND, REPEAT-FLOWERING

'Orange Mist' has flowers that are orange-salmon to yellow-orange. They are extremely large, with a 4 in (10 cm) diameter. They have a cupped form and are fragrant. The foliage is matt green and disease resistant. Although the plant has a dwarf growth habit, it provides an overwhelming number of clusters. This

'Orange Mist'

rose was never introduced into commerce for the rose-buying public; it was grown mainly as a greenhouse variety for cut flowers. ZONES 6–11.

Boerner, USA, 1957

'Ma Perkins' × seedling

'ORANGE RUMBA'
MODERN, CLUSTER-FLOWERED/FLORIBUNDA, ORANGE BLEND, REPEAT-FLOWERING

This rose has ovoid buds that open to medium-sized flowers that are bright orange with red flushes. The double florets contain 35 petals. They are cupped and have a light fragrance. The blooms come in small clusters with a remarkable degree of abundance. The foliage is a glossy dark green on a medium-sized compact bush. It was never available commercially, but was grown as a cut flower to be sold by florists. ZONES 5–10.

Zieger, USA, 1962

Sport of 'Rumba'

'ORANGE SENSATION'
MODERN, CLUSTER-FLOWERED/FLORIBUNDA, ORANGE-RED, REPEAT-FLOWERING

These orange-vermilion-red flowers are flushed slightly darker at the edges. The double florets have 24 petals, are 3 in (8 cm) across and have a marked scent. The blooms come in wonderfully shaped clusters that are long lasting and weatherproof. The foliage is light green on a very vigorous bush that grows to about 3 ft (1 m) high with some spreading. It is beautiful from bud to fully open bloom, easily making it a winner at most international rose trial grounds. It needs little maintenance and care. **'Climbing Orange Sensation'**, which can be trained onto walls or pillars, is very similar to its parent, although it may be less inclined to repeat-flower. ZONES 5–10.

de Ruiter, The Netherlands, 1961

'Amor' × 'Fashion'

National Rose Society Gold Medal 1961, Golden Rose of The Hague 1968

'ORANGE SILK'
MODERN, CLUSTER-FLOWERED/FLORIBUNDA, ORANGE-RED, REPEAT-FLOWERING

These large, orange-vermilion flowers have a shallow cupped bloom form and come in large clusters on strong straight stems. They have a light fragrance. While the large flowers can have high centers and symmetry on occasions, they usually open rather loosely with little change in color. The foliage is dark glossy green on a vigorous bush. This rose repeats

'Climbing Orange Sensation'

'Orange Rumba'

'Orange Sweetheart'

'Orange Silk'

quickly and is easy to grow. It is a seedling from the Cluster-flowered Rose 'Orangeade'. ZONES 5–10.

McGredy, UK, 1968

'Orangeade' × ('Ma Perkins' × 'Independence')

'ORANGE SUNBLAZE'   MEIjikatar
syns 'Orange Meillandina', 'Sunblaze'
MODERN, MINIATURE, ORANGE-RED, REPEAT-FLOWERING

This rose has flowers are that brilliant orange, unmatched in the plant world for vividness. They are normally borne singly or in small clusters. The double flowers of 35 petals have a decorative cupped form that is complemented by the petite, pointed, matt light green foliage. The blooms are normally borne in small clusters of 1–5 florets. 'Orange Sunblaze' is an upright and compact rose with a fast repeat-bloom; it is an excellent choice to brighten up the garden and, when grown in a container, it can provide a long succession of small sprays of brilliant color all year round. ZONES 5–10.

Meilland, France, 1982

'Parador' × ('Baby Bettina' × 'Duchess of Windsor')

'ORANGE SUNSHINE'
MODERN, MINIATURE, ORANGE BLEND

'Orange Sunshine' seems to be incorrectly named, as the flowers are a coppery gold color. They are small, almost double with 18–20 petals, and open quickly from long buds to full blooms that show a central boss of stamens. There is quite a good fragrance—a rare thing in a Miniature bred over 30 years ago. Growth is compact and bushy. There can be a mildew problem at times,

'Orange Sunblaze'

especially on the stems, and repeat-bloom can be a little slow. The foliage is small and matt mid-green. ZONES 5–10.

Moore, USA, 1968

Sport of 'Bit o' Sunshine'

'ORANGE SWEETHEART'
MODERN, CLUSTER-FLOWERED/FLORIBUNDA, ORANGE-PINK, REPEAT-FLOWERING

When the ovoid buds open, they reveal large, clear orange-pink flowers. The double florets contain 20–25 petals and have a light fruity fragrance. The foliage is dark green on an upright, compact bush. This rose is just one of many great Cluster-flowered Roses from the master breeder, Gene Boerner, who helped pioneer the introduction and popularity of this class. Although it is no longer available to the rose-buying public, it can be seen in many historic old gardens and estates. ZONES 5–10.

Boerner, USA, 1952

Seedling of 'Pinocchio' × 'Fashion'

O

'Orangeade'

'Orangeade'

'Orchid Lace'

'ORANGE TRIUMPH'

MODERN, POLYANTHA, MEDIUM RED, REPEAT-FLOWERING

These fragrant, deep orange-red flowers are borne in very large clusters. The small florets have a cupped form and clusters are provided in abundance all year long. They last remarkably well, and are weather resistant. The foliage is glossy green on a compact, vigorous, winter-hardy plant that grows to 4–5 ft (1.2–1.5 m) tall. This rose is considered historically important because its wonderful characteristics have been successfully passed on to its many progeny. 'Climbing Orange Triumph' was introduced in 1945 by Leenders of Holland. It grows to some 10–12 ft (3–3.5 m) and can be easily trained to cover a fence, wall or railing. In 1953 Jacob Maarse from the USA introduced 'Orange Triumph Superba', an orange blend Polyantha. In 1960, F. Cant of England introduced an improved orange-red non-climbing Polyantha of 'Orange Triumph' called 'Orange Triumph Improved'. ZONES 4–10.

Kordes, Germany, 1937

'Eva' × 'Solarium'

Royal National Rose Society Gold Medal 1937

'ORANGEADE'

MODERN, CLUSTER-FLOWERED/FLORIBUNDA, ORANGE-RED, REPEAT-FLOWERING

These flowers are such a bright orange-red that the color can sometimes overwhelm the eye. The semi-double flowers have a light fragrance and are borne in magnificent clusters. With age the blooms grow a little darker, bringing an even stronger color contrast with the golden yellow stamens at the open bloom stage. It is a vigorous upright bush that grows to about 4–5 ft (1.2–1.5 m) tall in warmer climates, and is very tolerant of less than perfect growing conditions. 'Climbing Orangeade' (Waterhouse Nursery, UK, 1964) is a climbing sport. ZONES 5–10.

McGredy, UK, 1959

'Orange Sweetheart' × 'Independence'

National Rose Society Gold Medal 1959, Portland Gold Medal 1965

'ORANGES AND LEMONS'

MACoranlem

syn. 'Papagena'

MODERN, LARGE-FLOWERED/HYBRID TEA, ORANGE BLEND, REPEAT-FLOWERING

These flowers have distinctive stripes of yellow and orange, showing off the hand-painted qualities that have become the signature of this breeder. The blooms are full, with 24–40 petals, and are borne in wonderful clusters on strong straight stems. The bloom production is excellent in most climates. The foliage is a mahogany-tinted, glossy dark green and is resistant to all rose diseases. The plant habit is dominated by tall arching canes 6–10 ft (1.8–3 m) tall and it can be trained as a climber, a pillar or just left to form a giant fountain of color. 'Oranges and Lemons' is yet another example of the pioneering spirit and dreams of Sam McGredy. ZONES 4–10.

McGredy, New Zealand, 1992

'Roller Coaster' × 'New Year'

'Orange Triumph'

'ORCHID JUBILEE'   MORclilav

MODERN, CLIMBING MINIATURE, MAUVE, REPEAT-FLOWERING

The flowers of 'Orchid Jubilee' are a mauve blend and hold their color well under sunny conditions. The double flowers of up to two dozen petals are usually borne in small clusters. These are nicely set off by the small and mid-green foliage. The growth habit is decidedly climbing and slender, and there is a profusion of blooms all year long. Unfortunately, the flowers have no fragrance. It needs several years to establish before it begins to show its real potential and can assume a permanent place in the garden. 'Orchid Jubilee' is yet another of Moore's achievements in developing mauve climbing Miniature Roses for garden display. ZONES 5–10.

Moore, USA, 1992

('Little Darling' × 'Yellow Magic') × 'Make Believe'

'ORCHID LACE'   BENorchid

MODERN, MINIATURE, MAUVE, REPEAT-FLOWERING

The double flowers of this variety are mauve with pinkish tones. They have good exhibition form and can have a light fragrance. For a traditional Miniature the blooms are rather large, and this rose will surely fit the Patio classification if ever approved by the various registration authorities. It is marred by weak stems and necks too small to accommodate and support the Patio-sized blooms. The plant is also prone to mildew if not protected by regular spraying. 'Orchid Lace' is a valuable addition to the mauve color class, but the plant finish is unpredictable in some climates. Over-feeding, especially too much nitrogen, can cause the flowers to look coarse and ugly. ZONES 5–10.

Benardella, USA, 1995

Parentage unknown

'Oregold'

'OREGOLD'   TANolg

syns 'Anneliesse Rothenberger', 'Miss Harp', 'Silhouette'

MODERN, LARGE-FLOWERED/HYBRID TEA, DEEP YELLOW, REPEAT-FLOWERING

Deep golden yellow, double flowers with lots of substance and classic high centers with excellent symmetry are the hallmarks of this rose. The blooms have excellent holding capacity in cooler climates, lasting for weeks on the bush. The color is non-fading, but the blooms tend to open too quickly in warmer climates. There is a very light fragrance. The foliage is large, glossy and dark green on a tall, slightly spreading plant that is very disease resistant. While the bush may be slow in establishing itself the rewards are worth waiting for—an abundance of blooms with fast repeat. The seed parent is a granddaughter of 'Peace'. Still grown widely throughout the world, this rose has maintained its popularity because of its color and vigor. ZONES 5–10.

Tantau, Germany, 1975

'Piccadilly' × 'Colour Wonder'

All-America Rose Selection 1975

'ORIANA'

MODERN, LARGE-FLOWERED/HYBRID TEA, RED BLEND, REPEAT-FLOWERING

These flowers are a cherry red with a chalk white reverse. The florets are 5 in (12 cm) across and double, having 38 petals, and a light fragrance. They are borne singly on strong straight stems but open too quickly in all climates. The foliage is glossy green on a vigorous, upright plant with spreading characteristics. It is disease resistant and hardy. While the plant can produce exhibition-type blooms, the repeat cycle is slower than average for a Large-flowered Rose. The use of the granddaughter of 'Peace' as pollen parent resulted in the successful transmission of that classical high center to the blooms. ZONES 5–10.

Tantau, Germany, 1970

'Caramba' × 'Piccadilly'

'ORIENTAL CHARM'

MODERN, LARGE-FLOWERED/HYBRID TEA, MEDIUM RED, REPEAT-FLOWERING

Globular buds on this variety open to reveal bright orange-red flowers which are heavily veined with crimson, with golden yellow stamens providing the finishing artistic touch. The lightly fragrant florets are single, with 11 petals, and can be up to 3–4 in (8–10 cm) across. The flowers are quite different from any

'Oriana'

'Oranges and Lemons'

other single-petalled rose, as they re-semble large oriental poppies. The color is fleeting and fades rather rapidly after the blooms open. The foliage is glossy dark green on a vigorous upright plant. The genealogy of 'Oriental Charm' is rich in rose history—'Mme Butterfly' is a sport of 'Ophelia'; Floradora' is the pollen parent of 'Queen Elizabeth'; and 'Charlotte Armstrong' is one of the great Large-flowered Roses of the century. ZONES 5–10.

Duehrsen, USA, 1960

('Charlotte Armstrong' × 'Gruss an Teplitz') × ('Mme Butterfly' × 'Floradora')

'ORIENTAL DAWN'

MODERN, LARGE-FLOWERED/HYBRID TEA, YELLOW BLEND, REPEAT-FLOWERING

This is a strong-growing and healthy rose that carries blooms of creamy yellow petals that are heavily flushed and edged with rose pink. These slightly perfumed flowers are well formed and are pro-duced both singly and in small clusters on long, strong stems. They repeat fairly quickly. The foliage is dark green and glossy. 'Oriental Dawn' is a good rose for bedding. ZONES 5–9.

Suzuki, Japan, 1973

Parentage unknown

'Oriental Charm'

'Oriental Dawn'

'Osiria'

'Orpheline de Juillet'

'Othello'

'ORLÉANS ROSE'
MODERN, POLYANTHA, RED BLEND, REPEAT-FLOWERING

The vivid rosy crimson-red flowers of this rose have a white center. The small, semi-double florets have a light fragrance and are produced with abundance and good continuity. Because 'Orléans Rose' produces lots of small sprays that are often globular in form, it has been named 'Poly-Pompons' by some rose-lovers. The foliage is glossy green on a vigorous, upright, bushy plant. This rose put the Polyantha on the rose map of the world. Like Ophelia', it is of importance historically. It gave 22 spontaneous sports, including some famous varieties such as 'Miss Edith Cavell', 'Freudenfeurer', 'Coral Cluster', 'Juliana', 'Orange Queen' and 'Teschendorffs Jubilaumsrose', which have all been used successfully in breeding programs. ZONES 4–10.

Levavasseur, France, 1909

Thought to be a seedling from 'Mme Norbert Levavasseur'

'Oskar Scheerer'

'Oskar Cordel'

'ORMISTON ROY'
MODERN, MODERN SHRUB, DEEP YELLOW

This rose bears large, single-petalled flowers sporting a bright buttercup yellow color. There is a magnificent spring bloom but it is non-repeating. The foliage is light green, wrinkled and fernlike, on a bush that is generally very dense and low growing in most climates, reaching no higher than about 3 ft (1 m). In autumn and winter the large globular hips that develop are an attractive purple to black color, making for an attractive display in the garden when all else has finished blooming. ZONES 4–11.

Doorenbos, The Netherlands, 1953

Rosa spinosissima × *R. xanthina*

'ORNAMENT DE LA NATURE'
syns 'Anemone Ancienne', 'Ornement de la Nature'
OLD, GALLICA, MAUVE

This quite rare Gallica bears medium-sized, double flowers of lilac to violet-pink in, as the alternative name suggests, the style of an anemone. The numerous petals are whorled and convoluted. Otherwise, the features are those of a normal Gallica. ZONES 4–9.

Toutain, The Netherlands, pre-1814

Parentage unknown

'ORPHELINE DE JUILLET'
syn. 'July's Orphan'
OLD, GALLICA, MAUVE

The flowers of this rose are large and very double, and are crimson-purple shading to bright red in the center. It has an upright, rather tall and moderately vigorous growth habit. This is not a conventional Gallica as it has some Damask characteristics. The reason for the name is unclear. William Paul mentions it in *The Rose Garden* (1848), but he was not the raiser as it was listed in Vibert's catalogue in 1836. ZONES 4–9.

Pre-1836

Parentage unknown

'OSIRIA'
MODERN, LARGE-FLOWERED/HYBRID TEA, RED BLEND, REPEAT-FLOWERING

The long, pointed buds of 'Osiria' open to dark red flowers with a sparkling white reverse. In very warm climates the dark red does develop to a much blacker red tone. The large, very full, fragrant blooms contain more than 50 petals, and the flowers have classic Large-flowered form with high centers. The bloom size can be smaller in hot climates. The flowers generally come on short stems, which can be a serious handicap for the exhibitor. It is a vigorous, upright bush with good dark green foliage that has outstanding color and form but tends to be highly susceptible to powdery mildew. ZONES 5–11.

Kordes, Germany, 1978

'Snowfire' × seedling

'OSKAR CORDEL'
syn. 'Oscar Kordel'
OLD, HYBRID PERPETUAL, DEEP PINK, REPEAT-FLOWERING

This is a vigorous, upright shrub that bears very large, rounded, solitary cupped blooms with large petals. These are carried on long stems, making them good for cutting. The flowers are carmine, and there is a pleasing fragrance. It was named for the editor of a journal called *The Voss Gazette*. ZONES 5–9.

Lambert, Germany, 1897

'Merveille de Lyon' × 'André Schwartz'

'OSKAR SCHEERER'
MODERN, MODERN SHRUB, DARK RED, REPEAT-FLOWERING

The flowers on this variety are a very dark garnet red with contrasting prominent yellow stamens. The florets are large and semi-double and come in small clusters. There is no fragrance. The foliage is dark glossy green on a vigorous, upright-growing plant to about 6 ft (1.8 m) high with exceptional branching characteristics for increased bloom production. This rose is one of the first of the Modern Shrubs of medium vigor where the blooms are like Cluster-flowered Roses. It does survive most weather conditions and is truly weatherproof. ZONES 4–10.

Kordes, Germany, 1961

Parentage unknown

Royal National Rose Society Gold Medal 1961, Royal Horticultural Society Award of Merit 1962

'OTAGO'   MACnecta
MODERN, MINIATURE, ORANGE-RED, REPEAT-FLOWERING

The brilliant orange-salmon-red flowers of 'Otago' have symmetrical high centers. They are double, with about 35 petals, and fragrant. The blooms come predominantly in beautiful clusters of 6–10 in a wonderful profusion that covers the compact bush with vivid color. In most climates, the blooms last an unusually long time and with no loss of color. The mid-green foliage is semi-glossy. This is another great progeny from the seed parent 'Anytime', which is frequently used by Sam McGredy to give great additions to the world of Miniature Roses. Like 'Kaikoura', 'Wanaka' and 'Moana', to name just a few, they are all named after places in New Zealand. ZONES 5–10.

McGredy, New Zealand, 1978

'Anytime' × 'Minuetto'

'OTHELLO'
MODERN, MODERN SHRUB, DARK RED, REPEAT-FLOWERING

'Othello' has large, showy flowers that are deep blood red gradually turning purple with age. The blooms are well filled with petals and are reminiscent of the Hybrid Perpetuals. They have a very strong fragrance. This is a vigorous, upright bush growing to about 5 ft (1.5 m) high in most moderate climates, and it has an over-abundance of thorns. Although it is hardy, it can suffer from powdery mildew if left unprotected. Also known as an English Rose, this variety was aptly named for Shakespeare's Moor. **ZONES 4–11.**

Austin, UK, 1987

'Lilian Austin' × 'The Squire'

'OUR MOLLY' DICreason
MODERN, MODERN SHRUB, MEDIUM RED, REPEAT-FLOWERING

This charming, single-petalled rose bears flowers that are redcurrant red with a silvery white eye. The blooms are borne in massive clusters which, unfortunately, have no fragrance. The foliage is medium green on a plant with a tall, spreading habit. One of the delightful characteristics of this plant is the wonderful display of orange hips in autumn. It was named for a charming and prominent rosarian from Northern Ireland. **ZONES 4–10.**

Dickson, UK, 1994

Parentage unknown

Royal National Rose Society Trial Ground Certificate 1991, Glasgow Gold Medal 1996, The People's Choice Award in Glasgow 1996, Dublin Prize 1997, Belfast Prize 1997

'OUR ROSAMOND'
MODERN, LARGE-FLOWERED/HYBRID TEA, PINK BLEND, REPEAT-FLOWERING

These flowers are a mixture of silver and pink. The lightly fragrant, double florets have 35 petals and good classic Large-flowered form. They are borne one to a stem. The foliage is medium green, glossy and disease resistant on an upright-growing tall bush. **ZONES 5–11.**

Bell, Australia, 1983

Seedling of 'Daily Sketch' × 'Red Planet'

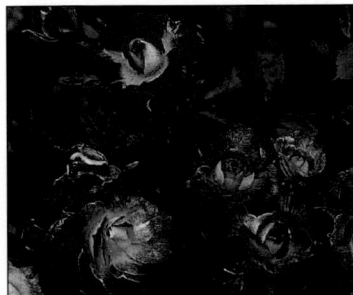

'Over the Rainbow'

'Oz Gold'

'Our Molly'

'OUT OF AFRICA' KORocken
MODERN, LARGE-FLOWERED/HYBRID TEA, ORANGE BLEND/APRICOT BLEND

This really is a lovely rose, with beautiful, glowing warm blooms. Their golden bases fade to apricot on the recurving petals and the pointed center is a darker bronze-apricot. It looks quite inspiring when planted together with 'Helpmekaar Roos' and 'Bernalene': you will have a glowing bed of bronze-apricot in your garden. 'Out of Africa' is a tall-growing plant that renews itself all the time with strong-growing basal stems, and these will provide further large candelabras of flowers. They are equally successful for both indoor arrangements and exhibitions, and there is a slight fragrance. **ZONES 5–11.**

Kordes, Germany

Parentage unknown

'OVER THE RAINBOW'
MODERN, MINIATURE, RED BLEND, REPEAT-FLOWERING

The use of the exquisite Cluster-flowered Rose 'Little Darling' as seed parent has produced 'Over the Rainbow', another

'Oz Gold'

'Our Rosamond'

prize-winning variety from Moore's stable. The small, well-shaped, double flowers are a deep scarlet red with bright yellow undersides. They possess good high-centered form and have a light fragrance. Foliage is semi-glossy and leathery in texture. This is a vigorous, upright bush that can grow tall in warm climates given the chance, but it is subject to mildew if unprotected. Evaluated as one of the best bicolored Miniatures, the blooms can be quite large in cooler climates. **ZONES 5–11.**

Moore, USA, 1972

'Little Darling' × 'Westmont'

American Rose Society Award of Excellence 1975

'OVERLOON'
MODERN, CLUSTER-FLOWERED/FLORIBUNDA, DEEP PINK, REPEAT-FLOWERING

Although it is nearly 50 years old, 'Overloon' is still a very good Cluster-flowered Rose. The bush is short to medium in height and very spreading. It is adorned with matt dark green, disease-resistant foliage that looks attractive as a backdrop when the clear rose pink flowers open from well-formed buds. The blooms are medium sized with

'Overloon'

about two dozen distinctive and attractive, very pointed petals. There is no fading of flower color, and the flowers are produced both singly and in small clusters with a fairly quick repeat. The blooms are produced in profusion. There are few good rosy pink Cluster-flowered Roses and 'Overloon' is one of them, although it is seldom seen in gardens today. **ZONES 5–9.**

Leenders, The Netherlands, 1949

'Irene' × 'Hebe'

'OZ GOLD'
MODERN, MINIATURE, ORANGE BLEND, REPEAT-FLOWERING

'Oz Gold' has golden yellow flowers with a touch of cerise on the outer petal edges. The florets have good exhibition form and are complemented by dark green, glossy foliage. The plant has a medium, vigorous, habit. The bloom color lasts well and it takes a few days for the cerise to pink color to develop on the edge of the petals. This is a generally healthy, vigorous-growing and self-cleaning plant. **ZONES 5–10**

McGredy, New Zealand, 1981

Parentage unknown

'Oz Gold'

O

'PACESETTER' SAVpace
MODERN, MINIATURE, WHITE, REPEAT-FLOWERING

'Pacesetter' has long pointed buds that open to pure white, fragrant flowers. The florets have consistent Large-flowered form. Indeed the form holds so well over days that this rose is an ideal candidate for rose shows and is perfect for cut flowers indoors. Bloom production is prolific once the plant has established itself. The elegant long stems add grace to charm. The foliage is dark green with a matt texture finish on an upright, compact bush. This rose was one of the first pure white Miniature Roses and ruled the show tables until the appearance of 'Snowbride'. It has maintained its popularity—many are still growing and showing this classic rose. ZONES 5–11.

Schwartz, USA, 1979

'Ma Perkins' × 'Magic Carrousel'

American Rose Society Award of Excellence 1981

'PACIFIC TRIUMPH'
MODERN, POLYANTHA, MEDIUM PINK, REPEAT-FLOWERING

The cupped flowers of this variety range from a salmon-pink to a medium pink. They are semi-double and have an easily detectable fragrance. The blooms tend to come in small clusters, often on stems a little too weak to support the whole mass. The handsome foliage is dark glossy green on a plant with a fairly compact habit. ZONES 5–10.

Heers, Australia, 1949

Sport of 'Orange Triumph'

'Pacesetter'

'Paddy McGredy'

'PADDY McGREDY' MACpa
MODERN, CLUSTER-FLOWERED/FLORIBUNDA, MEDIUM PINK, REPEAT-FLOWERING

The ovoid buds of this rose open to reveal large, deep rose pink to carmine flowers containing 33 petals. The flowers have classic Large-flowered form with high centers. They are occasionally borne one to a stem and there is a good strong fragrance. The foliage is leathery dark green, but it can be susceptible to black spot. 'Paddy McGredy' is a compact, vigorous bush that, when it was introduced, attracted a great deal of attention for its unique combination of Large-flowered and Cluster-flowered characteristics, hailed as a major breakthrough in rose breeding. Bloom production is excellent, with large trusses covering the bush so that the foliage is barely visible. It was named for the breeder's sister. ZONES 5–11.

McGredy, UK, 1962

'Spartan' × 'Tzigane'

National Rose Society Gold Medal 1961

'PADDY STEPHENS' MACclack
MODERN, LARGE-FLOWERED/HYBRID TEA, ORANGE BLEND, REPEAT-FLOWERING

This variety has flowers that are a lovely salmon-orange color with good exhibition-type form in spring but which tend to become smaller and flatter later in the growing season. The blooms are best at the fully open stage. The double florets, which have 15–25 petals and a light fragrance, are borne singly on stems

'Pacific Triumph'

that are usually straight and strong. The foliage is large, dark green and disease resistant on a compact bush. It looks its best in cool climates; in warmer zones the color fades rapidly. 'Paddy Stephens' was named for a rose grower from New Zealand. ZONES 5–10.

McGredy, New Zealand, 1991

'Solitaire' × {(['Tombola' × {'Elizabeth of Glamis' × ('Circus' × 'Golden Fleece')}] × 'Mary Sumner') × seedling}

'PAHEKA'
MODERN, LARGE-FLOWERED/HYBRID TEA, WHITE BLEND, REPEAT-FLOWERING

One of George Dawson's best roses, 'Paheka' produces flowers that are white with a slight tinge of the palest pink. They open slowly from very well-formed buds to large, full blooms that show stamens in the center. There are about two dozen broad petals of excellent substance. The growth is very tall and spreading, and is repeatedly covered with a profusion of flowers. 'Paheka' has no significant disease problems, and is an excellent rose for bedding or as a hedge. The fragrant blooms make wonderful cut flowers and keep their shape well. ZONES 5–9.

Dawson, Australia, 1980

Parentage unknown

'PAINTED MOON' DICpaint
MODERN, LARGE-FLOWERED/HYBRID TEA, RED BLEND, REPEAT-FLOWERING

This lightly fragrant rose displays an extraordinary color change with ageing. The flowers start off yellow turning pink from the tips of the petals, then the pink deepens to a red until finally the petals are totally crimson. The blooms are large, double with 40 petals and cupped. They are carried in wide sprays, which allows a range of ageing to provide a startling color display on the bush. The

'Paheka'

'Paddy Stephens'

'Painted Moon'

'Paleface'

foliage is semi-glossy and dark green on an upright bush with stocky growth characteristics. While it may have novelty appeal, it is also ideal for planting as a border or hedge. ZONES 5–10.

Dickson, UK, 1989

'Bonfire Night' × 'Silver Jubilee'

Royal National Rose Society Trial Ground Certificate 1989, Belfast Gold Medal 1993

'PAINTER'S PALETTE' MORpale
MODERN, MINIATURE, RED BLEND

From the master of Miniature Roses comes this little Moss-like plant with gaily striped flowers. The plant is taller than most Miniatures: it grows to knee height and spreads its vigorous branches to double that in width. When the flowers are in full bloom, the bush really has the appearance of a painter's palette spattered with red, white and pink; closer inspection reveals these to be striped floral rosettes. As the flowers age, the colors change, so these shrubs are fun to have in containers on the patio. Sadly, they lack fragrance. ZONES 4–11.

Moore, USA, 1984

Parentage unknown

'PALEFACE'
MODERN, LARGE-FLOWERED/HYBRID TEA, WHITE, REPEAT-FLOWERING

The oval and pointed buds of this variety open to almost pure white, semi-double flowers with up to two dozen petals with yellow bases. These blooms are large—to 5 in (12 cm) across—high centered or cupped, and show the stamens when open fully. There is a slight fragrance. The foliage is leathery, semi-glossy and dark green on the vigorous and upright bush. There is an excellent resistance to disease, but the flowers may be a little slow to repeat. ZONES 5–10.

Lindquist, USA, 1959

'Joanna Hill' × seedling

'PALLAS' HARvestal

MODERN, MINIATURE, LIGHT PINK, REPEAT-FLOWERING

The flowers of 'Pallas' are small but beautifully structured, allowing them to accommodate as many as 60 narrow petals in their petite rosettes. They slowly open to reveal a delightful array of petal tips. The young flowers are light buff in color, paling to white at the margins as the blooms expand. The first blooming is so prolific that one can scarcely see the ground beneath the plants, and the flowers continue to appear through the season to autumn. Unfortunately there is little fragrance. This is an excellent rose to grow in a container, in a group, as a petite hedge and to use wherever a small, neat plant is required. 'Pallas' is furnished with small, shiny and plentiful leaves. ZONES 5–10.

Harkness, UK, 1989

'Clarissa' × 'New Penny'

'PALMENGARTEN FRANKFURT' KORsilan

syns 'Beauce', 'Our Rosy Carpet'

MODERN, GROUND COVER, MEDIUM PINK, REPEAT-FLOWERING

This is an excellent Ground Cover Rose that grows to about 3 ft (1 m) in height and 4½ ft (1.3 m) in width. The plant is furnished with extremely healthy, semi-glossy, dark green foliage. The flowers are semi-double, and are made up of 15–20 strong rose pink petals that hold their color well. These are produced in dense clusters. The blooms completely cover the bush through the season from spring to autumn and have a very quick repeat cycle. 'Palmengarten Frankfurt'

'Pandora'

'Palmengarten Frankfurt'

'Pandemonium'

makes a wonderful bedding plant. It has also been found to be particularly suitable for use in difficult positions such as on banks and close to trees. It can also be trained as a tall or weeping standard. ZONES 5–9.

Kordes, Germany, 1988

Parentage unknown

Anerkannte Deutsche Rose 1992

'PANACHÉE DE LYON'

syns 'Rose du Roi Panachée', 'Striped Crimson Perpetual'

OLD, PORTLAND, PINK BLEND, REPEAT-FLOWERING

'Rose du Roi' was one of the early Portland Roses which were also known as the Perpetual Damasks, and it is sometimes classified as an early Hybrid Perpetual. 'Panachée de Lyon' is a striped version of 'Rose du Roi'—the fragrant flowers are pink with brilliant purple-red stripes. Unfortunately, however, it can sometimes revert to the original, which has red blooms. The attractive foliage is matt green. ZONES 4–9.

Dubreuil, France, 1895

Sport of 'Rose du Roi'

'PANDEMONIUM' MACpandem

syn. 'Claire Rayner'

MODERN, CLUSTER-FLOWERED/FLORIBUNDA, YELLOW BLEND, REPEAT-FLOWERING

This wonderfully named rose bears yellow flowers with random red stripes. The double blooms have 26–40 petals and a light musk fragrance. The overall look of the blooms is reminiscent of old-fashioned striped roses like 'Rosa Mundi' and 'Ferdinand Pichard', where the dominant feature is a flat, open bloom streaked and flecked with vibrant

'Pania'

orange and yellow. The foliage is small and mid-glossy green on a robust, bushy plant growing to about 2 ft (60 cm) in height. Although classified as a large Cluster-flowered Rose, this variety is more characteristic of a Modern Shrub as it tends to have a tall, arching growth habit. 'Pandemonium' shows strong evidence of the stripes which come from the pollen parent 'Stars 'n' Stripes', a striped Miniature from Ralph Moore. ZONES 5–11.

McGredy, New Zealand, 1988

'New Year' × (['Anytime' × 'Eyepaint'] × 'Stars 'n' Stripes')

Royal National Rose Society Trial Ground Certificate 1987

'PANDORA' HARwinner

MODERN, MINIATURE, NEAR WHITE, REPEAT-FLOWERING

The oval buds of this variety open into petite, light primrose yellow blooms, often crowded with a hundred tiny petals. They open fully to lovely, ivory white rosettes in sprays of 3–15 with remarkable freedom in summer and there is good continuity through to autumn. There is a light fragrance. In the garden, plantings of 'Pandora' can be used to form a group at the front of a border, in a bed and in containers. The plant is low, bushy and compact. As it has very few prickles, it is suitable for growing near pathways. It grows to an average size for a Miniature Rose. The mid-green leaves are small and semi-glossy. ZONES 4–9.

Harkness, UK, 1989

'Clarissa' × 'Darling Flame'

Royal National Rose Society Trial Ground Certificate 1989, Hradec Golden Rose 1991

'PANIA'

MODERN, LARGE-FLOWERED/HYBRID TEA, LIGHT PINK, REPEAT-FLOWERING

This rose was a worthy winner of the Gold Medal at the very first Trial of the New Zealand Rose Garden at Palmerston North. It has large, oval buds that open

'Pandemonium'

slowly to show particularly well-formed blooms of luminous, very soft clear rose pink. They hold their shape and lovely color extremely well, and appear with a quick repeat throughout the flowering season. The foliage is leathery, mid-green and very disease free, and covers this low and compact bush. In the garden 'Pania' is suitable for planting at the front of large beds. The attractive blooms, which are produced both singly and in small clusters, are excellent for cutting. ZONES 5–9.

McGredy, New Zealand, 1968

'Paddy McGredy' × ('Kordes' Perfecta' × 'Montezuma')

New Zealand Rose Garden Trial Gold Medal

'PAOLA' TANaloap

MODERN, LARGE-FLOWERED/HYBRID TEA, MEDIUM RED, REPEAT-FLOWERING

The flowers on this variety are a deep but bright red which looks attractive set against the plum-tinged foliage. The blooms have about 20 ruffled petals and no fragrance is detectable. The foliage is mid-green and fairly disease resistant. The medium-sized bush is upright in form. 'Paola' has good repeat-flowering characteristics, with blooms continuing to appear throughout the season. This is a good rose for borders, beds and hedges. ZONES 4–10.

Tantau, Germany, 1982

Parentage unknown

'Paprika'

'Papa Hémeray'

'Papa Meilland'

'PAPA GONTIER'
OLD, TEA, PINK BLEND, REPEAT-FLOWERING

The fragrant flowers of this rose are bright coppery pink with a carmine-red reverse. They are semi-double and loose. It can be rather wiry and twiggy, but in suitable conditions it can grow into a large shrub. This rose and 'Madame Hoste' are the parents of the well known 'Lady Hillingdon'. A climbing version of 'Papa Gontier' was introduced by Hosp in 1898. Many of the Tea Roses and the Large-flowered Roses mutate at some time from bush to climber, but the climbers tend to be less floriferous. Papa Gontier was a notable nurseryman in Montrouge in France. ZONES 4–9.

Nabonnand, France, 1883

Seedling of 'Duchess of Edinburgh'

'PAPA HÉMERAY'
OLD, CHINA, RED BLEND, REPEAT-FLOWERING

The flowers of this rose are an intense vermilion with white centers, and do not fade. The single blooms flower continuously throughout the season. It is a strong, low-growing shrub with an upright habit and few thorns. It is very suitable for bedding. ZONES 7–9.

Hémeray-Aubert, France, 1912

'Hiawatha' × 'Parson's Pink China'

'PAPA MEILLAND'   MEIsar,
MEIcesar

MODERN, LARGE-FLOWERED/HYBRID TEA, DARK RED, REPEAT-FLOWERING

The elegant, pointed buds of this rose open to reveal dark velvety crimson flowers of exquisite, classic Large-flowered form. The large, very fragrant blooms have about 35 petals. It always sends out one bloom per stem on strong, straight, long stems suitable for cutting for the home or for exhibition. The foliage is leathery, glossy and olive green on a vigorous, upright, tall plant. Unfortunately, it is quite susceptible to mildew and black spot, and it is not winter hardy, tending to die back in climates with even mild snowfall and frost. It was named by Alain Meilland as a fitting tribute to his grandfather Antoine (1844–1971). **'Climbing Papa Meilland'** (Stratford, Australia, 1970) is in every respect a clone of its parent. As the canes gain height and air circulation is improved, the mildew and black spot problems are minimized. It takes about 2 to 3 years to establish itself. ZONES 6–11.

Meilland, France, 1963

'Chrysler Imperial' × 'Charles Mallerin'

Baden-Baden Gold Medal 1962, James Alexander Gamble Fragrance Medal 1974, World Federation of Rose Societies Rose Hall of Fame 1988

'PAPAGENO'   MACgoofy
MODERN, LARGE-FLOWERED/HYBRID TEA, RED BLEND, REPEAT-FLOWERING

The well-formed buds on this rose open to large, cerise-red flowers striped with white. The moderately full flowers with 15–25 petals have a light scent and provide a dramatic display of blooms all year long. The foliage is large and light green on an upright, tall, vigorous, winter-hardy bush. It tends to do better in fertile soil and full sun, although it can tolerate partial sun. In warmer climates it needs

'Para Ti'

good drainage as well as mulching. This is a sister seedling to 'Pandemonium' using the breakthrough striped Miniature 'Stars 'n' Stripes'. It tends to grow more like a Hybrid Perpetual or Bourbon, sending out long, limber branches that can be pegged down to create a carpet effect. ZONES 4–10.

McGredy, New Zealand, 1990

'Freude' × (['Anytime' × 'Eyepaint'] × 'Stars 'n' Stripes')

'PAPI DELBARD'   DELaby
MODERN, LARGE-FLOWERED CLIMBER, APRICOT BLEND, REPEAT-FLOWERING

A number of warm colors make this rose very special: the many petals that form the cup of the open flower reflect a remarkable combination of yellow, orange and apricot, with an overall copper sheen. Add to this a fruity fragrance, and one can hardly think of a better shrub to adorn a fence or to form an informal hedge. 'Papi Delbard' is tall growing and vigorous, and since the branches are inclined to drop, it can form a graceful shrub. ZONES 5–12.

Delbard, France, 1995

Parentage unknown

'PAPILLON'
OLD, CHINA, MEDIUM RED, REPEAT-FLOWERING

This medium-sized China Rose bears rose red and purple flowers that are filled with many petals. The blooms have a classic shape and appear amid the mid-green foliage. It is not well known, and is very difficult to obtain. ZONES 7–9.

Dubourg, France, circa 1826

Parentage unknown

'PAPILLON'
OLD, CLIMBING TEA, PINK BLEND, REPEAT-FLOWERING

The flowers of this rose are coppery salmon-rose. They are medium-sized

'Papillon' (Dubourg)

and semi-double and have been compared to a group of butterflies on a bush—hence the name ('papillon' is French for 'butterfly'). It is a free-flowering bush with copper colored leaves. It is best grown as a pillar rose as it is quite a slow climber, and has been known not to climb at all! It is sometimes classified as a Noisette. ZONES 7–9.

Nabonnand, France, 1881

Tea Rose × Noisette Rose

'PAPRIKA'   TANprik
MODERN, CLUSTER-FLOWERED/FLORIBUNDA, ORANGE-RED, REPEAT-FLOWERING

When the long, pointed buds of this rose open, they reveal bright brick red or geranium red flowers with a very distinctive bluish zone at the base of the petals. The fragrant flowers are large and semi-double and are borne in large clusters or trusses against leathery, glossy, olive green foliage on a vigorous, upright bush that is 3 ft (1 m) high. The blooms are weatherproof, particularly against rain. In spite of competition in this color class of Cluster-flowered Roses this variety has managed to remain popular, even against the onslaught of recent introductions. It is ideal for a standard tree. ZONES 5–10.

Tantau, Germany, 1958

'Märchenland' × 'Red Favorite'

National Rose Society Gold Medal 1959, Golden Rose of The Hague 1961

'PARA TI'
syns 'For You', 'Pour Toi', 'Wendy'
MODERN, MINIATURE, WHITE, REPEAT-FLOWERING

The beautiful buds of this rose develop into flowers that are basically white, with the base tinted yellow. The blooms then tend to open more fully to a creamy white with just a hint of yellow-green at the base. The florets are barely semi-double with 15 petals and have no scent. The foliage is very glossy on an extremely bushy and dense plant. 'Para Ti' is an early classic example from Pedro Dot and shows his skills in evolving the Miniature Rose as a popular classification. It is regarded by many growers as a 'must have' for the garden. ZONES 4–10.

Dot, Spain, 1949

'Eduardo Toda' × 'Pompon de Paris'

'PARADE'
MODERN, LARGE-FLOWERED CLIMBER, DEEP PINK, REPEAT-FLOWERING

'Parade' has ovoid buds that open to deep rose pink flowers often described as

'Papillon' (Nabonnand)

'Parade'

'Parade'

a rich cerise, close to crimson, that glows like fine silk. The large, cupped-shaped blooms have 33 petals and are fragrant. They are borne in heavy clusters that often make the stems droop slightly. This is a hardy plant with glossy, dark green foliage that establishes itself rapidly and reaches a height of 10–12 ft (3–3.5 m). It prefers the pillar configuration to the spreading formation of classical climbers. It is a remarkably healthy free-blooming climber from the breeder perhaps best known for his Cluster-flowered Roses. ZONES 4–10.

Boerner, USA, 1953

Seedling of 'New Dawn' × 'Climbing World's Fair'

Royal Horticultural Society Award of Garden Merit 1993

'PARADISE' WEZeip
syn. 'Burning Sky'

MODERN, LARGE-FLOWERED/HYBRID TEA, MAUVE, REPEAT-FLOWERING

This rose has graceful, long, pointed buds that open to silvery lavender blooms with distinctive shading to ruby red at the edge of the petals. The large, fragrant, classically shaped blooms have 28 petals. The foliage is glossy dark green on an upright, tall plant that prefers warmer climates to develop the full color chrome and hue. However, intense sunshine can cause the edges of the petals to burn and lose substance. In winter climates, dieback is common. For those who like this color class, this rose is a must despite its faults. In moderate climates, it performs well throughout the year. ZONES 5–10.

Weeks, USA, 1978

'Swarthmore' × seedling

All-America Rose Selection 1979, Portland Gold Medal 1979

'Paradise'

'PARADOR' MEIchanso
syn. 'Tchin-Tchin'

MODERN, CLUSTER-FLOWERED/FLORIBUNDA, ORANGE-RED, REPEAT-FLOWERING

'Parador' bears vibrant neon orange-red blooms. They are very large—3–4 in (8–10 cm) across—cupped, and double with 20 petals, and there is no scent. The blooms are mainly borne in clusters of 3–15 flowers. The foliage is mid-green on a compact, very vigorous bush. It tends to dress itself with clusters, behaving more like a Cluster-flowered Rose than a Large-flowered Rose. ZONES 5–11.

Paolino, France, 1978

(['Sarabande' × MEIkim] × ['Alain' × 'Orange Triumph']) × 'Diablotin'

Tokyo Gold Medal 1978

'PARISER CHARME'
syn. 'Paris Charm'

MODERN, LARGE-FLOWERED/HYBRID TEA, MEDIUM PINK, REPEAT-FLOWERING

The ovoid buds of this rose open to salmon-pink flowers with a sweet perfume. The well-formed blooms are double with 28 petals and often large, with a 5 in (12 cm) diameter. They come in large-sized clusters that can weigh down the stems, especially after rain. The foliage is glossy dark green on a vigorous, upright plant. It is one of the more than

'Pariser Charme'

200 grandchildren bred from the Large-flowered Rose of the twentieth century, 'Peace'. ZONES 5–10.

Tantau, Germany, 1965

'Prima Ballerina' × 'Montezuma'

Anerkannte Deutsche Rose 1966

'PARKDIREKTOR RIGGERS'
MODERN, MODERN SHRUB, DARK RED, REPEAT-FLOWERING

The long, pointed buds of this rose open to reveal velvety crimson flowers with a small center of yellow stamens and a little white and purple at the base of the petals. The color is non-fading even in warm climates. The fragrant, semi-double blooms are borne in large clusters

'Parkdirektor Riggers'

of up to 50 blooms on a plant that can reach up to 12 ft (3.5 m) high by 6 ft (1.8 m) wide. The foliage is glossy dark green on a vigorous, climbing, spreading plant that is very disease resistant. This is one of the best *Kordesii* roses because of its freedom and abundance of flowers. When grown on a wall, it may suffer from mildew and black spot if left unprotected. ZONES 4–10.

Kordes, Germany, 1957

Rosa kordesii × 'Our Princess'

Anerkannte Deutsche Rose 1960

P

'PARKS' YELLOW TEA-SCENTED CHINA'

syns 'Old Yellow Tea', *Rosa × odorata ochroleuca, R. indica ochroleuca*
OLD, TEA, MEDIUM YELLOW, REPEAT-FLOWERING

This is one of the 4 'stud' China Roses from which the Teas and Noisettes were developed and which brought the repeat-flowering characteristic to modern roses. It was brought to England from China by J. D. Parks. It is considered to have been a hybrid between the wild China rose and *Rosa gigantea*, a Tea-scented wild climbing variety. 'Parks' Yellow Tea-scented China' is a short climber bearing straw yellow, double, loose flowers with a faint Tea scent. It was from this rose that the light yellow was introduced into the later Teas and Noisettes. It was lost for some time, no doubt having been superseded by better developments, and possibly also the victim of cold winters. ZONES 7–9.

From China, introduced by Parks, UK, 1824
Parentage unknown

'PARKZAUBER'
OLD, CENTIFOLIA, DARK RED

'Parkzauber' is a latter-day Centifolia from unusual parents. The double flowers are dark crimson. The leaves are dark and leathery on a medium to tall

'Parks' Yellow Tea-scented China'

'Parmelia'

bush with a vigorous, upright habit. The calyx and stems are very mossy, and it is listed by some rosarians as a Moss Rose. The name means 'Park Magic'. ZONES 4–9.

Kordes, Germany, 1956
'Independence' × 'Nuits de Young'

'PARKZIERDE'
OLD, BOURBON, DARK RED

The name of this variety means 'Park Adornment' and it is certainly an apt name. This late Bourbon Rose produces scarlet-crimson double, open flowers on very long stems. They are very suitable for cutting, but the blooms do fade rather quickly. The fragrant flowers are produced abundantly but briefly in early summer. 'Parkzierde' is a strong plant which grows to medium height. ZONES 5–9.

Lambert, Germany, 1911
Parentage unknown

'PARMELIA'
MODERN, LARGE-FLOWERED/HYBRID TEA, MEDIUM RED, REPEAT-FLOWERING

'Parmelia' produces long and pointed buds that open to flamingo red flowers with a classic form. The double blooms contain 24–30 petals and have no scent. The foliage is dark and glossy green on a

'Party Girl'

very vigorous, upright and compact plant. This sport carries many of the attributes of its award-winning 1944 All-America Rose Selection parent. ZONES 5–10.

Lennard, Australia, 1957
Sport of 'Mme Chiang Kai-Shek'

'PARMENTIER'
OLD, MOSS, MEDIUM PINK

'Parmentier' has rather small, globular flowers which are a vivid pink. They are very double, quartered and muddled in the old style. An attractive button eye is sometimes to be seen. This is a bushy, compact, low to medium plant with narrow foliage. There is some mossing. This variety is sometimes classified as a Hybrid Perpetual. It is quite difficult to come by. ZONES 5–10.

Robert, France, 1851 or Guillot, France, 1860
Parentage unknown

'PARTHENON'   DELbro
MODERN, LARGE-FLOWERED/HYBRID TEA, PINK BLEND, REPEAT-FLOWERING

This variety has flowers that are carmine-pink with a soft pastel yellow reverse. The cupped, double blooms have no fragrance. The foliage is a distinctive glossy bronze on a vigorous and upright plant. This rose has been all but forgotten amid the introductions of the latter part of the twentieth century. ZONES 5–10.

Delbard-Chabert, France, 1967
'Chic Parisien' × ('Bayadère' × 'Rome Glory')

'PARTY GIRL'
MODERN, MINIATURE, YELLOW BLEND, REPEAT-FLOWERING

'Party Girl' is perhaps the most famous of the Miniature Roses hybridized by the late Harm Saville of Rowley, Massachusetts, USA. This compact bush is adorned by apricot-yellow blooms with 23 petals of immaculate exhibition form. It prefers to send out large clusters of 10–18 florets that take several weeks to reach full maturity, adding grace and elegance to the garden all year long. In hot climates, the flowers appear to be almost white with a yellow base; in cooler and more moderate climate zones the blooms are characteristically yellow. This rose was named for Jan Shivers from Indiana who served as Chairman of the American Rose Society Prizes &

'Party Trick'

Award Committee and was well known at National Conventions to be quite a 'party girl' herself! ZONES 5–11.

Saville, USA, 1979
'Rise 'n' Shine' × 'Sheri Anne'
American Rose Society Award of Excellence 1982

'PARTY TRICK'   DICparty
MODERN, CLUSTER-FLOWERED/FLORIBUNDA, DEEP PINK, REPEAT-FLOWERING

The flowers of this variety have a deep pink color that is much lighter in sunny climates; they have a light fragrance. The florets are borne in medium-sized clusters on a vigorous, upright bush. It is a tall, upright bush with good disease resistance. ZONES 5–11.

Dickson, UK, 1994
Parentage unknown
Royal National Rose Society Certificate of Merit

'PARURE D'OR'   DELmir
MODERN, LARGE-FLOWERED CLIMBER, YELLOW BLEND, REPEAT-FLOWERING

The golden yellow flowers of this variety are edged orange-red. The florets can be either single petalled or sometimes semi-double, and they are medium sized. The foliage is dark and glossy green on a vigorous, climbing, spreading plant. The repeat-bloom cycle times are excellent throughout the year. When naming this rose the breeders borrowed the French word 'parure', meaning a suite of matching jewelry such as the celebrated set of emeralds (necklace, earrings, tiara, etc.) that belonged to Empress Josephine. ZONES 5–11.

Delbard-Chabert, France 1968
('Queen Elizabeth' × 'Provence') × (seedling of 'Sultane' × 'Mme Joseph Perraud')
Bagatelle Gold Medal 1968

'PASADENA TOURNAMENT'
syn. 'Red Cécile Brünner'
MODERN, CLUSTER-FLOWERED/FLORIBUNDA, MEDIUM RED

The long and pointed buds of this rose open to small and fragrant, double flowers with 36 velvety red petals. They are cupped in shape and supported by strong, long stems, which makes them good for cutting. 'Pasadena Tournament' is a vigorous bush rose from California that is covered with bronzy green foliage. ZONES 6–10.

Krebs, USA, 1942
'Cécile Brünner' × seedling

P

'PASCALI' LENip

syn. 'Blanche Pasca'

MODERN, LARGE-FLOWERED/HYBRID TEA, WHITE, REPEAT-FLOWERING

This variety has lightly fragrant, creamy clear white flowers that are double with 30 petals. They have classic exhibition-style form and are borne one to a stem, making them ideal for cutting or exhibition. They tend to be on the small side for a Large-flowered Rose. The foliage is dark green on a vigorous, compact bush. This rose is known for its disease resistance in all climates. Considering it was elevated to the Rose Hall of Fame by the Member Societies of the World Federation of Rose Societies, what other validation is needed that this rose is worth growing anywhere in the world?
ZONES 5–11.

Lens, Belgium, 1963

'Queen Elizabeth' × 'White Butterfly'

Golden Rose of The Hague 1963, National Rose Society Certificate of Merit 1963, Portland Gold Medal 1967, All-America Rose Selection 1969, World Federation of Rose Societies Rose Hall of Fame 1991

'PASSION'

MODERN, LARGE-FLOWERED/HYBRID TEA, MEDIUM RED, REPEAT-FLOWERING

'Passion' has long, pointed buds that open to fragrant scarlet-cerise flowers. They are very large at 5 in (12 cm) across and are borne in small clusters on tall, upright, strong stems. The foliage is glossy dark green on a very vigorous bush. This rose is just one of the many children bred from the mighty 'Peace' from the House of Meilland in France. It is also known as a Grandiflora as is 'Queen Elizabeth', which was introduced in the same year and was the very first variety of this classification. ZONES 5–11.

Gaujard, France, 1954

'Peace' × 'Alain'

'PASTEUR'

MODERN, LARGE-FLOWERED/HYBRID TEA, PINK BLEND, REPEAT-FLOWERING

The Gaujard family took over the business of Pernet-Ducher, the so-called 'Wizard of Lyon', and have continued as successful raisers ever since, although 'Pasteur' is not among those that have won universal acclaim and is currently available only in its native France. It has a large bloom, like many of its stablemates, opening from a long bud into a flower that is filled with broad petals in a lively shade of rose pink, flushed and veined with red. There is a

'Patio Charm'

light fragrance, and, after the main burst of flower, more blooms are produced during summer and autumn. It is a suitable rose for a bed, in a border and for cutting. The plant grows upright in habit, to a little below average height, and is furnished with large, glossy leaves. ZONES 4–9.

Gaujard, France, 1973

'Firmament' × 'Femina'

'PAT AUSTIN' AUSmum

MODERN, MODERN SHRUB, ORANGE-RED, REPEAT-FLOWERING

The flowers on this variety are large and double, and display a bright and vivid combination of color, rich copper on the upperside of the petals and pale coppery yellow on the underside. The deeply cupped nature of the open flowers ensures that the two contrasting tones catch the eye as the large petals expand. There is a sharp fruity fragrance, and flowers continue to appear through summer and autumn. For a shrub border, especially where a splash of bright and unusual color is required, this is a useful rose. The plant grows vigorously to average size for a shrub rose with a bushy, spreading habit and large, semi-glossy, deep green leaves. The raiser David Austin named it in appreciation of his wife. It is also classified as an English Rose. ZONES 4–9.

Austin, UK, 1995

Parentage unknown

'PAT JAMES' HARyoricks

MODERN, CLUSTER-FLOWERED/FLORIBUNDA, ORANGE BLEND, REPEAT-FLOWERING

This rose has an unusual combination of colors—nasturtium red on the upperside of the petal and light vermilion on the underside—which gives the flowers a degree of luminosity without any harshness of tone. The pointed buds, carried singly

'Pathfinder'

'Pasteur'

'Pat Austin'

or in clusters, open into neatly formed, cupped flowers of medium size and with a light fragrance. They have about 24 petals, which drop cleanly when they are spent. After the first flush is over, a good succession of bloom is maintained through summer and autumn, the late flowers being especially good. As a bedding or border rose, or when grown as a hedge, this is a very suitable variety. The plant grows vigorously up to average height with a bushy habit, and is furnished with dark, semi-glossy foliage. 'Pat James' was named to celebrate the golden wedding of Mr and Mrs Gordon James; it was a gift from him to thank her for so many happy and caring years. ZONES 4–9.

Harkness, UK, 1991

'Clarissa' × 'Amber Queen'

Baden-Baden Silver Medal 1995

'PATHFINDER' CHEwpobey

MODERN, GROUND COVER, ORANGE-RED, REPEAT-FLOWERING

This could be called a Patio Ground Cover Rose because it is very compact and extends along the ground about half as far again as its low height. The flowers are small, cupped, and are produced in well-filled clusters. They are vermilion, with cream on the underside of the petals, and show yellow stamens as they open wide. There is a light fragrance, and flowers continue to appear with little interruption through summer and autumn. There are many uses for a little rose like this, such as in beds, near the

front of borders, in a container or even in a hanging basket. The cushion-like plants are well furnished with small, shiny leaves. ZONES 4–9.

Warner, UK, 1993

('Anna Ford' × 'Little Darling') × 'Eyeopener'

Royal National Rose Society Trial Ground Certificate 1994, British Association of Rose Breeders, Breeders' Choice 1996

'PATIO CHARM' CHEwapri

MODERN, CLIMBING MINIATURE, APRICOT BLEND

Set against the dark green foliage of this rose, the dark orange-apricot flowers are very bright and attractive. They develop from long and pointed buds to give well-shaped, double blooms. The outer petals reflex as they mature. 'Patio Charm' can be trained against a wall or small trellis, and is propagated by budding. ZONES 5–10.

Warner, UK, 1994

'Laura Ford' × 'Anne Harkness'

'PATIO PRINCESS' POUlholm

syns 'Fashion', 'New Fashion'

MODERN, MODERN SHRUB, ORANGE-PINK, REPEAT-FLOWERING

The name 'Patio Princess' seems to be confined to New Zealand, where this shrub rose is treated as a climber and trained against fences, walls and pillars. The references to 'Fashion' are inappropriate, for neither in color nor form does it have the haunting beauty of the disease-prone American rose that originally bore the name. This rose bears closely packed clusters of medium-sized, semi-double blooms on upright, springy

'Pascali'

'Passion'

'Patriot'

'Patriot'

shoots. The flowers are a gentle shade of apricot-orange, lightly scented, and the plant continues to bear blooms through summer and autumn. As a shrub rose in a border, where it can be grown with shorter and more compact plants in front, this will add pleasing color tones. This variety grows quite vigorously, has arching stems and is furnished with mid-green foliage. ZONES 4–9.

Olesen, Denmark, 1989

'Mary Sumner' × seedling

'PATRICIA'
MODERN, LARGE-FLOWERED/HYBRID TEA, MEDIUM RED, REPEAT-FLOWERING

The flowers on this variety are a carmine flecked pink with an orange-yellow base to the petals. The florets are fragrant and have lovely color, particularly in autumn. The foliage is glossy dark green on a vigorous bush. This variety makes an ideal garden plant for the unending display of flowers throughout the year. ZONES 5–11.

Chaplin Bros Ltd, UK, 1932

Parentage unknown

'PATRICIA'   KORpatri
MODERN, CLUSTER-FLOWERED/FLORIBUNDA, APRICOT BLEND, REPEAT-FLOWERING

Although it is opular in Australia, this rose is only grown elsewhere as a cut-flower variety; 'Patricia' is at its best in warm climates. The flowers are a clear shade of salmon-pink, deeper on the petal rims and paler on the underside. They are of medium size with some 24 petals, and appear in clusters, becoming cupped to flat as they open out to make a bold show of color. The variety is excellent for cutting as the blooms last well, and it is also useful for beds and borders. It continues to produce flowers right through summer and autumn. There is a pleasing, if somewhat delicate fragrance. The plant grows tall and upright to average height, and it is furnished with rather broad, deep green leaves. Some authorities have questioned the parentage of this rose because it does not have the close resemblance in flower form and growth that is normally found in a sport. ZONES 5–9.

Kordes, Germany, 1972

Sport of 'Elizabeth of Glamis'

Orléans Gold Medal 1979

'PATRICIA MACOUN'
MODERN, RAMBLER, WHITE

The attractive flowers of this rose are white and double, but they are only moderately fragrant. Unfortunately they do not repeat-flower. *Rosa helenae* is a climbing rose which was found in China by the great collector and botanist E. H. Wilson, who named it for his wife. 'Patricia Macoun' probably inherited its glossy foliage and hardiness from the un-named other parent. Canadian breeders

'Patricia' (Kordes)

have concentrated on producing cold-tolerant roses using native species as parents. ZONES 3–9.

Central Experimental Farm, Canada, 1945

Rosa helenae × seedling

'PATRIOT'   JAClin
MODERN, LARGE-FLOWERED/HYBRID TEA, DARK RED, REPEAT-FLOWERING

Borne usually one to a stem but sometimes in threes, the flowers of this rose are very large, with up to 40 petals. They are dark red, but with a fragrance that is disappointingly light for a rose of this color and size. Flowers appear intermittently through summer and autumn. This makes a vigorous plant above average height, with a branching, spreading habit and a good covering of large, dark green, semi-glossy leaves. It needs a warm climate, and is only commercially available in Australia and India at the present time. ZONES 5–9.

Warriner, USA, 1991

'Showstopper' × 'Mr Lincoln'

'PAT'S CHOICE'   KORomega
MODERN, LARGE-FLOWERED/HYBRID TEA, ORANGE-RED, REPEAT-FLOWERING

According to Ludwig Taschner, this rose was noticed growing in the Pretoria trial grounds by a friend, Pat Martens, and

then marketed. It has proven to be a most rewarding rose, vigorous in growth and with a generous bloom production throughout the season. The large, shapely blooms appear in candelabra-like clusters, and will give the most exquisite exhibition flowers if deadheaded. They are a special coral crimson, which makes a bright show in the garden. There is a slight fragrance. ZONES 4–10.

Kordes, Germany, 1995

Seedling × 'Omega'

'PAUL CEZANNE'   JACdeli
MODERN, LARGE-FLOWERED/HYBRID TEA, YELLOW BLEND, REPEAT-FLOWERING

The flowers of this variety are made up of petals that are basically yellow and deep coral, but each one has a different combination of stripes or dots, and some petals are divided half and half between the two shades. Like 'Picasso', 'Old Master' and other curiously colored roses with their names linked to painters, this is an interesting rose and will make a talking point in the garden. The blooms are of medium size, full-petalled, and have a moderate fragrance. They appear singly or in clusters, on short stems, continuing through summer and autumn. It grows to average height with a bushy habit. Some growers consider 'Paul Cezanne' to be a Cluster-flowered Rose. ZONES 4–9.

Jackson and Perkins, USA, 1992

Parentage unknown

'PAUL CRAMPEL'
MODERN, POLYANTHA, ORANGE-RED, REPEAT-FLOWERING

The flowers of this variety are deep orange-scarlet, semi-double and appear

'Paul Cezanne'

'Patio Princess'

'Paul Ricault'

freely in big clusters. They are of small to medium size, without much fragrance, and after the first great flush of bloom there is a pause before they come back into flower, continuing to show color through the rest of summer and autumn. This, with other Polyantha Roses, was exceedingly popular for bedding until the 1950s, when the Cluster-flowered Roses found favor by reason of their bigger flowers, brighter colors and better resistance to mildew. 'Paul Crampel' has the further disadvantage of having flowers that sometimes revert to the parent from which it sported, giving a discordant spray of crimson blooms alongside the orange-scarlet ones. The plants grow upright to the average height for a Polyantha Rose, with light green leaves. It is named after the nurseryman who is also remembered for the famous geranium he introduced. ZONES 4–9.

Kersbergen, The Netherlands, 1930

Sport of 'Superb'

'PAUL GAUGUIN'   JACdebu
MODERN, LARGE-FLOWERED/HYBRID TEA, RUSSET, REPEAT-FLOWERING

This rose is grown for its novelty value, derived from the most unusual color combinations in the flowers. They are made up of deep russet and light salmon, varying in their proportions from bloom to bloom, and marked with random patterns of dots, stripes and patches. The flowering continues through summer and autumn, and plants sited where they will catch the eye of visitors are sure to provide a talking point. One specialist provides it in standard form, presumably with this in mind. The variety grows neatly and compactly with mid-green foliage, to below average height. It is considered by some to be a Cluster-flowered Rose. ZONES 4–9.

Parentage unknown

'PAUL LÉDÉ, CLIMBING'
OLD, CLIMBING TEA, APRICOT BLEND, REPEAT-FLOWERING

This rose is a sport of the bush form, 'Paul Lédé', which was one of Pernet-Ducher's Large-flowered/Hybrid Teas derived from the 'Persian Yellow' (*Rosa foetida*). This was a breakthrough in the early twentieth century, and the roses were known for a while as Pernetianas. They brought in the intense yellow, and unfortunately black spot. This climbing

'Paul Shirville'

form has flowers which have been variously described as soft peach-pink, yellow and apricot, carmine-pink and dawn yellow. They are fragrant and bloom freely and continuously. It has plentiful mid-green foliage. ZONES 5–9.

Lowe, UK, 1913

Sport 'Paul Lédé'

'PAUL NEYRON'
OLD, HYBRID PERPETUAL, MEDIUM PINK, REPEAT-FLOWERING

This is what many people think of as the 'cabbage rose', a name first given to the Centifolias by the English, who did not care for the alternative name of the roses of Provence. The fragrant flowers are very large, with as many as 50 petals; they are cupped and resemble peonies. It is a tall, upright, vigorous bush. ZONES 5–9.

Levet, France, 1869

'Victor Verdier' × 'Anna de Diesbach'

'PAUL NOËL'
MODERN, LARGE-FLOWERED CLIMBER, PINK BLEND, REPEAT-FLOWERING

The flowers of this rose are very double, and of medium to large size. They are a warm shade of rosy salmon-pink with a hint of yellow at the base and open wide to show a beautiful formation, with many ruffled petals jostling for space. The plant carries its blooms on short stems, singly or in small clusters, and they have a pleasing, delicate scent. The first flush is wonderfully prolific. It is suitable for fences, arches and pergolas. The plant is very vigorous, producing long, arching stems, and can grow further than the average extent of a Climber Rose. 'Paul Noël' has shiny, dark green foliage. ZONES 4–9.

Tanne, France, 1913

Rosa wichuraiana × 'Monsieur Tillier'

'Paul Gauguin'

'PAUL RICARD'   MEInivoz
syns 'Moondance', 'Paul Richard', 'Spirit of Peace', 'Summer's Kiss'
MODERN, LARGE FLOWERED/HYBRID TEA, YELLOW BLEND, REPEAT-FLOWERING

The flowers of this variety are large and very full, with about 40 broad petals; they open with high centers and maintain a wonderful symmetry of form. They are amber yellow, the color being richer in cool climates, and bleaching in warm ones to the extent that the outer petals become creamy buff with deeper amber tints in the heart of the bloom. The fragrance has been likened to spiced honey. It is good for cutting, as the blooms are on stiff stems and last well, and is very suitable for beds, borders and as a hedge. It grows vigorously with a freely branching, bushy habit to above average height, and has large mid- to dark green leaves. ZONES 4–9.

Meilland, France, 1994

('Hidalgo' × 'Mischief') × 'Ambassador'

Rome Gold Medal 1991

'PAUL RICAULT'
OLD, CENTIFOLIA, MEDIUM PINK, REPEAT-FLOWERING

This rose has been variously classified as a Centifolia, a hybrid Bourbon and a Hybrid Perpetual. It bears very full, flat, quartered flowers which are a rosy carmine color. The petals are reflexed at the edges and recurved in the center. There is a pleasant scent. It is a strong, thorny shrub with long arching canes. Bourbons were China-Damask crosses and Hybrid

'Climbing Paul Lédé'

Perpetuals were improved Bourbons, probably back-crossed, with Gallicas sometimes included. There was clearly a lot of breeding in this rose, but the official category of Centifolia seems unlikely, as it repeat-flowers. ZONES 4–9.

Portemer, France, 1845

Parentage unknown

'PAUL SHIRVILLE'   HARqueterwife
syns 'Heart Throb', 'Saxo'
MODERN, LARGE-FLOWERED/HYBRID TEA, ORANGE-PINK, REPEAT-FLOWERING

The official color coding is misleading, for this variety is rosy salmon-pink, lighter in tone on the petal reverse. The flowers on the first blooming are especially good, being large, high centered and well formed. They are double, borne either singly or in 3s, and have a sweet, enduring fragrance. Blooming continues through summer and autumn, but mid-season flowers are usually smaller. The variety makes a fine bed, hedge or standard rose. The semi-glossy leaves are large, purplish when young, maturing dark green, and are sometimes touched by seasonal mildew; they furnish a plant of vigorous, slightly spreading growth that reaches average height or less. ZONES 4–9.

Harkness, UK, 1983

Compassion' × 'Mischief'

Royal National Rose Society Edland Medal for Fragrance and Certificate of Merit 1982, New Zealand Fragrance Prize 1984, Courtrai Golden Rose 1989, Royal Horticultural Society Award of Garden Merit 1993

'Paul Neyron'

'Paul Neyron'

P

'PAUL TRANSON'
MODERN, LARGE-FLOWERED CLIMBER, ORANGE-PINK, REPEAT-FLOWERING

'Paul Transon' has medium-sized double blooms that open flat to show a charming formation, with the center petals infolded in a random, confused fashion while the outer ones slowly reflex. They are bright coppery pink, paling as they age, and there is a pleasant apple scent. After a prolific first flush a few flowers are likely to appear intermittently through summer and autumn, especially in warmer climates. This variety has the lax and arching stems of a rambler, which means it lends itself to being trained up arches, tall pillars, pergolas and similar structures. In growth it will extend slightly beyond the average expected of a climbing rose. The shiny, dark green foliage is plentiful and attractive. ZONES 4–9.

Barbier, France, 1900

Rosa wichuraiana × 'L'Ideal'

Royal Horticultural Society Award of Garden Merit 1993

'PAUL VERDIER'
OLD, HYBRID PERPETUAL, DEEP PINK, REPEAT-FLOWERING

This is a tall arching shrub with thorny canes, bearing blooms along their length in the usual Hybrid Perpetual and old European style. The more horizontal the canes, the more numerous the flowers. The blooms are medium to large, are globular and fragrant and come in a

'Paul Transon'

'Paul Transon'

lovely rich pink to light red color. It has a vigorous habit and makes a good pillar rose. It is sometimes classified with the Bourbons. ZONES 5–9.

Verdier, France, 1866

Parentage unknown

'PAULETTE'
MODERN, LARGE-FLOWERED/HYBRID TEA, DEEP PINK, REPEAT-FLOWERING

This variety was among the first of many seedlings of 'Peace' to be released. The flowers are large, full of petals and are well formed with high centers. They are bright rosy scarlet, with salmon tints close to the heart of the bloom, and are produced freely in summer on long sturdy stems, maintaining repeated cycles of growth and flower through summer and autumn, the late season show being especially good. There is a light and pleasing scent. This is a useful rose for beds and borders and as a hedge, for it grows vigorously with an upright habit, to above average height. The foliage is rich green. It does not appear to be commercially available. ZONES 4–9.

Meilland, France, 1946

'Peace' × 'Signora'

'PAULII'
syns *Rosa* ×*paulii* 'Rehder', *R. rugosa repens alba* 'Paul'
MODERN, MODERN SHRUB, WHITE

The parentage of this variety is botanically interesting, and as an early Ground

'Paulette'

'Paul's Early Blush'

Cover Rose its novelty value was high at the century's dawn. The clove-scented, medium-sized flowers are single and white, showing yellow stamens as they open. The folded petal tips give them a starry look, and they are borne in short-stemmed clusters on trailing shoots in summer. When grown from cuttings the growth is creeping and truly ground covering; budded plants tend to make mound-like, wide-spreading plants with arching, spiky stems. There are many vicious prickles. Though suitable for difficult sites where a tough utilitarian rose is required, and valued in cold climates for its hardiness, 'Paulii' has many more beautiful successors from which gardeners can choose today. ZONES 3–9.

Paul, UK, pre-1903

Believed to be *Rosa arvensis* × *R. rugosa*

'PAUL'S EARLY BLUSH'
syn. 'Mrs Harkness'
OLD, HYBRID PERPETUAL, LIGHT PINK, REPEAT-FLOWERING

The flowers of this rose are silvery pink and appear a little earlier in the season than most roses. An unusual feature is that flowers of two different shades may appear in the same cluster and even in the same flower. They are large, very double and scented. It is a medium-sized, thorny bush with thick stems and dark green foliage. John Harkness first exhibited his sport in 1890, naming it for his mother Mary Ann (1826–81). The two sports appear identical and originated about the same time. ZONES 5–9.

Paul, UK, 1893 and Harkness, UK, 1893

Sport of 'Heinreich Schultheiss'

'PAUL'S HIMALAYAN MUSK RAMBLER'
MODERN, RAMBLER, LIGHT PINK

This is an odd name. The true Himalayan Musk Rose or *Rosa moschata*

'Paulii'

'Paul's Himalayan Musk Rambler'

'Paul's Lemon Pillar'

nepalensis (syn. *R. brunonii*) has light green, narrow, long leaves and this rose is quite different, having duller and smaller foliage and a *R. multiflora* scent. This rose is considered to have been derived from this or from *R. filipes*, as it has the same thread-like flower stems. It is an enormous tree climber with long trailing stems. It flowers in summer. The small, lilac-pink, double flowers are produced in drooping clusters. ZONES 4–9.

Paul, UK, 1916

Parentage unknown

Royal Horticultural Society Award of Garden Merit 1993

'PAUL'S LEMON PILLAR'
MODERN, LARGE-FLOWERED CLIMBER, LIGHT YELLOW

The color coding has probably misled generations of gardeners, for the color of this variety is close to that of the pith of a lemon, not the outside of the fruit. The large, round buds show creamy yellow as the sepals part. When fully open the sweetly scented flowers are like cabbages, very large and with broad overlapping petals. They hold their form for a long time; indeed this rose was for many years a favorite with exhibitors. The flowers appear only in summer and are vulnerable to rain, which causes petals to stick and fail to open. This rose is best firmly attached to a large wall, where the stiff thick branches can be spread out. The large, dark green leaves are rather sparse, and the plant can grow almost twice as big as the average climber. ZONES 4–9.

Paul, UK, 1915

'Frau Karl Druschki' × 'Maréchal Niel'

National Rose Society Gold Medal 1915

'PAUL'S SCARLET CLIMBER'
MODERN, LARGE-FLOWERED CLIMBER, MEDIUM RED

Britain's Royal National Rose Society handbook *Roses To Enjoy* calls this a

Cluster-flowered Climber, which correctly describes its appearance, for it produces many medium-sized blooms in large sprays. The flowers have about 30 petals in a bright but not brash shade of medium red; they open loosely cupped and have a very light honey scent. They are borne so prolifically that in summertime beneath the massed effect of color the leaves are almost obscured from view. There is little or no repeat-flowering after this glorious show. 'Paul's Scarlet' is appropriate for use as a climber anywhere, as the stems are pliable and plentiful. The only problem is its liability to mildew, which means that potentially dry sites must be avoided. The plant grows vigorously to slightly more than average, with ample mid-green, semi-glossy foliage. ZONES 4–9.

Paul, UK, 1915

Seedling of 'Paul's Carmine Pillar', perhaps crossed with 'Rêve d'Or'

National Rose Society Gold Medal 1915, Bagatelle Gold Medal 1918

'PAX'
MODERN, MODERN SHRUB, WHITE, REPEAT-FLOWERING

'Commemorate peace by planting a bed of Pax' was the raiser's message to his customers in 1918. They would have required considerable space to plant a whole bed, for one plant will comfortably exceed the average dimensions of a shrub rose, producing a succession of cupped, semi-double blooms through summer and autumn. They are borne in large trusses of up to 50 medium to large-sized flowers, which open white from creamy buds and show golden

'Paul's Scarlet Climber'

'Paul's Scarlet Climber'

'Pax'

stamens and ruffled petals. There is a sweet fragrance, and the rose stands out well in a mixed border, for the pale flowers contrast beautifully with crisp dark foliage. ZONES 4–9.

Pemberton, UK, 1918

'Trier' × 'Sunburst'

National Rose Society Gold Medal 1918

'PEACE'
syns 'Béke', 'Fredsrosen', 'Gioia', 'Gloria Dei', 'Mme A. Meilland', 'Mme Antoine Meilland'

MODERN, LARGE-FLOWERED/HYBRID TEA, YELLOW BLEND, REPEAT-FLOWERING

This renowned rose set new standards of excellence for its vigor and beauty and also for its foliage, because it demonstrates that bush roses can attract the eye even when not in flower. The blooms are yellow flushed pink, full-petalled and rounded in form, with the ability to open slowly and look delightful at every stage. They have a pleasant scent, and maintain a good succession of bloom, seeming impervious to weather conditions and succeeding in a wide range of climates, though the yellow turns pale in hot conditions while the pink flushes become more pronounced. This is a splendid variety for beds, borders, hedges and for cutting, and it is one of the best roses to grow in standard form. The vigorous, shrub-like plants grow larger than average for a bush rose, and have glossy, rich green leaves. The raiser dedicated what he rightly considered his masterpiece to the memory of his mother, Claudia, but commercial pressures dictated a string of alternative names in countries other than his own. 'Climbing Peace' is offered for sale by several nurseries in the southern USA, South Africa, Australia and New Zealand but is rarely grown in cooler climates because for the plants to succeed, warm conditions are required. Where

'Peace 1902'

'Peace'

'Peace'

conditions suit it the variety can fulfil the catalogue's forecast of 'flower throughout the summer with peak levels reached in spring and fall'. It reaches a height of 15–20 feet (4.5–6 m). As a climbing sport of the bush form, it shares the same characteristics of flower and foliage but produces vigorous, long, clambering stems. The flowers are produced on side shoots off the wood that has been made in previous years, so an established plant will provide more bloom. ZONES 4–9.

Meilland, France, 1942

(['George Dickson' × 'Souvenir de Claudius Pernet'] × ['Joanna Hill' × 'Charles P. Kilham']) × 'Margaret McGredy'

Portland Gold Medal 1944, All-America Rose Selection 1946, American Rose Society Gold Medal 1947, National Rose Society Gold Medal 1947, The Hague Golden Rose 1965, World Federation of Rose Societies Hall of Fame World's Favorite Rose 1976, Royal Horticultural Society Award of Garden Merit 1993

'PEACE 1902'
OLD, TEA, LIGHT YELLOW, REPEAT-FLOWERING

This rose is apparently available only in Australia. It has attractive, classically Tea-shaped flowers made up of many very pale yellow petals. Each bloom unfurls to reveal a dark mass of stamens at the center. It has, of course, been overshadowed by the Meilland rose of 1945. It was presumably named to commemorate the end of the Boer War. ZONES 7–9.

Piper, Australia, 1902

Parentage unknown

'Peacekeeper'

'PEACEKEEPER' HARbella
syns 'The Peace Keeper', 'United Nations Rose'

MODERN, CLUSTER-FLOWERED/FLORIBUNDA, PINK BLEND, REPEAT-FLOWERING

Several light colors blend together in this rose, basically a mix of coral-pink, salmon and apricot tones on a yellow background, becoming light yellow as the blooms age. The flowers are fully double, and are carried in well-spaced clusters of up to 10. They open with neat centers, maintaining a rounded outline and good symmetry of form until the petals fall. The first flowering is very prolific, almost smothering the bush, and a good succession of bloom is maintained throughout summer and autumn. The flowers have a pleasant spicy fragrance, and this is a suitable garden rose for use in bedding schemes, to group in a border or to plant as a hedge. Individual blooms may be cut for use in small arrangements. The plant grows to average height with an upright, bushy habit and a good covering of light green, glossy foliage. 'Peacekeeper' was named to commemorate the golden jubilee of the United Nations and initially sold in aid of its work for children. ZONES 4–9.

Harkness, UK, 1995

'Dame of Sark' × 'Bright Smile'

Geneva Gold Medal 1995, The Hague First Class Certificate 1995

P

'Peach Blossom'

'Peachy Keen'

'PEACH BLOSSOM' AUSblossom
MODERN, MODERN SHRUB, LIGHT PINK, REPEAT-FLOWERING

The fragrant flowers of this variety are large for peach blossom, being of medium size, but it is quite well named, for the blooms come in big clusters on bowing stems, are blush pink with a light yellow base, and have just enough small petals to make up 2 or 3 rows surrounding the stamens, which show up handsomely in the depths of the flower. When sunlight catches the blooms it lends them an almost transparent quality. For a shrub border this makes an unusual and interesting item. It has a shrubby, spreading habit, grows to average size, and has mid-green glossy leaves. ZONES 4–9.

Austin, UK, 1990

'The Prioress' × 'Mary Rose'

'PEACH SPIRE' KORofaser
MODERN, LARGE-FLOWERED/HYBRID TEA, ORANGE BLEND, REPEAT-FLOWERING

This rose was chosen by Ludwig Taschner from his trial grounds in Pretoria for its tall, upright growth with branches that do not sag. The flowers are continuously produced on the top of the plant as well as on the side stems, so that the shrub never seems to be without blooms, even in autumn. In form, the blooms are very full, like a Large-flowered Rose, although they do not have a tightly pointed center. It has a wonderful combination of warm colors, mostly golden yellow flushed to peach on the outer petals. They make good cut flowers and exhibition roses, but have no fragrance. ZONES 4–11.

Kordes, Germany, 1994

Parentage unknown

'PEACHES 'N' CREAM'
MODERN, MINIATURE, PINK BLEND, REPEAT-FLOWERING

Tapered buds open up to light peach-pink, fragrant flowers with 52 petals of good Large-flowered exhibition form. It was certainly well named, as the blooms are a delicious blend of peachy pink and cream and look almost good enough to eat! This rose has so many petals that it may not open properly in cold damp climates. In warm climates it is a good show rose for exactly the opposite reasons. The plant is vigorous and compact, providing an ample supply of

'Pearl Drift'

blooms throughout the growing season. It is interesting to note that the parents are a well-known pair used previously by Ralph Moore. Yes, there is still gold to be found in that marriage! ZONES 5–10.

Woodcock, USA, 1976

'Little Darling' × 'Magic Wand'

American Rose Society Award of Excellence 1977

'PEACHY KEEN'
MODERN, MINIATURE, APRICOT BLEND, REPEAT-FLOWERING

The long, soft apricot-pink and cream pointed buds open to blooms which develop a stronger tones with age. These spectacular florets have consistent exhibition Large-flowered form and good color fastness. The petals tend to have lots of substance giving the blooms longevity in hot climates and the flowers last a long time when cut for indoors. This plant has a low growing style with more width than height so it is ideal for a border or ground cover. Here again, the use of 'Little Darling' and 'Sheri Anne' as parents, as borrowed from the Ralph Moore program, has resulted in yet another outstanding rose. ZONES 5–10.

Bennett, USA, 1979

'Little Darling' × 'Sheri Anne'

'PEARL DRIFT' LEGgab
MODERN, MODERN SHRUB, WHITE, REPEAT-FLOWERING

Clusters of long, pointed buds develop into large, semi-double pearly white flowers, opening wide like big saucers and showing their golden stamens. They are borne fairly close to the stems, have a pleasing scent, and appear with excellent continuity through summer and autumn. This graceful rose makes an excellent specimen plant, or it can be planted in a

mixed border or as a single-species bed; it will also make a good low hedge. The growth is vigorous and compact, with a somewhat spreading habit that is shorter than average for a shrub rose. The leaves are handsome, large and glossy, reddish when young and ageing to dark green. ZONES 4–9.

LeGrice, UK, 1980

'Mermaid' × 'New Dawn'

Royal National Rose Society Certificate of Merit 1979

'PEARL SEVILLANA' MEIchonar
MODERN, MODERN SHRUB, WHITE BLEND, REPEAT-FLOWERING

The flowers of this variety are pale pinkish-gray on the uppersides of the petals and pearly white on the undersides. The medium-sized flowers appear in well-spaced clusters and opening wide their dozen or so petals in such profusion as to move the catalogue writer to liken them to 'fleecy, shimmering clouds at dawn'! There is a slight fragrance, and there is a good display through summer and autumn. This is a good variety to group in a bed or border for massed color effect. It grows vigorously with an upright, bushy habit and has plentiful dark green foliage. ZONES 4–9.

Meilland, France, 1996

('Bonica' × 'Pascali') × 'Edelweiss'

'PEER GYNT' KORol
MODERN, LARGE-FLOWERED/HYBRID TEA, YELLOW BLEND, REPEAT-FLOWERING

This is quite a solid rose, with 50 broad petals composing each big rounded bloom. They are yellow, edged reddish pink, and appear with freedom on their first flush and with good continuity thereafter through summer and autumn, borne sometimes singly and sometimes in open clusters. They have a pleasing light scent, withstand bad weather well and in the garden will make a very satisfying bed, group or hedge or an effective standard. This rose does better in cool climates than in warm ones. It is well foliaged with large olive green leaves, and grows sturdily with a bushy, upright habit to average height or a little below. ZONES 4–9.

Kordes, Germany, 1968

'Colour Wonder' × 'Golden Giant'

Royal National Rose Society Certificate of Merit 1967, Belfast Gold Medal 1970

'Peaches 'n' Cream'

'Penelope' (Pemberton)

'Penelope' (Williams)

'PEGASUS'   AUSmoon

MODERN, MODERN SHRUB, DEEP YELLOW/
LIGHT YELLOW

The camellia-like flowers of 'Pegasus' are a rich yellow, fading to cream at the edges, and have a strong Tea fragrance. They are carried on clean, shiny foliage on a 3 ft (1 m) shrub with attractively arching growth. The blooms last well as cut flowers. ZONES 4–9.

Austin, UK

'Graham Thomas' × 'Pascali'

'PÉLISSON'

syn. 'Monsieur Pélisson'
OLD, MOSS, DARK RED

This short and tidy shrub to 4 ft (1.2 m) has stout, upright stems that are sparsely covered with dark green moss and few thorns. The leaves are small, dark green and coarsely serrated. For several weeks beginning in early summer, the small, round flower buds open to fragrant, fully double, medium-sized blooms with a distinct button center. Their color is purplish red, perhaps a little muddy and paler with age to pure pink. It is a healthy, yet little-known variety, which prefers a good, fertile soil. ZONES 5–9.

Vibert, France, 1848

Parentage unknown

'PENELOPE'

OLD, TEA, RED BLEND, REPEAT-FLOWERING

This rose bears red flowers with an ivory center. It has the conventional characteristics of the Tea Roses. It should not be confused with the well-known Modern Shrub of the same name. ZONES 7–9.

Williams, Australia, 1906

Parentage unknown

'PENELOPE'

MODERN, MODERN SHRUB, LIGHT PINK,
REPEAT-FLOWERING

This is a large, arching shrub with vigorous and disease-free growth. It flowers continuously through summer and into autumn and produces a lovely show of hips in winter. The trusses of double, medium-sized blooms are of a delicate light pink, fading to white with age. The blooms are sweetly scented. 'Penelope' makes an effective informal hedge, and is useful for growing over fences or walls. ZONES 3–11.

Pemberton, UK, 1924

'Ophelia' × seedling or possibly 'William Allen Richardson' or 'Trier'

National Rose Society Gold Medal 1925, Royal Horticultural Society Award of Garden Merit 1993

'PENNSYLVANIA'

MODERN, LARGE-FLOWERED/HYBRID TEA, PINK
BLEND, REPEAT-FLOWERING

Long, pointed buds open to semi-double, salmon-pink flowers with apricot centers and striped dark pink outer petals. The shapely, fragrant florets have high symmetrical centers. This rose is a sport of a very famous rose that was one of the ancestors of 'Peace'. ZONES 5–11.

Neuner, USA, 1934

Sport of 'Joanna Hill'

'PENNSYLVANIAN'

MODERN, LARGE-FLOWERED/HYBRID TEA,
ORANGE BLEND, REPEAT-FLOWERING

The elegant pointed buds of this rose open into quite large flowers composed of up to 30 petals, high centered in the young bloom. They are a blend of apricot and orange, fading a little as the flowers mature. There is a fruity fragrance. The first flush of bloom is excellent, and there is a respectable repeat-flowering. 'Pennsylvanian' is suitable for beds and borders and for cutting. It has an upright bushy habit and mid-green foliage. ZONES 5–9.

Ohlhus, USA, 1953

'Luna' × ('Mrs Pierre S. duPont' × 'Mrs Sam McGredy')

'PENNY LANE'   TALpen

MODERN, MINIATURE, LIGHT PINK,
REPEAT-FLOWERING

These flowers are a beautiful blending of cream and light pink with consistent exhibition Large-flowered form. The double florets with 26–30 petals have no scent. They are normally borne one bloom per long, straight stem. Foliage is mid-green and semi-glossy on an upright bush which has a tendency to mildew if unprotected. Bloom production is extremely good. ZONES 5–11.

Taylor, USA, 1992

'Party Girl' × 'Maids of Jubilee'

'Pennsylvanian'

'Pensioners' Voice'

'PENNY LANE'

MODERN, LARGE-FLOWERED CLIMBER, APRICOT
BLEND, REPEAT-FLOWERING

This is the first climber to be voted Rose of the Year in the UK. It is a significant addition to the range of repeat-blooming climbers, because of the old-fashioned nature of the flowers. They are filled with ruffled, informal petals which become larger and more beautiful as they expand. The color is pearly blush with light apricot in the depths of the fragrant flower. 'Penny Lane' blooms continuously through summer and autumn on long slender shoots, usually singly and sometimes in small clusters. The plant has flexible stems and grows vigorously to average height or more, making it ideal for pillars, pergolas, arches, walls and fences. The plentiful foliage is dark green and shiny. ZONES 5–10.

Harkness, UK, 1998

Seedling of 'New Dawn'

UK Rose of the Year 1998

'PENSIONERS' VOICE'   FRYrelax

MODERN, CLUSTER-FLOWERED/FLORIBUNDA,
APRICOT BLEND, REPEAT-FLOWERING

'Pensioners' Voice' bears well-spaced clusters of long buds that open into neatly formed flowers, like small-scale Large-flowered Roses, with high centers and becoming cupped as the petals reflex. They are quite large for a Cluster-flowered Rose and are basically orange-apricot, with vermilion-red flushes towards the margins of the petals. It is a very colorful rose, although some blooms tend to be overgrown by younger shoots. There is a pleasant fragrance, and flowering is maintained through summer and autumn. It is best suited for planting as a group in a border with shorter plants in front, to disguise its rather willowy, uneven habit. The healthy plant grows to average height with ample mid-green foliage. ZONES 4–9.

Fryer, UK, 1989

'Alexander' × 'Silver Jubilee'

National Rose Society Trial Ground Certificate 1989

P

'Penny Lane'

'PENTHOUSE'   MACsatur
syn. 'Pink Charm'

MODERN, LARGE-FLOWERED/HYBRID TEA, MEDIUM PINK, REPEAT-FLOWERING

The flowers of this variety are medium pink and fairly double with up to 24 large petals. They are borne singly or in small clusters, and open with neatly formed high centers, becoming cupped as the petals reflex. There is a pleasing fragrance, and flowers continue to appear through summer and autumn. It is suitable for grouping in a border, making a bushy plant of average height and having large matt leaves. There has been some confusion over two roses called 'Penthouse', both coming from the same raiser. The one described here is not as well known as the other one, which is a pink Large-flowered Rose with serrated petals also sold under the name 'West Coast', and code named MACngauru. ZONES 4–9.

McGredy, New Zealand, 1988
Seedling × 'Ferry Porsche'

'PEPITA'   KORkeilich

MODERN, MINIATURE, DEEP PINK, REPEAT-FLOWERING

Bred from the florist rose 'Garnette', 'Pepita' has very well-formed blooms made up of 40 deep pink petals, which open from attractive buds. The long-lasting, small flowers have great substance and are produced in small clusters that have no perfume. Although the flowers and buds keep very well when cut, there are not enough of them. The disease-free bush is covered with dark green foliage. ZONES 5–9.

Kordes, Germany, 1985
'Pink Delight' × ('Mercedes' × 'Garnette')

'Peppermint Twist'

'PEPPERMINT ICE'   BOSgreen

MODERN, CLUSTER-FLOWERED/FLORIBUNDA, GREEN, REPEAT-FLOWERING

Most rose color classifications do not recognize green, which is where this variety properly belongs. The rose is well named, for the flowers are a very creamy sort of green and are borne in clusters of up to 5 flowers, and sometimes singly, on rigid stems. They are of medium size, semi-double, and open cupped, retaining their cool color for a long time whether left on the bush or cut for floral arrangement. There is not much scent, although flowering continues through summer and autumn. This is a rose to plant for its unusual color; it has a neat and upright habit and mid-green, semi-glossy leaves. The name was chosen as the result of

a competition in the British magazine *Garden News*. ZONES 4–9.

Bossom, UK, 1991
'Anne Harkness' × 'Greensleeves'

'PEPPERMINT TWIST'   JACraw
syn. 'Red and White Delight'

MODERN, CLUSTER-FLOWERED/FLORIBUNDA, RED BLEND (STRIPED), REPEAT-FLOWERING

This rose was originally produced as 'Red and White Delight', but its name has since been changed to 'Peppermint Twist'. It is one of the parents of the award-winning Cluster-flowered Rose, 'Scentimental', the other parent being 'Playboy'. 'Peppermint Twist' is a fairly low-growing bush rose that produces white flowers with stripes of red and pink; the striping varies in its intensity. They develop from pointed buds that open fairly quickly to flat, perfumed blooms filled with 30 petals. These flowers appear in flushes that have a rather long period between them. This low and compact bush displays healthy, disease-resistant growth with mid-green, semi-glossy foliage. ZONES 5–9.

Christensen, USA, 1992
'Pinstripe' × 'Maestro'

'PERCEPTION'   HARzippee

MODERN, LARGE-FLOWERED/HYBRID TEA, PINK BLEND, REPEAT-FLOWERING

For size and fragrance combined this rose takes some beating. The blooms, which contain up to 60 broad petals, develop from plump buds into very large, high-centered blooms of symmetrical

form, holding their shape for a long time. The basic color is creamy vanilla, very noticeably stained with cherry pink towards the petal margins, and the fragrance is excellent. Blooming continues through summer and autumn; in the garden 'Perception' is suitable for a border, sited behind other plants since it is tall, and to grow for cutting, for the flowers come on long stiff stems. It grows vigorously with an upright, branching habit to above average height, and is furnished with large leathery leaves. The variety was selected by a group of rose lovers to be named and sold on behalf of Britain's Royal National Institute for the Blind. ZONES 4–9.

Harkness, UK, 1997
Parentage unknown
Geneva Gold Medal 1994

'PERCY THROWER'

MODERN, LARGE-FLOWERED/HYBRID TEA, MEDIUM PINK, REPEAT-FLOWERING

The well-formed flowers of 'Percy Thrower' are full-petalled, fairly large and low centered, shapely at first, then opening loosely and rather flat. They are clear pink, shading to silvery pink towards the petal margins. There is a light and pleasing fragrance, and blooms continue to appear through summer and autumn. It can be used for beds and borders, and as a cut rose it is good for home arrangements as the blooms last well. The plant grows vigorously and has a somewhat open, spreading habit to average height and has deep green glossy foliage. Percy Thrower was a highly respected English gardener, television broadcaster and writer. ZONES 4–9.

Lens, Belgium, 1964
'La Jolla' × 'Karl Herbst'
National Rose Society Trial Ground Certificate 1962

'PERDITA'   AUSperd

MODERN, MODERN SHRUB, APRICOT BLEND, REPEAT-FLOWERING

The medium to large-sized flowers of this rose are full-petalled and open cupped, becoming flat as the petals reflex. They are borne in close clusters

'Penthouse'

'Pepita'

'Penthouse'

'Perdita'

P

like a Cluster-flowered Rose, in a pretty shade of creamy blush with touches of apricot. After the initial blooming more flowers are produced through summer and autumn, when the color tends to be pinker. This makes a welcome addition to the flower border, thanks to its excellent fragrance. It grows shorter than the average size expected of a shrub rose, with plentiful dark green foliage. Perdita, meaning 'the abandoned one', is the name of the heroine of Shakespeare's play, *A Winter's Tale*. **ZONES 4–9.**

Austin, UK, 1983

'The Friar' × (seedling × 'Iceberg')

Royal National Rose Society Edland Medal for Fragrance and Trial Ground Certificate 1984

'PERFECT MOMENT' KORwilma
syn. 'Jack Dayson'

MODERN, LARGE-FLOWERED/HYBRID TEA, RED BLEND, REPEAT-FLOWERING

The flowers of this variety are rounded and full-petalled, of medium to large size, and are carried on stiff, upright stems. Their color is golden yellow on the lower part of the petals with a wide band of orange-red towards the margins, a dramatic combination. The brilliance of the color varies according to climate, needing sunshine but not too high a temperature, which is why this rose is particularly cherished in moderately warm countries. There is some fragrance, and flowers continue through summer and autumn. This plant is suitable for a bed, border and as a hedge, and, if they are cut at a young stage, the blooms are good for arrangements and to show. It grows vigorously to average height or more, with a bushy habit and glossy, dark green foliage. **ZONES 4–9.**

Kordes, Germany, 1991

'New Day' × seedling

All-America Rose Selection 1991

'Perfume Delight'

'Pergolèse'

'PERFUME DELIGHT'

MODERN, LARGE-FLOWERED/HYBRID TEA, MEDIUM PINK, REPEAT-FLOWERING

'Perfume Delight' has long pointed buds that open into large, well-formed blooms, full of broad petals. They are a vivid deep pink with a light purplish tone, paling towards the petal tips and lighter on the petal reverse. The flowers lose their centers and become loosely cupped, showing serrated petal edges, as they age. The sweet spicy fragrance can be excellent, but can become elusive in hot dry conditions. Flowering continues through summer and autumn, and the variety is a good choice for beds, borders and as a hedge and also for cutting, as it has long flower stems; it also withstands the effects of rain. The plant grows vigorously with an upright, bushy habit to average height and has large, dark green, leathery leaves. There is some liability to fungus troubles, so it is not reliably winter hardy in cooler climates. **ZONES 5–9.**

Swim and Weeks, USA, 1973

'Peace' × (['Happiness' × 'Chrysler Imperial'] × 'El Capitan')

All-America Rose Selection 1974

'PERGOLÈSE'

OLD, PORTLAND, MAUVE, REPEAT-FLOWERING

The flowers of this rose are smallish, flat and filled with petals that are quartered in the old rose style. They are very fragrant with a Damask scent. The color is a rich purple-crimson. It is a small to medium-sized, upright shrub with plenty of dark green foliage. The Portlands were produced by crossing the Chinas and the Damasks, and sometimes perhaps adding a bit of Gallica, which was probably the case with this rose. If it is pruned in the summer, it will repeat-flower. **ZONES 5–10.**

Robert-Moreau, France, 1860

Parentage unknown

'PERLA DE ALCAÑADA'

syns 'Baby Crimson', 'Pearl of Canada', 'Perle de Alcañada', 'Wheatcroft's Baby Crimson'

MODERN, MINIATURE, DEEP PINK, REPEAT-FLOWERING

Well-formed buds reveal bright pink double flowers which age to a reddish carmine color with a white base. Flower production is extremely good. The plant is a hardy, low growing bush that rarely grows above 10 in (25 cm) high. Developed in 1944, 'Perla de Alcañada' quickly became a cornerstone in the develop-

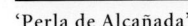

'Perla de Alcañada'

'Perfect Moment'

'Perla de Alcañada'

ment of modern Miniature Roses. The use of 'Rouletii' as the pollen parent brought into the usable genetic pool the earliest known Miniature Rose. Used by the House of Meilland as a basis for many of their Miniature introductions, this rose has earned its rightful place in rose history. **'Climbing Perla de Alcañada'** was developed by Pedro Dot in 1950. **ZONES 5–10.**

Dot, Spain, 1944

'Perle des Rouges' × 'Rouletii'

'PERLA DE MONTSERRAT'

MODERN, MINIATURE, PINK BLEND, REPEAT-FLOWERING

The flowers of this rose are pink in the center blending outwards to a paler pink on the edges of the petals. The blooms have about 18 petals and are grown in small clusters. The foliage is also small and medium green and the plant habit is very compact and dwarf. Perhaps best known as the first Miniature Rose, 'Perla de Montserrat' quickly became popular

because of its tiny size and its amazing vigor. It has all the charm of its pollen parent in producing perfectly shaped tiny flowers. It is a great candidate for small containers or rockeries. Here again, the significance of this classic rose in the history of Miniature Roses has been overlooked as modern Miniatures developed a fuller range of color and form. **ZONES 5–10.**

Dot, Spain, 1945

'Cécile Brünner' × 'Rouletii'

'PERLE DES BLANCHES'
syn. 'Ball of Snow'

OLD, NOISETTE, WHITE, REPEAT-FLOWERING

This rose has medium-sized, globular flowers which are creamy white changing to pure white as they age. When they are fully open the blooms have a camellia-like shape. There is a pleasing fragrance. The foliage is very handsome and nicely complements the flowers. **ZONES 5–9.**

Lacharmé, France, 1874

'Mlle Blanche Lafitte' × 'Sapho'

P

'Pernille Poulsen'

'Perle des Jardins'

'Perle d'Or'

'PERLE DES JARDINS'
OLD, TEA, LIGHT YELLOW, REPEAT-FLOWERING

This is an infuriating rose which is given to balling at the slightest hint of damp or humidity. It was a popular greenhouse rose in its day and well suited to that role. In a dry, sunny climate it can be superb. The large, fragrant flowers are straw yellow. They are full of petals which are pointed at first, opening flat in the Tea manner. It has a moderate growth habit, and the repeat-flowering depends on a dry spell. This rose is at its best in autumn. **'Climbing Perle des Jardins'** is similar to the bush, and is suitable for pergolas, arches and fences. ZONES 7–9.

Levet, France, 1874

Seedling of 'Madame Falcot'

'PERLE DES PANACHÉES'
syn. 'Cottage Maid'
OLD, GALLICA, MAUVE

The flowers of this rose are nearly white, with streaks and patches of crimson. They are loose and semi-double. Vibert produced many of these variegated Gallicas. It is a wiry bush with a suckering habit and grows to medium height. The young foliage is bronze at first, maturing to green. Vibert is said to have hated only two things—the grubs

that destroyed his roses and the English who defeated his beloved Napoleon. ZONES 4–9.

Vibert, France, 1845

Parentage unknown

'PERLE DES ROUGES'
MODERN, POLYANTHA, DARK RED, REPEAT-FLOWERING

This rose was an early and successful attempt to bring red into the Polyantha roses. The flowers are of medium size for the class, full of stiff petals with waved edges, shallowly cupped and opening like pompons. They display a bold crimson color lightened with bright cerise as the petals reflex; they appear in clusters with a prolific first flush of bloom and continue to produce flowers until the first winter frosts. There is little fragrance. Dwarf and compact in habit, the plant grows upright with a covering of small mid-green leaves. Though not apparently in commerce this item deserves a place in any garden of historic roses, as a reminder of the debt owed to the pioneer breeders around Lyon, who laid the foundations of today's Cluster-flowered bushes. ZONES 4–9.

Dubreuil, France, 1896

Parentage unknown

'PERLE D'OR'
syn. 'Yellow Cécile Brünner'
MODERN, POLYANTHA, YELLOW BLEND, REPEAT-FLOWERING

This is sometimes called a China Rose, being the result of an early cross between strains of Multiflora and Tea Roses. Clusters of up to 30 very small, urn-shaped buds open into double, narrow-petalled blooms of honey pink, showing light apricot in their confused centers as they expand. The variety's name, which translates as 'golden pearl', reflects the raiser's aspiration to obtain a yellow Polyantha rose. The synonym suggests a relationship with 'Cécile Brünner'—there is no connection. The flowers appear throughout summer and autumn and are borne on a spindly, free-branching dwarf shrub of upright habit that can become a substantial plant in warm climates. The blooms emit a pleasing light fragrance, and for button-holes and small floral arrangement this variety is a treasure. As a garden plant it has historic interest as well as intrinsic beauty, and is one to grow where it can be viewed. The leaflets are small, glossy and pointed and the whole plant, which looks quite frail, is surprisingly tough and long lived. The rose has long been credited to Dubreuil, but the *Journal des Roses* for 1900 states it was 'Developed by P. Rambaux in 1875 and released to commerce in 1883 by F. Dubreuil'. ZONES 4–9.

Rambaux, France, 1883

Possibly a seedling of *Rosa multiflora* × 'Mme Falcot'

Royal Horticultural Society Award of Garden Merit 1993

'PERNILLE POULSEN'
MODERN, CLUSTER-FLOWERED/FLORIBUNDA, MEDIUM PINK, REPEAT-FLOWERING

The blooms of this variety exhibit delicate shades of rose and coral pink, deepening towards the centers. They are fairly large for a Cluster-flowered Rose, are borne in clusters, with about 18 petals, and have a pleasant refreshing scent. After a free-flowering early flush a good succession of flowers is maintained through summer and autumn. In the garden this is a good plant for bedding and borders, and it is useful for cutting. 'Pernille Poulsen' has an upright, some-

what spreading habit, grows to average height or less, and is furnished with pointed, light to mid-green leaves. The name is that of the raiser's eldest daughter, herself now actively engaged with her husband, Mogens Olesen, in hybridizing roses. ZONES 4–9.

Poulsen, Denmark, 1965

'Ma Perkins' × 'Columbine'

'PERSIAN PRINCESS'
MODERN, MINIATURE, ORANGE-RED, REPEAT-FLOWERING

The beautifully shaped buds of this rose open to coral-red, double, fragrant blooms that come mainly in small clusters. The flower size can be a bit large in cooler climates. The foliage is small and dark green with a leathery texture. While the blooms have great color, performance and form, this rose is best enjoyed as a garden plant, as it provides a profusion of blossoms all year long. 'Persian Princess' is disease-resistant and has a dwarf, low growing habit suitable for a small space, border or container. ZONES 5–10.

Moore, USA, 1970

'Baccará' × 'Eleanor'

'PERSONALITY'
MODERN, LARGE-FLOWERED/HYBRID TEA, YELLOW BLEND, REPEAT-FLOWERING

The flowers of this variety are large, with up to 40 petals, and are carried usually one to a stem. They open from plump buds into high-centered flowers of golden yellow splashed with pink and crimson and have a pleasing Tea scent. With its continuity of bloom through summer and autumn, this is a suitable rose for a bed and to use in borders as well as for cutting. It grows vigorously with an upright habit to average height and is well furnished with leathery, glossy leaves. At present it does not appear to be commercially available. ZONES 4–9.

Morey, USA, 1960

'Peace' × 'Sutter's Gold'

'PETER BENJAMIN'
MODERN, LARGE-FLOWERED/HYBRID TEA, APRICOT BLEND, REPEAT-FLOWERING

This variety suits a warm climate, being grown exclusively in Australia, where it is recommended for exhibition. The

'Persian Princess'

P

'Petite Folie'

'Personality'

flowers, which are a pretty shade somewhere between coral and apricot-pink, are borne on long, strong stems, sometimes singly but quite often with 2 or 3 blooms together. They open with high centers, holding their form to a late stage, for they are composed of up to 40 firm petals. Flowering is maintained through summer and autumn, and there is a light fragrance. The plant grows vigorously with an upright habit to average height or more, and is covered with light green foliage. ZONES 5–9.

Allender, Australia, 1978

'Peter Frankenfeld' × 'Benjamin Franklin'

'PETER FRANKENFELD'
MODERN, LARGE-FLOWERED/HYBRID TEA, DEEP PINK, REPEAT-FLOWERING

'The excellence of form is unique in a rose of such immensity', says Ludwig Taschner of South Africa, one of the world's most knowledgeable rosarians. The deep rose pink flowers have a carmine tinge, and are large and well formed with high centers and maintaining a wonderful symmetry as the petals reflex. They have an agreeable fragrance. As an exhibition rose this is outstanding, because of the long-lasting nature of the flowers. They are long stemmed also, making them very suitable to grow for flower arrangement, and they can be used in beds and borders. Flowering

continues through summer and autumn on a vigorous, upright, free-branching plant that grows to average height or above and is well furnished with healthy deep olive green leaves. The variety is named after a comedian, a compatriot of the raiser. 'Climbing Peter Frankenfeld' (Allen, Australia, 1975) shares the good flower and foliage qualities of its parent bush rose, but does not appear to have enjoyed the wide distribution that might have been expected as it is grown today only in Australia. It seems to do well there, providing its deep cerise-pink pointed blooms very prolifically on long, strong stems. Maybe the existence of many recent pink climbers that are not sports has turned growers away from those that are, in view of some past experiences where the repeat-flowering ability of sports has proved inferior. In a warm climate like that of Australia this is evidently not a problem with this particular variety. ZONES 4–9.

Kordes, Germany, 1966

'Ballet' × 'Florex'

'PETIT FOUR'   INTerfour
MODERN, PATIO/DWARF CLUSTER-FLOWERED, MEDIUM PINK, REPEAT-FLOWERING

The flowers of 'Petit Four' are fairly small, semi-double, neatly formed and open like little powder puffs. They are clear pink with paler centers, have a light fragrance and are freely produced in short-stemmed clusters so they nestle close to the foliage. The succession of bloom through summer and autumn is excellent so that the plant is rarely out of bloom. As a bedding rose or to form a hedge or plant near the front of a border where a short-growing item is required this is a cheerful and most rewarding garden rose. 'Petit Four' is dwarf and cushiony in habit, and grows vigorously with small, mid-green glossy leaves. ZONES 4–9.

Ilsink, The Netherlands, 1982

Seedling of 'Marlena' × seedling

'PETITE DE HOLLANDE'
syns 'Petite Junon de Hollande', 'Pompon des Dames', *Rosa centifolia minor*
OLD, CENTIFOLIA, MEDIUM PINK

This short-growing and rather relaxed shrub to 4 ft (1.2 m) bears grayish green branches covered with reddish thorns and small, well-serrated, soft grayish green leaves. The small flowers are slightly cupped at first, then open flat to show a full set of layered petals often with a button eye. There is a fine scent, but blooms appear in early summer only. It makes a useful shrub or low hedge and is excellent in tubs or urns. ZONES 5–9.

The Netherlands, pre-1838

Parentage unknown

'PETITE FOLIE'   MEIherode
MODERN, MINIATURE, ORANGE BLEND, REPEAT-FLOWERING

'Petite Folie' has vermilion flowers with a carmine reverse. The florets are double, globular in form, and come in small trusses and they have a light fruity scent. The foliage is mid-green with a leathery texture. When it was introduced in 1968, no one quite knew what to make of it. However, it soon gained popularity for its attractive blooms, flower production and plant vigor. ZONES 5–10.

Meilland, France, 1968

('Dany Robin' × 'Fire King') × ('Cricri' × 'Perla de Montserrat')

'Peter Benjamin'

'PETITE LISETTE'
OLD, CENTIFOLIA, DEEP PINK

Similar to 'Petite de Hollande' in many ways, this rose is shorter in stature; it grows to no more than 3 ft (1 m) in height, and may be a little taller in very fertile soil. The soft leaves are gray-green, coarsely and heavily serrated and plentiful in number. They are a backdrop to the small flowers, which are full of deep rose pink petals when fully open. They are richly scented, mostly arranged in large clusters and appear in early summer only. 'Petite Lisette' is best planted in small groups, and also makes an excellent subject for growing in containers, or in smaller gardens. ZONES 5–9.

Vibert, France, 1817

Parentage unknown

'Petite Lisette'

'Petite de Hollande'

'Peter Frankenfeld'

P

'PETITE ORLÉANAISE'
syn. 'Petite de Orléanaise'
OLD, CENTIFOLIA, MEDIUM PINK

This variety is clearly a Centifolia, but has some affinity to the Gallicas. The grayish green wood has numerous thorns and is covered with an abundance of small, grayish green foliage, which can be a little coarse. The shrub is reasonably tidy in overall habit, and grows to about 4 ft (1.2 m) high. The flowers, which appear in mid-summer, are pompon-like when fully open. They are arranged in small clusters and are rich clear pink and well scented. 'Petite Orléanaise' is suitable for the smaller garden or for growing in containers. ZONES 5–9.
Circa 1900
Parentage unknown

'PETITE PENNY' MACjocel
syn. 'Dresselhuys'
MODERN, CLUSTER-FLOWERED/FLORIBUNDA, WHITE, REPEAT-FLOWERING

This little rose bears densely filled clusters of small white semi-double flowers, the number of petals varying from 6–14, on fairly short stiff stems. They have a very innocent look, being pure white, with frilled petals and opening like shallow saucers to display yellow stamens. There is some fragrance, and after a wonderfully prolific first flush the blooms repeat their flower through summer and autumn. It makes an excellent standard and is good for a bed or hedge, to edge the front of a border, or in a

container. It grows vigorously to average height with a bushy habit and bright green, semi-glossy leaves. ZONES 4–9.
McGredy, New Zealand, 1988
('Crépuscule' × seedling) × 'Royal Occasion'

'PETITE PINK SCOTCH'
syn. 'Petite Pink'
MODERN, MODERN SHRUB, MEDIUM PINK

This is what is termed a mystery rose, its true identity unknown. It was discovered in 1949 by Jackson M. Batchelor in the garden of a 1750s plantation home near Wilmington in North Carolina, USA. The name derives from his supposition that Scottish immigrants took it there, but the variety has no evident relationship to the Scots roses, being more likely a derivative of *Rosa wichuraiana*. It bears small, double, light pink rosettes on short stems along trailing branches, giving a most graceful effect in late spring. The lightly scented flowers do not repeat their bloom, but the low-growing, cascading plant covered in small shiny leaves remains attractive, and in milder climates it is almost evergreen. Apart from its usefulness as a ground-covering rose it is also good for an informal hedge. ZONES 4–9.
Parentage unknown

'PETITE RENONCULE VIOLETTE'
OLD, GALLICA, DARK RED

Gwen Fagan, in her search for old roses in Cape Province, South Africa, found a

'Petite Orléanaise'

'Petite Penny'

'Phantom'

'Pharaoh'

clump of this Gallica growing on an English settler's grave in Grahamstown cemetery. It was identified from Redouté's *Les Roses,* and although it was popular in French gardens of the nineteenth century, it had apparently become extinct. The shrubs are of medium size and inclined to sucker, and the leaves are dark green and brittle, dark red when young. The flowers appear on the ends of the many upright and thin branches in spring only. They are very dark maroon in color, but are distinguished by their unusual pompon shape, which resembles a buttercup. They have a sweet fragrance. ZONES 3–10.
Parentage unknown

'PFÄLZER GOLD' TANalzergo
syn. 'Moonlight Serenade'
MODERN, LARGE-FLOWERED/HYBRID TEA, DEEP YELLOW, REPEAT-FLOWERING

There is a puzzle about this rose, for the official description in *Modern Roses 10* says it is deep yellow and has 20 petals, but flowers seen on plants in Australia are medium yellow in bud then open quite pale, with blush tints appearing on the outer petals as they reflex. Also, they are more fully petalled. Maybe the change of climate accounts for this or else the identity has been confused, as can happen in horticulture when distances of much less than 11 000 miles (17 700 km) are involved. In Japan the blooms accord with the official entry, being deep yellow with high centers and symmetrical form. The variety flowers through summer and autumn, but lacks fragrance. It grows upright to average height and has glossy leaves. ZONES 4–9.
Tantau, Germany, 1981
Parentage unknown

'Pfälzer Gold'

'Phoebe'

'PHANTOM' MACatsan, MACcatsan
syns 'Phantom of the Opera', 'The Phantom'
MODERN, MODERN SHRUB, MEDIUM RED, REPEAT-FLOWERING

This handsome shrub carries long, arching growths of very large saucer-shaped scarlet-red flowers, which contrast well with the bright golden stamens. They are made up of up to 12 big petals, attractively waved and fluted, and have a light fragrance; blooming continues through summer and autumn. This variety can be used as an eye-catching plant for a border, as a specimen plant or as a weeping standard. It grows to average height with a wide spreading habit and is well furnished with large, mid-green, semi-glossy leaves. The parentage shown is from a New Zealand source; *Modern Roses 10* has it the other way round. ZONES 4–9.
McGredy, New Zealand, 1992
'Eyeopener' × 'Pandemonium'
New Zealand Novelty Award and Certificate of Merit 1992

'PHARAOH' MEIfiga
syns 'Farao', 'Pharaon'
MODERN, LARGE-FLOWERED/HYBRID TEA, ORANGE-RED, REPEAT-FLOWERING

Despite the haul of gold medals, this rose has never become widely grown in Britain, and today it seems to be commercially available only in Israel and Australia. The reason probably lies in the fact that although it holds its fiery scarlet color very well however fierce the climate, it does not bloom with sufficient freedom. It has plump buds that open into large, high-centered flowers made up of stiff petals that are reluctant to reflex and have little or no fragrance. More blooms appear sporadically through summer and autumn. This variety can be useful in beds and borders, and it is a good rose for cutting, as the stems are strong. The plant grows vigorously with an upright habit to average height and has dark, leathery, semi-glossy leaves. ZONES 4–9.
Meilland, France, 1967
('Happiness' × 'Independence') × 'Suspense'
Geneva Gold Medal 1967, Madrid Gold Medal 1967, The Hague Gold Medal 1967, Belfast Gold Medal 1969

'PHOEBE'
MODERN, LARGE-FLOWERED/HYBRID TEA, WHITE, REPEAT-FLOWERING

The color of this old variety is pale primrose shaded white, deeper in the center,

P

and occasionally almost pure white throughout. The flowers are fully double and high centered, becoming cupped as the long petals reflex. They are sweetly fragrant and are carried on long stiff stems, which makes them very useful for cutting. It is suitable for beds and borders, giving a succession of blooms through summer and autumn. The bush grows vigorously with an upright habit and a covering, rather sparse by modern standards, of large, deep green leaves. 'Phoebe' does not appear to be in commerce at the present time. **ZONES 4–9.**

Cant, UK, 1922

'Ophélia' × 'Verna Mackay'

National Rose Society Gold Medal 1921

'PHOEBE'S CHOICE'   BILice
MODERN, MINIATURE, PINK BLEND, REPEAT-FLOWERING

This plant produces small clusters of 3–4 blooms. They are pink with yellow edges ageing gracefully to white, especially in warm climates. The florets are double with 38 petals and have good exhibition form. The foliage is midgreen with reddish green prickles that slope downwards. The bush sets attractive orange hips in autumn. **ZONES 5–10.**

Bilson, USA, 1987

'Little Darling' × 'Over the Rainbow'

'PHOENIX'
MODERN, LARGE-FLOWERED/HYBRID TEA, DEEP PINK, REPEAT-FLOWERING

'Phoenix' has full-petalled flowers that open initially with high centers before

'Phyllis Bide'

'Phoebe's Choice'

becoming cupped as the petals reflex. They are cerise-pink, fairly large and have a strong fragrance. For a warm climate this variety serves as a suitable bedding and border rose, and it is good to cut as the flowers will open slowly indoors, casting their scent around the room. A succession of bloom is well maintained through summer and autumn on a plant that grows vigorously with an upright habit and is supplied with foliage that is large, leathery and glossy. The state of Arizona in the USA sponsored this rose, which bears the name of its capital city. **ZONES 5–9.**

Armstrong, USA, 1973

'Manitou' × 'Grand Slam'

'PHYLLIS BIDE'
MODERN, POLYANTHA, YELLOW BLEND, REPEAT-FLOWERING

This delightful climbing variety has some unusual features, notably its ability to produce flowers all through summer and autumn, an uncommon achievement for a climbing rose at the time it was introduced. The buds are like small cones and are carried in wide clusters on short stems. They open into fairly full rosette-shaped blooms of modest size, in a mixture of salmony pink and yellow shades. They are lightly scented, and their neat distribution within the cluster and overall on the plant is a pleasure to see. The plant grows vigorously with a branching habit and lax arching stems, making a splendid climber for fences, pillars and arches; it can also be used on a wall and

'Picasso'

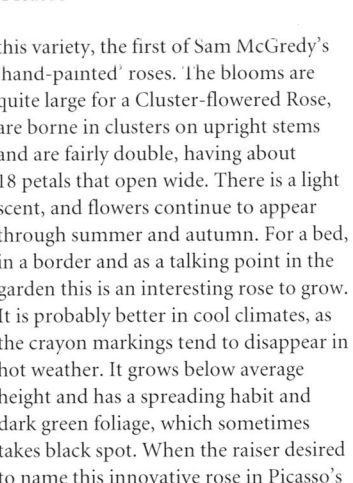

'Phoenix'

as a weeping standard. 'Phyllis Bide' grows to average height and can be pruned to form a sizeable shrub for training on a tripod or against a supporting post. The leaflets are plentiful, narrow and shiny. **ZONES 4–9.**

Bide, UK, 1923

'Perle d'Or' × 'William Allen Richardson' or 'Gloire de Dijon'

National Rose Society Gold Medal 1924, Royal Horticultural Society Award of Garden Merit 1993

'PICANINNI'   WRIpic
MODERN, MINIATURE, ORANGE BLEND, REPEAT-FLOWERING

Des Wright, Past President of the Federation of Rose Societies of South Africa and amateur rose breeder, created this rose that has become popular because of its carefree growth and continuous production of tiny flowers. The shapely, full blooms have deep orange petals with yellow undersides, and are sweetly scented. Their sturdy stems make them popular for exhibition, for posies or table arrangements. The vigorous plant is disease-resistant, and taller growing than most Miniatures. **ZONES 5–11.**

Wright, South Africa, 1991

'Bella Rosa' × 'Little Jackie'

'PICASSO'   MACpic
MODERN, CLUSTER-FLOWERED/FLORIBUNDA, PINK BLEND, REPEAT-FLOWERING

The 'crayon' marks on the blush and carmine petals are the sensational feature of

'Picasso'

this variety, the first of Sam McGredy's 'hand-painted' roses. The blooms are quite large for a Cluster-flowered Rose, are borne in clusters on upright stems and are fairly double, having about 18 petals that open wide. There is a light scent, and flowers continue to appear through summer and autumn. For a bed, in a border and as a talking point in the garden this is an interesting rose to grow. It is probably better in cool climates, as the crayon markings tend to disappear in hot weather. It grows below average height and has a spreading habit and dark green foliage, which sometimes takes black spot. When the raiser desired to name this innovative rose in Picasso's honor, he was rather taken aback by the artist's suggestion that McGredy pay him for the privilege! **ZONES 4–9.**

McGredy, UK, 1971

'Marlena' × ('Evelyn Fison' × [Orange Sweetheart' × 'Frühlingsmorgen])

Royal National Rose Society Certificate of Merit 1970, Belfast Gold Medal 1973, New Zealand Gold Medal 1973

'PICCADILLY'   MACar
MODERN, LARGE-FLOWERED/HYBRID TEA, RED BLEND, REPEAT-FLOWERING

This rose is loved for its bright bicolored flowers, which are scarlet on the inside and yellow on the outside of the petals. They open from pointed buds into large blooms with about 24 broad petals, which form high centers before reflexing to a cupped shape and then dropping

'Phyllis Bide'

'Piccadilly'

'Picture'

'Pierre B'

cleanly. Because the flowers are not as full as many Large-flowered Roses they are borne more freely, which adds to the variety's garden value, where it proves a marvellous bedding, border and hedge rose and also a fine standard. There is a light and pleasant scent, and flowering is well maintained through summer and autumn, bloom quality remaining high whatever the weather. The plant grows to average height with a well-spread bushy habit and a generous covering of handsome dark green glossy leaves, which are reddish when young. It was Reimer Kordes who, observing the 'bright lights' of this rose, suggested its name. ZONES 4–9.

McGredy, UK, 1959
'McGredy's Yellow' × 'Karl Herbst'
National Rose Society Certificate of Merit 1959, Madrid Gold Medal 1960, Rome Gold Medal 1960, Rotterdam Gold Medal, Nord-Rose Award

'PICCOLO'   TANolokip
syn. 'Piccola'
MODERN, CLUSTER-FLOWERED/FLORIBUNDA, ORANGE-RED, REPEAT-FLOWERING

Although this variety has the stature of a Patio Rose, the comparatively large size of the flowers means it fits better in the company of Cluster-flowered Roses wherever a low grower is required for a bed, in front of a border or to make a hedge. The very faintly scented flowers are fairly double and neatly formed and open cupped then become flat. They are

borne prolifically on short upright stems, giving a lively display of vivid tomato red close to the foliage on the first flush of bloom and maintaining a good succession through summer and autumn, performing well regardless of weather conditions. The plant grows to well below average height and has a bushy, spreading habit. It is furnished with large, glossy, dark green leaves that are purplish when young. ZONES 4–9.

Tantau, Germany, 1984
Parentage unknown

'PICTURE'
MODERN, LARGE-FLOWERED/HYBRID TEA, LIGHT PINK, REPEAT-FLOWERING

In the 1930s 'Picture' was a much sought after treasure, wanted for its exquisitely formed rose pink flowers. They have attractive camellia-like whorled centers that retain their shape for a long time while the outer petals gradually reflex. The result is indeed as pretty as a picture for the eye, though for the nose there is not much scent. To make a group in a border or to include in an historic collection this is a good rose to have, and 12 nurseries worldwide are still listing it even though over 60 years have elapsed since its introduction and its constitution is not as robust as it was. Flowering continues sporadically through summer and autumn on a plant that grows compactly to below average height and has a

trim, upright habit and light green matt leaves. 'Climbing Picture' (Swim, USA, 1942) is a decorative Large-flowered Rose of modest size, perfect for buttonholes and small flower arrangements. When this climbing sport was introduced, with it came the splendid opportunity of having quantities of these flowers out at the same time. It grows somewhat larger in extent than the average climbing rose, and is best on a wall where it can spread out and attach securely. In milder climates it is likely to produce flowers following the summer display, but elsewhere it is effectively a summer bloomer only. The most suitable site is one that receives sunshine and a reasonable amount of moisture, because mildew will soon prove troublesome if the roots are in dry soil. As with the bush form the flowers withstand bad weather well. ZONES 4–9.

McGredy, UK, 1932
Parentage unknown
National Rose Society Certificate of Merit 1932

'PIERRE B'
MODERN, LARGE-FLOWERED/HYBRID TEA, APRICOT, REPEAT-FLOWERING

This is one of the really good pure apricot roses. The shapely, ovoid buds open fairly quickly to double flowers containing 20–25 petals, produced on shortish stems. They form very beautiful, full blooms that show deep amber stamens. The petals have excellent substance. The apricot color in the full blooms pales a little at the edges but is still most attractive, and the rose has a very strong

'Pierre B'

perfume. The plant has a low to medium growth habit and dark green, semi-glossy foliage. This is a good rose for cutting, especially in the autumn when the color is much deeper. It was named after an employee of the breeder, who found it in a nursery row of 'Dr A. J. Verhage'. His surname was not disclosed, hence the 'B'. ZONES 5–11.

Brundrett, Australia, 1982
Sport of 'Dr A. J. Verhage'

'PIERRE DE RONSARD'
MEIviolin
syns 'Eden', 'Eden Rose 88', 'Grimpant Pierre de Ronsard'
MODERN, LARGE-FLOWERED CLIMBER, PINK BLEND, REPEAT-FLOWERING

This variety is a vigorous climber with flowers like an old-fashioned rose. They are large and full with over 40 petals and are shaped like round cabbages, opening to disclose a charming muddle of infolded petals. The basic color is creamy white, heavily suffused with lavender pink and carmine. The blooms repeat their flower through summer and autumn, and have a light fragrance. 'Pierre de Ronsard' will grow to the extent expected of an average climber and is suitable to grow on a wall or fence where the strong branching shoots can spread out, or it can be trained up a tall pillar or grown with support as a shrub. The leaves are large, bright green and semi-glossy. Pierre de Ronsard, who

'Pierre de Ronsard'

'Pierre de Ronsard'

'Piccolo'

lived from 1524–85, was a court poet in Scotland and France and was a very keen gardener. ZONES 4–9.

Meilland, France, 1987

('Danse des Sylphes' × 'Handel') × 'Climbing Pink Wonder'

'PIERRE DE ST CYR'
OLD, BOURBON, LIGHT PINK, REPEAT-FLOWERING

This is a conventional Bourbon with large, glossy, very double, cupped blooms. This variety is ideal for growing on a tall pillar, and as it flowers freely throughout summer and autumn, it is a lovely addition to any garden. Although one authority states that this rose is extinct, it is available by custom order in the USA. ZONES 5–9.

Plantier, France, 1838

Parentage unknown

'PIERRE NOTTING'
OLD, HYBRID PERPETUAL, DARK RED, REPEAT-FLOWERING

This rose has a very strong constitution which perhaps explains its longevity in

the catalogues. The flowers are a blackish red shaded blue-violet. Provided the season is fair, they are large and globular. They are disposed to ball badly in wet weather. It has an upright growth habit, and although it is a repeat-flowering rose, it can be unreliable in the autumn. Pierre Notting was a famous rose grower from Luxembourg. ZONES 5–9.

Portimer, France, 1863

Seedling of 'Alfred Colomb'

'PIERRINE' MICpie
MODERN, CLUSTER-FLOWERED/FLORIBUNDA, ORANGE-PINK, REPEAT-FLOWERING

This vigorous Miniature Rose grows taller than most other plants of its class. During summer, it is usually covered with perfect small blooms of Large-flowered shape that are popular with florists for small arrangements. The color is clear apricot, slightly darker on the undersides of the petals. Unfortunately, there is no fragrance. ZONES 5–11.

Williams, USA, 1988

'Tiki' × 'Party Girl'

'Pigalle'

'Pigalle'

'PIGALLE' MEIcloux
syns 'Chacock', 'Fakir', 'Jubilee 150', 'Pigalle 84'

MODERN, CLUSTER-FLOWERED/FLORIBUNDA, ORANGE BLEND, REPEAT-FLOWERING

Described by one of the few growers who supply it as 'a fun rose', 'Pigalle' bears creamy yellow flowers in which are blended shades of orange and orange-red. Shapely and full for a Cluster-flowered Rose, with some 40 petals, they are car-

ried in a huge candelabra on stems long and strong enough to provide an ample supply of blooms for cutting. There is no appreciable scent. It is suitable in beds and borders and as a hedge. It grows vigorously with a tall, bushy habit to above average height and has tough, mid-green semi-glossy leaves. ZONES 5–9.

Meilland, France, 1984

'Frenzy' × (['Zambra' × 'Suspense'] × 'King's Ransom')

'PILGRIM'

MODERN, LARGE-FLOWERED/HYBRID TEA,
DARK RED, REPEAT-FLOWERING

Plump buds on this variety develop into
large full-petalled blooms that open
cupped as the petals reflex. They are dark
crimson and yield a pleasant fragrance.
There is a good initial show of flower,
and the plant continues to produce a
succession of blooms through summer
and autumn. It is suitable for use in beds
and borders and as a hedge. The bush is
well clothed in dark, leathery foliage, and
it grows vigorously to average height
with an upright, bushy habit. At the
present time 'Pilgrim' does not appear to
be commercially available, indicating the
rose world thought it no improvement
on the pollen parent, 'Chrysler Imperial',
which is currently offered by over
60 nurseries worldwide. ZONES 4–9.

Armstrong, USA, 1970

Seedling × 'Chrysler Imperial'

'PILLARBOX'   CHEwaze

syns 'Pillar Box', 'Wardlip'

MODERN, CLUSTER-FLOWERED/FLORIBUNDA,
ORANGE-RED, REPEAT-FLOWERING

The eye is drawn to this rose by the vivid
vermilion color, a very pure shade. The
blooms are moderately full, with about

20 petals, and of medium size. They
open cupped in close clusters at the top
of long, rather gaunt stems and have
little fragrance. After the first flowering,
further blooms appear with good continuity through summer and autumn.
This variety's best place in the garden
is as a group in a border. It grows vigorously with an angular branching habit
to above average height and is provided
with mid-green, semi-glossy leaves.
'Pillarbox' was named in connection
with the Liverpool Garden Festival of
1984, which received sponsorship from
the British Post Office. ZONES 4–9.

Warner, UK, 1986

'Alexander' × ('Galway Bay' × 'Elizabeth of
Glamis')

'PIMLICO 81'   MEIdujaran

syns 'Pimlico 82'

MODERN, CLUSTER-FLOWERED/FLORIBUNDA,
MEDIUM RED, REPEAT-FLOWERING

The large flowers on this variety are fully
double, made up of several rows of small
crisp petals that are prettily waved at the
edges. They are a medium, kindly shade
of red, showing yellow stamens as they
open out. There is little or no appreciable fragrance. Blooms appear through
summer and autumn, making this a very

'Pilgrim'

'Pimlico 81'

'Pillarbox'

'Pink Bells'

suitable rose for a bed and for borders
and hedging. Despite its gold medal,
awarded after two years of growing trials
that testify to its all-round garden worth,
it is surprisingly little known, perhaps
because the color is not arresting enough
to make it stand out. The plant grows
vigorously with a bushy habit and has
large, dark glossy leaves. ZONES 4–9.

Meilland, France, 1980

('Tamago' × 'Fidelio') × ('Charleston' ×
'Lili Marlene')

Belfast Gold Medal 1983

'PIÑATA'

syn. 'Furedaiko'

MODERN, LARGE-FLOWERED CLIMBER,
YELLOW BLEND, REPEAT-FLOWERING

The flowers of this cheerful climber
undergo a remarkable transformation.
They are borne in clusters of 4 or 5 urn-
shaped buds, and after they have opened
with elegant high centers, the petals reflex and begin to change color, the initial
citrus yellow gradually being overlaid
with vermilion from the margins downwards, finishing as the petals age an overall pale shade of scarlet with patches of
pinky red. There is a little fragrance, and
the plant continues to produce flowers
through summer and autumn. It makes
a useful climbing plant for a fence, wall,
pillar or arch, growing more slowly and
less extensively than the average climbing rose. It provides its best flowers
where there is some shade or in cool
weather conditions, yet it needs a warm
climate as it is not hardy enough to withstand prolonged frost periods. 'Piñata' in
Spanish American means 'brawl' or
'scrap', perhaps with reference to the apparent contest within the flower as one
color overcomes the other. ZONES 6–10.

Suzuki, Japan, 1974

Parentage unknown

'Pincushion'

'Pink Cameo'

'PINCUSHION'

MODERN, MINIATURE, MEDIUM PINK,
REPEAT-FLOWERING

This unique low and spreading, bushy
Miniature Rose is adorned with large,
glossy mid-green, disease-resistant foliage. The very double, crowded flowers
come in small to medium-sized, well-
shaped clusters that color the plant with
masses of very soft and attractive rose
pink petals. They open freely from oval
buds and develop into very flat blooms
with an old-fashioned look. They have a
fairly quick repeat. 'Pincushion' makes a
good pot plant or a very attractive low
border. It also makes a lovely bushy
standard. ZONES 5–9.

Kordes, Germany, 1988

Parentage unknown

'PINK BASSINO'

syn. 'Korbasren'

MODERN, MODERN SHRUB, PINK BLEND,
REPEAT-FLOWERING

It is difficult to know whether to call this
a ground cover rose or a shrub rose, because although it spreads up to twice as
wide as it is high it is not procumbent.
The 5-petalled flowers are light pink with
a prominent white eye and are borne in
clusters on firm, slim stems quite close to
the foliage. They open like saucers to
display golden stamens and have a guileless, innocent air in their simplicity.
There is a light fragrance and, after the
prolific initial display, blooming continues throughout summer and autumn.
'Pink Bassino' is very suitable for
borders, and in parks it is used for beds
and landscaping. It grows vigorously to
below average height with a well-spread
habit. The foliage is plentiful, bright
green and shiny, reddish when young.
ZONES 4–9.

Kordes, Germany, 1993

Seedling of Rosa wichuraiana × 'Robin Redbreast'
Royal National Rose Society Trial Ground
Certificate 1992, Anerkannte Deutsche Rose 1993

'PINK BELLS'   POUbells

MODERN, GROUND COVER, DEEP PINK

These cheerful, bright rose pink flowers
are even more beautiful when the
blooms are fully opened. The florets are
double with 35 petals and have a light
fragrance. The blooms are very weatherproof, with cycles lasting from late spring
until early autumn. The foliage is small
and mid-green with a semi-glossy look
and the plant has a spreading habit,

'Pink Bassino'

making it ideal for use as a ground cover or low fence. 'Pink Bells' is an innovation in the development of Miniature Roses. ZONES 5–10.

Poulsen, Denmark, 1983

'Mini Poul' × 'Temple Bells'

'PINK CAMEO'
MODERN, CLIMBING MINIATURE, MEDIUM PINK, REPEAT-FLOWERING

The small, double, rich rose pink flowers are produced in clusters with the centers a little darker. The florets have about 20 petals and a light fragrance. The foliage is a rich, semi-glossy green. This plant can be tall in warm climates reaching as high as 5 ft (1.5 m) in certain zones. 'Pink Cameo' is one of the best

Climbing Miniatures developed so far, lending itself to twining its long branches along a low fence to create a spectacular effect. Developed from an early Large flowered Rose as seed parent and a pollen parent, 'Zee', never commercially introduced, this Climbing Miniature was the first of many climbers developed by Moore. ZONES 5–10.

Moore, USA, 1954

('Soeur Thérèse' × 'Skyrocket') × 'Zee'

'PINK CASCADE'   MORcade
MODERN, CLIMBING MINIATURE, MEDIUM PINK, REPEAT-FLOWERING

The medium pink, double (35 petals) flowers of 'Pink Cascade' have a decorative form and a light fragrance. The

florets are borne in profusion on a vigorous, climbing plant which can be trained into various shapes. The foliage is semi-glossy, mid- to dark green on a plant with a spreading habit. This series of climbers, introduced by Moore, do not crawl outwards, but rather arch outwards to form a mound about 3ft (1m) high. This growth habit is ideal on a bank or at the top of a wall where the plant can drape over the edge. This rose has also been used as a hanging basket with great success. The two other members of the series are 'Red Cascade' and 'Orange Cascade'. ZONES 5–11.

Moore, USA, 1981

(Rosa wichuraiana × 'Floradora') × 'Magic Dragon'

'Pink Cascade'

'Pink Favorite'

'Pink Chiffon'

'Pink Cloud'

'Pink Chimo'

'PINK CHIFFON'

MODERN, CLUSTER-FLOWERED/FLORIBUNDA,
LIGHT PINK, REPEAT-FLOWERING

This Cluster-flowered Rose resembles
the Old Garden Roses in the way its light
pink blooms are crowded with petals.
There are usually over 50 of them, folded
against one another to create confused
centers as the large flowers develop a
cupped and finally a flat shape as they
expand. The old flowers turn pale, especially in hot weather, but retain deeper
pink tones in the depths of the bloom.
They are produced in well-filled clusters
and have a pleasing spicy fragrance. This
is a pretty variety to group in a border,
but it needs calm sunny conditions for
best results as the blooms are easily
spoiled by rain. The plant grows vigorously with a bushy, rather spreading
habit to below average height and has
dark green glossy leaves. ZONES 5–9.

Boerner, USA, 1956

'Fashion' × 'Fantasia'

'PINK CHIMO'   INTerchimp

syn. 'Pink Panoramic'

MODERN, GROUND COVER, MEDIUM PINK,
REPEAT-FLOWERING

Once well established this plant produces
long arching stems that trail under their

own weight, extending twice as far in
all directions as its height. It produces
great numbers of small, medium pink,
5-petalled flowers, copiously on its first
blooming and with a respectable showing through the rest of summer and
autumn, so that the plant is rarely without some color. As a rose for parks and
environmental areas where a tough, easy
grower is needed it is very suitable, but
for general garden use there are more recent varieties of neater habit and greater
aesthetic appeal. 'Pink Chimo' makes a
rugged, prickly, hummocky plant with a
dense covering of mid-green semi-glossy
foliage, and is generally very healthy.
ZONES 4–9.

Ilsink, The Netherlands, 1990

Seedling × 'Immensee'

'PINK CLOUD'

MODERN, LARGE-FLOWERED CLIMBER,
MEDIUM PINK, REPEAT-FLOWERING

The genes of 'New Dawn' have contributed to scores of modern Climbers,
through both parents in the case of 'Pink
Cloud'. The large flowers are fairly full in
an attractive shade of deep rose pink
with a darker center, are borne in clusters, and open out into a cupped form.
There is a Tea fragrance, and after a

splendid first blooming the plant flowers
intermittently through summer and
autumn. The growth is about the average
to be expected of a climber, and the variety makes a very suitable choice for
walls, fences, pillars and arches or it can
be kept pruned and made to form a substantial shrub. It is vigorous and has an
upright, rather stiff branching habit and
a good covering of robust glossy foliage.
ZONES 4–9.

Boerner, USA, 1952

'New Dawn' × a red dwarf seedling of
'New Dawn'

'PINK DELIGHT'   LENpi

MODERN, MINIATURE, LIGHT PINK,
REPEAT-FLOWERING

These pastel pink blooms have a beautiful color tone at all stages—from bud all
the way until fully opened. The flowers
tend to be larger in cooler climates. They
have exhibition Large-flowered form
with lots of petals that open slowly maintaining the lovely color until it shatters.
This is a low growing plant with a tendency to mildew, unless given adequate
protection. ZONES 5–10.

Lens, Belgium, 1982

Parentage unknown

'PINK FAVORITE'

syn. 'Pink Favourite'

MODERN, LARGE-FLOWERED/HYBRID TEA,
MEDIUM PINK, REPEAT-FLOWERING

Those who recall 'Juno' remember a
flower of heartstopping beauty—but the

plant underneath never grew much. By
crossing it with a vigorous strain the
raiser hoped to recapture that beauty,
'Pink Favorite' being the creditable result. The flowers, borne singly, in threes
or in candelabra fashion, are long,
elegant and high centered, in a rather
cold color, somewhere between bright
rose and china pink. Although there are
only about 24 petals, they are so con-
trived as to make the flowers look full
and so firm that the variety has proved
most successful for exhibitors, as well as
a good garden rose for beds and borders.
The fragrance is elusive, pleasant to some
noses, negligible to others. It flowers
freely through summer and autumn,
stands bad weather well and does best in
cooler climates. Its habit is free branching, somewhat splayed, and the leaves are
beautiful, bright, long, smooth and polished. Though often praised for its good
health, it shows recent signs of vulner-
ability to rust. ZONES 4–9.

Von Abrams, USA, 1956

'Juno' × ('George Arends' × 'New Dawn')

Portland Gold Medal 1957

'PINK GROOTENDORST'

MODERN, HYBRID RUGOSA, MEDIUM PINK,
REPEAT-FLOWERING

This variety carries clusters of many
small frilly petalled rosettes, in appearance rather like a dianthus. They are fully
double and a refreshing shade of rose
pink, but have very little scent; they are
charming for use in small flower arrangements, lasting many days. The
dainty flowers are borne on a plant that
entirely lacks their charm, being a gaunt
and prickly shrub with small, rather

'Pink Delight'

'Pink Grootendorst'

'Pink Grootendorst'

'Pink La Sevillana'

pallid, coarse leaves. In a border it will provide color and interest throughout the growing season, for the plant is hardly ever out of flower through summer and autumn. It grows to average height and has an exemplary record for good health. ZONES 4–9.

Grootendorst, The Netherlands, 1923

Sport of 'F. J. Grootendorst'

Royal Horticultural Society Award of Garden Merit 1993

'PINK GRUSS AN AACHEN'
syn. 'Rosa Gruss an Aachen'

MODERN, CLUSTER-FLOWERED/FLORIBUNDA, ORANGE-PINK, REPEAT-FLOWERING

This sport shares the characteristics of its parent, being a Cluster-flowered Rose with an old-fashioned look, but whereas the original is listed by over 70 growers around the world the sport is offered by only seven. The difference lies in the color of the fragrant blooms, which are a blend of pale yellow and light salmon-pink. The character of the silky petalled flowers accords well with summer-flowering Old Garden Roses, and if the variety is planted with them it guarantees there will be some additional color, for the bushes will bloom on through summer and autumn. The growth is short and rather spreading, with a covering of dark green leathery leaves. ZONES 4–9.

Kluis and Koning, The Netherlands, 1929

Sport of 'Gruss an Aachen'

'PINK HEATHER'

MODERN, MINIATURE, LIGHT PINK, REPEAT-FLOWERING

The flowers of 'Pink Heather' are a delicate shade of lavender-pink to white. They are double with 45 petals, fragrant

and are borne in clusters. The foliage is very small and glossy green on a vigorous, low growing, compact bush. This rose is best known for its remarkable profusion of bloom and its distinctive perfume. The blooms tend to hold their color well in most climates and the bush is rarely without color throughout the growing season, as it has a very fast repeat cycle. It is best used as border plant. This is yet another offspring from that remarkable cross of the rambler, *Rosa wichuraiana* and the Cluster-flowered rose, 'Floradora', (which was a parent of 'Queen Elizabeth'). ZONES 5–11.

Moore, USA, 1959

(*Rosa wichuraiana* × 'Floradora') × ('Violette' × 'Zee')

'PINK ICEBERG'

MODERN, CLUSTER-FLOWERED/FLORIBUNDA, PINK BLEND, REPEAT-FLOWERING

This rose is a sport of 'Iceberg', which occurred in a garden in Hobart. It has all the good qualities of its parent, being disease resistant, with light green foliage and a light perfume. Like 'Iceberg', it flowers almost continuously over a long period. Its flowers are in varying shades from pink to white, often with a hand-painted appearance. The flowers fade with age and may be lighter in hot weather. The stamens are generally orange-pink and the filaments retain this color as the flowers age. Some flowers may be entirely white with yellow stamens, as in 'Iceberg'. It is an attractive rose and is a perfect choice for standard or bush. ZONES 5–10.

Weatherly, Australia, 1997

Sport of 'Iceberg'

'Pink Heather'

'PINK JOY'

MODERN, MINIATURE, DEEP PINK, REPEAT-FLOWERING

Globular buds open to reveal well-shaped, deep pink flowers with a scent described as sweet violet. The florets are small on a dwarf plant. There is a moderate profusion of bloom all through the growing season. Although the plant is healthy, it can mildew without proper protection. This rose is best used as a container-grown plant or in a border. It is interesting to note that 'Pink Joy' is the result of an incestuous cross, and bears the color and partial form of its parent which is considered one of the 3 earliest known Miniature Roses. More modern Miniatures have since replaced this old time favorite. ZONES 5–11.

Moore, USA, 1953

'Oakington Ruby' × 'Oakington Ruby'

'PINK KARDINAL'

MODERN, LARGE-FLOWERED/HYBRID TEA, DEEP PINK, REPEAT-FLOWERING

This rose has all the strengths of its parent, except for color which is a hard pink that fades to a dirty shade. The blooms are of true exhibition form. They are a little small in the summer for exhibition purposes but are superb in spring and autumn. 'Kardinal' and 'Pink Kardinal' are some of the first roses to flower in spring and continue until early winter

when the best flowers of the year are produced. Each bloom contains 50 petals with superb substance. The bush is of medium height and stocky. ZONES 5–10.

Stratford, Australia, 1995

Sport of 'Kardinal'

'PINK LA SEVILLANA'
MEIgeroka

syns 'Pink La Sevilliana', 'Pink Sevillana', 'Rosy La Sevillana'

MODERN, CLUSTER-FLOWERED/FLORIBUNDA, MEDIUM PINK, REPEAT-FLOWERING

This sport resembles its parent in all respects save color, which is deep pink in the young flowers, lightening with age. It bears clusters of up to 5 small to medium-sized, lightly fragrant blooms on long, flexible stems. They are made up of 12 or so petals, open with neat centers, and become cupped as they mature. Flowers are generously produced on the first flush, and a succession of color is well maintained through summer and autumn. 'Pink La Sevillana' makes a useful plant for a mixed border and is particularly successful as a hedge. The plant is spreading and hedge-like in habit, growing to average height and having dense, dark green, glossy foliage. ZONES 4–9.

Meilland, France, 1985

Sport of 'La Sevillana'

Baden-Baden Gold Medal 1985, Anerkannte Deutsche Rose 1986

'Pink Joy'

'Pink Kardinal'

'Pink Iceberg'

P

'PINK LÉDA'

syn. 'Painted Damask'
OLD, DAMASK, MEDIUM PINK

There are two forms of 'Léda', different only in color—one is white and the other is pink. They both have the intense Damask fragrance and although classed as Summer Damasks, there can be later flowers. They are both luxuriant shrubs. This rose is thought to have originated in France. The blooms are clear pink. The white form originated in England. It opens cream and then becomes suffused with blush, later turning crimson on the edges of the petals. In Greek mythology, Leda was seduced by Zeus who took the form of a swan. She became the mother of Helen of Troy. ZONES 4–9.

Pre-1844

Parentage unknown

'PINK LUSTRE'

MODERN, LARGE-FLOWERED/HYBRID TEA,
LIGHT PINK, REPEAT-FLOWERING

There is some luminosity about the light pink color of this rose, which explains the raiser's choice of name. The blooms are large, with up to 50 petals, and open with high centers. There is a satisfying fragrance but the flowers are not borne very freely, appearing after the first flush only intermittently through summer and autumn. The form and size of the blooms make them useful to exhibitors, despite occasional split centers and their tendency to open fast and lose color in hot

weather. This variety is useful in a bed or border, though it is commercially offered at the present time only in the USA, due probably to a deterioration in its constitution. It has an upright, bushy habit and a rather sparse provision of dark, glossy, leathery textured leaves. ZONES 4–9.

Verschuren, The Netherlands, 1957

'Peace' × 'Dame Edith Helen'

'PINK MASTERPIECE'

MODERN, LARGE-FLOWERED/HYBRID TEA,
PINK BLEND, REPEAT-FLOWERING

This plant bears elegant buds of clear shell pink on long firm stems; the buds develop into big flowers of about 40 petals, high centered at first then becoming rounded and cupped as the petals reflex. There are deeper pink tones within the open flower, which is enlivened by a touch of yellow at the petal base. The flowers yield a pleasant fragrance and, after the main flush, more appear through summer and autumn. This variety can be used for cutting as well as in beds and borders. It grows vigorously with an upright habit to average height. ZONES 4–9.

Boerner, USA, 1962

Seedling of 'Serenade' × 'Kate Smith'

'PINK MEIDILAND'   MEIpoque

syn. 'Schloss Heidegg'
MODERN, MODERN SHRUB, PINK BLEND,
REPEAT-FLOWERING

This is one of several amenity shrubs produced by the Meilland firm, and is

'Pink Masterpiece'

recommended as ideal for roadside planting and for green spaces in urban developments. It makes a vigorous, bushy plant with a dense covering of foliage, producing umbrella-like panicles with up to 20 lightly scented blooms. The pointed red buds open to medium-sized cupped blooms of deep pink, showing white eyes around the yellow stamens at the center. The color becomes paler as the flowers age, before dropping their petals cleanly. After the first prolific flush, more blooms follow on through summer and autumn. The height of the plant is less than average and the leaves are leathery and shiny and reddish green when young. ZONES 4–9.

Meilland, France, 1985

'Anne de Bretagne' × 'Nirvana'

Anerkannte Deutsche Rose 1987

'PINK MEILLANDINA'   MEIjidiro

syn. 'Pink Sunblaze'
MODERN, MINIATURE, MEDIUM PINK,
REPEAT-FLOWERING

These medium pink flowers have a distinctive gold center to the bloom and a rosette-type form. They are borne singly or in small clusters and there is no fragrance. The plant has small, pointed, mid-green foliage and a reliable succession of tiny flowers. It is mainly sold as small container grown plants and can be grown indoors for a while before planting out in the garden. ZONES 5–10.

Meilland, France, 1982

Parentage unknown

'Pink Parfait'

'Pink Meidiland'

'Pink Léda'

'Pink Lustre'

'Pink Panther'

'PINK PANTHER'   MEIcapinal

syns 'Aachener Dom', 'Panthere Rose'
MODERN, LARGE-FLOWERED/HYBRID TEA,
PINK BLEND, REPEAT-FLOWERING

In warm climates there is not so much difference in the colors within the flowers of this variety, apart from a deepening of the azalea pink tone near the petal margins, but cooler conditions show a marked contrast, the rims appearing as a definite rose red. The blooms at their best are beautiful, being large and high centered and having 40 or more petals, they can be borne singly, in clusters or in candelabra form. The flowers, which continue to appear through summer and autumn, have a light fruity scent and last well, coming to resemble peonies before the waved and fluted petals finally fall. This rose looks its best in a warm climate, because rain can mark the blooms. A vigorous plant, it is useful for beds, borders and hedges, growing to average height with an upright, bushy habit and having bronzy, glossy leaves. ZONES 5–9.

Meilland, France, 1982

MEIgurami × MEInaregi

The Hague Gold Medal 1981

'PINK PARFAIT'

MODERN, CLUSTER-FLOWERED/FLORIBUNDA,
PINK BLEND, REPEAT-FLOWERING

For a supply of buttonhole roses on a well-tempered plant, 'Pink Parfait' takes some beating. Clusters of 3 or more carmine buds open to light pink flowers of medium to large size, the shades of pink varying according to season and climate, sometimes with traces of peach-pink.

Each loosely double bloom is neatly formed with a coiled center, the outer petals reflexing in symmetrical fashion. The initial display is prolific, and the variety maintains an excellent succession of flowers through summer and autumn, though they tend to fly open and lose color quickly in hot weather. There is a light sweet scent, and for the garden this gives splendid value in a bed or border. It grows sturdily with an upright, bushy habit to slightly less than average height, with a flowing outline, and is well supplied with matt, mid-green foliage. ZONES 4–9.

Swim, USA, 1960

'First Love' × 'Pinocchio'

Baden-Baden Gold Medal 1959, Portland Gold Medal 1959, All-America Rose Selection 1961, National Rose Society Gold Medal 1962

'PINK PEACE'   MEIbil
MODERN, LARGE-FLOWERED/HYBRID TEA, MEDIUM PINK, REPEAT-FLOWERING

The color of the flowers of this variety is an arresting, rather hard and dusty deep pink, and it shows up from a long way off, for the blooms, of some 60 broad petals, are among the largest produced in quantity on any rose. They are carried on stiff stems, have a sweet strong fragrance and last well when cut. On opening out they display a well-filled cupped form, and carry a very narrow but distinct line of blush white along their petal rims. 'Pink Peace' is very suitable for a bed or border, but the strong color means it has to be sited so as not to clash with other garden items. Reflowering after the first flush continues through summer and autumn, with remarkable freedom considering the size of the flowers. The plant is vigorous, growing upright to more than average height, and it has large, leathery, matt leaves. Whereas over 50 nurseries offer the bush form of 'Pink Peace', those supplying **Climbing Pink Peace** (MEIbilsar; Meilland, France, 1968) can probably be numbered on the fingers of one hand. Two reasons can be suggested for this. First, a number of good pink climbers that were not sports were already established at the time of its introduction, such as 'Aloha', 'Pink Cloud' and 'Pink Perpetue', and they could be relied on to give much more

'Pink Perpetue'

flower per square meter of growth. Second, the color of 'Pink Peace' is strident and not easy to mix with other roses whether old or modern. Whatever the reason, and despite its vigor, the climbing form of 'Pink Peace' has never become widely grown. ZONES 4–9.

Meilland, France, 1959

('Peace' × 'Monique') × ('Peace' × 'Mrs John Laing')

Geneva Gold Medal 1959, Rome Gold Medal 1959

'PINK PEARL'   KORmasyl
syn. 'Fee'
MODERN, LARGE-FLOWERED/HYBRID TEA, LIGHT PINK, REPEAT-FLOWERING

This variety bears full-petalled flowers of medium size that open with neatly formed centers and develop slowly as the outer petals reflex to create a bloom of elegance and symmetry. The scented pearly blush blooms, which appear through summer and autumn, are borne on very long stems, perfect for cutting, and indeed this rose was named to mark the 30th anniversary of the National Association of Flower Arrangement Societies in the UK. 'Pink Pearl' needs a sunny place and free circulation of air, partly because shade will draw the plant up and make it lanky, and also because an open site reduces the risk of mildew. It grows well above average height with a narrow, upright habit and has rich dark green foliage. ZONES 4–9.

Martens, Germany, 1989

Sport of 'Congratulations'

'Pink Perpetue'

'PINK PERPETUE'
MODERN, CLUSTER-FLOWERED CLIMBER, MEDIUM PINK, REPEAT-FLOWERING

This rose is a warm and pleasing shade of rose pink. It flowers a lot, grows well and is easy to train and generally healthy, which explains why it has maintained its popularity for well over 30 years. The blooms are of medium size, rounded in form, and with up to 36 petals symmetrically arranged to form a cup. They are spaced neatly over the plant in short-stemmed clusters, have a light and pleasing scent and continue to carry their blooms through summer and autumn so effectively that it is unusual for there to be no color on the plant during this time. 'Pink Perpetue' can be used on a wall, fence, pillar, arch and even a pergola if the gardener is patient, for it extends itself by steady rather than rapid progress. It does not resent being pruned. 'Pink Perpetue' is a vigorous, stiff and free-branching grower, well furnished with dark leathery leaves. The name requires no French accents, as Walter Gregory chose it simply for its pleasing sound. ZONES 4–9.

Gregory, UK, 1965

'Danse du Feu' × 'New Dawn'

National Rose Society Certificate of Merit 1964

'PINK PETTICOAT'
MODERN, MINIATURE, PINK BLEND, REPEAT-FLOWERING

Pointed buds open to give creamy white double (33 petals) flowers edged with

'Climbing Pink Peace'

coral-pink. The florets have a light scent and good high centered Large-flowered form. The blooms tend to be larger than the normal Miniature size and this rose perhaps should be classified as a miniflora or Patio. Even in hot climates the blooms hold both their form and color well. The color combination is even more spectacular when the blooms are fully open. The plant is a very tall, upright bush with dark green, glossy foliage and is disease-resistant. 'Pink Petticoat' is extremely vigorous, producing large clusters on tall, strong straight stems. The flowers are excellent for cutting. ZONES 4–11.

Strawn, USA, 1979

'Neue Revue' × 'Sheri Anne'

American Rose Society Award of Excellence 1980

'Pink Petticoat'

P

'Pink Puff'

'Pink Porcelain'

'Pink Rosette'

'PINK PORCELAIN' TINporce
MODERN, MINIATURE, LIGHT PINK,
REPEAT-FLOWERING

As you might expect from the name, the flowers are a light shell pink with slightly softer tones on the outer petals. They have perfect high centered form and are suitable for exhibition. The porcelain-like blooms come on long stems with very attractive foliage. The blooms tend to be long lasting but can suffer from color loss in very hot weather turning to almost white. The plant has an upright, medium growth habit and is very suitable for growing in a container. It is a prolific bloomer. 'Pink Porcelain' is another prime example of the pioneering work of Dee Bennett and her use of her favorite breeding Large-flowered, 'Futura', as seed parent. ZONES 5–11.

Bennett, USA, 1983

'Futura' × 'Avandel'

'PINK POWDERPUFF' MORpuff
MODERN, LARGE-FLOWERED CLIMBER, LIGHT PINK,
REPEAT-FLOWERING

This remarkable but so far little known variety was introduced by the raiser as a new hybrid of *Rosa bracteata*, a species that has produced surprising diversity among its descendants. The flowers are quite large for a climber, and are carried in clusters of 3 or more. They are light pink, paling slightly as they mature, and are crammed with 100 or more infolded petals like an old-fashioned rose. There is a good fragrance, and blooms continue to appear in summer and autumn after the prolific initial flush. This variety can be used as a general purpose climber for a wall, fence, arch or pergola, growing vigorously to average height or more with a tall, spreading habit and large, semi-glossy leaves. ZONES 5–9.

Moore, USA, 1990

'Lulu' × 'Muriel'

'PINK PROSPERITY'
MODERN, MODERN SHRUB, LIGHT PINK,
REPEAT-FLOWERING

This variety bears its dainty small to medium-sized flowers in big strong-stemmed clusters. They have many small petals, of which the outer ones are blush pink and the remainder clear pink with deeper shadings; the petals lie back layer upon layer as the blooms open like shallow saucers. There is a musky fragrance. It is useful in borders and for hedging, growing very vigorously with an upright habit to average extent or more. It has attractive dark green leaves. ZONES 4–9.

Bentall, UK, 1931

Seedling of 'Prosperity'

'PINK PUFF'
MODERN, CLUSTER-FLOWERED/FLORIBUNDA,
LIGHT PINK, REPEAT-FLOWERING

Offered apparently only in Australia today, this American-raised rose seems

'Pink Robusta'

never to have been widely distributed. It bears clusters of double flowers in a gentle shade of rose pink, with a light and pleasant sweet fragrance. They open from long buds into quite large, well-formed blooms, and continue in flower through summer and autumn. This rose is suitable for beds and borders where a short plant is wanted, for it grows vigorously with an upright habit to below average height. The leaves are bronzy green and semi-glossy and have a leathery texture. ZONES 4–9.

Boerner, USA, 1965

Seedling of 'Pinocchio' × (seedling of 'Red Pinocchio' × 'Garnette')

'PINK ROBIN'
MODERN, MODERN SHRUB, PINK BLEND

Louis Lens is well known as the raiser of 'Pascali', one of the world's best loved white Large-flowered Roses, but his breeding work has included the use of unusual species, resulting in some fascinating shrub roses of diverse character. Among them is this one, derived from *Rosa helenae*, a rampant wild climbing rose with white flowers from China. 'Pink Robin' bears generously filled clusters of semi-double pink blooms, small to medium in size, that open like saucers and have a pleasant light fragrance. They are produced in summer only on a stiff upright plant with a well-spread habit, growing vigorously to about half as tall again as the average shrub rose and with a good covering of grayish green leaves. For collectors of the unusual this is a novel and interesting variety for the rose garden. ZONES 4–9.

Lens, Belgium, 1992

Parentage unknown

'Pink Roundelay'

'PINK ROBUSTA' KORpinrob
syn. 'The Seckford Rose'
MODERN, MODERN SHRUB, MEDIUM PINK,
REPEAT-FLOWERING

This rose owes much of its rugged character to 'Robusta', its pollen parent, which was raised from *Rosa rugosa*. The flowers are a warm shade of rose pink and appear in large, well-spaced clusters above the foliage on stiff upright stems. They are semi-double, loosely formed and quite big, so that when they open out in cupped form there is a telling display of color which shows up from a distance. In a public park, or as a hedge or a group in a garden border this is a noticeable rose giving excellent value, as it flowers over a long period through summer and autumn, has a pleasing scent and makes sturdy vigorous growth to average height. It has a good health record and is well furnished with large, medium to dark green leaves. ZONES 4–9.

Kordes, Germany, 1986

('Zitronenfalter' × 'Cläre Grammerstorf') × 'Robusta'

Royal National Rose Society Certificate of Merit 1987

'PINK ROSETTE'
MODERN, CLUSTER-FLOWERED/FLORIBUNDA,
LIGHT PINK, REPEAT-FLOWERING

The plump buds on this variety look rather small, but they belie their appearance by opening into medium-sized blooms of some 50 petals that are borne in sprays. They are a warm shade of rose pink, deeper in the heart of the flower, and develop as the name promises into cupped flowers of rosette form, the petals so arrayed one row upon another that they look artificial, like roses on ladies' hats. There is a little fragrance, and a good succession of bloom is maintained through summer and autumn. 'Pink Rosette' is excellent for cutting, and in the garden makes a suitable item for a border or a bed or hedge; it performs best in a warm climate. The plant grows with a sprawling habit to below average height and has a covering of dark green, leathery leaves. ZONES 4–9.

Krebs, USA, 1948

Parentage unknown

'PINK ROUNDELAY'
MODERN, LARGE-FLOWERED/HYBRID TEA,
DEEP PINK, REPEAT-FLOWERING

This rose was sported from the well-known 'Roundelay' 19 years after it was introduced. The very attractive flowers are double and filled with 40 very deep

'Pink Sensation'

P

'Pink Silk'

'Pink Triumph'

pink petals. They open to give a high-centered form that flattens out to quartered centers. The foliage is matt dark green and very profuse. The disease resistance of this bush is really good, and there is copious flower production that repeats rapidly. 'Pink Roundelay' is a good rose for cutting as the oval buds open flowly and hold well at the full bloom stage. At this final stage, the blooms could be mistaken for one of David Austin's English Roses. There is a good fragrance. ZONES 5–9.

Taylor, Australia, 1973

Sport of 'Roundelay'

'PINK SENSATION'

MODERN, LARGE-FLOWERED/HYBRID TEA, MEDIUM PINK, REPEAT-FLOWERING

The flowers of 'Pink Sensation' are fairly large, opening from urn-shaped buds into high-centered blooms of about 30 petals that become waved as they reflex and diffuse a slight fragrance. The color is an even and rather hard shade of rose pink, deeper than its parent 'Pink Lady'. The blooms are carried on stiff stems and open slowly, making them very suitable for cutting, for which purpose this variety has been cultivated as a commercial glasshouse rose. It needs warm conditions to perform well, and is suitable for borders and beds. There is a good repetition of flower and growth through summer and autumn, the plant growing with an upright, bushy habit and having glossy foliage. ZONES 4–9.

Bos, USA, 1958

Sport of 'Pink Lady'

'PINK SILK'

MODERN, LARGE-FLOWERED/HYBRID TEA, MEDIUM PINK, REPEAT-FLOWERING

This English-bred rose is offered today only in Australia, where it is regarded as a useful variety for garden display and exhibition. The flowers are large and high centered, with about 40 broad petals, and open from pinky red buds to flowers of carmine rose, nearer to deep pink than the medium pink color allocated to them by officialdom and having a lustrous sheen. They have a pleasing light fragrance, and the plant continues to produce them through summer and autumn. It grows freely with a bushy habit to average height and has a covering of mid-green leaves. ZONES 4–9.

Gregory, UK, 1972

'Pink Parfait' × seedling

New Zealand Gold Medal 1974

'PINK SYMPHONY' MEItonse

syns 'Pink Symphonie', 'Pretty Polly', 'Sweet Sunblaze'

MODERN, MINIATURE, LIGHT PINK, REPEAT-FLOWERING

Elegantly shaped buds open to light, cardinal pink flowers with a light scent. The initial high-centered form disappears rapidly as the blooms move quickly to the fully open stage. Bloom production is excellent, covering the bush with flowers all year long. The glossy, dark green foliage is disease resistant. It is a medium-sized, compact bush. ZONES 4–10.

Meilland, France, 1987

'Darling Flame' × 'Air France'

Glasgow Gold Medal 1992

'PINK TRIUMPH'

MODERN, MINIATURE, MEDIUM PINK, REPEAT-FLOWERING

The medium pink color of these flowers sometimes merges into bright orange in warmer climate zones. The florets are very double (48 petals), fragrant and have high centers suitable for exhibition. The blooms are borne singly on strong, straight stems with petite foliage. The flowers last a long time especially when cut for indoors, as the large number of petals guarantees the longevity of the blooms, which take their time opening fully. This plant can occasionally suffer from mildew; however, it is a vigorous bush that is easy to maintain and produces a long series of flowers all season long. 'Pink Triumph' will certainly add grace and charm to the garden. ZONES 5–10.

Jolly, USA, 1983

'Operetta' × 'Bonny'

'PINK WAVE' MATtgrow

MODERN, MODERN SHRUB, MEDIUM PINK, REPEAT-FLOWERING

Though classified in *Modern Roses 10* as

'Pinkie'

a Cluster-flowered Rose, this variety is offered as a Ground Cover Rose by the raiser. It carries loosely double blooms of light pink with a satiny sheen in short-stemmed clusters, borne on long spreading stems. They have a pleasant light fragrance, and continue to appear through summer and autumn. 'Pink Wave' is useful in a mixed border and for sloping ground where a low shrubby plant of some substance is wanted. The plant grows vigorously with arching stems and has a bushy, sprawling habit, to below the height of an average shrub rose but spreading wider. The leaves are plentiful, semi-glossy and mid-green. ZONES 4–9.

Mattock, UK, 1983

'Moon Maiden' × 'Eye Paint'

'PINK WONDER' MEIhartfor

syn. 'Kalinka'

MODERN, CLUSTER-FLOWERED/FLORIBUNDA, LIGHT PINK, REPEAT-FLOWERING

The 30 nurseries listing this rose all grow it as 'Kalinka'. It is particularly popular in Australia, South Africa and continental Europe, but is not offered at all in Britain and America. Pointed salmon-pink buds develop into semi-double flowers of charming informal character. They are borne sometimes singly, sometimes in clusters, have a light scent, and after the main flush continue to show color through summer and autumn. As a border rose or in a container this variety makes a useful item to brighten up the garden, and the growth is sufficiently dense for it to become an effective hedge. The plant grows with a bushy, spreading habit to average height and is furnished with glossy, deep green leaves and stems that have few thorns. **'Climbing Pink Wonder'** (MEIhartforsar; Meilland, France, 1976) is sold, like the bush, under its synonym. It makes a vigorous plant, growing in extent to the average height of a climber and having an extended period of flower, continuing after the main flush to show color through summer and autumn. Because the growth is rather stiff it is easier to grow it on a wall or fence where it can be firmly

attached, but it can also be trained on a tall pillar, arch or pergola. The comparative thornlessness of the bush form is a particularly welcome asset in the climber, because it eases the task of pruning. ZONES 4–9.

Meilland, France, 1970

'Zambra' × ('Sarabande' × ['Goldilocks' × 'Fashion'])

Madrid Gold Medal 1969, Belfast Gold Medal 1972

'PINKIE'

MODERN, POLYANTHA, MEDIUM PINK, REPEAT-FLOWERING

'Pinkie' has been classed as both a Cluster-flowered Rose and a Miniature, but the Polyantha group fits this dainty item well. The small to medium-sized flowers, made up of 12 or more petals, are borne in large trusses. They are of that delicate rose pink color with a salmon touch termed neyron rose, are pleasantly scented and open cupped. In cool climates the plant stays very dwarf, but in milder conditions its proportions become like those of a small shrub. Flowering continues through summer and autumn, and there are many ways of using the variety in the garden, in a container for example, in any small space or to edge the front of a border or grow as a short-stemmed standard. The growth is low and bushy and the leaves, which normally have 7 leaflets, are semi-glossy, bright green and soft in texture. The film *Pinkie* inspired the name of the rose. Although it was introduced with less of

'Climbing Pink Wonder'

'Pink Symphony'

a fanfare than the bush from which it sported, **'Climbing Pinkie'** (Dering, USA, 1952) is today more widely grown. The scented flowers are borne very freely on stems that bow under the weight of so much blossom. The visual effect of all the many nodding pink rosettes massed together is most appealing, and blooming continues with remarkable constancy through summer and autumn. This rose makes many shoots, growing with a dense habit to the average height. It is easy to train and manage and is particularly useful for a pillar or arch or to plant near a footpath, where its near thornlessness is a boon to all who pass by. This variety can also be trimmed back and grown as a cascading shrub. ZONES 4–9.

Swim, USA, 1947

'China Doll' × seedling

All-America Rose Selection 1948

'PINOCCHIO'

syn. 'Rosenmärchen'

MODERN, CLUSTER-FLOWERED/FLORIBUNDA, ORANGE-PINK, REPEAT-FLOWERING

The flowers of this variety are very full of petals, are borne in close clusters of up to 20, and are of medium size. They open with a salmon-pink base, which as the blooms develop becomes suffused with yellow and carmine, sometimes to spectacular effect. The old flowers are like big rosettes and often become mottled. There is a light fruity scent, and the

'Pioneer'

'Pinwheel'

'Pinocchio'

succession of flower is well maintained through summer and autumn. This was once a prime choice for gardeners, until it passed its genes on to the likes of 'Masquerade' and 'Fashion' and other popular descendants. It is still an attractive rose in its own right, and space should certainly be found for it in any historic rose collection. The plant grows upright with a fairly compact habit to below average height and with leathery foliage. ZONES 4–9.

Kordes, Germany, 1940

'Eva' × 'Geheimrat Duisberg'

Portland Gold Medal 1942, National Rose Society Certificate of Merit 1949

'PINSTRIPE' MORpints

MODERN, MINIATURE, RED BLEND, REPEAT-FLOWERING

A wide variety of vivid red and white stripes distinguish this rose; in fact no two blooms look alike. The well-formed double (35 petals) florets are fragrant. The blooms are extremely long lasting with small color differences developing as they move to fully open. The most beautiful bloom stage is when the florets are fully open, revealing their distinctive color striping. The florets are borne singly or in small clusters of 3–5 blooms. The dense foliage is mid-green and disease resistant and the plant has a low mounded habit. It is easy to maintain and in the garden setting, this rose is truly eye catching. 'Pinstripe' represents

'Playgirl'

a revolutionary step in hybridizing, in that Moore has successfully demonstrated the transmission of striped genes to Miniature Roses. ZONES 5–11.

Moore, USA, 1986

'Pinocchio' × seedling #33

'PINWHEEL'

MODERN, MINIATURE, PINK BLEND, REPEAT-FLOWERING

These pink and yellow flowers of 'Pinwheel' are best at the fully open stage, because the florets have very few petals and seldom have form. The color fades quickly in hot weather. The foliage is small, mid-green and pointed and is fairly disease resistant. This is a low growing plant suitable for borders or containers. This decorative rose has all but disappeared from the marketplace; it has been overtaken by the superior modern Miniatures. ZONES 5–10.

Moore, USA, 1979

Sport of 'Jeanie Williams'

'PIONEER'

MODERN, LARGE-FLOWERED/HYBRID TEA, MEDIUM RED, REPEAT-FLOWERING

The flowers of this rose are borne on stiff upright stems, usually singly or sometimes in 3s. The large flowers are very full with up to 50 broad petals and they open with high centers, the petals reflexing to provide a symmetrical flower of classic form, 'well built' in the words of the raiser. The color is an even and clear shade of red, and there is a good fragrance. Flowering continues through summer and autumn and, although the main appeal of the variety is to exhibitors on account of its form and lasting qualities, in the garden it is useful for beds and borders. The plant grows freely with a bushy, upright habit and is well furnished with attractive, small dark green leaves. ZONES 4–9.

LeGrice, UK, 1970

Parentage unknown

'PIXIE HAT' KORlamber

MODERN, CLUSTER-FLOWERED/FLORIBUNDA, DARK RED, REPEAT-FLOWERING

Because of its superb performance in his trial grounds, Taschner selected this rose for the South African market. He called it 'Pixie Hat' for its brilliant red, single flowers. This medium-sized plant produces up to 100 small flowers on a single stem. As this stem bends outwards, new flowering shoots spring up from the center of the bush. The show continues

'Pleasure'

right through the summer and into winter in warm climates. There is no fragrance. ZONES 4–9.

Kordes, Germany, 1993

Parentage unknown

'PLAYBOY'

syn. 'Cheerio'

MODERN, CLUSTER-FLOWERED/FLORIBUNDA, RED BLEND, REPEAT-FLOWERING

Originating in northern Scotland, this rose has proved a real sun lover, for it is most popular in warm climates where the bright orange-yellow flowers with scarlet shading attain a size and intensity of color not so evident at home. The blooms are almost single, and open from clusters of pointed buds to display their flamboyant tones and reveal attractive golden stamens. The petals hold their color surprisingly well, and drop cleanly when the blooms are spent. There is only a light scent but in all other respects this rose is a model performer, quick to reflower as summer and autumn advance, excellent for beds, borders and hedges and serviceable as a cut flower. The plant is vigorous with a bushy, free-branching habit, growing a little below average height and with an ample covering of dark glossy foliage. The original name, 'Cheerio', was soon abandoned in favor of one that suits the ambience of the rose so well. ZONES 4–9.

Cocker, UK, 1976

'City of Leeds' × ('Chanelle' × 'Piccadilly')

Royal National Rose Society Trial Ground Certificate 1975, Portland Gold Medal 1989

'PLAYGIRL' MORplag

MODERN, CLUSTER-FLOWERED/FLORIBUNDA, MEDIUM PINK, REPEAT-FLOWERING

Ralph Moore used 'Playboy' in his hybridizing, hoping that its splendid foliage and freedom of flower might be transmitted to his own seedlings. With this variety he achieved his aim, and it makes such a perfect partner that finding the right name for it surely gave him little pause for thought. The color of 'Playgirl' is a ladylike if not demure shade of pink, being a bright and strong color that, as the simple flowers open out like saucers, serves to emphasize the contrast with the yellow stamens. They are freely borne through summer and autumn, and serve almost limitless purposes in the garden, in beds, borders, as hedges or for tubs and exhibition. There is not much scent, so it must be the color that attracts bees to the flowers so often. The plant grows

'Playboy'

vigorously with a dense and bushy habit to average height, and has plentiful semi-glossy foliage. **ZONES 4–9.**
Moore, USA, 1986
'Playboy' × 'Angel Face'

'PLAYGOLD' MORplaygold
MODERN, MINIATURE, ORANGE BLEND, REPEAT-FLOWERING

The pointed buds of this rose open to bright orange, single-petalled flowers with a slight red on the petal's edge and a yellow halo. The blooms change to soft pink and orange as they age. They have a light fragrance and are borne singly and in small loose clusters. The foliage is small, glossy mid-green on a low growing spreading bush which grows to 15–18 in (38–45 cm) tall and is generally disease resistant and easy to maintain. It is interesting to note the use of the Cluster-flowered Rose 'Playboy', hybridized by Cocker of Scotland as the seed parent, to ensure retention of the single-petalled form and dominance of the coppery orange color. **ZONES 5–10.**
Moore, USA, 1997
'Playboy' × 'Sequoia Gold'
American Rose Society Award of Excellence 1998

'PLAYTIME' MORplati
MODERN, CLUSTER-FLOWERED/FLORIBUNDA, ORANGE-RED, REPEAT-FLOWERING

Advertised as a companion to 'Playgirl', this variety has not shared its popularity even though it enjoys a high score of 7.8, meaning it is considered 'good', in the Roses in Review rating of the American Rose Society. (Both 'Playboy' and 'Playgirl' are in the 'excellent' class on 8.1.) The flowers of 'Playtime' are of medium to large size for a Cluster-flowered Rose, with single blooms of bright orange-red borne in clusters. The plant repeats its flowering through summer and autumn, and is good for beds and borders. It grows sturdily to average height with a bushy habit and is well supplied with glossy leaves. **ZONES 4–9.**
Moore, USA, 1990
'Playboy' × 'Old Master'

'PLEASURE' JACpif
MODERN, CLUSTER-FLOWERED/FLORIBUNDA, MEDIUM PINK, REPEAT-FLOWERING

There is much warmth in the rosy salmon-pink color of this rose, which bears large, lightly fragrant flowers in rather close sprays of up to 7 blooms. They have over 30 petals and open cupped, displaying to advantage the pink tones, which are intensified in the depths of the flower. When fully developed the flowers have an old-fashioned look, with the petals infolded at the center, and ruffled at the margins. As a garden plant this is an excellent variety for beds and borders, and after its initial prolific blooming it continues to bear flowers right through summer and autumn. The plant grows compactly to average height or less with a rounded, bushy habit, and is well furnished with dark green leaves. **ZONES 4–9.**
Warriner, USA, 1988
('Merci' × 'Fabergé') × 'Intrigue'
All-America Rose Selection 1990

'PLEINE DE GRÂCE' LENgra
MODERN, MODERN SHRUB, WHITE

This variety covers itself with large panicles, each one composed of up to 24 single flowers. They are creamy white and single, giving off the pervasive aroma typical of *Rosa filipes*, and make

'Pleine de Grâce'

an amazing show for a short period in summer. Space permitting, this is well worth including in the garden on account not only of its beauty, but because of the rarity and innovative nature of the cross. It makes a fine specimen plant and could be allowed to romp in a wild garden. The plant grows with a bushy, spreading habit to above average height and twice as wide as it is tall, so it does need space. The leaves are a yellowish green. The name, meaning 'full of grace', is a happy choice for this rose. **ZONES 4–9.**
Lens, Belgium, 1983
'Ballerina' × *Rosa filipes*

P

'Plum Duffy'

'Plum Crazy'

'Plentiful'

'PLENTIFUL'

MODERN, CLUSTER-FLOWERED/FLORIBUNDA,
DEEP PINK, REPEAT-FLOWERING

The flowers of this variety are deep pink on the inside of the petals and a shade lighter on the reverse. They are large for a Cluster-flowered Rose, with over 70 petals, open like big rosettes, and are borne in well-filled clusters. As they open they are cupped, then they develop into quartered flowers with an old-fashioned look with the petals intricately folded in a manner that is wonderful to see. There is only a light fragrance. After the initial display the plant continues to flower through summer and autumn. In the garden it is a neat and tidy performer in beds and borders, and is wonderful to cut for small arrangements. The growth is shorter than average, vigorous and branching, and the plant has abundant mid-green, glossy foliage. ZONES 4–9.

LeGrice, UK, 1961

Parentage unknown

'PLUM CRAZY'   AROgraju

MODERN, LARGE-FLOWERED/HYBRID TEA, MAUVE,
REPEAT-FLOWERING

This variety is another in the long series of 'hopefully blue' roses, being deep lavender, shading to mauve at the petal edges. The color is attractive in the young blooms but tends to become 'muddy' as they age. The flowers are fairly large, with up to 36 petals, and maintain good symmetry of form, opening with high centers before becoming cupped. There is a pleasant sweet scent and the flowers stand bad weather well.

After the first flush a succession of flowers is maintained through summer and autumn, making 'Plum Crazy' suitable for use in beds and borders, though it has never become popular. The plant is bushy in growth, not very free in producing new basal stems and has dark green matt foliage, which is not proof against mildew. ZONES 4–9.

Christensen, USA, 1985

('Ivory Tower' × 'Angel Face') × 'Blue Nile'

'PLUM DUFFY'

MODERN, MINIATURE, MAUVE, REPEAT-FLOWERING

The oval buds of this rose open to deep plum-colored flowers that have a light fragrance. The double florets have 25 petals, and can have high, well-formed centers in some climates. However, the average stem length is very short for exhibition purposes. The foliage is dark green and disease resistant and the plant has a compact growth habit, making it an ideal container-grown bush. The repeat bloom cycle is fast and the color holds well even in the heat. It is slow to establish and may take several seasons to become fully productive. ZONES 5–11.

Bennett, USA, 1978

'Magic Carrousel' × 'Magic Carrousel'

'POËMA'

MODERN, RAMBLER, MEDIUM PINK,
REPEAT-FLOWERING

This rose bears huge clusters, with sometimes as many as 100 blossoms, of delightful, small bright pink flowers that become light pink as they age. During summer and autumn there is some

'Poetry in Motion'

recurrence of bloom. The plant grows vigorously to average height and is well suited for pillars, arches and trellises or wherever it has free circulation of air around it. The variety can also be trimmed and grown as a substantial shrub. It is a vigorous grower with attractive foliage, dark green and bright, and is a rare item, its known commercial distribution currently limited to nurseries in Oregon in the USA, and Germany. ZONES 4–9.

Brada, Czechoslovakia, 1933

'Tausendschön' × 'Farbenkönigin'

'POETRY IN MOTION'   HARelan

MODERN, LARGE-FLOWERED/HYBRID TEA,
YELLOW BLEND, REPEAT-FLOWERING

The flowers on this variety are large with over 30 big petals, opening with high centers, and usually borne individually on long stems. They become cupped and rounded in form, the petals reflexing slowly and maintaining an excellent symmetry within the bloom. The color is light yellow in the bud stage, becoming creamy primrose in the outer petals as the flower develops, the inner petals remaining yellow and showing golden highlights. The flowering period extends through summer and autumn and the late season blooms have particularly fine coloring. There is a strong, fruity scent, and for beds, borders and as a standard this makes a very effective garden rose, one that gives flowers suitable for cutting thanks to their lasting quality and long stems. The plant grows vigorously with a bushy, branching habit and is well endowed with large, leathery matt foliage. ZONES 4–9.

Harkness, UK, 1997

Parentage unknown

Courtrai Silver Medal 1995, British Association of Rose Breeders Breeders' Choice 1997, Royal National Rose Society British Rose Award 1998

'Poker Chip'

'POKER CHIP'

MODERN, MINIATURE, RED BLEND,
REPEAT-FLOWERING

Red flowers with a striking yellow reverse open from pointed buds. The double, fragrant florets have 28 petals and well-formed, high centers suitable for exhibition. The striking blooms are similar to 'Over The Rainbow' but are slightly bigger in size and have fewer petals. This is excellent as a cut flower or for exhibition as the form holds well over long periods. The foliage is glossy dark green and disease-resistant on a vigorous, compact bush loaded with blooms all season long. This color combination provides a great focal point in any garden. ZONES 5–11.

Saville, USA, 1979

'Sheri Anne' × ('Yellow Jewel' × seedling of 'Tamango')

'POLAREIS'

syn. 'Polaris'
MODERN, LARGE-FLOWERED CLIMBER, WHITE

This little-known Rambler produces clusters of snow white, double blooms. They are very fragrant. The foliage is glossy pale green and covers this very vigorous plant. The spring bloom is very profuse, but there is no repeat. 'Polareis' shows little influence from the Wild Rose parent, *Rosa foetida bicolor*. ZONES 5–9.

Horvarth, USA, 1939

(*Rosa wichuraiana* × *R. setigera*) × *R. foetida bicolor*

'POLARSTERN'   TANlarpost

syns 'Evita', 'Polar Star'
MODERN, LARGE-FLOWERED/HYBRID TEA, WHITE,
REPEAT-FLOWERING

The creamy buds on this variety open to very big, high-centered white flowers on tall, strong stems. This rose creates a commanding presence in the garden, partly because its color shows up so well, partly because of the freedom with which the flowers are borne, and partly because of its sturdy, vigorous growth. For a bed where a big plant is required it is a good choice, and it fits in well with other roses in mixed borders. There is not much scent, but it withstands wet weather better than most pale varieties and continues to bloom through summer and autumn. It has an upright, free-branching habit to above average height and has dark green matt leaves. ZONES 4–9.

Tantau, Germany, 1982

Parentage unknown

Royal National Rose Society Certificate of Merit 1985, UK Rose of the Year 1985

'Polarstern'

'Polynesian Sunset'

'Pompon Blanc Parfait'

'POLKA' MEItosier

syns 'Lord Byron', 'Polka 91', 'Scented Dawn', 'Twilight Glow'

MODERN, LARGE-FLOWERED CLIMBER, ORANGE BLEND, REPEAT-FLOWERING

There is an old-fashioned air about this rose, due to the way it opens wide and flat with the short petals reflexing one layer upon another. The blooms are double, of medium to large size, and are carried singly or in small clusters on stiff stems. The color is coppery salmon, fading to salmon pink as the petals expand but retaining copper tones in the depths of the flower. There is only a light scent, which is a pity in a flower of such warm and welcoming appearance, although blooming continues through summer and autumn. 'Polka' is ideal for pillars, walls and fences where a shorter than average climber is required. The growth is vigorous and rather shrubby, not rampant, and the plant has a good coverage of glossy foliage. ZONES 4–9.

Meilland, France, 1992

'Golden Showers' × 'Lichtkönigin Lucia'

'POLO CLUB' AROtigy

syn. 'Cherry Gold'

MODERN, LARGE-FLOWERED/HYBRID TEA, YELLOW BLEND, REPEAT-FLOWERING

Although classed as a Large-flowered Rose, this variety has much of the appearance of a Cluster-flowered Rose, bearing some flowers singly but many flowers in small clusters. The lightly scented blooms are of modest size, made up of 24–36 petals, and opening with tight centers that soon develop into loosely cupped flowers as the spoon-shaped petals reflex. The fleeting nature of the flowers is compensated for by their abundance and continuity in bloom, and above all because of the vivid color, the inside of each petal having a border of scarlet prettily veined with the yellow that occupies the remainder of their inner surface and the whole of the reverse. It is a pity that such a delightful rose should be so hard to obtain today, only one nursery in India still listing it, for it would brighten the beds and borders of any garden. The bush grows vigorously with an upright, bushy habit, taller than average, and with dark green semi-glossy foliage. ZONES 4–9.

Christensen, USA, 1986

'Gingersnap' × 'Young Quinn'

'POLYNESIAN SUNSET'

MODERN, LARGE-FLOWERED/HYBRID TEA, ORANGE-PINK, REPEAT-FLOWERING

Often the long buds of this variety are borne in clusters, so that some consider this a Cluster-flowered Rose. The buds part to reveal sizeable full-petalled flowers of salmon-pink with an orange cast, sometimes decribed as coral pink. They are high centered when they first open but soon acquire a dainty, informal character as the petals reflex in attractively random fashion. There is a fruity fragrance, and flowers continue to appear through summer and autumn. This is a cheerful, unassuming garden rose for general purposes, growing to above average height with a vigorous, bushy habit and leathery leaves. ZONES 4–9.

Boerner, USA, 1965

Seedling of 'Diamond Jubilee' × 'Hawaii'

'POMPON'

syn. 'Pompon Panachée'

OLD, GALLICA, WHITE/STRIPED

The flowers of this rose are double, and have a cream base striped with dark pink. It has been compared with 'Georges Vibert', a well-known striped Gallica with similar features. The plant grows to medium height and has very small leaves and wiry stems. The flowers have a pompon style. ZONES 5–10.

Robert-Moreau, France, 1858

Parentage unknown

'POMPON BLANC PARFAIT'

OLD, ALBA, WHITE

Not entirely typical of Alba Roses, 'Pompon Blanc Parfait' is an upright-growing shrub to about 4 ft (1.2 m) that makes many stiff, relatively thornless stems. These bear closely-packed, smooth, semi-glossy, light grayish green leaves, and in early summer flowers emerge from plump round buds. These are arranged in tight bunches, with each rosette-like, soft lilac-pink, fragrant flower opening flat. This rose continues to flower for a longer season than most other Albas, and is suitable for a herbaceous border or a shrubbery. ZONES 5–9.

Verdier, France, 1876

Parentage unknown

'POMPON DE PARIS'

OLD, CHINA, MEDIUM PINK/DEEP PINK, REPEAT-FLOWERING

This rose bears clusters of fully double, upright pink flowers. It was very popular in Victorian times when it was grown in containers. It is very dwarf and is said to be identical to 'Rouletii', the original Miniature Rose rediscovered by Major Roulet in Switzerland in 1918, but there are differences in cultivation. It is an almost evergreen bush that is tiny and thorny. 'Climbing Pompon de Paris' is probably a sport of a Miniature Rose that grew in France up to the late 1830s and then was lost. If that is correct, how surprising it is that the sport of a Miniature can prove so vigorous, for this variety, after a slowish start, can exceed the average extent expected of a climber. The lightly scented blooms, opening from well-filled clusters of light red buds, are rich carmine-pink, fading to a paler tone in strong sunshine. They make perfect rosettes, with many small petals laid back row upon row. The blooms come early, and there is not usually any significant later bloom. A good site for this rose is on a wall where the stems, heavy with many leaves and flower clusters, can be well anchored. The tiny leaves are mid-green and very numerous. ZONES 4–9.

Possibly France, circa 1839

Parentage unknown

'PONCTUÉE'

syn. 'Ma Ponctuée'

OLD, MOSS, PINK BLEND

The flowers of this rose are rose pink, spotted white. They are semi-double and of medium size. It flowers only once. The bush is also of medium size. This rose is probably extinct. ZONES 4–9.

Moreau-Robert, France, 1847

Parentage unknown

'Pompon'

'Polka'

'Polo Club'

'POPCORN'

MODERN, MINIATURE, WHITE, REPEAT-FLOWERING

The ovoid buds of 'Popcorn' open to pure white flowers with golden yellow stamens and look just like freshly burst popcorn. The florets have only 13–15 petals and display an informal decorative form that is at its best when fully open. They have a fragrance that improves in warmer climates. The blooms are borne in clusters on a vigorous, completely disease-resistant plant that is furnished with fern-like foliage. It has an upright habit and is self-cleaning—there is no need to deadhead spent blooms as the blooms fall off and the next cycle starts immediately. Its sport, 'Gourmet Popcorn', is an even more vigorous plant with larger clusters and a better overall shape. ZONES 4–11.

Morey, USA, 1973

'Katharina Zeimet' × 'Diamond Jewel'

'POPPY FLASH'   MEllena

syn. 'Rusticana'

MODERN, CLUSTER-FLOWERED/FLORIBUNDA, ORANGE-RED, REPEAT-FLOWERING

The name 'Poppy Flash' indicates the bright red color of this rose, which is lightened by a streak of golden yellow on some of the petals. The color deepens from bright vermilion to pale scarlet as the loosely cupped blooms age. The medium-sized flowers are borne in close clusters, and there is a light fruity scent. The initial display of bloom is prolific and flowers appear through summer and autumn with good continuity. The plant grows vigorously with a bushy habit to average height and has semi-glossy, bronzy leaves. **'Climbing Poppy Flash'** (MEIlenasar; Paolino, France, 1975) is popular in warmer countries where it is sold commercially only under the synonym 'Climbing Rusticana'. It serves a similar purpose in the garden to that of the bush variety, in that it provides a hot color tone where required but at a higher level. Planting the climber behind a group of bushes of the same type would provide a hot spot indeed. 'Climbing Poppy Flash' grows to average height, flowers freely on the first flush with sporadic later offerings and is comparatively thornless. ZONES 4–9.

Meilland, France, 1972

('Dany Robin' × 'Fire King') × ('Alain' × 'Mutabilis')

Geneva Gold Medal 1970, Royal National Rose Society Trial Ground Certificate 1970, Rome Gold Medal 1972

'Popcorn'

'Popcorn'

'Portrait'

'Portland Trailblazer'

'PORTHOS, CLIMBING'   LAPadsar

MODERN, CLUSTER-FLOWERED CLIMBER, ORANGE-RED, REPEAT-FLOWERING

The bush form of this climbing rose was introduced in 1971 but no date is officially recorded for the climber, which appears to be on sale today only in France and Italy. It bears well-filled clusters of bright red flowers on short stiff stems in summertime, with a sporadic showing late in summer and in autumn. The blooms are double, of small to medium size and open cupped and rather flat. They last well, but there is not very much fragrance. The plant is best suited to walls, fences and pillars, growing sturdily to average height and has shiny dark green leaves. ZONES 4–9.

Laperrière, France, post-1971

Parentage unknown

'PORTLAND TRAILBLAZER'

syn. 'Big Chief'

MODERN, LARGE-FLOWERED/HYBRID TEA, DARK RED, REPEAT-FLOWERING

If such a creature as a Jekyll and Hyde rose exists, this could be it. Seen on the show bench, seemingly the size of footballs, the blooms evoke gasps of envy from fellow exhibitors and admiration from the public. But it is likely to disappoint the general gardener because those flowers are the fruits of expert cultivation, and even with the necessary skill the reward is likely to be only a few blooms of any sort. The long-stemmed flowers are rich deep crimson, high centered with firm broad petals but with little fragrance. The plant grows upright and leggy, a little taller than the average bush and has large, brittle leaves. A disillusioned New Zealander summed it up by using the synonym 'Big Chief of a very small tribe'. ZONES 4–9.

Dickson, UK, 1978

'Ernest H. Morse' × 'Red Planet'

'Climbing Porthos'

'Pot o' Gold'

'PORTRAIT'   MEYpink

syn. 'Stéphanie de Monaco'

MODERN, LARGE-FLOWERED/HYBRID TEA, PINK BLEND, REPEAT-FLOWERING

The double flowers of this variety have attractively muddled centers as they open, with many petals folded against one another in the heart of the bloom. They are large and develop showing rose pink in the depths of the flower and pale pink towards the edges of the petals, the two shades toning in well together. As the fragrant blooms are carried on long stiff stems they are good for cutting, and make a prominent group in a bed or border, providing a good succession of bloom through summer and autumn. It grows vigorously and upright to average height or more with a free-branching, shapely habit and has glossy dark green leaves. When 'Portrait' was voted worthy of one of the highest accolades in the rose world it was the first time the prize had gone to an amateur raiser. ZONES 4–9.

Meyer, USA, 1971

'Pink Parfait' × 'Pink Peace'

All-America Rose Selection 1972

'POT O' GOLD'   DICdivine

MODERN, LARGE-FLOWERED/HYBRID TEA, MEDIUM YELLOW, REPEAT-FLOWERING

This variety is well named, for the yellow flowers have a hint of ochreous gold about them. They are of medium size with about 30 petals, borne sometimes singly but quite often in an open cluster of several flowers and developing from pointed buds into cupped, rather flat, neatly formed blooms. These appear on the plant through summer and autumn, the early and later flowers being of particularly good quality. There is a delightful scent, and for small arrangements 'Pot o' Gold' is a treasure. It is also very suitable for beds and borders, and it makes a fine standard. It grows compactly and vigorously with a spreading habit to a little below average height and has ample mid-green foliage. ZONES 4–9.

Dickson, UK, 1980

'Eurorose' × 'Whisky Mac'

Royal National Rose Society Certificate of Merit 1979, British Association of Rose Breeders, Breeders' Selection 1980

'POTTER & MOORE'   AUSpot

MODERN, MODERN SHRUB, MEDIUM PINK, REPEAT-FLOWERING

This variety is a kindly shade of rose pink, bearing full-petalled blooms that open cupped, diffusing a pronounced fragrance. They are freely produced on their first flush and continue to bloom through summer and autumn. In the garden they are suitable for a border, particularly in association with Old Garden Roses. The soft texture of the petals means that the blooms can be affected by damp weather and fail to open properly. The plant grows shorter than the average shrub rose, with a shrubby habit. Potter & Moore is a British company specializing in toiletries, and the variety's launch coincided with the release of their new 'Rose' range. ZONES 4–9.

Austin, UK, 1988

'Wife of Bath' × seedling

'Potter & Moore'

'POTTON HERITAGE'   HARsprice
MODERN, LARGE-FLOWERED/HYBRID TEA, RED BLEND, REPEAT-FLOWERING

This rose bears big flowers of 30 or more petals, well formed with high centers. There are several colors in the flower, which displays a two-toned effect due to the contrast of the inside of the petals, a warm cherry-red, with the outside, which is yellow shading to pink. The flowers have a sweet scent and repeat-bloom, after the main flush, through summer and autumn. As they are carried on long stems they are suitable for cutting, and look well in a bed or border. It is vigorous and free branching, growing to average height, and has dark glossy leaves. The name commemorates Britain's largest makers of timber frame components for rural-style houses. ZONES 4–9.

Harkness, UK, 1987

'Precious Platinum' × 'Dr A. J. Verhage'

Prague Certificate of Merit 1989

POULBRIGHT
MODERN, CLUSTER-FLOWERED/FLORIBUNDA, ORANGE-RED, REPEAT-FLOWERING

There is something curious about this rose: it was raised in Denmark, received a Gold Medal in Britain, was launched there under its code name, never received a commercial name, and then rapidly passed out of general circulation, surviving today solely in the list of the Indian firm of K. S. Gopalaswamiengar and Son. Why its eclipse was so sudden is puzzling, for it is a good variety—perhaps the existence of other good reds accounts for it. The very lightly scented, bright scarlet flowers are fairly double, of medium size, and are borne in well-filled clusters. The bush gives an excellent display of flowers through summer and autumn, and is a good subject for beds, borders and hedges. The plant grows with a vigorous, upright, bushy habit to average height and has bright green leaves. ZONES 4–9.

Poulsen, Denmark, 1985

'Royal Occasion' × 'Matangi'

Royal National Rose Society Gold Medal 1982

'POULSEN'S BEDDER'
syn. 'Poulsen's Grupperose'
MODERN, CLUSTER-FLOWERED/FLORIBUNDA, LIGHT PINK, REPEAT-FLOWERING

'A lovely clean refreshing pink' was the contemporary description of this neat-growing rose, shorter in habit than most

of the Poulsen varieties between the two world wars. The medium-sized, semi-double flowers are borne in clusters of several together, and open loosely cupped. As the name implies, this is an excellent rose for a bed of one variety where a short grower is required, and it is also suitable to make a hedge or border in front of other plants. There is a light scent, and after the first flush flowers continue to appear in cycles of growth and bloom through summer and autumn; they withstand bad weather well. The bush grows vigorously with an upright, compact habit and has bronzy green leaves. ZONES 4–9.

Poulsen, Denmark, 1948

'Orléans Rose' × 'Talisman'

National Rose Society Certificate of Merit 1946, Portland Gold Medal

'POULSEN'S DELIGHT'
syn. 'Fru Julie Poulsen'
MODERN, CLUSTER-FLOWERED/FLORIBUNDA, LIGHT PINK, REPEAT-FLOWERING

This variety bears big well-filled trusses of simple roses, usually with 7 petals or fewer, on firm upright stems. The blooms open cupped in a delicate shade of apple blossom pink. The first flowering is prolific, creating an effective massed color effect and making this a very suitable variety for a hedge or bed or to plant in a border. After a pause the plant comes again into bloom, to give more color in summer and autumn. It grows vigorously with an upright habit to average height and an adequate covering of dark glossy foliage. At the present time it does not appear that this rose is commercially available. ZONES 4–9.

Poulsen, Denmark, 1948

'Else Poulsen' × seedling

National Rose Society Certificate of Merit 1946

'POULSEN'S PEARL'
MODERN, CLUSTER-FLOWERED/FLORIBUNDA, LIGHT PINK, REPEAT-FLOWERING

This is a rose of distinct character, producing a wonderful show of saucer-shaped, single, pearl pink flowers marked at the center with showy reddish stamens. The flowers are well scented, and appear in widely spaced clusters on strong, wiry stems. After the first flush more blooms are produced through summer and autumn. For gardeners who enjoy unusual roses this is a treasure, with an ethereal quality about it that moved one devotee to describe it as 'the rose that always lifts my soul'. The plant

POULbright

'Poulsen's Bedder'

'Poulsen's Delight'

is healthy and hardy, growing vigorously with a bushy, upright habit to average height or less and with light to mid-green, semi-glossy leaves. ZONES 4–9.

Poulsen, Denmark, 1949

'Else Poulsen' × seedling

'POULSEN'S YELLOW'
MODERN, CLUSTER-FLOWERED/FLORIBUNDA, MEDIUM YELLOW, REPEAT-FLOWERING

This variety appears to be listed today by only 2 nurseries in California in the USA, but 60 years ago gardeners were falling over one another in their eagerness to obtain it, the reason being that it was the first true yellow Cluster-flowered Rose. The flowers, borne in short-stemmed clusters, have about 17 waved petals, and open buttercup yellow before paling to cream as they age. They continue blooming through summer and autumn, and have been extensively used in past years for planting in beds, borders and as low hedges. Growth is shorter than average, with a bushy spreading habit, and the light flower color shows well against the dark glossy foliage, which is affected by seasonal mildew. ZONES 4–9.

Poulsen, Denmark, 1938

'Mrs W. H. Cutbush' × 'Gottfried Keller'

National Rose Society Gold Medal 1937

'POURPRE DU LUXEMBOURG'
OLD, MOSS, MAUVE

The medium-sized, double flowers of this rose are deep purple with carmine shadings. They are borne on a conventional Centifolia-Moss-type shrub. It would be very hard to come by and is definitely one for the serious collector. Alexandre Hardy (1787–1876) was the

'Poulsen's Pearl'

chief horticulturalist at the Luxembourg Gardens in Paris. His most famous rose was the white Damask 'Madame Hardy'. ZONES 4–9.

Hardy, France, 1848

Parentage unknown

'PRAIRIE DAWN'
MODERN, MODERN SHRUB, MEDIUM PINK, REPEAT-FLOWERING

The Morden Experimental Farm in Manitoba has sought to raise hardier roses, able to withstand Canadian winters, and 'Prairie Dawn' is one of the fruits of that work. The flowers are a warm shade of luminous pink, of medium size and full-petalled. On the current season's wood they repeat their bloom after the main summer flush. The plant grows vigorously with an upright habit, to rather taller than average height and has dark green glossy leaves. It is very hardy. ZONES 3–9.

Morden, Canada, 1959

'Prairie Youth' × ('Ross Rambler' × ['Dr W. Van Fleet' × *Rosa pimpinellifolia altaica*])

P

'PRAIRIE FIRE'

MODERN, MODERN SHRUB, MEDIUM RED, REPEAT-FLOWERING

This shrub carries enormous clusters of up to 50 blooms on long canes. They make a colorful impact, being of middling size, opening their 7 petals to show flat cardinal red blooms with blush white eyes and yellow stamens. There is a light, Old Garden Rose fragrance. The cross is botanically of interest, and a collection of roses representative of different strains ought to include it. It deserves a place in the shrub border on its own merits, for the plant continues to give some bloom after the main flush, and as a plant it is very vigorous, making an erect shrub of above average height with tough olive green glossy foliage and a high degree of frost hardiness. ZONES 3–9.

Phillips, USA, 1960

'Red Rocket' × *Rosa arkansana*

'PRAIRIE HARVEST'

MODERN, MODERN SHRUB, LIGHT YELLOW, REPEAT-FLOWERING

This variety bears its medium yellow, double flowers from summer to autumn. The blooms are large, with 43 overlapping petals each, are fragrant, and are borne in clusters of 1–5. 'Prairie Harvest' is a very hardy, upright bushy grower that is disease resistant and has leathery, glossy foliage. It is a good plant for borders or for use as a specimen. ZONES 4–9.

Buck, USA, 1985

'Carefree Beauty' × 'Sunsprite'

'Président de Sèze'

'Président Leopold Senghor'

'PRAIRIE PRINCESS'

MODERN, MODERN SHRUB, ORANGE-PINK, REPEAT-FLOWERING

The large, semi-double blooms on this rose are a light coral-pink and have some scent. They appear with good continuity from summer to autumn on a vigorous shrub with an upright growth habit and leathery, dark green foliage. This variety, which is disease resistant, is a good choice for borders. ZONES 4–9.

Buck, USA, 1972

'Carrousel' × ('Morning Stars' × 'Suzanne')

'PRECIOUS PLATINUM'

syns 'Opa Pötschke', 'Red Star'

MODERN, LARGE-FLOWERED/HYBRID TEA, MEDIUM RED, REPEAT-FLOWERING

This rose has cardinal red double blooms that are full and high centered and have thick-textured petals. Slightly fragrant, they are produced in quantity from spring to autumn on long stems and make excellent cut flowers. This vigorous variety has glossy green foliage that is highly resistant to fungal disease. It can be planted singly or massed, or it can be used as a standard. ZONES 4–9.

Dickson, UK, 1974

'Red Planet' × 'Franklin Englemann'

'PRÉSENCE'   DELprat

syn. 'Present'

MODERN, LARGE-FLOWERED/HYBRID TEA, LIGHT PINK, REPEAT-FLOWERING

'Presence' has large, pink double flowers with light undersides. They have a fruity

'Pretty Jessica'

'Pretty Lady'

fragrance and 38 petals. This bushy, upright grower has matt mid-green foliage and is a good bedding choice. ZONES 4–9.

Delbard, France, 1970

'Dr Albert Schweitzer' × ('Michèle Meilland' × 'Bayadère')

'PRÉSIDENT DE SÈZE'

syn. 'Madame Hébert'

OLD, GALLICA, MAUVE

This beautiful Gallica bears two-toned flowers that are pale lilac-pink around the edges and crimson in the center. The color deepens with age. The cup-shaped blooms are double, tend to be convex and are borne in clusters. It is a loose, upright, medium to tall bush. ZONES 4–9.

Mme Hébert, France, 1828

Parentage unknown

Royal Horticultural Society Award of Garden Merit 1993

'PRÉSIDENT DUTAILLY'

syn. 'Charlemagne'

OLD, GALLICA, MAUVE, REPEAT-FLOWERING

This rather late Gallica bears reddish purple flowers with deeper centers and lighter lilac-rose edges. They are large and open flat. The bush has an upright growth habit and reaches medium height. Judging from its appearance and a disposition to produce late flowers, it seems this rose may have some Portland in it. ZONES 4–9.

Dubreuil, France, 1888

Parentage unknown

'PRESIDENT HERBERT HOOVER'

syn. 'President Hoover'

MODERN, LARGE-FLOWERED/HYBRID TEA, PINK BLEND, REPEAT-FLOWERING

'President Herbert Hoover' has long, pointed blooms that are colored orange,

'President Herbert Hoover'

'Precious Platinum'

rose and gold and have a lighter reverse. They are borne on long stems and have a spicy fragrance. The leathery green foliage is sparse but is healthy, and appears on an extremely vigorous variety that is good for cutting. ZONES 4–9.

Coddington, USA, 1930

'Sensation' × 'Souvenir de Claudius Pernet'

National Rose Society Gold Medal 1934, American Rose Society John Cook Medal 1935

'PRÉSIDENT LEOPOLD SENGHOR'   MEIluminac

syn. 'Président L. Senghor'

MODERN, LARGE-FLOWERED/HYBRID TEA, DARK RED, REPEAT-FLOWERING

This dark red rose has cupped, double blooms with 25 petals that open from conical buds. They have a slight fragrance. It is a vigorous bushy plant with large glossy dark green foliage. ZONES 4–9.

Meilland, France, 1979

([{'Scarlet Knight' × 'Samourai'} × {'Crimson Wave' × 'Imperator'}] × ['Pharaoh' × 'Pharoah']) × ('Pharaoh' × 'Pharoah')

'PRESIDENT LINCOLN'

OLD, HYBRID PERPETUAL, DARK RED, REPEAT-FLOWERING

This is by no means a well-known rose and it is difficult to obtain. The flowers are vermilion-red touched with crimson. They are very large, full and imbricated. The foliage is dark green on a vigorous plant. The parent, 'Lord Raglan', is still in cultivation. It was a seedling of the famous 'Géant des Batailles'. ZONES 4–9.

Granger-Lévêque, France, 1862

Seedling of 'Lord Raglan'

'PRETORIA'   KORhagon

MODERN, LARGE-FLOWERED/HYBRID TEA, DEEP PINK, REPEAT-FLOWERING

This tall-growing rose has a great amount of healthy foliage and a willingness to produce many perfect buds on long sturdy stems. These open into full, well-shaped flowers with dark, almost shining pink petals. A bed of these large roses provides a brilliant show throughout the growing season. The flowers have a sweet fragrance, which makes them useful for indoor displays. ZONES 5–10.

Kordes, Germany, 1992

Seedling × 'Kardinal'

'PRETTY IN PINK'   DICumpteen

MODERN, GROUND COVER, LIGHT PINK, REPEAT-FLOWERING

The clusters of medium, cupped blooms on this variety are a soft shell pink. They are borne throughout summer and

'Precious Platinum'

autumn and are fragrant. It is a prostrate plant with vigorous stems of mid-green foliage. A tremendous contribution to environmental planting, it is remarkably resistant to disease and is propagated by budding or from cuttings. **ZONES 4–9.**

Dickson, UK, 1996

('Minipol' × seedling) × 'Grouse'

Royal National Rose Society Trial Ground Certificate 1994

'PRETTY JESSICA' AUSjess
MODERN, MODERN SHRUB, DEEP PINK, REPEAT-FLOWERING

Also classified as an English Rose, 'Pretty Jessica' produces rosettes of medium-sized, pink flowers with 41 petals. They have a strong, Old Garden Rose scent. It is a bushy variety with a low-growing habit that is very suitable for a small garden. The foliage is mid-green and is not overly disease resistant. **ZONES 4–9.**

Austin, UK, 1983

'Wife of Bath' × seedling

'Pride 'n' Joy'

'PRETTY LADY' SCRivo
MODERN, CLUSTER-FLOWERED/FLORIBUNDA, LIGHT PINK, REPEAT-FLOWERING

The flowers of this variety are light pink and semi-double. The blooms are very large, reaching as much as 4 in (10 cm) across when fully open. This variety has many prickles and medium-sized, dark green, semi-glossy foliage. **ZONES 5–10.**

Scrivens, UK, 1997

(Seedling × [*Rosa davidii elongata* × seedling]) × (['Troika' × 'Alpine Sunset'] × 'Freedom')

'PREZIOSA' MEIhimper
syn. **'Indian Song'**
MODERN, LARGE-FLOWERED/HYBRID TEA, PINK BLEND, REPEAT-FLOWERING

This rose has large, high-centered, very double flowers. They have a slight scent and are rose colored with gold undersides. It is an upright, vigorous grower with dark green glossy foliage. **ZONES 4–9.**

Meilland, France, 1971

'Radar' × 'Karl Herbst'

'Pride of Maldon'

'Preziosa'

'PRIDE 'N' JOY' JACmo
MODERN, MINIATURE, ORANGE BLEND, REPEAT-FLOWERING

This rose has ovoid buds which open to bright, medium orange flowers with an orange-cream reverse that fades to salmon-pink. The double (30-35 petals) florets have a fruity fragrance and can have good, high, well-formed centers that tend to open too quickly for exhibition. The foliage is dark green and disease-resistant. This spreading, compact bush blooms profusely all year long. It is a wonderful cut flower because of the contrast of the bright orange color against the foliage. This is one of the few Miniature Roses recognized by All-America Rose Society as worthy of the award. It was hybridized by the master of Cluster-flowered Roses, the late Bill Warriner of Jackson & Perkins. **ZONES 5–11.**

Warriner, USA, 1991

'Chattem Centennial' × 'Prominent'

All-America Rose Selection 1992

'Preziosa'

'PRIDE OF ENGLAND'
HARencore
MODERN, LARGE-FLOWERED/HYBRID TEA, DARK RED, REPEAT-FLOWERING

'Pride of England' bears beautifully formed blooms of pure blood red. They have a slight fragrance. It is a strong healthy plant. **ZONES 4–9.**

Harkness, UK, 1998

Parentage unknown

'PRIDE OF MALDON' HARwonder
MODERN, CLUSTER-FLOWERED/FLORIBUNDA, ORANGE BLEND, REPEAT-FLOWERING

The pointed buds on this rose open to reddish orange, cupped flowers with orange-yellow undersides. They darken in color as they age, and are borne in small sprays. **ZONES 4–9.**

Harkness, UK, 1990

'Southampton' × 'Wandering Minstrel'

Royal National Rose Society Trial Ground Certificate 1988, ÖRP Baden 1991, Glasgow Silver Medal 1994

P

'Prima Ballerina'

'Primevère'

'Prince Arthur'

'Prince Camille de Rohan'

'PRIMA BALLERINA'

syns 'Première Ballerine', 'Primaballerina'

MODERN, LARGE-FLOWERED/HYBRID TEA, DEEP PINK, REPEAT-FLOWERING

This rose produces heavily scented, semi-double, rose pink medium-sized blooms. The glossy foliage and vigorous, upright habit make it suitable for bedding. Although it is prone to mildew, it is still an important contributor to the development of modern roses. ZONES 4–9.

Tantau, Germany, 1957

Seedling × 'Peace'

National Rose Society Trial Ground Certificate 1957

'PRIMA DONNA'

syn. 'Toboné'

MODERN, LARGE-FLOWERED, DEEP PINK, REPEAT-FLOWERING

The deep fuchsia pink, double blooms of this variety, which is sometimes classified

---

as a Grandiflora, have 27 petals. They are fragrant and appear in succession through summer and autumn. It is a vigorous plant with large, semi-glossy mid-green foliage and, although described as a garden rose, it appears to be more popular as a forcing plant in the greenhouse. ZONES 4–9.

Shiakawa, Japan, 1984

(Seedling × 'Happiness') × 'Prominent'

All-America Rose Selection 1988, Portland Gold Medal 1992

'PRIMEVÈRE'

syn. 'Primrose'

OLD, LARGE-FLOWERED CLIMBER, YELLOW BLEND

This is a very vigorous non-repeating Climber and trailer, which grows in the *Rosa wichuraiana* manner. The large, primrose to canary yellow flowers are double and are borne in clusters of 4–5 blooms. They are slightly fragrant. The stems are long and the foliage is rich green and glossy. ZONES 5–9.

Barbier, France, 1920

Rosa wichuraiana × 'Constance'

'PRINCE ARTHUR'

syn. 'Triomphe de Caen'

OLD, HYBRID PERPETUAL, MEDIUM RED, REPEAT-FLOWERING

This is a vigorous plant with smaller flowers than its putative parent, but it is said to be better formed. The crimson flowers are long-lasting, although they tend to hang down a bit. With good cultivation, this rose repeats well in the

---

'Prince Meillandina'

autumn. It may be hard to obtain these days. Prince Arthur of Connaught was a son of Queen Victoria. ZONES 5–9.

Cant, UK, 1875

'Général Jacqueminot' × seedling

'PRINCE CAMILLE DE ROHAN'

syn. 'La Rosière, Climbing'

OLD, HYBRID PERPETUAL, DARK RED, REPEAT-FLOWERING

With such distinguished parentage, you would expect this rose to be a good one, and the blooms indeed merit great praise; they are fragrant, deep red, very double, with about 100 petals, large, imbricated and cupped. The growth habit can be sprawling, becoming more upright with age. However, there is a fault upon which all agree—the weak stems cannot fully support the weight of the flowers. It is sometimes repeat-flowering. ZONES 5–9.

Verdier, France, 1861

Possibly 'Général Jacqueminot' × 'Géant des Batailles'

'PRINCE CHARLES'

OLD, BOURBON, MAUVE

This medium to tall Bourbon is not unlike the more well-known 'Bourbon Queen'. Large, deep green leaves adorn almost thornless stems on this vigorous bush. The well-scented, loose, semi-double flowers are crimson or bright cherry in color. There may also be some purple and some veining in the flowers, leading to the American Rose Society color attribution. There are few flowers after mid-summer. ZONES 5–9.

Hardy, France, 1842

Parentage unknown

'PRINCE FRÉDERIC'

OLD, GALLICA, MAUVE

This rose has large, red, fragrant flowers on a tall-growing plant of the Gallica

'Prince Napoléon'

---

style. It is by no means common, but is available in England and Denmark. ZONES 4–9.

Probably Parmentier, France, 1840

Parentage unknown

'PRINCE MEILLANDINA'

MEIrutral

syns 'Prince Sunblaze', 'Red Sunblaze'

MODERN, MINIATURE, DARK RED, REPEAT-FLOWERING

This rose has dark currant red flowers that vary to bright orange depending on the climate. The double florets with 15–25 petals have no fragrance, and a large number of clusters covers the bush with color and vibrancy. 'Prince Meillandina' has very dependable vigor and bloom production. It is a good garden variety that is disease resistant and easy to maintain. ZONES 5–10.

Meilland, France, 1988

'Parador' × 'Mogral'

'PRINCE NAPOLÉON'

OLD, BOURBON, PINK BLEND, REPEAT-FLOWERING

'Prince Napoléon' is now a collector's rose and rarely to be found. It has bright rose, very double flowers on a conventional Bourbon bush. It was named for the son of Napoléon III. ZONES 5–9.

Pernet, France, 1864

Parentage unknown

'PRINCEPS'

MODERN, LARGE-FLOWERED CLIMBER, MEDIUM RED

This climbing rose bears its very large red flowers in summer. They have only a slight fragrance. It is most suitable for growing on pillars and low fences. ZONES 4–9.

Clark, Australia, 1942

Parentage unknown

'Prince Charles'

'Princeps'

'Princess Michiko'

'Princess' (Laperrière)

'PRINCESS'

MODERN, LARGE-FLOWERED/HYBRID TEA,
ORANGE-RED, REPEAT-FLOWERING

Large vermilion blooms with good
exhibition form are produced on this
relatively small bush that only grows
3 ft (1 m) high in most climates. The
double florets have a faint fragrance
and bloom production is somewhat
sparse. This variety may make the
exhibitor happy, but does not give a
very good display in the garden.
ZONES 5–10.

Laperrière, France, 1964

('Peace' × 'Magicienne') × ('Independence' ×
'Radar')

'PRINCESS'   INTerprince

MODERN, CLUSTER-FLOWERED/FLORIBUNDA,
WHITE, REPEAT-FLOWERING

The attractive white, weatherproof
blooms of 'Princess' have 26–40
petals and are borne in large clusters.
They are medium sized with a hint of
fragrance. The foliage is glossy dark
green and disease resistant and the
plant is a tall, upright, vigorous bush.
ZONES 5–11.

Ilsink, The Netherlands, 1993

'Pink Delight' × seedling

'PRINCESS ALICE'   HARtanna

syns 'Brite Lites', 'Zonta Rose'

MODERN, CLUSTER-FLOWERED/FLORIBUNDA,
MEDIUM YELLOW, REPEAT-FLOWERING

'Princess Alice' is an upright-growing
bush rose with rounded, double yellow

flowers containing 22–28 petals.
Medium-sized and slightly scented,
the blooms are borne in many-flowered
sprays from spring to autumn. The
healthy foliage is mid-green and semi-
glossy. It grows best in cooler climates.
ZONES 4–9.

Harkness, UK, 1985

'Judy Garland' × 'Anne Harkness'

Dublin Gold Medal 1984, Royal National
Rose Society Trial Ground Certificate 1985,
Courtrai and Tokyo Certificates of Merit
1985, Orléans Prize 1987, The Hague Silver
Medal 1990

'PRINCESS CHICHIBU'

MODERN, CLUSTER-FLOWERED/FLORIBUNDA,
PINK BLEND, REPEAT-FLOWERING

This rose has large, double flowers with
30 petals. They are borne in clusters
and have a slight scent. 'Princess
Chichibu' is a healthy, medium-sized
variety. ZONES 4–9.

Harkness, UK, 1971

('Vera Dalton' × 'Highlight') × 'Merlin'

Baden-Baden and Hamburg Silver
Medals 1973

'PRINCESS MARGARET OF ENGLAND'   MEIlister, MEIlisia

syn. 'Princesse Margaret d'Angleterre'

MODERN, LARGE-FLOWERED/HYBRID TEA,
MEDIUM PINK, REPEAT-FLOWERING

'Princess Margaret of England' has
large, high-centered, double, lightly

'Princess Alice'

scented flowers. Phlox-pink in color,
they are borne singly or in clusters
in spring; in autumn they appear singly
and have a more intense tone. This
vigorous, free-flowering upright bush
has leathery, dark green foliage.
**'Climbing Princess Margaret of Eng-
land'** is suitable for walls and pillars. This
is the second rose named for Princess
Margaret. The first was from Benjamin
Cant in 1932. ZONES 4–9.

Meilland, France, 1968

'Queen Elizabeth' × ('Peace' × 'Michèle
Meilland')

Portland Gold Medal 1977

'PRINCESS MICHAEL OF KENT'   HARlightly

MODERN, CLUSTER-FLOWERED/FLORIBUNDA,
MEDIUM YELLOW, REPEAT-FLOWERING

The long, pointed buds on 'Princess
Margaret of Kent' open into rounded,
fully double, yellow, fragrant flowers
that are borne singly or in clusters.
With 38 petals each, they are long
stemmed and appear from spring to
autumn. This neat, compact bush has
healthy, glossy green foliage and
looks good in clumps in big borders.
ZONES 4–9.

Harkness, UK, 1981

'Manx Queen' × 'Alexander'

Royal National Rose Society Certificate of Merit
1979, Belfast Certificate of Merit 1981, Orléans
Prize 1983

'PRINCESS MICHIKO'

MODERN, CLUSTER-FLOWERED/FLORIBUNDA,
ORANGE BLEND

The large flowers of 'Princess Michiko',
borne in small clusters, have some scent.
Semi-double with 15 petals each, they
are copper-orange with a yellowish eye.
This bushy plant with glossy foliage is
good for bedding and as a standard.
ZONES 4–9.

Dickson, UK, 1966

'Circus' × 'Spartan'

'PRINCESS OF WALES'

OLD, HYBRID PERPETUAL, LIGHT PINK,
REPEAT-FLOWERING

This rare rose bears large blooms of
bright crimson to pink. They are double
and well-formed. The Princess was Princess Alexandra, the wife of Edward VII.
There were two other roses of the name,
Laxton's pink Hybrid Perpetual of 1871
and Henry Bennett's Tea of 1822, both
probably lost. ZONES 5–9.

Paul, UK, 1864

Parentage unknown

'PRINCESS OF WALES'

HARdinkum

MODERN, CLUSTER-FLOWERED/FLORIBUNDA,
WHITE, REPEAT-FLOWERING

The color impact of this rose is stunning,
due to the quantity of fragrant blooms in
each cluster. Held close to the foliage, the
cream buds open to pure white and continue through summer and autumn.
With a dense, leafy and compact habit to
below average height, it is ideal for beds,
borders and hedges. In April 1977 Robert
and Philip Harkness presented this rose
to Princess Diana and, in accordance
with her wishes, it is sold to benefit the
British Lung Association. ZONES 4–9.

Harkness, UK, 1997

Parentage unknown

'Princess Michael of Kent'

'Princess Margaret of England'

P

'PRINCESS ROYAL'   DICroyal
MODERN, LARGE-FLOWERED/HYBRID TEA,
APRICOT BLEND, REPEAT-FLOWERING

This bushy variety has large, full, apricot
blooms with 26–40 petals. Borne mostly
singly on stiff, very thorny stems, they
have a slight fragrance. It is a healthy
plant with medium-sized, semi-glossy
green foliage. ZONES 4–9.

Dickson, UK, 1992

'Tequila Sunrise' × seedling

'PRINCESSE ADÉLAIDE'
OLD, MOSS, LIGHT PINK

'Princesse Adélaide is a medium bush
with dark green foliage, which is often
variegated. The large, double flowers are
soft pink, are often variegated, with a
pleasing scent. They are not very mossy.
This rose is similar to the Gallicas, in which
class it is sometimes placed. ZONES 4–9.

Laffay, France, 1845

Parentage unknown

'Princesse de Nassau'

'Pristine'

'PRINCESSE DE MONACO'
MEImagarmic

syns 'Grace Kelly', 'Preference', 'Princesse
Grace', 'Princess of Monaco', 'Princesse
Grace de Monaco'

MODERN, LARGE-FLOWERED/HYBRID TEA, WHITE,
REPEAT-FLOWERING

The large high-centered blooms of
'Princesse de Monaco' are white edged
with pink. They continue through
summer and autumn, are very fragrant
and are double, with 35 petals. The dark
glossy foliage and upright growth make
this a good garden rose; it is also popular
on the exhibition table. ZONES 4–9.

Meilland, France, 1982

'Ambassador' × 'Peace'

'PRINCESSE DE NASSAU'
syn. 'Autumnalis'
OLD, NOISETTE, LIGHT YELLOW

This rose is more generally known as
'Autumnalis' and is a form of the Musk
Rose related to 'Blush Noisette'. Graham
Thomas has equated it with Laffay's
'Princesse de Nassau'. It is a medium
climber or rambler, and bears sprays of
small, creamy yellowish, double flowers,
nicely scented in the musk way. There
are few prickles and the stems grow in a
zig-zag (similar to another Noisette
'Aimée Vibert'). It does not flower until
late summer but continues to bloom for
a while. The plant is a little tender.
ZONES 7–9.

Laffay, France, 1835

Parentage unknown

'PRINCESSE DE SAGAN'
OLD, CHINA, DARK RED, REPEAT-FLOWERING

This moderate shrub bears deep cherry
red maroon, double flowers, which are
somewhat cupped with sporadic extra
petals. The solitary flowers are well held
on long stems at the ends of thin branches.
This rose would be hard to come by now,
but could be 'discovered' in old locations.
It was named for Jeanne Alexandrine
Marguerite Seillière, Princess de Sagan,
who died in 1905. ZONES 7–9.

Dubreuil, France, 1887

Parentage unknown

'Princesse de Sagan'

'Priscilla Burton'

'PRINCESSE LAMBALLE'
syn. 'Princesse de Lamballe'
OLD, ALBA, WHITE

Not a great deal is known about this
rose, except by a few of the cognoscenti.
Many Albas were in cultivation at
one time but have since been lost with
the coming of the repeat-flowering
roses. This rose has pure white, double
cupped flowers on a conventional blue-
green-leafed Alba bush. There seems to
be a touch of Musk Rose in it. The
flowers are sometimes flesh tinted.
ZONES 4–9.

Pre-1848

Parentage unknown

'PRINCESSE LOUISE'
OLD, SEMPERVIRENS, WHITE

Rosa sempervirens, a tender wild
rambler from southern Europe and
northern Africa, has been used to
create a number of hybrids, notably
'Adélaïde d'Orleans' and 'Félicité-
Perpétue', both vigorous once-flowering
ramblers with small, double white
flowers. This rose is considered to be
intermediate between them. Its flowers
are creamy white, with the back petals
shaded rose. ZONES 5–9.

Jacques, France, 1829

Hybrid of *Rosa sempervirens*

'PRINCESSE MARIE'
OLD, SEMPERVIRENS, MEDIUM PINK

This rose, from the same stable as
'Princesse Louise' and others created by
Jacques, bears bright pink flowers in very
large clusters. The other parent was pos-

'Princesse de Monaco'

sibly a Noisette. *Rosa sempervirens* is also
thought to be involved with the Ayrshire
Ramblers. ZONES 4–9.

Jacques, France, 1829

Hybrid of *Rosa sempervirens*

'PRISCILLA BURTON'   MACrat
MODERN, CLUSTER-FLOWERED/FLORIBUNDA,
RED BLEND, REPEAT-FLOWERING

From spring to autumn this free-
flowering bush rose bears cupped, semi-
double bicolored blooms in shades of
pale to deep pink, purple and cerise. Produced in clusters, they have 10 petals
each and are fragrant. It is vigorous and
upright in habit with glossy dark green
foliage. ZONES 4–9.

McGredy, NZ, 1978

'Old Master' × seedling

Royal National Rose Society President's
International Trophy 1976

'PRISTINE'   JACpico
MODERN, LARGE-FLOWERED/HYBRID TEA, WHITE,
REPEAT-FLOWERING

The long buds of this rose open to
huge high-centered almost white
blooms that are shaded light pink.
The 25–30 petals are overlapping and
there is a light scent. The colors are
unfading under all climatic conditions.
This healthy plant has deep green
leathery foliage and strong upright
stems. It is ideal for bedding and is
suitable for exhibiting. ZONES 4–9.

Warriner, USA, 1978

'White Masterpiece' × 'First Prize'

Portland Gold Medal 1979, Royal National Rose
Society Edland Fragrance Medal 1979

'Princesse Adélaide'

'Princess Royal'

'PRIVÉ'

syn. 'Lifirane'

MODERN, LARGE-FLOWERED/HYBRID TEA,
MEDIUM PINK, REPEAT-FLOWERING

This sport of the forcing variety 'Sonia'
is similar to its parent except for the
flowers, which are cherry red and semi-
double. 'Privé' has double flowers with
an excellent shape; the outer petals curve
back when the blooms open fully. They
are held singly or in small clusters amid
glossy dark green foliage. There is a slight
scent. ZONES 5–9.

Meilland, France, 1988

Sport of 'Sonia'

'Privé'

'PROFESSEUR JEAN BARNARD'   DELjaber

MODERN, LARGE-FLOWERED/HYBRID TEA,
DARK RED, REPEAT-FLOWERING

This rose, which is a good choice for
bedding, has very large dark red flowers.
Appearing through summer and autumn,
they have 25–30 petals and are lightly
fragrant. 'Professeur Jean Barnard' is a
vigorous, bushy plant with abundant
dark green foliage. ZONES 4–9.

Delbard-Chabert, France, 1989

('Charles Mallerin' × 'Divine') × ('Tropicana' ×
['Rome Glory' × 'Impeccable'])

'Professeur Jean Barnard'

'Prominent'

'Prosperity'

'Proud Land'

'PROLIFERA DE REDOUTÉ'
OLD, CENTIFOLIA, MEDIUM PINK

This medium to tall, lax shrub to about 6 ft (1.8 m) high is made up of very dark green, prickly stems. These are covered in coarse, dark green foliage. At first, the deep rose pink, very double flowers are cabbage-like, then open flat and are very fragrant. 'Prolifera de Redouté' would be a most agreeable shrub were it not for its propensity for proliferation (another bud growing through the center of the flower). It is more suitable for a larger collection, rather than for general garden use. ZONES 4–10.

France, pre-1824

Parentage unknown

'PROMINENT' KORp
syn. 'Korp'

MODERN, LARGE-FLOWERED, ORANGE-RED, REPEAT-FLOWERING

'Prominent' has large pointed buds that develop into bright orange-red blooms with 33 petals. Sometimes classified as a Grandiflora, they have an almost perfect form, are medium sized and are slightly fragrant. This free-flowering variety has an upright growth habit and matt green foliage. ZONES 4–9.

Kordes, Germany, 1971

'Colour Wonder' × 'Zorina'

Royal National Rose Society Certificate of Merit 1970, Portland Gold Medal 1977, All-America Rose Selection 1977

'Prospero'

'PROSPERITY'
MODERN, MODERN SHRUB, WHITE, REPEAT-FLOWERING

Large clusters of creamy white, fragrant blooms open from pale pink buds. Blooms are produced in profusion from early summer. The foliage is glossy green and the growth habit is medium and slightly lax. A good shrub or pillar rose, it requires feeding in mid-summer to encourage autumn color. ZONES 4–9.

Pemberton, UK, 1919

'Marie-Jeanne' × 'Perle des Jardins'

Royal Horticultural Society Award of Garden Merit 1994

'PROSPERO' AUSpero
MODERN, MODERN SHRUB, DARK RED, REPEAT-FLOWERING

A bush rather than a shrub, 'Prospero' produces large, deep crimson, fragrant blooms that turn a deep purple. They have 40 small petals. Not very robust, this variety requires feeding and spraying to obtain a maximum return. It is also classified as an English Rose. ZONES 4–9.

Austin, UK, 1982

'The Knight' × seedling

'PROUD LAND'
MODERN, LARGE-FLOWERED/HYBRID TEA, DARK RED, REPEAT-FLOWERING

'Proud Land' has deep red flowers that are very double with 60 petals. They have a considerable scent and appear with good continuity through summer and autumn. It has an upright growing habit and leathery, dark green foliage that is reasonably healthy. ZONES 4–9.

Morey, USA, 1969

'Chrysler Imperial' × seedling

'PROUD TITANIA' AUStania
MODERN, MODERN SHRUB, WHITE

An early variety in this family of roses from David Austin, 'Proud Titania' is

'Proud Titania'

also classified as an English Rose, and it can claim origins in the blend of Old and Modern Garden Roses. Although it is still listed by several growers the raisers have discontinued it, possibly because of its susceptibility to disease. It produces large, double blooms with 35 petals that are flat, creamy white and very fragrant. There is some doubt as to its repeat-flowering ability. The foliage is small and semi-glossy. ZONES 4–9.

Austin, UK, 1982

Seedling × seedling

'PUCKER UP' TINpuck
MODERN, MINIATURE, ORANGE-RED, REPEAT-FLOWERING

Small buds open to bright orange-red to lipstick red flowers depending on climatic conditions. The florets are double with 23 petals, and have a light fragrance and great exhibition form. The blooms which can develop a dark overlay in the outer petals are borne singly or in small clusters on a tall, upright plant. They generally have long stems (with an occasional crooked peduncle) with complementary mid-green, semi-glossy foliage. The growth habit is a bit gangly but the plant is vigorous, healthy and clean. This rose has won Best Bloom at the American Rose Society National Convention. ZONES 4–11.

Bennett, USA, 1984

'Futura' × 'Avendel'

'PUDSEY BEAR' BEDchild
MODERN, LARGE-FLOWERED/HYBRID TEA, DEEP YELLOW, REPEAT-FLOWERING

This variety bears its medium-sized, deep yellow blooms very freely from summer to autumn. They have some scent. It grows to medium height and is covered with ample dark green foliage. 'Pudsey Bear' was named to raise funds for a children's charity. ZONES 4–9.

Chessum, UK, 1996

Parentage unknown

'PUPPY LOVE' SAVapop
MODERN, MINIATURE, ORANGE BLEND, REPEAT-FLOWERING

Opening from elegantly pointed buds, the small flowers of this rose are an attractive color combination of pink, coral and orange. The double florets have a light fragrance and high well-formed centers suitable for exhibition. This is one of the first roses to bloom in the spring and it has excellent shape and color. With only 23 petals, the bloom

'Pucker Up'

P

'Purple Splendour'

matures very slowly and so holds its exhibition form. This is a favorite with floral arrangers because of its lovely bud form and eye catching color, set against lush, dark green foliage. It has an upright, compact growth habit and is clean and easy to maintain. 'Puppy Love' is a good choice for a border or in a container. ZONES 5–11.

Schwartz, USA, 1978

'Zorina' × seedling

'PURE BLISS' DICtator
MODERN, LARGE-FLOWERED/HYBRID TEA, PINK BLEND, REPEAT-FLOWERING

This aptly named variety has large blooms that are an extremely pretty blend of soft pink. Appearing throughout summer and autumn, they are well formed and have a slight scent. The growth is moderate, but very bushy and healthy. 'Pure Bliss' is a good bedding plant that is also suitable for growing as a standard. ZONES 4–9.

Dickson, UK, 1995

'Elina' × ('Silver Jubilee' × ['Typhoon' × 'Maxi'])

Belfast Gold Medal 1997, Genoa Silver Medal 1994

'PUREZZA'
syns *Rosa banksiae* 'The Pearl', 'Purezza'
MODERN, RAMBLER, WHITE, REPEAT-FLOWERING

Large clusters of very small, double, white blooms are borne on this thornless rambling variety. They are fragrant and appear with good continuity from summer to autumn. 'Purezza' is an extremely vigorous grower with healthy leathery foliage. ZONES 6–10.

Mansuino, Italy, 1961

'Tom Thumb' × *Rosa banksiae lutescens*

Rome Gold Medal 1960

'PURPLE BEAUTY'
MODERN, LARGE-FLOWERED/HYBRID TEA, MAUVE, REPEAT-FLOWERING

This variety, which is a favorite on the exhibitor's bench, has very large, red-purple flowers with 30 petals. They have some fragrance and are produced through summer and autumn. 'Purple Beauty' has an upright growth habit and leathery, dark green foliage. ZONES 4–9.

Gandy, UK, 1979

'Eminence' × 'Tyrius'

'PURPLE BUTTONS'
MODERN, MODERN SHRUB, MAUVE BLEND, REPEAT-FLOWERING

This recent introduction from the Californian breeder, Kim Rupert, forms a

'Purple Cloud'

neat, dense shrub. It bears many double blooms filled with deep mauve petals. ZONES 5–9.

Rupert, USA, 1998

Parentage unknown

'PURPLE CLOUD'
MODERN, LARGE-FLOWERED/HYBRID TEA, MAUVE BLEND, REPEAT-FLOWERING

Perhaps the nearest rose to purple in color, 'Purple Cloud' produces large, well-formed flowers with pointed petals. They open slowly to show a high-centered form that is filled with 40–50 petals. The fragrance is strong, as is the case in most roses of this color. The flowers are produced in profusion and the foliage is matt dark green and disease free, but the stems are short. Repeat-bloom is good. Since the growth is of medium height and bushy, 'Purple Cloud' is good for use on standards. The buds are also good for cutting because they hold their shape well without fading. ZONES 5–9.

Keisei, Japan, 1993

Parentage unknown

'PURPLE DAWN' BRIdawn
MODERN, MINIATURE, MAUVE, REPEAT-FLOWERING

The urn-shaped buds of this rose open to velvety mauve flowers with 25 petals. They are borne singly or in small clusters and have a light fragrance. The bloom size may be a bit big for a traditional Miniature and this is certainly a contender for the Patio classification. The color does not fade even in strong sunlight. The flower form is high centered with lots of substance to the petals, making it ideal as a cut flower for the home or for exhibition at rose shows. It has a vigorous, tall and upright habit, and provides an attractive dash of color in the garden. ZONES 5–10.

Bridges, USA, 1991

'Party Girl' × seedling

'Purezza'

'PURPLE SPLENDOUR'
MODERN, CLUSTER-FLOWERED/FLORIBUNDA, MAUVE, REPEAT-FLOWERING

Small clusters of glowing purple, double, large flowers with 26 petals are borne on 'Purple Splendour' throughout summer and autumn. They have a slight scent. It is suitable for beds. ZONES 4–9.

LeGrice, UK, 1976

'News' × 'Overture'

'PURPLE TIGER' JACpurr
syn. 'Impressionist'
MODERN, CLUSTER-FLOWERED/FLORIBUNDA, MAUVE, REPEAT-FLOWERING

This innovative variety has blooms with remarkable coloring, that is, very deep purple and then striped and flecked with white and mauve-pink. Produced in small clusters from summer to autumn, they are open, with 26-40 petals, and have some fragrance. The foliage, which is glossy green, grows on a short bush that is almost thornless. 'Purple Tiger' is a good bedding variety that is unfortunately very prone to black spot. ZONES 4–9.

Christensen, USA, 1991

'Intrigue' × 'Pinstripe'

'PURPUREA PLENA'
OLD, SCOTS, MAUVE

The Scots Roses (*Rosa pimpinellifolia* or *R. spinossissima*) were quite in vogue in the nineteenth century, particularly in cottage gardens. Many forms were developed from the single, creamy white wild type from about 1800. Most of these are now lost, although collections are still held by enthusiasts in Scotland and also at the Royal National Rose Society Garden at St. Albans. They are extremely hardy, prickly, low growing and once-only (early) flowering. 'Purpurea Plena' is a double purple variety and would not be easy to find. It displays a large number of characteristic black seeds. Kordes has developed some of the taller Pimpinellifolias into the hardy 'Frühlings' group. They will not grow in warm, humid climates, but do well in poor soil and even at the seashore. ZONES 3–8.

Early nineteenth century

Parentage unknown

'PZAZZ' POUzazz
MODERN, PATIO/DWARF CLUSTER-FLOWERED, RED BLEND, REPEAT-FLOWERING

This Patio Rose has medium-sized double blooms that are striped pink-cerise, turning as they age to a softer pink with cerise. A disease-resistant, repeat-flowering variety, it has glossy light green foliage and is a good choice for small flowerbeds and containers. ZONES 4–9.

Poulsen, Denmark, 1996

Parentage unknown

'Pure Bliss'

'Puppy Love'

'Purple Tiger'

QR

'Quaker Star'

'Queen Charlotte'

'Queen Elizabeth'

'QUAKER STAR'   DICperhaps

MODERN, LARGE-FLOWERED/HYBRID TEA, ORANGE-PINK, REPEAT-FLOWERING

'Quaker Star' has very full flowers with 40 petals that are orange with a silver reverse, then age to salmon with orange edges to the petals. They are borne mostly singly throughout summer and autumn; unfortunately they have little fragrance. It is a bushy plant with a short growth habit and healthy, glossy, mid-green foliage. It is sometimes classified as a Grandiflora. ZONES 4–9.

Dickson, UK, 1991

'Anisley Dickson' × seedling

Royal National Rose Society Certificate of Merit 1989

'QUATRE SAISONS BLANC MOUSSEUX'

syns 'Perpetual White Moss', 'Rosier de Thionville'

OLD, MOSS, WHITE, REPEAT-FLOWERING

This Moss Rose of distinction makes a tidy and upright, yet bushy shrub to some 5 ft (1.5 m) with stout stems well clothed in dark purplish green, stubbly moss and slightly mossy, mid-green foliage. The flower buds, which are also well covered with moss, are arranged in small clusters on short stalks and open to white and fairly full, medium-sized flowers. They lose some of their early promise as they mature, but their lack of significant

beauty is compensated for by their profusion, fragrance and constant renewal through summer and autumn. ZONES 5–9.

Laffay, France, pre-1837

Sport of 'Quatre Saisons'

'QUEEN CHARLOTTE'

HARubondee

MODERN, LARGE-FLOWERED/HYBRID TEA, ORANGE-PINK, REPEAT-FLOWERING

This tall, upright grower has flowers of salmon-red with a yellow base and a reverse of pink-red, ageing paler. High centered, the blooms are borne singly from summer to autumn and have a slight fragrance. The foliage is large, dark green and semi-glossy on a good bedding variety. ZONES 4–9.

Harkness, UK, 1989

'Basildon Bond' × 'Silver Jubilee'

Royal National Rose Society Trial Ground Certificate 1987, Hradec First Prize 1991

'QUEEN ELIZABETH'

syns 'Queen of England', 'The Queen Elizabeth Rose'

MODERN, CLUSTER-FLOWERED/FLORIBUNDA, MEDIUM PINK, REPEAT-FLOWERING

Called a Grandiflora in some countries, this remarkable variety has maintained its popularity for over 40 years; it is a grower's dream as it produces a high percentage of saleable plants. It has large, pointed, medium pink blooms that have

'Climbing Queen Elizabeth'

a high center. They appear throughout summer and autumn and are double, with 38 petals. A vigorous plant that, with light pruning, develops into an impressive shrub, it can be cut down hard in mid-winter about once every 6 years to rejuvenate it. Its large, glossy, dark green, leathery foliage is relatively resistant to disease, and it is an ideal variety for large borders, as a specimen plant or for hedging. The Queen Mother granted permission for her name to be associated with this rose on condition that it should be named in full—The Queen Elizabeth Rose. Any modification does not therefore carry the same validity. **'Climbing Queen Elizabeth'** (syns 'Climbing The Queen Elizabeth Rose', 'Grimpant Queen Elizabeth'; Whisler, USA, 1957), the summer-flowering climbing variety, has somewhat suspect flower production. In all other respects it is similar to its parent. ZONES 4–9.

Lammerts, USA, 1954

'Charlotte Armstrong' × 'Floradora'

Portland Gold Medal 1954, National Rose Society President's International Trophy 1955, All-America Rose Selection 1955, American Rose Society Gold Medal 1957, Golden Rose of The Hague 1968, World's Favorite Rose 1979

'QUEEN FABIOLA'

syn. 'Fabiola'

MODERN, LARGE-FLOWERED/HYBRID TEA, ORANGE-RED, REPEAT-FLOWERING

Named after the Queen of Belgium, 'Queen Fabiola' is more brightly colored than its parent. The oval buds open to large, double flowers made up of three dozen petals that give a high center. There is a slight fragrance, and the blooms look fine against the profuse, leathery and semi-glossy foliage. Flower production is very good with quick repeat. The variety is vigorous and compact, although there may be a mildew in autumn. 'Queen Fabiola' is an excellent rose for

'Queen Fabiola'

cutting as the blooms open slowly but, like 'Montezuma', they can bleach to a dull orange color and tend to hang onto the bush for too long. ZONES 5–9.

Hazenberg, Belgium, 1961

Sport of 'Montezuma'

'QUEEN MARGRETHE'

POUlskov, POUskul

syns 'Dronning Margrethé', 'Enchantment', 'Königin Margrethe', 'Queen Margarethe'

MODERN, MODERN SHRUB, LIGHT PINK, REPEAT-FLOWERING

'Queen Margrethe' is a relatively new shrub rose that bears light pink, double, medium-sized flowers with two dozen petals and an old-fashioned quartered form. They are carried in small clusters, and resemble the English Roses of David Austin. There is a slight fragrance. The small, glossy mid-green foliage covers this shortish, bushy and compact rose. This neat, rounded shrub flowers repeatedly from spring to late autumn. Many breeders are now creating roses with an old-fashioned form. ZONES 5–10.

Poulsen, Denmark, 1991

Seedling × 'Egeskov'

New Zealand Gold Medal 1993

'QUEEN MOTHER'   KORquemu

syn. 'Queen Mum'

MODERN, PATIO/DWARF CLUSTER-FLOWERED, LIGHT PINK, REPEAT-FLOWERING

This extremely free-flowering plant bears small clusters of loose, soft pink blooms throughout summer and autumn. They are slightly fragrant. 'Queen Mother' is a healthy plant with a slightly lax growth habit that develops into a shrubby grower; it has glossy dark green foliage. ZONES 4–9.

Kordes, Germany, 1991

Parentage unknown

Royal Horticultural Society Award of Garden Merit 1994

'Queen Margrethe'

'Queen Mother'

'Queen of Bedders'

'Queen of Hearts'

'QUEEN NEFERTITI' AUSap
MODERN, MODERN SHRUB, LIGHT YELLOW, REPEAT-FLOWERING

'Queen Nefertiti', a variable variety, produces yellow flowers with a 'muddy brown' edge to the petals from summer to autumn. The blooms have some fragrance. The plant forms a tidy shrub and is propagated by budding. It is also classified as an English Rose. ZONES 4–9.

Austin, UK, 1988

'Lilian Austin' × 'Chaucer'

'QUEEN OF BEDDERS'
OLD, BOURBON, DEEP PINK, REPEAT-FLOWERING

The fragrant flowers of this rose are a rich crimson and the plant flowers freely until autumn. It is a very compact Bourbon and so is very suitable at the front of borders. The stronger shoots should be shortened to encourage the bedding propensity. ZONES 5–9.

Standish & Nobel, UK, 1871

Seedling of 'Sir Joseph Paxton'

'QUEEN OF BOURBONS'
syns 'Bourbon Queen', 'Reine des Iles Bourbon', 'Souvenir de la Princesse de Lamballe'

OLD, BOURBON, PINK BLEND, REPEAT-FLOWERING

This rose is a well-known old favorite and is still grown widely. The rose pink flowers are semi-double, loose and cupped; they are well scented but do not repeat well. Although the plant can grow tall, it is best pruned to a bushy shrub. It has plenty of foliage and is very strong; it will survive even if it is neglected. This is most suitable for planting in a cottage garden. ZONES 5–9.

Mauget, France, 1834

Parentage unknown

'QUEEN OF HEARTS'
MODERN, LARGE-FLOWERED CLIMBER, MEDIUM PINK, REPEAT-FLOWERING

This vigorous summer-flowering climber bears globular buds that develop into rich pink, double, fragrant flowers. It has

'Queen of Bourbons' (rosehips)

'Queen of Bourbons'

dark foliage which contributes to a very vigorous climber that is a good choice for growing on walls. ZONES 4–9.

Clark, Australia, 1920

'Gustave Grünerwald' × 'Rosy Morn'

'QUEEN OF THE MUSKS'
MODERN, MODERN SHRUB, PINK BLEND, REPEAT-FLOWERING

The open flowers of this variety are a deep blush and white. They appear with good continuity from summer to autumn and they have a very strong fragrance. 'Queen of the Musks' is a little-known shrub rose. It has dark ivy-green foliage and is a useful rose in borders and as a specimen plant. ZONES 4–9.

Paul, UK, 1913

Parentage unknown

'QUEEN PARADE'
MODERN, MINIATURE, MEDIUM PINK, REPEAT-FLOWERING

'Queen Parade' produces rose pink blooms on a small bushy plant. The buds are small and shapely and open slowly to small, double, well-formed flat flowers of 25–30 petals. The flowers last well on the plant. The Parade series consists of over a dozen varieties that Poulsen has called the Rosa Nova series, all excellent pot plants with good continuity of bloom. The plant is disease free. ZONES 5–10.

Poulsen, Denmark, 1992

Parentage unknown

'Queen Parade'

'RACHEL BOWES LYON'
HARlacal

MODERN, MODERN SHRUB, YELLOW BLEND, REPEAT-FLOWERING

This low, bushy grower bears clusters of peach-pink flowers with a yellow reverse. Flat and open, the medium-sized blooms have 14 petals and some fragrance. The small to mid-sized foliage is mid-green on a plant with small prickles. It is suitable for borders and hedges. ZONES 4–9.

Harkness, UK, 1981

'Kim' × (['Orange Sensation' × 'Allgold'] × Rosa californica)

Courtrai Silver Medal 1980

'RADIANCE'
syn. 'Pink Radiance'

MODERN, LARGE-FLOWERED/HYBRID TEA, LIGHT PINK, REPEAT-FLOWERING

This vigorous grower has large, globular, cupped blooms of rose pink with a lighter reverse. The semi-double flowers have 23 petals and a considerable Damask fragrance. Suitable for bedding, this variety has a vigorous growth habit and large, leathery, very healthy foliage. 'Climbing Radiance' was introduced in 1926 by Griffing in Florida. ZONES 4–9.

Cook, USA, 1908

'Enchanter' × 'Cardinal'

'Radiance'

Q
R

'Climbing Radiance'

'RADIO TIMES' AUSsal

MODERN, MODERN SHRUB, MEDIUM PINK,
REPEAT-FLOWERING

This variety is one of David Austin's best
recent introductions; it is also classified
as an English Rose. The name was
chosen to celebrate the 70th anniversary
of the British magazine *Radio Times*.
Throughout the warmer months, this
shrub repeatedly bears gentle rose pink,
double blooms with a strong fragrance.
They have many petals that give a formal
rosette arrangement; the outer petals reflex as the flowers mature. **ZONES 5–10.**

Austin, UK, 1994

Parentage unknown

'Radox Bouquet'

'Radway Sunrise'

'Ragtime'

'RADOX BOUQUET' HARmusky

syn. 'Rosika'

MODERN, CLUSTER-FLOWERED/FLORIBUNDA,
MEDIUM PINK, REPEAT-FLOWERING

The very fragrant blooms of this variety
are produced in small clusters, with
1–3 soft pink blooms per cluster. The
medium-sized, cupped flowers have
30 petals each. The foliage is large, glossy
and mid-green on an upright plant that
is useful for bedding and for grouping in
borders. It is repeat-flowering and has
large dark prickles. **ZONES 4–9.**

Harkness, UK, 1981

('Alec's Red' × 'Piccadilly') × ('Southampton' ×
['Cläre Grammerstorf' × 'Frühlingsmorgen'])

Geneva Coupe de Parfum 1980, Belfast Fragrance
Prize 1983, Belfast Certificate of Merit 1983,
Courtrai Certificate of Merit 1983

'RADWAY SUNRISE'

syn. 'Morning Colors'

MODERN, MODERN SHRUB, ORANGE BLEND,
REPEAT-FLOWERING

This rose scored highly for health and
general effect in the UK trials, and was
one of the earliest successful attempts to
harness the extraordinary color genes of
'Masquerade' in a shrub rose. The young
flowers, carried in large trusses, are
yellow with cerise-pink at the edges of
the petals and change to deep cherry red

'Radway Sunrise'

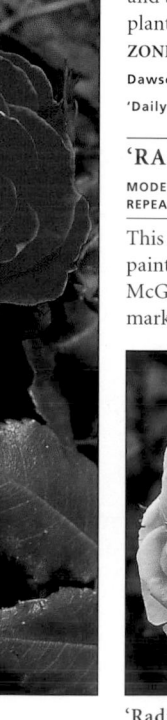

'Radio Times'

'Rainbow Robe'

as they age. Composed of 7 fairly large
petals, they open cupped to show reddish
gold stamens and have a modest scent. In
the garden, this stalwart plant makes a
colorful addition to shrub borders, and
continues in bloom through summer
and autumn. It grows with a vigorous,
free-branching and bushy habit to above
average height for a shrub rose, and is
furnished with dark green, leathery
leaves. It was so named because the
Waterhouse nursery was at Radway
Green in Cheshire, England. **ZONES 4–9.**

Waterhouse Nursery Ltd, UK, 1962

'Masquerade' × seedling

Royal National Rose Society Trial Ground
Certificate 1962

'RAE DUNGAN'

MODERN, LARGE-FLOWERED/HYBRID TEA,
YELLOW BLEND, REPEAT-FLOWERING

'Rae Dungan' has long, pointed buds
that open into creamy yellow flowers
edged with deep pink. The large, double
blooms have a considerable fragrance,
and the foliage is dark on a vigorous
plant that makes a good bedding rose.
ZONES 4–9.

Dawson, Australia, 1971

'Daily Sketch' × 'Fred Streeter'

'RAGTIME' MACcourlod

MODERN, MINIATURE, PINK BLEND,
REPEAT-FLOWERING

This rose is one of the earliest 'hand-
painted' Miniature Roses created by Sam
McGredy. The flowers all have different
markings, ranging from bright red and

'Rae Dungan'

pink and yellows with white tip edges as
the blooms age. The blooms are at their
most beautiful when fully open, displaying their dynamic range of color combinations against bright yellow stamens.
The flowers can come singly, but the
plant prefers to send out small clusters. It
is an attractive, compact bush making a
real splash in any garden. **ZONES 5–11.**

McGredy, New Zealand, 1984

'Mary Sumner' × seedling

'RAINBOW'

OLD, TEA, PINK BLEND, REPEAT-FLOWERING

'Papa Gontier' has intense pink flowers
with a carmine-red reverse with yellow
shades. The blooms of 'Rainbow' are
striped and flashed in the same colors,
which no doubt inspired the name. The
scented blooms are semi-double and
loose. It is a strong plant with stiff stems
suitable for cutting. This rose appears to
be available only in the USA. There was
an 'Improved Rainbow' (1896), but it
seems to have been lost. **ZONES 7–9.**

Sievers, USA, 1889

Sport of 'Papa Gontier'

'RAINBOW NATION' DELstricol

syn. 'Camille Pissarro'

MODERN, CLUSTER-FLOWERED/FLORIBUNDA,
YELLOW BLEND, REPEAT-FLOWERING

South Africa, a land of many races and
cultures, is sometimes known as the
'Rainbow Nation'. This spectacular
Cluster-flowered Rose has been chosen
as a reminder that different peoples can
live together peacefully. It is a vigorous

'Radio Times'

'Rainbow Robe'

and healthy shrub of medium height that gives a continuous display of flowers as the trusses appear throughout the year. The full blooms are blotched and striped with orange, red and yellow. If they are cut for indoor display, they give a long-lasting and very joyful arrangement. They are unbeatable for bedding schemes or in containers. **ZONES 5–11.**

Delbard, France, 1996

Parentage unknown

'RAINBOW ROBE'
MODERN, LARGE-FLOWERED/HYBRID TEA, MAUVE, REPEAT-FLOWERING

The color of this rose is an unusual shade of mauve-purple, which turns to red as the flowers age. It is as though the blooms darken when exposed to the sun, although the uppersides of the petals remain a paler color. The blooms are large, high centered and extremely fragrant, but production is below average with a slow repeat. The matt dark green foliage covers this relatively short and upright bush. **ZONES 5–9.**

Kordes, Germany, 1991

Parentage unknown

'RAINBOW'S END'   SAValife
MODERN, MINIATURE, YELLOW BLEND, REPEAT-FLOWERING

This rose is one of the most beautiful Miniature Roses ever created. The blooms are deep yellow with red edges, ageing to a red all over. The blending of the yellow and red is truly eye catching and usually draws murmurs of appreciation from everyone. The double florets with 35 petals have no fragrance. The foliage is small, dark green and glossy on an upright, compact, dense bush covered with blooms at all stages. This compact rounded growth habit makes it ideal as a container-grown plant. This rose is still ranked one of the most popular Miniature Roses. Recently, a climbing version was introduced. **ZONES 4–11.**

Saville, USA, 1984

'Rise 'n' Shine' × 'Watercolor'

American Rose Society Award of Excellence 1986

'Rainbow's End'

'Ralph's Creeper'

'Ramona'

'Ralph's Creeper'

'Raubritter'

'Rambling Rector'

'Rambling Rector'

'RALPH'S CREEPER' MORpapplay
syns 'Creepy', 'Glowing Carpet', 'Highveld Sun'

MODERN, MODERN SHRUB/GROUND COVER, RED BLEND, REPEAT-FLOWERING

This repeat-flowering ground cover has the potential to be used in a variety of situations in the garden. The flowers are deep orange-red with a bright yellow eye, with a reverse of bright yellow and white ageing to pinkish red. Loose and medium sized, the semi-double blooms, with 15 petals, are borne in sprays of 10–15. A moderate apple blossom fragrance and small, healthy, matt, dark green foliage is a bonus. If the blooms are not dead-headed then a crop of small round red fruit will be produced in autumn. This spreading plant is suitable for garden banks, window boxes, pots and hanging baskets. ZONES 4–9.

Moore, USA, 1987

'Papoose' × 'Playboy'

'RAMBLING RECTOR'
MODERN, RAMBLER, WHITE

Although its origins are unknown, this rose is probably very old and must surely have started life in a vicarage garden. 'Rambling Rector' has an intense scent and semi-double, white flowers. Not suitable for a small garden, it will ramble extensively through trees, bearing masses of small clusters in summer. ZONES 5–9.

Pre-1912

Possibly *Rosa multiflora* × *R. moschata*

Royal Horticultural Society Award of Garden Merit 1993

'RAMONA'
syn. 'Red Cherokee'

MODERN, MODERN SHRUB, MEDIUM RED, REPEAT-FLOWERING

'Ramona' is a vigorous, bushy, slightly lax plant with glossy foliage that is suitable for a border or as a specimen plant. It flowers early in summer with occasional bloom in autumn, and has large, single, fragrant blooms with 5 petals that are carmine-crimson. ZONES 4–9.

Dietrich and Turner, USA, 1913

Sport of 'Anemone'

'RAPHAEL'
OLD, MOSS, WHITE

The flowers of this rose are pinkish and well mossed. They do repeat-flower, but only very slightly. 'Raphael' is available only from a few specialist suppliers. ZONES 4–9.

Robert, France, 1856

Parentage unknown

'RAUBRITTER'
MODERN, MODERN SHRUB, LIGHT PINK

'Raubritter' bears clusters of light pink, double, globular flowers. The foliage is leathery and wrinkled. Although occasionally listed as a climber, this rose is more often grown as a sprawling shrub or ground cover. Only summer flowering, it is quite spectacular. ZONES 4–9.

Kordes, Germany, 1936

'Daisy Hill' × 'Solarium'

'RAY OF SUNSHINE' COCclare
MODERN, MODERN SHRUB, MEDIUM YELLOW, REPEAT-FLOWERING

The pointed buds of this variety open into clear bright unfading yellow, small semi-double blooms with 15 petals. Cupped and fragrant, they are borne in small sprays of 3–9. The foliage is small, dark green and glossy on a low, bushy plant that is suitable for small borders, pots and window boxes. ZONES 4–9.

Cocker, UK, 1988

'Sunsprite' × ('Cläre Grammerstorf' × 'Frühlingsmorgen')

R

'Red Ace'

'Red American Beauty'

'RAYMOND CHENAULT'

MODERN, MODERN SHRUB, MEDIUM RED,
REPEAT-FLOWERING

The large, bright red semi-double blooms
of 'Raymond Chenault' have 16 petals
and are borne in clusters. They have a
slight fragrance and are repeat-flowering.
The plant is vigorous and slightly lax,
and has dark glossy foliage that is disease
resistant. It is a good pillar rose that will
also grow on pergolas or as a large shrub.
ZONES 4–9.

Kordes, Germany, 1960

Rosa kordesii × 'Montezuma'

National Rose Society Trial Ground Certificate
1961

'RAZZLE DAZZLE'   JACraz

MODERN, CLUSTER-FLOWERED/FLORIBUNDA,
RED BLEND, REPEAT-FLOWERING

The clusters of medium-sized blooms on
this variety are double with 25 petals and
have a slight fragrance. They are red with
a reverse of white, 3 in (8 cm) across and
appear from summer to autumn. This
bushy grower has dark, leathery foliage
and is suitable for bedding. ZONES 4–9.

Warriner, USA, 1977

Parentage unknown

Portland Gold Medal 1978

'REBECCA CLAIRE'

MODERN, LARGE-FLOWERED/HYBRID TEA,
ORANGE-PINK, REPEAT-FLOWERING

The scented blooms of this rose are borne
singly or in small clusters during summer and autumn. Large and well formed,
they are double with 28 petals and coppery orange edged with light coral. The
upright, vigorous plant has glossy mid-
green foliage that is disease resistant. It
is a good bedding variety. ZONES 4–9.

Law, UK, 1986

'Blessings' × 'Redgold'

Royal National Rose Society President's
International Trophy, RNRS Edland Fragrance
Medal 1980

'Raymond Chenault'

'RECONCILIATION'   HARtillery

MODERN, LARGE-FLOWERED/HYBRID TEA,
APRICOT BLEND, REPEAT-FLOWERING

A true blend with nice perfume, 'Recon-
ciliation' has peachy blush flowers with a
hint of buff. The classically well-formed
blooms are borne singly or in small clusters and are repeat-flowering. A bushy
plant with disease-resistant dark green
foliage, it makes a good bedding plant
and is suitable for use as a standard; it is
also superb as a cut flower. ZONES 4–9.

Harkness, UK, 1995

'Basildon Bond' × 'Rosemary Harkness'

'RED ACE'   AmRUda

syn. 'Amanda'

MODERN, MINIATURE, DARK RED,
REPEAT-FLOWERING

The flowers of this variety are an attractive, dark, velvety crimson red and are
borne in large clusters on strong,
healthy, straight stems. The blooms are
at their best when fully open, when they
display their rich golden yellow stamens.
This is an upright, compact bush that is
winter hardy and relatively disease free.
The sprays are so beautiful that they are
constant winners at the Royal National
Rose Society shows in the UK, especially
when displayed as groups of 5 and 12
sprays. ZONES 4–10.

de Ruiter, The Netherlands, 1982

'Scarletta' × seedling

'RED ALERT'   MORalert

MODERN, MINIATURE, MEDIUM RED,
REPEAT-FLOWERING

The pointed buds of 'Red Alert' open to
double, medium red, 35-petalled flowers
with a slightly lighter reverse. They have
a light fragrance and are usually borne
singly or in small sprays of 3–5 blooms.

'Ray of Sunshine'

The gorgeous red bloom color provides a
real bright spot in the garden's range of
colors. The flower form is typically
Large-flowered and has good substance.
This is a wonderful garden variety as the
color is there all year long. The foliage is
medium sized and semi-glossy green on
a plant with an upright, medium growth
habit. The best feature of this rose is the
dependable color come wind, rain or
sunshine. ZONES 5–11.

Moore, USA, 1990

'Orangeade' × 'Rainbow's End'

'RED AMERICAN BEAUTY'

MODERN, LARGE-FLOWERED/HYBRID TEA,
MEDIUM RED, REPEAT-FLOWERING

'Red American Beauty' has ovoid buds
that open into large, high-pointed
blooms with 30–35 petals that are scarlet
to rose red and produced on long stems.
The fragrant flowers appear continuously
from summer to autumn. The dark,
leathery foliage appears on an upright,
bushy, vigorous grower. ZONES 5–9.

Morey, USA, 1959

'Happiness' × 'San Fernando'

R

'Red Blanket'

'Red Bells'

'Red Chief'

'Red Cross'

'Red Beauty'

'RED BEAUTY'

MODERN, MINIATURE, DARK RED,
REPEAT-FLOWERING

'Red Beauty' has dark red flowers that have a stunning yellow base to the petals. The florets are double with 35 petals and have a light fragrance and good overall exhibition form. The color is non-fading and holds well in most climates and the blooms tend to hold their form for a long time, because of the generous petal count. The dark green foliage is small to medium sized. The plant can send up some magnificent large sprays that have won at national rose shows both in the USA and the UK. It created a sensation when it was first introduced in 1981 in America, where gardeners raved about this wonderful new addition to the red Miniature class. It is still grown extensively today and is still winning prizes. ZONES 5–11.

Williams, USA, 1981

'Starburst' × 'Over the Rainbow'

'RED BELLS'   POUlred

MODERN, MINIATURE/GROUND COVER,
MEDIUM RED

This vigorous ground-cover variety has a spreading growth habit but, unfortunately, is only summer flowering. The small, double, mid-red blooms have 35 petals, are produced in large clusters and have a slight fragrance. The foliage is small, mid-green, semi-glossy and very healthy. ZONES 4–9.

Poulsen, Denmark, 1983

'Mini-Poul' × 'Temple Bells'

'RED BLANKET'   INTercel, INTercell

MODERN, MODERN SHRUB, DEEP PINK,
REPEAT-FLOWERING

'Red Blanket' is a very bushy ground cover with dull deep pink, semi-double small blooms. They are borne in small clusters and are slightly fragrant, and occur on the bush from summer through to autumn. This variety has small dark

green glossy foliage and lots of medium-sized thorns, and is vigorous to a height of 3–4 ft (1–1.2 m). ZONES 4–9.

Ilsink, The Netherlands, 1979

'Yesterday' × seedling

Royal Horticultural Society Award of Garden Merit 1993

'RED CASCADE'   MOOrcap

MODERN, CLIMBING MINIATURE, DARK RED,
REPEAT-FLOWERING

On this variety pointed buds open to an abundance of deep red, cupped, fragrant flowers containing about 40 petals. The foliage is small and leathery in texture. The plant habit is prostrate or cascading, allowing it to be used as a ground cover, in a hanging basket or draped over a wall. It is susceptible to powdery mildew if left unprotected. This rose is a garden favorite that provides a great splash of brilliant color. ZONES 5–11.

Moore, USA, 1976

(Rosa wichuraiana × 'Floradora') × 'Magic Dragon'

American Rose Society Award of Excellence 1976

'RED CHIEF'

MODERN, LARGE-FLOWERED/HYBRID TEA,
MEDIUM RED, REPEAT-FLOWERING

'Red Chief' produces very large, medium red, high-centered flowers with 35 petals. They are extremely fragrant and repeat their bloom. An exhibition variety, it has a bushy, upright, vigorous growth habit and dark green, leathery foliage. ZONES 4–9.

Armstrong, USA, 1967

Seedling × 'Chrysler Imperial'

'RED CROSS'   MEIsoyris

MODERN, LARGE-FLOWERED/HYBRID TEA,
MEDIUM RED, REPEAT-FLOWERING

This rose bears double blooms with many attractively scalloped, rich velvety red petals, which develop from long and

R

pointed buds. The flowers are produced in great abundance and have a quick repeat. They are good for cutting and there is a fragrance. The foliage is dark green, plentiful and disease free. Sales of this rose benefit the Red Cross. **ZONES 5–9.**

Meilland, France, 1998

Parentage unknown

'RED DEVIL'   DICam

syn. 'Coeur d'Amour'

MODERN, LARGE-FLOWERED/HYBRID TEA, MEDIUM RED, REPEAT-FLOWERING

'Red Devil' has been described as the most perfectly shaped big Large-flowered Rose that has ever appeared on the show bench. The bright scarlet-crimson blooms with a lighter reverse have 72 petals and high centers; they also have a good scent and are repeat-flowering. The foliage is a glossy deep green on a vigorous plant that, although primarily an exhibition variety, is also strong enough to make a spectacular bedding plant. **ZONES 4–9.**

Dickson, UK, 1970

'Silver Lining' × 'Prima Ballerina'

Royal National Rose Society Certificate of Merit 1965, Japan Gold Medal 1967, Belfast Gold Medal 1969, Portland Gold Medal 1970

'RED FAN'

MODERN, LARGE-FLOWERED/HYBRID TEA, ORANGE-RED, REPEAT-FLOWERING

This medium to tall, very spreading, vigorous bush rose bears moderately large flowers that have over 24 orange-red

'Red Flush'

'Red Devil'

petals, which unfold from oval buds. They hold their color well and are carried amid abundant, mid-green, semi-glossy foliage. The flowers are produced in very large numbers with a quick repeat. Sadly, there is almost no fragrance and black spot can be a problem in autumn. **ZONES 5–9.**

Keisei, Japan, 1991

Parentage unknown

'RED FAVORITE'   TANschweigru

syns 'Holländerin', 'Red Favourite', 'Salut à la Suisse', 'Schweizer Gruss'

MODERN, CLUSTER-FLOWERED/FLORIBUNDA, MEDIUM RED, REPEAT-FLOWERING

'Red Favorite' has semi-double flowers with 13 petals that are medium in size and have a slight fragrance. The blooms, which are velvety ox-blood red, are produced in medium-sized clusters. The foliage is dark green, leathery and glossy on a vigorous, moderate-height healthy plant that is suitable for bedding and makes a nice standard head. **ZONES 4–9.**

Tantau, Germany, 1954

'Karl Weinhausen' × 'Cinnabar'

Anerkannte Deutsche Rose 1950, National Rose Society Certificate of Merit 1952

'RED FLUSH'

MODERN, MINIATURE, MEDIUM RED, REPEAT-FLOWERING

The ovoid buds of this rose open to medium red flowers containing almost 50 petals. The florets are cupped and are

'Red Devil'

'Red Fan'

'Red Favorite'

surrounded by matt green foliage. The double blooms come largely in clusters, and look their best when fully open because of the contrasting golden yellow stamens; bloom production is excellent. It is a very small, compact and upright bush that is best grown in a container or used as a border. This rose has somehow lost its initial popularity as many new more modern Miniatures have offered the same color combination with better form and growth habit. **ZONES 5–10.**

Schwartz, USA, 1978

Parentage unknown

American Rose Society Award of Excellence 1978

'RED GLORY'

MODERN, CLUSTER-FLOWERED/FLORIBUNDA, MEDIUM RED, REPEAT-FLOWERING

The rounded clusters of single blooms with 11 petals on this variety are cherry to rose red and have a slight fragrance. A repeat-flowering variety with sufficient vigor to qualify as a hedge variety, 'Red Glory' is also good on pillars or on low fences. It has a very vigorous, tall, bushy growth habit and leathery, semi-glossy foliage. **ZONES 4–9.**

Swim, USA, 1958

'Gay Lady' × ('Pinocchio' × 'Floradora')

'RED HEAD'

MODERN, LARGE-FLOWERED/HYBRID TEA, ORANGE-RED, REPEAT-FLOWERING

This tall and upright variety produces flowers that are a rich and unusual

orange-red with undertones of deep coral-orange. The disease-resistant bush has very thorny canes that bear large, mid-green, semi-glossy foliage. The buds are large and oval and open to double blooms of 20–25 petals. They hold their color well, especially when picked for indoor use. **ZONES 5–9.**

Dickson, UK, 1983

Parentage unknown

'RED IMP'

syns 'Maid Marion', 'Mon Tresor', 'Montresor'

MODERN, MINIATURE, DARK RED, REPEAT-FLOWERING

Tiny deep crimson flat flowers develop from attractive ovoid buds on this variety. They contain almost 50 petals and are a smaller size than traditional Miniatures; in fact, this rose is more of a micro-miniature. The fragrance is greatly affected by climate and temperature. A dwarf, low-growing plant with small foliage, it is a favorite among floral arrangers for its diminutive size and great form although it has fallen in popularity in recent years. It grows to only 9–10 in (23–25 cm) in height. In spring the buds often tend to turn brown and die without opening. This rose is one of the classic micro-miniature roses of the early 1950s; it was bred from 'Tom Thumb'. **ZONES 5–10.**

deVink, The Netherlands, 1951

'Ellen Poulsen' × 'Tom Thumb'

'Red Head'

R

'Red Masterpiece'

'Red Lion'

'Red Nella'

'Red Pat'

R

'RED LION'

MODERN, LARGE-FLOWERED/HYBRID TEA,
MEDIUM RED, REPEAT-FLOWERING

'Red Lion' has double red flowers that
become rose red as they develop. High
centered and large, with 38 petals and to
5 in (13 cm) wide, they have a moderate
scent and repeat their bloom from summer to autumn. It is a variety that was
and still is grown exclusively for the
show bench. ZONES 4–9.

McGredy, UK, 1964

'Kordes' Perfecta' × 'Detroiter'

National Rose Society Trial Ground Certificate
1964

'RED MASTERPIECE'   JACder

MODERN, LARGE-FLOWERED/HYBRID TEA,
DARK RED, REPEAT-FLOWERING

The deep red, double flowers of this variety have high centers and are very large

and extremely fragrant. 'Red Masterpiece' has large, dark green, leathery foliage on a plant that is vigorous, upright
and repeat-flowering and which is suitable for bedding. ZONES 4–9.

Warriner, USA, 1974

('Siren' × 'Chrysler Imperial') × ('Carrousel' ×
'Chrysler Imperial')

'RED MEIDILAND'   MEIneble

syn. 'Rouge Meillandécor'

MODERN, MODERN SHRUB, RED BLEND,
REPEAT-FLOWERING

'Red Meidiland' is a vigorous, prostrate
plant with single, medium-sized cupped
flowers that are red with a white eye and
have little fragrance. They are repeat-
flowering and borne in clusters of 7–15.
The disease-resistant, medium-sized foliage is glossy deep green and there are
small, globular, red hips in autumn. A
good plant for borders, banks, pots, window boxes and as a standard, this variety
has been described by the raisers as being
very hardy. ZONES 3–9.

Meilland, France, 1989

'Sea Foam' × ('Picasso' × 'Eyepaint')

'RED MINIMO'   RUImired

MODERN, MINIATURE, DARK RED,
REPEAT-FLOWERING

This micro-miniature boasts red semi-
double flowers with 15–20 petals that are
borne in clusters. They have no fragrance
but a decorative form. The foliage is
small, dark green and semi-glossy on a

plant with a low and bushy habit. It produces quite a number of blooms for its
size and so is frequently used in floral
arrangements. This rose is the 'generic'
red potted Miniature Rose to be found in
most supermarkets—shoppers buy
them, bring them home and then after
blooming often throw them away!
ZONES 5–11.

de Ruiter, The Netherlands, 1987

Parentage unknown

'RED NELLA'

MODERN, LARGE-FLOWERED/HYBRID TEA, MAUVE/
LIGHT RED, REPEAT-FLOWERING

The name of this rose was derived by re-
versing the breeder's name. It bears light
sparkling red, slightly fragrant flowers
that have a good form. They are double
and come singly or in small clusters on a
tall, upright plant. There is a heavier display of blooms in spring than the rest of
the year. It is a good choice for overall
garden display. ZONES 5–10.

Allender, Australia, 1991

Parentage unknown

'RED PAT'

MODERN, MINIATURE, MEDIUM RED,
REPEAT-FLOWERING

This is a small and bushy Miniature Rose
that produces small clusters of bright
red, semi-double flowers that have a
central boss of golden stamens. There are
10–15 petals of good substance and, as
with most roses with few petals, hips will
be produced if spent blooms are not removed. These hips look attractive among
the later flowers. The quick-repeating
blooms are borne in large numbers amid
the small, mid-green, semi-glossy leaves.
'Red Pat' makes a nice compact pot
plant, but is also useful as a low border.
The flowers are bright, simple and unsophisticated. ZONES 5–9.

1990

Parentage unknown

'RED PETER'

MODERN, LARGE-FLOWERED/HYBRID TEA,
LIGHT RED, REPEAT-FLOWERING

'Red Peter' produces flowers that are
large, light crimson in color and filled
with about 40 petals that give an exhibition form. The blooms open slowly
from large, well-formed buds, and are
some of the first to flower in spring. The
repeat-bloom is particularly quick and
there is a slight fragrance. The plant has
a medium to tall growth habit with an
abundant covering of dark green, semi-
glossy foliage. It has a superb resistance
to disease. ZONES 5–9.

Gregory, UK, 1970

Sport of 'Peter Frankenfeld'

'RED PLANET'

MODERN, LARGE-FLOWERED/HYBRID TEA,
DARK RED, REPEAT-FLOWERING

An extremely popular rose, 'Red Planet'
has crimson, double flowers with 35
petals and considerable fragrance but
which are lacking in good form. The
glossy foliage appears on a healthy plant
that is repeat-flowering and is a reliable
bedding variety. ZONES 4–9.

Dickson, UK, 1970

'Red Devil' × seedling

Royal National Rose Society President's
International Trophy 1969

'Red Peter'

'Red Planet'

'Red Meidiland'

'RED QUEEN'

syn. 'Liebestraum'

MODERN, LARGE-FLOWERED/HYBRID TEA,
MEDIUM RED, REPEAT-FLOWERING

The ovoid buds on 'Red Queen' open to large, red, double flowers with little scent. They bloom from summer through to autumn. The foliage is dark green on an upright and vigorous plant that is suitable for bedding. ZONES 4–9.

Kordes, Germany, 1968

'Colour Wonder' × 'Liberty Bell'

Royal National Rose Society Trial Ground Certificate 1968

'RED RADIANCE'

MODERN, LARGE-FLOWERED/HYBRID TEA,
DEEP PINK, REPEAT-FLOWERING

'Red Radiance' has light crimson blooms that are a mutation of the once popular pink Large-flowered Roses and which still obtain some favor with a few nurseries. The flowers are very fragrant with Damask overtones and repeat their bloom from summer to autumn. The plant has healthy foliage and a vigorous growth habit. ZONES 4–9.

Gude Bros, USA, 1916

Sport of 'Radiance'

'Red Rascal'

'RED RASCAL'   JACbed

MODERN, MODERN SHRUB, MEDIUM RED,
REPEAT-FLOWERING

This pretty shrub has small, red, double flowers with 35 petals that are borne in sprays of 2–5. Repeat-flowering, they are cupped and have a slight fragrance. The mid-sized, red to brown thorns and the small, mid-green, semi-glossy foliage appears on a bushy grower that is suitable to plant in borders or to use as a specimen. ZONES 4–9.

Warriner, USA, 1986

Parentage unknown

'Red Queen'

R

'RED RIBBON'

MODERN, CLUSTER-FLOWERED/FLORIBUNDA, MEDIUM RED, REPEAT-FLOWERING

This short and stocky Cluster-flowered Rose bears trusses of medium red, semi-double flowers of good substance. The blooms have 10–15 clear crimson red petals, and are produced in small to medium-sized, well-spaced clusters. The foliage is dark green and semi-glossy, and the flower production is good with a fairly quick repeat. There is good resistance to disease. 'Red Ribbon' makes a nice low border if planted close together, giving a long-lasting display without fading. There is very little perfume. ZONES 5–9.

McGredy, New Zealand, 1973

Parentage unknown

'Red Rock'

'RED RIBBONS' KORtemma

syns 'Chilterns', 'Fiery Sunsation', 'Mainaufeuer'

MODERN, MODERN SHRUB/GROUND COVER, MEDIUM RED, REPEAT-FLOWERING

This vigorous ground cover with its bright scarlet flowers has been well recognized in the principle rose-growing countries. The open, medium-sized flowers are semi-double with 10 petals, have a slight scent and are produced in small clusters from summer through to autumn. Bright green, healthy foliage and vigorous strong growth make this a very good new introduction that is ideal to cover banks and is a good subject for pillars and as a standard. ZONES 4–9.

Kordes, Germany, 1990

Parentage unknown

Baden-Baden Gold Medal 1991

'RED ROCK' MEIlusam

syns 'Lusamba', 'Lusambo', 'Red Rocky'

MODERN, LARGE-FLOWERED/HYBRID TEA, MEDIUM RED, REPEAT-FLOWERING

This repeat-flowering variety has large, cherry red, double flowers with 35 petals. The open blooms are overlapping, 5 in (13 cm) wide and are slightly fragrant. The foliage is dark green on a plant with an extremely vigorous growth habit. ZONES 4–9.

Meilland, France, 1973

('Royal Velvet' × 'Chrysler Imperial') × 'Pharaoh'

'Red Ribbon'

'RED ROSAMINI' RUIredro

MODERN, MINIATURE, DARK RED, REPEAT-FLOWERING

The bright deep red flowers of 'Red Rosamini' are borne in small clusters on an attractive small plant. The blooms have decorative form but tend to open rather too quickly. However, bloom production is excellent all year long. This rose is one of the hardiest in the garden, surviving the coldest of winters. It is vigorous and can be used as a border or in a hanging basket. ZONES 4–11.

de Ruiter, The Netherlands, 1987

Parentage unknown

'RED RUGOSTAR'

syn. 'Magseed'

MODERN, HYBRID RUGOSA, MEDIUM RED

This shrub rose has very bright flowers. They are crimson-red, semi-double and

'Red Rosamini'

'Red Rugostar'

'Red Ribbons'

open fully to show a boss of golden stamens. The stems are clothed with grayish green leaves. 'Red Rugostar' can be propagated by budding. ZONES 5–10.

Moore, USA, 1997

Parentage unknown

'RED SHADOWS' SAVmore

MODERN, MINIATURE, DARK RED, REPEAT-FLOWERING

This is a most rewarding little rose that can be grown in beds or containers. The compact shrub is carefree and grows quickly to medium height or taller and produces flowers throughout summer and into autumn. The flowers are of medium size and open from fat buds into perfectly formed rosettes of luminous red; the edges of the petals are flushed a much darker, almost black color. Because the flowers are particularly long lasting, they make popular cut and exhibition blooms. They have no fragrance. ZONES 5–11.

Saville, USA, 1984

'Tamango' × 'Sheri Anne'

'RED SIMPLICITY' JACsimpl

syn. 'Red Iceberg'

MODERN, MODERN SHRUB, MEDIUM RED, REPEAT-FLOWERING

This extremely free-flowering hedge rose has large, bright red blooms that blacken near the petal edges and which are borne in small clusters. Repeat-flowering, they are semi-double with 15–25 petals and

'Red Simplicity'

R

are slightly fragrant. A vigorous, upright plant that is slightly spreading, 'Red Simplicity' has medium-sized, semi-glossy, mid-green foliage. ZONES 4–9.

Warriner, USA, 1991

Seedling × 'Sun Flare'

'RED SPLENDOUR'   DAVona
MODERN, CLUSTER-FLOWERED/FLORIBUNDA, DARK RED, REPEAT-FLOWERING

'Europeana' has very distinct, very dark red flowers with a hint of purple, so it requires considerable imagination to describe this sport as having even deeper red blooms. The foliage is also almost purple. ZONES 4–9.

Davies, UK, 1979

Sport of 'Europeana'

'RED SUCCESS'   MEirodium
MODERN, LARGE-FLOWERED/HYBRID TEA, RED BLEND, REPEAT-FLOWERING

Very full and large, with 40–45 petals, the large, blood red blooms of this variety have a base of cardinal red. They appear from summer to autumn on a vigorous, upright-growing plant, and have a slight fragrance. ZONES 4–9.

Paolino, France, 1976

('Tropicana' × MEialto) × ([MEibrem × 'Zambra'] × 'Tropicana')

'RED TRAIL'   INTerim
MODERN, MODERN SHRUB/GROUND COVER, MEDIUM RED, REPEAT-FLOWERING

This exuberantly strong grower has bright red blooms with a yellow eye that

'Redcoat'

are slightly scented. Small and semi-double, the flowers are borne in clusters along vigorous spreading stems with bright green plentiful foliage that is very healthy. A valuable plant to cover banks, 'Red Trail' also makes a good standard. ZONES 4–9.

Ilsink, The Netherlands, 1991

Parentage unknown

'RED WAGON'   MORdan
MODERN, MINIATURE, MEDIUM RED, REPEAT-FLOWERING

Bright scarlet red flowers with 23 petals are usually borne in clusters on this plant. There is no fragrance. The foliage is dark green and glossy on a vigorous, compact bush. The overall effect in the garden that this rose provides is a grand splash of color that is, however, subject to fading in warm climates. 'Red Wagon' suffers from being nitrogen sensitive—too much nitrogen causes ugly green vegetative centers in the blooms. It really is just another red Miniature, although it is a good grower that looks very pleasant in a hanging basket. ZONES 5–11.

Moore, USA, 1980

'Little Darling' × 'Little Chief'

'RED WONDER'
MODERN, CLUSTER-FLOWERED/FLORIBUNDA, DARK RED, REPEAT-FLOWERING

The globular buds of 'Red Wonder' open to double blooms with 28 dark red petals that have excellent substance. They are cupped at first then open to very large,

'Red Wagon'

'Redgold'

'Red Success'

nicely fragrant flowers that are borne in small to large clusters. Large, leathery, semi-glossy foliage covers this tall, disease-resistant bush. ZONES 5–9.

de Ruiter, The Netherlands, 1954

'Better Times' × Cluster-flowered seedling

National Rose Society Trial Ground Certificate 1954

'REDCOAT'   AUScoat
syn. 'Red Coat'
MODERN, CLUSTER-FLOWERED/FLORIBUNDA, MEDIUM RED, REPEAT-FLOWERING

The medium-sized, single flowers of 'Redcoat' have 10 petals and are borne in small clusters of 1–5. Slightly fragrant, they are a moderate red in color. It has hooked, brown thorns, dark green foliage and a bushy growth habit. ZONES 4–9.

Austin, UK, 1973

Seedling × 'Golden Showers'

'REDGOLD'   DICor
syns 'Alinka', 'Rouge et Or'
MODERN, CLUSTER-FLOWERED/FLORIBUNDA, YELLOW BLEND, REPEAT-FLOWERING

This repeat-flowering variety has gold flowers that are edged with deep pink.

'Redouté'

'Red Wonder'

The medium-sized blooms appear in large clusters and have a slight fragrance. The foliage is deep green on a vigorous, upright-growing plant that is a very good bedding variety. ZONES 4–9.

Dickson, UK, 1971

(['Karl Herbst' × 'Masquerade'] × 'Faust') × 'Piccadilly'

Royal National Rose Society Certificate of Merit 1966, Portland Gold Medal 1969, All-America Rose Selection 1971

'REDOUTÉ'   AUSpale
syn. 'Margaret Roberts'
MODERN, MODERN SHRUB, LIGHT PINK, REPEAT-FLOWERING

Generally acclaimed as one of the most successful roses in this class, and also known as an English Rose, this repeat-flowering variety has soft pink, open, cupped blooms that are large but which have little scent. It is a medium-sized shrub that is well furnished with disease-resistant, matt green foliage on very vigorous twiggy growth. 'Redouté' is a good subject for a specimen plant or to group in borders. ZONES 4–9.

Austin, UK, 1992

Sport of 'Mary Rose'

R

'Regatta' (Meilland)

'Reine des Centfeuilles'

'Reine des Violettes'

'Refulgence'

'REFULGENCE'
OLD, SWEET BRIAR, MEDIUM RED

The beautiful blooms on this rose are
scarlet-crimson when young. They open
fully to show gold stamens at the centers.
As they age, the petals develop purplish
tones. The leaves have a very sweet
fragrance, and the semi-double blooms,
borne in a single flush in summer, are
larger than those of most Sweet Briars.
'Refulgence' is a long-lived, vigorous-
growing variety, good for planting in
mixed borders, hedges or wild gardens,
and it makes an upright, arching, rather
open shrub of average height or more.
ZONES 4–9.

Paul, UK, 1909

Rosa eglanteria × unknown

'REGATTA'   JACette
MODERN, LARGE-FLOWERED/HYBRID TEA, WHITE, REPEAT-FLOWERING

The large flowers of this variety are a
weatherproof white with good exhibition
form. The blooms are filled with almost
50 petals and are usually carried one to a
stem. There is a strong fragrance and the
the plant is furnished with mid-green
foliage. This 'Regatta' was bred for the
cut-flower industry, and it should not
be confused with the light pink Large-
flowered Rose from Meilland that shares
the same name. ZONES 5–10.

Warriner, USA, 1986

'Bernadette' × 'Coquette'

'REGATTA'   MEInimo
syns 'Penny Coelen', 'Prestige de Lyon',
'21 Again!'
MODERN, LARGE-FLOWERED/HYBRID TEA, LIGHT PINK, REPEAT-FLOWERING

The flowers of this rose are a lovely clear
light pink. They are large and double,
filled with 26–40 petals, and have a good
fragrance. The stems have very few
prickles and the the foliage tends to be
large and dark green with a matt finish.
'Regatta' produces an abundance of
blooms which continue throughout the
year on a tall and upright-growing bush
that has very good disease resistance.
ZONES 5–10.

Meilland, France, 1992

MEIgurami × (MEInaregi × MEIdragelac)

Geneva Fragrance Award 1989

'REGENSBERG'   MACyoumis, MACyou
syns 'Buffalo Bill', 'Young Mistress'
MODERN, CLUSTER-FLOWERED/FLORIBUNDA, PINK BLEND, REPEAT-FLOWERING

The large, semi-double flowers of this
variety have 21 petals and are pink edged
white with a white center and a reverse of
white. Cupped to flat and having a fruity
fragrance, they are 4 in (10 cm) wide and
have yellow stamens. A very short bushy
plant with luxuriant, mid-green foliage
and one of the most successful of the
'hand-painted' varieties, 'Regensberg' is
sometimes erroneously classed as a Patio
Rose although the large foliage belies this

description. A remarkable bedding variety, it is also highly successful as a well-
rounded standard. ZONES 4–9.

McGredy, New Zealand, 1979

'Geoff Boycott' × 'Old Master'

British Association of Rose Breeders 1979,
Baden-Baden Gold Medal 1980, Belfast
Certificate of Merit 1981

'REINE BLANCHE'
OLD, MOSS, WHITE

The double white flowers of this lovely
rose have creamy centers and a green
button eye. They are produced on a short
to medium bush that is plentifully endowed with light green moss and foliage.
A possible fault would be that the weak
flower stems cause the blooms to nod a
little. ZONES 4–9.

Robert, France, 1857

Parentage unknown

'REINE DES CENTFEUILLES'
OLD, CENTIFOLIA, MEDIUM PINK

The scented flowers of this rose are some
2½ in (6 cm) across when fully open and
are packed full of rather fimbriated
bright pink petals, creating a charming
effect. It flowers in early mid-summer.
The plant grows to a height of some 5 ft
(1.5 m), and can be frustratingly disorderly in growth habit at times. It is amply
endowed with mid-green grayish foliage
and has a generous number of spiteful
prickles. This little-known rose is especially useful for the wilder garden due to
its sheer quantity of flowers. ZONES 4–9.

Belgium, 1824

Parentage unknown

'REINE DES VIOLETTES'
syn. 'Queen of the Violets'
OLD, HYBRID PERPETUAL, MAUVE, REPEAT-FLOWERING

This well-known and popular rose is
oddly classed as a Hybrid Perpetual,
although it looks like a Bourbon. It
makes a medium to tall, full bush with
Gallica-like purple flowers fading to violet, filled with 75 quilled and quartered
petals, each with a button eye. It flowers
in summer and repeats in autumn and is
nicely scented. The foliage is smooth
green and is almost thornless. The vigor
of this bush has enabled it to survive successfully through the years, and it is one
of the 'musts'. 'Pius IX' is no longer
available. ZONES 5–9.

Millet-Mallet, France, 1860

Seedling of 'Pius IX'

'REINE FRANCE'
MODERN, LARGE-FLOWERED/HYBRID TEA, MEDIUM PINK, REPEAT-FLOWERING

The large, oval buds of this rose open
slowly to well-formed, rather flat blooms
that are filled with 40 or more strong
mid-pink petals. There is a good
fragrance, and the blooms hold their
shape and color well without fading,
which makes them a good choice for
cutting. This disease-resistant bush is of
medium size and is covered with matt
mid-green foliage. Repeat-flowering is
rather sparse and slow; it is a pity that
'Reine France' does not live up to its
name. ZONES 5–9.

Delbard, France, 1966

Parentage unknown

'Regensberg'

'Regensberg'

'Reine Marie Henriette'

'Reine France'

clusters of up to 12, and if not dead-headed, small red hips appear amid the late flowers. The mid-green foliage is glossy, medium sized and abundant with good disease resistance. The leaves are often retained well into winter. This is a good rose for planting on banks, in large parks and on median strips. **ZONES 5–9.**

Meilland, France, 1993

Parentage unknown

'REMBRANDT'
OLD, PORTLAND, ORANGE-RED, REPEAT-FLOWERING

This rose has vigorous growth in the Damask style and flowers over a long period. The large full flowers, which come on long stalks, are vermilion shaded carmine and are occasionally striped. It only needs to be pruned every few years, after the summer flowering, and it tends to flower more if the stems are allowed to lie flat. **ZONES 5–9.**

Moreau-Robert, France, 1883

Parentage unknown

'REINE MARIE HENRIETTE'
MODERN, LARGE-FLOWERED CLIMBER, MEDIUM RED, REPEAT-FLOWERING

Marie-Henriette was Queen of the Belgians, and her rose has worn well; it is still grown despite its considerable thorniness. The loose flowers, which are borne in clusters, are a pure cherry red color. There is some autumn repeat-flowering, although the main flush is produced in summer. It should be lightly pruned. 'Reine Marie Henriette' is notable as having been one of the parents of the beautiful 'Belle Portugaise', the other being *Rosa gigantea*. **ZONES 7–9.**

Levet, France, 1878

'Mme Bérard' × 'Général Jacqueminot'

'REINE OLGA DE WÜRTEMBERG'
OLD, NOISETTE, MEDIUM RED, REPEAT-FLOWERING

Like all the Noisettes, this rose is a strong climber. The crimson flowers, set among dark green foliage, are medium sized, double and fragrant, but they can be spoiled by strong sunshine. This rose is worth having as the color is uncommon among Noisettes, although it is not found widely. **ZONES 7–9.**

Nabonnand, France, 1881

Parentage unknown

'REINE VICTORIA'
syn. 'La Reine Victoria'
OLD, BOURBON, MEDIUM PINK, REPEAT-FLOWERING

'Reine Victoria' displays rich pink blooms that have a tint of mauve in the

pink. They are very double, with up to 40 silky textured petals, and cupped. The spring flush is particularly profuse and from then on flowering is spasmodic. In autumn, the flowers are produced on very long stems. The growth is strong and upright with plentiful, close-jointed, matt pale green foliage. It produces long canes that are ideal for espalier work. Both the variety and its sport, 'Mme Pierrerogers', are prone to black spot, although both are fragrant and good for cutting. This rose was named for Queen Victoria. **ZONES 5–9.**

Labruyère, France, 1872

Parentage unknown

'RELAX'
MODERN, MODERN SHRUB, ORANGE RED

This tall yet rather gaunt shrub with semi-glossy foliage bears large, single blooms of fiery orange-red mixed with yellow with yellow undersides. They occur singly and in clusters of 2 or 3 along the canes of the previous season's growth. There is no perfume and, like its parent, no repeat-bloom. 'Relax' is prone to black spot and is probably at its best in warm, dry climates. **ZONES 5–9.**

Meilland, France, 1979

Hybrid of *Rosa foetida bicolor*

'RELAX MEILLANDECOR'
MEIdarwet
syn. 'Relax Meidiland'
MODERN, GROUND COVER, PINK BLEND, REPEAT-FLOWERING

This variety, with a spread of 4–5 ft (1.2–1.5 m), carries medium-sized semi-double blooms with about 10 watermelon pink petals. They are produced in

'Relax'

'Rembrandt'

'Relax Meillandecor'

R

'REMEMBER ME' COCdestin
syn. 'Remember'
MODERN, LARGE-FLOWERED/HYBRID TEA,
ORANGE BLEND, REPEAT-FLOWERING

This rose, which can justifiably be described as probably the deepest copper variety presently available, has in addition a subtle blend of yellow. It has single or small clusters of double, large, cupped flowers with 20 petals and has little fragrance. The raisers are undetermined as to its type, but Large-flowered is probably closer than Cluster-flowered. The foliage, which is dark and glossy, is small for the type, but the spreading plant is bushy and makes for a good bedding variety and a marvelous standard. ZONES 4–9.

Cocker, UK, 1984

'Ann Letts' × ('Dainty Maid' × 'Pink Favorite')

Belfast Gold Medal 1986, Royal National Rose Society James Mason Gold Medal 1995, Royal Horticultural Society Award of Garden Merit 1993

'REMEMBRANCE' HARxampton
MODERN, CLUSTER-FLOWERED/FLORIBUNDA,
MEDIUM RED, REPEAT-FLOWERING

The large clusters of cupped, bright red medium-sized blooms with 32 petals on

'Remember Me'

this variety have a slight fragrance. The foliage is dark green and glossy on a bushy plant that is truly repeat-flowering. 'Remembrance' is a healthy rose that is equally appropriate in a bed or as a standard. ZONES 4–9.

Harkness, UK, 1992

'Trumpeter' × 'Southampton'

Glasgow Gold Medal 1995

'RENAE'
MODERN, CLUSTER-FLOWERED CLIMBER,
MEDIUM PINK, REPEAT-FLOWERING

This repeat-flowering climber or rambler has clusters of medium-sized double flowers with 43 petals. They are mid-pink in color and have a considerable scent. The small, glossy foliage is very healthy on a vigorous plant this is a suitable subject for pergolas and arches and as a weeping standard. ZONES 4–9.

Moore, USA, 1954

'Étoile Luisante' × 'Sierra Snowstorm'

'RENAISSANCE'
MODERN, LARGE-FLOWERED/HYBRID TEA,
ORANGE BLEND, REPEAT-FLOWERING

The brilliant orange-red flowers of this variety are double and develop from

'René André'

'Renae'

long, pointed buds. There is a moderate fragrance, and the blooms are followed by rounded hips. The reasonably prickly stems are furnished with glossy light green leaves. 'Renaissance' can be propagated by budding. ZONES 5–10.

Gaujard, France, 1986

Seedling × 'Pampa'

'RENAISSANCE' HARzart
MODERN, LARGE-FLOWERED/HYBRID TEA, WHITE,
REPEAT-FLOWERING

A very highly scented variety, 'Renaissance' has pale blush pink flowers with a center of coral. The perfectly formed blooms are loose, giving a less formal appearance to a sophisticated color. This repeat-flowering, bushy plant performs well in beds, as a standard and as a cut flower. ZONES 4–9.

Harkness, UK, 1994

Parentage unknown

Belfast Fragrance Award 1995, Glasgow Silver Medal 1996, Glasgow Fragrance Award 1996

'RENDEZ-VOUS' LUCdod
MODERN, MODERN SHRUB, MEDIUM PINK

This medium-sized shrub has semi-double, medium blooms that are very

fragrant. A bushy, healthy, free-flowering variety with matt green foliage, its repeat-blooming ability is doubtful. It is suitable for planting in large borders. ZONES 4–9.

Lucas, UK, 1981

Rosa wichuraiana × 'Alain Blanchard'

'RENÉ ANDRÉ'
MODERN, RAMBLER, APRICOT BLEND

The first decade of the twentieth century saw a great surge in the breeding of the Ramblers from Rosa wichuraiana and R. multiflora. This rose is not common, but it is freely available. Even more lax than others of its kind, it is suitable for hanging in trees, where it will grow to great heights. The stems will hang, carrying small flowers in a mixture of coppery pink and yellow fading to soft pink. It will sometimes repeat a little. ZONES 5–9.

Barbier, France, 1901

Rosa wichuraiana × 'L'Idéal'

'RÉNÉ D'ANJOU'
OLD, MOSS, DEEP PINK

The buds of this rose are usually arranged in small clusters and are liberally clothed with bronzy brown moss. They appear in mid-summer and open to flowers of exquisite beauty. Each bloom is up to 3½ in (9 cm) across and is made up of many small crumpled petals that are randomly arranged to form flattish, fragrant cushions of a most lovely soft silvery pink. It has a bushy and upright habit and reaches 5 ft (1.5 m) high. The stems are covered in soft bronzy stubble and there are few thorns of consequence. The leaves are reddish when young, becoming dark green, serrated and leathery when older. This outstanding rose is worthy of more attention. It is extremely healthy and is also tolerant of most soils. ZONES 4–9.

Robert, France, 1853

Parentage unknown

'RENNY' MORreny
MODERN, MINIATURE, MEDIUM PINK,
REPEAT-FLOWERING

'Renny' has pointed buds that open to medium rose pink flowers with a lighter reverse. The florets are double with 25 petals, old fashioned in form and with a moderate fragrance. The flower size, however, is large and so this rose fits into the Patio class. The soft blending of pink and coral of the blooms is very pleasing to the eye. The blooms have a unique

'Remember Me'

form that is more of a star shape, somewhat reminiscent of a poinsettia. They bloom in large sprays, making for a striking display in the garden. The foliage is dark green and glossy on a clean and easy to maintain plant. ZONES 5–11.

Moore, USA, 1989

'Anytime' × 'Renae'

'REPANDIA' KORsami
syn. 'Kordes' Rose Repandia'
MODERN, MODERN SHRUB/GROUND COVER, LIGHT PINK

A flat, spreading plant with light pink semi-double flowers, 'Repandia' unfortunately is only summer flowering. The fragrant blooms are borne on a low-growing plant that will spread to 5 ft (1.5 m) and is one of the earliest of the modern Ground Cover Roses. It is furnished with small, glossy dark green foliage. ZONES 4–9.

Kordes, Germany, 1983

'The Fairy' × Seedling of *Rosa wichuraiana*

Anerkannte Deutsche Rose 1986

'RESTLESS'
MODERN, LARGE-FLOWERED/HYBRID TEA, MEDIUM RED, REPEAT-FLOWERING

This strongly fragranced variety was probably so named because it flowers continuously, nearly all year round in

'Rétro'

'Rêve de Paris'

warm climates. The flat blooms are semi-double, with 10–15 dark crimson petals that open quickly from slim, long buds to full blooms that show the stamens. The habit is extremely tall and upright and is covered with masses of matt mid-green foliage. 'Restless' is a superbly disease-resistant, vigorous bush rose that would make an excellent free-flowering tall hedge for a large estate. Attractive hips are produced if the spent blooms are not removed, although they do not seem to curtail the flowering very much. ZONES 5–9.

Clark, Australia, 1938

Parentage unknown

'RÉTRO' MEIbalani
MODERN, MODERN SHRUB, MEDIUM PINK, REPEAT-FLOWERING

Although classified as a Modern Shrub, 'Rétro' could just as well be a Ground Cover Rose. It is a low bush with extremely spreading canes that grow almost horizontally in all directions. These shoots are very thorny and produce an abundance of soft rose pink blooms in fragrant clusters with a fairly quick repeat. There are 60–70 petals per flower that form a quartered arrange-

'Rêve de Paris'

ment; they are so double that very few hips are produced, which helps with the repeat regardless of whether or not spend heads are removed. The foliage is very dark green, semi-glossy and very abundant. 'Rétro' grows at least twice as wide as it does high, which makes it a good rose for planting on banks and difficult sites where it will form an impenetrable barrier. The variety can also be trained as a very bushy standard, but care must be taken with the thorns if it is to be planted close to pathways. ZONES 5–9.

Meilland, France, 1980

Parentage unknown

'RÊVE DE PARIS' MEIloïse
MODERN, LARGE-FLOWERED/HYBRID TEA, ORANGE-PINK, REPEAT-FLOWERING

This short and stocky grower bears large, semi-double flowers that are glowing coral-salmon in color. There is good petal substance, and the flowers are produced in abundance with a quick repeat. The foliage is mid-green and semi-glossy,

'Renny'

and there are no disease problems. The blooms are ideal for cutting, since the color shows up well under artificial light. ZONES 5–10.

Meilland, France, 1985

Parentage unknown

'RÊVE D'OR'
OLD, NOISETTE, MEDIUM YELLOW, REPEAT-FLOWERING

The name of this rose means 'golden dream' or, more correctly, 'dream of gold'. The large, semi-double flowers are buff yellow, fragrant, frilly and quartered. The plant climbs to great heights and has strong branching stems, large hooked red thorns and plentiful foliage. It is a handsome rose and in 1878 it produced a well-known sport, 'William Allen Richardson', which is more orange in color. ZONES 7–9.

Ducher, France, 1869

Seedling of 'Mme Schultz'

'RÉVEIL DIJONNAIS'
MODERN, LARGE-FLOWERED CLIMBER, RED BLEND, REPEAT-FLOWERING

A remarkable rose that is equally as happy as a climber or as a shrub, this variety has brilliant cerise-scarlet flowers with yellow centers and a yellowish

'Restless'

'Rêve d'Or'

R

reverse. Semi-double, cupped and having some scent, they are produced in abundance and in clusters on short stems from early to mid-summer with occasional blooms in autumn. 'Réveil Dijonnais' is a vigorous plant with thick, glossy bronze foliage. ZONES 4–9.

Buatois, France, 1931

'Eugène Fürst' × 'Constance'

Portland Gold Medal 1929

'REVEREND H. D'OMBRAIN'
OLD, BOURBON, MEDIUM RED, REPEAT-FLOWERING

This rose is not easily available. The large, full, silvery carmine flowers are borne on a small to medium-sized bush. It can be prone to mildew, but this may depend on location and circumstance. It was named for the Reverend Henry Honeywood D'Ombrain, who was co-founder and first secretary of the (Royal) National Rose Society. ZONES 5–9.

Margottin, France, 1863

Parentage unknown

'REYNOLDS HOLE'
OLD, HYBRID PERPETUAL, MEDIUM RED, REPEAT-FLOWERING

'Reynolds Hole' was considered lost, but in the 1990s James Naylor, president of the Royal National Rose Society, noticed

a rose that answered its description while visiting the old family home of Reynolds Hole, Nottinghamshire. It bears deep reddish pink, fully double, fragrant blooms on a shrubby plant with arching, prickly stems. The deep grayish green leaves may need protection against black spot. Samuel Reynolds Hole served as curate and vicar for 40 years at Caunton. He helped to found the National Rose Society in 1876, becoming its first president. He was appointed Dean of Rochester in 1887 and died, still holding both offices, in 1904. ZONES 5–9.

Paul, UK, 1872

Seedling of 'Duke of Edinburgh'

'RHEINAUPARK'   KOReipark
MODERN, MODERN SHRUB, MEDIUM RED, REPEAT-FLOWERING

This rose has wrinkled foliage and thorny stems on an upright, bushy, vigorous plant. It is excellent for hedging or as a specimen. The clusters of medium red, semi-double large blooms with 20 petals are slightly scented. 'Rheinaupark' requires little maintenance. ZONES 3–9.

Kordes, Germany, 1983

('Gruss an Bayern' × seedling) × Seedling of *Rosa rugosa*

'Rheinaupark'

'RHODOLOGUE JULES GRAVEREAUX'
OLD, TEA, PINK BLEND, REPEAT-FLOWERING

This Tea Rose is of moderate height and scent and bears yellowish pink flowers. It has been preserved possibly for its association with Gravereaux, creator of the famous Roseraie de l'Haÿ outside Paris in 1899, where he attempted to collect all the known roses of the day. It is still a remarkable garden of considerable beauty and contains an enormous collection. Rhodologue is probably best translated at 'Rose Master'. ZONES 7–9.

Fontes, France, 1908

'Marie van Houtte' × 'Mme Abel Chatenay'

'RHONDA'
MODERN, LARGE-FLOWERED CLIMBER, MEDIUM PINK

This variety has large, double blooms that have 20 petals, are carmine rose and have a slight fragrance. The foliage is dark and glossy on a vigorous plant with climbing stems. There is some doubt as

to its repeat-flowering ability, but it is a good subject for growing on walls and pillars. ZONES 4–9.

Lissemore, USA, 1968

'New Dawn' × 'Spartan'

'RINA HUGO'   DORviso, PEKvizo
MODERN, LARGE-FLOWERED/HYBRID TEA, DEEP PINK, REPEAT-FLOWERING

Rina Hugo is a popular South African singer. This very vigorous, strong plant grows quickly to medium height or taller. An abundance of bloom is produced continuously. The flowers are very large with the classical pointed centers and outward-rolling petals of Large-flowered Roses, and the color is an outstanding, shocking pink. 'Rina Hugo' is a startling rose that is long lasting when cut or used for exhibition. ZONES 4–11.

Dorieux, France, 1993

Parentage unknown

'RING OF FIRE'   MORfire
MODERN, MINIATURE, YELLOW BLEND, REPEAT-FLOWERING

The flowers on this variety are a glowing yellow blended orange with a reverse yellow fading to a lighter tone. The florets have almost 60 petals. Occurring one per stem or in sprays, the blooms have a light fragrance. Flower production is excellent, so there is abundant color in the garden all season long. The foliage is mid-green and semi-glossy and the plant is vigorous, tall and upright. In cold climates the hardiness is questionable, but in general the plant is easy to grow and maintain. This rose retains many of the good qualities of its seed parent, 'Pink Petticoat'. ZONES 6–11.

Moore, USA, 1986

'Pink Petticoat' × 'Gold Badge'

American Rose Society Award of Excellence 1987

'RINGLET'
MODERN, LARGE-FLOWERED CLIMBER, PINK BLEND, REPEAT-FLOWERING

This climbing variety is repeat-flowering. It produces clusters of single blooms that are white tipped pink and lilac. 'Ringlet' is a healthy plant with considerable vigor. ZONES 4–9.

Clark, Australia, 1922

'Ernest Morel' × 'Betty Berkeley'

'Reverend H. d'Ombrain'

'Ringlet'

'Ring of Fire'

R

'Ripples'

'RIO SAMBA'   JACrite

MODERN, LARGE-FLOWERED/HYBRID TEA,
YELLOW BLEND, REPEAT-FLOWERING

'Rio Samba' has large blooms of yellow
fading to peach pink that are mostly
borne singly. They are double, with
15–25 petals, and have a slight fragrance.
This repeat-flowering variety has medium-
sized, dark green, matt foliage on an upright, bushy plant that is suitable for
bedding. It has some thorns. ZONES 4–9.

Warriner, USA, 1991

Seedling × 'Sunbright'

All-America Rose Selection 1993

'RIPPLES'

MODERN, CLUSTER-FLOWERED/FLORIBUNDA,
MAUVE, REPEAT-FLOWERING

The semi-double flowers with 18 wavy
petals on 'Ripples' are large and slightly
fragrant. They are a lovely lilac-lavender
color and appear in clusters, adding
novelty to the flower border. The foliage
is small and matt green, and is relatively
disease resistant. ZONES 4–9.

LeGrice, UK, 1971

('Tantau's Surprise' × 'Marjorie LeGrice') ×
(seedling × 'Africa Star')

'RISE 'N' SHINE'

syns 'Golden Meillandina', 'Golden
Sunblaze'

MODERN, MINIATURE, MEDIUM YELLOW,
REPEAT-FLOWERING

'Rise 'n' Shine' has long pointed buds
that open to rich medium yellow flowers

with 35 petals. They have classical Large-
flowered form and a light fragrance. The
foliage is glossy dark green and disease
resistant on a compact, medium bush
that is easy to grow. This superior rose
is well known all over the world for its
brilliant yellow blooms with good exhibition form; for over 20 years, it has set
the standard by which all other yellows
are judged. It was the top exhibition
Miniature in the USA during the decade
following its introduction, but has since
been replaced by other more popular
varieties produced after 1990. Interestingly, the name of the rose was intended
to be 'Dorothy Hamill' to honor the
Olympic figure skating champion, but
she rejected the offer. ZONES 5–11.

Moore, USA, 1977

'Little Darling' × 'Yellow Magic'

American Rose Society Award of Excellence 1978

'RITA APPLEGATE'   TINrita

MODERN, MINIATURE, LIGHT YELLOW,
REPEAT-FLOWERING

The flowers on this variety are a delicate
light yellow with a deeper yellow center.
The fragrant, double florets, which contain 26–40 petals and have good high-
centered form, are borne singly on good
strong stems. The color of the blooms
can fade to almost white in excessive
heat. The flowers hold their classic
Large-flowered form for days, making
this a suitable variety for exhibitors. The
foliage is mid-green and semi-glossy on a

tall, upright plant. In cooler climates the
bloom size can be larger, making this a
candidate for the Patio classification.
ZONES 5–10.

Bennett, USA, 1997

'Pink Porcelain' × seedling

'RITA LEVI MONTALCINI'

BARlev

MODERN, CLUSTER-FLOWERED/FLORIBUNDA,
APRICOT BLEND, REPEAT-FLOWERING

The fragrant flowers of this variety are
a pleasing blend of light shades, with
flushes of apricot against a background
of creamy pink. They are of medium
size, full of petals and are carried in close
clusters. Bloom production is maintained through summer and autumn.
It has a good health record, grows to
above average height and has large and
leathery, semi-glossy leaves. ZONES 4–9.

Barni, Italy, 1991

Parentage unknown

Geneva Gold Medal 1991, Glasgow Certificate of
Merit 1997

'RITTER VON BARMSTEDE'

MODERN, MODERN SHRUB, MEDIUM PINK,
REPEAT-FLOWERING

An extremely vigorous plant usually described as a shrub, this variety is more
commonly used in the garden as a
climber. Its medium-sized blooms with
20 petals appear in clusters of 30–40 and
are a hard pink color, and they are produced very freely. The foliage is glossy

'Rise 'n' Shine'

mid-green but it is prone to mildew and
has virtually no scent. An important
plant in the history and development of
modern climbers, 'Ritter von Barmstede'
is repeat-flowering. ZONES 4–9.

Kordes, Germany, 1959

Parentage unknown

'RITZ'

MODERN, CLUSTER-FLOWERED/FLORIBUNDA,
MEDIUM RED, REPEAT-FLOWERING

This repeat-flowering bedding variety
has large, semi-double flowers with
16 petals that are bright scarlet. They
have a slight perfume and appear on a
vigorous, well-branched plant with dark,
glossy foliage. ZONES 4–9.

Gaujard, France, 1961

Parentage unknown

National Rose Society Trial Ground Certificate
1962

'Roaming'

'Riverview Centennial'

'Robert le Diable'

'Robin Hood'

'RIVAL DE PAESTUM'
OLD, TEA, WHITE, REPEAT-FLOWERING

This Tea Rose is difficult to obtain these days. The small, Tea-scented flowers are fully double, ivory white tinted pink and tend to nod. It has plenty of dark green foliage on a short, twiggy bush. Paestum, a town in Italy, was credited by Virgil in his Georgics with the twice-bearing roses, considered to refer to the Autumn Damasks. ZONES 7–9.

Béluze, France, 1841

Parentage unknown

'RIVERS' GEORGE IV'
syns 'George IV', 'King George IV'
OLD, CHINA, DARK RED, REPEAT-FLOWERING

Thomas Rivers Jnr. (1798–1877) described how this rose 'was raised from seed by myself about 20 years ago, and contributed more than anything to make me an enthusiastic rose cultivator'. He became a celebrated and much-loved rosarian, whose catalogues and book *The Rose Amateur's Guide* furnish valuable information on roses of the period. This rose seems to be no longer in existence. The records say it was lax and twiggy, but capable of being grown with support to form a pillar. It had large cupped flowers of reddish crimson with touches of dark maroon, showing up well against purple-tinted foliage. ZONES 6–10.

Rivers, UK, circa 1817

Thought to be a hybrid of Damask and China

'RIVERVIEW CENTENNIAL'
syns 'Riverview', 'The Riverview Centennial Rose'
MODERN, LARGE-FLOWERED/HYBRID TEA, DARK RED, REPEAT-FLOWERING

Named after the centenary of a school in Sydney, Australia, 'Riverview Centennial' bears large, oval buds that develop slowly into large, very well-formed blooms of dark red. Filled with 40–50 petals, the flowers have good substance and last very well. The growth is tall and upright with large, matt, deep green foliage. Throughout summer the blooms are produced in profusion, both singly and in small clusters, on very long stems that are good for cutting. Particularly good, long-lasting blooms appear in autumn. There is a slight fragrance. ZONES 5–9.

Armstrong, USA, 1980

Parentage unknown

'ROAMING'
MODERN, LARGE-FLOWERED/HYBRID TEA, DEEP PINK, REPEAT-FLOWERING

This large-flowered variety, described by the breeder as having 'reddish pink shades', has double flowers with 24 petals that open from pointed buds. The foliage is matt green and healthy. It is suitable for bedding. ZONES 4–9.

Sanday, UK, 1970

'Vera Dalton' × 'Tropicana'

Royal National Rose Society Trial Ground Certificate 1970

'ROB ROY'   COrob
MODERN, CLUSTER-FLOWERED/FLORIBUNDA, DARK RED, REPEAT-FLOWERING

The dark red, medium-sized, double blooms on 'Rob Roy' have 30 petals and a good classical Cluster-flowered form. They are slightly fragrant and are 4 in (10 cm) wide. The foliage is glossy and healthy on an average-sized plant that is suitable for bedding and also makes a good standard. ZONES 4–9.

Cocker, UK, 1971

'Evelyn Fison' × 'Wendy Cussons'

Royal National Rose Society Trial Ground Certificate 1969

'ROBERT DUNCAN'
OLD, HYBRID PERPETUAL, PINK BLEND, REPEAT-FLOWERING

This rare rose can only be obtained by custom order. It is a conventional, vigorous Hybrid Perpetual with large flowers. The pink petals are notably concave, and the blooms are suitable for both garden and exhibition use. The number of Hybrid Perpetuals produced in the nineteenth century was very large; most are now lost, having been superseded by later, and better, roses. ZONES 5–9.

Dickson, UK, 1897

Parentage unknown

'ROBERT LE DIABLE'
OLD, GALLICA, MAUVE BLEND

This rose bears fragrant flowers made up of many petals. When fully open, they reflex around the edge of the flowers to create a flat cushion effect. If the shape is unusual then the color is even more so, for it varies within each bloom from deepest purple to softest lilac, mottled or splashed with bright red. In very dry weather, the colors intensify and deepen. It is a sizeable, lax shrub, growing as broad as it is tall, which in good soil can be up to 4 ft (1.2 m) high. The arching

'Rob Roy'

thorny stems are covered with narrow, dark green leaves. Few roses have such intensely colored flowers; these, combined with its semi-recumbent stature, make this an asset to any garden. ZONES 4–9.

France, pre-1837

Parentage unknown

'ROBERT LÉOPOLD'
OLD, MOSS, PINK BLEND, REPEAT-FLOWERING

The fragrant flowers of this rose have a background of orange-yellow and are flushed salmon and pink, but are not in any way gaudy. They can attain a size of up to 3 in (8 cm) in diameter. The blooms first appear in early summer and there is an occasional second crop in autumn. It is a shortish, tidy, bushy shrub to 4 ft (1.2 m) high. The stems are unarmed, and are covered in gingery green and stubbly moss, as are the leaf stalks and flower buds. The leaves are bronzy when young, ageing to light green. This handsome shrub, one of only a few Moss Roses raised in the twentieth century, would not be out of place in any modern garden. ZONES 5–9.

Buatois, France, 1941

Parentage unknown

'ROBIN HOOD'
syn. 'Robin des Bois'
MODERN, MODERN SHRUB, MEDIUM RED, REPEAT-FLOWERING

With its pleasant shrub style, 'Robin Hood' is very free flowering and is also repeat-flowering. The simple, small, cherry red blooms are produced in large clusters and are slightly fragrant. A vigorous, dense, compact grower that does well in borders or as a specimen plant, this variety's chief claim to fame is that it was one of the parents of 'Iceberg'. ZONES 4–9.

Pemberton, UK, 1927

Seedling × 'Miss Edith Cavell'

'Robert Léopold'

'Rob Roy'

'Robusta' (Kordes), far right, with 'Iceberg' (white, above 'Robusta'), and, on the left, 'Casino' (yellow) and 'Compassion' (pink)

'ROBIN RED BREAST' INTerrob
syn. 'Robin Redbreast'

MODERN, PATIO/DWARF CLUSTER-FLOWERED, RED BLEND, REPEAT-FLOWERING

The small, single blooms of this variety, which appear in clusters, are dark red with a white eye and a reverse of silver. They have no fragrance but they do appear with good continuity from summer to autumn. It is a small, healthy, vigorous plant with bushy growth and lots of thorns that is suitable for pots and small borders and can also be used as a short standard. ZONES 4–9.

Interplant, The Netherlands, 1983

Seedling × 'Eyepaint'

'ROBINA' KORxenna

MODERN, LARGE-FLOWERED/HYBRID TEA, MEDIUM RED, REPEAT-FLOWERING

Only grown by Treloar Nurseries in Victoria, Australia, this bright red rose carries its double flowers on upright stems. They have the classic Large-flowered form, and are usually borne singly. The foliage is glossy light green. ZONES 5–10.

Kordes, Germany, 1988

Parentage unknown

'ROBUSTA'

OLD, BOURBON, MEDIUM RED, REPEAT-FLOWERING

The well-scented, rosette-style flowers of 'Robusta' are large, flat and quartered.

They are fiery crimson in color, fading to purple, and are borne in clusters. It is an upright, open bush with large foliage. There are two other roses with the name 'Robusta'—a Climbing Tea, possibly extinct, and a modern Hybrid Rugosa from Kordes in 1979. ZONES 5–9.

Soupert et Notting, Luxembourg, 1877

Parentage unknown

'ROBUSTA' KORgosa
syn. 'Kordes' Rose Robusta'

MODERN, HYBRID RUGOSA, MEDIUM RED, REPEAT-FLOWERING

This extremely vigorous, repeat-flowering shrub carries all the characteristics of a Hybrid Rugosa, including a multitude of thorns. The large, crimson, single blooms with 5 petals are produced in small clusters and have a moderate fragrance. 'Robusta' is suited to large hedges if it is allowed to grow naturally, although in some countries it is cut down every winter to produce a medium-sized bush. Very healthy and with glossy dark green, leathery foliage, it is happier in cooler climates. ZONES 3–9.

Kordes, Germany, 1979

Seedling × Rosa rugosa

Anerkannte Deutsche Rose 1980, Royal National Rose Society Certificate of Merit 1980

'Robusta' (Soupert et Notting)

'ROCHESTER CATHEDRAL'

HARoffen, HARroffen

MODERN, MODERN SHRUB, MEDIUM PINK, REPEAT-FLOWERING

'Rochester Cathedral' has mid-pink, medium to large blooms that are double and have 58 petals. They appear in clusters from summer to autumn and are scented. The leathery, dark, matt foliage appears on a very vigorous plant that is dense, spreading and healthy and is a good subject for a specimen plant or in shrub borders. ZONES 4–9.

Harkness, UK, 1987

(Seedling × [{'Orange Sensation' × 'Allgold'} × Rosa californica]) × 'Frank Naylor'

'Robin Red Breast'

'Robina'

R

'ROD STILLMAN'

syn. 'Red Stillman'

MODERN, LARGE-FLOWERED/HYBRID TEA,
LIGHT PINK, REPEAT-FLOWERING

This variety has light pink flowers that
are flushed with orange at the base. Extremely fragrant, they are large and have
35 petals. Vigorous in growth and with
dark foliage and well-shaped blooms,
'Rod Stillman' is repeat-flowering and
is suitable for bedding. ZONES 4–9.

Hamilton, Australia, 1948

'Ophelia' × 'Editor McFarland'

'RODEO'

MODERN, CLUSTERED-FLOWERED/FLORIBUNDA,
ORANGE-RED, REPEAT-FLOWERING

The large, double, bright scarlet blooms
on 'Rodeo' are borne in clusters of up
to 10. They have a slight fragrance and
appear from summer to autumn. The
healthy, light green foliage is borne on
a bushy, low-growing plant. ZONES 4–9.

Kordes, Germany, 1960

'Obergärtner Wiebicke' × 'Spartan'

National Rose Society Trial Ground Certificate
1960

'Rod Stillman'

'RODEO DRIVE'   AROcore

syn. 'Sunset Strip'

MODERN, LARGE-FLOWERED/HYBRID TEA,
MEDIUM RED, REPEAT-FLOWERING

The large, double blooms with 32 petals
on 'Rodeo Drive' are bright deep red,
high centered but have only a slight
fragrance. The flowers are usually borne
singly on a bushy medium-sized plant
with large, semi-glossy mid-green foliage
and reddish thorns that age to light
brown. ZONES 4–9.

Christensen, USA, 1986

'Merci' × 'Pharaoh'

'RÖDHÄTTE'

syn. 'Red Riding Hood'

MODERN, CLUSTER-FLOWERED/FLORIBUNDA,
MEDIUM RED, REPEAT-FLOWERING

The flowers of 'Rödhätte' are deep cherry
red, semi-double and large; they appear
in big clusters from summer to autumn
but have no scent. It is a compact, bushy
grower with rich green foliage that is
suitable for bedding. ZONES 4–9.

Poulsen, Denmark, 1912

'Mme Norbert Levavasseur' × 'Richmond'

'Rodeo'

'Roger Lambelin'

'Roi de Siam'

'RÖDINGHAUSEN'

MODERN, MODERN SHRUB, MEDIUM RED,
REPEAT-FLOWERING

The flowers of 'Rödinghausen' are small
with waved petals in a bright orange-red
shade; they are carried in tight clusters of
up to 15 blooms, which makes a bright
color impact. There is little scent, although the display is repeated through
summer and autumn. This variety can be
used for a group in a border or bed, or to
make a sturdy hedge. The plant is free
branching and vigorous, with uneven,
spiky and spreading growth of average
height for a shrub rose. It is furnished
with ample shiny bright green foliage.
Rödinghausen is a city in Germany.
ZONES 4–9.

Noack, Germany, 1987

Parentage unknown

Anerkannte Deutsche Rose 1988

'ROGER LAMBELIN'

OLD, HYBRID PERPETUAL, RED BLEND,
REPEAT-FLOWERING

The flowers of this bush are a bizarre
crimson fading to maroon, with the 30
petals edged in white. It grows to a medium height, but needs good soil. Most
authorities recommend 'Baron Girod de
l'Ain' in preference to this rose; striped
and picoteed sports are always liable to
revert to the original, or vice versa.
'Fisher Holmes' lacks the white edge but
has received glowing reports. ZONES 5–9.

Schwartz, France, 1890

Sport of 'Fisher Holmes'

'ROI DE SIAM'

OLD, CLIMBING TEA, MEDIUM RED

This rose, although an early introduction, is still available from specialist
sources. The large, semi-double, rather
muddled flowers have rich pink tones. It
cannot be far removed from the original
'stud' roses, 'Parks' Yellow' and 'Hume's

'Roller Coaster'

'Rodeo Drive'

Blush'. The growth is tall and not bushy
and the flowering is said to be less than
enthusiastic. ZONES 7–9.

Laffay, France, 1825

Parentage unknown

'ROLLER COASTER'   MACminmo

syn. 'Minnie Mouse'

MODERN, MINIATURE, RED BLEND,
REPEAT-FLOWERING

'Roller Coaster' has striped red blend
flowers that are really a beautiful random
mixture of red, creamy yellow and white;
no two flowers are identical. The florets
are semi-double with 6–14 petals, have a
light fragrance and tend to grow in small
clusters of 10–12 blooms. The bloom
cycle is fast with the fully open flowers
being the most beautiful stage, providing
a wonderful carpet of bold color mix-
tures. The foliage is small, mid-green and
glossy on a tall, upright, vigorous plant.
In semi-tropical climates this rose can
grow like a shrub and has a gangly habit
if left untended. However, the spreading
habit makes it an ideal choice for containers, against a wall, or in a raised bed
where it can spill over. This rose was
popular in Australia, where it first appeared as 'Minnie Mouse'. ZONES 5–10.

McGredy, New Zealand, 1987

('Anytime' × 'Eyepaint') × 'Stars 'n' Stripes'

'ROMA'

MODERN, LARGE-FLOWERED/HYBRID TEA,
PINK BLEND, REPEAT-FLOWERING

This rose has all the attributes of its parent, except that the color is deep salmon-
pink with paler undersides. The oval
buds open fairly quickly to large, double
blooms made up of 25–30 petals that
give a high-centered form with a slight
scent. They last well, even when cut for
indoor display. The dark green, leathery
foliage is plentiful and healthy, and covers
this vigorous and upright bush. The
abundant blooms occur both singly and
in small clusters and give a quick repeat.
'Roma' is only available in Australia,
where it is one of the most free-flowering
and healthy of all roses. ZONES 5–9.

Spronk, Australia, 1970

Sport of 'Duet'

'ROMAN HOLIDAY'   LINro

MODERN, CLUSTER-FLOWERED/FLORIBUNDA,
RED BLEND, REPEAT-FLOWERING

A free- and repeat-flowering variety,
'Roman Holiday' has orange blooms
turning to blood red and with a yellow
base. Double with 28 petals and with

high centers, the medium blooms are borne in clusters and are fragrant. The foliage is dark green and leathery on a vigorous plant with a bushy, low-growing habit. ZONES 4–9.

Lindquist, USA, 1966

('Pinkie' × 'Independence') × 'Circus'

All-America Rose Selection 1967

'ROMANCE' TANezamor

syn. 'Romanze'

MODERN, MODERN SHRUB, MEDIUM PINK, REPEAT-FLOWERING

This bushy shrub has medium pink, double flowers with 20 petals. They have a slight fragrance and appear continuously from summer to autumn. The foliage is medium, dark green, semi-glossy and healthy on a plant that is most suited to use in borders. ZONES 4–9.

Tantau, Germany, 1985

Parentage unknown

Baden-Baden Gold Medal 1985, Anerkannte Deutsche Rose 1986, Golden Rose of The Hague 1992

'ROMANTIC HEDGEROSE'

KORworm

MODERN, CLUSTER-FLOWERED/FLORIBUNDA, MEDIUM PINK, REPEAT-FLOWERING

An extremely free-flowering, vigorous plant, 'Romantic Hedgerose' has rich rosy pink double blooms with a good form. Strong, healthy foliage appears on a repeat-blooming plant that unfortunately has little scent. However, it is a valuable variety for use in hedges and borders. ZONES 4–9.

Kordes, Germany, 1994

Parentage unknown

Glasgow Certificate of Merit 1977

'ROMEO'

MODERN, LARGE-FLOWERED CLIMBER, DARK RED

This old climber produces small clusters of deep red, well-formed, double flowers with a modicum of scent. It has vigorous, climbing growth that is slightly lax, which makes it suitable for arches and pergolas. Unfortunately, it is summer flowering only, and it can suffer from mildew. ZONES 4–9.

Easlea, UK, 1919

Parentage unknown

'Romance'

'ROOI ROSE' KORhood

MODERN, LARGE-FLOWERED/HYBRID TEA, MEDIUM RED, REPEAT FLOWERING

Every year, on its birthday, the South African magazine *Rooi Rose* (Red Rose) gives a bunch of 100 roses to a woman of its choice. It was therefore fitting to name this special rose in honor of the magazine. 'Rooi Rose' is a vigorous shrub that is quick to reach its full height, which is medium to tall for a bush rose. It produces well-shaped, full flowers that repeat in quick succession. With their long stems, they make excellent cut flowers that last a long time indoors and are also good for exhibition. The color is dark velvety red, but unfortunately there is only a light fragrance. ZONES 4–9.

Kordes, Germany, 1993

Parentage unknown

'ROSA MUNDI'

syns *Rosa gallica rosa mundi* 'Weston', *R. gallica variegata* 'Thory', *R. gallica versicolor* 'Linnaeus', *R. mundi*

OLD, GALLICA, PINK BLEND

The name of this rose can mean either 'rose of the world' or 'Rosamund's', a woman said to have been an unfortunate mistress of Henry II. It is a striped form of the type and sometimes reverts to it, and is pale pink splashed with crimson. It is sometimes confused with the Damask 'York and Lancaster' (also called 'Versicolor'), which is inferior. The branches in these roses tend to flop over under the weight of the flowers, and definitely need support. This can be solved by pruning halfway in early spring,

'Rosalie Coral'

'Romeo'

giving a better effect. 'Rose Mundi' can grow to a medium to tall height and is suitable for low hedging. ZONES 4–9.

First mentioned 1581

Sport of 'Apothecary's Rose'

Royal Horticultural Society Award of Garden Merit 1993

'ROSABELL' COCceleste

MODERN, CLUSTER-FLOWERED/FLORIBUNDA, MEDIUM PINK, REPEAT-FLOWERING

Incurved blooms give this variety an old-fashioned appearance. Bright rose pink, the medium-sized full blooms are borne in clusters on a free-flowering, low-growing plant. With its glossy mid-green foliage it is a good subject for small beds, pots and as a short standard. ZONES 4–9.

Cocker, UK, 1986

Seedling × 'Darling Flame'

'ROSALI' TANilasor

syn. 'Rosali 83'

MODERN, CLUSTER-FLOWERED/FLORIBUNDA, MEDIUM PINK, REPEAT-FLOWERING

The medium pink blooms with 20 petals on 'Rosali' are produced in small clusters; they have no scent. The average-sized foliage is mid-green and glossy on a repeat-flowering, bushy plant that is good for bedding. ZONES 4–9.

Tantau, Germany, 1983

Parentage unknown

'Rosa Mundi'

'Rosali'

'ROSALIE CORAL' CHEwallop

syns 'Rocketear', 'Rosilia'

MODERN, CLIMBING MINIATURE, ORANGE BLEND, REPEAT-FLOWERING

On 'Rosalie Coral', clear orange double flowers with 15–25 petals open to reveal a yellow 'eye' that has some shading. In cooler climates, the deep orange color has a distinctive circle of gold surrounding the stamens. The blooms have a light fragrance and are borne in small clusters amid glossy mid-green foliage with just a few prickles. This spectacular plant grows 6 ft (1.8 m) or more. ZONES 5–10.

Warner, UK, 1992

('Elizabeth of Glamis' × ['Galway Bay' × 'Sutter's Gold']) × 'Anna Ford'

Royal National Rose Society Trial Ground Certificate 1990

'Roma'

R

'Rose à Parfum de l'Haÿ'

'Rosamunde'

'Rose de Meaux'

'ROSAMUNDE'   KORmunde
MODERN, CLUSTER-FLOWERED/FLORIBUNDA, MEDIUM PINK, REPEAT-FLOWERING

A short-growing but very free-flowering variety, 'Rosamunde' has deep pink and salmon, medium-sized blooms. The flowers have a light scent and are produced in small clusters from summer through to autumn. This variety is most suited to use in small beds and pots. ZONES 4–9.

Kordes, Germany, 1975

Parentage unknown

'ROSARIUM UETERSEN'
KORtersen

syn. 'Uetersen'

MODERN, LARGE-FLOWERED CLIMBER, DEEP PINK, REPEAT-FLOWERING

When this rose is enjoying its main flush the color impact is powerful, thanks to the enormous number of deep rose pink flowers, some borne singly and some in great clusters. Well over 100 overlapping petals are packed into medium to large flowers that open wide and almost flat, admitting tints of silvery pink as they age. There is a light sweet fragrance, and after the main glorious flush some blooms appear intermittently in late summer and autumn. 'Rosarium Uetersen' grows well on a wall, fence, pillar or arch. It is very hardy and withstands bad weather well. The growth is quite vigorous, and the leaves are large, glossy and plentiful. ZONES 3–9.

Kordes, Germany, 1977

'Karlsruhe' × seedling

'ROSE À PARFUM DE L'HAŸ'
syn. 'Parfum de l'Haÿ'

MODERN, HYBRID RUGOSA, MEDIUM RED, REPEAT-FLOWERING

This very vigorous rose has flowers of cherry carmine red that turn blue in heat. The blooms are large and extremely fragrant and appear with good continuity from summer to autumn. The foliage, which is not particularly rugose, or wrinkled, is matt green; in some gardens it is very prone to mildew. Occasionally this variety's nomenclature can be confused with the famous scented Hybrid Rugosa 'Roseraie de l'Haÿ'. It is a subject for shrubberies or as a specimen plant. ZONES 3–9.

Gravereaux, France, 1901

('Summer Damask' × 'Général Jacqueminot') × Rosa rugosa

'ROSE BRADWARDINE'
OLD, SWEET BRIAR, MEDIUM PINK, REPEAT-FLOWERING

This is one of the lesser-grown Penzance hybrids. In 1890 Lord Penzance, an English judge, began to raise a number of hybrids from the Sweet Briar (Rosa rubiginosa, formerly R. eglanteria) in order to obtain repeat-flowering Sweet Briar types with better flowers. He used Hybrid Perpetuals, Bourbons and R. foetida ('Persian Yellow') as pollen parents. A few of them are still grown today, although it may be hard to find this one. It has rose pink, single flowers and an apple scent, a characteristic of the Briar. 'Rose Bradwardine' is tall and hardy, and makes a good hedge. It was named for a character in Sir Walter Scott's novel Waverley. ZONES 5–8.

Penzance, UK, 1894

Parentage unknown

'ROSE CASCADE'   DELcouro
MODERN, GROUND COVER, DEEP PINK

Known for its potential as a ground cover, 'Rose Cascade' bears clusters of bright pink, single flowers centered by a glowing boss of golden stamens. The foliage is glossy green. It is not a popular variety, and is only listed by two European growers. ZONES 5–10.

Delbard, France, 1995

Parentage unknown

'ROSE D'AMOUR'
syns Rosa virginiana plena, 'St Mark's Rose', 'The St Mark's Rose'

OLD, MISCELLANEOUS, DEEP PINK, REPEAT-FLOWERING

This large shrub, which grows considerably high and wide, is probably a hybrid of the wild single type, perhaps crossed with Rosa carolina. Almost thornless, it bears numerous small, dainty pink flowers over a long period from midsummer. A mature, free-standing bush of this rose is a magnificent sight. It is very similar to 'Rose d'Orsay', named for a Third Empire dandy who wore it in his buttonhole. ZONES 5–9.

Pre-1759

Thought to be a hybrid of Rosa virginiana

Royal Horticultural Society Award of Garden Merit 1993

'ROSE DE MEAUX'
syns 'Pompon Rose', Rosa centifolia pomponia 'Lindley', R. dijoniensis, R. pomponia 'Roessig', R. pulchella 'Willdenow'

OLD, CENTIFOLIA, MEDIUM PINK

In cultivation since it was first recorded in 1789, this summer-flowering rose bears small, double, pink flowers that have been compared with a dianthus, the

'Rosarium Uetersen'

'Rose Cascade'

petals being frilled rather than pompon-like. Erect and dwarf, it is suitable for small pot culture. In the Dark Ages, the Irish Saint Fiacre settled at Meaux and cultivated a garden. He became the patron saint of gardeners and the Abbey at Meaux held his relics. There is also a white form of this rose. ZONES 4–9.

Cultivated 1789

Parentage unknown

'ROSE DE RESHT'
OLD, DAMASK, DEEP PINK, REPEAT-FLOWERING

The flowers of 'Rose de Resht' are arranged in tight clusters or bunches and are borne close to the foliage, each on short necks. The fully double, scented blooms are 1½ in (35 mm) across; they are cushion shaped when fully open and are freely produced from mid-summer to autumn. The color is rich fuchsia-red with hints of purple, sometimes paler in hot sun. It is a compact, dense shrub with dark green wood and a few stubby thorns, and grows up to 3 ft (1 m) high. The foliage is profuse, dark grayish green, rounded and durable. This is an outstanding rose which is quite easy to grow. ZONES 5–9.

From Rasht (Iran) to Europe via Lindsay, UK, 1940

Parentage unknown

Royal Horticultural Society Award of Garden Merit 1993

'ROSE DES MAURES'
syn. 'Sissinghurst Castle'
OLD, GALLICA, DARK RED

Harold Nicolson and Vita Sackville-West created the famous Sissinghurst Castle Garden in Kent, and are said to have found this rose when they were clearing the grounds in 1930. The plum-colored flowers are semi-double, with the usual Gallica style of growth. ZONES 4–9.

The Netherlands, perhaps early nineteenth century, re-introduced 1947

Parentage unknown

'Rose de Resht'

'ROSE DES PEINTRES'
syns 'Centfeuille des Peintres', Rosa × centifolia major
OLD, CENTIFOLIA, MEDIUM PINK

This rather sprawling, tall plant is very similar to Rosa × centifolia and has fully double, clear pink, fragrant flowers that show a center green button eye. The name refers to the beautiful Dutch flower paintings of the eighteenth century, which made considerable use of the Centifolias (Roses of Provence), themselves a Dutch creation according to rose lore. They were the 100-petalled roses that the English called 'cabbage roses'. ZONES 4–9.

Pre-1838

Parentage unknown

'ROSE D'HIVERS'
OLD, DAMASK, WHITE, REPEAT-FLOWERING

'Rose D'Hivers' is classed as a Damask but it is rather unusual, being a twiggy little bush with dainty, small white flowers with pinkish center petals. It is repeat-flowering, so presumably it has an affinity with the autumn-flowering

'Rose des Peintres'

Damasks. It is said to have been brought to England from abroad by Miss Nancy Lindsay in the 1930s. The name implies winter flowers. ZONES 4–9.

Parentage unknown

'ROSE DU ROI'
syn. 'Lee's Crimson Perpetual'
OLD, PORTLAND, MEDIUM RED, REPEAT-FLOWERING

The fragrant flowers of this rose are arranged in tight clusters and produced continuously from mid-summer to autumn. They are fully double, although loosely formed, sometimes showing a few yellow stamens when fully open. The soft red color is mottled and smudged purple. It is a sturdy shrub to 3 ft (1 m) high with thorny dark green stems and

plentiful small, dark grayish green foliage. This was one of the first Portlands to be introduced and it has certainly stood the test of time with distinction. It makes an excellent container plant. ZONES 5–9.

Ecoffay, France, 1819

Parentage unknown

'ROSE DU ROI À FLEURS POURPRES'
OLD, PORTLAND, MAUVE, REPEAT-FLOWERING

This is an alleged sport of 'Rose du Roi'; it is said to be more vigorous than its parent; the flowers are also said to be bigger and more purple than 'Rose du Roi'. Graham Thomas raises doubts, writing that it bears no resemblance to the original. The photo supports Thomas' view. ZONES 5–9.

Possibly Varangot, France, 1844

Said to be a sport of 'Rose du Roi'

'ROSE EDOUARD'
syns 'Rose Dubreuil', 'Rose Neumann'
OLD, BOURBON, MEDIUM PINK, REPEAT-FLOWERING

This rose is said to have been found growing on Reunion Island by a settler, M. Edouard Perichon, in the vicinity of hedges of 'Autumn Damask' and 'Parsons' Pink China'. It had characteristics of both the Damask and the China, and cuttings were brought to France by M. Neumann. Second generation seedlings were grown, some having the repeat-flowering character of the Chinas. So the Bourbons came into being and, through them, the ever-flowering Modern Garden Roses. 'Rose Edouard' itself, or the form distributed as such, has bright pink, double to semi-double blooms on a tallish, lax bush. ZONES 5–9.

Perichon, France, circa 1821

Perhaps 'Autumn Damask' × 'Parson's Pink'

'Rose des Maures'

'Rose du Roi'

R

'ROSE GAUJARD' GAUmo

MODERN, LARGE-FLOWERED/HYBRID TEA, RED
BLEND, REPEAT-FLOWERING

The large flowers of 'Rose Gaujard' are
cherry red with a reverse of pale pink and
silvery white. Very double with 80 petals,
the high-centered blooms are cupped,
have a light scent and are produced from
summer through to autumn. The foliage
is large, leathery and glossy on a big,
vigorous plant that has maintained its
popularity for many years and appears
to be capable of going on forever. The
'Peace' input is very evident in this respectable bedding rose. ZONES 4–9.

Gaujard, France, 1957

'Peace' × Seedling of 'Opera'

Royal National Rose Society Gold Medal 1958

'ROSE GILARDI' MORose

MODERN, MINIATURE, RED BLEND,
REPEAT-FLOWERING

'Rose Gilardi' has deep red and pink
striped flowers with a similar reverse.
The florets are double with 12–15 petals,

'Rose Marie, Climbing'

have a light fragrance and a decorative
informal form. The blooms are borne in
small clusters and reveal their moss
background with a profusion of soft
prickles all down the stems. This is a vigorous, compact bush with a tendency to
spread outwards rather than grow upwards. The color quality of the blooms is
best in full sun—shading only reduces
the intensity of the red and white colors.
It is suitable for planting in a hanging
basket. This rose was named to honor a
well-known rosarian from San Francisco
who has served as the American Rose
Society's District Director. ZONES 4–10.

Moore, USA, 1987

'Dortmund' × (['Fairy Moss' × ('Little Darling' ×
'Ferdinand Pichard')] × seedling)

'ROSE HILLS RED'

MODERN, MINIATURE, DARK RED,
REPEAT-FLOWERING

The pointed buds on 'Rose Hills Red'
open to reveal deep red double flowers
with about 30 petals each. The florets

'Rose Hills Red'

'Rose-Marie Viaud'

'Rose Window'

open too quickly, but are at their best
when fully open and showing off their
yellow stamens. The foliage is leathery,
glossy and mid-green on a vigorous,
upright plant and the repeat cycle is fast.
This is an excellent red Miniature for the
garden but it has unfortunately lost
popularity due to the influx of many
clones with similar characteristics.
ZONES 5–11.

Moore, USA, 1978

(*Rosa wichuraiana* × 'Floradora') × 'Westmont'

'ROSE MARIE, CLIMBING'

MODERN, LARGE-FLOWERED CLIMBER, MEDIUM
PINK

This is a climbing mutation of a once
popular Large-flowered Rose but it is
virtually extinct now. The clear, fragrant,
rose pink double flowers are borne in
clusters. A plant for a warm wall, it has
dark green, glossy foliage. ZONES 4–9.

Pacific Rose Co., Australia, 1927

Sport of 'Rose Marie'

'ROSE-MARIE VIAUD'

MODERN, RAMBLER, MAUVE

This rose is almost thornless and makes
great arching shoots from which the
large clusters of flowers hang down in
mid-summer. This is similar to its

'Roselina'

'Roselina'

'Rose Window'

parent, except that the small, semi-double
flowers are a different shade, changing
from cerise when opening to a bluer violet and gray. ZONES 5–9.

Igoult, France, 1924

Seedling of 'Veilchenblau'

'ROSE PARADE'

MODERN, CLUSTER-FLOWERED/FLORIBUNDA,
PINK BLEND, REPEAT-FLOWERING

Ovoid buds on this variety open into
clusters of coral-peach to pink, double
and cupped blooms. The flowers are
large and have some fragrance. A compact, vigorous, bushy plant, it has dark
leathery foliage. It is suitable for bedding
and as a short standard. ZONES 4–9.

Williams, USA, 1974

'Sumatra' × 'Queen Elizabeth'

All-America Rose Selection 1975

'ROSE WINDOW'

MODERN, MINIATURE, ORANGE BLEND,
REPEAT-FLOWERING

'Rose Window' has ovoid, pointed buds
that open to bright orange-yellow
flowers with a broad edging of deep red.
The double florets with 15–20 petals
have a light fragrance. The blooms have
typical Large-flowered exhibition style,
and the deep red edge adds to their visual
appeal. The blooms tend to remain at the
exhibition stage rather longer than most
varieties and hence its reputation for
winning at rose shows. In cooler climates, however, the blooms approach
the Patio size and it is a rare person who
won't want to take a much closer look.
The foliage is dark green on a spreading,
bushy, vigorous plant. This rose was perfectly named—there are times when one
can see through the rose just as if it was a
real window. ZONES 5–10.

Williams, USA, 1978

Seedling × 'Over the Rainbow'

'ROSELINA' KORsaku

syns 'Playtime', 'Rosalina'

MODERN, HYBRID RUGOSA, PINK BLEND,
REPEAT-FLOWERING

This Hybrid Rugosa has a semi-prostrate
habit and is repeat-flowering. The single
blooms are mid-pink and medium in
size and are borne in small clusters. Described as being very tough and healthy
and with typical rugose, or wrinkled, foliage, this is a good plant for landscaping
in smaller gardens. ZONES 4–9.

Kordes, Germany, 1992

Parentage unknown

Belfast Crystal Prize 1995

'Rose Gaujard'

R

'Rosendorf Sparrieshoop'

'Rosemary Harkness'

'Rosenelfe'

'ROSEMARY HARKNESS'

HARrowbond

MODERN, LARGE-FLOWERED/HYBRID TEA, ORANGE-PINK, REPEAT-FLOWERING

The beautiful double blooms with 35 petals on 'Rosemary Harkness' have a good form and are orange-salmon with an orange-yellow reverse. They are very fragrant and repeat their bloom from summer to autumn. A modern Large-flowered Rose that makes a good bedding variety or is suitable for use as a standard, it has large, dark semi-glossy foliage on a bushy plant. ZONES 4–9.

Harkness, UK, 1985

'Compassion' × ('Basildon Bond' × 'Grandpa Dickson')

Belfast Gold Medal 1987, Belfast Fragrance Award 1987, Glasgow Fragrance Award 1991, Auckland Fragrance Award 1995

'ROSEMARY ROSE'

MODERN, CLUSTER-FLOWERED/FLORIBUNDA, DEEP PINK, REPEAT-FLOWERING

The very large clusters of deep pink flowers on this variety are double, camellia shaped and medium in size. When first introduced it intrigued the rose world with its deep coppery foliage and, although maintaining its popularity in some nurseries, its tendency to mildew made this a variety that has lost its popular appeal. It is a good bedding variety with a vigorous, bushy growth habit but it is disappointing when used as a standard. ZONES 4–9.

de Ruiter, The Netherlands, 1954

'Gruss an Teplitz' × Seedling of a Cluster-flowered Rose

Royal National Rose Society Gold Medal 1954, Rome Gold Medal 1954

'ROSENDORF SPARRIESHOOP' KORdibor

MODERN, MODERN SHRUB, LIGHT PINK, REPEAT-FLOWERING

This pretty, medium-sized shrub produces clusters of bright pale pink, semi-double blooms with 15 petals and with an apple scent. Repeat-flowering and very healthy, it is a bushy shrub that will grow equally happily in groups in a border or as a specimen plant. ZONES 4–9.

Kordes, Germany, 1988

Parentage unknown

'ROSENELFE'

syn. 'Rose Elf'

MODERN, CLUSTER-FLOWERED/FLORIBUNDA, MEDIUM PINK, REPEAT-FLOWERING

This repeat-flowering variety, which is suitable for bedding, bears small to medium pink blooms that are double, with

'Rosemary Rose'

many petals, and scented. The large clusters of flowers appear on a medium-sized, thin bush with leathery, glossy foliage. ZONES 4–9.

Kordes, Germany, 1939

'Else Poulsen' × 'Sir Basil McFarland'

'ROSENFEE'

MODERN, CLUSTER-FLOWERED/FLORIBUNDA, LIGHT PINK, REPEAT-FLOWERING

Big clusters of large open blooms that are rose pink then turn salmon with age are borne on this repeat-flowering variety. They have a slight fragrance. 'Rosenfee' is a medium-sized bush with good healthy foliage that is suitable for bedding. ZONES 4–9.

Boerner, USA, 1967

Parentage unknown

'ROSENPROFESSOR SIEBER'

KORparesni

MODERN, CLUSTER-FLOWERED/FLORIBUNDA, MEDIUM PINK, REPEAT-FLOWERING

The medium-sized flowers of this cultivar are a pure and even shade of salmon-rose, and are filled with rather short petals that form an attractive cupped shape as the blooms mature. They are borne through summer and autumn, sometimes singly but usually in clusters, and have a pleasing Wild Rose scent. In the garden, 'Rosenprofessor Sieber' makes a suitable item for beds and borders, or to form a hedge. The plant grows bushily with good vigor to average height, and is well clothed in glossy dark green foliage. The variety is named in recognition of Professor Josef Sieber, who has dedicated many years of his life to roses. ZONES 4–9.

Kordes, Germany, 1997

Parentage unknown

Anerkannte Deutsche Rose 1996

'ROSENRESLI' KORresli

syn. 'Love's Song'

MODERN, MODERN SHRUB, DEEP PINK, REPEAT-FLOWERING

The deep pink, fragrant flowers with salmon tones on this rose are large, with 26–40 petals, and are borne in medium-sized clusters. This vigorous, repeat-flowering plant has dark green glossy foliage and is suitable as a big shrub, on pillars or on walls. ZONES 4–9.

Kordes, Germany, 1986

('New Dawn' × 'Prima Ballerina') × seedling

Anerkannte Deutsche Rose 1984

'ROSENSTADT ZWEIBRÜCKEN' KORstatis

syns 'Morningrose', 'Rosenstadt'

MODERN, MODERN SHRUB, PINK BLEND, REPEAT-FLOWERING

This variety has large, open blooms with 20 petals that are deep bright pink with a yellow base but have little scent. A showy shrub that is remarkably hardy, it has deep green healthy foliage and is a good subject for borders and as a specimen plant. ZONES 3–9.

Kordes, Germany, 1989

Parentage unknown

'Rosendorf Sparrieshoop'

'Rosenfee'

R

'Rosenprofessor Sieber'

'ROSERAIE DE L'HAŸ'
MODERN, HYBRID RUGOSA, DARK RED, REPEAT-FLOWERING

Probably the most widely grown and certainly the most popular of all the Rugosa family, this rose is a typical Rugosa with vigorous, very thorny stems that is very healthy and is repeat-flowering. The big open flowers in small clusters are an intense crimson-purple with cream stamens and the scent is memorable, a rich concentration of cloves and honey.

'Roseraie de l'Haÿ' is probably the finest in its class and is useful in many situations, but it is most excellent as a hedge plant; a group of specimen plants in a wild garden will add color and scent. An unusual feature for this type of rose is that it does not have any hips. ZONES 4–9.

Cochet-Cochet, France, 1901

Said to be a sport of *Rosa rugosa rubra*

Royal Horticultural Society Award of Garden Merit 1993

'ROSEROMANTIC' KORsommer
MODERN, CLUSTER-FLOWERED/FLORIBUNDA, WHITE, REPEAT-FLOWERING

'Roseromantic' bears large clusters of well-spaced palest pink single flowers that are 2 in (5 cm) across. They have a slight fragrance. The flowers completely cover the bush, which grows much taller than it does wide. The foliage is plentiful, small, dark and glossy on a very spreading bush. If spent flowers are not removed a good crop of small, round hips is produced in clusters, these looking very attractive against the later flowers. This rose makes a very good low, spreading border or dwarf hedge that can also provide a light and airy effect when planted among bulbs and perennials of a similar color. ZONES 4–9.

Kordes, Germany, 1984

Seedling × 'Tornado'

Baden-Baden Gold Medal 1982

'ROSETTE DELIZY'
OLD, TEA, YELLOW BLEND, REPEAT-FLOWERING

This colorful rose has flowers containing cadmium-yellow, apricot, brick red and carmine tones. The large, well-formed blooms may appear garish to some. It repeats well and the colors are more vibrant in cooler months. ZONES 7–9.

Nabonnand, France, 1922

'General Galliéni' × 'Comtesse Bardi'

'ROSEVILLE COLLEGE'
MODERN, LARGE-FLOWERED/HYBRID TEA, ORANGE-PINK, REPEAT-FLOWERING

The large, very double blooms of this rose contain 55 petals of a warm orange-pink color. The flower production can be sparse and the repeat cycle somewhat slow. There is some fragrance. The profuse foliage is disease resistant, deep green and slightly wrinkled on a small to medium-sized, stocky plant. It was named after a girls' high school in Sydney, Australia. ZONES 5–10.

Bell, Australia, 1990

'Yellow Pages' × 'Silver Jubilee'

'Rosette Delizy'

'Rosenresli'

'Rosenstadt Zweibrücken'

'Roseraie de l'Haÿ'

'Roseraie de l'Haÿ' (hip)

'Roseville College'

'Roseromantic'

R

'ROSIE LARKIN'   FRYyippee

syn. 'Rosy Larkin'

MODERN, MODERN SHRUB, MAUVE, REPEAT-FLOWERING

This low-growing, lavender rose produces masses of slightly fragrant single blooms in good succession from summer through to autumn. A neat, tidy plant that is almost compact, it is suitable for small gardens, window boxes and pots. **ZONES 4–9.**

Fryer, UK, 1993

Parentage unknown

'ROSINA'

syns 'Josephine Wheatcroft', 'Yellow Sweetheart'

MODERN, MINIATURE, MEDIUM YELLOW, REPEAT-FLOWERING

The double flowers of this variety have 16 petals, are a pleasing sunflower yellow and are fragrant; the clear, bright color is at its best in cooler climates. The foliage is glossy light green on a dwarf, compact plant that grows 8–12 in (20–30 cm) high. The blooms appear in small clusters. This rose needs protection from black spot, but it is weatherproof and is a popular Miniature for borders and containers in the UK. This classic Miniature

'Rosmarin '89'

from the hybridizing program of early pioneer Pedro Dot is still a favorite for the garden. **ZONES 4–10.**

Dot, Spain, 1935

'Eduardo Toda' × 'Rouletti'

'ROSMARIN'

syn. 'Rosemarin'

MODERN, MINIATURE, PINK BLEND, REPEAT-FLOWERING

The globular buds of 'Rosmarin' open to reveal flowers that are a soft pink with a light red reverse. The florets are double, have a light fragrance and are decorative in form. The flowers change their color composition from light pink in cool weather to light red in warm, intermediate temperatures, which produces a fascinating blend. The foliage is light glossy green on a very compact plant that is always in bloom. **ZONES 5–10.**

Kordes, Germany, 1989

'Tom Thumb' × 'Dacapo'

'ROSMARIN '89'   KORfanto

syn. 'Rosmarin '90'

MODERN, MINIATURE, DEEP PINK, REPEAT-FLOWERING

'Rosmarin '89' is a very bushy, spreading Miniature Rose producing large, well-

'Rosmarin '89'

'Rosy Carpet'

shaped clusters of rich pink, double blooms each containing 60–70 petals. The flowers are produced very freely and continuously and are particularly long lasting, and they are excellent for cutting for indoor use. If planted very close together, this rose makes a very nice little border. It should not be confused with the Kordes' variety 'Rosmarin', which was introduced in 1965. This can be difficult, as the older rose is still grown in many gardens and is an excellent rose. **ZONES 5–9.**

Kordes, Germany, 1990

Parentage unknown

'ROSY CARPET'   INTercarp

syn. 'Matador'

MODERN, MODERN SHRUB, DEEP PINK, REPEAT-FLOWERING

This is one of the first introductions to prove that the Modern Garden Rose is a valuable plant to enhance the environment as a subject for landscaping. 'Rosy Carpet' has open, single, medium blooms with 5 petals. Deep pink in color, they are fragrant and are produced in clusters continuously from summer through to autumn. The dark green glossy foliage and a semi-spreading

'Rosy Carpet'

'Rosy Cushion'

growth habit makes for a plant that was and still is used in big planting schemes. **ZONES 4–9.**

Interplant, The Netherlands, 1984

'Yesterday' × seedling

'ROSY CHEEKS'

MODERN, LARGE-FLOWERED/HYBRID TEA, RED BLEND, REPEAT-FLOWERING

The large, fragrant blooms with 35 petals on 'Rosy Cheeks' are red with a reverse of yellow. The foliage is dark, glossy and disease resistant on a repeat-flowering bedding variety that has potential as an exhibition bloom. **ZONES 4–9.**

Anderson, UK, 1975

Seedling × 'Irish Gold'

'ROSY CUSHION'   INTerall

MODERN, MODERN SHRUB, LIGHT PINK, REPEAT-FLOWERING

This repeat-flowering shrub has the potential to be a very prolific ground cover, and it has extremely good disease resistance. The small, light pink single blooms with 7–8 petals are borne in large clusters and have a slight fragrance. Dark green, very glossy foliage and medium prickles appear on a good rose for environmental planting. **ZONES 4–9.**

Ilsink, The Netherlands, 1979

'Yesterday' × seedling

Golden Rose of The Hague 1985, Royal Horticultural Society Award of Garden Merit 1993

'ROSY DAWN'

MODERN, MINIATURE, YELLOW BLEND, REPEAT-FLOWERING

'Rosy Dawn' has ovoid buds that open to creamy yellow flowers edged deep carmine pink. The double florets with 28 petals have a light Tea fragrance and good Large-flowered exhibition form, which is fleeting. The blooms tend to come in small sprays and add real vitality to any garden—this brightly colored plant attracts a lot of attention. The glossy green foliage is small to medium on an attractive, vigorous, large bush. This is another rose developed from an incestuous relationship. **ZONES 5–10.**

Bennett, USA, 1982

'Magic Carrousel' × 'Magic Carrousel'

'ROSY FUTURE'   HARwaderox

MODERN, CLUSTER-FLOWERED/FLORIBUNDA, DEEP PINK, REPEAT-FLOWERING

This short-growing variety has small, double blooms with 15–25 petals. The fragrant flowers, which are carmine in color, repeat-bloom rapidly. There are few thorns and small dark green, semi-glossy foliage on 'Rosy Future', an upright plant that is a good subject for pots, small borders and small beds. ZONES 4–9.

Harkness, UK, 1991

'Radox Bouquet' × 'Anna Ford'

Courtrai Gold Medal 1989, Glasgow Silver Medal 1993

'ROSY HIT' POUlmar
MODERN, MINIATURE, ORANGE BLEND, REPEAT-FLOWERING

This rose prefers a sunny position and is a vigorous plant that grows taller than usual for its class. It blooms generously throughout summer until winter. The medium-sized blooms are exquisitely colored from the opening yellow buds to the unfolded blooms with their orange-pink centers. They are borne either singly or in clusters and are popular for exhibition, indoor arrangements or for planting in containers. ZONES 5–11.

Poulsen, Denmark, 1994

Parentage unknown

'ROSY MANTLE'
MODERN, LARGE-FLOWERED CLIMBER, MEDIUM PINK, REPEAT-FLOWERING

'Rosy Mantle' has large, fragrant, double blooms with a good Large-flowered

'Rosy Dawn'

'Roter Champagner'

'Rosy Mantle'

shape. They are a warm, rosy pink and are produced with good succession from summer through to autumn. The dark foliage is a perfect foil for a variety that is equally at home growing on a wall or on a pillar. The flowers are very good for cutting. ZONES 4–9.

Cocker, UK, 1968

'New Dawn' × 'Prima Ballerina'

Royal National Rose Society Trial Ground Certificate 1970

'ROTE MAX GRAF' KORmax
syn. 'Red Max Graf'
MODERN, MODERN SHRUB, MEDIUM RED

Ovoid buds on this variety open into large, single, bright medium red flowers with 6 petals. Produced in clusters, they appear only in summer and are fragrant. An extremely vigorous, prostrate plant, it has dark leathery foliage that is almost wrinkled. 'Rote Max Graf' is a valuable variety in large plantings, with the bright scarlet blooms making a distinctive feature on a big plant. ZONES 4–9.

Kordes, Germany, 1980

Rosa kordesii × seedling

Baden-Baden Gold Medal 1981

'Rouge Meilland'

'ROTE MOZART' KORtragfei
syn. 'Red Mozart'
MODERN, MODERN SHRUB, ORANGE-RED, REPEAT-FLOWERING

The large clusters of fragrant, red, single blooms on 'Rote Mozart' are borne on a well-shaped, rotund, vigorous plant. Its small leaves and robust flowering make it a useful plant as a specimen or in large borders. ZONES 4–9.

Kordes, Germany, 1989

Sport of 'Mozart'

'ROTER CHAMPAGNER'
syn. 'Pétillante'
MODERN, LARGE-FLOWERED/HYBRID TEA, MEDIUM RED, REPEAT-FLOWERING

The pointed buds of this variety open to large, double flowers of exhibition form. They are slightly fragrant and have up to 60 crimson petals, but are slow to repeat. They last well when cut. Matt dark green foliage covers this vigorous and upright plant. ZONES 5–9.

Tantau, Germany, 1963

Parentage unknown

'ROTES MEER'
syns 'Exception', 'Purple Pavement'
MODERN, HYBRID RUGOSA, MEDIUM RED, REPEAT-FLOWERING

This rose bears fragrant, carmine-red, semi-double flowers, usually in clusters. The blooms continue through summer and autumn. Sizeable red hips appear late in the season. The shrub has a dense habit with prickly stems and small, semi-glossy leaves. ZONES 4–9.

Baum, Germany, 1983

Seedling of 'White Hedge'

'ROUGE ADMIRABLE'
OLD, GALLICA, DEEP PINK

This rose may be difficult to obtain. A plant at the Sangerhausen rosarium bears this name, but does not match the old description. William Paul, in his *Rose*

'Rote Max Graf'

Garden, listed 471 Gallicas in the first edition (1848) and 87 in the tenth edition (1903). This one may just have survived! ZONES 4–9.

Vibert, France, 1825

Parentage unknown

'ROUGE MEILLAND' MEImalyna
syns 'New Rouge Meilland', 'Rouge Meilland 84'
MODERN, LARGE-FLOWERED/HYBRID TEA, MEDIUM RED, REPEAT-FLOWERING

'Rouge Meilland' has large, medium red flowers with 40 petals that have very little scent. A vigorous, repeat-flowering variety, it has dark, semi-glossy foliage and an upright growth habit. ZONES 4–9.

Meilland, France, 1982

(['Queen Elizabeth' × 'Karl Herbst'] × 'Pharaoh') × 'Antonia Ridge'

'ROUGE MOSS'
syn. 'Rougemoss'
MODERN, CLUSTER-FLOWERED/FLORIBUNDA, ORANGE-RED, REPEAT-FLOWERING

This vigorous, dwarf plant has small, orange-red, double, fragrant blooms that are produced from summer to autumn. It is suitable for pots and small borders and has leathery foliage. ZONES 4–9.

Moore, USA, 1972

'Rumba' × hybrid of a Moss Rose

R

'ROULETII'

syn. *Rosa rouletii* 'Correvon'
OLD, CHINA, MEDIUM PINK, REPEAT-FLOWERING

This rose was found growing in a pot in a window in Switzerland by M. Roulet and introduced by M. Correvon of Geneva. A similar rose was grown in England early in the nineteenth century and was known as 'Miss Lawrance's Rose', Mary Lawrance being an early flower illustrator. Many varieties were grown up until mid-Victorian times, but they died out with the introduction of the Polyanthas. 'Rouletii' sparked new interest and many, though not all, of the Miniatures of today are descended from this rose. It is very tiny, a 'micro-miniature', with rose pink flowers half a thumb width in diameter, and it is repeat-flowering. There is disagreement as to whether or not it is 'Pompon de Paris'. ZONES 7–9.

Correvon, Switzerland, 1922

Considered to be *Rosa chinensis minima*

'ROUNDELAY'

MODERN, LARGE-FLOWERED/HYBRID TEA, DARK RED, REPEAT-FLOWERING

'Roundelay' has dark red, double, high-centered blooms with 38 petals that open flat in small clusters. They are fragrant and repeat their bloom on a very vigor-

'Rouletii'

'Roundelay'

ous plant with dark foliage. Once popular, and known as a Grandiflora in America, it is used for bedding. ZONES 4–9.

Swim, USA, 1954

'Charlotte Armstrong' × 'Floradora'

Geneva Gold Medal 1954, National Rose Society Trial Ground Certificate 1958

'ROXIE'   RESox

MODERN, LARGE-FLOWERED/HYBRID TEA, MEDIUM RED, REPEAT-FLOWERING

The double, well-formed, lightly fragrant blooms of 'Roxie' have up to 40 petals. Usually they are carried singly, but are sometimes formed in small open clusters. A useful item in beds and borders, it makes a prickly bush of average height with matt mid-green foliage. ZONES 5–9.

Sheldon, USA, 1995

'Sheer Bliss' × 'Headliner'

'ROYAL ALBERT HALL'

MODERN, LARGE-FLOWERED/HYBRID TEA, RED BLEND, REPEAT-FLOWERING

The large, wine red blooms of this variety have a reverse of gold, 32 petals and a classic form. They have a considerable attar of roses fragrance and are high centered. The medium-sized plant is bushy and has dark foliage. ZONES 4–9.

Cocker, UK, 1972

'Fragrant Cloud' × 'Postillion'

'ROYAL AMETHYST'   DEVmorada

MODERN, LARGE-FLOWERED/HYBRID TEA, MAUVE, REPEAT-FLOWERING

Pointed buds open into large, double flowers with 32 petals on this rose. Borne singly, they are lavender in color and have a fruity scent. The foliage is glossy mid-green on an tall, upright plant with henna-colored thorns. The globular fruits are tangerine orange. ZONES 4–9.

DeVor, USA, 1989

'Angel Face' × 'Blue Moon'

Portland Gold Medal and Fragrance Award 1996

'Royal Canadian'

'ROYAL BASSINO'   KORfungo

MODERN, MODERN SHRUB, MEDIUM RED, REPEAT-FLOWERING

This improved form of the original repeat-flowering ground-cover has scarlet semi-double blooms borne in moderate clusters that have a light scent. It is a plant for the smaller garden; it produces color throughout the season and has a great resistance to disease. ZONES 4–9.

Kordes, Germany, 1990

Parentage unknown

'ROYAL BLUSH'   SIEroyal

MODERN, MODERN SHRUB, LIGHT PINK

'Royal Blush' resulted from a cross between an Alba and a rose of the *Rosa kordesii* line. The result is a hardy shrub with lovely old-fashioned flowers: they are large, quartered and very full of petals. The color is pale to flesh pink on the undersides and the lightest of blush pinks in the heart of each flower. There is a good fragrance, and the plant blooms for several weeks during summer. 'Royal Blush' is very suitable for a shrub border where larger plants are required, being half as big again as an average shrub rose. The grayish leaves are plentiful. ZONES 4–9.

Sievers, Germany, 1988

Parentage unknown

'ROYAL BONICA'   MEIdomac,

MEImodac

syn. 'Royal Bonnika'

MODERN, MODERN SHRUB, MEDIUM PINK, REPEAT-FLOWERING

This sport of 'Bonica' has blooms similar to its parent. They are a deep shade of rose pink, and the ageing flowers have

'Royal Bassino'

less tendency to fade and there are rather more petals and the blooms are larger. They appear through summer and autumn. There is a slight scent. It is a fine variety for beds and borders, and forms a good hedge. It grows vigorously, and has mid-green, semi-glossy foliage. ZONES 5–9.

Meilland, France, 1994

Sport of 'Bonica'

Belfast Certificate of Merit 1996

'ROYAL CANADIAN'

MODERN, LARGE-FLOWERED/HYBRID TEA, MEDIUM RED, REPEAT-FLOWERING

Glossy, leathery foliage on this robust, upright-growing plant make this a good variety for bedding. The large, scarlet, double flowers have 35 petals, are cupped and are fragrant. ZONES 4–9.

Morey, USA, 1968

Seedling × 'Talisman'

'ROYAL DANE'   POUmidor

syn. 'Troika'

MODERN, LARGE-FLOWERED/HYBRID TEA, ORANGE BLEND, REPEAT-FLOWERING

The remarkable orange-copper flowers have red outer petals and a classic form. They are very fragrant, are 6 in (10 cm) wide and appear from summer to autumn. Large, dark, glossy foliage appears on an extremely vigorous, upright, tall-growing plant that is a very good bedding variety in cool temperate climates but can grow to considerable height if encouraged in very mild environments. ZONES 4–9.

Poulsen, Denmark, 1971

('Tropicana' × ['Baccará' × 'Princesse Astride']) × 'Hanne'

Royal National Rose Society James Mason Medal 1992, Royal Horticultural Society Award of Garden Merit 1993

'ROYAL FLUSH'

MODERN, LARGE-FLOWERED CLIMBER, PINK BLEND, REPEAT-FLOWERING

Medium-sized blooms that are cream with the edges blending to pink open from ovoid buds on this repeat-flowering variety. The flowers are semi-double, cupped and fragrant and the foliage is dark and leathery on vigorous climbing growth. 'Royal Flush' is suitable for growing on pillars and walls. ZONES 4–9.

Fuller, USA, 1970

'Little Darling' × 'Suspense'

'Royal Dane'

'ROYAL GOLD'

MODERN, LARGE-FLOWERED CLIMBER, MEDIUM YELLOW, REPEAT-FLOWERING

The very double golden yellow blooms with 35 petals on 'Royal Gold' are cupped and large. Borne singly or in small clusters and having a considerable fruity fragrance, they appear from summer to autumn. The foliage is glossy and very healthy and the growth habit vigorous on a climber that enjoys a warm low wall or pillar in a sheltered environment. ZONES 4–9.

Morey, USA, 1957

'Climbing Goldilocks' × 'Lydia'

'ROYAL HIGHNESS'

syns 'Königliche Hoheit', 'Königlicht Hoheit'

MODERN, LARGE-FLOWERED/HYBRID TEA, LIGHT PINK, REPEAT-FLOWERING

The large, very light soft pink double blooms with 43 petals on 'Royal Highness' have high centers and are very fragrant. A strong, upright, bushy

'Royal Highness'

'Royal Gold'

grower, it is repeat-flowering and has dark, glossy, leathery foliage. It is a superb bedding variety. ZONES 5–9.

Swim, USA, 1962

'Virgo' × 'Peace'

Portland Gold Medal 1960, Madrid Gold Medal 1962, All-America Rose Selection 1963, AARS David Fuerstenberg Prize 1964

'ROYAL MARBRÉE'

OLD, GALLICA, MAUVE

The flowers of this rose open violet-crimson and fade to carmine; they are spotted with pink. This is a tall, vigorous shrub in the Gallica style that unfortunately has not been highly regarded. *Marbrée* means 'mottled'. ZONES 4–9.

Perhaps from Belgium, introduced to France pre-1837

Parentage unknown

'ROYAL OCCASION'

syn. 'Montana'

MODERN, CLUSTER-FLOWERED/FLORIBUNDA, ORANGE-RED, REPEAT-FLOWERING

The long, pointed buds of this rose open into semi-double, large, lightly fragranced flowers with 20 orange-scarlet petals. A healthy, repeat-flowering bedding rose, it has glossy deep green foliage and an upright habit. ZONES 4–9.

Tantau, Germany, 1974

'Walzertraum' × 'Europeana'

Anerkannte Deutsche Rose 1974

'ROYAL PARADE'

MODERN, MINIATURE, MEDIUM PINK, REPEAT-FLOWERING

Another of the 'Rosa Nova' series bred by Poulsen of Denmark for sale as potted

'Royal Salute'

plants, 'Royal Parade' is intended for use indoors in well-lit rooms. The plant is very small and compact with tiny foliage and shapely little buds that open to flat blooms filled with 25–30 petals. The flowers are pretty at all stages of development, and last a long time both on the bush and when cut for decoration. It is ideal for pots, window boxes and for small beds; the plant is a little small for use in the open garden. It rarely exceeds 12 in (30 cm) tall and wide. Although the disease resistance is good, the rose may be a little prone to black spot. ZONES 5–9.

Poulsen, Denmark, 1992

Parentage unknown

'ROYAL PHILHARMONIC'

HARdeed

MODERN, LARGE-FLOWERED/HYBRID TEA, WHITE, REPEAT-FLOWERING

'Royal Philharmonic' has been described as the leading white Large-flowered Rose of this era, leaving 'Virgo' and 'Pascali' redundant. The beautifully formed flowers have a good classical shape and a remarkable scent, and repeat their bloom. Disease-resistant foliage and strong growth has made this variety distinct and popular. ZONES 4–9.

Harkness, UK, 1997

Parentage unknown

'Royal Parade'

'Royal Occasion'

'ROYAL SALUTE' MACros

syn. 'Rose Baby'

MODERN, MINIATURE, MEDIUM RED, REPEAT-FLOWERING

The flowers of this rose are usually rose red, but in some climates such as England's they are a deep rose pink. The double florets have 30 petals and are borne in clusters. They tend to cover the compact, vigorous bush with dark green foliage, providing a dazzling display. The blooms are at their best when fully open, putting on an eye-catching performance in the garden. One of the first Miniatures introduced by the master hybridizer of Large-flowered and Cluster-flowered Roses, Sam McGredy, its popularity was limited to Great Britain where it was introduced to commemorate the Silver Jubilee of Queen Elizabeth II. ZONES 5–10.

McGredy, New Zealand, 1976

'New Penny' × 'Marlena'

Royal National Rose Society Trial Ground Certificate 1972, British Association of Rose Breeders, Breeders' Selection 1977

'ROYAL SCARLET'

MODERN, LARGE-FLOWERED/HYBRID TEA, MEDIUM RED, REPEAT-FLOWERING

This variety, which repeats its bloom from summer to autumn, has high-centered, large, scarlet red flowers that

'Royal William'

'Royal Scarlet'

'Roydon Hall'

are fragrant. The foliage is glossy and the bush, which is suitable for bedding, is vigorous and healthy. **ZONES 4–9.**

Kraus, Canada, 1966

'McGredy's Scarlet' × 'Christian Dior'

'ROYAL SHOW'

MODERN, LARGE-FLOWERED/HYBRID TEA, MEDIUM RED, REPEAT-FLOWERING

The medium red, double flowers of 'Royal Show' have 27 petals. Large and pointed, they are slightly fragrant and appear from summer to autumn. A vigorous, bushy plant, it has glossy foliage and is suitable for bedding. **ZONES 4–9.**

Gregory, UK, 1973

'The Queen Elizabeth Rose' × seedling

'ROYAL WILLIAM'   KORzaun

syns 'Duftzauber '84', 'Fragrant Charm '84', 'Leonora Christine'

MODERN, LARGE-FLOWERED/HYBRID TEA, DARK RED, REPEAT-FLOWERING

This exceptional variety has dark red, fragrant flowers with a velvety sheen. The large blooms have 35 petals and are repeat-flowering. The foliage is dark green, semi-glossy and disease resistant, and the growth habit is free and bushy. It is a good bedding variety. **ZONES 4–9.**

Kordes, Germany, 1984

'Feuerzauber' × seedling

Royal National Rose Society Trial Ground Certificate 1985, Rose of the Year 1987, Royal Horticultural Society Award of Garden Merit 1993

'Royal Show'

'ROYDON HALL'

MODERN, CLUSTER-FLOWERED/FLORIBUNDA, MEDIUM RED, REPEAT-FLOWERING

This free-flowering, repeat-blooming plant has medium red, double flowers with 35 petals but with little fragrance. The small clusters of blooms are produced on a plant with a bushy growth habit and mid-green, semi-glossy foliage. **ZONES 4–9.**

Scrivens, UK, 1983

'City of Leeds' × ('Paprika' × 'Rose Gaujard')

R

'RUBAIYAT'

MODERN, LARGE-FLOWERED/HYBRID TEA, DEEP
PINK, REPEAT-FLOWERING

The long, pointed buds of 'Rubaiyat'
become large, high-centered, double
flowers that are rose red with lighter
undersides. Very fragrant, they appear
on a vigorous, upright-growing plant
with dark green, leathery foliage. It is
suitable for exhibition and as a bedding
variety. ZONES 4–9.

McGredy, UK, 1946

('McGredy's Scarlet' × 'Mrs Sam McGredy') ×
(seedling × 'Sir Basil McFarland')

Portland Gold Medal 1945, All-America Rose
Selection 1947, National Rose Society Certificate
of Merit 1949

'Ruby' (Tantau)

'Ruby' (de Ruiter)

'Rugspin'

'RUBENS'

OLD, TEA, WHITE, REPEAT-FLOWERING

The flowers of this rose are creamy
white, shaded with rose, and have pale
gold centers. They are full, large and cup
shaped, and come quite early in the season. The plant is mildew free. If there is a
fault, it is that the blooms are a little pen-
dant. This rose is of conventional Tea
style and growth. ZONES 7–9.

Robert and Moreau, France, 1859

Parentage unknown

'RUBY'

MODERN, POLYANTHA, MEDIUM RED,
REPEAT-FLOWERING

This little-known Polyantha Rose carries
rich red flowers that appear in small,
well-spaced clusters on a neat bush
against the matt, mid-green foliage. The
plant is rather slow to repeat, and there
can be mildew problems in spring and
autumn. The flowers keep well on the
bush, finally fading to a dull red hue.
They also last well when cut; in fact
many Polyanthas like this one, such as
'Doris Ryker', are being grown again in
The Netherlands for the cut-flower market. ZONES 5–9.

de Ruiter, The Netherlands, 1932

Parentage unknown

'Rubens'

'Rugelda'

'RUBY'

MODERN, LARGE-FLOWERED/HYBRID TEA,
MEDIUM RED, REPEAT-FLOWERING

This rose should not be confused with
the Polyantha Rose of the same name;
neither variety is particularly well
known, and this one seems to be only
available to Australian gardeners. It bears
large, oval buds that open very slowly to
huge flat blooms that are filled with a
hundred or so tightly packed, intense
orange-red petals. They last a long time
on both the bush and indoors without
losing color, and are excellent for cutting,
even if removed at an advanced stage.
The blooms are so filled with petals that
they are not very attractive; however,
they become a little more attractive as
they open more fully. The growth is tall
and upright, and the abundant flowers
are borne amid the dark green, semi-
glossy, disease-free foliage. ZONES 5–9.

Tantau, Germany, 1989

Parentage unknown

'RUBY ANNIVERSARY'

HARbonny

MODERN, CLUSTER-FLOWERED/FLORIBUNDA,
MEDIUM RED, REPEAT-FLOWERING

This very free-flowering, low-growing
bushy variety produces ruby red, double,
small flowers in medium-sized clusters
from summer to autumn. They have
some scent. A superb plant for pots,
small borders and low hedges, it has
small, shiny foliage. ZONES 4–9.

Harkness, UK, 1993

Parentage unknown

Belfast Gold Medal 1995, Royal National Rose
Society Certificate of Merit 1995

'RUBY MAGIC'   MORrubi, MORuby

MODERN, MINIATURE, MEDIUM RED,
REPEAT-FLOWERING

The medium red, double, lightly fragrant
flowers on 'Ruby Magic' have 20 petals,

'Ruby Anniversary'

'Ruhm von Steinfurth'

'Ruby Wedding'

and are borne singly or in small clusters
of 3–5 blooms. They have a decorative
form and provide a good color display in
the garden. The foliage is small and
semi-glossy green on an upright, vigorous and prolific bush that is clean and
easy to maintain. This is an attractive
rose but there are many contenders in
this color class and 'Ruby Magic' does
not have sufficient novelty to outclass its
competitors. ZONES 5–10.

Moore, USA, 1986

'Orangeade' × 'Pinstripe'

'RUBY WEDDING'

MODERN, LARGE-FLOWERED/HYBRID TEA,
DARK RED, REPEAT-FLOWERING

This respectable bedding variety bears
large, deep red flowers with 44 petals.
'Ruby Wedding' repeats its bloom but
the flowers have little scent. It is a bushy
plant with a slightly spreading growth
habit. ZONES 4–9.

Gregory, UK, 1979

'Mayflower' × seedling

'RUGA'

syn. *Rosa* × *ruga* 'Lindley'
OLD, AYRSHIRE, WHITE

The Ayrshires are a class of Ramblers developed early in the nineteenth century.
They are hybrids of the wild field rose
Rosa arvensis (thought by many to be
Shakespeare's Musk Rose). The Earl of
Loudon in Ayrshire is said to have
started them. They make tall, vigorous
climbers and ramblers and mostly bear
small, non-repeat-flowering, white
flowers. 'Ruga' has good scent and its
double, cupped flowers are small and
flesh colored, fading to creamy white.
ZONES 5–9.

Italy, pre-1830

Thought to be *Rosa arvensis* × China or Tea Rose

'RUGELDA'   KORruge

MODERN, HYBRID RUGOSA, YELLOW BLEND,
REPEAT-FLOWERING

'Rugelda' has mid-green wrinkled foliage
on a vigorous shrub that can be grown as
a specimen plant or in groups in borders.
The light yellow, double blooms are medium in size and have 25 petals. They
have little scent. ZONES 4–9.

Kordes, Germany, 1992

Parentage unknown

Anerkannte Deutsche Rose 1992

'RUGOSA MAGNIFICA'

MODERN, HYBRID RUGOSA, MAUVE,
REPEAT-FLOWERING

This fragrant variety produces reddish
lavender flowers. They are double, but
still show their golden stamens when
fully open. Orange-red hips follow in
autumn. The vigorous growth is spreading and very hardy. ZONES 5–10.

Van Fleet, USA, 1905

Parentage unknown

'RUGSPIN'

MODERN, HYBRID RUGOSA, DARK RED,
REPEAT-FLOWERING

The scarlet-crimson, single flowers of
this shrub rose have a bold central boss
of golden yellow stamens. This gives an
attractive display when it is in bloom,
ideal for mixed borders or bedding
schemes. The bushy growth is made up
of prickly stems and glossy green, typically rugose foliage. ZONES 5–10.

Petersen, Denmark, circa 1960

Parentage unknown

'RUHM VON STEINFURTH'

syn. 'Red Druschki'

OLD, HYBRID PERPETUAL, MEDIUM RED,
REPEAT-FLOWERING

The name of this rose translates to mean
'glory of Steinfurth'. Late in date for a
Hybrid Perpetual, it has long, pointed
buds and red, double, fragrant flowers
containing 34 petals. They are cupped
and large. It is a vigorous plant with
dark, leathery foliage, and is a desirable
cut-flower rose. ZONES 5–9.

Weigand and Schultheis, Germany, 1920

'Frau Karl Druschki' × 'Ulrich Brünner Fils'

'RUMBA'

syn. 'Rhumba'

MODERN, CLUSTER-FLOWERED/FLORIBUNDA, RED
BLEND, REPEAT-FLOWERING

An extremely free-flowering Cluster-
flowered Rose, 'Rumba' bears large
clusters of small to medium, cupped,

'Russelliana'

'Rush'

reddish flowers with yellow centers. A
medium-sized, repeat-flowering variety,
it has a slight spicy fragrance. Disease resistant, it is a vigorous, bushy plant with
glossy dark, leathery foliage. ZONES 4–9.

Poulsen, Denmark, 1960

'Masquerade' × ('Poulsen's Bedder' ×
'Floradora')

National Rose Society Certificate of Merit 1959

'RUNNING MAID'   LENramp

MODERN, MODERN SHRUB, MAUVE,
REPEAT-FLOWERING

The single, fragrant blooms on 'Running
Maid' are lilac-red with a white eye. Medium to small with 5 petals, they are
borne in clusters of 2–32 from summer
to autumn. The foliage is reddish green
and spreading. It is good for banks, borders or in large pots. ZONES 4–9.

Lens, Belgium, 1982

Rosa multiflora × (R. wichuraiana ×
'Violet Hood')

Lyon Rose of the Century 1983, Düsseldorf Gold
Medal 1987

'RUSH'   LENmobri

MODERN, MODERN SHRUB, PINK BLEND,
REPEAT-FLOWERING

This bushy shrub bears its single blooms
with 5 petals in clusters of 3–32 from
summer to autumn. Pink with a white
eye, they have a fruity fragrance. It is upright-growing with pale green foliage.
ZONES 4–9.

Lens, Belgium, 1983

('Ballerina' × 'Britannia') × Rosa multiflora

Lyon Rose of the Century 1982, Monza Gold
Medal 1982, Rome Gold Medal 1982, Bagatelle
Gold Medal 1986, The Hague Gold Medal 1988

'RUSKIN'

syn. 'John Ruskin'

MODERN, HYBRID RUGOSA, DARK RED

This big Hybrid Rugosa has deep crimson, double flowers with 50 petals and a

'Ruskin'

'Rustica'

'Ruyton'

good fragrance. They are cupped and
large, but their repeat-flowering ability is
open to doubt. The foliage is large, rich
green and leathery on a strong, bushy
variety to 5 ft (1.5 m) in height. Plant it
in groups, as a specimen plant or as
hedging material. ZONES 4–9.

Van Fleet, USA, 1928

'Souvenir de Pierre Leperdrieux' × 'Victor Hugo'

'RUSSELLIANA'

syns 'Old Spanish Rose', 'Russell's Cottage
Rose', 'Scarlet Grevillea', 'Souvenir de la
Bataille de Marengo'

OLD, MISCELLANEOUS, MAUVE

The flowers of 'Russelliana' are magenta,
fading to mauve. They are fully double
and flat and are borne in clusters. This
strong-growing variety has rather coarse
foliage and can grow to great heights. It
is well worth a place in the garden.
ZONES 5–9.

Pre-1837

Possibly Rosa multiflora Hybrid × Rosa setigera

'RUSTICA'   MEIvilanic

syns 'Stadt Basel', 'Ville de Bâle'

MODERN, CLUSTER-FLOWERED/FLORIBUNDA,
YELLOW BLEND, REPEAT-FLOWERING

The very long buds of 'Rustica' produce
flowers of a yellow-peach blend with a
reverse of buff yellow-orange. They are
cupped and double with 35 petals, are
borne in clusters of 1–14 and have a
slight fragrance. The dark, semi-matt
foliage appears on a repeat-flowering

plant that is semi-recumbent. A good
bedding variety, it is also nice when
grown as a standard. ZONES 4–9.

Meilland, France, 1981

('Queen Elizabeth' × seedling) × 'Sweet Promise'

'RUTH LEUWERIK'

MODERN, CLUSTER-FLOWERED/FLORIBUNDA,
MEDIUM RED, REPEAT-FLOWERING

The large, bright red double flowers with
30 petals on 'Ruth Leuwerik' are very
fragrant. They appear in clusters on a
rose that has maintained considerable
popularity. The bronze foliage is healthy
on a vigorous, bushy plant. ZONES 4–9.

de Ruiter, UK, 1961

'Käthe Duvigneau' × 'Rosemary Rose'

National Rose Society Trial Ground Certificate
1960

'RUYTON'

syn. 'Ruyton Girl's School'

MODERN, LARGE-FLOWERED/HYBRID TEA,
MEDIUM PINK

'Ruyton' was named after a girls' school
in Victoria, Australia. The flowers are
soft pink and are borne singly or in small
clusters of up to 3 per stem. The slim,
long and pointed buds open to fragrant
flowers with up to 25 petals. 'Ruyton'
grows with an upright habit to medium
height, and is covered with glossy dark
green leaves with broad leaflets. The new
growth is purplish. ZONES 5–9.

Bell, Australia, 1989

'Mount Shasta' × 'Prima Ballerina'

'Rumba'

R

'SAARBRÜCKEN'

MODERN, MODERN SHRUB, MEDIUM RED, REPEAT-FLOWERING

The large flowers of this rose are borne in clusters of up to 20. The scarlet-red, semi-double blooms flower only in summer and have a delicate scent. It is a vigorous, bushy shrub with healthy dark green foliage that looks wonderful in a border. 'Saarbrücken' is an easy to grow variety. ZONES 4–9.

Kordes, Germany, 1959

Parentage unknown

'SACHA'   SPEkes

syn. 'Our Sacha'

MODERN, LARGE-FLOWERED/HYBRID TEA, MEDIUM RED, REPEAT-FLOWERING

'Sacha' is essentially a cut-flower rose that enjoys a reputation for consistency. The parent, 'Calibra', is a good-quality variety grown under glass, as is its muta-

'Sadlers Wells'

tion 'Sacha'. The blooms are medium red and are produced quite prolifically on the bush. ZONES 5–10.

Spek, The Netherlands, 1996

Sport of 'Calibra'

'SACHSENGRUSS'

syns 'Saxon's Greeting', 'Tendresse'

OLD, HYBRID PERPETUAL, LIGHT PINK, REPEAT-FLOWERING

The well-formed flowers of this rose are a soft flesh pink color. The blooms are very large. The growth habit and style of the plant is vigorous. ZONES 5–9.

Neubert, 1912

'Frau Karl Druschki' × 'Mme Jules Gravereaux'

'SADLERS WELLS'

MODERN, MODERN SHRUB, PINK BLEND, REPEAT-FLOWERING

This free-flowering Modern Shrub still has its admirers. The semi-double

'Sachsengruss'

'Sadlers Wells'

'Sacha'

flowers, which are produced in large clusters, are silvery pink laced with cherry red and are sweetly scented. The foliage is healthy and the bush has a moderate growth habit. The repeat cycle is good, making this a useful variety in borders. The flowers last a long time when cut. Sadlers Wells was the former name of England's Royal Ballet. ZONES 4–9.

Beales, UK, 1983

'Penelope' × 'Rose Gaujard'

'SAFFEX ROSE'   KORgreyel

MODERN, CLUSTER-FLOWERED/FLORIBUNDA, MAUVE BLEND, REPEAT-FLOWERING

Saffex is a South African organization that involves itself with the protection of the natural environment. The rose named for it is very special because of its gorgeous color and finely shaped blooms; they are just perfect for exhibition purposes and, of course, for the cut-flower trade. With this there is a lovely fragrance. The fat, pointed, dark pink buds open to blooms with tight, shocking pink centers, and as the petals curl back they reveal a creamy silver sheen on the undersides. This bush grows vigorously to a medium height and is easy to maintain because of its good health. It repeats its flowers from spring until autumn so that 'Saffex Rose' is always a joy in the garden. ZONES 4–9.

Kordes, Germany, 1993

Parentage unknown

'SAFRANO'

OLD, TEA, APRICOT BLEND, REPEAT-FLOWERING

This is one of the early Teas and is somewhat remarkable, in that the parentage is known. This is because it was the result

'Saarbrücken'

'Safrano'

of hand pollination, an innovative process at that time. The large, fragrant, semi-double flowers are apricot-yellow or saffron. The plant, which is repeat-flowering and resists weather damage, used to be very popular as a buttonhole rose. 'Safrano' is best kept out of full sun, as the blooms can fade badly to an off-white color. ZONES 7–9.

Beauregard, France, 1839

'Parks' Yellow' × 'Mme Desprez'

'SAGA'

MODERN, MODERN SHRUB, WHITE, REPEAT-FLOWERING

Opinion is divided as to the most appropriate classification for this rose, and it is often listed as a Cluster-flowered Rose. The creamy white, semi-single small blooms contain 12 petals and are slightly fragrant. They are produced in clusters on a vigorous, rounded bush that has a good repeat cycle. The foliage is healthy and dark green and sets off the flowers nicely. This rose is most at home when planted in groups in borders. ZONES 4–9.

Harkness, UK, 1974

'Rudolph Timm' × ('Chanelle' × 'Piccadilly')

Royal National Rose Society Trial Ground Certificate 1972

'ST BONIFACE'   KORmatt

MODERN, CLUSTER-FLOWERED/FLORIBUNDA, ORANGE-RED, REPEAT-FLOWERING

The bright orange flowers of this plant have neatly arranged petals that give good symmetry and form. Each bloom has 35 petals, and there is a light fragrance. There is an abundance of shiny green, disease-resistant foliage on this low-growing, vigorous bush. The plant needs to be regularly deadheaded to promote the next cycle of large-clustered blooms. **ZONES 5–11.**

Kordes, Germany, 1982

'Diablotin' × 'Traumerei'

Royal National Rose Society Certificate of Merit 1981

'ST BRUNO' LANpipe
MODERN, CLUSTER-FLOWERED/FLORIBUNDA, DEEP YELLOW, REPEAT-FLOWERING

The weatherproof flowers of this rose are deep amber-yellow and carried in wide sprays. They are high centered, and have a refreshing perfume. The foliage is mid-green and semi-glossy on a small plant with an uneven growth habit. 'St Bruno' was named for a well-known brand of pipe tobacco in the UK. **ZONES 5–10.**

Sealand Nursery, UK, 1985

'Arthur Bell' × 'Zambra'

Edland Fragrance Medal 1986

'ST CECELIA' AUSmit
MODERN, MODERN SHRUB, MEDIUM YELLOW, REPEAT-FLOWERING

Plump buds open to give this variety deeply cupped flowers of blush pink to light apricot. They age gracefully to cream and have a strong myrrh fragrance. Throughout summer and autumn, they are borne singly or in small sprays of 3–12 amid the small, matt mid-green foliage. 'St Cecelia' is free blooming, but needs protection from rust and mildew. It is also classified as an English Rose. **ZONES 5–10.**

Austin, UK, 1987

'Wife of Bath' × seedling

'St Patrick'

'St Patrick'

'St Boniface'

'ST CHRISTOPHER' HARcogent
MODERN, LARGE-FLOWERED/HYBRID TEA, DEEP YELLOW, REPEAT-FLOWERING

This rose has flowers with an unusually warm tone of glowing gold and they cover this vigorous and easy-to-grow plant. 'St Christopher' is destined to become a popular garden variety in the UK. Overall, the plant has a luxurious and healthy appearance. **ZONES 5–10.**

Harkness, UK, 1996

Parentage unknown

Belfast Gold Medal 1998

'ST DUNSTAN'S ROSE' KIRshru
MODERN, MODERN SHRUB, LIGHT YELLOW, REPEAT-FLOWERING

This rose has a superb perfume. It was named to commemorate the 75th anniversary of the foundation of the War Blind Association in the UK. Its young, lemon yellow flowers open to very full, quartered blooms of pure white with soft yellow in the centers. There are 50 or more slightly quilled petals. Glossy pale green leaves cover this compact bush, and there is a profusion of bloom. It is excellent for use in bridal work, where an old-fashioned look is needed. It may need protection against fungus. **ZONES 5–10.**

Kirkham, UK, 1991

Parentage unknown

'ST HELENA' CANlish
syn. 'Union-Rose St Helena'
MODERN, CLUSTER-FLOWERED/FLORIBUNDA, MEDIUM PINK, REPEAT-FLOWERING

This variety was named to raise funds for the St Helena Hospice in Colchester,

'St Hughs'

'St Bruno'

England, which opened in 1988; it also marked the birthday of the island of St Helena, which celebrated 150 years as a crown colony in 1984. The blooms have 20 large, medium lilac-pink petals, and are borne amid the glossy mid-green foliage on this small, upright plant. It has a rounded shape that is pleasing to the eye and the weatherproof blooms give a fine fragrance. **ZONES 5–11.**

Cant, UK, 1983

'Jubilant' × 'Prima Ballerina'

'ST HUGHS' KORhug
MODERN, LARGE-FLOWERED/HYBRID TEA, MEDIUM YELLOW, REPEAT-FLOWERING

The large flowers of 'St Hughs' are creamy yellow and contain 35 petals. There is only a slight fragrance. The bush is free flowering and has a good repeat-flowering cycle. It is a healthy, medium-sized plant with medium green, semi-glossy foliage that makes a very good bedding variety. **ZONES 4–9.**

Kordes, Germany, 1987

Seedling × seedling

'ST JOHN' HARbilbo
MODERN, CLUSTER-FLOWERED/FLORIBUNDA, WHITE, REPEAT-FLOWERING

Each flower of this rose has 15–25 clear white petals, which look attractive against the glossy green leaves. The flowers are borne in small clusters with just a hint of perfume on this low-growing plant with spreading tendencies. There are a few prickles on the stems. **ZONES 5–11.**

Harkness, UK, 1995

'Prima' × 'Grace Abounding'

'St Nicholas'

'ST NICHOLAS'
OLD, DAMASK, DEEP PINK

This upright-growing, sturdy shrub with green-gray wood and numerous sharp hooked thorns has mid- to dark green foliage, which is a little sparse on the lower branches. The pointed buds with feathery sepals unfold to semi-double flowers about 2½ in (6.5 cm) across, displaying a prominent array of golden yellow stamens. The blooms are fragrant and are silvery deep pink, remaining attractive as they pale to softer pink with age, and they are carried in well-filled clusters. Coming into flower in mid-summer, this rose should not be deadheaded because the autumn crop of red hips is very attractive. **ZONES 5–10.**

James, UK, 1950

Possibly a Damask × Gallica

S

'ST PATRICK' WEKamanda
MODERN, LARGE-FLOWERED/HYBRID TEA, YELLOW BLEND, REPEAT-FLOWERING

The golden yellow flowers of this rose are chartreuse green on the outer petals. The blooms are fully double, with 30–35 petals that give excellent, high-pointed centers suitable for exhibition, although summer heat is needed to bring out the best features of color and form. The foliage is mid-green and plentiful with good disease-resistant characteristics. Born from two great exhibition varieties, 'St Patrick' is one of the few top award winners from an amateur breeder. **ZONES 5–11.**

Strickland, USA, 1995

'Brandy' × 'Gold Medal'

All-America Rose Selection 1996

'ST PAULI'

MODERN, CLUSTER-FLOWERED/FLORIBUNDA,
YELLOW BLEND, REPEAT-FLOWERING

The blooms of 'St Pauli' are golden
yellow with red to pink edges that slowly
become fused with age. The flowers have
only 15 petals, but are reasonably large—
3 in (7 cm) across—borne in large, attractive clusters with a light perfume. It
is a vigorous and upright bush with disease-resistant, glossy dark green foliage.
ZONES 5–10.

Kordes, Germany, 1958

'Masquerade' × 'Karl Herbst'

'ST SWITHUN' AUSwith

MODERN, MODERN SHRUB, LIGHT PINK,
REPEAT-FLOWERING

The large, fragrant, pale pink flowers
of 'St Swithun' are very full, with about
40 petals. They are borne in profusion in
small clusters and the repeat-bloom is
rapid, which makes this a welcome addition to any garden. The foliage is mid-
green, semi-glossy and abundant on a
bushy growing plant that is also classified
as an English Rose. ZONES 5–10.

Austin, UK, 1993

('Mary Rose' × 'Chaucer') × 'C. F. Meyer'

'SALET'

OLD, MOSS, MEDIUM PINK, REPEAT-FLOWERING

This is an accommodating compact and
sturdy shrub to about 3 ft (1 m) tall in

'St Pauli'

most soils. Its stems are moderately
thorny and sparsely covered with light-
colored, reddish, mossy stubble. The
buds are also mossy, but not excessively
so, and develop into clear bright pink
flowers that have a multitude of fluted,
narrow petals to give an overall muddled
effect, often with a central button. They
are about 2½ in (6.5 cm) across, very
fragrant and are produced continuously
either singly or in small clusters from
mid-summer through to early winter.
The leaves are small, bright green and
soft to touch. ZONES 5–10.

Lacharmé, France, 1854

Parentage unknown

'SALITA' KORmorlet

MODERN, LARGE-FLOWERED CLIMBER, ORANGE
BLEND, REPEAT-FLOWERING

'Salita' bears clusters of light orange-red,
medium-sized blooms that are slightly
fragrant. It is a moderately vigorous
climber, and looks very effective growing
on walls or pillars. It also makes an attractive shrub. ZONES 4–9.

Kordes, Germany, 1987

Parentage unknown

'SALLY HOLMES'

MODERN, MODERN SHRUB, WHITE,
REPEAT-FLOWERING

This extremely popular, medium-sized
shrub rose has large, open, creamy white

'St Swithun'

'Salet'

flowers with only 5 petals. There is a
lovely fragrance. It has large, glossy, deep
green leaves on stiff upright stems. If
pruned lightly, it will develop into a well-
structured plant about 6 ft (1.8 m) high.
'Sally Holmes' is ideal as a specimen
plant or in groups in borders. ZONES 4–9.

Holmes, UK, 1976

'Ivory Fashion' × 'Ballerina'

Royal National Rose Society Trial Ground
Certificate 1975, Belfast Certificate of Merit
1979, Baden-Baden Gold Medal 1980, Glasgow
Fragrance Award 1993, Portland Gold Medal
1993

'SALLY'S ROSE' CANrem

MODERN, LARGE-FLOWERED/HYBRID TEA, PINK
BLEND, REPEAT-FLOWERING

The rounded double blooms of 'Sally's
Rose' are creamy pink with apricot tints
and are very appealing. The lightly
scented blooms are borne on a bushy
plant with dark green, glossy foliage.
This is a very good bedding variety that
was named by the raiser to celebrate his
daughter's 21st birthday. ZONES 4–9.

Cant, UK, 1994

'Amber Queen' × 'Remember Me'

Glasgow Fragrance Award 1997

'SALMON SORBET'

MODERN, CLUSTER-FLOWERED/FLORIBUNDA,
PINK BLEND, REPEAT-FLOWERING

This short, stocky Cluster-flowered Rose
with mid-green, semi-glossy foliage produces flowers that are soft salmon-pink
striped with white: a subdued combination compared with most striped roses.
They are produced in small clusters from

'Sally Holmes'

pointed buds, and open cupped at first,
becoming flat at the full bloom stage.
Flower production is below average for a
bush rose, with rather slow repeat. The
disease resistance is fair, although black
spot sometimes occurs in autumn. In
spite of the unusual color, 'Salmon Sorbet' has not become popular. ZONES 5–10.

Bear Creek Nurseries, USA, 1991

Parentage unknown

'SALMON SPIRE' KORturnus

MODERN, LARGE-FLOWERED/HYBRID TEA,
ORANGE-PINK, REPEAT-FLOWERING

This is an exceptionally vigorous Large-
flowered Rose that produces sturdy
straight stems to form very tall shrubs.
It is useful to employ as a backdrop for
lower beds or as a hedge, and if it is tied
to a support it can be grown as a climber.
The flowers are produced continuously
on the tops of the center and side
branches, so that there always seems to
be color on the shrub. In this case, the
blooms are pure salmon-pink and
emerge from long buds to give large,
open flowers with firm petals. They have
a strong fragrance, which adds to their
value as cutting and exhibition blooms.
ZONES 4–9.

Kordes, Germany, 1993

Parentage unknown

'SALMON SPRITE'

MODERN, CLUSTER-FLOWERED/FLORIBUNDA,
ORANGE-PINK, REPEAT-FLOWERING

The large, fragrant double blooms of this
rose contain 40 petals. They are salmon

'Salmon Sorbet'

'Sally's Rose'

suffused with strawberry and are produced in big clusters, with up to 15 blooms per spray. 'Salmon Sprite' is an upright grower with dark green, very shiny, healthy foliage. ZONES 4–9.

LeGrice, UK, 1964

Seedling × 'Jiminy Cricket'

'SALMON SUNSATION'

KORpapie

MODERN, GROUND COVER, ORANGE-PINK, REPEAT-FLOWERING

This rose has healthy, shiny foliage and masses of bright blooms. The small, double roses cover the plant intermittently throughout summer and are a lovely deep salmon, but they are not fragrant. For banks and along road verges, for containers and as a standard, 'Salmon Sunsation' has proven its worth. ZONES 4–9.

Kordes, Germany

Parentage unknown

'SAMANTHA'   JACanth, JACmantha

MODERN, LARGE-FLOWERED/HYBRID TEA, MEDIUM RED, REPEAT-FLOWERING

The medium-sized red flowers of this rose have high centers and a good shape. There is some scent. It is a vigorous, bushy variety with dark green, leathery foliage and a good repeat cycle. This is a bedding variety that can also be displayed on the show table. ZONES 4–9.

Warriner, USA, 1974

'Bridal Pink' × seedling

'Samantha'

'San Diego'

'Salmon Sprite'

'SAMBA'   KORcapas

MODERN, CLUSTER-FLOWERED/FLORIBUNDA, YELLOW BLEND, REPEAT FLOWERING

The medium-sized, globular blooms of 'Samba' are golden yellow suffused with red, becoming fiery red as they age. They are borne in clusters on a low bush. The foliage is glossy and relatively healthy. ZONES 4–9.

Kordes, Germany, 1964

Parentage unknown

'SAN ANTONIO'

MODERN, LARGE-FLOWERED/HYBRID TEA, ORANGE-RED, REPEAT-FLOWERING

The large, double blooms of this rose are orange-red and there is little fragrance. It makes up for this shortcoming, however, by its vigor and its good repeat cycle. The leaves are large and leathery. Planted in groups in borders, this rose will produce splashes of color. In the USA it is known as a Grandiflora Rose. ZONES 4–9.

Armstrong, USA, 1967

'Roundelay' × 'El Capitan'

'SAN DIEGO'

MODERN, LARGE-FLOWERED/HYBRID TEA, MEDIUM YELLOW, REPEAT-FLOWERING

The large, high-centered blooms of this rose are light yellow and contain 50 petals. The foliage is leathery and healthy on a vigorous, upright bush with a compact structure. ZONES 4–9.

Armstrong, USA, 1968

'Helen Traubel' × 'Tiffany'

'Samba'

'Sander's White Rambler'

'SAN JOSE SUNSHINE'   FOUsun

MODERN, MINIATURE, DEEP YELLOW, REPEAT-FLOWERING

This variety has pointed buds that open to deep golden yellow flowers with orange highlights. They are fragrant, double and age to light yellow. They have good Large-flowered exhibition form and are borne singly or in small sprays. The foliage is matt mid-green on a spreading, medium to tall bush. It is an attractive variety because of its vigor and bloom production. While the original color is stunning, the blooms tend to suffer from rain spots and age to an unattractive color. This rose was named to honor the American Rose Society National Convention of 1991 in San Jose, California. ZONES 5–10.

Jacobs, USA, 1991

('Rise 'n' Shine' × 'Redgold') × 'Summer Madness'

'Sandra'

'Sander's White Rambler'

'SANDER'S WHITE RAMBLER'

MODERN, RAMBLER, WHITE

This *wichuraiana*-type Rambler has small, white, rosette-style flowers that are borne in large clusters. The blooms have a fruity fragrance. The foliage is bright green and glossy. Although it is a little late in flowering, it is very reliable and is one of the better Ramblers. It can also be grown as an extended ground cover. Like the majority of the Ramblers, it flowers only once in the season. ZONES 5–9.

Possibly from Belgium, introduced by Sander, UK, 1912

Parentage unknown

Royal Horticultural Society Award of Garden Merit 1993

'SANDRA'   SandKOR

MODERN, LARGE-FLOWERED/HYBRID TEA, ORANGE-PINK, REPEAT-FLOWERING

The pure salmon blooms of 'Sandra' are high centered and contain 35 petals. There is a slight fragrance. It is an upright, bushy grower that has a good repeat cycle. It is a popular cut-flower variety. ZONES 4–9.

Kordes, Germany, 1981

'Mercedes' × seedling

S

'Sangria'

'Sandringham Centenary'

'SANDRINGHAM CENTENARY'

syns 'Sandringham Century', 'Sandy'

MODERN, LARGE-FLOWERED/HYBRID TEA, ORANGE-PINK, REPEAT-FLOWERING

'Sandringham Centenary' bears deep salmon-pink, semi-double flowers with 22 high-centered petals. The scented blooms are borne singly. The foliage is dark and glossy on an upright, vigorous, healthy plant. This good cut-flower rose is also ideal for bedding. ZONES 4–9.

Wisbech Plant Co., UK, 1980

'Queen Elizabeth' × 'Baccará'

'SANGERHAUSEN'

MODERN, MODERN SHRUB, DEEP PINK, REPEAT-FLOWERING

The large, deep pink, semi-double blooms of this rose are slightly fragrant. It is a medium-sized shrub with large, leathery, wrinkled foliage that is a good specimen shrub. It also looks great planted in groups in borders. ZONES 4–9.

Kordes, Germany, 1938

'Ingar Olsson' × 'Eva'

'SANGRIA'   MEiestho

MODERN, CLUSTER-FLOWERED/FLORIBUNDA, ORANGE-RED, REPEAT-FLOWERING

Although described as a Cluster-flowered Rose in Europe, 'Sangria' is catalogued in

'Sanguinea'

the USA as a forcing variety. The semi-double, orange-red blooms have 15 wavy petals, and are produced in large trusses. It is a vigorous plant with dark green, healthy foliage. ZONES 4–9.

Meilland, France, 1966

'Fire King' × ('Happiness' × 'Independence')

Geneva Gold Medal 1966, The Hague Gold Medal 1966

'SANGUINEA'

syns 'Bengal Cramoisi Double', 'Blood-red China', *Rosa indica cruenta*, 'Rose de Bangale'

OLD, CHINA, DARK RED, REPEAT-FLOWERING

'Sanguinea' bears single velvety, purplish crimson flowers with quilled petals. These can be enjoyed over a long period, as it flowers continuously from summer to autumn. It is a short, twiggy China Rose with a weak, spreading growth habit. ZONES 7–9.

Pre-1824

Parentage unknown

'SANKA'

syn. 'Enchantment'

MODERN, LARGE-FLOWERED/HYBRID TEA, ORANGE BLEND, REPEAT-FLOWERING

The orange-red flowers of this bush have the classic urn-shape that gardeners have come to expect from Large-flowered

Roses. They have paler centers, which fade to light pink as the blooms open fully, and are borne either singly or in small clusters. The upright growth is covered by large, glossy green leaves. ZONES 5–10.

Keisei, Japan, 1986

Parentage unknown

'SANS SOUCI'

MODERN, CLUSTER-FLOWERED/FLORIBUNDA, WHITE, REPEAT-FLOWERING

Little is known of 'Sans Souci' except that it won a gold medal at Baden-Baden in 1996, and that it was bred by Rose Barni of Italy. It can be propagated by budding. ZONES 5–10.

Barni, Italy, 1995

Parentage unknown

Baden-Baden Gold Medal 1996

'SANTA CATALINA'

MODERN, CLUSTER-FLOWERED CLIMBER, LIGHT PINK, REPEAT-FLOWERING

This rose bears clusters of light pink, semi-double flowers containing 18 petals. Occasionally there is a deeper flush of pink in the flowers. The medium-sized blooms have a slight fragrance. ZONES 4–9.

McGredy, UK, 1970

'Paddy McGredy' × 'Heidelberg'

'Sanka'

'SANTA CLAUS'   POUlclaus

MODERN, MINIATURE, DARK RED, REPEAT-FLOWERING

'Santa Claus' has long, shaped buds that open to well-formed, dark red flowers that hold their color in very hot climates even under the full midday sun. The double florets with 15–25 petals have a light fragrance. The blooms can have classical Large-flowered exhibition form, but this is fleeting because of the small number of petals. However, in some cooler climates the form can hold for days. The blooms are borne mainly in spectacularly large clusters of 10–15. The foliage is an attractive, dark glossy green on a vigorous, upright, compact plant. It is nearly always in bloom and has a very fast repeat cycle. Its one draw-back is that it is highly susceptible to spider mites. It looks best as a mass planting, providing a constant display of color. ZONES 5–10.

Olesen, Denmark, 1991

Cluster-flowered seedling × Miniature seedling

'SANTA FÉ'

MODERN, LARGE-FLOWERED/HYBRID TEA, ORANGE-PINK, REPEAT-FLOWERING

The flowers of 'Santa Fé' are deep salmon-pink, double with 25–30 petals, and large. They have paler undersides and there is a moderate perfume. The color is a little deeper than its parent, 'Mischief'. The bush is of average height with mid-green, semi-glossy foliage. 'Santa Fé' is not nearly as good as either parent, and it is no longer available in many countries. ZONES 5–10.

McGredy, UK, 1967

'Mischief' × 'Tropicana'

'SANTA ROSA'

OLD, TEA, DEEP PINK, REPEAT-FLOWERING

Although larger, this rose is said to resemble the rather small and dainty

'Santa Catalina'

'Sanka'

'Santa Fé'

'Saratoga'

'Hermosa'. It inclines to the Chinas, with which it is sometimes classed. The flowers are produced continuously and are rich rosy red, shading to coppery red. The raiser claimed that it had considerable resistance to mildew and rust, however, it is rarely seen nowadays. There is another 'Santa Rosa', a Cluster-flowered Rose introduced in 1954. ZONES 7–9.

Burbank, USA, 1899

'Hermosa' × 'Bon Silène'

'SANTANA' TANklesant
MODERN, LARGE-FLOWERED CLIMBER, MEDIUM RED, REPEAT-FLOWERING

'Santana' bears medium red, semi-double blooms containing 20 petals. The plant has a good repeat cycle, ensuring a steady supply of blooms, but unfortunately there is little scent. The foliage is medium green and glossy on a moderate-sized plant. This is a great rose for walls and pillars. ZONES 4–9.

Tantau, Germany, 1985

Parentage unknown

'SARABANDE' MEIhand, MEIrabande
MODERN, CLUSTER-FLOWERED/FLORIBUNDA, ORANGE-RED, REPEAT-FLOWERING

The flowers of this rose are a brilliant orange-red. The slightly fragrant, semi-double blooms have 13 petals and are borne in large trusses on a low, bushy plant with semi-glossy foliage. It is an ideal bedding variety that makes a good standard. This is one of the great roses from the House of Meilland, as the many

awards testify. **'Climbing Sarabande'** (MEIhandsar; Meilland, France, 1968; Japan Gold Medal 1968), is perfect for pillars and pergolas and looks wonderful against a warm wall. ZONES 4–9.

Meilland, France, 1957

'Cocorico' × 'Moulin Rouge'

Bagatelle Gold Medal 1957, Geneva Gold Medal 1957, Rome Gold Medal 1957, Portland Gold Medal 1958, All-America Rose Selection 1960

'SARAH' MEIframis, MEImafris
syns 'Drottning Silvia', 'Gardin de Bagatelle', 'Jardins de Bagatelle', 'Karl Heinz Hanisch', 'Queen Silvia'
MODERN, LARGE-FLOWERED/HYBRID TEA, WHITE, REPEAT-FLOWERING

This lovely rose bears fragrant, double, creamy blush flowers containing 40 petals. It is a robust plant with dense, mid-green foliage and a well-formed bushy appearance. This is quite a versatile plant—it is a good bedding variety that is equally presentable when grown as a standard. ZONES 4–9.

Meilland, France, 1986

('Queen Elizabeth' × 'Eleg') × MEIdragelac

Geneva Gold Medal 1984, Bagatelle Fragrance Award 1984, Poitiers Gold Medal 1986, Madrid Fragrance Award 1986, Genoa Gold Medal 1987

'SARAH ARNOT'
MODERN, LARGE-FLOWERED/HYBRID TEA, MEDIUM PINK, REPEAT-FLOWERING

The flowers of 'Sarah Arnot' are warm rose pink. The double, high-centered blooms contain 25 petals and have a wonderful fragrance. The foliage is leath-

'Sarah Arnot'

ery on a vigorous and upright plant. This is a reliable bedding variety that can also be shown to advantage on the show bench. ZONES 4–9.

Croll, UK, 1957

'Ena Harkness' × 'Peace'

National Rose Society Gold Medal 1957

'SARAH VAN FLEET'
MODERN, HYBRID RUGOSA, MEDIUM PINK, REPEAT-FLOWERING

The lilac-pink, open, medium-sized flowers of this rose are produced in small clusters and look quite spectacular when in full flower. This is an extremely free-flowering and vigorous shrub, and it is very thorny. The upright habit makes it suitable for the back of the border or as a specimen plant. It is furnished with handsome, wrinkled, dull green foliage and can sometimes be prone to mildew and rust in autumn. It has virtually no fragrance and does not set hips, which is unusual for a Hybrid Rugosa. The plethora of large sharp thorns make it a good hedge to discourage intruders. ZONES 4–9.

Van Fleet, USA, 1926

Reported to be Rosa rugosa × 'My Maryland'

'SARATOGA'
MODERN, CLUSTER-FLOWERED/FLORIBUNDA, WHITE, REPEAT-FLOWERING

This popular rose has ovoid buds opening into large white blooms that are borne in small clusters. The double flowers are 4 in (10 cm) wide, have 33 petals and are reminiscent of gardenias. There is a lovely fragrance. It is a vigorous, bushy, short grower with glossy, leathery foliage that makes a good bedding rose or standard. ZONES 4–9.

Boerner, USA, 1963

'White Bouquet' × 'Princess White'

All-America Rose Selection 1964

'Sarah van Fleet'

'Santana'

'Sarabande'

'Climbing Sarabande'

S

'SATCHMO'

MODERN, CLUSTER-FLOWERED/FLORIBUNDA,
ORANGE-RED, REPEAT-FLOWERING

The brilliant scarlet, double flowers of
'Satchmo' contain 25 petals, and are
borne in small clusters. They have a
slight fragrance. The foliage is dark and
leathery on a plant with a bushy habit
and a good repeat cycle. It is suitable as a
bedding rose and also looks effective as a
standard. It was named for the great jazz
man Louis Armstrong, who died in 1971.
ZONES 4–9.

McGredy, UK, 1970

'Evelyn Fison' × 'Diamant'

Golden Rose of The Hague 1975

'SATELLITE'   DELsatel

MODERN, LARGE-FLOWERED/HYBRID TEA,
ORANGE-RED, REPEAT-FLOWERING

'Satellite' bears large, orange-red, double
blooms that contain 28 petals. The
medium-sized flowers are fragrant. The

'Scarlet Knight'

'Scabrosa'

foliage is mid-green and semi-glossy on a
healthy plant with a good repeat cycle. It
is a reliable bedding rose. ZONES 4–9.

Delbard, France, 1982

(['Tropicana' × 'Samouri'] × ['Tropicana' ×
('Rome Glory' × 'Impeccable')]) × 'Grenada'

'SATINA'   TANinat

syn. 'Silky Cloud'

MODERN, MODERN SHRUB, MEDIUM PINK,
REPEAT-FLOWERING

This is a robust, free-flowering shrub
that bears clusters of deep pink, medium-sized, semi-double blooms. They
are only slightly fragrant. It is a rounded
plant with lax growth and deep green,
shiny foliage, and is a good subject for
landscape purposes. ZONES 4–9.

Tantau, Germany, 1992

Parentage unknown

'SAVOY HOTEL'   HARvintage

syns 'Integrity', 'Vercors', 'Violette Niestlé'

MODERN, LARGE-FLOWERED/HYBRID TEA, LIGHT
PINK, REPEAT-FLOWERING

The large, light pink flowers of 'Savoy
Hotel' have deeper undersides. The high-

'Scarlet Knight'

'Savoy Hotel'

centered blooms have a slight fragrance.
This is a free-flowering rose with medium-sized, bushy growth and dark
green, semi-glossy, healthy foliage. In
temperate climates it is a first-class bedding rose, and a good choice for grouping in mixed borders. ZONES 4–9.

Harkness, UK, 1989

'Silver Jubilee' × 'Amber Queen'

Dublin Gold Medal 1988, Dortmund Gold Medal
1991, Royal Horticultural Society Award of
Garden Merit 1994, Portland Gold Medal 1998

'SCABROSA'

syns *Rosa rugosa scabrosa*, 'Rugosa
Superba', 'Superba'

MODERN, HYBRID RUGOSA, MAUVE,
REPEAT-FLOWERING

This rose was discovered by Harkness
probably before 1939. It has large,
mauve-pink, single flowers that contain
only 5 petals. They are borne in small
clusters, and the plant is almost always in
bloom. The scent has been described as
being like a carnation. This free-growing
shrub is good as a hedge. The wrinkled
foliage is light green, and in autumn
large, round red hips appear. ZONES 4–9.

Introduced by Harkness, UK, 1950

Parentage unknown

Royal Horticultural Society Award of Garden
Merit 1993

'Satchmo'

'Satellite'

'Scarlet Gem'

'SCARLET GEM'   MEIdo

syn. 'Scarlet Pimpernel'

MODERN, MINIATURE, ORANGE-RED,
REPEAT-FLOWERING

This rose has ovoid buds that open
to give orange-scarlet flowers with 58
petals. They have a lovely cupped form
and a light fragrance, and because of the
high petal count the flowers are quite
long lasting. The foliage is dark glossy
green on a dwarf, compact bush that
grows 12–15 in (30–38 cm) high. This
is a vigorous little grower with attractive
foliage and bloom color. It looks wonderful in a border or when planted in a
container. ZONES 5–10.

Meilland, France, 1961

('Moulin Rouge' × 'Fashion') × ('Perla de
Montserrat' × 'Perla de Alcañada')

'SCARLET KNIGHT'   MEIelec

syn. 'Samourai'

MODERN, LARGE-FLOWERED/HYBRID TEA,
MEDIUM RED, REPEAT-FLOWERING

The crimson-scarlet, double blooms of
'Scarlet Knight' are cupped and slightly
fragrant. It has leathery, dark foliage on
a vigorous plant with an upright, bushy
habit that is a good bedding variety.
'Climbing Scarlet Knight' (syn. 'Climbing Samourai; Jack, Australia, 1972) is a
vigorous rose that is very suitable for
walls and pillars. ZONES 4–9.

Meilland, France, 1966

('Happiness' × 'Independence') × 'Sutter's Gold'

Madrid Gold Medal 1966

'SCARLET MEIDILAND'

MEIkrotal

syn. 'Scarlet Meillandécor'

MODERN, MODERN SHRUB, MEDIUM RED,
REPEAT-FLOWERING

The small, light cherry-red blooms of
this rose have dark carmine-pink undersides. The blooms are semi-double with
20 petals and are borne in large clusters.
There is very little fragrance. This is a
prostrate, spreading plant with dark
green, medium-sized foliage. It is suitable for landscaping, covering low walls
and for hanging baskets. It also makes an
effective ground cover. ZONES 4–9.

Meilland, France, 1987

MEItiraca × 'Clair Matin'

Frankfurt Gold Medal 1989

'SCARLET MOSS'   MORcarlet

MODERN, MINIATURE, MEDIUM RED,
REPEAT-FLOWERING

The flowers on 'Scarlet Moss' are an
intense scarlet-red. The blooms are

semi-double with no scent and are borne in small sprays of 3–10. The foliage is wrinkled and the sepals are very mossy. The plant is an upright, tall bush. While not a true moss Miniature, this rose has been acclaimed as the reddest of them all. Impressive in the garden setting, it provides an eye-catching display, but care must be taken with the thorns. ZONES 4–11.

Moore, USA, 1988

('Dortmund' × miniature Moss seedling) × ('Dortmund' × striped miniature Moss seedling)

'SCARLET PATIO'　KORtingle
MODERN, MINIATURE, MEDIUM RED, REPEAT-FLOWERING

This rose forms a neat and compact bush with very dark green, glossy and disease-resistant foliage. The blooms are an intense scarlet color, and are made up of up to two dozen petals that open flat to show golden stamens. The flowers have excellent substance and last extremely well without fading. They are produced in large, well-spaced clusters. 'Scarlet Patio' is an ideal rose for pots or for small beds and borders; the rich flower color is enhanced by the very glossy leaves. The flower production is high and there is a quick repeat. ZONES 5–10.

Kordes, Germany, 1993

Parentage unknown

'Scarlet Meidiland'

'Scarlet Queen Elizabeth'

'SCARLET QUEEN ELIZABETH'　DICel
MODERN, CLUSTER-FLOWERED/FLORIBUNDA, ORANGE-RED, REPEAT-FLOWERING

'Scarlet Queen Elizabeth' bears clusters of medium-sized flowers of flame scarlet. There is a very delicate scent. The foliage is dark and extremely healthy. It is a useful bedding variety that has a good repeat cycle. ZONES 4–9.

Dickson, UK, 1963

('Korona' × seedling) × 'Queen Elizabeth'

National Rose Society Trial Ground Certificate 1963, Golden Rose of The Hague 1973

'SCARLET SHOWERS'
MODERN, LARGE-FLOWERED CLIMBER, MEDIUM RED, REPEAT-FLOWERING

This sparkling red, repeat-flowering rose with copious dark green, shiny foliage is suitable for walls or pillars. There is very little fragrance. ZONES 4–9.

Gandy, UK, 1980

'Golden Showers' × 'Chrysler Imperial'

'SCARLET SUNBLAZE'
MEIcubasi

syn. 'Scarlet Meillandina'

MODERN, MINIATURE, DARK RED, REPEAT-FLOWERING

Dark velvety red flowers with beautiful contrasting bright yellow stamens make this a spectacular rose. The bloom size is

'Scented Air'

large so it is a contender for the Patio classification. The florets are double with 20 petals and have no fragrance. Bloom production is profuse so this plant is always in color, dazzling visitors to the garden with the massive display of clusters of scarlet (verging on orange) flowers. The repeat cycle is fast on a clean plant that is easy to maintain. The foliage is matt dark green on a compact bush. ZONES 5–10.

Meilland, France, 1982

'Tamango' × ('Baby Bettina' × 'Duchess of Windsor')

'SCENTED AIR'
MODERN, CLUSTER-FLOWERED/FLORIBUNDA, ORANGE-PINK, REPEAT-FLOWERING

This rose has a particularly lovely fragrance. The flowers are large, double and salmon-pink. They are borne in small clusters on a free-flowering, medium-sized bushy plant with hand-some, large, healthy leaves. It is a very good bedding rose. ZONES 4–9.

Dickson, UK, 1965

Seedling of 'Spartan' × 'Queen Elizabeth'

Royal National Rose Society Certificate of Merit 1965, Belfast Gold Medal 1967, Golden Rose of The Hague 1971

'Scarlet Patio'

'Scarlet Sunblaze'

'SCENTIMENTAL'　WEKplapep
MODERN, CLUSTER-FLOWERED/FLORIBUNDA, RED BLEND, REPEAT-FLOWERING

This is a striped Cluster-flowered Rose—the red and pink together create a startling visual impact. It is a bushy, free-flowering, vigorous plant with healthy, large, luxurious foliage. 'Scentimental' is a very modern-looking bedding rose that also makes a good standard. It has a fine fragrance. ZONES 4–9.

Carruth, USA, 1996

'Playboy' × 'Peppermint Twist'

All-America Rose Selection 1997

'SCENTSATIONAL'　SAVascent
MODERN, MINIATURE, MAUVE, REPEAT-FLOWERING

With a name like this you would expect a fabulous fragrance, and you get it! The double, mauve flowers are edged pink with cream undersides. They are borne one to a stem and have a high centered form suitable for exhibition. In spite of the low petal count, the form is main-tained for days. When fully open the blooms have magnificent golden stamens providing a beautiful contrast to the mauve reflexed petals. The foliage is semi-glossy, mid-green with only a few

'Scentimental'

S

'Schoolgirl'

'Schoener's Nutkana'

prickles on the stems. It is an upright, vigorous bush that has a tendency to spread in warmer climates. The hybridizer, Harm Saville, used 'Lavender Jade' with its heavy Damask fragrance to re-introduce fragrance into his Miniatures. It is suitable for hot climates. ZONES 5–11.

Saville, USA, 1995

'Lavender Jade' × 'Silverado'

'SCEPTER'D ISLE'   AUSland
MODERN, MODERN SHRUB, LIGHT PINK, REPEAT-FLOWERING

This rose is also classified as an English Rose. It bears large, light pink, double blooms that have a lovely scent. It is a shrubby plant with a good repeat cycle for large borders. ZONES 4–9.

Austin, UK, 1996

Parentage unknown

'SCHARLACHGLUT'
syns 'Scarlet Fire', 'Scarlet Glow'
MODERN, MODERN SHRUB, DARK RED

The bright scarlet-crimson flowers of this variety make a real splash of brilliant color in mid-summer. The blooms are large, open and semi-double. There is a crop of large, orange-red, round hips in autumn, making it an attractive plant all year round. It is a rampant, free-growing shrub with a slightly lax habit. The ample foliage is dark green and healthy. Although it flowers only once, it is a good subject in large borders. ZONES 4–9.

Kordes, Germany, 1952

'Poinsettia' × 'Alika'

Royal Horticultural Society Award of Garden Merit 1993

'Schneezwerg'

'SCHERZO'   MEIpuma
MODERN, CLUSTER-FLOWERED/FLORIBUNDA, RED BLEND, REPEAT-FLOWERING

The flowers of 'Scherzo' are bright scarlet with a white and crimson reverse. The double blooms contain 40 petals and are borne in large clusters. They have very little perfume. The foliage is dark green on a bushy plant with a good repeat cycle. This is a reliable bedding plant that also makes a well-formed standard. ZONES 4–9.

Meilland, France, 1975

'Tamango' × 'Frenzy'

Belfast Gold Medal 1975

'SCHNEELICHT'
MODERN, HYBRID RUGOSA, WHITE, REPEAT-FLOWERING

This rose has very large, pure white, single blooms that are borne in clusters. They are slightly fragrant. It is a very vigorous climbing plant with an abundance of thorns, making it an ideal subject for planting as an impenetrable hedge. The plant is very hardy and floriferous and has been successfully used as a ground cover. The name means 'snow light'. ZONES 4–10.

Geschwind, Hungary, 1894

Rosa rugosa × Rosa phoenicea

'SCHNEESTURM'   TANmurse
syn. 'Blenheim'
MODERN, MODERN SHRUB, WHITE, REPEAT-FLOWERING

This rose bears large clusters of lightly fragrant, small, white and pink flowers. It is a healthy plant for the smaller garden

'Schneewalzer'

and is also useful on banks and borders, where it forms an effective ground cover. In a large container, and for a year or two in a sizeable hanging basket, it is particularly attractive. ZONES 4–9.

Tantau, Germany, 1990

Parentage unknown

Royal National Rose Society President's International Trophy 1992

'SCHNEEWALZER'   TANrezlaw
syn. 'Snow Waltz'
MODERN, LARGE-FLOWERED CLIMBER, WHITE

The oval buds of this rose open to large, double white flowers. They have a classic Large-flowered form and the outer petals curl back when fully open; there is some cream shading at the center of the blooms. Borne singly or in small clusters, the flowers appear on upright growth amid the mid-green foliage. ZONES 5–10.

Tantau, Germany, 1987

Parentage unknown

'SCHNEEZWERG'
syns 'Snow Dwarf', 'Snowdwarf'
MODERN, HYBRID RUGOSA, WHITE, REPEAT-FLOWERING

Snow white flowers with golden stamens are the hallmark of this semi-double rose. The weatherproof blooms are borne from summer through to autumn in small clusters of 3–10 on strong stems. The foliage is typically glossy, disease resistant and rugosa-like on a vigorous, medium-sized bush growing to a height of about 3 ft (1 m). It has some spreading characteristics. If dead blooms are not removed during the growing season, attractive orange hips appear that make for an usual display of blooms and hips in autumn. ZONES 4–10.

Lambert, Germany, 1912

Possibly Rosa rugosa × hybrid of a Polyantha

Royal Horticultural Society Award of Garden Merit 1993

'Scharlachglut'

'SCHOENER'S NUTKANA'
MODERN, MODERN SHRUB, MEDIUM PINK

The fragrant, single-petalled flowers of this rose are a clear cerise-rose pink and 4 in (10 cm) in diameter. The foliage is medium green and the canes are almost thornless. Its growing habit is dominated by arching canes on a vigorous bush that reaches about 6 ft (1.8 m) high and 3 ft (1 m) wide. This versatile rose can tolerate poor soil conditions, shady areas in the garden and cold winters. ZONES 4–10.

Schoener, USA, 1930

Rosa nutkana × 'Paul Neyron'

'SCHOOLGIRL'
MODERN, LARGE-FLOWERED CLIMBER, APRICOT BLEND, REPEAT-FLOWERING

The large flowers of this rose reach 4 in (10 cm) across. They have extremely beautiful form and are apricot-orange, a rare color in climbers. The blooms are strongly fragrant and weatherproof. It has a stiff, vigorous growth habit and reaches a height of about 10 ft (3 m). The foliage is rather sparse and poorly covers the plant. 'Schoolgirl' can be successfully used either as a pillar or climber for a fence, wall or trellis, and it can be cultivated in a wide range of soils and climates. ZONES 5–10.

McGredy, UK, 1964

'Coral Dawn' × 'Belle Blonde'

'SCHWARZE MADONNA'
KORschwama
syns 'Barry Fearn', 'Black Madonna'
MODERN, LARGE-FLOWERED/HYBRID TEA, DARK RED, REPEAT-FLOWERING

This is a very dark crimson rose with a classic shape but little scent. The healthy foliage clothes a plant of moderate vigor. It is a good bedding variety and is also popular as a cut flower. ZONES 4–9.

Kordes, Germany, 1992

Parentage unknown

'Scherzo'

'Scharlachglut'

'Schwarze Madonna'

S

'SCHWEIZER GOLD'

syn. 'Swiss Gold'

**MODERN, LARGE-FLOWERED/HYBRID TEA, LIGHT
YELLOW, REPEAT-FLOWERING**

The ovoid buds of this rose open to light
yellow flowers with deeper centers. The
fragrant, double florets are borne singly
on long, straight, strong stems that are
suitable for exhibition. The foliage is
large, light green and matt on a vigorous,
compact bush. **ZONES 4–9.**

Kordes, Germany, 1975

'Peer Gynt' × 'King's Ransom'

Baden-Baden Gold Medal 1972

'SCORCHER'

MODERN, LARGE-FLOWERED CLIMBER, DARK RED

The lightly fragrant flowers of this
rose can range from a brilliant scarlet-

'Schweizer Gold'

'Sea Foam'

'Scrabo'

crimson to a deep strawberry or cherry
red. The early season bloom is magnificent, but there are only a few later
flushes. The florets are semi-double and
4 in (10 cm) across. Large, wrinkled foliage adorns the vigorous bush, which can
be trained as a climber or pillar reaching
about 10 ft (3 m) high. Hybridized by
one of Australia's most distinguished
breeders of the first half of the twentieth
century, 'Scorcher' may well have an
honored place in the hearts of many
Aussies despite fierce competition in this
classification from later introductions
such as 'Altissimo' or 'Danse du Feu'.
'Scorcher' is a cheerful addition to any
garden. **ZONES 5–10.**

Clark, Australia, 1922

'Mme Abel Chatenay' × seedling

'SCRABO'

**MODERN, CLUSTER-FLOWERED/FLORIBUNDA,
ORANGE-PINK, REPEAT-FLOWERING**

The flowers of this variety are crimson-
pink with salmon hues and a yellowish
base. The strongly perfumed, double
blooms have classic high centers and are
borne in medium-sized clusters. When
they are fully open the blooms tend to
take a flat form, and show off their delightful stamens. The foliage is light
green on a plant of medium height.
Regretfully, competition in this color
class for Cluster-flowered Roses has become fierce and the popularity of this
rose has waned. **ZONES 4–10.**

Dickson, UK, 1968

'Celebration' × 'Elizabeth of Glamis'

'Scorcher'

'Scorcher'

'SEA FOAM'

**MODERN, MODERN SHRUB, WHITE,
REPEAT-FLOWERING**

The flowers of this rose are white to
cream and are borne in small clusters.
The double florets have a delicate
fragrance. The foliage is small, glossy and
dark green on a very vigorous plant that
tends to climb or trail, or is just semi-
prostrate on the ground. It has been used
extensively as a ground cover, as the
canes are rarely longer than about 3 ft
(1 m); this is not enough to be a true
climber, but it can be used as a weeping
standard. The blooms cannot sustain bad
weather conditions and this rose is more
suitable for warmer climates with low
rainfall. There is another 'Sea Foam',
bred by William Paul in 1919, which is
said to be a seedling of 'Mermaid'.
ZONES 5–11.

Schwartz, USA, 1964

(['White Dawn' × 'Pinocchio'] × ['White Dawn' ×
'Pinocchio']) × ('White Dawn' × 'Pinocchio')

Rome Gold Medal 1963, American Rose Society
David Fuerstenberg Prize 1968

'SEA PEARL'

syn. 'Flower Girl'

**MODERN, CLUSTER-FLOWERED/FLORIBUNDA, PINK
BLEND, REPEAT-FLOWERING**

The long, pointed buds of this rose open
to soft pink flowers with a flushed pink
and yellow reverse. They are 4–5 in
(10–12 cm) across, semi-double with
24 petals, and well formed and come in
clusters or trusses of 5 or more on strong
straight stems. The blooms have a decided Large-flowered form in the early
stages of opening, but they open wide
with a change in color to a blend of orange and salmon-pink with a peach-pink
reverse, fading with age. Eventually they
become flecked with red. Although the
flowers are weatherproof, they are not
sunproof and the delicate coral-pink and
cream colors tend to bleach under the
hot sun. The foliage is dark green on a
tall, upright bush. **ZONES 4–10.**

Dickson, UK, 1964

'Kordes' Perfecta' × 'Montezuma'

Royal National Rose Society Certificate of Merit
1964, Belfast Frizzell Award 1966

'Sea Pearl'

S

'SEABREEZE' LEMsea
MODERN, MINIATURE, MEDIUM PINK,
REPEAT-FLOWERING

This variety has short, pointed buds that
open to pale lilac-pink flowers borne in
Clustered-flowered-like clusters. The
double florets with 35 petals have a light
fragrance. There is always a steady supply
of blooms on a vigorous bush with mid-
green foliage that can be susceptible to
mildew if left unprotected. The flowers
are airy and fluffy and have an informal
decorative form. Their color may vary
greatly depending on the climate, all the
way from a light pink that lasts a long
time and then slowly fades to a foamy
pink, or from pink to white to a dirty
brown. This is a good garden variety in
warm climates. ZONES 5–10.

Lemrow, USA, 1976

'White Fairy' × seedling

'SEAFARER' HARtilion
MODERN, CLUSTER-FLOWERED/FLORIBUNDA,
ORANGE-RED, REPEAT-FLOWERING

This variety has flowers that begin as
dark orange buds and open to reveal
vivid orange-red tints. The large florets
are cupped, double and scented, and are
borne in clusters of 3–5 on short stems.
The blooms are weatherproof. The foliage is mid- to dark green on a compact
bush with red prickles. 'Seafarer' was
named to recognize the work of The
Marine Society, whose founder, Jonas
Hanway, died in 1786. ZONES 4–10.

Harkness, UK, 1986

'Amy Brown' × 'Judy Garland'

'SEAGULL'
MODERN, RAMBLER, WHITE

'Seagull' is a vigorous Rambler with pure
white, semi-double flowers showing
golden stamens. They are borne in clusters and have the characteristic Multiflora perfume. This rose and 'Thalia',
descended from *Rosa multiflora* from
1895, were considered the best white
Ramblers until they were challenged by
those descended from *R. wichuraiana*,
notably 'Sander's White', which were less
susceptible to mildew. ZONES 4–10.

Pritchard, UK, 1907

Rosa multiflora × 'Général Jacqueminot'

Royal Horticultural Society Award of Garden
Merit 1993

'Seaspray'

'Seashell'

'SEALING WAX'
syn. *Rosa moyesii* 'Sealing Wax'
MODERN, MODERN SHRUB, MEDIUM PINK

'Sealing Wax' is one of the best of the
Rosa moyesii hybrids as it produces a
huge crop of bright red, flagon-shaped
hips that persist for a long time. The
flowers, however, are not as spectacular
as those of *R. moyesii*, yet the growth is
more manageable, which makes 'Sealing
Wax' the better rose for a small garden.
This variety likes a cool climate similar
to its natural Himalayan habitat. The
growth can burn in hot climates and it
seems to need higher altitudes to fruit
well. It is a spectacular plant in autumn
and the hips are excellent for indoor displays. ZONES 5–10.

Royal Horticultural Society, UK, 1938

Hybrid of *Rosa moyesii*

'Seagull'

'Seabreeze'

'Sealing Wax'

'SEASHELL' KORshel
MODERN, LARGE-FLOWERED/HYBRID TEA,
ORANGE-PINK, REPEAT-FLOWERING

The short, pointed buds of 'Seashell'
open to burnt orange, double flowers
with 48 petals. In some climates the
blooms tend to be a clear shade of coral-
pink, sometimes deeper at the edges of
the petals and seemingly lit with gold.
They have a light fragrance. The bloom
form has received praise for its beauty—
the frilled petals overlap with the regu-
larity of tiles on a roof. The foliage is
mid-green and fairly disease resistant. It
is an upright, healthy, vigorous bush,
and is easy to grow. ZONES 4–10.

Kordes, Germany, 1976

Seedling × 'Colour Wonder'

All-America Rose Selection 1976

'SEASPRAY' MACnew
MODERN, MINIATURE, PINK BLEND,
REPEAT-FLOWERING

'Seaspray' has pale pink semi-double
flowers with a red flush towards the petal
edges. They have a strong fragrance. The
blooms tend to come in clusters on a
low, spreading plant covered with bright
green foliage. The flowers are plentiful
and the plant is easy to maintain and
is always clean and healthy. In some
climates the color can be exquisite—a
unique combination of palest pink
flushed darker pink on the edges of the
petals. It can be used as a ground cover
as it is profuse in bloom on strong, lateral canes. ZONES 5–10.

McGredy, New Zealand, 1982

'Anytime' × 'Moana'

S

'Selfridges'

'Seliata'

'Senator Burda'

'SEATTLE SCENTSATION'

SAVaseat

MODERN, MINIATURE, PINK BLEND, REPEAT-FLOWERING

'Seattle Scentsation' has flowers that are a delightful mixture of yellow, apricot and pink. The double florets contain 15–25 petals and are very fragrant, and they are borne both singly and in small clusters. The color has been described as mouth-watering, but it is less tolerant of heat and there is some fading to washed pink. The foliage is dark, semi-glossy green on a tall, upright, vigorous bush with no prickles. This is the second in the fragrant series introduced by Harm Saville and has more perfume than 'Scentsational'. The bloom form is not of exhibition quality—it has sufficient petals but less substance than its sister seedling. ZONES 5–10.

Saville, USA, 1996

'Lavender Jade' × 'New Zealand'

'SEBBASTIAN KNEIPP'

KORpastato

syn. 'Amoretto'

MODERN, LARGE-FLOWERED/HYBRID TEA, APRICOT BLEND, REPEAT-FLOWERING

The pale apricot-pink flowers of this rose open from plump and pointed buds in summer. They are either borne singly or in clusters of up to three; the many petals are arranged to give a confused center, which is a much darker color than the reflexed outer petals when fully open. The dark foliage makes an attractive foil to these bright blooms. ZONES 5–10.

Kordes, Germany, 1997

Parentage unknown

'SECRET'   HILaroma

MODERN, LARGE-FLOWERED/HYBRID TEA, PINK BLEND, REPEAT-FLOWERING

The seductively fragrant, light pink flowers of this rose are edged with deep pink. The large, double blooms contain 26–40 petals and are borne singly on strong, straight stems. They have classic Large-flowered form with high symmetrical centers, and are suitable for cutting or exhibition. The blooms are attractive at all stages. The foliage is mid-green and semi-glossy on a tall bush. The plant, which derives its vigor from the award-winning seed parent 'Pristine', has a super fragrance that never fails to attract visitors to the garden. It prefers cooler climates. ZONES 4–10.

Tracy, USA, 1992

'Pristine' × 'Friendship'

All-America Rose Selection 1994

'Sebbastian Kneipp'

'SELFRIDGES'   KORpriwa

syn. 'Berolina'

MODERN, LARGE-FLOWERED/HYBRID TEA, DEEP YELLOW, REPEAT-FLOWERING

The amber-yellow flowers on 'Selfridges', which open from long pointed buds, deepen in color as the blooms age. The large florets have 35 petals and good high-centered form. There is a sweet Tea fragrance. The foliage is semi-glossy green and disease resistant. This is an extremely vigorous plant growing to a height of 7–10 ft (2–3 m). Large canes develop each year and will not produce flowers until the next season. This rose should be treated as a shrub and pruned more severely to produce better flowering results. ZONES 4–10.

Kordes, Germany, 1984

Parentage unknown

Anerkannte Deutsche Rose 1986

'SELIATA'

MODERN, LARGE-FLOWERED/HYBRID TEA, RED BLEND, REPEAT-FLOWERING

The growth of this rose is medium to tall and upright, and covered with glossy dark green leaves. The double flowers are usually produced one to a stem and have 20–25 rich orange-red petals. They emerge from shapely buds and there is a yellow base to the petals. 'Seliata' is slightly vulnerable to black spot. It is mainly available in Australia only, and is seldom seen in gardens. It is, however, quite a good rose: a profuse repeat-bloomer with flowers that are suitable for cutting. ZONES 5–10.

1986

Parentage unknown

'SENATOR BURDA'   MEIvestal

syns 'Dreams Come True', 'Spirit of Youth', 'Victor Hugo'

MODERN, LARGE-FLOWERED/HYBRID TEA, DARK RED, REPEAT-FLOWERING

This rose has brilliant currant-red flowers that are borne one bloom to a stem. They are large and double, containing 26–40 petals, and there is a strong fragrance. The foliage is large, mid-green and semi-glossy on a vigorous, upright, tall plant. The bloom production is excellent and the long-stemmed flowers are suitable for cutting or exhibition. ZONES 5–10.

Meilland, France, 1988

('Karl Herst' × ['Royal Velvet' × 'Suspense']) × 'Erotika'

L'Haÿ Fragrance Award 1985

'SÉNÉGAL'

MODERN, LARGE-FLOWERED CLIMBER, DARK RED, REPEAT-FLOWERING

The very dark red flowers on this variety are borne on an extremely vigorous bush that can reach 10 ft (3 m) high. 'Sénégal' has all but disappeared from commerce, but it can still be located in many French rose gardens. ZONES 5–10.

Mallerin, France, 1944

Parentage unknown

'SEQUOIA GOLD'   MORsegold

MODERN, MINIATURE, MEDIUM YELLOW, REPEAT-FLOWERING

The flowers of this rose are a bright medium yellow fading with age to a lighter yellow. The florets are double with 30 petals and have a fruity fragrance. They have typical high-pointed centers suitable for exhibition and come in small clusters of 3–7 flowers. The foliage is medium glossy green on a plant with a low-growing, spreading habit. Because the bloom cycle is fast, the plant is covered with blooms all season long. In the heat of summer, the color can fade rather rapidly. This rose was named to celebrate the 50th anniversary of the establishment of the Sequoia Nursery in Visalia, California. ZONES 5–11.

Moore, USA, 1986

('Little Darling' × 'Lemon Delight') × 'Gold Badge'

American Rose Society Award of Excellence 1987

'Sequoia Gold'

'Sexy Rexy'

'Shakespeare Festival'

'SERRATIPETALA'

syns 'Fimbriata à Pétales Frangés', *Rosa chinensis serratipetala*, 'Rose Oeillet de Saint Arquey Vilfray'

OLD, CHINA, PINK BLEND, REPEAT-FLOWERING

This is a very unusual rose, as it has the usual sparse China growth but is considerably taller and bushier. The flowers are carnation-like with fringed and serrated petals. They repeat throughout the season, but the blooms are fewer and smaller in the later months. The flowers can vary in color from deep red to pink in cool weather. Attributed to Jacques but 'rediscovered' in France in 1912, this rose was promoted with great *eclat*. It is generally described as a curiosity, but it is well worth a place in the garden. However, the Grootendorst range of Hybrid Rugosas, with similar carnation-type flowers, are better. ZONES 7–9.

Jacques, France, 1831

Parentage unknown

'SEVEN SEAS'

MODERN, CLUSTER-FLOWERED/FLORIBUNDA, MAUVE, REPEAT-FLOWERING

This rose has large, lilac flowers with a pleasing fragrance. The double blooms are up to 4 in (10 cm) in diameter; they contain 26 petals and are borne in small trusses. The foliage is large, glossy matt green on a low, compact-growing plant. 'Seven Seas' is a great addition to the mauve Cluster-flowered class. Using the pollen parent 'Sterling Silver', the breeder has successfully increased the lower petal count of its seed mother 'Lilac Charm' and still retained the low growth habit of the pollen parent. ZONES 5–10.

Harkness, UK, 1973

'Lilac Charm' × 'Sterling Silver'

Royal National Rose Society Trial Ground Certificate 1970

'Shadow'

'SEVEN SISTERS'

syns *Rosa cathayensis platyphylla*, *R. multiflora platyphylla*

OLD, MISCELLANEOUS, PINK BLEND

This is a form of *Rosa multiflora* with similar growth, larger leaves and bigger double flowers. The trusses can bear up to 7 flowers ranging from deep cerise-purple to pale mauve or even off-white; each flower is a different shade of color and changes as it ages. The growth is very vigorous and it can cover a large area. It is perhaps better on a wall in cooler areas, as it needs some protection from frosts. ZONES 5–9.

Japan, 1817

Parentage unknown

'SEVILLIANA'

MODERN, MODERN SHRUB, PINK BLEND, REPEAT-FLOWERING

The pointed, ovoid buds of this rose open to light claret-rose flowers with a yellow base. The fragrant, semi-double blooms, which contain 15–20 petals, are slightly cupped and are borne in large solid trusses. The foliage is tinted copper on an upright shrub-type bush that reaches about 4 ft (1.2 m) high. The plant is in constant bloom and is winter hardy. If it is left to set fruit, it produces masses of bright red hips. The late Griffith Buck is well known in America for his pioneering work in creating a line of winter-hardy shrubs. ZONES 4–10.

Buck, USA, 1976

('Vera Dalton' × 'Dornröschen') × (['World's Fair' × 'Floradora'] × 'Applejack')

'SEXY REXY' MACrexy

syn. 'Heckenzauber'

MODERN, CLUSTER-FLOWERED/FLORIBUNDA, MEDIUM PINK, REPEAT-FLOWERING

'Sexy Rexy' has medium to light pink flowers that are borne on very strong

'Serratipetala'

straight stems in large clusters. The fragrant, double blooms have 40 petals, and the flower form is more like that of a camellia, opening flat with a nice colorful finish. The trusses last for weeks and the repeat cycle is fast, although for continuous blooming the plant requires some deadheading to stimulate the next bloom cycle. The foliage is small and mid-green on a compact, healthy, disease-resistant bush. This is a great contribution to the development of colorfast, productive and easily maintained Cluster-flowered Roses. ZONES 5–11.

McGredy, New Zealand, 1984

'Seaspray' × 'Dreaming'

New Zealand Gold Medal 1984, Royal National Rose Society Certificate of Merit 1985, Glasgow Gold Medal 1989, Auckland Gold Medal 1990, Portland Gold Medal 1990, Royal Horticultural Society Award of Garden Merit 1993, RNRS James Mason Gold Medal 1996

'SHADOW'

MODERN, LARGE-FLOWERED/HYBRID TEA, DARK RED, REPEAT-FLOWERING

This rose gives a reasonable display of very dark red, strongly perfumed flowers with a rather slow repeat. The bush is of medium height with matt dark green, disease-resistant foliage. Throughout summer, urn-shaped buds open to double blooms that contain up to two dozen petals; the flowers are good for cutting in the bud stage. ZONES 5–10.

Dawson, Australia, 1966

Parentage unknown

'SHAKESPEARE FESTIVAL'

MODERN, MINIATURE, MEDIUM YELLOW, REPEAT-FLOWERING

On this variety, pointed buds open to clear yellow flowers with 45 petals, good exhibition form and a marked tea scent. The flowers tend to be large and have been compared with a zinnia-type bloom

in certain cooler climates. The foliage is matt green on a compact bush. This plant provides a good harvest of blooms on a regular bloom cycle. Unfortunately it is not as popular with American growers as it once was, as other more attractive yellows have appeared since this one was introduced. This rose is the result of a self-pollinated seedling. ZONES 5–11.

Moore, USA, 1979

'Golden Angel' × 'Golden Angel'

'SHANNON' MACnon

MODERN, LARGE-FLOWERED/HYBRID TEA, MEDIUM PINK, REPEAT-FLOWERING

The bright medium pink flowers on 'Shannon' have 58 petals. The blooms are large, to 5 in (12 cm) in diameter, and have a globular form, although on occasions a high-centered bloom may be produced. The foliage is dark and rounded on an upright plant reaching 3–4 ft (1–1.2 m) high. It tends to be a late bloomer and prefers warmer climates, where bloom production is increased. The flowers are long lasting on the bush. The plant should be frequently deadheaded to encourage the next bloom cycle. ZONES 5–11.

McGredy, UK, 1965

'Queen Elizabeth' × 'McGredy's Yellow'

'Seven Sisters'

'Shannon'

'SHARIFA ASMA'   AUSreef
syn. 'Sharifa'

MODERN, MODERN SHRUB, LIGHT PINK,
REPEAT-FLOWERING

The flowers of this rose are a nearly
translucent blush pink with just a touch
of gold at the base. They are shallow
cupped with a petal count somewhere
between 50–100, and show a perfect
rosette-like form at the fully opened
stage. It has a honey-like fragrance. The
petals can quickly dehydrate under hot,
sunny conditions. The foliage is mid-
green on a short, upright plant reaching
a height of 4 ft (1.2 m). It was named for
a member of the Omani royal family.
ZONES 4–10.

Austin, UK, 1989

'Mary Rose' × 'Admired Miranda'

'SHARON LOUISE'

MODERN, LARGE-FLOWERED/HYBRID TEA, WHITE,
REPEAT-FLOWERING

The ovoid buds of 'Sharon Louise' open
to near white, double flowers with a pale

'Sharon Louise'

'Sheer Bliss'

blush pink center. The delicately fragrant
blooms are borne one to a stem, and
have good flower form suitable for cutting for indoors. Flower production is
profuse and the repeat cycle is fairly fast.
The foliage is dark leathery green on a
vigorous, upright plant that can reach
3–5 ft (1–1.5 m) high. It prefers a warm
and sunny climate, where it will provide
an abundance of bloom, and makes a
neat hedge or border. Good soil is an
advantage in growing this rose, as is a
regular mulch and frequent watering.
ZONES 5–11.

Parkes, Australia, 1968

'Queen Elizabeth' × 'Virgo'

'SHEELAGH BAIRD'

MODERN, POLYANTHA, PINK BLEND,
REPEAT-FLOWERING

The weatherproof flowers of this rose are
shell pink overlaid with rich rose pink
with yellow at the base. The blooms are
full and large and are borne in large
trusses. As is the case with most
Polyanthas, the trusses can become too
heavy for the small diameter stems and
the sprays tend to droop, especially after
a light rain shower. The foliage is medium green on a vigorous, upright plant.
ZONES 4–10.

Cant, UK, 1934

Parentage unknown

'SHEER BLISS'   JACtro

MODERN, LARGE-FLOWERED/HYBRID TEA, WHITE
BLEND, REPEAT-FLOWERING

This variety has urn-shaped flowers
that are white with just a hint of pink. In
cool climates, however, there is a deeper

'Shell Queen'

shade of pink in the centers. The
double florets contain 35 petals and are
large, to 4–5 in (10–12 cm) across. They
have a detectable spicy fragrance. The
exhibition-type blooms are naturally
borne singly on strong straight stems.
The foliage is long, thin and matt on an
upright plant with a spreading habit that
is a vigorous grower, sending up many
stems. Its show-winning perfection has
made this rose popular with florists for
use in wedding bouquets. 'Sheer Bliss'
is one of the many prize-winning roses
hybridized by the late Bill Warriner of
Jackson & Perkins. ZONES 5–10.

Warriner, USA, 1985

'White Masterpiece' × 'Grand Masterpiece'

Japan Gold Medal 1984, All-America Rose
Selection 1987

'SHEER ELEGANCE'   TWObe

MODERN, LARGE-FLOWERED/HYBRID TEA,
ORANGE-PINK, REPEAT-FLOWERING

'Sheer Elegance' has pointed buds that
open to soft pink flowers with dark pink
edges to the petals. The large, cupped,
double florets contain 43 petals, and are
borne singly on strong straight stems.
There is a strong musk fragrance. In
cooler climates the flower form is classical, with the petals reflexing to give a
symmetrical shape to the blooms; in
warm climates the form is not as good,
but this is compensated for by an improvement in the color of the blooms.
The foliage is large, dark green and
glossy on a tall, upright, disease-resistant
plant. An easy rose to grow, it is one of
many All-America Rose Selection Large-
flowered Roses hybridized by Jerry
Twomey from San Diego, California.
ZONES 5–10.

Twomey, USA, 1989

'Pristine' × 'Fortuna'

All-America Rose Selection 1991, Portland Gold
Medal 1994

'Sharifa Asma'

'Sheila's Perfume'

'SHEILA MACQUEEN'

HARwotnext

MODERN, CLUSTER-FLOWERED/FLORIBUNDA,
WHITE, REPEAT-FLOWERING

The unique-colored flowers of this rose
are an unusual chartreuse-green with an
apricot and ginger tint at certain times of
the year, a major reason for growing it.
The 24-petaled blooms, which have a
slight peppery fragrance, come in small
sprays of 3–9 flowers per stem and have a
cupped form. The sparse foliage is semi-
glossy mid-green on an upright plant of
average height. The long-lasting flowers
are excellent for cutting. It is a hardy
plant and can withstand a wide range of
climatic conditions and soils. It has a
lanky habit and needs other plants
around it to hide this. This rose is popular with floral arrangers. ZONES 4–11.

Harkness, UK, 1988

'Greensleeves' × 'Letchworth Garden City'

'SHEILA'S PERFUME'   HARsherry

MODERN, CLUSTER-FLOWERED/FLORIBUNDA,
YELLOW BLEND, REPEAT-FLOWERING

'Sheila's Perfume' has yellow flowers
edged red, with a flower form and size
that could pass for a Large-flowered Rose.
The weatherproof, semi-double blooms
with 20 petals are fragrant. They are
borne singly and in clusters on strong,
short stems. The foliage is dark, semi-
glossy green, often too plentiful and
certainly disease resistant. This medium-
sized compact bush tends to spread in
warm climates, and it is one of the finest
roses ever raised by the breeder. It was
named to honor his wife. ZONES 4–11.

Sheridan, UK, 1985

'Peer Gynt' × ('Daily Sketch' × ['Paddy McGredy'
× 'Prima Ballerina'])

Edland Fragrance Award 1981, Royal National
Rose Society Torridge Award 1991, Glasgow
Silver Medal 1989, Glasgow Fragrance Award
1989

'SHELL QUEEN'

MODERN, LARGE-FLOWERED/HYBRID TEA,
LIGHT PINK, REPEAT-FLOWERING

The double flowers of 'Shell Queen' are
shell pink fading to almost white. The
blooms are borne in small clusters of
3–6 on strong, straight stems and can
have classical form at certain times of the
season. Known as a Grandiflora Rose in
the USA, the plant has no scent. The foliage is mid-green on a tall, upright plant.
This rose is grown mainly in Australia.
ZONES 5–10.

Allen, Australia, 1961

Sport of 'Queen Elizabeth'

'SHELLY'

MODERN, LARGE-FLOWERED/HYBRID TEA,
PINK BLEND, REPEAT-FLOWERING

There is a unique combination of colors
and shades in the flowers of this rose—
pale pink with cyclamen-pink shadings
and a striped reverse of pale pink and
silver. The large, semi-double blooms
contain 20–25 petals with decorative
form. They are borne in sprays of 5–6
and have a light sweet fragrance. The
foliage is dark green, glossy and disease
resistant on a medium-sized, compact
plant bearing slightly hooked prickles.
ZONES 5–10.

Meville, Australia, 1988

Sport of 'Francine'

'SHERI ANNE' MORsheri

MODERN, MINIATURE, ORANGE-RED,
REPEAT-FLOWERING

'Sheri Anne' has long, pointed buds that
reveal beautifully shaped orange-red
flowers with a yellow base to the petals.
The florets are semi-double containing
17 petals and are fragrant. The foliage is
glossy green and leathery on a vigorous,
upright bush. This rose has been used
extensively by breeders all over the world
as it has proven to be an extremely good
parent. Described as one of the pillars of
modern rose breeding from Moore, this
decorative little rose has a delicate touch
of yellow on the reverse of its petals and
will make an enthusiastic follower of all
who grow it because it does well even
without attention. The bloom repeat
cycle is good, but it can get black spot if
left unprotected. 'Sheri Anne' is a major
achievement for Moore, in that its

'Sheri Anne'

'Shona'

parents and grandparents have successfully transmitted their desirable qualities
to all of their offspring. ZONES 5–10.

Moore, USA, 1973

'Little Darling' × 'New Penny'

American Rose Society Award of Excellence 1975

'SHINE ON' DICtalent

syn. 'Just Happy'

MODERN, PATIO/DWARF CLUSTER-FLOWERED,
ORANGE-PINK, REPEAT-FLOWERING

Bright, shapely, weatherproof, orange-
coral blooms of excellent form and substance cover this sturdy bush. It always
performs well, but the flower size qualifies it as a Patio Rose rather than a Miniature. The flower color is vivid and it
shines even on the darkest days. This
rose is certainly one of the best of its
kind introduced to date. Colin Dickson,
who continued the fine work of his
father, Pat Dickson, considers this one
of his best efforts. ZONES 4–10.

Dickson, UK, 1995

'Sweet Magic' × (seedling × 'Mini Pol')

'SHINING HOUR' JACyef

MODERN, LARGE-FLOWERED/HYBRID TEA,
DEEP YELLOW, REPEAT-FLOWERING

The attractive ovoid buds on 'Shining
Hour' open to reveal deep bright yellow,
double flowers containing 33 petals. The
cupped blooms have high symmetrical
centers and a moderate fruity fragrance,
and are borne both one to a stem and in
small sprays of 3–5 flowers. The foliage is
large, dark green and semi-glossy on an
upright bush. Bill Warriner crossed two
of his creations to produce this wonderful rose, which is known as a Grandiflora

'Shocking Blue'

in America. It has retained the colorfast
yellow of the Cluster-flowered 'Sun
Flare' and the tall growth habit of the
seed parent, the Large-flowered
'Sunbright'. ZONES 5–11.

Warriner, USA, 1989

'Sunbright' × 'Sun Flare'

All-America Rose Selection 1991

'SHIRALEE'

MODERN, LARGE-FLOWERED/HYBRID TEA,
YELLOW BLEND, REPEAT-FLOWERING

The flowers of 'Shiralee' are yellow
flushed orange to soft salmon. The
fragrant blooms are extremely large and
can reach 6 in (15 cm) across in moderate climates. They have a good high-
centered form suitable for exhibition and
are also wonderful as cut flowers for indoors. The dark green foliage is disease
resistant and the upright bush grows to
medium height. ZONES 4–10.

Dickson, UK, 1965

Seedling × 'Kordes' Perfecta'

Japan Gold Medal 1964

'SHOCKING BLUE' KORblue

MODERN, CLUSTER-FLOWERED/FLORIBUNDA,
MAUVE, REPEAT-FLOWERING

'Shocking Blue' has heavily perfumed
flowers that are a rich lilac-mauve color.
The double blooms have classic Large-
flowered exhibition form, that is, high
centers with symmetrical outlines. They
are borne in wide sprays against the
backdrop of large, glossy foliage. It is a
very vigorous grower reaching 3–4 ft
(1–1.2 m) tall. This variety has a number
of advantages that somehow contradict
themselves: the color is not as good for
effective contrast against the dark green
foliage, and although it is free flowering
the spent blooms need to be removed to
encourage the next bloom cycle to begin,
otherwise the repeat cycle can be slow.
This rose has been used extensively by

'Shiralee'

other breeders to attempt to transmit its
superior color qualities and growth habit
to their seedlings. ZONES 4–10.

Kordes, Germany, 1974

Seedling × 'Silver Star'

'SHOCKING SKY' KORgenda

MODERN, CLUSTER-FLOWERED/FLORIBUNDA,
MAUVE BLEND, REPEAT-FLOWERING

This rose has firm petals that are deep
crimson. As the flowers unfold, the
uppersides reflect a silver sheen. The
stems are sturdy and the cut flowers long
lasting. It makes a healthy, vigorous
plant of medium height. ZONES 4–9.

Kordes, Germany, 1994

Parentage unknown

'SHONA' DICdrum

MODERN, CLUSTER-FLOWERED/FLORIBUNDA,
ORANGE-PINK, REPEAT-FLOWERING

'Shona' has fragrant, medium coral pink,
double flowers with 23 petals. The
weatherproof blooms are borne in small
tight clusters. The foliage is mid-green
and semi-glossy on a compact bush that
tends to sprawl a little. ZONES 5–10.

Dickson, UK, 1982

'Bangor' × 'Anabell'

Royal National Rose Society Trial Ground
Certificate 1979

'Shining Hour'

S

'Showtime'

'Shot Silk'

'SHOT SILK'
MODERN, LARGE-FLOWERED/HYBRID TEA, PINK
BLEND, REPEAT-FLOWERING

The cherry-cerise flowers on 'Shot Silk' shade to golden yellow at the bases. The fragrant double blooms have 27 petals with classic high centers. This old favorite of rose growers in the early part of the twentieth century has a truly inspired name, for there is something silky about the texture of the petals. This vigorous, upright plant has slightly curled, glossy dark green foliage. In the 1920s, during its greatest popularity, this rose was planted because of the healthy glossy leaves and the novel bloom color. Today's choice of Large-flowered Roses, particularly since the advent of 'Peace' in 1945, has meant that 'Shot Silk' has lost some of its appeal. Nevertheless, it is still grown in some parts of the world. **'Climbing Shot Silk'** (Knight, Australia, 1931; Royal Horticultural Society Award of Garden Merit 1993) can reach 10 ft (3 m) high. Few climbers in this unique color range have both fragrance and healthy foliage. ZONES 5–10.

Dickson, UK, 1924

Seedling of 'Hugh Dickson' × 'Sunstar'

National Rose Society Gold Medal 1923

'SHOW GIRL, CLIMBING'
MODERN, LARGE-FLOWERED CLIMBER, MEDIUM
PINK, REPEAT-FLOWERING

This Climber can reach heights of more than 15 ft (4.5 m). The medium pink

'Climbing Show Girl'

blooms tend to fade in warm, sunny climates. Many growers have declared this sport to be more productive than the original Large-flowered Rose, as the canes are strong, thick and long. In some climates, the bush prefers to grow more canes rather than produce blooms. The foliage has a tendency to suffer from mildew and black spot in damp climates. ZONES 5–11.

Chaffin, USA, 1949

Sport of 'Show Girl'

'SHOWBIZ' TANweieke
syns 'Bernhard Däneke Rose', 'Ingrid Weibull'

MODERN, CLUSTER-FLOWERED/FLORIBUNDA,
MEDIUM RED, REPEAT-FLOWERING

'Showbiz' has bright and bold medium red flowers that are produced in fairly large clusters of 10–30 blooms on very strong basal canes. The semi-double florets with 20 petals have no fragrance. The clusters can last several weeks on the bush before they need to be removed in order to encourage the next cycle. The foliage is dark, glossy green and disease free on a plant with a low, compact habit that reaches 2–4 ft (60 cm–1.2 m) in height. This rose is one of the best choices from the menu for a low-growing red Cluster-flowered Rose with grace, color and poise. ZONES 4–10.

Tantau, Germany, 1981

Parentage unknown

All-America Rose Selection 1985

'Showbiz'

'SHOWER OF GOLD'
MODERN, RAMBLER, MEDIUM YELLOW

This rose is a quarter *Rosa wichuraiana* and three-quarters Large-flowered Rose with a dash of 'Persian Yellow' (*R. foetida*). The fragrant, large, rosette-shaped flowers are deep yellow, fading to white, and appear in clusters. The foliage is glossy and fern-like and the plant, while vigorous, does not repeat-flower. It is readily available in New Zealand, but elsewhere it unfortunately seems to have lost the popularity it enjoyed between the wars. ZONES 5–9.

Paul, UK, 1910

'Jersey Beauty' × 'Instituteur Sirdey'

'SHOWTIME'
MODERN, LARGE-FLOWERED/HYBRID TEA,
MEDIUM PINK, REPEAT-FLOWERING

The flowers of this rose are true medium pink with a lovely fruity fragrance. The double blooms have high centers with good overall symmetry of form and are suitable for exhibition. The flower form can hold for days, both in the garden or in the home. The plant grows to about 4–6 ft (1.2–1.8 m) tall depending on the climate, and the foliage is glossy green, leathery in texture and disease resistant. 'Showtime' prefers full sun, fertile soil and plenty of water, and rewards these conditions with frequent blooms. It is a favorite among many American exhibitors. ZONES 5–10.

Lindquist, USA, 1969

'Kordes' Perfecta' × 'Granada'

'SHREVEPORT' KORpesh
MODERN, LARGE-FLOWERED/HYBRID TEA,
ORANGE BLEND, REPEAT-FLOWERING

The ovoid buds of this rose open to reveal blended orange and salmon-pink

'Shreveport'

flowers with 50 petals. The blooms have good symmetrical form with high centers and are generally borne on strong, straight stems in small clusters of 3–5 flowers. There is a light Tea scent. The foliage is large and mid-green and has small prickles that are hooked downwards. The plant, which is known as a Grandiflora in America, is tall and upright. It was named to honor the city of Shreveport, which is home to the American Rose Society and its extensive rose gardens. ZONES 5–11.

Kordes, Germany, 1981

'Zorina' × 'Uwe Seeler'

All-America Rose Selection 1982

'SHROPSHIRE LASS'
MODERN, MODERN SHRUB, LIGHT PINK

'Shropshire Lass' has fragrant, single-petalled blooms that are blushed pink. They are large, to 5 in (12 cm) across. This rose grows like a large shrub or climber but is more compact in habit, and has lush, mid-green foliage. It is tough and winter hardy. In earlier times it would have been classified as an Alba; however, the breeder has chosen to classify it along with his English Roses although it is not repeat-flowering. With this 1968 creation, David Austin honors the English countryside where he has lived all his life. ZONES 4–10.

Austin, UK, 1968

'Mme Butterfly' × 'Mme Legras St Germain'

'SI'
MODERN, MINIATURE, WHITE, REPEAT-FLOWERING

This rose has the smallest flowers of any known Miniature and qualifies as the first member of the micro-miniature class. The tiny pink buds are no larger than a grain of wheat and open to tiny semi-double, white to light pink flowers. It has a dwarf habit and is disease resistant, and is best planted in a container as its

'Si'

'Shropshire Lass'

'Silva' (KEIromo)

unbelievable beauty and charm are a delightful novelty. The tiny florets are a favorite with floral arrangers and add petiteness and delicacy to a design. 'Si' is still grown extensively throughout the world although it is now over 40 years old. ZONES 5–10.

Dot, Spain, 1957

'Perla de Monsterrat' × ('Anny' × 'Tom Thumb')

'SIGNATURE'   JACnor
MODERN, LARGE-FLOWERED/HYBRID TEA, DEEP PINK, REPEAT-FLOWERING

The sharply pointed, wine red buds on this variety slowly unfurl into deep pink blooms with impeccable high centers. This is a splendid symmetrical, three-dimensional rose worthy of competing with all the best show winners. The petal sheen bounces the color outwards in a dazzling display of color chrome and hue. The large florets are 5 in (12 cm) in diameter, double with 50 petals and have a fruity fragrance. The foliage is large, dark green and somewhat susceptible to mildew and black spot if left unprotected, on a vigorous, medium-sized, compact bush. In cool wet climates the foliage can drop off if it becomes diseased. Praised for its qualities of color, size and form, 'Signature' can proudly take its place along with 'Peace' in the evolutionary development of high-quality Large-flowered Roses. ZONES 5–11.

Warriner, USA, 1996

'Honor' × 'First Federal Renaissance'

'SIGNORA'
syn. 'Signora Piero Puricelli'
MODERN, LARGE-FLOWERED/HYBRID TEA, ORANGE BLEND, REPEAT-FLOWERING

The long, pointed buds of this rose open to orange-apricot blooms that slowly become suffused with gold while the outer petals turn magenta-pink. The double blooms contain 27 petals, are cupped and have a tea fragrance. The foliage is glossy dark green, sometimes red tinted, on a very vigorous, upright plant. The breeder also created two other popular roses, the deep pink 'Gloria di Roma' and the huge dawn pink 'Eterna Giovanezza'. ZONES 5–11.

Aicardi, Italy, 1936

'Julian Potin' × 'Sensation'

Portland Gold Medal 1937

'SILENT NIGHT'
MODERN, LARGE-FLOWERED/HYBRID TEA, YELLOW BLEND, REPEAT-FLOWERING

'Silent Night' has creamy yellow flowers overlaid with soft salmon-pink. The double, well-formed blooms have a pleasant fragrance, and are borne either one to a stem or in small clusters. The foliage is glossy green on a very attractive medium-sized bush with excellent bloom production throughout the growing season. The name has nothing whatsoever to do with the famous Christmas carol; in fact, McGredy's sponsor for his 1969 introduction was a British mattress maker. ZONES 5–10.

McGredy, UK, 1969

'Daily Sketch' × 'Hassan'

Geneva Gold Medal 1969

'SILK BUTTON'   KORzeito
MODERN, MINIATURE, WHITE, REPEAT-FLOWERING

This tall-growing Miniature Rose is vigorous and healthy, and produces many flowers on its long, slender stems. The rose is therefore popular among flower arrangers and exhibitors. The buds unfold to cup-shaped, cream young flowers that eventually open fully to tight-centered rosettes. Unfortunately, there is no fragrance. Flowers like this are always useful in the garden to lighten up and relieve brighter colors. ZONES 4–9.

Kordes, Germany, 1991

Seedling × 'Europa'

'SILK HAT'   AROsilha, AROsilma
MODERN, LARGE-FLOWERED/HYBRID TEA, MAUVE, REPEAT-FLOWERING

The red-purple flowers of 'Silk Hat' have cream undersides, creating almost

'Silva' (Meilland)

a fuchsia petal front look. The double blooms have 45 petals and are symmetrically formed with high centers. The large petal count means the blooms have good staying power, lasting weeks in moderate climates. They are borne singly on strong straight stems and are weatherproof. There is a light perfume. The foliage is large and matt mid-green on a medium-sized, compact bush. The plant is slow to establish but, once settled, the flower production is good to excellent. ZONES 5–10.

Christensen, USA, 1986

'Ivory Tower' × ('Night 'n' Day' × 'Plain Talk')

'SILVA'   MEIcham
MODERN, LARGE-FLOWERED/HYBRID TEA, PINK BLEND, REPEAT-FLOWERING

When the long, pointed buds of this rose open, they reveal yellowish salmon shaded, double flowers. The well-formed, lightly fragrant blooms have 38 petals with symmetrical high centers and are borne singly, with an occasional small spray, on long, straight, strong stems. The foliage is firm, dark and glossy green on a vigorous, upright plant. Its free-flowering habit over the long growing season makes 'Silva' an ideal

'Silent Night'

'Silk Hat'

candidate for the garden. There is another 'Silva' (KEIromo) which is an orange-pink Large-flowered Rose. ZONES 5–10.

Meilland, France, 1964

'Peace' × 'Confidence'

The Hague Gold Medal 1964, Royal National Rose Society Trial Ground Certificate 1967

'SILVER ANNIVERSARY'
JAClav
syn. 'Heather'
MODERN, LARGE-FLOWERED/HYBRID TEA, MAUVE, REPEAT-FLOWERING

This variety has medium lavender flowers with a hint of yellow at the bases. The double, urn-shaped, exhibition-type blooms have 25–30 petals and a heavy damask fragrance. They are borne singly on long, straight, sturdy stems. The foliage is large and dark green on a tall, upright plant that is susceptible to mildew if left unprotected. There is another rose by the same name from Olesen of Denmark introduced in 1994; it is a lovely white Large-flowered Rose with 41 petals and the flowers tend to come in small clusters. ZONES 5–10.

Christensen, USA, 1990

'Crystalline' × 'Shocking Blue'

'Signature'

'SILVER JUBILEE'
MODERN, LARGE-FLOWERED/HYBRID TEA,
PINK BLEND, REPEAT-FLOWERING

The fragrant flowers on this famous rose are silvery pink with darker undersides. The double blooms with 33 petals have perfect form and high centers that unfurl gracefully to reveal a portrait in absolute symmetry. They are large, to about 5 in (12 cm) in diameter in cool climates. The foliage is glossy dark green on a vigorous, medium-sized bush with very good bloom production. This rose has received praise worldwide for its beauty in color, form and vigor. It was named to mark the 25th anniversary of the reign of Queen Elizabeth II. There is no doubt that this was Alex Cocker's greatest masterpiece. ZONES 5–10.

Cocker, UK, 1978

(['Highlight' × 'Colour Wonder'] × ['Parkdirektor Riggers' × 'Piccadilly']) × 'Mischief'

Royal National Rose Society President's International Trophy 1977, Belfast Gold Medal 1980, Portland Gold Medal 1981, James Mason Gold Medal 1985, Royal Horticultural Society Award of Garden Merit 1993

'SILVER LINING'
MODERN, LARGE-FLOWERED/HYBRID TEA,
PINK BLEND, REPEAT-FLOWERING

The variations in color of the silvery pink flowers on 'Silver Lining' are caused by

'Silver Jubilee'

'Silver Lining'

the climate. The color can range from brighter colors to bicolors of pink and silver, most people finding the color very attractive. The double blooms contain 30 petals and are quite large, at 5 in (12 cm) across. They are fragrant and have classic Large-flowered form with good symmetry and good overall shape. The foliage is dark green and polished on a vigorous, medium-sized bush. ZONES 5–10.

Dickson, UK, 1958

'Karl Herbst' × seedling of 'Eden Rose'

National Rose Society Gold Medal 1958, Portland Gold Medal 1964

'SILVER MOON'
MODERN, LARGE-FLOWERED CLIMBER, WHITE

The long, pointed buds of this rose open to reveal creamy white flowers with an amber base and darker stamens. The blooms are semi-double with 20 petals, large to 5 in (12 cm) across and have a light fragrance. The foliage is large, leathery and glossy green on a very vigorous plant that easily grows to 20 ft (6 m) high. In spite of providing only one bloom cycle, it is worth the space for the magnificent early season flowers. ZONES 4–10.

Van Fleet, USA, 1910

(Rosa wichuraiana × 'Devoniensis') × R. laevigata

'Simon Robinson'

'Silver Moon'

'SILVER STAR'   KORbido
MODERN, LARGE-FLOWERED/HYBRID TEA, MAUVE,
REPEAT-FLOWERING

'Silver Star' has lovely lavender flowers with a pleasing perfume. The double, well-formed blooms are large, to about 5 in (12 cm) in diameter. They tend to open quite quickly and fade rather rapidly, especially in the heat. The foliage is dark green on a medium-sized, compact bush. This rose makes an ideal garden planting, but often sulks if temperatures soar. ZONES 5–10.

Kordes, Germany, 1966

'Sterling Silver' × seedling of 'Magenta'

Belfast Fragrance Award 1968

'SILVER WEDDING'
MODERN, LARGE-FLOWERED/HYBRID TEA, MAUVE,
REPEAT-FLOWERING

This variety has delicately fragrant flowers that are lavender-lilac fading with age to soft lilac. The large blooms are 4 in (10 cm) across and cupped and are borne mainly in small clusters. The foliage is semi-glossy and mid-green on an upright, vigorous bush. There are two other roses with the same name: a 1921 sport of 'Ophelia' that was introduced by the Amling Company in the USA, and a Large-flowered Rose with pearly white flowers introduced by Gregory in the UK in 1976. ZONES 5–10.

Leenders, The Netherlands, 1965

'Sterling Silver' × seedling

'SILVERADO'   AROgrewod
MODERN, LARGE-FLOWERED/HYBRID TEA, MAUVE,
REPEAT-FLOWERING

'Silverado' has soft silver flowers blushed ruby at the edges of the petals and with

'Simplex'

white undersides. The eye-catching color is often compared with 'Paradise'. The double florets contain 28 petals and have high centers and excellent symmetry. The exhibition-type blooms are borne singly on very strong straight stems, but the form can be fleeting as the blooms tend to open too fast. In spring the flowers are large, but they tend to shrink down in size as the day-time temperatures rise. There is a light fragrance. The foliage is a lovely dark lush green on a tall, vigorous, upright bush bearing large prickles that are hooked downwards. ZONES 5–11.

Christensen, USA, 1987

('Ivory Tower' × 'Angel Face') × 'Paradise'

'SILVERHILL'   TALsilver
MODERN, MINIATURE, PINK BLEND,
REPEAT-FLOWERING

The double flowers of this rose are pink with a mauve tint blending and cream undersides containing 26–40 petals. They are fragrant and have good Large-flowered form. The bloom size, however, is very large, making it a candidate for the patio-sized Miniature classification, although in very warm climates the bloom size is smaller, and has the dimensions more expected of a Miniature. The flowers come on long, crooked stems with a bent peduncle due to bloom weight. The disease-free foliage can also be large. The plant is angular, tall and upright and has a spreading habit so it needs plenty of room. ZONES 5–11.

Taylor, USA, 1997

'Azure Sea' × seedling

'SIMON FRASER'
MODERN, MODERN SHRUB, MEDIUM PINK,
REPEAT-FLOWERING

The single-petalled flowers on 'Simon Fraser' are a clear medium pink. The slightly fragrant blooms come in small clusters and can be single or semi-double, with 6–14 petals, depending on the climate. The foliage is dark green and semi-glossy on an upright plant with some prickles that is extremely winter hardy. ZONES 3–10.

Ogilvie, Canada, 1992

('Bonanza' × ['Arthur Bell' × ['Red Dawn' × 'Suzanne']]) × ('Single Kordesii' × ['Red Dawn' × 'Suzanne'] × 'Champlain')

'SIMON ROBINSON' TRObwich
MODERN, MINIATURE, MEDIUM PINK,
REPEAT-FLOWERING

The variety bears fragrant, single-petalled flowers with 5 petals that are medium pink and are borne in clusters of 10–60 blooms depending on the climate. The foliage is dark, glossy green on a compact, low bush. If not for the thorns and foliage, this rose can look like any annual or perennial in the garden. It provides a profusion of bloom all season long and deserves a prominent spot. This delightful rose was the result of using two of Ralph Moore's favorite parents. ZONES 5–10.

Robinson. UK. 1982

Rosa wichuraiana × 'New Penny'

'SIMPLEX'
MODERN, MINIATURE, WHITE, REPEAT-FLOWERING

Long, pointed apricot buds on 'Simplex' open to small, creamy white 5-petalled blooms complemented by attractive yellow stamens. The florets have a light fragrance and come in large sprays at the end of strong, straight stems. Simple beauty and elegance are truly the hall-marks of this rose. The foliage is small and leathery on a vigorous, compact bush and the plant is easy to grow and maintain. On occasions the growth can be a bit leggy, and grooming the plant to a desired shape and size is rewarded by a profusion of new stems loaded with blooms. This rose is ideal for growing in a container. Preferred by floral designers, it always adds a touch of grace to any design. ZONES 5–10.

Moore, USA, 1961

(*Rosa wichuraiana* × 'Floradora') × seedling

'SIMPLICITY' JACink
MODERN, CLUSTER-FLOWERED/FLORIBUNDA,
MEDIUM PINK, REPEAT-FLOWERING

The long, pointed buds of this rose open to reveal clear medium pink flowers. The semi-double blooms contain 18 petals and have a decorative form. They can be quite large in certain climates, reaching 4 in (10 cm) across. They always come in medium-sized clusters and have a light fragrance. The foliage is mid-green, and is resistant to pests and diseases. 'Simplicity' is healthy and easy to grow and maintain; growers in the USA have taken to growing it as a hedgerow for an attractive landscape design. ZONES 5–11.

Warriner, USA, 1978

'Iceberg' × seedling

New Zealand Gold Medal 1976

'Single Cherry' (rosehips)

'Simplicity'

'SINCERELY YOURS' MORdort
MODERN, MINIATURE, MEDIUM RED,
REPEAT-FLOWERING

The medium red flowers on 'Sincerely Yours' are borne in small clusters and have been described as a miniature 'Dortmund' right down to the prickly stems. The blooms have 6–14 petals complemented by lush, disease-free foliage on a compact bush. This is a well-behaved plant and a profuse bloomer, providing great color in the garden. It is best employed as a border plant, as it is nearly always in bloom and each red bloom lasts for weeks. ZONES 5–11.

Moore, USA, 1991

'Sheri Anne' × 'Dortmund'

American Rose Society Award of Excellence 1992

'SINGIN' IN THE RAIN' MACivy
syns 'Love's Spring', 'Spek's Centennial'
MODERN, CLUSTER-FLOWERED/FLORIBUNDA,
APRICOT BLEND, REPEAT-FLOWERING

The flowers of this rose are an apricot-copper that just lights up any garden. The moderately full florets have 25–30 petals and a light fragrance, and are borne in large clusters. The foliage is glossy dark green on a medium, upright, free-branching plant that is always in bloom, providing a colorful display all year long. It is easy to grow, and is resistant to mildew and black spot. Both floral arrangers and exhibitors admire this rose for its vibrant color and wonderful inflorescence. ZONES 5–11.

McGredy, New Zealand, 1991

'Sexy Rexy' × 'Pot o' Gold'

Royal National Rose Society Gold Medal 1991,
All-America Rose Selection 1995

'SINGLE CHERRY'
OLD, SCOTS, MEDIUM RED

This is one of few roses to have survived from the many cultivated forms of *Rosa spinosissima*, a low-growing rose native

'Single Cherry'

'Sir Alec Rose'

to higher latitudes of the northern hemisphere. Many were developed in the early years of the nineteenth century, but few now survive. They were hardy and flowered early, but once only, and a multitude of colors and shapes were created. 'Single Cherry' has intense red flowers. If pruned, this rose can form a dense mass of blooms in its short season. It makes a low, prickly bush. ZONES 4–7.

Early nineteenth century

Variant of *Rosa spinosissima*

'SIR ALEC ROSE'
MODERN, CLUSTER-FLOWERED/FLORIBUNDA,
DEEP PINK, REPEAT-FLOWERING

This variety could easily be classed as a climbing rose since the bush is very strong growing and produces long canes in autumn that are topped with small clusters of flowers. The large and deep green foliage is plentiful, and makes a nice backdrop to the deep rose pink flowers that are touched with coral-pink. The blooms are double with about 20 petals of good substance. Flowers appear profusely in spring, but the later flushes are diminished because of the strong autumn growth. There is some fragrance, and disease resistance is good. 'Sir Alec Rose' was the first man to sail single handed around the world. ZONES 5–10.

Treloar Roses, Australia, 1965

Parentage unknown

'SIR CEDRIC MORRIS'
MODERN, LARGE-FLOWERED CLIMBER, WHITE

'Sir Cedric Morris' has small buds that open to reveal globular, single-petalled, white flowers with prominent golden anthers. They are borne in large clusters containing as many as 20–40 blooms and have a sweet and pervading fragrance. In the summer bloom cycle the huge clusters are evenly spaced in mass profusion.

'Singin' in the Rain'

The foliage is elongated and finely toothed with the stems armed with many thorns. The large prickles are derived from the seed parent. It is a very vigorous grower that blooms only in summer; however, the masses of blooms in the one lavish crop are well worth the wait. It sets hips, which provide a spectacular autumn display of bright orange fruit. ZONES 4–10.

Morris, UK, 1980

Rosa glauca × seedling

'SIR CLOUGH' AUSclough
syn. 'Sir Glaugh'
MODERN, MODERN SHRUB, DEEP PINK,
REPEAT-FLOWERING

The slender stems of this rose are topped off by large, saucer-shaped, semi-double blooms that open from small, globular buds that are a colorfast deep pink. The foliage is unique, showing a thick covering of arrow-like leaves on a plant that grows to about 5 ft (1.5 m) high and blooms throughout the year. This rose prefers well-drained soil if it is to achieve the best results. It was named after Sir Clough William-Ellis, architect and creator of Portmeirion. ZONES 4–10.

Austin, UK, 1983

'Chaucer' × 'Conrad F. Meyer'

S

'Sir Walter Raleigh'

'Sir Walter Raleigh'

'Sir Harry Pilkington'

'SIR EDWARD ELGAR'

AUSprima

MODERN, MODERN SHRUB, MEDIUM RED/LIGHT
RED, REPEAT-FLOWERING

'Sir Edward Elgar' has crimson-cerise flowers that contain 40–50 petals and are borne one to a stem. The flower form is cupped at first, with the large blooms finally becoming a wonderful flat masterpiece. The foliage is mid-green and semi-glossy on an upright bush reaching 3–4 ft (1–1.2 m) high. This rose was bred from two of David Austin's previous successes in this classification and was named to honor the famous English composer noted for his compositions for royal occasions. ZONES 5–10.

Austin, UK, 1992

'Mary Rose' × 'The Squire'

'SIR FREDERICK ASHTON'

MODERN, LARGE-FLOWERED/HYBRID TEA, WHITE,
REPEAT-FLOWERING

The full flowers of this variety are almost pure white but for a hint of lemon at the base of each petal. This rose has all the stunning attributes of its parent, including a great fragrance. The growth habit is upright and stoutly vigorous and the blooms are borne on strong, straight stems. The foliage is dark green and leathery in texture. It was discovered by Peter Beales in his garden in Norfolk. He named it to celebrate the 80th birthday of Sir Frederick Ashton, Director of the Royal National Ballet at Covent Garden, London. ZONES 5–10.

Beales, UK, 1985

Sport of 'Anna Pavlova'

'SIR HARRY PILKINGTON'

TANema

syn. 'Melina'

MODERN, LARGE-FLOWERED/HYBRID TEA,
MEDIUM RED, REPEAT-FLOWERING

The fragrant, blood red flowers of this rose have darker shades at the petal edges as the blooms age. The double florets have 30 petals. They are large, to 5 in (12 cm) across, and are borne singly. The foliage is dark green on a vigorous, medium-sized bush. This healthy rose produces plenty of blooms throughout the growing season. ZONES 5–10.

Tantau, Germany, 1974

'Inge Horstmann' × 'Sophia Loren'

'SIR LANCELOT'

MODERN, CLUSTER-FLOWERED/FLORIBUNDA,
APRICOT BLEND, REPEAT-FLOWERING

'Sir Lancelot' has apricot-yellow, semi-double, fragrant flowers with salmon-pink hues, fading with age. The compact bush covers itself with clusters of blooms all year and has small, matt green foliage. It may need protection against black spot. This rose was one of the first breeding efforts by Jack Harkness to be sold commercially. ZONES 5–10.

Harkness, UK, 1967

'Vera Dalton' × 'Woburn Abbey'

Royal National Rose Society Trial Ground
Certificate 1966

'SIR THOMAS LIPTON'

MODERN, HYBRID RUGOSA, WHITE,
REPEAT-FLOWERING

This rose bears pure white flowers on a plant that is best described as a small

'Sir Lancelot'

rambler reaching 6–8 ft (1.8–2.4 m) tall. It has a vigorous, spreading habit and dark, leathery foliage. The strongly perfumed blooms are double and have a good cupped form, and appear with good continuity from summer to autumn. ZONES 4–10.

Van Fleet, USA, 1900

Rosa rugosa alba × 'Clotilde Soupert'

'SIR WALTER RALEIGH'

AUSspry

MODERN, MODERN SHRUB, MEDIUM PINK,
REPEAT-FLOWERING

'Sir Walter Raleigh' has rich creamy pink flowers with a form that has been likened to a peony. The florets have over 40 petals, have a cupped form and sport golden stamens in the center. The large blooms are borne singly and are very fragrant. The foliage is dark green and semi-glossy on an upright, extremely vigorous plant that blooms throughout the year. It is extremely hardy and can withstand harsh winter conditions. This rose can be used for a border, low fence and even as a trained pillar, spilling out its heavy fragrance in most climates. It was named by David Austin to commemorate the founding of the first English-speaking colony in America. ZONES 4–10.

Austin, UK, 1985

'Lilian Austin' × 'Chaucer'

'SIR WINSTON CHURCHILL'

MODERN, LARGE-FLOWERED/HYBRID TEA,
ORANGE-PINK, REPEAT-FLOWERING

This bush rose produces large, high-centered, double flowers filled with 45 salmon-pink petals that are orange in the centers. There is a strong fragrance. The glossy dark green foliage on this vigorous and upright plant is a nice backdrop to the single flowers, which are sometimes carried in small clusters.

'Sir Edward Elgar'

The bloom is adequate with a rather slow repeat, and the disease resistance is good. 'Sir Winston Churchill' is still a good bedding variety, but has vanished from most catalogues. A tendency of the blooms to ball in wet climates may be the reason for its disappearance. ZONES 5–10.

Dickson, UK, 1955

Seedling × 'Souvenir de Denier van der Gon'

National Rose Society Gold Medal 1955

'SIREN'

MODERN, CLUSTER-FLOWERED/FLORIBUNDA,
ORANGE-RED, REPEAT-FLOWERING

This is still an excellent bedding rose even after over 40 years in commerce. The oval buds open to bright scarlet-red, semi-double flowers of 18 petals. They are quite large and profusely born in well-spaced, fragrant clusters, lasting particularly well without fading. The dark green, leathery and semi-glossy foliage covers this vigorous and compact bush, which is quick to repeat its flowers in summer. There can be black spot at times. 'Siren' was one of the first fiery red bush roses bred from the famous variety 'Independence'. Nowadays, 'Independence' is in the pedigree of almost all red Cluster-flowered Roses. 'Siren' deserves its gold medal from the National Rose Society, and was planted widely as a bedding rose in the 1950s and 1960s. ZONES 5–10.

Kordes, Germany, 1953

('Baby Château' × 'Else Poulsen') ×
'Independence'

National Rose Society Gold Medal 1952

'SKYROCKET'

syn. 'Wilhelm'

MODERN, MODERN SHRUB, DARK RED,
REPEAT-FLOWERING

The long, pointed buds of this rose open to semi-double blooms with 20 deep red petals. They appear in fragrant clusters of

'Siren'

'Sir Winston Churchill'

'Sleigh Bells'

'Slater's Crimson China'

10–50 amid large, leathery, dark green leaves. The growth is vigorous and spreading; huge heads of flowers continue during autumn. It is a good rose for hedges and mixed borders. ZONES 5–9.

Kordes, Germany, 1934

'Robin Hood' × 'J. C. Thornton'

Royal Horticultural Society Award of Garden Merit 1993

'SLATER'S CRIMSON CHINA'
syns 'Belfield', 'Chinese Monthly Rose', 'Old Crimson China', *Rosa chinensis semperflorens*
OLD, CHINA, MEDIUM RED, REPEAT-FLOWERING

This is one of several roses brought to Europe from the Orient, which were then crossed with the once-flowering old European roses. Many hybrids were raised, giving rise in due course to the current wide range of repeat-blooming varieties. Its small, open, semi-double crimson blooms are of a shade not previously known in Europe and are borne constantly on a low-growing, open, twiggy bush with small, red-tinted leaves. Long believed extinct, it was rediscovered by rosarian Richard Thomson at Belfield in Bermuda in 1956. ZONES 7–9.

Circa 1790

Parentage unknown

'SLEIGH BELLS'
MODERN, LARGE-FLOWERED/HYBRID TEA, WHITE, REPEAT-FLOWERING

The oval buds of this rose open to give clear white blooms with creamy centers.

They are very strongly fragranced, decorative and double, with 40 or more petals. The flowers tend to be large and sometimes occur in small clusters amid the leathery and glossy dark foliage. 'Sleigh Bells' is a very vigorous, upright bush. ZONES 6–11.

Howard, USA, 1950

'Captain Thomas' × 'Eternal Youth'

'SMARTY' INTersmart
MODERN, MODERN SHRUB, LIGHT PINK, REPEAT-FLOWERING

This remarkable rose bears small, almost single flowers with 7–10 light pink petals. They are borne mainly in medium-sized clusters amid the matt, bright green foliage. The repeat-bloom is fast, and there is no need to remove spent blooms to promote the next bloom cycle. 'Smarty' is a low-growing, wide-spreading, hardy and vigorous bush that is easy to grow; it makes an ideal ground cover. There are many small prickles. ZONES 5–11.

Ilsink, The Netherlands, 1979

'Yesterday' × seedling

'SMITH'S PARISH'
OLD, TEA, RED BLEND, REPEAT-FLOWERING

'Smith's Parish' has creamy white flowers that occasionally have a red stripe on some of the petals. The foliage is light green. This rose seems to have a connection with 'Five-Colored Rose', a slender plant with the same multi-colored flowers discovered by Robert Fortune in China and recorded by him in 1847. Many tender roses lost elsewhere over the years have been preserved in gardens in Bermuda, possibly due to its equable climate, and have been re-introduced by nurseries in other areas. ZONES 5–10.

Parentage unknown

'SMOOTH ANGEL' HADangel
MODERN, LARGE-FLOWERED/HYBRID TEA, APRICOT BLEND, REPEAT-FLOWERING

This variety is a member of a series that were bred specifically for their thornless stems, which bear matt mid-green leaves. The apricot flowers blend to cream at the edges with a glowing apricot-yellow

center. They are double, with 36 petals, cupped, borne one to a stem and have a strong, sweet fragrance. 'Smooth Angel' displays medium growth with a slightly spreading habit. ZONES 5–11.

Davidson, USA, 1986

'Smooth Sailing' × 'Royal Flush'

'SMOOTH LADY' HADlady
MODERN, LARGE-FLOWERED/HYBRID TEA, MEDIUM PINK, REPEAT-FLOWERING

The thornless stems of this rose hold very glossy mid-green leaves and small clusters of spicy fragranced, medium pink flowers. They are double with about 21 petals that give a loose, urn-shaped flower form. 'Smooth Lady' produces attractive orange hips in autumn and winter on the tall and upright stems. ZONES 5–11.

Davidson, USA, 1986

'Smooth Sailing' × (['Polly' × 'Peace'] × 'Circus')

'SMOOTH MELODY' HADmelody
MODERN, CLUSTER-FLOWERED/FLORIBUNDA, RED BLEND, REPEAT-FLOWERING

'Smooth Melody' carries oval buds that open to give reddish flowers with white centers, white undersides and red edges, ageing darker. The blooms are double, with about two dozen petals, loosely urn shaped and have a heavy fruity fragrance. They are produced in small sprays of 3 or 4 amid the semi-glossy, dark green and disease resistant foliage. ZONES 5–11.

Davidson, USA, 1990

'Royal Flush' × 'Smooth Lady'

'SMOOTH PERFUME'
HADperfume
MODERN, LARGE-FLOWERED/HYBRID TEA, LIGHT PINK, REPEAT-FLOWERING

The pointed buds of this rose open to give light pink to very light mauve, heavily fragranced flowers. They are urn shaped, double with about 30 petals, and

have good symmetry. The semi-glossy foliage has excellent disease resistance, and it covers the thornless stems; 'Smooth Perfume' is one of a series of smooth-stemmed roses bred by the Californian rosarian Harvey Davidson. The medium-sized plant has a bushy habit. ZONES 5–11.

Davidson, USA, 1990

('Smooth Sailing' × 'Medallion') × 'Blue Moon'

'SMOOTH PRINCE' HADprince
MODERN, LARGE-FLOWERED/HYBRID TEA, MEDIUM RED, REPEAT-FLOWERING

This thornless variety is the product of a cross between two other thornless roses from the same series bred by Harvey Davidson. The oval buds open to reveal deep pink-red flowers with a great fruity fragrance. They are double with 27 petals that give an exceptional exhibition form, and are borne singly amid the semi-glossy, mid-green foliage. 'Smooth Prince' has a superior resistance to disease, and is considered a great garden variety with no problems or major faults. Oblong hips are produced in autumn, although they do not set seed. ZONES 5–11.

Davidson, USA, 1990

'Smooth Sailing' × 'Old Smoothie'

'Smooth Prince'

S

'Smooth Melody'

'SMOOTH SATIN' HADsatin
MODERN, LARGE-FLOWERED/HYBRID TEA,
MEDIUM PINK, REPEAT-FLOWERING

The flowers of this rose are medium pink and age gracefully to peach with a very pleasant fragrance. They are filled with up to 40 petals, and are borne one to a stem amid the large, glossy green foliage, which has excellent disease resistance. Like the other members of this series bred by Harvey Davidson, the stems have no thorns. 'Smooth Satin' has an upright and tall habit. ZONES 5–11.

Davidson, USA, 1994

'Smooth Lady' × 'Smooth Sailing'

'SMOOTH VELVET' HADvelvet
MODERN, LARGE-FLOWERED/HYBRID TEA,
DARK RED, REPEAT-FLOWERING

This variety is a sister seedling to 'Smooth Lady'. It bears large, cup-shaped blooms that are a lovely dark red and with a light damask fragrance. They are double, filled with 42 petals, and are borne amid the matt light green foliage. Medium orange hips follow the flowers in autumn on this tall and upright plant. 'Smooth Velvet' shows good resistance to disease. ZONES 5–11.

Davidson, USA, 1986

('Smooth Sailing' × [('Polly' × 'Peace'} × 'Circus']) × 'Red Devil'

'SNO'
MODERN, MINIATURE, WHITE, REPEAT-FLOWERING

This variety has snow white flowers with 48 petals, good exhibition form and a strong fragrance. The foliage is narrow

'Sno'

'Sno'

and light green on a plant that is low but spreading. For most of the season the bush is covered with blossoms, permeating the garden with a strong scent. If planted in a container it tends to flow elegantly over the rim. It can also be used in a hanging basket to allow the perfume to be enjoyed more easily. This rose is not quite dense enough to recommend it as a ground cover. Some nurseries have offered it under the name 'Snow'. Hybridized by an amateur grower from Santa Ana, California, 'Sno' has remained popular since its introduction. ZONES 5–10.

Meredith, USA, 1982

Seedling × 'Gold Pin'

'SNOW BALLET' CLAysnow
syn. 'Snowballet'
MODERN, MODERN SHRUB, WHITE,
REPEAT-FLOWERING

This interesting shrub produces very large, pure white blooms with 45 petals and a light fragrance. They are produced throughout the warmer months in small and large clusters amid the small and glossy dark green foliage. This disease-resistant plant does not grow tall but prefers to spread outwards to create a ground-cover effect. 'Snow Ballet' is a prize-winning variety, but is gradually losing its popularity due to keen competition from some of the white-flowered ground covers from Europe. ZONES 4–10.

Clayworth, New Zealand, 1977

'Sea Foam' × 'Iceberg'

Baden-Baden Gold Medal 1980

'Snow Bride'

'Snow Carpet'

'SNOW BRIDE'
syn. 'Snowbride'
MODERN, MINIATURE, WHITE, REPEAT-FLOWERING

Lovely creamy white flowers with excellent Large-flowered form make this rose suitable for exhibition. The florets occur one to a stem or in large clusters. As the petals reflex in a classical manner the form is maintained for days. This rose has won many prizes at shows all over the USA and in the UK. The foliage is small, dark green and glossy on a compact, vigorous plant. This outstanding white Miniature has been popular for more than 16 years because of its ability to consistently produce beautiful weatherproof blossoms on a healthy plant. In some climates, it may need some protection from powdery mildew. ZONES 4–10.

Jolly, USA, 1982

'Avendel' × 'Zinger'

American Rose Society Award of Excellence 1983

'SNOW CARPET' MACcarpe
syn. 'Blanche Neige'
MODERN, MINIATURE, WHITE, REPEAT-FLOWERING

The small, pompon-style, snow white flowers on this variety have just a hint of cream in cooler climates. The blooms have 55 petals and a light fragrance. This rose was a major breakthrough in the development of Miniature ground covers with a sprawling, vigorous habit and dainty foliage. It generally forms giant mounds of informal flowers against a background of small, mid-green foliage. When it is first transplanted it may sulk for a while, but it will establish itself within months. It has also been used as a weeping tree rose. ZONES 5–10.

McGredy, New Zealand, 1980

'New Penny' × 'Temple Bells'

Royal National Rose Society Trial Ground Certificate 1978, Baden-Baden Gold Medal 1982, Royal Horticultural Society Award of Garden Merit 1993

'SNOW MAGIC'
MODERN, MINIATURE, WHITE, REPEAT-FLOWERING

'Snow Magic' has short, pointed buds that open to light pink decorative flowers with 45 petals that fade rather quickly to pure white. The fragrant florets are similar to 'Popcorn', although not as refined. The bush is at its prettiest when all the flowers are fully open. The foliage is small on a spreading plant that is suitable as a ground cover. Bloom production is exceptional; a bush in full bloom looks much like a snowdrift. ZONES 4–11.

Moore, USA, 1976

Parentage unknown

'Snow Magic'

'Snow Meillandina'

'SNOW MEILLANDINA'
MEIgovin
syn. 'Snow Sunblaze'
MODERN, MINIATURE, WHITE, REPEAT-FLOWERING

This dwarf and very spreading rose is ideal for hanging baskets. The very double flowers with 40–50 petals are pure white in color with a touch of yellow at the bases. They open slowly from oval buds to flat, full blooms that are abundant, long lasting and have a quick repeat. There is good disease resistance, and the stems are covered with many small thorns. 'Snow Meillandina' is inclined to produce very full flowers in spring that have coarse, vegetative centers, which is the reason why it is being replaced for pot culture by a newer Meilland variety called 'Bridal Meillandina'. ZONES 5–10.

Meilland, France, 1991

Sport of 'Lady Sunblaze'

'SNOW OWL' UHLensch
syns 'Schnee-Eule', 'White Pavement'
MODERN, MODERN SHRUB, WHITE,
REPEAT-FLOWERING

This extremely rugged and hardy shrub grows with a dense and compact habit to a height of about 3 ft (1 m). The bloom cycles are fast with an excellent repeat. 'Snow Owl' gives a great display of red hips that appear in autumn after the flat, white, strongly perfumed flowers have faded. ZONES 4–10.

Uhl, Germany, 1989

Parentage unknown

'SNOW TWINKLE' MORsno
MODERN, MINIATURE, WHITE, REPEAT-FLOWERING

The double flowers of this rose are snow white and have good high centers suitable for exhibition. There is a light fragrance. The foliage is small and mid-green on a bushy plant. The blooms have sufficient petals to hold their elegant

'Snow Twinkle'

'Snowline'

'Snowflake'

'Snow Twinkle'

'Snowy Cupido'

shape on the bush or when picked, and come in sprays with a good floriferous shape. **ZONES 5–10.**

Moore, USA, 1987

('Little Darling' × 'Yellow Magic') × 'Magic Carrousel'

'SNOW WHITE'
MODERN, LARGE-FLOWERED/HYBRID TEA, WHITE, REPEAT-FLOWERING

The long, pointed buds of this variety open to pristine white blooms with good fragrance. They are large, double and have exceptional exhibition form. The leathery, dark green foliage has good disease-resistant characteristics, and it covers this vigorous, compact, medium-sized bush. The variety is very hardy. **ZONES 4–10.**

Hill, USA, 1941

'Joanna Hill' × 'White Briarcliff'

'SNOWDON'
MODERN, HYBRID RUGOSA, WHITE, REPEAT-FLOWERING

This dense, leafy and shapely plant bears white, fully double flowers that have a rosette-like form. The best crop of flowers occurs in spring, and blooming thereafter is somewhat intermittent. It is also classified as an English Rose. **ZONES 5–10.**

Austin, UK, 1989

Parentage unknown

'SNOWFIRE'
MODERN, LARGE-FLOWERED/HYBRID TEA, RED BLEND, REPEAT-FLOWERING

The oval buds of this variety open to give enormous, bright red flowers that have white undersides. These double blooms have a near-perfect exhibition form, and

are borne amid the large, dark green and leathery foliage. It is a vigorous grower that develops into a tall, upright bush. Overall, this is a hardy, spectacular performer with eye-catching color. **ZONES 5–10.**

Kordes, Germany, 1970

'Detroiter' × 'Liberty Bell'

'SNOWFLAKE'
MODERN, RAMBLER, WHITE

This vigorous Rambler produces clusters of double white blooms. It is a conventional lax *Rosa wichuraiana* hybrid with dark glossy foliage. As it has been superseded by better types, it is now only available from a few outlets. There are three other roses with the name 'Snowflake': a Tea Rose from 1890, a Large-flowered Rose from Kordes in 1970 and a Miniature from 1977. **ZONES 5–9.**

Cant, UK, 1922

Parentage unknown

National Rose Society Gold Medal 1921

'SNOWLINE'
syn. 'Edelweiss'
MODERN, CLUSTER-FLOWERED/FLORIBUNDA, WHITE, REPEAT-FLOWERING

This classic rose from the 1960s gives medium-sized, pure white or creamy blooms that have a light fragrance. Double, with 31 petals, they are produced freely in large trusses on this low-growing plant with glossy dark foliage. As it grows to about 3 ft (1m) high, it is an ideal bedding or border selection. **ZONES 5–10.**

Poulsen, Denmark, 1970

Parentage unknown

Royal National Rose Society Trial Ground Certificate 1970

'SNOWY CUPIDO'   RUIdiggel
MODERN, MINIATURE, WHITE, REPEAT-FLOWERING

'Snowy Cupido' has been bred specifically to flower under low light indoors. This small, compact bush has small, dull matt green, disease-resistant foliage. Small and shapely buds open slowly to

well-formed blooms of 30–35 petals. Ideal for the long winter months when there is little in flower outdoors, they are purchased in pots in the bud stage and often discarded in spring. **ZONES 5–10.**

de Ruiter, The Netherlands, 1992

Parentage unknown

S

'SOARING WINGS' KORwings
MODERN, LARGE-FLOWERED/HYBRID TEA, ORANGE BLEND, REPEAT-FLOWERING

The oval buds of this plant open to give deep dusky orange blooms filled with 65 petals. The large blooms have an excellent exhibition form. Matt mid-green leaves cover this vigorous and upright grower that has moderate resistance to disease. The blooms tend to be produced on short stems, so they are not much use for cutting. ZONES 5–10.

Kordes, Germany, 1978

'Colour Wonder' × seedling

'SODŌRI-HIMÉ'
syn. 'La Blancheur'
MODERN, LARGE-FLOWERED/HYBRID TEA, WHITE, REPEAT-FLOWERING

The large, pure white, weatherproof flowers of this variety have excellent symmetry. They are very suitable for exhibition and have such a light scent that it may not be detected in warm climates. The leaves are dark green and disease resistant on a compact, medium-sized bush that has a good overall architecture and dressing. ZONES 5–10.

Onodera, Japan, 1975

'White Knight' × 'White Prince'

'Sodōri-Himé'

'SOEUR THÉRÈSE'
syn. 'Sister Thérèse'
MODERN, LARGE-FLOWERED/HYBRID TEA, YELLOW BLEND, REPEAT-FLOWERING

The long, pointed buds of 'Soeur Thérèse' open to golden yellow flowers that are flushed and edged with carmine red. They are double with about two dozen petals, cupped and have a light fragrance. The foliage is bronze and leathery in texture, and it covers a vigorous, bushy rose. Roy Shepherd in the USA crossed *Rosa spinosissima altaica* with 'Soeur Thérèse' to produce the repeat-blooming shrub 'Golden Wings', which has large, single-petalled flowers. ZONES 5–10.

Guillot, France, 1931

('Général Jacqueminot' × 'Juliet') × 'Souvenir de Claudius Pernet'

'SOFTEE' MORfree
MODERN, MINIATURE, WHITE, REPEAT-FLOWERING

This novel Miniature Rose has creamy white decorative flowers with about 35 petals that tend to open quickly to the fully open stage. The florets have a light fragrance. The stems have very few thorns and no prickles, and the foliage is small and medium green on a spreading, compact bush. White pompon-like flowers borne in clusters cover the bush, making it a very attractive garden plant. There is a climbing sport of this rose that can be successfully trained on a veranda or over a handrail to stunning effect. ZONES 5–10.

Moore, USA, 1983

Parentage unknown

'SOFTLY SOFTLY' HARkotur
MODERN, CLUSTER-FLOWERED/FLORIBUNDA, PINK BLEND, REPEAT-FLOWERING

The flowers of this cultivar are pink to creamy pink depending on the climate it

'Soleil d'Or'

is grown in. The blooms are double, with 35 petals, large and have a light fragrance. The foliage is an attractive olive green. 'Softly Softly' is considered by some to be a Large-flowered Rose. The variety was named after a very popular television series in the UK during the 1980s. ZONES 5–10.

Harkness, UK, 1977

'White Cockade' × (['Highlight' × 'Colour Wonder'] × ['Parkdirektor Riggers' × 'Piccadilly'])

'SOLDIER BOY'
MODERN, LARGE-FLOWERED CLIMBER, MEDIUM RED, REPEAT-FLOWERING

'Soldier Boy' has single-petalled, deep scarlet flowers with yellow stamens; it resembles 'Altissimo', another great Climber, but it is more crimson. While it makes a good addition to the pillar class, it did not inherit the great fragrance of its pollen parent 'Guinée'. If a deeper red, single-petalled Climber is preferred, then try 'Sweet Sultan', a much-admired plant from the UK. 'Soldier Boy' is a very vigorous grower and repeats well. ZONES 5–10.

LeGrice, UK, 1953

Seedling × 'Guinée'

National Rose Society Trial Ground Certificate 1953

'SOLEIL D'OR'
MODERN, LARGE-FLOWERED/HYBRID TEA, YELLOW BLEND, REPEAT-FLOWERING

This rose is remarkable because it was the first of the class of Pernetianas now incorporated into the Large-flowered Roses. A breakthrough was made in introducing the deep yellow and range of

'Softly Softly'

'Softee'

'Soaring Wings'

orange shades of its wild parent to the Modern Garden Roses. The foliage is rich green, with ferny leaves similar to *Rosa foetida*. The deep orange-yellow to tawny gold-shaded red flowers are very large, double, cupped and flattish, with muddled centers. Unfortunately, a propensity to black spot was transmitted to many of its class; this has now almost been bred out and the new colors are part of the heritage of Modern Large- and Cluster-flowered Roses. **ZONES 5–9.**

Pernet-Ducher, France, 1900

(Seedling of 'Antoine Ducher' × *Rosa foetida persiana*) × Large-flowered Rose

'SOLFATERRE'

syn. 'Solfatare'

OLD, NOISETTE, MEDIUM YELLOW,
REPEAT-FLOWERING

'Solfaterre' is a vigorous Noisette climber that, like its parent, will ascend into a tree. The fragrant, light sulfur-yellow flowers are large, double and flattish and are produced freely. Too much sun will bleach them and this should be borne in mind when siting the plant. **ZONES 7–9.**

Boyau, France, 1843

Seedling of 'Lamarque'

'SOLITAIRE'   MACyefre

MODERN, LARGE-FLOWERED/HYBRID TEA,
YELLOW BLEND, REPEAT-FLOWERING

The large blooms are similar to the famous 'Peace', especially in shape and color. A vigorous and tall grower, 'Solitaire' reaches 6–8 ft (2–2.5 m) high by 3–4 ft (1–1.2 m) wide. The fragrant blooms are weatherproof. **ZONES 5–10.**

McGredy, New Zealand, 1987

'Freude' × 'Benson & Hedges Gold'

Royal National Rose Society President's International Trophy 1985

'Solitaire'

'Solfaterre'

'Sommermärchen'

'Sommerduft'

'Sombreuil'

'Sonia'

'Sonja Horstman'

'SOLITAIRE'

MODERN, CLUSTER-FLOWERED/FLORIBUNDA,
MEDIUM PINK, REPEAT-FLOWERING

'Solitaire' is a beautifully colored rose from Cants of Colchester. Its flowers are coral-pink with silvery undersides and they are large, double and slightly fragrant. The bush grows vigorously and has glossy, dark green foliage. ZONES 5–9.

Cant, UK, 1970

'Queen Elizabeth' × 'Elysium'

'SOLITUDE' POUlbero

MODERN, LARGE-FLOWERED/HYBRID TEA,
ORANGE BLEND, REPEAT-FLOWERING

The bicolored flowers of this variety are orange and yellow with 26–40 petals, and the outer petals are frilly. The double blooms come in large clusters on tall, straight stems, which are good for cutting but unfortunately are sometimes not strong enough to support the flowers in the garden. The color is an attractive attention point in the garden, although it can often burn in hot climates. Under some conditions 'Solitude' lacks vigor, and bloom production diminishes after the first spring flush. It is not winter hardy. ZONES 7–11.

Olesen, Denmark, 1991

'Selfridges' × seedling

All-America Rose Selection 1993

'SOMBREUIL'

syn. 'Colonial White'
OLD, CLIMBING TEA, WHITE, REPEAT-FLOWERING

The flowers of this rose typify the old rose style. They are white, with an occasional touch of rose and yellow. The flat, quilled, quartered and very double blooms can probably best be described as refined. They are well scented. The plant climbs to a moderate height. Mlle de Sombreuil was a heroine of the French Revolution, who is reputed to have drunk a glass of the blood of an aristocrat to prove her father's non-aristocratic status. This rose is among the hardier of the Teas. ZONES 7–9.

Robert, France, 1850

Seedling of 'Gigantesque'

'SOMMERDUFT' TANfudermos

syn. 'Summer Fragrance'
MODERN, LARGE-FLOWERED/HYBRID TEA,
DARK RED, REPEAT-FLOWERING

The large, double flowers of this plant are a deep dark red with a good scent. They have about 20 petals that give a good exhibition form in moderate climates. 'Sommerduft' is furnished with dark green, semi-glossy leaves that have good disease-resistant characteristics. ZONES 5–11.

Tantau, Germany, 1986

Parentage unknown

'SOMMERMÄRCHEN' KORpinka

syns 'Berkshire', 'Pink Sensation', 'Summer Fairy Tales', 'Xenia'
MODERN, MODERN SHRUB, DEEP PINK,
REPEAT-FLOWERING

This vigorous grower can also be considered a ground cover rose as it makes a shallow pyramid of itself, spreading twice as far as its modest height. It is suitable for the front of a large bed or grouped by itself. The medium-sized, semi-double flowers are carried freely in clusters through summer and autumn on long, arching stems. They are deep cherry pink, with gold stamens, and have a pleasing scent. The dark glossy leaves make this an attractive plant. ZONES 4–9.

Kordes, Germany, 1991

'Weisse Immensee' × seedling
Royal National Rose Society Trial Ground Certificate 1992, Baden-Baden, Geneva and Glasgow Gold Medals 1996

'SONG OF PARIS'

syn. 'Saphir'
MODERN, LARGE-FLOWERED/HYBRID TEA, MAUVE,
REPEAT-FLOWERING

The silvery lavender color is best in cool climates. The large blooms have good exhibition form and a great fragrance. Dark green and leathery foliage covers this tall and upright plant that gives a prolific bloom in moderate climates. The variety is not winter hardy. ZONES 6–11.

Delbard and Chabert, France, 1964

'Holstein' × 'Bayadère'

'SONIA' MEIhelvet

syns 'Sonia Meilland', 'Sweet Promise'
MODERN, LARGE-FLOWERED/HYBRID TEA,
PINK BLEND, REPEAT-FLOWERING

This is probably the most popular greenhouse rose in the world. It bears salmon-pink flowers that are suffused with coral to yellow as they emerge from the elegant, long buds. The blooms are large, with a strong fruity fragrance, but the color can fade in hot climates. It has thick, attractive, dark green foliage. It may also need protection from fungal diseases. 'Sonia' was one of the top money earners for the House of Meilland. It prefers full sun and rich well-drained soil. ZONES 5–11.

Meilland, France, 1974

'Zambra' × ('Baccarà' × 'White Knight')

'SONJA HORSTMANN'

MODERN, LARGE-FLOWERED/HYBRID TEA,
MEDIUM RED, REPEAT-FLOWERING

Both this rose and 'Adolf Horstmann' are named after members of a large German nursery. The shapely buds open to well-formed blooms filled with 25–30 crimson petals. They are good for cutting and retain their color and fragrance well. The dark green, semi-glossy and disease-free foliage forms a good backdrop to the many single blooms, which are sometimes carried several to a stem. There is a fairly quick repeat. ZONES 5–9.

Kordes, Germany, 1967

Parentage unknown

'Song of Paris'

'Sophie's Perpetual'

'Soupert et Notting'

'SONNENKIND' KORhitom
syn. 'Perestroika'

MODERN, PATIO/DWARF CLUSTER-FLOWERED, DEEP YELLOW, REPEAT-FLOWERING

The flowers on this rose are a bright deep, colorfast yellow. The well-formed florets have about 40 petals and a very light fragrance. The foliage is small, semi-glossy green on a vigorous, compact bush. This is one of several Patio Roses introduced by Kordes of Germany, who are famous for their attention to vigor, disease resistance and vitality of color. 'Sonnenkind' is now considered one of the best yellow Patio Roses with its bright, almost golden yellow Large-flowered blooms. ZONES 5–10.

Kordes, Germany, 1987

Seedling × 'Goldmarie'

'SONNENSCHIRN' TANmirsch
syn. 'Broadlands'

MODERN, MODERN SHRUB, LIGHT YELLOW, REPEAT-FLOWERING

The pale creamy yellow flowers of this rose are borne profusely in big clusters that have a sweet fresh scent. The blooms are double and cupped. 'Sonnenschirn' blooms throughout the year in warm climates, and the plant is a dense and spreading, vigorous bush that is suitable as a ground cover since it grows to no more than 2 ft (60 cm) high. ZONES 4–10.

Tantau, Germany, 1993

Parentage unknown

Royal National Rose Society President's International Trophy 1995, British Association of Rose Breeders, Breeders' Selection 1996

'SONORA'
MODERN, CLUSTER-FLOWERED/FLORIBUNDA, YELLOW BLEND, REPEAT-FLOWERING

The oval buds of this cultivar open to give buff yellow flowers that are flushed with pink, often with red stripes on the undersides. The large and fragrant blooms have 30 petals that form a cupped shape. The plant is a profuse bloomer with flowers lasting a long time on the bush or when cut. This green-house variety performs equally well outdoors in the garden. It is a vigorous, tall and upright bush covered with disease-resistant, dark green leaves. ZONES 5–10.

Boerner, USA, 1962

'Orange Mist' × 'Mayday'

'SOPHIE DE MARSILLY'
OLD, ALBA, PINK BLEND

The flowers of 'Sophie de Marsilly' are large and globular. They are blush

colored and have rose centers and can, on occasion, be striped. There can also be a little mossing, and some have classified this rose as a Moss. It is a vigorous, upright bush in the Alba style but does have more prickles than most Albas. Clearly there has been some hybridization, but the Alba features seem predominant. ZONES 4–9.

Pre-1848

Parentage unknown

'SOPHIE'S PERPETUAL'
syns 'Bengal Centifolia', 'Dresden China', 'Paul's Dresden China'

OLD, CHINA, PINK BLEND, REPEAT-FLOWERING

This 'discovered' rose was re-introduced in 1960, having been found and named for Countess Beckendorf by rosarian Humphrey Brooke. The flowers, which are globular and somewhat cupped, are a pale blush pink color overlaid with cerise-crimson, particularly on the outer petals. The scent is good and the bush repeats continually. It can be grown as a shrub or moderate climber and is almost thornless. The foliage is dark green. ZONES 7–9.

Pre-1928

Parentage unknown

'SORCERER' SAVasorc
MODERN, MINIATURE, MEDIUM RED, REPEAT-FLOWERING

These small flowers are a bright medium red and contain 15–25 petals. They are borne one to a stem and are complemented by small, mid-green, semi-glossy foliage. The plant has an upright habit and grows to a medium height of about 16–20 in (40–50 cm). The bloom form is more decorative than exhibition-style, and the flowers are excellent for cutting as they stay fresh for a long time with hardly any fading—this makes them very popular with floral designers. 'Sorcerer'

'Sonnenschirn'

is a strong, nicely shaped plant suitable for growing in containers as well as in beds. It needs minimal care and is very clean. ZONES 5–11.

Saville, USA, 1994

'Gingersnap' × 'Rainbow's End'

'SOUPERT ET NOTTING'
OLD, MOSS, DEEP PINK, REPEAT-FLOWERING

'Soupert et Notting' deserves attention on account of its repeat-flowering and short stature, never attaining heights of over 3 ft (1 m), even in good soil. The shrub is formed by numerous thin and upright shoots, which are sparsely adorned with brownish green moss. The foliage is small and bright grayish-green, and the flower buds are moderately mossy and arranged in small clusters. Relatively small for a Moss Rose, the flowers are 1½–2 in (4–5 cm) across, initially cupped then flat, very full but tidily formatted and fragrant. ZONES 5–10.

Pernet Père, France, 1874

Parentage unknown

'SOUTH SEAS'
syn. 'Mers du Sud'

MODERN, LARGE-FLOWERED/HYBRID TEA, ORANGE-PINK, REPEAT-FLOWERING

There are two opinions about this upright variety: some people rave about the

'Sonora'

'South Seas'

very large, coral-pink blooms, while others find them loose and informal. They are double, with up to 48 petals, cupped to flat in shape and fragrant. The color tends to fade to silvery white with age. The blooms come on long, straight stems, and while the plant is vigorous, flowering is somewhat shy. ZONES 5–11.

Morey, USA, 1962

'Rapture' × seedling of a Large-flowered Climber

'SOUTHAMPTON'
syn. 'Susan Ann'

MODERN, CLUSTER-FLOWERED/FLORIBUNDA, APRICOT BLEND, REPEAT-FLOWERING

This variety was selected by the Civic Authority in Southampton, England to bear the name of the port. Its flowers have about 28 apricot petals, which form a pleasing shape, and are carried in moderate-sized clusters on a tall and spreading bush. 'Southampton' is well regarded in the UK for its color and vigor, and it even does well in hot climates as the flowers do not fade with age. The foliage is glossy green and disease resistant. ZONES 5–11.

Harkness, UK, 1971

('Ann Elizabeth' × 'All Gold') × 'Yellow Cushion'

Royal National Rose Society Trial Ground Certificate 1971, Baden-Baden Silver Medal 1973, Belfast Gold Medal 1974, Royal Horticultural Society Award of Garden Merit 1993

'South Seas'

S

'Souvenir de Brod'

'Southern Cross' (Jack)

'SOUTHERN BELLE'

MODERN, LARGE-FLOWERED/HYBRID TEA, PINK BLEND, REPEAT-FLOWERING

Long, pointed, oval buds open deep pink flowers with white undersides. They are double with great exhibition form and come singly or in small clusters. There is a light fragrance. This upright, spreading bush has large, semi-glossy green leaves and long, narrow prickles. ZONES 5–11.

Swim, USA, 1981

'Pink Parfait' × 'Phoenix'

'SOUTHERN CROSS'

MODERN, LARGE-FLOWERED/HYBRID TEA, MEDIUM PINK, REPEAT-FLOWERING

The clear medium pink, double flowers of this rose tend to be globular in most climates. They are usually borne singly on this medium-sized and upright bush with good fragrance. It was hybridized by one of Australia's most notable breeders. ZONES 5–10.

Clark, Australia, 1931

'Joseph Hill' × 'General MacArthur'

'SOUTHERN CROSS'

MODERN, CLUSTER-FLOWERED/FLORIBUNDA, DEEP YELLOW, REPEAT-FLOWERING

This rose is very similar to its award-winning parent in most respects, with the exception of its flower color, which is daffodil yellow. The lightly fragranced blooms are well shaped and medium sized, with petals that reflex when the flower is fully open to show a dark mass of stamens at the center. 'Southern Cross' gives upright growth. ZONES 5–10.

Jack, Australia, 1977

Sport of 'Redgold'

'SOUTHERN DELIGHT'

MORdashin

MODERN, MINIATURE, YELLOW BLEND, REPEAT-FLOWERING

'Southern Delight' has bright yellow flowers edged with red that age to pink and yellow. The double florets with 15–25 petals have a light fragrance and usually occur in small clusters on strong stems. The foliage is semi-glossy and

'Souvenir' (Grootendorst)

mid-green on a large, upright bush. This rose is not as prolific as many of Moore's other creations and the flower form is fleeting due to a low petal count. However, the large plant does produce an abundance of exhibition-type blooms in the first flush of spring and late in autumn. Its is fairly free of disease. ZONES 5–10.

Moore, USA, 1991

'Little Darling' × 'Rise 'n' Shine'

'SOUVENIR'

MODERN, LARGE-FLOWERED/HYBRID TEA, DEEP YELLOW, REPEAT-FLOWERING

The pointed buds of this variety open to give gorgeous golden yellow, double flowers with 36–42 petals. They have an informal shape and a good fragrance, mostly borne one to a stem. The color fades under hot sun. Although 'Souvenir' is a vigorous and tall grower, it is not at all hardy. ZONES 7–11.

Pierson, USA, 1930

Sport of 'Talisman'

'SOUVENIR' EuroGROOT

syn. 'Sunny Sky'

MODERN, CLUSTER-FLOWERED/FLORIBUNDA, DEEP PINK/MAUVE, REPEAT-FLOWERING

The small clusters of buds on this bush rose open to red petals that unfurl to deep pink, double flowers. The pink is sometimes so rich, they take on a mauve glow. 'Souvenir' has upright stems covered with glossy green foliage. It is suitable for a mixed border or bedding scheme. ZONES 5–10.

Grootendorst, The Netherlands, 1991

Parentage unknown

'SOUVENIR D'ALPHONSE LAVALLÉE'

OLD, HYBRID PERPETUAL, DARK RED, REPEAT-FLOWERING

This floriferous rose bears dark velvety crimson to maroon flowers that are susceptible to burning in hot sun. They have a rich scent. A rather sprawling shrub, it makes a tall plant if tethered, or it can be grown as a short climber. It is somewhat similar to 'Souvenir du Docteur Jamain'. Alphonse Lavallée was an amateur dendrologist and one-time President of the French National Horticultural Society. He died in 1884. ZONES 5–9.

Verdier, France, 1884

Parentage unknown

'SOUVENIR DE BROD'

syn. 'Erinnerung an Brod'

OLD, HYBRID PERPETUAL, RED BLEND, REPEAT-FLOWERING

This rose was named in memory of a town in Bosnia. Its dark crimson, flat blooms are very double, very full and heavy with perfume and are best seen in partial shade where the colors remain constant. A long, floriferous blooming occurs in mid-summer. This is one of the most stunning cut flowers, especially just after the buds open. It is a healthy shrub that will reach 6–7 ft (1.8–2.1 m) and is quite winter hardy. It is popular in Germany. ZONES 4–10.

Geschwind, Hungary, 1886

Rosa setigera × seedling of 'Châteaubriand'

'SOUVENIR DE CHRISTOPHE COCHET'

MODERN, HYBRID RUGOSA, MEDIUM PINK, REPEAT-FLOWERING

Soft pink, semi-double flowers with pale yellow anthers and brisk sepals adorn this rose throughout summer. They are large with a lovely scent and in autumn, large red hips are formed. 'Souvenir de Christophe Cochet' is a vigorous grower with typical, wrinkled, Rugosa-looking leaves. It is winter hardy. ZONES 4–10.

Cochet-Cochet, France, 1894

Parentage unknown

'Souvenir de Christophe Cochet' (hips)

'Souvenir d'Alphonse Lavallée'

'SOUVENIR DE CLAUDIUS DENOYEL'

MODERN, LARGE-FLOWERED CLIMBER, DARK RED, REPEAT-FLOWERING

The long, pointed buds of this rose open to rich crimson-red flowers tinted with scarlet. They are very large, cupped in shape and fragrant. This is a fairly vigorous climber, although the bloom is not particularly profuse, especially after the initial spring flush. It can be used on a pillar, pergola or on a wall. ZONES 5–10.

Chambard, France, 1920

'Château de Clos Vougeot' × 'Commandeur Jules Gravereaux'

Royal Horticultural Society Award of Garden Merit 1993

'SOUVENIR DE JEANNE BALANDREAU'

syn. 'Souvenir de Mme Jeanne Balandreau'
OLD, HYBRID PERPETUAL, MEDIUM RED, REPEAT-FLOWERING

This rose bears very big, rich crimson flowers with pink and vermilion stripes. It is a medium to tall vigorous plant that is almost thornless and has bright green leaves. Some authorities specify this rose as 'Mme Jeanne Balandreau'. It is now uncommon, but can still be ordered from good nurseries. ZONES 5–9.

Vilin and Robichon, France, 1899

Sport of 'Ulrich Brunner Fils'

'SOUVENIR DE LA MALMAISON'

syn. 'Queen of Beauty'
OLD, BOURBON, LIGHT PINK, REPEAT-FLOWERING

This, the most famous and possibly the most beautiful of the Bourbon Roses, was named for Empress Josephine's famous home in Paris. The fragrant flowers are large, quartered and very double. They are pale flesh pink, becoming paler with age. The blooms ball in wet weather, a

'Climbing Souvenir de la Malmaison'

'Souvenir de Mme Léonie Viennot'

'Souvenir de Mme Boullet'

general complaint in the Old Garden Roses and one from which the Modern Roses are a good deal freer. The repeat-flowering plant is low growing and bushy. This rose caused such a stir that it is said that Mme Béluze used to hide at the window at night to watch for thieves who might try to steal cuttings. 'Climbing Souvenir de la Malmaison' (Bennett, UK, 1938) grows to about 6 ft (1.8 m) high. It should be kept out of the rain otherwise it will produce a great crop of balled, unopened blooms. ZONES 5–9.

Béluze, France, 1843

'Mme Desprez' × Tea Rose

'SOUVENIR DE LA REINE D'ANGLETERRE'

OLD, HYBRID PERPETUAL, MEDIUM PINK, REPEAT-FLOWERING

This rose was named to mark a visit to Paris by Queen Victoria in 1855. The parent, 'La Reine', was one of the first Hybrid Perpetuals, a large, globular-flowered rose that is pink to lilac in color. Its progeny has bright silvery pink flowers that are big and are held upright on the stems. It grows very tall and is suitable for a wall or trellis. All the Hybrid Perpetuals are rather coarse by modern standards, but it is remarkable how soon they were produced after the coming of the China Roses to Europe. ZONES 5–9.

Cochet Frères, France, 1855

'La Reine' × seedling

'SOUVENIR DE MME AUGUSTE CHARLES'

OLD, BOURBON, MEDIUM PINK, REPEAT-FLOWERING

The flowers of this rose are small and compact. They are full of petals and somewhat resemble a camellia. The color is between flesh and rosy pink. It is a tall, lax plant in the Bourbon manner and has

'Souvenir de Mlle Juliet de Bricard'

'Souvenir de Mme Breuil'

rather coarse leaves. It is most suitable for a column or perhaps for tying down. ZONES 5–9.

Moreau et Robert, France, 1866

Parentage unknown

'SOUVENIR DE MME BOULLET'

MODERN, LARGE-FLOWERED/HYBRID TEA, DEEP YELLOW, REPEAT-FLOWERING

Long and pointed buds reveal deep yellow flowers that cover this rose in summer. They are large, well formed and full, and come mostly one per stem. The color tends to fade in hot climates. 'Souvenir de Mme Boullet' is vigorous with a tendency to spread rather than grow tall. It is not hardy. 'Climbing Souvenir de Madame Boullet' is a sport discovered by the Californian rose breeders Howard and Smith in 1930. It retains all the desirable characteristics of the parent, except that it can be trained on to walls and pillars. ZONES 7–11.

Pernet-Ducher, France, 1921

'Sunburst' × seedling

'SOUVENIR DE MME BREUIL'

syns 'Souvenir de Mme Breuill', 'Souvenir de Mme Bruel'
OLD, BOURBON, DEEP PINK, REPEAT-FLOWERING

The flowers of 'Souvenir de Mme Breuil' are deep cerise or magenta-pink, and the style is reminiscent of 'Mme Isaac Pereire'. It is quite a vigorous plant with bright green, slightly glossy foliage that appears to be available only in Australia and New Zealand. ZONES 5–9.

Pre-1889

Parentage unknown

'SOUVENIR DE MME H. THURET'

OLD, HYBRID PERPETUAL, PINK BLEND, REPEAT-FLOWERING

This interesting rose was an attempt to introduce the Pernetiana yellow into the Hybrid Perpetuals (see 'Soleil d'Or').

It has the habit of 'Frau Karl Druschki', and is suitable for a low pillar. The main feature is the color, which is quite novel in a Hybrid Perpetual: it is a coppery salmon-pink. The foliage is rich pink and the growth is vigorous. Bred by M. Texier and introduced by Nabonnand, this rose might be hard to find but it is well worth the search. ZONES 5–9.

Nabonnand, France, 1922

'Frau Karl Druschki' × 'Lyon Rose'

'SOUVENIR DE MME LÉONIE VIENNOT'

OLD, CLIMBING TEA, YELLOW BLEND, REPEAT-FLOWERING

This rose is a Tea climber par excellence that will go high into trees and is very long lived. The large, loosely shaped flowers are light rose pink in color with yellow and coppery orange tints and perhaps a little gold. Some find the color just a little harsh and reminiscent of 'Lorraine Lee'. It starts flowering early with a long period and an occasional later repeat. It flowers on the old wood, so the less pruning the better but there will always be plenty of very old wood to cut out. This rose is highly recommended. ZONES 7–9.

Bernaix, France, 1898

'Gloire de Dijon' × seedling

'SOUVENIR DE MLLE JULIET DE BRICARD'

MODERN, POLYANTHA, LIGHT PINK, REPEAT-FLOWERING

Small, pale pink flowers appear in lovely large trusses on this rose, which is very characteristic of Polyanthas. These blooms have a delicate, light fragrance and a globular flower form. They are borne amid the glossy dark green, fairly disease resistant foliage, which covers this vigorous, medium-sized bush. ZONES 5–11.

Delepine, France, 1934

'Cécile Brünner' × 'Yvonne Rabier'

S

'Souvenir de Victor Landeau'

'Souvenir de Philemon Cochet'

'Souvenir de Thérèse Lovet'

'SOUVENIR DE PHILEMON COCHET'

MODERN, HYBRID RUGOSA, WHITE, REPEAT-FLOWERING

The flowers of this sport resemble the parent in every way, except that they have a greatly increased complement of petals and are not as prolific. The white blooms with a rose center are so double that they resemble perfect spheres when fully opened. The variety is not as prolific as the parent. Philemon Cochet was the brother of the breeder. ZONES 4–10.

Cochet-Cochet, France, 1899

Sport of 'Blanc Double de Coubert'

'SOUVENIR DE PIERRE NOTTING'

OLD, TEA, YELLOW BLEND, REPEAT-FLOWERING

'Maman Cochet' is notable for its very long pointed buds and big flowers, and this rose surpasses its parent. The color is apricot-yellow and there is good Tea fragrance. A winning feature is the longevity of the blooms, although they can be terribly spoilt by rain and humidity. In other respects it is a vigorous shrub like its parent with soft, rich green foliage. ZONES 7–9.

Soupert and Notting, Luxembourg, 1902

'Maréchal Niel' × 'Maman Cochet'

'SOUVENIR DE PIERRE VIBERT'

OLD, MOSS, RED BLEND

The fully double flowers of this rose are deep violet with red and carmine shades. The blooms are large and well scented, and there are a few late blooms. The growth is short and somewhat loose. It is not now often seen but is available and should be in every Moss collection. ZONES 4–9.

Moreau et Robert, France, 1867

Parentage unknown

'SOUVENIR DE ST ANNE'S'

OLD, BOURBON, LIGHT PINK, REPEAT-FLOWERING

This sport was discovered in the garden of St Anne's: a property of Lady Ardilaun near Dublin. Graham Thomas recounts that it was preserved for many years by Lady Moore of Rathfarnham in Dublin. This rose has fewer petals than its parent and stands up better to rain, but it is less spectacular. However, it is more fragrant, the scent residing, according to Thomas, in the many stamens. It makes a very bushy, quite tall shrub. ZONES 5–9.

Hilling, UK, 1950

Sport of 'Souvenir de la Malmaison'

Royal Horticultural Society Award of Garden Merit 1993

'Souvenir de St Anne's'

'SOUVENIR DE THÉRÈSE LOVET'

OLD, TEA, DEEP RED, REPEAT-FLOWERING

The deep rather dull crimson color of this variety's flowers is not all that usual in the Teas, and a comparison with 'Francis Dubreuil' springs to mind. The plant enjoys vigorous growth and has dark green foliage and big hooked thorns. This rose needs a hot climate. It is very popular in Australia. ZONES 7–9.

Levet, France, 1886

'Adam' × 'Safrano à Fleurs Rouges'

'SOUVENIR DE VICTOR LANDEAU'

OLD, BOURBON, MEDIUM RED, REPEAT-FLOWERING

This is now a somewhat obscure rose and would not be easy to find. It bears large flowers in plentiful clusters. It is said to be vigorous and has handsome, dark green foliage. It should not be confused with 'Souvenir de Victoire Landeau', a Hybrid Perpetual from the same stable in 1884 that is now even more obscure. ZONES 5–9.

Moreau et Robert, France, 1890

Parentage unknown

'SOUVENIR D'ELISE VARDON'

OLD, TEA, WHITE BLEND, REPEAT-FLOWRING

This is a moderately strong-growing Tea Rose with somewhat delicate, tender flowers. The medium-sized flowers are very double and fragrant. The color is not really white, though it can fade to white; it has been variously described as chamois, bronzish cream, bronzish pink and creamy fawn. ZONES 7–9.

Marest, France, 1855

Parentage unknown

'SOUVENIR DU DOCTEUR JAMAIN'

OLD, HYBRID PERPETUAL, DARK RED, REPEAT-FLOWERING

The blooms of this rose are dark wine colored with purple shades. The petals have considerable substance and verge on black. They are very fragrant. It is a tall-growing shrub that can be grown against a wall, but should be located to avoid strong sunlight, which is apt to burn the flowers. This rose needs plenty of nourishment to ensure good growth and reliable repeat-flowering. ZONES 5–9.

Lacharme, France, 1865

Seedling of 'Charles Lefèbvre'

'SOUVENIR D'UN AMI'

OLD, TEA, LIGHT PINK, REPEAT-FLOWERING

The cupped, double and intensely fragrant flowers of 'Souvenir d'un Ami' are pale rose tinted with salmon. The bush is vigorous and tall. This was one of the best-loved roses of Victorian England, because of its hardiness and ease of cultivation. The name means 'in remembrance of a friend', which sounds romantic, but it has been said that the friend was only the person who negotiated the deal between the amateur raiser and the distributor. ZONES 7–9.

Belot-Defougère, France, 1846

Parentage unknown

'Souvenir d'Elise Vardon'

'Souvenir du Docteur Jamain'

'Sparkling Scarlet'

'Souvenir d'un Ami'

'SPANGLES' GANspa

MODERN, CLUSTER-FLOWERED/FLORIBUNDA, LIGHT PINK, REPEAT-FLOWERING

The speckled pale pink, scented blooms of this rose have 15–25 petals. Medium sized, they are borne in large clusters on stems that have many prickles. 'Spangles' has light green, semi-glossy foliage, is moderately disease resistant. ZONES 5–10.

Gandy, UK, 1994

'Florence Nightingale' × 'Silver Jubilee'

Royal National Rose Society Trial Ground Certificate 1992

'SPARKLING SCARLET'

MEIhaiti, MEIhati
syn. 'Iskra'

MODERN, CLUSTER-FLOWERED CLIMBER, MEDIUM RED, REPEAT-FLOWERING

The bright scarlet-red flowers of 'Sparkling Scarlet' have a strong fruity scent. They also have 13 petals per bloom and are of medium size. This variety makes a wonderful display with its large clusters on strong stems that seem to last a long time. It grows to about 10 ft (3.5 m) high by about 5 ft (1.5 m) wide. ZONES 4–11.

Meilland, France, 1970

'Danse des Sylphes' × 'Zambra'

Paris Gold Medal 1969

'SPARRIESHOOP'

MODERN, MODERN SHRUB, LIGHT PINK, REPEAT-FLOWERING

Named for the village where Kordes' have their now famous nursery,

'Sparrieshoop' has long, pointed buds that open to almost single, sweetly perfumed flowers that are borne in large trusses of apple blossom pink. They are large and sweetly fragrant with many golden yellow stamens. The bush tends to cover itself with flowers all season long. The vigorous growth habit permits the long canes, which are bronze when young, to be trained as either a short climber or a big spreading shrub; it seems to have inherited its rampant growth from its Sweet Briar parent, 'Magnifica'. The glossy dark foliage is subject to mildew if not protected. 'Sparrieshoop' has enjoyed well over 40 years of popularity right around the world. ZONES 4–11.

Kordes, Germany, 1953

('Baby Château' × 'Else Poulsen') × 'Magnifica'

Portland Gold Medal 1971

'Speaker Sam'

'Spartan'

'SPARTAN'

syn. 'Aparte'

MODERN, CLUSTER-FLOWERED/FLORIBUNDA, ORANGE-RED, REPEAT-FLOWERING

The pointed buds of this cultivar open to give vibrant orange-red to reddish coral flowers that have good symmetry and shape. These large blooms are either produced singly or in small clusters, and they have a strong fragrance. They provide a stunning display amid the glossy dark green leaves that adorn this vigorous bush. In spite of all the awards gained by this variety, it failed to win the prestigious All-America Rose Selection; the introducers therefore gave 'Spartan' extra publicity, which included colored pages in both *Time Magazine* and *The Saturday Evening Post*. In the years that followed its introduction, it has been used extensively as a breeding parent with much success. ZONES 5–11.

Boerner, USA, 1955

'Geranium Red' × 'Fashion'

National Rose Society President's International Trophy 1954, Portland Gold Medal 1955, American Rose Society David Fuerstenberg Prize 1957, ARS National Gold Certificate 1961

'Sparrieshoop'

'Sparrieshoop'

'SPEAKER SAM'

MODERN, LARGE-FLOWERED/HYBRID TEA, YELLOW BLEND, REPEAT-FLOWERING

This rose is one of 24 sports of the famous 'Peace', which was introduced in 1945. It bears light yellow flowers that are edged with red. In all other respects, it is similar to its parent. ZONES 5–11.

Dean, USA, 1962

Sport of 'Peace'

'SPECIAL ANGEL'

MODERN, MINIATURE, MAUVE, REPEAT-FLOWERING

The blooms of this rose are mauve gently tipped with pink. The double florets contain 15–25 petals and have a light scent. They are high centered and are produced singly on long, strong, straight stems. The foliage is dark green and semi-glossy on an upright, vigorous, well-behaved plant. It may take a while to establish itself. It was dedicated to children with Downs Syndrome, as each child is truly a 'Special Angel'. ZONES 5–10.

Stoddard, USA, 1992

'Jean Kenneally' × ('Rise 'n' Shine' × 'Acey Deucy')

'Spangles'

'SPECTABILE'
syn. 'Spectabilis'
OLD, SEMPERVIRENS, MAUVE,
REPEAT-FLOWERING

This early rambler is less rampant than
'Félicité-Perpétue' and 'Adélaïde
d'Orléans' but is more dainty and flowers
later. The blooms are small, rose pink
rosettes with lilac shades. Some say the
scent is like primroses. The foliage is
dark and almost evergreen. ZONES 6–9.

Pre-1846

Possibly *Rosa sempervirens* × Noisette hybrid

'SPECTACULAR'
syns 'Danse du Feu', 'Mada'
MODERN, LARGE-FLOWERED CLIMBER,
ORANGE-RED, REPEAT-FLOWERING

The oval buds of this rose open to scarlet-
red, fragrant flowers with 33 petals that
have a cupped to flat shape. They occur
mainly in clusters against glossy bronze
foliage. 'Spectacular' is free flowering
and maintains a colorful display all season long. It is very hardy, even tolerating
shade, but is susceptible to black spot if
left unprotected. It will climb to about
8–10 ft (2.5–3.5 m) high. ZONES 4–10.

Mallerin, France, 1953

'Paul's Scarlet Climber' × seedling of *Rosa
multiflora*

'Spencer'

'SPENCER'
OLD, HYBRID PERPETUAL, LIGHT PINK,
REPEAT-FLOWERING

'Spencer' bears satin pink flowers with
outer petals reflexed with white. They are
cupped, flat and very double, befitting
the Hybrid Perpetual class. They are so
full, however, that they open badly in
rain. It is a medium-sized shrub in the
style of its progenitor 'Merveille de Lyon'
and is presumably liable to sport back to
it. ZONES 5–9.

Paul, UK, 1892

Sport of 'Merveille de Lyon'

'SPICE'
OLD, CHINA, LIGHT PINK, REPEAT-FLOWERING

This rose is one of the Bermuda 'mystery' roses. The middle of the pale pink,
semi-double flowers has loose petals.
There is a spicy perfume. It is a low-
growing, small bush of the China type,
and is a candidate for the identity of the
'lost' 'Hume's Blush'. ZONES 7–9.

Parentage unknown

'SPICE DROP'   SAVswet
MODERN, MINIATURE, ORANGE-PINK,
REPEAT-FLOWERING

Small salmon-pink buds on this variety
open to salmon-pink flowers with 35

'Spice Drop'

petals. The double florets have good-
quality exhibition-type form and are carried one to a stem. The attractive,
well-formed flowers literally cover the
tiny bush with color and are borne
throughout the flowering season. The
dwarf, compact plant is well furnished
with foliage that is small, semi-glossy and
dark green. This rose is one of those preferred by floral artists for their Miniature
Rose designs. It is best grown in a container, where it will be easy to keep
clean. 'Spice Drop' is a winner in every
respect and its popularity is guaranteed.
ZONES 5–10.

Saville, USA, 1982

('Sheri Anne' × 'Glenfiddich') × (seedling of a
Moss Rose × ['Sarabande' × 'Little Chief'])

'SPICE TWICE'   JACable
MODERN, LARGE-FLOWERED/HYBRID TEA,
ORANGE BLEND, REPEAT-FLOWERING

'Spice Twice' bears oval, pointed buds
that open to give this rose coral-orange,
lightly scented flowers which have lighter
undersides. The blooms are large and
double with 30 petals: most are quite
decorative, and there is an occasional
one of exhibition standard. The color
tends to fade rapidly in hot climates.
This vigorous, medium-sized bush is furnished with dark green and very disease-
resistant (especially to black spot)
foliage. ZONES 5–11.

Zary, USA, 1997

Parentage unknown

'SPICED COFFEE'   MACjuliat
syns 'Old Spice', 'Vidal Sassoon'
MODERN, LARGE-FLOWERED/HYBRID TEA, RUSSET,
REPEAT-FLOWERING

This variety is a real novelty rose that can
attract attention on account of its unusual color. In cool climates, the color is
more pink and lavender; in hot climates,
the color is at its best—a real putty tone.
The very fragrant blooms only have
15–25 petals and are borne amid the
matt green leaves. The variety is mainly
of interest to floral arrangers because of
the color. Unfortunately, it lacks sufficient vigor, and diseases such as mildew
and black spot can be a major problem.
'Spiced Coffee' seems to have inherited
some of its elegance from its award-
winning seed parent 'Harmonie'.
ZONES 5–11.

McGredy, New Zealand, 1990

'Harmonie' × 'Big Purple'

British Association of Rose Breeders, Breeders'
Selection 1994

'Spirit of Peace'

'SPIRIT OF PEACE'   JACstine
MODERN, LARGE-FLOWERED/HYBRID TEA,
YELLOW BLEND, REPEAT-FLOWERING

The attractive apricot-yellow flowers of
this cultivar open with a pink tinge
where the sunshine strikes the emerging
petals. These large double blooms are
filled with 26–40 petals and are borne
on long, straight stems with a hint of
fragrance. The foliage is dark green and
semi-glossy and there are some prickles
on the stems. 'Spirit of Peace' usually
makes a rather tall and spreading bush.
It should not be confused with the variety bred by Meilland, which although it
is better known as 'Paul Ricard' also has
'Spirit of Peace' as one of its synonyms.
'Paul Ricard' was introduced in 1994.
ZONES 5–10.

Warriner, USA, 1992

'Pristine' × seedling

'SPLENDENS'
syns 'Ayrshire Splendens', *Rosa arvensis
splendens*
OLD, AYRSHIRE, WHITE

Rosa arvensis, the rose of the field, is
native to southern England and is considered by some authorities to have been
Shakespeare's Musk Rose. This rose is
one of a number of scramblers and ramblers that were developed from it in the
early nineteenth century. The synonym
'Ayrshire Splendens' comes from the Earl
of Loudon in Ayrshire, who was involved
in its development. This rambling variety
is possibly the best of the hybrids, with
loose white flowers with hints of pink.
Like its parent, it tolerates shade. Perhaps
its most interesting feature is its scent,
which has been likened to myrrh, a scent
that is also found in the Albas 'Belle
Amour' and 'Belle Isis' and in some of
the modern David Austin roses, notably
'Constance Spry'. 'Splendens' flowers
only once and has very lax growth.
ZONES 5–9.

Pre-1837

Hybrid of *Rosa arvensis*

'SPLENDENS'
syns 'Frankfurt', *Rosa gallica splendens*
OLD, GALLICA, MEDIUM RED

This Old Garden Rose has semi-double,
crimson blooms with purplish overtones.
They have an excellent contrasting mass
of golden yellow stamens at the centers.
In the garden, this is a colorful rose near
the back of any mixed border. ZONES 5–10.

Pre-1583

Parentage unknown

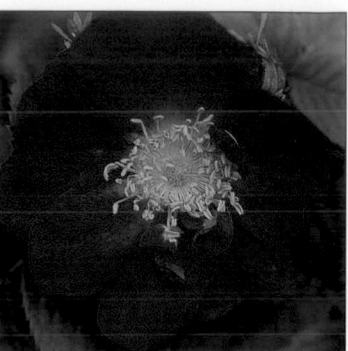

'Splendens' (syn. 'Frankfurt')

'Spiced Coffee'

S

'Spectacular'

'Spring Song'

'Spong'

'Squatters Dream'

'SPONG'

OLD, CENTIFOLIA, MEDIUM PINK

A dwarfish type Centifolia, this variety has little pink flowers that are fragrant and rather more open than pompons with randomly arranged centers. These are borne in sizeable clusters and flower only once in early summer. A notable fault of the blooms is that they do not drop after fading; instead, they remain on the plant, which necessitates deadheading if the plant is to remain tidy. It makes a good and healthy bush for the front of a border or among herbaceous plants. It is also good in tubs or urns, and the grayish green, prickly stems are covered by similar-colored, medium-sized, serrated leaves. The rather plebeian name is said to be that of a gardener who took it up. 'Rose de Meaux' and 'Petite de Hollande' are better medium pink Centifolia Roses. ZONES 4–9.

France, circa 1805

Parentage unknown

'SPRING SONG'

MODERN, MODERN SHRUB, DEEP PINK, REPEAT-FLOWERING

The fragrant flowers on this low-growing shrub are a rich carmine-pink. They are semi-double and appear freely on this vigorous bush, which has gracefully arching canes. 'Spring Song' prefers fertile soil conditions, good drainage and a mulch layer to perform at its best. The variety should not be confused with

another using the same name—a salmon-hued Miniature Rose from Ralph Moore. ZONES 5–10.

Riethmuller, Australia, 1954

Seedling of 'Gartendirektor Otto Linne'

'SQUATTERS DREAM'

MODERN, MODERN SHRUB, MEDIUM YELLOW, REPEAT-FLOWERING

The bright medium yellow flowers on this variety become much lighter with age. Single and moderately fragrant, they look attractive against the dark bronze-green leaves. This bush has a dwarf growth habit. ZONES 7–10.

Clark, Australia, 1923

Rosa gigantea seedling × *Rosa gigantea* seedling

'STACEY SUE'

MODERN, MINIATURE, LIGHT PINK, REPEAT-FLOWERING

'Stacey Sue' has short, pointed buds that open to soft pink flowers with almost 60 petals. The florets have a light fragrance and a rosette-type form. They are produced in clusters on strong stems that cover the bushy plant. This healthy plant has small, glossy green foliage and repeats quickly, but has a tendency to spread if not groomed. It can create a beautiful mound of sprays with lovely light pink flowers, but it is not widely known outside the UK. ZONES 5–11.

Moore, USA, 1976

'Ellen Poulsen' × 'Fairy Princess'

Royal Horticultural Society Award of Garden Merit 1993

'Stämmler'

'STADT ROSENHEIM'

MODERN, MODERN SHRUB, ORANGE-RED, REPEAT-FLOWERING

The orange-red, fragrant flowers of 'Stadt Rosenheim' are double, medium sized and come in clusters of up to 10 amid the glossy light green, abundant foliage. The plant has a vigorous and upright habit. This is one of the many brightly colored shrub roses bred by the firm of Kordes in the 1960s: all were hardy to winter cold and produced good displays of long-lasting flowers each summer. It is little known outside of Germany. ZONES 4–10.

Kordes, Germany, 1961

Parentage unknown

Anerkannte Deutsche Rose 1960

'STAINLESS STEEL'   WElkblusi

MODERN, LARGE-FLOWERED/HYBRID TEA, MAUVE, REPEAT-FLOWERING

This rose is well named, as it produces clear silvery gray-lavender flowers. Each large, well-formed bloom has 35–40 petals and is borne mostly singly, but there are a few clusters. They are very fragrant, which is the case with most roses of this color, and last well, so are good for picking. The foliage is large and abundant, mid-green and semi-glossy, and its growth habit is tall and vigorous. The flower production is good and it is quick to repeat. The color is unlike that

of any other rose, and it combines well with most roses with mauve shades. ZONES 5–11.

Carruth, USA, 1991

'Blue Nile' × 'Silverado'

'STÄMMLER'

OLD, HYBRID PERPETUAL, MEDIUM PINK, REPEAT-FLOWERING

This interesting cross has produced a strong, more reliable repeat-flowering Hybrid Perpetual with crimson-pink flowers at such a late date. The bush makes medium growth and is very floriferous. Hybrid Perpetuals, however, are somewhat passé and this rose would be quite difficult to come by these days. ZONES 5–9.

Tantau, Germany, 1933

'Victor Verdier' × 'Arabella'

'STANWELL PERPETUAL'

OLD, SCOTS, WHITE, REPEAT-FLOWERING

This rose was found as a seedling in a garden in Stanwell, and what an extraordinary find it was. It has the habit and leaves of the Scots Roses and very much more of the repeat-flowering features of the Autumn Damasks. It bears pale blush pink flowers that are double, flat and quilled and which have quartered petals. It flowers repeatedly, if not exactly perpetually, and has a delicious fragrance. This is a lax, thorny bush of medium to

'Stanwell Perpetual'

'Stacey Sue'

'Star Trail'

'Starlet'

tall height. The foliage is small, ferny and burnet-like with 9 leaflets; the stems are very prickly. Old wood should be cut from the base each season to stimulate new growth. ZONES 4–9.

Lee, UK, 1838

Possibly a repeat-flowering Damask × Scots

'STAR DELIGHT' MORstar
MODERN, HYBRID RUGOSA, MEDIUM PINK, REPEAT-FLOWERING

The buds of this rose are pointed and open to rose pink, single flowers with white bases and silvery pink undersides. They are usually produced in fragrant clusters of 3–5 blooms amid the semi-glossy, medium-sized foliage, which is an unusual olive blue-green shade. An upright, bushy and tall plant, 'Star Delight' is one of the roses bred by Ralph Moore in his efforts to bring more variety into Modern Garden Roses. ZONES 4–10.

Moore, USA, 1990

'Yellow Jewel' × Rosa rugosa magnifica

'STAR OF WALTHAM'
OLD, HYBRID PERPETUAL, MEDIUM RED, REPEAT-FLOWERING

The rich crimson flowers of this rose fade to magenta, with an occasional white stripe. The scent is good and there are autumn flowers. It is a medium-sized bush with an upright and bushy growth habit. On the debit side, it must be admitted that there is a tendency to unreliability and the buds will not open in wet weather. It is not commonly available. ZONES 5–9.

Paul, UK, 1875

Parentage unknown

'STAR TRAIL'
MODERN, MINIATURE, APRICOT BLEND

This good little Miniature Rose carries most attractive, flat, well-formed blooms of 20–25 apricot-flushed, yellow-orange

'Stardust'

petals. The variety is small, compact and disease resistant with an abundant supply of short-stemmed flowers over a long period. The foliage is small and glossy dark green. The flowers are good for cutting at the bud stage as they hold well and their color lasts a long time. There is very little scent. ZONES 5–9.

Meilland, France, 1976

Parentage unknown

'STARDUST'
MODERN, GROUND COVER, MEDIUM YELLOW, REPEAT-FLOWERING

'Stardust' is an attractive Ground Cover Rose which has creamy yellow buds, opening to lighter yellow flowers with a darker center. The delicately formed double flowers are complemented by small, glossy mid-green foliage. ZONES 5–10.

Interplant, Holland, 1995

Parentage unknown

'STARGAZER'
MODERN, CLUSTER-FLOWERED/FLORIBUNDA, ORANGE-BLEND, REPEAT-FLOWERING

The flowers of 'Stargazer' are vivid orange-pink with a distinct creamy eye. They are small and single, with 9 petals, and come in large clusters on a low bushy plant. The blooms look straight upwards, so the name is very appropriate. There is a slight fragrance. The foliage is small and matt mid-green. 'Stargazer' is a bright little rose with great visual appeal; a number of plants should be planted close together for maximum effect. It has not become as popular as it deserves to be. ZONES 5–11.

Harkness, UK, 1977

'Marlena' × 'Kim'

Royal National Rose Society Certificate of Merit 1976

'Starina'

'STARGLO'
MODERN, MINIATURE, WHITE, REPEAT-FLOWERING

On this variety beautiful long, pointed buds reveal white flowers with just a hint of red, which gives this rose a fresh look. Another feature are the fully open blooms with yellow stamens, where a unique pointed star outline appearance adds to their beauty. The florets are double with 32 petals, have a light scent and have high exhibition-type centers; they are borne singly on long straight stems. The foliage is small and leathery in texture on a vigorous, upright bush that has a sprawling habit if left ungroomed. In some climates it may be slow to establish, but the wait is well worth it because it is particularly hardy and disease resistant. Here again the use of the pink Cluster-flowered Rose 'Little Darling' has been successful in producing another award-winning variety. ZONES 4–11.

Williams, USA, 1973

'Little Darling' × 'Jet Trail'

American Rose Society Award of Excellence 1975

'STARINA' MEIgabi, MEIgali
MODERN, MINIATURE, ORANGE-RED, REPEAT-FLOWERING

The blooms on 'Starina' are bright orange-scarlet-vermilion and are borne singly or in small clusters. They are beautifully formed exhibition-type, double florets and are complemented by small,

'Starglo'

glossy green foliage. It has a dwarf habit and is a classical Miniature Rose of the twentieth century, defining the standard for what is expected of Miniature Roses. Its popularity has spread all over the world and it is regarded as the 'Peace' of Miniature Roses. ZONES 5–10.

Meilland, France, 1965

('Dany Robin' × 'Fire King') × 'Perla de Montserrat'

Japan Gold Medal 1968, Anerkannte Deutsche Rose 1971

'STARLET'
MODERN, CLUSTER-FLOWERED/FLORIBUNDA, MEDIUM YELLOW, REPEAT-FLOWERING

This is a lovely little rose with soft yellow coloring. The pointed buds open to very double blooms each with 60 petals. They are high centered, medium sized and are borne both singly and in small clusters. The petals are attractively pointed and the blooms have a light perfume. The flowers are produced continuously, and they are wonderful for cutting as they open slowly and keep their color well. The foliage is glossy dark green, leathery and disease free. This vigorous, spreading plant reaches a low to medium height, which makes it an excellent rose for bedding and for borders; it can also be combined effectively with many bulbs and perennials. ZONES 5–11.

Swim, USA, 1957

'Goldilocks' × seedling

'Star Delight'

'Stargazer'

S

'STARS 'N' STRIPES'
MODERN, MINIATURE, RED BLEND,
REPEAT-FLOWERING

This rose has long, pointed buds that open to reveal flowers that are an evenly striped carmine red and white. The florets have 21 petals, a sweet fragrance and are borne in clusters. The foliage is light to mid-green on a tall, upright bush, making it an ideal choice as a hedge. With this rose, Moore achieved his wish to introduce striping into the Miniature breeding line. His search began by crossing the Cluster-flowered 'Little Darling' with the Hybrid Perpetual 'Ferdinand Pichard', to produce a key seedling he named Striped #14. Using 'Little Chief' as a seed parent and Striped #14 as the pollen parent, Moore produced the first step in evolving striped Miniatures. That rose was destined to become 'Stars 'n' Stripes' and was introduced in time to help celebrate the bicentennial of the United States in 1976. Needless to say, it has played an important role in developing other striped varieties. ZONES 5–10.

Moore, USA, 1975

'Little Chief' × ('Little Darling' × 'Ferdinand Pichard')

'STEFFI GRAF'   HELgraf
MODERN, LARGE-FLOWERED/HYBRID TEA,
MEDIUM PINK, REPEAT-FLOWERING

The plump buds of this bush rose open to perfectly formed, tight-centered,

urn-shaped flowers on upright stems. The blooms are mostly borne singly. The color is light pink, although there are touches of deep pink, especially around the petal edges. The foliage is dark green. ZONES 5–10.

Hetzel, Germany, 1993

Parentage unknown

'STELLA'
MODERN, LARGE-FLOWERED/HYBRID TEA,
PINK BLEND, REPEAT-FLOWERING

This has been a popular rose for exhibition and garden display since the 1960s. The large buds open to soft rose pink blooms tinged with cream at the centers and edged deeper pink on the outer petals. They are double, with 36 petals, high centered and large, produced both singly and in clusters. The color combination is subtle, soft and very pleasing, and there is a slight fragrance. The foliage is dark and leathery covering a vigorous, upright plant with good flower production and a fairly quick repeat. It makes a good bedding rose and has won quite a few 'best rose' awards. ZONES 5–10.

Tantau, Germany, 1958

'Horstmann's Jubilaümrose' × 'Peace'

National Rose Society Gold Medal 1960

'STELLA ELIZABETH'
MODERN, MINIATURE, WHITE, REPEAT-FLOWERING

The creamy white, double flowers with 35 petals on 'Stella Elizabeth' have a pink

'Stars 'n' Stripes'

'Stella Elizabeth'

'Stella'

'Steffi Graf'

edge to the petals. The blooms have a light fragrance and are borne in small clusters. The foliage is small and glossy mid-green green on a semi-vigorous bush that is clean and disease free. This rose is a floriferous bloomer, covering the entire bush in spring and late autumn. Its fast repeat-bloom cycle makes it a wonderful garden display plant; the plant also looks great in containers or in small spaces. ZONES 5–10.

Moore, USA, 1983

Seedling × seedling

'STEPHANIE DIANE'
MODERN, LARGE-FLOWERED/HYBRID TEA,
MEDIUM RED, REPEAT-FLOWERING

The double flowers of 'Stephanie Diane' are scarlet-red. They have 35 high-centered petals, and are large—to 5 in (12 cm) across. The flower production is fair and although the repeat is fairly slow, this is compensated for by a sweet fragrance. It is a moderately vigorous and upright plant with mid-green, semi-glossy foliage. 'Stephanie Diane' is a good rose for cutting as the large flowers open slowly and hold well. It is also a useful rose for exhibitors. ZONES 5–10.

Bees, UK, 1971

'Fragrant Cloud' × 'Cassandra'

'STEPHANIE JO'
MODERN, LARGE-FLOWERED/HYBRID TEA,
LIGHT PINK, REPEAT-FLOWERING

This tall-growing rose with healthy, mid-green, semi-glossy foliage carries

'Stephanie Jo'

'Stephanie Diane'

well-formed flowers that are very pale pink. The 25–30 petals of good substance open slowly from long buds, and release some fragrance. The blooms are produced in profusion, both singly and in small clusters, and have a quick repeat. They are good for cutting. 'Stephanie Jo' is one of the best roses raised in Australia. The breeder, Bill Allender, is a very keen rose exhibitor and judge. ZONES 5–9.

Allender, Australia, 1995

Sport of 'Sylvia'

'STEPHENS' BIG PURPLE'
STEbigpu

syns 'Big Purple', 'Nuit d'Orient'

MODERN, LARGE-FLOWERED/HYBRID TEA,
MAUVE BLEND, REPEAT-FLOWERING

This rose was bred by the late Pat Stephens of Te Awamatu, New Zealand. Both Paddy and his wife were leading rose exhibitors for a great many years. 'Stephens' Big Purple' is the deepest purple of all Large-flowered Roses; the large and oval buds open slowly to reveal double flowers with 35 petals. They are very fragrant and are produced on long stems on a tall, upright bush with large, matt mid-green, healthy foliage. This is a good producer but a little slow to repeat. It can be up to exhibition standard in cool weather and is a good rose for cutting where its unique color and strong perfume can be appreciated indoors. ZONES 5–10.

Stephens, New Zealand, 1985

Seedling × 'Purple Splendour'

'Stephens' Big Purple'

S

'Strawberry Swirl'

'Sterling Silver'

'Strawberry Crush'

'Stroller'

'STERLING SILVER'

MODERN, LARGE-FLOWERED/HYBRID TEA,
MAUVE BLEND, REPEAT-FLOWERING

This variety was one of the first of the
silvery mauve roses. The color is very
beautiful, quite different from all other
varieties, and the petals unfold from
long, pointed buds to form double
flowers with good substance. They are
high centered, cupped and strongly
scented at the full bloom stage, and they
usually appear in small clusters. Sadly,
the flower production is not high and
the repeat is rather slow. The foliage is
glossy, large and disease-free on this
rather short and upright plant, although
it is still worth growing for its unique
color, which is much more blue than
most mauve roses. The blooms are good
for cutting, looking best in silver and
pewter containers. ZONES 5–11.

Fisher, USA, 1957

Seedling × 'Peace'

'STRAWBERRY CRUSH'

MODERN, CLUSTER-FLOWERED/FLORIBUNDA,
MEDIUM RED, REPEAT-FLOWERING

This is one of the best Cluster-flowered
Roses for bedding purposes, because the
foliage is a most attractive red in the
early stages before it slowly turns to rich
green; it is very plentiful, glossy and
disease-free. The flowers occur in small

to large, well-shaped clusters and are a
luminous clear scarlet color. The buds
are particularly attractive and open to
medium-sized, slightly fragrant flowers
that are full, have excellent substance
and last very well without fading. The
flowering is very profuse and there is
rapid repeat. 'Strawberry Crush' is very
eye-catching when used as a bedding
rose, and is also splendid as a standard.
ZONES 5–10.

Dickson, UK, 1974

'Bridal Pink' × 'Franklin Englemann'

'STRAWBERRY SWIRL'

MODERN, MINIATURE, RED BLEND,
REPEAT-FLOWERING

The oval buds on this rose open to
blooms with 48 petals that are red mixed
with white and are reminiscent of the
Gallica 'Rosa Mundi', although the form
is like a Large-flowered Rose. The florets
are double and display their moss character with many fine prickles on the
stems. It is a spreading bush that puts out
long and arching canes, which the flowers
grow along. This rose is ideal for planting
on a bank or in a hanging basket. The
unique color combination delighted
many rosarians by the random swirling
effect across the petals. ZONES 5–10.

Moore, USA, 1978

'Little darling' × seedling of a Miniature Rose

'STRETCH JOHNSON'

MACfirwal

syns 'Rock 'n' Roll', 'Tango'

MODERN, MODERN SHRUB, RED BLEND,
REPEAT-FLOWERING

This is one of Sam McGredy's best hand-
painted roses: the flowers are brilliant
orange-scarlet with yellow centers and an
attractive suffusion of orange through
the petals. The undersides of the 15 petals
are silvery orange. The blooms come in
small and large clusters on a tall, almost
climbing bush. The foliage is mid-green,
semi-glossy, close jointed and very profuse. In autumn, large shoots appear
from the base bearing large heads of
colorful blooms. Like all the hand-
painted roses, it produces its best flowers
in autumn or during cool weather. It is
excellent as an eye-catching pillar rose.
ZONES 4–11.

McGredy, New Zealand, 1988

'Sexy Rexy' × 'Maestro'

Royal National Rose Society Gold Medal 1988,
Glasgow Silver Medal 1992, Golden Rose of The
Hague 1993, Royal Horticultural Society Award
of Garden Merit 1993

'STRING OF PEARLS'

RUIstringperl

MODERN, MINIATURE, ORANGE-PINK,
REPEAT-FLOWERING

Fern-like, bright green foliage, tiny buds
and flowers, make this small and dainty
shrub ideal for containers or confined
spaces. Tiny round buds appear all over
the plant and open to full, pearl-colored
flowers, becoming darker pink in the sun
so the shrub looks like one big posy. Unfortunately, it has no scent. ZONES 4–9.

de Ruiter, The Netherlands, 1991

Parentage unknown

'STROLLER'

MODERN, CLUSTER-FLOWERED/FLORIBUNDA,
RED BLEND, REPEAT-FLOWERING

'Stroller' was one of the first richly
bicolored Cluster-flowered Roses bred
by Pat Dickson. The buds are slim and
open to loose flowers of mid-cerise with
gold undersides. They are double and
come in small and large, lightly perfumed
clusters. The old flowers lose their rich
color rather quickly. The foliage is matt
mid-green on a bushy plant. ZONES 5–10.

Dickson, UK, 1968

'Manx Queen' × 'Happy Event'

Royal National Rose Society Certificate of Merit
1969

'SUE LAWLEY'   MACspash,

MACsplash

syn. 'Spanish Shawl'

MODERN, CLUSTER-FLOWERED/FLORIBUNDA,
RED BLEND, REPEAT-FLOWERING

This rose has medium red flowers with
light pink edges and silvery pink undersides, which add to the hand-painted effect. There are 20 petals and the clusters
of 3–7 blooms are lightly scented. The
matt foliage is red when young, ageing to
bright green, on a tall and very bushy
plant. There are many small prickles.
The flowering is profuse, with very rapid
repeat and the disease resistance is very
good. The color contrast is at its best in
cool weather. ZONES 5–10.

McGredy, New Zealand, 1980

(['Little Darling' × 'Goldilocks'] × [{'Evelyn
Fison' × ('Coryana' × 'Tantau's Triumph')} ×
{'John Church' × 'Elizabeth of Glamis'}]) ×
('Evelyn Fison' × ['Orange Sweetheart' ×
'Frühlingsmorgen'])

Royal National Rose Society Certificate of Merit
1977, New Zealand Gold Medal 1981

'Stretch Johnson'

'Stretch Johnson'

'Suitor'

'Suitor'

'SUE RYDER' HARlino
MODERN, CLUSTER-FLOWERED/FLORIBUNDA,
ORANGE-PINK, REPEAT-FLOWERING

The double blooms of 'Sue Ryder' are rich
salmon-orange shading to yellow at the
bases. They have about 20 petals, are
cupped, medium sized and produced in
large clusters. The flowers retain their
color well. There is very little fragrance.
The medium-sized foliage is mid-green
and glossy on a bushy plant. This is an
excellent bedding rose as it repeats very
quickly. ZONES 5–10.

Harkness, UK, 1980

('Southampton' × 'Colour Wonder') ×
('Parkdirektor Riggers' × 'Piccadilly')

Royal National Rose Society Trial Ground
Certificate 1978

'SUGAR ELF'
MODERN, CLIMBING MINIATURE, PINK BLEND,
REPEAT-FLOWERING

'Sugar Elf' has long, pointed buds that
open to reveal semi-double pink and
gold blend flowers with 15 petals and a
light fragrance. The foliage is glossy and
has a leathery texture on a plant with a
spreading habit. However, the vigor is
mostly spent on spreading growth immediately following the spring bloom,
and the repeat-bloom is poor. This rose
is often trained as a climber or displayed
in a hanging basket, where the canes arch
downwards in a graceful manner. It is
fairly disease free. ZONES 5–10.

Moore, USA, 1974

(Rosa wichuraiana × 'Floradora') × 'Debbie'

'SUITOR'
MODERN, POLYANTHA, MEDIUM PINK,
REPEAT-FLOWERING

This dwarf Polyantha produces rose pink
flowers of over 24 petals, and are borne
in clusters of 10–20 that are small and
strongly perfumed—unusual in a
Polyantha. The flower production is
good and repeat-bloom is rapid, and the
foliage is matt mid-green with few prickles. There is very little mildew. 'Suitor'
makes a nice little dwarf hedge as the
flowers keep their color well and last a
long time. ZONES 5–10.

Clark, Australia, 1942

'Alice Amos' × unknown

'SUMA' HARsuma
MODERN, GROUND COVER, MEDIUM RED,
REPEAT-FLOWERING

This sister seedling of 'Nozomi' has
many petalled, rose red blooms that

'Suma'

'Sue Lawley'

'Summer Blush'

pale with age. The spring crop is particularly lovely and covers the entire bush,
followed by a lesser summer bloom and
spasmodic bloom in the autumn. The
canes are very prostrate on the ground
and hug the soil, yet there is a dense
covering of small foliage, which makes
this is an excellent rose for cascading
over rocks or walls. The thin canes are
very pliable and easy to manipulate, so
the rose can also be trained upwards as a
little climber on a pole. 'Suma' will never
exceed 12 in (30 cm) in height, but it can
grow 4 ft (1.2 m) across, so it should be
given enough space. ZONES 5–10.

Onodera, Japan, 1989

Parentage unknown

Royal Horticultural Society Award of Garden
Merit 1993

OLD, ALBA, DEEP PINK

Rolf Sievers has crossed forms of *Rosa
alba* with those of *R. kordesii* to produce
a number of Alba Roses. The summer
flowers of this variety are medium red in
color, which is interesting since all other
Alba Roses are white or shades of pink.
The blooms open to show centers of
incurved petals; there are 30–40 petals
altogether. 'Summer Blush' is disease
resistant, and tough, healthy foliage covers this gracefully arching plant. There
is a very strong perfume. Winter hardiness is extremely good, which makes it
very suitable for Canada, the northern
USA and northern Europe. ZONES 4–9.

Sievers, Germany, 1988

Parentage unknown

'Sugar Elf'

'Sue Ryder'

S

'SUMMER BREEZE'

MODERN, CLUSTER-FLOWERED/FLORIBUNDA,
MEDIUM PINK, REPEAT-FLOWERING

The semi-double blooms of 'Summer Breeze' are produced with great freedom in small to large clusters on a very strong, bushy and spreading plant. The 20 soft rose pink petals give the flowers great substance, and they last a long time without fading. Flower production is very high and the repeat bloom is quick. The glossy, rich green foliage is extremely plentiful and free from disease. 'Summer Breeze' is a near-perfect standard, a good hedge rose where a shortish variety is needed and makes a very colorful border, looking great when mixed with bulbs and perennials. ZONES 5–11.

Kordes, Germany, 1987

Parentage unknown

'SUMMER BREEZE' KORelasting

MODERN, CLUSTER-FLOWERED CLIMBER, DEEP PINK,
REPEAT-FLOWERING

This new climbing rose bears large single to semi-double flowers with wide petals that open like saucers, displaying attractive golden stamens at the center. The flowers are a vibrant shade of deep rose pink and have a pleasing sweet fragrance. After the first flush blooming is maintained through summer and autumn, and in the garden this is a climber that will answer many purposes, being suitable for walls, fences, arches, pergolas and tall pillars. It makes a vigorous grower and has a freely branching habit. It is well furnished with glossy mid-green foliage. ZONES 4–9.

Kordes, Germany, 1998

Parentage unknown

'SUMMER DAMASK'

syn. *Rosa* × *damascena*
OLD, DAMASK, MEDIUM PINK

It is said that this rose was introduced into Europe from Asia Minor in the sixteenth century, but it was probably there much earlier. It is considered to be a cross between *Rosa gallica* and *R. phoenicea* and has double, pink or white flowers, sometimes striped, that are borne in clusters. They are intensely fragrant. The growth is upright, like a Gallica but stronger and somewhat lax. There are many forms of this rose, which are considered under their varietal names. ZONES 4–9.

Sixteenth century

Parentage unknown

'SUMMER DREAM' JACshe

MODERN, LARGE-FLOWERED/HYBRID TEA, APRICOT
BLEND, REPEAT-FLOWERING

The double, apricot-pink flowers of this rose have 30 petals to form medium-sized blooms with high centers and good exhibition form. They are usually borne singly on long stems so are good for cutting, and there is also a slight fruity fragrance. 'Summer Dream' has matt mid-green foliage on a plant with an upright growth habit. The repeat cycle is good and the plant has excellent resistance to disease. ZONES 5–10.

Warriner, USA, 1987

'Sunshine' × seedling

'SUMMER FASHION' JACale

syn. 'Arc de Triomphe'
MODERN, CLUSTER-FLOWERED/FLORIBUNDA,
YELLOW BLEND, REPEAT-FLOWERING

The color of this rose is really quite beautiful: the 20 or so petals are light yellow and edged with soft salmon-pink, and as the flower ages the pink spreads over the yellow. The fragrant, double flowers are large for a Cluster-flowered Rose and are borne both singly and in small, well-shaped clusters. The foliage is large, mid-green, abundant and semi-glossy, and covers a bush that is a little on the small side. The repeat-flowering is a little slow, but 'Summer Fashion' always attracts attention because of its unusual, attractive color. It makes a good standard rose and is suitable as a low border. ZONES 5–10.

Warriner, USA, 1986

'Precilla' × 'Bridal Pink'

'SUMMER HOLIDAY'

MODERN, LARGE-FLOWERED/HYBRID TEA,
ORANGE-RED, REPEAT-FLOWERING

This is a much better rose than its parent 'Superstar'. The long, pointed buds open to flowers that are an intense orange-scarlet, and the clear color holds well on the bush without fading. The fragrant, double blooms have about 50 high-centered petals, and are produced on very long stems. It is a very vigorous, bushy plant with abundant, semi-glossy, dark green foliage. The flower production is profuse and continuous and there are no disease problems. This rose makes an excellent hedge. ZONES 5–11.

Gregory, UK, 1967

'Superstar' × seedling

Royal National Rose Society Trial Ground
Certificate 1968

'SUMMER LADY' TANyoal

MODERN, LARGE-FLOWERED/HYBRID TEA,
PINK BLEND, REPEAT-FLOWERING

The slender, velvety cream-pink buds of this plant open to give deeper pink blooms overlaid with a salmon tint deep into the center of the bloom. They have an excellent, high-centered form, but lack enough petals to hold perfection for long. The lush green foliage is plentiful, and there is a nice perfume. ZONES 5–10.

Tantau, Germany, 1993

Parentage unknown

'SUMMER QUEEN'

MODERN, LARGE-FLOWERED/HYBRID TEA,
WHITE BLEND, REPEAT-FLOWERING

This very pale pink sport of 'Queen Elizabeth' has all the vigor, glossy, healthy foliage and freedom of flower of its parent. The double blooms are made up of 38 pale shell pink petals to form high-centered to cupped flowers up to 4 in (10 cm) across. They are produced both singly and in small and large, well-spaced clusters. The very pale color looks very handsome against the very dark

'Summer Breeze'

'Summer Breeze'

'Summer Dream'

'Summer Holiday'

'Summer Fashion'

'Summer Queen'

S

green foliage. The flower production is excellent with a quick repeat and there are no disease problems. It is a very tall and upright bush with thick canes—an excellent rose for cutting as the flowers are produced on very long stems and are attractive at all stages of their development. ZONES 5–11.

Deforge, Belgium, 1964

Sport of 'Queen Elizabeth'

'SUMMER SNOW'
MODERN, CLUSTER-FLOWERED/FLORIBUNDA, WHITE, REPEAT-FLOWERING

It is unusual for a bush rose to have sported from a climbing rose, but this is the case with 'Summer Snow', which sported two years after the climber was introduced. The white, slightly scented flowers are large for a Cluster-flowered Rose, reaching 3 in (8 cm) across, and are borne in large, well-spaced clusters. The abundant foliage is very pale green on a plant with a low and very bushy growth habit. Mildew can be a problem in damp weather. This rose makes a nice bushy border or low hedge, and is also useful in groups among bulbs and perennials. ZONES 5–10.

Perkins, USA, 1938

Sport of 'Climbing Summer Snow'

'SUMMER SONG'
syn. 'Chanson d'Eté'

MODERN, CLUSTER-FLOWERED/FLORIBUNDA, ORANGE BLEND, REPEAT-FLOWERING

This rose changes color in the manner of its parent: the blooms open to apricot-orange with yellow shades, then mature to a peachy coral. They are semi-double

'Summer Song'

'Summertime'

with 12 petals, and are produced in small clusters with some fragrance. The repeat-bloom is very slow, and the low bush is covered with glossy foliage. ZONES 5–10.

Dickson, UK, 1962

Seedling × 'Masquerade'

'SUMMER SUNSHINE'
syn. 'Soleil d'Eté'

MODERN, LARGE-FLOWERED/HYBRID TEA, DEEP YELLOW, REPEAT-FLOWERING

The oval buds of 'Summer Sunshine' open to lightly fragrant flowers that are a brilliant yellow color. They are double, with 24 petals, high centered to cupped, and up to 5 in (12 cm) across. It is usually the first rose to bloom each spring and one of the last to finish in early winter. It also opens very quickly in summer heat and reaches its peak production and performance in the cool autumn months where the red tints in the outer petals are much more pronounced. The foliage is leathery, very dark green and semi-glossy, and growth is upright and bushy. There is only a little mildew in the autumn. 'Summer Sunshine' is one of the best yellow roses for bedding and for borders. ZONES 5–11.

Swim, USA, 1962

'Buccaneer' × 'Lemon Chiffon'

'SUMMER WINE'   KORizont
MODERN, LARGE FLOWERED CLIMBER, DEEP PINK/MEDIUM PINK, REPEAT-FLOWERING

This climbing rose has charming flowers of coral-pink with very prominent red stamens. The semi-double, very fragrant blooms are produced in clusters and they hold well if picked in the bud stage; they

'Summer Wine'

'Summer Sunshine'

'Summer Sunshine'

show up well against the dark green foliage. It is a very vigorous, tall and upright plant and is excellent for pillars, tripods, pergolas or arches where its unsophisticated flowers can act as a contrast to double varieties. ZONES 5–10.

Kordes, Germany, 1984

Parentage unknown

Royal National Rose Society Trial Ground Certificate 1982, Royal Horticultural Society Award of Garden Merit 1993

'SUMMERTIME'
MODERN, LARGE-FLOWERED/HYBRID TEA, DEEP YELLOW, REPEAT-FLOWERING

There are two roses with this name: one bred by Boerner in 1957 that has pink, very double flowers, and this one from Tantau in 1983. The double, rich yellow blooms which are tinged with red have about 24 petals, and are produced in small clusters. The flowers open rather quickly in summer heat amid the abundant, dark green foliage. 'Summertime' is a fine yellow bedding rose. There is a slight perfume and good disease resistance. ZONES 5–10.

Tantau, Germany, 1983

Parentage unknown

'SUN FLARE'   JACjem
syn. 'Sunflare'

MODERN, CLUSTER-FLOWERED/FLORIBUNDA, MEDIUM YELLOW, REPEAT-FLOWERING

The long, pointed buds of 'Sun Flare' open to flat, medium yellow, double

'Sun Flare'

flowers with 20-30 petals, showing attractive stamens. They are borne in small to medium-sized, well-spaced clusters of 3–15 blooms with a slight fragrance. The foliage is small, glossy and disease-free. This is a superb rose for a low hedge or for bedding and makes an ideal standard. If spent blooms are not removed, a large crop of round red hips are produced. The awards prove that it is a very good rose for exhibiting. **'Climbing Sun Flare'**, introduced in 1987, is a welcome addition to the small list of yellow climbers. With its glossy foliage and ample flowers, it makes an excellent rose for pergolas, tripods or poles. ZONES 5–10.

Warriner, USA, 1981

'Sunsprite' × seedling

Japan Gold Medal 1981, All-America Rose Selection 1983, Portland Gold Medal 1985

'Summer Snow'

S

'Sunblest'

'Sun Goddess'

'Sun King'

'SUN GODDESS' JACdash
syn. 'Rose of Wagga Wagga'
MODERN, LARGE-FLOWERED/HYBRID TEA,
DEEP YELLOW, REPEAT-FLOWERING

The synonym given to this rose by
Swane's Nurseries in Australia refers to
the New South Wales town of Wagga
Wagga. The flowers are a clear lemon
yellow, faintly edged with pink. The
blooms are produced on long strong
stems, each bloom containing 28 petals.
There is a moderate fragrance. The
abundant foliage is dark green and the
plant has an upright growth habit. This
is a good healthy rose that is excellent for
bedding as the flowers keep their color
well and are nicely complemented by the
attractive foliage. ZONES 6–9.
Warriner, USA, 1993
'Sunbright' × seedling

'SUN KING'
MODERN, LARGE-FLOWERED/HYBRID TEA,
MEDIUM YELLOW, REPEAT-FLOWERING

This is a rose of unusual color—a deep
chrome yellow. The lovely buds are long
and pointed and open rather quickly to
double flowers, which contain 45 high-
centered petals. The blooms are up to
4 in (10 cm) across and appear amid the
abundant dark green, very glossy foliage
on a vigorous, upright, fairly thorny
plant. The flower production is good and
the repeat cycle is quick. This is one of
the first roses to flower in the spring, and
it continues to flower until winter in
warm climates. The slender buds are
lovely even though they open quite
quickly. There are no disease problems.
ZONES 5–10.
Meilland, France, 1954
'Peace' × 'Duchesse de Talleyrand'

'SUNBABY'
MODERN, CLUSTER-FLOWERED/FLORIBUNDA, DEEP
YELLOW, REPEAT-FLOWERING

This is a very short-growing rose that
produces bright yellow, well-formed
flowers. These are small for a Cluster-
flowered Rose. They appear singly and
in small clusters and show up well
against the mid-green, semi-glossy
foliage. It is a very dense bush with no
disease problems; it makes a lovely rose
for pots and window boxes. It also makes
an attractive, very low border to other
varieties if a number of bushes are
planted close together. ZONES 5–10.
Kordes, Germany, 1987
Parentage unknown

'Sunblaze Baron'

'SUNBEAM' KORdoselba
MODERN, LARGE-FLOWERED/HYBRID TEA,
APRICOT BLEND, REPEAT-FLOWERING

The buds of 'Sunbeam' open slowly to
particularly well-formed, medium-sized,
double flowers with 30–40 petals, which
hold their color and form well. There is a
slight fragrance. The foliage is large, dark
green and semi-glossy, and covers this
shortish bush. Although the repeat-
bloom is rather slow, this is a good rose
for cutting as flowers are attractive at all
stages. It is a fine rose for bedding, and is
also grown under glass for the cut-flower
trade. ZONES 5–10.
Kordes, Germany, 1987
Parentage unknown

'SUNBLAZE BARON' NEItifran
syns 'Baron Meillandina', 'Baron Sunblaze'
MODERN, MINIATURE, RED BLEND,
REPEAT-FLOWERING

These blooms are bicolored: the 40 petals
are cream and heavily margined with
deep pink-red. The flowers are very full
and borne singly in small clusters. This is
a very compact and bushy plant, which is
ideal in pots or containers. The flower
production is very high, with a quick repeat. There is also a good resistance to
disease. The flowers are good for indoor
display if cut at the bud stage. ZONES 5–10.
Meilland, France, 1989
'Magic Carrousel' × (['Alain' × *Rosa chinensis*] ×
['Medar' × 'Caprice'])

'SUNBLEST'
syn. 'Landora'
MODERN, LARGE-FLOWERED/HYBRID TEA,
DEEP YELLOW, REPEAT-FLOWERING

This is one of the best yellow roses: it
bears copious supplies of mid- to deep
yellow, very well-shaped flowers that
contain 38 pointed petals. The slightly
fragrant, double blooms are up to 5 in
(12 cm) across and the color is very

attractive at all times. The stems are of
medium length, which makes this good
for cutting. The blooms last well on this
strong, tall and healthy bush with pale
green, very glossy foliage. The disease resistance is good for a yellow rose, but
there can be some black spot. **'Climbing
Sunblest'** is an excellent sport with lush
pale green foliage and excellent flower
production. It is a strong plant that is
suitable on pillars, tripods or fences.
ZONES 5–10.
Tantau, Germany, 1970
Seedling × 'King's Ransom'
Japan Gold Medal 1971, Royal National Rose
Society Trial Ground Certificate 1972, New
Zealand Gold Medal 1973

'SUNBRIGHT'
MODERN, LARGE-FLOWERED/HYBRID TEA,
MEDIUM YELLOW, REPEAT-FLOWERING

The long, pointed buds of 'Sunbright'
open to double flowers that contain
28 petals. They are medium yellow and
open flat. The blooms are large—up to
4 in (10 cm) across—and have a light
fragrance. The upright bush grows to
medium height and has abundant, mid-
green, disease-resistant foliage. It makes
a good bedding rose where a clear yellow
flower is required. ZONES 5–10.
Warriner, USA, 1984
Seedling × 'New Day'

'SUNDERLAND SUPREME'
NOSsun
MODERN, LARGE-FLOWERED/HYBRID TEA,
LIGHT PINK/PINK BLEND, REPEAT-FLOWERING

Very few roses bred in the 1980s have a
Hybrid Perpetual as a parent, although
there appears to be little of 'Paul Neyron'
in 'Sunderland Supreme' except for the
huge flowers. These are light pink,
shaded dark pink on the petal edges, and
are filled with 30–40 petals with good
exhibition form. There is a slight scent.
The foliage is medium-sized, mid-green
and semi-glossy on a tall and spreading
plant. The flower production is good for
the first flush, but there are rather long
spells between flushes. This rose can produce superb exhibition blooms in the
cool weather of autumn. ZONES 5–10.
Greensitt, UK, 1986
'Paul Neyron' × 'Royal Highness'

'SUNDOWNER' MACche, MACcheup
MODERN, LARGE-FLOWERED/HYBRID TEA,
APRICOT BLEND, REPEAT-FLOWERING

'Sundowner' is an enormous grower and
produces very long-stemmed flowers

'Sunbaby'

'Sunbeam'

'Sunhit'

'Sunmaid'

'Sunlit'

'Sunny'

'SUNLIT'

MODERN, LARGE-FLOWERED/HYBRID TEA, APRICOT BLEND, REPEAT-FLOWERING

One of Alister Clark's best roses, 'Sunlit' bears the richest apricot flowers, which are double, globular and are borne in great profusion for an enormous length of time. This rose even flowers well into winter in mild climates. It has a low to medium growth habit with a abundance of mid-green foliage. There are no disease problems. In 1937, there were very few apricot roses as rich in color as 'Sunlit', and because of its color and freedom of bloom, it is still a popular rose. ZONES 5–10.

Clark, Australia, 1937

Parentage unknown

'SUNMAID'

MODERN, MINIATURE, YELLOW BLEND, REPEAT-FLOWERING

These flowers are a bright combination of yellow and orange that looks spectacular against the dark glossy foliage. The yellow color deepens in full sun. The florets come mainly in clusters of 4–10 blooms. This low, compact grower is a good choice for a border or in a mass planting. It has a tendency to mildew and rust if left unprotected. It is often regarded by many rosarians as the best multicolored Miniature Rose. ZONES 5–10.

Spek, The Netherlands, 1972

Parentage unknown

'SUNNY'

MODERN, CLUSTER-FLOWERED/FLORIBUNDA, MEDIUM YELLOW, REPEAT-FLOWERING

Ralph Moore is considered the greatest breeder of Miniature Roses in the world today. His 'Halo series' roses have colorful eyes in the center of the flowers. 'Sunny' has pointed, yellow flowers that are overlaid with red. Semi-double, they open to pale yellow, and are small and fragrant. The foliage is leathery, mid-green and glossy on a vigorous, upright and bushy plant. ZONES 5–11.

Moore, USA, 1952

Seedling × 'Goldilocks'

that are apricot-orange with yellow bases to the petals. The very fragrant, double blooms have 35 petals of excellent form, and are borne amid the healthy, mid-green foliage on this very upright-growing bush, which is a little prone to mildew during autumn. Its long stems and bright color make 'Sundowner' an excellent rose for cutting for indoor display. It is also a wonderful rose to use with fruit and berries for autumn interior decoration. ZONES 5–10.

McGredy, New Zealand, 1978

'Bond Street' × 'Peer Gynt'

All-America Rose Selection 1979

'SUNDRA'   GAlsu

MODERN, CLUSTER-FLOWERED/FLORIBUNDA, DARK RED, REPEAT-FLOWERING

The dark red color and good petal texture of this rose is inherited from 'Lilli Marleen'. 'Sundra' produces pointed buds that mature to semi-double, cupped flowers, which are quite large for a Cluster-flowered Rose. The flowers are very fragrant, which is unusual in red Cluster-flowered Roses as they are not known for their scent. The foliage is glossy and the plant has a vigorous and bushy growth habit. 'Sundra' is an excellent little rose makes a good low border; it is also a great bedding rose for a spot where a low-grower is required. ZONES 5–10.

Gaujard, France, 1968

'Club' × 'Lilli Marleen'

'SUNDUST'

MODERN, MINIATURE, YELLOW BLEND, REPEAT-FLOWERING

Soft apricot, pointed buds on 'Sundust' open to lighter apricot to buff yellow, double flowers with 23 petals. They have

a fruity fragrance. The color of the flowers can be preserved longer if it is planted in partial shade. The foliage is light green on a compact bush that is probably best suited to growing in a container. Like many yellow Miniatures, this rose has lost some popularity due to the fierce competition of introductions during the last decade. ZONES 5–10.

Moore, USA, 1977

'Golden Glow ' × 'Magic Wand'

'SUNHIT'   POUlsun

MODERN, MINIATURE, DEEP YELLOW, REPEAT-FLOWERING

The large flowers of this cultivar have a fine form and are produced abundantly in well-spaced, quick-repeating clusters. There are about two dozen well-rounded petals of good substance, which hold their deep yellow color well. The leaves are glossy dark green, covering this compact and upright plant. 'Sunhit' makes a good, disease-resistant pot plant, which is also eye-catching in a small bed or border. ZONES 5–10.

Poulsen, Denmark, 1994

Parentage unknown

'Sundra'

'Sundust'

'Sunderland Supreme'

'Sundowner'

S

'SUNNY AFTERNOON' TALsun
MODERN, MINIATURE, YELLOW BLEND, REPEAT-FLOWERING

The beautiful pointed buds of 'Sunny Afternoon' open to light yellow flowers with the outer petal edges carrying a pinkish apricot tinge. The color holds well with very little fading in strong sunlight, although the pink and apricot can become more pronounced. The double blooms (15–25 petals) are borne one per stem and have good high centers that can hold for days. The size of the flowers is that of a true Miniature, and the equally small mid-green, semi-glossy foliage gracefully complements the blooms. It is a tall, upright, vigorous bush and is susceptible to powdery mildew if left unprotected. This rose is a bright addition to the garden with superior growth and flowering characteristics over many in its color class. ZONES 5–11.

Taylor, USA, 1995

'Party Girl' × 'Elina'

'SUNNY HONEY'
MODERN, CLUSTER-FLOWERED/FLORIBUNDA, APRICOT BLEND, REPEAT-FLOWERING

This rose produces flowers of an unusual and most attractive blend of apricot and peach tones: a lovely luminous color that is just that bit different. There is a shading of red on the outer petals, and the fragrant, double flowers—large for a Cluster-flowered Rose—have 22 petals and are produced in clusters of 3–7 amid the large, dark and disease-free foliage. The plant is a moderately sized, compact

bush, and its flowers look especially lovely in an indoor arrangement where the color glows under artificial light. 'Sunny Honey' is very popular in New Zealand and Australia, but it does not seem to be freely available in other countries. It is an excellent rose for beds and borders. ZONES 5–11.

Dickson, UK, 1972

'Happy Event' × 'Elizabeth of Glamis'

'SUNNY JUNE'
MODERN, MODERN SHRUB, DEEP YELLOW, REPEAT-FLOWERING

This first-class shrub rose has many pointed buds that open quickly to single, medium-sized flowers of deep canary yellow with amber stamens. They are produced in small to large clusters with a slight spicy fragrance. The flowering is continuous from spring to late autumn, and if the buds are picked when tight, they last well indoors. The growth is strong and upright. 'Sunny June' can be used as a large shrub or trained on a pillar; the deep yellow flowers show up very well against the profuse, glossy green foliage. It is one of the best repeat-flowering, yellow shrub roses available. ZONES 5–10.

Lammerts, USA, 1952

'Crimson Glory' × 'Captain Thomas'

'SUNNY MORNING'
MODERN, MINIATURE, MEDIUM YELLOW, REPEAT-FLOWERING

The long and pointed buds of 'Sunny Morning' open to deep creamy yellow,

'Sunny June'

'Sunny Morning'

'Sunny Honey'

'Sunrise Sunset'

double blooms of 35 neatly arranged petals. They are small and flat—1½ in (3 cm) across—with quite a pleasant fragrance. The plant is upright and bushy with a plentiful, fast-repeating display of well-spaced flowers. The buds are good for cutting. 'Sunny Morning' makes a good low border if planted close together, and has a good resistance to disease. ZONES 5–10.

Moore, USA, 1974

'Golden Glow' × 'Peachy White'

'SUNNY SKY'
MODERN, LARGE-FLOWERED/HYBRID TEA, YELLOW BLEND, REPEAT-FLOWERING

This rose is a clear coppery yellow color that is most attractive. The buds are shapely and open slowly to very double, attractive full blooms with excellent substance. The flowers are quite durable and hold their color well. It is a medium-sized plant with healthy, dark green foliage and an upright habit of growth. Both the flower production and the repeat-bloom are very good. 'Sunny Sky' is an excellent cut-flower variety for growing under glass, but also makes a wonderful garden rose. It lasts a long time when cut. ZONES 5–10.

Kordes, Germany, 1996

Parentage unknown

'SUNNY SOUTH'
MODERN, LARGE-FLOWERED/HYBRID TEA, PINK BLEND, REPEAT-FLOWERING

'Sunny South' and 'Lorraine Lee' are Alister Clark's best roses. 'Sunny South' grows very tall and is extremely vigorous. The plant is particularly free flowering over a very long period. The large blooms are rose pink, flushed with carmine and have a pronounced yellow base to each petal. They are semi-double with 15–20 petals, cupped at first then opening flat. The foliage is large, rich green and semi-

'Sunrose'

'Sunny Sky'

glossy, and is a nice backdrop to the large clusters of flowers. 'Sunny South' makes a superbly disease-resistant hedge rose. The variety is sometimes classified as a Grandiflora. ZONES 5–10.

Clark, Australia, 1918

'Gustau Grünerwald' × 'Betty Berkeley'

'SUNNY TODAY'
MODERN, CLUSTER-FLOWERED/FLORIBUNDA, DEEP YELLOW, REPEAT-FLOWERING

As this variety was bred from three deep yellow roses, it is not surprising that 'Sunny Today' has blooms of the same color. They are double, with 20–25, high-centered petals, 3½ in (9 cm) across and fragrant. Dark green and glossy foliage covers the moderate and bushy, disease-resistant growth. The plant begins its profuse flowering in early spring, quickly followed by repeat-blooms. ZONES 5–10.

Whisler, USA, 1970

('Summer Sunshine' × 'Gold Cup') × 'Isobel Harkness'

'SUNRISE SUNSET'
MODERN, LARGE-FLOWERED/HYBRID TEA, PINK BLEND, REPEAT-FLOWERING

This rose produces flowers that are a blend of pink, cream and lavender. The large, oval buds open to double flowers with 30 well-formed petals that give excellent substance. There is a slight fragrance. The foliage is dark, glossy and leathery on a plant with a strong and upright growth habit. The flower production is a little sparse and the plants take rather a long time to repeat, but the blooms can be of exhibition standard. The color is particularly rich in cool autumn weather. ZONES 5–11.

Swim and Weeks, USA, 1971

('Tiffany' × seedling) × 'Rouge Meilland'

'Sunny Today'

S

'Sunseeker'

'SUNROSE'

**MODERN, CLUSTER-FLOWERED/FLORIBUNDA,
ORANGE-PINK, REPEAT-FLOWERING**

This rose bears shapely, rich salmon-orange flowers that have excellent substance. The well-formed blooms are 3 in (8 cm) across and hold their color well on this low and spreading, disease-free bush with a good repeat cycle. This is a fine bedding rose, and its luminous color makes it attractive when cut. **ZONES 5–10.**

McGredy, New Zealand, 1973

Parentage unknown

'SUNSEEKER' DICracer
syns ' Duchess of York', 'Sarah Duchess of York'

**MODERN, CLUSTER-FLOWERED/FLORIBUNDA,
ORANGE-RED, REPEAT-FLOWERING**

This recent introduction has bright orange-red flowers suffused with sulfur yellow. They are small yet filled with about 25–40 petals, and are borne in small clusters on a very low bush amid mid-green, semi-glossy foliage. There is a light scent. This is a lovely little rose for pots or window boxes, and also makes a free-flowering border that provides bright color over a long period. There are no disease problems. **ZONES 5–10.**

Dickson, UK, 1994

'Little Prince' × 'Gentle Touch'

Royal National Rose Society Trial Ground Certificate 1991, Belfast Gold Medal 1994, Glasgow Silver Medal 1994

'SUNSET'
OLD, TEA, DEEP YELLOW, REPEAT-FLOWERING

This fragrant Tea Rose does not always open well: if the weather is wet, the blooms will simply ball and rot. The flowers are much deeper in color than its parent: they are orange-yellow, filled with 50–60 petals, cupped and very large. When they do open well, they are superb. It is very tall and spreading in warm climates, but much less robust in cooler areas and has plentiful, dark green foliage that is prone to mildew. Like its parent, 'Sunset' can be magnificent if weather conditions are right. Both roses were grown for many years under glass for the florist trade early this century. It used to be common for brides to carry bouquets of yellow Tea Roses. **ZONES 5–10.**

Henderson, USA, 1883

Sport of 'Perle des Jardins'

'Sunset Celebration'

'SUNSET BOULEVARD'
HARbabble

**MODERN, CLUSTER-FLOWERED/FLORIBUNDA,
ORANGE-PINK, REPEAT-FLOWERING**

Launched as the 'Rose of the Year' at the Hampton Court Flower Show in 1997, 'Sunset Boulevard' has very well-shaped buds that open to glowing apricot-orange flowers, which are borne in small clusters. The rose has only a moderate fragrance, but the substance is excellent. It is a low, compact, very free-flowering bush with a rapid repeat. There are no disease problems. It makes an excellent bedding rose and is also suitable for the front of the border. **ZONES 5–11.**

Harkness, UK, 1997

'Harold MacMillan' × 'Fellowship'

Royal National Rose Society Trial Ground Certificate 1996, UK Rose of the Year 1997

'SUNSET CELEBRATION'
FRYxotic

syns 'Chantoli', 'Exotic', 'Warm Wishes'

**MODERN, LARGE-FLOWERED/HYBRID TEA,
ORANGE-PINK, REPEAT-FLOWERING**

The peachy salmon blooms of this cultivar are of medium to large size with neatly formed high centers. Although the petals number fewer than 30, they are wide and substantial, opening slowly to

'Sunset Boulevard'

create a long-lasting and shapely flower. They are usually carried singly, sometimes in a wide cluster, and are fragrant and good for cutting. In the garden, this is a good subject for a bed of one variety and to group in a border. It continues to produce flowers through summer and autumn, and seems unaffected by wind and rain. The plants grow vigorously with a bushy habit to average height or more, with ample dark foliage. **ZONES 4–9.**

Fryer, UK, 1994

'Pot o' Gold' × (seedling × 'Cheshire Life')

Royal National Rose Society Trial Ground Certificate 1993, Belfast Gold Medal 1996, Golden Rose of the Hague 1997, All-America Rose Selection 1998

'Sunset Song'

'Sunsprite'

'Sunsprite'

'SUNSET SONG' COCasun

MODERN, LARGE-FLOWERED/HYBRID TEA, APRICOT BLEND/ORANGE BLEND, REPEAT-FLOWERING

This tall and upright grower produces large heads of flowers on long stems. The pointed buds open to double flowers with 45 petals of good form. The blooms are produced both singly and several to a cluster; they are apricot-orange in color, and last well. There is some fragrance. The abundant foliage is glossy and light olive green. In autumn, large candelabra-like growth appears with side shoots long enough for cutting. ZONES 5–10.

Cocker, UK, 1981

('Sabine' × 'Circus') × 'Sunblest'

Royal National Rose Society Trial Ground Certificate 1979

'SUNSHINE'

MODERN, POLYANTHA, ORANGE BLEND, REPEAT-FLOWERING

This small-growing rose is an unusual color for a Polyantha: it has small, oval, attractive buds that open to clusters of double, golden orange flowers. They are fragrant, and last well when cut. Glossy and abundant foliage covers this bush, which needs to be planted close together in groups for maximum effect as a low border to edge to taller varieties. The small clusters of flowers are quite charming. ZONES 5–10.

Robichon, France, 1927

Parentage unknown

'SUNSILK'

MODERN, CLUSTER-FLOWERED/FLORIBUNDA, MEDIUM YELLOW, REPEAT-FLOWERING

The slightly fragrant flowers of 'Sunsilk' are lemon yellow. They are double, with 30 petals, and are large for a Cluster-flowered Rose—up to 4 in (10 cm) across. The plant has a medium-sized and bushy growth habit, and the dark green foliage acts as an effective foil to the flowers. It is excellent for borders or bedding. It does not appear to be available in many countries outside the UK. ZONES 5–10.

Fryer, UK, 1974

'Pink Parfait' × seedling of 'Redgold'

Belfast Gold Medal 1976

'Super Fairy'

'SUNSPRAY' AROrasp

MODERN, MINIATURE, DEEP YELLOW, REPEAT-FLOWERING

'Sunspray' has long, ovoid, pointed buds that open to reveal bright deep yellow flowers with 16 petals. The florets have a light Tea fragrance and are set against complementary semi-glossy, dark green foliage on a vigorous, upright bush. The blooms are borne singly or in clusters. This rose is best suited to cooler climates where the color can be shown at its best. The bush stands out in the garden because of its lovely bright yellow blooms. It is easy to grow, very disease resistant and constantly in color. ZONES 5–10.

Christensen, USA, 1981

'Gingersnap' × 'Magic Carrousel'

'SUNSPRITE' KOResia

syns 'Friesia', 'Korresia'

MODERN, CLUSTER-FLOWERED/FLORIBUNDA, DEEP YELLOW, REPEAT-FLOWERING

This rose is one of the best deep yellow Cluster-flowered Roses. The attractive, oval buds open to flat, double flowers with 28 very symmetrically arranged petals. These large blooms are intense rich yellow, extremely fragrant and are produced in great quantities; the repeat-blooming is extremely fast. The foliage is abundant, dark green and very glossy on a plant with a short to medium, stocky habit. The open blooms shatter rather quickly, which makes them unsuitable for cutting, although deadheading keeps the bush neat and tidy. This is one of the best of all bedding roses, and makes a very colorful low hedge as well as a standard. ZONES 5–11.

Kordes, Germany, 1977

'Friedrich Wörlein' × 'Spanish Sun'

Baden-Baden Gold Medal 1972, James Alexander Gamble Fragrance Award 1979, James Mason Memorial Medal 1989

'SUPER DOROTHY' HELdoro

MODERN, RAMBLER, MEDIUM PINK, REPEAT-FLOWERING

This rose causes a sensation whenever it is seen: the blooms are similar to those of 'Dorothy Perkins', but it continues to bloom through summer and autumn, which makes 'Super Dorothy' a wonderful weeping rose. The pink flowers come in small clusters and last well on the bush. It is not quite as vigorous as 'Dorothy Perkins', but this does not matter because of the freedom of flower. 'Super Dorothy' has become popular in Europe since its introduction, and has now been introduced into the USA and Australia. It looks wonderful on pillars, tripods and arbors as its repeat-flowering provides color for much longer than any other rambling rose. ZONES 5–10.

Hetzel, Germany, 1986

'Dorothy Perkins' × unidentified repeat-flowering rose

'SUPER EXCELSA' HELexa

MODERN, RAMBLER, DARK RED, REPEAT-FLOWERING

This rose has all the good qualities of 'Excelsa', with the added bonus of repeat-flowering through summer and autumn. The crimson-red flowers appear in small clusters and its vigorous and pliable growth makes it perfect for training over arches and pergolas. Unfortunately, there is some mildew at times. 'Super Excelsa' is also suitable for pillars, and is excellent when grafted onto a weeping rose. ZONES 5–10.

Hetzel, Germany, 1986

'Excelsa' × unidentified repeat-flowering rose

Anerkannte Deutsche Rose 1992

'SUPER FAIRY' HELSvfair

MODERN, RAMBLER, LIGHT PINK, REPEAT-FLOWERING

The flowers of 'Super Fairy' are light pink, double with 15–25 petals and are borne in large clusters. The fragrant blooms are 1½ in (35 mm) across. The foliage is medium green and glossy on a strong plant that grows to 3 ft (1 m) high and has long pliable canes. Flowering is continuous, which is very rare in a rambling rose. This is one of the repeat-flowering Ramblers raised by Karl Helzel; others include 'Super Dorothy' and 'Super Excelsa'. ZONES 4–11.

Hetzel, Germany, 1992

Parentage unknown

'SUPER SPARKLE' HELfels

MODERN, RAMBLER, DARK RED, REPEAT-FLOWERING

Karl Hetzel has bred a number of repeat-flowering Ramblers, which is a major advance because almost all Ramblers currently available flower only once. All are becoming popular in Europe for use as weeping roses. 'Super Sparkle' produces crimson-scarlet, double flowers of 15–25 petals. These blooms are 2 in (5 cm) across and are carried in very large clusters that have some fragrance. Medium-sized, glossy dark green foliage covers this strong, disease-resistant variety. 'Super Sparkle' can be used on pillars, tripods, arches and pergolas and wherever a bright crimson rose is needed. ZONES 5–10.

Hetzel, Germany, 1996

Parentage unknown

'Superb Tuscan'

'Superb Tuscan'

'SUPER SUN'

MODERN, LARGE-FLOWERED/HYBRID TEA,
MEDIUM YELLOW, REPEAT-FLOWERING

This rose has all the good qualities of 'Piccadilly', except that the color is maize yellow. The double flowers have 28 high-centered petals, and open to large blooms of 4–5 in (10–12 cm) in diameter. The medium bush has glossy foliage that is tinted red when young. It is vigorous and upright, and bloom production is good with quick repeat. ZONES 5–10.

Bentley, UK, 1967

Sport of 'Piccadilly'

Royal National Rose Society Trial Ground
Certificate 1968

'SUPERB TUSCAN'

syn. 'Tuscany Superb'
OLD, GALLICA, MAUVE

This very old rose has larger leaves and flowers than its parent. The semi-double, maroon-purple flowers have pronounced yellow stamens. It is a medium-sized, upright plant with small dark green leaves. It will sucker freely unless grafted with the union above the ground. The origin of this beautiful old rose is lost in antiquity. ZONES 4–9.

Rivers, UK, pre-1837

Sport of 'Tuscany'

Royal Horticultural Society Award of Garden
Merit 1993

'SURPASSE TOUT'

syn. 'Cérisette la Jolie'
OLD, GALLICA, MEDIUM RED

Many Gallicas were selected in the early nineteenth century before the later Bourbons and Hybrid Perpetuals with repeat-flowering characteristics ended the fashion. This one has deep cerise-maroon flowers and is fragrant. The flowers are full with a button eye. It is said to be rather sparse and leggy and grows to medium height. ZONES 4–9.

The Netherlands, pre-1832

Parentage unknown

'SURPASSING BEAUTY OF WOOLVERSTONE'

syn. 'Woolverstone Church Rose'
OLD, HYBRID PERPETUAL, DARK RED

This 'found' rose, discovered by Humphrey Brooke in a churchyard of Woolverstone Church in Suffolk, England, was re-introduced by Peter Beales. It is a vigorous semi-climber with early, blowzy, deep red, very fragrant flowers. ZONES 5–9.

Parentage unknown

'SURREY'   KORlanum

syns 'Sommerwind', 'Vent d'Eté'
MODERN, GROUND COVER, LIGHT PINK,
REPEAT-FLOWERING

This excellent Ground Cover Rose grows much wider than it does tall: up to 3 ft (1 m) tall and 4 ft (1.2 m) wide. The plant smothers itself with great clusters of soft pink, double blooms that deepen to rose pink in the heart of the flower. They show up well against the small, dark green, disease-resistant foliage. 'Surrey' is very popular in the UK, where it is used with very pleasing results when planted in large drifts in front of taller-growing varieties. Most of the varieties named after English counties are bred in Denmark or Germany. ZONES 5–10.

Kordes, Germany, 1988

'The Fairy' × seedling

Royal National Rose Society Gold Medal 1987,
Royal Horticultural Society Award of Garden
Merit 1993

'SUSAN'   KORkilt

MODERN, LARGE-FLOWERED/HYBRID TEA,
MEDIUM PINK, REPEAT-FLOWERING

One of many cut-flower varieties produced by Kordes, 'Susan' is suitable for both cut-flower production under glass and for garden display. It produces shapely buds that open slowly to very fragrant flowers that are pale to mid-pink, flushed deeper pink in cool weather. The blooms hold their color well. This strong and upright plant flowers profusely. The healthy, dark green foliage is very resistant to disease. This is also an excellent rose for bedding. ZONES 5–11.

Kordes, Germany, 1996

Parentage unknown

'Surpasse Tout'

'SUSAN HAMPSHIRE'   MEInatac

MODERN, LARGE-FLOWERED/HYBRID TEA,
LIGHT PINK, REPEAT-FLOWERING

This is a very good garden rose with vigorous, upright growth and ample foliage. The very fragrant, rich pink, double flowers, with 40 petals, are large and globular. It makes an ideal bedding rose because the plants are well foliaged to ground level and the rich rose pink color holds well in all weather conditions. The strong scent is also a great asset. Susan Hampshire is a prominent television star in the UK. ZONES 5–11.

Paolino, France, 1972

('Monique' × 'Symphonie') × 'Maria Callas'

'SUSAN JELLICOE'   HORkeepog

MODERN, CLUSTER-FLOWERED/FLORIBUNDA, WHITE
BLEND, REPEAT-FLOWERING

This variety bears large, shapely flowers with 25–40 petals that are a fresh blend of soft creamy pink. They are borne both

'Susan'

singly and in small, very fragrant clusters. The abundant foliage is semi-glossy and mid-green on a plant with an upright and bushy habit. 'Susan Jellicoe' makes a good bedding plant, and is also suitable in a border. ZONES 5–10.

Horner, USA, 1994

'Keepsake' × 'Pot O' Gold'

'Susan Jellicoe'

'Susan Hampshire'

'Surrey'

S

'SUSAN LOUISE'
MODERN, MODERN SHRUB, LIGHT PINK, REPEAT-FLOWERING

'Susan Louise' is a repeat-flowering form of 'Belle Portugaise', and is credited to Charles Adams of San Jose, California. The large floppy blooms are a light flesh pink. It flowers very spectacularly, but only briefly in summer. 'Susan Louise' is rather tender and is suitable only for warm climates. It seems to have caught on only in Australia, where it is readily available. ZONES 7–9.

Adams, USA, 1929

Seedling of 'Belle Portugaise'

'SUSAN MASSU' KORad
syn. 'Susan'

MODERN, LARGE-FLOWERED/HYBRID TEA, YELLOW BLEND, REPEAT-FLOWERING

This rose is often confused with the Kordes cut-flower variety introduced in 1992. The flowers are an unusual blend of soft yellow and rich salmon-pink. They open fairly quickly from large, oval buds to very durable, full blooms that keep their color well. They are shapely and attractive being large, cupped and double, with up to 40 petals, and the fragrance is quite strong. 'Susan Massu' has dark green, leathery foliage and the bushy plant grows to medium height. It makes a fine bedding rose and the color is attractive both at close quarters and from a distance. ZONES 5–10.

Kordes, Germany, 1970

'Colour Wonder' × 'Liberty Bell'

Baden-Baden Gold Medal 1968

'SUSPENSE' MEIfan
MODERN, LARGE-FLOWERED/HYBRID TEA, RED BLEND, REPEAT-FLOWERING

One of the earliest red and yellow bicolored roses, 'Suspense' bears lightly fragrant flowers that are Turkey red with yellow undersides. They are very large, very double, with 50–60 high-centered petals, and very long lasting. The foliage is large, leathery and glossy and growth is upright. Unfortunately, it does not produce many flowers and the repeat cycle is very slow, although the full blooms are extremely beautiful and very useful at rose shows. ZONES 5–10.

Meilland, France, 1960

'Henri Mallerin' × ('Happiness' × 'Floradora')

'SUSSEX' POUlave
syn. 'Apricot Cottage Rose'

MODERN, GROUND COVER, APRICOT BLEND, REPEAT-FLOWERING

This is one of the series of roses named after English counties introduced by Mattocks of Oxford from various conti-nental breeders. The flowers of 'Sussex' are attractive apricot buff, double with about two dozen petals, small and cupped. They come in both small and large clusters, and are produced over a very long period on this low and spreading bush. The foliage is small, mid-green and plentiful. 'Sussex' is suitable for use as a low border and for forming mounds where a soft color is required. ZONES 5–10.

Poulsen, Denmark, 1991

Parentage unknown

'SUTTER'S GOLD'
MODERN, LARGE-FLOWERED/HYBRID TEA, ORANGE BLEND, REPEAT-FLOWERING

This is one of the great roses of the 1950s. Bred from 'Charlotte Armstrong', which is noted for its very long elegant buds, 'Sutter's Gold' has inherited the slim bud and flower form of that parent. The color is gold and orange overlaid with Indian red. It opens to rather a loose full bloom of 30 petals that form high-centered, large and very fragrant flowers. They open very quickly in summer heat. The copious foliage is very dark green and leathery on an upright and vigorous plant. Its many awards are testimony to its great qualities, and it is no surprise that is still grown in most countries of the world after 50 years in commerce. **'Climbing Sutter's Gold'** is a first class climbing rose with magnificent rich dark green, leathery foliage. ZONES 5–10.

Swim, USA, 1950

'Charlotte Armstrong' × 'Signora'

Portland Gold Medal 1946, Bagatelle Gold Medal 1948, All-America Rose Selection 1950, National Rose Society Certificate of Merit 1951, James Alexander Gamble Fragrance Medal 1966

'Susan Massu'

'Sussex'

'Susan Louise'

'Swan'

'Climbing Sutter's Gold'

'Suzon Lotthé, Climbing'

'SUZON LOTTHÉ, CLIMBING'
MODERN, LARGE-FLOWERED CLIMBER, PINK BLEND, REPEAT-FLOWERING

This rose has peach-pink and cream blooms that open fully to well-formed, high-centered flowers to 5 in (12 cm) across. They are very full, with 60 petals of a soft pearly pink flushed with deep lavender pink at the petal edges. They are very fragrant with a true Damask perfume, a feature inherited from the Hybrid Perpetual 'Mrs John Laing'. The blooms are produced on long stems and retain their color well; flower production is particularly good in autumn when the color deepens at the edges. The foliage is matt mid-green on a strong plant with pale stems and very few thorns. It is suitable on a pillar, tripod or fence, and is also good against the wall of a house where its perfume can be appreciated from inside. ZONES 4–11.

Trimper, Australia, 1964

('Peace' × 'Signora') × 'Mrs John Laing'

'SWAN' AUSwhite
MODERN, MODERN SHRUB, WHITE BLEND, REPEAT-FLOWERING

The lightly fragrant blooms of 'Swan' are extra large and contain at least 60 petals. The color is cream in the bud stage, then open to show soft primrose yellow at the centers of the flowers with cream shading on the outer petals; the whole flower becomes cream as it ages. It is at its best in warm, dry weather because the petals spot in the rain or after heavy dews. The bush is extremely strong and healthy and has large, glossy pale green foliage. 'Swan' is a magnificent rose for large arrangements as it holds its color and form when cut. In cold areas, the bush is much smaller with a consequent diminishing in the number of flowers. The variety can be easily recognized by the very quilled petals. In warm climates, it can be grown effectively on a pillar or tripod; it can also look good trained horizontally along a wall or fence where flower production is even greater. 'Swan' is also classified as an English Rose. ZONES 5–10.

Austin, UK, 1987

S

'SWAN LAKE'

syn. 'Schwanensee'

MODERN, LARGE-FLOWERED CLIMBER, WHITE BLEND, REPEAT-FLOWERING

The well-shaped buds of this rose open slowly to double, well-formed, fragrant blooms with 50 pale pink petals. They are produced on long stems and are suitable for exhibition. Flowering is continuous, although the most shapely and long lasting blooms are seen in autumn. The plant has a moderately vigorous growth habit and the foliage is mid-green, abundant and disease-free. It is ideal for pillars, tripods and fences. ZONES 4–11.

McGredy, UK, 1968

'Memoriam' × 'Heidelberg'

'SWANY' MEIburonac

MODERN, GROUND COVER, WHITE, REPEAT-FLOWERING

The oval buds on this variety open to pure white, cup-shaped flowers with an astonishing 95 petals. The blooms come in clusters that can cover the entire bush. The foliage is glossy bronze on a very vigorous, spreading plant. 'Swany' was probably the forerunner of the shrub 'Bonica' from the same breeder. It makes an ideal ground cover, even on a steep bank where the canes can tumble downwards. It derives its spreading habit from the species seed parent. ZONES 4–11.

Meilland, France, 1978

Rosa sempervirens × 'Mlle Marthe Carron'

Royal Horticultural Society Award of Garden Merit 1994

'SWARTHMORE' MEItaras

MODERN, LARGE-FLOWERED/HYBRID TEA, PINK BLEND, REPEAT-FLOWERING

The flowers of 'Swarthmore' are a subtle blend of several shades of pink and light red with a wash of mauve-pink. They are large and double with 50 petals that form a high center and a good exhibition form. There is some perfume. The blooms are produced on long stems and last well when cut, but flower production is average with long gaps between flushes. The foliage is dark green, leathery and abundant, and covers a tall, vigorous bush. The stems are very dark. ZONES 5–10.

Meilland, France, 1963

('Independence' × 'Rouge Meilland') × 'Peace'

'SWEET AFTON'

MODERN, LARGE-FLOWERED/HYBRID TEA, WHITE BLEND/LIGHT PINK, REPEAT-FLOWERING

The flowers of this rose are very pale pink. They develop from elegant, long,

'Swan'

'Sweet Dream'

pointed buds, and open to very fragrant, double, high-centered flowers that are 5 in (12 cm) across. The disease-resistant foliage is dark green and leathery on a plant with a tall, bushy and spreading growth habit. This is a lovely rose for cutting. ZONES 5–10.

Armstrong, USA, 1964

('Charlotte Armstrong' × 'Signora') × ('Alice Stern' × 'Ondine')

'SWEET CHARIOT' MORchari

syn. 'Insolite'

MODERN, MINIATURE, MAUVE, REPEAT-FLOWERING

'Sweet Chariot' has lavender to purple blend flowers that age to a superb mixture of lavender hues. The florets have 40 petals, and come in large clusters that take several weeks to bloom out. One very distinguishing feature of this rose is its overpowering perfume: no matter where it is planted in the garden the heavy Damask fragrance can be detected. The foliage is small and mid-green on an upright, vigorous, spreading plant. This rose is excellent in a hanging basket, as the canes arch downwards to cover the container and the clusters hang out, spreading their fragrance in the surrounding air. ZONES 5–10.

Moore, USA, 1984

'Little Chief' × 'Violette'

'SWEET DREAM' FRYminicot

syn. 'Sweet Dreams'

MODERN, CLUSTER-FLOWERED/FLORIBUNDA, APRICOT BLEND, REPEAT-FLOWERING

This variety has very well-formed blooms of soft peachy apricot that are borne both singly and in large clusters; they have a strong, sweet scent. It is a small, cushion-like bush with extremely

'Swany'

'Swarthmore'

'Sweet Chariot'

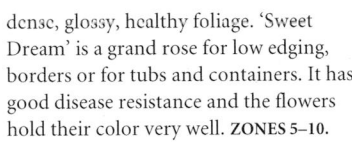

dense, glossy, healthy foliage. 'Sweet Dream' is a grand rose for low edging, borders or for tubs and containers. It has good disease resistance and the flowers hold their color very well. ZONES 5–10.

Fryer, UK, 1988

Seedling × (['Anytime' × 'Liverpool Echo'] × ['New Penny' × seedling])

British Association of Rose Breeders Rose of the Year 1988, Belfast Certificate of Merit 1990, Royal Horticultural Society Award of Garden Merit 1993

'SWEET FAIRY'

MODERN, MINIATURE, LIGHT PINK, REPEAT-FLOWERING

The lilac-rose pink, cupped flowers with 57 petals on this variety are very small, qualifying this rose as a micro-miniature. The foliage is small and dark green on a vigorous plant to only 6–8 in (15–20 cm) high. The blooms open flat with pointed petals arranged into a rosette shape. This is one of the earliest Miniature Roses hybridized using the classic early variety 'Tom Thumb' as a seed parent. 'Sweet Fairy' has become somewhat obscure because of popular taste in more modern Miniature Roses. ZONES 5–10.

de Vink, The Netherlands, 1946

'Tom Thumb' × seedling

'SWEET HOME'

MODERN, LARGE-FLOWERED/HYBRID TEA, DEEP PINK, REPEAT-FLOWERING

The flowers of 'Sweet Home' are a clear deep pink; they are double with 35 petals

'Sweet Home'

'Sweet Inspiration'

that form a high center at first, then open to a cupped form. The large blooms are produced in both small and large, well-shaped clusters and have excellent substance. There is some fragrance on this vigorous, bushy plant with dark, disease-resistant foliage. ZONES 5–10.

Meilland, France, 1969

('Jolie Madame' × 'Baccarà') × ('Baccarà' × 'Jolie Madame')

'SWEET INSPIRATION' JACsim

MODERN, CLUSTER-FLOWERED/FLORIBUNDA, MEDIUM PINK, REPEAT-FLOWERING

This well-named rose produces large quantities of very clear medium pink flowers with 25 petals that are cream at the bases. They are large—to 4 in (10 cm) across—with cream at the base of each petal. These have good substance and are borne in small and large clusters

S

'Sweet Magic'

'Sweet Juliet'

'Sweet Nell'

'Swiss Fire'

that last well on the bush with very little fading. The foliage is mid-green and matt, and there are very few thorns. 'Sweet Inspiration' is a bushy, strong and upright plant that is excellent for both bedding and borders, since the flower production is prolific and continuous. ZONES 5–10.

Warriner, USA, 1993

'Sunflare' × 'Simplicity'

All-America Rose Selection 1993

'SWEET JULIET'   AUSleap
MODERN, MODERN SHRUB, APRICOT BLEND, REPEAT-FLOWERING

This rose has small buds that open to large, very cupped flowers that form many-petalled rosettes with a distinct button eye. They are soft, delicate apricot fading to almost white at the petal edges, and have a strong Tea-like fragrance. The foliage has very pointed, pale green leaflets with a brownish tinge, and covers a very upright and strong shrub, which produces a thicket of canes in autumn. It is a great pity that many of these late growths do not flower, since the spring

flush is most prolific; if it flowered as well in autumn as in spring, this would be one of the best David Austin varieties. It is also classified as an English Rose. ZONES 5–10.

Austin, UK, 1989

'Graham Thomas' × 'Admired Miranda'

Belfast Fragrance Award 1992

'SWEET MAGIC'   DICmagic
MODERN, PATIO/DWARF CLUSTER-FLOWERED, ORANGE BLEND, REPEAT-FLOWERING

This variety has orange-gold pointed buds that open to reveal bright orange flowers with golden highlights. The florets are semi-double with 15–25 petals, have no fragrance and open quickly to flat flowers displaying prominent stamens. The medium-sized flowers are produced in wonderful clusters on a neat, well-rounded bush with dark green shiny foliage that is a perfect complement to the bright florets. This plant is easy to grow, healthy and weatherproof. It does well in containers, borders and patios. The centerpiece of the Royal National Rose Society Rose Festival in 1986 was a

massive display of 'Sweet Magic', which captured the audience because of its intensity of color and grace. ZONES 5–10.

Dickson, UK, 1986

'Peek A Boo' × 'Bright Smile'

Royal National Rose Society Trial Ground Certificate 1986, RNRS Rose of The Year 1987, Royal Horticultural Society Award of Garden Merit 1993

'SWEET MEMORIES'   WHAmemo
MODERN, PATIO/DWARF CLUSTER-FLOWERED, LIGHT YELLOW, REPEAT-FLOWERING

The flowers of this rose are produced in large clusters of soft lemon with a distinctive, old-fashioned and quartered look. The bloom production is prolific and free, and there is a light scent. Light green, disease-resistant foliage covers the plant, which grows to about 1–2 ft (30–60 cm) high in moderate climates. It is suitable for a container or for planting in a border. ZONES 5–11.

Sport of 'Sweet Dream'

'SWEET NELL'   COCavoter
MODERN, CLUSTER-FLOWERED/FLORIBUNDA, ORANGE BLEND, REPEAT-FLOWERING

The double, large flowers of 'Sweet Nell' have 35 orange petals, and have a slight fragrance. It has mid-green, semi-glossy foliage and an upright growth habit that is quite disease resistant. The flower production is good with a quick repeat. This is a good rose for beds and borders, but it does not seem to be readily available outside the UK. ZONES 5–10.

Cocker, UK, 1983

'Anne Cocker' × ('Mischief' × [('Sabine' × 'Circus') × ('Superstar' × 'Circus')])

'SWEET REVENGE'   TINrevenge
syn. 'Pat O'Brien'
MODERN, MINIATURE, ORANGE-RED, REPEAT-FLOWERING

These flowers are a soft orange with a blush of deep orange. The double florets

have 26–40 petals and a light scent. They are borne singly and occasionally in small clusters on long stems. The foliage is medium dark green and semi-glossy on a tall, vigorous bush. It is resistant to disease but lacks winter hardiness. This is mainly a garden variety and produces occasional exhibition blooms. It was originally called 'Pat O'Brien' who was married to Dee Bennett's daughter, Sue. After their divorce, Sue re-named it 'Sweet Revenge'! ZONES 5–10.

Bennett, USA, 1996

'Tony Jacklin' × 'Pucker Up'

'SWEET SUNSATION'   KORfisro
MODERN, GROUND COVER, LIGHT PINK, REPEAT-FLOWERING

Landscape architects love the new 'Sunsation' roses, because of their shiny, healthy foliage and the way they hug the ground to give low-maintenance coverage of large public spaces. When necessary, this plant can be clipped with ordinary shears, but because it is thorny, the bed it is planted in should, for easy management, not be too wide. 'Sweet Sunsation' bears soft pink flowers that are larger than other Ground Cover Roses. It has no fragrance. ZONES 4–11.

Kordes, Germany, 1991

Parentage unknown

'SWEET SURRENDER'
MODERN, LARGE-FLOWERED/HYBRID TEA, MEDIUM PINK, REPEAT-FLOWERING

The double flowers of 'Sweet Surrender' are clear silvery pink. They are 5 in (12 cm) across, and have 40 petals to form the shape of a cup; there is a strong Tea Rose fragrance. The foliage is dark, leathery and disease-free on a plant with a strong growth habit and above-average flower production with a quick repeat-bloom. Its parent, 'Tiffany', also received an All-America Rose Selection award. Both roses have a strong perfume, long stems and beautifully shaped flowers of a good strong color. ZONES 5–11.

Weeks, USA, 1983

Seedling × 'Tiffany'

All-America Rose Selection 1983

'SWEET VIVIEN'
MODERN, CLUSTER-FLOWERED/FLORIBUNDA, PINK BLEND, REPEAT-FLOWERING

This is a very compact-growing, bushy rose suitable for use as a low border or edging to a rose bed. The flowers are clear pink, shading to yellow at the center of the flower. The blooms are

'Swinging Sixties'

'Sweetie Pie'

'Symphony'

semi-double with 17 petals, quite large and are produced in small clusters on short stems. If spent blooms are not removed, large, pear-shaped hips are produced. It is not readily available outside the USA. **ZONES 5–10.**

Raffel, USA, 1961

'Little Darling' × 'Odorata'

'SWEETHEART' COCapeer
MODERN, LARGE-FLOWERED/HYBRID TEA, MEDIUM PINK, REPEAT-FLOWERING

The buds of 'Sweetheart' are oval and very attractive; they open to medium pink, double flowers with 50 high-centered petals that are usually borne singly on very long stems. They are very fragrant and hold their rich color very well. The foliage is large, prolific and mid-green on a tall, upright and bushy plant that repeats quickly. This is a good rose for bedding and for borders; its double flowers are excellent for cutting, with the strong scent an added bonus. **ZONES 5–10.**

Cocker, UK, 1980

'Peer Gynt' × ('Fragrant Cloud' × 'Gay Gordons')

Belfast Fragrance Award 1982

'SWEETIE PIE'
MODERN, LARGE-FLOWERED/HYBRID TEA, LIGHT PINK, REPEAT-FLOWERING

This very attractive rose has the same strong, upright growth of its parent. It also has the same abundance of dark green foliage and long-stemmed flowers, but the color is much richer. The blooms are light pink shaded with a deep lavender-pink that turns to ruby at the petal edges. They are about 4 in (10 cm) across with very high centers. There is a slight fragrance. With its unusual color and very long stems, this is a good rose for cutting; the 55-petalled blooms last very well when used for indoor decoration. **ZONES 5–10.**

Hyde, USA, 1971

Sport of 'Swarthmore'

'SWINGING SIXTIES'
MODERN, CLUSTER-FLOWERED/FLORIBUNDA, YELLOW BLEND, REPEAT-FLOWERING

'Swinging Sixties' produces clusters of very colorful flowers that change from yellow to orange then red as they mature. They are 3 in (8 cm) across and there is a

'Sydney Linton'

little scent. The bush is small to medium in size, which makes it excellent for a low border where a blend of bright color is required. The flower production is a little sparse, and the repeat rather slow. **ZONES 5–10.**

USA, 1996

Parentage unknown

'SWISS FIRE' HUBar
MODERN, LARGE-FLOWERED/HYBRID TEA, ORANGE-RED, REPEAT-FLOWERING

The flowers of this rose open from plump buds into large, full-petalled blooms, initially with high centers but becoming cupped as the broad petals reflex. They display lively shades of fiery red with geranium red but unfortunately fail to derive any great benefit from the parental fragrance genes, having no more than a light spicy aroma. Blooming continues through summer and autumn. This is a useful plant for beds and near the front of borders, though it does not appear to be commercially available at the present time. The plant grows with an upright, bushy habit to below average height and has matt dark green foliage. **ZONES 4–9.**

Huber, Switzerland, 1975

'Fragrant Cloud' × 'Ena Harkness'

'SYBIL HIPKIN'
MODERN, LARGE-FLOWERED/HYBRID TEA, DEEP YELLOW, REPEAT-FLOWERING

This is one of the best yellow roses bred in Australia. The buds are long and pointed, and open to well-formed blooms that contain 35–40 clear and unfading, yellow petals. Flowering is profuse and continuous, and there is a slight perfume. The disease-resistant foliage is large, plentiful and glossy, and flowers are produced on long stems with rather plum-colored wood. The buds are particularly good for cutting, since they

'Sybil Hipkin'

open slowly for a yellow rose and keep well. The autumn flush is very long lasting and rich in color. **ZONES 5–10.**

Dawson, Australia, 1972

Parentage unknown

'SYDNEY LINTON'
OLD, HYBRID PERPETUAL, DEEP PINK, REPEAT-FLOWERING

'Sydney Linton' was found at Hay, in New South Wales, Australia. It is a remarkable rose, with flowers not unlike those of 'Paul Neyron'. The many petals form a flat and full bloom of remarkable size, with the form of a peony. After an enormous spring flush, odd blooms are produced right through summer and autumn and give some scent. The foliage is large and dark green and cover this very tall and upright plant. This is one of the best of all Hybrid Perpetuals and was named after the first Bishop of the Riverina, who occupied Bishop's Lodge in the latter part the nineteenth century. **ZONES 5–10.**

Australia

Parentage unknown

'SYDONIE'
syn. 'Sidonie'
OLD, HYBRID PERPETUAL, MEDIUM PINK, REPEAT-FLOWERING

This rose has brilliant soft pink flowers that are flat and quartered and are borne in clusters. They have muddled centers and frilled petals. It is a small to medium bush and looks in some ways more like a Portland. It has the characteristic Damask fragrance and is said to be susceptible to black spot. **ZONES 5–9.**

Dorisy, France, 1846

Seedling of 'Belle de Trianon'

'SYMPATHIE'
syn. 'Sympathy'
MODERN, LARGE-FLOWERED CLIMBER, MEDIUM RED, REPEAT-FLOWERING

This variety bears clusters of lightly scented, blood red flowers, each with 20 or more petals that develop to a fairly large size and open cupped. The intensely deep, yet bright color stands out beautifully against the background of rich green shiny foliage. The first flush of

bloom is prolific, but the later repeats in summer are rather sporadic; repeat-flowering improves later in the season to give a good autumn display. 'Sympathie' descends from the raiser's Kordesii line and is a vigorous, fast-growing and adaptable plant; it produces long, arching stems and is very well suited to fences, walls and pergolas. **ZONES 4–9.**

Kordes, Germany, 1964

'Wilhelm Hansmann' × 'Don Juan'

Anerkannte Deutsche Rose 1966

'SYMPHONY' AUSlett
syns 'Allux Symphony', 'Symphonie'
MODERN, MODERN SHRUB, LIGHT YELLOW, REPEAT-FLOWERING

This variety produces medium-sized flowers composed of over 40 small petals, usually in close clusters. They open to a medium shade of yellow, paler towards the petal edges, then become rosette shaped as the petals expand and finally age to pink. They have a very pleasing fragrance and continue to appear through summer and autumn, being happiest in warmer weather. 'Symphony' is suitable for planting as a cheerful group near the front of a shrub border or for a bed. It grows upright with a fairly compact, bushy habit to below average height and has plentiful shiny foliage. It was named for the Allux commercial enterprise in connection with the Breast Cancer Fund for Wales. The variety is also classified as an English Rose. **ZONES 4–9.**

Austin, UK, 1986

'The Knight' × 'Yellow Cushion'

'Sympathie'

'Sydonie'

T

'TABARIN'

MODERN, CLUSTER-FLOWERED/FLORIBUNDA, MEDIUM PINK, REPEAT-FLOWERING

This is a colorful bicolor variety, having buttercup yellow on the lower petal area and clear red towards the margins. The buds are carried in small clusters and open into semi-double, cupped blooms of medium to large size with good scent. There is a good continuity of flower through summer and autumn, and in its heyday this lively, free-flowering rose was popular for use in beds and borders, and to make a hedge; it does not appear to be in cultivation today. 'Tabarin' grows with moderate vigor and a bushy, compact habit to average height, and has small, glossy light green leaves. Its name is a word used for a striped fabric, with reference to the variegated nature of the flowers. ZONES 4–9.

Gaujard, France, 1956

'Opéra' × 'Masquerade'

Royal National Rose Society Certificate of Merit 1957

'TABOO' TANelorak

syns 'Barkarole', 'Grand Château'

MODERN, LARGE-FLOWERED/HYBRID TEA, DARK RED, REPEAT-FLOWERING

The flowers of this variety are long and slender and are made up of broad petals that form high centers in classic Large-

'Tabarin'

'Taboo'

'Tamara'

flowered style. They are among the darkest red roses to be found, and as they are carried on long stems they provide plenty of blooms for cutting; they have a moderate scent. The succession of bloom is well maintained through summer and autumn and, with all these points in its favor, 'Taboo' should be a most desirable variety. Unfortunately, it has a poor habit of growth, the plant appearing splayed and lopsided, which greatly reduces its value as a rose for beds and borders. It is best grown in a cutting garden where the flowers can be taken but the plant does not continually confront the eye. It grows vigorously and unevenly to above average height and has large, dark glossy leaves. ZONES 4–9.

Evers, Germany, 1988

Parentage unknown

'TABRIS' KORtabris

syn. 'Raspberry Ice'

MODERN, CLUSTER-FLOWERED/FLORIBUNDA, PINK BLEND, REPEAT-FLOWERING

When the same name is used for different roses, confusion ensues. The rose 'Raspberry Ice' sold in most parts of the world is codenamed KORweiso and is also called 'Hannah Gordon'. But the less well known KORtabris, sold as 'Tabris', is also known as 'Raspberry Ice'. Both look similar, having semi-double,

'Talisman'

'Climbing Talisman'

cupped blooms of creamy blush white, edged with cherry red. However, with 'Tabris' the colors appear to contrast more harshly and the plant grows larger, so that as well as being used in beds, borders and as a hedge, it may be grown into a big shrub or semi-climber in warm climates. The flowers are lightly scented and continue in production through summer and autumn. The variety grows vigorously with an upright habit and is well furnished with rich green foliage. ZONES 4–9.

Kordes, Germany, 1986

Parentage unknown

Portland Gold Medal 1995

'TALISMAN'

MODERN, LARGE-FLOWERED/HYBRID TEA, YELLOW BLEND, REPEAT-FLOWERING

This variety was one of the few pre-1939 Large-flowered Roses to retain its popularity for many years after the war. In its favor is the wonderful freedom of flower, the ability to bloom again quickly, a neat bedding habit and a pretty combination of colors—for in its 30 petals can be found scarlet, pink, copper and gold shades mixed up together. The flowers show beautifully coiled centers as the petals begin to part, then they open out like saucers to reveal the stamens. In the young stage, the blooms make wonderful buttonholes; they were formerly cultivated as cut-flower roses, their straight, springy stems making them admirably suited for that purpose. They have a sweet fruity scent. This is a good rose to grow both for horticultural and historical reasons. The plant is moderately vigorous and has an upright, narrow habit, growing to average height or less with light green, leathery, semi-glossy leaves. **'Climbing Talisman'** (Western, USA, 1930) gives a splendid first flush of bloom followed by occasional flowers later in the season. It produces long, arching stems and grows to slightly more than the extent normally expected of a climber, with flowers and leaves identical to those of the bush form. ZONES 4–9.

Montgomery, USA, 1929

'Ophélia' × 'Souvenir de Claudius Pernet'

American Rose Society Gold Medal 1929, ARS John Cook Gold Medal 1932

'TALL STORY' DICkooky

MODERN, CLUSTER-FLOWERED/FLORIBUNDA, MEDIUM YELLOW, REPEAT-FLOWERING

This variety is often listed as a Ground Cover Rose, but it grows rather like a

shallow pyramid. The medium-sized blooms have a cool look, resembling butter fresh from the dairy. They are semi-double, borne in neatly spaced sprays on graceful arching stems and appear on the plant at various levels, giving a wonderfully airy effect. There is a pleasing scent, and flowers are produced with good succession through summer and autumn. 'Tall Story' is a lovely rose to use where a specimen plant is needed for a small space. It can also be grouped in a border or bed. By the nature of the growth, the bush will be amply adorned with bright green glossy leaves to the ground. It has a spreading habit. ZONES 4–9.

Dickson, UK, 1984

'Sunsprite' × 'Yesterday'

Royal Horticultural Society Award of Garden Merit 1993

'TAMARA' KORmador

MODERN, CLUSTER-FLOWERED/FLORIBUNDA, APRICOT BLEND, REPEAT-FLOWERING

This rose bears beautifully formed, soft creamy champagne pink flowers in large clusters. The medium-sized blooms open slowly to reveal 40 or more slightly ruffled petals. The stems are long and there are very few thorns, so this is a great rose for cutting. There is some fragrance on this very bushy rose, which reaches low to medium height. The flower production is high, and the repeat cycle is quick. It is excellent under glass, and for bedding schemes and borders in the open garden. ZONES 5–10.

Kordes, Germany, 1990

Parentage unknown

'TAMBOURINE' HARdolly

MODERN, CLUSTER-FLOWERED/FLORIBUNDA, ORANGE BLEND, REPEAT-FLOWERING

This bright little rose bears many clusters of medium-sized, semi-double yellow flowers that gradually turn to orange-red before dropping. A group of plants undergoing this change creates a flamboyant effect; it is a very suitable and noticeable variety for a bed, border or as a low and colorful hedge. There is a light scent, and good continuity of bloom is maintained through summer and autumn. 'Tambourine' grows vigorously, making many shoots of a compact habit to below average height. Its foliage is shiny and rich green. ZONES 4–9.

Harkness, UK, 1998

Parentage unknown

British Association of Rose Breeders, Breeders' Choice 1998

'TAMORA' AUStamora

MODERN, MODERN SHRUB, APRICOT BLEND, REPEAT-FLOWERING

Reddish orange buds on this variety open into fairly large flowers of apricot-yellow, deeper in their hearts and paling towards the margins. They are made up of over 40 silky textured petals that are arranged layer upon layer in an old-fashioned style; the petals finally part to form a deep cup in the center of the blooms. There is a sharp fragrance, and flowers continue to appear through summer and autumn. 'Tamora' is suitable for a group in a shrub border and is especially recommended for warm climates. It is vigorous, rather spreading in habit and grows to below the average height of a shrub rose. The foliage is small, dark and semi-glossy. 'Tamora' is also classified as an English Rose. ZONES 4–9.

Austin, UK, 1983

'Chaucer' × 'Conrad Ferdinand Meyer'

'TANAGRA' GActa

MODERN, LARGE-FLOWERED/HYBRID TEA, ORANGE-RED, REPEAT-FLOWERING

The long, pointed buds of 'Tanagra' open into large, full-petalled, high-centered blooms that become cupped as the petals expand. They are a rich shade of orange-red and carry a pleasant light fragrance. There is a prolific first flush of bloom; after that, the plant maintains a good succession of bloom through summer and autumn. Because the flowers are usually carried singly on long stems and hold their form well, they are excellent for cutting and can be grown specifically for that purpose anywhere in the garden, especially in beds and borders or as a hedge. The plant grows vigorously with an upright habit to average height or less, and has soft matt foliage. The tanagra, or tanager, is a fiery colored bird native to North America. ZONES 4–9.

Gaujard, France, 1969

'Queen Elizabeth' × 'Tropicana'

'TANGERINE' CHEwmarywarn

MODERN, CLIMBING MINIATURE, ORANGE-RED, REPEAT-FLOWERING

The color of this rose is a bright and attractive shade of orange-vermilion. The pointed buds open into saucer-shaped, neatly formed flowers of few petals, which show yellow stamens. These are carried profusely in clusters at all levels on the plant, which maintains a good continuity of bloom through summer and autumn, although there is little

'Tambourine'

'Tanagra'

scent. The variety is suitable for fences, pillars and low walls, but only in warmer climates as it is not reliably winter hardy. It grows vigorously and densely to a little below the average extent of a Climbing Miniature, with many shiny, pointed leaves. ZONES 6–10.

Warner, UK, 1999

'Mary Sumner' × 'Warm Welcome'

'TANIA VERSTAK'

MODERN, LARGE-FLOWERED/HYBRID TEA, MEDIUM RED, REPEAT-FLOWERING

This rose was named after a former Miss Australia, who has since created one of the loveliest gardens in Australia; the rose named after her does not do her justice! The large buds open to huge blooms of 60 dull red petals. The flowers come on long stems on an upright bush and ball in cool wet weather. There is some fragrance. Although the flower production is sparse, given dry weather conditions the flowers can be lovely; they last very well when cut. The foliage is light green, dull and profuse. ZONES 5–10.

Armbrust, Australia, 1962

'Charlotte Armstrong' × 'Rouge Meilland'

'TANYA'

syns 'Majeure', 'Majore'

MODERN, LARGE-FLOWERED/HYBRID TEA, ORANGE BLEND, REPEAT-FLOWERING

This variety, which is suited to mild climates, was once widely grown for cutting, although it is little seen nowadays. It produces large, long and pointed buds that open into big, slightly fragrant flowers in a positive shade of tangerine-apricot with hints of salmon—'almost like a raw steak' as one grower puts it. The blooms, which are well formed, high centered and have nearly 50 petals, are usually borne singly on long, elegant stems and hold their shape for a long time. They are therefore valued for the

'Tamora'

'Tangerine'

'Tania Verstak'

'Tapis Jaune'

cut-flower market, which relies on their ability to produce successive crops of flowers through summer and autumn. 'Tanya' is an upright grower to above average height with abundant, large, firm foliage. It demands extra care if it is to perform well. ZONES 5–9.

Combe, France, 1959

'Peace' × ('Peace' × 'Orange-Nassau')

'TAPIS JAUNE' RUgul

syns 'Golden Penny', 'Goldpenny', 'Guletta'

MODERN, MINIATURE, MEDIUM YELLOW, REPEAT-FLOWERING

Often known as 'Guletta', 'Tapis Jaune' carries double flowers of about 20 yellow petals. These blooms are small and are produced both singly and in clusters of 3–5 amid the glossy dark green leaves. The growth is low and compact. 'Tapis Jaune' flowers very profusely, and there is a quick repeat and good disease resistance. The clear yellow color does not fade, and the blooms have a good substance with a thick petal texture. It is a wonderful rose for pots, small beds and low borders. ZONES 5–10.

de Ruiter, The Netherlands, 1973

'Rosy Jewel' × 'Allgold'

'TAPIS VOLANT' LENplat

MODERN, MODERN SHRUB, PINK BLEND, REPEAT-FLOWERING

This is an example of innovative breeding on the part of Louis Lens, here unit-

'Tapis Volant'

ing the genes of *Rosa wichuraiana* and *R. multiflora* with other strains. The resultant shrub is a low, wide plant bearing masses of small, pinky white blooms. They are produced in clusters of 7–36, and some sprays continue to appear later in summer when the initial generous flush is over. There is a fruity fragrance. This is an interesting rose to have for its botanical value, and an attractive plant for the garden in its own right. It grows vigorously with a spreading, trailing habit and is well furnished with plentiful reddish green foliage and red-brown prickles. The name means 'flying carpet'. ZONES 4–9.

Lens, Belgium, 1982

(*Rosa luciae* × seedling) × (*R. multiflora adenochaeta* × 'Ballerina')

Kortrijk Gold Medal 1987

'Taupo'

'Tarantella'

'TARANTELLA' KORantel
MODERN, LARGE-FLOWERED/HYBRID TEA, YELLOW
BLEND, REPEAT-FLOWERING

This is a variety with flowers of noble
proportions that are able to open and
stand in the high temperatures that greet
it, for it is now offered only by Australian
nurseries. The flowers are composed of
50 or more petals, and are usually borne
one to a stem. They are high centered
and a blend of creamy yellow and pink.
There is a slight fragrance, and flowers
appear through summer and autumn. It
is useful for cutting as well as for planting in beds and borders. It grows with an
upright habit to average height or less, and
has glossy mid-green leaves. ZONES 4–9.

Kordes, Germany, 1985

'Colour Wonder' × 'Vienna Charm'

'TARRAWARRA'
MODERN, POLYANTHA, PINK BLEND, REPEAT-
FLOWERING

This variety started out as a seedling at
the Nieuwesteeg nursery in Victoria,

Australia. The flowers are produced in
great abundance in small to large clusters
of 10–40 blooms. They are small, only
1 in (2.5 cm) or so across, and contain
28 pale salmon-pink petals that open
fully to cream, with just a trace of salmon
at the edges. At the center is a boss of
golden stamens—a very refreshing effect.
'Tarrawarra' forms a small, rounded
plant with dense, dark green, rough-
textured foliage. It makes an excellent
border or low hedge and flowers continuously from spring until late autumn.
For maximum effect, the bush needs to
be planted in groups close together.
ZONES 5–10.

Nieuwesteeg, Australia, 1992

Parentage unknown

'TASSIN'
MODERN, LARGE-FLOWERED/HYBRID TEA, MEDIUM
RED, REPEAT-FLOWERING

Tassin, near Lyon, was the site of the
Meilland nursery for many years. Despite the occupation of France during
World War II, the nursery still managed
to nurture a few new roses—'Tassin'
among them. It is a full-petalled variety
with large flowers of medium red that
last well. There is a satisfying fragrance.
As a garden rose in beds and borders, as
well as for cutting, it is a useful item, the
growth being vigorous and the habit upright to about average height. The leaves
are strong and leathery. It enjoys warm
conditions, and is offered solely by nurseries in Australia at the present time.
ZONES 5–9.

Meilland, France, 1942

'National Flower Guild' × 'Lemania'

'Tarrawarra'

'Tassin'

'TATJANA' KORtat
syn. 'Rosenthal'
MODERN, LARGE-FLOWERED/HYBRID TEA, DARK
RED, REPEAT-FLOWERING

Like many other dark red roses, the
petals of this rose reflect the sunlight to
give a shimmer of velvet. The blooms are
rounded in form, made up of rather
short petals and are most neatly formed,
opening cupped and yielding a rich
scent. They may be carried singly or in
candelabra fashion, usually with long
stems. They are well suited for borders,
continuing in bloom through summer
and autumn. The plant grows vigorously
with a bushy, upright and dense habit to
above average height, and has large, dark
green, semi-glossy leaves. ZONES 4–9.

Kordes, Germany, 1970

'Liebeszauber' × 'Präsident Dr H. C. Schroder'

'TAUPO' MACmisech
MODERN, CLUSTER-FLOWERED/FLORIBUNDA,
ORANGE-PINK, REPEAT-FLOWERING

This is a 'halfway-house' rose, with
flowers the size of a Large-flowered
Rose borne in a Cluster-flowered fashion. The blooms are neatly formed with
about 40 petals, in which apricot-yellow
and orange are suffused with orange-red
at the petal margins, all paling to rosy
salmon shades as the blooms age. There
is a slight scent. 'Taupo' gives a prolific
early display then bears further blooms
at intervals through summer and
autumn. It is useful as a hedge rose and
in a border, and provides plenty of individual blooms for small arrangements.
The plant grows very vigorously to above
average height, is furnished with light
green leaves and has a good health
record. Taupo is the name of New Zealand's largest lake. ZONES 4–9.

McGredy, New Zealand, 1978

'Liverpool Echo' × 'Irish Mist'

'TAUSENDSCHÖN'
syn. 'Thousand Beauties'
MODERN, RAMBLER, PINK BLEND

This strong Rambler bears loose clusters
of quite large, double, pink flowers with
white centers. The stems are nearly
thornless. Its ancestry includes the red
Hybrid Perpetual 'Général Jacqueminot'
and 'Pâquerette', the first dwarf
Polyantha. It sported a dwarf form,

'Tausendschön'

'Tatjana'

'Tea Rambler'

'Tchin-Tchin'

'Baby Tausendschön' (syn. 'Echo') in 1914, which is the parent of many useful Polyantha pot roses. Both forms flower only once. ZONES 5–9.

Schmidt, Germany, 1906

'Daniel Lacombe' × 'Weiser Herumstreicher'

'TCHIN-TCHIN'   MEIkinosi
syn. 'Parador'

MODERN, LARGE-FLOWERED/HYBRID TEA, YELLOW BLEND, REPEAT-FLOWERING

The flowers of this variety are golden yellow and quite large, so that as their 30 petals expand into a symmetrical cupped form they display a bold expanse of color. The blooms do not have much fragrance, but they stand bad weather well and repeat their bloom satisfactorily through summer and autumn. 'Tchin-Tchin', which is useful for beds and borders and has flowers that last well when cut for arrangements, grows to average height and has dark green, leathery leaves. The raisers brought out two roses known as 'Tchin-Tchin' with the synonym 'Parador' in the same year, which has confused many growers and gardening writers. One is an orange-red Cluster-flowered Rose, and the other yellow—described here. ZONES 5–10.

Paolino, France, 1978

(['Zambra' × 'Suspense'] × 'King's Ransom') × ('Kabuki' × 'Dr A. J. Verhage')

'TEA RAMBLER'
MODERN, RAMBLER, ORANGE-PINK

One of the early hybrids from the famous 'Engineer's Rose', this variety has quite large, semi-double, pink flowers with shades of orange. They are borne in profusion in early summer and are fragrant, befitting the Tea strain. It is a vigorous climbing rose that is less prone to mildew than might be expected. This is a very worthwhile rose to plant, but it must be given enough space. ZONES 5–9.

Paul, UK, 1904

'Crimson Rambler' × Tea Rose

'TEAR DROP'
MODERN, MINIATURE, WHITE, REPEAT-FLOWERING

The single to semi-double flowers of this rose have 6–14 white petals and very prominent yellow stamens. The florets are flat and the same size as those seen on a Patio Rose. The blooms have a light fragrance and look like a white cloud over the ground. The foliage is small and glossy mid-green on a low, hardy plant that flowers all season long, and is shaped like a dinner plate. The weather-proof blossoms seem to have an air of innocence about them, and are admired for their rather simple form and beauty. 'Tear Drop' is ideal for tiny beds, at the front of a border or even in a small container for the patio. ZONES 4–11.

Dickson, UK, 1988

'Pink Spray' × 'Bright Smile'

'TEDDY BEAR'   SAVabear
MODERN, MINIATURE, RUSSET, REPEAT-FLOWERING

The oval buds of this variety open to terracotta-colored flowers with lighter undersides, ageing to mauve-pink. The florets are double with 28 petals, urn shaped with Large-flowered form, and have a light fragrance. These blooms are borne either singly or in small sprays of 3–5 amid the dark green and semi-glossy foliage on an upright and vigorous plant. This rose represented a major break-through in color, particularly as the open bloom shows its brown petals with deep golden stamens in the center; the color is certainly unique and people seem to either instantly like it or hate it! The blooms are long lasting when cut for the home or left on the bush. It has a nice rounded growth habit, but the plant can suffer from mildew if left unprotected. ZONES 4–11.

Saville, USA, 1989

'Sachet' × 'Rainbow's End'

'TELSTAR'
MODERN, CLUSTER-FLOWERED/FLORIBUNDA, ORANGE BLEND, REPEAT-FLOWERING

It seemed a good idea in July 1962 to name a new rose for the first transatlantic communications satellite, and of the two, it is the rose that has lasted longer. It takes after 'Masquerade' in having semi-double blooms that open yellow, change to rose red and finally deep crimson. They are larger than those of 'Masquerade' and open out flat, so that when several are together in a cluster, the color effect is most eye-catching. The reddish stamens also are noticeable, and are attractive to bees. There is a pleasing fragrance, and flowering continues through summer and autumn. 'Telstar' makes a good hedge or bed and looks well in a mixed border, although it needs careful placing as it has such strident color. The plant grows strongly with an upright habit to above average height, and it is furnished with dark green leaves. ZONES 4–9.

Gandy, UK, 1962

'Rosemary Gandy' × 'Masquerade'

'TEMPLE BELLS'
MODERN, CLIMBING MINIATURE, WHITE, REPEAT-FLOWERING

Large, white single flowers with beautiful yellow stamens are the hallmark of this rose. The florets are borne in trusses and have just a hint of fragrance. It is a very vigorous and spreading plant, but needs about two seasons to become well-established before it really performs. In some climates it has been used as a ground cover rather than as a climber, and with good results. The use of *Rosa wichuraiana* as a seed parent has given 'Temple Bells' the ability to ramble, climb and crawl along the ground. ZONES 5–10.

Morey, USA, 1971

Rosa wichuraiana × 'Blushing Jewel'

'TENDER BLUSH'
OLD, ALBA, LIGHT PINK

With rounded, double blooms that emerge from plump buds, 'Tender Blush' is a pretty light pink rose with a creamy shade to the petals when fully open. The foliage is dark green. Like most Albas, this variety is easy to grow, even in semi-shade. ZONES 5–10.

Sievers, Germany, 1988

Parentage unknown

'Tender Blush'

'Telstar'

'Teddy Bear'

'TENDER LOVING CARE'
BOSpeabay

MODERN, CLUSTER-FLOWERED/FLORIBUNDA, MEDIUM PINK, REPEAT-FLOWERING

The warm rose pink blooms of this variety have the graceful shape of 'Pearl Drift' as they open to a wide, saucer-like shape. They are borne in large clusters and are made up of about 20 substantial petals, so last well when cut. There is a pleasant fragrance, and blooming is well maintained through summer and autumn. This makes a suitable bedding rose, hedge or border plant, growing up to average height with an upright habit. It has dark green, semi-glossy foliage, and was named to promote the Greenwich and Bexley Cottage Hospice in Kent, England. ZONES 4–9.

Bossom, UK, 1995

'Pearl Drift' × ('Dublin Bay' × seedling)

'TENDER NIGHT' MEIlaur
syns 'Florian', 'Sankt Florian'

MODERN, CLUSTER-FLOWERED/FLORIBUNDA, MEDIUM RED, REPEAT-FLOWERING

This variety creates a bold show, bearing its currant red flowers in large, showy

'Tender Night'

trusses. They are of medium to large size, are made up of about 24 petals and carry a slight fruity fragrance. The hard petal texture enables the blooms to withstand hot sun better than many reds. This is a well-behaved rose for a bed, low hedge or to plant near the front of a border. It grows sturdily with a compact, upright habit to average height or less, and has leathery, medium-sized, semi-glossy foliage. **'Climbing Tender Night'** (MEIlaursar; syn. 'Climbing Florian'; 1976) resembles the parent rose in all respects, except that it only gives a limited amount of flower after the main flush. In growth, it is strong and arching to slightly more than the average extent expected of a Cluster-flowered Climber. ZONES 4–9.

Meilland, France, 1971

'Tamango' × ('Fire King' × 'Banzai')

Rome Gold Medal 1971

'TEQUILA' MEIgavesol

MODERN, CLUSTER-FLOWERED/FLORIBUNDA, ORANGE BLEND, REPEAT-FLOWERING

The flowers of this rose are colorful Indian red on the uppersides and golden

'Tequila'

orange shading to yellow on the undersides, which gives them a lively, vibrant tone. They are of medium size, neatly formed with about 18 petals and are carried in small, even clusters that are produced freely during the initial flush. They continue to appear through summer and autumn and there is only a slight scent. 'Tequila' is especially good for hedges and for containers. It is also suitable for beds and borders. It grows vigorously to average height and has plentiful dark green foliage. ZONES 4–9.

Meilland, France, 1982

'Poppy Flash' × ('Rumba' × [MEIkim × 'Fire King'])

'TEQUILA SUNRISE' DICobey
syn. 'Beaulieu'

MODERN, LARGE-FLOWERED/HYBRID TEA, RED BLEND, REPEAT-FLOWERING

An asset of this variety is its ability to keep on flowering, for it is rare during summer and autumn not to find several of its bright yellow and red blooms cheering up the garden. The flowers are of medium size, rounded in form, and are made up of broad, bright yellow petals that are randomly tipped and margined with red. They are carried sometimes singly and quite often in wide, candelabra-type sprays, which afford plenty of blooms for flower arranging. They open slowly, taking on a cupped form; they should be deadheaded because the old petals discolor. For beds, borders and hedges, this is a popular rose. It grows vigorously with a bushy, free-branching habit to average height, and is furnished with glossy dark green leaves. ZONES 4–9.

Dickson, UK, 1989

'Bonfire Night' × 'Freedom'

Royal National Rose Society Gold Medal 1988, Belfast Gold Medal 1991, Glasgow Silver Medal 1991, Royal Horticultural Society Award of Garden Merit 1993

'Texas' (Poulsen)

'Texas' (Kordes)

'TEXAS' POUltex
syn. 'Golden Piccolo'

MODERN, MINIATURE, MEDIUM YELLOW, REPEAT-FLOWERING

The bright medium yellow flowers of this rose are unfading, even in strong sunlight. They are double with good high centers suitable for exhibition and can have a light fragrance. The foliage is small, matt mid-green on a very upright, tall plant. This vigorous bush gives a high yield of blooms, borne one to a stem throughout the season. 'Texas', one of the best colorfast yellows on the Miniature Rose scene, is generally disease resistant and hardy. ZONES 5–10.

Poulsen, Denmark, 1984

Parentage unknown

'TEXAS'

MODERN, LARGE-FLOWERED/HYBRID TEA, YELLOW BLEND, REPEAT-FLOWERING

This fragrant variety is grown under glass for the cut-flower trade. The buds are long and pointed with a spiral form. They open to 15–20 large, bright yellow petals tinged with deep salmon-orange, and this color pervades the whole flower when it is fully open. The blooms have remarkable substance and are quite long lasting when picked. In the garden, the bush is very short in growth, and has poor flower production with a slow repeat cycle. There are also problems with black spot and mildew; this is really a greenhouse rather than an outdoor rose. ZONES 5–10.

Kordes, Germany, 1992

Parentage unknown

'TEXAS CENTENNIAL'

MODERN, LARGE-FLOWERED/HYBRID TEA, RED BLEND, REPEAT-FLOWERING

It was a lucky Texan who noticed these distinctive, vibrantly colored flowers growing on 'President Herbert Hoover'. This proved to be a marketable, and valuable, mutation. The color is deep strawberry red with some gold shading, lighter in the center of the blooms and becoming a gentler blend of pink, red and orange as the petals age. The flowers resemble those of the parent in form, being of medium size, prettily coiled as the buds open loosely with reflexing petals. They are held upright on long, straight stems and have a sweet spicy fragrance, which makes them excellent subjects for buttonholes and for cutting though they need to be taken young or they will fly open quickly. 'Texas Centennial' makes a

'Tequila Sunrise'

'Texas' (Poulsen)

T

wonderful hedge, screening or border plant. In growth, it is similar to the parent rose though it is not as tall, growing vigorously and upright to above average height and having large, leathery leaves. ZONES 4–9.

Watkins, USA, 1935

Sport of 'President Herbert Hoover'

Portland Gold Medal 1935

'THALIA'
MODERN, RAMBLER, WHITE

'Thalia' was also known as the 'White Rambler' and was well regarded until it was replaced by the better 'Sander's White', so it is not much seen today. The flowers are small, double and well scented, and are borne in clusters. In Greek mythology, Thalia was the Muse of comedy and pastoral poetry. ZONES 4–10.

Schmitt, France, 1895

Rosa multiflora × 'Pâquerette'

'THE ALEXANDRA ROSE'
AUSday

syn. 'Alexandra Rose'

MODERN, MODERN SHRUB, PINK BLEND, REPEAT-FLOWERING

This variety has simple 5-petalled flowers of beautiful coloring, yellow towards the center of the flowers and rose red towards the petal rims, fading to rose pink as the blossoms age. They are of medium size, borne in large clusters and are slightly fragrant, and there is continual production throughout summer and autumn. This is a useful addition to the mixed shrub border, where its gentle colors and guileless flower character will harmonize readily with other plants. It grows vigorously and with reasonable compactness to average height and is well endowed with mid-green, semi-glossy foliage. ZONES 4–9.

Austin, UK, 1993

('Shropshire Lass' × 'Shropshire Lass') × 'Heritage'

'The Bishop'

'Texas Centennial'

'The Bride'

'THE BISHOP'
syn. 'Le Rosier Évêque'
OLD, CENTIFOLIA, MAUVE

Although sometimes grouped with Gallica Roses, this ancient rose has many features that are characteristic of Centifolias. In growth habit, it is fairly upright and dense with thorny stems and dark green foliage. The flowers are flat when fully opened and are composed of many evenly layered, bluish purple and magenta petals that have hints of lilac and gray: a most unusual combination that gives an almost violet effect when viewed from a distance. The individual blooms can be as much as 3 in (8 cm) across; they appear in mid-summer and are arranged in small, fragrant clusters fairly close to the foliage. ZONES 4–9.

Listed by François, France, 1790

Parentage unknown

'THE BRIDE'
OLD, TEA, WHITE, REPEAT-FLOWERING

'Catherine Mermet' has flesh pink blooms and has produced several sports. This one is said to be an improvement on the parent, with better shaped flowers and a more floriferous habit. It has a hint of pale lilac-pink in it, particularly on the petal edges. ZONES 7–9.

May, USA, 1885

Sport of 'Catherine Mermet'

'THE COMPASS ROSE'
KORwisco

MODERN, MODERN SHRUB, WHITE, REPEAT-FLOWERING

This is a graceful shrubby plant, and against its dark leaves nestle clusters of blush white semi-double blooms that open cupped with clean crisp petals and show off the prominent orange-yellow stamens in their hearts. The flowers have good fragrance and are very freely borne from summer to autumn. It grows with a

'Thalia'

'The Countryman'

'The Compass Rose'

'The Dark Lady'

spreading habit to slightly below average height with ample shiny foliage. This rose takes its name from the symbol of the Anglican Communion, and its launch marked the 1400th anniversary of the landing in Kent of St Augustine. ZONES 4–9.

Kordes, Germany, 1997

Parentage unknown

Royal National Rose Society Edland Medal for Fragrance 1995

'THE COUNTRYMAN'   AUSman
syn. 'Countryman'

MODERN, MODERN SHRUB, MEDIUM PINK, REPEAT-FLOWERING

This distinctive rose from David Austin, which is also classified as an English Rose, brings a reinfusion of Portland genes into Modern Garden Roses. Its medium-sized flowers are deceptive, for to the eye it does not at first appear they can hold as many as 40 petals. They are peony-like when young in a warm shade of deep pink and open like large loose rosettes, with a good fragrance. Normally there are two distinct flushes of bloom, in summer and in autumn, and additional intermittent blooms can be encouraged if old flowers are removed. 'The Countryman' is suitable for a border, but due to its undisciplined and tangled growth some flowers become

half-hidden in the foliage. It is remarkably healthy and grows vigorously to below average height, having a covering of medium green matt leaves that are soft to the touch. ZONES 4–9.

Austin, UK, 1987

'Lilian Austin' × 'Comte de Chambord'

'THE DARK LADY'   AUSbloom
syn. 'Dark Lady'

MODERN, MODERN SHRUB, DARK RED, REPEAT-FLOWERING

The flowers of this variety are dark red; they are very full, with over 40 petals to make up a fairly large bloom. When the petals part, the blooms show some resemblance to tree peonies in form, becoming purplish as they age. A few flowers are usually borne together in a small cluster, and their combined weight may cause the stems to bow. There is a sharp fragrance. This is an interesting rose to grow in a border, though it may require special care to thrive; if it is planted in a raised bed the flowers can be better appreciated. It is from David Austin and is also classified as an English Rose. It grows upright with a bushy habit to less than average height and has dark green, semi-glossy leaves. ZONES 4–9.

Austin, UK, 1991

'Mary Rose' × 'Prospero'

T

'The Fairy'

'The Fairy'

'The Friar'

'THE DOCTOR'

MODERN, LARGE-FLOWERED/HYBRID TEA, MEDIUM PINK, REPEAT-FLOWERING

In its heyday this rose's huge satiny pink blooms were one of the most familiar sights in the garden, standing out because of their size and also because the color is so confident and cheering. It is surprising that fewer than 30 petals, albeit very big ones, make up those flowers, because their rounded, blowzy heads give such an impression of fullness. The scent, too, is wonderful, being strong and sweet and likened to verbena. The plant is not so impressive; because it fails to make new wood freely, there is only limited summer bloom after the first flush though there is usually a good display in autumn. It grows to below average height and has attractive but rather sparse shiny foliage. 'The Doctor' deserves a place in the garden for reasons of history, scent and sentiment, for in its name is preserved the memory of the great rosarian Dr J. H. Nicolas, French by birth, who became an American citizen and was honored by the growers of America. ZONES 4–9.

Howard, USA, 1936

'Mrs J. D. Eisele' × 'Los Angeles'

National Rose Society Gold Medal 1938

'THE FAIRY'

syns 'Fairy', 'Féerie'
MODERN, POLYANTHA, LIGHT PINK, REPEAT-FLOWERING

Although this rose comes into bloom later than almost any other, once it starts it provides a prolific show for weeks on end. The rosette-shaped flowers are made up of scores of tiny petals, and are carried in dainty sprays all over the bush in an even tone of light rose pink. Even during rare intervals through summer and autumn when not in flower the plant remains attractive, forming hummocks of small, bright, pointed leaves. 'The Fairy' has all manner of uses: as a low hedge, to front a border, trail over a low wall, occupy a small space or planted

'The Doctor'

in a container. Its only failing is a lack of fragrance. If kept pruned it will stay quite dwarf, or it can achieve the stature of a small shrub by being allowed to grow unchecked; it is also excellent as a weeping standard. 'Climbing The Fairy' has all the characteristics of the bush form except that it produces long, arching stems and is capable of extending nearly half as far again as an average climber. It is not a rapid grower, and the continuity of bloom is not maintained as successfully as with the bush form. ZONES 4–9.

Bentall, UK, 1932

'Paul Crampel' × 'Lady Gay'

Royal Horticultural Society Award of Garden Merit 1993

'THE FRIAR'

MODERN, MODERN SHRUB, LIGHT PINK, REPEAT-FLOWERING

The flowers of this variety are blush edged white, and open from plump pointed buds to reveal small petals enfolded one against another in an old-fashioned style without any particular pattern or symmetry in their arrangement. They are scented and continue appearing throughout summer and autumn on an upright, dark-leaved shrub that grows with moderate vigor to less than average height. Although less successful in cooler climates, 'The Friar' clearly improves its performance in sunshine, and is popular as a rose for the shrub border in Australia, New Zealand and parts of the USA. It takes its name, as do several others in these pages prefaced by the definite article, from a character in Chaucer's *The Canterbury Tales*. 'The Friar' is from David Austin and is also classified as an English Rose. ZONES 4–9.

Austin, UK, 1969

'Ivory Fashion' × seedling

'The Herbalist'

'THE GARLAND'

syn. 'Wood's Garland'
OLD, MISCELLANEOUS, WHITE

A characteristic of this rose is the way it carries many clusters of tiny buds upright on bowing shoots. They appear for a glorious burst of bloom in high summer, covering the plant with a wealth of small, semi-double blooms that open flat to display a mixture of shades—blush pink, very pale yellow and white. The flowers have a light scent. The plant makes vigorous growth, producing many shoots, and is suitable for pergolas, covering unsightly objects and in places where it can romp unhindered. The leaflets are small and dark.

Wells, UK, 1835

Rosa moschata × *R. multiflora*

Royal Horticultural Society Award of Garden Merit 1993

'THE HERBALIST'   AUSsemi

syn. 'Herbalist'
MODERN, MODERN SHRUB, DEEP PINK, REPEAT-FLOWERING

The flowers of this variety are of medium to large size, with about 12 petals, in that shade of deep pink that borders on light red. They are carried in small clusters and open saucer shaped, showing attractive golden stamens, and blooms continue to appear through summer and autumn, making this a very desirable plant for the garden border. It grows sturdily with a neat, bushy, rather spreading habit to a little less than average height and is furnished with semi-glossy foliage. The raiser, David Austin, chose the name on account of the rose's likeness to 'Officinalis', the 'Apothecary's' Rose', but it unfortunately lacks the powerful fragrance of that variety. It is also classified as an English Rose. ZONES 4–9.

Austin, UK, 1991

Seedling × 'Louise Odier'

'THE HOLT'   MEHsherry

MODERN, MODERN SHRUB, DEEP PINK, REPEAT-FLOWERING

The flowers are small and carried freely in abundant clusters on tall stems, creating a dense wall of flower and foliage. They are fuchsia pink, semi-double and neatly formed, become cupped as they open, and yield an appreciable and pleasant fragrance. Though late to come into its first flush of bloom, 'The Holt' is remarkably free with its flowers during the rest of summer and autumn, and would

'The Holt'

'The Knight'

be ideal as a short, dividing hedge or screen or to group in a border. The raiser intended it to serve as a Patio Rose, for which purpose it seems disproportionately tall, but there are many useful applications for so vigorous and well foliaged a plant. It grows with an upright habit to a little below average height and has abundant dark green, healthy, glossy leaves. ZONES 4–9.

Mehring, UK, 1994

Parentage unknown

Glasgow Gold Medal 1997

'THE KNIGHT'
MODERN, MODERN SHRUB, DARK RED, REPEAT-FLOWERING

The breeding line of this variety includes the Gallica Rose 'Tuscany', which is reflected in its color, deep reddish crimson turning to purple and mauve. The form of the flowers is like that of Old Garden Roses, with up to 80 petals arrayed in layers and folding in against each other. There is good fragrance, and some repeat-flowering in the course of summer and autumn. Although it is still being offered for sale, principally in warmer countries, the raiser has suggested that on health grounds more recent varieties will give better garden value. 'The Knight' grows to below average height and has dark leaves. It is from David Austin and is also classified as an English Rose. ZONES 4–9.

Austin, UK, 1969

'Chianti' × seedling

'THE LADY' FRYjingo
MODERN, LARGE-FLOWERED/HYBRID TEA, YELLOW BLEND, REPEAT-FLOWERING

Having hybridized a pair of Cluster-flowered Roses, the raiser must have been pleasantly surprised to find this Large-flowered Rose among the resultant seedlings, with its high center and exhibition quality. The blooms are honey yellow with some salmon shading on the petals, and are carried sometimes singly, sometimes in wide-spaced clusters, but always on long stems so that they are a great standby for flower arrangement. There is a light scent and the production of quality blooms through summer and autumn is remarkably good, the big flowers seeming impervious to the effects of wind and rain. In the garden this is a most useful border rose. The habit is rather uneven, which detracts from its value for bedding. 'The Lady' grows vigorously to average height and has a covering of medium green, semi-glossy leaves. The name is that of a British magazine, and this rose was named to mark its centenary. ZONES 4–9.

Fryer, UK, 1985

'Pink Parfait' × 'Redgold'

Royal National Rose Society Trial Ground Certificate 1982, Baden-Baden Gold Medal 1987, Royal Horticultural Society Award of Garden Merit 1993

'THE McCARTNEY ROSE'
MEIzeli

syns 'McCartney Rose', 'Paul McCartney', 'Sweet Lady', 'The MacCartney Rose'

MODERN, LARGE-FLOWERED/HYBRID TEA, MEDIUM PINK, REPEAT-FLOWERING

The color of the flowers of this variety is a rich deep pink, and a most satisfying heavy fragrance comes out of them. The blooms have up to 40 petals, forming a

'The Optimist'

high center in the young flowers, which become cupped as they develop. There is a good continuity of bloom through summer and autumn, and in the garden this is a neat grower for a bed or border. The growth of the plant is vigorous and upright, to about average height, though the mid-green, semi-glossy leaves are likely to be prone to black spot in a bad year. This rose was named for the celebrated ex-Beatle. ZONES 4–9.

Meilland, France, 1991

('Nirvana' × 'Papa Meilland') × 'First Prize'

Bagatelle Fragrance Prize 1988, Geneva Gold Medal 1988, Le Roeuix Gold Medal and Fragrance Prize 1988, Madrid Fragrance Prize 1988, Monza Gold Medal and Fragrance Prize 1988, Paris Gold Medal 1988, Belfast Fragrance Prize 1993, Durbanville Fragrance Prize 1993, Paris Fragrance Prize 1993

'THE NUN' AUSnun
syn. 'Candida'

MODERN, MODERN SHRUB, WHITE, REPEAT-FLOWERING

The lightly fragrant flowers of this rose at their best have a beautiful and unusual form, like that of a tulip, with the stamens seen peeping up from the depths of the cup. They are almost pure white and are held on slim stems well apart in open sprays 'giving', says the raiser, 'an effect of dainty purity', though he goes on to mention that due to the fragile nature of the construction the petals do not always remain in place. It is therefore in spells of warm, settled weather that this variety is at its best. The plant continues to show color through summer and autumn and makes an interesting addition to the rose border, where it will grow to the size of an average shrub rose. ZONES 4–9.

Austin, UK, 1987

Seedling of 'The Prioress'

'THE OPTIMIST'
syn. 'Sweet Repose'

MODERN, CLUSTER-FLOWERED/FLORIBUNDA, YELLOW BLEND, REPEAT-FLOWERING

The blooms of this cheerful rose are a blend of gentle colors, being maize-yellow flushed with carmine-pink and becoming more pink as the flowers mature. They are of medium size, have about 30 petals, are carried in well-spaced clusters on strong stems and open with firm centers, becoming cupped as they develop and yielding a sweet fragrance. For its general good qualities, of freedom of bloom through summer and autumn, ability to withstand bad weather, neat bedding habit and serviceability as a rose for hedges, borders and for cutting, this variety deservedly received a gold medal in its British trials. 'The Optimist' grows sturdily with a bushy, upright habit to average height and has plentiful dark leathery foliage. ZONES 4–9.

de Ruiter, The Netherlands, 1955

'Golden Rapture' × seedling of a Cluster-flowered Rose

National Rose Society Gold Medal 1955

'The Nun'

'The Lady'

'THE PILGRIM'   AUSwalker
syns 'Gartenarchitekt Günther Schulze', 'Pilgrim'

MODERN, MODERN SHRUB, MEDIUM YELLOW, REPEAT-FLOWERING

These softly textured blooms are beautifully formed, made up of scores of small infolded petals that form an intricately constructed flat flower with rich hints of yellow in their young centers, paling to creamy buff. They are carried in clusters on strong stems, have a pleasing scent and continue to appear through summer and autumn. 'The Pilgrim' is from David Austin and is also classified as an English Rose. It is an excellent rose to plant in a border, either as a specimen plant or in a group, where it will prove useful for cutting for small arrangements. It grows vigorously with a compact and graceful habit to average height and is amply furnished with polished-looking mid-green foliage. **ZONES 4–9.**

Austin, UK, 1991

'Graham Thomas' × 'Yellow Button'

'THE PRINCE'   AUSvelvet

MODERN, MODERN SHRUB, DARK RED, REPEAT-FLOWERING

The flower is everything in this variety. The inky buds are hard and round and open into rich deep crimson blooms of intricate construction like wide, shallow rosettes, full of petals folded against their neighbors as they strive to open out. The crimson tones soon change to royal purple, and there is an Old Garden Rose scent. 'The Prince' is best sited where the unusual character of the blooms can be enjoyed but where the plant is not readily in view, for the weak flower stems and poor constitution are serious visual drawbacks in its overall performance. Given a warm climate and good cultivation it can thrive, but it needs the dedication of a connoisseur. The plant grows to about half the height of an average shrub rose and has a skimpy provision of dark leaves. It is from David Austin and is also classified as an English Rose. **ZONES 4–9.**

Austin, UK, 1990

'Lilian Austin' × 'The Squire'

'THE PRIORESS'

MODERN, MODERN SHRUB, LIGHT PINK, REPEAT-FLOWERING

This variety bears clusters of medium-sized flowers that are made up of about 24 petals, the globular form of the young blooms resembling that of the Bourbon Rose recorded in the parentage. The flowers are pearly pink and become cupped on opening, revealing prominent and attractive stamens. There is a light fragrance, and good continuity of bloom is maintained through summer and autumn. 'The Prioress' is from David Austin and is also classified as an English Rose. It is suitable for a mixed bed or border, where it will make a vigorous bush with an upright habit to about average height. The leaves are fairly large and mid- to dark green. **ZONES 4–9.**

Austin, UK, 1969

'Reine Victoria' × seedling

'THE REEVE'   AUSreeve

MODERN, MODERN SHRUB, DEEP PINK, REPEAT-FLOWERING

The flowers of this rose are intensely dark pink. They are very full, with almost 60 petals, and are borne sometimes singly, sometimes in small clusters. In the bud and young flower stages they are globe shaped with incurving petals, and open cupped like blowzy peonies. They have a good fragrance and blooming continues through summer and autumn. Because it has a lax, trailing character the plant is suitable to grow where it can be allowed to form a tangled group in a mixed border, or allowed to run over a low retaining wall. It grows to about half the height of an average shrub rose with an untidy, spreading habit, and has prickly stems and a provision of small, rough-textured dark foliage that is reddish when young. It is from David Austin and is also classified as an English Rose. **ZONES 4–9.**

Austin, UK, 1979

'Lilian Austin' × 'Chaucer'

'THE SQUIRE'   AUSire, AUSquire
syn. 'Country Squire'

MODERN, MODERN SHRUB, DARK RED, REPEAT-FLOWERING

Judged by the flowers alone, this could be considered one of the world's loveliest red roses. It is from David Austin and is also classified as an English Rose. The deeply cupped blooms look sumptuous, with over 100 petals perfectly arranged to create a quartered-rosette effect as they expand. There is also a good fragrance, but it is sad to record that the plant is unworthy of so fine a flower. It makes a somewhat leggy bush, stingy with its blooms and sparse with its foliage, and not proof against fungus troubles on the leaves it has. Siting the variety in the garden is therefore a problem; one answer is to grow it in a moveable container so that it can be given extra feeding, and when good flowers come they can be made a focal point and enjoyed. 'The Squire' is an open, bushy shrub of less than average height with dark rough-textured foliage. **ZONES 4–9.**

Austin, UK, 1977

'The Knight' × 'Château de Clos Vougeot'

'THE SUN'

MODERN, CLUSTER-FLOWERED/FLORIBUNDA, ORANGE-PINK, REPEAT-FLOWERING

The sunniest note of these semi-double flowers is struck by the yellow stamens, which are visible almost as soon as the buds open. The blooms themselves are salmon-orange, and they are quite large for a Cluster-flowered Rose. There is a light fragrance, and good continuity of bloom through summer and autumn. 'The Sun' has been popular for planting in beds, borders and as a hedge, but at the present time it does not appear to be in commerce. It grows vigorously with an upright habit to average height or more and has plentiful shiny, olive green foliage. This rose was sponsored by *The Sun*, the London mass-circulation daily newspaper. **ZONES 4–9.**

McGredy, New Zealand, 1972

('Little Darling' × 'Goldilocks') × 'Irish Mist'

Madrid Gold Medal 1973

'The Reeve'

'The Prioress'

'The Pilgrim'

'The Prince'

'The Squire'

'THE TEMPTATIONS' WEKaq
MODERN, LARGE-FLOWERED/HYBRID TEA, PINK
BLEND, REPEAT-FLOWERING

This variety's flowers have the classic
symmetry of form of the best Large-
flowered Roses, and though they are not
extra large, being composed of up to 30
broad petals, they make the best of what
they have. The color is an appealing
blend of orchid pink tones, paler in the
center of the petals. There is a light fruity
scent and, once the main flush is over,
flowers continue to appear in summer
and autumn, the late blooms being finer
in quality and color. 'The Temptations'
is useful for exhibition and cutting,
blooms usually being produced one to a
stem, and is suitable in the garden as a
hedge and for beds and borders. It grows
with moderate vigor and an upright
habit to average height or more and has
dark green, semi-glossy leaves. The sing-
ing group for which it was named has
been responsible for many hits. ZONES 5–9.

Winchel, USA, 1993

'Paradise' × 'Admiral Rodney'

American Rose Center Gold Medal 1989

'THE WIFE OF BATH' AUSbath
syn. 'Wife of Bath'
MODERN, MODERN SHRUB, PINK BLEND,
REPEAT-FLOWERING

This variety is from David Austin and is
also classified as an English Rose. It bears
medium-sized flowers of old-fashioned
character that are deep rose pink on the
uppersides of the petals and blush pink
on the undersides. They open with the
petals tightly folded to show their deeper
tones, and as the blooms expand they become looser in form and lighter in color.
There is a strong myrrh scent, and the
continuity of flower through summer
and autumn is well maintained. 'The
Wife of Bath' can be used in a bed or
border, yet it will suit a container as it is
a comparatively short grower that forms
a bushy, twiggy plant to below average
height. It has small, mid-green leaves.
ZONES 4–9.

Austin, UK, 1969

'Mme Caroline Testout' × ('Ma Perkins' ×
'Constance Spry')

'THE YEOMAN' AUSyeo
MODERN, MODERN SHRUB, ORANGE-PINK,
REPEAT-FLOWERING

The flowers of this variety have a touch
of pale apricot in the heart of their rosy
pink petals, which gives them a pleasing
translucent quality. They are full petalled

'The Wife of Bath'

'The Sun'

'The Temptations'

and become cupped as they open, giving
off a strong frangrance of myrrh. There
is a prolific first flush of bloom, after
which sporadic flowers may appear until
autumn brings another respectable display. This is not a very strong-growing
rose, but it will reward good cultivation
and in fertile soil can make a handsome
addition to the shrub border. It may be
expected to grow lower than average
height with a compact habit and large
mid-green leaves. It is from David Austin
and is also classified as an English Rose.
ZONES 4–9.

Austin, UK, 1969

'Ivory Fashion' × ('Constance Spry' × 'Monique')

'The Yeoman'

'The Wife of Bath'

'THELMA'
MODERN, RAMBLER, ORANGE-PINK

This rose has flowers of an unusual color
for a Rambler. They are coral-pink suffused with deep carmine, semi-double
and borne in small to medium-sized
clusters. Individual flowers are large—to
3 in (8 cm) wide—and slightly fragrant.
The pliable canes, which have very few
prickles, make 'Thelma' ideal for growing over arches and pergolas. With so
many white and pale pink Ramblers
available, this orange-pink variety is a
welcome addition because of its stronger
color. Unfortunately, there is very little
repeat-bloom. The vigorous and climbing growth is reliably disease resistant.
ZONES 5–10.

Easlea, UK, 1927

Rosa wichuraiana × 'Paul's Scarlet Climber'

'THÉRÈSE BAUER'
MODERN, MODERN SHRUB, MEDIUM PINK

This is an interesting addition to the
small group of *Rosa setigera* hybrids, par-

'Thérèse Bauer'

ticularly as it has inherited Hybrid
Rugosa genes from its parent 'Hansa'.
'Thérèse Bauer' has very vigorous, upright growth as might be expected in a
hybrid, and bears clusters of large, medium pink, semi-double flowers. There
is, unfortunately, only a slight scent.
ZONES 4–10.

Ludwig, USA, 1963

('Hansa' × *Rosa setigera*) × *Rosa setigera*

'Tiffany'

'Tiffany'

'Thérèse Bugnet'

'THÉRÈSE BUGNET'

syn. 'Teresa Bugnet'

MODERN, HYBRID RUGOSA, MEDIUM PINK, REPEAT-FLOWERING

This is a vigorous, hardy plant whose complicated breeding line includes some of the wild roses best able to withstand Canadian winters. The flowers are quite large, being made up of some 36 wavy, folded, soft-textured petals. They are reddish pink, paling as they age, open out like shallow saucers and have an excellent sweet fragrance. Like most Rugosa hybrids, this one continues in bloom all through summer and autumn. The flowers are good to cut, while the near absence of prickles on the flower stalks is an added benefit. 'Thérèse Bugnet' grows easily and vigorously, and for a shrub border where minimal attention can be given and substantial growth is required it is an excellent choice. It reaches above average height and has long, rather smooth leaves not characteristic of a Rugosa. The raiser named it for a close member of the family. ZONES 3–9.

Bugnet, Canada, 1950

([Rosa acicularis × R. rugosa kamtchatica] × [R. amblyotis × R. rugosa plena]) × 'Betty Bland'

'THÉRÈSE DE LISIEUX'

ORAblan

syn. 'St Thérèse de Lisieux'

MODERN, LARGE-FLOWERED/HYBRID TEA, WHITE, REPEAT-FLOWERING

Theresa Martin was made a saint many years after her death in 1896; she was famous for helping the poor. To commemorate the centenary of her death, this rose was introduced by the Carmelite Monastery in Victoria, Australia. 'Thérèse de Lisieux' produces double white flowers with over 24 petals with a delicate blush of soft shell pink at the edges. The blooms are carried in profusion, both singly and in small clusters, and there is a quick repeat. This upright bush is covered with glossy deep green, disease-resistant foliage. ZONES 5–10.

Orard, France, 1992

Parentage unknown

'THISBE'

MODERN, MODERN SHRUB, LIGHT YELLOW, REPEAT-FLOWERING

This is one of the loveliest of the shrub roses. The flowers are borne close together in the cluster, so that in full bloom the effect is that of a fluffy cloud of chamois yellow. They open like rosettes with many small petals, showing amber stamens and imparting a light sweet fragrance. After a generous first flush of bloom more flowers are produced at intervals through summer and autumn, and in the garden this is a lovely shrub for a border, preferably by a path so that its unostentatious beauty can be enjoyed. The plant grows vigorously with a bushy, upright habit to average height and is well furnished with semi-glossy, olive green leaves. ZONES 4–9.

Pemberton, UK, 1918

Sport of 'Daphne'

'Thérèse de Lisieux'

'THOR'

MODERN, LARGE-FLOWERED CLIMBER, DARK RED

This rose was the outcome of a program to raise hardier climbers, and it produces a large crop of bright red flowers in summertime that bloom for about 4 weeks and intensify their color as they age. The blooms are borne singly in small clusters, appear at different levels on the plant and have a rich spicy scent. 'Thor' is not widely offered in commerce, because its brief period of flower is a sales deterrent; however, it is a worthwhile variety, being very vigorous and capable of extending twice as far or more as the average climber. The leaves are large, dark and glossy and have an excellent health record. ZONES 3–9.

Horvath, USA, 1940

('Alpha' × Rosa xanthina) × 'President Coolidge'

'THUNDER CLOUD'

MODERN, MINIATURE, ORANGE-RED, REPEAT-FLOWERING

The oval buds of this rose open to reveal clouded-over, orange-red flowers somewhat reminiscent of storm clouds at sunset. The florets have almost 70 petals and are borne mainly in clusters. Glossy leathery green foliage covers this dwarf, upright bush. The blooms are very impressive as large sprays. They have good longevity, providing a brilliance of color in the garden, although individually, the blooms are very informal and mediocre. The plant is not winter hardy, and repeat-flowering has been reported to be poor in warm climates. ZONES 6–10.

Moore, USA, 1979

'Little Chief' × 'Fire Princess'

'TIAMO'

MODERN, LARGE-FLOWERED/HYBRID TEA, DARK RED, REPEAT-FLOWERING

Kordes has produced a number of excellent pink and red roses for the cut-flower trade. This one is a dark red cut-flower rose, which produces very beautifully formed buds that open slowly to medium-sized blooms containing 35 petals. 'Tiamo' has a very long vase life and retains its lovely dark red color until petal fall. Flower production is excellent and there is a very quick repeat on this medium to tall bush, which gives strong and healthy growth. This is a good garden rose in warm climates, but the stems do not grow as long as those grown under glass. It makes a good bedding variety. ZONES 5–10.

Kordes, Germany, 1992

Sport of 'Calibra'

'TIDEWATER'   BRItide

MODERN, MINIATURE, WHITE, REPEAT-FLOWERING

The pointed buds of this rose open to white flowers with a slight pink tinge. The double blooms have about 30 petals and are very fragrant. They have good high centers. The bloom size can be larger than the traditional Miniature, so this is a candidate for the Patio classification. Because the petals have good substance, the flowers tend to be long lasting both on the bush and as cut flowers. The foliage is matt mid-green on a spreading bushy plant. This rose likes cool climates where the color can be maintained. Powdery mildew can be a problem and proper protective spraying is recommended. It was named to honor the rose society in Tidewater, Virginia, USA. ZONES 5–10.

Bridges, USA, 1991

'Jennifer' × seedling

'TIFFANY'

MODERN, LARGE-FLOWERED/HYBRID TEA, PINK BLEND, REPEAT-FLOWERING

The flowers of this variety are large and full petalled and formed in the classical Large-flowered style, with high centers

'Thisbe'

'Thunder Cloud'

'Tiamo'

'Tiger Cub'

'Timeless'

and maintaining wonderful symmetry of form as the petals reflex. They combine rose pink and rosy salmon shades, with hints of gold at the petal base, and are carried on long firm stems, sometimes singly and sometimes in clusters. They have good fragrance and are excellent for cutting, though they may spoil in rain. 'Tiffany' is an excellent choice for beds and borders or to form a hedge, and blooms with commendable freedom through summer and autumn. The plant grows vigorously and upright to above average height and has plentiful deep green glossy foliage. **'Climbing Tiffany'** (Lindquist, USA, 1958) has the same lovely fragrant flowers as found on the bush form, although it is less popular. It produces vigorous, arching stems, ideal for training over a support. ZONES 4–9.

Lindquist, USA, 1954

'Charlotte Armstrong' × 'Girona'

Portland Gold Medal 1954, All-America Rose Selection 1955, Gamble Fragrance Medal 1962

'TIFFIE'
MODERN, MINIATURE, LIGHT PINK, REPEAT-FLOWERING

The long and pointed buds of this variety open to soft pink flowers in cool climates, and apricot flowers in warmer areas. The flowers have high centers that are suitable for exhibition in spite of the low petal count (15–20 petals), but the blooms can be fleeting in warm climates. They are normally borne one to a stem and tend to become larger in cool temperatures. The foliage is mid-green on an upright bush; the delicate, shell pink

blooms are the plant's best asset, but repeat-flowering is poor. 'Tiffie' is most admired by floral arrangers. It is a great plant for containers and it is one of the first to bloom in the spring. ZONES 5–10.

Bennett, USA, 1979

'Little Darling' × 'Over The Rainbow'

'TIGER CUB'   POUlcub
MODERN, PATIO/DWARF CLUSTER-FLOWERED, YELLOW BLEND/STRIPED, REPEAT-FLOWERING

This well-named variety produces semi-double flowers of 20–25 petals that are striped and flecked orange-yellow and crimson on a cream background. The plant is small and compact with small, mid-green, semi-glossy foliage. The blooms are produced both singly and in small clusters, and there is very little perfume. 'Tiger Cub' certainly makes an interesting and unusual plant in containers, beds or borders. ZONES 5–10.

Poulsen, Denmark, 1996

Parentage unknown

'TIGRIS'   HARprier
MODERN, MODERN SHRUB, YELLOW BLEND

The flowers of this curious rose are canary yellow with a red eye at the base of the many small petals, which is noticeable as they unfold. When fully open the little rosettes resemble powder puffs in shape. There is no scent, and the flowering period does not extend beyond summer. The growth is very distinctive, because the influence of the *Rosa persica* parent is evident in the springy, wiry, prickly stems, the variation in shape of the leaves and the cushiony, ground-

'Till Uhlenspiegel'

hugging habit. As the first hardy hybrid of *R. persica*, this is an obvious item to include in a botanical rose collection, and it has garden merit for its unique flowers. The plant is low and compact, less than half the size of an average shrub rose. 'Tigris' was raised at the same time as another *R. persica* seedling, and Margaret Harkness suggested the names 'Tigris' and 'Euphrates' for them as an acknowledgment of their Near Eastern ancestry. ZONES 4–9.

Harkness, UK, 1985

Hulthemia persica × 'Trier'

'TIKI'
MODERN, CLUSTER-FLOWERED/FLORIBUNDA, PINK BLEND, REPEAT-FLOWERING

The fragrant flowers of this variety are quite large and their 30 petals give them the shape of Large-flowered Roses, high centered at first, becoming cupped as they age. They are a blend of light shell pink and pearly cream and are produced freely, usually in clusters but sometimes singly. Flowering continues through summer and autumn, some of the finest roses being produced in cooler spells. This rose is a good choice for planting in beds, borders and as a hedge, where the pale coloring of the blooms contrasts beautifully with its dark foliage. It grows vigorously with an upright, bushy habit to average height. In Maori mythology, Tiki was the creator of the first man; Sam McGredy named the rose after a visit to New Zealand. ZONES 4–9.

McGredy, UK, 1964

'Mme Léon Cuny' × 'Spartan'

'TILL UHLENSPIEGEL'
OLD, SWEET BRIAR, RED BLEND

Although it is classed with the Sweet Briars, this variety has little in common with them, for in both flower and foliage it takes after its Cluster-flowered seed parent. It bears, in enormous clusters,

saucer-like blooms of bright carmine with white eyes that flower profusely in early summer. They do not repeat-bloom and the scent is slight. It grows larger than average with a vigorous, free-branching habit and has dark green glossy leaves. ZONES 4–9.

Kordes, Germany, 1950

'Holstein' × 'Magnifica'

'TIMELESS'   JACecond
MODERN, LARGE-FLOWERED/HYBRID TEA, DEEP PINK/LIGHT RED, REPEAT-FLOWERING

As the blooms of this variety unfold, the colors veer between deep pink and medium red, the inside surface of the petal being deeper than the outside. It is a warm mixture, and the sizeable flowers display a lot of it as they open to reveal perfectly formed high centers on upright, strong stems. They open slowly, keeping their symmetrical shape thanks to the firm texture of the 30 or so petals, but the fragrance is only slight. The blooms continue through summer and autumn and this is a dependable rose for a bed, border or hedge. It grows sturdily with an upright habit to average height and has dark, semi-glossy foliage. ZONES 4–9.

Zary, USA, 1996

Seedling × 'Kardinal'

All-America Rose Selection 1997

'Tiffie'

'Tiki'

T

'TINEKE'

MODERN, LARGE-FLOWERED/HYBRID TEA, WHITE, REPEAT-FLOWERING

This rose is widely grown for the florists' market. It carries plump pointed buds with a greenish tint that develop into large flowers of almost pure creamy white, made up of about 50 broad petals. They are high centered, open slowly to a cupped form and are borne on strong straight stems, ideal for cutting. 'Tineke' needs a warm climate, because the blooms are blemished by cold wind and rain. It produces new flower stems readily, giving excellent continuity of bloom through summer and autumn. The plant is very vigorous, growing to average height or more with a cover of large, semi-glossy, dark green leaves. ZONES 4–9.

Select Roses BV, The Netherlands, 1989

Parentage unknown

'TINKERBELL'   SUNtink

MODERN, MINIATURE, LIGHT PINK, REPEAT-FLOWERING

The petals of these soft pink flowers reflex back gracefully to form an almost porcelain-like rose. The florets have outstanding Large-flowered form and are borne one to a stem as well as in clusters on long, straight stems. It has a strong fragrance. The foliage is glossy green on a tall, upright bush. Gardeners are recommended to remove the central bud on the clusters, so that all flowers come into bloom at the same time: this gives a colorful umbrella effect. ZONES 5–10.

Schuurman, New Zealand, 1992

'White Dream' × 'Evelien'

'Tineke'

'Tinkerbell'

'TINO ROSSI'   MEicelna

MODERN, LARGE-FLOWERED/HYBRID TEA, MEDIUM PINK, REPEAT-FLOWERING

The flowers of this variety are of medium to large size, rounded in form, and well filled with over 50 petals. In color they are a rather cool shade of light salmony pink, with pretty rose pink veining. There is an excellent fragrance and good continuity of flowering is maintained through summer and autumn. This rose is very suitable for use in beds and borders, to grow as a hedge and as a source of cut flowers. It grows vigorously with a bushy, upright habit to average height and has an ample coverage of semi-glossy, medium green foliage. The variety was named as a tribute to the celebrated singer. ZONES 4–9.

Meilland, France, 1990

'Pink Panther' × ('Dream' × 'Jardins de Bagatelle')

Bagatelle Fragrance Award 1989

'TINTINARA'   DICuptight

MODERN, LARGE-FLOWERED/HYBRID TEA, LIGHT RED, REPEAT-FLOWERING

This variety has big flowers borne on well-spaced clusters, of the type that in the USA are termed Grandifloras. They have about 24 petals and open with a high-centered form, becoming cupped. The color is unusual, being poppy red with the inner petals a lighter porcelain rose, and there is a light fragrance. 'Tintinara' gives a prolific first flowering, followed by further cycles of growth and bloom through summer and autumn, making it a good performer as a bedding

'Tip Top'

'Titian'

and border rose or to form a hedge. It makes a strong, upright plant to above average height and is densely clothed in large glossy leaves. On being asked why he named this after an obscure township in South Australia, the raiser said he had never heard of the place and had chosen to call it 'Tintinara' simply because it sounded good. ZONES 4–9.

Dickson, UK, 1995

'Melody Maker' × (seedling × 'Bright Smile')

The Hague Gold Medal 1994

'TINY STARS'   TRAstar

MODERN, MINIATURE, RED BLEND, REPEAT-FLOWERING

These single to semi-double flowers with 5–12 petals narrowly edged with red are small enough to be considered for the micro-miniature classification. Blooms come singly and in small clusters of 3–4 amid the matt mid-green foliage on a low-growing bush. It has no thorns. The plant needs a while to establish itself before it can perform well with a profusion of flowers. It is interesting to note that this rose is the result of self-pollination. ZONES 5–10.

Travis, USA, 1986

'Magic Carrousel' × 'Magic Carrousel'

'TINY TOT'   BENtintot, BENtot

MODERN, MINIATURE, APRICOT BLEND, REPEAT-FLOWERING

The tiny, fat buds of this variety open into bright yellow, perfectly shaped, full flowers with tight centers and petals that curl back to form points. The sun brings out overtones of orange and apricot. Since the blooms are carried on long, slender stems, they may be cut for indoor display and exhibition. The growth is very vigorous and willingly produces successive crops of flowers. These small shrubs therefore make colorful plants for pots and bedding. There is no fragrance. ZONES 5–11.

Benardella, USA, 1990

Parentage unknown

'TIP TOP'   TANope

MODERN, CLUSTER-FLOWERED/FLORIBUNDA, ORANGE-PINK, REPEAT-FLOWERING

In stature this rose belongs with the Patio Roses, but the flowers and leaves are proportionately too large for it to sit happily with the other members of this recent group and it is better regarded as a truncated Cluster-flowered Rose. As such it is a convenient rose to edge a border or to put in a small bed by itself, or

'Titian'

to use as a dwarf hedge. The medium-sized flowers are semi-double and open saucer shaped, showing their stamens. The fresh-looking, rosy salmon blooms are carried close to the plant in short-stemmed clusters. There is a slight scent, and the continuity of bloom through summer and autumn is well maintained. The plant grows with a low, spreading habit and has deep green leaves that provide ample cover at the start of the season but often suffer loss through black spot. ZONES 4–9.

Tantau, Germany, 1963

Parentage unknown

'TIPSY IMPERIAL CONCUBINE'

OLD, TEA, PINK BLEND, REPEAT-FLOWERING

This rose was brought to England from China by Hazel Le Rougetel, who attests the name to be the translation from the Chinese. To quote the introducer, the eminent rosarian and nurseryman of Attleborough in Norfolk, it 'has large double flowers of soft pink, subtly overlaid with tones of yellow and red … [it is] very free flowering.' It makes a low-growing bush that flowers continuously. There is only a slight scent. ZONES 7–9.

Beales, UK, 1989

Parentage unknown

'TITIAN'

MODERN, CLUSTER-FLOWERED/FLORIBUNDA, DEEP PINK, REPEAT-FLOWERING

This variety has well-formed flowers of deep carmine pink, though their brilliance is such that they have the remarkable property of appearing scarlet when caught by the sun and viewed from a distance. They open out rather flat, and the color tone intensifies as the large, full-petalled blooms age. Flowers continue to appear through the growing season, the autumn bloom being especially fine, and there is a light scent. Although classified as a Cluster-flowered Rose the plant takes on the dimensions of a shrub or pillar in warm areas, growing vigorously with an upright, arching habit to above average height; it is easy to grow in a border, with or without support. The foliage is rounded and mid-green. ZONES 4–9.

Riethmuller, Australia, 1950

Parentage unknown

T

'Tintinara'

T

'Tom Brown'

'Tom Thumb'

'Tivoli'

'TIVOLI' POUlduce
syn. 'Tivoli Gardens'
MODERN, LARGE-FLOWERED/HYBRID TEA, MEDIUM YELLOW, REPEAT-FLOWERING

These flowers are of medium to large size and consist of up to 40 petals. The blooms are rounded in form and are borne sometimes singly, sometimes in small clusters. The color is clear yellow, a positive but gentle shade. There is a light fragrance, and blooms are produced with good continuity through summer and autumn. 'Tivoli' is a dependable variety for a bed or border, or to plant as a hedge. It grows vigorously with a compact, free-branching habit up to average height and has large, dark green semi-glossy foliage. This Danish-raised variety is named after one of Copenhagen's main attractions. ZONES 4–9.

Poulsen, Denmark, 1996

Parentage unknown

'TOBY TRISTAM'
MODERN, RAMBLER, WHITE

Scores of pointed buds appear closely together in big trusses on this variety, and when they open their 5-petalled flowers wide, the overall effect is like seeing many golden-hearted, tiny saucers. The blooms are creamy white; their great profusion lasts only for a short period in summer, but where space is available this is a horticultural delight, very suitable for growing up a tree or in a wild garden. It grows with arching, clambering stems and mid-green foliage up to three times the extent of an average climbing rose. In autumn, there are small orange hips. This rose is perhaps a *Rosa multiflora* seedling, but little seems to be known about the parentage. ZONES 4–9.

Hillier, UK, circa 1970

Parentage unknown

'TOM BROWN'
MODERN, CLUSTER-FLOWERED/FLORIBUNDA, RUSSET, REPEAT-FLOWERING

The flowers of this rose are a curious color, being orange-brown on the inside of the petals and brownish red on the reverse. The blooms are fairly large, with about 30 petals, and well formed, opening neatly cupped. They have a good scent and continue to bloom through summer and autumn, being borne sometimes singly and sometimes in big clusters. This is a variety for planting where its strangeness can be appreciated, and it is also useful to have a group for cutting since it can be used with telling effect in arrangements. 'Tom Brown' grows vigorously with a bushy habit to average height and has leathery dark leaves. ZONES 4–9.

LeGrice, UK, 1964

Seedling (involving *Rosa californica*) × 'Amberlight'

'TOM THUMB'
syn. 'Peon'
MODERN, MINIATURE, RED BLEND, REPEAT-FLOWERING

These semi-double flowers are a plain deep crimson with a white center and are complemented by light green, leathery

'Toby Tristam'

foliage on a dwarf plant. The world owes much to Spain's Pedro Dot and Holland's Jan de Vink who pioneered the breeding of Miniatures. Originally called 'Peon', it was re-christened 'Tom Thumb' by Robert Pyle. The rose really caught the imagination of the public in 1936. Subsequently, 'Tom Thumb' has been used extensively by modern hybridizers to pass on the genetic traits of Miniature habits. While it may look plain alongside the glamorous Modern Miniatures of the late twentieth century, it is still well worth growing. The plant is extremely dwarf, reaching only 4–6 in (10–15 cm) high. It is a free-flowering rose and repeats well. ZONES 5–10.

de Vink, The Netherlands, 1936

'Rouletii' × 'Gloria Mundi'

'TOM TOM'
MODERN, CLUSTER-FLOWERED/FLORIBUNDA, DEEP PINK, REPEAT-FLOWERING

This variety bears clusters of red-pink flowers composed of about 24 petals. They are large by comparison with the size of the plant, and open with high centers like small-scale Large-flowered Roses before opening out flat. They have a light spicy scent and after the main flush they continue to appear through summer and autumn, the late season flowering being especially good. The plant grows with a compact habit and is excellent for bedding where a short grower is required, or to edge a border.

The growth is vigorous and the habit upright and bushy, to below average height. It is well furnished with deep green matt foliage. ZONES 4–9.

Lindquist, USA, 1957

'Improved Lafayette' × 'Floradora'

'TOM WOOD'
OLD, HYBRID PERPETUAL, MEDIUM RED, REPEAT-FLOWERING

This rose bears large, rather dull cherry red, double flowers. It is a reasonably short-growing bush with a good constitution that is apparently free of mildew. The plant repeat-flowers well in autumn, but seems to be available only in Europe. ZONES 5–10.

Dickson, UK, 1896

Parentage unknown

'TOMMY BRIGHT'
MODERN, CLUSTER-FLOWERED/FLORIBUNDA, MEDIUM RED, REPEAT-FLOWERING

This greenhouse rose does not appear to be currently offered for sale to the general public. The blooms are carried in large, well-spaced clusters on strong, upright stems. They are fairly large, open cupped to show an even shade of scarlet red and are well filled with up to 40 petals. There is a light fragrance, and the production of blooms throughout summer and autumn is well maintained. In a warm climate 'Tommy Bright' would be suitable to cultivate out of doors in a cutting garden, the individual blooms being ideal for buttonholes and small arrangements. It grows vigorously to above average height and has leathery foliage. ZONES 5–9.

Boerner, USA, 1961

Seedling of 'Chatter' × 'Garnette Supreme'

'TONIMBUK'
MODERN, LARGE-FLOWERED/HYBRID TEA, MEDIUM PINK/LIGHT PINK, REPEAT-FLOWERING

This rose produces very pale pink flowers with lovely form. The color is a little deeper than 'Royal Highness', and the long, elegant buds open slowly to blooms that contain about 35 petals. They are of

'Tom Tom'

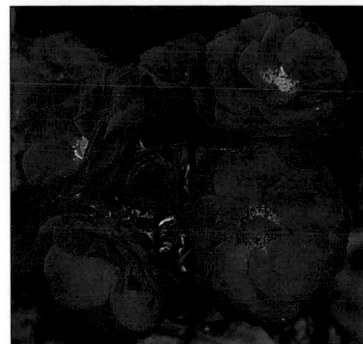

'Tommy Bright'

'Tonimbuk'

good exhibition form, wonderful for cutting and have a strong perfume. The flower production is high and the repeat-flowering cycle is rapid on this tall and upright plant. The foliage is dark green and semi-glossy. 'Tonimbuk' is a good rose that has been overlooked in the pale pink color class. It is only available in Australia, but would do well in other parts of the world with similar climates. ZONES 5–10.

Dawson, Australia, 1984

Parentage unknown

'TONY JACKLIN'

MODERN, CLUSTER-FLOWERED/FLORIBUNDA, ORANGE-PINK, REPEAT-FLOWERING

This Cluster-flowered Rose enjoyed wide popularity for many years on account of its good all-round garden qualities. The flowers are double, with about 30 petals, and open with high centers like small-scale Large-flowered Roses, becoming cupped as the petals reflex. The color is salmon-red, luminous without being harsh. The blooms are large and have a pleasant light fragrance, while the continuity of flower through summer and autumn is well maintained. This is a dependable variety to use for beds, borders and hedges, the plant being vigorous and growing with a bushy, free-branching habit to average height and having healthy, olive green, semi-glossy foliage. The name honors a well-known British golfer. ZONES 4–9.

McGredy, New Zealand, 1972

'City of Leeds' × 'Irish Mist'

Madrid Gold Medal 1972, Portland Gold Medal 1986

'TOO HOT TO HANDLE'

MODERN, CLUSTER-FLOWERED CLIMBER, MEDIUM RED, REPEAT-FLOWERING

Although listed as a climber, this variety can also be treated as a shrub. It bears big clusters of semi-double blooms in a rich blood red that, as they open, reveal creamy yellow stamens in their centers which contrast beautifully with the bright color of the petals. There is a slight fragrance, and the blooms continue to appear through summer and autumn, sometimes on short and sometimes on long stems so that the flowers appear at different levels on the plant. The versatile nature of this rose means that it can either be allowed to stand freely in a mixed border as a shrub of average proportions, or attached to a support to form a modest-sized climber. It

can be pruned as required, and makes a vigorous plant with a dense cover of leathery, glossy foliage. ZONES 4–9.

McGredy, New Zealand, 1996

'Waiheke' × 'Eyeopener'

British Association of Rose Breeders, Breeders' Choice 1996

'TOORENBURG'   KORkojotie

MODERN, CLUSTER-FLOWERED/FLORIBUNDA, APRICOT BLEND, REPEAT-FLOWERING

This rose was one of a number of unnamed varieties selected for trial in Taschner's Pretoria nursery for South African conditions. It proved to be such a good performer that it was given the name of a local artist and released for the South African rose market. The shrubs are of medium size, neat and compact, and produce flushes of roses throughout summer into autumn. These are medium sized and have a beautiful shape with compact, spiralled centers surrounded by whorls of warm pink outer petals. Sometimes there are apricot or fawn overtones. The flowers are very long lasting and are therefore ideal for cutting and exhibiting, but they are not fragrant. ZONES 4–9.

Kordes, Germany, 1995

Parentage unknown

'TOP MARKS'   FRYministar

MODERN, MINIATURE, MEDIUM RED, REPEAT-FLOWERING

What a perfect name for this rose! It has flowers that are a sparkling vibrant vermilion, which hold their color well in sunny climates. Although the florets have an informal look, they cover the bush with an attractive mass of color. The plant is very hardy but it can suffer from black spot if left unprotected. 'Top Marks' has been a consistent winner at rose trials in Europe where it has captured the attention of the rose-growing public. ZONES 4–10.

Fryer, UK, 1992

Parentage unknown

Geneva Certificate of Merit 1990, Royal National Rose Society Gold Medal and Rose of the Year 1992, Baden-Baden Gold Medal

'TOPAZ JEWEL'   MORyelrug

syns 'Gelbe Dagmar Hastrup', 'Rustica 91', 'Yellow Dagmar Hastrup', 'Yellow Fru Dagmar Hartopp'

MODERN, HYBRID RUGOSA, MEDIUM YELLOW, REPEAT-FLOWERING

Though not the first yellow Hybrid Rugosa as sometimes claimed, this variety is the most suitable one for the

average garden. It grows lower than the average shrub rose with a spreading, free-branching habit and carries primrose yellow flowers that open to display creamy gold stamens. They are made up of some 24 attractively curled petals and develop into wide, loosely cupped blooms with a pleasing fruity fragrance. 'Topaz Jewel', which makes a valuable addition to the shrub border as a specimen plant or group, has somewhat uneven and untidy growth and a tendency for some blooms to be hidden in new foliage, so it is less effective in a bed by itself. The foliage is matt, rugged and rich green but not as proof against disease as most Hybrid Rugosas, nor does the plant produce the typical Hybrid Rugosa hips. ZONES 4–9.

Moore, USA, 1987

'Golden Angel' × 'Belle Poitevine'

'TOPROSE'   COCgold

syn. 'Dania'

MODERN, CLUSTER-FLOWERED/FLORIBUNDA, DEEP YELLOW, REPEAT-FLOWERING

The distinction between the Cluster-flowered and Large-flowered Roses seems to disappear when 'Toprose' is on view, for it carries fairly large, full-petalled blooms of classic Large-flowered form at the top of long stems and, though sometimes borne singly, they often appear in a close group of 3. The color is a bright, shining and even shade of yellow. There is a light scent, and the continuity of bloom through summer

'Toprose'

and autumn is well maintained. This variety is best suited for a group in a border or as a hedge. The plant grows vigorously to average height and has handsome bright green leaves. ZONES 4–9.

Cocker, UK, 1991

(['Chinatown'] × 'Golden Masterpiece'] × 'Adolf Horstmann') × 'Yellow Pages'

Baden-Baden Gold Medal 1987, Belfast and Glasgow Certificates of Merit 1993

'TOPSI'

MODERN, CLUSTER-FLOWERED/FLORIBUNDA, ORANGE-RED, REPEAT-FLOWERING

Only a handful of nurseries now offer this beautiful rose which, when new, caused a sensation by reason of its color, a luminous orange-scarlet of startling brightness. The semi-double blooms appear in short-stemmed clusters and look large against this low-growing plant. They are freely produced and open like saucers. The plant puts much of its energy into making new flowering shoots; however, this led to its decline, insufficient ripened wood being made to prevent die-back in hard winters. 'Topsi' is best enjoyed in a small bed or container where it can be given good treatment, including preventive spraying against rust and black spot. It has a very short, spreading growth habit and large, mid-green leaves. ZONES 4–9.

Tantau, Germany, 1972

'Fragrant Cloud' × 'Fire Signal'

Royal National Rose Society President's International Trophy 1972

'Tony Jacklin'

'Top Marks'

T

'TORCH OF LIBERTY' MORtorch

MODERN, MINIATURE, ORANGE-RED, REPEAT-FLOWERING

The flowers of this rose are orange-red with silver undersides. The florets are double with 20 petals, have a light fragrance and are produced in abundance with an exhibition-type form. The foliage is semi-glossy and mid-green on a upright bush. Ralph Moore sent all his first-year royalties from this rose to The Statue of Liberty Fund. ZONES 5–10.

Moore, USA, 1986

'Orangeade' × 'Golden Angel'

'TORNADO' KORtor

MODERN, CLUSTER-FLOWERED/FLORIBUNDA, ORANGE-RED, REPEAT-FLOWERING

This dependable, bright, free-flowering rose grows vigorously with an upright, bushy habit and carries its semi-double blooms in showy clusters close to the plant on short, rigid stems. The flowers are orange-red, dark and bright and open cupped, giving a glimpse of bright golden stamens within the center petals. Little scent can be detected, but in other respects—continuity of bloom through summer and autumn, ability to shrug off bad weather and the way the spent flowers drop their petals cleanly—this is a well-behaved garden item for use in beds, borders, as a low hedge and in containers, growing to average height and having shiny dark green foliage. ZONES 4–9.

Kordes, Germany, 1973

Anerkannte Deutsche Rose 1972

'Europeana' × 'Marlena'

'Torch of Liberty'

'Torvill & Dean'

'TORVILL & DEAN' LANtor

MODERN, LARGE-FLOWERED/HYBRID TEA, PINK BLEND, REPEAT-FLOWERING

It was a public relations coup on the raiser's part to secure news headlines about this rose within hours of the Olympic medal success of Jayne Torvill and Christopher Dean. And it is aptly named for, as one writer puts it, 'pink and gold dance together across the petals'. The flowers are large and rounded, composed of 36 pale yellow petals on which appear flushes of the palest salmony pink. There is a light scent and flowers appear through summer and autumn, looking their best in cool climates. It is suitable for beds, borders or to form a hedge. It grows vigorously with an upright habit to average height and has deep green, semi-glossy foliage. ZONES 4–9.

Sealand, UK, 1984

'Grandpa Dickson' × 'Alexander'

'TOSCANA' KORkunde

MODERN, LARGE-FLOWERED/HYBRID TEA, MEDIUM RED, REPEAT-FLOWERING

This is one of the first red cut-flower varieties produced by the Kordes firm. The fragrant flowers are medium to large and bear long, elegant buds that open slowly to pure red, 25-petalled blooms with great substance. They have a long vase life; the stems are very long if grown under greenhouse conditions. There are a few small thorns. The plant has a high flower production with a rapid repeat. ZONES 5–10.

Kordes, Germany, 1992

Parentage unknown

'Tornado'

'Toulouse-Lautrec'

'TOUCH OF CLASS' KRIcarlo

syns 'Marachal Le Clerc', 'Maréchal le Clerc'

MODERN, LARGE-FLOWERED/HYBRID TEA, ORANGE-PINK, REPEAT-FLOWERING

The flowers of this variety are large and beautifully formed, with high centers surrounded by many petals in a neat and symmetrical arrangement. The color is an attractive combination of pale creamy pink suffused with coral pink. As the blooms slowly open they hold their centers for a long time, yielding a light Tea fragrance, and because they are produced on long stems they are excellent to cut. The flowers continue blooming very satisfactorily through summer and autumn, achieving their best quality in cooler temperatures. This is a good garden rose to use in a bed, border or as a hedge, growing vigorously and upright to above average height and being well furnished with large dark green leaves that are reddish when young and are sometimes touched by seasonal mildew. ZONES 4–9.

Kriloff, France, 1984

'Micäela' × ('Queen Elizabeth' × 'Romantica')

All-America Rose Selection 1986, Portland Gold Medal 1988

'TOULOUSE-LAUTREC' MEIrevolt

MODERN, LARGE-FLOWERED/HYBRID TEA, MEDIUM YELLOW, REPEAT-FLOWERING

The flowers of this rose are large and very full, with over 40 petals. They are formed in old-fashioned style with a random arrangement of the petals, which gives them a soft outline and a rather fluffy effect, and have a pleasing scent. Usually the blooms are borne one to a stem and they continue to appear through summer and autumn. 'Toulouse-Lautrec' is suitable for a mixed bed or border or to make a hedge. It grows

'Touch of Class'

'Tour de Malakoff'

strongly to average height with a bushy habit and has medium to dark green glossy foliage. It was named for the French artist. ZONES 4–9.

Meilland, France, 1993

'Ambassador' × ('King's Ransom' × 'Sunblest')

Monza Fragrance Prize 1993

'TOUR DE MALAKOFF'

OLD, CENTIFOLIA, MAUVE

A tall, lax-growing shrub attaining a height of 6 ft (1.8 m) or more in rich soil, 'Tour de Malakoff' has grayish green, moderately thorny stems that are covered with a profusion of medium-sized, mid- to dark green leaves. The fragrant flowers are fully double, quite large—up to 4 in (10 cm) in diameter—and flat in shape when fully open. Their color is most unusual especially on the outer petal edges: magenta flushed purple with lilac and grayish highlights. The outer petals reflex as the flower matures, and when fully open, golden stamens show through to add to the overall luminosity. It can be used as a wall plant or pillar rose or can be grown on a tripod. ZONES 4–10.

Soupert and Notting, Luxembourg, 1856

Possibly a Bourbon × a Gallica

'TOURBILLON' DELnolli

MODERN, CLUSTER-FLOWERED/FLORIBUNDA, PINK BLEND, REPEAT-FLOWERING

The flowers of this variety are colorful, opening to show pink on the insides of the petals and yellow on the undersides. They are neatly formed and loosely double, becoming cupped and quite sizeable as they expand. There is a light sweet fragrance, and more flower clusters are produced through summer and autumn. This is a useful garden rose for beds and borders, though it does not appear to be available commercially. It grows with an upright habit to below average height and has small, semi-glossy leaves. The name means 'swirl', alluding to the effect of the two colors mingling in the young blooms. ZONES 4–9.

Delbard, France, 1981

'Zambra' × (['Orléans Rose' × 'Goldilocks'] × ['Spartan' × 'Fashion'])

'TOURNAMENT OF ROSES' JACient

syns 'Berkeley', 'Poesie'

MODERN, LARGE-FLOWERED/HYBRID TEA, MEDIUM PINK, REPEAT-FLOWERING

In America, where this variety is widely grown, it is called a Grandiflora, an appropriate name for such a stalwart grower whose big clusters of sizeable flowers carried on firm stems are very noticeable in the rose garden. The blooms have a neat symmetry and show contrasting tones of pink as the petals unfold, deep pink on their outer surfaces and creamy pink within. There is a light spicy scent and an excellent continuity of bloom is maintained through summer and autumn, the color being particularly fine in warmer weather. It is a good variety for a hedge, group or bed, being very vigorous and growing upright to above average height with glossy green leaves. The name refers to the annual rose parade held in Pasadena, and this rose was launched to mark its centenary. ZONES 4–9.

Warriner, USA, 1988

'Impatient' × seedling

All-America Rose Selection 1989

'TOWER BRIDGE'   HARavis

MODERN, LARGE-FLOWERED/HYBRID TEA, DEEP PINK, REPEAT-FLOWERING

The color of the flowers on this variety is deep magenta, and to the eye it appears closer to purple than pink. The flowers have old-fashioned appeal also, opening from fat buds into big blooms full of petals with quartered centers and a strong sweet fragrance. The plant puts a great deal of strength into the flowers, which means that after the initial flush there is a pause before the next cycle of bloom comes to fruition, but after that a good display is maintained through the rest of summer and autumn. The flowers last well when cut. 'Tower Bridge' is very suitable for a group in a border, preferably close to a path so that its scent can be enjoyed; it grows sturdily with an upright habit to average height or less and has large dark leaves. This rose was named to celebrate the centenary of the opening of London's famous landmark. ZONES 4–9.

Harkness, UK, 1995

Parentage unknown

'TOY BALLOON'

MODERN, MINIATURE, DARK RED, REPEAT-FLOWERING

The oval buds of this rose open to reveal velvety red blooms with 48 petals, good centers and a lovely light fragrance. When fully open, the flowers look more like balloons than roses. They are very long lasting and the color holds well, particularly in partial shade. The foliage is dark green on a spreading bush.

'Toy Balloon'

'Tradescant'

Bloom production is prolific, especially for a Miniature Rose with Moss parentage, and since the plant tends to sprawl, it is best used in a hanging basket where the sprays can cascade over the edge of the container. ZONES 5–10.

Moore, USA, 1979

'Fairy Moss' × 'Fire Princess'

'TOY CLOWN'

MODERN, MINIATURE, RED BLEND, REPEAT-FLOWERING

These semi-double flowers, with 12–20 petals, are a blushed white deeply rimmed with carmine and have exceptionally good exhibition-type form. The foliage is small and leathery on a vigorous plant that produces an abundance of flowers throughout the growing season. When the blooms finally open, they reveal a flat form with contrasting yellow stamens. ZONES 5–10.

Moore, USA, 1966

'Little Darling' × 'Magic Wand'

American Rose Society Award of Excellence 1975

'TRACEY WICKHAM'

MODERN, MINIATURE, YELLOW BLEND, REPEAT-FLOWERING

The flowers of this rose are bright yellow and edged with red. The florets are double with 30 petals and have a light fragrance. They are borne singly or in small clusters. The blooms are a bit large for a Miniature, so this plant would be better treated as a Patio Rose. The foliage is semi-glossy and mid-green on an upright bush. 'Tracey Wickham' has been described as a miniature form of 'Redgold'. While the flowers have good potential exhibition form, the petals tend to move a little too fast to hold the form for long. It was named to honor a well-known Australian swimmer. ZONES 5–10.

Welsh, Australia, 1984

'Avandel' × 'Redgold'

'Tracey Wickham'

'Tourbillon'

'Tradition'

'TRADE WINDS'

MODERN, LARGE-FLOWERED/HYBRID TEA, RED BLEND, REPEAT-FLOWERING

There is a lively contrast between the dark red color of the inside petal surfaces of the large flowers on this variety and the silvery white reverse, which becomes accentuated as the flowers develop. They are made up of over 50 petals and open with high centers, holding their form for a long time. There is a good fragrance, and more flowers are produced through summer and autumn. 'Trade Winds' is a strong plant both in constitution and color tone, serving well for hedges, beds and borders and providing in addition a useful source of long-stemmed roses for flower arrangement. It grows vigorously to above average height and has glossy deep green foliage. ZONES 4–9.

Von Abrams, USA, 1964

('Multnomah' × seedling) × ('Carrousel' × seedling)

'TRADESCANT'   AUSdir

MODERN, MODERN SHRUB, DARK RED, REPEAT-FLOWERING

The flowers of 'Tradescant' are of medium size, open out almost flat and are carried in small clusters. They are deep wine crimson to purple with a handsome bloom on their petals, which number upwards of 40 and are folded tightly against one another, giving a quartered effect. There is a good fragrance, and blooms continue to appear through summer and autumn. This rose is suit-

'Tournament of Roses'

able near the front of a shrub border where, given good cultivation, it will grow to about half the size of an average shrub rose with a low, arching, spreading habit and a complement of dark green, semi-glossy leaves. In warm climates the stems grow long enough to be trained on pillars. It is from David Austin and is also classified as an English Rose. ZONES 4–9.

Austin, UK, 1993

'Prospero' × ('Charles Austin' × 'Gloire de Ducher')

'TRADITION'

MODERN, LARGE-FLOWERED/HYBRID TEA, MEDIUM RED, REPEAT-FLOWERING

Formerly much praised as a greenhouse variety, this rose does not appear to be commercially available today. It bears rich scarlet-crimson flowers that hold their color without fading and use their 36 broad petals to good effect, building a high-centered bloom of symmetry and grace. The firm petals ensure the blooms have a lengthy vase life, but also condemn it to being almost entirely scentless. As with greenhouse varieties in general, the cycles of growth and flower succeed each other fairly rapidly, ensuring a good supply of bloom through summer and autumn. The plant grows vigorously with long stems and a free-branching habit to average height, and is supplied with matt, dark green leaves that are reddish when young. ZONES 4–9.

Kordes, Germany, 1965

'Schlösser's Brillant' × 'Don Juan'

'Träumland'

'Travemünde'

'TRADITION 95'   KORkeltin
MODERN, CLUSTER-FLOWERED CLIMBER, MEDIUM RED, REPEAT-FLOWERING

This is a vigorous climber that displays clusters of many bright crimson-scarlet blooms. These are of medium size, semi-double with rather short petals and open cupped, revealing in the center glimpses of bright golden stamens. They hold their color tone well and carry a light fragrance, and flowering continues through summer and autumn. 'Tradition 95' can be used effectively on walls, fences, arches and pergolas, where it will grow strongly, capable of exceeding the normal extent of a climber but not resenting pruning as necessary. The attractive foliage is bright green, shiny and plentiful. ZONES 4–9.

Kordes, Germany, 1995

Parentage unknown

'TRÄUMEREI'   KORrei, ReiKOR
syns 'Dreaming', 'Reverie'
MODERN, CLUSTER-FLOWERED/FLORIBUNDA, ORANGE BLEND, REPEAT-FLOWERING

The color of this well-behaved rose is a pure coral-orange, and the flowers develop from long slender buds into rounded, low-centered blooms with neatly formed hearts, holding their form but dropping off the plant quickly and cleanly when they are spent. They are carried sometimes singly, sometimes in a cluster, have good fragrance, continue in bloom through summer and autumn and tolerate bad weather. This variety is very suitable for bedding and borders or to make a hedge, as it grows vigorously with a bushy, free-branching habit to average height. There is a dense covering of

reddish young leaves that become dark green with age. The synonyms are translations of the German name, which is the title of a piano work by Robert Schumann. ZONES 5–10.

Kordes, Germany, 1974

'Colour Wonder' × seedling

'TRÄUMLAND'
syn. 'Dreamland'
MODERN, CLUSTER-FLOWERED/FLORIBUNDA, LIGHT PINK, REPEAT-FLOWERING

Each little flower of this variety is daintily formed, with their 20 petals laid back to form a shallow saucer and acting as a frame for the attractive golden stamens. Lightly fragrant, the blooms are a gentle shade of peach pink and are carried in clusters that seem large in relation to the plant, which grows short and compact. Continuity of bloom is well maintained through summer and autumn. This rose used to be favored for mass planting in beds or for the front of a border, but after 40 years it has almost disappeared from nursery lists. The habit is upright and bushy, to below average height, and the plant has dark leathery leaves. ZONES 4–9.

Tantau, Germany, 1958

'Tantau's Triumph Improved' × 'Fashion'

'TRAVEMÜNDE'   KORrantu
MODERN, CLUSTER-FLOWERED/FLORIBUNDA, MEDIUM RED, REPEAT-FLOWERING

The flowers of this very deep red rose are carried in crowded clusters, giving a very rich and colorful effect. They are full petalled, of middling size and are carried on strong stems, but there is little fragrance. During summer and autumn the conti-

nuity of bloom is well maintained, and the flowers resist bad weather well. Because the variety is so dark it merits a site where it can be viewed from a distance and where it will be lit up by the sun. The bush grows strongly with an upright, bushy habit to average height and has dark green leaves that are reddish when young. The rose was named for a town in North Germany. ZONES 4–9.

Kordes, Germany, 1968

'Lilli Marleen' × 'Ama'

Anerkannte Deutsche Rose 1966

'TRAVERSER'
MODERN, LARGE-FLOWERED CLIMBER, YELLOW BLEND

Among the many varieties raised by Alister Clark was one by this name, described as bearing clusters of well-shaped, semi-double blooms in yellow and cream that cover the plant in early in the season. 'Traverser' was said to be a very strong and vigorous grower, which is typical behavior for Clark's Gigantea hybrids. Those descriptions were written over 60 years ago, and although a plant that sounds similar still grows at the raiser's old home, there appears to be some uncertainty as to whether it is the same item or not; currently only two nurseries in Australia are offering it. It needs a frost-free environment. ZONES 7–11.

Clark, Australia, 1928

Hybrid of Rosa gigantea

'TRAVESTI'
MODERN, CLUSTER-FLOWERED/FLORIBUNDA, YELLOW BLEND, REPEAT-FLOWERING

This rose bears small clusters of medium-sized flowers that are most neatly formed in the young stage with tightly coiled centers. They are double and become cupped, displaying a vivid mix of yellow and orange with an overlay of cherry red. Some of their beauty is lost as the petals age, but if cut young they are delightful to use in floral arrangements and they have some fragrance, too. 'Travesti' has a good record of flowering on through summer and autumn, and its even bedding habit makes it well suited for grouping in borders and to make a short hedge. The plant grows with a bushy, branching habit to average height or less and has small, dark, semi-glossy leaves. ZONES 4–9.

de Ruiter, The Netherlands, 1965

'Orange Sensation' × 'Circus'

Royal National Rose Society Certificate of Merit 1966

'TRAVIATA'
MODERN, LARGE-FLOWERED/HYBRID TEA, RED BLEND, REPEAT-FLOWERING

This is a strikingly pretty rose, made up of some 30 wavy petals that are bright red over much of their petal area save for prominent white patches towards the base. The blooms, which are quite large, open with high centers before developing a loosely cupped shape. They have a satisfying fragrance, and continue in production through summer and autumn, the late season blooms being particularly fine. This variety is very suitable for beds and borders. It grows vigorously with a bushy habit to average height, making plenty of basal shoots, and is furnished with bronze-green, leathery leaves. ZONES 4–9.

Meilland, France, 1962

'Baccará' × ('Independence' × 'Grand'mère Jenny')

'TREASURE TROVE'
MODERN, RAMBLER, APRICOT BLEND

'Kiftsgate' is a form of Rosa filipes that grows to enormous proportions; it was found and grown at Kiftsgate Court in Gloucestershire in England. 'Treasure Trove' is a chance seedling of it found by John Treasure in his garden in Staffordshire. The felicitous name was suggested by Graham Thomas. It is an enormous climber that bears large trusses of medium-sized, cupped, semi-double flowers with 23 petals. The blooms are apricot, mauve, pink and cream, and are strongly scented. ZONES 7–9.

Treasure, UK, 1977

'Kiftsgate' × China Rose (possibly 'Old Blush')

'TREVOR GRIFFITHS'   AUSold
MODERN, MODERN SHRUB, MEDIUM PINK, REPEAT-FLOWERING

These flowers are quite large and well filled with petals that are somewhat randomly and informally arranged, giving the effect of an old-fashioned rose. They are a warm and deepish shade of rose pink, have a pleasing scent and appear through summer and autumn. The plant has a spreading habit, growing to about average height, with rough-textured, dark green leaves. 'Trevor Griffiths' is a good rose for a border. It was named for the celebrated New Zealand rosarian whose enthusiasm, writings and photography have brought numerous under-appreciated varieties to notice. It is also classified as an English Rose. ZONES 4–9.

Austin, UK, 1994

'Wife of Bath' × 'Hero'

'Träumerei'

'Travesti'

'TRICKSTER' BRItrick
MODERN, MINIATURE, RED BLEND, REPEAT-FLOWERING

This Miniature Rose has very fragrant, bright red flowers with white undersides. The double florets contain 28–30 petals, and are borne one to a stem. The flower form is high centered, and the blooms can be large in some cooler climates. It has attractive, small, semi-glossy green foliage on a medium-sized, compact and rounded bush that tends to produce lots of blooms throughout the growing season while remaining a well-behaved plant. This is an ideal choice for the garden wherever a bright red is called for. Unfortunately, the color can fade in warm climates. ZONES 5–11.

Bridges, USA, 1995

'Jennifer' × 'Red Beauty'

'TRICOLORE'
syn. 'Reine Marguerite'
OLD, GALLICA, PINK BLEND

This medium-sized conventional Gallica Rose is one of the hundreds introduced in the early nineteenth century. The flowers are deep pink to crimson and are fringed at the edges, dotted and mottled white; the petal edges can be lilac. Descriptions of the color of this rose vary widely; Gallicas tend to fade to different shades during their brief flowering period. There is another 'Tricolore', an early Rambler (1863) with, it is said, similar-colored flowers, although it does not seem to be in commerce any more. ZONES 4–9.

Lahaye Père, France, 1827

Parentage unknown

'TRICOLORE DE FLANDRE'
OLD, GALLICA, PINK BLEND

This Gallica resembles the better known 'Camaieux'. The double flowers are pale pink, heavily striped with purple and have a pleasing perfume. The plant is upright but not very tall and has been recommended for growing in a pot. It can revert to monochrome, and flowers only once. ZONES 4–9.

Van Houtte, Belgium, pre-1846

Parentage unknown

'TRIER'
MODERN, RAMBLER, WHITE, REPEAT-FLOWERING

This rose is an upright bush or short climber with small leaves and small, creamy yellow flowers with a rosy flush. They are almost single. There are much better short climbing roses, but this rose is of considerable historical interest for rosarians. In England, the Reverend Joseph Pemberton crossed 'Trier' with a series of other roses to create a group of Modern Shrubs called the Hybrid Musks. They became, and remain, very successful and popular. ZONES 5–9.

Lambert, Germany, 1904

Probably a self-seedling of 'Aglaia'

'TRINITY'
OLD, TEA, WHITE, REPEAT-FLOWERING

This is one of the Bermuda 'mystery' roses, preserved or developed in the benign climate and remoteness of the islands over the years. 'Trinity' is a pure white, semi-double rose with dark green foliage on a plant of medium to tall height. It was named for the churchyard where it was found. ZONES 7–9.

Well established in Bermuda

Parentage unknown

'TRINITY' MACredparap
MODERN, MODERN SHRUB, DARK RED, REPEAT-FLOWERING

This makes a lowly shrub plant, bearing large trusses of small dark red flowers. They have about 24 petals and are initially formed like miniature Large-flowered Roses, before opening cupped and showing gold stamens. There is only a slight fragrance, but the continuity of bloom through summer and autumn is excellent. 'Trinity' is a suitable item for ground cover, on sloping sites and near the front of borders, or to fill small spaces. It produces strong, arching stems but at times the trusses are too heavy for them, causing the heads of flower to lie upon the ground. The plant makes a dense creeping mound of modest dimensions and has many small, dark green semi-glossy leaves. ZONES 4–9.

McGredy, New Zealand, 1994

'Sexy Rexy' × 'Eyeopener'

'TRINKET'
MODERN, MINIATURE, MEDIUM PINK, REPEAT-FLOWERING

The lovely pink buds of this rose open to small, phlox pink flowers that fade fast to a bland pink that hangs on for days. The bloom size is very small so qualifies this rose as a micro-miniature. The double flowers have excellent substance and are produced in abundance, complemented by attractive dark green foliage on a dwarf bush. Favored by floral arrangers, this rose is frequently a part of most Miniature arrangements entered for competition. 'Trinket' was one of many seedlings bred from 'Floradora'. ZONES 4–11.

Moore, USA, 1965

(Rosa wichuraiana × 'Floradora') × 'Magic Wand'

'TRIODENE' KORituscha
MODERN, CLUSTER-FLOWERED/FLORIBUNDA, PINK BLEND, REPEAT-FLOWERING

Named for a pharmaceutical product that uses a pink rose as a logo, 'Triodene' is a medium-sized shrub that is vigorous and disease resistant. It carries clusters of large, semi-double blooms for most of the growing season. They make good cut

'Traviata'

flowers, since the petals are strong and last well. The pink color is difficult to describe: it is a blend of warm pink, salmon and coral. There is a slight fragrance. ZONES 5–11.

Kordes, Germany, 1996

Parentage unknown

'TRIOLET' ORAdon
syn. 'Tanned Beauty'
MODERN, LARGE-FLOWERED/HYBRID TEA, APRICOT BLEND, REPEAT-FLOWERING

Of all the Modern Garden Roses, this one probably displays the most impressive color combinations: the tan-colored buds open to flowers of perfect Large-flowered shape with tight centers of cream; the undersides of the outer petals are tan. These outer petals curl back as the bloom matures. The vigorous shrub produces flowers that are suitable for exhibition or indoor display. They appear through summer, and in autumn the color seems more intense because of the hips and autumn leaves. Anothe plus for this rose is its very good fragrance. ZONES 5–11.

Orard, France, 1995

Parentage unknown

'TRIOMPHE DE L'EXPOSITION'
OLD, HYBRID PERPETUAL, MEDIUM RED, REPEAT-FLOWERING

This is a very tall-growing Hybrid Perpetual bearing large, crimson-purple flowers. It is very vigorous, making big long canes with ample foliage. It is

'Trier'

sweetly scented and looks every inch an Old Garden Rose. It took first prize at the Universal Exposition of 1855 in Paris. ZONES 5–9.

Margottin, France, 1855

Parentage unknown

'TRIOMPHE DU LUXEMBOURG'
OLD, TEA, PINK BLEND, REPEAT-FLOWERING

This strong Tea Rose bears very double, salmon-pink flowers that change to buff pink with age. It was one of the more celebrated roses of its time and was very expensive, retailing at 35 francs in 1836. Its full name would have been 'Triomphe of the Luxembourg Gardens', which are in Paris and where Alexandre Hardy was the chief horticulturist. Some writers erroneously substitute 'de' for 'du' in the name. ZONES 7–9.

Hardy, France, circa 1835

Parentage unknown

'Triomphe du Luxembourg'

'Tricolore de Flandre'

'Treasure Trove'

'TROILUS'   AUSoil

MODERN, MODERN SHRUB, APRICOT BLEND, REPEAT-FLOWERING

This variety bears large flowers made up of 40 or more petals that lie back row upon row, showing a dainty array of petal tips. They are often borne in large, heavy clusters. The blooms are cream and honey with a hint of apricot They have a pleasing scent. 'Troilus' is suitable for a shrub border, faring best in warm climates where the honey-apricot color is enriched; in cooler regions it is recommended for the greenhouse. The plant grows sturdily with an upright habit to average height and has large, dark green, semi-glossy leaves. It is also classified as an English Rose. ZONES 4–9.

Austin, UK, 1983

('Duchesse de Montebello' × 'Chaucer') × 'Charles Austin'

'TROPICAL TWIST'   JACorca

MODERN, MINIATURE, APRICOT BLEND, REPEAT-FLOWERING

The pointed buds of 'Tropical Twist' open to coral-orange-apricot flowers with yellow undersides. As the flowers age, the color changes dramatically to an intense coral-pink with cream undersides. The double blooms have 25–30 high-centered petals and are borne singly or in small clusters. In cool climates, the flowers tend to be borne in sprays. The long stems are surrounded by glossy dark green foliage on a vigorous, tall, disease-resistant bush. ZONES 5–10.

Walden, USA, 1997

AROmifi × 'Pink Polyantha'

American Rose Society Award of Excellence 1997

'Trumpeter'

'TROPICANA'   TANorstar

syn. 'Super Star'

MODERN, LARGE-FLOWERED/HYBRID TEA, ORANGE-RED, REPEAT-FLOWERING

This rose was significant at its time of introduction because of its pure rosy vermilion color, which had a luminous quality superior to anything found in a Large-flowered Rose before. The flowers are substantial and well formed, borne sometimes singly and sometimes in wide-spaced candelabra heads. There is a light scent. As a cut flower and for exhibition, it is very useful and continues to produce flowers very satisfactorily through summer and autumn, the mid-season ones often appearing with ragged edges to the petals. 'Tropicana' is used in beds and borders, though its growth habit tends to be uneven and it is liable to mildew readily wherever the circulation of air is limited. The plant grows vigorously with a lanky habit to average height or above, and has rather small matt leaves. **'Climbing Tropicana'** (TANgosar, TANgostar; syn. 'Climbing Super Star'; Boerner, USA, 1971) has never become popular, though in a position where there is plenty of air circulating through the plant, such as a pergola or open fence, it can make strong arching growth and being capable of extending somewhat further than the average climbing rose. ZONES 4–9.

Tantau, Germany, 1960

(Seedling × 'Peace') × (seedling × 'Alpine Glow')

National Rose Society President's International Trophy 1960, Portland Gold Medal 1961, All-America Rose Selection 1963, American Rose Society Gold Medal 1967

'Troilus'

'Trumpeter'

'Climbing Tropicana'

'TROPICO SUNBLAZE'

MEIglassol

syn. 'Tropico Meillandina'

MODERN, MINIATURE, MEDIUM YELLOW, REPEAT-FLOWERING

This rose has large, pale yellow, double flowers of over 50 petals; the outer petals are a lighter yellow than the center of the flower. These develop from oval buds into well-formed, flat, usually single blooms. The bush is compact with glossy dark green foliage and a profusion of repeat-blooms in summer. This is ideal in containers or in a small bed. ZONES 5–10.

Meilland, France, 1990

('Rise 'n' Shine' × 'Tapis Jaune') × 'Gold Badge'

'TRUMPETER'   MACtrum

MODERN, CLUSTER-FLOWERED/FLORIBUNDA, ORANGE-RED, REPEAT-FLOWERING

The admirable qualities that have justly earned a haul of awards for 'Trumpeter' include the freedom with which it produces its showy clusters of bright red flowers throughout the season, and the manner in which it displays them on a neatly habited, clean-foliaged plant. The blooms are of medium size, full petalled and open loosely cupped, standing all kinds of weather and falling cleanly when they are spent. Their only drawback is that the scent is light. It is excellent in beds, borders, as a low hedge and in standard form. It grows vigorously, making plenty of new shoots, with an upright, bushy habit to below average height and with a plentiful covering of deep green leaves. The name is a reference to Louis Armstrong, in whose honor the seed parent 'Satchmo' was named. ZONES 4–9.

McGredy, New Zealand, 1977

'Satchmo' × seedling

New Zealand Star of the South Pacific 1977, Portland Gold Medal 1981, Royal National Rose Society James Mason Gold Medal 1991, Royal Horticultural Society Award of Garden Merit

'Tropicana'

'Tropico Sunblaze'

'Tumbling Waters'

'TUMBLING WATERS'   POUltumb

MODERN, CLUSTER-FLOWERED/FLORIBUNDA, WHITE, REPEAT-FLOWERING

The raiser seems unsure whether to call this variety a bush or a shrub rose. It produces cascades of neatly formed white blooms with remarkable continuity throughout summer and autumn. They are of medium size, semi-double and open cupped, showing yellow stamens and exuding a light sweet fragrance. 'Tumbling Waters' makes a hummocky, spreading plant after the manner of a ground-cover rose except that it is not procumbent enough to be truly so described. It is ideal for mixed borders, performs well in containers and makes a graceful umbrella standard. The white flowers show up effectively against the rich green foliage. ZONES 4–9.

Poulsen, Denmark, 1997

Parentage unknown

'TURBO'   MEIrozrug

syns 'Turbo Meidiland', 'Turbo Rugostar'

MODERN, HYBRID RUGOSA, MEDIUM PINK, REPEAT-FLOWERING

This interesting fusion of Rugosa and Large-flowered varieties has resulted in a tough, hardy plant that grows to the average height of a shrub rose. The flowers have upwards of 20 petals and are of medium to large size, with a light scent. They are fuchsia pink, a warm and positive shade, with a white rim at the base of the petals, and reveal golden stamens as they open loosely cupped. After a good initial display, flowering continues through summer and autumn. It is a useful addition to mixed borders, growing with a vigorous, upright habit into a bushy, prickly stemmed plant with light green, semi-glossy leaves. ZONES 4–9.

Meilland, France, 1994

('Frau Dagmar Hastrup' × 'Manou Meilland') × 'Pink Grootendorst'

T

'TUSCANY'
syn. 'The Old Velvet Rose'
OLD, GALLICA, MAUVE

'Tuscany' is a very old rose, which bears semi-double, maroon-purple flowers on a medium-sized, upright bush. One of the plant's most attractive features is the show of yellow stamens. It is probable that this is the 'Velvet Rose' described by herbalist John Gerard in 1596.
ZONES 4–10.

Possibly of Italian origin, pre-1596

Parentage unknown

'TUTU MAUVE'
MODERN, CLUSTER-FLOWERED/FLORIBUNDA, MAUVE, REPEAT-FLOWERING

The flowers of this variety are fairly large for a Cluster-flowered Rose and are made up of 30 petals. They open from small clusters of plump buds into rounded blooms that become cupped and display a range of unconventional color with mauve and rose shading on a magenta base. The flowers are produced over a long period through summer and autumn and have a light fragrance. It is suitable for planting in mixed beds and borders, being best in warm climates for the texture of the petals is such that they do not enjoy cold or wet conditions. The bush grows with moderate vigor and a bushy habit to below average height.
ZONES 4–9.

Delbard-Chabert, France, 1963

Parentage unknown

Madrid Gold Medal 1962

'TWILIGHT MIST'
syn. 'Yuguri'
MODERN, LARGE-FLOWERED/HYBRID TEA, PINK BLEND, REPEAT-FLOWERING

'Twilight Mist' bears large, full flowers that open with tight, pointed centers, becoming rounded and cupped as the petals slowly expand. The color is a

delightful blend of gentle pastel colors, the petal margins carrying flushes of light rosy pink and pale carmine on a creamy background. There is a light scent and flowers continue to appear through summer and autumn. 'Twilight Mist' is a useful item in beds and borders, and is fine to cut for indoor decoration. It grows with a bushy habit to average height and is supplied with mid-green, semi-glossy leaves. ZONES 4–9.

Suzuki, Japan, 1987

Parentage unknown

'TWINKLE TWINKLE'
MODERN, MINIATURE, APRICOT BLEND, REPEAT-FLOWERING

The pointed buds of this variety open to micro-miniature, double white flowers with 23 apricot-edged petals. These blooms have a faint Tea fragrance and are borne one to a stem. The foliage is semi-glossy and mid-green on an upright bush. This tiny, decorative Miniature is certainly a novelty—the star-shaped flowers are a most attractive blend of cream, pink and soft apricot-orange. As the blooms age, the pink coloration becomes more pronounced. 'Twinkle Twinkle' has good growth characteristics, producing lots of blooms on slender, elegant stems. The plant is subject to mildew if left unprotected. ZONES 5–10.

Bennett, USA, 1981

'Contempo' × 'Sheri Anne'

'TYNWALD' MATtwyt
MODERN, LARGE-FLOWERED/HYBRID TEA, WHITE, REPEAT-FLOWERING

Borne usually one to a stem, the 60-petalled, cool creamy white flowers of this variety have ivory yellow in their hearts. They are large and open out rather flat, with the petal edges curling back. Considering the size of flowers, the succession of bloom is well maintained through summer and autumn, and there is a refreshing fragrance. This is a dependable rose for beds, borders or as a hedge, and the slowly opening flowers on their long firm stems are very suitable for cutting. The plant grows vigorously with an upright habit to above average height, and is furnished with large dark green leaves. It was named to mark the millennium year of Tynwald, the Isle of Man Parliament in the UK, which is the oldest continuous legislature in the world.
ZONES 4–9.

Mattock, UK, 1979

'Peer Gynt' × 'Isis'

'Typhoon'

'Twinkle Twinkle'

'TYPHOON'
syn. 'Taifun'
MODERN, LARGE-FLOWERED/HYBRID TEA, ORANGE BLEND, REPEAT-FLOWERING

These flowers are a combination of salmon and orange tints with a hint of yellow at the base of the petals. The blooms have about 36 petals and open slowly. They have a splendid scent, and seem impervious to bad weather. It is an excellent bedding and border rose or it can be used as a hedge, and the flowers are good for cutting. It grows vigorously with a bushy habit to average height with crisp shiny dark leaves. ZONES 4–9.

Kordes, Germany, 1972

'Dr A. J. Verhage' × 'Colour Wonder'

Royal National Rose Society Certificate of Merit 1972, Belfast Certificate of Merit 1974

'TYRIANA'
MODERN, LARGE-FLOWERED/HYBRID TEA, DEEP PINK, REPEAT-FLOWERING

The plump buds of this rose open out into large, well-formed flowers made up of some 40 petals. They are a warm shade of rosy pink and open cupped with a pleasing scent. It is unusually free flowering for so large a bloom, and repeats its display through summer and autumn. It is particularly suitable for a hedge as well as for beds and borders. It makes vigorous growth with an upright, free-branching habit to above average height and has large, leathery dark leaves. ZONES 4–9.

Meilland, France, 1963

('Rouge Meilland' × 'Independence') × 'Paris-Match'

'Tzigane'

'Tzigane'

'TZIGANE'
syn. 'Tiz'
MODERN, LARGE-FLOWERED/HYBRID TEA, RED BLEND, REPEAT-FLOWERING

These strikingly beautiful blooms are large and well formed with broad petals and open with high centers, becoming cupped. The petals are bright scarlet red inside and chrome yellow outside, as startling a bicolor as may be imagined. There is some fragrance. 'Tzigane' is perhaps grown more for sentiment and historic interest today, but it can still surprise the onlooker with its beauty. As a plant it is a moderate performer, not free with its new wood, and is apt to die-back in hard winters. It grows with an upright habit to below average height and has glossy foliage that resembles the color of a copper beech. A tzigane is a Hungarian gypsy dance. ZONES 4–9.

Meilland, France, 1951

'Peace' × 'J. B. Meilland'

'Tuscany'

'Tutu Mauve'

'Twilight Mist'

UV

'ULRICH BRUNNER FILS'

syn. 'Ulrich Brunner'

OLD, HYBRID PERPETUAL, DEEP PINK, REPEAT-FLOWERING

'Paul Neyron' is the quintessential giant-flowered, big Hybrid Perpetual of the nineteenth century and still flaunts its 'neyron' pink flowers. This rose, its off-spring, has bright cerise-red, large, cupped, fragrant flowers of the same style. The bush is upright and vigorous. Ulrich Brunner, the son, was a rosarian of Lausanne. ZONES 5–9.

Levet, France, 1881

Seedling of 'Paul Neyron'

'UNA'

MODERN, RAMBLER, LIGHT YELLOW

This rose is best described as a short rambler, but it can go further on a wall. The foliage resembles that of the dog rose. The flowers are almost single and are large, opening creamy buff and fading to creamy white. There is a delicious scent. The parentage is very unusual, and the Tea Rose parent may have been 'Gloire de Dijon'. There is only one flowering, but it is followed by a crop of large hips. It appears now to be available commercially only in France. ZONES 5–9.

Paul, UK, 1900

Tea Rose × *Rosa canina*

'Ulrich Brunner Fils'

'UNCLE JOE'

syns 'El Toro', 'Toro'

MODERN, LARGE-FLOWERED/HYBRID TEA, DARK RED, REPEAT-FLOWERING

The flowers of this dark red variety are extremely large and full, with high centers and symmetrical Large-flowered form. They are so long lasting that it becomes a fault, because the old petals hang on and become unsightly. Flowers continue to appear through summer and autumn, and some noses are able to detect a little fragrance. 'Uncle Joe' is vigorous and performs best in sunny climates, for the broad petals are likely to stick together and fail to open in cool or wet conditions. It lasts for ages as a cut flower; the rose 'Goliath', a mainstay of the export flower trade in India, is reputed to be this rose under another name. The plant grows vigorously with an upright habit to above average height and has large, dark leathery leaves. ZONES 4–9.

Kern, USA, 1972

(['Mirandy' × 'Charles Mallerin'] × seedling)

'UNCLE MERC'

MODERN, CLUSTER-FLOWERED/FLORIBUNDA, MEDIUM PINK, REPEAT-FLOWERING

'Uncle Merc' is a Cluster-flowered form with flowers that are a blend of pinks.

'UNICEF'

'Uncle Joe'

'Uncle Walter'

They are produced singly and in clusters on a bushy, medium-sized plant with matt mid-green foliage. Disease resistance is good. Buds are shapely and open to medium-sized blooms of 20 petals. There is a slight fragrance and repeat-bloom is rather slow. ZONES 5–10.

Parentage unknown

'UNCLE WALTER' MACon

MODERN, LARGE-FLOWERED/HYBRID TEA, MEDIUM RED, REPEAT-FLOWERING

The flowers of this variety are crimson scarlet, high centered and fairly large, with about 30 wide petals, and open rather loosely on very tall stems. They are often carried in open clusters, and the effect overall is more like a big shrub than a Large-flowered bush. Disbudding produces better quality flowers. There is a light fragrance, and continuity of bloom is maintained through summer and autumn. 'Uncle Walter' needs careful placing or it will dominate its neighbors; towards the back of a border is a suitable place, or it could be treated as a climber and grown on a support. It grows very vigorously with a tall, free-branching habit to well above average height. The leaves are large, crimson when young, then maturing to bronze-green, and plentiful. Raiser Sam McGredy named the rose for his uncle, Walter Johnston, who looked after the nursery during his infancy. ZONES 4–9.

McGredy, UK, 1963

'Detroiter' × 'Heidelberg'

National Rose Society Certificate of Merit 1963, Scandinavia Nord-Rose Award

'UNICEF' COCjojo

syn. 'The Audrey Hepburn Rose'

MODERN, CLUSTER-FLOWERED/FLORIBUNDA, ORANGE BLEND, REPEAT-FLOWERING

These flowers are carried in upright sprays and contain quite an assortment

'Uncle Merc'

'Unique Blanche'

'Uwe Seeler'

of orange, peach and apricot-yellow shades, with deep rose red flushes along the margins of the petals as they mature. They are of medium size, full petalled with neat tight centers, and open loosely cupped. There is a slight scent. This is a suitable rose for a hedge, bed or border, growing with an upright habit to average height or less and having ample rich green foliage. It was named for the United Nations' Children's Fund. ZONES 4–9.

Cocker, UK, 1993

'Anne Cocker' × 'Remember Me'

Glasgow Certificate of Merit 1995

'UNIQUE BLANCHE'

syns 'Blanche Unique', *Rosa centifolia alba*, 'Unica Alba', 'Vièrge de Clery', 'White Provence'

OLD, CENTIFOLIA, WHITE

This typical Centifolia—a lax shrub to about 4 ft (1.2 m)—has darkish wood with plentiful thorns and dark green, deeply serrated foliage. The flowers are creamy white to pure white and are made up of many rather narrowly fluted petals, giving a distinctly ragged appearance when fully open. Sometimes these petals are folded inwards within the center to form a button in the middle of the flower; at other times they open up to show off a few yellow stamens. Each very fragrant bloom is usually about 3 in (8 cm) across and they appear on the bush rather later than most other once-flowering roses. 'Unique Blanche' is well named; it is the only pure white Centifolia now in common use. ZONES 5–10.

UK, 1775

Possibly a sport of 'Cabbage Rose'

'UNIQUE PANACHÉE'

syn. 'Unique Blanche de Panachée'

OLD, CENTIFOLIA, WHITE BLEND

The Unique Roses were sports of the old Cabbage Rose, the 'Rose of Province'.

The first was pure white. This one is also white, with the flowers being faintly striped rose and lilac. They are double, globular and large. The shrub, which is now not often seen, is not very elegant, being rather sprawling, and the flowers spoil badly in rain. Panachée means striped or variegated. ZONES 4–9.

Caron, France, 1821

Sport of 'Unique Rouge'

'UWE SEELER' KORsee

syns 'Gitta Grummer', 'Orange Vilmorin', 'Rainer Maria Rilke'

MODERN, CLUSTER-FLOWERED/FLORIBUNDA, ORANGE BLEND, REPEAT-FLOWERING

The color of this rose is a luminous salmon-orange. The fairly full flowers are formed with high centers like Large-flowered Roses; they are borne singly or in small clusters and fulfil the requirements of a modern Cluster-flowered Rose by blooming freely and dropping their spent petals cleanly. They have a pleasant fragrance and appear with good continuity through summer and autumn. 'Uwe Seeler' is useful for bedding, grouping in a border or as a hedge. It grows vigorously with an upright, bushy habit to average height and has dense semi-glossy foliage that is reddish when young. ZONES 4–9.

Kordes, Germany, 1970

'Queen Elizabeth' × 'Color Wonder'

'VALENCIA' KOReklia

syns 'New Valencia', 'Valeccia', 'Valencia 89'

MODERN, LARGE-FLOWERED/HYBRID TEA, APRICOT BLEND, REPEAT-FLOWERING

The light copper-yellow blooms of this variety are among the purest in this color

'Valerie June'

'Valentine Heart'

'Valencia'

in the rose garden. They are fairly large, full of petals, usually borne singly on long stems and open with high centers in classic Large-flowered Rose form, becoming cupped before the petals fall. They have a sweet enduring fragrance, and there is a good continuity of bloom through summer and autumn. A fine rose for the border and for cutting, 'Valencia' has a somewhat splayed and uneven growth habit which makes it less appropriate for a bed or hedge. It grows vigorously with a rather open aspect to average height and is adorned with rich green, leathery leaves. ZONES 4–9.

Kordes, Germany, 1989

Parentage unknown

Durbanville Gold Medal 1988, Royal National Rose Society Edland Fragrance Medal 1989, RNHS Certificate of Merit 1989

'VALENTINE HEART' DICogle

syns 'St Andrew's', 'Tinon'

MODERN, CLUSTER-FLOWERED/FLORIBUNDA, MEDIUM PINK/PINK BLEND, REPEAT-FLOWERING

There are only 20 or so petals in the flowers of this variety, but their tight centers encompass a wide range of subtle colors to charming effect. The buds are the palest of scarlets, opening with blush pink on the insides of the petals and then taking on variable hues of rosy lilac and pink, giving a wonderful depth to the flowers. There is a pleasing fragrance, and blooms are produced with good continuity throughout summer and autumn. 'Valentine Heart' is a good rose for a bed or the front of a border, where its fresh and cheerful appearance can be readily enjoyed, and can be drawn on for

'Vanguard'

buttonholes and small flower arrangements. The plant grows bushily with a slightly spreading habit to below average height and has dark foliage. ZONES 4–9.

Dickson, UK, 1990

'Shona' × 'Pot o' Gold'

Geneva Gold Medal 1988, Royal National Rose Society Certificate of Merit 1988, Belfast Certificate of Merit 1992

'VALERIE JUNE'

MODERN, LARGE-FLOWERED/HYBRID TEA, LIGHT PINK, REPEAT-FLOWERING

This pale pink rose was bred from two varieties of a similar color. It produces pale pink blooms of perfect exhibition form. They have 40 petals, good substance and a strong fragrance. The plant, however, is rather small and not very productive; there are long intervals between flushes. This is a rose for exhibition purposes and it can produce blooms of superlative quality. ZONES 5–10.

Allender, Australia, 1982

'Royal Highness' × 'Alice'

'VALETA'

MODERN, CLUSTER-FLOWERED/FLORIBUNDA, ORANGE-RED, REPEAT-FLOWERING

The trusses of this variety are large and bold, filled with up to 20 blooms like a small-scale Large-flowered Rose. They are full petalled and open cupped, showing a beautiful orange-red tone with vermilion shading. There is little fragrance but a good continuity of bloom is maintained through summer and autumn, making this a most noticeable, free-flowering rose to use where a hot color is wanted for bedding, as a group in a border or for a hedge. The flowers last exceptionally well when cut, and indeed the variety is a good subject to grow in the greenhouse. It grows vigorously with an upright habit to average height with dark foliage. ZONES 4–9.

de Ruiter, The Netherlands, 1960

'Signal Red' × 'Fashion'

'Valeta'

'VAN ARTEVELDE'

OLD, GALLICA, DEEP PINK

This is a little-known rose. The flowers are crimson-purple with markings of slate and lilac. They are cupped and quartered in the Old Garden Rose style. It is a small to medium shrub. ZONES 5–9.

Probably Parmentier, Belgium, pre-1847

Parentage unknown

'VANGUARD'

MODERN, HYBRID RUGOSA, ORANGE-PINK, REPEAT-FLOWERING

This is an untypical Rugosa cross that bears very large, pale orange-apricot to salmon flowers that open with a confused arrangement of petals. They have an excellent fragrance, and repeat-bloom through summer and autumn. 'Vanguard' requires careful placing in the garden because it can grow twice the height of the average shrub rose; the back of a shrub border is suitable, or it can be used to make a dense high hedge. It is tolerant of poorer soil and grows vigorously with an upright habit, with plentiful light glossy foliage that is burnished and wrinkled. ZONES 3–9.

Stevens, USA, 1932

(Rosa wichuraiana × R. rugosa alba) × 'Eldorado'

American Rose Society Dr W. Van Fleet Medal 1933, American Rose Society David Fürstenberg Prize 1934

U

V

'Vanilla'

'Varlon'

'Varlon'

'Vanilla'

'Vanity'

'VANILLA'   KORplasina

syn. 'Our Vanilla'

MODERN, CLUSTER-FLOWERED/FLORIBUNDA, WHITE (SHADED GREEN), REPEAT-FLOWERING

This greenhouse rose has attracted notice by reason of its unusual coloring: the flowers are creamy white with a distinct green patina. They are fairly small and are made up of firm petals that unfold very slowly, meanwhile holding the blooms in an attractive shape for a very long time. As is usual with hard-petalled florists' roses, no fragrance is detectable. 'Vanilla' can be cultivated under glass for the benefit of having the flowers to cut and as a talking point for visitors, but it is not recommended for the garden except in warm climates. It continues to bear blooms through summer and autumn and grows to average height or more, with leathery leaves. ZONES 5–9.

Kordes, Germany, 1994

Parentage unknown

'VANITY'

MODERN, MODERN SHRUB, DEEP PINK, REPEAT-FLOWERING

This is a plant that seems unsure of its identity; classified as a shrub, the trailing character of the stems makes it easier to treat as a short climber. The medium-sized blooms are deep pink, with only a few rather untidily arranged petals, and open to show yellow stamens. The lightly scented flowers are usually borne in wide clusters on long, arching stems, and repeat-bloom through summer and autumn. It can be included in a shrub border, where it will spread and eventually become a substantial undisciplined thicket, or it can be trained against a wall, fence or pillar, making an effective climbing plant. The foliage is semi-glossy and rather sparse. ZONES 4–9.

Pemberton, UK, 1920

'Château de Clos Vougeot' × seedling

'VARIEGATA DI BOLOGNA'

OLD, BOURBON, RED BLEND, REPEAT-FLOWERING

These fragrant flowers are white, striped purplish red; they are double and globular and are borne in clusters. There are few repeat flowers after the main summer flush. The plant is tall and lax and needs good cultivation, without which it is susceptible to black spot. It will occasionally sport back to the parent. The foliage is somewhat coarse and sparse. It can be grown as a short climber or pruned to a bush. ZONES 5–9.

Bonfiglioli & Son, Italy, 1909

Sport of 'Victor Emmanuel'

'VARLON'

syn. 'Ilona'

MODERN, LARGE-FLOWERED/HYBRID TEA, MEDIUM RED, REPEAT-FLOWERING

This is primarily a rose for greenhouses, bearing medium- to large-sized flowers of rich Turkey red. They are made up of 40 petals and are neatly formed, opening slowly. There is little fragrance but flower production through summer and autumn is well maintained. It does not appear to be available commercially, but in former years it was a top florists' rose and worth trying out of doors in warm climates. It grows vigorously with a bushy habit to above average height with glossy, leathery foliage. ZONES 4–9.

Verbeek, The Netherlands, 1973

'Miracle' × ('Romantica' × 'Edith Piaf')

'VEILCHENBLAU'

syns 'Blue Rambler', 'Blue Rosalie', 'Violet Blue'

MODERN, RAMBLER, MAUVE

This is a very popular Rambler in the *Rosa multiflora* style—it is vigorous, semi-rigid and almost thornless; it has fresh green leaves. The fragrant flowers, taking after the 'male' parent, are violet streaked with white, fading to gray. They are small, semi-double and incurved, and show prominent yellow stamens. This is the best known of the three similar violet-purple ramblers, the others being 'Rose-Marie Viaud' and 'Violette'. It flowers early in the season. ZONES 5–9.

Schmidt, Germany, 1909

'Crimson Rambler' × 'Souvenir de Brod'

Royal Horticultural Society Award of Garden Merit 1993

'VELUTINIFLORA'

syn. 'Velutinaeflora'

OLD, GALLICA, DARK RED

'Velutiniflora' is a short-growing Gallica with pointed buds with unusual downy sepals, opening to single, 5-petalled flowers of rich rosy-purple. There is a prominent boss of golden stamens. The rough-textured foliage is dense, close-jointed and matt gray-green, and the stems are quite thorny. The single blooms are attractive but short lived, and there is no repeat. Like most Gallicas, 'Velutiniflora' will sucker if planted with the bud-union below ground level, and it makes an attractive thicket. It is winter hardy, but there may be mildew in autumn. ZONES 5–10.

Pre-1872

Parentage unknown

'VELVET FRAGRANCE'

FRYperdee

syn. 'Velours Parfumé'

MODERN, LARGE-FLOWERED/HYBRID TEA, DARK RED, REPEAT-FLOWERING

These flowers are among the deepest reds grown today, their velvety petal texture being apparent when sun lights the blooms. They are large and high centered, with over 40 long petals, and are often borne singly or sometimes several together in a wide spray, in either case on stems are long enough to cut for indoor decoration. There is good continuity of bloom through summer and autumn and, as the name and awards testify, the flowers carry a satisfying fragrance. 'Velvet Fragrance' looks well planted as a group. It grows strongly with an upright, rather lanky habit to above average height and has large, dark green, semi-glossy leaves. ZONES 4–9.

Fryer, UK, 1988

Seedling × seedling

Royal National Rose Society Edland Fragrance Award 1988, RNRS Trial Ground Certificate 1988, Baden-Baden Fragrance Award 1990

'Veilchenblau'

'Variegata di Bologna'

'Veilchenblau'

V

'Velvet Fragrance'

'VELVET HOUR'
MODERN, LARGE-FLOWERED/HYBRID TEA, DARK RED, REPEAT-FLOWERING

The blooms of this variety are a rich dark blood red and are carried firmly on strong tall stems. They are of modest size for a Large-flowered Rose and neatly formed in the young blooms. As they open the edges of the reflexing petals furl into points, giving a spiky effect. There is a sweet scent, and the continuity of bloom through summer and autumn is satisfactorily maintained. 'Velvet Hour' can be used for beds and borders and as a hedge, and is certainly an asset to have for cutting, as the blooms last well. It grows with an upright habit to above average height and has a respectable covering of dark green, semi-glossy foliage. **ZONES 4–9.**
LeGrice, UK, 1978
Parentage unknown

'VENUSTA PENDULA'
OLD, AYRSHIRE, WHITE

The origin of this rose is unknown, but it was re-introduced by Kordes in Germany in 1928. For a short account of the

'Velutiniflora'

'Velvet Hour'

Ayrshire Roses, see 'Splendens'. This is a moderately rampant climber or rambler that bears clusters of small, white flushed pink, double flowers that practically smother the plant in its short flowering season. There is practically no scent. If grown through a tree, for which it is eminently suitable, the effect is in fact pendulous and *venusta* (Latin for beautiful). ZONES 4–9.

Parentage unknown

'VERA JOHNS'   KORvera
MODERN, LARGE-FLOWERED/HYBRID TEA, ORANGE-RED, REPEAT-FLOWERING

The oval buds of this rose open to large flowers of exquisite form and color. Because these flowers are produced so profusely, 'Vera Johns' has remained popular for longer than most roses. The flower is probably at its best when half open, with the central petals scrolled and pointed, and the outer petals rolling back; all the petals show shades of light

'Verdi'

orange and salmon, which are beautifully blended. The medium to tall shrub has handsome, glossy foliage and is a strong grower, so it is a successful bedder. The flowers are long lasting when cut, so are good for exhibition. This rose excels in all respects except for fragrance, which is only slight. ZONES 4–10.

Kordes, Germany, 1977

Seedling × 'Prominent'

'VERDI'
MODERN, MODERN SHRUB, MAUVE BLEND, REPEAT-FLOWERING

Only very few nurseries list this rose, which is a Modern Shrub with a strong scent similar to that of *Rosa moschata*, the Musk Rose. The pinkish mauve flowers are borne in massed sprays, covering the shiny green foliage on an upright plant. 'Verdi' needs to be well cared for if it is to flower well. ZONES 5–10.

Lens, Belgium, 1984

'Mr Bluebird '× 'Violet Hood'

'Versailles'

'Verschuren'

'Vesper'

'VERSAILLES'   DELset
syn. 'Castel'
MODERN, LARGE-FLOWERED/HYBRID TEA, LIGHT PINK, REPEAT-FLOWERING

This variety has light pink, double blooms that develop from ovoid buds. It is an average-sized bush with an upright growth habit and dark green, glossy, leathery leaves. The soft, cupped, slightly fragrant blooms are formed freely and are found in typical Large-flowered formations. 'Versailles' suffers from mildew and black spot late in the season, so it is best to prevent these with a sound eradication program from the beginning of the season. At its release it was a winner of many awards, although it has been overlooked greatly by professional growers; it is not now widely grown, and as it was not released in all countries, it will be difficult to find plants in many nurseries. ZONES 5–11.

Delbard-Chabert, France, 1967

('Queen Elizabeth' × 'Provence') × ('Michèle Meilland' × 'Bayadère')

Baden-Baden Gold Medal 1965, Bagatelle Gold Medal 1966, Geneva Gold Medal 1966

'VERSCHUREN'
MODERN, LARGE-FLOWERED/HYBRID TEA, LIGHT PINK, REPEAT-FLOWERING

This Large-flowered Rose forms classically formed blooms that are medium pink in the urn-shaped stage, then mellow out to a gentle light pink as they open more fully. The variegated mid-green leaves are splashed with pale yellow—a rare and highly valued characteristic. ZONES 5–10.

Verschuren, The Netherlands, 1904

Parentage unknown

'VESPER'
MODERN, CLUSTER-FLOWERED/FLORIBUNDA, ORANGE BLEND, REPEAT-FLOWERING

Another of the unusually colored Cluster-flowered Roses bred by the late Edward LeGrice, 'Vesper' produces striking apricot-brown flowers. They develop from well-shaped buds to give small to large, very well-spaced clusters. Each bloom is semi-double and has 20 petals. There is a slight fragrance. Green and leathery foliage covers this short and stocky bush. The spring and autumn flushes are most appealing, although the flowers fade rather quickly in summer. The small leaves are blue-gray and the disease resistance is average, with some susceptibility to black spot and mildew early in the season. Pruning should be

'Vestey's Pink Tea'

carefully done to achieve a good, well-rounded bush that will bring pleasure in spring. 'Vesper' is a good rose for cutting. ZONES 5–10.

LeGrice, UK, 1966

Parentage unknown

Royal National Rose Society Trial Ground Certificate 1967

'VESTEY'S PINK TEA'
OLD, TEA, MEDIUM PINK, REPEAT-FLOWERING

This rose was rediscovered in Lady Vestey's garden, although the original name is not known. 'Vestey's Pink Tea' forms a medium-sized, spreading bush with rather large, curved thorns and mid-green, semi-glossy foliage that is very free of disease. The flowers are deep rose pink with a cream base to each petal; a suffusion of cream runs through the pink. There are 30–40 petals, forming a full flower that is attractively cupped. The buds are well shaped and the blooms keep their color well. This variety will flower continuously in mild climates with the best flowers usually seen in autumn and winter. There is a typical Tea Rose scent. ZONES 5–10.

Parentage unknown

'VESTEY'S YELLOW TEA'
OLD, TEA, LIGHT YELLOW, REPEAT-FLOWERING

This Tea Rose was reintroduced into commerce from Lady Vestey's garden. The original name has been lost. 'Vestey's Yellow Tea' is an unusual rose, since it produces masses of loose, semi-double flowers of 10–15 petals, and there are a few petals in the center of the flower. The blooms are medium to large in size, and are produced in small clusters. In warm weather, the blooms are cream and fade to white, but in cool weather they are a most attractive soft yellow; the same color as 'McGredy's Yellow'. The bush is tall and very spreading with an abundance of mid-green, semi-glossy foliage. There is a slight perfume. 'Vestey's Yellow Tea' covers itself with flowers from ground level upwards; it is an excellent rose to plant in groups for continuous color. ZONES 5–10.

Parentage unknown

'VESUVIUS'
MODERN, LARGE-FLOWERED/HYBRID TEA, DARK RED, REPEAT-FLOWERING

The dark red single flowers, made up of 6 petals, are found on a strong, vigorous bush that has a light style of growth with thinner type of wood. The health of the

V

plant is good, and with its upright habit it is easy to maintain and prune. The flowers are produced in a show, starting with pleasant, long, pointed buds that develop into large flowers. It is not widely grown and it may be difficult to find, as there are better options. ZONES 5–10.

McGredy, UK, 1923

Parentage unknown

'VI'S VIOLET'   MORvi
MODERN, MINIATURE, MAUVE, REPEAT-FLOWERING

These soft lavender flowers fade very quickly—before the bloom even opens fully. The blooms are double and have a light fragrance, appearing amid the matt mid-green foliage that is subject to mildew and other fungi. This plant is a compact, upright bush, which has no resistance whatsoever to disease. Frequent spraying is absolutely essential to maintain a healthy plant. ZONES 5–10.

Moore, USA, 1991

Seedling × 'Angel Face'

'VICK'S CAPRICE'
OLD, HYBRID PERPETUAL, PINK BLEND, REPEAT-FLOWERING

The flowers of this rose contain 25 petals. They are lilac rose, often striped white and carmine, and are cupped, large and fragrant. The blooms are inclined to ball in wet weather. The plant has a bushy and compact habit and can revert to the original, as is the way with such sports. It

'Vestey's Yellow Tea'

'Victor Emmanuel'

'Victor Borge'

is noticeably shorter in growth than the parent, which is a 'La Reine'-type of Hybrid Perpetual. The Hybrid Perpetuals were extremely various because of their complex hybridity, and the experts used to divide them into 12 distinct groups. ZONES 5–9.

Vick, USA, 1891

Sport of 'Archiduchesse Elisabeth d'Aûtriche'

'VICKY MARFÁ'
MODERN, LARGE-FLOWERED/HYBRID TEA, MEDIUM PINK, REPEAT-FLOWERING

These pink, high-pointed flowers have a yellow center. The double blooms with 32 petals are fragrant and repeat-flower often. The strong flower stems form part of a vigorous, upright, compact bush that is easy to prune in winter. Disease can be kept under control with normal chemical applications. This variety is not widely grown. ZONES 5–10.

Dot, Spain, 1958

('Soraya' × 'Ellinor LeGrice') × 'Henri Mallerin'

'VICOMTESSE PIERRE DU FOU'
MODERN, LARGE-FLOWERED CLIMBER, ORANGE-PINK, REPEAT-FLOWERING

This rampant climber needs ample space and sunlight to produce its best blooms, which have a very fragrant, unfading scent. The large, double flowers are red and age to a deeper orange-pink color. The strongly wooded plant is easy to

'Vick's Caprice'

prune because of its wealth of growth, although the framework will have to be carefully planned and priority must be given to carefully training lateral canes at pruning to produce the best early blooms. It will repeat-flower in good conditions, which is unusual for a climber of this period. Growth is vigorous, and the foliage is large, glossy and bronze. This variety is not widely grown, and is found only in specialist catalogues. ZONES 6–11.

Sauvageot, France, 1923

'L'Ideal' × 'Joseph Hill'

'VICTOR BORGE'   POUlvue
syn. 'Michael Crawford'
MODERN, LARGE-FLOWERED/HYBRID TEA, ORANGE BLEND, REPEAT-FLOWERING

This rose was named after two very talented people and is better known in some countries as 'Michael Crawford'. The bush is healthy and vigorous and is a medium to tall grower with a good coverage of leaves and resistance to mildew in warm areas. The well-shaped buds open to large salmon-orange flowers with a brushing of light peach. They are fully double and are carried singly or in small clusters, and there is some fragrance but it can be washed out in damp weather. If the bush is well fed it is disease free. The repeat-flowering is spontaneous, which allows the plant to produce large splashes of color in the garden provided it is planted in full sun. ZONES 5–10.

Poulsen, Denmark, 1995

Parentage unknown

Courtrai Certificate of Merit 1990, Belfast Certificate of Merit 1992

'Vicky Marfá'

'VICTOR EMMANUEL'
OLD, BOURBON, DEEP RED, REPEAT-FLOWERING

This moderately vigorous bush bears large, double, richly colored velvety black blooms. It would be very hard to find these days, and is more celebrated as a parent of 'Variegata di Bologna'. Victor Emmanuel II (1820–78, King of Sardinia) was also the first king of unified Italy. Some rosarians say this rose is a Hybrid Perpetual. ZONES 5–9.

Guillot Père, France, 1859

Parentage unknown

'VICTOR HUGO'
OLD, HYBRID PERPETUAL, DEEP RED, REPEAT-FLOWERING

The flowers of 'Victor Hugo' are double and contain 30 petals. They are carmine-red shaded purple, globular and of medium size. It is said to require very good cultivation, and is available from only a few specialist growers. There are also a Bourbon and a Meilland Large-flowered Rose with the same name. Victor Hugo

V

'Victoriana'

'Victoria Gold'

'Victoria Gold'

was a famous French writer who lived from 1802–85. This was the breeder's last rose. ZONES 5–10.

Schwartz, France, 1884

'Charles Lefèbvre' × seedling

'VICTORIA GOLD'

MODERN, CLUSTER-FLOWERED/FLORIBUNDA, DEEP YELLOW, REPEAT-FLOWERING

This rose, introduced by the Rose Society of Victoria, Australia, in honor of their centenary, carries well-formed buds that open to 3 in (8 cm) flowers, which hold their color extremely well—much better than those of either parent. It is one of the first roses to flower in the spring and flowers right through the season and well into winter. The blooms occur in small clusters and are an intense golden yellow that is deeper towards the edges of the petals in the same manner as 'Gold Medal'. They are very good for cutting. 'Victoria Gold' is a tall and very bushy plant with glossy, healthy, rich green foliage. The variety could easily join with

'Friesia' and 'Gold Badge' to make a trio of the best bright yellow Cluster-flowered Roses in commerce today. ZONES 5–10.

Welsh, Australia, 1999

'Gold Medal' × seedling of 'Gold Badge'

'VICTORIANA'

MODERN, CLUSTER-FLOWERED/FLORIBUNDA, ORANGE BLEND, REPEAT-FLOWERING

This unusual rose has its best flowers in cooler regions and tends to lose its special individuality in the heat of summer. The very dark burnt orange blooms have a brown appearance, with the centers of the flowers a lighter shade—it is certainly evocative of this timeless era. The plant itself grows into a vigorous low bush and is an ideal choice for a patio or small standard rose, as well as being ideal for a low border or mass planting in an area that is to be kept short. Health is good and with some preventive measures it can remain free of disease all season. Many rose nurseries do not grow this

bush, as it is hard to find growth that will be suitable for propagation. 'Victoriana' is slightly fragrant and has a good repeat-flowering. ZONES 5–10.

LeGrice, UK, 1977

Parentage unknown

'VIKING QUEEN'

MODERN, LARGE-FLOWERED CLIMBER, MEDIUM PINK, REPEAT-FLOWERING

'Viking Queen' is not widely grown. The deep to mid-pink flowers are large, fully double, with 60 petals and have a strong fragrance. They are borne in clusters and there is some stem length for cutting; the blooms will fill a bowl easily. The glossy dark green healthy growth keeps the flowers coming and repeat-flowering is good. As a climbing rose it has strength and vigor that is manageable, while pruning is easy and it produces a great deal of growth throughout the season. Disease resistance is fair. ZONES 4–11.

Phillips, USA, 1963

'White Dawn' × 'L. E. Longley'

'Victoriana'

'VILLE DE LONDRES'

OLD, GALLICA, DEEP PINK

This rose seems to be available only in Europe. It bears double, medium-sized flowers that are a lovely cerise-pink color. They are fragrant. The plant has a compact growth habit. François Joyaux believes the rose sold by this name may be 'La Gloire des Jardins' (Descemet, France, pre-1815). ZONES 4–9.

Possibly Vibert, France, pre-1850

Parentage unknown

'VINCENT GODSIFF'

OLD, CHINA, MEDIUM RED, REPEAT-FLOWERING

This is a short, twiggy China Rose peculiar to Bermuda and was found in Mr Godsiff's garden at Fairhaven, Paget. It is semi-double and deep pink in color. 'Vincent Godsiff' is available from a few specialist American growers. Interestingly, many odd China seedlings are to be found in cemeteries and such places in suitable climates. ZONES 7–9.

Parentage unknown

'VINO DELICADO'

MODERN, LARGE-FLOWERED/HYBRID TEA, MAUVE, REPEAT-FLOWERING

This classically formed Large-flowered Rose has mauve flowers that are tinged on the outside with tones of darker purple. The color is a novelty and is difficult to match in the garden bed. The well-formed buds open quickly to full blown flowers that exude a slight rose fragrance. It is an upright-growing bush with large, leathery foliage. 'Vino Delicado' is one of a number of rose plants developed to widen the spectrum of the *Rosa* color range towards blue. It had its part to play but other roses, such as 'Paradise' and 'Blue Moon', grow and perform in a better way. ZONES 5–10.

Raffel, USA, 1972

Seedling × 'Mauve Melodee'

'VINTAGE VISALIA'   MORlu

MODERN, CLUSTER-FLOWERED/FLORIBUNDA, MEDIUM PINK, REPEAT-FLOWERING

'Vintage Visalia' was released by Ralph Moore in 1992 but it has not gained great popularity. The Old Garden Rose form of the flowers is pleasant; the full blooms are mid-pink, the outer petals showing a darker shade of pink. They are slightly fragrant, have over 41 petals and are borne mostly singly. The upright growth has a pleasing style that is enhanced by the dark glossy leaves. Disease must be monitored and, as with the rest

'Vino Delicado'

V

'Violet Carson'

'Violette'

of the rose garden, will need to be maintained with an active control program especially against red spider mite. The plant suits individual or block planting and is better placed in an old rose-style bed where the full benefit of its blooms can be seen. It is not freely available all over the world. ZONES 4–11.

Moore, USA, 1992

'Pink Petticoat' × 'Lulu'

'VIOLACÉE'
OLD, MOSS, MAUVE

This is now a very rare rose, and should not to be confused with 'Violacea' (syn. 'La Belle Sultane'), a very desirable Gallica. The flowers are purple, shaded violet to grayish pink. They are full and large. ZONES 4–9.

Soupert and Notting, Luxembourg, 1876

Shows strong affinity to *Rosa gallica*

'VIOLAINE'
MODERN, LARGE-FLOWERED/HYBRID TEA, MAUVE, REPEAT-FLOWERING

This 1960s Large-flowered Rose is now difficult to find, and the only listed nursery supplier is in Israel. The large blooms are a mauve shade and feature good high-centered buds. The very fragrant flowers are free and repeat well during the season on a vigorous, strong bush with leathery foliage that is easy to prune. Better suited to warmer and drier areas, 'Violaine' has been outdated and is

now grown by collectors of roses rather than the general gardener. 'Simone', its pollen parent, was popular during the 1960s as it had unusual parchment gray petals that it has passed down to its progeny. ZONES 4–10.

Gaujard, France, 1968

'Eminence' × 'Simone'

'VIOLET CARSON' MACio
MODERN, CLUSTER-FLOWERED/FLORIBUNDA, ORANGE-PINK/PINK BLEND REPEAT-FLOWERING

'Violet Carson' produces masses of blooms throughout the season. The light-petalled, strong salmon-pink blooms open from classically styled buds and are produced in clusters in large heads. It is a vigorous, low-growing bush that is quick to repeat-flower. The plant needs protection from mildew to ensure its health and vigor, as it does not suffer from black spot. Pruning in winter is an easy task on the short stout growth. It is an ideal plant for hedging and border plantings, providing a mass of color that will endure and be very rewarding with little input and maximum joy. 'Violet Carson' has dark green, glossy foliage and is suited to most climates, especially hotter regions, and it is very widely grown all over the world. ZONES 5–10.

McGredy, New Zealand, 1964

'Mme Léon Cuny' × 'Spartan'

Royal National Rose Society Certificate of Merit 1963

'Violinista Costa'

'VIOLETTE'
MODERN, RAMBLER, MAUVE

This is a wonderfully free-growing climber. The flowers have two rows of deep violet petals that are quite showy. The flowers appear abundantly in the first flush of bloom and it does not flower again, as it concentrates on its growth for the next year. It is a healthy, vigorous grower that suffers only a little mildew late in the season on new shoots. At pruning the long canes should be trained horizontally for the best quality blooms and most pleasing effect. A great climber for walls and trellis work, 'Violette' has few thorns and light green shiny leaves. ZONES 4–11.

Turbat, France, 1921

Parentage unknown

'VIOLETTE PARFUMÉE'
DORient

syn. 'Melodie Parfumée'

MODERN, LARGE-FLOWERED/HYBRID TEA, MAUVE BLEND, REPEAT-FLOWERING

The bluish green foliage of this upright bush rose combines well with the mauve-pink flowers. These are double and urn-shaped with tight centers, opening out flat as the flowers mature to show golden yellow stamens. ZONES 5–10.

Dorieux, France, 1995

Parentage unknown

Baden-Baden Fragrance Award 1995, Bagatelle Gold Medal 1995, Bagatelle Fragrance Award 1995

'VIOLINISTA COSTA'
MODERN, LARGE-FLOWERED/HYBRID TEA, RED BLEND, REPEAT-FLOWERING

The red to darker red flowers of 'Violinista Costa' have an open Cluster-flowered style and a loose form. The small-growing bush has lots of thorns on the stems. Disease resistance is fair but will need attention to keep it from developing mildew on its young shoots in cooler weather. Despite this it is a very reliable rose that suits a range of situations and growing habits; it can be used as a standard as well as a bush, providing a spectacle when in full flower. A remarkable characteristic of this rose is that after deadheading or pruning, one's hands smell delightfully of rose water. ZONES 5–10.

Camprubi, Spain, 1936

'Sensation' × 'Shot Silk'

'Violaine'

'Violinista Costa'

'Violette Parfumée'

'VIRGINIA' PEKwhina

MODERN, LARGE-FLOWERED/HYBRID TEA, WHITE, REPEAT-FLOWERING

This vigorous shrub grows to a medium height with glossy bright green leaves. The growth is very resistant to disease, especially fungus. Large pure white flowers are carried in clusters, which gives 'Virginia' the appearance of a Cluster-flowered Rose. The variety can produce show-quality single blooms if disbudded at an early stage. There is no fragrance. ZONES 5–10.

Pekmez, France, 1994

Sport of 'Anna'

'VIRGO'

syn. 'Virgo Liberationem'

MODERN, LARGE-FLOWERED/HYBRID TEA, WHITE, REPEAT-FLOWERING

'Virgo' produces some of the finest classic white Large-flowered Roses available and is a plant that is well worth growing. The tall, high-pointed buds open out to fully double white flowers of great purity and perfection. The upright bush has a tall nature and thick, light green leaves with a susceptibility to mildew, which should be prevented with sprayings of fungicide early in the growing season. The freedom and repeat-flowering frequency of this bush is similar to the older Large-flowered varieties, although it has been outshone in recent years by other roses that bloom in a shorter time and

with less fungus disease. However 'Virgo' is worth growing and is a plant that is freely available in all rose nurseries. ZONES 5–10.

Mallerin, France, 1947

'Blanche Mallerin' × 'Neige Parfum'

National Rose Society Gold Medal 1949

'VISTA' SAValav

MODERN, MINIATURE, MAUVE, REPEAT-FLOWERING

These soft lavender flowers have 15–25 petals. The lightly fragrant blooms have high centers suitable for exhibition. They are borne singly and in small clusters. The color shows little sign of fading, and the flowers last well, both when cut for indoors or left on the bush. The foliage is mid-green and semi-glossy on a compact, prolific, well-rounded bush. It is very suitable as a container-grown plant. Bright orange hips cover the bush in the winter, making this an even more attractive addition to the garden. ZONES 5–10.

Saville, USA, 1994

'Sachet' × 'Copper Sunset'

'VITAL'

MODERN, LARGE-FLOWERED/HYBRID TEA, DARK RED, REPEAT-FLOWERING

This is a really good cut-flower rose for growing under glass or for garden display. The buds are slim and elegant and open very slowly to a profusion of well-formed, deep red blooms of 25–30 petals. The substance is good so the long-

'Virgo'

'Vital'

'Vivacious'

'Vivid'

stemmed blooms last for a very long time when cut. 'Vital' is an excellent bedding rose for warm, dry climates. The blooms show up well against the shiny dark green, disease-resistant foliage, and there is a very quick repeat. ZONES 5–10.

Kordes, Germany, 1996

Sport of 'Corvette'

'VITAL SPARK' COCacert

MODERN, CLUSTER-FLOWERED/FLORIBUNDA, APRICOT BLEND, REPEAT-FLOWERING

'Vital Spark' is a mid-sized, bushy grower with slightly glossy leaves that cover the bush well. The double flowers are a golden color and have a pink blushing, especially in cooler climates. They are composed of 35 petals and have a slight fragrance. Disease can be kept in check with normal preventive measures, which is all that is needed. ZONES 5–10.

Cocker, UK, 1982

('Anne Cocker' × ['Sabine' × 'Circus']) × 'Yellow Pages'

Royal National Rose Society Trial Ground Certificate 1978

'VIVACIOUS'

MODERN, CLUSTER-FLOWERED/FLORIBUNDA, MEDIUM PINK, REPEAT-FLOWERING

'Vivacious' produces large, mid-pink flowers that are fragrant and double. The Large-flowered-type blooms are found in clusters on a healthy, free-growing bush. It is ideal for mass plantings, as the growth will spread. Disease control is recommended for the best blooms and a healthy bush. ZONES 5–10.

Gregory, UK, 1971

'Tropicana' × seedling

'Vogelpark Walsrode'

'Vital Spark'

'VIVID'

OLD, BOURBON, MAUVE/LIGHT RED

'Vivid' bears very bright, fully double flowers that are magenta to magenta-pink. They are fragrant. This is a tall, upright, rather prickly shrub that is very vigorous. It has been recommended as being suitable for a pillar or trellis, as is the case for many Bourbons. It repeats only occasionally. ZONES 5–9.

Paul, UK, 1853

Parentage unknown

'VOGELPARK WALSRODE'

KORlomet

syn. 'Kookaburra'

MODERN, MODERN SHRUB, LIGHT PINK, REPEAT-FLOWERING

The color is a delicate shade of light pink, fading to a pale blush as the blooms open wide, showing golden stamens. They are fairly full, of medium to large size, and borne very freely in clusters at different levels on the plant, creating a delightful effect. There is a sweet light fragrance, and flowering is well maintained through summer and particularly good again in autumn. In a shrub border or as a specimen plant or in a bed, this is an attractive garden rose, complemented by plentiful light green shiny foliage. It is a vigorous, robust shrub of average height and spreading habit. The mouthful of a name was too much for an Australian grower, who, realising it referred to an aviary, considered 'Kookaburra' more acceptable. ZONES 4–9.

Kordes, Germany, 1991

Parentage unknown

Anerkannte Deutsche Rose 1989

'VOGUE'

MODERN, CLUSTER-FLOWERED/FLORIBUNDA, PINK
BLEND, REPEAT-FLOWERING

'Vogue' has a sweet scent that endures
and so is irresistible to many growers.
The loose, semi-double, cherry pink
flowers appear in clusters; when fully
open the blooms have a flat nature. The
color fades over the flowers' life and can
tend to be washed out. The bush is vigorous, with minimal care needed to keep it
healthy throughout the year. This variety
has good repeat-flowering on a medium-
sized, vigorous, upright plant with glossy
foliage. It is available through some specialist rose nurseries now but has been
surpassed, as many newer varieties offer
much more. ZONES 5–10.

Boerner, USA, 1951

'Pinocchio' × 'Crimson Glory'

Portland Gold Medal 1950, Geneva Gold Medal
1950, National Rose Society Certificate of Merit
1951, All-America Rose Selection 1952

'VOL DE NUIT'   DELrio

syn. 'Night Flight'

MODERN, LARGE-FLOWERED/HYBRID TEA, MAUVE,
REPEAT-FLOWERING

The lovely mauve tones of 'Vol de Nuit'
have pleased many rose growers since its
introduction in 1970; the flower color is
strong, with some paler toning towards
the outer edges of the petals as the
blooms age. The fully double blooms repeat well and are found in ones and twos
with good long stems for picking. The
vigorous, upright bush has good disease
resistance that is easy to maintain, form-

'Von Scharnhorst'

'Vogue'

ing a strong framework for good production of flowers. Care must be taken in
protecting the flowers from the harsher
early season weather, as the blooms' delicate nature can sometimes be spoilt by
adverse weather. ZONES 5–11.

Delbard, France, 1970

('Holstein' × ['Bayadère' × 'Prélude']) × 'Saint-
Exupery'

Rome Gold Medal 1970

'VOLCANO'

MODERN, LARGE-FLOWERED/HYBRID TEA, DEEP
PINK, REPEAT-FLOWERING

Bright cherry red blooms are produced
on 'Volcano', and the name certainly
suits! The fruity scented blooms are very
large, carrying around 25 petals, and last
well when cut. The strong growth produces a fine plant that prunes easily
every year. Repeat-flowering is average,
and the plant needs to be monitored for
diseases. The dark, strong foliage can be
attractive to birds, who may damage it.
Well rated by the American Rose Society
when released, the variety is not now
widely grown and has been outclassed by
newer varieties. ZONES 5–11.

Moro, Italy, 1950

'Charles P. Kilham' × 'Rome Glory'

'VOLUNTEER'   HARquaker

MODERN, CLUSTER-FLOWERED/FLORIBUNDA,
YELLOW BLEND, REPEAT-FLOWERING

This low-growing Cluster-flowered Rose
has medium, glossy light green foliage.
The cream yellow flowers have a pink
brushing on the outside petals that tends
to fade over time and is less obvious in
warmer climates. The health and vigor
make this plant an honest performer
with good repeat-flowerings throughout
the entire season. The double flowers are
found in large sprays and, while the mature bush is only low, they cover the
bush well with bloom. Health is good and
it only requires attention when the season
encourages the development of fungus
disease. The slight fragrance is only
noticeable in warm weather. ZONES 5–11.

Harkness, UK, 1985

'Dame of Sark' × 'Silver Jubilee'

Paris, Silver Medal 1982

'Voodoo'

'Volcano'

'VON SCHARNHORST'

MODERN, MODERN SHRUB, LIGHT YELLOW,
REPEAT-FLOWERING

Walter Schultheis of Germany specializes
in rare roses, and his nursery appears to
be the sole source of this one, which is
among the last of Lambert's many creations. The buds and young flowers are
sulfur yellow, then pale to yellowish
white as they open out. They are semi-
double, have a light fragrance and continue to appear through summer and
autumn on strong, free-branching, vigorous growth that can attain about twice
the average height for a shrub rose. In
the garden, 'Von Scharnhorst' looks well
in a mixed border among other shrubs.
Its ancestry is unusual: 'Gottfried Keller'
has 'Persian Yellow' on both sides of its
parentage. ZONES 4–8.

Lambert, Germany, 1921

'Frau Karl Druschki' × 'Gottfried Keller'

'VOODOO'   AROmiclea

MODERN, LARGE-FLOWERED/HYBRID TEA, ORANGE
BLEND, REPEAT-FLOWERING

'Voodoo' has vibrant salmon-red, orange
and yellow-orange flowers that are crisp
and clear and of exhibition form. They
are fully double with 35 petals and have
little or no scent. The bush grows to

'Vol de Nuit'

medium height and has an upright
nature and a quickness to reshoot after
flowering. The glossy leaves are thick and
hard with good resistance to disease, and
the abundant thorns protect the stocky,
tough plant. Black spot will need to be
watched for late in the season when the
best blooms are being produced. It is an
ideal plant for a massed individual planting as the color can be difficult to blend.
It is available widely from rose nurseries
that have comprehensive lists. ZONES 5–11.

Christensen, USA, 1984

(['Camelot' × 'First Prize'] × 'Typhoo Tea') ×
'Lolita'

All-America Rose Selection 1986

V

WXYZ

'WAIHEKE' MACwaihe
syn. 'Waikiki'

MODERN, LARGE-FLOWERED/HYBRID TEA,
ORANGE-PINK, REPEAT-FLOWERING

This rose produces a lovely spectacle of
medium orange and pinkish blooms on
good stems. The blooms, which are easily
picked for display, are usually solitary
but can sometimes be found in small
clusters of 5–9 and carry a lovely spicy
fragrance. The outside petals on the
double flowers reflex well, and in cooler
weather are darker pink on the edges.
The health of 'Waiheke' is good and only
normal rose maintenance is needed to
keep its leaves and flowers in first-class
order. Glossy leaves and quick repeat-
flowering make this variety a good addition to any garden. ZONES 5–10.

McGredy, New Zealand, 1987

'Tony Jacklin' × 'Young Quinn'

'WALDFEE'

OLD, HYBRID PERPETUAL, MEDIUM RED,
REPEAT-FLOWERING

It is extraordinary that a Hybrid Perpetual Rose should be produced at this
late date. It has not really caught on,
however, and is available from only a few
outlets. The flowers are large and come
in small clusters. They are fragrant,
camellia shaped and blood red in color.
The foliage is glossy on a plant with a
vigorous growth habit. It can almost
reach the height of a short climber. A
waldfee is a wood fairy. ZONES 5–9.

Kordes, Germany, 1960

'Independence' × 'Mrs John Laing'

'Waiheke'

'Warley Jubilee'

'WALKO' DELde

MODERN, CLUSTER-FLOWERED/FLORIBUNDA,
DARK RED, REPEAT-FLOWERING

This dark crimson rose from the 1950s
is now largely overlooked as more reliable and hardy varieties have emerged.
The double flowers with 23 petals are
fragrant and are found in clusters over
the medium-sized bush. The growth
habit is upright and with repeat-flowering is able to produce a good framework
for pruning in winter. 'Walko' is rarely
grown. ZONES 5–9.

Delbard-Chabert, France, 1957

('Incendie' × 'Holstein') × 'Rouge Chabert'

'WANAKA' MACinca
syns 'Longleat', 'Young Cale'

MODERN, MINIATURE, ORANGE-RED,
REPEAT-FLOWERING

The flowers of this rose are such a
dazzling orange-red that they resemble
small begonias, although at a distance
'Wanaka' has also been likened to a red
geranium. The double flowers with
40 petals have a light fragrance and do
not fade, even in strong sunlight. They
come in large clusters on strong stems
that cover the surface of the plant. Sam
McGredy once called this rose his best
Miniature, but that was in the 1980s; his
later creations have certainly caused him
to re-evaluate that statement. However,
this rose has everything going for it:
color, vigor and vitality and it is easy
to grow. ZONES 5–10.

McGredy, New Zealand, 1978

'Anytime' × 'Trumpeter'

'Waldfee'

'Wapiti'

'WANDERING MINSTREL'
HARquince
syn. 'Daniel Gélin'

MODERN, CLUSTER-FLOWERED/FLORIBUNDA,
ORANGE-PINK, REPEAT-FLOWERING

A large-flowering Cluster-flowered Rose
that changes color according to the temperature, 'Wandering Minstrel' bears
orange-pink blooms that intensify with
yellow as cooler weather slows the flower
formation and growth of the bush.
Although only a small grower, it is fine
in borders and is ideal for banks or rockeries. Small clusters of double blooms
with 28 petals cover the bush all season;
it is a good repeat-bloomer and has a
moderate scent. Disease will need to be
watched for as the small growth encourages this, and some preventive measures
should be taken early and late in the
season to ensure bush growth and bloom
quality is kept at its best. ZONES 5–10.

Harkness, UK, 1986

'Dame of Sark' × 'Silver Jubilee'

Courtrai Silver Medal 1989, Glasgow Certificate
of Merit 1989

'WAPITI' MEInagre
syns 'Dazzla', 'Dazzler', 'Laurence Olivier',
'Striking'

MODERN, CLUSTER-FLOWERED/FLORIBUNDA,
RED BLEND, REPEAT-FLOWERING

This rose was released under several
different names that suited the different
markets into which it was introduced.
The loose flowers, with two or so rows of
petals that give a ruffled effect, open flat
in large clusters of color. The bright red
flowers give a good show and cover the
bush well when in full bloom. Their perfume is slight and they are not ideal for
cutting; 'Wapiti' is better suited to mass
plantings in the garden. Disease resistance is good, but the bush will need attention to keep it healthy throughout the
season. It is also an ideal plant for a bor-

'Walko'

'Warm Welcome'

der or area that is in need of brightening
up, but it is not widely grown and could
prove difficult to find. ZONES 5–10.

Meilland, France, 1988

Parentage unknown

Geneva Gold Medal 1987, Monza Gold Medal
1987, Rome Gold Medal 1987

'WARLEY JUBILEE'

MODERN, CLUSTER-FLOWERED/FLORIBUNDA,
MEDIUM PINK, REPEAT-FLOWERING

This sport bears clusters of medium-
sized, bright salmon-pink flowers that
have about 30 loosely opening petals.
There is a light scent, and the blooms
continue to appear through summer and
autumn on a bushy, rather spreading
plant of below average height. There are
many light green, semi-glossy leaves.
This rose is suitable for bedding schemes
or to edge a border. It was introduced by
Warley Roses to celebrate the silver jubilee of their firm. ZONES 5–9.

Warley Roses, UK, 1986

Sport of 'Warrior'

'WARM WELCOME' CHEwizz

MODERN, CLIMBING MINIATURE, ORANGE-RED,
REPEAT-FLOWERING

'Warm Welcome' bears fragrant, single
to semi-double, orange-vermilion
flowers with yellow bases. They come in
clusters at all levels on the plant, so that
it is covered from head to toe. The foliage is dark green and semi-glossy and
adorns this relatively tall, upright plant
that should be trained as a climber. It is
disease free and reliable, and can be used
as a pillar or to brighten up a fence. This
rose was a breakthrough in hybridizing
because it is a free-blooming, low-
maintenance Climbing Miniature with
small flowers and foliage. ZONES 5–10.

Warner, UK, 1992

'Elizabeth of Glamis' × (['Galway Bay' ×
'Sutter's Gold'] × 'Anna Ford')

Royal National Rose Society President's
International Trophy 1988, Royal Horticultural
Society Award of Garden Merit 1993

'WARRAWEE'

MODERN, LARGE-FLOWERED/HYBRID TEA,
MEDIUM PINK, REPEAT-FLOWERING

Introduced in Australia and named after
a suburb of Sydney, 'Warrawee' has
quaint flowers that open to show the
stamens clearly. The light pink, double
blooms are large and have a good Large-
flowered exhibition style and an enduring fragrance. The vigorous bush grows
into a small shrub with glossy foliage that
prunes well into a nice shape, but must

W

be looked after to ensure that it remains disease free. 'Warrawee' is best described as an early Tea Rose and, although not widely grown, it is still popular with people who like this type of rose; for that reason it will always have a following. It is not widely grown and some difficulty may be had in obtaining plants outside Australia. ZONES 5–10.

Fitzhardinge, Australia, 1935

'Padre' × 'Reverend F. Page-Roberts'

'WARRIOR'

MODERN, CLUSTER-FLOWERED/FLORIBUNDA, ORANGE-RED, REPEAT-FLOWERING

This fully double variety has lovely flowers that shine out from the garden bed. The bright scarlet-red blooms are found on short stems in small clusters, opening to give a slight glimpse of the stamens. The prolifically produced, quality blooms are good for cutting and repeat well if the bush is pruned and deadheaded when necessary. The light green foliage is healthy and robust, with a good tolerance to disease and other seasonal problems. ZONES 5–10.

LeGrice, UK, 1977

'City of Belfast' × 'Ronde Endiablee'

Royal National Rose Society Trial Ground Certificate 1977

'WARWICK CASTLE'   AUSlian

MODERN, MODERN SHRUB, DEEP PINK, REPEAT-FLOWERING

The beautiful, fully double flowers of this variety have the true appeal and charm of the Old Garden Roses it was bred to complement. The rich pink, scented blooms open flat without showing the stamens and have a perfection that is a delight to display in the house. Also classified as an English Rose, the medium-sized shrub has an upright habit and forms a solid bush that is both resistant to disease and easy to prune. The flowers

'Warrawee'

'Watercolor'

'Water Music'

are found from spring onwards and it is quick to repeat all season. 'Warwick Castle' has been replaced by many newer releases that offer more disease resistance and improved flowering habits. However, it is worth growing and will always be rewarding. ZONES 5–10.

Austin, UK, 1986

'The Reeve' × 'Lilian Austin'

'WARWICKSHIRE'   KORkandel

MODERN, MODERN SHRUB, PINK BLEND, REPEAT-FLOWERING

The 5-petalled flowers of this rose are small, borne very freely in short-stemmed clusters and make a noticeable impact because of their shape and coloring. They open like saucers to display creamy blush centers fringed with deep reddish pink. The effect is quite strange; the shrub seems to watch you with its many white eyes. There is little scent, and flowering continues through summer and autumn. Rain can dim the brilliance of the blooms, making them look tired and jaded. In the garden, this variety can be used where a low, spreading shrub is required, since it grows well below average height; it could almost be considered a Ground Cover Rose, because it is nearly twice as wide as it is high. There is a good complement of deep green foliage. ZONES 5–9.

Kordes, Germany, 1991

Parentage unknown

'WATER MUSIC'

MODERN, LARGE-FLOWERED CLIMBER, DEEP PINK

Bred by Australian Ron Bell, 'Water Music' is a large climbing rose that produces deep pink, double flowers with 20 petals early in the season. The flowers are darker on the petal edges, fading as they age, and are slightly fragrant. This variety grows well in the warm climate of Australia, but is largely unknown in the rest

'Warwick Castle'

'Water Music'

'Warrior'

of the world. The disease resistance is good on a spreading plant with medium-sized, glossy dark green foliage. 'Water Music' is an example of a rose that has been released by an Australian breeder into his local market without a large distribution network. ZONES 5–10.

Bell, Australia, 1982

'Handel' × seedling

'WATERCOLOR'

syn. 'Watercolour'

MODERN, MINIATURE, MEDIUM PINK, REPEAT-FLOWERING

The long, pointed buds of this rose open to reveal flowers that are a beautiful blend of light and deep pink. The blooms are double, with about two dozen petals, and have a light fragrance. The flower form is a typical exhibition style and tends to hold well even on sunny days, usually in sprays of 3–5 flowers, but one bloom per stem can occur in warm climates. The foliage is large and glossy dark green on a vigorous, upright plant that is healthy and easy to maintain. ZONES 5–10.

Moore, USA, 1975

'Rumba' × ('Little Darling' × 'Red Germain')

'WATERMELON ICE'   JACair

MODERN, MODERN SHRUB, PINK BLEND, REPEAT-FLOWERING

The color of this rose is variable, beginning lavender pink and gradually paling to blush, so that in each of its flower-filled sprays there are several shades visible together. The semi-double blooms open to shallow cups that reveal golden yellow stamens. There is little fragrance. The variety maintains a good continuity of flower through summer and autumn,

'Warrior'

'Waverley Garden Club'

forming a low and spreading mound well below the average height for a shrub rose; it is twice as wide as it is high, and is well provided with deep green, semi-glossy leaves. 'Watermelon Ice' is well suited for growing individually, near the front of a border, or in a container. ZONES 4–9.

Jackson & Perkins, USA, 1996

Seedling of 'The Fairy'

'WAVERLEY GARDEN CLUB'

MODERN, LARGE-FLOWERED/HYBRID TEA, PINK BLEND, REPEAT-FLOWERING

This rose has blooms of 40–45 petals in a blend of pinks. The basic color is cerise-pink mottled with paler pinks. The very double blooms are produced both singly and in small clusters amid unusual and distinctive, grayish green foliage. There are many very small prickles on the new growth with an occasional large thorn. The disease-resistant plant is bushy and spreading, with abundant, quick-repeating flowers in summer. ZONES 5–10.

Dawson, Australia, 1983

(['Stella' × 'Columbine'] × 'Prima Ballerina') × (seedling of 'Sabrina' × 'Golden Giant')

'Welwyn Garden Glory'

'Wedding Day'

'Wedding Day' (hips)

'Wedding Ring'

'WEDDING DAY'

syn. 'English Wedding Day'
MODERN, RAMBLER, WHITE

Rosa sinowilsonii was discovered in China in 1904; it is a single, white, vigorous rose. 'Wedding Day' is an improved version with rampant growth and clear green foliage. The flowers are larger and are white with pronounced orange stamens. They come in big trusses and have a citrus scent. ZONES 7–9.

Stern, UK, 1950

Rosa sinowilsonii × seedling

'WEDDING RING'

MODERN, LARGE-FLOWERED/HYBRID TEA, MEDIUM YELLOW, REPEAT-FLOWERING

This relatively rare, compact-growing bush is vigorous and strong, making an ideal plant for the edge of a bed or a low border. The large, fragrant, medium yellow flowers have 25–35 petals and carry a slight fragrance. Disease resistance is fair, although the plant will need to be maintained if grown in a prone area. 'Wedding Ring' has glossy dark green, leathery foliage. ZONES 5–10.

Shepherd, USA, 1956

'Ville de Paris' × 'Mrs Sam McGredy'

'WEE BARBIE' JELbar

MODERN, MINIATURE, WHITE, REPEAT-FLOWERING

The globular buds of this rose reveal creamy white flowers with almost 45 petals; these blooms are repeatedly produced mainly as big clusters of 10–20 fragrant flowers, which make a lovely bouquet when cut for the home. The foliage is dark green on a bushy, vigorous-growing plant that is easy to maintain and is disease resistant. The popularity of this rose seems to be confined to the UK. ZONES 5–10.

Jellyman, UK, 1980

Parentage unknown

'WEE BETH'

MODERN, MINIATURE, ORANGE BLEND, REPEAT-FLOWERING

This variety has pointed, mossy buds that open to pinkish salmon flowers with about a dozen petals. These come mainly in small clusters and have a Sweet Briar fragrance. The foliage is small and dark green and covers a compact bush that is

'Wee Beth'

vigorous and easy to grow. 'Wee Beth' gets its charm from the lovely orange blend, single-petalled blooms that are displayed through summer. ZONES 5–10.

Cherry, Australia, 1981

'Orange Silk' × 'Fairy Moss'

'WEE JOCK' COCabest

MODERN, PATIO/DWARF CLUSTER-FLOWERED, MEDIUM RED, REPEAT-FLOWERING

The pointed buds of 'Wee Jock' open to deep crimson-red flowers with almost 50 petals and Large-flowered form. These generally occur as small clusters and have a light fragrance. The small, glossy green foliage is borne in profusion on this compact, vigorous bush that is easy to maintain. It is best in a small bed or at the front of a border; the bright red flowers on this well-shaped bush make it a welcome garden plant. ZONES 4–11.

Cocker, UK, 1980

'National Trust' × 'Wee Man'

'WEE MAN'

syns 'Silken Carpet', 'Tapis de Soie'
MODERN, MINIATURE, MEDIUM RED, REPEAT-FLOWERING

The flowers of this cultivar are single, scarlet-red with golden stamens, and are beautifully staged in well-spaced clusters. There is a light fragrance. The foliage is glossy green on a compact plant that branches well and provides a more than average bloom for a rose of this size. For a wonderful effect, mass plant 'Wee Man' in a bed or row. ZONES 5–10.

McGredy, New Zealand, 1974

'Little Flirt' × 'Marlena'

'WEE MATT' MACweemat

syns 'Waitmata', 'Waitemata'
MODERN, MINIATURE, MEDIUM RED, REPEAT-FLOWERING

The flowers of this rose are filled with many bright red petals. The blooms

'Wee Matt'

occur mainly as small clusters of 6–10, and repeat-flowering is excellent. The foliage is large and broad on this clean and compact bush, which is suitable as a Miniature standard. The availability of 'Wee Matt' is restricted in most countries except for Australia. ZONES 5–10.

McGredy, New Zealand, 1978

Parentage unknown

'WEETWOOD'

MODERN, RAMBLER, LIGHT PINK

The delicately scented, medium-sized blooms of this rose have a delightful, old-fashioned character. They are full of petals that open in a random fashion, incurved at first and later reflexing to form a quartered rosette. The plant is very vigorous with arching branches; they may extend up to three times as far as an average Rambler. The flowers appear freely in summer amid deep green, medium-sized leaves. ZONES 4–9.

Bawden, UK, 1983

Seedling of 'Debutante'

'WEISSE IMMENSEE' KORweirim

syns 'Kordes' Rose Weiss Immensee', 'Lac Blanc', 'Partridge'
MODERN, MODERN SHRUB, WHITE

This is a wonderful ground-covering rose to grow on a bank or in a terraced garden where it can be seen at its best. The single, 5-petalled flowers start out a light shade of pink, but quickly fade to white as they age and cover the bush well. They are very fragrant and appear on a spreading plant with a mass of healthy, glossy dark green foliage. Long canes run along the ground and can become easily entwined among other garden plants. This bush is very hardy and will need little attention to keep it clean and disease free. Flowering is early and it will not repeat. ZONES 5–10.

Kordes, Germany, 1982

'The Fairy' × seedling of *Rosa wichuraiana*

Royal National Rose Society Certificate of Merit 1984

'WELWYN GARDEN GLORY'

HARzumber

syn. 'Garden Glory'
MODERN, LARGE-FLOWERED/HYBRID TEA, APRICOT BLEND, REPEAT-FLOWERING

This rose was named after the Welwyn Garden City project, which was started in the 1920s in the UK. The idea was that this garden city would be a far more desirable place to live, and indeed a better place to garden. The glowing amber

'Wendy'

flowers have prettily frilled petals and are borne, usually singly on long stems, throughout the flowering season on this medium-growing bush. The color is at its richest in the center of each flower and pales towards the outer petal edges. The glossy leaves are disease resistant, and the growth is upright and is easily shaped. ZONES 5–10.

Harkness, UK, 1996

Parentage unknown

'WENDY' SUNwend
MODERN, MINIATURE, WHITE, REPEAT-FLOWERING

The very double, sunken-centered flowers of this rose appear in large clusters that cover the whole bush throughout summer. Like many white roses, the blooms are easily damaged by rain. 'Wendy' does not respond well to harsh climates, so will need the protection of a fairly shaded spot. ZONES 6–10.

Schuurman, New Zealand, 1993

'White Dream' × seedling

'WENDY CUSSONS'
MODERN, LARGE-FLOWERED/HYBRID TEA, MEDIUM RED, REPEAT-FLOWERING

'Wendy Cussons' bears fully double, medium red flowers which are evenly distributed over the whole plant and exude a strong fragrance. They are high centered and large, with 30 petals, and the foliage is glossy and dark on a well-branched plant. Health and vigor are strong points of the bush, and in warm climates it can become difficult to control with rampant growth and little bloom. It is an ideal plant for cool areas with climates that hinder vigorous growth and promote the full intensity of the beautiful flowers. **'Climbing Wendy Cussons'** (Gregory and Follen, UK, 1967) was released in Germany. ZONES 5–10.

Gregory & Son Ltd, UK, 1963

Probably 'Independence' × 'Eden Rose'

National Rose Society President's International Trophy 1959, Golden Rose of The Hague 1964, Portland Gold Medal 1964

'WENLOCK' AUSwen
MODERN, MODERN SHRUB, MEDIUM RED, REPEAT-FLOWERING

This cultivar has a wonderful scent that is fitting for a crimson-red rose. The fully double flowers are found on short stems and the bush is an ideal choice for a border or low hedge as it does not become obtrusive in the garden. The flowers turn cerise with age. The repeat-flowering is quick and it produces a mass of bloom to

'Western Sun'

'Wendy Cussons'

start the flowering season in spring. 'Wenlock' is upright with a good shape, pruning easily into a small shrub. Care is needed to keep it disease free and healthy all season as the large leaves can become infected in cool regions. Also classified as an English Rose, it is freely available at most rose nurseries. ZONES 5–10.

Austin, UK, 1984

'The Knight' × 'Glastonbury'

'WEST COAST' MACnauru
syns 'Metropolitan', 'Penthouse'
MODERN, LARGE-FLOWERED/HYBRID TEA, MEDIUM PINK, REPEAT-FLOWERING

This variety is a Large-flowered Rose bred by Sam McGredy in New Zealand. The slightly scented, medium pink flowers are double and are found singly or in small clusters on a strong bush. The repeat-flowering is good and the plant is reasonably disease resistant, although it will need attention in areas that are prone to disease. 'West Coast' is a bushy grower with matt light green foliage. It is not widely grown and is available from only a few North American nurseries. ZONES 5–10.

McGredy, New Zealand, 1987

(['Yellow Pages' × 'Kabuki'] × 'Golden Gate') × (Poulsen seedling × 'Picasso')

'WESTERLAND' KORlawe, KORwest
MODERN, CLUSTER-FLOWERED/FLORIBUNDA, APRICOT BLEND, REPEAT-FLOWERING

The bright apricot-orange flowers of 'Westerland' are a colorful addition to any garden. The double blooms have a ruffled look, the petals having slightly serrated edges, and there is a pleasant scent. Clusters of the flowers appear regularly on the bush, with a short time between repeat-flowerings. This vigorous, upright bush grows to medium height and has large, soft, dark green foliage that can suffer from disease.

'Westfalenpark'

'Wedding Day'

'Westerland'

'Westerland' is widely grown and is freely available in those countries where it has been released. ZONES 5–10.

Kordes, Germany, 1969

'Friedrich Worlein' × 'Circus'

Anerkannte Deutsche Rose 1974, Royal Horticultural Society Award of Garden Merit 1993

'WESTERN SUN'
MODERN, LARGE-FLOWERED/HYBRID TEA, DEEP YELLOW, REPEAT-FLOWERING

This rose produces deep yellow flowers on a strong bush with dark foliage. The fully double flowers are large, with a purity of color that is a joy to behold. The small bush is prone to disease early and late in the season. The finest examples of the flower are in late summer and autumn when the color and form develop and mature slowly. They are ideal to cut if short stems are required. ZONES 5–10.

Poulsen, Denmark, 1965

Seedling of 'Golden Scepter' × 'Golden Sun'

'Westerland'

'WESTFALENPARK' KORplavi
syns 'Chevreuse', 'Kordes' Rose Westfalenpark'
MODERN, MODERN SHRUB, APRICOT BLEND, REPEAT-FLOWERING

This shrub rose is suitable for mass planting and gives a spectacle in vast areas like public parks or roadside plantings. 'Westfalenpark' has large, double, apricot flowers that are scented. The bush has big, glossy dark green foliage and a spreading nature that will require some attention if it is to be planted into a confined space. Rarely grown, it is only available from a few specialist nurseries. ZONES 5–10.

Kordes, Germany, 1987

Seedling × 'Las Vegas'

W

'White Bells'

'Whipped Cream'

'WHIPPED CREAM'
MODERN, MINIATURE, WHITE, REPEAT-FLOWERING

The globular buds of this variety open quickly to double, white, informal flowers that are touched with cream in the centers. The fully opened blooms are even more attractive because of their golden yellow stamens. The foliage is small and light green on a vigorous, upright bush with very healthy canes. In cool climates the blooms can be a bit large, which makes it more of a Patio size; in warm climates the bush can sometimes sprawl, and is also prone to attack by spider mites. The blooms are not very fast to repeat. ZONES 5–10.

Moore, USA, 1968

(*Rosa wichuraiana* × 'Carolyn Dean') × 'White King'

'WHISKY MAC'   TANky
syn. 'Whisky'

MODERN, LARGE-FLOWERED/HYBRID TEA, YELLOW BLEND, REPEAT-FLOWERING

This delightful rose produces wonderful, rich apricot-yellow blooms. The fully double flowers are found singly or in small groups all through the flowering season. 'Whisky Mac' has an open style of growth with a slightly spreading nature; it makes a stout bush that has a good covering of thorns. The disease resistance is only fair, however, and the bush needs attention during the cooler months to prevent fungal disease spoiling the leaves. By far the best blooms are produced in cool climates, where the color is intensified by the slowness of the developing flowers. **'Climbing Whisky Mac'** (ANDmac; syn. 'Climbing Whisky';

'Whisky Mac'

Anderson's Rose Nurseries, UK, 1985) has bronze-yellow flowers, vigorous growth and good disease resistance. ZONES 5–10.

Tantau, Germany, 1967

Parentage unknown

'WHITE ANGEL'
MODERN, MINIATURE, WHITE, REPEAT-FLOWERING

The dainty buds of this rose open to reveal very attractive, small white flowers with pointed petals. There is a light fragrance and the foliage is a complementary light green. The vigorous dwarf bush is a true example of what a Miniature plant should look like: very petite in every characteristic. 'White Angel' is short in stature but is very branched, which adds to its ability to produce many more blooms than normal. This rose has lost much of its popularity now that more attractive white Miniature Roses have been introduced. The parentage is an award-winning cross of a Rambler with a Cluster-flowered Rose. ZONES 5–10.

Moore, USA, 1971

(*Rosa wichuraiana* × 'Floradora') × ('Little Darling' × seedling of a red Miniature Rose)

American Rose Society Award of Excellence 1975

'WHITE BATH'
syns 'Clifton Moss', *Rosa centifolia albo-muscosa*, *R. muscosa alba*, 'Shailer's White Moss'

OLD, MOSS, WHITE

The common Moss is pink; this variety is a white sport that can revert in part or in whole on the bush. 'White Bath' has very bright flowers that are fully double,

'White Angel'

fragrant and arranged in small, tight clusters. A distinguishing feature is a purple smudge or two showing through from under the surface of the leaves. It is a shrub of medium size and vigor, generously clothed on the stems and buds with ginger-colored, stubbly moss—the main reason for growing it. The rounded foliage is grayish dark green and soft to the touch. This lovely rose shows a clear affinity to the Damasks. ZONES 4–9.

Shailer, UK, 1788

Sport of *Rosa centifolia muscosa*

Royal Horticultural Society Award of Garden Merit 1993

'WHITE BELLA ROSA'
syn. 'Bella Weisse'

MODERN, CLUSTER-FLOWERED/FLORIBUNDA, WHITE, REPEAT-FLOWERING

This small-growing rose has all the features of its parent, the only difference being the color of its flowers. These are semi-double and white with a tinge of pink in cool weather. They open flat and show the stamens clearly. Known as a good parent for breeding, neither 'Bella Rosa' nor its progeny are widely grown. Disease resistance is good and it needs only minimal care during the season. Better varieties exist and should be sought instead. ZONES 5–10.

Kordes, Germany, 1990

Sport of 'Bella Rosa'

'WHITE BELLS'   POUlwhite
MODERN, MINIATURE, WHITE

This rose is a counterpart clone to 'Pink Bells' and 'Red Bells', both with the same parentage and growth habit. It has white flowers with creamy lemon centers that fade with age. The lightly fragrant blooms have 35 petals, and these are set against the small, very glossy green foliage on a spreading plant. 'White Bells' tends to grow larger than its sister seedlings, as it

'White Bella Rosa'

sends out long, disease-resistant canes with many flowers. It needs a season to establish and then it performs in an exceptional manner. Flowers appear freely over an extended period in late spring and summer. The plant has been used successfully as both a weeping standard and a ground cover. Winter die-back is minimal in warm climates. ZONES 5–10.

Poulsen, Denmark, 1983

'Mini-Poul' × 'Temple Bells'

'WHITE BLUSH'   SIEwhite
MODERN, MODERN SHRUB, WHITE

This is part of a series of hardy hybrids raised by Rolf Sievers using Alba Roses and those derived from *Rosa kordesii*. In summer, it bears pure white flowers of old-fashioned character with many petals. They have a pleasing scent and are carried in clusters on a leafy and upright plant. It grows considerably taller and wider than an average shrub rose. ZONES 4–9.

Sievers, Germany, 1988

Parentage unknown

'WHITE BOUQUET'
MODERN, CLUSTER-FLOWERED/FLORIBUNDA, WHITE, REPEAT-FLOWERING

'White Bouquet' produces clear white, double flowers with a good size and form. They have a spicy fragrance, are gardenia shaped and appear in irregular clusters. It has largely been overlooked in recent times and newer varieties are grown in its place. This is unfortunate as the plant grows healthily with dark glossy, disease-resistant foliage. ZONES 5–10.

Boerner, USA, 1956

'Glacier' × seedling of 'Pinocchio'

All-America Rose Selection 1957

'WHITE BUTTERFLY'
MODERN, LARGE-FLOWERED/HYBRID TEA, WHITE, REPEAT-FLOWERING

This prolifically flowering, white Large-flowered Rose is best suited to hot

'White Bath'

'White Bella Rosa'

W

'White Christmas'

'White Dream'

'White Cécile Brünner'

'White Butterfly'

The glossy leaves are small and cover the growth well; they are resistant to disease and need little attention to keep them producing worthwhile growth for the next year. The white blooms are found early in the season, so it is best to prepare some good lateral canes while pruning in winter. The double, gardenia-shaped, fragrant flowers with 35 petals are produced in clusters. It is only available from specialist rose growers. ZONES 5–9.

Longley, USA, 1949

'New Dawn' × 'Lily Pons'

'WHITE DOROTHY'
syn. 'White Dorothy Perkins'
MODERN, RAMBLER, WHITE

The parent of this variety, with its sprays of pink flowers, is perhaps the best known of the very lax Ramblers; it was created by Jackson and Perkins in the USA in 1901, the seed parent being 'Mme Gabriel Luizet'. Both the parent and the sport are, however, subject to mildew. ZONES 5–9.

Cant, UK, 1908

Sport of 'Dorothy Perkins'

'WHITE DREAM'   LENblank, LENvir
syn. 'Sentinel'
MODERN, MINIATURE, WHITE, REPEAT-FLOWERING

The pure white flowers of this variety contain 35 petals and have good high centers, which show Large-flowered form. They have a light scent and occur

mainly in small clusters. Although the flowers tend to be larger than expected for a Miniature Rosé, they have good shape from bud to bloom. 'White Dream' is a vigorous low grower with a tendency to sprawl if left to itself. It is commonly grown in England and New Zealand. The bloom form is almost as good as 'Pacesetter' and 'Starglo'. ZONES 5–10.

Lens, Belgium, 1982

Parentage unknown

'WHITE ENSIGN'
syn. 'Monty's White Tea'
MODERN, LARGE-FLOWERED/HYBRID TEA, WHITE, REPEAT-FLOWERING

The flowers of this rose have a very Tea-like form. From nicely shaped buds they open to very double, flat, white, many-petalled flowers with a cream center. There is some fragrance. The foliage is healthy, mid-green and plentiful, and the production of flowers is very good. It enjoys vigorous and bushy growth and there are no disease problems. This is an excellent rose for picking as the creamy buff color in the center of the flowers holds its color well and looks lovely in arrangements. It is a popular rose for planting in beds and borders and for use among bulbs and perennial plants. ZONES 5–10.

McGredy, UK, 1925

Parentage unknown

conditions or those of a greenhouse. The long, pointed buds open to large, double, fragrant blooms that have pale chartreuse inner petals and continue to hold a cupped center when fully open. The growth habit is bushy and vigorous and produces blooms continuously all season. The foliage is leathery. ZONES 5–10.

Spanbauer, USA, 1954

'Ophelia' × 'Curly White'

American Rose Society John Cook Medal 1957

'WHITE CÉCILE BRÜNNER'
MODERN, POLYANTHA, WHITE, REPEAT-FLOWERING

This sweet little bush produces some of the best posy flowers possible. A small-growing plant, it is a delight for those who persist in growing it. The small, creamy white blooms are double and have a slight scent, and are found on short stems among delicate leaves. Sometimes the bush will not perform well, while in other situations it will grow extremely easily and produce flowers all season. The growth needs some attention to disease during cool weather as the tight growth tends to encourage health problems. ZONES 5–10.

Fraque, 1909

Sport of 'Cécile Brünner'

'WHITE CHRISTMAS'
MODERN, LARGE-FLOWERED/HYBRID TEA, WHITE, REPEAT-FLOWERING

Bred in 1953, this Large-flowered Rose is still popular today. The fully double, high-centered flowers have around 50 petals in each bloom but suffer badly from botrytis in rain and damp weather. The compact, upright bush is vigorous and produces its fragrant blooms all through the season. The light green foliage is leathery. ZONES 5–10.

Howard and Smith, USA, 1953

'Sleigh Bells' × seedling

'WHITE COCKADE'
MODERN, LARGE-FLOWERED CLIMBER, WHITE, REPEAT-FLOWERING

'White Cockade' is a robust climber that produces a mass of white, double blooms in the first flush of the season; they exude a sweet subtle scent. The growth is vigorous and healthy and requires minimal attention for disease and other problems. Flowering is almost entirely at the beginning of the season, and it produces only a limited show during the remainder of the year. The strong growth is easy to prune and can be very effective for covering walls and fences that will hold its weight. The legacy of 'New Dawn' is evident in this offspring with its glossy leaves and classic flowers. ZONES 5–9.

Cocker, UK, 1969

'New Dawn' × 'Circus'

Royal Horticultural Society Award of Garden Merit 1993

'WHITE DAWN'
MODERN, LARGE-FLOWERED CLIMBER, WHITE

'White Dawn' has many similarities to 'New Dawn'. The low, climbing growth is vigorous and is covered generously with thorns to deter the unwelcome.

'White Bouquet'

'White Ensign'

'White Ensign'

'White Dorothy', showing some sprays reverting to its pink parent

W

'WHITE FAIRY'

syn. 'Wirruna White Fairy'
MODERN, POLYANTHA, WHITE, REPEAT-FLOWERING

This relatively hardy and free-flowering variety carries large clusters of pompon-like blooms. These are pure white, each with a boss of golden stamens at the center. The backdrop of dark green foliage gives this bush rose a pleasing appearance. 'White Fairy' can be used in bedding schemes. ZONES 4–10.

1988

Parentage unknown

'WHITE FLOWER CARPET'

NOAschnee

syns 'Emera Blanc', 'Opalia', 'Schneeflocke'
MODERN, CLUSTER-FLOWERED/FLORIBUNDA, WHITE, REPEAT-FLOWERING

'White Flower Carpet' has small, double blooms that provide good cover on the bush. The plant is low growing. Disease resistance is reasonably good and it needs little attention if it is to remain healthy all season. This variety is good for mass planting on a bank or bed where low height is a consideration. 'White Flower Carpet' is freely available and is commonly grown from cuttings instead of from a grafted plant. ZONES 5–10.

Noack, Germany, 1991

'Immensee' × 'Margaret Merrill'

Anerkannte Deutsche Rose 1991, Royal National Rose Society Gold Medal 1991, Golden Rose of The Hague 1995, Glasgow Certificate of Merit 1996

'White Maman Cochet'

'White Maman Cochet' (thorns)

'White Madonna'

'WHITE GEM'   MEIturusa
MODERN, MINIATURE, WHITE, REPEAT-FLOWERING

The long and pointed buds of this rose open to soft ivory flowers that are shaded with pale tan and are filled with an overwhelming 90 petals. The petals reflex beautifully to give that perfect exhibition form so admired at rose shows. Both blooms and foliage can be larger in cool climates, and the flowers have a light fragrance and are borne singly or in clusters at all times. The leaves are large and glossy dark green, and adorn this upright, vigorous bush that reaches an average height. 'White Gem' has not been received well in the USA; there are many other superior whites, so it has been relegated to a common garden variety. ZONES 5–10.

Meilland, France, 1976

'Darling Flame' × 'Jack Frost'

'WHITE GROOTENDORST'

MODERN, HYBRID RUGOSA, WHITE, REPEAT-FLOWERING

This lovely Hybrid Rugosa forms a medium garden shrub and provides a pleasant change to the way the rose bed looks. The growth is branching and upright, forming a good framework for the flowers, which are found all over the bush and repeat throughout the season. The semi-double flowers are white; the petals have a frilled edge that is quite charming. Disease resistance is good and will remain so all season with little

'White Lightnin'

attention. The best blooms appear early in the season and at the end just before winter knocks. 'White Grootendorst' is one of a group of plants that have sported from one parent; they are all good and it is well worth growing them together. This plant is best suited to cool climates as it does not do well in very hot conditions. ZONES 5–10.

Eddy, USA, 1962

Sport of 'Pink Grootendorst'

'WHITE KNIGHT'   MEban

syn. 'Message'
MODERN, LARGE-FLOWERED/HYBRID TEA, WHITE, REPEAT-FLOWERING

This award-winning Large-flowered Rose has some of the most lovely classic-style blooms ever produced, and it is sure to delight. The large, clear white flowers are double and high-centered with 33 petals, on a tall and upright plant that is easily maintained. The buds can sometimes show a greenish tinge, but this quickly disappears as the flowers open. 'White Knight' is prone to mildew and requires attention to keep it performing well all season. It responds to a light summer pruning to produce a flower spectacle in autumn. It has leathery, light green foliage and is well recommended. ZONES 5–10.

Meilland, France, 1955

('Virgo' × 'Peace') × 'Virgo'

All-America Rose Selection 1958

'WHITE LIGHTNIN'   AROwhif

MODERN, LARGE-FLOWERED/HYBRID TEA, WHITE, REPEAT-FLOWERING

This rose produces large, double blooms with 30 petals on a strong, vigorous, upright-growing bush. The flowers are pure white and open in classic Large-flowered style. The scent is strong, lasting the entire life of the flowers. Picking is easy and the blooms look wonderful in a vase. The

'White Flower Carpet'

'White Knight'

'White Fairy'

bush is healthy and able to resist most diseases with minimal attention through the season. Repeat-flowering is quick and it is a good addition to any garden. ZONES 5–10.

Swim, USA, 1980

'Angel Face' × 'Misty'

All-America Rose Selection 1981

'WHITE MADONNA'

MODERN, MINIATURE, WHITE, REPEAT-FLOWERING

The long buds of this rose open to give white to pale pink flowers with a loose decorative form. The double flowers have more than 30 petals and come in small, lightly fragranced clusters. In cool climates the blooms are light pink and tend to increase in size. The glossy green foliage has a leathery texture. 'White Madonna' is an upright and vigorous plant with an awkward growth habit. The repeat-bloom cycle is fast and continuous, and the plant survives winter weather well. ZONES 4–10.

Moore, USA, 1973

(*Rosa wichuraiana* × 'Floradora') × ('Little Darling' × red Miniature Rose)

'WHITE MAMAN COCHET'

OLD, TEA, WHITE, REPEAT-FLOWERING

Both the parent and the sport are very vigorous and strong plants that can grow into large shrubs. This one has white flowers—but not entirely so, as pink flushing is common. The buds are very long and big, and the blooms have been described as blowzy. They ball badly in wet weather. **'Climbing White Maman Cochet'** (Knight, Australia, 1907) is a vigorous climbing version of the bush that bears flowers that are inclined towards yellow. It is suitable only for a warm climate and seems very popular in Australia. ZONES 7–9.

Cook, USA, 1896

Sport of 'Maman Cochet'

W

'WHITE MARY MacKILLOP'

MODERN, LARGE-FLOWERED/HYBRID TEA, WHITE, REPEAT-FLOWERING

This sport is identical to its parent except the flowers are white. The bush is dense and compact with an abundance of glossy rich green foliage. Shapely buds open to well-formed blooms of 30–35 petals of good substance. The flowers occur in profusion both singly and in small clusters, with an extremely quick repeat. 'White Mary MacKillop' and its parent are good for bedding schemes and borders. Although the stems are short, they are sturdy. ZONES 5–10.

Swane's Nursery, Australia, 1988

Sport of 'Mary MacKillop'

'WHITE MASTERPIECE'

JACmas

MODERN, LARGE-FLOWERED/HYBRID TEA, WHITE, REPEAT-FLOWERING

This variety produces large, high-pointed flowers that are borne singly atop a moderate bush. The blooms are not freely produced and mark in bad weather. Slightly fragrant and of double form, they have a greenish tinge that is lost in warm climates, although it can carry through in the fully open bloom in cooler climates. Disease control should be carried out all season as the bush will not produce its best blooms unless it is maintained. Exquisite flowers are produced on this plant. ZONES 5–10.

Boerner, USA, 1969

Parentage unknown

'White Meidiland'

'White Meidiland'

'WHITE MEIDILAND'

MEIcoublan

syns 'Alba Meidiland', 'Blanc Meillandécor'

MODERN, MODERN SHRUB, WHITE, REPEAT-FLOWERING

Originally released as a Ground Cover Rose, this unusual plant is one of a series introduced by Meilland of France for landscaping. It is largely disease free and for that reason is ideally suited for roadways and gardens that receive little care. The flowers are very full, with 40 petals, appearing in flushes each year to cover the bush in a mass of white. Pruning is not normally practised in the usual way, but a general reduction of plant size is performed each winter. It has a spreading growth habit and is clothed with medium-sized, glossy dark green foliage. ZONES 5–10.

Meilland, France, 1986

'Temple Bells' × MEIgurami

'WHITE MEILLANDINA'

MEIblam

syn. 'Yorkshire Sunblaze'

MODERN, MINIATURE, WHITE, REPEAT-FLOWERING

The white, semi-double, medium-sized flowers of this rose have no fragrance, but they combine well with the small and light green foliage on the compact bush. 'White Meillandina' is a prolific bloomer that is very disease resistant, so it is an ideal choice for growing in a container. As one of the popular 'Sunblaze' series introduced by the House of Meilland in France, this

'White Pet'

'White Masterpiece'

'White Mary MacKillop'

'White Meillandina'

variety is an attractive addition to any garden because it gives a profusion of color all year long. ZONES 5–10.

Meilland, France, 1984

'Katharina Zeimet' × 'White Gem'

American Rose Society Top Garden Rose in Proof of the Pudding Survey 1991

'WHITE MRS FLIGHT'

syn. 'White Flight'

MODERN, RAMBLER, WHITE

This sport of 'Mrs F. W. Flight' is rather more vigorous and bears single, pure white flowers. Peter Beales has doubts as to whether it is actually a sport as generally supposed. ZONES 5–9.

Rockford, 1916

Sport of 'Mrs F. W. Flight'

'WHITE NEW DAWN'

syns 'New Dawn White', 'Weisse New Dawn'

MODERN, LARGE-FLOWERED CLIMBER, WHITE, REPEAT-FLOWERING

Apart from being white instead of blush, this variety has the same characteristics as its parent. The sweetly fragrant flowers are loosely double, cupped and open in graceful clusters through summer and autumn. They look clean and fresh whatever the weather. In the garden, 'White New Dawn' is wonderful for fences, pillars, arches, pergolas and walls, and for clothing unsightly objects. Its stems are vigorous and pliable with a good covering of shiny leaves. It can be kept pruned and grown as a shrub or hedge, or allowed to run up to twice the average extent of a climber. ZONES 4–9.

1959

Sport of 'New Dawn'

'WHITE OUT'   MACwhitout

MODERN, MINIATURE, WHITE, REPEAT-FLOWERING

The buds of this variety open to pale pink then mature to small, white, rosette-shaped flowers that are borne in clusters and cover a compact, healthy bush. They are very fragrant, and their small size qualifies this rose as a micro-miniature. The plant is prolific, clean and easy to maintain. A basket of 'White Out' was chosen as the best Miniature entry in the 1994 Rose World Convention held in Christchurch, New Zealand. ZONES 5–10.

McGredy , New Zealand, 1988

'Sexy Rexy' × 'Popcorn'

'WHITE PET'

syn. 'Little White Pet'

MODERN, POLYANTHA, WHITE, REPEAT-FLOWERING

'White Pet' is sometimes classified as a Dwarf Sempervirens, and makes a compact shrub, bearing flowers all through the season. The fully double flowers are white with a pink tinge on the buds that sometimes continues during cool weather. When fully open, the flowers have a pompon look and are easily cut for display. The strong, vigorous growth is complemented by glossy leaves, and there is good disease resistance. The bush is great for borders and also does well as a standard or patio. Widely propagated by Old Garden Rose nurseries, it is easily grown and is an asset to any garden. 'Climbing White Pet' (Corboeuf, France, 1894) is also available. ZONES 5–10.

Henderson, USA, 1879

Sport of 'Félicité-Perpétue'

Royal Horticultural Society Award of Garden Merit 1993

W

'White Rose of York'

'White Rose of York'

'White Radox Bouquet'

'White Spray'

'WHITE QUEEN ELIZABETH'
syn. 'Blanc Queen Elizabeth'

MODERN, CLUSTER-FLOWERED/FLORIBUNDA, WHITE, REPEAT-FLOWERING

'White Queen Elizabeth' is a bud sport from the well-known Large-flowered Rose 'Queen Elizabeth'. It inherits all the characteristics of its parent: strong, disease-resistant growth, vigor, and free flower production. This fragrant rose also has the same flower formation, rather informal and open, but differs in color, which is white with the faintest tinge of cream. This makes it interesting but not striking as it lacks the brightness usually found in a white rose. It is a tall grower and is best planted at the back of a rose bed. ZONES 5–10.

Banner, UK, 1965

Sport of 'Queen Elizabeth'

'WHITE RADOX BOUQUET'

MODERN, MODERN SHRUB, WHITE, REPEAT-FLOWERING

This large-growing shrub is a sport of its better-known parent, 'Radox Bouquet'. The fully double, fragrant flowers with 50 petals are white with a hint of pink in the bud. They are borne in sprays of five or more. The glossy leaves are healthy and growth is vigorous, providing ample stems for cutting and next year's frame while the plant matures into a large specimen or shrub. Disease control is rarely needed in warm climates but is advisable in cooler, damp areas. ZONES 5–10.

Melville Nurseries Pty Ltd, Australia, 1988

Sport of 'Radox Bouquet'

'WHITE ROSE OF YORK'
syns 'Bonnie Prince Charlie's Rose', 'Jacobite Rose', 'La Rose de York'

OLD, ALBA, WHITE

This very famous rose is also a first-rate garden plant. It is an elegantly shaped shrub to 6 ft (2 m) tall with a luxuriant covering of grayish green foliage. The large, more or less double flowers are borne several together once only in summer, but they have pure white petals that surround a prominent boss of brilliant yellow stamens. The fragrance is very strong; 'White Rose of York' is one of two roses cultivated at Kazanlik in Bulgaria to make attar of roses. A fine crop of oval, scarlet hips appears in autumn. Some consider it to be the same rose as 'Alba Maxima'. ZONES 5–10.

Pre-1597

Probably *Rosa corymbifera* × *R. gallica*

'WHITE SIMPLICITY' JACsnow

MODERN, CLUSTER-FLOWERED/FLORIBUNDA, WHITE, REPEAT-FLOWERING

This free-flowering bush is disease resistant and healthy in most conditions, suffering only in weather that is ideal for disease. The large, double white flowers open flat to show the stamens clearly. Repeat-flowering is quick and the plant's growth habit makes it an outstanding specimen for a border or hedge. Widely grown, 'White Simplicity' is readily available from rose nurseries. ZONES 5–10.

Warriner, USA, 1991

Parentage unknown

'WHITE SPARRIESHOOP'
syn. 'Weisse aus Sparrieshoop'

MODERN, MODERN SHRUB, WHITE, REPEAT-FLOWERING

This rose shares the characteristics of its parent in all respects except for the color, which is a clear white. The saucer-shaped blooms are quite large with a few waved petals, and reveal golden stamens. They have a pleasing fragrance and continue to give a good display through summer and autumn. As a free-flowering shrub rose of average height and width, 'White Sparrieshoop' makes a handsome border or specimen plant. It grows vigorously with an upright, bushy habit and is well furnished with leathery, glossy foliage that is reddish when young. ZONES 4–9.

Kordes, Germany, 1962

Sport of 'Sparrieshoop'

'WHITE SPRAY'

MODERN, CLUSTER-FLOWERED/FLORIBUNDA, WHITE, REPEAT-FLOWERING

'White Spray' is a free-flowering bush that is not dissimilar to its parent, 'Iceberg'. The flowers are borne in clusters all over the bush and have a stem length that is useful for cutting. Its health is good, and it only requires disease control early in the season. The well-formed, white flowers are double and carry a slight fragrance. Released in 1968, this rose has been overshadowed by its parent. ZONES 5–10.

LeGrice, UK, 1968

Seedling × 'Iceberg'

'WHITE TAUSENDSCHÖN'

MODERN, RAMBLER, WHITE

This rose is similar to its parent, but has somewhat lighter green foliage. Sometimes there is a little pink in the flowers. It is more readily available in Australia and New Zealand than elsewhere, but is by no means common as there are better roses in its class. ZONES 5–9.

Paul, UK, 1913

Sport of 'Tausendschön'

'WHITE WINGS'

MODERN, LARGE-FLOWERED/HYBRID TEA, WHITE, REPEAT-FLOWERING

The flowers of 'White Wings', which are borne in clusters, do indeed look like white wings, as they turn and angle from each other when fully open. The 5-petalled flowers open flat to show chocolate-colored anthers, and have a sweet scent. The foliage is leathery on a moderately vigorous, upright-growing, medium-sized plant that is easy to cultivate. The American Rose Society rated it as 7.7 when it was released, which helped make it popular at that time. Rarely grown now, it is still available from specialist rose nurseries. ZONES 5–10.

Krebs, USA, 1947

'Dainty Bess' × seedling

'White Sparrieshoop'

'White Simplicity'

'White Queen Elizabeth'

W

'Wichmoss'

'Wienerwald'

'WHOOPI' SAVawhoop

MODERN, MINIATURE, RED BLEND,
REPEAT-FLOWERING

Harm Saville created this Miniature Rose
to honor movie star Whoopi Goldberg,
and it is one of the most interesting
recent introductions of its type. Its fat,
round buds open slowly to full flowers
with pointed centers and rows of heart-
shaped petals that bend stiffly outwards.
The foliage is dark green and semi-glossy
on a medium-sized bush that is not vigorous by most standards and not winter
hardy. It has a slower repeat-bloom cycle
than most Miniature Roses, but the
beautiful color is worth waiting for. The
flowers have a spicy fragrance. The beauty
of the rose lies in the combination of
white petal bases and carmine-flushed
tips. Unfortunately, there is no scent.
'Whoopi' is a small, medium-sized and
healthy shrub that grows vigorously to
produce successive crops of pickable
buds and flowers; they are also good for
exhibition. ZONES 5–11.

Saville, USA, 1991

('Yellow Jewel' × 'Tamango') × 'Party Girl'

'WHY NOT' MORwhy

MODERN, MINIATURE, RED BLEND,
REPEAT-FLOWERING

The small, single flowers of this rose are
bright fire-engine red with very prominent contrasting yellow eyes. The blooms
are small and have a light fragrance, and
combine well against the small, matt
mid-green foliage on an upright bush.
'Why Not' makes a wonderful feature in

the garden because it provides a focal
point of color. The repeat-bloom cycle
is fast and quite abundant. When Ralph
Moore, the hybridizer, was asked by a
visitor to his nursery if he was going to
introduce this rose he seemed unsure,
so the visitor asked 'Why not?' and a rose
name was born. ZONES 5–10.

Moore, USA, 1983

'Golden Angel' × seedling

'WICHMOSS'

MODERN, RAMBLER, LIGHT PINK

The result of an attempt to produce a
Rambler with mossed buds, 'Wichmoss'
rambles well in the lax manner usual
for *Rosa wichuraiana*, and has fragrant
flowers. The moss is said to be very susceptible to mildew. The flowers are pale
pink and semi-double fading to creamy
white. There do not appear to have been
other attempts in this direction, though
Ralph Moore in California has produced
many mossed Miniatures. This is a very
interesting rose to have in the garden.
ZONES 5–9.

Barbier, France, 1911

Rosa wichuraiana × 'Salet'

'WICKWAR'

MODERN, MODERN SHRUB, LIGHT PINK

Rosa soulieana is an unusual Wild Rose
introduced to Europe from western
China in 1896. It bears clusters of large,
single, white flowers that are followed
by a crop of yellow-orange hips. The
blooms are very fragrant. This seedling
has pink flowers and is not as big, but it
retains the other interesting qualities
of the parent. It makes a large bush
with grayish green leaflets and many
prickles, and appears to be available only
in England and France from specialist
growers. ZONES 7–9.

Steadman, UK, 1960

Seedling of *Rosa soulieana*

'WIENER CHARME' KORschaprat

syns 'Charme de Vienne', 'Charming
Vienne', 'Vienna Charm'

MODERN, LARGE-FLOWERED/HYBRID TEA,
ORANGE BLEND, REPEAT-FLOWERING

'Wiener Charme' produces fine coppery
orange, high-centered flowers on a stout
bush. An upright plant, it grows well
in most conditions providing repeat-

'Wild Flower'

flowering all season. Its long stems and
good bud shape make it an ideal cut-
flower variety for the garden, and it provides blooms that last well. The large,
double flowers with 27 petals have a
tinge of pink in the cooler parts of the
season, but have little scent. It is tall and
has dark foliage. ZONES 5–10.

Kordes, Germany, 1963

'Chantré' × 'Golden Sun'

'WIENERWALD'

syn. 'Vienna Woods'

MODERN, LARGE-FLOWERED/HYBRID TEA,
ORANGE-PINK, REPEAT-FLOWERING

This variety has medium pink, double
flowers with a lovely fragrance and texture. The outer petals have a stronger
dark pink tone that is intensified
with cool weather. They are fragrant.
'Wienerwald' grows into a medium-sized
bush with upright and vigorous growth,
stout stems and large, dark green, leathery foliage. The plant is not particularly

'White Wings'

healthy and requires attention to produce good blooms and growth all season.
It is not widely grown and may be difficult to find, although it does well in hot,
dry climates. ZONES 5–9.

Kordes, Germany, 1974

'Colour Wonder' × seedling

'WILD FLOWER' AUSwing

syn. 'Wildflower'

MODERN, MODERN SHRUB, LIGHT YELLOW,
REPEAT-FLOWERING

Also classified as an English Rose, this
variety has creamy yellow, single flowers
that open flat to show golden stamens.
The blooms cover the bush well, repeating all season. A small-growing shrub, it
has a spreading habit and is ideal for edges
or borders. It is susceptible to disease
and is therefore not popular. 'Wild
Flower' has been left off many growers'
lists and is rarely grown. ZONES 5–10.

Austin, UK, 1986

'Lilian Austin' × ('Canterbury' × 'Golden Wings')

'White Wings'

'Why Not'

'Wiener Charme'

W

'WILDFEUER'
syn. 'Wildfire'
MODERN, MODERN SHRUB, MEDIUM RED

This rose with its bright red large semi-double flowers is hard to find nowadays but it is still most attractive and worth growing. ZONES 5–10.

Kordes, Germany, 1953

'WILDFIRE'
MODERN, CLUSTER-FLOWERED/FLORIBUNDA, MEDIUM RED, REPEAT-FLOWERING

This rose produces bright scarlet, single blooms with 8–10 petals in large, lightly fragrant clusters. The vigorous, bushy, compact shrub is easily maintained. Disease needs to be controlled. ZONES 5–10.

Swim, USA, 1955

'World's Fair' × 'Pinocchio'

'Wildfeuer'

'William and Mary'

'WILL SCARLET'
MODERN, MODERN SHRUB, MEDIUM RED, REPEAT-FLOWERING

This variety has bright red, semi-double flowers that open flat to clearly show the stamens. The color fades to cerise as the flowers age. The continuous flowering of these attractive blooms make it a colorful sight in the garden. This vigorous, up-right-growing shrub is disease resistant, but like many roses it can succumb when bad conditions prevail. 'Will Scarlet' is widely grown although its richness of tone is best suited to cool climates. ZONES 5–9.

Hilling, UK, 1948

Sport of 'Skyrocket'

National Rose Society Trial Ground Certificate 1957

'William Allen Richardson'

'William Grant'

'WILLIAM ALLEN RICHARDSON'
OLD, NOISETTE, YELLOW BLEND, REPEAT-FLOWERING

The growth of this rose is less vigorous than that of the parent but the flowers are much deeper in color, being deep orange-yellow. Medium in size and borne freely, they are neat and quartered in shape. Although it lacks fragrance, this rose has retained considerable popularity and is widely grown. ZONES 7–9.

Ducher, France, 1878

Seedling of 'Rêve d'Or'

'WILLIAM AND MARY'
MODERN, MODERN SHRUB, PINK BLEND

This variety was bred by Peter Beales and was one of the first three shrub roses that he introduced. An interesting rose, it has inherited the vigorous growth of 'Constance Spry'. The flowers are strongly scented, large and fully double, with the loose, informal blooms decorating the bush in true old-fashioned style. The deep silvery pink petals are highlighted with carmine and are produced both singly and in clusters. A lovely show of bloom appers in early summer. The growth is strong and upright and it can be used as a small climber. The matt green foliage blends well with herbaceous plants, and its informal growth also mixes well in a shrub border. It flowers poorly in warm climates. ZONES 5–10.

Beales, UK, 1988

Seedling of 'Constance Spry'

'WILLIAM BAFFIN'
MODERN, MODERN SHRUB, DEEP PINK, REPEAT-FLOWERING

This is a tough and hardy rose suitable for those colder areas where most roses

'Will Scarlet'

'William Lobb'

cannot thrive. The beautiful loose blooms are semi-double and strawberry pink with a touch of white towards the centers, which are lit up by golden stamens, and appear in clusters of up to 30 from summer to autumn. There is little fragrance. 'William Baffin' can be grown as a specimen shrub, planted to form an impenetrable hedge or trained on a support as a climber. The plant is very vigorous, with upright, slightly arching stems embellished with robust, glossy and healthy foliage. The name commemorates the famous explorer who sought the Northwest Passage. ZONES 3–9.

Svejda, Canada, 1983

Rosa kordesii × seedling

'WILLIAM GRANT'
OLD, GALLICA, DEEP PINK, REPEAT-FLOWERING

When this gorgeous Gallica is in full bloom during summer it gives an abundance of rich pink, single to semi-double, cupped flowers. They are carried in small clusters and open flat to show a central boss of golden yellow stamens. The rose has a climbing habit and a wonderful perfume. It was found by William Grant—one of the contributors to this book—growing on a fence by an abandoned petrol station in Oregon, USA. The nursery that propagated it named it after its finder. ZONES 5–10.

Parentage unknown

'WILLIAM LOBB'
syns 'Duchesse d'Istrie', 'Old Velvet Moss'
OLD, MOSS, MAUVE

Deservedly one of the most popular Moss Roses, 'William Lobb' grows vigorously to 8 ft (2.5 m). Its long, firm stems, covered in grayish brown moss, have many stout thorns and are overlaid with dark gray-green, medium-sized and coarse, well-serrated foliage. The buds have a lot of soft, mid- to dark green moss. The semi-double flowers are almost ragged in structure but charming nevertheless, especially when fully open and displaying the centers of golden yellow stamens that contrast so beautifully with the purplish petals which have a lavender-pink reverse. Deep down near the base, each petal is flecked with white. There is a strong scent and the flowers appear in mid-summer in great profusion. It is useful as both a tall shrub or small climber on walls, trellises and arches. It will need support. ZONES 5–10.

Laffay, France, 1855

Parentage unknown

W

'Wiltshire'

'WILLIAM R. SMITH'

syns 'Blush Maman Cochet', 'Charles Dingee', 'Jeannette Heller', 'Maiden's Blush', 'President Smith', 'President William R. Smith'

OLD, TEA, PINK BLEND, REPEAT-FLOWERING

The flowers of this rose are creamy white flushed with pink; there is also some buff and gold. They are double and long lasting on the medium-sized, compact plant, which is hardier than most and has been said to thrive in most locations. A friend of Bagg's is said to have sold this rose to Hill's Nursery in Indiana for $500, which he kept, but he also sold it to others under a multitude of different names. ZONES 7–9.

Bagg, USA, 1908

'Maman Cochet' × 'Mme Hoste'

'WILLIAM SHAKESPEARE'

AUSroyal

MODERN, MODERN SHRUB, DARK RED, REPEAT-FLOWERING

Also classified as an English Rose, 'William Shakespeare' produces attractive, rich crimson flowers and was created by David Austin to develop the red strain in this series. It is not, however, one of the better varieties in the line as it is prone to rust and black spot, which is hard to control. The rosette-formed flowers have a rich, Damask scent and are borne in sprays of 3–7. This tall, upright plant has large, semi-glossy, dark green foliage and red thorns. ZONES 5–10.

Austin, UK, 1987

'The Squire' × 'Mary Rose'

'WILLIAM III'

OLD, SCOTS, MAUVE

The Scots Roses were quite in vogue in the early nineteenth century, but most are now lost; this is one of the few survivors. It is a dwarf bush that suckers strongly, making a vigorous and prickly thicket. The small, spicy scented flowers with 15 petals are magenta-crimson, fading to lilac-pink with age. There are black hips in autumn and plenty of seeds. ZONES 4–9.

Parentage unknown

'WILLIAMS' DOUBLE YELLOW'

syn. 'Double Yellow Scots Rose'
OLD, SCOTS, MEDIUM YELLOW

This rose has double yellow flowers, no doubt inherited from *Rosa foetida*. The

'William Shakespeare'

'Wimi'

'William III'

'Williams' Double Yellow'

blooms are small and very fragrant, and are seen in profusion in spring. The foliage is tiny on a very twiggy plant. ZONES 4–9.

Williams, UK, 1828

Rosa foetida × *R. pimpinellifolia*

'WILTSHIRE' KORmuse

MODERN, MODERN SHRUB, MEDIUM PINK, REPEAT-FLOWERING

The flowers of this variety are bright pink, of medium size, fairly full of petals, borne in clusters and have an open cupped shape. Because they appear on a plant with a low, untidy habit they are easily overgrown by younger shoots, so

their full beauty is not always easy to appreciate. There is a light fragrance, and flowering is well maintained through summer and autumn. In the garden, 'Wiltshire' can be used as a ground-cover plant towards the front of a border, to trail over a wall or to use in a substantial container. The habit is low, and the plant spreads about twice as far as its height. The foliage is plentiful and shiny. ZONES 4–9.

Kordes, Germany, 1993

'Partridge' × seedling

Royal National Rose Society Certificate of Merit 1991, British Association of Rose Breeders, Breeders' Choice 1993, Glasgow Certificate of Commendation 1994

'WIMI' TANrowisa

syn. 'Willy Millowitch Rose'
MODERN, LARGE-FLOWERED/HYBRID TEA, PINK BLEND, REPEAT-FLOWERING

The flowers of this lovely rose are pink blended with soft creamy white at the centers and medium pink at the outer edges of the petals. The effect these colors give is quite striking. 'Wimi' is a vigorous bush that reaches a medium size, and it has a fair resistance to disease. 'Wimi' has not been introduced globally, so it may prove a difficult plant to obtain. ZONES 5–9.

Tantau, Germany, 1982

Parentage unknown

'Winsome'

'Windrush'

'Wini Edmunds'

'WINCHESTER CATHEDRAL'

AUScat

syn. 'Winchester'

MODERN, MODERN SHRUB, WHITE,
REPEAT-FLOWERING

This variety is identical to its parent
in every way except color. The white
blooms are bright and free, but sometimes revert on the bush to pink, like its
parent, or both pink and white. This is
either an endearing habit or a nuisance,
depending on the individual taste of the
grower. The frequency of flowering and
the wonderful loose blooms make this
plant ideal for any garden; it is untroubled
by disease right through the year.
'Winchester Cathedral' has a habit like
that of an Old Garden Rose, which
makes it easy to prune and grow. It
is also classified as an English Rose.
ZONES 5–9.

Austin, UK, 1988

Sport of 'Mary Rose'

'WIND CHIMES'

MODERN, RAMBLER, MEDIUM PINK,
REPEAT-FLOWERING

This Rambler will grow into a large,
dense mass that is ideal for covering
walls or the sides of buildings. The pink,
double flowers are borne in clusters all
over the canes in the early part of the
growing season. They appear almost entirely in this flush, and although there
will be more bloom over the rest of the
season it is nothing like this first flush.
The growth is long and slender with attractive green canes that freely branch

out from the bush. The plant is healthy
and vigorous and needs little attention.
'Wind Chimes' is not widely grown,
and is only available through specialist
nurseries. ZONES 5–9.

Lester Rose Gardens, USA, pre-1946

Parentage unknown

'WINDFLOWER'   AUScross

MODERN, MODERN SHRUB, LIGHT PINK,
REPEAT-FLOWERING

Related to the Alba Roses, this variety
carries flowers that are a kindly shade of
light pink. They are daintily formed with
scalloped petals that incurve at the tips,
which give the kind of charming, rather
frail effect commonly associated with
anemones (meaning 'windflowers' in
Greek). These flowers are held on wiry
stems, have a pleasant scent and continue
blooming through summer and autumn.
'Windflower' is appropriate for planting
in a mixed border and associates well
with other flowers. It grows upright to
average height for a shrub rose, with
mid-green foliage. ZONES 5–9.

Austin, UK, 1994

'Shropshire Lass' × seedling

'WINDRUSH'   AUSrush

MODERN, MODERN SHRUB, LIGHT YELLOW,
REPEAT-FLOWERING

This is a large shrub that bears lovely soft
yellow, semi-double blooms. Although
they fade a little when fully open, the
stamens are clearly visible at this stage
and their dark color is a striking contrast
to the light-colored petals. It repeats

quickly, and because the shrub is vigorous there are few times in the summer
when it is without flowers. 'Windrush'
must be deadheaded regularly to achieve
a continuous bloom, but if this process
is relaxed near the start of autumn the
plant will produce an abundant crop of
rosehips. It is a strong plant with good
disease resistance. The variety is also
classified as an English Rose. ZONES 5–9.

Austin, UK, 1984

Seedling × ('Canterbury' × 'Golden Wings')

'WINI EDMUNDS'

MODERN, LARGE-FLOWERED/HYBRID TEA,
RED BLEND, REPEAT-FLOWERING

The bright red, double flowers of 'Wini
Edmunds' have lighter pink and white
undersides. The blooms have classic
Large-flowered form and are ideal for the
show bench, particularly as they are long
lasting. The color becomes more intense
in cool weather, and growers in warmer
climates may therefore be a little disappointed with the flowers during the
summer heat. It is a strong grower with
tough, dark green foliage that is slightly
prone to black spot, so it should be
monitored all season so that the best
blooms are produced. ZONES 5–9.

McGredy, New Zealand, 1973

'Red Lion' × 'Hanne'

'WINNING COLORS'   TWOwin

MODERN, LARGE-FLOWERED/HYBRID TEA,
ORANGE BLEND, REPEAT-FLOWERING

This rose is a vibrant and unusual red
and orange combination; it is very eye
catching. The fully double, cupped
flowers have a musk fragrance and are
borne in small clusters on this medium-
sized bush. 'Winning Colors' is a vigorous plant with healthy, glossy green
foliage. ZONES 5–10.

Twomey, USA, 1989

'Gingersnap' × 'Marina'

'Wise Portia'

'WINNIPEG PARKS'

MODERN, MODERN SHRUB, DEEP PINK,
REPEAT-FLOWERING

The pointed buds of this rose open
into cupped, deep pink-red flowers of
medium size. The blooms have a velvety
texture and are neatly formed with about
20 petals that show yellow stamens. They
are borne singly or in small sprays and
have a slight fragrance. Although the
blooms do not last long, they give a good
succession of flowers through summer
and autumn. Because it is very frost
hardy, 'Winnipeg Parks' is a useful, medium-sized rose to grow in cold climates.
This shrubby plant is well covered with
matt mid-green leaves, which have a reddish tinge when young. ZONES 3–9.

Collicut, Canada, 1990

('Prairie Princess' × 'Cuthbert Grant') ×
(seedling × 'Morden Cardinette')

'WINSOME'   SAVawin

MODERN, MINIATURE, MAUVE, REPEAT-FLOWERING

The purple-red flowers of 'Winsome'
have over 40 petals. They have no scent,
nor do they fade, and are borne singly on
this upright bush with semi-glossy, mid-
green foliage. The blooms can be larger
in cool climates where a darker shading
effect on the petals makes the rose even
more attractive. When fully open, the
quality of the flowers is further enhanced
by the bright golden yellow stamens. It
is an extremely vigorous plant and also
self-cleaning: spent blooms fall off by
themselves before the next bloom cycle
begins. This award-winning rose has a
previous American Rose Society award
winner as its seed parent. ZONES 5–10.

Saville, USA, 1884

'Party Girl' × 'Shocking Blue'

American Rose Society Award of Excellence 1985

'WINTER MAGIC'   FOUmagic

MODERN, MINIATURE, MAUVE, REPEAT-FLOWERING

The long, shapely buds of this rose open
to flowers of an unusual color—light
lavender-gray with golden stamens. The
double flowers hold about 30 petals and
have a strong Tea fragrance. In hot climates a hint of russet may creep into the
petals, and in all conditions the blooms
appear on long stems that are suitable for
cutting since they are long lasting. People
either love or hate this color, and it is
popular with floral arrangers simply because it is unique. The foliage is mid-
green and semi-glossy, and covers this
tall, upright plant. It is easy to grow,
but can suffer from mildew if left

'Winchester Cathedral'

'Winnipeg Parks'

W

'Work of Art'

'World's Fair Salute'

unprotected. 'Winter Magic' has interesting parents; the seed parent is a top yellow Miniature from California, and the pollen parent is a highly rated, exhibition-standard Large-flowered Rose from France. **ZONES 5–10.**

Jacobs, USA, 1986

'Rise 'n' Shine' × 'Blue Nile'

'WISE PORTIA'   AUSport
MODERN, MODERN SHRUB, MAUVE, REPEAT-FLOWERING

Introduced in 1982, 'Wise Portia' is one of the earliest in David Austin's English Rose group. The flowers open to pinky mauve but have a large variation of tone over the season; the best blooms are produced in cool weather. The bush is a poor grower and there is a great need to keep disease under control, as it is susceptible to all the common fungus problems. It requires treatment and nurturing all season long to make it perform well and produce its best blooms. The rewards for the gardener are wonderful; when cut, the long-lasting blooms fill a room with their strong fragrance. It was named for the heroine of Shakespeare's *The Merchant of Venice*. **ZONES 5–9.**

Austin, UK, 1982

'The Knight' × 'Glastonbury'

'WISHING'   DICkerfuffle
syn. 'Georgie Girl'
MODERN, CLUSTER-FLOWERED/FLORIBUNDA, MEDIUM PINK/ORANGE-PINK, REPEAT-FLOWERING

'Wishing' bears flowers that are a mixture of apricot and pink, although pink is the dominant color of the two. The medium-sized, lightly scented blooms are borne in clusters. They are double but not too full, and cover this low-growing bush repeatedly through the warmer months. It is not susceptible to disease, but it is always wise to take preventive measures. **ZONES 5–9.**

Dickson, UK, 1985

'Silver Jubilee' × 'Bright Smile'

Royal National Rose Society Certificate of Merit 1984, Belfast Certificate of Merit 1986, Glasgow Certificate of Merit 1988

'WISTFUL'   SAVawist
MODERN, MINIATURE, MAUVE, REPEAT-FLOWERING

This easy to maintain rose has stately, pointed buds that open to small, pink-mauve flowers with paler edges. The high-centered blooms are suitable for exhibition; the petals have good substance and can sustain their Large-flowered form for days. This color is unique, quite

unlike any other mauve variety. In hot climates the petals can acquire a reddish haze. Small, dark glossy green foliage clothes a disease-resistant, upright, vigorous bush with a well-rounded and compact appearance. **ZONES 5–11.**

Saville, USA, 1995

'Sachet' × 'Rainbow's End'

'WOBURN ABBEY'
MODERN, CLUSTER-FLOWERED/FLORIBUNDA, ORANGE BLEND, REPEAT-FLOWERING

The orange flowers of this cultivar have an intense yellow glow in cool weather. They are fully double and form freely on short stems all over the small-growing plant. They are good for cutting, and the repeat cycle is good. The leathery, glossy mid-green foliage covers this tough, disease-resistant plant. 'Woburn Abbey' takes its name from the stately home of the Dukes of Bedford. **ZONES 5–9.**

Sidey and Cobley, UK, 1962

'Masquerade' × 'Fashion'

National Rose Society Trial Ground Certificate 1961

'WOBURN GOLD'
MODERN, CLUSTER-FLOWERED/FLORIBUNDA, DEEP YELLOW, REPEAT-FLOWERING

'Woburn Gold' is not widely grown. It is similar to its parent in every way, except for the color. Deep yellow flowers are borne all through summer on this strong, medium-sized, disease-resistant bush. It is an attractive rose, but the color is not particularly striking. As a result, its popularity has never been great. **ZONES 5–9.**

Robinson, Australia, 1970

Sport of 'Woburn Abbey'

'WOMAN'S DAY'
MODERN, CLUSTER-FLOWERED/FLORIBUNDA, PINK BLEND, REPEAT-FLOWERING

The pale creamy flowers have a strong pink edge on the petal and look their

best when the weather is cool, so that the flowers have a long time to develop. The bush has a compact habit, which makes it ideal for hedging and for border plantings, and the vigorous growth is disease resistant; it only needs care when grown in difficult conditions. 'Woman's Day' is not widely available, and should not be confused with the 1966 release of the same name which was also from Australia and named after a popular women's magazine. **ZONES 5–9.**

Welsh, Australia, 1993

Parentage unknown

'WOMAN'S VALUE'   KORvalue
MODERN, LARGE-FLOWERED/HYBRID TEA, PINK BLEND, REPEAT-FLOWERING

One of the most rewarding roses of the last two decades, this rose will undoubtedly remain popular into the next century. The shrub is vigorous and very healthy, and repeatedly produces numerous new blooms so that there are always buds and flowers to cut for display; it is a joy to bring these flowers indoors at the bud stage and watch them open slowly to perfectly shaped, full, soft pink flowers with a lovely fragrance. **ZONES 4–9.**

Kordes, Germany, 1984

('Sonia' × [('Dr A. J. Verhage' × 'Colour Wonder') × 'Zorina']) × 'Asso di Cuori'

'Woman's Day'

'Wishing'

'WORK OF ART'   MORart
MODERN, CLIMBING MINIATURE, ORANGE BLEND, REPEAT-FLOWERING

The short buds of this variety open to orange, urn-shaped blooms with undersides that are blended with yellow. They are double, with about 35 petals, come in small clusters and can be larger with high centers in cool climates. The flowers hold their form for a long time. It is a very vigorous climber reaching 6 ft (1.8 m) high, and has long canes that can be fanned out to achieve a larger area of color. This is a great plant in the garden; the color is truly a work of art! **ZONES 6–10.**

Moore, USA, 1989

Seedling of a yellow Climbing Miniature × 'Gold Badge'

'WORLD'S FAIR SALUTE'
MODERN, LARGE-FLOWERED/HYBRID TEA, MEDIUM RED, REPEAT-FLOWERING

This handsome rose bears large, medium red flowers with high centers. They have a sweet fragrance. The plant has a strong, upright growth habit and is easy to maintain. It is no longer widely grown, however, so may be quite difficult to obtain. **ZONES 5–9.**

Morey, USA, 1964

'Mardi Gras' × 'New Yorker'

'Woburn Abbey'

'Woburn Gold'

'WORTHWHILE'

MODERN, LARGE-FLOWERED/HYBRID TEA,
ORANGE BLEND, REPEAT-FLOWERING

The pointed buds of 'Worthwhile' open
to double, pink and salmon flowers that
only have a light fragrance. The stem
lengths make the blooms just right for
cutting, and they last well indoors. It is a
hardy plant with a tall growth habit and
a fair resistance to disease. This is definitely a worthwhile rose, producing
many beautiful flowers throughout the
warmer months. ZONES 5–9.

LeGrice, UK, 1973

'Gavotte' × 'Vienna Charm'

'X-RATED' TINx

MODERN, MINIATURE, PINK BLEND,
REPEAT-FLOWERING

'X-Rated' has flowers that are a wonderful creamy white with a blush of soft
coral to pink. The lightly fragrant,
double blooms have 26–40 high-
centered petals and are borne singly.
The combination of attractively colored
blooms on long stems make this a popular choice for garden display and exhibition. It has small, glossy mid-green
foliage on a medium-sized, vigorous
bush with an angular habit. It tends to be
rather wide, so plenty of room must be
given when planting in beds. It is susceptible to powdery mildew and constantly
needs protection by frequent spraying. It
was named to have a rose begin with the
letter 'X'. ZONES 5–10.

Bennett, USA, 1994

'Tiki' × 'Baby Katie'

'Worthwhile'

'XAVIER OLIBO'

OLD, HYBRID PERPETUAL, DEEP RED,
REPEAT-FLOWERING

'Xavier Olibo' is almost an exact version
of the parent, but the flowers are a much
darker red. They are spectacular, but the
plant must be well grown and requires
some care. ZONES 5–9.

Lacharmé, France, 1865

Sport of 'Général Jacqueminot'

'YAKIMOUR' MEIpsilon

MODERN, LARGE-FLOWERED/HYBRID TEA,
RED BLEND, REPEAT-FLOWERING

This rose is not available to most gardeners. It bears double, medium red flowers
with a full complement of petals that are
slightly paler on the undersides, showing
just a hint of gold. The foliage is glossy
bright green and covers a vigorous, tidy
bush with a fast repeat bloom. Unfortunately, it is prone to black spot and
mildew. ZONES 5–9.

Meilland, France, 1980

Parentage unknown

Baden-Baden Gold Medal 1985

'YANKEE DOODLE' YanKOR

MODERN, LARGE-FLOWERED/HYBRID TEA,
YELLOW BLEND, REPEAT-FLOWERING

This German-bred rose has all the appeal
of an Old Garden Rose with the added
advantage of repeat-flowering. The large
buds open to full, rich yellow and peachy
pink flowers; the outer petals turn and
hold the center of the blooms in place.
They are borne either singly or in small
clusters and have no scent, and can be

'Yakimour'

'Xavier Olibo'

'Yellow Butterfly'

ruined in wet weather. The glossy leaves
are slightly prone to disease, particularly
in cooler weather when there can be a
problem with black spot. This lovely rose
was an award winner in 1976, and still
retains its popularity after more than
three decades. ZONES 5–9.

Kordes, Germany, 1965

'Colour Wonder' × 'King's Ransom'

All-America Rose Selection 1976

'YELLOW BANTAM'

MODERN, MINIATURE, LIGHT YELLOW,
REPEAT-FLOWERING

The tiny pointed lemon buds of this rose
open to small yellow to white flowers.
They are so small that this rose qualifies
as a micro-miniature. The blooms are
double with 25 petals and have a light
fragrance. The bloom form is decorative.
It is a dwarf bush growing no higher than
10 in (25 cm) and is recommended as a
container-grown plant where it enjoys
being pot bound just as orchids do. Unfortunately 'Yellow Bantam' has become
obscure in the USA due to the ready
availability of more modern roses in this
color class. ZONES 5–10.

Moore, USA, 1960

(Rosa wichuraiana × 'Floradora') ×
'Fairy Princess'

'YELLOW BUTTERFLY'

MORwings

MODERN, MODERN SHRUB, LIGHT YELLOW,
REPEAT-FLOWERING

'Yellow Butterfly' bears delicate, golden
yellow flowers from pinkish buds

'Yellow Bantam'

'Yellow Button'

through summer. These blooms are single
with very little scent, and adorn this
sprawling bush. The leaves are glossy.
Ralph Moore is better known for his
wonderful Miniature Roses. ZONES 5–9.

Moore, USA, 1989

'Ellen Poulsen' × 'Yellow Jewel'

'YELLOW BUTTON' AUSlow

MODERN, MODERN SHRUB, YELLOW BLEND,
REPEAT-FLOWERING

'Yellow Button' was an early introduction from David Austin, and it showed
the world where he wanted to go in his
rose breeding program. It produces
yellow, rosette-shaped blooms, and
these open to a wonderful flower that is
excellent for cutting. The form holds
well, so it is ideal for posies and hand-
held arrangements. The low bush, however, is not strong and succumbs to
disease easily, so it needs a lot of work
to keep it healthy. For this reason, it has
been removed from many rose growers'
lists and is not now widely available.
ZONES 5–9.

Austin, UK, 1975

'Wife of Bath' × 'Chinatown'

'YELLOW CHAMPAGNER'

MODERN, CLUSTER-FLOWERED/FLORIBUNDA,
YELLOW BLEND, REPEAT-FLOWERING

The beautiful flowers of 'Yellow
Champagner' have a lovely classic shape.
Their many petals open deep yellow with
orange-yellow tight centers. As the
flowers mature, they fade to light
yellow and pale cream and the outer

W
X
Y

petals reflex. The glossy dark green foliage is a lovely complement to the flowers. ZONES 5–10.

1986

Parentage unknown

'YELLOW CHARLES AUSTIN'

AUSyel

MODERN, MODERN SHRUB, LIGHT YELLOW, REPEAT-FLOWERING

This rose is identical to its parent in every way except for the color of the flowers, which are fully double, clear yellow and have a full rosette shape. There is a good perfume and the blooms keep well, as long as they are cut when it is cool. The bush is healthy but needs to be maintained when conditions are cool and damp, usually early and late in the season. The growth habit is strong, and in warm climates the plant can grow quite large; summer pruning reduces growth and encourages more flowers. It is not widely available. 'Yellow Charles Austin' is also classified as an English Rose. ZONES 5–9.

Austin, UK, 1981

Sport of 'Charles Austin'

'YELLOW CUSHION'

MODERN, CLUSTER-FLOWERED/FLORIBUNDA, MEDIUM YELLOW, REPEAT-FLOWERING

The pointed buds of 'Yellow Cushion' open to large, fragrant, double flowers of

'Yellow Charles Austin'

'Yellow Champagner'

'Yellow Pages'

about two dozen petals. They have good substance and are produced, not very freely, in small, well-spaced clusters amid the glossy mid-green, leathery foliage. There is only a slow repeat, but the flowers hold well without fading. The bush is small, compact and reliably disease resistant. ZONES 5–10.

Armstrong, USA, 1966

'Fandango' × 'Pinocchio'

'YELLOW DOLL'

MODERN, MINIATURE, LIGHT YELLOW, REPEAT-FLOWERING

'Yellow Doll' produces pointed buds that open to reveal yellow to cream flowers with almost 55 narrow petals. The fragrant florets have high centers: a typical characteristic of Large-flowered roses. The flowers tend to last for quite a long time due to their high petal count, and the bright yellow color pales with age. The foliage is a leathery, glossy green on a medium-sized bush. Moore's use of 'Zee', derived from an early cross of the Rambler 'Carolyn Dean' with the Miniature 'Tom Thumb', consistently gave its offspring a reasonable probability to be a climber and a bushy habit. In this case the bushy habit prevailed, but a climbing counterpart also became available. ZONES 5–10.

Moore, USA, 1962

'Golden Glow' × 'Zee'

'Yellow Pinocchio'

'YELLOW FAIRY'   POUlfair

MODERN, MODERN SHRUB, MEDIUM YELLOW, REPEAT-FLOWERING

'Texas' is a yellow Miniature Rose, and the concept of breeding it with 'The Fairy' in hopes of creating a dainty yellow shrublet was a good one. The result is slightly disappointing because 'Yellow Fairy' lacks much of the grace and charm of its pollen parent. The flowers are small, made up of a dozen or so small petals, formed like rosettes and are borne very freely in sprays. They are a pleasing shade of medium yellow when the flowers are young, but they turn brown with age and may fail to open altogether in wet weather. The growth is uneven, and although many arching stems are produced the overall effect appears wispy due to insufficient leaf cover. As an example of an interesting cross, a place in the rose garden for this rose can be justified; it grows below average height with small, light green, semi-glossy leaves. ZONES 5–9.

Olesen, Denmark, 1988

'Texas' × 'The Fairy'

Madrid Gold Medal 1988

'YELLOW MEILLANDINA'

MEltrisical

syn. 'Yellow Sunblaze'

MODERN, MINIATURE, YELLOW BLEND, REPEAT-FLOWERING

The petal edges of these fragrant yellow flowers are touched with pink. The florets have 20 petals. The foliage is medium, semi-glossy dark green on a well-behaved compact bush. Like all the other roses from the House of Meilland in the 'Sunblaze' series, it is best grown in a container. This is a profuse bloomer and very easy to grow. ZONES 5–10.

Meilland, France, 1982

('Poppy Flash' × ['Charleston' × 'Allgold']) × 'Gold Coin'

'Yellow Cushion'

'YELLOW PAGES'

MODERN, LARGE-FLOWERED/HYBRID TEA, YELLOW BLEND, REPEAT-FLOWERING

This rose produces lovely mid-yellow blooms with a delicate scent that are borne either singly or in small clusters. It has tough, glossy leaves with slight disease resistance. The variety is medium sized, stout and bushy, but like its parent 'Peer Gynt' it is not robust enough to allow a carefree season. ZONES 5–9.

McGredy, UK, 1971

'Arthur Bell' × 'Peer Gynt'

Royal National Rose Society Trial Ground Certificate 1971

'YELLOW PINOCCHIO'

MODERN, CLUSTER-FLOWERED/FLORIBUNDA, MEDIUM YELLOW, REPEAT-FLOWERING

When this vigorous rose was released in 1949, it was rated 6.2 by the American Rose Society. Its fully double, yellow, medium-sized flowers open from tight buds into cup-shaped blooms with a slight fragrance. The repeat cycle is fair, and the bush responds well to deadheading. Not a widely grown plant, it may be difficult to obtain. ZONES 5–9.

Boerner, USA, 1949

'Goldilocks' × 'Marionette'

National Rose Society Certificate of Merit 1952

Y

'YELLOW QUEEN ELIZABETH'

syn. 'Queen Elisabeth Jaune'

MODERN, LARGE-FLOWERED/HYBRID TEA, MEDIUM YELLOW, REPEAT-FLOWERING

This yellow sport of 'Queen Elizabeth' carries on many of the parent's strengths. The yellow blooms have a creamy golden tone when the weather is cooler. It is a good, healthy plant that, with encouragement, can be kept free of black spot and mildew during the flowering season. It is not as widely grown as its parent, but makes an attractive yellow bush for the garden. ZONES 5–9.

Vlaeminck, Belgium, 1964

Sport of 'Queen Elizabeth'

'Yellow Queen Elizabeth'

'YESTERDAY'

syn. 'Tapis d'Orient'

MODERN, POLYANTHA, MEDIUM PINK, REPEAT-FLOWERING

This rose has won many awards and is well recommended for the garden; its semi-double flowers are borne in clusters that make a beautiful spectacle when in full bloom. They are mid- to violet-pink and the buds are a darker shade against the open flowers. The blooms last well when cut. This medium-sized shrub with thin and vigorous, disease-free growth forms an attractive round bush. Rows of 'Yesterday' look very effective in the garden. ZONES 5–9.

Harkness, UK, 1974

('Phyllis Bide' × 'Shepherd's Delight') × 'Ballerina'

Royal National Rose Society Certificate of Merit 1972, Monza Gold Medal 1974, Baden-Baden Gold Medal 1976, Anerkannte Deutsche Rose 1978, Royal Horticultural Society Award of Garden Merit 1993

'YESTERYEAR' HARwoey

syn. 'Lotsa Fragrance'

MODERN, LARGE-FLOWERED/HYBRID TEA, APRICOT BLEND, REPEAT-FLOWERING

This variety produces shapely blooms of over two dozen peachy apricot petals. They develop from well-formed buds and retain their color well. There is a

'Yesterday'

'Yolande d'Aragon'

quick repeat and a very strong fragrance. The abundant blooms are mainly produced singly on long stems, which makes them good for cutting. The disease-resistant growth is vigorous with glossy dark green foliage. 'Yesteryear' is a good rose for bedding and also does well in borders. ZONES 5–10.

Harkness, UK, 1994

Seedling of 'Just Joey'

'YOLANDE D'ARAGON'

OLD, HYBRID PERPETUAL, MAUVE, REPEAT-FLOWERING

The very full and large flowers of 'Yolande d'Aragon' are bright purple-pink. They are produced in big clusters and are very fragrant. There is a good autumn repeat, provided deadheading, summer pruning and feeding are carried out. The bush is of moderate height with upright growth and the foliage is light green. Yolande was the wife of Louis II of Anjou and the Two Sicilies. Considering its antiquity it is in remarkably plentiful supply, being available from a large

'Yesterday'

number of outlets. Some authorities classify it as a Perpetual Damask (Portland). The first Hybrid Perpetuals were developed from the Portlands. ZONES 5–9.

Vibert, France, 1843

Parentage unknown

'YORK AND LANCASTER'

syns *Rosa damascena versicolor*, 'Versicolor', 'York et Lancastre'

OLD, DAMASK, PINK BLEND

A lanky, lax-growing shrub of branching habit, 'York and Lancaster' has grayish green wood armed with hooked, sharp thorns. The many leaves are also grayish green and have a soft texture. The blooms are carried on long stalks in nodding, loose clusters, each raggedly semi-double and about 2½ in (6.5 cm) across. Their color is variable, some consisting of soft mid-pink and others consistently white; both shades may even be present in the same flower. The variety is very fragrant, but a little shy in its yield of flowers. Historically it is very interesting, but it is not a rose to overly enhance the average garden. ZONES 5–10.

Pre-1629

Parentage unknown

'YORKSHIRE' KORbarkeit

MODERN, GROUND COVER, WHITE, REPEAT-FLOWERING

This variety bears small clusters of semi-double white flowers that open wide like saucers. They have fluted petals and prominent golden stamens. There is a pleasant light fragrance, and the blooms continue to appear through summer and autumn nestling on short stems against a background of glossy dark green leaves on this compact, cushiony plant. The habit of growth is low and wide, and the plant is small enough to use in a sizeable container or to group in a border or bed. 'Yorkshire' grows vigorously and

Y

'Yorkshire Bank'

produces many shoots. This name had to be given to a white rose, because that became the emblem of the royal house of York in the early fifteenth century and has been associated with the county of Yorkshire ever since. **ZONES 4–9.**

Kordes, Germany, 1998

Parentage unknown

'YORKSHIRE BANK'   RUtrulo
syn. 'True Love'

MODERN, LARGE-FLOWERED/HYBRID TEA, NEAR WHITE, REPEAT-FLOWERING

The double flowers of 'Yorkshire Bank' are a rich creamy pale yellow paling to white. They display attractive stamens when fully open. The glossy leaves have some disease resistance, but the plant will need some care through the season to help it produce a bountiful supply of lovely blooms. The parentage should have resulted in a hugely successful cross

but this has not been the case. It is not widely grown, but is available in most countries. **ZONES 5–9.**

de Ruiter, The Netherlands, 1979

'Pascali' × 'Peer Gynt'

Geneva Gold Medal 1979, New Zealand Gold Medal 1979

'York and Lancaster' (hip)

'York and Lancaster'

Y

'Youki San'

'Young at Heart'

'Youth of the World'

'Young at Heart'

'Young Quinn'

'YOUKI SAN'   MEIdona
syn. 'Mme Neige'
MODERN, LARGE-FLOWERED/HYBRID TEA, WHITE,
REPEAT-FLOWERING

This rose bears large and unusual, semi-double flowers that open flat to reveal pure white petals and striking gold and red stamens. It is a low-growing plant that is best suited to warm, dry climates where mildew and black spot are easily kept at bay. At the time of introduction, 'Youki San' was widely used in floral decorations . It is well worth growing. ZONES 5–9.

Meilland, France, 1965

'Lady Sylvia' × 'White Knight'

Baden Baden Gold Medal 1964

'YOUNG AT HEART'
MODERN, LARGE-FLOWERED/HYBRID TEA,
APRICOT BLEND, REPEAT-FLOWERING

The shapely, fully double flowers of this rose are a long-lasting soft apricot-pink, and have a strong fragrance. The plant has an upright growth habit with glossy, dark green foliage. It needs to be monitored in cool, damp weather when disease resistance is poorest. 'Young at Heart' produces vigorous canes from basal growth, so pruning is easy. It was introduced as Australian Rose of the Year in 1989. It is becoming more difficult to obtain. ZONES 5–9.

Armstrong, USA, 1988

Parentage unknown

'YOUNG QUINN'   MACbern
syn. 'Yellow Wonder'
MODERN, LARGE-FLOWERED/HYBRID TEA,
MEDIUM YELLOW, REPEAT-FLOWERING

The oval buds of 'Young Quinn' open to double blooms of about 30 large petals that are of good substance. The full blooms are borne singly on tall stems amid the huge, glossy rich green, attractive leaves. The profuse flowers are edged with pink as they age, and keep very well when cut. 'Young Quinn' is a good, disease-resistant rose for a tall hedge or for the back of a rose bed. ZONES 5–10.

McGredy, New Zealand, 1975

'Peer Gynt' × 'Kiskadee'

Belfast Gold Medal 1978

'YOUTH OF THE WORLD'
MODERN, LARGE-FLOWERED/HYBRID TEA,
MEDIUM RED, REPEAT-FLOWERING

This variety is one of the very few Russian-bred roses available outside of the former Soviet Union. The huge blooms are very large and very full, with 60 or more tightly packed, very deep pink or light red petals. The flowers are very long lasting, but they may ball in wet weather. This tall and upright bush carries large, dull matt green, disease-resistant foliage. The flower production is low with slow repeat, although there is some perfume. ZONES 5–10.

Russia, 1962

Parentage unknown

Y

'YVES PIAGET' MEIvildo
syns 'Queen Adelaide', 'The Royal Brompton Rose'

MODERN, LARGE-FLOWERED/HYBRID TEA, DEEP PINK, REPEAT-FLOWERING

This rose was released under the name 'Queen Adelaide' in some countries. The fully double, pink flowers are very sweetly scented and have an old rose charm about them. 'Yves Piaget' is a medium-sized shrub with stout growth and produces blooms all season. The resistance to disease is good in warm, dry climates, but it is prone to black spot in cool, damp weather. This unusual plant is well worth growing for the scent alone. ZONES 5–9.

Meilland, France, 1985

(['Pharaoh' × 'Peace'] × ['Chrysler Imperial' × 'Charles Mallerin']) × 'Tamango'

Geneva Gold Medal and Fragrance Award 1982, Le Roeulx Gold Medal and Fragrance Award 1982, Belfast Fragrance Award 1986, Bagatelle Fragrance Award 1992

'YVONNE RABIER'
MODERN, POLYANTHA, WHITE, REPEAT-FLOWERING

This cultivar produces some of the best white flowers of the Polyantha Roses. They are double and are borne in clusters that cover the bush when in full bloom. The leaves are disease resistant, although some control may be needed in those areas that are constantly damp; it grows well in warmer climates. 'Yvonne Rabier' makes an ideal patio standard and, as it is quite low, it is also wonderful for edging a rose bed. ZONES 5–9.

Turbat, France, 1910

Rosa wichuraiana × unidentified Polyantha Rose

Royal Horticultural Society Award of Garden Merit 1993

'ZAMBRA' MEIalfi
MODERN, CLUSTER-FLOWERED/FLORIBUNDA, ORANGE BLEND, REPEAT-FLOWERING

The bright orange flowers of 'Zambra' open flat; the blooms have only a few petals that almost make up two rows and show the stamens off well. There is a slight scent. The bush is susceptible to mildew and black spot and growers who are not careful will soon have a plant that is bare of leaves and in a poor state.

'Zara Hore-Ruthven'

Better varieties are available. In its heyday it created a great sensation because the color was so bright and unusual. 'Climbing Zambra' (MEIalfisar; 1969) is not too rampant, and can easily be managed if grown on a wall or fence. ZONES 5–9.

Meilland, France, 1961

('Goldilocks' × 'Fashion') × ('Goldilocks' × 'Fashion')

Bagatelle Gold Medal 1961, National Rose Society Certificate of Merit 1961, Rome Gold Medal 1961

'ZARA HORE-RUTHVEN'
MODERN, LARGE-FLOWERED/HYBRID TEA, MEDIUM PINK, REPEAT-FLOWERING

This strong-growing bush was an early release and showed Clark's love for large-growing, free-formed roses with both character and style. The medium-pink flowers have a slight fragrance and hold well when picked. ZONES 5–9.

Clark, Australia, 1932

'Mme Abel Chatenay' × 'Scorcher'

'Zambra'

'Yvonne Rabier'

'Yves Piaget'

'ZEBRA'   BENraar

MODERN, LARGE-FLOWERED/HYBRID TEA, RED BLEND, REPEAT-FLOWERING

This is one of those contentious roses that rosarians either love or detest. It is, however, a valuable garden shrub, because it is healthy, vigorous and floriferous. The startling combination of white and shocking pink stripes on the large flowers makes it difficult to accommodate in a garden with more gentle colors; it may have to be grown on its own where the medium-sized shrubs can produce their display unrivalled. The long-stemmed flowers can also be cut for vase and exhibition. ZONES 5–11.

Benardella, USA, 1995

'Lorena' × 'Tinseltown'

'ZENOBIA'

OLD, MOSS, MEDIUM PINK

This is a vigorous rose bearing large, double, satin pink flowers. They are very fragrant, and resemble those of a Hybrid Perpetual. It flowers only in summer. It

is a medium to tall, somewhat lanky plant and is quite prickly, as one would expect in a Moss. ZONES 4–9.

Paul, UK, 1892

Parentage unknown

'ZÉPHIRINE DROUHIN'

syns 'Belle Dijonnaise', 'Charles Bonnet', 'Ingegnoli Prediletta', 'Mme Gustave Bonnet'

OLD, BOURBON, MEDIUM PINK, REPEAT-FLOWERING

This thornless rose can be grown as a pillar rose, over an arch, or as a moderate to large, open shrub. The fragrant, medium-sized flowers are semi-double and loose petalled. They are cerise-pink with a white base. This vigorous plant is easy to cultivate. 'Kathleen Harrop' is a pink sport of this rose. Both make good hedge roses but should be kept away from walls for fear of black spot. ZONES 5–10.

Bizot, France, 1868

Parentage unknown

Royal Horticultural Society Award of Garden Merit 1993

'Zwergkönig 78'

'Zwergkönig 78'

'Zéphirine Drouihn'

'Zweibrücken'

'ZIGEUNERBLUT'

syn. 'Gipsy Blood'
OLD, BOURBON, DARK RED

This rose mirrors its wild parent except in the shape of the flowers, which are double, cup shaped, cerise-purple and appear in clusters. The full blossoms reflex upon opening and the wiry canes are armed with prickles. Once blooming, the open, arching shrub has attractive, dark green foliage. It is best in a woodland setting or trained behind lower shrubs. The 6 ft (1.8 m) bush is another creation of a Bohemian hybridizer who strove to create winter-hardy roses. This one is no exception. ZONES 5–10.

Geschwind, Hungary, 1890

Rosa alpina × 'Ile de Bourbon'

'ZINGER'

MODERN, MINIATURE, MEDIUM RED, REPEAT-FLOWERING

'Zinger' has long, pointed, elegant buds that open to medium bright red flowers with contrasting golden stamens. The florets have 11 petals and are fragrant. The blooms come one to a stem but more often in small clusters and they do not burn even in hot climates. The bloom cycle is fast on a prolific plant. Its vigorous, spreading habit can be used to advantage especially in rock gardens. 'Zorina', the Cluster-flowered seed parent, is commonly used in the hybridization of large roses, and here it has been used with great success as 'Zinger' won the prestigious American Rose Society Award of Excellence. ZONES 5–10.

Schwartz, USA, 1978

'Zorina' × 'Magic Carrousel'

American Rose Society Award of Excellence 1979

'ZOÉ'

syn. 'Moussue Partout'
OLD, MOSS, MEDIUM PINK

The flowers of 'Zoé' are rose pink, globular and well mossed on a conventional plant. It is generally available. ZONES 4–9.

Pradel, France, 1861

Parentage unknown

'ZWEIBRÜCKEN'

MODERN, MODERN SHRUB, DARK RED, REPEAT-FLOWERING

This rose was introduced in 1955 following an outstanding performance at the German Rose Trials. It shows a very

'Zinger'

vigorous climbing habit covered with deep crimson, fully double flowers. The blooms last well in the garden, but they do not have a long life when picked and taken indoors. ZONES 5–9.

Kordes, Germany, 1955

Rosa kordesii × 'Independence'

Baden-Baden Bronze Medal 1956

'ZWERGKÖNIG 78'   KORkönig

syn. 'Dwarf King'

MODERN, MINIATURE, DARK RED, REPEAT-FLOWERING

'Zwergkönig 78' has fragrant, cupped, carmine flowers with 25 petals. The foliage is glossy green on a vigorous, compact, hardy bush only 8–10 in (20–25 cm) high. The original 'Zwergkönig' was the darkest of the Miniatures with its ruffled flowers almost black-red. This new rose has the reputation of being stronger and easier to grow and with a much brighter color tone. ZONES 5–10.

Kordes, Germany, 1978

Parentage unknown

'ZWERKÖNIGIN 82'   KORwerk

syn. 'Dwarf Queen 82'

MODERN, MINIATURE, MEDIUM PINK, REPEAT-FLOWERING

The original 'Dwarf King' had a consort introduced in 1955. This newer rose has a pink consort also: 'Zwergkönigin 82'. Apart from the color difference, it is similar in every way to 'Zwergkönig 78'. This rose grows taller than most Miniatures and is a wonderful tidy bush that produces long stems with beautifully shaped blooms. ZONES 5–10.

Kordes, Germany, 1982

KORkönig × 'Sunday Times'

Reference Table

This table presents a simple description of the roses in this book to help you select a rose that suits your tastes. The group the rose belongs to is given in the individual text entries; more information on the classification of roses can be found in the chapter 'The Rose and Its Heritage'. Further information on many of the terms used in this table can be found in the Glossary; flower shape is explained in detail in the chapter 'Cultivating Roses'. The colors given in the table reflect the general color classification given in the headings to the individual text entries. A fuller description can be found in the individual entries.

NAME	BLOOM COLOR	FLOWER SIZE	FLOWER TYPE	FLOWER SHAPE	FRAGRANCE AMOUNT	FLOWERING HABIT	FLOWERING INCIDENCE	PETAL SHAPE
WILD ROSES								
Rosa acicularis nipponensis	deep pink	small	single	open	moderate	small clusters	once	plain
Rosa arkansana	medium pink	small	single	open	slight	corymb	once	plain
Rosa arvensis	white	medium	single	flat	slight	small clusters	once	plain
Rosa banksiae normalis	white	small	single	open	moderate	corymb	once	plain
Rosa beggeriana	white	medium	single	flat	none	corymb	once	plain
Rosa blanda	medium pink	medium	single	open	slight	small clusters	once	plain
Rosa bracteata	white	large	single	cupped	none	singly	repeat	plain
Rosa brunonii	white	medium	single	flat	moderate	corymb	once	plain
Rosa californica	light pink	medium	single	flat	none	corymb	once	plain
Rosa canina	light pink	medium	single	open	moderate	small clusters	once	plain
Rosa carolina	medium pink	medium	single	flat	none	singly	once	plain
Rosa chinensis	medium pink/ dark red	medium	single	open	none	singly	repeat	plain
Rosa cinnamomea	mauve	medium	single	open	moderate	singly	once	plain
Rosa × coryana	deep pink	medium	single	open	none	small clusters	once	plain
Rosa davidii	light pink	medium	single	open	none	corymb	once	plain
Rosa ecae	deep yellow	small	single	flat	none	singly	once	plain
Rosa eglanteria	light pink	small	single	open	moderate	small clusters	once	plain
Rosa elegantula 'Persetosa'	medium pink	small	single	open	slight	small clusters	once	plain
Rosa fedtschenkoana	white	medium	single	flat	moderate	small clusters	once	plain
Rosa filipes	white	small	single	open	moderate	corymb	once	plain
Rosa foetida	medium yellow	medium	single	open	moderate	singly	once	plain
Rosa foliolosa	medium pink	small	single	open	slight	singly	once	plain
Rosa forrestiana	deep pink	small	single	flat	none	small clusters	once	plain
Rosa gallica	deep pink	medium	single	open	strong	small clusters	once	plain
Rosa gentiliana	white	small	single	flat	none	large clusters	once	plain
Rosa gigantea	white	large	single	flat	strong	small clusters	once	plain
Rosa giraldii	medium pink	small	single	flat	none	small clusters	once	plain
Rosa glauca	medium pink	small	single	flat	slight	small clusters	once	plain
Rosa helenae	white	medium	single	open	moderate	corymb	once	plain
Rosa hemisphaerica	medium yellow	medium	double	open	slight	small clusters	once	plain
Rosa holodonta	light pink	medium	single	open	slight	small clusters	once	plain
Rosa hugonis	medium yellow	medium	single	open	slight	singly	once	plain
Rosa × kochiana	deep pink	small	single	flat	none	small clusters	once	plain
Rosa laevigata	white	large	single	open	slight	singly	once	plain
Rosa longicuspis	white	medium	single	flat	slight	corymb	once	plain
Rosa × macrantha 'Macrantha'	light pink/ white	medium	single	open	moderate	small clusters	once	plain
Rosa maximowicziana	white	medium	single	flat	none	corymb	once	plain
Rosa micrantha	light pink	small	single	open	slight	small clusters	once	plain
Rosa moschata	white	medium	single	flat	strong	corymb	once	plain
Rosa moyesii	medium red	medium	single	flat	none	singly	once	plain
Rosa mulliganii	white	medium	single	flat	moderate	corymb	once	plain

NAME	BLOOM COLOR	FLOWER SIZE	FLOWER TYPE	FLOWER SHAPE	FRAGRANCE AMOUNT	FLOWERING HABIT	FLOWERING INCIDENCE	PETAL SHAPE
Rosa multiflora	white	small	single	flat	slight	corymb	once	plain
Rosa nitida	medium pink	medium	single	flat	moderate	small clusters	once	plain
Rosa nutkana	medium pink	medium	single	flat	slight	singly	once	plain
Rosa omeiensis	white	small	single	flat	none	singly	once	plain
Rosa pendulina	deep pink/ mauve	medium	single	flat	none	small clusters	once	plain
Rosa phoenicia	white	small	single	open	none	corymb	once	plain
Rosa pisocarpa	medium pink	small	single	flat	none	small clusters	once	plain
Rosa pomifera	medium pink	medium	single	open	slight	small clusters	once	plain
Rosa primula	light yellow	small	single	flat	strong	singly	once	plain
Rosa roxburghii	medium pink	medium	double to full	rosette	slight	singly	repeat	plain
Rosa rugosa	mauve	medium	single	flat	strong	small clusters	repeat	plain
Rosa sempervirens	white	medium	single	open	slight	corymb	once	plain
Rosa sericea	white	small	single	flat	none	singly	once	plain
Rosa sericea pteracantha	white	small	single	flat	none	singly	once	plain
Rosa setigera	deep pink	medium	single	open	none	corymb	once	plain
Rosa setipoda	light pink	medium	single	open	moderate	corymb	once	plain
Rosa sherardii	deep pink	medium	single	flat	moderate	small clusters	once	plain
Rosa sicula	deep pink to white blend	small	single	flat	slight	singly	once	plain
Rosa soulieana	white	small	single	open	moderate	corymb	once	plain
Rosa spinosissima	white	small	single	open	none	singly	once	plain
Rosa stellata mirifica	mauve	small	single	open	slight	singly	once	plain
Rosa sweginzowii	medium pink	small	single	flat	slight	small clusters	once	plain
Rosa tomentosa	light pink	medium	single	open	strong	small clusters	once	plain
Rosa virginiana	medium pink	medium	single	open	slight	small clusters	open	plain
Rosa webbiana	medium pink	small	single	flat	moderate	singly	once	plain
Rosa wichuraiana	white	medium	single	open	slight	corymb	once	plain
Rosa willmottiae	mauve	small	single	open	slight	singly	once	plain
Rosa woodsii	medium pink	medium	single	open	none	small clusters	once	plain
Rosa xanthina	medium yellow	small	single	open	slight	small clusters	once	plain
CULTIVARS								
A Country Woman	dark red	medium	double to full	high-centered	moderate	small clusters	repeat	plain
A Longs Pédoncules	light pink	small	very full	quartered	strong	large clusters	once	plain
Aalsmeer Gold	deep yellow	large	double	high-centered	slight	small clusters	repeat	plain
Abailard	pink blend	medium	very full	rosette	moderate	small clusters	once	plain
Abbaye de Cluny	apricot blend	large	double to full	high-centered	slight	singly	repeat	reflexed
Abbeyfield Rose	deep pink	large	double to full	high-centered	slight	small clusters	repeat	reflexed
Abbotswood	medium pink	medium	semi-double	cupped	strong	small clusters	once	plain
Abigaile	pink blend	large	double to full	high-centered	none	small clusters	repeat	reflexed
Abraham Darby	orange-pink	large	very full	cupped	strong	small clusters	repeat	plain
Acapulco	red blend	large	double to full	high-centered	slight	small clusters	repeat	plain
Acey Deucy	medium red	small	double to full	high-centered	slight	small clusters	repeat	reflexed
Achievement	deep pink	small	double to full	flat	none	large clusters	once	plain
Acidalie	white	large	very full	globular	moderate	small clusters	repeat	plain

NAME	BLOOM COLOR	FLOWER SIZE	FLOWER TYPE	FLOWER SHAPE	FRAGRANCE AMOUNT	FLOWERING HABIT	FLOWERING INCIDENCE	PETAL SHAPE
Adair Roche	pink blend	large	double to full	high-centered	slight	small clusters	repeat	reflexed
Adam	medium pink	large	very full	globular	slight	singly	repeat	plain
Adam Messerich	medium red	medium	semi-double	cupped	moderate	small clusters	repeat	plain
Adam's Smile	deep pink	small	double to full	high-centered	none	small clusters	repeat	reflexed
Adélaïde d'Orléans	white	small	semi-double	cupped	moderate	small clusters	once	reflexed
Adèle Prévost	light pink	large	very full	rosette	moderate	small clusters	once	plain
Admiral Rodney	pink blend	large	double to full	high-centered	strong	small clusters	repeat	reflexed
Adolf Horstmann	yellow blend	large	double to full	high-centered	slight	singly	repeat	reflexed
Adventure	orange-red	large	very full	high-centered	slight	small clusters	repeat	reflexed
Aennchen von Tharau	white	medium	double to full	cupped	slight	small clusters	once	plain
Africa Star	mauve	large	very full	cupped	moderate	small clusters	repeat	reflexed
Afterglow	orange blend	medium	double to full	cupped	slight	small clusters	repeat	frilled
Agatha	light pink	medium	double to full	rosette	moderate	small clusters	once	reflexed
Agatha Christie	pink	large	double to full	high-centered	moderate	small clusters	repeat	plain
Agathe Incarnata	medium pink	medium	double to full	quartered	strong	small clusters	once	plain
Age Tendre	deep pink	large	double to full	high-centered	none	singly	repeat	reflexed
Agéna	orange-pink	large	double to full	high-centered	slight	singly	repeat	reflexed
Aglaia	light yellow	small	double to full	flat	slight	large clusters	once	plain
Agnes	light yellow	medium	double to full	open	moderate	singly	repeat	ruffled
Agnes Bernauer	light pink	large	double to full	high-centered	strong	singly	repeat	reflexed
Agreement	pink blend	large	double to full	high-centered	none	small clusters	repeat	reflexed
Ahoi	orange-red	medium	double to full	open	none	large clusters	repeat	plain
Aïcha	deep yellow	large	semi-double	open	strong	small clusters	once	plain
Aimable Amie	deep pink	medium	double to full	rosette	moderate	small clusters	once	plain
Aimable Rouge	deep pink	large	double to full	high-centered	moderate	singly	repeat	reflexed
Aimée Vibert	white	medium	double to full	cupped	strong	umbel	repeat	plain
Akebono	yellow blend	large	double to full	high-centered	none	singly	repeat	reflexed
Alain	medium red	medium	semi-double	open	slight	large clusters	repeat	plain
Alain Blanchard	mauve	medium	semi-double	cupped	moderate	small clusters	once	plain
Alamein	orange-red	large	semi-double	flat	slight	small clusters	repeat	plain
Alba Maxima	white	medium	double to full	open	slight	small clusters	once	plain
Alba Meidiland	white	medium	double to full	cupped	none	small clusters	repeat	plain
Alba Semi-plena	white	medium	semi-double	flat	slight	large clusters	once	plain
Alba Suaveolens	white	medium	semi-double	flat	strong	large clusters	once	plain
Albéric Barbier	white	medium	double to full	cupped	moderate	small clusters	once	plain
Albertine	orange-pink	medium	double to full	cupped	moderate	small clusters	once	plain
Alchymist	apricot blend	large	very full	flat	moderate	small clusters	once	plain
Aldo	orange blend	medium	semi-double	open	none	small clusters	repeat	reflexed
Alec's Red	medium red	large	double to full	high-centered	moderate	singly	repeat	reflexed
Alexander	orange-red	large	double to full	high-centered	none	small clusters	repeat	reflexed
Alexander Hill Gray	deep yellow	large	double to full	quartered	moderate	singly	repeat	plain
Alexander MacKenzie	red blend	medium	double to full	open	moderate	small clusters	repeat	plain
Alexander von Humboldt	medium red	medium	semi-double	open	slight	large clusters	repeat	plain
Alexandre Girault	pink blend	large	double to full	cupped	moderate	small clusters	once	plain
Alexandre Laquement	mauve	medium	double to full	cupped	moderate	small clusters	once	plain
Alfred Colomb	pink blend	large	double to full	globular	strong	small clusters	repeat	reflexed
Alfred de Dalmas	light pink	medium	semi-double	cupped	slight	small clusters	repeat	plain
Alice Amos	pink blend	small	single	cupped	none	large clusters	repeat	plain
Alida Lovett	light pink	large	double to full	open	slight	small clusters	once	plain
Alika	medium red	large	semi-double	open	moderate	small clusters	once	plain
Alister Clark	light pink	large	double to full	cupped	moderate	small clusters	repeat	reflexed
Alister Stella Gray	light yellow	medium	double to full	flat	moderate	small clusters	repeat	plain
All That Jazz	orange-pink	medium	semi-double	open	moderate	small clusters	repeat	plain
Allegro	orange-red	large	double to full	cupped	slight	small clusters	repeat	reflexed
Allelulia	red blend	large	double to full	high-centered	none	singly	repeat	reflexed
Allen Chandler	medium red	large	semi-double	cupped	slight	small clusters	repeat	plain
Allgold	medium yellow	large	double to full	flat	slight	large clusters	repeat	reflexed
Allotria	orange-red	large	double to full	flat	none	large clusters	repeat	plain
Allspice	medium yellow	large	double to full	high-centered	moderate	singly	repeat	reflexed
Almost Sunset	yellow blend	medium	semi-double	high-centered	moderate	singly	repeat	plain
Aloha	medium pink	large	very full	rosette	moderate	singly	repeat	plain
Alouette	orange-pink	medium	semi-double	cupped	slight	large clusters	repeat	plain
Alpine Sunset	apricot blend	large	double to full	high-centered	moderate	singly	repeat	reflexed
Altissimo	medium red	large	single	cupped	slight	small clusters	repeat	plain
Amadis	dark red	medium	double to full	open	none	small clusters	once	reflexed
Amalia	dark red/ light red	large	double to full	high-centered	none	small clusters	repeat	reflexed
Amanda	medium yellow	large	double to full	high-centered	slight	small clusters	repeat	reflexed
Amatsu-Otome	yellow blend	large	double to full	high-centered	slight	small clusters	repeat	reflexed
Amatsu Pink	pink blend	large	double to full	high centered	none	small clusters	repeat	reflexed
Ambassador	orange blend	large	double to full	cupped	none	small clusters	repeat	plain
Amber Nectar	apricot blend	small	double to full	cupped	slight	large clusters	repeat	plain
Amber Queen	apricot blend	medium	double to full	cupped	slight	small clusters	repeat	ruffled
Ambossfunken	red blend	large	double to full	open	slight	singly	repeat	plain
Ambridge Rose	apricot blend	medium	double to full	cupped	strong	small clusters	repeat	plain
Ambrosia	orange blend	large	single	flat	none	large clusters	repeat	plain
Amélia	medium pink	large	double to full	rosette	strong	small clusters	once	plain
America	orange-pink	large	double to full	cupped	strong	small clusters	repeat	reflexed
American Beauty	deep pink	large	double to full	cupped	strong	singly	repeat	reflexed
American Heritage	yellow blend	large	double to full	high-centered	none	singly	repeat	reflexed
American Home	dark red	large	double to full	cupped	strong	singly	repeat	reflexed
American Pillar	pink blend	small	single	cupped	none	large clusters	once	reflexed
American Pride	dark red	large	double to full	high-centered	none	singly	repeat	ruffled
Americana	medium red	large	double to full	high-centered	slight	singly	repeat	reflexed
Améthyste	mauve	small	double to full	flat	none	large clusters	once	plain
Amiga Mia	medium pink	large	double to full	high-centered	moderate	singly	repeat	reflexed
Amore	medium pink	medium	double to full	cupped	moderate	large clusters	repeat	plain
Amorette	white	small	double to full	high-centered	none	large clusters	repeat	reflexed
Amorosa	white	large	double to full	high-centered	moderate	singly	repeat	reflexed
Amsterdam	orange-red	large	semi-double	cupped	none	small clusters	repeat	plain
Amy Johnson	medium pink	large	double to full	cupped	slight	small clusters	repeat	plain
Amy Robsart	deep pink	medium	single	cupped	moderate	singly	once	ruffled
Anabell	orange blend	large	double to full	high-centered	moderate	small clusters	repeat	reflexed
Anaïs Ségalas	pink blend	medium	very full	rosette	moderate	small clusters	once	plain
Anastasia	white	large	double to full	high-centered	none	singly	repeat	reflexed
Andalusien	medium red	medium	double to full	cupped	none	small clusters	repeat	reflexed
Andenken an Alma de l'Aigle	light pink	medium	semi-double	cupped	moderate	small clusters	repeat	plain
André Leroy d'Angers	medium red	large	double to full	cupped	moderate	singly	repeat	plain
Andrea Stelzer	light pink	large	double to full	high-centered	none	small clusters	repeat	reflexed
Andrewsii	medium pink	small	semi-double	cupped	moderate	small clusters	once	plain
Anemone	light pink	large	single	flat	none	singly	repeat	plain
Angel Darling	mauve	small	single	open	slight	small clusters	repeat	ruffled
Angel Face	mauve	large	double to full	cupped	strong	small clusters	repeat	ruffled
Angela	deep pink	medium	double to full	cupped	none	small clusters	repeat	reflexed
Angela Rippon	medium pink	small	double to full	cupped	slight	small clusters	repeat	reflexed
Angelina	pink blend	large	single	open	moderate	small clusters	repeat	plain
Angelique	orange blend	large	double to full	high-centered	slight	singly	repeat	reflexed
Angelita	white	small	very full	cupped	none	small clusters	repeat	reflexed
Angel's Blush	apricot blend	small	double to full	high-centered	slight	small clusters	repeat	reflexed
Anita	pink blend	large	double to full	high-centered	slight	small clusters	repeat	reflexed
Anita Charles	orange-pink	small	double to full	high-centered	moderate	small clusters	repeat	reflexed
Ann Aberconway	apricot blend	large	double to full	cupped	slight	small clusters	repeat	plain
Ann Endt	dark red	medium	single	flat	strong	small clusters	repeat	plain
Anna de Diesbach	deep pink	medium	double to full	cupped	strong	singly	repeat	plain
Anna Ford	orange blend	small	semi-double	open	slight	large clusters	repeat	reflexed
Anna Livia	orange-pink	large	double to full	open	slight	small clusters	repeat	reflexed
Anna Louisa	light pink	medium	double to full	cupped	slight	large clusters	repeat	reflexed
Anna Olivier	pink blend	large	double to full	high-centered	moderate	small clusters	repeat	ruffled

NAME	BLOOM COLOR	FLOWER SIZE	FLOWER TYPE	FLOWER SHAPE	FRAGRANCE AMOUNT	FLOWERING HABIT	FLOWERING INCIDENCE	PETAL SHAPE
Anna Pavlova	light pink	large	double to full	high-centered	strong	small clusters	repeat	reflexed
Anna Zinkeisen	light yellow	large	double to full	rosette	moderate	small clusters	repeat	plain
Anne Cocker	orange-pink	medium	double	high-centered	none	small clusters	repeat	reflexed
Anne de Bretagne	deep pink	medium	double to full	high-centered	none	small clusters	repeat	reflexed
Anne Diamond	apricot blend	medium	double to full	cupped	none	small clusters	repeat	plain
Anne Harkness	apricot blend	medium	double to full	cupped	none	truss	repeat	ruffled
Anne Letts	pink blend	large	double to full	high-centered	none	small clusters	repeat	reflexed
Anne-Marie de Montravel	white	small	double to full	globular	slight	large clusters	repeat	frilled
Anne Marie Trechslin	deep pink	large	double to full	high-centered	moderate	small clusters	repeat	reflexed
Anne Morrow Lindbergh	pink blend	large	double to full	high-centered	slight	singly	repeat	reflexed
Anne of Geierstein	dark red	small	single	open	strong	small clusters	once	plain
Anneka	yellow blend	medium	double to full	cupped	moderate	singly	repeat	reflexed
Anne's Delight	medium pink	small	double to full	high-centered	none	singly	repeat	reflexed
Annie Vibert	white blend	medium	double to full	cupped	moderate	large clusters	repeat	plain
Annie's Song	orange-pink	medium	double to full	high-centered	slight	large clusters	repeat	reflexed
Another Chance	white	large	double to full	cupped	slight	singly	repeat	reflexed
Anthony Meilland	medium yellow	large	double to full	cupped	slight	small clusters	repeat	ruffled
Antigone	yellow blend	large	double to full	high-centered	moderate	singly	repeat	reflexed
Antigua	apricot blend	large	double to full	high-centered	slight	singly	repeat	reflexed
Antike 89	pink blend	large	very full	globular	slight	small clusters	repeat	plain
Antique	red blend	medium	double to full	cupped	none	small clusters	repeat	reflexed
Antique Rose	medium pink	medium	double to full	high-centered	slight	singly	repeat	reflexed
Antique Silk	white	large	double to full	high-centered	none	small clusters	repeat	reflexed
Antoine Rivoire	light pink	large	double to full	rosette	slight	singly	repeat	reflexed
Antonia Ridge	medium red	large	double to full	high-centered	slight	singly	repeat	reflexed
Antonine d'Ormois	light pink	medium	double to full	pompons	moderate	small clusters	once	plain
Anusheh	red blend	medium	double to full	rosette	slight	small clusters	repeat	plain
Anytime	orange-pink	small	single	open	none	small clusters	repeat	plain
Apart	mauve blend	medium	semi-double	open	moderate	small clusters	repeat	ruffled
Apfelblüte	white	medium	single	open	none	large clusters	repeat	plain
Apogée	orange blend	large	double to full	cupped	slight	small clusters	repeat	reflexed
Apollo	medium yellow	large	double to full	high-centered	slight	singly	repeat	reflexed
Apothecary's Rose	deep pink	medium	semi-double	open	strong	small clusters	once	plain
Apple Blossom	light pink	small	double to full	open	slight	truss	once	ruffled
Applejack	pink blend	large	semi-double	flat	strong	small clusters	repeat	plain
Appreciation	medium red	large	double to full	cupped	slight	small clusters	repeat	reflexed
Apricot Delight	apricot blend	large	double to full	high-centered	moderate	small clusters	repeat	reflexed
Apricot Gem	apricot blend	medium	double to full	high-centered	none	small clusters	repeat	reflexed
Apricot Nectar	apricot blend	large	double to full	cupped	moderate	small clusters	repeat	reflexed
Apricot Queen	apricot blend	large	double to full	open	slight	small clusters	repeat	reflexed
Apricot Silk	apricot blend	large	double to full	high-centered	slight	small clusters	repeat	reflexed
Apricot Summer	apricot blend	small	double to full	rosette	none	small clusters	repeat	plain
Apricot Sunblaze	orange-red	small	double to full	flat	moderate	large clusters	repeat	reflexed
April Hamer	pink blend	large	double to full	high-centered	moderate	singly	repeat	reflexed
Aquarius	pink blend	medium	double to full	high-centered	slight	small clusters	repeat	reflexed
Arabian Nights	orange-pink	large	double to full	cupped	none	small clusters	repeat	reflexed
Aramis	dark red	medium	semi-double	cupped	moderate	small clusters	repeat	plain
ARC Angel	orange blend	large	double to full	high-centered	slight	small clusters	repeat	reflexed
Archduke Charles	red blend	medium	double to full	cupped	moderate	small clusters	repeat	plain
Archiduc Joseph	pink blend	large	very full	quartered	moderate	small clusters	repeat	reflexed
Archiduchesse Elizabeth d'Autriche	medium pink	large	double to full	flat	slight	small clusters	repeat	plain
Arctic Sunrise	white	small	double to full	flat	none	large clusters	repeat	plain
Ardoisée de Lyon	mauve	large	double to full	quartered	strong	singly	repeat	plain
Ards Beauty	medium yellow	medium	double to full	cupped	moderate	small clusters	repeat	reflexed
Ards Rover	dark red	large	double to full	globular	strong	singly	once	reflexed
Arethusa	yellow blend	medium	double to full	cupped	none	small clusters	repeat	reflexed
Arianna	pink blend	large	double to full	high-centered	slight	singly	repeat	reflexed
Arielle Dombasle	orange blend	large	double	high-centered	slight	small clusters	repeat	plain
Aristide Briand	mauve	small	semi-double	open	none	large clusters	once	plain
Aristobule	deep pink	medium	double to full	quartered	moderate	small clusters	once	plain
Arizona	orange blend	large	double to full	high-centered	moderate	small clusters	repeat	reflexed
Arizona Sunset	yellow blend	small	double to full	cupped	slight	small clusters	repeat	reflexed
Armada	medium pink	medium	double to full	cupped	moderate	small clusters	repeat	reflexed
Arnold	medium red	medium	single	open	slight	small clusters	repeat	plain
Arrillaga	light pink	large	double to full	high-centered	strong	singly	repeat	reflexed
Arthur Bell	medium yellow	large	double to full	cupped	moderate	small clusters	repeat	plain
Arthur de Sansal	mauve	medium	very full	rosette	strong	small clusters	repeat	plain
Arthur Hillier	deep pink	large	single	open	none	small clusters	once	plain
Artistic	orange blend	medium	semi-double	open	moderate	small clusters	repeat	plain
Artistry	orange blend	large	double to full	high-centered	slight	small clusters	repeat	reflexed
Aruba	medium red	medium	double to full	high-centered	none	singly	repeat	reflexed
Aschermittwoch	white blend	large	double to full	open	none	small clusters	once	reflexed
Ascot	apricot blend	large	double to full	open	none	small clusters	repeat	ruffled
Aspen	medium yellow	small	semi-double	open	slight	small clusters	repeat	plain
Assemblage des Beautés	dark red	medium	very full	flat	strong	small clusters	once	plain
Assiniboine	medium red	medium	semi-double	open	slight	small clusters	repeat	plain
Asso di Cuori	dark red	large	double to full	high-centered	none	singly	repeat	reflexed
Asta von Parpart	mauve	medium	double to full	rosette	slight	large clusters	once	ruffled
Astra	medium pink	small	double to full	high-centered	none	small clusters	repeat	reflexed
Astra Desmond	yellow blend	small	semi-double	open	moderate	truss	once	plain
Astrée	pink blend	large	double to full	high-centered	strong	singly	repeat	reflexed
Astrid Lindgren	light pink	medium	double to full	cupped	slight	truss	repeat	reflexed
Athena	white blend	large	double to full	high-centered	none	singly	repeat	reflexed
Atlantic Star	orange-pink	large	double to full	high-centered	slight	small clusters	repeat	reflexed
Atlantis	mauve	large	single	flat	none	small clusters	repeat	plain
Auckland Metro	white blend	large	double to full	rosette	moderate	small clusters	repeat	ruffled
Audie Murphy	medium red	large	double to full	open	slight	small clusters	repeat	reflexed
Audrey Hepburn	light pink	large	double to full	high-centered	moderate	small clusters	repeat	reflexed
August Seebauer	deep pink	large	double to full	high-centered	none	small clusters	repeat	reflexed
Auguste Gervais	apricot blend	large	double to full	cupped	moderate	small clusters	once	plain
Auguste Renoir	medium pink	large	very full	cupped	strong	singly	repeat	reflexed
Augustine Guinoisseau	white blend	large	double to full	globular	strong	small clusters	repeat	reflexed
Aunty Dora	mauve	medium	semi-double	cupped	none	small clusters	repeat	plain
Auria Sunblaze	deep yellow	small	double to full	high-centered	none	small clusters	repeat	reflexed
Australia Felix	pink blend	medium	semi-double	cupped	moderate	small clusters	repeat	reflexed
Australian Bicentennial	medium red	large	double to full	high-centered	moderate	small clusters	repeat	reflexed
Australian Centre Gold	medium yellow	medium	semi-double	flat	moderate	small clusters	repeat	plain
Australian Gold	apricot blend	medium	double to full	high-centered	slight	small clusters	repeat	reflexed
Autumn	orange blend	large	double to full	high-centered	strong	singly	repeat	reflexed
Autumn Damask	medium pink	medium	double to full	cupped	strong	small clusters	repeat	plain
Autumn Delight	white	large	semi-double	flat	moderate	large clusters	repeat	plain
Autumn Kiss	medium pink	small	double to full	cupped	slight	small clusters	repeat	reflexed
Autumn Magic	orange blend	small	double to full	high-centered	none	small clusters	repeat	reflexed
Autumn Sunblaze	orange-red	small	semi-double	cupped	none	small clusters	repeat	reflexed
Autumn Sunlight	orange-red	large	double to full	cupped	moderate	small clusters	repeat	reflexed
Autumn Sunset	apricot blend	medium	double to full	cupped	strong	large clusters	repeat	reflexed
Avalanche Rose	medium red	medium	double to full	cupped	slight	small clusters	repeat	reflexed
Avandel	yellow blend	small	double to full	cupped	moderate	small clusters	repeat	reflexed
Ave Maria	orange-pink	large	double to full	high-centered	moderate	small clusters	repeat	reflexed
Aviateur Blériot	yellow blend	small	double to full	cupped	moderate	small clusters	once	plain
Avignon	medium yellow	medium	double to full	cupped	moderate	small clusters	repeat	reflexed
Avocet	orange blend	large	semi-double	open	moderate	small clusters	repeat	ruffled
Avon	dark red	large	double to full	high-centered	strong	small clusters	repeat	reflexed
Awakening	light pink	medium	double to full	cupped	moderate	small clusters	repeat	reflexed
Awareness	medium pink	large	double to full	high-centered	slight	small clusters	repeat	reflexed
Ayrshire Queen	dark red	small	semi-double	open	slight	small clusters	once	plain

NAME	BLOOM COLOR	FLOWER SIZE	FLOWER TYPE	FLOWER SHAPE	FRAGRANCE AMOUNT	FLOWERING HABIT	FLOWERING INCIDENCE	PETAL SHAPE
Aztec	orange-red	large	double to full	cupped	moderate	small clusters	repeat	reflexed
Azure Sea	mauve	large	double to full	high-centered	slight	small clusters	repeat	reflexed
Babe	pink blend	small	semi-double	cupped	none	small clusters	repeat	plain
Baby Alberic	light yellow	small	double to full	flat	slight	small clusters	repeat	plain
Baby Baccarà	orange-red	small	double	open	slight	singly	repeat	plain
Baby Betsy McCall	light pink	small	double to full	open	slight	small clusters	repeat	reflexed
Baby Bettina	orange-red	small	double to full	cupped	slight	small clusters	repeat	reflexed
Baby Bio	deep yellow	medium	double to full	cupped	none	small clusters	repeat	reflexed
Baby Blanket	light pink	small	double to full	open	slight	small clusters	repeat	reflexed
Baby Cécile Brünner	light pink	small	double to full	flat	slight	large clusters	repeat	plain
Baby Darling	apricot blend	small	double to full	cupped	none	small clusters	repeat	reflexed
Baby Eclipse	light yellow	small	semi-double	open	slight	small clusters	repeat	plain
Baby Faurax	mauve	small	double to full	rosette	slight	large clusters	repeat	plain
Baby Gold Star	deep yellow	small	semi-double	open	slight	small clusters	repeat	plain
Baby Grand	medium pink	small	double to full	quartered	slight	small clusters	repeat	reflexed
Baby Jayne	medium pink	small	double to full	cupped	slight	small clusters	repeat	reflexed
Baby Katie	pink blend	small	double to full	high-centered	none	small clusters	repeat	reflexed
Baby Love	deep yellow	small	double to full	open	slight	small clusters	repeat	ruffled
Baby Masquerade	red blend	small	semi-double	flat	slight	small clusters	repeat	reflexed
Baby Pinocchio	pink blend	small	double	open	moderate	small clusters	repeat	plain
Baccará	orange-red	medium	double to full	flat	none	small clusters	repeat	reflexed
Ballade	light pink	medium	double to full	open	none	small clusters	repeat	reflexed
Ballerina	medium pink	small	single	open	slight	large clusters	repeat	plain
Ballet	deep pink	large	double to full	high-centered	none	small clusters	repeat	reflexed
Baltimore Belle	light pink	medium	double to full	cupped	moderate	large clusters	once	plain
Bambula	orange-pink	large	double to full	open	slight	small clusters	repeat	reflexed
Bantry Bay	medium pink	large	double to full	cupped	slight	small clusters	repeat	reflexed
Banzai '83	yellow blend	large	double to full	open	slight	small clusters	repeat	reflexed
Barbara Bush	pink blend	large	double to full	cupped	moderate	small clusters	repeat	reflexed
Barby	medium pink	large	double to full	high-centered	none	singly	repeat	reflexed
Baron de Bonstetten	dark red	large	double to full	flat	strong	singly	repeat	reflexed
Baron de Wassenaer	deep pink	medium	double to full	cupped	strong	small clusters	once	reflexed
Baron Girod de l'Ain	red blend	large	double to full	cupped	moderate	small clusters	repeat	ruffled
Baron J.B.Gonella	pink blend	large	double to full	cupped	moderate	small clusters	repeat	plain
Baronne Edmond de Rothschild	red blend	large	double to full	cupped	strong	small clusters	repeat	reflexed
Baronne Henriette de Snoy	pink blend	large	very full	quartered	moderate	small clusters	repeat	reflexed
Baronne Prévost	medium pink	large	double to full	flat	moderate	singly	repeat	plain
Baroness Rothschild	light pink	large	double to full	cupped	none	singly	repeat	plain
Baroque	mauve	small	semi-double	open	moderate	small clusters	repeat	plain
Basildon Bond	apricot blend	medium	double to full	cupped	moderate	small clusters	repeat	reflexed
Bassino	medium red	small	single	open	none	small clusters	repeat	plain
Basye's Blueberry	medium pink	small	single	open	moderate	small clusters	once	plain
Basye's Purple Rose	mauve	large	single	open	slight	small clusters	repeat	plain
Baxter Beauty	apricot blend	medium	semi-double	cupped	moderate	singly	repeat	plain
Bayadère	apricot blend	large	very full	quartered	slight	singly	repeat	reflexed
Bazaar	medium pink	medium	semi-double	high-centered	strong	small clusters	repeat	plain
Beau Narcisse	mauve	small	double to full	globular	moderate	small clusters	once	plain
Beaute	apricot blend	large	double to full	high-centered	moderate	small clusters	repeat	reflexed
Beautiful Britain	orange-red	medium	semi-double	cupped	slight	small clusters	repeat	reflexed
Beauty of Rosemawr	pink blend	small	double to full	cupped	slight	small clusters	repeat	plain
Beauty Secret	medium red	small	double to full	high-centered	slight	small clusters	repeat	reflexed
Begonia	pink blend	large	double to full	high-centered	none	small clusters	repeat	ruffled
Behold	medium yellow	small	double to full	high-centered	none	small clusters	repeat	reflexed
Bel Ange	medium pink	large	double to full	high-centered	moderate	small clusters	repeat	reflexed
Belami	orange-pink	large	double to full	high-centered	moderate	small clusters	repeat	reflexed
Belinda (Tantau)	orange blend	medium	double to full	high-centered	slight	small clusters	repeat	reflexed
Belinda (Bentall)	medium pink	small	semi-double	cupped	moderate	large clusters	repeat	ruffled
Belinda's Dream	medium pink	large	double to full	cupped	moderate	small clusters	repeat	reflexed
Bella Donna	light pink	medium	double to full	flat	strong	small clusters	once	plain
Bella Minijet	yellow blend	small	double to full	cupped	none	small clusters	repeat	reflexed
Bella Rosa	medium pink	medium	double to full	cupped	slight	small clusters	repeat	reflexed
Bellard	light pink	medium	very full	quartered	strong	small clusters	once	plain
Belle Amour	light pink	medium	semi-double	cupped	strong	small clusters	once	plain
Belle Blonde	medium yellow	large	double to full	high-centered	moderate	singly	repeat	reflexed
Belle de Crécy	mauve	medium	double to full	flat	moderate	small clusters	once	plain
Belle de Ségur	light pink	medium	double to full	cupped	strong	small clusters	once	plain
Belle des Jardins	mauve blend	medium	very full	globular	strong	small clusters	once	plain
Belle d'Orléans	orange-red	large	double to full	cupped	none	small clusters	repeat	reflexed
Belle Epoque	orange blend	large	double to full	high centered	moderate	small clusters	repeat	reflexed
Belle Isis	light pink	medium	very full	rosette	strong	small clusters	once	plain
Belle Lyonnaise	light yellow	large	double to full	quartered	moderate	small clusters	repeat	reflexed
Belle of Berlin	medium pink	large	double to full	high-centered	slight	singly	repeat	reflexed
Belle Poitevine	medium pink	large	semi-double	flat	moderate	small clusters	repeat	plain
Belle Portugaise	light pink	large	semi-double	open	moderate	small clusters	once	plain
Belle sans Flatterie	mauve blend	medium	double to full	quartered	moderate	small clusters	once	plain
Belle Story	light pink	large	double to full	open	moderate	small clusters	repeat	reflexed
Belle Vichysoise	light pink	small	double to full	cupped	moderate	large clusters	repeat	plain
Belle Virginie	mauve blend	medium	double to full	rosette	moderate	small clusters	once	plain
Bellona	medium yellow	large	double to full	high-centered	none	small clusters	repeat	reflexed
Belvedere	medium pink	small	double to full	flat	strong	large clusters	once	plain
Ben-Hur	medium red	large	double to full	high-centered	moderate	small clusters	repeat	reflexed
Bendigold	orange-red	medium	double to full	cupped	slight	small clusters	repeat	reflexed
Bengale Rouge	medium red	extra large	double to full	open	none	small clusters	repeat	plain
Bengali	orange-red	medium	double to full	cupped	slight	small clusters	repeat	reflexed
Benita	deep yellow	medium	double to full	open	slight	small clusters	repeat	ruffled
Benjamin Franklin	light pink	large	double to full	high-centered	slight	singly	repeat	reflexed
Bennett's Seedling	white	medium	double to full	flat	slight	small clusters	once	plain
Benson and Hedges Gold	yellow blend	medium	double to full	high-centered	slight	small clusters	repeat	reflexed
Benvenuto	medium red	medium	semi-double	open	slight	small clusters	repeat	reflexed
Bérénice	red blend	large	very full	globular	strong	small clusters	once	plain
Berkeley Beauty	mauve blend	small	double to full	high-centered	none	singly	repeat	reflexed
Berlin	orange blend	large	single	open	slight	large clusters	repeat	plain
Bermuda Kathleen	medium red	medium	single	cupped	none	small clusters	repeat	plain
Bernina	white	medium	double to full	high-centered	slight	small clusters	repeat	reflexed
Bernstein-Rose	deep yellow	medium	double to full	rosette	slight	small clusters	repeat	plain
Bert Mulley	medium pink	small	double to full	cupped	moderate	large clusters	repeat	plain
Beryl Bach	yellow blend	large	double to full	cupped	moderate	small clusters	repeat	reflexed
Best Wishes	red blend	large	double to full	cupped	slight	small clusters	repeat	reflexed
Betsy McCall	orange-pink	large	double to full	open	moderate	small clusters	repeat	reflexed
Betsy Ross	dark red	large	double to full	high-centered	moderate	small clusters	repeat	reflexed
Bettina	orange-pink	large	double to full	high-centered	slight	small clusters	repeat	reflexed
Betty Harkness	orange blend	medium	double to full	cupped	moderate	large clusters	repeat	reflexed
Betty Prior	medium pink	medium	single	cupped	none	small clusters	repeat	plain
Betty Uprichard	apricot blend	large	double to full	cupped	strong	small clusters	repeat	reflexed
Beverly Hills	orange blend	large	double to full	high-centered	none	small clusters	repeat	reflexed
Bewitched	medium pink	large	double to full	high-centered	moderate	singly	repeat	reflexed
Bianco	white	small	double to full	cupped	none	small clusters	repeat	reflexed
Bibi Maizoon	deep pink	medium	very full	cupped	strong	small clusters	repeat	plain
Bicolette	red blend	large	double to full	high-centered	none	singly	repeat	plain
Biddulph Grange	red blend	medium	double to full	open	none	small clusters	repeat	plain
Big Ben	dark red	large	double to full	high-centered	strong	singly	repeat	reflexed
Big John	medium red	small	double to full	high-centered	none	small clusters	repeat	reflexed
Bijou d'Or	deep yellow	small	double to full	cupped	slight	small clusters	repeat	reflexed
Bill Slim	orange-pink	large	double to full	cupped	slight	small clusters	repeat	reflexed
Bill Temple	white blend	large	double to full	high-centered	slight	small clusters	repeat	reflexed
Bill Warriner	orange-pink	medium	double to full	cupped	slight	small clusters	repeat	reflexed

NAME	BLOOM COLOR	FLOWER SIZE	FLOWER TYPE	FLOWER SHAPE	FRAGRANCE AMOUNT	FLOWERING HABIT	FLOWERING INCIDENCE	PETAL SHAPE
Billard et Barré	medium yellow	large	very full	cupped	moderate	small clusters	repeat	reflexed
Billy Boiler	medium red	medium	semi-double	cupped	moderate	small clusters	once	plain
Bing Crosby	orange blend	large	double to full	cupped	slight	singly	repeat	reflexed
Birmingham Post	deep pink	large	double to full	cupped	moderate	small clusters	repeat	reflexed
Birthday Present	dark red	large	double to full	high-centered	strong	small clusters	repeat	reflexed
Bishofsstadt Paderborn	orange-red	large	semi-double	open	moderate	small clusters	repeat	plain
Bishop Darlington	apricot blend	large	semi-double	cupped	moderate	small clusters	repeat	plain
Bit o' Spring	pink blend	small	double to full	high-centered	moderate	small clusters	repeat	reflexed
Bit o' Sunshine	deep yellow	small	double to full	open	slight	small clusters	repeat	reflexed
Black Beauty	dark red	large	double to full	cupped	none	small clusters	repeat	reflexed
Black Boy	dark red	large	double to full	cupped	moderate	small clusters	once	plain
Black Garnet	dark red	large	double to full	high-centered	none	small clusters	repeat	reflexed
Black Ice	dark red	large	double to full	cupped	none	small clusters	repeat	reflexed
Black Jack	dark red	small	double to full	high-centered	slight	small clusters	repeat	reflexed
Black Jade	dark red	small	double to full	high-centered	none	small clusters	repeat	reflexed
Black Magic	dark red	large	double to full	cupped	strong	small clusters	once	reflexed
Black Prince	dark red	large	double to full	cupped	strong	small clusters	repeat	reflexed
Black Velvet	dark red	large	double to full	high-centered	moderate	singly	repeat	reflexed
Blairii No. 1	medium pink	medium	double to full	flat	strong	small clusters	once	reflexed
Blairii No. 2	light pink	medium	double to full	flat	strong	small clusters	once	reflexed
Blanc de Vibert	white	medium	double to full	cupped	strong	small clusters	repeat	plain
Blanc Double de Coubert	white	large	semi-double	open	strong	small clusters	repeat	plain
Blanche de Belgique	white	large	very full	flat	strong	small clusters	once	plain
Blanche Lafitte	white blend	medium	double to full	cupped	moderate	small clusters	repeat	plain
Blanche Moreau	white	large	double to full	cupped	strong	small clusters	repeat	plain
Blanchefleur	white	medium	very full	cupped	strong	small clusters	once	plain
Blaze	medium red	medium	semi-double	cupped	slight	large clusters	repeat	plain
Blessings	orange-pink	large	double to full	cupped	slight	small clusters	repeat	reflexed
Bleu Magenta	mauve	small	double to full	cupped	slight	small clusters	once	plain
Blizzard	white	small	double to full	cupped	none	small clusters	repeat	reflexed
Bloomer Girl	orange-pink	small	double to full	cupped	slight	small clusters	repeat	reflexed
Bloomfield Abundance	light pink	small	double to full	rosette	slight	small clusters	repeat	plain
Bloomfield Courage	red blend	small	single	cupped	none	large clusters	once	plain
Bloomfield Dainty	medium yellow	small	single	open	moderate	small clusters	repeat	plain
Bloomin' Easy	medium red	medium	semi-double	cupped	moderate	singly	repeat	plain
Blossomtime	medium pink	large	double to full	high-centered	moderate	small clusters	repeat	reflexed
Blue Bajou	mauve blend	large	double to full	cupped	slight	small clusters	repeat	plain
Blue Boy	mauve	large	double to full	high-centered	strong	small clusters	once	reflexed
Blue Diamond	mauve	large	double to full	cupped	slight	small clusters	repeat	reflexed
Blue Moon	mauve	large	double to full	cupped	strong	small clusters	repeat	reflexed
Blue Nile	mauve	large	double to full	high-centered	strong	small clusters	repeat	reflexed
Blue Parfum	mauve	large	double to full	high-centered	strong	small clusters	repeat	reflexed
Blue Peter	mauve blend	small	semi-double	cupped	slight	small clusters	repeat	plain
Blue River	mauve blend	large	double to full	high-centered	strong	small clusters	repeat	reflexed
Bluesette	mauve	small	very full	flat	slight	large clusters	repeat	plain
Blumenschmidt	yellow blend	medium	double to full	cupped	slight	small clusters	repeat	reflexed
Blumenwunder	deep pink	medium	semi-double	open	none	large clusters	repeat	plain
Blush Boursault	pink blend	medium	very full	globular	none	small clusters	once	reflexed
Blush Damask	light pink	medium	double to full	cupped	strong	small clusters	once	plain
Blush Hip	light pink	medium	double to full	flat	strong	small clusters	once	plain
Blush Noisette	white	small	semi-double	cupped	moderate	large clusters	repeat	plain
Blush Rambler	light pink	small	semi-double	flat	slight	large clusters	once	ruffled
Blushing Lucy	light pink	small	semi-double	cupped	moderate	large clusters	repeat	plain
Bob Hope	medium red	large	double to full	high-centered	moderate	singly	repeat	reflexed
Bob Woolley	apricot blend	large	very full	high-centered	slight	singly	repeat	reflexed
Bobbie James	white	small	single	cupped	strong	large clusters	once	plain
Bobby Charlton	pink blend	extra large	double to full	high-centered	strong	singly	repeat	reflexed
Bobby Dazzler	apricot blend	large	very full	cupped	slight	small clusters	repeat	reflexed
Bon Silène	deep pink	medium	double to full	cupped	strong	small clusters	repeat	plain
Bon Silène Blanc	light yellow	medium	double to full	cupped	moderate	small clusters	repeat	plain
Bonfire	medium red	small	double to full	open	slight	large clusters	once	plain
Bonfire Night	red blend	large	semi-double	globular	slight	small clusters	repeat	reflexed
Bonica	medium pink	medium	semi-double	open	none	small clusters	repeat	plain
Bonn	orange-red	medium	semi-double	open	moderate	large clusters	repeat	plain
Bonnie Hamilton	orange-red	medium	double to full	high-centered	slight	small clusters	repeat	reflexed
Bonny	medium pink	small	double to full	globular	slight	small clusters	repeat	plain
Bonsoir	medium pink	extra large	double to full	high-centered	strong	small clusters	repeat	reflexed
Border King	medium red	small	semi-double	open	none	truss	repeat	plain
Border Queen	orange-pink	medium	single	cupped	none	truss	repeat	ruffled
Borderer	pink blend	medium	semi-double	cupped	slight	small clusters	repeat	ruffled
Bordure Rose	pink blend	large	double to full	cupped	none	small clusters	repeat	reflexed
Born Free	orange-red	small	double to full	open	none	small clusters	repeat	reflexed
Botanica	light pink	medium	double	high-centered	strong	large clusters	repeat	plain
Botzaris	white	medium	very full	quartered	strong	small clusters	once	plain
Bougainville	pink blend	medium	very full	cupped	slight	small clusters	repeat	plain
Boule de Neige	white	medium	double to full	flat	strong	small clusters	repeat	plain
Bouquet de Venus	light pink	medium	double to full	quartered	strong	small clusters	once	plain
Bouquet d'Or	yellow blend	large	very full	cupped	strong	small clusters	repeat	reflexed
Bourbon Rose	red/pink/purple	medium	double to full	rosette	moderate	small clusters	repeat	plain
Bourgogne	medium red	medium	single	cupped	moderate	small clusters	once	plain
Bow Bells	deep pink	medium	double to full	cupped	slight	small clusters	repeat	plain
Boy O Boy	medium red	medium	single	cupped	none	large clusters	repeat	plain
Boys' Brigade	medium red	small	single	open	none	large clusters	repeat	plain
Bradley Craig	orange-red	medium	double to full	cupped	slight	small clusters	repeat	reflexed
Brandenburg	orange-red	large	double to full	high-centered	none	small clusters	repeat	reflexed
Brandy	apricot blend	large	double to full	high-centered	slight	singly	repeat	reflexed
Brasilia	red blend	large	double to full	high-centered	slight	singly	repeat	reflexed
Brass Band	apricot blend	medium	very full	cupped	slight	small clusters	repeat	ruffled
Brass Ring	orange blend	small	double to full	flat	none	large clusters	repeat	reflexed
Brave Heart	medium pink	medium	double to full	high-centered	moderate	small clusters	repeat	reflexed
Breath of Life	apricot blend	large	double to full	cupped	slight	small clusters	repeat	ruffled
Breathless	deep pink	extra large	double to full	high-centered	slight	singly	repeat	reflexed
Bredon	apricot blend	medium	double to full	rosette	moderate	small clusters	repeat	plain
Breeze Hill	apricot blend	large	very full	cupped	moderate	small clusters	once	plain
Brenda	light pink	small	single	open	moderate	small clusters	once	plain
Brenda Colvin	light pink	small	single	open	strong	corymb	once	plain
Brennus	dark red	medium	double to full	cupped	slight	small clusters	once	ruffled
Bridal Pink	medium pink	medium	double to full	high-centered	moderate	small clusters	repeat	reflexed
Bridal White	white	medium	double to full	high-centered	slight	small clusters	repeat	reflexed
Bride	light pink	large	double to full	high-centered	moderate	small clusters	repeat	reflexed
Bride's Dream	light pink	large	double	high-centered	slight	singly	repeat	plain
Brigadoon	pink blend	extra large	double to full	high-centered	moderate	small clusters	repeat	reflexed
Bright Beauty	orange-red	large	double to full	high-centered	slight	singly	repeat	reflexed
Bright Fire	dark red	large	semi-double	cupped	slight	small clusters	repeat	plain
Bright Melody	medium red	large	double to full	cupped	slight	small clusters	repeat	reflexed
Bright Smile	medium yellow	medium	semi-double	flat	slight	small clusters	repeat	plain
Brilliant Meillandina	orange	small	semi-double	cupped	none	large clusters	repeat	reflexed
Brisbane Blush	red blend	large	double to full	high-centered	moderate	small clusters	repeat	reflexed
Britannia	red blend	small	single	open	none	large clusters	repeat	plain
Broadway	yellow blend	large	double to full	high-centered	strong	singly	repeat	reflexed
Bronze Masterpiece	apricot blend	extra large	double to full	high-centered	moderate	singly	repeat	reflexed
Brother Cadfael	medium pink	medium	double to full	cupped	strong	small clusters	repeat	plain
Brown Velvet	russet	medium	double to full	flat	slight	small clusters	repeat	reflexed
Brownie	russet	large	double to full	flat	slight	small clusters	repeat	reflexed
Buccaneer	medium yellow	large	double to full	cupped	moderate	small clusters	repeat	reflexed
Buff Beauty	apricot blend	medium	double to full	cupped	moderate	small clusters	repeat	plain

NAME	BLOOM COLOR	FLOWER SIZE	FLOWER TYPE	FLOWER SHAPE	FRAGRANCE AMOUNT	FLOWERING HABIT	FLOWERING INCIDENCE	PETAL SHAPE
Buffalo Gal	deep pink	medium	semi-double	flat	strong	small clusters	repeat	ruffled
Buisman's Triumph	medium pink	medium	semi-double	open	slight	small clusters	repeat	plain
Bullata	medium pink	medium	double to full	globular	strong	small clusters	once	plain
Bulls Red	medium red	large	double to full	high-centered	none	singly	repeat	reflexed
Burbank	medium pink	large	double to full	cupped	moderate	small clusters	repeat	reflexed
Burgundian Rose	pink blend	small	double to full	rosette	slight	small clusters	once	plain
Burma Star	apricot blend	large	double to full	cupped	slight	small clusters	repeat	reflexed
Burnaby	light yellow	large	double to full	high-centered	slight	small clusters	repeat	reflexed
Burning Love	medium red	large	double to full	cupped	moderate	small clusters	repeat	reflexed
Butterscotch	russet	large	double to full	cupped	slight	small clusters	repeat	reflexed
Buttons	pink blend	small	double to full	globular	none	singly	repeat	plain
Buttons 'n' Bows	deep pink	small	double to full	high-centered	slight	small clusters	repeat	reflexed
By Appointment	apricot blend	medium	double to full	cupped	slight	small clusters	repeat	reflexed
Cabbage Rose	medium pink	large	very full	cupped	strong	small clusters	once	plain
Cadillac	orange-pink	medium	double to full	high-centered	none	singly	repeat	reflexed
Café	russet	large	very full	flat	slight	small clusters	repeat	plain
Café Olé	russet	small	very full	cupped	moderate	small clusters	repeat	reflexed
Caid	orange blend	medium	double to full	cupped	slight	small clusters	repeat	reflexed
Cairngorm	orange blend	medium	double to full	cupped	slight	small clusters	repeat	reflexed
Cajun Spice	orange-red	large	semi-double	open	none	singly	repeat	plain
Cal Poly	medium yellow	small	double to full	cupped	slight	small clusters	repeat	reflexed
Caldwell Pink	medium pink	small	double to full	rosette	none	large clusters	repeat	plain
Calgold	deep yellow	small	double to full	high-centered	slight	small clusters	repeat	reflexed
Calocarpa	medium pink	medium	single	open	strong	small clusters	repeat	plain
Camaieux	mauve	medium	double to full	rosette	strong	small clusters	once	plain
Camaieux Fimbriata	mauve	medium	double	cupped	moderate	small clusters	once	plain
Camara	orange-red	large	double to full	high-centered	slight	singly	repeat	reflexed
Cambridgeshire	red blend	small	semi-double	cupped	none	large clusters	repeat	plain
Camélia Rose	light pink	medium	double to full	rosette	none	small clusters	repeat	plain
Camelot	orange-pink	extra large	double to full	cupped	moderate	small clusters	repeat	reflexed
Cameo	orange-pink	medium	double to full	cupped	none	large clusters	repeat	plain
Camp David	dark red	large	double to full	high-centered	moderate	singly	repeat	reflexed
Camphill Glory	pink blend	large	double to full	high-centered	slight	singly	repeat	reflexed
Can-Can	orange blend	large	double to full	high-centered	moderate	small clusters	repeat	ruffled
Canary	yellow blend	large	double to full	cupped	none	small clusters	repeat	reflexed
Canary Bird	deep yellow	small	single	open	none	singly	once	plain
Candella	red blend	large	double to full	high-centered	none	singly	repeat	reflexed
Candeur Lyonnaise	light yellow	extra large	double to full	cupped	none	singly	repeat	reflexed
Candlelight	deep yellow	large	double to full	high-centered	slight	singly	repeat	reflexed
Candy Cane	pink blend	small	semi-double	cupped	none	small clusters	repeat	plain
Candy Flo	apricot blend	large	double to full	cupped	none	small clusters	repeat	reflexed
Candy Rose	red blend	medium	double to full	cupped	slight	large clusters	repeat	plain
Candy Stripe	pink blend	large	double to full	high-centered	slight	small clusters	repeat	reflexed
Candy Sunblaze	deep pink	medium	double to full	high-centered	slight	small clusters	repeat	reflexed
Cannes Festival	yellow blend	large	double to full	cupped	slight	singly	repeat	reflexed
Cantabrigiensis	light yellow	medium	single	cupped	slight	singly	once	plain
Canterbury	medium pink	large	semi-double	open	moderate	small clusters	repeat	plain
Cape Cod	light pink	medium	single	open	none	large clusters	repeat	plain
Capitaine Basroger	red blend	large	double to full	cupped	strong	small clusters	once	plain
Capitaine John Ingram	mauve	medium	double to full	pompons	strong	small clusters	once	plain
Capri	orange-pink	large	double to full	high-centered	slight	small clusters	repeat	reflexed
Caprice	pink blend	small	double to full	cupped	slight	singly	repeat	reflexed
Capriole	medium pink	medium	semi-double	open	none	large clusters	repeat	plain
Captain Christy	light pink	large	double to full	globular	none	small clusters	once	reflexed
Captain Harry Stebbings	deep pink	large	double to full	high-centered	strong	singly	repeat	reflexed
Captain Samuel Holland	medium red	medium	double to full	open	slight	small clusters	repeat	plain
Captain Thomas	white	large	single	open	moderate	small clusters	repeat	plain
Captain Watkins	medium pink	medium	semi-double	open	none	small clusters	repeat	frilled
Cara Mia	medium red	large	double to full	high-centered	moderate	singly	repeat	reflexed
Carabella	yellow blend	small	single	open	slight	large clusters	repeat	plain
Cardinal de Richelieu	mauve	large	very full	cupped	strong	small clusters	once	plain
Cardinal Hume	mauve blend	medium	semi-double	cupped	slight	large clusters	repeat	plain
Cardinal Song	medium red	large	very full	high-centered	slight	singly	repeat	reflexed
Carefree Beauty	medium pink	medium	semi-double	open	slight	small clusters	repeat	plain
Carefree Delight	pink blend	medium	single	open	none	large clusters	repeat	plain
Carefree Wonder	pink blend	large	double to full	cupped	none	small clusters	repeat	ruffled
Careless Love	pink blend	large	double to full	cupped	strong	small clusters	repeat	reflexed
Careless Moment	pink blend	small	double to full	high-centered	slight	small clusters	repeat	reflexed
Caribbean	apricot blend	large	double to full	cupped	moderate	small clusters	repeat	plain
Carina	medium pink	large	double to full	high-centered	moderate	singly	repeat	reflexed
Carla	orange-pink	large	double to full	high-centered	slight	singly	repeat	reflexed
Carmen	medium red	large	single	flat	strong	small clusters	repeat	plain
Carnaval	red blend	large	double to full	open	none	small clusters	repeat	plain
Carnival Parade	yellow blend	small	double to full	high-centered	slight	small clusters	repeat	reflexed
Carol	pink blend	large	double to full	high-centered	slight	singly	repeat	reflexed
Carol Amling	medium pink	medium	double to full	open	none	small clusters	repeat	plain
Carol Ann	orange-pink	small	double to full	cupped	none	large clusters	repeat	plain
Carol-Jean	deep pink	small	double to full	cupped	slight	small clusters	repeat	reflexed
Carole Joy	medium red	large	double to full	cupped	moderate	small clusters	repeat	reflexed
Caroline Marniesse	white blend	medium	double to full	globular	moderate	large clusters	repeat	plain
Carrot Top	orange blend	small	double to full	high-centered	none	small clusters	repeat	reflexed
Carrousel	medium red	medium	double to full	open	moderate	small clusters	repeat	reflexed
Cary Grant	orange blend	large	double to full	high-centered	strong	singly	repeat	reflexed
Casa Blanca	white	medium	semi-double	open	none	small clusters	repeat	plain
Casanova	light yellow	large	double to full	high-centered	moderate	singly	repeat	reflexed
Cascabel	red blend	medium	double	globular	none	small clusters	repeat	reflexed
Casino	light yellow	large	double to full	high-centered	slight	singly	repeat	reflexed
Casque d'Or	medium yellow	large	double to full	high-centered	slight	small clusters	repeat	reflexed
Cassandra	medium red	large	double to full	high-centered	slight	singly	repeat	reflexed
Cassandre	medium red	medium	double to full	open	slight	small clusters	repeat	ruffled
Castle of Mey	orange blend	medium	double to full	high-centered	slight	small clusters	repeat	reflexed
Caterpillar	light pink	small	semi-double	open	none	truss	repeat	plain
Cathedral	apricot blend	large	double to full	cupped	slight	small clusters	repeat	reflexed
Cathedral Splendour	orange-pink	medium	semi-double	high-centered	moderate	small clusters	repeat	reflexed
Catherine de Würtemberg	light pink	large	very full	globular	slight	small clusters	once	ruffled
Catherine Deneuve	orange-pink	large	double to full	high-centered	strong	singly	repeat	reflexed
Catherine Guillot	deep pink	large	double to full	cupped	strong	small clusters	repeat	plain
Catherine McAuley	medium yellow	medium	double to full	cupped	none	small clusters	repeat	reflexed
Catherine Mermet	light pink	large	double to full	high-centered	moderate	small clusters	repeat	reflexed
Catherine Seyton	light pink	small	single	open	moderate	small clusters	once	plain
Cavalcade	red blend	medium	double to full	high-centered	strong	small clusters	repeat	reflexed
Cécile Brünner	light pink	small	double to full	flat	moderate	large clusters	repeat	plain
Cécile Lens	medium pink	small	semi-double	open	none	small clusters	repeat	reflexed
Cee Dee Moss	pink blend	medium	semi-double	cupped	slight	small clusters	repeat	plain
Celebrity	deep yellow	large	double to full	high-centered	moderate	singly	repeat	reflexed
Celestial	light pink	medium	double to full	open	strong	small clusters	once	plain
Célina	mauve	medium	semi-double	flat	moderate	small clusters	once	ruffled
Céline Delbard	orange blend	large	double to full	cupped	none	small clusters	repeat	reflexed
Céline Forestier	light yellow	large	very full	flat	strong	small clusters	repeat	plain
Celsiana	light pink	medium	semi-double	cupped	moderate	small clusters	once	plain
Centenaire de Lourdes	medium pink	medium	semi-double	cupped	none	large clusters	repeat	plain
Centenary	medium pink	medium	semi-double	cupped	none	large clusters	repeat	plain
Centifolia	medium pink	medium	double	flat	strong	small clusters	once	plain
Centifolia Muscosa	medium pink	large	double	flat	moderate	small clusters	once	plain
Centifolia Variegata	pink blend	large	very full	rosette	strong	small clusters	once	plain
Central Park	apricot blend	small	double to full	open	slight	small clusters	repeat	plain

NAME	BLOOM COLOR	FLOWER SIZE	FLOWER TYPE	FLOWER SHAPE	FRAGRANCE AMOUNT	FLOWERING HABIT	FLOWERING INCIDENCE	PETAL SHAPE
Centurion	dark red	large	double to full	cupped	slight	small clusters	repeat	plain
Century Two	medium pink	large	double to full	cupped	moderate	singly	repeat	reflexed
Cerise Bouquet	deep pink	medium	double to full	open	moderate	large clusters	repeat	plain
Cerys Ann	yellow blend	large	double to full	high-centered	slight	singly	repeat	reflexed
Césonie	deep pink	large	double to full	cupped	strong	small clusters	once	plain
Chablis	white	large	double to full	high-centered	slight	singly	repeat	reflexed
Champagne	yellow blend	extra large	double to full	high-centered	slight	singly	repeat	reflexed
Champagne Cocktail	yellow blend	medium	double to full	cupped	moderate	small clusters	repeat	ruffled
Champagne Pearl	apricot blend	large	semi-double	cupped	slight	large clusters	repeat	plain
Champion	yellow blend	large	double to full	high-centered	moderate	singly	repeat	reflexed
Champion of the World	medium pink	large	double to full	cupped	strong	singly	repeat	plain
Champlain	dark red	medium	double to full	cupped	slight	large clusters	repeat	plain
Champneys' Pink Cluster	light pink	small	double to full	cupped	strong	large clusters	repeat	plain
Champs-Elysées	dark red	large	double to full	cupped	slight	singly	repeat	reflexed
Chanelle	orange-pink	large	double to full	cupped	slight	small clusters	repeat	reflexed
Chaplin's Pink Climber	medium pink	large	semi-double	flat	slight	large clusters	once	reflexed
Chaplin's Pink Companion	light pink	medium	double to full	open	moderate	large clusters	repeat	plain
Charisma	red blend	medium	double to full	high-centered	slight	small clusters	repeat	reflexed
Charles Albanel	medium red	medium	double to full	cupped	moderate	small clusters	repeat	plain
Charles Austin	apricot blend	medium	very full	rosette	moderate	small clusters	repeat	plain
Charles de Gaulle	mauve blend	large	double to full	cupped	strong	small clusters	repeat	reflexed
Charles de Lapisse	light pink	large	double to full	cupped	slight	small clusters	repeat	reflexed
Charles de Mills	mauve	large	very full	quartered	strong	small clusters	once	plain
Charles Gater	medium red	extra large	double to full	globular	moderate	singly	repeat	ruffled
Charles Lawson	deep pink	large	double to full	cupped	moderate	small clusters	repeat	plain
Charles Lefèbvre	dark red	large	very full	cupped	moderate	singly	repeat	ruffled
Charles Mallerin	dark red	large	double to full	flat	strong	singly	repeat	reflexed
Charles Rennie Mackintosh	pink blend	medium	double to full	globular	strong	small clusters	repeat	plain
Charleston	yellow blend	large	very full	high-centered	slight	small clusters	repeat	reflexed
Charlie's Aunt	pink blend	large	very full	high-centered	moderate	singly	repeat	reflexed
Charlotte (Duehrsen)	orange-pink	large	very full	cupped	moderate	small clusters	repeat	plain
Charlotte (Austin)	light yellow	large	very full	cupped	moderate	small clusters	repeat	plain
Charlotte Armstrong	deep pink	large	double to full	high-centered	moderate	small clusters	repeat	reflexed
Charlotte Rampling	medium red	large	double to full	high-centered	strong	small clusters	repeat	reflexed
Charmian	medium pink	medium	very full	cupped	strong	small clusters	repeat	ruffled
Chasin' Rainbows	red blend	small	double to full	high-centered	slight	small clusters	repeat	plain
Château de Chenonceaux	medium pink	large	double to full	flat	none	small clusters	repeat	reflexed
Château de Clos Vougeot	dark red	large	very full	cupped	strong	small clusters	repeat	reflexed
Châtelaine	orange-pink	large	double to full	high-centered	moderate	small clusters	repeat	reflexed
Chattem Centennial	orange-red	small	double to full	cupped	slight	small clusters	repeat	reflexed
Chaucer	medium pink	large	double to full	cupped	strong	small clusters	repeat	plain
Chelsea Belle	medium red	small	double to full	high-centered	moderate	singly	repeat	reflexed
Chénédolé	orange-red	large	double	cupped	moderate	small clusters	once	reflexed
Cherish	orange-pink	large	double to full	high-centered	slight	small clusters	repeat	reflexed
Cherry Brandy	orange blend	large	double to full	high-centered	moderate	singly	repeat	reflexed
Cherry Meillandecor	red blend	small	single	open	none	small clusters	repeat	plain
Cherry Sunblaze	medium red	small	double to full	cupped	none	small clusters	repeat	reflexed
Cherry-Vanilla	pink blend	extra large	double to full	cupped	moderate	small clusters	repeat	reflexed
Cherub	pink blend	small	semi-double	cupped	slight	truss	once	plain
Cheshire Life	orange-red	large	double to full	high-centered	slight	singly	repeat	reflexed
Chevy Chase	dark red	small	very full	flat	slight	large clusters	once	plain
Chianti	mauve blend	large	double to full	cupped	strong	small clusters	once	ruffled
Chic	pink blend	medium	very full	cupped	slight	small clusters	repeat	reflexed
Chica	light pink	small	double	open	moderate	singly	repeat	plain
Chicago Peace	pink blend	extra large	double to full	high-centered	slight	small clusters	repeat	reflexed
Chick-A-Dee	medium pink	small	double to full	high-centered	slight	small clusters	repeat	reflexed
Child's Play	white	small	double to full	high-centered	moderate	small clusters	repeat	reflexed
Chimo	medium red	small	single	cupped	slight	singly	repeat	plain
China Doll	medium pink	medium	double to full	cupped	slight	truss	repeat	plain
Chinatown	deep yellow	large	double to full	cupped	strong	small clusters	repeat	reflexed
Chiquita	dark red	small	semi-double	flat	slight	singly	repeat	reflexed
Chivalry	red blend	large	double to full	flat	none	singly	repeat	reflexed
Chloris	light pink	medium	double to full	flat	strong	small clusters	once	ruffled
Choo-Choo Centennial	light pink	small	double to full	high-centered	slight	small clusters	repeat	reflexed
Chorus	orange-red	large	double to full	cupped	slight	small clusters	repeat	reflexed
Christian Dior	medium red	large	double to full	high-centered	slight	singly	repeat	reflexed
Christine, Climbing	deep yellow	large	double to full	high-centered	moderate	small clusters	repeat	reflexed
Christine Wright	medium pink	large	semi-double	cupped	moderate	small clusters	repeat	plain
Christopher	medium red	small	double to full	cupped	none	small clusters	repeat	reflexed
Christopher Columbus (Meilland)	orange blend	large	double to full	high-centered	slight	singly	repeat	reflexed
Christopher Columbus (Poulsen)	pink blend	large	double to full	high-centered	slight	singly	repeat	reflexed
Chromatella	light yellow	medium	very full	globular	moderate	small clusters	repeat	plain
Chrysler Imperial	dark red	extra large	double to full	high-centered	strong	small clusters	repeat	reflexed
Church Mouse	russet	small	double to full	cupped	slight	small clusters	repeat	reflexed
Cicely Lascelles	orange-pink	large	semi-double	open	slight	small clusters	repeat	plain
Cider Cup	orange blend	small	double to full	high-centered	slight	small clusters	repeat	reflexed
Cinderella	white	small	very full	flat	moderate	small clusters	repeat	reflexed
Circus	yellow blend	medium	double to full	high-centered	moderate	small clusters	repeat	reflexed
City Girl	pink blend	medium	semi-double	open	moderate	small clusters	repeat	plain
City of Auckland	orange blend	large	double to full	high-centered	strong	singly	repeat	reflexed
City of Belfast	orange-red	medium	double to full	cupped	none	truss	repeat	reflexed
City of Benalla	orange-pink	large	double to full	high-centered	slight	singly	repeat	reflexed
City of Birmingham	dark red	medium	semi-double	flat	none	small clusters	repeat	plain
City of Bradford	orange-red	medium	semi-double	cupped	slight	large clusters	repeat	ruffled
City of Goulburn	yellow blend	medium	double to full	cupped	none	small clusters	repeat	ruffled
City of Hereford	medium pink	large	double to full	high-centered	strong	singly	repeat	reflexed
City of Leeds	orange-pink	large	semi-double	cupped	slight	small clusters	repeat	reflexed
City of London	light pink	large	double to full	cupped	strong	small clusters	repeat	reflexed
City of Newcastle Bicentennial	medium red	large	double to full	high-centered	strong	singly	repeat	reflexed
City of Pretoria	apricot blend	medium	semi-double	open	slight	truss	repeat	plain
City of Wangaratta	medium red	large	double to full	high-centered	moderate	singly	repeat	reflexed
City of Warwick	russet	large	double to full	high-centered	slight	singly	repeat	reflexed
City of Worcester	medium red	large	double to full	high-centered	moderate	singly	repeat	reflexed
City of York	white	large	semi-double	cupped	moderate	large clusters	repeat	plain
Clair Matin	medium pink	medium	semi-double	cupped	moderate	large clusters	repeat	plain
Claire Jacquier	light yellow	medium	double to full	flat	moderate	large clusters	once	ruffled
Claire Rose	medium pink	large	very full	flat	strong	small clusters	repeat	ruffled
Claret Cup	red blend	small	double to full	globular	moderate	large clusters	repeat	plain
Clarissa	apricot blend	small	double to full	high-centered	slight	large clusters	repeat	reflexed
Clarita	orange-red	large	double to full	high-centered	slight	singly	repeat	reflexed
Class Act	white	large	semi-double	cupped	slight	small clusters	repeat	ruffled
Classic Sunblaze	medium pink	small	double to full	high-centered	slight	small clusters	repeat	reflexed
Classic Touch	light pink	large	double to full	high-centered	slight	singly	repeat	reflexed
Claude Monet	red blend	large	double to full	high-centered	slight	small clusters	repeat	reflexed
Claus Groth	orange blend	large	double to full	open	strong	small clusters	once	plain
Cleo	light pink	large	double to full	high-centered	slight	singly	repeat	reflexed
Cliffs of Dover	white	small	single	open	none	small clusters	repeat	plain
Climentina	light pink	large	double to full	high-centered	slight	singly	repeat	reflexed
Clio	light pink	large	very full	globular	moderate	singly	repeat	reflexed
Clivia	orange blend	large	double to full	high-centered	moderate	singly	repeat	reflexed
Clos Fleuri Blanc	white	large	double to full	cupped	slight	small clusters	repeat	plain
Clos Vougeot	medium red	medium	double to full	cupped	none	small clusters	repeat	plain

NAME	BLOOM COLOR	FLOWER SIZE	FLOWER TYPE	FLOWER SHAPE	FRAGRANCE AMOUNT	FLOWERING HABIT	FLOWERING INCIDENCE	PETAL SHAPE
Clotilde Soupert	white	medium	very full	cupped	none	large clusters	repeat	ruffled
Clytemnestra	orange-pink	small	semi-double	open	moderate	large clusters	repeat	ruffled
Coalite Flame	orange-red	extra large	very full	high-centered	slight	singly	repeat	reflexed
Cockadoo	medium red	medium	double to full	open	none	small clusters	repeat	plain
Cocktail	red blend	medium	single	open	slight	small clusters	repeat	plain
Cocktail '90	yellow blend	large	semi-double	open	none	singly	repeat	plain
Coco	yellow blend	medium	double to full	cupped	moderate	small clusters	repeat	reflexed
Cocorico	orange-red	medium	semi-double	cupped	none	small clusters	repeat	ruffled
Cocorico 1989	pink blend	medium	semi-double	open	slight	small clusters	repeat	plain
Cognac	apricot blend	large	double to full	cupped	none	small clusters	repeat	reflexed
Colchester Beauty	deep pink	medium	semi-double	high-centered	strong	singly	repeat	reflexed
Colibri	orange blend	small	double to full	flat	slight	small clusters	repeat	reflexed
Colibri 79	orange blend	small	double to full	flat	slight	small clusters	repeat	reflexed
Colin's Salmon	pink blend	large	double	high-centered	moderate	small clusters	repeat	reflexed
Collegiate 110	medium yellow	medium	semi-double	open	none	truss	repeat	plain
Collegiate Pride	medium red	large	double to full	high-centered	slight	singly	repeat	reflexed
Color Magic	pink blend	large	double to full	flat	slight	small clusters	repeat	reflexed
Colorama	red blend	large	double to full	cupped	moderate	small clusters	repeat	reflexed
Colour Wonder	orange blend	large	double to full	high-centered	slight	small clusters	repeat	reflexed
Columbia	medium pink	large	double to full	globular	strong	small clusters	repeat	reflexed
Columbine	yellow blend	medium	double to full	high-centered	strong	small clusters	repeat	reflexed
Columbus	deep pink	large	double to full	high-centered	none	small clusters	repeat	reflexed
Columbus Queen	pink blend	large	double to full	high-centered	slight	small clusters	repeat	reflexed
Comanche	orange-red	large	double to full	high-centered	slight	small clusters	repeat	reflexed
Command Performance	orange-red	large	double to full	high-centered	strong	small clusters	repeat	reflexed
Commandant Beaurepaire	pink blend	medium	double to full	cupped	moderate	small clusters	once	reflexed
Communis	medium pink	medium	very full	cupped	strong	small clusters	once	plain
Compassion	orange-pink	large	double to full	open	moderate	small clusters	repeat	reflexed
Complicata	pink blend	medium	single	open	strong	small clusters	once	plain
Comte Boula de Nanteuil	mauve	large	double to full	flat	strong	small clusters	once	plain
Comte de Chambord	pink blend	large	very full	flat	strong	small clusters	repeat	ruffled
Comte de Nanteuil	pink blend	large	double to full	flat	strong	small clusters	once	plain
Comtesse Cécile de Chabrillant	pink blend	large	very full	globular	moderate	singly	repeat	reflexed
Comtesse de Lacépède	light pink	large	double to full	cupped	moderate	small clusters	once	plain
Comtesse de Murinais	white	large	double to full	flat	strong	small clusters	once	ruffled
Comtesse de Rocquigny	white	medium	double to full	cupped	strong	small clusters	repeat	plain
Comtesse du Caÿla	orange blend	medium	semi-double	open	slight	small clusters	repeat	plain
Comtesse Riza du Parc	medium pink	large	double to full	globular	moderate	small clusters	repeat	plain
Comtesse Vandal	pink blend	large	double to full	high-centered	slight	small clusters	repeat	reflexed
Concertino	orange-red	medium	double to full	cupped	slight	small clusters	repeat	plain
Concerto	medium red	medium	semi-double	cupped	slight	small clusters	repeat	plain
Condesa de Sástago	pink blend	large	double to full	cupped	moderate	small clusters	repeat	reflexed
Conditorum	dark red	medium	semi-double	open	strong	small clusters	once	plain
Confetti	red blend	medium	double to full	high-centered	slight	small clusters	repeat	reflexed
Confidence	pink blend	large	double to full	high-centered	moderate	singly	repeat	reflexed
Congratulations	orange-pink	large	double to full	high-centered	slight	small clusters	repeat	reflexed
Conqueror's Gold	yellow blend	medium	semi-double	cupped	slight	small clusters	repeat	plain
Conrad Ferdinand Meyer	light pink	large	double to full	cupped	strong	small clusters	repeat	reflexed
Conservation	pink blend	small	semi-double	cupped	slight	small clusters	repeat	reflexed
Constance	medium yellow	large	double to full	high-centered	slight	singly	repeat	reflexed
Constance Finn	light pink	large	double to full	cupped	moderate	large clusters	repeat	reflexed
Constance Spry	light pink	large	double to full	cupped	strong	small clusters	once	plain
Contrast	pink blend	large	double to full	high-centered	moderate	small clusters	repeat	reflexed
Cooper's Burmese	white	large	single	open	slight	small clusters	once	plain
Copacabana	orange-red	medium	double to full	cupped	slight	small clusters	repeat	reflexed
Copenhagen	medium red	large	double to full	high-centered	moderate	small clusters	repeat	reflexed
Coppélia	orange blend	medium	double to full	cupped	slight	small clusters	repeat	reflexed
Copper Gem	apricot blend	large	double to full	cupped	slight	small clusters	repeat	reflexed
Copper Pot	orange blend	large	semi-double	cupped	slight	large clusters	repeat	reflexed
Copper Sunset	orange blend	small	double to full	high-centered	slight	small clusters	repeat	reflexed
Coquette des Alpes	white	medium	double to full	cupped	slight	small clusters	repeat	plain
Coquette des Blanches	white	medium	double to full	flat	moderate	small clusters	repeat	plain
Cora Marie	medium red	large	double	open	none	singly	repeat	plain
Coral Cluster	orange-pink	small	double to full	cupped	none	large clusters	repeat	ruffled
Coral Dawn	medium pink	large	double to full	cupped	moderate	small clusters	repeat	reflexed
Coral Satin	orange-pink	large	double to full	high-centered	moderate	small clusters	repeat	reflexed
Coral Spire	medium pink	large	semi-double	high-centered	none	small clusters	repeat	reflexed
Coral Treasure	orange blend	small	double to full	high-centered	none	small clusters	repeat	reflexed
Coralie	light pink	medium	double to full	cupped	moderate	small clusters	once	ruffled
Coralin	orange-red	small	double to full	high-centered	none	small clusters	repeat	reflexed
Cordelia	apricot blend	large	double to full	high-centered	moderate	singly	repeat	reflexed
Cordon Bleu	apricot blend	large	double to full	cupped	moderate	small clusters	repeat	reflexed
Cordula	orange-red	medium	double to full	cupped	slight	small clusters	repeat	plain
Cornelia	pink blend	medium	double to full	rosette	strong	large clusters	repeat	plain
Cornsilk	light yellow	small	double to full	high-centered	slight	singly	repeat	reflexed
Coronado	red blend	large	double to full	high-centered	moderate	singly	repeat	reflexed
Coronation Gold	apricot blend	large	double to full	cupped	slight	small clusters	repeat	reflexed
Coronet	dark red	large	semi-double	cupped	none	small clusters	repeat	plain
Corrie	deep pink	large	double to full	high-centered	none	singly	repeat	reflexed
Corso	orange blend	large	double to full	high-centered	slight	singly	repeat	reflexed
Corvette	orange-red	large	double to full	high-centered	none	small clusters	repeat	reflexed
Corylus	medium pink	medium	single	open	slight	small clusters	repeat	plain
Cosette	medium pink	medium	very full	flat	slight	small clusters	repeat	plain
Cosimo Ridolfi	mauve	medium	double to full	cupped	strong	small clusters	once	plain
Cosmic	orange blend	small	double to full	high-centered	slight	small clusters	repeat	reflexed
Cottage Garden	orange blend	medium	double to full	open	none	small clusters	repeat	plain
Cottage Rose	medium pink	medium	very full	cupped	slight	small clusters	repeat	ruffled
Cottontail	white	small	double to full	flat	slight	large clusters	repeat	ruffled
Countess of Stradbroke	dark red	large	double to full	globular	strong	small clusters	repeat	reflexed
Country Dancer	deep pink	large	double to full	cupped	moderate	small clusters	repeat	reflexed
Country Joy	pink blend	small	double to full	cupped	slight	small clusters	repeat	reflexed
Country Lady	orange blend	large	double to full	open	slight	singly	repeat	reflexed
Country Living	light pink	large	double to full	cupped	moderate	small clusters	repeat	ruffled
Countrywoman	medium yellow	large	double to full	globular	moderate	small clusters	repeat	reflexed
Coup de Foudre	orange-red	medium	double to full	cupped	none	small clusters	repeat	reflexed
Coup d'Hébé	deep pink	large	very full	cupped	strong	small clusters	repeat	plain
Courtoisie	orange blend	large	double to full	cupped	moderate	small clusters	repeat	reflexed
Courtship	medium pink	large	double to full	cupped	none	singly	repeat	reflexed
Courvoisier	deep yellow	large	double to full	high-centered	moderate	small clusters	repeat	reflexed
Cramoisi Picoté	red blend	medium	very full	pompons	moderate	small clusters	once	plain
Cramoisi Supérieur	medium red	small	double to full	cupped	none	large clusters	repeat	plain
Crazy Quilt	red blend	small	double to full	flat	none	small clusters	repeat	reflexed
Cream Delight	light pink	large	double to full	high-centered	slight	singly	repeat	reflexed
Cream Gold	medium yellow	small	double to full	high-centered	none	small clusters	repeat	reflexed
Cream Puff	pink blend	small	semi-double	open	slight	small clusters	repeat	reflexed
Crépuscule	apricot blend	medium	double to full	open	slight	small clusters	repeat	plain
Cressida	apricot blend	large	very full	cupped	strong	small clusters	repeat	ruffled
Crested Jewel	medium pink	medium	semi-double	high-centered	slight	small clusters	once	reflexed
Crested Moss	medium pink	medium	double to full	cupped	strong	small clusters	once	ruffled
Cricket	orange blend	small	double to full	globular	slight	small clusters	repeat	reflexed
Cricri	orange blend	small	double to full	cupped	none	small clusters	repeat	reflexed
Crimson Cascade	dark red	medium	double to full	flat	slight	small clusters	repeat	reflexed
Crimson Conquest	dark red	large	semi-double	open	none	small clusters	repeat	reflexed

NAME	BLOOM COLOR	FLOWER SIZE	FLOWER TYPE	FLOWER SHAPE	FRAGRANCE AMOUNT	FLOWERING HABIT	FLOWERING INCIDENCE	PETAL SHAPE
Crimson Descant	medium red	large	double to full	cupped	slight	small clusters	repeat	reflexed
Crimson Globe	dark red	large	double to full	globular	strong	small clusters	once	ruffled
Crimson Glory	dark red	large	double to full	cupped	strong	singly	repeat	reflexed
Crimson Moss	dark red	medium	double to full	flat	moderate	small clusters	once	ruffled
Crimson Rambler	medium red	small	semi-double	open	none	truss	once	ruffled
Crimson Rosette	dark red	medium	double to full	rosette	slight	large clusters	repeat	plain
Crimson Shower	medium red	small	double to full	pompons	slight	large clusters	repeat	plain
Crimson Wave	medium red	large	double to full	flat	slight	small clusters	repeat	reflexed
Criterion	pink blend	large	double to full	high-centered	moderate	singly	repeat	reflexed
Crumble Bar	deep yellow	medium	double to full	cupped	slight	large clusters	repeat	reflexed
Crystal Palace	apricot blend	medium	double to full	open	moderate	small clusters	repeat	ruffled
Crystalline	white	large	double to full	high-centered	moderate	small clusters	repeat	reflexed
Cuddles	orange-pink	small	double to full	high-centered	slight	small clusters	repeat	reflexed
Cuisse de Nymphe Emué	medium pink	medium	double to full	cupped	strong	small clusters	once	ruffled
Cupcake	medium pink	small	double to full	high-centered	none	small clusters	repeat	reflexed
Cupid	light pink	large	single	open	none	large clusters	once	ruffled
Curiosity	red blend	large	double to full	cupped	slight	small clusters	repeat	reflexed
Cuthbert Grant	dark red	medium	semi-double	cupped	slight	small clusters	repeat	plain
Cymbaline	light pink	large	double to full	flat	strong	small clusters	repeat	ruffled
Dagmar Späth	white	large	semi-double	cupped	none	large clusters	repeat	plain
D'Aguesseau	medium red	medium	double to full	quartered	moderate	small clusters	once	ruffled
Daily Mail Scented Rose	red blend	large	double to full	cupped	strong	small clusters	repeat	reflexed
Daily Sketch	pink blend	large	double to full	high-centered	moderate	small clusters	repeat	reflexed
Dainty Bess	light pink	large	single	cupped	moderate	small clusters	repeat	frilled
Dainty Dinah	orange-pink	small	semi-double	open	slight	small clusters	repeat	plain
Dainty Maid	pink blend	small	single	open	none	small clusters	repeat	plain
Dairy Maid	light yellow	medium	single	open	none	large clusters	repeat	plain
Dale Farm	orange-red	large	double to full	cupped	moderate	small clusters	repeat	reflexed
Dallas	red blend	large	double to full	high-centered	none	singly	repeat	reflexed
Dame Blanche	white	large	single	open	none	large clusters	once	plain
Dame de Coeur	medium red	large	double to full	high-centered	moderate	singly	repeat	reflexed
Dame Edith Helen	medium pink	large	very full	high-centered	strong	singly	repeat	reflexed
Dame of Sark	orange blend	large	double to full	flat	slight	small clusters	repeat	reflexed
Dame Prudence	light pink	medium	very full	flat	strong	small clusters	repeat	plain
Dame Wendy	medium pink	large	double to full	cupped	slight	small clusters	repeat	reflexed
Danaë	light yellow	medium	double to full	cupped	slight	large clusters	repeat	plain
Dance of Joy	medium red	large	double to full	cupped	moderate	small clusters	repeat	reflexed
Daniel Lacombe	yellow blend	medium	double to full	cupped	slight	small clusters	once	plain
Danse des Sylphes	orange-red	medium	double to full	globular	none	small clusters	repeat	reflexed
Daphné	medium pink	medium	very full	pompons	strong	small clusters	once	plain
Dapple Dawn	light pink	large	single	open	none	large clusters	repeat	plain
Darling Flame	orange-red	small	double to full	high-centered	slight	small clusters	repeat	reflexed
David Thompson	medium red	medium	double to full	open	strong	small clusters	repeat	ruffled
David Whitfield	medium pink	large	double to full	high-centered	moderate	small clusters	repeat	reflexed
Dawn Chorus	orange blend	large	double to full	high-centered	none	small clusters	repeat	reflexed
Dawson	medium pink	large	double to full	cupped	slight	large clusters	once	plain
Dawson's Delight	deep pink	extra large	double to full	high-centered	slight	singly	repeat	reflexed
Day Light	apricot blend	medium	double to full	cupped	none	small clusters	repeat	reflexed
Daybreak	medium yellow	medium	semi-double	open	strong	small clusters	repeat	plain
Daydream	light pink	large	semi-double	open	slight	small clusters	repeat	ruffled
Dazzler	yellow blend	small	double to full	high-centered	slight	small clusters	repeat	reflexed
De Candolle	light pink	large	very full	cupped	slight	small clusters	once	plain
De la Grifferaie	deep pink	medium	double to full	cupped	moderate	truss	once	plain
De la Maître-École	mauve	large	double to full	quartered	strong	small clusters	once	reflexed
De Meaux	medium pink	small	double to full	pompons	moderate	small clusters	once	ruffled
Dearest	pink blend	large	double to full	flat	slight	small clusters	repeat	reflexed
Debbie Thomas	red blend	large	double to full	high-centered	slight	singly	repeat	reflexed
Deb's Delight	pink blend	medium	double to full	cupped	moderate	small clusters	repeat	reflexed
Début	red blend	small	double to full	high-centered	none	singly	repeat	plain
Debutante	light pink	medium	double to full	open	moderate	small clusters	once	plain
Declic	mauve blend	medium	semi-double	cupped	slight	large clusters	repeat	plain
Decor Arlequin	apricot blend	medium	semi-double	cupped	none	small clusters	repeat	plain
Dee Bennett	orange blend	small	double to full	high-centered	slight	small clusters	repeat	reflexed
Deep Secret	dark red	large	double to full	high-centered	strong	singly	repeat	reflexed
Deep Velvet	dark red	small	double to full	high-centered	slight	small clusters	repeat	reflexed
Delambre	deep pink	medium	double to full	quartered	strong	small clusters	repeat	ruffled
Delicado	orange-pink	large	double to full	high-centered	slight	singly	repeat	reflexed
Delicata	light pink	large	semi-double	open	moderate	small clusters	repeat	plain
Delicious	medium pink	medium	double to full	high-centered	slight	small clusters	repeat	reflexed
Delille	white	medium	semi-double	open	moderate	small clusters	once	ruffled
Della Balfour	apricot blend	large	double to full	high-centered	slight	small clusters	repeat	reflexed
Demokracie	dark red	small	semi-double	open	slight	large clusters	repeat	plain
Denise Grey	light pink	medium	semi-double	open	slight	large clusters	repeat	plain
Dentelle de Bruxelles	light pink	medium	semi-double	high-centered	moderate	small clusters	repeat	plain
Dentelle de Malines	medium pink	medium	semi-double	high-centered	slight	small clusters	once	plain
Denver's Dream	orange blend	small	double to full	flat	none	small clusters	repeat	reflexed
Deschamps	medium red	large	double to full	open	slight	small clusters	repeat	ruffled
Desert Charm	dark red	small	double to full	high-centered	slight	small clusters	repeat	reflexed
Desert Peace	yellow blend	large	double to full	high-centered	slight	small clusters	repeat	reflexed
Deuil de Paul Fontaine	mauve	medium	double to full	cupped	moderate	small clusters	repeat	ruffled
Devoniensis	white	large	double to full	quartered	slight	small clusters	repeat	reflexed
Diablotin	medium red	large	semi-double	open	none	small clusters	repeat	reflexed
Diadem	medium pink	medium	double to full	high-centered	none	small clusters	repeat	reflexed
Diamant	orange-red	large	double to full	high-centered	slight	small clusters	repeat	reflexed
Diamond Jubilee	light yellow	extra large	double to full	cupped	moderate	singly	repeat	reflexed
Diana	medium yellow	medium	double to full	flat	slight	small clusters	repeat	reflexed
Diane	yellow blend	large	double to full	high-centered	none	singly	repeat	reflexed
Diapason	medium pink	large	double to full	globular	moderate	small clusters	repeat	reflexed
Dick Koster	deep pink	small	double to full	cupped	none	small clusters	repeat	plain
Dickson's Flame	orange-red	large	double to full	high-centered	slight	large clusters	repeat	reflexed
Dicky	orange-pink	medium	double to full	flat	slight	small clusters	repeat	reflexed
Die Welt	orange blend	large	double to full	high-centered	slight	singly	repeat	reflexed
Dimples	light yellow	medium	semi-double	cupped	slight	small clusters	repeat	ruffled
Diorama	yellow blend	large	double to full	high-centered	moderate	singly	repeat	reflexed
Directeur Alphand	mauve	large	double to full	cupped	strong	singly	repeat	ruffled
Dirigent	medium red	medium	semi-double	open	slight	large clusters	repeat	reflexed
Disco Dancer	orange-red	medium	semi-double	open	slight	small clusters	repeat	plain
Distant Drums	mauve	large	double to full	cupped	strong	small clusters	repeat	ruffled
Dr A. J. Verhage	deep yellow	large	double to full	high-centered	moderate	singly	repeat	ruffled
Doctor Dick	orange-pink	large	very full	high-centered	slight	singly	repeat	reflexed
Dr Eckener	pink blend	large	semi-double	cupped	moderate	small clusters	repeat	ruffled
Dr Edward Deacon	orange blend	large	double to full	globular	moderate	small clusters	repeat	reflexed
Doctor Grill	orange-pink	large	double to full	quartered	slight	small clusters	repeat	reflexed
Dr Harry Upshall	pink blend	medium	double to full	cupped	moderate	small clusters	repeat	plain
Dr Huey	dark red	medium	semi-double	open	slight	small clusters	once	plain
Dr J. H. Nicholas	medium pink	large	very full	globular	moderate	small clusters	repeat	reflexed
Dr Jackson	medium red	medium	single	flat	none	singly	repeat	plain
Dr John Snow	white	large	double to full	high-centered	moderate	singly	repeat	reflexed
Dr McAlpine	deep pink	medium	double to full	high-centered	strong	small clusters	repeat	reflexed
Dr W. Van Fleet	light pink	medium	double to full	open	moderate	small clusters	once	reflexed
Dolce Vita	orange-pink	large	double to full	high-centered	slight	singly	repeat	reflexed
Dolly	orange-pink	medium	double to full	open	none	small clusters	repeat	plain
Dolly Parton	orange-red	extra large	double to full	high-centered	strong	singly	repeat	reflexed
Domstadt Fulda	dark red	medium	double to full	flat	none	small clusters	repeat	plain
Don Juan	dark red	large	double to full	cupped	strong	small clusters	repeat	reflexed
Don Marshall	dark red	small	double to full	high-centered	slight	small clusters	repeat	reflexed
Donald Prior	medium red	large	semi-double	cupped	moderate	large clusters	repeat	plain
Donau	mauve	medium	semi-double	flat	slight	small clusters	once	plain
Doncasteri	deep pink	medium	single	flat	none	small clusters	once	plain

NAME	BLOOM COLOR	FLOWER SIZE	FLOWER TYPE	FLOWER SHAPE	FRAGRANCE AMOUNT	FLOWERING HABIT	FLOWERING INCIDENCE	PETAL SHAPE
Donna Marie	white	small	very full	cupped	none	large clusters	once	plain
Doris Downes	pink blend	extra large	semi-double	cupped	moderate	small clusters	once	reflexed
Doris Tysterman	orange blend	large	double to full	high-centered	slight	small clusters	repeat	reflexed
Dornröschen	pink blend	large	double to full	open	moderate	small clusters	repeat	plain
Dorola	deep yellow	small	double to full	cupped	moderate	small clusters	repeat	plain
Dorothy Dennison	light pink	small	double to full	cupped	moderate	large clusters	once	ruffled
Dorothy Peach	yellow blend	large	double to full	high-centered	moderate	singly	repeat	reflexed
Dorothy Perkins	light pink	small	double to full	cupped	moderate	large clusters	once	ruffled
Dorothy Wheatcroft	medium red	large	semi-double	open	slight	large clusters	repeat	plain
Dortmund	medium red	large	single	open	slight	small clusters	repeat	plain
Double Charm	yellow blend	medium	double to full	high-centered	none	large clusters	repeat	plain
Double Delight	red blend	large	double to full	high-centered	strong	small clusters	repeat	reflexed
Double Joy	orange-pink	small	double to full	high-centered	slight	small clusters	repeat	reflexed
Double Treat	yellow blend	small	double to full	cupped	slight	small clusters	repeat	plain
Double White	white	small	double to full	cupped	moderate	small clusters	once	plain
Douceur Normande	medium pink	medium	single	open	none	small clusters	repeat	ruffled
Dove	light pink	large	double to full	cupped	slight	small clusters	repeat	ruffled
Dream	light pink	large	double to full	high-centered	none	small clusters	repeat	reflexed
Dream Girl	pink blend	large	double to full	cupped	strong	small clusters	repeat	reflexed
Dream Lover	light pink	small	double to full	high-centered	none	singly	repeat	reflexed
Dream Time	medium pink	large	double to full	high-centered	moderate	small clusters	repeat	reflexed
Dreamer	medium pink	small	double to full	cupped	none	small clusters	repeat	reflexed
Dreamglo	red blend	small	double to full	high-centered	none	small clusters	repeat	reflexed
Dreaming Parade	orange blend	small	double to full	cupped	none	small clusters	repeat	reflexed
Dreaming Spires	deep yellow	medium	double to full	high-centered	strong	small clusters	repeat	reflexed
Dresden	white	large	very full	high-centered	strong	singly	repeat	reflexed
Dresden Doll	light pink	small	semi-double	flat	slight	small clusters	repeat	plain
Drummer Boy	dark red	small	semi-double	cupped	slight	small clusters	repeat	plain
Dublin Bay	medium red	large	double to full	high-centered	moderate	small clusters	repeat	reflexed
Duc de Cambridge	mauve	medium	double to full	cupped	moderate	small clusters	once	ruffled
Duc de Fitzjames	dark red/ deep pink	medium	double to full	cupped	strong	small clusters	once	ruffled
Duc de Guiche	mauve	medium	double to full	quartered	strong	small clusters	once	plain
Duc de Sussex	light pink	medium	double to full	open	strong	small clusters	once	ruffled
Duc de Valmy	mauve	large	double to full	cupped	moderate	small clusters	once	plain
Ducher	white	medium	double to full	flat	none	small clusters	repeat	reflexed
Duchess of Portland	medium red	large	semi-double	cupped	moderate	small clusters	repeat	plain
Duchess of Wellington	light yellow	large	semi-double	open	slight	small clusters	repeat	reflexed
Duchesse d'Angoulême	light pink	large	double to full	cupped	strong	small clusters	once	ruffled
Duchesse d'Auerstädt	yellow	large	double to full	quartered	slight	small clusters	repeat	reflexed
Duchesse de Berry	pink blend	large	double to full	cupped	moderate	small clusters	once	plain
Duchesse de Brabant	light pink	medium	double to full	cupped	moderate	small clusters	repeat	plain
Duchesse de Buccleugh	red blend	medium	double to full	cupped	moderate	small clusters	once	plain
Duchesse de Cambacérès	mauve blend	large	double to full	open	strong	small clusters	repeat	plain
Duchesse de Grammont	white	small	double to full	cupped	none	large clusters	repeat	plain
Duchesse de Montebello	pink	medium	double to full	cupped	strong	small clusters	once	plain
Duchesse de Rohan	pink blend	large	very full	flat	strong	singly	once	ruffled
Duchesse de Verneuil	pink blend	large	double to full	cupped	strong	small clusters	once	ruffled
Duet	medium pink	large	double to full	cupped	none	small clusters	repeat	ruffled
Duftrausch	medium pink	extra large	very full	flat	strong	singly	repeat	reflexed
Duke of Edinburgh	dark red	large	double to full	cupped	strong	singly	repeat	reflexed
Duke of Wellington	dark red	large	double to full	cupped	strong	singly	repeat	reflexed
Duke of Windsor	orange blend	large	double to full	high-centered	strong	singly	repeat	reflexed
Duke of York	pink blend	medium	double to full	open	none	small clusters	repeat	plain

NAME	BLOOM COLOR	FLOWER SIZE	FLOWER TYPE	FLOWER SHAPE	FRAGRANCE AMOUNT	FLOWERING HABIT	FLOWERING INCIDENCE	PETAL SHAPE
Duke Sunblaze	deep pink	small	double to full	high-centered	none	small clusters	repeat	reflexed
Dundee Rambler	white	medium	semi-double	flat	slight	large clusters	once	plain
Duplex	medium pink	small	semi-double	open	slight	small clusters	once	ruffled
Dupontii	white	small	single	flat	strong	truss	once	plain
Dupuy Jamain	medium red	large	double to full	cupped	moderate	singly	repeat	ruffled
Dusky Maiden	dark red	medium	single	open	slight	small clusters	repeat	plain
Düsterlohe	deep pink	medium	single	open	slight	small clusters	once	plain
Dusty Rose	mauve	small	very full	high-centered	moderate	small clusters	repeat	reflexed
Dutch Gold	medium yellow	large	double to full	high-centered	moderate	small clusters	repeat	reflexed
Dynamite	dark red	large	double to full	cupped	slight	small clusters	repeat	reflexed
Earl of Eldon	orange blend	medium	double to full	flat	moderate	small clusters	once	ruffled
Earth Song	deep pink	large	double to full	cupped	moderate	small clusters	repeat	reflexed
Earthquake	red blend	small	double to full	cupped	none	small clusters	repeat	plain
Easlea's Golden Rambler	yellow blend	large	double to full	cupped	moderate	small clusters	once	ruffled
Easter Morning	white	small	very full	high-centered	slight	small clusters	repeat	reflexed
Easy Going	medium yellow	large	double to full	cupped	moderate	small clusters	repeat	ruffled
Echo	pink blend	large	semi-double	cupped	none	truss	repeat	plain
Éclair	dark red	small	double to full	quartered	moderate	small clusters	repeat	ruffled
Eclipse	light yellow	large	double to full	open	moderate	singly	repeat	reflexed
Eddie's Crimson	medium red	large	semi-double	flat	none	small clusters	once	plain
Eddie's Jewel	medium red	large	single	flat	none	large clusters	once	plain
Eden Rose	deep pink	large	double to full	cupped	strong	singly	repeat	reflexed
Edith Bellenden	medium pink	small	single	open	slight	small clusters	once	plain
Edith Clark	medium red	large	double to full	globular	slight	small clusters	repeat	reflexed
Edith Holden	russet	medium	semi-double	open	slight	large clusters	repeat	reflexed
Editor McFarland	medium pink	large	double to full	high-centered	strong	singly	repeat	reflexed
Editor Stewart	medium red	large	semi-double	open	none	small clusters	repeat	plain
Edna Marie	light pink	small	double to full	high-centered	slight	small clusters	repeat	reflexed
Eglantyne	light pink	large	very full	flat	strong	small clusters	repeat	ruffled
Egoli	deep yellow	large	double	high-centered	slight	small clusters	repeat	plain
Eiffel Tower	medium pink	large	double to full	high-centered	moderate	singly	repeat	reflexed
Ekstase	dark red	large	double to full	high-centered	strong	singly	repeat	reflexed
El Capitan	medium red	large	double to full	high-centered	slight	small clusters	repeat	reflexed
Electron	deep pink	large	double to full	high-centered	moderate	singly	repeat	reflexed
Elegance (Brownell)	medium yellow	large	double to full	open	moderate	small clusters	repeat	plain
Elégance (Buyl)	pink blend	large	double to full	globular	moderate	small clusters	repeat	plain
Elegant Beauty	light yellow	large	double to full	high-centered	none	singly	repeat	reflexed
Elegy	orange-red	large	double to full	globular	slight	singly	repeat	reflexed
Elfin Charm	pink blend	small	very full	cupped	moderate	small clusters	repeat	plain
Elfinglo	mauve	small	double	cupped	none	large clusters	repeat	reflexed
Elie Beauvillain	medium pink	large	double to full	cupped	slight	small clusters	repeat	reflexed
Elina	light yellow	large	double to full	high-centered	slight	singly	repeat	reflexed
Élisa Boëlle	white	large	double to full	cupped	strong	singly	repeat	ruffled
Eliza	medium pink	medium	double to full	high-centered	none	small clusters	repeat	reflexed
Eliza Dorothy	medium yellow	large	double to full	high-centered	moderate	singly	repeat	reflexed
Elizabeth Arden	white	large	double to full	high-centered	strong	singly	repeat	reflexed
Elizabeth Harkness	light yellow	large	double to full	high-centered	moderate	singly	repeat	reflexed
Elizabeth of Glamis	orange-pink	large	double to full	flat	slight	small clusters	repeat	reflexed
Elizabeth Taylor	deep pink	large	double to full	high-centered	moderate	singly	repeat	reflexed
Ellen	apricot blend	large	double to full	cupped	strong	small clusters	repeat	plain
Ellen Poulsen	medium pink	medium	double to full	open	slight	large clusters	repeat	plain
Ellen Willmott	yellow blend	large	single	cupped	none	small clusters	repeat	ruffled
Ellinor LeGrice	medium yellow	large	double to full	cupped	moderate	singly	repeat	reflexed
Elmhurst	pink blend	large	double to full	high-centered	moderate	singly	repeat	reflexed
Elmshorn	deep pink	small	double to full	cupped	slight	large clusters	repeat	reflexed
Else Poulsen	medium pink	medium	semi-double	flat	slight	large clusters	repeat	reflexed
Elveshörn	medium pink	medium	double to full	globular	slight	small clusters	repeat	plain
Elysium	medium pink	large	double to full	high-centered	moderate	small clusters	repeat	reflexed

NAME	BLOOM COLOR	FLOWER SIZE	FLOWER TYPE	FLOWER SHAPE	FRAGRANCE AMOUNT	FLOWERING HABIT	FLOWERING INCIDENCE	PETAL SHAPE
Emanuel	apricot blend	large	very full	flat	strong	small clusters	repeat	ruffled
Embassy	pink blend	large	double to full	high-centered	slight	singly	repeat	reflexed
Ember	orange-red	small	double to full	flat	none	singly	repeat	reflexed
Embers	medium red	large	double to full	high-centered	moderate	small clusters	repeat	reflexed
Emily	light pink	large	double to full	open	moderate	singly	repeat	reflexed
Emily Gray	deep yellow	large	double to full	open	moderate	small clusters	once	reflexed
Emily Louise	deep yellow	small	single	open	slight	large clusters	repeat	plain
Éminence	mauve	large	double to full	high-centered	strong	small clusters	repeat	reflexed
Emmie Gray	medium red	medium	single	flat	none	small clusters	repeat	plain
Emotion	pink blend	large	double to full	cupped	strong	small clusters	repeat	ruffled
Empereur du Maroc	red	small	very full	quartered	strong	small clusters	repeat	ruffled
Empress Joséphine	medium pink	large	semi-double	open	moderate	small clusters	once	ruffled
Empress Michiko	light pink	medium	double to full	high-centered	strong	small clusters	repeat	reflexed
Ena Baxter	medium pink	medium	double to full	high-centered	slight	small clusters	repeat	reflexed
Ena Harkness	medium red	large	double to full	high-centered	strong	singly	repeat	reflexed
Enchantress	white	large	very full	cupped	moderate	small clusters	repeat	ruffled
Enfant de France	light pink	large	double to full	quartered	strong	singly	repeat	ruffled
English Elegance	pink blend	large	double to full	open	slight	small clusters	repeat	plain
English Garden	apricot blend	large	very full	flat	slight	small clusters	repeat	reflexed
English Holiday	yellow blend	large	double to full	cupped	moderate	small clusters	repeat	plain
English Miss	light pink	medium	double to full	open	moderate	small clusters	repeat	plain
Eos	red blend	medium	single	open	none	small clusters	once	plain
Erfurt	pink blend	medium	semi-double	flat	strong	small clusters	repeat	plain
Ernest H. Morse	medium red	large	double to full	high-centered	strong	singly	repeat	reflexed
Ernest's Blue	mauve	large	double to full	high-centered	strong	small clusters	repeat	reflexed
Erotika	dark red	large	double to full	high-centered	strong	singly	repeat	reflexed
Escapade	mauve	large	semi-double	cupped	slight	large clusters	repeat	plain
Eskimo	white	medium	double to full	high-centered	none	small clusters	repeat	reflexed
Esme Euvrard	light pink	large	semi-double	high-centered	slight	singly	repeat	plain
Especially For You	medium yellow	large	double to full	high-centered	strong	small clusters	repeat	reflexed
Espéranza	medium red	large	double to full	open	none	small clusters	repeat	reflexed
Essex	medium pink	small	single	cupped	none	small clusters	repeat	plain
Esther	pink blend	medium	double to full	open	strong	small clusters	once	ruffled
Esther Geldenhuys	orange-pink	large	double to full	high-centered	moderate	singly	repeat	reflexed
Estima	orange blend	small	double to full	high-centered	none	small clusters	once	plain
Etain	orange-pink	medium	double to full	open	slight	large clusters	repeat	reflexed
Éterna	light pink	large	double to full	high-centered	slight	small clusters	repeat	reflexed
Ethel	light pink	small	double to full	cupped	none	small clusters	once	plain
Ethel Austin	deep pink	large	double to full	high-centered	slight	small clusters	repeat	reflexed
Ethel Dawson	medium red	large	double to full	high-centered	slight	small clusters	repeat	reflexed
Etna	dark red	large	very full	cupped	strong	small clusters	once	ruffled
Étoile de Hollande	medium red	large	double to full	cupped	strong	small clusters	repeat	plain
Etoile de Lyon	medium yellow	large	double to full	globular	moderate	singly	repeat	reflexed
Étude	deep pink	medium	semi-double	open	moderate	small clusters	repeat	ruffled
Eugene de Beauharnais	mauve	medium	double to full	cupped	slight	small clusters	repeat	reflexed
Eugène Fürst	deep red	large	double to full	globular	moderate	singly	repeat	ruffled
Eugène Verdier	deep pink	medium	very full	cupped	moderate	small clusters	once	reflexed
Eugénie Guinoiseau	medium red	medium	double to full	flat	moderate	small clusters	once	ruffled
Euphoria	yellow blend	medium	single	saucer-shaped	slight	small clusters	repeat	plain
Euphrates	pink blend	small	single	open	none	small clusters	once	ruffled
Euphrosyne	medium pink	small	double to full	flat	strong	large clusters	once	plain
Europa	medium pink	medium	double to full	flat	none	small clusters	repeat	reflexed
Europeana	red	large	double to full	rosette	slight	small clusters	repeat	reflexed
Eurorose	yellow blend	medium	double to full	cupped	none	small clusters	repeat	plain
Eurostar	medium yellow	large	very full	cupped	moderate	small clusters	repeat	reflexed
Eutin	dark red	medium	double to full	cupped	slight	large clusters	repeat	plain
Eva	red blend	medium	single	cupped	slight	truss	repeat	plain
Evangeline	pink blend	small	single	flat	moderate	small clusters	once	plain
Evelyn	apricot blend	large	very full	rosette	strong	small clusters	repeat	ruffled

NAME	BLOOM COLOR	FLOWER SIZE	FLOWER TYPE	FLOWER SHAPE	FRAGRANCE AMOUNT	FLOWERING HABIT	FLOWERING INCIDENCE	PETAL SHAPE
Evelyn Fison	medium red	large	double to full	open	slight	small clusters	repeat	reflexed
Evening Star	white	large	double to full	flat	slight	small clusters	repeat	reflexed
Evensong	orange-pink	large	double to full	cupped	none	singly	repeat	reflexed
Everest	white	extra large	double to full	high-centered	moderate	singly	repeat	reflexed
Everest Double Fragrance	light pink	large	double to full	cupped	moderate	small clusters	repeat	reflexed
Excellenz von Schubert	deep pink	small	double to full	cupped	none	large clusters	repeat	plain
Excelsa	medium red	small	double to full	cupped	none	small clusters	once	plain
Exciting	medium red	large	semi-double	open	none	singly	repeat	plain
Exploit	deep pink/ medium red	medium	double to full	cupped	none	small clusters	repeat	reflexed
Explorer's Dream	orange-pink	small	double to full	open	none	small clusters	repeat	reflexed
Eyecatcher	pink blend	medium	double to full	high-centered	moderate	small clusters	repeat	reflexed
Eyeopener	medium red	small	single	open	none	small clusters	repeat	plain
Eyepaint	red blend	medium	single	open	slight	large clusters	repeat	plain
F. J. Grootendorst	medium red	small	very full	cupped	slight	large clusters	repeat	plain
Fabvier	medium red	medium	semi-double	open	moderate	small clusters	repeat	reflexed
Fair Bianca	white	medium	very full	flat	moderate	small clusters	repeat	plain
Fair Dinkum	pink blend	small	double to full	high-centered	slight	singly	repeat	reflexed
Fair Play	mauve	medium	semi-double	open	slight	large clusters	repeat	plain
Fairhope	light yellow	small	double to full	high-centered	slight	singly	repeat	reflexed
Fairlane	light yellow	small	double to full	high-centered	slight	small clusters	repeat	reflexed
Fairy Changeling	medium pink	small	double to full	pompons	slight	small clusters	repeat	plain
Fairy Damsel	dark red	small	double to full	flat	none	small clusters	repeat	plain
Fairy Dancers	apricot blend	medium	double to full	high-centered	moderate	small clusters	repeat	reflexed
Fairy Moss	medium pink	small	semi-double	flat	none	small clusters	repeat	reflexed
Fairy Prince	medium red	small	double to full	cupped	slight	small clusters	repeat	plain
Fairy Princess	light pink	small	very full	cupped	none	small clusters	repeat	plain
Fairy Snow	white	small	double to full	cupped	none	small clusters	repeat	plain
Fairy Tale	light pink	small	double to full	flat	none	small clusters	repeat	reflexed
Fairyland	light pink	small	double to full	cupped	moderate	small clusters	repeat	plain
Falkland	white	small	semi-double	cupped	slight	small clusters	once	plain
Fancy Princess	deep pink	extralarge	double to full	high-centered	moderate	singly	repeat	reflexed
Fandango	orange-red	large	semi-double	open	moderate	small clusters	repeat	plain
Fanny Bias	medium pink	large	double to full	globular	moderate	small clusters	once	plain
Fantasia (Kordes)	pink blend	medium	double	open	strong	singly	repeat	plain
Fantasia (Dickson)	medium yellow	large	double	globular	moderate	singly	repeat	reflexed
Fantin-Latour	light pink	large	double to full	flat	strong	small clusters	once	plain
Fascination	orange-pink	large	double to full	high-centered	none	singly	repeat	reflexed
Fashion	pink blend	large	double to full	open	moderate	small clusters	repeat	reflexed
Fashion Flame	orange-pink	small	double to full	high-centered	slight	small clusters	repeat	reflexed
Faust	yellow blend	medium	double to full	open	slight	large clusters	repeat	reflexed
Fee	light pink	large	double to full	high-centered	slight	small clusters	repeat	reflexed
Felicia	pink blend	medium	double to full	cupped	strong	large clusters	repeat	plain
Félicité Bohain	deep pink	medium	double to full	quartered	strong	small clusters	once	ruffled
Félicité Parmentier	light pink	medium	very full	flat	strong	small clusters	once	plain
Félicité-Perpétue	white	small	very full	rosette	moderate	large clusters	once	plain
Felicity Kendal	orange-pink	large	double to full	high-centered	none	small clusters	repeat	reflexed
Fellenberg	medium red	large	double to full	cupped	slight	small clusters	repeat	reflexed
Femina	orange-pink	large	double	open	moderate	small clusters	repeat	plain
Ferdinand Pichard	red blend	large	double to full	cupped	moderate	small clusters	repeat	plain
Ferdy	deep pink	small	double to full	cupped	none	small clusters	once	plain
Feria	orange-pink	large	double to full	globular	moderate	singly	repeat	reflexed
Ferline	medium red	large	double to full	high-centered	slight	singly	repeat	reflexed
Ferry Porsche	medium red	large	double to full	high-centered	slight	small clusters	repeat	reflexed
Fervid	orange-red	large	single	open	slight	small clusters	repeat	ruffled
Festival	red blend	small	semi-double	open	none	small clusters	repeat	reflexed
Feu Pernet-Ducher	medium yellow	large	double to full	globular	slight	small clusters	repeat	reflexed
Feuerwerk	orange blend	medium	semi-double	cupped	none	small clusters	repeat	plain
Feuerzauber	orange-red	large	double to full	high-centered	none	singly	repeat	reflexed
Feverball	medium red	medium	double to full	high-centered	moderate	small clusters	repeat	plain

NAME	BLOOM COLOR	FLOWER SIZE	FLOWER TYPE	FLOWER SHAPE	FRAGRANCE AMOUNT	FLOWERING HABIT	FLOWERING INCIDENCE	PETAL SHAPE
Fidélio	orange-red	medium	double to full	high-centered	slight	small clusters	repeat	plain
Fiesta	red blend	large	double to full	high-centered	moderate	singly	repeat	reflexed
Fiesta Gold	yellow blend	small	double to full	cupped	slight	small clusters	repeat	reflexed
Fiesta Ruby	medium red	small	double to full	high-centered	slight	small clusters	repeat	reflexed
Figurine	white	small	double to full	high-centered	slight	small clusters	repeat	ruffled
Fimbriata	light pink	small	semi-double	open	strong	small clusters	repeat	frilled
Finale	orange blend	large	double to full	high-centered	none	small clusters	repeat	reflexed
Financial Times Centenary	deep pink	large	very full	globular	strong	small clusters	repeat	plain
Fiona	dark red	small	double to full	open	slight	small clusters	repeat	plain
Fire Festival	yellow blend	small	double to full	cupped	none	small clusters	repeat	reflexed
Fire King	orange-red	medium	very full	flat	moderate	small clusters	repeat	reflexed
Fire Princess	orange-red	small	double to full	cupped	none	small clusters	repeat	reflexed
Firecracker	medium red	large	semi-double	open	moderate	small clusters	repeat	reflexed
Firefly	orange blend	small	double to full	open	slight	small clusters	repeat	reflexed
Fireworks	red blend	small	double to full	high-centered	slight	small clusters	repeat	reflexed
First Edition	orange-pink	medium	double to full	cupped	slight	small clusters	repeat	reflexed
First Federal Gold	deep yellow	large	double to full	high-centered	moderate	singly	repeat	reflexed
First Kiss	pink blend	large	semi-double	cupped	slight	small clusters	repeat	reflexed
First Lady	deep pink	large	semi-double	cupped	slight	singly	repeat	reflexed
First Light	light pink	small	single	flat	moderate	large clusters	repeat	plain
First Love	light pink	large	double to full	high-centered	slight	small clusters	repeat	reflexed
First Prize	pink blend	extra large	double to full	high-centered	slight	singly	repeat	reflexed
Fisher Holmes	dark red	large	double to full	globular	moderate	small clusters	repeat	plain
Fisherman's Friend	dark red	large	very full	cupped	moderate	small clusters	repeat	ruffled
Five-Colored Rose	white	medium	semi-double	cupped	none	small clusters	repeat	plain
Flair	orange-pink	medium	double to full	cupped	none	small clusters	repeat	reflexed
Flame Sunblaze	medium red	small	double to full	flat	none	small clusters	repeat	reflexed
Flamenco	light pink	large	double to full	cupped	slight	small clusters	repeat	reflexed
Flaming Beauty	red blend	large	double to full	high-centered	slight	singly	repeat	reflexed
Flaming Peace	red blend	large	double to full	high-centered	moderate	singly	repeat	reflexed
Flaming Sunset	orange blend	large	double	high-centered	none	small clusters	repeat	plain
Flamingo	light pink	large	double to full	high-centered	slight	singly	repeat	reflexed
Flammentanz	medium red	extra large	double to full	high-centered	moderate	small clusters	once	reflexed
Flashlight	orange-red	large	double to full	high-centered	moderate	small clusters	repeat	reflexed
Fleur Cowles	light yellow	large	double to full	high-centered	moderate	small clusters	repeat	reflexed
Flora (Maarse)	orange-pink	large	double to full	high-centered	strong	singly	repeat	reflexed
Flora (Jacques)	mauve	medium	double to full	cupped	moderate	large clusters	once	reflexed
Floradora	orange-red	medium	double to full	cupped	slight	large clusters	repeat	plain
Florence	light pink	medium	semi-double	globular	moderate	small clusters	repeat	plain
Florence Mary Morse	medium red	large	semi-double	open	none	truss	repeat	plain
Flower Carpet	deep pink	medium	semi-double	cupped	none	small clusters	repeat	plain
Flower Power	orange-red	medium	double	cupped	moderate	small clusters	repeat	plain
Flutterbye	yellow blend	large	single	open	moderate	small clusters	repeat	plain
Flying Colors	red blend	small	semi-double	flat	none	small clusters	repeat	reflexed
Flying Doctor	orange-red	medium	double to full	high-centered	none	singly	repeat	reflexed
Foliacée	medium pink	large	double to full	globular	strong	small clusters	once	plain
Folies-Bergère	yellow blend	large	double to full	high-centered	moderate	singly	repeat	reflexed
Folklore	orange blend	large	double to full	high-centered	moderate	small clusters	repeat	reflexed
Folksinger	yellow blend	large	double to full	cupped	moderate	small clusters	repeat	reflexed
Forever Young	pink blend	small	double to full	high-centered	none	singly	repeat	reflexed
Fornarina	pink blend	medium	double to full	cupped	moderate	small clusters	once	plain
Fortune Cookie	apricot blend	small	double to full	flat	none	small clusters	repeat	reflexed
Fortune Teller	mauve	large	double to full	high-centered	strong	singly	repeat	reflexed
Fortune's Double Yellow	yellow blend	medium	double to full	cupped	moderate	small clusters	once	plain
Fortuniana	white	medium	single	flat	moderate	singly	once	plain
Forty-niner	red blend	large	double to full	high-centered	slight	singly	repeat	reflexed
Fountain	medium red	large	double to full	high-centered	strong	small clusters	repeat	reflexed
Fountain Square	white	large	double to full	high-centered	none	small clusters	repeat	reflexed
Foxy Lady	orange-pink	small	double to full	cupped	none	small clusters	repeat	reflexed
Fragrance	deep pink	large	double to full	high-centered	strong	singly	repeat	reflexed
Fragrant Cloud	orange-red	large	double to full	high-centered	strong	singly	repeat	reflexed
Fragrant Delight	orange-pink	medium	double to full	cupped	strong	small clusters	repeat	ruffled
Fragrant Dream	apricot blend	large	double to full	cupped	strong	small clusters	repeat	reflexed
Fragrant Gold	deep yellow	large	semi-double	cupped	moderate	small clusters	repeat	reflexed
Fragrant Hour	orange-pink	large	double to full	high-centered	strong	small clusters	repeat	reflexed
Fragrant Plum	mauve	large	double to full	cupped	strong	large clusters	repeat	reflexed
Fragrant Surprise	apricot blend	large	very full	cupped	moderate	small clusters	repeat	plain
Français	orange-pink	medium	semi-double	cupped	none	large clusters	repeat	plain
France Inter	medium red	large	double to full	high-centered	slight	singly	repeat	reflexed
Frances Phoebe	white	large	very full	high-centered	none	singly	repeat	reflexed
Francesca	apricot blend	large	single	flat	slight	small clusters	repeat	plain
Francine Austin	white	small	double to full	pompons	slight	large clusters	repeat	plain
Francis Dubreuil	dark red	medium	double to full	cupped	strong	small clusters	repeat	plain
Francis E. Lester	white	medium	single	flat	moderate	large clusters	once	plain
François Coppée	dark red	large	double to full	globular	strong	singly	repeat	reflexed
François Foucard	medium yellow	medium	semi-double	open	moderate	small clusters	once	plain
François Guillot	white	medium	double to full	cupped	none	small clusters	once	plain
François Juranville	orange-pink	medium	double to full	flat	moderate	small clusters	once	plain
Frank Naylor	red blend	small	single	flat	moderate	large clusters	repeat	plain
Franklin Englemann	dark red	large	double to full	high-centered	none	large clusters	repeat	reflexed
Frau Astrid Späth	deep pink	medium	semi-double	cupped	slight	large clusters	repeat	plain
Frau Dagmar Hartopp	medium pink	medium	single	open	slight	small clusters	repeat	plain
Frau Karl Druschki	white	large	double to full	high-centered	none	singly	repeat	reflexed
Fräulein Octavia Hesse	light yellow	small	semi-double	cupped	moderate	small clusters	once	plain
Fred Edmunds	orange blend	large	double to full	cupped	strong	singly	repeat	plain
Fred Gibson	apricot blend	large	double to full	open	slight	singly	repeat	plain
Fred Howard	yellow blend	large	double to full	high-centered	slight	singly	repeat	plain
Fred Loads	orange-red	large	single	open	moderate	small clusters	repeat	plain
Frederic Mistral	light pink	extra large	very full	globular	strong	small clusters	repeat	reflexed
Freedom	deep yellow	large	double to full	high-centered	moderate	singly	repeat	reflexed
Freegold	deep yellow	small	double to full	cupped	moderate	small clusters	repeat	reflexed
Freiherr von Marschall	medium red	large	double to full	flat	strong	small clusters	once	plain
Freisinger Morgenröte	orange blend	large	double to full	cupped	moderate	small clusters	repeat	reflexed
French Lace	white	large	double to full	open	slight	small clusters	repeat	reflexed
French Perfume	yellow blend	large	very full	high-centered	strong	singly	repeat	plain
Frensham	dark red	medium	semi-double	open	slight	truss	repeat	plain
Frenzy	red blend	medium	double to full	globular	moderate	small clusters	repeat	plain
Fresh Pink	light pink	medium	double to full	cupped	slight	large clusters	repeat	plain
Freude	orange-red	medium	semi-double	open	moderate	singly	repeat	plain
Friedrich Heyer	orange blend	large	single	open	moderate	large clusters	once	plain
Friend for Life	pink blend	small	semi-double	open	slight	large clusters	repeat	plain
Friendship	deep pink	large	double to full	cupped	strong	singly	repeat	reflexed
Frilly Dilly (Murray)	deep pink	small	very full	open	slight	small clusters	repeat	plain
Frilly Dilly (Cocker)	light pink	small	very full	open	slight	small clusters	repeat	plain
Frisco	medium yellow	medium	double to full	open	slight	small clusters	repeat	plain
Fritz Nobis	pink blend	medium	double to full	cupped	strong	truss	once	plain
Frolic	medium pink	medium	double to full	cupped	moderate	small clusters	repeat	plain
Frontier Twirl	pink blend	large	double to full	cupped	moderate	small clusters	repeat	reflexed
Frosty	white	small	semi-double	cupped	moderate	large clusters	once	plain
Frühlingsanfang	white	large	single	open	moderate	small clusters	once	plain
Frühlingsduft	pink blend	large	double to full	cupped	strong	small clusters	once	reflexed
Frühlingsgold	medium yellow	large	single	open	moderate	small clusters	once	plain
Frühlingsmorgen	pink blend	medium	single	open	none	small clusters	once	plain
Frühlingsschnee	white	large	semi-double	open	slight	small clusters	once	plain
Frühlingszauber	medium pink	medium	semi-double	cupped	slight	small clusters	once	plain

NAME	BLOOM COLOR	FLOWER SIZE	FLOWER TYPE	FLOWER SHAPE	FRAGRANCE AMOUNT	FLOWERING HABIT	FLOWERING INCIDENCE	PETAL SHAPE
Fruité	orange blend	large	double to full	open	moderate	small clusters	repeat	reflexed
Fuchsia Meidiland	deep pink	medium	semi-double	cupped	none	small clusters	repeat	reflexed
Fugue	dark red	large	double to full	cupped	none	small clusters	repeat	reflexed
Fulgurante	medium red	large	double to full	high-centered	none	singly	repeat	reflexed
Fulton MacKay	yellow blend	large	double to full	high-centered	moderate	small clusters	repeat	reflexed
Futura	mauve	medium	double to full	high-centered	slight	small clusters	repeat	reflexed
Fyvie Castle	pink blend	large	double to full	cupped	moderate	small clusters	repeat	reflexed
Gabriel Noyelle	apricot blend	medium	double to full	cupped	moderate	small clusters	repeat	plain
Gabriella	medium red	medium	double to full	high-centered	none	small clusters	repeat	reflexed
Gail Borden	pink blend	large	double to full	high-centered	moderate	small clusters	repeat	reflexed
Galaxy	dark red	small	double to full	high-centered	none	small clusters	repeat	reflexed
Galia	orange-red	large	double to full	cupped	none	singly	repeat	reflexed
Galway Bay	orange-pink	large	double to full	cupped	slight	small clusters	repeat	reflexed
Garden Charm	medium red	medium	semi-double	open	none	small clusters	repeat	plain
Garden Party	white	large	double to full	high-centered	slight	small clusters	repeat	reflexed
Gardenia	white	large	double to full	cupped	slight	small clusters	once	plain
Garnette	dark red	medium	double to full	cupped	none	small clusters	repeat	reflexed
Gärtendirektor Otto Linne	deep pink	small	double to full	pompons	none	large clusters	repeat	plain
Gartenzauber	medium red	large	double to full	cupped	slight	small clusters	repeat	reflexed
Gary Lineker	orange blend	medium	semi-double	cupped	slight	large clusters	repeat	plain
Gavnø	orange blend	medium	double to full	cupped	none	small clusters	repeat	reflexed
Gavotte	pink blend	extra large	double to full	high-centered	moderate	singly	repeat	reflexed
Gay Debutante	pink blend	extra large	double to full	cupped	slight	singly	repeat	reflexed
Gay Princess	light pink	large	double to full	cupped	slight	small clusters	repeat	reflexed
Gay Vista	light pink	small	single	open	slight	large clusters	repeat	plain
Géant des Batailles	medium red	large	very full	flat	strong	small clusters	repeat	plain
Gee Gee	light yellow	small	double	cupped	moderate	small clusters	repeat	plain
Geisha	medium pink	medium	semi-double	high-centered	none	small clusters	repeat	reflexed
Gem	medium pink	large	semi-double	high-centered	moderate	small clusters	repeat	reflexed
Gene Boerner	medium pink	medium	double to full	high-centered	none	small clusters	repeat	reflexed
Général Galliéni	red blend	medium	double to full	cupped	moderate	small clusters	repeat	plain
Général Jacqueminot	red blend	large	double to full	open	strong	small clusters	repeat	reflexed
Général Kléber	medium pink	medium	double to full	cupped	strong	small clusters	once	plain
General MacArthur, Climbing	deep pink	large	double to full	cupped	strong	small clusters	repeat	reflexed
Général Schablikine	orange-pink	medium	double to full	quartered	moderate	small clusters	repeat	plain
General Testard	red blend	small	semi-double	flat	none	large clusters	once	plain
General Washington	dark red	large	very full	flat	moderate	singly	once	reflexed
Gentle Maid	mauve	small	double to full	rosette	none	small clusters	repeat	plain
Gentle Touch	light pink	medium	double to full	open	slight	small clusters	repeat	reflexed
Geoff Hamilton	light pink	large	very full	quartered	moderate	small clusters	repeat	ruffled
Geordie	russet	large	double to full	cupped	moderate	small clusters	repeat	reflexed
Georg Arends	medium pink	large	double to full	high-centered	strong	small clusters	repeat	reflexed
George Dickson	medium red	large	double to full	high-centered	moderate	singly	repeat	reflexed
Georges Vibert	red blend	medium	very full	flat	strong	small clusters	once	ruffled
Georgette	medium pink/deep pink	small	double to full	high-centered	none	singly	repeat	reflexed
Geraldine	orange blend	medium	double to full	open	slight	small clusters	repeat	reflexed
Geranium	medium red	small	single	flat	none	small clusters	once	plain
Geranium Red	orange-red	medium	very full	quartered	moderate	small clusters	repeat	ruffled
Gerbe Rose	light pink	large	double to full	cupped	slight	small clusters	once	ruffled
Gerdo	apricot blend	medium	double to full	high-centered	none	small clusters	repeat	reflexed
Germania-Africana	orange blend	large	semi-double	high-centered	strong	small clusters	repeat	plain
Germiston Gold	deep yellow	large	double to full	open	strong	small clusters	repeat	ruffled
Gertrude Jekyll	medium pink	large	double to full	rosette	moderate	small clusters	repeat	reflexed
Gertrude Raffel	deep pink	medium	semi-double	open	slight	large clusters	repeat	plain
Geschwind's Nordlandrose	medium pink	medium	very full	open	none	small clusters	once	plain
Geschwind's Orden	mauve	medium	very full	pompons	none	small clusters	once	ruffled
Geschwind's Schönste	dark red	medium	double to full	flat	none	small clusters	once	plain
Ghislaine de Féligonde	light yellow	small	double to full	cupped	slight	large clusters	repeat	reflexed
Gidget	orange-pink	small	semi-double	cupped	slight	small clusters	repeat	plain
Giggles	medium pink	small	semi-double	cupped	slight	small clusters	repeat	plain
Gilbert Becaud	yellow blend	large	double to full	high-centered	slight	singly	repeat	reflexed
Gilda (Geschwind)	dark red/mauve	medium	double to full	high-centered	none	small clusters	once	plain
Gilda (Pearce)	light pink	medium	full	high-centered	strong	small clusters	repeat	plain
Gina (Kriloff)	dark red	medium	single	high-centered	slight	large clusters	repeat	plain
Gina (Kordes)	dark red	small	double to full	high-centered	none	small clusters	repeat	plain
Gina Lollobrigida	deep yellow	extra large	very full	cupped	slight	singly	repeat	reflexed
Ginger	orange blend	medium	double to full	cupped	moderate	small clusters	repeat	reflexed
Ginger Meggs	orange blend	large	double to full	cupped	slight	small clusters	repeat	reflexed
Ginger Rogers	orange-pink	large	double to full	cupped	slight	small clusters	repeat	reflexed
Ginger Toddler	orange blend	medium	double	open	moderate	small clusters	repeat	plain
Gingerbread Man	apricot blend	small	double to full	quartered	slight	small clusters	repeat	plain
Gingernut	russet	medium	double to full	high-centered	moderate	small clusters	repeat	reflexed
Gingersnap	orange blend	large	double to full	open	slight	small clusters	repeat	ruffled
Gipsy Boy	dark red	medium	semi-double	flat	slight	small clusters	repeat	reflexed
Gitte	apricot blend	large	double to full	high-centered	strong	singly	repeat	reflexed
Givenchy	red blend	medium	double to full	high-centered	moderate	small clusters	repeat	reflexed
Glad Tidings	dark red	medium	double to full	cupped	none	large clusters	repeat	reflexed
Gladsome	medium pink	small	single	flat	slight	large clusters	once	plain
Glamis Castle	white	medium	very full	cupped	strong	small clusters	repeat	plain
Glastonbury	red blend	large	double to full	rosette	moderate	small clusters	repeat	reflexed
Glenara	deep pink	extra large	semi-double	open	slight	small clusters	repeat	reflexed
Glendora	apricot blend	large	double to full	cupped	moderate	small clusters	repeat	reflexed
Glenfiddich	deep yellow	large	double to full	cupped	slight	small clusters	repeat	reflexed
Glengarry	orange-red	large	double to full	high-centered	slight	small clusters	repeat	reflexed
Glenn Dale	light yellow	large	double to full	cupped	slight	large clusters	once	plain
Glenshane	medium red	small	semi-double	rosette	slight	truss	repeat	plain
Gletscher	mauve	large	double to full	high-centered	strong	small clusters	repeat	reflexed
Gloire de Bruxelles	mauve	large	double to full	rosette	strong	singly	repeat	plain
Gloire de Chédane-Guinoisseau	medium red	large	double to full	cupped	moderate	singly	repeat	plain
Gloire de Dijon	orange-pink	large	double to full	globular	moderate	small clusters	repeat	plain
Gloire de Ducher	dark red	extra large	double to full	globular	moderate	singly	repeat	plain
Gloire de France	light pink	medium	double to full	quartered	strong	small clusters	once	plain
Gloire de Guilan	light pink	medium	double to full	quartered	strong	small clusters	once	reflexed
Gloire des Jardins	mauve	medium	double to full	cupped	moderate	small clusters	once	plain
Gloire des Mousseuses	medium pink	medium	double to full	cupped	strong	small clusters	once	reflexed
Gloire des Polyantha	medium pink	small	double to full	cupped	none	truss	repeat	plain
Gloire des Rosomanes	medium red	extra large	semi-double	cupped	moderate	large clusters	repeat	plain
Gloire d'Un Enfant d'Hiram	medium red	large	double to full	cupped	moderate	singly	repeat	plain
Gloire Lyonnaise	white	extra large	very full	flat	moderate	small clusters	once	plain
Gloria Mundi	orange-red	small	double to full	rosette	none	large clusters	repeat	plain
Gloriana 97	mauve	medium	double	cupped	slight	small clusters	repeat	plain
Glory Be	deep yellow	small	double to full	cupped	none	small clusters	repeat	plain
Glory of Edsell	light pink	small	single	flat	none	singly	once	plain
Glowing	pale yellow	medium	double to full	open	slight	small clusters	repeat	quilled
Glowing Amber	red blend	small	double to full	high-centered	none	small clusters	repeat	reflexed
Goethe	mauve blend	medium	single	open	slight	small clusters	once	plain
Gold Badge	medium yellow	large	double to full	cupped	slight	small clusters	repeat	ruffled
Gold Coin	deep yellow	small	double to full	open	slight	small clusters	repeat	reflexed
Gold Country	medium yellow	small	double to full	high-centered	moderate	small clusters	repeat	reflexed
Gold Crown	deep yellow	large	double	high-centered	moderate	singly	repeat	plain

NAME	BLOOM COLOR	FLOWER SIZE	FLOWER TYPE	FLOWER SHAPE	FRAGRANCE AMOUNT	FLOWERING HABIT	FLOWERING INCIDENCE	PETAL SHAPE
Gold Fever	medium yellow	medium	double to full	cupped	moderate	small clusters	repeat	reflexed
Gold Glow	deep yellow	large	very full	rosette	slight	singly	repeat	ruffled
Gold Medal	medium yellow	large	double to full	high-centered	slight	small clusters	repeat	reflexed
Gold Reef	deep yellow	medium	double	high-centered	slight	small clusters	repeat	plain
Gold Rush	yellow blend	large	double to full	cupped	moderate	small clusters	once	reflexed
Goldbusch	medium yellow	large	semi-double	cupped	slight	small clusters	repeat	ruffled
Golden Angel	deep yellow	small	very full	globular	moderate	small clusters	repeat	plain
Golden Anniversary	deep yellow	large	double to full	cupped	slight	singly	repeat	reflexed
Golden Bettina	deep yellow	medium	double	flat	moderate	small clusters	repeat	plain
Golden Celebration	deep yellow	large	very full	rosette	moderate	small clusters	repeat	plain
Golden Century	orange blend	medium	double to full	cupped	moderate	small clusters	repeat	reflexed
Golden Chersonese	medium yellow	small	single	cupped	slight	small clusters	once	plain
Golden Choice	medium yellow	large	double to full	high-centered	strong	small clusters	repeat	reflexed
Golden Dawn	medium yellow	large	double to full	high-centered	moderate	singly	repeat	reflexed
Golden Days	deep yellow	large	double to full	cupped	slight	singly	repeat	plain
Golden Delight	medium yellow	large	very full	cupped	moderate	small clusters	repeat	reflexed
Golden Fleece	medium yellow	large	double to full	cupped	strong	large clusters	repeat	reflexed
Golden Friendship	medium yellow	large	double to full	high-centered	slight	small clusters	repeat	reflexed
Golden Gardens	medium yellow	small	double to full	cupped	none	small clusters	repeat	plain
Golden Giant	deep yellow	extra large	double to full	high-centered	slight	singly	repeat	reflexed
Golden Girl	medium yellow	large	double to full	high-centered	moderate	small clusters	repeat	reflexed
Golden Gloves	deep yellow	medium	double to full	cupped	slight	small clusters	repeat	reflexed
Golden Halo	medium yellow	small	double to full	cupped	slight	small clusters	repeat	reflexed
Golden Handshake	deep yellow	small	semi-double	open	slight	small clusters	repeat	plain
Golden Harvest	deep yellow	large	double to full	high-centered	slight	singly	repeat	reflexed
Golden Holstein	deep yellow	medium	semi-double	cupped	slight	small clusters	repeat	ruffled
Golden Jubilee	medium yellow	medium	double to full	high-centered	moderate	small clusters	repeat	reflexed
Golden Masterpiece	medium yellow	large	double to full	high-centered	slight	small clusters	repeat	reflexed
Golden Moments	deep yellow	large	double to full	high-centered	strong	singly	repeat	reflexed
Golden Ophelia	medium yellow	medium	double to full	high-centered	slight	singly	repeat	reflexed
Golden Scepter	deep yellow	large	double to full	high-centered	slight	small clusters	repeat	reflexed
Golden Showers	medium yellow	large	semi-double	cupped	moderate	small clusters	repeat	plain
Golden Slippers	yellow blend	medium	double to full	cupped	slight	small clusters	repeat	reflexed
Golden State	deep yellow	large	double to full	cupped	moderate	small clusters	repeat	ruffled
Golden Surprise	deep yellow	medium	double to full	cupped	slight	small clusters	repeat	reflexed
Golden Times	medium yellow	medium	very full	high-centered	slight	small clusters	repeat	reflexed
Golden Vision	medium yellow	large	semi-double	open	slight	small clusters	once	reflexed
Golden Wedding	deep yellow	medium	double to full	high-centered	none	small clusters	repeat	reflexed
Golden Wings	light yellow	large	single	cupped	slight	small clusters	repeat	plain
Golden Years	medium yellow	medium	very full	cupped	slight	small clusters	repeat	plain
Goldener Olymp	deep yellow	large	double to full	cupped	slight	small clusters	repeat	frilled
Goldener Sommer 83	medium yellow	large	double to full	open	slight	small clusters	repeat	plain
Goldfinch	light yellow	medium	semi-double	open	slight	large clusters	once	reflexed
Goldilocks	medium yellow	medium	double to full	globular	slight	small clusters	repeat	plain
Goldmarie 82	deep yellow	large	double to full	high-centered	slight	large clusters	repeat	frilled
Goldstar	deep yellow	medium	double to full	high-centered	slight	small clusters	repeat	reflexed
Goldstern	medium yellow	large	double to full	cupped	none	small clusters	repeat	reflexed
Goldtopas	medium yellow	medium	double to full	high-centered	slight	small clusters	repeat	reflexed
Goldy	deep yellow	large	double to full	high-centered	moderate	singly	repeat	reflexed

NAME	BLOOM COLOR	FLOWER SIZE	FLOWER TYPE	FLOWER SHAPE	FRAGRANCE AMOUNT	FLOWERING HABIT	FLOWERING INCIDENCE	PETAL SHAPE
Golestan	orange-red	large	double to full	high-centered	none	small clusters	repeat	reflexed
Goliath	orange blend	extra large	double to full	high-centered	slight	singly	repeat	reflexed
Good As Gold	deep yellow	small	double to full	open	moderate	small clusters	repeat	plain
Gordon's College	orange-pink	medium	double to full	high-centered	slight	small clusters	repeat	reflexed
Gourmet Pheasant	medium red	small	semi-double	open	none	large clusters	repeat	plain
Gourmet Popcorn	white	small	semi-double	flat	slight	truss	repeat	plain
Goya	white	large	double to full	high-centered	slight	small clusters	repeat	reflexed
Grace Abounding	white	medium	semi-double	cupped	moderate	large clusters	repeat	plain
Grace Darling	white	medium	double to full	globular	slight	small clusters	repeat	plain
Grace de Monaco	light pink	large	double to full	high-centered	strong	singly	repeat	reflexed
Graceland	medium yellow	large	double to full	cupped	none	small clusters	repeat	reflexed
Gracilis	medium red	medium	semi-double	flat	none	small clusters	once	plain
Grafin Sonja	pink blend	medium	double to full	high-centered	slight	small clusters	repeat	reflexed
Graham Thomas	deep yellow	large	double to full	cupped	slight	small clusters	repeat	plain
Granada	red blend	large	double to full	high-centered	moderate	small clusters	repeat	reflexed
Grand Hotel	medium red	large	double to full	cupped	none	small clusters	repeat	reflexed
Grand Masterpiece	medium red	large	double to full	high-centered	none	singly	repeat	reflexed
Grand Nord	white	large	double to full	high-centered	slight	singly	repeat	reflexed
Grand Siècle	pink blend	large	double to full	cupped	slight	small clusters	repeat	reflexed
Grandma's Pink	medium pink	medium	very full	cupped	none	small clusters	repeat	plain
Grandmaster	apricot blend	large	semi-double	open	moderate	small clusters	repeat	plain
Grand'mère Jenny	yellow blend	large	double to full	high-centered	moderate	singly	repeat	reflexed
Granny's Bonnet	pink blend	medium	double to full	cupped	none	small clusters	repeat	plain
Great Maiden's Blush	light pink	medium	double to full	flat	strong	small clusters	once	plain
Great News	mauve	large	double to full	open	strong	singly	repeat	ruffled
Great Venture	yellow blend	large	double to full	high-centered	strong	singly	repeat	reflexed
Great Western	mauve	large	double to full	globular	moderate	large clusters	once	plain
Green Diamond	pink	small	double to full	cupped	none	small clusters	repeat	plain
Green Fire	deep yellow	medium	semi-double	flat	slight	small clusters	repeat	plain
Green Ice	white	small	double to full	cupped	none	small clusters	repeat	plain
Green Rose	green	small	double to full	open	none	small clusters	repeat	plain
Green Snake	white	small	single	open	slight	large clusters	once	plain
Greenalls Glory	pink blend	large	semi-double	open	slight	small clusters	repeat	plain
Greenmantle	red blend	medium	single	open	moderate	small clusters	once	ruffled
Greensleeves	green	large	semi-double	flat	none	small clusters	repeat	plain
Grey Dawn	mauve	large	double to full	high-centered	slight	small clusters	repeat	reflexed
Griseldis	medium pink	large	double to full	flat	none	small clusters	repeat	plain
Grootendorst Supreme	dark red	small	double to full	open	slight	small clusters	repeat	frilled
Gros Choux d'Hollande	light pink	large	very full	cupped	strong	small clusters	once	plain
Gros Provins Panaché	mauve	large	double to full	open	strong	small clusters	once	plain
Grouse 2000	light pink	small	single	flat	slight	singly	repeat	plain
Gruss an Aachen	light pink	large	double to full	open	slight	small clusters	repeat	ruffled
Gruss an Berlin	medium red	large	double to full	high-centered	slight	singly	repeat	plain
Gruss an Coburg	apricot blend	medium	double to full	globular	strong	singly	repeat	plain
Gruss an Freundorf	dark red	medium	single	high-centered	strong	truss	once	plain
Gruss an Teplitz	medium red	medium	double to full	cupped	strong	small clusters	repeat	ruffled
Gruss an Zabern	white	medium	double to full	flat	moderate	small clusters	once	plain
Guiding Spirit	deep pink	small	double to full	flat	slight	large clusters	repeat	plain
Guillaum Gillemot	medium red	extra large	double to full	globular	none	singly	repeat	plain
Guinée	dark red	large	double to full	globular	strong	small clusters	repeat	plain
Guinevere	medium pink	large	double to full	high-centered	slight	singly	repeat	reflexed
Guitare	orange blend	medium	double to full	globular	strong	small clusters	repeat	plain
Gütersloh 85	medium red	medium	double to full	cupped	none	small clusters	repeat	plain
Guy de Maupassant	medium pink	medium	very full	cupped	strong	small clusters	repeat	plain
Guy Laroche	red blend	large	double to full	high-centered	slight	singly	repeat	reflexed
Gwen Fagan	light pink	medium	double	rosette	moderate	small clusters	repeat	plain

NAME	BLOOM COLOR	FLOWER SIZE	FLOWER TYPE	FLOWER SHAPE	FRAGRANCE AMOUNT	FLOWERING HABIT	FLOWERING INCIDENCE	PETAL SHAPE
Gwen Mayor	apricot blend	large	double to full	high-centered	slight	small clusters	repeat	reflexed
Gwen Nash	pink blend	large	semi-double	cupped	slight	small clusters	once	plain
Gwen Swane	medium pink	small	double to full	flat	slight	small clusters	repeat	plain
Gypsy	orange-red	large	double to full	cupped	slight	small clusters	repeat	plain
Gypsy Jewel	deep pink	small	very full	high-centered	none	small clusters	repeat	reflexed
Gypsy Moth	orange-pink	medium	double to full	high-centered	none	small clusters	repeat	reflexed
Hadley, Climbing	medium red	large	double to full	high-centered	strong	singly	repeat	reflexed
Hakuun	white	medium	semi-double	cupped	slight	small clusters	repeat	reflexed
Halali	deep pink	large	semi-double	cupped	none	small clusters	repeat	plain
Halo Dolly	pink blend	small	semi-double	open	none	small clusters	repeat	plain
Halo Rainbow	pink blend	small	single	open	slight	small clusters	repeat	plain
Halo Star	orange blend	small	single	open	none	small clusters	repeat	plain
Halo Today	orange-pink	small	semi-double	open	none	small clusters	repeat	plain
Hamburger Phoenix	medium red	large	semi-double	cupped	none	small clusters	repeat	plain
Hampshire	medium red	small	single	flat	none	small clusters	repeat	plain
Hand in Hand	orange-red	small	double to full	rosette	none	small clusters	repeat	plain
Handel	red blend	medium	double to full	open	none	small clusters	repeat	plain
Hannah Gordon	pink blend	medium	semi-double	cupped	slight	small clusters	repeat	plain
Hanne	medium red	large	double to full	high-centered	strong	singly	repeat	reflexed
Hansa	medium red	large	double to full	open	strong	small clusters	repeat	plain
Hansa-Park	mauve	medium	double to full	open	slight	small clusters	repeat	reflexed
Hansaland	dark red	medium	semi-double	cupped	slight	small clusters	repeat	plain
Happenstance	light yellow	medium	single	cupped	slight	small clusters	repeat	plain
Happiness	medium red	large	double to full	high-centered	slight	singly	repeat	reflexed
Happy	medium red	small	semi-double	rosette	none	truss	repeat	plain
Happy Child	medium yellow	large	very full	cupped	strong	small clusters	repeat	plain
Happy Day	red blend	large	double to full	cupped	slight	singly	repeat	reflexed
Happy Days	pink blend	medium	double to full	high-centered	slight	small clusters	repeat	reflexed
Happy Thought	orange-pink	small	double to full	open	slight	small clusters	repeat	plain
Happy Wanderer	medium red	medium	double to full	cupped	slight	small clusters	repeat	plain
Harewood	white	small	semi-double	cupped	slight	large clusters	repeat	plain
Harison's Yellow	dark yellow	small	semi-double	cupped	moderate	small clusters	once	plain
Harlekin	pink blend	large	double to full	cupped	moderate	small clusters	repeat	plain
Harmonie	orange-pink	large	double to full	high-centered	strong	small clusters	repeat	reflexed
Harold Macmillan	orange-red	medium	double to full	cupped	slight	small clusters	repeat	reflexed
Harriny	medium pink	large	double to full	high-centered	strong	small clusters	repeat	reflexed
Harry Edland	mauve	large	double to full	cupped	strong	small clusters	repeat	reflexed
Harry Wheatcroft	yellow blend	extra large	double to full	high-centered	slight	singly	repeat	reflexed
Harvest Fayre	orange blend	medium	double to full	cupped	slight	small clusters	repeat	plain
Harvest Home	medium pink	large	semi-double	cupped	slight	small clusters	repeat	ruffled
Hawa Mahal	orange-pink	large	double to full	cupped	moderate	small clusters	repeat	plain
Hawaii	orange-red	large	double to full	high-centered	strong	small clusters	repeat	reflexed
Hawkeye Belle	white	large	double to full	high-centered	strong	small clusters	repeat	reflexed
Headliner	pink blend	large	double to full	high-centered	slight	singly	repeat	reflexed
Heart of Gold	yellowblend/ deep yellow	large	double to full	flat	strong	small clusters	repeat	plain
Heartbeat	orange blend	large	double	globular	moderate	small clusters	repeat	plain
Heartbeat 97	apricot blend	medium	double	high-centered	slight	large clusters	repeat	reflexed
Heartbreaker	pink blend	small	double to full	high-centered	slight	small clusters	repeat	reflexed
Heartland	orange-pink	small	double to full	high-centered	slight	small clusters	repeat	reflexed
Hearts A'Fire	dark red	small	double to full	high-centered	slight	singly	repeat	reflexed
Heat Wave	orange-red	large	double to full	cupped	slight	small clusters	repeat	plain
Heather Austin	red blend	medium	double to full	cupped	moderate	small clusters	repeat	plain
Heather Honey	apricot blend	large	double to full	cupped	moderate	small clusters	repeat	plain
Heaven	white	large	double to full	high-centered	slight	singly	repeat	reflexed
Heavenly Rosalind	pink blend	medium	single	open	slight	small clusters	repeat	plain
Hebe (Leenders)	deep pink	medium	semi-double	open	moderate	small clusters	repeat	plain
Hebe (Dickson)	orange-pink	large	double to full	high-centered	moderate	singly	repeat	reflexed
Hébé's Lip	white	medium	semi-double	cupped	moderate	small clusters	once	plain
Hector Deane	red blend	large	double to full	high-centered	strong	singly	repeat	reflexed
Heidekind	dark red	large	double to full	open	slight	small clusters	repeat	plain
Heidekönigin	light pink	medium	double to full	open	slight	small clusters	repeat	plain
Heidelberg	medium red	large	double to full	high-centered	slight	small clusters	repeat	reflexed
Heideröslein	yellow blend	medium	single	flat	moderate	large clusters	repeat	ruffled
Heideschnee	white	small	single	flat	none	large clusters	repeat	ruffled
Heidesommer	white	medium	semi-double	open	moderate	large clusters	repeat	plain
Heidi	medium pink	small	semi-double	open	none	large clusters	repeat	plain
Heike	medium yellow	large	semi-double	open	moderate	small clusters	repeat	reflexed
Heinrich Münch	medium pink	extra large	very full	globular	moderate	singly	once	reflexed
Heinrich Schultheis	light pink	large	very full	high-centered	strong	singly	once	reflexed
Heinz Erhardt	medium red	medium	double to full	open	slight	small clusters	repeat	plain
Heinzelmännchen	medium red	large	double to full	cupped	slight	small clusters	repeat	plain
Heirloom	mauve	medium	semi-double	cupped	strong	small clusters	repeat	plain
Helen Knight	medium yellow	small	single	cupped	none	small clusters	once	plain
Helen Naudé	white blend	large	semi-double	high-centered	slight	small clusters	repeat	plain
Helen Traubel	pink blend	large	double to full	cupped	moderate	singly	repeat	plain
Helena	light yellow	large	double	high-centered	moderate	small clusters	repeat	plain
Hello	medium red	small	semi-double	open	slight	large clusters	repeat	plain
Helmut Schmidt	medium yellow	large	double to full	high-centered	slight	singly	repeat	reflexed
Helpmekaar Roos	apricot blend	large	semi-double	open	moderate	small clusters	repeat	plain
Henkell Royal	medium red	large	double to full	high-centered	strong	singly	repeat	reflexed
Henri Barruet	pink blend	medium	double to full	cupped	slight	large clusters	once	plain
Henri Fouquier	medium pink	medium	double to full	flat	strong	small clusters	once	plain
Henri Martin	medium red	medium	double to full	flat	strong	large clusters	once	plain
Henry Fonda	deep yellow	large	double to full	high-centered	slight	small clusters	repeat	reflexed
Henry Hudson	white	medium	double to full	cupped	strong	small clusters	repeat	plain
Henry Kelsey	medium red	medium	double to full	cupped	moderate	large clusters	repeat	plain
Henry Nevard	dark red	extra large	double to full	cupped	strong	singly	repeat	plain
Her Majesty	medium pink	extra large	very full	high-centered	slight	singly	repeat	reflexed
Herbstfeuer	dark red	large	semi-double	open	moderate	small clusters	repeat	plain
Herero	red blend	medium	double	open	none	small clusters	repeat	plain
Heritage	light pink	medium	double to full	cupped	strong	small clusters	repeat	plain
Herman Steyn	red blend	large	semi-double	open	slight	small clusters	repeat	plain
Hermosa	light pink	small	double to full	globular	slight	small clusters	repeat	plain
Hero	medium pink	large	double to full	cupped	strong	small clusters	repeat	plain
Heroïca	dark red	large	double to full	high-centered	slight	singly	repeat	reflexed
Heroïne de Vaucluse	medium pink	large	very full	quartered	strong	small clusters	repeat	plain
Hertfordshire	deep pink	small	single	flat	none	large clusters	repeat	plain
Hi Ho	orange-pink	small	double to full	flat	none	large clusters	repeat	reflexed
Hiawatha	red blend	small	single	cupped	none	large clusters	once	plain
Hidalgo	medium red	extra large	double to full	cupped	strong	singly	repeat	reflexed
High Esteem	pink blend	extra large	very full	high-centered	strong	singly	repeat	reflexed
High Hopes	medium pink	medium	double to full	high-centered	slight	small clusters	repeat	reflexed
High Noon	medium yellow	medium	semi-double	cupped	moderate	small clusters	repeat	plain
High Sheriff	orange-red	medium	double to full	high-centered	strong	small clusters	repeat	reflexed
High Summer	orange-red	large	double to full	cupped	none	small clusters	repeat	plain
Highdownensis	medium red	small	single	open	none	small clusters	once	plain
Highfield	light yellow	medium	double to full	open	moderate	small clusters	repeat	reflexed
Highlight	orange-red	medium	double to full	open	moderate	small clusters	repeat	plain
Hilda Heinemann	red blend	large	semi-double	open	moderate	small clusters	repeat	plain
Hilda Murrell	medium pink	large	very full	globular	moderate	small clusters	repeat	plain
Himmelsauge	mauve	large	double to full	cupped	strong	small clusters	once	plain
Hinrich Gaede	orange blend	extra large	double to full	high-centered	moderate	singly	repeat	reflexed
Hippolyte	mauve	medium	very full	rosette	strong	small clusters	once	plain
Hippolyte Jamain	deep pink	large	double to full	globular	moderate	singly	repeat	plain
Hiroshima's Children	yellow blend	medium	double to full	high-centered	slight	small clusters	repeat	reflexed

NAME	BLOOM COLOR	FLOWER SIZE	FLOWER TYPE	FLOWER SHAPE	FRAGRANCE AMOUNT	FLOWERING HABIT	FLOWERING INCIDENCE	PETAL SHAPE
Hoagy Carmichael	medium red	large	double to full	high-centered	slight	singly	repeat	reflexed
Hofgärtner Kalb	pink blend	medium	double to full	high-centered	moderate	small clusters	repeat	reflexed
Hokey Pokey	apricot blend	small	double to full	high-centered	slight	singly.	repeat	reflexed
Hollie Roffey	medium pink	small	double to full	rosette	slight	small clusters	repeat	plain
Holsteinperle	orange-pink	large	very full	flat	none	singly	repeat	plain
Holtermann's Gold	medium yellow	medium	double to full	cupped	moderate	small clusters	repeat	plain
Holy Toledo	apricot blend	small	double to full	flat	none	small clusters	repeat	reflexed
Hombre	pink blend	small	very full	high-centered	slight	small clusters	repeat	reflexed
Homère	pink blend	large	very full	cupped	moderate	small clusters	repeat	ruffled
Honey Bunch	yellow blend	small	double to full	cupped	moderate	large clusters	repeat	plain
Honey Chile	light pink	medium	double to full	cupped	slight	small clusters	repeat	plain
Honey Favorite	light pink	large	double to full	open	slight	small clusters	repeat	plain
Honeyflow	pink blend	small	single	open	moderate	truss	repeat	plain
Honigmond	medium yellow	medium	double to full	rosette	slight	small clusters	repeat	plain
Honor	white	large	double to full	open	slight	singly	repeat	reflexed
Honorable Lady Lindsay	pink blend	medium	double to full	open	none	small clusters	repeat	reflexed
Honoré de Balzac	pink blend	extra large	very full	cupped	moderate	singly	repeat	plain
Honorine de Brabant	pink blend	large	double to full	cupped	moderate	small clusters	repeat	plain
Hoot Owl	red blend	small	single	open	none	small clusters	repeat	plain
Horace Vernet	dark red	large	double to full	high-centered	strong	singly	repeat	reflexed
Horstmann's Rosenresli	white	large	double to full	open	moderate	small clusters	repeat	plain
Hot Chocolate	russet	medium	double to full	cupped	none	small clusters	repeat	plain
Hot Lips	orange-pink	small	double to full	high-centered	slight	small clusters	repeat	reflexed
Hot Pewter	orange-red	large	double to full	high-centered	slight	singly	repeat	reflexed
Hot Shot	orange-red	small	double to full	high-centered	none	small clusters	repeat	reflexed
Hot Tamale	yellow blend	small	double to full	high-centered	slight	small clusters	repeat	reflexed
Hugh Dickson	medium red	extra large	double to full	high-centered	strong	small clusters	repeat	reflexed
Hugh Watson	orange-pink	extra large	very full	flat	moderate	small clusters	repeat	plain
Hugo Roller	yellow blend	medium	double to full	cupped	slight	small clusters	repeat	plain
Huguenot 300	orange blend	medium	semi-double	high-centered	none	truss	repeat	plain
Hula Girl	orange blend	small	double to full	high-centered	moderate	small clusters	repeat	reflexed
Hula Hoop	pink blend	medium	semi-double	flat	none	small clusters	repeat	plain
Hume's Blush Tea-scented China	light pink	medium	double to full	open	strong	small clusters	repeat	plain
Hunter	medium red	medium	double to full	globular	moderate	small clusters	repeat	plain
Hurdy Gurdy	red blend	small	double to full	open	none	small clusters	repeat	plain
Ice White	white	medium	double to full	open	moderate	small clusters	repeat	reflexed
Iceberg	white	medium	double to full	open	slight	large clusters	repeat	reflexed
Iced Ginger	orange blend	large	double to full	cupped	slight	small clusters	repeat	reflexed
Iced Parfait	light pink	large	double to full	cupped	slight	small clusters	repeat	reflexed
Ida Elizabeth	medium red	large	double to full	high-centered	none	singly	repeat	reflexed
Iga 83 München	medium red	medium	double to full	cupped	none	small clusters	repeat	plain
Ile de France	red blend	small	semi-double	flat	slight	large clusters	once	plain
Ilse Haberland	medium pink	extra large	double to full	high-centered	moderate	small clusters	repeat	reflexed
Ilse Krohn Superior	white	large	double to full	high-centered	strong	small clusters	repeat	reflexed
Imagination	apricot blend	large	double to full	high-centered	none	small clusters	repeat	reflexed
Immensee	light pink	small	single	flat	moderate	small clusters	repeat	plain
Immortal Juno	deep pink	large	very full	globular	moderate	small clusters	repeat	plain
Imp	red blend	medium	double to full	cupped	none	small clusters	repeat	plain
Impatient	orange-red	medium	semi-double	cupped	none	small clusters	repeat	plain
Impératrice Eugénie	mauve	medium	double to full	globular	strong	small clusters	once	plain
Impératrice Farah	white	large	double to full	high-centered	none	small clusters	repeat	reflexed
Improved Cécile Brünner	orange-pink	medium	double to full	high-centered	slight	small clusters	repeat	reflexed
In the Pink	medium pink	medium	very full	globular	moderate	small clusters	repeat	plain
Ina	white	small	double to full	high-centered	slight	singly	repeat	reflexed
Incognito	mauve	small	double to full	high-centered	slight	singly	repeat	reflexed

NAME	BLOOM COLOR	FLOWER SIZE	FLOWER TYPE	FLOWER SHAPE	FRAGRANCE AMOUNT	FLOWERING HABIT	FLOWERING INCIDENCE	PETAL SHAPE
Independence	orange-red	large	double to full	cupped	slight	small clusters	repeat	plain
Indian Summer	orange blend	large	double to full	high-centered	strong	small clusters	repeat	reflexed
Indigo	mauve	medium	double to full	rosette	strong	small clusters	repeat	plain
Ingrid Bergman	dark red	medium	double to full	high-centered	slight	singly	repeat	reflexed
Inner Wheel	pink blend	medium	double to full	high-centered	none	small clusters	repeat	reflexed
Innocence (Chaplin Brothers)	white	large	semi-double	open	moderate	small clusters	repeat	ruffled
Innocence (Saville)	white	large	double	open	slight	small clusters	repeat	plain
International Herald Tribune	mauve blend	medium	double to full	cupped	slight	truss	repeat	plain
Interview	orange pink	large	double to full	high-centered	slight	singly	repeat	reflexed
Intervilles	medium red	large	semi-double	cupped	moderate	small clusters	repeat	plain
Intrigue	mauve	large	double to full	high-centered	strong	small clusters	repeat	plain
Invincible	dark red	large	double to full	open	slight	small clusters	repeat	plain
Ipsilanté	mauve	medium	double to full	quartered	strong	small clusters	once	plain
Irène	deep pink	medium	double to full	cupped	none	small clusters	repeat	plain
Irene of Denmark	white	medium	double to full	cupped	moderate	small clusters	repeat	plain
Irène Watts	white	medium	double to full	rosette	moderate	small clusters	repeat	plain
Irish Elegance	orange blend	large	single	flat	none	small clusters	repeat	plain
Irish Gold	medium yellow	large	double to full	high-centered	moderate	small clusters	repeat	plain
Irish Mist	orange-pink	large	double to full	high-centered	none	small clusters	repeat	reflexed
Irish Rich Marbled	red blend	small	single	open	slight	small clusters	once	plain
Irresistible	white	small	double to full	high-centered	moderate	small clusters	repeat	reflexed
Isabel de Ortiz	pink blend	extra large	double to full	high-centered	moderate	singly	repeat	reflexed
Isabella Gray	deep yellow	large	double to full	globular	moderate	small clusters	repeat	plain
Isabella Skinner	medium pink	medium	double to full	high-centered	none	small clusters	once	reflexed
Isabelle de France	orange-red	large	double to full	high-centered	slight	singly	repeat	reflexed
Isobel Derby	pink blend	extra large	double to full	cupped	moderate	small clusters	repeat	reflexed
Isobel Harkness	deep yellow	large	double to full	high-centered	moderate	singly	repeat	reflexed
Ispahan	medium pink	medium	double to full	open	strong	small clusters	once	plain
Ita Buttrose	orange-pink	large	double to full	high-centered	none	singly	repeat	reflexed
Ivory Fashion	white	large	semi-double	cupped	slight	small clusters	repeat	plain
Ivory Palace	white	small	very full	high-centered	slight	small clusters	repeat	reflexed
J. P. Connell	light yellow	medium	double	high-centered	strong	small clusters	repeat	plain
Jacaranda	medium pink	large	double to full	high-centered	slight	singly	repeat	reflexed
Jack Frost	white	large	double to full	high-centered	moderate	small clusters	repeat	reflexed
Jackie	light yellow	small	very full	high-centered	slight	small clusters	repeat	reflexed
Jacqueline du Pré	white	large	semi-double	open	moderate	small clusters	repeat	plain
Jacqueline Nebout	medium pink	medium	double to full	high-centered	moderate	small clusters	repeat	reflexed
Jadis	medium pink	large	double to full	high-centered	strong	singly	repeat	reflexed
Jamaica	medium red	large	semi-double	cupped	moderate	small clusters	repeat	plain
James Mason	medium red	large	semi-double	flat	strong	small clusters	once	plain
James Mitchell	deep pink	medium	double to full	quartered	moderate	small clusters	once	plain
James Veitch	mauve	medium	double to full	flat	moderate	singly	repeat	plain
Jane Asher	medium red	small	very full	globular	none	large clusters	repeat	plain
Jane Isobella Linton	pink blend	medium	very full	quartered	moderate	small clusters	repeat	plain
Janet B. Wood	white	small	semi-double	open	slight	small clusters	once	plain
Janet Morrison	deep pink	large	semi-double	open	moderate	small clusters	repeat	reflexed
Janet's Pride	pink blend	medium	semi-double	flat	moderate	small clusters	once	plain
Janice Heyes	light pink	large	double to full	high-centered	moderate	singly	repeat	reflexed
Janina	orange blend	medium	double to full	high-centered	none	small clusters	repeat	reflexed
Janna	pink blend	small	double to full	cupped	none	small clusters	repeat	plain
Jaquenetta	apricot blend	large	semi-double	cupped	slight	small clusters	repeat	ruffled
Jardins de Bagatelle	white	large	double to full	high-centered	moderate	singly	repeat	reflexed
Jason	deep pink	large	double to full	high-centered	none	small clusters	repeat	reflexed
Jaune Desprez	yellow blend	large	double to full	cupped	moderate	small clusters	repeat	plain
Jayne Austin	medium yellow	medium	very full	cupped	moderate	small clusters	repeat	plain
Jazz	orange blend	medium	double to full	high-centered	slight	small clusters	repeat	reflexed
Jean Bach Sisley	pink blend	medium	double to full	high-centered	slight	small clusters	repeat	reflexed

NAME	BLOOM COLOR	FLOWER SIZE	FLOWER TYPE	FLOWER SHAPE	FRAGRANCE AMOUNT	FLOWERING HABIT	FLOWERING INCIDENCE	PETAL SHAPE
Jean de la Lune	deep yellow	medium	double to full	cupped	slight	small clusters	repeat	plain
Jean Ducher	orange-pink	medium	double to full	cupped	slight	small clusters	repeat	plain
Jean Giono	yellow blend	large	double to full	high-centered	slight	small clusters	repeat	reflexed
Jean Guichard	pink blend	medium	double to full	cupped	moderate	small clusters	once	plain
Jean Kenneally	apricot blend	small	double to full	high-centered	slight	small clusters	repeat	reflexed
Jean Mermoz	medium pink	small	very full	cupped	slight	large clusters	repeat	plain
Jean Rameau	deep pink	large	very full	cupped	strong	small clusters	repeat	plain
Jean Rosenkrantz	orange-red	large	double to full	high-centered	strong	singly	repeat	reflexed
Jean Soupert	dark red	large	very full	rosette	moderate	singly	repeat	plain
Jeanie	white blend	large	double	high-centered	moderate	singly	repeat	plain
Jeanie Williams	red blend	small	double to full	high-centered	slight	small clusters	repeat	reflexed
Jeanne D'Arc	white	medium	double to full	flat	moderate	small clusters	once	plain
Jeanne de Montfort	medium pink	medium	semi-double	flat	moderate	small clusters	once	plain
Jeanne LaJoie	medium pink	small	double to full	high-centered	none	small clusters	repeat	reflexed
Jeannie Deans	dark red	small	semi-double	open	moderate	small clusters	once	plain
Jennifer	pink blend	small	double to full	high-centered	slight	small clusters	repeat	reflexed
Jenny Brown	orange-red	large	single	open	moderate	small clusters	repeat	plain
Jenny Duval	mauve	medium	double to full	open	strong	small clusters	once	ruffled
Jenny Wren	apricot blend	small	double to full	flat	strong	large clusters	repeat	ruffled
Jenny's Rose	light pink	medium	semi-double	open	strong	small clusters	repeat	plain
Jens Munk	medium pink	large	semi-double	open	moderate	small clusters	repeat	plain
Jersey Beauty	light yellow	large	single	open	strong	small clusters	once	plain
Jessie Clark	medium pink	extra large	single	open	none	small clusters	once	plain
Jessika	orange-pink	large	double to full	high-centered	moderate	small clusters	repeat	plain
Jet Trail	white	small	double to full	high-centered	none	small clusters	repeat	reflexed
Jewel Box	pink blend	small	double	cupped	slight	small clusters	repeat	plain
Joanna Hill	light yellow	large	double to full	high-centered	strong	small clusters	repeat	plain
Joasine Hanet	mauve	medium	double to full	quartered	strong	small clusters	repeat	plain
Jocelyn	russet	large	double to full	quartered	none	small clusters	repeat	plain
Johann Strauss	pink blend	large	double to full	globular	strong	small clusters	repeat	reflexed
John Cabot	medium red	medium	semi-double	open	none	small clusters	repeat	plain
John Clare	deep pink	medium	double to full	open	slight	small clusters	repeat	plain
John Davis	medium pink	medium	double to full	cupped	strong	small clusters	repeat	plain
John F. Kennedy	white	large	double to full	high-centered	slight	small clusters	repeat	reflexed
John Franklin	medium red	medium	double to full	open	slight	small clusters	repeat	plain
John Hopper	pink blend	large	very full	cupped	moderate	singly	repeat	plain
John S. Armstrong	dark red	large	double to full	cupped	slight	small clusters	repeat	reflexed
John Waterer	dark red	large	double to full	high-centered	moderate	small clusters	repeat	reflexed
Johnnie Walker	apricot blend	large	semi-double	high-centered	strong	small clusters	repeat	reflexed
Joie de Vivre	pink blend	extra large	double to full	high-centered	moderate	small clusters	repeat	reflexed
Jolly Roger	orange blend	medium	semi-double	cupped	slight	small clusters	repeat	plain
Josephine Baker	dark red	medium	double	open	slight	small clusters	repeat	plain
Josephine Bruce	dark red	large	double to full	open	moderate	small clusters	repeat	reflexed
Joseph's Coat	red blend	medium	double	open	slight	small clusters	repeat	plain
Joy of Health	medium pink	medium	double to full	cupped	none	small clusters	repeat	plain
Joy of Life	red blend	large	double to full	high-centered	none	singly	repeat	reflexed
Joybells	medium pink	large	double to full	high-centered	slight	small clusters	repeat	ruffled
Joyce Edmonds	orange-pink	large	double to full	cupped	none	small clusters	repeat	plain
Joyce Northfield	orange blend	large	double to full	high-centered	slight	small clusters	repeat	plain
Joycie	orange blend	small	double to full	high-centered	moderate	small clusters	repeat	reflexed
Joyfulness	apricot blend	large	double	cupped	slight	large clusters	repeat	plain
Jubilant	light pink	medium	double to full	cupped	slight	small clusters	repeat	plain
Jude the Obscure	medium yellow	large	very full	globular	strong	small clusters	repeat	plain
Judy Fischer	medium pink	small	double to full	high-centered	none	small clusters	repeat	reflexed
Judy Garland	yellow blend	medium	double to full	open	none	small clusters	repeat	reflexed
Jules Margottin	medium pink	large	very full	flat	slight	singly	repeat	plain
Julia Mannering	light pink	small	single	open	moderate	singly	once	plain
Julia's Rose	russet	medium	double to full	open	slight	small clusters	repeat	plain
Julie	dark red	large	double to full	cupped	moderate	singly	repeat	reflexed
Julie de Mersan	medium pink	medium	double to full	globular	moderate	small clusters	once	plain
Julie Y	orange-red	large	double to full	open	slight	singly	repeat	plain
Juliet	pink blend	large	double to full	cupped	moderate	singly	once	plain
Julischka	medium red	medium	double to full	open	slight	small clusters	repeat	plain
June Bride	white	large	double to full	high-centered	slight	small clusters	repeat	reflexed
June Laver	deep yellow	small	double to full	high-centered	none	small clusters	repeat	reflexed
June Park	deep pink	large	double to full	high-centered	strong	small clusters	repeat	reflexed
June Time	light pink	small	very full	pompons	none	small clusters	repeat	plain
June Whitfield	pink blend	large	double to full	cupped	slight	small clusters	repeat	plain
Junior Geisha	orange-red	medium	double	high-centred	slight	large clusters	repeat	plain
Junior Miss	light pink	medium	semi-double	high-centered	slight	small clusters	repeat	plain
Juno	light pink	medium	very full	flat	strong	small clusters	once	plain
Just For You	deep pink	medium	double to full	high-centered	none	small clusters	repeat	reflexed
Just Joey	orange blend	extra large	double to full	open	moderate	small clusters	repeat	ruffled
Kabuki	deep yellow	medium	double to full	high-centered	slight	singly	repeat	reflexed
Kagayaki	red blend	large	double to full	high-centered	none	small clusters	repeat	reflexed
Kaikoura	orange blend	small	double to full	high-centered	none	small clusters	repeat	reflexed
Kaiserin Auguste Viktoria	white	large	very full	high-centered	slight	small clusters	repeat	reflexed
Kakwa	white	medium	double	open	strong	small clusters	once	plain
Kambala	apricot blend	large	double to full	high-centered	moderate	singly	repeat	reflexed
Kardinal	medium red	large	double to full	high-centered	none	singly	repeat	reflexed
Karen Blixen	white	large	double to full	high-centered	slight	small clusters	repeat	reflexed
Karen Julie	orange-red	large	double to full	high-centered	none	singly	repeat	reflexed
Karen Poulsen	medium red	medium	single	cupped	none	large clusters	repeat	plain
Karl Förster	white	large	double to full	high-centered	slight	small clusters	repeat	reflexed
Karl Herbst	medium red	extra large	very full	high-centered	slight	singly	repeat	reflexed
Karlsruhe	deep pink	large	double to full	cupped	slight	small clusters	repeat	plain
Karoo Rose	orange-red	medium	double	open	moderate	small clusters	repeat	plain
Kassel	orange-red	large	semi-double	cupped	slight	small clusters	repeat	reflexed
Katharina Zeimet	white	small	double to full	cupped	slight	truss	repeat	plain
Kathleen	light pink	small	single	open	slight	large clusters	repeat	plain
Kathleen Ferrier	orange-pink	medium	semi-double	cupped	slight	small clusters	repeat	plain
Kathleen Harrop	light pink	medium	semi-double	open	moderate	small clusters	repeat	plain
Kathryn McGredy	orange-pink	large	double to full	high-centered	slight	singly	repeat	reflexed
Kathryn Morley	light pink	medium	very full	cupped	slight	small clusters	repeat	plain
Kathy	medium red	small	double to full	high-centered	slight	small clusters	repeat	reflexed
Kazanlik	deep pink	medium	double to full	open	strong	small clusters	once	plain
Keepit	light pink	large	double to full	high-centered	moderate	singly	repeat	reflexed
Keepsake	pink blend	large	double to full	high-centered	slight	small clusters	repeat	reflexed
Keith Kirsten	orange-red	large	semi-double	cupped	none	small clusters	repeat	plain
Kent	white	small	semi-double	flat	slight	large clusters	repeat	plain
Kentucky Derby	dark red	large	double to full	high-centered	slight	singly	repeat	reflexed
Kerry Gold	yellow blend	medium	double to full	globular	none	large clusters	repeat	reflexed
Kerryman	pink blend	large	double to full	cupped	slight	small clusters	repeat	plain
Kew Rambler	medium pink	small	single	open	slight	truss	once	plain
Kiese	medium red	medium	semi-double	open	slight	small clusters	once	plain
Kiftsgate	white	small	single	open	moderate	truss	once	plain
Kim	medium yellow	large	double to full	cupped	slight	small clusters	repeat	reflexed
Kimono	pink blend	large	double to full	flat	moderate	small clusters	repeat	reflexed
Kind Regards	medium red	medium	double to full	cupped	none	small clusters	repeat	ruffled
King Arthur	orange-pink	large	double to full	cupped	slight	small clusters	repeat	reflexed
King Richard	mauve	small	single	cupped	moderate	large clusters	repeat	plain
King's Ransom	deep yellow	large	double to full	high-centered	slight	small clusters	repeat	reflexed
Kirsten Poulsen	medium red	medium	single	open	none	large clusters	repeat	plain
Kiskadee	medium yellow	large	double to full	high-centered	slight	small clusters	repeat	reflexed
Kiss	orange-pink	medium	double to full	high-centered	none	small clusters	repeat	reflexed
Kitty Kininmonth	deep pink	large	semi-double	cupped	slight	small clusters	repeat	plain
Klaus Störtebeker	medium red	large	double to full	high-centered	slight	singly	repeat	reflexed
Kleopatra	red blend	large	double to full	high-centered	slight	singly	repeat	reflexed

NAME	BLOOM COLOR	FLOWER SIZE	FLOWER TYPE	FLOWER SHAPE	FRAGRANCE AMOUNT	FLOWERING HABIT	FLOWERING INCIDENCE	PETAL SHAPE
Koba	orange-red	medium	double to full	cupped	slight	small clusters	repeat	plain
Kölner Karneval	mauve	large	double to full	cupped	slight	small clusters	repeat	reflexed
Königin Beatrix	orange blend	large	double to full	high-centered	moderate	singly	repeat	reflexed
Königin von Dänemark	medium pink	medium	very full	quartered	strong	small clusters	once	plain
Konrad Adenauer	dark red	large	double to full	cupped	strong	small clusters	repeat	reflexed
Konrad Henkel	medium red	large	double to full	high-centered	slight	small clusters	repeat	reflexed
Kordes' Brillant	orange blend	large	double to full	cupped	slight	large clusters	repeat	plain
Kordes' Perfecta	pink blend	extra large	very full	high-centered	slight	singly	repeat	reflexed
Kordes' Perfecta Superior	medium pink	extra large	very full	high-centered	slight	singly	repeat	reflexed
Korona	orange-red	medium	double to full	cupped	none	small clusters	repeat	plain
KORliam	yellow blend	large	double to full	open	slight	small clusters	repeat	plain
Korovo	medium pink	large	double to full	high-centered	moderate	singly	repeat	reflexed
Ko's Yellow	yellow blend	small	double to full	high-centered	slight	small clusters	repeat	reflexed
Kristin	red blend	medium	double to full	high-centered	none	small clusters	repeat	reflexed
Kristo Pienaar	yellow blend	large	semi-double	high-centered	none	small clusters	repeat	plain
Kronprincessin Viktoria	white	medium	very full	quartered	moderate	small clusters	repeat	plain
Kwinana	red blend	small	single	open	slight	small clusters	repeat	plain
L. D. Braithwaite	dark red	large	very full	flat	slight	small clusters	repeat	plain
La Belle Distinguée	medium red	small	double to full	flat	slight	small clusters	once	plain
La Belle Sultane	dark red	medium	semi-double	flat	slight	small clusters	once	plain
La Biche	white	large	very full	cupped	moderate	singly	repeat	plain
La Bonne Maison	pink blend	medium	single	cupped	moderate	small clusters	repeat	plain
La Follette	medium pink	large	semi-double	cupped	moderate	small clusters	repeat	plain
La France	light pink	large	very full	globular	strong	small clusters	repeat	reflexed
La Jolla	pink blend	extra large	double to full	high-centered	slight	singly	repeat	reflexed
La Louise	dark red	medium	semi-double	open	moderate	small clusters	once	plain
La Maculée	red blend	medium	semi-double	cupped	strong	small clusters	once	plain
La Marne	pink blend	small	single	flat	none	large clusters	repeat	plain
La Marseillaise	dark red	large	double to full	high-centered	moderate	singly	repeat	reflexed
La Mortola	white	large	single	flat	strong	truss	once	plain
La Neige	white	medium	double to full	cupped	moderate	small clusters	once	plain
La Noblesse	light pink	medium	very full	flat	strong	small clusters	once	plain
La Paloma 85	white	medium	double to full	high-centered	slight	small clusters	repeat	reflexed
La Perla	light pink	medium	double to full	high-centered	none	small clusters	repeat	reflexed
La Perle	light yellow	large	double to full	flat	strong	small clusters	once	plain
La Plus Belle des Ponctuées	pink blend	medium	double to full	flat	strong	small clusters	once	plain
La Reine	medium pink	large	very full	cupped	moderate	small clusters	repeat	plain
La Sévillana	orange-red	medium	semi-double	cupped	none	large clusters	repeat	ruffled
La Ville de Bruxelles	deep pink	large	double to full	quartered	strong	small clusters	once	plain
L'Abondance	white	medium	double to full	cupped	slight	small clusters	once	plain
Lace Cascade	white	large	double to full	cupped	slight	small clusters	repeat	plain
Lady Alice Stanley	pink blend	large	very full	cupped	strong	singly	repeat	reflexed
Lady Barbara	orange blend	medium	double to full	open	slight	small clusters	repeat	plain
Lady Curzon	medium pink	large	single	flat	moderate	small clusters	repeat	plain
Lady Diana	light pink	medium	double to full	high-centered	slight	small clusters	repeat	reflexed
Lady Elgin	yellow blend	large	double to full	cupped	slight	small clusters	repeat	reflexed
Lady Gay	orange-pink	medium	double to full	globular	slight	small clusters	once	plain
Lady Godiva	light pink	small	double to full	globular	slight	large clusters	once	plain
Lady Hillingdon	yellow blend	medium	semi-double	cupped	moderate	singly	repeat	plain
Lady Huntingfield	medium yellow	large	double to full	cupped	slight	small clusters	repeat	plain
Lady Iliffe	medium red	large	double to full	high-centered	strong	singly	repeat	reflexed
Lady in Red	medium red	small	double to full	high-centered	none	small clusters	repeat	reflexed
Lady Like	pink blend	large	double to full	cupped	slight	singly	repeat	reflexed
Lady MacRobert	apricot blend	medium	double to full	cupped	slight	large clusters	repeat	plain
Lady Mann	pink blend	medium	double to full	cupped	slight	small clusters	repeat	reflexed
Lady Mary Fitzwilliam	light pink	large	double to full	high-centered	slight	small clusters	repeat	reflexed
Lady Mavis Pilkington	yellow blend	large	double to full	high-centered	moderate	singly	repeat	reflexed
Lady Meilland	orange-pink	large	double to full	high-centered	none	singly	repeat	reflexed
Lady Mitchell	medium red	medium	very full	cupped	moderate	small clusters	repeat	reflexed
Lady of Sky	orange-red	large	double to full	high-centered	slight	small clusters	repeat	reflexed
Lady of the Dawn	light pink	large	semi-double	open	slight	small clusters	repeat	plain
Lady Penzance	orange-pink	small	single	cupped	strong	small clusters	once	plain
Lady Rachel	white	medium	double to full	high-centered	moderate	small clusters	repeat	reflexed
Lady Roberts	apricot blend	large	very full	globular	moderate	singly	repeat	plain
Lady Romsey	white	medium	double to full	high-centered	moderate	small clusters	repeat	reflexed
Lady Rose	orange-pink	large	double to full	high-centered	moderate	singly	repeat	reflexed
Lady Stuart	light pink	large	double to full	globular	moderate	small clusters	repeat	plain
Lady Sunblaze	light pink	medium	very full	high-centered	none	small clusters	repeat	reflexed
Lady Sylvia	light pink	large	double to full	high-centered	strong	singly	repeat	reflexed
Lady Taylor	orange-red	medium	double to full	high-centered	slight	small clusters	repeat	reflexed
Lady Trent	orange blend	large	double to full	high-centered	moderate	singly	repeat	reflexed
Lady Vera	pink blend	large	double to full	high-centered	slight	small clusters	repeat	reflexed
Lady Waterlow	pink blend	large	semi-double	high-centered	moderate	small clusters	repeat	reflexed
Lady X	mauve	large	double to full	high-centered	none	singly	repeat	reflexed
Lafayette	deep pink	medium	semi-double	cupped	slight	small clusters	repeat	plain
Lafter	yellow blend	large	semi-double	open	slight	singly	repeat	reflexed
Lagerfeld	mauve	large	double to full	high-centered	strong	small clusters	repeat	reflexed
L'Aimant	medium pink	medium	double to full	cupped	strong	small clusters	repeat	reflexed
Lamarque	white	medium	double to full	rosette	strong	small clusters	repeat	plain
Lambada	orange-pink	large	semi-double	open	none	small clusters	repeat	plain
Lancashire	medium red	large	double to full	high-centered	strong	small clusters	repeat	reflexed
Lancôme	deep pink	large	double to full	high-centered	none	singly	repeat	reflexed
Laneii	medium red	medium	double to full	globular	moderate	small clusters	once	plain
Langford Light	white	small	semi-double	open	slight	small clusters	repeat	plain
Lanvin	light yellow	large	double to full	high-centered	slight	small clusters	repeat	reflexed
Las Vegas	orange blend	large	double to full	high-centered	slight	small clusters	repeat	reflexed
Laughter Lines	pink blend	large	semi-double	open	slight	small clusters	repeat	plain
Laura	orange blend	large	double to full	high-centered	slight	singly	repeat	reflexed
Laura Ashley	mauve	small	single	flat	slight	large clusters	repeat	plain
Laura Chantal	pink blend	small	semi-double	open	strong	small clusters	repeat	plain
Laura Ford	medium yellow	small	double to full	high-centered	slight	small clusters	repeat	reflexed
Lauré Davoust	light pink	small	double to full	cupped	slight	truss	once	plain
Laurette	light pink	large	double to full	cupped	slight	small clusters	repeat	plain
Lavaglut	dark red	medium	double to full	globular	slight	small clusters	repeat	plain
Lavender Crystal	mauve	medium	double	high-centered	moderate	small clusters	repeat	ruffled
Lavender Dream	mauve	medium	semi-double	open	none	small clusters	repeat	plain
Lavender Jewel	mauve	small	double to full	high-centered	slight	small clusters	repeat	reflexed
Lavender Lace	mauve	small	double to full	rosette	slight	small clusters	repeat	plain
Lavender Lassie	mauve	medium	double to full	high-centered	strong	small clusters	repeat	reflexed
Lavender Mist	mauve	large	double to full	high-centered	slight	small clusters	repeat	reflexed
Lavender Pinocchio	mauve	large	double to full	open	slight	small clusters	repeat	plain
Lavendula	mauve	large	double to full	high-centered	strong	small clusters	repeat	reflexed
Lawinia	medium pink	large	double to full	cupped	slight	small clusters	repeat	plain
Lawrence Johnston	medium yellow	large	semi-double	open	moderate	small clusters	repeat	plain
Le Cid	medium red	large	double to full	open	moderate	small clusters	repeat	plain
Le Havre	medium red	large	very full	globular	strong	singly	repeat	plain
Le Rêve	light yellow	large	semi-double	open	moderate	small clusters	once	plain
Le Rouge et Le Noir	dark red	large	double to full	high-centered	none	small clusters	repeat	reflexed
Le Soleil	orange-red	small	double	open	slight	small clusters	repeat	plain
Le Vésuve	pink blend	medium	double to full	cupped	none	small clusters	repeat	reflexed
Leander	apricot blend	medium	very full	flat	moderate	small clusters	repeat	plain
Leaping Salmon	orange-pink	medium	double to full	high-centered	strong	small clusters	repeat	reflexed
Léda	white	medium	double to full	flat	moderate	small clusters	once	plain
Legacy Jubilee	yellow blend	large	double to full	high-centered	moderate	singly	repeat	reflexed
Legend	medium red	large	double to full	high-centered	slight	singly	repeat	reflexed

NAME	BLOOM COLOR	FLOWER SIZE	FLOWER TYPE	FLOWER SHAPE	FRAGRANCE AMOUNT	FLOWERING HABIT	FLOWERING INCIDENCE	PETAL SHAPE
Lelia Laird	orange blend	small	double to full	high-centered	moderate	small clusters	repeat	reflexed
Lemon Blush	light yellow	medium	double to full	rosette	moderate	small clusters	once	plain
Lemon Delight	medium yellow	small	semi-double	open	none	small clusters	repeat	plain
Lemon Elegance	medium yellow	large	double to full	high-centered	slight	singly	repeat	reflexed
Lemon Glow	medium yellow	extra large	double to full	high-centered	moderate	singly	repeat	reflexed
Lemon Honey	light yellow	large	double to full	high-centered	slight	small clusters	repeat	reflexed
Lemon Sherbet	light yellow	large	double to full	high-centered	slight	singly	repeat	reflexed
Lemon Spice	light yellow	large	double to full	high-centered	strong	small clusters	repeat	reflexed
Len Turner	red blend	large	double to full	high-centered	slight	small clusters	repeat	reflexed
Leon Lecomte	deep pink	medium	very full	rosette	moderate	small clusters	once	plain
Léonardo de Vinci	light pink	large	very full	cupped	none	small clusters	repeat	plain
Léonie Lamesch	orange blend	small	semi-double	open	none	large clusters	repeat	plain
Léonor de March	dark red	large	double to full	high-centered	moderate	small clusters	repeat	reflexed
Léontine Gervais	apricot blend	large	double to full	open	moderate	small clusters	once	plain
Les Amoureux de Peynet	deep pink	medium	semi-double	open	slight	large clusters	repeat	plain
Les Sjulin	pink blend	large	double to full	cupped	moderate	small clusters	repeat	plain
Leslie's Dream	red blend	large	double to full	cupped	none	small clusters	repeat	plain
Leuchtstern	pink blend	medium	single	open	slight	large clusters	once	plain
Leverkusen	light yellow	medium	double to full	high-centered	slight	small clusters	once	reflexed
Leveson Gower	orange-pink	large	very full	quartered	slight	small clusters	repeat	reflexed
Lichtkönigin Lucia	medium yellow	medium	semi-double	cupped	moderate	small clusters	repeat	plain
Liebeszauber	medium red	large	double to full	cupped	none	small clusters	repeat	plain
Lifestyle	pink blend	small	double to full	open	none	singly	repeat	plain
Lights of Broadway	red blend	small	very full	flat	none	singly	repeat	plain
Lilac Charm	mauve	medium	single	cupped	slight	small clusters	repeat	plain
Lilac Rose	pink blend	large	double to full	rosette	moderate	small clusters	repeat	plain
Lilac Time	mauve	medium	double to full	high-centered	moderate	small clusters	repeat	reflexed
Lilian Austin	orange-pink	large	double to full	flat	moderate	small clusters	repeat	plain
Lilian Baylis	light yellow	medium	double to full	rosette	slight	small clusters	repeat	reflexed
Lilli Marleen	medium red	medium	double to full	open	slight	small clusters	repeat	plain
Lillian Gibson	medium pink	large	double	open	strong	large clusters	once	plain
Lily Freeman	medium pink	medium	single	flat	moderate	small clusters	repeat	plain
Lime Kiln	white	small	semi-double	cupped	slight	large clusters	once	plain
Limelight	light yellow	large	double to full	high-centered	slight	small clusters	repeat	reflexed
Limona	white	large	double	open	slight	singly	repeat	plain
Lincoln Cathedral	orange blend	large	double to full	high-centered	slight	singly	repeat	reflexed
Linda Campbell	medium red	medium	semi-double	cupped	none	large clusters	repeat	plain
Linda Thomson	deep pink	medium	semi-double	open	moderate	large clusters	repeat	ruffled
Linden Heath	medium pink	medium	semi-double	flat	none	large clusters	repeat	plain
Linville	white blend	medium	double to full	high-centered	moderate	singly	repeat	reflexed
Lisa Marée	deep pink	large	double to full	open	moderate	singly	repeat	ruffled
Liselle	orange blend	large	double to full	high-centered	slight	small clusters	repeat	reflexed
Little Artist	red blend	small	semi-double	open	none	small clusters	repeat	plain
Little Bo-Peep	medium pink	small	double to full	open	none	small clusters	repeat	plain
Little Buckaroo	medium red	small	double to full	open	slight	small clusters	repeat	plain
Little Darling	yellow blend	medium	double to full	high-centered	moderate	small clusters	repeat	reflexed
Little Eskimo	white	small	very full	high-centered	none	small clusters	repeat	reflexed
Little Flirt	red blend	small	double to full	high-centered	slight	small clusters	repeat	reflexed
Little Gem	deep pink	small	double to full	cupped	strong	small clusters	repeat	reflexed
Little Girl	orange-pink	small	double to full	high-centered	none	small clusters	repeat	plain
Little Jackie	orange blend	small	double to full	open	moderate	small clusters	repeat	plain
Little Linda	light yellow	small	semi-double	high-centered	none	small clusters	repeat	reflexed
Little Opal	light pink	small	full	high-centered	slight	small clusters	repeat	plain
Little Paradise	mauve	medium	double to full	high-centered	none	singly	repeat	plain
Little Rambler	light pink	small	double to full	flat	strong	large clusters	repeat	plain
Little Red Devil	medium red	small	double to full	cupped	none	small clusters	repeat	frilled
Little Scotch	light yellow	medium	very full	high-centered	slight	small clusters	repeat	reflexed
Little Sizzler	medium red	medium	double to full	cupped	none	large clusters	repeat	plain
Little Sunset	pink blend	small	double to full	high-centered	none	small clusters	repeat	reflexed
Little Tiger	red blend	small	very full	high-centered	none	small clusters	repeat	reflexed
Little Wallace	pink blend	medium	double to full	high-centered	none	small clusters	repeat	reflexed
Little Woman	pink blend	medium	double to full	high-centered	none	small clusters	repeat	reflexed
Lively	deep pink	large	double to full	high-centered	strong	singly	repeat	reflexed
Liverpool Echo	orange-pink	large	double to full	high-centered	slight	small clusters	repeat	reflexed
Liverpool Remembers	orange-red	large	double to full	high-centered	moderate	singly	repeat	reflexed
Livin' Easy	orange blend	medium	double to full	open	slight	small clusters	repeat	plain
Living Fire	orange blend	medium	double to full	rosette	slight	small clusters	repeat	plain
L'Obscurité	dark red	medium	semi-double	open	moderate	small clusters	once	plain
Lola Montez	medium red	large	double	open	none	small clusters	repeat	plain
Lolita	apricot blend	large	double to full	high-centered	slight	small clusters	repeat	reflexed
Lollipop	medium red	small	double to full	flat	none	small clusters	repeat	plain
Long John Silver	white	extra large	double to full	cupped	moderate	small clusters	once	plain
Lord Gold	deep yellow	large	double to full	high-centered	none	small clusters	repeat	reflexed
Lord Penzance	yellow blend	small	single	open	moderate	small clusters	once	plain
Lord Raglan	dark red	extra large	very full	high-centered	strong	singly	repeat	plain
Lordly Oberon	light pink	large	double to full	cupped	strong	small clusters	repeat	plain
L'Oréal Trophy	orange blend	large	double to full	high-centered	none	singly	repeat	reflexed
Lorena	medium pink	large	double to full	high-centered	none	small clusters	repeat	reflexed
Lorraine Lee	pink blend	medium	double to full	cupped	moderate	singly	repeat	plain
Lotte Günthart	medium red	large	very full	pompons	none	small clusters	repeat	plain
L'Ouche	pink blend	medium	double to full	cupped	slight	small clusters	repeat	plain
Louis de Funès	orange blend	large	double to full	high-centered	none	small clusters	repeat	reflexed
Louis Gimard	medium pink	large	very full	globular	moderate	small clusters	once	plain
Louis Philippe	red blend	medium	double to full	globular	none	small clusters	repeat	plain
Louis van Houtte	dark red	extra large	very full	high-centered	strong	singly	repeat	plain
Louis XIV	dark red	medium	double to full	open	slight	small clusters	repeat	plain
Louisa Jane	mauve	large	double to full	cupped	strong	small clusters	repeat	plain
Louisa Stone	apricot blend	medium	very full	quartered	none	small clusters	repeat	plain
Louise Cretté	white	extra large	very full	high-centered	slight	singly	repeat	reflexed
Louise d'Arzens	white	medium	double to full	cupped	slight	small clusters	repeat	plain
Louise Gardner	yellow blend	medium	double to full	high-centered	none	small clusters	repeat	reflexed
Louise Odier	deep pink	medium	very full	cupped	moderate	small clusters	repeat	plain
Love	red blend	large	double to full	high-centered	none	small clusters	repeat	reflexed
Love Me	white	small	double to full	open	none	small clusters	repeat	plain
Love Potion	mauve	medium	double to full	cupped	moderate	small clusters	repeat	ruffled
Lovely Fairy	deep pink	small	semi-double	cupped	slight	truss	repeat	plain
Lovely Lady	medium pink	large	double to full	high-centered	slight	singly	repeat	plain
Lovely Louise	apricot blend	medium	double to full	open	none	small clusters	repeat	reflexed
Lovers' Meeting	orange blend	large	double to full	high-centered	slight	small clusters	repeat	reflexed
Loving Memory	medium red	large	double to full	high-centered	none	small clusters	repeat	reflexed
Loving Touch	apricot blend	medium	double to full	high-centered	none	singly	repeat	reflexed
Lübeck	orange red	medium	double to full	cupped	slight	small clusters	repeat	plain
Lucetta	apricot blend	large	semi-double	open	slight	small clusters	repeat	ruffled
Lucky Charm	yellow blend	small	double to full	high-centered	none	small clusters	repeat	reflexed
Lucky Lady	light pink	large	double to full	high-centered	none	small clusters	repeat	reflexed
Lucky Piece	pink blend	large	double to full	high-centered	slight	small clusters	repeat	reflexed
Lucy Ashton	white	small	single	flat	moderate	small clusters	once	plain
Lucy Bertram	red blend	small	single	flat	moderate	small clusters	once	plain
Lucy Cramphorn	orange-red	extra large	double to full	high-centered	moderate	singly	repeat	reflexed
Luis Desamero	light yellow	small	double to full	high-centered	slight	small clusters	repeat	reflexed
Lulu	orange-pink	medium	double to full	high-centered	none	small clusters	repeat	reflexed
Lustige	red blend	large	double to full	high-centered	slight	small clusters	repeat	reflexed
Lutin	pink blend	small	semi-double	flat	none	large clusters	repeat	plain
Lyda Rose	white	medium	semi-double	open	none	small clusters	repeat	plain
Lydia	deep yellow	medium	semi-double	cupped	slight	small clusters	repeat	reflexed
Lykkefund	white	small	semi-double	cupped	strong	large clusters	once	plain
Lynette	white	large	double to full	high-centered	none	small clusters	repeat	reflexed
Lynn Anderson	pink blend	large	double to full	high-centered	none	singly	repeat	reflexed

NAME	BLOOM COLOR	FLOWER SIZE	FLOWER TYPE	FLOWER SHAPE	FRAGRANCE AMOUNT	FLOWERING HABIT	FLOWERING INCIDENCE	PETAL SHAPE
Lynne Gold	medium yellow	small	double to full	open	none	small clusters	repeat	plain
Lyon Rambler	deep pink	small	semi-double	open	none	truss	once	plain
Lyon Rose	orange-pink	large	double to full	high-centered	moderate	singly	repeat	reflexed
Lyric	medium pink	medium	double to full	cupped	slight	large clusters	repeat	plain
Ma Perkins	pink blend	medium	double to full	high-centered	moderate	small clusters	repeat	plain
Ma Tulipe	dark red	large	semi-double	cupped	moderate	small clusters	repeat	plain
Mab Grimwade	yellow blend	large	double to full	open	none	small clusters	repeat	reflexed
Mabel Morrison	white	large	double to full	cupped	slight	singly	once	plain
McGredy's Sunset	orange blend	large	double to full	globular	moderate	small clusters	repeat	reflexed
McGredy's Yellow	medium yellow	large	double to full	cupped	slight	small clusters	repeat	reflexed
MACspice	mauve	small	semi-double	open	none	large clusters	repeat	plain
Madam President	pink blend	large	very full	high centered	none	small clusters	repeat	reflexed
Mme Abel Chatenay	pink blend	medium	double to full	high-centered	slight	singly	repeat	reflexed
Mme Alfred Carrière	white	large	full	globular	strong	small clusters	repeat	plain
Mme Alfred de Rougement	light pink	medium	full	cupped	none	small clusters	repeat	plain
Mme Alice Garnier	pink blend	small	double to full	cupped	moderate	large clusters	once	plain
Mme Antoine Mari	pink blend	large	double to full	open	slight	small clusters	repeat	plain
Mme Arthur Oger	medium pink	large	double to full	cupped	moderate	small clusters	repeat	plain
Mme Bérard	orange blend	large	double to full	cupped	slight	small clusters	repeat	plain
Mme Berkeley	pink blend	large	double to full	cupped	slight	small clusters	repeat	plain
Mme Boll	deep pink	large	double to full	cupped	moderate	singly	repeat	plain
Mme Bollinger	orange-pink	medium	double to full	high-centered	slight	small clusters	repeat	reflexed
Mme Bravy	white	large	double to full	cupped	moderate	small clusters	repeat	plain
Mme Butterfly	light pink	large	double to full	cupped	strong	small clusters	repeat	reflexed
Mme Caroline Testout	medium pink	large	double to full	cupped	slight	singly	repeat	reflexed
Mme Charles	yellow blend	large	double to full	globular	slight	small clusters	repeat	plain
Mme Charles Baltet	light pink	large	very full	cupped	strong	small clusters	repeat	plain
Mme Cornélissen	white	medium	double to full	flat	strong	small clusters	repeat	plain
Mme de la Rôche-Lambert	mauve	medium	double to full	globular	strong	small clusters	once	plain
Mme de Sancy de Parabère	light pink	large	double to full	rosette	none	small clusters	once	plain
Mme de Sévigné	pink blend	large	double to full	globular	moderate	small clusters	repeat	plain
Mme de Tartas	light pink	large	double to full	cupped	slight	small clusters	repeat	plain
Mme de Watteville	yellow blend	large	double to full	cupped	strong	small clusters	repeat	plain
Mme d'Hebray	pink blend	medium	double to full	cupped	strong	small clusters	once	plain
Mme Dieudonné	red blend	large	double to full	high-centered	moderate	singly	repeat	reflexed
Mme Doré	light pink	large	very full	cupped	moderate	small clusters	repeat	plain
Mme Driout	pink blend	large	very full	quartered	moderate	small clusters	repeat	reflexed
Mme Edouard Herriot	orange blend	large	semi-double	cupped	slight	small clusters	repeat	reflexed
Mme Edouard Ory	deep pink	medium	double to full	globular	moderate	small clusters	once	plain
Mme Emilie Charron	medium pink	large	very full	cupped	slight	small clusters	repeat	plain
Mme Ernst Calvat	medium pink	large	very full	cupped	strong	small clusters	repeat	ruffled
Mme Eugène Résal	pink blend	medium	semi-double	cupped	none	small clusters	repeat	plain
Mme Falcot	medium yellow	large	double to full	cupped	moderate	small clusters	repeat	plain
Mme Fernandel	deep pink	medium	double to full	cupped	none	small clusters	repeat	reflexed
Mme Gabriel Luizet	light pink	large	double to full	quartered	moderate	singly	repeat	plain
Mme Georges Bruant	white	large	double to full	cupped	moderate	small clusters	repeat	plain
Mme Georges Delbard	dark red	large	double to full	high-centered	none	singly	repeat	reflexed
Mme Grégoire Staechelin	pink blend	large	double to full	open	moderate	small clusters	once	ruffled
Mme Hardy	white	medium	double to full	flat	strong	small clusters	once	plain
Mme Henri Guillot	red blend	large	double to full	cupped	slight	small clusters	repeat	reflexed
Mme Isaac Pereire	deep pink	large	very full	cupped	strong	small clusters	repeat	plain
Mme Jean Dupuy Perraud	yellow blend	large	double to full	cupped	moderate	small clusters	repeat	reflexed
Mme Joseph	yellow blend	large	double to full	cupped	moderate	small clusters	repeat	reflexed
Mme Joseph Schwartz	white	medium	double to full	cupped	moderate	small clusters	repeat	plain
Mme Jules Bouché	white	large	double to full	cupped	slight	singly	repeat	plain
Mme Jules Gravereaux	apricot blend	large	very full	cupped	moderate	small clusters	repeat	plain
Mme Jules Thibaud	orange-pink	medium	double to full	rosette	slight	large clusters	repeat	plain
Mme Knorr	medium pink	medium	double to full	cupped	strong	small clusters	repeat	plain
Mme Kriloff	yellow blend	large	double to full	globular	moderate	singly	repeat	reflexed
Mme Laurette Messimy	deep pink	medium	double to full	cupped	none	small clusters	repeat	plain
Mme Lauriol de Barny	light pink	large	double to full	quartered	strong	small clusters	once	plain
Mme Legras de St Germain	white	large	very full	rosette	strong	small clusters	once	plain
Mme Léon Pain	pink blend	large	double to full	cupped	moderate	small clusters	repeat	reflexed
Mme Line Renaud	medium red	large	double to full	high-centered	strong	singly	repeat	reflexed
Mme Lombard	orange-pink	large	very full	globular	slight	small clusters	repeat	plain
Mme Louis Laperrière	medium red	large	double to full	high-centered	strong	small clusters	repeat	reflexed
Mme Louis Lévêque	medium pink	large	double to full	globular	strong	small clusters	once	plain
Mme Marie Curie	deep yellow	large	double to full	high-centered	slight	small clusters	repeat	reflexed
Mme Moreau	pink blend	large	double to full	cupped	strong	small clusters	once	plain
Mme Pierre Oger	pink blend	large	double to full	cupped	slight	small clusters	repeat	plain
Mme Plantier	white	medium	double to full	flat	strong	small clusters	once	plain
Mme Scipion Cochet (Bernaix)	pink blend	large	double to full	cupped	moderate	singly	repeat	plain
Mme Scipion Cochet (Cochet)	mauve	large	double to full	cupped	slight	small clusters	repeat	plain
Mme Souchet	pink blend	large	double to full	cupped	moderate	small clusters	repeat	plain
Mme Souveton	pink blend	medium	double to full	cupped	slight	small clusters	repeat	plain
Mme Victor Verdier	medium red	large	very full	flat	strong	singly	once	plain
Mme Violet	mauve	medium	double to full	high-centered	none	small clusters	repeat	reflexed
Mme Wagram, Comtesse de Turenne	pink blend	large	full	open	moderate	small clusters	repeat	plain
Mme William Paul	deep pink	medium	double to full	cupped	moderate	small clusters	repeat	plain
Mme Zöetmans	white	large	very full	flat	moderate	small clusters	once	plain
Madeleine Selzer	light yellow	medium	double to full	cupped	strong	truss	once	plain
Madelon	orange-red	large	double to full	cupped	slight	small clusters	repeat	reflexed
Mlle Annie Wood	medium red	large	double to full	open	moderate	singly	repeat	plain
Mlle Blanche Lafitte	light pink	large	double to full	flat	moderate	small clusters	repeat	plain
Mlle Claire Truffaut	medium pink	medium	double to full	cupped	strong	small clusters	repeat	plain
Mlle Franziska Krueger	orange-pink	large	very full	cupped	slight	small clusters	repeat	reflexed
Mlle Marie Dauvesse	medium pink	large	double to full	cupped	moderate	small clusters	repeat	plain
Mlle Marie Drivon	pink blend	medium	double to full	cupped	moderate	small clusters	repeat	plain
Mlle Marthe Carron	white	small	semi-double	open	none	large clusters	once	plain
Madhatter	medium yellow	small	double to full	cupped	moderate	small clusters	repeat	reflexed
Madiba	mauve	large	double	open	moderate	small clusters	repeat	plain
Maestro	red blend	medium	double to full	open	slight	small clusters	repeat	reflexed
Magali	deep pink	medium	double to full	open	slight	small clusters	repeat	reflexed
Magenta	mauve	large	double to full	cupped	strong	large clusters	repeat	reflexed
Maggie	medium red	large	very full	cupped	moderate	small clusters	repeat	plain
Maggie Barry	pink blend	large	double to full	high-centered	slight	singly	repeat	reflexed
Magic	medium red	medium	double to full	high-centered	none	singly	repeat	reflexed
Magic Carpet	mauve	small	semi-double	flat	none	large clusters	repeat	plain
Magic Carrousel	red blend	small	double to full	high-centered	slight	small clusters	repeat	plain
Magic Dragon	dark red	small	double to full	open	none	small clusters	repeat	plain
Magic Lantern	orange	large	double to full	cupped	slight	small clusters	repeat	reflexed
Magic Meidiland	medium pink	medium	very full	cupped	none	small clusters	repeat	plain

NAME	BLOOM COLOR	FLOWER SIZE	FLOWER TYPE	FLOWER SHAPE	FRAGRANCE AMOUNT	FLOWERING HABIT	FLOWERING INCIDENCE	PETAL SHAPE
Magic Sunset	orange blend	large	double to full	rosette	slight	small clusters	repeat	plain
Magna Charta	medium pink	large	double to full	globular	moderate	singly	repeat	plain
Magnifica	mauve	large	double to full	open	moderate	small clusters	repeat	plain
Mahina	apricot blend	large	double to full	high-centered	moderate	singly	repeat	reflexed
Maiden's Blush	white	medium	double to full	globular	strong	small clusters	once	plain
Maigold	deep yellow	large	semi-double	cupped	moderate	small clusters	once	ruffled
Mainauperle	dark red	large	double to full	high-centered	moderate	singly	repeat	reflexed
Majorette	medium red	medium	double to full	open	none	small clusters	repeat	plain
Mala Rubinstein	medium pink	large	double to full	high-centered	slight	small clusters	repeat	reflexed
Malaga	deep pink	large	double to full	high-centered	strong	singly	repeat	reflexed
Malcolm Sargent	medium red	medium	double to full	open	slight	singly	repeat	reflexed
Maman Cochet	pink blend	large	double to full	high-centered	moderate	singly	repeat	reflexed
Mamita	medium red	large	double to full	cupped	strong	singly	repeat	reflexed
Mandarin (Boerner)	medium red	medium	semi-double	high-centered	moderate	large clusters	repeat	reflexed
Mandarin (Kordes)	orange-red	small	double	cupped	slight	small clusters	repeat	plain
Manettii	light pink	medium	double to full	open	none	small clusters	once	plain
Mannheim	dark red	large	double to full	open	none	small clusters	repeat	plain
Manning's Blush	white	small	double to full	cupped	moderate	small clusters	once	reflexed
Manou Meilland	mauve	large	double to full	high-centered	moderate	small clusters	repeat	reflexed
Many Happy Returns	pink blend	large	semi-double	cupped	slight	small clusters	repeat	ruffled
Manx Queen	orange blend	medium	semi-double	open	none	large clusters	repeat	plain
Many Thanks	apricot blend	small	double to full	cupped	slight	small clusters	repeat	reflexed
Marbrée	red blend	medium	double to full	flat	slight	small clusters	repeat	plain
Marcel Bourgoin	mauve	medium	double to full	open	moderate	small clusters	once	plain
Marcella	orange blend	medium	double	open	slight	small clusters	repeat	plain
Märchenkönigin	light pink	extra large	double to full	high-centered	slight	singly	repeat	reflexed
Märchenland	orange blend	medium	semi-double	open	slight	large clusters	repeat	plain
Marchesa Boccella	light pink	medium	double to full	flat	moderate	small clusters	repeat	plain
Marchioness of Londonderry	light pink	extra large	double to full	high-centered	strong	singly	repeat	reflexed
Marchioness of Lorne	pink blend	large	double to full	cupped	strong	singly	repeat	reflexed
Marchioness of Salisbury	dark red	large	double to full	high-centered	moderate	singly	repeat	reflexed
Marcia Gandy	red blend	large	double to full	cupped	strong	small clusters	repeat	reflexed
Marco Polo	light pink	large	double	high-centered	moderate	singly	repeat	plain
Maréchal Davoust	medium pink	large	double to full	cupped	moderate	small clusters	once	plain
Maréchal Foch	deep pink	medium	semi-double	open	moderate	small clusters	repeat	plain
Maréchal Niel	medium yellow	large	double to full	cupped	moderate	small clusters	repeat	plain
Margaret	pink blend	large	very full	high-centered	slight	small clusters	repeat	reflexed
Margaret Merril	white	large	double to full	high-centered	strong	small clusters	repeat	plain
Margaret Turnbull	yellow blend	large	double to full	cupped	slight	small clusters	repeat	reflexed
Margaret Wasserfall	white blend	large	full	star-shaped	moderate	small clusters	repeat	plain
Margo Koster	orange blend	small	semi-double	open	none	large clusters	repeat	plain
Marguerite Hilling	medium pink	large	single	open	slight	small clusters	repeat	plain
Maria Lisa	pink blend	small	single	open	none	large clusters	once	plain
Maria Mathilda	white	small	double to full	cupped	moderate	large clusters	repeat	plain
Maria Teresa Bordas	medium pink	large	very full	high-centered	moderate	singly	repeat	reflexed
Mariandel	medium red	medium	semi-double	open	slight	small clusters	repeat	plain
Marie-Antoinette	mauve	large	double to full	cupped	slight	small clusters	repeat	reflexed
Marie de Blois	medium pink	medium	double to full	cupped	moderate	small clusters	once	plain
Marie de Bourgogne	medium pink	large	double to full	cupped	moderate	small clusters	once	plain
Marie de Saint Jean	white	medium	double to full	cupped	moderate	small clusters	repeat	plain
Marie Dermar	light yellow	medium	double to full	cupped	slight	small clusters	repeat	plain
Marie d'Orléans	medium pink	large	double to full	flat	slight	small clusters	repeat	plain
Marie Gouchault	medium red	small	double to full	flat	slight	truss	once	plain
Marie-Jeanne	white	medium	double to full	rosette	slight	large clusters	repeat	plain
Marie Lambert	white	medium	double to full	cupped	slight	small clusters	repeat	plain
Marie Leonida	white	medium	double	quartered	slight	small clusters	repeat	plain
Marie Louise	medium pink	large	very full	flat	strong	singly	once	reflexed
Marie Pavié	white	medium	double to full	cupped	none	small clusters	repeat	plain
Marie Robert	pink blend	medium	double to full	flat	moderate	small clusters	repeat	plain
Marie van Houtte	pink blend	large	very full	high-centered	moderate	singly	repeat	plain
Marietta Silva Tarouca	medium pink	small	double to full	open	none	large clusters	once	frilled
Marijke Koopman	medium pink	medium	double to full	open	moderate	small clusters	repeat	reflexed
Marilyn	light pink	small	very full	rosette	none	small clusters	repeat	plain
Marina	orange blend	medium	double to full	open	moderate	large clusters	repeat	reflexed
Marinette	medium pink	large	double to full	cupped	slight	small clusters	repeat	plain
Marion Harkness	yellow blend	large	double to full	cupped	slight	small clusters	repeat	reflexed
Marionette	white blend	small	double	flat	moderate	small clusters	repeat	plain
Marjorie Atherton	medium yellow	large	double to full	high-centered	slight	singly	repeat	plain
Marjorie Chase	apricot blend	large	full	open	moderate	small clusters	repeat	plain
Marjorie Fair	red blend	small	single	flat	slight	truss	repeat	plain
Marjorie Marshall	apricot blend	large	double to full	flat	slight	large clusters	repeat	plain
Marjorie May	orange-pink	large	double to full	cupped	slight	small clusters	repeat	plain
Marjory Palmer	medium pink	medium	double to full	open	slight	small clusters	repeat	reflexed
Mark Sullivan	orange-pink	large	double to full	high-centered	moderate	small clusters	repeat	reflexed
Marlena	medium red	medium	semi-double	flat	none	large clusters	repeat	plain
Marmalade	orange blend	large	very full	cupped	slight	small clusters	repeat	reflexed
Marondo	medium pink	medium	double to full	open	none	small clusters	repeat	plain
Marquise de Balbiano	mauve	large	double to full	cupped	moderate	small clusters	repeat	plain
Marry Me	medium pink	small	double	flat	slight	small clusters	rpeeat	plain
Martha	pink blend	medium	double to full	open	slight	small clusters	repeat	plain
Martha Gonzales	medium red	medium	double to full	cupped	none	small clusters	repeat	plain
Martha's Vineyard	deep pink	medium	double to full	open	slight	small clusters	repeat	plain
Martin Frobisher	light pink	medium	double to full	cupped	moderate	small clusters	repeat	plain
Martini	dark red	medium	double to full	open	strong	small clusters	repeat	plain
Martone	pink blend	medium	double to full	high-centered	slight	small clusters	repeat	reflexed
Mary	orange-pink	small	semi-double	cupped	none	large clusters	repeat	ruffled
Mary Adair	apricot blend	small	double to full	cupped	slight	small clusters	repeat	reflexed
Mary Cave	medium yellow	large	double to full	cupped	slight	small clusters	repeat	plain
Mary Delahunty	dark red	large	double to full	high-centered	moderate	singly	repeat	reflexed
Mary Donaldson	medium pink	medium	double to full	high-centered	strong	small clusters	repeat	reflexed
Mary Guthrie	medium pink	small	single	open	moderate	large clusters	repeat	plain
Mary Hart, Climbing	medium red	medium	double to full	flat	moderate	small clusters	repeat	reflexed
Mary Hayley Bell	medium pink	medium	double to full	rosette	moderate	small clusters	repeat	plain
Mary Jean	apricot blend	extra large	double to full	cupped	strong	singly	repeat	reflexed
Mary Kay	light pink	small	double	open	slight	small clusters	repeat	plain
Mary MacKillop	pink blend	medium	double to full	cupped	none	small clusters	repeat	reflexed
Mary Manners	white blend	large	double to full	cupped	strong	small clusters	repeat	reflexed
Mary Marshall	orange blend	small	double to full	cupped	slight	small clusters	repeat	reflexed
Mary Matthews	light pink	medium	double	high-centered	slight	singly	repeat	plain
Mary Pope	yellow blend	large	double to full	cupped	none	small clusters	repeat	plain
Mary Queen of Scots	white	small	single	flat	slight	singly	once	plain
Mary Rose	medium pink	large	very full	cupped	strong	small clusters	repeat	plain
Mary Sumner	orange-red	medium	semi-double	cupped	slight	small clusters	repeat	reflexed
Mary Wallace	medium pink	extra large	semi-double	cupped	moderate	small clusters	once	reflexed
Mary Webb	apricot blend	large	very full	cupped	strong	small clusters	repeat	plain
Marylène	medium pink	large	double to full	cupped	slight	small clusters	repeat	reflexed
Mascara	mauve blend	small	double	high-centered	slight	small clusters	repeat	plain
Mascotte	medium pink	large	double to full	high-centered	moderate	singly	repeat	reflexed
Masquerade	red blend	medium	semi-double	open	slight	small clusters	repeat	reflexed
Master Hugh	deep pink	small	single	open	slight	small clusters	once	plain
Matador	orange blend	medium	double	high-centered	slight	small clusters	repeat	plain
Matangi	red blend	large	double to full	open	slight	small clusters	repeat	plain

NAME	BLOOM COLOR	FLOWER SIZE	FLOWER TYPE	FLOWER SHAPE	FRAGRANCE AMOUNT	FLOWERING HABIT	FLOWERING INCIDENCE	PETAL SHAPE
Mateo's Silk Butterflies	medium pink	medium	double to full	open	none	small clusters	repeat	plain
Matilda	white	large	semi-double	open	none	small clusters	repeat	ruffled
Matterhorn	white	large	double to full	high-centered	none	small clusters	repeat	reflexed
Matthias Meilland	medium red	large	double to full	cupped	none	small clusters	repeat	reflexed
Maude Sumner	orange blend	medium	double	high-centered	none	singly	repeat	plain
Maureen Lipman	orange-pink	large	full	cupped	moderate	small clusters	repeat	plain
Maurice Bernardin	medium red	large	double to full	globular	strong	singly	repeat	plain
Mauve Melodée	mauve	large	double to full	cupped	moderate	small clusters	repeat	reflexed
Max Colwell	orange-red	small	double to full	flat	slight	small clusters	repeat	reflexed
Max Graf	pink blend	medium	single	open	slight	small clusters	once	plain
May Queen	medium pink	large	semi-double	cupped	strong	small clusters	once	plain
Mayor of Casterbridge	light pink	medium	very full	cupped	moderate	small clusters	repeat	plain
Mazeppa	red blend	medium	double to full	open	moderate	small clusters	once	plain
Mécène	pink blend	medium	double to full	cupped	moderate	small clusters	once	plain
Medallion	apricot blend	large	double to full	open	moderate	small clusters	repeat	plain
Medeo	white	medium	double to full	high-centered	none	small clusters	repeat	reflexed
Meg	apricot blend	large	semi-double	open	moderate	small clusters	repeat	ruffled
Meg Merrilies	deep pink medium red	small	semi-double	open	moderate	small clusters	once	plain
Megan Louise	pink blend	large	double to full	high-centered	moderate	small clusters	repeat	reflexed
Megiddo	orange-red	large	double to full	cupped	slight	small clusters	repeat	reflexed
Meillandina	medium red	small	double to full	cupped	none	small clusters	repeat	reflexed
Melody	light pink	medium	double	open	slight	small clusters	repeat	plain
Melody Maker	orange-red	large	very full	cupped	none	small clusters	repeat	plain
Memento	red blend	large	double to full	cupped	none	small clusters	repeat	reflexed
Memoire	white	large	double to full	cupped	moderate	singly	repeat	reflexed
Memoriam	light pink	extra large	very full	high-centered	moderate	singly	repeat	reflexed
Memory Bells	deep pink	small	double	high-centered	slight	small clusters	repeat	plain
Memory Lane (Moore)	light pink	small	very full	cupped	slight	small clusters	repeat	plain
Memory Lane (Pearce)	apricot blend	medium	double	urn-shaped	slight	large clusters	repeat	reflexed
Menja	medium pink	small	single	cupped	slight	large clusters	repeat	plain
Mercedes	orange-red	medium	double to full	high-centered	slight	small clusters	repeat	reflexed
Mermaid	light yellow	large	single	open	moderate	small clusters	repeat	plain
Merry England	medium red	large	double to full	globular	strong	singly	repeat	reflexed
Merveille de Lyon	white	large	double to full	cupped	slight	singly	repeat	plain
Meteor (Geschwind)	deep pink	large	double to full	cupped	strong	small clusters	repeat	plain
Meteor (Kordes)	orange-red	medium	double to full	cupped	none	small clusters	repeat	reflexed
Mevrouw G. A. van Rossem	orange blend	large	double to full	cupped	moderate	singly	repeat	reflexed
Mevrouw Nathalie Nypels	medium pink	medium	semi-double	open	moderate	small clusters	repeat	plain
Mevrouw van Straaten van Nes	medium red	medium	semi-double	open	none	small clusters	repeat	ruffled
Mexicana	red blend	large	double to full	high-centered	moderate	small clusters	repeat	reflexed
Michelangelo	orange blend	large	double to full	high-centered	none	small clusters	repeat	reflexed
Michèle Meilland	light pink	large	double to full	cupped	slight	small clusters	repeat	reflexed
Michelle Joy	orange-pink	extra large	double to full	cupped	none	singly	repeat	reflexed
Micrugosa	light pink	large	single	high-centered	slight	singly	repeat	plain
Micrugosa Alba	white	large	single	high-centered	slight	singly	repeat	plain
Midas Touch	deep yellow	large	double to full	high-centered	slight	small clusters	repeat	reflexed
Mignonette	light pink	small	double to full	globular	none	large clusters	repeat	plain
Mikado	red blend	medium	double to full	high-centered	slight	singly	repeat	reflexed
Milestone	red blend	large	double to full	cupped	slight	singly	repeat	reflexed
Milkmaid	white	small	semi-double	open	moderate	large clusters	repeat	plain
Millie Walters	orange-pink	small	double to full	cupped	slight	small clusters	repeat	reflexed
Milord	medium red	large	double to full	high-centered	strong	singly	repeat	reflexed
Milrose	medium pink	large	semi-double	cupped	slight	small clusters	repeat	reflexed
Mini Magic	red blend	small	double to full	cupped	none	small clusters	repeat	reflexed
Minijet	medium pink	small	double to full	cupped	none	small clusters	repeat	reflexed

NAME	BLOOM COLOR	FLOWER SIZE	FLOWER TYPE	FLOWER SHAPE	FRAGRANCE AMOUNT	FLOWERING HABIT	FLOWERING INCIDENCE	PETAL SHAPE
Minilights	medium yellow	small	single	flat	none	small clusters	repeat	plain
Minna	white	small	semi-double	open	moderate	small clusters	once	plain
Minnehaha	light pink	small	semi-double	open	slight	large clusters	once	plain
Minnie Francis	deep pink	large	double to full	open	moderate	small clusters	repeat	plain
Minnie Pearl	pink blend	small	double to full	high-centered	slight	small clusters	repeat	reflexed
Minnie Watson	light pink	large	semi-double	cupped	slight	small clusters	repeat	reflexed
Minuette	red blend	medium	double to full	flat	slight	small clusters	repeat	reflexed
Mio Mac	deep yellow	medium	double	high-centered	slight	small clusters	repeat	plain
Miranda	medium pink/ light pink	medium	very full	cupped	moderate	small clusters	repeat	plain
Mirandy	dark red	large	double to full	globular	strong	small clusters	repeat	reflexed
Mirato	medium pink	medium	double to full	flat	none	large clusters	repeat	plain
Mireille Mathieu	orange-red	large	double	high-centered	slight	small clusters	repeat	plain
Miriam Wilkins	light pink	large	double to full	high-centered	moderate	singly	repeat	reflexed
Miriana	medium red	large	double to full	cupped	none	singly	repeat	reflexed
Mischief	orange-pink	large	double to full	high-centered	moderate	singly	repeat	reflexed
Miss All-American Beauty	deep pink	large	double to full	cupped	moderate	singly	repeat	reflexed
Miss All-Australian Beauty	deep pink	large	double to full	cupped	slight	small clusters	repeat	reflexed
Miss Cynthia Forde	deep pink	large	double to full	open	moderate	small clusters	repeat	reflexed
Miss Daisy	deep yellow	small	very full	flat	slight	small clusters	repeat	reflexed
Miss Edith Cavell	dark red	small	semi-double	cupped	none	small clusters	repeat	plain
Miss Flippins	medium red	small	double to full	high-centered	none	singly	repeat	reflexed
Miss Lowe	medium red	medium	single	flat	none	small clusters	repeat	plain
Miss Marion Manifold	medium red	large	double to full	globular	moderate	small clusters	repeat	ruffled
Mission Bells	pink blend	large	double to full	high-centered	moderate	singly	repeat	reflexed
Mr Bluebird	mauve	small	semi-double	cupped	none	large clusters	repeat	plain
Mr Chips	yellow blend	large	double to full	high-centered	none	small clusters	repeat	reflexed
Mr E. E. Greenwell	orange-pink	large	semi-double	flat	none	small clusters	repeat	plain
Mister Lincoln	dark red	large	double to full	cupped	strong	small clusters	repeat	reflexed
Mrs Aaron Ward	yellow blend	large	double to full	high-centered	moderate	singly	repeat	reflexed
Mrs Albert Nash	dark red	large	double to full	cupped	slight	small clusters	repeat	reflexed
Mrs Alston's Rose	red blend	small	semi-double	open	none	large clusters	repeat	plain
Mrs Anthony Waterer	dark red	medium	semi-double	open	strong	small clusters	repeat	plain
Mrs B. R. Cant	medium pink	large	double to full	cupped	moderate	singly	repeat	ruffled
Mrs Bushby	deep pink	medium	double to full	flat	slight	singly	once	plain
Mrs Doreen Pike	medium pink	medium	very full	flat	moderate	large clusters	repeat	plain
Mrs Dudley Cross	yellow blend	large	double to full	cupped	slight	small clusters	repeat	reflexed
Mrs F. W. Flight	deep pink	large	semi-double	open	none	small clusters	once	plain
Mrs F. W. Sandford	light pink	large	double to full	cupped	moderate	small clusters	repeat	plain
Mrs Foley Hobbs	pink blend	large	double to full	cupped	slight	small clusters	repeat	reflexed
Mrs Fred Danks	mauve	large	semi-double	open	moderate	small clusters	repeat	reflexed
Mrs Georgia Chobe	light pink	large	double to full	high-centered	none	singly	repeat	reflexed
Mrs Harold Alston	medium pink	large	double to full	cupped	slight	small clusters	repeat	reflexed
Mrs Herbert Stevens	white	large	double to full	high-centered	moderate	singly	repeat	reflexed
Mrs Hugh Dettmann	apricot blend	large	double to full	cupped	slight	small clusters	repeat	reflexed
Mrs Iris Clow	light pink	medium	double to full	open	moderate	small clusters	repeat	reflexed
Mrs John Laing	medium pink	large	double to full	cupped	strong	small clusters	repeat	reflexed
Mrs Mary Thomson	pink blend	large	semi-double	open	strong	large clusters	repeat	reflexed
Mrs Myles Kennedy	pink blend	large	double to full	cupped	none	small clusters	repeat	plain
Mrs Norman Watson	deep pink	large	double to full	cupped	slight	small clusters	repeat	reflexed
Mrs Oakley Fisher	deep yellow	large	single	open	slight	small clusters	repeat	plain
Mrs Paul	light pink	medium	double to full	flat	slight	small clusters	once	plain
Mrs Pierre S. duPont	medium yellow	large	double to full	high-centered	moderate	small clusters	repeat	reflexed
Mistress Quickly	medium pink	small	double to full	flat	slight	large clusters	repeat	plain

NAME	BLOOM COLOR	FLOWER SIZE	FLOWER TYPE	FLOWER SHAPE	FRAGRANCE AMOUNT	FLOWERING HABIT	FLOWERING INCIDENCE	PETAL SHAPE
Mrs R. M. Finch	medium pink	medium	double to full	cupped	none	large clusters	repeat	plain
Mrs Reynolds Hole	pink blend	large	very full	cupped	moderate	small clusters	repeat	ruffled
Mrs Richard Turnbull	white blend	extra large	single	open	none	small clusters	once	plain
Mrs Sam McGredy	orange-pink	large	double to full	high-centered	slight	singly	repeat	reflexed
Mrs Wakefield Christie-Miller	pink blend	large	double to full	globular	slight	small clusters	repeat	plain
Misty	white	large	double to full	cupped	moderate	small clusters	repeat	reflexed
Mixed Marriage	light pink	large	full	open	slight	small clusters	repeat	plain
Model of Perfection	orange blend	large	double to full	cupped	slight	small clusters	repeat	reflexed
Modern Art	red blend	large	double to full	high-centered	slight	singly	repeat	reflexed
Mojave	orange blend	large	double to full	high-centered	moderate	singly	repeat	reflexed
Moje Hammarberg	mauve	large	double to full	open	strong	small clusters	repeat	plain
Molineux	deep yellow	large	double to full	rosette	strong	small clusters	repeat	plain
Molly McGredy	red blend	large	double to full	high-centered	slight	truss	repeat	reflexed
Molly Sharman-Crawford	white	large	double to full	high-centered	moderate	small clusters	repeat	reflexed
Mon Cheri	red blend	large	double to full	cupped	slight	small clusters	repeat	reflexed
Mona Lisa	pink blend	large	double to full	cupped	strong	small clusters	repeat	reflexed
Moncton	light pink	large	double to full	open	strong	small clusters	repeat	plain
Mondiale	pink blend	large	double to full	cupped	slight	singly	repeat	reflexed
Monika	pink blend	large	double to full	high-centered	slight	singly	repeat	reflexed
Monique	orange-pink	large	double to full	high-centered	strong	singly	repeat	reflexed
Monsieur A. Maillé	red blend	large	double to full	cupped	strong	small clusters	repeat	plain
Monsieur Cordeau	deep pink	large	double to full	cupped	strong	small clusters	repeat	plain
Monsieur Tillier	orange-pink/ pink blend	large	double to full	open	slight	small clusters	repeat	plain
Montezuma	orange-pink	large	double to full	high-centered	slight	small clusters	repeat	reflexed
Moon River	mauve	medium	double to full	cupped	moderate	small clusters	repeat	reflexed
Moonbeam	apricot blend	medium	semi-double	open	moderate	small clusters	repeat	ruffled
Moonlight	light yellow	medium	semi-double	flat	moderate	small clusters	repeat	plain
Moonsprite	light yellow	medium	double to full	cupped	strong	small clusters	repeat	plain
Moore's Yellow	medium yellow	small	double to full	cupped	slight	small clusters	repeat	reflexed
Morden Blush	light pink	small	double to full	flat	none	small clusters	repeat	plain
Morden Centennial	medium pink	small	double to full	open	slight	large clusters	repeat	plain
Morden Fireglow	orange-red	medium	double to full	cupped	slight	small clusters	repeat	plain
Morden Ruby	pink blend	large	double to full	open	none	small clusters	repeat	plain
Morgengruss	orange-pink	large	double to full	open	strong	small clusters	repeat	reflexed
Morgenrot	red blend	medium	single	flat	slight	small clusters	repeat	plain
Morletii	mauve	medium	double to full	open	none	small clusters	once	plain
Morning Blush	light yellow	medium	semi-double	open	moderate	small clusters	once	plain
Morning Jewel	medium pink	large	semi-double	open	moderate	small clusters	repeat	reflexed
Moth	mauve	large	semi-double	open	slight	small clusters	repeat	plain
Mother's Love	pink blend	medium	double to full	high-centered	moderate	small clusters	repeat	reflexed
Mothersday	dark red	medium	double to full	globular	none	large clusters	repeat	plain
Moulin Rouge	medium red	medium	double to full	cupped	slight	small clusters	repeat	reflexed
Mount Hood	white	large	double to full	cupped	slight	small clusters	repeat	reflexed
Mount Shasta	white	large	double to full	cupped	slight	small clusters	repeat	reflexed
Mountbatten	medium yellow	large	double to full	cupped	slight	small clusters	repeat	reflexed
Mousseux du Japon	mauve	medium	semi-double	cupped	slight	small clusters	once	plain
Movie Star	pink blend	medium	double	high-centered	moderate	singly	repeat	reflexed
Mozart	pink blend	small	single	open	slight	large clusters	repeat	plain
Multiflore de Vaumarcus	light pink	medium	semi-double	cupped	slight	large clusters	repeat	plain
München	dark red	large	semi-double	open	slight	small clusters	repeat	plain
Mutabilis	yellow blend	medium	single	open	none	small clusters	repeat	plain
My Choice	pink blend	large	double to full	high-centered	moderate	singly	repeat	reflexed
My Girl	orange blend	large	double to full	open	none	small clusters	repeat	plain
My Granny	medium pink	small	double	rosette	none	small clusters	repeat	plain
My Joy	medium pink	large	double to full	high-centered	moderate	singly	repeat	reflexed
My Love	dark red	large	double to full	high-centered	strong	singly	repeat	reflexed
My Pleasure	medium red	medium	double to full	high-centered	moderate	small clusters	repeat	reflexed
My Valentine	dark red	small	very full	high-centered	none	small clusters	repeat	reflexed
Myra Stegman	orange-pink	large	double	open	none	small clusters	repeat	plain
Myriam	light pink	large	very full	cupped	strong	small clusters	repeat	reflexed
Nana Mouskouri	white	large	double to full	high-centered	slight	small clusters	repeat	reflexed
Nancy Gardiner	orange-pink	small	full	high-centered	slight	small clusters	repeat	reflexed
Nancy Hayward	medium red	extra large	single	open	none	small clusters	repeat	plain
Nancy Steen	pink blend	large	double to full	flat	moderate	small clusters	repeat	reflexed
Narrow Water	light pink	small	semi-double	cupped	moderate	large clusters	repeat	plain
National Trust	dark red	large	double to full	high-centered	none	singly	repeat	reflexed
Nearly Wild	medium pink	medium	single	open	slight	small clusters	repeat	plain
Nellie Neil	white	large	double to full	high-centered	slight	singly	repeat	reflexed
Némésis	dark red	medium	double to full	pompons	none	small clusters	repeat	plain
Neon	orange blend	large	very full	high-centered	moderate	singly	repeat	reflexed
Nestor	medium red	large	very full	flat	slight	small clusters	once	plain
Neue Revue	red blend	large	double to full	high-centered	strong	small clusters	repeat	reflexed
Nevada	white	large	single	flat	moderate	singly	repeat	plain
Neville Gibson	medium pink	large	double to full	high-centered	slight	small clusters	repeat	reflexed
New Beginning	orange blend	medium	very full	cupped	none	small clusters	repeat	reflexed
New Daily Mail	dark red	large	semi-double	cupped	none	small clusters	repeat	plain
New Dawn	light pink	large	double to full	cupped	moderate	small clusters	repeat	reflexed
New Day	medium yellow	large	double to full	high-centered	strong	singly	repeat	reflexed
New Face	yellow blend	small	single	open	slight	large clusters	repeat	plain
New Horizon	orange blend	medium	double to full	cupped	none	small clusters	repeat	reflexed
New Penny	orange-red	small	double to full	flat	moderate	small clusters	repeat	reflexed
New Star	medium yellow	large	double to full	high-centered	slight	small clusters	repeat	reflexed
New Year	orange blend	large	double to full	high-centered	slight	singly	repeat	reflexed
New Yorker	medium red	large	double to full	high-centered	moderate	singly	repeat	reflexed
New Zealand	light pink	large	double to full	high-centered	moderate	small clusters	repeat	reflexed
Newport Fairy	pink blend	small	single	open	none	large clusters	once	plain
News	mauve	large	semi-double	open	slight	truss	repeat	plain
Niccolo Paganini	medium red	medium	double to full	cupped	none	small clusters	repeat	reflexed
Nice Day	orange-pink	small	double to full	flat	slight	large clusters	repeat	reflexed
Nicole	white	large	double to full	high-centered	slight	small clusters	repeat	reflexed
Nicolette	apricot blend	large	semi-double	high-centered	none	singly	repeat	plain
Nigel Hawthorne	pink blend	medium	single	open	slight	small clusters	once	plain
Night	dark red	large	double to full	high-centered	strong	singly	repeat	reflexed
Night Light	deep yellow	medium	double to full	open	moderate	small clusters	repeat	reflexed
Nightingale	pink blend	large	double to full	high-centered	slight	singly	repeat	reflexed
Nikki	orange blend	medium	semi-double	open	none	small clusters	repeat	reflexed
Nina Weibull	dark red	medium	double to full	open	none	small clusters	repeat	reflexed
Niphetos	white	large	double to full	cupped	moderate	small clusters	repeat	plain
Nobilo's Chardonnay	medium yellow	large	double to full	high-centered	slight	small clusters	repeat	reflexed
Noble Antony	medium red	large	very full	globular	moderate	small clusters	repeat	plain
Noblesse	orange-red	extra large	double to full	high-centered	slight	singly	repeat	reflexed
Noëlla Nabonnand	dark red	large	double to full	open	moderate	small clusters	once	plain
Nora Cunningham	light pink	large	semi-double	cupped	slight	small clusters	repeat	reflexed
Norfolk	medium yellow	medium	double to full	rosette	slight	small clusters	repeat	plain
Norris Pratt	medium yellow	large	double to full	cupped	none	small clusters	repeat	reflexed
Northamptonshire	white	small	double to full	open	none	small clusters	repeat	reflexed
Northern Lights	yellow blend	large	double to full	high-centered	strong	small clusters	repeat	reflexed
Norwich Castle	orange blend	large	double to full	cupped	slight	small clusters	repeat	ruffled
Norwich Union	medium yellow	large	double to full	cupped	strong	small clusters	repeat	reflexed
Nouveau Vulcain	mauve	medium	double to full	cupped	moderate	small clusters	once	plain
Nova Zembla	white	large	double to full	cupped	strong	small clusters	repeat	reflexed
Nozomi	light pink	small	single	flat	none	large clusters	once	plain

NAME	BLOOM COLOR	FLOWER SIZE	FLOWER TYPE	FLOWER SHAPE	FRAGRANCE AMOUNT	FLOWERING HABIT	FLOWERING INCIDENCE	PETAL SHAPE
Nuits de Young	dark red	medium	double to full	open	strong	small clusters	once	plain
Nur Mahal	medium red	medium	semi-double	open	strong	large clusters	repeat	plain
Nuria de Recolons	white	large	double to full	high-centered	slight	small clusters	repeat	reflexed
Nymphenburg	orange-pink	large	semi-double	flat	moderate	large clusters	repeat	plain
Nyveldt's White	white	large	single	open	strong	small clusters	repeat	plain
Oakington Ruby	medium red	small	double to full	open	none	small clusters	repeat	plain
Oakmont	pink blend	large	double to full	flat	moderate	small clusters	repeat	plain
Octavia Hill	medium pink	medium	very full	cupped	moderate	small clusters	repeat	reflexed
Octavius Weld	pink blend	large	double to full	cupped	moderate	small clusters	repeat	reflexed
Oeillet Flamand	pink blend	medium	double to full	flat	strong	small clusters	once	plain
Oeillet Panachée	pink blend	small	double to full	flat	moderate	small clusters	once	plain
Oeillet Parfait	pink blend	medium	double to full	open	moderate	small clusters	once	plain
Oklahoma	dark red	large	double to full	high-centered	strong	singly	repeat	reflexed
Olave Baden-Powell	medium red	large	double to full	cupped	slight	small clusters	repeat	reflexed
Old Blush	medium pink	medium	double to full	open	slight	small clusters	repeat	plain
Old Glory	medium red	medium	double to full	high-centered	none	small clusters	repeat	reflexed
Old John	orange-red	medium	semi-double	open	slight	small clusters	repeat	plain
Old Master	red blend	large	semi-double	open	slight	small clusters	repeat	plain
Old Port	mauve	medium	double to full	quartered	moderate	small clusters	repeat	reflexed
Oldtimer	orange blend	large	double to full	high-centered	slight	small clusters	repeat	reflexed
Olé	orange-red	medium	double to full	high-centered	moderate	small clusters	repeat	reflexed
Olive	medium red	large	double to full	high-centered	moderate	small clusters	repeat	reflexed
Olympiad	medium red	large	double to full	high-centered	slight	small clusters	repeat	reflexed
Olympic Torch	red blend	medium	double to full	high-centered	none	small clusters	repeat	reflexed
Olympic Triumph	red blend	large	double to full	globular	none	small clusters	repeat	reflexed
Omar Khayyám	light pink	small	very full	quartered	strong	small clusters	once	plain
Ombrée Parfaite	mauve	medium	double to full	rosette	strong	small clusters	once	plain
Ondella	orange-red	large	double to full	open	none	small clusters	repeat	reflexed
Onkaparinga	apricot blend	medium	very full	cupped	strong	small clusters	repeat	plain
Opal Brünner	light pink	small	double	open	slight	large clusters	once	plain
Open Arms	light pink	small	semi-double	open	moderate	large clusters	repeat	plain
Opening Night	red blend	large	double to full	high-centered	slight	singly	repeat	reflexed
Opera	red blend	extra large	double to full	cupped	moderate	singly	repeat	reflexed
Ophelia	light pink	large	double to full	open	strong	small clusters	repeat	reflexed
Orange Bunny	orange-red	medium	semi-double	cupped	slight	small clusters	repeat	plain
Orange Cascade	orange blend	small	double to full	open	slight	small clusters	repeat	plain
Orange Fire	orange-pink	small	double to full	cupped	none	small clusters	repeat	reflexed
Orange Flame	orange-red	large	double to full	high-centered	moderate	small clusters	repeat	reflexed
Orange Honey	orange blend	small	double to full	cupped	moderate	small clusters	repeat	reflexed
Orange Mist	orange blend	medium	double to full	high-centered	slight	small clusters	repeat	reflexed
Orange Rumba	orange blend	medium	double to full	cupped	slight	small clusters	repeat	reflexed
Orange Sensation	orange-red	large	double to full	cupped	moderate	small clusters	repeat	reflexed
Orange Silk	orange-red	large	double to full	cupped	slight	small clusters	repeat	reflexed
Orange Sunblaze	orange-red	medium	double to full	cupped	slight	small clusters	repeat	reflexed
Orange Sunshine	orange blend	small	double to full	cupped	moderate	small clusters	repeat	reflexed
Orange Sweetheart	orange-pink	large	double to full	cupped	slight	small clusters	repeat	reflexed
Orange Triumph	medium red	small	semi-double	cupped	slight	large clusters	repeat	plain
Orangeade	orange-red	medium	semi-double	cupped	slight	small clusters	repeat	reflexed
Oranges and Lemons	orange blend	large	full	high-centered	slight	small clusters	repeat	plain
Orchid Jubilee	mauve	medium	double to full	open	none	small clusters	repeat	plain
Orchid Lace	mauve	medium	double to full	high-centered	slight	small clusters	repeat	reflexed
Oregold	deep yellow	large	double to full	high-centered	slight	singly	repeat	reflexed
Oriana	red blend	large	double to full	high-centered	slight	singly	repeat	reflexed
Oriental Charm	medium red	large	semi-double	open	slight	small clusters	repeat	reflexed
Oriental Dawn	yellow blend	large	double to full	cupped	moderate	singly	repeat	reflexed
Orléans Rose	red blend	small	semi-double	open	slight	small clusters	repeat	plain
Ormiston Roy	deep yellow	large	single	flat	slight	small clusters	once	plain
Ornament de la Nature	mauve	large	very full	cupped	strong	small clusters	once	plain
Orpheline de Juillet	mauve	medium	double to full	pompons	moderate	small clusters	once	plain
Osiria	red blend	large	double to full	high-centered	moderate	singly	repeat	reflexed
Oskar Cordel	deep pink	large	double to full	cupped	moderate	singly	repeat	plain
Oskar Scheerer	dark red	large	double to full	open	none	large clusters	repeat	reflexed
Otago	orange-red	medium	double to full	high-centered	slight	small clusters	repeat	reflexed
Othello	dark red	large	double to full	cupped	strong	small clusters	repeat	plain
Our Molly	medium red	medium	single	open	none	large clusters	repeat	plain
Our Rosamond	pink blend	large	double to full	high-centered	slight	singly	repeat	reflexed
Out of Africa	orange blend	large	double	high-centered	slight	small clusters	once	reflexed
Over the Rainbow	red blend	small	double to full	high-centered	slight	small clusters	repeat	reflexed
Overloon	deep pink	medium	double to full	open	none	small clusters	repeat	reflexed
Oz Gold	orange blend	small	double to full	cupped	none	small clusters	repeat	plain
Pacesetter	white	medium	double to full	high-centered	moderate	small clusters	repeat	reflexed
Pacific Triumph	medium pink	small	semi-double	cupped	slight	large clusters	repeat	plain
Paddy McGredy	medium pink	large	double to full	cupped	moderate	small clusters	repeat	reflexed
Paddy Stephens	orange blend	extra large	double to full	cupped	slight	singly	repeat	reflexed
Paheka	white blend	large	double to full	high-centered	moderate	small clusters	repeat	reflexed
Painted Moon	red blend	large	double to full	cupped	slight	small clusters	repeat	reflexed
Painter's Palette	red blend	medium	double	open	slight	small clusters	once	plain
Paleface	white	large	semi-double	cupped	slight	small clusters	repeat	plain
Pallas	light pink	small	double	rosette	slight	small clusters	repeat	plain
Palmengarten Frankfurt	medium pink	medium	semi-double	open	none	small clusters	repeat	reflexed
Panachée de Lyon	pink blend	large	semi-double	flat	strong	small clusters	repeat	plain
Pandemonium	yellow blend	medium	double to full	cupped	slight	small clusters	repeat	reflexed
Pandora	white	medium	very full	rosette	slight	small clusters	repeat	plain
Pania	light pink	large	double to full	high-centered	slight	singly	repeat	reflexed
Paola	medium red	large	double to full	open	slight	small clusters	repeat	plain
Papa Gontier	pink blend	large	semi-double	open	slight	small clusters	repeat	plain
Papa Hémeray	red blend	small	single	open	none	large clusters	repeat	plain
Papa Meilland	dark red	large	double to full	high-centered	strong	small clusters	repeat	reflexed
Papageno	red blend	large	double to full	open	slight	small clusters	repeat	reflexed
Papi Delbard	apricot blend	large	double	cupped	moderate	small clusters	repeat	plain
Papillon (Dubourg)	medium red	medium	full	open	none	small clusters	repeat	plain
Papillon (Nabonnand)	pink blend	medium	semi-double	cupped	slight	small clusters	repeat	plain
Paprika	orange-red	large	semi-double	open	slight	large clusters	repeat	plain
Para Ti	white	small	semi-double	open	none	small clusters	repeat	plain
Parade	deep pink	large	double to full	cupped	moderate	small clusters	repeat	plain
Paradise	mauve	large	double to full	high-centered	slight	small clusters	repeat	reflexed
Parador	orange-red	large	double to full	cupped	none	small clusters	repeat	reflexed
Pariser Charme	medium pink	large	double to full	high-centered	strong	small clusters	repeat	reflexed
Parkdirektor Riggers	dark red	medium	semi-double	open	slight	large clusters	repeat	plain
Parks' Yellow Tea-scented China	medium yellow	large	double to full	cupped	moderate	small clusters	repeat	reflexed
Parkzauber	dark red	large	double to full	globular	moderate	small clusters	once	plain
Parkzierde	dark red	large	double to full	cupped	moderate	small clusters	once	plain
Parmelia	medium red	large	double to full	high-centered	none	small clusters	repeat	reflexed
Parmentier	medium pink	large	double to full	globular	moderate	singly	once	plain
Parthenon	pink blend	large	double to full	cupped	none	small clusters	repeat	reflexed
Party Girl	yellow blend	small	double to full	high-centered	slight	small clusters	repeat	reflexed
Party Trick	deep pink	medium	double	open	slight	small clusters	repeat	plain
Parure d'Or	yellow blend	medium	semi-double	open	none	small clusters	repeat	plain
Pasadena Tournament	medium red	small	double	cupped	moderate	small clusters	once	plain
Pascali	white	medium	double to full	high-centered	none	small clusters	repeat	reflexed
Passion	medium red	large	double to full	cupped	moderate	small clusters	repeat	reflexed
Pasteur	pink blend	large	double to full	high-centered	none	singly	repeat	reflexed
Pat Austin	orange-red	large	very full	cupped	strong	small clusters	repeat	plain
Pat James	orange blend	medium	double to full	cupped	moderate	small clusters	repeat	reflexed
Pathfinder	orange-red	medium	single	flat	none	small clusters	repeat	plain
Patio Charm	apricot blend	small	double to full	cupped	slight	small clusters	repeat	reflexed
Patio Princess	orange-pink	medium	double to full	open	none	small clusters	repeat	reflexed

NAME	BLOOM COLOR	FLOWER SIZE	FLOWER TYPE	FLOWER SHAPE	FRAGRANCE AMOUNT	FLOWERING HABIT	FLOWERING INCIDENCE	PETAL SHAPE
Patricia (Chaplin Bros Ltd)	medium red	large	double to full	high-centered	moderate	small clusters	repeat	reflexed
Patricia (Kordes)	apricot blend	medium	double	cupped	slight	small clusters	repeat	plain
Patricia Macoun	white	medium	semi-double	open	none	large clusters	once	plain
Patriot	dark red	large	double to full	cupped	slight	singly	repeat	reflexed
Pat's Choice	orange-red	large	double	cupped	slight	small clusters	repeat	plain
Paul Cezanne	yellow blend	large	double to full	cupped	none	small clusters	repeat	reflexed
Paul Crampel	orange-red	medium	double to full	cupped	none	large clusters	repeat	plain
Paul Gauguin	russet	large	double to full	cupped	none	small clusters	repeat	reflexed
Paul Ledé	apricot blend	large	double to full	cupped	moderate	singly	repeat	reflexed
Paul Neyron	medium pink	large	double to full	cupped	strong	singly	repeat	plain
Paul Noël	pink blend	medium	double to full	cupped	none	small clusters	repeat	plain
Paul Ricard	yellow blend	large	double to full	cupped	moderate	small clusters	repeat	reflexed
Paul Ricault	medium pink	large	double to full	quartered	strong	singly	repeat	plain
Paul Shirville	orange-pink	large	double to full	high-centered	strong	small clusters	repeat	reflexed
Paul Transon	orange-pink	medium	double to full	flat	moderate	small clusters	repeat	plain
Paul Verdier	deep pink	large	double to full	cupped	moderate	singly	repeat	plain
Paulette	deep pink	large	very full	high-centered	slight	singly	repeat	reflexed
Paulii	white	medium	single	flat	moderate	small clusters	repeat	reflexed
Paul's Early Blush	light pink	large	double to full	high-centered	strong	singly	repeat	reflexed
Paul's Himalayan Musk Rambler	light pink	small	semi-double	rosette	slight	large clusters	once	plain
Paul's Lemon Pillar	light yellow	large	full	high-centered	strong	singly	once	reflexed
Paul's Scarlet Climber	medium red	medium	semi-double	open	slight	large clusters	once	plain
Pax	white	large	semi-double	flat	moderate	large clusters	repeat	plain
Peace	yellow blend	large	double to full	cupped	slight	small clusters	repeat	reflexed
Peace 1902	light yellow	medium	full	high-centered	slight	small clusters	repeat	plain
Peacekeeper	pink blend	medium	double to full	cupped	moderate	small clusters	repeat	reflexed
Peach Blossom	light pink	medium	semi-double	open	slight	large clusters	repeat	plain
Peach Spire	orange blend	large	full	open	none	small clusters	repeat	plain
Peaches'n' Cream	pink blend	small	double to full	high-centered	slight	small clusters	repeat	reflexed
Peachy Keen	apricot blend	small	double to full	high-centered	slight	small clusters	repeat	reflexed
Pearl Drift	white	medium	semi-double	open	slight	small clusters	repeat	plain
Pearl Sevillana	white blend	medium	semi-double	open	slight	small clusters	repeat	ruffled
Peer Gynt	yellow blend	large	double to full	high-centered	slight	singly	repeat	reflexed
Pélisson	dark red	medium	double to full	flat	moderate	small clusters	once	plain
Penelope (Williams)	red blend	medium	double to full	cupped	slight	small clusters	repeat	plain
Penelope (Pemberton)	light pink	medium	semi-double	open	moderate	truss	repeat	plain
Pennsylvania	pink blend	large	semi-double	high-centered	strong	small clusters	repeat	reflexed
Pennsylvanian	orange blend	large	double to full	cupped	moderate	small clusters	repeat	reflexed
Penny Lane (Taylor)	light pink	small	double to full	high-centered	none	singly	repeat	reflexed
Penny Lane (Harkness)	apricot blend	large	double	cupped	moderate	small clusters	repeat	ruffled
Pensioners' Voice	apricot blend	large	double to full	high-centered	moderate	small clusters	repeat	reflexed
Penthouse	medium pink	large	double to full	high-centered	moderate	small clusters	repeat	reflexed
Pepita	deep pink	small	double to full	cupped	none	small clusters	repeat	reflexed
Peppermint Ice	green	medium	semi-double	cupped	slight	small clusters	repeat	reflexed
Peppermint Twist	red blend	large	very full	flat	slight	small clusters	repeat	reflexed
Perception	pink blend	large	double to full	high-centered	moderate	small clusters	repeat	reflexed
Percy Thrower	medium pink	large	double to full	high-centered	moderate	small clusters	repeat	reflexed
Perdita	apricot blend	medium	very full	cupped	moderate	small clusters	repeat	plain
Perfect Moment	red blend	medium	double to full	high-centered	slight	singly	repeat	reflexed
Perfume Delight	medium pink	large	double to full	cupped	strong	small clusters	repeat	plain
Pergolèse	mauve	medium	very full	cupped	moderate	small clusters	repeat	plain
Perla de Alcañada	deep pink	small	semi-double	open	none	small clusters	repeat	plain
Perla de Montserrat	pink blend	small	semi-double	open	none	small clusters	repeat	plain
Perle des Blanches	white	medium	double to full	cupped	moderate	small clusters	repeat	plain
Perle des Jardins	light yellow	large	very full	globular	moderate	small clusters	repeat	plain
Perle des Panachées	mauve	medium	double to full	open	moderate	small clusters	once	plain
Perle des Rouges	dark red	small	double to full	cupped	none	large clusters	repeat	ruffled
Perle d'Or	yellow blend	small	double to full	open	slight	large clusters	repeat	plain
Pernille Poulsen	medium pink	large	semi-double	open	slight	small clusters	repeat	plain
Persian Princess	orange-red	small	double to full	cupped	slight	small clusters	repeat	reflexed
Personality	yellow blend	large	double to full	high-centered	moderate	singly	repeat	reflexed
Peter Benjamin	apricot blend	large	double to full	high-centered	moderate	small clusters	repeat	reflexed
Peter Frankenfeld	deep pink	large	double to full	high-centered	none	small clusters	repeat	reflexed
Petit Four	medium pink	medium	semi-double	cupped	moderate	small clusters	repeat	reflexed
Petite de Hollande	medium pink	small	double to full	flat	moderate	small clusters	once	plain
Petite Folie	orange blend	small	double to full	high-centered	slight	small clusters	repeat	reflexed
Petite Lisette	deep pink	small	double to full	rosette	strong	small clusters	once	plain
Petite Orléanaise	medium pink	small	double to full	pompons	strong	small clusters	once	plain
Petite Penny	white	small	semi-double	open	moderate	large clusters	repeat	frilled
Petite Pink Scotch	medium pink	small	double	rosette	slight	small clusters	once	plain
Petite Renoncule Violette	dark red	medium	double	pompon	moderate	small clusters	once	plain
Pfälzer Gold	deep yellow	large	double to full	cupped	none	small clusters	repeat	reflexed
Phantom	medium red	large	semi-double	flat	slight	large clusters	repeat	plain
Pharaoh	orange-red	large	double to full	high-centered	moderate	singly	repeat	reflexed
Phoebe	white	large	double to full	high-centered	moderate	small clusters	repeat	reflexed
Phoebe's Choice	pink blend	small	double to full	high-centered	none	small clusters	repeat	reflexed
Phoenix	deep pink	small	double to full	rosette	slight	small clusters	repeat	plain
Phyllis Bide	yellow blend	small	double to full	rosette	none	large clusters	repeat	plain
Picaninni	orange blend	small	full	open	strong	small clusters	repeat	plain
Picasso	pink blend	large	semi-double	open	none	small clusters	repeat	plain
Piccadilly	red blend	large	double to full	high-centered	none	small clusters	repeat	reflexed
Piccolo	orange-red	medium	double to full	open	none	small clusters	repeat	reflexed
Picture	light pink	large	double to full	high-centered	slight	small clusters	repeat	reflexed
Pierre B	apricot	large	double to full	high-centered	moderate	singly	repeat	reflexed
Pierre de Ronsard	pink blend	extra large	very full	globular	slight	small clusters	repeat	ruffled
Pierre de St Cyr	light pink	large	very full	cupped	moderate	small clusters	repeat	plain
Pierre Notting	dark red	large	double to full	globular	moderate	singly	repeat	plain
Pierrine	orange-pink	medium	double	high-centered	none	singly	repeat	plain
Pigalle	orange blend	large	double to full	high-centered	none	small clusters	repeat	reflexed
Pilgrim	dark red	large	double to full	high-centered	moderate	singly	repeat	reflexed
Pillarbox	orange-red	medium	double to full	open	slight	small clusters	repeat	reflexed
Pimlico 81	medium red	large	double to full	cupped	none	small clusters	repeat	ruffled
Piñata	yellow blend	large	double to full	high-centered	none	small clusters	repeat	reflexed
Pincushion	medium pink	small	double to full	flat	none	large clusters	repeat	plain
Pink Bassino	pink blend	small	single	open	none	truss	repeat	plain
Pink Bells	deep pink	small	double to full	rosette	slight	small clusters	repeat	plain
Pink Cameo	medium pink	small	double to full	cupped	none	small clusters	repeat	plain
Pink Cascade	medium pink	small	double to full	flat	none	small clusters	repeat	plain
Pink Chiffon	light pink	medium	double to full	cupped	moderate	large clusters	repeat	plain
Pink Chimo	medium pink	small	single	cupped	none	singly	repeat	plain
Pink Cloud	medium pink	large	double to full	cupped	moderate	large clusters	repeat	reflexed
Pink Delight	light pink	small	double to full	high-centered	none	small clusters	repeat	reflexed
Pink Favorite	medium pink	large	double to full	high-centered	slight	small clusters	repeat	reflexed
Pink Grootendorst	medium pink	small	double to full	open	slight	large clusters	repeat	frilled
Pink Gruss an Aachen	orange-pink	large	double to full	cupped	slight	small clusters	repeat	reflexed
Pink Heather	light pink	small	double to full	rosette	slight	large clusters	repeat	plain
Pink Iceberg	pink blend	medium	double to full	cupped	slight	large clusters	repeat	reflexed
Pink Joy	deep pink	small	double to full	high-centered	moderate	small clusters	repeat	reflexed
Pink Kardinal	deep pink	large	double to full	high-centered	none	singly	repeat	reflexed
Pink La Sevillana	medium pink	medium	semi-double	open	none	small clusters	repeat	ruffled
Pink Léda	medium pink	medium	double to full	flat	moderate	small clusters	once	plain
Pink Lustre	light pink	large	double to full	high-centered	strong	singly	repeat	reflexed
Pink Masterpiece	pink blend	large	double to full	high-centered	moderate	singly	repeat	reflexed
Pink Meidiland	pink blend	medium	single	open	none	small clusters	repeat	plain
Pink Meillandinda	medium pink	medium	double to full	cupped	none	small clusters	repeat	reflexed
Pink Panther	pink blend	large	double to full	high-centered	slight	small clusters	repeat	ruffled

NAME	BLOOM COLOR	FLOWER SIZE	FLOWER TYPE	FLOWER SHAPE	FRAGRANCE AMOUNT	FLOWERING HABIT	FLOWERING INCIDENCE	PETAL SHAPE
Pink Parfait	pink blend	large	double to full	cupped	slight	small clusters	repeat	reflexed
Pink Peace	medium pink	extra large	very full	cupped	strong	singly	repeat	reflexed
Pink Pearl	light pink	large	double to full	high-centered	slight	singly	repeat	reflexed
Pink Perpetue	medium pink	medium	double to full	globular	slight	small clusters	repeat	plain
Pink Petticoat	pink blend	medium	double to full	high-centered	slight	small clusters	repeat	reflexed
Pink Porcelain	light pink	small	double to full	high-centered	slight	small clusters	repeat	reflexed
Pink Powderpuff	light pink	large	very full	high-centered	strong	small clusters	repeat	reflexed
Pink Prosperity	light pink	small	double to full	open	moderate	truss	repeat	plain
Pink Puff	light pink	large	double to full	high-centered	moderate	small clusters	repeat	reflexed
Pink Robin	pink blend	small	semi-double	saucer	slight	small clusters	once	plain
Pink Robusta	medium pink	large	semi-double	open	slight	small clusters	repeat	plain
Pink Rosette	light pink	medium	double to full	rosette	slight	small clusters	repeat	plain
Pink Roundelay	deep pink	large	double to full	high-centered	slight	small clusters	repeat	reflexed
Pink Sensation	medium pink	large	double to full	high-centered	slight	small clusters	repeat	reflexed
Pink Silk	medium pink	large	double to full	high-centered	none	singly	repeat	reflexed
Pink Symphony	light pink	medium	double to full	open	slight	small clusters	repeat	plain
Pink Triumph	medium pink	small	double to full	high-centered	none	singly	repeat	reflexed
Pink Wave	medium pink	medium	semi-double	open	moderate	small clusters	repeat	reflexed
Pink Wonder	light pink	medium	double to full	cupped	slight	small clusters	repeat	reflexed
Pinkie	medium pink	medium	semi-double	cupped	moderate	large clusters	repeat	plain
Pinocchio	orange-pink	small	double to full	cupped	slight	large clusters	repeat	reflexed
Pinstripe	red blend	small	double to full	high-centered	none	small clusters	repeat	reflexed
Pinwheel	pink blend	small	semi-double	cupped	slight	small clusters	repeat	plain
Pioneer	medium red	large	double to full	high-centered	moderate	small clusters	repeat	reflexed
Pixie Hat	dark red	medium	single	high-centered	none	large clusters	repeat	plain
Playboy	red blend	large	single	open	none	small clusters	repeat	plain
Playgirl	medium pink	medium	single	open	none	small clusters	repeat	plain
Playgold	orange blend	small	semi-double	open	slight	small clusters	repeat	plain
Playtime	orange-red	medium	single	flat	none	small clusters	repeat	plain
Pleasure	medium pink	large	double to full	cupped	none	small clusters	repeat	ruffled
Pleine de Grâce	white	small	single	open	strong	large clusters	repeat	plain
Plentiful	deep pink	large	very full	flat	none	small clusters	repeat	plain
Plum Crazy	mauve	large	double to full	high-centered	moderate	small clusters	repeat	reflexed
Plum Duffy	mauve	small	double to full	high-centered	slight	singly	repeat	reflexed
Poëma	medium pink	medium	double to full	cupped	none	large clusters	repeat	plain
Poetry in Motion	yellow blend	large	double to full	cupped	moderate	singly	repeat	reflexed
Poker Chip	red blend	medium	double to full	high-centered	strong	small clusters	repeat	reflexed
Polareis	white	medium	double to full	open	strong	small clusters	repeat	plain
Polarstern	white	medium	double to full	high-centered	none	small clusters	repeat	reflexed
Polka	orange blend	large	double to full	cupped	moderate	small clusters	repeat	ruffled
Polo Club	yellow blend	medium	double to full	cupped	slight	small clusters	repeat	reflexed
Polynesian Sunset	orange-pink	large	double to full	high-centered	moderate	small clusters	repeat	reflexed
Pompon	white/striped	small	double to full	pompons	moderate	small clusters	once	plain
Pompon Blanc Parfait	white	small	very full	pompons	strong	small clusters	once	plain
Pompon de Paris	medium pink/ deep pink	small	double to full	open	none	small clusters	repeat	plain
Ponctuée	pink blend	medium	semi-double	open	moderate	small clusters	once	plain
Popcorn	white	small	semi-double	open	moderate	small clusters	repeat	reflexed
Poppy Flash	orange-red	large	double to full	cupped	moderate	small clusters	repeat	reflexed
Porthos	orange-red	medium	double to full	cupped	none	small clusters	repeat	reflexed
Portland Trailblazer	dark red	extra large	double to full	high-centered	moderate	singly	repeat	reflexed
Portrait	pink blend	large	double to full	cupped	moderate	small clusters	repeat	reflexed
Pot o' Gold	medium yellow	medium	double to full	flat	strong	small clusters	repeat	plain
Potter & Moore	medium pink	large	double to full	cupped	moderate	small clusters	repeat	plain
Poulbright	orange-red	medium	double to full	cupped	slight	small clusters	repeat	plain
Potton Heritage	red blend	large	double to full	high-centered	moderate	small clusters	repeat	reflexed
Poulsen's Bedder	light pink	large	semi-double	open	slight	truss	repeat	plain
Poulsen's Delight	light pink	medium	single	open	none	truss	repeat	plain
Poulsen's Pearl	light pink	medium	single	open	none	truss	repeat	plain
Poulsen's Yellow	medium yellow	medium	semi-double	open	strong	large clusters	repeat	plain
Pourpre du Luxembourg	mauve	medium	double to full	cupped	moderate	small clusters	once	plain
Prairie Dawn	medium pink	medium	double to full	open	none	small clusters	repeat	plain
Prairie Fire	medium red	medium	single	open	moderate	large clusters	repeat	plain
Prairie Harvest	light yellow	large	double to full	open	moderate	large clusters	repeat	plain
Prairie Princess	orange-pink	large	semi-double	open	slight	small clusters	repeat	plain
Precious Platinum	medium red	large	double to full	high-centered	none	small clusters	repeat	reflexed
Présence	light pink	large	double	high-centered	moderate	small clusters	repeat	plain
Président de Sèze	mauve	large	double to full	flat	strong	small clusters	once	plain
Président Dutailly	mauve	large	double to full	rosette	strong	small clusters	once	plain
President Herbert Hoover	pink blend	large	double to full	cupped	moderate	small clusters	repeat	reflexed
Président Leopold Senghor	dark red	large	double to full	cupped	none	small clusters	repeat	reflexed
President Lincoln	dark red	large	double to full	cupped	moderate	singly	repeat	plain
Pretoria	deep pink	large	full	cupped	moderate	small clusters	repeat	plain
Pretty in Pink	light pink	medium	double to full	cupped	moderate	large clusters	repeat	reflexed
Pretty Jessica	deep pink	medium	very full	rosette	strong	small clusters	repeat	plain
Pretty Lady	light pink	medium	semi-double	open	none	small clusters	repeat	plain
Preziosa	pink blend	large	double to full	high-centered	slight	small clusters	repeat	reflexed
Pride 'n' Joy	orange blend	medium	double to full	high-centered	moderate	small clusters	repeat	reflexed
Pride of England	dark red	large	double to full	high-centered	slight	small clusters	repeat	reflexed
Pride of Maldon	orange blend	medium	semi-double	open	slight	small clusters	repeat	plain
Prima Ballerina	deep pink	large	double to full	cupped	moderate	singly	repeat	reflexed
Prima Donna	deep pink	large	double to full	high-centered	slight	small clusters	repeat	reflexed
Primevère	yellow blend	large	double to full	cupped	slight	small clusters	once	plain
Prince Arthur	medium red	medium	double to full	pompons	moderate	small clusters	repeat	plain
Prince Camille de Rohan	dark red	large	very full	cupped	strong	small clusters	repeat	reflexed
Prince Charles	mauve	large	semi-double	open	slight	small clusters	once	ruffled
Prince Fréderic	mauve	medium	double to full	rosette	moderate	small clusters	once	plain
Prince Meillandina	dark red	medium	double to full	cupped	none	small clusters	repeat	reflexed
Prince Napoléon	pink blend	large	double to full	cupped	moderate	small clusters	repeat	plain
Princeps	medium red	large	semi-double	open	slight	small clusters	once	reflexed
Princess (Laperrière)	orange-red	large	double	urn-shaped	slight	singly	repeat	plain
Princess (Ilsink)	white	medium	double	open	slight	large clusters	repeat	reflexed
Princess Alice	medium yellow	medium	double to full	open	slight	large clusters	repeat	reflexed
Princess Chichibu	pink blend	large	double to full	cupped	slight	small clusters	repeat	plain
Princess Margaret of England	medium pink	large	double to full	high-centered	slight	singly	repeat	reflexed
Princess Michael of Kent	medium yellow	large	double to full	high-centered	slight	small clusters	repeat	reflexed
Princess Michiko	orange blend	medium	semi-double	cupped	none	small clusters	repeat	reflexed
Princess of Wales	light pink	large	double to full	cupped	slight	large clusters	repeat	reflexed
Princess of Wales	white	large	double to full	cupped	moderate	singly	repeat	plain
Princess Royal	apricot blend	large	double to full	cupped	slight	singly	repeat	reflexed
Princesse Adélaïde	light pink	medium	double to full	cupped	moderate	small clusters	once	plain
Princesse de Monaco	white	large	double to full	high-centered	slight	small clusters	repeat	reflexed
Princesse de Nassau	light yellow	medium	double to full	cupped	moderate	large clusters	repeat	plain
Princesse de Sagan	dark red	medium	double to full	cupped	none	small clusters	repeat	plain
Princesse Lamballe	white	medium	double to full	flat	moderate	small clusters	once	plain
Princesse Louise	white	large	double to full	cupped	none	large clusters	once	plain
Princesse Marie	medium pink	medium	double to full	cupped	none	large clusters	once	plain
Priscilla Burton	red blend	medium	semi-double	open	moderate	small clusters	repeat	plain
Pristine	white	large	double to full	high-centered	moderate	small clusters	repeat	reflexed
Privé	medium pink	large	double to full	high-centered	moderate	small clusters	repeat	reflexed
Professeur Jean Barnard	dark red	extra large	double to full	cupped	slight	singly	repeat	reflexed
Prolifera de Redouté	medium pink	large	very full	globular	strong	small clusters	once	plain
Prominent	orange-red	large	double to full	cupped	slight	small clusters	repeat	reflexed

NAME	BLOOM COLOR	FLOWER SIZE	FLOWER TYPE	FLOWER SHAPE	FRAGRANCE AMOUNT	FLOWERING HABIT	FLOWERING INCIDENCE	PETAL SHAPE
Prosperity	white	small	semi-double	open	moderate	large clusters	repeat	plain
Prospero	dark red	large	double to full	rosette	strong	small clusters	repeat	plain
Proud Land	dark red	large	very full	high-centered	moderate	singly	repeat	reflexed
Proud Titania	white	large	double to full	flat	strong	small clusters	repeat	plain
Pucker Up	orange-red	small	double to full	high-centered	slight	small clusters	repeat	reflexed
Pudsey Bear	deep yellow	medium	double to full	high-centered	none	small clusters	repeat	reflexed
Puppy Love	orange blend	small	double to full	high-centered	slight	small clusters	repeat	reflexed
Pure Bliss	pink blend	large	double to full	high-centered	moderate	small clusters	repeat	reflexed
Purezza	white	small	double to full	pompons	moderate	truss	repeat	plain
Purple Beauty	mauve	large	double to full	high-centered	moderate	small clusters	repeat	reflexed
Purple Buttons	mauve blend	small	double to full	pompons	slight	large clusters	repeat	plain
Purple Cloud	mauve blend	large	double to full	high-centered	strong	small clusters	repeat	reflexed
Purple Dawn	mauve	small	double to full	high-centered	slight	small clusters	repeat	reflexed
Purple Splendour	mauve	large	double to full	cupped	slight	small clusters	repeat	reflexed
Purple Tiger	mauve	large	double to full	high-centered	slight	small clusters	repeat	reflexed
Purpurea Plena	mauve	medium	double	cupped	slight	small clusters	once	plain
Pzazz	red blend	medium	double to full	cupped	slight	small clusters	repeat	plain
Quaker Star	orange-pink	large	double to full	high-centered	none	small clusters	repeat	reflexed
Quatre Saisons Blanc Mousseux	white	medium	double to full	cupped	strong	small clusters	repeat	plain
Queen Charlotte	orange-pink	large	double to full	high-centered	slight	singly	repeat	reflexed
Queen Elizabeth	medium pink	large	double to full	cupped	moderate	small clusters	repeat	plain
Queen Fabiola	orange-red	large	double to full	high-centered	slight	small clusters	repeat	reflexed
Queen Margrethe	light pink	medium	double to full	cupped	slight	small clusters	repeat	plain
Queen Mother	light pink	small	double to full	cupped	slight	small clusters	repeat	plain
Queen Nefertiti	light yellow	medium	double to full	rosette	moderate	small clusters	repeat	plain
Queen of Bedders	deep pink	medium	double to full	rosette	moderate	small clusters	repeat	plain
Queen of Bourbons	pink blend	large	semi-double	cupped	strong	small clusters	once	plain
Queen of Hearts	medium pink	large	double to full	cupped	moderate	small clusters	repeat	reflexed
Queen of the Musks	pink blend	medium	double to full	open	strong	large clusters	repeat	plain
Queen Parade	soft pink	small	double	flat	slight	small clusters	repeat	plain
Rachel Bowes Lyon	yellow blend	medium	semi-double	flat	moderate	large clusters	repeat	plain
Radiance	light pink	large	double to full	cupped	strong	small clusters	repeat	reflexed
Radio Times	medium pink	medium	very full	cupped	strong	small clusters	repeat	plain
Radox Bouquet	medium pink	large	double to full	cupped	strong	small clusters	repeat	reflexed
Radway Sunrise	orange blend	large	single	cupped	slight	truss	repeat	plain
Rae Dungan	yellow blend	large	double to full	high-centered	moderate	small clusters	repeat	reflexed
Ragtime	pink blend	small	very full	cupped	none	small clusters	repeat	plain
Rainbow	pink blend	large	semi-double	open	moderate	small clusters	repeat	reflexed
Rainbow Nation	yellow blend	medium	double	open	slight	truss	repeat	plain
Rainbow Robe	mauve	large	double to full	high-centered	strong	small clusters	repeat	reflexed
Rainbow's End	yellow blend	small	double to full	high-centered	none	small clusters	repeat	reflexed
Ralph's Creeper	red blend	medium	semi-double	open	moderate	large clusters	repeat	plain
Rambling Rector	white	small	semi-double	open	strong	large clusters	once	plain
Ramona	medium red	large	single	open	slight	small clusters	repeat	plain
Raphael	white	medium	double to full	cupped	moderate	small clusters	once	plain
Raubritter	light pink	medium	semi-double	globular	moderate	truss	once	plain
Ray of Sunshine	medium yellow	small	semi-double	cupped	slight	small clusters	repeat	plain
Raymond Chenault	medium red	large	semi-double	open	slight	small clusters	repeat	reflexed
Razzle Dazzle	red blend	medium	double to full	high-centered	slight	small clusters	repeat	reflexed
Rebecca Claire	orange-pink	large	double to full	cupped	strong	small clusters	repeat	reflexed
Reconciliation	apricot blend	large	double to full	high-centered	moderate	small clusters	repeat	reflexed
Red Ace	dark red	small	double to full	high-centered	slight	small clusters	repeat	reflexed
Red Alert	medium red	small	double to full	high-centered	slight	small clusters	repeat	reflexed
Red American Beauty	medium red	large	double to full	high-centered	strong	singly	repeat	reflexed
Red Beauty	dark red	small	double to full	high-centered	slight	small clusters	repeat	reflexed
Red Bells	medium red	small	double to full	flat	slight	large clusters	once	reflexed
Red Blanket	deep pink	small	semi-double	open	slight	small clusters	repeat	plain
Red Cascade	dark red	small	double to full	cupped	slight	small clusters	repeat	plain

NAME	BLOOM COLOR	FLOWER SIZE	FLOWER TYPE	FLOWER SHAPE	FRAGRANCE AMOUNT	FLOWERING HABIT	FLOWERING INCIDENCE	PETAL SHAPE
Red Chief	medium red	large	double to full	high-centered	strong	singly	repeat	reflexed
Red Cross	medium red	medium	double to full	cupped	moderate	small clusters	repeat	reflexed
Red Devil	medium red	large	very full	high-centered	moderate	singly	repeat	reflexed
Red Fan	orange-red	extra large	double to full	cupped	slight	singly	repeat	reflexed
Red Favorite	medium red	medium	semi-double	cupped	slight	truss	repeat	reflexed
Red Flush	medium red	small	double to full	cupped	none	small clusters	repeat	reflexed
Red Glory	medium red	large	semi-double	flat	slight	large clusters	repeat	plain
Red Head	orange-red	large	double to full	cupped	moderate	small clusters	repeat	reflexed
Red Imp	dark red	small	very full	flat	slight	large clusters	repeat	plain
Red Lion	medium red	large	double to full	high-centered	moderate	small clusters	repeat	reflexed
Red Masterpiece	dark red	large	double to full	high-centered	strong	small clusters	repeat	reflexed
Red Meidiland	red blend	medium	single	cupped	none	small clusters	repeat	plain
Red Minimo	dark red	small	semi-double	open	none	small clusters	repeat	plain
Red Nella	light red	large	double to full	high-centered	slight	singly	repeat	reflexed
Red Pat	medium red	small	semi-double	open	slight	small clusters	repeat	plain
Red Peter	light red	large	double	cupped	slight	small clusters	repeat	plain
Red Planet	dark red	large	double to full	high-centered	strong	singly	repeat	reflexed
Red Queen	medium red	large	double to full	high-centered	none	singly	repeat	reflexed
Red Radiance	deep pink	large	double to full	open	strong	small clusters	repeat	reflexed
Red Rascal	medium red	small	double to full	cupped	slight	small clusters	repeat	reflexed
Red Ribbon	medium red	medium	semi-double	cupped	slight	small clusters	repeat	reflexed
Red Ribbons	medium red	medium	semi-double	flat	slight	large clusters	repeat	plain
Red Rock	medium red	large	double to full	open	slight	singly	repeat	reflexed
Red Rosamini	dark red	small	double to full	cupped	none	small clusters	repeat	reflexed
Red Rugostar	medium red	medium	semi-double	open	slight	small clusters	repeat	plain
Red Shadows	dark red	small	double	rosette	none	small clusters	repeat	plain
Red Simplicity	medium red	large	semi-double	cupped	slight	small clusters	repeat	ruffled
Red Splendour	dark red	medium	double to full	rosette	slight	large clusters	repeat	plain
Red Success	red blend	large	very full	high-centered	slight	singly	repeat	reflexed
Red Trail	medium red	small	semi-double	open	none	small clusters	repeat	plain
Red Wagon	medium red	small	double to full	open	none	small clusters	repeat	plain
Red Wonder	dark red	large	double to full	cupped	moderate	large clusters	repeat	reflexed
Redcoat	medium red	large	single	open	slight	small clusters	repeat	plain
Redgold	yellow blend	medium	double to full	open	slight	large clusters	repeat	reflexed
Redouté	light pink	large	very full	cupped	slight	small clusters	repeat	reflexed
Refulgence	medium red	large	semi-double	open	strong	small clusters	once	plain
Regatta (Warriner)	white	large	double to full	high-centered	strong	singly	repeat	reflexed
Regatta (Meilland)	light pink	large	double to full	high-centered	moderate	singly	repeat	reflexed
Regensberg	pink blend	large	semi-double	open	slight	large clusters	repeat	ruffled
Reine Blanche	white	medium	double to full	cupped	strong	small clusters	once	plain
Reine des Centfeuilles	medium pink	medium	very full	rosette	strong	small clusters	once	reflexed
Reine des Violettes	mauve	large	double to full	rosette	strong	small clusters	repeat	plain
Reine France	medium pink	large	double to full	cupped	slight	small clusters	repeat	reflexed
Reine Marie Henriette	medium red	large	double	cupped	moderate	small clusters	repeat	plain
Reine Olga de Würtemberg	medium red	large	double to full	flat	moderate	small clusters	repeat	reflexed
Reine Victoria	medium pink	large	double	cupped	strong	small clusters	repeat	plain
Relax	orange-red	large	single	open	none	small clusters	once	plain
Relax Meillandecor	pink blend	medium	double to full	open	none	large clusters	repeat	reflexed
Rembrandt	orange-red	medium	double to full	quartered	moderate	small clusters	repeat	reflexed
Remember Me	orange blend	large	double to full	open	slight	small clusters	repeat	reflexed
Remembrance	medium red	large	double to full	cupped	slight	small clusters	repeat	reflexed
Renae	medium pink	medium	double to full	open	moderate	large clusters	repeat	plain
Renaissance (Gaujard)	orange blend	large	double	high-centered	moderate	small clusters	repeat	plain
Renaissance (Harkness)	white	large	double	loose	strong	small clusters	repeat	plain
Rendez-vous	medium pink	large	double to full	high-centered	moderate	small clusters	repeat	reflexed
René André	apricot blend	medium	semi-double	cupped	moderate	small clusters	once	plain
Réné d'Anjou	deep pink	medium	double to full	globular	strong	small clusters	once	plain

NAME	BLOOM COLOR	FLOWER SIZE	FLOWER TYPE	FLOWER SHAPE	FRAGRANCE AMOUNT	FLOWERING HABIT	FLOWERING INCIDENCE	PETAL SHAPE
Renny	medium pink	medium	double to full	rosette	moderate	small clusters	repeat	reflexed
Repandia	light pink	medium	semi-double	open	moderate	large clusters	repeat	plain
Restless	medium red	large	semi-double	cupped	moderate	small clusters	repeat	reflexed
Rétro	medium pink	medium	double to full	open	none	small clusters	repeat	reflexed
Rêve de Paris	orange-pink	large	double to full	high-centered	slight	small clusters	repeat	reflexed
Rêve d'Or	medium yellow	medium	double to full	open	moderate	small clusters	repeat	reflexed
Réveil Dijonnais	red blend	large	semi-double	cupped	moderate	small clusters	repeat	reflexed
Reverend H. d'Ombrain	medium red	medium	double to full	flat	moderate	small clusters	repeat	reflexed
Reynolds Hole	medium red	medium	double to full	open	moderate	small clusters	repeat	reflexed
Rheinaupark	medium red	large	semi-double	open	slight	small clusters	repeat	reflexed
Rhodologue Jules Gravereaux	pink blend	large	double to full	cupped	slight	small clusters	repeat	reflexed
Rhonda	medium pink	large	double to full	cupped	slight	small clusters	repeat	reflexed
Rina Hugo	deep pink	large	double	high-centered	slight	small clusters	repeat	reflexed
Ring of Fire	yellow blend	small	very full	rosette	slight	small clusters	repeat	plain
Ringlet	pink blend	small	single	open	slight	large clusters	repeat	plain
Rio Samba	yellow blend	large	double to full	open	slight	small clusters	repeat	reflexed
Ripples	mauve	medium	semi-double	open	slight	small clusters	repeat	ruffled
Rise 'n' Shine	medium yellow	small	double to full	high-centered	moderate	small clusters	repeat	reflexed
Rita Applegate	light yellow	small	double to full	high-centered	moderate	small clusters	repeat	reflexed
Rita Levi Montalcini	apricot blend	medium	double to full	cupped	slight	small clusters	repeat	reflexed
Ritter von Barmstede	medium pink	medium	double to full	open	none	large clusters	repeat	plain
Ritz	medium red	large	semi-double	open	slight	small clusters	repeat	plain
Rival de Paestum	white	large	double to full	cupped	moderate	small clusters	repeat	reflexed
Rivers' George IV	dark red	medium	double to full	open	none	small clusters	once	plain
Riverview Centennial	dark red	large	double to full	high-centered	slight	small clusters	repeat	reflexed
Roaming	deep pink	large	double to full	high-centered	none	small clusters	repeat	reflexed
Rob Roy	dark red	medium	double	high-centered	slight	small clusters	repeat	plain
Robert Duncan	pink blend	extra large	very full	high-centered	moderate	small clusters	repeat	reflexed
Robert le Diable	mauve blend	medium	double to full	cupped	strong	small clusters	once	reflexed
Robert Léopold	pink blend	large	double to full	cupped	moderate	small clusters	repeat	reflexed
Robin Hood	medium red	medium	semi-double	flat	slight	large clusters	repeat	plain
Robin Red Breast	red blend	small	single	open	none	small clusters	repeat	plain
Robina	medium red	medium	double to full	high-centered	none	singly	repeat	reflexed
Robusta (Soupert et Notting)	medium red	large	single	rosette	moderate	small clusters	repeat	plain
Robusta (Kordes)	medium red	medium	single	open	moderate	small clusters	repeat	plain
Rochester Cathedral	medium pink	medium	very full	cupped	moderate	small clusters	repeat	reflexed
Rod Stillman	light pink	large	double to full	high-centered	moderate	singly	repeat	reflexed
Rodeo	orange-red	large	double to full	cupped	slight	small clusters	repeat	reflexed
Rodeo Drive	medium red	large	double to full	high-centered	slight	singly	repeat	reflexed
Rödhätte	medium red	large	semi-double	open	none	large clusters	repeat	plain
Rödinghausen	medium red	medium	double to full	open	none	small clusters	repeat	plain
Roger Lambelin	red blend	medium	double to full	cupped	moderate	small clusters	repeat	ruffled
Roi de Siam	medium red	large	double to full	cupped	slight	small clusters	repeat	plain
Roller Coaster	red blend	small	semi-double	open	none	small clusters	repeat	plain
Roma	pink blend	large	double	high-centered	slight	small clusters	repeat	plain
Roman Holiday	red blend	medium	double to full	high-centered	moderate	small clusters	repeat	reflexed
Romance	medium pink	medium	double	cupped	slight	small clusters	repeat	reflexed
Romantic Hedgerose	medium pink	medium	double to full	open	none	small clusters	repeat	plain
Romeo	dark red	large	double to full	high-centered	slight	small clusters	repeat	reflexed
Rooi Rose	medium red	large	full	high-centered	slight	small clusters	repeat	plain
Rosa Mundi	pink blend	medium	semi-double	cupped	moderate	singly	once	plain
Rosabell	medium pink	medium	double to full	cupped	slight	small clusters	repeat	reflexed
Rosali	medium pink	medium	double to full	open	none	small clusters	repeat	reflexed
Rosalie Coral	orange blend	medium	double to full	cupped	slight	small clusters	repeat	reflexed
Rosamunde	medium pink	medium	double to full	cupped	slight	small clusters	repeat	reflexed
Rosarium Uetersen	deep pink	medium	very full	cupped	moderate	small clusters	repeat	reflexed
Rose à Parfum de l'Haÿ	medium red	large	double to full	globular	strong	small clusters	repeat	plain
Rose Bradwardine	medium pink	small	single	open	moderate	small clusters	once	plain
Rose Cascade	deep pink	medium	single	open	none	large clusters	repeat	plain
Rose d'Amour	deep pink	small	double to full	open	slight	small clusters	once	plain
Rose de Meaux	medium pink	small	double to full	pompons	moderate	small clusters	once	ruffled
Rose de Rescht	deep pink	medium	double to full	rosette	strong	small clusters	repeat	plain
Rose des Maures	dark red	medium	semi-double	open	moderate	small clusters	once	plain
Rose des Peintres	medium pink	medium	double to full	flat	strong	small clusters	once	plain
Rose d'Hivers	white	medium	double to full	cupped	slight	small clusters	repeat	plain
Rose du Roi	medium red	medium	double to full	pompons	strong	small clusters	repeat	plain
Rose du Roi à Fleurs Pourpres	mauve	medium	double to full	pompons	strong	small clusters	repeat	plain
Rose Edouard	medium pink	medium	double to full	cupped	strong	small clusters	repeat	plain
Rose Gaujard	red blend	large	double to full	high-centered	slight	small clusters	repeat	reflexed
Rose Gilardi	red blend	small	semi-double	open	none	small clusters	repeat	plain
Rose Hills Red	dark red	small	double to full	open	none	small clusters	repeat	reflexed
Rose Marie, Climbing	medium pink	extra large	double to full	cupped	moderate	small clusters	repeat	reflexed
Rose-Marie Viaud	mauve	small	double to full	cupped	moderate	large clusters	once	plain
Rose Parade	pink blend	large	double to full	cupped	moderate	small clusters	repeat	reflexed
Rose Window	orange blend	small	semi-double	cupped	slight	small clusters	repeat	reflexed
Roselina	pink blend	medium	single	open	slight	small clusters	repeat	plain
Rosemary Harkness	orange-pink	large	double to full	cupped	strong	small clusters	repeat	reflexed
Rosemary Rose	deep pink	medium	double to full	rosette	moderate	truss	repeat	plain
Rosendorf Sparrieshoop	light pink	medium	semi-double	cupped	slight	small clusters	repeat	plain
Rosenelfe	medium pink	medium	double to full	high-centered	moderate	small clusters	repeat	reflexed
Rosenfee	light pink	medium	double to full	cupped	slight	small clusters	repeat	reflexed
Rosenprofessor Sieber	medium pink	medium	double	cupped	moderate	small clusters	repeat	plain
Rosenresli	deep pink	large	double to full	cupped	strong	small clusters	repeat	reflexed
Rosenstadt Zweibrücken	pink blend	medium	double	cupped	none	small clusters	repeat	ruffled
Roseraie de l'Haÿ	dark red	large	semi-double	open	strong	small clusters	repeat	plain
Roseromantic	white	large	single	open	slight	small clusters	repeat	plain
Rosette Delizy	yellow blend	large	double to full	cupped	moderate	small clusters	repeat	plain
Roseville College	orange-pink	large	double to full	high-centered	slight	small clusters	repeat	reflexed
Rosie Larkin	mauve	small	single	open	slight	small clusters	repeat	plain
Rosina	medium yellow	small	semi-double	open	slight	small clusters	repeat	plain
Rosmarin	pink blend	small	double to full	globular	slight	small clusters	repeat	plain
Rosmarin '89	deep pink	small	double to full	cupped	slight	small clusters	repeat	reflexed
Rosy Carpet	deep pink	small	single	open	slight	large clusters	repeat	plain
Rosy Cheeks	red blend	large	double to full	cupped	strong	small clusters	repeat	reflexed
Rosy Cushion	light pink	small	single	open	slight	large clusters	repeat	plain
Rosy Dawn	yellow blend	small	double to full	high-centered	slight	small clusters	repeat	reflexed
Rosy Future	deep pink	small	double	open	moderate	large clusters	repeat	reflexed
Rosy Hit	orange blend	medium	semi-double	open	slight	small clusters	repeat	plain
Rosy Mantle	medium pink	large	double to full	cupped	moderate	small clusters	repeat	reflexed
Rote Max Graf	medium red	medium	single	open	moderate	small clusters	repeat	plain
Rote Mozart	orange-red	small	semi-double	cupped	slight	large clusters	repeat	plain
Roter Champagner	medium red	large	double to full	high-centered	none	small clusters	repeat	reflexed
Rotes Meer	medium red	medium	semi-double	open	slight	small clusters	repeat	plain
Rouge Admirable	deep pink	medium	double to full	rosette	strong	small clusters	once	plain
Rouge Meilland	medium red	large	double to full	high-centered	none	small clusters	repeat	reflexed
Rouge Moss	orange-red	medium	double	open	moderate	small clusters	repeat	plain
Rouletii	medium pink	small	semi-double	open	none	small clusters	repeat	plain
Roundelay	dark red	large	double to full	high-centered	moderate	small clusters	repeat	reflexed
Roxie	medium red	large	double to full	cupped	slight	small clusters	repeat	reflexed
Royal Albert Hall	red blend	large	double to full	high-centered	strong	singly	repeat	reflexed
Royal Amethyst	mauve	large	double to full	high-centered	strong	singly	repeat	reflexed
Royal Bassino	medium red	medium	single	open	slight	large clusters	repeat	plain
Royal Blush	light pink	medium	double to full	flat	moderate	small clusters	once	plain

NAME	BLOOM COLOR	FLOWER SIZE	FLOWER TYPE	FLOWER SHAPE	FRAGRANCE AMOUNT	FLOWERING HABIT	FLOWERING INCIDENCE	PETAL SHAPE
Royal Bonica	medium pink	medium	double to full	cupped	slight	small clusters	repeat	plain
Royal Canadian	medium red	large	double to full	cupped	moderate	small clusters	repeat	reflexed
Royal Dane	orange blend	large	double to full	high-centered	strong	singly	repeat	reflexed
Royal Flush	pink blend	medium	double to full	cupped	slight	small clusters	repeat	reflexed
Royal Gold	medium yellow	large	double to full	cupped	moderate	small clusters	repeat	reflexed
Royal Highness	light pink	large	double to full	high-centered	strong	singly	repeat	reflexed
Royal Marbrée	mauve	medium	very full	rosette	moderate	small clusters	once	plain
Royal Occasion	orange-red	medium	semi-double	cupped	slight	small clusters	repeat	reflexed
Royal Parade	medium pink	small	double	flat	slight	small clusters	repeat	plain
Royal Philharmonic	white	large	double to full	high-centered	slight	small clusters	repeat	reflexed
Royal Salute	medium red	small	double to full	cupped	none	small clusters	repeat	reflexed
Royal Scarlet	medium red	large	double to full	high-centered	moderate	singly	repeat	reflexed
Royal Show	medium red	large	double to full	high-centered	slight	singly	repeat	reflexed
Royal William	dark red	large	double to full	high-centered	moderate	singly	repeat	reflexed
Roydon Hall	medium red	large	double to full	cupped	none	small clusters	repeat	reflexed
Rubaiyat	deep pink	large	double to full	high-centered	strong	singly	repeat	reflexed
Rubens	white	large	double to full	cupped	moderate	singly	repeat	plain
Ruby (de Ruiter)	medium red	medium	double to full	high-centered	none	small clusters	repeat	reflexed
Ruby (Tantau)	medium red	large	double to full	flat	none	small clusters	repeat	reflexed
Ruby Anniversary	medium red	medium	double to full	open	slight	small clusters	repeat	plain
Ruby Magic	medium red	small	double to full	cupped	slight	small clusters	repeat	reflexed
Ruby Wedding	dark red	large	double to full	cupped	none	small clusters	repeat	reflexed
Ruga	white	large	double to full	cupped	slight	corymb	once	plain
Rugelda	yellow blend	medium	double to full	cupped	slight	small clusters	repeat	ruffled
Rugosa Magnifica	mauve	large	double to full	open	moderate	small clusters	repeat	plain
Rugspin	dark red	large	single	open	moderate	small clusters	repeat	plain
Ruhm von Steinfurth	medium red	large	double to full	cupped	moderate	singly	repeat	reflexed
Rumba	red blend	medium	double to full	cupped	slight	small clusters	repeat	reflexed
Running Maid	mauve	medium	single	open	strong	large clusters	repeat	plain
Rush	pink blend	medium	single	open	moderate	large clusters	repeat	plain
Ruskin	dark red	large	double to full	cupped	strong	small clusters	repeat	reflexed
Russelliana	mauve	medium	very full	flat	moderate	large clusters	once	plain
Rustica	yellow blend	large	double to full	cupped	slight	small clusters	repeat	reflexed
Ruth Leuwerik	medium red	medium	double to full	open	moderate	small clusters	repeat	reflexed
Ruyton	medium pink	large	double	open	moderate	singly	once	plain
Saarbrücken	medium red	large	semi-double	open	slight	large clusters	repeat	plain
Sacha	medium red	large	double to full	high-centered	none	small clusters	repeat	reflexed
Sachsengruss	light pink	extra large	double to full	high-centered	moderate	small clusters	repeat	reflexed
Sadlers Wells	pink blend	medium	semi-double	open	slight	large clusters	repeat	ruffled
Saffex Rose	mauve blend	medium	full	cupped	moderate	small clusters	repeat	reflexed
Safrano	apricot blend	large	semi-double	open	moderate	small clusters	repeat	plain
Saga	white	small	semi-double	open	slight	small clusters	repeat	plain
St Boniface	orange-red	medium	double to full	flat	slight	large clusters	repeat	reflexed
St Bruno	deep yellow	large	double to full	high-centered	strong	large clusters	repeat	reflexed
St Cecilia	medium yellow	medium	double to full	cupped	strong	small clusters	repeat	plain
St Christopher	deep yellow	medium	double to full	high-centered	moderate	small clusters	repeat	reflexed
St Dunstan's Rose	light yellow	medium	double to full	rosette	strong	small clusters	repeat	plain
St Helena	medium pink	medium	semi-double	quartered	slight	large clusters	repeat	ruffled
St Hughs	medium yellow	large	double to full	cupped	slight	small clusters	repeat	plain
St John	white	medium	double to full	cupped	slight	small clusters	repeat	reflexed
St Nicholas	deep pink	medium	semi-double	cupped	strong	small clusters	repeat	plain
St Patrick	yellow blend	large	double to full	high-centered	slight	small clusters	repeat	reflexed
St Pauli	yellow blend	medium	semi-double	open	slight	large clusters	repeat	reflexed
St Swithun	light pink	large	double to full	rosette	strong	small clusters	repeat	plain
Salet	medium pink	medium	double to full	cupped	strong	small clusters	repeat	plain
Salita	orange blend	medium	double to full	open	slight	small clusters	repeat	reflexed
Sally Holmes	white	large	single	open	slight	large clusters	repeat	plain
Sally's Rose	pink blend	medium	double to full	high-centered	slight	small clusters	repeat	reflexed
Salmon Sorbet	pink blend	large	double to full	high-centered	moderate	small clusters	repeat	reflexed

NAME	BLOOM COLOR	FLOWER SIZE	FLOWER TYPE	FLOWER SHAPE	FRAGRANCE AMOUNT	FLOWERING HABIT	FLOWERING INCIDENCE	PETAL SHAPE
Salmon Spire	orange-pink	large	semi-double	open	strong	small clusters	repeat	plain
Salmon Sprite	orange-pink	large	double to full	high-centered	strong	small clusters	repeat	reflexed
Salmon Sunsation	orange-pink	small	double	high-centered	none	small clusters	repeat	plain
Samantha	medium red	medium	double to full	high-centered	slight	small clusters	repeat	reflexed
Samba	yellow blend	medium	double to full	cupped	moderate	small clusters	repeat	reflexed
San Antonio	orange-red	large	double to full	cupped	slight	small clusters	repeat	reflexed
San Diego	medium yellow	large	double to full	high-centered	moderate	small clusters	repeat	reflexed
San Jose Sunshine	deep yellow	medium	double to full	high-centered	slight	small clusters	repeat	reflexed
Sander's White Rambler	white	small	double to full	rosette	moderate	large clusters	once	plain
Sandra	orange-pink	large	double to full	high-centered	slight	singly	repeat	reflexed
Sandringham Centenary	orange-pink	large	double to full	cupped	moderate	singly	repeat	ruffled
Sangerhausen	deep pink	large	semi-double	cupped	slight	large clusters	repeat	plain
Sangria	orange-red	medium	semi-double	open	none	truss	repeat	ruffled
Sanguinea	dark red	medium	single	globular	none	small clusters	repeat	plain
Sanka	orange blend	large	double to full	high-centered	none	small clusters	repeat	reflexed
Sans Souci	white	medium	double to full	cupped	slight	small clusters	repeat	reflexed
Santa Catalina	light pink	medium	semi-double	cupped	slight	small clusters	repeat	reflexed
Santa Claus	dark red	small	double to full	cupped	slight	large clusters	repeat	reflexed
Santa Fé	orange-pink	large	double to full	high-centered	slight	small clusters	repeat	reflexed
Santa Rosa	deep pink	large	full	globular	slight	small clusters	repeat	plain
Santana	medium red	medium	semi-double	open	none	small clusters	repeat	reflexed
Sarabande	orange-red	medium	semi-double	cupped	slight	large clusters	repeat	plain
Sarah	white	small	double to full	cupped	strong	singly	repeat	reflexed
Sarah Arnot	medium pink	large	double to full	cupped	moderate	small clusters	repeat	reflexed
Sarah van Fleet	medium pink	large	semi-double	cupped	strong	small clusters	repeat	reflexed
Saratoga	white	large	double to full	cupped	moderate	small clusters	repeat	reflexed
Satchmo	orange-red	medium	double to full	high-centered	slight	small clusters	repeat	reflexed
Satellite	orange-red	large	double to full	high-centered	strong	singly	repeat	reflexed
Satina	medium pink	medium	semi-double	open	slight	small clusters	repeat	reflexed
Savoy Hotel	light pink	large	double to full	high-centered	slight	singly	repeat	reflexed
Scabrosa	mauve	large	single	open	moderate	small clusters	repeat	plain
Scarlet Gem	orange-red	small	very full	cupped	slight	small clusters	repeat	plain
Scarlet Knight	medium red	large	double to full	cupped	slight	small clusters	repeat	reflexed
Scarlet Meidiland	medium red	small	semi-double	open	none	large clusters	repeat	plain
Scarlet Moss	medium red	small	semi-double	open	none	small clusters	repeat	plain
Scarlet Patio	medium red	small	double to full	flat	none	small clusters	repeat	reflexed
Scarlet Queen Elizabeth	orange-red	large	double to full	globular	slight	small clusters	repeat	plain
Scarlet Showers	medium red	large	double to full	open	slight	small clusters	repeat	reflexed
Scarlet Sunblaze	dark red	medium	double	cupped	none	small clusters	repeat	reflexed
Scented Air	orange-pink	large	double to full	high-centered	strong	small clusters	repeat	reflexed
Scentimental	red blend	large	double to full	high-centered	strong	small clusters	repeat	reflexed
Scentsational	mauve	medium	semi-double	open	strong	singly	repeat	reflexed
Scepter'd Isle	light pink	medium	double to full	cupped	strong	small clusters	repeat	plain
Scharlachglut	dark red	large	single	open	none	small clusters	repeat	plain
Scherzo	red blend	large	double to full	high-centered	none	small clusters	repeat	reflexed
Schneelicht	white	large	single	open	slight	small clusters	repeat	plain
Schneesturm	white	medium	double to full	open	light	large clusters	repeat	plain
Schneewalzer	white	large	double to full	cupped	none	small clusters	repeat	reflexed
Schneezwerg	white	small	semi-double	flat	none	small clusters	repeat	plain
Schoener's Nutkana	medium pink	large	single	open	moderate	small clusters	once	plain
Schoolgirl	apricot blend	large	double to full	flat	strong	small clusters	repeat	reflexed
Schwarze Madonna	dark red	large	double to full	high-centered	none	small clusters	repeat	reflexed
Schweizer Gold	light yellow	large	double to full	high-centered	moderate	singly	repeat	reflexed
Scorcher	dark red	large	semi-double	open	slight	small clusters	once	plain
Scrabo	orange-pink	large	double to full	high-centered	moderate	small clusters	repeat	reflexed
Sea Foam	white	medium	double to full	rosette	slight	small clusters	repeat	plain
Sea Pearl	pink blend	large	double to full	high-centered	slight	small clusters	repeat	reflexed
Seabreeze	medium pink	small	double to full	cupped	slight	small clusters	repeat	plain
Seafarer	orange-red	large	double to full	cupped	slight	small clusters	repeat	reflexed

NAME	BLOOM COLOR	FLOWER SIZE	FLOWER TYPE	FLOWER SHAPE	FRAGRANCE AMOUNT	FLOWERING HABIT	FLOWERING INCIDENCE	PETAL SHAPE
Seagull	white	small	semi-double	open	moderate	corymb	once	plain
Sealing Wax	medium pink	small	single	open	none	small clusters	once	plain
Seashell	orange-pink	large	double to full	cupped	slight	singly	repeat	reflexed
Seaspray	pink blend	medium	semi-double	open	strong	small clusters	repeat	plain
Seattle Scentsation	pink blend	large	double to full	open	strong	small clusters	repeat	plain
Sebbastian Kneipp	apricot blend	large	double to full	open	slight	singly	repeat	plain
Secret	pink blend	large	double to full	high-centered	strong	singly	repeat	reflexed
Selfridges	deep yellow	large	double to full	high-centered	moderate	singly	repeat	reflexed
Seliata	red blend	large	double	high-centered	slight	singly	repeat	plain
Senator Burda	dark red	large	double to full	high-centered	strong	singly	repeat	reflexed
Sénégal	dark red	large	double to full	open	slight	small clusters	repeat	reflexed
Sequoia Gold	medium yellow	small	double to full	high-centered	moderate	small clusters	repeat	reflexed
Serratipetala	pink blend	medium	double to full	cupped	none	small clusters	repeat	frilled
Seven Seas	mauve	large	double to full	open	moderate	small clusters	repeat	reflexed
Seven Sisters	pink blend	medium	double to full	open	moderate	truss	once	reflexed
Sevilliana	pink blend	large	semi-double	cupped	moderate	large trusses	repeat	reflexed
Sexy Rexy	medium pink	medium	double to full	rosette	slight	large clusters	repeat	plain
Shadow	dark red	large	double to full	high-centered	strong	singly	repeat	reflexed
Shakespeare Festival	medium yellow	medium	double to full	high-centered	moderate	small clusters	repeat	reflexed
Shannon	medium pink	large	double to full	globular	none	singly	repeat	reflexed
Sharifa Asma	light pink	large	double to full	cupped	strong	small clusters	repeat	plain
Sharon Louise	white	large	double to full	cupped	slight	small clusters	repeat	reflexed
Sheelagh Baird	pink blend	large	double to full	cupped	none	truss	repeat	plain
Sheer Bliss	white	large	double to full	high-centered	moderate	singly	repeat	reflexed
Sheer Elegance	orange-pink	large	double to full	cupped	moderate	singly	repeat	reflexed
Sheila MacQueen	white	medium	double to full	cupped	slight	small clusters	repeat	ruffled
Sheila's Perfume	yellow blend	large	semi-double	open	strong	singly	repeat	reflexed
Shell Queen	light pink	large	double to full	globular	none	small clusters	repeat	plain
Shelly	pink blend	large	semi-double	open	moderate	small clusters	repeat	reflexed
Sheri Anne	orange-red	small	semi-double	cupped	moderate	small clusters	repeat	reflexed
Shine On	orange-pink	medium	double to full	high-centered	none	small clusters	repeat	reflexed
Shining Hour	deep yellow	large	double to full	high-centered	moderate	singly	repeat	reflexed
Shiralee	yellow blend	large	double to full	high-centered	moderate	singly	repeat	reflexed
Shocking Blue	mauve	large	double to full	high-centered	strong	small clusters	repeat	reflexed
Shocking Sky	mauve blend	medium	semi-double	high-centered	slight	small clusters	repeat	plain
Shona	orange-pink	medium	double to full	cupped	slight	small clusters	repeat	reflexed
Shot Silk	pink blend	large	double to full	high-centered	moderate	small clusters	repeat	reflexed
Show Girl, Climbing	medium pink	large	double to full	high-centered	slight	small clusters	repeat	reflexed
Showbiz	medium red	medium	semi-double	cupped	none	large clusters	repeat	ruffled
Shower of Gold	medium yellow	medium	double to full	rosette	moderate	small clusters	once	plain
Showtime	medium pink	large	double to full	high-centered	moderate	singly	repeat	reflexed
Shreveport	orange blend	large	double to full	high-centered	slight	small clusters	repeat	reflexed
Shropshire Lass	light pink	large	single	open	slight	small clusters	once	ruffled
Si	white	small	semi-double	open	none	singly	repeat	plain
Signature	deep pink	large	double to full	high-centered	slight	singly	repeat	reflexed
Signora	orange blend	large	double to full	cupped	moderate	small clusters	repeat	reflexed
Silent Night	yellow blend	large	double to full	high-centered	moderate	singly	repeat	reflexed
Silk Button	white	small	double	cupped	none	small clusters	repeat	plain
Silk Hat	mauve	extra large	double to full	high-centered	slight	singly	repeat	reflexed
Silva	pink blend	large	double to full	high-centered	slight	singly	repeat	reflexed
Silver Anniversary	mauve	large	double to full	high-centered	strong	singly	repeat	reflexed
Silver Jubilee	pink blend	large	double to full	high-centered	slight	small clusters	repeat	reflexed
Silver Lining	pink blend	large	double to full	high-centered	moderate	singly	repeat	reflexed
Silver Moon	white	large	semi-double	flat	slight	small clusters	once	plain
Silver Star	mauve	large	double to full	cupped	strong	small clusters	repeat	reflexed
Silver Wedding	mauve	large	double to full	cupped	slight	small clusters	repeat	reflexed
Silverado	mauve	large	double to full	high-centered	slight	singly	repeat	reflexed
Silverhill	pink blend	medium	double to full	high-centered	slight	singly	repeat	reflexed
Simon Fraser	medium pink	medium	semi-double	open	slight	small clusters	repeat	plain
Simon Robinson	medium pink	small	single	open	moderate	large clusters	repeat	plain
Simplex	white	small	single	flat	slight	small clusters	repeat	plain
Simplicity	medium pink	large	semi-double	flat	slight	small clusters	repeat	reflexed
Sincerely Yours	medium red	medium	semi-double	open	none	small clusters	repeat	plain
Singin' in the Rain	apricot blend	medium	double to full	cupped	light	large clusters	repeat	reflexed
Single Cherry	medium red	small	single	open	moderate	small clusters	once	plain
Sir Alec Rose	deep pink	medium	double	open	slight	small clusters	repeat	plain
Sir Cedric Morris	white	small	single	flat	strong	large clusters	once	plain
Sir Clough	deep pink	large	semi-double	open	moderate	small clusters	repeat	plain
Sir Edward Elgar	medium red	medium	double to full	cupped	slight	singly	repeat	reflexed
Sir Frederick Ashton	white	large	double to full	high-centered	strong	small clusters	repeat	reflexed
Sir Harry Pilkington	medium red	large	double to full	high-centered	slight	singly	repeat	reflexed
Sir Lancelot	apricot blend	large	semi-double	cupped	slight	small clusters	repeat	plain
Sir Thomas Lipton	white	large	double to full	cupped	strong	small clusters	repeat	plain
Sir Walter Raleigh	medium pink	extra large	double to full	cupped	strong	singly	repeat	plain
Sir Winston Churchill	orange-pink	large	double to full	high-centered	strong	singly	repeat	reflexed
Siren	orange-red	large	semi-double	open	moderate	small clusters	repeat	reflexed
Skyrocket	dark red	medium	semi-double	open	moderate	large clusters	repeat	plain
Slater's Crimson China	medium red	small	semi-double	open	none	singly	repeat	plain
Sleigh Bells	white	large	double to full	open	strong	singly	repeat	reflexed
Smarty	light pink	small	single	open	none	large clusters	repeat	plain
Smith's Parish	red blend	medium	semi-double	cupped	none	small clusters	repeat	plain
Smooth Angel	apricot blend	large	double to full	cupped	strong	singly	repeat	reflexed
Smooth Lady	medium pink	medium	double to full	open	moderate	small clusters	repeat	reflexed
Smooth Melody	red blend	medium	double to full	open	strong	small clusters	repeat	plain
Smooth Perfume	light pink	large	double to full	high-centered	strong	singly	repeat	reflexed
Smooth Prince	medium red	large	double	urn-shaped	strong	singly	repeat	plain
Smooth Satin	medium pink	large	double to full	cupped	moderate	singly	repeat	reflexed
Smooth Velvet	dark red	large	double to full	cupped	slight	singly	repeat	reflexed
Sno	white	medium	double to full	high-centered	strong	small clusters	repeat	reflexed
Snow Ballet	white	large	double to full	cupped	slight	small clusters	repeat	reflexed
Snow Bride	white	small	double to full	high-centered	slight	small clusters	repeat	reflexed
Snow Carpet	white	small	double to full	open	light	small clusters	repeat	plain
Snow Magic	white	small	double to full	cupped	slight	small clusters	repeat	reflexed
Snow Meillandina	white	medium	double to full	flat	none	small clusters	repeat	reflexed
Snow Owl	white	medium	double to full	open	strong	small clusters	repeat	plain
Snow Twinkle	white	small	double to full	high-centered	light	small clusters	repeat	reflexed
Snow White	white	large	double to full	high-centered	moderate	small clusters	repeat	reflexed
Snowdon	white	large	double	rosette	slight	small clusters	repeat	plain
Snowfire	red blend	large	double to full	cupped	slight	small clusters	repeat	reflexed
Snowflake	white	medium	double	high-centered	strong	small clusters	once	plain
Snowline	white	medium	double to full	cupped	slight	large trusses	repeat	ruffled
Snowy Cupido	white	small	double to full	cupped	slight	small clusters	repeat	reflexed
Soaring Wings	orange blend	large	double to full	high-centered	moderate	small clusters	repeat	reflexed
Sodōri-Himé	white	large	double to full	high-centered	slight	small clusters	repeat	reflexed
Soeur Thérèse	yellow blend	large	double to full	cupped	slight	small clusters	repeat	reflexed
Softee	white	small	double to full	cupped	slight	small clusters	repeat	reflexed
Softly Softly	pink blend	large	double to full	cupped	slight	small clusters	repeat	reflexed
Soldier Boy	medium red	large	single	open	none	small clusters	repeat	plain
Soleil d'Or	yellow blend	large	double to full	cupped	moderate	small clusters	repeat	reflexed
Solfaterre	medium yellow	large	double to full	cupped	moderate	small clusters	repeat	reflexed
Solitaire (Cant)	medium pink	large	double to full	cupped	slight	small clusters	repeat	reflexed
Solitaire (McGredy)	yellow blend	large	double	urn-shaped	moderate	singly	repeat	plain
Solitude	orange blend	large	double to full	cupped	slight	large clusters	repeat	ruffled
Sombreuil	white	large	double to full	flat	strong	small clusters	repeat	plain
Sommerduft	dark red	large	double to full	cupped	strong	small clusters	repeat	reflexed
Sommermärchen	deep pink	medium	semi-double	flat	slight	large clusters	repeat	plain

NAME	BLOOM COLOR	FLOWER SIZE	FLOWER TYPE	FLOWER SHAPE	FRAGRANCE AMOUNT	FLOWERING HABIT	FLOWERING INCIDENCE	PETAL SHAPE
Song of Paris	mauve	large	double to full	high-centered	slight	small clusters	repeat	reflexed
Sonia	pink blend	large	double to full	high-centered	moderate	small clusters	repeat	reflexed
Sonja Horstman	medium red	medium	double to full	flat	none	singly	repeat	reflexed
Sonnenkind	deep yellow	medium	double to full	flat	slight	small clusters	repeat	reflexed
Sonnenschirn	light yellow	medium	semi-double	cupped	none	large clusters	repeat	plain
Sonora	yellow blend	large	double to full	cupped	moderate	small clusters	repeat	reflexed
Sophie de Marsilly	pink blend	large	double to full	globular	moderate	small clusters	once	plain
Sophie's Perpetual	pink blend	small	double	globular	moderate	small clusters	repeat	plain
Sorcerer	medium red	small	double to full	open	none	singly	repeat	reflexed
Soupert et Notting	deep pink	large	double to full	globular	strong	small clusters	repeat	plain
South Seas	orange-pink	extra large	double to full	cupped	slight	singly	repeat	reflexed
Southampton	apricot blend	medium	double to full	cupped	slight	small clusters	repeat	reflexed
Southern Belle	pink blend	large	double to full	high-centered	slight	small clusters	repeat	reflexed
Southern Cross (Clark)	medium pink	medium	double	globular	moderate	singly	repeat	plain
Southern Cross (Jack)	deep yellow	small	double to full	open	slight	small clusters	repeat	reflexed
Southern Delight	yellow blend	small	double to full	cupped	slight	small clusters	repeat	reflexed
Souvenir (Pierson)	deep yellow	medium	double to full	flat	moderate	small clusters	repeat	reflexed
Souvenir (Grootendorst)	deep pink/mauve	medium	double	open	slight	small clusters	repeat	plain
Souvenir d'Alphonse Lavallée	dark red	medium	double to full	cupped	strong	small clusters	repeat	plain
Souvenir de Brod	red blend	large	double to full	quartered	moderate	small clusters	repeat	plain
Souvenir de Christophe Cochet	medium pink	large	semi-double	open	moderate	small clusters	repeat	plain
Souvenir de Claudius Denoyel	dark red	large	double to full	cupped	moderate	small clusters	repeat	plain
Souvenir de Jeanne Balandreau	medium red	large	double to full	globular	moderate	small clusters	repeat	reflexed
Souvenir de la Malmaison	light pink	large	double to full	quartered	strong	small clusters	repeat	plain
Souvenir de la Reine d'Angleterre	medium pink	large	double to full	cupped	moderate	small clusters	repeat	reflexed
Souvenir de Mme Auguste Charles	medium pink	small	double	quartered	slight	small clusters	repeat	plain
Souvenir de Mme Boullet	deep yellow	large	double to full	cupped	slight	small clusters	repeat	reflexed
Souvenir de Mme Breuil	deep pink	large	double to full	cupped	moderate	small clusters	repeat	plain
Souvenir de Mme H. Thuret	pink blend	extra large	double to full	cupped	moderate	singly	repeat	reflexed
Souvenir de Mme Léonie Viennot	yellow blend	large	double to full	cupped	moderate	small clusters	repeat	plain
Souvenir de Mlle Juliet de Bricard	light pink	medium	very full	globular	slight	large clusters	repeat	plain
Souvenir de Philemon Cochet	white	large	double to full	open	strong	small clusters	repeat	plain
Souvenir de Pierre Notting	yellow blend	large	very full	cupped	moderate	small clusters	repeat	plain
Souvenir de Pierre Vibert	red blend	medium	double to full	cupped	strong	small clusters	once	plain
Souvenir de St Anne's	light pink	large	semi-double	open	moderate	small clusters	repeat	plain
Souvenir de Thérèse Lovet	deep red	medium	double to full	open	none	small clusters	repeat	reflexed
Souvenir de Victor Landeau	medium red	large	double to full	globular	moderate	singly	repeat	reflexed
Souvenir d'Elise Vardon	white	large	double to full	globular	slight	small clusters	repeat	plain
Souvenir du Docteur Jamain	dark red	medium	double to full	cupped	moderate	small clusters	repeat	plain
Souvenir d'un Ami	light pink	large	double to full	cupped	moderate	small clusters	repeat	reflexed
Spangles	light pink	medium	double to full	cupped	moderate	large clusters	repeat	reflexed
Sparkling Scarlet	medium red	medium	semi-double	open	moderate	small clusters	repeat	plain
Sparrieshoop	light pink	large	single	flat	moderate	large clusters	repeat	ruffled
Spartan	orange-red	large	double to full	high-centered	moderate	small clusters	repeat	reflexed
Speaker Sam	yellow blend	large	double to full	cupped	slight	small clusters	repeat	reflexed
Special Angel	mauve	small	double to full	high-centered	slight	small clusters	repeat	reflexed
Spectabile	dark red	small	double to full	cupped	strong	large clusters	once	ruffled
Spectacular	orange-red	medium	double to full	flat	slight	large clusters	repeat	reflexed
Spencer	light pink	large	double to full	cupped	slight	singly	repeat	plain
Spice	light pink	medium	double to full	open	none	small clusters	repeat	plain
Spice Drop	orange-pink	small	double to full	high-centered	slight	small clusters	repeat	reflexed
Spice Twice	orange blend	large	double to full	high-centered	moderate	singly	repeat	reflexed
Spiced Coffee	russet	large	double to full	high-centered	moderate	small clusters	repeat	reflexed
Spirit of Peace	yellow blend	large	double to full	cupped	moderate	singly	repeat	reflexed
Spirit of Peace	yellow blend	large	double to full	cupped	moderate	small clusters	repeat	reflexed
Splendens (Pre-1837)	white	large	double	globular	strong	small clusters	once	plain
Splendens (Pre-1583)	medium red	medium	double to full	globular	strong	large clusters	once	reflexed
Spong	medium pink	small	double to full	rosette	strong	small clusters	once	plain
Spring Song	deep pink	medium	semi-double	open	moderate	small clusters	repeat	plain
Squatters Dream	medium yellow	large	single	open	moderate	small clusters	repeat	plain
Stacey Sue	light pink	small	double to full	flat	none	small clusters	repeat	plain
Stadt Rosenheim	orange-red	medium	double to full	cupped	moderate	small clusters	repeat	reflexed
Stainless Steel	mauve	large	semi-double	high-centered	strong	small clusters	repeat	reflexed
Stämmler	medium pink	large	very full	high-centered	strong	singly	repeat	reflexed
Stanwell Perpetual	white	medium	double to full	quartered	slight	small clusters	repeat	plain
Star Delight	medium pink	medium	single	flat	slight	small clusters	repeat	plain
Star of Waltham	medium red	medium	double to full	globular	moderate	small clusters	repeat	reflexed
Star Trail	apricot blend	small	double	flat	slight	small clusters	once	plain
Stardust	white	medium	double to full	cupped	strong	small clusters	repeat	reflexed
Stargazer	orange-red	medium	single	open	slight	large clusters	repeat	plain
Starglo	white	small	double to full	high-centered	slight	small clusters	repeat	reflexed
Starina	orange-red	small	double to full	high-centered	none	small clusters	repeat	reflexed
Starlet yellow	medium	medium	very full	high-centered	slight	small clusters	repeat	reflexed
Stars 'n' Stripes	red blend	small	double to full	high-centered	moderate	small clusters	repeat	plain
Steffi Graf	medium pink	large	double to full	high-centered	none	singly	repeat	reflexed
Stella	pink blend	large	double to full	high-centered	slight	small clusters	repeat	reflexed
Stella Elizabeth	white	small	double to full	cupped	slight	small clusters	repeat	reflexed
Stephanie Diane	medium red	large	double to full	high-centered	none	singly	repeat	reflexed
Stephanie Jo	light pink	large	double to full	high-centered	slight	singly	repeat	reflexed
Stephens' Big Purple	mauve blend	large	double to full	flat	strong	singly	repeat	reflexed
Sterling Silver	mauve blend	large	double to full	cupped	strong	small clusters	repeat	reflexed
Strawberry Crush	medium red	medium	double to full	cupped	slight	small clusters	repeat	reflexed
Strawberry Swirl	red blend	small	double to full	rosette	none	small clusters	repeat	plain
Stretch Johnson	red blend	medium	semi-double	cupped	slight	small clusters	repeat	reflexed
String of Pearls	orange-red	medium	semi-double	high-centered	slight	small clusters	repeat	plain
Stroller	red blend	large	double to full	open	none	truss	repeat	plain
Sue Lawley	red blend	medium	semi-double	open	slight	small clusters	repeat	plain
Sue Ryder	orange-pink	medium	double to full	cupped	none	large clusters	repeat	reflexed
Sugar Elf	pink blend	small	semi-double	open	slight	small clusters	repeat	reflexed
Suitor	medium pink	small	semi-double	open	none	large clusters	repeat	plain
Suma	medium red	small	double to full	rosette	none	large clusters	repeat	plain
Summer Blush	deep pink	medium	double to full	cupped	slight	small clusters	once	plain
Summer Breeze (Kordes, 1987)	medium pink	medium	semi-double	cupped	none	small clusters	repeat	plain
Summer Breeze (Kordes, 1998)	deep pink	large	semi-double	saucer	moderate	large clusters	repeat	plain
Summer Damask	medium pink	medium	double to full	cupped	strong	corymb	once	plain
Summer Dream	apricot blend	medium	double	high-centered	slight	small clusters	repeat	reflexed
Summer Fashion	yellow blend	large	double to full	open	moderate	small clusters	repeat	plain
Summer Holiday	orange-red	large	double to full	high-centered	moderate	singly	repeat	reflexed
Summer Lady	pink blend	large	double to full	high-centered	strong	singly	repeat	reflexed
Summer Queen	white blend	large	double to full	globular	slight	small clusters	repeat	plain
Summer Snow	white	large	double to full	cupped	slight	large clusters	repeat	reflexed
Summer Song	orange blend	large	semi-double	open	slight	small clusters	repeat	reflexed
Summer Sunshine	deep yellow	large	double to full	high-centered	slight	small clusters	repeat	reflexed
Summer Wine	medium pink	large	single	open	moderate	small clusters	repeat	plain
Summertime	deep yellow	large	double to full	cupped	slight	singly	repeat	reflexed

NAME	BLOOM COLOR	FLOWER SIZE	FLOWER TYPE	FLOWER SHAPE	FRAGRANCE AMOUNT	FLOWERING HABIT	FLOWERING INCIDENCE	PETAL SHAPE
Sun Flare	medium yellow	medium	double to full	flat	slight	small clusters	repeat	reflexed
Sun Goddess	deep yellow	large	double to full	high-centered	slight	small clusters	repeat	reflexed
Sun King	medium yellow	large	double to full	high-centered	moderate	small clusters	repeat	reflexed
Sunbaby	deep yellow	small	double to full	cupped	none	small clusters	repeat	reflexed
Sunbeam	apricot blend	large	double to full	cupped	slight	small clusters	repeat	reflexed
Sunblaze Baron	red blend	medium	double	high-centered	slight	small clusters	repeat	plain
Sunblest	deep yellow	large	double to full	high-centered	slight	small clusters	repeat	reflexed
Sunbright	medium yellow	large	double to full	flat	slight	small clusters	repeat	reflexed
Sunderland Supreme	light pink/ pink blend	medium	double to full	cupped	slight	small clusters	repeat	reflexed
Sundowner	apricot blend	large	double to full	high-centered	strong	small clusters	repeat	reflexed
Sundra	dark red	large	semi-double	cupped	strong	small clusters	repeat	plain
Sundust	yellow blend	small	double to full	high-centered	moderate	small clusters	repeat	reflexed
Sunhit	deep yellow	medium	double to full	cupped	slight	large clusters	repeat	reflexed
Sunlit	apricot blend	large	double to full	globular	slight	small clusters	repeat	reflexed
Sunmaid	yellow blend	small	double to full	rosette	none	small clusters	repeat	plain
Sunny	medium yellow	small	semi-double	open	moderate	small clusters	repeat	plain
Sunny Afternoon	yellow blend	small	double to full	open	slight	small clusters	repeat	reflexed
Sunny Honey	apricot blend	large	double to full	flat	moderate	small clusters	repeat	plain
Sunny June	deep yellow	medium	single	cupped	slight	large clusters	repeat	plain
Sunny Morning	medium yellow	small	double to full	flat	moderate	small clusters	repeat	reflexed
Sunny Sky	yellow blend	medium	double to full	high-centered	slight	small clusters	repeat	reflexed
Sunny South	pink blend	medium	semi-double	open	moderate	small clusters	repeat	reflexed
Sunny Today	deep yellow	medium	double to full	high-centered	slight	small clusters	repeat	reflexed
Sunrise Sunset	pink blend	large	double to full	high-centered	slight	singly	repeat	reflexed
Sunrose	orange-pink	medium	double to full	open	none	small clusters	repeat	plain
Sunseeker	orange-red	small	double to full	flat	slight	small clusters	repeat	reflexed
Sunset	deep yellow	large	double to full	cupped	moderate	small clusters	repeat	plain
Sunset Boulevard	orange-pink	medium	double to full	high-centered	slight	small clusters	repeat	reflexed
Sunset Celebration	orange-pink	large	double	high-centered	moderate	singly	repeat	plain
Sunset Song	apricot blend/ orange blend	large	double to full	high-centered	slight	small clusters	repeat	reflexed
Sunshine	orange blend	small	double to full	cupped	moderate	small clusters	repeat	reflexed
Sunsilk	medium yellow	large	double to full	open	slight	small clusters	repeat	reflexed
Sunspray	deep yellow	small	semi-double	cupped	slight	small clusters	repeat	reflexed
Sunsprite	deep yellow	large	double to full	flat	strong	small clusters	repeat	reflexed
Super Dorothy	medium pink	small	double to full	rosette	moderate	large clusters	repeat	plain
Super Excelsa	dark red	small	double to full	cupped	moderate	large clusters	repeat	plain
Super Fairy	light pink	small	double to full	cupped	moderate	large clusters	repeat	plain
Super Sparkle	dark red	medium	double to full	open	slight	large clusters	repeat	plain
Super Sun	medium yellow	large	double to full	high-centered	none	singly	repeat	reflexed
Superb Tuscan	mauve	medium	double to full	open	strong	small clusters	once	plain
Surpasse Tout	medium red	large	double to full	flat	strong	small clusters	once	plain
Surpassing Beauty of Wolverstone	dark red	large	double to full	open	strong	singly	repeat	plain
Surrey	light pink	medium	double to full	open	none	large clusters	repeat	plain
Susan	medium pink	large	double to full	high-centered	moderate	singly	repeat	reflexed
Susan Hampshire	light pink	large	double to full	globular	strong	singly	repeat	reflexed
Susan Jellicoe	white blend	large	double to full	cupped	strong	small clusters	repeat	reflexed
Susan Louise	light pink	medium	double to full	open	slight	small clusters	repeat	plain
Susan Massu	yellow blend	large	double to full	cupped	moderate	small clusters	repeat	reflexed
Suspense	red blend	large	double to full	high-centered	slight	singly	repeat	reflexed
Sussex	apricot blend	medium	double to full	open	none	truss	repeat	plain
Sutter's Gold	orange blend	large	double to full	high-centered	strong	singly	repeat	reflexed
Suzon Lotthé, Climbing	pink blend	large	double to full	high-centered	strong	singly	repeat	reflexed
Swan	white blend	extra large	double to full	rosette	slight	small clusters	repeat	plain
Swan Lake	white blend	large	double to full	cupped	slight	small clusters	repeat	reflexed
Swany	white	medium	very full	cupped	none	small clusters	repeat	reflexed

NAME	BLOOM COLOR	FLOWER SIZE	FLOWER TYPE	FLOWER SHAPE	FRAGRANCE AMOUNT	FLOWERING HABIT	FLOWERING INCIDENCE	PETAL SHAPE
Swarthmore	pink blend	large	double to full	high-centered	slight	singly	repeat	reflexed
Sweet Afton	white blend/ light pink	large	double to full	high-centered	strong	singly	repeat	reflexed
Sweet Chariot	mauve	small	double to full	pompons	strong	large clusters	repeat	plain
Sweet Dream	apricot blend	medium	double to full	cupped	moderate	large clusters	repeat	plain
Sweet Fairy	light pink	small	double to full	cupped	moderate	small clusters	repeat	plain
Sweet Home	deep pink	large	double to full	cupped	slight	singly	repeat	reflexed
Sweet Inspiration	medium pink	large	double to full	open	none	large clusters	repeat	plain
Sweet Juliet	apricot blend	medium	very full	cupped	moderate	small clusters	repeat	plain
Sweet Magic	orange blend	small	double to full	open	none	small clusters	repeat	plain
Sweet Memories	light yellow	medium	double to full	cupped	moderate	large clusters	repeat	plain
Sweet Nell	orange blend	large	double to full	flat	slight	small clusters	repeat	reflexed
Sweet Revenge	orange-red	small	double to full	flat	slight	singly	repeat	reflexed
Sweet Sunsation	light pink	medium	double	cupped	none	small clusters	repeat	plain
Sweet Surrender	medium pink	large	double to full	cupped	strong	singly	repeat	reflexed
Sweet Vivien	pink blend	large	semi-double	open	slight	small clusters	repeat	plain
Sweetheart	medium pink	large	double to full	high-centered	moderate	singly	repeat	reflexed
Sweetie Pie	light pink	large	double to full	high-centered	slight	singly	repeat	reflexed
Swinging Sixties	yellow blend	medium	double	open	none	small clusters	repeat	plain
Swiss Fire	orange-red	large	double to full	high-centered	slight	singly	repeat	reflexed
Sybil Hipkin	deep yellow	large	double to full	high-centered	slight	singly	repeat	reflexed
Sydney Linton	deep pink	large	double to full	flat	slight	singly	repeat	plain
Sydonie	medium pink	medium	very full	quartered	strong	small clusters	repeat	plain
Sympathie	medium red	medium	double to full	high-centered	strong	small clusters	repeat	reflexed
Symphony	light yellow	medium	double to full	rosette	strong	small clusters	repeat	reflexed
Tabarin	medium pink	large	semi-double	open	moderate	small clusters	repeat	reflexed
Taboo	dark red	large	double to full	high-centered	moderate	singly	repeat	reflexed
Tabris	pink blend	medium	semi-double	open	slight	small clusters	repeat	ruffled
Talisman	yellow blend	medium	double to full	flat	moderate	small clusters	repeat	reflexed
Tall Story	medium yellow	medium	semi-double	open	slight	small clusters	repeat	plain
Tamara	apricot blend	medium	double to full	high-centered	slight	small clusters	repeat	reflexed
Tambourine	orange blend	large	double to full	open	slight	small clusters	repeat	reflexed
Tamora	apricot blend	medium	very full	cupped	strong	small clusters	repeat	ruffled
Tanagra	orange-red	large	double to full	high-centered	slight	singly	repeat	reflexed
Tangerine	orange-red	small	semi-double	saucer	slight	small clusters	repeat	plain
Tania Verstak	medium red	large	double to full	flat	slight	small clusters	repeat	reflexed
Tanya	orange blend	large	double to full	high-centered	moderate	singly	repeat	reflexed
Tapis Jaune	medium yellow	small	double to full	open	none	small clusters	repeat	reflexed
Tapis Volant	pink blend	medium	single	open	moderate	large clusters	repeat	plain
Tarantella	yellow blend	extra large	very full	high-centered	slight	singly	repeat	reflexed
Tarrawarra	pink blend	small	semi-double	open	slight	large clusters	repeat	plain
Tassin	medium red	large	double to full	high-centered	strong	small clusters	repeat	reflexed
Tatjana	dark red	large	double to full	cupped	strong	small clusters	repeat	reflexed
Taupo	orange-pink	large	double to full	flat	slight	small clusters	repeat	reflexed
Tausendschön	pink blend	large	double to full	cupped	slight	large clusters	once	plain
Tchin-Tchin	yellow blend	large	double to full	cupped	none	small clusters	repeat	reflexed
Tea Rambler	orange-pink	large	double to full	cupped	moderate	small clusters	once	reflexed
Tear Drop	white	small	semi-double	flat	slight	small clusters	repeat	plain
Teddy Bear	russet	small	double to full	high-centered	slight	small clusters	repeat	reflexed
Telstar	orange blend	medium	semi-double	open	moderate	small clusters	repeat	plain
Temple Bells	white	medium	single	open	slight	small clusters	repeat	plain
Tender Blush	light pink	medium	double to full	rounded	moderate	small clusters	once	plain
Tender Loving Care	medium pink	large	double to full	open	moderate	large clusters	repeat	plain
Tender Night	medium red	large	double to full	flat	slight	large trusses	repeat	reflexed
Tequila	orange blend	large	double to full	open	slight	small clusters	repeat	reflexed
Tequila Sunrise	red blend	large	double to full	cupped	slight	small clusters	repeat	ruffled
Texas (Poulsen)	medium yellow	small	double	high-centered	slight	small clusters	repeat	reflexed
Texas (Kordes)	yellow blend	large	double to full	high-centered	moderate	small clusters	repeat	reflexed
Texas Centennial	red blend	large	double to full	cupped	moderate	small clusters	repeat	reflexed
Thalia	white	small	semi-double	open	moderate	large clusters	once	plain

NAME	BLOOM COLOR	FLOWER SIZE	FLOWER TYPE	FLOWER SHAPE	FRAGRANCE AMOUNT	FLOWERING HABIT	FLOWERING INCIDENCE	PETAL SHAPE
The Alexandra Rose	pink blend	small	single	open	slight	large clusters	repeat	plain
The Bishop	mauve	medium	double to full	rosette	moderate	small clusters	once	plain
The Bride	white	large	double to full	high-centered	moderate	small clusters	repeat	reflexed
The Compass Rose	white	medium	semi-double	cupped	strong	small clusters	repeat	plain
The Countryman	medium pink	medium	double to full	rosette	strong	small clusters	repeat	plain
The Dark Lady	dark red	large	double to full	flat	moderate	small clusters	repeat	plain
The Doctor	medium pink	extra large	double to full	open	strong	small clusters	repeat	reflexed
The Fairy	light pink	small	double to full	rosette	none	large clusters	repeat	plain
The Friar	light pink	medium	semi-double	open	strong	small clusters	repeat	plain
The Garland	white	small	semi-double	flat	slight	small clusters	once	plain
The Herbalist	deep pink	medium	semi-double	flat	slight	small clusters	repeat	plain
The Holt	deep pink	small	double to full	open	moderate	large clusters	repeat	plain
The Knight	dark red	medium	very full	flat	moderate	small clusters	repeat	plain
The Lady	yellow blend	large	double to full	high-centered	slight	small clusters	repeat	reflexed
The McCartney Rose	medium pink	large	double to full	cupped	strong	small clusters	repeat	reflexed
The Nun	white	large	semi-double	cupped	slight	small clusters	repeat	plain
The Optimist	yellow blend	medium	double to full	high-centered	moderate	large clusters	repeat	reflexed
The Pilgrim	medium yellow	medium	double to full	rosette	moderate	small clusters	repeat	plain
The Prince	dark red	medium	double to full	rosette	strong	small clusters	repeat	plain
The Prioress	light pink	medium	double to full	cupped	moderate	small clusters	repeat	plain
The Reeve	deep pink	large	double to full	cupped	strong	small clusters	repeat	plain
The Squire	dark red	large	double to full	rosette	strong	small clusters	repeat	plain
The Sun	orange-pink	large	semi-double	open	slight	small clusters	repeat	plain
The Temptations	pink blend	large	double to full	high-centered	slight	small clusters	repeat	reflexed
The Wife of Bath	pink blend	medium	semi-double	cupped	strong	small clusters	repeat	plain
The Yeoman	orange-pink	medium	double to full	cupped	strong	small clusters	repeat	plain
Thelma	orange-pink	large	semi-double	open	slight	small clusters	once	plain
Thérèse Bauer	medium pink	large	semi-double	open	slight	small clusters	once	plain
Thérèse Bugnet	medium pink	large	double to full	open	moderate	small clusters	repeat	plain
Thérèse de Lisieux	white	large	double to full	high-centered	slight	small clusters	repeat	reflexed
Thisbe	light yellow	medium	full	rosette	slight	large clusters	repeat	plain
Thor	dark red	large	very full	flat	slight	small clusters	once	reflexed
Thunder Cloud	orange-red	small	double to full	high-centered	none	large clusters	repeat	reflexed
Tiamo	dark red	medium	double to full	high-centered	none	singly	repeat	reflexed
Tidewater	white	medium	double to full	high-centered	strong	singly	repeat	reflexed
Tiffany	pink blend	large	double to full	high-centered	strong	small clusters	repeat	reflexed
Tiffie	light pink	small	double to full	high-centered	moderate	singly	repeat	reflexed
Tiger Cub	yellow blend/ striped	small	semi-double	open	none	small clusters	repeat	plain
Tigris	yellow blend	small	semi-double	rosette	none	small clusters	once	plain
Tiki	pink blend	large	double to full	high-centered	none	small clusters	repeat	reflexed
Till Uhlenspiegel	red blend	large	single	open	slight	small clusters	once	plain
Timeless	deep pink	large	double to full	high-centered	slight	small clusters	repeat	reflexed
Tineke	white	large	double to full	high-centered	none	singly	repeat	reflexed
Tinkerbell	light pink	small	double to full	cupped	none	small clusters	repeat	reflexed
Tino Rossi	medium pink	large	double to full	flat	moderate	small clusters	repeat	reflexed
Tintinara	light red	large	double to full	high-centered	slight	small clusters	repeat	reflexed
Tiny Stars	red blend	small	semi-double	cupped	none	small clusters	repeat	plain
Tiny Tot	apricot blend	small	double	open	none	small clusters	repeat	reflexed
Tip Top	orange-pink	medium	semi-double	cupped	slight	small clusters	repeat	plain
Tipsy Imperial Concubine	pink blend	medium	double to full	globular	slight	small clusters	repeat	reflexed
Titian	deep pink	large	double to full	flat	slight	small clusters	repeat	reflexed
Tivoli	medium yellow	large	double to full	globular	slight	small clusters	repeat	reflexed
Toby Tristam	white	small	single	open	moderate	truss	once	plain
Tom Brown	russet	large	double to full	high-centered	strong	small clusters	repeat	reflexed
Tom Thumb	red blend	small	semi-double	open	none	small clusters	repeat	plain
Tom Tom	deep pink	large	double	high-centered	slight	small clusters	repeat	plain
Tom Wood	medium red	large	double to full	cupped	moderate	small clusters	repeat	reflexed
Tommy Bright	medium red	large	double to full	cupped	slight	large clusters	repeat	reflexed

NAME	BLOOM COLOR	FLOWER SIZE	FLOWER TYPE	FLOWER SHAPE	FRAGRANCE AMOUNT	FLOWERING HABIT	FLOWERING INCIDENCE	PETAL SHAPE
Tonimbuk	medium pink/ light pink	large	double to full	high-centered	strong	small clusters	repeat	reflexed
Tony Jacklin	orange-pink	large	double to full	high-centered	slight	small clusters	repeat	reflexed
Too Hot to Handle	medium red	large	semi-double	open	slight	large clusters	repeat	reflexed
Toorenburg	apricot blend	medium	double	globular	none	small clusters	repeat	plain
Top Marks	medium red	small	double to full	globular	slight	small clusters	repeat	plain
Topaz Jewel	medium yellow	large	double to full	cupped	moderate	small clusters	repeat	plain
Toprose	deep yellow	large	double to full	high-centered	slight	large clusters	repeat	reflexed
Topsi	orange-red	medium	semi-double	open	slight	small clusters	repeat	reflexed
Torch of Liberty	orange-red	small	double to full	open	slight	small clusters	repeat	reflexed
Tornado	orange-red	medium	semi-double	cupped	slight	small clusters	repeat	reflexed
Torvill & Dean	pink blend	large	double to full	rounded	slight	small clusters	repeat	reflexed
Toscana	medium red	large	double to full	flat	slight	small clusters	repeat	reflexed
Touch of Class	orange-pink	large	double to full	high-centered	slight	small clusters	repeat	reflexed
Toulouse-Lautrec	medium yellow	large	double to full	rosette	moderate	singly	repeat	plain
Tour de Malakoff	mauve	large	double to full	rosette	strong	small clusters	once	plain
Tourbillon	pink blend	large	double to full	open	slight	small clusters	repeat	reflexed
Tournament of Roses	medium pink	large	double to full	high-centered	slight	large clusters	repeat	reflexed
Tower Bridge	deep pink	large	double to full	high-centered	strong	singly	repeat	reflexed
Toy Balloon	dark red	medium	double to full	high-centered	moderate	small clusters	repeat	reflexed
Toy Clown	red blend	small	semi-double	open	none	small clusters	repeat	reflexed
Tracey Wickham	yellow blend	small	double to full	high-centered	slight	small clusters	repeat	reflexed
Trade Winds	red blend	large	double to full	high-centered	strong	singly	repeat	reflexed
Tradescant	dark red	medium	very full	rosette	moderate	small clusters	repeat	plain
Tradition	medium red	large	double to full	high-centered	none	singly	repeat	reflexed
Tradition 95	medium red	medium	semi-double	open	slight	large clusters	repeat	plain
Träumerei	orange blend	medium	double to full	cupped	strong	small clusters	repeat	reflexed
Träumland	light pink	medium	double to full	cupped	slight	small clusters	repeat	reflexed
Travemünde	medium red	medium	double to full	flat	none	large clusters	repeat	reflexed
Traverser	yellow blend	large	semi-double	open	slight	small clusters	once	reflexed
Travesti	yellow blend	medium	double to full	cupped	moderate	small clusters	repeat	reflexed
Traviata	red blend	large	double to full	high-centered	moderate	small clusters	repeat	reflexed
Treasure Trove	apricot blend	medium	double to full	cupped	strong	truss	once	plain
Trevor Griffiths	medium pink	large	very full	rosette	strong	small clusters	repeat	plain
Trickster	red blend	small	double	high-centered	strong	singly	repeat	reflexed
Tricolore	pink blend	large	double to full	rosette	moderate	small clusters	once	plain
Tricolore de Flandre	pink blend	small	double to full	rosette	moderate	small clusters	once	plain
Trier	white	small	semi-double	open	moderate	large clusters	repeat	plain
Trinity	white	large	semi-double	open	slight	singly	repeat	reflexed
Trinity	dark red	small	double to full	open	slight	small clusters	repeat	plain
Trinket	medium pink	small	double to full	flat	none	small clusters	repeat	reflexed
Triodene	pink blend	large	semi-double	open	slight	small clusters	repeat	plain
Triolet	apricot blend	large	semi-double	open	strong	small clusters	repeat	plain
Triomphe de l'Exposition	medium red	large	very full	rosette	moderate	small clusters	repeat	plain
Triomphe du Luxembourg	pink blend	large	double to full	cupped	moderate	small clusters	repeat	plain
Troilus	apricot blend	large	very full	cupped	strong	small clusters	repeat	plain
Tropical Twist	apricot blend	small	double to full	high-centered	none	small clusters	repeat	reflexed
Tropicana	orange-red	large	double to full	high-centered	slight	small clusters	repeat	reflexed
Tropico Sunblaze	medium yellow	small	double to full	flat	slight	singly	repeat	reflexed
Trumpeter	orange-red	medium	double to full	cupped	slight	small clusters	repeat	reflexed
Tumbling Waters	white	medium	semi-double	cupped	slight	large clusters	repeat	reflexed
Turbo	medium pink	large	double to full	open	slight	small clusters	repeat	reflexed
Tuscany	mauve	large	semi-double	flat	moderate	small clusters	once	plain
Tutu Mauve	mauve	large	double to full	high-centered	slight	small clusters	repeat	reflexed
Twilight Mist	pink blend	large	double to full	cupped	slight	small clusters	repeat	reflexed
Twinkle Twinkle	apricot blend	small	double to full	flat	slight	singly	repeat	reflexed
Tynwald	white	large	very full	globular	strong	singly	repeat	reflexed
Typhoon	orange blend	large	double to full	globular	strong	singly	repeat	reflexed

NAME	BLOOM COLOR	FLOWER SIZE	FLOWER TYPE	FLOWER SHAPE	FRAGRANCE AMOUNT	FLOWERING HABIT	FLOWERING INCIDENCE	PETAL SHAPE
Tyriana	deep pink	large	double to full	high-centered	moderate	singly	repeat	reflexed
Tzigane	red blend	large	double to full	cupped	moderate	small clusters	repeat	reflexed
Ulrich Brunner Fils	deep pink	large	double to full	cupped	strong	small clusters	repeat	reflexed
Una	light yellow	medium	semi-double	open	slight	small clusters	once	plain
Uncle Joe	dark red	extra large	very full	high-centered	none	singly	repeat	reflexed
Uncle Merc	medium pink	medium	double	open	slight	singly	repeat	plain
Uncle Walter	medium red	large	double to full	high-centered	slight	singly	repeat	reflexed
UNICEF	orange blend	medium	double to full	cupped	slight	small clusters	repeat	reflexed
Unique Blanche	white	large	double to full	cupped	strong	small clusters	once	reflexed
Unique Panachée	white blend	medium	double to full	cupped	strong	small clusters	once	plain
Uwe Seeler	orange blend	large	semi-double	high-centered	moderate	small clusters	repeat	reflexed
Valencia	apricot blend	extra large	double to full	high-centered	moderate	singly	repeat	reflexed
Valentine Heart	medium pink/ pink blend	large	double to full	flat	strong	small clusters	repeat	reflexed
Valerie June	light pink	large	double to full	high-centered	slight	small clusters	repeat	reflexed
Valeta	orange-red	medium	double to full	open	none	truss	repeat	reflexed
Van Artevelde	deep pink	large	double to full	rosette	strong	small clusters	once	plain
Vanguard	orange-pink	extra large	double to full	rosette	moderate	small clusters	repeat	plain
Vanilla	white (shaded green)	medium	double to full	high-centered	none	small clusters	repeat	reflexed
Vanity	deep pink	medium	single	open	strong	large clusters	repeat	plain
Variegata di Bologna	red blend	large	double to full	cupped	moderate	small clusters	once	reflexed
Varlon	medium red	large	double to full	flat	none	singly	repeat	reflexed
Veilchenblau	mauve	small	semi-double	cupped	moderate	large clusters	once	plain
Velutiniflora	dark red	medium	single	open	slight	small clusters	once	plain
Velvet Fragrance	dark red	large	double to full	high-centered	strong	small clusters	repeat	reflexed
Velvet Hour	dark red	medium	double to full	cupped	moderate	small clusters	repeat	reflexed
Venusta Pendula	white	small	semi-double	open	slight	large clusters	once	plain
Vera Johns	orange-red	large	double	high-centered	slight	small clusters	repeat	reflexed
Verdi	mauve blend	medium	double to full	open	moderate	large clusters	repeat	plain
Versailles	light pink	medium	double to full	cupped	slight	small clusters	repeat	reflexed
Verschuren	light pink	medium	double to full	cupped	slight	small clusters	repeat	reflexed
Vesper	orange blend	medium	double to full	flat	slight	small clusters	repeat	reflexed
Vestey's Pink Tea	medium pink	medium	double to full	cupped	slight	small clusters	repeat	plain
Vestey's Yellow Tea	light yellow	medium	double to full	open	moderate	small clusters	repeat	plain
Vesuvius	dark red	large	single	open	moderate	small clusters	repeat	plain
Vi's Violet	mauve	small	double to full	flat	moderate	small clusters	repeat	reflexed
Vick's Caprice	pink blend	large	double to full	cupped	moderate	small clusters	repeat	plain
Vicky Marfá	medium pink	large	double to full	high-centered	moderate	small clusters	repeat	reflexed
Vicomtesse Pierre du Fou	orange-pink	large	double to full	flat	strong	small clusters	repeat	reflexed
Victor Borge	orange blend	large	double to full	high-centered	slight	small clusters	repeat	reflexed
Victor Emmanuel	deep red	large	double to full	cupped	moderate	small clusters	once	reflexed
Victor Hugo	deep red	large	double to full	high-centered	strong	singly	repeat	reflexed
Victoria Gold	deep yellow	medium	double to full	cupped	slight	small clusters	repeat	ruffled
Victoriana	orange blend	large	double to full	cupped	slight	small clusters	repeat	ruffled
Viking Queen	medium pink	large	double to full	globular	strong	large clusters	repeat	reflexed
Ville de Londres	deep pink	medium	double to full	rosette	moderate	small clusters	once	plain
Vincent Godsiff	medium red	medium	semi-double	cupped	none	small clusters	repeat	plain
Vino Delicado	mauve	large	double to full	high-centered	slight	small clusters	repeat	reflexed
Vintage Visalia	medium pink	large	very full	rosette	slight	small clusters	repeat	plain
Violacée	mauve	medium	very full	cupped	strong	small clusters	once	plain
Violaine	mauve	large	double to full	high-centered	strong	singly	repeat	reflexed
Violet Carson	orange-pink/ pink blend	medium	double to full	high-centered	slight	large clusters	repeat	reflexed
Violette	mauve	small	very full	cupped	moderate	large clusters	once	plain
Violette Parfumée	mauve blend	large	double to full	cupped	strong	singly	repeat	reflexed
Violinista Costa	red blend	large	double to full	high-centered	moderate	singly	repeat	reflexed
Virginia	white	large	double	high-centered	none	small clusters	repeat	plain
Virgo	white	large	double to full	high-centered	slight	singly	repeat	reflexed
Vista	mauve	small	double to full	high-centered	slight	small clusters	repeat	reflexed
Vital	dark red	large	double	cupped	slight	small clusters	repeat	plain
Vital Spark	apricot blend	medium	double to full	flat	slight	small clusters	repeat	reflexed
Vivacious	medium pink	large	double to full	cupped	slight	small clusters	repeat	reflexed
Vivid	mauve	large	very full	cupped	moderate	small clusters	repeat	reflexed
Vogelpark Walsrode	light pink	medium	full	open	slight	small clusters	repeat	plain
Vogue	pink blend	large	double to full	high-centered	slight	small clusters	repeat	reflexed
Vol de Nuit	mauve	large	double to full	cupped	strong	small clusters	repeat	reflexed
Volcano	deep pink	extra large	double to full	cupped	moderate	singly	repeat	reflexed
Volunteer	yellow blend	large	double to full	high-centered	slight	small clusters	repeat	reflexed
Von Scharnhorst	light yellow	medium	semi-double	open	slight	small clusters	repeat	plain
Voodoo	orange blend	large	double to full	high-centered	moderate	singly	repeat	reflexed
Walheke	orange-pink	large	double to full	high-centered	slight	small clusters	repeat	reflexed
Waldfee	medium red	large	double to full	rosette	slight	small clusters	repeat	reflexed
Walko	dark red	medium	double to full	flat	moderate	small clusters	repeat	reflexed
Wanaka	orange-red	small	double to full	rosette	slight	large clusters	repeat	reflexed
Wandering Minstrel	orange-pink	medium	double to full	rosette	slight	small clusters	repeat	plain
Wapiti	red blend	medium	semi-double	open	none	large clusters	repeat	ruffled
Warley Jubilee	medium pink	medium	double	high-centered	slight	small clusters	repeat	plain
Warm Welcome	orange-red	small	semi-double	open	moderate	large clusters	repeat	plain
Warrawee	medium pink	large	double to full	high-centered	moderate	small clusters	repeat	reflexed
Warrior	orange-red	large	double to full	open	slight	truss	repeat	reflexed
Warwick Castle	deep pink	large	very full	rosette	strong	small clusters	repeat	plain
Warwickshire	pink blend	small	single	open	none	large clusters	repeat	plain
Water Music	deep pink	medium	semi-double	open	slight	small clusters	repeat	plain
Watercolor	medium pink	small	double to full	high-centered	slight	small clusters	repeat	reflexed
Watermelon Ice	pink blend	medium	double to full	open	slight	small clusters	repeat	plain
Waverley Garden Club	pink blend	large	double to full	high-centered	slight	small clusters	repeat	reflexed
Wedding Day	white	medium	single	open	strong	truss	once	plain
Wedding Ring	medium yellow	large	double to full	high-centered	slight	small clusters	repeat	reflexed
Wee Barbie	white	small	very full	globular	moderate	large clusters	repeat	reflexed
Wee Beth	orange blend	small	single	open	moderate	large clusters	repeat	plain
Wee Jock	medium red	small	double to full	flat	slight	small clusters	repeat	reflexed
Wee Man	medium red	small	semi-double	flat	slight	small clusters	repeat	plain
Wee Matt	medium red	small	double to full	rosette	moderate	small clusters	repeat	plain
Weetwood	light pink	medium	double to full	open	slight	large clusters	once	plain
Weisse Immensee	white	small	single	flat	moderate	large clusters	repeat	plain
Welwyn Garden Glory	apricot blend	large	double to full	high-centered	strong	small clusters	repeat	reflexed
Wendy	white	small	double to full	flat	none	small clusters	repeat	reflexed
Wendy Cussons	medium red	large	double to full	high-centered	strong	small clusters	repeat	reflexed
Wenlock	medium red	large	double to full	cupped	strong	small clusters	repeat	plain
West Coast	medium pink	large	double to full	flat	slight	small clusters	repeat	reflexed
Westerland	apricot blend	large	double to full	cupped	strong	small clusters	repeat	reflexed
Western Sun	deep yellow	large	double to full	high-centered	none	singly	repeat	reflexed
Westfalenpark	apricot blend	large	double to full	cupped	moderate	small clusters	repeat	reflexed
Whipped Cream	white	small	double to full	high-centered	none	small clusters	repeat	reflexed
Whisky Mac	yellow blend	large	double to full	high-centered	moderate	small clusters	repeat	reflexed
White Angel	white	small	double to full	high-centered	slight	small clusters	repeat	reflexed
White Bath	white	medium	double to full	cupped	strong	small clusters	once	plain
White Bella Rosa	white	medium	double to full	flat	slight	large clusters	repeat	reflexed
White Bells	white	small	double to full	rosette	slight	small clusters	repeat	reflexed
White Blush	white	medium	double to full	flat	moderate	small clusters	once	plain
White Bouquet	white	large	double to full	rosette	moderate	small clusters	repeat	reflexed
White Butterfly	white	large	double to full	cupped	moderate	singly	repeat	reflexed
White Cécile Brünner	white	small	double to full	rosette	slight	large clusters	repeat	plain
White Christmas	white	medium	double to full	high-centered	moderate	small clusters	repeat	reflexed
White Cockade	white	large	double to full	cupped	moderate	small clusters	repeat	reflexed
White Dawn	white	medium	double to full	open	moderate	small clusters	repeat	reflexed
White Dorothy	white	small	double to full	rosette	slight	large clusters	once	plain

NAME	BLOOM COLOR	FLOWER SIZE	FLOWER TYPE	FLOWER SHAPE	FRAGRANCE AMOUNT	FLOWERING HABIT	FLOWERING INCIDENCE	PETAL SHAPE
White Dream	white	small	double to full	high-centered	slight	small clusters	repeat	reflexed
White Ensign	white	large	double to full	flat	slight	small clusters	repeat	reflexed
White Fairy	white	small	semi-double	cupped	moderate	large clusters	repeat	plain
White Flower Carpet	white	medium	semi-double	cupped	slight	small clusters	repeat	plain
White Gem	white	medium	very full	high-centered	slight	small clusters	repeat	reflexed
White Grootendorst	white	small	semi-double	open	slight	small clusters	repeat	frilled
White Knight	white	large	double to full	high-centered	none	small clusters	repeat	reflexed
White Lightnin	white	large	double to full	flat	moderate	small clusters	repeat	reflexed
White Madonna	white	small	double to full	high-centered	slight	small clusters	repeat	reflexed
White Maman Cochet	white	large	double to full	high-centered	slight	small clusters	repeat	reflexed
White Mary MacKillop	white	medium	double to full	flat	slight	small clusters	repeat	reflexed
White Masterpiece	white	extra large	double to full	high-centered	slight	singly	repeat	reflexed
White Meidiland	white	medium	very full	flat	none	small clusters	repeat	plain
White Meillandina	white	small	semi-double	flat	none	small clusters	repeat	plain
White Mrs Flight	white	medium	semi-double	open	slight	large clusters	once	plain
White New Dawn	white	medium	double to full	cupped	moderate	large clusters	repeat	reflexed
White Out	white	small	double to full	cupped	slight	small clusters	repeat	reflexed
White Pet	white	small	double to full	rosette	none	large clusters	repeat	plain
White Queen Elizabeth	white	large	double to full	globular	slight	small clusters	repeat	plain
White Radox Bouquet	white	large	very full	rosette	moderate	small clusters	repeat	plain
White Rose of York	white	large	double to full	cupped	moderate	small clusters	once	plain
White Simplicity	white	large	semi-double	cupped	none	small clusters	repeat	ruffled
White Sparrieshoop	white	large	semi-double	open	slight	large clusters	repeat	plain
White Spray	white	small	double to full	high-centered	moderate	large clusters	repeat	reflexed
White Tausendschön	white	large	double to full	cupped	slight	large clusters	repeat	reflexed
White Wings	white	large	single	flat	slight	large clusters	repeat	plain
Whoopi	red blend	small	double to full	high-centered	moderate	small clusters	repeat	reflexed
Why Not	red blend	small	single	open	slight	small clusters	repeat	plain
Wichmoss	light pink	medium	semi-double	cupped	slight	large clusters	once	reflexed
Wickwar	light pink	medium	single	flat	strong	small clusters	once	plain
Wiener Charme	orange blend	extra large	double to full	high-centered	moderate	singly	repeat	reflexed
Wienerwald	orange-pink	large	double to full	high-centered	moderate	small clusters	repeat	reflexed
Wild Flower	light yellow	small	single	open	slight	singly	repeat	plain
Wildfire	medium red	large	semi-double	open	slight	small clusters	repeat	plain
Will Scarlet	medium red	small	double to full	cupped	slight	large clusters	repeat	ruffled
William Allen Richardson	yellow blend	medium	double to full	rosette	moderate	small clusters	repeat	plain
William and Mary	pink blend	large	double to full	cupped	strong	small clusters	once	plain
William Baffin	deep pink	large	semi-double	open	none	small clusters	repeat	plain
William Grant	deep pink	medium	semi-double	cupped	slight	small clusters	repeat	plain
William Lobb	mauve	large	semi-double	open	strong	small clusters	once	plain
William R. Smith	pink blend	large	double to full	high-centered	slight	small clusters	repeat	reflexed
William Shakespeare	dark red	large	double to full	rosette	strong	small clusters	repeat	plain
William III	mauve	small	semi-double	open	moderate	small clusters	once	plain
Williams' Double Yellow	medium yellow	medium	semi-double	open	strong	small clusters	once	plain
Wiltshire	medium pink	small	double to full	rosette	none	large clusters	repeat	plain
Wimi	pink blend	large	double to full	high-centered	strong	small clusters	repeat	reflexed
Winchester Cathedral	white	medium	double to full	cupped	moderate	small clusters	repeat	plain
Wind Chimes	medium pink	small	single	open	strong	large clusters	repeat	plain
Windflower	light pink	medium	double to full	cupped	moderate	small clusters	repeat	plain
Windrush	light yellow	large	semi-double	open	strong	small clusters	repeat	ruffled
Wini Edmunds	red blend	large	double to full	high-centered	moderate	singly	repeat	reflexed

NAME	BLOOM COLOR	FLOWER SIZE	FLOWER TYPE	FLOWER SHAPE	FRAGRANCE AMOUNT	FLOWERING HABIT	FLOWERING INCIDENCE	PETAL SHAPE
Winning Colors	orange blend	medium	very full	cupped	moderate	small clusters	repeat	reflexed
Winnipeg Parks	deep pink	medium	semi-double	cupped	slight	small clusters	repeat	plain
Winsome	mauve	medium	double to full	high-centered	none	small clusters	repeat	reflexed
Winter Magic	mauve	medium	double to full	cupped	moderate	small clusters	repeat	reflexed
Wise Portia	mauve	large	very full	cupped	strong	small clusters	repeat	plain
Wishing	medium pink	medium	double to full	cupped	slight	small clusters	repeat	reflexed
Wistful	mauve	small	double to full	open	slight	small clusters	repeat	reflexed
Woburn Abbey	orange blend	large	double to full	cupped	moderate	large clusters	repeat	reflexed
Woburn Gold	deep yellow	large	double to full	cupped	moderate	large clusters	repeat	reflexed
Woman's Day	pink blend	large	double to full	open	slight	small clusters	repeat	reflexed
Woman's Value	pink blend	large	full	open	slight	small clusters	repeat	plain
Work of Art	orange blend	medium	double to full	high-centered	slight	small clusters	repeat	reflexed
World's Fair Salute	medium red	large	double to full	high-centered	moderate	singly	repeat	reflexed
Worthwhile	orange blend	extra large	double to full	high-centered	slight	singly	repeat	reflexed
X-Rated	pink blend	small	double to full	high-centered	slight	singly	repeat	plain
Xavier Olibo	deep red	large	double to full	cupped	strong	small clusters	repeat	plain
Yakimour	red blend	large	double to full	high-centered	strong	small clusters	repeat	plain
Yankee Doodle	yellow blend	large	double to full	cupped	slight	small clusters	repeat	reflexed
Yellow Bantam	light yellow	small	double to full	open	none	small clusters	repeat	plain
Yellow Butterfly	light yellow	medium	single	open	none	small clusters	repeat	plain
Yellow Button	yellow blend	medium	very full	rosette	slight	large clusters	repeat	plain
Yellow Champagner	yellow blend	medium	double to full	high-centered	slight	small clusters	repeat	plain
Yellow Charles Austin	light yellow	medium	very full	rosette	slight	small clusters	repeat	plain
Yellow Cushion	medium yellow	large	double to full	flat	moderate	small clusters	repeat	reflexed
Yellow Doll	light yellow	small	very full	high-centered	moderate	small clusters	repeat	reflexed
Yellow Fairy	medium yellow	small	semi-double	open	slight	large clusters	repeat	plain
Yellow Meillandina	yellow blend	small	double to full	open	moderate	small clusters	repeat	reflexed
Yellow Pages	yellow blend	large	double to full	high-centered	moderate	singly	repeat	reflexed
Yellow Pinocchio	medium yellow	medium	double to full	cupped	slight	large clusters	repeat	reflexed
Yellow Queen Elizabeth	medium yellow	large	double to full	globular	none	small clusters	repeat	plain
Yesterday	medium pink	small	semi-double	open	slight	truss	repeat	plain
Yesteryear	apricot blend	large	double to full	cupped	slight	small clusters	repeat	reflexed
Yolande d'Aragon	mauve	large	very full	flat	strong	small clusters	repeat	plain
York and Lancaster	pink blend	medium	double to full	open	moderate	small clusters	once	plain
Yorkshire	white	medium	semi-double	saucer	slight	small clusters	repeat	plain
Yorkshire Bank	white	large	double to full	high-centered	moderate	small clusters	repeat	reflexed
Youki San	white	large	double to full	flat	strong	small clusters	repeat	reflexed
Young at Heart	apricot blend	medium	double to full	high-centered	moderate	small clusters	repeat	reflexed
Young Quinn	medium yellow	large	double to full	flat	slight	singly	repeat	reflexed
Youth of the World	medium red	extra large	double to full	cupped	slight	small clusters	repeat	plain
Yves Piaget	deep pink	large	double to full	rosette	strong	singly	repeat	plain
Yvonne Rabier	white	small	semi-double	open	none	large clusters	repeat	plain
Zambra	orange blend	large	semi-double	flat	slight	small clusters	repeat	plain
Zara Hore-Ruthven	medium pink	large	double to full	cupped	slight	small clusters	repeat	reflexed
Zebra	red blend	large	double to full	cupped	none	small clusters	repeat	plain
Zenobia	medium pink	large	double to full	globular	strong	small clusters	once	plain
Zéphirine Drouhin	medium pink	large	semi-double	open	strong	small clusters	repeat	reflexed
Zigeunerblut	dark red	large	double to full	cupped	strong	small clusters	repeat	reflexed
Zinger	medium red	small	semi-double	flat	moderate	small clusters	repeat	plain
Zoé	medium pink	medium	double to full	flat	strong	small clusters	once	plain
Zweibrücken	dark red	large	double to full	open	slight	large clusters	repeat	reflexed
Zwergkönig 78	dark red	small	double to full	rosette	none	small clusters	repeat	plain
Zwerkönigin 82	medium pink	small	double to full	rosette	none	small clusters	repeat	plain

Notable Rose Breeders

Peter Harkness

Hundreds of breeders have been responsible for the roses included in this book. For many centuries gardeners have collected rosehips, sown the seeds and checked the resulting seedlings, hoping to find an improved form that would add something special to the range of varieties already in existence. Not until 1691 was it established that plants possess a sex life, having male and female parts.

More than a century elapsed before rose growers in France began to take advantage of this knowledge, and even then the process was random, haphazard and poorly recorded, so that breeders could only guess at the parentage of their seedlings. Once they learned to keep proper records and work through previously selected parents, they became able to direct their efforts to particular ends—though they needed luck as well as skill, for it has been said that two roses can combine their genes in 250 million different ways. The plethora of new colors, shapes, and qualities of fragrance, health, hardiness, freedom of bloom and thornlessness within the modern rose is the combined fruit of their successes—and of their good fortune. A few noteworthy breeders of recent times are listed here:

Aicardi, Domenico (Italy). Aicardi was active in San Remo between the 1930s and the 1950s. His Large-flowered/Hybrid Tea 'Signora' from 1936 is still grown and loved and has proved a useful parent.
Archer, William (England). Archer's firm, W. E. B. Archer & Daughter was in Sellindge, Kent and was active from the 1920s to the 1940s. He pursued unusual lines, and had commercial successes with the single Large-flowered/Hybrid Teas 'Dainty Bess' (1925) and 'Ellen Willmott' (1936), and 'Golden Crest', a charming restrained Climber from 1948.
Armstrong, David (USA). Armstrong was active between 1963 and 1972, at Armstrong Nurseries, Ontario, California. With Herb Swim, he raised the Large-flowered/Hybrid Tea 'Eiffel Tower' (1963) and the Cluster-flowered/Floribunda 'Joseph's Coat' (1964). Some of his own roses are the Large-flowered/Hybrid Teas 'Aquarius' (1971) and 'Kentucky Derby' (1972). His Cluster-flowered/Floribunda 'Yellow Cushion' (1966) proved a useful parent rose for other breeders.
Austin, David (England). Austin began raising roses in the 1960s at his nursery in Albrighton. His aim was to create repeat-flowering old style roses, popularly termed 'English Roses'. Some of his successes include shrubs 'Leander' (1982), 'Mary Rose' (1983), 'Graham Thomas' (1983), 'Heritage' (1984), 'Gertrude Jekyll' (1986), 'L. D. Braithwaite' (1988), 'Molineux' (1994). He also bred the climbing shrub 'Constance Spry' (1961), the graceful 'Francine Austin' (1988) and 'Mrs Doreen Pike' (1994).
Barbier (France). Barbier Bros & Co. of Orléans was active from 1900 to 1933. They raised Wichuraiana Climbers, Polyanthas, Hybrid Perpetuals and Large-flowered/Hybrid Teas. Their enduring achievements include 'Albéric Barbier' (1900), 'Paul Transon' (1900), 'Léontine Gervais' (1903), 'François Juranville' (1906), 'Alexandre Girault' (1909), 'Albertine' (1927) and the curious, mildew-prone 'Wichmoss' (1911).

Basye, Dr Robert (USA). Basye has been active since the 1940s in Texas. He is an innovative raiser of interspecies crosses, aiming for health, hardiness and thornlessness. He has also endowed a chair for research work. Some of his achievements include the shrubs 'Basye's Purple' (1968), 'Basye's Blueberry' (1982) and 'Belinda's Dream' (1988).
Benardella, Frank (USA). Benardella has been raising roses since the 1980s. He is a specialist in Miniatures and created 'Black Jade' (1985), 'Jennifer' (1985), 'Old Glory' (1988) and 'Figurine' (1991). In recent years, he has concentrated on developing striped Large-flowered/Hybrid Teas.
Bennett, Dee (USA). Bennett began raising roses in the 1970s in Chula Vista, California. She was a specialist in Miniatures; her breeding work includes 'Angel Dust' (1978), 'Hot Shot' (1982), 'Jean Kenneally' (1984) and many others.
Bennett, Henry (England). Bennett was active in the 1870s and 1880s in Wiltshire and Middlesex. He pioneered modern methods of planned parent selection, working with Teas and Hybrid Perpetuals to create Large-flowered/Hybrid Teas, including the valuable future parent roses 'Lady Mary Fitzwilliam' (1882) and 'Mrs John Laing' (1887).
Bentall, Ann (England). Bentall was active in the 1920s and the 1930s in Essex, following Pemberton. She raised the shrubs 'The Fairy' (1932) and 'Buff Beauty' (1939), and discovered 'Ballerina' ('a chance seedling') in 1937.
Boerner, Gene (USA). 'Papa Floribunda' was active from the 1940s until 1966 with Jackson & Perkins Nursery, Newark, New York. He utilized Kordes' 'Pinocchio' and Hybrid Polyanthas with brilliant results, which were achieved by working on a large scale, sowing a quarter of a million seeds each year. His successes include the Cluster-flowered/Floribundas 'Goldilocks' (1945), 'Lavender Pinocchio' (1948), 'Fashion' (1949), 'Masquerade' (1949) and 'Apricot Nectar' (1965). He raised 'Diamond Jubilee' (1947), a yellow rose with scent and health.
Bossom, Bill (England). Bossom has been working with roses since the 1980s in Enfield, Middlesex. His varied output includes the Cluster-flowered/Floribundas 'Peppermint Ice' (1991) and 'Tender Loving Care' (1995).
Brownell, Dr Walter and Mrs (USA). The Brownells were active between the 1920s and the 1950s in Rhode Island. They worked to develop hardier roses and are remembered for the Climbers 'Elegance' (1937), 'Golden Glow' (1937) and the Large-flowered/Hybrid Tea 'Lafter' (1948).
Buck, Griffith (USA). Buck worked with roses between the 1950s and the 1990s in Iowa, and aimed to breed hardier garden roses. His versatile output includes the shrubs 'Applejack' (1973), 'Summer Wind' (1975) and 'Carefree Beauty' (1977).
Cant (England). The breeding work of Cant spans from 1875 to the present day, with B. R. Cant, Frank Cant and currently Cants of Colchester under Roger Pawsey. They have produced over 130 named varieties; the enduring highlights of these are the climbing roses

'Blush Rambler' (1903) and 'Cupid' (1915), and the Large-flowered/Hybrid Teas 'Mrs Oakley Fisher' (1921), 'Just Joey' (1972), 'Alpine Sunset' (1973) and 'Goldstar' (1983).
Carruth, Tom (USA). Carruth has been raising roses since the 1980s with Weeks Roses Inc., Ontario, California. His output includes Cluster-flowered/Floribunda 'Columbus' (1991), the shrub 'Flutterbye' (1996) and the Miniature 'Heartbreaker' (1990).
Christensen, Jack (USA). Christensen succeeded Swim at Armstrongs and has been active since the 1970s. With Herb Swim, he raised the Large-flowered/Hybrid Tea 'Brandy' (1981). His notable successes include the Large-flowered/Hybrid Teas 'Gold Medal' (1982), 'Voodoo' (1986), 'Midas Touch' (1992), and the Miniatures 'Cricket' (1978) and 'Holy Toledo' (1980).
Clark, Alister (Australia). Clark worked with roses from the 1910s to the 1940s in Bulla, Victoria. He had over 120 releases, including many vigorous but tender Climbers with *Rosa gigantea* behind them, such as 'Kitty Kininmonth' (1922), and 'Nancy Hayward' (1937), and the Tea Rose 'Lorraine Lee' (1924). He also bred the tough and popular Climber 'Black Boy' (1919).
Cocker, Alec and Ann (Scotland). The Cockers have been active since the 1960s with James Cocker & Son, Aberdeen. They have a large output, and are notable for Large-flowered/Hybrid Teas 'Alec's Red' (1970), 'Silver Jubilee' (1977), 'Remember Me' (1984) and 'Abbeyfield Rose' (1985), the Cluster-flowered/Floribundas 'Anne Cocker' and 'Rob Roy' (1971), 'Playboy' (1976), 'Toprose' (1991), 'Gordon's College' (1992) and 'Friend for Life' (1993), the Patio 'Conservation' (1988), and the Climbers 'Morning Jewel' (1968) and 'White Cockade' (1968). Alec Cocker obtained a rare seed of *Rosa persica* in the 1960s and began breeding work using it.
Croix, Paul (France). Active from the 1950s to the present time in Bourg-Argental, Loire, Croix has produced prize-winning bushes and some climbing roses, but they are little known outside Europe.
Davidson, Harvey (USA). Davidson has been working with roses since the 1980s in Orinda, California. He aims for thornlessness, mostly with Large-flowered/Hybrid Teas, his 'Smooth Angel' (1986) and 'Smooth Velvet' (1986) being the most widely grown.
Delbard, Georges and Chabert, André (France). Active from the 1950s to today and trading in Paris, their varieties are best suited to warm climates. Some of their successes are 'Centenaire de Lourdes' (1958), 'Diablotin' (1961), 'Gingersnap' (1978), 'Lancôme' (1973) and the fragrant lilac 'Dioressence' (1984). They also produced the excellent single red Climber 'Altissimo' in 1966.
De Ruiter, Gerrit, Gijs, Leendert etc. (The Netherlands). Active from the 1920s to the present in Hazerswoude, they have a big output, notably the Polyanthas 'Gloria Mundi' (1929), 'Cameo' (1932), 'De Ruiter's Herald' (1949), the Cluster-flowered/Floribundas 'Rosemary Rose' (1954), 'Sweet Repose' (1955), 'Orange Sensation' (1961), 'Europeana' (1963), and the unusual "Compacta Seven Dwarfs" roses (1954–56).

Dickson, George, Alex, Pat and Colin (Northern Ireland). The Dicksons have been going since the 1880s in Hawlmark and Newtownards. Their successes read like a roll call of famous names, including the first National Rose Society Gold Medal winner 'Mrs W. J. Grant' (1895), the Large-flowered/Hybrid Teas 'Betty Uprichard' (1922), 'Shot Silk' (1924), 'Dame Edith Helen' (1926), 'Grandpa Dickson' (1966), 'Red Devil' (1970), 'Freedom' (1984), 'Elina' (1985) and 'Lovely Lady' (1986), and the Cluster-flowered/Floribundas 'Dickson's Flame' (1958) and 'Anisley Dickson' (1983) (both Royal National Rose Society President's International Trophy winners). Their pioneer work with Patio Roses include 'Peek a Boo' (1981), 'Sweet Magic' (one of several Dickson-raised UK Roses of the Year) (1987), 'Cider Cup' (1988) and 'Marry Me' (1998).

Dickson, Hugh (Northern Ireland). Hugh Dickson was active from the 1900s up to the 1930s in Belfast. He is noted for 'Hugh Dickson' (1905).

Dot, Pedro and Simon (Spain). The Dots have been raising roses since the 1920s near Barcelona, and are famous for the Large-flowered/Hybrid Tea 'Condesa de Sastago' (1932), the shrub 'Nevada' (1927) and the Climber 'Mme Grégoire Staechelin' (1927). Their pioneer work with Miniature Roses produced 'Rosina' (1935), 'Baby Gold Star' (1940), 'Pour Toi' (1946) and 'Coralin' (1955).

Ducher, Jean-Claude and Veuve (France). Active between the 1850s and the 1880s in the Lyon region, Ducher also tutored Joseph Pernet-Ducher. His enduring successes include the Noisettes 'Rêve d'Or' (1869) and 'William Allen Richardson' (1878), the Tea 'Anna Olivier' (1872), and the Polyantha 'Cécile Brünner' (1880).

Fryer, Gareth (England). Active since the 1970s with Fryer's Roses in Knutsford, Cheshire, Fryer is noted for the classic Large-flowered/Hybrid Teas 'Bobby Charlton' (1974), 'The Lady' (1985), 'Velvet Fragrance' (1988), 'Belle Epoque' (1994), 'Warm Wishes' (1994), 'Bride' (1995) and 'Especially for You' (1996), the Cluster-flowered/Floribunda 'Sunsilk' (1974), the Patios 'Sweet Dream' (1988) and 'Top Marks' (1992), the shrub 'Biddulph Grange' (1988), and the Climber 'Crimson Cascade' (1991).

Gaujard, Jean (France). Gaujard succeeded Pernet-Ducher and has been active since the 1920s in the Lyon region. He raised many Large-flowered/Hybrid Teas suited to warm climates and his popular successes include 'Opéra' (1950) and 'Rose Gaujard' (1957).

Geschwind, Rudolf (Austria-Hungary). Geschwind was active between the 1860s and 1910, and aimed to breed for hardiness. He had a large output of up to 140 varieties, although his work is sometimes credited to others. The Rambler 'Theano' (1895), and the Bourbons 'Gruss an Teplitz' (1897) and 'Gipsy Boy' (1909) are still grown.

Gregory, Walter (England). Between the 1950s and the 1970s, with C. Gregory & Son, Chilwell, Nottingham, Gregory's most successful roses have been the Large-flowered/Hybrid Tea 'Wendy Cussons' (1959) and the Climber 'Pink Pérpetué' (1965).

Guillot, Jean-Baptiste (France). Guillot was active from 1850s to the 1880s in the Lyon region. He is famous as the raiser of the first Large-flowered/Hybrid Tea 'La France' (1867), the Tea 'Catherine Mermet' (1869), the first Polyantha 'Pâquérette' (1875), and the first pink Polyantha 'Gloire des Polyantha' (1887).

Hardy, Eugène (France). During the 1820s and 1830s Hardy was director of the Jardins de Luxembourg, Paris. His fragrant white Damask 'Mme Hardy' (1832) is widely grown, as is the Tea 'Bon Silène' (circa 1837). He raised the first known *Rosa persica* hybrid with 'Hardii' about 1836.

Harkness, Jack (England). Harkness was involved with raising roses from the 1960s to the 1990s with R. Harkness & Co. Ltd, Hitchin. Looking for health and

fragrance, his wide range includes the Large-flowered/Hybrid Teas 'Alexander' (1972), 'Rosemary Harkness' (1985) and 'Savoy Hotel' (1989), the Cluster-flowered/Floribundas 'Escapade' (1967), 'Margaret Merril' (1977), 'Anne Harkness' (1980), 'Mountbatten' (1982)—the first UK Rose of the Year— 'Amber Queen' (1984), 'City of London' (1988), 'Fellowship' (1992), 'Sunset Boulevard' (1997), 'Betty Harkness' and 'Easy Going' (1998), the Patio 'Anna Ford' (1980), the Climbers 'Compassion' (1973) and 'Penny Lane' (1998), the Polyanthas 'Yesterday' (1974) and 'Marjorie Fair' (1978), and the shrubs 'Armada' (1988) and 'Jacqueline du Pré' (1989). His pioneering work with *Rosa persica* produced 'Tigris' (1985), 'Euphrates' (1986) and 'Nigel Hawthorne' (1989).

Hetzel, Karl (Germany). Hetzel has been raising roses since the 1970s in Beutelsbach. He has recently developed an innovative line of repeat-flowering Ramblers such as 'Super Dorothy' and 'Super Excelsa' (1986), and 'Super Fairy' (1992).

Hill, E. Gurney and Joseph H. (USA). The Hills have been active since the 1900s in Richmond, Indiana. Their large output includes the vigorous, fragrant Large-flowered/Hybrid Teas 'General MacArthur' (1905), 'Richmond' (1905) and 'Joanna Hill' (1928). The last two have proved important parents.

Holmes, Richard (England). During the 1960s and the 1970s in Stockport, Cheshire, Holmes had wonderful success with the Cluster-flowered/Floribunda 'Fred Loads' (1967) and the shrub 'Sally Holmes' (1976).

Horner, Colin (England). Since the 1970s Horner has worked in Stansted, Essex. His most successful variety to date is the Cluster-flowered/Floribunda 'Champagne Cocktail' (1985).

Howard, Fred (USA). Howard was active from the 1910s to the 1950s with Howard & Smith, Montebello, California. He is best remembered for his sweet-scented bright pink 'The Doctor' (1936).

Ilsink, Peter (The Netherlands). With Interplant, Leersum, Ilsink has worked since the 1970s to raise many graceful shrub roses, including 'Red Blanket', 'Rosy Cushion' and 'Smarty' (1979), 'Robin Redbreast' (1983), 'Lavender Dream' (1985), 'Eyeopener' (1987) and 'Euphoria', which was developed from a *Rosa persica* line in 1998.

Jolly, Betty and Nelson (USA). The Jollys have been working with roses since the 1970s. They are specialists in Miniatures, 'Chattem Centennial' (1979) and 'Arizona Sunset' (1985) being among their most successful.

Kordes, Wilhelm, Reimer and Willi (Germany). The Kordes firm has been active since the 1900s with W. Kordes Sohne, Sparrieshoop. Their versatile output includes several mold-breaking masterworks, such as the Large-flowered/Hybrid Teas 'Geheimrat Duisberg' (syn. 'Golden Rapture') (1933), 'Crimson Glory' (1935), 'Independence' (1950), 'Perfecta' (1957) and 'Royal William' (1984), the Polyantha 'Orange Triumph' (1937), and the Cluster-flowered/Floribundas 'Pinocchio' (1947), 'Korona' (1955), 'Iceberg' (1958), 'Lili Marlene' (1959), 'Friesia' (1977) and 'Anna Livia' (1985). Kordes also produced a hardy strain of shrub roses with 'Frühlingsgold' (1937) and others; and derived *Rosa kordesii* from seed of the supposedly infertile 'Max Graf' leading to 'Dortmund' (1955) and 'Leverkusen' (1955). Other roses include 'Westerland' (1969), 'Grouse' (1984), 'Surrey' (1985) and 'Roselina' (syn. 'Playtime') (1992).

Kriloff, Michel (France). Kriloff has been active from 1950s to the 1990s in Antibes. He has a large output, of which Large-flowered/Hybrid Teas 'Lucy Cramphorn' (1960), 'Touch of Class' (1984) (an All-America Rose Selection winner) and 'Tabriz' (1986) have perhaps gained the greatest international recognition.

Lambert, Peter (Germany). Between the 1890s and the 1920s in Trier, Lambert produced a wide output.

The survivors include the Large-flowered/Hybrid Tea 'Frau Karl Druschki' (1901), the Polyanthas 'Léonie Lamesch' (1899) and 'Katharina Zeimet' (1901), and the shrub 'Trier' (1904), an ancestor of many Modern Garden Roses.

Lammerts, Dr Walter (USA). During the 1940 and the 1950s in Livermore, California, Lamments had major success with the Large-flowered/Hybrid Teas 'Charlotte Armstrong' (1940), 'Show Girl' (1946) and 'Chrysler Imperial' (1952), the Grandiflora 'Queen Elizabeth' (1954), the Climbers 'High Noon' (1946) and 'Golden Showers' (1957), and the Polyantha 'China Doll' (1946).

Leenders (The Netherlands). From the 1900s to the 1970s in Tegelen, Leenders produced a large output. His enduring successes include the Large-flowered/Hybrid Tea 'Comtesse Vandal' (1932) and the Cluster-flowered/Floribunda 'Nathalie Nypels' (1919).

LeGrice, Edward and Bill (England). The LeGrices have been active since 1930. Based in Norfolk, their innovative crosses include novel color blends. They have had commercial success with the Large-flowered/Hybrid Teas 'My Choice' (1958) and 'Great News' (1973), the Cluster-flowered/Floribundas 'Dainty Maid' (1937), 'Allgold' (1956), 'Lilac Charm' (1962) and 'News' (1968), and the shrub 'Pearl Drift' (1980), bred from 'Mermaid'. Edward LeGrice declared that 'People have to play for safety if they want a living, and that is quite the wrong way for a hybridist.'

Lens, Louis (Belgium). Lens has been raising roses since the 1930s in Wavre-Notre-Dame. His commercial successes include the Large-flowered/Hybrid Teas 'Dame de Coeur' (1958) and 'Pascali' (1961). He has produced innovative crosses, such as the Ground Cover 'Green Snake' (1985) (*Rosa arvensis* × *R. wichuraiana*), and the shrubs 'Running Maid' (1982) and 'Pink Robin' (1993) (*R. helenae* hybrid).

Mallerin, Charles (France). A heating engineer by profession, Mallerin was active between the 1920s and 1960 in Varce, Pont-de-Claix, Isère. He raised over 130 varieties and tutored Francis Meilland. The Large-flowered/Hybrid Teas 'Mrs Pierre S. du Pont' (1929), 'Virgo' (1947), 'Beaute' (1953) and 'Isabelle de France' (1956), and the Climbers 'Guinée' (1938), 'Spectacular' (1954) and 'Danse des Sylphes' (1959) are among his notable creations.

Marciel, Stanley and Jeanne (USA). The Marciels have been active since the 1980s and are based in Aptos, California. They raised the shrub rose 'First Light' (All-America Rose Selection winner 1998) for DeVor Nursery.

Mattock, John & successors (England). The varied output of Mattock includes the Large-flowered/Hybrid Tea 'Tynwald' (1979), the Climber 'Dreaming Spires' (1973), and the shrubs 'Pink Wave' (1983) and 'Northamptonshire' (1990). They have been raising roses since the 1960s.

McCann, Sean (Ireland). Since the 1960s in Dublin, McCann has been known as a lecturer and garden writer with practical experience as a raiser of Miniatures. His roses include 'Kiss 'n' Tell' (1989), 'Lovers Only' (1989) and 'Lady in Red' (1990).

McGredy, Sam II, III and IV (Northern Ireland and New Zealand). The McGredy firm has been going since the 1890s with S. McGredy & Son, Portadown up to 1972, and McGredy Roses International, Auckland. They have a huge output which includes household names and major innovations, such as the Large-flowered/Hybrid Teas 'Mrs Herbert Stevens' (1910), 'Emma Wright', 'The Queen Alexandra Rose' (1918), 'Mrs Henry Morse' (1919), 'Charles P. Kilham' (1926), 'Mrs Sam McGredy' (1929), 'Picture' (1932), 'McGredy's Yellow' (1933), 'Hector Deane' (1938), 'Cynthia Brooke' (1942), 'Piccadilly' (1959), 'Mischief' (1961), 'Olympiad' (1983) and 'New Zealand' (1990), the Cluster-flowered/Floribundas 'Elizabeth of Glamis' (1964), 'Arthur Bell' (1965), 'Evelyn Fison' and 'Paddy

McGredy' (1962) and 'Trumpeter' (1977), the Miniature 'Snow Carpet' (1980), the Climbers 'Casino' (1963), 'Schoolgirl' (1964), 'Handel' (1965), 'Bantry Bay' (1967) and 'Dublin Bay' (1976), color breaks such as 'Grey Pearl' (1945), and many 'hand-painted' roses including 'Picasso' (1971), 'Eyepaint' (1975), 'Maestro' (1980) and 'Oranges and Lemons' (1992).

Mehring, Bernard (England). Mehring has been active since the 1990s raising roses for Eurosa, Woodley, Berkshire. His aims include health and thornlessness. He is known for the Cluster-flowered/Floribunda 'Golden Hope', the Climber 'Jane Eyre' (1998), and the Patio Rose 'Make a Wish' (1996).

Meilland, Francis, Marie-Louisette and Alain; and Paolino, Marie-Louise (France). Since the 1930s, as Meilland, latterly Meilland-Richardier, Tassin and Cap d'Antibes, the House of Meilland has become a household name. Meilland is famous for the mold-breaking Large-flowered/Hybrid Tea 'Mme A. Meilland' (1942)—better known as 'Peace'—of which Francis reported that the original seedling had been 'a weak plant'! Many major successes since include Large-flowered/Hybrid Teas 'Charles Mallerin' (1951), 'Grand'mère Jenny' (1950), 'Eden Rose' (1950), 'Bettina' (1953), 'Papa Meilland' (1963) and 'The McCartney Rose' (1991), the cut-flower roses 'Baccarà' (1954) and 'Sonia' (1974), the Miniatures 'Darling Flame' (1971), 'Colibri' (1958) and 'Orange Sunblaze' (1981), the Ground Cover 'Swany' (1977), the shrub 'Bonica' (1981), the Cluster-flowered/Floribunda 'La Sévillana' (1982), the Climber 'Clair Matin' (1960), and the recent 'Romantica' series of roses with old-style flowers.

Miller, Alvin (USA). During the 1890s up to the 1910s while with the Jackson & Perkins Co. in Newark, New York, Miller raised the Rambler 'Dorothy Perkins' (1901), one of the few roses that is an international household name.

Moore, Ralph (USA). Moore has been working with roses since the 1920s at his Sequoia Nursery, in Visalia, California. He specializes in Miniatures, many raised using his seedling Rambler 'Zee'. His successes include 'Bit o' Sunshine' (1956), 'Mr Bluebird' (1960), 'Magic Carrousel' (1962), 'Stars 'n' Stripes' (1975), 'Stacey Sue' (1976), 'Rise 'n' Shine' (1977), the innovative Moss Miniature 'Dresden Doll' (1975), and the 1990s 'Halo' series that have red petal bases, which make a ring around the stamens.

Morey, Dennison (USA). Between the 1950s and the 1970s with General Bionomics Inc., Santa Rosa, California, Morey created the Large-flowered/Hybrid Tea 'King's Ransom' (1961), which was the best yellow for years. He also created the popular Miniature 'Popcorn' (1973), the Climber 'Royal Gold' (1957), and the fascinating, creeping Climbing Miniature 'Temple Bells' (1971).

Noack, Werner (Germany). Noack's Rosen, Gütersloh has been active since the 1970s, raising bush, climbing and especially Ground Cover and shrub roses, notably 'Flower Carpet' and 'White Flower Carpet' (1991).

Norman, Albert (England). A diamond setter by profession, Norman raised roses between the 1910s and the 1950s in Normandy, Surrey. He had success with the Large-flowered/Hybrid Tea 'Ena Harkness', the Cluster-flowered/Floribunda 'Frensham' (1946), and his uniquely late-flowering Rambler 'Crimson Shower' (1951).

Olesen, Mogens and Pernille (Denmark). See Poulsen.

Onodera, Toru (Japan). A geologist by profession, Onodera has been active since the 1960s in Urawa. He produced the outstanding novel Climbing Miniature 'Nozomi' (1968), and its seedling 'Suma' (1989).

Pal, J. Benjamin (India). During the 1950s up to the 1980s, Pal raised mostly Large-flowered/Hybrid Teas popular in India but little known elsewhere; among them are 'Princess of India' (1980) and 'Nandini' (1983).

Paolino, Marie-Louise (France). See Meilland.

Paul, George and George Laing (England). Between the 1870s and the 1910s in Cheshunt, the Pauls produced a wide range of roses. They are noted for the Large-flowered/Hybrid Teas 'Cheshunt Hybrid' (1872), 'Goldfinch' (1907) and 'Paul's Lemon Pillar' (1915).

Paul, William and Arthur William (England). During the 1850s until the 1920s in Waltham Cross, the Pauls had a large output including the climbing roses 'Mermaid' (1918) and 'Paul's Scarlet Climber' (1916). They introduced the Large-flowered/Hybrid Tea 'Ophelia' (1912).

Pemberton, Rev. Joseph (England). Between the 1900s and the 1920s in Essex, Pemberton raised delightful shrub roses of Noisette, Polyantha, Tea and Large-flowered/Hybrid Tea ancestry such as 'Moonlight' (1913), 'Penelope' (1924) and 'Cornelia' (1925).

Penzance, Lord (England). During the 1890s, Penzance raised in Surrey a range of Sweet Briar hybrids, 'Lady Penzance' being perhaps the best for its scented foliage. Still widely grown are 'Amy Robsart', 'Lady Penzance', 'Lord Penzance' and 'Meg Merrilies', all from 1894.

Pernet-Ducher, Joseph (France). Succeeding Jean-Claude and Veuve Ducher, Pernet-Ducher was active from the 1870s up to the 1920s in the Lyon region. His many Large-flowered/Hybrid Teas include the commercially successful 'Mme Caroline Testout' (1890), 'Antoine Rivoire' and 'Mme Abel Chatenay' (1893) and the novel orange-gold 'Soleil d'Or' (1900), whereby the bright colors of *Rosa foetida* came into the Large-flowered/Hybrid Teas. The yellow 'Rayon d'Or' followed in 1910 and the coral-pink 'Mme Edouard Herriot' in 1913. He was known as 'The Wizard of Lyon'.

Poulsen, Dines, Svend, Niels, and Olesen, Mogens and Pernille (Denmark). The Poulsen firm has been active since the 1900s. Dines raised the Polyantha 'Ellen Poulsen' and the novel Polyantha/Large-flowered cross 'Rödhätte' (1912). Svend, seeking hardy roses, developed the Cluster-flowered/Floribundas 'Else Poulsen' and 'Kirsten Poulsen' (1924), 'Poulsen's Yellow' (1938), 'Rumba' (1958) and many more. Among Niels' roses are the Cluster-flowered/Floribundas 'Chinatown' (1963), 'Pernille Poulsen' (1965) and the Large-flowered/Hybrid Tea 'Troika' (1972). The Olesens have a wonderfully diverse output, with Large-flowered/Hybrid Teas 'Ingrid Bergman' (1984) and 'Modern Art' (1985), the Cluster-flowered/Floribundas 'Christopher Columbus' (striped) (1992), 'Fredensborg' (1995), a novel range of Patios, old-style roses such as 'Queen Margrethe' (1995), and the Miniatures including 'White Bells' (1980), 'Pink Bells' and 'Red Bells' (1983).

Prior, D. (England). During the 1920s and the 1930s in Colchester, Essex, Prior raised Polyanthas and two outstanding Cluster-flowered/Floribundas still widely grown, 'Betty Prior' (1935) and 'Donald Prior' (1938).

Robinson, Herbert (England). Between the 1920s up to the 1950s at Hinckley, Leicestershire, Robinson produced some notable Large-flowered/Hybrid Teas including 'Christopher Stone' and 'Phyllis Gold' (1935), the brilliant yellow 'Lydia' (1949), and 'Doreen' (1951).

Robinson, Thomas (Guernsey). Active during the 1980s, Robinson concentrated on Miniatures, one of the most striking being his creeping mini-shrub 'Simon Robinson' (1982) (*Rosa wichuraiana* × 'New Penny')

Saville, Harmon (USA). Saville has been raising roses since the 1970s. With Nor' East Roses, in Rowley, Massachusetts, he has raised many Miniatures, both for garden and exhibition, including 'Party Girl' (1979), 'Little Jackie' and 'Minnie Pearl' (1982), the lavender-toned 'Winsome' (1984), 'Raindrops' (1990) and 'Teddy Bear' (1990). He has also created Moss Miniatures such as 'Single's Better' (1985).

Scrivens, Len (England). Scrivens has been active since the 1970s. He is known for the yellow Patio Rose 'Baby Love' (1993), a shrub-like, free-flowering, well-foliaged and healthy plant from the *Rosa davidii elongata* line.

Simpson, Nola (New Zealand). Simpson is a computer scientist who has been raising roses in Palmerston North since the 1970s. Her varied output includes what may be the only rose named for a cat—the Large-flowered/Hybrid Tea 'Hamish' (1979)—and the Cluster-flowered/Floribunda 'Hot Chocolate' (1986), which won a New Zealand Gold Medal.

Smith, Ted (England). Smith is a former railwayman who has been working with roses since the 1970s in Sandiacre, Nottinghire. His gold medal successes include Cluster-flowered/Floribundas 'Baby Bio' (1976) and 'Summer Serenade' (1986).

Suzuki, Seizo (Japan). Suzuki has been active since the 1960s with Keisei Nurseries, Yachiyo-Shi. He holds an extensive species collection, from which he obtained the remarkable shrub 'Ferdy' (1984) and the prize-winning Large-flowered/Hybrid Teas 'Olympic Torch' (1966) and 'Mikado' (1984).

Svejda, Felicitas (Canada). Using Kordesii and Rugosa roses to obtain winter hardy shrubs and Climbers, Svejda worked with the Canadian Department of Agriculture from the 1960s to the 1980s. Her successes include 'John Cabot' (1978), 'William Baffin' (1983), 'Henry Kelsey' (1984) and 'John Davis' (1986).

Swim, Herb (USA). Between the 1930s and the 1970s, Swim raised roses with Armstrong and Weeks. His many superb varieties include 22 All-America Rose Selection winners. His notable Large-flowered/Hybrid Teas include 'Tallyho' (1948), 'Fandango' (1950), 'Sutter's Gold' (1950), 'First Love' and 'Helen Traubel' (1951), 'Buccaneer' (1952), 'Montezuma' (1955), 'Garden Party' (1959), 'Summer Sunshine' (1962), and with Weeks 'Royal Highness' (1962), 'Mister Lincoln' (1964), and with Ellis 'Double Delight' (1977). His Cluster-flowered/Floribundas include 'Circus' (1956), 'Pink Parfait' (1960), and with Armstrong 'Joseph's Coat' (1969).

Tantau, Mathias and Mathias Jnr (Germany). For over 80 years, the Tantau family has produced a wide range, which includes many first-rate garden roses such as the Large-flowered/Hybrid Teas 'Prima Ballerina' (1957), 'Tropicana' (1960), 'Fragrant Cloud' (1963), 'Blue Moon' (1964), 'Whisky Mac' (1967) and 'Polar Star' (1982), the Cluster-flowered/Floribundas 'Paprika' (1958) and 'Topsi' (1972), the Miniature 'Baby Masquerade' (1956), the shrub 'Broadlands' (1993), and the Climbers 'City of York' (1945) and 'Lawinia' (1980). The remarkable shrub 'Cerise Bouquet' (1958) (often attributed wrongly to Kordes) is also a Tantau rose.

Teranishi, Kikuo (Japan). Teranishi has been active since the 1950s in the Itami Rose Nursery. He is perhaps best known internationally for the exhibition Large-flowered/Hybrid Tea 'Amatsu-Otome' (1960), and the lavender 'Mme Violet' (1981).

Twomey, Jerry (USA). Twomey has worked since the 1980s in Leucadia, California aiming for healthy garden roses. He has produced the All-America Rose Selection winners 'Sheer Elegance' (1989) and 'All That Jazz' (1991).

Tysterman, Bill (England). During the 1960s to the 1980s with Wisbech Plant Co., Tysterman produced a limited but high-quality output, including the Large-flowered/Hybrid Teas 'Doris Tysterman' (1975), 'Dutch Gold' (1978) and the strange parchment-colored 'Julia's Rose' (1980); he also raised the Cluster-flowered/Floribunda 'Fragrant Delight' (1978).

Van Fleet, Walter (USA). A physician by profession, Van Fleet raised roses between the 1890s and the 1920s, latterly with the Department of Agriculture. He aimed to produce healthy roses using species, and is famous for 'American Pillar' (1902), 'Silver Moon' (1910), 'Dr W. Van Fleet' (1910) and 'Mary Wallace' (1924).

Verbeek, Gijsbert (The Netherlands). Between the 1940s and the 1960s in Aalsmeer, Verbeek created his famous, wavy-petalled yellow Large-flowered/Hybrid Tea 'Dr A. J. Verhage' (1963), an important parent of other roses.

Verdier, Eugène (France). From the period between the 1860s and the 1890s in Paris, Verdier raised 222 hybrids of which the Hybrid Perpetual 'Prince Camille de Rohan' (1861) is perhaps the best known survivor.

Verschuren, Jacques and Hens (The Netherlands). Active from the 1910s to the 1940s, the Verschurens were, respectively, raisers of the famous Large-flowered/Hybrid Teas 'Golden Scepter' (syn. 'Spek's Yellow') (1950) and the fragrant, deep red 'Etoile de Hollande' (1919).

Vibert, Jean-Pierre (France). During the period from the 1810s to the 1840s in Angers, Vibert was responsible for the Bourbon 'Gloire des Rosomanes' (1825), the Noisette 'Aimée Vibert' (1828) and the Damask 'La Ville de Bruxelles' (1849) among some 600 others.

Viraraghavan, M. S. (India). Viraraghavan has been raising roses since the 1980s, pursuing innovative work with Indian species, including *Rosa clinophylla,* which tolerates wet ground. His named varieties, including the Large-flowered/Hybrid Tea 'Nefertiti' (1985), are not generally known outside India.

Von Abrams, Gordon (USA). During the 1950s and the 1960s in Oregon, and later in Davis, California, Von Abrams was involved with Peterson and Deering. Von Abrams is best known for the Large-flowered/Hybrid Teas 'Pink Favorite' (1956) and 'Memoriam' (1961), and the Cluster-flowered/Floribunda 'Golden Slippers' (1961).

Warner, Chris (England). Warner is an innovative breeder of Climbing Miniatures, including 'Laura Ford' (1990), 'Warm Welcome' (1991), 'Niceday' (1994), 'Good as Gold' (1995) and 'Open Arms' (1996), the repeat-flowering 'Little Rambler' (1995), the Ground Cover 'Pathfinder' (1993), and the shrub 'Laura Ashley' (1991). He has been active since the 1980s in Devon, and later in Shropshire.

Warriner, Bill (USA). Since the 1950s, and mostly with Jackson & Perkins, Warriner created over 150 varieties, including 18 All-America Rose Selection winners. His Large-flowered/Hybrid Teas include 'Pristine' (1978), 'Honor' (1980), 'Sheer Bliss' (1985) and 'Brigadoon' (1991), and his Cluster-flowered/Floribundas include 'Intrigue' (1982), 'Simplicity' (1978) and 'Tournament of Roses' (1988). He also produced the Climber 'America' (1976).

Weeks, Ollie (USA). During the 1950s until the 1980s in Chino, California, Weeks produced the Large-flowered/Hybrid Teas 'Oklahoma' (1964), 'Arizona' (1975), 'Paradise' (1978), and jointly with Swim 'Royal Highness' (1962), 'Mister Lincoln' (1964) and 'Angel Face' (1968).

Williams, Ernest D. (USA). Williams has been raising roses since the 1960s in Dallas, Texas. He specializes in Miniatures; those currently offered include 'Hula Girl' (1975), 'Dreamglo' (1978), 'Red Beauty' (1981) and the colorful single 'Oriental Simplex' (1987).

Zary, Keith (USA). Since the mid-1980s Zary has been with Bear Creek Gardens, raising garden and cut-flower varieties. His Ground Cover Rose 'Magic Carpet' (with Warriner) (1992) became UK Rose of the Year in 1996.

Glossary

Abscission layer A layer of tissue on a plant stem where a leaf or fruit is shed.

Achene A small, dry and hard fruit that contains a single seed.

Acid (of soils) Containing relatively little lime, to give a pH reaction of less than 7. A very acid soil is described as 'sour'.

Alkaline (of soils) Containing a great deal of calcium (lime) to give a pH reaction of more than 7. Some gardeners refer to alkaline soils as 'sweet'.

Alternate (of leaves) Arising, one by one, first from one side of the stem and then the other. Whether the leaves are alternate or opposite is an important aid in plant identification. Most leaf arrangements called 'alternate' are in fact spiral.

Anther The part of the stamen that actually contains the pollen, released when the anther opens.

Apex The growing tip of a shoot; the uppermost part of any plant organ, or the part furthest from its stalk or base. The plural of apex is apices.

Aphid Member of the order Aphididae of small sap-sucking insects with delicate translucent bodies, often infesting foliage in large numbers and weakening the plant. Aphids secrete a sugary 'honeydew' eaten by ants, which in return protect the aphids from other predators.

Arbor A structure, usually freestanding, designed to be covered with climbing plants to provide shade. The term is more or less interchangeable with pergola.

Aromatic Having a strong, usually pleasant but not just sweet smell. Aromatic plants often have resin glands on their stems and leaves, releasing the strongest aroma when the sun is hottest; many others contain essential oils in tiny leaf cavities, releasing their aroma when foliage is crushed or bruised.

Attar of roses The essential oil of rose petals.

Axil The 'armpit' of a leaf; that is, the angle between the leaf base and the stem, where there is usually a bud which may elongate to produce a lateral branch, a flower, or a group of flowers—these are then termed axillary.

Balled, Balling (of flowers) A disfiguration of rose flowers caused by the clinging together of the petals in damp weather, so that the blooms fail to open.

Bare-root Any plant bought with an exposed root system, not in a container.

Bark The protective surface layer of the trunk or branches of a tree or shrub, generated from a layer of dividing cells at the bark-wood interface (cambium) and often from additional layers of dividing cells (cork cambium).

Basal (of branches, leaves, etc.) Springing directly from the base of the plant rather than from an aerial stem; or may simply mean the opposite of apical, as in the basal lobes of a leaf.

Bedding (of plants) A plant, usually short or low growing, suitable for a mass-planting display of flowers or foliage.

Bicolored (of flowers) Having two different shades of color on the same flower, often sharply contrasting.

Blend (of flowers) Having two or more shades of color on the same flower, but without the contrast of a bicolored bloom.

Bloom A general term for a flower, or any inflorescence or portion of an inflorescence that has the appearance of a flower; a coating of whitish or bluish wax on a leaf, stem or fruit.

Blossom Much the same as *bloom*.

Boss The cluster of stamens at the flower center.

Branch Any plant stem arising from the primary stem in a lateral position, including flowering stems, though most commonly used for the lateral shoots of a tree which become thick and woody.

Bristle An outgrowth from any plant organ (leaf, stem, fruit etc.) that is thicker and stiffer than a hair but thinner and weaker than a prickle or thorn.

Bud An immature flower before its petals have unfolded; the embryonic stage of a leafy shoot before it expands. Sometimes called 'eye' or 'bud eye'.

Bud union The position on the rootstock where the bud was inserted.

Budding A form of grafting in which a (vegetative) bud of the desired clone (scion) is inserted in a slit in the bark of the stock plant.

Bush A bush rose, as distinct from a climbing or shrub rose, is a conventional, more or less upright plant suitable for both formal and informal displays.

Calyx The outermost whorl of enclosing organs in a flower, often green and leafy in contrast to the colored petals.

Cane A branch or stem that is slender, straight and not very woody, usually produced by a single season's growth.

Carpel The basic female organ of the flower, containing the ovary, in which the seeds develop, a stigma, which receives pollen, and frequently a style, an elongated section between ovary and stigma. The carpels of a flower are collectively called the pistil.

Chalk A kind of soft, porous limestone that on weathering produces very fine, powdery, alkaline soil in which many garden plants are difficult to grow. Chalk soils are common in parts of the UK.

Clay A major component of soils, consisting of very fine particles of mineral origin that swell and become sticky when they take up water. A high proportion of clay in a soil makes it difficult to dig and impedes both root penetration and drainage.

Climber A plant with stems too long and flexible to be self-supporting. Climbing roses may be trained to a support such as a pergola, trellis or arch, or even onto larger shrubs and trees.

Cloche A miniature, portable greenhouse placed over plants in the open ground to protect them from cold or encourage early development. Traditionally made from two or four pieces of glass in a wire frame, but can be simply a wire frame clad in transparent polythene.

Clone A group of plants propagated asexually (that is, by cuttings, grafting, layering, etc.) from a single individual and thus genetically all identical. Named cultivars of roses are always clonal—that is, each cultivar consists of a single clone—but a clone need not be named as a cultivar.

Common name The name by which a plant is commonly known by non-botanists, though many plants that are not well known or have only a short history of cultivation lack a common name. Common names vary from country to country or even from person to person, whereas botanical (scientific) names are used internationally.

Compost Material resulting from the breakdown by fungi and bacteria of waste organic matter such as leaves, grass clippings, vegetable peelings, animal manure and many other items—used in gardens as fertilizer and for improvement of soil texture. The term is also used for soilless growing mixes used for potting indoor plants.

Compound (of any plant organ) Consisting of smaller, simple units—thus a compound leaf consists of two to many leaflets arranged in regular fashion (see *pinnate*).

Conservatory A glassed-in area for growing frost-tender plants, usually attached to or forming part of a house.

Cool-temperate (of climates) Those in the cooler half of the temperate zones, essentially those regions between about 40 and 60 degrees latitude though extending closer to the equator in highlands and large continental landmasses of the northern hemisphere. Regions between 60 degrees north and the Arctic Circle are usually termed subarctic.

Corolla The whole collection of petals that forms the eye-catching part of a flower.

Corymb A type of inflorescence with a flat top.

Creeper A plant that makes long shoots that grow along the ground or up a wall.

Cross Another name for a hybrid, though somewhat vaguer in meaning.

Cultivar A variety of plant which has arisen or been selected in the course of cultivation, commonly as the result of hybridization. It may be propagated by any means that preserves its distinctive character, and the Code of Nomenclature states that it must not be named in Latin but should be given in Roman type with single quotes, for example, 'Iceberg', 'Jeanne d'Arc'. Cultivars that arose before this ruling and were given Latin names are treated similarly, giving rise to such names as 'Alba Maxima'. Most cultivars represent single clones and are propagated from cuttings or by budding.

Cultivated (of plants) Domesticated for use in gardens or agriculture, with the implication that cultivation techniques appropriate to the plant have been worked out.

Cutting A piece of stem or root cut from a plant and used for propagation, producing roots and new growth if kept in a suitable environment; (of flowers) the process of removing flowers from a plant for display elsewhere.

Deadhead To remove dead flowers, with the twofold aim of tidying up the plant and to promote flowering, preventing it wasting energy in unwanted seed.

Deciduous Losing all the leaves each year, growing a fresh set later. Typically the leaves drop in autumn, sometimes assuming brilliant colors before they do so, and new leaves grow in spring.

Dieback The death of the tips of shoots or branches, often progressing downward with time until the whole plant dies—mostly caused by diseases or pests attacking the root system, preventing uptake of sufficient water to support the foliage.

Disease An ailment of a plant caused by an infectious micro-organism, either fungal, bacterial or viral, or by a defect of environment such as a mineral deficiency in the soil, or an air pollutant. Infestations of most insects and other fauna are not regarded as diseases, except maybe for nematodes (eelworms) and some gall-producing insects.

Dormant (of plants) In a state of non-growth, usually leafless or with leaves and stems having died back to the ground, thus evading winter cold or a dry season; (of seeds) in a state adapted to long-term survival and in which germination is not readily initiated. Seed dormancy can be broken in a variety of ways, including stratifying and scarifying of the seeds.

Double (of flowers) Having more than the 'natural' number of petals. The extra petals are in most cases mutated stamens, and where all of these are completely transformed the flower is apt to be sterile. Double rose flowers are divided into three categories: semi-double (10–20 petals), double (20–40 petals) and very double (over 40 petals).

Downy (of leaves, fruits) Having a coating of fine, short hairs, as on the skin of a peach.

Embryo The earliest detectable stage of a seedling enclosed in the developing seed, shortly after fertilization; or the plantlet that can be observed when a mature seed is dissected.

Entire (of leaves) Having margins that are smooth, not toothed, scalloped, lobed or dissected in any way.

Erect Standing up almost vertically, applied to stems, branches, leaves or inflorescences.

Escape A plant that is on the away to becoming naturalized, having 'escaped' from cultivation.

Essential oil An aromatic oil found in minute cavities in the leaves or flowers of plants. Plants are harvested and distilled to obtain commercial quantities of certain oils, used for perfumery and food flavoring. So-called because each type of oil was said to be the 'essence' of a particular fragrance. The essential oil of rose petals is known as attar of roses, and it is a precious commodity.

Evergreen Any plant that retains foliage all year. Evergreen plants do drop old leaves, though not until after the new ones have been formed and usually only a few at a time.

Exhibition rose A high-quality flower suitable for competitive display at a rose exhibition.

Exotic A plant that is not native to the country or region in which it is grown, though the term is often used to signify any kind of plant seen as strange, alluring or glamorous.

Eye See *bud*.

Family The next major unit of classification above the level of genus. A plant family may consist of few to many genera, or in rare cases of a single genus only. The Rosaceae family contains over 50 genera, including the genus *Rosa*.

Fertile (of soils) Containing an abundance of the mineral nutrients (chiefly nitrogen, phosphorus and potassium) necessary for good plant growth, as well as decomposed organic materials producing a good tilth and moisture retention; (of plants and flowers) possessing fully functioning sexual organs, ensuring successful production of fruit or seed.

Fertilizer Anything added to the soil to maintain or increase its fertility. Fertilizer may be organic, that is, derived from once-living matter, as are manure, compost, and bone meal; or inorganic (artificial), such as sulphate of ammonia or superphosphate, which are prepared in chemical factories.

Fibrous root A fine, young root, usually one of very many. These are the roots that take up moisture and nourishment from the soil.

Filament The stalk of a stamen, which carries the anther.

Floret Much the same as *flower*, usually small and carried in clusters.

Flower The organ of reproduction of the flowering plants. They are normally composed of three parts: the calyx, the corolla, and the sexual organs proper, the male stamens and the female carpels.

Flush The period of flowering.

Frame A miniature greenhouse, designed mainly for propagation. The traditional style is an enclosed bed with wood to a height of about 16 in (40 cm) with an old window across the top. A hot frame is heated, a cold one not.

Frost hardy (of plants) Able to survive winter frosts without damage to leaves (in the case of evergreens) or of dormant stems, buds or roots (in the case of deciduous plants). Frost hardiness is a relative concept, in that many plants able to survive a frost of 20°F (−7°C) in, say, southern England would be killed outright by the −30°F (−34°C) frosts experienced in northern USA. See Hardiness Zone Map on page 21.

Frost tender (of plants) Damaged or killed by even the lightest winter frosts.

Fruit The part of the plant which contains the seeds.

Full (of flowers) Used to describe a double bloom that is packed with many petals.

Fungal disease Any of a great number of diseases of plants caused by a fungal organism.

Fungi (plural of fungus) A very large group of organisms, now considered to belong to a kingdom separate from both plants and animals, with vegetative bodies consisting of fine, almost invisible threads, or single cells, or even aggregations of naked protoplasm (the slime molds). Many fungi produce more conspicuous spore-bearing organs, as in the mushrooms, toadstools and puffballs. Fungi, unlike green plants, cannot synthesize their food from soil minerals but must utilize organic foods that have been synthesized by other organisms: they may feed either on dead matter (saprophytes) or living plants or animals (parasites). Many plant diseases are caused by parasitic fungi, but saprophytic fungi play a vital role in breaking down dead plant material, channeling it back into the nutrient cycle.

Genera Plural of genus.

Genus The next major unit of plant classification above species—thus a group of species with many features in common may be grouped together and named as a genus. The name given to a genus is of Latin form (or Latinized Greek). A genus name can stand on its own, referring then to all its members, but a species name must always consist of two words, the first being the genus name. All roses belong to the genus *Rosa*, which consists of about 140 species including *Rosa canina* and *R. rugosa*.

Glabrous (of leaves, stems, fruits etc.) Smooth, lacking any covering of hairs, scales or bristles.

Gland In botany used for a variety of plant organs, mainly very small, associated with the secretion of any fluid such as nectar, resin, oil or even water. Most flowers have one or more nectar glands (or nectaries) secreting nectar as the 'bait' for pollinating birds or insects, but nectar glands can also be found on leaves or stems of some plants.

Glaucous (of leaves and stems) Bluish gray or whitish, usually due to a thin coating or 'bloom' of wax which reflects light strongly.

Globular Approximately spherical in shape.

Grafting A method of propagation which involves the uniting of a piece of stem of a desirable plant, the scion, to that of a less desirable but hardier one, the stock or rootstock, to give a stronger root system than the scion would have naturally. Roses are grafted by budding.

Greenhouse A structure, traditionally roofed and clad with glass but now often with polythene sheeting, designed to trap the sun's heat and thus allow warmth-loving plants to be grown in cool climates. Supplementary heating may be provided. Now synonymous with 'glasshouse'.

Ground cover An extensive planting of a single type of low-growing plants.

Growing season The time of year in which a particular plant makes its maximum growth of stems and foliage; usually late spring and summer.

Habit (or growth habit) The complete picture of the way a plant grows; a certain variety may be described as being of 'compact', 'weeping' or 'upright' habit, for instance.

Habitat The environment in which a plant is usually found growing—the concept of habitat encompasses many factors, the most important being climate and soils, but microclimate is also significant, as are a plant's interactions with all the other plants, animals and micro-organisms present.

Hardiness In a wide sense, the ability to withstand adverse conditions, but in gardening the use of this term has narrowed to mean frost hardiness, at least in those parts of the world where frost is a major factor in determining what plants can be grown. The opposite of hardy is tender.

Hedge A close planting of trees or shrubs, their branches intertwining and serving as a barrier or fence. Hedges can be almost any height or width, depending on the plant used, but the typical garden hedge is 5–10 ft (1.5–3 m) high and composed of a single variety.

Heel A sliver of old wood retained at the base of a *cutting*. It is traditional in taking cuttings of carnations and roses.

Hemisphere Any half of the earth's surface, but most commonly taken to mean the northern or southern hemisphere, divided by the equator—though in earlier times an equally significant distinction was seen to be that between the eastern (Europe, Asia, Africa) and western (Americas) hemispheres. Climatically, there is a considerable difference between the northern and southern temperate zones, the latter having milder winters for equivalent latitudes due to the greater extent of oceans and the unimpeded circulation of their currents.

High-centered (of flowers) Used to describe rose flowers that have a classical shape, with the inner petals tightly arranged so that they retain their point until fully open. Also known as pointed.

Hip The fruit of the rose, also called a rosehip. Some roses are sterile and are incapable of producing hips.

Horticulture The art and science of gardening. Commercial horticulture is traditionally distinguished from agriculture in covering fruit, flower and small-scale vegetable growing, as well as the nursery industry, whereas agriculture covers broad-acre farming activities.

House plant Any kind of plant that can be grown for ornamental purposes inside a house.

Humus The organic content of soil, in nature derived mostly from fallen leaves, twigs, bark, and dead roots. These are broken down by insects and other ground fauna at the same time as they are being decomposed by fungi and bacteria. Earthworms are important in distributing humus throughout the topsoil. The humus content of soil can be enriched with many organic materials, including manure, compost, dead leaves, peat, and composted sawdust or pine bark. Humus returns nutrients to the soil and improves its texture and water retentiveness.

Hybrid A plant originating from the cross-pollination, either in the wild or as the result of matchmaking by the gardener, of two different species. If hybrids are crossed, the resulting plants may carry the genes of several species.

In situ Applied to the sowing of seeds or rooting of cuttings directly in the ground where they are to grow.

Incurved (of leaves, petals, leaf margins, etc.) Curving upward and inward, toward the center or base of the organ in question. The opposite is recurved, which means curving downward and outward.

Indigenous Of plant species in relation to any country or geographical region: native to that region—that is, growing there in the wild and believed always to have occurred there in the wild (at least for the span of human history).

Indoor (of plant cultivation) Within any enclosed structure, such as a house, conservatory or green-house, that a person can enter (thus excluding frames and cloches). Indoor cultivation both avoids winter frosts and raises temperatures in the growing season.

Inflorescence The structure that carries the flowers. Inflorescences are described as 'terminal' when they grow at the ends of shoots, or axillary, when they arise in the axils of the leaves.

Invasive (of plant species) Apt to spread rapidly, either by self-sown seedlings or by rhizomes or stolons, crowding out or smothering other garden plants or native vegetation.

Lax Weak-stemmed and consequently of rather floppy habit. The opposite of erect or stiff.

Layering A method of propagation by which a branch of a plant is bent down to the ground where it takes root; the rooted section can then be severed from its parent and transplanted. It is most useful for plants that can be slow or reluctant to root from cuttings; some plants will layer themselves naturally.

Leader The central growing shoot of a young tree or shrub, which eventually thickens to form the main stem or trunk of the mature plant.

Leaf The primary photosynthetic organ of green plants above the level of mosses.

Leaflet One of the several leaves into which a compound leaf such as a rose leaf is divided. A leaf has a bud in its axil; a leaflet does not.

Lime Compounds of calcium (principally calcium carbonate and calcium hydroxide) added to soil to make it more alkaline, and also to improve the structure of clay soil.

Loam Soil of light texture, with a low clay content and roughly equal proportions of silt and sand (defined as the medium and large particle sizes of mineral soil), usually with a good humus content as well. Loams are valued as garden soils, being easily worked and allowing good root penetration, though varying in fertility.

Manure The dung of animals, used as fertilizer. Like all materials of organic origin it adds humus to the soil but may also be a rich source of nitrogen and sometimes phosphorus, depending on which animal it comes from and their diet at the time.

Margin The edge of any flat organ such as a leaf or petal. Features of the leaf margin such as teeth are important in plant identification.

Mediterranean (of plant distributions) Countries bordering the Mediterranean Sea, or at least those parts of them that are climatically influenced by the Mediterranean—for example, the southeastern thirds respectively of France and Spain, most of Italy, all the southern Balkans and much of Turkey. Only a narrow fringe of the coast and mountains of North Africa is truly Mediterranean. The Mediterranean climate is characteristically mild and wet in winter but hot and dry in summer. Similar climates exist in other parts of the world, notably California, central Chile, western South Africa and coastal southern Australia, all of which are often termed 'Mediterranean'.

Midrib The main central vein of a leaf; the central stalk to which the leaflets of a pinnate leaf are attached.

Mildew Certain kinds of fungi that form fine webs on the surfaces of organic materials, or on the leaves

of live plants. Mildews thrive in warm, humid conditions and mainly affect plants that are not adapted to such conditions. Downy mildews are virulent plant diseases.

Miniature Rose Having all growth reduced in pro-portion to give a small bush about 14 in (35 cm) tall.

Moss Some roses have a moss-like growth on their sepals, which in some varieties extends down the flower stem. They are known as Moss Roses.

Mulch A blanket spread over the bare surface of soil to block the loss of moisture and to discourage the growth of weeds. Most mulches are of such organic matter as manure, compost, straw, bark chips, etc. which eventually rot and add humus to the soil, thus enhancing its fertility. Inorganic materials such as pebbles may also be also used.

Mutation See *sport*.

Native Much the same as *indigenous*: a term denoting the relationship of a plant species to a particular geographical region.

Naturalized (of a plant species) Behaving like a native plant of a particular geographical region, though originally introduced from a distant region, either as a cultivated plant or accidentally as a weed. *R. laevigata* 'Cherokee Rose', has become so natural-ized in southern USA that it is considered indigenous.

Neutral (of soils) Neither acid nor alkaline, that is having a pH of 7.

Node The point on a stem, often with a slight swelling, where a leaf is attached.

Nutrient In respect to plant growth, nutrients are the water-soluble substances taken up by the roots. The major nutrients, required in high concentration, are the elements nitrogen, phosphorus and potassium, while the minor nutrients include the elements iron, magnesium, calcium, manganese, zinc, boron, sulfur and molybdenum. These do not actually form the plant 'food', which consists of carbohydrates manufactured by photosynthesis from water and carbon dioxide, using the sun's energy, but they all have key positions in the protein and enzyme molecules essential to plant growth.

Organic matter Material derived from things that were once alive, such as manure and compost, and which breaks down to form humus. The addition of organic matter improves the structure and fertility of any soil.

Ornamental A plant grown purely for its aesthetic attractions, rather than for food or any other economic use.

Oval, Ovoid Egg-shaped in outline, with the widest point closer to the base than the apex.

Ovary The lowest part of a carpel, containing the embryonic seeds (ovules).

Panicle A loose and branching inflorescence, sometimes arranged around a short stem.

Peat The preserved and compressed remains of dead bog plants, usually either sphagnum moss or sedges. The natural acidity of some bogs prevents the dead plant material from decaying, so that it accumulates and over time forms thick deposits. Peat is extracted from these deposits and used for many purposes, including horticultural uses. It is termed moss peat (or peat moss) when derived mainly from sphagnum, or sedge peat when formed from sedges.

Peduncle A flower stalk, supporting either a flower or a whole cluster of flowers.

Pendent or pendulous Hanging, sometimes applied to flower clusters.

Perennial In botany, any plant that lives for three or more years; roses are woody perennials, in contrast to herbaceous perennials which have no woody above-ground parts.

Pergola A structure built in the garden, usually with walls or posts and a roof of open beams, on which climbing plants can be grown. A pergola may be

circular or square, or elongated and open at the ends, forming a passageway.

Persistent A structure that stays on the plant after it serves its purpose, instead of falling off. The sepals of the rose which stay on the ripening rose hip are an example.

Pest Any of various kinds of fauna that infest garden plants, or disturb a garden. Insect pests are of most concern in gardens, causing much damage to prized plants, also slugs and snails. Diseases differ from pests in being caused by micro-organisms such as fungi and bacteria, or minute internal fauna such as eelworms.

Petals The whorl of enclosing organs of a flower that comes between sepals and stamens; the most colorful and conspicuous part of most flowers. The petals collectively form the corolla.

Petiole The stalk of a leaf. The stalk of a leaflet of a compound leaf is termed the petiolule.

pH The scale on which the acidity or alkalinity of soil is measured. It ranges from 1, an acid of fearsome strength, to 14, an alkali of equal ferocity, with 7 being the neutral point. Most garden soils fall somewhere between about pH 5.5 and 8.6.

Picking See *cutting* (of flowers).

Pillar rose Any vigorous climbing rose suitable for training up a pillar.

Pinch out The operation of removing the tip of a growing shoot, usually with the fingers, to encourage lateral shoots to grow and make the plant develop a bushier habit.

Pinnate (of leaves) Compound and consisting of leaflets arranged on either side of a central stalk or rachis, as in a rose leaf. From the Latin *pinna*, meaning 'a feather'.

Pointed See *high-centered*.

Pollen The tiny grains of plant substance containing genetic material, which unite with the embryonic seeds contained in the ovary to create the fruit and hence a new generation of flowering plants—a process termed pollination. The transfer is usually carried out by insects, but can also be carried out by nectar-eating birds and sometimes by the wind.

Pollination The act of transference of pollen from the anther of one flower to the stigma of another.

Pompon (of flowers) Small and rounded, very double flowers filled with masses of tiny petals.

Potpourri A mix of sweet-smelling dried herbs and petals, usually placed in a bowl or a small muslin bag to perfume a room. Rose petals and lavender flowers are common ingredients.

Prickle A sharp-pointed projection from a stem, leaf or fruit. Prickles are not as strong or as robust as thorns, but are thicker and stiffer than bristles.

Proliferous (of flowers, leaves, hips, etc.) Produced in an abundance.

Propagate To intentionally multiply a particular plant, whether by sowing seed, taking cuttings, grafting, budding, or using tissue culture techniques in a laboratory.

Prostrate A plant of low-growing, ground-hugging growth habit.

Pruning The art of cutting off parts of a plant to encourage more of the sort of growth the gardener desires, or to maintain a compact habit of growth.

Quartered (of flowers) Very double flowers in which the center petals are folded and packed into four distinct quarters.

Raceme A type of inflorescence, where the flowers are arranged around an elongated stem, each flower having a separate stalk.

Rambler A climbing rose with very long and flexible canes bearing large bunches of small blooms. Very few rambling roses are repeat-flowering.

Receptacle The expanded portion of a flower, which bears the sepals, petals, stamens and carpels.

Recurrent See *repeat-flowering*.

Reflexed (of leaves, leaf-tips, sepals etc.) Bent sharply downwards or backwards.

Remontant See *repeat-flowering*.

Repeat-flowering Any plant that produces more than one flush of flowers during the same growing season, though not necessarily continuously.

Revert To return to normal, as when a sport starts to produce the same growth as its parent.

Root The underground parts of a plant, which anchor it in position and take up water and nutrients from the soil.

Rootstock The understock of a grafted plant; the base of a perennial where the roots grow.

Rosehip See *hip*.

Rosette (of flowers) Very double flowers with many overlapping petals of different sizes.

Rust fungus Any of a large group of plant-parasitic fungi characterized by the production of tiny but profuse spore-bodies that erupt from the host plant's leaves or stems, usually yellow, orange or rusty brown in color.

Sand The coarsest of the mineral components of soils, easily detected as grit by rubbing a pinch of soil between the fingers. Most sand is almost pure silica (quartz), one of the hardest and most insoluble minerals and containing no plant nutrients. Washed sand has many horticultural uses.

Scientific name The internationally recognized Latin name of a plant which may be descriptive of a feature of the plant, or commemorate some person connected with it. The name of a species consists of two parts, the genus name and the species name. The system was first devised by the Swedish botanist Linnaeus in 1753.

Scion In grafting, the piece of plant stem of the desired variety that is grafted onto the rooted stock (or rootstock). The scion subsequently grows, comprising all the branches, flowers and fruit of the desired variety.

Seed The organ of dispersal of flowering plants. Seeds are not immortal, and it is not worth saving leftover seeds for the following year; the percentage that will germinate decreases markedly.

Seedling A plant grown from seed; the offspring of a named variety.

Self-sow, self-seed A plant's habit of shedding seeds around itself which germinate without the gardener's assistance.

Semi-double (of flowers) Having more than the 'natural' number of petals, but with stamens still showing in the center. Semi-double roses usually have between 10–20 petals; more than this number, and the flower is classed as double.

Serrated (of leaf margins) Toothed, but with the teeth all forward-pointing, as the teeth of a saw.

Shoot Any aerial part of a plant that bears leaves, though in normal usage a shoot is an actively elongating stem or branch.

Shrub A rose of more informal stature than a bush rose. Not all shrub roses are necessarily large.

Simple (of leaves) Not compound, in the strict botanical meaning, though a heavily dissected leaf would not normally be called simple.

Single (of flowers) Having only a single row of petals. Single roses usually have five petals.

Soft-wooded (of plants) Having stems and branches lacking very strong woody tissue, usually with a core of pith.

Solitary (of flowers) Not grouped into a cluster but appearing singly.

Species A population of wild plants that are sufficiently alike to carry the same name, and which will freely breed with one another to give rise to offspring like themselves. The honor of naming a species goes to the scientist who discovers or describes it. Rose species are known as Wild Roses.

Sport A mutation that causes a plant to produce a different form of growth. When propagated, the sport gives rise to a new variety.

Spreading A plant which grows much wider than it does tall, perhaps with mainly horizontal branches.

Stalk, stem The two terms are almost interchangeable, but in horticulture a stem usually has leaves growing from its sides while a stalk does not.

Stamen The basic male organ in a flower. The stamens usually form the next whorl in from the whorl of petals. A stamen typically consists of a filament or stalk bearing at its tip the anther, the hollow organ containing the pollen.

Standard A tree or shrub with a single, rather tall stem before the branches begin. Roses have to be trained to the form artificially. A half-standard has a shorter stem than usual.

Stem The main body of a plant, that connects the roots to the leaves and flowers, or any part of it. Trunks, branches and twigs are all stems.

Sterile Incapable of bearing seeds or pollen or both. A plant may produce perfectly normal flowers but not mature fertile seed due to some aberration in its genetic make up, something which often occurs in hybrids; or the reproductive parts of the flower may have been transformed into the extra petals of a double flower.

Stigma The upper part of a carpel with specialized receptive cells on its surface, often slightly sticky and hence able to capture pollen grains from visiting insects or birds, or wind-borne pollen. The chemical environment of the stigma allows the pollen grain to germinate, sending a fine tube down through the style of the carpel, this tube containing the pollen parent's genetic material which then impregnates the ovules, resulting in seeds.

Stock In grafting or budding, the rooted plant (rootstock) onto which the scion is grafted. Any subsequent regrowth from the stock must be trimmed off as soon as it appears, otherwise it will rob food and water from the more desirable scion.

Stratify A technique used to break the dormancy of seeds that need a period of cold before they can germinate. In its simplest form, it involves bundling them up in damp sphagnum moss or peat and putting them in a refrigerator for a few weeks.

Strike The emergence of roots of a cutting.

Subarctic (of regions) The coolest parts of the northern temperate zone, close to the Arctic Circle.

Subshrub A perennial with more or less permanent aboveground but hardly woody stems.

Subtropical Applied to regions of the world usually no more than 5 to 10 degrees higher in latitude than the Tropics of Cancer or Capricorn and enjoying a climate that is virtually tropical.

Sucker A shoot or stem that arises from the roots or trunk base of a tree or shrub or, undesirably, from the understock of a grafted specimen.

Synonym (usually abbreviated to 'syn.') A scientific or common name that, though no longer accepted, still lingers in use, *Rosa arkansana* syn. *R. suffulta*.

Temperate Strictly speaking, those regions lying between the tropic of Capricorn and the Arctic Circle and between the Tropic of Cancer and the Antarctic Circle, known as the north and south temperate zones respectively. Used in a more general way to refer to climates without extremes of heat or cold. Often subdivided approximately into cool-temperate, warm-temperate, and subtropical, the latter applying to regions no more than 5 to 10 degrees of latitude beyond the tropics.

Tender Commonly taken to mean *frost tender*.

Terminal (of inflorescences and flowers) Appearing at the end of a shoot, as with rose inflorescences.

Thorn A thorn is a short lateral branch with a sharp point. Technically, roses do not have thorns, but prickles, which are outgrowths of the bark. In this book, however, thorns are used to describe large, often hooked prickles that are thick, strong and potentially harmful.

Toothed (of leaves) with teeth or serrations on the margin, as in rose leaves. In botanical usage toothing is distinguished as dentate, with teeth pointing straight out, or serrate, with teeth pointing forward as in a saw.

Trellis A structure or arrangement of wires or rods held up by posts or frames, specifically for the support of climbing plants. It may be freestanding in a garden, or attached to the wall of a house.

Tropical (of regions) Lying anywhere between the Tropic of Capricorn and the Tropic of Cancer, in what was once known as the 'torrid zone'—defined as the part of the globe in which the sun is directly overhead at least once each year.

Turkey Red A bright red color seen in fabric dyed with madder or alizarin.

Upright A growth habit in which at least the main branches grow more or less vertically.

Variegated Variegated plants have patterns of other colors as well as green on their leaves, and usually grow less strongly than their plain-leafed counterparts, as they have less chlorophyll. They are usually the result of cultivation and are sometimes caused by viruses.

Variety Strictly speaking, a variety is a group of plants arising in the wild that are reasonably different from the norm of their species. Garden rose varieties created by plant breeders are correctly called cultivars, but in this book the terms are used interchangeably.

Vein Any one of the strands of conducting tissue visible through the surface of a leaf or flower petal. The primary vein is often called the midvein or midrib and secondary veins are alternatively called lateral veins.

Warm-temperate (of climates) Usually applied to the upper-middle parts of the temperate zones, between about 30 and 40 degrees of latitude, where at least in coastal areas frost is absent or very light. See *cool-temperate* and *subtropical*.

Weed Any plant that is unwanted and a nuisance in the context of a particular environment, whether it be a garden, a cultivated field, a pasture or in natural woodland or forest. In natural vegetation weeds are almost by definition exotic to the region, but in gardens they may include some native plants. Weeds cause much economic loss and there is a large industry devoted to their control. They compete with cultivated plants for water, nutrients and sunlight as well as contaminating harvested crops, or spoiling the aesthetics of ornamental plantings.

Weeping Used mostly for trees and shrubs with pendulous branches or branchlets.

Wild garden A low-maintenance planting scheme that imitates nature, in that the plants are left to take care of themselves. Such areas are often designed to encourage wild animals and native plants, which is sometimes known as conservation gardening.

Wood The tissue laid down inside the bark cylinder by the dividing cells of the cambium layer. It consists largely of a cellulose framework with the denser carbohydrate lignin deposited in the cell walls. The living outer part (sapwood) is the main tissue by which water and dissolved nutrients are conducted upward from the roots. In gardening 'wood' is used with various qualifying adjectives to indicate the stage of maturity of a plant's stems, branches or twigs, as in 'new wood', 'old wood', 'previous year's wood', and so on.

× (multiplication sign) A sign placed within the Latin name of a plant to indicate that the plant is of hybrid origin, whether natural or artificial; as in *Rosa × coryana*.

Bibliography

Ackland, Dianne, *The Australian Rose Directory Second Edition*, Melbourne, Australia, 1996.

Allison, Sally, *Climbing and Rambling Roses*, Moa Beckett, Auckland, 1993.

American Rose Society, *The American Rose Annual*, 1916–present.

Andrews, Henry, *Roses: A Monograph*, London, 1804–28.

Austin, David, *The Heritage of the Rose*, Antique, Suffolk, 1988.

—— *Old Roses and English Roses*, Antique, Suffolk, 1992.

—— *Shrub Roses and Climbing Roses*, Antique, Suffolk, 1993.

—— *David Austin's English Roses*, Little, Brown, Boston, 1996.

Beales, Amanda, *Old-Fashioned Roses*, Cassell, London, 1990.

Beales, Peter, *Twentieth-Century Roses*, Collins/Harvill, London, 1988.

—— *Visions of Roses*, Little, Brown, New York, 1996.

—— *Classic Roses*, Harvill Press, London, 1997.

Bois, Eric & Trechslin, Anne-Marie, *Roses*, Nelson, London, 1962.

Browne et al, *Rose Gardening*, Pantheon, New York, 1995.

Buist, Robert, *The Rose Manual*, Buist, Philadelphia, 1844.

Bunyard, Edward A., *Old Garden Roses*, Collingridge, London, 1936.

Cairns, Thomas, ed. *Modern Roses 10*, American Rose Society, Shreveport, 1993.

Canadian Rose Society, *Canadian Rose Annual*, 1955–present.

Christopher, Thomas, *In Search of Lost Roses*, Summit Books, New York, 1989.

Clarke, Ethne, *Making a Rose Garden*, Weidenfeld, London, 1991.

Coats, Peter, *Roses*, G. P. Putnam, New York, 1962.

Coggiatti, Stelvio, *The Language of Roses*, Gallery Books, New York, 1986.

Cooper, Tuppy & Davidson, Lee, *Roses in Bermuda*, Bermuda Publ., Hamilton, 1997.

Cruse, Eleonore, *Roses*, Hachette Livre, Paris, 1997.

Curtis, Henry, *Beauties of the Rose*, Goombridge, London, 1850–53.

Delbard, Henri, *A Passion for Roses*, Thames & Hudson, London 1996.

Dickerson, Brent, *The Old Rose Advisor*, Timber Press, Portland, 1992.

Dobson, Beverley & Schneider, Peter, *Combined Rose List*, Mantua, 1998.

Druit, Liz, *The Organic Rose Garden*, Taylor, Dallas, 1996.

Druit, Liz & Shoup, G. Michael, *Landscaping with Antique Roses*, Taunton Press, Newtown, 1992.

Edland, Henry C., *Pocket Encyclopaedia of Roses* (3rd ed.), Blandford, London, 1970.

Ellwanger, Henry B., *The Rose*, Dodd, Mead, New York, 1882.

Fagan, Gwen, *Roses of the Cape of Good Hope*, Breestraat, Cape Town, 1988.

Fisher, John, *The Companion to Roses*, Viking, New York, 1986.

Gault, S. Millar & Synge, Patrick, *The Dictionary of Roses in Colour*, Michael Joseph, London, 1971.

Geschwind, Rudolf, *Die Hybridation und Samlingszucht der Rosen*, Hugo Voigt, Leipzig, 1885.

Gibson, Michael, *The Book of the Rose*, Macdonald, London, 1980.

—— *Shrub Roses, Climbers, and Ramblers*, Collins, London, 1981.

—— *Fifty Favourite Roses*, Cassell, London, 1995.

Gore, Catherine F., *The Book of Roses*, H. Colburn, London, 1838.

Gravereaux, Jules, *Les Roses de L'Impératrice Joséphine*, Editions D'Art, Paris, 1912.

Griffiths, Trevor, *The Book of Old Roses*, Michael Joseph, London, 1984.

—— *The Book of Classic Old Roses*, Michael Joseph, London, 1986.

—— *A Celebration of Old Roses*, Viking, Auckland, 1990.

—— *Old-Fashioned Roses—150 Favorites*, Trafalgar Square, N. Pomfret, 1995.

Grimm, Hedi & Wernt, *Die Rosensammlung zu Wilhelmshohe*, Kassel, 1987.

Harkness, Jack, *Roses*, J. M. Dent, London, 1978.

—— *The Makers of Heavenly Roses*, Souvenir Press, London, 1985.

—— *Rose Classes*, British Association of Rose Breeders, Suffolk, 1989.

Harkness, Peter, *Modern Garden Roses*, Justin Knowles, Devon, 1987.

—— *The Photographic Encyclopedia of Roses*, Gallery Books, New York, 1991.

Hole, Dean, *A Book About Roses*, Blackwood, Edinburgh, 1869.

Howells, John, *The Rose and the Clematis*, Garden Art, Suffolk, 1996.

Indian Rose Federation, *Indian Rose Annuals —Vols I–XIV*, Jabalpur, 1984–present.

Irvine, Susan, *Garden of a Thousand Roses*, Hyland House, Melbourne, 1992.

—— *A Hillside of Roses*, 1994.

—— *Fragrant Roses*, Hyland House, Melbourne, 1996.

—— *Rose Gardens of Australia*, Viking, Melbourne, 1997.

Jacob, Anny, *Rosen-Portrats*, Maniascriptum, Leipzig, 1997.

Jacob, A. & Grimm, Hedi & Wernt, *Alte Rosen und Wildrosen*, Eugen Ulmner, Stuttgart, 1990.

Jager, August, *Rosenlexicon*, DDR, Leipzig, 1960.

Jekyll, Gertrude & Mawley, Edward, *Roses for English Gardens*, Country Life, London, 1902.

Joyaux, François, *La Rose de France*, Imprimerie, Paris, 1998.

Keays, Ethelyn Emery, *Old Roses*, Macmillan, New York, 1936.

Krussmann, Gerd, *The Complete Book of Roses*, Timber, Portland, 1981.

Lancaster, Roy, *Travels in China*, Antique, Suffolk, 1989.

Lang, Ingomar, *Rosenverzeichnis Rosarium Sangerhausen*, Rosarium, Sangerhausen, 1988.

Le Rougetel, Hazel, *A Heritage of Roses*, Unwin Hyman, London, 1988.

Lester, Francis E., *My Friend the Rose*, Mt Pleasant, Harrisburg, 1942.

Lindley, John, *Rosarum Monographia*, J. Ridgway, London, 1820.

Macoboy, Stirling, *The Ultimate Rose Book*, Harry Abrams, New York, 1993.

Macself, A. J., *The Rose Grower's Treasury*, Collingridge, London, 1934.

Mansfield, T. C., *Roses in Colour and Cultivation*, Collins, London, 1943.

Mattock, John, *Identifying Roses*, Chartwell, Seacacus, 1994.

McFarland, J. Horace, *Modern Roses III*, McFarland Co., Harrisburg, 1947.

—— *Roses of the World in Color*, Houghton, Boston, 1947.

McGredy, Sam & Jennett, Sean, *A Family of Roses*, Dodd, Mead, New York, 1971.

Miessler, Herbert, *Miessler's Rosenlexikon* (2 vols), Rosenfreund, Weinheim, 1996.

Moody, Mary, *The Illustrated Encyclopedia of Roses*, Timber, Portland, 1992.

Muetze, Wilhelm & Schneider, C. K., *Das Rosenbuch*, Verlag, Berlin, 1924.

Nichols, J. H., *A Rose Odyssey*, Doubleday, New York, 1937.

Nietner, Theodor E., *Die Rose*, Wiegandt et al, Berlin, 1880.

Nottle, Trevor, *Growing Old-Fashioned Roses*, Kangaroo Press, Kenthurst, 1984.

—— *Roses for Every Garden*, ACP Publishers, Sydney, 1995.

Osborne, Robert, *Hardy Roses*, Garden Way, Pownal, 1991.

Pal, B. P., *The Rose in India*, Indian Council, New Delhi, 1966.

Park, Bertram, *The Guide to Roses*, Collins, London, 1956.

Parsons, Alfred, *A Garden of Roses*, Salem House, Topsfield, 1987.

Paterson, Allen, *The History of the Rose*, Collins, London, 1956.

Pemberton, Joseph H., *Roses: Their Cultivation*, Longmans, London, 1920.

Phillips, Roger & Rix, Martyn, *Roses*, Random House, New York, 1988.

—— *The Quest for the Rose*, BBC Books, London, 1993.

Pinney, Margaret E., *The Miniature Rose Book*, Van Nostrand, Princeton, 1964.

Redouté, Pierre Joseph, *Les Roses*, Firmin Didot, Paris, 1817–1824.

Rehder, Alfred, *Manual of Cultivated Trees and Shrubs*, Macmillan, New York, 1927.

Rivers, Thomas, *Rose Amateur's Guide* (4th ed.), Longman, London, 1846.

Rose, Graham & King, Peter, *The Love of Roses*, Quiller Press, London, 1990.

Roses Anciennes France, *Bulletins*, 1997.

Ross, Deane M., *A Manual of Heritage Roses*, Ross Roses, South Australia, 1989.

Royal National Rose Society, *The Rose Annual*, 1907–80.

Rumsey, Heather, *Old-fashioned Roses for Australian Gardens*, Macmillan, Melbourne, 1990.

Sala, Orietta, *Old-fashioned Roses*, Beazley, London, 1991.

—— *The World's Best Roses*, Prentice Hall, New York, 1993.

Scanniello, Stephen, *A Year of Roses*, Henry Holt, New York, 1996.

Scanniello, Stephen & Bayard, Tania, *Roses of America*, Henry Holt, New York, 1990.

Scarman, John, *Gardening with Old Roses*, Harper-Collins, London, 1996.

Schneider, Peter, *Peter Schneider on Roses*, Macmillan, New York, 1995.

Shepherd, Roy E., *History of the Rose*, Macmillan, New York, 1954.

Simon, Leon, *Noms de Roses* (2nd ed.), Library of Horticulture, Paris, 1906.

Sinclair, Alan & Thodey, Rosemary, *Gardening with Old Roses*, Cassell, London, 1993.

Steen, Nancy, *The Charm of Old Roses*, AH/AW Reed, Wellington, 1966.

Stevens, G. A., *Climbing Roses*, Macmillan, New York, 1933.

Swane, Valerie, *Growing Roses*, Kangaroo Press, Kenthurst, 1992.

Taylor, Barbara Lea, *Old-Fashioned Roses*, David Bateman, Auckland, 1993.

Testu, Charlotte, *Les Roses Anciennes*, Flammarion, Paris, 1984.

Thomas, George C., *Practical Book of Outdoor Rose Growing*, J. P. Lippincott, Philadelphia, 1914.

—— *Roses for all American Climates*, Macmillan, New York, 1924.

Thomas, Graham Stuart, *The Art Of Gardening with Roses*, Henry Holt, New York, 1991.

—— *The Graham Stuart Thomas Rose Book*, Saga/Timber, Portland, 1994.

Thomas, H. H., *The Rose Book*, Cassel, London, 1913.

Vecera, Ludvik, *Classic Roses*, Hamlyn, London, 1971.

Verein Deutscher Rosenfreunde, *Rosenjahrbuch*, VDR, Baden-Baden, 1950.

Verrier, Suzanne, *Rosa Rugosa*, Capability, Wisconsin 1991.

—— *Rosa Gallica*, Capability, Wisconsin 1995.

Warner, Christopher, *Climbing Roses*, Justin Knowles, Devon, 1987.

Welch, David, *Roses*, Collingridge, London, 1988.

Welch, William C., *Antique Roses for the South*, Taylor, Dallas, 1990.

Wesselhoeft, Johannes, *Der Rosenfreund*, B. F.Voigt, Weimar, 1873.

Wheatcroft, Harry, *In Praise of Roses*, Henry Regnery, Chicago, 1970.

Willmott, Ellen A., *The Genus Rosa*, J. Murray, London, 1910–14.

Wilson, Helen Van Pelt, *Climbing Roses*, M. Barrows, New York, 1955.

Young, Norman, *The Complete Rosarian*, St Martins, New York, 1971.

Zuzek et al, *Roses for the North*, University Press, St Paul, 1995.

Index to the Roses